Best Books for Middle School and Junior High Readers

GRADES 6–9
Third Edition

Catherine Barr

Children's and Young Adult Literature Reference

LIBRARIES UNLIMITED

AN IMPRINT OF ABC-CLIO, LLC
Santa Barbara, California • Denver, Colorado • Oxford, England

Library of Congress Cataloging-in-Publication Data

Barr, Catherine, 1951–
  Best books for middle school and junior high readers : grades 6–9 / Catherine Barr. — Third edition.
    pages cm. — (Children's and young adult literature reference)
  ISBN 978-1-59884-782-6 (hardback) 1. Middle school students—Books and reading—United States. 2. Junior high school students—Books and reading—United States. 3. Preteens—Books and reading— United States. 4. Teenagers—Books and reading—United States. 5. Children's literature—Bibliography. 6. Young adult literature—Bibliography. 7. Middle school libraries—United States—Book lists. 8. Junior high school libraries—United States—Book lists. I. Title.
  Z1037.G482   2013
  011.62—dc23   2013011588

ISBN: 978-1-59884-782-6

17 16 15 14 13   1 2 3 4 5

Libraries Unlimited
An Imprint of ABC-CLIO, LLC

ABC-CLIO, LLC
130 Cremona Drive, P.O. Box 1911
Santa Barbara, California 93116-1911

This book is printed on acid-free paper ∞
Manufactured in the United States of America

Contents

CONTENTS

The Arts and Entertainment

History and Geography

Philosophy and Religion

Society and the Individual

Guidance and Personal Development

Physical and Applied Sciences

Recreation and Sports

Major Subjects Arranged Alphabetically

Preface

Librarians and other specialists in children's literature have available, through print and online sources, a large number of bibliographies that recommend books suitable for young people. Unfortunately, these sources vary widely in quality and usefulness. The Best Books series was created to furnish authoritative, reliable, and comprehensive bibliographies for use in libraries that collect materials for readers from preschool through grade 12. The series now consists of three volumes: *Best Books for Children*, *Best Books for Middle School and Junior High Readers*, and *Best Books for High School Readers*.

Best Books for Middle School and Junior High Readers, Third Edition is a continuation of *Best Books for Children, Ninth Edition* (Libraries Unlimited, 2010) and its supplement (Libraries Unlimited, 2013). *Best Books for Middle School and Junior High Readers* supplies information on books recommended for readers in grades 6 through 9 or roughly ages 11 through 15. *Best Books for Children* contains books recommended for preschool through grade 6 readers and *Best Books for High School Readers, Third Edition* (Libraries Unlimited, 2013) covers grades 9 through 12.

As every librarian knows, reading levels are elastic. There is no such thing, for example, as a seventh-grade book. Instead there are only seventh-grade readers who, in their diversity, can represent a wide range of reading abilities and interests. This bibliography contains a liberal selection of entries that, one hopes, will accommodate readers in these grades and make allowance for their great range of tastes and reading competencies. By the ninth grade, a percentage of the books read should be at the adult level. Keeping this in mind, about one fifth of the entries in this volume are adult books suitable for young adult readers (they are designated by reading level grades of 6–12, 7–12, and 8–12 within the entries). At the other end of the spectrum, there are also many titles that are suitable for readers below the sixth grade (indicated by grade level designations such as 4–7, 4–8, 4–9, 5–7, and 5–8 within the entries). This has resulted in a slight duplication of titles in this book with those in *Best Books for Children*. Similarly, there is a slight overlap with *Best Books for High School Readers*.

In selecting books for inclusion, deciding on their arrangement, and collecting the information supplied on each, it was the editors' intention to reflect the current needs and interests of young readers while keeping in mind the latest trends and curricular emphases in today's schools.

General Scope and Criteria for Inclusion

Of the 14,028 titles listed in *Best Books for Middle School and Junior High Readers*, 13,583 are individually numbered entries and 445 are cited within the annotations as additional recommended titles by the same author (often these are titles that are part of an extensive series). It should be noted that some series are so extensive that, because of space limitations, only representative titles are included.

Excluded from this bibliography are general reference works, such as dictionaries and encyclopedias, except for a few single-volume works that are so heavily illustrated and attractive that they can also be used in the general circulation collection. Also excluded are professional books for librarians and teachers and mass market series books.

For most fiction and nonfiction, a minimum of two recommendations were required from the current reviewing sources consulted for a title to be considered for listing. However, there were a number of necessary exceptions. For example, in some reviewing journals only a few representative titles from extensive nonfiction series are reviewed even though others in the series will also be recommended. In such cases a single favorable review was enough for inclusion. This also held true for some of the adult titles suitable for young adult readers where, it has been found, reviewing journals tend to be less inclusive than with juvenile titles. Again, depending on the strength of the review, a single positive one was sufficient for inclusion. As well as favorable reviews, additional criteria such as availability, currency, accuracy, usefulness, and relevance were considered.

An asterisk following a review citation denotes an outstanding recommendation from that source.

Many awards are also cited.

Sources Used

A number of current and retrospective sources were used in compiling this bibliography. Book reviewing journals consulted were *Booklist, Library Media Connection, School Library Journal*, and *VOYA (Voice of Youth Advocates)*. Other sources used include *Bulletin of the Center for Children's Books, Horn Book*, and *Horn Book Guide*. Reviews in issues of these journals were read and evaluated from July 2008 through early 2013, when this book's coverage ends.

Uses of This Book

Best Books for Middle School and Junior High Readers was designed to help librarians and media specialists with four vital tasks: (1) evaluating the adequacy of existing collections; (2) building new collections or strengthening existing holdings; (3) providing reading guidance to young adults; and (4) preparing bibliographies and reading lists. To increase the book's usefulness, particularly in preparation of bibliographies or suggested reading lists, titles are arranged under broad areas of interest or, in the case of nonfiction works, by curriculum-oriented subjects rather than the Dewey Decimal classification (suggested Dewey classification numbers are nevertheless provided within nonfiction entries). The subject arrangement corresponds roughly to the one used in *Best Books for Children*, minus its large section on picture books.

Some arbitrary decisions were made concerning placement of books under specific subjects. For example, books of experiments and projects in general science are placed under "Physical and Applied Sciences—Experiments and Projects," whereas books of experiments and projects on a specific branch of science (e.g., physics) appear under that branch. It is hoped that use of cross-references in the Subject/Grade Level Index will help guide the user in this regard.

Audio and ebook versions are indicated with the symbols ⌒ and e. Lexile reading levels are also provided where available. Additional information about Lexile measures is available at lexile.com.

Arrangement

In the Table of Contents, subjects are arranged by the order in which they appear in the book. Following the Table of Contents is a listing of Major Subjects Arranged Alphabetically, which provides entry numbers as well as page numbers for easy access. Following the main body of the text, there are three indexes. The Author Index cites authors and editors, titles, and entry numbers (joint authors and editors are listed separately). The Title Index gives the book's entry number. Works of fiction in both of these indexes are indicated by (F) following the entry number. Finally, an extensive Subject/Grade Level Index lists entry numbers under hundreds of subject headings with specific grade-level suitability given for each entry. The following codes are used to identify general grade levels:

IJ   (Intermediate-Junior High) suitable for upper elementary and lower middle school

J   (Junior High) suitable for middle school and junior high

JS   (Junior-Senior High) suitable for junior high and senior high

Entries

A typical entry contains the following information where applicable: (1) author, joint author, or editor; (2) title and subtitle; (3) specific grade levels given in parentheses; (4) adapter or translator; (5) indication of illustrations; (6) publication date; (7) publisher and price of hardbound edition (LB = library binding); (8) International Standard Book Number (ISBN) of hardbound edition; (9) paperback publisher (paper) and price (if no publisher is listed it is the same as the hardbound edition); (10) ISBN of paperback edition; (11) annotation; (12) awards; (13) audio version; (14) ebook version; (15) Lexile; (16) review citations; (17) Dewey Decimal classification number.

Review Citations

Review citations are given for the following journals:

Booklist (BL)
Booklist Online (BLO)
Bulletin of the Center for Children's Books (BCCB)
Book Report (BR)
Horn Book (HB)
Horn Book Guide (HBG)
Library Media Connection (LMC)
School Library Journal (SLJ)
VOYA (Voice of Youth Advocates) (VOYA)

Additional Pointers for Users

For series that contain an extensive number of titles -- numbered graphic novel series, for example — only a representative number of books are listed. For more complete listings of titles, it is suggested that the user consult author or publisher Web sites, or the Web sites of such online booksellers as Amazon (amazon.com) and Barnes and Noble (bn.com).

All graphic novels are collected in one section, which includes graphic adaptations of classics such as *Moby Dick.*

Anthologies of short stories on a single subject are found under that subject (an anthology of science fiction short stories will be listed under "Science Fiction," for example), but general anthologies or collections by a single author on diverse subjects are listed in the "Short Stories and General Anthologies" section.

Similarly, books of experiments and projects on a specific subject in science are placed under that subject, but general science project books are in the section "Physical and Applied Sciences — Experiments and Projects."

Books of criticism about individual authors, even though they contain some biographical information, are placed in the "Literary History and Criticism" section.

Books on World War II are found in the "World War II and Holocaust" section but books on internal conditions in the United States during this period are found in the United States history section under "World War II."

Books on the history of specific ethnic groups (for example, books that are historical accounts of African American slavery) are generally found in the "Ethnic Groups and Prejudice" section.

Acknowledgments

Many people were involved in the preparation of this bibliography. In particular, we are grateful to Barbara Ittner of Libraries Unlimited and to Christine McNaull, who makes production of this book possible. Thanks are also due to Kristina Strain and Jane Higgins for their contributions.

Catherine Barr

Literary Forms

Fiction

Adventure and Survival Stories

1 Aaron, Chester. *Lackawanna* (6–9). 1986, HarperCollins LB $11.89 (978-0-397-32058-5). In Depression New York, the youthful Lackawanna gang sets out to find a member who has been kidnapped. (Rev: BL 2/15/86; SLJ 4/86; VOYA 6/86)

2 Aaron, Chester. *Out of Sight, Out of Mind* (6–9). 1985, HarperCollins LB $11.89 (978-0-397-32101-8). Twins with psychic powers are pursued by foreign agents who want their secret. (Rev: VOYA 12/85)

3 Adams, W. Royce. *Me and Jay* (5–8). 2001, Rairarubia paper $10.99 (978-1-58832-021-6). Two 13-year-olds meet with trouble at every turn when they venture into forbidden territory in search of a hidden pond. (Rev: BL 1/1–15/02)

4 Aguiar, Nadia. *The Lost Island of Tamarind* (7–10). 2008, Feiwel & Friends $17.95 (978-031238029-8). Part mystery, part fantasy, part survival story, this tale tells of 13-year-old Maya and her two young siblings who survive a storm aboard their parents' marine research boat and end up in a fantasy world full of danger and magic. e Lexile 880L (Rev: BLO 10/29/08; LMC 3–4/09; SLJ 10/1/08; VOYA 12/08)

5 Aiken, Joan. *Midnight Is a Place* (7–10). Series: Wolves Chronicles. 1974, Scholastic paper $2.95 (978-0-590-45496-4). In Victorian England, two young waifs are cast adrift in a hostile town when their guardian's house burns.

6 Aiken, Joan. *Midwinter Nightingale* (5–8). Series: Wolves Chronicles. 2003, Delacorte $15.95 (978-0-385-73081-5). Dido Twite and Simon, Duke of Battersea, continue their adventures in this eighth installment in the series, protecting a dying king, searching for a missing coronet, and defeating an evil baron. (Rev: BL 6/1–15/03; HBG 10/03; SLJ 6/03)

7 Alexander, Lloyd. *The Golden Dreams of Carlo Chuchio* (5–8). 2007, Henry Holt $17.95 (978-0-8050-8333-0). The final book by the late Alexander takes Carlo along the Road of Golden Dreams in search of treasure. (Rev: BCCB 10/07; BL 7/07; HB 9–10/07; LMC 2/08; SLJ 8/07)

8 Alexander, Lloyd. *The Xanadu Adventure* (5–8). 2005, Button $16.99 (978-0-525-47371-8). Vesper Holly, accompanied by friends and guardians, sets off for Asia Minor to search for an artifact in the ancient city of Troy but soon finds herself in the clutches of her nemesis, Dr. Desmond Helvitius. (Rev: BL 2/1/05*; SLJ 2/05)

9 Allende, Isabel. *Kingdom of the Golden Dragon* (7–12). 2004, HarperCollins $19.99 (978-0-06-058942-4). Yetis, high in the Himalayas, help 16-year-old Alexander in his fight against American corporate villains in this sequel to *City of the Beasts*. (Rev: BL 2/15/04; SLJ 4/04)

10 Anderson, M. T. *Whales on Stilts!* (5–7). 2005, Harcourt $15.00 (978-0-15-205340-6). Twelve-year-old Lily Gefelty enlists the help of two friends to foil a plan to take over the world using an army of mind-controlled whales on stilts; a fast-paced adventure full of tongue-in-cheek fun. (Rev: BL 2/15/05*; SLJ 5/05)

11 Anderson, Scott. *Unknown Rider* (6–9). 1995, Dennoch paper $12.50 (978-0-9644521-0-7). Combining fact and fiction, this is the story of fighter pilot Rick Wedon — his training, experiences in officer school, and his missions. (Rev: VOYA 8/96)

12 Asai, Carrie. *The Book of the Sword* (6–12). Series: Samurai Girl. 2003, Simon & Schuster paper $6.99 (978-0-689-85948-9). Heaven abandons her adoptive family when her brother is murdered in the middle of her arranged wedding and devotes herself to studying to be a samurai and avenging her brother. (Rev: SLJ 8/03)

13 Ashby, John. *Sea Gift* (6–8). 2003, Clarion $15.00 (978-0-395-77603-2). Lauchie and his friends set off on an exciting treasure hunt on the coast of Cape Breton Island after they discover a pistol and letter dating to 1632. (Rev: BL 9/15/03; SLJ 12/03)

14 Ashley, Bernard. *Break in the Sun* (6–9). 1980, Phillips $26.95 (978-0-87599-230-3). Patsy Bleigh runs away on a ship belonging to a theatrical company.

15 Ashley, Bernard. *A Kind of Wild Justice* (6–9). 1978, Phillips $26.95 (978-0-87599-229-7). Ronnie is threatened by the same gang that made his father a criminal.

16 Avi. *Captain Grey* (5–8). 1993, Morrow paper $4.95 (978-0-688-12234-8). In 1783, young Kevin is captured by pirates. A reissue.

17 Avi. *Windcatcher* (4–7). 1991, Avon paper $4.99 (978-0-380-71805-4). Eleven-year-old Tony dreads a summer by the sea, but ends up finding a sailing adventure. (Rev: BCCB 5/91; BL 3/1/91; HB 5–6/91; SLJ 4/91)

18 Baccalario, Pierdomenico. *Star of Stone* (5–9). Trans. from Italian by Leah D. Janeczko. Series: Century Quartet. 2010, Random House $16.99 (978-0-375-85896-3); LB $19.99 (978-0-375-95896-0). Harvey, Elettra, Mistral, and Sheng are led all around Manhattan by tricky clues left by an eccentric professor in this action-packed sequel to *Ring of Fire* (2009). Also use *City of Wind* (2011). ⌒ ℮ (Rev: SLJ 11/1/10)

19 Baird, Thomas. *Finding Fever* (6–8). 1982, HarperCollins $12.95 (978-0-06-020353-5). Kidnappers make off with Benny's sister's dog, and Benny sets out to investigate.

20 Bancks, Tristan. *Mac Slater vs. the City* (5–8). 2011, Simon & Schuster $15.99 (978-1-4169-8576-1). Eighth-grader Mac and his friend Paul are excited to travel to New York City to compete in a Coolhunter competition but find more challenges than expected. (Rev: BLO 3/25/11; SLJ 4/11)

21 Bauer, Hans, and Catherine Masciola. *Fishtale* (4–7). Illus. by Catherine Masciola. 2012, Amazon Children's $16.99 (978-076146223-1). In the Mississippi bayou, 12-year-old Sawyer — with his sister and friends — sets out to find a legendary catfish that may have his widowed mother's missing wedding ring. ⌒ ℮ (Rev: BL 10/15/12; LMC 5–6/13; SLJ 1/13)

22 Bawden, Nina. *Rebel on a Rock* (6–8). 1978, HarperCollins LB $13.89 (978-0-397-32140-7). Jo reluctantly believes that her stepfather is a spy for a cruel dictator.

23 Becker, Helaine. *Trouble in the Hills* (8–12). 2011, Fitzhenry & Whiteside paper $9.95 (978-1-55455-174-3). Reckless after an argument with his father, Cam sets off into the mountains on his bike; nonstop adventure ensues as he has an accident, meets a girl who has escaped from kidnappers, and must deal with drug runners. (Rev: LMC 10/12; SLJ 6/12)

24 Bernardo, Anilú. *Jumping Off to Freedom* (7–10). 1996, Arte Publico paper $9.95 (978-1-55885-088-0). The story of four refugees, including teenage David, on a harrowing voyage from Cuba to Florida on a raft. (Rev: BL BL 5/1/96; SLJ 7/96; VOYA 6/96; VOYA 6/96)

25 Blackwood, Gary. *Around the World in 100 Days* (6–9). 2010, Dutton $16.99 (978-0-525-42295-2). Phineas Fogg's 17-year-old son Harry races against time in 1891 to prove the worth of his newfangled steam-powered motor car. (Rev: BL 11/1/10; SLJ 12/1/10)

26 Blades, Ann. *A Boy of Tache* (6–9). 1995, Tundra paper $5.95 (978-0-88776-350-2). A Canadian novel of a boy's trek through the wilderness to save his grandfather's life.

27 Bledsoe, Lucy Jane. *The Antarctic Scoop* (4–7). 2003, Holiday House $16.95 (978-0-8234-1792-6). In this fast-paced adventure story, 12-year-old Victoria, a shy girl with ambitious dreams, wins a trip to Antarctica but discovers during her travels that the real goal of the contest sponsor is to develop and exploit the icy continent. (Rev: BL 1/1–15/04; SLJ 1/04)

28 Bodeen, S. A. *The Compound* (7–12). 2008, Feiwel & Friends $16.95 (978-0-312-37015-2). Eli and members of his family have lived in an elaborate underground shelter for years, believing that the world as they knew it was destroyed. But was it? Or did Eli's wealthy father have other reasons for building the compound? (Rev: BL 4/15/08; SLJ 7/08)

29 Bodett, Tom. *Williwaw* (5–8). 1999, Random House paper $5.50 (978-0-375-80687-2). The story of two youngsters — 13-year-old September Crane and her 12-year-old brother Ivan — and their life in the wilds of Alaska, where they are often left alone by their fisherman father. (Rev: BCCB 6/99; BL 4/1/99; HBG 10/99; SLJ 5/99)

30 Bondoux, Anne-Laure. *The Princetta* (6–9). 2006, Bloomsbury $17.95 (978-1-58234-924-4). Malva, the Princetta of Galnicia, flees the strictness of her parents and her arranged marriage and boards a ship, hoping to find freedom in a new land. (Rev: BL 9/1/06; SLJ 12/06)

31 Brand, Max. *Dan Barry's Daughter* (7–12). 1976, Amereon LB $25.95 (978-0-88411-516-8). Harry is an accused murderer who, though innocent, is forced to hide. One of many recommended westerns by this prolific author.

32 Bray, Libba. *Beauty Queens* (8–12). 2011, Scholastic $18.99 (978-0-439-89597-2). When a plane carrying teen pageant contestants crashes on a remote island, the survivors face big challenges — and learn a lot about themselves and each other in the process. YALSA Amazing Audiobooks Top Ten 2012. ⌒ ℮ Lexile HL690L (Rev: BL 5/1/11; HB 7–8/11; SLJ 7/11*; VOYA 6/11)

33 Bruchac, Joseph. *Bearwalker* (5–8). Illus. by Sally Wern Comport. 2007, HarperCollins $15.99 (978-0-06-112309-2). Thirteen-year-old Baron, Native American and not as tall as he would like, comes into his own on a class trip to the Adirondacks as he draws on strengths that were not apparent to his classmates. (Rev: BL 9/15/07; SLJ 8/07)

34 Bruchac, Joseph. *The Return of Skeleton Man* (5–8). Illus. by Sally Wern Comport. 2006, HarperCollins $15.99 (978-0-06-058090-2). Molly, the Mohawk teen who survived a terrifying kidnapping in *Skeleton Man* (2001), discovers her nemesis is back. (Rev: BL 9/15/06; SLJ 8/06)

35 Bruchac, Joseph. *Wolf Mark* (7–12). 2011, Lee & Low $17.95 (978-1-60060-661-8). When Luke's father is kidnapped, Luke must use unusual abilities to rescue him; a fast-paced adventure combining Native American lore, supernatural elements, and high-tech devices. **e** Lexile 810L (Rev: BL 10/1/11; LMC 1–2/12*; SLJ 9/1/11)

36 Buckley, Michael. *The Cheerleaders of Doom* (4–7). Illus. by Ethen Beavers. Series: NERDS. 2011, Abrams $14.95 (978-141970024-8). When Gertie, a former member of the National Espionage, Rescue, and Defense Society, disrupts the multi-verse with her cheerleading aspirations, Wheezer and the other NERDS swing into action; the third volume in the series. ∩ (Rev: BL 12/1/11; SLJ 2/12)

37 Buckley, Michael. *M Is for Mama's Boy* (4–7). Illus. by Ethen Beavers. Series: NERDS. 2010, Abrams $14.95 (978-0-8109-8986-3). The 5th-grade NERDS team is back to deal with more outrageous behavior by supervillain Simon. ∩ Lexile 780L (Rev: BL 9/15/10; LMC 1–2/11; SLJ 12/1/10)

38 Buckley, Michael. *NERDS: National Espionage, Rescue, and Defense Society* (4–7). Illus. by Ethen Beavers. Series: NERDS. 2009, Abrams $14.95 (978-0-8109-4324-7). Former cool kid Jackson Jones now finds himself among the school's nerd population, but he soon learns that the unassuming geeks whom he so recently delighted in tormenting are actually members of a top-secret spy ring that is attempting to stop the insidious Dr. Jigsaw from destroying the world. The second and third volumes in the series are *M Is for Mama's Boy* (2010) and *The Cheerleaders of Doom* (2011). ∩ Lexile 760L (Rev: BL 10/15/09; LMC 1–2/11; SLJ 12/09)

39 Bunting, Eve. *Someone Is Hiding on Alcatraz Island* (5–8). 1986, Berkley paper $5.99 (978-0-425-10294-7). A boy and a young woman ranger are trapped by a gang of thugs on Alcatraz. (Rev: BL 7/88)

40 Bunting, Eve. *SOS Titanic* (6–9). 1996, Harcourt paper $6.00 (978-0-15-201305-9). During his voyage on the *Titanic*, 15-year-old Barry O'Neill learns about the inequities of the class system and the true meaning of heroism. (Rev: BL 3/15/96; SLJ 4/96; VOYA 6/96)

41 Butler, Geoff. *The Hangashore* (6–8). 1998, Tundra $15.95 (978-0-88776-444-8). A picture book for older children about a stubborn, self-righteous magistrate from England who changes his mind about a slow-witted local boy and his own role in the Newfoundland community after the boy saves his life. (Rev: HBG 3/99; SLJ 2/99)

42 Butler, William. *The Butterfly Revolution* (7–12). 1961, Ballantine paper $6.50 (978-0-345-33182-3). A frightening story of problems in a boys' camp told in diary form by one of the campers.

43 Campbell, Eric. *The Place of Lions* (6–9). 1991, Harcourt $17.00 (978-0-15-262408-8). When their plane crashes over the Serengeti, Chris and his injured father must learn a lesson in survival while surrounded by poachers and a pride of lions. (Rev: BL 11/15/91; SLJ 11/91)

44 Carman, Patrick. *Eve of Destruction* (6–9). 2012, HarperCollins $17.99 (978-006210182-2). The seven teens introduced in *Dark Eden* (2011) return to Fort Eden in hopes of finding a cure for the side effects they have been suffering since eliminating their crippling phobias. ∩ **e** Lexile HL770L (Rev: BL 3/1/12; SLJ 5/1/12)

45 Carman, Patrick. *Floors* (4–7). 2011, Scholastic $16.99 (978-0-545-25519-6). Charged with taking care of the magical Whippet Hotel, Leo and his dad must protect the place from a foreboding future hinted at by mysterious clues. **e** Lexile 870L (Rev: BL 10/15/11; SLJ 11/1/11)

46 Cavanagh, Helen. *Panther Glade* (5–8). 1993, Simon & Schuster paper $16.00 (978-0-671-75617-8). Bill spends a summer in Florida with his great-aunt Cait. He's afraid of the Everglades and alligators, but he comes to appreciate Indian history and crafts. (Rev: BL 6/1–15/93; SLJ 6/93; VOYA 10/93)

47 Caveney, Philip. *Prince of Explorers* (7–10). Illus. by Jonny Duddle. Series: Sebastian Darke. 2010, Delacorte $17.99 (978-038573469-1). Accompanied by tiny warrior Cornelius and snarky buffalope Max, Sebastian works his way through dense jungle to find the lost city of Mendip, facing danger at every turn. **e** (Rev: BLO 4/15/10; SLJ 5/10)

48 Caveney, Philip. *Prince of Pirates* (7–10). Series: Sebastian Darke. 2009, Delacorte $16.99 (978-038573468-4); LB $19.99 (978-038590466-7). In the second book in the series, Sebastian Darke and his sidekicks try out the pirate life and sail off in search of treasure. Lexile 830L (Rev: BL 4/1/09; VOYA 10/09)

49 Cole, Stephen. *Thieves till We Die* (8–11). 2007, Bloomsbury $16.95 (978-1-59990-082-7). Nathaniel Coldhart sends his band of teen outlaws on another action-packed adventure (after 2006's *Thieves Like Us*), this time to steal a priceless sword. (Rev: BL 5/1/07; SLJ 5/07)

5

50 Conly, Jane Leslie. *Murder Afloat* (5–8). 2010, Hyperion/Disney $17.99 (978-142310416-2). In the 1870s privileged 14-year-old Benjamin is kidnapped and put to work aboard an oyster ship in this suspenseful high seas adventure. (Rev: BL 12/1/10; HB 11–12/10; LMC 1–2/11; SLJ 3/1/11)

51 Cooney, Caroline B. *Flash Fire* (7–10). 1995, Scholastic paper $14.95 (978-0-590-25253-9). A girl's wish for a more exciting life comes true when a fire sweeps the wealthy Los Angeles neighborhood where she lives. (Rev: BL 11/1/95; SLJ 12/95; VOYA 12/95)

52 Cooney, Caroline B. *Flight No. 116 Is Down* (7–10). 1992, Scholastic paper $14.95 (978-0-590-44465-1). With a lightning pace, the author depicts the drama and human interest inherent in disaster. (Rev: BL 1/15/92; SLJ 2/92)

53 Couloumbis, Audrey. *Maude March on the Run! or, Trouble Is Her Middle Name* (5–7). 2007, Random House $15.99 (978-0-375-83246-8). In this action-packed sequel to *The Misadventures of Maude March*, 16-year-old Maude and her 12-year-old sister, both orphans, are pursued by the law after Maude is unjustly accused of multiple crimes. (Rev: SLJ 1/07)

54 Creech, Sharon. *The Wanderer* (5–9). Illus. by David Diaz. 2000, HarperCollins LB $17.89 (978-0-06-027731-4). In this Newbery Honor Book, 13-year-old Sophie, her two cousins, and three uncles sail across the Atlantic to England in a 45-foot yacht. (Rev: BCCB 4/00*; BL 4/1/00; HB 5–6/00; HBG 10/00; SLJ 4/00*)

55 Crocker, Carter. *Last of the Gullivers* (5–7). 2012, Philomel $16.99 (978-039924231-1). Twelve-year-old orphan Michael is a boy headed for trouble until he finds purpose when he discovers a village full of Lilliputians and is entrusted with their care. ℮ Lexile 750L (Rev: BL 2/1/12; HB 9–10/12; SLJ 2/12)

56 Cummings, Priscilla. *The Journey Back* (7–10). 2012, Dutton $16.99 (978-052542362-1). Fourteen-year-old Digger Griswald has many adventures when he escapes from a juvenile detention center and heads toward home to protect his mother from his abusive father. ℮ Lexile 810L (Rev: BL 12/1/12; LMC 5–6/13; SLJ 1/13)

57 DeFelice, Cynthia. *Lostman's River* (5–7). 1994, Macmillan LB $15.00 (978-0-02-726466-1). Tyler's trust is betrayed when he takes an eccentric scientist to a secret rookery in the Everglades and the man reveals himself to be an unscrupulous plume hunter. (Rev: BCCB 6/94; BL 5/15/94; HB 9–10/94; SLJ 7/94)

58 Demers, Barbara. *Willa's New World* (5–8). 2000, Coteau paper $6.95 (978-1-55050-150-6). An adventure story set in Canada around 1800 in which 15-year-old Willa is sent to a trading post on Hudson's Bay. (Rev: BL 9/15/00; SLJ 9/00)

59 Docherty, Jimmy. *The Ice Cream Con* (6–10). 2008, Scholastic $16.99 (978-0-545-02885-1). Jake, who lives in a bad section of Glasgow, is tired of getting mugged and spreads a rumor about a bodyguard called the Big Baresi in this fun, vulgar, action-packed story. (Rev: BL 5/1/08; SLJ 6/08)

60 Doder, Joshua. *A Dog Called Grk* (5–8). 2007, Delacorte $14.99 (978-0-385-73359-5). In this fast-paced adventure, 12-year-old Londoner Tim, trying to help the Stanislavian ambassador's family — and dog — becomes enmeshed in international political intrigue. A sequel is *Grk and the Pelotti Gang* (2007). (Rev: BL 1/1–15/07; SLJ 3/07)

61 Dowd, John. *Rare and Endangered: A Caribbean Island Eco-Adventure* (6–8). 2000, Peachtree paper $5.95 (978-1-56145-217-0). While tagging turtles on an exotic island, Jim and Julia must save themselves and their friend Miles from evil poachers. (Rev: SLJ 7/00; VOYA 6/00)

62 Doyle, Bill, and David Borgenicht. *Everest* (4–8). Illus. by Yancey Labat. Series: Worst-Case Scenario Ultimate Adventure. 2011, Chronicle $12.99 (978-0-8118-7123-5). Readers are invited to participate in the decision-making process in this choose-your-own-adventure style story of a team trying to summit Mount Everest. ℮ (Rev: SLJ 6/11)

63 Doyle, Roddy. *Wilderness* (5–7). 2007, Scholastic $16.99 (978-0-439-02356-6). Johnny and Tom must find their mother in frozen Lapland when her dogsled team is lost; meanwhile the boys' half sister is reunited with her own mother, who left her family long ago. (Rev: BL 11/15/07; HB 1–2/08; SLJ 11/07)

64 Draper, Penny. *Terror at Turtle Mountain* (4–7). 2006, Coteau paper $7.95 (978-1-55050-343-2). In Canada's Northwest Territory in 1903, a 13-year-old girl participates in frantic efforts to rescue victims of a rock slide; an action-packed novel based on a real-life incident. (Rev: SLJ 10/06)

65 Eames, Brian. *The Dagger Quick* (4–7). 2011, Simon & Schuster $15.99 (978-1-4424-2311-4). Kitto, a 12-year-old with a clubfoot, finds himself setting out to sea with his long-lost pirate uncle in this fast-paced adventure set in the 17th century. ℮ Lexile 690L (Rev: LMC 11–12/11; SLJ 8/11)

66 Easton, Kelly. *Aftershock* (7–10). 2006, Simon & Schuster $16.95 (978-1-4169-0052-8). Mute and in shock after seeing his parents die in a car crash, Adam hitchhikes from Idaho to Rhode Island, his life flashing through his mind as he makes his way home. (Rev: BL 12/15/06; SLJ 12/06)

67 Ewing, Lynne. *Drive-By* (5–8). 1996, HarperCollins paper $4.99 (978-0-06-440649-9). When Tito's brother is killed in a gang-related shooting, he is bullied and threatened by the gang to reveal where his brother hid a cache of stolen money. (Rev: SLJ 8/96)

68 Fama, Elizabeth. *Overboard* (4–8). 2002, Cricket $15.95 (978-0-8126-2652-0). Fourteen-year-old Emily struggles to save her own life and that of a boy named

Isman when a ferry sinks off the coast of Sumatra. (Rev: BCCB 6/02; BL 7/02; HBG 10/02; SLJ 7/02)

69 Fardell, John. *The Flight of the Silver Turtle* (5–8). 2006, Putnam $15.99 (978-0-399-24382-0). The same crew from *The 7 Professors of the Far North* (2005) must find an antigravity machine before the villains discover it, in an exciting chase around Europe. (Rev: BL 12/15/06; SLJ 10/06)

70 Ferraiolo, Jack D. *Sidekicks* (6–9). 2011, Abrams/ Amulet $16.95 (978-0-8109-9803-2). Middle-schooler Scott, aka Bright Boy, is proud of his role as a sidekick of superhero Phantom Justice until an unfortunate exposure on live TV complicates his situation and makes him question his purpose. ∩ ℮ Lexile 620L (Rev: BL 4/15/11; LMC 10/11; SLJ 7/11*)

71 Ferris, Jean. *Song of the Sea* (7–9). Series: American Dreams. 1996, Avon paper $3.99 (978-0-380-78199-7). In the second title of this adventure series, set on the sea and in the Yucatan in 1814, privateer Raider Lyons lies near death as a result of wounds inflicted by the evil Captain Lawrence of the British navy and longs for the love of Rosie. (Rev: VOYA 10/96)

72 Fields, T. S. *Danger in the Desert* (5–7). 1997, Rising Moon $12.95 (978-0-87358-666-5); paper $6.95 (978-0-87358-664-1). A survival story about two boys who endure great hardships when they are left without food or supplies in the desert. (Rev: HBG 3/98; SLJ 11/97)

73 Fleck, Earl. *Chasing Bears: A Canoe-Country Adventure* (5–8). Illus. by author. 1999, Holy Cow paper $12.95 (978-0-930100-90-2). An adventure story set near the Minnesota-Canada border that involves Danny, a 12-year-old who is on a canoe trip with his father and older brother. (Rev: SLJ 12/99)

74 Fleischman, Paul. *The Half-a-Moon Inn* (5–7). Illus. by Kathryn Jacobi. 1991, HarperCollins paper $5.99 (978-0-06-440364-1). A young mute boy sets out to find his mother in a violent snowstorm.

75 Fleischman, Sid. *The Ghost in the Noonday Sun* (5–7). Illus. by Warren Chappell. 1989, Scholastic paper $3.50 (978-0-590-43662-5). This pirate story features all the standard ingredients — a shanghaied boy, a villainous captain, and buried treasure. (Rev: VOYA 8/89)

76 Fleischman, Sid. *The Whipping Boy* (5–7). 1986, Greenwillow $16.99 (978-0-688-06216-3). Prince Brat and his whipping boy, Jemmy, who takes the blame for all the bad things the prince does, find their roles reversed when they meet up with CutWater and Hold-Your-Nose Billy. Newbery Medal 1987. (Rev: BCCB 3/86; BL 3/1/86; SLJ 5/86)

77 Flores-Galbis, Enrique. *Raining Sardines* (6–9). 2007, Roaring Brook $16.95 (978-1-59643-166-9). A dramatic, operatic adventure set in pre-revolutionary Cuba, where young Ernestina and Enriquito ultimately triumph over an evil landowner after encountering

much danger and magic. (Rev: BCCB 6/07; BL 4/1/07; SLJ 4/07)

78 Freedman, Benedict, and Nancy Freedman. *Mrs. Mike* (7–12). 1968, Berkley paper $5.99 (978-0-425-10328-9). Based on a true story, this tells of Kathy, her love for her Mountie husband Mike, and her hard life in the Canadian Northwest.

79 Frost, Helen. *Diamond Willow* (6–9). 2008, Farrar $16.00 (978-0-374-31776-8). A survival story in diamond-shaped poems about 12-year-old Diamond Willow, a part-Athabascan girl caught with her blind dog in a blizzard in Alaska; she's saved with the help of her ancestral spirits. (Rev: BL 6/1–15/08; SLJ 6/08)

80 Garland, Sherry. *The Silent Storm* (4–7). 1993, Harcourt $14.95 (978-0-15-274170-9). Alyssa, who has lost both of her parents in a violent storm and has become mute because of the trauma, hears that another hurricane is approaching. (Rev: BCCB 4/93; BL 6/1–15/93; SLJ 7/04)

81 George, Jean Craighead. *Julie of the Wolves* (5–8). Illus. by John Schoenherr. 1974, HarperCollins LB $16.89 (978-0-06-021944-4); paper $5.99 (978-0-06-440058-9). Julie (Inuit name, Miyax) begins a trek across frozen Alaska and is saved only by the friendship of a pack of wolves. Newbery Medal 1973.

82 George, Jean Craighead. *Julie's Wolf Pack* (5–7). Series: Julie of the Wolves. 1997, HarperCollins LB $18.89 (978-0-06-027407-8). Kapu, leader of the pack, is captured by researchers in this continuing story of Julie and her wolf friends. (Rev: BL 9/1/97; HBG 3/98; SLJ 9/97; VOYA 6/98)

83 George, Jean Craighead. *Shark Beneath the Reef* (7–9). 1989, HarperCollins $13.95 (978-0-06-021992-5); paper $5.99 (978-0-06-440308-5). The story of a young Mexican boy who is torn between becoming a shark fisherman like his father or going to college to be a marine biologist. (Rev: BL 6/1/89; SLJ 6/89; VOYA 6/89)

84 George, Jean Craighead. *The Talking Earth* (6–8). 1983, HarperCollins paper $5.99 (978-0-06-440212-5). A young Seminole girl spends three months in the Everglades alone. (Rev: BL 11/1/88)

85 George, Jean Craighead. *Water Sky* (6–8). 1987, HarperCollins paper $6.99 (978-0-06-440202-6). A boy is sent by his father to an Eskimo whaling camp to learn survival techniques. (Rev: BL 2/1/87)

86 Gilman, David. *The Devil's Breath* (7–12). Series: Danger Zone. 2008, Delacorte $16.99 (978-038573560-5); LB $19.99 (978-038590546-6). In this action-packed adventure tale, 15-year-old Max Gordon embarks on a search for his missing father in the Namibian desert; the first installment in a series. ∩ (Rev: BL 11/1/08; SLJ 10/1/08)

87 Gilman, David. *Ice Claw* (7–12). Series: Danger Zone. 2010, Delacorte $15.99 (978-0-385-73561-2);

LB $18.99 (978-0-385-90547-3). During an extreme sports competition in the French Pyrenees, 15-year-old Max Gordon becomes embroiled in a complex plot involving a Basque monk and a potential ecological disaster. ℮ Lexile 810L (Rev: BL 2/15/10; SLJ 5/10)

88 Golden, Christopher, and Tim Lebbon. *The Sea Wolves* (7–10). Illus. by Greg Ruth. Series: Secret Journeys of Jack London. 2012, HarperCollins $16.99 (978-006186320-2). An action-packed story in which 18-year-old Jack London is captured by werewolf pirates. ℮ (Rev: BL 2/1/12; SLJ 2/12)

89 Golding, Julia. *Cat O'Nine Tails* (5–8). Series: Cat Royal Adventures. 2009, Roaring Brook $16.99 (978-159643445-5). Cat and her friends are kidnapped and pressed into service in the British Navy and must use guile and courage to survive as they travel to the New World, where Cat becomes engaged to a Creek Indian. Lexile 760L (Rev: BL 11/1/09; SLJ 11/09; VOYA 2/10)

90 Golding, William. *Lord of the Flies* (8–12). 1999, Viking paper $15.00 (978-0-14-028333-4). When they are marooned on a deserted island, a group of English schoolboys soon lose their civilized ways.

91 Goodman, Joan Elizabeth. *Paradise* (7–12). 2002, Houghton Mifflin $16.00 (978-0-618-11450-4). The fictionalized story of Marguerite de la Rocque, who in 1536, after being left on Canada's Isle of Demons by her explorer uncle, struggled to survive along with her maid and the young man she loved. (Rev: BL 11/15/02; HBG 3/03; SLJ 12/02; VOYA 12/02)

92 Gordon, Amy. *Return to Gill Park* (5–8). Series: Gill Park. 2006, Holiday $16.95 (978-0-8234-1998-2). This oddball sequel to *The Gorillas of Gill Park* (2006) finds Willy Wilson on the trail of vandals determined to destroy the beauty of the park he now owns. (Rev: BL 5/15/06; SLJ 4/06)

93 Gourley, Catherine, ed. *Read for Your Life: Tales of Survival from the Editors of Read Magazine* (5–8). Series: Best of Read. 1998, Millbrook paper $5.95 (978-0-7613-0344-2). This is a collection of excellent survival stories from 50 years of *Read,* a literary magazine for middle and high school students. (Rev: BL 8/98)

94 Graf, Mike. *Bryce and Zion: Danger in the Narrows* (5–8). Illus. by Marjorie Leggitt. Series: Adventures with the Parkers. 2006, Fulcrum paper $9.95 (978-1-55591-532-2). On a vacation in the national parks of southern Utah, 10-year-old twins James and Morgan Parker learn about the delicate ecology of the area, rescue an injured hiker, and come to the aid of their father when he slips and falls in the Narrows; a fact-filled adventure story with full-color photographs and nature sketches. (Rev: SLJ 12/06)

95 Grant, Katy. *Hide and Seek* (5–8). 2010, Peachtree $15.95 (978-1-56145542-3). Chase, 14, enjoys geocaching (using a GPS to locate hidden items) and exploring in the Arizona mountains with his dog; one day

he stumbles on two abducted boys and becomes embroiled in their plight. Lexile 700L (Rev: BL 10/1/10; LMC 11–12/10; SLJ 9/1/10)

96 Grant, Michael. *The Call* (5–8). Series: The Magnificent 12. 2010, HarperCollins $16.99 (978-006183366-3). An ordinary, fearful 12-year-old finds himself pitted against the Pale Queen in this tongue-in-cheek story about overcoming phobias; the first installment in a series. Also use *The Trap*. ℮ Lexile 710L (Rev: BL 11/15/10*)

97 Grant, Michael. *The Key* (5–8). Series: Magnificent 12. 2012, HarperCollins $16.99 (978-006183370-0). In this third volume in the action-packed series, 12-year-old Mack continues his mission to find a dozen 12-year-olds with special powers, at the same time encountering danger, challenges — and achievement; a sequel to *The Call* (2010) and *The Trap* (2011). ℮ Lexile 750L (Rev: BL 10/1/12; SLJ 9/12)

98 Green, Tim. *Pinch Hit* (6–8). 2012, HarperCollins $16.99 (978-006201246-3). Tween movie star Trevor and Little League player Sam, who lead very different lives, discover they are identical twins who were separated at birth, and decide to trade places. ℮ Lexile 730L (Rev: BL 3/15/12; SLJ 3/12; VOYA 2/12)

99 Greenburg, Dan. *Claws* (6–9). 2006, Random House $15.95 (978-0-375-83410-3). A fast-paced story about 14-year-old Cody, on the run from an abusive mother and finding new challenges at a tiger ranch in Texas. (Rev: BL 6/1–15/06; LMC 8–9/06; SLJ 7/06)

100 Gross, Philip. *The Lastling* (8–12). 2006, Clarion $16 (978-0-618-65998-2). Melding themes of the environment, adventure, and personal growth, this exciting story is about Paris — a privileged 14-year-old on a hunting expedition in the Himalayas with her uncle — who befriends a 12-year-old monk-to-be named Tahr and sets in motion a horrifying episode with a young yeti. (Rev: LMC 2/07*; SLJ 12/06)

101 Gutman, Dan. *Getting Air* (5–8). 2007, Simon & Schuster $15.99 (978-0-689-87680-6). Thirteen-year-old Jimmy and five others prevent a hijacking, survive a plane crash, and find themselves faced with surviving in a Canadian forest; girl scout lore comes to their aid and they even find time to build a half-pipe for skateboarding. (Rev: BL 7/07; SLJ 6/07)

102 Gutman, Dan. *Mission Unstoppable* (5–8). Illus. Series: The Genius Files. 2011, HarperCollins $16.99 (978-0-06-182764-8); LB $17.89 (978-0-06-182765-5). Twin geniuses Coke and Pepsi McDonald, 12, are pursued by nefarious government agents while on a cross-country road trip with their parents. ℮ (Rev: BL 12/1/10; LMC 8–9/11; SLJ 3/1/11)

103 Harlow, Joan Hiatt. *Star in the Storm* (4–7). 2000, Simon & Schuster $16.00 (978-0-689-82905-5). This novel, set in Newfoundland in 1912, tells how a girl and her dog save a ship full of stranded passengers. (Rev:

BCCB 3/00; BL 1/1–15/00; HB 3–4/00; HBG 10/00; SLJ 4/00)

104 Harper, Jo. *Delfino's Journey* (6–12). 2001, Texas Tech Univ. $15.95 (978-0-89672-437-2). Delfino and Salvador travel from Mexico to the United States in search of a new life but face many difficult challenges in this novel that interweaves Aztec folklore and information on illegal immigration. (Rev: BL 4/15/01; HBG 10/01)

105 Harris, M. G. *Invisible City* (6–8). Series: The Joshua Files. 2010, Walker $16.99 (978-0-8027-2095-5). After his father is murdered, Joshua continues his archaeological work searching for mysterious Mayan artifacts in this action-filled adventure that also involves possible alien abduction. Lexile 640L (Rev: BL 5/1/10; LMC 8–9/10; SLJ 7/10)

106 Harrison, Michael. *It's My Life* (6–8). 1998, Holiday $15.95 (978-0-8234-1363-8). Martin's mother and her lover conspire to "kidnap" Martin to collect a ransom in this British thriller that is told alternately by Martin and his friend, Hannah. (Rev: BCCB 3/98; BL 3/1/98; HB 5–6/98; HBG 9/98; SLJ 4/98; VOYA 8/98)

107 Haugaard, Erik C. *Under the Black Flag* (5–7). 1994, Roberts Rinehart paper $8.95 (978-1-879373-63-1). Fourteen-year-old William is captured by the pirate Blackbeard and held for ransom in this 18th-century yarn. (Rev: BL 4/1/94; HB 9–10/94; SLJ 5/94)

108 Hausman, Gerald. *Tom Cringle: Battle on the High Seas* (6–8). Illus. by Tad Hills. 2000, Simon & Schuster $16.95 (978-0-689-82810-2). This action novel set in the Caribbean in 1812 tells how an English boy becomes involved in battles, mutinies, an earthquake, and a shipwreck. (Rev: BCCB 7–8/00; BL 11/1/00; HBG 3/01; SLJ 11/00; VOYA 12/00)

109 Hausman, Gerald. *Tom Cringle: The Pirate and the Patriot* (6–8). Illus. by Tad Hills. 2001, Simon & Schuster $16.00 (978-0-689-82811-9). Tom Cringle, a 14-year-old lieutenant in the Royal Navy, fights pirates, braves storms, and conquers slave traders in this sequel to *Tom Cringle: Battle on the High Seas* (2000). (Rev: BL 9/15/01; HBG 3/02; SLJ 10/01)

110 Hawks, Robert. *The Richest Kid in the World* (4–8). 1992, Avon paper $2.99 (978-0-380-76241-5). Josh is kidnapped and taken to the estate of billionaire Grizzle Welch. (Rev: SLJ 5/92)

111 Herlong, M. H. *The Great Wide Sea* (6–10). 2008, Viking $16.99 (978-067006330-7). Not long after their mother's death, three brothers find themselves stranded on an island in the Bahamas when their unpredictable father disappears in an ocean storm. YALSA Top Ten 2010. Lexile 660L (Rev: BL 11/15/08; HB 1–2/09; SLJ 3/1/09)

112 Hesse, Karen. *Safekeeping* (8–11). 2012, Feiwel & Friends $17.99 (978-125001134-3). Radley, 17, is in Haiti when the American president is assassinated and martial law is imposed, with many dissenters imprisoned; she returns home to find her parents are gone, and she and a girl named Celia head overland toward Canada. ⌒ e Lexile 720L (Rev: BL 8/12; LMC 1–2/13; SLJ 8/12; VOYA 12/12)

113 Hesse, Karen. *Stowaway* (5–8). 2000, Simon & Schuster $17.95 (978-0-689-83987-0). Told by an 11-year-old stowaway, this adventurous sea story tells of Captain Cook's two-and-a-half-year voyage around the world beginning in 1768. (Rev: BL 12/15/00; HB 1–2/01; HBG 3/01; SLJ 11/00; VOYA 4/01)

114 Higgins, F. E. *The Black Book of Secrets* (5–7). 2007, Feiwel & Friends $14.95 (978-0-312-36844-9). Joe Zabbidou takes the confessions of everyone in the remote village of Pagus Parvus, collecting them in a black book. Ludlow Fitch, a desperate boy on the run from cruel parents, acts as Joe's scribe, a dangerous position in a dangerous world. (Rev: BL 10/15/07; HB 1–2/08; LMC 4–5/08; SLJ 4/08)

115 Higgins, Jack, and Justin Richards. *Death Run* (5–8). Series: Rich and Jade. 2008, Putnam $16.99 (978-039925081-1). Teenage twins Rich and Jade travel around the world with their secret-agent dad in this action-packed, fast-paced sequel to 2007's *Sure Fire*. e Lexile HL660L (Rev: BL 9/1/08; SLJ 12/08; VOYA 8/08)

116 Higgins, Jack, and Justin Richards. *First Strike* (5–8). Series: Rich and Jade. 2010, Putnam $16.99 (978-039925240-2). When two disparate sets of villains invade the White House with designs on stealing nuclear launch codes, the British twins Rich and Jade and their secret-agent father again save the day. (Rev: BLO 6/10; VOYA 8/10)

117 Higgins, Jack, and Justin Richards. *Sharp Shot* (5–8). Series: Rich and Jade. 2009, Putnam $16.99 (978-0-399-25239-6). In this action-packed volume, the third in a series, twins Jade and Rich find themselves on a dangerous mission to thwart an evil plot after they're attacked by one of their secret agent dad's old enemies. Lexile HL730L (Rev: BLO 11/1/09; SLJ 3/10)

118 Higgins, Jack, and Justin Richards. *Sure Fire* (6–9). Series: Rich and Jade. 2007, Putnam $16.99 (978-0-399-24784-2). When their mother dies suddenly, 15-year-old twins Rich and Jade move to London with their long-absent, secret-agent father, and they soon get caught up in his life of nonstop action. (Rev: BL 10/1/07; SLJ 2/08)

119 Higgins, Simon. *Moonshadow: Rise of the Ninja* (4–7). 2010, Little, Brown $15.99 (978-0-316-05531-4). Moonshadow is forced to test his skills as a ninja when Silver Wolf's warriors attack in this story set in Japan in the time of the samurai. Lexile 840L (Rev: BL 6/10; LMC 8–9/10; SLJ 8/10)

120 Higson, Charlie. *Blood Fever: A James Bond Adventure* (5–8). Series: Young Bond. 2006, Hyperion $16.95 (978-0-7868-3662-8). Even at 13, Bond is having adventures: this one finds him on the island of Sardinia, caught up in an art-theft mystery and rescuing a girl in peril. (Rev: SLJ 6/06)

121 Hilgartner, Beth. *A Murder for Her Majesty* (5–8). 1986, Houghton Mifflin paper $6.95 (978-0-395-61619-2). Alice disguises herself as a boy to escape her father's murderers. (Rev: BCCB 9/86; SLJ 10/86)

122 Hill, David. *Running Hot* (5–8). 2007, Simply Read paper $9.95 (978-1-894965-52-1). A group of students clearing forest trees in rural New Zealand suddenly find themselves threatened by a raging fire. (Rev: SLJ 4/07)

123 Hinton, S. E. *The Outsiders* (7–10). 1967, Viking $17.99 (978-0-670-53257-5). Two rival gangs — the "haves" and "have-nots" — fight it out on the streets of an Oklahoma city. (Rev: BL 11/15/97)

124 Hinton, S. E. *Rumble Fish* (7–10). 1975, Dell paper $5.99 (978-0-440-97534-2). Rusty-James loses everything he loves most — including his brother.

125 Hinton, S. E. *Tex* (7–10). 1979, Dell paper $5.50 (978-0-440-97850-3). Tex and his 17-year-old older brother encounter problems with family, sex, and drugs.

126 Hinton, S. E. *That Was Then, This Is Now* (7–10). 1971, Viking $17.99 (978-0-670-69798-4). Bryon discovers that his "brother" Mark is a drug pusher.

127 Hobbs, Will. *The Big Wander* (7–10). 1992, Avon paper $5.95 (978-0-380-72140-5). Clay Lancaster, 14, and his brother Mike are on a "big wander," their last trip together before Mike goes away to college. (Rev: BL 10/15/92*; SLJ 11/92)

128 Hobbs, Will. *Far North* (7–12). 1996, Morrow $17.99 (978-0-688-14192-9). Fifteen-year old Gabe, his school roommate, and an elderly Native American are stranded in the Canadian wilderness. The boys survive even after the death of the wise old man. (Rev: BL 7/96; SLJ 9/96; VOYA 2/97)

129 Hobbs, Will. *Ghost Canoe* (6–8). 1997, Morrow $16.99 (978-0-688-14193-6); paper $5.99 (978-0-380-72537-3). Mystery, plenty of action, murder, Spanish treasure, and a dangerous villain are some of the elements in this historical adventure set on the northwest coast of Washington state. (Rev: BL 5/1/97; SLJ 4/97; VOYA 8/97)

130 Hobbs, Will. *Jackie's Wild Seattle* (5–8). 2003, HarperCollins LB $16.89 (978-0-06-051631-4). In the aftermath of September 11, 2001, Shannon, 14, and her younger brother spend an exciting and healing summer in Seattle with their animal rescuer uncle. (Rev: BL 6/1–15/03; HBG 4/04; SLJ 5/03; VOYA 8/03)

131 Hobbs, Will. *Jason's Gold* (5–9). 1999, Morrow $17.99 (978-0-688-15093-8). In this sharply realistic novel, 15-year-old Jason leaves Seattle in 1897 and, with a dog he has saved, heads for the Klondike and gold. (Rev: BL 8/99; HB 9–10/99; HBG 3/00; SLJ 11/99)

132 Hobbs, Will. *Leaving Protection* (7–12). 2004, HarperCollins $19.99 (978-0-688-17475-0). An exciting novel about a 16-year-old boy, his work on an Alaskan salmon trawler, and the secret plans of its skipper. (Rev: BL 3/1/04; SLJ 4/04)

133 Hobbs, Will. *The Maze* (6–12). 1998, Morrow $19.99 (978-0-688-15092-1). After living in a series of foster homes and detention centers, Rick escapes to Canyonlands National Park in Utah where he is befriended by a loner who helps him find himself. (Rev: BL 9/1/98; HBG 3/99; SLJ 10/98; VOYA 2/99)

134 Hobbs, Will. *Wild Man Island* (7–10). 2002, HarperCollins LB $16.89 (978-0-06-029810-4); paper $5.99 (978-0-380-73310-1). An adventure story in which 14-year-old Andy becomes stranded on a remote Alaska island, faces many dangers, and tests his dead archaeologist father's theories about the earliest prehistoric immigrants to America. (Rev: BL 4/15/02; HB 7–8/02; HBG 10/02; SLJ 5/02; VOYA 6/02)

135 Hokenson, Terry. *The Winter Road* (6–9). 2006, Front St $16.95 (978-1-932425-45-1). In this survival story, licensed pilot Willa, 17, flies her uncle's plane without permission and crash-lands in the freezing Canadian wilderness. (Rev: BL 6/1–15/06; HB 5–6/06; LMC 11–12/06; SLJ 5/06)

136 Holman, Felice. *Slake's Limbo* (5–9). 1974, Macmillan paper $4.99 (978-0-689-71066-7). Thirteen-year-old Artemis Slake finds an ideal hideaway for four months in the labyrinth of the New York City subway. (Rev: BL 6/1/88)

137 Horowitz, Anthony. *Snakehead: An Alex Rider Adventure* (6–8). Series: Alex Rider. 2007, Philomel $17.99 (978-0-399-24161-1). This seventh title in the series follows Alex as he's reunited with his godfather, Ash, and goes on a mission for the Australian Secret Intelligence Service that brings him face to face with a terrorist organization. (Rev: BL 9/15/07; SLJ 1/08)

138 Houston, James. *Frozen Fire* (6–8). Illus. by author. 1977, Macmillan paper $4.95 (978-0-689-71612-6). An Eskimo boy, Kayak, and his white friend set out to find Kayak's father, a prospector who has disappeared. A sequel is *Black Diamond*.

139 Hunt, L. J. *The Abernathy Boys* (5–7). 2004, HarperCollins LB $16.89 (978-0-06-029259-1). Young Bud and Temple Abernathy survive an eventful journey through the desert in this fictionalized version of a real expedition in the early 20th century. (Rev: BL 1/1–15/04; SLJ 3/04)

140 Hyde, Dayton O. *Mr. Beans* (5–7). 2000, Boyds Mills $14.95 (978-1-56397-866-1). In a small town in Oregon in the early 1940s, bully Mugsy wrongfully accuses a tame bear of attacking him, and timid Chirp frees the bear and takes off with him on a wilderness journey. (Rev: BL 11/15/00; HBG 10/01; SLJ 1/01; VOYA 4/01)

141 Hyland, Hilary. *The Wreck of the Ethie* (4–7). Illus. by Paul Bachem. 1999, Peachtree paper $7.95 (978-1-56145-198-2). Told through the eyes of two youngsters, this is a novelization of a true incident in which a dog saved passengers after their ship sank off the coast of Newfoundland. (Rev: SLJ 4/00)

142 Jacobson, Jennifer Richard. *Small as an Elephant* (4–7). 2011, Candlewick $15.99 (978-0-7636-4155-9). Abandoned in Maine by his bipolar mother, 11-year-old Jack sets out for his Boston home determined to escape detection by adults. ∩ **e** Lexile 790L (Rev: BL 6/1/11; HB 3–4/11; SLJ 4/11; VOYA 2/11)

143 Jaramillo, Ann. *La Línea* (5–8). 2006, Roaring Brook $16.95 (978-1-59643-154-6). Miguel, 15, and his sister Elena, 13, survive a terrifying journey across the border (la linea) from Mexico to California to join their parents. (Rev: BCCB 5/06; BL 3/15/06*; HBG 10/06; LMC 10/06; SLJ 4/06; VOYA 4/06)

144 Jennings, Richard W. *The Pirates of Turtle Rock* (5–8). 2008, Houghton Mifflin $16.00 (978-0-618-98793-1). A modern-day Florida girl falls for a young pirate and the two embark on a treasure hunt for an ancient Caribbean artifact; a novel full of humor and adventure. (Rev: BL 4/15/08; SLJ 8/08)

145 Jinks, Catherine. *Evil Genius* (7–10). 2007, Harcourt $17.00 (978-0-15-205988-0). By age 13, Cadel's illegal computer hacking skills have landed him in the secretive Axis Institute for World Domination, where he's surrounded by aspiring villains but questions his own commitment to the cause. (Rev: BL 5/15/07; SLJ 7/07)

146 Jinks, Catherine. *Genius Squad* (7–10). 2008, Harcourt $17.00 (978-0-15-205985-9). In this fast-paced sequel to *Evil Genius* (2007), 15-year-old Cadel and his friend Sonja join teen computer hackers enlisted to expose an evil corporation. (Rev: BL 6/1–15/08; SLJ 6/08)

147 Jinks, Catherine. *The Genius Wars* (7–10). Series: Genius Trilogy. 2010, Harcourt $17 (978-015206619-2). The trilogy that began with *Evil Genius* (2007) and *Genius Squad* (2008) reaches an ingenious conclusion as Cadel, who has a new family with a police detective as stepfather, travels in search of Prosper English, determined to stop his evil plots. ∩ **e** Lexile 750L (Rev: BL 10/15/10; HB 9–10/10; VOYA 10/10)

148 Johnson, Annabel, and Edgar Johnson. *The Grizzly* (5–7). Illus. by Gilbert Riswold. 1964, HarperCollins paper $4.95 (978-0-06-440036-7). A perceptive story of a father-son relationship in which David, on a camping trip, saves his father's life when a grizzly bear attacks.

149 Johnson, Maureen. *Girl at Sea* (8–11). 2007, HarperTeen $15.99 (978-0-06-054144-6). Clio, 17, is crushed to learn she must spend the summer with her father and his girlfriend sailing on the Mediterranean, but soon discovers that she's part of a treasure hunt. (Rev: BCCB 10/07; BL 7/07; SLJ 6/07)

150 Jung, Mike. *Geeks, Girls, and Secret Identities* (4–7). Illus. by Mike Maihack. 2012, Scholastic $16.99 (978-0-545-33548-5). Vincent, 12, contends with the realization that his superhero idol Captain Stupendous and his crush Polly are the same person even as they work to save Vincent's kidnapped mother. **e** Lexile 790L (Rev: BL 10/15/12; LMC 1–2/13; SLJ 12/12)

151 Karr, Kathleen. *Born for Adventure* (6–9). 2007, Marshall Cavendish $16.99 (978-0-7614-5348-2). While accompanying explorer Henry Morton Stanley on a trip to Africa in 1887, young Tom encounters disease, danger, and disaster. (Rev: BCCB 6/07; BL 4/1/07; LMC 10/07; SLJ 7/07)

152 Kehret, Peg. *Earthquake Terror* (4–7). 1998, Puffin paper $5.99 (978-0-14-038343-0). A violent earthquake strikes the small island on which 12-year-old Jonathan is alone with his younger sister, Abby. (Rev: BCCB 3/96; BL 1/1–15/96; SLJ 2/96)

153 Kelley, Ann. *Lost Girls* (8–12). 2012, Little, Brown $17.99 (978-0-316-09062-9). In 1974 a group of Amelia Earhart cadets and their young troop leader find themselves in severe difficulties on an island off the coast of Thailand in the face of a fierce storm. **e** (Rev: LMC 8–9/12*; SLJ 9/12; VOYA 4/12)

154 Kessler, Cristina. *Trouble in Timbuktu* (7–12). 2009, Philomel $17.99 (978-039924451-3). The history and culture of the city of Timbuktu are an integral part of this novel about Malian twins Ahmed and Ayisha, who embark on a dangerous journey to foil the attempt of two American thieves trying to steal valuable ancient manuscripts. Lexile 900L (Rev: BL 12/15/08; LMC 8–9/09; SLJ 3/1/09; VOYA 6/09)

155 Kinch, Michael. *The Fires of New Sun* (8–12). Series: Blending Time. 2012, Flux paper $9.95 (978-07387307-6-9). After surviving their journey to Africa in the mid-21st century, teens Jaym, Reya, and D'Shay work against treason and violence to unite the native peoples. **e** (Rev: BL 1/1/12; SLJ 4/12; VOYA 2/12)

156 King, Wesley. *The Vindico* (5–8). 2012, Putnam $16.99 (978-0-399-25654-7). A troupe of aging super-villains kidnaps five teens to train as their successors, but James, Lana, Hayden, Emily, and Sam resist their fates when they see the destruction they will be creating. **e** Lexile 700L (Rev: BL 5/15/12; HB 7–8/12; SLJ 8/1/12)

157 Klavan, Andrew. *If We Survive* (8–11). 2012, Thomas Nelson $14.99 (978-159554795-8). Revolution in a Central American country propels 16-year-old Will and his friends, who have just finished a Christian outreach mission, into a desperate bid to escape. ⌒ ℮ (Rev: BL 11/15/12; SLJ 3/13)

158 Konigsburg, E. L. *From the Mixed-Up Files of Mrs. Basil E. Frankweiler* (5–7). Illus. by author. 1967, Macmillan $17.00 (978-0-689-20586-6). Adventure, suspense, detection, and humor are involved when 12-year-old Claudia and her younger brother elude the security guards and live for a week in New York's Metropolitan Museum of Art. Newbery Medal winner, 1968.

159 Korman, Gordon. *The Abduction* (4–7). Series: Kidnapped. 2006, Scholastic paper $4.99 (978-0-439-84777-3). A fast-paced thriller, the opening volume of a new series, in which 15-year-old Aiden works with the FBI to rescue his 11-year-old sister Meg, who was abducted while on her way home from school and is meanwhile resisting her captors. The second volume is *The Search* (2006). (Rev: BL 8/06; SLJ 9/06)

160 Korman, Gordon. *Chasing the Falconers* (4–7). 2005, Scholastic paper $4.99 (978-0-439-65136-3). In this fast-paced adventure, Aiden and Meg Falconer must evade pursuers as they work to gather evidence that will prove their parents' innocence of treason. (Rev: BL 5/15/05; SLJ 8/05)

161 Korman, Gordon. *Zoobreak* (4–7). Series: Swindle. 2009, Scholastic $16.99 (978-054512499-7). When Savannah finds her missing pet monkey Cleo at a floating animal zoo, she and her friends plan a rescue mission; a sequel to *Swindle* (2008). ⌒ ℮ Lexile 700L (Rev: BL 11/1/09; LMC 11–12/09; SLJ 11/09; VOYA 10/09)

162 Kress, Nancy. *Flash Point* (7–10). 2012, Viking $17.99 (978-067001247-3). Desperate for money to help with her sick grandmother and younger sister, 16-year-old Amy signs up for a reality TV show — and surprising stress. ℮ Lexile HL680L (Rev: BL 11/15/12; LMC 1–2/13; SLJ 2/13; VOYA 10/12)

163 LaFevers, R. L. *Theodosia and the Staff of Osiris* (5–8). 2008, Houghton Mifflin $16 (978-061892764-7). Brainy 11-year-old Theodosia solves the puzzles of misplaced mummies and ancient curses — all the while coping with a conniving grandmother and a father in prison — in this witty first-person tale set in Edwardian England. ⌒ ℮ Lexile 750L (Rev: BL 11/15/08; SLJ 12/08)

164 Lamensdorf, Len. *The Crouching Dragon* (6–9). 1999, Seascape $19.95 (978-0-9669741-5-7). In this novel set in a French coastal town in 1959, 14-year-old William and his friends secretly renovate a crumbling castle called the Crouching Dragon. (Rev: BL 9/1/99; VOYA 12/99)

165 Lamensdorf, Len. *The Raging Dragon* (6–9). Series: Will to Conquer. 2002, Seascape $22.95 (978-0-9669741-7-1). William and Louise become embroiled in exciting events in 1960s Paris, including an effort to counter Algerian terrorists, in this sequel to *The Crouching Dragon* (1999). (Rev: BL 10/1/02; SLJ 10/02)

166 Lee, Norman. *Camel Rider* (5–7). 2007, Charlesbridge $15.95 (978-1-58089-314-5). Two boys — a 12-year-old Australian named Adam and Walid, a camel driver from Bangladesh — find themselves alone in the desert during a Middle Eastern war and must struggle to survive; told in alternating first-person narratives, this is an exciting story that also shows how people with no common language can learn to communicate. (Rev: BL 9/1/07; SLJ 7/07)

167 Lee, Tanith. *Piratica II: Return to Parrot Island* (7–10). Series: Piratica. 2006, Dutton $17.99 (978-0-525-47769-3). The second action-packed installment in the series finds Art the pirate queen leaving her husband behind on dry land as she sails the seas on behalf of the government — and perhaps with the opportunity to vanquish old enemies. (Rev: BL 12/15/06; SLJ 4/07)

168 Lester, Alison. *The Snow Pony* (6–12). 2003, Houghton Mifflin $15.00 (978-0-618-25404-0). Fourteen-year-old Dusty's love for Snow Pony lightens the problems of her life in this novel set on an Australian cattle ranch. (Rev: BL 3/15/03; HBG 10/03; SLJ 4/03; VOYA 6/03)

169 Little, Kimberley Griffiths. *Enchanted Runner* (5–7). 1999, Avon $15.00 (978-0-380-97623-2). Twelve-year-old Kendall, who is half Native American, hopes to excel in running as his ancestors did, and is given an unusual opportunity to test himself. (Rev: BCCB 9/99; BL 9/1/99; HBG 3/00; SLJ 12/99)

170 London, C. Alexander. *We Are Not Eaten by Yaks* (5–8). Series: An Accidental Adventure. 2011, Philomel $12.99 (978-0-399-25487-1). When their mother goes missing, 11-year-old twins Oliver and Celia journey with their father to Tibet, where they encounter many dangerous adventures. Also use *We Dine with Cannibals* (2011). ⌒ Lexile 760L (Rev: BL 1/1–15/11; SLJ 4/11)

171 London, C. Alexander. *We Dine with Cannibals* (5–8). Illus. by Jonny Duddle. Series: An Accidental Adventure. 2011, Philomel $12.99 (978-039925488-8). Their explorer father drags 11-year-old twins Celia and Oliver deep into the Amazon in search of El Dorado and their mother in this humorous sequel to *We Are Not Eaten by Yaks* (2011). ℮ Lexile 700L (Rev: BL 11/1/11; SLJ 1/12)

172 Lourie, Peter. *The Lost Treasure of Captain Kidd* (5–8). 1996, Shawangunk paper $10.95 (978-1-885482-03-7). Friends Killian and Alex set out to discover Captain Kidd's treasure buried on the banks of the Hudson River centuries ago. (Rev: BL 2/15/96; SLJ 6/96)

173 Lu, Marie. *Legend* (7–12). 2011, Putnam $17.99 (978-0-399-25675-2). In a future, dystopian California the lives of 15-year-old Day (who commits crimes to help the needy) and June (clever and privileged, with military training) intersect as she hunts for Day and uncovers scary secrets. ∩ ℮ Lexile HL710L (Rev: BL 10/15/11*; HB 11–12/11; LMC 1–2/12*; SLJ 10/1/11)

174 Lupica, Mike. *Hero* (6–9). 2010, Philomel $17.99 (978-0-399-25283-9). Zach's special agent father has died, but Zach has inherited his superpowers and must risk his own life now. (Rev: BL 10/1/10; SLJ 12/1/10)

175 McCaughrean, Geraldine. *The Death-Defying Pepper Roux* (5–8). 2010, HarperCollins LB $17.89 (978-0-06-183666-4). Believing his aunt's prediction that he will die at the age of 14, young Pepper Roux first runs away to sea and then has a series of exciting adventures; set in France. ∩ Lexile 920L (Rev: BL 11/1/09*; HB 1–2/10; LMC 5–6/10; SLJ 1/10)

176 McCaughrean, Geraldine. *The White Darkness* (7–10). 2007, HarperCollins $16.99 (978-0-06-089035-3). Symone is thrilled when her uncle Victor offers to take her on a trip to the South Pole, since her "hero" is Captain Laurence "Titus" Oates, who traveled there in 1911 as part of Robert Scott's expedition. But the trip — and her uncle's obsession — turn out to be more than she bargained for. Printz Award 2008. ∩ (Rev: BL 12/1/06; HB 3–4/07; SLJ 4/07)

177 McFadden, Deanna. *Robinson Crusoe: Retold from the Daniel Defoe Original* (4–7). Illus. by Jamel Akib. Series: Classic Starts. 2006, Sterling $4.95 (978-1-4027-2664-4). The 1719 original text is retold in brief, accessible sentences that portray Crusoe and Friday as equals. (Rev: BL 2/15/06)

178 McNicoll, Sylvia. *Last Chance for Paris* (6–9). 2008, Fitzhenry & Whiteside paper $11.95 (978-1-55455-061-6). Zanna, 14, who had hoped to be in Paris with her mom, ends up instead in the Canadian wilderness searching for her lost twin brother with the help of a wolf puppy. (Rev: BL 3/1/08; SLJ 5/08)

179 MacPhail, Catherine. *Underworld* (7–10). 2005, Bloomsbury $16.95 (978-1-58234-997-8). Five British teens with very different personalities find themselves trapped in a cave on a remote Scottish island; adding to their predicament is their fear of a giant worm reputed to inhabit the caves. (Rev: BL 7/05; SLJ 7/05; VOYA 8/05)

180 Maddox, Jake. *Blizzard!* (5–9). Illus. by Sean Tiffany. Series: A Jake Maddox Sports Story. 2009, Stone Arch LB $23.99 (978-1-4342-1206-1). Two teen boys are on their way to an awards dinner when a catastrophic blizzard challenges their survival skills; suitable for reluctant readers, this easy-reading novel includes large black-and-white illustrations. (Rev: SLJ 6/1/09)

181 Maddox, Jake. *Shipwreck!* (5–9). Illus. by Sean Tiffany. Series: A Jake Maddox Sports Story. 2009, Stone Arch LB $23.99 (978-1-4342-1207-8). When their whale-watching boat sinks, three teens must use their wits to survive sweltering heat, storms, and even a shark attack; suitable for reluctant readers, this easy-

reading novel includes large black-and-white illustrations. (Rev: SLJ 6/1/09)

182 Malaghan, Michael. *Greek Ransom* (4–7). 2010, Andersen paper $9.99 (978-1-84270-786-9). When their archaeologist parents are kidnapped on a Greek island, Nick and Callie must rescue them in an action-packed adventure that includes hidden treasure, exciting chases, and even an earthquake and a monster. (Rev: BL 4/15/10; SLJ 2/10)

183 Marsden, John. *The Dead of Night* (6–10). Series: Tomorrow. 1997, Houghton Mifflin $16.00 (978-0-395-83734-4). In this sequel to *Tomorrow, When the War Began* (1996), the teenage group continues its guerrilla activities against their enemy, a country that has invaded their homeland, Australia. (Rev: HBG 3/98; SLJ 11/97; VOYA 2/98)

184 Marsden, John. *A Killing Frost* (7–12). Series: Tomorrow. 1998, Houghton Mifflin $17.00 (978-0-395-83735-1). In this third episode of an adventure series about a group of Australian teens who fight an enemy that has occupied their country, five young people carry out a plan to sink a container ship. (Rev: BCCB 4/98; BL 5/15/98; HB 7–8/98; HBG 9/98; SLJ 6/98; VOYA 6/98)

185 Marsden, John. *The Other Side of Dawn* (8–12). Series: Tomorrow. 2002, Houghton Mifflin $16.00 (978-0-618-07028-2). Ellie's exploits are at the center of this action-packed seventh and final installment in the Tomorrow series, which leaves Ellie back home after peace has been declared, trying to adjust to postwar life. (Rev: BCCB 10/02; BL 10/15/02; HB 11/02; HBG 3/03; SLJ 10/02; VOYA 2/03)

186 Marsden, John. *Tomorrow, When the War Began* (8–12). 1995, Houghton Mifflin $16.00 (978-0-395-70673-2). A girl and her friends return from a camping trip in the bush to find that Australia has been invaded and their families taken prisoner. (Rev: BL 4/15/95; SLJ 6/95)

187 Marsden, John. *While I Live* (8–12). Series: Ellie Chronicles. 2007, Scholastic $16.99 (978-0-439-78318-7). Ellie is back on her farm after the upheavals of the Tomorrow series, but new violence soon disrupts her life again; knowledge of the previous series will enhance understanding of this new story arc. (Rev: BCCB 6/07; HB 5–6/07; LMC 10/07; SLJ 5/07)

188 Mass, Wendy. *Jeremy Fink and the Meaning of Life* (5–8). 2006, Little, Brown $15.99 (978-0-316-05829-2). Just before his 13th birthday, Jeremy Fink receives a package from his dead father containing a locked box but no keys; Jeremy and Liz set off on a tour of New York City in search of the keys and meet a number of characters with different views on the meaning of life. (Rev: BL 12/15/06; SLJ 12/06)

189 Mazer, Harry. *Snow Bound* (5–7). 1987, Dell $21.50 (978-0-8446-6240-4); paper $5.50 (978-0-440-96134-

5). Tony and Cindy survive for several days after being trapped in a snow storm. (Rev: BL 9/1/89)

190 Messner, Kate. *Capture the Flag* (5–7). 2012, Scholastic $16.99 (978-0-545-39539-7). Seventh-graders Anne, José, and Henry discover that they are all descendants of the Silver Jaguar Society as they investigate the theft of the original Star Spangled Banner. **e** Lexile 700L (Rev: BLO 8/12; LMC 1–2/13; SLJ 10/12)

191 Meyer, L. A. *Bloody Jack: Being an Account of the Curious Adventures of Mary "Jacky" Faber, Ship's Boy* (6–9). 2002, Harcourt $17.00 (978-0-15-216731-8). Orphaned by the plague, Mary Faber disguises herself as a boy and signs up to work on the *HMS Dolphin* to escape life on the streets of 18th-century London. Odyssey Honor Recording 2008. ⌒ (Rev: BL 3/1/03; HB 1–2/03; HBG 3/03; SLJ 9/02; VOYA 12/02)

192 Meyer, L. A. *Curse of the Blue Tattoo: Being an Account of the Misadventures of Jacky Faber, Midshipman and Fine Lady* (6–9). 2004, Harcourt $17.00 (978-0-15-205115-0). Forced to leave her ship after being exposed as a girl, Jacky Faber enrolls in an elite Boston girls' school but frustrates all attempts to make a lady out of her in this sequel to *Bloody Jack* (2002). Odyssey Honor Recording 2009. ⌒ (Rev: BL 5/15/04*; HB 7–8/04; SLJ 7/04; VOYA 8/04)

193 Meyer, L. A. *In the Belly of the Bloodhound: Being an Account of a Particularly Peculiar Adventure in the Life of Jacky Faber* (8–11). Series: Bloody Jack. 2006, Harcourt $17.00 (978-0-15-205557-8). Jacky Faber, girl pirate, is kidnapped along with her classmates from the Lawson Peabody School for Young Girls in Boston; they find themselves on a slave ship bound for North Africa and Jacky must devise an escape plan. Odyssey Honor Recording 2010. ⌒ (Rev: BL 11/1/06; SLJ 1/07)

194 Meyer, L. A. *The Mark of the Golden Dragon: Being an Account of the Further Adventures of Jacky Faber, Jewel of the East, Vexation of the West, and Pearl of the South China Sea* (8–11). Series: Bloody Jack Adventure. 2011, Harcourt $16.99 (978-054751764-3). Thinking Jacky Faber is dead after a typhoon in the South China Sea in 1807, a heartbroken Jaimy Fletcher heads for London even as Jacky has various adventures also on her way there. ⌒ **e** Lexile 1000L (Rev: BL 12/1/11)

195 Meyer, L. A. *Mississippi Jack: Being an Account of the Further Waterborne Adventures of Jacky Faber, Midshipman, Fine Lady, and the Lily of the West* (8–11). Series: Bloody Jack. 2007, Harcourt $17.00 (978-0-15-206003-9). Jacky has plenty of outsized adventures as she travels down the Mississippi in search of her true love in this latest installment. (Rev: BL 11/1/07; SLJ 12/07)

196 Meyer, L. A. *Rapture of the Deep: Being an Account of the Further Adventures of Jacky Faber, Soldier, Sailor, Mermaid, Spy* (7–12). Series: Bloody Jack Adventure. 2009, Harcourt $17 (978-0-15-206501-0). On

her way to her wedding in 1806, Jacky is forced by the British Navy to head for the Caribbean to search for a sunken treasure ship. YALSA Amazing Audiobooks Top Ten 2011. ⌒ (Rev: BL 9/1/09; SLJ 12/09)

197 Meyer, L. A. *Under the Jolly Roger: Being an Account of the Further Nautical Adventures of Jacky Faber* (7–10). Series: Bloody Jack. 2005, Harcourt $17.00 (978-0-15-205345-1). In this volume full of adventure, plucky 15-year-old Jacky Faber — last seen in *Bloody Jack* (2002) and *Curse of the Blue Tattoo* (2004) — travels from Boston to England in 1804 in search of her true love but ends up taking control of a British warship. (Rev: BL 8/05; SLJ 9/05; VOYA 8/05)

198 Meyer, L. A. *The Wake of the Lorelei Lee: Being an Account of the Further Adventures of Jacky Faber, on Her Way to Botany Bay* (8–11). Series: Bloody Jack Adventure. 2010, Harcourt $17 (978-054732768-6). Hopeful that she can start a profitable career with her new ship, Jacky arrives in London only to find herself accused of piracy and sentenced to servitude in Australia; the 8th volume in the series. YALSA Amazing Audiobooks Top Ten 2012. ⌒ **e** Lexile 970L (Rev: BL 9/15/10; VOYA 8/10)

199 Miklowitz, Gloria D. *After the Bomb* (7–12). 1987, Scholastic paper $2.50 (978-0-590-40568-3). This novel describes the experiences of a group of young people after an atomic bomb falls on Los Angeles. (Rev: BL 6/15/86; SLJ 9/85; VOYA 8/85)

200 Miklowitz, Gloria D. *Camouflage* (8–10). 1998, Harcourt $16.00 (978-0-15-201467-4). When 14-year-old Kyle visits northern Michigan to spend a summer with his father, he becomes involved in a government-hating militia movement in which his father is a general. (Rev: BCCB 5/98; HBG 9/98; SLJ 4/98; VOYA 10/98)

201 Miller, Kirsten. *Kiki Strike: Inside the Shadow City* (5–8). 2006, Bloomsbury $16.95 (978-1-58234-960-2). A complex story featuring adventurous and multitalented 12-year-old girls exploring the subterranean levels of New York City. (Rev: BL 7/06; HBG 10/06; LMC 10/06; SLJ 6/06; VOYA 8/06)

202 Miller, Kirsten. *Kiki Strike: The Darkness Dwellers* (5–8). 2013, Bloomsbury $17.99 (978-159990736-9). In Paris Betty Bent rescues Kiki Strike from her evil aunt and the two become involved in a subterranean adventure. **e** (Rev: BL 12/15/12)

203 Milway, Alex. *The Curse of Mousebeard* (4–7). Series: Mousehunter Trilogy. 2010, Little, Brown $15.99 (978-0-316-07744-6). In this followup to 2009's *The Mousehunter,* Emiline and her friends find themselves in the lost land of mice known as Norgammon as they seek a way to free Mousebeard from his curse. **e** (Rev: BLO 5/15/10; SLJ 6/10)

204 Mitchelhill, Barbara. *Storm Runners* (4–8). 2008, Andersen paper $9.95 (978-18427064-0-4). In this thrilling read, global warming turns out to be a conspiracy masterminded by villains, and it's up to 10-year-old Ally and her older sister to save the next city on the bad guys' "hit list"— Edinburgh, Scotland. Lexile 630L (Rev: BL 11/1/08)

205 Mitchell, Nancy. *Global Warning: Attack on the Pacific Rim!* (5–8). Illus. by Darren Wiebe and Ryan T. Fong. Series: The Changing Earth Trilogy. 1999, Lightstream paper $5.95 (978-1-892713-02-5). A thrilling adventure story about Jenny Powers, a wheelchair-bound youngster, who must warn the authorities of an impending biological disaster at her school. (Rev: SLJ 10/99)

206 Moodie, Craig. *Into the Trap* (4–8). 2011, Roaring Brook $15.99 (978-1-59643-585-8). An action-packed story set off the coast of Maine and featuring 12-year-old Eddie, who enlists a summer visitor to help in catching the person who has been stealing his family's lobsters. **e** Lexile 600L (Rev: BL 7/11; SLJ 8/11)

207 Morey, Walt. *Angry Waters* (6–9). 1990, Blue Heron paper $7.95 (978-0-936085-10-4). A hostile 15-year-old boy is unwillingly paroled to a family farm, where he comes to terms with himself. (Rev: VOYA 8/90)

208 Morey, Walt. *Death Walk* (6–10). 1991, Blue Heron $13.95 (978-0-936085-18-0). After being stranded in the Alaskan wilderness, a teenage boy must learn to survive in the harsh climate while on the run from killers. (Rev: BL 6/1/91; SLJ 6/91)

209 Morpurgo, Michael. *Kensuke's Kingdom* (4–7). 2003, Scholastic paper $16.95 (978-0-439-38202-1). A boy washed onto a seemingly deserted island finds a friend in a Japanese soldier who has lived there since World War II. (Rev: BL 2/15/03; HB 5–6/03; HBG 10/03; SLJ 3/03; VOYA 6/03)

210 Morris, Deborah. *Teens 911: Snowbound, Helicopter Crash and Other True Survival Stories* (7–12). 2002, Health Communications paper $12.95 (978-0-7573-0039-4). Five stories that portray teens facing emergencies (being stranded, in helicopter crashes, rescuing residents of burning houses, and so forth) are followed by postscripts and survival quizzes. (Rev: SLJ 2/03; VOYA 2/03)

211 Moulton, Erin E. *Flutter: The Story of Four Sisters and One Incredible Journey* (4–7). 2011, Philomel $16.99 (978-0-399-25515-1). Guided by Vermont folklore, Maple, 9, and her sister Dawn undertake a daring trek into the heart of the mountains to gather water from a mysterious well, hoping to save their premature baby sister's life. (Rev: BLO 5/1/11; SLJ 7/11)

212 Mowat, Farley. *Lost in the Barrens* (7–9). 1985, Bantam paper $5.50 (978-0-553-27525-4). Two boys lost in the wilderness of northern Canada must fight for survival.

213 Mowll, Joshua. *Operation Storm City* (6–8). Illus. Series: The Guild Trilogy. 2009, Candlewick $16.99

(978-0-7636-4224-2). Doug and Becca set out to deliver a secret code to their parents, who are in China searching for the lost city of Ur-Can; set in the 1920s and full of intrigue, this includes many foldouts and added features. Lexile 780L (Rev: BLO 7/09; SLJ 8/09; VOYA 8/09)

214 Mowll, Joshua. *Operation Typhoon Shore* (8–12). Illus. by author, et al. Series: The Guild of Specialists. 2006, Candlewick $15.99 (978-0-7636-3122-2). In 1920, siblings Doug and Becca sail through a typhoon on their uncle's ship while seeking the gyrolabe that may offer a clue to their parents' disappearance; the second installment in the series. (Rev: BL 1/1–15/07; SLJ 3/07)

215 Muller, Rachel Dunstan. *Squeeze* (5–8). Series: Orca Sports. 2010, Orca paper $9.95 (978-1-55469-324-5). Four teens embark on a caving expedition with disastrous results in this suspenseful story full of betrayal and teen drama. **e** Lexile HL640L (Rev: BL 11/1/10; SLJ 10/1/10)

216 Mullin, Mike. *Ashfall* (8–12). 2011, Tanglewood $16.95 (978-1-933718-55-2). Alex, 15, goes on a dangerous search for his family after a supervolcano erupts in Yellowstone Park; this action-packed story combines survival, science fiction, and romance. **e** Lexile 750L (Rev: BL 10/1/11; HB 1–2/12; LMC 1–2/13; SLJ 11/1/11; VOYA 12/11)

217 Myers, Edward. *Survival of the Fittest* (6–9). 2000, Montemayor paper $11.95 (978-0-9674477-2-8). Rus and his cousins survive a plane crash in the Peruvian rainforest and set off through the dangerous terrain in search of help. (Rev: SLJ 1/01)

218 Napoli, Donna Jo. *North* (4–7). 2004, Greenwillow $16.99 (978-0-06-057987-6). Twelve-year-old Alvin, an African American boy fascinated by explorer Matthew Henson, sets off for the Arctic and, with the help of several adults along the way, makes the long and complex journey safely. (Rev: BL 3/1/04; SLJ 5/04)

219 Nolan, Peggy. *The Spy Who Came in from the Sea* (4–8). 1999, Pineapple $14.95 (978-1-56164-186-4). In this adventure story set in World War II Florida, 14-year-old Frank, who has a reputation for lying, is not believed when he claims to have seen a German sub off the coast. (Rev: HBG 3/00; SLJ 1/00)

220 Nordin, Sofia. *In the Wild* (4–7). Trans. from Swedish by Maria Lundin. 2005, Groundwood $15.95 (978-0-88899-648-0). Set in Sweden, this is an adventure story featuring 6th-grade outcast Amanda and bully Philip, who become lost and must rely on their own resources to survive. (Rev: SLJ 10/05)

221 O'Dell, Scott. *The Black Pearl* (7–9). 1967, Houghton Mifflin $17.00 (978-0-395-06961-5). Young Ramon dives into a forbidden cave to collect a fabulous black pearl that in time seems to bring a curse to his family.

15

222 O'Dell, Scott. *Black Star, Bright Dawn* (5–8). 1988, Houghton Mifflin $18.00 (978-0-395-47778-6). An Inuit girl decides to run the 1,197-mile sled dog race called the Iditarod. (Rev: BCCB 6/88; BL 4/1/88; SLJ 5/88; VOYA 6/88)

223 O'Dell, Scott. *Island of the Blue Dolphins* (5–8). 1960, Houghton Mifflin $16.00 (978-0-395-06962-2); paper $6.50 (978-0-440-43988-2). An Indian girl spends 18 years alone on an island off the coast of California in the 1800s. A sequel is *Zia* (1976). Newbery Medal 1961. (Rev: BL 3/1/88)

224 Olshan, Matthew. *Finn* (8–12). 2001, Bancroft $19.95 (978-1-890862-13-8); paper $14.95 (978-1-890862-14-5). Teenage Chloe, who has suffered an abusive childhood, and a pregnant Hispanic girl set off to find new lives in a Huck Finn-like adventure full of insight and social commentary. (Rev: BL 4/1/01; SLJ 4/01; VOYA 4/01)

225 Parkinson, Curtis. *Storm-Blast* (4–8). 2003, Tundra paper $7.95 (978-0-88776-630-5). On a sailing trip in the Caribbean, three teens become stranded in a small dinghy and must use their resources to survive. (Rev: SLJ 10/03; VOYA 8/03)

226 Patneaude, David. *The Last Man's Reward* (5–8). 1996, Albert Whitman LB $15.99 (978-0-8075-4370-2). In this adventure, a group of boys agree to a pact rewarding the last to leave the neighborhood. (Rev: BL 6/1–15/96; SLJ 7/96)

227 Patneaude, David. *A Piece of the Sky* (5–8). 2007, Albert Whitman $15.95 (978-0-8075-6536-0). In Oregon to help his grandfather settle into an assisted-living residence, 14-year-old Russell and his new friend Phoebe, pursued by a sinister character, set off on an unexpectedly dangerous meteorite search. (Rev: SLJ 5/07)

228 Paulsen, Gary. *Brian's Hunt* (6–9). 2003, Random House $14.95 (978-0-385-74647-2). This story of Brian's return to the wilderness at the age of 16, his care for a wounded dog, and his distress over the fate of his Cree friends will please Hatchet fans. (Rev: BCCB 2/04; BL 1/1–15/04; SLJ 12/03)

229 Paulsen, Gary. *Brian's Winter* (5–9). 1996, Delacorte $15.95 (978-0-385-32198-3). In a reworking of the ending of *Hatchet,* in which Brian Robeson is rescued after surviving a plane crash, this novel tells what would have happened had Brian had to survive a harsh winter in the wilderness. (Rev: BL 12/15/95; SLJ 2/96; VOYA 2/97)

230 Paulsen, Gary. *Canyons* (7–10). 1991, Dell paper $5.99 (978-0-440-21023-8). Blennan becomes obsessed with the story of a young Indian boy murdered by white men 100 years before. (Rev: SLJ 9/90)

231 Paulsen, Gary. *The Haymeadow* (6–9). 1992, Dell paper $4.99 (978-0-440-40923-6). A 14-year-old boy takes sheep out to pasture for the summer in this story about a boy who is trying to gain acceptance by his father. (Rev: BL 5/15/92*; SLJ 6/92)

232 Paulsen, Gary. *The River* (5–10). 1991, Delacorte $15.95 (978-0-385-30388-0). In this sequel to *Hatchet*, Paulsen takes the wilderness adventure beyond self-preservation and makes teen Brian responsible for saving someone else. (Rev: BL 5/15/91)

233 Paulsen, Gary. *The Voyage of the Frog* (6–8). 1989, Orchard $15.95 (978-0-531-05805-3). Alone on a 22-foot sailboat, a 14-year-old boy survives a 9-day sea ordeal. (Rev: BL 3/1/89; SLJ 1/89; VOYA 2/89)

234 Paver, Michelle. *Gods and Warriors* (5–8). 2012, Dial $16.99 (978-0-8037-3877-5). A bronze dagger is at the heart of this tale of adventure featuring 12-year-old Hylas and his journeys around the Mediterranean in the Bronze Age. ℰ Lexile 680L (Rev: BL 8/12; LMC 3–4/13; SLJ 10/12; VOYA 12/12)

235 Peck, Robert Newton. *Arly's Run* (6–9). 1991, Walker $16.95 (978-0-8027-8120-8). Orphaned Arly escapes from an early 19th-century Florida work farm and journeys to Moore Haven, where shelter has been arranged for him. (Rev: BL 12/15/91; SLJ 2/92)

236 Peterson, P. J. *Wild River* (4–7). 2009, Delacorte $14.99 (978-0-385-73724-1); LB $17.99 (978-0-385-90656-2). When a kayaking trip with his older brother turns dangerous, 12-year-old Ryan must make life-or-death decisions in this exciting, harrowing tale. ℰ Lexile 420L (Rev: BL 8/09; SLJ 9/09)

237 Petrucha, Stefan. *Teen, Inc.* (8–10). 2007, Walker $16.95 (978-0-8027-9650-9). Jaiden, 14, is being raised by a corporation after being orphaned as a baby, and he's coming to discover that his "parent" is harming his community in this action-packed eco-thriller. (Rev: BL 12/1/07; SLJ 12/07)

238 Pfeffer, Susan Beth. *The Dead and the Gone* (8–12). 2008, Harcourt $17.00 (978-0-15-206311-5). A tilt in the moon's orbit sends Earth into environmental and social chaos, and Alex, Bri, and Julie must fend for themselves and find food, safety, and shelter when their parents disappear. (Rev: BL 5/15/08; SLJ 8/08)

239 Philbrick, Rodman. *Max the Mighty* (6–9). 1998, Scholastic $16.95 (978-0-590-18892-0); paper $6.99 (978-0-590-57964-3). Maxwell Kane and his new friend Worm, who is being abused by her stepfather, run away in a cross-country search for Worm's real father. (Rev: BL 6/1–15/98; HB 7–8/98; HBG 9/98; SLJ 4/98; VOYA 6/98)

240 Pilling, Ann. *The Year of the Worm* (5–7). 2000, Lion paper $7.50 (978-0-7459-4294-0). Lonely Peter Wrigley, who is mourning his father's death, gets his chance to become a hero when he uncovers a group of birds'-nest poachers in this English novel set in the Lake District. (Rev: SLJ 3/01)

241 Potter, Ellen. *The Kneebone Boy* (4–8). 2010, Feiwel & Friends $16.99 (978-0-312-37772-4). Otto, Lucia, and Max Hardscrabble, three idiosyncratic children, have many adventures while looking for their long-absent mother in a British seaside town. ℮ Lexile 850L (Rev: BL 9/15/10; HB 9–10/10; LMC 11–12/10; SLJ 9/1/10)

242 Pratchett, Terry. *Nation* (7–10). 2008, HarperCollins $16.99 (978-0-06-143301-6). In this survival tale, a tidal wave leaves survivors of very different backgrounds to re-create civilization and consider what it is they treasure and why. (Rev: BL 8/08)

243 Ransome, Arthur. *Swallows and Amazons* (4–7). Illus. by author. 1985, Godine paper $14.95 (978-0-87923-573-4). These adventures of the four Walker children have been read for many years. A reissue. Others in the series *Swallowdale* (1985); *Peter Duck* (1987).

244 Ransome, Arthur. *Winter Holiday* (4–7). Illus. by author. 1989, Godine paper $14.95 (978-0-87923-661-8). Further adventures of the Swallows and Amazons. A reissue. A sequel is *Coot Club*.

245 Rees, Celia. *Pirates!* (7–10). 2003, Bloomsbury $17.95 (978-1-58234-816-2). Horrified by the prospect of an arranged marriage to a plantation owner, teenage Nancy and a close slave friend run off and join a pirate crew in this swashbuckling adventure set in the 18th century. (Rev: BCCB 1/04; BL 12/15/03*; HBG 4/04; SLJ 10/03*)

246 Reichs, Kathy. *Seizure* (6–9). 2011, Penguin $17.99 (978-159514394-5). In this action-packed sequel to *Virals* (2010), Tory and her friends put their heads together to save their parents' jobs. (Rev: BL 12/15/11; SLJ 1/12)

247 Repp, Gloria. *Mik-Shrok* (4–8). Illus. by Jim Brooks. 1998, Bob Jones Univ. paper $7.49 (978-1-57924-069-1). A married missionary couple journey to a remote Alaska village in 1950, where they begin their work and, in time, acquire a dog team led by Mik-Shrok. (Rev: BL 3/1/99)

248 Richards, Justin. *The Chaos Code* (7–10). 2007, Bloomsbury $16.95 (978-1-59990-124-4). Matt's father is missing, and Matt must travel through time and kingdoms to find him in this fast-paced tale. ⌒ (Rev: BL 10/15/07)

249 Richardson, V. A. *The Moneylender's Daughter* (5–8). 2006, Bloomsbury $17.95 (978-1-58234-885-8). In this exciting sequel to *The House of Windjammer* (2003), Adam Windjammer sets sail for America, finds himself burdened with more responsibility on the death of his uncle, and is preoccupied with thoughts of Jade van Helsen, daughter of the man who brought his family to the brink of ruin. (Rev: BL 6/1–15/06; SLJ 9/06)

250 Riordan, Rick. *The Maze of Bones* (4–8). Series: The 39 Clues. 2008, Scholastic $12.99 (978-054506039-4);

LB $12.99 (978-054509054-4). Part adventure story, part online gaming platform, this book kicks off a ten-title series with the story of orphans Amy and Dan, who decipher clues and puzzles in their round-the-world quest. ⌒ ℮ Lexile 610L (Rev: BL 10/15/08; LMC 5–6/09; SLJ 11/1/08*)

251 Rochman, Hazel, and Darlene Z. McCampbell, eds. *Leaving Home* (7–12). 1997, HarperCollins LB $16.89 (978-0-06-024874-1). These 16 stories by well-known writers describe various forms of leaving home, from immigration to a new country to running away or taking a trip. (Rev: BL 1/1–15/97; SLJ 3/97*)

252 Rodkey, Geoff. *Deadweather and Sunrise* (6–8). 2012, Putnam $16.99 (978-039925785-8). An entertaining pirate romp in which 13-year-old Egbert, son of a planter in the Caribbean, battles to protect a hidden treasure from a wealthy villain with a lovely daughter. ℮ Lexile 940L (Rev: BL 6/12; SLJ 6/12)

253 Rodman, Sean. *Infiltration* (7–12). 2011, Orca LB $16.95 (978-155469986-5); paper $9.95 (9781554699858). Abandoned-buildings explorer Bex feels threatened when a newcomer devises a plan more dangerous and exciting than he could have imagined. ℮ Lexile HL570L (Rev: BL 10/15/11; SLJ 3/12)

254 Rollins, James. *Jake Ransom and the Howling Sphinx* (5–8). 2011, HarperCollins $16.99 (978-0-06-147382-1). An evil mummified creature delivers an ominous message to siblings Jake and Kady, who must fight for their lives in this fast-paced archaeological time-travel thriller. ⌒ ℮ Lexile 700L (Rev: LMC 11–12/11; SLJ 10/1/11; VOYA 8/11)

255 Rossell, Judith. *Jack Jones and the Pirate Curse* (4–7). 2007, Walker $15.95 (978-0-8027-9661-5). Jack inherits the family curse and finds himself suddenly facing a band of vengeful pirates he knows he must fight with brain rather than brawn. (Rev: BL 4/1/07; SLJ 6/07)

256 Ruckman, Ivy. *Night of the Twisters* (6–8). 1984, HarperCollins paper $5.99 (978-0-06-440176-0). An account based on actual events about children who survive a devastating series of tornadoes.

257 Salisbury, Graham. *Night of the Howling Dogs* (5–8). 2007, Random House $16.99 (978-0-385-73122-5). Dylan, an 8th-grader from Hilo, Hawaii, goes on a trip to the coast with his scout troop to camp in the shadow of a volcano and faces a bully and natural disasters. ⌒ (Rev: BL 8/07; HB 9–10/07; SLJ 8/07)

258 Schrefer, Eliot. *The School for Dangerous Girls* (8–11). 2009, Scholastic $16.99 (978-054503528-6). Angela, 15, uncovers what is happening to the "hopeless cases" at her Colorado reform school in this suspenseful novel about cruelty and punishment. (Rev: BL 2/1/09; LMC 5–6/09; SLJ 2/1/09)

259 Scrimger, Richard. *Into the Ravine* (6–9). 2007, Tundra paper $9.95 (978-0-88776-822-4). Jules, Chris,

17

and Cory build a raft and float down the town creek in this adventure that has all the elements boys could want — including bullies, cute girls, and jewel thieves; the action will appeal to reluctant readers. (Rev: BL 11/1/07; SLJ 1/08)

260 Shahan, Sherry. *Death Mountain* (5–8). 2005, Peachtree $15.95 (978-1-56145-353-5). In this gripping thriller, 14-year-old Erin uses her survival skills to rescue her new friend Mae and navigate their way through a mountain wilderness to safety. (Rev: SLJ 11/05; VOYA 2/06)

261 Shahan, Sherry. *Ice Island* (4–7). 2012, Delacorte $15.99 (978-038574154-5); LB $18.99 (978-037599009-0). Thirteen-year-old Tatum finds herself on a scary dogsled trip in this survival story full of facts about Alaska. e (Rev: BL 3/1/12; LMC 5–6/12; SLJ 1/12)

262 Shusterman, Neal. *Dissidents* (7–10). 1989, Little, Brown $13.95 (978-0-316-78904-2). A teenage boy joins his mother, the American ambassador in Moscow, and becomes involved in a spy caper. (Rev: BL 8/89; SLJ 10/89)

263 Simmons, Kristen. *Article 5* (7–12). 2012, Tor $17.99 (978-076532958-5). In a postwar America where Moral Statutes have replaced the Bill of Rights, 17-year-old Ember, usually non-confrontational, is perplexed when her former boyfriend arrests her mother for noncompliance. ∩ e Lexile HL660L (Rev: BL 3/15/12; LMC 8–9/12; SLJ 5/1/12; VOYA 4/12)

264 Skurzynski, Gloria, and Alane Ferguson. *Cliff-Hanger* (4–7). Series: Mysteries in Our National Parks. 1999, National Geographic $15.95 (978-0-7922-7036-2). In Mesa Verde National Park, the Landon family encounters two problems — a foster care girl named Lucky, who is deceitful, and a rampaging cougar. (Rev: BL 4/15/99; HBG 10/99; SLJ 5/99)

265 Smelcer, John. *The Great Death* (6–8). 2009, Henry Holt $15.99 (978-080508100-8). Native Alaskan sisters Maura and Millie struggle to survive after an epidemic brought by white men wipes out the population of their village. ∩ (Rev: BL 7/09; LMC 10/09; SLJ 11/09)

266 Smelcer, John. *The Trap* (6–9). 2006, Henry Holt $15.95 (978-0-8050-7939-5). Johnny, a young Native American, sets out to find his grandfather, who is caught in an animal trap in the Alaskan wilderness. (Rev: HB 11–12/06; SLJ 10/06)

267 Smith, Cotton. *Dark Trail to Dodge* (7–10). 1997, Walker $20.95 (978-0-8027-4158-5). Eighteen-year-old Tyrel Bannon faces unusual problems on his first cattle drive when rustlers attack and plan on taking no prisoners. (Rev: BL 6/1–15/97; VOYA 8/97)

268 Smith, Roland. *Cryptid Hunters* (5–8). 2005, Hyperion $15.99 (978-0-7868-5161-4). Thirteen-year-old twins Marty and Grace find themselves in an action-packed adventure in the Congo. (Rev: BL 2/1/05; SLJ 5/05)

269 Smith, Roland. *Eruption* (5–8). Series: Storm Runners. 2012, Scholastic $16.99 (978-054508174-0). While in Mexico pursuing a missing circus act, Chase and his dad end up a hair too close to an erupting volcano and a few wild animals. (Rev: BL 3/15/12)

270 Smith, Roland. *Peak* (8–11). 2007, Harcourt $17.00 (978-0-15-202417-8). Aptly named Peak joins his father in Tibet, where he may become the youngest person (at 14) to climb Mount Everest; this is an exciting, multilayered adventure story. ∩ (Rev: BL 4/1/07; HB 5–6/07; SLJ 6/07)

271 Smith, Roland. *Storm Runners* (5–8). Series: Storm Runners. 2011, Scholastic $16.99 (978-0-545-08175-7). Chase, 13, is well prepared for the challenges posed by a hurricane, a bus accident, and escaped zoo animals in this exciting, fast read. (Rev: BL 4/15/11; SLJ 4/11)

272 Soto, Gary. *Crazy Weekend* (4–7). 1994, Scholastic paper $13.95 (978-0-590-47814-4). Two boys are being pursued by some crooks in this fast-moving adventure story. (Rev: BCCB 7–8/94; SLJ 3/94)

273 Sperry, Armstrong. *Call It Courage* (5–8). Illus. by author. 1968, Macmillan $16.95 (978-0-02-786030-6); paper $4.99 (978-0-689-71391-0). The "Crusoe" theme is interwoven with this story of a Polynesian boy's courage in facing the sea he feared. Newbery Medal 1941.

274 Springer, Nancy. *Lionclaw* (5–8). Series: Tales of Rowan Hood. 2002, Putnam $16.99 (978-0-399-23716-4). Gentle, music-loving Lionel abandons his timidity when Rowan Hood is captured, but, despite his newfound courage, his father still refuses to accept him in this sequel to *Rowan Hood: Outlaw Girl of Sherwood Forest* (2001). (Rev: BL 10/1/02; HBG 10/03; SLJ 10/02; VOYA 12/02)

275 Springer, Nancy. *Outlaw Princess of Sherwood* (4–7). Series: Tales of Rowan Hood. 2003, Putnam $16.99 (978-0-399-23721-8). The third installment of this series features Princess Ettarde, whose father has hatched a dastardly plot to lure Etty away from Sherwood Forest. (Rev: BL 12/1/03; HBG 4/04; SLJ 9/03)

276 Steer, Dugald, ed. *Pirateology: The Sea Journal of Captain William Lubber* (4–7). Illus. by Yvonne Gilbert. 2006, Candlewick $19.99 (978-0-7636-3143-7). An authentic-looking large-format scrapbook chronicling the pirate-chasing adventures of a sea captain of old, complete with treasure maps and a working compass. (Rev: BL 7/06; SLJ 12/06)

277 Stenhouse, Ted. *Murder on the Ridge* (5–8). 2006, Kids Can $16.95 (978-1-55337-892-1); paper $6.95 (978-1-55337-893-8). Will and Arthur, a white boy and an Indian boy who are friends despite the prejudices of 1950s Canada, investigate a World War I mystery in the latest installment in the series that started with *Across* *the Steel River* (2001) and *A Dirty Deed* (2003). (Rev: BL 5/15/06)

278 Stevenson, Robin. *Dead in the Water* (5–8). Series: Orca Sports. 2008, Orca paper $9.95 (978-1-55143-962-4). While at sea as part of a sailing camp, Simon ends up a captive on a boat full of poachers in this thriller for reluctant readers. (Rev: BL 3/15/08)

279 Stewart, A. C. *Ossian House* (6–8). 1976, Phillips LB $26.95 (978-0-87599-219-8). An 11-year-old boy inherits a mansion in Scotland and sets out alone to live there for the summer.

280 Stewart, Trenton Lee. *The Mysterious Benedict Society and the Perilous Journey* (4–7). Illus. by Diana Sudyka. Series: The Mysterious Benedict Society. 2008, Little, Brown $16.99 (978-0-316-05780-6). Reynie, Kate, Sticky, and Constance have many adventures as they travel to rescue Mr. Benedict from the evil Mr. Curtain in this action-packed sequel to *The Mysterious Benedict Society* (2007). (Rev: BL 3/15/08; SLJ 5/08)

281 Strickland, Brad. *The House Where Nobody Lived* (5–8). Series: Lewis Barnavelt. 2006, Dial $16.99 (978-0-8037-3148-6). Lewis befriends David, whose family has moved into a creepy, long-abandoned house, which may be haunted; with help from Uncle Jonathan and a neighborhood witch, Lewis confronts magic and danger. (Rev: BL 1/1–15/07; SLJ 1/07)

282 Sullivan, Paul. *The Unforgiving Land* (7–10). 1996, Fireworks paper $9.99 (978-0-88092-256-2). A white trader gives guns and bullets to a group of Inuit, causing a breakdown in the delicate harmony between nature and humankind and destruction of the Inuit way of life. (Rev: VOYA 8/96)

283 Swarthout, Glendon, and Kathryn Swarthout. *Whichaway* (7–10). 1997, Rising Moon paper $6.95 (978-0-87358-676-4). A reissue of an exciting story about a boy whose character is tested when he is trapped with two broken legs on top of a windmill in an isolated area of Texas. (Rev: HBG 3/98; VOYA 2/98)

284 Taylor, Theodore. *The Cay* (5–8). 1987, Doubleday $16.95 (978-0-385-07906-8); paper $4.95 (978-0-380-00142-2). A blind boy and an old black sailor are shipwrecked on a coral island. (Rev: BL 9/1/89)

285 Taylor, Theodore. *Ice Drift* (4–7). 2005, Harcourt $16.00 (978-0-15-205081-8). Inuit brothers Alika, 14, and Sulu, 10, struggle to survive over the months that they are trapped on an ice floe that is slowly floating south in the Greenland Strait. (Rev: BL 2/1/05; SLJ 1/05)

286 Taylor, Theodore. *The Odyssey of Ben O'Neal* (6–8). Illus. by Richard Cuffari. 1991, Avon paper $3.99 (978-0-380-71026-3). Action and humor are skillfully combined in this story of a trip by Ben and his friend Tee to England at the turn of the 20th century. Two others in the series *Teetoncey; Teetoncey and Ben O'Neal* (both 1981).

287 Thomas, Jane Resh. *Blind Mountain* (4–7). 2006, Clarion $15.00 (978-0-618-64872-6). Forced to go on a hiking trip with his bossy father in the mountainous Montana wilderness, 12-year-old Sam finds himself in charge of their survival when his father is temporarily blinded by a branch. (Rev: BL 12/1/06; SLJ 12/06)

288 Thomas, Jane Resh. *Courage at Indian Deep* (5–7). 1984, Houghton Mifflin paper $6.95 (978-0-395-55699-3). A young boy must help save a ship caught in a sudden storm.

289 Thompson, Julian. *The Grounding of Group Six* (8–12). 1983, Avon paper $3.99 (978-0-380-83386-3). Five 16-year-olds think they are being sent to an exclusive school but actually they have been slated for murder.

290 Tomlinson, Theresa. *Voyage of the Snake Lady* (6–9). 2007, Eos $16.99 (978-0-06-084739-5). Myrina and her fellow women warriors must come to the aid of Iphigenia, the daughter of Agamemnon, in this sequel to *The Moon Riders* that draws on ancient Greek mythology. (Rev: BL 11/15/07; SLJ 3/08)

291 Torrey, Michele. *Voyage of Ice* (4–7). Series: Chronicle of Courage. 2004, Knopf LB $17.99 (978-0-375-92381-4). In 1851, 15-year-old Nick signs on as a hand aboard the whaler *Sea Hawk* and soon discovers unexpected hardships, including struggling to survive in the Arctic. (Rev: BL 5/15/04; SLJ 7/04)

292 Townsend, John Rowe. *The Islanders* (7–10). 1981, HarperCollins $11.95 (978-0-397-31940-4). Two strangers washed up on a remote island are regarded as enemies by the inhabitants. **e**

293 Townsend, John Rowe. *Kate and the Revolution* (7–10). 1983, HarperCollins LB $12.89 (978-0-397-32016-5). A 17-year-old girl is attracted to a visiting prince and then the adventure begins.

294 Ullman, James R. *Banner in the Sky* (7–9). 1988, HarperCollins LB $12.89 (978-0-397-30264-2); paper $6.99 (978-0-06-447048-3). The thrilling story of a boy's determination to conquer a challenging Swiss mountain. (Rev: SLJ 2/88)

295 Umansky, Kaye. *Solomon Snow and the Stolen Jewel* (4–7). 2007, Candlewick $12.99 (978-0-7636-2793-5). In this sequel to *Solomon Snow and the Silver Spoon* (2005), Solomon and Prudence set out to help Prudence's father escape from a prison ship and become caught up in a plot to steal a cursed ruby. (Rev: BL 4/15/07; SLJ 7/07)

296 Volponi, Paul. *Hurricane Song* (7–12). 2008, Viking $15.99 (978-0-670-06160-0). Miles and his father find themselves in the middle of the chaos following Hurricane Katrina when they head to the New Orleans Superdome for shelter. (Rev: BL 5/1/08; SLJ 8/08)

297 Wallace, Bill. *Danger in Quicksand Swamp* (4–7). 1989, Holiday $16.95 (978-0-8234-0786-6). While searching for buried treasure, Ben and Jake become stranded on an island near Quicksand Swamp. (Rev: BL 1/1/90; SLJ 10/89)

298 Wallace, Bill. *Trapped in Death Cave* (5–8). 1984, Holiday $16.95 (978-0-8234-0516-9). Gary is convinced his grandpa was murdered to secure a map indicating where gold is buried.

299 Walters, Eric. *Northern Exposures* (5–8). 2008, Fitzhenry & Whiteside paper $11.95 (978-1-55455-107-1). In this fast-paced novel, a 13-year-old boy finds himself on an adventure when he wins a trip to photograph polar bears and gets involved with poachers; this will appeal to reluctant readers. (Rev: SLJ 2/09)

300 Watson, Jude. *In Too Deep* (4–7). Series: 39 Clues. 2009, Scholastic $12.99 (978-054506046-2); LB $12.99 (978-054509064-3). Amy and Dan travel to Australia searching for clues to their parents' disappearance while battling threats from humans and animals in this sixth installment in the series. ⌒ e Lexile 550L (Rev: BL 1/1/10)

301 Westerfeld, Scott. *Leviathan* (7–10). Illus. by Keith Thompson. 2009, Simon & Schuster $19.99 (978-1-4169-7173-3). An exciting steampunk adventure set in an alternate 1914 and featuring Prince Alek, son of the assassinated Archduke Ferdinand and a member of the technologically innovative Clankers, and Deryn, a girl from opposing Darwinist England masquerading as a boy in order to fly on the giant airship *Leviathan*. ALA Notable Books 2010; YALSA Popular Paperbacks for Young Adults Top Ten 2011. e Lexile 790L (Rev: BL 8/09; HB 11–12/09; SLJ 9/09)

302 Weyn, Suzanne. *Empty* (5–8). 2010, Scholastic $17.99 (978-054517278-3). In this dystopian story, three teens struggle to survive in a world thrown into chaos by global warming and lack of petroleum. (Rev: BL 10/15/10; LMC 3–4/11; SLJ 1/1/11)

303 Whittaker, Dorothy Raymond. *Angels of the Swamp* (6–8). 1991, Walker $17.95 (978-0-8027-8129-1). Two teenage orphans who manage to survive on an island off the Florida coast discover they're not alone. (Rev: BL 1/15/92; SLJ 4/92)

304 Wild, K. *Firefight* (7–10). 2009, Scholastic $16.99 (978-043987176-1). Super-strong Freedom Smith must defeat an evil gang of kidnappers; world travel, action, the supernatural, and even romance combine in this exciting story, a sequel to *Fight Game* (2007). Lexile HL640L (Rev: BLO 3/24/09; SLJ 8/09)

305 Wilkins, Kay. *A Scaly Tale* (4–7). Illus. by Ailin Chambers. Series: Ripley's Bureau of Investigation. 2010, Ripley paper $4.99 (978-18939515-2-5). After a half-man, half-reptile creature is spotted in the Florida Everglades, Ripley's Bureau of Investigation sends a team with special powers to look into the matter. e Lexile 820L (Rev: BL 9/1/10)

306 Williams, Michael. *The Genuine Half-Moon Kid* (7–10). 1994, Dutton $15.99 (978-0-525-67479-5). Like questing Jason in Greek mythology, 18-year-old South African Jay Watson sets out with some friends to find a yellow wood box left him by his grandfather. (Rev: BL 6/1–15/94)

307 Wilson, N. D. *Leepike Ridge* (4–7). 2007, Random House $15.99 (978-0-375-83873-6). Eleven-year-old Tom must use his survival skills when he finds himself trapped in a series of caves where he meets Reg, who's been trapped for three years, and discovers mysterious carvings on the wall. (Rev: BL 5/15/07; HB 5–6/07; LMC 10/07; SLJ 5/07)

308 Withers, Pam. *Camp Wild* (7–9). Series: Orca Currents. 2005, Orca paper $7.95 (978-1-55143-361-5). For reluctant readers, this is the story of 14-year-old Wilf, who must learn to work with others to succeed in his escape from summer camp. (Rev: SLJ 10/05; VOYA 10/05)

309 Withers, Pam. *First Descent* (8–12). 2011, Tundra $17.95 (978-177049257-8). In this adventure-filled book, whitewater daredevil Rex, 17, succeeds in kayaking an uncharted Colombian river — and avoiding guerrillas and paramilitary forces — with the help of a native young woman named Myriam. e Lexile 830L (Rev: BL 10/15/11; SLJ 1/12; VOYA 12/11)

310 Woods, Brenda. *Saint Louis Armstrong Beach* (4–7). 2011, Penguin $16.99 (978-0-399-25507-6). When Hurricane Katrina arrives, 12-year-old clarinet-playing Saint Louis Armstrong Beach makes plans to get the dog he loves, Shadow, to safety. e Lexile 660L (Rev: BL 11/15/11; HB 11–12/11; LMC 1–2/12*; SLJ 10/1/11*)

311 Wynne-Jones, Tim. *The Maestro* (6–8). 1996, Orchard LB $17.99 (978-0-531-08894-4). This moving novel describes a boy's maturation in the wilderness of northern Ontario and his friendship with a gifted musician. (Rev: BL 12/15/96*; SLJ 1/97; VOYA 4/97)

312 Yolen, Jane, and Robert J. Harris. *The Rogues* (6–10). Series: Scottish Quartet. 2007, Philomel $18.99 (978-0-399-23898-7). In the late 18th century, Roddy Macallan's family is forced to leave its Scottish tenant farm; Roddy goes back to retrieve a treasure and finds himself in big trouble, from which he is saved by a rogue named Alan Dunbar; historical facts are found throughout the adventure, which ends in North America. (Rev: BL 9/15/07; SLJ 9/07)

313 Young, E. L. *The Black Sphere* (5–8). Illus. Series: STORM. 2009, Dial $16.99 (978-0-8037-3268-1). Three 14-year-olds — Andrew, Will, and Gaia — save the day in this thriller featuring high-tech intrigue and budding romance. (Rev: BL 2/1/09; SLJ 9/09; VOYA 3/09)

314 Zindel, Paul. *Reef of Death* (7–12). 1998, HarperCollins $15.95 (978-0-06-024728-7). A tale of terror about two teens, a monster creature that lives on an Australian reef, and a mad geologist who has a torture chamber on her freighter. (Rev: BL 3/1/98; HBG 9/98; SLJ 3/98; VOYA 4/98)

Animal Stories

315 Adler, C. S. *More Than a Horse* (5–7). 1997, Clarion $15.00 (978-0-395-79769-3). Leeann and her mother move to a dude ranch in Arizona, where the young girl develops a love of horses. (Rev: BCCB 3/97; BL 3/15/97; SLJ 4/97)

316 Adler, C. S. *One Unhappy Horse* (5–7). 2001, Clarion $16.00 (978-0-618-04912-7). Set on a small ranch near Tucson, this novel features 12-year-old Jan, her horse, Dove, an old lady in a retirement home, and Jan's new friend, Lisa. (Rev: BL 3/1/01; HBG 10/01; SLJ 4/01)

317 Adler, C. S. *That Horse Whiskey!* (6–8). 1996, Avon paper $3.99 (978-0-380-72601-1). Lainey, 13, disappointed that she didn't get a horse for her birthday, works at a stable training a stubborn horse and falls for a city boy. (Rev: BL 11/1/94; SLJ 11/94; VOYA 12/94)

318 Alter, Judith. *Callie Shaw, Stable Boy* (5–8). 1996, Eakin $16.95 (978-1-57168-092-1). During the Great Depression, Callie, disguised as a boy, works in a stable and uncovers a race-fixing racket. (Rev: BL 2/1/97; SLJ 8/97)

319 Alter, Judith. *Maggie and a Horse Named Devildust* (5–7). 1989, Ellen C. Temple paper $5.95 (978-0-936650-08-1). Maggie is determined to ride her spirited horse in the Wild West show in this historical horse story. (Rev: BL 4/15/89)

320 Alter, Judith. *Maggie and the Search for Devildust* (5–7). 1989, Ellen C. Temple paper $5.95 (978-0-936650-09-8). Maggie, a gorgeous girl of the Old West, sets out to find her horse, which has been stolen. (Rev: BL 10/1/89)

321 Appelt, Kathi. *The Underneath* (4–8). Illus. by David Small. 2008, Atheneum $16.99 (978-1-4169-5058-5). Newborn kittens, a bloodhound named Ranger, and a water snake find safety together in this story set in the mysterious bayous of East Texas. Newbery Honor 2009. (Rev: BL 5/15/08; SLJ 6/08)

322 Armstrong, William H. *Sounder* (6–10). 1969, HarperCollins LB $17.89 (978-0-06-020144-9); paper $5.99 (978-0-06-440020-6). The moving story of an African American sharecropper, his family, and his devoted coon dog, Sounder. A sequel is *Sour Land* (1971). Newbery Medal 1970.

323 Bagnold, Enid. *National Velvet* (5–8). Illus. by Ted Lewin. 1985, Avon paper $4.99 (978-0-380-71235-9).

The now-classic story of Heather Brown and her struggle to ride in the Grand National. A reissue. (Rev: BL 12/15/85)

324 Bastedo, Jamie. *Tracking Triple Seven* (5–7). 2001, Red Deer paper $9.95 (978-0-88995-238-6). Benji, a teenage boy grieving his mother's death, becomes involved with biologists tracking grizzly bears near his father's mine in Canada. (Rev: BL 2/1/02)

325 Benchley, Peter. *Jaws* (8–12). 1974, Doubleday paper $6.99 (978-0-449-21963-8). The best-selling novel about a small Long Island town and the creature that became a threat to its beaches.

326 Blom, Jen J. *Possum Summer* (4–7). Illus. by Omar Rayyan. 2011, Holiday House $17.95 (978-0-8234-2331-6). Eleven-year-old Princess ("P") misses her father when he is stationed in Iraq, and ignoring his advice about wild animals she rescues a baby possum on their Oklahoma ranch. (Rev: BL 5/1/11; SLJ 6/11)

327 Brooke, Lauren. *Heartland: Coming Home* (4–7). 2000, Scholastic paper $4.99 (978-0-439-13020-2). When her mother dies, Amy works through her grief by helping horses with behavioral problems in this novel set on a Virginia horse farm. (Rev: BL 9/15/00)

328 Brown, Paul. *Wolf Pack of the Winisk River* (6–12). 2009, Lobster paper $10.95 (978-189755010-6). Told in free verse from a wolf's point of view, this story takes the reader into the life of a wolf pack. (Rev: BL 4/15/09; LMC 10/09; SLJ 12/09)

329 Burgess, Melvin. *The Cry of the Wolf* (5–8). 1994, Morrow $17.99 (978-0-397-30693-0). Young Ben Tilley insists that wolves run past his farm in rural Surrey, even though they have supposedly been gone from England for 500 years. (Rev: BL 10/15/92; SLJ 9/92)

330 Burnford, Sheila. *Bel Ria* (7–12). 2006, Random House $17.95 (978-1-59017-211-7). Set in France during World War II, this is a novel about a poodle's amazing adventures.

331 Carlson, Nolan. *Summer and Shiner* (5–8). 1992, Hearth paper $6.95 (978-0-9627947-4-2). In a small Kansas town in the 1940s, 12-year-old Carley adopts a raccoon called Shiner. (Rev: BL 9/15/92)

332 Cleary, Beverly. *Strider* (5–9). 1991, Morrow LB $17.89 (978-0-688-09901-5). In this sequel to the 1984 Newbery winner *Dear Mr. Henshaw*, Leigh Botts is beginning high school and still writing in his diary, with his beloved dog, Strider, by his side. (Rev: BCCB 10/91; BL 7/91*; HB 9–10/91; SLJ 9/91)

333 DeJong, Meindert. *Along Came a Dog* (4–7). Illus. by Maurice Sendak. 1958, HarperCollins paper $5.95 (978-0-06-440114-2). The friendship of a timid, lonely dog and a toeless little red hen is the basis for a very moving story, full of suspense.

334 Eckert, Allan W. *Incident at Hawk's Hill* (6–8). Illus. by John Schoenherr. 1995, Bantam paper $6.99 (978-0-316-20948-9). A 6-year-old boy wanders away from home and is nurtured and protected by a badger.

335 Gallico, Paul. *The Snow Goose* (7–12). 1941, Knopf $15.00 (978-0-394-44593-9); paper $9.99 (978-0-7710-3250-9). A hunchbacked artist and a young child nurse a wounded snow goose back to health, and it later returns to protect them in this large, illustrated 50th anniversary edition of the classic tale. (Rev: BL 9/15/92)

336 George, Jean Craighead. *The Cry of the Crow* (5–7). 1980, HarperCollins paper $5.99 (978-0-06-440131-9). Mandy finds a helpless baby crow in the woods and tames it.

337 George, Jean Craighead. *Frightful's Mountain* (5–8). 1999, Dutton $18.99 (978-0-525-46166-1). Frightful, the falcon in *My Side of the Mountain,* is the central character in this novel in which she has difficult and enjoyable adventures in the wild. (Rev: BL 9/1/99; HBG 3/00; SLJ 9/99; VOYA 6/00)

338 Ghent, Natale. *No Small Thing* (5–8). 2005, Candlewick $15.00 (978-0-7636-2422-4). Nathaniel and his siblings struggle to keep their horse while their single mother struggles to keep her family afloat. (Rev: BL 3/1/05; SLJ 4/05)

339 Ghent, Natale. *Piper* (5–7). 2001, Orca paper $6.95 (978-1-55143-167-3). The love and attention young Wesley showers on a tiny Australian shepherd puppy helps her recover from the death of her father. (Rev: BL 3/1/01)

340 Gipson, Fred. *Old Yeller* (6–9). Illus. by Carl Burger. 1956, HarperCollins $23.00 (978-0-06-011545-6); paper $5.99 (978-0-06-440382-5). A powerful story set in the Texas hill country about a 14-year-old boy and the ugly stray dog he comes to love. Also use *Savage Sam* (1976).

341 Graeber, Charlotte. *Grey Cloud* (6–8). 1979, Macmillan $8.95 (978-0-02-736690-7). Tom and Orville become friends when they train pigeons for a big race.

342 Hall, Elizabeth. *Child of the Wolves* (4–7). 1996, Houghton Mifflin $16.00 (978-0-395-76502-9). Granite, a Siberian husky pup, must survive in the wilderness when he is separated from his family. (Rev: BCCB 3/96; BL 4/1/96; VOYA 6/96)

343 Hall, Lynn. *The Soul of the Silver Dog* (5–8). 1992, Harcourt $16.95 (978-0-15-277196-6). A handicapped dog bonds with his new teenage owner living in a troubled family. (Rev: BL 4/15/92; SLJ 6/92)

344 Heinz, Brian. *Cheyenne Medicine Hat* (4–8). Illus. by Gregory Manchess. 2006, Creative Editions $18.95 (978-1-56846-181-6). The story of a summer in the life of a wild mustang mare as she tries to keep her band safe from predators — both animal and human. (Rev: SLJ 11/06)

345 Henkes, Kevin. *Protecting Marie* (5–7). 1995, Greenwillow $19.99 (978-0-688-13958-2). Fanny is afraid that she will lose her pet dog if her temperamental father decides the dog must go. (Rev: BCCB 3/95; BL 3/15/95; HB 7–8/95; SLJ 5/95*)

346 Henry, Marguerite. *King of the Wind* (5–8). Illus. by Wesley Dennis. 1990, Macmillan $17.95 (978-0-02-743629-7). The story of the famous stallion Godolphin Arabian, ancestor of Man O'War and founder of the Thoroughbred breed. Also use *Black Gold* and *Born to Trot* (both 1987). Newbery Medal 1949.

347 Henry, Marguerite. *Mustang, Wild Spirit of the West* (6–8). Illus. by Robert Lougheed. 1992, Macmillan paper $4.99 (978-0-689-71601-0). An excellent horse story written by a master.

348 High, Linda O. *Hound Heaven* (5–8). 1995, Holiday $15.95 (978-0-8234-1195-5). More than anything in the world, Silver Iris wants a dog, but her grandfather won't allow it. (Rev: BCCB 12/95; SLJ 11/95; VOYA 2/96)

349 Holland, Isabelle. *Toby the Splendid* (6–8). 1987, Walker $13.95 (978-0-8027-6674-8). An intense argument arises between mother and daughter when young Janet buys a horse and wants to start riding. (Rev: BL 4/1/87; SLJ 4/87; VOYA 8/89)

350 Howard, Jean G. *Half a Cage* (6–8). 1978, Tidal $5.50 (978-0-930954-07-9). Ann's pet monkey causes so many problems she wonders if she should give it away.

351 Hunter, Erin. *Seekers: The Quest Begins* (5–8). Series: Seekers. 2008, HarperCollins $16.99 (978-0-06-087122-2). Readers are introduced to three bear cubs — a polar bear, a black bear, and a grizzly — in this first installment in a series about survival and the realities of bear life in the wild and in captivity. (Rev: BL 5/15/08)

352 Jimenez, Juan Ramon. *Platero y Yo / Platero and I* (5–7). Trans. by Myra Cohn Livingston and Joseph F. Dominguez. Illus. by Antonio Frasconi. 1994, Clarion $16.00 (978-0-395-62365-7). Using both Spanish and English texts, this book contains excerpts from the prose poem about a writer and his donkey. (Rev: BL 6/1–15/94) [863]

353 Jones, Adrienne. *The Hawks of Chelney* (7–9). 1978, HarperCollins $13.95 (978-0-06-023057-9). A young outcast and his girlfriend try to understand the hawks and their habits.

354 Kehret, Peg. *Ghost Dog Secrets* (5–7). 2010, Dutton $16.99 (978-0-525-42178-8). The ghost of an abused dog helps 6th-grader Rusty locate and save other abused dogs in this slightly creepy story with a strong, believable protagonist. Lexile 730L (Rev: BL 10/1/10; LMC 1–2/11; SLJ 9/1/10; VOYA 8/10)

355 Kipling, Rudyard. *The Jungle Book: The Mowgli Stories* (4–7). Illus. by Jerry Pinkney. 1995, Morrow

$25.99 (978-0-688-09979-4). Eight stories about Mowgli are reprinted with 18 handsome watercolors. (Rev: BCCB 6/96; BL 10/15/95; SLJ 11/95)

356 Kjelgaard, James A. *Big Red* (6–9). 1956, Holiday $17.95 (978-0-8234-0007-2); paper $5.50 (978-0-553-15434-4). This is the perennial favorite about Danny and his Irish setter. Continued in *Irish Red* and *Outlaw Red*. (Rev: BL 9/1/89)

357 Kjelgaard, James A. *Snow Dog* (6–8). 1983, Bantam paper $4.99 (978-0-553-15560-0). In the wilderness, a snow dog fights for survival. A sequel is *Wild Trek*.

358 Kjelgaard, James A. *Stormy* (6–8). 1983, Bantam paper $5.50 (978-0-553-15468-9). Alan is helped to accept his father's being sent to prison through love for a retriever named Stormy.

359 Levin, Betty. *Look Back, Moss* (5–8). 1998, Greenwillow $15.00 (978-0-688-15696-1). Young Moss, disturbed by his mother's lack of attention and his own weight problems, welcomes an injured sheepdog into the family. (Rev: BCCB 10/98; BL 8/98; HB 1–2/99; HBG 3/99; SLJ 11/98)

360 Lippincott, Joseph W. *Wilderness Champion* (7–9). 1944, HarperCollins $11.95 (978-0-397-30099-0). This novel, now almost 50 years old, tells about a most unusual hound dog.

361 Lowry, Lois. *Stay! Keeper's Story* (5–8). 1997, Houghton Mifflin $16.00 (978-0-395-87048-8). A dog named Keeper narrates this story about his puppyhood and the three different masters he has had. (Rev: BL 11/1/97; HBG 3/98; SLJ 10/97)

362 Malterre, Elona. *The Last Wolf of Ireland* (5–7). 1990, Houghton Mifflin $15.00 (978-0-395-54381-8). Devin and his friend Katey hide wolf pups when the pups are threatened. (Rev: BCCB 10/90; BL 9/15/90*; SLJ 10/90)

363 Martin, Ann M. *Everything for a Dog* (5–8). 2009, Feiwel & Friends $16.99 (978-0-312-38651-1). Three separate story lines introduce Bone, a dog who has suffered through losing more than one home; Sunny, a dog who comforts her young master after his brother's death; and a boy named Henry who longs to have a dog. (Rev: BL 6/1–15/09)

364 Morey, Walt. *Gentle Ben* (5–8). 1991, Puffin paper $6.99 (978-0-14-036035-6). A warm story of deep trust and friendship between a boy and an Alaskan bear.

365 Morey, Walt. *Scrub Dog of Alaska* (4–8). 1989, Blue Heron paper $7.95 (978-0-936085-13-5). A pup, abandoned because of his small size, turns out to be a winner. Also use *Kavik the Wolf Dog* (1977).

366 Morey, Walt. *Year of the Black Pony* (5–8). Illus. by Fredrika Spillman. 1989, Blue Heron paper $6.95 (978-0-936085-14-2). A family story about a boy's love for his pony in rural Oregon at the turn of the 20th century.

367 Morgan, Clay. *The Boy Who Spoke Dog* (5–8). 2003, Dutton $15.99 (978-0-525-47159-2). Marooned on an island dominated by two warring dog packs, Jack, a young cabin boy, feels very much alone until he develops a friendship with a border collie named Moxie. (Rev: BL 1/1–15/04; SLJ 1/04; VOYA 6/04)

368 Morpurgo, Michael. *Shadow* (6–9). 2012, Feiwel & Friends $16.99 (978-0-312-60659-6). The loss of his dog continues to haunt Afghan refugee Aman, 14, even as he is in a British prison awaiting deportation back to his homeland; is there really hope he will get Shadow back? ∩ Lexile 780L (Rev: BL 9/15/12; HB 11–12/12; LMC 3–4/13; SLJ 11/12)

369 Mowat, Farley. *The Dog Who Wouldn't Be* (4–7). Illus. by Paul Galdone. 1957, Bantam paper $4.99 (978-0-553-27928-3). The humorous story of Mutt, a dog of character and personality, and his boy.

370 Mukerji, Dhan Gopal. *Gay-Neck: The Story of a Pigeon* (4–8). Illus. by Boris Artzybasheff. 1968, Dutton $16.99 (978-0-525-30400-5). A boy from India's brave carrier pigeon is selected to perform dangerous missions during World War I. Newbery Medal 1928.

371 Myers, Anna. *Red-Dirt Jessie* (4–7). 1992, Walker $13.95 (978-0-8027-8172-7). In this tale of the Depression era in Oklahoma, 12-year-old Jessie helps keep her family together. (Rev: BCCB 10/92; BL 1/15/93; HB 1–2/93; SLJ 11/92*)

372 Naylor, Phyllis Reynolds. *Saving Shiloh* (4–7). 1997, Simon & Schuster $15.00 (978-0-689-81460-0). In this sequel to the Newbery Medal-winning *Shiloh* and *Shiloh Season*, Marty again encounters the evil Judd Travers, who has been accused of murder. (Rev: BL 9/1/97*; HB 9–10/97; HBG 3/98; SLJ 9/97)

373 Naylor, Phyllis Reynolds. *Shiloh* (4–8). 1991, Macmillan $16.00 (978-0-689-31614-2). When a beagle follows him home, Marty, from a West Virginia family with a strict code of honor, learns a painful lesson about right and wrong. Newbery Medal 1992. (Rev: BCCB 10/91; BL 12/1/91*; HB 1–2/92; SLJ 9/91)

374 Naylor, Phyllis Reynolds. *Shiloh Season* (4–8). 1996, Simon & Schuster $15.00 (978-0-689-80647-6). The evil Judd Travers wants his dog back from the Prestons in this sequel to *Shiloh* (1991). (Rev: BCCB 12/96; BL 11/15/96*; HB 11–12/96; SLJ 11/96)

375 Nuzum, K. A. *The Leanin' Dog* (4–7). 2008, HarperCollins $15.99 (978-0-06-113934-5). A starving dog appears at the door of an unhappy 11-year-old girl's wilderness home. ∩ (Rev: BCCB 11/08; BL 11/15/08; SLJ 10/08)

376 O'Hara, Mary. *My Friend Flicka* (7–12). 1988, HarperCollins paper $6.00 (978-0-06-080902-7). This story about Ken McLaughlin and the filly named Flicka is continued in *Thunderhead, Son of Flicka*.

377 Oppel, Kenneth. *Darkwing* (6–9). 2007, Eos $16.99 (978-0-06-085054-8). In this story set 65 million years ago, Dusk is different from the rest of his colony of chiropters — he's the first bat with the ability to fly and use echo vision — and he uses his abilities to save the colony from other changing species. (Rev: BL 9/1/07; SLJ 9/07)

378 Paley, Jane. *Hooper Finds a Family: A Hurricane Katrina Dog's Survival Tale* (3–7). Illus. 2011, HarperCollins $15.99 (978-0-06-201103-9). A personable yellow Lab orphaned by Hurricane Katrina narrates this inspiring story about adjusting to new surroundings in New York City. ℮ Lexile 540L (Rev: BL 7/11; SLJ 7/11)

379 Parker, Cam. *A Horse in New York* (4–8). 1989, Avon paper $2.75 (978-0-380-75704-6). To save Blue, the horse she rode at summer camp, from destruction, Tiffin has to convince her parents to board him for the winter. (Rev: BL 12/15/89)

380 Peterson, Shelley. *Sundancer* (6–9). 2007, Key Porter paper $7.95 (978-1-55263-842-2). Bird is the only one at Saddle Creek Farm who can handle the new horse, Sundancer, and her work with him helps her through her own personal and family problems. (Rev: BL 8/07)

381 Peyton, K. M. *The Team* (7–9). 1976, HarperCollins $12.95 (978-0-690-01083-1). Ruth is determined to own the special show pony that is for sale.

382 Platt, Chris. *Moon Shadow* (4–7). 2006, Peachtree $14.95 (978-1-56145-382-5). When a wild mustang mare dies giving birth near her Nevada home, 13-year-old Callie vows to raise and train the foal. (Rev: BL 11/1/06; SLJ 1/07)

383 Pyron, Bobbie. *A Dog's Way Home* (4–7). 2011, HarperCollins $16.99 (978-0-06-198674-1); LB $17.89 (978-0-06-198673-4). Told in alternating chapters by Abby, an 11-year-old girl, and Tam, a beloved dog trying to find his way home after the accident in which they both were injured, this tense story ends happily. ∩ (Rev: BL 2/15/11; SLJ 4/11; VOYA 4/11)

384 Rawlings, Marjorie Kinnan. *The Yearling* (6–9). Illus. by N. C. Wyeth. 1983, Macmillan paper $5.95 (978-0-02-044931-7). The classic story of Joss and the orphaned fawn he adopts. (Rev: BL 9/1/89)

385 Salten, Felix. *Bambi: A Life in the Woods* (5–8). 1926, Pocket paper $4.99 (978-0-671-66607-1). The growing to maturity of an Austrian deer.

386 Sewell, Anna. *Black Beauty* (7–9). 1974, Airmont paper $1.50 (978-0-8049-0023-2). The classic sentimental story about the cruelty and kindness experienced by a horse in Victorian England.

387 Sherlock, Patti. *Four of a Kind* (5–9). 1991, Holiday $13.95 (978-0-8234-0913-6). Andy's grandfather agrees to lend him money to buy a pair of horses, and he sets his sights on winning the horse-pulling contest at a state fair. (Rev: BL 12/1/91; SLJ 10/91)

388 Smiley, Jane. *A Good Horse* (4–8). 2010, Knopf $16.99 (978-037586229-8); LB $19.99 (978-037596228-8). Thirteen-year-old Abby worries that her colt Jack might be the offspring of a stolen mare at the same time that she is dealing with the sale of her prized Black George. ℮ (Rev: BL 10/15/10; HB 11–12/10; SLJ 12/1/10)

389 Smiley, Jane. *Pie in the Sky* (4–8). Illus. by Elaine Clayton. 2012, Knopf $16.99 (978-0-375-86968-6); LB $19.99 (978-037596968-3). Ninth-grader Abby tackles various horse problems in this story set in 1960s California; the fourth in a series. ℮ (Rev: BLO 10/1/12; HB 9–10/12; SLJ 9/12; VOYA 8/12)

390 Snelling, Lauraine. *The Winner's Circle* (5–8). Series: Golden Filly. 1995, Bethany House paper $5.99 (978-1-55661-533-7). In this horse story, Trish Evanston, a high school senior who is also a jockey and Triple Crown winner, is being stalked by a mystery man who sends her threatening notes. (Rev: SLJ 10/95; VOYA 4/96)

391 Springer, Nancy. *A Horse to Love* (4–8). 1987, HarperCollins $11.95 (978-0-06-025824-5). Erin's parents buy her a horse hoping that this will help cure her shyness. (Rev: BL 3/87; SLJ 3/87)

392 Sullivan, Paul. *Legend of the North* (7–12). 1995, Fireworks paper $9.99 (978-0-88092-308-8). Set in northern Canada, this novel contains two narratives, the first about a young wolf's struggle for dominance within the pack, and the second about an elderly Inuit and his survival in the harsh tundra regions. (Rev: BL 1/1–15/96; VOYA 4/96)

393 Taylor, Theodore. *Tuck Triumphant* (4–7). 1991, Avon paper $5.99 (978-0-380-71323-3). A 1950s novel about a blind dog in a loving family and the deaf Korean boy they adopt. (Rev: BL 2/1/91)

394 Terhune, Albert Payson. *Lad: A Dog* (7–9). 1993, Puffin paper $7.99 (978-0-14-036474-3). The classic story of a beautiful collie. The beginning of a lengthy series now all out of print.

395 Townsend, Wendy. *The Sundown Rule* (4–7). 2011, Namelos $18.95 (978-1-60898-099-4). Louise's father is on assignment in Brazil and she must live with relatives in a housing development, far from the woods and the animals that Louise so loves. Lexile 750L (Rev: SLJ 4/11)

396 Wedekind, Annie. *Wild Blue: The Story of a Mustang Appaloosa* (4–7). 2009, Feiwel & Friends $12.99 (978-0-312-38424-1). Josiah helps a mustang return to her Idaho home. (Rev: BL 6/1–15/09; SLJ 5/09)

397 Wells, Ken. *Rascal: A Dog and His Boy* (5–8). Illus. by Christian Slade. 2010, Knopf $16.99 (978-037586652-4); LB $19.99 (978-037596652-1). A playful beagle puppy named Rascal learns how to be an alert, responsive dog when his young owner, Meely, is in danger, in this novel set in the Louisiana bayou. Lexile 720L (Rev: BL 9/1/10; LMC 1–2/11)

398 Wilbur, Frances. *The Dog with Golden Eyes* (4–7). 1998, Milkweed paper $6.95 (978-1-57131-615-8). Cassie befriends a white dog that turns out to be an arctic wolf, and she must find his owners before he becomes a target for the police or hunters. (Rev: BCCB 9/98; BL 9/1/98; HBG 3/99; SLJ 7/98; VOYA 8/98)

Classics

Europe

GENERAL AND MISCELLANEOUS

399 de Cervantes, Miguel, and Martin Jenkins. *Don Quixote* (5–8). Illus. by Chris Riddell. 2009, Candlewick $27.99 (978-0-7636-4081-1). Suitably lighthearted, this is a faithful and nicely illustrated retelling of the story of Don Quixote and his exploits. (Rev: BL 4/15/09)

400 Dumas, Alexandre. *The Count of Monte Cristo* (8–12). 1996, Random House $25.95 (978-0-679-60199-9). The classic French novel about false imprisonment, escape, and revenge.

401 Dumas, Alexandre. *The Three Musketeers* (8–12). 1984, Dodd paper $5.95 (978-0-553-21337-9). A novel of daring and intrigue in France. Sequels are *The Man in the Iron Mask* and *Twenty Years After* (available in various editions).

402 Maupassant, Guy de. *The Best Short Stories of Guy de Maupassant* (7–12). 1968, Amereon $26.95 (978-0-88411-589-2). The French master is represented by 19 tales including "The Diamond Necklace."

403 Verne, Jules. *Around the World in Eighty Days* (7–12). 1996, Puffin paper $4.99 (978-0-14-036711-9). Phileas Fogg and servant Passepartout leave on a world trip in this 1873 classic adventure. (Rev: SLJ 7/96)

404 Verne, Jules. *A Journey to the Center of the Earth* (7–12). 1984, Penguin paper $7.00 (978-0-14-002265-0). A group of adventurers enter the Earth through a volcano in Iceland. First published in French in 1864.

405 Verne, Jules. *Twenty Thousand Leagues Under the Sea* (7–12). 1990, Viking paper $5.99 (978-0-14-036721-8). Evil Captain Nemo captures a group of underwater explorers. First published in 1869. A sequel is *The Mysterious Island* (1988 Macmillan).

406 Wyss, Johann. *The Swiss Family Robinson* (6–9). 1999, Bantam paper $4.99 (978-0-440-41594-7). One of many editions of the classic survival story, first published in 1814, of a family marooned on a deserted island.

GREAT BRITAIN AND IRELAND

407 Barrie, J. M. *Peter Pan* (5–8). 1995, NAL paper $4.95 (978-0-451-52088-3). The classic tale of the boy who wouldn't grow up and of his adventures with the Darling children. (Rev: BL 12/15/87)

408 Barrie, J. M. *Peter Pan* (5–7). 2000, Chronicle $19.95 (978-0-8118-2297-8). Using illustrations from 15 different artists, this is an unusual, unabridged edition of Barrie's classic fantasy. (Rev: BL 11/1/00; HBG 3/01; SLJ 12/00)

409 Brontë, Charlotte. *Jane Eyre* (6–12). Illus. by Kathy Mitchell. Series: Illustrated Junior Library. 1983, Putnam $19.99 (978-0-448-06031-6); paper $4.95 (978-0-553-21140-5). The immortal love story of Jane and Mr. Rochester.

410 Brontë, Charlotte, and Amy Corzine. *Jane Eyre, The Graphic Novel: Original Text* (7–10). Illus. by John M. Burns. Series: Classical Comics. 2009, Classical Comics paper $16.95 (978-190633247-1). Drawing directly from Brontë's text, this graphic-novel adaptation offers an appealing introduction to the story; back matter includes material on Brontë's life. (Rev: BL 3/1/09)

411 Burnett, Frances Hodgson. *The Secret Garden* (5–8). 1999, Scholastic paper $4.99 (978-0-439-09939-4). An easily read classic about a spoiled girl relocated to England and the unusual friendship she finds there.

412 Carroll, Lewis. *Alice in Wonderland and Through the Looking Glass* (4–7). Illus. by John Tenniel. 1963, Putnam $18.99 (978-0-448-06004-0). One of many recommended editions of these enduring fantasies.

413 Carroll, Lewis. *Alice Through the Looking-Glass* (4–7). Illus. by Helen Oxenbury. 2005, Candlewick $24.99 (978-0-7636-2892-5). Faithful to the original text, Oxenbury's inviting artwork will draw young readers; a companion to her award-winning *Alice's Adventures in Wonderland* (1999). (Rev: BL 12/15/05*; HBG 4/06; SLJ 12/05)

414 Carroll, Lewis. *Alice's Adventures in Wonderland* (5–7). 2000, Chronicle $19.95 (978-0-8118-2274-9). This oversize edition of the complete text of Carroll's classic features illustrations from 29 artists. (Rev: BL 11/1/00; HBG 3/01; SLJ 11/00)

415 Carroll, Lewis. *Alice's Adventures in Wonderland* (5–12). Illus. by Iassen Ghiuselev. 2003, Simply Read $29.95 (978-1-894965-00-2). Interesting illustrations by Ghiuselev that interpret incidents and characters in a different way highlight this new edition of an old classic. (Rev: BL 2/1/04; SLJ 6/04)

416 Carroll, Lewis. *Through the Looking Glass, and What Alice Found There* (4–7). Illus. by John Tenniel.

1977, St. Martin's $14.95 (978-0-312-80374-2). The sequel to *Alice's Adventures in Wonderland*. One of many editions.

417 Chaucer, Geoffrey. *Canterbury Tales* (4–8). Adapted by Barbara Cohen. Illus. by Trina Schart Hyman. 1988, Lothrop $26.99 (978-0-688-06201-9). Several of the popular stories are retold with handsome illustrations by Trina Schart Hyman. (Rev: BL 9/1/88; SLJ 8/88)

418 Dickens, Charles. *A Christmas Carol* (6–8). Illus. by Trina Schart Hyman. 1983, Holiday $18.95 (978-0-8234-0486-5). A handsome edition of this classic illustrated by Trina S. Hyman.

419 Dickens, Charles. *Great Expectations* (8–12). 1998, NAL paper $4.95 (978-0-451-52671-7). The story of Pip and his slow journey to maturity and fortune.

420 Doyle, Arthur Conan. *The Adventures of Sherlock Holmes* (7–12). 1981, Avon paper $2.95 (978-0-380-78105-8). A collection of 12 of the most famous stories about this famous sleuth.

421 Doyle, Arthur Conan. *The Complete Sherlock Holmes: All 4 Novels and 56 Stories* (7–12). 1998, Bantam paper $13.90 (978-0-553-32825-7). In two volumes, all the stories and novels involving Holmes and his foil Watson.

422 Doyle, Arthur Conan. *Sherlock Holmes: The Complete Novels and Stories* (8–12). 1986, Bantam paper $6.95 (978-0-553-21241-9). A handy collection in two volumes of all the writings about Holmes and Watson. (Rev: BL 3/15/87)

423 Grahame, Kenneth. *The Wind in the Willows* (4–7). Illus. by E. H. Shepard. 1983, Macmillan $19.95 (978-0-684-17957-5). The classic that introduced Mole, Ratty, and Mr. Toad. Two of many other editions are: illus. by Michael Hague (1980, Henry Holt); illus. by John Burningham (1983, Viking).

424 Grant, Alan. *The Strange Case of Dr. Jekyll and Mr. Hyde* (5–8). Illus. by Cam Kennedy. 2008, Tundra paper $11.95 (978-08877688-2-8). In this condensed adaptation of Robert Louis Stevenson's classic tale, Grant and Kennedy bring their comic sensibilities to bear with concise, fast-paced text and brilliant, atmospheric illustrations. (Rev: BL 9/1/08; SLJ 11/08; VOYA 8/08)

425 Kipling, Rudyard. *Captains Courageous* (7–10). 1964, Amereon LB $20.95 (978-0-88411-818-3). The story of a spoiled teenager who learns about life from common fishermen who save him when he falls overboard from an ocean liner.

426 Stevenson, Robert Louis. *The Black Arrow* (7–12). 1998, Tor paper $3.99 (978-0-8125-6562-1). Set against the War of the Roses, this is an adventure story involving a young hero, Dick Shelton. First published in 1888.

427 Stevenson, Robert Louis. *Dr. Jekyll and Mr. Hyde* (7–12). 1990, Buccaneer LB $16.95 (978-0-89968-552-6). This 1886 horror classic involves a drug-induced change of personality. One of several editions.

428 Stevenson, Robert Louis. *The Strange Case of Dr. Jekyll and Mr. Hyde* (5–8). Series: Whole Story. 2003, Barnes & Noble paper $3.95 (978-1-59308-054-9). Using lively ink-and-watercolor illustrations, this book offers the complete text of the classic in an attractive format. (Rev: BL 5/1/00; HBG 10/00)

429 Stevenson, Robert Louis. *Treasure Island* (5–9). Illus. by N. C. Wyeth. Series: Scribner Storybook Classic. 2003, Simon & Schuster $18.95 (978-0-689-85468-2). This picture-book adaptation of the classic story features beautiful paintings by N. C. Wyeth. (Rev: BL 8/03; HBG 4/04)

430 Wilde, Oscar. *The Picture of Dorian Gray* (6–12). 2001, Viking $25.99 (978-0-670-89494-9). Informative sidebars and bright illustrations amplify many of the more esoteric aspects of Wilde's classic story about the young man who never ages. (Rev: BL 5/15/01; HBG 10/01; SLJ 8/01; VOYA 8/01)

431 Wilde, Oscar, and Ian Edginton. *The Picture of Dorian Gray* (8–12). Illus. by I. N. J. Culbard. 2009, Sterling paper $14.95 (978-141141593-5). This graphic-novel interpretation of the classic story will serve as an introduction for reluctant readers. (Rev: BL 4/1/09)

United States

432 Alcott, Louisa May. *Little Women* (5–9). 1947, Putnam $21.99 (978-0-448-06019-4). One of the many fine editions of this enduring story. Two sequels are *Little Men* and *Jo's Boys*.

433 Camfield, Gregg, ed. *Mark Twain* (6–9). Illus. by Sally Wern Comport. Series: Stories for Young People. 2005, Sterling LB $14.95 (978-1-4027-1178-7). A collection of five stories by Mark Twain, plus a brief biography and glossary notes. (Rev: SLJ 10/05)

434 Cooper, James Fenimore. *The Last of the Mohicans* (8–12). 1986, Macmillan paper $4.95 (978-0-553-21329-4). This is the second of the classic Leatherstocking Tales. The others are *The Pioneers, The Prairie, The Pathfinder,* and *The Deerslayer* (all available in various editions). (Rev: BL 1/87)

435 Crane, Stephen. *The Red Badge of Courage* (8–12). 1991, Airmont paper $2.50 (978-0-8049-0003-4). The classic novel of a young man who explored the meanings of courage during the Civil War.

436 Henry, O. *The Gift of the Magi* (5–8). Illus. by Carol Heyer. 1994, Ideals $14.95 (978-1-57102-003-1). The classic story of unselfish love at Christmas gets some handsome illustrations. Another fine edition is illustrated by Kevin King (1988, Simon & Schuster). (Rev: BL 8/94)

437 London, Jack. *The Sea-Wolf* (7–12). 1958, Macmillan $15.95 (978-0-02-574630-5). Wolf Larsen helps a ne'er-do-well and a female poet find their destinies in the classic that was originally published in 1904.

438 Lovecraft, H. P. *Nyarlathotep* (8–12). Illus. by Chuck BB. 2009, Boom! $14.99 (978-193450665-3). A graphic and disturbing rendering of the horrifying 1920 prose poem. (Rev: BL 3/15/09; SLJ 7/09)

439 Needle, Jan. *Moby Dick* (6–9). Illus. by Patrick Benson. 2006, Candlewick $21.99 (978-0-7636-3018-8). Commentary and illustrations enhance this adaptation of Melville's classic sea story. (Rev: BL 11/1/06; LMC 4–5/07; SLJ 4/07)

440 Poe, Edgar Allan. *Edgar Allan Poe* (6–9). Ed. by Andrew Delbanco. Illus. by Gerard DuBois. 2006, Sterling $14.95 (978-1-4027-1515-0). This collection of five well-known stories by Poe, including "The Fall of the House of Usher" and "The Cask of Amontillado," is enhanced by general information about Poe and his writing, an introduction to each tale, and a glossary. (Rev: BL 11/1/06; SLJ 2/07)

441 Poe, Edgar Allan. *Edgar Allan Poe's Tales of Death and Dementia* (5–8). Illus. by Gris Grimly. 2009, Simon & Schuster $18.99 (978-1-4169-5025-7). A highly illustrated adaptation of four of Poe's thrillingly macabre stories. (Rev: BL 9/1/09; SLJ 9/09)

442 Poe, Edgar Allan. *Edgar Allan Poe's Tales of Mystery and Madness* (7–12). Illus. by Gris Grimly. 2004, Simon & Schuster $17.95 (978-0-689-84837-7). Striking artwork brings to life four of Edgar Allan Poe's classic mystery tales, presented here in abridged form. (Rev: BL 10/15/04*; SLJ 10/04)

443 Schmidt, Gary D. *Pilgrim's Progress* (4–7). Illus. by Barry Moser. 1994, Eerdmans $22.00 (978-0-8028-5080-5). A simple retelling of the classic in which Christian leaves his home to find the Celestial City. (Rev: BL 11/1/94; SLJ 12/94)

444 Sinclair, Upton, and Peter Kuper. *The Jungle* (7–12). Series: Classics Illustrated. 2010, Papercutz $9.99 (978-156163-404-0). Kuper's graphic-novel adaptation brings new life to Sinclair's 1906 classic about the meatpacking industry and the plight of immigrant workers. (Rev: BL 6/18/10; LMC 10/10)

445 Twain, Mark. *The Adventures of Huckleberry Finn* (7–12). 1993, Random House $16.50 (978-0-679-42470-3). One of many editions of this classic.

446 Twain, Mark. *A Connecticut Yankee in King Arthur's Court* (7–12). 1988, Morrow $25.99 (978-0-688-06346-7); paper $4.95 (978-0-553-21143-6). Through a time-travel fantasy, a swaggering Yankee is plummeted into the age of chivalry. First published in 1889. (Rev: BL 2/15/89)

447 Twain, Mark. *The Prince and the Pauper* (7–12). 1996, Andre Deutsch $9.95 (978-0-233-99081-1); paper $2.50 (978-0-8049-0032-4). A king and a poor boy switch places in 16th-century England. First published in 1881.

448 Twain, Mark. *Pudd'nhead Wilson* (7–12). 1966, Airmont paper $2.50 (978-0-8049-0124-6). In the Midwest of over 100 years ago, a black servant switches her baby with a white couple's child to ensure that he gets a fair chance at life.

449 Twain, Mark. *Tom Sawyer Abroad [and] Tom Sawyer, Detective* (7–12). 1981, Univ. of California $50.00 (978-0-520-04560-6). Two sequels to *The Adventures of Tom Sawyer,* both involving Tom and Huck.

Contemporary Life and Problems

General and Miscellaneous

450 Abrahams, Peter. *Robbie Forester and the Outlaws of Sherwood Street* (5–8). 2012, Philomel $16.99 (978-039925502-1). Robyn, a 7th-grader, receives a charm bracelet as thanks for a good deed and finds that she has special powers that help in her mission to fight injustice in her Brooklyn neighborhood. ℮ (Rev: BL 2/1/12; LMC 8–9/12; SLJ 2/12)

451 Ackley, Amy. *Sign Language* (7–10). 2011, Viking $16.99 (978-0-670-01318-0). Reeling from her father's death from cancer, Abby, 12, slowly grows out of her grief and begins accepting her life after tragedy. ∩ ℮ Lexile HL730L (Rev: BL 8/11; SLJ 9/1/11)

452 Adler, C. S. *Always and Forever Friends* (5–7). 1990, Avon paper $3.99 (978-0-380-70687-7). Wendy, at 11, is having a painful struggle making new friends after Meg moves away until she meets Honor, who is African American and very hesitant about accepting Wendy. (Rev: BCCB 4/88; BL 4/1/88; SLJ 4/88)

453 Adler, C. S. *The Magic of the Glits* (5–7). Illus. by Ati Forberg. 1987, Avon paper $2.50 (978-0-380-70403-3). Jeremy, age 12, takes care of 7-year-old Lynette for the summer. A reissue of the 1979 edition. Also use *Some Other Summer* (1988).

454 Airgood, Ellen. *Prairie Evers* (4–7). 2012, Penguin $15.99 (978-0-399-25691-2). Former homeschooler Prairie adjusts to her new home and the novelty of public school even as she misses her grandmother and finds a new friend. (Rev: BL 8/12; LMC 1–2/13; SLJ 9/12)

455 Alexander, Jill S. *The Sweetheart of Prosper County* (7–10). 2009, Feiwel & Friends $16.99 (978-0-312-54856-8). Funny characters populate this likable story about 15-year-old Austin, a girl who learns to look inward for the confidence to stand up to a boy who bullies her, and decides to enter a rooster in the local poultry competition. ∩ Lexile 710L (Rev: BL 8/09; SLJ 9/09)

456 Almond, David. *Click* (7–10). 2007, Scholastic $16.99 (978-0-439-41138-7). Ten well-known authors collaborate to form this compelling well-crafted novel (written to support Amnesty International) about a character named George "Gee" Keane — a famous photojournalist but something of a mystery man. (Rev: BL 9/15/07; SLJ 10/07)

457 Almond, David. *My Name Is Mina* (4–7). 2011, Delacorte $15.99 (978-0-385-74073-9); LB $18.99 (978-0-375-98964-3). This prequel to *Skellig* (1998) explores the life of homeschooled Mina, who lives next door to Michael, and her imaginative fascination with language and nature. (Rev: BL 9/15/11*; SLJ 11/1/11)

458 Amato, Mary. *Guitar Notes* (6–9). 2012, Egmont $15.99 (978-1-60684-124-2). Cellist Lyla and guitar player Tripp, two very different but talented students, come to appreciate each other when they share a music practice room. **e** (Rev: BL 7/12; LMC 8–9/12; SLJ 10/12)

459 Anderson, Jodi Lynn. *Love and Peaches* (8–11). 2008, HarperTeen $16.99 (978-0-06-073311-7); LB $17.89 (978-0-06-073312-4). Friends Leeda, Murphy, and Birdie return to Darlington Orchard, where they face jilted boyfriends, inheritances, heartbreak, and goodbyes. (Rev: SLJ 4/1/09)

460 Anderson, Jodi Lynn. *Peaches* (8–11). 2005, HarperCollins LB $16.89 (978-0-06-073306-3). Three teenage girls from diverse backgrounds forge lasting bonds during a summer picking peaches in a Georgia orchard. (Rev: BL 10/1/05; SLJ 8/05; VOYA 2/06)

461 Anderson, Mary. *The Unsinkable Molly Malone* (7–10). 1991, Harcourt $16.95 (978-0-15-213801-1). Molly, 16, sells her collages outside New York's Metropolitan Museum, starts an art class for kids on welfare, and learns that her boyfriend is rich. (Rev: BL 11/15/91; SLJ 12/91)

462 Andrews, Jesse. *Me and Earl and the Dying Girl* (8–11). 2012, Abrams $16.95 (978-1-4197-0176-4). High school loner Greg's life changes when he befriends Rachel, who is dying from leukemia, in this surprisingly humorous novel. YALSA Top Ten Best Fiction for Young Adults 2013. **e** Lexile 820L (Rev: BL 3/1/12*; SLJ 7/12)

463 Anthony, Joelle. *The Right and the Real* (8–11). 2012, Putnam $17.99 (978-039925525-0). After she refuses to join her father's cult, 17-year-old Jamie is thrown out of her home and must fend for herself. **e** (Rev: BL 4/1/12; LMC 10/12; SLJ 5/1/12)

464 Antieau, Kim. *Ruby's Imagine* (6–10). 2008, Houghton Mifflin $16.00 (978-061899767-1). Ruby, 17, lives in New Orleans but is in tune with nature, and when Hurricane Katrina overwhelms the city Ruby heeds her grandmother rather than her instincts and ends up learning some family secrets. Lexile 540L (Rev: BL 11/15/08; LMC 3–4/09; SLJ 12/08)

465 Appelt, Kathi. *Keeper* (4–7). Illus. by August Hall. 2010, Simon & Schuster $16.99 (978-1-4169-5060-8). Ten-year-old Keeper believes her absent mother is a mermaid and sets off in a boat, in the company of her dog and a seagull, to find her. ⌒ Lexile 770L (Rev: BL 6/10; HB 9–10/10; LMC 10/10; SLJ 7/10)

466 Applegate, Katherine. *Home of the Brave* (5–8). 2007, Feiwel & Friends $16.95 (978-0-312-36765-7). Young refugee Kek, who barely escaped death in Sudan, where his brother and father were murdered, finds a new home — and culture shock — in Minnesota. ⌒ (Rev: BCCB 2/08; BL 7/07; HB 11–12/07; SLJ 10/07)

467 Archer, Lily. *The Poison Apples* (7–10). 2007, Feiwel & Friends $16.95 (978-0-312-36762-6). Three 15-year-old girls — Molly, Reena, and Alice — who have been shipped off to boarding school are united in their hatred for their new stepmothers in this funny novel full of pop-culture references. (Rev: BL 10/15/07; SLJ 9/07)

468 Armstrong, Alan. *Looking for Marco Polo* (4–7). Illus. by Tim Jessell. 2009, Random House $16.99 (978-0-375-83321-2); LB $19.99 (978-0-375-93321-9). Eleven-year-old Mark hears many stories about famed explorer Marco Polo when recovering from an asthma attack while searching for his missing father in the Gobi Desert. Lexile 830L (Rev: BL 8/09; SLJ 12/09)

469 Asher, Jay, and Carolyn Mackler. *The Future of Us* (8–12). 2011, Penguin $18.99 (978-1-59514-491-1). In 1996 Emma and Josh discover their future selves on Facebook and perhaps the chance to change their destinies. ⌒ **e** (Rev: BL 10/15/11*; HB 1–2/12; SLJ 11/1/11)

470 Ashton, Victoria. *Confessions of a Teen Nanny* (8–12). 2005, HarperCollins LB $16.89 (978-0-06-077524-7). Hired as a temporary nanny for an 8-year-old child prodigy, 16-year-old Adrienne finds herself being manipulated by her charge's older sister. (Rev: BL 8/05; SLJ 7/05)

471 Bailey, Em. *Shift* (7–11). 2012, Egmont $16.99 (978-160684358-1). Olive, who is recovering from a suicide attempt, is suspicious of new student Miranda and her apparent devotion to popular Katie; could Miranda be a shape-shifter? **e** (Rev: BLO 6/12; HB 5–6/12; LMC 8–9/12; SLJ 6/12)

472 Bancks, Tristan. *Mac Slater Hunts the Cool* (5–8). 2010, Simon & Schuster $15.99 (978-1-4169-8574-7). Is Mac truly cool? He feels like an outsider at his Australian school, but when he enters a contest to come up with the next cool trend, he gets a chance to prove that outsiders can be cool too. Lexile 690L (Rev: BL 4/1/10; LMC 8–9/10; SLJ 3/10)

473 Banks, Kate. *Friends of the Heart/Amici del Cuore* (6–9). 2005, Farrar $16.00 (978-0-374-32455-1). Lucrezia looks back a few years to the idyllic summer she and her childhood friend spent an idyllic summer in a seaside Italian village until tragedy struck. (Rev: BL 12/1/05)

474 Barkley, Brad, and Heather Hepler. *Scrambled Eggs at Midnight* (7–10). 2006, Dutton $16.99 (978-0-525-47760-0). Unhappy with the nomadic life she lives with her mother, 15-year-old Calliope finds friendship and romance and learns about herself in the process. (Rev: BL 6/1–15/06; LMC 1/07; SLJ 5/06)

475 Barshaw, Ruth McNally. *Ellie McDoodle: New Kid in School* (4–7). Illus. by author. 2008, Bloomsbury $12.99 (978-159990238-8). In 6th grade at a new school Ellie McDoodle tackles finding friends, horrible school lunches, and various other trials and tribulations recounted through sketches, cartoons, and engaging text. Lexile 510L (Rev: BLO 8/08)

476 Bateson, Catherine. *Stranded in Boringsville* (5–8). 2005, Holiday House $16.95 (978-0-8234-1969-2). Twelve-year-old Rain's life is turned upside down when she and her mother move from cosmopolitan Melbourne to a small Australian town in the middle of nowhere; but she finds a good friend in her neighbor Daniel. (Rev: BL 12/1/05; SLJ 2/06; VOYA 2/06)

477 Bauer, A. C. E. *Gil Marsh* (8–11). 2012, Random House $15.99 (978-037586933-4); LB $18.99 (978-037596933-1). Track star Gil, 17, travels to the grave of his friend (and former rival) Enko and considers the meaning of life and death in this retelling of the ancient story of Gilgamesh. **e** (Rev: BL 2/15/12; LMC 3–4/12; SLJ 2/12)

478 Bauer, Joan. *Best Foot Forward* (6–9). 2005, Penguin $16.99 (978-0-399-23474-3). In this funny sequel to *Rules of the Road* (1998), 17-year-old Jenna finds it difficult to juggle her high school studies, her alcoholic father, her declining grandmother, and her part-time job at the shoe store, where she has been appointed a supervisor. (Rev: BCCB 6/05; BL 5/1/05; HB 5–6/05; SLJ 6/05; VOYA 6/05)

479 Bauer, Joan. *Hope Was Here* (7–9). 2000, Putnam $16.99 (978-0-399-23142-1). When she and her aunt move to Wisconsin, 16-year-old Hope is pleasantly surprised and becomes involved in politics while working in a diner. (Rev: BL 9/15/00; HB 9–10/00; HBG 3/01; SLJ 11/00*; VOYA 2/01)

480 Bauer, Marion Dane. *On My Honor* (5–7). 1986, Houghton Mifflin $15.00 (978-0-89919-439-4); paper $4.99 (978-0-440-46633-8). A powerful story in which 12-year-old Joel faces telling his parents that his friend Tony has drowned in the river they promised never to swim. (Rev: BCCB 10/86; BL 9/1/86; SLJ 11/86)

481 Beam, Matt. *Can You Spell Revolution?* (5–8). 2008, Dutton $17.99 (978-0-525-47998-7). New student Clouds McFadden brings together four unlikely classmates to overthrow the lousy administration at Laverton Middle School, using strategies gleaned from history. (Rev: BL 12/1/08; SLJ 1/09)

482 Bell, Cathleen Davitt. *Little Blog on the Prairie* (5–8). 2010, Bloomsbury $16.99 (978-1-59990-286-9). Sentenced to spend a summer at a frontier family history camp in Wyoming, 13-year-old Gen sneaks in a cell phone and reports her experiences back to friends at home even as she becomes more comfortable with the life of 1890. ⋒ **e** Lexile 820L (Rev: BL 4/1/10; SLJ 5/10)

483 Bell, Joanne. *Breaking Trail* (5–7). 2005, Groundwood $15.95 (978-0-88899-630-5); paper $6.95 (978-0-88899-662-6). Becky's dreams of training a dog team to participate in the Junior Quest fade when her father grows increasingly depressed, but a sled trip back to the family's cabin offers a chance to make those dreams come true. (Rev: SLJ 10/05)

484 Bell, Juliet. *Kepler's Dream* (5–7). 2012, Putnam $16.99 (978-039925645-5). Ella goes to live with her estranged grandmother in Albuquerque while her mother is being treated for cancer and finds herself learning about family history and investigating a mystery. (Rev: BL 5/15/12*; LMC 11–12/12; SLJ 5/1/12)

485 Bell, Krista Blakeney. *Who Cares?* (6–8). 2011, Kane/Miller paper $4.99 (978-1-61067-046-3). In Australia Toby and Rhys find themselves thrown together for a week's vacation, and both boys dread it because they each have a secret they must keep. Lexile 870L (Rev: LMC 3–4/12; SLJ 12/1/11)

486 Bennet, Olivia. *The Allegra Biscotti Collection* (5–8). Illus. 2010, Sourcebooks paper $8.99 (978-1-4022-4391-2). Eighth-grader Emma adopts an alter ego, Allegra Biscotti, to represent her fashion designs for the likes of *Vogue* in this entertaining book full of Emma's sketches. (Rev: BL 12/15/10; SLJ 12/1/10)

487 Benway, Robin. *Audrey, Wait!* (8–11). 2008, Penguin $16.99 (978-159514191-0). Audrey's ex-boyfriend Even, a rock singer, writes a song about their breakup and she suddenly finds herself a reluctant celebrity. Lexile 760L (Rev: BL 8/08; SLJ 8/08)

488 Berk, Josh. *The Dark Days of Hamburger Halpin* (6–9). 2010, Knopf LB $19.99 (978-0-375-95699-7). Will Halpin has left his "deaf school" and is trying to fit into regular high school; he befriends a geeky classmate named Devon and together the two misfits investigate the death of a star quarterback in this darkly funny novel. ⋒ **e** Lexile 820L (Rev: BL 12/15/09; LMC 3–4/10; SLJ 1/10)

489 Berlin, Eric. *The Puzzler's Mansion* (4–7). Series: Puzzling World of Winston Breen. 2012, Putnam $16.99 (978-039925697-4). Winston and other puzzle fiends journey to a mansion owned by a man offering rewards for the solvers of word, number, logic, and grouping puzzles in this third volume in the series. **e** (Rev: BLO 7/12)

490 Bernard, Virginia. *Eliza Down Under: Going to Sydney* (5–8). Series: Going To. 2000, Four Corners paper

$7.95 (978-1-893577-02-2). This novel deals with Eliza's adventures in Australia when she accompanies her mother to the 2000 Olympic Games in Sydney. (Rev: SLJ 3/00)

491 Blacker, Terence. *Boy2Girl* (6–9). 2005, Farrar $16.00 (978-0-374-30926-8). After the death of his mother, American-born Sam is sent to London to live with relatives; on a dare from his cousin, Sam shows up for his first day of school dressed as a girl. (Rev: BCCB 3/05; BL 3/1/05; SLJ 3/05; VOYA 4/05)

492 Blatchford, Claire H. *Nick's Secret* (5–7). 2000, Lerner LB $14.95 (978-0-8225-0743-7). When 13-year-old Nick, who is deaf, is summoned to a motel by Darryl Smythe and his gang of vandals, the boy knows he is in for trouble. (Rev: BL 9/15/00; HBG 3/01; SLJ 12/00; VOYA 2/01)

493 Blexbolex. *People* (4–12). Trans. from French by Claudia Bedrick. Illus. by author. 2011, Enchanted Lion $19.95 (978-1-59270-110-0). A stimulating look at the similarities and differences in our lives, pairing, for example, a contortionist and a plumber, a bystander and a rescuer, a partygoer and a hermit. (Rev: HB 9–10/11; SLJ 9/1/11)

494 Bloor, Edward. *A Plague Year* (8–11). 2011, Knopf $15.99 (978-0-375-85681-5); LB $18.99 (978-037595681-2). Ninth-grader Tom Coleman documents the impact on his small Pennsylvania town of September 11, 2001, a rash of meth addiction, and a July 2002 mining accident. e Lexile HL590L (Rev: BLO 10/1/11; SLJ 12/1/11)

495 Bodett, Tom. *Norman Tuttle on the Last Frontier: A Novel in Stories* (8–10). 2004, Knopf LB $17.99 (978-0-679-99031-4). In this coming-of-age story presented in interconnected episodes, klutzy Alaskan teenager Norman Tuttle experiences many firsts — first job, first date, first hunting expedition — and his relationship with his father evolves. (Rev: BL 12/1/04; SLJ 12/04; VOYA 12/04)

496 Boles, Philana Marie. *Little Divas* (5–8). 2006, HarperCollins LB $16.89 (978-0-06-073300-1). Twelve-year-old Cass is facing a lot of change in her life: her parents' divorce, living with her father, a new friend, a first kiss, and perhaps a new school. (Rev: BL 4/1/06; SLJ 1/06)

497 Boll, Rosemarie. *The Second Trial* (6–9). 2010, Second Story paper $11.95 (978-1-897187-72-2). Thirteen-year-old Danny's father goes to jail for beating his wife, and when Danny and his mother and sister must assume new identities and move to another town he spirals out of control, skipping school, bullying, and stealing. (Rev: LMC 11–12/10; SLJ 5/11)

498 Brande, Robin. *Evolution, Me and Other Freaks of Nature* (6–9). 2007, Knopf $15.99 (978-0-375-84349-5). Mena's views on evolution, gays, and other topics are challenged by her peers, parents, and church. (Rev: BL 6/1–15/07; HB 9–10/07; SLJ 10/07)

499 Brande, Robin. *Fat Cat* (8–11). 2009, Knopf $16.99 (978-0-375-84449-2); LB $19.99 (978-0-375-94449-9). A science research project motivates overweight high school junior Cat to take on a prehistoric lifestyle and thereby lose pounds and for the first time attract male attention. ⌒ e (Rev: BL 10/15/09; SLJ 1/10)

500 Brashares, Ann. *Forever in Blue: The Fourth Summer of the Sisterhood* (8–11). Series: The Sisterhood of the Traveling Pants. 2007, Delacorte $18.99 (978-0-385-72936-9). The four girls of *The Sisterhood of the Traveling Pants* are growing up, exploring love and life, and recognizing their ability to succeed without the pants in this final book in the series. ⌒ (Rev: BL 12/15/06; SLJ 2/07)

501 Brashares, Ann. *The Sisterhood of the Traveling Pants* (6–9). 2001, Delacorte $14.95 (978-0-385-72933-8). Four teenage girls who are spending the summer apart pin their hopes on a pair of jeans that seems to magically fit and flatter them all. (Rev: BCCB 12/01; BL 8/01; HB 11–12/01; HBG 3/02; SLJ 8/01*; VOYA 10/01)

502 Bredsdorff, Bodil. *Alek* (4–7). Trans. from Danish by Elisabeth Kallick Dyssegaard. Series: Children of Crow Cove. 2012, Farrar $16.99 (978-0-374-31269-5). In this final book in the series, Doup adopts his real name of Alek and travels to Last Harbor to be with his lovesick brother Ravnar; there he works at an inn, uncovers shipwreckers, and rescues a girl. e Lexile 830L (Rev: BL 6/12; HB 7–8/12; SLJ 8/1/12)

503 Brian, Kate. *Megan Meade's Guide to the McGowan Boys* (8–11). 2005, Simon & Schuster $14.95 (978-1-4169-0030-6). Megan does not want to move to South Korea with her military parents and chooses instead to stay with the McGowans, a family with seven sons, requiring adjustments all round. (Rev: BL 9/15/05; SLJ 11/05; VOYA 12/05)

504 Brinkerhoff, Shirley. *Second Choices* (6–8). Series: Nikki Sheridan. 2000, Bethany paper $5.99 (978-1-56179-880-3). Nikki Sheridan finds comfort in her Christian values as she faces her parents' divorce, telling the father of her child about his paternity, and an incident of school violence in this sixth and final installment in the series. (Rev: BL 3/1/01)

505 Brody, Jessica. *52 Reasons to Hate My Father* (8–12). 2012, Farrar $16.99 (978-0-374-32303-5). Lexi, 18, can't wait to get her hands on her multimillion-dollar trust fund, but when she wrecks a brand-new Mercedes convertible her father decides it's time for her to learn the value of money — through performing menial jobs for a whole year. e Lexile 790L (Rev: BL 7/12; SLJ 9/12; VOYA 8/12)

506 Brody, Jessica. *My Life Undecided* (7–10). 2011, Farrar $16.99 (978-0-374-39905-4). Famous for her bad decision-making skills, Brooklyn, 15, decides to start a blog and let her readers guide her through life. e Lexile 840L (Rev: BLO 8/11; SLJ 6/11; VOYA 8/11)

507 Brooks, Bruce. *Everywhere* (5–8). 1990, HarperCollins LB $16.89 (978-0-06-020729-8). Eleven-year-old Dooley, who is African American, helps a 10-year-old white boy live through the emotional trauma of waiting to see if his beloved grandfather will recover from a heart attack. (Rev: BCCB 10/90; BL 10/15/90*; SLJ 9/90*)

508 Brown, Jason Robert, and Dan Elish. *13* (5–7). 2008, HarperCollins $15.99 (978-006078749-3); LB $16.89 (978-006078750-9). In this humorous coming-of-age story, Evan finds himself relocated halfway across the country — from comfortable New York City to the middle of Indiana— and grappling with the social terrain of his new school and preparations for his bar mitzvah speech. (Rev: BL 9/1/08)

509 Brugman, Alyssa. *Finding Grace* (6–12). 2004, Dell LB $17.99 (978-0-385-90142-0). College-bound Rachel is hired to care for a brain-injured woman named Grace and in the process learns some valuable lessons about both Grace and herself. (Rev: BL 9/15/04; SLJ 11/04; VOYA 12/04)

510 Buckley, Kristen. *Thirteen Reasons Why* (8–11). 2007, Penguin $16.99 (978-1-59514-171-2). Clay Jenson describes his thoughts as he listens to cassette tapes bearing the voice of his dead classmate, Hannah, who describes events and circumstances that led to her suicide. ∩ (Rev: BL 9/1/07; SLJ 11/07)

511 Buffie, Margaret. *Winter Shadows* (7–10). 2010, Tundra $19.95 (978-0-88776-968-9). High school senior Cass, unhappy and resentful of her stepmother, finds a diary written by Beatrice in the mid-19th century, who also is grappling with an unpleasant stepmother — and the two form a bond that transcends time. (Rev: BL 11/15/10; SLJ 12/1/10)

512 Burch, Christian. *The Manny Files* (6–9). 2006, Simon & Schuster $15.95 (978-1-4169-0039-9). A fun, creative male nanny, or "manny," takes charge of the Dalinger children and bonds with 3rd-grader Keats, while older sister Lulu is unimpressed and puts the manny on mock trial. ∩ (Rev: BL 5/1/06; LMC 11–12/06; SLJ 7/06)

513 Burg, Shana. *Laugh with the Moon* (4–7). 2012, Delacorte $16.99 (978-038573471-4); LB $19.99 (978-038590469-8). Clare, 13, is still grieving for her mother when her doctor father takes her to Malawi, where he works in a hospital; there Clare contends with everyday hardships but finds friendship and comfort. e Lexile 740 (Rev: BL 6/12; LMC 10/12; SLJ 6/12)

514 Burton, Rebecca. *Leaving Jetty Road* (8–11). 2006, Knopf $15.95 (978-0-375-83488-2). Three Australian high school girls decide to become vegetarians, a choice that affects each in a different way and becomes

more critical as Lise has serious anorexia. (Rev: BL 6/1–15/06; LMC 10/06; SLJ 8/06)

515 Butcher, Kristin. *Cheat* (5–8). 2010, Orca LB $16.95 (978-1-55469-275-0); paper $9.95 (978-1-55469-274-3). Eager for acclaim, school newspaper reporter Laurel is disappointed when her story about school cheating is poorly received. (Rev: BL 12/15/10; SLJ 2/11/11)

516 Butcher, Kristin. *The Runaways* (5–8). 1998, Kids Can $16.95 (978-1-55074-413-2). During an unsuccessful attempt to run away from home, young Nick Battle meets Luther, a homeless man, and through this friendship gains insights into poverty in America. (Rev: BL 4/15/98; HBG 10/98; SLJ 4/98)

517 Butler, Dori Hillestad. *The Truth about Truman School* (5–8). 2008, Albert Whitman $15.95 (978-0-8075-8095-0). Zebby and Amr start an alternative, online school newspaper and soon learn that not all postings are fit to print in this story told from many characters' points of view. (Rev: BL 3/15/08; SLJ 5/08)

518 Buyea, Rob. *Mr. Terupt Falls Again* (4–7). 2012, Delacorte $16.99 (978-0-385-74205-4); LB $19.99 (978-037599038-0). Mr. Terupt's students are now in 6th grade and are dealing with coming-of-age problems even as they help their teacher plan his wedding. e Lexile 680L (Rev: BLO 12/15/12; SLJ 11/12; VOYA 12/12)

519 Byars, Betsy. *The Pinballs* (5–7). 1977, HarperCollins LB $16.89 (978-0-06-020918-6). Three misfits in a foster home band together to help lessen their problems.

520 Byrd, Sandra. *Island Girl* (5–8). Series: Friends for a Season. 2005, Bethany House paper $9.99 (978-0-7642-0020-5). Confused by changes in her family situation, 13-year-old Meg spends a summer with her grandparents on an Oregon island where she meets and befriends Tia. (Rev: BL 10/1/05)

521 Cabot, Meg. *Being Nikki* (7–10). Series: Airhead. 2009, Scholastic $16.99 (978-054504056-3). Romance, suspense, and comedy (and a touch of science fiction) are intertwined in this second book about the ordinary teen whose brain has been transplanted into a famous model's body. ∩ Lexile 800L (Rev: BL 4/15/09; SLJ 1/10)

522 Cabot, Meg. *How to Be Popular* (6–9). 2006, HarperTempest $16.99 (978-0-06-088012-5). Steph is determined no longer to be the class klutz and studies a book she finds titled *How to Be Popular*, surprising everyone with the results. (Rev: BL 9/15/06)

523 Cadnum, Michael. *Flash* (8–11). 2010, Farrar $16.99 (978-0-374-39911-5). On a tense day in Albany, California, five young people deal with various acute personal problems. (Rev: BL 5/1/10; HB 7–8/10; LMC 8–9/10; SLJ 6/10)

524 Caletti, Deb. *The Secret Life of Prince Charming* (8–11). 2009, Simon & Schuster $16.99 (978-141695940-

3). Quinn, 17, and her sisters Sprout and Frances take a road trip to visit their father's former wives and girlfriends and to learn why men do the things they do. ⋂ Lexile 760L (Rev: BL 4/1/09; HB 7–8/09; SLJ 6/1/09; VOYA 10/09)

525 Caletti, Deb. *Wild Roses* (7–10). 2005, Simon & Schuster $15.95 (978-0-689-86766-8). Seventeen-year-old Cassie finds life with her stepfather — an unstable violinist and composer — difficult at the best of times, but things go from bad to worse when she falls for one of his music students. (Rev: BCCB 10/05; BL 10/1/05; SLJ 11/05*; VOYA 12/05)

526 Calhoun, Dia. *Eva of the Farm* (5–7). Illus. by Kate Slater. 2012, Simon & Schuster $16.99 (978-1-4424-1700-7). Twelve-year-old Eva's family farm in Washington state is endangered when their crops fail and her younger brother gets sick, and she tries selling her poems to help make ends meet. ℮ Lexile 840L (Rev: LMC 1–2/13; SLJ 8/1/12)

527 Calloway, Cassidy. *Confessions of a First Daughter* (7–10). 2009, HarperTeen paper $8.99 (978-0-06-172439-8). Eighteen-year-old Morgan Abbott thinks that life as the First Daughter of the United States is trying enough as it is, but when her mother, the president, asks her to temporarily fill her shoes, Morgan finds that her life is about to get considerably more complicated. ℮ (Rev: BL 7/09; SLJ 12/09; VOYA 8/09)

528 Calonita, Jen. *Paparazzi Princess* (6–10). Series: Secrets of My Hollywood Life. 2009, Little, Brown $16.99 (978-0-316-03064-9). Finding it difficult to cope with the impending end of her long-running show, teen TV star Kaitlin spends time with two publicity-hungry party girls until she finally realizes that their life is not satisfying. (Rev: SLJ 6/1/09; VOYA 6/09)

529 Calonita, Jen. *Reality Check* (7–10). 2010, Little, Brown $16.99 (978-0-316-04554-4). The friendship between four Long Island teenage girls does not survive when a media executive scout offers them their own reality TV show. ℮ Lexile HL690L (Rev: BL 4/15/10; SLJ 10/1/10; VOYA 8/10)

530 Calonita, Jen. *Secrets of My Hollywood Life: On Location* (7–12). 2007, Little, Brown $16.99 (978-0-316-15439-0). Kaitlin is a likable Hollywood starlet whose life gets tricky when she has to make a movie co-starring her ex-boyfriend and her biggest enemy. (Rev: SLJ 7/07)

531 Calonita, Jen. *Sleepaway Girls* (7–10). 2009, Little, Brown $16.99 (978-031601717-6). Samantha has the time of her life at summer camp as a counselor in training. Lexile 710L (Rev: BL 5/1/09; SLJ 6/1/09)

532 Carlson, Melody. *Glamour* (7–10). Series: On the Runway. 2011, Zondervan paper $9.99 (978-031071790-4). Erin and Paige are filming Fashion Week in the Bahamas for their reality TV show as ro-mantic problems intrude, their friend Fran has cancer, and Mollie awaits the arrival of her baby. ℮ (Rev: BL 4/15/11)

533 Carlson, Ron. *The Speed of Light* (4–7). 2003, HarperTempest LB $16.89 (978-0-06-029825-8). Baseball, science experiments, and the mysteries of the universe occupy Larry and his two best friends during the summer before junior high. (Rev: BL 8/03; HBG 4/04; SLJ 7/03; VOYA 10/03)

534 Carlyle, Carolyn. *Mercy Hospital: Crisis!* (5–8). 1993, Avon paper $3.50 (978-0-380-76846-2). Three friends volunteer at a local hospital. (Rev: SLJ 7/93)

535 Caseley, Judith. *The Kissing Diary* (5–8). 2007, Farrar $16.00 (978-0-374-36346-8). After her parents' divorce, 12-year-old Rosie keeps a diary in which she describes problems at home and at school and her crush on Robbie Romano. (Rev: BL 8/07; SLJ 11/07)

536 Chandler, Ann. *Siena Summer* (7–10). 2009, Orca paper $12.95 (978-189658017-3). Angela spends a summer in Italy and rescues a doomed horse that she later rides in Siena's annual race. (Rev: BL 5/1/09)

537 Chase, Paula. *Don't Get It Twisted* (7–10). Series: Del Rio Bay Clique. 2007, Dafina paper $9.95 (978-0-7582-1861-2). Friends (and enemies) gossiping, IMing, and flirting fill the pages of this second novel about freshman Mina and her friends, full of slick, slangy dialogue and pop-culture references. ⋂ (Rev: BL 1/1–15/08)

538 Cheripko, Jan. *Rat* (7–12). 2002, Boyds Mills $16.95 (978-1-59078-034-3). Fifteen-year-old Jeremy faces difficult choices in this novel that looks at moral questions against a backdrop of basketball. (Rev: HBG 10/03; SLJ 8/02)

539 Chocolate, Deborah M. *NEATE to the Rescue!* (4–7). Series: NEATE. 1992, Just Us Bks. paper $3.95 (978-0-940975-42-2). A 13-year-old African American girl and her friends help out when her mother's seat on the local council is put in doubt by a racist. (Rev: BCCB 3/93; BL 3/15/93)

540 Choyce, Lesley. *Rat* (5–8). Series: Orca Soundings. 2012, Orca LB $16.95 (978-145980301-5); paper $9.95 (9781459803008). Colin finally rebels against the bullying at school in this novel suitable for reluctant readers. ℮ Lexile 580L (Rev: BLO 9/15/12; LMC 5–6/13)

541 Christopher, Lucy. *Flyaway* (5–8). 2011, Scholastic $16.99 (978-0-545-31771-9). Thirteen-year-old Isla's deep connection with birds and nature helps her when her father is in the hospital and she befriends a boy with leukemia. ALA Notable Books 2012. ⋂ ℮ Lexile HL580L (Rev: BL 8/11*; SLJ 12/1/11*; VOYA 8/11)

542 Cirrone, Dorian. *Prom Kings and Drama Queens* (6–9). 2008, HarperTeen $16.99 (978-0-06-114372-4). Emily writes for the school newspaper but is still a social outcast; this begins to change as she starts to date her popular next-door neighbor. (Rev: SLJ 3/08)

543 Citra, Becky. *Missing* (7–10). 2011, Orca paper $9.95 (978-1-55469-345-0). When her father gets a job at a ranch, 8th-grader Thea finds friends in an abused horse and in a classmate named Van who helps her unravel a mystery about a young girl who disappeared in the 1950s. e Lexile 670L (Rev: BL 5/1/11; LMC 10/11; SLJ 9/1/11; VOYA 4/11)

544 Clark, Catherine. *Frozen Rodeo* (8–12). 2003, HarperCollins LB $16.89 (978-0-06-623008-5). What starts out as a dull summer has its high points for P.F. (Peggy Fleming) Farrell as she enjoys a teen romance, foils a robbery, and even finds time to help deliver her mother's baby. (Rev: BL 2/15/03; HBG 10/03; SLJ 3/03; VOYA 4/03)

545 Clark, Catherine. *How Not to Run for President* (5–8). 2012, Egmont $15.99 (978-160684101-3). After he saves a candidate's life, Aidan is brought along on the campaign trail, where he learns firsthand how the fickle media game works. e Lexile 600L (Rev: BL 2/1/12; LMC 3–4/12; SLJ 1/12)

546 Clements, Andrew. *Extra Credit* (4–7). Illus. by Mark Elliot. 2009, Atheneum $16.99 (978-1-4169-4929-9). Abby, 11, becomes pen pals with a student in Afghanistan. (Rev: BCCB 9/09; BL 6/1–15/09; HB 7/09)

547 Clements, Andrew. *The Report Card* (4–7). 2004, Simon & Schuster $15.95 (978-0-689-84515-4). Nora, a bright 5th-grader, deliberately gets low grades in a bid to boost her friend Stephen's self-esteem, but her plans backfire. (Rev: BL 2/15/04; SLJ 3/04)

548 Clements, Andrew. *The School Story* (4–7). 2001, Simon & Schuster $16.00 (978-0-689-82594-1). Two 12-year-old girls tackle the task of getting a book by a new author published. (Rev: BCCB 7–8/01; BL 6/1–15/01; HB 7–8/01; HBG 10/01; SLJ 6/01)

549 Clements, Andrew. *A Week in the Woods* (4–8). 2002, Simon & Schuster $16.95 (978-0-689-82596-5). Mark, a lonely 5th-grader, and a forceful teacher test each other — and Mark's survival skills — on a week-long camping trip. (Rev: BCCB 1/03; BL 10/1/02; HBG 3/03; SLJ 11/02)

550 Clipston, Amy. *Reckless Heart* (6–9). 2012, Zondervan paper $9.99 (978-031071984-7). Under stress over her responsibilities as the oldest sibling when there is illness in the family, Amish good girl Lydia rebels by drinking beer and befriending a non-Amish neighbor. e (Rev: BL 7/12; VOYA 8/12)

551 Cobb, Katie. *Happenings* (6–10). 2002, HarperCollins LB $15.89 (978-0-06-028928-7). Kelsey and her classmates start a protest against their AP English teacher that spirals out of control, causing conflict between Kelsey and her guardian brother. (Rev: BL 3/1/02; HBG 10/02; SLJ 3/02; VOYA 2/02)

552 Cochrane, Mick. *Fitz* (8–12). 2012, Knopf $16.99 (978-0-375-85683-9); LB $19.99 (978-037595683-6). Fifteen-year-old Fitz's volatile mix of bitterness and longing boils over, and he kidnaps the father he's never known at gunpoint. ∩ e Lexile 750L (Rev: BL 12/1/12; SLJ 12/12)

553 Cochrane, Mick. *The Girl Who Threw Butterflies* (6–9). 2009, Knopf $16.99 (978-037585682-2); LB $19.99 (978-037595682-9). While trying to deal with her father's recent death, Molly tries out for the boys' baseball team, where she encounters both rejection and potential romance. ∩ e Lexile 750L (Rev: BL 3/15/09; HB 5–6/09; SLJ 3/1/09)

554 Cohen, Tish. *The Invisible Rules of the Zoe Lama* (4–7). 2007, Dutton $15.99 (978-0-525-47810-2). This playfully illustrated story about 7th-grader Zoë describes her busy life at home and at school, offering advice and organizing projects and lives. (Rev: BL 10/1/07; SLJ 8/07)

555 Cohen, Tish. *Little Black Lies* (8–12). 2009, Egmont $16.99 (978-1-60684-033-7); LB $19.99 (978-1-60684-046-7). When high school junior Sara Black allows her snobbish classmates to believe that she has just transferred to her upper-crust Boston school from London, England, this lie puts her father — the school's new janitor and obsessive-compulsive disorder victim — in a precarious position. and jeopardizes her relationship with him. e (Rev: BL 11/1/09; SLJ 12/09; VOYA 12/09)

556 Cole, Stephen. *Thieves Like Us* (8–11). 2006, Bloomsbury $16.95 (978-1-58234-653-3). Jonah Wish, a member of a gang of teenage thieves, finds himself questioning the morality of certain activities. (Rev: BL 4/1/06)

557 Colfer, Eoin. *Benny and Babe* (6–8). 2001, O'Brien paper $7.95 (978-0-86278-603-8). On a visit to his grandfather, Benny, 13, makes a new friend, and he and Babe have money-making and other, more dangerous adventures. (Rev: SLJ 3/02)

558 Colfer, Eoin. *Benny and Omar* (5–8). 2001, O'Brien paper $7.95 (978-0-86278-567-3). Benny, a young Irish lad, has trouble adjusting to his new life in Tunisia until he befriends Omar, a local orphan without a home, and the two have some exciting and amusing adventures. (Rev: BL 8/01; SLJ 12/01)

559 Collard, Sneed B, III. *Flash Point* (7–10). 2006, Peachtree $16.95 (978-156145385-6). Luther, a high school sophomore, has turned away from sports and is now interested in birds of prey and the environment but this new focus threatens to alienate many in his logging community; when his girlfriend's beloved falcon is shot, this fast-paced story becomes even more exciting. **e** (Rev: SLJ 12/06)

560 Collins, Yvonne, and Sandy Rideout. *Introducing Vivien Leigh Reid: Daughter of the Diva* (7–10). 2005, St. Martin's $11.95 (978-0-312-33837-4). Sent to Ireland to spend the summer on the set of her actress mother's latest film, 15-year-old Leigh Reid wins a bit part in the movie, develops a crush on a costar, and finally begins to build a meaningful relationship with her mom. (Rev: BL 6/1–15/05; SLJ 9/05)

561 Collins, Yvonne, and Sandy Rideout. *The New and Improved Vivien Leigh Reid: Diva in Control* (7–10). 2007, Griffin paper $9.95 (978-0-312-35828-0). Despite her determination to make her life better, Leigh continues to face challenges in both her personal and professional lives in this third book in the series. (Rev: SLJ 3/07)

562 Collins, Yvonne, and Sandy Rideout. *Now Starring Vivien Leigh Reid: Diva in Training* (8–12). 2006, Griffin paper $9.95 (978-0-312-33839-8). In this sequel to the witty *Introducing Vivien Leigh Reid: Daughter of the Diva* (2005), 16-year-old Leigh lands a role in a soap opera and initially adopts a prima donna attitude that threatens her friendships and her job. (Rev: SLJ 1/06; VOYA 4/06)

563 Coman, Carolyn. *Many Stones* (7–12). 2000, Front St $15.95 (978-1-886910-55-3). A year after her sister was murdered there, Berry reluctantly travels with her father to South Africa to attend her memorial in this novel set during the proceedings of the Truth and Reconciliation Commission. (Rev: BL 11/1/00; HB 1–2/01; HBG 3/01; SLJ 11/00*; VOYA 2/01)

564 Comerford, Lynda B. *Rissa Bartholomew's Declaration of Independence* (3–7). 2009, Scholastic $16.99 (978-0-545-05058-6). Everything seems to be different as 6th grade starts, and Clarissa copes (with wry humor) with changes at school and at home. (Rev: BCCB 6/09; BL 5/15/09; SLJ 6/09)

565 Conrad, Pam. *Our House: The Stories of Levittown* (4–7). Illus. by Brian Selznick. 1995, Scholastic paper $14.95 (978-0-590-46523-6). A series of fictional vignettes trace the history of the middle-class community of Levittown, New York. (Rev: BCCB 12/95; BL 1/1–15/96; HB 11–12/95; SLJ 11/95)

566 Cook, Eileen. *Unraveling Isobel* (8–10). 2012, Simon & Schuster $16.99 (978-144241327-6). Isobel, 17, begins to worry she's losing her mind when she and her mother move to her new husband's spooky mansion. **e** Lexile HL700L (Rev: BL 3/1/12; HB 1–2/12; VOYA 2/12)

567 *Cool Like That* (7–10). Series: So for Real. 2010, Kensington paper $9.95 (978-07582344-2-1). Gia had high hopes for her relationship with Ricky while attending a summer program at Columbia but Ricky is being cautious and she soon finds herself intrigued by

Rashad; the fourth in the series, this book stands alone. **e** (Rev: BL 2/1/10)

568 Cooney, Caroline B. *Hit the Road* (6–9). 2006, Delacorte LB $17.99 (978-0-385-90174-1). When Brit's parents leave the 16-year-old with her grandmother, they have no idea the brand-new driver will be setting off on a road trip to get the elderly woman and her two friends to their 65th college reunion. (Rev: BL 3/15/06*; SLJ 5/06)

569 Cooney, Caroline B. *Janie Face to Face* (7–10). 2013, Delacorte $17.99 (978-038574206-1); LB $20.99 (978-037599039-7). In this series conclusion, Janie and her friends are dogged by a writer who's eager to tell the story of her kidnapping to the world. **e** Lexile HL660L (Rev: BL 12/15/12; SLJ 2/13)

570 Cooper, Ilene. *Angel in My Pocket* (5–8). 2011, Feiwel & Friends $16.99 (978-0-312-37014-5). A magical coin travels from middle-schooler Bette to three classmates who also are suffering a variety of problems in this novel about friendship, magic, and transformation. Lexile 810L (Rev: BLO 2/15/11; LMC 5–6/11; SLJ 3/1/11; VOYA 6/11)

571 Coriell, Shelley. *Welcome, Caller, This Is Chloe* (8–12). 2012, Abrams Amulet $16.95 (978-1-4197-0191-7). Chloe copes with problems at home and the sudden alienation of her two best friends by joining her school's failing radio station, where she is given her own show. **e** (Rev: SLJ 6/12)

572 Corriveau, Art. *How I, Nicky Flynn, Finally Get a Life (and a Dog)* (4–7). 2010, Abrams $16.95 (978-081098298-7). The gift of a former seeing-eye dog coaxes depressed 11-year-old Nicky Flynn to meet people and explore his new Boston neighborhood. Lexile 670L (Rev: BL 3/1/10; LMC 11–12/10; SLJ 5/10)

573 Couloumbis, Audrey. *Not Exactly a Love Story* (8–11). 2012, Random House $16.99 (978-0-375-86783-5); LB $19.99 (978-037596783-2). After his dog dies and his parents get divorced, 15-year-old Vinnie finds himself living in Long Island and conducting a rocky relationship with a cute girl. 🎧 **e** (Rev: BL 12/1/12; LMC 5–6/13; SLJ 11/12; VOYA 12/12)

574 Crabtree, Julie. *Discovering Pig Magic* (5–8). 2008, Milkweed $16.95 (978-1-57131-683-7); paper $6.95 (978-1-57131-684-4). Thirteen-year-old Matilda and her friends Ariel and Nicki try using magic to resolve the problems they face. (Rev: BCCB 1/09; SLJ 6/09)

575 Crane, Dede. *Poster Boy* (8–12). 2009, Groundwood $17.95 (978-0-88899-855-2). When his younger sister is diagnosed with late-stage cancer, 16-year-old Gray Fallon's focus changes from parties and fun to an obsessive crusade against chemicals and toxins. Lexile 700L (Rev: BL 8/09; LMC 5–6/10; SLJ 12/09)

576 Craven, Margaret. *I Heard the Owl Call My Name* (7–12). 1973, Dell paper $6.99 (978-0-440-34369-1). A terminally ill Anglican priest and his assignment in a coastal Indian community in British Columbia. The nonfiction story behind this book is told in *Again Calls the Owl*.

577 Crew, Linda. *Brides of Eden: A True Story Imagined* (7–12). 2001, HarperCollins LB $15.89 (978-0-06-028751-1). Teenage Eva Mae Hurt describes the influence that magnetic preacher Joshua Creffield has on a group of women, who renounce their families and their everyday lives to follow his lead in this book based on fact, set in early 20th-century Oregon. (Rev: BCCB 2/01; BL 12/15/00; HB 3–4/01; HBG 10/01; SLJ 2/01; VOYA 6/01)

578 Crutcher, Chris. *Athletic Shorts: 6 Short Stories* (8–12). 1991, Greenwillow $18.99 (978-0-688-10816-8). These short stories focus on themes important to teens, such as sports, father-son friction, insecurity, and friendship. (Rev: BL 10/15/91; SLJ 9/91*)

579 Cuevas, Michelle. *The Masterwork of a Painting Elephant* (3–7). Illus. by Ed Young. 2011, Farrar $15.99 (978-0-374-34854-0). An artistic elephant named Birch and a boy abandoned as a baby, Pigeon Jones, become fast friends and travel together in search of their loved ones. (Rev: BL 9/1/11; SLJ 12/1/11)

580 Cummings, Priscilla. *Red Kayak* (6–9). 2004, Penguin $15.99 (978-0-525-47317-6). Brady's longtime friendship with J.T. and Digger is tested after a childish prank results in the death of a neighbor's child. (Rev: BL 9/1/04; SLJ 9/04; VOYA 10/04)

581 Cummings, Priscilla. *What Mr. Mattero Did* (6–9). 2005, Dutton $16.99 (978-0-525-47621-4). Three 7th-grade girls thoughtlessly accuse their music teacher of inappropriate behavior and are overwhelmed by the consequences. (Rev: BL 7/05; SLJ 8/05)

582 Curtis, Vanessa. *Zelah Green: One More Little Problem* (7–10). 2012, IPG/Egmont paper $7.99 (978-14052405-4-3). Zelah Green, first seen in 2011 and still suffering from obsessive compulsive disorder, is back in this novel about the summer Caro moves in and stirs things up. ℮ (Rev: BL 3/1/12; VOYA 2/12)

583 Dahl, Lesley. *The Problem with Paradise* (6–9). 2006, Delacorte $15.95 (978-0-385-73335-9). Fourteen-year-old Casey isn't excited about spending the summer on a small tropical island with her naturalist father and new stepfamily but storms, an interesting boy, and mild adventure await her there. (Rev: BL 11/15/06; SLJ 1/07)

584 Damico, Gina. *Croak* (7–10). 2012, Houghton Mifflin paper $8.99 (978-05476083-2-7). Lex, a 16-year-old with delinquent tendencies, discovers her uncle is the Grim Reaper when she goes to live with him for a summer in this novel that blends humor and mystery. ∩ ℮ (Rev: BL 3/15/12; SLJ 4/12; VOYA 12/11)

585 Danziger, Paula, and Ann M. Martin. *P. S. Longer Letter Later* (5–8). 1998, Scholastic paper $16.95 (978-0-590-21310-3). This novel consists of letters between two recently separated girlfriends — one who is adjusting well and the other who is facing family problems after her father loses his job and the family must change its lifestyle. (Rev: BL 6/1–15/98; HBG 10/98; SLJ 5/98; VOYA 8/98)

586 De Gramont, Nina. *Every Little Thing in the World* (8–11). 2010, Simon & Schuster $16.99 (978-1-4169-8013-1). Sent to a summer camp in Canada, 16-year-olds Sydney, who has just discovered she is pregnant, and her friend Natalia explore Sydney's options. ℮ Lexile 870L (Rev: BL 3/15/10; SLJ 4/10)

587 de la Cruz, Melissa. *Girl Stays in the Picture* (8–12). 2009, Simon & Schuster $16.99 (978-141696096-6). Gossip columns, news items, and parodies of real celebrities enliven this story of teens on a movie shoot in Saint-Tropez. (Rev: BL 7/09; SLJ 8/09)

588 de la Peña, Matt. *We Were Here* (7–12). 2009, Delacorte $17.99 (978-0-385-73667-1); LB $20.99 (978-0-385-90622-7). Thoughtful 16-year-old Miguel escapes from a California juvenile detention center with two other teens, and they become friends as they struggle to find a way to live. ℮ (Rev: BL 9/1/09; HB 11–12/09; SLJ 12/09; VOYA 12/09)

589 De Vigan, Delphine. *No and Me* (8–11). 2010, Bloomsbury $16.99 (978-1-59990-479-5). A moving book set in Paris about 13-year-old Lou's decision to invite a vagrant 18-year-old girl into her home, a home that has been unhappy since the death of Lou's younger sister. (Rev: BL 8/10; LMC 8–9/10; SLJ 7/10)

590 Dean, Carolee. *Forget Me Not* (7–10). 2012, Simon & Schuster $16.99 (978-1-4424-3254-3). Aspiring actress Ally struggles with depression and self-loathing when a compromising photo of her goes viral in this novel written in verse and with a plot twist involving ghosts. ℮ Lexile HL720L (Rev: BLO 11/1/12; SLJ 12/12; VOYA 12/12)

591 Deaver, Julie Reece. *Say Goodnight Gracie* (8–10). 1988, HarperCollins $15.00 (978-0-06-021418-0); paper $6.99 (978-0-06-447007-0). When her best friend Jimmy dies in an accident, Morgan struggles with her grief. (Rev: SLJ 2/88)

592 DeFelice, Cynthia. *The Light on Hogback Hill* (4–8). 1993, Macmillan paper $15.00 (978-0-02-726453-1). When 11-year-olds Hadley and Josh discover that the Witch Woman of Hogback Hill is really a shy, deformed woman, they help her find the courage to return to town. (Rev: BCCB 12/93; BL 11/1/93; SLJ 11/93)

593 Denman, K. L. *Mirror Image* (5–8). Series: Currents. 2007, Orca $14.95 (978-1-55143-667-8); paper $8.95 (978-1-55143-667-4). Popular Lacey and Sable, an immigrant to Canada from Bosnia who is a loner, could not be more different, and the girls are initially disappointed to be paired for an art project. (Rev: BL 3/15/07)

594 Devillers, Julia. *Lynn Visible* (7–10). 2010, Dutton $16.99 (978-0-525-47691-7). Lynn's 9th-grade classmates mock her flamboyant clothes until she is chosen as the "It Girl" for an online magazine. Lexile HL560L (Rev: BL 3/1/10; SLJ 4/10)

595 Dionne, Erin. *Models Don't Eat Chocolate Cookies* (6–8). 2009, Dial $16.99 (978-080373296-4). Overweight 13-year-old Celeste decides to take action when her aunt enters her in the Miss Husky Peach Pageant. ℮ Lexile 690L (Rev: BL 3/1/09; SLJ 4/1/09)

596 Dionne, Erin. *Notes from an Accidental Band Geek* (5–8). 2011, Dial $16.99 (978-0-8037-3564-4). Ambitious 9th-grader Elsie has her heart set on becoming a French horn player in an orchestra and is surprised to find that she actually enjoys playing the melliphone in the school's marching band despite her initial resistance. (Rev: BL 11/1/11; SLJ 10/1/11)

597 Dionne, Erin. *The Total Tragedy of a Girl Named Hamlet* (4–7). 2010, Dial $16.99 (978-0-803-73298-8). It's not easy for socially uncertain 8th-grader Hamlet when her genius 7-year-old sister Desdemona starts attending her middle school; however an audition for *A Midsummer Night's Dream* reveals Hamlet's acting abilities. ℮ Lexile 750L (Rev: BL 1/1/10; LMC 5–6/10; SLJ 2/10)

598 Dowell, Frances O'Roark. *The Kind of Friends We Used to Be* (4–7). 2009, Atheneum $16.99 (978-1-4169-5031-8). Kate and Marylin, whose friendship fell apart in *The Secret Language of Girls* (2005), are now in 7th grade and still heading in separate directions. ∩ (Rev: BCCB 5/09; BL 3/1/09; SLJ 3/09)

599 Doyle, Roddy. *A Greyhound of a Girl* (7–12). 2012, Abrams $16.95 (978-141970168-9). Covering several generations of an Irish family, this story features sassy 12-year-old Mary, her mother Scarlett, grandmother Emer, and Tansey, her great-grandmother, now a ghost. ℮ Lexile 500L (Rev: BL 3/15/12*; HB 5–6/12; LMC 8–9/12; SLJ 8/12)

600 Draper, Sharon M. *The Battle of Jericho* (7–10). 2003, Simon & Schuster $16.95 (978-0-689-84232-0). Sixteen-year-old Jericho is initially thrilled when he's asked to pledge for membership in the Warriors of Distinction club, but subsequent events turn chilling. (Rev: BL 6/1–15/03; HBG 4/04; SLJ 6/03; VOYA 8/03)

601 Draper, Sharon M. *Darkness Before Dawn* (8–12). Series: Hazelwood High. 2001, Simon & Schuster $16.95 (978-0-689-83080-8). Keisha Montgomery copes with many issues — the suicide of her ex-boyfriend, a new relationship, date rape, and more in this novel set at Hazelwood High. (Rev: BCCB 3/01; BL 1/1–15/01; HBG 10/01; SLJ 2/01; VOYA 8/01)

602 Draper, Sharon M. *Double Dutch* (7–10). 2002, Simon & Schuster $16.00 (978-0-689-84230-6). Eighth-graders Delia and Randy both have secrets — Delia can't read and Randy's father has disappeared, leaving him on his own. (Rev: BCCB 10/02; BL 9/1/02; HBG 10/02; SLJ 6/02; VOYA 8/02)

603 Draper, Sharon M. *Just Another Hero* (7–10). 2009, Simon & Schuster $16.99 (978-141690700-8). Bullying, family problems, drug addiction, thefts, and worries about school and college challenge the students introduced in *The Battle of Jericho* (2003) and *November Blues* (2007). ∩ (Rev: BL 6/1–15/09; SLJ 7/1/09)

604 Dunlop, Eileen. *Finn's Search* (4–7). 1994, Holiday $14.95 (978-0-8234-1099-6). Two Scottish boys try to save a gravel pit from local developers. (Rev: BCCB 12/94; BL 10/1/94; SLJ 10/94)

605 DuPrau, Jeanne. *Car Trouble* (7–10). 2005, Greenwillow LB $16.89 (978-0-06-073674-3). Seventeen-year-old Duff Pringle has various car and people adventures on the road from Virginia to a promised job in California. (Rev: BL 8/05; SLJ 10/05; VOYA 10/05)

606 Easton, Kelly. *To Be Mona* (8–11). 2008, Simon & Schuster $16.99 (978-141696940-2). Hampered by her life with a bipolar mother, 17-year-old Sage envies gorgeous class president Mona and overlooks friend Vern's devotion in favor of the attentions of the manipulative Roger; with an afterword about bipolar disorder and abusive relationships. ℮ (Rev: BL 11/15/08; LMC 3–4/09; SLJ 1/1/09)

607 Easton, Kelly. *White Magic: Spells to Hold You* (8–11). 2007, Random House $15.99 (978-0-375-83769-2). After moving to Los Angeles, Chrissie befriends Yvonne (a self-proclaimed witch) and Karen, who welcome her to their coven in this book that is more about friendship than magic. (Rev: BL 6/1–15/07; HB 9–10/07; SLJ 12/07)

608 Edgar, Elsbeth. *The Visconti House* (4–7). 2011, Candlewick $16.99 (978-0-7636-5019-3). Laura, who wants to fit in in her 8th-grade class, and Leon, a new student, become friends as they work together to unravel the history of Laura's supposedly haunted house; set in Australia. ℮ Lexile 650L (Rev: BL 2/1/11; SLJ 2/1/11; VOYA 4/11)

609 Ehrenberg, Pamela. *Ethan, Suspended* (7–10). 2007, Eerdmans $16.00 (978-0-8028-5324-0). After being suspended from school, Ethan is sent to live with his grandparents in inner-city Washington, D.C., where he's one of the very few white students and learns about segregation, poverty, making new friends, and falling in love. (Rev: BL 5/15/07; SLJ 7/07)

610 Ehrenhaft, Daniel. *Friend Is Not a Verb* (7–10). 2010, HarperCollins $16.99 (978-0-06-113106-6). Music helps Henry (Hen) cope with a breakup with his girlfriend, a close friendship with Emma that may lead somewhere, and the mysterious disappearance and reappearance of his sister. ∩ ℮ (Rev: BL 3/1/10; SLJ 5/10)

611 Ehrenhaft, Daniel. *That's Life, Samara Brooks* (6–8). 2010, Delacorte $15.99 (978-0-385-73434-9); LB

$18.99 (978-0-385-90441-4). A funny, fast-paced story about 13-year-old adoptee Samara, her efforts to fit in at school (running a blackjack table in the cafeteria?), and the aftermath that involves DNA and discussions of religion versus science. ⌒ (Rev: BL 1/1/10; SLJ 5/10)

612 Elkeles, Simone. *How to Ruin My Teenage Life* (7–10). Series: How to Ruin a Summer Vacation. 2007, Flux paper $8.95 (978-0-7387-1019-8). In this follow-up to *How to Ruin a Summer Vacation* (2006), Amy's life in Chicago with her Israeli father is full of irritating people, including her dad — who badly needs a girlfriend, her mother and her new husband and forthcoming baby, and a nerdy new guy in her apartment building. (Rev: SLJ 7/07)

613 Elkeles, Simone. *How to Ruin Your Boyfriend's Reputation* (8–12). 2009, Flux paper $9.95 (978-0-7387-1897-8). Seventeen-year-old Amy's scheme to spend some face time with her long-distance boyfriend lands her in boot camp with the Israeli Defense Force. ℮ Lexile HL750L (Rev: SLJ 12/09; VOYA 2/10)

614 Ellerbee, Linda. *Girl Reporter Blows Lid Off Town!* (4–7). Series: Get Real. 2000, HarperCollins LB $14.89 (978-0-06-028245-5). Casey Smith, a 6th-grade reporter, discovers the thrill of tracking down stories and getting at the truth in this lighthearted story set in a small town in the Berkshires. Also use *Girl Reporter Sinks School!* (Rev: BL 3/1/00; HBG 10/00; SLJ 6/00)

615 Ellsworth, Loretta. *In a Heartbeat* (8–12). 2010, Walker $16.99 (978-0-8027-2068-9). Figure skater Eagan, 16, dies in a fall and her heart is given to ailing 14-year-old Amelia, a procedure that affects both girls as they describe in alternating chapters. ℮ Lexile HL580L (Rev: BL 1/1–15/10; LMC 3–4/10; SLJ 2/10)

616 Epstein, Robin. *God Is in the Pancakes* (7–10). 2010, Dial $16.99 (978-0-803-73382-4). While working as a candy striper, 15-year-old Grace becomes friends with a man suffering from Lou Gehrig's disease, who eventually asks her to help him die. ⌒ ℮ (Rev: BL 5/15/10; LMC 10/10; SLJ 5/10; VOYA 8/10)

617 Fagan, Deva. *Fortune's Folly* (5–7). 2009, Holt $17.95 (978-0-8050-8742-0). Seventeen-year-old Fortunata becomes a fortune teller to support herself and her father and finds herself in a pickle when her predictions threaten her father's life. (Rev: BCCB 9/09; BL 4/1/09; SLJ 7/09)

618 Farrar, Josh. *A Song for Bijou* (4–8). 2013, Walker $16.99 (978-0-8027-3394-8). A beautiful Haitian girl who moved to Brooklyn after the earthquake instantly wins 7th-grader Alex's heart, but he must learn about her family's strict dating rules and together they face bullies and misunderstandings. ℮ Lexile 750L (Rev: BLO 7/5/13; LMC 5–6/13; SLJ 2/13; VOYA 12/12)

619 Feldman, Jody. *The Gollywhopper Games* (4–7). Illus. by Victoria Jamieson. 2008, Greenwillow $16.99 (978-0-06-121450-9). Gil Goodson is determined to

win the Gollywhopper Games, sponsored by the Golly Toy and Game Company, in this engaging novel that includes the puzzles that Gil must solve to be victorious. (Rev: BL 12/1/07; SLJ 3/08)

620 Feldman, Jody. *The Seventh Level* (5–8). 2010, Greenwillow $16.99 (978-0-06-195105-3). Eager for acceptance into his middle school's secret society, the Legend, Travis is thrilled when he begins receiving the clues and puzzles that, if solved, will grant him admittance. ℮ Lexile 630L (Rev: BL 5/1/10; SLJ 10/1/10)

621 Fergus, Maureen. *Recipe for Disaster* (7–9). 2009, Kids Can $18.95 (978-1-55453-319-0); paper $8.95 (978-1-55453-320-6). The funny, lighthearted story of 9th-grader Francie, who loves to cook and spend time with her friend Holly until a new girl at school threatens to come between them. Lexile 1130L (Rev: BL 8/09; SLJ 9/09)

622 Fifty Cent, and Laura Moser. *Playground* (7–10). 2011, Penguin $17.99 (978-1-59514-434-8). After a violent act, troubled and overweight black teen Butterball finds himself being egged on to perpetrate more violence by his peers. ⌒ ℮ Lexile 900L (Rev: BLO 10/1/11; SLJ 11/1/11)

623 Finch, Susan. *The Intimacy of Indiana* (8–12). 2001, Tudor $5.95 (978-0-936389-79-0). Readers follow three teens through the trials of their senior year in high school in small-town Indiana — SATs, college finance, romance, drugs, and of course parents. (Rev: BL 7/01)

624 Fink, Mark. *The Summer I Got a Life* (7–9). 2009, WestSide $16.95 (978-1-934813-12-6). Fifteen-year-old Andy Crenshaw is understandably upset when his Hawaiian vacation gets scrapped for a two-week visit to his uncle's farm in Wisconsin, but things take a turn for the better when he meets Laura, a spirited beauty who is confined to a wheelchair. Lexile HL690L (Rev: BL 9/15/09; SLJ 12/09; VOYA 2/10)

625 Fleischman, Paul. *Seek* (7–12). 2001, Cricket $16.95 (978-0-8126-4900-0). For a school autobiography project, 17-year-old Rob makes a recording of important sounds in his life, including the voice of the father he never knew. (Rev: BCCB 11/01; BL 12/15/01; HB 11–12/01; HBG 3/02; SLJ 9/01*; VOYA 12/01)

626 Fletcher, Ralph. *Flying Solo* (5–8). 1998, Clarion $16.00 (978-0-395-87323-6). This novel answers the question, "What would a 6th-grade class do if their substitute teacher fails to appear and they are left alone for a whole day?" (Rev: BCCB 9/98; BL 8/98*; HB 11–12/98; HBG 3/99; SLJ 10/98)

627 Fletcher, Ralph. *One O'Clock Chop* (8–10). 2007, Henry Holt $16.95 (978-0-8050-8143-5). In 1973, 14-year-old Matt falls for his gorgeous first cousin Jazzy, who ends up breaking his heart. (Rev: BL 9/15/07; SLJ 10/07)

628 Flinn, Alex. *Diva* (8–11). 2006, HarperTempest $15.99 (978-0-06-056843-6). Caitlin (last seen in the

2005 *Breathing Underwater*) deals with her past abusive relationship, weight issues, troubles with her mom, and her dream of attending a performing arts school for opera. (Rev: BL 10/1/06; SLJ 11/06)

629 Fogelin, Adrian. *The Big Nothing* (7–9). 2004, Peachtree $14.95 (978-1-56145-326-9). Thirteen-year-old Justin has a miserable home life and generally feels abandoned until neighbor Jemmie starts paying attention to him and he discovers he has a talent for playing the piano; this novel shares a setting and some with characters from *Crossing Jordan* (2000) and *My Brother's Hero* (2002). (Rev: BL 12/15/04; SLJ 12/04)

630 Fogelin, Adrian. *The Real Question* (7–10). 2006, Peachtree $15.95 (978-1-56145-383-2). Fisher Brown, 16, is just under too much pressure — from his counselor dad, academic stress, a sick dog, and so forth — and on an impulse he sets off to do an out-of-town roofing job with a carefree guy named Lonny. (Rev: LMC 3/07; SLJ 11/06)

631 Foley, John. *A Mighty Wall* (7–10). 2009, Flux paper $9.95 (978-073871448-6). Jordan's junior year in high school is all about rock climbing, friends, drinking, and sex—until an accident changes everything. e (Rev: BL 3/1/09; SLJ 6/1/09)

632 Franco, Betsy. *Metamorphosis: Junior Year* (7–10). Illus. by Tom Franco. 2009, Candlewick $16.99 (978-0-7636-3765-1). After the sudden departure of his drug-addicted sister, high school junior, poet, and artist Ovid finds himself the sole focus of his suddenly over-attentive parents in this contemporary novel that finds its inspiration in Roman mythology. ∩ Lexile HL740L (Rev: BL 9/1/09; SLJ 12/09; VOYA 2/10)

633 Frank, Lucy. *The Homeschool Liberation League* (5–8). 2009, Dial $16.99 (978-0-8037-3230-8). Eighth-grader Katya is disappointed when home schooling does not turn out to give her the freedom she desires, and she sets out — with the help of a cute violin player named Milo — to change this. (Rev: BCCB 9/09; BLO 5/27/09; HB 9/09; SLJ 8/09)

634 Frank, Lucy. *Lucky Stars* (4–7). 2005, Simon & Schuster $16.95 (978-0-689-85933-5). Kira, a talented singer with a feisty character, arrives in New York City to find that her father has plans that don't fit in with her own. (Rev: BL 5/15/05; SLJ 7/05)

635 Franklin, Emily, and Brendan Halpin. *Tessa Masterson Will Go to Prom* (8–12). 2012, Walker $16.99 (978-080272345-1); paper $9.99 (978-08027235-9-8). The forthcoming prom is a catalyst to local scandal as high school senior Luke invites his best friend Tessa and she reveals that she is in fact lesbian and intends to bring a female date. e (Rev: BL 4/1/12; LMC 5–6/12; SLJ 4/12; VOYA 12/11)

636 Fraustino, Lisa Rowe. *The Hole in the Wall* (5–8). 2010, Milkweed $16.95 (978-157131696-7). Strip mining has ruined their environment and 11-year-old twins

Sebby and Barbara wonder if some of the strange things they are seeing are real in this novel that blends ecology and science fiction. (Rev: BL 12/15/10; LMC 3–4/11)

637 Frederick, Heather Vogel. *Home for the Holidays* (6–10). 2011, Simon & Schuster $15.99 (978-144240685-8). The mother-daughter book club's girls cope with imperfections in their plans for relaxing holiday vacations. e Lexile 840L (Rev: BLO 12/15/11; SLJ 10/1/11)

638 Frederick, Heather Vogel. *The Mother-Daughter Book Club* (4–7). 2007, Simon & Schuster $15.99 (978-0-689-86412-4). Four very different 6th-grade girls join a book club where they will read *Little Women* with their mothers. (Rev: BL 6/1–15/07; SLJ 8/07)

639 Frederick, Heather Vogel. *Much Ado About Anne* (5–8). 2008, Simon & Schuster $15.99 (978-0-689-85566-5). Seventh-graders Cassidy, Megan, Jess, and Emma are reading books by Lucy Maud Montgomery with their mothers and using insights gained there in dealing with various problems; a sequel to *The Mother-Daughter Book Club* (2007). (Rev: SLJ 11/08)

640 Fredericks, Mariah. *Crunch Time* (8–11). 2006, Simon & Schuster $15.95 (978-0-689-86938-9). Four members of a private SAT study group — who have formed emotional attachments as they study — find themselves under suspicion of cheating. (Rev: BL 1/1–15/06; SLJ 1/06; VOYA 12/05)

641 Fredericks, Mariah. *Fame* (5–8). Illus. by Liselotte Watkins. Series: In the Cards. 2008, Atheneum $15.99 (978-0-689-87656-1). Eve tries out for the 8th-grade play only after the tarot cards tell her it could lead to fame in this sequel to *In the Cards: Love* (2007). (Rev: BL 1/1–15/08; SLJ 8/08)

642 Fredericks, Mariah. *Life* (5–8). Series: In the Cards. 2008, Simon & Schuster $16.99 (978-068987658-5). Syd narrates this well-written stand-alone volume in a tarot-reading series as the three best friends seek answers about their daily lives. Lexile NC560L (Rev: BL 9/1/08; SLJ 8/08)

643 Freymann-Weyr, Garret. *The Kings Are Already Here* (7–10). 2003, Houghton $15.00 (978-0-618-26363-9). Phebe's love of ballet dominates her life until she travels to Geneva to visit her father and meets Nikolai, a 16-year-old refugee who is obsessed with chess. (Rev: BL 2/15/03; HB 3–4/03; HBG 10/03; SLJ 4/03; VOYA 4/03)

644 Friedman, Aimee. *The Year My Sister Got Lucky* (7–10). 2008, Scholastic $16.99 (978-0-439-92227-2). When Katie and Michaela's parents move them from New York City to the Adirondacks, Katie is crushed and angry, while Michaela adapts and thrives. (Rev: BL 12/1/07; SLJ 3/08)

645 Friend, Catherine. *Barn Boot Blues* (4–7). 2011, Marshall Cavendish $16.99 (978-0-7614-5930-9). Twelve-year-old Taylor is miserable when her family moves from Minneapolis to a rural farm, but her innate sense of humor helps her make new friends at school. **e** (Rev: HB 11–12/11; LMC 1–2/12; SLJ 12/1/11)

646 Friend, Natasha. *For Keeps* (8–11). 2010, Viking $16.99 (978-0-670-01190-2). Josie's life is changing as she navigates her junior year — she has a serious boyfriend, and her mother also has found someone; and then the father she has never met comes back to town and shakes things up. **e** (Rev: BL 1/1–15/10; HB 5–6/10; SLJ 4/10; VOYA 4/10)

647 Friesen, Gayle. *The Isabel Factor* (7–10). 2005, Kids Can $16.95 (978-1-55337-737-5). Anna's best friend Zoe breaks her arm and, for the first time in years, Anna finds herself running her own life. (Rev: BL 9/1/05; SLJ 11/05)

648 Frost, Helen. *Hidden* (6–9). 2011, Farrar $16.99 (978-0-374-38221-6). Six years after the event, Darra and Wren meet at a summer camp and recall when Darra's father inadvertently kidnapped Wren, who was then trapped in Darra's garage for several days; this story is told in verse. ALA Notable Books 2012. ⌂ Lexile HL670L (Rev: BL 4/1/11; LMC 8–9/11*; SLJ 6/11; VOYA 6/11)

649 Fry, Erin. *Losing It* (7–9). 2012, Amazon Children's $16.99 (978-0-7614-6220-0). After his mother's death and his father's subsequent stroke, overweight 8th-grader Bennett finds himself living with a aunt and uncle, and is surprised to discover that a healthy diet and cross-country running bring him contentment and purpose. **e** (Rev: BLO 10/1/12; LMC 5–6/13; SLJ 11/12; VOYA 12/12)

650 Funke, Cornelia. *The Thief Lord* (6–9). 2002, Scholastic $19.99 (978-0-439-40437-2). Inspired by their dead mother's stories of the wonders of Venice, two boys run away from Hamburg and find an unusual home under the protection of a young Venetian thief. (Rev: BCCB 11/02; BL 10/15/02; HB 11–12/02; HBG 3/03; SLJ 10/02*; VOYA 4/03)

651 Gallagher, Diana G. *Guilty! The Complicated Life of Claudia Cristina Cortez* (4–7). Illus. by Brann Garvey. Series: Claudia Cristina Cortez. 2008, Stone Arch LB $23.93 (978-1-59889-838-5); paper $5.95 (978-1-59889-881-1). Claudia and are friend Monica are accused of stealing $10 in this novel that will attract reluctant readers. Also use *Whatever!* (2008), in which the girls in Claudia's club must decide whether a boy can join and *Camp Can't* (2008), about Claudia's efforts to become a junior counselor. (Rev: SLJ 1/08)

652 Gallagher, Diana G. *Vote! The Complicated Life of Claudia Cristina Cortez* (5–7). Illus. by Brann Garvey. Series: Claudia Cristina Cortez. 2008, Stone Arch LB $23.93 (978-1-4342-0770-8); paper $5.95 (978-1-4342-0866-8). Claudia and her classmates deal with the ups and downs of a class election in this visually appealing story for reluctant readers that includes a dis-

cussion guide and Internet links. (Rev: LMC 5/09; SLJ 2/09)

653 Gantos, Jack. *Heads or Tails: Stories from the Sixth Grade* (5–8). 1994, Farrar $16.00 (978-0-374-32909-9). A collection of eight unusual short stories about 6th-grader Jack, a born survivor who overcomes amazing obstacles in this book set in Fort Lauderdale. (Rev: BCCB 7–8/94; HB 7–8/94; SLJ 6/94*)

654 Gantos, Jack. *Jack on the Tracks: Four Seasons of Fifth Grade* (5–7). 1999, Farrar $16.00 (978-0-374-33665-3). An episodic novel (the fourth about Jack Henry) in which Jack, a preadolescent, has several innocent adventures while growing up. (Rev: BCCB 9/99; BL 9/1/99; HB 11–12/99; HBG 3/00; SLJ 10/99; VOYA 2/00)

655 George, Madeleine. *Looks* (7–10). 2008, Viking $16.99 (978-067006167-9). High school seniors Meghan, who is fat, and Aimee, who is razor thin, form an unlikely alliance as they seek revenge against the popular and cruel Cara in this tense story. Best Books for Young Adults 2009. (Rev: BL 9/15/08*; HB 7–8/08; SLJ 5/08; VOYA 10/08)

656 German, Carol. *A Midsummer Night's Dork* (4–7). 2004, HarperCollins $15.99 (978-0-06-050718-3). In this sequel to *Dork on the Run* (2002), 6th-grader Jerry's class puts on an Elizabethan fair and Jerry has to stand up to another bully, even if it means making a fool of himself. (Rev: BL 2/1/04; SLJ 3/04)

657 Gilbert, Barbara Snow. *Paper Trail* (7–10). 2000, Front St $16.95 (978-1-886910-44-7). A thought-provoking story of a boy torn between family loyalties and connections to a cult known as the Soldiers of God. (Rev: BL 7/00; HB 7–8/00; HBG 9/00; SLJ 8/00)

658 Giles, Gail. *Dark Song* (7–11). 2010, Little, Brown $16.99 (978-0-316-06886-4). In this timely riches-to-rags story, well-heeled Ames's family lands on skid row, and the 15-year-old takes up with 22-year-old criminally inclined Marc. **e** Lexile HL570L (Rev: BL 9/1/10; SLJ 10/1/10; VOYA 10/10)

659 Gilson, Jamie. *Thirteen Ways to Sink a Sub* (4–7). Illus. by Linda Strauss Edwards. 1982, Lothrop $15.95 (978-0-688-01304-2). The girls in Room 4A challenge the boys to see who can first make their substitute teacher cry. A sequel is *4B Goes Wild* (1983).

660 Givner, Joan. *Ellen Fremedon* (5–7). 2004, Groundwood $15.95 (978-0-88899-557-5). When her family seeks to block a proposed housing development, 12-year-old Ellen Fremedon, an aspiring novelist, must set aside her summer project to cope with the repercussions. (Rev: BL 11/15/04)

661 Givner, Joan. *Ellen Fremedon, Journalist* (5–7). 2005, Groundwood $15.95 (978-0-88899-668-8). In this appealing sequel to *Ellen Fremedon* (2004), young Ellen uncovers some shocking stories when she starts a newspaper in quiet Partridge Cove. (Rev: BL 11/1/05; SLJ 2/06)

662 Going, K. L. *King of the Screwups* (7–12). 2009, Harcourt $17.00 (978-015206258-3). Straight athlete Liam's love of fashion and fun irks his strict father, so Liam moves in with his cross-dressing uncle — "Aunt Pete" — and tries to fit in in his new environment. Lexile HL690L (Rev: BL 4/15/09; SLJ 4/1/09*)

663 Golds, Cassandra. *The Museum of Mary Child* (5–8). 2009, Kane/Miller $16.99 (978-1-935279-13-6). Sad teen Heloise, who longs for love, finds a doll under the floorboards of her bedroom and runs away from home when her unloving godmother threatens it. Lexile 840L (Rev: BLO 8/09; LMC 1–2/10; SLJ 12/09)

664 Goldschmidt, Judy. *The Secret Blog of Raisin Rodriguez* (6–9). 2005, Penguin $12.99 (978-1-59514-018-0). Uprooted from her familiar life in California and trying to adjust to her new digs in Philadelphia, 13-year-old Raisin Rodriguez keeps old friends up to date on what's happening in her life through a frank blog that she does not intend to become public. (Rev: BCCB 5/05; BL 3/1/05; SLJ 5/05)

665 Goldschmidt, Judy. *Will the Real Raisin Rodriguez Please Stand Up?* (6–8). 2007, Penguin $12.99 (978-1-59514-058-6). Raisin, still in 7th grade, travels back home to visit her dad in Berkeley and is jealous to see that her two best friends have made a friendship with another girl; this third installment in the humorous series is also delivered in blogging/texting format. (Rev: SLJ 7/07)

666 Gonzalez, Julie. *Wings* (8–11). 2005, Delacorte LB $17.99 (978-0-385-90253-3). A suspenseful story in which Ben is convinced he will someday sprout wings and take to the sky despite evidence to the contrary. (Rev: BCCB 4/05; BL 3/15/05; SLJ 8/05; VOYA 4/05)

667 Goobie, Beth. *Before Wings* (7–10). 2001, Orca $16.95 (978-1-55143-161-1). An absorbing story that centers on the counselors at a summer camp and on 15-year-old Adrien's past illness and present mystical experiences. (Rev: BL 3/15/01; HB 3–4/01; HBG 10/01; SLJ 4/01; VOYA 4/01)

668 Goobie, Beth. *The Lottery* (7–12). 2002, Orca $15.95 (978-1-55143-238-0). As the lottery winner, 15-year-old Sal must spend the year doing the bidding of a sinister student group, the Shadow Council. (Rev: BL 1/1–15/03; HBG 10/03; SLJ 3/03; VOYA 2/03)

669 Grace, Amanda. *In Too Deep* (7–11). 2012, Flux paper $9.95 (978-07387260-0-7). An effort to make her best friend Nick jealous backfires when high school senior Sam allows a rumor to proliferate. e Lexile 730L (Rev: BL 2/1/12; LMC 5–6/12; SLJ 3/12)

670 Grant, Vicki. *Hold the Pickles* (5–8). Series: Orca Currents. 2012, Orca LB $16.95 (978-155469921-6); paper $9.95 (978-155469920-9). A puny 15-year-old eager for a chance to earn some money dresses up as a hot dog at a food fair, making him a prime target for bullies; for reluctant readers, this action-packed story also involves a mystery. e Lexile HL580L (Rev: BL 3/1/12; LMC 8–9/12; SLJ 5/1/12)

671 Grant, Vicki. *Nine Doors* (5–9). Series: Orca Currents. 2009, Orca LB $16.95 (978-1-55469-074-9); paper $9.95 (978-1-55469-073-2). When Emery and Richard play pranks on their neighbors, they get more than they bargained for and end up in serious trouble; for reluctant readers. Lexile HL470L (Rev: BL 5/15/09; SLJ 8/09)

672 Green, Tim. *Unstoppable* (5–8). 2012, HarperCollins $16.99 (978-0-06-208956-4). Harrison, a 13-year-old who has had a tough life in a series of foster homes, finally gets lucky and is placed with a loving couple and even a football coach! But his stardom on the field comes to a crashing halt. ⋒ e Lexile 730L (Rev: BL 9/1/12; SLJ 8/1/12; VOYA 8/12)

673 Greene, Constance C. *A Girl Called Al* (5–7). Illus. by Byron Barton. 1991, Puffin paper $5.99 (978-0-14-034786-9). The friendship between two 7th-graders and their apartment building superintendent is humorously and deftly recounted.

674 Greenwald, Lisa. *My Life in Pink and Green* (4–7). 2009, Abrams $16.95 (978-0-8109-8352-6). Twelve-year-old Lucy's family's pharmacy is in serious financial trouble until Lucy has the idea to turn part of it into an eco-spa. e Lexile 680L (Rev: BL 2/15/09; SLJ 4/1/09)

675 Gregory, Deborah. *Wishing on a Star* (5–8). Series: The Cheetah Girls. 1999, Hyperion paper $3.99 (978-0-7868-1384-1). A light novel about five girls in New York City who form a singing group, the Cheetah Girls, and are soon signed up for an important gig. (Rev: SLJ 1/00)

676 Griffin, Adele. *The Julian Game* (8–12). 2010, Penguin $16.99 (978-0-399-25460-4). Scholarship student Raye is eager to make friends at her elite school and agrees to help the popular Ella with Mandarin — and with an ill-advised Facebook attempt at revenge. e Lexile HL700L (Rev: BL 8/10; SLJ 10/1/10; VOYA 10/10)

677 Grunwell, Jeanne Marie. *Mind Games* (5–8). 2003, Houghton Mifflin $15.00 (978-0-618-17672-4). Six very different 7th-graders get to know each other as they collaborate on a science fair project in this inventive novel sprinkled with press clippings and project notes. (Rev: BL 5/15/03; HB 5–6/03; HBG 10/03; LMC 10/03; SLJ 5/03)

678 Gurtler, Janet. *Who I Kissed* (8–11). 2012, Sourcebooks paper $9.99 (978-1-4022-7-054-3). When a boy she kissed dies of anaphylactic shock, Samantha finds herself isolated from her peers. e Lexile HL590L (Rev: BL 10/15/12; SLJ 11/12)

679 Gutman, Dan. *The Million Dollar Putt* (6–8). 2006, Hyperion LB $14.99 (978-1-4395-9681-4). Birdie, a 12-year-old loner with asthma, is the perfect coach for Bogie, a blind golfer who hopes to win a tournament with a $1 million prize. (Rev: SLJ 9/06)

680 Gutman, Dan. *The Talent Show* (4–7). 2010, Simon & Schuster $15.99 (978-1-4169-9003-1). A small Kansas town decides to hold a talent show to renew their spirits after a destructive tornado; however, even as the show takes place and the students have picked a favorite another tornado affects the outcome. ℯ Lexile 800L (Rev: BL 6/10; LMC 11–12/10; SLJ 8/10)

681 Haber, Melissa Glenn. *The Pluto Project* (7–10). 2006, Dutton $17.99 (978-0-525-47721-1). Alan Green acts cool and indifferent to cover up his emotions after his mother's death, but a new love interest and a spy game that turns realistic force him to confront his feelings. (Rev: BL 7/06; SLJ 7/06)

682 Haddix, Margaret Peterson. *Leaving Fishers* (6–9). 2008, Paw Prints $14.99 (978-1-4395-2932-4). High-schooler Dorrie becomes innocently involved in a religious cult called Fishers of Men and soon finds that getting out is difficult; first published in 1997. (Rev: BL 12/15/97; BR 5–6/98; SLJ 10/97; VOYA 2/98)

683 Hagerup, Klaus. *Markus and the Girls* (6–9). Trans. by Tara Chace. 2009, Front St $17.95 (978-159078520-1). In this funny sequel to *Markus and Diana* (2006), 8th-graders Markus and Sigmund attempt to win a girl's heart by staging a production of *Romeo and Juliet*; set in Norway. (Rev: BLO 3/24/09; HB 5–6/09; SLJ 9/09; VOYA 8/09)

684 Hahn, Mary Downing. *Daphne's Book* (6–8). 1983, Houghton Mifflin $15.00 (978-0-89919-183-6). The story of a friendship between two very different girls.

685 Hall, Barbara. *Tempo Change* (7–12). 2009, Delacorte $16.99 (978-038573607-7); LB $19.99 (978-038590585-5). High school sophomore Blanche hopes her band's gig at a music festival will help her meet her long-lost father. ℯ (Rev: BL 7/09; SLJ 10/09)

686 Hall, Katy, and Lisa Eisenberg. *The Paxton Cheerleaders: Go for It, Patti!* (4–7). 1994, Simon & Schuster paper $3.50 (978-0-671-89490-0). Four 7th-grade girls from different backgrounds make the cheerleading team in their junior high school. (Rev: BL 2/1/95)

687 Halpern, Julie. *Have a Nice Day* (8–12). 2012, Feiwel & Friends $16.99 (978-0-312-60660-2). After being treated for depression, Anna struggles to readjust to life outside a mental hospital — and to cope with her parents' failing marriage — in this sequel to 2007's *Get Well Soon*. ℯ Lexile 870L (Rev: BL 11/1/12; LMC 3–4/13; SLJ 10/12)

688 Han, Jenny. *Shug* (5–8). 2006, Simon & Schuster $14.95 (978-1-4169-0942-2). Annemarie Wilcox, a 7th-grader better known as Shug, faces numerous challenges in addition to the usual middle-school problems:

a gorgeous older sister, squabbling parents, a fight with her best friend, and a crush on Mark that doesn't seem to be reciprocated. (Rev: BL 2/15/06; SLJ 5/06)

689 Harkrader, Lisa. *The Adventures of Beanboy* (4–7). Illus. by author. 2012, Houghton Mifflin $9.99 (978-054755078-7). Thirteen-year-old Tucker's creation of a superhero sidekick for a comic book competition leads to a big boost in his own confidence in and out of school. ℯ Lexile 670L (Rev: BL 3/1/12; SLJ 2/12*)

690 Harper, Suzanne. *The Juliet Club* (8–12). 2008, Greenwillow $16.99 (978-006136691-8); LB $17.89 (978-006136692-5). In this light, modern-day Shakespearean tale set in Verona, Italy, six teens — three American and three Italian — study and perform scenes from *Romeo and Juliet* — that mirror the events of their own lives. Lexile 830L (Rev: BL 8/08; SLJ 7/08; VOYA 6/08)

691 Harrington, Jane. *Four Things My Geeky-Jock-of-a-Best-Friend Must Do in Europe* (5–8). 2006, Darby Creek LB $15.95 (978-1-58196-041-9). From the European cruise she is taking with her mother, 13-year-old Brady reports via letter on her progress in meeting her must-dos — which include wearing a revealing bikini and meeting a "code-red Euro-hottie." (Rev: SLJ 6/06)

692 Hartinger, Brent. *Project Sweet Life* (6–9). 2009, HarperTeen $16.99 (978-006082411-2). In this comedy of errors, three 15-year-old boys — Dave, Victor, and Curtis — opt to avoid their parent-mandated summer jobs with a mixture of lighthearted deceit and amusing get-rich-quick schemes. ℯ Lexile 740L (Rev: BL 10/1/08; SLJ 4/1/09; VOYA 4/09)

693 Hartman, Brett. *Cadillac Chronicles* (8–12). 2012, Cinco Puntos $16.95 (978-1-935955-41-2). On a mission to find his absent father, 16-year-old Alex sets off on a road trip with an elderly African American man named Lester. ℯ Lexile HL650L (Rev: BL 12/15/12; SLJ 9/12*)

694 Hathaway, Jill. *Slide* (8–12). 2012, HarperCollins $17.99 (978-006207790-5). Vee has an ability to slide into the minds of others, and when she witnesses a murder in this way she struggles to solve this without revealing her secret. ℯ (Rev: BL 4/1/12; HB 3–4/12; SLJ 3/12)

695 Hautman, Pete. *All-In* (7–10). 2007, Simon & Schuster $15.99 (978-1-4169-1325-2). Seventeen-year-old Denn, the poker prodigy last seen in *Stone Cold* (1998), finds his luck deserting him in this fast-action story. (Rev: BL 5/1/07; HB 7–8/07; SLJ 7/07)

696 Hautman, Pete. *Blank Confession* (8–11). 2010, Simon & Schuster $16.99 (978-1-4169-1327-6). Bullying, drugs, and violence are themes in this story about a 16-year-old named Shayne who walks into a police station and confesses to murder. (Rev: BL 10/1/10; SLJ 12/1/10)

697 Hautman, Pete. *What Boys Really Want* (8–11). 2012, Scholastic $17.99 (978-054511315-1). Adam borrows liberally from Lita's blog for his self-published advice book for boys, endangering their friendship. ℮ (Rev: BL 12/15/11; HB 3–4/12; VOYA 2/12)

698 Hawkins, Aaron R. *The Year Money Grew on Trees* (5–8). 2010, Houghton Mifflin $16 (978-0-547-27977-0). Fourteen-year-old Jackson learns a lot about farming — and about himself — when his manipulative neighbor promises him the deed to his son's apple orchard — if he can sell $8,000 worth of fruit in the first year. ℮ Lexile 810L (Rev: BL 9/15/10; LMC 3–4/11; SLJ 10/1/10)

699 Haworth-Attard, Barbara. *My Life from Air-Bras to Zits* (8–10). 2009, Flux paper $9.95 (978-0-7387-1483-7). Tenth-grader Teresa chronicles her life in this entertaining diary-style narrative by taking readers on an A to Z trip through her myriad social and domestic challenges. (Rev: SLJ 3/1/09)

700 Hazuka, Tom. *Last Chance for First* (8–11). 2008, Brown Barn paper $8.95 (978-0-9798824-0-1). Robby, a high school junior, faces a lot of challenges: unfavorable comparisons with his older brother, an attraction to an unpopular girl, problems with his coach and a soccer teammate. . . . (Rev: BL 6/1–15/08; SLJ 9/08)

701 Headley, Justina Chen. *Girl Overboard* (7–11). 2008, Little, Brown $16.99 (978-0-316-01130-3). Super-rich Chinese American Syrah learns more about her family's heritage and about the satisfaction in helping others when she uses her family's power to help a sick friend. (Rev: BL 1/1–15/08; SLJ 2/08)

702 Hendrickson, Dave. *Cracking the Ice* (8–11). 2011, WestSide $16.95 (978-193481355-3). In 1968 African American Jessie Stackhouse confronts racism when he wins a hockey scholarship to a New Hampshire prep school. Lexile HL770L (Rev: BLO 12/15/11; LMC 8–9/12)

703 Heneghan, James. *Payback* (6–9). 2007, Groundwood $16.95 (978-0-88899-701-2). When fellow new student Benny commits suicide because of the torment he was subjected to by bullies, Charley blames himself for not helping and feels he has to make amends. (Rev: BL 5/1/07; SLJ 9/07)

704 Henkes, Kevin. *Bird Lake Moon* (5–7). 2008, Greenwillow $15.99 (978-0-06-147076-9). Unsettled because his parents are divorcing, Mitch hopes to move into the empty house next door and is annoyed when the family who owns it turns up; he decides to trick them into thinking their dead son is haunting them, a choice that has consequences when he becomes friends with the son. ∩ (Rev: BL 3/15/08; SLJ 3/08)

705 Henkes, Kevin. *Olive's Ocean* (5–8). 2003, Greenwillow LB $16.89 (978-0-06-053544-5). During a summer at the beach, Martha, an aspiring writer, wrestles with a classmate's sudden death, has her first whiff of romance, and gets to know her family and herself better. Newbery Honor 2004. (Rev: BL 9/1/03*; HB 11–12/03*; HBG 4/04; SLJ 8/03*)

706 Henson, Heather. *Dream of Night* (4–8). 2010, Simon & Schuster $15.99 (978-1-4169-4899-5). Twelve-year-old Shiloh slowly learns to trust others with the help of her foster mother and Dream of Night, a horse that has also suffered and that offers its own perspective. ℮ Lexile 470L (Rev: BLO 4/15/10; LMC 8–9/10; SLJ 4/10)

707 Henson, Heather. *Here's How I See It, Here's How It Is* (5–7). 2009, Atheneum $16.99 (978-1-4169-4901-5). Twelve-year-old Junebug is a budding actress working at her parents' summer stock theater but suddenly circumstances change and she faces a number of problems including her parents' separation and a boy with Asperger's syndrome. (Rev: BCCB 6/09; BL 4/1/09; SLJ 6/09)

708 Herbach, Geoff. *Nothing Special* (7–10). 2012, Sourcebooks paper $9.99 (978-1-4022-6-507-5). In this often funny sequel to *Stupid Fast* (2011), high school football player Felton Reinstein frets over the disappearance of his younger brother Andrew and sets out to find him. ℮ Lexile 630L (Rev: BL 6/12; SLJ 7/12; VOYA 6/12)

709 Herrera, Juan Felipe. *Cinnamon Girl: Letters Found Inside a Cereal Box* (6–9). 2005, HarperCollins LB $16.89 (978-0-06-057985-2). In free verse, 13-year-old Yolanda struggles to cope with the impact of 9/11 and the uncertainties in her life that this shock has revived. (Rev: BL 8/05; SLJ 11/05)

710 Hershey, Mary. *The One Where the Kid Nearly Jumps to His Death and Lands in California* (7–10). 2007, Penguin $15.99 (978-1-59514-150-7). Thirteen-year-old Stump, so named because one of his legs was amputated below the knee after a skiing accident, expects a difficult summer with his father and his new wife but in addition to dealing with his dad, he falls for a soap opera star and learns to swim. (Rev: BL 5/1/07; SLJ 3/07)

711 Hiaasen, Carl. *Chomp* (5–8). 2012, Knopf $16.99 (978-037586842-9); LB $19.99 (978-037596842-6). A reality TV show called "Expedition Survival" sparks an exciting environmental adventure when the star disappears in the Everglades. ∩ ℮ Lexile 800L (Rev: BL 11/15/11; HB 3–4/12; LMC 5–6/12*; SLJ 3/12*)

712 Hiaasen, Carl. *Flush* (5–8). 2005, Knopf LB $18.99 (978-0-375-92182-7). Noah Underwood and his younger sister Abbey set out to prove their father was justified in sinking a floating casino because it was polluting. (Rev: BL 8/05; SLJ 9/05)

713 High, Linda Oatman. *Sister Slam and the Poetic Motormouth Road Trip* (8–12). 2004, Bloomsbury $16.95 (978-1-58234-948-0). Laura Rose Crapper, a.k.a. Sister Slam, and her friend Twig head for New York, where they meet a handsome boy named Jake. (Rev: BL 5/1/04; SLJ 5/04)

714 Hobbs, Valerie. *Defiance* (4–7). 2005, Farrar $16.00 (978-0-374-30847-6). An elderly neighbor named Pearl — and her cow — become valuable friends to 11-year-old Toby, who does not want to tell his parents that his cancer is back. (Rev: BL 8/05; SLJ 9/05)

715 Hollings, Anastasia. *Beautiful World* (7–10). 2009, HarperTeen paper $8.99 (978-006143532-4). Amelia Warner wants a place in New York society and is determined to get it by hook or by crook in this first installment in a chick-lit series. e (Rev: BL 7/09)

716 Holm, Jennifer L. *Eighth Grade Is Making Me Sick: Ginny Davis's Year in Stuff* (5–8). Illus. by Elicia Castaldi. 2012, Random House $15.99 (978-0-375-86851-1); LB $18.99 (978-0-375-96851-8). In this moving and funny sequel to *Middle School Is Worse Than Meatloaf* (2007), Ginny relates through a variety of formats — notes, poems, emails, and other ephemera — her ambitions for the year and the problems that arise when her stepfather loses his job, her brother Henry gets in trouble, and a new baby is on the way. (Rev: BL 9/1/12; SLJ 10/12)

717 Holm, Jennifer L. *Middle School Is Worse Than Meatloaf: A Year Told through Stuff* (5–8). Illus. by Elicia Castaldi. 2007, Atheneum $12.99 (978-0-689-85281-7). Receipts, notes, cards, magazine clippings, and other "stuff" tell of an eventful year in Ginny's life that includes bad hair days, iffy report cards, her mother's remarriage, and other tragedies. (Rev: BL 10/15/07; SLJ 9/07)

718 Holmes, Elizabeth. *The Normal Kid* (5–7). 2012, Carolrhoda $17.95 (978-0-7613-8085-6). In alternating first-person narratives, 5th-graders Sylvan and Charity describe their efforts to be accepted and recognize that the other students feel the same way. e Lexile 780L (Rev: BL 11/1/12; LMC 3–4/13; SLJ 9/12)

719 Holt, Kimberly Willis. *When Zachary Beaver Came to Town* (5–9). 1999, Henry Holt $16.95 (978-0-8050-6116-1). Thirteen-year-old Toby Wilson learns the value of love and friendship when he gets to know Zachary Beaver, a 643-pound teen who has been abandoned by his guardian. (Rev: BCCB 12/99; BL 9/15/99; HB 11–12/99; HBG 3/00; SLJ 11/99*; VOYA 12/99)

720 Holtwijk, Ineke. *Asphalt Angels* (8–12). Trans. by Wanda Boeke. 1999, Front St $15.95 (978-1-886910-24-9). When a homeless boy in the slums of Rio de Janeiro joins a street gang, the Asphalt Angels, for protection from corrupt police officers, pedophiles, and other homeless people, he finds himself being drawn into a life of crime. (Rev: BL 8/99; HBG 4/00; SLJ 9/99; VOYA 12/99)

721 Honeycutt, Natalie. *Josie's Beau* (5–7). 1988, Avon paper $2.95 (978-0-380-70524-5). Beau's mother doesn't want him fighting, so Josie offers to say she's the one who fights — but the lie backfires. (Rev: BCCB 12/87; BL 12/1/87; SLJ 12/87)

722 Horvath, Polly. *One Year in Coal Harbor* (5–7). 2012, Random House $16.99 (978-037586970-9); LB $19.99 (978-037596970-6). Primrose Squarp works to make a match for her Uncle Jack, befriends foster child Ked, and writes a cookbook with Ked's help in this sequel to *Everything on a Waffle* (2001). ♫ e Lexile 880L (Rev: BL 7/12; HB 9–10/12; LMC 11–12/12; SLJ 8/12)

723 Hossack, Sylvie. *Green Mango Magic* (4–7). 1999, Avon $14.00 (978-0-380-97613-3). Maile, who lives alone with her grandmother in Hawaii since her father abandoned her, finds a friend in Brooke, from Seattle, who is a recovering cancer patient. (Rev: BCCB 12/98; BL 5/1/99; HBG 10/99; SLJ 2/99; VOYA 8/99)

724 House, Silas, and Neela Vaswani. *Same Sun Here* (5–8). 2012, Candlewick $15.99 (978-076365684-3). Twelve-year-old Meena, an immigrant from India living in Chinatown, New York, with her struggling parents, and 12-year-old River, an unemployed Kentucky coal miner's son, become pen pals and through letters and e-mails share their problems and aspirations. e Lexile 890L (Rev: BL 3/1/12; LMC 8–9/12; SLJ 4/12*)

725 Houts, Michelle. *The Beef Princess of Practical County* (6–9). 2009, Delacorte $16.99 (978-038573584-1); LB $19.99 (978-038590568-8). Twelve-year-old Libby learns that cattle are not pets when she raises two steers to show at the county fair in this entertaining look at rural life. Lexile 810L (Rev: BL 4/1/09; SLJ 6/1/09)

726 Howe, James. *The Misfits* (5–8). 2001, Simon & Schuster $16.00 (978-0-689-83955-9). A group of 7th-grade social misfits challenge the so-called norms at their school by running for student council and instituting a no-names-calling day. (Rev: BCCB 1/02; BL 11/15/01; HB 11–12/01; HBG 3/02; SLJ 11/01; VOYA 12/01)

727 Hudson, Wade. *Anthony's Big Surprise* (5–7). Series: NEATE. 1998, Just Us Bks. paper $3.95 (978-0940975736). Interracial tensions erupt in junior high school when some African American students are suspended and Anthony, who is also trying to cope with a family crisis, must deal with both problems. (Rev: SLJ 6/99)

728 Hughes, Mark Peter. *Lemonade Mouth* (8–11). 2007, Delacorte $15.99 (978-0-385-73392-2). Five teens in the band Lemonade Mouth take turns — tied together by a fan's comments — telling the story of their rise to fame (and their various stumbles) at Opoquonsett High in Rhode Island. (Rev: BCCB 6/07; BL 2/15/07; SLJ 5/07)

729 Huntley, Amy. *The Everafter* (8–11). 2009, HarperCollins $16.99 (978-0-06-177679-3); LB $17.89 (978-0-06-177680-9). Working from the afterlife, 17-year-old Maddy Stanton attempts to unravel the mystery of how she met her untimely demise. ⌒ **e** Lexile HL680L (Rev: BL 8/09; SLJ 12/09; VOYA 12/09)

730 Ingold, Jeanette. *Mountain Solo* (6–9). 2003, Harcourt $17.00 (978-0-15-202670-7). After an unsuccessful violin concert, 16-year-old Tess flees to her father's home in Montana where she meets Frederick, another violinist, and reviews her love of music, her past life, and her goals for the future. (Rev: BL 12/1/03; SLJ 11/03)

731 Ishizaki, Hiroshi. *Chain Mail: Addicted to You* (6–9). Trans. from Japanese by Richard Kim. 2007, TokyoPop paper $7.99 (978-1-59816-581-4). This is the story of Sawako, a lonely and troubled Japanese teen who collaborates with strangers on the Internet to write a story about a girl in danger. (Rev: SLJ 7/07)

732 Jacobson, Jennifer Richard. *The Complete History of Why I Hate Her* (7–9). 2010, Simon & Schuster $16.99 (978-0-6898-7800-8). Waitressing in Maine for the summer, 17-year-old Nola is initially bedazzled by her new friend Carly but has already become disenchanted when her younger sister, who is fragile from a long battle with cancer, arrives and falls under Carly's spell. **e** Lexile 670L (Rev: BL 2/15/10; LMC 5–6/10; SLJ 8/10)

733 Jenkins, A. M. *Out of Order* (8–10). 2003, HarperCollins LB $16.89 (978-0-06-623969-9). Sophomore Colt relies on his good looks and athletic prowess to pull him through, but failing grades place him in the company of a brainy girl and his attitudes begin to change. (Rev: BL 9/1/03; HB 11–12/03; HBG 4/04; SLJ 9/03*; VOYA 10/03)

734 Jennings, Patrick. *The Beastly Arms* (5–7). 2001, Scholastic paper $16.95 (978-0-439-16589-1). A dreamy 6th-grader who pictures animals in everything he sees, discovers a world of real beasts when he and his mother move to the Beastly Arms. (Rev: BCCB 10/01; BL 5/1/01; HB 7–8/01; HBG 10/01; SLJ 4/01)

735 Jennings, Richard W. *The Great Whale of Kansas* (5–9). 2001, Houghton Mifflin $15.00 (978-0-618-10228-0). When a boy finds a prehistoric whale fossil in his backyard, the discovery brings unexpected consequences. (Rev: HB 9–10/01; HBG 3/02; SLJ 8/01; VOYA 2/02)

736 Johnson, Angela. *Bird* (6–10). 2004, Penguin $16.99 (978-0-8037-2847-9). Heartbroken when her stepfather abandons the family, 13-year-old Bird travels from Cleveland to Alabama to find him and bring him home and instead finds unexpected friendship. (Rev: BL 9/1/04; SLJ 9/04; VOYA 2/05)

737 Johnson, Maureen. *The Last Little Blue Envelope* (8–11). 2011, HarperTeen $16.99 (978-0-06-197679-7). Eager to continue the scavenger hunt that will offer up clues to her late great aunt's personality, Ginny travels to London in this sequel to *13 Little Blue Enve-*

lopes (2005). ⌒ **e** Lexile HL670L (Rev: BL 5/1/11; HB 5–6/11; SLJ 8/11; VOYA 4/11)

738 Johnson, Maureen. *Scarlett Fever* (8–10). 2010, Scholastic $16.99 (978-0-439-89928-4). In this follow-up to 2008's *Suite Scarlett,* life at the Hopewell Hotel has reverted to its usual humdrum pace, and 15-year-old Scarlett is desperate for something to break the ennui even as she handles various crises. ⌒ **e** Lexile 710L (Rev: BLO 12/8/09; HB 3–4/10; SLJ 1/10; VOYA 8/10)

739 Johnson, Maureen. *Suite Scarlett* (7–12). 2008, Scholastic $16.99 (978-0-439-89927-7). When Scarlett turns 15, she's "given" the Empire Suite in the family's rundown hotel to care for; the suite comes with Mrs. Amberson, an unusual long-term guest, and here this zany adventure involving four siblings begins. (Rev: BL 6/1–15/08)

740 Johnson, Maureen. *13 Little Blue Envelopes* (8–11). 2005, HarperCollins LB $17.89 (978-0-06-054142-2). On a trip through Europe following instructions left to her in 13 letters written by her Aunt Peg before her death, 17-year-old Ginny learns about Peg's past and about herself. (Rev: BL 9/15/05; SLJ 10/05; VOYA 10/05)

741 Johnson, Peter. *The Amazing Adventures of John Smith, Jr. AKA Houdini* (5–7). 2012, HarperCollins $15.99 (978-006198890-5). Thirteen-year-old John "Houdini" Smith writes a novel that describes his life in Providence, Rhode Island, his family problems, and his efforts to make money raking leaves. **e** Lexile 950L (Rev: BL 1/12; SLJ 4/12*)

742 Jones, Carrie. *Girl, Hero* (7–10). 2008, Flux $16.95 (978-0-7387-1051-8). High school freshman Lili writes letters to John Wayne, confiding to this hero her worries about her perhaps-gay father, her mother's new boyfriend who likes to drink, her own romantic interests, school challenges, and so forth. Lexile HL700L (Rev: BLO 9/15/08; SLJ 1/1/09)

743 Jones, Patrick. *Stolen Car* (8–12). 2008, Walker $16.99 (978-080279700-1). Enraged by the shabby behavior of the older boy for whom she neglected her friends, 15-year-old Danielle steals his car and takes off on a road trip with BFF Ashley. **e** (Rev: BL 11/15/08; LMC 1–2/09; SLJ 12/08; VOYA 2/09)

744 Jordan, Rosa. *The Goatnappers* (6–9). 2007, Peachtree $14.95 (978-1-56145-400-6). Justin is thrilled to be the first freshman picked for the varsity baseball team, but must also cope with his newly reappeared father and with the goat he and others have liberated from its abuser; a sequel to *Lost Goat Lane* (2004). (Rev: BL 5/1/07; SLJ 9/07)

745 Juby, Susan. *Another Kind of Cowboy* (8–11). 2007, HarperTeen $16.99 (978-0-06-076517-0). A horse story with a male protagonist, this novel set in Vancouver centers on Alex, who is 16 and questioning his sexuality, and on Cleo, a fellow dressage student who needs a friend. (Rev: BL 12/1/07; HB 1–2/08; SLJ 2/08)

746 Juby, Susan. *Getting the Girl: A Guide to Private Investigation, Surveillance, and Cookery* (8–10). 2008, HarperTeen $16.99 (978-006076525-5); LB $17.89 (978-006076527-9). Goodhearted Sherman Mack sets out to protect the reputations of girls in his school through a combination of sleuthing, persuasion, and ultimately standing up for his beliefs in this quirky first-person story. ℮ (Rev: BL 10/1/08; HB 9–10/08; SLJ 11/1/08)

747 Jukes, Mavis. *Getting Even* (5–7). 1988, Knopf paper $4.50 (978-0-679-86570-4). Maggie seems unable to stop the nasty pranks of classmate Corky, and receives differing advice from her divorced parents. (Rev: BCCB 5/88; BL 4/1/88; SLJ 5/88)

748 Kain, P. G. *Picture Perfect* (5–8). Series: Commercial Breaks. 2012, Aladdin paper $6.99 (978-14169978-7-0). Teen actress Cassie recognizes that the "picture perfect" commercials she appears in are far from the reality of her home life. ℮ Lexile 1240L (Rev: BLO 6/12; SLJ 1/13; VOYA 12/12)

749 Kantor, Melissa. *The Breakup Bible* (8–10). 2007, Hyperion $15.99 (978-0-7868-0962-2). Jen turns to a book called *The Breakup Bible* after Max, the editor at her school's newspaper, dumps her for another girl. (Rev: BL 7/07)

750 Karasyov, Carrie, and Jill Kargman. *Bittersweet Sixteen* (7–10). 2006, HarperCollins $15.99 (978-0-06-077844-6). Laura learns who her true friends are when new girl Sophie starts at her school and everyone starts planning their 16th-birthday parties. (Rev: SLJ 10/06)

751 Karasyov, Carrie, and Jill Kargman. *Summer Intern* (7–12). 2007, HarperCollins $16.99 (978-0-06-115375-4). In this entertaining novel, hardworking Kira gets a summer internship at a national fashion magazine in New York City and learns about both fashion and office politics. (Rev: SLJ 6/07)

752 Kaye, Amy. *The Real Deal: Unscripted* (7–12). 2004, Dorchester paper $5.99 (978-0-8439-5315-2). Claire juggles a potential Broadway career, a romance with a teen star, and the needs of her newfound half-sister, all under the glare of reality TV cameras. (Rev: SLJ 5/04)

753 Kephart, Beth. *Undercover* (7–10). 2007, Harper-Collins $16.99 (978-0-06-123893-2). Sensitive soul Elisa writes love letters for boys to give to their girl-friends as she deals with problems at home and tries to find solace in nature and her love of ice skating; her growing friendship with Theo gives her hope. ☊ (Rev: BL 10/15/07; SLJ 10/07)

754 Kerz, Anna. *Better Than Weird* (4–7). 2011, Orca paper $9.95 (978-1-55469-362-7). Sixth-grader Aaron struggles to calm his excitable behavior, deal with a bully, and to make some friends in advance of the arriv-

al of the father he has not seen in eight years. ℮ Lexile 560L (Rev: BL 4/1/11; SLJ 5/11; VOYA 4/11)

755 Key, Watt. *Alabama Moon* (6–9). 2006, Farrar $17.00 (978-0-374-30184-2). Moon, 10, is raised in the forest by a Vietnam vet father who trusts nobody; when his father dies, Moon's life changes dramatically — he is taken into custody and repeatedly escapes before he finally finds friends. ☊ (Rev: BL 11/1/06; HB 9–10/06; SLJ 9/06)

756 Key, Watt. *Dirt Road Home* (7–10). 2010, Farrar $16.99 (978-0-374-30863-6). Eager to get out of the state home for juvenile delinquents, 14-year-old Hal tries to behave amid the pervasive gang violence and hopes that his father will quit drinking. ℮ Lexile HL540L (Rev: BL 6/10; HB 9–10/10; LMC 11–12/10; SLJ 11/1/10; VOYA 12/10)

757 Kherdian, David. *The Revelations of Alvin Toll-iver* (5–7). 2001, Hampton Roads paper $7.95 (978-1-57174-255-1). Twelve-year-old Alvin is fascinated with nature and the great outdoors, and finds some unusual adult friends who introduce him to nature's charms. (Rev: BL 12/1/01; SLJ 3/02)

758 Kimmel, Elizabeth Cody. *Lily B. on the Brink of Paris* (5–8). 2006, HarperCollins $16.99 (978-0-06-083948-2). Lily B.'s latest diary entries record the cultural sights of Paris, where the 13-year-old travels with her French class. (Rev: BL 1/1–15/07; SLJ 1/07)

759 Kittle, Katrina. *Reasons to Be Happy* (7–10). 2011, Sourcebooks paper $7.99 (978-1-4022-6-020-9). When her movie star parents spiral downward — her mother with cancer, her father with alcohol — Hannah's aunt takes her on a trip to Ghana, hoping to arrest Hannah's own descent into bulimia. ℮ Lexile 690L (Rev: BL 10/1/11; LMC 3–4/12; SLJ 12/1/11)

760 Klass, David. *Dark Angel* (8–11). 2005, Farrar $17.00 (978-0-374-39950-4). Seventeen-year-old Jeff's family has hidden the existence of his older brother, a murderer who has been in jail; when Troy is released and comes home to live, Jeff's life is turned upside down. (Rev: BL 9/15/05; SLJ 10/05; VOYA 10/05)

761 Kline, Lisa Williams. *The Princesses of Atlantis* (5–7). 2002, Cricket $16.95 (978-0-8126-2855-5). Twelve-year-old Arlene experiences ups and downs in her friendship with Carly, with whom she is writing a novel about two princesses. (Rev: BL 4/15/02; HBG 10/02; SLJ 7/02)

762 Klinger, Shula. *The Kingdom of Strange* (6–9). 2008, Marshall Cavendish $16.99 (978-0-7614-5395-6). Fourteen-year-old Thisbe works on her writing skills by recording her thoughts — on life and on writing — in a journal. (Rev: BL 5/1/08; LMC 10/08)

763 Kluger, Steve. *My Most Excellent Year: A Novel of Love, Mary Poppins, and Fenway Park* (8–12). 2008, Dial $16.99 (978-0-8037-3227-8). The freshman year of three diverse Boston-area teenagers is filled with romance, good works, sexual awakenings, sports, and more, as revealed in this collection of entries that includes letters, poems, e-mails, and other artifacts. (Rev: BL 3/15/08; SLJ 4/08)

764 Knowles, Jo. *Pearl* (7–9). 2011, Henry Holt $16.99 (978-0-8050-9207-3). When her grandfather Gus dies, Bean's whole family structure comes into question and she turns to her friend Henry. **e** Lexile HL610L (Rev: BL 9/15/11; LMC 11–12/11; SLJ 9/1/11)

765 Koertge, Ron. *The Heart of the City* (5–7). 1998, Orchard LB $16.99 (978-0-531-33078-4). Apprehensive about moving to the big city of Los Angeles, 10-year-old Joy soon finds a friend in a young African American girl and together they fight the takeover of an abandoned house by hoods. (Rev: BCCB 4/98; BL 4/1/98; HBG 10/98)

766 Koertge, Ron. *Shakespeare Makes the Playoffs* (6–9). 2010, Candlewick $15.99 (978-0-7636-4435-2). After focusing exclusively on baseball and his girlfriend Mira, Kevin revives his interest in poetry when his father gives him a new journal; full of poems by Kevin and his new friend Amy. (Rev: BL 1/1/10; HB 3–4/10; SLJ 2/10)

767 Konigsburg, E. L. *The Mysterious Edge of the Heroic World* (5–7). 2007, Simon & Schuster $16.99 (978-1-4169-4972-5). Amedeo Kaplan hopes to make a name for himself by discovering something important; could he have the opportunity as he and his new friend William help to clean out the home of Mrs. Aida Zender, a former opera singer? Blending humor and mystery, this story has an added layer of Holocaust history. ⌒ (Rev: BL 9/15/07; SLJ 9/07)

768 Konigsburg, E. L. *The Outcasts of 19 Schuyler Place* (4–8). 2004, Simon & Schuster $16.95 (978-0-689-86636-4). Rescued from summer camp by aging uncles, Margaret is dismayed to find that their prized garden sculptures are endangered in this absorbing, amusing, and thought-provoking novel. (Rev: BL 12/15/03*; HB 3–4/04; SLJ 1/04*)

769 Konigsburg, E. L. *The View from Saturday* (5–7). 1996, Simon & Schuster $16.00 (978-0-689-80993-4). A complicated tale about four 6th-graders who are contestants in an Academic Bowl competition. Newbery Medal 1997. (Rev: BCCB 11/96; BL 10/15/96; SLJ 9/96*)

770 Korman, Gordon. *Schooled* (6–9). 2007, Hyperion $15.99 (978-0-7868-5692-3). When his grandmother becomes ill, 13-year-old Cap is removed from the farm commune where he has grown up and been homeschooled, and must deal with a whole new world at the local junior high; the often-funny story is told from various perspectives. (Rev: BL 8/07*; LMC 11/07; SLJ 8/07)

771 Korman, Gordon. *The Twinkie Squad* (5–7). 1992, Scholastic paper $13.95 (978-0-590-45249-6). A bossy,

insecure 6th-grader and a defender of weaker kids are sentenced to the school's Special Discussion Group. (Rev: BCCB 11/92; BL 9/15/92; SLJ 9/92)

772 Korman, Gordon. *Ungifted* (5–8). 2012, HarperCollins $16.99 (978-0-06-174266-8); LB $17.89 (978-0-06-174268-2). Delinquent Donovan finds himself wrongly assigned to the gifted kids' school, where he joins the robotics team and discovers hidden talents. ⌒ **e** Lexile 730L (Rev: BL 7/12; SLJ 10/12; VOYA 6/12)

773 Koss, Amy Goldman. *Poison Ivy* (7–10). 2006, Roaring Brook $16.95 (978-1-59643-118-8). Multiple voices tell the story of the mock trial of the three bullies who have been making unpopular Ivy's life a misery. (Rev: BL 2/15/06; SLJ 3/06; VOYA 4/06)

774 Kraft, Erik P. *Miracle Wimp* (8–11). Illus. by author. 2007, Little, Brown $16.99 (978-0-316-01165-5). In often humorous anecdotes with accompanying drawings, Tom Mayo describes a year of his high school life as he deals with school and bullies, makes friends, gets his license, and finds a girlfriend. (Rev: BL 6/1–15/07; SLJ 10/07)

775 Kraus, Daniel. *The Monster Variations* (8–12). 2009, Delacorte $16.99 (978-038573733-3); LB $19.99 (978-038590659-3). James remembers the summer he was 12 and the wave of violence that swept his small town, terrifying him and his friends. (Rev: BLO 6/1/09; LMC 10/09; SLJ 11/09)

776 Kraut, Julie. *Slept Away* (7–10). 2009, LB $11.99 (978-038590661-6); paper $8.99 (978-038573737-1). Very urban Laney Parker, 15, has a hard time adapting when she is sent to a summer camp in the Pennsylvania countryside. (Rev: BL 7/09; SLJ 8/09)

777 Kropp, Paul. *The Countess and Me* (6–9). 2002, Fitzhenry & Whiteside $14.95 (978-1-55041-680-0). Young Jordan, eager to fit in at his new school, must decide whether to betray his eccentric neighbor to a group of delinquent boys. (Rev: BL 10/1/02; SLJ 11/02)

778 LaBan, Elizabeth. *The Tragedy Paper* (7–12). 2013, Knopf $17.99 (978-037587040-8); LB $20.99 (978-037597040-5). A suspenseful story set in a private school with traditions that affect the students' studies and romantic relationships. ⌒ **e** (Rev: BL 11/15/12*; SLJ 2/13; VOYA 12/12)

779 Lamm, Drew. *Bittersweet* (8–11). 2003, Clarion $15.00 (978-0-618-16443-1). When Taylor's grandmother, who has essentially raised her, falls ill, artist Taylor suddenly finds she lacks creativity and is unsure of her other relationships. (Rev: BCCB 2/04; BL 11/15/03; HBG 4/04; SLJ 12/03; VOYA 12/03)

780 Langan, John. *Search for Safety* (7–12). Series: Bluford. 2006, Townsend paper $4.95 (978-1-59194-070-8). Sophomore Ben is new at Bluford High and must find someone to talk to about his abusive home life before it is too late; suitable for reluctant readers. (Rev: SLJ 7/07)

781 Langan, Paul. *The Fallen* (7–12). Series: Bluford. 2006, Townsend paper $4.95 (978-1-59194-066-1). Martin Luna starts his sophomore year at Bluford High with the goal of avoiding the gang conflicts that took his brother's life; suitable for reluctant readers. (Rev: SLJ 7/07)

782 Langan, Paul. *Shattered* (7–12). Series: Bluford. 2006, Townsend paper $4.95 (978-1-59194-069-2). When Darcy's ex-boyfriend returns to town, the 11th-grader must come to terms with her past; suitable for reluctant readers. (Rev: SLJ 7/07)

783 Langston, Laura. *The Trouble with Cupid* (4–8). 2008, Fitzhenry & Whiteside paper $11.95 (978-1-55455-059-3). Eighth-grader Erin is asked to train the school's mascot for a dog food contest and finds the job more complicated and educational than she had expected; the gorgeous Zach Cameron is going to help, though. (Rev: SLJ 2/09; VOYA 6/08)

784 Larson, Kirby. *Hattie Big Sky* (7–10). 2006, Delacorte $17.99 (978-0-385-73313-7). Hattie Brooks, a 16-year-old orphan, inherits a Montana homestead from her uncle, and learns to farm the land and make a home for herself despite the many difficulties she faces. Newbery Honor 2007. (Rev: BL 9/1/06; SLJ 11/06*)

785 Leader, Jessica. *Nice and Mean* (5–7). 2010, Aladdin paper $6.99 (978-1-4169-9160-1). Middle-schoolers Sachi and Marina are very different and get off to a bad start when they work together on a video project. **e** Lexile 680L (Rev: BL 7/10; LMC 11–12/10)

786 Leavitt, Lindsey. *Princess for Hire* (5–8). 2010, Hyperion $16.99 (978-142312192-3). Fifteen-year-old Desi is offered a chance to escape her humdrum life — to "sub" for real princesses — but soon learns this is harder than it seems. Lexile 670L (Rev: BLO 3/1/10; SLJ 5/10)

787 Lecesne, James. *Absolute Brightness* (8–12). 2008, HarperTeen $17.99 (978-0-06-125627-1). A gay teenager disappears from a small New Jersey town in this multilayered, well-written novel. (Rev: SLJ 3/08; VOYA 4/08)

788 Lenhard, Elizabeth. *It's a Purl Thing* (6–9). Series: Chicks with Sticks. 2005, Dutton $16.99 (978-0-525-47622-1). Four Chicago high school girls from diverse backgrounds become friends when they join a class at KnitWit, a local yarn shop. (Rev: BL 10/15/05; SLJ 2/06)

789 Lennon, Stella, and Melissa Kantor. *Invisible I* (7–10). Series: The Amanda Project. 2009, HarperCollins $16.99 (978-0-06-174212-5). Callie is facing enough problems at home when she finds herself implicated in defacing the vice principal's car. She is sure her friend Amanda was the perpetrator, but where is Amanda now? ∩ **e** (Rev: BL 8/09; LMC 1–2/10; SLJ 9/09)

790 Levithan, David. *Wide Awake* (8–11). 2006, Knopf $16.95 (978-0-375-83466-0). When a recount is de-manded after a gay Jewish man is elected president, Duncan — with his boyfriend Jimmy — joins the millions who protest and learns a lot about himself, his beliefs and feelings. (Rev: BL 9/15/06; SLJ 9/06)

791 Lewis, J. Patrick. *The Last Resort* (6–9). Illus. by Roberto Innocenti. 2002, Creative $17.95 (978-1-56846-172-4). Noted poet J. Patrick Lewis uses word play and inventive characters to tell the story of an artist looking for inspiration, in this picture book for older readers full of thought-provoking images. (Rev: BL 2/1/03; HBG 3/03)

792 Lewis, Wendy. *Graveyard Girl* (7–10). 2000, Red Deer paper $7.95 (978-0-88995-202-7). While looking back at her high school yearbook, Ginger reminisces about her classmates and vignettes reveal their stories of marriage, achievement, and lost romance. (Rev: BL 1/1–15/01; SLJ 5/01; VOYA 6/01)

793 Lichtman, Wendy. *Do the Math: Secrets, Lies, and Algebra* (5–9). 2007, HarperCollins $16.99 (978-0-06-122955-8). Tess, 13, applies mathematical principles to all situations in her life including a cheating classmate, untrustworthy friends, and a potential murder. (Rev: BCCB 9/07; SLJ 12/07)

794 Lichtman, Wendy. *The Writing on the Wall* (6–9). Series: Do the Math. 2008, Greenwillow $16.99 (978-006122958-9); LB $17.89 (978-006122959-6). Algebra whiz Tess uses her skills to crack a secret graffiti code that may be linked to a classroom fire in this sequel to 2007's *Secrets, Lies, and Algebra*. **e** Lexile 1050L (Rev: BL 9/1/08; SLJ 10/1/08)

795 Lieb, Josh. *I Am a Genius of Unspeakable Evil and I Want to Be Your Class President* (5–7). 2009, Penguin $15.99 (978-1-59514-240-5). Overweight, apparently slow but secretly genius 7th-grader Oliver Watson takes on his arch nemesis — his father — by running for class president, a move secretly motivated by a desire for Dad's affection. ∩ **e** Lexile 780L (Rev: BL 10/15/09; SLJ 10/09; VOYA 12/09)

796 Linko, Gina. *Flutter* (7–12). 2012, Random House $16.99 (978-037586996-9); LB $19.99 (978-037596996-6). A suspenseful story about 17-year-old Emery, who suffers seizures that lead her into adventure and romance. **e** (Rev: BL 11/15/12; LMC 1–2/13; SLJ 1/13; VOYA 8/12)

797 Littman, Sarah Darer. *Life, After* (6–9). 2010, Scholastic $16.99 (978-054515144-3). Growing unrest in Buenos Aires compels Daniela and her Jewish family to move to suburban New York, where she struggles to make friends and deal with the problems plaguing her parents. Sydney Taylor Book Honor 2011. **e** Lexile 850L (Rev: BL 8/10; SLJ 11/10; VOYA 8/10)

798 Lockhart, E. *The Disreputable History of Frankie Landau-Banks* (7–12). 2008, Hyperion $16.99 (978-0-7868-3818-9). In her sophomore year at Alabaster Prep, Frankie shakes up her boyfriend's all-male secret club, the Loyal Order of the Basset Hounds, and brings much-needed change to her elite boarding school; combining humor and social commentary, this is an appealing book full of wordplay. ⌒ (Rev: BL 1/1–15/08; HB 5–6/08; LMC 10/08; SLJ 3/08)

799 Lord, Cynthia. *Rules* (4–7). 2006, Scholastic $15.99 (978-0-439-44382-1). Catherine is a likable 12-year-old struggling to cope with the family challenges posed by her younger autistic brother. Newbery Honor 2007. (Rev: BL 2/15/06; SLJ 4/06)

800 Lord, Cynthia. *Touch Blue* (4–7). 2010, Scholastic $16.99 (978-0-545-03531-6). When the state of Maine threatens to close an island school for lack of pupils, the families take in foster children, and 11-year-old Tess must adjust to the arrival of 13-year-old Aaron. ⌒ Lexile 750L (Rev: BL 8/10; HB 11–12/10; SLJ 9/1/10)

801 Lowry, Brigid. *Guitar Highway Rose* (8–12). 2003, Holiday $16.95 (978-0-8234-1790-2). Set in Australia, this story of two teens who run away from home presents the voices of various characters including teachers, family, and friends. (Rev: BL 2/15/04; HBG 4/04; SLJ 12/03; VOYA 4/04)

802 Lubar, David. *Hidden Talents* (5–9). 1999, Tor $16.95 (978-0-312-86646-4). Five misfits, who are attending the last-resort Edgeview Alternative School, become friends and discover extrasensory talents they can use against the school bully. (Rev: BL 9/15/99; HBG 10/99; SLJ 11/99; VOYA 10/99)

803 Luddy, Karon. *Spelldown: The Big-Time Dreams of a Small-Town Word Whiz* (5–8). 2007, Simon & Schuster $15.99 (978-1-4169-1610-9). Mentored by her Latin teacher, 13-year-old Karlene manages to win the spelling championship in her rural South Carolina county and moves on to competitions at the state and national levels. (Rev: BL 1/1–15/07; LMC 8–9/07; SLJ 2/07)

804 Ludwig, Elisa. *Pretty Crooked* (7–10). 2012, HarperCollins $17.99 (978-0-06-206606-0). A newcomer to a prep school for wealthy kids, artist's daughter Willa tries to even the score by stealing from her well-heeled and often bullying classmates and distributing the spoils among the poorer ones. ℮ (Rev: BL 1/1/12; SLJ 7/12; VOYA 12/11)

805 Lundquist, Jenny. *Seeing Cinderella* (4–7). 2012, Simon & Schuster $15.99 (978-1-4424-4550-5). Callie is most unhappy to be starting 6th grade wearing ugly glasses — until she discovers that they have given her amazing abilities to "read" other people. ℮ Lexile 680L (Rev: SLJ 5/1/12; VOYA 6/12)

806 Lurie, April. *The Latent Powers of Dylan Fontaine* (8–12). 2008, Delacorte $15.99 (978-0-385-73125-6). Sixteen-year-old Dylan's problems include separated parents, a brother doing drugs, his own arrest for shoplifting, and his best friend Angie appearing unaware of his romantic interest; humor adds to the appeal of this story. (Rev: BL 4/1/08; SLJ 9/08)

807 Lyga, Barry. *The Astonishing Adventures of Fanboy and Goth Girl* (8–11). 2006, Houghton Mifflin $16.95 (978-0-618-72392-8). Fanboy confides in his friend Goth girl and creates his own comic book as a way of escaping the violence he experiences at school. (Rev: BL 9/1/06; SLJ 11/06)

808 Lyons, Kelly Starling. *Eddie's Ordeal* (5–8). 2004, Just Us Bks. paper $3.95 (978-0-940975-16-3). When Eddie's grades slip, his father makes him quit baseball. (Rev: BL 2/1/05)

809 McCall, Guadalupe Garcia. *Summer of the Mariposas* (7–12). 2012, Lee & Low $19.95 (978-1-60060-900-8). Magical realism and traditional Latin American folkloric characters combine with a family story as five sisters decide to return a drowned man's body to his family in Mexico. ℮ Lexile 840L (Rev: BL 11/15/12; LMC 5–6/13; SLJ 11/12*; VOYA 12/12)

810 McCullough, Kathy. *Don't Expect Magic* (7–11). 2011, Delacorte $17.99 (978-0-385-74012-8). Still reeling from her mother's death, Delaney, 15, moves to California to live with her dad, and is much surprised to learn that he is a fairy godmother — and that she may well have the same powers. But how will this impact her life? ℮ Lexile 800L (Rev: LMC 3–4/12; SLJ 6/12; VOYA 2/12)

811 McDonald, Abby. *The Anti-Prom* (8–11). 2011, Candlewick $16.99 (978-0-7636-4956-2). Bliss, Jolene, and Meg, students who barely know each other, all arrive at the prom with different problems — but they offer support where they can. ⌒ ℮ Lexile HL720L (Rev: BL 4/1/11; SLJ 6/11; VOYA 6/11)

812 MacDonald, Amy. *Too Much Flapdoodle!* (5–8). Illus. by Cat B. Smith. 2008, Farrar $16.95 (978-0-374-37671-0). Parker, 12, suffers a severe shock to his urban self when he goes to spend the summer on a ramshackle farm without Internet and cell service and nothing to do but chores. (Rev: BL 12/15/08; SLJ 11/08)

813 MacDonald, Anne Louise. *Seeing Red* (5–8). 2009, Kids Can $17.95 (978-1-55453-291-9); paper $8.95 (978-1-55453-292-6). Thirteen-year-old Frankie wonders if he has supernatural powers as he discovers new talents — for working with horses and disabled children, helping injured birds, and making friends. (Rev: BL 3/1/09; LMC 10/09; SLJ 8/09)

814 McDowell, Beck. *This Is Not a Drill* (6–9). 2012, Penguin $17.99 (978-0-399-25794-0). A tense story in which high school students Jake and Emery find themselves dealing with a hostage crisis. ℮ (Rev: BL 10/15/12; LMC 1–2/13; SLJ 11/12)

815 McElligott, Matthew, and Larry Tuxbury. *Benjamin Franklinstein Lives!* (4–7). Illus. by Matthew McElligott. Series: Benjamin Franklinstein. 2010, Putnam $12.99 (978-0-399-25229-7). Science whiz Victor's expectations of winning the school science fair are dashed when a lightning strike revives a dormant Ben

Franklin, who had been in secret suspended animation. A sequel is *Benjamin Franklinstein Meets the Fright Brothers* (2011). ℰ Lexile 590L (Rev: BL 9/1/10; LMC 11–12/10; SLJ 11/1/10)

816 MacLean, Jill. *The Nine Lives of Travis Keating* (5–8). 2008, Fitzhenry & Whiteside paper $11.95 (978-1-55455-104-0). Eleven-year-old Travis misses his mother and his old life but soon finds new purpose when he finds a tribe of feral cats who need care and protection. (Rev: BLO 11/19/08; SLJ 3/09)

817 MacLean, Jill. *The Present Tense of Prinny Murphy* (5–8). 2010, Fitzhenry & Whiteside paper $11.95 (978-1-55455-145-3). In Fiddler's Cove, Newfoundland, Prinny Murphy faces many challenges — an alcoholic mother who no longer lives at home, a distant father, loss of her best friend, bullying — but when she reads Virginia Euwer Wolff's *Make Lemonade* she recognizes a kindred spirit and resolves to conquer her problems. Lexile 700L (Rev: BL 12/15/10; LMC 11–12/10; SLJ 7/10; VOYA 8/10)

818 McNeal, Laura. *Dark Water* (8–12). 2010, Knopf $16.99 (978-0-375-84973-2); LB $19.99 (978-0-375-94973-9). Troubled 15-year-old Pearl seduces a mute migrant worker and faces difficult choices when wildfires approach her California town and threaten her uncle's ranch. ℰ (Rev: HB 1–2/11; SLJ 10/1/10; VOYA 12/10)

819 McNeal, Laura, and Tom McNeal. *The Decoding of Lana Morris* (8–11). 2007, Knopf $15.99 (978-0-375-83106-5). Lana suffers through the circumstances of her foster home — four special needs kids, a foster father who behaves inappropriately — until she gets an art kit that appears to have magical powers. (Rev: BCCB 7–8/07; BL 4/1/07; SLJ 6/07)

820 McNicoll, Sylvia. *A Different Kind of Beauty* (7–10). 2004, Fitzhenry & Whiteside $15.95 (978-1-55005-059-2); paper $8.95 (978-1-55005-060-8). Elizabeth, who is training a puppy as a guide dog, and Kyle, whose diabetes has left him blind, attend the same high school without knowing each other. (Rev: SLJ 8/04; VOYA 8/04)

821 Maldonado, Torrey. *Secret Saturdays* (6–9). 2010, Putnam $16.99 (978-0-399-25158-0). In a tough area of New York City, 12-year-old Justin, half Puerto Rican and half African American, is worried about his best friend Sean's behavior and eventually discovers that Sean is embarrassed because his father is in jail. ℰ Lexile HL580L (Rev: BL 3/15/10; LMC 5–6/10; SLJ 6/10)

822 Mancusi, Marianne. *Gamer Girl* (6–10). 2008, Dutton $16.99 (978-052547995-6). Manga drawing and the online game Fields of Fantasy help Maddy cope with her parents' divorce, unpopularity in her new school, and rejection by boys, but she eventually finds the courage to reach out to others. Lexile HL660L (Rev: BL 11/15/08; SLJ 1/09)

823 Mankell, Henning. *A Bridge to the Stars* (6–9). 2007, Delacorte $15.99 (978-0-385-73495-0). Set in Sweden in the 1950s, this novel centers on Joel and his single father; their shaky relationship is cemented one night when Joel risks his life on a dare. (Rev: BL 12/1/07; HB 1–2/08; LMC 1/08; SLJ 1/08)

824 Margolis, Leslie. *Boys Are Dogs* (4–7). 2008, Bloomsbury $15.99 (978-1-59990-221-0). Sixth-grader Annabelle is struggling to cope at her new school and discovers that the training manual that came with her new, rambunctious puppy offers useful advice. ∩ (Rev: BCCB 11/08; SLJ 11/08)

825 Marks, Graham. *Radio Radio* (8–11). 2004, Bloomsbury paper $11.99 (978-0-7475-5939-9). A group of London club kids goes up against both the government and some unsavory competitors when they set up a pirate radio station. (Rev: BL 1/1–15/05; SLJ 1/05)

826 Martineau, Diane. *The Wall on 7th Street* (6–8). 2005, Llewellyn paper $7.95 (978-0-7387-0715-0). An unlikely friendship between a 12-year-old boy and a homeless man helps the boy deal with his parents' divorce and results in a plan to save 7th Street from the gang that has ruled there. (Rev: SLJ 1/06)

827 Martinez, Jessica. *Virtuosity* (8–11). 2011, Simon & Schuster $16.99 (978-1-4424-2052-6). Carmen, 17, is a talented violinist and on the eve of an international competition she decides to tackle her dependence on anti-anxiety medication, her controlling mother, and her growing affection for her competitor Jeremy. ℰ Lexile HL710L (Rev: BL 12/1/11; LMC 1–2/12; SLJ 10/1/11)

828 Mass, Wendy. *Heaven Looks a Lot like the Mall* (7–10). 2007, Little, Brown $16.99 (978-0-316-05851-3). Thanks to a poorly aimed dodge ball, 16-year-old Tessa has a near-death experience and looks back on her life in free verse. (Rev: BL 10/15/07; SLJ 9/07)

829 Mass, Wendy. *Thirteen Gifts* (4–7). 2011, Scholastic $16.99 (978-0-545-31003-1). This story of Tara's summer in Willow Falls combines magic, mystery, and quirky characters. ∩ ℰ Lexile 720L (Rev: BL 8/11; SLJ 9/1/11*)

830 Matson, Morgan. *Second Chance Summer* (7–12). 2012, Simon & Schuster $16.99 (978-1-4169-9067-3). When her father is diagnosed with pancreatic cancer, the family decides to spend the summer together at their Poconos lake house, and Taylor finds herself in the company of her former best friend and her first boyfriend after an absence of five years. ℰ Lexile 1020L (Rev: BL 8/12*; SLJ 7/12*; VOYA 8/12)

831 Maude, Rachel. *Poseur* (8–12). Series: Poseur. 2008, Little, Brown paper $9.99 (978-0-316-06583-2). Charlotte, Janie, Petra, and Melissa — who attend an expensive private school in Los Angeles — are assigned to work together on creating their own clothing line. (Rev: BL 3/3/08; SLJ 3/08)

832 Maynard, Joyce. *The Cloud Chamber* (6–9). 2005, Simon & Schuster $16.95 (978-0-689-87152-8). In 1950s Montana, 14-year-old Nate finds a friend in his science project partner Naomi as he struggles to cope with his father's apparent suicide attempt and subsequent hospitalization, his mother's withdrawal, and the needs of his younger sister. (Rev: BL 7/05; SLJ 7/05; VOYA 2/06)

833 Mazer, Norma Fox. *Mrs. Fish, Ape, and Me, the Dump Queen* (6–9). 1981, Avon paper $3.50 (978-0-380-69153-1). Joyce has been hurt by supposed friends but somehow she trusts the school custodian, Mrs. Fish.

834 Mechling, Lauren, and Laura Moser. *Foreign Exposure: The Social Climber Abroad* (7–10). 2007, Houghton Mifflin paper $8.99 (978-0-618-66379-8). Sixteen-year-old Mimi visits a friend in London and soon finds herself immersed in the celebrity gossip scene. (Rev: SLJ 6/07)

835 Mendle, Jane. *Better Off Famous?* (7–12). 2007, St. Martin's paper $8.95 (978-0-312-36903-3). On a visit to New York from Alabama, 16-year-old Annie, a talented violinist, unexpectedly wins a part on a TV series and becomes an instant celebrity — and an instant brat. (Rev: SLJ 2/08)

836 Mikaelsen, Ben. *Ghost of Spirit Bear* (6–9). 2008, HarperCollins $16.99 (978-0-06-009007-4). In this sequel to *Touching Spirit Bear* (2001), Peter and Cole are back from exile on an Alaskan island and now face the rigors of high school life. ∩ (Rev: BL 6/1–15/08; SLJ 8/08)

837 Mikaelsen, Ben. *Touching Spirit Bear* (6–9). 2001, HarperCollins $16.99 (978-0-380-97744-4). Cole, an angry and violent 15-year-old, is sentenced according to Native American tradition to a year of solitude on an island in Alaska. (Rev: BCCB 5/01; BL 1/1–15/01; HBG 10/01; SLJ 2/01; VOYA 6/01)

838 Minter, J. *Inside Girl* (8–12). 2007, Bloomsbury paper $8.95 (978-1-59990-086-5). Flan, younger sister of popular Patch Flood of the Insiders series, tries to escape her high-society world by transferring to a public school, but soon her ultra-rich friends show up to blow her cover. (Rev: BL 7/07; SLJ 7/07)

839 Miranda, Megan. *Fracture* (8–12). 2012, Walker $17.99 (978-080272309-3). After a near-death experience, Delaney, 17, finds herself fascinated by and able to predict impending death. **e** (Rev: BL 12/15/11; SLJ 2/12; VOYA 12/11)

840 Moeyaert, Bart. *Hornet's Nest* (8–10). Trans. from Dutch by David Colmer. 2000, Front St $15.95 (978-1-886910-48-5). Translated from Dutch, this is a fablelike story of Susanna's efforts to solve some of the problems in her life and her village. (Rev: BL 9/15/00; HB 11–12/00; HBG 3/01; SLJ 11/00)

841 Moriarty, Jaclyn. *The Murder of Bindy Mackenzie* (8–11). 2006, Scholastic $16.99 (978-0-439-74051-7).

Humor and mystery are combined in this story about the precocious Bindy, whose perfectionism has lost her many friends; her growth through this story is shown in diary entries, assignments, and other documents. (Rev: BL 10/15/06; HB 1–2/07*; SLJ 1/07)

842 Morris, Taylor. *Class Favorite* (5–8). 2007, Simon & Schuster paper $5.99 (978-1-4169-3598-8). It's hard enough being an 8th-grader, but Sara has to endure countless public embarrassments at her school — still, this hilarious book shows how this unflappable girl keeps trying to climb the social ladder in spite of it all. (Rev: SLJ 3/08)

843 Moss, Marissa. *Vote 4 Amelia* (4–7). Illus. by author. 2007, Simon & Schuster $9.99 (978-1-4169-2789-1). Amelia is running for secretary and her friend Carly for president; they didn't expect the campaign to be so intense and Amelia's diary entries are — as always — humorous and revealing. (Rev: SLJ 9/07)

844 Murdock, Catherine Gilbert. *Dairy Queen* (6–9). 2006, Houghton Mifflin $16.00 (978-0-618-68307-9). Fifteen-year-old D.J., who comes from an uncommunicative family, has quietly taken over the work of the family dairy farm, but when she decides to try out for the football team she suddenly becomes the focus of attention. (Rev: BL 4/1/06; SLJ 4/06)

845 Murphy, Pat. *The Wild Girls* (5–8). 2007, Viking $16.99 (978-0-670-06226-3). Joan and best friend Sarah (who calls herself Fox) love to explore in the woods and to write — a pastime that wins them spots at a writing camp and an outlet for their frustrations with their family lives. ∩ (Rev: BL 10/1/07; SLJ 11/07)

846 Myers, Edward. *Far from Gringo Land* (7–10). 2010, Clarion $17 (978-0-547-05630-2). Rick, a teenager from Colorado, gets more than he bargained for when he moves to Mexico for a summer job and experiences culture shock. **e** Lexile 990 (Rev: BL 11/15/09; LMC 1–2/10; SLJ 12/09)

847 Myers, Walter Dean. *All the Right Stuff* (8–12). 2012, Amistad $17.99 (978-006196087-1). After his father is killed, 16-year-old Paul volunteers at a soup kitchen and there learns much about civil liberties while also building relationships with his Harlem neighbors. ∩ **e** (Rev: BL 2/15/12; HB 5–6/12; SLJ 5/1/12; VOYA 4/12)

848 Myers, Walter Dean. *Checkmate* (5–8). 2011, Scholastic $16.99 (978-0-439-91627-1). Zander and his middle-school friends in Harlem intervene when their chess-star classmate Sidney is caught trying to buy drugs. (Rev: BL 9/1/11; SLJ 10/1/11)

849 Myers, Walter Dean. *The Cruisers* (5–8). 2010, Scholastic $15.99 (978-0-439-91626-4). The four low-achieving 8th-grade creators of *The Cruiser* alternative newspaper are assigned the roles of peacekeepers during a Civil War unit with interesting results; set in a Harlem school for the gifted and talented. ∩ Lexile 810L (Rev: BL 9/1/10*; LMC 1–2/11; SLJ 10/1/10)

850 Myers, Walter Dean. *A Star Is Born* (5–8). Series: The Cruisers. 2012, Scholastic $17.99 (978-043991628-8). LaShonda's costume designs provide her an opportunity to leave the group home behind — but can she be parted from her younger, autistic brother? ∩ Lexile 810L (Rev: BL 7/12; LMC 3–4/13; SLJ 8/12)

851 Myracle, Lauren. *Eleven* (4–7). 2004, Dutton $16.99 (978-0-525-47165-3). Covering Winnie's life from her 11th birthday to her 12th, this novel reveals typical friendship and family tensions. (Rev: BL 4/15/04; SLJ 2/04)

852 Myracle, Lauren. *The Fashion Disaster That Changed My Life* (5–8). 2005, Dutton $15.99 (978-0-525-47222-3). Through her diary and instant messages, Allison relates the turmoil of 7th grade, from her humiliating first-day arrival with her mother's underwear clinging to her pants to her problems making and keeping friends. (Rev: BL 9/15/05; SLJ 7/05)

853 Myracle, Lauren. *Thirteen* (6–9). 2008, Dutton $15.99 (978-0-525-47896-6). In this installment — following *Eleven* (2004) and *Twelve* (2007) — Winnie is 13 and busy with friends, boys, and family (including a new baby sister — and an older sister leaving for college). (Rev: BL 1/1–15/08; SLJ 7/08)

854 Na, An. *Wait for Me* (8–11). 2006, Penguin $15.99 (978-0-399-24275-5). Unable to meet her mother's expectations, Korean American high school senior Mina resorts to lies and plans for escape, but when Ysrael, with whom she has fallen in love, is blamed for Mina's actions she must make a difficult choice. (Rev: BL 3/15/06*; SLJ 7/06)

855 Nash, Naomi. *I Am So Jinxed!* (8–12). 2006, Dorchester paper $5.99 (978-0-8439-5405-0). Vick Marotti gives up her Goth girl ways and gets in a relationship with a cute senior guy, but things are still far from perfect in her life; a sequel to *You Are So Cursed!* (2004). (Rev: SLJ 5/06)

856 Naylor, Phyllis Reynolds. *All But Alice* (5–8). 1992, Macmillan $15.95 (978-0-689-31773-6). Alice, now a 7th grader and still motherless, deals with the challenges of friendship and popularity. (Rev: BCCB 5/92; BL 3/1/92; HB 7–8/92; SLJ 5/92*)

857 Naylor, Phyllis Reynolds. *Faith, Hope, and Ivy June* (5–8). 2009, Delacorte $16.99 (978-0-385-73615-2). Seventh-graders Ivy June and Catherine trade lives for two weeks — Kentucky mountain vs. modern suburb — and track their experiences in journals. ∩ (Rev: BCCB 9/09; BL 5/15/09; HB 9/09; LMC 10/09; SLJ 10/09; VOYA 8/09)

858 Nelson, Blake. *Paranoid Park* (8–11). 2006, Viking $15.99 (978-0-670-06118-1). The narrator of this title, a 16-year-old skateboarder, is involved in the death of

security officer and must deal with his feelings of confusion, fear, and the decision to confess or not. (Rev: BL 9/1/06; SLJ 11/06)

859 Neri, G. *Ghetto Cowboy* (5–8). Illus. by Jesse Joshua Watson. 2011, Candlewick $15.99 (978-0-7636-4922-7). African American Cole, 12, finally pushes his mother over the edge and she drives him from Detroit to Philadelphia where he will live with the father he has never met — who turns out to be an inner city cowboy. Odyssey Honor Recording 2012. ∩ e Lexile 660L (Rev: BL 9/15/11; LMC 11–12/11; SLJ 10/1/11)

860 Ness, Patrick. *A Monster Calls* (7–10). Illus. by Jim Kay. 2011, Candlewick $16.99 (978-0-7636-5559-4). Thirteen-year-old Conor's mother is dying and he is plagued by nightmares; then one night a monster wakes him and tells him three hard-to-fathom stories, finally asking Conor for a story that embodies the truth; a moving story about facing loss. ALA Notable Books 2012; YALSA Top Ten Best Fiction for Young Adults 2012. ∩ e Lexile 730L (Rev: BL 7/11; HB 9–19/11; LMC 1–2/12*; SLJ 9/1/11*)

861 Nichols, Travis. *Matthew Meets the Man* (6–9). Illus. by author. 2012, Roaring Brook $15.99 (978-159643545-2). Matt, 15, aspires to being a drummer and wowing his new girlfriend, though his progress toward these goals seem to be thwarted by adults. e Lexile 770L (Rev: BL 3/1/12; SLJ 2/12)

862 Nields, Nerissa. *Plastic Angel* (7–10). 2005, Scholastic $17.95 (978-0-439-70913-2). Thirteen-year-olds Randi and Gellie become friends despite their differences and form a band called Plastic Angel. (Rev: BL 8/05; SLJ 9/05; VOYA 2/06)

863 Noël, Alyson. *Saving Zoë* (7–10). 2007, St. Martin's paper $8.95 (978-0-312-35510-4). Fifteen-year-old Echo's world fell apart when her older sister Zoë was murdered; when she gets Zoë's diaries, however, she discovers just how many risks her sister had been taking and is able to start healing herself and her family. (Rev: SLJ 12/07; VOYA date)

864 Nolan, Han. *When We Were Saints* (7–10). 2003, Harcourt $17.00 (978-0-15-216371-6). After his grandfather's death, Archie, 14, is overwhelmed by a need to find God and, with his religious friend Clare, sets off on a pilgrimage to the Cloisters in New York. (Rev: BL 10/1/03; HBG 4/04; SLJ 11/03; VOYA 12/03)

865 Oaks, J. Adams. *Why I Fight* (8–12). 2009, Simon & Schuster $16.99 (978-141691177-7). Since the age of 12, Wyatt has been traveling with his drifter uncle named Spade and earning money with his fists. Lexile 770L (Rev: BL 4/15/09; SLJ 7/1/09; VOYA 6/09)

866 Obed, Ellen Bryan. *Twelve Kinds of Ice* (4–7). Illus. by Barbara McClintock. 2012, Houghton Mifflin $16.99 (978-061889129-0). A family in Maine celebrates the different kinds of ice that take them through the winter. ALA Notable Books 2013. Lexile 870L (Rev: BL 10/1/12*; HB 11–12/12; LMC 10/12; SLJ 12/12)

867 O'Connell, Tyne. *Pulling Princes* (7–10). 2004, Bloomsbury $16.95 (978-1-58234-957-2). Calypso Kelly, a 15-year-old from LA, finds it difficult to fit in at her posh English boarding school. (Rev: SLJ 12/04; VOYA 4/05)

868 O'Keefe, Susan Heyboer. *My Life and Death by Alexandra Canarsie* (7–10). 2002, Peachtree $14.95 (978-1-56145-264-4). Allie, a lonely teenager, finds a friend and a mystery when she starts going to strangers' funerals. (Rev: HBG 10/02; SLJ 9/02; VOYA 4/02)

869 Oppel, Kenneth. *Half Brother* (7–10). 2010, Scholastic $17.99 (978-0-545-22925-8). In 1970s Canada 13-year-old Ben's psychologist father brings home a young chimp that will be raised as a member of the family. ⌒ **e** Lexile 680L (Rev: BL 9/1/10; HB 9–10/10; LMC 11–12/10; SLJ 9/1/10*; VOYA 12/10)

870 Orlev, Uri. *The Song of the Whales* (5–8). Trans. by Hillel Halkin. 2010, Houghton Mifflin $16 (978-054725752-5). Living in Jerusalem, Mikha'el becomes close to his grandfather and joins him on nightly dream journeys; as the old man's health fails he passes his ability as a dream master on to his grandson. (Rev: BL 3/1/10*; SLJ 5/10)

871 Ostow, Micol. *Gettin' Lucky* (6–9). 2007, Simon & Schuster paper $5.99 (978-1-4169-3536-0). A breezy book about Cass, a girl who has it all until her best friend kisses her boyfriend, forcing her to make new friends. (Rev: SLJ 7/07)

872 Ostow, Micol. *So Punk Rock (and Other Ways to Disappoint Your Mother)* (8–12). Illus. by David Ostow. 2009, Flux paper $9.95 (978-073871471-4). This is a funny and affecting story about four New Jersey Jewish teens and the ways in which their band's success affects their lives. (Rev: BL 6/1–15/09*; SLJ 11/09)

873 Ostow, Micol. *Westminster Abby* (6–9). Series: Students Across the Seven Seas. 2005, Penguin paper $6.99 (978-0-14-240413-3). Sent to study in London for the summer, Abby has a great time and learns a lot about herself. (Rev: BL 8/05; SLJ 6/05)

874 Padian, Maria. *Brett McCarthy: Work in Progress* (6–9). 2008, Knopf $15.99 (978-0-375-84675-5). In 8th grade, Brett's life changes; although she's still good at soccer and her studies, her friendship with Diane is disrupted and her beloved grandmother has cancer. (Rev: SLJ 2/08)

875 Papademetriou, Lisa. *Drop* (7–12). 2008, Knopf $15.99 (978-037584244-3); LB $18.99 (978-037594244-0). Three Las Vegas teens band together to try to beat the system at the roulette tables, one to pay off gambling debts, one to escape family problems, and one to prove her mathematical theories in this tense, fast-paced novel. Lexile 690L (Rev: BL 12/1/08; LMC 3–4/09; SLJ 12/08; VOYA 4/09)

876 Paratore, Coleen Murtagh. *The Cupid Chronicles* (5–9). 2006, Simon & Schuster $15.95 (978-1-4169-0867-8). Now that her mother is married, Willa puts her considerable energies into the campaign to save the town library, and somehow romance keeps intruding; a sequel to *The Wedding Planner's Daughter* (2005). ⌒ (Rev: SLJ 4/07)

877 Paratore, Coleen Murtagh. *From Willa, with Love* (6–9). 2011, Scholastic $16.99 (978-0-545-09405-4). Making the best of summer without her best friend and boyfriend, 14-year-old Willa helps plan a wedding, meets an interesting new boy, copes with various problems, and keeps a list of the books she has read. **e** Lexile 690L (Rev: BL 8/11; SLJ 8/11)

878 Parkinson, Siobhan. *Something Invisible* (4–7). 2006, Roaring Brook $16.95 (978-1-59643-123-2). Jake, a self-absorbed 11-year-old, learns a lot about family and friendship over a summer that involves tragedy. (Rev: BL 3/1/06; SLJ 4/06; VOYA 6/06)

879 Paterson, Katherine. *Bridge to Terabithia* (6–8). Illus. by Donna Diamond. 1977, HarperCollins LB $16.89 (978-0-690-04635-9); paper $6.99 (978-0-06-440184-5). Jess becomes a close friend of Leslie, a new girl in his school, and suffers agony after her accidental death. Newbery Medal 1978. (Rev: SLJ 1/00)

880 Paulsen, Gary. *The Glass Cafe* (6–8). 2003, Random House $12.95 (978-0-385-32499-1). Tony, 12, has an unusual mother who allows him to draw the women at the Kitty Kat Club, a situation that does not please social services. (Rev: BL 9/1/03; HBG 10/03; SLJ 6/03; VOYA 8/03)

881 Paulsen, Gary, and Jim Paulsen. *Road Trip* (3–7). 2013, Random House $12.99 (978-038574191-0); LB $15.99 (978-037599031-1). Fourteen-year-old Ben and his father — along with the family dog Atticus — have many adventures on a trip to adopt a rescued dog from a shelter; written by Paulsen and his son, this book is narrated in part by Atticus. ⌒ **e** Lexile 700L (Rev: BL 12/15/12; SLJ 2/13; VOYA 2/13)

882 Pavlcin, Karen. *Perch, Mrs. Sackets, and Crow's Nest* (4–7). 2007, Alma Little $16.95 (978-1-934617-00-7). Ten-year-old Andy Parker dreads the idea of a summer in the country but in the end finds he really enjoys it. (Rev: SLJ 12/07)

883 Pearce, Jackson. *Purity* (8–12). 2012, Little, Brown $17.99 (978-031618246-1). Shelby, 16, struggles to find balance between living a morally pure life and fulfilling her mother's dying wish to live "without restraint." **e** (Rev: BL 5/1/12; LMC 8–9/12; SLJ 5/1/12)

884 Pearsall, Shelley. *All of the Above* (5–8). 2006, Little, Brown $15.99 (978-0-316-11524-7). In this inspiring, fact-based novel, a 7th-grade math teacher challenges his students to build the world's largest tetrahedron and ends up involving the whole community;

alternating chapters are narrated by the teacher and four of the students. (Rev: BL 9/1/06; SLJ 9/06)

885 Perkins, Lynne Rae. *All Alone in the Universe* (5–8). 1999, Greenwillow $16.99 (978-0-688-16881-0). Debbie is crushed when her friend of many years drops her for another, but she has the courage to adjust and reach out to others. (Rev: BCCB 10/99; BL 9/1/99*; HB 9–10/99; HBG 3/00; SLJ 10/99)

886 Perkins, Mitali. *Extreme American Makeover* (7–10). Series: First Daughter. 2007, Dutton $16.99 (978-0-525-47800-3). Sixteen-year-old Sameera is the adopted Pakistani daughter of the Republican candidate for president and finds herself half enjoying and half hating efforts to make her over for public scrutiny. (Rev: BL 5/15/07; SLJ 6/07)

887 Perkins, Mitali. *White House Rules* (7–10). Series: First Daughter. 2008, Dutton $16.99 (978-0-525-47951-2). Sameera, the adopted Pakistani daughter of President Righton, livens up the White House with a blog (that readers can actually access), parties for her friends, and her thoughts on politics; the sequel to *Extreme American Makeover* (2007). (Rev: BL 2/1/08; SLJ 2/08)

888 Peters, Kimberly Joy. *Painting Caitlyn* (8–11). 2006, Lobster paper $9.95 (978-1-897073-40-7). Fourteen-year-old Caitlyn feels alone and depressed about her life until she starts dating an older boy named Tyler. But when Tyler starts controlling her and the relationship becomes abusive, Caitlyn must make a choice. (Rev: BL 9/15/06; SLJ 9/06)

889 Pixley, Marcella. *Freak* (6–9). 2007, Farrar $16.00 (978-0-374-32453-7). Miriam — already a talented poet in 7th grade but unpopular because of her social awkwardness — eventually lashes out at her bullies. (Rev: BL 9/15/07; SLJ 11/07)

890 Polisner, Gae H. *The Pull of Gravity* (6–9). 2011, Farrar $16.99 (978-0-374-37193-7). When their friend Scooter dies, teens Nick and his friend Jaycee set out to find Scooter's long-absent father and return a signed first edition of *Of Mice and Men*. e Lexile L690L (Rev: BL 6/1/11; LMC 10/11; SLJ 6/11; VOYA 6/11)

891 Pollack, Jenny. *Klepto: Best Friends, First Love, and Shoplifting* (8–11). 2006, Viking $16.99 (978-0-670-06061-0). In the early 1980s, Julie Prodsky, a 14-year-old drama major at New York's High School of Performing Arts, meets cool Julie Braverman and sets out on a career of "getting" rather than buying. (Rev: BL 2/15/06; SLJ 4/06)

892 Potter, Ellen. *The Humming Room* (4–7). 2012, Feiwel & Friends $16.99 (978-031264438-2). Sent to live with an estranged uncle on a remote island, 12-year-old orphan Roo finds a frail cousin named Phillip, a wild boy, and a walled-off and abandoned garden; inspired by Frances Hodgson Burnett's *The Secret Garden*.

e Lexile 800L (Rev: BL 2/1/12*; LMC 8–9/12; SLJ 5/1/12)

893 Potter, Ellen. *Slob* (4–7). 2009, Philomel $16.99 (978-0-399-24705-7). Twelve-year-old Owen is smart and fat and carries around a tragic memory. (Rev: BCCB 9/09; BL 6/1–15/09; SLJ 7/09*)

894 Preller, James. *Before You Go* (7–10). 2012, Feiwel & Friends $16.99 (978-0-312-56107-9). Haunted by the death of his little sister, Jude, 16, is sent reeling when tragedy strikes again, lashing out at work and at his erstwhile love interest. e Lexile 740L (Rev: BL 7/12; SLJ 10/12)

895 Prinz, Yvonne. *The Vinyl Princess* (7–11). 2010, HarperCollins $16.99 (978-0-06-171583-9). Allie, 16, blogs about music, collects vinyl, and works in a record store while dreaming of romance, which proves rocky. e Lexile 850L (Rev: BL 11/1/09; LMC 3–4/10; SLJ 2/10)

896 Quick, Matthew. *Sorta Like a Rock Star* (9–12). 2010, Little, Brown $16.99 (978-0-316-04352-6). Tirelessly optimistic despite her desperate condition, homeless teen Amber seeks to inspire and uplift those around her until she encounters an obstacle even she can't cope with. ⋒ e Lexile 1030L (Rev: BL 8/10; SLJ 5/10; VOYA 10/10)

897 Rallison, Janette. *How to Take the Ex Out of Ex-boyfriend* (7–10). 2007, Putnam $15.99 (978-0-399-24617-3). This funny novel follows Giovanna as she is torn between being loyal to her brother, who is running for student body president, and her boyfriend, the other candidate's campaign manager. (Rev: SLJ 7/07)

898 Rallison, Janette. *Revenge of the Cheerleaders* (7–9). 2007, Walker $16.95 (978-0-8027-8999-0). Chelsea's cheerleader persona is resented by her younger sister, a sullen 15-year-old Goth, and her sister's boyfriend, a singer with a heavy-metal group. (Rev: BL 1/15/08; SLJ 3/08)

899 Randle, Kristen D. *Slumming* (8–11). 2003, HarperTempest LB $16.89 (978-0-06-001023-2). Three Mormon high school seniors decide to befriend the friendless and invite them to the school prom. (Rev: BCCB 9/03; BL 8/03; HB 7–8/03; HBG 4/04; SLJ 8/03; VOYA 8/03)

900 Ray, Delia. *Here Lies Linc* (5–8). 2011, Knopf $16.99 (978-0-375-86757-6); LB $19.99 (978-0-375-96756-6). Eager to impress his new classmates, formerly home-schooled 12-year-old Linc throws himself into the Adopt-a-Grave project and finds out some unexpected facts about his own family. (Rev: BL 9/1/11; SLJ 9/1/11)

901 Rayban, Chloe. *Hollywood Bliss: My Life So Far* (5–8). Series: Hollywood Bliss. 2007, Bloomsbury $16.95 (978-1-59990-093-3). Hollywood's famous and super-rich mom is getting married in an over-the-top ceremony — and Hollywood is gaining a new step-brother in this glamorous and funny sequel to *Holly-wood Bliss: My Life Starring Mum* (2006). (Rev: BL 7/07; SLJ 2/08)

902 Rayburn, Tricia. *The Melting of Maggie Bean* (6–8). 2007, Simon & Schuster paper $5.99 (978-1-4169-3348-9). Maggie discovers her inner strength and gains confidence as she loses unwanted pounds with the goal of joining her school's synchronized swim team. (Rev: SLJ 7/07)

903 Rayburn, Tricia. *Ruby's Slippers* (4–7). 2010, Aladdin paper $6.99 (978-1-4169-8701-7). A Wizard of Oz-inspired tale in which 7th-grader Ruby is swept from her rural Kansas home to a new life in Florida filled with new electronics and culture, a grandmother, and typical middle school politics. e Lexile 790L (Rev: BL 6/10; LMC 11–12/10)

904 Reisfeld, Randi, and H. B. Gilmour. *What the Dog Said* (6–8). 2012, Bloomsbury $16.99 (978-159990702-4). Grieving for their police officer father, killed in a drive-by shooting, Grace and Regan get a shelter dog that offers lots of useful advice to Grace. e Lexile 690L (Rev: BLO 2/15/12; LMC 5–6/12; SLJ 3/12; VOYA 12/11)

905 Resau, Laura. *The Indigo Notebook* (7–10). 2009, Delacorte $16.99 (978-0-385-73652-7); LB $19.99 (978-0-385-90614-2). It's move number 15 (to Ecuador), and 15-year-old Zeeta is heartily tired of their itinerant life; helping an American teenager find his birth parents brings her interest as she becomes involved in a mysterious adventure that involves magical realism. (Rev: BL 11/1/09; SLJ 12/09)

906 Resau, Laura. *Red Glass* (7–10). 2007, Delacorte $15.99 (978-0-385-73466-0). Sixteen-year-old Sophie, a girl beset by trepidations, befriends 6-year-old Pablo, whose parents died trying to cross the border illegally, and decides to take him back to see his relatives in Mexico with life-changing results. (Rev: BL 9/15/07; SLJ 10/07)

907 Rettig, Liz. *My Desperate Love Diary* (8–12). 2007, Holiday House $16.95 (978-0-8234-2033-9). Wittily written in diary format, this book tells the story of Kelly Ann, a 15-year-old British girl with family problems who finds herself obsessed with a boy who doesn't return her feelings, while a caring boy waits on the sidelines. (Rev: SLJ 7/07)

908 Reynolds, Marilyn. *Love Rules: True-to-Life Stories from Hamilton High* (8–12). Series: True-to-Life. 2001, Morning Glory $18.95 (978-1-885356-75-8); paper $9.95 (978-1-885356-76-5). Lynn, a white high school senior, learns about prejudice as she dates an African American football player and supports her lesbian friend Kit. (Rev: BL 8/01; HBG 3/02; SLJ 9/01; VOYA 10/01)

909 Rhodes, Jewell Parker. *Ninth Ward* (5–8). 2010, Little, Brown $15.99 (978-0-316-04307-6). Plucky 12-year-old Lanesha, who lives in New Orleans's Ninth Ward, draws on her special gifts when Hurricane Katrina arrives. Coretta Scott King Author Honor 2011; ALA Notable Books 2011. ∩ (Rev: BL 5/1/10; LMC 10/10; SLJ 8/10)

910 Ritter, John H. *Under the Baseball Moon* (7–10). 2006, Philomel $16.99 (978-0-399-23623-5). Andy and his friend Glory lean on each other for support as they both pursue their dreams; he wants to be a famous musician and she wants to be a professional softball player. ∩ (Rev: BL 8/06*; SLJ 10/06)

911 Rivers, Karen. *The Encyclopedia of Me* (6–9). 2012, Scholastic $16.99 (978-0-545-31028-4). Grounded for the summer, 13-year-old Tink writes a comic, detailed encyclopedia of her life using an A to Z format. e Lexile 760L (Rev: BL 7/12; HB 9–10/12; SLJ 12/12*)

912 Robinson, Sharon. *Safe at Home* (4–7). 2006, Scholastic $16.99 (978-0-439-67197-2). Still shaken by the sudden death of his father, 10-year-old Elijah Breeze must cope with culture shock when his mother moves him from suburban Connecticut to New York City's Harlem and he attends a coed summer baseball camp. (Rev: SLJ 10/06)

913 Rodrigues, Carmen. *34 Pieces of You* (8–11). 2012, Simon & Schuster $16.99 (978-144243906-1). Three friends try to piece together the truth about Ellie's death from a drug and alcohol overdose. e Lexile HL690L (Rev: BL 10/1/12; SLJ 1/13; VOYA 10/12)

914 Romain, Trevor. *Under the Big Sky* (4–7). 2001, HarperCollins LB $14.89 (978-0-06-029495-3). Encouraged by his grandfather, a young boy searches far and wide for the secret of life. (Rev: BL 8/01; HBG 10/01; SLJ 8/01)

915 Roter, Jordan. *Camp Rules* (7–9). 2007, Dutton $15.99 (978-0-525-47803-4). Penny can't crack the cliques at all-girls Fern Lake Camp, which she attends for the first time as a 16-year-old. (Rev: BL 7/07; SLJ 6/07)

916 Rottman, S. L. *Out of the Blue* (8–11). 2009, Peachtree $16.95 (978-1-56145-499-0). Newly moved to Minot Air Force Base in North Dakota, 15-year-old Stu Ballentyne is compelled to act when he witnesses child abuse first hand, and the experience draws him out of his loneliness and isolation. Lexile 660L (Rev: BL 12/1/09; SLJ 10/09)

917 Rubens, Michael. *Sons of the 613* (8–10). 2012, Clarion $16.99 (978-0-547-61216-4). Preparations for Isaac's bar mitzvah take an unusual turn when his parents take off for Italy, leaving him in the care of his older brother Josh. e (Rev: BL 11/15/12; SLJ 12/12; VOYA 10/12)

918 Rudetsky, Seth. *My Awesome/Awful Popularity Plan* (7–10). 2012, Random House $16.99 (978-037586915-

0); LB $19.99 (978-037596915-7). Justin, who is gay, Jewish, and longing to become popular, agrees to some perilous ploys in this story full of believable self-deprecation and humor. (Rev: BL 1/1/12; VOYA 2/12)

919 Ruditis, Paul. *Everyone's a Critic (Drama!)* (6–9). Series: Drama! 2007, Simon & Schuster paper $8.99 (978-1-4169-3392-2). The students we met in *The Four Dorothys* (2007) now eagerly await the arrival at Orion Academy's summer drama camp of Hartley Blackstone, a famous director; narrator Bryan enjoys watching all the behind-the-scenes drama. (Rev: BL 1/1–15/08; SLJ 12/07)

920 Rushton, Rosie. *Friends, Enemies* (6–8). 2004, Hyperion $15.74 (978-0-7868-5177-5). Four teenage girls, longtime friends, begin to have doubts about each other after a newcomer named Hannah is reluctantly accepted into their circle in this fast-paced novel set in Britain. (Rev: BL 12/15/04; SLJ 2/05)

921 Ryan, Darlene. *Pieces of Me* (8–12). 2012, Orca paper $12.95 (978-14598008-0-9). Teenager Maddie, living on the streets, connects with a young man named Q, and together they find themselves looking after an abandoned 6-year-old boy. e Lexile HL580L (Rev: BL 10/1/12; SLJ 2/13; VOYA 10/12)

922 Ryan, Darlene. *Saving Grace* (7–12). 2006, Orca $14.95 (978-1-55143-668-5). Evie, 15, soon regrets that she gave up her baby and persuades the child's father to help her kidnap Brianna (now named Grace) and head for a new life in Montreal. (Rev: SLJ 4/07)

923 Rylander, Chris. *The Fourth Stall* (4–7). 2011, HarperCollins $15.99 (978-0-06-199496-8). Sixth-graders Mac and Vince run a successful business helping fellow students with everything from tests to defense against bullies, but find their friendship tested when they confront a real challenge. (Rev: BL 2/15/11; LMC 5–6/11; SLJ 9/1/11; VOYA 12/11)

924 Rylant, Cynthia. *God Went to Beauty School* (4–8). 2003, HarperCollins LB $15.89 (978-0-06-009434-8). God indulges in a lot of mortal activities, some fairly wacky, in this collection of thought-provoking poems. (Rev: BL 8/03; HB 7–8/03*; HBG 10/03; SLJ 6/03; VOYA 8/03)

925 Sachs, Marilyn. *The Bears' House* (4–7). Illus. by Louis Glanzman. 1987, Avon paper $2.99 (978-0-380-70582-5). A poor girl escapes from reality by living in a fantasy in her classroom. A reissue of the 1971 edition.

926 Sales, Leila. *Mostly Good Girls* (8–12). 2010, Simon & Schuster $16.99 (978-1-4424-0679-7). Witty, sometimes whiny Violet narrates this story of two private-school friends growing apart as they contend with boys, PSATs, and school politicking. e Lexile 820L (Rev: BL 10/15/10; SLJ 10/1/10*)

927 Schaefer, Laura. *The Secret Ingredient* (4–7). Illus. 2011, Simon & Schuster $15.99 (978-1-4424-1959-9). Annie, 14 and in her last summer before high school,

gets her friends to help her compete in a scone baking contest to win a vacation in London; a sequel to *The Teashop Girls* (2008). e Lexile 710L (Rev: BL 6/1/11; SLJ 8/11)

928 Schaefer, Laura. *The Teashop Girls* (5–8). Illus. by Sujean Rim. 2008, Simon & Schuster $15.99 (978-1-4169-6793-4). Annie and her friends try a variety of business strategies to help save Annie's grandmother's teashop in this book full of tea trivia. (Rev: BL 12/1/08)

929 Schmatz, Pat. *Bluefish* (6–9). 2011, Candlewick $15.99 (978-0-7636-5334-7). Eighth-grader Travis finds help with his reading problems when he and his grandfather move to a new town and he meets outgoing Vida (aka Velveeta) and a compassionate teacher. ALA Notable Books 2012. ∩ e Lexile HL600L (Rev: BLO 10/15/11; HB 11–12/11; LMC 11–12/11; SLJ 12/1/11*)

930 Schmidt, René. *Leaving Fletchville* (7–9). 2008, Orca paper $9.95 (978-1-55143-945-7). Eighth-grader Brandon is a difficult loner until three black siblings arrive at school and he decides to help them hide the fact that they have no parents; for reluctant readers. Lexile HL660L (Rev: SLJ 2/1/09; VOYA 2/09)

931 Schroeder, Lisa. *The Day Before* (8–10). 2011, Simon & Schuster $16.99 (978-1-4424-1743-4). Sixteen-year-old Amber, about to meet her birth parents for the first time, hopes for one last happy day at the beach — and there she meets Cade, a handsome teen also facing a crisis; a novel told in verse. e Lexile HL560L (Rev: BL 6/1/11; SLJ 8/11)

932 Schroeder, Lisa. *It's Raining Cupcakes* (4–7). 2010, Simon & Schuster $15.99 (978-1-4169-9084-0). As her mother opens a cupcake shop, 12-year-old Isabel longs to travel and pins her hopes on a baking contest; with recipes. e Lexile 640L (Rev: BLO 2/15/10; SLJ 2/10)

933 Schroeder, Lisa. *Sprinkles and Secrets* (4–7). 2011, Simon & Schuster $15.99 (978-1-4424-2263-6). Sophie's dreams of becoming an actress are on the verge of coming true, but can she appear in a commercial advertising the competitor to her best friend Isabel's shop? A sequel to *It's Raining Cupcakes* (2010). (Rev: SLJ 10/1/11)

934 Schumacher, Julie. *The Unbearable Book Club for Unsinkable Girls* (8–11). 2012, Delacorte $16.99 (978-038573773-9); LB $19.99 (978-038590685-2). A mother-daughter book club provides the framework for 15-year-old Adrienne and her friends' adventures during a humid summer in Delaware. (Rev: BL 8/12; SLJ 6/12)

935 Schwartz, Ellen. *Stealing Home* (4–7). 2006, Tundra $8.95 (978-0-88776-765-4). Joey, a biracial 9-year-old baseball fan living in the Bronx, is orphaned with his mother's death and moved to live with his Jewish maternal grandparents in Brooklyn, where he must cope with a startlingly different world. (Rev: BL 9/1/06; SLJ 10/06)

936 Scott, Elizabeth. *Between Here and Forever* (8–12). 2011, Simon & Schuster $16.99 (978-1-4169-9484-8). Her beautiful older sister Tess is in a coma after a car accident and Abby, 17, is desperate to help her recovery — to the point of asking handsome Eli to spend time with Tess. ℮ Lexile HL760L (Rev: BL 5/15/11; SLJ 6/11; VOYA 6/11)

937 Scott, Kieran. *This Is So Not Happening* (8–12). Series: He's So/She's So Trilogy. 2012, Simon & Schuster $16.99 (978-141699955-3). Ally tries to remain supportive of her boyfriend Jake when they learn that a summer fling with Chloe resulted in pregnancy. ℮ Lexile HL670L (Rev: BL 7/12A; VOYA 4/12)

938 Selzer, Adam. *How to Get Suspended and Influence People* (6–9). 2007, Delacorte $15.99 (978-0-385-73369-4). Gifted student Leon, 13, makes an "artistic and frank" sex education video that includes artistic nudes and poems about masturbation — and that gets him suspended before "free speech" prevails. (Rev: BCCB 5/07; BL 1/1–15/07; SLJ 3/07)

939 Senate, Melissa. *Theodora Twist* (8–11). 2006, Delacorte $15.95 (978-0-385-73301-4). Dora, a teen star with a wild past, moves in with average teen Emily and her family, with a reality show TV crew monitoring their every move. (Rev: BL 5/15/06; SLJ 2/07)

940 Shaw, Susan. *The Boy in the Basement* (6–9). 2004, Penguin $16.99 (978-0-525-47223-0). Locked in the basement for years by his abusive father, 12-year-old Charlie one day escapes his domestic prison but finds himself totally unequipped to deal with his newfound freedom. (Rev: BL 11/15/04; SLJ 11/04; VOYA 12/04)

941 Shulman, Polly. *Enthusiasm* (7–10). 2006, Penguin $15.99 (978-0-399-24389-9). A romantic comedy of errors featuring Jane and Ashleigh, both fans of Jane Austen, who get roles in a play at the local boys' prep school. (Rev: BL 1/1–15/06*; SLJ 3/06; VOYA 4/06)

942 Shura, Mary Francis. *The Josie Gambit* (5–7). 1986, Avon paper $2.50 (978-0-380-70497-2). Josie's friend Tory behaves in an inexplicable way to his new friend Greg. (Rev: BCCB 5/86; SLJ 9/86)

943 Silberberg, Alan. *Milo: Sticky Notes and Brain Freeze* (5–8). Illus. by author. 2010, Simon & Schuster $15.99 (978-1-4169-9430-5). The death of 12-year-old Milo's mother overshadows all the normal trials and tribulations of middle school in this novel that interweaves humor and pain. ℮ (Rev: HB 11–12/10; LMC 11–12/11; SLJ 9/1/10*)

944 Simone, Ni-Ni. *No Boyz Allowed* (8–12). 2012, Kensington paper $9.95 (978-0-7582-4-193-1). Foster child Gem, 16, struggles to adjust as she moves into a new home and seeks new friends at school. ℮ (Rev: BL 8/12; LMC 3–4/13; SLJ 11/12)

945 Smith, Andrew. *Ghost Medicine* (8–12). 2008, Feiwel & Friends $17.95 (978-0-312-37557-7). Following the death of his brother and then of his mother, 16-year-old Troy finds comfort in a camping trip, spending time with his friends, and practicing "ghost medicine," but also must deal with the bullying son of the sheriff. (Rev: LMC 3–4/09; SLJ 9/1/08)

946 Smith, Andrew. *Stick* (8–11). 2011, Feiwel & Friends $17.99 (978-0-312-61341-9). Stick is a tall, skinny 13-year-old who has a deformed ear and relies on his older brother Bosten for protection from bullies until Bosten's homosexuality is revealed and he must flee from their home. ⌂ ℮ Lexile HL750L (Rev: BL 9/1/11; HB 1–2/12; SLJ 12/1/11)

947 Smith, Sherri L. *Sparrow* (7–10). 2006, Delacorte $15.95 (978-0-385-73324-3). Orphaned when she was little, African American teen Kendall searches for an estranged aunt after her grandmother dies but her search does not progress as she hoped. (Rev: BL 6/1–15/06; SLJ 10/06)

948 Smith, Yeardley. *I, Lorelei* (5–8). 2009, HarperCollins $16.99 (978-0-06-149344-7). In diary entries addressed to her dead cat, 11-year old Lorelei talks about her parents' failing marriage, her friends at her private school in Washington, D.C., a cute boy named Bo, and her efforts to land a role in the school play. (Rev: BL 1/1–15/09; SLJ 3/09)

949 Snyder, Zilpha Keatley. *The Egypt Game* (5–7). Illus. by Alton Raible. 1967, Dell paper $5.99 (978-0-440-42225-9). Humor and suspense mark an outstanding story of city children whose safety, while playing at an unsupervised re-creation of an Egyptian ritual, is threatened by a violent lunatic.

950 Sonnenblick, Jordan. *After Ever After* (6–9). 2010, Scholastic $16.99 (978-0-439-83706-4). Jeffrey, the younger brother who had leukemia in *Drums, Girls and Dangerous Pie* (2005), is now in 8th grade and he and his friend Tad struggle with all the usual young teen angst as well as the long-lasting effects of chemotherapy and radiation. ⌂ (Rev: BL 12/15/09*; HB 3–4/10; LMC 3–4/10; SLJ 1/10)

951 Sonnenblick, Jordan. *Curveball: The Year I Lost My Grip* (8–10). 2012, Scholastic $17.99 (978-054532069-6). Former star athlete Pete, 13, finds a new outlet and a deepened connection to his ailing grandfather through photography. ⌂ ℮ Lexile 800L (Rev: BL 2/1/12*; LMC 5–6/12; SLJ 4/12*)

952 Sonnenblick, Jordan. *Drums, Girls and Dangerous Pie* (6–9). 2004, Turning Tide $15.95 (978-0-9761030-1-1). A moving, often funny story about 8th-grader Steven and the impact on his life and his family of his younger brother's leukemia. (Rev: BL 9/15/05; SLJ 10/04)

953 Sonnenblick, Jordan. *Zen and the Art of Faking It* (5–8). 2007, Scholastic $16.99 (978-0-439-83707-1).

Adopted from China as a child and tired of moving to new schools, 8th-grader San Lee decides to play the role of a Zen master when he arrives in Pennsylvania. (Rev: BL 10/1/07; HB 11–12/07; LMC 1/08; SLJ 10/07)

954 Spinelli, Jerry. *Smiles to Go* (6–10). 2008, Harper-Collins $16.99 (978-0-06-028133-5). The discovery that protons decay unsettles high school freshman Will Tuppence, causing him to take a new look at all sorts of things, including his little sister Tabby and his best friends Mi-Su and BT. (Rev: BL 2/15/08; SLJ 5/08)

955 Springer, Nancy. *Blood Trail* (6–8). 2003, Holiday $16.95 (978-0-8234-1723-0). A suspenseful story about a boy afraid to reveal what he knows about his friend's murder. (Rev: BL 5/1/03; HBG 10/03; SLJ 5/03; VOYA 8/03)

956 Springstubb, Tricia. *What Happened on Fox Street* (4–7). 2010, HarperCollins $15.99 (978-0-06-198635-2). Although she still misses her dead mother, 10-year-old Mo is fairly happy with life on Fox Street until the summer her friend Mercedes seems to change and her father receives an interesting offer for their house. ∩ e (Rev: BL 9/1/10*; HB 9–10/10; SLJ 9/1/10)

957 Staples, Suzanne Fisher. *Under the Persimmon Tree* (7–10). 2005, Farrar $17.00 (978-0-374-38025-0). The stories of Najmal, a brave young Afghani refugee, and Nusrat, an American woman helping with a refugee school, intersect as they wait for news of their loved ones in the chaos of the 2001 Afghan War. (Rev: BL 7/05*; SLJ 7/05; VOYA 10/05)

958 Stead, Rebecca. *Liar and Spy* (5–7). 2012, Random House $15.99 (978-0-385-73743-2); LB $18.99 (978-0-385-90665-4). Coping with his father's job loss, his mother's double shifts at work, and bullies at school, 7th-grader Georges is pleased to meet a neighbor boy who wants his help investigating a mystery. ∩ e Lexile 670L (Rev: BL 6/12; HB 9–10/12; LMC 3–4/13*; SLJ 9/12*; VOYA 10/12)

959 Stead, Rebecca. *When You Reach Me* (4–7). 2009, Random $15.99 (978-0-385-73742-5). Sixth-grader Miranda receives notes from someone she believes knows the future. Newbery Medal 2010; Boston Globe–Horn Book Fiction 2010; ALA Notable Books 2010. ∩ e (Rev: BCCB 9/09; BL 6/1–15/09*; HB 7/09; LMC 10/09; SLJ 7/09*)

960 Steele, J. M. *The Taker* (8–11). 2006, Hyperion $15.99 (978-0-7868-4930-7). Carly's SAT scores are not good enough to get her into Princeton as her family expects, so she accepts an offer to cheat next time she takes the test, a decision that has wide-ranging repercussions. (Rev: BL 10/1/06; SLJ 12/06)

961 Stolz, Mary. *The Bully of Barkham Street* (4–8). Illus. by Leonard Shortall. 1963, HarperCollins paper $6.99 (978-0-06-440159-3). Eleven-year-old Martin goes through a typical phase of growing up — feel-

ing misunderstood. Also use *A Dog on Barkham Street* (1960).

962 Stork, Francisco X. *Last Summer of the Death Warriors* (8–12). 2010, Scholastic $17.99 (978-0-545-15133-7). This complex tale features 17-year-olds Pancho, who seeks to avenge his sister's death, and D.Q., who is dying of brain cancer, as they contemplate the meaning of being a "Death Warrior." ∩ e Lexile HL640L (Rev: BL 2/1/10*; HB 3–4/10; LMC 3–4/10; SLJ 3/10)

963 Strasser, Todd. *Famous* (7–12). 2011, Simon & Schuster $15.99 (978-1-4169-7511-3). Budding paparazzo Jamie, 16, must decide how much to reveal of what she has learned about starlet Willow Twine's life. e Lexile 800L (Rev: BL 5/1/11; LMC 5–6/11; SLJ 5/11; VOYA 2/11)

964 Strohmeyer, Sarah. *Smart Girls Get What They Want* (8–11). 2012, HarperCollins $17.99 (978-0-06-195340-8). Smart girl Gigi and her sophomore friends set out to become popular with mixed results. e Lexile HL820L (Rev: BLO 6/12; SLJ 7/12; VOYA 2/12)

965 Strong, Jeremy. *Stuff: The Life of a Cool Demented Dude* (6–8). Illus. by Matthew S. Armstrong. 2007, HarperTempest $15.99 (978-0-06-084105-8). This entertaining story about a British teen nicknamed "Stuff" who has a chaotic home life and an equally complicated love life; the only thing that keeps him sane is the anonymous weekly comic strip he writes for a school publication. (Rev: SLJ 7/07)

966 Supplee, Suzanne. *Somebody Everybody Listens To* (8–11). 2010, Dutton $16.99 (978-0-525-42242-6). Plucky country-star wannabe Retta heads for Nashville and succeeds despite having to sleep in her car at first. e Lexile 830L (Rev: BL 6/10; SLJ 10/1/10)

967 Sutherland, Tui T. *This Must Be Love* (7–10). 2004, HarperCollins LB $16.89 (978-0-06-056476-6). Shakespearean plots are interwoven in this tale of Helena and Hermia, best friends in a modern New Jersey high school, and the comedy of errors that is their romantic life. (Rev: BCCB 1/05; SLJ 9/04)

968 Sweeney, Joyce. *The Guardian* (7–9). 2009, Henry Holt $16.95 (978-080508019-3). Hunter is abused by his foster mother and bullied at school until he begins praying to an angel, Gabriel. When a real-life Gabriel, Hunter's biological father, shows up, Hunter finds himself in danger. (Rev: BL 4/1/09; HB 5–6/09; SLJ 6/1/09; VOYA 8/09)

969 Tanen, Sloane. *Are You Going to Kiss Me Now?* (8–11). 2011, Sourcebooks paper $8.99 (978-1-4022-5-461-1). High school junior Fran wins an essay contest and sets off to travel to Africa to a charity event with five celebrities; but the plane crashes and she finds herself stranded on an island learning the assets and foibles of her companions. e Lexile HL700L (Rev: BL 4/1/11; SLJ 6/11; VOYA 6/11)

970 Tanzman, Carol M. *dancergirl* (8–10). 2011, Harle-quinTeen paper $9.99 (978-03732104-0-4). Ali Ruffino initially enjoys her Internet fame as "dancergirl," but the story turns grimmer as she discovers a video camera outside her bedroom window. ℮ (Rev: BL 2/1/12; LMC 8–9/12; SLJ 3/12)

971 Tashjian, Janet. *The Gospel According to Larry* (7–10). 2001, Henry Holt $16.95 (978-0-8050-6378-3). When Josh (a.k.a. "Larry") publishes his anticonsumer-ism worldview on the Web, he develops a cult follow-ing and discovers the dark side of fame. (Rev: BCCB 1/02; BL 11/1/01; HB 1–2/02*; HBG 3/02; SLJ 10/01; VOYA 12/01)

972 Tashjian, Janet. *Larry and the Meaning of Life* (8–12). 2008, Henry Holt $16.95 (978-080507735-3). In this third book in the series, Josh/Larry falls in with a mysterious guru named Gus and finds himself having a series of bizarre adventures. ♫ Lexile 760L (Rev: BL 9/1/08; SLJ 12/08; VOYA 2/09)

973 Tashjian, Janet. *My Life as a Book* (4–7). Illus. by Jake Tashjian. 2010, Henry Holt $16.99 (978-0-8050-8903-5). Derek spends a summer at reading camp and, to his surprise, learns to love books. (Rev: BL 8/10*; LMC 8–9/10; SLJ 8/10)

974 Tashjian, Janet. *Vote for Larry* (7–10). 2004, Henry Holt $16.95 (978-0-8050-7201-3). In this sequel to *The Gospel According to Larry* (2001), our young hero de-cides to run for president of the United States. (Rev: BL 5/1/04; HB 7–8/04; SLJ 5/04; VOYA 6/04)

975 Teller, Janne. *Nothing* (7–12). 2010, Simon & Schuster $16.99 (978-1-4169-8579-2). A group of 7th-grade students struggle to defuse a classmate's existen-tial crisis in this compelling novel translated from Dan-ish. Printz Honor 2011; Batchelder Honor 2011; ALA Notable Books 2011. ♫ ℮ (Rev: BL 12/1/09*; LMC 3–4/10; SLJ 4/10)

976 Thesman, Jean. *In the House of the Queen's Beasts* (6–8). 2001, Viking $11.99 (978-0-670-89288-4). Two diffident 14-year-old girls, Emily and Rowan, share their secrets and develop a tentative friendship in a se-cluded tree house. (Rev: BCCB 6/01; BL 2/15/01; SLJ 3/01; VOYA 4/01)

977 Tigelaar, Liz. *Pretty Tough* (7–12). 2007, Penguin paper $8.99 (978-1-59514-112-5). Krista and Charlie Brown are sisters but very different — one popular, one solitary; when they are both chosen for the soccer team they must work together. (Rev: BCCB 2/08; SLJ 9/07)

978 Timberlake, Amy. *That Girl Lucy Moon* (5–8). 2006, Hyperion $15.99 (978-0-7868-5298-7). When her mother takes off on an extended photography as-signment, Lucy Moon is left without her biggest ally in her campaigns for animal rights, social justice, and, now, for the liberation of a sledding hill. (Rev: SLJ 9/06)

979 Tolan, Stephanie S. *Applewhites at Wit's End* (5–8). 2012, HarperCollins $15.99 (978-006057938-8). Fac-ing foreclosure, the eccentric Applewhites decide to turn their rambling property into a retreat for fellow artists; humor and mystery are blended with bouncy ac-tion. ℮ Lexile 840L (Rev: BL 5/1/12; SLJ 6/12)

980 Townsend, Wendy. *Lizard Love* (6–12). 2008, Front St $17.95 (978-1-932425-34-5). Grace, a country girl living in Manhattan, is thrilled to discover a city pet store that is stocked with reptiles and that becomes a refuge from the pressures of school and life. (Rev: BL 5/1/08; SLJ 8/08)

981 Tracey, Rhian. *When Isla Meets Luke Meets Isla* (8–10). 2004, Bloomsbury paper $9.95 (978-0-7475-6344-0). Told from alternating points of view, this is the story of troubled teens Isla and Luke — a Scottish girl who has just moved to England and a son of a newly divorced, obsessive mother — and the support and af-fection they give to each other. (Rev: SLJ 2/04)

982 Trigiani, Adriana. *Viola in Reel Life* (7–10). 2009, HarperTeen $16.99 (978-0-06-145102-7). Ninth-grader Viola feels neglected after her parents, documentary filmmakers, send her to a boarding school while they film in Afghanistan; but after making friends and get-ting involved in activities, she warms to her new school and finds a potential new romantic interest. ℮ Lexile 820L (Rev: BL 8/09; SLJ 9/09; VOYA 12/09)

983 Trigiani, Adriana. *Viola in the Spotlight* (7–10). 2011, HarperTeen $16.99 (978-0-06-145105-8). In this sequel to *Viola in Reel Life* (1999) Viola is back home in Brooklyn with her parents and looking forward to the summer, but things don't turn out as she expected and she has to find different ways to fill her days. ℮ Lexile 730L (Rev: BL 6/1/11; SLJ 9/1/11; VOYA 8/11)

984 Trueit, Trudi. *Julep O'Toole: What I Really Want to Do Is Direct* (5–7). 2007, Dutton $16.99 (978-0-525-47781-5). Julep auditions for the school play to earn extra English credit but ends up as assistant director in this enjoyable third installment in the series. (Rev: SLJ 6/07)

985 Tulloch, Richard. *Freaky Stuff* (5–8). Illus. by Shane Nagle. 2007, Walker $16.95 (978-0-8027-9623-3). Funny illustrations are included in this sequel to *Weird Stuff* (2006), in which Brian is unhappy with a TV se-ries based on his favorite books and the effect the show has on his little brother. (Rev: SLJ 6/07)

986 Tullson, Diane. *Riot Act* (6–9). Series: Orca Sound-ings. 2012, Orca LB $16.95 (978-1-4598-0140-0); paper $9.95 (978-1-4598-0139-4). Daniel, 17, and his best friend Nick find themselves taking part in looting following a hockey game, and Daniel must deal with guilt when he is taken for a hero; suitable for reluctant readers. ℮ Lexile HL540L (Rev: BL 6/12; SLJ 11/12)

987 Turetsky, Bianca. *The Time-Traveling Fashionista* (5–8). Illus. by Sandra Suy. 2011, Little, Brown $17.99

(978-0-316-10542-2). Seventh-grader Louise tries on a vintage dress for the school dance and finds herself whisked back in time — to a glamorous life on the *Titanic*; this first volume in a series includes full-color illustrations of elegant gowns. e Lexile 860L (Rev: BL 4/1/11; HB 3–4/12; SLJ 4/11; VOYA 6/11)

988 Vail, Rachel. *If You Only Knew* (4–7). Series: Friendship Ring. 1998, Scholastic paper $14.95 (978-0-590-03370-1). In this book shaped like a CD, Zoe Grandon, a 7th grader, gives up a boy she likes to pursue a friendship. (Rev: BCCB 10/98; BL 10/15/98; HBG 3/99; SLJ 10/98; VOYA 6/99)

989 Vail, Rachel. *Not That I Care* (4–7). Series: Friendship Ring. 1998, Scholastic paper $14.95 (978-0-590-03476-0). For a classroom presentation on 10 items that reveal who you are, Morgan Miller remembers crucial incidents in her life but, in her final report, glosses over the truth. (Rev: BCCB 12/98; BL 11/15/98; HBG 3/99; SLJ 12/98; VOYA 6/99)

990 Vail, Rachel. *Please, Please, Please* (4–7). Series: Friendship Ring. 1998, Scholastic paper $14.95 (978-0-590-00327-8). CJ Hurley has to overcome a controlling mother in order to hang out with her friends in this book shaped like a CD. (Rev: BCCB 10/98; BL 10/15/98; HBG 3/99; SLJ 12/98; VOYA 6/99)

991 van de Ruit, John. *Spud* (8–12). 2007, Penguin paper $16.99 (978-1-59514-170-5). Attending an elite boys boarding school in Australia in 1990, 13-year-old Spud describes in diary form his problems with his classmates and his family as well as his thoughts on Mandela's release from prison; the fast-paced humor of this novel will get readers past the unfamiliar vocabulary and sports. (Rev: BL 9/15/07; SLJ 12/07)

992 van de Ruit, John. *Spud — The Madness Continues . . .* (8–12). 2008, Penguin $16.99 (978-159514190-3). In this humorous sequel to *Spud* (2007), Spud is still at his South African boarding school and dealing with puberty, a changing voice, racism, and particularly useless adults. (Rev: BLO 10/1/08; LMC 3/08)

993 Van Draanen, Wendelin. *Flipped* (5–8). 2001, Knopf $14.95 (978-0-375-81174-6). In 2nd grade Julianna was infatuated with Bryce, but now, six years later, the situation is reversed in this story told from each viewpoint in alternating chapters. (Rev: BCCB 1/02; BL 12/15/01; HBG 3/02; SLJ 11/01*; VOYA 12/01)

994 Vande Velde, Vivian. *Deadly Pink* (6–9). 2012, Harcourt $16.99 (978-0-547-73850-5). Grace, 14, becomes worried when her older sister refuses to leave the virtual reality game in which she has ensconced herself, a world where men are voiceless and women have all the control. e Lexile 850L (Rev: BL 6/12; LMC 5–6/13; SLJ 7/12; VOYA 4/12)

995 Vande Velde, Vivian. *Remembering Raquel* (8–11). 2007, Harcourt $16.00 (978-0-15-205976-7). In text, emails, and blogs, classmates and others remember Raquel, a high-school freshman who died in a car accident, and learn that there was more to her than met the eye; this will appeal to reluctant readers. (Rev: BL 11/15/07; HB 1–2/08; LMC 2/08; SLJ 12/07)

996 Vaught, Susan. *Freaks Like Us* (7–12). 2012, Bloomsbury $16.99 (978-159990872-4). Jason, a high schooler with schizophrenia, investigates when one of his fellow disturbed students disappears. e Lexile 890L (Rev: BL 10/1/12; HB 9–10/12; LMC 1–2/13*; VOYA 12/12)

997 Vaupel, Robin. *My Contract with Henry* (5–8). 2003, Holiday $16.95 (978-0-8234-1701-8). An 8th-grade Thoreau project brings a group of outsider students together as they learn about the environment, the simple life, and each other. (Rev: BL 7/03; HBG 10/03; SLJ 7/03; VOYA 10/03)

998 Vega, Denise. *Access Denied (And Other Eighth Grade Error Messages)* (6–8). 2009, Little, Brown $16.99 (978-031603448-7). Now in 8th grade, Erin is determined to recover from the humiliation of 7th-grade—when her private blog was made public—and meet boys, make new friends, and update her look; a sequel to *Click Here (To Find Out How I Survived Seventh Grade)* (2005). Lexile 620L (Rev: BLO 5/27/09; SLJ 10/09)

999 Velasquez, Gloria. *Ankiza* (7–12). Series: Roosevelt High School. 2000, Piñata $16.95 (978-1-55885-308-9); paper $9.95 (978-1-55885-309-6). African American Ankiza learns about prejudice when she starts dating a white boy. (Rev: SLJ 4/01; VOYA 8/01)

1000 Vivian, Siobhan. *A Little Friendly Advice* (7–9). 2008, Scholastic $16.99 (978-0-545-00404-6). Ruby, 16, has been a quiet girl, prepared to accept advice from her friends no matter how self-serving or ill-advised; the gift of a Polaroid camera gives Ruby the chance to look at things differently and she learns a lot about her family and friends. (Rev: BL 6/1–15/08; SLJ 2/08)

1001 Volponi, Paul. *The Hand You're Dealt* (8–11). 2008, Atheneum $16.99 (978-1-4169-6935-8). A raw and gritty coming-of-age page-turner about grief, family, and Texas Hold 'Em poker, featuring Huck Porter, a young man determined to avenge his father. (Rev: BL 8/08)

1002 Vrettos, Adrienne Maria. *Skin* (8–11). 2006, Simon & Schuster $16.95 (978-1-4169-0655-1). Fourteen-year-old Donnie tells the story of his parents' unhappy marriage and his older sister's death from anorexia. (Rev: BL 3/1/06; SLJ 6/06)

1003 Waite, Judy. *Forbidden* (8–11). 2006, Simon & Schuster $16.95 (978-0-689-87642-4). As one of the Chosen girls in the True Cause cult led by Howard, 16-year-old Elinor does not question her life until Outsider Jaime appears. (Rev: BCCB 2/06; BL 4/15/06; SLJ 3/06)

1004 Walters, Eric. *Branded* (6–8). Series: Orca Currents. 2010, Orca LB $16.95 (978-1-55469-268-2); paper $9.95 (978-1-55469-267-5). The prospect of school uniforms brings diverse reactions in this easy read for reluctant readers. e Lexile HL600L (Rev: BL 4/1/10; SLJ 5/10)

1005 Walters, Eric. *In a Flash* (6–9). 2008, Orca $16.95 (978-155469035-0); paper $9.95 (978-155469034-3). A high school boy enjoys organizing flash mobs, eventually planning one to protest his new school principal's unpopular policies in this novel for reluctant readers. (Rev: BLO 12/8/08; SLJ 3/1/09)

1006 Walters, Eric. *Special Edward* (5–8). 2009, Orca $16.95 (978-1-55469-096-1); paper $9.95 (978-1-55469-092-3). Eddy, a lazy sophomore, figures that if he can get himself into special ed class, he won't have to work so hard. (Rev: BL 5/15/09; SLJ 9/09)

1007 Walters, Eric. *Stuffed* (8–12). Series: Orca Soundings. 2006, Orca $14.95 (978-1-55143-519-0). Ian gets even more of a reaction than he bargained for when he and his friends boycott a fast-food restaurant. (Rev: SLJ 10/06)

1008 Walters, Eric. *Visions* (7–10). 2012, Fitzhenry & Whiteside paper $9.95 (978-1-55455-122-4). After their father's death, 12-year-old twins Rob and Mark join their scientist mother on a trip to an Arctic island and learn much about Inuit mystic and everyday life while enjoying various adventures — and seeing their father's ghost. Lexile 630L (Rev: BL 5/15/12; SLJ 8/1/12)

1009 Warner, Sally. *It's Only Temporary* (5–7). Illus. by author. 2008, Viking $15.99 (978-0-670-06111-2). With sketches and lists, 12-year-old Skye reviews her problems in her journal when she is sent to live with her grandmother after her brother has a bad accident. (Rev: BL 6/1–15/08; SLJ 8/08)

1010 Wasserman, Robin. *Hacking Harvard* (8–11). 2007, Simon & Schuster paper $8.99 (978-1-4169-3633-6). Eric, Max, and Schwarz set out to hack into Harvard's admissions computer system and get their classmate Clay (who is definitely not Harvard material) admitted to the university. (Rev: BL 1/1–15/08; SLJ 1/08)

1011 Waysman, Dvora. *Back of Beyond: A Bar Mitzvah Journey* (5–7). 1996, Pitspopany paper $4.95 (978-0-943706-54-2). On a trip to Australia, a 12-year-old Jewish boy becomes involved in the Aborigine culture and witnesses a ritual of manhood similar to a bar mitzvah. (Rev: SLJ 5/96)

1012 Wedekind, Annie. *A Horse of Her Own* (5–7). 2008, Feiwel & Friends $16.95 (978-0-312-36927-9). At horse camp, Jane is surrounded by girls who come from wealthy families and who have horses of their own, a fact that bothers her until she wins an important competition. (Rev: BL 5/15/08; SLJ 8/08)

1013 Weingarten, Lynn. *The Secret Sisterhood of Heartbreakers* (8–11). 2012, HarperTeen $17.99 (978-006192618-1). Reeling from a bad breakup, Lucy is intrigued by the appearance of three magical girls who offer to cure her heartbreak. e (Rev: BLO 12/15/11; SLJ 3/12; VOYA 12/11)

1014 Weingarten, Lynn. *Wherever Nina Lies* (8–12). 2009, Scholastic $16.99 (978-054506631-0). Ellie, 16, sets out on a road trip to find her missing older sister and encounters romance and mystery in this compelling read. YALSA Popular Paperbacks for Young Adults Top Ten 2011. Lexile HL780L (Rev: BL 2/15/09; SLJ 8/09)

1015 Wells, Tina. *The Secret Crush* (4–8). Illus. by Michael Segawa. Series: Mackenzie Blue. 2010, HarperCollins $10.99 (978-0-06-158311-7). Seventh-grader Mackenzie Blue hopes to catch the attention of cute Landon, and the school's forthcoming rock-and-roll musical seems a good opportunity. e (Rev: SLJ 5/10)

1016 Whitaker, Alecia. *The Queen of Kentucky* (7–10). 2012, Little, Brown $17.99 (978-031612506-2). New high school freshman Ricki Jo tries to reinvent herself as Ericka but finds popularity elusive in this novel set in rural Kentucky. e Lexile 860L (Rev: BL 10/15/11; SLJ 1/12)

1017 Willey, Margaret. *A Summer of Silk Moths* (7–10). 2009, Flux paper $9.95 (978-0-7387-1540-7). Seventeen-year-old Pete and Nora overcome their initial animosity as they realize sobering truths about their pasts in this contemplative story with a nature preserve setting. (Rev: BLO 11/16/09; LMC 11–12/09; SLJ 1/10)

1018 Williams, Maiya. *The Fizzy Whiz Kid* (5–8). 2010, Abrams $16.95 (978-081098347-2). Suddenly plunked down among the children of movie stars, producers, and makeup artists, midwesterner Mitchell wins over his new classmates when he lands a spot in a TV commercial. e (Rev: BL 3/1/10; SLJ 5/10)

1019 Willner-Pardo, Gina. *Prettiest Doll* (4–7). 2012, Clarion $16.99 (978-054768170-2). After a childhood of beauty pageant successes, 13-year-old Olivia is feeling overwhelmed when asked to sing; she takes to the road with Danny, a 15-year-old with his own problems. e Lexile 680L (Rev: BL 7/12; HB 1–2/13; SLJ 2/13; VOYA 8/12)

1020 Wilson, Jacqueline. *Candyfloss* (4–7). Illus. by Nick Sharratt. 2007, Roaring Brook $14.95 (978-1-59643-241-3). Flossie, busy helping her divorced dad at his restaurant while her mother and stepfather are in Australia, must also deal with old and new friends at school in this story set in England. (Rev: BL 10/1/07; HB 9–10/07; LMC 11/07; SLJ 9/07)

1021 Winerip, Michael. *Adam Canfield: The Last Reporter* (5–8). 2009, Candlewick $16.99 (978-0-7636-2342-5). Featuring teen journalist Adam and his coeditor sidekick Jennifer, this third installment in a series builds upon themes of enterprise, journalistic ethics, and budding romance. ⌒ Lexile 710L (Rev: BLO 10/15/09; SLJ 10/09; VOYA 12/09)

1022 Winerip, Michael. *Adam Canfield of the Slash* (4–7). 2005, Candlewick $15.99 (978-0-7636-2340-1). As editors of the *Slash*, the Harris Elementary/Middle School student newspaper, Adam and Jennifer chase scoops and tackle ethical questions. (Rev: BL 5/1/05; SLJ 3/05)

1023 Winerip, Michael. *Adam Canfield, Watch Your Back!* (5–8). Series: Adam Canfield. 2007, Candlewick $15.99 (978-0-7636-2341-8). Adam of *Adam Canfield of the Slash* has even more on his plate in this sequel: writing for the school newspaper, exposing an unfair science fair, and even facing down high school muggers. (Rev: BL 4/1/08; SLJ 12/07)

1024 Winters, Ben H. *The Secret Life of Ms. Finkleman* (5–8). 2010, HarperCollins $16.99 (978-0-06-196541-8). Brainy 7th-grader Bethesda investigates her music teacher and uncovers an unsuspected past as a punk rocker, resulting in an unusual school concert. Lexile 910L (Rev: BL 11/15/10; LMC 3–4/11; SLJ 11/1/10)

1025 Wise, Rachel. *Read All About It!* (5–7). Series: Dear Know-It-All. 2012, Simon & Schuster paper $5.99 (978-144244402-7). Seventh-grade Samantha is thrilled to be named the school newspaper's advice columnist but less happy to realize that her best friend Hailey is crushing on Sam's own romantic target. e (Rev: BLO 6/12; LMC 1–2/13)

1026 Wiseman, Rosalind. *Boys, Girls and Other Hazardous Materials* (7–10). 2010, Putnam $17.99 (978-0-399-24796-5). Freshman Charlie finds new and old friends in high school and learns about romance and social pressure while navigating bullies and cliques. e Lexile HL660L (Rev: BL 12/15/09; SLJ 1/10; VOYA 4/10)

1027 Wittlinger, Ellen. *Blind Faith* (7–10). 2006, Simon & Schuster $15.95 (978-1-4169-0273-7). Her mother's grief following the death of her grandmother causes 15-year-old Elizabeth to struggle with questions of faith even as she finds some solace in the new boy across the street. (Rev: BL 6/1–15/06; HB 7–8/06; SLJ 9/06)

1028 Wittlinger, Ellen. *Gracie's Girl* (4–7). 2000, Simon & Schuster $16.95 (978-0-689-82249-0). Bess and her best friend Ethan, both middle schoolers, get involved with a homeless old lady. (Rev: BCCB 2/01; BL 9/15/00; HBG 3/01; SLJ 11/00; VOYA 10/01)

1029 Wittlinger, Ellen. *Razzle* (7–12). 2001, Simon & Schuster $17.00 (978-0-689-83565-0). New on Cape Cod, Kenyon becomes friends with an offbeat girl named Razzle — until he falls for beautiful Harley — in this mutilayered and appealing novel. (Rev: BCCB 10/01; BL 11/1/01; HB 11–12/01; HBG 3/02; SLJ 9/01; VOYA 10/01)

1030 Wolff, Virginia Euwer. *True Believer* (7–12). Series: Make Lemonade. 2001, Simon & Schuster $17.00 (978-0-689-82827-0). Poverty and violence are continuing forces in this sequel to *Make Lemonade*, in which LaVaughn fosters her college ambitions and finds romance. YPL National Book Award 2001; Printz Honor 2002. ⌒ (Rev: BL 6/1–15/02; HB 1–2/01; HBG 10/01; SLJ 1/01; VOYA 4/01)

1031 Wolitzer, Meg. *The Fingertips of Duncan Dorfman* (5–8). 2011, Dutton $16.99 (978-0-525-42304-1). Three middle-school students learn about themselves as they spend time at the Youth Scrabble Tournament. ALA Notable Books 2012. e (Rev: BL 9/15/11; LMC 1–2/12; SLJ 9/1/11)

1032 Wood, Maryrose. *My Life the Musical* (8–12). 2008, Delacorte $15.99 (978-0-385-73278-9). Emily and Philip, both 16, have seen the musical "Aurora" umpteen times; what will they do if the show closes? (Rev: BL 2/20/08; SLJ 5/08)

1033 Woods, Brenda. *A Star on the Hollywood Walk of Fame* (7–9). 2010, Putnam $16.99 (978-0-399-24683-8). A disparate group of 10th-grade Los Angeles students tell their stories in response to their teacher's creative writing assignment. e Lexile HL620L (Rev: BL 1/1–15/10; LMC 3–4/10; SLJ 7/10)

1034 Woodson, Jacqueline. *After Tupac and D Foster* (6–9). 2008, Putnam $15.99 (978-0-399-24654-8). In Queens, New York, in the early 1960s, three 11-year-old African American girls become fast friends partly through their mutual adoration of the music of Tupac Shakur, a bond they share until his death in 1996. Newbery Honor 2009; ALA Notable Books 2009. (Rev: BL 1/1/08; HB 1–2/08; LMC 10/08; SLJ 4/08; VOYA 2/08)

1035 Wunder, Wendy. *The Probability of Miracles* (7–12). 2011, Penguin $17.99 (978-1-59514-368-6). After seven years of battling cancer, 16-year-old Cam learns that nothing more can be done and heads with her mother and sister to Promise, Maine, where miracles are known to happen; a quirky, often funny novel. ⌒ e Lexile HL800L (Rev: BL 12/1/11; LMC 3–4/12; SLJ 12/1/11*)

1036 Wynne-Jones, Tim. *Rex Zero: The Great Pretender* (4–7). Series: Rex Zero. 2010, Farrar $16.99 (978-0-374-36260-7). Rex, now 12, is unhappy that his family has moved across town yet determined to start middle school with his old friends, however difficult that may be; set in 1963 Ottawa against a backdrop of civil rights turmoil. e Lexile 610L (Rev: BL 12/1/10; HB 11–12/10; SLJ 10/1/10)

1037 Wynne-Jones, Tim. *A Thief in the House of Memory* (7–10). 2005, Farrar $17.00 (978-0-374-37478-5). Sixteen-year-old Dec can barely recall the events surrounding his mother's sudden disappearance six years earlier until the death of an intruder in the family home reawakens forgotten memories. (Rev: BCCB 5/05; BL 3/1/05; HB 5–6/05; SLJ 4/05; VOYA 6/05)

1038 Wyshynski, Sue. *Poser* (6–9). 2010, Walker $16.99 (978-080272063-4); paper $8.99 (978-08027209-4-8). Tallulah gets off to a bad start at her new high school, lying about her skills at surfing; however, a new friend rescues her from her doldrums and she recovers and even finds romance. e (Rev: BLO 8/10; SLJ 8/10)

1039 Zadoff, Allen. *My Life, the Theater, and Other Tragedies* (7–12). 2011, Egmont $16.99 (978-1-60684-036-8). High school theater "technie" Adam is drawn to an attractive young actress and overcomes his shyness even as he begins to come to terms with his father's death two years before. ∩ e Lexile HL500L (Rev: BL 5/1/11; HB 5–6/11; SLJ 7/11; VOYA 4/11)

1040 Zarr, Sara. *Once Was Lost* (8–10). 2009, Little, Brown $16.99 (978-0-316-03604-7). A 13-year-old girl is missing and 15-year-old Samara begins to question her faith. Best Books for Young Adults 2010. ∩ e (Rev: BL 11/15/09*; SLJ 11/09)

1041 Zemser, Amy Bronwen. *Dear Julia* (7–10). 2008, Greenwillow $16.99 (978-0-06-029458-8); LB $17.89 (978-006029459-5). Two unlikely young women — Elaine, 16, and Lucinda — forge a friendship built on shared family quirks and their separate quests for fulfillment and renown in this lighthearted exploration of feminist themes. Lexile 780L (Rev: BL 9/1/08; SLJ 1/1/09; VOYA 2/09)

1042 Zevin, Gabrielle. *Because It Is My Blood* (8–11). 2012, Farrar $17.99 (978-0-374-38074-8). In 2083, 17-year-old Anya is released from Liberty Children's Facility (after the events of 2011's *All These Things I've Done*) and must figure out what to do about her back-stabbing, unreliable, criminally inclined family. ∩ e Lexile 640L (Rev: BL 8/12; SLJ 9/12; VOYA 8/12)

1043 Zielin, Lara. *The Waiting Sky* (8–11). 2012, Putnam $16.99 (978-0-399-25686-8). Seventeen-year-old Jane is guilt-ridden when she leaves her alcoholic mother for the summer and goes to work with her brother's tornado-chasing team in this novel that also features potential romance. e (Rev: BL 10/1/12; HB 7–8/12; SLJ 8/1/12; VOYA 8/12)

1044 Zindel, Lizabeth. *Girl of the Moment* (7–10). 2007, Viking $16.99 (978-0-670-06210-2). Being a celebrity's assistant isn't all it's cracked up to be, as Lily learns when she takes a job working for the ultra-famous, ultra-rich Sabrina Snow. (Rev: BL 3/15/07; SLJ 6/07)

1045 Zucker, Naomi. *Callie's Rules* (4–7). 2009, Egmont $15.99 (978-160684027-6). Callie, 11, is a smart kid who tries to understand what's necessary to fit in in middle school but feels compelled, along with her family, to take a stand when her school decides to ban "satanic" Halloween celebrations. A sequel is *Write On, Callie Jones* (2010). (Rev: BL 9/1/09; SLJ 8/09)

Ethnic Groups and Problems

1046 Abdel-Fattah, Randa. *Does My Head Look Big in This?* (7–10). 2007, Scholastic $16.99 (978-0-439-91947-0). Amal is a Muslim Palestinian growing up in Australia, where family, friends, and strangers all react in different ways to her decision to veil herself in the traditional hijab. (Rev: BCCB 9/07; BL 7/07; LMC 11–12/07; SLJ 6/07)

1047 Abdel-Fattah, Randa. *Ten Things I Hate About Me* (7–10). 2009, Scholastic $16.99 (978-054505055-5). In this humorous story about fitting in and finding who you really are, 16-year-old Jamilah — known as Jamie at school — is a Lebanese Australian Muslim who isn't comfortable telling her friends who she really is and hides her identity by dying her hair blond and wearing blue contact lenses. Lexile HL720L (Rev: BL 12/1/08; SLJ 2/1/09; VOYA 6/09)

1048 Abraham, Susan Gonzales, and Denise Gonzales Abraham. *Cecilia's Year* (4–7). 2004, Cinco Puntos $16.95 (978-0-938317-87-6). Inspired by the real-life story of the authors' mother, this is the story of a 14-year-old Hispanic American girl's determination to defy cultural tradition and continue her schooling in Depression-era New Mexico. (Rev: BL 1/1–15/05; SLJ 4/05)

1049 Abraham, Susan Gonzales, and Denise Gonzales Abraham. *Surprising Cecilia* (6–9). Series: Latino Fiction for Young Adults. 2005, Cinco Puntos $16.95 (978-0-938317-96-8). In this appealing sequel to *Cecilia's Year*, set in the Rio Grande Valley during the Depression, the title character gets a chance to move to El Paso to further her education but is given little encouragement at home to do so. (Rev: BL 11/15/05; SLJ 1/06)

1050 Adler, Emily, and Alex Echevarria. *Sweet 15* (7–10). 2010, Marshall Cavendish $16.99 (978-0-7614-5584-4). Destiny Lozada is not sure she wants to have a quinceañera but she also does not want to disappoint her Puerto Rican family. (Rev: BLO 3/1/10; LMC 8–9/10; SLJ 7/10)

1051 Alegria, Malin. *Crossing the Line* (7–12). Series: Border Town. 2012, Scholastic/Point paper $5.99 (978-054540240-8). An appealing first novel in a series featuring Latina teen Fabiola and her younger sister Alexis as they deal with the family restaurant, small town life close to the Mexican border, school life, and a mystery. e Lexile 680L (Rev: BL 5/15/12; LMC 5–6/13*; SLJ 6/12)

1052 Alegría, Malín. *Estrella's Quinceañera* (7–10). 2006, Simon & Schuster $14.95 (978-0-689-87809-1). Planning for her 15th birthday celebration, Mexican American Estrella finds herself balancing her hopes against reality. (Rev: BL 2/15/06; SLJ 4/06)

1053 Alvarez, Julia. *Finding Miracles* (8–11). 2004, Knopf LB $17.99 (978-0-375-82760-0). Sixteen-year-old Milly Kaufman, rescued as a child from a strife-torn Latin American nation, is encouraged to return to her native country and learn more about her family roots. (Rev: BL 10/15/04; SLJ 10/04; VOYA 12/04)

1054 Alvarez, Julia. *How Tía Lola Learned to Teach* (4–7). Series: Tía Lola. 2010, Knopf $15.99 (978-0-375-86460-5); LB $18.99 (978-0-375-96460-2). In this sequel to *How Tía Lola Came to (Visit) Stay* (2001), Miguel and Juanita's Dominican aunt is teaching at their school and worrying about her soon-to-expire visa. ⏾ (Rev: BL 12/1/10; HB 1–2/11; LMC 3–4/11; SLJ 11/1/10)

1055 Angell, Judie. *One-Way to Ansonia* (7–10). 2001, iUniverse paper $12.95 (978-0-595-15830-0). In novel format this is the story of a young Russian girl's experience in this country around the turn of the century; originally published in 1985. (Rev: BL 1/1/86; SLJ 12/85; VOYA 2/86)

1056 Bailey-Williams, Nicole. *A Little Piece of Sky* (7–12). 2002, Broadway paper $9.95 (978-0-7679-1216-7). Song Byrd is an African American girl who rises above her very difficult circumstances in this realistic and compelling novel. (Rev: VOYA 4/03)

1057 Barnes, Derrick. *We Could Be Brothers* (5–8). 2010, Scholastic $17.99 (978-054513573-3). African American 8th-graders Robeson and Pacino come from different backgrounds but recognize their common aims as they confront Tariq, a threatening classmate. Lexile HL600L (Rev: BL 11/15/10; VOYA 4/11)

1058 Barrett, William E. *The Lilies of the Field* (8–12). 1988, Warner paper $5.99 (978-0-446-31500-5). A young black man, Homer Smith, helps a group of German nuns to achieve their dream.

1059 Barth-Grozinger, Inge. *Something Remains* (8–11). Trans. by Anthea Bell. 2006, Hyperion $16.99 (978-0-7868-3880-6). This book is based on the true story of a 12-year-old Jewish boy named Erich Levi and what life was like for him and his family, dealing with prejudice and persecution, during Hitler's first years in power. (Rev: BL 9/1/06; SLJ 12/06)

1060 Baskin, Nora Raleigh. *The Truth about My Bat Mitzvah* (5–8). 2008, Simon & Schuster $15.99 (978-1-4169-3558-2). Caroline, daughter of a Jewish mother and Christian father, has never been a practicing Jew but when her grandmother dies and leaves her a Star of David necklace — and her best friend Rachel is preparing for her bat mitzvah at the same time — she begins to acknowledge this part of her identity. (Rev: BL 3/15/08; SLJ 4/08)

1061 Bavati, Robyn. *Dancing in the Dark* (7–11). 2013, Flux paper $9.99 (978-073873477-4). Ditty's love of ballet leads her to defy the edicts of her ultra-Orthodox Jewish family and at age 17 must make a difficult final choice. ⓔ Lexile HL750L (Rev: BL 2/15/13; LMC 8–9/13; SLJ 2/13; VOYA 2/13)

1062 Bernier-Grand, Carmen T. *In the Shade of the Nispero Tree* (4–7). 1999, Orchard LB $16.99 (978-0-531-33154-5). Prejudice and racism separate two friends in this story set in Ponce, Puerto Rico, during 1961. (Rev: BCCB 3/99; BL 4/1/99; HBG 10/99; SLJ 3/99)

1063 Bertrand, Diane Gonzales. *Sweet Fifteen* (8–12). 1995, Arte Publico paper $9.95 (978-1-55885-133-7). While making a party dress for Stefanie Bonilla, age 14, Rita Navarro falls in love with her uncle and befriends her widowed mother, maturing in the process. (Rev: BL 6/1–15/95; SLJ 9/95)

1064 Blume, Judy. *Iggie's House* (4–7). 1970, Dell paper $4.99 (978-0-440-44062-8). An African American family moves into Iggie's old house.

1065 Bosse, Malcolm. *Ganesh* (7–9). 1981, HarperCollins LB $11.89 (978-0-690-04103-3). A young boy from India has difficulty fitting into the American Midwest and its ways.

1066 Bush, Lawrence. *Rooftop Secrets: And Other Stories of Anti-Semitism* (6–9). 1986, American Hebrew Cong. paper $9.95 (978-0-8074-0314-3). In each of these eight short stories, some form of anti-Semitism is encountered by a young person. (Rev: SLJ 11/86)

1067 Canales, Viola. *Orange Candy Slices and Other Secret Tales* (6–12). 2001, Arte Publico paper $9.95 (978-1-55885-332-4). Life on the Texas-Mexico border is the focus of this collection of coming-of-age short stories. (Rev: VOYA 6/02)

1068 Carlson, Lori Marie, ed. *American Eyes: New Asian-American Short Stories for Young Adults* (8–12). 1994, Henry Holt $15.95 (978-0-8050-3544-5). These stories present widely varied answers to the question, What does it mean to Asian American adolescents to grow up in a country that views them as aliens? (Rev: BL 1/1/95; SLJ 1/95; VOYA 5/95)

1069 Carlson, Lori Marie, ed. *Voices in First Person: Reflections on Latino Identity* (7–12). Illus. by Flavio Morais. 2008, Simon & Schuster $16.99 (978-141696212-0). This book explores the experiences of Latinos in America through a variety of fictional monologues, poems, and short stories focusing on themes of heartbreak, prejudice, identity, and pride. ⓔ (Rev: BL 10/1/08; HB 7–8/08; LMC 11–12/08; SLJ 8/08; VOYA 8/08)

1070 Cervantes, Jennifer. *Tortilla Sun* (4–7). 2010, Chronicle $16.99 (978-0-8118-7015-3). Izzy, 12, spends a summer in New Mexico with her grandmother and learns about her father and her cultural heritage. (Rev: BLO 5/1/10; LMC 8–9/10; SLJ 6/10)

1071 Chambers, Veronica. *Quinceañera Means Sweet 15* (6–9). 2001, Hyperion LB $16.49 (978-0-7868-2426-7). Fourteen-year-old Brooklyn friends Marisol and Magdalena look ahead to their quinceanera coming-of-age parties with anticipation and some frustration. (Rev: BCCB 5/01; HBG 10/01; SLJ 6/01)

1072 Chase, Paula. *So Not the Drama* (7–10). Series: Del Rio Bay Clique. 2007, Kensington paper $9.95 (978-0-7582-1859-9). Mina deals with issues of popularity and prejudice at her high school, where students of all races and many backgrounds intermingle but don't always get along. (Rev: BL 2/1/07)

1073 Cheng, Andrea. *Honeysuckle House* (4–7). 2004, Front St $16.95 (978-1-886910-99-7). The problems of immigration and adjustment to new cultures are shown in this story of two girls of Chinese heritage, told in the girls' alternating voices. (Rev: BL 4/1/04; HB 7–8/04; SLJ 6/04)

1074 Childress, Alice. *A Hero Ain't Nothin' but a Sandwich* (7–10). 2000, Putnam paper $5.99 (978-0-698-11854-6). Benjie's life in Harlem, told from many viewpoints, involves drugs and rejection. (Rev: BL 10/15/88)

1075 Cofer, Judith Ortiz. *Call Me María* (6–10). 2004, Scholastic $16.95 (978-0-439-38577-0). Initially María mourns the loss of her island landscape when she moves from Puerto Rico to the mainland, but gradually she adapts, makes new friends, and writes new poetry; the appealing format includes poems and letters. (Rev: BL 12/1/04; HB 1–2/05; LMC 3/05; SLJ 11/04)

1076 Cofer, Judith Ortiz. *If I Could Fly* (7–10). 2011, Farrar $16.99 (978-0-374-33517-5). When 15-year-old Doris's mother moves back to Puerto Rico, and her father is often absent, the girl finds comfort in a neighbor's pigeons. ℮ Lexile 820L (Rev: BL 5/1/11; HB 5–6/11; SLJ 6/11; VOYA 6/11)

1077 Cofer, Judith Ortiz. *An Island Like You* (7–12). 2008, Paw Prints paper $15.99 (978-1-4395-0880-0). Stories of Puerto Rican immigrant children experiencing the tensions between two cultures. (Rev: BL 2/15/95*; SLJ 7/95)

1078 Cruz, Maria Colleen. *Border Crossing* (4–8). 2003, Arte Publico paper $9.95 (978-1-55885-405-5). Ceci, 12, can't understand why her Mexican father won't speak Spanish or talk about his home, so she decides to go and investigate. (Rev: BL 11/15/03; SLJ 2/04)

1079 Curtis, Christopher Paul. *The Watsons Go to Birmingham — 1963* (4–8). 1995, Delacorte $16.95 (978-0-385-32175-4); paper $6.50 (978-0-440-41412-4). An African American family returns to Alabama from Michigan to place their troubled son with his grandmother in this novel set in the 1960s. (Rev: BL 8/95; SLJ 10/95*; VOYA 12/95)

1080 Daswani, Kavita. *Indie Girl* (7–10). 2007, Simon & Schuster paper $8.99 (978-1-4169-4892-6). Indira, who lives in Los Angeles, is thrilled to get a job for a fashion editor (even if she's only babysitting) until she discovers the woman is prejudiced against Indians. (Rev: BL 10/15/07; SLJ 12/07)

1081 Davis, Tanita S. *Mare's War* (6–9). 2009, Knopf $16.99 (978-037585714-0); LB $19.99 (978-037595714-7). During a summer-long road trip, teen sisters Octavia and Tali learn about their unconventional grandmother's days in the African American battalion of the Women's Army Corps. Coretta Scott King Author Honor 2010. ℮ Lexile 830L (Rev: BLO 5/27/09; LMC 11–12/09; SLJ 7/1/09; VOYA 6/09)

1082 Easton, Kelly. *Hiroshima Dreams* (7–10). 2007, Dutton $16.99 (978-0-525-47821-8). Lin's Japanese mother wants their family to be more American but when her grandmother, Obaachan, arrives from Japan, she reminds them of their heritage. (Rev: BL 9/15/07; SLJ 12/07)

1083 Ellison, James W. *Finding Forrester* (7–12). 2000, Newmarket paper $9.95 (978-1-55704-479-2). This inspiring novel tells how a reclusive author helps a promising inner-city African American youth to develop his writing skills. (Rev: SLJ 9/01; VOYA 6/01)

1084 English, Karen. *Francie* (5–8). 1999, Farrar $17.00 (978-0-374-32456-8). Francie, a black girl growing up in segregated Alabama, places her family in danger when she helps a friend who is escaping a racist employer. (Rev: BCCB 10/99; BL 10/15/99; HB 9–10/99; HBG 3/00; SLJ 9/99; VOYA 2/00)

1085 Felin, M. Sindy. *Touching Snow* (8–10). 2007, Atheneum $16.99 (978-1-4169-1795-3). Karina, 13, and her two Haitian sisters are referred to social services when their stepfather brutally beats Enid, the oldest sister, in this novel that shows the tensions in an immigrant family and the often unfulfilled aspirations. (Rev: BL 5/15/07; HB 7–8/07; SLJ 9/07)

1086 Flake, Sharon G. *Who Am I Without Him?* (6–12). 2004, Hyperion $15.99 (978-0-7868-0693-5). Funny, moving, and truthful, these 10 short stories deal with growing up black in today's society. (Rev: BL 4/15/04*; HB 7–8/04; SLJ 5/04; VOYA 6/04)

1087 Flake, Sharon G. *You Don't Even Know Me: Stories and Poems About Boys* (7–10). 2010, Disney/Jump at the Sun $16.99 (978-1-4231-0014-0). In prose and free-verse poetry, African American teens talk about their experiences in all areas of life in this companion to *Who Am I Without Him?* (2007). ℮ (Rev: BL 12/15/09; SLJ 5/10)

1088 Fleischman, Paul. *Seedfolks* (4–8). 1997, HarperCollins LB $15.89 (978-0-06-027472-6). Thirteen people from many cultures explain why they have planted gardens in a vacant lot in Cleveland, Ohio. (Rev: BCCB 7–8/97; BL 5/15/97; HB 5–6/97; SLJ 5/97*; VOYA 6/97)

1089 Flores, Bettina R. *Chiquita's Diary* (6–9). 1995, Pepper Vine paper $13.50 (978-0-9625777-7-2). Twelve-year-old Chiquita is determined to break out of the poverty that her widowed Mexican American mother endures, and she makes a start by becoming a mother's helper. (Rev: BL 2/15/96)

1090 Fogelin, Adrian. *Crossing Jordan* (5–8). Illus. by Suzy Schultz. 2000, Peachtree $14.95 (978-1-56145-215-6). Set in contemporary Florida, this novel tells how 12-year-old Cass must keep her friendship with African American Jemmie a secret from her racist father. (Rev: BCCB 4/00; HBG 10/00; SLJ 6/00)

1091 Friedman, Robin. *The Importance of Wings* (7–9). 2009, Charlesbridge $15.95 (978-158089330-5). Roxanne is fascinated by her new next-door neighbor, Liat, who is also Israeli American but seems more proud of her heritage, in this story set in 1980s Staten Island. Sydney Taylor Book Award 2010. Lexile 650L (Rev: BL 5/15/09; SLJ 7/1/09)

1092 Gallo, Donald R., ed. *Join In: Multiethnic Short Stories by Outstanding Writers for Young Adults* (7–12). 1995, Bantam paper $5.99 (978-0-440-21957-6). Seventeen stories concerning the problems teenagers of various ethnic backgrounds have living in the United States. (Rev: BL 1/15/94; SLJ 11/93; VOYA 10/93)

1093 Garland, Sherry. *Shadow of the Dragon* (6–12). 1993, Harcourt $10.95 (978-0-15-273530-2); paper $6.00 (978-0-15-273532-6). Danny Vo has grown up American since he emigrated from Vietnam as a child. Now traditional Vietnamese ways, the new American culture, and skinhead prejudice clash, resulting in his cousin's death. (Rev: BL 11/15/93*; SLJ 11/93; VOYA 12/93)

1094 Gonzalez, Christina Diaz. *The Red Umbrella* (6–10). 2010, Knopf $16.99 (978-0-375-86190-1). Lucia and her brother are uprooted from their comfortable life in Cuba and sent to live in Nebraska during the Communist revolution of the 1960s. **e** (Rev: BLO 7/10; LMC 8–9/10; SLJ 5/10; VOYA 6/10)

1095 Green, Richard G. *Sing, Like a Hermit Thrush* (6–9). 1995, Ricara paper $12.95 (978-0-911737-01-1). A young Native American teenager growing up on the Six Nations Reserve is confused by his gift of seeing events before they happen. (Rev: BL 4/15/96)

1096 Griffis, Molly Levite. *Simon Says* (6–12). 2004, Eakin $22.95 (978-1-57168-836-1). It's 1942, and 11-year-old Jewish refugee Simon, shipped from Poland to live with an American family five years earlier, is remembering his past amid signs of rising anti-Semitism in his adopted Oklahoma home; a sequel to *The Rachel Resistance* (2001) and *The Feester Filibuster* (2002). (Rev: BL 11/1/04; SLJ 1/05)

1097 Grimes, Nikki. *Jazmin's Notebook* (6–10). 1998, Dial $15.99 (978-0-8037-2224-8). The journal of 14-year-old Jazmin, who writes about her tough, tender, and angry life in Harlem in the 1960s, living with her sister after her mother is hospitalized with a breakdown and her father has died. (Rev: BL 9/15/98; HBG 9/98; SLJ 7/98; VOYA 10/98)

1098 Guy, Rosa. *The Friends* (7–10). 1995, Random House paper $5.99 (978-0-440-22667-3). Phyllisia, a

newcomer to Harlem, finds a friend in the unusual Edith Jackson; first published in 1973.

1099 Hamilton, Virginia. *A White Romance* (8–12). 1987, Scholastic paper $4.50 (978-0-590-13005-9). A formerly all-black high school becomes integrated and social values and relationships change. (Rev: SLJ 1/88; VOYA 2/88)

1100 Hayes, Rosemary. *Mixing It* (7–12). 2007, Frances Lincoln paper $7.95 (978-1-84507-495-1). Fatimah, a Muslim, rescues a boy from a church bombing and exposes her family to unwanted attention in this novel set in England. (Rev: BL 1/1–15/08)

1101 Hernandez, Irene B. *Across the Great River* (7–10). 1989, Arte Publico paper $9.95 (978-0-934770-96-5). The harrowing story of a young Mexican girl and her family, who enter the United States illegally. (Rev: BL 8/89; SLJ 8/89)

1102 Hernandez, Irene B. *The Secret of Two Brothers* (7–10). 1995, Arte Publico paper $9.95 (978-1-55885-142-9). An action-packed story about two Mexican American boys who meet many challenges. Especially appealing to those whose first language is Spanish or for reluctant readers. (Rev: BL 10/1/95; SLJ 11/95)

1103 Hernández, Jo Ann Yolanda. *White Bread Competition* (7–12). 1997, Arte Publico paper $9.95 (978-1-55885-210-5). The effects of winning a spelling bee on Luz Rios and her Hispanic American family in San Antonio are explored in a series of vignettes. (Rev: BL 1/1–15/98; SLJ 8/98; VOYA 4/98)

1104 Herrera, Juan Felipe. *Downtown Boy* (5–8). 2005, Scholastic $16.99 (978-0-439-64489-1). This poignant free-verse novel, narrated by 10-year-old Juanito, offers an unflinching look at what life was like for Chicano migrant workers and their families in 1950s California. (Rev: BL 12/15/05; SLJ 1/06; VOYA 4/06)

1105 Hirsch, Odo. *Have Courage, Hazel Green!* (4–7). 2006, Bloomsbury $15.95 (978-1-58234-659-5). Independent-minded Hazel Green and her friends must mend some fences when her plan to shame a neighbor into apologizing for a blatant act of ethnic prejudice backfires. (Rev: BL 6/1–15/06; SLJ 8/06)

1106 Ingold, Jeanette. *Paper Daughter* (6–9). 2010, Harcourt $17 (978-0-1520-5507-3). After her journalist father is killed in an accident, 16-year-old Maggie Chen seeks clues to his past and uncovers some family secrets; information about the Chinese Exclusion Act and the lives of Chinese Americans in the early 20th century is woven into the story. **e** Lexile HL800L (Rev: BL 3/1/10; LMC 10/10; SLJ 4/10; VOYA 10/10)

1107 Irwin, Hadley. *Kim / Kimi* (7–10). 1987, Penguin paper $5.99 (978-0-14-032593-5). A half-Japanese teenager brought up in an all-white small town sets out to explore her Asian roots. (Rev: BL 3/15/87; SLJ 5/87; VOYA 6/87)

1108 Jimenez, Francisco. *The Circuit: Stories from the Life of a Migrant Child* (5–10). 1997, Univ. of New Mexico paper $11.95 (978-0-8263-1797-1). Eleven moving stories about the lives, fears, hopes, and problems of children in Mexican migrant worker families. (Rev: BL 12/1/97)

1109 Jimenez, Francisco. *Reaching Out* (7–12). 2008, Houghton Mifflin $16 (978-061803851-0). In this fictionalized autobiography young Jimenez struggles to rise beyond his immigrant migrant farm family and succeed in college. Belpré Honor 2009; ALA Notable Books 2009. **e** Lexile 910L (Rev: BL 8/08*; LMC 1–2/09; SLJ 12/08; VOYA 10/08)

1110 Johnson, Angela. *Toning the Sweep* (7–12). 1993, Scholastic paper $6.99 (978-0-590-48142-7). This novel captures the innocence, vulnerability, and love of human interaction, as well as the melancholy, self-discovery, and introspection of an African American adolescent. (Rev: BL 4/1/93*; SLJ 4/93*)

1111 Johnston, Tony. *Any Small Goodness: A Novel of the Barrio* (4–7). Illus. by Raul Colon. 2001, Scholastic paper $16.95 (978-0-439-18936-1). Eleven-year-old Arturo Rodriguez, whose Mexican family is new to Los Angeles, describes family life, school, celebrations, and dangers. (Rev: BL 9/15/01; HBG 3/02; SLJ 9/01; VOYA 10/01)

1112 Johnston, Tony. *Bone by Bone by Bone* (6–9). 2007, Roaring Brook $16.95 (978-1-59643-113-3). David, a 9-year-old white boy, and Malcolm, an 8-year-old black boy, are best friends in a small town in Tennessee in the 1950s, but David's father forbids the relationship. (Rev: BL 8/07; LMC 11/07; SLJ 10/07)

1113 Jones, Traci L. *Standing against the Wind* (6–9). 2006, Farrar $16.00 (978-0-374-37174-6). Being raised by her aunt in an impoverished city neighborhood, African American Patrice struggles to overcome her environment in order to succeed. (Rev: BL 7/06; SLJ 11/06)

1114 Jordan, Dream. *Hot Girl* (7–10). 2008, St. Martin's paper $9.95 (978-031238284-1). Troubled 14-year-old African American Kate's resolve to stick with her new foster family is threatened when smooth-talking Naleejah takes her in, gives her a makeover, and teaches her how to win her crush's affection. **e** Lexile HL660L (Rev: BLO 11/19/08; SLJ 4/1/09; VOYA 12/08)

1115 Karim, Sheba. *Skunk Girl* (7–10). 2009, Farrar $16.95 (978-037437011-4). Muslim Nina, 16, comes from the only Pakistani American family in town, and struggles with her parents' strict rules and expectations and her own hairiness. Lexile 840L (Rev: BL 4/15/09; SLJ 4/1/09; VOYA 4/10)

1116 Krech, Bob. *Rebound* (8–11). 2006, Marshall Cavendish $16.99 (978-0-7614-5319-2). In a school where Polish kids wrestle and African American kids play basketball, a student named Ray Wisniewski challenges the status quo and tries out for basketball, dealing with racism on and off the court. (Rev: BL 9/1/06; LMC 2/07; SLJ 12/06)

1117 Laird, Elizabeth. *Kiss the Dust* (6–10). 1992, Penguin $6.99 (978-0-14-036855-0). A docunovel about a refugee Kurdish teen caught up in the 1984 Iran-Iraq War. (Rev: BL 6/15/92)

1118 Lamba, Marie. *What I Meant . . .* (6–9). 2007, Random House $16.99 (978-0-375-84091-3). Sangeet's strict Indian father and crazy aunt make her life in an American suburb very complicated, especially when Sangeet gets caught going out on a date. (Rev: BL 7/07; SLJ 11/07)

1119 Lee, Harper. *To Kill a Mockingbird* (8–12). 1977, HarperCollins $23.00 (978-0-397-00151-4). A lawyer in a small Southern town defends an African American man wrongfully accused of rape.

1120 Lee, Lauren. *Stella: On the Edge of Popularity* (5–7). 1994, Polychrome $10.95 (978-1-879965-08-9). A Korean American girl has to choose between being popular and being loyal to her Korean culture. (Rev: BCCB 7–8/94; SLJ 9/94)

1121 Lee, Marie G. *F Is for Fabuloso* (6–9). 1999, Avon $15.95 (978-0-380-97648-5). A sensitive story about Jin-Ha, a Korean girl, and the troubles she and her parents face in the United States. (Rev: BL 9/15/99; HBG 4/00)

1122 Lee, Marie G. *Necessary Roughness* (7–12). 1996, HarperCollins LB $14.89 (978-0-06-025130-7). Chan, a Korean American football enthusiast, and his twin sister, Young, encounter prejudice when their family moves to a small Minnesota community. (Rev: BL 1/1–15/97; SLJ 1/97; VOYA 6/97)

1123 Lester, Julius. *Long Journey Home* (6–8). 1998, Viking paper $6.99 (978-0-14-038981-4). Six based-on-fact stories concerning slaves, ex-slaves, and their lives in a hostile America.

1124 Lester, Julius. *This Strange New Feeling* (7–9). 2006, Penguin $16.99 (978-0-8037-3172-1). Three stories about black couples and the meaning of freedom; originally published in 1982.

1125 Levitin, Sonia. *Strange Relations* (8–11). 2007, Knopf $15.99 (978-0-375-83751-7). Fifteen-year-old Marne, from a secular Jewish family, visits her conservative Jewish relatives in Hawaii and comes to appreciate their differences. Sydney Taylor Book Award 2008. (Rev: BL 6/1–15/07; SLJ 5/07)

1126 Lipsyte, Robert. *The Brave* (8–12). 1991, HarperCollins paper $5.99 (978-0-06-447079-7). A Native American heavyweight boxer is rescued from drugs, pimps, and hookers by a tough but tender ex-boxer/New York City cop. (Rev: BL 10/15/91; SLJ 10/91*)

1127 Lipsyte, Robert. *The Chief* (7–10). 1995, Harper-Collins paper $6.50 (978-0-06-447097-1). Sonny Bear can't decide whether to go back to the reservation, continue boxing, or become Hollywood's new Native American darling. Sequel to *The Brave*. (Rev: BL 6/1–15/93; VOYA 12/93)

1128 López, Lorraine M. *Call Me Henri* (6–9). 2006, Curbstone $17.95 (978-1-931896-27-6). Enrique, a Latino middle-school student, does his best to juggle all the responsibilities on his plate — including school and caring for baby triplets — and does so with very little help until a medical emergency raises him to hero status; but just when things are looking promising, more troubles loom. (Rev: SLJ 8/06)

1129 Lord, Bette Bao. *In the Year of the Boar and Jackie Robinson* (6–8). 1984, HarperCollins paper $5.99 (978-0-06-440175-3). A young Chinese girl finds that the world of baseball helps her adjust to her new home in America.

1130 Ly, Many. *Roots and Wings* (6–10). 2008, Delacorte $15.99 (978-0-385-73500-1). Fourteen-year-old Grace learns about her Cambodian heritage when she and her mother travel to Florida for her grandmother's funeral. (Rev: BL 3/15/08; SLJ 7/08)

1131 Lynch, Janet Nichols. *Messed Up* (7–10). 2009, Holiday House $17.95 (978-082342185-5). Part Cheyenne, part Mexican R.D. tries to make it on his own when the only reliable adult in his life dies and he must navigate life in an unstable school and a violent neighborhood. Lexile 780L (Rev: BL 4/1/09; SLJ 8/09; VOYA 8/09)

1132 McCall, Guadalupe Garcia. *Under the Mesquite* (7–10). 2011, Lee & Low $18.95 (978-1-60060-429-4). After Lupita's mother is diagnosed with cancer, the teen finds herself assuming greater responsibility for her seven younger siblings in this Mexican American family story told in verse; includes a glossary of Spanish terms. Belpré Author Award 2012; ALA Notable Books 2012; YALSA Top Ten Best Fiction for Young Adults 2012. e Lexile 990L (Rev: BL 10/1/11; LMC 1–2/12; SLJ 10/1/11)

1133 McDonald, Janet. *Brother Hood* (7–12). 2004, Farrar $16.00 (978-0-374-30995-4). Nate Whitely, a 16-year-old student at a prestigious boarding school, finds himself straddling two very different cultures as he seeks to remain loyal to his Harlem roots. (Rev: BL 9/1/04; SLJ 11/04; VOYA 2/05)

1134 McMullan, Margaret. *Cashay* (7–10). 2009, Houghton Mifflin $15.00 (978-054707656-0). Cashay's younger sister is killed in gang-related violence in their housing project, and Cashay is helped by a white mentor as her mother returns to drug taking. e Lexile 700L (Rev: BLO 5/27/09; SLJ 8/09)

1135 Magoon, Kekla. *Camo Girl* (5–8). 2011, Simon & Schuster $15.99 (978-1-4169-7804-6). Biracial 6th-grader Ella, an outsider unhappy with her skin tone, is pleased when popular Bailey moves to town and befriends her, but anxious to keep her friendship with the troubled Z. e Lexile 600L (Rev: BL 2/1/11; LMC 11–12/11; SLJ 1/1/11)

1136 Magoon, Kekla. *Fire in the Streets* (6–10). 2012, Aladdin $15.99 (978-1-4424-2230-8). African American Maxie, 14, gets involved with the Black Panthers in this compelling novel set in 1968 Chicago. e Lexile 650L (Rev: BL 7/12*; HB 9–10/12; LMC 1–2/13*; SLJ 9/12)

1137 Marino, Jan. *The Day That Elvis Came to Town* (7–10). 1993, Avon paper $3.50 (978-0-380-71672-2). In this tale of southern blacks, Wanda is thrilled when a room in her parents' boarding house is rented to Mercedes, who makes her feel pretty and smart — and who once went to school with Elvis Presley. (Rev: BL 12/15/90*; SLJ 1/91*)

1138 Markle, Sandra. *The Fledglings* (6–9). 1998, Boyds Mills paper $9.95 (978-1-56397-696-4). With her parents dead, Kate, 14, runs away to live with her Cherokee grandfather and immerses herself happily in his world. (Rev: BL 6/15/92)

1139 Martinez, Victor. *Parrot in the Oven: Mi Vida* (7–10). 1996, HarperCollins LB $16.89 (978-0-06-026706-3). Through a series of vignettes, the story of Manuel, a teenage Mexican American, unfolds as he grows up in the city projects with an abusive father and a loving mother. (Rev: BL 10/15/96; SLJ 11/96)

1140 Meminger, Neesha. *Shine, Coconut Moon* (7–10). 2009, Simon & Schuster $16.99 (978-141695495-8). An Indian American girl realizes how vital her heritage is to her in the months following 9/11. Lexile HL740L (Rev: BL 2/15/09; SLJ 4/1/09)

1141 Meriwether, Louise. *Daddy Was a Number Runner* (7–12). 1986, Feminist paper $16.59 (978-1-55861-442-0). The story of Frances, a black girl, growing up in Harlem during the Depression.

1142 Miklowitz, Gloria D. *The War Between the Classes* (7–10). 1986, Dell paper $4.99 (978-0-440-99406-0). A Japanese American girl finds that hidden prejudices and bigotry emerge when students in school are divided into four socioeconomic groups. (Rev: BL 4/15/85; SLJ 8/85; VOYA 6/85)

1143 Mobin-Uddi, Asma. *My Name Is Bilal* (4–7). Illus. by Barbara Kiawk. 2005, Boyds Mills $15.95 (978-1-59078-175-3). When they start at a new school, Muslim Bilal and his sister Ayesha balance pride in their own heritage and their desire to blend in. (Rev: BL 8/05; SLJ 8/05)

1144 Mohr, Nicholasa. *El Bronx Remembered: A Novella and Stories* (7–9). 1993, HarperCollins paper $5.99 (978-0-06-447100-8). These 12 stories set in the Bronx reflect the general Puerto Rican experience in New York.

1145 Mohr, Nicholasa. *Going Home* (6–8). 1986, Puffin paper $6.99 (978-0-14-130644-5). The young heroine finds a boyfriend and spends a summer in her family's home in Puerto Rico in this sequel to *Felita*. (Rev: BL 7/86; SLJ 8/86)

1146 Mohr, Nicholasa. *Nilda* (7–9). 1986, Publico paper $11.95 (978-0-934770-61-3). The story of a 12-year-old Puerto Rican girl growing up in the New York barrio.

1147 Moodley, Ermila. *Path to My African Eyes* (6–9). 2007, Just Us Bks $15.95 (978-1-933491-09-7). Thandi, 14, and her family move from South Africa to California, and she finds that her classmates' misconceptions about her background — as well as the natural culture shock — make it hard for her to adjust to her new home. (Rev: BL 11/15/07; SLJ 12/07)

1148 Moore, Yvette. *Freedom Songs* (6–12). 1991, Penguin paper $5.99 (978-0-14-036017-2). In 1968, Sheryl, 14, witnesses and then experiences acts of prejudice while visiting relatives in North Carolina. (Rev: BL 4/15/91; SLJ 3/91)

1149 Myers, Walter Dean. *Autobiography of My Dead Brother* (8–11). Illus. by Christopher Myers. 2005, HarperCollins LB $16.89 (978-0-06-058292-0). In this compelling novel of teenage life in contemporary Harlem, Jessie watches helplessly as his friend Rise drifts away from him, dragged down in a whirlpool of drugs and crime. (Rev: BL 6/1–15/05; SLJ 8/05; VOYA 10/05)

1150 Myers, Walter Dean. *The Dream Bearer* (5–8). 2003, HarperCollins LB $24.00 (978-0-06-054277-1). David, 12 and living in Harlem, gains valuable insights about his heritage and his ambitions when he gets to know an old man who calls himself a "dream bearer." (Rev: BL 7/03; HBG 4/04; SLJ 6/03; VOYA 6/03)

1151 Myers, Walter Dean. *Fast Sam, Cool Clyde, and Stuff* (7–10). 1995, Peter Smith $20.75 (978-0-8446-6798-0); paper $6.99 (978-0-14-032613-0). Three male friends in Harlem join forces to found the 116th Street Good People.

1152 Myers, Walter Dean. *145th Street: Stories* (5–9). 2000, Delacorte $15.95 (978-0-385-32137-2). A Harlem neighborhood is the setting for this collection of short stories dealing with a wide range of human emotions. (Rev: BL 12/15/99; HB 3–4/00; HBG 10/00; SLJ 4/00)

1153 Myers, Walter Dean. *Scorpions* (7–9). 1988, HarperCollins LB $18.89 (978-0-06-024365-4). Gang warfare, death, and despair are the elements of this story set in present-day Harlem. (Rev: BL 9/1/88; SLJ 9/88; VOYA 8/88)

1154 Myers, Walter Dean. *Slam!* (8–12). 1996, Scholastic paper $15.95 (978-0-590-48667-5). Although Slam is successful on the school's basketball court, his personal life has problems caused by difficulties fitting into an all-white school, a very sick grandmother, and a friend who is involved in drugs. (Rev: BL 11/15/96; SLJ 11/96; VOYA 2/97)

1155 Myers, Walter Dean. *The Young Landlords* (7–10). 1979, Penguin paper $6.99 (978-0-14-034244-4). A group of African American teenagers take over a slum building in Harlem.

1156 Na, An. *The Fold* (6–10). 2008, Putnam $16.99 (978-0-399-24276-2). Sixteen-year-old Korean American Joyce Park longs to be beautiful like her gorgeous older sister, but when her aunt offers to pay for eyelid surgery that will make her look more Western, Joyce finds the decision very difficult. ☊ (Rev: BL 3/15/08; SLJ 3/08)

1157 Namioka, Lensey. *April and the Dragon Lady* (7–12). 1994, Harcourt $10.95 (978-0-15-276644-3). A Chinese American high school junior must relinquish important activities to care for her ailing grandmother and struggles with the constraints of a traditional female role. (Rev: BL 3/1/94; SLJ 4/94; VOYA 6/94)

1158 Namioka, Lensey. *Yang the Third and Her Impossible Family* (4–7). Illus. by Kees de Kiefte. 1996, Bantam paper $4.50 (978-0-440-41231-1). Mary, part of a Chinese family newly arrived in Seattle, is embarrassed by her parents' old-country ways in this humorous story. (Rev: BCCB 5/95; BL 4/15/95; SLJ 8/95)

1159 Neufeld, John. *Edgar Allan* (6–8). 1968, Phillips $26.95 (978-0-87599-149-8). Michael's family adopts a 3-year-old African American boy and the signs of bigotry begin.

1160 Nislick, June Levitt. *Zayda Was a Cowboy* (4–7). 2005, Jewish Publication Soc. paper $9.95 (978-0-8276-0817-7). A Jewish grandfather tells his grandchildren about his exploits as a cowboy when he first arrived in America from Eastern Europe; an epilogue gives background and there is a glossary and a bibliography. (Rev: BL 8/05*)

1161 Okimoto, Jean D. *Talent Night* (6–10). 1995, Scholastic paper $14.95 (978-0-590-47809-0). In this story, Rodney Suyama, 17, wants to be the first Japanese American rapper and to date beautiful Ivy Ramos. (Rev: BL 6/1–15/95; SLJ 5/95)

1162 Olsen, Sylvia. *The Girl with a Baby* (6–10). 2004, Sono Nis paper $7.95 (978-1-55039-142-8). A biracial girl of white and Indian parents wants to stay in school and raise her baby but finds it difficult. (Rev: BL 3/15/04; SLJ 7/04)

1163 Olsen, Sylvia. *White Girl* (7–10). 2005, Sono Nis paper $8.95 (978-1-55039-147-3). When her mother marries a native Canadian, 15-year-old Josie feels anger at being moved to a reservation where she is taunted for being different, but she eventually works past her resentment and begins to appreciate the larger family of which she is now a part. (Rev: BCCB 9/05; BL 4/15/05*; SLJ 7/05; VOYA 6/05)

1164 Osa, Nancy. *Cuba 15* (6–10). 2003, Delacorte $15.95 (978-0-385-72021-2). Violet Paz, who considers herself totally American, is surprised when her grandmother insists that she celebrate a traditional coming-of-age ceremony. (Rev: BL 7/03*)

1165 Ostow, Micol. *Emily Goldberg Learns to Salsa* (8–11). 2006, Penguin $16.99 (978-1-59514-081-4). When Emily's grandmother dies, Emily visits Puerto Rico — where her mother grew up — for the first time, and is amazed by a culture so foreign to her yet part of her heritage. (Rev: BL 12/15/06; SLJ 1/07)

1166 Pagliarulo, Antonio. *A Different Kind of Heat* (7–10). 2006, Delacorte LB $9.99 (978-0-385-90319-6). Luz Cordero's anger about life in general and her brother's violent death in particular begins to abate when she finds friendship at the St. Therese Home for Boys and Girls and faces the truth. (Rev: BL 4/1/06; SLJ 12/06)

1167 Park, Linda Sue. *Project Mulberry* (5–8). 2005, Clarion $16.00 (978-0-618-47786-9). Working on a silkworm project with her friend Patrick, Korean American Julia also learns about prejudices and friendship. (Rev: BL 8/05; SLJ 5/05)

1168 Pellegrino, Marge. *Journey of Dreams* (6–10). 2009, Frances Lincoln $15.95 (978-1-84780-061-9). Eleven-year-old Tomasa's family is reunited in Arizona after escaping violent persecution in their Mayan village. Lexile 740L (Rev: BL 8/09; SLJ 8/09)

1169 Perkins, Mitali. *Secret Keeper* (7–12). 2009, Delacorte $16.99 (978-038573340-3); LB $19.99 (978-038590356-1). In the mid -1970s, 16-year-old Asha Gupta and her family make a difficult move from India to the United States, where Indian tradition and Asha's dreams for herself clash when she meets the boy next door, and attempts to rescue her older sister from a horrible arranged marriage. ℮ Lexile 800L (Rev: BL 12/15/08; SLJ 3/1/09)

1170 Pinkney, Andrea Davis. *Hold Fast to Dreams* (5–8). 1995, Morrow $16.00 (978-0-688-12832-6). A bright, resourceful African American girl faces problems when she finds she is the only black student in her new middle school. (Rev: BCCB 5/95; BL 2/15/95; HB 9–10/95; SLJ 4/95)

1171 Pitts, Paul. *Racing the Sun* (5–7). 1988, Avon paper $6.99 (978-0-380-75496-0). Brandon begins to understand his Navajo heritage after his grandfather comes to live with him. (Rev: BL 9/15/88; SLJ 2/89)

1172 Porte, Barbara Ann. *Something Terrible Happened* (6–10). 1994, Orchard LB $17.99 (978-0-531-08719-0). Part white, part West Indian, Gillian, 12, must adjust to living with her deceased father's "plain white" relatives when her mother contracts AIDS. (Rev: BL 9/15/94; SLJ 10/94; VOYA 10/94)

1173 Roseman, Kenneth. *The Other Side of the Hudson: A Jewish Immigrant Adventure* (5–8). Series: Do-It-Yourself Adventure. 1993, UAHC paper $11.95 (978-0-8074-0506-2). Using an interactive format, readers can choose various destinations for a young male Jewish immigrant after he arrives in New York City from Germany in 1851. (Rev: SLJ 6/94)

1174 Savage, Deborah. *Kotuku* (7–12). 2002, Houghton Mifflin $16.00 (978-0-618-07456-3). Struggling to recover from the death of her best friend, 17-year-old Wim throws herself into her job at a Cape Cod riding stable, but visitors from afar prompt her to delve into the mystery surrounding her Maori heritage. (Rev: BL 5/15/02; HBG 10/02; SLJ 3/02; VOYA 4/02)

1175 Schorr, Melissa. *Goy Crazy* (8–11). 2006, Hyperion $15.99 (978-0-7868-3852-3). Rachel, a 15-year-old Jewish girl facing typical teen challenges, dates a popular basketball player from a Catholic school and hides this from her parents while at the same time questioning her own beliefs. (Rev: BL 10/1/06; SLJ 10/06)

1176 Schraff, Anne. *The Stranger* (8–11). Series: Urban Underground. 2010, Saddleback Educational paper $8.95 (978-16165126-6-8). Meeting cute Naomi makes 16-year-old Ernesto's return to the barrio where he was born more palatable; suitable for reluctant readers. ∩ (Rev: BL 4/1/11; VOYA 4/11)

1177 Sebestyen, Ouida. *On Fire* (7–12). 1985, Little, Brown $12.95 (978-0-87113-010-5). Tater leaves home with his brother Sammy and takes a mining job where he confronts labor problems in this sequel to the author's powerful *Words by Heart.* (Rev: BL 5/15/85; SLJ 4/85; VOYA 8/85)

1178 Sebestyen, Ouida. *Words by Heart* (5–7). 1979, Little, Brown $15.95 (978-0-316-77931-9). Race relations are explored when an African American family moves to an all-white community during the Reconstruction era. (Rev: BL 6/1/88)

1179 Sharif, Medeia. *Bestest. Ramadan. Ever* (7–10). 2011, Flux paper $9.95 (978-0-7387-2-323-5). A coming-of-age story about Almira, a 16-year-old Muslim girl trying to balance her family's pressures and her longing to fit in at school. ℮ Lexile 760L (Rev: BL 7/11; LMC 11–12/11; SLJ 11/1/11)

1180 Shea, Pegi Deitz. *Tangled Threads: A Hmong Girl's Story* (6–8). 2003, Clarion $15.00 (978-0-618-24748-6). Mai, a Hmong refugee newly arrived in the United States, is initially overwhelmed by her Americanized cousins and her new surroundings in this novel that conveys much information about Hmong culture. (Rev: BL 9/15/03; SLJ 11/03)

1181 Singer, Isaac Bashevis. *The Power of Light: Eight Stories for Hanukkah* (7–10). 1980, Avon paper $2.50 (978-0-380-60103-5). Eight stories of the Festival of Lights that span centuries of Jewish history.

1182 Singer, Marilyn, ed. *Face Relations: 11 Stories About Seeing Beyond Color* (7–12). 2004, Simon & Schuster $17.95 (978-0-689-85637-2). This collection of 11 original short stories by well-known authors explores the issues of racial identity and race relations in American high schools. (Rev: BL 8/04*; SLJ 6/04; VOYA 8/04)

1183 Smith, Sherri L. *Hot, Sour, Salty, Sweet* (5–7). 2008, Delacorte $15.99 (978-0-385-73417-2). As her grandmothers, one Chinese American and one African American, argue over food and family, Ana's junior high graduation party gets more and more complicated. (Rev: BL 2/1/08; SLJ 4/08)

1184 Son, John. *Finding My Hat* (4–8). Series: First Person Fiction. 2003, Scholastic $16.95 (978-0-439-43538-3). Autobiography plays a large part in this frank, often funny novel about the son of Korean immigrants growing up in America in the 1970s and 1980s. (Rev: BL 11/15/03; HBG 4/04; LMC 11–12/03; SLJ 10/03)

1185 Soto, Gary. *Facts of Life* (5–8). 2008, Harcourt $16.00 (978-0-15-206181-4). Soto offers 10 new stories about important events in the lives of Latino tweens and teens living in California. (Rev: BL 3/1/08; SLJ 7/08)

1186 Soto, Gary. *Local News* (4–7). 1993, Harcourt $14.00 (978-0-15-248117-9). This collection of 13 short stories deals with a number of Mexican American youngsters at home, school, and play. (Rev: BL 4/15/93; HB 7–8/93*)

1187 Soto, Gary. *Petty Crimes* (5–8). 1998, Harcourt $17.00 (978-0-15-201658-6). Ten short stories about Mexican American teenagers in California's Central Valley deal with some humorous situations but more often with gangs, violence, and poverty. (Rev: BL 3/15/98; HBG 10/98; SLJ 5/98)

1188 Soto, Gary. *Taking Sides* (6–9). 1991, Harcourt $17.00 (978-0-15-284076-1). Lincoln Mendoza moves from his inner-city San Francisco neighborhood to a middle-class suburb and must adjust to life in a new high school. (Rev: BL 12/1/91; SLJ 11/91)

1189 Spinelli, Jerry. *Maniac Magee* (5–7). 1990, Little, Brown $15.95 (978-0-316-80722-7). This thought-provoking Newbery Medal winner (1991) tells the story of an amazing white boy who runs away from home and suddenly becomes aware of the racism in his town. (Rev: BL 6/1/90*; SLJ 6/90)

1190 Starke, Ruth. *Noodle Pie* (5–7). 2010, Kane/Miller $15.99 (978-1-935279-25-9). Andy, an 11-year-old Australian boy, keeps a diary during his visit to Vietnam, the place of his father's birth, recording all the interesting cultural differences and the fun he has with his cousin Minh as they work to revamp the family's restaurant. Lexile 770L (Rev: BLO 3/15/10; LMC 8–9/10; SLJ 5/10)

1191 Stepto, Michele, ed. *African-American Voices* (7–12). Series: Writers of America. 1995, Millbrook LB $23.90 (978-1-56294-474-2). Selections by W. E. B. Du Bois, Toni Morrison, Ralph Ellison, and others, plus traditional chants, speeches, and poetry. (Rev: BL 5/15/95; SLJ 3/95)

1192 Stering, Shirley. *My Name Is Seepeetza* (5–10). 1997, Douglas & McIntyre paper $5.95 (978-0-88899-165-2). Told in diary form, this autobiographical novel about a 6th-grade Native American girl tells of her heartbreak at the terrible conditions at her school, where she is persecuted because of her race. (Rev: BL 3/1/97)

1193 Taylor, Mildred D. *The Road to Memphis* (7–12). 1990, Dial $18.99 (978-0-8037-0340-7). Set in 1941, this is a continuation of the story of the Logans, a poor black southern family who were previously featured in *Roll of Thunder, Hear My Cry* and *Let the Circle Be Unbroken*. (Rev: BL 5/15/90; SLJ 1/90; VOYA 8/90)

1194 Uchida, Yoshiko. *Journey Home* (7–9). 1978, Macmillan paper $4.99 (978-0-689-71641-6). A Japanese American family return to their ordinary life after being relocated during World War II.

1195 Vaught, Susan. *Stormwitch* (7–10). 2005, Bloomsbury $16.95 (978-1-58234-952-7). Sixteen-year-old Ruba Cleo, transplanted in 1969 to a Mississippi Gulf Coast town from Haiti, wants to strike back at the racism and hostility she encounters by calling on the voodoo skills she learned in her native land. (Rev: BCCB 3/05; BL 2/15/05; SLJ 5/05; VOYA 2/05)

1196 Veciana-Suarez, Ana. *Flight to Freedom* (6–9). 2002, Scholastic $16.95 (978-0-439-38199-4). In her diary, Yara describes her old life in Cuba and her new life in 1960s Miami with all the attendant problems of new immigrants and teen development. (Rev: BCCB 2/03; BL 11/15/02; HB 1–2/03; HBG 3/03; SLJ 10/02; VOYA 2/03)

1197 Vogiel, Eva. *Invisible Chains* (5–8). 2000, Judaica $19.95 (978-1-880582-57-2). In 1948, 14-year-old Frumie is sent with her crippled younger sister, Judy, to a boarding school for religiously observant Jewish girls. (Rev: BL 7/00; HBG 10/00)

1198 Volponi, Paul. *Response* (6–9). 2009, Viking $15.99 (978-067006283-6). African American Noah, 17, finds himself a reluctant center of attention when he is beaten up by a gang of Italian Americans who are charged with a hate crime. e Lexile HL880L (Rev: BL 11/15/08; LMC 5–6/09; SLJ 3/1/09; VOYA 4/09)

1199 Volponi, Paul. *Rooftop* (8–11). 2006, Viking $15.99 (978-0-670-06069-6). As teen cousins Clay and Addison struggle to overcome their drug problems, Addison is shot dead by a white police officer and Clay must cope with the aftermath of the shooting. (Rev: BL 4/15/06*; SLJ 8/06)

1200 Walters, Eric. *War of the Eagles* (5–7). 1998, Orca $14.00 (978-1-55143-118-5); paper $7.95 (978-1-55143-099-7). During the opening months of the war against Japan, a West Coast Canadian boy witnesses the growing prejudice against Japanese Canadians and also becomes aware of his own Indian heritage. (Rev: BL 12/15/98; HBG 3/99; SLJ 12/98)

1201 Winston, Sherri. *The Kayla Chronicles* (5–9). 2008, Little, Brown $16.99 (978-0-316-11430-1). African American Kayla alienates her friend Rosalie when she joins her Florida high school's hip-hop dance team. (Rev: BL 2/1/08; SLJ 4/08)

1202 Wiseman, Eva. *No One Must Know* (4–7). 2004, Tundra paper $8.95 (978-0-88776-680-0). Thirteen-year-old Alexandra, who's been raised as a Catholic in Canada, learns that her parents are really Jewish Holocaust survivors. (Rev: BL 1/1–15/05; SLJ 6/05)

1203 Wishinsky, Frieda. *Queen of the Toilet Bowl* (7–9). Series: Orca Currents. 2005, Orca paper $7.95 (978-1-55143-364-6). For reluctant readers, this is the story of high school student Renata, who immigrated to the United States from Brazil with her mother and now faces — and conquers — bullying by a classmate. (Rev: SLJ 10/05; VOYA 10/05)

1204 Woodson, Jacqueline. *Behind You* (7–12). 2004, Putnam $15.99 (978-0-399-23988-5). In this sequel to *If You Come Softly* (1998), Jeremiah, though dead from a policeman's bullet, watches over the people he left behind. (Rev: BL 2/15/04; HB 5–6/04; SLJ 6/04; VOYA 6/04)

1205 Woodson, Jacqueline. *From the Notebooks of Melanin Sun* (6–10). 1995, Scholastic paper $5.99 (978-0-590-45881-8). A 13-year-old African American boy's mother announces that she loves a fellow student, a white woman. (Rev: BL 4/15/95; SLJ 8/95)

1206 Wright, Bil. *When the Black Girl Sings* (7–10). 2008, Simon & Schuster $16.99 (978-1-4169-3995-5). When adopted Lahni (who has grown up in a white family and attended a mostly white private school) discovers gospel music, she also finds a new pride in her identity. (Rev: BL 2/1/08; SLJ 1/08)

1207 Wright, Richard. *Rite of Passage* (7–12). 1994, HarperCollins paper $6.99 (978-0-06-447111-4). This newly discovered novella, written in the 1940s, concerns a gifted 15-year-old who runs away from his loving Harlem home and survives on the streets with a violent gang. (Rev: BL 1/1/94; SLJ 2/94; VOYA 4/94)

1208 Yee, Paul. *Learning to Fly* (6–10). 2008, Orca $16.95 (978-155143955-6); paper $9.95 (978-155143953-2). Chinese immigrant Jason, 17, bonds with Native American "Chief"— and falls in with a pot-smoking crowd — to escape prejudice and feeling like an outsider in his small Canadian town. € Lexile HL540L (Rev: BL 10/1/08; LMC 3–4/09; SLJ 3/1/09; VOYA 10/08)

1209 Yep, Laurence. *Dragonwings* (7–9). 1975, HarperCollins LB $16.89 (978-0-06-026738-4); paper $6.99 (978-0-06-440085-5). At the turn of the 20th century, a young Chinese boy in San Francisco becomes an aviation pioneer. (Rev: BL 3/1/88)

1210 Yep, Laurence. *Dream Soul* (5–8). 2000, Harper-Collins LB $14.89 (978-0-06-028309-4). In this sequel to *Star Fisher* (1991), the Lees, a family of Chinese immigrants who live in Clarksburg, West Virginia, in 1927, face conflicts when the children want to celebrate Christmas. (Rev: BCCB 12/00; BL 12/1/00)

1211 Yep, Laurence, ed. *American Dragons: Twenty-Five Asian American Voices* (7–12). 1995, HarperCollins paper $7.99 (978-0-06-440603-1). Autobiographical stories, poems, and essays about children whose parents come from China, Japan, Korea, and Tibet, struggling to find "an identity that isn't generic." (Rev: BL 5/15/93; SLJ 7/93; VOYA 10/93)

1212 Yoo, Paula. *Good Enough* (7–10). 2008, Harper-Teen $16.99 (978-0-06-079085-1). In her senior year of high school, Patti must juggle pressure to be the "Perfect Korean Daughter" with college applications, a crush on a musician, and racist comments from school bullies; reluctant readers will enjoy the humor. (Rev: BL 11/15/07; SLJ 2/08)

Family Life and Problems

1213 Abbott, Hailey. *The Bridesmaid* (6–9). 2005, Delacorte $7.95 (978-0-385-73220-8). Abby Beaumont, 15-year-old daughter of parents who run a wedding planning service and jaundiced by the whole idea, watches with wry amusement as her older sister falls into the trap. (Rev: BCCB 9/05; BL 4/15/05; SLJ 4/05)

1214 Aciman, André. *Baby* (8–11). 2007, Front St $16.95 (978-1-59078-502-7). After her alcoholic mother disappears again, 15-year-old Baby finds herself in another foster home; this time, though, it turns out to be a real refuge, with an older couple who race sled dogs. (Rev: BL 9/1/07; SLJ 11/07)

1215 Ackermann, Joan. *In the Space Left Behind* (7–10). 2007, HarperCollins $16.99 (978-0-06-072255-5). Fifteen-year-old Colm's mother has married for the third time and is threatening to sell the family home when Colm's long-lost father shows up and offers to pay $70,000 if Colm will accompany him on a cross-country road trip. (Rev: BL 10/1/07; SLJ 12/07)

1216 Adler, C. S. *Ghost Brother* (5–8). 1990, Houghton Mifflin $15.00 (978-0-395-52592-0). After his older brother dies in an accident, 11-year-old Wally finds comfort in his ghost. (Rev: BCCB 5/90; BL 5/15/90; SLJ 5/90; VOYA 8/90)

1217 Adler, C. S. *The Lump in the Middle* (6–10). 1991, Avon paper $3.50 (978-0-380-71176-5). Kelsey, the middle child, struggles for her identity after Dad loses his job. (Rev: BL 10/1/89; SLJ 10/89; VOYA 2/90)

1218 Adler, C. S. *The No Place Cat* (5–8). 2002, Clarion $15.00 (978-0-618-09644-2). Twelve-year-old Tess runs away from home only to find that life with her father and new stepfamily had its good side after all. (Rev: BCCB 4/02; HBG 10/02; SLJ 3/02)

1219 Adler, C. S. *One Sister Too Many* (5–7). 1989, Macmillan paper $3.95 (978-0-689-71521-1). Casey and her reunited family are being driven crazy by the newest addition — a colicky baby. (Rev: BCCB 3/89; BL 3/15/89; SLJ 4/89)

1220 Adler, C. S. *The Shell Lady's Daughter* (7–10). 2004, iUniverse paper $10.95 (978-0-595-33912-9). Kelly's mother has emotional problems and attempts suicide; first published in 1983.

1221 Adoff, Jaime. *Jimi and Me* (8–11). 2005, Hyperion $15.99 (978-0-7868-5214-7). Struggling to recover from the shock of his father's brutal murder, Keith, a biracial teen who loves the music of Hendrix, moves from Brooklyn to Ohio and discovers that his father had another son, named Jimi. (Rev: BL 10/1/05; SLJ 9/05)

1222 Almond, David. *Slog's Dad* (4–7). Illus. by Dave McKean. 2011, Candlewick $15.99 (978-0-7636-4940-1). A young boy grieving after his father's death meets a stranger he believes to be his dad returned with his legs intact. (Rev: BL 3/15/11; SLJ 5/11; VOYA 6/11)

1223 Alphin, Elaine Marie. *Picture Perfect* (6–9). 2003, Carolrhoda $15.95 (978-0-8225-0535-8). When his friend Teddy disappears, Ian, son of the principal, wonders if his father might be involved. (Rev: BL 8/03; SLJ 10/03)

1224 Altebrando, Tara. *Dreamland Social Club* (7–12). 2011, Dutton $16.99 (978-0-525-42325-6). Jane and her brother, who have been living in Europe with their father, return to the United States when they inherit a house on Coney Island and there they learn secrets about their dead mother. ⌂ ℮ (Rev: BLO 5/1/11; LMC 11–12/11; SLJ 7/11; VOYA 6/11)

1225 Alvarez, Julia. *How Tía Lola Came to (Visit) Stay* (4–7). 2001, Knopf $15.95 (978-0-375-80215-7). Aunt Lola from the Dominican Republic comes to visit 10-year-old Miguel and his family in Vermont and everywhere she goes she spreads friendliness, enthusiasm, stories, and surprise parties. (Rev: BCCB 4/01; BL 2/15/01; HBG 10/01; SLJ 3/01)

1226 Alvarez, Julia. *How Tía Lola Ended Up Starting Over* (4–7). Series: Tía Lola. 2011, Knopf $15.99 (978-037586914-3); LB $18.99 (978-037596914-0). Tía Lola starts a bed-and-breakfast with the help of the children, but it seems that someone wants the business to fail; who can be wishing them ill in this mystery set in Vermont and featuring Latino families? (Rev: BL 11/1/11)

1227 Alvarez, Julia. *How Tía Lola Saved the Summer* (4–7). Series: Tía Lola. 2011, Knopf $15.99 (978-0-375-86727-9); LB $18.99 (978-0-375-96727-6). Tía Lola saves the day when three unwelcome girls and their father visit Miguel's Vermont farmhouse, creat-

ing a summer camp atmosphere. (Rev: BL 5/1/11; SLJ 7/11)

1228 Amateau, Gigi. *A Certain Strain of Peculiar* (6–9). 2009, Candlewick $16.99 (978-076363009-6). Fed up with life, 13-year-old Mary runs away to her grandmother's farm in Alabama and learns from the older woman's wisdom and experience. Lexile 830L (Rev: BL 5/1/09; SLJ 11/09; VOYA 6/09)

1229 Amateau, Gigi. *Claiming Georgia Tate* (8–12). 2005, Candlewick $15.99 (978-0-7636-2339-5). When her beloved and protective grandmother dies, 12-year-old Georgia Tate finds herself at the mercy of her sexually abusive father in this novel set in the 1970s. (Rev: SLJ 6/05; VOYA 6/05)

1230 Amato, Mary. *The Naked Mole Rat Letters* (4–7). 2005, Holiday $16.95 (978-0-8234-1927-2). Through emails and diary entries, readers learn about Frankie's fear that her father is becoming involved in a new romance. (Rev: BL 6/1–15/05; SLJ 8/05)

1231 Anfousse, Ginette. *A Terrible Secret* (7–12). Trans. from French by Jennifer Hutchison. 2001, Lorimer paper $4.99 (978-1-55028-704-2). A new neighbor, Ben, helps Maggie to recover from the death of her Down syndrome brother. (Rev: SLJ 9/01)

1232 Atkinson, Elizabeth. *I, Emma Freke* (4–7). 2010, Carolrhoda $16.95 (978-0-7613-5604-2). Twelve-year-old Emma, tall and uncertain, learns a lot about herself when she is invited to a family reunion of the father she has never met. (Rev: BL 11/1/10; SLJ 2/1/11*)

1233 Auch, M. J. *Guitar Boy* (5–8). 2010, Henry Holt $16.99 (978-0-8050-9112-0). When his mother suffers a brain injury and his father throws him out, 13-year-old Travis's love of guitars and music helps him to survive and even contribute to restoring his family. ⌂ Lexile 750L (Rev: BL 11/1/10; LMC 11–12/10; SLJ 9/1/10)

1234 Austen, Catherine. *Walking Backward* (6–9). 2009, Orca paper $9.95 (978-1-55469-147-0). In this realistic story of grief, 12-year-old Josh must adjust to his mother's death in an accident. Lexile 840L (Rev: BL 10/15/09; LMC 1–2/10; SLJ 2/10)

1235 Banks, Kate. *Walk Softly, Rachel* (7–10). 2003, Farrar $16.00 (978-0-374-38230-8). When Rachel, 14, reads her dead brother's diary she discovers that his life was not the ideal she had thought. (Rev: BL 10/15/03; HBG 4/04; SLJ 9/03*; VOYA 2/04)

1236 Baptiste, Tracey. *Angel's Grace* (5–8). 2005, Simon & Schuster $15.95 (978-0-689-86773-6). Thirteen-year-old Grace, who has always felt different, embarks on a search for the man she believes is her biological father. (Rev: BL 2/1/05; SLJ 3/05)

1237 Barkley, Brad, and Heather Hepler. *Jars of Glass* (7–10). 2008, Dutton $16.99 (978-052547911-6). Sisters Chloe, 15, and Shana, 15, react differently when their artist mother is suddenly committed to a mental institution and their father turns to alcohol to cope. **e** (Rev: BLO 12/11/08; SLJ 12/08; VOYA 12/08)

1238 Baron, Kathi. *Shattered* (8–10). 2009, WestSide $16.95 (978-1-934813-08-9). When Cassie's father, in a fit of rage at his own father, shatters her vintage violin on the day of her debut performance with the Chicago Youth Orchestra, the 14-year-old virtuoso heads for her grandfather's house and uncovers the disturbing genesis of her father's fury. Lexile HL660L (Rev: BLO 8/20/09; SLJ 12/09)

1239 Barwin, Gary. *Seeing Stars* (6–12). 2002, Stoddart paper $7.95 (978-0-7737-6227-5). A quirky story about a boy who has been brought up in strange circumstances and who now wants the truth about his father and his family. (Rev: BL 7/02; SLJ 5/02)

1240 Bauer, Cat. *Harley, Like a Person* (7–10). 2000, Winslow $16.95 (978-1-890817-48-0); paper $6.95 (978-1-890817-49-7). Unhappy with her distant mother and an alcoholic father, Harley Columba becomes convinced that she is an adopted child. (Rev: BL 6/1–15/00; HB 5–6/00; HBG 9/00; SLJ 5/00)

1241 Bauer, Joan. *Almost Home* (5–8). 2012, Viking $16.99 (978-0-670-01289-3). With help from various members of the community 6th-grader Sugar and her mother are able to bounce back from homelessness and depression. **e** Lexile 590L (Rev: BL 8/12; HB 9–10/12; LMC 3–4/13*; SLJ 10/12)

1242 Bauer, Joan. *Backwater* (7–10). 1999, Putnam $18.99 (978-0-399-23141-4). When 16-year-old Ivy Breedlove begins working on her family history, the trail leads to the New York State Adirondacks and eccentric, talented Aunt Jo. (Rev: BL 5/15/99; HB 7–8/99; HBG 9/99; SLJ 6/99; VOYA 8/99)

1243 Bauer, Joan. *Rules of the Road* (6–10). 1998, Putnam $20.99 (978-0-399-23140-7). Jenna Boller is the confident, smart, and moral heroine of this novel that deals with the effects of alcoholism on a family and a girl's growing friendship with a wealthy, elderly woman. (Rev: BL 2/1/98; HB 5–6/98; HBG 9/98; SLJ 3/98*; VOYA 6/98)

1244 Bauer, Joan. *Stand Tall* (5–7). 2002, Putnam $16.99 (978-0-399-23473-6). Tree, a tall 7th grader, has a lot of challenges in this nonetheless humorous novel: his height, his lack of athletic ability, shuffling between his divorced parents' homes, and his veteran grandfather's ailments, to name just a few. (Rev: BCCB 10/02; BL 9/15/02; HB 11–12/02; HBG 3/03; SLJ 8/02)

1245 Bauer, Marion Dane. *Shelter from the Wind* (5–9). 2010, Marshall Cavendish $16.99 (978-0-7614-5687-2). Originally published in 1975, this is a story of a girl coming to terms with upheaval in her family including alcoholism, divorce, and remarriage. (Rev: LMC 8–9/10)

1246 Bawden, Nina. *Granny the Pag* (5–8). 1996, Clarion $16.00 (978-0-395-77604-9). Catriona is embarrassed by her grandmother's eccentric ways, such as riding motorbikes and wearing leather jackets, but that doesn't mean she wants to live with her parents instead. (Rev: BCCB 3/96; BL 4/1/96; HB 9–10/96; SLJ 4/96*; VOYA 6/96)

1247 Belton, Sandra. *Store-Bought Baby* (7–10). 2006, Greenwillow $15.99 (978-0-06-085086-9). The death of her adopted older brother forces Leah to face issues of love, jealousy, and what it means to truly be a family. (Rev: BL 5/1/06; HB 5–6/06; LMC 3/07; SLJ 6/06)

1248 Benedict, Helen. *The Opposite of Love* (7–12). 2007, Viking $16.99 (978-0-670-06135-8). Seventeen-year-old Madge, who never knew her Jamaican dad and has an irresponsible illegal-alien British mom, faces prejudice in her Pennsylvania town but helps an abandoned black foster kid. (Rev: BL 9/1/07; SLJ 3/08)

1249 Berry, James. *A Thief in the Village and Other Stories* (7–12). 1988, Penguin paper $5.99 (978-0-14-034357-1). Nine stories about a teenager in Jamaica and everyday life on the Caribbean island. (Rev: BL 4/15/88)

1250 Birdsall, Jeanne. *The Penderwicks at Point Mouette* (4–7). 2011, Knopf $16.99 (978-0-375-85851-2); LB $19.99 (978-0-375-95851-9). Father, his new wife, and young son are away in England and Rosalind is in New Jersey, so Skye finds herself in an unaccustomed role as OAP (oldest available Penderwick) when the three younger sisters go to Maine with Aunt Claire. (Rev: BL 5/1/11; SLJ 7/11)

1251 Birdsall, Jeanne. *The Penderwicks on Gardam Street* (4–7). Series: The Penderwicks. 2008, Knopf $15.99 (978-0-375-84090-6). The loving, close Penderwick sisters, who were introduced in *The Penderwicks*, are loath to see their widower father start dating again and come up with a plan to discourage him. (Rev: BL 5/1/08; SLJ 3/08)

1252 Birdsall, Olivia. *Notes on a Near-Life Experience* (6–12). 2007, Delacorte $15.99 (978-0-385-73370-0). Mia is 15 when her parents separate and her life changes dramatically; although she finds it hard to cope at first, she does — with some help — adapt and is happy to spark some interest in her brother's friend Julian. (Rev: BCCB 3/07; SLJ 3/07)

1253 Birdseye, Tom. *Tucker* (5–8). 1990, Holiday $16.95 (978-0-8234-0813-9). A story set in rural Kentucky of a young boy reunited with his younger sister after seven years of separation caused by divorce. (Rev: BL 7/90; SLJ 6/90)

1254 Blacker, Terence. *Parent Swap* (6–9). 2006, Farrar $16 (978-0-374-35752-8). Thirteen-year-old Danny is fed up with his ex-rocker dad and absent mother, so he answers an ad for "ParentSwap," a secret London agency promising kids a better life with a new set of parents; eventually Danny catches on to the true nature of this business and his role in it — an unknowing star of a new reality TV show. (Rev: SLJ 8/06)

1255 Blume, Judy. *It's Not the End of the World* (5–8). 1972, Dell paper $5.50 (978-0-440-44158-8). Twelve-year-old Karen's world seems to end when her parents are divorced and her older brother runs away.

1256 Bond, Nancy. *Truth to Tell* (6–8). 1994, Macmillan $17.95 (978-0-689-50601-7). A 14-year-old girl finds herself on her way to New Zealand with her mother and not really understanding the reason for the relocation. (Rev: BL 4/15/94; SLJ 6/94; VOYA 8/94)

1257 Bondoux, Anne-Laure. *Life as It Comes* (7–10). Trans. by Y. Mauder. 2007, Delacorte $15.99 (978-0-385-90390-5). After their parents are killed in a car crash, two French sisters — 15-year-old Mado and 20-year-old Patty — find adapting to a new life difficult, especially when Patty becomes pregnant. (Rev: BCCB 4/07; BL 3/1/07; SLJ 3/07)

1258 Bowers, Laura. *Beauty Shop for Rent: . . . Fully Equipped, Inquire Within* (6–9). 2007, Harcourt $17.00 (978-0-15-205764-0). Fifteen-year-old Abbey's life changes dramatically when strong, smart Gena takes over Abbey's grandmother's beauty shop. (Rev: BL 9/15/07; SLJ 4/07)

1259 Brandis, Marianne. *The Tinderbox* (6–8). 2003, Tundra paper $9.95 (978-0-88776-626-8). In Canada in 1830, 14-year-old Emma and her younger brother, recently orphaned in a fire, must decide whether to trust a woman who claims a family relationship. (Rev: BL 9/1/03; SLJ 2/04)

1260 Briant, Ed. *Choppy Socky Blues* (8–11). 2010, Flux paper $9.95 (978-0-73871-897-2). Fourteen-year-old Jason's interest in a girl fascinated with karate prompts him to approach his father, a martial arts teacher whom he has not seen since his parents' difficult divorce; set in England. (Rev: BL 4/15/10; LMC 8–9/10; SLJ 5/10; VOYA 10/10)

1261 Bridgers, Sue Ellen. *Home Before Dark* (7–10). 1998, Replica LB $29.95 (978-0-7351-0053-4). A migrant worker and his family settle down in a permanent home.

1262 Bridgers, Sue Ellen. *Notes for Another Life* (7–12). 1981, Replica $29.95 (978-0-7351-0044-2). A brother and sister cope with a frequently absent mother and a mentally ill father. (Rev: BL 9/1/85; SLJ 10/85; VOYA 4/86)

1263 Brokaw, Nancy Steele. *Leaving Emma* (4–7). 1999, Clarion $15.00 (978-0-395-90699-6). When Emma's best friend moves away and her father is sent to work overseas, the young girl is left with a mother who suffers from bouts of depression. (Rev: BCCB 3/99; BL 3/1/99; HBG 10/99; SLJ 5/99)

1264 Brooks, Kevin. *Martyn Pig* (7–10). 2002, Scholastic $16.95 (978-0-439-29595-6). When Martyn's abusive father dies during a drunken argument, Martyn and a friend dispose of the body, setting off a complicated, suspenseful, and often amusing string of events. (Rev: BCCB 9/02; BL 5/1/02; HBG 10/02; SLJ 5/02*)

1265 Brown, Susan Taylor. *Hugging the Rock* (5–8). 2006, Tricycle $15.95 (978-1-58246-180-9). In this poignant novel told in free-verse poetry, Rachel describes the difficulties she and her dad have in coping after her mother's departure. (Rev: SLJ 9/06)

1266 Bryant, Ann. *One Mom Too Many! Book No. 1* (4–7). Series: Step-Chain. 2003, Lobster paper $3.95 (978-1-894222-78-5). Sarah, 12, is not pleased to discover that both her divorced parents have found new romantic interests. (Rev: SLJ 5/04)

1267 Bryant, Ann. *You Can't Fall for Your Stepsister* (4–7). Series: Step-Chain. 2003, Lobster paper $3.95 (978-1-894222-77-8). Ollie, 13, thinks he may be falling in love with his stepsister Frankie, but she ends up becoming his new best friend. (Rev: SLJ 5/04)

1268 Buffie, Margaret. *Out of Focus* (7–10). 2006, Kids Can $16.95 (978-1-55337-955-3); paper $6.95 (978-1-55337-956-0). Sixteen-year-old Bernie moves his alcoholic mother and younger siblings into a lake cabin in hopes of keeping the family together. (Rev: LMC 3/07; SLJ 10/06)

1269 Bunting, Eve. *Is Anybody There?* (4–7). 1990, HarperCollins paper $6.99 (978-0-06-440347-4). Marcus is both scared and angry after his latchkey disappears and things are stolen. (Rev: BCCB 10/88; BL 12/15/88; SLJ 12/88)

1270 Bunting, Eve. *Surrogate Sister* (7–10). 1984, HarperCollins LB $13.89 (978-0-397-32099-8). A 16-year-old girl copes with a pregnant mother who has offered to be a surrogate mother for a childless couple.

1271 Burch, Robert. *Ida Early Comes over the Mountain* (4–8). 1990, Puffin paper $5.99 (978-0-14-034534-6). The four motherless Sutton children find a new and most unusual housekeeper in Ida.

1272 Burtinshaw, Julie. *Adrift* (6–8). 2002, Raincoast paper $7.95 (978-1-55192-469-4). David, 14, and his younger sister Laura have exciting adventures when they rebel against the adults' plans for their future after their mother is hospitalized for depression. (Rev: SLJ 1/03; VOYA 12/02)

1273 Butler, Dori Hillestad. *Yes, I Know the Monkey Man* (5–7). 2009, Peachtree $16.95 (978-1-56145-479-2). This tense sequel to *Do You Know the Monkey Man?* (2005) flips the narrative to T.J., the discovered twin, as she struggles to connect with her recently found mom and sister and deal with her father's deception. (Rev: BLO 6/16/09; LMC 10/09; SLJ 7/09)

1274 Byalick, Marcia. *It's a Matter of Trust* (7–9). 1995, Browndeer paper $5.00 (978-0-15-200240-4). Erika's father confesses to a white-collar crime, and this novel traces the effects of this confession on the family, particularly on 16-year-old Erika and her relations with boyfriend Greg. (Rev: SLJ 12/95; VOYA 2/96)

1275 Calonita, Jen. *Belles* (7–12). 2012, Little, Brown $17.99 (978-031609113-8). Isabelle's world is upended when her ailing grandmother — her only guardian — is placed in a nursing home, and the 15-year-old is sent to live with distant relatives. ☊ ℮ Lexile 730L (Rev: BL 4/1/12; SLJ 4/12)

1276 Cardenas, Teresa. *Letters to My Mother* (5–8). Trans. by David Unger. 2006, Groundwood paper $6.95 (978-0-88899-721-0). In unhappy letters to her dead mother, a 10-year-old Cuban girl describes cruelty and prejudice at the hands of her relatives. (Rev: BL 5/1/06; SLJ 8/06)

1277 Carlson, Melody. *Just Ask* (8–12). Series: Diary of a Teenage Girl. 2005, Multnomah paper $12.99 (978-1-59052-321-6). A family tragedy shakes the faith of 16-year-old Kim, who's been struggling to live a Christian life. (Rev: SLJ 12/05)

1278 Carmichael, Clay. *Wild Things* (5–8). 2009, Front St. $18.95 (978-1-59078-627-7). After her mother dies, 11-year-old Zoe goes to live with her sculptor uncle Henry and gradually learns to trust people with the help of a feral cat who alternates narrating with Zoe. ALA Notable Books 2010. (Rev: BL 4/15/09; VOYA 8/09)

1279 Cassidy, Cathy. *Indigo Blue* (5–8). 2005, Viking $15.99 (978-0-670-05927-0). As her family life slowly disintegrates, 11-year-old Indigo tries her best to conceal the truth from her friends at school in this realistic story set in Britain. (Rev: BL 10/1/05; SLJ 11/05)

1280 Chaltas, Thalia. *Because I Am Furniture* (8–12). 2009, Viking $16.99 (978-0-670-06298-0). This novel in verse tracks the development of 14-year-old Anke, the only one of the three siblings in her family to escape her father's abuse, as she gains sufficient confidence to challenge him. Best Books for Young Adults 2010. (Rev: LMC 8–9/09; SLJ 6/1/09; VOYA 4/09)

1281 Chambers, Veronica. *Marisol and Magdalena: The Sound of Our Sisterhood* (5–9). 1998, Hyperion LB $15.49 (978-0-7868-2385-7). Hispanic American Marisol is sent to live with her grandmother in Panama for a year, and hopes to track down her absent father. (Rev: BL 10/1/98; SLJ 12/98)

1282 Charlton-Trujillo, E. E. *Feels Like Home* (8–10). 2007, Delacorte $15.99 (978-0-385-73332-8). Two siblings in South Texas — 17-year-old Michelle (Mickey) and her older brother — come together after their father's death and, after some false starts, find a way to heal. (Rev: SLJ 7/07)

1283 Chayil, Eishes. *Hush* (8–12). 2010, Walker $16.99 (978-0-8027-2088-7). Gittel, 17 and soon to enter into

an arranged marriage, is determined to disobey tradition and speak out about sex abuse in her Hasidic community, in memory of her friend who committed suicide several years before. YALSA Best Fiction for Young Adults; Sydney Taylor Book Honor 2011. ℮ (Rev: 10/15/10; LMC 1–2/11; SLJ 9/1/10; VOYA 12/10)

1284 Cheaney, J. B. *The Middle of Somewhere* (5–8). 2007, Knopf $15.99 (978-0-375-83790-6). Put in charge of her learning disabled brother while her mother recovers from knee surgery, 12-year-old Ronnie Sparks comes under even greater pressure when she and her brother accompany their grandfather on a trip to Kansas. (Rev: BL 3/15/07; SLJ 7/07)

1285 Cheng, Andrea. *Brushing Mom's Hair* (7–10). Illus. by Nicole Wong. 2009, Boyds Mills $17.95 (978-1-59078-599-7). This novel in verse follows 15-year-old dancer Ann through her mother's ultimately successful battle with breast cancer. (Rev: BL 9/1/09; SLJ 10/09)

1286 Christian, Mary Blount. *Growin' Pains* (6–8). 1985, Penguin paper $3.95 (978-0-317-63785-4). With the help of a disabled neighbor, Ginny Ruth continues to develop her writing talent in spite of her mother's objections. (Rev: BL 2/1/86)

1287 Clarke, Judith. *One Whole and Perfect Day* (8–10). 2007, Front St $16.95 (978-1-932425-95-6). Lily, 16, finally gets what she longs for — a single day when her irritating and eccentric family comes together happily — in this gentle novel set in Australia. Printz Honor 2008. (Rev: BL 5/1/07; HB 5–6/07; SLJ 8/07)

1288 Cleary, Beverly. *Sister of the Bride* (6–9). 1963, Morrow $19.89 (978-0-688-31742-3); paper $6.99 (978-0-380-72807-7). A young girl becomes too involved with the plans for her sister's wedding.

1289 Cleaver, Vera. *Sweetly Sings the Donkey* (6–9). 1985, HarperCollins LB $12.89 (978-0-397-32157-5). Fourteen-year-old Lily Snow and her family hope that their inheritance in Florida will help them financially but this is not to be. (Rev: BL 10/1/85)

1290 Cleaver, Vera, and Bill Cleaver. *Dust of the Earth* (7–9). 1975, HarperCollins $13.95 (978-0-397-31650-2). Fern and her family face problems when they move to a farm in South Dakota. (Rev: BL 3/1/89)

1291 Cleaver, Vera, and Bill Cleaver. *Queen of Hearts* (7–9). 1978, HarperCollins $14.00 (978-0-397-31771-4). Wilma must take care of her grandmother whom she really dislikes.

1292 Clements, Andrew. *Things Hoped For* (8–11). 2006, Philomel $16.99 (978-0-399-24350-9). Gwen lives with her grandfather in New York City and studies violin at the Manhattan School of Music; when her grandfather disappears, Gwen teams up with Robert, a fellow music student, to solve the mystery. A sequel to *Things Not Seen* (2002). ☊ (Rev: BL 8/06; SLJ 11/06)

1293 Cohn, Rachel. *The Steps* (4–7). 2003, Simon & Schuster $16.95 (978-0-689-84549-9). Annabel resents the complexity of her family life as she reluctantly sets out to visit her father and his new wife, baby, and stepchildren in Australia, but she gradually learns to accept the situation in this humorous portrayal. (Rev: BCCB 2/03; BL 1/1–15/03; HB 5–6/03; HBG 10/03; SLJ 2/03*)

1294 Cohn, Rachel. *Two Steps Forward* (6–8). 2006, Simon & Schuster $15.95 (978-0-689-86614-2). In this sequel to *The Steps*, 14-year-old stepsisters Annabel and Lucy, as well as their stepbrothers Ben and Wheaties, provide alternate views of their four blended families and the tensions, humor, and feelings that arise. (Rev: SLJ 5/06)

1295 Cohn, Rachel. *You Know Where to Find Me* (8–11). 2008, Simon & Schuster $15.99 (978-0-689-87859-6). Miles turns to drugs following her cousin Laura's suicide in this story full of complicated families and relationships. (Rev: BL 4/1/08; SLJ 3/08)

1296 Collier, James Lincoln. *Outside Looking In* (6–8). 1990, Avon paper $2.95 (978-0-380-70961-8). Fergie and his sister hate the nomadic life their parents lead and long to settle down. (Rev: BL 4/1/87; SLJ 5/87; VOYA 10/87)

1297 Collins, Yvonne, and Sandy Rideout. *The Black Sheep* (8–12). 2007, Hyperion $15.99 (978-1-4231-0156-7). Sick of her boring Manhattan lifestyle, 15-year-old Kendra agrees to be on a reality show where she switches lives with Maya, who comes from a hippie family that's all about saving otters. (Rev: BL 5/15/07; SLJ 9/07)

1298 Colman, Hila. *Rich and Famous Like My Mom* (6–9). 1988, Bantam paper $5.50 (978-0-5175-6836-1). Cassandra is growing up in the shadow of her mother, a world-famous rock star. (Rev: BL 6/15/88)

1299 Coman, Carolyn. *What Jamie Saw* (5–8). 1995, Front St $15.95 (978-1-886910-02-7). In this novel seen through the eyes of a young boy, a mother and her family flee her physically abusive husband. (Rev: BCCB 12/95; BL 12/15/95*; SLJ 12/95*)

1300 Connor, Leslie. *Crunch* (5–8). 2010, HarperCollins $16.99 (978-0-06-169229-1); LB $17.89 (978-0-06-169233-8). When his parents are stranded on vacation, 14-year-old Dewey must help his older sister look after their three younger siblings and at the same time run their dad's bicycle repair shop and solve the mystery of missing parts. Lexile HL490L (Rev: BL 4/1/10; HB 7–8/10; LMC 11–12/10; SLJ 5/10)

1301 Connor, Leslie. *Waiting for Normal* (5–7). 2008, HarperCollins $15.99 (978-0-06-089088-9). Addie lives in a trailer with her mother and looks forward to visits with her stepfather and half sisters, whose life is far more "normal." ALA Notable Books 2009. (Rev: BL 4/1/08; SLJ 2/08)

1302 Cooley, Beth. *Shelter* (7–10). 2006, Delacorte $15.95 (978-0-385-73330-4). Lucy and her mother and little brother go from affluence to a homeless shelter after Lucy's father dies, and Lucy must learn to adjust to new circumstances and improve her life. (Rev: BCCB 1/07; BL 1/1–15/07; SLJ 12/06)

1303 Cooney, Caroline B. *A Friend at Midnight* (6–9). 2006, Delacorte $15.95 (978-0-385-73326-7). Despite her Christian beliefs, Lily has a hard time forgiving her father for his neglect of herself and her siblings, and her resentment grows when her big sister wants him to be a part of her wedding. (Rev: BL 12/15/06; LMC 2/07; SLJ 11/06)

1304 Cooney, Caroline B. *Whatever Happened to Janie?* (6–10). 1993, Dell paper $5.50 (978-0-440-21924-8). Janie, 15, after discovering she's a missing child on a milk carton, returns to her birth family, which has been searching for her since her kidnapping at age three. Sequel to *The Face on the Milk Carton*. (Rev: BL 6/1–15/93; SLJ 6/93; VOYA 8/93)

1305 Corcoran, Barbara. *I Am the Universe* (6–8). 1993, Harcourt paper $23.40 (978-0-15-300366-0). With an indifferent father at home and her mother seriously ill in the hospital, Katherine and her older brother take care of the house. (Rev: BL 10/1/86; SLJ 10/86; VOYA 12/86)

1306 Corcoran, Barbara. *The Potato Kid* (5–8). 1993, Avon paper $3.50 (978-0-380-71213-7). In spite of her protests, Ellis must look after an underprivileged girl her mother takes in for the summer. (Rev: BCCB 11/89; BL 11/15/89; HB 1–2/90; SLJ 10/89; VOYA 2/90)

1307 Cotten, Cynthia. *Fair Has Nothing to Do with It* (4–7). 2007, Farrar $16.00 (978-0-374-39935-1). Upset by the death of his grandfather, 12-year-old Michael focuses his energies on an art project to honor his memory. (Rev: BL 4/1/07; SLJ 6/07)

1308 Couloumbis, Audrey. *Getting Near to Baby* (5–9). 1999, Putnam $17.99 (978-0-399-23389-0). When their baby sister dies and their mother sinks into a depression, 12-year-old Willa Jo and Little Sister go to live with a bossy aunt in this story set in North Carolina. (Rev: BCCB 11/99; BL 11/1/99; HB 11–12/99; HBG 3/00; SLJ 10/99; VOYA 2/00)

1309 Couloumbis, Audrey. *Love Me Tender* (5–8). 2008, Random House $16.99 (978-0-375-83839-2). Thirteen-year-old Elvira initially questions her future when after a fight, her father leaves for Vegas to compete in an Elvis-impersonation contest and her pregnant mother takes Elvira and her younger sister to Memphis to reunite with her family. (Rev: BL 2/15/08; SLJ 4/08)

1310 Couvillon, Jacques. *The Chicken Dance* (6–9). 2007, Bloomsbury $16.95 (978-1-59990-043-8). In this poignantly funny story set in the late 1970s, 11-year-old Don's skill at judging chickens brings him welcome acceptance but also triggers some unhappy discoveries. ∩ (Rev: BCCB 11/07; SLJ 11/07)

1311 Creech, Sharon. *Replay* (4–7). 2005, HarperCollins LB $16.89 (978-0-06-054020-3). Twelve-year-old Leo untangles some of the secrets of his boisterous Italian American family when he finds his father's boyhood journal. (Rev: BCCB 11/05; BL 9/1/05*; HBG 4/06; LMC 3–4/06; SLJ 9/05; VOYA 12/05)

1312 Creech, Sharon. *Walk Two Moons* (7–9). 1994, HarperCollins LB $17.89 (978-0-06-023337-2). The story of Sal, 13, who goes to Idaho with her grandparents to be with her mother, who has been killed in a bus accident. (Rev: BL 11/15/94; SLJ 10/94*; VOYA 2/95)

1313 Curtis, Vanessa. *The Taming of Lilah May* (6–9). 2012, Frances Lincoln paper $8.99 (978-184780149-4). The disappearance of her older brother, Jay, has thrown Lilah May's family into turmoil and the 15-year-old feels constantly angry. (Rev: BLO 6/12; LMC 1–2/13; SLJ 8/1/12)

1314 Dalton, Annie, and Maria Dalton. *Invisible Threads* (8–11). 2006, Delacorte LB $17.99 (978-0-385-90303-5). In alternating chapters, Carrie Ann describes her need to find her birth mother and Naomi, the birth mother, talks about her pregnancy and the decision to give up her baby. (Rev: BL 4/1/06; SLJ 4/06)

1315 Darrow, Sharon. *Trash* (8–11). 2006, Candlewick $16.99 (978-0-7636-2624-2). The sad story of two abandoned siblings—Sissy Lexie and Boy—who suffer through abuse, poverty, depression, and death; written in rhythmic prose and free verse. (Rev: BL 12/1/06; SLJ 10/06)

1316 Day, Karen. *Tall Tales* (5–8). 2007, Random House $15.99 (978-0-375-83773-9). As she starts school in yet another new town, 12-year-old Meg conceals her father's alcoholism and abuse, afraid it will frighten off potential friends. (Rev: BL 4/1/07; SLJ 6/07)

1317 De Goldi, Kate. *The 10 p.m. Question* (7–12). 2010, Candlewick $15.99 (978-0-7636-4939-5). Frankie, 12, worries about many things until free-thinking Sydney, veteran of 22 schools, makes him question his priorities; set in New Zealand. ∩ Lexile 830L (Rev: BL 8/10*; HB 11–12/10; LMC 1–2/11; SLJ 9/1/10; VOYA 12/10)

1318 Deaver, Julie Reece. *Chicago Blues* (6–10). 1995, HarperCollins $15.95 (978-0-06-024675-4). Two sisters are forced to make it on their own because of an alcoholic mother and experience struggle, success, and eventual forgiveness. (Rev: BL 9/1/95; SLJ 8/95; VOYA 12/95)

1319 Deedy, Carmen A. *The Last Dance* (7–10). 1995, Peachtree $16.95 (978-1-56145-109-8). A picture book for young adults that tells of the abiding love through the years of husband and wife Ninny and Bessie. (Rev: BL 1/1–15/96; SLJ 1/96)

1320 DeFelice, Cynthia. *Wild Life* (4–7). 2011, Farrar $16.99 (978-0-374-38001-4). When his parents are posted to Iraq, 12-year-old Erik is sent to his grandparents in North Dakota; unhappy there, he strikes out on his own with his newly adopted dog and manages to survive a time in the wilderness. Lexile 860L (Rev: BLO 6/21/11; LMC 10/11; SLJ 6/11)

1321 Delacre, Lulu. *Salsa Stories* (4–7). 2000, Scholastic paper $16.99 (978-0-590-63118-1). After each of her relatives tells a childhood story about a favorite food, Carmen Teresa records them and supplies appropriate recipes. (Rev: BCCB 5/00; BL 5/1/00; HBG 10/00; SLJ 3/00; VOYA 6/00)

1322 Dellasega, Cheryl. *Sistrsic92 (Meg)* (7–10). Illus. by Tyler Beauford. Series: Bloggrls. 2009, Marshall Cavendish $16.99 (978-0-7614-5456-4). When Meg's older, perfect sister Cara develops an eating disorder, plain, average Meg feels even more isolated from her family and confides her woes to her blog. (Rev: BL 10/1/09; SLJ 1/10; VOYA 2/10)

1323 Derby, Sally. *Kyle's Island* (5–8). 2010, Charlesbridge $16.95 (978-1-58089-316-9). Heartbroken that this will be the last summer at his family's lake cottage — his parents have just divorced — 13-year-old Kyle spends much of his time nursing his anger and fishing with an elderly neighbor who helps him deal with his unhappiness. Lexile 670L (Rev: BL 12/15/09; LMC 5–6/10; SLJ 1/10)

1324 Dessen, Sarah. *What Happened to Goodbye* (8–12). 2011, Viking $19.99 (978-0-670-01294-7). After her parents' bitter divorce, 17-year-old Mclean has been living with her father, moving from town to town and reinventing herself in each location. ∩ e Lexile HL760L (Rev: BL 5/1/11; HB 7–8/11; SLJ 6/11; VOYA 6/11)

1325 Deuker, Carl. *High Heat* (5–8). 2003, Houghton Mifflin $16.00 (978-0-618-31117-0). Even his baseball prowess seems to desert Shane when his father commits suicide and he must move to a tough new neighborhood and school. (Rev: BL 8/03; HBG 10/03; SLJ 7/03; VOYA 8/03)

1326 Deuker, Carl. *Runner* (7–10). 2005, Houghton Mifflin $16.00 (978-0-618-54298-7). Living on a weather-beaten sailboat on Puget Sound with his alcoholic father, high school senior Chance Taylor gets mixed up in some shady dealings to help pay the family bills. (Rev: BL 6/1–15/05; SLJ 6/05; VOYA 8/05)

1327 Doherty, Berlie. *Holly Starcross* (6–10). 2002, HarperCollins LB $17.89 (978-0-06-001342-4). Holly is forced to choose between her mother's new family and her long-lost father in this dramatic British novel. (Rev: BCCB 12/02; BL 11/1/02; HB 9–10/02; HBG 3/03; SLJ 8/02)

1328 Donaldson, Julia. *Running on the Cracks* (6–9). 2009, Henry Holt $16.99 (978-080509054-3). After her parents die in a plane crash, 15-year-old Leonora Watts-Chan rejects living with her aunt and ogling uncle in England and heads to Scotland in search of her Chinese grandparents. **e** (Rev: BL 7/09; SLJ 12/09)

1329 Doody, Margaret Anne. *The Annotated Anne of Green Gables* (7–12). 1997, Oxford $49.95 (978-0-19-510428-8). A biography of Lucy Maud Montgomery and notes and annotations explaining references to the places, people, and settings add to this edition of Montgomery's novel. (Rev: SLJ 3/98; VOYA 6/98)

1330 Doucet, Sharon Arms. *Fiddle Fever* (4–7). 2000, Clarion $15.00 (978-0-618-04324-8). Felix disobeys his mother, who hates fiddle playing, and builds one out of a cigar box and practices in secret. (Rev: BL 9/1/00; HB 9–10/00; HBG 3/01; SLJ 10/00)

1331 Dowd, Siobhan. *Solace of the Road* (8–12). 2009, Random House $17.99 (978-0-375-84971-8); LB $20.99 (978-0-375-94971-5). Holly Hogan, 14, assumes an alter-ego and escapes from her London foster home to reunite with her mother in Ireland, learning a valuable lesson about herself along the way. ☊ **e** Lexile HL650L (Rev: BL 10/1/09*; SLJ 10/09)

1332 Dowell, Frances O'Roark. *Chicken Boy* (4–7). 2005, Simon & Schuster $15.95 (978-0-689-85816-1). A new friend called Henry brings some comfort into Tobin's sad life. (Rev: BL 5/15/05*; SLJ 7/05*)

1333 Dowell, Frances O'Roark. *Dovey Coe* (4–7). 2000, Simon & Schuster $16.00 (978-0-689-83174-4). The mountain country of North Carolina in 1928 is the setting of this story of a plucky girl who cares for her siblings and who gets involved in a murder trial. (Rev: BL 4/15/00; HBG 10/00; SLJ 5/00; VOYA 6/00)

1334 Doyle, Eugenie. *Stray Voltage* (5–7). 2002, Front St $16.95 (978-1-886910-86-7). The electrical problems in Ian's family barn reflect the flickering, unpredictable relationships at home, but a wise teacher helps Ian to cope with his circumstances. (Rev: BCCB 1/03; BL 1/1–15/03*; HBG 3/03; SLJ 10/02*; VOYA 2/03)

1335 Draper, Sharon M. *Forged by Fire* (7–10). 1997, Simon & Schuster $16.95 (978-0-689-80699-5). Nine-year-old African American Gerald Nickelby must leave the comfort of his aunt's home to live with a neglectful mother, her daughter Angel, and husband Jordan, who is secretly sexually abusing young Angel. A companion volume to *Tears of a Tiger.* (Rev: BL 2/15/97; SLJ 3/97; VOYA 6/97)

1336 Duble, Kathleen Benner. *Bravo Zulu, Samantha!* (5–8). 2007, Peachtree $14.95 (978-1-56145-401-3). Twelve-year-old Samantha unwillingly spends the summer with her grandparents but her retired Air Force grandfather turns out to have an exciting secret. (Rev: BL 6/1–15/07; SLJ 6/07)

1337 Dunmore, Helen. *Brother Brother, Sister Sister* (5–8). 2000, Scholastic paper $4.50 (978-0-439-11322-9). Written in diary format, this is the story of Tanya, once

an only child and now surrounded by babies after her mother has quadruplets. (Rev: SLJ 8/00)

1338 Durrant, Sabine. *Cross Your Heart, Connie Pickles* (6–9). 2007, HarperTempest $16.99 (978-0-06-085479-9). This engaging story of Connie's quest to find a husband for her widowed mother is written in appealing diary format. (Rev: SLJ 6/07)

1339 Elkeles, Simone. *How to Ruin a Summer Vacation* (8–10). 2006, Flux paper $8.95 (978-0-7387-0961-1). Amy, 16, enters a whole new world when she goes to Israel for the summer with her father and must share a room with a cousin she's neverr met. (Rev: SLJ 12/06)

1340 Elliott, Zetta. *Bird* (4–8). Illus. by Shadra Strickland. 2008, Lee & Low $19.95 (978-1-60060-241-2). Bird, an African American boy struggling with his brother's death from drugs, finds solace in drawing and the understanding of his uncle in this novel in verse. Coretta Scott King/John Steptoe New Talent Author Award; ALA Notable Books 2009. (Rev: BL 11/1/08; LMC 3–4/09)

1341 Ellis, Sarah. *Out of the Blue* (5–7). 1995, Simon & Schuster paper $15.00 (978-0-689-80025-2). Twelve-year-old Megan discovers that she has a 24-year-old half-sister whom her mother gave up for adoption years ago. (Rev: BCCB 4/95; BL 5/1/95; HB 7–8/95; SLJ 5/95)

1342 Ellison, Elizabeth Stow. *Flight* (4–8). 2008, Holiday House $16.95 (978-082342128-2). Caught between her unresponsive, oblivious parents and her older brother Evan who's coping with a learning disability, 12-year-old Samantha struggles to advocate for Evan and eventually discovers that her mother is hiding her own disability — that she cannot read. Lexile 710L (Rev: BLO 11/1/08; SLJ 11/1/08)

1343 Ephron, Delia. *Frannie in Pieces* (7–10). 2007, HarperCollins $16.99 (978-0-06-074716-9). Frannie, devastated by her father's death, discovers a magical jigsaw puzzle that he made before his death and that allows Frannie to see him again. ☊ (Rev: BL 11/1/07; SLJ 10/07)

1344 Ernst, Kathleen. *Highland Fling* (6–9). 2006, Cricket $15.95 (978-0-8126-2742-8). Tanya, a budding documentary filmmaker, must overcome her negativity as she attends a Scottish heritage festival with her recently divorced mom. (Rev: BL 4/15/06; SLJ 6/06)

1345 Erskine, Kathryn. *Quaking* (8–10). 2007, Philomel $16.99 (978-0-399-24774-3). Fourteen-year-old Matilda's resistance gradually breaks down as she settles into her new, Quaker foster home; community differences over antiwar protests threaten this new ease. (Rev: BL 5/1/07; HB 7–8/07; SLJ 7/07)

1346 Eulo, Elena Yates. *Mixed-Up Doubles* (8–11). 2003, Holiday $16.95 (978-0-8234-1706-3). In this poignant yet funny story of a tennis-playing family hit by divorce, middle child Hank, 14, narrates the effects on the children. (Rev: BCCB 7–8/03; BL 5/15/03; HBG 4/04; SLJ 7/03; VOYA 6/03)

1347 Ferber, Brenda. *Julia's Kitchen* (5–8). 2006, Farrar $16.00 (978-0-374-39932-0). Eleven-year-old Cara Segal's faith is tested when her mother and sister die in a house fire while Cara is sleeping over at a friend's home. Sydney Taylor Book Award 2007. (Rev: BL 2/1/06; SLJ 4/06)

1348 Fine, Anne. *The Book of the Banshee* (6–9). 1992, Little, Brown $13.95 (978-0-316-28315-1). English teenager Will Flowers's younger sister, Estelle, has become a banshee, and he decides his family life is like an account of World War I he is reading. (Rev: BL 12/1/91*)

1349 Flake, Sharon G. *Begging for Change* (7–12). 2003, Hyperion $15.99 (978-0-7868-0601-0). Raspberry resorts to stealing from a friend when her mother is hospitalized after being hit in the head and her addicted father reappears on the scene in this sequel to *Money Hungry* (2001). (Rev: BL 8/03*; HBG 4/04; SLJ 7/03; VOYA 6/03)

1350 Fleischman, Paul. *Rear-View Mirrors* (7–10). 1986, HarperCollins $12.95 (978-0-06-021866-9). After her father's death, Olivia relives through memory a summer when she and her estranged father reconciled. (Rev: BL 3/1/86; SLJ 5/86; VOYA 8/86)

1351 Fleischman, Sid. *Bo and Mzzz Mad* (5–7). 2001, Greenwillow LB $15.89 (978-0-06-029398-7). When his father dies, 12-year-old Bo accepts an invitation from relatives despite a longstanding family feud. (Rev: BL 5/15/01*; HB 5–6/01; HBG 10/01; SLJ 5/01)

1352 Fletcher, Ralph. *Fig Pudding* (5–7). 1995, Clarion $15.00 (978-0-395-71125-5). A year that brings both tragedy and hilarity in the life of a family of six children. (Rev: BCCB 5/95; BL 5/15/95; SLJ 7/95)

1353 Flinn, Alex. *Nothing to Lose* (7–12). 2004, HarperCollins $16.99 (978-0-06-051750-2). At age 17, Michael returns home after being a runaway for a year to find that his mother is on trial for the murder of his abusive father. (Rev: BL 3/15/04; HB 5–6/04; SLJ 3/04; VOYA 6/04)

1354 Fogelin, Adrian. *Anna Casey's Place in the World* (6–8). 2001, Peachtree $14.95 (978-1-56145-249-1). Twelve-year-old orphan Anna must adjust to her new foster home and begin to make friends. (Rev: BL 10/15/01; HBG 3/02; SLJ 12/01; VOYA 12/01)

1355 Fogelin, Adrian. *My Brother's Hero* (5–8). 2002, Peachtree $14.95 (978-1-56145-274-3). When Ben and his family travel to Florida for a vacation, Ben meets a girl named Mica, whose life he finds exciting and mysterious. (Rev: BL 2/1/03; HBG 10/03; SLJ 2/03)

1356 Fogelin, Adrian. *Sister Spider Knows All* (6–9). 2003, Peachtree $14.95 (978-1-56145-290-3). A sensitive and humorous novel narrated by Rox, 12, who is

doing OK being brought up by her financially strapped grandmother and cousin John until John brings home a rich girlfriend who sees things differently. (Rev: BCCB 2/04; BL 12/15/03; SLJ 12/03)

1357 Foggo, Cheryl. *One Thing That's True* (5–8). 1998, Kids Can $16.95 (978-1-55074-411-8). Roxanne is heartbroken when her older brother runs away after learning that he is adopted. (Rev: BCCB 5/98; BL 2/15/98; HBG 10/98; SLJ 4/98)

1358 Forbes, Kathryn. *Mama's Bank Account* (7–10). 1968, Harcourt paper $11.00 (978-0-15-656377-2). The story, told in vignettes, of a loving Norwegian family and of Mama's mythical bank account.

1359 Fox, Paula. *The Eagle Kite* (6–10). 1995, Orchard LB $16.99 (978-0-531-08742-8). Liam goes through a tangle of denial, anger, shame, grief, and empathy after learning that his father is dying of AIDS. His mother says he got it from a blood transfusion, but Liam remembers seeing his father embrace a young man two years before. (Rev: BL 2/1/95*; SLJ 4/95*; VOYA 5/95)

1360 Fox, Paula. *The Village by the Sea* (5–8). 1988, Orchard $15.95 (978-0-531-05788-9). Emma is staying with an aunt and uncle while her father has heart surgery, and the three interact in complex ways. Also use the reissued *A Likely Place* (1997). (Rev: BCCB 7–8/88; BL 9/1/88; HB 9–10/88; SLJ 8/88; VOYA 10/88)

1361 Frechette, Carole. *In the Key of Do* (6–9). 2003, Red Deer paper $9.95 (978-0-88995-254-6). Past and present are interwoven in this story of two girls in Montreal whose family circumstances bring them together. (Rev: BL 6/1–15/03; SLJ 6/03; VOYA 10/03)

1362 French, Simon. *Where in the World* (5–8). 2003, Peachtree $14.95 (978-1-56145-292-7). A move from Germany to Australia is difficult for Ari, a talented young violinist who spends time living in the past while trying to find ways to cope with the present. (Rev: BL 12/1/03; HBG 4/04; SLJ 12/03*)

1363 Friend, Natasha. *Bounce* (6–9). 2007, Scholastic $16.99 (978-0-439-85350-7). Thirteen-year-old Evyn has a hard time adjusting to six new stepsiblings, a pregnant stepmother, and a new home and school — until she decides to let things bounce. (Rev: BL 11/1/07; SLJ 9/07)

1364 Friend, Natasha. *Lush* (7–10). 2006, Scholastic $16.99 (978-0-439-85346-0). Thirteen-year-old Sam writes anonymous letters to an older student at school, sharing the truth about her family life and her father's alcoholism, and asking for advice. (Rev: BL 11/1/06; SLJ 12/06)

1365 Friesen, Gayle. *Janey's Girl* (6–9). 1998, Kids Can $16.95 (978-1-55074-461-3). When Claire and her mother visit her mother's hometown in rural British Columbia, the young girl meets her father for the first time and begins to find out truths about her family's past. (Rev: HBG 3/99; SLJ 11/98)

1366 Friesen, Gayle. *Losing Forever* (7–10). 2002, Kids Can $16.95 (978-1-55337-031-4). As her mother prepares to remarry, 9th-grader Jes is still coping with her parents' divorce, her changing relationships with her friends, and her beautiful soon-to-be stepsister. (Rev: BCCB 11/02; BL 1/1–15/03; HBG 3/03; SLJ 11/02; VOYA 2/03)

1367 Gantos, Jack. *I Am Not Joey Pigza* (5–8). 2007, Farrar $16.00 (978-0-374-39941-2). Joey's father returns to the Pigza family with lottery winnings, a new name, and promises of a new future based on a diner. ∩ (Rev: BL 8/07; SLJ 9/07)

1368 Gantos, Jack. *Jack Adrift: Fourth Grade Without a Clue* (4–7). 2003, Farrar $16.00 (978-0-374-39987-0). In this prequel to the four previous books, Jack Henry is 9 and has just moved to Cape Hatteras where he has comic experiences and more serious conversations with his dad. (Rev: BL 8/03; HB 11–12/03; HBG 4/04; SLJ 9/03)

1369 Garland, Sherry. *Rainmaker's Dream* (6–9). 1997, Harcourt paper $6.00 (978-0-15-200652-5). After her family falls apart, 13-year-old Caroline runs away to a Wild West show where she discovers a secret about her mother's identity. (Rev: BL 4/1/97; SLJ 6/97; VOYA 8/97)

1370 Garsee, Jeannine. *Before, After, and Somebody in Between* (8–11). 2007, Bloomsbury $16.95 (978-1-59990-022-3). This is a problem novel in which 14-year-old Martha — smart, sensitive, and musically gifted — copes with an alcoholic mother, poverty and violence, foster care, and ill-advised sex but finds hope at the end of it all. (Rev: BL 8/07; SLJ 10/07)

1371 Gates, Doris. *Blue Willow* (5–8). 1940, Penguin paper $6.99 (978-0-14-030924-9). An easily read novel about a poor girl and the china plate that belonged to her mother. (Rev: BCCB 12/99)

1372 Gates, Susan. *Beyond the Billboard* (5–8). 2007, Harcourt $16.00 (978-0-15-205983-5). Ford and Firebird, 13-year-old twins, have grown up secluded from the modern world but their lives are about to change as secrets are revealed. (Rev: BL 6/1–15/07; SLJ 8/07)

1373 Geithner, Carole. *If Only* (5–8). 2012, Scholastic $16.99 (978-0-545-23499-3). This novel about grief features 8th-grader Corinna learning to navigate the first year after her mother's death from cancer. ℮ Lexile 810L (Rev: BL 3/15/11; LMC 5–6/12; SLJ 3/12)

1374 Giff, Patricia Reilly. *Pictures of Hollis Woods* (5–7). 2002, Random House $15.95 (978-0-385-32655-1). Twelve-year-old Hollis Woods has finally found a foster home where she feels safe, but when the artist who takes her in begins to suffer from dementia, Hollis finds herself in the position of caregiver. Newbery Honor

2003. (Rev: BCCB 12/02; BL 10/15/02; HB 1–2/03; HBG 3/03; SLJ 9/02)

1375 Gilliland, Hap, and William Walters. *Flint's Rock* (5–7). 1996, Roberts Rinehart paper $8.95 (978-1-879373-82-2). Flint, a young Cheyenne, faces problems when he moves with his parents from the reservation to Butte, Montana. (Rev: BCCB 5/96; BL 5/1/96)

1376 Gilmore, Rachna. *Mina's Spring of Colors* (4–7). 2000, Fitzhenry & Whiteside $14.95 (978-1-55041-549-0); paper $8.95 (978-1-55041-534-6). Mina is happy when her grandfather comes from India, but with his arrival comes a culture clash that troubles the girl. (Rev: BL 6/1–15/00; SLJ 9/00; VOYA 12/00)

1377 Givner, Joan. *Ellen's Book of Life* (5–8). 2008, Groundwood $17.95 (978-088899853-8). When Ellen's mother dies, Ellen seeks out her birth mother and is introduced to Judaism in this multilayered first-person narrative, the third in a series. (Rev: BL 10/15/08; SLJ 1/1/09)

1378 Going, K. L. *Saint Iggy* (8–11). 2006, Harcourt $17.00 (978-0-15-205795-4). Sixteen-year-old Iggy Corso, who lives in public housing with his drug-addicted parents, faces expulsion from school and decides to make something of himself. ∩ (Rev: BL 9/15/06; HB 11–12/06; SLJ 9/06)

1379 Golding, Theresa Martin. *The Secret Within* (5–8). 2002, Boyds Mills $16.95 (978-1-56397-995-8). Eighth-grader Carly's secret is that her father is abusive and a criminal; the neighbors in the family's new town help her and her mother to finally escape his grip. (Rev: BL 9/15/02; HBG 3/03; SLJ 8/02; VOYA 2/03)

1380 Goobie, Beth. *Something Girl* (5–8). 2005, Orca paper $7.95 (978-1-55143-347-9). Fifteen-year-old Sophie tries to hide the fact that her mother is an alcoholic and her father abusive in this book for reluctant readers. (Rev: BL 7/05; SLJ 12/05)

1381 Goobie, Beth. *Who Owns Kelly Paddik?* (7–10). Series: Orca Soundings. 2003, Orca paper $7.95 (978-1-55143-239-7). Kelly, 15, slowly comes to realize that she is not alone as she recovers from the sexual abuse inflicted by her father. (Rev: SLJ 11/03)

1382 Goodman, Joan Elizabeth. *Songs from Home* (5–7). 1994, Harcourt paper $4.95 (978-0-15-203591-4). Anna discovers the truth about her father, who has become a drifter in Italy singing for tips in restaurants. (Rev: BCCB 12/94; BL 9/1/94; SLJ 10/94)

1383 Grant, Vicki. *B Negative* (7–10). Series: Orca Soundings. 2011, Orca LB $16.95 (978-155469842-4); paper $9.95 (9781554698417). Eighteen-year-old Paddy discovers his blood type doesn't match his family's when he gets a physical prior to joining the army; for reluctant readers. ℮ Lexile HL510L (Rev: BLO 2/15/11)

1384 Grant, Vicki. *Comeback* (6–10). Series: Orca Soundings. 2010, Orca LB $16.95 (978-1-55469-311-5); paper $9.95 (978-1-55469-310-8). Upset when her father's plane goes down, Ria runs away from her mother's home with her 5-year-old brother and faces many challenges; for reluctant readers. **ℓ** Lexile HL550L (Rev: BL 4/15/10; SLJ 4/10)

1385 Greene, Stephanie. *The Lucky Ones* (5–8). 2008, Greenwillow $16.99 (978-0-06-156586-1). Twelve-year-old Cecile wants things the way they were before her parents began fighting and her sister became interested in boys in this coming-of-age novel set during a summer vacation on an island. (Rev: BL 10/1/08; SLJ 11/08)

1386 Greenfield, Eloise. *Sister* (5–7). Illus. by Moneta Barnett. 1974, HarperCollins $15.99 (978-0-690-00497-7); paper $5.99 (978-0-06-440199-9). Four years in an African American girl's life, as revealed through scattered diary entries, during which she shows maturation, particularly in her attitude toward her sister.

1387 Greer, Daphne. *Maxed Out* (6–9). Series: Orca Currents. 2012, Orca LB $16.95 (978-155469982-7); paper $9.95 (9781554699810). After his father's death, young Max finds himself looking after his family, including his disabled older brother; for reluctant readers. **ℓ** Lexile HL450L (Rev: BL 3/1/12; SLJ 5/1/12)

1388 Gregory, Nan. *I'll Sing You One-O* (5–8). 2006, Clarion $16.00 (978-0-618-60708-2). Twelve-year-old Gemma is overwhelmed when relatives — including a twin brother — turn up to take her from the foster home she's come to love, and she becomes convinced that an angel will save the day. (Rev: BL 8/06; SLJ 10/06*)

1389 Grimes, Nikki. *Dark Sons* (5–8). 2005, Hyperion $15.99 (978-0-7868-1888-4). Alternating between biblical times and contemporary New York, free-verse narratives express the frustrations of Ishmael — son of Abraham, who must wander the desert with his rejected mother — and of Sam, whose father has left his mother for a young white woman. (Rev: BL 8/05*; SLJ 11/05; VOYA 10/05)

1390 Grimes, Nikki. *The Road to Paris* (4–7). 2006, Putnam $15.99 (978-0-399-24537-4). Half-white and half-black, 9-year-old Paris suddenly finds herself separated from her older brother Malcolm and living with a foster family in a mostly white neighborhood. Coretta Scott King Author Honor 2007. ∩ (Rev: BL 8/06; SLJ 12/06)

1391 Hahn, Mary Downing. *As Ever, Gordy* (5–8). 1998, Houghton Mifflin $15.00 (978-0-395-83627-9). After his grandmother's death, 13-year-old Gordy must move back to his hometown to live with his older brother, and there he finds himself in a downward spiral. A sequel to *Stepping on Cracks* and *Following My Own Footsteps*. (Rev: BCCB 6/98; BL 5/1/98; HBG 10/98; SLJ 7/98; VOYA 4/99)

1392 Hall, Barbara. *Dixie Storms* (7–12). 1990, Harcourt $15.95 (978-0-15-223825-4). Dutch's troubled relationships within her family worsen when cousin Norma comes to stay. (Rev: BL 5/1/90; SLJ 9/90)

1393 Hall, Barbara. *The Noah Confessions* (8–12). 2007, Random House $15.99 (978-0-385-73328-1). The compelling story of Lynnie, a 16-year-old girl who comes to terms with her family's secret past when she reads a letter written by her deceased mother. (Rev: SLJ 6/07)

1394 Hamilton, Virginia. *Plain City* (5–7). 1993, Scholastic paper $13.95 (978-0-590-47364-4). Buhlaire's life changes dramatically when the father she believed to be dead unexpectedly arrives in town. (Rev: BCCB 11/93; BL 9/15/93*; SLJ 11/93*)

1395 Hamilton, Virginia. *Second Cousins* (5–8). 1998, Scholastic paper $14.95 (978-0-590-47368-2). In this sequel to *Cousins*, 12-year-old Cammy learns a secret during a family reunion in her small Ohio town. (Rev: BCCB 11/98; BL 8/98; HB 1–2/99; HBG 3/99; SLJ 11/98; VOYA 2/99)

1396 Hansen, Joyce. *One True Friend* (4–7). 2001, Clarion $14.00 (978-0-395-84983-5). Amir's correspondence with his friend Doris comforts him as he tries to fulfill a deathbed promise to his mother to keep his family together. (Rev: BCCB 12/01; BL 12/15/01; HBG 3/02; SLJ 12/01; VOYA 10/01)

1397 Harmon, Michael. *Skate* (7–10). 2006, Knopf $15.95 (978-0-375-87516-8). Facing foster care and separation from his younger brother Sammy, Ian takes Sammy and the two run away, heading across Washington State to find their long-absent father. (Rev: BL 11/15/06; SLJ 12/06)

1398 Harness, Cheryl. *Just for You to Know* (5–8). 2006, HarperCollins $17.99 (978-0-06-078313-6). Life is turned upside down for 13-year-old Carmen Cathcart, an aspiring artist, when her mother dies during childbirth. (Rev: SLJ 9/06)

1399 Harrar, George. *Parents Wanted* (6–9). 2001, Milkweed $17.95 (978-1-57131-632-5); paper $6.95 (978-1-57131-633-2). Andy Fleck, a foster child with ADD, sabotages his own adoption by accusing his prospective father of abuse. (Rev: BL 12/15/01; HBG 3/02; SLJ 11/01)

1400 Harrison, Mette Ivie. *The Monster in Me* (5–8). 2003, Holiday $16.95 (978-0-8234-1713-1). A caring foster family and her growing enjoyment in running make Natalie, 13, more optimistic about life. (Rev: BL 4/1/03; HBG 10/03; SLJ 6/03; VOYA 10/03)

1401 Harrison, Troon. *Goodbye to Atlantis* (7–10). 2002, Stoddart paper $7.95 (978-0-7737-6229-9). Stella, 14, whose mother died of cancer, initially resents being stuck with her father's girlfriend as a traveling companion. (Rev: BL 9/1/02; SLJ 4/02)

1402 Hartnett, Sonya. *What the Birds See* (7–12). 2003, Candlewick $15.99 (978-0-7636-2092-9). A beautifully written complex story featuring three missing children and a lonely and fearful boy who is fascinated by three children who move in next door. (Rev: BCCB 3/03; BL 4/15/03; HB 5–6/03; HBG 10/03; SLJ 5/03; VOYA 6/03)

1403 Hathorn, Libby. *Thunderwith* (7–10). 1991, Little, Brown $15.95 (978-0-316-35034-1). This story of an unhappy 15-year-old girl and a beautiful dingolike dog she finds is set in the Australian rain forest. (Rev: BL 9/1/91; SLJ 5/91*)

1404 Hausman, Gerald, and Uton Hinds. *The Jacob Ladder* (5–8). 2001, Orchard paper $15.95 (978-0-531-30331-3). This story of a young Jamaican who struggles valiantly to cope with poverty, a charismatic but neglectful father, and the problems of growing up is based on the youth of coauthor Uton Hinds. (Rev: BL 5/1/01; HBG 3/02; SLJ 4/01; VOYA 6/01)

1405 Helget, Nicole, and Nate LeBoutillier. *Horse Camp* (5–8). 2012, Egmont $15.99 (978-160684351-2). Twins Percy and Penny, 12, grudgingly adjust to farm life with their uncle in Minnesota after their mother is arrested. (Rev: BL 5/15/12*; SLJ 6/12)

1406 Heneghan, James, and Norma Charles. *Bank Job* (5–7). 2009, Orca paper $9.95 (978-1-55143-855-9). A gripping read about three foster children who will resort to robbery to stay together. (Rev: BL 5/15/09)

1407 Henkes, Kevin. *The Birthday Room* (5–7). 1999, Greenwillow $19.99 (978-0-688-16733-2). Ben travels to Oregon with his mother to visit Uncle Ian who was responsible for Ben's losing his little finger in an accident. (Rev: BCCB 9/99; BL 7/99; HB 9–10/99; HBG 3/00; SLJ 10/99)

1408 Hermes, Patricia. *You Shouldn't Have to Say Goodbye* (5–8). 1982, Scholastic paper $3.25 (978-0-590-43174-3). A moving novel about a girl whose mother is dying of cancer.

1409 Herschler, Mildred Barger. *The Darkest Corner* (5–9). 2000, Front St $17.95 (978-1-886910-54-6). In this novel set in the Deep South of the 1960s, 10-year-old Teddy is shocked to discover that her beloved dad participated in the lynching of her best friend's father. (Rev: BL 1/1–15/01; HBG 3/01; SLJ 2/01; VOYA 2/01)

1410 Hicks, Betty. *Get Real* (6–9). 2006, Roaring Brook $16.95 (978-1-59643-089-1). Best friends Destiny and Jil come from very different families and Dez is puzzled but supporting when Jil fixates on her birth mother. (Rev: BL 10/15/06; SLJ 1/07)

1411 Hicks, Betty. *Out of Order* (4–7). 2005, Roaring Brook $15.95 (978-1-59643-061-7). In alternating chapters, four new stepsiblings relate the problems — and the fun — they have had adjusting to life together. (Rev: BL 9/15/05; SLJ 10/05; VOYA 12/05)

1412 High, Linda O. *Maizie* (4–8). 1995, Holiday $14.95 (978-0-8234-1161-0). Maizie, a survivor, succeeds in spite of being abandoned by her mother and left with an alcoholic father. (Rev: BCCB 4/95; BL 4/15/95; HB 5–6/95; SLJ 4/95)

1413 Hill, Kirkpatrick. *Do Not Pass Go* (6–9). 2007, Simon & Schuster $15.99 (978-1-4169-1400-6). Deet must deal with new family pressures when his stepfather is sent to jail for drug possession. (Rev: BL 12/15/06; SLJ 3/07)

1414 Hinton, S. E. *Taming the Star Runner* (7–12). 1989, Bantam paper $5.50 (978-0-440-20479-4). A tough delinquent is sent to his uncle's ranch to be straightened out and there he falls in love with Casey, who is trying to tame a wild horse named Star Runner. (Rev: BL 10/15/88; SLJ 10/88; VOYA 12/88)

1415 Hirahara, Naomi. *1001 Cranes* (4–7). 2008, Delacorte $15.99 (978-0-385-73556-8). Twelve-year-old Angela reluctantly spends the summer with her Japanese American grandparents, where she learns to cope with her parents' separation while creating origami for the family business. (Rev: BL 8/08; SLJ 8/08)

1416 Hirsch, Odo. *Darius Bell and the Glitter Pool* (4–7). 2010, Kane/Miller $15.99 (978-193527965-5). Broke and desperate, Darius's once wealthy family has nothing to give to the community as its annual thank you, until an earthquake reveals a hidden cave that may provide the answer; set in Australia. Lexile 770L (Rev: BL 9/1/10; LMC 3–4/11)

1417 Hite, Sid. *The King of Slippery Falls* (6–9). 2004, Scholastic $16.95 (978-0-439-34257-5). Sixteen-year-old adoptee Lewis Hinton believes he may be a descendant of French royalty, and the whole town of Slippery Falls follows the story. (Rev: BCCB 7–8/04; BL 4/15/04; SLJ 5/04; VOYA 8/04)

1418 Hoffman, Alice. *Green Angel* (6–12). 2003, Scholastic $16.95 (978-0-439-44384-5). Fifteen-year-old Green, so-called for her gardening skills, is the only member of her family to survive a major disaster. (Rev: BL 4/15/03; HB 3–4/03; HBG 10/03; SLJ 3/03*; VOYA 4/03)

1419 Holcomb, Jerry Kimble. *The Chinquapin Tree* (5–9). 1998, Marshall Cavendish $14.95 (978-0-7614-5028-3). Faced with being sent back to their abusive mother, three youngsters head for the wilderness in this survival story set in Oregon. (Rev: BL 5/1/98; HBG 10/98; SLJ 5/98)

1420 Holeman, Linda. *Raspberry House Blues* (6–10). 2000, Tundra paper $6.95 (978-0-88776-493-6). Poppy's search for her birth mother looks hopeful for a while when she spends a summer in Winnipeg. (Rev: SLJ 12/00; VOYA 2/01)

1421 Hollyer, Belinda. *Secrets, Lies, and My Sister Kate* (6–9). 2009, Holiday House $16.95 (978-082342179-4). When her older sister's teenage rebellion goes too far, 12-year-old Mini relies on a friend to help bring her back home to the family. Lexile 890L (Rev: BL 2/15/09; SLJ 4/1/09)

1422 Holmes, Elizabeth. *Tracktown Summer* (5–8). 2009, Dutton $16.99 (978-0-525-47946-8). Spending summer with his newly separated and remote father, 12-year-old Jake turns to a 14-year-old neighbor called Adrian for company and eventually discovers the reasons for his strange behavior — he is protecting his mentally ill father. (Rev: BCCB 7–8/09; BL 5/15/09; SLJ 7/09; VOYA 8/09)

1423 Holt, Kimberly Willis. *Keeper of the Night* (6–10). 2003, Henry Holt $16.95 (978-0-8050-6361-5). Isabel, a 13-year-old who lives on Guam, tells the story of her mother's suicide and the family's subsequent grief. (Rev: BL 4/15/03; HB 5–6/03; HBG 10/03; SLJ 5/03*; VOYA 6/03)

1424 Holt, Kimberly Willis. *My Louisiana Sky* (6–9). 1998, Henry Holt $16.95 (978-0-8050-5251-0). When Tiger Ann's caring grandmother dies, the young girl is tempted to leave her retarded parents and relocate to Baton Rouge to live with an aunt. (Rev: BCCB 6/98; BL 4/15/98; HB 7–8/98*; HBG 9/98; SLJ 7/98; VOYA 8/98)

1425 Honeycutt, Natalie. *Twilight in Grace Falls* (5–9). 1997, Orchard LB $17.99 (978-0-531-33007-4). A moving novel about the closing of a lumber mill that brings unemployment to 11-year-old Dasie Jenson's father. (Rev: BCCB 6/97; BL 3/15/97*; HB 7–8/97; SLJ 5/97; VOYA 8/97)

1426 Hood, Ann. *How I Saved My Father's Life (And Ruined Everything Else)* (6–8). 2008, Scholastic $16.99 (978-0-439-92819-9). Twelve-year-old Madeline knows that it was her prayers that saved her father from a terrible accident, so she goes to work on becoming religious enough to pray her parents back together. (Rev: BL 12/15/07; SLJ 7/08)

1427 Horrocks, Anita. *What They Don't Know* (7–9). 1999, Stoddart paper $8.95 (978-0-7737-6001-1). After Hannah discovers a family secret that involves her identity, she heads down a path of self-destruction that her older sister tries to stop. (Rev: BL 11/1/99; SLJ 8/99; VOYA 10/99)

1428 Horvath, Polly. *The Canning Season* (6–9). 2003, Farrar $16.00 (978-0-374-39956-6). Thirteen-year-old Ratchet is sent to live with twin great aunts in Maine in this complex and dark tale that includes some strong language and will appeal to readers interested in adult characters. (Rev: BL 4/1/03; HB 5–6/03*; HBG 10/03; SLJ 5/03*; VOYA 8/03)

1429 Horvath, Polly. *The Corps of the Bare-Boned Plane* (6–9). 2007, Farrar $17.00 (978-0-374-31553-5). Teen cousins Jocelyn and Meline move to British Columbia to live with their wealthy uncle after the deaths of their

parents, where they try to cope with their grief. (Rev: BL 6/1–15/07; HB 9–10/07; LMC 1/08; SLJ 9/07)

1430 Horvath, Polly. *Northward to the Moon* (5–8). 2010, Random House LB $20.99 (978-0-375-96110-6). Jane recounts her family's varied experiences as, after their stepfather is fired from his teaching job, they travel back from Saskatchewan to Massachusetts in this sequel to *My One Hundred Adventures* (2008). ∩ e Lexile 750L (Rev: BL 11/15/09; HB 1–2/10; LMC 3–4/10; SLJ 2/10)

1431 Hunter, Evan. *Me and Mr. Stenner* (5–8). 1976, HarperCollins $11.95 (978-0-397-31689-2). Abby's attitudes toward her new stepfather gradually change from resentment to love.

1432 Hyde, Catherine Ryan. *The Year of My Miraculous Reappearance* (7–10). 2007, Knopf $15.99 (978-0-375-83257-4). In the void created by her alcoholic mother with her constantly changing boyfriends, Cynnie, 13, treasures her relationship with her young brother; when he is taken away, Cynnie sinks into alcoholism herself. (Rev: BCCB 7–8/07; BL 3/1/07; LMC 4–5/07; SLJ 4/07)

1433 James, Brian. *The Heights* (8–12). 2009, Feiwel & Friends $16.99 (978-031236853-1). Privileged Catherine and her stepbrother Henry, a Mexican orphan, share a doomed passion for each other in this contemporary retelling of *Wuthering Heights* set in San Francisco. Lexile 900L (Rev: BL 5/1/09; HB 5–6/09; LMC 8–9/09; SLJ 7/1/09)

1434 Jarrow, Gail. *If Phyllis Were Here* (5–7). 1989, Avon paper $2.75 (978-0-380-70634-1). Libby, age 11, has to learn to adjust to living without her best friend — her grandmother who moves to Florida. (Rev: BL 10/15/87; SLJ 9/87)

1435 Jarzab, Anna. *The Opposite of Hallelujah* (8–12). 2012, Delacorte $16.99 (978-038573836-1); LB $19.99 (978-038590724-8). Carolina uses untruths to cope with her confusion of her sister's decision to enter a convent, and years later to suddenly leave it. (Rev: BL 10/1/12*; VOYA 12/12)

1436 Johnson, Angela. *Heaven* (6–10). 1998, Simon & Schuster $16.00 (978-0-689-82229-2). Marley, a 14-year-old African American girl, is devastated when she learns that she is adopted and that the couple she has regarded as her mother and father are really her aunt and uncle. (Rev: BCCB 12/98; BL 9/15/98; HBG 3/99; SLJ 10/98; VOYA 2/99)

1437 Johnson, Angela. *Songs of Faith* (5–8). 1998, Orchard LB $16.99 (978-0-531-33023-4). Doreen is a child of divorce who is particularly upset by her younger brother's problems adjusting after their father moves away. (Rev: BCCB 6/98; BL 2/15/98; HBG 10/98; SLJ 3/98; VOYA 6/98)

1438 Johnson, Peter. *What Happened* (7–12). 2007, Front St $16.95 (978-1-932425-67-3). A hit-and-run accident reveals long-concealed relationships between the parents of Duane on one side and Kyle and the un-named narrator on the other side in this novel about troubled young people facing difficult choices. (Rev: BL 5/1/07; SLJ 6/07)

1439 Johnston, Lindsay Lee. *Soul Moon Soup* (5–7). 2002, Front St $15.95 (978-1-886910-87-4). When homeless Phoebe and her mother hit bottom, Phoebe goes to live with her grandmother and slowly learns to value her own resources in this story told in verse. (Rev: BCCB 2/03; BL 11/15/02; HB 1–2/03; HBG 3/03; SLJ 11/02)

1440 Jones, Kimberly K. *Sand Dollar Summer* (5–8). 2006, Simon & Schuster $15.95 (978-1-4169-0362-8). Annalise's summer in Maine with her mother and younger, often-mute brother Free takes a dramatic turn when a hurricane hits their island. (Rev: BL 5/15/06; HBG 10/06; LMC 1/07; SLJ 6/06*)

1441 Jones, Traci L. *Silhouetted by the Blue* (5–8). 2011, Farrar $16.99 (978-0-374-36914-9). Serena, an African American 7th-grader, must finally ask for help when her father does not recover from his depression after her mother's death. Lexile 720L (Rev: BL 6/1/11; HB 7–8/11; SLJ 8/11*)

1442 Jongman, Mariken. *Rits* (7–9). Trans. by Wanda Boeke. 2008, Front St $17.95 (978-1-59078-545-4). Rits befriends a neighbor named Rita when family circumstances force him to move in with his unemployed uncle in this novel translated from the Dutch. (Rev: BL 4/15/08; SLJ 5/08)

1443 Joosse, Barbara M. *Pieces of the Picture* (5–8). 1989, HarperCollins LB $12.89 (978-0-397-32343-2); paper $3.50 (978-0-06-440310-8). Emily is not happy when she and her mother move to Wisconsin after her father's death to earn a livelihood running an inn. (Rev: BL 6/1/89; SLJ 4/89)

1444 Kadohata, Cynthia. *Outside Beauty* (6–9). 2008, Atheneum $16.99 (978-0-689-86575-6). Four sisters — Shelby, Maddie, Lakey, and Marilyn — are sent to live with their respective fathers after their beautiful mother is in an accident; but the girls need each other and go to great lengths to get back together. (Rev: BL 6/1–15/08; SLJ 7/08)

1445 Kearney, Meg. *The Girl in the Mirror: A Novel in Poems and Journal Entries* (7–12). Series: Karen and Michael Braziller Books. 2012, Persea paper $15 (978-0-89255-385-3). Poems and journal entries document Lizzie's grief over the death of her adoptive father and her search for her birth mother in this sequel to *The Secret of Me* (2007). (Rev: BLO 3/1/12; HB 7–8/12; SLJ 6/12; VOYA 6/12)

1446 Kearney, Meg. *The Secret of Me* (7–10). 2005, Persea $17.95 (978-0-89255-322-8). Lizzie, 14, is disappointed that her family won't discuss her adoption with her and her obsession with this secret affects her whole life; a novel told in verse. (Rev: BCCB 1/06; SLJ 1/06)

1447 Kehret, Peg. *Runaway Twin* (5–8). 2009, Dutton $16.99 (978-0-525-42177-1). Thirteen-year-old Sunny Skyland leaves her Nebraska foster home for Washington state on a quest to find the twin sister from whom she was separated ten years before. Lexile 740L (Rev: BLO 8/09; SLJ 12/09; VOYA 12/09)

1448 Kehret, Peg. *Sisters Long Ago* (5–8). 1992, Pocket paper $3.99 (978-0-671-78433-1). While surviving a near drowning, Willow has a glimpse of herself living another life in ancient Egypt. (Rev: SLJ 3/90)

1449 Kelly, Tom. *Finn's Going* (6–9). 2007, Greenwillow $16.99 (978-0-06-121453-0). When his identical twin brother dies, 10-year-old Danny feels that his very existence reminds others of their loss, and he runs away to the island where the family last vacationed together and there finally starts to overcome his grief. (Rev: BL 5/1/07; SLJ 6/07)

1450 Kelsey, Marybeth. *Tracking Daddy Down* (4–7). 2008, HarperCollins $16.99 (978-0-06-128842-5). Eleven-year-old Billie knows her father and uncle have robbed a bank and she hopes to persuade them to surrender. (Rev: LMC 3/09; SLJ 12/08)

1451 Kennedy, Marlane. *The Dog Days of Charlotte Hayes* (4–7). 2009, Greenwillow $15.99 (978-0-06-145241-3); LB $16.89 (978-0-06-145242-0). Eleven-year-old Charlotte, no dog lover, nonetheless works to find a better home for the St. Bernard her family neglects. *e* Lexile 790L (Rev: BL 2/15/09; SLJ 4/1/09)

1452 Kephart, Beth. *House of Dance* (7–10). 2008, HarperTeen $16.99 (978-0-06-142928-6). Fifteen-year-old Rosie's grandfather is dying, and she decides to bring back his youth by throwing a party with ballroom dancing. (Rev: BL 6/1–15/08; SLJ 7/08)

1453 Klass, David. *You Don't Know Me* (6–9). 2001, Farrar $17.00 (978-0-374-38706-8). John, 14, retreats into his own world when faced with abuse from his mother's boyfriend. (Rev: BCCB 2/01; BL 3/1/01; HB 7–8/01; HBG 10/01; SLJ 3/01; VOYA 6/01)

1454 Klein, Norma. *Breaking Up* (7–10). 1981, Avon paper $2.50 (978-0-380-55830-8). While visiting her divorced father in California, Alison falls in love with her best friend's brother.

1455 Klein, Norma. *Mom, the Wolfman and Me* (5–8). 1972, Avon paper $3.50 (978-0-380-00791-2). Brett's mother is single but the Wolfman is becoming more than a steady boyfriend.

1456 Klise, Kate. *Deliver Us from Normal* (5–8). 2005, Scholastic $16.95 (978-0-439-52322-6). Charles Harrisong, 11, is embarrassed by his abnormal family life in Normal, Illinois, and horrified when his parents decide to move them all to a houseboat off the Alabama coast. (Rev: BL 3/1/05; SLJ 5/05)

1457 Klise, Kate. *Far from Normal* (5–8). 2006, Scholastic $16.99 (978-0-439-79447-3). In this sequel to *Deliver Us from Normal* (2005), the Harrisong family makes a deal with the devil when a retailing giant threatens to sue over disparaging remarks made about the chain in a book written by Charles. (Rev: BL 10/15/06; VOYA 4/07)

1458 Knowles, Jo. *See You at Harry's* (6–9). 2012, Candlewick $16.99 (978-076365407-8). Twelve-year-old Fern's life goes from difficult to chaotic when tragedy hits her dysfunctional family. ALA Notable Books 2013. ⌒ e Lexile HL600L (Rev: BL 7/12; HB 9–10/12; LMC 10/12; SLJ 5/1/12; VOYA 4/12)

1459 Koertge, Ron. *Strays* (7–10). 2007, Candlewick $16.99 (978-0-7636-2705-8). After the death of his parents, 16-year-old Ted is placed in foster care and initially finds comfort in talking to animals but gradually learns to trust his roommates and other human beings. (Rev: BL 5/1/07; HB 7–8/07; SLJ 7/07)

1460 Kogler, Jennifer Anne. *Ruby Tuesday* (8–10). 2005, HarperCollins LB $16.89 (978-0-06-073957-7). The world of 13-year-old Ruby Tuesday Sweet is turned upside down when her father is arrested for the murder of a bookie. (Rev: BCCB 5/05; SLJ 4/05; VOYA 8/05)

1461 Krishnaswami, Uma. *Naming Maya* (5–8). 2004, Farrar $16.00 (978-0-374-35485-5). On a trip to India with her mother, 12-year-old Maya learns some important lessons about herself and the real reasons for the breakup of her parents' marriage. (Rev: BL 4/1/04; HB 7–8/04; SLJ 6/04; VOYA 6/04)

1462 Kuipers, Alice. *Lost for Words* (8–12). 2010, HarperCollins $16.99 (978-0-06-142922-4). Sophie, 16, finally begins to move on from her sister's death with help from her journal, a new friend, and a kind therapist. e Lexile HL650L (Rev: SLJ 5/10; VOYA 8/10*)

1463 LaFleur, Suzanne. *Eight Keys* (4–7). 2011, Random House $16.99 (978-0-385-74030-2); LB $19.99 (978-0-385-90833-7). Twelve-year-old orphan Elise is having trouble adapting to middle school when she discovers keys to rooms that her late father designed, which help her cope. (Rev: BL 9/1/11; SLJ 8/11)

1464 LaFleur, Suzanne. *Love, Aubrey* (4–7). 2009, Random House $15.99 (978-038573774-6); LB $18.99 (978-038590686-9). When her mother disappears after her father and sister die in a car accident, 11-year-old Aubrey struggles to cope. ⌒ (Rev: BL 8/09*; SLJ 9/09)

1465 Lantz, Francess. *Someone to Love* (7–10). 1997, Avon $14.00 (978-0-380-97477-1). Sara's secure family life changes when her parents decide to adopt the yet-unborn child of Iris, an unmarried teen. (Rev: BL 4/15/97)

1466 Leavitt, Martine. *Heck, Superhero!* (7–9). 2004, Front St $16.95 (978-1-886910-94-2). In this surprisingly upbeat tale, 13-year-old talented artist Heck, left homeless after the sudden disappearance of his mentally ill mother, wanders the streets in search of her. (Rev: BL 10/1/04; SLJ 10/04)

1467 Les Becquets, Diane. *Season of Ice* (8–12). 2008, Bloomsbury $16.95 (978-1-59990-063-6). When her father disappears one day, 17-year-old Genesis must deal not only with grief but also with helping to support her stepbrothers in this novel set in wintry northern Maine. (Rev: BL 1/1–15/08; HB 5–6/08; SLJ 4/08)

1468 Levoy, Myron. *The Witch of Fourth Street and Other Stories* (4–7). 1991, Peter Smith $19.75 (978-0-8446-6450-7); paper $5.99 (978-0-06-440059-6). Eight stories about growing up poor on the Lower East Side of New York City.

1469 Lewis, Beverly. *Whispers down the Lane* (5–8). Series: Summerhill Secrets. 1995, Bethany paper $5.99 (978-1-55661-476-7). An Amish girl agrees to hide Lissa, who has run away from her father's abusive treatment. (Rev: BL 9/1/95; SLJ 2/96)

1470 Lindbergh, Anne. *The Worry Week* (5–7). Illus. by Kathryn Hewitt. 1985, Harcourt $12.95 (978-0-15-299675-8); paper $2.95 (978-0-380-70394-4). Left alone with her sisters for a week in Maine, 11-year-old "Legs" spends most of her time tending to and worrying about her siblings. (Rev: BL 6/1/85; HB 9–10/85; SLJ 8/85)

1471 Little, Kimberley Griffiths. *The Healing Spell* (5–8). 2010, Scholastic $17.99 (978-0-545-16559-4). A healer in the Louisiana bayou gives 12-year-old Livie a spell to help coax her mother out of a coma. Lexile 800L (Rev: BL 6/10; LMC 8–9/10; SLJ 11/1/10)

1472 Love, D. Anne. *Picture Perfect* (6–9). 2007, Simon & Schuster $16.99 (978-0-689-87390-4). When Phoebe's mother decides to leave Texas and take a job in Nevada, Phoebe's life begins to change; she must deal with her dad befriending an attractive widow, her brother getting in trouble with the law, and her first love. (Rev: BL 5/1/07; SLJ 6/07)

1473 Lowenstein, Sallie. *Waiting for Eugene* (6–9). 2005, Lion Stone $19.00 (978-0-9658486-5-7). Twelve-year-old Sara Goldman's father suffers from mental illness and often retreats into memories of his nightmarish experiences in France during World War II. (Rev: BL 12/1/05; SLJ 11/05)

1474 Lowry, Lois. *Autumn Street* (7–9). 1980, Houghton Mifflin $16.00 (978-0-395-27812-3); paper $5.50 (978-0-440-40344-9). With her father away, Elizabeth and her mother and older sister move in with her grandmother. (Rev: BL 12/15/89)

1475 Lowry, Lois. *Find a Stranger, Say Goodbye* (7–10). 1978, Houghton Mifflin $18.00 (978-0-395-26459-1). A college-bound girl decides to find her natural mother.

1476 Lowry, Lois. *Rabble Starkey* (6–9). 1987, Houghton Mifflin $16.00 (978-0-395-43607-3). The story of a friendship between two girls (Rabble and Veronica), their 6th-grade year, and their many experiences with family and friends. (Rev: BL 3/15/87; SLJ 4/87; VOYA 4/87)

1477 Lowry, Lois. *Us and Uncle Fraud* (6–9). 1984, Houghton Mifflin $16.00 (978-0-395-36633-2). Uncle Claude visits his sister and her four children and an experience in human relations begins.

1478 Luger, Harriett. *Bye, Bye, Bali Kai* (5–7). 1996, Harcourt paper $5.00 (978-0-15-200863-5). Suzie's family hits rock bottom when they are evicted and forced to live in an abandoned building. (Rev: BCCB 3/96; BL 6/1–15/96; SLJ 6/96; VOYA 6/96)

1479 Lupica, Mike. *Miracle on 49th Street* (5–8). 2006, Philomel $17.99 (978-0-399-24488-9). The life of pro basketball star Josh Cameron is turned upside down when 12-year-old Molly Parker turns up claiming to be his daughter. ⋒ (Rev: BL 9/1/06; SLJ 11/06)

1480 Lurie, April. *Dancing in the Streets of Brooklyn* (5–9). 2002, Delacorte LB $17.99 (978-0-385-90066-9). Judy, from a Norwegian immigrant family, is devastated to learn that the man she knows as "Pa" is not her birth father in this novel set in 1944. (Rev: BCCB 12/02; BL 11/15/02; HBG 3/03; SLJ 9/02)

1481 Lynch, Chris. *The Big Game of Everything* (7–10). 2008, HarperTeen $16.99 (978-006074034-4); LB $17.89 (978-006074035-1). Jock and his younger brother Egon spend a summer working at their grandfather's golf course and learn the importance of integrity versus material gain. Lexile 830L (Rev: BL 9/1/08; HB 9–10/08; SLJ 10/1/08; VOYA 8/08)

1482 Lyon, Annabel. *All-Season Edie* (5–7). 2008, Orca paper $8.95 (978-1-55143-713-2). Edie, 11, flirts with witchcraft as a solution to her family's problems and to aid her in her quest for coolness; this is a fast-paced first-person narrative full of humor. (Rev: BL 3/1/08)

1483 Lytton, Deborah. *Jane in Bloom* (5–8). 2009, Dutton $16.99 (978-0-525-42078-1). When 12-year-old Jane's "perfect" older sister Lizzie dies of anorexia, Jane's parents separate and the girl is left to cope by herself — which she does with the aid of a babysitter, a puppy, a digital camera, and a new friend. ❤ Lexile HL540L (Rev: BL 2/15/09; SLJ 5/1/09)

1484 McCord, Patricia. *Pictures in the Dark* (7–10). 2004, Bloomsbury $16.95 (978-1-58234-848-3). Set in the 1950s, this is the story of two sisters, one 12 and the other 15, and how their mother gradually sank into insanity. (Rev: BL 5/15/04; HB 7–8/04; SLJ 5/04)

1485 MacCullough, Carolyn. *Drawing the Ocean* (8–11). 2006, Roaring Brook $16.95 (978-1-59643-092-1). Sadie, a gifted 16-year-old artist, wants to fit in and be popular at her new school but finds it hard when her dead twin brother still haunts her and she's drawn to an outcast poet named Ryan. (Rev: BL 11/15/06; LMC 2/07; SLJ 2/07)

1486 McDonald, Janet. *Off-Color* (7–12). 2007, Farrar $16.00 (978-0-374-37196-8). When her single mother gets a job on the other side of Brooklyn, 15-year-old Cameron has to leave her white neighborhood and move to the projects, where she learns about diversity and a secret about her absentee father. (Rev: BL 8/07; SLJ 3/08)

1487 McDonald, Janet. *Spellbound* (7–12). 2001, Farrar $16.00 (978-0-374-37140-1). Despite enormous obstacles, 16-year-old African American mother Raven decides to enter a spelling bee in hopes of going to college. (Rev: BCCB 10/01; BL 11/1/01; HB 1–2/02; HBG 3/02; SLJ 9/01; VOYA 10/01)

1488 Mack, Tracy. *Birdland* (7–10). 2003, Scholastic $16.95 (978-0-439-53590-8). Jed's family has not recovered from the death of his brother Zeke, and Jed finds some comfort in videotaping their neighborhood and finding links to Zeke through the poems and journal he left. Sidney Taylor Book Honor 2003. (Rev: BL 10/15/03*; SLJ 10/03)

1489 McKay, Hilary. *Caddy Ever After* (6–9). 2006, Simon & Schuster $15.95 (978-1-4169-0930-9). The youngest members of the Casson family narrate this funny, moving fourth installment in the series, which focuses on Caddy's proposed marriage to someone other than Darling Michael. (Rev: BL 6/1–15/06; HB 7–8/06; SLJ 7/06)

1490 McKay, Hilary. *Caddy's World* (4–7). 2012, Simon & Schuster $16.99 (978-144244105-7). In this prequel to the series about the Casson family, 12-year-old Caddy is thrown for a loop when her newest sibling, Rose, is born prematurely and her mother decamps for the hospital, leaving her father to look after the family. ❤ Lexile 770L (Rev: BL 5/1/12*; HB 3–4/12; SLJ 3/12*; VOYA 2/12)

1491 McKay, Hilary. *Forever Rose* (4–7). 2008, Simon & Schuster $16.99 (978-1-4169-5486-6). Rose, part of the flighty and dramatic Casson family, gets her own book in the series, in which she and her friends cook up a dangerous adventure and her family unveils a series of surprises. (Rev: BL 4/1/08; SLJ 5/08)

1492 McKay, Hilary. *Indigo's Star* (5–8). 2004, Simon & Schuster $15.95 (978-0-689-86563-3). In this sequel to *Saffy's Angel* (2002), Saffy's younger siblings — 12-year-old Indigo and 8-year-old Rose — take a stand against school bullies with the help of a lonely young American called Tom. (Rev: BL 9/15/04; SLJ 9/04*)

1493 McKay, Hilary. *Permanent Rose* (6–9). 2005, Simon & Schuster $15.95 (978-1-4169-0372-7). This third volume of a fast-paced series about the eccentric and colorful Casson family finds all four children — Cadmium, Indigo, Saffron, and Rose — struggling with their individual crises during a hot summer in England. (Rev: BCCB 6/05; BL 5/15/05; HB 7–8/05; SLJ 6/05; VOYA 12/05)

1494 McKay, Hilary. *Saffy's Angel* (4–7). 2002, Simon & Schuster $16.00 (978-0-689-84933-6). Saffron learns she was adopted into her artistic family and travels to Italy in search of her roots. (Rev: BCCB 5/02; BL 5/15/02; HB 7–8/02*; HBG 10/02; SLJ 5/02)

1495 Mackel, Kathy. *Boost* (6–9). 2008, Dial $16.99 (978-080373240-7). In this action-filled glimpse into teen competitive sports, elite basketball player Savvy and her sister, cheerleader Callie, cope with family problems and the pressures to always be faster, stronger, and better. e (Rev: BL 10/1/08; LMC 1–2/09; SLJ 9/1/08*; VOYA 10/08)

1496 McKinnon, Hannah Roberts. *Franny Parker* (5–8). 2009, Farrar $16.00 (978-0-374-32469-8). Animal-loving Franny, 12, has been expecting another long hot Oklahoma summer with the usual activities, but then a boy and his mother move in next door and she learns about a different kind of life. (Rev: BCCB 9/09; BL 4/1/09; SLJ 7/09*)

1497 McKinnon, Hannah Roberts. *The Properties of Water* (4–7). 2010, Farrar $16.99 (978-0-0374-36145-). When her older sister Marni is paralyzed in a diving accident, 12-year-old Lacey's life is turned upside down. (Rev: BL 11/1/10; SLJ 12/1/10)

1498 MacLachlan, Patricia. *All the Places to Love* (5–8). 1994, HarperCollins LB $18.89 (978-0-06-021099-1). This picture book celebrates the love found in an extended rural family and the joy that a new arrival brings. (Rev: BCCB 7–8/94; BL 6/1–15/94*; SLJ 6/94)

1499 MacLachlan, Patricia. *Cassie Binegar* (4–7). 1982, HarperCollins paper $5.99 (978-0-06-440195-1). Cassie is not happy with the disorder in her family situation.

1500 Mansfield, Creina. *Cherokee* (5–8). 2001, O'Brien paper $7.95 (978-0-86278-368-6). Gene's wonderful life with his jazz musician grandfather, Cherokee, comes to an end when his aunt decides he needs a home and an education. (Rev: SLJ 11/01)

1501 Marchetta, Melina. *Saving Francesca* (8–10). 2004, Knopf LB $17.99 (978-0-375-92982-3). Unhappy with life at her new Australian high school, Francesca desperately needs the help and support of her mother, who is struggling with her own battle against depression. (Rev: BL 10/1/04; SLJ 9/04; VOYA 10/04)

1502 Marino, Jan. *For the Love of Pete* (5–8). 1994, Avon paper $3.50 (978-0-380-72281-5). Three devoted servants take Phoebe on a journey to find the father she has never met. (Rev: BCCB 7–8/93; BL 6/1–15/93; SLJ 5/93*)

1503 Martin, Nora. *The Eagle's Shadow* (6–9). 1997, Scholastic paper $15.95 (978-0-590-36087-6). Twelve-year-old Clearie is sent to live with Tlingit relatives in Alaska and comes to accept the desertion by her mother. (Rev: BL 8/97; HBG 3/98; SLJ 10/97; VOYA 4/98)

1504 Martin, Patricia A. *Travels with Rainie Marie* (5–7). 1997, Hyperion LB $16.49 (978-0-7868-2212-6). When there is no one to care for her and her five brothers and sisters, Rainie Marie is afraid that her bossy aunt will try to split up the family among various relatives. (Rev: BL 5/15/97; SLJ 7/97)

1505 Martinez, Arturo O. *Pedrito's World* (5–7). 2007, Texas Tech Univ. $16.95 (978-0-89672-600-0). In rural south Texas in 1941, 6-year-old Pedrito describes the important things in his life — his first day of school, the death of a friend, a Christmas celebration, his first words of English. (Rev: BL 5/1/07)

1506 Martinez, Jessica. *The Space Between Us* (8–12). 2012, Simon & Schuster $16.99 (978-144242055-7). Amelia, 17, has been looking after her irresponsible younger sister for years, and now finds herself reluctantly accompanying a pregnant Charly to Canada for a year. e Lexile HL640L (Rev: BL 11/1/12; SLJ 4/13; VOYA 2/13)

1507 Mason, Simon. *Moon Pie* (5–8). 2011, Random House $16.99 (978-038575235-0); LB $19.99 (978-038575237-4). Martha, 11, looks after her little brother Tug after her mother's death as her father struggles with his drinking. e (Rev: BL 11/15/11; HB 11–12/11)

1508 Masterman-Smith, Virginia. *First Mate Tate* (7–9). 2000, Marshall Cavendish $14.95 (978-0-7614-5075-7). When her father's gambling brings the family close to financial ruin, First Mate Tate thinks up daring schemes to keep her family afloat. (Rev: BL 10/15/00; HBG 3/01; SLJ 9/00)

1509 Matas, Carol. *Sparks Fly Upward* (4–8). 2002, Clarion $15.00 (978-0-618-15964-2). Set in Manitoba in the early 20th century, this is the story of 12-year-old Rebecca, a Jewish girl, and her life with a Ukrainian foster family. (Rev: BCCB 7–8/02; BL 4/1/02; HBG 10/02; SLJ 3/02)

1510 Matthews, Kezi. *Flying Lessons* (5–7). 2002, Cricket $16.95 (978-0-8126-2671-1). A girl in a small southern town bonds with an eclectic bunch of adults after the airplane in which her mother was traveling disappears. (Rev: BL 12/15/02; HB 1–2/03; HBG 3/03; SLJ 12/02; VOYA 6/03)

1511 Matthews, Kezi. *John Riley's Daughter* (6–9). 2000, Front St $15.95 (978-0-8126-2775-6). Memphis feels responsible when her mentally disabled aunt, Clover, runs off in this story of tangled family ties. (Rev: BCCB 6/00; HB 7–8/00; HBG 9/00; SLJ 7/00)

1512 Mazer, Norma Fox. *After the Rain* (7–10). 1987, Avon paper $5.99 (978-0-380-75025-2). Rachel gradually develops a warm relationship with her terminally ill grandfather who is noted for his bad temper. (Rev: BL 5/1/87; SLJ 5/87; VOYA 6/87)

1513 Mazer, Norma Fox. *D, My Name Is Danita* (6–8). 1991, Scholastic $13.95 (978-0-590-43655-7). The latest in this light series presents an interesting premise:

Girl meets boy who turns out to be her older half-brother. (Rev: BL 4/1/91; SLJ 3/91)

1514 Mazer, Norma Fox. *Downtown* (7–10). 1984, Avon paper $4.95 (978-0-380-88534-3). Pete, 15, the son of anti-war demonstrators who are in hiding, faces problems when his mother reappears and wants to be part of his life.

1515 Mazer, Norma Fox. *Missing Pieces* (7–10). 1995, Morrow $16.00 (978-0-688-13349-8). A 14-year-old seeks a missing part of her life by looking for a father who abandoned her. (Rev: BL 4/1/95; SLJ 4/95*; VOYA 5/95)

1516 Mazer, Norma Fox. *What I Believe* (5–8). 2005, Harcourt $16.00 (978-0-15-201462-9). When Vicki's father loses his job and the family's fortunes go into free fall, Vicki finds the resulting changes hard to accept and reveals in her poems and journal her coping strategies. (Rev: BL 9/15/05; SLJ 10/05)

1517 Mead, Alice. *Junebug in Trouble* (5–8). 2002, Farrar $16.00 (978-0-374-33969-2). Young Junebug and his mother move out of the housing projects, but Junebug continues to get into the trouble his mother was hoping to avoid. (Rev: BCCB 6/02; BL 4/15/02; HB 5–6/02; HBG 10/02; SLJ 3/02)

1518 Mead, Alice. *Madame Squidley and Beanie* (4–7). 2004, Farrar $16.00 (978-0-374-34688-1). Ten-year-old Beanie's mother has chronic fatigue syndrome and her illness is affecting the 5th-grader's life. (Rev: BL 4/15/04; SLJ 6/04)

1519 Michaels, Rune. *Nobel Genes* (6–9). 2010, Simon & Schuster $16.99 (978-1-4169-1259-0). A young boy struggles to satisfy the demands of his manic-depressive mother, who claims he was conceived with sperm from a Nobel Prize winner; the truth that eventually emerges is even more unsettling. **e** Lexile 940L (Rev: BL 8/10; LMC 11–12/10; SLJ 11/1/10; VOYA 10/10)

1520 Miles, Betty. *Just the Beginning* (6–8). 1978, Avon paper $2.50 (978-0-380-01913-7). Being relatively poor in an upper-class neighborhood causes problems for 13-year-old Catherine Myers.

1521 Modiano, Patrick. *Catherine Certitude* (4–7). Trans. by William Rodarmor. Illus. by Jean-Jacques Sempé. 2001, Godine $17.95 (978-0-87923-959-6). An adult Catherine reminisces about her life as a youngster in Paris — living with her father, puzzling over his job, going to ballet classes, eating in restaurants — in this stylishly illustrated chapter book delivered in picture-book format. (Rev: BL 12/15/01; HBG 3/02; SLJ 2/02)

1522 Monninger, Joseph. *Wish* (5–8). 2010, Delacorte $17.99 (978-0-385-73941-2); LB $20.99 (978-0-385-90788-0). Fifteen-year-old Bee sets out to give her little brother Tommy, an 11-year-old with cystic fibrosis, the experience of a lifetime — a chance to swim with sharks. **e** (Rev: BL 12/1/10*; SLJ 1/1/11)

1523 Montgomery, L. M. *Anne of Green Gables* (7–9). 1995, Puffin paper $4.99 (978-0-14-036741-6). This is a reissue of the classic Canadian story of Anne and how she was gradually accepted in a foster home. Her story continued in *Anne of Avonlea, Anne of the Island, Anne of Windy Poplars, Anne's House of Dreams,* and *Anne of Ingleside.*

1524 Montgomery, L. M. *Christmas with Anne and Other Holiday Stories* (4–7). 1996, McClelland & Stewart $12.95 (978-0-7710-6204-9). A collection of 16 short pieces and stories (two from the Anne of Green Gables books) that deal with Christmas. (Rev: BL 9/1/96)

1525 Montgomery, L. M. *Emily of New Moon* (7–9). 1986, Bantam paper $4.99 (978-0-553-23370-4). Beginning when Emily is only 11, this trilogy continues in *Emily Climbs* and *Emily's Quest* and tells about the making of a writer. These are reissues.

1526 Monthei, Betty. *Looking for Normal* (5–8). 2005, HarperCollins LB $16.89 (978-0-06-072506-8). Annie, 12, and her younger brother are sent to live with their grandparents after their father kills their mother and then himself; unfortunately, life does not improve as they must cope with Grandma's drinking and abuse and Grandpa's indifference. (Rev: BL 6/1–15/05; SLJ 4/05)

1527 Moore, Ishbel. *Daughter* (6–12). 1999, Kids Can $16.95 (978-1-55074-535-1). Sylvie struggles to cope with her parents' divorce and her mother's Alzheimer's disease in this moving story. (Rev: BCCB 12/99; BL 11/15/99; HBG 4/00; SLJ 11/99)

1528 Mori, Kyoko. *One Bird* (8–12). 1996, Fawcett paper $6.50 (978-0-449-70453-0). A coming-of-age story set in Japan about 15-year-old girl Megumi, who loses her mother yet finds people who understand and love her. (Rev: BL 10/15/95; SLJ 11/95; VOYA 2/96)

1529 Mourlevat, Jean-Claude. *The Pull of the Ocean* (5–8). Trans. by Y. Mauder. 2006, Delacorte $15.95 (978-0-385-73348-9). In this modern version of "Tom Thumb," Yann — the smallest and youngest of seven — leads his six older brothers (three sets of twins) away from their dismal home to the ocean that's far to the west, meeting many characters along the way. Batchelder Award 2007. (Rev: BL 12/1/06; SLJ 1/07*)

1530 Murray, Kirsty. *The Secret Life of Maeve Lee Kwong* (6–9). Series: Children of the Wind. 2008, Allen & Unwin paper $8.95 (978-18650873-7-5). When 13-year-old Maeve's mother dies, the Chinese-Irish girl considers her options and sets out on a quest to find her unknown father, traveling from Australia to Hong Kong and Ireland. (Rev: BLO 8/08; SLJ 5/08; VOYA 8/08)

1531 Murray, Martine. *How to Make a Bird* (8–12). 2010, Scholastic $16.99 (978-0-439-66951-1). Manon, 17, travels from the Australian countryside to Melbourne, where she hopes to come to terms with family tragedies. **e** (Rev: BL 4/15/10; LMC 8–9/10; SLJ 8/10)

1532 Myracle, Lauren. *Peace, Love, and Baby Ducks* (8–12). 2009, Dutton $16.99 (978-052547743-3). Privileged Atlanta teen sisters Anna and Carly deal with boys, looks, and emerging belief systems as they navigate family and school life. ⌒ Lexile HL630L (Rev: BL 4/15/09; HB 7–8/09; SLJ 8/09; VOYA 8/09)

1533 Nelson, Jandy. *The Sky Is Everywhere* (8–11). 2010, Dial $17.99 (978-0-8037-3495-1). When Lennie's popular older sister suddenly dies, the 17-year-old struggles to fill her shoes — which include a fiancé and the lead role in Romeo and Juliet. ⌒ ℮ (Rev: BL 1/1–15/10; HB 3–4/10; SLJ 3/10; VOYA 8/10)

1534 Nelson, Theresa. *Earthshine* (5–9). 1994, Orchard LB $17.99 (978-0-531-08717-6). "Slim" decides to live with her father and his lover, who is dying of AIDS. At a support group, she meets Isaiah, whose pregnant mother also has AIDS. (Rev: BL 9/1/94; SLJ 9/94*; VOYA 10/94)

1535 Nelson, Theresa. *Ruby Electric* (5–8). 2003, Simon & Schuster $16.95 (978-0-689-83852-1). The movie script she is writing brings 12-year-old Ruby needed relief from the realities of her life. (Rev: BL 7/03; HB 7–8/03; HBG 10/03; SLJ 6/03*; VOYA 10/03)

1536 Newman, John. *Mimi* (4–7). 2011, Candlewick $15.99 (978-0-7636-5415-3). Mimi's mother was killed in an accident and everyone in the family — even the dog — is having trouble dealing with this; the fact that Mimi was adopted from China is mentioned in passing. (Rev: BLO 9/1/11; SLJ 9/1/11)

1537 Nicholls, Sally. *Season of Secrets* (5–8). 2011, Scholastic $16.99 (978-0-545-21825-2). Sisters Hannah and Molly are sent to live with their grandparents in northern England after their mother's death, and there they cope very differently with their grief, Molly increasingly absorbed in an inner world. ℮ Lexile 620L (Rev: BL 12/15/10; HB 1–2/11; LMC 5–6/11; SLJ 2/1/11)

1538 Nielsen, Susin. *Dear George Clooney, Please Marry My Mom* (5–8). 2010, Tundra $18.95 (978-0-88776-977-1). Fed up with her phony new stepmom, and her mother's out-of-control dating, 12-year-old Violet decides that George Clooney would be the perfect dad replacement. ℮ (Rev: BL 9/1/10; SLJ 9/1/10; VOYA 10/10)

1539 Nielsen, Susin. *The Reluctant Journal of Henry K. Larsen* (5–8). 2012, Tundra $17.95 (978-177049372-8). Thirteen-year-old Henry is advised by a therapist to keep a journal as he tries to cope with the upheaval in his family after his older brother kills a school bully and then himself. ℮ Lexile 630L (Rev: BLO 9/15/12; SLJ 1/13*; VOYA 12/12)

1540 Nixon, Joan Lowery. *Maggie Forevermore* (5–8). 1987, Harcourt $13.95 (978-0-15-250345-1). In this sequel to *Maggie, Too* and *And Maggie Makes Three* (both o.p.), 13-year-old Maggie resents spending Christmas with her father and his new wife in California. (Rev: BCCB 4/87; BL 3/1/87; SLJ 3/87)

1541 Nuzum, K. A. *A Small White Scar* (6–9). 2006, HarperCollins $15.99 (978-0-06-075639-0). Will, 15, tries to leave home to become a cowboy, but things get complicated when his brother Denny, who has Down syndrome, follows him. (Rev: BL 8/06; SLJ 8/06*)

1542 Oates, Joyce Carol. *Freaky Green Eyes* (7–10). 2003, HarperCollins LB $17.89 (978-0-06-623757-2). Franky, 15, recounts the tensions between her artist mother and her abusive, controlling father and the buildup to her mother's eventual disappearance. (Rev: BL 12/1/03; HB 11–12/03; HBG 4/04; SLJ 10/03; VOYA 10/03)

1543 O'Connor, Sheila. *Sparrow Road* (5–8). 2011, Putnam $16.99 (978-0-399-25458-1). Raine, 12, ends up meeting her estranged father when she accompanies her mother to a remote artists' retreat for the summer. ℮ Lexile 530L (Rev: BL 7/11*; LMC 10/11; SLJ 7/11)

1544 Olson, Gretchen. *Call Me Hope* (4–7). 2007, Little, Brown $15.99 (978-0-316-01236-2). Beaten down by her mother's verbal abuse, 11-year-old Hope screws up the courage to confront her mother and tell her how badly she has been hurt by the name calling. (Rev: BL 3/15/07; SLJ 5/07)

1545 Omololu, C. J. *Dirty Little Secrets* (7–10). 2010, Walker $16.99 (978-0-8027-8660-9). High school sophomore Lucy is determined to hide the fact that her mother is a hoarder, and when she finds her mother dead from an asthma attack amid the stacks of junk, Lucy decides to take drastic action. ⌒ ℮ Lexile 890L (Rev: BL 10/1509; LMC 3–4/10; SLJ 2/10)

1546 Oughton, Jerrie. *Perfect Family* (6–9). 2000, Houghton Mifflin $15.00 (978-0-395-98668-4). Set in a small town in North Carolina in the 1950s, this is the story of a girl named Welcome, an unwanted pregnancy, and the family that loves and supports her. (Rev: BL 4/15/00; HBG 9/00; SLJ 4/00; VOYA 6/00)

1547 Palmer, Robin. *Yours Truly, Lucy B. Parker: Girl vs. Superstar* (5–7). 2010, Putnam $15.99 (978-0-399-25489-5). Plagued by family, friendship, and puberty problems, 12-year-old Lucy writes to Dr. Maude, a famous psychologist, for advice about handling her complicated life. Lexile 1080L (Rev: BL 6/10; LMC 8–9/10; SLJ 4/10)

1548 Paratore, Coleen Murtagh. *Willa by Heart* (6–9). Series: Wedding Planner's Daughter. 2008, Simon & Schuster $15.99 (978-1-4169-4076-0). In this third installment in the series, Willa has a busy summer helping to plan two weddings, preparing to become a big sister, and worrying about a beautiful new girl in town. (Rev: BL 2/1/08; SLJ 4/08)

1549 Park, Barbara. *The Graduation of Jake Moon* (5–8). 2000, Simon & Schuster $15.00 (978-0-689-83912-2). Jake Moon finds it impossible to cope with his grandfather's gradual disintegration from Alzheimer's disease. (Rev: BCCB 12/00; BL 6/1–15/00; HB 9–10/00; HBG 3/01; SLJ 9/00)

1550 Parkinson, Siobhan. *Blue like Friday* (4–7). 2008, Roaring Brook $16.95 (978-1-59643-340-3). In Ireland, tweens Olivia and Hal are unlikely friends but Olivia helps Hal to accept his mother's fiancé. (Rev: BL 3/1/08; SLJ 6/08)

1551 Paterson, Katherine. *Come Sing, Jimmy Jo* (6–10). 1985, Avon paper $3.99 (978-0-380-70052-3). The family decides it's time to include James in their singing group. (Rev: BL 9/1/87; SLJ 4/85)

1552 Paterson, Katherine. *Jacob Have I Loved* (6–10). 1980, HarperCollins LB $17.89 (978-0-690-04079-1); paper $6.99 (978-0-06-440368-9). A story set in the Chesapeake Bay region about the rivalry between two sisters. Newbery Medal 1981.

1553 Paterson, Katherine. *Park's Quest* (4–7). 1989, Puffin paper $5.99 (978-0-14-034262-8). A boy searches for the cause of his father's death in Vietnam. (Rev: BCCB 4/88; HB 7–8/88; SLJ 5/88)

1554 Paterson, Katherine. *The Same Stuff as Stars* (5–7). 2002, Clarion $15.00 (978-0-618-24744-8). An unhappy 11-year-old Angel and her younger brother Bernie are sent to live with their father's grandmother, where Angel finds comfort in a mysterious man who introduces her to astronomy. (Rev: BCCB 10/02; BL 9/15/02; HB 9–10/02; HBG 3/03; SLJ 8/02*)

1555 Patneaude, David. *Framed in Fire* (6–9). 1999, Albert Whitman LB $15.99 (978-0-8075-9098-0). Peter Larson, who lives with his mother and verbally abusive stepfather, discovers that his mother has lied to him about the death of his real father and sets out to find the truth. (Rev: BCCB 5/99; HBG 9/99; SLJ 4/99)

1556 Patterson, Janci. *Chasing the Skip* (7–10). 2012, Henry Holt $16.99 (978-0-8050-9391-9). Abandoned by her neglectful mother, 15-year-old Ricki finds herself chasing bail jumpers with the bounty hunter father she hardly knows. e Lexile HL620L (Rev: BL 10/15/12; LMC 3–4/13; SLJ 11/12)

1557 Paul, Dominique. *The Possibility of Fireflies* (7–10). 2006, Simon & Schuster $15.95 (978-1-4169-1310-8). Ellie, 14, lives with an abusive, alcoholic mother and a rebellious older sister but tries to make right choices and looks for support from a neighbor named Leo. (Rev: BL 11/15/06; SLJ 11/06)

1558 Paulsen, Gary. *The Winter Room* (6–8). 1989, Watts LB $16.99 (978-0-531-08439-7). A quiet novel about an 11-year-old boy growing up on a farm in Minnesota. (Rev: BL 11/1/89; SLJ 10/89; VOYA 12/89)

1559 Pearsall, Shelley. *All Shook Up* (5–8). 2008, Knopf $15.99 (978-0-375-83698-5). Josh's divorced dad has a new girlfriend and a new job as an Elvis impersonator, much to Josh's horror. (Rev: BL 5/1/08; SLJ 7/08)

1560 Peck, Richard. *Father Figure* (7–10). 1996, Puffin paper $6.99 (978-0-14-037969-3). Jim and his younger brother are sent to live in Florida with a father they scarcely know.

1561 Peck, Robert Newton. *Bro* (7–9). 2004, HarperCollins $16.99 (978-0-06-052974-1). When his parents' sudden death forces 9-year-old Tug to return to his grandfather's ranch, the scene of an earlier trauma, the boy's older brother, Bro, escapes from a prison labor camp to rescue him; a compelling story set in 1930s Florida. (Rev: BL 3/15/04; SLJ 8/04; VOYA 6/04)

1562 Peck, Robert Newton. *A Day No Pigs Would Die* (7–9). 1973, Knopf $25.00 (978-0-394-48235-4); paper $5.50 (978-0-679-85306-0). A Shaker farm boy in Vermont must give up his pet pig to help his family. (Rev: BL 3/1/89)

1563 Pfeffer, Susan Beth. *Blood Wounds* (8–12). 2011, Harcourt $16.99 (978-0-547-49638-2). Willa's settled life begins to fall apart when her estranged biological father sets out on a murderous rampage. e Lexile HL620L (Rev: BL 9/15/11; SLJ 8/11; VOYA 12/11)

1564 Pfeffer, Susan Beth. *Devil's Den* (4–7). 1998, Walker $15.95 (978-0-8027-8650-0). Joey faces the pain of rejection when he seeks out his real father, discovers he is not wanted by him, and must accept living permanently with his mom and loving stepfather. (Rev: BCCB 5/98; BL 5/15/98; HBG 10/98; SLJ 6/98)

1565 Prose, Francine. *Bullyville* (7–9). 2007, HarperTeen $16.99 (978-0-06-057497-0). Eighth-grader Bart faces extreme bullying when he gets a scholarship to Bailywell prep school not long after his father dies in the September 11 attacks. (Rev: BL 9/1/07; SLJ 8/07)

1566 Provoost, Anne. *My Aunt Is a Pilot Whale* (6–9). Trans. by Ria Bleumer. 1995, Women's paper $12.95 (978-0-88961-202-0). A story of family relationships and friendship but also of incest. (Rev: BL 3/1/95)

1567 Resau, Laura. *What the Moon Saw* (6–9). 2006, Delacorte $15.95 (978-0-385-73343-4). Fourteen-year-old Clara travels from Maryland to a remote part of Mexico to visit her father's parents for the first time and learns a lot about her family and herself while there. (Rev: BL 10/15/06; LMC 2/07; SLJ 9/06)

1568 Reynolds, Marilyn. *Baby Help: True-to-Life Series from Hamilton High* (8–12). Series: Hamilton High. 1998, Morning Glory $15.95 (978-1-885356-26-0); paper $8.95 (978-1-885356-27-7). Partner-abuse is explored in this novel about a teenage mother who is living with a difficult boyfriend and his unsympathetic mother. (Rev: BL 2/1/98; HBG 9/98; SLJ 3/98; VOYA 6/98)

1569 Reynolds, Marilyn. *Shut Up!* (8–12). 2008, Morning Glory $15.96 (978-193253893-9); paper $9.95 (978-193253888-5). Seventeen-year-old Mario desperately attempts to get help when he finds his brother is being abused by his aunt's boyfriend in this inspiring story of a strong family coping with conflict. **e** (Rev: BL 11/15/08; SLJ 2/1/09; VOYA 12/08)

1570 Rinn, Miriam. *The Saturday Secret* (4–7). 1998, Alef Design Group paper $7.95 (978-1-881283-26-3). Jason's resentment and anger at having to obey the strict rules imposed by his devout Orthodox Jewish stepfather are made more intense because of his grief at the death of his beloved father. (Rev: BL 10/1/98; SLJ 2/99)

1571 Rodowsky, Colby. *That Fernhill Summer* (5–8). 2006, Farrar $16.00 (978-0-374-37442-6). When her grandmother becomes ill, biracial teen Kiara confronts family problems and develops relationships with two white cousins she didn't know existed. (Rev: BL 4/15/06; SLJ 6/06)

1572 Rosenthal, Betsy R. *Looking for Me* (4–7). 2012, Houghton Mifflin $15.99 (978-054761084-9). The fourth of 12 children in a Jewish family in 1936 Baltimore, 11-year-old Edith finds it difficult to establish her own identity. **e** (Rev: BL 4/15/12; SLJ 4/12)

1573 Rottman, S. L. *Shadow of a Doubt* (7–10). 2003, Peachtree $14.95 (978-1-56145-291-0). Shadow is newly 15 and entering high school when his brother Daniel, who has been missing for years, reappears on the scene, suspected of murder. (Rev: BCCB 1/04; BL 11/15/03; HBG 4/04; SLJ 1/04; VOYA 12/03)

1574 Russo, Marisabina. *A Portrait of Pia* (5–8). 2007, Harcourt $17.00 (978-0-15-205577-6). Overwhelmed by her brother's schizophrenia and her mother's new boyfriend, 12-year-old Pia, already a talented artist, travels to Italy to meet her long-absent father and learns how to love her family despite its flaws. (Rev: BL 4/1/07; SLJ 8/07)

1575 Ryan, Darlene. *Rules for Life* (7–12). 2004, Orca paper $7.95 (978-1-55143-350-9). Sixteen-year-old Izzy, whose mother died two years earlier, has difficulty coming to terms with her father's decision to remarry; suitable for reluctant readers. (Rev: BCCB 2/05; SLJ 3/05; VOYA 6/05)

1576 Ryan, Pam Muñoz. *Paint the Wind* (4–7). 2007, Scholastic $16.99 (978-0-439-87362-8). On the death of her grandmother — who has been a distant and strict guardian — orphaned 11-year-old Maya is sent to relatives in Wyoming, where she learns about the love of horses and family. (Rev: BL 11/15/07; LMC 1/08; SLJ 11/07)

1577 Sachs, Marilyn. *Baby Sister* (7–10). 1986, Avon paper $3.50 (978-0-380-70358-6). Penny is torn between her admiration for her older sister and the realization that she is really selfish. (Rev: BL 2/15/86; SLJ 8/86; VOYA 8/86)

1578 Sachs, Marilyn. *Just Like a Friend* (6–9). 1990, Avon paper $2.95 (978-0-380-70964-9). The friendship between a mother and a daughter falls apart when fa-

ther has a heart attack. (Rev: BL 10/15/89; SLJ 12/89; VOYA 12/89)

1579 St. Anthony, Jane. *Grace Above All* (5–7). 2007, Farrar $16.00 (978-0-374-39940-5). In this gentle story set in the 1960s, 13-year-old Grace expects to have a boring summer watching over her siblings but a neighboring boy and Great Aunt Hilda provide unexpected interest. (Rev: BL 5/15/07; SLJ 7/07)

1580 Salmansohn, Karen. *Wherever I Go, There I Am* (4–7). Illus. by author. Series: Alexandra Rambles On! 2002, Tricycle $12.95 (978-1-58246-079-6). Alexandra's journal reveals her angst about issues such as scary movies and becoming a teenager. (Rev: HBG 3/03; SLJ 2/03)

1581 Sand-Eveland, Cyndi. *A Tinfoil Sky* (6–8). 2012, Tundra $17.95 (978-1-77049-294-3). Twelve-year-old Mel has been living with her mother in their car until her mom is caught shoplifting and Mel must move in with her grandmother. **e** (Rev: BL 3/1/12; SLJ 3/12; VOYA 4/12)

1582 Savage, Deborah. *Summer Hawk* (7–10). 1999, Houghton Mifflin $16.00 (978-0-395-91163-1). In this coming-of-age story, 15-year-old Taylor has trouble relating to her mother and father, shuns the company of Rail Bogart, the other smart kid in her school, and showers her attention and affection on a young hawk she rescues. (Rev: BCCB 6/99; BL 3/1/99; HBG 9/99; SLJ 4/99; VOYA 4/99)

1583 Seagraves, Donny Bailey. *Gone from These Woods* (4–7). 2009, Delacorte $15.99 (978-0-385-73629-9). With help from a school counselor, Daniel — whose father is an abusive alcoholic — tries to come to terms with the hunting accident in which he shot and killed his beloved uncle. (Rev: BCCB 9/09; BLO 5/27/09; SLJ 9/09)

1584 Sebestyen, Ouida. *Far from Home* (7–10). 1980, Little, Brown $15.95 (978-0-316-77932-6). An orphaned boy is taken in by a couple who run a boardinghouse and there he uncovers secrets about his family's past.

1585 Seidler, Tor. *Brothers Below Zero* (5–8). 2002, HarperCollins LB $15.89 (978-0-06-029180-8). Artistic Tim, overwhelmed by his athletic younger brother, eventually runs away to the place he has felt most valued. (Rev: BCCB 3/02; BL 1/1–15/02; HBG 10/02; SLJ 4/02)

1586 Shafer, Audrey. *The Mailbox* (5–7). 2006, Delacorte $15.95 (978-0-385-73344-1). Twelve-year-old Gabe, who has been happy with Uncle Vernon after years in foster care, is shocked when he comes home to find Uncle Vernon dead. ∩ (Rev: SLJ 11/06)

1587 Shearer, Alex. *The Great Blue Yonder* (5–8). 2002, Clarion $15.00 (978-0-618-21257-6). Twelve-year-old Harry, who has died in an accident, experiences afterlife on the Other Side and has the opportunity to review his relations with other family members. (Rev: BCCB 6/02; HBG 10/02; SLJ 4/02; VOYA 6/02)

1588 Sheinmel, Courtney. *All the Things You Are* (5–8). 2011, Simon & Schuster $15.99 (978-1-4169-9717-7). Twelve-year-old Carly's mother is arrested for embezzling, and this has an impact on the whole family, particularly affecting Carly's school life. (Rev: BLO 6/21/11; SLJ 7/11)

1589 Sheinmel, Courtney. *My So-Called Family* (5–8). 2008, Simon & Schuster $15.99 (978-1-4169-5785-0). Thirteen-year-old Leah sets out to discover her father — an anonymous sperm donor — and her four recently revealed half-siblings, one of whom is about her age. (Rev: BCCB 10/08; BL 11/15/08; SLJ 12/08)

1590 Shimko, Bonnie. *Letters in the Attic* (7–12). 2002, Academy Chicago $23.50 (978-0-89733-511-9). Twelve-year-old Lizzie and her mother move to upstate New York after her father leaves home, and there Lizzie finds new attachments and a new understanding of her mother's behavior. (Rev: VOYA 4/03)

1591 Shusterman, Neal. *What Daddy Did* (7–10). 1991, Little, Brown paper $15.95 (978-0-316-78906-6). A young boy recounts the story of how his father murdered his mother and how he ultimately comes to understand and forgive him. (Rev: BL 7/91; SLJ 6/91)

1592 Simmons, Michael. *Vandal* (7–10). 2006, Roaring Brook $16.95 (978-1-59643-070-9). In a story laced with tragedy, 16-year-old guitar player Will struggles to forge a relationship with his destructive older brother. (Rev: BL 7/06; HB 7–8/06; LMC 11–12/06; SLJ 6/06)

1593 Slate, Joseph. *Crossing the Trestle* (5–8). 1999, Marshall Cavendish $14.95 (978-0-7614-5053-5). Set in West Virginia in 1944, this novel centers on 11-year-old Petey and the problems he and his family face after their father is killed in an accident. (Rev: BCCB 12/99; BL 1/1–15/00; HBG 3/00; SLJ 10/99)

1594 Smith, Anne Warren. *Sister in the Shadow* (7–10). 1986, Avon paper $2.75 (978-0-380-70378-4). In competition with her successful younger sister, Sharon becomes a live-in baby-sitter, with unhappy results. (Rev: BL 5/1/86; SLJ 5/86; VOYA 8/86)

1595 Snyder, Laurel. *Bigger Than a Bread Box* (5–8). 2011, Random House $16.99 (978-0-375-86916-7); LB $19.99 (978-037596916-4). Twelve-year-old Rebecca turns to a magical bread box for help in putting her fractured family back together. ∩ e Lexile 680L (Rev: BL 10/1/11; SLJ 9/1/11)

1596 Sones, Sonya. *One of Those Hideous Books Where the Mother Dies* (7–12). 2004, Simon & Schuster $15.95 (978-0-689-85820-8). In this free-verse novel, a high schooler, after the death of her mother, is sent to live with her father, a famous movie actor whom she detests. (Rev: BL 5/1/04*; SLJ 8/04)

1597 Sonnenblick, Jordan. *Notes from the Midnight Driver* (8–11). 2006, Scholastic $16.99 (978-0-439-75779-9). Unhappy about his parents' separation, 16-year-old Alex drives drunk and ends up with a sentence of 100 hours of community service at a nursing home, during which he ends up learning some very valuable life lessons from an older man named Solomon. (Rev: BL 10/1/06; SLJ 10/06)

1598 Sparks, Beatrice, ed. *Finding Katie: The Diary of Anonymous, a Teenager in Foster Care* (7–10). 2005, Avon paper $5.99 (978-0-06-050721-3). In this angst-filled fictional diary, Katie, a teenager living on a California estate, makes it clear that money and privilege do nothing to ensure a happy life. (Rev: SLJ 10/05)

1599 Spollen, Anne. *The Shape of Water* (7–10). 2008, Flux paper $9.95 (978-0-7387-1101-0). Fifteen-year-old Magda initially grieves her artistic mother's death by committing arson and imagining talking fish. (Rev: BLO 6/17/08; SLJ 6/08)

1600 Springer, Nancy. *Separate Sisters* (5–7). 2001, Holiday $16.95 (978-0-8234-1544-1). Two teenage girls deal with the divorce of their parents in different ways. (Rev: BCCB 2/02; BL 2/1/02; HB 3–4/02; HBG 10/02; SLJ 2/02; VOYA 4/02)

1601 Stacey, Cherylyn. *How Do You Spell Abducted?* (4–8). 1996, Red Deer paper $7.95 (978-0-88995-148-8). When their divorced father abducts Deb, Paige, and Cory, the three youngsters must escape from his home in the U.S. and make their way back to their mother in Canada. (Rev: SLJ 12/96)

1602 Stauffacher, Sue. *Harry Sue* (5–8). 2005, Knopf LB $17.99 (978-0-375-93274-8). Both her parents are in prison and 11-year-old Harry Sue Clotkin acts as tough as she can in the face of a difficult life with her grandmother. (Rev: BL 5/1/05; SLJ 8/05)

1603 Stevenson, Robin. *Escape Velocity* (7–10). 2011, Orca paper $12.95 (978-15546986-6-0). After her father has a stroke, 15-year-old Lou is sent to live with her mother, a writer who abandoned her when she was only a few days old. e Lexile HL630L (Rev: BL 12/1/11; LMC 1–2/12; SLJ 1/12)

1604 Strauss, Linda Leopold. *Really, Truly, Everything's Fine* (5–8). 2004, Marshall Cavendish $15.95 (978-0-7614-5163-1). Life changes dramatically for 14-year-old Jill Rider when her father is arrested for jewelry theft. (Rev: BL 5/15/04; SLJ 7/04)

1605 Summers, Laura. *Desperate Measures* (4–7). 2011, Putnam $16.99 (978-0-399-25616-5). Vicky, 13, her mentally disabled twin sister Rhianna, and their younger brother Jamie run away to their aunt's cottage to avoid being split up by the foster care system. (Rev: LMC 11–12/11; SLJ 7/11)

1606 Swanson, Julie A. *Going for the Record* (7–12). 2004, Eerdmans paper $8.00 (978-0-8028-5273-1). High school soccer star Leah Weiczynkowski finds herself torn between family responsibilities and her sports aspirations when her father is diagnosed with terminal cancer. (Rev: BL 9/1/04*; SLJ 8/04; VOYA 10/04)

1607 Sweeney, Joyce. *Headlock: A Novel* (8–10). 2006, Henry Holt $16.95 (978-0-8050-8018-6). Kyle, 18, wants to become a professional wrestler but must put his dream aside when his grandmother becomes ill. (Rev: BL 11/1/06; SLJ 11/06)

1608 Talbert, Marc. *The Purple Heart* (5–8). 1992, HarperCollins $14.95 (978-0-06-020428-0); paper $3.50 (978-0-380-71985-3). Luke's father has returned from Vietnam an anguished, brooding war hero, and Luke loses his father's Purple Heart, leading to confrontation and reconciliation. (Rev: BL 12/15/91*; SLJ 2/92)

1609 Thesman, Jean. *The Last April Dancers* (7–10). 1987, Avon paper $2.75 (978-0-380-70614-3). Catherine tries to recover from the guilt caused by her father's suicide through friendship and love of a neighboring boy. (Rev: BL 9/15/87; SLJ 10/87; VOYA 10/87)

1610 Thomson, John. *A Small Boat at the Bottom of the Sea* (5–7). 2005, Milkweed $16.95 (978-1-57131-657-8); paper $6.95 (978-1-57131-656-1). Upset and angry when he's sent to spend the summer with his ex-con uncle and dying aunt on Puget Sound, 12-year-old Donovan begins to develop a closer relationship with his uncle as his vacation progresses. (Rev: SLJ 10/05; VOYA 4/06)

1611 Tilly, Meg. *Porcupine* (5–8). 2007, Tundra $15.95 (978-0-88776-810-1). Jacqueline and her younger brother and sister go to Canada to live with a great-grandmother after their father dies in Afghanistan. (Rev: BL 11/15/07; SLJ 12/07)

1612 Torres, Laura. *Crossing Montana* (7–10). 2002, Holiday $16.95 (978-0-8234-1643-1). Callie sets off on a journey across Montana in search of her missing grandfather, and in the process finds out the truth about her father's death. (Rev: BCCB 10/02; BL 8/02; HBG 10/02; SLJ 7/02; VOYA 8/02)

1613 Trembath, Don. *The Popsicle Journal* (7–12). 2001, Orca paper $6.95 (978-1-55143-185-7). Fledgling journalist Harper Winslow finds himself torn between professional responsibility and family loyalty when his sister is involved in a DUI auto accident while his father is running for mayor. (Rev: SLJ 7/02; VOYA 4/02)

1614 Trueman, Terry. *Cruise Control* (7–10). 2004, HarperCollins LB $16.89 (978-0-06-623961-3). High school senior Paul McDaniel is a star athlete, but he's filled with rage over his brother's disabilities and his father's desertion; a companion to *Stuck in Neutral* (2000). (Rev: BCCB 11/04; BL 3/15/05; SLJ 1/05; VOYA 10/04)

1615 Underdahl, S. T. *The Other Sister* (7–12). 2007, Flux paper $8.95 (978-0-7387-0933-8). The happy, secure life of 15-year-old Josey Muller is turned upside

down when her parents tell her that she has an older sister, conceived when they were in high school and given up for adoption. (Rev: SLJ 3/07)

1616 Valgardson, W. D. *Frances* (6–10). 2000, Groundwood $15.95 (978-0-88899-386-1); paper $5.95 (978-0-88899-397-7). Growing up in Manitoba, young Frances probes into her Icelandic background and uncovers many family secrets, past and present. (Rev: BL 9/1/00; HBG 3/01; SLJ 9/00; VOYA 2/01)

1617 Van Draanen, Wendelin. *Runaway* (6–9). 2006, Knopf $15.95 (978-0-375-83522-3). After Holly's mother dies of a drug overdose, Holly initially goes to foster homes but decides that being on her own is better; she keeps a journal as she makes her way to Los Angeles, struggling to find food, shelter, and warmth. (Rev: BL 9/1/06; SLJ 9/06)

1618 Van Steenwyk, Elizabeth. *Three Dog Winter* (5–8). 1987, Walker $13.95 (978-0-8027-6718-9). A story of dog racing, this family tale tells of 12-year-old Scott and his Malamute, Kaylah. (Rev: BL 2/1/88; SLJ 12/87)

1619 Velasquez, Gloria. *Rina's Family Secret* (8–12). Series: Roosevelt High School. 1998, Arte Publico paper $9.95 (978-1-55885-233-4). Puerto Rican teenager Rina cannot endure life with her alcoholic stepfather, and so moves in with her grandmother. Also use *Tyrone's Betrayal*. 2006, Arte Publico paper $9.95 (978-1-55885-233-4). Puerto Rican teenager Rina cannot endure life with her alcoholic stepfather, and so moves in with her grandmother. Also use *Tyrone's Betrayal* (2006). (Rev: BL 8/98; SLJ 10/98)

1620 Viglucci, Patricia C. *Sun Dance at Turtle Rock* (5–7). 1996, Patri paper $4.95 (978-0-9645914-9-3). The child of a racially mixed marriage feels uncomfortable when he visits his white grandfather. (Rev: BL 4/15/96)

1621 Villareal, Ray. *My Father, the Angel of Death* (5–8). 2006, Piñata paper $9.95 (978-1-55885-466-6). Newly relocated to Texas and unhappy with his home life, Jesse Baron wonders what life would be like if his dad were not the well-known wrestler called the Angel of Death; suitable for reluctant readers. (Rev: SLJ 10/06)

1622 Vincent, Zu. *The Lucky Place* (7–10). 2008, Front St $17.95 (978-1-932425-70-3). Cassie struggles with the reality of having a stepfather as well as an "Old Daddy," especially when her stepfather becomes ill. (Rev: BL 5/1/08; SLJ 5/08)

1623 Voigt, Cynthia. *Dicey's Song* (5–9). 1982, Macmillan $17.95 (978-0-689-30944-1). This story of Dicey's life with her "Gram" in Maryland won a Newbery Medal (1983). Preceding it was *Homecoming* (1981) and a sequel is *A Solitary Blue* (1983). (Rev: BL 12/15/89)

1624 Waldorf, Heather. *Grist* (7–10). 2006, Red Deer paper $9.95 (978-0-88995-347-5). Sixteen-year-old Charlie decides to spend the summer with her grandmother at Lake Ringrose, Ontario, and discovers some secrets about her past while there. (Rev: BL 11/1/06; SLJ 1/07)

1625 Walker, Pamela. *Pray Hard* (5–8). 2001, Scholastic paper $15.95 (978-0-439-21586-2). After Amelia Forest's father dies in an airplane accident for which she feels responsible, her life and that of her family fall apart. ∩ (Rev: BL 3/1/01; HBG 10/01; SLJ 7/01; VOYA 8/01)

1626 Wallace, Bill. *Beauty* (5–7). 1988, Holiday $16.95 (978-0-8234-0715-6). Luke finds the adjustment difficult when he and his mother go to live on his grandfather's Oklahoma farm. (Rev: BCCB 11/88; BL 2/1/89; SLJ 10/88)

1627 Wallace, Bill. *True Friends* (4–7). 1994, Holiday $15.95 (978-0-8234-1141-2). Everything in Courtney's life becomes a shambles and she must rely on her new friend Judy to help her. (Rev: BCCB 11/94; BL 10/15/94; SLJ 10/94)

1628 Wallace, Rich. *Perpetual Check* (8–11). 2009, Knopf $15.99 (978-037584058-6); LB $18.99 (978-037594058-3). Brothers Zeke and Randy face off against each other in chess while growing closer and making important discoveries about life. **e** Lexile 750L (Rev: BL 1/1–15/09; SLJ 2/1/09; VOYA 6/09)

1629 Walsh, Marissa. *A Field Guide to High School* (7–9). 2007, Delacorte $14.99 (978-0-385-73410-3). When Andie's perfect sister Claire leaves for college she gives Andie a field guide, full of advice on how to navigate the world of private high school. (Rev: BL 6/1–15/07; SLJ 9/07)

1630 Watson, Renée. *What Momma Left Me* (5–8). 2010, Bloomsbury $16.99 (978-1-59990-446-7). African American Serenity, 13, tells how she and her brother cope when they go to live with their grandparents after their mother dies and their father disappears. (Rev: BL 5/1/10; LMC 10/10; SLJ 8/10; VOYA 8/10)

1631 Weeks, Sarah. *My Guy* (4–7). 2001, HarperCollins LB $14.89 (978-0-06-028370-4). Guy and Lana agree on only one thing — they don't want to become part of a blended family — and they set out to make sure it won't happen. (Rev: BCCB 6/01; BL 8/01; HB 7–8/01; HBG 10/01; SLJ 5/01)

1632 Weissenberg, Fran. *The Streets Are Paved with Gold* (7–9). 1990, Harbinger paper $6.95 (978-0-943173-51-1). Debbie is from a poor immigrant Jewish family and she is ashamed to bring her friends home. (Rev: BL 8/90; SLJ 8/90)

1633 Welch, Sheila Kelly. *Waiting to Forget* (6–9). 2011, Namelos $18.95 (978-1-60898-114-4); paper $9.95 (978-1-60898-115-1). Told in two narratives — Now and Then, this is the compelling story of T.J. and his younger sister, who have suffered tumultuous lives in foster care and who now face more turmoil as Angela lies in a coma. **e** (Rev: BL 12/1/11; LMC 3–4/12*; SLJ 12/1/11)

1634 Wenberg, Michael. *Seattle Blues* (5–8). 2009, WestSide $16.95 (978-1-934813-04-1). When unhappy 13-year-old Maya, spending a reluctant summer with her grandmother in Seattle, finds a musical instrument hidden in the attic she also finds the key to growing into a happier person. (Rev: BLO 1/14/09; SLJ 7/09)

1635 Werlin, Nancy. *The Rules of Survival* (7–10). 2006, Dial $16.99 (978-0-8037-3001-4). Written as a letter to his younger sister Emmy, Matt tells the story of their abusive mother, their everyday struggles to stay safe, and their search for an adult who is willing to help free them from the situation. (Rev: BL 8/06; SLJ 9/06)

1636 White, Ellen Emerson. *The President's Daughter* (7–10). 2008, Feiwel & Friends paper $8.99 (978-0-312-37488-4). Meg Powers, 16, is not pleased when her mother runs for and wins the presidency; an update of a book first published in 1984. (Rev: BL 8/08)

1637 White, Ellen Emerson. *White House Autumn* (7–10). 1985, Avon paper $2.95 (978-0-380-89780-3). The daughter of the first female president of the United States feels her family is coming apart after an assassination attempt on her mother. (Rev: BL 11/1/85; SLJ 2/86; VOYA 4/86)

1638 White, Ruth. *Belle Prater's Boy* (5–9). 1996, Farrar $17.00 (978-0-374-30668-7). Set in Appalachia in the 1950s, this moving, often humorous story tells about Gypsy and her unusual cousin Woodrow, who hides a secret involving his mother's disappearance. (Rev: BL 4/15/96; SLJ 4/96*)

1639 White, Ruth. *A Month of Sundays* (6–8). 2011, Farrar $16.99 (978-0-374-39912-2). When her mother takes off to make a fresh start, 14-year-old Garnet finds a surprisingly supportive friend in her Aunt June, sister of the father she never met. **e** (Rev: BL 8/11*; LMC 1–2/12; SLJ 10/1/11)

1640 White, Ruth. *Tadpole* (5–8). 2003, Farrar $16.00 (978-0-374-31002-8). In this novel set in 1950s Appalachia, uncertain 10-year-old Carolina finds her own strengths when her 13-year-old cousin Tadpole arrives, running away from an abusive uncle. (Rev: BL 5/1/03; HB 5–6/03; HBG 10/03; SLJ 3/03*)

1641 Whittemore, Jo. *Odd Girl In* (5–7). 2011, Simon & Schuster paper $6.99 (978-1-4424-1284-2). Unruly Alex, 12, and her older twin brothers are enrolled in a good behavior program after one prank too many, and, despite the various challenges, the whole experience turns out well in this novel full of humor. **e** (Rev: SLJ 3/1/11)

1642 Wilder, Laura Ingalls. *Little House in the Big Woods* (4–7). Illus. by Garth Williams. 1953, HarperCollins LB $17.89 (978-0-06-026431-4); paper $6.99 (978-0-06-440001-5). Outstanding story of a log-cabin family in Wisconsin in the late 1800s. Also use *By the Shores of Silver Lake; Farmer Boy; Little House on the Prairie; Long Winter; On the Banks of Plum Creek; These Happy Golden Years* (all 1953); *Little Town on the Prairie* (1961); *The First Four Years* (1971).

1643 Williams, Carol Lynch. *Glimpse* (8–11). 2010, Simon & Schuster $16.99 (978-1-4169-9730-6). In free verse, Williams tells the story of two sisters who together face the difficulties of living with an alcoholic, prostitute mother; when Lizzie attempts suicide, the younger Hope plumbs her memories of abuse. **e** Lexile 630L (Rev: BL 4/15/10; LMC 10/10; SLJ 8/10)

1644 Williams, Suzanne Morgan. *Bull Rider* (7–10). 2009, Simon & Schuster $16.99 (978-141696130-7). Fourteen-year-old Cam enters a bull-riding competition to win prize money to help with his brother's rehabilitation from injuries suffered in Iraq. **e** (Rev: BL 1/1–15/09; SLJ 4/1/09)

1645 Williams-Garcia, Rita. *P.S. Be Eleven* (4–7). 2013, Amistad $16.99 (978-006193862-7). Delphine and her younger sisters are back in Brooklyn where they find things changed — Pa has a girlfriend, Uncle Darnell is back from Vietnam but is not the same, and 6th grade poses new challenges for Delphine, who shares them with her mother in California; the sequel to *One Crazy Summer* (2010). ∩ **e** Lexile 770L (Rev: BL 2/15/13*; HB 5–6/13; SLJ 6/13)

1646 Willis, Patricia. *The Barn Burner* (5–8). 2000, Clarion $15.00 (978-0-395-98409-3). In 1933, 14-year-old Ross, a runaway, becomes involved with the Warfield family whose father is away looking for work. (Rev: BCCB 5/00; BL 4/15/00; HBG 10/00; SLJ 7/00)

1647 Wilson, Jacqueline. *Cookie* (4–7). Illus. by Nick Sharratt. 2009, Roaring Brook $16.99 (978-1-59643-534-6). Beauty Cookson and her mother flee the abusive, boorish yet wealthy Mr. Cookson and start a new life of their own in this endearing tale of redemption. ∩ Lexile 680L (Rev: BL 9/1/09; LMC 11–12/09; SLJ 10/09)

1648 Wilson, Nancy Hope. *Mountain Pose* (5–7). 2001, Farrar $17.00 (978-0-374-35078-9). Ellie is surprised to inherit her grandmother's farm, but when she reads the diaries left for her she begins to understand more about her family. (Rev: BCCB 6/01; BL 8/01; HB 7–8/01; HBG 10/01; SLJ 4/01*; VOYA 6/01)

1649 Wolff, Virginia Euwer. *Make Lemonade* (7–12). Series: Make Lemonade. 1993, Henry Holt $17.95 (978-0-8050-2228-5). Rooted in the community of poverty, this story offers a penetrating view of the conditions that foster ignorance, destroy self-esteem, and challenge strength. (Rev: BL 6/1–15/93*; SLJ 7/93*; VOYA 10/93)

1650 Wood, Maryrose. *The Unseen Guest* (4–7). Series: The Incorrigible Children of Ashton Place. 2012, HarperCollins $15.99 (978-006179118-5). The three children raised by wolves threaten to undo their years of training by nanny Penelope and return to the wild. ∩ **e** (Rev: BL 3/15/12*; SLJ 4/12; VOYA 4/12)

1651 Woodson, Jacqueline. *Hush* (5–9). 2002, Putnam $15.99 (978-0-399-23114-8). A girl and her family are relocated in the witness protection program after her father, a police officer, testifies against fellow cops in a case that involves racial prejudice. (Rev: BCCB 3/02; BL 1/1–15/02; HB 1–2/02; HBG 10/02; SLJ 2/02*; VOYA 2/02)

1652 Woodson, Jacqueline. *Miracle's Boys* (6–10). 2000, Putnam $15.99 (978-0-399-23113-1). Twelve-year-old African American LaFayette, growing up in a poor inner-city environment, is cared for by his oldest brother who is also responsible for the troubled middle brother, Charlie. (Rev: BL 2/15/00; HB 3–4/00; HBG 9/00; SLJ 5/00; VOYA 4/00)

1653 Woodson, Jacqueline. *Peace, Locomotion* (4–7). 2009, Putnam $15.99 (978-0-399-24655-5). In letters to his little sister Lili, who is living in a separate foster home, 12-year-old Lonnie describes his life and his fears for his foster brother who is away at war. Odyssey Honor Recording 2010. ∩ (Rev: BCCB 1/09; BL 12/15/08; HB 1/09; LMC 5/09; SLJ 1/09)

1654 Woodworth, Chris. *When Ratboy Lived Next Door* (4–8). 2005, Farrar $16.00 (978-0-374-34677-5). Twelve-year-old Lydia takes an instant dislike to her new neighbor Willis and his pet raccoon, but as she gains a better understanding of the family dynamics that make the boy who he is, she also gains valuable insights into her strained relationship with her mother. (Rev: BCCB 2/05; BL 1/1–15/05; SLJ 3/05)

1655 Wylie, Sarah. *All These Lives* (8–12). 2012, Farrar $17.99 (978-0-374-30208-5). On the assumption that she has nine lives, 16-year-old Dani aims to give her remaining ones to her twin sister Jena, who has leukemia. **e** Lexile 800L (Rev: LMC 11–12/12*; SLJ 7/12; VOYA 8/12)

1656 Zarr, Sara. *How to Save a Life* (8–12). 2011, Little, Brown $17.99 (978-0-316-03606-1). Seventeen-year-old Jill is still struggling to deal with her father's sudden death when her mother announces that she plans to adopt a baby and that the expectant Mandy will be coming to live with them until the delivery; told from the perspectives of the two troubled teens. YALSA Top Ten Best Fiction for Young Adults 2012. ∩ **e** Lexile HL710L (Rev: BL 11/1/11*; HB 1–2/12; SLJ 12/1/11*; VOYA 12/11)

Physical and Emotional Problems

1657 Abbott, Tony. *Firegirl* (5–8). 2006, Little, Brown $15.99 (978-0-316-01171-6). Tom, already an outsider at his Catholic school, bravely befriends a girl scarred by burns even when his classmates ostracize and ridicule her. (Rev: BL 7/06; SLJ 7/06)

1658 Arnold, Elana K. *Sacred* (8–11). 2012, Delacorte $17.99 (978-038574211-5); LB $20.99 (978-037599042-7). Scarlett struggles with anorexia and depression after her older brother dies, and finds some solace in her beloved horse and a strange boy named Will. ℮ (Rev: BL 10/15/12; SLJ 3/13; VOYA 2/13)

1659 Baskin, Nora Raleigh. *Anything But Typical* (4–7). 2009, Simon & Schuster $15.99 (978-1-4169-6378-3). This deftly told story centers on Jason, an autistic 6th-grader who can create dynamic stories and relationships on paper but is painfully at a loss in social situations. ALA Notable Books 2010. ∩ (Rev: BCCB 4/09; BL 2/1/09; HB 5/09; SLJ 3/09)

1660 Bingham, Kelly. *Shark Girl* (7–10). 2007, Candlewick $16.99 (978-0-7636-3207-6). When she's attacked by a shark and loses an arm, 15-year-old Jane feels divorced from her former popular self and has trouble adjusting to her new life. (Rev: BL 5/1/07; SLJ 6/07)

1661 Blackstone, Matt. *A Scary Scene in a Scary Movie* (6–9). 2011, Farrar $16.99 (978-0-374-36421-2). An unexpected new friend gets obsessive-compulsive Rene, 14, out of his shell in this believable story. ℮ Lexile 850L (Rev: BL 8/11; SLJ 8/11)

1662 Blume, Judy. *Deenie* (5–8). 1982, Dell paper $5.50 (978-0-440-93259-8). Instead of becoming a model, Deenie must cope with scoliosis and wearing a back brace.

1663 Borris, Albert. *Crash into Me* (8–12). 2009, Simon & Schuster $16.99 (978-141697435-2). Four suicidal teenagers set off on a road trip planning to kill themselves when they reach their destination, but things change along the way. Lexile HL530L (Rev: BL 5/15/09; SLJ 8/09; VOYA 12/09)

1664 Brooks, Bruce. *Vanishing* (5–8). 1999, HarperCollins LB $14.89 (978-0-06-028237-0). A challenging novel about a hospitalized girl who gives up eating so she can't be sent home to her dysfunctional family, and the boy she meets who is in remission from a fatal disease. (Rev: BL 5/15/99; HB 5–6/99; HBG 10/99; SLJ 6/99; VOYA 10/99)

1665 Brothers, Meagan. *Debbie Harry Sings in French* (8–12). 2008, Henry Holt $16.95 (978-0-8050-8080-3). Johnny, who has struggled with alcohol and bullies who think he is gay, is encouraged by his girlfriend to pursue his passion and sing in drag. (Rev: BL 4/1/08; SLJ 9/08)

1666 Brown, Kay. *Willy's Summer Dream* (6–9). 1989, Harcourt $13.95 (978-0-15-200645-7). Willy lacks confidence because he is a slow learner. (Rev: BL 2/1/90; SLJ 12/89)

1667 Bryson, Bill. *Choices* (7–10). 2007, Roaring Brook $16.95 (978-1-59643-217-8). Kathleen finds herself switching between realities after her brother is killed on his way to pick her up; when she meets Luke, this

"phase shifting" takes on more meaning. (Rev: BL 9/1/07; SLJ 10/07)

1668 Buchanan, Dawna Lisa. *The Falcon's Wing* (6–9). 1992, Orchard paper $16.99 (978-0-531-08586-8). A teenage girl learns to understand and defend her retarded cousin. (Rev: BL 2/1/92; SLJ 4/92)

1669 Buckley, James. *The Very Ordered Existence of Merilee Marvelous* (5–8). 2007, Greenwillow $16.99 (978-0-06-123197-1). Marilee, a bright young girl with Asperger's syndrome, enjoys order in her life until a new boy in town — Biswick, who has fetal alcohol syndrome — decides to attach himself to her. (Rev: BL 9/1/07; SLJ 10/07)

1670 Butts, Nancy. *Cheshire Moon* (5–7). 1996, Front St $14.95 (978-1-886910-08-9). A friendless deaf girl grieves for a cousin who has drowned at sea in this novel in an island setting. (Rev: BL 10/15/96; SLJ 11/96; VOYA 4/97)

1671 Byars, Betsy. *The Summer of the Swans* (5–7). Illus. by Ted Coconis. 1970, Puffin paper $5.99 (978-0-14-031420-5). The story of a 14-year-old named Sara — moody, unpredictable, and on the brink of womanhood — and how her life changes when her younger, mentally retarded brother disappears. Newbery Medal 1971.

1672 Carter, Anne Laurel. *In the Clear* (4–7). 2001, Orca paper $6.95 (978-1-55143-192-5). A 12-year-old Canadian polio survivor in the 1950s works through her fears and struggles to recapture her lost childhood. (Rev: BL 11/15/01; SLJ 1/02)

1673 Castan, Mike. *Fighting for Dontae* (6–12). 2012, Holiday $16.95 (978-082342348-4). A tough Mexican American kid with gang connections learns the value of kindness when he begins helping a severely disabled kid in his special education class. Lexile 750L (Rev: BL 7/12; LMC 3–4/13; SLJ 5/1/12*)

1674 Chappell, Crissa-Jean. *Total Constant Order* (7–10). 2007, HarperTeen $16.99 (978-0-06-088605-9). Plagued by obsessive-compulsive behavior, 9th-grader Frances (called Fin) finds some relief when she meets Thayer, who has ADD, and starts seeing a new therapist. (Rev: BL 11/15/07; SLJ 1/08)

1675 Cleaver, Vera, and Bill Cleaver. *Me Too* (7–9). 1973, HarperCollins $13.95 (978-0-397-31485-0); paper $2.95 (978-0-06-440161-6). Linda is convinced that she can make her slightly retarded sister normal.

1676 Coffelt, Nancy. *Listen* (8–11). 2009, WestSide $16.95 (978-1-934813-07-2). In alternating narratives, this compelling, fast-paced novel introduces 18-year-old orphan Will, whose lonely life intersects with those of troubled 14-year-old Kurt and middle-aged schizophrenic Carrie. Lexile HL770L (Rev: BL 9/1/09; SLJ 12/09)

1677 Cole, Barbara. *Alex the Great* (8–12). 1989, Rosen LB $12.95 (978-0-8239-0941-4). The events leading up to Alex's drug overdose are told first by Alex and then by her friend, Deonna. (Rev: VOYA 8/89)

1678 Cooner, Donna. *Skinny* (7–10). 2012, Scholastic $17.99 (978-0-545-42763-0). Obese Ever, 15, realizes that self-hatred is her biggest problem after gastric bypass surgery helps her drop over a hundred pounds. ∩ ℮ Lexile 670L (Rev: BL 10/15/12; LMC 1–2/13; SLJ 10/12; VOYA 8/12)

1679 Cormier, Robert. *The Bumblebee Flies Anyway* (7–12). 1983, Dell paper $4.99 (978-0-440-90871-5). A terminally ill boy and his gradual realization of his situation.

1680 Crane, E. M. *Skin Deep* (7–10). 2008, Delacorte $16.99 (978-0-385-73479-0). Andrea, 16, befriends a woman named Honora, who is dying of cancer but teaches the unhappy girl a lot about life. (Rev: BL 1/1–15/08; SLJ 5/08)

1681 Cummings, Priscilla. *Blindsided* (6–10). 2010, Dutton $16.99 (978-0-525-42161-0). Natalie, 14, is losing her eyesight and struggles to accept this reality and learn special skills at her new school for the blind. ℮ Lexile 710L (Rev: BL 6/10; LMC 10/10; SLJ 7/10; VOYA 8/10)

1682 Davis, Rebecca Fjelland. *Jake Riley: Irreparably Damaged* (7–10). 2003, HarperCollins LB $16.89 (978-0-06-051838-7). Lainey, a farm girl, struggles to cope with her friend Jake, a 15-year-old with frightening emotional problems. (Rev: BL 9/1/03; HBG 10/03; SLJ 7/03; VOYA 10/03)

1683 de la Peña, Matt. *I Will Save You* (8–11). 2010, Delacorte $16.99 (978-038573827-9); LB $19.99 (978-038590719-4). Seventeen-year-old Kidd flees his group home and struggles to find a new life at the beach, but the past soon catches up with him; a tense and complex tale. (Rev: BL 12/15/10; LMC 5–6/11)

1684 Denenberg, Barry. *Mirror, Mirror on the Wall: The Diary of Bess Brennan* (4–8). Series: Dear America. 2002, Scholastic paper $10.95 (978-0-439-19446-4). When she comes home at weekends, 12-year-old Bess, who has lost her sight, shares her new life and school experiences with her twin sister, in this novel set in the Depression that includes many details of how the blind cope. (Rev: BL 10/1/02; HBG 3/03; SLJ 10/02)

1685 Denman, K. L. *Me, Myself and Ike* (7–10). 2009, Orca paper $12.95 (978-1-55469-086-2). Encouraged to commit suicide by his antagonistic companion Ike, who is in reality the result of a schizophrenia-induced hallucination, 17-year-old Kit, once popular and even-tempered, becomes increasingly insular and paranoid. ℮ (Rev: BL 11/1/09; SLJ 12/09; VOYA 12/09)

1686 Dewey, Jennifer Owlings. *Borderlands* (7–12). 2002, Marshall Cavendish $14.95 (978-0-7614-5114-3). When Jamie, an unhappy 17-year-old, is hospital-ized after a suicide attempt she finds new friends and slowly comes to terms with her difficult relationship with her parents. (Rev: BL 9/1/02; HBG 10/02; SLJ 7/02)

1687 Diersch, Sandra. *Ceiling Stars* (7–12). Series: SideStreets. 2004, Lorimer paper $4.99 (978-1-55028-834-6). The close friendship of two high school girls is put to the test when one falls victim to mental illness and begins acting strangely; suitable for reluctant readers. (Rev: SLJ 1/05)

1688 Diezeno, Patricia. *Why Me? The Story of Jenny* (7–10). 1976, Avon paper $3.50 (978-0-380-00563-5). A young rape victim doesn't know how to cope.

1689 Dooley, Sarah. *Livvie Owen Lived Here* (6–9). 2010, Feiwel & Friends $16.99 (978-0-312-61253-5). Ninth-grader Livvie's autistic behavior has forced her family to move many times, but Livvie longs to find the perfect home. ∩ ℮ (Rev: BL 8/10; LMC 11–12/10; SLJ 9/1/10; VOYA 10/10)

1690 Doyle, Malachy. *Georgie* (6–10). 2002, Bloomsbury $13.95 (978-1-58234-753-0). Georgie, 14, who has buried horrible memories under a cloak of isolation, slowly learns to trust his teacher and recovers his sanity. (Rev: BCCB 11/02; BL 9/1/02; SLJ 7/02; VOYA 12/03)

1691 Draper, Sharon M. *Out of My Mind* (5–8). 2010, Simon & Schuster $16.99 (978-1-4169-7170-2). Intelligent 10-year-old Melody, who has cerebral palsy, describes the frustrations of her life, which are somewhat alleviated when she gets a specially adapted computer and can interact with students in a regular classroom. ∩ ℮ Lexile 700L (Rev: BL 1/1/10*; HB 3–4/10; LMC 5–6/10; SLJ 3/10)

1692 Draper, Sharon M. *Tears of a Tiger* (7–10). 1994, Atheneum $16.95 (978-0-689-31878-8). A star basketball player is killed in an accident after he and his friends drink and drive. The driver, who survives, is depressed and ultimately commits suicide. (Rev: BL 11/1/94; SLJ 2/95)

1693 Dreyer, Ellen. *The Glow Stone* (8–12). 2006, Peachtree $15.95 (978-1-56145-370-2). When 15-year-old Phoebe begins to suspect that her uncle's death was not an accident, she journeys into a metaphorical and actual cave. (Rev: SLJ 7/06)

1694 Edwards, Johanna. *The Next Big Thing* (8–12). 2005, Berkley paper $14.00 (978-0-425-20028-5). Kat, determined to lose weight to win the heart of her online boyfriend, lands a spot on a reality TV makeover show but finds in the end that she likes herself just the way she is. (Rev: SLJ 11/05)

1695 Ellis, Ann Dee. *This Is What I Did* (6–9). 2007, Little, Brown $16.99 (978-0-316-01363-5). After witnessing a violent encounter between his best friend Zyler and Zyler's abusive father, Logan struggles to cope and finds comfort in a new friendship, help from a counselor, and a part in the school play; this novel will appeal to reluctant readers. (Rev: BL 5/15/07; SLJ 10/07)

1696 Erskine, Kathryn. *Mockingbird* (4–7). 2010, Philomel $15.99 (978-0-399-25264-8). Ten-year-old Caitlin, who has Asperger's syndrome and recently lost her older brother in a school shooting, struggles to find closure. National Book Award 2010; ALA Notable Children's Books 2011. ∩ e Lexile 630L (Rev: BL 2/15/10; HB 3–4/10; LMC 5–6/10; SLJ 4/10)

1697 Farnes, Catherine. *Snow* (5–9). 1999, Bob Jones Univ $6.49 (978-1-57924-199-5). A thoughtful novel about an albino girl's problems being accepted, even among students who profess to have Christian charity. (Rev: BL 7/99)

1698 Fensham, Elizabeth. *Helicopter Man* (6–9). 2005, Bloomsbury $15.95 (978-1-58234-981-7). Twelve-year-old Peter's journal entries reveal the difficulties of living with a single parent who is schizophrenic; set in Australia. (Rev: BL 8/05; SLJ 6/05; VOYA 6/05)

1699 Fields, Terri. *After the Death of Anna Gonzales* (7–12). 2002, Henry Holt $16.95 (978-0-8050-7127-6). A collection of poems written by her friends reveals the terrible aftermath of a teenager's suicide. (Rev: BL 12/15/02; HBG 3/03; SLJ 11/02; VOYA 12/02)

1700 Flake, Sharon G. *Pinned* (8–12). 2012, Scholastic $17.99 (978-0-545-05718-9). Struggling reader and championship wrestler Autumn is determined to make inroads with the team's brilliant manager Adonis, who was born without legs, in this story about African American teens told in alternating chapters. ∩ e Lexile HL460L (Rev: BL 10/15/12; HB 11–12/12; LMC 3–4/13; SLJ 9/12)

1701 Fraustino, Lisa Rowe, ed. *Don't Cramp My Style: Stories About That Time of the Month* (8–12). 2004, Simon & Schuster $15.95 (978-0-689-85882-6). This collection of stories about girls' menstrual periods includes fiction about different places, cultures, and times. (Rev: BL 3/1/04; HB 3–4/04; SLJ 4/04; VOYA 4/04)

1702 Friend, Natasha. *Perfect* (6–9). 2004, Milkweed $16.95 (978-1-57131-652-3); paper $6.95 (978-1-57131-651-6). Thirteen-year-old Isabelle Lee struggles to recover from an eating disorder that began shortly after the death of her father. (Rev: BL 1/1–15/05; SLJ 12/04)

1703 Galante, Cecilia. *Hershey Herself* (5–8). 2008, Aladdin paper $5.99 (978-1-4169-5463-7). While living at a shelter for battered women with her mother and younger sister, Hershey discovers real friends and a real talent. (Rev: BL 5/15/08)

1704 Gantos, Jack. *Joey Pigza Loses Control* (4–7). 2000, Farrar $16.00 (978-0-374-39989-4). Joey, a hyperactive kid, tries to please his father but goes haywire when his father destroys his medication in this Newbery Honor Book. (Rev: BCCB 9/00*; BL 9/1/00*; HB 9–10/00; HBG 3/01; SLJ 9/00; VOYA 2/01)

1705 Gantos, Jack. *Joey Pigza Swallowed the Key* (4–8). 1998, Farrar $16.00 (978-0-374-33664-6). Joey, who suffers from attention deficit disorder, causes so much trouble that he is sent to a special education center, where he learns to cope with his problem. (Rev: BCCB 11/98; BL 12/15/98; HB 11–12/98; HBG 3/99; SLJ 12/98*; VOYA 2/99)

1706 Gantos, Jack. *What Would Joey Do?* (5–8). 2002, Farrar $16.00 (978-0-374-39986-3). Hyperactive Joey is nearly overwhelmed by the antics of his parents, his dying grandmother, and the needs of his blind home-school partner, but manages to cope in his own unusual way in this final installment in the Joey Pigza trilogy. (Rev: BCCB 11/02; BL 10/1/02*; HB 11–12/02; HBG 3/03; SLJ 9/02*; VOYA 12/02)

1707 Garden, Nancy. *Endgame* (8–12). 2006, Harcourt $16 (978-0-15-205416-8). While awaiting his murder trial, 15-year-old Gray Wilton reveals in a series of interviews with his lawyer the extreme bullying, both physical and emotional, that finally drove him to take a gun to school. (Rev: SLJ 5/06*)

1708 Geus, Mireille. *Piggy* (6–10). Trans. by Nancy Forest-Flier. 2008, Front St $14.95 (978-159078636-9). Told in the first-person voice of 12-year-old Lizzy, who has autism, this story recounts the constant teasing Lizzy faces everyday until she forms an unlikely friendship with Peggy, which leads to complications of its own. Lexile HL390L (Rev: BLO 11/19/08; HB 1–2/09; LMC 1–2/09; SLJ 1/1/09)

1709 Going, K. L. *Fat Kid Rules the World* (8–12). 2003, Putnam $17.99 (978-0-399-23990-8). An unlikely but beneficial friendship develops between suicidal, 300-pound Troy and dropout punk rock guitarist Curt. (Rev: BCCB 6/03*; BL 5/15/03*; HB 7–8/03; HBG 10/03; SLJ 5/03*; VOYA 6/03)

1710 Gonzalez, Ann. *Running for My Life* (8–10). 2009, WestSide $16.95 (978-193481300-3). Andrea turns to running as a way to cope with her mother's schizophrenia, but still suffers from anxiety and nightmares. Lexile HL520L (Rev: BL 5/1/09; SLJ 7/1/09)

1711 Goobie, Beth. *The Dream Where the Losers Go* (7–12). 2006, Orca paper $8.95 (978-1-55143-455-1). Skey finds herself institutionalized after a suicide attempt, but she doesn't know what caused her actions, just that she travels in tunnels in both her sleep and waking hours; a disturbing but compelling book about the ways in which we survive traumas. (Rev: SLJ 6/06)

1712 Gould, Marilyn. *Golden Daffodils* (5–7). 1991, Allied Crafts paper $10.95 (978-0-9632305-1-5). Janis adjusts to her impairment resulting from cerebral palsy.

1713 Gould, Marilyn. *The Twelfth of June* (5–8). 1994, Allied Crafts LB $12.95 (978-0-9632305-4-6). Janis, who has cerebral palsy, is suffering the first pangs of adolescence and is still fighting the battle to be treated like other girls her age, in this sequel to *Golden Daffodils* (1982). (Rev: SLJ 11/86; VOYA 12/86)

1714 Gourlay, Candy. *Tall Story* (6–9). 2011, Random House $16.99 (978-038575217-6). Bernardo, who is 8 feet tall at the age of 16, leaves the Philippines to join his mother and his diminutive 13-year-old half-sister in London, where he gets treatment for his gigantism. ALA Notable Books 2012. (Rev: BL 1/1/11*; HB 5–6/11; SLJ 3/1/11*)

1715 Greene, Shep. *The Boy Who Drank Too Much* (7–9). 1979, Dell paper $5.50 (978-0-440-90493-9). At one time Buff's main concern was sports, now it's alcohol.

1716 Griffin, Adele. *Where I Want to Be* (7–10). 2005, Penguin $15.99 (978-0-399-23783-6). In alternating chapters, teenage sisters Lily and Jane tell about their relationship and the mental illness that led to Jane's tragic death. (Rev: BCCB 3/05; BL 2/15/05*; HB 3–4/05; SLJ 4/05; VOYA 4/05)

1717 Hall, Liza F. *Perk! The Story of a Teenager with Bulimia* (6–9). 1997, Gurze paper $10.95 (978-0-936077-27-7). The story of Priscilla, who binges on food then vomits, her disapproving parents, and her crush on an unsuitable boy. (Rev: BL 9/15/97; SLJ 4/98; VOYA 4/98)

1718 Halpern, Julie. *Get Well Soon* (8–12). 2007, Feiwel & Friends $16.95 (978-0-312-36795-4). Anna is sent to a psychiatric hospital for her depression and anxiety, and in letters to her best friend—full of profanity, sarcasm, and humor—she describes her experiences there. (Rev: BL 10/15/07; LMC 4–5/08; SLJ 10/07)

1719 Halpin, Brendan. *Forever Changes* (8–11). 2008, Farrar $16.95 (978-037432436-0). Cystic fibrosis sufferer Brianna ponders the meaning of life, and the futility of planning a future she likely won't live to see. Lexile 890L (Rev: BL 10/15/08; SLJ 11/1/08; VOYA 6/08)

1720 Hamilton, Virginia. *The Planet of Junior Brown* (7–9). 1971, Macmillan paper $4.99 (978-0-02-043540-2). A 300-pound misfit is taken care of by his friends.

1721 Harrar, George. *Not as Crazy as I Seem* (7–10). 2003, Houghton Mifflin $15.00 (978-0-618-26365-3). Devon, 15, is frustrated by his obsessive-compulsive disorder and the different responses of his peers, his parents, and his doctor. (Rev: BL 2/15/03; HBG 10/03; SLJ 4/03; VOYA 6/03)

1722 Hautman, Pete. *Invisible* (7–10). 2005, Simon & Schuster $15.95 (978-0-689-86800-9). It's clear to the reader from the beginning that there's something odd about the friendship between 17-year-old Doug Hanson and his only friend Andy, and the mystery unravels as Doug's state of mind deteriorates through the course of the book. (Rev: BL 6/1–15/05; SLJ 6/05; VOYA 8/05)

1723 Hautman, Pete. *Sweetblood* (8–12). 2003, Simon & Schuster $16.95 (978-0-689-85048-6). Sixteen-year-

old Lucy, an insulin-dependent diabetic, links her condition with her interest in vampires. (Rev: BL 5/1/03*; HB 7–8/03; HBG 10/03; SLJ 7/03; VOYA 10/03)

1724 Helfman, Elizabeth. *On Being Sarah* (7–9). 1992, Albert Whitman LB $14.99 (978-0-8075-6068-6). Based on the life of a real person, this is the story of wheelchair-bound Sarah, 12, who has cerebral palsy, cannot vocalize, and communicates through Blissymbols. (Rev: BL 12/15/92; SLJ 1/93)

1725 Hesse, Karen. *The Music of Dolphins* (6–9). 1996, Scholastic paper $5.99 (978-0-590-89798-3). An intriguing novel about a young girl who has been raised by dolphins and, after being returned to the world of humans, longs for her life in the sea. (Rev: BL 10/15/96; SLJ 11/96*; VOYA 2/97)

1726 Heuston, Kimberley. *The Book of Jude* (6–9). 2008, Front St $17.95 (978-1-932425-26-0). While living with her family in Prague in 1989, Jude suffers a breakdown triggered in part by the political unrest she sees around her. (Rev: BL 4/15/08; SLJ 8/08)

1727 Hoekstra, Molly. *Upstream: A Novel* (7–12). 2001, Tudor paper $15.95 (978-0-936389-86-8). This story of a 16-year-old girl's struggle with anorexia gives a clear idea of the psychological problems associated with this illness. (Rev: SLJ 12/01)

1728 Houtman, Jacqueline Jaeger. *The Reinvention of Edison Thomas* (5–8). 2010, Front St $17.95 (978-1-59078-708-3). Eddy is bright and loves science and inventing but has great difficulty getting along with the other students and is often the butt of pranks. Lexile 780L (Rev: BL 4/1/10; LMC 10/10; SLJ 6/10)

1729 Howe, James. *A Night Without Stars* (5–7). 1983, Avon paper $2.95 (978-0-380-69877-6). A novel about a young girl's hospitalization and serious operation.

1730 Howe, James. *The Watcher* (8–12). 1997, Simon & Schuster $16.00 (978-0-689-80186-0). The lives of three troubled teens converge in a horrific climax in this novel of child abuse. (Rev: BL 6/1–15/97; SLJ 5/97; VOYA 8/97)

1731 Hughes, Monica. *The King's Shadow* (7–10). 2003, Fitzhenry & Whiteside paper $9.95 (978-1-55005-056-1). In spite of his leukemia, Mike goes on a secret hunting trip; originally published in 1983.

1732 Hurwin, Davida Wills. *A Time for Dancing* (7–12). 1995, Puffin paper $6.99 (978-0-14-038618-9). A powerful story of two friends, one of whom is diagnosed with lymphoma. Their friendship becomes a story of saying good-bye and death. (Rev: BL 11/1/95*; SLJ 10/95; VOYA 12/95)

1733 Hyde, Catherine Ryan. *Diary of a Witness* (7–10). 2009, Knopf $16.99 (978-037585684-6). Will gets pushed to the breaking point by school bullies and the death of his younger brother. The story is told through entries in Will's friend Ernie's diary. Lexile HL510L (Rev: BLO 5/27/09; SLJ 9/09)

1734 James, Brian. *Life Is But a Dream* (7–10). 2012, Feiwel & Friends $16.99 (978-031261004-3). Artistic Sabrina, 16, is hospitalized for serious mental problems and things go from bad to worse when co-patient Alec persuades her to stop taking her medication. ℮ Lexile 740L (Rev: BL 4/15/12; SLJ 3/12)

1735 Johnson, Angela. *Humming Whispers* (8–12). 1995, Orchard LB $16.99 (978-0-531-08748-0). Sophy, 14, reveals the impact of her 24-year-old sister Nicole's schizophrenia on the lives of those who love her. (Rev: BL 2/15/95; SLJ 4/95; VOYA 5/95)

1736 Johnson, Harriet McBryde. *Accidents of Nature* (8–11). 2006, Henry Holt $16.95 (978-0-8050-7634-9). Set in 1970, this is the story of Jean, a teen with cerebral palsy who attends a camp for the disabled and discovers new possibilities for living her life. ∩ (Rev: BL 7/06; LMC 1/07; SLJ 5/06*)

1737 Jonsberg, Barry. *Dreamrider* (8–11). 2008, Knopf $15.99 (978-0-375-84457-7). Overweight Michael, starting at a new school yet again, is bullied and miserable; the only respite he finds is in his "lucid dreams," which he can control — can he use his dreams to control life too? (Rev: BL 2/15/08; SLJ 7/08)

1738 Jung, Reinhardt. *Dreaming in Black and White* (5–8). Trans. from German by Anthea Bell. 2003, Penguin $15.99 (978-0-8037-2811-0). A boy with disabilities has waking dreams in which he travels back to Nazi Germany and suffers at the hands of his classmates, teachers, and eventually his father, in this compelling novel translated from German. (Rev: BCCB 9/03; BL 5/15/03; HB 9–10/03*; HBG 4/04; SLJ 8/03)

1739 Kachur, Wanda G. *The Nautilus* (5–7). 1997, Peytral paper $7.95 (978-0-9644271-5-0). A compassionate novel about a girl's rehabilitation after receiving spinal cord injuries in an automobile accident. (Rev: SLJ 9/97)

1740 Knowles, Jo. *Lessons from a Dead Girl* (8–11). 2007, Candlewick $16.99 (978-0-7636-3279-3). When Leah dies in an accident, Laine recalls their complicated relationship, including Leah's blackmail, threatening to reveal their "practice" sexual encounters. (Rev: BL 12/1/07; LMC 1/08; SLJ 12/07)

1741 Koertge, Ron. *Stoner and Spaz* (8–12). 2002, Candlewick $15.99 (978-0-7636-1608-3). An unlikely romance between a 16-year-old boy with cerebral palsy and a girl who is constantly stoned brings benefits to both of them. (Rev: BCCB 3/02; BL 5/1/02*; SLJ 4/02)

1742 Koss, Amy Goldman. *Side Effects* (8–11). 2006, Roaring Brook $16.95 (978-1-59643-167-6). Isabelle, 15, is diagnosed with lymphoma and is scared that she might miss out on all the things she wants to do but she makes it through. (Rev: BL 9/15/06; SLJ 9/06)

1743 Kwasney, Michelle D. *Itch* (5–8). 2008, Henry Holt $16.95 (978-0-8050-8083-4). When Itch and her grandmother move from Florida to Ohio, Itch makes friends with a popular girl who has a sad secret. (Rev: BL 4/15/08; SLJ 9/08)

1744 Lachtman, Ofelia Dumas. *Leticia's Secret* (5–8). 1997, Arte Publico $14.95 (978-1-55885-205-1); paper $7.95 (978-1-55885-209-9). Rosario, from a Mexican American family, shares many adventures with her cousin, the pretty Leticia, and is devastated to learn that she has a fatal disease. (Rev: SLJ 1/98)

1745 Lafaye, A. *Water Steps* (4–7). 2009, Milkweed $16.95 (978-1-57131-687-5); paper $6.95 (978-1-57131-686-8). Terrified of water since seeing her family drown as a little girl, 11-year-old Kyna finds she must spend the summer at Lake Champlain with her adoptive parents, who are trying to help her overcome her fears. ∩ Lexile 790L (Rev: BL 3/15/09; SLJ 9/09)

1746 Lascarso, Laura. *Counting Backwards* (8–11). 2012, Atheneum $16.99 (978-1-4424-0690-2). Committed to a juvenile psychiatric correctional facility, Taylor, 16, eventually learns to deal with the problems posed by her alcoholic mother and distant, Seminole father. ℮ Lexile 730L (Rev: BLO 8/12; LMC 1–2/13; SLJ 9/12; VOYA 8/12)

1747 Levoy, Myron. *Alan and Naomi* (7–9). 1977, HarperCollins paper $5.99 (978-0-06-440209-5). Alan tries to reach Naomi, whose mind has been warped by memories of the Holocaust. (Rev: BL 10/1/97)

1748 Lipsyte, Robert. *One Fat Summer* (7–12). 1991, HarperCollins paper $5.99 (978-0-06-447073-5). Bobby Marks is 14, fat, and unhappy in this first novel of three that traces Bobby's career through his first year of college. (Rev: BL 1/1–15/98)

1749 Littman, Sarah Darer. *Purge* (7–10). 2009, Scholastic $16.99 (978-054505235-1). Janie, 16, confronts her bulimia as well as other psychological problems while at a rehab facility for eating disorders. Lexile 950L (Rev: BLO 2/9/09; LMC 5–6/09; SLJ 7/1/09)

1750 McBay, Bruce, and James Heneghan. *Waiting for Sarah* (7–10). 2003, Orca paper $7.95 (978-1-55143-270-0). After becoming disabled in a car accident, Mike suffers from depression and withdrawal until he gets to know 8th-grader Sarah. (Rev: BL 9/15/03; SLJ 10/03; VOYA 12/03)

1751 McCormick, Patricia. *Cut* (7–10). 2000, Front St $16.95 (978-1-886910-61-4). In a hospital that treats teens with serious issues, including drugs and anorexia, Callie participates in group therapy and tries to face her own self-mutilation. (Rev: BL 1/1–15/01; HB 11–12/00; HBG 3/01; SLJ 12/00; VOYA 2/01)

1752 McDaniel, Lurlene. *Breathless* (7–10). 2009, Delacorte $10.99 (978-038573459-2); LB $13.99 (978-038590458-2). This moving story about a champion diver who learns he has bone cancer is told from his perspective and from those of three other teens who all struggle with Travis's desire for assisted suicide. (Rev: BL 7/09; SLJ 4/1/09)

1753 McDaniel, Lurlene. *How Do I Love Thee? Three Stories* (6–10). 2001, Bantam $9.95 (978-0-553-57154-7). Three dramatic stories combine young romance and critical illness with clever twists of plot. (Rev: BL 10/15/01; HBG 3/02; SLJ 11/01; VOYA 12/01)

1754 McDaniel, Lurlene. *Saving Jessica* (7–10). 1996, Bantam paper $4.99 (978-0-553-56721-2). When Jessica is stricken with kidney failure, her boyfriend, Jeremy, volunteers to donate one of his but his parents, fearful that he will die, refuse permission. (Rev: VOYA 4/96)

1755 McDaniel, Lurlene. *To Live Again* (5–9). 2001, Bantam paper $4.99 (978-0-553-57151-6). After three years of remission from leukemia, 16-year-old Dawn has a stroke that produces a terrible bout of depression. (Rev: BL 3/1/01)

1756 Maclean, John. *Mac* (8–12). 1987, Avon paper $2.95 (978-0-380-70700-3). A high school sophomore's life falls apart after he is sexually assaulted by a doctor during a physical exam. (Rev: BL 10/1/87; SLJ 11/87)

1757 Marino, Jan. *Eighty-Eight Steps to September* (5–7). 1989, Avon paper $2.95 (978-0-380-71001-0). Amy and Robbie have the usual sibling rivalry, until Robbie develops leukemia. (Rev: BCCB 5/89; BL 8/89)

1758 Martin, Ann M. *A Corner of the Universe* (6–8). 2002, Scholastic paper $15.95 (978-0-439-38880-1). Hattie recalls the summer she became 12, when a mentally disabled uncle came to stay with her family. Newbery Honor Book, 2003. (Rev: BCCB 2/03; BL 12/1/02; HB 1–2/03*; HBG 3/03; SLJ 9/02*; VOYA 12/02)

1759 Mathis, Sharon. *Teacup Full of Roses* (7–12). 1987, Puffin paper $5.99 (978-0-14-032328-3). For mature teens, a novel about the devastating effects of drugs on an African American family.

1760 Miller, Sarah. *Miss Spitfire: Reaching Helen Keller* (8–11). 2007, Atheneum $16.99 (978-1-4169-2542-2). A fictionalized account of Annie Sullivan's first experiences and struggles with her famous student. ⌒ (Rev: BL 8/07; LMC 11/07; SLJ 7/07)

1761 Mitchard, Jacquelyn. *All We Know of Heaven* (8–12). 2008, HarperTeen $16.99 (978-0-06-134578-4). Inspired by a true but almost unbelievable story, this novel centers on a girl who is mistaken for her dead best friend after a terrible car accident; Maureen has to deal not only with learning to walk and talk again, but also with her guilt about her friend Bridget's death. (Rev: BL 3/15/08; SLJ 6/08)

1762 Morgenroth, Kate. *Echo* (7–10). 2007, Simon & Schuster $15.99 (978-1-4169-1438-9). Justin finds it

hard to cope with his brother's accidental death and on the one-year anniversary of the tragedy he relives the day — again and again. (Rev: BL 11/15/06; LMC 4–5/07; SLJ 2/07)

1763 Neufeld, John. *Lisa, Bright and Dark* (7–9). 1969, Phillips $26.95 (978-0-87599-153-5). Her friend notices that Lisa is gradually sinking into mental illness but her parents seem indifferent.

1764 Nicholls, Sally. *Ways to Live Forever* (3–7). 2008, Scholastic $16.99 (978-0-545-06948-9). Eleven-year-old Sam tells a poignant first-person story of his losing struggle with leukemia. ALA Notable Books 2009. (Rev: BCCB 11/08; BL 11/15/08; HB 9/09;1/09; SLJ 11/08)

1765 Nolan, Han. *Crazy* (7–10). 2010, Houghton Mifflin $17 (978-0-15-205109-9). Fifteen-year-old Jason's mother has died and he must cope alone with his mentally ill father; fear of his father and for his own sanity are alleviated when his predicament is discovered and he is sent to foster care. (Rev: BL 8/10*; HB 11–12/10; SLJ 9/1/10)

1766 Oates, Joyce Carol. *After the Wreck I Picked Myself Up, Spread My Wings, and Flew Away* (7–10). 2006, HarperCollins $16.99 (978-0-06-073525-8). After her mother dies in a car crash, 15-year-old Jenna moves in with her aunt's family and struggles to cope with feelings of guilt and loss. ⌒ (Rev: BL 7/06; LMC 4–5/07; SLJ 10/06)

1767 Oke, Janette, and Laurel Oke Logan. *Dana's Valley* (7–12). 2001, Bethany House paper $11.95 (978-0-7642-2451-5). Erin, 10 years old and part of a happy Christian family, has her faith tested when her beloved older sister is diagnosed with leukemia. (Rev: VOYA 2/02)

1768 Orr, Wendy. *Peeling the Onion* (8–12). 1997, Holiday $16.95 (978-0-8234-1289-1); paper $4.99 (978-0-440-22773-1). An automobile accident leaves Anna with a broken back, debilitating pain, physical and mental handicaps, and questions about what to do with her life. (Rev: BL 4/1/97; SLJ 5/97*; VOYA 10/97)

1769 Page, Katherine Hall. *Club Meds* (6–10). 2006, Simon & Schuster paper $6.99 (978-1-4169-0903-3). Jack has ADHD and depends on the drug Ritalin to function, but as he enters 9th grade he is forced by bully Chuck Williams to hand over a quota of the drug each week; Jack teams up with fellow ADHD sufferer and "Club Meds" (kids who have to take medications) member Mary to deal with this problem. (Rev: BL 8/06; SLJ 8/06)

1770 Paley, Sasha. *Huge* (7–9). 2007, Simon & Schuster $15.99 (978-1-4169-3517-9). Wil and April, both overweight teenage girls, meet as roommates at Wellness Canyon Camp, and change in ways they didn't expect. (Rev: BL 5/15/07; SLJ 12/07)

1771 Paulsen, Gary. *The Monument* (6–9). 1991, Delacorte $15.00 (978-0-385-30518-1). A 13-year-old girl's friendship with an artist who is hired to create a monument in her small town transforms her. (Rev: BL 9/15/91; SLJ 10/91*)

1772 Peck, Richard. *Remembering the Good Times* (7–10). 1986, Bantam paper $5.50 (978-0-440-97339-3). A strong friendship between two boys and a girl is destroyed when one of them commits suicide. (Rev: BL 3/1/85)

1773 Pixley, Marcella. *Without Tess* (8–12). 2011, Farrar $16.99 (978-0-374-36174-7). Lizzie, 15, reflects on the life and death of her older sister Tess, whose fantasies as a child morphed into full-fledged mental illness as a teen. ℮ Lexile 790L (Rev: BLO 11/15/11; HB 1–2/12; LMC 1–2/12; SLJ 11/1/11*)

1774 Platt, Kin. *The Ape Inside Me* (6–8). 1979, HarperCollins LB $11.89 (978-0-397-31863-6). Eddie and Debbie work together to try and curb their terrible tempers.

1775 Ross, Jeff. *Coming Clean* (7–12). 2012, Orca LB $16.95 (978-145980332-9); paper $9.95 (978-145980331-2). Aspiring DJ Rob becomes caught up in a world of drugs and betrayal, with unhappy consequences; for reluctant readers. ℮ Lexile HL500L (Rev: BLO 10/15/12; SLJ 4/13)

1776 Ruckman, Ivy. *The Hunger Scream* (7–10). 1983, Walker $14.95 (978-0-8027-6514-7). Lily starves herself to become a popular member of the in-crowd.

1777 Ryan, Darlene. *Five Minutes More* (7–10). 2009, Orca paper $12.95 (978-155469006-0). D'Arcy has trouble adjusting after the death of her father, who suffered from ALS; the idea that he killed himself makes everything worse. Lexile HL570L (Rev: BLO 4/14/09; VOYA 6/09)

1778 Sanchez, Alex. *Bait* (7–10). 2009, Simon & Schuster $16.99 (978-141693772-2). When Diego ends up in juvenile court, his parole officer helps him get to the source of his anger problems—namely, being sexually abused by his stepfather. Lexile HL630L (Rev: BL 5/15/09; SLJ 7/1/09*; VOYA 8/09)

1779 Sandell, Lisa Ann. *A Map of the Known World* (7–10). 2009, Scholastic $16.99 (978-054506970-0). After her brother Nate dies in a car crash, 14-year-old Cora becomes close to Nate's best friend, who survived the crash, and learns that there was an artistic, thoughtful side to Nate that she had never seen. Lexile 800L (Rev: BL 4/1/09; SLJ 6/1/09)

1780 Schindler, Holly. *A Blue So Dark* (8–11). 2010, Flux paper $9.95 (978-0-73871-926-9). When 15-year-old Aura's mentally ill mother finally enters a catatonic state of schizophrenia, Aura realizes she can't care for her on her own. ℮ (Rev: BL 5/1/10*; LMC 8–9/10; SLJ 6/10)

1781 Schmidt, Tiffany. *Send Me a Sign* (8–12). 2012, Walker $16.99 (978-080272840-1). Superstitious 17-year-old Mia consults horoscopes and tarot cards when she is diagnosed with leukemia and allows them to guide her behavior. ℮ (Rev: BL 10/15/12; SLJ 2/13)

1782 Scoppettone, Sandra. *Long Time Between Kisses* (7–10). 1982, HarperCollins $12.95 (978-0-06-025229-8). A 16-year-old brings together a victim of multiple sclerosis and his fiance.

1783 Scott, Elizabeth. *Miracle* (7–10). 2012, Simon & Schuster $16.99 (978-1-4424-1706-9). Megan, the sole survivor of an airplane crash, remains haunted by the ghosts of the four passengers who died, and finds herself unable to fit back into her old life in this portrait of a teen with emotional damage who eventually finds solace. ℮ Lexile HL750L (Rev: BLO 6/12; LMC 11–12/12; SLJ 7/12)

1784 Seidler, Tor. *The Silent Spillbills* (5–8). 1998, HarperCollins LB $14.89 (978-0-06-205181-3). Katrina faces problems trying to overcome her stuttering but stands up to her tyrannical grandfather to help save from extinction a rare bird known as the silent spillbill. (Rev: BCCB 1/99; BL 12/15/98; HBG 3/99; SLJ 4/99)

1785 Selznick, Brian. *Wonderstruck* (4–8). Illus. by author. 2011, Scholastic $29.99 (978-0-545-02789-2). Two parallel stories set 50 years apart involve lonely children who've lost their hearing and run off to New York City to discover themselves; Ben's story unfolds in text, Rose's in pictures. ALA Notable Books 2012. Lexile 830L (Rev: BL 8/11*; HB 9–10/11; SLJ 8/11*; VOYA 10/11)

1786 Shaw, Susan. *Black-Eyed Suzie* (7–9). 2002, Boyds Mills $15.95 (978-1-56397-729-9); paper $4.95 (978-1-56397-701-5). In the pages of her diary and with the help of hospital staff, Suzie struggles to recover emotionally from her mother's physical abuse. (Rev: BCCB 9/02; BL 5/15/02; HBG 10/02; VOYA 8/02)

1787 Sheinmel, Courtney. *Positively* (6–10). 2009, Simon & Schuster $15.99 (978-141697169-6). This is 13-year-old Emmy's first-person account of coming to accept living with AIDS. (Rev: BL 7/09; SLJ 1/10)

1788 Shreve, Susan. *The Lovely Shoes* (5–8). 2011, Scholastic $16.99 (978-0-439-68049-3). In 1950s Ohio 14-year-old Franny, a girl with a curled-in foot and clunky orthopedic shoes — and a beautiful, fashion-obsessed mother, goes to Italy to see shoe designer Salvatore Ferragamo and finds the attention she deserves. Lexile 1030L (Rev: HB 9–10/11; SLJ 10/1/11)

1789 Shyer, Marlene Fanta. *Welcome Home, Jellybean* (5–8). 1978, Macmillan paper $4.99 (978-0-689-71213-5). Twelve-year-old Neil encounters a near-tragic situation when his older retarded sister comes home to stay.

1790 Smith, Jennifer E. *The Comeback Season* (6–9). 2008, Simon & Schuster $15.99 (978-1-4169-5213-8). Two friends with painful problems (a deceased parent and a cancer diagnosis) help each other through compassion and a love of baseball. (Rev: BL 3/1/08)

1791 Snyder, Zilpha Keatley. *The Witches of Worm* (5–8). Illus. by Alton Raible. 1972, Dell paper $5.50 (978-0-440-49727-1). A deeply disturbed girl believes that her selfish and destructive acts are caused by bewitchment.

1792 Spencer, Katherine. *Saving Grace* (8–11). 2006, Harcourt $15.00 (978-0-15-205740-4). Grace is emotionally lost and heading down a dangerous path after her brother, Matt, dies in a car accident. Help comes in the form of a girl named Philomena who guides her back to God. (Rev: BCCB 11/06; BL 1/1–15/07; SLJ 10/06)

1793 Strachan, Ian. *The Flawed Glass* (5–8). 1990, Little, Brown $14.95 (978-0-316-81813-1). Physically disabled Shona makes friends with an American boy on an island off the Scottish coast. (Rev: BCCB 11/90; BL 12/1/90; SLJ 1/91)

1794 Stratton, Allan. *Leslie's Journal* (8–12). 2000, Annick $19.95 (978-1-55037-665-4); paper $8.95 (978-1-55037-664-7). A new teacher reads Leslie's journal and learns about her boyfriend's abusive behavior. (Rev: HBG 10/01; SLJ 4/01; VOYA 2/01)

1795 Striegel, Jana. *Homeroom Exercise* (4–7). 2002, Holiday $16.95 (978-0-8234-1579-3). A 12-year-old who dreams of becoming a professional dancer is diagnosed with juvenile rheumatoid arthritis. (Rev: BL 3/1/02; HBG 10/02; SLJ 6/02; VOYA 8/02)

1796 Tan, Shaun. *The Red Tree* (6–12). 2003, Simply Read $15.95 (978-0-9688767-3-2). This arresting picture book for older readers portrays a girl searching for meaning in a frightening world, with a glimmer of hope that grows as the book reaches its conclusion. (Rev: BL 5/1/03)

1797 Tashjian, Janet. *Fault Line* (8–12). 2003, Henry Holt $16.95 (978-0-8050-7200-6). Becky, 17, happy and enjoying doing comedy routines, finds her life changing when she falls for Kip, whose apparent self-confidence hides his abusive nature. (Rev: BL 9/1/03; HB 9–10/03; HBG 4/04; SLJ 10/03; VOYA 10/03)

1798 Taylor, Michelle A. *The Angel of Barbican High* (7–12). 2002, Univ. of Queensland paper $15.95 (978-0-7022-3251-0). Jez feels responsible for the death of her boyfriend and pours out her guilt in her poems, which reveal that she is close to suicide. (Rev: SLJ 8/02)

1799 Tokio, Mamelle. *More Than You Can Chew* (8–10). 2003, Tundra paper $9.95 (978-0-88776-639-8). Anorexic 17-year-old Marty Black faces an uphill struggle as she begins treatment for her eating disorder but tackles it with some humor. (Rev: BL 1/1–15/04; SLJ 6/04; VOYA 8/04)

1800 Toten, Teresa. *The Game* (7–12). 2001, Red Deer paper $7.95 (978-0-88995-232-4). A dramatic story

about Dani, a suicidal girl who finds friendship and succor at a clinic for troubled adolescents. (Rev: BL 2/15/02; VOYA 4/02)

1801 Trembath, Don. *Lefty Carmichael Has a Fit* (8–12). 2000, Orca paper $6.95 (978-1-55143-166-6). When 15-year-old Lefty discovers that he is an epileptic, he develops a fearful, cautious lifestyle that his friends and family try to change. (Rev: BL 1/1–15/00; SLJ 2/00; VOYA 4/00)

1802 Trueman, Terry. *Inside Out* (7–10). 2003, HarperCollins LB $16.89 (978-0-06-623963-7). An absorbing story about a schizophrenic teenager who is held hostage in a robbery attempt. (Rev: BL 9/1/03; HBG 4/04; SLJ 9/03; VOYA 10/03)

1803 Trueman, Terry. *Life Happens Next* (8–12). 2012, HarperTeen $17.99 (978-006202803-7). Cerebral palsy sufferer Shawn, almost 15, forges a strong bond with Debi, who has Down syndrome, when the woman and her dog move in with his family; the sequel to *Stuck in Neutral* (2001). 🎧 e (Rev: BL 12/1/12; HB 11–12/12; VOYA 6/12)

1804 Trueman, Terry. *Stuck in Neutral* (6–10). 2000, HarperCollins LB $16.89 (978-0-06-028518-0). Fourteen-year-old Shawn, whose severe cerebral palsy does not hamper his great intelligence, fears that his father may be planning to put him out of his misery. (Rev: BL 7/00*; HB 5–6/00; HBG 10/00; SLJ 7/00; VOYA 12/00)

1805 Tullson, Diane. *Riley Park* (7–12). 2009, LB $16.95 (978-155469124-1); paper $9.95 (978-155469123-4). After a night of partying and fighting, friends Darius and Corbin are attacked in a park. Darius dies and Corbin is seriously injured. A suspenseful offering for reluctant readers. Lexile HL480L (Rev: BL 5/1/09; SLJ 10/09)

1806 Tullson, Diane. *Zero* (8–11). 2007, Fitzhenry & Whiteside paper $9.95 (978-1-55041-950-4). While at a boarding school for the arts, Kas becomes anorexic and manages to hide her problem from everyone until she nearly dies. (Rev: BL 4/15/07; SLJ 6/07)

1807 Waite, Judy. *Shopaholic* (6–10). 2003, Simon & Schuster $16.95 (978-0-689-85138-4). Unhappy Taylor, a British 14-year-old, allows herself to fall in with glamorous Kat's plans despite her reservations. (Rev: BL 5/1/03; HBG 10/03; SLJ 7/03; VOYA 8/03)

1808 Waldorf, Heather. *Tripping* (8–12). 2009, Red Deer paper $12.95 (978-088995426-7). Rainey, who has a prosthetic leg, sets off on an Outward Bound-type trip across Canada and learns about herself, her mother, and her fellow travelers. YALSA Popular Paperbacks for Young Adults Top Ten 2012. Lexile HL780L (Rev: BL 5/1/09; SLJ 5/1/09)

1809 Weatherly, Lee. *Kat Got Your Tongue* (8–10). 2007, Random House $15.99 (978-0-385-75117-9). After being hit by a car, Kat doesn't remember who she is and struggles with her new identity and relationships with her mother and friends. (Rev: BL 8/07; SLJ 9/07)

1810 Wersba, Barbara. *Fat: A Love Story* (8–12). 1987, HarperCollins $11.95 (978-0-06-026400-0). Rita Formica, fat and unhappy, falls for rich, attractive Robert. (Rev: BL 6/1/87; SLJ 8/87; VOYA 6/87)

1811 White, Andrea. *Window Boy* (5–8). 2008, Bright Sky $17.95 (978-193397914-4). Twelve-year-old Sam invents a relationship with his hero Winston Churchill to help him cope with cerebral palsy and a difficult family life in 1968 England. Lexile 700L (Rev: BLO 8/08; SLJ 10/1/08)

1812 White, Ruth. *Memories of Summer* (7–12). 2000, Farrar $16.00 (978-0-374-34945-5). Lyric is devastated when her older sister, Summer, must be hospitalized for her schizophrenia in this novel set in 1955. (Rev: BL 9/1/00; HB 9–10/00; HBG 3/01; SLJ 8/00*; VOYA 12/00)

1813 White, Ruth. *Weeping Willow* (7–10). 1992, Farrar paper $5.95 (978-0-374-48280-0). This uplifting novel conveying hill country life is about a girl who overcomes abuse to make her own way. (Rev: BL 6/15/92; SLJ 7/92)

1814 Wilson, Dawn. *Saint Jude* (8–12). 2001, Tudor $15.95 (978-0-936389-68-4). Taylor, who is bipolar, makes friends and learns to cope with her illness while in an outpatient program at St. Jude Hospital. (Rev: BL 11/1/01; SLJ 11/01)

1815 Wolff, Virginia Euwer. *Probably Still Nick Swansen* (7–12). 1988, Henry Holt $14.95 (978-0-8050-0701-5). Nick, a 16-year-old victim of slight brain dysfunction, tells his story of rejection and separation. (Rev: BL 11/15/88; SLJ 12/88; VOYA 6/89)

1816 Wolfson, Jill. *Cold Hands, Warm Heart* (8–10). 2009, Henry Holt $17.95 (978-080508282-1). When a 14-year-old gymnast dies, her organs are transplanted, affecting many people in profound ways. Lexile HL760L (Rev: BL 3/15/09; SLJ 5/1/09; VOYA 6/09)

1817 Woodruff, Joan L. *The Shiloh Renewal* (7–10). 1998, Black Heron $22.95 (978-0-930773-50-2). Sandy, who has been mentally and physically disabled since an automobile accident, tries to regain basic skills, recover from the brain trauma, and straighten out her life in this novel that takes place on a small farm near Shiloh National Park in Tennessee. (Rev: VOYA 12/98)

1818 Woodson, Jacqueline. *Beneath a Meth Moon* (8–11). 2012, Penguin $16.99 (978-039925250-1). After becoming hooked on crystal meth in the aftermath of Hurricane Katrina, Laurel, 15, now struggles to overcome her addiction. YALSA Quick Picks for Reluctant Young Adult Readers 2013. ⌒ ℮ Lexile HL730L (Rev: BL 12/15/11; HB 3–4/12; SLJ 2/12*)

1819 Yeomans, Ellen. *Rubber Houses* (6–12). 2007, Little, Brown $15.99 (978-0-316-10647-X). This novel in verse follows Kit's grief when her younger brother, with whom she shared a love of baseball, is diagnosed with and then dies of cancer. (Rev: BCCB 2/07; BL 1/1–15/07; SLJ 3/07)

1820 Young, Janet Ruth. *My Beautiful Failure* (8–11). 2012, Atheneum $16.99 (978-141695489-7). Billy Morrison, a high school sophomore whose father has suffered from severe depression, signs up to volunteer on a suicide hotline and soon finds himself fascinated by a regular young woman caller named Jenney. ℮ Lexile HL670L (Rev: BL 11/15/12; LMC 3–4/13; SLJ 2/13)

1821 Zarr, Sara. *Sweethearts* (8–12). 2008, Little, Brown $16.99 (978-0-316-01455-7). Jenna has remade herself in an attempt to forget her troubled childhood, but when Cameron — who suffered abuse along with Jenna long ago — reappears in her life, her past seems to come back with him. ⌒ (Rev: BL 1/1–15/08; HB 5–6/08; SLJ 4/08)

1822 Zevin, Gabrielle. *Memoirs of a Teenage Amnesiac* (6–10). 2007, Farrar $17.00 (978-0-374-34946-2). After a head injury, Naomi, a high school junior, can't remember anything that's happened since 6th grade and struggles with her present and past life, a new romance, and her parents' separation. (Rev: BL 9/1/07; SLJ 10/07)

1823 Zimmer, Tracie Vaughn. *Reaching for the Sun* (5–8). 2007, Bloomsbury $14.95 (978-1-59990-037-7). Seventh-grader Josie faces daunting troubles: school, loneliness, cerebral palsy, and her rural area's development; a new, science-loving neighbor becomes a friend and Josie redefines her relationship with her mother in this appealing verse novel. (Rev: BL 1/1–15/07; SLJ 3/07)

Personal Problems and Growing into Maturity

1824 Adams, Lenora. *Baby Girl* (7–10). 2007, Simon & Schuster paper $6.99 (978-1-4169-2512-5). Sheree, a pregnant runaway, exchanges letters with her mother expressing anguish over her life, which has included neglect, drugs, and disappointment. (Rev: BL 3/1/07)

1825 Adler, C. S. *Willie, the Frog Prince* (4–7). 1994, Clarion $15.00 (978-0-395-65615-0). Willie's inability to accept responsibility almost causes the loss of his dog, Booboo. (Rev: BL 4/15/94; SLJ 6/94)

1826 Aker, Don. *Stranger at Bay* (6–9). 1998, Stoddart paper $5.95 (978-0-7736-7468-4). Set in a town on the Bay of Fundy in Canada, this novel tells about Randy Forsythe's adjustment to a new home and stepmother while coping with a gang of bullies who want him to steal drugs from his father, who is a pharmaceutical salesman. (Rev: SLJ 7/98)

1827 Alexie, Sherman. *The Absolutely True Diary of a Part-Time Indian* (7–10). 2007, Little, Brown $16.99 (978-0-316-01368-0). Arnold Spirit, a teenager on the Spokane Indian reservation, expects obstacles when he switches to a privileged white school but finds there are challenges at home too. ∩ (Rev: BL 8/07; HB 1–2/08; LMC 1/08; SLJ 9/07)

1828 Allen, Crystal. *How Lamar's Bad Prank Won a Bubba-Sized Trophy* (5–8). 2011, HarperCollins $16.99 (978-0-06-199272-8). Bowling is an important anchor in the difficult life of 13-year-old African American Lamar, but it threatens to undercut his best efforts in this humorous novel about young teen love and emotions. ∩ e Lexile 550L (Rev: BL 3/1/11; SLJ 2/1/11; VOYA 4/11)

1829 Allen, M. E. *Gotta Get Some Bish Bash Bosh* (7–10). 2005, HarperCollins LB $16.89 (978-0-06-073201-1). When he's dumped by his girlfriend Sandi, the 14-year-old narrator resolves to cultivate a brand-new image in this entertaining novel set in Britain. (Rev: BL 1/1–15/05; SLJ 4/05; VOYA 2/05)

1830 Almond, David. *The Fire-Eaters* (6–8). 2004, Delacorte $15.95 (978-0-385-73170-6). In 1962, 12-year-old Bobby Burns grows increasingly troubled by his father's deteriorating health, the growing threat of another world war, and his clashes at school with a cruel teacher. (Rev: BCCB 5/04; BL 3/15/04; HB 5–6/04; SLJ 5/04; VOYA 10/04)

1831 Almond, David. *The Savage* (6–9). Illus. by Dave McKean. 2008, Candlewick $17.99 (978-0-7636-3932-7). After Blue Baker's father dies, the boy is urged to write a story about his feelings, and creates a feral child living in the woods and killing people who come too close, a story that begins to seem all too real. Best Books for Young Adults 2009. (Rev: BL 9/15/08; HB 9–10/08; LMC 3–4/09; SLJ 12/08)

1832 Alphin, Elaine Marie. *Simon Says* (8–12). 2002, Harcourt $17.00 (978-0-15-216355-6). Charles, a brooding 16-year-old artist, is determined to remain nonconformist when he starts attending a boarding school for the arts in this thoughtful novel. (Rev: BCCB 6/02; BL 4/15/02; HBG 10/02; SLJ 6/02)

1833 Amato, Mary. *Invisible Lines* (5–8). Illus. by Antonio Caparo. 2009, Egmont $15.99 (978-1-60684-010-8); LB $18.99 (978-1-60684-043-6). Soccer and science are safe havens for 7th-grader Trevor, who lives in a grim housing project but attends a school for the privileged and has trouble fitting in. Lexile 650L (Rev: BL 11/1/09; SLJ 11/09)

1834 Anderson, Laurie Halse. *Speak* (8–12). 1999, Farrar $16.00 (978-0-374-37152-4). A victim of rape, high school freshman Mellinda Sordino finds that her attacker is again threatening her. Printz Honor 2000; Margaret A. Edwards Award 2009. (Rev: BL 9/15/99; HB 9–10/99; HBG 4/00; SLJ 10/99; VOYA 12/99)

1835 Anderson, Mary. *Tune in Tomorrow* (7–9). 1985, Avon paper $2.50 (978-0-380-69870-7). Jo is fixated on two soap opera characters whom she later meets in real life.

1836 *Annie's Baby: The Diary of Anonymous, a Pregnant Teenager* (6–10). 1998, Avon paper $5.99 (978-0-380-79141-5). In diary format, this is the story of 14-year-old Annie, her love for an abusive rich boyfriend, and her rape and subsequent pregnancy. (Rev: SLJ 7/98; VOYA 6/98)

1837 Ashley, Bernard. *All My Men* (7–9). 1978, Phillips $26.95 (978-0-87599-228-0). In this English story, Paul pays a heavy price to be part of the "in" crowd.

1838 Ashley, Bernard. *Little Soldier* (8–12). 2002, Scholastic $16.95 (978-0-439-22424-6). Young Kaninda Bulumba is rescued from the incredible violence taking place in his native country only to find himself confronting gang violence in his new neighborhood in London. (Rev: BCCB 7–8/02; BL 5/1/02; HBG 10/02; SLJ 6/02*; VOYA 8/02)

1839 Ashley, Bernard. *Terry on the Fence* (6–8). 1977, Phillips $26.95 (978-0-87599-222-8). Unhappy at home, Terry unwillingly becomes a member of a street gang.

1840 Atkinson, Elizabeth. *From Alice to Zen and Everyone in Between* (5–7). 2008, Carolrhoda $16.95 (978-0-8225-7271-8). Alice moves to a new suburb with her dad and quickly becomes friends with Zen, but when school starts she realizes he's part of the wrong crowd. (Rev: BL 5/1/08; SLJ 9/08)

1841 Auch, Mary Jane. *Seven Long Years Until College* (4–7). 1991, Holiday $13.95 (978-0-8234-0901-3). Natalie runs away from home to join her older sister at college. (Rev: BCCB 1/92; SLJ 10/91)

1842 Avi. *A Place Called Ugly* (6–9). 1995, Avon paper $6.99 (978-0-380-72423-9). A 14-year-old boy protests the tearing down of a beach cottage to build a hotel.

1843 Axelrod, Amy. *Your Friend in Fashion, Abby Shapiro* (5–7). Illus. by author. 2011, Holiday House $17.95 (978-0-8234-2340-8). In 1959, 11-year-old Abby has a hard time making the transition from girlhood to womanhood, and leans on her close-knit Jewish extended family for support and guidance while sharing her problems in letters to Jackie Kennedy. Lexile 710L (Rev: BL 4/15/11; SLJ 4/11)

1844 Bagert, Brod. *Hormone Jungle: Coming of Age in Middle School* (5–8). 2006, Maupin House $23.95 (978-0-929895-87-1). The scrapbook of Christina Curtis's middle-school years tells the story of the poetry war that erupted in sixth grade and of the changing relationships between the young people as they learned more about each other. (Rev: SLJ 6/06)

1845 Barnholdt, Lauren. *The Secret Identity of Devon Delaney* (4–7). 2007, Aladdin Mix paper $5.99 (978-1-

105

4169-3503-2). The lies that Devon tells while spending the summer at her grandmother's house come back to bite her when her new friend Lexi moves to Devon's town and attends Devon's middle school. (Rev: BL 8/07; SLJ 8/07)

1846 Bartek, Mary. *Funerals and Fly Fishing* (4–7). 2004, Henry Holt $16.95 (978-0-8050-7409-3). A visit to the grandfather he has never met gives Brad Stanislawski new confidence to deal with the classmates at his new school. (Rev: SLJ 8/04)

1847 Baskin, Nora Raleigh. *All We Know of Love* (7–10). 2008, Candlewick $16.99 (978-076363623-4). Sixteen-year-old Natalie Gordon sets off on a bus trip from Connecticut to Florida to find the mother who abandoned her four years ago, and learns lessons about herself, and about love, along the way. Lexile NC660L (Rev: BL 10/15/08; SLJ 9/1/08; VOYA 8/08)

1848 Baskin, Nora Raleigh. *The Summer Before Boys* (5–8). 2011, Simon & Schuster $15.99 (978-1-4169-8673-7). When her mother is deployed to Iraq, Julia, 12, moves in with her friend Eliza's family but the girls' close bond is threatened by Julia's crush on a boy. **e** Lexile 720L (Rev: BL 3/1/11; HB 5–6/11; SLJ 4/11)

1849 Bateson, Catherine. *The Boyfriend Rules of Good Behavior* (6–8). 2006, Holiday House $16.95 (978-0-8234-2026-1). Millie learns to make adjustments as her mother finds a new boyfriend and circumstances alter yet again in this Australian import full of Down Under flavor. (Rev: SLJ 11/06)

1850 Bauer, A. C. E. *No Castles Here* (4–7). 2007, Random House $15.99 (978-0-375-83921-4). A magical book, a Big Brother, and a school chorus rescue 11-year-old Augie Boretski from feeling completely lost in his life of poverty and loneliness in Camden, New Jersey. (Rev: BL 12/1/07; SLJ 10/07)

1851 Bauer, Joan. *Close to Famous* (5–8). 2011, Viking $16.99 (978-0-670-01282-4). Slow learner and talented baker Foster, 12, and her mother flee her mother's abusive boyfriend to start a new life in West Virginia, where she learns to read and gets the chance to market her baked goods. YALSA Best Fiction for Young Adults 2012. **e** Lexile 540L (Rev: BL 1/1–15/11; HB 1–2/11; LMC 5–6/11; SLJ 3/1/11)

1852 Bawden, Nina. *The Peppermint Pig* (6–8). 1975, HarperCollins LB $13.89 (978-0-397-31618-2). A brother and sister save a pig that they soon regard as a pet but they find something terrible is going to happen to it.

1853 Beaudoin, Sean. *Going Nowhere Faster* (8–12). 2007, Little, Brown $16.99 (978-0-316-01415-1). Stan Smith, 17, has a high IQ and showed promise when he was younger but now spends his time working in a video store, inventing dreadful screenplay scenarios, avoiding his embarrassing hippie parents, and worrying

about a stalker; a darkly comic story with a satisfying resolution. (Rev: BCCB 5/07; HB 5–6/07; SLJ 4/07)

1854 Bell, William. *Death Wind* (7–12). 2002, Orca paper $7.95 (978-1-55143-215-1). After running away from her unhappy home when she thinks she may be pregnant, Allie returns to find that a tornado has devastated her town. (Rev: SLJ 10/02; VOYA 12/02)

1855 Benjamin, Carol Lea. *The Wicked Stepdog* (4–7). Illus. by author. 1982, Avon paper $2.50 (978-0-380-70089-9). Louise is in the midst of puberty problems and her father's remarriage.

1856 Bertrand, Diane Gonzales. *Trino's Choice* (6–9). 1999, Arte Publico $16.95 (978-1-55885-279-2); paper $9.95 (978-1-55885-268-6). A Latino boy growing up in a Texas trailer park succumbs to the offer of a hood who offers him chance at quick cash, but in time it leads to tragedy. (Rev: BL 6/1–15/99; VOYA 4/00)

1857 Bertrand, Diane Gonzales. *Trino's Time* (6–12). 2001, Arte Publico $14.95 (978-1-55885-316-4); paper $14.95 (978-1-55885-317-1). In this sequel to *Trino's Choice* (1999), things begin to look better for Trino's family as Trino gets a job and starts enjoying school. (Rev: BL 11/1/01; SLJ 7/01; VOYA 12/01)

1858 Betancourt, Jeanne. *Kate's Turn* (5–8). 1992, Scholastic $13.95 (978-0-590-43103-3). This story of the young ballerina Kate, who decides the price of fame is too high, shows the grueling, often painful life of a dancer. (Rev: BL 1/1/92; SLJ 2/92)

1859 Billerbeck, Kristin. *Perfectly Dateless* (8–12). 2010, Revell paper $9.99 (978-08007343-9-8). Can Daisy find a date in time for the prom despite her weird parents and her social ineptitude? A funny story about high school problems. **e** (Rev: BL 7/10)

1860 Billingsley, ReShonda Tate. *With Friends Like These* (7–12). Series: African American Christian Teen Fiction. 2007, Pocket paper $9.95 (978-1-4165-2562-2). The four girls we first met in *Nothing but Drama* (2006) now become enemies in their efforts to get on a TV show. (Rev: BL 4/1/07)

1861 Block, Francesca Lia. *Echo* (8–12). 2001, HarperCollins LB $14.89 (978-0-06-028128-1). A series of interconnected stories set in glamorous Los Angeles follows the maturing of an unhappy young girl called Echo, who feels neglected by her talented parents and seeks attention where she can find it. (Rev: BCCB 10/01; BL 8/01; HB 9–10/01; HBG 3/02; SLJ 8/01; VOYA 10/01)

1862 Bloor, Edward. *Tangerine* (7–10). 1997, Harcourt $17.00 (978-0-15-201246-5); paper $4.99 (978-0-590-43277-1). Although he wears thick glasses, Paul is able to see clearly the people around him, their problems and their mistakes, as he adjusts to his new home in Tangerine County, Florida. (Rev: BL 5/15/97; SLJ 4/97; VOYA 8/97)

1863 Bloss, Josie. *Albatross* (8–11). Series: Band Geek. 2010, Flux paper $9.95 (978-0-73871-476-9). Tess, a 16-year-old French horn player lacking in self-confidence, falls for pianist Micah despite his abusive and manipulative behavior. Lexile HL680L (Rev: BLO 1/1–15/10; LMC 5–6/10; SLJ 3/10)

1864 Bloss, Josie. *Faking Faith* (7–10). 2011, Flux paper $9.95 (978-0-7387-2-757-8). Shunned after inappropriate postings on the Internet, Dylan seeks new friends on a fundamentalist network, creating a new version of herself named Faith. ℮ Lexile HL790L (Rev: BLO 10/15/11; SLJ 12/1/11; VOYA 12/11)

1865 Blount, Patty. *Send* (8–10). 2012, Sourcebooks paper $8.99 (978-14022733-7-7). Dan, 18 years old and a former bully, has been trying to keep a low profile at school but comes into the limelight when he stops a beating. ℮ Lexile HL550L (Rev: BLO 8/12; VOYA 12/12)

1866 Blume, Judy. *Here's to You, Rachel Robinson* (6–8). 1993, Dell paper $5.50 (978-0-440-40946-5). This sequel to *Just As Long As We're Together* is full of multidimensional characters. (Rev: BL 9/1/93; SLJ 11/93; VOYA 12/93)

1867 Blume, Judy. *Just as Long as We're Together* (6–8). 1987, Dell paper $5.50 (978-0-440-40075-2). A student entering junior high faces problems involving weight, friendships, and a family that is disintegrating. (Rev: BL 8/87; VOYA 2/88)

1868 Blume, Judy. *Then Again, Maybe I Won't* (5–8). 1971, Dell paper $4.99 (978-0-440-48659-6). Thirteen-year-old Tony faces many problems when his family relocates to suburban Long Island.

1869 Blume, Judy. *Tiger Eyes* (7–10). 1981, Dell paper $5.99 (978-0-440-98469-6). A girl struggles to cope with her father's violent death. (Rev: BL 7/88)

1870 Boock, Paula. *Dare Truth or Promise* (8–12). 1999, Houghton Mifflin $15.00 (978-0-395-97117-8). Two girls, Willa and Louise, attend a New Zealand high school and, though they are opposites in many ways, they fall in love. (Rev: BL 9/15/99; HB 9–10/99; HBG 4/00; SLJ 11/99; VOYA 10/99)

1871 Book, Rick. *Necking with Louise* (7–12). 1999, Red Deer paper $7.95 (978-0-88995-194-5). Set in Saskatchewan in 1965, this is a book of stories about Eric Anderson's 16th year, when he has his first date, plays in a championship hockey game, has a summer job, and reacts to his family and the land on which he lives. (Rev: BL 10/15/99*; SLJ 3/00)

1872 Borntrager, Mary Christner. *Rebecca* (7–12). 1989, Herald paper $8.99 (978-0-8361-3500-8). A coming-of-age novel about an Amish girl and her attraction to a Mennonite young man. (Rev: SLJ 11/89)

1873 Bottner, Barbara. *Nothing in Common* (7–10). 1986, HarperCollins $12.95 (978-0-06-020604-8).

When Mrs. Gregori dies, both her daughter and Melissa Warren, a teenager in the household where Mrs. Gregori worked, enter a period of grief. (Rev: VOYA 2/87)

1874 Bradley, Kimberly Brubaker. *Leap of Faith* (4–7). 2007, Dial $16.99 (978-0-8037-3127-1). Abigail finds herself attracted to the new ideas she's learning at the Catholic school where she ended up after being expelled from public school. (Rev: BCCB 9/07; BL 7/07; SLJ 8/07)

1875 Branscum, Robbie. *Johnny May Grows Up* (6–8). 1987, HarperCollins $11.95 (978-0-06-020606-2). Johnny May, a spunky mountain girl, has no money to continue her schooling after 8th grade. (Rev: BL 10/1/87; SLJ 12/87)

1876 Brashares, Ann. *Girls in Pants: The Third Summer of the Sisterhood* (8–12). Series: Sisterhood of the Traveling Pants. 2005, Delacorte LB $18.99 (978-0-385-90919-8). It's summer again for the four friends and they manage to get together for a weekend before they leave for separate colleges; the pants continue their travels. (Rev: BL 12/15/04*; SLJ 1/05; VOYA 2/05)

1877 Brashares, Ann. *3 Willows: The Sisterhood Grows* (6–10). Series: Sisterhood. 2009, Delacorte $18.99 (978-038573676-3); LB $21.99 (978-038590628-9). The author of *The Sisterhood of the Traveling Pants* introduces Ama, Jo, and Polly, who are about to enter high school and face different but typical challenges. ∩ ℮ Lexile 700L (Rev: BL 2/15/09; HB 3–4/09; LMC 5–6/09; SLJ 1/1/09)

1878 Brezenoff, Steve. *Brooklyn, Burning* (8–12). 2011, Carolrhoda/Lab $17.95 (978-0-7613-7526-5). Sixteen-year-old Kid, overcoming the loss of Felix who disappeared, establishes an important new relationship in Scout in this sexually ambiguous novel set among homeless young people in Brooklyn. ℮ Lexile 760L (Rev: BL 9/1/11; HB 11–12/11; SLJ 9/1/11; VOYA 8/11)

1879 Brian, Kate. *Fake Boyfriend* (7–10). 2007, Simon & Schuster $16.99 (978-1-4169-1367-2). A fast-paced, humorous read about Vivi and Lane's efforts to help their friend Izzy, whose boyfriend has turned undependable just before the senior prom; they naturally turn to the Internet and MySpace. (Rev: SLJ 1/08)

1880 Bridgers, Sue Ellen. *Keeping Christina* (7–10). 1998, Replica LB $29.95 (978-0-7351-0042-8). Annie takes sad newcomer Christina under her wing, but she turns out to be a liar and troublemaker, which creates conflicts with Annie's family, friends, and boyfriend. (Rev: BL 7/93; SLJ 7/93)

1881 Bridgers, Sue Ellen. *Permanent Connections* (8–12). 1998, Replica LB $29.95 (978-0-7351-0043-5). When Rob's behavior gets out of control, the teenager is sent to his uncle's farm to cool off. (Rev: BL 2/15/87; SLJ 3/87; VOYA 4/87)

107

1882 Brooks, Martha. *Traveling On into the Light* (7–12). 1994, Orchard LB $16.99 (978-0-531-08713-8). Stories about runaways, suicide, and desertion, featuring romantic, sensitive, and smart teenage outsiders. (Rev: BL 8/94; SLJ 8/94*; VOYA 10/94)

1883 Bruchac, Joseph. *The Way* (6–8). 2007, Darby Creek $16.95 (978-1-58196-062-4). Cody, a Native American teenager who is used to being bullied, feels empowered when his uncle teaches him about his ancestors' traditions and the art of self-defense. (Rev: BL 10/1/07; SLJ 11/07)

1884 Brugman, Alyssa. *Walking Naked* (7–12). 2002, Allen & Unwin $17.95 (978-1-86508-822-8). A tragic tale in which a member of a 10th-grade elite group finds peer pressure more important than her growing friendship with the class outcast. (Rev: BCCB 4/04; BL 2/1/04; HB 7–8/04; SLJ 7/04; VOYA 4/03)

1885 Bulion, Leslie. *Uncharted Waters* (4–8). 2006, Peachtree $14.95 (978-1-56145-365-8). Jonah's summer of self-discovery following a dismal school year includes a heroic rescue at sea and excelling at his true talent. (Rev: SLJ 6/06)

1886 Bunting, Eve. *Doll Baby* (5–10). Illus. by Catherine Stock. 2000, Clarion $15.00 (978-0-395-93094-6). A simple, direct narrative in which 15-year-old Ellie explains how being pregnant and having a baby radically changed her life. (Rev: BL 11/1/00; HB 9–10/00; HBG 3/01; SLJ 10/00)

1887 Bunting, Eve. *If I Asked You, Would You Stay?* (8–10). 1984, HarperCollins LB $12.89 (978-0-397-32066-0). Two lonely people find comfort in love for each other.

1888 Burch, Robert. *Queenie Peavy* (5–7). 1987, Penguin paper $5.99 (978-0-14-032305-4). Queenie, whose father is in prison, is growing up a defiant, disobedient girl in rural Georgia in the 1930s.

1889 Bush, Penelope. *Alice in Time* (7–10). 2011, Holiday $17.95 (978-0-8234-2329-3). After falling from a merry-go-round, 14-year-old Alice wakes up in her 7-year-old body and gets a rare opportunity to reevaluate her life, her relationships with family members, and her own behavior. Lexile 830L (Rev: BL 4/1/11; SLJ 7/11)

1890 Cabot, Meg. *Pants on Fire* (8–12). 2007, Harper-Tempest $16.99 (978-0-06-088015-6). Katie, 16, is a bit loose with the truth, and a bit loose with the guys; when her former best friend Tommy — who exposed some cheaters in the past — returns to town she finds herself reviewing her behavior. 𝛀 (Rev: BL 5/1/07; SLJ 8/07)

1891 Caldwell, V. M. *The Ocean Within* (5–7). 1999, Milkweed paper $6.95 (978-1-57131-624-0). Elizabeth, who is on her third set of foster parents since she was orphaned five years before, has built walls of silence around herself that are impossible to penetrate.

(Rev: BCCB 1/00; BL 9/1/99; HBG 3/00; SLJ 11/99; VOYA 4/00)

1892 Caldwell, V. M. *Runt* (5–7). 2006, Milkweed $16.95 (978-1-57131-662-2); paper $6.95 (978-1-57131-661-5). Runt, a 13-year-old who is trying to cope with his mother's death and his new living arrangements, becomes close to Mitch, who is dying of cancer. (Rev: SLJ 7/06)

1893 Caletti, Deb. *The Queen of Everything* (8–12). 2002, Simon & Schuster paper $5.99 (978-0-7434-3684-7). Jordan's life is turned upside-down by her grandmother's death, her father's new romance, and her own sexual experimentation. (Rev: BCCB 1/03; BL 11/15/02; SLJ 11/02; VOYA 2/03)

1894 Calonita, Jen. *Secrets of My Hollywood Life: A Novel* (6–12). 2006, Little, Brown $16.99 (978-0-316-15442-0). Kaitlin needs a break from celebrity and enrolls, incognito, at a friend's high school where she establishes a new persona — complete with new boyfriend — until a coincidental visit from her costar blows her cover. (Rev: SLJ 6/06)

1895 Cameron, Ann. *Colibri* (5–8). 2003, Farrar $17.00 (978-0-374-31519-1). Twelve-year-old Rosa, who was kidnapped from her Mayan village when she was four, seeks to escape from the abusive "uncle" who is exploiting her. (Rev: BCCB 10/03; BL 10/1/03*; HB 9–10/03; HBG 4/04; SLJ 10/03*)

1896 Cantor, Jillian. *The Life of Glass* (7–12). 2010, HarperCollins $16.99 (978-0-06-168651-1). Melissa, 14, is still grieving for her father while she struggles to adjust to her mother's new beau, get along with her sister, and make sense of her feelings for her friend Ryan. e Lexile 860L (Rev: BL 12/15/09; SLJ 5/10; VOYA 6/10)

1897 Carr, Dennis, and Elise Carr. *Welcome to Wahoo* (8–11). 2006, Bloomsbury $16.95 (978-1-58234-696-0). Snooty socialite Victoria gets a taste of what it means to be an outsider when she is forced to transfer to a small-town high school in Nebraska. (Rev: BL 7/06; SLJ 6/06)

1898 Carter, Alden R. *Dogwolf* (7–10). 1994, Scholastic paper $13.95 (978-0-590-46741-4). In this coming-of-age novel, Pete realizes that a dogwolf that he's set free must be found and killed before it harms a human. (Rev: BL 1/1/95; SLJ 4/95; VOYA 2/95)

1899 Carter, Scott William. *The Last Great Getaway of the Water Balloon Boys* (8–11). 2010, Simon & Schuster $16.99 (978-1-4169-7156-6). Charlie, 16, unwisely renews a friendship with the wayward Jake and the two embark on a series of unfortunate adventures that involve theft, car racing, drug use, and violence. (Rev: BLO 4/1/10; LMC 5–6/10; SLJ 4/10)

1900 Caseley, Judith. *Praying to A. L.* (5–8). 2000, Greenwillow $15.95 (978-0-688-15934-4). After her father dies, 12-year-old Sierra transfers all her love to a portrait of Abraham Lincoln given to her by her father. (Rev: BL 5/15/00; HBG 10/00; SLJ 6/00)

1901 Cassidy, Anne. *Looking for JJ* (8–11). 2007, Harcourt $17.00 (978-0-15-206190-6). Alice was called Jennifer Jones during the disturbed childhood that came to an abrupt end when she murdered another child; now Alice, released from prison, hopes to lead a new life. ∩ (Rev: BL 10/1/07; LMC 1/08; SLJ 10/07)

1902 Castellucci, Cecil. *Boy Proof* (7–10). 2005, Candlewick $15.99 (978-0-7636-2333-3). Sixteen-year-old Victoria, who prefers to be known as Egg, is smart, cool, and totally in control until Max Carter enters her life and breaks the shell. (Rev: BCCB 2/05; BL 2/15/05; HB 5–6/05; SLJ 4/05; VOYA 4/05)

1903 Chan, Gillian. *Glory Days and Other Stories* (7–10). 1997, Kids Can $16.95 (978-1-55074-381-4). Five stories about young people at Elmwood High School, each of whom faces problems because of decisions that have been made. (Rev: BL 1/1–15/98; SLJ 10/97)

1904 Chan, Gillian. *Golden Girl and Other Stories* (7–10). 1997, Kids Can $14.95 (978-1-55074-385-2). Short stories about students in a high school, with details of their pleasures, pains, and concerns. (Rev: BL 9/15/97; SLJ 11/97)

1905 Chandler, Kristen. *Girls Don't Fly* (7–10). 2011, Viking $16.99 (978-067001331-9). After getting dumped by her boyfriend, Myra pours herself into cormorant research, hoping to win a trip to the Galapagos islands. ∩ ℮ Lexile HL590L (Rev: BL 10/15/11; HB 1–2/12; SLJ 1/12; VOYA 10/11)

1906 Cheng, Andrea. *Where Do You Stay?* (4–7). 2011, Boyds Mills $17.95 (978-1-59078-707-6). After Jerome's mother dies, the 11-year-old goes to live with an aunt and cousins, struggling to adjust to his new setting with the help of a homeless man who shares his love of music. Lexile 590L (Rev: BL 3/15/11; SLJ 5/11)

1907 Chin, Michael. *Free Throw* (7–12). 2001, PublishAmerica paper $24.95 (978-1-58851-166-9). Basketball and romance play major roles in the life of high school sophomore Mike Weaver. (Rev: VOYA 4/02)

1908 Choldenko, Gennifer. *If a Tree Falls at Lunch Period* (6–8). 2007, Harcourt $17.00 (978-0-15-205753-4). The mean girls at Kirsten's private school are making her life miserable, but things start to look up when Walk, a new kid from the inner city, enrolls in her class; chapters alternate between Kirsten's and Walk's points of view. ∩ (Rev: BL 10/1/07; HB 9–10/07; LMC 1/08; SLJ 8/07)

1909 Clairday, Robynn. *Confessions of a Boyfriend Stealer* (8–11). 2005, Delacorte paper $7.95 (978-0-385-73242-0). In entries from a blog, 16-year-old Gen, high school junior and aspiring documentary filmmaker, describes her growing disillusion with her best friends CJ and Tasha. (Rev: BL 9/15/05; SLJ 9/05)

1910 Clark, Catherine. *The Alison Rules* (7–12). 2004, HarperCollins LB $16.89 (978-0-06-055981-6). Reeling from her mother's death, high school sophomore Alison retreats into herself and creates sets of rules to help her cope; the arrival of a new student called Patrick finally brings her out of her shell. (Rev: BL 10/15/04; SLJ 8/04; VOYA 12/04)

1911 Clarke, Judith. *Night Train* (8–11). 2000, Henry Holt $16.95 (978-0-8050-6151-2). Luke Leman, an Australian teenager, finds that he is cracking under scholastic and family pressures and thinks he might be going insane. (Rev: BCCB 5/00; BL 6/1–15/00; HBG 9/00; SLJ 5/00)

1912 Clarke, Nicole. *Spin City* (6–9). 2006, Dunlap paper $6.99 (978-0-448-44123-8). Kiyoka, a nonconformist / go-getter / pop-culture-loving teen, has taken an internship at *Flirt* fashion magazine in New York City where she works hard but hasn't gotten the big break assignment she is anticipating, so she decides to try her hand at music composition — a true passion — which produces both disappointing and triumphant results. (Rev: SLJ 8/06)

1913 Cleary, Beverly. *Dear Mr. Henshaw* (4–7). Illus. by Paul O. Zelinsky. 1983, Morrow LB $16.89 (978-0-688-02406-2). A Newbery Medal winner (1984) about a boy who pours out his problems in letters to a writer he greatly admires.

1914 Cleaver, Vera, and Bill Cleaver. *Ellen Grae* (6–8). 1967, HarperCollins LB $12.89 (978-0-397-30938-2). Ellen Grae, an imaginative girl, finds it impossible to assimilate the story of the death of her friend Ira's parents. Included in this volume is the sequel *Lady Ellen Grae*.

1915 Cleaver, Vera, and Bill Cleaver. *Grover* (6–9). 1987, HarperCollins $13.95 (978-0-397-31118-7). The death of his beloved mother seems more than Grover can handle. A reissue.

1916 Cleaver, Vera, and Bill Cleaver. *Hazel Rye* (6–9). 1983, HarperCollins LB $13.89 (978-0-397-31952-7); paper $3.95 (978-0-06-440156-2). Eleven-year-old Hazel rents the Poole family a small house in a citrus grove.

1917 Clements, Andrew. *Troublemaker* (5–8). Illus. by Mark Elliott. 2011, Atheneum $16.99 (978-1-4169-4930-5). When his older brother Mitchell gets out of jail a changed character, 6th-grader Clay also decides to reform, but finds it harder than expected. ∩ Lexile 730L (Rev: BL 6/1/11; HB 7–8/11; LMC 1–2/12; SLJ 7/11)

1918 Clipston, Amy. *Roadside Assistance* (7–11). 2011, Zondervan paper $9.99 (978-0-310-71-981-6). Car lover Emily, 17, struggles with her loss of faith and feelings of inadequacy when her mother dies and she and her father move in with her wealthy aunt. ℮ (Rev: BL 5/1/11; SLJ 7/11; VOYA 6/11)

109

1919 Cohen, Miriam. *Robert and Dawn Marie 4Ever* (6–9). 1986, HarperCollins $11.95 (978-0-06-021396-1). Robert, a street waif, finds a new home and forms a friendship with Dawn Marie, a young girl whose mother disapproves of Robert. (Rev: BL 11/1/86; SLJ 12/86; VOYA 12/86)

1920 Cohn, Rachel. *Pop Princess* (8–12). 2004, Simon & Schuster $15.95 (978-0-689-85205-3). Sixteen-year-old Wonder Blake has a wry understanding of the changes affecting her life when she is offered a recording contract. (Rev: BCCB 4/04; BL 1/1–15/04; SLJ 3/04; VOYA 8/04)

1921 Colasanti, Susane. *Take Me There* (7–10). 2008, Viking $17.99 (978-0-670-06333-8). Three high school students in New York — Rhiannon, James, and Nicole — deal with family problems, school, and romantic entanglements in this compelling story told in three alternating narratives. (Rev: BL 8/08; SLJ 9/08)

1922 Cole, Brock. *The Goats* (6–9). 1987, Farrar paper $5.95 (978-0-374-42575-3). Two misfits at summer camp find inner strength and self-knowledge when they are cruelly marooned on an island by fellow campers. (Rev: BL 11/15/87; SLJ 11/87; VOYA 4/88)

1923 Coleman, Rowan. *Ruby Parker Hits the Small Time* (6–9). 2007, HarperCollins $15.99 (978-0-06-077628-2). Ruby, 13, a child star on a British soap opera, must deal with jealous peers, divorcing parents, and fans who look to her for advice in this appealing, fast-paced novel. (Rev: BCCB 3/07; BL 2/1/07; SLJ 4/07)

1924 Collard, Sneed B, III. *Dog Sense* (5–8). 2005, Peachtree $14.95 (978-1-56145-351-1). Unhappy after moving from sunny California to a small town in Montana, 13-year-old Guy Martinez finds solace in time spent with his dog, Streak, and a newfound friend named Luke. (Rev: BL 10/15/05; SLJ 11/05)

1925 Collier, Kristi. *Throwing Stones* (7–10). 2006, Henry Holt $16.95 (978-0-8050-7614-1). In the year 1923, Andy begins high school and dreams of being a basketball star like his late brother, hoping that it will help his parents cope with his death, but a bet could ruin his plan. (Rev: BL 9/1/06; SLJ 11/06)

1926 Conford, Ellen. *Hail, Hail Camp Timberwood* (5–7). Illus. by Gail Owens. 1978, Little, Brown $14.95 (978-0-316-15291-4). Thirteen-year-old Melanie's first summer at camp.

1927 Conford, Ellen. *You Never Can Tell* (7–9). 1984, Little, Brown $14.95 (978-0-316-15267-9). Katie's soap opera heartthrob enters her high school.

1928 Conly, Jane Leslie. *Crazy Lady!* (5–8). 1993, HarperCollins LB $18.89 (978-0-06-021360-2). In a city slum, Vernon forms a friendship with an eccentric woman and helps her care for her disabled teenage son. Newbery Honor 1994; ALA Notable Children's Books 1994; ALA Best Books for Young Adults 1994. (Rev: BCCB 7–8/93; BL 5/15/93*; SLJ 4/93*)

1929 Cooney, Caroline B. *Summer Nights* (7–12). 1992, Scholastic paper $3.25 (978-0-590-45786-6). At a farewell party, five high school girls look back on their school years and their friendship. (Rev: SLJ 1/89)

1930 Cooper, Rose. *Gossip from the Girls' Room* (5–8). Illus. by author. 2011, Delacorte $12.99 (978-0-385-73947-4); LB $15.99 (978-0-385-90791-0). Sixth-grader Sophia's attempts to bring down a popular girl at school by posting gossipy blogs go awry. e (Rev: BL 1/1–15/11; SLJ 3/1/11)

1931 Corcoran, Barbara. *You Put Up with Me, I'll Put Up with You* (6–8). 1989, Avon paper $2.50 (978-0-380-70558-0). A somewhat self-centered girl moves with her mother to a new community and has problems adjusting. (Rev: BL 3/15/87; SLJ 3/87; VOYA 4/87)

1932 Cormier, Robert. *The Chocolate War* (7–12). 1993, Dell paper $3.99 (978-0-440-90032-0). A chocolate sale in a boys' private school creates power struggles. Followed by *Beyond the Chocolate War.*

1933 Cormier, Robert. *The Rag and Bone Shop* (8–10). 2001, Delacorte $15.95 (978-0-385-72962-8). Shy, introverted 13-year-old Jason is a suspect in the murder of a 7-year-old girl in this dark and suspenseful story that features an ambitious and ruthless detective. (Rev: BCCB 12/01; BL 7/01; HB 11–12/01; HBG 3/02; SLJ 9/01; VOYA 10/01)

1934 Cormier, Robert. *Tunes for Bears to Dance To* (6–12). 1992, Dell paper $5.50 (978-0-440-21903-3). In a stark morality tale set in a Massachusetts town after World War II, Henry, 11, is tempted, corrupted, and redeemed. (Rev: BL 6/15/92; SLJ 9/92)

1935 Cormier, Robert. *We All Fall Down* (8–12). 1991, Dell paper $5.50 (978-0-440-21556-1). Random violence committed by four high school seniors is observed by the Avenger, who also witnesses the budding love affair of one of the victims of the attack. (Rev: BL 9/15/91*; SLJ 9/91*)

1936 Coryell, Susan. *Eaglebait* (6–9). 1989, Harcourt $14.95 (978-0-15-200442-2). An unpopular teenage nerd thinks he has found a friend in a new science teacher. (Rev: BL 11/1/89; SLJ 6/90)

1937 Cossi, Olga. *The Magic Box* (7–9). 1990, Pelican $14.95 (978-0-88289-748-6). Mara cannot seem to give up smoking until her mother, a former smoker, develops throat cancer. (Rev: BL 10/15/90; SLJ 8/90; VOYA 8/90)

1938 Craig, Jeremy. *The Straits* (6–9). 2009, Flux paper $9.95 (978-073871444-8). Jim turns to gambling in his struggle to survive after a hurricane that killed his mother and sister. (Rev: BLO 4/14/09)

1939 Crocker, Nancy. *Billie Standish Was Here* (6–9). 2007, Simon & Schuster $16.99 (978-1-4169-2423-4). Billie, an unhappy 11-year-old, befriends her elderly neighbor Miss Lydia, and they rely on each other as they navigate some major personal and natural upheavals. (Rev: BL 6/1–15/07; SLJ 7/07)

1940 Cross, Gillian. *Tightrope* (7–12). 1999, Holiday $16.95 (978-0-8234-1512-0). To take her mind off the hours she spends caring for her invalid mother, Ashley begins to hang out with a local street gang. (Rev: BCCB 12/99; BL 9/15/99; HBG 4/00; SLJ 10/99; VOYA 4/00)

1941 Crowe, Carole. *Waiting for Dolphins* (6–12). 2000, Boyds Mills $16.95 (978-1-56397-847-0). Still recovering from her father's death in a boating incident, Molly must also adjust to her mother's new love interest. (Rev: BL 3/1/00; HBG 9/00; SLJ 4/00; VOYA 6/00)

1942 Crutcher, Chris. *The Sledding Hill* (8–11). 2005, HarperCollins LB $17.89 (978-0-06-050244-7). Not even death can separate teenage friends Billy Bartholomew and Eddie Proffit in this thought-provoking novel that not only features author Crutcher but also a controversial novel called *Warren Peace*. (Rev: BL 5/1/05; SLJ 6/05; VOYA 6/05)

1943 Cumbie, Patricia. *Where People like Us Live* (7–12). 2008, HarperCollins $16.99 (978-0-06-137597-2). When her family moves to a depressed town in Wisconsin, Libby makes friends with a girl named Angie and soon discovers that Angie is being sexually abused by her stepfather. (Rev: BL 4/1/08; SLJ 6/08)

1944 Danziger, Paula. *Can You Sue Your Parents for Malpractice?* (6–9). 1998, Putnam paper $4.99 (978-0-698-11688-7). Lauren, 14 years old, faces a variety of problems both at home and at school.

1945 Danziger, Paula. *Remember Me to Harold Square* (6–9). 1999, Putnam paper $5.99 (978-0-698-11694-8). Kendra gets to know attractive Frank when they participate in scavenger hunts in New York City. (Rev: BL 10/1/87; SLJ 11/87; VOYA 12/87)

1946 Daoust, Jerry. *Waking Up Bees: Stories of Living Life's Questions* (7–12). 1999, Saint Mary's paper $6.95 (978-0-88489-527-5). In this collection of 10 short stories, young Christians find answers to life's dilemmas in their faith. (Rev: VOYA 4/00)

1947 Davis, Tanita S. *A La Carte* (7–10). 2008, Knopf $15.99 (978-0-375-84815-5). African American high school senior Lainey hopes to become a celebrity vegetarian chef; when her best friend Simeon disappears with $500 of her money, Lainey is alone in the kitchen and with her thoughts. (Rev: BL 8/08)

1948 Day, Karen. *A Million Miles from Boston* (5–8). 2011, Random House $15.99 (978-0-385-73899-6); LB $18.99 (978-0-385-90763-7). Lucy, 12, contends with her dad's new girlfriend, the shifting social landscape, and a pesky boy from back home who's popped up at their summer vacation home in Maine. (Rev: BL 3/15/11; LMC 10/11; SLJ 6/11)

1949 de Guzman, Michael. *Finding Stinko* (5–8). 2007, Farrar $16.00 (978-0-374-32305-9). On the run from his latest and worst set of foster parents, Newboy, an elective mute, finds new voice with a ventriloquist's dummy; a compelling book of survival on the streets. (Rev: BL 4/15/07; SLJ 6/07)

1950 De Palma, Toni. *Under the Banyan Tree* (6–9). 2007, Holiday $16.95 (978-0-8234-1965-4). Irena, 15 but seeming younger, runs away from home after her mother leaves and tries to make a better life for herself working at the Banyan Tree Motel in Key West. (Rev: BL 8/07; SLJ 7/07)

1951 De Vries, Anke. *Bruises* (6–10). Trans. by Stacey Knecht. 1996, Front St $15.95 (978-1-886910-03-4). This novel, set in Holland, tells of the friendship between a sympathetic boy, Michael, and Judith, a disturbed, abused young girl. (Rev: BL 4/1/96; SLJ 6/96; VOYA 6/96)

1952 Dean, Carolee. *Comfort* (7–10). 2002, Houghton Mifflin $15.00 (978-0-618-13846-3). Fourteen-year-old Kenny persists in his dreams of making something of himself in spite of his mother's conflicting desires. (Rev: HBG 10/02; SLJ 3/02*; VOYA 4/02)

1953 Deckers, Amber. *Ella Mental: And the Good Sense Guide* (6–9). 2006, Simon & Schuster paper $5.99 (978-1-4169-1322-1). Fourteen-year-old Ella brings her high standards of morality and her offbeat sense of humor to bear as she attempts to help her British mates deal with very serious problems while struggling with her own interest in Toby. (Rev: SLJ 7/06)

1954 Dee, Barbara. *Just Another Day in My Insanely Real Life* (4–7). 2006, Simon & Schuster $15.95 (978-1-4169-0861-6). Cassie must deal with the fallout from her parents' divorce, with her irresponsible older sister and demanding little brother, and with her former best friends in this novel about an all-too-real situation. (Rev: BL 5/15/06; SLJ 8/06)

1955 Dee, Barbara. *Solving Zoe* (4–7). 2009, Simon & Schuster $15.99 (978-1-4169-6128-4). Zoe drifts in a sea of bright students and fading friends until her talent for codes and puzzles unlocks her new direction. (Rev: BCCB 6/09; BL 6/1–15/09; SLJ 6/09)

1956 Dee, Barbara. *This Is Me from Now On* (5–8). 2010, Aladdin paper $5.99 (978-14169941-4-5). Seventh-grader Evie is fascinated by the new girl next door, who lives totally by her own rules. e (Rev: BLO 11/15/10)

1957 DeKeyser, Stacy. *Jump the Cracks* (5–8). 2008, Flux paper $9.95 (978-0-7387-1274-1). Victoria, 15, sees a little boy being mistreated at a train station and ends up taking him to Georgia — an originally compassionate act that she soon finds will have huge complications. (Rev: BL 3/1/08; SLJ 9/08)

1958 Delaney, Mark. *Pepperland* (8–12). 2004, Peachtree $14.95 (978-1-56145-317-7). In this poignant coming-of-age novel set in 1980, 16-year-old Pamela Jean tries to cope with the pain of her mother's death from cancer. (Rev: BL 12/1/04; SLJ 11/04; VOYA 10/04)

1959 Deriso, Christine Hurley. *Do-Over* (5–8). 2006, Delacorte LB $17.99 (978-0-385-90350-9). Between the recent death of her mother and the move to a new school, 7th-grader Elsa is having a hard time of it, but things look up when her mother mysteriously appears one night and grants her do-over power. (Rev: SLJ 8/06)

1960 Deriso, Christine Hurley. *. . . Then I Met My Sister* (8–10). 2011, Flux paper $9.95 (978-0-7387-2-581-9). Summer learns important truths when she receives her dead sister Shannon's diary; it seems her sister wasn't as perfect as everyone thought. **e** Lexile HL680L (Rev: BL 5/1/11; SLJ 4/11; VOYA 4/11)

1961 Dessen, Sarah. *Dreamland* (8–10). 2000, Viking $16.99 (978-0-670-89122-1). After her sister runs away, Caitlin's life comes apart and she descends into drugs and sex. (Rev: BL 11/1/00*; HB 9–10/00; HBG 3/01; SLJ 9/00)

1962 Dessen, Sarah. *Just Listen* (8–11). 2006, Viking $17.99 (978-0-670-06105-1). Annabel is shunned by her friends after being seen in a compromising situation with her best friend's boyfriend. (Rev: BL 3/15/06; SLJ 5/06; VOYA 4/06)

1963 Dessen, Sarah. *Keeping the Moon* (6–10). 1999, Viking $17.99 (978-0-670-88549-7). Colie, a 15-year-old girl with little self-esteem, spends a summer with an eccentric aunt and finds a kind of salvation in a friendship with two waitresses and the love of a shy teenage artist. (Rev: BL 9/1/99; HBG 4/00; SLJ 9/99; VOYA 12/99)

1964 Dessen, Sarah. *Lock and Key* (8–12). 2008, Viking $18.99 (978-0-670-01088-2). After a life of experiencing abandonment, 17-year-old Ruby moves in with her older sister Cora and her husband, starts attending a private school, and slowly learns to trust others and make friends. (Rev: BL 2/1/08; SLJ 5/08)

1965 Dessen, Sarah. *Someone Like You* (7–12). 1998, Viking $17.99 (978-0-670-87778-2). Young Halley discovers that her best friend Scarlett is pregnant and Scarlett's boyfriend has been killed in an accident. (Rev: BL 5/15/98; HB 7–8/98; HBG 9/98; SLJ 6/98; VOYA 8/98)

1966 Dessen, Sarah. *That Summer* (7–12). 1996, Orchard LB $17.99 (978-0-531-08888-3). Haven is 15 and 5 feet 11, and to make matters worse, she has to be bridesmaid at her picture-perfect sister's wedding. (Rev: BL 10/15/96*; SLJ 10/96; VOYA 12/96)

1967 Dooley, Sarah. *Body of Water* (6–9). 2011, Feiwel & Friends $16.99 (978-0-312-61254-2). Ember, 12, and her Wiccan family are homeless after their trailer home burns, and Ember struggles with various problems including the fact that her friend Anson may have set the fire. 🎧 **e** Lexile 940L (Rev: BL 10/1/11; LMC 1–2/12; SLJ 12/1/11)

1968 Douglas, Lola. *True Confessions of a Hollywood Starlet* (8–10). 2005, Penguin $16.99 (978-1-59514-035-7). Teen movie star Morgan Carter, on the mend from a drug overdose in Hollywood, adopts a new identity when she is sent to a midwestern high school in this credible and amusing novel. (Rev: BCCB 2/06; SLJ 12/05; VOYA 4/06)

1969 Dowell, Frances O'Roark. *The Second Life of Abigail Walker* (4–7). 2012, Atheneum $16.99 (978-1-4424-0593-6). Abigail, 11, is overweight and bullied until an encounter with a fox spurs her to view her life in a different way. **e** Lexile 740L (Rev: BL 9/15/12*; LMC 1–2/13; SLJ 10/12)

1970 Doyle, Malachy. *Who Is Jesse Flood?* (6–9). 2002, Bloomsbury $14.95 (978-1-58234-776-9). Unhappy 14-year-old Jesse struggles to cope with his parents and his loneliness in his Northern Ireland hometown. (Rev: BCCB 12/02; BL 10/1/02; SLJ 10/02*)

1971 Draper, Sharon M. *Romiette and Julio* (6–10). 1999, Simon & Schuster $16.00 (978-0-689-82180-6). An updated version of Romeo and Juliet set in contemporary Cincinnati involving a Hispanic American boy, an African American girl, street gangs, and, in this case, a happy ending. (Rev: BL 9/15/99; HBG 4/00; SLJ 9/99; VOYA 12/99)

1972 Dreyer, Ellen. *Speechless in New York: Going to New York* (5–8). Series: Going To. 2000, Four Corners paper $7.95 (978-1-893577-01-5). Jessie is beset with personal problems when she flies to New York from Minnesota with the Prairie Youth Chorale. (Rev: SLJ 3/00)

1973 Ellis, Deborah. *Looking for X* (6–9). 2000, Douglas & McIntyre paper $7.95 (978-0-88899-382-3). Khyber, a waif who is considered a loner by her classmates, is wrongfully accused of vandalism. (Rev: BCCB 9/00; BL 5/15/00; HB 7–8/00; HBG 9/00; SLJ 7/00)

1974 Ellis, Sarah. *Pick-Up Sticks* (5–8). 1992, Macmillan LB $15.00 (978-0-689-50550-8). A disgruntled teen learns a lesson in life after being sent to live with relatives. (Rev: BL 1/15/92; SLJ 3/92*)

1975 Emerson, Kevin. *Carlos Is Gonna Get It* (4–7). 2008, Scholastic $16.99 (978-0-439-93525-8). A group of 7th-graders plan a prank on their special-needs classmate during a wilderness trip, but their plan backfires when they become lost in the forest during a lightning storm. (Rev: BCCB 11/08; BL 10/1/08; SLJ 12/08)

1976 Emond, Stephen. *Happyface* (7–10). Illus. by author. 2010, Little, Brown $16.99 (978-0-316-04100-3). In this quirky journal-style offering, awkward, talented teen Happyface records his life — his painful past, his determination to make a fresh start, and the smile he wears to hide the truth. (Rev: LMC 11–12/09; SLJ 3/10; VOYA 6/10)

1977 Erlings, Fridrik. *Benjamin Dove* (5–8). 2007, North-South $15.95 (978-0-7358-2150-7); paper $7.95

(978-0-7358-2149-1). Set in Iceland, this story of four boys' friendship ends in violence when some of the friends take tragically wrong turns in their lives. (Rev: BL 2/1/08; SLJ 12/07)

1978 Esckilsen, Erik E. *The Last Mall Rat* (7–10). 2003, Houghton Mifflin $15.00 (978-0-618-23417-2). Bored and penniless, 15-year-old Mitch agrees to harass rude shoppers. (Rev: BL 4/1/03; HBG 4/04; SLJ 6/03; VOYA 6/03)

1979 Evangelista, Beth. *Gifted* (5–8). 2005, Walker $16.95 (978-0-8027-8994-5). George R. Clark is gifted and colossally unpopular with most of his classmates, so he is uneasy about going on his 8th-grade science field trip without his principal-father to protect him from the bullies; funny and real. (Rev: BL 12/15/05*; HBG 4/06; LMC 11–12/05; SLJ 1/06; VOYA 10/05)

1980 Evans, Douglas. *So What Do You Do?* (5–8). 1997, Front St $14.95 (978-1-886910-20-1). Two middle-schoolers help their beloved former teacher who has become a homeless drunk. (Rev: BCCB 3/98; BL 11/1/97; HBG 3/98; SLJ 1/98; VOYA 2/98)

1981 Evans, Mari. *I'm Late: The Story of LaNeese and Moonlight and Alisha Who Didn't Have Anyone of Her Own* (7–12). Illus. by Varnette Honeywood. 2006, Just Us Bks $14.95 (978-1-933491-00-4). Using an authentic voice and effective line drawings, Evans interweaves stories about pregnancy, loneliness, and bad decisions as experienced by three African American teenagers and shows their growth as they learn to make better choices. (Rev: SLJ 7/06)

1982 Eyerly, Jeannette. *Someone to Love Me* (7–10). 1987, HarperCollins LB $11.89 (978-0-397-32206-0). An unpopular high school girl is seduced by the school's glamour boy and decides, when she finds she is pregnant, to keep the child. (Rev: BL 2/1/87; SLJ 4/87; VOYA 4/87)

1983 Facklam, Margery. *The Trouble with Mothers* (6–8). 1991, Avon paper $2.95 (978-0-380-71139-0). Troy is angered when the town censors target his mother's historical novel. (Rev: BL 3/1/89; SLJ 5/89; VOYA 6/89)

1984 Fergus, Maureen. *Exploits of a Reluctant (but Extremely Goodlooking) Hero* (8–10). 2007, Kids Can $16.95 (978-1-55453-024-3). A nameless 13-year-old narrator records his comments on life on a tape recorder; this is a funny story about a self-centered kid who eventually learns a little about sensitivity. (Rev: HB 5–6/07; LMC 10/07; SLJ 4/07)

1985 Ferris, Jean. *Across the Grain* (8–12). 1993, Topeka LB $16.35 (978-0-7857-0723-3). Paige and his elder sister head to a community in the desert where they take jobs in a restaurant. (Rev: BL 11/15/90)

1986 Ferris, Jean. *Bad* (7–10). 1998, Farrar paper $4.95 (978-0-374-40475-8). Dallas gains self knowledge when she is sent to a women's correctional center for six months and meets gang members, drug dealers, a 14-year-old prostitute, and other unfortunates. (Rev: BL 10/1/98; SLJ 12/98; VOYA 2/99)

1987 Ferris, Jean. *Of Sound Mind* (6–9). 2001, Farrar $16.00 (978-0-374-35580-7). High school senior Theo, who is the only hearing member of his demanding family, finds support and romance when he meets Ivy, who also can both hear and sign. (Rev: BCCB 10/01; BL 9/15/01; HB 11–12/01; HBG 3/02; SLJ 9/01; VOYA 10/01)

1988 Ferry, Charles. *A Fresh Start* (7–10). 1996, Proctor paper $8.95 (978-1-882792-18-4). This novel explores the problems of troubled teens in a summer-school program for young alcoholics. (Rev: SLJ 5/96; VOYA 10/96)

1989 Filichia, Peter. *What's in a Name?* (7–12). 1988, Avon paper $2.75 (978-0-380-75536-3). Rose is so unhappy with her foreign-sounding last name that she decides to change it. (Rev: BL 3/1/89; VOYA 4/89)

1990 Fitzhugh, Louise. *Harriet the Spy* (6–8). 2001, Random House paper $5.99 (978-0-440-41679-1). The story of a girl whose passion for honesty gets her into trouble. Followed by *The Long Secret*.

1991 Flack, Sophie. *Bunheads* (8–12). 2011, Little, Brown $17.99 (978-0-316-12653-3). Five years into her career with the Manhattan Ballet, 19-year-old Hannah begins to realize how much she's given up to be where she is, and meeting Jacob makes her question her sacrifices. ℮ (Rev: BL 10/15/11; SLJ 10/1/11; VOYA 10/11)

1992 Flake, Sharon G. *A Freak Like Me* (5–9). 1999, Hyperion paper $5.99 (978-0-7868-1307-0). In her inner-city middle school, Maleeka Madison is picked on by classmates because she is poorly dressed, darker than the others, and gets good grades. (Rev: BL 9/1/98; SLJ 11/98)

1993 Fletcher, Christine. *Tallulah Falls* (8–11). 2006, Bloomsbury $16.95 (978-1-58234-662-5). At the age of 17, unhappy Tallulah (formerly known as Debbie) runs away from home looking for her older friend Maeve, who has bipolar disease and has left Oregon for Florida; on the way, Tallulah becomes stranded in Tennessee and finds a haven working in a veterinary clinic. (Rev: BL 4/1/06; SLJ 6/06)

1994 Fletcher, Ralph. *Spider Boy* (5–8). 1997, Houghton Mifflin $16.00 (978-0-395-77606-3). Bobby — nicknamed Spider Boy because he knows so much about spiders — has trouble adjusting to his new life in the town of New Paltz, New York. (Rev: BCCB 4/97; BL 6/1–15/97; HB 7–8/97; SLJ 7/97)

1995 Flinn, Alex. *Breathing Underwater* (7–12). 2001, HarperCollins $18.99 (978-0-06-029198-3). In this harrowing account of domestic violence, the sins of the father are reflected in troubled teen Nick Andreas's savage treatment of his girlfriend, Caitlin. (Rev: BCCB 7–8/01; BL 8/01; HBG 10/01; SLJ 5/01; VOYA 6/01)

1996 Fogelin, Adrian. *The Sorta Sisters* (5–8). Illus. by author. 2007, Peachtree $14.95 (978-1-56145-424-2). Anna, a foster child who lives in Tallahassee, Florida, corresponds with Mica, who lives with her alcoholic father on a boat in the Florida Keys, and their friendship brings them both solace. (Rev: BL 1/1–15/08; SLJ 12/07)

1997 Fogelin, Adrian. *Summer on the Moon* (5–8). 2012, Peachtree $15.95 (978-1-56145-626-0). Socko, 13, and his mother move from the gritty inner city to the suburbs, where they will look after an elderly relative, but the situation there is not as simple or satisfactory as they hoped. Lexile 630L (Rev: BL 4/15/12*; LMC 11–12/12; SLJ 7/12)

1998 Foon, Dennis. *Double or Nothing* (6–12). 2000, Annick $17.95 (978-1-55037-627-2); paper $6.95 (978-1-55037-626-5). High school senior Kip feels secure that he has saved enough money for college until he meets King, a magician and con artist who takes advantage of Kip's love of gambling. (Rev: BL 8/00; HBG 9/00; SLJ 9/00)

1999 Fox, Paula. *Monkey Island* (5–8). 1991, Watts LB $16.99 (978-0-531-08562-2). A homeless, abandoned 11-year-old boy in New York City contracts pneumonia and is cared for by a homeless African American teenager and retired teacher, who share their place in the park with him. (Rev: BCCB 10/91*; BL 9/1/91*; HB 9–10/91*; SLJ 8/91)

2000 Fox, Paula. *Western Wind* (5–9). 1993, Orchard LB $17.99 (978-0-531-08652-0). At first resentful of being sent to spend a summer with her grandmother on a Maine island, Elizabeth gradually adjusts and learns a great deal about herself. (Rev: BCCB 9/93; BL 10/15/93; SLJ 12/93*; VOYA 12/93)

2001 Franco, Betsy, ed. *Things I Have to Tell You: Poems and Writing by Teenage Girls* (7–12). Photos by Nina Nickles. 2001, Candlewick paper $8.99 (978-0-7636-1035-7). Teen girls reveal their aspirations, fears, and frustrations in this appealing collection of poems, stories, and essays. (Rev: BL 3/15/01; HB 5–6/01; HBG 10/01; SLJ 5/01; VOYA 10/01)

2002 Fredericks, Mariah. *The True Meaning of Cleavage* (7–10). 2003, Simon & Schuster $15.95 (978-0-689-85092-9). High school freshman Jess describes her friend Sari's obsession with an older student in this novel of sexuality, betrayal, and self-image. (Rev: BCCB 3/03; BL 3/15/03*; HB 7–8/03; HBG 10/03; SLJ 2/03; VOYA 4/03)

2003 Freeman, Martha. *1,000 Reasons Never to Kiss a Boy* (7–10). 2007, Holiday $16.95 (978-0-8234-2044-5). Sixteen-year-old Jane actually comes up with only 40+ reasons not to kiss boys before she gets over her

first boyfriend and finds reasons to love and kiss again; a funny, light novel. (Rev: BL 8/07; SLJ 10/07)

2004 Freeman, Martha. *The Year My Parents Ruined My Life* (6–9). 1997, Holiday $15.95 (978-0-8234-1324-9). Twelve-year-old Kate has many problems adjusting to her new home in a small Pennsylvania town and longs to return to the suburbs of Los Angeles, her friends, and dreamy boyfriend. (Rev: BL 12/1/97; HBG 3/98; SLJ 12/97)

2005 Freymann-Weyr, Garret. *My Heartbeat* (8–12). 2002, Houghton Mifflin $15.00 (978-0-618-14181-4). Fourteen-year-old Ellen is in love with James, but James and her older brother Link are also involved. (Rev: BCCB 5/02; BL 6/1–15/02; HB 5–6/02*; HBG 10/02; SLJ 4/02; VOYA 4/02)

2006 Friel, Maeve. *Charlie's Story* (8–10). 1997, Peachtree $14.95 (978-0-561-45167-1). Charlie, who was abandoned by her mother as a child, now lives with her father in Ireland and, at age 14, is facing a group of bullies at school who accuse her of a theft and cause a terrible field hockey incident. (Rev: BL 1/1–15/98; VOYA 2/98)

2007 Friesen, Gayle. *Men of Stone* (5–8). 2000, Kids Can $16.95 (978-1-55074-781-2). While Ben Conrad traces his own family roots, he confronts a local bully in this story of a boy's journey to maturity. (Rev: HBG 3/01; SLJ 10/00; VOYA 2/01)

2008 Friesen, Jonathan. *The Last Martin* (5–7). 2011, Zondervan $14.99 (978-0-310-72080-5). Convinced that he is about to die because of a family curse, 13-year-old Martin starts to exhibit increasingly reckless behavior but also finds himself making new friends who try to help him; a story full of humor. **e** (Rev: SLJ 5/11*)

2009 Frizzell, Colin. *Chill* (7–10). 2006, Orca paper $8.95 (978-1-55143-507-7). Chill, a talented artist with a crippled leg, has a very low opinion of the new English teacher, Mr. Sfinkter, and shows this in a mural he paints at the front of the school; suitable for reluctant readers. (Rev: SLJ 3/07)

2010 Froese, Deborah. *Out of the Fire* (8–11). 2002, Sumach paper $7.95 (978-1-894549-09-7). Sixteen-year-old Dayle is badly burned at a riotous bonfire party and spends the painful months that follow reassessing her feelings about friends and family. (Rev: BL 7/02; SLJ 8/02)

2011 Frost, Helen. *Keesha's House* (6–10). 2003, Farrar $16.00 (978-0-374-34064-3). Keesha reaches out to other teens in trouble as they describe their problems in brief, poetic vignettes. (Rev: BL 3/1/03; HBG 10/03; SLJ 3/03*; VOYA 4/03)

2012 Gabhart, Ann H. *Bridge to Courage* (6–8). 1993, Avon paper $3.50 (978-0-380-76051-0). Luke is afraid of bridges and walks away from the initiation rites of the elite Truelanders, who then shun him. Luke finally learns self-confidence in this deftly plotted tale. (Rev: BL 5/15/93; VOYA 10/93)

2013 Galante, Cecilia. *The Patron Saint of Butterflies* (6–10). 2008, Bloomsbury $16.95 (978-1-59990-249-4). Honey and Agnes are whisked away from the religious commune in which they have grown up and are amazed to discover the world that has always existed around them. (Rev: BL 4/15/08; SLJ 6/08)

2014 Gale, Emily. *Girl Out Loud* (7–10). 2012, Scholastic $17.99 (978-0-545-30438-2). Kass, a 15-year-old who is not pretty and has no particular talents, contends with her father's dramatic mood swings and desire for his daughter to be famous. e (Rev: BL 6/12; SLJ 7/12; VOYA 6/12)

2015 Gallagher, Liz. *The Opposite of Invisible* (8–10). 2008, Random House $15.99 (978-0-375-84152-1). Should Alice return the affections of popular, football-playing Simon or remain true to her friend Julian (Jewel), an artistic loner who also has feelings for her? ∩ (Rev: BL 11/15/07; LMC 4–5/08; SLJ 5/08)

2016 Garcia, Cristina. *I Wanna Be Your Shoebox* (5–8). 2008, Simon & Schuster $16.99 (978-1-4169-6229-8). Thirteen-year-old Yumi is part Cuban, part Japanese, and part Jewish, and it is only when her terminally ill grandfather, a Russian Jew, tells her his life story that she begins to understand her own identity. (Rev: BL 8/08)

2017 Garden, Nancy. *The Year They Burned the Books* (7–12). 1999, Farrar $17.00 (978-0-374-38667-2). High school senior Jamie Crawford's problems as editor of the school newspaper under attack by a right-wing group are compounded when she realizes that she is a lesbian and falling in love with Tessa, a new girl in school. (Rev: BL 8/99; HBG 4/00; SLJ 9/99; VOYA 12/99)

2018 Gardner, Graham. *Inventing Elliot* (5–9). 2004, Dial $16.99 (978-0-8037-2964-3). Despite efforts to avoid bullies at his new high school, 14-year-old Elliot Sutton finds himself embroiled with the Guardians, a group that metes out punishment to those it deems "losers." (Rev: BL 5/15/04; SLJ 3/04; VOYA 4/04)

2019 Garfinkle, D. L. *Storky: How I Lost My Nickname and Won the Girl* (8–11). 2005, Penguin $16.99 (978-0-399-24284-7). In journal entries, 14-year-old Mike Pomerantz chronicles the troubles and unexpected joys of his first year in high school. (Rev: BCCB 5/05; BL 3/15/05; SLJ 3/05)

2020 Gauthier, Gail. *Happy Kid!* (6–9). 2006, Penguin $16.99 (978-0-399-24266-3). Kyle starts 7th grade with a negative attitude that is sometimes lightened and sometimes reinforced by the advice in a book his mother gives him called *Happy Kid!* (Rev: BL 4/1/06; SLJ 7/06)

2021 George, Madeleine. *The Difference between You and Me* (8–11). 2012, Viking $16.99 (978-067001128-5). Jesse, a 15-year-old lesbian and political activist, is having a secret relationship with Emily, who is student council vice president and dating a star football player; tensions rise as they take opposite sides on a new superstore. e Lexile 1020L (Rev: BL 3/15/12; HB 3–4/12; LMC 8–9/12; SLJ 6/12)

2022 Gephart, Donna. *How to Survive Middle School* (5–8). 2010, Delacorte $15.99 (978-038573793-7); LB $18.99 (978-038590701-9). Used to being bullied and grieving the loss of his best friend Elliott, 13-year-old David Greenberg finds a new ally in Sophie who boosts his popularity by promoting his YouTube videos. e (Rev: BL 3/1/10; SLJ 6/10)

2023 Gephart, Donna. *Olivia Bean, Trivia Queen* (4–7). 2012, Delacorte $16.99 (978-038574052-4); LB $19.99 (978-037598952-0). Olivia's desire to see her father, who now lives in California, fuels her determination to compete in "Kids' Week" on *Jeopardy*; then her father will really appreciate her? (Rev: BL 5/15/12; SLJ 3/12)

2024 Gervay, Susanne. *Butterflies* (8–11). 2011, Kane/Miller paper $6.99 (978-1-61067-043-2). Katherine, now nearly 18, was severely burned as a child and has undergone many surgeries; she has tried to live a normal life and questions whether one last operation will do the trick. Set in Australia. Lexile 540L (Rev: BLO 11/15/11; LMC 1–2/12; SLJ 11/1/11*)

2025 Gilbert, Barbara Snow. *Broken Chords* (8–12). 1998, Front St $15.95 (978-1-886910-23-2). As she prepares for the piano competition that could lead to a place at Juilliard, Clara has doubts about the lifetime of sacrifice that a career in music would require. (Rev: BL 12/15/98; HB 11–12/98; HBG 3/99; SLJ 12/98; VOYA 2/99)

2026 Gilbert, Barbara Snow. *Stone Water* (5–9). 1996, Front St $15.95 (978-1-886910-11-9). Fourteen-year-old Grant must decide if he will honor his ailing grandfather's wish to help him commit suicide. (Rev: BL 12/15/96; SLJ 12/96*; VOYA 4/97)

2027 Giles, Gail. *Right Behind You* (8–11). 2007, Little, Brown $15.99 (978-0-316-16636-2). Four years after killing a child by setting him on fire, 14-year-old Kip is released from a juvenile mental facility and must try to start over in a new place with a new name. (Rev: BL 10/15/07; LMC 1/08; SLJ 9/07)

2028 Godden, Rumer. *An Episode of Sparrows* (7–10). 1993, Pan Books paper $16.95 (978-0-330-32779-4). In postwar London two waifs try to grow a secret garden. (Rev: SLJ 6/89)

2029 Goldbach, Veronica. *Deep in the Heart of High School* (6–9). 2009, Farrar $16.95 (978-037432330-1). Three girls in a San Antonio high school marching band deal with their individual problems — diet, shyness and loss, and divorce. (Rev: BLO 6/19/09; SLJ 6/1/09)

2030 Golding, Theresa Martin. *Kat's Surrender* (5–8). 1999, Boyds Mills $16.95 (978-1-56397-755-8). Thirteen-year-old Kat misses her deceased mother terribly, but she tries to hide it in her friendships for an old man and a wacky girl. (Rev: BL 10/15/99; HBG 3/00; SLJ 11/99; VOYA 4/00)

2031 Gonzalez, Gabriela, and Gaby Triana. *Backstage Pass* (6–12). 2004, HarperCollins LB $16.89 (978-0-06-056018-8). Desert McGraw, 16-year-old daughter of an aging rock star, moves to Miami and longs more than anything for normalcy in her life. (Rev: BL 7/04; SLJ 8/04)

2032 Gonzalez, Julie. *Ricochet* (7–9). 2007, Delacorte $17.99 (978-0-385-73228-4). While playing a game of Russian roulette, Connor's best friend Daniel is killed, and Connor, who was a part of the game, must deal with guilt and grief. (Rev: BL 4/1/07; LMC 4–5/07; SLJ 4/07)

2033 Gordon, Amy. *The Gorillas of Gill Park* (4–7). 2003, Holiday $16.95 (978-0-8234-1751-3). Shy, lonely Willie comes into his own when he spends the summer with his eccentric Aunt Bridget and meets her zany neighbors. (Rev: BL 6/1–15/03; HBG 10/03; SLJ 5/03)

2034 Gordon, Amy. *The Secret Life of a Boarding School Brat* (5–7). 2004, Holiday House $16.95 (978-0-8234-1779-7). Lydia, already unhappy about her parents' divorce and her grandmother's death, becomes even more miserable at her new boarding school and chronicles her woes in her diary. (Rev: HB 7–8/04; SLJ 8/04)

2035 Gorman, Carol. *Games: A Tale of Two Bullies* (4–7). 2007, HarperCollins $16.99 (978-0-06-057027-9). Instead of suspending Mick and Boot for fighting, their principal requires them to play board games together; after a rocky start punctuated with petty crimes, the boys explore a hidden tunnel together, discovering that they both cope with alcoholic, abusive fathers. (Rev: BL 1/1–15/07; SLJ 1/07)

2036 Grab, Daphne. *Alive and Well in Prague, New York* (7–10). 2008, HarperCollins $16.99 (978-0-06-125670-7). Matisse's father becomes ill and the family moves from Manhattan to a tiny town in upstate New York, resulting in culture shock and resentment until Matisse learns to appreciate her new school and surroundings. (Rev: BL 5/15/08; SLJ 6/08)

2037 Grace, Amanda. *But I Love Him* (8–12). 2011, Flux paper $9.95 (978-07387259-4-9). The compelling story of how A-student and track star Ann's life spirals downward after she falls for Connor, a young man with a troubled past. ℮ (Rev: BL 5/1/11; LMC 8–9/11; VOYA 4/11)

2038 Grant, Vicki. *Dead-End Job* (7–12). 2005, Orca paper $7.95 (978-1-55143-378-3). Frances finds her life coming apart at the seams after she meets an emotionally disturbed loner named Devin; suitable for reluctant readers. (Rev: SLJ 11/05)

2039 Grant, Vicki. *Pigboy* (5–9). Series: Orca Currents. 2006, Orca $14.95 (978-1-55143-666-1); paper $8.95 (978-1-5314-3643-8). Certain that his classmates' teasing will reach a new high, Dan Hogg dreads the field trip to a pig farm, but he deals well with the challenges that await him as he faces off with an escaped convict; suitable for reluctant readers and gripping enough for others. (Rev: SLJ 12/06)

2040 Gray, Dianne E. *Holding Up the Earth* (5–8). 2000, Houghton Mifflin $15.00 (978-0-618-00703-5). Sarah, a foster child now living on a Nebraska farm, does some research and uncovers stories of the many generations of women who preceded her on the farm and their struggles and problems. (Rev: BL 1/1–15/01; HB 9–10/00; HBG 3/01; SLJ 10/00)

2041 Greene, Bette. *I've Already Forgotten Your Name, Philip Hall!* (4–7). Illus. by Leonard Jenkins. 2004, HarperCollins $15.99 (978-0-06-051835-6). A little white lie that strains her relationship with her best friend, Philip Hall, is only one of the dramas Beth Lambert must deal with in this story set in small-town Arkansas. (Rev: BL 5/1/04; HB 3–4/04; SLJ 3/04; VOYA 6/04)

2042 Greene, Constance C. *Monday I Love You* (7–10). 1988, HarperCollins $11.95 (978-0-06-022183-6). An overdeveloped bust is just one of the problems 15-year-old Grace faces. (Rev: BL 7/88; VOYA 8/88)

2043 Greenman, Catherine. *Hooked* (8–11). 2011, Delacorte $16.99 (978-0-385-74008-1); LB $19.99 (978-038590822-1). Thea's pregnancy brings new stress to her relationship with Will, which has survived his going to college and their moving in together. (Rev: BL 8/11; SLJ 10/1/11; VOYA 8/11)

2044 Griffin, Adele. *My Almost Epic Summer* (7–10). 2006, Penguin $15.99 (978-0-399-23784-3). Irene, 14, who is spending the summer babysitting, learns about friendship when she takes up with the beautiful and manipulative Starla. (Rev: BL 2/15/06; SLJ 4/06; VOYA 4/06)

2045 Grimes, Nikki. *Bronx Masquerade* (7–12). 2002, Dial $16.99 (978-0-8037-2569-0). Eighteen high school English students enjoy the weekly open-mike opportunity to express themselves in poetry and prose, revealing much about their lives and their maturing selves. (Rev: BCCB 3/02; BL 2/15/02; HB 3–4/02; HBG 10/02; SLJ 1/02; VOYA 2/02)

2046 Grimes, Nikki. *Planet Middle School* (5–8). 2011, Bloomsbury $15.99 (978-1-59990-284-5). African American Joylin, 12, copes with changes to her body and social relationships as she goes through puberty. (Rev: BL 9/15/11; SLJ 12/1/11*)

2047 Grove, Vicki. *Reaching Dustin* (5–8). 1998, Putnam paper $6.99 (978-0-698-11839-3). As part of a 6th-grade assignment, Carly must get to know Dustin Groat, the class outcast, and as she learns more about him and his family, she realizes that her attitudes toward him in the past have helped create his problems. (Rev: BCCB 3/98; BL 5/1/98; SLJ 5/98)

2048 Haas, Jessie. *Will You, Won't You?* (5–8). 2000, Greenwillow LB $15.89 (978-0-06-029197-6). Mad (short for Madison) is a shy middle-schooler who comes out of her shell during a summer she spends with her wise grandmother in the country. (Rev: BCCB 10/00; BL 2/1/01; HBG 3/01; SLJ 10/00)

2049 Haddix, Margaret Peterson. *Just Ella* (7–12). 2008, Paw Prints $14.99 (978-1-4352-7937-7). The story of Cinderella after the ball, when she finds out that castle life with Prince Charming isn't all it's cut out to be, meets a social activist tutor, and rethinks her priorities in life; first published in 1999. (Rev: BL 9/1/99; SLJ 9/99; VOYA 12/99)

2050 Haines, J. D. *Vision Quest: Journey to Manhood* (6–9). 1999, Arrowsmith paper $11.95 (978-0-9653119-0-8). A 13-year-old boy is mentored by his Native American grandfather when he and his mother move from gang-ridden Chicago to the wilderness of Oklahoma. (Rev: BL 9/1/99)

2051 Halpin, Brendan. *How Ya Like Me Now* (7–10). 2007, Farrar $16.00 (978-0-374-33495-6). After his mom finally checks into rehab, Eddie moves to Boston to live with his aunt, uncle, and cousin Alex; there he deals with a totally new school and social environment and begins to blossom. (Rev: BL 5/1/07; SLJ 7/07)

2052 Hantz, Sara. *The Second Virginity of Suzy Green* (8–10). 2007, Llewellyn paper $9.95 (978-0-7387-1139-3). Suzy decides to turn over a new leaf when her sister dies and her family moves to a new town in Australia, even joining her school's virginity club and befriending the good students. (Rev: BL 10/1/07; SLJ 12/07)

2053 Hartinger, Brent. *The Order of the Poison Oak* (7–10). 2005, HarperCollins LB $16.89 (978-0-06-056731-6). Anxious to escape the "gay kid" label, 16-year-old Russel Middlebrook and two of his friends sign up to be counselors at a summer camp for young burn victims; a sequel to *Geography Club* (2003). (Rev: BCCB 3/05; BL 1/1–15/05; SLJ 4/05; VOYA 4/05)

2054 Hartry, Nancy. *Watching Jimmy* (5–8). 2009, Tundra $16.95 (978-0-88776-871-2). Carolyn saw the "accident" that left her friend Jimmy brain-damaged and she keeps her mouth shut until she just can't keep quiet anymore. (Rev: BL 6/1–15/09; SLJ 6/09)

2055 Harvey-Fitzhenry, Alyxandra. *Waking* (7–10). 2006, Orca paper $8.95 (978-1-55143-489-6). Since her mother's suicide, 16-year old Beauty has withdrawn into herself, but a new classmate, Luna, manages to reach her and Beauty soon finds the confidence to paint again and to take hesitant steps toward love. (Rev: SLJ 7/06)

2056 Hawks, Robert. *The Twenty-Six Minutes* (6–10). 1988, Square One paper $4.95 (978-0-938961-03-1). Two teenage misfits join an anti-nuclear protest group. (Rev: SLJ 11/88; VOYA 4/89)

2057 Haworth-Attard, Barbara. *Theories of Relativity* (8–11). 2005, Henry Holt $16.95 (978-0-8050-7790-2). When his mother sends him packing to make room for her latest boyfriend, 16-year-old Dylan Wallace struggles to survive on the streets without resorting to a life of crime. (Rev: BL 11/1/05; SLJ 11/05; VOYA 2/06)

2058 Head, Ann. *Mr. and Mrs. Bo Jo Jones* (7–12). 1973, Signet paper $4.99 (978-0-451-16319-6). The perennial favorite about two teenagers madly in love but unprepared for the responsibilities of parenthood.

2059 Heide, Florence Parry. *Growing Anyway Up* (6–8). 1976, HarperCollins $12.95 (978-0-397-31657-1). Florence is shy when confronted with new situations but an aunt helps her conquer her fears.

2060 Hemphill, Stephanie. *Things Left Unsaid* (8–12). 2005, Hyperion $16.99 (978-0-7868-1850-1). In this powerful free-verse novel, good girl Sarah Lewis becomes bored with her predictable life and adopts defiant Robin's bad habits, until Robin attempts suicide and Sarah must review her priorities. (Rev: BCCB 7–8/05; BL 5/1/05; HB 5–6/05; SLJ 2/05; VOYA 10/04)

2061 Henderson, Aileen K. *Treasure of Panther Peak* (4–7). 1998, Milkweed paper $6.95 (978-1-57131-619-6). Twelve-year-old Ellie Williams gradually adjusts to her new home when her mother, fleeing an abusive husband, moves to Big Bend National Park to teach in a one-room school. (Rev: BL 12/1/98; HBG 3/99; VOYA 8/99)

2062 Hepler, Heather. *The Cupcake Queen* (6–9). 2009, Dutton $16.99 (978-0-525-42157-3). Penny, 14, recounts the anxieties and enigmas of her life as the new girl in a small seaside town, including her first boyfriend and her parents' separation. ℮ Lexile 710L (Rev: BL 9/15/09; LMC 11–12/09)

2063 Herbach, Geoff. *Stupid Fast* (8–11). 2011, Sourcebooks paper $9.99 (978-1-4022-5-630-1). Social outcast Felton's fortunes take a turn for the better when he discovers hitherto unimagined athletic ability, but problems do remain. ∩ ℮ Lexile 670L (Rev: BL 5/1/11; LMC 10/11; SLJ 8/11)

2064 Herrick, Steven. *The Wolf* (7–10). 2007, Front St $17.95 (978-1-932425-75-8). Sixteen-year-old Lucy, who lives in the shadow of her abusive father, and 15-year-old Jake, who comes from a loving household, find romance when they set out to discover whether the howling heard at night is a wolf or a dog. (Rev: BL 5/1/07; HB 5–6/07; SLJ 4/07*)

2065 High, Linda O. *The Summer of the Great Divide* (5–8). 1996, Holiday $15.95 (978-0-8234-1228-0). With the political events of 1969 as a backdrop,

13-year-old Wheezie sorts herself out at her relatives' farm. (Rev: BCCB 7–8/96; BL 6/1–15/96; SLJ 4/96)

2066 High, Linda Oatman. *Planet Pregnancy* (7–12). 2008, Front St $16.95 (978-1-59078-584-3). Written in free verse, this is the story of 16-year-old Sahara, a teen from a small Texas town coping with pregnancy, her emotions, and the difficult decision she must make. (Rev: BL 8/08)

2067 Hill, David. *Time Out* (6–9). 2001, Cricket $15.95 (978-0-8126-2899-9). Kit is training for a race when a serious accident seems to send him into a parallel universe, where people and circumstances are eerily familiar. (Rev: BCCB 11/01; HBG 3/02; SLJ 10/01; VOYA 2/02)

2068 Hite, Sid. *A Hole in the World* (7–9). 2001, Scholastic $16.95 (978-0-439-09830-4). When Paul spends the summer on a Virginia farm, he is introduced to hard work and to the memory of a man who committed suicide the year before. (Rev: BCCB 11/01; BL 11/15/01; HBG 3/02; SLJ 10/01; VOYA 10/01)

2069 Hite, Sid. *I'm Exploding Now* (8–12). 2007, Hyperion $16.99 (978-0-7868-3757-1). Sixteen-year-old Max Whooten is disgruntled with life until he travels from Manhattan to Woodstock to bury his cat on his aunt's property and there finds some interest in life; Max's diary entries are intense and often funny. (Rev: SLJ 11/07)

2070 Hobbs, Valerie. *The Last Best Days of Summer* (4–8). 2010, Farrar $16.99 (978-0-374-34670-6). Twelve-year-old Lucy is tugged in two directions — she wants to join the "in" crowd at school and yet she does not want to abandon her neighbor Eddie, who has Down syndrome and will be attending the same school. ℮ Lexile 570L (Rev: BL 4/1/10*; LMC 5–6/10; SLJ 4/10)

2071 Holeman, Linda. *Mercy's Birds* (6–10). 1998, Tundra paper $5.95 (978-0-88776-463-9). Fifteen-year-old Mercy lives a life of loneliness and hurt as she cares for a depressed mother and an alcoholic aunt while working after school in a flower shop. (Rev: BL 12/15/98; SLJ 3/99; VOYA 12/98)

2072 Holland, Isabelle. *The Man Without a Face* (7–10). 1972, HarperCollins paper $5.99 (978-0-06-447028-5). Charles's close relations with his reclusive tutor lead to a physical experience.

2073 Holmes, Sara Lewis. *Letters from Rapunzel* (5–8). 2007, HarperCollins $15.99 (978-0-06-078073-9). In letters to an unknown correspondent, Cadence — who calls herself Rapunzel — describes her father's depression and her sense of being alone. (Rev: SLJ 2/07)

2074 Hopkins, Cathy. *Mates, Dates, and Cosmic Kisses* (6–10). 2003, Simon & Schuster paper $5.99 (978-0-689-85545-0). Teen anxieties about dating, friendship, and making decisions fill this funny novel about Izzy's attraction to a boy — and how her friends help her cope. (Rev: BL 2/1/03; SLJ 4/03)

2075 Hopkins, Cathy. *Mates, Dates, and Inflatable Bras* (6–10). 2003, Simon & Schuster paper $4.99 (978-0-689-85544-3). Lucy, 14, is concerned about her lack of development but, with the help of her friends, she is able to accept herself and even attract a cute boy. Other titles in this series include *Mates, Dates, and Designer Divas* (2003). (Rev: BL 2/1/03; SLJ 4/03)

2076 Hopkins, Cathy. *Mates, Dates, and Mad Mistakes* (6–9). 2004, Simon & Schuster paper $5.99 (978-0-689-86722-4). Izzie is ready for some rebellion anyway, but when Josh turns up her infatuation leads her into embarrassing territory. (Rev: SLJ 10/04)

2077 Hopkins, Cathy. *Mates, Dates, and Sequin Smiles* (6–9). 2004, Simon & Schuster paper $5.99 (978-0-689-86723-1). The prospect of braces sends Nesta into a funk, so she joins an acting class and there meets a cute guy named Luke. (Rev: SLJ 9/04)

2078 Horrocks, Anita. *Almost Eden* (5–8). 2006, Tundra paper $9.95 (978-0-88776-742-5). Elsie is a Mennonite girl who must deal with her mother's depression, the onset of puberty, and religious doubts in this story set in Canada in the 1960s. (Rev: BL 5/15/06)

2079 Horvath, Penny. *Everything on a Waffle* (5–7). 2001, Farrar $16.00 (978-0-374-32236-6). Eleven-year-old Primrose Squarp does not believe her parents drowned during a storm. In the meantime she is moved from pillar to post, ending up as a foster child to an elderly couple. (Rev: BCCB 3/01*; BL 2/15/01; HB 5–6/01*; HBG 10/01; SLJ 4/01; VOYA 6/01)

2080 Horvath, Polly. *The Vacation* (5–7). 2005, Farrar $16.00 (978-0-374-30870-4). When his parents go to Africa as missionaries, 12-year-old Henry is taken on an eye-opening, cross-country trip by his eccentric maiden aunts, Magnolia and Pigg; comedy and weirdness ensue. (Rev: BCCB 10/05; BL 6/05; HB 7–8/05; SLJ 8/05*)

2081 Howe, James. *Addie on the Inside* (5–8). 2011, Atheneum $16.99 (978-1-4169-1384-9). Seventh grade brings a combination of challenges for Addie Carle in this verse companion to *The Misfits* (2001) and *Totally Joe* (2005). ℮ (Rev: BL 6/1/11; SLJ 8/11*)

2082 Howe, James. *Totally Joe* (6–9). 2005, Simon & Schuster $15.95 (978-0-689-83957-3). At the age of 12, Joe knows he is gay and this is reflected in his "alphabiography" (in which he must present his life from A to Z), which shows him to be a generally happy person despite some bullying. (Rev: BL 8/05; SLJ 11/05; VOYA 12/05)

2083 Howe, Norma. *Blue Avenger and the Theory of Everything* (8–10). Series: Blue Avenger. 2002, Cricket $17.95 (978-0-8126-2654-4). David Schumacher (a.k.a. Blue Avenger) faces a dilemma as he seeks to save his girlfriend from eviction. (Rev: BCCB 7–8/02; BL 5/15/02; HBG 3/03; SLJ 7/02; VOYA 12/02)

118

2084 Howe, Norma. *God, the Universe, and Hot Fudge Sundaes* (7–10). 1986, Avon paper $2.50 (978-0-380-70074-5). A 16-year-old girl would like to share her mother's born-again faith but can't.

2085 Howell, Simmone. *Notes from the Teenage Underground* (8–11). 2007, Bloomsbury $16.95 (978-1-58234-835-3). Gem, 17, sets out to make an original film but has problems with her friends and makes discoveries about herself along the way. (Rev: BL 6/1–15/07; SLJ 4/07)

2086 Hrdlitschka, Shelley. *Dancing Naked* (7–12). 2001, Orca $6.95 (978-1-55143-210-6). Finding herself pregnant after her first sexual encounter, 16-year-old Kia walks away from an abortion at the last minute and must draw on her inner strength to deal with the consequences of that decision. (Rev: BL 3/15/02; SLJ 3/02*)

2087 Hrdlitschka, Shelley. *Disconnected* (7–12). 1999, Orca paper $6.95 (978-1-55143-105-5). The lives of Tanner, a hockey-playing teen who has recurring dreams of trying to escape an underwater attacker, and Alex, a boy escaping his father's abuse, connect in a most unusual way. (Rev: BL 4/1/99; SLJ 6/99; VOYA 6/99)

2088 Hughes, Mark Peter. *I Am the Wallpaper* (6–9). 2005, Delacorte LB $17.99 (978-0-385-90265-6). Tired of being overshadowed by her older and prettier sister, 13-year-old Floey Packer decides it's time to give herself a radical makeover. (Rev: BCCB 9/05; BL 3/1/05; SLJ 5/05; VOYA 8/05)

2089 Huser, Glen. *Stitches* (7–10). 2003, Groundwood paper $9.95 (978-0-88899-578-0). Disfigured Chantelle and much-bullied Travis support each other through the difficult years of junior high school. (Rev: BCCB 2/04; HB 11–12/03*; HBG 4/04; SLJ 12/03; VOYA 4/04)

2090 Huser, Glen. *Touch of the Clown* (7–10). 1999, Groundwood $15.95 (978-0-88899-343-4). Neglected sisters Barbara and Livvy get a new lease on life when they meet the eccentric Cosmo, who runs a teen clown workshop. (Rev: SLJ 11/99; VOYA 10/99)

2091 Ingold, Jeanette. *Pictures, 1918* (6–9). 1998, Harcourt $16.00 (978-0-15-201802-3). In this novel set in the final days of World War I, 16-year-old Asa faces many personal problems but finds release when he becomes an apprentice to the local portrait photographer. (Rev: BCCB 10/98; VOYA 2/99)

2092 Irwin, Hadley. *The Lilith Summer* (6–8). 1979, Feminist paper $8.95 (978-0-912670-52-2). Twelve-year-old Ellen learns about old age when she "lady sits" with 77-year-old Lilith Adams.

2093 Jahn-Clough, Lisa. *Me, Penelope* (8–10). 2007, Houghton Mifflin $16.00 (978-0-618-77366-4). Penelope (called Lopi) is trying to lose her virginity, and her good friend Toad helps her out while also helping Lopi make sense of her difficult past. (Rev: BL 4/1/07; HB 5–6/07; SLJ 7/07)

2094 James, Brian. *A Perfect World* (7–10). 2004, Scholastic $16.95 (978-0-439-67364-8). Haunted by the suicide of her father, Lacie Johnson follows mindlessly in the footsteps of her best friend Jenna, but when she meets Benji and falls in love, she realizes that Jenna is not a real friend at all. (Rev: BL 1/1–15/05; SLJ 1/05)

2095 Jellen, Michelle. *Spain or Shine* (6–9). Series: Students Across the Seven Seas. 2005, Penguin paper $6.99 (978-0-14-240368-6). A semester in Spain helps to bring 16-year-old Elena Holloway out of her shell. (Rev: BL 12/1/05; SLJ 1/06)

2096 Jimenez, Francisco. *Breaking Through* (6–12). 2001, Houghton Mifflin $16.00 (978-0-618-01173-5). In this sequel to *The Circuit: Stories from the Life of a Migrant Child* (2001), 14-year-old Francisco recounts his efforts to improve his lot in life and describes his school and romantic experiences. (Rev: BCCB 1/02; BL 9/1/01; HB 11–12/01; HBG 3/02; SLJ 9/01; VOYA 12/01)

2097 Johnson, Angela. *The First Part Last* (6–12). 2003, Simon & Schuster $15.95 (978-0-689-84922-0). Sixteen-year-old single-parent Bobby is overwhelmed and exhausted, but he loves his baby daughter. (Rev: BL 9/1/03*; HB 7–8/03; HBG 10/03; SLJ 6/03*; VOYA 6/03)

2098 Johnson, Angela. *Sweet, Hereafter* (8–11). 2010, Simon & Schuster $16.95 (978-0-689-87385-0). African American teen Shoogy (Sweet) has left her home and moved into a cabin with Curtis when the army summons him for another tour in Iraq, a prospect he cannot face; the final volume in the trilogy that began with *Heaven* (1998) and *The First Part Last* (2003). ℮ Lexile 750L (Rev: BL 12/1/09; HB 3–4/10; LMC 5–6/10; SLJ 1/10)

2099 Johnson, Lissa Halls. *Fast Forward to Normal* (6–10). Series: Brio Girls. 2001, Bethany paper $5.99 (978-1-56179-952-7). Becca, one of a quartet of high school juniors who call themselves the Brio Girls, isn't happy with her parents' idea of adopting the Guatemalan boy they have been fostering. Also in this series is *Stuck in the Sky* (2001). (Rev: BL 10/15/01)

2100 Johnson, LouAnne. *Muchacho* (8–12). 2009, Knopf $15.99 (978-0-375-86117-8); LB $18.99 (978-0-375-96117-5). A serious girlfriend and his love of reading are two major factors in stopping Mexican American high school junior Eddie Corazon's slide into juvenile delinquency. YALSA Amazing Audiobooks Top Ten 2011. ∩ Lexile 1250L (Rev: LMC 11–12/09; SLJ 9/09; VOYA 12/09)

2101 Jones, Jada. *Holding Back* (6–10). Series: Juicy Central. 2012, Saddleback Educational paper $8.95 (978-16165177-5-5). This title in the series suitable for reluctant readers features African American Nishell, 16, who is conflicted about her longing for Jackson. Also in this series set in an inner-city high school is *Keepin' Her Man* (2012). ℮ Lexile HL350L (Rev: BL 4/1/12)

2102 Jones, Patrick. *Cheated* (7–12). 2008, Walker $16.95 (978-0-8027-9699-8). This disturbing story about a teenager surrounded by people who cheat — and worse— spirals downward into drunken violence. (Rev: BL 3/15/08; SLJ 4/08)

2103 Jones, Patrick. *Things Change* (8–11). 2004, Walker $16.95 (978-0-8027-8901-3). Johanna, age 16, has her first boyfriend, Paul, a disturbed boy, in this novel about dating, violence, and the problems of falling in love. (Rev: BL 5/1/04; SLJ 5/04; VOYA 6/04)

2104 Jonsberg, Barry. *Am I Right or Am I Right?* (7–10). 2007, Knopf $15.99 (978-0-375-83637-4). Calma, 16, has a lot to cope with: her friend Vanessa, who is being abused; her long-absent father's return; her mother's behavior; and her crush on the gorgeous Jason. The interesting format and Calma's humor lighten the drama. (Rev: BL 1/1–15/07; SLJ 2/07)

2105 Joyce, Graham. *TWOC* (8–12). 2007, Viking $16.99 (978-0-670-06090-0). Matt's brother, who taught Matt how to steal cars (TWOC equals "take without consent"), dies in a car accident. When he appears as a ghost to Matt, Matt becomes so difficult that he is sent to a camp for troubled teens for a life-changing weekend. (Rev: BL 4/1/07; SLJ 3/07)

2106 Juby, Susan. *Alice, I Think* (8–12). 2003, HarperTempest LB $16.89 (978-0-06-051544-7). Alice, a quirky 15-year-old who has been homeschooled, enters public school and narrates in her diary all her new experiences. (Rev: BCCB 9/03; BL 8/03; HB 7–8/03; HBG 10/03; SLJ 7/03; VOYA 8/03)

2107 Juby, Susan. *Alice MacLeod, Realist at Last* (8–11). 2005, HarperCollins LB $16.89 (978-0-06-051550-8). It's an eventful summer for unconventional 16-year-old Alice McLeod, who breaks up with her boyfriend, gets and loses jobs, attracts three new male admirers, and sees her activist mom packed off to jail — all with dark good humor. (Rev: BL 4/15/05; HB 9–10/05; SLJ 9/05)

2108 Kane, Kim. *Pip: The Story of Olive* (5–8). 2009, Random $15.99 (978-0-385-75171-1). When her friend Mathilda drops her, lonely Olive suddenly finds she has a twin sister called Pip, who is as bright and adventurous as Olive is pale and retiring; with Pip beside her, Olive decides to look for the father she never met. (Rev: BCCB 7–8/09; SLJ 7/09)

2109 Kaplow, Robert. *Alessandra in Between* (8–12). 1992, HarperCollins LB $13.89 (978-0-06-023298-6). A young heroine has a lot on her mind, including her grandfather's deteriorating health, her friendships, and an unrequited love. (Rev: BL 9/15/92; SLJ 9/92)

2110 Kassem, Lou. *Secret Wishes* (6–8). 1989, Avon paper $2.95 (978-0-380-75544-8). A girl summons up her resources to try to lose weight to be a cheerleader. (Rev: BL 4/15/89; SLJ 4/89)

2111 Katcher, Brian. *Playing with Matches* (8–11). 2008, Delacorte $15.99 (978-0-385-73544-5). Katcher combines humor and a serious teen dilemma in this story of geeky 17-year-old Leon who gets involved with Melody, who bears facial scars resulting from an accident, but then drops her to date the popular Amy. (Rev: BL 8/08)

2112 Kaye, Marilyn. *The Atonement of Mindy Wise* (6–9). 1991, Harcourt $15.95 (978-0-15-200402-6). A Jewish girl reviews a year's worth of sins on Yom Kippur and realizes she isn't as bad as she thought. (Rev: BL 6/15/91)

2113 Kaye, Marilyn. *Cassie* (6–9). 1987, Harcourt paper $4.95 (978-0-15-200422-4). A shoplifting incident forces Cassie to examine her values. A companion volume is *Lydia*, about Cassie's older sister. (Rev: SLJ 12/87)

2114 Kaye, Marilyn. *Real Heroes* (5–7). 1993, Avon paper $3.50 (978-0-380-72283-9). Kevin finds he is in the middle of a situation involving quarrels between parents and between best friends, and a controversy about a teacher who is HIV positive. (Rev: BCCB 5/93; BL 4/1/93)

2115 Keene, Carolyn. *Love Times Three* (5–8). Series: River Heights. 1991, Pocket paper $3.50 (978-0-671-96703-1). Nikki has a crush on Tim, but Brittany wants him too. (Rev: BL 12/15/89)

2116 Kehoe, Stasia Ward. *Audition* (7–11). 2011, Viking $17.99 (978-0-670-01319-7). Sara, 16, leaves her rural Vermont home to study ballet and becomes involved in an unfortunate affair with a dancer and choreographer; this coming-of-age novel offers many details of the world of dance. e (Rev: BL 11/1/11; SLJ 10/1/11; VOYA 10/11)

2117 Kennen, Ally. *Beast* (8–12). 2006, Scholastic $16.99 (978-0-439-86549-4). Stephen, 17, has faced many challenges — a criminal father, a series of foster families, arrest for theft and arson — and now he must rid himself of the huge crocodile his father gave him; this suspenseful novel full of dark humor is set in Britain. (Rev: LMC 2/07; SLJ 11/06)

2118 Kerr, Dan. *Candy on the Edge* (5–8). 2002, Coteau paper $8.95 (978-1-55050-189-6). Candy, an 8th grader, finds herself drawn into a world of crime as she makes new friends and falls for Ramon. (Rev: SLJ 5/02)

2119 Kerr, M. E. *Dinky Hocker Shoots Smack!* (6–9). 1989, HarperCollins paper $6.99 (978-0-06-447006-3). Overweight and underloved Dinky finds a unique way to gain her parents' attention in this humorous novel.

2120 Kerr, M. E. *Gentlehands* (7–12). 1990, HarperCollins paper $5.99 (978-0-06-447067-4). Buddy Boyle wonders if the grandfather he has recently grown to love is really a Nazi war criminal in this novel set on the eastern tip of Long Island.

2121 Kerr, M. E. *The Son of Someone Famous* (7–10). 1991, HarperCollins paper $3.95 (978-0-06-447069-8). In chapters alternately written by each, two teenagers in rural Vermont write about their friendship and their problems.

2122 Kerr, M. E. *What I Really Think of You* (7–10). 1982, HarperCollins $13.00 (978-0-06-023188-0); paper $3.50 (978-0-06-447062-9). The meeting of two teenagers who represent two kinds of religion — the evangelical mission and the TV pulpit. (Rev: BL 9/1/95)

2123 Ketchum, Liza. *Blue Coyote* (7–12). 1997, Simon & Schuster $16.00 (978-0-689-80790-9). High school junior Alex Beekman denies that he is gay, but, in time, he realizes the truth about himself. (Rev: BL 6/1–15/97; SLJ 5/97; VOYA 8/97)

2124 Killien, Christi. *Artie's Brief: The Whole Truth, and Nothing But* (5–7). 1989, Avon paper $2.95 (978-0-380-71108-6). Sixth-grader Artie deals with the suicide of his older brother. (Rev: BL 5/15/89)

2125 Kimmel, Elizabeth Cody. *Lily B. on the Brink of Love* (5–8). 2005, HarperCollins LB $16.89 (978-0-06-075543-0). In this charming sequel to *Lily B. on the Brink of Cool* (2003), the title character, an aspiring writer and advice columnist for her school paper, needs counsel herself when she falls in love. (Rev: BL 10/1/05; SLJ 7/05)

2126 Kimmel, Elizabeth Cody. *Spin the Bottle* (5–7). 2008, Dial $16.99 (978-0-8037-3191-2). Phoebe gets a small part in a middle-school play and must deal with spin-the-bottle games, the popular crowd, and changing friendships. (Rev: BL 5/1/08; SLJ 6/08)

2127 Kinney, Jeff. *Diary of a Wimpy Kid* (5–8). Series: Diary of a Wimpy Kid. 2007, Abrams $14.95 (978-0-8109-9313-6). Greg Heffley writes in his very funny journal about the highlights — and the frequent low moments — of his first year in middle school. (Rev: BL 4/1/07; SLJ 4/07; VOYA 4/07)

2128 Klass, David. *Home of the Braves* (8–12). 2002, Farrar $18.00 (978-0-374-39963-4). Joe's plans for his senior year in high school are changed by the arrival of a Brazilian student who threatens Joe's position as soccer star and steals his would-be girlfriend too. (Rev: BCCB 12/02; BL 9/1/02; HB 1–2/03; HBG 3/03; SLJ 9/02)

2129 Klass, Sheila Solomon. *The Uncivil War* (6–9). 1997, Holiday $15.95 (978-0-8234-1329-4). An engaging novel about a 6th-grade girl who wants to get control of her life, which includes dealing with a lifelong weight problem and the pending birth of a sibling. (Rev: BL 2/15/98; HBG 9/98; SLJ 4/98)

2130 Koertge, Ron. *The Arizona Kid* (8–12). 1989, Avon paper $3.99 (978-0-380-70776-8). Teenage Billy discovers that his uncle Wes is gay and learns about rodeos as well as the nature of love when he meets an outspoken girl named Cara. (Rev: BL 5/1/88; SLJ 6/88; VOYA 10/88)

2131 Koertge, Ron. *Boy Girl Boy* (8–11). 2005, Harcourt $16.00 (978-0-15-205325-3). Longtime friends Elliot, Teresa, and Larry find that their lives and their relationships change dramatically with high school graduation. (Rev: BL 9/1/05*; VOYA 12/05)

2132 Koertge, Ron. *Confess-O-Rama* (7–9). 1996, Orchard LB $17.99 (978-0-531-08865-4). Beset with problems about his mother and his new school, Tony unburdens himself on Confess-O-Rama, a telephone hot line, only to discover he has told all to the school's weirdo, who then makes Tony her new project. (Rev: BL 10/1/96; SLJ 9/96*; VOYA 12/96)

2133 Koertge, Ron. *The Harmony Arms* (7–9). 1992, Avon paper $3.99 (978-0-380-72188-7). Gabriel and his father have gone to Los Angeles to break into the movies. By summer's end, Gabriel has embarked on his first romance and confronted death for the first time. (Rev: BL 10/15/92; SLJ 8/92*)

2134 Koja, Kathe. *Buddha Boy* (6–10). 2003, Farrar $16.00 (978-0-374-30998-5). Justin is intrigued by "Buddha Boy," a new student whose appearance and beliefs make him the target of bullies. (Rev: BL 2/15/03; HB 5–6/03; HBG 10/03; SLJ 2/03; VOYA 4/03)

2135 Koja, Kathe. *Straydog* (7–10). 2002, Farrar $16.00 (978-0-374-37278-1). Rachel, a lonely teenager who enjoys writing, is devastated when her favorite dog at the animal shelter is put to sleep, and her anger affects the people closest to her. (Rev: BL 4/15/02; HB 5–6/02; HBG 10/02; SLJ 4/02; VOYA 6/02)

2136 Konigsburg, E. L. *Jennifer, Hecate, Macbeth, William McKinley, and Me, Elizabeth* (6–8). 1967, Macmillan $16.00 (978-0-689-30007-3). Elizabeth finds a new friend in Jennifer, an unusual girl who is interested in witchcraft.

2137 Korman, Gordon. *The Juvie Three* (7–10). 2008, Hyperion $15.99 (978-142310158-1). Troubled kids Terence, Arjay, and Gecko are given a second chance by a kindhearted social worker named Doug; when Doug ends up comatose the three band together to conceal his absence from the authorities. ⌒ Lexile NC730L (Rev: BL 11/15/08; LMC 1–2/09; SLJ 12/08; VOYA 10/08)

2138 Kornblatt, Marc. *Izzy's Place* (4–7). 2003, Simon & Schuster $16.95 (978-0-689-84639-7). Summer with his grandmother proves more rewarding than 10-year-old Henry anticipated as he makes friends and gains a new outlook on life. (Rev: BL 6/1–15/03; HBG 10/03; SLJ 7/03)

2139 Koss, Amy Goldman. *The Girls* (5–9). 2000, Dial $17.99 (978-0-8037-2494-5). In chapters narrated by different protagonists, this book tells of Maya who has been dropped for no apparent reason from a clique of five popular girls in the middle school she attends.

(Rev: BCCB 6/00; BL 8/00; HB 7–8/00; HBG 10/00; SLJ 6/00)

2140 Kowitt, H. N. *The Loser List* (4–7). Illus. by author. 2011, Scholastic $9.99 (978-0-545-24004-8). Seventh-grader Danny Shine finds himself in trouble when he ends up on the Loser List in the girls' bathroom, and then befriends a bully in detention. Lexile 480L (Rev: BL 3/15/11; LMC 10/11; SLJ 4/11)

2141 Kowitt, H. N. *Revenge of the Loser* (4–7). Illus. by author. 2012, Scholastic paper $9.99 (978-05453992-6-5). Jealous 7th-grader Danny finally finds a flaw in seemingly perfect new kid Ty but his attempts to exploit it go off track; the diary-style narrative is peppered with cartoons. (Rev: BLO 5/15/12; SLJ 6/12)

2142 Krantz, Hazel. *Walks in Beauty* (6–9). 1997, Northland paper $6.95 (978-0-87358-671-9). The story of a 15-year-old Navajo girl and how she copes with such adolescent woes as popularity, boyfriends, prom dates, and family problems. (Rev: BL 8/97; HBG 3/98; SLJ 10/97)

2143 Krech, R.W. *Love Puppies and Corner Kicks* (5–8). 2010, Dutton $16.99 (978-0-525-42197-9). American Andrea DiLorenzo, 13, moves to Scotland and initially has trouble making friends and is distressed when her stutter returns; however, her soccer skills help her overcome her loneliness and adjust to her new life. ℮ Lexile 530L (Rev: LMC 1–2/10; SLJ 4/10)

2144 Kropp, Paul. *Moonkid and Liberty* (6–9). 1990, Little, Brown $13.95 (978-0-316-50485-0). The teen-age son and daughter of two hippies try to sort out their lives and plan for their future. (Rev: BL 6/15/90; SLJ 4/90; VOYA 6/90)

2145 Kropp, Paul. *Moonkid and Prometheus* (6–8). 1998, Stoddart paper $5.95 (978-0-7736-7465-3). In this sequel to *Moonkid and Liberty,* Moonkid takes on the job of tutoring a black student, Prometheus, in reading and Pro in turn teaches Moonkid techniques in basketball. (Rev: BL 6/1–15/98; SLJ 10/98)

2146 Krumgold, Joseph. *Onion John* (5–8). Illus. by Symeon Shimin. 1959, HarperCollins LB $17.89 (978-0-690-04698-4); paper $5.99 (978-0-06-440144-9). A Newbery Medal winner (1960) about a boy's friendship with an old man. Also use the Newbery winner . . . *And Now Miguel* (1954).

2147 Kurland, Morton L. *Our Sacred Honor* (7–12). 1987, Rosen LB $12.95 (978-0-8239-0692-5). A story from two points of view about a pregnant teenage girl, her boyfriend, and their decision for abortion. (Rev: SLJ 6/87)

2148 Kyi, Tanya Lloyd. *My Time as Caz Hazard* (8–12). 2004, Orca paper $7.95 (978-1-55143-319-6). Caz Hazard — who faces problems at home and at school — strikes up a friendship with Amanda and is drawn into a series of antisocial activities, one of which leads

to the suicide of a classmate. (Rev: SLJ 3/05; VOYA 2/05)

2149 Lang, Diane, and Michael Buchanan. *The Fat Boy Chronicles* (6–9). 2010, Sleeping Bear paper $9.95 (978-1-58536-543-2). Jimmy chronicles in his diary his first year at a new high school, describing the constant bullying and his efforts to lose weight. (Rev: BL 7/10; SLJ 12/1/10)

2150 Larimer, Tamela. *Buck* (7–10). 1986, Avon paper $2.50 (978-0-380-75172-3). The friendship between runaway Buck and Rich is threatened when Buck becomes friendly with Rich's girlfriend. (Rev: BL 4/87; SLJ 6/87; VOYA 4/87)

2151 LaRochelle, David. *Absolutely, Positively Not* (7–10). 2005, Scholastic $16.95 (978-0-439-59109-6). A funny and sensitive first-person portrayal of a 16-year-old's efforts to deny his homosexuality. (Rev: BL 7/05*; SLJ 9/05; VOYA 10/05)

2152 Laser, Michael. *Cheater* (7–10). 2008, Dutton $16.99 (978-0-525-47826-3). When Karl is drawn into a secret cheating ring at his high school, he is found out by the evil assistant principal and faces challenges to his morality from all sides. (Rev: BL 3/1/08; SLJ 5/08)

2153 Lawson, Julie. *Turns on a Dime* (5–8). 1999, Stoddart paper $7.95 (978-0-7737-5942-8). In this sequel to *Goldstone* (1998), set in British Columbia, 11-year-old Jo faces many new situations, including finding a boyfriend, discovering that she is adopted, and learning that her beloved babysitter is pregnant. (Rev: SLJ 6/99)

2154 Le Guin, Ursula K. *Very Far Away from Anywhere Else* (7–10). 2004, Harcourt paper $6.95 (978-0-15-205208-9). In his friendship for Natalie, Owen finds the fulfillment he seeks; first published in 1976.

2155 Lean, Sarah. *A Dog Called Homeless* (4–7). 2012, HarperCollins $16.99 (978-0-06-212220-9). A large dog, a disabled boy, and a homeless man help 5th-grader Cally start to communicate again as she recovers from her mother's death a year earlier. ℮ Lexile 660L (Rev: BL 9/1/12*; HB 9–10/12; SLJ 12/12)

2156 Lekich, John. *King of the Lost and Found* (6–9). 2007, Raincoast paper $9.95 (978-1-55192-802-9). Wimpy Raymond, a 10th-grader with embarrassing health problems, finds that his social status changes when he is put in charge of the school's lost-and-found and becomes business partners with popular Jack. (Rev: BL 11/15/07; SLJ 11/07)

2157 Lemieux, Michele. *Stormy Night* (4–8). Illus. by author. 1999, Kids Can $15.95 (978-1-55074-692-1). A long picture book in which a young girl who can't sleep ponders questions that are common to preteen girls. (Rev: BL 12/1/99; HBG 3/00; SLJ 12/99)

2158 Lenhard, Elizabeth. *Chicks with Sticks (Knitwise)* (7–10). Series: Chicks with Sticks. 2007, Dutton $16.99 (978-0-525-47838-6). Now in their final year of high school (and in the final book of the series), the knitting friends must deal with family problems and plans for the future; includes four knitting projects. (Rev: BL 11/1/07; SLJ 12/07)

2159 Les Becquets, Diane. *Love, Cajun Style* (8–11). 2005, Bloomsbury $16.95 (978-1-58234-674-8). Romance seems to be in the air in Lucy Beauregard's Louisiana town, spicing her interest in Dewey, son of the artist who has just opened an art gallery. (Rev: BL 9/15/05*; SLJ 10/05; VOYA 10/05)

2160 Lester, Alison. *The Quicksand Pony* (5–8). 1998, Houghton Mifflin $15.00 (978-0-395-93749-5). In this novel set in Australia, 17-year-old Joycie fakes a drowning and seeks a new life in the bush with her infant son, but two young girls stumble on the truth nine years later. (Rev: BCCB 10/98; BL 12/15/98; HB 1–2/99; HBG 3/99; SLJ 10/98; VOYA 2/99)

2161 Lester, Joan Steinau. *Black, White, Other: In Search of Nina Armstrong* (7–10). 2011, Zondervan $15.99 (978-0-310-72763-7). Nina, 15, learns about her great-great-grandmother's escape from slavery even as she herself struggles with her multiracial background and her parents' divorce. **e** (Rev: BL 10/15/11; SLJ 12/1/11; VOYA 8/11)

2162 Levoy, Myron. *A Shadow Like a Leopard* (7–9). 2000, iUniverse paper $12.95 (978-0-595-09355-7). The story of an unlikely friendship between a streetwise Puerto Rican punk and a wheelchair-ridden artist, this was first published in 1981.

2163 Levy, Elizabeth. *Cheater, Cheater* (5–8). 1994, Scholastic paper $3.50 (978-0-590-45866-5). Lucy Lovello has been labeled a cheater and even her teachers don't trust her. When she finds her best friend cheating, she faces a moral dilemma. (Rev: BL 10/1/93; SLJ 10/93; VOYA 12/93)

2164 Lewis, Beverly. *Catch a Falling Star* (5–8). Series: Summerhill Secrets. 1995, Bethany paper $5.99 (978-1-55661-478-1). An Amish boy faces excommunication when he begins paying too much attention to a non-Amish girl. (Rev: BL 3/15/96)

2165 Lewis, Beverly. *Night of the Fireflies* (5–8). Series: Summerhill Secrets. 1995, Bethany House paper $5.99 (978-1-55661-479-8). In this sequel to *Catch a Falling Star* (1995), Levi, an Amish boy, tries to save his young sister, who has been struck by a car. (Rev: BL 3/15/96)

2166 Linker, Julie. *Disenchanted Princess* (8–10). 2007, Simon & Schuster paper $8.99 (978-1-4169-3472-1). West's father is in prison and West is sent from her ritzy life in Beverly Hills to remote Possum Grape, Arkansas, to live with her aunt's family. (Rev: BL 7/07; SLJ 8/07)

2167 Lisle, Janet Taylor. *Sirens and Spies* (7–10). 2003, Aladdin paper $4.99 (978-0-689-84457-7). Elsie discovers that her beloved music teacher, originally from France, was an accused collaborator who had a child by

a German soldier; originally published in 1985. (Rev: BL 5/15/85; SLJ 8/85; VOYA 12/85)

2168 Littke, Lael. *Loydene in Love* (8–10). 1986, Harcourt $13.95 (978-0-15-249888-7). A high school junior from a small town gets a different view of life when she visits Los Angeles for the summer. (Rev: BL 2/15/87; SLJ 3/87)

2169 Littke, Lael. *Shanny on Her Own* (6–9). 1985, Harcourt $12.95 (978-0-15-273531-9). Shanny is sent to live with an aunt in rural Idaho to counteract her developing punkiness. (Rev: BL 1/1/86; SLJ 12/85; VOYA 4/86)

2170 Littman, Sarah Darer. *Confessions of a Closet Catholic* (4–7). 2005, Dutton $15.99 (978-0-525-47365-7). Since she made friends with Mac, a Catholic girl, 11-year-old Justine has been questioning her Jewish faith. Sidney Taylor Book Award 2006. (Rev: SLJ 1/05)

2171 Littman, Sarah Darer. *Want to Go Private?* (7–10). 2011, Scholastic $17.99 (978-0-545-15146-7). Shy, insecure Abby retreats to Chezteen.com for solace, and there meets the attractive and sexy Luke; this cautionary tale contains graphic sexual emails. **e** Lexile HL750L (Rev: BL 9/15/11; SLJ 11/1/11)

2172 Liu, Cynthea. *Paris Pan Takes the Dare* (5–7). 2009, Putnam $16.99 (978-0-399-25043-9). New girl Paris Pan, a 12-year-old Chinese American, is pleased to be asked to join a clique but distressed when she hears about The Dare. (Rev: BLO 5/27/09; SLJ 8/09)

2173 Lockhart, E. *The Boyfriend List* (8–11). 2005, Delacorte LB $17.99 (978-0-385-90238-0). After her disastrous social life triggers a series of panic attacks, 15-year-old Ruby consults a psychiatrist. (Rev: BCCB 3/05; BL 4/1/05; SLJ 4/05)

2174 Lockhart, E. *Dramarama* (8–12). 2007, Hyperion $15.99 (978-0-7868-3815-8). Sarah and her gay friend Demi find their true selves and the fun of musical theater at drama camp. (Rev: BL 4/1/07; SLJ 7/07)

2175 London, Kelli. *Cali Boys* (8–11). 2012, Kensington paper $9.95 (978-0-7582-6129-8). A fast-paced story involving two African American girls in Los Angeles: teen model Kassidy, who attracts boys like fleas, and Jacobi, who is creative and does well academically but is less successful in other areas. **e** (Rev: SLJ 5/1/12; VOYA 6/12)

2176 Lopez, Diana. *Confetti Girl* (4–7). 2009, Little, Brown $15.99 (978-0-316-02955-1). Sixth-grader Lina Flores, living in Texas, struggles to cope with her mother's death, her best friend's problems, her schoolwork, and typical middle-school friendship and romantic challenges; this coming-of-age story is sprinkled with Spanish phrases. (Rev: BL 5/15/09; SLJ 7/09)

2177 Love, D. Anne. *Defying the Diva* (7–10). 2008, Simon & Schuster $16.99 (978-1-4169-5209-1). When

Haley publishes a piece about diva Camilla in the school newspaper's gossip column, Camilla retaliates with force, leaving Haley friendless. (Rev: BL 3/15/08; SLJ 5/08)

2178 Lowry, Brigid. *Things You Either Hate or Love* (8–11). 2006, Holiday $16.95 (978-0-8234-2004-9). The funny, compelling story of 15-year-old Georgia, a creative misfit whose quest to earn enough money for a concert ticket leads to valuable learning experiences in life and love; set in Australia, this novel includes journal entries that discuss Georgia's weight problems. (Rev: BL 4/15/06; SLJ 4/06)

2179 Lowry, Lois. *A Summer to Die* (7–10). 1977, Houghton Mifflin $16.00 (978-0-395-25338-0). Meg is confused and dismayed by her older sister's death. (Rev: BL 7/88)

2180 Lowry, Lois. *Taking Care of Terrific* (7–9). 1983, Houghton Mifflin $16.00 (978-0-395-34070-7). A baby-sitting job leads to all sorts of hectic adventures for 14-year-old Enid.

2181 Lubar, David. *Dunk* (8–12). 2002, Clarion $15.00 (978-0-618-19455-1). Over the course of a summer, troubled young Chad learns a lot about himself and his anger. (Rev: BCCB 12/02; BL 9/1/02; HB 11–12/02; HBG 3/03; SLJ 8/02*)

2182 Lubar, David. *Sleeping Freshmen Never Lie* (8–11). 2005, Dutton $16.99 (978-0-525-47311-4). Aspiring writer Scott Hudson chronicles the highs and lows of his freshman year in high school. (Rev: BCCB 10/05; BL 5/15/05; SLJ 7/05*; VOYA 6/05)

2183 Lynch, Chris. *Who the Man* (6–9). 2002, HarperCollins $15.99 (978-0-06-623938-5). Thirteen-year-old Earl Pryor's ideas about manhood are turned upside-down when he sees how his father reacts to problems in his marriage. (Rev: BCCB 1/03; BL 11/15/02; HBG 10/03; SLJ 12/02; VOYA 2/03)

2184 Mac, Carrie. *Crush* (8–12). 2006, Orca $14.95 (978-1-55143-521-3); paper $7.95 (978-1-55143-526-8). While spending the summer with her older sister Joy in New York City, Hope discovers some surprises about both Joy (drug use and a live-in boyfriend) and herself (an apparent crush on a lesbian babysitting client); for reluctant readers. (Rev: SLJ 8/06)

2185 McCall, Edith. *Better Than a Brother* (6–9). 1988, Walker $14.85 (978-0-8027-6783-7). Hughie turns to her friend Jerry for help when she loses her new gold locket. (Rev: SLJ 5/88)

2186 McClintock, Norah. *Back* (5–8). 2009, Orca LB $16.95 (978-1-55143-991-4); paper $9.95 (978-1-55143-989-1). The compelling story of Jojo, who returns from prison to an unwelcoming community. (Rev: BL 4/15/09)

2187 McDaniel, Lurlene. *The Girl Death Left Behind* (6–9). 1999, Bantam paper $4.99 (978-0-553-57091-5).

A touching story of a girl's adjustment to the sudden death of her parents and starting a new life living with relatives. (Rev: SLJ 3/99; VOYA 4/99)

2188 McDaniel, Lurlene. *I'll Be Seeing You* (6–9). 1996, Bantam paper $4.99 (978-0-553-56718-2). Carley's face has been disfigured by the removal of a tumor and she tries to keep this secret from a blind boy with whom she has fallen in love. (Rev: BL 7/96; SLJ 12/96)

2189 McDaniel, Lurlene. *Telling Christina Goodbye* (6–10). 2002, Bantam paper $4.99 (978-0-533-57087-4). Tucker, who had been driving recklessly, is the only person uninjured in the accident that kills Christina. (Rev: BL 3/15/02; SLJ 7/02)

2190 MacDonald, Caroline. *Speaking to Miranda* (7–10). 1992, HarperCollins LB $13.89 (978-0-06-021103-5). Set in Australia and New Zealand, Ruby, 18, leaves her boyfriend, travels with her father, and gradually decides to explore the mysteries of her life: Who was her mother? Who is her family? Who is she? (Rev: BL 12/15/92*; SLJ 10/92)

2191 McDonald, Janet. *Harlem Hustle* (8–11). 2006, Farrar $16.00 (978-0-374-37184-5). When he raps, Eric is known as "Hustle" (and he hustles on the street, too, stealing), in this novel about a young man struggling to make it against tough odds. (Rev: BL 12/1/06; HB 9–10/06; SLJ 10/06*)

2192 McDonald, Joyce. *Swallowing Stones* (7–10). 1997, Bantam paper $4.99 (978-0-440-22672-7). When Michael accidentally kills a man with his rifle, he and his friend decide to hide the gun and feign ignorance. (Rev: BL 10/15/97; SLJ 9/97; VOYA 12/97)

2193 MacKall, Dandi Daley. *Crazy in Love* (8–12). 2007, Dutton $16.99 (978-0-525-47780-8). Seventeen-year-old Mary Jane finally gets together with Jackson House and the two become an item; soon, however, Mary-Jane must decide whether to have sex with Jackson, recognizing that saying no might jeopardize their relationship. (Rev: SLJ 2/07)

2194 Mackey, Weezie Kerr. *Throwing Like a Girl* (7–10). 2007, Marshall Cavendish $16.99 (978-0-7614-5342-0). Ella adjusts to her new home in Dallas by playing on a softball team and dating a senior named Nate. (Rev: BL 3/15/07; SLJ 5/07)

2195 Mackler, Carolyn. *The Earth, My Butt, and Other Big Round Things* (7–10). 2003, Candlewick $15.99 (978-0-7636-1958-9). Virginia, a privileged New York 15-year-old, struggles with her weight, her lack of self confidence, her family, the absence of her best friend, and her aspiring boyfriend. (Rev: BL 9/1/03; HB 9–10/03; HBG 4/04; SLJ 9/03)

2196 Mackler, Carolyn. *Vegan Virgin Valentine* (8–12). 2004, Candlewick $16.99 (978-0-7636-2155-1). High school senior Mara Valentine, a classic overachiever, is right on schedule with her short-term goals for her future when Vivian comes to live with Mara's family. (Rev: BL 6/1–15/04; SLJ 8/04; VOYA 10/04)

2197 MacLachlan, Patricia. *The Facts and Fictions of Minna Pratt* (5–7). 1988, HarperCollins paper $6.99 (978-0-06-440265-1). A budding young cellist on the verge of adolescence experiences her first boyfriend. (Rev: BCCB 4/88; BL 6/15/88; SLJ 6–7/88)

2198 MacLachlan, Patricia. *Unclaimed Treasures* (5–8). 1984, HarperCollins paper $6.99 (978-0-06-440189-0). A romantic story of a young girl finding herself.

2199 McNaughton, Janet. *To Dance at the Palais Royale* (7–10). 1999, Stoddart paper $5.95 (978-0-7736-7473-8). The story of the loneliness and growing maturity of Aggie Maxwell who leaves her home in Scotland at age 17 to become a domestic servant with her sister in Toronto. (Rev: SLJ 5/99; VOYA 10/99)

2200 McVeity, Jen. *On Different Shores* (6–10). 1998, Orchard LB $17.99 (978-0-531-33115-6). The problems of a teenage Australian girl surface when the guerrilla environmental group to which she belongs is caught and a crisis develops over a beached whale. (Rev: BCCB 11/98; BL 11/15/98; HBG 3/99; SLJ 3/99; VOYA 10/98)

2201 McVoy, Terra Elan. *Pure* (8–11). 2009, Simon & Schuster $16.99 (978-141697872-5). When one girl in their group of friends breaks the promise symbolized by her purity ring, 15-year-old Tabitha is shocked and forced to examine her friendship and her faith. Lexile 970L (Rev: BL 4/1/09; SLJ 9/09)

2202 Maguire, Gregory. *Oasis* (7–10). 1996, Clarion $15.00 (978-0-395-67019-4). This story of grief and guilt involves 13-year-old Hand, his adjustment to his father's sudden death, and his mother's efforts to save the motel her husband had managed. (Rev: BL 9/15/96; SLJ 11/96; VOYA 2/97)

2203 Mahy, Margaret. *The Catalogue of the Universe* (8–12). 1987, Scholastic paper $2.75 (978-0-590-42318-2). Through their friendship, Angela, who longs to meet her absent father, and Tycho, who believes he is physically ugly, find tenderness and compassion. (Rev: BL 3/15/86; SLJ 4/86; VOYA 12/86)

2204 Makris, Kathryn. *A Different Way* (7–10). 1989, Avon paper $2.95 (978-0-380-75728-2). A newcomer in a Texas high school wonders if acceptance by the in-crowd is worth the effort. (Rev: BL 10/15/89)

2205 Malloy, Brian. *Twelve Long Months* (8–12). 2008, Scholastic $17.99 (978-0-439-87761-9). Molly meets many challenges when she moves from a Minnesota high school to Columbia University, including finding out that the boy she loves is gay. (Rev: BL 8/08; SLJ 8/08)

2206 Mandabach, Brian. *. . . Or Not?* (7–10). 2007, Llewellyn $16.95 (978-0-7387-1100-3). From her 8th-grade classmates' point of view, Cassie is a contrarian

— she rejects cell phones but loves vinyl records, she won't shave her legs, nor will she stand for the Pledge of Allegiance, and above all she's against the U.S. reaction to 9/11. (Rev: BL 9/15/07; SLJ 3/08)

2207 Manning, Sara. *French Kiss* (8–11). Series: Diary of a Crush. 2006, Penguin paper $6.99 (978-0-14-240632-8). Edie, a 16-year-old English teen, falls in love with Dylan, a brooding art student, in this first volume in a trilogy. (Rev: BL 7/06)

2208 Margolis, Leslie. *Fix* (7–12). 2006, Simon & Schuster paper $6.99 (978-1-4169-2456-2). Two sisters take different stands when their mother wants them to get nose jobs. (Rev: SLJ 10/06)

2209 Marineau, Michele. *Lean Mean Machines* (7–12). 2001, Red Deer paper $7.95 (978-0-88995-230-0). Canadian teen Jeremy Martucci befriends Laure, the new girl at his high school, but senses she's keeping a painful secret. (Rev: SLJ 11/01; VOYA 8/01)

2210 Marino, Peter. *Dough Boy* (7–10). 2005, Holiday House $16.95 (978-0-8234-1873-2). Fifteen-year-old Tristan, a child of divorce, is unfazed by his weight until Kelly, the health-obsessed daughter of his mother's boyfriend, starts picking on him. (Rev: BL 11/15/05; SLJ 11/05; VOYA 2/06)

2211 Mass, Wendy. *Every Soul a Star* (5–8). 2008, Little, Brown $16.99 (978-0-316-00256-1). Three quite different young teens meet at a wilderness camp to view a spectacular solar eclipse and find themselves much changed by the experience. ⌒ (Rev: BL 12/1/08; HB 11/08; LMC 5/09; SLJ 11/08)

2212 Mass, Wendy. *Finally* (4–7). 2010, Scholastic $16.99 (978-0-545-05242-9). Rory's long-nurtured dreams about what she'll do when she turns 12 turn out to be full of pitfalls in this light, funny story about confidence and insecurity. ⌒ (Rev: BL 2/1/10; SLJ 7/10)

2213 Matthews, Phoebe. *Switchstance* (7–10). 1989, Avon paper $2.95 (978-0-380-75729-9). After her parents' divorce, Elvy moves in with her grandmother and forms friendships with two very different boys. (Rev: VOYA 2/90)

2214 Mazer, Anne, ed. *Working Days: Stories About Teenagers and Work* (6–12). 1997, Persea paper $9.95 (978-0-89255-224-5). An anthology of 15 varied, multicultural short stories about teenagers at their jobs. (Rev: BL 7/97; HBG 3/98; SLJ 9/97; VOYA 12/97)

2215 Mazer, Harry. *Hey, Kid! Does She Love Me?* (7–12). 1986, Avon paper $2.95 (978-0-380-70025-7). Stage-struck Jeff falls in love with a woman who was once an aspiring actress in this romance that contains some sexually explicit language.

2216 Mazer, Norma Fox, and Harry Mazer. *Bright Days, Stupid Nights* (7–10). 1993, Bantam paper $3.50 (978-0-553-56253-8). Charts the course of four youths who are brought together for a summer newspaper internship. (Rev: BL 6/15/92; SLJ 7/92)

2217 Miles, Betty. *The Real Me* (6–8). 1975, Avon paper $2.75 (978-0-380-00347-1). Barbara rebels against all the restrictions placed on her life because she is a girl.

2218 Miller-Lachmann, Lyn. *Hiding Places* (8–12). 1987, Square One paper $4.95 (978-0-938961-00-0). Mark runs away from his suburban home and ends up in a shelter in New York City. (Rev: SLJ 5/87)

2219 Mills, Claudia. *Makeovers by Marcia* (4–7). Series: West Creek Middle School. 2005, Farrar $16.00 (978-0-374-34654-6). Marcia learns that beauty is more than skin deep — and that there are more important things than the school dance — when she gives makeovers to the women in a nursing home. (Rev: BL 3/1/05; SLJ 2/05)

2220 Moiles, Steven. *The Summer of My First Pediddle* (7–9). 1995, Fireworks paper $9.99 (978-0-88092-122-0). Set in a small Illinois town during 1953, this is 14-year-old Brad Thatcher's story of how he weathered two firsts in his life — first love and his first encounter with prejudice after his father is investigated during the McCarthy hearings. (Rev: VOYA 2/96)

2221 Moore, Peter. *Caught in the Act* (8–11). 2005, Viking $16.99 (978-0-670-05990-4). Honor student Ethan Lederer is having trouble keeping his grades up and his problems multiply when he falls for Lydia, a Goth-type who turns out to be alarmingly manipulative. (Rev: BCCB 6/05; BL 3/1/05; HB 3–4/05; SLJ 5/05; VOYA 4/05)

2222 Moranville, Sharelle Byars. *The Snows* (7–10). 2007, Henry Holt $16.95 (978-0-8050-7469-7). The stories of four 16-year-old characters in the Snow family (Jim, Cathy, Jim's daughter Jill, and Jill's daughter Mona), spanning the years 1931 to 2006 and describing key events in their adolescent lives, come together at a funeral. (Rev: BL 8/07; LMC 2/08; SLJ 9/07)

2223 Morgan, Nicola. *Chicken Friend* (5–7). 2005, Candlewick $15.99 (978-0-7636-2735-5). When her family moves to the country, Becca tries too hard to be cool and winds up in trouble in this story told from a believable pre-teen point of view. (Rev: BL 3/1/05; SLJ 4/05)

2224 Moriarty, Jaclyn. *The Year of Secret Assignments* (8–12). 2004, Scholastic $16.95 (978-0-439-49881-4). A rollicking year in the lives of three Australian high school girls — Lydia, Emily, and Cassie — is chronicled in their correspondence with male pen pals at a rival school. (Rev: BCCB 4/04; BL 1/1–15/04; HB 3–4/04; SLJ 3/04; VOYA 6/04)

2225 Morris, Taylor. *Blowout* (5–8). Illus. by Anne Keenan Higgins. Series: Hello, Gorgeous! 2011, Grosset & Dunlap paper $6.99 (978-04484552-6-6). Mickey, 13, is sure her ship has come in when she gets a job working at her mother's salon, but she finds getting in

with the popular crowd isn't as easy as she'd hoped. (Rev: BL 4/1/11)

2226 Morris, Winifred. *Liar* (7–10). 1996, Walker $15.95 (978-0-8027-8461-2). Fourteen-year-old Alex starts life over on his grandparents' farm in Oregon, but there are many obstacles, including school bullies, a hostile principal, and an unloving grandfather. (Rev: BL 12/1/96; SLJ 1/97; VOYA 12/96)

2227 Moskowitz, Hannah. *Gone, Gone, Gone* (8–12). 2012, Simon & Schuster paper $9.99 (978-14424075-3-4). September 11 and the sniper shootings in the District of Columbia area form a backdrop for this story about teens Craig and Lio, their personal problems, and their potential romantic relationship. Stonewall Honor Book 2013. ℮ (Rev: BL 4/1/12; VOYA 4/12)

2228 Moss, Marissa. *Amelia's Boy Survival Guide* (4–7). Illus. by author. Series: Amelia's Notebooks. 2012, Simon & Schuster $9.99 (978-144244084-5). After starting off 8th grade with confidence, Amelia finds herself reeling from an unexpected crush. (Rev: BLO 4/1/12)

2229 Murdoch, Patricia. *Exposure* (8–12). Series: Orca Soundings. 2006, Orca $14.95 (978-1-55143-523-7). Revenge is the theme of this story about a girl who uses incriminating photographs to get back at a classmate who has been tormenting her; for reluctant readers. (Rev: SLJ 10/06)

2230 Murdock, Catherine Gilbert. *Front and Center* (7–10). Series: Dairy Queen. 2009, Houghton Mifflin $16 (978-0-618-95982-2). Now in her junior year, basketball star D.J. is pressured by adults to choose the "right" college and navigates a tricky social life in this well-written, final volume in the trilogy. ∩ ℮ Lexile 980L (Rev: BL 10/1/09; HB 9–10/09; SLJ 9/09; VOYA 12/09)

2231 Murdock, Catherine Gilbert. *The Off Season* (7–10). 2007, Houghton Mifflin $16.00 (978-0-618-68695-7). The unconventional D.J., first introduced to readers in 2006's *Diary Queen*, is now a junior in high school and must juggle work on her family's diary farm, playing on her school football team, and her first boyfriend. ∩ (Rev: BCCB 9/07; BL 4/15/07; HB 7–8/07; SLJ 4/07*)

2232 Murphy, Claire Rudolf. *Free Radical* (7–10). 2002, Clarion $15.00 (978-0-618-11134-3). Luke, a baseball star in Fairbanks, Alaska, is stunned when his mother turns herself in for her role in a fatal bombing more than 30 years before. (Rev: BCCB 6/02; BL 3/15/02; HBG 10/02; SLJ 3/02; VOYA 6/02)

2233 Myers, Walter Dean. *Lockdown* (7–10). 2010, Amistad $16.99 (978-0-06-121480-6); LB $17.89 (978-0-06-121481-3). Determined not to sink deeper into a criminal life, 14-year-old African American Reese tries to control his behavior during his time at a juvenile corrections facility. Coretta Scott King Author Honor 2011. ∩ Lexile 730L (Rev: BL 12/1/09; HB 3–4/10; SLJ 2/10; VOYA 2/10)

2234 Myers, Walter Dean. *Shooter* (7–12). 2004, HarperCollins $15.99 (978-0-06-029519-6). Told from many viewpoints, this is the story of a high school senior who commits suicide after shooting a star football player and injuring several others. (Rev: BL 2/15/04*; HB 5–6/04; SLJ 5/04; VOYA 6/04)

2235 Myers, Walter Dean. *Won't Know Till I Get There* (7–10). 1982, Penguin paper $5.99 (978-0-14-032612-3). A young subway graffiti artist is sentenced to help out in a senior citizens' home.

2236 Myracle, Lauren. *ttyl* (6–10). 2004, Abrams $15.95 (978-0-8109-4821-1). This story of three 10th-graders and their lives is told through instant messages. (Rev: BL 5/15/04; SLJ 4/04; VOYA 6/04)

2237 Naylor, Phyllis Reynolds. *Alice in the Know* (7–10). 2006, Simon & Schuster $15.95 (978-0-689-87092-7). Alice, now 16, must find work for the summer, longs for more family contact, and copes with the often embarrassing teen rites of passage. (Rev: BL 5/1/06; HB 7–8/06; SLJ 8/06)

2238 Naylor, Phyllis Reynolds. *Alice on Her Way* (7–10). 2005, Simon & Schuster $15.95 (978-0-689-87090-3). Alice, now almost 16 and hoping to get her driver's license, protests the idea of attending a sex class at church, but finds to her surprise that it's interesting and informative. (Rev: BL 7/05; SLJ 5/05; VOYA 8/05)

2239 Naylor, Phyllis Reynolds. *Cricket Man* (7–9). 2008, Atheneum $16.99 (978-1-4169-4981-7). Thirteen-year-old Kenny spends his summer saving crickets from his family's pool, building his self-confidence, and nursing a desire to save his depressed 16-year-old neighbor in a story that combines humor with the heavier issues of depression and teen pregnancy. (Rev: BL 8/08)

2240 Naylor, Phyllis Reynolds. *Dangerously Alice* (7–11). Series: Alice. 2007, Simon & Schuster $15.99 (978-0-689-87094-1). Alice is worried that she's being labeled a prude at school but is reluctant to "go all the way" with her boyfriend Tony in this installment in the Alice series. (Rev: BL 4/1/07; HB 7–8/07; SLJ 8/07; VOYA 4/07)

2241 Nelson, Blake. *Destroy All Cars* (8–11). 2009, Scholastic $17.99 (978-054510474-6). Following 17-year-old James through his junior year, this novel describes his early obsessions with environmental threats and base consumerism (and his ex-girlfriend) and his gradual development of a less austere attitude. (Rev: BL 6/1–15/09)

2242 Nelson, R. A. *Days of Little Texas* (8–10). 2009, Knopf $16.99 (978-037585593-1); LB $19.99 (978-037595593-8). Ronald Earl, a 16-year-old evangelist, begins to question his faith as he becomes obsessed by the ghost of a girl he failed to cure in this well-written,

thought-provoking novel. ∩ (Rev: BL 6/1–15/09; SLJ 10/09)

2243 Nelson, Suzanne. *The Sound of Munich* (6–10). 2006, Penguin paper $6.99 (978-0-14-240576-5). While Siena studies in Munich, she looks for the individual who enabled her father to escape from East Germany. (Rev: SLJ 6/06)

2244 Nelson, Theresa. *The Beggar's Ride* (6–8). 1992, Orchard LB $17.99 (978-0-531-08496-0). A compelling chronicle of a runaway's time on the tawdry boardwalks of Atlantic City. (Rev: BL 11/1/92; SLJ 11/92*)

2245 Neri, G. *Chess Rumble* (5–8). Illus. by Jesse Joshua Watson. 2007, Lee & Low $18.95 (978-1-58430-279-7). Marcus learns to channel his anger — over his sister's death and his father's absence — into chess, and tells about it in free verse. ALA Notable Books 2008. (Rev: BL 1/1–15/08; SLJ 11/07)

2246 Neville, Emily C. *It's Like This, Cat* (7–9). 1963, HarperCollins LB $17.89 (978-0-06-024391-3); paper $5.99 (978-0-06-440073-2). A New York City 14-year-old boy has more in common with his cat than his father. Newbery Medal, 1964.

2247 Newbery, Linda. *Sisterland* (8–12). 2004, Random House $15.95 (978-0-385-75026-4). This powerful story of love, anger, and guilt includes many generations and countries and revolves around Hilly, a contemporary British teen who is love with a Palestinian. (Rev: BL 3/1/04; HB 3–4/04; SLJ 4/04; VOYA 4/04)

2248 Nielsen, Susin. *Word Nerd* (4–8). 2008, Tundra $18.95 (978-0-88776-875-0). Twelve-year-old Ambrose, tired of moving and suffering bullies, makes friends with a 25-year-old ex-con neighbor who introduces him to Scrabble and broadens his horizons. (Rev: BCCB 9/08; BLO 12/30/08; SLJ 12/08)

2249 Noe, Katherine Schlick. *Something to Hold* (4–7). 2011, Clarion $16.99 (978-0-547-55813-4). In the early 1960s Kitty, 11, contends with being one of few white children on an Indian reservation, struggling to make friends while learning about discrimination; includes a map, author's note, glossary, and pronunciation guide. (Rev: BL 10/1/11; SLJ 11/1/11)

2250 Noël, Alyson. *Kiss and Blog* (7–9). 2007, St. Martin's paper $8.95 (978-0-312-35509-8). Friends Winter and Sloane have a pact and when Sloane reneges, Winter gets revenge through her blog. (Rev: SLJ 6/07)

2251 Nolan, Han. *Pregnant Pause* (8–12). 2011, Harcourt $16.99 (978-0-15-206570-6). Pregnant and married at 16, Elly learns that she needs to rely on herself rather than undependable adults. **e** Lexile 820L (Rev: BL 8/11; SLJ 9/1/11*; VOYA 10/11)

2252 Norris, Shana. *Something to Blog About* (7–10). 2008, Abrams $15.95 (978-0-8109-9474-4). Libby is horrified when her 10th-grade classmate Angel posts Libby's diary entries on the Web for all to see, and it's all made worse by the fact that her mother is dating Angel's father. (Rev: BL 2/8/08; SLJ 5/08)

2253 Palacio, R. J. *Wonder* (5–8). 2012, Knopf $15.99 (978-037586902-0); LB $18.99 (978-037596902-7). Augie Pullman, a 10-year-old with facial abnormalities who has been homeschooled, is sent to a private school in Manhattan with repercussions for himself and others. YALSA Amazing Audiobooks Top Ten 2013; ALA Notable Books 2013. ⌒ e (Rev: BL 2/1/12*; HB 7–8/12; SLJ 2/12*)

2254 Paratore, Coleen Murtagh. *Mack McGinn's Big Win* (4–7). 2007, Simon & Schuster $15.99 (978-1-4169-1613-0). Mack is unhappy about his family's move to a new neighborhood and jealous of the attention his older brother gets for his athletic abilities, until a heroic act on Mack's part changes perceptions. (Rev: BL 7/07; SLJ 8/07)

2255 Park, Barbara. *Beanpole* (7–9). 1983, Avon paper $2.95 (978-0-380-69840-0). On her 13th birthday Lillian, who is extra tall for her age, makes three wishes and they seem to be coming true.

2256 Parkinson, Siobhan. *Second Fiddle* (4–7). 2007, Roaring Brook $16.95 (978-1-59643-122-5). Mags and Gillian attempt to track down Gillian's father in the hopes that he will help finance her education at a music school in England. (Rev: BCCB 6/07; BL 2/15/07; HB 3–4/07; SLJ 6/07)

2257 Parry, Rosanne. *Heart of a Shepherd* (4–7). 2009, Random House $15.99 (978-0-375-84802-5); LB $18.99 (978-0-375-94802-2). In this heartwarming faith-based coming-of-age story, 11-year-old Brother learns a lot about ranching in eastern Oregon — and himself — when his courageous father is deployed to Iraq. ⌒ e (Rev: BL 2/15/09; HB 5–6/09*; SLJ 3/1/09)

2258 Pascal, Francine. *The Ruling Class* (8–11). 2004, Simon & Schuster $14.95 (978-0-689-87332-4). Brutally harassed by bullies at her new high school in Dallas, 16-year-old Twyla Gay briefly considers dropping out but decides instead to seek revenge. (Rev: BCCB 12/04; BL 1/1–15/05; SLJ 12/04)

2259 Patterson, James, and Chris Tebbetts. *Middle School: Get Me out of Here!* (4–7). Illus. by Laura Park. 2012, Little, Brown $15.99 (978-031620671-6). When his mother loses her job, she and Rafe move in with Grandma and the 7th-grader must attend a new school. ⌒ (Rev: BL 5/1/12; SLJ 6/12)

2260 Paulsen, Gary. *The Amazing Life of Birds: (The Twenty-Day Puberty Journal of Duane Homer Leech)* (5–7). 2006, Random House $13.95 (978-0-385-74660-1). Having a bad time with the onset of puberty and its accompanying embarrassments — amusingly confided in his journal — 12-year-old Duane identifies with a baby bird developing in a nest outside his window. (Rev: SLJ 10/06)

2261 Paulsen, Gary. *The Boy Who Owned the School* (6–9). 1990, Orchard paper $15.95 (978-0-531-05865-7). Jacob's main object in life is to be as invisible as possible and to avoid trouble. (Rev: BL 4/1/90; SLJ 4/90; VOYA 6/90)

2262 Paulsen, Gary. *Brian's Return* (5–8). 1999, Delacorte $15.95 (978-0-385-32500-4). Brian, the hero of *Brian's Winter,* becomes so disheartened with life at school away from the wilderness that he decides to leave society behind forever. (Rev: BL 2/1/99; HB 1–2/99; HBG 10/99; SLJ 2/99)

2263 Paulsen, Gary. *The Car* (6–9). 1994, Harcourt $17.00 (978-0-15-292878-0). The cross-country adventures of Terry, 14, and Waylon, a 45-year-old Vietnam vet who sometimes suffers flashback memories and becomes violent. (Rev: BL 4/1/94; SLJ 5/94; VOYA 6/94)

2264 Paulsen, Gary. *The Cookcamp* (5–7). 1991, Orchard paper $15.95 (978-0-531-05927-2). After a 5-year-old boy discovers his mother is having an affair, he is sent off to northern Minnesota in this World War II story. (Rev: BCCB 3/91; BL 3/1/91; HB 3–4/91; SLJ 2/91*)

2265 Paulsen, Gary. *Crush: The Theory, Practice, and Destructive Properties of Love* (5–8). Series: Liar, Liar. 2012, Random House $12.99 (978-038574230-6); LB $15.99 (978-037599054-0). Too scared to ask Tina Zabinski for a date, 14-year-old Kevin decides to investigate how relationships work and launches a series of often ill-fated romance projects, including a speed dating night at school; a companion to *Liar, Liar* and *Flat Broke* (both 2011). ⌒ e (Rev: BL 4/15/12; HB 5–6/12; LMC 10/12; SLJ 4/12)

2266 Paulsen, Gary. *Dancing Carl* (7–9). 1987, Puffin paper $3.95 (978-0-685-19101-9). A young boy recalls his friendship with Carl, a troubled man who is an expert ice skater.

2267 Paulsen, Gary. *Flat Broke: The Theory, Practice and Destructive Properties of Greed* (5–8). Series: Liar, Liar. 2011, Random House $12.99 (978-0-385-74002-9); LB $15.99 (978-0-385-90818-4). When his allowance is cut off because of his behavior in *Liar Liar* (2011), 14-year-old Kevin schemes up some clever ways to make money that don't always go over so well with his customers. ⌒ e Lexile 810L (Rev: BL 6/1/11; HB 9–10/11; SLJ 7/11)

2268 Paulsen, Gary. *The Island* (7–10). 1988, Orchard paper $17.95 (978-0-531-05749-0). A 15-year-old boy finds peace and a meaning to life when he explores his own private island. (Rev: BL 3/15/88; SLJ 5/88; VOYA 6/88)

2269 Paulsen, Gary. *Liar, Liar* (5–8). Series: Liar, Liar. 2011, Random House $12.99 (978-0-385-74001-2); LB $15.99 (978-038590817-7). Fourteen-year-old Kevin lies to make life easier until he finally gets in too deep and has to work out a way to extricate himself. ⌒ (Rev: BL 3/1/11; HB 3–4/11; LMC 8–9/11; SLJ 6/11)

2270 Paulsen, Gary. *Notes from the Dog* (4–7). 2009, Random House $15.99 (978-0-385-73845-3); LB $18.99 (978-0-385-90730-9). Fourteen-year-old Finn overcomes his shyness as he befriends his new neighbor, 24-year-old breast cancer survivor Johanna, who inspires him with her enthusiasm for life. ℮ Lexile 760L (Rev: BL 8/09; LMC 11–12/09; SLJ 9/09; VOYA 10/09)

2271 Paulsen, Gary. *Paintings from the Cave: Three Novellas* (5–9). 2011, Random House $15.99 (978-0-385-74684-7); LB $18.99 (978-0-385-90921-1). Lonely children trying to overcome abuse or neglect use various strategies in these three stories that reflect the author's own difficult childhood. ℮ Lexile 880L (Rev: LMC 5–6/12; SLJ 12/1/11)

2272 Paulsen, Gary. *Popcorn Days and Buttermilk Nights* (8–12). 1989, Penguin paper $4.99 (978-0-14-034204-8). Carley finds adventure after he is sent to his Uncle David's farm in Minnesota to sort himself out.

2273 Paulsen, Gary. *Sisters / Hermanas* (8–10). Trans. by Gloria de Aragón Andújar. 1993, Harcourt $10.95 (978-0-15-275323-8); paper $6.00 (978-0-15-275324-5). The bilingual story of two girls, age 14, in a Texas town, one an illegal Mexican immigrant prostitute, the other a superficial blond cheerleader. (Rev: BL 1/1/94; SLJ 1/94; VOYA 12/93)

2274 Paulsen, Gary. *Tracker* (7–9). 1984, Bradbury paper $3.95 (978-0-317-62280-5). John's encounters with nature help him accept the approaching death of his grandfather.

2275 Perkins, Lynne Rae. *Criss Cross* (6–9). 2005, Greenwillow LB $17.89 (978-0-06-009273-3). In a series of intersecting vignettes, a group of young teenage friends tell about their experiences on the difficult road to adulthood in this sequel to *All Alone in the Universe* (1999). Newbery Medal 2006. (Rev: BL 10/15/05*; SLJ 9/05; VOYA 10/05)

2276 Peters, Julie Anne. *It's Our Prom (So Deal with It)* (8–11). 2012, Little, Brown $17.99 (978-031613158-2). Plans for the senior prom get interesting — and a bit fractious — when lesbian Azure and bisexual Luke are appointed to the planning committee. ℮ (Rev: BL 4/15/12; LMC 8–9/12; SLJ 4/12; VOYA 4/12)

2277 Peterseil, Tehila. *The Safe Place* (5–8). 1996, Pitspopany $16.95 (978-0-943706-71-9); paper $12.95 (978-0-943706-72-6). A moving story of an Israeli girl and the problems she faces at school because of a learning disability. (Rev: SLJ 12/96)

2278 Peterson, Lois. *Disconnect* (7–10). Series: Orca Currents. 2012, Orca LB $16.95 (978-145980144-8); paper $9.95 (978-145980143-1). Suitable for reluctant readers, this is the story of Daria, who depends heav-

ily on her cell phone when she is moved far from her friends — with potentially fatal results. ℮ Lexile 430L (Rev: BL 10/15/12; LMC 5–6/13; SLJ 3/13; VOYA 2/13)

2279 Petrucha, Stefan. *Split* (7–10). 2010, Walker $16.99 (978-0-8027-9372-0). Wade has trouble dealing with the death of his mother, and as a high school senior develops two quite different and separate personalities; the serious Wade is skilled with computers while the wayward Wade is a musician who gets in debt to gangsters. Lexile HL610L (Rev: BL 2/15/10; LMC 5–6/10; SLJ 3/10)

2280 Pfeffer, Susan Beth. *Kid Power* (6–9). 1988, Scholastic paper $2.99 (978-0-590-42607-7). A group of youngsters join together to do jobs for money.

2281 Philbrick, Rodman. *The Fire Pony* (5–8). 1996, Scholastic paper $14.95 (978-0-590-55251-6). Rescued from a foster home by his half-brother Joe, Roy hopes that life will be better on the ranch where Joe finds work. (Rev: BCCB 7–8/96; BL 5/1/96; HB 7–8/96; SLJ 9/96; VOYA 10/96)

2282 Philbrick, Rodman. *Freak the Mighty* (7–10). 1993, Scholastic paper $16.95 (978-0-590-47412-2). When Maxwell Kane, the son of Killer Kane, becomes friends with Kevin, a new boy with a birth defect, he gains a new interest in school and learning. (Rev: BL 12/15/93; SLJ 12/93*; VOYA 4/94)

2283 Phillips, Wendy. *Fishtailing* (7–12). 2010, Coteau paper $14.95 (978-15505041-1-8). Four teens — Natalie, Tricia, Kyle, and Miguel — with a range of problems describe their lives in first-person free verse writing assignments; these are accompanied by teacher critiques. (Rev: BL 10/15/10; LMC 3–4/11)

2284 Plaisted, Caroline. *10 Things to Do Before You're 16* (7–9). 2006, Simon & Schuster paper $5.99 (978-1-4169-2460-9). London teens Beth and Anna aim to become gorgeous goddesses for their 16th birthdays and create a list of key tasks, which don't all go smoothly. (Rev: SLJ 8/06)

2285 Platt, Kin. *Crocker* (7–10). 1983, HarperCollins $11.95 (978-0-397-32025-7). Dorothy is attracted to a new boy in school.

2286 Platt, Randall B. *The Cornerstone* (8–12). 1998, Catbird $21.95 (978-0-945774-40-2). Using flashbacks, this novel tells about the growth of a tough 15-year-old charity case at summer camp on a scholarship in 1944, where he meets a Navy man on medical leave who changes his life. (Rev: VOYA 2/99)

2287 Plum-Ucci, Carol. *What Happened to Lani Garver* (8–12). 2002, Harcourt $17.00 (978-0-15-216813-1). Claire, a popular 16-year-old who is battling private demons, finds support and a cause in a newly arrived, curiously androgynous student who disturbs her friends. (Rev: BCCB 11/02; BL 8/02; HBG 10/03; SLJ 10/02*; VOYA 12/02)

2288 Polacco, Patricia. *Bully* (3–7). Illus. by author. 2012, Putnam $17.99 (978-039925704-9). New kids in 6th grade Lyla and Jamie give each other support through the online bullying they suffer from other students. ℮ Lexile 630L (Rev: BL 12/1/12; LMC 3–4/13; SLJ 8/12)

2289 Polikoff, Barbara Garland. *Why Does the Coqui Sing?* (5–8). 2004, Holiday $16.95 (978-0-8234-1817-6). Thirteen-year-old Luz and her brother Rome have trouble adjusting when they move from Chicago to Puerto Rico with their mother and stepfather. (Rev: BL 5/15/04; SLJ 6/04)

2290 Porter, Tracey. *A Dance of Sisters* (5–8). 2002, HarperCollins LB $17.89 (978-0-06-029239-3). When a young ballet dancer's dreams are dashed, she is comforted by her sister. (Rev: BCCB 1/03; BL 2/15/03; HBG 3/03; SLJ 1/03)

2291 Powell, Randy. *Swiss Mist* (6–9). 2008, Farrar $16.95 (978-037437356-6). This low-key coming-of-age novel follows Milo from 5th to 10th grade, through his parents' divorce and his move to a new home and school, learning along the way that life and other people aren't always what they seem. Lexile 720L (Rev: BL 12/1/08; HB 1–2/09; SLJ 12/08; VOYA 12/08)

2292 Preller, James. *Bystander* (5–8). 2009, Feiwel & Friends $16.99 (978-0-312-37906-3). Seventh-grader Eric moves to a new town and is quickly befriended by the charismatic school bully, prompting him to question the morality of his own bystander status. ℮ Lexile HL600L (Rev: BL 10/1/09; LMC 10/09; SLJ 1/10; VOYA 2/10)

2293 Prosek, James. *The Day My Mother Left* (6–12). 2007, Simon & Schuster $15.99 (978-1-4169-0770-1). Jeremy's mother leaves his family to be with another man, and over the next few difficult years Jeremy finds some comfort being outside and sketching birds. ∩ (Rev: BCCB 2/07; BL 4/15/07; LMC 8–9/07; SLJ 3/07)

2294 Prue, Sally. *The Devil's Toenail* (7–10). 2004, Scholastic $16.95 (978-0-439-48634-7). Thirteen-year-old Stevie Saunders, still trying to recover from a brutal bullying incident that left him scarred, enters a new school determined to endear himself. (Rev: BCCB 9/04; BL 4/15/04; SLJ 8/04)

2295 Quigley, Sarah. *TMI* (7–10). 2009, Dutton $16.99 (978-052547908-6). Becca, 15, learns the hard way that blogs are not private and that gossip can hurt people deeply. (Rev: BL 4/1/09; VOYA 12/09)

2296 Quintero, Sofia. *Efrain's Secret* (8–11). 2010, Knopf $16.99 (978-0-375-84706-6). Latino star student Efrain, 17, turns to dealing drugs to earn tuition money for an Ivy League college. Lexile 780L (Rev: BL 3/1/10*; LMC 8–9/10; SLJ 6/10)

2297 Rainfield, Cheryl. *Scars* (8–11). 2010, WestSide $16.95 (978-1-93481332-4.). Kendra, now 15 and hid-ing her habit of cutting herself, was sexually abused when she was younger and is sure her attacker is following her; her deepening relationship with classmate Meghan gives her support. YALSA Quick Picks for Reluctant Young Adult Readers 2011. Lexile HL560L (Rev: BL 3/1/10; LMC 10/10; SLJ 5/10; VOYA 4/10)

2298 Rayburn, Tricia. *Maggie Bean Stays Afloat* (6–9). 2008, Aladdin Mix paper $5.99 (978-1-4169-6264-9). Now that Maggie has lost all her excess weight (in *The Melting of Maggie Bean*), things change, including her friends and her confidence. (Rev: BL 4/15/08)

2299 Reed, Don C. *The Kraken* (6–10). 1997, Boyds Mills paper $7.95 (978-1-56397-693-3). In Newfoundland in the late 1800s, a boy struggles to survive against the impersonal rich and the harsh environment. (Rev: BL 3/15/95; SLJ 2/95)

2300 Reid, Kimberly. *My Own Worst Frenemy* (8–11). Series: Landgon Prep Academy. 2011, Kensington paper $9.95 (978-0-7582-6740-5). At a new exclusive school, street-savvy Chanti finds herself suspected of theft and must identify the real perpetrator and clear her own name. ℮ (Rev: SLJ 12/1/11)

2301 Reinhardt, Dana. *Harmless* (7–12). 2007, Random House $15.99 (978-0-385-74699-1). Anna and Emma have been friends forever when Mariah enters the picture and widens their horizons, leading them, however, into a lie that has wide repercussions. ∩ (Rev: BCCB 2/07; BL 12/1/06; LMC 4–5/07; SLJ 3/07)

2302 Reinhardt, Dana. *The Summer I Learned to Fly* (5–8). 2011, Random House $15.99 (978-0-385-73954-2); LB $18.99 (978-0-385-90792-7). In the summer of 1986, 13-year-old Drew (aka Birdie) finally finds a friend in runaway Emmett, and he helps her cope with the fact that her widowed mother is dating. ∩ ℮ Lexile 750L (Rev: BL 6/1/11; HB 7–8/11; LMC 11–12/11; SLJ 6/11; VOYA 6/11)

2303 Reynolds, Marilyn. *Detour for Emmy* (8–12). 1993, Morning Glory paper $8.95 (978-0-930934-76-7). Emmy is a good student and a hunk's girlfriend, but her home life includes a deserter father and an alcoholic mother. Emmy's pregnancy causes more hardship when she keeps the baby. (Rev: BL 10/1/93; SLJ 7/93; VOYA 12/93)

2304 Reynolds, Marilyn. *If You Loved Me: True-to-Life Series from Hamilton High* (8–12). 1999, Morning Glory paper $8.95 (978-1-885356-55-0). Seventeen-year-old Lauren, born to a drug-addicted mother now deceased, vows to abstain from drugs and sex, but the latter is particularly difficult because of an insistent boyfriend. (Rev: BL 9/1/99; HBG 4/00; VOYA 2/00)

2305 Reynolds, Marilyn. *Telling: True-to-Life Series from Hamilton High* (7–10). 1996, Morning Glory paper $8.95 (978-1-885356-03-1). Twelve-year-old Cassie is confused and embarrassed when her adult neighbor makes sexual advances towards her. (Rev: BL 4/1/96; SLJ 5/96; VOYA 6/96)

2306 Reynolds, Marilyn. *Too Soon for Jeff* (8–12). 1994, Morning Glory $15.95 (978-0-930934-90-3); paper $8.95 (978-0-930934-91-0). Jeff's hopes of going to college on a debate scholarship are put in jeopardy when his girlfriend happily announces she's pregnant. Jeff reluctantly prepares for fatherhood. (Rev: BL 9/15/94; SLJ 9/94; VOYA 12/94)

2307 Rhue, Morton. *The Wave* (7–10). 1981, Dell paper $5.50 (978-0-440-99371-1). A high school experiment to test social interaction backfires when an elitist group is formed.

2308 Rosenberg, Liz. *Heart and Soul* (8–12). 1996, Harcourt $11.00 (978-0-15-200942-7). It is only when Willie helps a troubled Jewish classmate that she is able to straighten out her own problems. (Rev: BL 6/1–15/96; VOYA 8/96)

2309 Rottman, S. L. *Head Above Water* (6–9). 1999, Peachtree $14.95 (978-1-56145-185-2). Skye's efforts to care for her mentally disabled brother, to work toward a swimming scholarship, and to deal with a violent boyfriend threaten to overwhelm her in this arresting novel. (Rev: BL 11/15/99; HBG 4/00)

2310 Rottman, S. L. *Hero* (5–8). 1997, Peachtree $14.95 (978-1-56145-159-3). When his home life becomes unbearable, Sean is sent to Carbondale Ranch, where his sense of self-worth gradually grows. (Rev: BL 12/1/97; HBG 3/98; SLJ 12/97; VOYA 12/97)

2311 Rottman, S. L. *Rough Waters* (7–12). 1998, Peachtree $14.95 (978-1-56145-172-2). After the deaths of their parents, teenage brothers Gregg and Scott move to Colorado to live with an uncle who runs a white-water rafting business. (Rev: BL 5/1/98; HBG 9/98; SLJ 8/98; VOYA 8/98)

2312 Roy, James. *Max Quigley: Technically Not a Bully* (4–7). Illus. by author. 2009, Houghton $12.95 (978-0-547-15263-9). Max Quigley is a bully, although he doesn't see himself this way, and he is forced to spend time with smart but nerdy classmate Triffin in hopes that each will learn from the other. (Rev: BCCB 6/09; BL 3/15/09; HB 5/09)

2313 Ruby, Laura. *Bad Apple* (8–12). 2009, HarperTeen $16.99 (978-0-06-124330-1). Tola (Cenerentola) Riley, a high school junior, struggles to tell the truth when she and her art teacher are accused of having an affair. (Rev: BL 11/15/09; LMC 11–12/09; SLJ 12/09)

2314 Rumley, Crickett. *Never Sit Down in a Hoopskirt and Other Things I Learned in Southern Belle Hell* (8–11). 2011, Egmont paper $8.99 (978-1-60684-131-0). Rebellious Jane — back home in Bienville, Alabama, after being thrown out of her 13th boarding school — is unexpectedly chosen as one of her Gulf town's Magnolia Maids, where she helps empower other outsiders

and gradually gains acceptance. **e** (Rev: BL 5/1/11; SLJ 6/11; VOYA 4/11)

2315 Runyon, Brent. *Surface Tension: A Novel in Four Summers* (8–11). 2009, Knopf $16.99 (978-037584446-1); LB $19.99 (978-037594446-8). This novel records how Luke changes over the summers he spends at his family's lake cabin from the ages of 13 to 16. Lexile HL720L (Rev: BL 2/15/09; SLJ 4/1/09)

2316 Rupp, Rebecca. *After Eli* (5–8). 2012, Candlewick $15.99 (978-0-7636-5810-6). Three years after his older brother's death in Iraq, 14-year-old Daniel finally finds some solace. ⌒ **e** Lexile 1020L (Rev: BL 9/15/12*; HB 11–12/12; SLJ 9/12)

2317 Ryan, Amy Kathleen. *Vibes* (7–9). 2008, Houghton Mifflin $16 (978-061899530-1). Sarcastic misfit Kristi learns to accept herself and her body, and to open up to those around her through a budding romance and the return of her estranged father. Lexile 770L (Rev: BLO 9/1/08; SLJ 12/08; VOYA 10/08)

2318 Ryan, Mary C. *The Voice from the Mendelsohns' Maple* (5–7). Illus. by Irena Roman. 1990, Little, Brown $13.95 (978-0-316-76360-8). Penny tries to cope with many problems, including finding out the identity of the woman who is hiding in the neighbor's maple tree. (Rev: SLJ 12/89)

2319 Ryan, P. E. *In Mike We Trust* (8–12). 2009, HarperTeen $16.99 (978-006085813-1). Gay-but-closeted Garth, 15, tries to free himself from the complications created by lies cooked up by his exploitative Uncle Mike. Lexile HL690L (Rev: BL 2/15/09; SLJ 3/1/09)

2320 Ryan, P. E. *Saints of Augustine* (8–11). 2007, HarperTempest $16.99 (978-0-06-085810-0). Charlie and Sam's close friendship was abruptly severed a year ago but their respective problems — including Charlie's use of drugs and Sam's worries about his sexuality — finally bring them together again. (Rev: BL 7/07; SLJ 10/07)

2321 Ryan, Tom. *Way to Go* (8–11). 2012, Orca paper $12.95 (978-145980077-9). Danny, 17, is pretty sure he is gay but aims to test this during a summer in his tiny Nova Scotia town. **e** (Rev: BLO 6/12; LMC 11–12/12; SLJ 6/12)

2322 Rylant, Cynthia. *Missing May* (5–8). 1992, Orchard LB $15.99 (978-0-531-08596-7). Caring about each other is the tender message in this story of 12-year-old Summer, who, along with her uncle, must cope with the death of her beloved aunt. Newbery Medal 1993. (Rev: BCCB 3/92*; BL 2/15/92*; HB 3–4/92; SLJ 3/92*)

2323 Sachar, Louis. *Small Steps* (5–8). 2006, Delacorte LB $18.99 (978-0-385-90333-2). Two years after being released from Camp Green Lake, African American 17-year-old Armpit is home in Texas and trying to find good work, which is hard when you have a record, when X-Ray turns up with an interesting proposal; a sequel to *Holes* (1998). (Rev: BL 1/1–15/06*; SLJ 1/06; VOYA 2/06)

2324 Sachs, Marilyn. *Almost Fifteen* (6–8). 1988, Avon paper $2.95 (978-0-380-70357-9). A light story of a practical girl, her boyfriends, and her impractical parents. (Rev: BL 6/15/87; SLJ 5/87)

2325 Sachs, Marilyn. *Class Pictures* (7–9). 1980, Avon paper $2.95 (978-0-380-61408-0). The friendship from kindergarten through high school between two girls is recalled through old class pictures.

2326 Sachs, Marilyn. *Fourteen* (7–9). 1983, Avon paper $2.95 (978-0-380-69842-4). First love comes to Rebecca by way of a new neighbor.

2327 Saenz, Benjamin Alire. *He Forgot to Say Goodbye* (8–11). 2008, Simon & Schuster $16.99 (978-1-4169-6228-1). Ramiro, from the poor section of El Paso, becomes friends with privileged Jake, the two fatherless young men forming a bond that is stronger than class or circumstance. (Rev: BL 4/15/08)

2328 Saldana, Rene. *The Whole Sky Full of Stars* (8–12). 2007, Random House $15.99 (978-0-385-73053-2). Barry agrees to a risky boxing match to help pay off a friend's gambling debt — and to help his own family after his father's death. (Rev: BCCB 5/07; BL 3/15/07; SLJ 5/07)

2329 Salinger, J. D. *The Catcher in the Rye* (7–12). 1951, Little, Brown $25.95 (978-0-316-76953-2). For mature readers, the saga of Holden Caulfield and his three days in New York City. (Rev: BL 10/1/88)

2330 Sawyer, Kim Vogel. *Katy's Debate* (5–8). Series: Katy Lambright. 2010, Zondervan paper $9.99 (978-0-310-71923-6). Katy, a Mennonite, is adjusting to high school and enjoying the debating team when she learns her father is considering remarriage. Can she dissuade him? In *Katy's Homecoming* (2011), Katy struggles to find a balance between her modest religion and popularity at school. *Katy's Decision* (2011) is the fourth book in the series. (Rev: SLJ 8/11)

2331 Say, Allen. *The Sign Painter* (5–9). 2000, Houghton Mifflin $17.00 (978-0-395-97974-7). An Asian American youth who wants to be a serious artist gets a job painting signboards scattered through the desert. (Rev: BL 10/1/00; HB 9–10/00; HBG 3/01; SLJ 9/00)

2332 Schmidt, Gary D. *Trouble* (7–10). 2008, Clarion paper $16.00 (978-0-618-92766-1). A multilayered novel in which Henry's brother dies after being hit by a truck driven by a classmate, a Cambodian immigrant named Chay; Henry later finds himself accepting a ride from Chay and the two learn more about each other. (Rev: BL 3/1/08; SLJ 4/08)

2333 Schraff, Anne. *To Catch a Dream* (6–10). Series: Urban Underground. 2010, Saddleback Educational paper $8.95 (978-16165126-9-9). Abel, 16, struggles to achieve his ambition of becoming a chef in the face of many obstacles. Lexile HL630L (Rev: BL 8/11)

2334 Schreck, Karen Halvorsen. *Dream Journal* (7–10). 2006, Hyperion $15.99 (978-1-4231-0105-5). Sixteen-year-old Livy's dream journal records the happy times before her mother became terminally ill, and before Livy tried to renew her friendship with Ruth with "fun" that turns into tragedy. (Rev: SLJ 11/06)

2335 Schumacher, Julie. *The Book of One Hundred Truths* (5–8). 2006, Delacorte $15.95 (978-0-385-73290-1). While spending the summer with her grandparents at the Jersey shore, 12-year-old Thea finds herself baby-sitting her younger cousin Jocelyn and struggling to keep private the truths she is listing in her diary. (Rev: BL 11/1/06)

2336 Scott, Elizabeth. *Something, Maybe* (8–11). 2009, Simon & Schuster $16.99 (978-141697865-7). Hannah — the child of a famous playboy and an Internet sex celebrity — is unsure about romance and about her relationship with her father. Lexile HL760L (Rev: BL 2/15/09; SLJ 5/1/09)

2337 Scott, Elizabeth. *Stealing Heaven* (7–10). 2008, HarperTeen $16.99 (978-0-06-112280-4). Dani, weary from the life of crime she and her mother have long lived, yearns for normalcy when they move to the town of Heaven. (Rev: BL 4/15/08; SLJ 8/08)

2338 Scott, Kieran. *I Was a Non-Blonde Cheerleader* (7–10). 2005, Penguin $16.99 (978-0-399-24279-3). As a brunette, Annisa has a hard time fitting in at her new high school where almost everybody else is blond. (Rev: BL 1/1–15/05; SLJ 1/05; VOYA 4/05)

2339 Scott, Kieran. *A Non-Blonde Cheerleader in Love* (8–12). 2007, Putnam $16.99 (978-0-399-24494-0). Annisa's cheerleading squad goes coed in this sequel to *I Was a Non-Blonde Cheerleader* (2005) and *Brunettes Strike Back* (2006). (Rev: BL 8/07; SLJ 6/07)

2340 Sebestyen, Ouida. *Out of Nowhere* (6–9). 1994, Orchard LB $17.99 (978-0-531-08689-6). The story of the bonding into a sort of family of a quirky group of characters, among them Harley, 13, who's left home; his dog Ishmael; Bill, a junk collector; and May, the "queen of clean." (Rev: BL 4/1/94; SLJ 3/94; VOYA 4/94)

2341 Sefton, Catherine. *Island of the Strangers* (7–9). 1985, Harcourt $12.95 (978-0-15-239100-3). City kids from Belfast clash with town toughs in this novel set on an island off Northern Ireland. (Rev: BL 1/1/86; SLJ 1/86)

2342 Selvadurai, Shyam. *Swimming in the Monsoon Sea* (8–11). 2005, Tundra $18.95 (978-0-88776-735-7). In Sri Lanka in 1980, Amrith's expected quiet summer is enlivened by the arrival from Canada of his cousin Niresh, a boy with whom he soon falls in love but who does not share his feelings. (Rev: BL 9/15/05*; SLJ 11/05)

2343 Seymour, Tres. *The Revelation of Saint Bruce* (7–12). 1998, Orchard paper $16.95 (978-0-531-30109-8). Because of his honesty, Bruce is responsible for the expulsion of several friends from school. (Rev: BL 10/15/98; HBG 3/99; SLJ 9/98; VOYA 2/99)

2344 Shanahan, Lisa. *The Sweet, Terrible, Glorious Year I Truly, Completely Lost It* (7–10). 2007, Delacorte $15.99 (978-0-385-75316-2). In this coming-of-age novel set in small-town Australia, 14-year-old Gemma deals with her emotional family, her sister's wedding, the school play, and shifting romantic attractions. (Rev: BL 8/07; SLJ 8/07)

2345 Shaw, Liane. *Fostergirls* (8–12). 2011, Second Story paper $11.95 (978-1-897187-90-6). Foster child Sadie, 15, is in her 13th home and determined to keep a low profile until she reaches 16 and can seek emancipation. (Rev: SLJ 12/1/11)

2346 Shaw, Susan. *Safe* (7–10). 2007, Dutton $16.99 (978-0-525-47829-4). Thirteen-year-old Tracy, whose mother died when she was 3, is overwhelmed by fears after she is raped by the older brother of a classmate. (Rev: BL 9/15/07; SLJ 12/07)

2347 Shaw, Tucker. *Confessions of a Backup Dancer* (8–12). 2004, Simon & Schuster paper $8.99 (978-0-689-87075-0). Seventeen-year-old Kelly Kimball, a talented dancer, suddenly finds herself thrust into a close relationship with pop diva Darcy Barnes; in this journal-like novel, Kelly dishes the dirt on Darcy and the diva's entourage. (Rev: BL 9/15/04; SLJ 8/04)

2348 Sheldon, Dyan. *Planet Janet* (6–10). 2003, Candlewick $14.99 (978-0-7636-2048-6). Janet pours out to her diary the frustrations she and her friend Disha face in their dealings with family and friends in this entertaining novel set in London. (Rev: BCCB 3/03; BL 3/15/03; HBG 4/04; SLJ 5/03)

2349 Shoup, Barbara. *Stranded in Harmony* (7–10). 1997, Hyperion LB $18.49 (978-0-7868-2284-3). Lucas, an 18-year-old popular senior in high school, is discontented until he meets and becomes friendly with an older woman. (Rev: BL 7/97; HBG 3/98; SLJ 6/97*)

2350 Shreve, Susan. *Kiss Me Tomorrow* (5–8). 2006, Scholastic $16.99 (978-0-439-68047-9). Alyssa (aka Blister) is not having a good 7th grade; she feels abandoned by best friend Jonah although she's quick to help him when he's in trouble; she is unhappy about her mother's new boyfriend; and she worries about everything else from clothes to sex. (Rev: BL 9/15/06; SLJ 10/06)

2351 Shulman, Mark. *Scrawl* (7–10). 2010, Roaring Brook $16.99 (978-1-59643-417-2). Todd, an 8th-grade bully, gets caught vandalizing school property and is sentenced to detention and writing journal entries — which proves quite revealing. ℮ Lexile 650L (Rev: BLO 8/10; LMC 11–12/10*; SLJ 11/1/10; VOYA 10/10)

2352 Shura, Mary Francis. *The Sunday Doll* (5–7). 1988, Avon paper $2.95 (978-0-380-70618-1). Thirteen-year-old Emmy is miffed when the family won't tell her what has happened to upset her older sister Jayne, until she learns that Jayne's boyfriend has committed suicide. (Rev: BCCB 7–8/88; BL 7/88; SLJ 8/88)

2353 Shyer, Marlene Fanta. *The Rainbow Kite* (6–8). 2002, Marshall Cavendish $15.95 (978-0-7614-5122-8). Matthew tells of his gay brother Bennett's "coming out," a process that began painfully but ended happily when Bennett was accepted by his family and friends. (Rev: BCCB 12/02; BL 12/15/02; HBG 3/03; SLJ 11/02; VOYA 6/03)

2354 Siebold, Jan. *My Nights at the Improv* (4–8). 2005, Whitman $14.95 (978-0-8075-5630-6). Lizzie, a shy 8th-grader whose father died two years before, learns how to speak out by eavesdropping on an improvisational theater class, in the process also learning about bullying Vanessa. (Rev: BCCB 7–8/05; SLJ 11/05)

2355 Silverman, A. O. *Mirror Mirror: Twisted Tales* (5–8). 2002, Scholastic paper $15.95 (978-0-439-29593-2). Disturbing stories serve as metaphors for the problems of drug use, divorce, homelessness, and other ills. (Rev: BL 9/1/02; HBG 10/02; SLJ 8/02; VOYA 6/02)

2356 Silvey, Anita, ed. *Help Wanted: Short Stories About Young People Working* (6–12). 1997, Little, Brown $16.95 (978-0-316-79148-9). A collection of 12 short stories by such writers as Michael Dorris, Norma Fox Mazer, and Gary Soto that deal with teenagers at work. (Rev: BL 11/1/97; HBG 3/98; SLJ 11/97; VOYA 12/97)

2357 Simon, Charnan. *Plan B* (8–12). Series: Surviving Southside. 2011, Lerner/Darby Creek LB $27.93 (978-076136149-7); paper $7.95 (9780761361633). High schoolers Lucy and Luke struggle with difficult decisions when Lucy becomes pregnant; suitable for reluctant readers. Lexile HL430L (Rev: BL 5/1/11; SLJ 4/11)

2358 Singer, Marilyn, ed. *Stay True: Short Stories for Strong Girls* (7–12). 1998, Scholastic paper $16.95 (978-0-590-36031-9). There are 11 new short stories in this collection that explores the problems girls face growing up and how they discover inner strength. (Rev: BL 4/1/98; HB 3–4/98; SLJ 5/98; VOYA 4/98)

2359 Slepian, Jan. *The Broccoli Tapes* (5–8). 1989, Scholastic paper $3.50 (978-0-590-43473-7). Sara uses tapes during her stay in Hawaii to keep up with her class oral history project. (Rev: BCCB 4/89; BL 4/15/89; SLJ 4/89; VOYA 6/89)

2360 Smith, Jennifer E. *You Are Here* (8–11). 2009, Simon & Schuster $15.99 (978-141696799-6). Sixteen-year-old Emma, who has always felt detached from her family, discovers she had a twin brother who died when they were newly born; she and a friend Peter set off on a road trip to visit her brother's grave and learn about each other on the way. (Rev: BL 6/1–15/09; SLJ 8/09)

133

2361 Smith, Kirsten. *The Geography of Girlhood* (8–11). 2006, Little, Brown $16.99 (978-0-316-16021-6). High schooler Penny documents in verse her unhappy family, school, and friendship experiences, all overshadowed by her mother's abandonment when she was young. (Rev: BCCB 5/06; BL 2/1/06; SLJ 5/06)

2362 Sonenklar, Carol. *My Own Worst Enemy* (5–8). 1999, Holiday $15.95 (978-0-8234-1456-7). In this first-person narrative, Eve Belkin finds there is a price to pay when she outdoes herself to be popular in her new school. (Rev: BL 5/15/99; HBG 9/99; SLJ 8/99; VOYA 10/99)

2363 Sones, Sonya. *What My Mother Doesn't Know* (6–10). 2001, Simon & Schuster $17.00 (978-0-689-84114-9). Sophie, 14, expresses her feelings about falling in and out of love in a poetic narrative that is humorous and romantic. (Rev: BCCB 12/01; BL 11/1/01; HBG 10/02; SLJ 10/01; VOYA 10/01)

2364 Soto, Gary. *Accidental Love* (7–10). 2006, Harcourt $16.00 (978-0-15-205497-7). Something clicks when 14-year-old Marisa meets wimpy Rene and she is inspired to transfer to his school, where, despite complications, she finds herself blossoming socially and academically — and enjoying her first love. (Rev: BL 1/1–15/06; SLJ 1/06; VOYA 2/06)

2365 Soto, Gary. *Buried Onions* (8–12). 1997, Harcourt $17.00 (978-0-15-201333-2). A junior college dropout, 19-year-old Eddie is trying to support himself in this story set in the barrio of Fresno, California. (Rev: BL 11/15/97; HBG 3/98; SLJ 1/98; VOYA 10/97)

2366 Soto, Gary. *Hey, 13!* (6–8). 2011, Holiday House $16.95 (978-082342395-8). Thirteen stories offer different perspectives on being 13 years old, many of them featuring Latinos in California. ℮ (Rev: BL 9/15/11; LMC 1–2/12; SLJ 1/12)

2367 Soto, Gary. *Mercy on These Teenage Chimps* (5–8). 2007, Harcourt $16.00 (978-0-15-206022-0). Friends Ronnie Gonzalez and Joey Rios have just turned 13 and are wrestling with physical and emotional changes. (Rev: BL 12/1/06; SLJ 2/07)

2368 Soto, Gary. *The Pool Party* (4–7). Illus. by Robert Casilla. 1992, Delacorte $13.95 (978-0-385-30890-8). Rudy, part of a Mexican American family, has growing-up problems. (Rev: SLJ 6/93)

2369 Spencer, Katherine. *More Than Friends* (7–10). 2008, Harcourt paper $6.95 (978-01520574-6-6). Teenage Grace is determined to overcome the self-destructive behavior she adopted after her brother's death in this story with a romantic twist; a sequel to *Saving Grace* (2006). (Rev: BL 8/08; VOYA 4/08)

2370 Spinelli, Jerry. *Eggs* (4–7). 2007, Little, Brown $15.99 (978-0-316-16646-1). Two troubled children — 9-year-old David and 13-year-old Primrose — forge an unlikely friendship. (Rev: BL 4/1/07; SLJ 7/07)

2371 Spinelli, Jerry. *Hokey Pokey* (7–12). 2013, Knopf $15.99 (978-037583198-0); LB $18.99 (978-037593198-7). Jack comes to the unwelcome realization that he is growing up and will soon be leaving the wonderful world of Hokey Pokey. ∩ ℮ Lexile HL600L (Rev: BL 11/1/12; HB 5–6/13; LMC 5–6/13; SLJ 1/13*; VOYA 12/12)

2372 Spinelli, Jerry. *Jason and Marceline* (7–10). 2000, Little, Brown paper $6.99 (978-0-316-80662-6). Jason, now in the 9th grade, sorts out his feelings toward girls in general and Marceline in particular. Preceded by *Space Station Seventh Grade*. (Rev: BL 1/1/87; SLJ 2/87)

2373 Spinelli, Jerry. *Love, Stargirl* (7–10). 2007, Knopf $16.99 (978-0-375-81375-7). In this sequel to the 2000 novel, 15-year-old Stargirl has moved to Pennsylvania and writes letters to her former boyfriend Leo, describing her new life and the very varied friends she has made in her new home. ∩ (Rev: BL 8/07; HB 9–10/07; SLJ 9/07)

2374 Spinelli, Jerry. *Space Station Seventh Grade* (6–8). 2000, Little, Brown paper $6.99 (978-0-316-80605-3). Jason has many adventures, mostly hilarious, during his 7th-grade year.

2375 Spinelli, Jerry. *Stargirl* (6–9). 2000, Knopf $15.95 (978-0-679-88637-2). When the unusual Stargirl appears at Mica High School, things change and social relationships are questioned. (Rev: BL 6/1–15/00; HB 7–8/00; HBG 3/01; SLJ 8/00)

2376 Spinelli, Jerry. *Wringer* (4–7). 1997, HarperCollins LB $17.89 (978-0-06-024914-4). A sensitive boy must participate in the massacre of thousands of pigeons released at an annual fair. (Rev: BL 9/1/97*; HB 9–10/97; HBG 3/98; SLJ 9/97*)

2377 Stanley, Diane. *A Time Apart* (6–9). 1999, Morrow $15.95 (978-0-688-16997-8). A 13-year-old girl discovers she has inner strengths when she spends a summer with her father on an archaeological project to replicate an Iron Age village in England. (Rev: BCCB 10/99; BL 6/1–15/99; HBG 4/00; SLJ 9/99)

2378 Stevenson, Robin. *Impossible Things* (5–7). 2008, Orca paper $8.95 (978-1-55143-736-1). Cassidy befriends a new girl in town who claims to have magical powers in the hopes that she can become magical too and overpower mean girls and bullies. (Rev: BL 4/15/08; SLJ 8/08)

2379 Stevenson, Robin. *Out of Order* (8–11). 2007, Orca paper $8.95 (978-1-55143-693-7). Sophie, newly slim, is starting high school in a new town and is attracted to classmate Zelia's wild ways until Zelia attempts suicide in this novel about self-perception, sexual identity, and self-respect. (Rev: BL 1/1–15/08)

2380 Stewart, Jennifer J. *The Bean King's Daughter* (5–7). 2002, Holiday $15.95 (978-0-8234-1644-8). Phoebe, a 12-year-old heiress, reluctantly learns about herself and her young stepmother while at an Arizona ranch. (Rev: BL 9/1/02; HBG 10/02; SLJ 7/02)

2381 Stewart, Kiera. *Fetching* (5–8). 2011, Hyperion/Disney $16.99 (978-1-4231-3845-7). Olivia applies dog training principles to the "pack" of mean cliquish kids at her middle school, but finds that the results are not quite what she expected. ℮ Lexile 740L (Rev: BL 10/15/11; SLJ 11/1/11; VOYA 12/11)

2382 Stone, Phoebe. *The Boy on Cinnamon Street* (4–7). 2012, Scholastic $16.99 (978-054521512-1). Diminutive 7th-grader Louise, who has suffered tragedy in her life and lives with her grandparents, finds herself opening up when her friend Reni helps her with the mystery of a secret admirer. ℮ Lexile 720L (Rev: BL 3/1/12*; HB 1–2/12; LMC 3–4/12; SLJ 1/12; VOYA 2/12)

2383 Strasnick, Lauren. *Nothing Like You* (8–10). 2009, Simon & Schuster paper $16.99 (978-1-4169-8264-7). After her mother's death, high school senior Holly Hirsch puts her self-worth aside to seek acceptance in the arms of a popular, handsome guy who hides their relationship from everyone he knows. ℮ (Rev: BL 9/15/09; SLJ 10/09)

2384 Strasser, Todd. *Boot Camp* (8–12). 2007, Simon & Schuster $15.99 (978-1-4169-0848-7). After several warnings about his behavior (dating a teacher), Garrett's parents decide to send the 15-year-old to a disciplinary boot camp; Garrett's descriptions of the mental and physical abuse he undergoes at this camp are realistic. (Rev: BL 8/07; LMC 11–12/07; SLJ 4/07)

2385 Strasser, Todd. *Can't Get There from Here* (7–12). 2004, Simon & Schuster $15.95 (978-0-689-84169-9). A teenage girl who has been thrown out by an abusive mother tries to survive on the streets of New York City. (Rev: BL 3/15/04; SLJ 3/04; VOYA 6/04)

2386 Strasser, Todd. *CON-fidence* (5–8). 2002, Holiday $16.95 (978-0-8234-1394-2). Shy Lauren falls under the spell of the dazzling Celeste, failing to perceive Celeste's underlying motives. (Rev: BCCB 2/03; BL 4/15/03; HBG 10/03; SLJ 1/03; VOYA 4/03)

2387 Strauss, Peggy Guthart. *Getting the Boot* (8–12). Series: Students Across the Seven Seas. 2005, Penguin paper $6.99 (978-0-14-240414-0). A light story about popular high school junior Kelly Brandt's summer as an exchange student in Italy. (Rev: BL 5/15/05; SLJ 8/05)

2388 Summer, Jane. *Not the Only One: Lesbian and Gay Fiction for Teens* (7–12). 2004, Alyson paper $13.95 (978-1-55583-834-8). This revised edition includes 10 new stories featuring gay and lesbian teens. (Rev: BL 12/15/04; VOYA 2/05)

2389 Supplee, Suzanne. *Artichoke's Heart* (7–10). 2008, Dutton $16.99 (978-0-525-47902-4). Overweight Rosemary is trying to deal with kids at school teasing her when her mother is diagnosed with cancer. (Rev: BL 5/1/08; SLJ 8/08)

2390 Swallow, Pamela Curtis. *It Only Looks Easy* (4–7). 2003, Millbrook $15.95 (978-0-7613-1790-6). Kat's problems start when her dog is hit by a car and she "borrows" a bicycle to get to the vet only to have it stolen from her. (Rev: BL 4/15/03; HBG 10/03; SLJ 4/03)

2391 Sweeney, Joyce. *Waiting for June* (8–11). 2003, Marshall Cavendish $15.95 (978-0-7614-5138-9). High school senior Sophie is pregnant, reluctant to disclose the identity of the father, and in danger in this complex, suspenseful novel. (Rev: BL 9/1/03; HBG 4/04; SLJ 10/03; VOYA 4/04)

2392 Tamar, Erika. *The Things I Did Last Summer* (7–9). 1994, Harcourt $10.95 (978-0-15-282490-7). A teenager spending the summer on Long Island with his pregnant stepmother loses his virginity when he meets a deceptive older woman. (Rev: BL 3/15/94; SLJ 4/94; VOYA 6/94)

2393 Tan, Shaun. *Lost and Found: Three by Shaun Tan* (5–10). Illus. by author. 2011, Scholastic $21.99 (978-0-545-22924-1). A beautifully illustrated collection of three stories first published in Australia and dealing with loss. ALA Notable Books 2012. (Rev: BL 4/1/11; HB 5–6/11; SLJ 4/11*)

2394 Tarshis, Lauren. *Emma-Jean Lazarus Fell in Love* (5–7). 2009, Dial $16.99 (978-0-8037-3321-3). Emma-Jean is a bright 7th-grader who applies logic even to matters of the heart. (Rev: BL 5/15/09; SLJ 7/09)

2395 Tharp, Tim. *The Spectacular Now* (8–12). 2008, Knopf $16.99 (978-037585179-7); LB $19.99 (978-037595179-4). Part comedic, part poignant, this novel explores the often reckless life of Sutter, a high school party boy, and the hurt and denial driving him. ⌒ ℮ Lexile HL790L (Rev: BL 11/15/08; SLJ 12/08)

2396 Thesman, Jean. *Cattail Moon* (6–9). 1994, Avon paper $4.50 (978-0-380-72504-5). Julia, 14, is at odds with her mother, who wants to transform her from a classical musician into a cheerleader. (Rev: BL 4/1/94; SLJ 5/94; VOYA 8/94)

2397 Thesman, Jean. *Couldn't I Start Over?* (7–10). 1989, Avon paper $2.95 (978-0-380-75717-6). Growing up in a caring family situation, teenager Shiloh still faces many problems in her coming of age. (Rev: BL 11/15/89; VOYA 2/90)

2398 Thomas, Joyce Carol. *When the Nightingale Sings* (6–8). 1992, HarperCollins paper $3.95 (978-0-06-440524-9). Marigold's only joy in her stepfamily is singing, which leads her to audition for a Baptist church choir, where she discovers self-worth, her family, and happiness. (Rev: BL 1/1/93; SLJ 2/93)

2399 Thompson, Julian. *Facing It* (7–9). 1989, Avon paper $2.95 (978-0-380-84491-3). An accident ruins the baseball chances of the star at Camp Raycroft. A reissue.

2400 Thompson, Julian. *Philo Fortune's Awesome Journey to His Comfort Zone* (8–12). 1995, Hyperion $16.95 (978-0-7868-0067-4). A story of a youth who discovers the possibilities of the man he might become. (Rev: BL 5/1/95; SLJ 5/95; VOYA 2/96)

2401 Todd, Pamela. *The Blind Faith Hotel* (8–12). 2008, Simon & Schuster $16.99 (978-141695494-1). After getting caught shoplifting, defiant 14-year-old Zoe is assigned community service at a nature center and finally comes to appreciate her new surroundings in the rural Midwest, aided by a budding romance with fellow miscreant Todd. ❂ Lexile 780L (Rev: BL 10/15/08; SLJ 12/08; VOYA 2/09)

2402 Tolan, Stephanie S. *Listen!* (4–7). 2006, Harper-Collins $15.99 (978-0-06-057925-8). Lonely after the death of her mother and the departure of her best friend for the summer, 12-year-old Charley finds solace in a stray dog. (Rev: BL 4/1/06)

2403 Torres, Laura. *November Ever After* (8–12). 1999, Holiday $16.95 (978-0-8234-1464-2). Still recovering from her mother's death, 16-yer-old Amy discovers that her best friend, Sara, is a lesbian and in love with a girl in her class. (Rev: BL 12/1/99; HBG 4/00; SLJ 1/00)

2404 Toten, Teresa. *The Onlyhouse* (5–8). 1996, Red Deer paper $7.95 (978-0-88995-137-2). Eleven-year-old Lucija, whose family was originally from Croatia, relocates to a new house in suburban Toronto after several years in a dense downtown neighborhood with a large immigrant population, and must adjust to a new school, peer pressures, and bullies. (Rev: SLJ 7/96)

2405 Townley, Roderick. *Sky: A Novel in 3 Sets and an Encore* (7–10). 2004, Simon & Schuster $16.95 (978-0-689-85712-6). Angered by his father's opposition to his interest in jazz, 15-year-old Sky runs away from home and moves in with the blind jazz pianist whose life he saved. (Rev: BL 8/04; SLJ 7/04)

2406 Tracy, Kristen. *Bessica Lefter Bites Back* (4–7). 2012, Delacorte $16.99 (978-038574069-2); LB $19.99 (978-037598961-2). Bessica's iffy social standing goes from bad to worse when her friend lets fly a rumor about a nasty foot fungus even as she must work out a strategy for sharing mascot duty. ❂ Lexile 550L (Rev: BL 2/15/12; LMC 8–9/12; SLJ 3/12; VOYA 4/12)

2407 Tracy, Kristen. *The Reinvention of Bessica Lefter* (4–7). 2011, Delacorte $15.99 (978-0-385-73688-6); LB $18.99 (978-0-385-90634-0). Eager to shuck off her elementary school persona, Bessica decides on a series of brash and ill-fated attempts to change her appearance in time for the beginning of 6th grade. ❂ Lexile 570L (Rev: BL 1/1–15/11; SLJ 3/1/11)

2408 Trembath, Don. *The Tuesday Cafe* (6–9). 1996, Orca paper $6.95 (978-1-55143-074-4). Harper Winslow, a disaffected, wealthy teenager, learns about life and grows up when he is forced to join a local writing group called "The Tuesday Cafe." (Rev: BL 8/97; SLJ 9/96; VOYA 2/97)

2409 Trueman, Terry. *7 Days at the Hot Corner* (8–11). 2007, HarperTempest $16.99 (978-0-06-057494-9). The "hot corner" of the title is third base, Scott's position on the varsity baseball team, which is threatened when Scott fears he may have contracted AIDS while tending to an injured teammate and friend who is gay. (Rev: BCCB 4/07; BL 2/1/07; SLJ 4/07)

2410 Tullson, Diane. *Edge* (7–10). 2003, Fitzhenry & Whiteside paper $6.95 (978-0-7737-6230-5). Tired of being bullied, Marlie Peters, 14, joins a group of other outcast students only to realize that they are involved in a dangerous plot. (Rev: BL 3/1/03; SLJ 10/03; VOYA 6/03)

2411 Vail, Rachel. *Ever After* (5–9). 1994, Orchard LB $16.99 (978-0-531-08688-9). Fourteen-year-old Molly is trying to act maturely but always seems to mess things up. (Rev: BCCB 4/94; BL 3/1/94; HB 5–6/94, 7–8/94; SLJ 5/94*; VOYA 6/94)

2412 Vail, Rachel. *Gorgeous* (7–10). Series: Avery Sisters Trilogy. 2009, HarperTeen $16.99 (978-0-06-089046-9). Ninth-grader Allison longs to be attractive and is stunned when she becomes a finalist in a teen magazine model contest. ❂ Lexile 740L (Rev: BL 8/09; HB 7–8/09; SLJ 7/1/09; VOYA 8/09)

2413 Vail, Rachel. *If We Kiss* (7–10). 2005, HarperCollins LB $16.89 (978-0-06-056915-0). Fourteen-year-old Charlie struggles with feelings of guilt after she kisses Kevin, who just happens to be her best friend's steady. (Rev: BCCB 5/05; BL 3/15/05; HB 7–8/05; SLJ 5/05)

2414 Vail, Rachel. *Lucky* (7–10). 2008, HarperTeen $16.99 (978-0-06-089043-8). Fourteen-year-old Phoebe's family has never had to worry about money, so when her mother loses her job, Phoebe's new reality changes how she looks at the world and how her friends look at her. (Rev: BL 3/1/08; SLJ 4/08)

2415 Vail, Rachel. *You, Maybe: The Profound Asymmetry of Love in High School* (8–11). 2006, HarperCollins $15.99 (978-0-06-056917-4). Smart, secure teen Josie's confidence is shattered when a boy she casually "hooks up" with gains her trust and then breaks her heart. (Rev: BL 5/1/06; HB 5–6/06; SLJ 7/06)

2416 van Diepen, Allison. *Snitch* (7–10). 2007, Simon & Schuster paper $6.99 (978-1-4169-5030-1). Julia is reluctantly caught up in the world of gang violence when she falls in love with a Crip in this cautionary tale. (Rev: BL 1/1–15/08)

2417 Van Tol, Alex. *Oracle* (5–8). Series: Orca Currents. 2012, Orca LB $16.95 (978-145980133-2); paper $9.95 (978-145980132-5). Fourteen-year-old Owen is upset that Kamryn has a crush on his older brother, and sets out to win her himself with the aid of an advice Web site he creates; for reluctant readers. **e** Lexile 410L (Rev: BLO 10/15/12; SLJ 3/13; VOYA 2/13)

2418 Vande Velde, Vivian. *Curses, Inc.: And Other Stories* (6–10). 1997, Harcourt $16.00 (978-0-15-201452-0). In the title story in this collection of tales with surprise endings, Bill Essler thinks he has found the perfect way to get even with his girlfriend, who humiliated him, by utilizing a web site, Curses, Inc. (Rev: SLJ 6/97*; VOYA 6/97)

2419 Vega, Denise. *Rock On: A Story of Guitars, Gigs, Girls, and a Brother (Not Necessarily in That Order)* (8–12). 2012, Little, Brown $17.99 (978-031613310-4). Orion Taylor, 16, is just starting to feel optimistic about himself and his future as a musician but his older brother's unexpected return from college upsets this new worldview. **e** (Rev: BL 3/15/12; SLJ 3/12)

2420 Velasquez, Gloria. *Tommy Stands Alone* (7–10). 1995, Arte Publico paper $9.95 (978-1-55885-147-4). An engaging story about a Latino gay teen who is humiliated and rejected but finds understanding from a Chicano therapist. (Rev: BL 10/15/95; SLJ 11/95; VOYA 12/95)

2421 Vernick, Audrey. *Water Balloon* (4–7). 2011, Clarion $16.99 (978-0-547-59554-2). Thirteen-year-old Marley is having a tough summer — her parents have separated and she must move into her father's home; her friends seem to have changed — until she meets a new boy who offers friendship and maybe more. **e** Lexile 630L (Rev: SLJ 10/1/11*; VOYA 10/11)

2422 Violi, Jen. *Putting Makeup on Dead People* (8–12). 2011, Hyperion $16.99 (978-142313481-7). Donna takes an internship at a funeral home as a way of working through her father's death and she finds the science and art of the job fascinating. **e** Lexile HL820L (Rev: BL 10/15/11; LMC 10/11; VOYA 6/11)

2423 Vivian, Siobhan. *Same Difference* (8–11). 2009, Scholastic $16.99 (978-054500407-7). Sixteen-year-old Emily takes a summer art course in Philadelphia and finds many differences from — and similarities to — her life in privileged suburbia. Lexile HL740L (Rev: BL 5/1/09; SLJ 5/1/09; VOYA 6/09)

2424 Volponi, Paul. *Crossing Lines* (7–12). 2011, Viking $16.99 (978-0-670-01214-5). Adonis is protective of his status as a football player and realizes too late that he could have acted to protect transgendered Alan from the cruelty of others. **e** Lexile 810L (Rev: BL 5/1/11; SLJ 11/1/11; VOYA 4/11)

2425 Volponi, Paul. *Homestretch* (7–10). 2009, Simon & Schuster $16.99 (978-1-4169-3987-0). When his father's behavior becomes unbearable after his mother is killed in an accident, high school senior Gas runs away and finds work at a horse track with the help of young Mexicans, a group his bigoted father blamed for his mother's death. (Rev: BL 9/15/09; SLJ 12/09)

2426 Volponi, Paul. *Rikers High* (8–11). 2010, Viking $16.99 (978-0-670-011070-). Martin attends high school at Rikers Island while he is waiting for his trial date; this book gives a good description of life in jail and will appeal to male reluctant readers. YALSA Quick Picks for Reluctant Young Adult Readers 2011. **e** Lexile 790L (Rev: BL 12/1/09; LMC 3–4/10; SLJ 1/10)

2427 Walker, Paul R. *The Method* (8–12). 1990, Harcourt $14.95 (978-0-15-200528-3). A candid novel about a 15-year-old boy, his acting aspirations, and his sexual problems. (Rev: BL 8/90; SLJ 6/90)

2428 Wallace, Bill. *Aloha Summer* (7–9). 1997, Holiday $15.95 (978-0-8234-1306-5). Fourteen-year-old John Priddle moves with his family to Hawaii in 1925 and finds less than the island paradise he expected. However, his friendship with a Hawaiian classmate brings new meaning to his life. (Rev: BL 10/1/97; HBG 3/98; SLJ 10/97; VOYA 12/97)

2429 Wallace, Rich. *Losing Is Not an Option* (6–10). 2003, Knopf $15.95 (978-0-375-81351-1). Nine stories follow Ron, a high school athlete, through coming-of-age experiences including family problems, budding sexual attractions, and competition with his peers. (Rev: BL 8/03; HB 9–10/03; HBG 4/04; SLJ 9/03; VOYA 10/03)

2430 Walliams, David. *The Boy in the Dress* (4–7). Illus. by Quentin Blake. 2009, Penguin $15.99 (978-1-59514-299-3). British 12-year-old Dennis discovers he's interested in fashion — and enjoys wearing dresses — in this funny story that includes some slapstick moments but also some difficult ones with his father and brother. Stonewall Honor 2011. (Rev: BL 11/1/09; SLJ 12/09)

2431 Walpole, Peter. *The Healer of Harrow Point* (4–7). 2000, Hampton Roads paper $11.95 (978-1-57174-167-7). A novel of love and compassion about a boy who is promised a hunting trip for his twelfth birthday but wonders if he can kill a deer, particularly after seeing one killed by poachers and after meeting Emma, who can heal animals with her touch. (Rev: SLJ 10/00)

2432 Walters, Eric. *Sketches* (7–10). 2008, Viking $15.99 (978-0-670-06294-2). Runaway Dana, 14, finds solace at Sketches, an art center for homeless teens in Toronto. (Rev: BL 1/1–15/08; SLJ 4/08)

2433 Waltman, Kevin. *Nowhere Fast* (8–12). 2002, Scholastic paper $7.99 (978-0-439-41424-1). After stealing a car for joyriding, teenagers Gary and Wilson become entrapped in the activities of a former teacher with a dangerous agenda. (Rev: BL 2/1/03; SLJ 4/03; VOYA 4/03)

2434 Wardlaw, Lee. *101 Ways to Bug Your Friends and Enemies* (5–8). 2011, Dial $16.99 (978-0-8037-3262-9). Eighth grade proves challenging to "Sneeze" Wyatt as he attends some classes at high school, falls for Hayley who unfortunately is in love with someone else, and a golfer bullies him. **e** Lexile 600L (Rev: BLO 10/15/11; SLJ 10/1/11)

2435 Wartski, Maureen C. *My Name Is Nobody* (7–10). 1988, Walker $15.95 (978-0-8027-6770-7). A victim of child abuse survives a suicide attempt and is given a second chance by a tough ex-cop. (Rev: BL 2/1/88; SLJ 3/88; VOYA 4/88)

2436 Wasserman, Robin. *Lust* (8–11). Series: Seven Deadly Sins. 2005, Simon & Schuster paper $7.99 (978-0-689-87782-7). In an entertaining opening volume of a soap-opera-like series, several sex-obsessed high school seniors in a small California town ruthlessly scheme to win the girl or guy of their dreams. (Rev: BL 12/1/05; SLJ 1/06)

2437 Weaver, Beth Nixon. *Rooster* (7–12). 2001, Winslow $16.95 (978-1-58837-001-3). In the 1960s, 15-year-old Kady is growing up in a confusing mix of poverty at home on a struggling orange grove, a devoted but disabled neighboring child, and a wealthy boyfriend who introduces her to marijuana. (Rev: BL 7/01; HB 7–8/01; HBG 10/01; SLJ 6/01; VOYA 2/02)

2438 Weaver, Will. *Full Service* (7–10). 2005, Farrar $17.00 (978-0-374-32485-8). Paul, a sheltered Christian 15-year-old, discovers hippies, alcohol, and sex when he takes a job at a gas station in the summer of 1965. (Rev: BL 9/1/05; SLJ 11/05; VOYA 10/05)

2439 Weinheimer, Beckie. *Converting Kate* (7–10). 2007, Viking $16.99 (978-0-670-06152-5). Her parents' divorce and her father's death have led Kate, 16, to question her faith in the religious sect in which she has grown up, and a move to Maine exposes her to a world outside her strict upbringing. (Rev: BCCB 3/07; BL 3/1/07; SLJ 4/07)

2440 Wenberg, Michael. *Stringz* (6–9). 2010, WestSide $16.95 (978-1-934813-33-1). Fourteen-year-old Jace's cello is his most prized possession and brings him the rewards that have been so lacking in his difficult life. Lexile HL760L (Rev: BL 6/10; LMC 11–12/10; SLJ 9/1/10; VOYA 8/10)

2441 Wetter, Bruce. *The Boy with the Lampshade on His Head* (5–8). 2004, Simon & Schuster $16.95 (978-0-689-85032-5). Painfully shy, 11-year-old Stanley Krakow maintains a low profile but a rich inner life until he makes friends with an abused girl and finds the inner strength to be a real hero. (Rev: BL 5/1/04; SLJ 8/04)

2442 Whelan, Gloria. *Listening for Lions* (6–9). 2005, HarperCollins LB $16.89 (978-0-06-058175-6). Rachel, the orphaned daughter of missionary parents, gets pulled into an elaborate scheme to get her money-grubbing neighbors reinstated in the will of an ailing Englishman. (Rev: BCCB 9/05; BL 5/15/05*; HB 9–10/05; SLJ 8/05; VOYA 8/05)

2443 Whittenberg, Allison. *Life Is Fine* (8–12). 2008, Delacorte $15.99 (978-0-385-73480-6). Samara, a sad, neglected 15-year-old, develops a crush on a substitute teacher who introduces her to poetry. (Rev: BL 1/1–15/08; SLJ 2/08)

2444 Wieler, Diana. *RanVan: The Defender* (7–12). 1997, Douglas & McIntyre $16.95 (978-0-88899-270-3). Orphaned Rhan Van, who lives with his grandmother in a city apartment, begins hanging out in bad company and soon finds he is vandalizing school and private property. (Rev: BL 2/1/98; SLJ 3/98)

2445 Wilhelm, Doug. *Falling* (7–10). 2007, Farrar $17.00 (978-0-374-32251-9). Two troubled teens — Matt, whose first year in high school is ruined by his brother's heroin addiction, and Katie — connect through the Internet in this coming-of-age story set in Vermont. (Rev: BL 3/15/07; SLJ 7/07)

2446 Wilkins, Ebony Joy. *Sellout* (7–10). 2010, Scholastic $17.99 (978-0-545-10928-4). Socially uncertain African American NaTasha's parents have moved her to a privileged high school in New Jersey, but a summer with her grandmother in Harlem and volunteering at a crisis center in the Bronx help her adjust her preconceptions. **e** Lexile 720L (Rev: BL 9/1/10; LMC 10/10; SLJ 8/10)

2447 Wilkinson, Lili. *The Not Quite Perfect Boyfriend* (8–11). 2012, IPG/Allen & Unwin paper $8.99 (978-17423776-5-0). A lighthearted story about Australian Midge, 16, who invents a boyfriend. **e** (Rev: BL 3/15/12; SLJ 2/12)

2448 Williams, Carol Lynch. *Waiting* (8–11). 2012, Simon & Schuster $16.99 (978-144244353-2). Still grieving for her older brother Zach, London seeks comfort from two quite different boys, knowing she must make a choice; a novel told in free verse. **e** (Rev: BL 7/12; HB 7–8/12; SLJ 6/12; VOYA 6/12)

2449 Williams, Laura E. *Slant* (5–8). 2008, Milkweed $16.95 (978-1-57131-681-3); paper $6.95 (978-1-57131-682-0). Lauren, an 8th-grader and Korean American adoptee, wants to have surgery to make her eyes more Western in this compelling story of identity, culture, and belonging. (Rev: BLO 1/13/09; LMC 3–4/09; SLJ 12/08)

2450 Williams, Lori Aurelia. *Shayla's Double Brown Baby Blues* (7–12). 2003, Pulse $17.00 (978-0-689-85670-9). In this sequel to *When Kambia Elaine Flew in from Neptune* (2000), 13-year-old Shayla must cope with problems including the arrival of a new half-sister, her friend Kambia's traumatic and abusive past, and her friend Lemm's alcoholism. (Rev: BL 7/01; HB 9–10/01; SLJ 8/01)

2451 Williams, Lori Aurelia. *When Kambia Elaine Flew in from Neptune* (7–12). 2001, Pulse paper $17.00 (978-0-689-84593-2). In this first-person narrative, 12-year-old Shayla adjusts to the unhappy departure from the family of her older sister and finds escape in her friendship with an imaginative girl named Kambia. (Rev: BL 2/15/00)

2452 Willner-Pardo, Gina. *The Hard Kind of Promise* (5–7). 2010, Clarion $16 (978-0-547-24395-5). In kindergarten Sarah and Marjorie promised to be friends forever, but by 7th grade Marjorie's oddness jeopardizes Sarah's chances for popularity. **e** Lexile 670L (Rev: BL 8/10; HB 7–8/10; SLJ 8/10)

2453 Wilson, Budge. *Sharla* (7–10). 1998, Stoddart paper $6.95 (978-0-7736-7467-7). A run-in with a polar bear, adjusting to a new school, trying to make friends, and getting used to severe weather are some of the problems 15-year-old Sharla faces when she moves with her family from Ottawa to Churchill, a small community in northern Manitoba. (Rev: SLJ 8/98)

2454 Wilson, Jacqueline. *Kiss* (7–10). 2010, Roaring Brook $16.99 (978-1-59643-242-0). At age 14, Sylvie has always assumed that she will eventually marry her best friend Carl, but with high school things change and Carl appears to be more interested in his new friend Paul. ∩ **e** Lexile HL680L (Rev: BL 2/1/10; HB 3–4/10; LMC 5–6/10; SLJ 3/10)

2455 Wilson, Johnniece M. *Poor Girl* (5–7). 1992, Scholastic $13.95 (978-0-590-44732-4). A first-person story about Miranda, who spends the summer trying to earn money for contact lenses before the fall. (Rev: BCCB 4/92; BL 8/92; SLJ 4/92)

2456 Winton, Tim. *Lockie Leonard, Human Torpedo* (6–8). 1992, Little, Brown $13.95 (978-0-316-94753-4). Set in Australia, the story of a 14-year-old surfer and his confusion as he begins a more intimate relationship with his girlfriend. (Rev: BL 12/15/91; SLJ 12/91)

2457 Withrow, Sarah. *What Gloria Wants* (7–10). 2005, Groundwood paper $6.95 (978-0-88899-692-3). Gloria always seems to be a step behind her best friend Shawna, so Gloria initially exults when she is first to land a boyfriend. (Rev: BCCB 11/05; BL 12/1/05; HB 1–2/06; SLJ 2/06; VOYA 12/05)

2458 Wittlinger, Ellen. *Hard Love* (8–12). 1999, Simon & Schuster paper $8.00 (978-0-689-84154-5). Two outsiders, John, a high school junior and fan of "zines," and Marisol, a self-proclaimed virgin lesbian, form an unusual relationship in this well-crafted novel that explores many teenage problems. (Rev: BL 10/1/99*; HB 7–8/99; HBG 9/99; SLJ 7/99; VOYA 8/99)

2459 Wittlinger, Ellen. *Sandpiper* (8–12). 2005, Simon & Schuster $16.95 (978-0-689-86802-3). Her promiscuous past has severely tarnished 16-year-old Sandpiper's reputation, but when she develops a friendship with Walker, both troubled teens begin to make some important discoveries about the ways in which the past is shaping their future. (Rev: BL 6/1–15/05; SLJ 7/05; VOYA 8/05)

2460 Wittlinger, Ellen. *Zigzag* (8–12). 2003, Simon & Schuster $16.95 (978-0-689-84996-1). A summer

cross-country car trip with her recently widowed aunt and two cousins poses many challenges for 17-year-old Robin. (Rev: BL 9/1/03; HB 7–8/03; HBG 4/04; SLJ 8/03; VOYA 10/03)

2461 Wojciechowska, Maia. *Shadow of a Bull* (5–8). Illus. by Alvin Smith. 1964, Macmillan $16.95 (978-0-689-30042-4). Manolo, surviving son of a great bullfighter, has his own "moment of truth" when he faces his first bull. Newbery Medal 1965.

2462 Wolfson, Jill. *Home, and Other Big, Fat Lies* (5–7). 2006, Henry Holt $16.95 (978-0-8050-7670-7). Shuttled through the foster care system for much of her life, 11-year-old Whitney isn't expecting much out of her latest stop with a family in remote northern California, but her interest in nature — and some new friendships — open her eyes to the importance of fighting for what you believe in. (Rev: SLJ 12/06)

2463 Wolfson, Jill. *What I Call Life* (5–8). 2005, Henry Holt $16.95 (978-0-8050-7669-1). Five young girls — all refugees from troubled families — find friendship and strength during their stay in a group home run by a wise Knitting Lady. (Rev: BCCB 9/05; BL 11/1/05; HBG 4/06; LMC 4–5/06; SLJ 9/05; VOYA 12/05)

2464 Wong, Joyce Lee. *Seeing Emily* (6–9). 2005, Abrams $16.95 (978-0-8109-5757-2). This appealing free-verse novel chronicles the coming of age of 16-year-old Emily Wu, a promising artist and the daughter of Chinese immigrants. (Rev: BCCB 11/05; SLJ 12/05)

2465 Woodson, Jacqueline. *The House You Pass on the Way* (6–9). 1997, Puffin paper $5.99 (978-0-14-250191-7). A young girl from an interracial marriage feels left out and becomes a loner until she falls in love with a girl cousin who comes to visit. (Rev: BL 8/97; SLJ 10/97; VOYA 10/97)

2466 Wright, Betty R. *The Summer of Mrs. MacGregor* (5–8). 1986, Holiday $15.95 (978-0-8234-0628-9). Meeting an exotic teenager who calls herself Mrs. Lillina MacGregor helps Linda solve her problem of jealousy toward her older sister. (Rev: BCCB 12/86; BL 11/1/86; SLJ 11/86; VOYA 4/87)

2467 Wright, Bil. *Putting Makeup on the Fat Boy* (7–10). 2011, Simon & Schuster $16.99 (978-1-4169-3996-2). Gay teen Carlos is on track for a career as a makeup artist but first must contend with a jealous boss, his sister's thuggish boyfriend, and his own crush on a boy at school. YALSA Popular Paperbacks for Young Adults Top Ten 2013. **e** Lexile 820L (Rev: BL 9/1/11; LMC 1–2/12; SLJ 7/11)

2468 Wyss, Thelma Hatch. *Ten Miles from Winnemucca* (6–8). 2002, HarperCollins $15.95 (978-0-06-029783-1). When his mother and new husband leave on their honeymoon, 16-year-old Martin decides to take a break from his new stepbrother and starts a new life for himself in Idaho. (Rev: BCCB 7–8/02; BL 2/1/02; HB 7–8/02; HBG 10/02; SLJ 6/02; VOYA 2/02)

2469 Yang, J. A. *Exclusively Chloe* (6–10). 2009, Penguin paper $7.99 (978-014241226-8). A "makeunder" allows 16-year-old Chinese American Chloe to escape the constant attention her adoptive parents' celebrity has imposed on her. (Rev: BL 7/09)

2470 Yang, Margaret. *Locked Out* (6–9). 1996, Tudor $17.95 (978-0-936389-40-0). Gina is outraged and goaded into activism when she learns that the principal of her school, in an effort to curb smoking, has closed all the bathrooms except those close to his office. (Rev: SLJ 5/96)

2471 Yee, Lisa. *Absolutely Maybe* (7–10). 2009, Scholastic $16.99 (978-043983844-3). This is a mostly humorous tale about high school junior Maybe (short for Maybelline, her mother's favorite mascara), who leaves her soon-to-be-married-again mother's home and heads for California to search for her biological father. **e** Lexile HL570L (Rev: BL 12/1/08; HB 3–4/09)

2472 Yee, Lisa. *Warp Speed* (4–7). 2011, Scholastic $16.99 (978-0-545-12276-4). Marley, a shy wallflower geek who loves Star Trek and suffers bullying, must chart a new course for himself when his speed and agility catch the coach's eye and Marley becomes a star athlete. Lexile HL620L (Rev: BL 2/15/11; HB 3–4/11; SLJ 5/11)

2473 Yoo, David. *The Detention Club* (5–8). 2011, HarperCollins $16.99 (978-0-06-178378-4). Sixth-grader Peter's zany scheme to boost his faltering popularity lands him in detention in this humorous story about the challenges of middle school. **e** Lexile 880L (Rev: BL 8/11; HB 9–10/11; SLJ 10/1/11)

2474 Young, Ronder T. *Moving Mama to Town* (5–8). 1997, Orchard LB $18.99 (978-0-531-33025-8). Although his father is a gambler and a failure, Fred never loses faith in him in this story of a boy who must help support his family although he's only 13. (Rev: BL 6/1–15/97; HB 7–8/97; SLJ 6/97)

2475 Zalben, Jane Breskin. *Water from the Moon* (8–10). 1987, Random House paper $4.99 (978-0-440-22855-4). Nicky Berstein, a high school sophomore, tries too hard to make friends and is hurt in the process. (Rev: BL 5/15/87; SLJ 5/87; VOYA 8/87)

2476 Zeises, Lara M. *Contents Under Pressure* (6–9). 2004, Delacorte $15.95 (978-0-385-73047-1). In this appealing coming-of-age novel, 14-year-old Lucy experiences dramatic changes in her life when she starts to date Tobin. (Rev: BCCB 5/04; BL 3/15/04; HB 3–4/04; SLJ 4/04; VOYA 6/04)

2477 Zindel, Bonnie, and Paul Zindel. *A Star for the Latecomer* (7–10). 1980, HarperCollins $12.95 (978-0-06-026847-3). When her mother dies, Brooke is freed of the need to pursue a dancing career.

2478 Zindel, Lizabeth. *The Secret Rites of Social Butterflies* (7–10). 2008, Viking $16.99 (978-0-670-06217-1). At her new girls' school in New York City, Maggie breaks into the popular clique and soon finds that betrayal is her new friends' pastime. (Rev: BL 5/15/08)

2479 Zinnen, Linda. *The Truth About Rats, Rules, and Seventh Grade* (5–7). 2001, HarperCollins LB $15.89 (978-0-06-028800-6). Larch, who faces multiple problems at home and at school, tries to live her life by a set of unemotional rules, but a friendly stray dog and the discovery of the truth about her father's death make these rules hard to keep. (Rev: BCCB 6/01; BL 4/1/01*; HBG 10/01; SLJ 2/01)

2480 Zolotow, Charlotte, ed. *Early Sorrow: Ten Stories of Youth* (8–12). 1986, HarperCollins $12.95 (978-0-06-026936-4). This excellent collection of 12 adult stories about growing up is a companion piece to *An Overpraised Season* (o.p.), another anthology about adolescence. (Rev: BL 10/1/86; SLJ 1/87; VOYA 2/87)

2481 Zusak, Markus. *Underdogs* (7–10). 2012, Scholastic $19.99 (978-054535442-4). This volume featuring brothers Cameron and Ruben Wolfe collects three novels: *The Underdog, Fighting Ruben Wolfe,* and *Getting the Girl.* **e** Lexile HL610L (Rev: BLO 2/15/12; LMC 5–6/12)

World Affairs and Contemporary Problems

2482 Abelove, Joan. *Go and Come Back* (8–10). 1998, Puffin paper $5.99 (978-0-14-130694-0). The story of two female anthropologists studying a primitive Peruvian Indian village, written from the perspective of Alicia, one of the village teenagers. (Rev: BL 3/1/98; SLJ 3/98*; VOYA 10/98)

2483 Adoff, Jaime. *Names Will Never Hurt Me* (7–10). 2004, Dutton $16.99 (978-0-525-47175-2). As their high school marks the first anniversary of the shooting death of a fellow student, four very different teenagers express their feelings about school, their classmates, and themselves. (Rev: BCCB 4/04; BL 4/1/04; HB 7–8/04; SLJ 4/04; VOYA 4/04)

2484 Akbarpour, Ahmad. *Good Night, Commander* (5–8). Illus. by Morteza Zahedi. 2010, Groundwood $17.95 (978-0-88899-989-4). Childlike illustrations accompany this account of a young Iranian boy's devastating wartime experiences. (Rev: BL 5/1/10; LMC 8–9/10; SLJ 5/1/10)

2485 Alvarez, Julia. *Return to Sender* (6–9). 2009, Random House $16.99 (978-037585838-3); LB $19.99 (978-037595838-0). After 11-year-old Tyler's father is injured in an accident, the family must hire illegal immigrants, who have their own serious family problems, to help run their Vermont dairy farm in this thoughtful novel told from both Tyler's point of view and that of the young Mexican daughter. Belpré Medal 2010;

ALA Notable Books 2010. 🎧 **e** Lexile 890L (Rev: BL 12/1/08; LMC 5–6/09; SLJ 2/1/09)

2486 Bledsoe, Lucy Jane. *Cougar Canyon* (5–8). 2001, Holiday $16.95 (978-0-8234-1599-1). A family story and environmental tale about a 13-year-old girl named Izzy who fights to save a cougar in the local park. (Rev: BCCB 2/02; BL 2/1/02; HBG 3/02; SLJ 2/02; VOYA 4/02)

2487 Budhos, Marina. *Ask Me No Questions* (7–10). 2006, Simon & Schuster $16.95 (978-1-4169-0351-2). Fourteen-year-old Nadira describes the legal and emotional upheavals her family faces as Bangladeshis living illegally in the United States. (Rev: BCCB 3/06; BL 12/15/05*; HB 3–4/06; SLJ 4/06; VOYA 2/06)

2488 Carmi, Daniella. *Samir and Yonatan* (4–8). Trans. from Hebrew by Yael Lotan. 2000, Scholastic paper $15.95 (978-0-439-13504-7). Samir, a young Palestinian, is sent to a Jewish hospital for surgery and there he meets some Jewish contemporaries. (Rev: BCCB 4/00; BL 2/1/00; HBG 10/00; SLJ 3/00; VOYA 6/00)

2489 Castaneda, Omar S. *Among the Volcanoes* (7–10). 1996, Bantam paper $4.50 (978-0-440-91118-0). Set in a remote Guatemalan village, this story is about a Mayan woodcutter's daughter, Isabel, who is caught between her respect for the old ways and her yearning for something more. (Rev: BL 5/15/91; SLJ 3/91)

2490 Clinton, Cathryn. *A Stone in My Hand* (6–12). 2002, Candlewick $15.99 (978-0-7636-1388-4). Eleven-year-old Maalak's father is killed in the violence of 1988 Gaza, and she must worry about her brother's future. (Rev: BL 9/15/02; HBG 3/03; SLJ 11/02*; VOYA 2/03)

2491 Collins, Pat Lowery. *The Fattening Hut* (8–12). 2003, Houghton Mifflin $15.00 (978-0-618-30955-9). Fourteen-year-old Helen sets off on a dangerous journey, running away from the tropical tribe that requires her to undergo female circumcision before her impending marriage. (Rev: BL 11/1/03; HBG 4/04; SLJ 11/03; VOYA 2/04)

2492 Cooney, Caroline B. *Diamonds in the Shadow* (8–12). 2007, Delacorte $15.99 (978-0-385-73261-1). Jared and Mopsy have different experiences when their family hosts a refugee family from Sierra Leone. (Rev: BL 9/1/07; SLJ 9/07)

2493 Covington, Dennis. *Lasso the Moon* (7–10). 1996, Bantam $20.95 (978-0-385-30991-2). After April and her divorced doctor father move to Saint Simons Island, April takes a liking to Fernando, an illegal alien from El Salvador being treated by her father. (Rev: BL 1/15/95; SLJ 3/95; VOYA 4/95)

2494 Cowan, Jennifer. *Earthgirl* (8–11). 2009, Groundwood $17.95 (978-088899889-7); paper $12.95 (978-088899890-3). A fast-food lunch tossed out a window spurs 16-year-old Sabine to environmental activism and

she starts a successful blog and becomes involved in a relationship with Vray, a passionate eco-warrior. (Rev: BL 6/1–15/09; SLJ 6/1/09*)

2495 Craig, Colleen. *Afrika* (7–12). 2008, Tundra paper $9.95 (978-0-88776-807-1). Kim, a 13-year-old who has grown up in Canada, travels to South Africa with her journalist mother, a white South African, to cover the Truth and Reconciliation Commission hearings; while there she learns about her father's African roots and finds out why her mother left him. (Rev: BL 6/1–15/08; SLJ 7/08)

2496 D'Adamo, Francesco. *Iqbal: A Novel* (4–7). 2003, Simon & Schuster $15.95 (978-0-689-85445-3). The sad story of the death of Iqbal, the young child labor activist, is brought to life through the fictional narrative of a young Pakistani girl who worked with him in the carpet factories. (Rev: BL 11/1/03; HB 11–12/03; HBG 4/04; SLJ 11/03)

2497 Davis, Jenny. *Checking on the Moon* (6–9). 1991, Orchard LB $17.99 (978-0-531-08560-8). A 13-year-old, forced to spend the summer in a run-down Pittsburgh neighborhood with a grandmother she has never met, discovers community activism and her own abilities. (Rev: BL 9/15/91; SLJ 10/91*)

2498 Dixon, Peter. *Hunting the Dragon* (8–12). 2010, Hyperion $15.99 (978-1-4231-2498-6). Eighteen-year-old Billy becomes a passionate defender of the rights of dolphins after working on a tuna boat. (Rev: LMC 8–9/10; SLJ 6/10)

2499 Doherty, Berlie. *The Girl Who Saw Lions* (6–12). 2008, Roaring Brook $16.95 (978-1-59643-377-9). Abela, 9, and Rosa, 13, tell their contrasting stories in alternating chapters. Abela is an AIDS orphan in Tanzania, whose uncle plans to sell her for adoption in England; in London, Rosa is unhappy when she learns that her single-parent mother plans to adopt a child. (Rev: BL 2/15/08; SLJ 7/08)

2500 Ellis, Deborah. *Mud City* (4–7). Series: Breadwinner Trilogy. 2003, Douglas & McIntyre $15.95 (978-0-88899-518-6). Feisty Afghan refugee Shauzia sets off on her own, dreaming of a life of freedom in France and prepared to dress as a boy and beg, but circumstances force her back to the camp on the Pakistan border in this final novel in the trilogy. (Rev: BL 11/15/03; HBG 4/04; SLJ 11/03)

2501 Ellis, Deborah, and Eric Walters. *Bifocal* (7–10). 2007, Fitzhenry & Whiteside $18.95 (978-1-55455-036-4). When a Muslim student is arrested, suspected of being a terrorist, his school is abuzz, and various groups take sides. (Rev: BL 1/1–15/08; SLJ 3/08)

2502 Farish, Terry. *The Good Braider* (8–12). 2012, Amazon Children's $17.99 (978-0-7614-6267-5). Viola, 16, remembers in free-verse poems her difficult experiences in Sudan, harrowing escape overland to Egypt, and being received as a refugee in Portland, Maine. **e**

141

Lexile HL630L (Rev: BL 7/12*; HB 9–10/12; LMC 1–2/13; SLJ 9/12*; VOYA 10/12)

2503 Flegg, Aubrey. *The Cinnamon Tree* (7–10). 2002, O'Brien paper $7.95 (978-0-86278-657-1). The horror of the injuries inflicted by landmines is brought to life in this story of a girl who loses a leg and goes on to teach others about the dangers of these weapons. (Rev: BL 8/02; SLJ 8/02)

2504 Fox, Paula. *Lily and the Lost Boy* (6–9). 1987, Watts LB $17.99 (978-0-531-08320-8). Using the tiny island of Thasos in Greece as a setting the author tells a story of the maturation of a 12-year-old American girl and her older brother. (Rev: BL 7/87; VOYA 2/88)

2505 French, S. Terrell. *Operation Redwood* (5–7). 2009, Abrams $16.95 (978-0-8109-8354-0). Twelve-year-old Julian tries to save historic redwoods with a little help from his friends. (Rev: BLO 5/28/09; HB 7/09; SLJ 7/09)

2506 Golio, Janet, and Mike Golio. *A Present from the Past* (6–8). 1995, Portunus paper $8.95 (978-0-9641330-5-1). In this blend of fact and fiction, Sarah and her friend become concerned about their environment after they discover some petroglyphs. (Rev: BL 1/1–15/96)

2507 Griffin, Paul. *Ten Mile River* (8–12). 2008, Dial $16.99 (978-0-8037-3284-1). Ray, 14, and José, 15, live together in an abandoned building in west Harlem and survive on odd jobs and what they can steal; when they meet the lovely Trini, complications of romance and opportunity test their friendship. (Rev: BL 6/1–15/08; SLJ 9/08)

2508 Guest, Jacqueline. *War Games* (7–10). 2009, Orca $16.95 (978-155277036-8); paper $9.95 (978-155277035-1). His strict soldier father is in Afghanistan, and 15-year-old Ryan enjoys a freer life and ample access to computer war games while at the same time recognizing the dangers his father faces. (Rev: BL 6/1–15/09; SLJ 12/09)

2509 Henry, April. *Torched* (8–11). 2009, Putnam $16.99 (978-039924645-6). Ellie, 16, is recruited by the FBI to infiltrate and report on an ecoterrorism group, the Mother Earth Defenders; action, romance, and an environmental message combine for an exciting read. Lexile HL710L (Rev: BL 2/15/09; SLJ 4/1/09)

2510 Hentoff, Nat. *The Day They Came to Arrest the Book* (7–10). 1983, Dell paper $5.50 (978-0-440-91814-1). Some students at George Mason High think *Huckleberry Finn* is a racist book.

2511 Hesse, Karen. *Phoenix Rising* (6–8). 1994, Henry Holt $16.95 (978-0-8050-3108-9). A 13-year-old and her grandmother on a Vermont farm hope to avoid radiation contamination from a nuclear plant. They are visited by Boston evacuees, one of them a boy with whom the girl falls in love. (Rev: BL 5/15/94; SLJ 6/94*; VOYA 8/94)

2512 Hiaasen, Carl. *Hoot* (5–8). 2002, Knopf $15.95 (978-0-375-82181-3). Roy Eberhart, the new kid in Coconut Cove, finds himself embroiled in a battle to save some owls. Newbery Honor 2003. (Rev: BCCB 11/02; BL 10/15/02; HB 11–12/02; HBG 3/03; SLJ 8/02)

2513 Ho, Minfong. *Rice Without Rain* (7–12). 1990, Lothrop $17.99 (978-0-688-06355-9). Jinda, a 17-year-old girl, experiences personal tragedy and the awakening of love in this novel set during revolutionary times in Thailand during the 1970s. (Rev: BL 7/90; SLJ 9/90)

2514 Hobbs, Will. *Crossing the Wire* (5–8). 2006, HarperCollins $15.99 (978-0-06-074138-9). Victor, a teenage Mexican boy who is the sole support for his family, decides to risk the dangerous crossing into the United States in search of work. ◯ (Rev: BL 5/1/06; SLJ 5/06; VOYA 4/06)

2515 Holmes, Sara Lewis. *Operation Yes* (5–8). 2009, Scholastic $16.99 (978-054510795-2). Miss Loupe uses improv acting in her 6th-grade class at an Air Force base school, and she is rewarded by her students' loyal support when her brother goes missing in Afghanistan. ◯ (Rev: BL 9/15/09*; HB 11–12/09; SLJ 11/09)

2516 Hopkins, Ellen. *Crank* (8–12). 2004, Simon & Schuster paper $6.99 (978-0-689-86519-0). In this debut novel written in verse, Hopkins introduces readers to Kristina Snow and how the high school junior became addicted to crystal meth. (Rev: BL 11/15/04; SLJ 11/04; VOYA 2/05)

2517 James, Brian. *Tomorrow, Maybe* (7–12). 2003, Scholastic paper $6.99 (978-0-439-49035-1). Living a hard life on the streets of New York, 15-year-old Gretchen, a.k.a. Chan, finds a purpose when she takes charge of an 11-year-old in the same predicament. (Rev: LMC 10/03; SLJ 6/03; VOYA 8/03)

2518 Jennings, Richard W. *Stink City* (5–8). 2006, Houghton Mifflin $16.00 (978-0-618-55248-1). Cade Carlsen, heir to his family's successful — but smelly — catfish bait business, becomes an anti-fishing activist. (Rev: BL 10/15/06)

2519 Kilbourne, Christina. *Dear Jo: The Story of Losing Leah . . . and Searching for Hope* (6–8). 2007, Lobster paper $9.95 (978-1-897073-51-3). A cautionary tale that maintains its readability, this novel focuses on two 12-year-old girl with online boyfriends; one friend disappears, and the other copes by keeping a diary and helping to catch the predator. (Rev: SLJ 7/07)

2520 Kilbourne, Christina. *They Called Me Red* (8–12). 2008, Lobster $10.95 (978-189707388-9). This is a dark story about human trafficking in which an American teen is sold by his Vietnamese stepmother into a Cambodian brothel after his father dies. (Rev: BLO 12/30/08)

2521 Koss, Amy Goldman. *The Not-So-Great Depression* (5–7). 2010, Roaring Brook paper $9.99 (978-1-59643-613-8). When her divorced mother is laid off,

14-year-old Jacki and her siblings face losing their privileged private-school life; the subtitle, *In Which the Economy Crashes, My Sister's Plans Are Ruined, My Mom Goes Broke, My Dad Grows Vegetables, and I Do Not Get a Hamster,* fills in some of the rest of the story. ℮ Lexile 810L (Rev: BL 3/15/10; HB 5–6/10; LMC 5–6/10; SLJ 5/10)

2522 Laird, Elizabeth, and Sonia Nimr. *A Little Piece of Ground* (6–9). 2006, Haymarket paper $9.95 (978-1-931859-38-7). Karim, 12, and his friends hope to create a soccer field in Ramallah so they have a place to escape from the war surrounding them. (Rev: BL 10/15/06)

2523 Levine, Anna. *Running on Eggs* (5–9). 1999, Front St $15.95 (978-0-8126-2875-3). The story of two girls — one Jewish and the other Palestinian — and a friendship that withstands cultural and political differences. (Rev: BCCB 11/99; BL 1/1–15/00; HBG 3/00; SLJ 12/99; VOYA 2/00)

2524 Levithan, David. *Love Is the Higher Law* (8–12). 2009, Knopf $15.99 (978-037583468-4); LB $18.99 (978-037593468-1). Three New York City teens — Claire, Peter, and Peter's potential boyfriend Jasper — witness the events of September 11, 2001, and become close as they deal with the experience. (Rev: BL 6/1–15/09; LMC 11–12/09; SLJ 9/09)

2525 Levitin, Sonia. *The Return* (6–10). 1987, Fawcett paper $5.99 (978-0-449-70280-2). Seen from the viewpoint of a teenage girl, this is the story of a group of African Jews who journey from Ethiopia to the Sudan to escape persecution. (Rev: BL 4/15/87; SLJ 5/87; VOYA 6/87)

2526 Lynch, Janet Nichols. *Peace Is a Four-Letter Word* (7–10). 2005, Heyday paper $9.95 (978-1-59714-014-0). The carefully ordered life of high school cheerleader Emily Rankin is shattered when a history teacher inspires her to get involved in the peace movement on the eve of the Gulf War. (Rev: BL 10/1/05; SLJ 10/05)

2527 McDaniel, Lurlene. *Baby Alicia Is Dying* (8–10). 1993, Bantam paper $4.99 (978-0-553-29605-1). In an attempt to feel needed, Desi volunteers to care for HIV-positive babies and discovers a deep commitment in herself. (Rev: BL 10/1/93; SLJ 7/93; VOYA 8/93)

2528 Mankell, Henning. *Secrets in the Fire* (4–8). 2003, Annick $14.95 (978-1-55037-801-6); paper $7.95 (978-1-55037-800-9). This is the true story of Sofia, a courageous Mozambican girl who lost both legs — and her sister — when a landmine exploded. (Rev: BL 12/15/03*; SLJ 5/04)

2529 Martin, Nora. *Perfect Snow* (8–12). 2002, Bloomsbury $16.95 (978-1-58234-788-2). Ben feels strong and confident when he participates in the violent intolerance of the local white supremacists until he meets Eden, a new — and Jewish — girl at school, in this novel set in a small Montana community. (Rev: BL 8/02; SLJ 9/02)

2530 Mosher, Richard. *Zazoo* (6–9). 2001, Clarion $16.00 (978-0-618-13534-9). Zazoo, a French girl adopted from Vietnam, comes to understand the complexities of her adoptive Grand-Pierre's past in this absorbing, multilayered novel. (Rev: BL 12/15/01; HBG 3/02; SLJ 11/01*; VOYA 10/01)

2531 Mulligan, Andy. *Trash* (6–9). 2010, Random House $16.99 (978-0-385-75214-5); LB $19.99 (978-0-385-75215-2). Third World garbage scavengers Rat, Raphael, and Gardo discover a mysterious bag and are drawn into a mystery that involves danger and exposes political corruption and exploitation of the poor. YALSA Top Ten Best Fiction for Young Adults 2011. ℮ Lexile 850L (Rev: BL 9/15/10; HB 11–12/10; LMC 5–6/11; SLJ 10/1/10*)

2532 Nelson, Blake. *They Came from Below* (7–12). 2007, Tor $17.95 (978-0-7653-1423-9). Steve and Dave initially seem to be two cute boys, but Emily and Reese come to realize that they are actually creatures from another world intent on persuading humans to save the oceans from pollution. (Rev: BCCB 9/07; SLJ 8/07)

2533 Neville, Emily C. *The China Year* (5–8). 1991, HarperCollins $15.95 (978-0-06-024383-8). Henri, 14, has left his New York City home, school, and friends to go to Peking University for a year with his father. (Rev: BL 5/1/91; SLJ 5/91)

2534 Newman, Leslea. *October Mourning: A Song for Matthew Shepard* (8–12). 2012, Candlewick $15.99 (978-0-7636-5807-6). In a novel consisting of 68 poems, Newman tells from multiple perspectives the story of the savage beating and subsequent death of gay 21-year-old Matthew Shepard in 1998. Stonewall Honor 2013. ∩ (Rev: BL 9/15/12*; HB 9–10/12; LMC 3–4/13*; SLJ 11/12)

2535 Nye, Naomi Shihab. *Going Going* (7–10). 2005, Greenwillow LB $16.89 (978-0-06-029366-6). Angered by the exodus of small businesses from her hometown, 16-year-old Florrie launches a grassroots campaign against the giant chain stores that she believes are responsible. (Rev: BCCB 7–8/05; BL 4/1/05; HB 7–8/05; SLJ 5/05; VOYA 10/05)

2536 Paulsen, Gary. *Sentries* (8–12). 1986, Penguin paper $3.95 (978-0-317-62279-9). The stories of four different young people are left unresolved when they are all wiped out by a superbomb. (Rev: BL 5/1/86; SLJ 8/86; VOYA 8/86)

2537 Perera, Anna. *Guantanamo Boy* (7–12). 2011, Albert Whitman $17.99 (978-080753077-1). Based on a true story, this novel is about 15-year-old Khalid's experiences when he — a normal British Muslim teen — is captured during a visit to relatives in Pakistan and turned over to the U.S. authorities as a possible terrorist. ℮ Lexile 900L (Rev: BL 9/1/11*; LMC 11–12/11*)

2538 Pitcher, Annabel. *My Sister Lives on the Mantelpiece* (7–10). 2012, Little, Brown $17.99 (978-

031617690-3). Ten-year-old Jamie's family has fallen apart in the aftermath of his sister's death in a terrorist bombing, and his only friend seems to be a Muslim friend named Sunya — something he must keep secret from his father. ALA Notable Books 2013. 🎧 ℮ (Rev: BL 9/15/12*; LMC 8–9/12; SLJ 8/1/12*)

2539 Prose, Francine. *After* (8–10). 2003, HarperCollins LB $17.89 (978-0-06-008082-2). A school district hires an over-the-top crisis counselor to impose order in the name of safety after a massacre at a nearby high school. (Rev: HB 5–6/03; HBG 10/03; SLJ 5/03; VOYA 6/03)

2540 Resau, Laura. *Star in the Forest* (4–8). 2010, Delacorte $14.99 (978-0-385-73792-0). After her father is deported to Mexico as an illegal immigrant, 11-year-old Zitlally turns to her trailer-park neighbor Crystal and the two girls care for an abandoned dog that Zitlally believes holds the key to her father's return. ℮ Lexile 780L (Rev: BL 2/1/10*; HB 3–4/11; LMC 5–6/10; SLJ 2/10)

2541 Rochman, Hazel, ed. *Somehow Tenderness Survives: Stories of Southern Africa* (8–12). 1988, HarperCollins $12.95 (978-0-06-025022-5); paper $5.99 (978-0-06-447063-6). Ten stories by such writers as Nadine Gordimer about growing up in South Africa. (Rev: BL 8/88; SLJ 12/88; VOYA 12/88)

2542 Rosen, Roger, and Patra McSharry, eds. *Border Crossings: Emigration and Exile* (8–12). Series: Icarus World Issues. 1992, Rosen LB $21.95 (978-0-8239-1364-0); paper $8.95 (978-0-8239-1365-7). Twelve fiction and nonfiction selections that illustrate the lives of those affected by geopolitical change. (Rev: BL 11/1/92)

2543 Ruby, Lois. *Skin Deep* (8–12). 1994, Scholastic paper $14.95 (978-0-590-47699-7). Dan, the frustrated new kid in town, falls in love with popular senior Laurel, but he destroys their relationship when he joins a neo-Nazi skinhead group. (Rev: BL 11/15/94*; SLJ 3/95; VOYA 12/94)

2544 Senzai, N. H. *Shooting Kabul* (4–7). 2010, Simon & Schuster $16.99 (978-1-4424-0194-5). Fadi's little sister Mariam is lost when the family flees Afghanistan in July 2001, and they continue to search for her even as they deal with a new life in the United States and the backlash after September 11. ℮ Lexile 800L (Rev: BL 6/10; LMC 10/10; SLJ 6/10; VOYA 8/10)

2545 Sitomer, Alan Lawrence. *Homeboyz* (7–10). 2007, Hyperion $16.99 (978-1-4231-0030-0). When his little sister Tina is gunned down by gang members, 17-year-old Teddy quickly seeks revenge and ends up arrested for attempted homicide in this novel that looks at the causes of inner-city violence; the third volume in the trilogy that started with *The Hoopster* (2005) and *Hip-Hop High School* (2006). (Rev: BL 7/07; LMC 10/07; SLJ 8/07)

2546 Sleator, William. *Test* (7–10). 2008, Abrams $16.95 (978-0-8109-9356-3). In a near-future United States, Ann discovers that a test that high school students must pass is part of a larger, corrupt government plan. (Rev: BL 5/1/08; SLJ 7/08)

2547 Stanley, Diane. *Saving Sky* (5–8). 2010, HarperCollins $15.99 (978-0-06-123905-2). Living on a New Mexico ranch, 7th-grader Sky is isolated from the terrorism affecting the nation until her friend Kareem finds himself under suspicion. (Rev: BL 6/10*; SLJ 9/1/10)

2548 Strasser, Todd. *If I Grow Up* (7–10). 2009, Simon & Schuster $16.99 (978-141692523-1). This story follows DeShawn's life in the projects from the ages of 12 to 28, and his efforts to resist the lure of gangs. ℮ Lexile 650L (Rev: BL 1/1–15/09; LMC 8–9/09; SLJ 2/1/09; VOYA 12/08)

2549 Stratton, Allan. *Borderline* (8–11). 2010, HarperTeen $16.99 (978-0-06-145111-9); LB $17.89 (978-0-06-145112-6). In this culturally charged thriller, young Muslim Sami copes with faith-based bullying at school and his father's increasingly cold behavior, until his family is groundlessly accused of terrorism by the FBI. ℮ Lexile HL560L (Rev: BL 1/1–15/10; SLJ 3/10)

2550 Temple, Frances. *Grab Hands and Run* (6–12). 1993, Orchard LB $16.99 (978-0-531-08630-8). Jacinto opposes the oppressive government of El Salvador. When he disappears, his wife, Paloma, and their son, 12-year-old Felipe, try to escape to freedom in Canada. (Rev: BL 5/1/93*; SLJ 4/93*)

2551 Temple, Frances. *Tonight, by Sea* (6–10). 1995, Orchard LB $16.99 (978-0-531-08749-7). A docunovel about Haitian boat people who struggle for social justice and attempt harrowing escapes to freedom. (Rev: BL 3/15/95; SLJ 4/95)

2552 Walliams, David. *Mr. Stink* (4–7). Illus. by Quentin Blake. 2010, Penguin $15.99 (978-159514332-7). Twelve-year-old Chloe befriends a smelly tramp despite her mother's crusade to clean up the streets in this funny British book. 🎧 ℮ Lexile 730L (Rev: BL 11/15/10*; LMC 1–2/11; SLJ 1/1/11)

2553 Williams, Dar. *Lights, Camera, Amalee* (5–7). 2006, Scholastic $16.99 (978-0-439-80352-6). A modest inheritance from a grandmother she barely knew gives 12-year-old Amalee the funds she needs to make a documentary about endangered species. (Rev: SLJ 9/06)

2554 Woods, Brenda. *Emako Blue* (7–10). 2004, Penguin $15.99 (978-0-399-24006-5). After Emako, a talented singer, is mistakenly killed in a drive-by shooting in Los Angeles, her surviving friends — Eddie, Jamal, and Monteroy — share their thoughts about what she meant to them. (Rev: BL 7/04; SLJ 7/04)

2555 Zenatti, Valérie. *A Bottle in the Gaza Sea* (7–12). Trans. by Adriana Hunter. 2008, Bloomsbury $16.95 (978-1-59990-200-5). A Jewish girl in Israel puts a message in a bottle that is thrown into the sea and makes its way to Naïm, a Palestinian in Gaza; Tal and Naïm correspond and develop a relationship despite the wide gulf between their peoples. Sidney Taylor Book Award 2009. (Rev: BL 4/1/08; SLJ 5/08)

Fantasy

2556 Abbott, Ellen Jensen. *Watersmeet* (7–10). 2009, Marshall Cavendish $16.99 (978-076145536-3). Abisina, 14, learns to love those who are different from her when she travels to Watersmeet, a more diverse environment than her home of Vranille. (Rev: BLO 3/11/09; LMC 8–9/09; SLJ 8/09; VOYA 8/09)

2557 Abbott, Tony. *Kringle* (5–8). 2005, Scholastic $14.99 (978-0-439-74942-8). In early Britain a 12-year-old orphan named Kringle battles dark forces and discovers his true destiny. (Rev: BCCB 12/05; BL 10/15/05; HBG 4/06; SLJ 10/05; VOYA 2/06)

2558 Abouzeid, Chris. *Anatopsis* (6–8). 2006, Dutton $16.99 (978-0-525-47583-5). Princess Anatopsis, an immortal with magical powers, questions her mother's plans for her future and considers the plight of the mere mortals in her land. (Rev: BCCB 4/06; SLJ 3/06; VOYA 4/06)

2559 Adams, Richard. *Tales from Watership Down* (7–12). 1996, Avon paper $7.99 (978-0-380-72934-0). Nineteen tales keep readers abreast of developments on Watership Down and provide information on the exploits of El-ahrairah, the rabbit folk hero. (Rev: BL 9/1/96; SLJ 1/97)

2560 Adams, Richard. *Watership Down* (7–12). 1996, Scribner $30.00 (978-0-684-83605-8); paper $16 (978-0-7432-7770-9). In this fantasy first published in 1974, a small group of male rabbits sets out to find a new home.

2561 Adler, C. S. *Good-bye Pink Pig* (5–7). 1986, Avon paper $2.75 (978-0-380-70175-9). Shy Amanda takes comfort in the make-believe world of her miniature pink pig — away from the elegant world of her mother and easygoing life of her brother — until trouble enters her real and imaginary worlds and she learns to assert herself. (Rev: BCCB 2/86; BL 12/15/85)

2562 Adler, C. S. *Help, Pink Pig!* (5–7). 1991, Avon paper $2.95 (978-0-380-71156-7). Unsure of herself with her mother, Amanda retreats into the world of her miniature pink pig. (Rev: BL 5/1/90; SLJ 5/90)

2563 Adlington, L. J. *Cherry Heaven* (8–11). 2008, Greenwillow $16.99 (978-0-06-143180-7). In a strange world where cities and towns war against each other and hide disturbing secrets, three girls tell about their lives — one as a slave, two sisters as new citizens of the town of Meander. A companion to *The Diary of Pelly*

D. (Rev: BCCB 6/08; BL 12/15/07; HB 3–4/08; LMC 10/08; SLJ 3/08)

2564 Aguirre, Ann, and Jaclyn Dolamore, et al. *Corsets and Clockwork: 13 Steampunk Romances* (8–11). Ed. by Trisha Telep. 2011, Running Press paper $9.95 (978-0-7624-4-092-4). With contributions by such authors as Tessa Gratton, Frewin Jones, and Caitlin Kittredge, this is a strong collection of steampunk romances. e (Rev: BL 5/1/11; SLJ 6/11; VOYA 6/11)

2565 Alcock, Vivien. *The Haunting of Cassie Palmer* (5–8). 1997, Houghton Mifflin paper $6.95 (978-0-395-81653-0). Cassie finds she is blessed with second sight.

2566 Alexander, Alma. *Cybermage* (7–10). Series: Worldweavers. 2009, Eos $17.99 (978-006083961-1). Thea tackles new challenges at Wandless Academy, including new powers, old friends, and mysteries; the third volume in the trilogy. e (Rev: BLO 2/2/09; SLJ 8/09)

2567 Alexander, Alma. *Gift of the Unmage* (7–10). Series: Worldweavers Trilogy. 2007, HarperTeen $16.99 (978-0-06-083955-0). Thea, the seventh child of two seventh children, unexpectedly shows no magical ability until Grandma Spider uncovers her power as a dream weaver and Thea enters Wandless Academy for remedial magic. (Rev: BCCB 6/07; BL 3/1/07; SLJ 8/07)

2568 Alexander, Alma. *Spellspam* (7–10). Series: Worldweavers. 2008, Eos $17.99 (978-0-06-083958-1). E-mails that cast spells on unsuspecting people are endangering computer users around the world; can Thea use her magic to stop them? (Rev: BL 2/8/08; SLJ 7/08)

2569 Alexander, Lloyd. *The Iron Ring* (6–9). 1997, Puffin paper $7.99 (978-0-14-130348-2). When he loses in a dice game, Tamar must fulfill a promise to journey to the kingdom of King Jaya in this fantasy based on Indian mythology. (Rev: BL 5/15/97; SLJ 5/97*; VOYA 10/97)

2570 Alexander, Lloyd. *The Rope Trick* (4–7). 2002, Dutton $16.99 (978-0-525-47020-5). A young magician sets out on a challenging journey to master the difficult rope trick. (Rev: BCCB 1/03; BL 10/15/02; HB 11–12/02; HBG 3/03; SLJ 9/02; VOYA 12/02)

2571 Alexander, R. C. *Unfamiliar Magic* (5–8). 2010, Random House $17.99 (978-0-375-85854-3). Desi, a young witch whose mother has left on a mysterious quest, must fend for herself with only a cat in human form for companionship. Lexile 650L (Rev: BL 4/15/10; LMC 8–9/10; SLJ 4/10)

2572 Allen, Will. *Swords for Hire: Two of the Most Unlikely Heroes You'll Ever Meet* (5–8). Illus. by David Michael Beck. 2003, CenterPunch paper $6.95 (978-0-9724882-0-4). A spoof of a fantasy in which inexperienced warrior 16-year-old Sam Hatcher and his eccentric mentor Rigby Skeet set off to rescue King Olive, who has been unseated by his evil brother. (Rev: BCCB 6/03; SLJ 8/03)

2573 Almond, David. *Clay* (6–9). 2006, Delacorte $15.95 (978-0-385-73171-3). Themes of religion, art and the nature of evil are predominant in this tale of two English boys who create a modern-day Frankenstein-like monster. (Rev: BCCB 9/06; BL 6/1–15/06; HB 7–8/06; LMC 8–9/06; SLJ 8/06)

2574 Almond, David. *Skellig* (5–8). 1999, Delacorte $16.95 (978-0-385-32653-7). Michael discovers a ragged man in his garage existing on dead flies in this novel that is part fantasy, part mystery, and part family story. (Rev: BL 2/1/99*; HB 5–6/99; HBG 10/99; SLJ 2/99)

2575 Alter, Stephen. *Ghost Letters* (5–8). 2008, Bloomsbury $16.95 (978-1-58234-739-4). Gil tosses a message in a bottle into the sea off the Massachusetts coast and receives a reply from a boy living 100 years in the past; fantasy and the supernatural combine for a chilling and thrilling story. (Rev: BL 1/1–15/08; SLJ 5/08)

2576 Alton, Steve. *The Firehills* (6–9). 2005, Carolrhoda $15.95 (978-1-57505-798-9). Sam, Charley, and Amergin — three teens with magical powers — do battle against a group of evil fairies known as the Sidhe. (Rev: BL 10/1/05; SLJ 1/06; VOYA 10/05)

2577 Alton, Steve. *The Malifex* (5–8). 2002, Carolrhoda LB $14.95 (978-0-8225-0959-2). Sam's vacation in contemporary England is complicated by a Wiccan's daughter, the release of the ghost of Merlin's apprentice, and a battle between good and evil. (Rev: BL 9/1/02; HBG 10/03; SLJ 11/02)

2578 Amoss, Berthe. *Lost Magic* (5–7). 1993, Hyperion $14.95 (978-1-56282-573-7). Fantasy and history mingle in this story set in the Middle Ages about a young girl who knows how to use both healing herbs and magic. (Rev: BL 11/1/93)

2579 Andersen, Jodi. *May Bird and the Ever After* (4–7). Illus. by Leonid Gore. 2005, Simon & Schuster $15.95 (978-0-689-86923-5). After falling into a lake near her home, 10-year-old May Bird finds herself in Ever After, a fantasy underworld inhabited by the souls of the dead. (Rev: BCCB 12/05; BL 10/15/05; HBG 4/06; SLJ 12/05; VOYA 12/05)

2580 Anderson, Jodi Lynn. *May Bird, Warrior Princess* (4–7). Series: May Bird. 2007, Atheneum $16.99 (978-0-689-86925-9). Three years after returning from the land of the dead, May Bird and Somber Kitty return to Ever After after falling from a rooftop in the final installment in this inventive fantasy series. (Rev: BL 11/1/07; SLJ 10/07)

2581 Anderson, Jodi Lynn. *Tiger Lily* (8–11). 2012, HarperTeen $17.99 (978-0-06-200325-6). In Neverland Tiger Lily, 15, must choose between her tribe's wishes and her burgeoning crush on Peter Pan. ⌂ ℮ Lexile 850L (Rev: BL 4/15/12; SLJ 7/12*; VOYA 2/12)

2582 Anderson, John David. *Standard Hero Behavior* (6–9). 2007, Clarion $16.00 (978-0-618-75920-0).

There's a shortage of heroes in Highsmith, and someone needs to fight the giants and ogres, so Mason sets out to find a hero to save the day. (Rev: BL 10/15/07; SLJ 1/08)

2583 Anderson, M. T. *The Chamber in the Sky* (5–8). Series: Norumbegan Quartet. 2012, Scholastic $17.99 (978054533493-8). Brian and Gregory make a last-ditch effort to save the Norumbegans from their enemies by finding a lost chamber in this final installment in the series. ℮ Lexile 680L (Rev: BLO 6/12)

2584 Anderson, M. T. *The Empire of Gut and Bone* (5–8). Series: Norumbegan Quartet. 2011, Scholastic $17.99 (978-0-545-13884-0). In the land of New Norumbega, Brian and Gregory plead with the lazy, snooty inhabitants — who live inside an alien body — to resist the Thusser invasion of Vermont; the third volume in the series. (Rev: BL 5/1/11; SLJ 7/11)

2585 Anderson, M. T. *The Suburb Beyond the Stars* (5–8). 2010, Scholastic $17.99 (978-0-545-13882-6). Brian and Gregory discover that Prudence is missing, a strange suburb has appeared near her Vermont home, time is not working properly, and the Thussers threaten destruction; a sequel to *The Game of Sunken Places* (2004). Lexile 620L (Rev: BL 6/10; LMC 11–12/10; SLJ 7/10)

2586 Anderson, R. J. *Faery Rebels: Spell Hunter* (7–10). 2009, HarperCollins $16.99 (978-006155474-2). The fairy world of Oakenwyld is dying and a hunter named Knife sets out to save the Oakenfolk, involving herself with humans in the process. (Rev: BL 7/09; SLJ 8/09; VOYA 8/09)

2587 Appelbaum, Susannah. *The Hollow Bettle* (4–7). 2009, Knopf $16.99 (978-0-375-85173-5). Eleven-year-old Ivy sets out to find her missing uncle, a healer, in this first installment in a fantasy involving magic, herbs, and poisons. (Rev: BL 6/1–15/09; 12/09; LMC 10/09)

2588 Appelbaum, Susannah. *The Tasters Guild* (4–7). Illus. by Jennifer Taylor. Series: Poisons of Caux. 2010, Knopf $16.99 (978-0-375-85174-2); LB $19.99 (978-0-375-95174-9). In this exciting second installment, Poison Ivy and her friends battle new dangers as they work to save King Verdigris. (Rev: BL 11/15/10; SLJ 8/10)

2589 Arbuthnott, Gill. *The Keepers' Tattoo* (5–8). 2010, Scholastic $17.99 (978-0-545-17166-3). In a land called Archipelago, 15-year-old Nyssa and her twin brother bear tattoos that hold the secret to the ancient cult of the Keepers; but her brother is being held by the cruel Alaric, and Nyssa must rescue him. ℮ Lexile 790L (Rev: BLO 5/15/10; LMC 10/10; SLJ 7/10)

2590 Archer, E. *Geek Fantasy Novel* (5–8). 2011, Scholastic $17.99 (978-0-545-16040-7). Geeky Ralph, 14, visits his British cousins for the summer and discovers there exactly why his parents have always forbidden him to make wishes; a quirky, humorous fantasy. e Lexile 940L (Rev: BL 4/1/11; LMC 8–9/11; SLJ 11/1/11; VOYA 4/11)

2591 Arkin, Alan. *The Lemming Condition* (4–7). Illus. by Joan Sandin. 1989, HarperCollins paper $9.95 (978-0-06-250048-9). Bubber opposes the mass suicide of his companions in this interesting fable.

2592 Armstrong, Alan. *Whittington* (5–8). Illus. by S. D. Schindler. 2005, Random House LB $16.99 (978-0-375-92864-2). Happy to have found a place to live, Whittington the cat regales the other barnyard animals with tales of his famous forebears. (Rev: BL 5/15/05; SLJ 8/05*)

2593 Armstrong, Kelley. *The Awakening* (7–10). Series: Darkest Powers. 2009, HarperCollins $17.99 (978-006166276-8); LB $18.89 (978-006166280-5). This sequel to *The Summoning* (2008) finds Chloe on the run and enlisting the help of other teens who have supernatural powers. ⌒ e Lexile HL630L (Rev: BL 4/1/09; SLJ 9/09; VOYA 8/09)

2594 Armstrong, Kelley. *The Calling* (7–11). Series: Darkness Rising. 2012, HarperCollins $17.99 (978-006179705-7). Native American Maya and her friends, now aware of their supernatural powers, are being pursued by evil adults in this action-packed second volume in the series. ⌒ e Lexile HL570L (Rev: BL 2/1/12; SLJ 5/1/12; VOYA 12/1/12)

2595 Ashby, Amanda. *Fairy Bad Day* (7–10). 2011, Penguin paper $7.99 (978-0-14-241-259-6). Emma Jones, a sophomore at Burtonwood Academy, is mortified to be assigned to the task of fairy slaying instead of dragon slaying, especially when the new dragon killer-in-training turns out to be a very attractive young man. e Lexile 920L (Rev: BL 8/11; SLJ 8/11; VOYA 6/11)

2596 Ashby, Amanda. *Zombie Queen of Newbury High* (8–12). 2009, Penguin paper $7.99 (978-014241256-5). Mia accidentally turns her fellow high school students into flesh-eating zombies and escapes only with the help of handsome Chase, who works for the Department of Paranormal Containment. e Lexile HL810L (Rev: BL 4/1/09; SLJ 6/1/09; VOYA 2/09)

2597 Atwater-Rhodes, Amelia. *Hawksong* (7–10). 2003, Delacorte $9.95 (978-0-385-73071-6). A gripping fantasy about two young leaders who seek to end the long war between their peoples — avian shapeshifters and serpent shapeshifters — and are prepared to consider marriage for the sake of peace. (Rev: HBG 4/04; SLJ 8/03*; VOYA 6/03)

2598 Atwater-Rhodes, Amelia. *Midnight Predator* (7–9). 2002, Delacorte $9.95 (978-0-385-32794-7). In a world where humans are slaves to vampires, teen vampire hunter Turquoise and her colleague pose as slaves in order to defeat an evil tyrant. (Rev: BL 8/02; HBG 10/02; SLJ 5/02; VOYA 6/02)

2599 Augarde, Steve. *Celandine* (7–10). 2006, Random House $16.95 (978-0-385-75048-6). Celandine escapes the cruel boarding school she attends during World War I and returns to the village of the little people, the Various, that live near her family's farm where she discovers her special powers. (Rev: BL 8/06; SLJ 11/06)

2600 Augarde, Steve. *The Various* (4–8). 2004, Random House LB $17.99 (978-0-385-75037-0). Midge, a 12-year-old girl on vacation in the countryside, discovers a tribe of little people known as the Various, who are not as helpless as they seem. (Rev: BL 12/15/03; SLJ 3/04)

2601 Augarde, Steve. *Winter Wood* (7–10). Series: The Touchstone Trilogy. 2009, Random House $17.99 (978-038575074-5); LB $20.99 (978-038575075-2). Midge moves to Mill Farm and finally meets her great-aunt Celandine, who holds the key to the fate of the Various, a race of tiny winged people; the final volume in the trilogy, following *The Various* (2004) and *Celandine* (2006). Lexile 750L (Rev: BL 4/1/09; SLJ 6/1/09; VOYA 8/09)

2602 Augarde, Steve. *X-Isle* (7–10). 2010, Random House $17.99 (978-038575193-3). After a cataclysmic flood, young Baz and Ray find themselves on an island that purportedly offers survival and a future but in fact turns out to be an evil society run by the fanatical Preacher John; it's up to Baz and Ray to ensure their future. e (Rev: BL 6/10; LMC 10/10; SLJ 8/10)

2603 Auxier, Jonathan. *Peter Nimble and His Fantastic Eyes* (6–9). Illus. by author. 2011, Abrams $16.95 (978-1-4197-0025-5). Peter Nimble, a blind 10-year-old orphan — and skilled thief, acquires a mysterious box containing three pairs of eyes that launch him on a series of wondrous adventures. ⌒ e Lexile 790L (Rev: BLO 10/1/11; LMC 1–2/12; SLJ 10/1/11)

2604 Avi. *Bright Shadow* (5–8). 1994, Simon & Schuster paper $4.99 (978-0-689-71783-3). At the death of the great wizard, Morenna finds she possesses the last five wishes in the world. (Rev: SLJ 12/85)

2605 Avi. *The Man Who Was Poe* (7–10). 1991, Avon paper $6.99 (978-0-380-71192-5). When Edmund goes out to search for his missing mother and sister, he encounters Edgar Allan Poe in disguise as detective Auguste Dupin. (Rev: BL 10/1/89; SLJ 9/89; VOYA 2/90)

2606 Avi. *Strange Happenings: Five Tales of Transformation* (4–7). 2006, Harcourt $15.00 (978-0-15-205790-9). Shape-shifting and invisibility are among the transformations in this collection of five fantasy tales. (Rev: BL 3/15/06; SLJ 5/06)

2607 Babbitt, Natalie. *The Search for Delicious* (4–7). Illus. by author. 1969, Farrar $17.00 (978-0-374-36534-9). The innocent task of polling the kingdom's subjects for personal food preferences provokes civil war in a zestful spoof of taste and society.

147

2608 Bach, Shelby. *Of Giants and Ice* (4–7). 2012, Simon & Schuster $15.99 (978-1-4424-3146-1). At the Ever After School 11-year-old Rory, daughter of Hollywood parents, discovers that magic is the celebrity as she helps create a new fairy tale. ℮ Lexile 700L (Rev: BLO 8/12; LMC 1–2/13; SLJ 9/12)

2609 Bachmann, Stefan. *The Peculiar* (4–7). 2012, HarperCollins $16.99 (978-0-06-219518-0). After fairies lose the war with humans, half-fairy half-human changeling children Bartholomew and Hettie find themselves embroiled in mystery and intrigue in this steampunk fantasy. ⌒ ℮ Lexile 760L (Rev: BL 9/15/12; HB 11–12/12; LMC 3–4/13; SLJ 10/12)

2610 Baggott, Julianna. *The Prince of Fenway Park* (5–8). 2009, HarperCollins $16.99 (978-0-06-087242-7). Twelve-year-old Oscar Egg holds the power to lift the curse affecting the Boston Red Sox. (Rev: BL 5/15/09; SLJ 5/09)

2611 Baker, E. D. *The Dragon Princess* (5–8). Series: Tales of the Frog Princess. 2008, Bloomsbury $16.99 (978-159990194-7). In hopes of controlling an unfortunate flaw — she turns into a dragon whenever she's upset — 15-year-old princess Millie appeals to the Blue Witch for help in this lighthearted tale. ⌒ ℮ Lexile 820L (Rev: BLO 11/15/08; VOYA 12/08)

2612 Baker, E. D. *Dragon's Breath* (5–7). 2003, Bloomsbury $15.95 (978-1-58234-858-2). Esmeralda and Eadric help Aunt Grassina find ingredients needed to break the spell that turned Grassina's true love, Haywood, into an otter in this humorous sequel to *The Frog Princess* (2002). (Rev: BL 4/15/04; SLJ 12/03; VOYA 4/04)

2613 Baker, E. D. *Fairy Lies* (5–8). Series: Wings: A Fairy Tale. 2012, Bloomsbury $16.99 (978-159990550-1). Half-fairy Tamisin's half-goblin boyfriend Jak endeavors to rescue her when she's kidnapped by King Oberon in this fast-paced sequel to *Wings: A Fairy Tale* (2008). (Rev: BLO 2/15/12; LMC 3–4/12; SLJ 3/12; VOYA 2/12)

2614 Baker, E. D. *The Frog Princess* (5–8). 2002, Bloomsbury $15.95 (978-1-58234-799-8). When Princess Esmeralda kisses the frog, she turns into one herself in this humorous twist on the traditional saga. (Rev: BCCB 2/03; BL 11/15/02; SLJ 1/03; VOYA 12/02)

2615 Baker, E. D. *The Salamander Spell* (4–7). 2007, Bloomsbury $16.95 (978-1-59990-018-6). In this prequel to *The Frog Princess* (2002), 13-year-old Grassina is tired of being overshadowed by her older sister Chartreuse and, accompanied by her snake friend Pippa, runs away to the swamp where she discovers her powers, meets a young magician, and saves the kingdom from werewolves. (Rev: BL 9/15/07; SLJ 12/07)

2616 Baker, E. D. *The Wide-Awake Princess* (7–10). 2010, Bloomsbury $16.99 (978-1-59990-487-0). Annie, Sleeping Beauty's little sister, is left wide awake when the rest of the castle falls into its 100-year slumber, so it's up to her to save the day. Lexile 890L (Rev: BLO 4/15/10; LMC 8–9/10; SLJ 6/10)

2617 Baker, E. D. *Wings: A Fairy Tale* (5–8). 2008, Bloomsbury $16.95 (978-1-59990-193-0). Could Tamisin really be a goblin? When she grows wings, she realizes she must be from another world. (Rev: BL 5/15/08)

2618 Balog, Cyn. *Fairy Tale* (7–10). 2009, Delacorte $16.99 (978-038573706-7); LB $19.99 (978-038590644-9). Morgan learns that her long-term boyfriend is a fairy changeling and does not belong in her world. (Rev: BL 5/15/09; LMC 10/09; SLJ 12/09)

2619 Balog, Cyn. *Sleepless* (7–10). 2010, Delacorte $16.99 (978-0-385-73848-4). Romance and fantasy blend in this novel about a Sandman called Eron whose contract is up and who must return to human form; he is reluctant to hand over care of his beloved Julia's nightly sleep to Griffin, her recently deceased boyfriend. ℮ (Rev: LMC 10/10; SLJ 8/10)

2620 Banks, Kate. *The Magician's Apprentice* (5–8). Illus. by Peter Sís. 2012, Farrar $16.99 (978-037434716-1). A complex tale in which 16-year-old Baz becomes apprentice to a magician and makes a long and mystical trip through the desert learning about various truths. ⌒ ℮ Lexile 740L (Rev: BL 8/12; HB 9–10/12; SLJ 8/1/12)

2621 Banks, Lynne Reid. *Angela and Diabola* (5–8). 1997, Avon $15.95 (978-0-380-97562-4). A wicked romp that chronicles the lives of twins, the angelic Angela and the truly horrible and destructive Diabola. (Rev: SLJ 7/97)

2622 Banks, Lynne Reid. *The Key to the Indian* (4–8). Series: Indian in the Cupboard. 1998, Avon $16.00 (978-0-380-97717-8). In the fifth book of the Indian in the Cupboard series, Omri and Dad return to the time of Little Bear to help the Iroquois deal with European meddlers. (Rev: BL 11/15/98; HBG 3/99; SLJ 12/98)

2623 Banks, Lynne Reid. *The Mystery of the Cupboard* (4–8). Series: Indian in the Cupboard. 1993, HarperCollins paper $5.99 (978-0-380-72013-2). In this, the fourth book in the series, the young hero Omri uncovers a diary that reveals secrets about his magical cupboard. (Rev: BCCB 6/93; BL 4/1/93; HB 7–8/93; SLJ 6/93; VOYA 10/93)

2624 Banks, Lynne Reid. *The Return of the Indian* (5–7). Illus. by William Celdart. Series: Indian in the Cupboard. 1986, Doubleday $16.95 (978-0-385-23497-9); paper $5.99 (978-0-380-70284-8). Omri brings his plastic Indian figures to life and discovers that his friend Little Bear has been wounded and needs his help. (Rev: BL 9/15/86; HB 11–12/86; SLJ 11/86)

2625 Banner, Catherine. *The Eyes of a King* (7–11). Series: The Last Descendants. 2008, Random House $16.99 (978-0-375-83875-0). An intricate and many-layered fantasy in which teenaged Leo discovers that the true ruler of Malonia has been exiled to England. (Rev: BL 5/15/08; SLJ 8/08)

2626 Baratz-Logsted, Lauren. *Little Women and Me* (6–10). 2011, Bloomsbury $16.99 (978-1-59990-514-3). Present-day teen Emily March finds herself drawn into another world when she begins reading Louisa May Alcott's *Little Women*. ℮ Lexile 830L (Rev: BL 11/15/11; LMC 3–4/12; SLJ 10/1/11; VOYA 12/11)

2627 Barker, Clive. *Days of Magic, Nights of War* (7–12). Series: Abarat. 2004, HarperCollins $24.99 (978-0-06-029170-9). In the second installment in the series, Candy Quackenbush makes discoveries about herself and the islands of Abarat as she tries to stay one step ahead of the Lord of Midnight. (Rev: BL 9/1/04; SLJ 11/04)

2628 Barnes, Jennifer Lynn. *Fate* (6–9). 2009, LB $8.99 (978-038573537-7); paper $11.99 (978-038590519-0). This sequel to *Tattoo* (2007) finds Bailey about to graduate from high school and wrestling with the responsibilities that come with being half faerie and facing the loss of her best friends. ℮ (Rev: BL 3/15/09; VOYA 4/09)

2629 Barnes, Jennifer Lynn. *Nobody* (7–12). 2013, Egmont $17.99 (978-160684321-5). Claire, 15, has always kept a low profile and spent her life alone until she meets Nix, an attractive 17-year-old who has been sent to kill her but is now questioning why the Society has labeled Claire as dangerous. ⌒ ℮ Lexile HL710L (Rev: BL 1/13; LMC 5–6/13; SLJ 2/13)

2630 Barnes, Jennifer Lynn. *Tattoo* (8–11). 2007, Delacorte LB $11.99 (978-0-385-90363-9); paper $7.99 (978-0-385-73347-2). Four 15-year-old girls buy temporary tattoos and discover each of them now has a superpower that will help the quartet battle an ancient force that plans to create mayhem at their school dance. (Rev: BCCB 3/07; BL 1/1–15/07; SLJ 1/07)

2631 Barnhill, Kelly. *Iron Hearted Violet* (4–7). Illus. by Iacopo Bruno. 2012, Little, Brown $16.99 (978-0-316-05673-1). Princess Violet, a lover of good stories, and her friend Demetrius take on the legendary Nybbas in this well-crafted story. ⌒ ℮ (Rev: BL 11/1/12; HB 11–12/12; LMC 3–4/13; SLJ 12/12; VOYA 10/12)

2632 Barnhill, Kelly. *The Mostly True Story of Jack* (5–8). 2011, Little, Brown $16.99 (978-0-316-05670-0). Dumped with his aunt and uncle, Jack — who has considered himself virtually invisible up till now — soon realizes that there is something strange going on in Hazelwood, Iowa, and he is suddenly the center of attention. ⌒ ℮ Lexile 740L (Rev: BL 8/11*; LMC 10/11; SLJ 9/1/11; VOYA 8/11)

2633 Barnhouse, Rebecca. *Peaceweaver* (6–9). 2012, Random House $16.99 (978-037586766-8); LB $19.99 (978-037596766-5). In this stand-alone companion to the Norse *The Coming of the Dragon* (2010), 16-year-old Hild is sent to marry a neighboring king only to find

things are not as they seem and she must make difficult choices. ℮ Lexile 840L (Rev: BL 4/1/12; SLJ 5/1/12; VOYA 2/12)

2634 Barrett, Tracy. *Dark of the Moon* (7–10). 2011, Harcourt $16.99 (978-0-547-58132-3). The story of the minotaur is told from the perspective of his 15-year-old sister Ariadne, a lonely girl destined to be a goddess. ℮ Lexile 920L (Rev: BL 10/15/11; SLJ 8/11; VOYA 12/11)

2635 Barrett, Tracy. *King of Ithaka* (7–10). 2010, Henry Holt $16.99 (978-0-8050-8969-1). At the age of 16, Telemachos sets off from Ithaka to find his long-departed father Odysseus in this action-packed novel. ℮ Lexile 830L (Rev: BL 10/1/10; LMC 11–12/10; SLJ 11/1/10; VOYA 12/10)

2636 Barrett, Tracy. *On Etruscan Time* (5–8). 2005, Henry Holt $16.95 (978-0-8050-7569-4). Hector, 11, finds himself struggling to rescue an Etruscan boy from execution, in this time-travel fantasy set on an archaeological dig in Italy. (Rev: BL 6/1–15/05; SLJ 7/05)

2637 Barron, T. A. *The Ancient One* (6–9). 1992, Putnam $20.99 (978-0-399-21899-6). A fight to save a stand of Oregon redwoods occupies Kate, 13, in this time-travel fantasy. (Rev: BL 9/1/92; SLJ 11/92)

2638 Barron, T. A. *The Book of Magic* (6–9). Illus. by August Hall. 2011, Philomel $17.99 (978-0-399-24741-5). Barron includes maps, character sketches, timelines, a magical glossary, and other enhancements for fans of the Merlin saga in this companion volume. (Rev: BL 12/15/11; SLJ 10/1/11)

2639 Barron, T. A. *Doomraga's Revenge* (5–8). Series: Merlin's Dragon Trilogy. 2009, Philomel $16.99 (978-0-399-25212-9). The powerful dragon Basil tackles threats to Avalon while Merlin is preoccupied with personal woes; the middle volume in the trilogy. (Rev: BL 9/1/09; LMC 11–12/09; SLJ 9/09)

2640 Barron, T. A. *The Eternal Flame* (7–10). Series: Great Tree of Avalon. 2006, Philomel $19.99 (978-0-399-24213-7). This final book in the trilogy follows Tamwyn, Elli, and Scree as they make their final, dramatic efforts to fend off the evil Rhita Gawr. (Rev: BL 9/1/06; SLJ 11/06)

2641 Barron, T. A. *The Fires of Merlin* (7–10). Series: Lost Years of Merlin. 1998, Putnam $20.99 (978-0-399-23020-2). A complex sequel to *The Seven Songs of Merlin*, in which young Merlin once again faces the threat of the dragon Valdearg, who is preparing to conquer the land of Fincayra. (Rev: BL 9/1/98; HBG 3/99; SLJ 3/99; VOYA 2/99)

2642 Barron, T. A. *The Great Tree of Avalon* (6–12). Series: Great Tree of Avalon. 2004, Penguin $19.99 (978-0-399-23763-8). The fate of Avalon, which the Lady of the Lake has prophesied will be destroyed by the Dark Child, rests in the hands of two 17-year-old boys: Tamwyn and Scree. (Rev: BL 9/1/04*; SLJ 10/04)

149

2643 Barron, T. A. *The Lost Years of Merlin* (7–10). Series: Lost Years of Merlin. 1996, Putnam $19.99 (978-0-399-23018-9). The author has created a magical land populated by remarkable creatures in this first book of a trilogy about the early years of the magician Merlin. (Rev: BL 9/1/96; SLJ 9/96; VOYA 10/96)

2644 Barron, T. A. *The Merlin Effect* (6–9). 1994, Putnam $19.99 (978-0-399-22689-2). Kate, 13, accompanies her father, a King Arthur expert, to a remote lagoon where they search a sunken ship for the magical horn of Merlin. A sequel to *Heartlight* (1990) and *The Ancient One* (1992). (Rev: BL 11/1/94; SLJ 11/94; VOYA 12/94)

2645 Barron, T. A. *Merlin's Dragon* (7–10). Series: Merlin's Dragon Trilogy. 2008, Philomel $19.99 (978-039924750-7). Basil, a lizard-like creature with magical powers, sets off to track down Merlin and warn him of impending doom and, at the same time, find others like himself in this latest installment in Barron's Merlin saga. The second volume is *Doomraga's Revenge* (2009). Lexile 820L (Rev: BL 9/1/08; SLJ 9/1/08; VOYA 8/08)

2646 Barron, T. A. *The Mirror of Merlin* (7–10). Series: Lost Years of Merlin. 1999, Putnam $20.99 (978-0-399-23455-2). Young Merlin faces a deadly disease and confronts his future self as he continues his dangerous search for his sword. (Rev: BL 10/1/99; HBG 4/00; SLJ 10/99; VOYA 2/00)

2647 Barron, T. A. *The Seven Songs of Merlin* (7–10). Series: Lost Years of Merlin. 1997, Putnam $19.99 (978-0-399-23019-6). In this sequel to *The Lost Years of Merlin,* Emrys, who will become Merlin, must travel to the Otherworld to save his mother who has been poisoned. (Rev: BL 9/1/97; HBG 3/98; SLJ 9/97)

2648 Barron, T. A. *Shadows on the Stars* (7–10). Series: Great Tree of Avalon. 2005, Philomel $19.99 (978-0-399-23764-5). In the year 1002 Tamwyn, Elli, and Scree set off on separate quests to conquer the evil Rhita Gawr and save Avalon in this sequel to *Child of the Dark Prophecy* (2004). (Rev: BL 9/15/05; SLJ 12/05)

2649 Barron, T. A. *Tree Girl* (4–8). 2001, Putnam $14.99 (978-0-399-23457-6). Rowanna, 9, discovers she is descended from tree spirits after she is lured into the woods by a shape-shifting bear cub in this book for middle-graders. (Rev: BCCB 10/01; BL 11/1/01; HBG 3/02; SLJ 10/01; VOYA 10/01)

2650 Barron, T. A. *The Wings of Merlin* (7–10). Series: Lost Years of Merlin. 2000, Philomel $21.99 (978-0-399-23456-9). In this, the concluding volume of the saga, Merlin faces his most difficult decision. (Rev: BL 10/1/00; HBG 3/01; SLJ 11/00; VOYA 12/00)

2651 Barrowman, John, and Carole E. Barrowman. *Hollow Earth* (5–8). 2012, Aladdin $16.99 (978-144245852-9). Twelve-year-old twins Matt and Emily have the power to bring art to life, and this puts them in peril from ancient forces. ℮ Lexile 880L (Rev: BL 12/1/12; LMC 5–6/13; SLJ 1/13)

2652 Barry, Dave, and Ridley Pearson. *Peter and the Secret of Rundoon* (4–7). Illus. by Greg Call. Series: Starcatchers. 2007, Hyperion $18.99 (978-0-7868-3788-5). In this action-packed conclusion to the Starcatchers trilogy, Peter (Pan, that is) saves the world long before ever meeting Wendy and her siblings. (Rev: BL 11/15/07; SLJ 10/07)

2653 Barry, Dave, and Ridley Pearson. *Peter and the Shadow Thieves* (5–8). Illus. by Greg Call. 2006, Hyperion $18.99 (978-0-7868-3787-8). In this sequel to *Peter and the Starcatchers* (2005), the forever-young Peter and Tinker Bell race to foil the evil plans of Lord Ombra. (Rev: BL 6/1–15/06; SLJ 8/06; VOYA 8/06)

2654 Basye, Dale E. *Blimpo: The Third Circle of Heck* (4–7). Illus. by Bob Dob. Series: Heck. 2010, Random House $16.99 (978-037585676-1); LB $19.99 (978-037595676-8). Milton Fauster, 11, must help his sister Marlo, who is training as Satan's secretary, and his friend Virgil, who is consigned to the circle for overweight children, in this third installment in the humorous series. In *Fibble: The Fourth Circle of Heck,* set in the city of liars, Marlo wakes up in her younger brother Milton's body. (Rev: BLO 2/15/10)

2655 Basye, Dale E. *Rapacia: The Second Circle of Heck* (4–7). Illus. by Bob Dob. Series: Heck. 2009, Random House $16.99 (978-0-375-84077-7); LB $19.99 (978-0-375-94077-4). Marlo joins other young shoplifters in the second circle of Heck, where he is taunted by cool stuff he can never have. ᴖ (Rev: BL 5/15/11; SLJ 8/09)

2656 Basye, Dale E. *Snivel: The Fifth Circle of Heck* (4–7). Illus. by Bob Dob. Series: Heck. 2012, Random House $16.99 (978-037586834-4); LB $19.99 (978-037596834-1). Deceased Milton and Marlo Fauster save the world from Nikola Tesla's nefarious plot to come back to life. ℮ (Rev: BL 3/15/12; SLJ 3/12; VOYA 10/12)

2657 Bateman, Colin. *Running with the Reservoir Pups* (4–7). 2005, Delacorte LB $17.99 (978-0-440-42048-4). Eddie becomes involved with a gang of tough Belfast kids and ends up rescuing kidnapped babies from a horrible fate in this action-packed fantasy, the first installment in a trilogy. (Rev: BL 3/1/05; SLJ 1/05)

2658 Batson, Wayne Thomas. *The Rise of the Wyrm Lord* (6–8). Series: The Door Within. 2006, Tommy Nelson $16.99 (978-1-4003-0737-1). This is the second volume in a trilogy that weaves Christian undertones into the adventures of friends Aidan and Antoinette, who are called to unite a world called The Realm after the death of King Eliam, to rescue Aidan's friend Robby before he is pulled into the dark side, and to defeat the plans of the evil Paragor the Betrayer and his secret weapon, the Wyrm Lord. (Rev: SLJ 8/06)

2659 Bauer, A. C. E. *Come Fall* (4–7). 2010, Random House $15.99 (978-0-375-85825-3). Misfits Salman, Lu, and Blos become friends in 7th grade and deal with bullies, dysfunctional homes, and other problems with some input from Puck, Oberon, and Titania in this fantasy inspired by *A Midsummer Night's Dream.* ℯ (Rev: BL 7/10; LMC 10/10; SLJ 9/1/10)

2660 Bauer, Marion Dane. *Touch the Moon* (5–7). Illus. by Alix Berenzy. 1987, Houghton Mifflin $15.00 (978-0-89919-526-1). Angry when she doesn't get a real horse, Jennifer throws away her toy horse gift and learns a lesson in responsibility. (Rev: BCCB 9/87; BL 9/15/87; HB 9–10/87)

2661 Baum, L. Frank. *The Wonderful Wizard of Oz* (4–8). Illus. by W. W. Denslow. 2000, HarperCollins $24.99 (978-0-06-029323-9). A handsome facsimile of the 1900 publication on high-quality paper and featuring 24 original color plates and 130 two-color drawings. (Rev: BL 12/1/00)

2662 Baum, L. Frank. *The Wonderful Wizard of Oz: A Commemorative Pop-Up* (4–8). Illus. by Robert Sabuda. 2001, Simon & Schuster $24.95 (978-0-689-81751-9). An extraordinary pop-up version of the classic fantasy told in a condensed text. (Rev: BL 12/1/00; HB 9–10/00; HBG 3/01; SLJ 11/00)

2663 Beck, Ian. *The Secret History of Tom Trueheart* (4–7). 2007, HarperCollins $16.99 (978-0-06-115210-8). Twelve-year-old Tom Trueheart must try to track down his six older brothers when they mysteriously disappear, suspected victims of the enemy of storytelling. ⌒ (Rev: SLJ 2/07)

2664 Becker, Tom. *Darkside* (7–10). 2008, Scholastic $16.99 (978-0-545-03739-6). Darkside is a dangerous and magical underground London that Jonathan discovers is connected to his family (specifically, his mentally troubled father) in mysterious ways. (Rev: BL 2/1/08; SLJ 5/08)

2665 Bedard, Michael. *A Darker Magic* (6–8). 1987, Avon paper $2.95 (978-0-380-70611-2). An intricate fantasy about the strange effects of a magic show run by Professor Mephisto. (Rev: BL 9/1/87; SLJ 9/87)

2666 Beddor, Frank. *The Looking Glass Wars* (6–9). 2006, Dial $17.99 (978-0-8037-3153-0). When she is forced to flee from Wonderland by her evil aunt Redd, young Alyss Heart finds a home in Victorian Oxford, where she persuades Charles Dodgson to write her story and dreams of reclaiming her throne. The sequel is *Seeing Redd* (2007). ⌒ (Rev: BL 9/1/06; LMC 4/07; SLJ 10/06)

2667 Bedford, Martyn. *Flip* (7–10). 2011, Random House $16.99 (978-0-385-73990-0); LB $19.99 (978-038590808-5). Alex, 14, is shocked when he wakes up in the body of Flip, an athlete and his complete opposite, and struggles to understand this switch and to find a way back to his former self and his family. ⌒ ℯ Lexile

HL740L (Rev: BL 5/1/11; HB 5–6/11; LMC 10/11*; SLJ 6/11*; VOYA 4/11)

2668 Belden, Wilanne Schneider. *Mind-Hold* (6–9). 1987, Harcourt $14.95 (978-0-15-254280-1). After a violent earthquake, Carson and his sister, who has the gift of ESP, move into the desert hoping to find new friends. (Rev: BL 2/15/87; SLJ 3/87)

2669 Bell, Clare. *Ratha and Thistle-Chaser* (7–12). 2007, Penguin paper $8.99 (978-0-14-240944-2). Further adventures of the clan of intelligent cats and their search for new land in this continuation (first published in 1990) of *Ratha's Creature* (1983) and *Clan Ground* (1984). (Rev: BL 2/1/90; SLJ 6/90; VOYA 6/90)

2670 Bell, Hilari. *Crown of Earth* (5–8). Series: The Shield, Sword, and Crown. 2009, Simon & Schuster $16.99 (978-1-4169-0598-1). In this fast-paced standalone sequel to *Sword of Waters* (2008), Prince Edoran endeavors to save the life of the hostage Weasel by enlisting the help of his friend Arisa. Lexile 880L (Rev: BL 12/1/09; SLJ 10/09)

2671 Bell, Hilari. *Forging the Sword* (7–10). Series: Farsala Trilogy. 2006, Simon & Schuster $17.99 (978-0-689-85416-3). The final book in the Farsala trilogy finds Jiaan, Kavi, and Soraya fighting the Hrum with magic and a newly forged sword. (Rev: BL 12/15/06; SLJ 3/07)

2672 Bell, Hilari. *The Goblin Gate* (5–8). Series: The Goblin Wood. 2010, HarperTeen $16.99 (978-0-06-165102-1). Jeriah goes off in search of the spell that will open the gate to the otherworld and release his brother; the sequel to 2003's *The Goblin Wood.* ℯ Lexile 750L (Rev: HB 9–10/10; SLJ 10/1/10)

2673 Bell, Hilari. *The Last Knight: A Knight and Rogue Novel* (8–10). 2007, HarperCollins $16.99 (978-0-06-082503-4). Eighteen-year-old Sir Michael Sevenson, a throwback knight errant, and 17-year-old Fisk, his squire, have many adventures as they tangle with the less-noble-than-they-initially-thought Lady Ceciel; the narration alternates between the honest knight and the slippery squire in this blend of fantasy, adventure, and mystery, with humor and "magica" thrown in. (Rev: BL 10/1/07; HB 9–10/07; LMC 2/08; SLJ 9/07)

2674 Bell, Hilari. *The Prophecy* (6–9). 2006, Eos $15.99 (978-0-06-059943-0). Prince Perryn must find his true self while saving his father's kingdom from a dragon and a vicious traitor. (Rev: BL 6/1–15/06; SLJ 10/06)

2675 Bell, Hilari. *Shield of Stars* (5–8). Series: The Shield, the Sword and the Crown. 2007, Simon & Schuster $16.99 (978-1-4169-0594-3). Weasel, 14 and a reformed pickpocket, sets out to rescue Justice Holis, who has given him a home and a job, from the wicked ruler of Deorthas. (Rev: BL 5/15/07; SLJ 5/07)

2676 Bell, Hilari. *Traitor's Son* (7–12). Series: Raven Duet. 2012, Houghton Mifflin $16.99 (978-054719621-3). In this companion to *Trickster's Girl* (2011) set in

21st-century Alaska, Raven and Jase struggle to stop the bio-plague threatening the world's survival, requiring Jase to embrace his Native American roots. ☻ Lexile 840L (Rev: BL 2/15/12; SLJ 3/12; VOYA 2/12)

2677 Bell, Hilari. *Trickster's Girl* (7–10). 2010, Houghton Mifflin $16 (978-0-547-19620-6). Humans have caused untold damage to the ecosystem and terrorism is rife, so in the year 2098, 15-year-old Kelsa hopes to use her magic to heal these ills. (Rev: BL 12/15/10; SLJ 12/1/10)

2678 Bell, Hilari. *The Wizard Test* (5–8). 2005, HarperCollins LB $16.89 (978-0-06-059941-6). Fourteen-year-old Dayven is not thrilled when he learns he has magical abilities until he undergoes wizard training. (Rev: BL 2/1/05; SLJ 3/05)

2679 Bell, Ted. *Nick of Time* (5–8). 2008, St. Martin's $17.95 (978-0-312-38068-7). Villains from the past and present (that is, 1939) show up when plucky young Nick opens a sea chest washed up near his family's lighthouse. (Rev: BL 4/1/08; SLJ 5/08)

2680 Bellairs, John. *The Ghost in the Mirror* (5–8). 1994, Puffin paper $5.99 (978-0-14-034934-4). Fourteen-year-old Rose and white witch Mrs. Zimmerman are transported in time to 1828 on a secret mission. (Rev: SLJ 3/93)

2681 Bemis, John Claude. *The Nine Pound Hammer* (6–9). Series: Clockwork Dark. 2009, Random House $16.99 (978-037585564-1); LB $19.99 (978-037595564-8). Orphan Ray, 12, joins a traveling sideshow and discovers that its members have exceptionally strange abilities. ☊ Lexile 730L (Rev: BL 5/15/09; LMC 11–12/09; SLJ 10/09; VOYA 12/09)

2682 Bemis, John Claude. *The White City* (7–10). Series: Clockwork Dark. 2011, Random House $17.99 (978-037585568-9); LB $20.99 (978-037595568-6). Fans of the series will enjoy this steampunk finale set in Chicago's White City in 1893. ☻ Lexile 810L (Rev: BL 8/11)

2683 Bemis, John Claude. *The Wolf Tree* (7–10). Series: Clockwork Dark. 2010, Random House $16.99 (978-0-375-85566-5); LB $19.99 (978-0-375-95566-2). A Darkness is spreading over the land and Ray Cobb and the remaining Ramblers must cross into the Gloaming and try to stop the Gog's evil machine; the second book in the series. ☻ (Rev: BL 10/1/10; SLJ 12/1/10)

2684 Bennardo, Charlotte, and Natalie Zaman. *Sirenz* (8–10). 2011, Flux paper $9.95 (978-0-7387-2-319-8). Having made a deal with Hades, 17-year-old fashionistas Shar and Meg become Sirens and must lure a fashion designer into the Underworld. ☻ (Rev: BL 6/1/11; SLJ 11/1/11)

2685 Bennett, Cherie. *Love Never Dies* (7–10). Series: Teen Angels. 1996, Avon paper $3.99 (978-0-380-78248-2). In this fantasy, a teen angel is sent back to earth to help a rock star bent on self-destruction. (Rev: VOYA 6/96)

2686 Bennett, Holly. *The Bonemender* (6–9). 2005, Orca paper $7.95 (978-1-55143-336-3). When Gabrielle, a princess and healer, falls in love with Feolan, an elf, she sees little future for the romance because of the sharp differences between their basic natures. (Rev: BL 11/1/05; SLJ 12/05; VOYA 12/05)

2687 Bennett, Holly. *The Bonemender's Choice* (7–10). Series: Bonemender. 2007, Orca paper $8.95 (978-1-55143-718-7). Gabrielle and her elfen husband race to rescue young Matthieu and Madeline from pirates and from a spreading affliction called the Gray Veil in this third book in the series. (Rev: BL 11/1/07; SLJ 12/07)

2688 Bennett, Holly. *The Bonemender's Oath* (7–12). 2006, Orca paper $8.95 (978-1-55143-443-8). Gabrielle faces a new threat as she heads home from the war in this satisfying sequel to *The Bonemender* (2005). (Rev: SLJ 2/07)

2689 Bennett, Holly. *Shapeshifter* (7–10). 2010, Orca paper $12.95 (978-1-55469-158-6). Sive uses her shapeshifting ability to become a deer in the mortal world and escape from the evil Far Doirche, who seeks to exploit her magical voice; a fantasy based on an ancient Irish legend. Lexile 910L (Rev: BL 6/10; LMC 11–12/10; SLJ 10/1/10; VOYA 8/10)

2690 Bennett, Holly. *The Warrior's Daughter* (7–10). 2007, Orca paper $8.95 (978-1-55143-607-4). With its roots in Irish mythology, this tale about the courageous daughter of a famous warrior will satisfy readers in search of adventure; a pronunciation guide helps with the many Gaelic names. (Rev: LMC 8–9/07; SLJ 6/07)

2691 Benz, Derek, and Jon S. Lewis. *The Brimstone Key* (5–8). Series: Grey Griffins: The Clockwork Chronicles. 2010, Little, Brown $15.99 (978-0-316-04522-3). Max, Ernie, Natalia, and Hailey use their unusual powers to fight the clockworks — robots who are forming an army — at the Iron Bridge Academy; the first installment in a steampunk trilogy. (Rev: BLO 4/15/10; LMC 8–9/10; SLJ 8/10; VOYA 10/10)

2692 Berkeley, Jon. *The Lightning Key* (4–7). Illus. by Brandon Dorman. Series: The Wednesday Tales. 2009, HarperCollins $16.99 (978-0-06-075513-3). In this fast-moving conclusion to the trilogy Miles sets off in hot pursuit of the thieves who stole the powerful Tiger's Egg, having many adventures on the way. (Rev: SLJ 7/09; VOYA 2/09)

2693 Berkeley, Jon. *The Palace of Laughter: The Wednesday Tales No. 1* (4–7). Illus. by Brandon Dorman. Series: Julie Andrews Collection. 2006, HarperCollins $16.99 (978-0-06-075507-2). Miles Wednesday, an 11-year-old orphan, joins forces with a talking tiger and a diminutive angel named Little to rescue Little's mentor from the Palace of Laughter. (Rev: SLJ 8/06)

2694 Berman, Steve, ed. *Magic in the Mirrorstone* (8–11). 2008, Mirrorstone $14.95 (978-0-7869-4732-4). Fifteen authors — among them Holly Black and Nina Kiriki Hoffman — contribute fantasy stories on topics that interest teens (bullies, friendship, cheating boyfriends, and so forth). (Rev: BL 2/15/08; SLJ 3/08)

2695 Berry, Julie. *The Amaranth Enchantment* (6–8). 2009, Bloomsbury $16.99 (978-159990334-7). Orphaned Lucinda, on a mission to return a gemstone to a witch, faces danger, suitors, and magical creatures in this entertaining fantasy. ⌒ Lexile HL610L (Rev: BL 2/1/09; HB 5–6/09; LMC 3–4/09; SLJ 4/1/09; VOYA 6/09)

2696 Berry, Julie. *Secondhand Charm* (6–9). 2010, Bloomsbury $16.99 (978-1-59990-511-2). After serving as the village healer, 15-year-old Evie accepts the opportunity to study medicine at university only to find herself facing unexpected dangers. ℮ Lexile 680L (Rev: BLO 12/1/10; LMC 10/10; SLJ 1/1/11)

2697 Berry, Liz. *The China Garden* (8–12). 1996, HarperCollins paper $7.99 (978-0-380-73228-9). Mysterious occurrences involving villagers who appear to know Clare and a handsome young man on a motorcycle happen when she accompanies her mother to an estate named Ravensmere. (Rev: BL 3/15/96; SLJ 5/96; VOYA 6/96)

2698 Berryhill, Shane. *Chance Fortune and the Outlaws* (5–8). Series: Adventures of Chance Fortune. 2006, Tom Doherty Assoc. $17.95 (978-0-7653-1468-0). Despite his lack of superpowers, 14-year-old Josh Blevins manages to bluff his way into Burlington Academy for the Superhuman, and there discovers that evil is afoot. (Rev: SLJ 1/07)

2699 Bertagna, Julie. *Exodus* (6–10). 2008, Walker $16.95 (978-0-8027-9745-2). In 2100, when the rising waters of global warming threaten her island world, 15-year-old Mara persuades her people to journey to the new sky cities and seek refuge there; but when they arrive they find only rejection. (Rev: BL 2/15/08; SLJ 3/08)

2700 Bertagna, Julie. *Zenith* (6–10). 2009, Walker $16.99 (978-080279803-9). In a world nearly obliterated by global warming, Mara seeks out higher ground with a group of refugees; a sequel to *Exodus* (2008). Lexile 820L (Rev: BL 2/15/09*; SLJ 7/1/09)

2701 Bildner, Phil, and Loren Long. *The Barnstormers: Tales of Travelin' Nine Game 1* (4–7). Illus. by Loren Long. 2007, Simon & Schuster $9.99 (978-1-4169-1863-9). On the road with their late father's traveling baseball team, siblings Griffith, Ruby, and Graham discover a ragged baseball with magical powers. (Rev: BL 4/1/07; SLJ 4/07)

2702 Billingsley, Franny. *The Folk Keeper* (5–8). 1999, Simon & Schuster $16.00 (978-0-689-82876-8); paper $4.99 (978-0-689-84461-4). Orphaned Corinna dis-

guises herself as a boy to become a Folk Keeper, one who guards the fierce Folk who live underground. (Rev: BCCB 10/99; BL 9/1/99; HB 11–12/99; HBG 3/00; SLJ 10/99; VOYA 12/99)

2703 Binding, Tim. *Sylvie and the Songman* (5–8). Illus. by Angela Barrett. 2009, Random $15.99 (978-0-385-75157-5). Sylvie's composer father disappears, the animals lose their voices, and a villain arrives. (Rev: BL 6/1–15/09*; SLJ 10/09)

2704 Birney, Betty G. *The Princess and the Peabodys* (5–8). 2007, HarperCollins $15.99 (978-0-06-084720-3). Casey Peabody, a no-nonsense sports-loving 8th grader, is an unlikely constant companion for Princess Eglantine, who is accidentally released from 700 years of imprisonment, but the two do become good friends while efforts are made to return Egg to her medieval home. (Rev: BCCB 11/07; SLJ 1/08)

2705 Black, Holly. *Black Heart* (8–11). Series: Curse Workers. 2012, Simon & Schuster $17.99 (978-144240346-8). In this third volume in the series Cassel, who has strong transformation powers in a world in which magic is illegal, must choose between the Feds and the Mob, challenging his passion for Lila. ⌒ ℮ Lexile HL680L (Rev: BL 2/15/12; SLJ 4/12)

2706 Black, Holly. *Red Glove* (7–10). Series: Curse Workers. 2011, Simon & Schuster $17.99 (978-1-4424-0339-0). Cassel, 17, faces several challenges: he must cope with Lila, who is cursed to love him; he must try to solve his older brother's murder; and he must decide whether to work for the Feds or the Mob; the sequel to *White Cat* (2010). ⌒ ℮ Lexile HL660L (Rev: BL 4/1/11; SLJ 5/11; VOYA 6/11)

2707 Black, Holly. *Tithe: A Modern Faerie Tale* (8–12). 2002, Simon & Schuster $16.95 (978-0-689-84924-4). Sixteen-year-old Kaye's adventures include rescuing a knight, Roiben, and being caught up in the battles between faerie kingdoms. (Rev: BL 2/15/03; HBG 3/03; SLJ 10/02)

2708 Black, Holly. *Valiant: A Modern Tale of Faerie* (8–11). 2005, Simon & Schuster $16.95 (978-0-689-86822-1). In this dark fantasy featuring drugs and homeless teens in New York City, 17-year-old Val becomes involved with trolls and faeries. (Rev: BL 7/05; SLJ 6/05)

2709 Black, Holly. *White Cat* (7–10). Series: The Curse Workers. 2010, Simon & Schuster $17.99 (978-1-4169-6396-7). Cassel is a member of a family of curse workers — illegal practitioners who can change fate — but have they now turned on him? The first installment in a series. ℮ Lexile HL700L (Rev: BL 4/1/10; LMC 10/10; SLJ 6/10)

2710 Black, Jenna. *Glimmerglass* (8–11). 2010, St. Martin's paper $9.99 (978-03125759-3-9). On a quest to find her father in Avalon, 16-year-old Dana enters a realm sandwiched between modern London and the

153

fairy world, encountering danger and romance. **e** Lexile 880L (Rev: BLO 7/10; VOYA 10/10)

2711 Blackman, Malorie. *Naughts and Crosses* (8–11). 2005, Simon & Schuster $15.95 (978-1-4169-0016-0). Callum, a 15-year-old, pale-skinned Naught in a world dominated by the dark-skinned Crosses, falls in love with Sephy, daughter of the Cross politician for whom Callum's mother works. (Rev: BL 6/1–15/05*; SLJ 6/05; VOYA 8/05)

2712 Blackwood, Gary. *The Year of the Hangman* (6–9). 2002, Dutton $16.99 (978-0-525-46921-6). After the British have defeated the colonists and captured General Washington, a 15-year-old English boy faces questions of loyalty in this exciting alternate history. (Rev: BCCB 12/02; BL 8/02; HBG 3/03; SLJ 9/02*)

2713 Blackwood, Sage. *Jinx* (4–7). 2013, HarperCollins $16.99 (978-006212990-1). In a deep forest named the Unwald, a young orphan named Jinx who has various powers discovers a complex world full of magic. **e** Lexile HL620L (Rev: BL 2/15/13*; HB 5–6/13; SLJ 1/13*)

2714 Blair, Margaret Whitman. *Brothers at War* (4–7). 1997, White Mane paper $7.95 (978-1-57249-049-9). Two brothers and their friend Sarah find themselves transported back in time to the Battle of Antietam in 1862. (Rev: BL 8/97)

2715 Blake, Kendare. *Anna Dressed in Blood* (8–12). 2011, Tor $17.99 (978-0-7653-2865-6). Successful ghost hunter Cas, 17, surprisingly finds love when he meets a murderous teen ghost named Anna. **e** Lexile HL690L (Rev: BL 6/1/11; LMC 3–4/12*; SLJ 11/1/11*)

2716 Block, Francesca Lia. *I Was a Teenage Fairy* (8–12). 1998, HarperCollins LB $14.89 (978-0-06-027748-2). Barbie Marks, at 16 a successful model, sorts herself out with the help of a fairy named Mab, after her father leaves and she is molested by a photographer. (Rev: BL 10/15/98; HB 11–12/98; HBG 3/99; SLJ 12/98*; VOYA 10/98)

2717 Block, Francesca Lia. *The Waters and the Wild* (5–8). 2009, HarperTeen $16.99 (978-0-06-145244-4). Bee, 13 and a lonely misfit, believes she was switched at birth with the real Bee. Lexile 680L (Rev: BL 3/15/09; SLJ 7/09)

2718 Blubaugh, Penny. *Serendipity Market* (6–10). 2009, HarperCollins $16.99 (978-006146875-9); LB $17.89 (978-006146876-6). Mama Inez calls on storytellers from all over the world to tell their tales and get the earth back on track. **e** (Rev: BL 3/15/09; SLJ 4/1/09; VOYA 8/09)

2719 Bode, N. E. *The Slippery Map* (5–8). 2007, HarperCollins $16.99 (978-0-06-079108-7). Orphan Oyster R. Motel, 10, enters the imaginary world of Boneland and discovers that his parents are in danger and that the slippery map has fallen into the hands of evil Dark Mouth. (Rev: BL 11/1/07; SLJ 12/07)

2720 Bode, N. E. *The Somebodies* (5–8). Illus. by Peter Ferguson. 2006, HarperCollins $16.99 (978-0-06-079111-7). Fern and her best friend Howard are determined to foil the Blue Queen's plan to destroy the home of the Anybodies who live in a city beneath Manhattan; the final book in a fast-paced trilogy. (Rev: SLJ 9/06)

2721 Bondoux, Anne-Laure. *Vasco: Leader of the Tribe* (4–7). 2007, Delacorte $15.99 (978-0-385-73363-2). Vasco, a rat with hopes for the future, escapes extermination by humans and boards an ocean liner, where he encounters more obstacles before tackling a dangerous rainforest. (Rev: BL 12/1/07; LMC 1/08; SLJ 3/08)

2722 Booraem, Ellen. *Small Persons with Wings* (5–7). 2011, Dial $16.99 (978-0-8037-3471-5). When Mellie's family inherits a dilapidated inn, they find it swarming with fairy-like beings who are desperate to regain a magical moonstone. **e** Lexile 660L (Rev: BL 1/1–15/11; HB 3–4/11; LMC 11–12/11; SLJ 1/1/11*)

2723 Booraem, Ellen. *The Unnameables* (6–9). 2008, Harcourt $16.00 (978-015206368-9). Young orphaned artist Medford struggles with outcast status — and the fact that his artistry could get him exiled — on a fantastical island where only useful things have merit. **e** Lexile 690L (Rev: BL 11/15/08; HB 1–2/09; SLJ 11/1/08)

2724 Bosworth, Jennifer. *Struck* (7–10). 2012, Farrar $17.99 (978-037437283-5). Seventeen-year-old Mia's propensity for attracting lightning draws the attention of two competing cults in post-disaster Los Angeles. **e** (Rev: BL 5/1/12; HB 7–8/12; LMC 7–8/12; SLJ 6/12)

2725 Bouwman, H. M. *The Remarkable and Very True Story of Lucy and Snowcap* (5–7). 2008, Marshall Cavendish $16.99 (978-0-7614-5441-0). In 1787 on the fictional island of Tatenland, two 12-year-old girls — Lucy, a native Colay, and Snowcap, daughter of a British governor — investigate why the men have all been turned to stone. (Rev: BLO 10/7/08; LMC 3/09; SLJ 11/08)

2726 Bow, Erin. *Plain Kate* (6–9). 2010, Scholastic $17.99 (978-0-545-16664-5). When homeless young Kate, plain but a genius at carving wood, realizes she must leave her village she foolishly agrees to exchange her shadow for supplies for the journey and a single wish. ∩ **e** Lexile 630L (Rev: BL 10/15/10; HB 9–10/10; LMC 11–12/10; SLJ 10/1/10; VOYA 12/10)

2727 Bracken, Alexandra. *Brightly Woven* (7–10). 2010, Egmont $16.99 (978-1-60684-038-2). A wizard named Wayland whisks 16-year-old weaver Sydelle off on an action-packed effort to stop a war in this fantasy that features magic, romance, and danger. **e** Lexile HL760L (Rev: BL 3/15/10; LMC 10/10; SLJ 4/10)

2728 Bradbury, Ray. *The Illustrated Man* (7–12). 1990, Bantam paper $7.50 (978-0-553-27449-3). A tattooed man tells a story for each of his tattoos.

2729 Bray, Libba. *Going Bovine* (8–12). 2009, Delacorte $17.99 (978-0-385-73397-7); LB $20.99 (978-0-385-90411-7). After Cameron, 16, is diagnosed with "mad cow" disease, he finds himself transported by an angel of kinds who sends him on a quest to save mankind; similarities to Don Quixote will amuse readers who know the story. Printz Winner 2010. ∩ Lexile HL680L (Rev: BL 8/09*; HB 9–10/09; SLJ 9/09; VOYA 8/09)

2730 Bray, Libba. *A Great and Terrible Beauty* (8–12). 2003, Delacorte LB $17.99 (978-0-385-90161-1). Gemma, a troubled student in London, learns to control her visions and enter the Realms, a place of magic, in this multilayered novel that combines fantasy, mystery, and romance with a look at 19th-century manners. ∩ (Rev: BCCB 5/04; BL 11/15/03; SLJ 2/04; VOYA 4/04)

2731 Bray, Libba. *The Sweet Far Thing* (8–10). Series: Gemma Doyle. 2007, Delacorte $17.99 (978-0-385-73030-3). This final installment in the series finds Gemma wondering whom she can trust with the magic of the Realms even as the Realms themselves are transforming. ∩ (Rev: BL 11/15/07; SLJ 1/08)

2732 Breathed, Berkeley. *The Last Basselope: One Ferocious Story* (4–7). 2001, Little, Brown paper $5.95 (978-0-316-12664-9). In this imaginative picture book for older readers, Opus and his reluctant adventurers are after the nearly extinct basselope. (Rev: BCCB 1/93; BL 12/15/92; SLJ 1/93)

2733 Breen, M. E. *Darkwood* (5–8). 2009, Bloomsbury $16.99 (978-1-59990-259-3). Twelve-year-old Annie flees the home she has shared with her aunt and uncle and finds herself in an even less inviting world that is full of danger but may offer clues to her heritage. (Rev: BCCB 9/09; BL 5/15/09; SLJ 6/09; VOYA 10/09)

2734 Brennan, Herbie. *Faerie Lord* (6–8). Series: Faerie War Chronicles. 2007, Bloomsbury $18.95 (978-1-59990-120-6). Henry travels to the far reaches of the realm to stop a plague that threatens all its denizens. ∩ (Rev: BL 1/1–15/08; SLJ 1/08)

2735 Brennan, Herbie. *Faerie Wars* (6–8). 2003, Bloomsbury $17.95 (978-1-58234-810-0). Henry Atherton becomes involved with an escaped fairy crown prince in this complex tale of parallel worlds. (Rev: BL 4/15/03; HBG 10/03; SLJ 7/03; VOYA 6/03)

2736 Brennan, Herbie. *The Purple Emperor: Faerie Wars II* (6–8). 2004, Bloomsbury $17.95 (978-1-58234-880-3). In a sequel to *Faerie Wars* (2003) full of humor and adventure, Henry Atherton returns to the Faerie Realm to help royal siblings Pyrgus Malvae and Holly Blue. (Rev: BL 9/15/04; SLJ 12/04; VOYA 2/05)

2737 Brennan, Herbie. *Ruler of the Realm* (7–10). Series: The Faerie Wars Chronicles. 2006, Bloomsbury $18.95 (978-1-58234-881-0). This action-packed third installment of the series that blends fantasy and science fiction has Queen Blue investigating an office of peace

from the Faeries of the Night and Henry (a human) being abducted by aliens. (Rev: SLJ 2/07)

2738 Briceland, V. *The Buccaneer's Apprentice* (7–11). Series: The Cassaforte Chronicles. 2010, Flux paper $9.95 (978-0-73871895-8.). Escaping servitude, 17-year-old Nic has many adventures at sea in his quest to save the city of Cassaforte. Lexile 880L (Rev: BLO 3/1/10; LMC 8–9/10; SLJ 7/10)

2739 Briceland, V. *The Glass Maker's Daughter* (7–11). Series: The Cassaforte Chronicles. 2009, Flux paper $9.95 (978-073871424-0). Risa struggles to find her place in the medieval city of Cassaforte when she is not chosen to learn valuable enchantment secrets. Lexile 840L (Rev: BL 4/15/09; SLJ 7/1/09)

2740 Bridges, Robin. *The Gathering Storm* (7–10). 2012, Delacorte $17.99 (978-038574022-7); LB $20.99 (978-038590829-0). Romance, social mores, fantasy, and intrigue are combined in this story about 16-year-old Katerina, Duchess of Oldenburg, and her abilities as a necromancer. ℮ (Rev: BL 2/1/12; LMC 3–4/12; SLJ 2/12)

2741 Briggs, Andy. *Rise of the Heroes* (5–8). Series: Hero.com. 2009, Walker paper $7.99 (978-0-8027-9503-8). Downloading superpowers including flight and laser vision proves irresistible to four teens who find their new abilities challenging at first. Lexile 780L (Rev: BL 8/09; SLJ 9/09)

2742 Brockenbrough, Martha. *Devine Intervention* (7–12). 2012, Scholastic $17.99 (978-0-545-38213-7). Jerome, 17, messes everything up, even in the afterlife where he is struggling to succeed as a guardian angel but risks losing the soul of 16-year-old Heidi. ℮ Lexile 810L (Rev: LMC 11–12/12; SLJ 6/12)

2743 Brodien-Jones, Christine. *The Owl Keeper* (5–8). Illus. by Maggie Kneen. 2010, Delacorte $17.99 (978-0-385-73814-9); LB $20.99 (978-0-385-90710-1). Eleven-year-old Max partners with an unusual girl, Rose, who shares his appreciation of the silver owls that the High Echelon wants to destroy, and together they make a perilous journey seeking to fulfill a prophecy. ℮ Lexile 750L (Rev: BL 4/15/10; LMC 8–9/10; SLJ 5/10; VOYA 10/10)

2744 Brodien-Jones, Christine. *The Scorpions of Zahir* (5–8). Illus. by Kelly Murphy. 2012, Delacorte $17.99 (978-0-385-73933-7); LB $20.99 (978-038590783-5). Zagora and her archaeologist father head to Morocco to the ancient city of Zahir in this fantasy/adventure/mystery story featuring an evil scientist, giant scorpions, and long-extinct gazelles. ℮ (Rev: BL 8/12; LMC 1–2/13; SLJ 10/12)

2745 Brooks, Laurie. *Selkie Girl* (6–9). 2008, Knopf $15.99 (978-037585170-4); LB $18.99 (978-037595170-1). In this eloquent, haunting Celtic mythology-inspired tale, half-breed Elin struggles to belong, first in the terrestrial human world, and then in the aquatic world of the selkies. **e** Lexile 890L (Rev: BL 11/15/08; LMC 3–4/09; SLJ 12/08)

2746 Brown, Joseph F. *Dark Things* (6–9). 1995, Fireworks paper $9.99 (978-0-88092-110-7). A fantasy that spans 130 years, from the Civil War to the present, about a boy who never grows old and who possesses magical powers. (Rev: VOYA 4/96)

2747 Browne, N. M. *Silverboy* (6–9). 2007, Bloomsbury $16.95 (978-1-58234-780-6). Akenna and Tommo—a 15-year-old spellgrinder's apprentice—are fleeing the powers of the spellstones and the Protector, pursued by a flock of human-looking birds. (Rev: BL 2/1/07; LMC 8–9/07; SLJ 5/07)

2748 Browne, N. M. *Warriors of Alavna* (7–10). 2002, Bloomsbury $16.95 (978-1-58234-775-2). This historical fantasy pits 15-year-olds Dan and Ursula against invaders in Roman Britain. A sequel is *Warriors of Camlann* (2003). (Rev: BCCB 10/02; SLJ 1/03; VOYA 2/03)

2749 Bruchac, Joseph. *Dragon Castle* (5–8). 2011, Dial $16.99 (978-0-8037-3376-3). A 15-year-old Slovakian prince, Rashko, must contend with the arrival of a rogue army when his parents are away and finds himself relying on the power of an ancestor who slayed a dragon. **e** Lexile 850L (Rev: BLO 8/11; HB 9–10/11; LMC 1–2/12*; SLJ 8/11)

2750 Bruchac, Joseph. *Wabi: A Hero's Tale* (7–10). 2006, Dial $16.99 (978-0-8037-3098-4). A white great horned owl named Wabi has the power to transform himself into a human being and falls in love with an Abenaki girl named Dojihla. (Rev: BL 2/15/06; SLJ 4/06*; VOYA 4/06)

2751 Buckingham, Jane. *The Hound of Rowan* (6–9). Illus. by author. 2007, Random House $17.99 (978-0-375-83894-1). Max McDaniels attends Rowan Academy in New England, where apprentices learn magical skills, train to fight an unnamed enemy, and are paired with unusual animals. (Rev: BL 9/1/07; SLJ 3/08)

2752 Buckingham, Royce. *Goblins! An UnderEarth Adventure* (5–8). 2008, Putnam $16.99 (978-0-399-25002-6). Twelve-year-old Sam and his 17-year-old friend PJ, son of the only police officer in their small town, discover a scary underworld where goblins live. (Rev: SLJ 11/08)

2753 Buckley-Archer, Linda. *The Time Thief* (6–9). Series: Gideon Trilogy. 2007, Simon & Schuster $17.99 (978-1-4169-1527-0). Peter's father and Kate travel through time to save Peter but end up meeting him at age 41 instead of 12, the age he was at the end of *Gideon the Cutpurse* (2006). (Rev: BL 3/1/08; SLJ 2/08)

2754 Buffie, Margaret. *Angels Turn Their Backs* (7–9). 1998, Kids Can $16.95 (978-1-55074-415-6). When 15-year-old Addy moves with her mother to Winnipeg, she suffers panic attacks at the thought of going to a

new school and trying to make new friends, but she gets help from a ghost who speaks through a parrot. (Rev: BCCB 11/98; HBG 3/99; SLJ 11/98; VOYA 4/99)

2755 Buffie, Margaret. *The Finder* (6–10). Series: The Watcher's Quest. 2004, Kids Can $16.95 (978-1-55337-671-2). In the final volume of the trilogy, shape-changing heroine Emma Sweeny defies her training master and passes through a magical portal before she must get to four hidden power wands before they're found by the evil Eefa. (Rev: BL 10/15/04; SLJ 1/05; VOYA 2/05)

2756 Buffie, Margaret. *The Seeker* (5–8). 2002, Kids Can $16.95 (978-1-55337-358-2). Emma is involved in a quest to reunite her family and becomes embroiled in interplanetary intrigue and gaming in this sequel to *The Watcher* (2000). (Rev: BL 10/1/02; HBG 10/03; SLJ 11/02; VOYA 4/03)

2757 Buffie, Margaret. *The Watcher* (5–8). 2000, Kids Can $16.95 (978-1-55074-829-1). Sixteen-year-old Emma discovers that she is really a changeling, a Watcher, whose mission is to protect her younger sister from warring factions. (Rev: BL 11/1/00; HBG 3/01; SLJ 10/00; VOYA 2/01)

2758 Bullen, Allexandra. *Wish* (8–11). 2010, Scholastic $17.99 (978-0-545-13905-2). Three magical dresses aid — and complicate — Olivia's efforts to recover from the death of her twin sister Violet. **e** Lexile 1150 (Rev: BL 12/109; LMC 3–4/10; SLJ 1/10)

2759 Bunce, Elizabeth C. *A Curse as Dark as Gold* (7–10). 2008, Scholastic $17.99 (978-0-439-89576-7). Charlotte and her sister Rosie make a bargain with a man named Spinner to save themselves from a curse in this take on the Rumplestiltskin story. (Rev: BL 5/1/08; SLJ 5/08)

2760 Bunce, Elizabeth C. *Star Crossed* (8–11). 2010, Scholastic $17.99 (978-0-545-13605-1). Fleeing after a job goes wrong, teen thief Digger takes on the persona of Celyn, a lady's maid, in this intricate fantasy full of political intrigue and magic. Lexile 820L (Rev: BL 11/15/10; LMC 11–12/10; SLJ 1/1/11; VOYA 2/11)

2761 Bunting, Eve. *The Lambkins* (7–10). Illus. by Jonathan Keegan. 2005, HarperCollins LB $16.89 (978-0-06-059907-2). Kyle's offer to help a woman with a flat tire goes awry when she kidnaps him and shrinks him to the size of a Coke bottle. (Rev: BL 8/05; SLJ 8/05)

2762 Burden, Meg. *Northlander: Tales of the Borderlands* (5–8). Series: Tales of the Borderlands. 2007, Brown Barn paper $8.95 (978-0-9768126-8-5). Ellin, a Southling with healing powers and other mystical abilities, is torn between her homeland and her friends in the Northlands. (Rev: BL 1/1–15/08; SLJ 2/08)

2763 Burgis, Stephanie. *Renegade Magic* (6–10). Series: Kat, Incorrigible. 2012, Atheneum $16.99 (978-141699449-7). Kat, 12, struggles to get a grip on the magical talents she possesses in this fantasy set in 19th-century Bath, England, where the family has moved to find a suitable match for Kat's older sister. ℮ Lexile 790L (Rev: BL 3/15/12; SLJ 3/12)

2764 Burt, Marissa. *Storybound* (4–7). 2012, Harper-Collins $16.99 (978-006202052-9). Una Fairchild, 12, is magically transported to the Land of Story where she finds mystery and danger. (Rev: BL 3/15/12; SLJ 8/12)

2765 Buzbee, Lewis. *Bridge of Time* (5–8). 2012, Feiwel & Friends $17.99 (978-031238257-5). Best friends Lee Jones and Joan Lee, 8th-graders who discover their respective parents are divorcing, wish they could go back to an earlier, better time — and get more than they bargained for. ℮ (Rev: BL 4/1/12; SLJ 5/1/12)

2766 Buzbee, Lewis. *Steinbeck's Ghost* (5–8). 2008, Feiwel & Friends $17.95 (978-0-312-37328-3). Thirteen-year-old Travis is unhappy when his family moves to a new subdivision and he drifts back to his old neighborhood in Salinas, California, John Steinbeck's hometown; there he works to save the Steinbeck Library from closure and finds that characters from Steinbeck novels are coming to life. ∩ (Rev: BL 8/08; SLJ 9/08)

2767 Cabot, Meg. *Jinx* (6–10). 2007, HarperTeen $16.99 (978-0-06-083764-8). Unlucky Jinx is sent to live with her relatives in New York City, where she discovers her supernatural powers and that her cousin Tory has sinister intentions. ∩ (Rev: BL 9/1/07; SLJ 9/07)

2768 Cabot, Meg. *Underworld* (8–12). 2012, Scholastic $17.99 (978-054528411-0). John — the "deity of death" — takes Pierce to the Underworld, ostensibly to protect her from the Furies, but Pierce is determined to leave when she learns her family is in danger; the sequel to *Abandon* (2011). ∩ ℮ Lexile 850L (Rev: BL 6/12; SLJ 8/12; VOYA 8/12)

2769 Calhoun, Dia. *Aria of the Sea* (6–9). 2003, Farrar paper $7.95 (978-0-374-40454-3). In the kingdom of Windward, 13-year-old Cerinthe joins the Royal Dancing School and finds herself having to choose between her talents: dancing and healing. (Rev: SLJ 9/00)

2770 Calhoun, Dia. *Avielle of Rhia* (8–11). 2006, Marshall Cavendish $16.99 (978-0-7614-5320-8). Princess Avielle of Rhia has the physical characteristics of Dredonians (fearful doers of magic) but when all of her royal family is murdered she must use her magic to save the people of Rhia, despite their hatred toward her. (Rev: BL 10/1/06; LMC 2/07; SLJ 11/06)

2771 Calhoun, Dia. *Firegold* (7–12). 1999, Winslow $15.95 (978-1-890817-10-7). A fantasy in which a 13-year-old boy is persecuted in his village because of his different looks and behavior and is forced to travel to the Red Mountains, home of fierce barbarians. (Rev: BL 5/15/99; SLJ 6/99; VOYA 8/99)

2772 Carey, Janet Lee. *The Beast of Noor* (6–9). 2006, Simon & Schuster $16.95 (978-0-689-87644-8). Miles and his sister Hanna are impelled to break their family curse and defeat the Shriker, a vicious dog that feeds on human prey that was supposedly brought to the area by their ancestors. (Rev: BL 8/06; SLJ 11/06)

2773 Carey, Janet Lee. *Dragon's Keep* (7–10). 2007, Harcourt $17.00 (978-0-15-205926-2). Rosland discovers that she is part dragon and that she is destined to care for a brood of dragon children in this action-filled fantasy. ∩ (Rev: BCCB 5/07; BL 2/1/07; SLJ 4/07*)

2774 Carey, Janet Lee. *Dragonswood* (8–12). 2012, Dial $17.99 (978-080373504-0). Accused of witchcraft, Tess is offered protection by a mysterious warden in this fantastical romance set in 1192 and featuring dragons, humans, and fairies; a sequel to *Dragon's Keep* (2007). ℮ (Rev: BL 1/1/12; SLJ 1/12)

2775 Carey, Janet Lee. *Stealing Death* (7–10). 2009, Egmont $16.99 (978-1-60684-009-2); LB $19.99 (978-1-60684-045-0). After a tragic fire that kills his parents and brother, 17-year-old Kipp is on a mission to steal the sack in which the Gwali collects souls of the dead, hoping to keep his other loved ones from dying. Lexile 710L (Rev: BL 9/15/09; SLJ 9/09; VOYA 10/09)

2776 Carman, Patrick. *Rivers of Fire* (5–8). Series: Atherton. 2008, Little, Brown $16.99 (978-0-316-16672-0). The planet of Atherton is still in trouble, and Edgar, Samuel, and Isabel fight to save it in this continuation of the story that began in *The House of Power*. (Rev: BL 5/15/08; SLJ 8/08)

2777 Carmody, Isobelle. *Alyzon Whitestarr* (7–10). 2009, Random House $17.99 (978-037583938-2); LB $20.99 (978-037593938-9). A concussion endows Alyzon Whitestarr with amazing abilities that will perhaps enable her to save her unusual family from disaster; set in Australia, this is a multilayered story full of mystery and romance. (Rev: BL 6/1–15/09; SLJ 11/09)

2778 Carmody, Isobelle. *Winter Door* (7–12). Series: Gateway Trilogy. 2006, Random House $16.95 (978-0-375-83018-1). In this second installment in the trilogy, Rage attempts to combat an unusually severe winter while also dealing with a bully; readers will want to read the first volume before tackling this one. (Rev: SLJ 7/06)

2779 Carroll, Michael. *The Ascension: A Super Human Clash* (5–8). Series: Super Human. 2011, Philomel $16.99 (978-0-399-25624-0). Villain Krodin returns in this second installment in the series and is conquered by the teenage superheroes after plenty of struggle and fast-paced action. Lexile 680L (Rev: SLJ 8/11)

2780 Carroll, Thomas. *The Colony* (4–7). 2000, Sunstone $18.95 (978-0-86534-295-8). Fifth-grader Tony and his bullying arch-enemy Lawrence are shrunk to the size of ants by a Navajo charm and in their new environment join opposing forces. (Rev: HBG 3/01; SLJ 7/00)

2781 Carson, Rae. *The Girl of Fire and Thorns* (8–12). 2011, Greenwillow $17.99 (978-0-06-202648-4). In a fantasy medieval world 16-year-old Elisa, a princess forced into an arranged marriage, grows into a strong woman worthy of the magical gem she carries in her navel. YALSA Top Ten Best Fiction for Young Adults 2012. ∩ e Lexile 730L (Rev: BL 10/1/11; SLJ 8/11*)

2782 Carter, Scott William. *Wooden Bones* (4–7). 2012, Simon & Schuster $15.99 (978-1-4424-2751-8). After Pinocchio becomes a real boy, he realizes he has the power to bring wood to life, which endangers both him and his father, Gepetto. e (Rev: LMC 1–2/13; SLJ 8/1/12)

2783 Cashore, Kristin. *Fire* (8–12). 2009, Dial $17.99 (978-0-8037-3461-6). A prequel to *Graceling*, this book focuses on the beautiful Fire, who, like the other inhabitants of the Dells, is part monster and has supernatural powers. e Lexile 870L (Rev: BL 9/15/09*; HB 9–10/09; LMC 11–12/09; SLJ 8/09)

2784 Cast, P. C., and Kristin Cast. *Lenobia's Vow* (8–11). Series: House of Night. 2012, St. Martin's $12.99 (978-125000024-8). Sixteen-year-old Lenobia, posing as her dead half-sister, is on her way to marriage to a rich man in New Orleans in this romantic historical fantasy featuring an evil bishop, a handsome horse trainer, and vampyres. (Rev: BLO 3/15/12)

2785 Catanese, P. W. *Dragon Games* (5–8). Series: The Books of Umber. 2010, Simon & Schuster $16.99 (978-1-4169-7521-2). Lord Umber and his ward Happenstance travel to Sarnica in an attempt to sate an unquenchable thirst for knowledge about dragons and a disregard for looming danger. ∩ e Lexile 740L (Rev: BLO 12/1/09; SLJ 7/10)

2786 Catanese, P. W. *Happenstance Found* (6–9). Series: The Books of Umber. 2009, Aladdin $16.99 (978-141697519-9). Happenstance, who has no memory but does have mysterious powers, is taken in by Lord Umber and tasked with evading an evil enemy and saving Earth. ∩ Lexile NC700L (Rev: BL 4/1/09; HB 1–2/09; SLJ 5/1/09)

2787 Catanese, P. W. *The Mirror's Tale: A Further Tales Adventure* (4–7). 2006, Simon & Schuster paper $4.99 (978-1-4169-1251-4). When their father decides to separate his mischievous 13-year-old twin sons for the summer, they switch places and one is sent to the castle of his aunt and uncle where he discovers and falls under the spell of a bewitching mirror. (Rev: SLJ 8/06)

2788 Catmull, Katherine. *Summer and Bird* (5–8). 2012, Dutton $16.99 (978-0-525-95346-3). Set in the world of Down, this complex fantasy features young sisters Summer and Bird who separately search for their missing parents in an alternate world. e Lexile 760L (Rev: BL 9/15/12*; SLJ 11/12; VOYA 10/12)

2789 Caveney, Philip. *Prince of Fools* (7–12). Series: Sebastian Darke. 2008, Delacorte $15.99 (978-0-385-73467-7). Would-be (but not very funny) jester Sebastian, 17 and half-elf, travels with his (quite funny) buffalope and the tiny Captain Cornelius, to the court of King Septimus in hopes of gaining employment; along the way they rescue a princess and find themselves embroiled in intrigue. (Rev: BL 3/15/08; SLJ 9/08)

2790 Chan, Gillian. *The Carved Box* (5–8). 2001, Kids Can $16.95 (978-1-55074-895-6). The acquisition of a dog and a carved box ease the transition for orphaned Callum, 15, who has moved from Scotland to Canada to live with his uncle, in this novel which has an element of fantasy that comes to the fore in the dramatic ending. (Rev: BL 10/01; HBG 3/02; SLJ 10/01; VOYA 4/02)

2791 Charnas, Suzy McKee. *The Kingdom of Kevin Malone* (7–10). 1993, Harcourt $16.95 (978-0-15-200756-0). This novel melds the world of the teenage problem novel with that of fantasy in a story that pokes gentle fun at the conventions of fantasy fiction. (Rev: BL 6/1–15/93; SLJ 1/94; VOYA 8/93)

2792 Childs, Tera Lynn. *Goddess Boot Camp* (7–10). 2009, Dutton $16.99 (978-052542134-4). Teenage Phoebe is a real goddess — a descendant of Nike — who first appeared in *Oh. My. Gods* (2008). Here she suffers through goddess boot camp on a Greek island. Lexile 710L (Rev: BLO 4/23/09; SLJ 7/1/09)

2793 Childs, Tera Lynn. *Sweet Venom* (7–10). 2011, HarperCollins $17.99 (978-006200181-8). Sixteen-year-old Grace discovers that she and her previously unknown sisters are descendants of Medusa charged with protecting humanity from all manner of mythological monsters. A sequel is *Sweet Shadows* (2012). e Lexile 780L (Rev: BL 10/1/11; SLJ 2/12; VOYA 10/11)

2794 Chima, Cinda Williams. *The Demon King* (6–10). Series: Seven Realms. 2009, Hyperion $17.99 (978-1-4231-1823-7). A rich and varied fantasy featuring one-time thief Han Alister, owner of magic silver cuffs, and Princess Raisa, who rebels against many aspects of the royal court; their lives intersect as they face danger and challenge; the first installment in the series. ∩ e Lexile 760L (Rev: HB 1–2/10; LMC 1–2/10; SLJ 12/09)

2795 Chima, Cinda Williams. *The Wizard Heir* (8–11). 2007, Hyperion $17.99 (978-1-4231-0487-2). When Seph's magical mishaps (he has had no wizard training) lead to a death, he's sent to a boys' school named the Havens, where he's offered training but at a cost Seph must reject; a companion to *The Warrior Heir* (2006). (Rev: BL 5/15/07; SLJ 12/07)

2796 Choldenko, Gennifer. *No Passengers Beyond This Point* (5–8). 2011, Dial $16.99 (978-0-8037-3534-7). Three children sent to live in Colorado find themselves in a disconcerting alternate reality, and their determination to support each other is what pulls them through. ∩ e (Rev: BL 2/1/11; HB 1–2/11; LMC 5–6/11; SLJ 2/1/11; VOYA 4/11)

2797 Churchyard, Kathleen. *Bye for Now: A Wisher's Story* (4–7). 2011, Egmont $15.99 (978-1-60684-190-7). Robin, 11, is not enjoying her birthday and wishes she could be someone else; the next day she wakes up in

London in the body of 11-year-old Fiona, who has quite a different life — but is it better? **e** (Rev: BL 9/1/11; SLJ 12/1/11)

2798 Ciddor, Anna. *Night of the Fifth Moon* (5–8). 2008, Allen & Unwin paper $9.95 (978-1-74114-814-5). Set in ancient Ireland and filled with beautiful imagery, this engaging novel tells the story of Ket, who must leave his family and struggle for the chance to become a druid. (Rev: SLJ 5/09; VOYA 10/08)

2799 Clare, Cassandra. *City of Glass* (8–11). Series: Mortal Instruments. 2009, Simon & Schuster $17.99 (978-141691430-3). Clary uncovers secrets about her family as she continues to seek a cure for her mother in this multilayered story; the third installment in the series. ⌒ **e** Lexile 760L (Rev: BL 3/1/09; SLJ 7/1/09; VOYA 4/09)

2800 Clare, Cassandra. *Clockwork Angel* (8–12). Series: The Infernal Devices. 2010, Simon & Schuster $19.99 (978-1-4169-7586-1). In Victorian England, 16-year-old Tessa Gray is kidnapped by the sinister Dark Sisters, who want to use her powers for their own diabolical purposes. **e** Lexile HL780L (Rev: BL 8/10; LMC 1–2/11; SLJ 10/1/10; VOYA 8/10)

2801 Clare, Cassandra. *Clockwork Prince* (8–12). Series: The Infernal Devices. 2011, Simon & Schuster $19.99 (978-141697588-5). Tessa, 16, searches for answers about her identity and works to dismantle the clockwork army amid a richly imagined steampunk setting in this sequel to *Clockwork Angel* (2010). ⌒ **e** Lexile HL790L (Rev: BL 11/15/11; SLJ 1/12; VOYA 12/11)

2802 Clayton, Emma. *The Whisper* (5–8). 2012, Scholastic $17.99 (978-054531772-6). Telepathic twins Mika and Ellie endeavor to halt the evil that is dividing the population into the poor on one side of The Wall and the megalomaniacs on the other side in this sequel to *The Roar* (2009). **e** (Rev: BL 3/1/12; SLJ 3/12)

2803 Cle, Troy. *The Marvelous Effect* (6–9). Series: Marvelous World. 2007, Simon & Schuster $14.99 (978-1-4169-3958-0). Louis goes to an amusement park one day and receives special powers to fight the Galonious Imperial Evil in a video-game like battle. (Rev: BL 7/07; LMC 10/07; SLJ 11/07)

2804 Clement-Davies, David. *Fell* (7–12). 2007, Abrams $19.95 (978-0-8109-1185-7). Alina travels through Transylvania with Fell, a wolf, to defeat Lord Vladeran and his dark powers in order to save the natural world; a sequel to *The Sight*. ⌒ (Rev: BL 10/15/07; SLJ 1/08)

2805 Clement-Davies, David. *The Telling Pool* (6–9). 2005, Abrams $19.95 (978-0-8109-5758-9). In this historical fantasy set in 12th-century England, young Rhodri Falcon must defeat the evil sorceress who has cast a spell on his father. (Rev: BCCB 1/06; BL 10/1/05; SLJ 11/05; VOYA 12/05)

2806 Clement-Moore, Rosemary. *Highway to Hell* (8–10). Series: Maggie Quinn: Girl vs. Evil. 2009, Delacorte $16.99 (978-038573463-9); LB $19.99 (978-038590462-9). Magic, legends, and religion mix while Maggie and Lisa are on vacation in south Texas. (Rev: BL 3/15/09; SLJ 4/1/09; VOYA 2/09)

2807 Coakley, Lena. *Witchlanders* (7–10). 2011, Atheneum $16.99 (978-1-4424-2004-5). Witchlander Ryder and Baen Prince Falpian are enemies but share a mystical bond as they struggle to spare the lives of their countrymen. **e** Lexile HL690L (Rev: BL 10/15/11; LMC 1–2/12; SLJ 12/1/11*; VOYA 8/11)

2808 Cody, Matthew. *Powerless* (5–8). 2009, Knopf $15.99 (978-0-375-85595-5); LB $18.99 (978-0-375-95595-2). When Daniel, 12, arrives in Noble's Green he soon learns that all the other kids have superpowers that they will lose when they turn 13. Can Daniel use his intelligence to prevent this? ⌒ **e** Lexile 800L (Rev: BL 10/15/09; LMC 11–12/09; SLJ 1/10)

2809 Cody, Matthew. *Super* (5–8). 2012, Knopf $16.99 (978-0-375-86894-8); LB $19.99 (978-037596894-5). Despite his lack of superpowers, 13-year-old Daniel has proved quite effective in the past; now he seems to be acquiring powers as others are losing them. What is going on? ⌒ **e** (Rev: BLO 12/1/12; LMC 1–2/13*; SLJ 12/12)

2810 Coleman, Alice Scovell. *Engraved in Stone* (4–7). Illus. by Anjal Ren e Armand. 2003, Tiara Bks $14.95 (978-0-9729846-0-7). A prince and princess who will do anything to avoid their planned marriage set off on a quest to get their fate changed in this humorous fantasy. (Rev: SLJ 12/03)

2811 Colfer, Eoin. *The Arctic Incident* (6–9). Series: Artemis Fowl. 2002, Hyperion $16.99 (978-0-7868-0855-7). Another madcap adventure in which Artemis and Captain Holly combine their talents to combat forces as diverse as the Russian mafia and a band of dangerous smugglers. (Rev: BCCB 7–8/01; BL 5/1/02; HBG 10/02; SLJ 7/02; VOYA 8/02)

2812 Colfer, Eoin. *Artemis Fowl* (6–9). Series: Artemis Fowl. 2001, Hyperion $16.95 (978-0-7868-0801-4). Twelve-year-old genius and adventurous criminal entrepreneur Artemis Fowl captures a fairy investigator, with lively and hilarious results. (Rev: BL 4/15/01; HB 7–8/01; HBG 10/01; SLJ 5/01; VOYA 8/01)

2813 Colfer, Eoin. *Artemis Fowl: The Last Guardian* (5–8). 2012, Disney/Hyperion $18.99 (978-142316161-5). In this series conclusion, genius Artemis Fowl finds himself up against his familiar — and deadly — rival Opal for the final time. Odyssey Honor Recording 2013. ⌒ **e** (Rev: BLO 10/15/12; SLJ 11/12; VOYA 10/12)

2814 Colfer, Eoin. *The Atlantis Complex* (5–8). Series: Artemis Fowl. 2010, Hyperion $17.99 (978-142312819-9). In this seventh title in the series, Artemis combats global warming while struggling to overcome a serious

159

case of the Atlantis Complex, an affliction that causes OCD, paranoia, and multiple personalities. ∩ **e** Lexile 900L (Rev: BL 10/1/10; VOYA 12/10)

2815 Colfer, Eoin. *The Eternity Code* (6–9). Series: Artemis Fowl. 2003, Hyperion $16.95 (978-0-7868-1914-0). An action-packed adventure in which Artemis creates an unauthorized groundbreaking supercomputer with fairy technology, which becomes a threat when it is stolen. (Rev: BL 6/1–15/03; HBG 10/03; SLJ 7/03)

2816 Colfer, Eoin. *The Lost Colony* (6–9). Series: Artemis Fowl. 2006, Hyperion $16.95 (978-0-7868-4956-7). Artemis, 14, faces new challenges when he must stop demons that are seeking their revenge on humans and threatening to expose the whole fairy world. (Rev: BL 11/1/06)

2817 Colfer, Eoin. *The Opal Deception* (6–9). Series: Artemis Fowl. 2005, Hyperion $16.95 (978-0-7868-5289-5). In the fourth volume of the series, Artemis, his mind wiped clean of memories about the fairy world, reverts to a life of crime and provides an easy target for his nemesis, Opal Koboi. (Rev: BL 5/15/05; SLJ 7/05)

2818 Colfer, Eoin. *The Time Paradox* (4–8). Series: Artemis Fowl. 2008, Hyperion $17.99 (978-1-4231-0836-8). Artemis travels back in time to retrieve a substance that will cure his mother's disease. ∩ **e** Lexile 780L (Rev: SLJ 10/1/08; VOYA 10/08)

2819 Collins, Suzanne. *Gregor and the Code of Claw* (5–9). Series: The Underland Chronicles. 2007, Scholastic $17.99 (978-0-439-79143-4). A mysterious prophecy makes Gregor question himself in this adventure-filled fifth title in the series. (Rev: SLJ 7/07)

2820 Collins, Suzanne. *Gregor and the Marks of Secret* (5–8). Series: The Underland Chronicles. 2006, Scholastic $16.99 (978-0-439-79145-8). Gregor, accompanied by his little sister Boots, joins forces with Queen Luxa to defend Underland from attacks by the rat army. (Rev: SLJ 9/06; VOYA 8/06)

2821 Collins, Suzanne. *Gregor the Overlander* (4–7). 2003, Scholastic $17.99 (978-0-439-43536-9). When his baby sister disappears into an air vent, 11-year-old Gregor doesn't hesitate to follow and finds himself in a whole new world, an Underland where an unexpected role awaits him. (Rev: BCCB 1/04; BL 11/15/03*; HB 9–10/03; HBG 9–10/03; LMC 11–12/03; SLJ 11/03; VOYA 10/03)

2822 Collins, Suzanne. *Mockingjay* (6–12). Series: Hunger Games. 2010, Scholastic $17.99 (978-1-439-02351-1). Katniss has survived the Hunger Games and is now being asked to serve as a kind of poster girl for the rebels hoping to oust the evil President Snow. ∩ **e** Lexile 800L (Rev: BLO 8/10*; HB 11–12/10; SLJ 10/1/10)

2823 Collodi, Carlo. *The Adventures of Pinocchio. Rev. ed.* (4–10). Trans. from Italian by M. A. Murray. Illus. by Roberta Innocenti. 2005, Creative Editions $19.95

(978-1-56846-190-8). Nineteenth-century European landscapes provide the backdrop for this appealing retelling of the classic story about the puppet that longed to become a little boy; a revision of the 1988 edition. (Rev: SLJ 12/05)

2824 Conly, Jane Leslie. *Racso and the Rats of NIMH* (5–7). Illus. by Leonard Lubin. 1986, HarperCollins LB $17.89 (978-0-06-021362-6). This sequel to the Newbery Medal winner involves once again the smart rodents who wish to live in peace in Thorn Valley. (Rev: BCCB 6/86; BL 6/1/86; SLJ 4/86)

2825 Constable, Kate. *The Singer of All Songs* (7–10). Series: Chanters of Tremaris. 2004, Scholastic $16.95 (978-0-439-55478-7). In this impressive fantasy, Calwyn, a novice priestess, is able to control all things cold and uses this power to fight an evil sorcerer. (Rev: BL 2/1/04*; SLJ 4/04; VOYA 4/04)

2826 Constable, Kate. *The Tenth Power* (7–10). Series: Chanters of Tremaris. 2006, Scholastic $16.99 (978-0-439-55482-4). Mourning the loss of her nine powers of chantment, 18-year-old Calwyn returns to Antaris to discover she must go in search of the key to the mysterious tenth, healing, power. (Rev: BL 3/15/06; SLJ 3/06)

2827 Constable, Kate. *The Waterless Sea* (8–11). Series: Chanters of Tremaris. 2005, Scholastic $16.95 (978-0-439-55480-0). In the second volume of the trilogy, Calwyn and her friends travel to the desolate Merithuran Empire on a mission to rescue some children with magical powers. (Rev: BL 5/15/05; SLJ 8/05; VOYA 8/05)

2828 Coombs, Kate. *The Runaway Dragon* (5–8). 2009, Farrar $16.99 (978-0-374-36361-1). With powerful friends in tow, 16-year-old Princess Meg courageously pursues her dragon, Laddy, through the far reaches of an enchanted forest while dodging the evil witch Malison in this sequel to *The Runaway Princess* (2006). **e** Lexile 780L (Rev: BL 9/1/09; HB 9–10/09; SLJ 9/09)

2829 Cooney, Caroline B. *Prisoner of Time* (6–10). Series: Time Travel. 1998, Laurel Leaf paper $5.50 (978-0-440-22019-0). In this conclusion to the trilogy, there is again a contrast between the lifestyles of today and those of 100 years ago as a girl is rescued from an unsuitable marriage. (Rev: BL 6/1–15/98; HBG 3/02; SLJ 5/98; VOYA 6/98)

2830 Cooper, Susan. *Green Boy* (4–8). 2002, Simon & Schuster $16.00 (978-0-689-84751-6). Two young boys discover a futuristic world in which natural resources are depleted and a war to save the environment is being waged. (Rev: BCCB 5/02; BL 3/1/02; HB 5–6/02; HBG 10/02; SLJ 2/02)

2831 Cooper, Susan. *King of Shadows* (5–8). Illus. by John Clapp. 1999, Simon & Schuster $16.00 (978-0-689-82817-1). Nat Field time-travels to 1599 London and assumes the child-actor role of Puck in *A Midsummer Night's Dream*. (Rev: BL 10/15/99*; HB 11–12/99; HBG 3/00; SLJ 11/99)

2832 Cooper, Susan. *Over Sea, Under Stone* (6–9). Series: The Dark Is Rising. 1966, Harcourt $18.00 (978-0-15-259034-5). Three contemporary children enter the world of King Arthur in this first volume of a series. Followed by *The Dark Is Rising* (1973), *Greenwitch* (1985), *The Grey King* (1975), and *Silver on the Tree* (1977). Margaret A. Edwards Award 2012.

2833 Cooper, Susan. *Silver on the Tree* (5–7). Series: The Dark Is Rising. 1980, Macmillan $18.00 (978-0-689-50088-6). In this fifth and last volume of a series, Will Stanton and his friends wage a final battle against the Dark, the powers of evil. The first four volumes are *Over Sea, Under Stone* (1966), *The Dark Is Rising* (1973), *The Grey King* (1975), and *Greenwitch* (1985). *The Grey King* won the 1976 Newbery Medal. Margaret A. Edwards Award 2012.

2834 Cooper, Susan. *Victory* (4–7). 2006, Simon & Schuster $16.95 (978-1-4169-1477-8). Homesick Molly finds her fate is intertwined with that of Sam, a child sailor of the 19th century who fought in the Battle of Trafalgar; chapters alternate between the present and the past. (Rev: BL 5/1/06; LMC 11/12/06; SLJ 7/06)

2835 Corder, Zizou. *Lionboy: The Truth* (5–8). 2005, Dial $16.99 (978-0-8037-2985-8). In the final installment in the trilogy, Charlie Ashanti, reunited with his parents in Morocco, is kidnapped by the Corporacy and put on a boat bound for the Caribbean, but the boy wonder calls on his animal friends for help. (Rev: BL 10/1/05; SLJ 9/05; VOYA 12/05)

2836 Cornish, D. M. *Foundling* (7–10). Series: Monster Blood Tattoo. 2006, Penguin $18.99 (978-0-399-24638-8). Rossamund Bookchild, a foundling boy with a girl's name, sets off from the orphanage to his new job as a lamplighter and finds himself in a perilous world (called Half-Continent) full of monsters. (Rev: BL 4/1/06*; SLJ 7/06*)

2837 Cornish, D. M. *Lamplighter* (7–10). Series: Monster Blood Tattoo. 2008, Putnam $19.99 (978-0-399-24639-5). In the second book of the trilogy that began with *Foundling*, Rossamund Bookchild is joined in his lamplighting by Threnody and the two face even more danger. (Rev: BL 4/15/08; SLJ 7/08)

2838 Coville, Bruce. *Goblins in the Castle* (5–7). 1992, Pocket paper $4.99 (978-0-671-72711-6). William, now 11, has grown up in Toad-in-a-Cage Castle and knows many of its secret passages. (Rev: BL 2/1/93)

2839 Coville, Bruce. *Juliet Dove, Queen of Love: A Magic Shop Book* (4–8). 2003, Harcourt $17.00 (978-0-15-204561-6). Life changes for shy Juliet, 12, when she is given an amulet and the boys suddenly come flocking to her side. (Rev: BL 1/1–15/04; HBG 4/04; SLJ 12/03)

2840 Coville, Bruce, ed. *A Glory of Unicorns* (5–8). 1998, Scholastic paper $16.95 (978-0-590-95943-8). A collection of stories by fantasy authors, including the editor and his wife, that deal with unicorns. (Rev: BL 6/1–15/98; HBG 10/98; SLJ 5/98; VOYA 8/98)

2841 Cowell, Cressida. *How to Train Your Dragon: By Hiccup Horrendous Haddock III: Translated from an Old Norse Legend by Cressida Cowell* (4–8). 2004, Little, Brown paper $10.95 (978-0-316-73737-1). The hilarious account of the fumbling efforts of nerdy Hiccup to capture and train a dragon and to take his rightful place as the next Warrior Chief. Also use *How to Be a Pirate: By Hiccup Horrendous Haddock III* (2005). (Rev: BL 4/15/04; SLJ 7/04)

2842 Cox, Judy. *The Mystery of the Burmese Bandicoot: The Tails of Frederick and Ishbu* (4–7). Illus. by Omar Rayyan. Series: The Tails of Frederick and Ishbu. 2007, Marshall Cavendish $16.99 (978-0-7614-5376-5). Rats Frederick and Ishbu escape their schoolroom cage and embark on an adventure that involves a shipwreck and a statue with the power to end the world. (Rev: BL 10/1/07; SLJ 12/07)

2843 Cremer, Andrea. *Nightshade* (7–11). 2010, Philomel $17.99 (978-0-399-25482-6). Werewolves Calla and Ren, both pack leaders, plan to marry, but when Shay, a human, arrives on the scene, Calla falls for him and risks everything. (Rev: BL 8/10; SLJ 12/1/10)

2844 Cremer, Andrea. *Rift* (7–11). Series: Nightshade. 2012, Philomel $18.99 (978-039925613-4). Ember wins her freedom from an arranged marriage when she joins the warrior branch of secret church society Conatus in this standalone prequel set in 1404 and featuring magic and romance. ⌒ e Lexile HL790L (Rev: BL 8/12; SLJ 8/1/12; VOYA 10/12)

2845 Cremer, Andrea. *Rise* (7–11). Series: Nightshade. 2013, Philomel $18.99 (978-039915960-2). In this second prequel, a followup to 2012's *Rift*, 16-year-old Ember must appease former boyfriend Alistair while working with the handsome Barrow to escape supernatural forces. e (Rev: BL 12/15/12; VOYA 4/13)

2846 Crew, Gary. *The Viewer* (5–9). Illus. by Shaun Tan. 2003, Lothian $16.95 (978-0-85091-828-1). A well-illustrated dark fantasy linked to world catastrophes caused by mankind, from religious persecution to atomic war. (Rev: SLJ 3/04)

2847 Crilley, Paul. *Rise of the Darklings* (5–8). Series: The Invisible Order. 2010, Egmont $16.99 (978-160684031-3); LB $19.99 (978-160684064-1). A fast-paced, multilayered fantasy in which 12-year-old Emily Snow — used to selling watercress on the streets of Victorian London — finds herself in the middle of an ancient war. ⌒ Lexile 650L (Rev: BLO 5/15/10; LMC 1–2/11; SLJ 10/1/10)

2848 Croggon, Alison. *The Crow: The Third Book of Pellinor* (7–10). Series: Pellinor. 2007, Candlewick $18.99 (978-0-7636-3409-4). Hem becomes a warrior in the fight against the Nameless One and goes in search of kidnapped Zelika in this third installment in the series. (Rev: BL 2/1/08; SLJ 2/08)

2849 Croggon, Alison. *The Naming* (7–10). 2005, Candlewick $17.99 (978-0-7636-2639-6). The life of 16-year-old Maerad, a slave, changes dramatically after she meets Cadvan, who tells her of her epic destiny. (Rev: BCCB 9/05; BL 5/1/05; SLJ 10/05*; VOYA 8/05)

2850 Croggon, Alison. *The Riddle: The Second Book of Pellinor* (7–10). Series: Pellinor. 2006, Candlewick $17.99 (978-0-7636-3015-7). In this second installment in the series, Maerad continues on her quest to find the Treesong, battling the Nameless One along the way, and discovering more about herself and her powers. (Rev: BL 11/1/06; LMC 4/07; SLJ 1/07)

2851 Croggon, Alison. *The Singing* (7–12). Series: Pellinor. 2009, Candlewick $19.99 (978-076363665-4). Maerad and her brother Hem combine their powers to retrieve the Treesong and conquer evil in this compelling final installment in the quartet. ⌐ e Lexile 900L (Rev: BL 3/1/09; SLJ 5/1/09)

2852 Cross, Gillian. *The Nightmare Game* (6–9). Series: Dark Ground. 2007, Dutton $18.99 (978-0-525-47923-9). The final volume in the trilogy is a multilayered blend of fantasy and mystery in which Robert and friends discover a frightening connection between their own world and the parallel underground world. (Rev: BL 1/1–15/08; LMC 1–2/08; SLJ 12/07)

2853 Cross, Gillian. *Pictures in the Dark* (5–8). 1996, Holiday $16.95 (978-0-8234-1267-9). A boy whose life is miserable uses supernatural means to escape the pressures. (Rev: BCCB 1/97; BL 1/1–15/97)

2854 Cross, Sarah. *Dull Boy* (7–10). 2009, Dutton $16.99 (978-052542133-7). Avery discovers he has superpowers and that there are others like him. Will they use their abilities for good or evil? Lexile 770L (Rev: BLO 4/14/09; SLJ 8/09)

2855 Crossley-Holland, Kevin. *King of the Middle March* (6–9). 2004, Scholastic $17.95 (978-0-439-26600-0). In the final volume of the trilogy that started with *The Seeing Stone* (2001), 16-year-old Arthur de Caldicot watches the disintegration of King Arthur's court in his seeing stone as he waits in Venice for the start of the Fourth Crusade. (Rev: BL 9/1/04*; SLJ 11/04)

2856 Curley, Marianne. *The Named* (7–11). 2002, Bloomsbury $16.95 (978-1-58234-779-0). Ethan and Isabel time-travel through history on a difficult quest in this first volume of a multilayered trilogy recounting the battle against the Order of Chaos. (Rev: BL 11/15/02; SLJ 1/03)

2857 Curry, Jane Louise. *The Black Canary* (5–8). 2005, Simon & Schuster $16.95 (978-0-689-86478-0). Twelve-year-old James, from a biracial family of musicians, resists pressure to develop his own musical abili-

ties until he travels back in time to Elizabethan London and discovers he is also talented. (Rev: BL 2/15/05*; SLJ 3/05)

2858 Cypess, Leah. *Mistwood* (6–9). 2010, HarperCollins $16.99 (978-0-06-195699-7). Though she has no memory of her past as a shape-shifter, Isabel is conscripted once again to use her powers to protect the royal family by the new prince, Rokan. (Rev: BL 4/1/10; SLJ 5/10; VOYA 6/10)

2859 D'Lacey, Chris. *Fire Star* (7–12). Series: The Dragon Trilogy. 2007, Scholastic $15.99 (978-0-439-84582-3). David Rain faces a major dragon challenge in this conclusion to the trilogy; readers familiar with the earlier books will enjoy this most. (Rev: SLJ 4/07)

2860 D'Lacey, Chris. *The Fire Within* (5–8). 2005, Scholastic $12.95 (978-0-439-67343-3). A multilayered fantasy in which British college student David Rain comes to board at the home of Liz Pennykettle and her daughter, Lucy, and discovers that the clay dragons crafted by Liz have magical properties. (Rev: SLJ 10/05)

2861 D'Lacey, Chris. *Icefire* (7–12). Series: The Dragon Trilogy. 2006, Scholastic $14.99 (978-0-439-67245-0). In this action-packed sequel to *The Fire Within* (2005), David researches dragons for an essay that might win him a trip to the Arctic. (Rev: SLJ 11/06)

2862 Dadey, Debbie, and Marcia T. Jones. *Leprechauns Don't Play Basketball* (5–8). Illus. by John S. Gurney. 1992, Scholastic paper $3.99 (978-0-590-44822-2). The Bailey Elementary 3rd grade thinks the gym teacher is a leprechaun. (Rev: BL 9/15/92)

2863 Dakin, Glenn. *The Society of Unrelenting Vigilance* (5–7). Series: Candle Man. 2009, Egmont $15.99 (978-1-60684-015-3); LB $18.99 (978-1-60684-047-4). Young Theo discovers he has the ability to melt people into puddles in this contemporary fast-paced adventure story with a Victorian feel. (Rev: BL 10/15/09; HB 1–2/10; LMC 11–12/09; SLJ 10/09)

2864 Datlow, Ellen, and Terri Windling, eds. *Swan Sister: Fairy Tales Retold* (5–10). 2003, Simon & Schuster $16.95 (978-0-689-84613-7). Retellings by well-known authors of traditional stories are inventive and entertaining. (Rev: BCCB 11/03; BL 9/15/03; HBG 4/04; SLJ 12/03)

2865 Datlow, Ellen, and Terri Windling, eds. *Troll's-Eye View: A Book of Villainous Tales* (5–8). 2009, Viking $16.99 (978-0-670-06141-9). The villains in fairy tales get a chance to tell their stories in this collection of varied, original tales and poems by authors including Neil Gaiman, Garth Nix, and Jane Yolen. ALA Notable Books 2010. (Rev: BCCB 7–8/09; BL 3/1/09; LMC 8–9/09; SLJ 4/09)

2866 Davidson, Jenny. *The Explosionist* (8–12). 2008, HarperTeen $17.99 (978-0-06-123975-5); LB $18.89 (978-0-06-123976-2). Set in 1938 in an alternate Scotland (Napoleon won at Waterloo and spiritualists work with scientists), this is the story of Sophie, a 15-year-old girl whose message from a psychic medium sends her into a political firestorm. ℮ Lexile 1010L (Rev: SLJ 10/1/08)

2867 Davies, Jocelyn. *A Fractured Light* (8–11). Series: Beautiful Dark Trilogy. 2012, HarperTeen $17.99 (978-006199067-0). Skye faces difficult decisions — to join the Rebellion with Asher or to try to redeem Devin, who betrayed her — in this turbulent sequel to 2011's *A Beautiful Dark.* ℮ (Rev: BLO 11/1/12; SLJ 1/13)

2868 Davis, Bryan. *Starlighter* (7–10). Series: Dragons of Starlight. 2010, Zondervan paper $9.99 (978-03107183-6-9). When Jason's brothers disappear, he's forced to believe in the sinister dragons he always doubted, and he ventures into a mysterious realm where he meets Koren, a slave struggling to save mankind; the first installment in a series. ℮ (Rev: BL 5/15/10; VOYA 8/10)

2869 de Alcantara, Pedro. *Backtracked* (8–11). 2009, Delacorte $15.99 (978-038573419-6); LB $18.99 (978-038590433-9). Tommy, a teenage drifter, travels through time while staying in New York City, experiencing the flu epidemic of 1918, the Depression, and World War II. ℮ Lexile HL570L (Rev: BL 1/1–15/09; SLJ 6/1/09)

2870 de Lint, Charles. *Dingo* (7–10). 2008, Penguin $11.99 (978-0-14-240816-2). Miguel falls in love with a girl who happens to be an Aboriginal shape-shifter and who, along with her twin, is in danger and needs Miguel's help. (Rev: BL 5/15/08; SLJ 8/08)

2871 de Lint, Charles. *Little (Grrl) Lost* (7–10). 2007, Viking $17.99 (978-0-670-06144-0). T.J., 14, misses her old friends and her horse after her family moves to the suburbs, but then she meets and befriends Elizabeth, a 16-year-old "Little" who is only 6 inches high but has an oversized personality. (Rev: BL 8/07; SLJ 11/07)

2872 de Lint, Charles. *The Painted Boy* (7–12). 2010, Viking $18.99 (978-0-670-01191-9). Now a member of the Yellow Dragon Clan, part-dragon high-schooler Jay Li finds an Arizona barrio where he can do good work. (Rev: BL 12/1/10; SLJ 12/1/10)

2873 De Mari, Silvana. *The Last Dragon* (5–8). Trans. by Shaun Whiteside. 2006, Hyperion $16.95 (978-0-7868-3636-9). To fulfill a prophecy in which he will play a key role, a young elf named Yorsh, the last of his kind in a world hostile to elves, sets off in search of the last dragon. (Rev: BL 11/1/06; SLJ 1/07)

2874 De Quidt, Jeremy. *The Toymaker* (5–8). 2010, Random House $16.99 (978-0-385-75180-3). Orphaned young Mathias finds a piece of paper that holds a valuable secret and must elude his various pursuers in this eerie adventure. ℮ Lexile 710L (Rev: BL 7/10*; HB 9–10/10; LMC 11–12/10; SLJ 10/1/10)

2875 de Saint-Exupéry, Antoine. *The Little Prince* (4–8). Trans. from French by Richard Howard. Illus. by author.

2009, Houghton Mifflin $35 (978-0-547-26069-3). This effective pop-up presentation will attract new readers to the classic story. (Rev: BL 12/15/09; SLJ 3/10)

2876 Dekker, Ted. *Chosen* (7–10). Series: The Lost Books. 2008, Thomas Nelson $12.99 (978-1-59554-359-2). A football game is used to choose four new forest guards who must find the seven lost Books of History. (Rev: BL 3/15/08)

2877 Del Vecchio, Gene. *The Pearl of Anton* (7–10). 2004, Pelican $16.95 (978-1-58980-172-1). In this complex, gripping fantasy, Jason inherits the Wizard's Stone when he turns 15, but the stone's powers cannot be realized until it is joined with the Pearl of Anton, which is hidden in a mountain cave and guarded by two fearsome beasts. (Rev: BL 6/1–15/04*; VOYA 10/04)

2878 Delany, Shannon. *Bargains and Betrayals* (7–10). Series: 13 to Life. 2011, St. Martin's paper $9.99 (978-03126091-6-0). Jessica struggles to maintain her equilibrium while locked away in a mental facility while Pietr makes an ill-advised agreement with the Russian mafia; for readers who have read the first two installments in the series. ℮ (Rev: BL 7/11)

2879 Delany, Shannon. *13 to Life* (7–10). Series: 13 to Life. 2010, St. Martin's paper $9.99 (978-0-312-60914-6). High school junior Jessica is still dealing with her mother's death in a car accident when strange events start happening in her town and she finds herself drawn to Pietr, the new guy at school, with whom she seems to share some kind of connection. ℮ (Rev: BL 6/10; SLJ 10/1/10)

2880 Deming, Sarah. *Iris, Messenger* (5–8). 2007, Harcourt $16.00 (978-0-15-205823-4). Iris is a miserable outcast whose life takes a turn for the better when the mythology book she gets for her birthday leads her to an amazing discovery. (Rev: SLJ 7/07)

2881 Derting, Kimberly. *The Pledge* (7–10). 2011, Simon & Schuster $16.99 (978-144242201-8). In a world where languages separate classes, 17-year-old Charlie learns that her linguistic abilities may be invaluable — and dangerous. (Rev: BL 12/1/11; SLJ 2/12)

2882 DeVita, James. *The Silenced* (8–12). 2007, HarperCollins $17.99 (978-0-06-078462-1). Under the new Zero Tolerance government, Marina attends a Youth Training Facility where she is educated under strict regulations but follows her heart and starts a resistance movement named the White Rose. (Rev: BL 6/1–15/07; SLJ 9/07)

2883 Diamand, Emily. *Raiders' Ransom* (4–8). 2009, Scholastic $17.99 (978-0-545-14297-7). In the early 23rd century, when global warming has put much of Great Britain underwater and at risk from attack by marauding Raiders, 13-year-olds Lilly and Zeph are from opposing tribes but must join forces to rescue the kidnapped daughter of the prime minister. ⌒ Lexile 720L (Rev: BL 12/1/09; LMC 11–12/09; SLJ 12/09)

2884 DiCamillo, Kate. *The Magician's Elephant* (4–7). Illus. by Yoko Tanaka. 2009, Candlewick $16.99 (978-0-7636-4410-9). Young orphan Peter Augustus Duchene learns from a fortune-teller that his younger sister Adele is still alive and sets off, with an elephant, to find her, facing many challenges along the way. ALA Notable Books 2010. (Rev: BCCB 11/09; BL 7/09*; HB 9/09; SLJ 8/09*; VOYA 8/09)

2885 Dickinson, Peter. *Angel Isle* (7–10). 2007, Random House $17.99 (978-0-385-74690-8). Maja and her companions make an arduous journey to find the Ropemaker so he can use his magic to defy the Watchers; a sequel to *The Ropemaker* (2001). (Rev: BL 10/15/07; HB 11–12/07; LMC 1/08; SLJ 11/07)

2886 DiTerlizzi, Tony. *A Hero for WondLa* (5–8). Illus. by author. 2012, Simon & Schuster $17.99 (978-141698312-5). Eva Nine, 12, who was raised underground by a robot, finds her way to New Attica, a seeming utopia; but she soon discovers a sinister underbelly. ⌂ ℮ (Rev: BL 3/15/12; SLJ 6/12; VOYA 6/12)

2887 DiTocco, Robyn, and Tony DiTocco. *Atlas' Revenge: Another Mad Myth Mystery* (7–12). 2005, Brainstorm $19.95 (978-0-9723429-2-6); paper $11.95 (978-0-9723429-3-3). PJ Allen, a carefree college senior, is called upon to travel to the world of mythology to complete the legendary Twelve Labors of Hercules and solve a cryptic riddle in this fast-paced novel full of legendary characters and literary references. (Rev: SLJ 6/05)

2888 Divakaruni, Chitra Banerjee. *The Mirror of Fire and Dreaming* (5–8). 2005, Roaring Brook $16.95 (978-1-59643-067-9). In this sequel to *The Conch Bearer* (2003), 12-year-old Anand continues his magic studies and travels back to Moghul times, where he encounters powerful sorcerers and evil jinns. (Rev: BL 9/1/05; SLJ 12/05)

2889 Dixon, Heather. *Entwined* (7–10). 2011, Greenwillow $17.99 (978-0-06-200103-0). In this dark version of a Grimm tale, Princess Azalea and her eleven sisters dance all night despite their mother's death, able to do so through the Keeper, whose intentions may not be kindly. ⌂ ℮ Lexile 740L (Rev: BL 2/1/11*; HB 5–6/11; SLJ 5/11; VOYA 4/11)

2890 Dolamore, Jaclyn. *Magic Under Glass* (7–10). 2010, Bloomsbury $16.99 (978-1-59990-430-6). Seventeen-year-old Nimira discovers that an automaton is in fact a trapped fairy prince and sets out to rescue him from the handsome sorcerer Hollin Parry. ℮ Lexile HL680L (Rev: BL 10/15/09*; LMC 3–4/10; SLJ 3/10)

2891 Dowell, Frances O'Roark. *Falling In* (4–7). 2010, Simon & Schuster $16.99 (978-1-4169-5032-5). Middle-schooler Isabelle Bean suddenly finds herself in an alternate world in which a frightening witch might be her grandmother Grete. ⌂ ℮ Lexile 850L (Rev: BL 1/1/10*; LMC 5–6/10; SLJ 4/10)

2892 Downer, Ann. *The Dragon of Never-Was* (4–7). Illus. by Omar Ryyan. 2006, Simon & Schuster $16.95 (978-0-689-85571-9). In this lively sequel to *Hatching Magic* (2003), 12-year-old Theodora Oglethorpe accompanies her father to Scotland to investigate the origin of a mysterious scale and there learns more about her own magical powers. (Rev: BL 6/1–15/06; SLJ 12/06)

2893 Downer, Ann. *Hatching Magic* (4–7). Illus. by Omar Rayyan. 2003, Simon & Schuster $16.95 (978-0-689-83400-4). A procession of a pet dragon, a wizard, and his archenemy travel through time from the 13th century to the 21st century, where an 11-year-old Bostonian becomes involved in their disputes. (Rev: BL 4/15/03; HB 7–8/03; HBG 10/03; SLJ 8/03)

2894 Doyle, Marissa. *Bewitching Season* (7–10). 2008, Henry Holt $16.95 (978-0-8050-8251-7). Set during the reign of Queen Victoria, this novel about twins Persephone and Penelope as they ready for their London debut combines historical romance with mystery and a touch of fantasy. (Rev: BL 1/1–15/08; LMC 11–12/08; SLJ 3/08)

2895 *Dr. Ernest Drake's Dragonology: The Complete Book of Dragons* (5–12). 2003, Candlewick $18.99 (978-0-7636-2329-6). Presented as the recently discovered research of a 19th-century scientist, this richly illustrated volume presents a very realistic encyclopedia of dragon facts and figures. (Rev: BL 4/15/04; SLJ 4/04)

2896 Drago, Ty. *The Undertakers: Rise of the Corpses* (4–7). 2011, Sourcebooks paper $10.99 (978-1-4022-4-785-9). Gifted with the ability to see zombies, 12-year-old Will joins the Undertakers, a group determined to thwart the zombies' evil plans. (Rev: BL 5/1/11; SLJ 7/11)

2897 Drexler, Sam, and Fay Shelby. *Lost in Spillville* (5–9). Series: Erika and Oz Adventures in American History. 2000, Aunt Strawberry paper $6.99 (978-0-9669988-1-8). Two teenagers accidentally are transported to the 1930s and must locate an important clock maker to be returned to the 1990s. (Rev: SLJ 11/00; VOYA 12/00)

2898 Druitt, Tobias. *Corydon and the Siege of Troy* (6–9). Series: Corydon Trilogy. 2009, Knopf $15.99 (978-037583384-7); LB $18.99 (978-037593384-4). This final installment in the trilogy continues the story of Corydon Panfoot and his adventures in a world of Greek mythology turned upside-down, with good monsters and evil gods. Lexile 710 (Rev: BL 2/15/09; SLJ 4/1/09; VOYA 4/09)

2899 Duane, Diane. *Deep Wizardry* (5–8). Series: Young Wizards. 2001, Magic Carpet Books LB $15.25 (978-0-613-36059-3); paper $6.95 (978-0-15-216257-3). Nita and Kit, the two young wizards of *So You Want to Be a Wizard*, again use their powers to prevent a great catastrophe. (Rev: HB 5–6/85)

2900 Duane, Diane. *So You Want to Be a Wizard* (5–8). Series: Young Wizards. 2003, Harcourt $16.95 (978-0-15-204738-2); paper $6.95 (978-0-15-216250-4). Nita and friends embark on a journey to retrieve the Book of Night with Moon.

2901 Duane, Diane. *A Wizard Alone* (6–10). Series: Young Wizards. 2002, Harcourt $17.00 (978-0-15-204562-3). The sixth book in the series of Nita and Kit's adventures in magic finds wizard Kit working on his own while Nita mourns the death of her mother. (Rev: BL 11/15/02; HBG 3/03; SLJ 2/03; VOYA 4/03)

2902 Duane, Diane. *Wizard's Holiday* (6–9). Series: Young Wizards. 2003, Harcourt $17.00 (978-0-15-204771-9). Plotlines alternate between teen wizards Nita and Kit's exploits on a distant planet and Nita's little sister and her father, who are hosting alien exchange students, as disaster approaches. (Rev: BL 1/1–15/04; SLJ 12/03)

2903 Duel, John. *Wide Awake in Dreamland* (5–8). 1992, Stargaze $15.95 (978-0-9630923-0-4). An evil warlock threatens to steal a 9-year-old's imagination unless the young boy can find a friendly wizard first. (Rev: BL 3/1/92; SLJ 5/92)

2904 Duey, Kathleen. *Skin Hunger* (7–10). Illus. by Sheila Rayyan. Series: A Resurrection of Magic. 2007, Atheneum $17.99 (978-0-689-84093-7). The story of Sadima, a teenage girl who can communicate with animals, as she lives with magician outlaws; interwoven with the story of Hahp, generations later, as he deals with attending a harsh wizardry school. ∩ (Rev: BL 6/1–15/07; HB 7–8/07; SLJ 11/07)

2905 Dunkle, Clare B. *Close Kin* (6–9). Series: Hollow Kingdom. 2004, Henry Holt $16.95 (978-0-8050-7497-0). In this sequel to *The Hollow Kingdom* (2003), Kate's younger sister Emily realizes the depth of her feelings for Seylin, who has gone in search of his elfin roots, and she sets off to find him. (Rev: BL 10/1/04; SLJ 10/04; VOYA 12/04)

2906 Dunkle, Clare B. *The Hollow Kingdom* (5–8). 2003, Henry Holt $16.95 (978-0-8050-7390-4). A beauty-and-the-beast story with a twist, in which Kate is persuaded to marry a goblin king and move to his underground world. (Rev: BL 11/15/03; HBG 4/04; SLJ 12/03)

2907 Dunkle, Clare B. *In the Coils of the Snake* (7–10). Series: Hollow Kingdom. 2005, Henry Holt $16.95 (978-0-8050-7747-6). When human girl Miranda learns she will not after all marry the new goblin king, she flees from the kingdom; this final volume in the trilogy is set 30 years after *Close Kin* (2004). (Rev: BL 1/1–15/06*; SLJ 10/05; VOYA 10/05)

2908 Dunlop, Eileen. *Websters' Leap* (4–7). 1995, Holiday $15.95 (978-0-8234-1193-1). In this time-slip fantasy, Jill gets involved with people who owned a Scottish castle 400 years before. (Rev: BL 10/1/95; SLJ 10/95)

2909 Dunmore, Helen. *Ingo* (5–8). 2006, HarperCollins $16.99 (978-0-06-081852-4). As they search for their missing father, 11-year-old Sapphire and her brother Conor find themselves torn between their home on England's Cornish coast and the Mer people and magical sea world of Ingo. (Rev: BCCB 10/06; BL 9/1/06; HBG 4/07; SLJ 8/06; VOYA 4/06)

2910 Dunmore, Helen. *The Tide Knot* (5–8). 2008, HarperCollins $16.99 (978-0-06-081855-5). Part-mermaid siblings Sapphire and Conor, introduced in *Ingo* (2006), must save humans from a huge tidal wave. (Rev: BL 1/1–15/08; HB 1/08; SLJ 2/08)

2911 DuPrau, Jeanne. *The City of Ember* (5–7). Series: Books of Ember. 2003, Random House LB $17.99 (978-0-375-92274-9). Lina and Doon work to find a way out of their isolated and decaying city, where the population is beginning to panic. (Rev: BL 4/15/03; HB 5–6/03; HBG 10/03; SLJ 5/03; VOYA 6/03)

2912 DuPrau, Jeanne. *The Diamond of Darkhold* (4–9). Series: Ember. 2008, Random $16.99 (978-0-375-85571-9). Lima and Doon return to Ember to search for a device that may offer hope, and to find food to support the residents of Sparks through the hard winter; the final installment in the series. ∩ (Rev: HB 9/08; SLJ 11/08)

2913 DuPrau, Jeanne. *The People of Sparks* (5–7). Series: Books of Ember. 2004, Random House $15.95 (978-0-375-82824-9). In this sequel to *The City of Ember*, Doon and Lina, plus the 400 people they have led from Ember to the surface of the Earth, seek aid from the people of Sparks. (Rev: BL 4/15/04; HB 7–8/04; SLJ 5/04)

2914 DuPrau, Jeanne. *The Prophet of Yonwood* (4–7). Series: Books of Ember. 2006, Random House $15.95 (978-0-375-87526-7). About 50 years before the time of the Embers series, 11-year-old Nickie hides out at her great-grandfather's estate in Yonwood, North Carolina, and thinks about good and evil as she watches her neighbors react to predictions of doom. ∩ (Rev: BL 5/15/06; SLJ 6/06; VOYA 4/06)

2915 Durst, Sarah Beth. *Enchanted Ivy* (7–12). 2010, Simon & Schuster $16.99 (978-1-4169-8645-4). Sixteen-year-old Lily's special admission test for Princeton University, engineered by her alumnus grandfather, in fact qualifies her to enter a parallel world full of magical creatures. ℮ (Rev: BLO 12/1/10; SLJ 12/1/10)

2916 Durst, Sarah Beth. *Ice* (7–10). 2009, Simon & Schuster $16.99 (978-1-4169-8643-0). The daughter of a scientist who studies polar bears in the Arctic, Cassie was raised believing that her mother was taken away by trolls; consequently, she agrees to marry the Polar Bear King if he will return her mother to her in this romantic fantasy. **e** (Rev: BL 9/1/09; LMC 11–12/09; SLJ 12/09)

2917 Durst, Sarah Beth. *Into the Wild* (6–9). 2007, Penguin $15.99 (978-1-59514-156-9). Rapunzel and her 12-year-old daughter Julie have escaped the enchanted forest known as the Wild and are trying to lead normal lives; but now the Wild is loose and Julie must rescue others before they become trapped in fairy tales. (Rev: BL 6/1–15/07; LMC 11/07; SLJ 9/07)

2918 Durst, Sarah Beth. *Vessel* (7–12). 2012, Simon & Schuster $16.99 (978-1-4424-2376-3). Sacrificial Liyana is abandoned by her clan when the goddess Bayla fails to take possession of her body, and she then finds herself facing new challenges in this exciting combination of fantasy, adventure, and romance. **e** Lexile HL630L (Rev: BL 10/1/12*; LMC 1–2/13; SLJ 12/12)

2919 Eaton, Jason Carter. *The Facttracker* (4–7). Illus. by Pascale Constantin. 2008, HarperCollins $15.99 (978-0-06-056434-6). The library turns into the "liebrary" when the town of Traäkerfaxx decides to deal in lies rather than facts in this imaginative and clever story. (Rev: BL 1/1–15/08; SLJ 3/08)

2920 Ebbitt, Carolyn Q. *The Extra-Ordinary Princess* (5–8). 2009, Bloomsbury $16.99 (978-1-59990-340-8). A younger, overlooked princess is thrust into the spotlight when an evil uncle tries to take over Gossling, leaving her to rescue her older siblings and save the kingdom. (Rev: BL 5/15/09; LMC 1–2/10; SLJ 9/09)

2921 Elliott, Zetta. *Ship of Souls* (6–9). 2012, AmazonEncore paper $9.95 (978-16121826-8-1). An urban fantasy in which 11-year-old African American D and his friends come across a magical bird, Nuru, that seeks help freeing the trapped souls in Manhattan's African Burial Ground. ∩ **e** (Rev: BL 2/15/12*; HB 7–8/12; SLJ 5/1/12)

2922 Ellis, Helen. *What Curiosity Kills* (8–11). Series: The Turning. 2010, Sourcebooks $14.99 (978-1-4022-3861-1). As 16-year-old Mary gradually turns into a cat she discovers that there are many cat people out at night and battles are looming between the domestic cats and the strays of New York City. **e** Lexile HL700L (Rev: BL 5/15/10; LMC 10/10)

2923 Else, Barbara. *The Traveling Restaurant: Jasper's Voyage in Three Parts* (4–7). 2012, Gecko $17.95 (978-187757903-5). When the powerful Lady Gall sets Jasper's family in her sights, the 12-year-old sets off on an epic search involving aspects of fantasy, time travel, mystery, and seafaring. (Rev: BLO 4/1/12; HB 5–6/12; SLJ 3/12)

2924 Ende, Michael. *The Neverending Story* (7–12). Trans. by Ralph Manheim. 1984, Penguin paper $15.00 (978-0-14-007431-4). An overweight boy with many problems enters the magic world of Fantastica in this charming fantasy.

2925 Estep, Jennifer. *Dark Frost* (7–10). Series: Mythos Academy. 2012, Kensington paper $9.95 (978-07582669-6-5). High school sophomore Gwen is on a mission to find the Helheim dagger and prevent Loki from unleashing havoc in this action-packed story with elements of romance and mythology. (Rev: BL 8/12)

2926 Etchemendy, Nancy. *The Power of Un* (4–7). 2000, Front St $14.95 (978-0-8126-2850-0). Gib, a young boy, meets a strange old man who gives him an "unner," which can send him back in time in this thought-provoking fantasy. (Rev: BCCB 7–8/00; BL 5/1/00; HBG 10/00; SLJ 6/00; VOYA 6/00)

2927 Ewing, Lynne. *Barbarian* (8–12). Series: Sons of the Dark. 2004, Hyperion $9.99 (978-0-7868-1811-2). Four gorgeous and immortal teens with magical powers escape slavery in the parallel universe of Nefandus and must deal with life in modern Los Angeles before fulfilling their destinies. (Rev: SLJ 10/04; VOYA 2/05)

2928 Ewing, Lynne. *Into the Cold Fire* (7–12). Series: Daughters of the Moon. 2000, Hyperion LB $9.99 (978-0-7868-0654-6). In this latest light-hearted tale about four Los Angeles girls with extraordinary powers, Serena is faced with a difficult choice: to succumb to the dark and seductive power of the Atrox or to remain loyal to her sister goddesses. (Rev: HBG 3/01; VOYA 6/01)

2929 Fagan, Deva. *The Magical Misadventures of Prunella Bogthistle* (4–8). 2010, Henry Holt $16.99 (978-0-8050-8743-7). Prunella isn't very successful as a witch, but during her quest to find the Mirable Chalice, she finds that she has other talents; plenty of details about life as a witch make this an entertaining read. Lexile 640L (Rev: LMC 8–9/10; SLJ 6/10; VOYA 6/10)

2930 Falls, Kat. *Rip Tide* (6–9). 2011, Scholastic $16.99 (978-0-545-17843-3). Ty and Gemma discover an entire submerged township filled with dead bodies in this compelling sequel to *Dark Life* (2010). ∩ **e** Lexile 780L (Rev: BL 9/1/11; SLJ 9/1/11; VOYA 8/11)

2931 Fantaskey, Beth. *Jessica's Guide to Dating on the Dark Side* (8–12). 2009, Harcourt $17.00 (978-015206384-9). Jessica learns she is a vampire princess when the Romanian boy to whom she was betrothed at birth shows up at her high school. ∩ **e** Lexile 700L (Rev: BL 3/1/09; SLJ 3/1/09; VOYA 6/09)

2932 Farjeon, Eleanor. *The Glass Slipper* (6–9). 1986, HarperCollins LB $11.89 (978-0-397-32181-0). A romantic retelling in prose of the Cinderella story. (Rev: BL 10/15/86)

2933 Farland, David. *Of Mice and Magic* (5–8). Illus. by Howard Lyon. Series: Ravenspell. 2005, Covenant Communications $16.95 (978-1-57734-918-1). Ben's magical mouse Amber turns Ben into a mouse and together the two set out to rescue the animals from the pet store. (Rev: SLJ 1/06)

2934 Farley, Terri. *Seven Tears into the Sea* (7–10). 2005, Simon & Schuster paper $6.99 (978-0-689-86442-1). Working at her clairvoyant grandmother's seaside inn for the summer, 17-year-old Gwen becomes attracted to Jesse, a strange boy with secrets. (Rev: BCCB 4/05; BL 4/1/05; SLJ 6/05; VOYA 6/05)

2935 Farmer, Nancy. *The Islands of the Blessed* (6–9). Series: Sea of Trolls Trilogy. 2009, Simon & Schuster $18.99 (978-1-4169-0737-4). In the conclusion to this fantasy trilogy, 14-year-old Jack faces challenges and adventures aplenty with his sidekick Thorgill, and arrives at a heightened understanding of his past and himself. ℮ Lexile 730L (Rev: BL 8/09*; HB 9–10/09; SLJ 10/09; VOYA 12/09)

2936 Farmer, Nancy. *The Land of the Silver Apples* (6–9). 2007, Atheneum $18.99 (978-1-4169-0735-0). In this sequel to *The Sea of Trolls* (2004), young poet Jack is faced with new revelations about his sister Lucy as he travels underground to the Land of the Silver Apples. (Rev: BL 8/07; HB 7–8/07; LMC 11/07; SLJ 8/07)

2937 Farmer, Nancy. *The Sea of Trolls* (6–9). 2004, Atheneum $17.95 (978-0-689-86744-6). In this thrill-packed Viking fantasy, 11-year-old Jack must embark on a dangerous quest into troll country to save his little sister's life. (Rev: BL 11/1/04; SLJ 10/04)

2938 Farrey, Brian. *The Vengekeep Prophecies* (4–7). Illus. by Brett Helquist. 2012, HarperCollins $16.99 (978-006204928-5). The Grimjink, a family of thieves in a medieval world, will prove to be saviors of the city of Vengekeep according to a prophecy woven into a tapestry. ℮ Lexile 780L (Rev: BL 12/1/12; SLJ 3/13)

2939 Favole, Robert J. *Through the Wormhole* (5–8). 2001, Flywheel $17.95 (978-1-930826-00-7). Detailed endnotes add historical weight to this story of Michael and Kate, who travel through time to 1778 to aid the Marquis de Lafayette and rescue one of Michael's ancestors. (Rev: BL 3/1/01; SLJ 4/01; VOYA 4/01)

2940 Federici, Debbie, and Susan Vaught. *L.O.S.T* (8–12). 2004, Llewellyn paper $9.95 (978-0-7387-0561-3). Fantasy and romance are intertwined in this fast-paced story about 17-year-old Bren, who is kidnapped by Jazz, 16-year-old Queen of the Witches, because she believes he is the long-prophesied Shadowalker. (Rev: SLJ 1/05)

2941 Fforde, Jasper. *The Last Dragonslayer* (7–10). Series: Chronicles of Kazam. 2012, Harcourt $16.99 (978-0-547-73847-5). Mystic retirement home manager Jennifer, 15, learns she's the last living dragonslayer in this captivating start to a series. (Rev: BL 8/12; SLJ 11/12*)

2942 Fienberg, Anna. *The Witch in the Lake* (5–8). 2002, Annick LB $18.95 (978-1-55037-723-1); paper $7.95 (978-1-55037-722-4). This story of magic and suspense in 16th-century Italy interweaves fantasy with facts about the time. (Rev: HBG 3/03; SLJ 8/02; VOYA 8/02)

2943 Findon, Joanne. *When Night Eats the Moon* (4–7). 2000, Red Deer paper $7.95 (978-0-88995-212-6). Her flute music and some magic take Holly, a Canadian girl visiting England, back to prehistoric times at Stonehenge when the locals are being threatened with a Celtic invasion. (Rev: BL 8/00; VOYA 6/00)

2944 Finnin, Ann. *The Sorcerer of Sainte Felice* (7–10). 2010, Flux paper $9.95 (978-0-73872070-8.). Rescued from the stake by a Benedictine abbot, 15-year-old Michael de Lorraine becomes a wizard's apprentice in this novel set in turbulent 15th-century France. ℮ (Rev: BL 6/10; LMC 10/10; SLJ 9/1/10; VOYA 6/10)

2945 Fisher, Catherine. *The Dark City* (8–11). Series: Relic Master. 2011, Dial $16.99 (978-0-8037-3673-3). Raffi, 16, travels with injured relic master Galen to the ruined city of Tasceron in search of an artifact that may save the world. ℮ Lexile HL540L (Rev: BL 5/1/11; SLJ 7/11)

2946 Fisher, Catherine. *Day of the Scarab* (6–9). Series: Oracle Prophecies. 2006, Greenwillow $16.99 (978-0-06-057163-4). The final volume of the complex trilogy set in an imaginary classical world. (Rev: BL 5/15/06; HB 5–6/06; SLJ 7/06)

2947 Fisher, Catherine. *Incarceron* (8–12). 2010, Dial $17.99 (978-0-803-73396-1). In a future world, the daughter of the warden of a prison called Incarceron joins forces with an escaping prisoner in a tense adventure. ∩ ℮ Lexile HL600L (Rev: BL 1/1–15/10*; HB 1–2/10*; LMC 1–2/10; SLJ 2/10)

2948 Fisher, Catherine. *The Oracle Betrayed* (5–8). 2004, Greenwillow $16.99 (978-0-06-057157-3). This suspenseful story set in an imaginary country that combines aspects of ancient Greece and ancient Egypt involves a young heroine, Mirany, on a dangerous quest. (Rev: BL 2/15/04; HB 3–4/04; SLJ 3/04; VOYA 4/04)

2949 Fisher, Catherine. *Snow-Walker* (6–9). 2004, HarperCollins $17.99 (978-0-06-072474-0). Gudrun, an evil witch and the title character of this fantasy novel that draws on Norse and Celtic legends, faces a stiff challenge from the people of Jarshold as they fight to oust her and restore the rightful rulers to the throne. (Rev: BL 9/1/04; SLJ 11/04)

2950 Fisher, Catherine. *The Sphere of Secrets* (5–8). Series: Oracle Prophecies Trilogy. 2005, Greenwillow LB $18.89 (978-0-06-057162-7). Alexos, introduced in *The Oracle Betrayed* (2004), embarks on a journey to the Well of Songs while his friend Mirany serves the Oracle. (Rev: BL 3/15/05; SLJ 3/05)

2951 Flanagan, John. *The Battle for Skandia* (4–7). Series: Ranger's Apprentice. 2008, Philomel $16.99 (978-0-399-24457-5). In book four of the series, Will is saved from death by Halt and Horace, Evanlyn is captured, and the Temujai army closes in. (Rev: BL 4/1/08)

2952 Flanagan, John. *The Burning Bridge* (5–8). Series: Ranger's Apprentice. 2006, Philomel $16.99 (978-0-399-24455-1). Will and his friend Horace again face war and find the safety of the kingdom depends on them. (Rev: BL 5/15/06; SLJ 8/06)

2953 Flanagan, John. *Halt's Peril* (5–8). Series: Ranger's Apprentice. 2010, Philomel $17.99 (978-039925207-5). In this ninth installment in the series, Will and Horace defy danger and save Halt by trusting each other and working together. ∩ e Lexile 800L (Rev: BL 9/15/10)

2954 Flanagan, John. *The Hunters* (4–8). Series: Brotherband Chronicles. 2012, Philomel $18.99 (978-039925621-9). In this sequel to 2012's *The Invaders*, Hal realizes he must engage in a one-on-one fight in order to defeat the villainous Zavac. ∩ e Lexile 780L (Rev: BL 10/15/12)

2955 Flanagan, John. *The Icebound Land* (4–7). Series: Ranger's Apprentice. 2007, Philomel $16.99 (978-0-399-24456-8). Will, the ranger's apprentice, and Princess Evanlyn are captives on a ship that takes them to Skandia to work as slaves; while the ranger Halt and knight-in-training Horace journey to rescue them but face many obstacles. (Rev: BL 6/1–15/07; SLJ 8/07)

2956 Flanagan, John. *The Kings of Clonmel* (5–8). Series: Ranger's Apprentice. 2010, Philomel $17.99 (978-039925206-8). Halt, Will, and Horace work against a cult religion called the Outsiders and they discover secrets from Halt's past in this eighth installment in the series. ∩ Lexile 830L (Rev: BLO 6/10; VOYA 6/10)

2957 Flanagan, John. *The Lost Stories* (5–8). Series: Ranger's Apprentice. 2011, Philomel $17.99 (978-039925618-9). A collection of nine stories that give the back story to the Ranger's Apprentice series. ∩ e (Rev: BL 11/15/11; SLJ 4/12)

2958 Flanagan, John. *The Outcasts* (5–9). Series: Brotherband Chronicles. 2011, Philomel $18.99 (978-039925619-6). In an alternate Scandinavia called Skandia outcasts Hal, Stig, and other 16-year-olds undertake military training and compete with each other in races at sea. ∩ e (Rev: BL 11/15/11*; SLJ 2/12)

2959 Flanagan, John. *The Ruins of Gorlan* (5–8). 2005, Philomel $15.99 (978-0-399-24454-4). Will becomes an apprentice ranger and plays a key role in protecting his kingdom in this memorable first installment in a new fantasy series. (Rev: BL 6/1–15/05*; SLJ 6/05)

2960 Flanagan, John. *The Siege of Macindaw* (4–8). Series: Ranger's Apprentice. 2009, Philomel $17.99 (978-039925033-0). Will, Horace, and a healer band together with the Skandians to reclaim Castle Macindaw and rescue Alyss in this sixth installment in the series. Also use *The Emperor of Nihon-Ja* (2011). ∩ e Lexile 850L (Rev: BLO 4/15/09)

2961 Flavin, Teresa. *The Blackhope Enigma* (5–7). 2011, Candlewick $15.99 (978-0-7636-5694-2). A mysterious 16th-century painting draws Sunni, 14, her stepbrother, and an art classmate into its labyrinthine embrace. e Lexile 690L (Rev: BL 9/15/11; LMC 11–12/11; SLJ 11/1/11)

2962 Flavin, Teresa. *The Crimson Shard* (5–7). 2012, Candlewick $15.99 (978-0-7636-6093-2). Sunni and Blaise find themselves transported to 18th-century London and must solve a mystery and work to find a way home in this sequel to *The Blackhope Enigma* (2011). e Lexile 700L (Rev: BL 10/1/12; SLJ 12/12)

2963 Fletcher, Charlie. *Ironhand* (5–8). Series: The Stoneheart Trilogy. 2008, Hyperion $16.99 (978-1-4231-0177-2). In this sequel to *Stoneheart*, George races against three gruesome veins that have appeared on his body as he takes the Hard Way and searches for the Stoneheart. (Rev: BL 4/15/08; SLJ 6/08)

2964 Fletcher, Charlie. *Silvertongue* (5–8). Series: Stoneheart Trilogy. 2009, Hyperion $16.99 (978-1-4231-0179-6). In this final book in the trilogy, George, 13, and Edie, 12, employ their newfound gifts — and receive help from statues come to life — in the fight against the Walker, the Last Knight, and the Ice Devil. (Rev: SLJ 6/1/09; VOYA 4/09)

2965 Fletcher, Charlie. *Stoneheart* (5–8). 2007, Hyperion $16.99 (978-1-4231-0175-8). At the Natural History Museum in London 12-year-old George stumbles upon a parallel world where good statues (or spits) and evil taints are at war. (Rev: BL 5/15/07; SLJ 8/07)

2966 Flinn, Alex. *Beastly* (7–10). 2007, HarperTeen $16.99 (978-0-06-087416-2). Popular, snooty Kyle is transformed into a beast when he insults a classmate in this modern adaptation of "Beauty and the Beast." (Rev: BL 2/1/08; SLJ 11/07)

2967 Flinn, Alex. *Bewitching* (8–11). Series: Kendra Chronicles. 2012, HarperTeen $17.99 (978-006202414-5). Teen witch Kendra begins her life during the plague in 1666, when she and her brother outwit an evil witch in a gingerbread house, and goes on to participate in the *Titanic* disaster (the Little Mermaid), Versailles (the Princess and the Pea), and an evil stepsister story. e (Rev: BL 1/1/12; HB 3–4/12; SLJ 3/12; VOYA 12/11)

2968 Flinn, Alex. *A Kiss in Time* (7–10). 2009, HarperTeen $16.99 (978-006087419-3); LB $17.89 (978-006087420-9). A fractured and lively Sleeping Beauty tale in which Princess Talia of Euphrasia is awakened after 300 years by young American Jack. ∩ (Rev: BL 5/15/09; HB 7–8/09; SLJ 8/09; VOYA 6/09)

2969 Foon, Dennis. *The Dirt Eaters* (5–10). Series: Longlight Legacy Trilogy. 2003, Annick $19.95 (978-1-55037-807-8); paper $9.95 (978-1-55037-806-1). In this well-written first installment of a trilogy, 15-year-old Roan finds himself torn between the peaceful ways of his upbringing and a desire to avenge a murderous attack on his village. (Rev: SLJ 1/04; VOYA 2/04)

2970 Forester, Victoria. *The Girl Who Could Fly* (4–7). 2008, Feiwel & Friends $16.95 (978-0-312-37462-4).

Piper McCloud can fly — an ability that unsettles her community — and she is taken to a school for children with unusual abilities, which she soon senses is not quite what it seems. (Rev: BL 6/1–15/08; SLJ 9/08)

2971 Fox, Helen. *Eager's Nephew* (5–8). 2006, Random House LB $17.99 (978-0-385-90904-4). In this sequel to *Eager* (2004), Eager the robot and his nephew Jonquil pay a forbidden visit to Eager's human friends, the Bells; mystery and adventure ensue. (Rev: BL 10/15/06; SLJ 1/07)

2972 Friesner, Esther. *Nobody's Princess* (6–10). 2007, Random House $16.99 (978-0-375-87528-1). The romantic, exciting, and dangerous childhood of Helen of Troy, whose face launched all those ships when she grew up. The sequel *Nobody's Prize* (2008) continues the story. (Rev: BCCB 7–8/07; BL 3/15/07; LMC 4–5/07; SLJ 7/07)

2973 Friesner, Esther. *Nobody's Prize* (8–12). 2008, Random House $16.99 (978-0-375-87531-1). Princess Helen of Sparta (the future Helen of Troy), longing for adventure, disguises herself as a boy and stows away on the *Argo* in this exciting sequel to *Nobody's Princess*. (Rev: BL 2/1/08; SLJ 6/08)

2974 Friesner, Esther. *Temping Fate* (7–10). 2006, Dutton $16.99 (978-0-525-47730-3). Unsuspecting teenager Ilana finds that her summer employer, Divine Relief Temp Agency, has genuine Greek gods and goddesses among its clientele. (Rev: BL 5/15/06; SLJ 8/06)

2975 Fromental, Jean-Luc. *Broadway Chicken* (5–8). Trans. by Suzi Baker. 1995, Hyperion LB $15.49 (978-0-7868-2048-1). A tale of success and failure with, yes, a dancing chicken as the protagonist. (Rev: BL 12/15/95; SLJ 2/96)

2976 Frost, Mark. *The Paladin Prophecy* (7–10). 2012, Random House $17.99 (978-0-375-87045-3); LB $20.99 (978-037597045-0). Will West, a clever 15-year-old who tries to maintain a low profile, finds himself thrust into the midst of a centuries-old struggle between good and evil. ☊ ℮ Lexile HL700L (Rev: BL 9/15/12; SLJ 10/12; VOYA 12/12)

2977 Funke, Cornelia. *Inkdeath* (8–12). 2008, Scholastic $24.99 (978-043986628-6). An old bookbinder brings characters both benevolent and evil to life in this plot-driven conclusion to Funke's popular trilogy. ☊ Lexile 830L (Rev: BL 11/1/08*; HB 1–2/09; SLJ 12/08; VOYA 12/08)

2978 Funke, Cornelia. *Inkheart* (6–12). 2003, Scholastic $24.99 (978-0-439-53164-1). Twelve-year-old Meggie, the key character in this complex novel, is the daughter of a bookbinder who can release fictional characters from their books. (Rev: BL 9/1/03; HBG 4/04; SLJ 10/03; VOYA 12/03)

2979 Funke, Cornelia. *Inkspell* (6–9). 2005, Scholastic $24.99 (978-0-439-55400-8). In this gripping sequel to *Inkheart*, the magical process is reversed and earlier

characters find themselves in a fictional world of violence. (Rev: BL 10/1/05*; SLJ 10/05; VOYA 10/05)

2980 Furey, Maggie. *Heart of Myrial* (7–12). Series: Shadowleague. 2000, Bantam paper $6.99 (978-0-553-57938-3). As catastrophic events threaten Myrial, a firedrake, a telepathic dragon, and a woman warrior seek to avert destruction. (Rev: VOYA 6/00)

2981 Gaiman, Neil. *Coraline* (5–8). Illus. by Dave McKean. 2002, HarperCollins LB $17.89 (978-0-06-623744-2). An Alice-in-Wonderland type of tale for older readers in which a girl finds an alternate world in the empty apartment next door. (Rev: BCCB 11/02; BL 8/02; HB 11–12/02; HBG 3/03; SLJ 8/02*)

2982 Gaiman, Neil. *The Graveyard Book* (6–10). Illus. by Dave McKean. 2008, HarperCollins $17.99 (978-006053092-1); LB $18.89 (978-006053093-8). After the murder of his family, a toddler wanders out of his house into a graveyard, where the residents agree to raise him and protect him from the killer. Newbery Medal 2009; Carnegie Medal; Hugo Best Novel Award 2009; ALA Notable Books 2009; Boston Globe–Horn Book Honor 2009. ☊ ℮ (Rev: BL 9/15/08*; HB 11–12/08; SLJ 10/1/08)

2983 Gaiman, Neil. *M Is for Magic* (7–10). Illus. by Teddy Kristiansen. 2007, HarperCollins $16.99 (978-0-06-118642-4). This collection of previously published stories (many from *Fragile Things*) includes twisted fairy tales, stories based on myth and legend (from aliens to the Holy Grail), and quirky illustrations. (Rev: BCCB 9/07; BL 4/15/07; SLJ 8/07)

2984 Galloway, Priscilla. *Truly Grim Tales* (7–12). 1998, Random House paper $NIS (978-0-440-22728-1). Familiar folk tales get new twists in this collection. (Rev: BL 9/15/95; SLJ 9/95)

2985 García, Laura Gallego. *The Legend of the Wandering King* (6–9). Trans. by Dan Bellm. 2005, Scholastic $16.95 (978-0-439-58556-9). Jealous of the carpet weaver who has bested him in the annual poetry competition for three consecutive years, an Arabian prince orders his rival to weave a carpet that chronicles the complete history of humankind. (Rev: BL 10/15/05; SLJ 10/05)

2986 García, Laura Gallego. *The Valley of the Wolves* (5–8). Trans. by Margaret Sayers Peden. 2006, Scholastic $16.99 (978-0-439-58553-8). Dana, 10, learns to use her magical powers at an academy of sorcery and wonders about the origins of her best friend and constant companion Kai, visible only to Dana. (Rev: BL 5/15/06; SLJ 6/06; VOYA 6/06)

2987 Gardner, Lyn. *Into the Woods* (4–7). Illus. by Mini Grey. 2007, Random House $16.99 (978-0-385-75115-5). After their mother's death, Storm and her sisters flee the evil Dr. DeWilde and his pack of wolves and find themselves facing many dangers that will be familiar to readers of fairy tales. (Rev: BL 5/1/07; HB 7–8/07; LMC 10/07; SLJ 6/07)

2988 Gardner, Sally. *I, Coriander* (7–10). 2005, Dial $16.99 (978-0-8037-3099-1). In a fantasy full of the atmosphere of 17th-century England, Coriander is the daughter of a human father and a fairy princess. (Rev: BL 8/05; SLJ 9/05; VOYA 10/05)

2989 Gardner, Sally. *Maggot Moon* (7–12). Illus. by Julian Crouch. 2013, Candlewick $16.99 (978-076366553-1). In a dystopian 1956 where the "impure" live in ghettos — grim but better than the camps — young Standish has knowledge that could bring down the Motherland. ⌒ e Lexile 690L (Rev: BL 1/13*; HB 3–4/13*; SLJ 3/13; VOYA 2/13)

2990 Garfield, Henry. *Tartabull's Throw* (7–10). 2001, Simon & Schuster $15.00 (978-0-689-83840-8). A 19-year-old baseball player and a mysterious young woman called Cassandra are the principal characters in this multifaceted story set in 1967 that entwines baseball, werewolves, romance, and suspense. (Rev: BL 5/15/01; HBG 10/01; SLJ 6/01; VOYA 8/01)

2991 Gear, W. Michael, and Kathleen O'Neal Gear. *Children of the Dawnland* (5–8). 2009, Starscape $17.95 (978-0-7653-2019-3). Twig dreams the future and sees danger for her world so she takes off on a daring journey to save her people. (Rev: BL 7/09)

2992 Gee, Maurice. *Salt* (7–10). 2009, Orca $18 (978-1-55469-209-5). This gripping, dark fantasy features Hari, a 17-year-old telepath who fights the oppressive ruling class that kidnapped his father; the first in a trilogy. Lexile 700L (Rev: LMC 1–2/10; SLJ 11/09)

2993 George, Jessica Day. *Dragon Flight* (6–9). 2008, Bloomsbury $16.95 (978-1-59990-110-7). In a world populated by people and dragons, orphan Creel is drawn into a war and a romance. (Rev: BL 5/15/08)

2994 George, Jessica Day. *Dragon Slippers* (6–9). 2007, Bloomsbury $16.95 (978-1-59990-057-5). After befriending a dragon, orphan Creel unwittingly acquires an intriguing pair of slippers with the power to determine the future of her kingdom. (Rev: BL 5/15/07; SLJ 10/07)

2995 George, Jessica Day. *Dragon Spear* (6–9). Series: Dragon Slippers. 2009, Bloomsbury $16.99 (978-159990369-9). Following *Dragon Slippers* (2007) and *Dragon Flight* (2008), this installment finds Creel and Luka searching for a kidnapped dragon queen. Lexile 920L (Rev: BLO 4/23/09)

2996 George, Jessica Day. *Princess of the Midnight Ball* (6–10). 2009, Bloomsbury $16.99 (978-159990322-4). Galen, a young soldier at the end of a long war in a fictional 19th century, falls in love with a princess and saves her and her 11 dancing sisters by using his talent for knitting. e Lexile 830L (Rev: BL 1/1–15/09; SLJ 4/1/09; VOYA 6/09)

2997 George, Jessica Day. *Sun and Moon, Ice and Snow* (7–10). 2008, Bloomsbury $16.95 (978-1-59990-109-1). Based on Norse myth, this is a story of a girl who lives in an ice palace with a white bear after being rejected by her mother. (Rev: BL 2/1/08; SLJ 3/08)

2998 George, Jessica Day. *Tuesdays at the Castle* (4–8). 2011, Bloomsbury $16.99 (978-1-59990-644-7). Princess Celie, 11, lives in a magical castle that has the power to change itself at will; it also has its favorite people and it comes to the aid of Celie when her parents are in danger. e Lexile 860L (Rev: LMC 1–2/12; SLJ 11/1/11)

2999 Gibbs, Stuart. *The Last Musketeer* (5–8). 2011, HarperCollins $16.99 (978-0-06-204838-7). On a trip to Paris 14-year-old Greg is whisked back to 1615 France, where he meets young Aramis, Porthos, and Athos and has adventures including a struggle against Richelieu. Lexile 700L (Rev: BL 10/15/11; LMC 1–2/12; SLJ 10/1/11)

3000 Gibsen, Cole. *Katana* (7–10). 2012, Flux paper $9.95 (978-07387304-0-0). Rileigh, 17, comes to believe she is channeling the spirit of an ancient samurai, who provides her with guidance and the tools to break out of her very ordinary life. e (Rev: BL 4/1/12; LMC 8–9/12; SLJ 3/12)

3001 Gier, Kerstin. *Ruby Red* (7–10). Trans. by Anthea Bell. 2011, Henry Holt $16.99 (978-0-8050-9252-3). Gwen, 16, is surprised to find that she carries the family's time-travel gene rather than her well-prepared cousin Charlotte, but she is soon having extraordinary adventures. ⌒ e Lexile HL680L (Rev: BL 4/15/11; LMC 10/11; SLJ 6/11)

3002 Gilmore, Rachna. *The Sower of Tales* (6–9). 2005, Fitzhenry & Whiteside $15.95 (978-1-55041-945-0). In a land where the Plainsfolk are nourished by stories, Calantha, who dreams of following in the footsteps of the Gatherer who harvests the story pods, must act to save them all. (Rev: BL 12/15/05; SLJ 1/06; VOYA 12/05)

3003 Going, K. L. *The Garden of Eve* (5–8). 2007, Harcourt $17.00 (978-0-15-205986-6). When Evie and her father move to a house with an enchanted apple orchard after Evie's mother dies, a ghost and a magical seed help to ease Evie's grief. ⌒ (Rev: BL 10/1/07; HB 11–12/07; LMC 1/08; SLJ 12/07)

3004 Golding, Julia. *The Glass Swallow* (7–10). 2011, Marshall Cavendish $17.99 (978-0-7614-5979-8). In a land where women cannot work, Rain hides her stained-glass designs; finally able to travel abroad, she finds herself in a chaotic country with some hope provided by a handsome falconer named Peri. e Lexile 760L (Rev: BL 9/1/11; LMC 3–4/12; SLJ 11/1/11)

3005 Golding, Julia. *The Gorgon's Gaze* (4–7). Series: Companions Quartet. 2007, Marshall Cavendish $16.99 (978-0-7614-5377-2). This sequel to *Secret of the Sirens* finds both Connie and the Society for the Protection of Mythical Creatures in danger. (Rev: BL 1/1–15/08)

3006 Golding, Julia. *Mines of the Minotaur* (5–8). Series: The Companions Quartet. 2008, Marshall Cavendish $16.99 (978-0-7614-5302-4). This installment in the series features Connie, a 13-year-old who has a gift for communicating with mythical creatures. (Rev: SLJ 10/1/08; VOYA 6/08)

3007 Goodman, Alison. *Eon: Dragoneye Reborn* (7–10). 2008, Viking $19.99 (978-067006227-0). A hypnotic tale about a 12-year-old girl who poses as a boy to compete to become the next apprentice to a dragon tamer, and who is pulled into the dangerous intrigues and political machinations of the Asian-inspired fantasy world in which the story takes place. (Rev: BL 12/15/08; LMC 5–6/09; SLJ 1/1/09)

3008 Goodman, Alison. *Eona* (7–10). Series: The Last Dragoneye. 2011, Viking $19.99 (978-0-670-06311-6). Eona (formerly disguised as a boy, Eon) faces both an internal struggle and a fierce battle for her homeland as she joins forces with the young Pearl Emperor; the sequel to *Eon* (2008). ∩ e Lexile 740L (Rev: BL 5/1/11; SLJ 7/11; VOYA 6/11)

3009 Gopnik, Adam. *The King in the Window* (5–8). 2005, Hyperion $19.95 (978-0-7868-1862-4). Mistaken by window wraiths as their king, 11-year-old Oliver Parker struggles to resist their efforts to pull him into their world. (Rev: BL 10/1/05; SLJ 11/05; VOYA 2/06)

3010 Gordon, Amy. *The Shadow Collector's Apprentice* (4–7). 2012, Holiday House $16.95 (978-082342359-0). In 1963, 12-year-old Cully Pennyacre, whose father has mysteriously disappeared leaving him with three aunts, takes a job with an antiques dealer who collects people's shadows. (Rev: BL 4/1/12; LMC 8–9/12; SLJ 4/12)

3011 Gordon, Lawrence. *User Friendly* (7–10). Series: Ghost Chronicles. 1999, Karmichael paper $11.95 (978-0-9653966-0-8). Frank, a teenage ghost in limbo, contacts Eddie through the computer to get help to free himself and his friend, a runaway slave, from the purgatory in which they are living. (Rev: BL 1/1–15/99; SLJ 1/99)

3012 Gordon, Roderick, and Brian Williams. *Freefall* (6–9). Series: Tunnels. 2010, Scholastic $18.99 (978-0-545-13877-2). Will, 14, and his friends meet the sinister Rebecca twins in their travels through a series of monster-filled subterranean tunnels; the third installment in the series that began with *Tunnels* (2008) and *Deeper* (2009). ∩ e Lexile HL590L (Rev: BL 6/10; SLJ 5/10)

3013 Gordon, Roderick, and Brian Williams. *Spiral* (7–10). Series: Tunnels. 2012, Scholastic $18.99 (978-054542961-0). Will, Chester, and Drake continue their struggle to prevent Earth's destruction even as the Styx institute "the phase," during which they use humans as egg incubators; new readers should tackle this series in

order. e Lexile 910L (Rev: BLO 6/12; SLJ 1/13; VOYA 6/12)

3014 Gordon, Roderick, and Brian Williams. *Tunnels: Book 1* (6–9). Series: Tunnels. 2008, Scholastic $17.99 (978-0-439-87177-8). Will, 14, and his friend Chester discover secret worlds beneath London when they investigate the disappearance of Will's archaeologist father; the first volume in a series. (Rev: BL 2/15/08; SLJ 3/08)

3015 Gormley, Beatrice. *Best Friend Insurance* (5–7). Illus. by Emily Arnold McCully. 1988, Avon paper $2.50 (978-0-380-69854-7). Maureen finds that her mother has been transformed into a new friend named Kitty. (Rev: SLJ 8/04)

3016 Goto, Hiromi. *Half World* (8–10). Illus. by Jillian Tamaki. 2010, Viking $16.99 (978-0-670-01220-6). Looking for her mother, 14-year-old Melanie Tamaki enters the Half World and finds herself in a gruesome realm of souls caught between life and death. e Lexile 710L (Rev: BL 3/1/10; HB 7–8/10; LMC 3–4/10; SLJ 4/10)

3017 Goto, Hiromi. *The Water of Possibility* (5–7). Illus. by Aries Cheung. Series: In the Same Boat. 2002, Coteau paper $8.95 (978-1-55050-183-4). Sayuri, 12, and her younger brother discover a magical world full of danger in this fantasy that includes many elements of Japanese folklore. (Rev: SLJ 8/02)

3018 Grant, K. M. *White Heat* (7–10). Series: The Perfect Fire. 2009, Walker $16.99 (978-0-8027-9695-0). In 13th-century France Raimon struggles to protect the mythical Blue Flame even as he worries about the fate of his love, Yolanda; the sequel to *Blue Flame* (2008). Lexile 820L (Rev: BL 3/15/10; HB 11–12/09; SLJ 1/10)

3019 Grant, Vicki. *The Puppet Wrangler* (6–8). 2004, Orca paper $6.95 (978-1-55143-304-2). A humorous, offbeat modern fantasy in which 12-year-old Telly, unfairly banished from home because of her older sister's misdeeds, finds herself befriending a live puppet from her aunt's television show. (Rev: BCCB 7–8/04; SLJ 8/04)

3020 Gray, Anne. *Rites of the Healer* (6–10). 2007, Sumach paper $11.95 (978-1-894549-59-2). This imaginative book tells the story of Dovella, a villager who is sent on a dangerous quest to find the source of a water supply shortage. (Rev: SLJ 3/08)

3021 Gray, Claudia. *Evernight* (8–11). 2008, HarperTeen $16.99 (978-0-06-128439-7). Bianca's new boarding school is populated with beautiful vampires, and she and her boyfriend Lucas face danger as they uncover the school's secrets. (Rev: BL 5/15/08; SLJ 6/08)

3022 Gray, Claudia. *Spellcaster* (7–10). 2013, HarperTeen $17.99 (978-006196120-5). Nadia, Mateo, and Verlaine, high school seniors, are determined to save

Captive's Sound from an evil sorceress. **e** (Rev: BL 12/15/12)

3023 Gray, Luli. *Falcon and the Carousel of Time* (4–7). 2005, Houghton Mifflin $15.00 (978-0-618-44895-1). Falcon, 13, and her Aunt Emily travel back to 1903 New York City in this novel that blends elements of *Timespinners* (2003) and the two previous Falcon novels. (Rev: BL 6/1–15/05; SLJ 7/05)

3024 Gray, Luli. *Falcon and the Charles Street Witch* (4–7). 2002, Houghton Mifflin $16.00 (978-0-618-16410-3). In this fantasy follow-up to 1995's *Falcon's Egg*, a 12-year-old girl becomes reacquainted with a dragon she released over New York City and befriends a witch who lives in Greenwich Village. (Rev: BL 3/15/02*; HBG 10/02; SLJ 4/02; VOYA 4/02)

3025 Greer, Gery, and Bob Ruddick. *Max and Me and the Time Machine* (5–8). 1983, HarperCollins paper $4.99 (978-0-06-440222-4). Steve and Max travel back in time to England during the Middle Ages.

3026 Griffin, Peni R. *Switching Well* (5–9). 1993, Penguin paper $5.99 (978-0-14-036910-6). Two girls from different centuries trade places but soon regret their decisions. (Rev: BCCB 7–8/93; BL 6/1–15/93*; SLJ 6/93*; VOYA 8/93)

3027 Gutman, Dan. *Abner and Me* (5–8). Series: Baseball Card Adventure. 2005, HarperCollins LB $17.89 (978-0-06-053444-8). Stosh and his mother travel back to visit the Battle of Gettysburg in an effort to learn more about baseball's origins. (Rev: BL 1/1–15/05)

3028 Gutman, Dan. *Babe and Me* (4–7). 2000, Avon $16.99 (978-0-380-97739-0). Joe and his dad time-travel to the 1932 World Series to witness a historic moment with hitter Babe Ruth. (Rev: BL 2/1/00; HBG 10/00; SLJ 2/00; VOYA 4/00)

3029 Gutman, Dan. *Honus and Me: A Baseball Card Adventure* (4–7). 1997, Avon paper $5.99 (978-0-380-78878-1). Young Joe Stoshack finds a magical baseball card that allows him to travel through time and participate in the 1909 World Series. (Rev: BL 4/15/97; SLJ 6/97)

3030 Gutman, Dan. *Jackie and Me: A Baseball Card Adventure* (4–7). 1999, Avon $16.99 (978-0-380-97685-0). While time-traveling to research a paper on Jackie Robinson, Joe Stoshack becomes an African American and experiences prejudice first hand. (Rev: BL 2/1/99; HBG 10/99; SLJ 3/99)

3031 Gutman, Dan. *Satch and Me* (4–7). Series: Baseball Card Adventure. 2005, HarperCollins LB $16.89 (978-0-06-059492-3). Stosh travels back to 1942 to establish whether Satchel Paige was the fastest pitcher in history and learns about racial discrimination in the process. (Rev: SLJ 2/06; VOYA 4/06)

3032 Habel, Lia. *Dearly, Departed* (7–10). 2011, Ballantine $16.99 (978-034552331-0). A steampunk fantasy involving zombies — set in the year 2195 but featuring a society more suited to Victorian England. ∩ **e** (Rev: BLO 11/15/11; SLJ 4/12)

3033 Haberdasher, Violet. *Knightley Academy* (4–8). 2010, Simon & Schuster $15.99 (978-1-4169-9143-4). Orphan Henry Grim becomes the first commoner to attend the prestigious Knightley Academy, which trains police and other public authorities in the Britonian Isles, and soon uncovers a plot to start war. **e** Lexile 860L (Rev: BL 2/15/10; SLJ 4/10)

3034 Haberdasher, Violet. *The Secret Prince* (5–8). Series: Knightley Academy. 2011, Aladdin $16.99 (978-1-4169-9145-8). Back at Knightley Academy and studying for their knighthood, Henry and his friends start a secret battle society and Henry learns about his parents and his destiny. Lexile 830L (Rev: BL 7/11; LMC 10/11; SLJ 8/11)

3035 Haddix, Margaret Peterson. *Claim to Fame* (7–9). 2009, Simon & Schuster $16.99 (978-1-4169-3917-7). Former child star Lindsay Scott, 16, now lives in self-imposed exile and is cursed with the disturbing ability to hear anything that is said about her throughout the entire world. ∩ Lexile 770L (Rev: SLJ 12/09; VOYA 2/10)

3036 Haddix, Margaret Peterson. *Escape from Memory* (6–9). 2003, Simon & Schuster $16.95 (978-0-689-85421-7). Under hypnosis, Kira reveals memories of another place in another time, one that threatens both herself and her mother. (Rev: BL 9/1/03; SLJ 3/04; VOYA 10/03)

3037 Haddix, Margaret Peterson. *Running Out of Time* (4–7). 1995, Simon & Schuster $16.95 (978-0-689-80084-9). Living in a historical site where the time is the 1840s, Jessie escapes into the present in this fantasy. (Rev: BCCB 11/95; BL 10/1/95; SLJ 10/95*)

3038 Hague, Michael, ed. *The Book of Dragons* (4–7). Illus. by author. 1995, Morrow $21.99 (978-0-688-10879-3). Seventeen classic tales about dragons by such authors as Tolkien and Kenneth Grahame are included in this interesting anthology. (Rev: BL 10/1/95; SLJ 10/95)

3039 Hale, Shannon. *Book of a Thousand Days* (7–10). Illus. by James Noel Smith. 2007, Bloomsbury $17.95 (978-1-59990-051-3). As punishment for refusing to marry, Lady Saren and her servant Dashti are sentenced to seven years in a sealed tower, where Dashti writes in her diary about their imprisonment, her secret love for a lord, and their escape; based on a fairy tale from the Brothers Grimm. ∩ (Rev: BL 9/15/07; SLJ 10/07)

3040 Hale, Shannon. *Enna Burning* (8–11). Series: Books of Bayern. 2004, Bloomsbury $17.95 (978-1-58234-889-6). In this companion to *The Goose Girl*, Enna returns to her home in the forest and learns to wield the power of fire, but she must struggle to use that power wisely without risking her life or those of her people. (Rev: BL 9/15/04; SLJ 9/04; VOYA 12/04)

3041 Hale, Shannon. *Forest Born* (7–10). Series: Books of Bayern. 2009, Bloomsbury $17.99 (978-1-59990-167-1). An engaging addition to the series, this stand-alone volume follows a girl named Rin who comes to understand the value of her own special gifts as she and others struggle to defeat the evil Selia. **e** Lexile 800L (Rev: BL 12/15/09; HB 9–10/09; LMC 10/09; SLJ 9/09)

3042 Hale, Shannon. *The Goose Girl* (6–10). Series: Books of Bayern. 2003, Bloomsbury $17.95 (978-1-58234-843-8). Crown Princess Ani, who can talk to the animals, is betrayed by her guards and disguises herself as a goose girl until she can reclaim her crown. (Rev: BL 8/03; HBG 4/04; SLJ 8/03*; VOYA 10/03)

3043 Hale, Shannon. *Palace of Stone* (6–9). Series: Princess Academy. 2012, Bloomsbury $16.99 (978-1-59990-873-1). Miri draws on everything she learned at Princess Academy to write a new school charter and argue for social change in this sequel to the first book. ∩ **e** Lexile 740L (Rev: BL 9/1/12; HB 9–10/12; SLJ 8/1/12; VOYA 10/12)

3044 Hale, Shannon. *Princess Academy* (6–9). 2005, Bloomsbury $16.95 (978-1-58234-993-0). Fantasy, feminism, adventure, and romance are combined in the story of 14-year-old Miri, prize student in the Princess Academy and advocate for the miners of the stone called *under*. Newbery Honor 2006. (Rev: BL 6/1–15/05; SLJ 8/05; VOYA 8/05)

3045 Hale, Shannon. *River Secrets* (7–10). Series: Books of Bayern. 2006, Bloomsbury $17.95 (978-1-58234-901-5). Razo, a teenage soldier from Bazo, is surprised to learn he's being sent on a mission to Tira after the war, to help keep peace. But someone is trying to sabotage the peace and Razo must figure out who. A sequel to *The Goose Girl* (2003) and *Enna Burning* (2004). (Rev: BL 9/15/06; SLJ 10/06*)

3046 Halpern, Jake, and Peter Kujawinski. *Dormia* (5–8). Illus. 2009, Houghton $17.00 (978-0-547-07665-2). All the action takes place when 12-year-old Alphonso falls asleep and enters a world called Dormia where he must use his special powers or Dormia will die. (Rev: BL 7/09; SLJ 9/09)

3047 Hamilton, Kersten. *Tyger Tyger* (7–10). 2010, Clarion $17 (978-0-547-33008-2). The lives of Teagan Wylltson and her disabled brother change dramatically when their cousin Finn Mac Cumhaill arrives in Chicago and the three are drawn into a dangerous mission. (Rev: BL 11/1/10; SLJ 12/1/10*)

3048 Hamilton, Kiki. *The Faerie Ring* (7–10). 2011, Tor $17.99 (978-0-7653-2722-2). A street urchin steals a ring that carries remarkable power — and responsibility — in this action-filled mix of faerie fantasy and

Victorian historical fiction. **e** (Rev: BL 10/15/11; SLJ 11/1/11)

3049 Hamilton, Virginia. *Justice and Her Brothers* (7–10). Series: The Justice Cycle. 1978, Scholastic paper $4.99 (978-0-590-36214-6). Four children with supernatural powers move in time in this complex novel. Sequels are *Dustland* (1980) and *The Gathering* (1981).

3050 Hand, Cynthia. *Hallowed* (7–10). 2012, Harper-Teen $17.99 (978-006199618-4). Part-angel Clara, 16, works to halt the predestined death of someone close to her as she contends with increasingly complex feelings toward her boyfriend Tucker. ∩ **e** (Rev: BL 1/1/12; VOYA 2/12)

3051 Hand, Cynthia. *Unearthly* (7–10). 2011, Harper-Teen $17.99 (978-006199616-0). Sixteen-year-old Clara is a quarter-angel whose half-angel mother supports her in her efforts to fulfill her destiny, moving the family from California to Wyoming where Clara meets the boy she has seen in her visions; the first book in a series. ∩ **e** (Rev: BL 12/1/10; SLJ 1/1/11; VOYA 2/12)

3052 Hanley, Victoria. *The Healer's Keep* (7–12). 2002, Holiday $17.95 (978-0-8234-1760-5). A princess, a former slave girl, and their companions battle evil in a land full of magic. (Rev: BCCB 1/03; HBG 3/03; SLJ 12/02; VOYA 2/03)

3053 Hanley, Victoria. *The Seer and the Sword* (6–10). 2000, Holiday $17.95 (978-0-8234-1532-8). Romance, court politics, battles, and suspense all are essential parts of this fantasy featuring Princess Torina and Prince Landen. (Rev: BCCB 2/01; BL 12/15/00; HBG 10/01; SLJ 3/01; VOYA 4/01)

3054 Haptie, Charlotte. *Otto and the Flying Twins* (4–7). 2004, Holiday $17.95 (978-0-8234-1826-8). In the City of Trees, Otto is shocked to discover his father is king of the magical Karmidee. The sequel is *Otto and the Bird Charmers* (2005). (Rev: BL 4/15/04; SLJ 6/04)

3055 Hardinge, Frances. *Fly by Night* (6–9). 2006, HarperCollins $16.99 (978-0-06-087627-2). Set in an oppressive medieval kingdom, this multilayered novel features Mosca Mye, 12, an orphan with courage and an usual ability — the gift of reading. ∩ (Rev: BL 8/06; SLJ SLJ 7/06)

3056 Hardinge, Frances. *Fly Trap* (5–8). 2011, Harper-Collins $16.99 (978-0-06-088044-6). Orphan Mosca, her goose, and con man Eponymous Clent journey to the city of Toll, which is divided into the parallel towns of Toll-by-Day and the scary Toll-by-Night. (Rev: BL 3/15/11; HB 5–6/11; SLJ 6/11; VOYA 6/11)

3057 Hardinge, Frances. *The Lost Conspiracy* (6–10). 2009, HarperCollins $16.99 (978-006088041-5); LB $17.89 (978-006088042-2). In the strange world of Gullstruck Island, Hathin and her sister Arilou are on the run from a mysterious force killing off the Lost people. ALA Notable Books 2010. Lexile 970L (Rev: BL 5/15/09; HB 9–10/09; LMC 3–4/10; SLJ 9/09)

3058 Hardinge, Frances. *Well Witched* (5–8). 2008, HarperCollins LB $17.89 (978-0-06-088039-2); paper $16.99 (978-0-06-088038-5). Ryan, Josh, and Chelle steal from a wishing well and discover that the act has given them undesirable wish-granting powers in this intriguing story. (Rev: BL 5/15/08; SLJ 8/08)

3059 Hardy, Janice. *The Shifter* (5–8). Series: The Healing Wars. 2009, HarperCollins $16.99 (978-0-06-174704-5); LB $17.89 (978-0-06-176177-5). Fifteen-year-old Nya and her younger sister have the ability to remove pain, but Nya's gift is more tenuous and puts her in danger. ℮ Lexile 630L (Rev: BL 10/15/09; HB 11–12/09; SLJ 1/10)

3060 Harland, Richard. *Worldshaker* (6–9). 2010, Simon & Schuster $16.99 (978-1-4169-9552-4). Privileged 16-year-old Col has a bright future in his traveling community until he meets a 14-year-old girl named Riff who has intruded into the Upper Deck and opens Col's eyes to the inequalities in his steampunk world. ℮ Lexile 640L (Rev: BL 5/15/10; LMC 8–9/10; SLJ 8/10)

3061 Harrison, Mette Ivie. *The Princess and the Bear* (7–10). 2009, HarperTeen $17.99 (978-0-06-155314-1). This unlikely love story is told from the points of view of King Richon and Chala, human/animal shape-shifters whose bond grows as they try to end war in their kingdom. ℮ Lexile 790L (Rev: SLJ 9/09; VOYA 8/09)

3062 Harrison, Mette Ivie. *The Princess and the Hound* (6–9). 2007, Eos $17.99 (978-0-06-113187-5). In a kingdom where magical communication with animals is forbidden, Prince George manages to hide his talent until he meets the Princess Beatrice and her beloved dog, Marit. (Rev: BCCB 6/07; BL 7/07; SLJ 9/07)

3063 Harrison, Michelle. *13 Curses* (6–9). 2011, Little, Brown $15.99 (978-0-316-04150-8). In the sequel to *13 Treasures* (2010), 13-year-old Rowan (now calling herself Red) searches for her young brother James in the dangerous fairy realm. ℮ Lexile 760L (Rev: BL 5/1/11; LMC 10/11*; SLJ 7/11; VOYA 8/11)

3064 Harrison, Michelle. *13 Treasures* (5–8). 2010, Little, Brown $15.99 (978-0-316-04148-5). Tanya, a 13-year-old whose sleep has been disrupted by fairies, is sent to stay with her grandmother at Elvesden Manor and there uncovers dark secrets that place her in danger. ℮ Lexile 770L (Rev: BL 4/1/10; SLJ 4/10)

3065 Hartinger, Brent. *Dreamquest: Tales of Slumberia* (4–8). 2007, Tom Doherty Assoc. $16.95 (978-0-7653-1397-3). Julie, 11, is suffering — her parents fight all day and she has nightmares every night — until she wakes up in Slumberia, where her dreams are created, and must escape while there's still a chance. (Rev: LMC 1/08*; SLJ 2/08)

3066 Hartley, A. J. *Darwen Arkwright and the Peregrine Pact* (5–8). Illus. by Emily Osborne. 2011, Penguin $16.99 (978-1-59514-409-6). Darwen, 11, receives a mysterious mirror that acts as a portal to another dimension full of battle and magic; his new friend Alexandra helps him make sense of all the mayhem. ℮ Lexile 810L (Rev: BLO 10/15/11; SLJ 12/1/11)

3067 Hartnett, Sonya. *The Ghost's Child* (8–12). 2008, Candlewick $16.99 (978-076363964-8). In this melancholic fantasy, elderly Matilda recounts the ill-fated romance of her youth to a mysterious young boy who turns out to have a connection to her past. ☊ Lexile 900L (Rev: BL 11/1/08*; LMC 3–4/09; SLJ 1/1/09; VOYA 2/09)

3068 Harvey, Alyxandra. *Stolen Away* (8–12). 2012, Walker $17.99 (978-0-8027-2189-1). Jo concocts a daring scheme to rescue her friend Eloise, 17, who has been kidnapped by a tyrannical fairy ruler. ℮ (Rev: LMC 5–6/12; SLJ 6/12; VOYA 4/12)

3069 Haskell, Merrie. *The Princess Curse* (5–8). 2011, HarperCollins $16.99 (978-0-06-200813-8). Based on the fairy tale about the dancing princesses, this story set in 15th-century Romania involves 13-year-old Reveka, apprentice to a herbalist, who tries to break the curse on the princesses of Sylvania. ℮ Lexile 790L (Rev: BL 10/15/11; SLJ 12/1/11)

3070 Haworth, Danette. *The Summer of Moonlight Secrets* (4–7). 2010, Walker $16.99 (978-0-8027-9520-5). Allie Jo, who lives at a rundown hotel, befriends resident skateboarder Chase and the two spend a summer helping Tara, a girl who is part sea creature and is in danger. Lexile 610L (Rev: BL 6/10; LMC 8–9/10; SLJ 7/10)

3071 Haydon, Elizabeth. *The Dragon's Lair* (6–9). Illus. by Jason Chan. Series: The Lost Journals of Ven Polypheme. 2008, Tor $17.95 (978-0-7653-0869-6). King Vandermere sends Ven and his friends to placate an angry dragon and avoid war in this story with sketches and excerpts from Ven's journals. (Rev: BLO 7/31/08; SLJ 10/1/08; VOYA 12/08)

3072 Haydon, Elizabeth. *The Floating Island* (6–9). Illus. by Brett Helquist. 2006, Tor $17.95 (978-0-7653-0867-2). The adventures of Ven Polypheme, a Nain (a dwarf-like creature) with a seafaring heritage; here he ends up fighting Fire Pirates, is rescued by a mermaid, and visits an inn populated by ghosts and other strange characters. (Rev: BL 9/1/06; SLJ 12/06)

3073 Haydon, Elizabeth. *The Thief Queen's Daughter* (6–9). Illus. by Jason Chan. Series: Lost Journals of Ven Polypheme. 2007, Tor $17.95 (978-0-7653-0868-9). King Vandermere sends Ven and four of his friends on a mission to the Gated City to solve the riddle of a mysterious light stone. (Rev: BL 5/15/07; SLJ 7/07)

3074 Hearn, Julie. *Sign of the Raven* (7–10). 2005, Simon & Schuster $16.95 (978-0-689-85734-8). Living with his grandmother in London while his mother recovers from cancer, 12-year-old Tom finds a portal into

FICTION: *Fantasy*

an 18th-century world far different from his own. (Rev: BCCB 12/05; HB 1–2/06; SLJ 11/05; VOYA 10/05)

3075 Helgerson, Joseph. *Horns and Wrinkles* (4–7). 2006, Houghton Mifflin $16.00 (978-0-618-61679-4). Mysterious events are taking place in Blue Wing, Minnesota — the nose of a bully named Duke turns into a rhino horn, and his parents turn to stone — and 12-year-old Claire is drawn into an adventure involving fairies and trolls. ◖ (Rev: BL 9/1/06; SLJ 9/06)

3076 Hemphill, Michael, and Sam Riddleburger. *Stonewall Hinkleman and the Battle of Bull Run* (5–7). 2009, Dial $16.99 (978-0-8037-3179-0). At yet another boring Civil War reenactment, 12-year-old Stonewall Hinkleman finds himself whisked back to the First Battle of Bull Run, where he must stop a companion time traveler from reversing the outcome of the war. (Rev: BL 4/15/09; SLJ 5/09)

3077 Hennesy, Carolyn. *Pandora Gets Jealous* (4–7). Series: Mythic Misadventures. 2008, Bloomsbury $12.95 (978-1-59990-196-1). A lighthearted take on the myth of Pandora in which Pandy takes a special box to school for show-and-tell. (Rev: BL 11/15/07; LMC 4–5/08; SLJ 3/08)

3078 Hess, Nina. *A Practical Guide to Monsters* (4–7). 2007, Mirrorstone $12.95 (978-0-7869-4809-3). A tongue-in-cheek field guide to common monsters, this companion to the series Knights of the Silver Dragon is geared toward young wizards and features detailed illustrations. (Rev: BL 1/1–15/08)

3079 Hieber, Leanna Renee. *Darker Still* (7–10). 2011, Sourcebooks paper $8.99 (978-14022605-2-0). Magically talented Natalie, 17, falls in love with a man in a painting and becomes engrossed in his world in this story set in 1880. ℮ Lexile 830L (Rev: BL 11/15/11; SLJ 1/12)

3080 Higgins, F. E. *The Eyeball Collector* (5–8). 2009, Feiwel & Friends $14.99 (978-0-312-56681-4). Young Hector Fitzbaudly seeks revenge for his father's death, setting out to track down the evil, one-eyed Gulliver Truepin. ℮ Lexile 950L (Rev: BL 9/15/09; HB 9–10/09; LMC 1–2/10; SLJ 11/09)

3081 Higgins, F. E. *The Lunatic's Curse* (5–8). 2011, Feiwel & Friends $15.99 (978-031256682-1). Rex's quest to solve his father's death leads him to the insane asylum on Lake Beluarum in this page-turner that includes an evil stepmother, steampunk aspects, and cannibalism. ℮ Lexile 810L (Rev: BL 8/11; LMC 11–12/11; SLJ 3/12)

3082 Higgins, Simon. *The Nightmare Ninja* (5–8). Series: Moonshadow. 2011, Little, Brown $15.99 (978-0-316-05533-8). Moonshadow contends with the altered emotional state of his former rival, now comrade, Snowhawk as he continues to dodge the evil advances of Silver Wolf's underlings; the second book in the series. (Rev: SLJ 9/1/11)

3083 Hightman, Jason. *The Saint of Dragons* (6–8). 2004, Morrow $16.99 (978-0-06-054011-1). Enrolled at an elite boarding school, 13-year-old Simon St. George is approached by a man claiming to be his father who asks for the boy's help in vanquishing the last surviving dragons; a sequel is *Samurai* (2006). (Rev: BL 8/04; SLJ 9/04)

3084 Highwater, Jamake. *Rama: A Legend* (5–9). 1997, Replica LB $24.95 (978-0-7351-0001-5). When he's wrongfully banished from his father's kingdom and his wife, Sita, is kidnapped, valiant Prince Rama charges back to avenge the evil that's befallen his world. (Rev: BL 11/15/94; SLJ 12/94; VOYA 2/95)

3085 Hill, C. J. *Slayers* (7–10). 2011, Feiwel & Friends $16.99 (978-031261414-0). Tori, 16, learns that she is a dragon slayer and that she and her fellow campers are training for a real battle against the beasts. ◖ ℮ Lexile 740L (Rev: BL 11/15/11; LMC 1–2/12; SLJ 2/12; VOYA 12/11)

3086 Hill, Laban Carrick. *Casa Azul: An Encounter with Frida Kahlo* (7–10). 2005, Watson-Guptill $15.95 (978-0-8230-0411-9). In this appealing novel, two country children roaming the streets of Mexico City in search of their mother are befriended by artist Frida Kahlo and introduced to the magical world in which she dwells. (Rev: BL 10/1/05; SLJ 9/05)

3087 Hill, Pamela Smith. *The Last Grail Keeper* (7–10). 2001, Holiday $17.95 (978-0-8234-1574-8). While visiting England with her mother, 16-year-old Felicity discovers she is an Arthurian "grail keeper" with magical powers. (Rev: BCCB 2/02; BL 11/15/01; HBG 3/02; SLJ 12/01; VOYA 6/02)

3088 Hill, Stuart. *Blade of Fire* (7–10). Series: The Icemark Chronicles. 2007, Scholastic $18.99 (978-0-439-84122-1). Charlemagne, the youngest child of Queen Thirrin and Oskan Witchfather, is now an adult and finds himself at war with his own sister, who has joined the evil forces of Scipio Bellorum. (Rev: BL 3/15/07; LMC 8–9/07; SLJ 6/07)

3089 Hill, Stuart. *The Cry of the Icemark* (8–11). Series: The Icemark Chronicles. 2005, Scholastic $18.95 (978-0-439-68626-6). In this sprawling military fantasy, 13-year-old Thirrin succeeds her fallen father as ruler of Icemark and sets off to forge alliances with werewolves, vampires, and talking snow leopards to help her defend her tiny country. (Rev: BCCB 4/05; BL 2/15/05; SLJ 5/05; VOYA 6/05)

3090 Hinwood, Christine. *The Returning* (9–11). 2011, Dial $17.99 (978-0-8037-3528-6). In a medieval time, Cam returns from war to his village missing one arm and with a strong desire to understand why his life was spared. Printz Honor 2012. ℮ Lexile 670L (Rev: BL 5/1/11; HB 5–6/11; LMC 10/11; SLJ 6/11; VOYA 6/11)

3091 Hite, Sid. *The Distance of Hope* (6–8). 1998, Henry Holt $16.95 (978-0-8050-5054-7). Young prince Yeshe embarks on a perilous journey to find the White Bean Lama who will help him save his diminishing eyesight. (Rev: BL 3/15/98; HBG 9/98; SLJ 5/98; VOYA 6/98)

3092 Hite, Sid. *Dither Farm* (6–10). 1992, Henry Holt $15.95 (978-0-8050-1871-4). An 11-year-old orphan is taken in by a farm family and discovers joys and miracles. (Rev: BL 5/15/92*; SLJ 5/92)

3093 Hoban, Russell. *The Mouse and His Child* (4–8). Illus. by David Small. 2001, Scholastic paper $16.99 (978-0-439-09826-7). A toy mouse and his child embark on a quest to become "self-winding" and have sometimes scary, sometimes humorous adventures in this enchanting fantasy first published in 1967 and now updated with new illustrations. (Rev: BL 12/1/01; HBG 3/02)

3094 Hocking, Amanda. *Lullaby* (6–9). Series: Watersong. 2012, St. Martin's $17.99 (978-125000565-6). Harper receives welcome help from handsome Daniel in her relentless quest to retrieve her sister Gemma from the sirens; the sequel to *Wake* (2012). ☊ ℮ (Rev: BL 12/1/12; LMC 5–6/13; VOYA 2/13)

3095 Hocking, Amanda. *Wake* (6–9). Series: Watersong. 2012, St. Martin's/Griffin $17.99 (978-1-250-00812-1). Teen swimming star Gemma finds herself lured by a seductive band of sirens in this compelling paranormal story. ☊ ℮ Lexile HL710L (Rev: BL 7/12; SLJ 11/12; VOYA 8/12)

3096 Hodges, Margaret. *Gulliver in Lilliput: From Gulliver's Travels by Jonathan Swift* (4–7). Illus. by Kimberly B. Root. 1995, Holiday $17.95 (978-0-8234-1147-4). The story of Gulliver in the land of the little people is retold with bright, detailed illustrations. (Rev: BCCB 6/95; BL 4/15/95; HB 7–8/95; SLJ 6/95*)

3097 Hoeye, Michael. *No Time Like Show Time* (5–8). Series: A Hermux Tantamoq Adventure. 2004, Putnam $14.99 (978-0-399-23880-2). Hermux the mouse investigates who is responsible for sending threatening letters to famous director Fluster Varmint. (Rev: SLJ 11/04)

3098 Hoeye, Michael. *The Sands of Time* (5–8). Series: A Hermux Tantamoq Adventure. 2002, Putnam $14.99 (978-0-399-23879-6). In this sequel to *Time Stops for No Mouse* (2002), the mouse watchmaker and a chipmunk friend believe that mice were once the slaves of cats. (Rev: HBG 3/03; SLJ 10/02; VOYA 12/02)

3099 Hoeye, Michael. *Time Stops for No Mouse* (5–9). Series: A Hermux Tantamoq Adventure. 2002, Putnam $14.99 (978-0-399-23878-9). Hermux Tantamoq, a mouse, leads a quiet life as a watchmaker until Linka Perflinger turns up and Hermux becomes entangled in mystery and suspense. (Rev: BL 3/15/02*; HB 7–8/02; HBG 10/02; SLJ 5/02; VOYA 6/02)

3100 Hoeye, Michael. *Time to Smell the Roses: A Hermux Tantamoq Adventure* (7–10). Series: Hermux Tantamoq Adventures. 2007, Putnam $15.99 (978-0-399-

24490-2). Our mouse detective must solve a mystery at Thorny End while planning his wedding to Linka Perflinger and dodging mutant bees. (Rev: BL 10/1/07)

3101 Hoffman, Alice. *Aquamarine* (4–7). 2001, Scholastic paper $16.95 (978-0-439-09863-2). Twelve-year-old friends Hailey and Claire find a lonely mermaid named Aquamarine, and they try to give her love and adventure. (Rev: BCCB 2/01; BL 3/1/01; HBG 10/01; SLJ 3/01; VOYA 4/01)

3102 Hoffman, Alice. *Green Witch* (7–12). 2010, Scholastic $17.99 (978-0-545-14195-6). Seventeen-year-old Green — first seen in *Green Angel* (2003) — is tending her garden and listening to stories of other survivors of her ruined civilization while she hopes to find her lost love. ℮ Lexile 740L (Rev: BL 1/1–15/10; LMC 3–4/10; SLJ 5/10)

3103 Hoffman, Mary. *Stravaganza: City of Flowers* (7–10). Series: Stravaganza. 2005, Bloomsbury $17.95 (978-1-58234-887-2). In the final volume of the trilogy, Sky Meadows, a 17-year-old biracial Londoner, travels back in time to 16th-century Talia, where many of the characters become involved in multilayered intrigue. (Rev: BL 3/1/05; SLJ 5/05)

3104 Hoffman, Nina Kiriki. *Thresholds* (5–7). 2010, Viking $15.99 (978-0-670-06319-2). Maya moves with her family to Oregon after her best friend's death and the 7th-grader becomes fascinated with her mysterious neighbors, eventually discovering the portal into a fantastical realm they are guarding. A sequel is *Meeting* (2011). ℮ Lexile 630L (Rev: BL 8/10; LMC 10/10; SLJ 9/1/10)

3105 Holt, K. A. *Brains for Lunch: A Zombie Novel in Haiku?!* (5–8). Illus. by Gahan Wilson. 2010, Roaring Brook $15.99 (978-1-59643-629-9). Irreverent, sometimes gross, haiku tell the humorous story of a middle school populated by zombies, humans, and blood-sucking chupacabras. (Rev: BL 6/10; LMC 11–12/10; SLJ 10/1/10)

3106 Hoobler, Dorothy, and Thomas Hoobler. *The Ghost in the Tokaido Inn* (6–12). 1999, Putnam $17.99 (978-0-399-23330-2). Set in 18th-century Japan, this is the story of 14-year-old Seikei, his dreams of becoming a samurai, and what happened after he saw a legendary ghost stealing a valuable jewel. (Rev: BL 6/1–15/99; HBG 4/00; SLJ 6/99; VOYA 10/99)

3107 Horowitz, Anthony. *Evil Star* (5–8). Series: The Gatekeepers. 2006, Scholastic $17.99 (978-0-439-67996-1). In the second installment of this action-packed fantasy series, 14-year-old Matt Freeman travels to Peru to learn more about the possible opening of another gate to the underworld. (Rev: BL 6/1–15/06; SLJ 7/06)

3108 Horowitz, Anthony. *Necropolis* (7–12). Series: Gatekeepers. 2009, Scholastic $17.99 (978-043968003-5). Fifteen-year-old Scarlet joins the other four teens struggling to defeat the Old Ones. ⌒ (Rev: BLO 6/16/09)

3109 Horowitz, Anthony. *Nightrise* (6–9). Series: The Gatekeepers. 2007, Scholastic $17.99 (978-0-439-68001-1). An organization called Nightrise is after telepathic twins Jamie and Scott, 14, in this third exciting volume in the struggle to keep the world safe from the Old Ones. ⌒ (Rev: SLJ 1/08)

3110 Horowitz, Anthony. *Return to Groosham Grange: The Unholy Grail* (5–8). Series: Groosham Grange. 2009, Philomel $16.99 (978-0-399-25063-7). In this funny and somewhat spooky tale, David competes with a new student to earn Groosham Grange's top prize, the magical cup known as the Unholy Grail; a sequel to *Groosham Grange* (2008). Lexile 690L (Rev: BL 8/09; SLJ 9/09; VOYA 8/09)

3111 Horowitz, Anthony. *The Switch* (5–8). 2009, Philomel $16.99 (978-0-399-25062-0). Rich kid Tad Spencer, 13, is not pleased when he finds himself in the body of Bob Snarby, son of carnival workers, until he starts to learn more about his old life. (Rev: BL 12/15/08; LMC 5/09; SLJ 3/09)

3112 Houck, Colleen. *Tiger's Quest* (7–12). 2011, Sterling $17.95 (978-1-4027-8404-0). Back home in Oregon after her breakup with Ren, an immortal shape-shifting tiger, Kelsey tries to forget him — until he shows up at her house and then is kidnapped; Kelsey must return to India to rescue him. The sequel to *Tiger's Curse* (2011). ⌒ Lexile 720L (Rev: BL 6/1/11; SLJ 8/11)

3113 Hoving, Isabel. *The Dream Merchant* (8–12). Trans. from Dutch by Hester Velmans. 2005, Candlewick $17.99 (978-0-7636-2880-2). An action-packed, intricately plotted adventure involving three young people in time travel and a world of collective dreams called *umaya*. (Rev: SLJ 1/06; VOYA 12/05)

3114 Howe, Norma. *Angel in Vegas* (6–9). 2009, Candlewick $16.99 (978-0-7636-3985-3). Hapless guardian angel Noah Sark's latest assignment takes him to the Las Vegas strip where he is to protect Barbra, a dead ringer for the late Princess Di, whose untimely death was the result of Noah's ineptitude on his last mission. Lexile 930L (Rev: BL 11/15/09; SLJ 12/09; VOYA 2/10)

3115 Howell, Troy. *The Dragon of Cripple Creek* (5–8). 2011, Abrams $19.95 (978-0-8109-9713-4). Kat, 12, falls into an abandoned mine chute in Colorado and discovers not only gold but an ancient dragon guarding the hoard; Kat inadvertently starts a 21st-century gold rush even as she seeks to protect the dragon and the environment. (Rev: BL 5/1/11; SLJ 7/11)

3116 Hubbard, Mandy. *Prada and Prejudice* (7–10). 2009, Penguin paper $8.99 (978-159514260-3). On a class trip to England, bumbling Callie has a bad fall and wakes up in the year 1815. She makes friends with Em-

ily, a girl about to be forced into an unfortunate marriage, and gains the affections of a young duke. (Rev: BL 5/15/09; SLJ 7/1/09)

3117 Hubbard, Mandy. *Ripple* (7–11). 2011, Penguin $16.99 (978-1-59514-423-2). Since the drowning death of her boyfriend, 18-year-old Lexi has discovered that she is a siren, with the gift of luring men to their fates. ℮ (Rev: BL 9/15/11; SLJ 9/1/11)

3118 Huff, Tanya. *The Second Summoning: The Keeper's Chronicles #2* (7–12). 2001, DAW paper $7.99 (978-0-88677-975-7). Claire, a Keeper entrusted with protecting Canada, allows an angel and a demon to enter with humorous results. (Rev: VOYA 12/01)

3119 Hughes, Carol. *Dirty Magic* (5–8). 2006, Random House $17.95 (978-0-375-83187-4). In a desperate attempt to save his little sister's life, 10-year-old Joe Brooks enters a shadowy world where ill children are held captive. (Rev: BL 10/1/06; SLJ 2/07)

3120 Hughes, Mark Peter. *A Crack in the Sky* (6–10). 2010, Delacorte $16.99 (978-0-385-73708-1). Eli, a 13-year-old with special powers, notices problems with his dome-city but his worries are ignored and his continuing investigations lead to him being sent for reeducation. ℮ Lexile 740L (Rev: BL 7/10; LMC 11–12/10; SLJ 10/1/10)

3121 Hughes, Monica, sel. *What If? Amazing Stories* (5–10). 1998, Tundra paper $6.95 (978-0-88776-458-5). Fourteen fantasy and science fiction short stories by noted Canadian writers are included in this anthology, plus a few related poems. (Rev: BL 2/15/99; SLJ 6/99; VOYA 6/99)

3122 Hulme, John, and Michael Wexler. *The Glitch in Sleep* (5–8). Series: Seems. 2007, Bloomsbury $16.95 (978-1-59990-129-9). When 12-year-old Becker gets a job at the Institute for Fixing and Repair, he discovers that the world as we know it is under the control of the Seems; a humorous and thought-provoking story with plenty of illustrations and lots of entertaining gadgets. (Rev: BL 11/15/07; LMC 1/08; SLJ 11/07)

3123 Humphreys, Chris. *Vendetta* (8–11). Series: Runestone Saga. 2007, Knopf $15.99 (978-0-375-83293-2). Fifteen-year-old Sky March heads to Corsica to find a way to free his cousin Kristin from his evil Norwegian grandfather's spell. (Rev: BL 8/07; SLJ 1/08)

3124 Hunter, Erin. *A Dangerous Path* (6–9). Series: Warriors. 2004, HarperCollins LB $17.89 (978-0-06-052564-4). In the fifth installment in the series, Fireheart, deputy leader of ThunderClan, worries about the future of all the cats in the forest now that Tigerstar has taken over the leadership of ShadowClan. (Rev: BL 8/04)

3125 Hunter, Erin. *Dawn* (6–9). Series: Warriors: The New Prophecy. 2006, HarperCollins LB $17.89 (978-0-06-074456-4). In the third volume of the series, humans are encroaching further into the habitat of the four cat clans and there is pressure to unite and seek a new home. (Rev: BL 12/1/05)

3126 Hunter, Erin. *Fire and Ice* (6–9). Series: Warriors. 2003, HarperCollins $16.99 (978-0-06-000003-5). Ex-kittypet Firepaw (now known as Fireheart) is eager to prove himself on his first mission — to bring WindClan back to their territory — but faces many obstacles. (Rev: BL 9/1/03; HBG 10/03; SLJ 9/03)

3127 Hunter, Erin. *Firestar's Quest* (6–9). Series: Warriors. 2007, HarperCollins $17.99 (978-0-06-113164-6). Leader of the ThunderClan and proud of the current era of peace, Firestar sets out on a dangerous journey to discover what happened to the SkyClan cats. (Rev: BL 9/15/07)

3128 Hunter, Erin. *Forest of Secrets* (6–9). Series: Warriors. 2003, HarperCollins $16.99 (978-0-06-000004-2). Firepaw suspects Tigerclaw of treachery and works to expose him in this exciting installment featuring a flood, a tragic death, and clan rivalries. (Rev: BL 9/15/03; SLJ 10/03)

3129 Hunter, Erin. *Into the Wild* (6–9). Series: Warriors. 2003, HarperCollins $16.99 (978-0-06-000002-8). A young cat named Firepaw, formerly a pet, becomes an apprentice in the ThunderClan of wild warrior cats, which is in the midst of a struggle to retain its territory. (Rev: BL 2/15/03; HBG 10/03; SLJ 5/03)

3130 Hunter, Erin. *Island of Shadows* (5–8). Series: Seekers: Return to the Wild. 2012, HarperCollins $16.99 (978-006199634-4). Bears Toklo, Lusa, and Kallik, missing their former companion Ujurak, encounter many dangers as they make a difficult journey home in this first volume in a new series that is a companion to the Seeker books. (Rev: BL 1/1/12)

3131 Hunter, Erin. *Moonrise* (6–9). Series: Warriors: The New Prophecy. 2005, HarperCollins LB $17.89 (978-0-06-074453-3). The cats of the StarClan take advice from a badger named Midnight and on the ensuing journey through the mountains meet a new and unusual tribe of cats. (Rev: BL 9/1/05)

3132 Hunter, Erin. *Rising Storm* (6–9). Series: Warriors. 2004, HarperCollins LB $17.89 (978-0-06-052562-0). In this fourth volume of the series, Fireheart the cat faces a number of daunting challenges in his new position as deputy leader of the ThunderClan. (Rev: BL 1/1–15/04; VOYA 4/04)

3133 Hunter, Erin. *The Sight* (5–7). Series: Warriors: The Power of Three. 2007, HarperCollins $16.99 (978-0-06-089201-2). Three kits — Hollypaw, Jaypaw, and Lionpaw — whose parents were members of the Thunderclan are endowed with special abilities in this series opener that follows the New Prophecy cycle. (Rev: BL 8/07; LMC 11–12/08)

3134 Hunter, Erin. *Sign of the Moon* (5–8). Series: Warriors, Omen of the Stars. 2011, HarperCollins $16.99 (978-006155518-3). Jayfeather prepares for a danger-ous journey that will reveal truth about the final battle as clan disputes continue; the fourth installment in this series. (Rev: BL 9/1/11)

3135 Hunter, Erin. *Sunset* (6–9). Series: Warriors: The New Prophecy. 2007, HarperCollins paper $6.99 (978-0-06-082771-7). The dead Tigerstar plots against Firestar; will Tigerstar's son Brambleclaw, Firestar's good friend, remain true to Firestar? (Rev: BL 2/1/08)

3136 Hunter, Mollie. *The Mermaid Summer* (5–8). 1988, HarperCollins $15.89 (978-0-06-022628-2). Eric Anderson refuses to recognize the power of the mermaid and leaves his Scottish fishing village after his boat is dashed to pieces on the rocks. (Rev: BCCB 5/88; BL 6/1/88; SLJ 6–7/88)

3137 Hunter, Mollie. *A Stranger Came Ashore* (7–9). 1977, HarperCollins paper $6.99 (978-0-06-440082-4). In this fantasy set in the Shetland Islands, a bull seal takes human form and comes ashore.

3138 Hussey, Charmain. *The Valley of Secrets* (4–7). Illus. by Christopher Crump. 2005, Simon & Schuster $16.95 (978-0-689-87862-6). A detailed, multifaceted novel about an orphan who inherits his great-uncle's estate and, through his uncle's journal, learns about the plight of the Amazon Indians. (Rev: BL 3/1/05; SLJ 2/05)

3139 Irving, Washington. *Rip Van Winkle and the Legend of Sleepy Hollow* (5–7). Illus. by Felix O. Darley. 1980, Sleepy Hollow $19.95 (978-0-912882-42-0). A handsome edition of these two classics.

3140 Iserles, Inbali. *The Tygrine Cat* (5–8). 2008, Candlewick $15.99 (978-0-7636-3798-9). Mati, the son of the slain queen of the Tygrine Cats, is being pursued by a killer sent by Suzerain in this feline fantasy. (Rev: BL 5/15/08)

3141 Jablonski, Carla. *Silent Echoes* (7–10). 2007, Penguin $16.99 (978-1-59514-082-1). Lucy, a 19th-century spiritualist, is astonished when she finds herself communicating with Lindsay, a modern-day teenager, in this time travel novel that will have readers learning about life in the 1880s. (Rev: BCCB 4/07; BL 3/1/07; SLJ 3/07)

3142 Jacques, Brian. *The Angel's Command: A Tale from the Castaways of the Flying Dutchman* (5–9). 2003, Putnam $23.99 (978-0-399-23999-1). This action-packed fantasy, set in the 17th century, is the sequel to *Castaways of the Flying Dutchman*. (Rev: BL 2/1/03; HB 3–4/03; HBG 10/03; SLJ 3/03; VOYA 4/03)

3143 Jacques, Brian. *The Bellmaker* (5–7). Series: Redwall. 1995, Putnam $24.99 (978-0-399-22805-6). This seventh tale in the series of animal fantasies features Mariel, a courageous, outspoken mouse. (Rev: BCCB 4/95; BL 4/1/95; HB 5–6/95; SLJ 8/95)

3144 Jacques, Brian. *Castaways of the Flying Dutchman* (5–9). 2001, Putnam $23.99 (978-0-399-23601-3). A mute boy stows away on the *Flying Dutchman*, a ship that is condemned to sail the seas forever, and there he meets the ghostly crew and the crazed captain in this story in which the boy has many adventures and eventually gains the power of speech and the gift of staying young forever. (Rev: BCCB 3/01; BL 3/1/01; HB 3–4/01; HBG 10/01; SLJ 3/01; VOYA 4/01)

3145 Jacques, Brian. *Doomwyte* (5–8). Illus. by David Elliot. Series: Redwall. 2008, Philomel $23.99 (978-039924544-2). In this latest installment in the series, two contemptible new villains are thwarted in their quest for the jeweled eyes of the Great Doomwyte Idol. ∩ Lexile 860L (Rev: BL 9/1/08)

3146 Jacques, Brian. *Eulalia!* (5–8). Series: Redwall. 2007, Philomel $23.99 (978-0-399-24209-0). Lord Asheye, Badger Lord of Salamandastron, wishes to find his successor in this satisfying installment in the long-running series. ∩ (Rev: BL 8/07; SLJ 5/08)

3147 Jacques, Brian. *High Rhulain* (5–8). Illus. by David Elliot. Series: Redwall. 2005, Philomel $23.99 (978-0-399-24208-3). In this eighteenth installment, ottermaid Tiria bravely journeys to the Green Isle to rescue otter kinsmen from evil wildcats. (Rev: BL 9/1/05; SLJ 9/05)

3148 Jacques, Brian. *The Legend of Luke: A Tale from Redwall* (5–8). Series: Redwall. 2000, Putnam $23.99 (978-0-399-23490-3). This book focuses on the building of the abbey, Martin's search for his father Luke, and Luke's heroic career. (Rev: BL 12/15/99; HBG 10/00; SLJ 2/00; VOYA 4/00)

3149 Jacques, Brian. *Loamhedge* (5–8). Series: Redwall. 2003, Putnam $23.99 (978-0-399-23724-9). As Redwall stalwarts including Bragoon and Sarobando seek a cure for a haremaid's ills at Loamhedge Abbey, Redwall itself comes under attack. (Rev: BL 9/15/03; HB 11–12/03; HBG 4/04; SLJ 10/03)

3150 Jacques, Brian. *The Long Patrol* (5–8). Series: Redwall. 1998, Putnam $23.99 (978-0-399-23165-0). In this tenth adventure, the villainous Rapscallions decide to attack the peaceful Abbey of Redwall. (Rev: BCCB 4/98; BL 12/15/97; HB 3–4/98; HBG 10/98; SLJ 1/98)

3151 Jacques, Brian. *Lord Brocktree* (5–8). Series: Redwall. 2000, Putnam $23.99 (978-0-399-23590-0). The villainous Ungatt Trunn and his Blue Hordes invade and capture the mountain fortress Salamandastron. (Rev: BCCB 9/00; BL 9/1/00; HB 9–10/00; HBG 3/01; SLJ 9/00)

3152 Jacques, Brian. *Mariel of Redwall* (5–7). Illus. by Gary Chalk. Series: Redwall. 1992, Putnam $24.99 (978-0-399-22144-6). Fourth in the saga of the animals of Redwall Abbey, this story tells how the great Joseph Bell is brought to the abbey. (Rev: BCCB 3/92; BL 1/15/92*; HB 9–10/92; SLJ 3/92)

3153 Jacques, Brian. *Marlfox* (5–8). Series: Redwall. 1999, Putnam $22.99 (978-0-399-23307-4). The fa-

mous tapestry depicting Martin and Warrior has been stolen from Redwall Abbey, and four young would-be heroes set out to recover it. (Rev: BL 12/15/98; HB 1–2/99; HBG 10/99; SLJ 4/99; VOYA 2/99)

3154 Jacques, Brian. *Martin the Warrior* (5–7). Illus. by Gary Chalk. Series: Redwall. 1994, Putnam $23.99 (978-0-399-22670-0). This volume tells how the mouse Martin the Warrior became the bold, courageous fighter that he is. (Rev: BCCB 1/94; BL 3/1/94; HB 9–10/94; SLJ 1/94)

3155 Jacques, Brian. *Mattimeo* (5–8). Series: Redwall. 1990, Putnam $23.99 (978-0-399-21741-8). The evil fox kidnaps the animal children of Redwall Abbey in this continuation of *Mossflower* (1988) and *Redwall* (1987). (Rev: BL 4/15/90; SLJ 9/90; VOYA 8/90)

3156 Jacques, Brian. *Mossflower* (5–7). Illus. by Gary Chalk. Series: Redwall. 1988, Putnam $24.99 (978-0-399-21549-0); paper $5.99 (978-0-380-70828-4). How a brave and resourceful mouse took power from the evil wildcat. (Rev: BCCB 12/88; BL 11/1/88; SLJ 11/88)

3157 Jacques, Brian. *Outcast of Redwall* (5–8). Series: Redwall. 1996, Philomel $24.99 (978-0-399-22914-5). This episode in the Redwall saga involves the badger Sunflash, his buddy Skarlath the kestrel, and their enemy the ferret Swartt Sixclaw. (Rev: BCCB 3/96; BL 3/1/96; SLJ 5/96; VOYA 10/96)

3158 Jacques, Brian. *The Pearls of Lutra* (5–8). Series: Redwall. 1997, Putnam $23.99 (978-0-399-22946-6). The evil marten Mad Eyes threatens the peaceful Redwall Abbey in this ninth book in the series. (Rev: BCCB 4/97; BL 2/15/97; SLJ 3/97*; VOYA 6/97)

3159 Jacques, Brian. *Rakkety Tam* (5–8). Illus. by David Elliot. Series: Redwall. 2004, Putnam $23.99 (978-0-399-23725-6). When Redwall is threatened by a murderous wolverine called Gulo the Savage, two warrior squirrels — Rakkety Tam McBurl and Wild Doogy Plumm — take action. (Rev: BL 9/15/04; SLJ 9/04)

3160 Jacques, Brian. *The Rogue Crew* (5–8). Illus. by Sean Rubin. Series: Redwall. 2011, Philomel $23.99 (978-039925416-1). Wearat returns to exact revenge in this satisfying, action-packed final installment of the Redwall series. (Rev: BL 5/1/11)

3161 Jacques, Brian. *The Sable Quean* (5–8). Illus. by Sean Charles Rubin. Series: Redwall. 2010, Philomel $23.99 (978-039925164-1). Buckler and other courageous Redwall creatures prepare to battle the evil Sable Quean when the abbey's young inhabitants start disappearing. ∩ (Rev: BLO 12/1/09; VOYA 12/09)

3162 Jacques, Brian. *Salamandastron* (5–7). Illus. by Gary Chalk. Series: Redwall. 1993, Putnam $23.99 (978-0-399-21992-4). These tales are centered on the badgers and hares of the castle of Salamandastron near the sea. (Rev: BCCB 7–8/93; BL 3/15/93; HB 5–6/93; SLJ 3/93)

3163 Jacques, Brian. *Taggerung* (5–8). Series: Redwall. 2001, Putnam $23.99 (978-0-399-23720-1). The 14th book in the series features an otter named Taggerung who was kidnapped from the abbey as a baby and raised by an outlaw ferret. (Rev: BL 8/01; HB 11–12/01; HBG 3/02; SLJ 10/01; VOYA 10/01)

3164 Jacques, Brian. *Triss* (5–8). 2002, Putnam $23.99 (978-0-399-23723-2). An action-packed installment in the Redwall series in which squirrel Triss, an escaped slave, meets up with the badger Sagax and his friend Scarum. (Rev: BL 9/1/02; HB 1–2/03; HBG 3/03; SLJ 10/02; VOYA 12/02)

3165 James, Mary. *Frankenlouse* (5–8). 1994, Scholastic paper $13.95 (978-0-590-46528-1). Nick, 14, is enrolled at Blister Military Academy, which is run by his father. He escapes into his own comic book creations featuring an insect named Frankenlouse. (Rev: BCCB 11/94; BL 10/15/94; SLJ 11/94; VOYA 12/94)

3166 James, Mary. *The Shuteyes* (4–7). 1994, Scholastic paper $3.25 (978-0-590-45070-6). Chester has some unusual experiences when he journeys to Alert, a land where no one sleeps. (Rev: SLJ 4/93)

3167 James, Syrie, and Ryan M. James. *Forbidden* (8–11). 2012, HarperTeen $8.99 (978-006202789-4). Happy to be settled in one place for her junior year, Claire finds herself having visions and learns, from new student Alec, that she is a half angel — and is in danger. e (Rev: BL 2/1/12; SLJ 3/12; VOYA 4/12)

3168 Jarvis, Robin. *The Whitby Witches* (4–7). Illus. by Jess Petersen. 2006, Chronicle $17.95 (978-0-8118-5413-9). Sent to live with their elderly Aunt Alice in the English seaside village of Whitby, 8-year-old Ben — who can see the invisible — and 12-year-old Jennet find themselves swept up in a struggle between good and evil. (Rev: BL 10/1/06; SLJ 10/06)

3169 Jenkins, A. M. *Night Road* (8–12). 2008, HarperTeen $16.99 (978-0-06-054604-5). Cole and Sandor, both hemovores (as these vampires prefer to be called), are assigned the project of helping young Gordon adjust to the difficult life of a vampire. (Rev: BL 5/15/08; SLJ 8/08)

3170 Jenkins, Jerry B., and Chris Fabry. *The Book of the King* (5–8). Series: The Wormling. 2007, Tyndale paper $5.99 (978-1-4143-0155-6). Owen discovers that there is another world beneath his family's bookstore and that he must battle with dragons to overcome evil forces. (Rev: BL 10/15/07)

3171 Jenkins, Martin. *Jonathan Swift's Gulliver* (5–8). Illus. by Chris Riddell. 2005, Candlewick $19.99 (978-0-7636-2409-5). A retelling of the classic tale using contemporary language and striking artwork. (Rev: BL 3/15/05; SLJ 3/05)

3172 Jennewein, James, and Tom S. Parker. *Sword of Doom* (6–9). 2010, HarperCollins $17.99 (978-0-06-144939-0). An entertaining sequel to *RuneWarriors*

(2008), in which Dane the Defiant has more adventures including a quest to retrieve a magical sword. ⌒ e Lexile 970L (Rev: LMC 3–4/10; SLJ 2/10)

3173 Jennings, Richard W. *Ghost Town* (5–8). 2009, Houghton $16.00 (978-0-547-19471-4). A teenager discovers a camera with the ability to photograph the dearly departed. (Rev: BL 6/1–15/09; HB 7/09; SLJ 9/09)

3174 Jinks, Catherine. *The Reformed Vampire Support Group* (8–12). 2009, Houghton Mifflin $17.00 (978-015206609-3). Nina's support group for vampires is thrown for a loop when one member is killed by a stake through the heart; a funny take on the modern vampire genre. YALSA Top Ten 2010. ⌒ e Lexile 750L (Rev: BL 1/1–15/09; HB 5–6/09; SLJ 3/1/09; VOYA 10/09)

3175 Johansen, K. V. *Nightwalker* (5–8). 2007, Orca paper $8.95 (978-1-55143-481-0). Thrown into the dungeon when it's discovered that he possesses a powerful magical ring, young Maurey escapes with the help of a baroness and travels to Talverdin in an effort to find out if he is a nightwalker. (Rev: BL 4/1/07; SLJ 9/07)

3176 Johnson-Shelton, Nils. *The Invisible Tower* (5–8). Series: Otherworld Chronicles. 2012, HarperCollins $16.99 (978-006207086-9). Ordinary kid Artie Kingfisher, 12, learns that he is actually King Arthur brought back to life in the 21st century and that he must save the world from disaster. ⌒ e (Rev: BL 3/1/12; SLJ 3/12; VOYA 2/12)

3177 Johnson, Christine. *Claire de Lune* (8–10). 2010, Simon & Schuster $16.99 (978-1-4169-9182-3). Claire discovers that she is destined to become a werewolf and face terrible danger in this fast-paced fantasy. e (Rev: BL 5/15/10; LMC 8–9/10; SLJ 4/10)

3178 Johnson, Jane. *The Shadow World: The Eidolon Chronicles* (4–7). Illus. by Adam Stower. Series: Eidolon Chronicles. 2007, Simon & Schuster $15.99 (978-1-4169-1783-0). The second book in the series finds Ben entering Eidolon to bring back his sister Ellie, who is being held by the evil Dodman. (Rev: BL 12/1/07; SLJ 11/07)

3179 Johnson, Kathleen Jeffrie. *A Fast and Brutal Wing* (8–11). 2004, Roaring Brook $16.95 (978-1-59643-013-6). In a series of e-mails, journal entries, and newspaper stories, three teens recount the mysterious and fantastic events that led to a Halloween disappearance. (Rev: BL 12/15/04; SLJ 12/04; VOYA 12/04)

3180 Jolley, Dan. *The Time Travel Trap* (4–8). Illus. by Matt Wendt. Series: Twisted Journeys. 2008, Lerner LB $27.93 (978-0-7613-9472-3); paper $7.95 (978-0-8225-8874-0). Readers can choose which way the plot will go in this time-travel adventure story. (Rev: SLJ 5/08)

3181 Jones, David. *Baboon* (6–9). 2007, Annick $21.95 (978-1-55451-054-2); paper $11.95 (978-1-55451-053-5). After a plane crash in Africa, Gerry, 14, finds himself in a baboon body, part of a baboon troop, and progressively becoming more baboon and less human; the baboon behavior is very realistic. (Rev: BL 5/1/07; SLJ 6/07)

3182 Jones, Diana Wynne. *Cart and Cwidder* (8–10). 1995, Greenwillow $15.00 (978-0-688-13360-3); paper $4.95 (978-0-688-13399-3). When his father dies, 11-year-old Moril becomes heir to the family's cwidder, a musical instrument that has magical powers.

3183 Jones, Diana Wynne. *The Crown of Dalemark* (6–9). Series: Dalemark Quartet. 1995, Greenwillow $17.00 (978-0-688-13363-4). Readers familiar with the first three books in this quartet will enjoy its conclusion about Noreth, a teen who believes she is destined to become queen, and Maewen, who is sent to impersonate her. New readers should start with book one. (Rev: BL 12/15/95; SLJ 8/96)

3184 Jones, Diana Wynne. *Enchanted Glass* (6–9). 2010, Greenwillow $16.99 (978-0-06-186684-5). Andrew Hope, a professor, inherits a manor from his magician grandfather and finds that life gets quite complicated when he moves in and a 12-year-old orphan named Aidan arrives seeking help; a humorous and intriguing fantasy. ∩ ℮ Lexile 790L (Rev: BL 2/15/10*; HB 5–6/10; LMC 3–4/10; SLJ 4/10)

3185 Jones, Diana Wynne. *House of Many Ways* (6–9). Series: Howl's Moving Castle. 2008, Greenwillow $17.99 (978-0-06-147795-9). Characters from *Howl's Moving Castle* and *Castle in the Air* populate this story about Charmain, who is sent to live in her great-uncle William's magical house and ends up helping to save High Norland. (Rev: BL 5/15/08; SLJ 6/08)

3186 Jones, Diana Wynne. *Howl's Moving Castle* (7–12). 1986, Greenwillow $16.95 (978-0-688-06233-0). A fearful young girl is changed into an old woman and in that disguise moves into the castle of Wizard Howl. (Rev: BL 6/1/86; SLJ 8/86; VOYA 8/86)

3187 Jones, Diana Wynne. *The Merlin Conspiracy* (6–10). 2003, HarperCollins LB $17.89 (978-0-06-052319-0). Three teenagers blessed with magical powers collaborate to save the islands of Blest, an alternate England, from attack by wizards in this complex novel full of humor. (Rev: BL 4/15/03; HB 5–6/03; HBG 10/03; SLJ 5/03; VOYA 8/03)

3188 Jones, Diana Wynne. *The Pinhoe Egg* (5–8). Series: Chrestomanci. 2006, Greenwillow $18.89 (978-0-06-113125-7). In this compelling addition to the Chrestomanci series, Marianne Pinhoe and Cat Chant find a strange egg with magical properties. ∩ (Rev: BL 9/15/06; SLJ 10/06)

3189 Jones, Diana Wynne. *The Time of the Ghost* (6–9). 1996, Greenwillow $15.00 (978-0-668-14598-5). Sally, the ghost of one of four sisters whose parents run a school for boys, tries to undo a bargain she made with

an evil goddess when she was young. (Rev: BL 8/96; SLJ 11/96; VOYA 4/97)

3190 Jones, Diana Wynne. *Unexpected Magic: Collected Stories* (5–10). 2004, Greenwillow $16.99 (978-0-06-055533-7). An exciting anthology of 16 tales of mystery and magic by a master of fantasy. (Rev: BL 4/15/04; SLJ 9/04)

3191 Jones, Diana Wynne. *Year of the Griffin* (7–10). 2000, Greenwillow LB $15.89 (978-0-06-029158-7). Pirates, assassins, and plain old magic are among the challenges faced by students at Wizard's University — including Elda, griffin daughter of the wizard Derk — in this sequel to the humorous *Dark Lord of Derkholm* (1998). (Rev: BL 11/1/00; HB 11–12/00; HBG 3/01; SLJ 10/00; VOYA 12/00)

3192 Jones, Frewin. *The Faerie Path* (6–9). 2007, HarperCollins $16.99 (978-0-06-087102-4). After a car accident on the eve of her 16th birthday, Anita wakes up to find that she is in Faerie and has been transformed into Princess Tania, who has been missing for 500 years; what's more, her boyfriend Evan (who was in the car with her) is now Edric, servant to a faerie lord. (Rev: BCCB 3/07; BL 1/1–15/07; SLJ 3/07)

3193 Jones, Frewin. *The Immortal Realm* (6–8). Series: The Faerie Path. 2009, HarperTeen $16.99 (978-0-06-087155-0). When members of the Faerie community become ill and even die, Tania sets out to save the kingdom in this fourth installment in the series. ℮ Lexile 720L (Rev: SLJ 8/09; VOYA 8/9)

3194 Jones, Frewin. *The Lost Queen* (6–9). Series: The Faerie Path. 2007, Eos $16.99 (978-0-06-087105-5). Tania, who lives a double life in the faerie world and the mortal world, goes in search of the long-lost Queen Titania in this sequel to *The Faerie Path*. (Rev: BL 11/1/07; SLJ 11/07)

3195 Jones, Frewin. *The Sorcerer King* (6–9). Series: Faerie Path. 2008, Eos $16.99 (978-0-06-087108-6). With their king kidnapped and the faerie people enslaved, Princess Tania, Queen Titania, and Edric go to war to save their culture and their world; the final volume in the trilogy. (Rev: BL 2/1/08; SLJ 2/08)

3196 Jones, Frewin. *Warrior Princess* (7–10). Series: Warrior Princess. 2009, Eos $16.99 (978-006087143-7). Branwen must choose between the pampered life of a princess and the dangerous life of a warrior in this action-paced story set in medieval Britain; the first in a series. Lexile 780L (Rev: BL 2/15/09; SLJ 2/1/09)

3197 Jones, Kimberly K. *The Genie Scheme* (4–7). 2009, Simon & Schuster $15.99 (978-1-4169-5554-2). When she acquires her personal genie, Janna, 12, learns that material possessions are not the best things to wish for. (Rev: BCCB 6/09; BL 3/15/09; SLJ 3/09)

3198 Jordan, Robert. *A Crown of Swords* (8–12). Series: Wheel of Time. 1996, Tor $29.95 (978-0-312-85767-7). In this seventh book of this series, Rand and his army of Aiel warriors prepare to do battle with the Dark One. (Rev: VOYA 2/97)

3199 Jordan, Sherryl. *The Hunting of the Last Dragon* (6–10). 2002, HarperCollins LB $15.89 (978-0-06-028903-4). In 14th-century England a monk records young peasant Jude's story of his quest, accompanied by a young Chinese woman, to kill a dragon. (Rev: BCCB 9/02; BL 4/15/02; HBG 10/02; SLJ 7/02)

3200 Jordan, Sherryl. *Secret Sacrament* (8–12). 2001, HarperCollins LB $17.89 (978-0-06-028905-8). In an ancient time, Gabriel trains at the Citadel to become a healer, hoping to intervene in the violence that surrounds him. (Rev: BCCB 3/01; BL 2/15/01; HBG 10/01; SLJ 2/01; VOYA 6/01)

3201 Jordan, Sherryl. *Time of the Eagle* (7–10). 2007, Eos $16.99 (978-0-06-059554-8). As the daughter of Gabriel Eshban Vala (hero of the 2001 *Secret Sacrament*, Avala is a healer and the Chosen One, who must bring about the uprising of the persecuted Shinali people. (Rev: BL 5/15/07; LMC 11/07; SLJ 9/07)

3202 Jordan, Sophie. *Vanish* (8–12). 2011, HarperCollins $17.99 (978-0-06-193510-7). In this sequel to the paranormal romance *Firelight* (2010), draki Jacinda must make difficult choices when her human lover Will reappears on the scene. ℮ (Rev: BL 10/1/11; SLJ 10/1/11)

3203 Kaaberbol, Lene. *The Serpent Gift* (6–9). Series: Shamer Chronicles. 2006, Henry Holt $17.95 (978-0-8050-7770-4). In this third book in the series, Dina and her family escape their Blackmaster father only to find themselves enslaved by the Foundation. (Rev: BL 5/15/06; HB 5–6/06; SLJ 1/07)

3204 Kaaberbol, Lene. *The Shamer's Daughter* (6–8). 2004, Henry Holt $16.95 (978-0-8050-7541-0). Dina has inherited her mother's powers as a Shamer, able to ferret out the shameful truths that others try to hide; the 10-year-old sees her gift as a burden until she's called upon to use her powers to save her mother's life. The sequel is *The Shamer's Signet* (2005). (Rev: BL 4/15/04; HB 5–6/04; SLJ 6/04; VOYA 6/04)

3205 Kaaberbol, Lene. *The Shamer's War* (6–10). Series: The Shamer's Chronicles. 2006, Henry Holt $17.95 (978-0-8050-7771-1). The final volume in this action-packed series featuring a battle between Prince Nicodemus and his acquisitive relative Drakan. (Rev: HB 11–12/06; SLJ 1/07)

3206 Kagawa, Julie. *The Lost Prince* (8–12). 2012, HarlequinTeen paper $9.99 (978-0-373-21-057-2). Ethan, 17, finds himself risking his life to save Kenzie as the fey mount a menacing attack against humankind. ∩ ℮ (Rev: BL 11/1/12; LMC 5–6/13; SLJ 12/12)

3207 Kalman, Maira. *Swami on Rye: Max in India* (4–8). 1995, Viking $14.99 (978-0-670-84646-7). A sophisticated comic novel about a dog who goes to India to find the meaning of life. (Rev: BL 10/15/95; SLJ 11/95)

3208 Kassem, Lou. *A Summer for Secrets* (5–7). 1989, Avon paper $2.95 (978-0-380-75759-6). Laura's ability to communicate with animals causes complications. (Rev: BL 10/1/89)

3209 Kate, Lauren. *Rapture* (8–11). Series: Fallen. 2012, Delacorte $17.99 (978-038573918-4); LB $20.99 (978-038590775-0). In this fourth book in the series, Luce and Daniel struggle to unravel the ancient mystery that threatens their love. ∩ ℮ (Rev: BL 8/12; VOYA 10/12)

3210 Kay, Elizabeth. *The Divide* (5–9). 2003, Scholastic $15.95 (978-0-439-45696-8). Felix, a 13-year-old with a heart problem, passes out while on a trip to Costa Rica and wakes up in a world full of mythical creatures. The sequel is *Back to the Divide* (2004). (Rev: BL 6/1–15/03; HBG 4/04; SLJ 9/03; VOYA 8/03)

3211 Kaye, Marilyn. *Here Today, Gone Tomorrow* (5–8). Series: Gifted. 2009, Kingfisher paper $7.99 (978-0-7534-6310-9). When her classmates begin mysteriously disappearing, clairvoyant Emily battles low self-esteem and bullying and uses her talents to save them. Lexile HL610L (Rev: BL 11/1/09; SLJ 10/09)

3212 Keaton, Kelly. *A Beautiful Evil* (8–10). 2012, Simon & Schuster $16.99 (978-144240927-9). A descendant of Medusa, Ari struggles to sublimate the evil urges she feels as Athena comes to steal her secret powers. ℮ Lexile 750L (Rev: BL 3/1/12; LMC 8–9/12; SLJ 5/1/12; VOYA 12/11)

3213 Keehn, Sally M. *Magpie Gabbard and the Quest for the Buried Moon* (5–8). 2007, Philomel $16.99 (978-0-399-24340-0). Thirteen-year-old Magpie Gabbard must fulfill a prophecy and put aside her cussedness in order to save the moon in this exuberant and complex tall tale. (Rev: BL 4/15/07; SLJ 2/07)

3214 Kelleher, Victor. *Brother Night* (7–9). 1991, Walker $16.95 (978-0-8027-8100-0). Rabon, 15, was raised by a foster father in a small town and ends up on a quest to the city with his dark, ugly twin, both learning about their heritage along the way. (Rev: BL 6/15/91; SLJ 5/91)

3215 Kelly, Jacqueline. *Return to the Willows* (4–7). Illus. by Clint Young. 2012, Henry Holt $19.99 (978-0-8050-9413-8). Toad, Mole, Rat, and Badger are back in this well-illustrated sequel to *The Wind in the Willows*. ℮ Lexile 890L (Rev: BL 10/15/12; SLJ 12/12)

3216 Kempton, Kate. *The World Beyond the Waves: An Environmental Adventure* (5–7). 1995, Portunus $14.95 (978-0-9641330-6-8); paper $8.95 (978-0-9641330-1-3). After being washed overboard during a violent storm, Sam visits a land where she meets ocean animals that have been misused by humans. (Rev: BL 4/15/95; SLJ 3/95)

3217 Kendall, Carol. *The Gammage Cup* (4–7). Illus. by Erik Blegvad. 1990, Harcourt paper $6.00 (978-0-15-230575-8). A fantasy of the Minnipins, a small people of the "land between the mountains."

3218 Kennedy, James. *The Order of Odd-Fish* (7–12). 2008, Delacorte $15.99 (978-0-385-73543-8). A 13-year-old girl is transported to a strange world where she will play a key role in this involved tale full of absurdities and eccentricities. (Rev: BCCB 7–8/08; BL 8/08; LMC 8/08; SLJ 9/08)

3219 Kerr, P. B. *The Blue Djinn of Babylon* (5–8). Series: Children of the Lamp. 2006, Scholastic $16.99 (978-0-439-67021-0). Philippa Gaunt, 12, is wrongly convicted of cheating and her twin John must rescue her in this action-packed sequel to *The Akhenatan Adventure* (2005). (Rev: BL 3/15/06; SLJ 3/06; VOYA 2/06)

3220 Kessler, Jackie Morse. *Loss* (7–10). Series: Riders of the Apocalypse. 2012, Houghton Mifflin paper $8.99 (978-05477121-5-4). Tricked into becoming one of the Four Horsemen of the Apocalypse, Billy, 15, confronts Death in order to avoid his fate. ℯ Lexile 850L (Rev: BL 3/1/12; SLJ 5/1/12)

3221 Kessler, Liz. *Emily Windsnap and the Monster from the Deep* (4–7). Series: Emily Windsnap. 2006, Candlewick $15.99 (978-0-7636-2504-7). Half-human and half-mermaid, Emily Windsnap enjoys an idyllic life on Allpoints Island until she inadvertently awakens an evil monster named Kraken; a sequel to *The Tail of Emily Windsnap* (2004). (Rev: BL 6/1–15/06; SLJ 7/06)

3222 Kessler, Liz. *Emily Windsnap and the Siren's Secret* (4–7). Illus. by Natacha Ledwidge. 2010, Candlewick $15.99 (978-0-7636-4374-4). Emily helps to resolve a dispute between the merpeople of Shiprock and human developers, and in the process finds some lost sirens and solves a mystery. ℯ Lexile 590L (Rev: BLO 3/1/10; SLJ 4/10)

3223 Kessler, Liz. *The Tail of Emily Windsnap* (4–7). Illus. by Sarah Gibb. Series: Emily Windsnap. 2004, Candlewick $15.99 (978-0-7636-2483-5). Twelve-year-old Emily Windsnap, who turns into a mermaid when she gets into the water, learns the truth about her parents. (Rev: BL 5/1/04; SLJ 6/04; VOYA 6/04)

3224 Kessler, Liz. *A Year Without Autumn* (4–7). 2011, Candlewick $15.99 (978-0-7636-5595-2). A ride in an old elevator transports 12-year-old Jenni into the future and provides unhappy news about her best friend Autumn's little brother; Jenni manages to return to the present and avert the accident that was in store. ℯ (Rev: BLO 11/15/11; LMC 1–2/12; SLJ 12/1/11)

3225 Kilworth, Garry. *Attica* (4–8). 2009, IPG/Atom paper $11.95 (978-1-904233-56-5). At the top of a house, step-siblings Jordy, Chloe, and Alex find themselves in a strange yet familiar — and threatening — new world. (Rev: BL 4/15/09; VOYA 10/09)

3226 Kimmel, Elizabeth Cody. *The Ghost of the Stone Circle* (5–8). 1998, Scholastic paper $15.95 (978-0-590-21308-0). Fourteen-year-old Cristyn, who is spending the summer in Wales with her historian father, discovers a ghost in the house her father has rented.

(Rev: BCCB 3/98; BL 4/15/98; HBG 10/98; SLJ 4/98; VOYA 8/98)

3227 Kimmel, Elizabeth Cody. *Suddenly Supernatural: Scaredy Kat* (5–7). 2009, Little, Brown $10.99 (978-0-316-06685-3). Can 13-year-old Kat, who can speak to the dead, and her friend Jac help the spirit of a young boy they find in an abandoned house? ⌒ (Rev: HB 3/09; SLJ 3/09)

3228 Kinde, Christa. *The Blue Door* (6–8). 2012, Zonderkidz $14.99 (978-031072419-3). Fourteen-year-old farm girl Prissie's life is changed when she realizes that she can see angels and that she has a role in a forthcoming spiritual struggle between good and evil. ℯ (Rev: BL 11/15/12; VOYA 12/12)

3229 Kindl, Patrice. *Goose Chase* (6–9). 2001, Houghton Mifflin $16.00 (978-0-618-03377-5). A lively romp in true fairy-tale style that involves an enchanted Goose Girl who must escape a difficult choice between two unappealing suitors. (Rev: BCCB 4/01; BL 4/15/01; HB 7–8/01; HBG 10/01; SLJ 4/01; VOYA 6/01)

3230 King-Smith, Dick. *The Roundhill* (5–7). 2000, Random House paper $4.99 (978-0-440-41844-3). In the English countryside in 1936, 14-year-old Evan meets a mysterious girl who seems to be the Alice of *Alice in Wonderland*. (Rev: BL 1/1–15/01; HBG 3/01; SLJ 12/00)

3231 Kirby, Matthew J. *Icefall* (5–8). 2011, Scholastic $17.99 (978-0-545-27424-1). In Viking times, Princess Solveig and her siblings are sent to a fortress on a fjord for safety during a war but soon realize that there is a traitor in their midst. ⌒ ℯ (Rev: BL 11/15/11; SLJ 11/1/11; VOYA 10/11)

3232 Kirov, Erica. *Magickeepers: The Eternal Hourglass* (5–8). 2009, Sourcebooks $16.99 (978-1-4022-1501-8). The son of a magician discovers magic is real in this melange of ancient underworld shadows and Las Vegas glitter. (Rev: LMC 10/09; SLJ 7/09)

3233 Kirwan-Vogel, Anna. *The Jewel of Life* (6–8). 1991, Harcourt $15.95 (978-0-15-200750-8). Young orphan Duffy travels to other worlds, brings back a precious cockatrice feather, and creates the Philosopher's Stone. (Rev: BL 6/15/91; SLJ 6/91)

3234 Kitanidis, Phoebe. *Whisper* (8–12). 2010, HarperCollins $16.99 (978-0-06-179925-9). Sisters Joy and Jessica both have the ability to hear others' thoughts, but they use this talent in quite different ways. (Rev: BLO 4/15/10; LMC 10/10; SLJ 6/10; VOYA 8/10)

3235 Kizer, Amber. *Meridian* (7–10). 2009, Delacorte $16.99 (978-0-385-73668-8); LB $19.99 (978-0-385-90621-0). After witnessing a traumatizing accident on her 16th birthday, Meridian's parents decide that it's time to inform their daughter that she is a Fenestra, an angel-like being who helps escort the dying to their final destinations. ℯ Lexile HL590L (Rev: BL 2/15/10; SLJ 12/09; VOYA 2/10)

3236 Kizer, Amber. *Wildcat Fireflies* (7–10). 2011, Delacorte $16.99 (978-0-385-73971-9); LB $19.99 (978-038590803-0). In this sequel to 2009's *Meridian,* Tens and the title character continue their search for other half-angels or Fenestras, and finds a compelling case in Juliet, who they assist. ∩ e Lexile HL630L (Rev: BL 9/1/11; SLJ 8/11; VOYA 8/11)

3237 Klass, David. *Timelock* (6–9). Series: The Caretaker Trilogy. 2009, Farrar $17.99 (978-0-374-32309-7). Jack travels to the future to save the Earth, which is threatened by global warming, and to save his father, who is being held by the Dark Lord; the concluding volume in the trilogy. e Lexile 830L (Rev: BL 8/09; SLJ 8/09)

3238 Kloepfer, John. *The Zombie Chasers* (4–7). Illus. by Steve Wolfhard. 2010, HarperCollins $15.99 (978-0-06-185304-3). This is a gruesomely humorous — and graphically illustrated — story of a zombified neighborhood in which only Zack, Rice, Zoe, and Madison are normal and must defend themselves against the hungry crowd. e Lexile 760L (Rev: BL 4/15/10; LMC 11–12/10; SLJ 11/1/10)

3239 Kluger, Jeffrey. *Nacky Patcher and the Curse of the Dry-Land Boats* (4–7). 2007, Philomel $18.99 (978-0-399-24604-3). When thief Nacky Patcher and orphan Teedie find a sailing ship floating in the lake, they try to persuade the hapless inhabitants of Yole to rally together to rebuild the vessel and escape their oppression by the cruel Baloo family. (Rev: BL 6/1–15/07; SLJ 7/07)

3240 Kluver, Cayla. *Legacy* (6–9). 2008, Forsooth $17.95 (978-0-9802089-7-9). In this romantic fantasy by a teen author, Princess Alera of Hytanica battles the requirement that she marry, while a boy named Narian, ostensibly from the enemy land of Cokyr, fights his destiny that he destroy Alera's kingdom. (Rev: BLO 6/17/08)

3241 Knox, Elizabeth. *Dreamquake: Book Two of the Dreamhunter Duet* (8–11). Series: Dreamhunter Duet. 2007, Farrar $19.00 (978-0-374-31854-3). Laura and her family are troubled by the government's dream-harvesting program in this follow-up to *Dreamhunter.* Printz Honor 2008. (Rev: BL 1/1–15/07; HB 3–4/07; SLJ 6/07)

3242 Knudsen, Michelle. *The Dragon of Trelian* (4–7). 2009, Candlewick $16.99 (978-0-7636-3455-1). Calen, a lonely magician's apprentice, and Meg, who is secretly caring for a baby dragon, join forces when they find their kingdom is in danger. (Rev: BCCB 9/09; BL 4/1/09; HB 5/09; LMC 8/09; SLJ 6/09)

3243 Knudsen, Michelle. *The Princess of Trelian* (4–7). 2012, Candlewick $16.99 (978-076365062-9). Meg struggles to clear her dragon's name after a rash of attacks plague Lourin. (Rev: BL 3/15/12; HB 5–6/12; VOYA 6/12)

3244 Knutsson, Catherine. *Shadows Cast by Stars* (8–11). 2012, Simon & Schuster $17.99 (978-1-4424-0191-4). In a future where plague has killed a large percent of the population, the blood of Native Americans, which has special properties, is much in demand and 16-year-old Cassandra and her family must flee to the Island, where Cassandra's special abilities come to the fore. e Lexile 670L (Rev: BL 5/15/12; LMC 10/12; SLJ 8/1/12; VOYA 6/12)

3245 Kogler, Jennifer Ann. *The Death Catchers* (7–10). 2011, Walker $16.99 (978-080272184-6). Morgan le Fay descendant Lizzy with supernatural powers discovers that she must protect Drake, a popular senior at her school who is a descendant of King Arthur. e Lexile 800L (Rev: BL 5/1/11; LMC 8–9/11; SLJ 2/12; VOYA 8/11)

3246 Koller, Jackie F. *If I Had One Wish . . .* (5–8). 1991, Little, Brown $14.95 (978-0-316-50150-7). When 8th-grader Alec is granted his wish that his little brother had never been born, he learns a lesson about charity, kindness, and old-fashioned family values. (Rev: BCCB 12/91; BL 11/1/91; SLJ 11/91)

3247 Konwicki, Tadeusz. *The Anthropos-Specter-Beast* (7–9). Trans. by George Korwin Rodziszewski and Audrey Korwin Rodziszewski. 1977, Phillips $26.95 (978-0-87599-218-1). Peter is transported to a remote place by the talking dog Sebastian.

3248 Korman, Gordon. *The Medusa Plot* (5–8). Series: The 39 Clues: Cahills vs. Vespers. 2011, Scholastic $12.99 (978-054529839-1). Amy and Dan Cahill combine their talents to rescue captured friends and family from the evil Vespers. ∩ e (Rev: BL 11/1/11; SLJ 4/12)

3249 Kortum, Jeanie. *Ghost Vision* (5–8). Illus. by Dugald Stermer. 1983, Scholastic paper $3.50 (978-0-614-19197-4). A Greenland Inuit realizes that his son has special mystical powers.

3250 Kostick, Conor. *Epic* (7–10). 2007, Viking $17.99 (978-0-670-06179-2). Readers who enjoy role-playing games will love this book, a fantasy that takes place on New Earth, where violence occurs only in the computer game Epic. (Rev: BL 3/1/07; SLJ 5/07)

3251 Kostick, Conor. *Saga* (7–10). 2008, Viking $18.99 (978-0-670-06280-5). The world of Saga is a virtual reality, role-playing game that has its players captive, and it is up to 15-year-old Ghost and Eric to stop the Dark Queen, who is using Saga to control New Earth. A sequel to *Epic.* (Rev: BL 5/15/08; SLJ 7/08)

3252 L'Engle, Madeleine. *An Acceptable Time* (8–12). 1989, Farrar $18.00 (978-0-374-30027-2). Polly O'Keefe time-travels (as her parents did years before in the Time trilogy) but this time to visit a civilization of Druids that lived 3,000 years ago. (Rev: BL 1/1/90; SLJ 1/90; VOYA 4/90)

3253 Lairamore, Dawn. *Ivy's Ever After* (5–8). 2010, Holiday House $16.95 (978-0-8234-2261-6). A well-meaning but somewhat cowardly dragon rescues a young, independent-minded princess from marrying an evil man. Lexile 980L (Rev: BL 5/15/10; SLJ 8/10)

3254 Lake, Nick. *Blood Ninja* (7–11). 2009, Simon & Schuster $16.99 (978-1-4169-8627-0). In 16th-century Japan teenage Taro is saved from certain death by a bite from a ninja vampire. ☪ Lexile 870L (Rev: BL 12/1/09; SLJ 12/09; VOYA 2/10)

3255 Lally, Soinbhe. *A Hive for the Honeybee* (8–12). 1999, Scholastic paper $16.95 (978-0-590-51038-7). An allegory about life and work that takes place in a beehive with such characters as Alfred, the bee poet, and Mo, a radical drone. (Rev: BL 2/1/99; HB 3–4/99; HBG 10/99; SLJ 5/99*; VOYA 4/99)

3256 Landy, Derek. *The Faceless Ones* (6–8). Series: Skulduggery Pleasant. 2009, HarperCollins $16.99 (978-0-06-124091-1). Skeleton detective Skulduggery and his 14-year-old sidekick Valkyrie cope with many false starts and red herrings as they endeavor to foil a plot to introduce evil beings— The Faceless Ones— into our world. ᴖ ☪ Lexile 680L (Rev: BL 8/09; SLJ 10/09)

3257 Landy, Derek. *Playing with Fire* (5–8). Series: Skulduggery Pleasant. 2008, HarperCollins $16.99 (978-0-06-124088-1). Skulduggery and 13-year-old Valkyrie (formerly known as Stephanie) must curb the evil Baron Vengeous, who plans to bring back to life a terrifying monster called the Grotesquery. (Rev: BL 6/1–15/08; SLJ 7/08)

3258 Landy, Derek. *Skulduggery Pleasant* (5–8). Series: Skulduggery Pleasant. 2007, HarperCollins $17.99 (978-0-06-123115-5). When she inherits her Uncle Gordon's property, plucky 12-year-old Stephanie finds herself swept into an adventure combining magic, mystery, and violence in which her companion is a skeleton named Skulduggery Pleasant. Odyssey Honor Recording 2008. ᴖ (Rev: BL 5/1/07; HB 7–8/07; SLJ 6/07)

3259 Langrish, Katherine. *The Shadow Hunt* (6–9). 2010, HarperCollins $16.99 (978-006111676-6). A medieval fantasy in which 13-year-old Wolf and a girl named Nest nurture an elf-child, unaware that dark forces are gathering around them. (Rev: BL 5/15/10*; SLJ 6/10)

3260 Langrish, Katherine. *Troll Mill* (5–8). 2006, HarperCollins LB $17.89 (978-0-06-058308-8). In this sequel to *Troll Fell* (2004), 15-year-old Peer Ulfsson, who still worries about his cruel uncles and is increasingly involved with Hilde, must help protect a half-selkie baby from trolls and other threats. (Rev: BCCB 3/06; BL 2/1/06*; HBG 10/06; LMC 2/07; SLJ 3/06; VOYA 2/06)

3261 Langton, Jane. *The Fledgling* (5–7). 1980, HarperCollins LB $17.89 (978-0-06-023679-3); paper $6.99 (978-0-06-440121-0). A young girl learns to fly with

her Goose Prince. A sequel is *The Fragile Flag* (1984). Also use *The Diamond in the Window* (1962).

3262 Larbalestier, Justine. *Magic or Madness* (8–11). 2005, Penguin $16.99 (978-1-59514-022-7). Australian 15-year-old Reason resists the idea of magic until she is transported from her grandmother's home to New York City and finds herself tackling new realities. (Rev: BCCB 3/05; BL 3/15/05*; SLJ 3/05; VOYA 2/05)

3263 Larbalestier, Justine. *Magic's Child* (8–11). Series: Magic or Madness. 2007, Penguin $16.99 (978-1-59514-064-7). Reason, now 15, pregnant, and on her own, struggles with her magical abilities in this final installment in the trilogy. (Rev: BCCB 6/07; BL 4/15/07; SLJ 5/07)

3264 Lasky, Kathryn. *Blood Secret* (6–10). 2004, HarperCollins LB $16.89 (978-0-06-000065-3). Silent since the sudden disappearance of her mother eight years earlier, 14-year-old Jerry Luna goes to live with a great-aunt where a trunk draws her into the time of the Spanish Inquisition and long-hidden secrets about her ancestors. (Rev: BL 10/1/04; SLJ 8/04; VOYA 10/04)

3265 Lasky, Kathryn. *The Capture* (5–8). 2003, Scholastic paper $5.99 (978-0-439-40557-7). Soren, a happy, well-adjusted young barn owl, falls from his nest and is stolen away by a group of owlet thieves bent on reeducation. (Rev: BL 9/15/03; SLJ 10/03)

3266 Lasky, Kathryn. *Daughters of the Sea: Hannah* (4–8). 2009, Scholastic $16.99 (978-0-439-78310-1). Orphan Hannah, 15, gets a job as a scullery maid in 19th-century Boston, meets a young artist who seems to have an incredible understanding of her, and on a trip to the coast starts to recognize how she reacts to the presence of water. ☪ Lexile 800L (Rev: BL 9/1/09; SLJ 10/09; VOYA 2/10)

3267 Lasky, Kathryn. *Lone Wolf* (5–8). Series: Wolves of the Beyond. 2010, Scholastic $15.99 (978-0-545-09310-1). A young wolf with a defective paw is adopted by a mother grizzly bear who teaches him various skills in this first installment in the series. ᴖ ☪ Lexile 890L (Rev: BL 12/1/09; LMC 3–4/10; SLJ 3/10)

3268 Lasky, Kathryn. *Lucy* (5–8). Series: Daughters of the Sea. 2012, Scholastic $17.99 (978-043978-312-5). Seventeen-year-old Lucy, who has been brought up in New York City by a minister and his ambitious wife, spends the summer in Bar Harbor, Maine, in 1899 and finds out about her sisters, her mother, and her affinity for the sea. ☪ (Rev: BLO 4/15/12)

3269 Lasky, Kathryn. *Shadow Wolf* (5–8). Series: Wolves of the Beyond. 2010, Scholastic $16.99 (978-0-545-09312-5). Deformed wolf Faolan struggles to accept his lot as a lowly "gnaw wolf" even as a rival challenges him at every turn. ☪ Lexile 870L (Rev: BL 12/1/10; SLJ 1/11)

3270 Law, Ingrid. *Savvy* (5–7). 2008, Dial $16.99 (978-0-803-73306-0). On her 13th birthday, Mibs is looking forward to following the pattern of the other Beaumont children and developing a supernatural "savvy" just as her father is hurt in an accident; Mibs and her siblings set off on an adventure-filled journey to be at his side. Newbery Honor 2009; ALA Notable Books 2009; Boston Globe–Horn Book Honor 2008. (Rev: BL 5/15/08*; LMC 10/08; SLJ 5/08; VOYA 2/09)

3271 Law, Ingrid. *Scumble* (5–8). 2010, Dial $16.99 (978-0-8037-3307-7). It's Ledge's turn to acquire an unusual power on his 13th birthday in this companion to *Savvy* (2008), and his new ability to create havoc has unwelcome results. ⌂ (Rev: BL 7/10*; HB 9–10/10; SLJ 9/1/10)

3272 Lawrence, Michael. *A Crack in the Line* (8–12). Series: Withern Rise. 2004, HarperCollins $15.99 (978-0-06-072477-1). Still mourning his mother's death, 16-year-old Alaric discovers how to travel to an alternate reality where his mother is still alive. (Rev: BL 6/1–15/04*; SLJ 8/04)

3273 Lawrence, Michael. *The Underwood See* (8–11). Series: Withern Rise. 2007, Greenwillow $16.99 (978-0-06-072483-2). Readers of the previous books in the series (*The Crack in the Line* and *Small Eternities*, 2004 and 2005 respectively) will enjoy this final volume in which Naia, now pregnant, returns to the Underwood See to have her child there. (Rev: BL 5/15/07; SLJ 10/07)

3274 Lawson, Julie. *Ghosts of the Titanic* (5–8). 2012, Holiday House $16.95 (978-082342423-8). Parallel plots and a neat time-travel sequence splice the stories of modern-day class clown Kevin with that of young 1912 seamen Angus, who's been given the grim job of recovering the *Titanic* victims' bodies, in this complex story. (Rev: BL 2/15/12; LMC 11–12/12; SLJ 3/12)

3275 Lawson, Robert. *Rabbit Hill* (4–7). Illus. by author. 1944, Puffin paper $5.99 (978-0-14-031010-8). A warm and humorous story about the small creatures of a Connecticut countryside — each with a distinct personality. Newbery Medal 1945.

3276 Laybourne, Emma. *Missing Magic* (4–7). 2007, Dial $16.99 (978-0-8037-3219-3). Ned, 11, is one of the few students at Leodwych who has no magic, but his practical abilities prove useful when he and two of his classmates are kidnapped. (Rev: BL 7/07; SLJ 9/07)

3277 Layefsky, Virginia. *Impossible Things* (5–8). 1998, Marshall Cavendish $14.95 (978-0-7614-5038-2). Twelve-year-old Brady has several personal and family problems to solve along with taking care of the dragon-like creature that he is hiding. (Rev: HBG 3/99; SLJ 11/98)

3278 Le Guin, Ursula K. *Gifts* (6–10). 2004, Harcourt $17.00 (978-0-15-205123-5). In this engaging fantasy, Gry and Orrec, two Uplanders with supernatural abilities, are hesitant to use their awesome powers for fear

that they will cause more harm than good. (Rev: BL 8/04*; SLJ 9/04; VOYA 12/04)

3279 Le Guin, Ursula K. *Powers* (8–12). Series: Annals of the Western Shore. 2007, Harcourt $17.00 (978-0-15-205770-1). The third book in the series continues the theme of a society based on slavery, with slave Gavir —who was kidnapped from his tribe as a child — running from his masters after his sister is raped. ⌂ (Rev: BL 10/1/07; HB 9–10/07; SLJ 9/07)

3280 Le Guin, Ursula K. *Voices* (7–10). 2006, Harcourt $17.00 (978-0-15-205678-0). Seventeen-year-old Memer resents the conquerors who oppress her land and ban books and writing and goes on a quest to get revenge; a thought-provoking companion to *Gifts*. ⌂ (Rev: BL 8/06; HB 9–10/06; LMC 3/07; SLJ 8/06*; VOYA)

3281 Le Guin, Ursula K. *A Wizard of Earthsea* (8–12). Series: Earthsea. 1968, Bantam paper $7.50 (978-0-553-26250-6). An apprentice wizard accidentally unleashes an evil power onto the land of Earthsea. Followed by *The Tombs of Atuan* and *The Farthest Shore*.

3282 Leavitt, Martine. *Keturah and Lord Death* (8–11). 2006, Front St $16.95 (978-1-932425-29-1). After Keturah becomes lost in the woods and encounters Lord Death she must use her storytelling skills to convince him to let her go and in the process he falls in love with her. (Rev: BL 9/15/06)

3283 Leeuwen, Joke van. *Eep!* (4–8). Trans. by Bill Nagelkerke. Illus. by author. 2012, Gecko paper $7.95 (978-18775790-7-3). A childless couple's discovery and stewardship of an odd bird-girl bonds them to others who've cared for the creature in this touching, quirky tale. (Rev: BL 3/1/12*; HB 5–6/12; SLJ 3/12)

3284 Legrand, Claire. *The Cavendish Home for Boys and Girls* (4–7). Illus. by Sarah Watts. 2012, Simon & Schuster $16.99 (978-1-4424-4291-7). Twelve-year-old Victoria, who strives for perfection, investigates the disappearance of her imperfect friend Lawrence and stumbles on some unpleasant secrets. ℮ Lexile 750L (Rev: BLO 11/1/12; SLJ 12/12)

3285 Lenahan, John. *Shadowmagic* (7–11). 2010, Independent paper $10.99 (978-1-90-554892-7). Conor is amazed to discover that he is a prince when he and his father are transported to Tir Na Nog and the Celtic past. ℮ (Rev: BL 2/1/10; SLJ 5/10)

3286 Leonard, Elmore. *A Coyote's in the House* (5–8). 2004, HarperEntertainment $22.00 (978-0-06-072882-3). A coyote named Antwan strikes up a friendship with a couple of pampered dogs from Hollywood. (Rev: BL 5/15/04*)

3287 Lerangis, Peter. *The Colossus Rises* (4–8). Series: Seven Wonders. 2013, HarperCollins $17.99 (978-006207040-1); paper $9.99 (978-00620704-2-5). Jack and three other young teens who have a rare genetic abnormality set off to find the artifacts from Atlantis that will save them. ∩ e Lexile 580L (Rev: BL 12/1/12; SLJ 3/13)

3288 Leszczynski, Diana. *Fern Verdant and the Silver Rose* (4–8). 2008, Knopf $15.99 (978-0-375-85213-8). When her botanist mother Lily is kidnapped, Fern uses her newly discovered talent for communicating with plants to search for her. (Rev: LMC 3/09; SLJ 2/09)

3289 Levine, Gail Carson. *Ever* (6–10). 2008, HarperCollins $16.99 (978-0-06-122962-6). Olus, a god, is in love with Kezi, a human girl who is fated to be sacrificed to Admat, the god of oaths. (Rev: BL 4/1/08; SLJ 6/08)

3290 Levine, Gail Carson. *Fairest* (7–10). 2006, HarperCollins paper $17.00 (978-0-06-073408-4). An unattractive 15-year-old girl gains confidence as she comes to recognize her own strengths in this imaginative fairy tale. ∩ (Rev: BL 7/06; SLJ 9/06)

3291 Levine, Gail Carson. *The Two Princesses of Bamarre* (4–7). 2001, HarperCollins LB $17.89 (978-0-06-029316-1). Princess Addie sets out on a quest to find a cure for the Grey Death, a sickness that is destroying her older sister. (Rev: BCCB 10/01; BL 4/15/01; HB 5–6/01; HBG 10/01; SLJ 5/01)

3292 Lewis, C. S. *The Lion, the Witch and the Wardrobe* (5–8). Series: Narnia. 1988, Macmillan LB $22.95 (978-0-02-758200-0). Four children enter the kingdom of Narnia through the back of an old wardrobe. A special edition illustrated by Michael Hague. The other six volumes in this series are *Prince Caspian, The Voyage of the Dawn Treader, The Silver Chair, The Horse and His Boy, The Magician's Nephew,* and *The Last Battle.*

3293 Lewis, C. S. *The Lion, the Witch and the Wardrobe: A Story for Children* (4–7). Illus. by Pauline Baynes. 1988, Macmillan paper $7.95 (978-0-02-044490-9). A beautifully written adventure featuring four children who go into the magical land of Narnia.

3294 Lewis, Richard. *The Demon Queen* (8–11). 2008, Simon & Schuster $15.99 (978-1-4169-6226-7). Jesse, who appears to all to be a regular high-schooler, has a mysterious past that is made clear when it is revealed that he must fight a demon queen to save the world. (Rev: BL 5/15/08)

3295 Lindbergh, Anne. *The Hunky-Dory Dairy* (5–7). Illus. by Julie Brinckloe. 1986, Harcourt $14.95 (978-0-15-237449-5); paper $2.75 (978-0-380-70320-3). Zannah visits a community magically removed from the 20th century and enjoys introducing the people to bubble gum, tacos, and other "modern" things. (Rev: BCCB 9/86; BL 4/1/86; SLJ 8/86)

3296 Lindbergh, Anne. *The Prisoner of Pineapple Place* (5–7). 1988, Harcourt $13.95 (978-0-15-263559-6); paper $2.95 (978-0-380-70765-2). Pineapple Place is invisible to everyone except the inhabitants, and some-

how finds itself landing in Connecticut. (Rev: BL 7/88; SLJ 8/88)

3297 Lindgren, Astrid. *Ronia, the Robber's Daughter* (4–7). 1985, Puffin paper $5.99 (978-0-14-031720-6). Ronia becomes friendly with the son of her father's rival in this fantasy.

3298 Link, Kelly, and Gavin J. Grant, eds. *Steampunk! An Anthology of Fantastically Rich and Strange Stories* (8–12). Illus. 2011, Candlewick $22.99 (978-0-7636-4843-5). History and technology blend in this collection of 14 steampunk stories by authors including Holly Black, Libba Bray, Garth Nix, and Cory Doctorow. e Lexile 940L (Rev: BL 11/1/11*; HB 9–10/11; LMC 3–4/12; SLJ 9/1/11*)

3299 Lisle, Holly. *The Ruby Key* (6–10). Series: Moon & Sun. 2008, Scholastic $16.99 (978-0-545-00012-3). Genna and Danrith discover that the local nightlings have hatched an evil plan to do away with the nocturnal humans in their village in this first installment in the series. (Rev: BL 5/15/08; SLJ 6/08)

3300 Lisle, Holly. *The Silver Door* (5–8). Series: Moon and Sun. 2009, Scholastic $17.99 (978-0-545-00014-7). Genna is training to become the Sunrider of prophecy and discovers a lost human city in this danger-laden sequel to *The Ruby Key* (2008). (Rev: BLO 5/27/09; HB 7/09)

3301 Lisle, Janet Taylor. *Highway Cats* (4–7). Illus. by David Frankland. 2008, Philomel $14.99 (978-0-399-25070-5). Against all odds, three kittens survive abandonment on the edge of a busy highway and meet up with a group of feral cats; the kittens' unusual abilities become apparent when the cats' scruffy piece of land comes under threat of development. ∩ (Rev: BL 7/08*; HB 9/08; LMC 1/09; SLJ 11/08)

3302 Littlefield, Bill. *The Circus in the Woods* (6–10). 2001, Houghton Mifflin $15.00 (978-0-618-06642-1). Mystery and fantasy are combined in this quiet, reflective story about a 13-year-old girl who finds a strange circus in the Vermont woods where she spends her summers. (Rev: BCCB 12/01; HBG 10/02; SLJ 11/01; VOYA 12/01)

3303 Livingston, Lesley. *Darklight* (7–10). 2010, HarperCollins $16.99 (978-0-06-157540-2). In this sequel to *Wondrous Strange* (2009), actress Kelley is transported from New York to the Otherworld where she faces many challenges — including resurrecting her relationship with her beloved Sonny. Lexile 880L (Rev: BL 12/15/09; LMC 3–4/10; SLJ 2/10)

3304 Livingston, Lesley. *Wondrous Strange* (7–10). Series: Wondrous Strange. 2009, HarperCollins $16.99 (978-006157537-2). Kelley, 17, is acting in a New York City production of "A Midsummer Night's Dream" when she discovers she has a connection to a magic faerie world inhabited by mystical creatures. e Lexile 840L (Rev: BL 1/1–15/09; HB 3–4/09; SLJ 1/1/09; VOYA 4/09)

3305 Llewellyn, Sam. *Darksolstice* (5–8). Series: Lyonesse. 2010, Scholastic $17.99 (978-0-439-93471-8). Idris Limpet journeys to Aegypt to rescue his sister Morgan and meets up with the future Knights of the Round Table in this second book in the series. Lexile 790L (Rev: BL 3/1/10; HB 5–6/10; SLJ 5/10)

3306 London, Dena. *Shapeshifter's Quest* (7–10). 2005, Dutton $16.99 (978-0-525-47310-7). Syanthe, a shapeshifting teenager, ventures outside the forest that has always been her home on a mission to unravel the secret of the king's black magic. (Rev: BL 10/1/05; SLJ 10/05; VOYA 8/05)

3307 Lott, Tim. *Fearless* (6–9). 2007, Candlewick $15.99 (978-0-7636-3637-1). In a dystopian future, orphan Little Fearless plans an escape from the workhouse in which she and a thousand other girls are imprisoned under the Controller. (Rev: BL 11/15/07; LMC 1/08; SLJ 3/08)

3308 Lovric, Michelle. *The Undrowned Child* (5–7). 2011, Delacorte $17.99 (978-0-385-73999-3); LB $20.99 (978-0-385-90814-6). Eleven-year-old Teo, an orphan adopted by two scientists, finds herself taking part in a battle to save 1899 Venice from destruction in this fantasy full of historical detail. ℮ Lexile 830L (Rev: BL 6/1/11; LMC 11–12/11; SLJ 8/11*)

3309 Lowry, Lois. *Gathering Blue* (5–9). 2000, Houghton Mifflin $16.00 (978-0-618-05581-4). In an inhospitable future world, young Kira must use her courage and her artistic talents. (Rev: BL 6/1–15/00*; HB 9–10/00; HBG 3/01; SLJ 8/00*)

3310 Lowry, Lois. *The Giver* (6–9). 1993, Houghton Mifflin $16.00 (978-0-395-64566-6). A dystopian fantasy in which Jonas receives his life assignment as Receiver of Memory and learns that a land with no war, poverty, fear, or hardship is also one where "misfits" are killed. (Rev: BL 4/15/93*; SLJ 5/93*; VOYA 8/93)

3311 Lowry, Lois. *Gossamer* (5–8). 2006, Houghton Mifflin $16.00 (978-0-618-68550-9). A spirit called Littlest One learns to mix memories that will heal people while they sleep. (Rev: BL 2/15/06; SLJ 5/06*; VOYA 8/06)

3312 Lowry, Lois. *Messenger* (6–10). 2004, Houghton Mifflin $16.00 (978-0-618-40441-4). In the Village where teenage Matty is a caregiver, the residents decide to build a wall to keep out undesirables in this fantasy filled with truth and symbolism. (Rev: BL 2/15/04*; HB 5–6/04; SLJ 4/04; VOYA 6/04)

3313 Lyga, Barry. *Wolverine: Worst Day Ever* (6–9). Illus. by Roland Boschi. 2009, Marvel $14.99 (978-078513757-3). Eric, who has the ability to become invisible, blogs about feeling out of place at the Xavier School for Gifted Students in this novel full of graphic elements. (Rev: BL 5/15/09; SLJ 10/09; VOYA 12/09)

3314 Lyon, George Ella. *Here and Then* (6–8). 1994, Orchard paper $15.95 (978-0-531-06866-3). Abby, 13, becomes connected across time to Eliza, a nurse she portrays in a Civil War reenactment, and goes back in time to help her. (Rev: BL 10/1/94; SLJ 10/94; VOYA 10/94)

3315 Lyon, Steve. *The Gift Moves* (6–9). 2004, Houghton Mifflin $15.00 (978-0-618-39128-8). In this quiet, futuristic novel set in an America devoid of wealth and materialism, Path Down the Mountain, a weaver's apprentice, and Bird Speaks, son of the local baker, strike up a friendship. (Rev: BL 6/1–15/04; SLJ 6/04; VOYA 6/04)

3316 Lyons, Mary E. *Knockabeg: A Famine Tale* (4–7). 2001, Houghton Mifflin $15.00 (978-0-618-09283-3). In order to protect the people of Knockabeg, faeries battle with the creatures who are causing the blight during the great Irish potato famine. (Rev: BL 11/15/01; HBG 3/02; SLJ 9/01; VOYA 10/01)

3317 Lytle, Robert A. *Three Rivers Crossing* (5–8). 2000, River Road $15.95 (978-0-938682-55-4). After he suffers an accident while fishing, 7th-grader Walker wakes to find he is in the 1820s village of his ancestors. (Rev: BL 5/15/00; SLJ 6/00)

3318 Maas, Sarah J. *Throne of Glass* (7–10). 2012, Bloomsbury $17.99 (978-1-59990-695-9). Teen assassin Celaena Sardothien has spent a year imprisoned in the salt mines when she is offered the chance to compete against soldiers and other men for the dubious privilege of being the king's champion — and for her eventual freedom. ℮ Lexile HL790L (Rev: BL 9/1/12; LMC 1–2/13*; SLJ 12/12)

3319 McAllister, M. I. *Urchin of the Riding Stars* (5–8). Series: Mismantle Chronicles. 2005, Hyperion $17.95 (978-0-7868-5486-8). When his mentor, Captain Crispin, is unjustly accused of slaying the infant prince of Mismantle, Urchin the squirrel is determined to find out who is responsible for the crime. (Rev: BL 10/1/05; SLJ 11/05; VOYA 2/06)

3320 Macaulay, David. *Baaa* (6–10). 1985, Houghton Mifflin paper $6.95 (978-0-395-39588-2). An allegory about the world after humans have left and intelligent sheep take control. (Rev: BL 9/1/85; SLJ 10/85)

3321 McBride, Lish. *Necromancing the Stone* (8–11). 2012, Henry Holt $16.99 (978-0-8050-9099-4). Having gained a conscience since 2010's *Hold Me Closer, Necromancer,* Sam returns to continue his work of sorting good from evil, still dogged by the evil Douglas. ⌒ ℮ Lexile HL720L (Rev: BL 12/1/12; SLJ 10/12)

3322 McBride, Regina. *The Fire Opal* (7–10). 2010, Delacorte LB $19.99 (978-0-385-90692-0). In late-16th-century Ireland, 14-year-old Maeve must retrieve a precious fire opal from the corpse goddess Uria in order to save the souls of her mother and sister. Lexile 970L (Rev: BL 5/15/10; LMC 8–9/10; SLJ 8/10)

3323 McCaffrey, Laura Williams. *Alia Waking* (5–7). 2003, Clarion $16.00 (978-0-618-19461-2). Alia, 12, and her best friend Kay long to be come "keenten," or warrior women. (Rev: BL 3/1/03; HBG 10/03; SLJ 6/03; VOYA 10/03)

3324 McCaffrey, Laura Williams. *Water Shaper* (6–9). 2006, Clarion $16.00 (978-0-618-61489-9). Princess Margot leaves her father's strict kingdom in an adventure-laden search for her true home. (Rev: BL 5/15/06; SLJ 7/06)

3325 McCaughrean, Geraldine. *A Pack of Lies* (5–7). 1990, Macmillan $16.95 (978-0-7451-1154-4). Stories told by mysterious M.C.C. Berkshire, who wanders into an antique store run by adolescent Ailsa and her mother. (Rev: BCCB 5/89)

3326 McCaughrean, Geraldine. *Peter Pan in Scarlet* (6–9). Illus. by Scott M. Fischer. 2006, Simon & Schuster $17.99 (978-1-4169-1808-0). In this authorized sequel to J. M. Barrie's *Peter Pan,* the adventure continues — at breakneck speed — for Peter, Wendy, John, and the Lost Boys as they return to Neverland. ☊ (Rev: BL 11/15/06; HB 1–2/07; LMC 4–5/07; SLJ 12/06*)

3327 MacCullough, Carolyn. *Always a Witch* (7–10). 2011, Clarion $16.99 (978-054722485-5). Witch Tamsin Greene travels back in time to 1887 to confront a villain and save her family in this sequel to *Once a Witch* (2009). ❤ Lexile HL800L (Rev: BLO 11/15/11; SLJ 2/12)

3328 MacCullough, Carolyn. *Once a Witch* (8–11). 2009, Clarion $16 (978-0-547-22399-5). Tamsin is bitter that her family's predisposition toward great talents has forsaken her, until a journey through time sets off a sinister chain of events and allows the edgy heroine to realize her true potential. ❤ Lexile HL790L (Rev: BL 10/1/09; SLJ 10/09; VOYA 10/09)

3329 McGann, Oisín. *The Gods and Their Machines* (8–11). 2004, Tor $19.95 (978-0-7653-1159-7). Fantasy and allegory are blended in this story about Chamus, a teenage Altiman fighter pilot trainee, whose denigration of the people of nearby Bartokhrin as ignorant religious fanatics is revised when a Bartokhrin girl helps him after his plane is forced to land near her home. (Rev: BL 12/15/04)

3330 McGowan, Keith. *The Witch's Guide to Cooking with Children* (6–9). Illus. by Yoko Tanaka. 2009, Henry Holt $15.99 (978-080508668-3). Eleven-year-old Sol and his younger sister Connie star in this contemporary retelling of Hansel and Gretel that is full of tension. ☊ ❤ (Rev: BL 7/09; LMC 10/09; SLJ 10/09)

3331 MacHale, D. J. *The Lost City of Faar* (5–8). Series: Pendragon. 2003, Simon & Schuster paper $5.99 (978-0-7434-3732-5). After saving Denduron from Saint Dane in *The Merchant of Death* (2002), 14-year-old Bobby must confront the shape-changer again in Cloral, a world covered by water. (Rev: SLJ 5/03)

3332 MacHale, D. J. *The Rivers of Zadaa* (5–8). Series: Pendragon. 2005, Simon & Schuster $14.95 (978-1-4169-0710-7). Bobby Pendragon teams up with Loor to foil the villainous Saint Dane's plan to cut off the water supply to Loor's people in Zadaa. (Rev: SLJ 7/05)

3333 McKinley, Robin. *The Blue Sword* (7–10). 1982, Greenwillow $16.99 (978-0-688-00938-0). The king of Damar kidnaps a girl to help in his war against the Northerners. A prequel to *The Hero and the Crown.* Newbery Medal 1985. (Rev: BL 12/15/89)

3334 McKinley, Robin. *The Door in the Hedge* (6–9). 2003, Firebird paper $6.99 (978-0-698-11960-4). Four tales, two of which originated in the folklore of the Grimm Brothers.

3335 McKinley, Robin. *Dragonhaven* (8–11). 2007, Putnam $17.99 (978-0-399-24675-3). Jake, who lives on the dragon preserve at Smokehill National Park, rescues and cares for an orphaned dragon in this realistic novel with an environmental message. (Rev: BL 10/1/07; HB 9–10/07; LMC 3/08; SLJ 9/07)

3336 McKinley, Robin. *Pegasus* (8–11). 2010, Putnam $18.99 (978-0-399-24677-7). Human Princess Sylvi, 12, discovers she can communicate telepathically with Ebon, her personal pegasus, signaling a potential new era of rapprochement between the two species. (Rev: BL 10/1/10; LMC 3–4/11; SLJ 12/1/10)

3337 McKinley, Robin. *Rose Daughter* (6–12). 1997, Greenwillow $16.95 (978-0-688-15439-4). As in her award-winning *Beauty,* (1955) the author returns to the Beauty and the Beast fairy tale in this outstanding reworking of the traditional story. (Rev: BL 8/97; HBG 3/98; SLJ 9/97; VOYA 2/98) [398.2]

3338 McKinley, Robin, and Peter Dickinson. *Fire: Tales of Elemental Spirits* (6–10). 2009, Putnam $19.99 (978-0-399-25289-1). Five well-crafted tales illustrate contacts between humans and supernatural beings associated with fire; a companion to *Water: Tales of Elemental Spirits* (2002). ❤ (Rev: BL 9/1/09; HB 11–12/09; LMC 11–12/09; SLJ 9/09; VOYA 12/09)

3339 McMann, Lisa. *Fade* (8–11). Series: Wake Trilogy. 2009, Simon & Schuster $15.99 (978-141695358-6). This gripping sequel to 2008's *Wake* has the heroine, Janie, exploring more deeply her dream-catching abilities and trying to solve a dangerous case of student abuse. ❤ Lexile 570L (Rev: BL 12/1/08; SLJ 5/1/09)

3340 McMann, Lisa. *Gone* (8–11). Series: Wake Trilogy. 2010, Simon & Schuster $16.99 (978-1-4169-7918-0). Janie faces tough decisions about her future as she struggles with her alcoholic mother and her father, also a dream-catcher, surprisingly comes into her life when he is in a coma; the final volume in the trilogy that began with *Wake* (2008) and *Fade* (2009). ❤ (Rev: BL 1/1–15/10; SLJ 2/10)

3341 McMann, Lisa. *The Unwanteds* (4–7). 2011, Simon & Schuster $16.99 (978-1-4424-0768-8). In a

189

dystopian land named Quill, Unwanted 13-year-olds with artistic abilities are purged from society; Alex, declared an Unwanted, finds himself in the magical land of Artime, where he learns new skills and worries about his twin brother Aaron, one of the Wanted. (Rev: BLO 9/1/11; SLJ 8/11)

3342 McMann, Lisa. *Wake* (8–10). Series: Wake. 2008, Simon & Schuster $15.99 (978-1-4169-5969-4). Janie, 17, feels both cursed and blessed by her ability to enter and experience other people's dreams; then she begins to learn how to use her skill to help herself and others, including a boy named Cabel whose dreams include her. (Rev: BL 4/15/08; LMC 8//08; SLJ 3/08)

3343 McNamee, Eoin. *City of Time* (5–8). Series: The Navigator Trilogy. 2008, Random House $16.99 (978-0-375-83912-2). The moon is inching toward Owen's home planet, causing panic and environmental changes, and Owen travels to the City of Time to try to set things right. (Rev: BL 5/15/08; SLJ 8/08)

3344 McNamee, Eoin. *The Ring of Five* (5–7). 2010, Random House $16.99 (978-0-385-73731-9). Unhappy young Danny Caulfield gets a chance to go to boarding school and is surprised to find himself at Wilson's Academy of the Devious Arts where he is trained to protect the Upper World from the Lower World. **e** Lexile 740L (Rev: BL 6/10; LMC 10/10; SLJ 6/10)

3345 McNaughton, Janet. *An Earthly Knight* (7–10). 2004, HarperCollins $15.99 (978-0-06-008992-4). In this romantic fantasy, 16-year-old Jennie in Scotland falls in love with an enchanted lord and their love is so strong that it shatters a powerful curse. (Rev: BL 2/15/04; SLJ 3/04)

3346 McNish, Cliff. *Angel* (7–10). 2008, Carolrhoda $16.95 (978-0-8225-8900-6). Freya's belief in angels has led her into trouble in the past; now, at the age of 14, she realizes that the angels are real. (Rev: BL 6/1–15/08; SLJ 6/08)

3347 McNish, Cliff. *Breathe: A Ghost Story* (4–8). 2006, Carolrhoda LB $15.95 (978-0-8225-6443-0). After the death of his father, young Jack moves with his mother to an old farmhouse in the English countryside, a home that they share with the spirits of four children and the Ghost Mother who enslaved them. (Rev: SLJ 11/06)

3348 McNish, Cliff. *The Silver Child* (6–9). 2005, Carolrhoda $15.95 (978-1-57505-825-2). Mysteriously drawn to a huge garbage dump known as Coldharbour, six children undergo fantastic transformations. (Rev: BCCB 4/05; BL 4/15/05; SLJ 6/05; VOYA 6/05)

3349 McNish, Cliff. *Silver City* (5–8). Series: Silver Sequence. 2006, Carolrhoda $15.95 (978-1-57505-926-6). As the fearsome Roar draws closer to the Earth, Milo, Thomas, Helen, and their friends use their magical powers to keep the threat at bay; a sequel to *The Silver Child* (2005). (Rev: BL 6/1–15/06; SLJ 9/06)

3350 McNish, Cliff. *Silver World* (5–8). Series: The Silver Sequence. 2007, Carolrhoda LB $15.95 (978-1-57505-897-9). In this third volume in the series, Milo and the other children of Coldharbour use their extraordinary powers to protect the Earth from being destroyed by the terrifying monster called "The Roar." (Rev: SLJ 6/07)

3351 McQuerry, Maureen Doyle. *The Peculiars* (7–12). 2012, Abrams/Amulet $16.95 (978-1-4197-0178-8). At the age of 18, long-fingered Lena sets out for Scree, a province where the Peculiars — including her long-lost father — may be living; on the journey she meets a young librarian and a handsome marshall. **e** (Rev: BL 5/15/12*; HB 7–8/12; LMC 11–12/12*; SLJ 11/12; VOYA 6/12)

3352 Madigan, L. K. *The Mermaid's Mirror* (8–10). 2010, Houghton Mifflin $16 (978-0-547-19491-2). Why does the sea call so strongly to Lena, even though her father, a former surfer, has forbidden her to swim in it? (Rev: BL 9/15/10*; SLJ 12/1/10)

3353 Mafi, Tahereh. *Shatter Me* (8–12). 2011, HarperTeen $17.99 (978-006208548-1). An "undesirable" girl whose touch causes pain and death meets Adam, who is immune to her curse and gives her hope for a less violent future. ∩ **e** Lexile HL650L (Rev: BL 10/15/11; LMC 3–4/12; SLJ 2/12)

3354 Maguire, Gregory. *What the Dickens* (6–9). 2007, Candlewick $15.99 (978-0-7636-2961-8). While seeking shelter from a storm, Gage tells his younger cousins an imaginative story about tooth fairies What-the-Dickens and Pepper. (Rev: BL 10/1/07; HB 9–10/07; LMC 1/08; SLJ 11/07)

3355 Mahoney, Karen. *The Wood Queen* (6–9). Series: Iron Witch. 2012, Flux paper $9.95 (978-07387266-2-5). In a bid to save the life of her mother, 17-year-old Donna must make a deal with Aliette, the Wood Queen. **e** (Rev: BL 3/1/12; SLJ 3/12; VOYA 2/12)

3356 Mahy, Margaret. *Maddigan's Fantasia* (5–8). 2007, Simon & Schuster $17.99 (978-1-4169-1812-7). When 12-year-old Garland's father is killed, messengers from the future arrive to urge her to travel to a far-off town in search of a solar converter that will prevent future catastrophe. (Rev: BL 12/15/07; HB 11–12/07; LMC 2/08; SLJ 11/07)

3357 Maizel, Rebecca. *Infinite Days* (8–12). Series: Vampire Queen. 2010, St. Martin's paper $9.99 (978-0-312-64991-3). Lenah Beaudonte, a vampire whose humanity has been restored thanks to the sacrifice of her lover, Rhode, did not believe she would ever be 16 or fall in love again, but she is having those experiences until her past comes back to haunt her. (Rev: BL 7/10; SLJ 12/1/10)

3358 Malley, Gemma. *The Declaration* (6–10). 2007, Bloomsbury $16.95 (978-1-59990-119-0). In a world where people exchange childlessness for immortality,

Surplus Anna should never have been born and lives a life of servitude. ⌒ (Rev: BL 11/15/07; SLJ 2/08)

3359 Malone, Marianne. *Stealing Magic* (4–7). Illus. by Greg Call. Series: A Sixty-Eight Rooms Adventures. 2012, Random House $16.99 (978-037586819-1); LB $19.99 (978-037596819-8). Sixth-graders Ruthie and Jack travel back in time to help a Jewish girl in 1937 Paris and a slave girl in antebellum Charleston, South Carolina, in this sequel to *The Sixty-Eight Rooms* (2010) involving the Thorne Rooms at the Art Institute of Chicago. ⌒ 𝐞 (Rev: BL 1/1/12; SLJ 2/12)

3360 Mantchev, Lisa. *Eyes Like Stars* (8–12). Series: Théâtre Illuminata. 2009, Feiwel & Friends $16.99 (978-031238096-0). The magical Théâtre Illuminata — where characters from Shakespeare's plays materialize from thin air — has been Beatrice's home since infancy, and she is determined to save it by putting on a blockbuster. The sequels are *Perchance to Dream* (2010) and *So Silver Bright* (2011). ⌒ Lexile HL740L (Rev: BL 5/15/09; LMC 10/09; SLJ 8/09; VOYA 8/09)

3361 Marchetta, Melina. *Finnikin of the Rock* (6–10). 2010, Candlewick $18.99 (978-0-7636-4361-4). In this rich, multilayered fantasy, 19-year-old Finnikin prepares to return from exile and, with the help of a mysterious young woman Evanjalin and other refugees, restore the kingdom of Lumatere to its former glory. YALSA Amazing Audiobooks Top Ten 2011. ⌒ Lexile 820L (Rev: BL 3/1/10*; HB 5–6/10; LMC 5–6/10; SLJ 3/10)

3362 Marillier, Juliet. *Cybele's Secret* (7–10). 2008, Knopf $16.99 (978-0-375-83365-6). Scholarly Paula, 17, accompanies her father on a trip to Istanbul to buy a treasured artifact, the remnant of a pagan cult, only to find herself in a dangerous and challenging position; a companion to *Wildwood Dancing* (2007). Best Books for Young Adults 2009. ⌒ (Rev: BL 7/08*; HB 11–12/08; LMC 11–12/08; SLJ 9/1/08; VOYA 12/08)

3363 Marillier, Juliet. *Shadowfell* (7–10). 2012, Knopf $16.99 (978-0-375-86954-9); LB $19.99 (978-037596954-6). Neryn, a 15-year-old with magical powers that she has kept secret, learns that she alone can save her homeland of Alban from destruction. 𝐞 Lexile 730L (Rev: BLO 10/15/12; LMC 1–2/13; SLJ 12/12; VOYA 12/12)

3364 Marillier, Juliet. *Wildwood Dancing* (8–11). 2007, Knopf $16.99 (978-0-375-83364-9). Five Transylvanian sisters live lives filled with magic, danger, and romance when they enter a portal into the Other Kingdom. (Rev: BCCB 3/07; BL 2/1/07; HB 3–4/07; LMC 4–5/07; SLJ 2/07*)

3365 Marr, Melissa. *Carnival of Souls* (8–12). 2012, HarperCollins $17.99 (978-0-06-165928-7). When she falls in love with a daimon she's supposed to fight, Mallory, 17, learns important truths about her real heritage and destiny. 𝐞 (Rev: BL 8/12; SLJ 10/12)

3366 Marr, Melissa. *Wicked Lovely* (7–12). 2007, HarperTeen $16.99 (978-0-06-121465-3). Aislinn, who can see fairies, is faced with a very difficult choice that involves all of humanity and faerie when the Summer King asks her to be his queen. (Rev: SLJ 7/07)

3367 Marriott, Zoe. *Daughter of the Flames* (7–11). 2009, Candlewick $17.99 (978-076363749-1). Zira, who is part Ruan and part Sedorne, is caught up in a battle between the two tribes in this sweeping story. (Rev: BL 2/15/09; LMC 8–9/09; SLJ 8/09; VOYA 4/09)

3368 Marriott, Zoë. *The Swan Kingdom* (6–9). 2008, Candlewick $16.99 (978-0-7636-3481-0). A fairy-tale-like fantasy in which 15-year-old Alexandra's mother is killed by a shapeshifter and her brothers changed into swans. Can Alexandra save them with her magic? (Rev: BL 1/1–15/08; SLJ 8/08)

3369 Marrone, Amanda. *The Multiplying Menace* (4–7). 2010, Aladdin paper $5.99 (978-1-4169-9033-8). Twelve-year-old Maggie's somewhat unpredictable magical talents cause her difficulties until she's sent to live with her grandmother and hones her skills. 𝐞 Lexile 760L (Rev: BL 8/10; LMC 10/10; SLJ 8/10)

3370 Marrone, Amanda. *Uninvited* (7–10). 2007, Simon & Schuster paper $8.99 (978-1-4169-3978-8). Jordan decides to clean up her act (really, her acting out with drugs and sex) when her vampire ex-boyfriend returns to haunt her. (Rev: BL 1/1–15/08; SLJ 11/07)

3371 Marsden, John. *Burning for Revenge* (8–12). Series: Tomorrow. 2000, Houghton Mifflin $17.00 (978-0-395-96054-7). Ellie and her four Australian friends attack an airfield held by the enemy in this continuing saga. (Rev: BL 10/1/00; HBG 3/01; SLJ 10/00)

3372 Marsden, John. *The Night Is for Hunting* (8–12). Series: Tomorrow. 2001, Houghton Mifflin $16.00 (978-0-618-07026-8). This sixth book in the Tomorrow series continues the action-packed story of a group of teenagers fighting to defend Australia against a band of invaders. (Rev: BCCB 2/02; BL 11/1/01; HBG 10/02; SLJ 10/01; VOYA 12/01)

3373 Marsh, Katherine. *The Night Tourist* (6–9). 2007, Hyperion $17.99 (978-1-4231-0689-0). Literate and erudite Jack finds he can see the dead after he is hit by a car and is led to another world via the New York subway and a girl called Euri; references to classic literature and mythology add depth to this story. (Rev: BL 11/1/07; SLJ 11/07)

3374 Martin, Rafe. *Birdwing* (5–8). 2005, Scholastic $16.99 (978-0-459-21167-7). This appealing fantasy picks up where "The Six Swans" by the Brothers Grimm ends, chronicling the story of Ardwin, the prince who was turned into a swan and then restored to human form apart from his left arm, which remains a swan's wing. (Rev: BCCB 12/05; BL 11/15/05; HB 1–2/06; SLJ 12/05; VOYA 12/05)

3375 Martini, Clem. *The Mob* (5–8). Series: Feather and Bone: The Crow Chronicles. 2004, Kids Can $16.95 (978-1-55337-574-6). As hundreds of crows of the Kinaar clan come together for their annual socialization at the Gathering Tree, internal conflicts threaten to tear the avian family apart in this first volume in a trilogy. (Rev: BL 10/1/04; SLJ 12/04)

3376 Mason, Timothy. *The Last Synapsid* (4–7). 2009, Delacorte $16.99 (978-0-385-73581-0). Before there were dinosaurs, there were reptiles called synapsids and two of them — plus a villain named Jenkins — travel through time to a tiny town in Colorado where Rob and Phoebe try to figure out how to send them back before something terrible happens. (Rev: BCCB 1/09; BLO 2/9/09; LMC 5/09; SLJ 6/09)

3377 Masson, Sophie. *Serafin* (5–8). 2000, Saint Mary's paper $5.50 (978-0-88489-567-1). After he saves Calou from being lynched as a witch, Frederick is forced to flee his 17th-century French village with Calou and soon afterward realizes that the girl is a matagot, a half-angel half-human creature. (Rev: SLJ 8/00)

3378 Masson, Sophie. *Snow, Fire, Sword* (6–9). 2006, HarperCollins $15.99 (978-0-06-079091-2). Teens Adi and Dewi must discern right from wrong in their quest to defeat a villainous sorcerer seeking to destroy the forces of good on their island nation of Jayanga. (Rev: BL 5/15/06; SLJ 10/06)

3379 Matas, Carol, and Perry Nodelman. *Out of Their Minds* (5–8). Series: Minds. 1998, Simon & Schuster $16.00 (978-0-689-81946-9). In this fantasy (the third in the series), Princess Lenora and Prince Coren journey to Andilla to marry but find that some force is upsetting The Balance. (Rev: HBG 3/99; SLJ 9/98; VOYA 2/99)

3380 Matthews, L. S. *A Dog for Life* (5–7). 2006, Delacorte $14.95 (978-0-385-73366-3). Tom is sick and Mouse the dog is banished on grounds of possible infection, so John and Mouse, who can communicate psychically, set out to find Mouse a new home. ⌒ (Rev: BL 12/1/06*; SLJ 10/06)

3381 Mebus, Scott. *Gods of Manhattan* (5–8). Series: Gods of Manhattan. 2008, Dutton $17.99 (978-0-525-47955-0). Rory discovers that he has the ability to see figures from New York history (such as Peter Stuyvesant and Babe Ruth) and that he must use this power to save Manhattan. (Rev: BL 5/15/08; SLJ 4/08)

3382 Mebus, Scott. *Spirits in the Park* (5–8). Series: Gods of Manhattan. 2009, Dutton $17.99 (978-0-525-42148-1). In Mannahatta, the spirit city that exists parallel to the real city, Rory — reluctantly — must find his missing father. (Rev: BLO 4/24/09; SLJ 9/09; VOYA 8/09)

3383 Meehan, Kierin. *Hannah's Winter* (5–8). 2009, Kane $15.95 (978-1-933605-98-2). Hannah, an Australian 12-year-old, finds herself enjoying her stay in Ja-

pan and, with her new friends Miki and Hiro, she investigates a mysterious riddle. (Rev: HB 5/09*; SLJ 3/09)

3384 Melling, O. R. *The Book of Dreams* (7–12). Series: The Chronicles of Faerie. 2009, Abrams $19.95 (978-0-8109-8346-5). Dana, a 13-year-old who is half faerie, now lives unhappily in Canada but travels to the land of Faerie to find the Book of Dreams. Lexile 670L (Rev: BL 10/1/09; SLJ 8/09; VOYA 6/09)

3385 Melling, O. R. *The Light-Bearer's Daughter* (7–11). Series: Chronicles of Faerie. 2007, Abrams $16.95 (978-0-8109-0781-2). In a forest in the fairy realm, 12-year-old Dana embarks on a dangerous mission to deliver a message to the fairy High King; and in contemporary Ireland activists work to save the forest from developers. (Rev: BL 5/15/07)

3386 Melling, O. R. *The Summer King* (8–11). 2005, Abrams $16.95 (978-0-8109-5969-9). Laurel visits her grandparents in Ireland a year after her twin sister's death and discovers a hidden world of fairies, who enlist her help to save their kingdom. (Rev: BL 4/15/06; SLJ 8/06)

3387 Melling, Orla. *The Druid's Tune* (6–10). 1993, O'Brien paper $9.95 (978-0-86278-285-6). Peter, a Druid lost in the 20th century, involves two teenagers in a time-travel spell that sends them back to Ireland's Iron Age. (Rev: BL 2/15/93)

3388 Meloy, Colin. *Under Wildwood* (4–8). Illus. by Carson Ellis. 2012, HarperCollins $17.99 (978-0-06-202471-8). Prue and Curtis discover a machinated sweatshop beneath Wildwood, where they're mistaken for deities and trusted with rescuing the children working there; the sequel to *Wildwood* (2011). ⌒ **e** Lexile 800L (Rev: BL 8/12; SLJ 11/12)

3389 Meloy, Colin. *Wildwood* (4–8). Illus. by Carson Ellis. 2011, HarperCollins $16.99 (978-0-06-202468-8). Twelve-year-old Prue enters the Wilderness in search of her brother, who's been abducted by crows, in this richly imagined fantasy. (Rev: BL 7/11; SLJ 8/11*)

3390 Meloy, Maile. *The Apothecary* (6–9). Illus. by Ian Schoenherr. 2011, Putnam $16.99 (978-0-399-25627-1). In 1952 London, 14-year-old Janie's family arrives from Hollywood and the teen soon finds herself embroiled in international intrigue with an element of magic. ⌒ **e** Lexile 740L (Rev: BL 9/1/11; LMC 3–4/12; SLJ 12/1/11)

3391 Messenger, Shannon. *Keeper of the Lost Cities* (4–7). 2012, Aladdin $16.99 (978-144244593-2). At the age of 12 Sophie Foster, who has always known that she is different, learns that she is in fact an elf. **e** (Rev: BL 11/1/12; LMC 3–4/13; SLJ 1/13)

3392 Messer, Stephen. *Windblowne* (4–7). 2010, Random House $16.99 (978-0-375-86195-6). Hoping to become a better kite-maker, Oliver seeks help from his Uncle Gilbert and his talking red kite; together they work to save the trees that support their treehouse village. Lexile 760L (Rev: BL 5/15/10; LMC 8–9/10; SLJ 6/10)

3393 Meyer, Kai. *Pirate Curse* (6–9). Trans. by Elizabeth D. Crawford. Series: Wave Walkers. 2006, Simon & Schuster $15.95 (978-1-4169-2421-0). This first book in the series features the adventures of Jolly, a 14-year-old girl who has the ability to walk on water. (Rev: BL 6/1–15/06; LMC 2/07; SLJ 6/06)

3394 Meyer, Kai. *Pirate Emperor* (6–9). Trans. from German by Elizabeth D. Crawford. Series: Wave Walkers. 2007, Simon & Schuster $16.99 (978-1-4169-2474-6). Readers of *Pirate Curse* will enjoy this sequel in which the magical pirate characters encounter thrilling battles and adventures. (Rev: SLJ 6/07)

3395 Meyer, Kai. *The Stone Light* (5–7). Trans. from German by Elizabeth D. Crawford. Series: The Dark Reflections Trilogy. 2006, Simon & Schuster $16.95 (978-0-689-87789-6). Desperately searching for help in their fight to free Venice from the evil Egyptian pharaoh, Merle travels on Vermithrax, the flying lion, to Hell in hopes of convincing Lucifer to ally himself with their cause; the sequel to *The Water Mirror* (2005). (Rev: BL 3/15/07; SLJ 1/07)

3396 Meyer, Kai. *The Water Mirror* (4–7). Trans. by Elizabeth D. Crawford. Series: Dark Reflections. 2005, Simon & Schuster $15.95 (978-0-689-87787-2). In an alternate Venice in danger of destruction, 14-year-old Merle, a plucky orphan, finds herself playing a central role; the first volume in a series noted for its setting; sequels are *The Stone Light* (2007) and *The Glass Word* (2008). ⌒ (Rev: BL 1/1–15/06; SLJ 11/05*; VOYA 12/05)

3397 Michael, Livi. *City of Dogs* (5–8). 2007, Putnam $16.99 (978-0-399-24356-1). Sam has always wanted a dog and is happy when Jenny comes to live with him, but Jenny's mission becomes overarching and she must take on friends and foes in this fantasy full of mythological references. (Rev: BCCB 11/07; LMC 11–12/07; SLJ 11/07)

3398 Miéville, China. *Un Lun Dun* (5–9). 2007, Del Rey $17.95 (978-0-345-49516-7). In contemporary London, Zanna and her friend Deeba find themselves on the edge of a strange Unlondon that is awaiting a chosen one. (Rev: SLJ 4/07*)

3399 Milford, Kate. *The Boneshaker* (5–8). 2010, Clarion $17 (978-0-547-24187-6). In 1913 Arcane, Missouri, 13-year-old Natalie is suspicious of the owner of a traveling medicine show who has many mysterious machines; but everyone else seems to be taken in by him. ⌒ **e** Lexile 900L (Rev: BL 5/15/10*; LMC 10/10; SLJ 6/10)

3400 Miller, Christopher, and Allan Miller. *Hunter Brown and the Secret of the Shadow* (4–7). Series: Codebearers. 2008, Warner $13.99 (978-1-59317-328-9). Pranksters Stretch and Hunter are transported to fan-

tastical Solandra, where they must fight amongst the Codebearers, battling evil and following the wisdom contained in a mysterious book. (Rev: BLO 11/1/08; SLJ 3/1/09)

3401 Miller, Kirsten. *All You Desire* (8–11). 2011, Penguin $17.99 (978-1-59514-323-5). Haven and Iain, both reincarnated, are in New York City on the trail of Beau Decker, a friend of Haven's who has gone missing; this sequel to *The Eternal Ones* (2010) has rich historical details. ⌒ **e** (Rev: BL 10/1/11; SLJ 11/1/11)

3402 Miller, Kirsten. *The Eternal Ones* (8–11). 2010, Penguin $17.99 (978-1-595-14308-2). This suspenseful tale mixes fantasy, mystery, and romance as 17-year-old Haven faces discrimination because of her visions of previous lives and flees from small-town Tennessee to New York City. ⌒ **e** Lexile HL760L (Rev: BL 6/10; LMC 11–12/10; SLJ 8/10)

3403 Mingle, Pamela. *Kissing Shakespeare* (7–12). 2012, Delacorte $17.99 (978-038574196-5); LB $20.99 (978-037599034-2). Kidnapped from her high school production of "The Taming of the Shrew," Miranda is whisked back to 1581 where her mission is to discourage young William Shakespeare from joining the priesthood. **e** (Rev: BL 9/15/12; SLJ 8/1/12; VOYA 10/12)

3404 Mitchard, Jacquelyn. *Look Both Ways* (7–10). Series: Midnight Twins. 2009, Penguin $16.99 (978-159514161-3). Twins Merry and Mallory, who can "see" the future and the past, try to sort out their latest cryptic vision with the help of Native American friends. ⌒ Lexile 710L (Rev: BL 2/15/09; SLJ 5/1/09)

3405 Mitchell, Todd. *The Traitor King* (7–10). 2007, Scholastic $16.99 (978-0-439-82788-1). Darren and Jackie discover their uncle in Maine is missing; their search for him leads to family secrets, magical powers, and an alternate world. (Rev: BL 6/1–15/07; LMC 10/07; SLJ 5/07)

3406 Mlynowski, Sarah. *Gimme a Call* (7–10). 2010, Delacorte $17.99 (978-0-385-73588-9); LB $20.99 (978-0-385-90574-9). When Devi's boyfriend dumps her just before senior prom, she decides to rewrite her own present by summoning her 14-year-old self and attempting to avert her current problems from happening in this light novel with a time travel twist. ⌒ **e** Lexile HL440L (Rev: BL 3/1/10; SLJ 3/10; VOYA 10/10)

3407 Moesta, Rebecca, and Kevin J. Anderson. *Crystal Doors* (6–9). 2006, Little, Brown $15.99 (978-0-316-01055-9). Fourteen-year-old cousins Gwen and Vic are transported to the island world of Elantya, where they find magic and conflict. (Rev: BL 7/06; LMC 2/07; SLJ 9/06)

3408 Molloy, Michael. *The House on Falling Star Hill* (4–8). 2004, Scholastic $16.95 (978-0-439-57740-3). While spending a vacation with his grandparents in a peaceful English village, Tim discovers an alternate world called Tallis and becomes involved in the turmoil taking place there. (Rev: BL 4/15/04; SLJ 4/04)

3409 Molloy, Michael. *The Time Witches* (5–8). 2002, Scholastic paper $4.99 (978-0-439-42090-7). The characters from *The Witch Trade* (2002) return in this sequel in which Abby, a Light Witch, and her friends must travel into the past to foil a plot hatched by the nefarious Wolfbane. (Rev: BL 1/1–15/03; SLJ 8/03)

3410 Mont, Eve Marie. *A Breath of Eyre* (8–10). 2012, Kensington paper $9.95 (978-07582694-8-5). Modern-day teen Emma finds herself trapped inside Jane Eyre's body after a lightning strike. e (Rev: BL 4/15/12; SLJ 4/12; VOYA 6/12)

3411 Moore, Perry. *Hero* (8–11). 2007, Hyperion $16.99 (978-1-4231-0195-6). Thom, who hides his developing superpowers and his homosexual feelings from his once superhero father, joins the League as an apprentice. (Rev: BL 8/07; HB 9–10/07; LMC 11/07; SLJ 9/07)

3412 Morden, Simon. *The Lost Art* (7–10). 2008, Random House $16.99 (978-0-385-75147-6). The world has entered a new dark age, with books and knowledge locked away, and it is up to Va and Benzamir Michael Mahmood to rescue them in this fantasy with action, suspense and romance. (Rev: BL 5/15/08; LMC 4–5/08; SLJ 11/08)

3413 Moredun, P. R. *The Dragon Conspiracy* (5–8). Series: World of Eldaterra. 2005, HarperCollins LB $17.89 (978-0-06-076664-1). A complex first installment in which a British schoolboy in 1910 must battle female dragons to save both our world and the magical parallel world of Eldaterra. (Rev: BL 6/1–15/05; SLJ 10/05)

3414 Moriarty, Jaclyn. *A Corner of White* (7–11). 2013, Scholastic $17.99 (978-054539736-0). Fourteen-year-old Madeleine, who lives in Cambridge, England, with her mother, and 15-year-old Elliot, who lives in the Kingdom of Cello, find they can communicate with each other by letters through a crack between their worlds, and share their concerns about their families. Boston Globe–Horn Book Honor 2013. ∩ e Lexile 800L (Rev: BL 2/15/13; HB 5–6/13; LMC 8–9/13; SLJ 5/13*; VOYA 6/13)

3415 Morpurgo, Michael. *Little Foxes* (6–9). 1987, David & Charles $15.95 (978-0-7182-3972-5). Two orphans — a boy and a fox — are helped by a swan in this magical story. (Rev: SLJ 9/87)

3416 Morris, Gerald. *The Legend of the King* (6–9). Series: The Squire's Tales. 2010, Houghton Mifflin $16 (978-0-547-14420-7). King Arthur's reign is under threat from Mordred and his White Horsemen, and Sir Terence and other knights prepare for battle. e Lexile 760L (Rev: BLO 11/15/10; HB 11–12/10; SLJ 10/1/10)

3417 Morris, Gerald. *Parsifal's Page* (5–8). 2001, Houghton Mifflin $16.00 (978-0-618-05509-8). Piers becomes a page to Parsifal and accompanies the inno-

cent young man on his quest to become a knight. (Rev: BCCB 4/01; BL 4/15/01; HB 5–6/01; HBG 10/01; SLJ 4/01; VOYA 6/01)

3418 Morris, Gerald. *The Princess, the Crone, and the Dung-Cart Knight* (6–9). 2004, Houghton Mifflin $17.00 (978-0-618-37823-4). In this absorbing Arthurian fantasy, 13-year-old Sarah enlists help from others in her quest to identify those who instigated the murderous riot that took the lives of her mother and their Jewish friend. (Rev: BCCB 3/04; BL 4/15/04; HB 5–6/04; SLJ 5/04; VOYA 6/04)

3419 Morris, Gerald. *The Savage Damsel and the Dwarf* (5–8). 2000, Houghton Mifflin $16.00 (978-0-395-97126-0). Sixteen-year-old Lady Lynet travels to Camelot, in the company of a dwarf, to ask King Arthur's aid in defeating her sister's suitor. (Rev: BL 3/1/00; HB 5–6/00; HBG 10/00; SLJ 5/00; VOYA 6/00)

3420 Moss, Jenny. *Shadow* (6–9). 2010, Scholastic $17.99 (978-0-545-03641-2). Orphan Shadow's true identity and destiny are revealed when she fails in her mission to keep her young queen alive. e (Rev: BL 2/15/10; LMC 3–4/10; SLJ 7/10)

3421 Moss, Marissa. *Mira's Diary: Lost in Paris* (4–7). Illus. by author. 2012, Sourcebooks $12.99 (978-1-4022-6606-5). Traveling with her father to Paris in search of her missing mother, Mira visits Notre Dame is transported to the 19th century where she meets Degas and learns about the Dreyfus affair. e Lexile 730L (Rev: BL 12/1/12; LMC 5–6/13; SLJ 10/12)

3422 Mull, Brandon. *Seeds of Rebellion* (5–8). Series: Beyonders. 2012, Aladdin $19.99 (978-141699794-8). Jason succeeds in traveling from Colorado back to Lyrian in this action-packed story and joins with Rachel and Galloran to fight the evil that is lurking. ∩ e (Rev: BL 2/1/12; SLJ 3/12)

3423 Mull, Brandon. *A World Without Heroes* (4–7). Series: Beyonders. 2011, Simon & Schuster $19.99 (978-1-4169-9792-4). Jason, 14, is transported into an alternate world called Lyrian where he meets another young American, Rachel, and the two set out on a quest to overthrow the evil emperor and find their way home. ∩ e Lexile 710L (Rev: BL 2/15/11; SLJ 3/1/11; VOYA 8/11)

3424 Muller, Rachel Dunstan. *The Solstice Cup* (5–8). 2009, Orca paper $9.95 (978-1-55469-017-6). On a visit to Northern Ireland, tween twins Breanne and Mackenzie ignore warnings about the fairies and find themselves transported into a scary Otherworld. (Rev: BL 5/15/09)

3425 Mullin, Caryl Cude. *A Riddle of Roses* (4–7). 2000, Second Story paper $6.95 (978-1-896764-28-3). Meryl, who has been expelled from school for a year, goes on a quest to Avalon to find her own wisdom. (Rev: BL 2/15/01; VOYA 4/01)

3426 Mullin, Caryl Cude. *Rough Magic* (7–10). 2009, Second Story paper $9.95 (978-1-897187-63-0). This fantasy based on Shakespeare's *The Tempest* is presented in five acts and tells the story of three generations of Caliban's family. Lexile HL610L (Rev: BL 8/09; LMC 3–4/10)

3427 Murdock, Catherine Gilbert. *Princess Ben* (8–11). 2008, Houghton Mifflin $16.00 (978-0-618-95971-6). The princess of the title (whose full name is Benevolence) must take on new responsibilities when her parents and her uncle are killed and she learns magic secrets. (Rev: BL 5/15/08; SLJ 6/08)

3428 Myers, Edward. *Storyteller* (6–9). 2008, Clarion $16.00 (978-0-618-69541-6). A 17-year-old storyteller sets off to seek his fortune, gathering stories from characters he meets and finding work, romance, and trouble — and in the process teaching the reader about the value of stories. (Rev: BL 8/08; SLJ 9/08)

3429 Myers, Walter Dean. *The Legend of Tarik* (6–9). 1991, Scholastic paper $3.50 (978-0-590-44426-2). Tarik, a black teenager in Africa of years ago, acquires a magic sword.

3430 Nation, Kaleb. *Bran Hambric: The Farfield Curse* (6–9). 2009, Sourcebooks $17.99 (978-1-4022-1857-6). Outsider 14-year-old Bran Hambric discovers he has magical powers in a land where magic is forbidden, and quickly sets about learning the truth about his real family, his past, and the unexplained gaps in his memory. ⌒ (Rev: BL 11/1/09; LMC 11–12/09; SLJ 10/09)

3431 Nayeri, Daniel, and Dina Nayeri. *Another Pan* (6–9). Series: Another. 2010, Candlewick $16.99 (978-0-7636-3712-5). While attending an elite prep school where their father is a professor, Wendy and John Darling discover a book which opens the door to other worlds, to Egyptian myths long thought impossible, and to the home of an age-old darkness. ℮ (Rev: BL 11/15/10; SLJ 12/1/10)

3432 Nesbet, Anne. *The Cabinet of Earths* (4–7). 2012, HarperCollins $16.99 (978-006196313-1). Full of mystery and magic, this book tells of 13-year-old Maya's relocation, with her family, to Paris, where she struggles to keep watch over her young brother while finding herself enchanted by the magical Cabinet of Earths. ℮ Lexile 800L (Rev: BL 1/1/12; HB 1–2/12; SLJ 5/1/12; VOYA 12/11)

3433 Neumeier, Rachel. *The City in the Lake* (8–11). 2008, Knopf $15.99 (978-0-375-84704-2). When Prince Cassiel disappears from the City in the Lake, so does the city's life and magic. Neill and Timou set off in search of him and learn about their heritage as they battle the forces that threaten the kingdom. (Rev: BL 5/15/08; SLJ 9/08)

3434 Newbound, Andrew. *Ghoul Strike!* (5–8). 2010, Scholastic $16.99 (978-054522938-8). Twelve-year-old ghost hunter Alannah Malarra is out of her depth when

she faces spirits from another dimension and must call in reinforcements. (Rev: BL 10/15/10; SLJ 1/1/11)

3435 Nicholson, William. *Noman* (7–10). Series: Noble Warriors. 2008, Harcourt paper $14.00 (978-0-15-206005-3). In the third book of this unusually contemplative trilogy, Seeker, Morning Star and the Wildman search for a new leader. (Rev: BL 5/15/08; SLJ 8/08)

3436 Nicholson, William. *Seeker* (6–9). 2006, Harcourt $17.00 (978-0-15-205768-8). This fantasy with a religious theme tells the story of Seeker, a 16-year old who tries to protect his religion from those who wish to destroy it; the sequel is *Jango* (2007). (Rev: BL 6/1–15/06; LMC 1/07; SLJ 8/06)

3437 Nielsen, Jennifer A. *The False Prince* (4–7). Series: Ascendance Trilogy. 2012, Scholastic $17.99 (978-054528413-4). Most of the royal family of Carthya is dead, and nobleman Conner seeks a child to impersonate the missing younger son and inherit the throne; the first volume in a trilogy. ⌒ ℮ Lexile 710L (Rev: BL 4/1/12; HB 3–4/12; LMC 8–9/12; SLJ 4/12)

3438 Nigg, Joseph. *How to Raise and Keep a Dragon* (5–10). Illus. by Dan Malone. 2006, Barron's $18.99 (978-0-7641-5920-6). This whimsical guide to the care and feeding of dragons offers tips for selecting just the right type of dragon, finding the correct equipment and supplies, establishing good modes of communication, and training for competitions. (Rev: SLJ 11/06)

3439 Nimmo, Jenny. *Charlie Bone and the Time Twister* (5–7). 2003, Scholastic $10.99 (978-0-439-49687-2). In 1916 Henry Yewbeam finds a strange marble and is transported to the present-day Bloor's Academy, where Charlie Bone tests his magical abilities in an effort to send him home. A sequel to *Midnight for Charlie Bone* (2003). (Rev: BL 9/15/03; HBG 4/04; SLJ 10/03)

3440 Nimmo, Jenny. *Griffin's Castle* (5–8). 1997, Orchard LB $17.99 (978-0-531-33006-7). When Dinah and her young mother, Rosalie, move into the rundown mansion owned by Rosalie's boyfriend, Dinah brings to life several carved animals for protection. (Rev: SLJ 6/97; VOYA 8/97)

3441 Nimmo, Jenny. *The Secret Kingdom* (4–7). 2011, Scholastic $16.99 (978-0-439-84673-8). Charlie Bone introduces this tale of his ancestor Timoken the Red King, who, with his sister Zobayda, finds himself in an action-packed fantasy adventure. The second volume in the series is *The Stones of Ravenglass* (2012). (Rev: BL 10/1/11; SLJ 9/1/11)

3442 Nix, Garth. *Above the Veil* (5–7). Series: The Seventh Tower. 2001, Scholastic paper $5.99 (978-0-439-17685-9). In episode four in this series, Tal and Milla continue their otherworldly adventures full of action, secrets, and surprising twists and turns. (Rev: SLJ 9/01)

3443 Nix, Garth. *Grim Tuesday* (5–8). Series: Keys to the Kingdom. 2004, Scholastic paper $7.99 (978-0-439-43655-7). Arthur Penhaligon returns in this second installment in the series to the house that holds an alternate universe and there must challenge the evil Grim Tuesday, who threatens to destroy everything; the next volume is *Drowned Wednesday* (2005). (Rev: SLJ 8/04)

3444 Nix, Garth. *Lady Friday* (6–9). Series: The Keys to the Kingdom. 2007, Scholastic $17.99 (978-0-439-70088-7). A funny, well-written tale in the popular but complex series that finds Arthur challenged by Lady Friday for control of the Middle House. (Rev: SLJ 6/07)

3445 Nix, Garth. *Lord Sunday* (5–8). Series: Keys to the Kingdom. 2010, Scholastic $17.99 (978-043970090-0). Arthur and his allies meet with great hardship and eventually triumph over the diabolical Lord Sunday in this series conclusion. ☊ ℮ Lexile 980L (Rev: BL 4/15/10)

3446 Nix, Garth. *Mister Monday* (5–8). Series: The Keys to the Kingdom. 2003, Scholastic paper $6.99 (978-0-439-55123-6). When 7th-grader Arthur Penhaligon receives a healing key from a mysterious stranger, the gift turns out to be a mixed blessing that brings illness and strange creatures seeking to reclaim the key. (Rev: BCCB 1/04; SLJ 12/03)

3447 Nix, Garth. *One Beastly Beast: Two Aliens, Three Inventors, Four Fantastic Tales* (5–7). Illus. by Brian Biggs. 2007, Eos $15.99 (978-0-06-084319-9). Four short stories accompanied by cartoonish illustrations for readers who enjoy fantasy that's not too far out or too scary. (Rev: BCCB 10/07; BL 7/07; SLJ 9/07)

3448 Nix, Garth. *Superior Saturday* (8–11). Series: Keys to the Kingdom. 2008, Scholastic $17.99 (978-043970089-4). In this sixth installment in the series, Arthur is revealed as heir to the kingdom and must obtain the Sixth Key from the powerful Saturday in the face of many challenges. ☊ ℮ Lexile 930L (Rev: BL 11/15/08; VOYA 8/08)

3449 Nix, Garth, and Sean Williams. *Troubletwisters* (4–7). 2011, Scholastic $16.99 (978-054525897-5). When their house mysteriously explodes, twins Jaide and Jack, 12, are sent to live with their previously unknown Grandma X, where they discover they have unusual talents, and that a power named The Evil is lurking. (Rev: BL 9/15/11)

3450 Noel, Alyson. *Fated* (8–11). Series: Soul Seekers. 2012, St. Martin's/Griffin $18.99 (978-0-312-66485-5). Daire, 16, learns the source of her bloody visions when she goes to live with her grandmother in Enchantment, New Mexico. ☊ ℮ Lexile 1060L (Rev: BL 6/12; SLJ 7/12)

3451 Noël, Alyson. *Blue Moon* (8–11). Series: The Immortals. 2009, St. Martin's paper $9.99 (978-031253276-5). In this sequel to *Evermore* (2008), 600-year-old Damen's powers are weakening and 16-year-old Ever knows she must save him from the evil perpetrated by the newly arrived Roman. ☊ (Rev: BL 7/09)

3452 Noël, Alyson. *Evermore* (8–10). Series: The Immortals. 2009, St. Martin's $8.95 (978-031253275-8). The first book in the Immortals series introduces Ever, who finds she has supernatural powers as a result of the car crash that killed the rest of her family. Lexile 940L (Rev: BL 2/1/09; SLJ 4/1/09)

3453 Noël, Alyson. *Shadowland* (8–11). Series: The Immortals. 2009, St. Martin's $17.99 (978-0-312-59044-4). Girlfriend (Ever) and boyfriend (Damen) have achieved immortality but at a cost — they are never allowed to touch each other. Lexile 960L (Rev: BLO 11/17/09; SLJ 2/10)

3454 Norcliffe, James. *The Boy Who Could Fly* (5–8). 2010, Egmont $16.99 (978-1-60684-084-9). Michael accepts an offer that allows him to fly, and to escape the miserable home for unwanted children where he lives, but is he really better off? Lexile 700L (Rev: BL 7/10; HB 9–10/10; SLJ 4/11)

3455 North, Pearl. *Libyrinth* (8–11). 2009, Tor $17.95 (978-076532096-4). In a distant future, Haly, who has the ability to hear books, finds herself between competing forces: the Libyrarians, who protect and preserve ancient books, and the Eradicants, who seek to destroy the printed word. (Rev: BLO 6/17/09; LMC 11–12/09; SLJ 9/09)

3456 Nyoka, Gail. *Mella and the N'anga: An African Tale* (5–8). 2006, Sumach paper $9.95 (978-1-894549-49-3). Mella, the daughter of a king in ancient Zimbabwe, with the help of the magical powers she learns from the spiritual adviser called N'anga, strives to save her father's life and realm. (Rev: BL 3/1/06; SLJ 7/06)

3457 O'Brien, Robert C. *Mrs. Frisby and the Rats of NIMH* (5–7). Illus. by Zena Bernstein. 1971, Macmillan $18.00 (978-0-689-20651-1); paper $5.50 (978-0-689-71068-1). Saga of a group of rats made literate and given human intelligence by a series of experiments, who escape from their laboratory to found their own community. Newbery Medal 1972.

3458 O'Dell, Kathleen. *The Aviary* (5–8). 2011, Knopf $15.99 (978-0-375-85605-1); LB $18.99 (978-0-375-95605-8). At the turn of the 20th century in Maine, solitary 11-year-old Clara discovers that there is a link between the birds in the aviary in the rose garden and the supposed drowning of five children some years before. (Rev: BL 10/1/11; SLJ 11/1/11)

3459 O'Hearn, Kate. *Kira* (6–8). Series: Shadow of the Dragon. 2009, Kane/Miller $16.99 (978-1-935279-05-1). Feisty sisters Kira, 12, and Elspeth, 7, escape from a tyrannical regime and rescue a baby dragon, starting a quest to save their kingdom. ☊ ℮ Lexile 680L (Rev: BL 10/15/09; LMC 1–2/10; SLJ 10/09)

3460 Okorafor-Mbachu, Nnedi. *The Shadow Speaker* (5–8). 2007, Hyperion $16.99 (978-1-4231-0033-1). West Africa is a very different place in 2070 in this futuristic tale in which Muslim Ejii, 15, shadow-speaks with the queen who had her father killed years earlier. (Rev: BL 3/1/08; SLJ 2/08)

3461 Okorafor-Mbachu, Nnedi. *Zahrah the Windseeker* (5–8). 2005, Houghton Mifflin $16.00 (978-0-618-34090-3). In this appealing debut novel, 13-year-old Zahrah, a "dada girl" readily identifiable by her telltale vine-entwined dreadlocks, struggles to come to terms with her magical powers. (Rev: BL 11/15/05; SLJ 12/05)

3462 Okorafor, Nnedi. *Akata Witch* (6–9). 2011, Viking $16.99 (978-0-670-01196-4). Twelve-year-old Sunny, an albino of Nigerian descent but born in New York City, moves back to West Africa with her family and discovers her magical powers. e Lexile HL590L (Rev: BL 5/1/11; HB 5–6/11; LMC 10/11; SLJ 6/11; VOYA 6/11)

3463 Oliver, Lauren. *Liesl and Po* (4–7). Illus. by Kei Acedera. 2011, HarperCollins $16.99 (978-0-06-201451-1). A young apothecary's apprentice accidentally switches a box of magic with a vessel containing Liesl's father's ashes, leading to an adventure full of ghosts. ⌒ e Lexile 830L (Rev: BL 9/1/11; SLJ 11/1/11*)

3464 Oliver, Lauren. *The Spindlers* (4–7). 2012, HarperCollins $16.99 (978-0-06-197808-1). Liza realizes that her little brother Patrick has been infiltrated by the Spindlers and that he will soon disintegrate and produce hundreds of new Spindlers; Liza is determined to save his soul. ⌒ e Lexile 840L (Rev: BL 7/12; LMC 3–4/13; SLJ 9/12*)

3465 O'Neal, Eilis. *The False Princess* (6–9). 2011, Egmont $16.99 (978-1-60684-079-5). The Princess of Thorvaldor learns at the age of 16 that she is in fact Sinda, a peasant girl swapped at birth to save the real infant from a curse . . . but Sinda has her own magic abilities. ⌒ e Lexile 860L (Rev: BL 6/1/11; HB 5–6/11; SLJ 6/11*)

3466 Oppel, Kenneth. *Starclimber* (6–10). 2009, HarperTeen $17.99 (978-006085057-9); LB $18.89 (978-006085058-6). Matt and Kate rocket into space aboard a Canadian spaceship in this exciting sequel to *Airborn* (2004) and *Skybreaker* (2005). e (Rev: BLO 6/16/09; SLJ 6/1/09*)

3467 Orgel, Doris. *The Princess and the God* (7–10). 1996, Orchard LB $16.99 (978-0-531-08866-1). A handsome retelling of the Cupid and Psyche myth in novel format, in which the power of pure love is shown conquering overwhelming obstacles. (Rev: BL 2/1/96; SLJ 4/96)

3468 Osborne, Mary Pope. *Haunted Waters* (6–8). 2006, Candlewick $14.99 (978-0-7636-2995-3). The story, based on an old fairy tale and beautifully written, of the troubled marriage of a mermaid and a human; by the author of the Magic Treehouse books. (Rev: SLJ 9/06)

3469 Osterweil, Adam. *The Amulet of Komondor* (5–7). 2003, Front St $15.95 (978-1-886910-81-2). Finding themselves in a parallel world of "Japanimations," Joe and Katie face a mighty challenge, worry about how to get home, and continue their real-world romance in this lighthearted fantasy with *anime*-style illustrations. (Rev: BL 11/15/03; HBG 4/04; SLJ 12/03)

3470 Owen, James A. *Here, There Be Dragons* (8–11). Series: Chronicles of Imaginarium Geographica. 2006, Simon & Schuster $9.99 (978-1-4169-1227-9). John, Jack, and Charles — English intellectuals who will one day be known as J. R. R. Tolkien, C. S. Lewis, and Charles Williams — sail to the Archipelago of Dreams to defeat the Winter King. (Rev: BL 12/15/06; LMC 2/07; SLJ 11/06)

3471 Owen, James A. *The Search for the Red Dragon* (8–11). Illus. by author. Series: Chronicles of the Imaginarium Geographica. 2008, Simon & Schuster $17.99 (978-1-4169-4850-6). In this sequel to *Here, There Be Dragons*, the caretakers of the Imaginarium must solve the mystery behind the disappearance of the Archipelago's children. (Rev: BL 4/15/08; SLJ 2/08)

3472 Oz, Amos. *Suddenly in the Depths of the Forest* (4–7). Trans. from Hebrew by Sondra Silverston. 2011, Houghton Mifflin $15.99 (978-0-547-55153-1). A multilayered story about two children — Maya and Matti — who set out despite their fears to find out why their village has been cursed and all the animals have disappeared; an allegorical fable about tolerance and redemption. e Lexile NC1260L (Rev: BL 2/15/11; HB 5–6/11; LMC 10/11*; SLJ 5/11; VOYA 4/11)

3473 Page, Jan. *Rewind* (7–10). 2005, Walker $16.95 (978-0-8027-8995-2). When he is injured in an accident while playing drums onstage, Liam finds himself back in time watching his parents as teenagers, when they had a band whose drummer was killed. (Rev: BL 9/1/05; SLJ 11/05; VOYA 10/05)

3474 Palmer, Robin. *Little Miss Red* (7–11). 2010, Penguin paper $7.99 (978-0-14-241123-0). A frothy romantic fairy tale in which 16-year-old, Jewish Sophie, on her way to visit her grandmother in Florida, meets bad boy Jack, who is charming but somehow scary. Lexile 890L (Rev: BL 2/1/10; SLJ 2/10; VOYA 4/10)

3475 Paolini, Christopher. *Eldest* (8–11). Series: Inheritance. 2005, Knopf LB $24.99 (978-0-375-92670-9). Eragon continues his training as a Dragon Rider while his cousin Roran is under threat in this second installment in the trilogy. (Rev: BL 8/05; SLJ 10/05; VOYA 12/05)

3476 Paolini, Christopher. *Eragon* (7–12). Series: Inheritance. 2003, Knopf LB $20.99 (978-0-375-92668-6). A 15-year-old boy called Eragon finds a stone that hatches a magnificent blue dragon, drawing him into a series of dangerous adventures as the two hunt killers and in turn are hunted. (Rev: BL 8/03*; HBG 4/04; SLJ 9/03; VOYA 8/03)

197

3477 Paolini, Christopher. *Inheritance* (7–12). Series: Inheritance Cycle. 2011, Knopf $27.99 (978-037585611-2); LB $30.99 (978-037595611-9). Young Dragon Rider Eragon is forced to do battle with King Galbatorix in order to free Alagaesia in this lengthy final volume in the series. YALSA Amazing Audiobooks Top Ten 2013. ∩ ℮ Lexile 1010L (Rev: BLO 11/1/11)

3478 Papademetriou, Lisa. *The Wizard, the Witch, and Two Girls from Jersey* (6–9). 2006, Penguin paper $8.99 (978-1-59514-074-6). Veronica and Heather find themselves transported into the fantasy world of a novel they're reading for a high school English class. (Rev: BL 5/15/06; LMC 2/07; SLJ 10/06)

3479 Park, Linda Sue. *Archer's Quest* (4–7). 2006, Clarion $16.00 (978-0-618-59631-7). An ancient Korean ruler suddenly appears in the New York State bedroom of 12-year-old Kevin and the two must work out how to get him back home before the Year of the Tiger ends. (Rev: BL 3/15/06; SLJ 5/06)

3480 Parkkola, Seita. *The School of Possibilities* (6–9). 2010, Sourcebooks $12.99 (978-1-4022-1835-4). "Difficult" 12-year-old Storm is sent to the horrendous School of Possibilities where he meets the feisty India and together they challenge authority. ℮ Lexile 650L (Rev: BLO 4/15/10; LMC 10/10; SLJ 7/10; VOYA 6/10)

3481 Patterson, James. *Angel* (6–9). Series: Maximum Ride. 2011, Little, Brown $17.99 (978-031603620-7). Max is getting over the departure of Fang and growing more interested in Dylan, who is designed to love her, when she once again must act to save the world. ∩ ℮ Lexile 700L (Rev: BLO 4/15/11)

3482 Patterson, James. *Maximum Ride: School's Out — Forever* (7–10). 2006, Little, Brown $16.99 (978-0-316-15559-5). In this sequel to *The Angel Experiment* (2004), Max and her fellow bird-humans try to integrate into mainstream society but must overcome unexpected danger and betrayal. (Rev: BL 5/15/06; SLJ 8/06)

3483 Patterson, James. *Maximum Ride: The Angel Experiment* (7–9). 2005, Little, Brown $16.99 (978-0-316-15556-4). An engaging tale about a group of children, part human and part bird, who escape from the lab where they were bred and now must track down one of their number who's been kidnapped. (Rev: BCCB 4/05; BL 2/1/05; SLJ 5/05; VOYA 4/06)

3484 Pattou, Edith. *East* (6–10). 2003, Harcourt $18.00 (978-0-15-204563-0). A great white bear carries Rose away from home to her destiny in this romantic novelization of the East o' the Sun and West o' the Moon fairy tale. (Rev: BL 9/1/03*; HBG 4/04; SLJ 12/03; VOYA 12/03)

3485 Paul, Donita K. *Dragonspell* (4–8). 2004, WaterBrook paper $12.99 (978-1-57856-823-9). Fourteen-year-old Kale is the protagonist of this classic quest tale, set in the world of Amara, with Christian overtones reminiscent of C. S. Lewis. (Rev: SLJ 11/04)

3486 Pauley, Kimberly. *Cat Girl's Day Off* (7–10). 2012, Lee & Low $17.95 (978-160060883-4). Natalie uses her ability to communicate with cats to solve a criminal celebrity impersonation case. ℮ Lexile 660L (Rev: BL 5/1/12; SLJ 4/12; VOYA 6/12)

3487 Pauley, Kimberly. *Sucks to Be Me: The All-True Confessions of Mina Hamilton, Teen Vampire (Maybe)* (7–10). 2008, Mirrorstone $14.95 (978-078695028-7). Sixteen-year-old Mina must decide between staying human and becoming a vampire in this light, often funny story. ℮ Lexile HL740L (Rev: BL 11/15/08; VOYA 10/08)

3488 Paver, Michelle. *Oath Breaker* (5–9). Series: Chronicles of Ancient Darkness. 2009, HarperCollins $16.99 (978-0-06-072837-3); LB $17.89 (978-0-06-072838-0). When Torak's friend is murdered by a soul-eater, he sets out to get revenge in this fifth book in the series. Lexile 660L (Rev: SLJ 8/09; VOYA 2/09)

3489 Paver, Michelle. *Soul Eater* (6–9). Illus. by Geoff Taylor. Series: Chronicles of Ancient Darkness. 2007, HarperCollins $16.99 (978-0-06-072831-1). The third book in the series finds Torak and Renn traveling north to rescue Wolf, who has been taken into the icy wilderness by Soul Eaters. (Rev: BL 3/15/07; SLJ 5/07)

3490 Paver, Michelle. *Spirit Walker* (6–9). Series: Chronicles of Ancient Darkness. 2006, HarperCollins LB $17.89 (978-0-06-072829-8). Young Stone Age survivor Torak seeks a remedy for the epidemic affecting the clans and is reunited with his beloved Wolf in this sequel to *Wolf Brother* (2005). (Rev: BL 2/15/06; SLJ 6/06; VOYA 2/06)

3491 Pearce, Jackson. *As You Wish* (8–10). 2009, HarperTeen $16.99 (978-006166152-5). Upset when her boyfriend declares that he is gay, 16-year-old Viola accidentally summons a genie and her wish to be popular comes true. But does she prefer the genie to her new status? (Rev: BLO 5/15/09; SLJ 1/10; VOYA 8/09)

3492 Pearce, Jackson. *Fathomless* (8–11). 2012, Little, Brown $17.99 (978-0-316-20778-2). This dark remake of Hans Christian Andersen's "Little Mermaid" features Celia, a triplet who can read people's pasts, and a mermaid named Lo. ℮ (Rev: BL 10/1/12; LMC 3–4/13; SLJ 12/12; VOYA 10/12)

3493 Pearce, Philippa. *Tom's Midnight Garden* (4–7). Illus. by Susan Einzig. 1959, Dell paper $6.99 (978-0-06-440445-7). When the clock strikes 13, Tom visits his garden and meets Hatty, a strange mid-Victorian girl.

3494 Peck, Dale. *The Drift House: The First Voyage* (8–11). 2005, Bloomsbury $16.95 (978-1-58234-969-5). The Oakenfield siblings are sent to live with their Uncle Farley in Canada, and when their uncle's ship-like home is swept away in a flood, they enjoy a magical journey on the Sea of Time. (Rev: BL 10/1/05; SLJ 11/05; VOYA 10/05)

3495 Peck, Dale. *The Lost Cities: A Drift House Voyage* (8–11). 2007, Bloomsbury $16.95 (978-1-58234-859-9). Siblings Susan and Charles, who first traveled the Sea of Time in *The Drift House: The First Voyage* (2005), are afloat again in this action-packed sequel, this time battling Vikings and a time jetty. (Rev: BL 4/1/07; SLJ 4/07)

3496 Peck, Richard. *Secrets at Sea* (4–7). Illus. by Kelly Murphy. 2011, Dial $16.99 (978-0-8037-3455-5). In the late 19th century Helena and her mouse siblings must conquer their fears as they accompany the Cranston family (whose house they live in) on an ocean voyage to Europe, meeting many new mice and people as they travel. (Rev: BL 9/1/11; SLJ 9/1/11)

3497 Pemberton, Bonnie. *The Cat Master* (5–8). 2007, Marshall Cavendish $16.99 (978-0-7614-5340-6). A dying Cat Master's telepathic message to his successor — indoor cat but formerly feral Buddy — is intercepted by the evil cat Jett, and Buddy and his friends must fight for justice to be fulfilled. (Rev: BL 6/1–15/07; SLJ 6/07)

3498 Perrin, Randy. *Time Like a River* (5–7). 1997, RDR $14.95 (978-1-57143-061-8). Margie travels back in time to find a cure for her mother's mysterious illness. (Rev: HBG 3/98; SLJ 3/98)

3499 Perro, Bryan. *The Mask Wearer* (4–7). Trans. by Y. Maudet. 2011, Delacorte $16.99 (978-0-385-73903-0); LB $19.99 (978-038590766-8). With the help of mythical animal friends, young Amos Daragon sets out on a quest to find four masks representing earth, wind, fire, and water and thereby defeat the evil threatening his land. e Lexile 800L (Rev: BL 2/15/11; LMC 8–9/11*; SLJ 4/11)

3500 Pierce, Tamora. *Bloodhound* (6–8). Series: Beka Cooper. 2009, Random House $18.99 (978-037581469-3); LB $21.99 (978-037591469-0). The second book in the series follows Beka in her first year as a police officer in a land of magic and romance with a medieval feel. ⌒ e Lexile HL730L (Rev: BL 3/1/09; HB 5–6/09; SLJ 5/1/09)

3501 Pierce, Tamora. *Briar's Book* (5–9). Series: Circle of Magic. 1999, Scholastic paper $15.95 (978-0-590-55359-9). In this fantasy, Briar, a former street urchin and petty thief, and his teacher, Rosethorn, search for the cause of a deadly plague that is sweeping through their land. (Rev: BL 2/15/99; HBG 10/99; SLJ 3/99; VOYA 6/99)

3502 Pierce, Tamora. *Cold Fire* (6–10). Series: The Circle Opens. 2002, Scholastic $16.95 (978-0-590-39655-4). Daja is studying in the chilly northern city of Kugisko, where her ability to handle fire comes in handy but also draws her into a relationship with an arsonist.

(Rev: BL 9/1/02; HB 7–8/02; HBG 10/02; SLJ 8/02; VOYA 6/02)

3503 Pierce, Tamora. *Daja's Book* (5–9). Series: Circle of Magic. 1998, Scholastic paper $15.95 (978-0-590-55358-2). Daja, a mage-in-training, uses her magical powers to create a living vine out of metal, and soon members of the nomadic Traders want to possess it. (Rev: BCCB 12/98; BL 12/1/98; HBG 3/99; SLJ 12/98; VOYA 2/99)

3504 Pierce, Tamora. *Lady Knight* (6–9). Series: Protector of the Small. 2002, Random House $16.95 (978-0-375-81465-5). Now a knight, Kel is disappointed when her first assignment is to command a refugee camp. Margaret A. Edwards Award 2013. (Rev: BL 10/1/02; HBG 3/03; SLJ 12/02; VOYA 2/03)

3505 Pierce, Tamora. *Magic Steps* (5–9). Series: The Circle Opens. 2000, Scholastic paper $16.95 (978-0-590-39588-5). Fourteen-year-old Sandry and her friend Pasco use their magic to stop the murders of local merchants. (Rev: BCCB 3/00; BL 3/1/00; HB 5–6/00; HBG 10/00; SLJ 4/00)

3506 Pierce, Tamora. *Mastiff* (6–9). Series: Beka Cooper. 2011, Random House $18.99 (978-0-375-81470-9); LB $21.99 (978-037591470-6). Beka Cooper and her sidekicks investigate the disappearance of a prince in this blend of mystery, romance, and fantasy; the final title in the series. ⌒ e Lexile 790L (Rev: BL 12/1/11; SLJ 12/1/11)

3507 Pierce, Tamora. *Melting Stones* (6–10). 2008, Scholastic $17.99 (978-054505264-1). Evvy helps to save the Battle Islands from mysterious environmental ailments by using her magical powers. ⌒ e Lexile 590L (Rev: BLO 5/27/09; LMC 5–6/09; SLJ 12/08; VOYA 12/08)

3508 Pierce, Tamora. *Shatterglass* (6–9). Series: The Circle Opens. 2003, Scholastic $16.95 (978-0-590-39683-7). Tris, 14, joins forces with another mage, Kethlun, whose glass-blowing skills help them solve a series of murders. (Rev: BL 3/1/03; HB 5–6/03; HBG 10/03; SLJ 7/03; VOYA 6/03)

3509 Pierce, Tamora. *Terrier* (7–10). 2006, Random House $18.95 (978-0-375-81468-6). Sixteen-year-old orphan Beka Cooper becomes a trainee (or Puppy) with the city guards (Dogs) and uses her magical abilities to good effect, relating her exploits in her journal. (Rev: BL 11/15/06; HB 1–2/07; SLJ 2/07*)

3510 Pierce, Tamora. *Trickster's Queen* (7–12). 2004, Random House LB $19.99 (978-0-375-81467-9). In this thrilling sequel to *Trickster's Choice*, Aly must call upon her magical powers to protect the Balitang children and ensure that one of them — Dove — ascends to the throne of the Copper Isles. (Rev: BCCB 10/04; BL 10/1/04; SLJ 9/04; VOYA 2/05)

3511 Pierce, Tamora. *Tris's Book* (5–9). Series: Circle of Magic. 1998, Scholastic paper $15.95 (978-0-590-

55357-5). Tris and her three fellow mages combine forces to fight the pirates who are threatening to destroy their home in this sequel to *Sandry's Book*. (Rev: BCCB 4/98; BL 8/98; HBG 10/98; SLJ 4/98; VOYA 8/98)

3512 Pierce, Tamora. *The Will of the Empress* (8–11). 2005, Scholastic $17.99 (978-0-439-44171-1). Bowing to the will of the Empress of Namorn, Sandry, accompanied by her mage friends from the Winding Circle, embarks on a perilous journey to visit her cousin, the empress; this stand-alone novel comes after the Circle of Magic and The Circle Opens quartets. (Rev: BCCB 1/06; BL 11/15/05*; HB 11–12/05; SLJ 11/05; VOYA 10/05)

3513 Pike, Aprilynne. *Destined* (6–9). 2012, HarperTeen $17.99 (978-006166812-8). In this action-packed final volume in the series that began with *Wings* (2009), Laurel and her friends conduct a final battle against Klea for the survival of Avalon. ∩ ℮ (Rev: BL 3/1/12; VOYA 4/12)

3514 Pike, Aprilynne. *Spells* (7–10). 2010, HarperTeen $16.99 (978-0-06-166806-7). In this sequel to *Wings* (2009), 16-year-old Laurel is studying at the faerie academy and feeling tensions between her two worlds and her romantic relationships. ∩ (Rev: BL 3/15/10*; SLJ 8/10; VOYA 8/10)

3515 Pike, Aprilynne. *Wings* (6–9). 2009, HarperTeen $16.99 (978-0-06-166803-6); LB $17.89 (978-006166804-3). When a wing-shaped flower begins to grow on her back, Laurel discovers that she is not human but faerie; a love triangle and threats from other supernatural beings add tension to the fantasy. ∩ Lexile 690L (Rev: BL 2/15/09; SLJ 7/1/09; VOYA 6/09)

3516 Pinkwater, Daniel. *The Yggyssey: How Iggy Wondered What Happened to All the Ghosts, Found Out Where They Went, and Went There* (6–9). Illus. by Calef Brown. 2009, Houghton Mifflin $16.00 (978-061859445-0). Iggy and her friends Neddie and Seamus end up in Underland while chasing ghosts through 1950s Los Angeles; a wacky sequel to *The Neddiad* (2007). ℮ Lexile 810L (Rev: BL 2/15/09; HB 3–4/09; LMC 10/09; SLJ 2/1/09)

3517 Plum, Amy. *Until I Die* (8–11). Series: Revenant Trilogy. 2012, HarperTeen $17.99 (978-006200404-8). In Paris, Kate and Vincent work against a dangerous supernatural power to maintain their affection for each other in this sequel to *Die for Me* (2011). ∩ ℮ (Rev: BLO 4/1/12; SLJ 6/12; VOYA 4/12)

3518 Popescu, Petru. *Birth of the Pack* (8–11). Series: Weregirls. 2007, Tor $12.95 (978-0-7653-1641-7). The members of the Weregirls soccer team find that they have magical powers to fight evil — and the mean girls at school. (Rev: BL 10/1/07; LMC 1/08; SLJ 12/07)

3519 Porte, Barbara Ann. *Hearsay: Tales from the Middle Kingdom* (5–8). 1998, Greenwillow $15.00 (978-0-

688-15381-6). Each of these 15 entertaining fantasies contains elements of Chinese folklore and culture. (Rev: BCCB 5/98; HBG 10/98; SLJ 6/98)

3520 Porter, Sarah. *Lost Voices* (7–10). 2011, Harcourt $16.99 (978-0-547-48250-7). During an attack by her abusive uncle, 14-year-old Luce falls from a cliff in an Alaskan fishing village and becomes a mermaid; in her new life she finds friendship but also horror as she learns how the mermaids extract vengeance against the humans who hurt them. ∩ ℮ Lexile 880L (Rev: BL 5/1/11; LMC 10/11*; SLJ 8/11; VOYA 10/12)

3521 Porter, Tracey. *Lark* (8–11). 2011, HarperTeen $15.99 (978-0-06-112287-3). After being kidnapped, raped, and murdered, 16-year-old Lark finds herself in limbo and seeks help from a young girl named Nyetta, who teams up with Lark's friend Eve and Eve's boyfriend. ℮ (Rev: BL 6/1/11; HB 5–6/11; LMC 8–9/11; SLJ 8/11; VOYA 8/11)

3522 Powell, Laura. *Burn Marks* (7–12). 2012, Bloomsbury $17.99 (978-1-59990-843-4). A story of discrimination against witchcraft set in an alternate London, England, and involving two teens from very different backgrounds. ℮ Lexile 770L (Rev: SLJ 7/12; VOYA 6/13)

3523 Pratchett, Terry. *A Hat Full of Sky* (6–10). 2004, HarperCollins $16.99 (978-0-06-058660-7). Witch-in-training Tiffany Aching battles a monster with help from the wee men and head witch Granny Weatherwax in the sequel to *The Wee Free Men*. Margaret A. Edwards Award 2011. (Rev: BCCB 5/04; BL 4/15/04; HB 7–8/04; SLJ 7/04; VOYA 6/04)

3524 Pratchett, Terry. *Wintersmith* (7–10). 2006, HarperTempest $16.99 (978-0-06-089031-5). Tiffany Aching, a 13-year-old witch, must find a way to bring back spring, with the help of her friends the Wee Free Men, after the god of winter falls in love with her and will do anything to keep her in his frozen world. (Rev: BL 9/1/06; SLJ 11/06)

3525 Prevost, Guillaume. *The Book of Time* (5–8). Trans. by William Rodarmor. Series: The Book of Time. 2007, Scholastic $16.99 (978-0-439-88375-7). Sam travels through time — to medieval Scotland, World War I France, and ancient Egypt — to find his missing father and finally discovers he's being held captive in Dracula's castle in this first installment in the series. ∩ (Rev: BCCB 9/07; BL 7/07; HB 9–10/07; SLJ 11/07)

3526 Prineas, Sarah. *Found* (4–7). Illus. by Antonio Javier Caparo. Series: The Magic Thief. 2010, HarperCollins $16.99 (978-0-06-137593-4). In the third book in the series, Conn is on the run after escaping from prison and heads for Dragon Mountain in an effort to save Wellmet from bad magic. Lexile 730L (Rev: LMC 8–9/10)

3527 Prineas, Sarah. *Winterling* (5–8). 2012, HarperCollins $16.99 (978-006192103-2). Fer accidentally travels to a magical but dangerous world full of strange creatures, where she learns a lot about her family and herself. ∩ ℮ Lexile 720L (Rev: BLO 11/15/11; SLJ 5/1/12)

3528 Prue, Sally. *Cold Tom* (4–8). 2003, Scholastic $15.95 (978-0-439-48268-4). Tom has disabilities that make him an outcast, and he flees from his elfin tribe to the city inhabited by demons (humans), where he is confronted with his human side. (Rev: BL 9/15/03; HB 7–8/03*; HBG 10/03; SLJ 9/03*; VOYA 10/03)

3529 Pullman, Philip. *The Amber Spyglass* (7–12). Series: His Dark Materials. 2000, Knopf $19.95 (978-0-679-87926-8). Lyra and Will are key figures in the battle between good and evil in this final volume in the prize-winning trilogy. (Rev: BL 10/1/00; HB 11–12/00; HBG 3/01; SLJ 10/00)

3530 Pullman, Philip. *The Golden Compass* (7–12). Series: His Dark Materials. 1996, Knopf $20.00 (978-0-679-87924-4). In this first book of a fantasy trilogy, young Lyra and her alter ego, a protective animal named Pantalaimon, escape from the child-stealing Gobblers and join a group heading north to rescue a band of missing children. (Rev: BL 3/1/96*; SLJ 4/96)

3531 Pullman, Philip. *Lyra's Oxford* (5–8). Illus. by John Lawrence. 2003, Knopf $10.95 (978-0-375-82819-5). This slim volume takes readers back to the world of Pullman's His Dark Materials trilogy, with maps, postcards, and other ephemera. (Rev: BL 2/1/04; SLJ 1/04; VOYA 6/04)

3532 Pullman, Philip. *Once Upon a Time in the North* (7–10). Illus. by John Lawrence. Series: His Dark Materials. 2008, Knopf $12.99 (978-0-375-84510-9). The story of how Lee Scoresby and bear lorke Byrnison — of the His Dark Materials trilogy — met for the first time in an arctic frontier town; a board game is included with the book. ∩ (Rev: BL 5/15/08; LMC 10/08; SLJ 8/08; VOYA 4/08)

3533 Pullman, Philip. *The Subtle Knife* (7–12). Series: His Dark Materials. 1997, Random House $20.00 (978-0-679-87925-1). In this second volume of a trilogy, Will and Lyra travel from world to world searching for the mysterious Dust and Will's long-lost father. (Rev: BL 7/97; HBG 3/98; SLJ 10/97)

3534 Purtill, Richard. *Enchantment at Delphi* (6–9). 1986, Harcourt $14.95 (978-0-15-200447-7). On a trip to Delphi, Alice finds herself transported back in time to the days of Apollo and other Greek gods. (Rev: SLJ 11/86)

3535 Quimby, Laura. *The Carnival of Lost Souls* (5–8). 2010, Abrams $16.95 (978-081098980-1). Orphaned Jack Carr, a Houdini aficionado, is happy to find a home with Professor Hawthorne but unhappy surprises await him. (Rev: BL 10/15/10; LMC 1–2/11; SLJ 12/1/10)

3536 Raedeke, Christy. *The Daykeeper's Grimoire* (7–10). Series: Prophecy of Days. 2010, Flux paper $9.95 (978-0-73871-576-6). Caity decodes a message she finds in a room in her parents' Scottish castle and is sent on a crucial mission that takes her around the world. ℮ (Rev: BL 5/15/10; LMC 8–9/10; SLJ 11/1/10)

3537 Rallison, Janette. *My Fair Godmother* (6–9). 2009, Walker $16.99 (978-080279780-3). After Savannah wishes for a fairy-tale life, her own fairy godmother appears, bringing with her adventure and romance and some funny predicaments. ℮ (Rev: BL 1/1–15/09)

3538 Randall, David. *Chandlefort: In the Shadow of the Bear* (7–12). 2006, Simon & Schuster $16.95 (978-0-689-87870-1). In this sequel to *Clovermead* (2004), the title character discovers she is really the royal Demoiselle Cerelune Cindertallow and the 13-year-old must learn a whole new way of living; a complex and multilayered fantasy. (Rev: SLJ 7/07)

3539 Reeve, Philip. *A Darkling Plain* (7–10). Series: The Hungry City Chronicles. 2007, Eos $18.99 (978-0-06-089055-1). Cities are still gobbling one another up in this final installment in the Hungry City Chronicles, and the reappearance of the Stalker Fang threatens all human beings on Earth. (Rev: BL 7/07; HB 9–10/07; SLJ 6/07)

3540 Reeve, Philip. *No Such Thing as Dragons* (4–7). 2010, Scholastic $16.99 (978-0-545-22224-2). A mute boy named Ansel apprenticed to a fraudulent dragon hunter is much surprised to discover that dragons do in fact exist — and are simply hungry animals. ℮ (Rev: BL 8/10; LMC 11–12/10; SLJ 9/1/10)

3541 Reiss, Kathryn. *Pale Phoenix* (7–10). 1994, Harcourt paper $3.95 (978-0-15-200031-8). Miranda Browne's parents take in an orphan girl who can disappear at will and who was the victim of a tragedy in a past life in Puritan Massachusetts. (Rev: BL 3/15/94; SLJ 5/94; VOYA 6/94)

3542 Renner, Ellen. *Castle of Shadows* (4–7). 2012, Houghton Mifflin $15.99 (978-054774446-9). In a fantastic kingdom in the 1850s Princess Charlie,11, sets out to find her missing mother and encounters mystery and adventure. (Rev: BL 3/15/12; SLJ 4/12*)

3543 Resnick, Mike. *Lady with an Alien: An Encounter with Leonardo da Vinci* (6–9). Series: Art Encounters. 2005, Watson-Guptill $15.95 (978-0-8230-0323-5). Elements of fantasy, time travel, history, art, and philosophy are all present in this novel about da Vinci and his supposed substitution of an alien for an ermine. (Rev: BL 11/1/05; SLJ 10/05)

3544 Rex, Adam. *Cold Cereal* (4–7). Illus. by author. 2012, HarperCollins $16.99 (978-006206002-0). A funny and complex fantasy involving humor, secret experiments, parallel stories, and engaging characters both fairy and real. ∩ ℮ (Rev: BL 2/1/12; SLJ 2/12*)

3545 Rhodes, Morgan. *Falling Kingdoms* (7–12). 2012, Penguin $18.99 (978-159514584-0). Princess Cleo finds she holds the fate of three kingdoms in her hands. ∩ **e** (Rev: BL 10/15/12; LMC 1–2/13; SLJ 3/13)

3546 Richardson, Bill. *After Hamelin* (4–8). 2000, Annick $19.95 (978-1-55037-629-6). In this entertaining fantasy that is a follow-up to the Pied Piper of Hamelin story, Penelope gets the gift of Deep Dreaming and is able to enter the Piper's secret world in the hope of rescuing the children. (Rev: BL 2/15/01; SLJ 4/01; VOYA 4/01)

3547 Richter, Jutta. *The Cat: Or, How I Lost Eternity* (5–8). Trans. by Anna Brailovsky. Illus. by Rotraut Susanne Berner. 2007, Milkweed $14 (978-157131676-9). Eight-year-old Christine is late for school every day because a talking alley cat waylays her and together they discuss everything from math to eternity. Batchelder Honor 2008; ALA Notable Books 2008. Lexile 720L (Rev: BL 3/1/08; SLJ 2/08)

3548 Riley, James. *Half Upon a Time* (5–9). 2010, Simon & Schuster $15.99 (978-1-4169-9593-7). Goodhearted but clumsy Jack and a sassy punk princess set off on a memorable quest to locate her mother, Snow White, in this zany fractured fairy tale. **e** (Rev: LMC 1–2/11; SLJ 3/1/11)

3549 Riordan, Rick. *The Last Olympian* (4–8). Series: Percy Jackson and the Olympians. 2009, Hyperion $17.99 (978-1-4231-0147-5). In this final installment in the series, demigod Percy is approaching his important 16th birthday as he moves to protect New York City. ∩ (Rev: BL 5/15/09*; HB 7/09; SLJ 6/09; VOYA 6/09)

3550 Riordan, Rick. *The Lightning Thief* (6–9). Series: Percy Jackson and the Olympians. 2005, Hyperion $17.95 (978-0-7868-5629-9). Perseus (aka Percy) Jackson, a New York 12-year-old with problems, has action-packed adventures after he is sent to Camp Half Blood — a summer camp for demigods — and discovers his father is Poseidon. (Rev: BL 9/15/05; SLJ 8/05*)

3551 Riordan, Rick. *The Lost Hero* (4–8). Series: Heroes of Olympus. 2010, Hyperion/Disney $18.99 (978-142311339-3). Teen demigods Piper, Leo, and Jason meet up at Camp Half-Blood and are sent on an urgent quest that takes them across the United States in three days. ∩ **e** Lexile 660L (Rev: BLO 10/1/10; HB 1–2/11; LMC 5–6/11; SLJ 2/1/11)

3552 Riordan, Rick. *The Mark of Athena* (5–8). Series: Heroes of Olympus. 2012, Disney/Hyperion $19.99 (978-142314060-3). In the third book in the series, the seven Greek and Roman demigod friends work together to combat threats to the known world. ∩ **e** Lexile 690L (Rev: BLO 10/1/12; SLJ 1/13)

3553 Riordan, Rick. *The Red Pyramid* (5–8). Series: The Kane Chronicles. 2010, Hyperion $17.99 (978-1-4231-1338-6). Carter, 14, and Sadie, 12, discover they are descended from Egyptian royalty as they hone their newly evident magical talents while searching for their Egyptologist father, who disappeared after releasing an enemy god from the Rosetta Stone. ∩ **e** Lexile 650L (Rev: BL 5/15/10*; HB 7–8/10; LMC 10/10; SLJ 6/10)

3554 Riordan, Rick. *The Sea of Monsters* (6–9). Series: Percy Jackson and the Olympians. 2006, Hyperion $17.95 (978-0-7868-5686-2). The 13-year-old son of Poseidon tries to save his friends and summer camp from danger in this second volume in the series. Also use *The Titan's Curse* (2007). ∩ (Rev: BL 7/06; HB 5–6/06; SLJ 5/06)

3555 Riordan, Rick. *The Serpent's Shadow* (5–8). Series: Kane Chronicles. 2012, Disney/Hyperion $19.99 (978-142314057-3). Siblings Carter and Sade work to defy the impending end of the world by using their magic against the chaos snake Apophis. ∩ **e** Lexile 690L (Rev: BLO 5/1/12; HB 9–10/12; SLJ 9/12)

3556 Riordan, Rick. *The Son of Neptune* (5–8). Series: Heroes of Olympus. 2011, Hyperion $19.99 (978-1-4231-4059-7). In this sequel to *The Lost Hero* (2010), Percy Jackson finds himself in Camp Jupiter, a modern refuge for demigods, where he makes friends with Hazel and Frank and together they set off to free Thanatos (Death) and then tackle bigger challenges. ∩ **e** (Rev: BLO 10/1/11; SLJ 12/1/11)

3557 Riordan, Rick. *The Throne of Fire* (5–8). Series: The Kane Chronicles. 2011, Hyperion $18.99 (978-1-4231-4056-6). Carter and Sadie must revive the sun god Ra in order to stop Apophis, the snake god of Chaos, from wreaking destruction. (Rev: BL 5/1/11; SLJ 6/11*)

3558 Roberts, Katherine. *Crystal Mask* (5–8). Series: The Echorium Sequence. 2002, Scholastic paper $15.95 (978-0-439-33864-6). The Singers, a group of people who maintain peace in the world through their unusual powers, are confronted by evildoers known as the Frazhin. Also use *Dark Quetzal* (2003). (Rev: BL 4/15/02; HBG 10/02; SLJ 3/02)

3559 Roberts, Laura Peyton. *Green* (5–8). 2010, Delacorte $16.99 (978-0-385-73558-2). Thirteen-year-old Lily succeeds her grandmother as Keeper of the Green Clan's gold in this clever, leprechaun-filled story. **e** Lexile 720L (Rev: BL 12/1/09; LMC 1–2/10; SLJ 2/10)

3560 Rodda, Emily. *The Golden Door* (6–9). 2012, Scholastic $16.99 (978-0-545-42990-0). When his two brothers fail to return from a dangerous battle with the skimmers, Rye feels it is up to him to follow. **e** Lexile 820L (Rev: BL 12/1/12; SLJ 12/12)

3561 Rodda, Emily. *The Key to Rondo* (4–7). 2008, Scholastic $16.99 (978-0-545-03535-4). A magic music box takes Leo and his cousin Mimi to the land of Rondo, home to fairy-tale characters and an evil queen. (Rev: BL 12/15/07; SLJ 4/08)

3562 Rodda, Emily. *The Wizard of Rondo* (4–7). 2009, Scholastic $16.99 (978-0-545-11516-2). Cousins Leo and Mimi return to the land of Rondo to find a missing wizard and in the process have a confrontation with the evil Blue Queen. (Rev: BL 10/1/09; SLJ 12/09)

3563 Rodgers, Mary, and Heather Hach. *Freaky Monday* (4–7). 2009, HarperCollins $15.99 (978-0-06-166478-6). Switching bodies presents some challenges and some welcome changes for a 13-year-old-girl and her teacher; a successor to 1972's *Freaky Friday*. (Rev: BLO 4/14/09; SLJ 6/09)

3564 Rollins, James. *Jake Ransom and the Skull King's Shadow* (5–8). 2009, HarperCollins $16.99 (978-0-06-147379-1). Jake Ransom and his older sister receive a package that may be linked to the disappearance of their archaeologist parents and find themselves transported into a strange and dangerous world. ∩ (Rev: BL 3/15/09; SLJ 9/09)

3565 Rossetti, Rinsai. *The Girl with Borrowed Wings* (7–12). 2012, Dial $17.99 (978-0-8037-3566-8). A Free shape-shifter brings new options to 17-year-old Frenenqer's tightly controlled life. **e** Lexile 680L (Rev: BL 9/15/12*; HB 7–8/12; SLJ 12/12; VOYA 8/12)

3566 Rowen, Michelle. *Reign Check* (7–10). Series: Demon Princess. 2010, Walker $16.99 (978-080272093-1). Nikki (half-human and half-demon princess) contends with the unsettling prophesy that she will destroy the world as she also discovers that her best friend is training as a demon-slayer and that the attractive foreign-exchange student is in fact the faery king; the sequel to *Reign or Shine* (2009). **e** (Rev: BL 5/15/10; SLJ 8/10)

3567 Rowling, J. K. *Harry Potter and the Chamber of Secrets* (4–8). 1999, Scholastic $22.99 (978-0-439-06486-6). During his second year at Hogwarts School of Witchcraft and Wizardry, Harry is baffled when he hears noises no one else can. (Rev: BCCB 9/99; BL 5/15/99*; HB 7–8/99; HBG 10/99; SLJ 7/99; VOYA 10/99)

3568 Rowling, J. K. *Harry Potter and the Deathly Hallows* (6–12). Illus. by Mary GrandPré. 2007, Scholastic $34.99 (978-0-545-01022-1). The seventh and final book in the series ties up all the plot threads and ends with an epilogue updating readers on the main characters 19 years later. Odyssey Honor Recording 2008; ALA Notable Books 2008. ∩ (Rev: BCCB 10/07; BL 8/07*; HB 9–10/07; SLJ 9/07)

3569 Rowling, J. K. *Harry Potter and the Goblet of Fire* (4–9). 2000, Scholastic $29.99 (978-0-439-13959-5). This, the fourth installment of Harry Potter's adventures, begins when Voldemort tries to regain the power he lost in his failed attempt to kill Harry. (Rev: BL 8/00*; HB 11–12/00; HBG 3/01; SLJ 8/00)

3570 Rowling, J. K. *Harry Potter and the Half-Blood Prince* (5–12). Illus. by Mary GrandPré. 2005, Scholastic LB $34.99 (978-0-439-78677-5). In this sixth and penultimate volume, Harry, now 16, begins mapping a strategy to defeat the evil Lord Voldemort. (Rev: BL 8/05*; SLJ 9/05; VOYA 10/05)

3571 Rowling, J. K. *Harry Potter and the Order of the Phoenix* (4–12). 2003, Scholastic LB $34.99 (978-0-439-56761-9). Adolescence, adult hypocrisy, and the deadly threat of Voldemort and his evil supporters combine to make Harry's fifth year at Hogwarts as eventful as ever. (Rev: BL 7/03; HB 9–10/03; HBG 10/03; SLJ 8/03; VOYA 8/03)

3572 Rowling, J. K. *Harry Potter and the Prisoner of Azkaban* (4–8). Illus. by Mary GrandPré. 1999, Scholastic $22.99 (978-0-439-13635-8). In this third thrilling adventure, a murderer has escaped from prison and is after our young hero. (Rev: BCCB 10/99; BL 9/1/99*; HB 11–12/99; HBG 3/00; SLJ 10/99)

3573 Rowling, J. K. *Harry Potter and the Sorcerer's Stone* (4–8). 1998, Scholastic $22.99 (978-0-590-35340-3). In this humorous and suspenseful story, 11-year-old Harry Potter attends the Hogwarts School for Witchcraft and Wizardry, where he discovers that he is a wizard just as his parents had been and that someone at the school is trying to steal a valuable stone with the power to make people immortal. (Rev: BCCB 11/98; BL 9/15/98; HB 1–2/99; HBG 3/99; SLJ 10/98; VOYA 12/98)

3574 Rowling, J. K. *The Tales of Beedle the Bard* (5–8). Illus. by author. 2008, Scholastic $12.99 (978-0-545-12828-5). Professor Dumbledore's collection of five fairy tales, which he bequeathed to Hermione; with Dumbledore's accompanying commentary. (Rev: BCCB 3/09; BL 1/1–15/09; HB 3/09; SLJ 3/09)

3575 Rubenstein, Gillian. *Foxspell* (7–9). 1996, Simon & Schuster $16.00 (978-0-689-80602-5). In this fantasy, a troubled boy is tempted by a fox spirit to receive peace and immortality if he will assume a fox shape forever. (Rev: BL 10/15/96; SLJ 9/96; VOYA 12/96)

3576 Ruby, Laura. *The Chaos King* (5–8). 2007, HarperCollins $16.99 (978-0-06-075258-3). In this sequel to *The Wall and the Wing* (2006), Gurl — called Georgie now that she has been reunited with her parents — and her friend Bug must put aside their temporary differences and cope with myriad challenges. ∩ (Rev: BCCB 9/07; SLJ 11/07)

3577 Russell, Barbara T. *The Taker's Stone* (7–12). 1999, DK $16.95 (978-1-78942-568-0). When 14-year-old Fischer steals some glowing red gemstones from a man at a campsite, he unleashes the terrible evil of Belial, some catastrophic weather, and the beginning of the end of the world. (Rev: VOYA 10/99)

3578 Russell, Christine, and Christopher Russell. *The Warrior Sheep Down Under* (4–7). 2012, Sourcebooks paper $6.99 (978-140226780-2). The five intrepid sheep head to Australia to rescue a ewe in this funny third adventure in the series. **e** Lexile 660L (Rev: BLO 6/12; SLJ 6/12)

3579 Rutkoski, Marie. *The Cabinet of Wonders* (5–8). Series: The Kronos Chronicles. 2008, Farrar $16.95 (978-0-374-31026-4). Sprinkled with tidbits of Bohemian history, this volume set in an alternate European Renaissance follows 12-year-old Petra as she works with the Roma to retrieve her father's eyes from an evil prince. ⌂ ℮ Lexile 720L (Rev: BL 7/08; HB 1–2/09; SLJ 10/1/08)

3580 Rutkoski, Marie. *The Celestial Globe* (5–8). Series: The Kronos Chronicles. 2010, Farrar $16.99 (978-0-374-31027-1). British spy John Dee helps Petra escape Prince Rodolfo, and subsequently enrolls her in magic classes instead of returning her home. Lexile 640L (Rev: BLO 4/15/10; SLJ 4/10)

3581 Rutkoski, Marie. *The Jewel of the Kalderash* (5–8). Series: Kronos Chronicles. 2011, Farrar $16.99 (978-037433678-3). Petra embarks on a daring quest to find who created the Gray Men, so she can free her father from this curse in this fast-paced series conclusion. ℮ Lexile 680L (Rev: BL 10/15/11)

3582 Rylant, Cynthia. *The Heavenly Village* (4–7). 1999, Scholastic paper $15.95 (978-0-439-04096-9). A special book about the Heavenly Village — a place where some people stay who are not sure about going to heaven — and about some of the people who live in this in-between world. (Rev: BL 12/1/99*; HBG 3/00; SLJ 3/00; VOYA 2/00)

3583 Sage, Angie. *Darke* (5–8). Illus. by Mark Zug. Series: Septimus Heap. 2011, HarperCollins $17.99 (978-006124242-7). Jenna and Septimus's 14th birthday celebration is interrupted when a new Darke Domaine opens up and the two — along with Beetle — are called to save the day; the 6th installment in the series. (Rev: BL 5/1/11)

3584 Sage, Angie. *Flyte* (5–8). Illus. by Mark Zug. Series: Septimus Heap. 2006, HarperCollins $17.99 (978-0-06-057734-6). In this fast-paced sequel to *Magyk* (2005), wizard Septimus must protect Princess Jenna from numerous dangers; a CD includes games. (Rev: BL 5/15/06; SLJ 6/06; VOYA 2/06)

3585 Sage, Angie. *Physik* (5–8). Series: Septimus Heap. 2007, HarperCollins $17.99 (978-0-06-057737-7). When Septimus Heap, apprenticed to a wizard, inadvertently releases the spirit of an evil queen who lived centuries earlier, the ill-tempered monarch unleashes chaos in the kingdom; the third book in the series. ⌂ (Rev: BL 4/1/07; SLJ 6/07)

3586 Sage, Angie. *Queste* (5–8). Series: Septimus Heap. 2008, HarperCollins $17.99 (978-0-06-088207-5). In the fourth book of the series, Septimus is sent on a dangerous Queste and tries to rescue his brother Nicko. (Rev: BL 5/15/08; SLJ 6/08)

3587 St. John, Lauren. *The Elephant's Tale* (5–8). Series: Legend of the Animal Healer. 2010, Dial $16.99 (978-0-8037-3291-9). Eleven-year-old Martine, who

can communicate with and heal animals, faces the possible loss of her grandmother's South African animal sanctuary in this action-filled final volume in the series. ℮ Lexile 880L (Rev: LMC 10/10; SLJ 7/10)

3588 St. John, Lauren. *The Last Leopard* (4–7). 2009, Dial $16.99 (978-0-8037-3342-8). In this third volume about a girl with a gift for healing animals, 11-year-old Martine is on a safari with her grandmother, and she and her best friend Ben must search for an elusive white leopard in grave danger from those who hunt it for its mystical powers. ℮ Lexile 920L (Rev: BL 2/15/09; SLJ 5/1/09)

3589 St. John, Lauren. *The White Giraffe* (5–8). Illus. by David Dean. 2007, Dial $16.99 (978-0-8037-3211-7). After the tragic death of her parents, 11-year-old Martine is sent to live with her grandmother on a large game preserve in South Africa, where she discovers her mystical gifts and exposes poachers who are hunting a rare white giraffe. (Rev: BL 6/1–15/07; LMC 11/07; SLJ 6/07)

3590 Salvatore, R. A., and Geno Salvatore. *The Stowaway* (5–8). Series: Stone of Tymora. 2008, Mirrorstone $17.95 (978-078695094-2). In this fantastical maritime tale, young orphan Maimum uses a magical stone to fend off pirates, beasts, and demons. ℮ (Rev: BL 11/15/08)

3591 Sampson, Fay. *Pangur Ban: The White Cat* (5–8). Series: Pangur Ban. 2003, Lion paper $7.95 (978-0-7459-4763-1). A Welsh cat and an Irish monk encounter princesses and mermaids in this fantasy set in the Middle Ages. (Rev: BL 5/15/03; SLJ 11/03)

3592 Sampson, Fay. *Shape-Shifter: The Naming of Pangur Ban* (5–8). Series: Pangur Ban. 2003, Lion paper $7.95 (978-0-7459-4762-4). A Welsh cat pursued by witches befriends an Irish monk in this first book in the series. (Rev: BL 5/15/03)

3593 Sanders, Stephanie S. *Hero in Disguise* (4–7). Series: Villain School. 2012, Bloomsbury $15.99 (978-1-59990-907-3); paper $6.99 (978-1-59990-906-6). The students at Villain School are suspicious that two new students are in fact spies from the Hero School. (Rev: BL 10/1/12; SLJ 12/12)

3594 Sanderson, Brandon. *Alcatraz Versus the Evil Librarians* (5–8). 2007, Scholastic $16.99 (978-0-439-92550-1). Alcatraz is a 13-year-old boy with unusual powers and a tendency to insert his own thoughts into the narrative, and the librarians are insidious censors of information; fast-paced antics ensure. (Rev: BCCB 2/08; HB 1–2/08; SLJ 11/07)

3595 Sanderson, Brandon. *Alcatraz Versus the Scrivener's Bones* (5–9). 2008, Scholastic $16.99 (978-0-439-92553-2). Alcatraz Smedry and his companions face many obstacles as they try to rescue his father from the Library of Alexandria; a pun-filled, humorous fantasy. (Rev: HB 11/08; SLJ 12/08; VOYA 10/08)

3596 Sargent, Pamela. *Farseed* (7–10). Series: Seed Trilogy. 2007, Tor $17.95 (978-0-7653-1427-7). The offspring of the genetically engineered humans sent to the planet Home to create a new society have split into two factions in this second book in the trilogy. (Rev: BL 3/15/07; LMC 11–12/07; SLJ 10/07)

3597 Saunders, Kate. *Beswitched* (5–8). 2011, Delacorte $16.99 (978-0-385-74075-3); LB $19.99 (978-0-375-98967-4). On her way to boarding school in England, 12-year-old Flora finds herself transported back to 1935 and discovers that her new dorm mates have summoned her. (Rev: BL 11/1/11*; SLJ 12/1/11)

3598 Schade, Susan. *Travels of Thelonious* (4–7). Illus. by Jon Buller. 2006, Simon & Schuster $14.95 (978-0-689-87684-4). This is the engaging, imaginative story of Thelonious, a squirrel who discovers the ruins of a city and searches for clues to the mystery of why humans disappeared. (Rev: BL 4/15/06; SLJ 7/06)

3599 Schaeffer, Susan F. *The Dragons of North Chittendon* (5–7). Illus. by Darcy May. 1986, Simon & Schuster paper $2.95 (978-0-685-14462-6). The story of Arthur, an unruly dragon, and his ESP relationship with the boy Patrick in a story of humans and dragons in and above North Chittendon, Vermont. (Rev: BL 8/86; SLJ 9/86)

3600 Schmidt, Gary D. *Straw into Gold* (5–8). 2001, Clarion $15.00 (978-0-618-05601-9). Two boys set off to find the answer to the king's riddle and thereby save the lives of rebels, only to discover much more than they had expected. (Rev: BCCB 9/01; HBG 10/01; SLJ 8/01; VOYA 2/02)

3601 Schmidt, Gary D. *What Came from the Stars* (6–9). 2012, Clarion $16.99 (978-0-547-61213-3). In an effort to save their civilization, the threatened people of Valorim send a necklace made of memories to Earth — and into the lunchbox of 12-year-old Tommy. ∩ ℮ Lexile 930L (Rev: BL 7/12; HB 9–10/12; LMC 1–2/13*; SLJ 9/12; VOYA 10/12)

3602 Scott, Deborah. *The Kid Who Got Zapped Through Time* (4–7). 1997, Avon $14.00 (978-0-380-97356-9). In this humorous time-travel fantasy, Flattop Kincaid is transported to England during the Middle Ages, where he becomes a serf. (Rev: BL 11/1/97; SLJ 9/97)

3603 Scott, Michael. *The Alchemyst: The Secrets of the Immortal Nicholas Flamel* (7–12). 2007, Delacorte $16.99 (978-0-385-73357-1). Fifteen-year-old twins Sophie and Josh find themselves caught up in a deadly, ancient struggle over a Codex, the Book of Abraham the Mage, that holds the promise of eternal youth. ∩ (Rev: BL 5/1/07; LMC 10/07; SLJ 5/07)

3604 Scott, Michael. *The Necromancer* (8–12). Series: The Secrets of the Immortal Nicholas Flamel. 2010, Delacorte $18.99 (978-038573531-5); LB $21.99 (978-038590516-9). In this fourth, action-packed installment, twins Sophie and Josh help the dying Nicholas

Flamel and his wife in their efforts to contain the monsters living on Alcatraz. ∩ ℮ Lexile 780L (Rev: BLO 6/10; SLJ 8/10; VOYA 8/10)

3605 Scott, Michael. *The Sorceress* (7–10). Series: The Secrets of the Immortal Nicholas Flamel. 2009, Delacorte $17.99 (978-038573529-2); LB $20.99 (978-038590515-2). Twins Josh and Sophie, along with Nicolas Flamel, are still on the run in this third book in the series. Shakespeare, Billy the Kid, and Gilgamesh are some of the characters that pop up along the journey. Lexile 840L (Rev: BLO 4/24/09; SLJ 7/1/09)

3606 Seabrooke, Brenda. *Stonewolf* (5–8). 2005, Holiday $16.95 (978-0-8234-1848-0). Young orphan Nicholas is taken captive by a group called the Synod but manages to escape, taking with him a sought-after secret formula. (Rev: BL 3/15/05; SLJ 3/05)

3607 Seidler, Tor. *Gully's Travels* (4–7). Illus. by Brock Cole. 2008, Scholastic $16.95 (978-0-5450-2506-5). Spoiled dog Gulliver's life of luxury is turned upside-down when his master falls for an allergic Frenchwoman and hands the dog over to the doorman; Gully takes off for Paris and other points east. (Rev: BL 9/1/08*; HB 9/08; LMC 1/09; SLJ 8/08)

3608 Selfors, Suzanne. *Coffeehouse Angel* (7–10). 2009, Walker $16.99 (978-0-8027-9812-1). Katrina helps a young man who turns out to be an angel, ready to grant her her heart's desire . . . once she figures out what that is. ℮ Lexile HL620L (Rev: BL 9/15/09; SLJ 8/09; VOYA 12/09)

3609 Selfors, Suzanne. *Fortune's Magic Farm* (4–7). Illus. by Catia Chien. 2009, Little, Brown $14.99 (978-0-316-01818-0). Ten-year-old Isabelle lives in a soggy place called Runny Cove but knows she came from a place called Nowhere; she leaves her home and finds herself on a journey to a magical place called Fortune's Farm. (Rev: BCCB 5/09; BL 3/15/09; SLJ 3/09)

3610 Selfors, Suzanne. *Saving Juliet* (7–10). 2008, Walker $16.95 (978-0-8027-9740-7). Mimi, a reluctant actress in her family's theater, is transported to medieval Verona, where she meets the real Juliet (and her Romeo). (Rev: BL 1/1–15/08; LMC 2/08; SLJ 3/08)

3611 Selfors, Suzanne. *The Sweetest Spell* (8–11). 2012, Walker $16.99 (978-0-8027-2376-5). Outcast Emmeline's life changes when she discovers she possesses the ability to make chocolate. ℮ (Rev: BL 9/15/12; LMC 10/12; SLJ 9/12; VOYA 4/12)

3612 Sensel, Joni. *The Farwalker's Quest* (5–8). 2009, Bloomsbury $16.99 (978-1-59990-272-2). Not long before the Namingfest in which Ariel expects to be selected as an apprentice Healtouch, Ariel and her friend Zeke find a telling dart that alters their futures. Lexile 660L (Rev: BL 2/15/09; SLJ 4/1/09)

3613 Sensel, Joni. *The Timekeeper's Moon* (5–8). 2010, Bloomsbury $16.99 (978-1-59990-457-3). In the future without technology or books introduced in *The Far-*

walker's Quest (2009), Ariel and her guardian, Scarl, follow a mysterious map, aware that success is vital. Lexile 700L (Rev: BL 2/1/10; LMC 5–6/10; SLJ 3/10)

3614 Shan, Darren. *Lord of the Shadows* (5–10). Series: Cirque du Freak. 2006, Little, Brown $15.99 (978-0-316-15628-8). In the 11th book in the series, part-vampire Darren faces off against Steve Leopard, leader of the Vampaneze, in a battle to determine who will be the next Lord of the Shadows. (Rev: SLJ 9/06)

3615 Sherman, Delia. *Changeling* (5–8). 2006, Viking $16.99 (978-0-670-05967-6). Neef, kidnapped as a baby by fairies, faces exile from her home in New York Between — an alternate Manhattan inhabited by elves, pixies, fairies, and other spirits — when she breaks the rules. (Rev: SLJ 10/06)

3616 Sherman, Delia. *The Freedom Maze* (7–10). 2011, Big Mouth paper $9.95 (978-19315203-0-0). In 1960, 13-year-old Sophie finds herself transported back to 1860 Louisiana and is mistaken for a slave. ⌒ ℮ (Rev: BLO 11/15/11; HB 1–2/12; VOYA 10/11)

3617 Sherman, Josepha. *Windleaf* (7–12). 1993, Walker $14.95 (978-0-8027-8259-5). Count Thierry falls in love with half-faerie Glinfinial, only to have her father, the Faerie Lord, steal her away. (Rev: BL 11/1/93*; SLJ 12/93; VOYA 2/94)

3618 Shetterly, Will. *Elsewhere* (8–12). 1991, Harcourt $16.95 (978-0-15-200731-7). Set in Bordertown, between the real world and Faerie world, home to runaway elves and humans, this is a fantasy of integration, survival, and coming of age. (Rev: BL 10/15/91; SLJ 11/91)

3619 Shetterly, Will. *Nevernever* (8–12). 1993, Tor paper $4.99 (978-0-8125-5151-8). This sequel to *Elsewhere* (1991) shows Wolfboy trying to protect Florida, the heir of Faerie, from gangs of Elves out to get her, while one of his friends is framed for murder. (Rev: BL 9/15/93; SLJ 10/93; VOYA 12/93)

3620 Shinn, Sharon. *The Dream-Maker's Magic* (7–10). 2006, Viking $16.99 (978-0-670-06070-2). In this novel set in the same world as *The Safe-Keeper's Secret* (2004) and *The Truth-Teller's Tale* (2005), Kellen, who was brought up as a boy, matures and offers comfort to her deformed and abused friend Gryffin who turns out to be the new Dream-Maker. (Rev: BL 5/15/06; SLJ 7/06)

3621 Shinn, Sharon. *The Safe-Keeper's Secret* (7–12). 2004, Viking $16.99 (978-0-670-05910-2). Truth and justice are themes in this fantasy about Fiona, a girl whose family has many secrets, and Reed, a boy without an identity, who was left as a baby with Fiona's mother. (Rev: BL 4/15/04; SLJ 6/04; VOYA 6/04)

3622 Shinn, Sharon. *The Truth-Teller's Tale* (7–10). 2005, Viking $16.99 (978-0-670-06000-9). Twin sisters Eleda and Adele are mirror images — Eleda can neither tell nor hear a lie, while Adele can be trusted to

keep secret anything she is told. (Rev: BCCB 9/05; BL 4/15/05*; SLJ 7/05; VOYA 8/05)

3623 Showalter, Gena. *Alice in Zombieland* (7–12). 2012, HarlequinTeen $18.99 (978-037321058-9). On her 16th birthday, Alice learns that her father was right and zombies do exist and she must avenge her family. ⌒ ℮ (Rev: BL 10/15/12)

3624 Showalter, Gena. *Intertwined* (7–10). 2009, Harlequin $15.99 (978-0-373-21002-2). Misdiagnosed as a schizophrenic, 16-year-old Aden Stone in fact has four souls with special powers living inside his body the complex plot involves vampires, werewolves, assorted magical beings, and a touch of romance. (Rev: BL 9/15/09; SLJ 12/09)

3625 Shulman, Polly. *The Grimm Legacy* (6–9). 2010, Putnam $16.99 (978-0-399-25096-5). Unhappy Elizabeth is cheered when she gets a job at the New York Circulating Material Repository and fascinated when she gets access to the Grimm Collection full of magical artifacts — until these pieces start disappearing. ℮ Lexile HL600L (Rev: BL 5/15/10; HB 7–8/11; LMC 10/10; SLJ 6/10; VOYA 6/10)

3626 Shusterman, Neal. *Dread Locks* (6–9). Series: Dark Fusion. 2005, Dutton $15.99 (978-0-525-47554-5). When Tara, with her thick golden hair and dark sunglasses, moves in next door to the family of 14-year-old Parker Baer, bad things start to happen in this novel based on the story of Medusa. (Rev: BL 6/1–15/05; SLJ 6/05; VOYA 6/05)

3627 Shusterman, Neal. *Duckling Ugly* (7–10). Series: Dark Fusion. 2006, Dutton $15.99 (978-0-525-47585-9). Apart from her ability to spell, Cara DeFido has no known attributes until she finds herself in a magic kingdom; her successes there prompt her to return home, however. (Rev: BL 2/1/06; SLJ 7/06)

3628 Shusterman, Neal. *Everwild* (7–10). Series: The Skinjacker Trilogy. 2009, Simon & Schuster $16.99 (978-1-4169-5863-5). Allie, Nick, and Mikey split up to pursue different and dangerous avenues in their quest to help the children of Everlost. (Rev: BLO 11/5/09; SLJ 12/09)

3629 Shusterman, Neal. *Red Rider's Hood* (6–9). 2005, Dutton $15.99 (978-0-525-47562-0). A dark variation on the Red Riding Hood story in which Red Rider, a 16-year-old boy, vows to seek revenge after a group of werewolves attack his grandmother and steal his beloved Mustang; this will appeal to reluctant readers. (Rev: BL 10/15/05; SLJ 12/05; VOYA 10/05)

3630 Shusterman, Neal. *Unwind* (6–9). 2007, Simon & Schuster $16.99 (978-1-4169-1204-0). Unwinds are teenagers whose organs are to be harvested in this disturbing story set after the Second Civil War. (Rev: BL 10/15/07; HB 3–4/08; LMC 1/08; SLJ 1/08)

3631 Silberberg, Alan. *Pond Scum* (4–7). 2005, Hyperion $15.99 (978-0-7868-5634-3). Ten-year-old Oliver gains a whole new appreciation for his animal neighbors after he finds a magical gem that allows him to assume the shape of various creatures. (Rev: BL 12/1/05; SLJ 11/05)

3632 Simner, Janni Lee. *Bones of Faerie* (7–10). 2009, Random House $16.99 (978-037584563-5); LB $19.99 (978-037594563-2). In a world devastated by a war between faeries and humans, 15-year-old Liza finds herself in danger when she discovers she's gained faerie powers. ℮ Lexile HL670L (Rev: BL 12/1/08; LMC 5–6/09; SLJ 4/1/09)

3633 Simner, Janni Lee. *Faerie Winter* (8–11). 2011, Random House $16.99 (978-0-375-86671-5); LB $19.99 (978-0-375-96671-2). The war between the fairy and human worlds has resulted in disaster for both sides and Liza, 16, learns that she may be able to help by stopping the Faerie Queen's evil plot; the sequel to *Bones of Faerie* (2009). ℮ Lexile HL680L (Rev: BL 6/1/11; SLJ 11/1/11; VOYA 8/11)

3634 Simner, Janni Lee. *Thief Eyes* (7–10). 2010, Random House $16.99 (978-0-375-86770-8). While in Iceland with her father, 16-year-old Haley discovers that she is related to the Hallgerd of Icelandic mythology and that this relationship is linked with her mother's disappearance. (Rev: BL 4/1/10; LMC 8–9/10; SLJ 5/10)

3635 Singleton, Linda Joy. *Last Dance* (6–8). Series: The Seer. 2005, Llewellyn paper $6.99 (978-0-7387-0638-2). Sabine goes in search of a possible cure for her desperately ill grandmother but is sidetracked by the ghost of a young girl who reportedly committed suicide. (Rev: SLJ 7/05)

3636 Singleton, Sarah. *Out of the Shadows* (8–10). 2008, Clarion $16.00 (978-061892722-7). A complicated plot makes knowledge of the time period's political and religious scheming necessary to fully understand this tale of friendship between a time-traveling faerie girl and a young Catholic teen in Elizabethan England. Lexile 770L (Rev: BL 12/1/08; LMC 3–4/09; SLJ 6/1/09)

3637 Skelton, Matthew. *Endymion Spring* (6–9). 2006, Delacorte $17.95 (978-0-385-73380-9). While visiting Oxford, England, an American teen discovers part of a rare, centuries-old book that holds many secrets and is sought by sinister forces. ⋒ (Rev: BL 6/1–15/06; LMC 4–5/07; SLJ 9/06)

3638 Skelton, Matthew. *The Story of Cirrus Flux* (4–7). 2010, Random House $17.99 (978-0-385-73381-6); LB $20.99 (978-0-385-90398-1). In this suspenseful fantasy set in 18th-century London and featuring steampunk-style gadgets, orphan Cirrus must protect a magical token left by his father. ⋒ ℮ Lexile 840L (Rev: BL 2/1/10; HB 5–6/10; LMC 5–6/10; SLJ 3/10)

3639 Slade, Arthur. *The Hunchback Assignments* (7–10). 2009, Random House $15.99 (978-0-385-73784-5); LB $18.99 (978-0-385-90694-4). A complex steampunk adventure set in Victorian London in which 14-year-old Modo, a shape-shifting hunchback, joins the Permanent Association, an organization formed to fight the evil Clockwork Guild. ⋒ (Rev: BL 8/09; LMC 11–12/09; SLJ 12/09)

3640 Slater, Adam. *Hunted* (7–10). 2011, Egmont $16.99 (978-1-60684-261-4). The barrier between the human world and a threatening underworld is deteriorating, and 14-year-old Callum, who is a "chime child," must fulfill his destiny. ℮ Lexile 750L (Rev: BL 11/15/11; SLJ 12/1/11; VOYA 10/11)

3641 Slepian, Jan. *Back to Before* (5–7). 1994, Scholastic paper $3.25 (978-0-590-48459-6). Cousins Linny and Hilary travel back to a time before Linny's mother's death and Hilary's parents' separation. (Rev: BCCB 9/93; BL 9/1/93*; SLJ 10/93)

3642 Smith, Clete Barrett. *Aliens on Vacation* (5–8). Illus. by Christian Slade. 2011, Hyperion/Disney $16.99 (978-1-4231-3363-6). Scrub is not pleased to find himself spending a summer at his eccentric grandmother's Washington State bed and breakfast, where he soon discovers things are not at all what they seem. (Rev: BL 5/1/11; SLJ 7/11)

3643 Smith, Gordon. *The Forest in the Hallway* (6–9). 2006, Clarion $16.00 (978-0-618-68847-0). On the 19th floor of her uncle's apartment building, Beatriz finds a path that leads her to a magical world on a quest to find her missing parents. (Rev: BL 11/15/06; SLJ 12/06)

3644 Smith, Jennifer E. *The Storm Makers* (4–7). Illus. by Brett Helquist. 2012, Little, Brown $16.99 (978-031617958-4). Twelve-year-olds Ruby and Simon move with their parents to a Wisconsin farm during a terrible drought, and discover that Simon's strange ties to the weather suggest he may be a very powerful Storm Maker. (Rev: BL 4/1/12; LMC 8–9/12; SLJ 6/12)

3645 Smith, L. J. *The Initiation and the Captive, Part 1* (7–10). Series: The Secret Circle. 2008, HarperTeen paper $8.99 (978-006167085-5). Cassie discovers that she is part witch — and that there are others like her — when she and her mother move to New Salem, Massachusetts. (Rev: BLO 3/5/09)

3646 Smith, Sherwood. *The Spy Princess* (5–8). 2012, Viking $17.99 (978-0-670-06341-3). In a medieval land full of magic, Princess Lilah dresses as a peasant boy and discovers that revolution is brewing. ℮ Lexile 700L (Rev: BL 8/12; LMC 1–2/13; SLJ 9/12)

3647 Smith, Sherwood. *Wren's Quest* (5–8). 1993, Harcourt $16.95 (978-0-15-200976-2). Wren takes time out from magician school to search for clues to her parentage. Sequel to *Wren to the Rescue* (1990). (Rev: BL 4/1/93*; SLJ 6/93)

3648 Smith, Sherwood. *Wren's War* (5–8). 1995, Harcourt $17.00 (978-0-15-200977-9). In this sequel to *Wren to the Rescue* and *Wren's Quest*, Princess Teressa struggles to control herself and her destiny when she finds her parents murdered. (Rev: BL 3/1/95*; SLJ 5/95)

3649 Sniegoski, Thomas E. *Legacy* (8–11). 2009, Delacorte $15.99 (978-0-385-73714-2); LB $18.99 (978-0-385-90648-7). When his mother is killed, 18-year-old Lucas changes his mind and agrees to take on his father's role as Seraph City superhero and crime fighter. (Rev: BL 9/1/09; SLJ 12/09)

3650 Sniegoski, Tom. *Quest for the Spark, Vol. 1* (4–7). Illus. by Jeff Smith. Series: Bone. 2011, Scholastic $22.99 (978-054514101-7); paper $10.99 (978-05451410-2-4). Tom Elm, 12, teams up with a motley crew after he receives a vision telling him to use his necklace to defeat the Nacht, a rogue dragon, in this (illustrated) text addition to the Bone graphic novel series. Lexile 790L (Rev: BL 1/1–15/11; SLJ 3/1/11)

3651 Sniegoski, Tom. *Quest for the Spark, Vol. 2* (4–7). Illus. by Jeff Smith. Series: Bone. 2012, Scholastic $22.99 (978-054514103-1); paper $10.99 (978-05451410-4-8). Twelve-year-old Tom proves himself a competent quest leader by obtaining a piece of the Spark that will defeat the evil Nacht. (Rev: BL 2/15/12; SLJ 3/1/12)

3652 Snyder, Laurel. *Any Which Wall* (4–7). Illus. by LeUyen Pham. 2009, Random $16.99 (978-0-375-85560-3). Four children discover a magic wall in a cornfield and have many adventures traveling through time. (Rev: BCCB 7–8/09; BL 5/15/09; HB 5/09; LMC 8/09; SLJ 6/09; VOYA 4/09)

3653 Somary, Wolfgang. *Night and the Candlemaker* (4–8). 2000, Barefoot Bks $16.99 (978-1-84148-137-1). In this allegory, a candle maker continues with his trade in spite of threats he receives from Night. (Rev: BL 9/15/00; HBG 10/01; SLJ 1/01)

3654 Spicer, Dorothy. *The Humming Top* (6–8). 1968, Phillips $26.95 (978-0-87599-147-4). An orphan finds she is able to predict future events.

3655 Spiegler, Louise. *The Amethyst Road* (8–11). 2005, Clarion $16.00 (978-0-618-48572-7). In this cautionary futuristic novel, siblings Serena and Willow, half-Gorgio and half-Yulang, struggle to survive the violence of their urban neighborhood and the ostracism caused by their mixed blood. (Rev: BL 12/1/05; SLJ 11/05; VOYA 2/06)

3656 Spinner, Stephanie. *Damosel: In Which the Lady of the Lake Renders a Frank and Often Startling Account of Her Wondrous Life and Times* (6–10). 2008, Knopf $16.99 (978-037583634-3); LB $19.99 (978-037593634-0). Elegantly told, this Arthurian-based tale tells of the Lady of the Lake's magical creation of the sword Excalibur and the loyal support of Twixt, a dwarf jester in Arthur's court. e Lexile 830L (Rev: BL 10/1/08; LMC 3–4/09; SLJ 12/08; VOYA 2/09)

3657 Spotswood, Jessica. *Born Wicked* (8–12). 2012, Putnam $17.99 (978-039925745-2). In an alternate New England in 1900, 16-year-old Cate and her sisters Maura and Tess struggle to keep their witchcraft secret in the face of the threatening Brotherhood. e (Rev: BL 1/1/12; LMC 8–9/12; SLJ 4/12; VOYA 4/12)

3658 Springer, Nancy. *Dussie* (5–8). 2007, Walker $16.95 (978-0-8027-9649-3). When she hits puberty, Dussie, a New York City 13-year-old named for her aunt Medusa, discovers she is a gorgon — and that the talkative snakes that have sprouted from her head may be an inconvenience, as is her ability to turn people to stone. (Rev: BL 11/15/07; SLJ 12/07)

3659 Stanley, Diane. *Bella at Midnight* (5–8). Illus. by Bagram Ibatoulline. 2006, HarperCollins LB $17.89 (978-0-06-077574-2). A fine retelling of the Cinderella story featuring a plucky Bella and a storytelling format. (Rev: BCCB 4/06; BL 2/1/06*; HB 3–4/06; HBG 10/06; LMC 2/07; SLJ 3/06*; VOYA 2/06)

3660 Stanley, Diane. *The Cup and the Crown* (5–8). 2012, HarperCollins $16.99 (978-0-06-196321-6). On a quest to find the Loving Cup, Molly — last seen in *The Silver Bowl* (2011) — discovers Harrowsgode, the mysterious city of her magical ancestors. e Lexile 790L (Rev: BL 11/1/12; HB 11–12/12; SLJ 10/12)

3661 Stanley, Diane. *The Silver Bowl* (5–8). 2011, HarperCollins $16.99 (978-0-06-157543-3). A young scullery maid chooses to share the visions she's been keeping silent when foretold events seem to threaten the royal family she works for. Lexile 700L (Rev: BL 4/15/11; SLJ 7/11*)

3662 Stead, Rebecca. *First Light* (5–8). 2007, Random House $15.99 (978-0-375-84017-3). On a scientific expedition to Greenland with his parents, 12-year-old Peter meets 14-year-old Thea, a member of a secret society that lives beneath the ice. (Rev: BL 4/15/07; SLJ 8/07)

3663 Steele, Mary Q. *Journey Outside* (5–8). Illus. by Rocco Negri. 1984, Peter Smith $21.75 (978-0-8446-6169-8); paper $5.99 (978-0-14-030588-3). Young Dilar, believing that his Raft People have been circling endlessly in their quest for a "Better Place," sets out to discover the origin and fate of his kind.

3664 Steer, Dugald A. *The Dragon's Eye* (5–8). Series: Dragonology Chronicles. 2006, Candlewick $15.99 (978-0-7636-2810-9). In the late 19th century, Daniel Cook, 12, and his sister Beatrice attend a dragon school run by Dr. Ernest Drake and accompany him on search for the important Dragon's Eye. (Rev: BL 1/1–15/07; SLJ 1/07)

3665 Stephens, John. *The Emerald Atlas* (4–7). Series: The Books of Beginning. 2011, Knopf $17.99 (978-0-375-86870-2); LB $20.99 (978-0-375-96870-9). Siblings Kate, Michael, and Emma have lived in a series of orphanages since their parents disappeared, and now they discover they can travel through time and must deal with both good and evil. ∩ e (Rev: BL 3/1/11; HB 3–4/11; LMC 5–6/11; SLJ 6/11*)

3666 Stephens, John. *The Fire Chronicle* (4–7). Series: Books of Beginning. 2012, Knopf $17.99 (978-0-375-86871-9); LB $20.99 (978-037596871-6). In this suspense-filled sequel to *The Emerald Atlas* (2011), Kate is transported to 1899 New York while Michael and Emma seek the second volume in the Books of Beginning. ∩ e Lexile 780L (Rev: BL 9/15/12; HB 11–12/12; SLJ 10/12*)

3667 Stewart, Paul. *The Immortals* (5–8). Illus. by Chris Riddell. Series: Edge Chronicles. 2010, Random House $19.99 (978-037583743-2); LB $22.99 (978-037593743-9). In this concluding volume in the exciting series, Nate Quarter flees for his life from the phraxmines of the Eastern Woods. e (Rev: BL 10/1/10)

3668 Stewart, Sean, and Jordan Weisman. *Cathy's Ring: If Found, Please Call 650-266-8263* (8–11). Illus. by author. Series: Cathy. 2009, Running Press $17.95 (978-076243530-2). The page-turning final volume in the trilogy features the familiar format (doodles and designs on each page) and Cathy is still in love with an immortal and running from assassins. (Rev: BL 4/15/09; SLJ 6/1/09)

3669 Stewart, Sharon. *Raven Quest* (5–8). 2005, Carolrhoda LB $15.95 (978-1-57505-894-8). Tok the raven seeks to restore his good name after being falsely accused of murder and sets off to find the legendary Grey Lords. (Rev: SLJ 1/06; VOYA 12/05)

3670 Stiefvater, Maggie. *Forever* (7–10). Series: Wolves of Mercy Falls. 2011, Scholastic $17.99 (978-0-545-25908-8). Grace and Sam face new threats to their love as human-werewolf-wolf tensions escalate; the third book in the trilogy. ∩ e Lexile 770L (Rev: BL 9/15/11; SLJ 9/1/11)

3671 Stiefvater, Maggie. *Linger* (8–11). 2010, Scholastic $17.99 (978-0-545-12328-0). In this sequel to *Shiver* (2009), Sam is close to leaving his werewolf status and achieving humanity, but his girlfriend Grace is now suffering from illnesses that may be related to a wolf bite; at the same time a new wolf pack member called Cole threatens the group's stability. ∩ e Lexile 800L (Rev: BL 6/10; HB 7–8/10; LMC 10/10; SLJ 8/10; VOYA 8/10)

3672 Stiefvater, Maggie. *The Scorpio Races* (8–12). 2011, Scholastic $17.99 (978-0-545-22490-1). The fictional island of Thisby is home to the famous Scorpio Races, in which 19-year-old Sean, riding a water horse, competes against Puck, the first girl to enter the race, who is riding a regular land horse. Printz Honor 2012; ALA Notable Books 2012; YALSA Top Ten Best Fiction for Young Adults 2012; Odyssey Honor Recording 2012. ∩ e Lexile 840L (Rev: BL 9/1/11*; HB 11–12/11*; LMC 3–4/12*; SLJ 11/1/11*)

3673 Stoffels, Karlijn. *Heartsinger* (7–9). Trans. by Laura Watkinson. 2009, Scholastic $16.99 (978-054506929-8). A deaf-mute orphan uses his beautiful singing voice to comfort the mourning in this otherworldly story translated from the Dutch. Lexile 1000L (Rev: BL 1/1–15/09; LMC 5–6/09; SLJ 3/1/09)

3674 Stone, David Lee. *The Shadewell Shenanigans* (6–9). Series: Illmoor Chronicles. 2006, Hyperion $16.99 (978-0-7868-3795-3). How to get rid of Groan Teethgrit and his barbarian sidekicks? The lords of Illmoor do their best in this funny, edgy final book of the series. (Rev: BL 5/15/06; LMC 2/05; SLJ 8/06)

3675 Stone, David Lee. *The Yowler Foul-up* (5–8). 2006, Hyperion $16.99 (978-0-7868-5597-1). A motley group of would-be heroes tries to stop a plot to turn the people of Dullitch into rocks in this sequel to *The Ratastrophe Catastrophe* (2004). (Rev: BL 4/15/06)

3676 Stone, Tamara Ireland. *Time Between Us* (7–12). 2012, Disney/Hyperion $17.99 (978-142315956-8). In 1995 Illinois 16-year-old Anna's ordinary life is changed forever when she meets Bennett, who has the ability to travel through space and time. ∩ e (Rev: BL 9/15/12; LMC 3–4/13; SLJ 2/13)

3677 Stratton, Allan. *The Grave Robber's Apprentice* (5–8). 2012, HarperCollins $16.99 (978-006197608-7). Grave robber Hans becomes aware of his royal heritage in this complex fantasy. (Rev: BL 5/15/12*; SLJ 3/12)

3678 Strickland, Brad. *The Curse of the Midions* (5–8). Series: Grimoire. 2006, Dial $12.99 (978-0-8037-3060-1). A trip to London with his parents goes terribly awry when Jarvey Midion finds himself transported to an alternate universe where he must confront the villainous wizard Tantalus Mideon. (Rev: BL 6/1–15/06; SLJ 11/06)

3679 Strickland, Brad. *Tracked by Terror* (5–8). Series: Grimoire. 2007, Dial $15.99 (978-0-8037-3061-8). This sequel to *Curse of the Midions* (2006) finds 12-year-old Jarvey and his friend Betsy navigating a haunted theater and being hunted by animals. (Rev: BL 11/15/07; LMC 11/07; SLJ 2/08)

3680 Stringer, Helen. *The Midnight Gate* (5–8). 2011, Feiwel & Friends $17.99 (978-0-312-38764-8). Paranormally gifted Belladonna and her friend Steve tackle a dangerous assignment involving a trip to the Land of the Dead. (Rev: BL 5/1/11; SLJ 5/11)

3681 Stringer, Helen. *Spellbinder* (5–8). 2009, Feiwel & Friends $17.99 (978-0-312-38763-1). The friendly, benevolent ghosts who populate Belladonna Johnson's world begin to disappear, and the 12-year-old enters the Land of the Dead to find out why. ∩ e Lexile 840L (Rev: BL 10/15/09; SLJ 10/09; VOYA 2/10)

3682 Stroud, Jonathan. *The Amulet of Samarkand* (6–12). Series: The Bartimaeus Trilogy. 2003, Hyperion $17.95 (978-0-7868-1859-4). Nathaniel, an apprentice magician, plots to steal an amulet and sets powerful forces in motion in this fantasy set in London. (Rev: BL 9/1/03*; HB 11–12/03; HBG 4/04; SLJ 1/04; VOYA 12/03)

3683 Stroud, Jonathan. *The Golem's Eye* (7–12). Series: The Bartimaeus Trilogy. 2004, Miramax $17.95 (978-0-7868-1860-0). In this sequel to *The Amulet of Samarkand*, 14-year-old Nathaniel, a magician's apprentice, joins forces with the mischievous djinni Bartimaeus to foil the evil plot of a golem. (Rev: BL 8/04; SLJ 10/04)

3684 Stroud, Jonathan. *Heroes of the Valley* (6–10). 2009, Hyperion $17.99 (978-142310966-2). A rollicking fantasy about Halli Sveinsson, the young descendent of a legendary Nordic hero, who finds himself on an epic journey to avenge his uncle's death, in the process spawning his own, brand-new legend. ∩ Lexile 770L (Rev: BL 12/1/08*; HB 1–2/09; LMC 8–9/09; SLJ 1/1/09*)

3685 Stroud, Jonathan. *The Ring of Solomon: A Bartimaeus Novel* (6–9). 2010, Hyperion $17.99 (978-1-4231-2372-9). The mischievous djinni Bartimaeus is at the court of King Solomon and meets up with Asmira, sent by the Queen of Sheba to steal Solomon's precious ring. YALSA Amazing Audiobooks Top Ten 2012. ∩ (Rev: BL 11/15/10*; SLJ 12/1/10*)

3686 Sutherland, Tui T. *Shadow Falling: Avatars Book Two* (7–9). Series: Avatars. 2007, Eos $16.99 (978-0-06-085146-0). Beings from different eras of history and prehistory threaten teens Gus, Tigre, Kali, and Diana in the second book in the series. (Rev: BL 12/1/07)

3687 Swados, Elizabeth. *Dreamtective: The Dreamy and Daring Adventures of Cobra Kite* (6–9). 1999, Genesis paper $5.95 (978-1-885478-54-2). A humorous and unusual adventure in which 12-year-old Cobra discovers she can visit other people's dreams. (Rev: SLJ 10/99)

3688 Sweeney, Joyce. *Shadow* (7–10). 1995, Bantam $20.95 (978-0-385-30988-2). Sarah's cat, Shadow, has mysteriously returned from the dead. Sarah and Cissy, the psychic housemaid, try to figure out why. (Rev: BL 7/94; SLJ 9/94; VOYA 10/94)

3689 Tanner, Lian. *Museum of Thieves* (4–7). 2010, Delacorte $17.99 (978-0-385-73905-4); LB $20.99 (978-0-385-90768-2). In a world where children are chained to their parents until a separation ceremony, 12-year-old Goldie manages to escape and finds herself playing an important role. ∩ (Rev: BL 10/1/10; SLJ 10/1/10)

3690 Tayler, Kassy. *Ashes of Twilight* (8–11). 2012, St. Martin's paper $9.99 (978-03126417-8-8). In this fast-paced dystopian novel set in the 2070s, 200 years after a comet hit the earth, 16-year-old Wren is a miner in a domed — and perhaps doomed — city. ∩ e (Rev: BL 11/15/12; LMC 3–4/13; SLJ 3/13; VOYA 4/13)

3691 Taylor, G. P. *The Shadowmancer Returns: The Curse of Salamander Street* (6–10). 2007, Putnam $17.99 (978-0-399-24346-2). This sequel to *Shadow-*

mancer follows Kate and Thomas as they avoid the evil Obadiah only to be caught in a trap, and Beadle and Raphah as they try to distinguish good from evil as they journey to London. (Rev: BL 5/15/07; SLJ 9/07)

3692 Taylor, Greg. *Killer Pizza* (5–8). 2009, Feiwel & Friends $14.99 (978-0-312-37379-5). Fourteen-year-old Toby's first summer job involves making pizza and hunting monsters. (Rev: BL 5/15/09; SLJ 9/09; VOYA 8/09)

3693 Taylor, Laini. *Daughter of Smoke and Bone* (8–12). 2011, Little, Brown $18.99 (978-0-316-13402-6). Prague high-schooler Karou copes with the disappearance of the chimaera who've become her family. YALSA Top Ten Best Fiction for Young Adults 2012. ∩ e Lexile 850L (Rev: BL 9/1/11; HB 11–12/11*; LMC 1–2/12; SLJ 11/1/11*)

3694 Taylor, Laini. *Days of Blood and Starlight* (8–12). 2012, Little, Brown $18.99 (978-0-316-13397-5). Karou, betrayed by Akiva in *Daughter of Smoke and Bone* (2011), must decide what to risk to avenge her people. ∩ e Lexile HL800L (Rev: BL 11/15/12; HB 1–2/13; SLJ 12/12; VOYA 12/12)

3695 Taylor, Laini. *Faeries of Dreamdark: Blackbringer* (5–8). 2007, Putnam $17.99 (978-0-399-24630-2). With the help of her band of crows, a faerie named Magpie must hunt down devils that the humans have released and keep the dark from consuming the world. (Rev: BL 5/15/07; SLJ 8/07)

3696 Taylor, Laini. *Silksinger* (7–10). Illus. by Jim Di Bartolo. Series: Dreamdark. 2009, Putnam $18.99 (978-0-399-24631-9). Full of fast-paced adventure, this second volume in the series has Magpie and the other fairies discovering long-lost clans as they try to save the world from destruction. ∩ Lexile 870L (Rev: BLO 8/20/09; SLJ 9/09)

3697 Telep, Trisha, ed. *The Eternal Kiss: 13 Vampire Tales of Blood and Desire* (8–12). 2009, Running Press paper $9.95 (978-0-7624-3717-7). Vampires of all kinds populate these diverse stories featuring comedy, romance, violence, mystery, and so forth. (Rev: BL 9/1/09; SLJ 12/09)

3698 Thesman, Jean. *The Other Ones* (7–9). 1999, Puffin paper $5.99 (978-0-14-131246-0). Bridget must decide if she should try to be a normal human or, because she possesses supernatural powers, remain part of the Other Ones. (Rev: BL 5/99; SLJ 6/99; VOYA 8/99)

3699 Thompson, Kate. *The Last of the High Kings* (7–10). 2008, Greenwillow $16.99 (978-0-06-117595-4). J.J. Liddy, introduced in *The New Policeman*, is now married and a father of four, one of whom is a fairy, having been traded for one of J.J.'s children at birth. (Rev: BL 5/15/08; SLJ 7/08)

3700 Thompson, Kate. *The New Policeman* (7–10). 2007, Greenwillow $16.99 (978-0-06-117427-8). J.J., hoping to grant his mother's wish for "more time," goes out into his Irish town to find out just where all the time has gone and discovers the land of eternal youth in this music-filled story. ALA Notable Books 2008. ∩ (Rev: BCCB 4/07; BL 2/1/07; HB 3–4/07; LMC 8–9/07; SLJ 3/07*)

3701 Thompson, Kate. *Only Human* (6–9). Series: Missing Link. 2006, Bloomsbury $16.95 (978-1-58234-651-9). Part human and part animal, characters in this second volume of the trilogy attempt to learn more about human evolution by hunting for the yeti. (Rev: BL 5/15/06; HB 5–6/06)

3702 Thompson, Kate. *Origins* (6–9). Series: Missing Link. 2007, Bloomsbury $16.95 (978-1-58234-652-6). In this final volume in the trilogy, the story alternates between Christie's life at the Fourth World laboratory in 2009 and a post-nuclear-disaster future in which Dogs and Cats have been at war. (Rev: BL 3/3/08; SLJ 12/07)

3703 Thompson, Paul B. *The Brightworking* (4–7). Series: The Brightstone Saga. 2012, Enslow $17.95 (978-0-7660-3950-6). Mikal, 11-year-old son of a blacksmith, is apprenticed to a powerful wizard in this appealing fantasy featuring political intrigue and a talking metal head. e Lexile 630L (Rev: LMC 11–12/12; SLJ 8/1/12; VOYA 6/12)

3704 Thomson, Jamie. *Dark Lord: The Early Years* (5–8). Illus. by Freya Hartas. 2012, Walker $16.99 (978-080272849-4). The evil Dark Lord of the Iron Tower of Despair wakes up in the body of a 12-year-old boy in a supermarket parking lot and finds himself facing a very different life, deprived of most of his magical powers. e Lexile HL780L (Rev: BL 9/1/12*; LMC 1–2/13; SLJ 2/13; VOYA 8/12)

3705 Thornton, Duncan. *Kalifax* (5–9). Illus. by Yves Noblet. 2000, Coteau paper $8.95 (978-1-55050-152-0). In this fantasy novel, young Tom, with the help of Grandfather Frost, saves the crew of his ship after it becomes trapped in ice. (Rev: SLJ 1/01)

3706 Thornton, Duncan. *The Star-Glass* (5–8). Illus. by Yves Noblet. 2004, Coteau paper $10.95 (978-1-55050-269-5). Tom and Jenny face new challenges in this sequel to the fantasies *Kalifax* and *Captain Jenny and the Sea of Wonders*. (Rev: SLJ 4/04; VOYA 6/04)

3707 Tiernan, Cate. *A Chalice of Wind* (8–11). Series: Balefire. 2005, Penguin paper $6.99 (978-1-59514-045-6). Thais discovers that she has a twin — and that she is a witch — when her father dies and she is sent to live in New Orleans. (Rev: BL 9/1/05; SLJ 8/05)

3708 Tiernan, Cate. *Darkness Falls* (8–11). 2012, Little, Brown $17.99 (978-031603593-4). In this sequel to *Immortal Beloved* (2010), immortal Nastasya — now 450 years old — struggles to escape her inner darkness and to forget the past. ∩ e Lexile 760L (Rev: BL 12/15/11; SLJ 2/12)

3709 Tiernan, Cate. *Night's Child* (7–12). Series: Sweep. 2003, Penguin paper $7.99 (978-0-14-250119-1). In

this 15th installment — a double-length, stand-alone novel — Moira, 15-year-old daughter of the powerful blood witch Morgan, learns about her heritage and faces danger and treachery as well as romance. (Rev: SLJ 2/04)

3710 Toft, Di. *Wolven* (5–8). 2010, Scholastic $16.99 (978-0-545-17109-0). Twelve-year-old Nat is devoted to his unconventional-looking dog, and is astonished when it suddenly morphs into a human boy. Lexile 860L (Rev: BLO 6/10; LMC 11–12/10; SLJ 8/10)

3711 Tolkien, J. R. R. *The Hobbit: Or, There and Back Again* (7–12). 1938, Houghton Mifflin $16.00 (978-0-395-07122-9); paper $7.99 (978-0-345-33968-3). In this prelude to *The Lord of the Rings*, the reader meets Bilbo Baggins, a hobbit, in a land filled with dwarfs, elves, goblins, and dragons.

3712 Tolkien, J. R. R. *Roverandom* (4–9). 1998, Houghton Mifflin $17.00 (978-0-395-89871-0); paper $12.95 (978-0-395-95799-8). This fantasy deals with a dog named Roverandom who has the misfortune of insulting a wizard and having to pay the consequences. (Rev: BL 7/98; SLJ 6/98; VOYA 10/98)

3713 Tolkien, J. R. R. *Unfinished Tales of Numenor and Middle-Earth* (8–12). Ed. by Christopher Tolkien. 2001, Houghton Mifflin $26.00 (978-0-618-15404-3); paper $14.95 (978-0-618-15405-0). A collection of previously unpublished fantasy writings by this English master.

3714 Tomlinson, Heather. *Aurelie: A Faerie Tale* (7–10). 2008, Henry Holt $16.95 (978-080508276-0). As gifted friends Aurelie, Garin, and Netta come of age in their intricate, fantastical world, they cope with distance, physical struggles, familial obligations, and a complex and ill-fated love story. e Lexile 780L (Rev: BL 9/1/08; HB 9–10/08; SLJ 12/08)

3715 Tomlinson, Heather. *The Swan Maiden* (6–10). 2007, Henry Holt $16.95 (978-0-8050-8275-3). Swan maiden Doucette, who only discovers her natural magic in her teens, is in love with the shepherd Jaume, who must complete a series of trials to win her hand in this story based on French fairy tales. (Rev: BL 10/1/07; SLJ 12/07)

3716 Tomlinson, Heather. *Toads and Diamonds* (8–12). 2010, Henry Holt $16.99 (978-0-8050-8968-4). Perrault's classic tale is reimagined in a fictional Indian land, where stepsisters Diribani and Tana have very different experiences as they use the gifts bestowed on them by a goddess. e Lexile 820L (Rev: BL 2/15/10*; LMC 5–6/10; SLJ 7/10)

3717 Townley, Roderick. *The Door in the Forest* (5–8). 2011, Knopf $16.99 (978-0-375-85601-3); LB $19.99 (978-0-375-95601-0). Fourteen-year-old Daniel, who cannot lie, and Emily, who has magical powers, travel from their town — which is being occupied by soldiers

— to a mysterious nearby island. **e** Lexile 600L (Rev: BL 3/1/11; HB 3–4/11; SLJ 3/1/11)

3718 Townley, Roderick. *Into the Labyrinth* (5–7). 2002, Simon & Schuster $16.95 (978-0-689-84615-1). In this sequel to *The Great Good Thing* (2001), Princess Sylvie and the other characters in their novel become exhausted as their popularity grows and they must rush from chapter to chapter; when the book goes digital, things spiral out of control and Sylvie must defeat an evil "bot" that threatens to destroy them. (Rev: BL 11/1/02; HBG 10/03; SLJ 10/02)

3719 Townsend, John Rowe. *The Fortunate Isles* (7–12). 1989, HarperCollins LB $13.89 (978-0-397-32366-1). Eleni and her friend Andreas seek the living god in this novel set in a mythical land. (Rev: BL 10/15/89; SLJ 10/89)

3720 Townsend, Tom. *The Trouble with an Elf* (5–8). Series: Fairie Ring. 1999, Fireworks paper $9.99 (978-0-88092-525-9). The adopted daughter of the king of the elves, Elazandra, journeys through a ring of mushrooms to the world of humans to stop the evil that will destroy both worlds. (Rev: SLJ 4/00)

3721 Trent, Tiffany. *The Unnaturalists* (6–9). 2012, Simon & Schuster $16.99 (978-1-4424-2206-3). In this steampunk fantasy set in the world New London, 16-year-old Vespa, a witch, teams up with Syrus, a Tinker, to save their world. **e** (Rev: BL 10/1/12; LMC 1–2/13; SLJ 8/1/12)

3722 Trivas, Tracy. *The Wish Stealers* (4–7). 2010, Simon & Schuster $16.99 (978-1-4169-8725-3). A girl named Griffin Penshine receives a box of stolen wishes — pennies dredged from a fountain — and attempts to reunite each one with its owner in order to escape misfortune. **e** Lexile 710L (Rev: BLO 11/15/09; LMC 10/10; SLJ 3/10)

3723 Tunnell, Michael O. *Moon without Magic* (6–9). 2007, Dutton $17.99 (978-0-525-47729-7). Aminah and her jinni travel through the Middle East searching for the lamp that once belonged to Aladdin in this sequel to *Wishing Moon* (2004). (Rev: LMC 1/08; SLJ 12/07)

3724 Tunnell, Michael O. *The Wishing Moon* (6–9). 2004, Penguin $17.99 (978-0-525-47193-6). Struggling to survive after the death of her parents, 14-year-old Aminah is begging for alms outside the sultan's palace when the sultan's daughter throws an old oil lamp at her, not realizing the lamp's magical properties. (Rev: BL 8/04; SLJ 7/04; VOYA 6/04)

3725 Turner, Ann W. *Rosemary's Witch* (5–8). 1991, HarperCollins paper $3.95 (978-0-06-440494-5). Rosemary discovers that her new home is haunted by the spirit of a girl named Mathilda, who's become a witch because of her pain and anger. (Rev: BL 4/1/91; SLJ 5/91*)

3726 Turner, Megan W. *The Queen of Attolia* (5–8). 2000, Greenwillow $15.95 (978-0-688-17423-1). In this sequel to *The Thief*, Gen, a slippery rogue, once more gets involved in the rivalry between two city states. (Rev: BL 4/15/00; HB 7–8/00; HBG 10/00; SLJ 5/00)

3727 Turner, Megan W. *The Thief* (5–8). 1996, Greenwillow $17.99 (978-0-688-14627-6). To escape life imprisonment, Gen must steal a legendary stone in this first-person fantasy set in olden days. (Rev: BCCB 11/96; BL 1/1–15/97; HB 11–12/96; SLJ 10/96; VOYA 6/97)

3728 Uehashi, Nahoko. *Moribito: Guardian of the Spirit* (6–9). Trans. by Cathy Hirano. 2008, Scholastic $17.99 (978-0-545-00542-5). Balsa, a 30-year-old woman, is hired to protect the son of the Mikado in this fantasy involving lots of magic and martial arts. Batchelder Award 2009. (Rev: BL 8/08; SLJ 9/08)

3729 Umansky, Kaye. *Clover Twig and the Magical Cottage* (4–7). Illus. by Johanna Wright. 2009, Roaring Brook $16.99 (978-1-59643-507-0). In this funny, clever tale, 11-year-old Clover gets work cleaning a witch's magical cottage and finds herself protecting the cottage from the witch's evil sister. Lexile 550L (Rev: BL 8/09; HB 9–10/09; LMC 11–12/09; SLJ 9/09)

3730 Umansky, Kaye. *Clover Twig and the Perilous Path* (4–7). Illus. by Johanna Wright. 2012, Roaring Brook $16.99 (978-1-59643-754-8). When Clover's baby brother disappears, she enlists the aid of her boss, the good witch Mrs. Eckles in this sequel to *Clover Twig and the Magical Cottage* (2009). **e** Lexile 570L (Rev: BL 8/12; SLJ 7/12)

3731 Ursu, Anne. *The Immortal Fire* (5–8). Series: Cronus Chronicles. 2009, Atheneum $16.99 (978-1-4169-0591-2). Thirteen-year-olds Charlotte and Zee take on the task of saving mankind in this action-packed final installment in a series that features many classical references. (Rev: BLO 4/24/09; SLJ 9/09)

3732 Ursu, Anne. *The Shadow Thieves* (5–8). 2006, Simon & Schuster $16.95 (978-1-4169-0587-5). A plot to reanimate the dead using the essence of living children is foiled by cousins Charlotte and Zee in this story of heroism and mythology that ranges from the Midwest to England to Hades. (Rev: BL 3/1/06; SLJ 4/06)

3733 Ursu, Anne. *The Siren Song* (5–8). Series: Cronus Chronicles. 2007, Atheneum $16.99 (978-1-4169-0589-9). Charlotte, just back from the Underworld (in 2007's *The Shadow Thieves*), goes on a cruise with her cousin Zee and finds herself battling Poseidon and the sea monster Ketos; the second installment in the series that uses elements of Greek mythology. (Rev: BL 11/1/07; HB 7–8/07; SLJ 8/07)

3734 Valente, Catherynne M. *The Girl Who Circumnavigated Fairyland in a Ship of Her Own Making* (5–8). Illus. by Ana Juan. 2011, Feiwel & Friends $16.99 (978-

0-312-64961-6). This quirky, imaginative story features 12-year-old September, who is carried off to Fairyland, where she has some wild and wonderful adventures among the unusual and sometimes sinister inhabitants there. ⌒ ℮ Lexile 920 (Rev: BL 4/15/11; HB 5–6/11; LMC 10/11; SLJ 5/11; VOYA 6/11)

3735 Valente, Catherynne M. *The Girl Who Fell Beneath Fairyland and Led the Revels There* (5–8). Illus. by Ana Juan. 2012, Feiwel & Friends $16.99 (978-0-312-64962-3). September, 13, realizes that her shadow is draining the magic from Fairyland Above and sets out to put things right in this sequel to *The Girl Who Circumnavigated Fairyland in a Ship of Her Own Making* (2011). ⌒ ℮ Lexile 950L (Rev: BL 10/1/12*; HB 11–12/12; SLJ 9/12)

3736 Van Belkom, Edo. *Lone Wolf* (5–8). 2005, Tundra paper $8.95 (978-0-88776-741-8). The four teen werewolves adopted by Ranger Brock in *Wolf Pack* (2004) defend their beloved woods against a corrupt developer. (Rev: SLJ 1/06; VOYA 4/06)

3737 Van Cleve, Kathleen. *Drizzle* (5–8). 2010, Dial $16.99 (978-0-8037-3362-6). Polly, an 11-year-old who can communicate with plants, lives on a rhubarb farm where it rains at the same time every Monday; when the rains stop, Polly must use her powers of logic and communication to solve the problem. ⌒ Lexile 650L (Rev: BL 3/1/10; SLJ 4/10)

3738 Van Eekhout, Greg. *Kid vs. Squid* (4–7). 2010, Bloomsbury $16.99 (978-1-59990-489-4). When a girl steals a shrunken head from the Museum of the Strange and Curious, Thatcher and Trudy chase the thief and end up saving a cursed civilization; a lighthearted fantasy full of humor. (Rev: BL 5/15/10; LMC 8–9/10; SLJ 7/10)

3739 Van Lowe, E. *Never Slow Dance with a Zombie* (7–10). 2009, Tor paper $8.99 (978-0-7653-2040-7). A satirically humorous zombie story in which 16-year-old Margot, who longs to be popular, gets her chance for stardom when nearly all her classmates are turned into zombies. ℮ Lexile 620L (Rev: BL 9/1/09; LMC 3–4/10; SLJ 1/10)

3740 Vande Velde, Vivian. *Now You See It . . .* (5–8). 2005, Harcourt $17.00 (978-0-15-205311-6). Wendy, 15, puts on a pair of sunglasses and a whole new fantasy world is revealed. (Rev: BL 1/1–15/05; SLJ 1/05)

3741 Vande Velde, Vivian. *Witch Dreams* (5–8). 2005, Marshall Cavendish $15.95 (978-0-7614-5235-5). Nyssa, a 16-year-old witch, seeks justice for her parents, who were murdered six years earlier. (Rev: BL 12/15/05; SLJ 11/05; VOYA 12/05)

3742 Vanderwal, Andrew H. *The Battle for Duncragglin* (5–7). 2009, Tundra $17.95 (978-0-88776-886-6). On a visit to Scotland, 12-year-old Alex and three Scottish children are transported back to a chaotic and dangerous time. (Rev: BL 4/15/09; SLJ 7/09; VOYA 8/09)

3743 Vansickle, Lisa. *The Secret Little City* (5–8). 2000, Palmae $15.95 (978-1-930167-11-7). When 11-year-old Mackenzie moves with her family to a small town in Oregon, she discovers a whole civilization of inch-high people living beneath the floorboards of her new room. (Rev: SLJ 8/00)

3744 Vaughn, Carrie. *Voices of Dragons* (7–10). 2010, HarperTeen $16.99 (978-0-06-179894-8). When 17-year-old Kay is rescued from a fall by a friendly dragon named Artegal, the two attempt to negotiate a peace agreement between the warring realms of humans and dragons. ℮ Lexile HL690L (Rev: BL 1/1–15/10; SLJ 3/10; VOYA 8/11)

3745 Vaught, S. R, and J. B. Redmond. *Assassin's Apprentice* (7–12). Series: Oathbreaker. 2009, Bloomsbury paper $10.99 (978-1-59990-162-6). When young Aron is chosen to join an elite team of assassins — the Stone Brothers — his considerable aptitude for magic becomes apparent; the first volume in a two-part fantasy set in the world of Eyrie. ℮ Lexile 1020L (Rev: SLJ 6/1/09; VOYA 8/09)

3746 Vaupel, Robin. *The Rules of the Universe by Austin W. Hale* (5–8). 2007, Holiday $16.95 (978-0-8234-1811-4). When Austin, 13, discovers that he can alter the molecular structures of people and animals, he conducts careful experiments to determine the limits of this power — and to see if he can save his dying grandfather. (Rev: BL 11/1/07)

3747 Verrillo, Erica. *Elissa's Odyssey* (5–8). Series: Phoenix Rising. 2008, Random House $16.99 (978-0-375-83948-1). The second book in the trilogy, following *Elissa's Quest*, finds Elissa in Alhamazar, her mysterious power to speak to animals expanding. (Rev: BL 5/15/08)

3748 Verrillo, Erica. *Elissa's Quest* (5–8). Series: Phoenix Rising. 2007, Random House $16.99 (978-0-375-83946-7). Thirteen-year-old Elissa struggles to control her destiny when she finds out that she is the princess of Castlemar and that her father the king plans to trade her to a desert warlord. (Rev: BL 6/1–15/07; LMC 10/07; SLJ 8/07)

3749 Verrillo, Erica. *World's End* (5–8). Series: Phoenix Rising. 2009, Random $16.99 (978-0-375-83950-4). Elissa must escape her father's plans for her in this satisfying final installment in the trilogy. (Rev: BLO 4/24/09; SLJ 9/09)

3750 Vick, Helen H. *Tag Against Time* (6–9). 1996, Harbinger $15.95 (978-1-57140-006-2); paper $9.95 (978-1-57140-007-9). In this third volume about Tag, our hero thinks it is time to leave the 1200s and the Hopi culture he has grown to love and return to the present. (Rev: SLJ 10/96; VOYA 2/97)

3751 Vick, Helen H. *Walker's Journey Home* (7–10). 1995, Harbinger $14.95 (978-1-57140-000-0); paper $9.95 (978-1-57140-001-7). Walker leads the Sinagua

213

Indians through treacherous challenges from both old enemies and new, and learns that greed and jealousy have been destructive forces throughout history. Sequel to *Walker of Time* (1993). (Rev: BL 8/95)

3752 Voake, Steve. *The Dreamwalker's Child* (5–8). 2006, Bloomsbury $16.95 (978-1-58234-661-8). After being hit by a car, Sam Palmer finds himself in the alternate world of Aurobon, where he learns of a deadly plot to wipe out human life on Earth using a virus transmitted by mosquitoes. (Rev: SLJ 8/06; VOYA 6/06)

3753 Voelkel, Jon, and Pamela Voelkel. *Middleworld* (5–8). Series: Jaguar Stones Trilogy. 2007, Smith & Kraus $17.95 (978-1-57525-561-3). Fourteen-year-old Max's parents disappear while working in Central America, and he searches for them with the help of local girl Lola and her knowledge of the mystical elements of Mayan culture. (Rev: BL 11/15/07; SLJ 10/07)

3754 Voigt, Cynthia. *The Wings of a Falcon* (7–12). 1993, Scholastic $15.95 (978-0-590-46712-4). Two boys escape from a remote island and face danger and adventure in this multilayered tale that includes themes of friendship, romance, and heroism. (Rev: SLJ 10/93*; VOYA 12/93)

3755 Wagner, Hilary. *Nightshade City* (5–8). Illus. by Omar Rayyan. Series: Nightshade Chronicles. 2010, Holiday House $17.95 (978-0-8234-2285-2). A city of intelligent rats prepares to overthrow its oppressive ruler. Lexile 800L (Rev: BL 9/15/10; LMC 3–4/11; SLJ 1/1/11; VOYA 12/10)

3756 Wagner, Hilary. *The White Assassin* (5–8). Illus. by Omar Rayyan. Series: Nightshade Chronicles. 2011, Holiday House $17.95 (978-0-8234-2333-0). Nightshade City's residents work to keep themselves safe from Billycan's devious and conniving ways in this fast-paced sequel to *Nightshade City* (2010). (Rev: BLO 10/15/11; SLJ 10/1/11)

3757 Walsh, Jill Paton. *A Chance Child* (7–9). 1978, Avon paper $1.95 (978-0-380-48561-1). In this English novel, a young boy who has been a prisoner all his life suddenly travels back in time. (Rev: BL 5/1/89)

3758 Walsh, Pat. *The Crowfield Curse* (5–8). 2010, Scholastic $16.99 (978-0-545-22922-7). In England in 1347, 14-year-old orphaned William comes across a hobgoblin and discovers he himself has magical powers, which must be put to good use; this suspenseful story is full of medieval details. ⌂ Lexile 840L (Rev: BL 10/15/10; LMC 11–12/10; SLJ 9/1/10*)

3759 Walsh, Pat. *The Crowfield Demon* (5–8). 2012, Scholastic $16.99 (978-054531769-6). In this sequel to *The Crowfield Curse* (2010), young William — who can see into the spirit world — must deal with a fallen angel threatening Crowfield Abbey and all therein. ℮ (Rev: BLO 4/1/12; SLJ 5/1/12) [800L]

3760 Wangerin, Walter, Jr. *The Book of the Dun Cow* (7–10). 1978, HarperCollins $12.95 (978-0-06-026346-1).

A farmyard fable with talking animals that retells the story of Chanticleer the Rooster.

3761 Ward, David. *Escape the Mask* (5–8). Series: The Grassland Trilogy. 2008, Abrams $15.95 (978-0-8109-9477-5). Coriko and Pippa escape the Spears, who have been keeping them as slaves, when the Spears are attacked by a mysterious group of warriors; but their adventures do not end there. (Rev: BL 4/15/08)

3762 Ward, Rachel. *Numbers* (8–12). 2010, Scholastic $17.99 (978-0-545-14299-1). When Jem, 15, realizes that all the tourists in line for the London Eye Ferris wheel are scheduled to die that day, she and her friend Spider take off, setting in motion a chain of events. ⌂ ℮ Lexile HL650L (Rev: BL 12/15/09; SLJ 1/10; VOYA 4/10)

3763 Warman, Jessica. *Between* (8–11). 2011, Walker $17.99 (978-0-8027-2182-2). Liz, newly 18, wakes up to find herself caught in the afterlife along with a loser named Alex, and together the two try to work out what caused their deaths. ℮ Lexile HL620L (Rev: BL 9/15/11*; HB 9–10/11; LMC 1–2/12; SLJ 9/1/11; VOYA 10/11)

3764 Waugh, Sylvia. *The Mennyms* (4–8). 1994, Greenwillow $16.00 (978-0-688-13070-1). When their owner dies, a family of rag dolls comes to life and takes over her house in this beginning volume of an extensive series. (Rev: BCCB 5/94; HB 7–8/94; SLJ 4/94)

3765 Weatherill, Cat. *Barkbelly* (4–7). Illus. by Peter Brown. 2006, Knopf $15.95 (978-0-375-83327-4). A wooden boy being raised by normal parents flees after he accidentally causes a tragedy and searches for his own family. (Rev: BL 5/15/06; SLJ 7/06)

3766 Weatherill, Cat. *Snowbone* (4–7). Illus. by Peter Brown. 2007, Knopf $15.99 (978-0-375-83328-1). Snowbone rallies her fellow Ashenpeakers (a race of wooden beings that are used as slaves) to escape their bondage and end slavery; a companion to *Barkbelly* (2006). (Rev: BL 6/1–15/07; SLJ 12/07)

3767 Weatherill, Cat. *Wild Magic* (4–7). 2008, Walker $16.99 (978-0-8027-9799-5). It seems that the Pied Piper (whose real name was Finn) was actually an elf and took the children from Hamelin in hopes of ridding himself of a curse. (Rev: BCCB 1/09; BL 12/1/08; LMC 1/09; SLJ 11/08)

3768 Weaver, Will. *Defect* (6–9). 2007, Farrar $16.00 (978-0-374-31725-6). David's defects include strange-looking, supersensitive ears and an even stranger set of wings that he tries to hide; when they are eventually discovered, he must deal with the repercussions of being different. (Rev: BCCB 9/07; BL 7/07; HB 9–10/07; SLJ 3/08)

3769 Weinberg, Karen. *Window of Time* (5–7). Illus. by Annelle W. Ratcliffe. 1991, White Mane paper $9.95 (978-0-942597-18-9). Ben climbs through a window and finds himself 125 years back in time. (Rev: SLJ 7/91)

3770 Weiss, M. Jerry, and Helen S. Weiss, eds. *Dreams and Visions: Fourteen Flights of Fancy* (7–10). 2006, Tor $19.95 (978-0-7653-1249-5). A collection of 14 appealing fantasy short stories by writers including Joan Bauer and Tamora Pierce; includes short biographies of the authors. (Rev: BL 4/15/06; SLJ 4/06)

3771 Wells, Rosemary. *On the Blue Comet* (5–8). Illus. by Bagram Ibatoulline. 2010, Candlewick $16.99 (978-0-7636-3722-4). The crash of 1929 hits 11-year-old Oscar's family hard and the young model train devotee, longing for his old set, discovers a magical train that allows him to visit different times and places. ⌒ (Rev: BL 7/10; HB 9–10/10; LMC 11–12/10; SLJ 9/1/10)

3772 Werlin, Nancy. *Extraordinary* (8–12). 2010, Dial $17.99 (978-0-8037-3372-5). Privileged Phoebe's best friend Mallory, and her mysterious half-brother Ryland, are both part fairy, and, as it turns out, they have secretive, sinister plans for their friend. ⌒ (Rev: BL 7/10; HB 9–10/10; LMC 1–2/11; SLJ 10/1/10*; VOYA 10/10)

3773 Werlin, Nancy. *Impossible* (7–11). 2008, Dial $17.99 (978-0-8037-3002-1). Magic and reality are intertwined in this tale of 17-year-old Lucy, who becomes pregnant after being raped by her date on prom night and decides to keep the baby even though she must rid herself and the unborn child of a curse. ⌒ € (Rev: BL 7/08*; HB 9–10/08; SLJ 9/1/08*; VOYA 8/08)

3774 Wersba, Barbara. *Walter: The Story of a Rat* (4–7). Illus. by Donna Diamond. 2005, Front St $16.95 (978-1-932425-41-3). Miss Pomeroy, a children's author, develops a friendship with a literary rat named Walter who shares her house in this thoughtful and sophisticated book. (Rev: BCCB 2/06; BL 11/15/05; SLJ 12/05)

3775 Weyn, Suzanne. *Reincarnation* (7–10). 2008, Scholastic $17.99 (978-0-545-01323-9). A fantasy in which a boy and girl are repeatedly reincarnated throughout history and manage to find each other over and over again although impediments to their love sadly also arise. (Rev: BL 6/1–15/08)

3776 Wharton, Thomas. *The Shadow of Malabron* (5–8). 2009, Candlewick $16.99 (978-0-7636-3911-2). A motorcycle crash transports a boy to a magical realm where all the world's stories originate in this imaginative, well-conceived novel about the battle between good and evil. € Lexile 830L (Rev: BL 2/15/10; LMC 1–2/10; SLJ 11/09)

3777 White, Amy Brecount. *Forget-Her-Nots* (7–10). 2010, HarperTeen $16.99 (978-0-06-167298-9); LB $17.89 (978-0-06-167299-6). While at boarding school 14-year-old Laurel learns that her affinity with flowers — and her ability to affect the lives of others through them — is something she has inherited. € (Rev: BL 1/1–15/10; SLJ 3/10; VOYA 6/10)

3778 White, T. H. *The Sword in the Stone* (7–12). 1993, Putnam $24.99 (978-0-399-22502-4). In this, the first part of *The Once and Future King,* the career of Wart is traced until he becomes King Arthur.

3779 Whitley, David. *The Midnight Charter* (7–10). 2009, Roaring Brook $16.99 (978-1-59643-381-6). In a society where lives are treated as a basic commodity, teens Lily and Mark — sold by their parents — take opposing attitudes to the prevailing system. ⌒ € Lexile 790L (Rev: BL 8/09; LMC 1–2/10; SLJ 10/09)

3780 Whitlock, Dean. *Raven* (6–9). 2007, Clarion $16.00 (978-0-618-70224-4). Raven, a 15-year-old bird mage, tries to rescue her mother, Roxaine, and reunite her with her new baby after the overlord Barron Cutter dies, leaving Roxaine vulnerable to the evil estate manager; a companion to *Sky Carver* (2005). (Rev: BL 5/15/07; SLJ 8/07)

3781 Whittemore, Jo. *Escape from Arylon* (5–8). Series: The Silverskin Legacy. 2006, Llewellyn paper $8.95 (978-0-7387-0869-0). Ainsley and Megan, neighbors with an uneasy friendship, find themselves transported through a portal to Arylon, where they meet many magical characters and must save the Staff of Lexiam from thieves. € (Rev: SLJ 6/06; VOYA 6/06)

3782 Wignall, K. J. *Blood* (7–11). Series: Mercian Trilogy. 2011, Egmont $16.99 (978-1-60684-220-1). Sixteen-year-old Will has been a vampire for nearly 800 years and now in the 21st century meets an attractive young runaway named Eloise and starts to investigate his past; the first volume in a trilogy. € (Rev: BL 9/1/11; HB 11–12/11; SLJ 8/11*)

3783 Wilce, Ysabeau S. *Flora Segunda: Being the Magical Mishaps of a Girl of Spirit, Her Glass-Gazing Sidekick, Two Ominous Butlers (One Blue), a House with Eleven Thousand Rooms, and a Red Dog* (6–9). Series: Tygers of Wrath. 2007, Harcourt $17.00 (978-0-15-205433-5). Flora, a plucky 13-year-old who lives in the gigantic, magical Crackpot Hall, enters a library she didn't know about and finds herself on a wild adventure. (Rev: BL 11/15/06; SLJ 2/07)

3784 Wilce, Ysabeau S. *Flora's Dare: How a Girl of Spirit Gambles All to Expand Her Vocabulary, Confront a Bouncing Boy Terror, and Try to Save Califa from a Shaky Doom (Despite Being Confined to Her Room)* (6–9). 2008, Harcourt $17 (978-015205427-4). In this followup to 2007's *Flora Segunda,* 14-year-old Flora and her friend Udo discover a giant squid threatening their fantastic, Spanish-inspired city, and use their familiarity with magic to end the treacherous earthquakes. Lexile 850L (Rev: BLO 8/08; HB 1–2/09; SLJ 1/1/09; VOYA 12/08)

3785 Wilks, Mike. *Mirrorscape* (6–9). 2009, Egmont $16.99 (978-1-60684-008-5); LB $19.99 (978-1-60684-040-5). In the land of Nem, young artist Mel discovers a magical world inside paintings known as

Mirrorscape and there finds adventure and danger. ∩ (Rev: BL 10/1/09; LMC 11–12/09; SLJ 12/09)

3786 Williams, Alex. *The Deep Freeze of Bartholomew Tullock* (5–8). 2008, Philomel $16.99 (978-0-399-25185-6). Never-ending snow has ruined the Breeze family's fan business and they find themselves in debt to the tyrannical Bartholomew Tullock; with their parents, young Madeline and Rufus succeed in finding the machine that has been causing the constant winter. (Rev: BCCB 11/08; BL 10/1/08; LMC 1/09; SLJ 1/09)

3787 Williams, Maiya. *The Golden Hour* (4–8). 2004, Abrams $16.95 (978-0-8109-4823-5). Thirteen-year-old Rowan and his 11-year-old sister Nina are sent to live with two great-aunts after the death of their mother and find themselves — with their new friends Xanthe and Xavier — transported through a time portal to 1789 Paris. (Rev: BL 3/15/04; SLJ 4/04; VOYA 6/04)

3788 Williams, Maiya. *The Hour of the Cobra* (4–7). 2006, Abrams $16.95 (978-0-8109-5970-5). Xanthe, Xavier, Rowan, and Nina time-travel to ancient Egypt and narrowly avoid altering history in this sequel to *The Golden Hour* (2004). (Rev: BL 5/15/06; SLJ 7/06; VOYA 6/06)

3789 Williams, Maiya. *The Hour of the Outlaw* (4–7). 2007, Abrams $16.95 (978-0-8109-9355-6). Xavier and Xanthe, Rowan and Nina travel back in time again — this time to the Old West during the California Gold Rush. (Rev: BL 1/1–15/08; SLJ 1/08)

3790 Williams, Mark London. *Trail of Bones* (5–8). Series: Danger Boy. 2005, Candlewick $9.99 (978-0-7636-2154-4). Eli, Thea, and Clyne — three characters of very different backgrounds — travel back in time from 2019 to early 19th-century America and become involved with Lewis and Clark and the plight of escaping slaves. (Rev: SLJ 7/05)

3791 Williams, Tad, and Deborah Beale. *The Dragons of Ordinary Farm* (4–7). Illus. by Greg Swearingen. 2009, HarperCollins $16.99 (978-0-06-154345-6). Tyler and Lucinda are staying with their great-uncle for the summer and discover the farm is full of mythical animals — dragons, unicorns, and more. (Rev: BLO 4/24/09; LMC 10/09)

3792 Willingham, Bill. *Down the Mysterly River* (4–7). Illus. by Mark Buckingham. 2011, Starscape $15.99 (978-0-7653-2792-5). Max, Boy Scout and sleuth, finds himself and three talking animals in a forest, being chased by the mysterious and sinister Blue Cutters. (Rev: BLO 9/1/11; SLJ 12/1/11)

3793 Wilson, N. D. *The Chestnut King* (4–7). Series: 100 Cupboards. 2010, Random House $16.99 (978-0-375-83885-9); LB $19.99 (978-0-375-93885-6). In this trilogy conclusion, young Henry finally meets the Chestnut King, who can help him to defeat the evil witch Nimiane. ∩ **e** Lexile 670L (Rev: BLO 2/1/10; SLJ 6/10)

3794 Wilson, N. D. *Dandelion Fire* (4–7). 2008, Random $16.99 (978-0-375-83883-5). In an attempt to learn more about his birth parents, Henry and his cousin Henrietta again explore the magical cupboards that lead to other worlds and run up against an evil witch and her powerful minion; a multilayered sequel to *100 Cupboards* (2007). ∩ (Rev: BLO 1/13/09; SLJ 1/09)

3795 Wilson, N. D. *The Dragon's Tooth* (5–8). Series: Ashtown Burials. 2011, Random House $16.99 (978-0-375-86439-1); LB $16.99 (978-0-375-86439-1). Cyrus and Antigone struggle to rescue their brother Dan from the clutches of Dr. Phoenix, who is performing experiments on him, in this fast-paced fantasy involving an ancient secret society. ∩ Lexile 640L (Rev: BL 10/15/11*; SLJ 11/1/11*)

3796 Wilson, N. D. *The Drowned Vault* (8–12). Series: Ashtown Burials. 2012, Random House $16.99 (978-0-375-86440-7); LB $19.99 (978-037596440-4). Cyrus and Antigone must evade the Transmortals and find Dr. Phoenix, regaining the Tooth of the Dragon; an action-packed sequel to *The Dragon's Tooth* (2011). ∩ **e** (Rev: BL 9/15/12; LMC 1–2/13; SLJ 10/12)

3797 Wilson, N. D. *100 Cupboards* (4–7). Series: 100 Cupboards. 2007, Random House $16.99 (978-0-375-83881-1). Henry, a timid 12-year-old, and his braver cousin Henrietta discover a wall of cupboards that lead to alternate worlds. (Rev: BL 12/1/07; HB 1–2/08; LMC 4–5/08; SLJ 4/08)

3798 Winterson, Jeanette. *Tanglewreck* (4–7). 2006, Bloomsbury $16.95 (978-1-58234-919-0). After "time tornadoes" upset the delicate balance of time and space in and around London, 11-year-old Silver embarks on a fantastic odyssey in search of the Timekeeper that, hopefully, can set things right again. (Rev: BL 10/1/06; SLJ 10/06; VOYA 8/06)

3799 Winthrop, Elizabeth. *The Battle for the Castle* (4–7). 1993, Holiday $16.95 (978-0-8234-1010-1). William and friend Jason time-travel to the Middle Ages, where they become involved in a struggle to prevent the return of evil as a ruling power. A sequel to *The Castle in the Attic* (1985). (Rev: BL 9/1/93; HB 7–8/93; SLJ 5/93)

3800 Winthrop, Elizabeth. *The Castle in the Attic* (5–7). 1985, Holiday $16.95 (978-0-8234-0579-4). In an effort to keep his sitter from returning to England, William miniaturizes her and then must find a way to undo the deed. (Rev: BCCB 10/85; BL 1/15/86; SLJ 2/86)

3801 Wollman, Jessica. *Second Skin: Appearances Can Be Deceiving* (8–11). 2009, Delacorte $8.99 (978-038573601-5); LB $11.99 (978-038590581-7). Sam steals the invisible second skin that bestowed popularity on Kylie and discovers what it's like to be on top of the high school heap. (Rev: BL 5/15/09; SLJ 10/09)

3802 Wood, Beverley, and Chris Wood. *Dog Star* (5–8). 1998, Orca paper $6.95 (978-0-89609-537-3). On a cruise to Alaska with his family, 13-year-old Jeff Beacon encounters a magical pet bull terrier who transports him back in time to the Juneau of 1932. (Rev: VOYA 8/98)

3803 Wood, Beverley, and Chris Wood. *Jack's Knife* (5–9). Series: A Sirius Mystery. 2006, Raincoast paper $7.95 (978-1-55192-709-1). This sequel to *Dog Star* (1998) finds Jack time-traveling with bull terrier Patsy Ann to 1930s Alaska to help solve a mystery at sea. (Rev: SLJ 5/06)

3804 Wooding, Chris. *Poison* (6–9). 2005, Scholastic $16.99 (978-0-439-75570-2). Poison sets out to rescue her little sister from the phaeries and faces many challenges in this rich gothic fantasy. (Rev: BL 8/05; SLJ 9/05; VOYA 12/05)

3805 Woodruff, Elvira. *Orphan of Ellis Island* (4–7). 1997, Scholastic paper $15.95 (978-0-590-48245-5). Left alone on Ellis Island, Dominic finds himself transported in time to the village in Italy his family came from. (Rev: BCCB 3/97; BL 6/1–15/97; SLJ 5/97)

3806 Wrede, Patricia C. *Across the Great Barrier* (5–8). Series: Frontier Magic. 2011, Scholastic $16.99 (978-0-545-03343-5). In the second volume of this series set in an alternate Wild West, 18-year-old Eff decides against magic school and joins an expedition to the wilderness beyond the Great Barrier. (Rev: BL 9/1/11; SLJ 9/1/11)

3807 Wrede, Patricia C. *Searching for Dragons* (6–10). Series: Enchanted Forest Chronicles. 1991, Harcourt $16.95 (978-0-15-200898-7). Cimorene goes on a quest with Mendanbar, king of the forest, to find the dragon king Kazul by borrowing a faulty magic carpet from a giant. (Rev: BL 10/1/91; SLJ 12/91)

3808 Wrede, Patricia C. *Talking to Dragons* (6–10). Series: Enchanted Forest Chronicles. 1993, Harcourt $16.95 (978-0-15-284247-5). The fourth book in the series opens 16 years after *Calling on Dragons* with King Menenbar still imprisoned in his castle by a wizard's spells. (Rev: BL 8/93; VOYA 12/93)

3809 Wrede, Patricia C. *Thirteenth Child* (5–8). 2009, Scholastic $16.99 (978-0-545-03342-8). Magical beasts appear on the western frontier in this American history fantasy with a global awareness vibe. (Rev: BCCB 9/09; BL 6/1–15/09; HB 7/09)

3810 Wrede, Patricia C., and Caroline Stevermer. *The Grand Tour or the Purloined Coronation Regalia: Being a Revelation of Matters of High Confidentiality and Greatest Importance, Including Extracts from the Intimate Diary of a Noblewoman and the Sworn Testimony of a Lady of Quality* (6–9). 2004, Harcourt $17.00 (978-0-15-204616-3). In this sequel to *Sorcery and Cecelia* (2003) set in 1817 and blending adventure, humor, fantasy, mystery, and romance, two English cousins, honeymooning in Europe with their husbands, uncover a plot by evil wizards to create a new empire. (Rev: BL 9/1/04; SLJ 11/04)

3811 Wrede, Patricia C., and Caroline Stevermer. *The Mislaid Magician or Ten Years After* (7–10). 2006, Harcourt $17.00 (978-0-15-205548-6). Two cousins investigate a wizard's disappearance in this novel set in 1828 in a magical version of England; this sequel to *Sorcery and Cecelia* (2003) and *The Grand Tour* (2004) is told in the form of letters. (Rev: BL 1/1–15/07; SLJ 1/07)

3812 Wright, Nina. *Homefree* (6–12). 2006, Flux paper $8.95 (978-0-7387-0927-7). Easter is having "astral experiences" in which she travels to her own past; could this have something to do with Homefree, an organization for teenagers with unusual talents? (Rev: SLJ 10/06)

3813 Wright, Randall. *The Silver Penny* (4–7). 2005, Henry Holt $16.95 (978-0-8050-7391-1). In this compelling fantasy set in the 19th century, Jacob — after breaking his leg and facing disability — receives from his great-grandfather a lucky silver penny that gives him access to a supernatural world. (Rev: BCCB 7–8/05; SLJ 8/05; VOYA 10/05)

3814 Wynne-Jones, Tim. *Some of the Kinder Planets* (5–8). 1995, Orchard LB $16.99 (978-0-531-08751-0). Nine imaginative stories about ordinary boys and girls in offbeat situations. (Rev: BCCB 5/95; BL 3/1/95*; HB 1–2/95, 5–6/95, 9–10/95; SLJ 4/95*)

3815 Yancey, Rick. *Alfred Kropp: The Seal of Solomon* (8–11). 2007, Bloomsbury $16.95 (978-1-59990-045-2). Alfred, awkward high school sophomore and descendant of Sir Lancelot, has many adventures as he struggles to battle the forces of evil in this sequel to *The Extraordinary Adventures of Alfred Kropp* (2005). ℮ (Rev: BL 5/15/07; SLJ 6/07)

3816 Yep, Laurence. *City of Ice* (5–8). Series: City Trilogy. 2011, Tor $16.99 (978-0-7653-1925-8). Scirye and her companions travel to the Arctic Circle in their quest to stop the evil Mr. Roland and dragon Badik from acquiring magical power; the sequel to *City of Fire* (2009). ℮ Lexile 890L (Rev: BL 6/1/11; SLJ 6/11)

3817 Yep, Laurence. *Dragon of the Lost Sea* (5–8). 1982, HarperCollins paper $6.99 (978-0-06-440227-9). Shimmer, a dragon, in the company of a boy, Thorn, sets out to destroy the villain Civet. (Rev: BL 4/15/04)

3818 Yep, Laurence. *Dragon Steel* (6–10). 1985, HarperCollins $12.95 (978-0-06-026748-3). The dragon princess Shimmer tries to save her people who are forced to work in an undersea volcano in this sequel to *Dragon of the Lost Sea*. (Rev: BL 5/15/85; SLJ 9/85; VOYA 8/85)

3819 Yolen, Jane. *Curse of the Thirteenth Fey: The True Tale of Sleeping Beauty* (5–8). 2012, Philomel $16.99 (978-0-399-25664-6). This retelling of the Sleeping Beauty story features 13-year-old Gorse, the 13th and youngest fey in her family — and a little accident-prone. ℮ Lexile 880L (Rev: BL 11/15/12; HB 11–12/12; LMC 1–2/13; SLJ 10/12; VOYA 4/13)

3820 Yolen, Jane. *Merlin* (5–8). Series: Young Merlin Trilogy. 1997, Harcourt $16.00 (978-0-15-200814-7). In this concluding volume of a trilogy, Hawk-Hobby (Merlin) escapes from his enemies with a young friend who will later become King Arthur. (Rev: BL 4/15/97; SLJ 5/97)

3821 Yolen, Jane. *The One-Armed Queen* (8–10). 1998, Tor $23.95 (978-0-312-85243-6). Scillia, the adopted daughter of Queen Jenna, is being groomed to rule when her younger brother decides that he should become king. (Rev: BL 10/1/98; VOYA 4/99)

3822 Yolen, Jane. *Passager* (4–7). Series: Young Merlin Trilogy. 1996, Harcourt $16.00 (978-0-15-200391-3). In medieval England, an abandoned 8-year-old boy named Merlin is taken in by a friendly man who becomes his master. Book two of the trilogy is *Hobby* (1996). (Rev: BL 5/1/96; HB 7–8/96; SLJ 5/96*)

3823 Yolen, Jane. *Snow in Summer* (6–9). 2011, Philomel $16.99 (978-0-399-25663-9). The story of Snow White is set in 1940s Appalachia and features an evil Stepmama and a group of seven miners. **e** (Rev: BL 11/15/11; HB 1–2/12; LMC 3–4/12*; SLJ 11/1/11)

3824 Yolen, Jane, and Adam Stemple. *Pay the Piper* (6–9). 2005, Tor $16.95 (978-0-7653-1158-0). Fourteen-year-old Callie discovers the secret of a member of the Brass Rat when the town's children disappear on Halloween night in this lighthearted version of the Pied Piper tale. (Rev: BL 6/1–15/05; SLJ 8/05; VOYA 8/05)

3825 Yolen, Jane, and Adam Stemple. *Trollbridge: A Rock n' Roll Fairy Tale* (6–9). 2006, Tor $16.95 (978-0-7653-1426-0). Moira, a princess and harpist, and three brothers from a popular band called the Griffsons, are transported to the strange wilderness world of Trollholm where they must rescue the other princesses from Aenmarr, a colossal troll. (Rev: BL 9/1/06; SLJ 8/06)

3826 Yolen, Jane, ed. *Dragons and Dreams* (6–10). 1986, HarperCollins $12.95 (978-0-06-026792-6). A collection of 10 fantasy and some science fiction stories that can be a fine introduction to these genres. (Rev: SLJ 5/86; VOYA 6/86)

3827 Yoshi. *The Butterfly Hunt* (5–8). 1991, Picture Book paper $14.95 (978-0-88708-137-8). In this fantasy, a young boy releases a butterfly and forevermore it becomes his own. (Rev: SLJ 6/91)

3828 Young, Steve. *15 Minutes* (5–8). 2006, HarperCollins $15.99 (978-0-06-072508-2). Casey, a 7th-grader who's always late for almost everything, discovers that his grandfather's watch gives him the power to go back 15 minutes. (Rev: SLJ 9/06)

3829 Zahler, Diane. *The Thirteenth Princess* (4–7). 2010, HarperCollins $15.99 (978-0-06-182498-2). Zita learns that she is a king's daughter and that her 12 sisters are under a magic spell. ∩ Lexile 850L (Rev: BL 12/15/09; LMC 8–9/10; SLJ 3/10)

3830 Zahn, Timothy. *Dragon and Herdsman: The Fourth Dragonback Adventure* (5–8). 2006, Tom Doherty Assoc. $17.95 (978-0-7653-1417-8). With the help of a shape-changing dragon and his friend Alison, 14-year-old Jack Morgan escapes from the Malison Ring. (Rev: SLJ 9/06; VOYA 6/06)

3831 Zappa, Ahmet. *The Monstrous Memoirs of a Mighty McFearless* (4–7). Illus. by author. 2006, Random House $12.95 (978-0-375-83287-1). Written and illustrated by the son of Frank Zappa, this rollicking fantasy follows Mini and Max McFearless, monsterminators who must rescue their father from kidnappers. ∩ (Rev: BL 5/15/06; SLJ 7/06)

3832 Zettel, Sarah. *Dust Girl* (6–9). Series: American Fairy Trilogy. 2012, Random House $17.99 (978-0-375-86938-9); LB $20.99 (978-0-375-96938-6). Callie discovers she's half-fairy when her human mother disappears in a dust storm and she receives a message from a mysterious presence in this fantasy set in 1935 Kansas. **e** Lexile 700L (Rev: HB 5–6/12; SLJ 6/12; VOYA 6/12)

3833 Zevin, Gabrielle. *Elsewhere* (7–10). 2005, Farrar $16.00 (978-0-374-32091-1). After dying of a head injury, 15-year-old Liz Hall does not adapt easily to afterlife in Elsewhere and at first spends a lot of time watching what's going on on Earth. (Rev: BL 8/05*; SLJ 10/05*)

3834 Zink, Michelle. *Prophecy of the Sisters* (7–10). Series: Prophecy of the Sisters. 2009, Little, Brown $17.99 (978-031602742-7). Twins Lia and Alice, 16, are at the center of a battle against the fallen angel Samael in this complex fantasy set in the late 1800s. (Rev: BL 5/15/09; SLJ 1/10; VOYA 10/09)

3835 Zuckerman, Linda. *A Taste for Rabbit* (6–10). 2007, Scholastic $16.99 (978-0-439-86977-5). This fable of civilized animals can be disturbing in its violence as a group of rabbits begins selling its young to hungry foxes. (Rev: BL 11/15/07; HB 11–12/07; LMC 1/08; SLJ 11/07)

Graphic Novels

3836 Abadzis, Nick. *Laika* (8–12). Illus. by author. 2007, Roaring Brook paper $17.95 (978-1-59643-101-0). A fictionalized account of the little dog named Laika, the first living creature launched into space by the Russians, and her trainer, Yelena Dubrovsky. (Rev: BL 9/1/07; SLJ 11/07)

3837 Abe, Yoshitoshi. *New Feathers* (6–9). Series: Haibane Renmei. 2006, Dark Horse $14.95 (978-1-59307-520-0). Rakka awakes as a member of the Haibane, angel-like people who live among humans in a walled city, with no recollection of her past. (Rev: BL 11/1/06)

3838 Akimoto, Nami. *Ultra Cute, Vol. 1* (5–8). Trans. from Japanese by Emi Onishi. Illus. by author. 2006, TokyoPop paper $9.99 (978-1-59532-956-1). Ami and Noa, more rivals than friends, compete with each other over two guys who are not as nice as they seem. (Rev: SLJ 7/06)

3839 Alexovich, Aaron. *Kimmie66* (8–12). Illus. by author. 2007, DC Comics paper $9.99 (978-1-4012-0373-3). In the technologically advanced 23rd century, Telly receives a suicide note from a friend — or is it from her friend's digital duplicate? (Rev: BL 1/1–15/08; SLJ 3/08)

3840 *All Star Comics: Archives, Vol. 11* (7–12). Illus. by Arthur Peddy and Bernard Sachs. Series: Archive Editions. 2005, DC Comics $49.95 (978-1-4012-0403-7). The final volume of the Archive Editions series continues the adventures of the Justice Society of America, a band of comic book superheroes that includes the Green Lantern, Flash, Wonder Woman, Atom, and Hawkman. (Rev: BL 7/05; SLJ 9/05)

3841 Altman, Steven-Elliot. *The Irregulars: . . . In the Service of Sherlock Holmes* (7–12). 2005, Dark Horse paper $12.95 (978-1-59307-303-9). In this suspenseful graphic novel, Holmes assigns the Baker Street Irregulars to find out who's responsible for a murder for which Dr. Watson has been charged. (Rev: BL 5/1/05)

3842 Ando, Natsumi, and Miyuki Kobayashi. *Kitchen Princess* (6–9). Illus. by Natsumi Ando. 2007, Ballantine paper $10.95 (978-0-345-49659-1). A student at a prestigious cooking academy is on the trail of a mysterious stranger from her past in this girls' manga. (Rev: BL 4/1/07; SLJ 9/07)

3843 Appignanesi, Richard. *A Midsummer Night's Dream* (8–12). Adapted by Richard Appignanesi. Illus. by Kate Brown. Series: Manga Shakespeare. 2008, Abrams paper $9.95 (978-0-8109-9475-1). A manga retelling of the comedy featuring fairies and lovers; illustrated by Kate Brown. (Rev: BL 3/15/08; SLJ 5/08)

3844 Aristophane. *The Zabime Sisters* (7–10). 2010, First Second paper $16.99 (978-1-59643-638-1). On the island of Guadeloupe, three teen sisters enjoy a summer day with adventures including smoking, sneaking a drink, stealing mangoes, and watching a fight. YALSA Great Graphic Novels Top Ten 2011. (Rev: BL 10/15/10; LMC 10/10; SLJ 11/10)

3845 Arni, Samhita. *Sita's Ramayana* (5–12). Illus. by Moyna Chitrakar. 2011, Groundwood $24.95 (978-155498145-8). With Patua scroll paintings, this graphic-novel retelling has Rama's beautiful wife as its main focus. ALA Notable Books 2012. (Rev: BL 9/15/11*; LMC 1–2/12*; SLJ 9/1/11*)

3846 Asamiya, Kia. *Dark Angel: The Path to Destiny* (8–12). Series: Dark Angel. 2000, CPM Comics paper $15.95 (978-1-56219-827-5). In this first volume of a series of graphic novels, a young swordsman named

Dark travels through time and different worlds to complete his moral journey. (Rev: BL 12/1/00)

3847 Avi. *City of Light, City of Dark: A Comic-Book Novel* (6–9). 1995, Orchard paper $8.99 (978-0-531-07058-1). In black-and-white comic book format, Sarah and her friend Carlos must save her father from the evil Underton and pay tribute to the Kurbs before Manhattan freezes. (Rev: BL 9/15/93; VOYA 2/94)

3848 Beddor, Frank, and Liz Cavalier. *Hatter M* (8–12). Illus. by Ben Templesmith. Series: Hatter M. 2008, Automatic Pictures paper $14.95 (978-098187370-1). Fans of Beddor's Looking Glass trilogy will enjoy this dark and complex story of Hatter Madigan and his search for Princess Alyss. (Rev: BL 1/1–15/09; VOYA 2/09)

3849 Beechen, Adam. *Robin: Teenage Wasteland* (8–11). Illus. by Freddie Williams. 2007, DC Comics paper $17.99 (978-1-4012-1480-7). A collection of nine issues of well-written comic book stories featuring the boy wonder. (Rev: BL 1/15/08)

3850 Beka. *Dance Class: So, You Think You Can Hip-Hop?* (4–8). Illus. by Crip. 2012, Papercutz $9.99 (978-159707254-0). A graphic novel in which dance students compete for the lead role in *Sleeping Beauty* while at the same time swooning over KT, the hip-hop teacher. (Rev: BL 3/15/12; LMC 10/12)

3851 Bilgrey, Marc, and Rob Vollmar. *Ghouls Gone Wild!* (6–8). Illus. by Exes. Series: Tales from the Crypt. 2007, Papercutz $12.95 (978-1-59707-083-6); paper $7.95 (978-1-59707-082-9). Four stories from the classic Tales from the Crypt series of the 1950s, with new illustrations. (Rev: BL 1/1–15/08; SLJ 3/08)

3852 Bishop, Debbie. *Black Tide: Awakening of the Key* (6–10). Illus. by Mike S. Miller. 2004, Angel Gate paper $19.99 (978-1-932431-00-1). In this gripping graphic novel, which collects the first eight issues of an ongoing comic book series, past and present collide when Justin Braddock embarks on a mission to solve a series of international murders. (Rev: BL 4/15/04)

3853 Blackman, Haden. *Clone Wars Adventures* (4–7). Series: Star Wars Clone Wars Adventures. 2006, Dark Horse paper $6.95 (978-1-59307-483-8). This fifth volume of the fantasy series, based on the TV cartoon show, includes four fast-paced stories of graphic novel action and adventure. (Rev: BL 6/1–15/06)

3854 Bradbury, Ray. *The Best of Ray Bradbury: The Graphic Novel* (6–12). 2003, iBooks paper $18.95 (978-0-7434-7476-4). Some of the best artists working in the graphic novels field have adapted Bradbury's works. (Rev: BL 2/1/04)

3855 Brennan, Michael. *Electric Girl, Vol. 2* (5–8). 2002, Mighty Gremlin paper $13.95 (978-0-9703555-1-5). In this graphic novel, Virginia, who can release bursts of electricity at will, locks horns with evil gremlin Oogleeoog. (Rev: BL 5/1/02; SLJ 5/02)

3856 Brooks, Terry. *Dark Wraith of Shannara* (6–9). Illus. by David Edwin. Series: Shannara. 2008, Del Rey paper $13.95 (978-0-345-49462-7). This graphic novel, which first recaps relevant Shannara history, takes place after the events of *The Wishsong of Shannara* (1988) as Jair uses the power of wishsong to continue to battle the Ildatch. (Rev: BL 3/15/08; SLJ 7/08)

3857 Brosgol, Vera. *Anya's Ghost* (7–12). Illus. by author. 2011, First Second paper $15.99 (978-159643552-0). Teenage Anya, embarrassed by her Russian immigrant family and failing to fit in at school, finds herself making friends with a ghost. YALSA Great Graphic Novels Top Ten 2012; ALA Notable Books 2012. (Rev: BL 3/15/11*; HB 7–8/11; SLJ 7/1/11*)

3858 Brown, Jeffrey. *Incredible Change-Bots* (8–12). 2007, Top Shelf paper $15.00 (978-1-891830-91-4). Change-Bots, who can morph from robots into vehicles, trash their own planet and then arrive on Earth with a continuing appetite for a fight in this funny, action-filled fantasy. (Rev: BL 11/15/07)

3859 Cabot, Meg. *The Merlin Prophecy* (6–8). Illus. by Jinky Coronado. 2007, TokyoPop paper $7.99 (978-0-06-117707-1). A graphic novel version of Meg Cabot's *Avalon High* (2006) about Ellie and her boyfriend Will, who is unaware that he's the reincarnation of King Arthur. (Rev: BL 9/1/07; SLJ 9/07)

3860 Cammuso, Frank. *Max Hamm, Fairy Tale Detective, Vol. 1* (8–12). Series: Fairy Tale Detectives. 2005, Nite Owl paper $14.95 (978-0-9720061-4-9). Max Hamm, a pig, is also a private eye in a cycle of pulp-novel-style stories involving fairy tale characters and much clever wordplay. (Rev: BL 8/05; SLJ 11/05)

3861 Campbell, Ross. *Shadoweyes* (8–12). Illus. by author. 2010, SLG paper $14.95 (978-159362189-6). In a future dystopia called Dranac, African American Scout Montana morphs into a superhero but may never have the chance to revert to normal. YALSA Popular Paperbacks for Young Adults Top Ten 2011. (Rev: BL 9/15/10*; VOYA 10/10)

3862 Carey, Mike. *Re-Gifters* (7–9). Illus. by Sonny Liew. 2007, DC Comics paper $9.99 (978-1-4012-0371-9). Jen Dik Seong, known as Dixie, and her friend Avril want to enter a hapkido (a martial art) tournament but when Dixie foolishly spends her entry fee on a gift for Adam she risks losing her chance to compete. (Rev: BL 6/1–15/07; LMC 11/07; SLJ 1/08)

3863 Carey, Mike, and Louise Carey. *Confessions of a Blabbermouth* (7–12). Illus. by Aaron Alexovich. 2007, Minx paper $9.99 (978-1-4012-1148-6). Blabbermouth is the name of Tasha's blog, and it's an appropriate name for an effective tool that lets important people in her life know how she's feeling; a humorous, well-illustrated graphic novel. (Rev: LMC 1/08; SLJ 11/07)

3864 Chantler, Scott. *The Annotated Northwest Passage* (8–12). Illus. by author. 2007, Oni $19.95 (978-1-932664-61-4). This action-packed graphic novel, set in northern Canada in 1755, tells of the fierce competition between the French, British, and other private interests to control the fur trade. (Rev: BL 8/07; SLJ 11/07)

3865 Chantler, Scott. *The Sign of the Black Rock* (4–7). Illus. by author. Series: Three Thieves. 2011, Kids Can $17.95 (978-155453416-6); paper $8.95 (978-15545341-7-3). Dessa and her fugitive friends spend a rainy night at the Black Rock Inn, evading detection by the Queen's soldiers, also guests at the inn, who've been sent to capture her; this second installment in the series focuses in part on the innkeeper and his shady activities. Lexile GN510L (Rev: BL 10/15/11; SLJ 11/1/11)

3866 Clamp. *Cardcaptor Sakura, vol. 1* (3–8). Illus. by author. 2010, Dark Horse paper $19.99 (978-15958252-2-3). Three previously published volumes in the series about 4th-grader Sakura and her efforts to save the universe are collected in this remastered and newly translated volume. (Rev: BLO 1/1–15/11)

3867 Clugston, Chynna. *Queen Bee* (5–8). 2005, Scholastic paper $8.99 (978-0-439-70987-3). In this humorous graphic novel about school cliques, Haley and Alexa, two middle school students with psychokinetic powers, battle each other to become the school's most popular girl. (Rev: BL 9/15/05; SLJ 1/06; VOYA 12/05)

3868 Colfer, Eoin, and Andrew Donkin. *Artemis Fowl: The Graphic Novel* (5–7). Illus. by Giovanni Rigano. 2007, Hyperion $18.99 (978-0-7868-4881-2); paper $9.99 (978-0-7868-4882-9). A well-illustrated graphic novel rendering of the 2001 novel about the 12-year-old genius and adventurous criminal entrepreneur Artemis Fowl. (Rev: BL 11/15/07; LMC 2/08; SLJ 1/08)

3869 Colfer, Eoin, and Andrew Donkin. *The Supernaturalist* (6–9). Illus. by Giovanni Rigano. 2012, Disney/Hyperion $19.99 (978-078684879-9). Paranormally gifted Cosmo, 14, teams up with two other "seers" who are able to spot the blue parasites that are draining the human race of its vitality. e Lexile GN500L (Rev: BL 12/15/12; LMC 3–4/13; SLJ 11/12)

3870 Conami, Shoko. *Shinobi Life, Vol. 1* (8–11). Illus. by Vicente Rivera. 2008, Tokyopop paper $9.99 (978-142781111-0). Beni finds herself being shadowed by a very cute time-traveling ninja in this first installment in the series. (Rev: BLO 1/13/09)

3871 Cover, Arthur Byron. *Macbeth* (6–9). Illus. by Tony Leonard Tamai. 2005, Penguin paper $9.99 (978-0-14-240409-6). This imaginative graphic novel adaptation transports Shakespeare's *Macbeth* to a futuristic setting in outer space. (Rev: BL 10/15/05; SLJ 3/06)

3872 Crilley, Mark. *Autumn* (7–9). Illus. by author. Series: Miki Falls. 2007, HarperTeen paper $7.99 (978-0-06-084618-3). In this manga sequel to *Spring* and *Summer* (both 2007), Miki and Hiro continue to break the rules of Hiro's Deliverer organization (a secret group whose members may not fall in love with humans) and decide to run away. (Rev: BL 2/8/08; SLJ 5/08)

3873 Crilley, Mark. *Brody's Ghost, Vol. 1* (7–12). Illus. by author. 2010, Dark Horse paper $6.99 (978-15958252-1-6). Brody's sad, directionless life changes when a teenage ghost enlists his aid to help her gain entrance into heaven. (Rev: BLO 9/1/10)

3874 Crilley, Mark. *Miki Falls: Summer* (7–12). Illus. by author. 2007, HarperTeen paper $7.99 (978-0-06-084617-X). This well-illustrated volume in the manga style follows Miki, a Japanese teen who falls in love with a superhuman entity. (Rev: SLJ 7/07)

3875 Crilley, Mark. *Spring* (4–7). Series: Miki Falls. 2007, HarperTempest paper $7.99 (978-0-06-084616-9). In this manga-style romance novel, high school senior Miki is determined to break through the defenses of the gorgeous but secretive new boy called Hiro. (Rev: BL 3/15/07; SLJ 7/07)

3876 d'Errico, Camilla, and Joshua Dysart. *Avril Lavigne's Make 5 Wishes, Vol. 2* (6–9). 2007, Del Rey paper $12.95 (978-0-345-50079-3). Hana gets through her family and school problems with the help of her imaginary friend (a version of pop star Avril Lavigne); but then genie/demon Romeo comes along and grants Hana five wishes that have disastrous results. (Rev: BL 8/07)

3877 David, Peter. *Final Exam* (6–9). Series: SpyBoy. 2005, Dark Horse paper $12.95 (978-1-59307-017-5). SpyBoy Alex Fleming faces off against a villainous substitute teacher who threatens to derail Alex's plans to attend his senior prom and graduate from high school. (Rev: BL 3/15/05)

3878 Davila, Claudia. *Luz Makes a Splash* (4–7). Illus. by author. Series: Future According to Luz. 2012, Kids Can $16.95 (978-155453762-4). Luz and her friends set out to solve problems associated with a drought and a company draining water from the local swimming hole. (Rev: BLO 10/15/12; LMC 5–6/13; SLJ 1/13)

3879 Davis, Jim. *Garfield: 30 Years of Laughs and Lasagna* (5–10). Illus. by author. 2008, Ballantine $35.00 (978-0-345-50379-4). A collection of the popular comic strip that centers on a grumpy, overweight cat. (Rev: BL 10/15/08; SLJ 1/09)

3880 de Saint-Exupéry, Antoine, and Joann Sfar. *The Little Prince* (5–9). Illus. by Joann Sfar. 2010, Houghton Mifflin $19.99 (978-054733802-6). A respectful graphic-novel retelling of Saint-Exupery's classic about a stranded pilot and a little boy who discuss matters of life and love. e (Rev: BL 9/15/10*; SLJ 11/10; VOYA 12/10)

3881 DeFilippis, Nunzio, and Christina Weir. *Play Ball* (6–9). Illus. by Jackie Lewis. 2012, Oni $19.99 (978-193496479-8). Dashiel and her family move to Arizona and she decides she will play baseball (not softball) despite the obstacles she faces. (Rev: BL 4/15/12; LMC 11–12/12)

3882 Dekker, Ted. *Chaos* (7–9). Illus. by author. Series: Lost Books. 2009, Thomas Nelson paper $15.99 (978-159554606-7). This fourth installment in the series continues the science fiction battle between the forces of good and evil as Johnis and his friends search for the seven books; the illustrations are integral to the fast-paced action. (Rev: BL 6/1–15/09; SLJ 5/09)

3883 Dekker, Ted. *Renegade* (7–9). Illus. by author. Series: Lost Books. 2009, Thomas Nelson paper $15.99 (978-159554605-0). The Christian flavor is very evident in this third time-traveling installment during which Billos makes a decision that affects them all. ∩ (Rev: BL 4/15/09; SLJ 5/09) [741.5]

3884 Dembicki, Matt, ed. *Trickster: Native American Tales: A Graphic Collection* (8–12). Illus. 2010, Fulcrum Publishing paper $22.95 (978-1-55591-724-1). More than 20 Native American tales are presented in appealing graphic-novel format, illustrated by a variety of artists. ALA Notable Books 2011. (Rev: BL 5/1/10*; LMC 11–12/10; SLJ 5/10) [398.2]

3885 Despeyroux, Denise. *Dark Graphic Tales by Edgar Allan Poe* (4–7). Illus. by Miquel Serratosa. 2012, Enslow LB $30.60 (978-076604086-1). Three Poe stories — "The Gold Bug," "The System of Doctor Tarr and Professor Fether," and "The Fall of the House of Usher" — are given effective graphic-novel treatment. (Rev: BL 11/15/12; SLJ 7/1/12; VOYA 10/12)

3886 Deutsch, Barry. *Hereville: How Mirka Met a Meteorite* (4–7). Illus. by author. 2012, Abrams $16.95 (978-141970398-0). In this sequel to *How Mirka Got Her Sword* (2010), the plucky 11-year-old Orthodox Jew must deal with a meteorite that is turned into a clone of herself. Sydney Taylor Book Award 2011. e Lexile GN300L (Rev: BL 11/15/12; HB 11–12/12; SLJ 11/12*)

3887 Dezago, Todd. *Spider-Man: The Terrible Threat of the Living Brain!* (5–8). Illus. by Jonboy Meyers, et al. Series: Spider-Man. 2006, ABDO LB $21.35 (978-1-59961-008-5). Spider-Man, with a little help from Flash, foils the theft of the Living Brain, a powerful robot-like computer. (Rev: SLJ 11/06)

3888 Dezago, Todd. *Spider-Man and Captain America: Stars, Stripes, and Spiders!* (5–8). Series: Spider-Man Team Up. 2006, ABDO LB $21.35 (978-1-59961-001-6). In this action-packed comic-book fantasy, superheroes Spider-Man and Captain America team up to battle the Grey Gargoyle. (Rev: SLJ 11/06)

3889 Dickens, Charles, and Loic Dauvillier. *Oliver Twist* (7–12). Illus. by Olivier Deloye. Series: Classics Illustrated Deluxe. 2012, Papercutz $24.99 (978-159707308-0); paper $19.99 (978-15970730-7-3). With a French adapter and illustrator, this graphic-novel version of the story about Oliver's hard childhood reflects the original. (Rev: BL 4/15/12; SLJ 1/13)

3890 Dixon, Chuck. *Nightwing: On the Razor's Edge* (8–12). Illus. by Greg Land and Drew Geraci. 2005, DC Comics paper $14.99 (978-1-4012-0437-2). Robin, Batman's former sidekick, now takes on the superhero identity of Nightwing and must defend himself against his foes. (Rev: SLJ 11/05)

3891 Dixon, Chuck. *Way of the Rat: The Walls of Zhumar* (7–12). 2003, CrossGeneration paper $15.95 (978-1-931484-51-0). Boon has stolen a scholar's magic ring and the Book of Hell and is now being chased by villains in this fantasy set in Asia and enhanced by dynamic illustrations. (Rev: BL 2/1/03)

3892 DuPrau, Jeanne, and Dallas Middaugh. *The City of Ember* (4–7). Illus. by Niklas Asker. 2012, Random House $18.99 (978-037586821-4); LB $21.99 (978-037596821-1). A graphic novel version of the first book in the successful series, in which Lina and Doon work to find a way out of their isolated and decaying city, where the population is beginning to panic. (Rev: BL 10/15/12; SLJ 11/12*)

3893 Eisner, Will. *Moby Dick* (6–12). 2001, NBM $15.95 (978-1-56163-293-0). A faithful retelling of Melville's famous novel in full-color graphic novel format. (Rev: BL 11/15/01; HBG 3/02; SLJ 1/02)

3894 Eisner, Will. *The Princess and the Frog: By the Grimm Brothers* (4–7). 1999, NBM $15.95 (978-1-56163-244-2). A retelling of the familiar fairy tale in graphic novel style. (Rev: BL 12/15/99; HBG 3/00) [398.2]

3895 Eisner, Will. *Will Eisner's The Spirit Archives, Vol. 12* (8–12). 2003, DC Comics $49.95 (978-1-4012-0006-0). This collection of comic strips covers the full 12-year career of the Spirit, a masked crime fighter. (Rev: BL 2/1/04)

3896 Emerson, Sharon. *Zebrafish* (5–8). Illus. by Renee Kurilla. 2010, Simon & Schuster $16.99 (978-1-4169-9525-8). Led by purple-haired Vita — the only one with any musical abilities — the members of a middle-school rock band prepare for a performance that will bring donations for the fight against cancer. (Rev: BL 3/15/10; LMC 10/10; SLJ 5/10)

3897 Espinosa, Rod. *Neotopia Color Manga* (6–12). Series: Neotopia. 2004, Antarctic paper $9.99 (978-1-932453-57-7). In the opening volume of the graphic novel series, Nalyn, a servant girl, takes over her spoiled mistress's responsibilities as grand duchess of Mathenia, but the going gets tough when Mathenia comes under attack from the evil empire of Krossos. (Rev: BL 12/1/04)

3898 Everheart, Chris. *Shadow Cell Scam* (4–8). Illus. by Arcana Studio. Series: The Recon Academy. 2009, Stone Arch $25.32 (978-1-4342-1166-8). Working together, four superpower-endowed teens confront danger and adversity when they're sent to protect the

launch of a Navy spy satellite in this thrilling graphic novel. (Rev: LMC 10/09; SLJ 9/09)

3899 *Fairy Tales of Oscar Wilde* (5–8). Illus. by P. Craig Russell. 1992, Nantier $15.95 (978-1-56163-056-1). Graphic novel treatment enlivens this retelling of two of Wilde's short stories. (Rev: BL 1/15/93)

3900 Fisher, Jane Smith. *WJHC: Hold Tight* (4–7). 2005, Wilson Place paper $11.95 (978-0-9744235-1-7). This graphic-novel sequel to *WJHC: On the Air* (2003) continues the adventures of six diverse teenage friends who launched a high school radio station, following them through a reality TV show, a celebrity fashion show, and a trip to a rock concert. (Rev: BL 11/1/05; SLJ 1/06)

3901 Fisher, Jane Smith. *WJHC: On the Air!* (4–8). 2003, Wilson Place paper $11.95 (978-0-9744235-0-0). Six episodes catalog the entertaining misadventures of a diverse band of teens who launch a high school radio station. (Rev: BL 2/1/04; VOYA 12/03)

3902 Ford, Christopher. *Stickman Odyssey, Vol. 1: An Epic Doodle* (5–8). Illus. by author. 2011, Philomel $12.99 (978-039925426-0). Banished by his evil stepmother, Zozimos has many adventures as he journeys home to reclaim his throne in this graphic-novel take on the *Odyssey*. (Rev: BL 6/1/11; SLJ 9/1/11)

3903 Frampton, Otis. *Oddly Normal, Vol. 1* (4–7). 2006, Viper paper $11.95 (978-0-9777883-0-9). Half-human and half-witch, unhappy 10-year-old Oddly Normal struggles to find a place where she fits in; a collection of four issues of a mini-series published by Viper Comics. Also use *Family Reunion* (2007). (Rev: BL 11/1/06)

3904 Friedman, Aimee. *Breaking Up* (8–11). Illus. by Christine Norrie. 2007, Scholastic paper $8.99 (978-0-439-74867-4). Romance, sex, and fashion at the Georgia O'Keeffe School for the Arts. (Rev: BL 3/15/07; SLJ 3/07)

3905 Friesen, Ray. *A Cheese Related Mishap and Other Stories* (5–8). 2005, Don't Eat Any Bugs paper $8.95 (978-0-9728177-6-9). This collection of zany tales full of entertaining characters and situations was created by a teenage author/illustrator. (Rev: BL 11/15/05; SLJ 3/06)

3906 Fujino, Moyamu. *The First King Adventure, Vol. 1* (4–8). Trans. from Japanese by Kay Bertrand. Illus. by author. 2004, ADV paper $9.99 (978-1-4139-0194-8). Prince Tiltu cannot succeed his father as king until he's made contracts with all of the spirit masters that inhabit the kingdom. (Rev: SLJ 7/05)

3907 Fujishima, Kosuke. *Oh My Goddess! Colors* (8–12). Illus. by author. 2009, Dark Horse paper $19.95 (978-1595822550). Four classic manga stories each focus on a goddess — Belldandy, Urd, Skuld, and Peorth — in this oversized volume that includes a thorough encyclopedia of the series. (Rev: BL 6/1–15/09)

3908 Fukushima, Haruka. *Orange Planet, Vol. 1* (8–11). Illus. by author. 2009, Del Rey paper $10.99 (978-034551338-0). In this *shojo* manga, Rui finds herself the object of much male interest — from her contemporaries and from a teacher. (Rev: BLO 4/30/09; SLJ 9/09)

3909 Gaiman, Neil. *Coraline* (4–7). Illus. by P. Craig Russell. 2008, HarperCollins LB $19.89 (978-0-06-082544-7); paper $18.99 (978-0-06-082543-0). This adaptation of the 2002 novel by the same name graphically captures Coraline's horror as her nightmares become real behind a strange door. (Rev: BL 3/15/08; SLJ 7/08)

3910 Gallardo, Adam. *Gear School* (4–7). Illus. by Nuria Peris. 2007, Dark Horse paper $7.95 (978-1-59307-854-6). Teresa, 13, is being trained to operate huge robotic attack machines called Gear when aliens attack and she and her classmates must defend themselves. (Rev: BL 11/15/07)

3911 Geary, Rick. *The Case of Madeleine Smith* (7–12). Illus. by author. Series: Treasury of Victorian Murder. 2006, NBM $15.95 (978-1-56163-467-5). Based on actual events in Victorian Glasgow, this story of an affair between an upper-class young woman and a merchant's son ends in murder. (Rev: BL 6/1–15/06; SLJ 9/06)

3912 Geary, Rick. *Great Expectations. Rev. ed.* (4–7). Illus. by author. Series: Classics Illustrated. 2008, Papercutz $9.95 (978-1-59707-097-3). The Dickens classic is retold in graphic novel format with illustrations that highlight the key parts of the story. (Rev: BL 3/15/08)

3913 Giallongo, Zack. *Broxo* (7–10). Illus. by author. 2012, First Second paper $16.99 (978-15964355-1-3). A multilayered graphic novel featuring Princess Zora, who is on a quest, and Broxo, a young warrior with no friends save his horned-beast companion Migo. (Rev: BL 9/15/12; LMC 3–4/13; SLJ 11/12; VOYA 10/12)

3914 Gownley, Jimmy. *The Meaning of Life . . . and Other Stuff* (3–7). Illus. by author. Series: Amelia Rules! 2011, Atheneum paper $10.99 (978-14169861-2-6). This seventh book in the Amelia Rules series finds the protagonist on the verge of puberty and yearning for simpler times. (Rev: BL 9/15/11)

3915 Gownley, Jimmy. *Superheroes* (4–7). Illus. by author. Series: Amelia Rules! 2007, Renaissance paper $14.95 (978-0-9712169-6-9). Amelia's life is a blend of comedy and angst as she faces life after her parents' divorce, a new neighborhood, and new friends. (Rev: BL 9/1/07)

3916 Grant, Alan. *Kidnapped: The Graphic Novel* (5–8). Illus. by Cam Kennedy. 2007, Tundra paper $11.95 (978-0-88776-843-9). A graphic novel adaptation of the story by Robert Louis Stevenson that captures the spirit of the original. (Rev: BL 10/1/07; SLJ 1/08)

3917 Grayson, Devin. *X-Men: Evolution: Hearing Things* (5–8). Illus. by UDON, et al. Series: X-Men Evolution. 2006, ABDO LB $21.35 (978-1-59961-053-5). In this comic-book adventure from the early years of the X-Men series, Jean Grey comes to grips with her telepathic and telekinetic powers. (Rev: SLJ 11/06)

3918 *Green Lantern* (4–10). Series: Showcase Presents. 2005, DC Comics paper $9.99 (978-1-4012-0759-5). A collection of black-and-white reprints of the early comics about the handsome crime fighter. (Rev: SLJ 5/06)

3919 Hague, Michael. *In the Small* (7–10). Illus. by author. 2008, Little, Brown $12.99 (978-0-316-01323-9). In a flash of blue light, the people of the earth are shrunk to a height of six inches or less, changing their lives and leaving them vulnerable to animals — even the household cat; a teen brother and sister seem to offer the only path to salvation. (Rev: BL 3/15/08; SLJ 5/08)

3920 Hale, Shannon, and Dean Hale. *Rapunzel's Revenge* (5–8). Illus. by Nathan Hale. 2008, Bloomsbury $18.99 (978-1-59990-070-4). In the Wild West, a girl called Rapunzel eventually escapes from a prison in a magic tree and uses her hair to gain revenge against the woman who kept her real mother a slave. ALA Notable Books 2009. (Rev: BL 9/1/08; HB 11–12/08; LMC 11–12/08*; SLJ 9/08)

3921 Harper, Charise Mericle. *Fashion Kitty Versus the Fashion Queen* (4–7). Illus. by author. 2007, Hyperion paper $8.99 (978-0-7868-3726-7). Superhero Fashion Kitty (Kiki Kittie's alter ego) continues to rescue victims of fashion emergencies in this funny sequel to *Fashion Kitty* (2005). (Rev: BCCB 7–8/07; SLJ 11/07)

3922 Heuvel, Eric. *A Family Secret* (7–12). Trans. from Dutch by Lorraine T. Miller. Illus. by author. 2009, Farrar $18.99. (978-0-374-32271-7). A contemporary teen learns from his grandmother about the Nazi occupation of the Netherlands and the difficult decisions that people had to make. (Rev: BL 9/15/09*; SLJ 5/10)

3923 Hicks, Faith Erin. *Friends with Boys* (8–12). Illus. by author. 2012, First Second paper $15.99 (978-15964355-6-8). After years of home-schooling, Maggie enters public high school where she must navigate all kinds of challenges, all the while accompanied by the ghost that haunts her. YALSA Great Graphic Novels Top Ten 2013. Lexile GN390L (Rev: BL 2/15/12; HB 5–6/12; LMC 8–9/12; SLJ 3/1/12*; VOYA 6/12)

3924 Hicks, Faith Erin. *The War at Ellsmere* (5–8). Illus. by author. 2008, SLG paper $12.95 (978-1-59362-140-7). The war is between wealthy snobs and a scholarship student at a classy boarding school, with a legendary unicorn thrown into this readable mix. (Rev: BL 3/1/09)

3925 Hinds, Gareth. *Beowulf* (6–9). 2007, Candlewick $21.99 (978-0-7636-3022-5). This atmospheric graphic novel treatment is abridged but faithful to the original themes. (Rev: BL 5/1/07; HB 7–8/07; LMC 10/07; SLJ 5/07)

3926 Hinds, Gareth. *King Lear* (7–10). Illus. by author. 2007, Thecomic.com $30.00 (978-1-893131-07-1); paper $15.95 (978-1-893131-06-4). This graphic adaptation of the Shakespeare play brings visual drama to the abridged story, adding interest to pull in reluctant readers. (Rev: BL 2/1/08)

3927 Hinds, Gareth. *The Merchant of Venice* (8–12). Illus. by author. 2008, Candlewick $21.99 (978-0-7636-3024-9); paper $11.99 (978-0-7636-3025-6). Gray, moody illustrations of characters in modern dress combine with a pared-down story to make this a very engaging version of the play. (Rev: BL 3/15/08; SLJ 5/08)

3928 Hinds, Gareth. *The Odyssey* (7–12). 2010, Candlewick $24.99 (978-0-7636-4266-2). Rich illustrations enhance this faithful graphic-novel rendering of the amazing adventures of Odysseus. Lexile GN840L (Rev: BL 9/15/10*; HB 11–12/10; LMC 11–12/10; SLJ 11/10; VOYA 2/11)

3929 Hino, Matsuri. *Captive Hearts, Vol. 2* (8–11). Illus. by author. Series: Captive Hearts. 2009, VIZ Media paper $8.99 (978-142151933-3). Megumi continues to do anything for Suzuka and her love in the second book in this manga series. (Rev: BLO 4/30/09)

3930 Horowitz, Anthony, and Antony Johnston. *Point Blank: The Graphic Novel* (6–9). Illus. by Kanako Damerum. Series: Alex Rider. 2008, Philomel paper $14.99 (978-0-399-25026-2). A graphic novel presentation of the adventure in which the young British spy infiltrates an exclusive Swiss boarding school. (Rev: BL 3/15/08)

3931 Horowitz, Anthony, and Antony Johnston. *Stormbreaker* (6–9). Illus. by Kanako Damerum. Series: Alex Rider. 2006, Philomel paper $14.99 (978-0-399-24633-3). In this manga-style graphic novel, the infamous young spy named Alex Rider is recruited to work for Britain's elite spy agency after the death of his uncle and must investigate the Stormbreaker computers; this is based on the movie rather than the novel by the same name. (Rev: BL 11/15/06; LMC 11/07)

3932 Hosler, Jay. *Clan Apis* (5–7). 2001, Active Synapse paper $15.00 (978-0-9677255-0-5). Nyuki, a honeybee, describes his hive's history and migration to a new location in a text presented in graphic novel style that includes information about bees and their environment. (Rev: BL 7/01)

3933 Hugo, Victor. *The Hunchback of Notre Dame* (5–12). Retold by Michael Ford. Illus. by Penko Gelev. Series: Graphic Classics. 2007, Barron's $15.99 (978-0-7641-5979-4). The classic story about the misshapen bell ringer is presented in graphic-novel format. (Rev: SLJ 5/07)

3934 Hurd, Damon, and Tatiana Gill. *A Strange Day* (8–12). 2005, Alternative Comics paper $3.95 (978-1-891867-74-3). This appealing graphic novella tells a story of instant attraction between two teens who share the same tastes in music. (Rev: BL 5/1/05)

3935 Igarashi, Daisuke. *Children of the Sea, Vol. 1* (7–12). Illus. by author. 2009, VIZ Media paper $14.99 (978-142152914-1). Fish are disappearing from aquariums around the world and strange children are simultaneously discovered living in the sea; young Ruka feels drawn to the aquarium and sets out to investigate. (Rev: BL 11/1/09*; VOYA 4/10)

3936 Ikezawa, Satomi. *Guru Guru Pon-Chan, Vol. 1* (5–12). Trans. from Japanese by Douglas Varenas. Illus. by author. 2005, Del Rey paper $10.95 (978-0-345-48095-8). In this whimsical shape-changing story, Ponta, a Labrador retriever puppy, nibbles on a newly invented "chit-chat" bone and turns into a human girl who comically retains doggy behavior. (Rev: SLJ 11/05)

3937 Ikumi, Mia. *Tokyo Mew Mew a la Mode, Vol. 1* (5–8). Trans. from Japanese by Yoohae Yang. Illus. by author. 2005, TokyoPop paper $9.99 (978-1-59532-789-5). In the opening volume of the Tokyo Mew Mew a la Mode series, 12-year-old Berry Shirayuki is shanghaied into a team of girl superheroes and soon finds herself doing battle with dragons and the evil Saint Rose Crusaders. (Rev: SLJ 11/05)

3938 Inzana, Ryan. *Ichiro* (7–10). Illus. by author. 2012, Houghton Mifflin $19.99 (978-054725269-8). Ichiro, son of an American soldier who died in battle and a Japanese mother, learns much about his heritage on a visit to his maternal grandfather in Hiroshima City. Lexile GN490L (Rev: BL 3/15/12; HB 3–4/12; LMC 11–12/12; SLJ 3/1/12)

3939 Irwin, Jane, and Jeff Berndt. *Vogelein: Clockwork Faerie* (5–12). 2003, Fiery Studios paper $12.95 (978-0-9743110-0-5). A beautiful 17th-century mechanical fairy who is immortal but depends on others to wind her up stars in this graphic novel. (Rev: BL 11/1/03)

3940 Jablonski, Carla. *Defiance* (7–10). Illus. by Leland Purvis. Series: Resistance. 2011, First Second paper $16.99 (978-15964329-2-5). Paul Tessier, 14, wants to join the French Resistance, and does work for them drawing maps, but he also feels he must look after his younger sister. Lexile GN300L (Rev: BL 6/1/11; HB 9–10/11; SLJ 9/1/11)

3941 Jablonski, Carla. *Resistance* (7–10). Illus. by Leland Purvis. Series: Resistance. 2010, First Second paper $16.99 (978-1-59643-291-8). Marie and Paul help Henri, who is Jewish, reunite with his deported parents in this graphic novel set in World War II. Sydney Taylor Book Honor 2011. Lexile GN190L (Rev: BL 3/15/10*; LMC 8–9/10; SLJ 5/10)

3942 Jablonski, Carla. *Victory* (7–10). Illus. by Leland Purvis. 2012, First Second paper $17.99 (978-159643293-2). The Allies are in Normandy and the Tessier siblings are all working in the Resistance in this final volume in the trilogy, in which Paris is finally liberated. (Rev: BL 6/12; HB 7–8/12; LMC 11–12/12; SLJ 1/13; VOYA 8/12)

3943 Jacques, Brian. *Redwall: The Graphic Novel* (4–7). Illus. by Bret Blevins. Series: Redwall. 2007, Philomel paper $12.99 (978-0-399-24481-0). Redwall makes an effective transition to the graphic novel format with this spirited adaptation. (Rev: BL 9/1/07; SLJ 9/07)

3944 Johns, Geoff. *The Flash, Vol. 2: The Road to Flashpoint* (8–12). Illus. by Scott Kolins. 2012, DC Comics paper $14.99 (978-14012344-8-5). This title provides backstory on the Flash's biggest foe, Eobard Thawne, while also introducing a new villain whose motorcycle travels as fast as the hero's. (Rev: BLO 10/15/12)

3945 Johns, Geoff. *Infinite Crisis* (7–12). 2006, DC Comics $24.99 (978-1-4012-0959-9). Adapted from the DC Comics miniseries, this is a novel of a nasty era for Superman, Batman, Wonderwoman, and other superheros known as the Justice League: already at odds with each other, being hunted down by cyborgs, and having to deal with parallel realities; fans familiar with DC back stories will appreciate this novel. (Rev: BL 11/15/06; SLJ 3/07)

3946 Johns, Geoff. *JSA: Black Reign* (7–12). Illus. by Rags Morales, et al. 2005, DC Comics paper $12.99 (978-1-4012-0480-8). In a setting reminiscent of present-day Iraq, superhero Black Adam fights for an unpopular cause and faces strong opposition from the people he's trying to help. (Rev: SLJ 11/05)

3947 Johns, Geoff. *Teen Titans: The Future Is Now* (5–8). Series: Teen Titans. 2005, DC Comics paper $9.99 (978-1-4012-0475-4). In volume four of the series, the title characters return from a mission into the future to learn that Robin's father died while they were away. (Rev: BL 3/15/06)

3948 Johns, Geoff, and Jeff Katz. *Blue and Gold* (6–12). Illus. by Norm Rapmund. 2008, DC Comics $24.99 (978-140121956-7). Booster Gold and Blue Beetle travel through time and encounter fellow superheroes in this engaging adventure. (Rev: BLO 2/9/09)

3949 Johnson, Dan Curtis, and J. H. Williams. *Snow: Batman* (6–12). 2007, DC Comics paper $14.99 (978-1-4012-1265-0). Early in his crime-fighting career, Batman confronts a superpowered villain named Mr. Freeze. (Rev: BL 5/15/07)

3950 Johnson, Nathan, and Matt Yamashita. *Ghostbusters: Ghost Busted* (6–10). Illus. by Chrissy Delk. 2008, Tokyopop $12.99 (978-142781459-3). Based on the 1984 movie about ghostbusting, this manga is filled with comedy, ghosts, and adventure. **e** (Rev: BL 1/1–15/09; LMC 8–9/09)

3951 Jolley, Dan. *My Boyfriend Bites* (7–10). Illus. by Alitha E. Martinez. Series: My Boyfriend Is a Monster. 2011, Lerner/Graphic Universe LB $29.27 (978-076135599-1); paper $9.95 (978-076137078-9). In this light paranormal romance Vanessa discovers that her janitor boyfriend Jean-Paul has a hidden side. Lexile GN360L (Rev: BL 10/15/11)

3952 Jones, Frewin. *Lamia's Revenge: The Serpent Awakes* (8–11). Illus. by Alison Acton. Series: The Faerie Path. 2009, Tokyopop paper $7.99 (978-006145694-7). Teen faerie princess Tania sets out to rescue her mortal parents in this manga version. (Rev: BLO 4/30/09)

3953 Joong-Ki, Park. *Shaman Warrior, Vol. 1* (7–12). Illus. by Park Joong Ki. 2007, Dark Horse paper $12.95 (978-1-59307-638-2). A battle-filled Korean manhwa tale featuring Shaman Warrior Master Yarong and his devoted servant Batu. (Rev: BL 8/07)

3954 Kanno, Aya. *Otomen, Vol. 1* (8–12). Illus. by author. 2009, VIZ Media paper $8.99 (978-1-4215-2186-2). Readers meet Asuka, a teenage boy who embraces his feminine side, in this first installment in the series. (Rev: BLO 2/9/09)

3955 Kawamura, Mika. *Panic X Panic, Vol. 1* (7–10). Illus. by author. 2010, Del Rey paper $10.99 (978-03455146-3-9). A race of evil demons locked up for millennia gets loose and begins to wreak havoc on mankind in this entertaining manga. (Rev: BLO 3/15/10)

3956 Kelly, Joe. *Justice League Elite, Vol. 1* (8–12). Illus. by Doug Mahnke and John Byrne. 2005, DC Comics paper $19.99 (978-1-4012-0481-5). Superman and other members of the Justice League clash with the rival Justice League Elite over strategies for dealing with evildoers. (Rev: BL 10/1/05; SLJ 11/05)

3957 Kesel, Barbara. *Meridian: Flying Solo* (7–12). Series: Meridian. 2003, CrossGeneration paper $9.95 (978-1-931484-54-1). Sephie inherits her father's position as first minister of Meridian, a floating city, and must use her magical powers to battle an evil uncle. (Rev: BL 4/1/03)

3958 Kibuishi, Kazu. *Copper* (5–8). 2010, Graphix paper $12.99 (978-0-545-09893-9). A collection of funny short stories, in graphic novel format, featuring a boy named Copper and his fraidy-cat talking dog Fred; with author comments on how he creates comic strips. (Rev: BL 12/1/09; LMC 3–4/10; SLJ 5/10)

3959 Kibuishi, Kazu. *The Last Council* (4–7). Illus. by author. Series: Amulet. 2011, Scholastic paper $10.99 (978-05452088-7-1). Emily and her friends arrive in the cloud city of Cielis and find themselves in a contest for a seat on the Guardian Council. Lexile GN400L (Rev: BL 10/15/11)

3960 Kibuishi, Kazu. *Prince of the Elves* (4–7). Illus. by author. Series: Amulet. 2012, Scholastic paper $12.99 (978-05452088-9-5). In the fifth book in the series, war is looming over the city of Cielis and Emily and her friends must meet the Elf King. Lexile 400L (Rev: BLO 9/15/12; SLJ 9/12)

3961 Kibuishi, Kazu. *The Stonekeeper* (4–7). Illus. by author. Series: Amulet. 2008, Scholastic $21.99 (978-0-439-84680-6); paper $9.99 (978-0-439-84681-3). Emily's father is killed in a car crash and her mother swallowed by a monster after opening a doorway to another world in this first volume in the series. (Rev: BL 12/1/07; LMC 2/08; SLJ 1/08)

3962 Kibuishi, Kazu. *The Stonekeeper's Curse* (4–7). Series: Amulet. 2009, Graphix $21.99 (978-0-439-84682-0). This sequel to *The Stonekeeper* (2007) has Emily and Navin searching for a remedy that will save their mother from poison, even as the evil Elf King is in pursuit. (Rev: BL 10/15/09; LMC 1–2/10; SLJ 11/09)

3963 Kim, Susan, and Laurence Klavan. *City of Spies* (4–7). Illus. by Pascal Dizin. 2010, First Second paper $16.99 (978-1-59643-262-8). Evelyn and her friend Tony expose Nazi spies in this story set in New York in 1942. (Rev: BL 3/15/10*; LMC 8–9/10; SLJ 5/10)

3964 Kindt, Matt. *2 Sisters* (8–12). 2004, Top Shelf paper $19.95 (978-1-891830-58-7). In this graphic novel thriller, set in Europe during World War II, Elle, a volunteer ambulance driver, is recruited as a spy and dispatched on perilous missions behind enemy lines. (Rev: BL 11/1/04)

3965 Kipling, Rudyard, and Lewis Helfand. *Kim* (5–8). Illus. by Rakesh Kumar. 2011, Campfire paper $9.99 (978-93800284-2-2). The classic story of the boy who becomes a spy is presented in graphic-novel format with accessible text and colorful illustrations. (Rev: BL 1/1–15/11; LMC 5–6/11)

3966 Kiyuouki, Satoko. *Shoulder-A-Coffin Kuro, Vol. 2* (8–11). Illus. by author. Series: Shoulder-A-Coffin Kuro. 2008, Yen paper $10.99 (978-075952901-4). Little Kuro seeks to rid herself of her coffin as she travels through an eerie land and encounters creepy and dangerous characters; an unusual manga full of humor. (Rev: BLO 1/13/09; SLJ 5/09)

3967 Knaak, Richard A. *Dragon Hunt* (7–10). Illus. by Jae-Hwan Kim. Series: Warcraft Sunwell. 2005, Tokyo-Pop paper $9.99 (978-1-59532-712-3). In the first volume of a graphic novel trilogy, Kalec, a shape-changing dragon, and Anveena race to reach the all-powerful Sunwell before the villainous Dar'khan can get to it. (Rev: BL 6/1–15/05; SLJ 7/05)

3968 Kobayashi, Jin. *School Rumble, Vol. 1* (7–12). Adapted by William Flanagan. 2006, Del Rey paper $10.95 (978-0-345-49147-3). This romantic manga-style comedy features high school student Tsukamoto Tenma, who has a crush on the oblivious Karasuma Oji and is meanwhile the object of Harima Kenji's desires. (Rev: SLJ 7/06)

3969 Kobayashi, Makoto. *Planet of the Cats* (5–8). Series: What's Michael? 2006, Dark Horse paper $9.95 (978-1-59307-525-5). In this 11th, concluding volume of the graphic novel series first published in Japan, Hanako, a human exobiologist, and her spaceship crew find themselves stranded on a planet ruled by house cats. (Rev: BL 9/1/06)

3970 Kobayashi, Makoto. *Sleepless Nights* (5–8). Series: What's Michael? 2005, Dark Horse paper $8.95

(978-1-59307-337-4). Volume ten of the continuing adventures of the house cat who has been described as "Japan's version of Garfield, Heathcliff, and Krazy Kat all rolled into one." (Rev: BL 9/1/05)

3971 Kovac, Tommy. *Wonderland* (4–8). Illus. by Sonny Liew. 2009, Disney $19.99 (978-1-4231-0451-3). A chaotic graphic Alice in Wonderland novel from the point of view of the terribly tidy maid, Mary Ann. (Rev: BCCB 6/09; BL 5/15/09; SLJ 5/09)

3972 Krueger, Jim. *Justice 1* (7–12). 2006, DC Comics $19.99 (978-1-4012-0969-8). Lex Luthor, the Riddler, and other villains join forces to eradicate the Justice League superheroes in this volume illustrated by the award-winning Alex Ross. (Rev: BL 11/15/06)

3973 Kubert, Joe. *Yossel: April 19, 1943: A Story of the Warsaw Ghetto Uprising* (8–12). 2003, iBooks $24.95 (978-0-7434-7516-7). In this graphic novel, Yossel and his friends fight to the death against their Nazi oppressors. (Rev: BL 2/1/04; SLJ 7/04)

3974 Kurata, Hideyuki. *Train + Train, Vol. 1* (8–11). Illus. by Tomomasa Takuma. 2007, Go! Comi paper $10.99 (978-1-933617-18-3). On the way to school on the distant planet of Deloca, Reiichi Sakakusa meets a wild teen named Arena, who changes his life. (Rev: BL 8/07)

3975 Kusakabe, Rei. *Nephylym, Vol. 2* (8–12). Illus. by author. Series: Nephylym. 2008, DrMaster paper $9.99 (978-159796182-0). Sexy yet cute creatures team with humans to battle Noir, the personification of negativity. (Rev: BLO 2/9/09)

3976 Kusakawa, Nari. *The Recipe for Gertrude* (6–9). 2006, DC Comics paper $9.99 (978-1-4012-1110-3). Gertrude, who looks like a teenage boy but is really a man-made demon built from parts of other demons, is searching for the recipe that made him with the help of a high school girl named Sahara. (Rev: BL 10/1/06; LMC 3/07; SLJ 11/06)

3977 Kwitney, Alisa. *Token* (8–10). Illus. by Joelle Jones. 2008, DC Comics paper $9.99 (978-140121538-5). Jewish 15-year-old Shira and her widowed father struggle to cope with their changing lives — which include Shira's father's relationship with his secretary and her own romance with a young Spaniard — in 1980s Miami Beach. (Rev: BL 11/15/08; LMC 5–6/09)

3978 Kye, Seung-Hui. *Recast* (8–11). 2006, TokyoPop $9.99 (978-1-59816-664-4). JDs grandfather, a master magician, is in danger of assassination in this action- and humor-filled manga. (Rev: BL 2/1/07)

3979 Kyoko, Ariyoshi. *The Swan* (6–9). 2004, DC Comics paper $9.95 (978-1-4012-0535-5). In this appealing shoujo — manga designed to appeal especially to girls — a young Japanese girl from a rural area seeks to realize her dreams of becoming a prima ballerina. (Rev: BL 2/15/05)

3980 L'Engle, Madeleine, and Hope Larson. *A Wrinkle in Time* (6–12). Illus. by Hope Larson. 2012, Farrar $19.99 (978-037438615-3). This graphic novel adaptation stays true to the breadth and spirit of L'Engle's original. YALSA Great Graphic Novels for Teens 2013. **e** Lexile 740L (Rev: BL 10/15/12*; LMC 5–6/13; SLJ 11/12)

3981 Larson, Hope. *Chiggers* (6–8). Illus. by author. 2008, Atheneum $17.99 (978-1-4169-3584-1); paper $9.99 (978-1-4169-3587-2). Summer is different this year for Abby, as last year's camp friendships shift and change. (Rev: BL 4/15/08; SLJ 7/08)

3982 Lat. *Kampung Boy* (8–11). 2006, Roaring Brook paper $16.95 (978-1-59643-121-8). This funny and eloquent autobiographical graphic novel follows the childhood of a Muslim boy named Mat as he grows up in a small Malaysian town in the 1950s, giving details on the traditions of his kampung (village), and ending with his departure to attend a boarding school. (Rev: BL 9/15/06; SLJ 11/06*)

3983 Lee, Stan. *The Fantastic Four, Vol. 1* (5–10). Illus. by Jack Kirby. 2009, Marvel paper $24.99 (978-0-7851-3710-8). This volume collects the first 10 stories about the four who returned to Earth with superhuman abilities after being exposed to cosmic rays. (Rev: BLO 4/30/09)

3984 Loeb, Jeph. *Hulk, Vol. 1: Red Hulk* (6–12). Illus. by Ed McGuinness. Series: Hulk. 2009, Marvel paper $19.99 (978-078512882-3). Good old-fashioned superhero action for Marvel comics fans. (Rev: BL 4/15/09)

3985 London, Jack. *The Call of the Wild: The Graphic Novel* (6–9). Ed. by Neil Kleid. Illus. by Alex Niño. Series: Puffin Graphics. 2006, Penguin paper $10.99 (978-0-14-240571-0). Jack London's classic tale in graphic format. (Rev: BL 4/1/06; SLJ 3/06)

3986 Love, Courtney, and D. J. Milky. *Princess Ai: Lumination, Vol. 2* (7–12). Trans. from Japanese by Kimiko Fujikawa and Yuki N. Johnson. Illus. by Misaho Kujiradou. 2005, TokyoPop paper $9.99 (978-1-59182-670-5). In volume two of the Princess Ai series, the title character, an aspiring rock star, turns ever more angelic as her music career begins to take off. (Rev: SLJ 11/05)

3987 Lovecraft, H. P., and I. N. J. Culbard. *At the Mountains of Madness* (7–12). Illus. by I. N. J. Culbard. 2012, Sterling paper $14.95 (978-14027804-2-4). An effective graphic novel adaptation of Lovecraft's dark novel about an expedition to the Antarctic. (Rev: BL 3/15/12)

3988 Lutes, Jason, and Nick Bertozzi. *Houdini: The Handcuff King* (6–9). 2007, Hyperion $16.99 (978-0-7868-3902-5). This graphic novel centers on Houdini's jump into the Boston River in 1908 and provides information on his character and achievements. (Rev: BCCB 6/07; BL 3/15/07; LMC 8–9/07; SLJ 7/07)

3989 Ma, Wing Shing. *Storm Riders: Invading Sun, Vol. 1* (8–12). 2003, ComicsOne paper $9.95 (978-1-58899-359-5). Martial arts and an alternate China are featured in this graphic novel about two expert fighters who set out to find their former master named Conquer. (Rev: BL 2/1/04)

3990 McCaffrey, Anne. *Dragonflight* (6–12). Adapted by Brynne Stephens. Series: Dragonriders of Pern. 1991, Eclipse Books $4.95 (978-1-56060-074-9). Book one of a three-part graphic novel based on *Dragonflight* from the Dragonriders of Pern series. (Rev: BL 9/1/91)

3991 McCann, Jim. *Return of the Dapper Men* (7–10). Illus. by Janet Lee. 2010, Archaia $24.95 (978-193238690-5). In a world where children live underground and robots inhabit houses overhead, time has stopped and is only restarted with the arrival of 314 Dapper Men. (Rev: BL 2/15/11*)

3992 McClintock, Norah. *I, Witness* (7–10). Illus. by Mike Deas. 2012, Orca paper $16.95 (978-15546978--9-2). Witnessing a murder poses questions for Boone — should he speak up or not? — and as things go from bad to worse, the conflicts deepen. Lexile HL270L (Rev: BL 11/15/12; SLJ 1/13; VOYA 2/13)

3993 McCloud, Scott. *The New Adventures of Abraham Lincoln* (7–10). 1998, Homage Comics paper $19.00 (978-1-887279-87-1). Time travel, an encounter with Abraham Lincoln, and an alien attempt to rule America are some of the adventures faced by a middle-school student when he is sent to detention. (Rev: BL 2/1/03)

3994 MacDonald, Fiona. *Dracula* (6–9). Illus. by Penko Gelev. Series: Graphic Classics. 2007, Barron's LB $15.99 (978-0-7641-6054-7). A graphic retelling of the classic story, with illustrations that will draw in reluctant readers plus a biography of Stoker, a history of vampires, and highlighting of SAT vocabulary words. (Rev: BL 2/8/08; SLJ 1/08)

3995 Marazano, Richard. *The Chimpanzee Complex, Vol. 1: Paradox* (7–12). Illus. by Jean-Michel Ponzio. 2009, Cinebook paper $13.95 (978-18491800-2-3). Young Sophia's astronaut mom becomes distracted by a sci-fi mystery: Buzz Aldrin and Neil Armstrong have returned from space more than 60 years after the Apollo XI mission. (Rev: BLO 3/15/10)

3996 Marder, Larry. *Beanworld: Wahoolazuma* (8–12). Illus. by author. Series: Beanworld. 2009, Dark Horse $19.95 (978-159582240-6). A collection of comics first published in the 1980s, *Wahoolazuma* features a world populated by beans who learn they are dependent on one another and on the environment. (Rev: BL 4/15/09)

3997 Marr, Melissa. *Sanctuary: Desert Tales, Vol. 1* (8–11). Illus. by Xian Nu Studio. Series: Wicked Lovely: Desert Tales. 2009, Tokyopop paper $9.99 (978-006149354-6). This first volume in a new manga trilogy is set in a world familiar to Marr's readers and features Rika, a faery living in the Mojave Desert who becomes involved with a mortal young man. ℮ (Rev: BLO 6/16/09; SLJ 7/09)

3998 Marunas, Nathaniel. *Manga Claus: The Blade of Kringle* (5–8). Illus. by Erik Craddock. 2006, Penguin $12.99 (978-1-59514-134-7). In this graphic novel Christmas tale, a disgruntled elf triggers a series of events that wrecks Santa's North Pole workshop and threatens to ruin Christmas for millions of children around the world. (Rev: BL 10/15/06; SLJ 10/06)

3999 Mashima, Hiro. *Fairy Tail, Vol. 1* (7–12). Trans. from Japanese by William Flanagan. Adapted by William Flanagan. Illus. by author. 2008, Del Rey paper $10.95 (978-0-345-50133-2). Lucy wants to join a wizards club called the Fairy Tail in this boisterous fantasy full of oddball characters; the first in a series. (Rev: SLJ 5/08)

4000 Mechner, Jordan. *Solomon's Thieves* (6–10). Illus. by Pham LeUyen and Alex Puvilland. 2010, First Second paper $12.99 (978-1-59643-391-5). The very existence of the Knights Templar is threatened and they must fight for their lives and their treasure in early 14th-century France. (Rev: BL 4/15/10; LMC 8–9/10; SLJ 7/10)

4001 Melville, Herman. *Moby Dick* (5–12). Retold by Sophie Furse. Illus. by Penko Gelev. Series: Graphic Classics. 2007, Barron's $15.99 (978-0-7641-5977-0). The classic story about the giant white whale is presented in graphic novel format. (Rev: SLJ 5/07)

4002 Misako Rocks!. *Biker Girl* (5–8). Illus. by author. 2006, Hyperion paper $7.99 (978-0-7868-3676-5). Aki, a shy, bookish girl, is transformed into a superhero after finding a discarded bicycle in her grandfather's garage. (Rev: BL 3/15/06; SLJ 9/06)

4003 Mizuno, Ryo. *Record of Lodoss War: The Grey Witch — Birth of a New Knight* (7–12). Illus. by Yoshihiko Ochi. Series: Grey Witch Trilogy. 2000, CPM Comics $15.95 (978-1-56219-928-9). This graphic novel is the second volume of the Grey Witch Trilogy and tells how Pam struggles to learn the identity of his father in a universe where gods, goddesses, and goblins exist. (Rev: BL 12/1/00)

4004 Monroe, Kevin. *El Zombo Fantasma* (7–10). 2005, Dark Horse paper $9.95 (978-1-59307-284-1). In this eye-popping superhero graphic novel, Mexican wrestler El Zombo Fantasma, murdered for throwing a match, seeks to avoid eternal damnation by becoming guardian angel to a feisty 10-year-old and tracking down his own killer. (Rev: BL 3/15/05; VOYA 8/05)

4005 Moore, Terry. *Spider-Man Loves Mary Jane: Sophomore Jinx* (7–9). Illus. by Craig Rousseau. Series: Spider-Man Loves Mary Jane. 2009, Marvel $19.99 (978-078513004-8). Mary Jane and Peter are sophomores in high school and dealing with everyday issues as well as some that are not-so-everyday. (Rev: BLO 5/27/09)

4006 Mori, Kaoru. *Shirley, Vol. 1* (7–10). Illus. by author. 2008, DC Comics paper $9.99 (978-1-4012-1777-8). Set in Edwardian England, this manga novel follows the life of an endearing 13-year-old orphan who gets a job as a maid for a cafe owner. (Rev: BLO 12/30/08)

4007 Morrison, Grant. *Vimanarama* (8–12). Illus. by Philip Bond. 2006, Vertigo paper $12.99 (978-1-4012-0496-9). In Bradford, England, Ali — 19-year-old son of Pakistani immigrants — and his arranged bride-to-be Sofia become embroiled in a battle against evil when an ancient spirit is released. (Rev: BL 2/1/06; SLJ 5/06)

4008 Mowll, Joshua. *Operation Red Jericho* (8–11). Series: Guild Trilogy. 2005, Candlewick $15.99 (978-0-7636-2634-1). In this first volume of a trilogy set in the early 20th century, teens Becca and Doug MacKenzie search for their parents, who disappeared in China, and document their exciting adventures. (Rev: BL 11/15/05; SLJ 12/05)

4009 Mucci, Tim. *The Odyssey* (5–8). Illus. by Emanuel Tenderini. 2010, Sterling paper $7.95 (978-1-4027-3155-6). This graphic novel emphasizes Odysseus's various adventures on his journey home — with Circe, Calypso, the cyclops, the sirens, and so forth. (Rev: BL 4/15/10*; LMC 10/10; SLJ 7/10)

4010 Mucha, Corinne. *Freshman: Tales of 9th Grade Obsessions, Revelations, and Other Nonsense* (7–10). Illus. by author. 2011, Zest paper $12.99 (978-09819733-6-4). Annie and her friends navigate the choppy waters of their freshman year at high school. (Rev: BLO 9/1/11; LMC 11–12/11)

4011 Murakami, Maki. *Kanpai! Vol. 1* (8–12). Trans. from Japanese by Christine Schilling. Illus. by author. 2005, TokyoPop paper $9.99 (978-1-59532-317-0). Yamada finds himself torn between his rigid training to be a monster guardian and his infatuation with attractive Taino Municipal Middle School classmate Nao. (Rev: SLJ 1/06)

4012 Muth, Jon. *Swamp Thing: Roots* (8–12). 1998, DC Comics paper $7.95 (978-1-56389-377-3). Visual images enhance this story of the supernatural elements that influence life in a small community. (Rev: BL 2/1/03)

4013 Neel, Julien. *Secret Diary* (4–7). Trans. by Carol Klio Burrell. Illus. by author. 2012, Lerner/Graphic Universe LB $27.93 (978-076138776-3); paper $8.95 (978-076138868-5). Lou, 12, contends with her shiftless single mom, the mean girls at school, and her timidity about dating in this appealing graphic novel. ℮ (Rev: BL 3/15/12; LMC 11–12/12; SLJ 7/1/12)

4014 Nelson, O. T., and Dan Jolley. *The Girl Who Owned a City* (6–9). Illus. by Joelle Jones. 2012, Lerner/Graphic Universe $29.27 (978-076134903-7); paper $9.95 (978-07613563-4-9). All the adults have been killed by a virus, and 10-year-old Lisa proves an effective leader of the children on her block in the face of rival gangs; a graphic-novel version of the 1975 novel. Lexile GN420L (Rev: BL 3/15/12; LMC 11–12/12; SLJ 3/1/12)

4015 Neri, Filippo. *Steam Park* (6–9). Illus. by Piero Ruggeri. 2007, Simply Read $16.95 (978-1-894965-63-7). A carnival turns sinister in this wordless, darkly humorous story in which children are saved from a menacing carnival worker by the attractions themselves. (Rev: BL 3/15/07)

4016 Nicieza, Fabian. *A Stake to the Heart* (8–12). 2004, Dark Horse paper $12.95 (978-1-59307-012-0). Angel's efforts to help Buffy and Dawn cope with their parents' problems backfire in this graphic novel that precedes the events of the TV show. (Rev: BL 6/1–15/04)

4017 Niles, Steve, and Scott Hampton. *Gotham County Line: Batman* (7–12). 2006, DC Comics paper $17.99 (978-1-4012-0905-6). Batman takes on a mysterious case of suburban murders, finds that logic (his usual method) is not leading to the solution this time, and must deal with the supernatural in this well-illustrated story. (Rev: BL 12/1/06)

4018 Nishiyama, Yuriko. *Harlem Beat* (8–12). 1999, To-kyoPop paper $9.95 (978-1-892213-04-4). Created and produced in Japan, this graphic novel follows the adventures of an urban, teenage boy who loves basketball. (Rev: BL 2/1/03)

4019 No, Yee-Jung. *Visitor, Vol. 1* (7–10). Trans. from Japanese by Jennifer Hahm. Illus. by author. 2005, To-kyoPop paper $9.99 (978-1-59532-342-2). On her first day at a new school, Hyo-Bin attracts a number of admirers, but she rebuffs them all, fearful that they could be harmed by the magical powers she's not yet learned to control. (Rev: SLJ 9/05)

4020 Nykko. *The Master of Shadows* (4–7). Trans. by Carol Kilo Burrell. Illus. by Bannister. Series: Else-Where Chronicles. 2009, Graphic Universe LB $27.93 (978-076134461-2); paper $6.95 (978-076134744-6). Max, Rebecca, Theo, and Noah must tackle the Master of Shadows in their continuing search for a way to escape the strange world of ElseWhere. (Rev: BL 4/15/09; LMC 10/09; SLJ 5/09) [741.5]

4021 Nykko. *The Shadow Spies. Bk. 2* (4–8). Illus. by Bannister. Series: The ElseWhere Chronicles. 2009, Lerner LB $27.93 (978-0-7613-4460-5); paper $6.95 (978-0-7613-3964-9). Max, Theo, Noah, and Rebecca enter a strange world called ElseWhere and must evade the Shadow Spies to get back home. (Rev: LMC 10/09; SLJ 5/09)

4022 O'Connor, George. *Athena: Grey-Eyed Goddess* (5–9). Illus. by author. 2010, Roaring Brook $16.99 (978-159643649-7); paper $9.99 (978-15964343-2-5). A graphic-novel retelling of the myths involving Athena, the Greek goddess of wisdom and war. (Rev: BL 5/1/10; SLJ 5/10)

4023 O'Connor, George. *Hades: Lord of the Dead* (6–9). Illus. by author. Series: Olympians. 2012, First Second $16.99 (978-159643761-6); paper $9.99 (978-15964343-4-9). A graphic-novel retelling of the story of Persephone and Hades. Lexile GN710L (Rev: BL 1/1/12; SLJ 3/1/12*; VOYA 4/10) [398.2]

4024 O'Connor, George. *Hera: The Goddess and Her Glory* (6–9). Illus. by author. 2011, First Second $16.99 (978-159643724-1); paper $9.99 (978-15964343-3-2). This graphic novel introduces the life of Hera, Zeus's powerful queen. Lexile GN650L (Rev: BL 5/1/11; SLJ 9/1/11; VOYA 10/11)

4025 O'Connor, George. *Zeus: King of the Gods* (5–9). Series: Olympians. 2010, First Second paper $9.99 (978-1-59643-431-8). The first of a series of graphic novels based on mythology, this is a good introduction to Zeus and his circle. (Rev: BL 1/1/10; LMC 8–9/10; SLJ 3/10) [741.5]

4026 O'Donnell, Liam. *Max Finder Mystery: Collected Casebook, Vol. 1* (4–7). Illus. by Michael Cho. 2009, Owlkids paper $9.95 (978-2-8957-9116-4). First published in *Owl Magazine*, this graphic novel collection includes 10 mysteries starring 7th-graders Max Finder and Alison Santos that invite the reader to help solve the case — answers and puzzles are included. Also use volumes 2 and 3. (Rev: BL 7/09)

4027 O'Donnell, Liam. *Soccer Sabotage* (4–7). Illus. by Mike Deas. Series: Graphic Guide Adventure. 2009, Orca paper $9.95 (978-1-55143-884-9). Why is their soccer team experiencing so many problems in the national under-18 tournament? Nadia and Devin investigate in this mystery full of soccer tips. (Rev: BL 3/1/09; SLJ 9/09)

4028 Okamoto, Kazuhiro. *Translucent, Vol. 1* (6–10). Trans. by Heidi Plechl. Illus. by author. Series: Translucent. 2007, Dark Horse paper $9.95 (978-1-59307-647-4). Quiet 8th-grader Shizuka is slowly becoming invisible as a result of a strange disease called the Translucent Syndrome but Mamoru — a possible romantic interest? — and Keiko both help her cope and give her hope for the future. (Rev: BL 2/13/08)

4029 Ono, Fuyumi. *Ghost Hunt, Vol. 3* (8–12). Trans. from Japanese by Akira Tsubasa. Illus. by Shiho Inada. 2006, Del Rey paper $10.95 (978-0-345-48626-4). Seventeen-year-old Naru and his paranormal detective agency investigate strange goings-on at the local high school. (Rev: SLJ 5/06)

4030 Park, Sang-Sun. *Ark Angels, Vol. 1* (6–12). Trans. from Japanese by Monica Seya. Illus. by author. 2005, TokyoPop paper $9.99 (978-1-59816-262-2). Three superhero sisters try to juggle being normal teenagers and saving the world from destruction. (Rev: SLJ 5/06)

4031 Patterson, James. *Maximum Ride, Vol. 1* (7–10). Illus. by NaRae Lee. Series: Maximum Ride. 2009, Yen paper $10.99 (978-075952951-9). A manga adaptation of the series by the same name, this story introduces readers to a group of mutant teenagers living in a dangerous world. **e** (Rev: BL 3/1/09; SLJ 5/09)

4032 Patterson, James, and Leopold Gout. *Alien Hunter* (5–8). Illus. by Klaus Lyngeled. 2008, Little, Brown paper $9.99 (978-0-316-00425-1). This action-packed graphic novel follows the exploits of Daniel, an orphaned alien who hunts evil extraterrestrials on Earth. (Rev: BL 10/1/08; SLJ 11/08; VOYA 6/08)

4033 Pérez, George. *Wonder Woman: Destiny Calling, Vol. 4* (8–12). Illus. by author, et al. 2006, DC Comics paper $19.99 (978-1-4012-0943-8). Collects the last five issues of Wonder Woman, in which she investigates the death of her publicist, reveals much about her early home on Themyscira, and must rescue Earth from the god Hermes. (Rev: SLJ 11/06)

4034 Petersen, David. *Mouse Guard: Fall 1152* (7–12). Illus. by Philip Jacobs. 2007, Archaia Studios $24.95 (978-1-932386-57-8). The excellent art will draw readers into this story of about three mice — Saxon, Kenzie and Lieam — who, as part of the Mouse Guard, patrol the Mouse Territories borders, and battle to keep the inhabitants safe. (Rev: BL 9/1/07; LMC 1/08)

4035 Petrucha, Stefan. *Nancy Drew: The Demon of River Heights* (4–9). Series: Nancy Drew, Girl Detective. 2005, Papercutz $12.95 (978-1-59707-004-1). The familiar heroine returns in graphic-novel format with this story in which Nancy, Bess, George discover the secret behind a legendary monster. (Rev: SLJ 8/05)

4036 Phelan, Matt. *The Storm in the Barn* (5–8). 2009, Candlewick $24.99 (978-0-7636-3618-0). In 1937 Kansas 11-year-old Jack faces many challenges — bullies, a sister with problems, and above all the hardships of the Dust Bowl — to which he may have a solution. ALA Notable Books 2010. (Rev: BL 8/09*; LMC 11–12/09; SLJ 9/09)

4037 Plessix, Michel. *The Wind in the Willows. Rev. ed.* (4–7). Illus. by author. Series: Classics Illustrated Deluxe. 2008, Papercutz $17.95 (978-1-59707-095-9); paper $13.95 (978-1-59707-096-6). The classic animal story, presented in a graphic format with beautiful illustrations. (Rev: BL 3/18/08)

4038 Poe, Marshall. *Sons of Liberty* (3–7). Illus. by Leland Purvis. Series: Turning Points. 2008, Simon & Schuster paper $7.99 (978-1-4169-5067-7). Young Nathaniel joins the cause of the American Revolution and even meets Samuel Adams and Paul Revere as he fights for the young nation. (Rev: LMC 1/09; SLJ 7/08)

4039 Pomplun, Tom, ed. *Arthur Conan Doyle* (8–11). Series: Graphic Classics. 2005, Eureka paper $11.95 (978-0-9746648-5-9). This revised edition adds several non-Holmes stories to the collection. (Rev: BL 9/15/05; SLJ 11/05; VOYA 4/06)

4040 Pomplun, Tom, ed. *Gothic Classics, vol. 14* (8–12). Illus. by Anne Timmons, et al. Series: Graphic Clas-

sics. 2007, Eureka paper $11.95 (978-0-9787919-0-2). Poe, Austen, and Radcliffe are only three of the authors whose works are adapted here with effective illustrations. (Rev: BL 9/1/07; SLJ 9/07)

4041 Pomplun, Tom, ed. *Graphic Classics: Edgar Allan Poe* (8–12). 2006, Eureka paper $11.95 (978-0-9746648-7-3). This is a graphic novel collection of classic Poe stories. (Rev: BL 6/1–15/06; LMC 1/07)

4042 Raicht, Mike. *Spider-Man: Kraven the Hunter* (5–8). Illus. by Jamal Igle, et al. Series: Spider-Man. 2006, ABDO LB $21.35 (978-1-59961-009-2). Spider-Man once again does battle with Kraven the Hunter, one of his oldest enemies. (Rev: SLJ 11/06)

4043 Raymond, Alex, and Don Moore. *Alex Raymond's Flash Gordon, Vol. 2* (8–12). 2004, Checker paper $19.95 (978-0-9741664-6-9). The second volume of the Flash Gordon series collects comic strips that first appeared in 1935 and 1936. (Rev: BL 10/1/04)

4044 Reed, Gary. *Mary Shelley's Frankenstein: The Graphic Novel* (7–10). Illus. by Frazer Irving. Series: Puffin Graphics. 2005, Penguin paper $10.99 (978-0-14-240407-2). This graphic novel adaptation accurately conveys the dominant themes of the classic. (Rev: BL 3/15/05; SLJ 9/05; VOYA 8/05)

4045 Reed, M. K. *Americus* (7–10). Illus. by Jonathan Hill. 2011, First Second $18.99 (978-159643768-5); paper $14.99 (978-15964360-1-5). On the verge of beginning high school, shy Neil finds the courage to stand up for what he likes when there is an effort to ban his favorite fantasy series from the local library. Lexile GN550L (Rev: BL 9/15/11; LMC 3–4/12*; SLJ 9/1/11)

4046 Renier, Aaron. *Spiral Bound: Top Secret Summer* (4–7). 2005, Top Shelf paper $14.95 (978-1-891830-50-1). This delightful graphic novel chronicles the summer adventures of the animal residents of the Town, a community with a monster in its pond. (Rev: BL 11/1/05)

4047 Renier, Aaron. *The Unsinkable Walker Bean* (5–8). Illus. by author. 2010, First Second paper $13.99 (978-159643453-0). Exciting action rules in this imaginative story of courageous young Walter's dangerous quest to return a pearl skull to the witches on the Mango Islands. (Rev: BL 6/1/10*; LMC 3–4/11; SLJ 9/10; VOYA 6/10)

4048 Rioux, Jo. *The Golden Twine* (4–7). Illus. by author. 2012, Kids Can $17.95 (978-155453636-8); paper $9.95 (978-15545363-7-5). Suri, an orphan living in a traveling caravan, is determined to prove herself a monster tamer. Lexile 260L (Rev: BL 8/12; LMC 5–6/13; SLJ 11/12)

4049 Robbins, Trina. *The Drained Brains Caper* (4–7). Illus. by Tyler Page. Series: Chicagoland Detective Agency. 2010, Lerner/Graphic Universe LB $29.27 (978-076134601-2); paper $6.95 (978-076135635-6). New to summer school, Megan, 13, soon becomes suspicious about the principal's motives and seeks help from computer genius Raf. The second volume is *The

Maltese Mummy (2011). Lexile GN390L (Rev: BL 9/15/10; LMC 1–2/11; SLJ 11/10)

4050 Rodi, Rob. *Crossovers* (5–12). 2003, CrossGeneration paper $15.95 (978-1-931484-85-5). This graphic novel is an entertaining look at a suburban family whose members possess a unique power. (Rev: BL 2/1/04)

4051 Roman, Dave. *Agnes Quill: An Anthology of Mystery* (8–10). Illus. by John Ho. 2006, SLG paper $10.95 (978-1-59362-052-3). Agnes — a girl with the ability to speak to the dead — investigates the supernatural and the gory in this anthology, illustrated by four different artists. (Rev: BL 2/1/07)

4052 Roman, Dave. *Astronaut Academy: Zero Gravity* (5–8). Illus. by author. 2011, First Second paper $9.99 (978-1-59643-620-6). Child space hero Hakata Soy enrolls in Astronaut Academy and meets danger in his first term when a robot doppelganger is sent to kill him. (Rev: BL 6/11; LMC 8–9/11; SLJ 5/1/11)

4053 Rosa, Don. *The Life and Times of Scrooge McDuck* (5–8). Illus. by author. 2010, Boom! $24.99 (978-1-60886-538-3). Rosa tells the story of Scrooge McDuck's origins in Scotland, exploits in America, and success in Africa, rendering him the world's richest duck and introducing many famous characters along the way. (Rev: BL 3/15/10*; SLJ 5/10)

4054 Rucka, Greg. *The Omac Project* (7–12). Illus. by Jesus Saiz and Cliff Richards. 2005, DC Comics paper $14.99 (978-1-4012-0837-0). Blue Beetle discovers that Max Lord, the millionaire who took over the surveillance camera Brother I, knows the identity of every superhero. (Rev: SLJ 5/06)

4055 Rucka, Greg, and Michael Lark. *The Quick and the Dead: Gotham Central* (7–12). 2006, Vertigo paper $14.99 (978-1-4012-0912-4). The police force of Gotham is the central focus here — rather than the masked and caped hero who typically comes to their aid in crime-fighting — partially the Bat-Signal has been removed from police HQ following a dispute with Batman. (Rev: BL 12/15/06)

4056 Russell, P. Craig. *The Birthday of the Infanta: Fairy Tales of Oscar Wilde, Vol. 3* (5–8). 1998, NBM $15.95 (978-1-56163-213-8). A graphic novel version of Wilde's fairy tale about the misshapen dwarf who dies of a broken heart. (Rev: BL 4/1/99)

4057 Russell, P. Craig. *The Fairy Tales of Oscar Wilde: The Devoted Friend, The Nightingale and the Rose* (5–8). Illus. by author. 2004, NBM $15.95 (978-1-56163-391-3). Two of Oscar Wilde's fairy tales — "The Devoted Friend" and "The Nightingale and the Rose" — are presented in a rich, picture-book-size graphic novel format. (Rev: BL 8/04; SLJ 11/04)

4058 Saenagi, Ryo. *Psychic Power Nanaki, Vol. 1* (7–12). Trans. from Japanese by Elina Ishikawa. Illus. by author. 2007, TokyoPop paper $9.99 (978-1-4278-0304-7). In this well-illustrated manga book, a Japanese teen acquires psychic powers and uses them to investigate ghosts and supernatural phenomena. (Rev: SLJ 3/08)

4059 Sahara, Mizu. *The Voices of a Distant Star* (7–10). 2006, TokyoPop paper $9.99 (978-1-59816-529-6). When Mikako, 15, leaves Earth to travel through space and fight Tarsians (an alien race), she stays in contact with her boyfriend, Noboru, through text messages; but years pass and he must decide if he can wait for her any longer. (Rev: BL 11/1/06)

4060 Sakai, Stan. *Usagi Yojimbo, Vol. 24: Return of the Black Soul* (8–12). Illus. by author. 2010, Dark Horse paper $16.99 (978-15958247-2-1). The genesis of the demon spirit that has haunted samurai rabbit Usagi for years is finally revealed in this installment in the long-running series. (Rev: BL 12/15/10)

4061 Sakai, Stan. *Usagi Yojimbo: Glimpses of Death, Vol. 20* (8–11). Series: Usagi Yojimbo. 2006, Dark Horse $15.95 (978-1-59307-549-1). This newest installment in the series finds the samurai rabbit granting a dying man's last request and embarking on a danger-filled quest to deliver a mysterious package to the man's daughter. (Rev: BL 11/1/06)

4062 Sakai, Stan. *Usagi Yojimbo: Travels with Jotaro, Vol. 18* (8–12). 2004, Dark Horse paper $15.95 (978-1-59307-220-9). In the 18th volume of the series, the title character, a rabbit samurai in feudal Japan, encounters a series of adventures while traveling with Jotaro, who is Usagi's son but doesn't know it. (Rev: BL 9/15/04; SLJ 10/04)

4063 Sakura, Tsukuba. *Land of the Blindfolded* (8–11). 2004, DC Comics paper $9.95 (978-1-4012-0524-9). This manga designed primarily for girls tells of two Japanese high school friends (boy and girl) who become close as they decide how to use their conflicting super powers. (Rev: BL 2/15/05)

4064 Sala, Richard. *Cat Burglar Black* (7–10). Illus. by author. 2009, First Second paper $16.99 (978-159643144-7). K (Katherine), already quite skilled as a burglar, finds herself investigating the motives of an art theft group she has been working with. (Rev: BL 7/09; LMC 11–12/09; SLJ 11/09)

4065 Schrag, Ariel, ed. *Stuck in the Middle: Seventeen Comics from an Unpleasant Age* (7–10). 2007, Viking $18.99 (978-0-670-06221-8). Is middle school really that bad? Yes, say these artists, who present their versions of this "unpleasant age" in various artistic styles. (Rev: BCCB 9/07; BL 3/15/07; LMC 11–12/07; SLJ 7/07)

4066 Schreiber, Ellen. *Blood Relatives* (6–9). Illus. by Rem. 2007, TokyoPop paper $7.99 (978-0-06-134081-9). Raven's perfect relationship with her vampire boyfriend is threatened when Claude and his Goth friends come to town. (Rev: BL 1/15/08; SLJ 1/08)

4067 Schweizer, Chris. *Crogan's Loyalty* (7–12). Illus. by author. 2012, Oni $14.99 (978-193496440-8). The

Crogan brothers — Charlie and Will — are divided over the American Revolution, one a Loyalist and one a rebel. (Rev: BL 3/15/12*)

4068 Schweizer, Chris. *Crogan's March* (7–12). Illus. by author. Series: The Crogan Adventures. 2009, Oni $14.95 (978-1-934964-24-8). Peter Crogan is a legionnaire fighting for France in North Africa in 1912 in this action-packed addition to the legends of this unusual family. (Rev: BL 3/15/10*; SLJ 5/10)

4069 Schweizer, Chris. *Crogan's Vengeance* (7–12). Illus. by author. 2008, Oni $14.95 (978-193496406-4). Catfish Crogan and his crewmates fight off pirates on the high seas in this adventure tale set in 1701. (Rev: BL 1/1–15/09; SLJ 5/09)

4070 Serling, Rod, and Mark Kneece. *Death's-Head Revisited* (7–10). Illus. by Chris Lie. Series: Twilight Zone. 2009, Walker $16.99 (978-080279722-3); paper $9.99 (978-080279723-0). A faithful adaptation of an episode of the *Twilight Zone* television show in which a former concentration camp guard is judged by the souls of the people he murdered. (Rev: BL 3/1/09; SLJ 5/09)

4071 Sfar, Joann. *The Rabbi's Cat* (8–12). 2005, Pantheon $21.95 (978-0-375-42281-2). The entertaining and sophisticated adventures of a talking cat who lives with a rabbi and his daughter in 1930s Algeria. (Rev: BL 7/05; SLJ 3/06)

4072 Shakespeare, William. *Julius Caesar* (8–12). Adapted by Richard Appignanesi. Illus. by Mustashrik. Series: Manga Shakespeare. 2008, Abrams paper $9.95 (978-081097072-4). Abridged text and expressive illustrations tell the story of the play with a manga twist. (Rev: BL 10/1/08*; SLJ 1/09) [741.5]

4073 Shakespeare, William, and John McDonald. *Macbeth: The Graphic Novel* (6–10). Illus. by Jon Haward. 2008, Classical Comics paper $16.95 (978-190633205-1). This dramatically illustrated, condensed version of the play is accompanied by background information to help students understand its plot, setting, characters and significance. (Rev: BL 1/1–15/09)

4074 Shakespeare, William, and Richard Appignanesi. *As You Like It* (8–10). Illus. by Chie Kutsuwada. 2009, Abrams paper $10.95 (978-081098351-9). A manga retelling of the play set in the forest of Arden. (Rev: BL 3/1/09; SLJ 3/09) [823]

4075 Shakespeare, William, and Steven Grant. *Hamlet* (8–10). Illus. by Tom Mandrake. Series: Classics Illustrated. 2009, Papercutz $9.95 (978-159707149-9). This graphic-novel adaptation gives an effective rendering of the key events and characters, and will be useful to supplement the play itself. (Rev: BL 6/1–15/09; LMC 10/09) [822]

4076 Shakespeare, William, et al. *The Tempest: The Graphic Novel; Original Text* (7–12). Illus. by Jon Haward. 2009, Classical Comics paper $16.95 (978-19063326-9-3). An effective graphic-novel version of

the story about magic and adventure on a desert island. (Rev: BL 3/15/10*)

4077 Shanower, Eric. *Adventures in Oz* (4–7). Illus. by author. 2007, IDW $75.00 (978-1-60010-071-0); paper $39.99 (978-1-933239-61-3). Dorothy and her friends from Oz return in this beautifully drawn collection of five graphic novel adventures. (Rev: BL 3/15/07; SLJ 3/07; VOYA 4/07)

4078 Shiga, Jason. *Meanwhile* (4–9). Illus. by author. 2010, Abrams $15.95 (978-0-8109-8423-3). A mad scientist asks a boy to test one of three inventions in this choose-your-own-adventure graphic novel. ALA Notable Books 2011; YALSA Great Graphic Novels Top Ten 2011. (Rev: BL 1/1/10*; SLJ 3/10)

4079 Shimizu, Aki. *Qwan, Vol. 1* (7–12). Trans. from Japanese by Mike Kief. Illus. by author. 2005, TokyoPop paper $9.99 (978-1-59532-534-1). This compelling graphic novel follows Qwan and his friend as they embark on a magical journey to uncover Qwan's destiny. (Rev: SLJ 7/05)

4080 Shone, Rob. *Greek Myths* (5–9). Illus. by author. Series: Graphic Mythology. 2006, Rosen LB $29.25 (978-1-4042-0801-8). "Jason and the Golden Fleece," "Icarus," and "The Labors of Hercules" are the three tales presented here in graphic novel format. (Rev: SLJ 9/06) [292.1]

4081 *Showcase Presents the House of Mystery, Vol. 1* (5–9). 2006, DC Comics paper $16.99 (978-1-4012-0786-1). A collection of relatively tame horror comics that first appeared in the 1960s, in black and white. (Rev: SLJ 7/06)

4082 Siddell, Thomas. *Orientation* (6–12). Illus. by author. Series: Gunnerkrigg Court. 2009, Archaia $26.95 (978-193238634-9). Antimony arrives at a creepy boarding school where things get odder every day in this webcomic collection, the first in a series. YALSA Great Graphic Novels for Teens 2010; Booklist Top 10 Graphic Novels for Youth. (Rev: BL 3/15/09*)

4083 Siddell, Thomas. *Research* (8–12). Illus. by author. Series: Gunnerkrigg Court. 2010, Archaia $26.95 (978-193238677-6). Antimony Carver and her friend Kat discover more intriguing mysteries, including a tomb of ancient robots, as they explore their unusual boarding school; the second volume in the series. (Rev: BL 5/1/10)

4084 Sierra, Sergio A. *Frankenstein by Mary Shelley* (7–11). Illus. by Meritxell Ribas. Series: Dark Graphic Novel. 2012, Enslow LB $25.26 (978-076604084-7). A graphic-novel adaptation of the classic novel with woodcut-inspired art. (Rev: BL 9/15/12; SLJ 7/12; VOYA 10/12)

4085 Simone, Gail. *Wonder Woman: Ends of the Earth* (8–12). Illus. by Aaron Lopresti. 2010, DC Comics paper $14.99 (978-14012213-7-9). Wonder Woman goes head-to-head against a powerful lord at the edge of existence. (Rev: BL 5/1/10)

4086 Singer, Bryan, and Justin Gray. *Superman Returns: The Prequels* (7–12). 2006, DC Comics paper $12.99 (978-1-4012-1146-2). *Superman Returns,* the film, is enhanced by these stories that occur in the five years before his return to Earth and involve his adoptive mother Martha, his nemesis Lex Luthor, and his heartbroken love interest Lois Lane; they also bridge some scenes from the 1978 *Superman* film for a better continuity. (Rev: BL 12/1/06)

4087 Siu-Chong, Ken. *Round One: Fight!* (6–9). Series: Street Fighter. 2004, DDP paper $9.99 (978-1-932796-08-7). The opening volume in the series brings to life the characters and action of the popular video game of the same name and will appeal to reluctant readers. (Rev: SLJ 7/05)

4088 Smith, Jeff. *Eyes of the Storm, Vol. 3* (4–8). Illus. by author. Series: Bone. 2006, Scholastic $19.99 (978-0-439-70625-4); paper $9.99 (978-0-439-70638-4). The final book in the first Bone trilogy, this comic-book fantasy has funny moments, suspense and dream sequences that fans will love. (Rev: SLJ 7/06)

4089 Smith, Jeff. *Old Man's Cave* (5–12). Illus. by author. Series: Bone. 2007, Scholastic $18.99 (978-0-439-70628-5); paper $9.99 (978-0-439-70635-3). Episode six of this series that combines goofy-looking characters with dramatic fantasy plots finds Phoney Bone and Thorn in grave danger. (Rev: BL 11/1/07)

4090 Smith, Jeff. *Shazam! The Monster Society of Evil* (7–12). 2007, DC Comics $29.99 (978-1-4012-1466-1). Young Billy Batson, an orphan living in unpleasant circumstances, only has to say Shazam to be transformed into Captain Marvel; but Billy is hampered by his own behavior and his younger sister and now faces an alien invasion and the Monster Society of Evil. (Rev: BL 10/15/07; SLJ 3/08)

4091 Smith, Jeff, and Tom Sniegoski. *Bone: Tall Tales* (6–12). 2010, Graphix $22.99 (978-0-545-14095-9). A collection of stories featuring the founder of Boneville, Big Johnson Bone, and his intrepid adventures. Lexile GN560L (Rev: BL 3/15/10; LMC 10/10; SLJ 7/10)

4092 Soo, Kean. *Jellaby* (4–7). Illus. by author. 2008, Hyperion $18.99 (978-1-4231-0337-0); paper $9.99 (978-1-4231-0303-5). A gentle purple monster changes the lives of 10-year-old Portia and her friend Jason. (Rev: BL 3/15/08; SLJ 1/08)

4093 Spiegelman, Art. *Little Lit: Folklore and Fairy Tale Funnies* (4–9). 2000, HarperCollins $19.95 (978-0-06-028624-8). In this presentation in graphic novel format, 15 different artists create brilliant variations on standard fairy and folk tales. (Rev: BL 1/1–15/01*; HB 9–10/00; HBG 3/01; SLJ 12/00) [398.2]

4094 Spradlin, Michael P. *Chase for the Chalice* (6–8). Illus. by Rainbow Buddy. Series: Spy Goddess. 2008,

TokyoPop paper $9.99 (978-0-06-136299-6). In this installment, the first in manga form and full of details about Japan, Rachel and her friends are on a mission to thwart Simon Blankenship. (Rev: BL 6/1–15/08; SLJ 9/08)

4095 Stanley, John. *Melvin Monster: The John Stanley Library* (6–12). Illus. 2009, Drawn & Quarterly $19.95 (978-189729963-0). Stanley's monster kid, Melvin, is funny and sympathetic in this reprinted comic book series. (Rev: BL 7/09; SLJ 11/09)

4096 Stanley, John, and Irving Tripp. *Color Special: Little Lulu* (7–12). 2006, Dark Horse paper $13.95 (978-1-59307-613-9). Little Lulu is back in vibrant color reproductions of selected stories from issues 4 through 86. (Rev: BL 10/1/06)

4097 Stanley, John, and Irving Tripp. *Miss Feeny's Folly and Other Stories: Little Lulu 21* (6–12). Illus. 2009, Dark Horse paper $14.95 (978-15958236-5-6). This 21st volume continues the meticulous reprinting of the delightful Little Lulu series. (Rev: BL 12/1/09)

4098 Stevenson, Robert Louis. *Treasure Island* (5–9). Illus. by Tim Hamilton. Series: Puffin Graphics. 2005, Puffin paper $10.99 (978-0-14-240470-6). Robert Louis Stevenson's adventure classic springs to life in this striking graphic novel adaptation that remains faithful to the original text. (Rev: SLJ 11/05)

4099 Stoker, Bram. *Dracula* (7–12). Adapted by Gary Reed. Illus. by Becky Cloonan. Series: Puffin Graphics. 2006, Puffin paper $10.99 (978-0-14-240572-7). A compelling graphic-novel version of the famous vampire story. (Rev: SLJ 3/06)

4100 Storrie, Paul D. *Made for Each Other* (7–10). Illus. by Eldon Cowgur. 2011, Lerner/Graphic Universe LB $29.27 (978-076135601-1); paper $9.95 (9780761370772). A saucy paranormal romance in graphic-novel format that features Maria and her new beau, Tom B. Stone, and a series of mysterious deaths. Lexile GN340L (Rev: BL 5/1/11; LMC 10/11*; SLJ 7/1/11)

4101 Storrie, Paul D. *Yu the Great: Conquering the Flood* (4–7). Illus. by Sandy Carruthers. Series: Graphic Myths and Legends. 2007, Lerner LB $26.60 (978-0-8225-3088-6). In this graphic novel adaptation of an ancient Chinese folk tale, the emperor Shun asks Yu to save China and its people from the floods that are ravaging the land. (Rev: BL 3/15/07; SLJ 5/07) [398.2]

4102 Sturm, James. *Satchel Paige: Striking Out Jim Crow* (6–12). Illus. by Rich Tommaso. 2007, Hyperion $16.99 (978-0-7868-3900-1); paper $9.99 (978-0-7868-3901-8). This graphic novel serves up a slice of segregated Southern history in which a fictional Negro League player named Emmet Wilson goes up against Paige — a high point in Wilson's life before he returns to farming. (Rev: BL 11/1/07; SLJ 1/08)

4103 Sugisaki, Yukiro. *Rizelmine* (8–12). Trans. from Japanese by Alethea Nibley and Athena Nibley. Illus. by author. 2005, TokyoPop paper $9.99 (978-1-59532-901-1). Fifteen-year-old Iwaki Tomonori rejects the advances of robot-like Rizel, who's become his bride by government decree. (Rev: SLJ 11/05)

4104 Sumerak, Marc, and Fred Van Lente. *Wolverine: Tales of Weapon X* (8–12). Illus. by Mark Robinson. 2009, Marvel $14.99 (978-078513936-2). Six lively comics combine humor and adventure with details of Wolverine's past. (Rev: BLO 6/16/09)

4105 Tada, Kaoru. *Itazura na Kiss, Vol. 2* (7–10). Illus. by author. 2010, DMP paper $16.95 (978-15697013-6-2). Kotoko continues naively trying to get Naoki to fall for her as they graduate from high school and start college; the second volume in the series. (Rev: BLO 9/1/10)

4106 Takada, Rie. *Gaba Kawa, Vol. 1* (8–12). Illus. by author. 2008, VIZ Media paper $8.99 (978-142152259-3). Rara is a high-school demon who falls in love with a human classmate in this funny yet sometimes disturbing story. (Rev: BLO 2/9/09)

4107 Takeuchi, Mick. *Bound Beauty* (8–11). Illus. by author. 2008, Go! Comi $10.99 (978-1-60510-008-1). This manga novel about a teenage matchmaker contains lots of great information about Japanese folklore, history, and traditions. (Rev: BLO 12/30/08)

4108 Tamaki, Mariko. *Emiko Superstar* (8–12). Illus. by Steve Rolston. 2008, DC Comics paper $9.99 (978-140121536-1). Asian Canadian Emiko discovers she can use performance art to be someone completely different from the geeky teen she believes she is. (Rev: BL 12/1/08; LMC 5–6/09; SLJ 11/08)

4109 Tan, Shaun. *The Arrival* (6–12). Illus. by author. 2007, Scholastic $19.99 (978-043989529-3). This wordless graphic novel tells the moving story of a man who migrates to a new country hoping to build a new life. Boston Globe–Horn Book Special Citation 2008; ALA Notable Books 2008. (Rev: BL 9/1/07*; SLJ 9/07)

4110 Tan, Shaun. *Tales from Outer Suburbia* (7–12). Illus. by author. 2009, Scholastic $19.99 (978-054505587-1). These fifteen diverse short tales are beautifully illustrated with Tan's evocative artwork. ALA Notable Books 2010. Lexile 1100L (Rev: BL 12/1/08; HB 3–4/09; LMC 5–6/09; SLJ 3/1/09*; VOYA 6/09)

4111 Taniguchi, Tomoko. *Call Me Princess* (5–8). Trans. from Japanese by Mutsumi Masuda and C. B. Cebulski. Illus. by author. 2003, CPM Manga paper $9.99 (978-1-58664-898-5). This graphic novel, set in Japan, centers on the young heroine's romantic attachments but gets a "G" rating. (Rev: SLJ 3/04)

4112 *Teen Titans: Jam Packed Action!* (4–8). 2005, DC Comics paper $7.99 (978-1-4012-0902-5). Two exciting technology-oriented stories are drawn from the Cartoon Network show. (Rev: SLJ 5/06)

4113 Telgemeier, Raina. *Drama* (6–9). Illus. by author. 2012, Scholastic $23.99 (978-054532698-8); paper $10.99 (978-05453269-9-5). Middle schooler Callie struggles to find her niche while serving on the stage crew for her school's production of "Moon over Mississippi." Stonewall Honor 2013; ALA Notable Books 2013; YALSA Great Graphic Novels Top Ten 2013; YALSA Popular Paperbacks for Young Adults Top Ten 2013. Lexile GN400L (Rev: BL 9/15/12*; HB 9–10/12; LMC 3–4/13; SLJ 11/12*; VOYA 10/12)

4114 TenNapel, Doug. *Bad Island* (6–10). Illus. by author. 2011, Graphix $24.99 (978-054531479-4); paper $12.99 (978-054531480-0). On a boat trip with his family, Reese finds himself washed up on an island inhabited by weird beings from a distant galaxy. (Rev: BL 3/15/11*; SLJ 11/1/11)

4115 TenNapel, Doug. *Cardboard* (5–8). Illus. by author. 2012, Scholastic $24.99 (978-054541872-0); paper $12.99 (978-05454187-3-7). A jobless father's meager birthday gift — a cardboard box that the two fashion into a boxer — comes alive for his son and mayhem ensues. (Rev: BL 3/15/12; HB 7–8/12; LMC 11–12/12; SLJ 9/12*; VOYA 6/12)

4116 TenNapel, Doug. *Ghostopolis* (5–8). Illus. by author. 2010, Scholastic $24.99 (978-0-545-21027-0); paper $14.99 (978-0-545-21-028-7). When Frank Gallows of the Supernatural Immigration Task Force accidentally transports him to the afterlife, young Garth Hale discovers he has hitherto unknown powers and is in danger from the sinister ruler of Ghostopolis. YALSA Quick Picks for Reluctant Young Adult Readers 2012; YALSA Great Graphic Novels Top Ten 2011. Lexile GN300L (Rev: BL 3/15/10; SLJ 7/10; VOYA 2/10)

4117 Tetzner, Lisa. *The Black Brothers* (6–9). Trans. by Peter F. Neumeyer. Illus. by Hannes Binder. 2004, Front St $16.95 (978-1-932425-04-8). This striking graphic novel adaptation of Lisa Tetzner's 1941 novel recounts the trials and tribulations of 13-year-old Giorgio, a young chimney sweep in 19th-century Europe whose friendship with the leader of a secret society called the Black Brothers ultimately leads him to happiness. (Rev: BL 9/1/04; SLJ 11/04; VOYA 2/05)

4118 Tinsley, Kevin, and Phil Singer. *Milk Cartons and Dog Biscuits* (7–12). 2004, Stickman Graphics paper $19.95 (978-0-9675423-4-8). People and elf-like creatures mingle in this adventure mystery about a state ranger who is searching for a runaway daughter. (Rev: BL 2/1/04)

4119 Tolkien, J. R. R. *The Hobbit; or, There and Back Again* (5–10). Adapted by Charles Dixon. 1990, Eclipse Books paper $12.95 (978-0-345-36858-4). The classic story of Bilbo Baggins and his companions is introduced to reluctant readers in this full-color graphic novel. (Rev: BL 9/1/91)

4120 Tomori, Miyoshi. *A Devil and Her Love Song, Vol. 1* (8–12). Illus. by author. 2012, VIZ Media paper $9.99 (978-14215416-4-8). Maria's reputation precedes her at her new school but her angelic voice contradicts her overly frank behavior, attracting the attention of two boys. (Rev: BL 4/15/12; SLJ 7/1/12)

4121 Toume, Kei. *Kurogane, Vol. 1* (7–12). Trans. from Japanese by Akira Tsubasa. Adapted by Alex Kent. Illus. by author. 2006, Del Rey paper $10.95 (978-0-345-49203-6). Jintetsu, with a steel body and a talking sword, sets out to avenge his father's death in this story set in feudal Japan. (Rev: SLJ 9/06)

4122 Toyoda, Minoru. *Love Roma, Vol. 1* (8–11). 2005, Del Rey paper $10.95 (978-0-345-48262-4). This delightful manga chronicles the budding romance of teenagers Hoshino and Negishi. (Rev: BL 10/15/05; SLJ 1/06)

4123 Tran, Thien, and Keith Giffen. *Road Trip* (6–9). Illus. by Cully Hamner. Series: Blue Beetle. 2007, DC Comics paper $12.99 (978-1-4012-1361-9). An alien scarab has attached itself to a young Latino named Jaime Reyes, giving him an armor-like shell and superhero abilities; in this second volume in the series, Jaime tries to find out more about what's happening to him. (Rev: BL 9/1/07)

4124 Trondheim, Lewis. *Mister O* (4–8). Illus. by author. 2004, NBM $13.95 (978-1-56163-382-1). Mister O, portrayed in wordless rectangular cartoons, is a round caricature who — à la Wile E. Coyote — can't seem conquer a chasm, no matter how many successful crossings he views. (Rev: SLJ 9/04)

4125 Trondheim, Lewis. *Tiny Tyrant* (4–7). Illus. by Fabrice Parme. 2007, Roaring Brook paper $12.95 (978-1-59643-094-5). Ethelbert, the diminutive and willful 6-year-old child-king of Portocristo, is used to getting his own way in this series of funny episodes. (Rev: BL 3/15/07; SLJ 9/07)

4126 Truman, Timothy, and Mark Schultz. *Star Wars Omnibus: Emissaries and Assassins* (6–12). Illus. by Tim Bradstreet. 2009, Dark Horse paper $24.95 (978-159582229-1). A collection of comics based on movies *Episode I* and *II*, with different styles of artwork and featuring favorite characters. (Rev: BLO 5/27/09)

4127 Tsuda, Masami. *Castle of Dreams: Stories from the Kare Kano Creator* (8–12). Illus. Series: Sorcerer. 2009, Tokyopop paper $12.99 (978-142781227-8). Teenage romance, fantasy, and modern life mix in this collection of sweet stories. (Rev: BLO 2/9/09)

4128 Tsukiji, Toshihiko. *Maburaho, Vol. 1* (8–12). Trans. from Japanese by Kay Bertrand. Illus. by Miki Miyashita. 2005, ADV paper $9.99 (978-1-4139-0293-8). Kazuki, a hapless magician-in-training, is pursued by three female students who know that he is destined to father a child who'll become a powerful wizard. (Rev: SLJ 7/05)

4129 Twain, Mark, and Jean David Morvan, et al. *The Adventures of Tom Sawyer* (5–8). Illus. by Severine Lefebvre. Series: Papercutz' Classics Illustrated Deluxe. 2009, Papercutz $17.95 (978-159707152-9); paper $13.95 (978-15970715-3-6). Bold manga-style illustrations enhance this adaptation that preserves the plot twists and tenor of the original story. (Rev: BL 1/1/10; SLJ 1/10)

4130 Type-Moon. *Fate/Stay Night* (8–11). Illus. by Dat Nishiwaki. Series: Fate/Stay Night. 2008, Tokyopop $9.99 (978-142781037-3). Emiya faces danger and evil forces in his ongoing fight for the powerful Holy Grail; an action-packed manga with mythological references. (Rev: BLO 1/21/09)

4131 Uderzo, Albert. *Asterix and the Actress* (4–7). Trans. by Anthea Bell and Derek Hockridge. 2001, Sterling $12.95 (978-0-7528-4657-6). These pun-filled, graphic novel exploits of Asterix the Gaul include a boisterous shared birthday with the rotund Obelix and a daring rescue of prisoners in a Roman jail. (Rev: BL 8/01)

4132 Ueda, Miwa. *Papillon, Vol. 1* (8–11). Illus. by author. 2008, Del Rey paper $10.95 (978-0-345-50519-4). High school student Ageha is always upstaged by her twin sister Hana in this manga novel until her sister steals the boy Ageha likes and she decides, with the encouragement of a friend and her school guidance counselor, that it's time to make a change. (Rev: BLO 12/8/08; SLJ 11/08)

4133 Urushibara, Yuki. *Mushishi, Vol. 1* (8–12). Adapted by William Flanagan. Illus. by author. 2007, Del Rey paper $10.95 (978-0-345-49621-8). Mushi are parasitic, supernatural beings that invade human victims, and Ginko's job is to control them in this compelling manga. (Rev: SLJ 7/07)

4134 Varon, Sara. *Bake Sale* (5–8). Illus. by author. 2011, First Second $19.99 (978-159643740-1); paper $16.99 (978-15964341-9-6). Cupcake, who runs a bakery and plays in a band, is thrilled when his friend Eggplant invites him to go to Istanbul and meet his idol, Turkish Delight. (Rev: BL 9/15/11; LMC 1–2/12; SLJ 11/1/11)

4135 Varon, Sara. *Robot Dreams* (6–12). Illus. by author. 2007, Roaring Brook paper $16.95 (978-1-59643-108-9). Poor lonely Dog is very happy when Robot arrives, but Dog doesn't realize Robot can't go swimming in this appealing almost-wordless graphic novel that provides both humor and poignancy. ALA Notable Books 2008. (Rev: BL 8/07; LMC 11/07; SLJ 9/07)

4136 Vollmar, Rob. *The Castaways* (6–9). Illus. by Pablo G. Callejo. 2007, ComicsLit $17.95 (978-1-56163-492-7). Tucker's life is changed when he meets a hobo on a freight train during the Great Depression; this new edition adds a color wash to the black-and-white illustrations as well as an epilogue. (Rev: BL 3/15/07; LMC 11–12/07; SLJ 5/07)

4137 Von Sholly, Pete. *Dead But Not Out! Pete Von Sholly's Morbid 2* (7–12). 2005, Dark Horse paper $14.95 (978-1-59307-289-6). Cheap horror movies are the target of this entertaining parody. (Rev: BL 3/15/05)

4138 Wagner, Josh. *Sky Pirates of Neo Terra* (4–7). Illus. by Camilla D'Errico. 2010, Image paper $17.99 (978-16070632-4-7). Billy sets out to thwart the Witch Queen's evil plans by rescuing her mechanic — his friend Ricket's dad. (Rev: BLO 1/1–15/11)

4139 Waid, Mark. *Legion of Super-Heroes: Teenage Revolution* (8–11). Illus. by Barry Kitson. 2005, DC Comics paper $14.99 (978-1-4012-0482-2). In this comic book vision of the future, teenage superheroes rebel against their parents' utopian government. (Rev: BL 1/1–15/06; SLJ 3/06)

4140 Waid, Mark. *Ruse: Inferno of Blue* (7–12). Illus. by Butch Guice. 2002, CrossGeneration paper $15.95 (978-1-931484-19-0). Mystery, action, and magical powers abound in this graphic novel set in an alternate universe and starring detective Simon Archard and sidekick Emma Bishop. (Rev: BL 8/02)

4141 Watts, Irene N. *Good-Bye Marianne* (3–7). Illus. by Kathryn E. Shoemaker. 2008, Tundra paper $12.95 (978-0-88776-830-9). Marianne, an 11-year-old Jewish girl first seen in *Remember Me* (2000), deals with various problems as the Nazis take over in 1937 Berlin in this affecting graphic novel. (Rev: BLO 9/24/08)

4142 Wein, Len. *Secret of the Swamp Thing* (7–12). Illus. by Berni Wrightson. 2005, DC Comics paper $9.99 (978-1-4012-0798-4). A collection of the first ten issues of the original comics about the legendary hero called Swamp Thing. (Rev: SLJ 5/06)

4143 Weing, Drew. *Set to Sea* (8–12). Illus. by author. 2010, Fantagraphics $16.99 (978-160699368-2). After years of glorifying the sea in his mind, the unnamed main character of this simple fable suddenly finds himself aboard a clipper bound for Hong Kong. YALSA Great Graphic Novels Top Ten 2011. (Rev: BL 10/15/10*)

4144 Wells, H. G. *The Invisible Man* (7–12). Retold by Terry Davis. Illus. by Dennis Calero. Series: Graphic Revolve. 2008, Stone Arch LB $23.93 (978-1-59889-831-6); paper $6.95 (978-1-59889-887-3). This somewhat altered retelling of Wells's story is concise and easy to understand. (Rev: SLJ 3/08)

4145 Wells, H. G. *The Time Machine* (7–12). Retold by Terry Davis. Illus. by Josée Alfonso and Ocampo Ruiz. Series: Graphic Revolve. 2008, Stone Arch LB $23.93 (978-1-59889-833-0); paper $6.95 (978-1-59889-889-7). Simpler in its retelling, this version of Wells's classic will attract a wide audience. (Rev: SLJ 3/08)

4146 West, David. *Mesoamerican Myths* (5–9). Illus. by Mike Taylor. Series: Graphic Mythology. 2006, Rosen LB $29.25 (978-1-4042-0802-5). Presented in graphic novel format are three tales from the mythology of Mexico and Central America — two creation stories and a hero tale. (Rev: SLJ 9/06) [398.2]

4147 Westerfeld, Scott, and Devin Grayson. *Shay's Story* (7–10). Illus. by Steven Cummings. Series: Uglies. 2012, Del Rey paper $10.99 (978-03455272-2-6). Shay must choose between the shallow perks of being beautiful and the realness of being an ordinary Ugly. Lexile GN510L (Rev: BL 3/15/12)

4148 *William Shakespeare's A Midsummer Night's Dream* (5–9). Illus. by Rod Espinosa. Series: Graphic Shakespeare. 2008, ABDO LB $19.95 (978-1-60270-191-5). An entertaining graphic version of *A Midsummer Night's Dream*, using dialogue from the play and featuring commentary on its plot, characters, themes, and other aspects. (Rev: SLJ 1/09)

4149 *William Shakespeare's Hamlet* (5–9). Illus. by Ben Dunn. Series: Graphic Shakespeare. 2008, ABDO LB $19.95 (978-1-60270-188-5). An entertaining graphic version of *Hamlet*, using dialogue from the play and featuring commentary on its plot, characters, themes, and other aspects. (Rev: SLJ 1/09)

4150 *William Shakespeare's King Lear* (5–9). Illus. by Ben Dunn. Series: Graphic Shakespeare. 2008, ABDO LB $19.95 (978-1-60270-189-2). An entertaining graphic version of *King Lear*, using dialogue from the play and featuring commentary on its plot, characters, themes, and other aspects. (Rev: SLJ 1/09)

4151 Williams, Rob. *Star Wars Rebellion: My Brother, My Enemy, Vol. 1* (8–12). Illus. by Brandon Badeaux. 2007, Dark Horse paper $14.95 (978-1-59307-711-2). This first volume in a new graphic novel series follows Luke Skywalker after he joins the rebellion and must decide whether to trust his old friend Tank, who is now an Imperial Officer. (Rev: BL 8/07)

4152 Willingham, Bill. *Robin: To Kill a Bird* (8–11). Illus. by Damion Scott. 2006, DC Comics paper $14.99 (978-1-4012-0909-4). In this Batman and Robin adventure, Robin learns to fight for himself as he's attacked by the Penguin's hit men. (Rev: BL 7/06)

4153 Winick, Judd. *Pedro and Me: Friendship, Loss, and What I Learned* (8–12). 2000, Henry Holt paper $16.00 (978-0-8050-6403-2). A graphic novel tribute to Pedro Zamora, an AIDS educator and actor who died of HIV complications at the age of 22. (Rev: BL 9/15/00; HB 11–12/00; HBG 3/01; SLJ 10/00)

4154 Wolfman, Marv. *The New Teen Titans Archives, Vol. 3* (7–12). 2006, DC Comics $49.99 (978-1-4012-1144-8). This collection includes the most popular stories from the 1980s comics that updated the 1960s tales about teen sidekicks of superheroes — Robin, Wonder Girl, Starfire, Cyborg, Raven, the Changeling, and Kid Flash. (Rev: BL 12/1/06)

4155 Wolfram, Amy. *Teen Titans: Year One* (5–8). Illus. by Karl Kerschl. 2008, DC Comics paper $14.99 (978-1-4012-1927-7). A collection of six comic book stories following five young friends (Robin, Wonder Girl, Kid Flash, Aqualad, and Speedy) as they join forces to defeat evil. (Rev: BLO 1/7/09)

4156 Wood, Don. *Into the Volcano* (4–7). Illus. by author. 2008, Scholastic $18.99 (978-0-439-72671-9). An action-packed graphic-novel thriller in which two brothers, Duffy and Sumo, find themselves inside an erupting volcano. (Rev: BCCB 11/08; BL 11/15/08; HB 9/08; LMC 1/09; SLJ 9/08)

4157 Wooding, Chris. *Pandemonium* (7–12). Illus. by Cassandra Diaz. 2012, Scholastic $22.99 (978-054525221-8); paper $12.99 (978-04398775-9-6). Peasant boy Seifer proves his merit when he's called on to impersonate the missing Prince Talon Pandemonium. Lexile GN460L (Rev: BL 3/15/12; LMC 5–6/12; SLJ 3/1/12*)

4158 Yagami, Yu. *Hikkatsu, Vol. 1* (6–10). Illus. by author. 2007, Go! Comi paper $10.99 (978-1-933617-29-9). A wacky manga story of a martial artist gone wild, karate-chopping small electrical appliances. (Rev: BL 1/1–15/08)

4159 Yamada, Norie. *Someday's Dreamers, Vol. 1* (8–12). Trans. from Japanese by Jeremiah Bourque. Illus. by Kumichi Yoshizuki. 2006, TokyoPop paper $9.99 (978-1-59816-178-6). Yume is a "magic user" who is paid by the government to use her skills for the good of others. (Rev: SLJ 9/06)

4160 Yolen, Jane. *Foiled* (6–10). Illus. by Mike Cavallaro. 2010, First Second paper $15.99 (978-1-59643-279-6). Reality morphs into fantasy (and black and white into color) when Aliera dons her fencing mask and wields her new ruby-handled foil; the first installment in a series. Lexile GN460L (Rev: BL 3/15/10; HB 7–8/10; LMC 8–9/10; SLJ 3/10)

4161 Yoshizaki, Mine. *Sgt. Frog, Vol. 1* (8–11). 2004, TokyoPop paper $9.99 (978-1-59182-703-0). In this *manga* work, a young brother and sister are dealing with an uninvited guest, an invader from another planet. (Rev: BL 3/15/04)

4162 Young-You, Lee. *Moon Boy* (6–9). 2006, Ice Kunion paper $10.95 (978-8-9527460-4-7). Myung-Ee meets and likes Yu-da, also realizes he too is a moon rabbit (a being hiding in human form); later she must rescue him from their predators, the moon foxes. (Rev: BL 9/15/06; SLJ 1/07)

4163 Yune, Tommy. *From the Stars* (7–12). 2003, DC Comics paper $9.95 (978-1-4012-0144-9). When an alien ship crashes on earth, Roy Fokker signs up to be a test pilot and then learns a great deal about alien technology. (Rev: BL 2/1/04)

4164 Zirkel, Huddleston. *A Bit Haywire* (4–7). 2006, Viper paper $11.95 (978-0-977788-35-4). Owen has many extraordinary powers, but he's having trouble figuring out how to control them. (Rev: BL 3/15/07)

4165 Zornow, Jeff. *The Legend of Sleepy Hollow* (5–7). Illus. by author. Series: Graphic Planet: Graphic Horror. 2008, ABDO LB $18.95 (978-1-60270-060-4). A graphic adaptation of the classic story with satisfyingly creepy illustrations. (Rev: BL 3/15/08; SLJ 5/08)

Historical Fiction and Foreign Lands

Prehistory

4166 Brennan, J. H. *Shiva Accused: An Adventure of the Ice Age* (6–9). 1991, HarperCollins LB $16.89 (978-0-06-020742-7). In this sequel to *Shiva* (o.p.), a prehistoric orphan girl is accused of murder by a rival tribe. (Rev: BL 8/91; SLJ 11/91)

4167 Brennan, J. H. *Shiva's Challenge: An Adventure of the Ice Age* (6–9). 1992, HarperCollins LB $16.89 (978-0-06-020826-4). In the third entry in the series, Cro-Magnon Shiva is spirited away by the shamanistic Crones to test her powers and see if she can survive the ordeals that will make her a Crone, too. (Rev: BL 12/15/92)

4168 Denzel, Justin. *Boy of the Painted Cave* (5–7). 1988, Putnam $17.99 (978-0-399-21559-9). The story of a boy who longs to be a cave artist, set in Cro Magnon times. (Rev: BL 11/1/88; SLJ 11/88)

4169 Dickinson, Peter. *A Bone from a Dry Sea* (7–10). 1993, Dell paper $4.99 (978-0-440-21928-6). The protagonists are Li, a girl in a tribe of "sea apes" living four million years ago, and Vinny, the teenage daughter of a modern-day paleontologist. (Rev: BL 2/1/93; SLJ 4/93*)

4170 Levin, Betty. *Thorn* (7–10). 2005, Front St $16.95 (978-1-932425-46-8). Thorn, a young boy with an atrophied leg, is befriended by Willow but still feels uncomfortable and plans his escape. (Rev: BL 12/15/05; SLJ 1/06)

4171 Paver, Michelle. *Wolf Brother* (6–9). Illus. by Geoff Taylor. Series: Chronicles of Ancient Darkness. 2005, HarperCollins LB $17.89 (978-0-06-072826-7). In the distant prehistoric past, 12-year-old Torak and his wolf cub companion set off on a perilous journey to destroy a demon-possessed bear. (Rev: BCCB 2/05; BL 3/1/05; SLJ 2/05)

4172 Williams, Susan. *Wind Rider* (6–9). 2006, HarperCollins $16.99 (978-0-06-087236-6). In Central Asia about 6,000 years ago, a teenage girl named Fern befriends and tames a horse, showing her tribe how useful the animals can be and challenging the standards set for women at that time. (Rev: BL 10/15/06; SLJ 11/06)

Ancient and Medieval History

GENERAL AND MISCELLANEOUS

4173 Cadnum, Michael. *Raven of the Waves* (7–10). 2001, Scholastic $17.95 (978-0-531-30334-4). In this gory tale set in the 8th century, 17-year-old Viking Lidsmod takes part in a bloodthirsty raid on an English community but later helps a boy who is taken captive. (Rev: BL 4/1/01; HB 9–10/01; HBG 3/02; SLJ 7/01; VOYA 8/01)

4174 Carter, Dorothy Sharp. *His Majesty, Queen Hatshepsut* (6–9). 1987, HarperCollins LB $16.89 (978-0-397-32179-7). A fictionalized biography of Queen Hatshepsut, daughter of Thutmose I and the only female pharaoh of Egypt. (Rev: SLJ 10/87; VOYA 12/87)

4175 Chen, Da. *Sword* (6–9). Series: Forbidden Tales. 2008, HarperCollins $16.99 (978-0-06-144758-7). Fifteen-year-old Miu Miu must avenge her father's murder at the hand of the emperor in this novel set in ancient China and featuring lots of martial arts. (Rev: BL 8/08)

4176 Gormley, Beatrice. *Poisoned Honey* (8–12). 2010, Knopf $16.99 (978-0-375-85207-7). Gormley reimagines the life of Mary Magdalene before she became a follower of Jesus Christ, with anecdotes about the evolution of Matthew the tax collector plus an author's note about various versions of Mary's story. e Lexile HL780L (Rev: BL 5/15/10; LMC 5–6/10; SLJ 2/10)

4177 Gregory, Kristiana. *Cleopatra VII: Daughter of the Nile* (5–8). Series: Royal Diaries. 1999, Scholastic paper $10.95 (978-0-590-81975-6). This mock-diary recounts various events in the life of 12-year-old Cleopatra who, even at that age, was involved in palace intrigue. (Rev: BL 1/1–15/00; HBG 3/00; SLJ 10/99)

4178 Harvey, Gill. *Orphan of the Sun* (6–9). 2006, Bloomsbury $16.95 (978-1-58234-685-4). Thirteen-year-old Meryt-Re, an orphaned girl living in ancient Egypt, is kicked out of her uncle's home and embarks on a road to self-discovery. (Rev: BL 7/06; LMC 10/06; SLJ 1/07)

4179 Hofmeyr, Dianne. *Eye of the Moon* (6–9). 2011, Aladdin paper $6.99 (978-1-4424-1-188-3). After the death of his mother, Prince Tuthmosis escapes from a villainous high priest with the help of an embalmer and his daughter Isikara, and the two journey across Egypt in search of help to regain the boy-king's throne. e Lexile 700L (Rev: BLO 7/11; LMC 11–12/11; SLJ 8/11)

4180 Lasky, Kathryn. *The Last Girls of Pompeii* (7–10). 2007, Viking $15.99 (978-0-670-06196-9). Julia and her slave (and best friend) Sura do not have bright futures in Pompeii but together they manage to escape the smothering ash of erupting Vesuvius. (Rev: BL 4/15/07; LMC 11–12/07; SLJ 8/07)

4181 Lloyd, Alison. *Year of the Tiger* (5–8). 2010, Holiday House $16.95 (978-0-8234-2277-7). In ancient China two 12-year-old boys from different backgrounds become friends amid turbulent times. Lexile 600L (Rev: BL 4/15/10; LMC 10/10; SLJ 6/10)

4182 McCaughrean, Geraldine. *Casting the Gods Adrift: A Tale of Ancient Egypt* (5–8). Illus. by Patricia D. Ludlow. 2003, Cricket $15.95 (978-0-8126-2684-1). History and fiction are intertwined in this well-illustrated, suspenseful novel about two boys who are content to be taken in by the Pharoah Akhenaten, and a father enraged by the Pharaoh's refusal to worship the traditional Egyptian gods. (Rev: BCCB 10/03; BL 10/15/03; HBG 4/04; SLJ 8/03)

4183 McCaughrean, Geraldine. *Not the End of the World* (7–10). 2005, HarperCollins LB $17.89 (978-0-06-076031-1). A harrowing but thought-provoking story of what it was really like aboard Noah's ark, with terrified animals and humans unhinged by their circumstances. (Rev: BL 8/05; SLJ 8/05*; VOYA 8/05)

4184 Miklowitz, Gloria D. *Masada: The Last Fortress* (7–10). 1998, Eerdmans $16.00 (978-0-8028-5165-9). The siege of Masada comes alive through the eyes of a young Jewish man and a Roman commander. (Rev: BCCB 10/98; BL 10/1/98; HBG 3/99; SLJ 12/98; VOYA 2/99)

4185 Pinsker, Marlee. *In the Days of Sand and Stars* (6–9). Illus. by Francois Thisdale. 2006, Tundra $22.95 (978-0-88776-724-1). Ten imagined stories about the lives of legendary women of the Bible such as Eve, Sarah, and Rachel. (Rev: BL 10/1/06; SLJ 1/07)

4186 Roberts, Judson. *Dragons from the Sea* (8–11). Series: Strongbow Saga. 2007, HarperCollins $16.99 (978-0-06-081300-0). In A.D. 845, a young Viking named Halfden, who is skilled at the longbow, joins the crew of the *Gull* and struggles to uphold his honor as he's involved in the violent invasion of France. (Rev: BL 5/15/07; SLJ 9/07)

4187 Roberts, Katherine. *I Am the Great Horse* (8–11). 2006, Scholastic $16.99 (978-0-439-82163-6). The life of Alexander the Great is related from the viewpoint of his famous horse, Bucephalus. (Rev: BL 10/15/06; SLJ 12/06)

4188 Shecter, Vicky Alvear. *Cleopatra's Moon* (7–10). 2011, Scholastic $18.99 (978-0-545-22130-6). Cleopatra's only daughter hopes for a royal future but her expectations are not realized in this compelling historical novel. ∩ (Rev: BL 8/11; HB 9–10/11; LMC 11–12/11; SLJ 8/11; VOYA 10/11)

4189 Silverberg, Selma Kritzer. *Naomi's Song* (6–9). 2009, Jewish Publication Society $14.00 (978-0-8276-0886-3). The story of Ruth and Naomi of Scripture, told from the older woman's point of view. Sydney Taylor Book Honor 2010. (Rev: BL 4/15/09)

4190 Speare, Elizabeth George. *The Bronze Bow* (7–10). 1961, Houghton Mifflin paper $6.95 (978-0-395-13719-2). A Jewish boy seeks revenge against the Romans who killed his parents, but finally his hatred abates when he hears the messages and teachings of Jesus. Newbery Medal 1962. (Rev: BL 9/1/95)

GREECE AND ROME

4191 Ford, Michael. *Birth of a Warrior* (5–8). 2008, Bloomsbury $16.99 (978-0-8027-9794-0). Lysander's Spartan heritage is in conflict with his fondness for the Helot villages with whom he grew up in this exciting, sometimes violent, sequel to *The Fire of Ares* (2008). (Rev: BLO 12/18/08; SLJ 2/09)

4192 Lawrence, Caroline. *The Charioteer of Delphi* (5–8). Series: Roman Mysteries. 2007, Roaring Brook $16.95 (978-1-59643-085-3). Flavia, Jonathan, Nubia, and Lupus find themselves involved in chariot racing in Rome. (Rev: BL 8/07)

4193 Lawrence, Caroline. *Gladiators from Capua* (5–8). Series: Roman Mysteries. 2005, Roaring Brook $16.95 (978-1-59643-074-7). In their search for Jonathan, who may be alive after all, Flavia, Lupus, and Nubia venture into the coliseum and witness gladiator fights. (Rev: BL 12/1/05; SLJ 2/06)

4194 Lawrence, L. S. *Escape by Sea* (6–9). 2009, Holiday House $16.95 (978-082342217-3). Sara, 16, and her father escape Carthage just as the Romans invade and take their chances at sea in this tale set at the end of the second Punic War. Lexile 640L (Rev: BL 4/15/09; SLJ 6/1/09)

4195 McLaren, Clemence. *Aphrodite's Blessings: Love Stories from the Greek Myths* (7–12). 2002, Simon & Schuster $16.00 (978-0-689-84377-8). The lot of women in ancient Greece comes to life in three stories, based on mythology, about Atalanta, Andromeda, and Psyche. (Rev: BL 3/1/02; HBG 10/02; SLJ 1/02; VOYA 4/02)

4196 Mitchell, Jack. *The Ancient Ocean Blues* (5–8). 2008, Tundra paper $9.95 (978-08877683-2-3). In 63 B.C. Greece, teenager Marcus Oppius arrives in Athens on an espionage mission for Julius Caesar. ℮ Lexile 800L (Rev: BLO 11/15/08; SLJ 5/1/09)

4197 Mitchell, Jack. *The Roman Conspiracy* (5–9). 2005, Tundra paper $8.95 (978-0-88776-713-5). In this compelling historical thriller set in the Roman Empire, young Aulus Spurinna travels to Rome in a desperate attempt to protect his homeland of Etruria from military pillagers. (Rev: SLJ 11/05)

4198 Napoli, Donna Jo. *The Great God Pan* (7–10). 2003, Random House $15.95 (978-0-385-32777-0). A beautifully written novel about the life and aspirations of Pan, who was half man and half goat. (Rev: BL 4/15/03; SLJ 6/03)

4199 Napoli, Donna Jo. *Sirena* (7–12). 1998, Scholastic $15.95 (978-0-590-38388-2). This romantic expansion of the Greek myth of the Sirens describes the dilemma of an immortal mermaid who loves a mortal. (Rev: BL 1/1–15/03; HBG 3/99; SLJ 10/98; VOYA 12/98)

4200 Rao, Sirish, and Gita Wolf. *Sophocles' Oedipus the King* (7–10). Illus. by Indrapramit Roy. 2004, Getty $18.95 (978-0-89236-764-1). This retelling of Sophocles' tragic tale of Oedipus is highlighted by the striking illustrations of Indrapromit Roy. (Rev: BL 1/1–15/05)

4201 Rubalcaba, Jill. *The Wadjet Eye* (5–8). 2000, Clarion $15.00 (978-0-395-68942-4). After mummifying his dead mother, Damon sets off to find his father and is later hired by Cleopatra as a spy in this action-filled novel set in the Roman Empire of 45 B.C. (Rev: BL 5/15/00; HBG 10/00; SLJ 6/00; VOYA 6/00)

4202 Scarrow, Simon. *Fight for Freedom* (5–8). 2012, Hyperion $16.99 (978-142315101-2). An exciting story set in ancient Rome about 10-year-old Marcus who is forced to become a gladiator but is determined to gain freedom and save his mother. ℮ (Rev: BL 4/15/12; LMC 5–6/12; SLJ 3/12)

4203 Sutcliff, Rosemary. *The Eagle of the Ninth* (7–12). 1993, Farrar paper $5.95 (978-0-374-41930-1). A reissue of the historical novel about the Roman legion that went to battle and disappeared.

MIDDLE AGES

4204 Alder, Elizabeth. *The King's Shadow* (7–12). 1995, Bantam paper $5.50 (978-0-440-22011-4). In medieval Britain, mute Evyn is sold into slavery, but as Earl Harold of Wessex's squire and eventual foster son, he chronicles the king's life and becomes a storyteller. (Rev: BL 7/95; SLJ 7/95)

4205 Avi. *Crispin: At the Edge of the World* (5–8). 2006, Hyperion $16.99 (978-0-7868-5152-2). In this compelling sequel to *Crispin: The Cross of Lead*, Bear, who Crispin now regards as a father, is seriously wounded and they make friends with a disfigured girl named Troth; Crispin now finds himself making decisions for the three. ∩ (Rev: BCCB 1/07; BL 9/15/06; HB 9–10/06; HBG 4/07; LMC 2/07; SLJ 10/06*; VOYA 10/06)

4206 Bell, Hilari. *Player's Ruse* (7–10). Series: Knight and Rogue. 2010, HarperTeen $17.99 (978-0-06-082509-6). Sir Michael and his squire Fisk visit a port town, Huckerston, in an effort to solve a maritime mystery and perhaps woo the fair Rosamund. Lexile 910L (Rev: BL 12/1/09; HB 1–2/10; SLJ 1/10; VOYA 2/10)

4207 Black, Kat. *A Templar's Apprentice* (6–9). 2009, Scholastic $17.99 (978-0-545-05654-0). This 14th-century adventure story follows diligent, likable Tormod as he travels around the world on a mission to deliver a parchment while pursued by the French Army. (Rev: BLO 4/9/09; LMC 10/09; SLJ 5/1/09)

4208 Cadnum, Michael. *Forbidden Forest* (7–10). 2002, Scholastic $17.95 (978-0-439-31774-0). The story of Little John's entry into Robin Hood's band of merry men is told from John's point of view and combines realistic descriptions of medieval life with adventure and romance. (Rev: BL 4/15/02; HB 7–8/02; HBG 10/02; SLJ 6/02; VOYA 4/02)

4209 Cadnum, Michael. *In a Dark Wood* (7–10). 1998, Orchard LB $18.99 (978-0-531-33071-5). The story of Robin Hood as seen through the eyes of the sheriff of Nottingham and his young squire, Hugh. (Rev: BL 3/1/98; HB 3–4/98; HBG 9/98; SLJ 4/98; VOYA 8/98)

4210 Cadnum, Michael. *The King's Arrow* (7–10). 2008, Viking $16.99 (978-0-670-06331-4). This story of young Simon, a nobleman who is present during the shooting of King William II with an arrow, will bring the harsh and intriguing Middle Ages to life for its readers. (Rev: BL 12/15/07; HB 3–4/08; LMC 10/08; SLJ 3/08)

4211 Cushman, Karen. *Catherine, Called Birdy* (6–9). 1994, Clarion $16.00 (978-0-395-68186-2). Life in the last decade of the 12th century as seen through the eyes of a teenage girl. (Rev: BL 4/15/94; SLJ 6/94*; VOYA 6/94)

4212 Cushman, Karen. *Matilda Bone* (4–8). 2000, Clarion $15.00 (978-0-395-88156-9). Set in the 14th century, this novel describes the development of Matilda, 13, who serves as an assistant to the local bone setter in exchange for food and shelter. (Rev: BCCB 12/00; BL 8/00; HB 11–12/00; HBG 3/01; SLJ 9/00*; VOYA 12/00)

4213 Cushman, Karen. *The Midwife's Apprentice* (7–12). 1995, Clarion $13.00 (978-0-395-69229-5). A homeless young woman in medieval England becomes strong as she picks herself up and learns from a midwife to be brave. (Rev: BL 3/15/95*; SLJ 5/95)

4214 Dana, Barbara. *Young Joan* (6–10). 1991, HarperCollins $17.95 (978-0-06-021422-7). A fictional account of Joan of Arc that questions how a simple French farm girl hears, assimilates, and acts upon a message from God. (Rev: BL 5/15/91*; SLJ 5/91)

4215 Decker, Timothy. *Run Far, Run Fast* (8–12). Illus. by author. 2007, Front St $17.95 (978-1-59078-469-3). In 14th-century Europe a young girl's mother tells her to "run far, run fast" to escape the plague; the stark illustrations and simple text add to the setting and the tension. (Rev: BL 9/15/07; SLJ 1/08)

4216 Goodman, Joan Elizabeth. *Peregrine* (7–10). 2000, Houghton Mifflin $16.00 (978-0-395-97729-3). Fifteen-year-old Lady Edith, who has lost her husband and baby, escapes her problems by going on a pilgrimage from England to the Holy Land. (Rev: BL 4/1/00; HBG 9/00; SLJ 5/00; VOYA 6/00)

4217 Grant, K. M. *Blaze of Silver* (6–9). Series: The de Granville Trilogy. 2007, Walker $16.95 (978-0-8027-

9625-7). Will is betrayed by Kamil and must save the king from an assassination plot in this sweeping story that horse-lovers will adore; the final book in the trilogy set in the time of the Crusades, following *Blood Red Horse* (2005) and *Green Jasper* (2006). (Rev: BL 2/1/07; SLJ 5/07)

4218 Grant, K. M. *Blood Red Horse* (6–9). 2005, Walker $16.95 (978-0-8027-8960-0). This epic historical novel chronicles the adventures of English brothers Gavin and William de Granville as they leave home to join the Third Crusade under the leadership of King Richard I. (Rev: BCCB 5/05; BL 4/1/05*; SLJ 5/05; VOYA 6/05)

4219 Grant, K. M. *Blue Flame* (7–10). Series: Perfect Fire. 2008, Walker $16.99 (978-080279694-3). Young lovers Raimon and Yolanda's religious differences suddenly become cause for conflict when a powerful beacon of Christ reappears in 13th-century France. Lexile 890L (Rev: BL 10/15/08*; HB 11–12/08; LMC 1–2/09; SLJ 12/08; VOYA 2/09)

4220 Grant, K. M. *Green Jasper* (5–9). Series: The de Granville Trilogy. 2006, Walker $16.95 (978-0-8027-8073-7). Will and Gavin, introduced in *Blood Red Horse* (2005), come home from the crusade to find England in chaos and Gavin's beloved Ellie abducted by Constable de Scabious; a multilayered medieval adventure story. (Rev: SLJ 6/06; VOYA 8/06)

4221 Gray, Elizabeth Janet. *Adam of the Road* (5–8). Illus. by Robert Lawson. 1942, Puffin paper $7.99 (978-0-14-032464-8). Adventures of a 13th-century minstrel boy. Newbery Medal 1943.

4222 Grey, Christopher. *Leonardo's Shadow: or, My Astonishing Life as Leonardo da Vinci's Servant* (7–10). 2006, Simon & Schuster $16.95 (978-1-4169-0543-1). Fifteen-year-old Giacomo, a servant to the great Leonardo da Vinci, wards off the artist's creditors while also trying to uncover the truth about his own origins. (Rev: BL 8/06; SLJ 10/06)

4223 Grove, Vicki. *Rhiannon* (6–9). 2007, Putnam $18.99 (978-0-399-23633-4). Rhiannon, her mother, and her grandmother care for the sick and outcast in their medieval Welsh village, even defending one against a murder charge, in this novel that beautifully captures the feel of the times. (Rev: BL 11/15/07; SLJ 12/07)

4224 Jinks, Catherine. *Babylonne* (8–12). 2008, Candlewick $18.99 (978-076363650-0). Sixteen-year-old Babylonne, daughter of Pagan Kidrouk, escapes her arranged marriage to an old man by teaming up with a priest in a daring journey through the 13th-century French countryside. (Rev: BL 10/15/08; HB 1–2/09; LMC 3–4/09; SLJ 12/08; VOYA 2/09)

4225 Jinks, Catherine. *Pagan's Vows* (8–10). 2005, Candlewick $16.99 (978-0-7636-2021-9). Seventeen-year-old Pagan Kidrouk, squire to Lord Roland, joins his master at the Abbey of St. Martin where they are to begin training as monks, but Pagan soon finds that he has trouble adjusting to all the rules of his new life. (Rev: BL 10/1/04; SLJ 9/04; VOYA 10/04)

4226 Karr, Kathleen. *Fortune's Fool* (7–12). 2008, Knopf $15.99 (978-0-375-84816-2). Set in 14th-century Germany, this story of a court jester in search of a new master is full of medieval flavor and humor. (Rev: BL 3/1/08; SLJ 7/08)

4227 Lasky, Kathryn. *Hawksmaid* (5–8). 2010, Harper-Collins $16.99 (978-0-06-000071-4). In 12th-century England Matty, who is a skilled falconer, teams up with Fynn (soon to become Robin Hood) to right some wrongs in this story about the young Maid Marian that blends history and fantasy. **e** Lexile 780L (Rev: BL 5/15/10; LMC 5–6/10; SLJ 7/10)

4228 Leeds, Constance. *The Silver Cup* (6–9). 2007, Viking $16.99 (978-0-670-06157-0). Anna's family takes in an orphaned Jewish girl in this novel that captures the danger and difficulties of everyday life in 1095 Germany. (Rev: BL 2/15/07; SLJ 7/07)

4229 McKenzie, Nancy. *Guinevere's Gamble* (6–10). Series: Chrysalis Queen Quartet. 2009, Knopf $16.99 (978-0-375-84346-4); LB $19.99 (978-0-375-94346-1). In the second installment in the series, Guinevere, 13, uses her wit to battle Morgan le Fey's conniving, sinister nature as she progresses toward maturity and eventual queendom. **e** Lexile 780L (Rev: SLJ 10/09; VOYA 10/09)

4230 Morressy, John. *The Juggler* (7–10). 1996, Henry Holt $16.95 (978-0-8050-4217-7). In this adventure story set in the Middle Ages, a young man regrets the bargain he has made with the devil to become the world's greatest juggler in exchange for his soul. (Rev: SLJ 6/96; VOYA 8/96)

4231 Morris, Gerald. *The Ballad of Sir Dinadan* (5–9). 2003, Houghton Mifflin $16.00 (978-0-618-19099-7). An amusing retelling from Arthurian legend that features the younger brother of Sir Tristram as a music lover and reluctant knight. (Rev: BL 5/1/03; HB 5–6/03; HBG 10/03; SLJ 4/03*; VOYA 6/03)

4232 Morris, Gerald. *The Squire, His Knight, and His Lady* (5–9). 1999, Houghton Mifflin $16.00 (978-0-395-91211-9). This is a retelling, from the perspective of a knight's squire, of the classic story of Sir Gawain and the Green Knight. (Rev: BL 5/1/99; HBG 10/99; SLJ 5/99; VOYA 8/99)

4233 Morris, Gerald. *The Squire's Tale* (5–9). 1998, Houghton Mifflin $16.00 (978-0-395-86959-8). The peaceful existence of 14-year-old Terence is shattered when he becomes the squire of Sir Gawain and becomes involved in a series of quests. (Rev: BL 4/15/98; HB 7–8/98; SLJ 7/98; VOYA 8/98)

4234 Napoli, Donna Jo. *Hush: An Irish Princess' Tale* (8–11). 2007, Atheneum $16.99 (978-0-689-86176-5). Melkorka, an Irish princess, is captured by Russian

slave traders and refuses to speak in this present-tense story set in the 10th century. (Rev: BL 11/1/07; SLJ 12/07)

4235 Pernoud, Regine. *A Day with a Miller* (4–7). Trans. by Dominique Clift. Illus. by Giorgio Bacchin. 1997, Runestone LB $22.60 (978-0-8225-1914-0). A description of the life of a miller and his family in the 12th century and how hydraulic energy was being introduced at that time. (Rev: HBG 3/98; SLJ 3/98)

4236 Pyle, Howard. *Otto of the Silver Hand* (6–8). Illus. by author. 1967, Dover paper $8.95 (978-0-486-21784-0). Life in feudal Germany, the turbulence and cruelty of robber barons, and the peaceful, scholarly pursuits of the monks are presented in the story of the kidnapped son of a robber baron.

4237 Reeve, Philip. *Here Lies Arthur* (7–10). 2008, Scholastic $17.99 (978-0-545-09334-7). The story of King Arthur is told from the viewpoint of young Gwyna, a peasant girl given shelter by Myrddin, the Merlin figure. ALA Notable Books 2009. (Rev: BL 8/08*; LMC 3–4/09*)

4238 Rosen, Sidney, and Dorothy S. Rosen. *The Magician's Apprentice* (5–8). 1994, Carolrhoda LB $19.95 (978-0-87614-809-9). An orphan in a French abbey in the Middle Ages is accused of having a heretical document in his possession and is sent to spy on Roger Bacon, the English scientist. (Rev: BL 5/1/94; SLJ 6/94)

4239 Russell, Christopher. *Hunted* (5–8). 2007, Harper-Collins $15.99 (978-0-06-084119-5). Set in the Middle Ages, this is the exciting tale of two teens who run away after being falsely accused of bringing the Black Death to the manor in which they work. (Rev: SLJ 6/07)

4240 Sauerwein, Leigh. *Song for Eloise* (8–10). 2003, Front St $15.95 (978-1-886910-90-4). In the Middle Ages, an unhappy wife falls for a passing troubadour in a rich text full of historical detail. (Rev: BL 12/1/03; HBG 4/04; SLJ 12/03; VOYA 4/04)

4241 Shulevitz, Uri. *The Travels of Benjamin of Tudela: Through Three Continents in the Twelfth Century* (4–7). 2005, Farrar $17.00 (978-0-374-37754-0). Based on Benjamin's diaries, this picture book, which is incredibly detailed in both illustrations and text, tells of his perilous journey through parts of Europe, the Mediterranean, and the Middle East. Sidney Taylor Book Honor 2006. (Rev: BL 3/15/05*; SLJ 4/05)

4242 Spradlin, Michael P. *Keeper of the Grail* (5–8). Series: The Youngest Templar. 2008, Putnam $17.99 (978-0-399-24763-7). Fourteen-year-old Tristan, who has been raised by monks, becomes a squire to a Templar knight and finds himself journeying to the Holy Land and returning with the Holy Grail; an action-packed, first-person narrative. The second and third books in the series are *Trail of Fate* (2009) and *Orphan of Destiny* (2010). ∩ Lexile 830L (Rev: BL 9/15/08; LMC 1–2/09; SLJ 2/1/09)

4243 Temple, Frances. *The Beduins' Gazelle* (7–10). 1996, Orchard LB $16.99 (978-0-531-08869-2). In this 14th-century adventure, a companion piece to *The Ramsey Scallop*, young scholar Etienne becomes involved in the lives of two lovers when he goes to Fez to study at the university. (Rev: BL 2/15/96; SLJ 4/96*; VOYA 12/96)

4244 Temple, Frances. *The Ramsay Scallop* (7–10). 1994, Orchard LB $19.99 (978-0-531-08686-5). In 1299, 14-year-old Elenor and her betrothed nobleman are sent on a chaste pilgrimage to Spain and hear the stories of their fellow travelers. (Rev: BL 3/15/94*; SLJ 5/94; VOYA 4/94)

4245 Thal, Lilli. *Mimus* (8–11). Trans. by John Brownjohn. 2005, Annick $19.95 (978-1-55037-925-9); paper $9.95 (978-1-55037-924-2). Prince Florin is taken captive and made a jester when the kingdom of Vinland overpowers Moltovia in this novel of the Middle Ages. (Rev: BL 9/1/05*; SLJ 12/05*; VOYA 2/06)

4246 Thomson, Sarah L. *The Dragon's Son* (7–12). 2001, Scholastic $17.95 (978-0-531-30333-7). This historical novel, based on Welsh legends about King Arthur, tells the stories of family members and others who were involved in Arthur's life. (Rev: BCCB 7–8/01; BL 5/1/01; HBG 10/01; SLJ 7/01; VOYA 6/01)

4247 Tingle, Rebecca. *Far Traveler* (7–10). 2005, Penguin $18.99 (978-0-399-23890-1). In this historical novel set in 10th-century England, 16-year-old Aelfwyn flees when her uncle, West Saxon King Edward, tells her she must marry one of his allies or enter a convent. (Rev: BCCB 3/05; BL 2/1/05; SLJ 2/05; VOYA 8/05)

4248 Tomlinson, Theresa. *The Forestwife* (8–12). 1995, Orchard LB $17.99 (978-0-531-08750-3). A Robin Hood legend with Marian as the benevolent Green Lady of the forest. (Rev: BL 3/1/95*; SLJ 3/95; VOYA 5/95)

4249 Wein, Elizabeth E. *A Coalition of Lions* (7–12). Series: The Winter Prince. 2003, Viking $16.99 (978-0-370-03618-2). In the 6th century, a princess named Goewin travels from Britain to Africa on her way to an arranged marriage, in this absorbing sequel to *The Winter Prince* (1993). (Rev: BCCB 4/03; BL 2/15/03; SLJ 4/03)

4250 Williams, Marcia. *Chaucer's Canterbury Tales* (4–8). 2007, Candlewick $16.99 (978-0-7636-3197-0). The exploits of Chaucer's pilgrims are recounted in age-appropriate double-page spreads that are alive with action and humor; the illustrations help to define the more difficult words. ALA Notable Books 2008. (Rev: BL 2/15/07; HB 3–4/07; LMC 8–9/07; SLJ 3/07*)

4251 Wright, Randall. *Hunchback* (6–9). 2004, Henry Holt $16.95 (978-0-8050-7232-7). Fourteen-year-old Hodge, a hunchbacked orphan in medieval times, dreams that one day he will be a servant to royalty, and when his dream comes true Hodge finds himself drawn

into a series of intrigues and adventures. (Rev: BCCB 6/04; BL 5/1/04; SLJ 4/04; VOYA 6/04)

Africa

4252 Badoe, Adwoa. *Between Sisters* (8–12). 2010, Groundwood $18.95 (978-0-88899-996-2); paper $12.95 (978-0-88899-997-9). Sixteen-year-old Ghanaian Gloria dreams of escaping a life of illiteracy, poverty, and AIDS in this poignant story, eventually befriending a young doctor who teaches her to read. (Rev: BL 10/1/10; HB 11–12/10; SLJ 10/1/10; VOYA 12/10)

4253 Burns, Khephra. *Mansa Musa: The Lion of Mali* (4–7). Illus. by Diane Dillon and Leo Dillon. 2001, Harcourt $18.00 (978-0-15-200375-3). Lavish illustrations complement this handsome, challenging book about Mansa Musa's journey from a rural village boyhood to becoming the king of Mali. (Rev: BL 12/1/01; HB 11–12/01; HBG 3/02; SLJ 10/01)

4254 De Graaf, Anne. *Son of a Gun* (6–9). 2012, Eerdmans paper $8 (978-0-8028-5406-3). In Liberia, 10-year-old Nopi and her 8-year-old brother Lucky are kidnapped and forced to become child soldiers, an experience that changes their lives. Batchelder Honor 2013; ALA Notable Books 2013. ⊖ Lexile 700L (Rev: LMC 10/12; SLJ 5/1/12)

4255 Ellis, Deborah. *The Heaven Shop* (5–8). 2004, Fitzhenry & Whiteside $16.95 (978-1-55041-908-5). The AIDS epidemic has a devastating impact on the family of Binti, a 13-year-old Malawi girl. (Rev: BL 9/1/04; SLJ 10/04)

4256 Farmer, Nancy. *A Girl Named Disaster* (6–10). 1996, Orchard paper $19.95 (978-0-531-09539-3). Set in modern-day Africa, this is the story, with fantasy undertones, of Nhamo, who flees from her home in Mozambique to escape a planned marriage and settles with her father's family in Zimbabwe. (Rev: BL 9/1/96; SLJ 10/96*; VOYA 12/96)

4257 Glass, Linzi Alex. *The Year the Gypsies Came* (8–11). 2006, Henry Holt $16.95 (978-0-8050-7999-9). An elderly Zulu watchman turns out to be young Emily's strongest anchor in this moving story about a 12-year-old in 1960s Johannesburg, whose life is changed when a family of Australian vagabonds arrives, bringing additional tensions. (Rev: BL 3/1/06; SLJ 5/06)

4258 Kent, Trilby. *Stones for My Father* (6–9). 2011, Tundra $19.95 (978-1-77049-252-3). Young Corlie finds the strength to survive great hardships during the Boer War and a generous Canadian soldier gives her hope for the future. ALA Notable Books 2012. ⊖ Lexile 970L (Rev: BL 7/11; SLJ 7/11)

4259 Kurtz, Jane. *The Storyteller's Beads* (5–8). 1998, Harcourt $15.00 (978-0-15-201074-4). Two Ethiopian refugees, one a girl from a traditional Ethiopian culture and the other a blind Jewish girl, overcome generations of prejudice against Jews when they face common danger as they flee war and famine during the 1980s. (Rev: BCCB 9/98; BL 5/1/98; HBG 10/98; SLJ 7/98; VOYA 10/98)

4260 Levitin, Sonia. *Dream Freedom* (5–9). 2000, Harcourt $17.00 (978-0-15-202404-8). A novel that graphically portrays the plight of Sudanese slaves, juxtaposed with the story of an American 5th-grade class that joins the fight to free them. (Rev: BL 11/1/00; HBG 3/01; SLJ 10/00; VOYA 12/00)

4261 MacColl, Michaela. *Promise the Night* (6–9). 2011, Chronicle $16.99 (978-081187625-4). Explores Beryl Markham's early life in Kenya, before she defied conventions and became the first person to fly solo across the Atlantic from east to west. ⌒ ℮ (Rev: BL 10/1/11; LMC 1–2/12; SLJ 1/12)

4262 McDaniel, Lurlene. *Angel of Hope* (7–10). 2000, Bantam paper $8.95 (978-0-553-57148-6). In this sequel to *Angel of Mercy,* Heather returns from missionary work in Uganda and, in her place, her younger, spoiled sister, Amber, continues the work in Africa. (Rev: BL 5/1/00; HBG 9/00)

4263 McKissack, Patricia C. *Never Forgotten* (4–8). Illus. by Leo Dillon. 2011, Random House $18.99 (978-0-375-84384-6); LB $21.99 (978-0-375-94453-6). Full of magical realism, this is the wrenching story, told in free verse, of a father left behind in West Africa after his son is taken to America in a slave ship. Coretta Scott King Author Honor 2012; ALA Notable Books 2012. ℮ (Rev: BL 9/1/11*; SLJ 9/1/11*)

4264 McKissack, Patricia C. *Nzingha: Warrior Queen of Matamba* (5–8). Series: Royal Diaries. 2000, Scholastic paper $10.95 (978-0-439-11210-9). Based on fact, this is the story of 17th-century African queen Nzingha who, in present-day Angola, resisted the Portuguese colonizers and slave traders. (Rev: BL 11/1/00; HBG 3/01; SLJ 12/00)

4265 Marsden, Carolyn, and Philip Matzigkeit. *Sahwira: An African Friendship* (5–8). 2009, Candlewick $15.99 (978-0-7636-3575-6). In Rhodesia in the late 1960s, Evan, son of a white American teacher, and Blessing, son of a Shona pastor, find their friendship is challenged by the political and racial tensions that surround them. (Rev: BCCB 7–8/09; BL 4/15/09; SLJ 5/09; VOYA 6/09)

4266 Marston, Elsa. *The Ugly Goddess* (5–8). 2002, Cricket $16.95 (978-0-8126-2667-4). In 523 B.C. Egypt, a 14-year-old Egyptian princess, a young Greek soldier who is in love with her, and an Egyptian boy become embroiled in a mystery adventure that blends fact, fiction, and fantasy. (Rev: BL 1/1–15/03; HBG 3/03; SLJ 12/02)

4267 Michael, Jan. *City Boy* (5–8). 2009, Clarion $16.00 (978-0-547-22310-0). In Malawi, after his parents' deaths from AIDS, Sam must swap his urban environment for his aunt's one-room hut. (Rev: BL 5/1/09; HB 9/09)

4268 Mwangi, Meja. *The Mzungu Boy* (5–8). 2005, Groundwood $15.95 (978-0-88899-653-4). In 1950s Kenya, a 12-year-old Kenyan boy becomes friendly with the white landowner's son despite both families' disapproval. (Rev: BL 8/05; SLJ 11/05)

4269 Naidoo, Beverley. *Burn My Heart* (7–12). 2009, Amistad $15.99 (978-006143297-2); LB $16.89 (978-006143298-9). In the turbulent Kenya of the 1950s, the tenuous friendship of a privileged white boy and a disenfranchised black boy — whose family has been accused of arson — unravels against a dramatic backdrop of prejudice and racial inequality. Lexile 740L (Rev: BL 10/1/08*; LMC 8–9/09; SLJ 2/1/09*; VOYA 4/09)

4270 Naidoo, Beverley. *No Turning Back* (5–9). 1997, HarperCollins $15.89 (978-0-06-027506-8). Jaabu, a homeless African boy, looks for shelter in contemporary Johannesburg. (Rev: BCCB 2/97; BL 12/15/96*; HB 3–4/97; SLJ 2/97; VOYA 10/97)

4271 Nanji, Shenaaz. *Child of Dandelions* (7–12). 2008, Front St $17.95 (978-1-932425-93-2). In 1972, the privileged life of 15-year-old Sabine, member of a wealthy Indian family, is turned upside down when President Idi Amin gives all Indians 90 days to leave the country. (Rev: BL 6/1–15/08; SLJ 5/08)

4272 Park, Linda Sue. *A Long Walk to Water: Based on a True Story* (6–9). 2010, Clarion $16 (978-0-547-25127-1). In alternating chapters, Park tells the grim stories of 11-year-old Salva's flight from Sudan in 1985 and of Nya's life in Sudan in 2008, when she must walk eight hours a day to fetch water for her family. (Rev: BL 9/1/10*; SLJ 11/1/10)

4273 Robert, Na'ima B. *Far from Home* (7–12). 2012, Frances Lincoln paper $8.99 (978-18478000-6-0). The turbulent history of the country now called Zimbabwe is illustrated in stories set in 1964 and 2000. (Rev: BLO 10/15/12; LMC 5–6/13; SLJ 2/13)

4274 Schrefer, Eliot. *Endangered* (8–12). 2012, Scholastic $17.99 (978-0-545-16576-1). Initially resentful of her mother's involvement with a Congolese bonobo sanctuary, 14-year-old Sophie comes to understand and appreciate the work when she spends the summer there, and when civil war breaks out she flees into the jungle with a young ape. ℮ Lexile 900L (Rev: BL 11/15/12; HB 1–2/13; LMC 1–2/13; SLJ 12/12; VOYA 12/12)

4275 Stolz, Joelle. *The Shadows of Ghadames* (6–10). 2004, Random House LB $17.99 (978-0-385-73104-1). In late-19th-century Libya, Malika dreads the restricted life her 12th birthday will bring, but her father's two wives defy convention and nurse a wounded man back to health within the women's community, opening new horizons for Malika. (Rev: BL 12/1/04*; SLJ 11/04)

4276 Stratton, Allan. *Chanda's Wars* (8–12). 2008, HarperTeen $17.99 (978-0-06-087262-5). Chanda, the

African AIDS orphan introduced in *Chanda's Secret,* tracks down her younger brother and sister after they are kidnapped and forced to become vicious child soldiers. (Rev: BL 12/1/07; HB 3–4/08; SLJ 3/08)

4277 Wein, Elizabeth E. *The Lion Hunter* (7–10). Series: The Mark of Solomon. 2007, Viking $16.99 (978-0-670-06163-1). To escape threats made against his aristocratic family, Telemakos (half-Ethiopian grandson of Britain's King Artos) and his young sister Athena are sent to a new community where new friendships are not what they seem in this first volume in a series set in 6th-century Africa and drawing on the author's preceding Arthurian-Aksumite cycle, which ended with *The Sunbird* (2004). (Rev: BL 6/1–15/07; HB 7–8/07; SLJ 9/07)

4278 Wein, Elizabeth E. *The Sunbird* (7–12). Series: The Winter Prince. 2004, Viking $16.99 (978-0-670-03691-2). Telemakos, grandson of noblemen, undertakes a perilous journey to the African kingdom of Aksum to find those responsible for allowing the plague to enter the kingdom in this third volume in the saga. (Rev: BL 6/1–15/04; HB 3–4/04; SLJ 5/04; VOYA 4/04)

4279 Williams, Michael. *Now Is the Time for Running* (7–12). 2011, Little, Brown $17.99 (978-0-316-07790-3). Deo's soccer skills prove to be the 14-year-old's salvation — and that of his mentally disabled brother — as they flee violence in Zimbabwe and seek a new life in South Africa. ℮ Lexile 650L (Rev: BL 9/15/11; HB 7–8/11; LMC 10/11; SLJ 9/1/11*)

4280 Yohalem, Eve. *Escape Under the Forever Sky* (5–8). 2009, Chronicle $16.99 (978-0-8118-6653-8). Lucy, 13-year-old daughter of the U.S. ambassador to Ethiopia, sneaks out of the house and is kidnapped; her survival skills help her when she manages to escape. (Rev: BL 5/1/09; SLJ 5/09)

4281 Zemser, Amy Bronwen. *Beyond the Mango Tree* (6–12). 1998, Greenwillow $14.95 (978-0-688-16005-0). Trapped in her home by a domineering mother, Sarina, a 12-year-old white American girl living in Liberia, befriends a gentle African boy named Boima. (Rev: BL 11/1/98; HB 11–12/98; HBG 3/99; SLJ 10/98; VOYA 4/99)

Asia and the Pacific

4282 Antieau, Kim. *Broken Moon* (6–9). 2007, Simon & Schuster $15.99 (978-1-4169-1767-0). Set in Pakistan, this story of Nadira and her younger brother, who is carried off to become a camel jockey, is disturbing yet not graphic in its descriptions of violence. (Rev: BL 12/15/06; HB 5–6/07; SLJ 5/07)

4283 Bosse, Malcolm. *The Examination* (8–12). 2008, Paw Prints $17.95 (978-1-4352-4634-8). During the Ming Dynasty, two very different Chinese brothers try to understand one another as they travel to Beijing,

where one brother hopes to pass a government examination. (Rev: BL 11/1/94*; SLJ 12/94)

4284 Bosse, Malcolm. *Tusk and Stone* (6–10). 1995, Front St $15.95 (978-1-886910-01-0). Set in 7th-century India, this story tells about a young Brahman who is separated from his sister and sold to the military as a slave, goes on to gain recognition and fame for his skills and bravery as a warrior, and ultimately discovers his true talents and nature as a sculptor and stonecarver. (Rev: BL 12/1/95; VOYA 2/96)

4285 Bradford, Chris. *Young Samurai: The Way of the Warrior* (6–9). 2009, Hyperion $16.99 (978-1-4231-1871-8). After his father's ship is attacked by ninjas, Jack is rescued by a samurai and masters martial arts in this adventure set in 17th-century Japan. ℮ Lexile 860L (Rev: BL 1/1–15/09; SLJ 4/1/09)

4286 Choi, Sook N. *Year of Impossible Goodbyes* (6–10). 1991, Houghton Mifflin $16.00 (978-0-395-57419-5). An autobiographical novel of two children in North Korea following World War II who become separated from their mother while attempting to cross the border into South Korea. (Rev: BL 9/15/91; SLJ 10/91*)

4287 Clarke, Judith. *Kalpana's Dream* (6–9). 2005, Front St $16.95 (978-1-932425-22-2). A visit from her Indian great-grandmother and a school essay assignment help Australian teen Neema to make some important discoveries about who she is. (Rev: BCCB 4/05; BL 5/1/05*; HB 1–2/06; SLJ 8/05; VOYA 8/05)

4288 Clarke, Judith. *The Winds of Heaven* (8–12). 2010, Henry Holt $16.99 (978-080509164-9). In 1950s Australia Clementine and her cousin Fan come from very different backgrounds and have similarly divergent lives. ℮ Lexile 910L (Rev: BL 10/15/10; HB 9–10/10; VOYA 8/10)

4289 Compestine, Ying Chang. *Revolution Is Not a Dinner Party* (6–9). 2007, Henry Holt $16.95 (978-0-8050-8207-4). Nine-year-old Ling, a privileged child growing up in China during the Cultural Revolution, learns her family's vulnerability to the political regime; based on Compestine's own youth. ALA Notable Books 2008. ∩ (Rev: BL 8/07; SLJ 8/07)

4290 Conlogue, Ray. *Shen and the Treasure Fleet* (5–8). 2007, Annick $21.95 (978-1-55451-104-4); paper $11.95 (978-1-55451-103-7). Shen and his sister Chang try to free their mother and learn their father's fate while at sea with Zheng He's "treasure fleet" in early 15th-century China. (Rev: BL 11/15/07)

4291 Crew, Gary. *Mama's Babies* (6–9). 2002, Annick $18.95 (978-1-55037-725-5); paper $6.95 (978-1-55037-724-8). Set in Australia in 1897, this absorbing story of cruelty toward foster children — told from the point of view of 9-year-old Sarah — is based on true stories of "baby farmer" mothers who killed their young charges. (Rev: BCCB 9/02; BL 8/02; HBG 10/02; SLJ 6/02; VOYA 8/02)

4292 Crew, Gary. *Troy Thompson's Excellent Poetry Book* (4–7). Illus. by Craig Smith. 2003, Kane/Miller $14.95 (978-1-929132-52-2). Troy Thompson, an 11-year-old Australian boy, uses different forms of poetry to express his feelings about various elements of his life, participating in a yearlong literature assignment and, we learn at the end, winning the grand prize. (Rev: SLJ 1/04)

4293 Ellis, Deborah. *The Breadwinner* (5–7). 2001, Groundwood $15.95 (978-0-88899-419-6). In Kabul under the strict rule of the Taliban, Parvana dresses as a boy so she can work to feed the remaining women in her family. (Rev: BL 3/1/01; HBG 10/01; SLJ 7/01; VOYA 6/01)

4294 Ellis, Deborah. *My Name Is Parvana* (5–8). Series: Breadwinner. 2012, Groundwood $16.95 (978-1-55498-297-4). Parvana is now 15 and uncooperative with her American captors in this sequel to the moving books about life in turbulent Afghanistan. **e** Lexile 670L (Rev: BL 10/15/12; SLJ 10/12*)

4295 Ellis, Deborah. *No Ordinary Day* (4–7). 2011, Groundwood $16.95 (978-1-55498-134-2). Valli, a poor Indian orphan who has a fear of lepers, is horrified to hear that she herself has the disease. ALA Notable Books 2012. (Rev: BL 11/1/11*; SLJ 9/1/11*)

4296 Frazier, Angie. *Everlasting* (8–10). 2010, Scholastic $17.99 (978-0-545-11473-8). In 1885 independent-minded 17-year-old Camille sets off across Australia in search of her long-lost mother, whose existence her father revealed before the shipwreck that killed him. **e** Lexile 790L (Rev: LMC 10/10; SLJ 9/1/10; VOYA 6/10)

4297 Garland, Sherry. *Song of the Buffalo Boy* (7–10). 1992, Harcourt paper $6.00 (978-0-15-200098-1). Loi, the spurned daughter of an American G.I. and a disgraced Vietnamese woman, escapes to Ho Chi Minh City to avoid an arranged marriage. (Rev: BL 4/15/06)

4298 Gratz, Alan. *Samurai Shortstop* (8–11). 2006, Dial $15.99 (978-0-8037-3075-5). Even though the samurai traditions have been outlawed, 16-year-old Toyo is educated in the ancient ways and applies his discipline to the game of baseball in this novel set in 1890 Tokyo. 🎧 (Rev: BL 4/15/06*; LMC 11–12/06; SLJ 7/06)

4299 Harrison, Troon. *The Horse Road* (4–7). 2012, Bloomsbury $16.99 (978-1-59990-846-5). In ancient central Asia horse-crazy Kalli, a young teen, must act to save her beloved horses from invaders; a history-rich novel with lots of detail. **e** Lexile 1050L (Rev: BL 8/12; LMC 10/12; SLJ 9/12)

4300 Haugaard, Erik C. *The Revenge of the Forty-Seven Samurai* (7–12). 1995, Houghton Mifflin $16.00 (978-0-395-70809-5). In a true story set in feudal Japan, a young servant is a witness to destiny when his master meets an unjust death. (Rev: BL 5/15/95; SLJ 4/95)

4301 Herrick, Steven. *Cold Skin* (8–12). 2009, Front St $18.95 (978-159078572-0). The murder of a pretty girl sets an Australian town on edge in this story set just after World War II. (Rev: BL 4/15/09; SLJ 5/1/09)

4302 Herrick, Steven. *The Simple Gift* (8–10). 2004, Simon & Schuster paper $14.95 (978-0-689-86867-2). In this compelling free-verse novel told in three voices, Australian 16-year-old Billy escapes an unhappy family life and takes up residence in an abandoned freight car where he finds both friendship and love. (Rev: BL 8/04; SLJ 9/04; VOYA 2/05)

4303 Ho, Minfong. *The Clay Marble* (5–9). 1991, Houghton Mifflin $12.00 (978-0-395-77155-6). After fleeing from her Cambodian home in the early 1980s, 12-year-old Dara is separated from her family during an attack on a refugee camp on the Thailand border. (Rev: BL 11/15/91; SLJ 10/91)

4304 Ho, Minfong. *Gathering the Dew* (6–9). 2003, Scholastic $16.95 (978-0-439-38197-0). Twelve-year-old Nakri loses her beloved sister to the brutal Khmer Rouge regime in Cambodia and starts a new life in America, determined to uphold her sister's dedication to dance. (Rev: BL 3/1/03; HB 5–6/03; SLJ 3/03)

4305 Hollyer, Belinda. *River Song* (5–8). 2008, Holiday $16.95 (978-0-8234-2149-7). Set in New Zealand, this story of a half-Maori girl torn between two cultures is infused with magical elements from Maori legend. (Rev: BL 5/1/08; SLJ 6/08)

4306 Hoobler, Dorothy, and Thomas Hoobler. *In Darkness, Death* (7–10). 2004, Putnam $16.99 (978-0-399-23767-6). Set in 18th-century Japan like the authors' previous *The Ghost in the Tokaido Inn* (1999), this novel tells how 14-year-old Seikei and his adopted father set out to discover who murdered a powerful warlord. (Rev: BL 5/1/04; SLJ 3/04; VOYA 4/04)

4307 Hoobler, Dorothy, and Thomas Hoobler. *A Samurai Never Fears Death* (6–9). Series: The Samurai Mysteries. 2007, Philomel $12.99 (978-0-399-24609-8). Seikei, who is now a samurai, must clear the name of a puppeteer implicated in a crime in this sequel to *The Ghost in the Tokaido Inn* (1999). (Rev: BL 3/15/07; SLJ 4/07)

4308 Hoobler, Dorothy, and Thomas Hoobler. *The Sword That Cut the Burning Grass* (5–8). Series: The Samurai Mysteries. 2005, Philomel $10.99 (978-0-399-24272-4). In this fourth book about the aspiring young samurai, Seikei tackles a challenging task involving the teenage emperor. (Rev: BL 5/1/05; SLJ 10/05)

4309 Huynh, Quang Nhuong. *The Land I Lost: Adventures of a Boy in Vietnam* (5–8). Illus. by Mai Vo Dinh. 1990, HarperCollins $15.89 (978-0-397-32448-4); paper $5.99 (978-0-06-440183-8). The story of a boy's growing up in rural Vietnam before the war.

4310 Kadohata, Cynthia. *A Million Shades of Gray* (7–12). 2010, Simon & Schuster $16.99 (978-1-4169-

1883-7). In 1975 Vietnam, Y'Tin, 13, survives a massacre and is able to find his favorite elephant, Lady, and take her deep into the jungle, but the stress of this flight lingers with him for years. ℮ Lexile 700L (Rev: BL 12/1/09; SLJ 3/10; VOYA 2/10)

4311 Kelly, Lynne. *Chained* (4–7). 2012, Farrar $16.99 (978-037431237-4). Hastin, 10, takes a job looking after a young elephant who is mistreated by a cruel circus owner in this moving story set in northern India. ℮ Lexile 770L (Rev: BL 6/12; HB 7–8/12; LMC 8/12*; SLJ 6/12)

4312 Khan, Rukhsana. *Wanting Mor* (5–8). 2009, Greenwood $17.95 (978-0-88899-858-3). This is a harrowing tale about a young Afghani girl, Jameela, who faces abuse, abandonment, and an orphanage after the death of her mother; based on a true story. (Rev: BCCB 9/09; BL 4/1/09; HB 7/09; LMC 10/09)

4313 Lasky, Kathryn. *Jahanara: Princess of Princesses* (4–8). Series: Royal Diaries. 2002, Scholastic paper $10.95 (978-0-439-22350-8). Princess Jaharana, the daughter of Shah Jahan (who built the Taj Mahal) writes detailed diary accounts of her 17th-century life, with rich descriptions of her surroundings, palace intrigues, and dealing with her family. (Rev: BL 1/1–15/03; HBG 3/03; SLJ 1/03)

4314 Lewis, Richard. *The Killing Sea: A Story of the Tsunami That Stunned the World* (6–9). 2006, Simon & Schuster $15.95 (978-1-4169-1165-4). This novel based on the devastating 2004 tsunami spares none of the horrifying details of the disaster as it follows survivors Ruslan and Sarah as they search for family and for help. (Rev: BL 12/15/06; SLJ 2/07)

4315 McKay, Sharon E. *Thunder over Kandahar* (7–12). Photos by Rafal Gerszak. 2010, Annick LB $21.95 (978-1-55451-267-6); paper $12.95 (978-1-55451-266-9). Two Afghan teens, Yasmine and Tamanna, are from very different backgrounds but become friends as they flee the Taliban. ⌒ (Rev: BL 12/1/10; SLJ 12/1/10)

4316 Marchetta, Melina. *Looking for Alibrandi* (8–10). 1999, Orchard LB $17.99 (978-0-531-33142-2). In this novel set in Sydney, Australia, teenage Josie Alibrandi is torn between her family's cultural ties to Italy and her Australian environment. (Rev: BL 2/15/99; HB 5–6/99; HBG 9/99; SLJ 7/99; VOYA 6/99)

4317 Master, Irfan. *A Beautiful Lie* (6–9). 2012, Albert Whitman $16.99 (978-0-8075-0597-7). As partition looms in 1947 India, 13-year-old Bilal tries to hide the bad news from his dying father. ⌒ ℮ Lexile 790L (Rev: BL 10/15/12; LMC 1–2/13; SLJ 10/12)

4318 Millard, Glenda. *A Small Free Kiss in the Dark* (7–10). 2010, Holiday House $16.95 (978-0-8234-2264-7). When war strikes unexpectedly, four unlikely allies — 12-year-old runaway Skip, homeless man Billy, 6-year-old Max, and teen mother Tia — flee their

Australian city. Lexile 840L (Rev: BL 3/1/10; LMC 10/10; SLJ 3/10)

4319 Newton, Robert. *Runner* (7–10). 2007, Knopf $15.99 (978-0-375-83744-9). Set in Australia in 1919, this novel is about 15-year-old Charlie and his dangerous efforts to lift himself and his mother from poverty. (Rev: BCCB 7–8/07; BL 4/15/07; SLJ 4/07)

4320 Park, Linda Sue. *Seesaw Girl* (4–7). 1999, Clarion $14.00 (978-0-395-91514-1). In 17th-century Korea, 12-year-old Jade Blossom wanders away from her aristocratic palace and discovers the reality and poverty of the world outside. (Rev: BCCB 12/99; BL 9/1/99; HBG 3/00; SLJ 9/99)

4321 Park, Linda Sue. *A Single Shard* (4–8). 2001, Clarion $15.00 (978-0-395-97827-6). This Newbery Medal winner describes a Korean boy's journey through unknown territory to deliver two valuable pots. (Rev: BCCB 3/01; BL 4/1/01*; HBG 10/01; SLJ 5/01*)

4322 Park, Linda Sue. *When My Name Was Keoko* (5–9). 2002, Clarion $16.00 (978-0-618-13335-2). A young brother and sister tell, in first-person accounts, what life was like during the Japanese occupation of Korea. (Rev: BCCB 5/02; BL 3/1/02; HB 5–6/02; HBG 10/02; SLJ 4/02)

4323 Paterson, Katherine. *The Master Puppeteer* (4–7). Illus. by Haru Wells. 1989, HarperCollins paper $5.99 (978-0-06-440281-1). Feudal Japan is the setting for this story about a young apprentice puppeteer and his search for a mysterious bandit.

4324 Paterson, Katherine. *Of Nightingales That Weep* (4–7). Illus. by Haru Wells. 1974, HarperCollins paper $6.99 (978-0-06-440282-8). A story set in feudal Japan tells of Takiko, a samurai's daughter, who is sent to the royal court when her mother remarries.

4325 Paterson, Katherine. *Rebels of the Heavenly Kingdom* (7–9). 1983, Avon paper $2.95 (978-0-380-68304-8). In 19th-century China a 15-year-old boy and a young girl engage in activities to overthrow the Manchu government.

4326 Paterson, Katherine. *The Sign of the Chrysanthemum* (5–7). Illus. by Peter Landa. 1973, HarperCollins LB $14.89 (978-0-690-04913-8); paper $5.99 (978-0-06-440232-3). At the death of his mother, a young boy sets out to find his samurai father in 12th-century Japan.

4327 Perkins, Mitali. *Bamboo People* (5–8). 2010, Charlesbridge $16.95 (978-1-58089-328-2). Contemporary Burma is seen through the perspectives of two protagonists — 15-year-old Chiko, reluctant soldier and son of an imprisoned doctor, and Tu Reh, a Karenni refugee. YALSA Top Ten Best Fiction for Young Adults 2011. ⌒ Lexile 680L (Rev: BL 5/15/10; HB 7–8/10; LMC 11–12/10; SLJ 11/1/10*)

4328 Place, Francois. *The Old Man Mad About Drawing* (5–8). Trans. by William Rodarmor. 2003, Godine

$19.95 (978-1-56792-260-8). In 19th-century Edo (now Tokyo), Tojiro, a 9-year-old orphan who sells rice cakes, becomes the assistant to a famous old artist. (Rev: BL 3/15/04*; HB 3–4/04; SLJ 5/04)

4329 Qamar, Amjed. *Beneath My Mother's Feet* (7–10). 2008, Atheneum $16.99 (978-1-4169-4728-8). Fourteen-year-old Nazia's life changes dramatically when her family's economic well-being spirals downward and she finds herself cleaning houses in this novel set in Karachi, Pakistan. (Rev: BL 8/08; SLJ 7/08)

4330 Reedy, Trent. *Words in the Dust* (5–8). 2011, Scholastic $17.99 (978-0-545-26125-8). Learning to read and the unexpected opportunity to have her cleft palate repaired give 13-year-old Afghani Zulaikha a new outlook on life. ∩ Lexile 670L (Rev: BL 1/1–15/11; LMC 5–6/11; SLJ 2/1/11)

4331 Roberts, Marion. *Sunny Side Up* (5–8). Illus. 2009, Random $15.99 (978-0-385-73672-5). An 11-year-old Australian girl struggles to balance a complex set of relationships that include divorced parents with newly emerging families, a long-lost grandmother and a best friend whose sudden interest in a boy threatens their pizza delivery business. (Rev: BCCB 2/09; BL 1/1–15/09; SLJ 2/09)

4332 Russell, Ching Yeung. *Child Bride* (4–7). 1999, Boyds Mills $15.95 (978-1-56397-748-0). Set in China in the early 1940s, this is the story of 11-year-old Ying, her arranged marriage, and an understanding bridegroom who allows her to go home to her ailing grandmother. (Rev: BL 3/1/99; HBG 10/99; SLJ 4/99)

4333 Russell, Ching Yeung. *Lichee Tree* (4–7). 1997, Boyds Mills $15.95 (978-1-56397-629-2). Growing up in China during the 1940s, Ying dreams of selling lichee nuts and visiting Canton. (Rev: BCCB 4/97; BL 3/15/97; SLJ 6/97)

4334 Say, Allen. *Tea with Milk* (4–8). 1999, Houghton Mifflin LB $17.00 (978-0-395-90495-4). A picture book about the author's mother, who was forced by her father to leave her California residence and return to the family's original home in Japan. (Rev: BCCB 6/99; BL 3/15/99*; HB 7–8/99; HBG 10/99; SLJ 5/99) [952]

4335 Sayres, Meghan Nuttall. *Anahita's Woven Riddle* (8–12). 2006, Abrams $16.95 (978-0-8109-5481-6). In early-20th-century Iran, Anahita, a teenage nomad, resists an arranged marriage and seeks a mate who can solve the riddles woven into her wedding carpet. (Rev: SLJ 1/07)

4336 Sheth, Kashmira. *Boys Without Names* (4–7). 2010, HarperCollins $15.99 (978-0-06-185760-7). Eleven-year-old Gopal's rural family cannot make ends meet and heads for Mumbai where the boy looks for work only to find himself a captive in a soul-crushing sweatshop. e Lexile 670L (Rev: BL 11/15/09; SLJ 1/10)

4337 Sheth, Kashmira. *Keeping Corner* (7–12). 2007, Hyperion $15.99 (978-0-7868-3859-2). A 12-year-old widow, Leela is forced to mourn in her family's home for a year but dreams of reforms that would allow her to get an education and a career in this story set in 1918 India. (Rev: BL 10/15/07; LMC 1/08; SLJ 12/07)

4338 Sheth, Kashmira. *Koyal Dark, Mango Sweet* (8–11). 2006, Hyperion $15.99 (978-0-7868-3857-8). At the age of 16, Jeeta, who lives in Mumbai (formerly Bombay), finds many of the traditions that preoccupy her mother to be old-fashioned and inappropriate. (Rev: BL 4/1/06; SLJ 4/06)

4339 Smith, Icy. *Half Spoon of Rice: A Survival Story of the Cambodian Genocide* (4–7). Illus. by Sopaul Nhem. 2010, East West Discovery Press $19.95 (978-0-9821675-8-8). Nine-year-old Nat relates his shocking experiences after the Khmer Rouge force millions to leave Phnom Penh and work in the fields; a moving picture book for older readers. (Rev: BL 12/15/09; LMC 5–6/10; SLJ 12/09)

4340 Snow, Maya. *Sisters of the Sword* (6–9). Series: Sisters of the Sword. 2008, HarperCollins $16.99 (978-0-06-124387-5). In 13th-century Japan two sisters — Kimi and Hana — disguise themselves as boys to attend samurai school and avenge their father, who was killed by their uncle; an action-packed first volume that offers good historical detail. (Rev: BL 6/1–15/08; SLJ 9/08)

4341 Sparrow, Rebecca. *The Year Nick McGowan Came to Stay* (8–11). 2008, Knopf $15.99 (978-0-375-84570-3). When Nick comes to live with her family after being kicked out of boarding school, Rachel finds out that under his cool, unapproachable exterior is a boy with serious problems; set in Australia in the late 1980s. (Rev: BL 4/15/08; SLJ 5/08)

4342 Sreenivasan, Jyotsna. *Aruna's Journeys* (4–7). 1997, Smooth Stone paper $6.95 (978-0-9619401-7-1). Aruna denies her Indian heritage until she spends a summer in Bangalore, India. (Rev: BL 7/97)

4343 Staples, Suzanne Fisher. *The House of Djinn* (7–12). 2008, Farrar $16.95 (978-0-374-39936-8). Set in Pakistan, this family drama (and follow-up to 1989's *Shabanu* and 1993's *Haveli*) about Mumtaz and Jameel, young cousins who are ordered to marry, shows the conflicts between generations in traditional Pakistani families. (Rev: BL 2/15/08; SLJ 4/08)

4344 Stone, Jeff. *Tiger* (6–9). Series: The Ancestors. 2005, Random House LB $17.99 (978-0-375-93071-3). Five young warrior monk trainees survive a deadly attack on their monastery and use their martial arts skills to avenge their beloved grandmaster, who was killed in the attack. (Rev: BCCB 2/05; BL 2/15/05; SLJ 2/05)

4345 Thomason, Mark. *Moonrunner* (4–8). 2009, Kane/Miller $15.95 (978-1-935279-03-7). In 1890s Australia, Casey, 12, copes with a difficult transition to a new home by befriending a spirited wild stallion that he decides to save from captivity at all costs. Lexile 620L (Rev: BL 4/15/09; SLJ 6/1/09)

4346 Vejjajiva, Jane. *The Happiness of Kati* (4–7). Trans. by Prudence Borthwick. 2006, Simon & Schuster $15.95 (978-1-4169-1788-5). Nine-year-old Kati's mother is dying and the identity of her father is a mystery in this story set in Thailand. (Rev: BL 5/15/06; SLJ 6/06)

4347 Venkatraman, Padma. *Climbing the Stairs* (6–9). 2008, Putnam $16.99 (978-0-399-24746-0). Vidya's life changes when her father is injured while protesting against the British occupation of India during World War II. (Rev: BL 4/15/08; SLJ 5/08)

4348 Venkatraman, Padma. *Island's End* (7–10). 2011, Putnam $16.99 (978-0-399-25099-6). Uido, 15, copes with the threats facing her people, who inhabit an island in the Bay of Bengal, and tries to provide the spiritual guidance they expect from her. Lexile 800L (Rev: BL 9/15/11*; LMC 11–12/11; SLJ 8/11*; VOYA 10/11)

4349 Whelan, Gloria. *Chu Ju's House* (6–9). 2004, HarperCollins $16.99 (978-0-06-050724-4). To save her baby sister, destined to be put up for adoption to comply with China's limits on a family's number of children, 14-year-old Chu Ju leaves home and is forced to fend for herself. (Rev: BCCB 5/04; BL 3/15/04; HB 5–6/04; SLJ 5/04; VOYA 10/04)

4350 Whelan, Gloria. *Goodbye, Vietnam* (5–8). 1992, Turtleback paper $11.65 (978-0-606-05848-3). Young Mai and her family escape from Vietnam to Hong Kong, suffering through a difficult boat journey; originally published in 1992. (Rev: BL 4/15/06; HB 1/93; SLJ 9/92)

4351 Whitesel, Cheryl Aylward. *Blue Fingers: A Ninja's Tale* (5–8). 2004, Clarion $15.00 (978-0-618-38139-5). In 16th-century Japan, 12-year-old Koji is trained to become a ninja warrior. (Rev: BL 3/15/04; SLJ 3/04)

4352 Whitesel, Cheryl Aylward. *Rebel: A Tibetan Odyssey* (5–8). 2000, HarperCollins $16.99 (978-0-688-16735-6). In Tibet about a century ago, a young boy named Thunder is sent to live with his uncle, an important lama in a Buddhist monastery. (Rev: BCCB 5/00; BL 4/15/00; HBG 3/01; SLJ 7/00)

4353 Wu, Priscilla. *The Abacus Contest: Stories from Taiwan and China* (5–8). 1996, Fulcrum $15.95 (978-1-55591-243-7). Six simple short stories explore life in a Taiwanese city. (Rev: BL 7/96; SLJ 6/96)

4354 Wulffson, Don. *The Golden Rat* (6–9). 2007, Bloomsbury $16.95 (978-1-59990-000-1). In 12th-century China, 16-year-old Baoliu is wrongly accused of murdering his stepmother; his father, although rejecting Baoliu, arranges for a stand-in to be executed in Baoliu's place and Baoliu must then make his own way in the world, eager to prove his innocence. (Rev: BL 9/1/07; SLJ 1/08)

4355 Yep, Laurence. *Dragons of Silk* (6–9). Series: Golden Mountain Chronicles. 2011, HarperCollins $16.99 (978-0-06-027518-1). This final installment in the series follows successive generations of women who work in the evolving silk industry in China and San Francisco. Lexile 830L (Rev: BL 10/15/11; HB 11–12/11; SLJ 11/1/11)

4356 Yep, Laurence. *Lady of Ch'iao Kuo: Warrior of the South* (5–8). Series: Royal Diaries. 2001, Scholastic $10.95 (978-0-439-16483-2). In this volume of the Royal Diaries series, the teenage Princess Redbird of the Hsien tribe must use her diplomatic skills to save the lives of both her own people and Chinese colonists in the 6th century A.D. Historical notes add background information. (Rev: BL 11/1/01)

4357 Yep, Laurence. *Mountain Light* (8–12). 1997, HarperCollins paper $8.99 (978-0-06-440667-3). Yep continues to explore life in 19th-century China through the experience of a girl, Cassia, her father and friends, and their struggle against the Manchus in this sequel to *The Serpent's Children* (1984). (Rev: BL 9/15/85; SLJ 1/87; VOYA 12/85)

Europe and the Middle East

4358 Abdel-Fattah, Randa. *Where the Streets Had a Name* (5–8). 2010, Scholastic $17.99 (978-0-545-17292-9). Thirteen-year-old Palestinian Hayaat faces checkpoints and curfews when she travels from Bethlehem to Jerusalem in search of some soil she hopes will bring relief to her sick grandmother. Lexile 740L (Rev: BL 10/1/10; HB 1–2/11; LMC 1–2/11; SLJ 11/1/10; VOYA 4/10)

4359 Almond, David. *Raven Summer* (7–12). 2009, Delacorte $16.99 (978-0-385-73806-4); LB $19.99 (978-0-385-90715-6). War and violence are at the heart of this novel set in northern England during the Iraq War, in which teenage Liam copes with an abandoned child, a Liberian refugee, and a prejudiced bully. Lexile HL480L (Rev: BL 9/15/09*; HB 11–12/09; LMC 11–12/09; SLJ 12/09; VOYA 12/09)

4360 Armstrong, Alan. *Raleigh's Page* (5–7). Illus. by Tim Jessell. 2007, Random House $16.99 (978-0-375-83319-9). As page to Walter Raleigh, 11-year-old Andrew learns about court life, becomes embroiled in intrigues, and has adventures that include visiting the New World. (Rev: BL 8/07; HB 11–12/07; LMC 11/07; SLJ 11/07)

4361 Avi. *Crispin: The End of Time* (5–8). 2010, HarperCollins $16.99 (978-0-06-174080-0); LB $17.89 (978-0-06-174082-4). Still heading for Iceland, Crispin leaves Troth at a convent that needs a healer and continues on alone, soon finding himself in danger from a group of traveling musicians. Lexile 690L (Rev: BL 4/15/10; HB 7–8/10; SLJ 6/10)

4362 Avi. *The Traitors' Gate* (6–9). 2007, Simon & Schuster $17.99 (978-0-689-85335-7). Victorian England comes to life in this story about 14-year-old John's efforts to save his father from debtors' prison and to find out why he's being spied on. ∩ (Rev: BCCB 7–8/07; BL 4/15/07; HB 9–10/07; SLJ 5/07)

4363 Bajoria, Paul. *The God of Mischief* (7–10). Illus. by Bret Bertholf. 2007, Little, Brown $16.99 (978-0-316-01091-7). Orphans Mog and Nick, the twin discovered in *The Printer's Devil* (2005), are sent to live with their uncle, Sir Septimus Cloy, at Kniveacres Hall and there have further spooky adventures and investigate their past; this series is set in early-19th-century England. (Rev: BL 1/1–15/07; HB 1–2/07; SLJ 3/07)

4364 Banks, Lynne Reid. *The Dungeon* (6–9). 2002, HarperCollins $16.99 (978-0-06-623782-4). Retribution is at the heart of this dark story about a bereaved 14th-century laird whose anger spurs him to abuse a Chinese child. (Rev: BL 10/1/02; HB 9/02; HBG 3/03; SLJ 12/02)

4365 Banks, Lynne Reid. *Tiger, Tiger* (5–8). 2005, Delacorte LB $17.99 (978-0-385-90264-9). Two tiger cubs arrive in Rome destined for different fates; Brute is trained to be a killer of men in the Colosseum while Boots becomes a pet for the caesar's daughter, a decision with dangerous consequences. (Rev: BL 5/15/05; SLJ 6/05)

4366 Baratz-Logsted, Lauren. *The Education of Bet* (8–11). 2010, Houghton Mifflin $16 (978-0-547-22308-7). In 19th-century England 16-year-old Elizabeth poses as her brother Will, who has joined the army, and takes his place at boarding school, hoping to gain an education but also facing quite a few challenges. (Rev: BL 5/1/10; SLJ 12/1/10)

4367 Baratz-Logsted, Lauren. *The Twin's Daughter* (7–11). 2010, Bloomsbury $16.99 (978-1-59990-513-6). Thirteen-year-old Lucy Sexton's peaceful, privileged life in Victorian London is upset when her mother's identical twin sister turns up, starting a series of events that ends in murder. ℮ Lexile 910L (Rev: BL 9/1/10; LMC 10/10; SLJ 12/1/10; VOYA 12/10)

4368 Barratt, Mark. *Joe Rat* (7–10). 2009, Eerdmans paper $9 (978-0-8028-5356-1). In 19th-century London orphan Joe escapes his bleak future in the sewers by choosing to trust his new friend Bess Farleigh and a madman who gives the two sanctuary. (Rev: HB 1–2/10; SLJ 10/09)

4369 Bawden, Nina. *The Real Plato Jones* (5–8). 1993, Clarion $15.00 (978-0-395-66972-3). British teen Plato Jones and his mother return to Greece for his grandfather's funeral, where Plato discovers that his grandfather may have been a coward and traitor while serving in the Greek Resistance. (Rev: BCCB 11/93; BL 10/15/93; SLJ 11/93*)

4370 Beaufrand, Mary Jane. *Primavera* (8–10). 2008, Little, Brown $16.99 (978-0-316-01644-5). While Sandro Botticelli uses Flora's sister Domenica as inspiration for his painting "Primavera," Flora plots an escape

from her powerful family and a future in a convent. (Rev: BL 1/1–15/08; LMC 1/08; SLJ 2/08)

4371 Blackwood, Gary. *Shakespeare Stealer* (5–8). 1998, NAL $16.99 (978-0-525-45863-0). A 14-year-old apprentice at the Globe Theater is sent by a rival theater company to steal Shakespeare's plays. (Rev: BL 6/1–15/98; HB 7–8/98; HBG 10/98; SLJ 6/98; VOYA 8/98)

4372 Blackwood, Gary. *Shakespeare's Spy* (5–8). 2003, Dutton $16.99 (978-0-525-47145-5). Romance and intrigue are at hand as Widge continues his career at the Globe Theatre in this sequel to *The Shakespeare Stealer* (1998) and *Shakespeare's Scribe* (2000). (Rev: BL 9/1/03; HB 11–12/03; HBG 4/04; SLJ 10/03)

4373 Bowler, Tim. *Playing Dead* (5–8). Series: Blade. 2009, Philomel $16.99 (978-0-399-25186-3). Full of British slang and violence, this speedily paced thriller features 14-year-old Blade, a street kid with an instinct for survival amid a culture of gangs. (Rev: BL 5/1/09; HB 5/09; LMC 10/09; SLJ 8/09; VOYA 6/09)

4374 Bradbury, Jennifer. *Wrapped* (7–10). 2011, Atheneum $16.99 (978-1-4169-9007-9). In early 19th-century England 17-year-old debutante Agnes discovers a jackal in an Egyptian mummy and becomes embroiled in international intrigue. ∩ ℮ Lexile 860L (Rev: BL 5/1/11; LMC 8–9/11*; SLJ 6/11; VOYA 6/11)

4375 Bradley, Kimberly Brubaker. *The Lacemaker and the Princess* (4–8). 2007, Simon & Schuster $16.99 (978-1-4169-1920-9). As the French Revolution gathers strength, a young lace maker becomes the companion of Princess Marie-Thérèse, daughter of Marie Antoinette and King Louis XVI, and witness the growing social unrest. (Rev: BL 4/15/07; SLJ 7/07)

4376 Burgis, Stephanie. *A Most Improper Magick* (6–10). Series: Unladylike Adventures of Kat Stephenson. 2010, Templar paper $5.99 (978-1848770072). Romance, historical fiction, literary allusions, and humor are interwoven in this story, set in England in the early 19th century, about 12-year-old Kat who seeks to use her magic powers to help her siblings. ℮ Lexile 740L (Rev: BL 2/15/10; LMC 11–12/10; SLJ 12/1/10)

4377 Buzbee, Lewis. *The Haunting of Charles Dickens* (5–8). Illus. by Greg Ruth. 2010, Feiwel & Friends $17.99 (978-0-312-38256-8). Twelve-year-old Meg searches the streets of 1862 London for her missing brother Orion, accompanied by a family friend, the famed author Charles Dickens. ℮ Lexile 910L (Rev: BL 11/1/10; LMC 1–2/11; SLJ 11/1/10; VOYA 2/11)

4378 Cadnum, Michael. *Peril on the Sea* (7–10). 2009, Farrar $16.95 (978-037435823-5). Sherwin, an 18-year-old crew member on Captain Fletcher's *Vixen*, is charged with recording the captain's memoirs as they fight the Spanish Armada in 1588. (Rev: BL 4/15/09; VOYA 10/09)

4379 Cadnum, Michael. *Ship of Fire* (6–8). 2003, Viking $16.99 (978-0-670-89907-4). Apprentice surgeon Thomas, 17, has to learn medicine and seafaring fast when he sails with Sir Francis Drake's fleet. (Rev: BL 9/15/03; SLJ 10/03)

4380 Cameron, Sharon. *The Dark Unwinding* (7–12). 2012, Scholastic $17.99 (978-0-545-32786-2). Katharine Tulman, 17, faces various challenges when she arrives at her uncle's estate in 1852, initially prepared to commit him to an asylum. **e** Lexile 890L (Rev: BLO 9/15/12; HB 11–12/12; LMC 1–2/13; SLJ 12/12; VOYA 12/12)

4381 Carter, Anne Laurel. *The Shepherd's Granddaughter* (7–12). 2008, Groundwood $17.95 (978-0-88899-902-3). Palestinian Amani, 15, witnesses the heartbreak and destruction of displacement firsthand in this story of the volatile Israeli-Palestinian conflict. **e** (Rev: BLO 10/7/08; LMC 5–6/09; SLJ 12/08)

4382 Cassidy, Cathy. *Scarlett* (5–8). 2006, Viking $16.99 (978-0-670-06068-9). Much to her surprise (and with some help from a mysterious boy), 12-year-old Scarlett actually enjoys living in Ireland with her father and his new family. (Rev: BL 12/1/06)

4383 Cheng, Andrea. *The Bear Makers* (6–9). 2008, Front St $16.95 (978-159078518-8). This affecting story of a family struggling to adapt to the new Soviet regime in post-World War II Hungary is told from the point of view of 11-year-old Kata, who has flashbacks to their time hiding from the Nazis. Lexile 500L (Rev: BL 12/1/08; LMC 1–2/09; SLJ 12/08)

4384 *Clay Man: The Golem of Prague* (5–8). Retold by Irene N. Watts. Illus. by Kathryn E. Shoemaker. 2009, Tundra $19.95 (978-0-88776-880-4). Told from the perspective of pensive 13-year-old Jacob, the story of the magical golem who protected the Jews of 16th-century Prague is illustrated in striking black-and-white drawings. **e** Lexile 780L (Rev: BLO 12/1/09; SLJ 3/10)

4385 Collins, Pat Lowery. *Hidden Voices: The Orphan Musicians of Venice* (8–10). 2009, Candlewick $17.99 (978-076363917-4). Set in an orphanage where composer Antonio Vivaldi teaches, this story is about three of his young students — Anetta, Rosalba, and Luisa — and their differing aspirations. Lexile 1040L (Rev: BL 4/15/09; HB 7–8/09; LMC 8–9/09; SLJ 5/1/09; VOYA 6/09)

4386 Conlon-McKenna, Marita. *Fields of Home* (6–10). 1997, Holiday paper $15.95 (978-0-8234-1295-2). In this sequel to *Under the Hawthorn Tree* (1990) and *Wildflower Girl* (1992), the Irish O'Driscoll family saga continues as Michael and Eily try to make progress in spite of the hard times in Ireland. (Rev: BCCB 7–8/97; BL 4/15/97; SLJ 6/97)

4387 Cooney, Caroline B. *Enter Three Witches* (8–11). 2007, Scholastic $16.99 (978-0-439-71156-2). A novel based on Shakespeare's play *Macbeth* in which the ac-

tion centers on 14-year-old Lady Mary, ward of Lord and Lady Macbeth. (Rev: BCCB 5/07; BL 3/1/07; HB 5–6/07; LMC 10/07; SLJ 5/07)

4388 Cooper, Michelle. *A Brief History of Montmaray* (7–10). 2009, Knopf $16.99 (978-0-375-85864-2); LB $19.99 (978-0-375-95864-9). On the invented island nation of Montmaray in 1936, Sophie FitzOsborne, niece to the rather nutty king, lives in a castle with her family and starts a diary in which she records the struggle to escape Nazi domination; romance, conspiracy, ghosts, murder — they're all here. ∩ **e** Lexile 1000L (Rev: BL 9/15/09*; HB 11–12/09; LMC 10/09; SLJ 12/09; VOYA 4/10)

4389 Cottrell Boyce, Frank. *Framed* (4–7). 2006, HarperCollins $16.99 (978-0-06-073402-2). Life changes dramatically for 9-year-old Dylan Hughes and his quiet Welsh village when priceless art from London's National Gallery is temporarily stored in a nearby quarry. ∩ (Rev: BL 9/1/06; SLJ 8/06*)

4390 Creech, Sharon. *The Castle Corona* (4–7). Illus. by David Diaz. 2007, HarperCollins $18.99 (978-0-06-084621-3). This lively and entertaining fairy tale set in medieval Italy follows a pair of orphaned peasant children named Pia and Enzio who become tasters for the royal family of Castle Corona. ∩ (Rev: BL 9/1/07; SLJ 10/07)

4391 Crowley, Suzanne. *The Stolen One* (8–12). 2009, Greenwillow $17.99 (978-006123200-8); LB $18.89 (978-006123201-5). Could Kat, an orphan, really be Mary Seymour, the daughter of Katherine Parr and Thomas Seymour? This tale of romance and court intrigue, set in Elizabethan England, is full of historical detail. Lexile HL740L (Rev: BL 5/1/09; HB 7–8/09; SLJ 8/09; VOYA 4/09)

4392 Cullen, Lynn. *I Am Rembrandt's Daughter* (8–12). 2007, Bloomsbury $16.95 (978-1-59990-046-9). The daughter of the famous artist feels adrift when her mother dies, leaving only her poor, unconventional father to raise her; Rembrandt's art and times are revealed in this compelling story. (Rev: BCCB 9/07; BL 4/15/07; LMC 1/08; SLJ 8/07)

4393 Curtis, Chara M. *No One Walks on My Father's Moon* (4–8). 1996, Voyage LB $16.95 (978-0-9649454-1-8). A Turkish boy is accused of blasphemy when he states that a man has walked on the moon. (Rev: BL 11/15/96)

4394 Cushman, Karen. *Alchemy and Meggy Swann* (4–8). 2010, Clarion $16 (978-0-547-23184-6). In Elizabethan England, 13-year-old Meggy, who needs sticks to walk, arrives in London to work with the father who abandoned her years before; as she adapts to city life she also comes to believe that her father is in serious trouble and determines to save him. Odyssey Honor Recording 2011. ∩ (Rev: BL 3/1/10*; LMC 10/10; SLJ 4/10)

4395 Cushman, Karen. *Will Sparrow's Road* (5–7). 2012, Clarion $16.99 (978-0-547-73962-5). In Elizabethan England young Will Sparrow has many adventures on the road and learns a lot about character. ⋒ ⓔ (Rev: BL 10/1/12; HB 11–12/12; LMC 11–12/12; SLJ 11/12)

4396 De Angeli, Marguerite. *The Door in the Wall* (5–7). Illus. by Marguerite De Angeli. 1990, Dell paper $5.50 (978-0-440-40283-1). Crippled Robin proves his courage in plague-ridden 19th-century London. Newbery Medal 1950.

4397 DeJong, Meindert. *Wheel on the School* (4–7). Illus. by Maurice Sendak. 1954, HarperCollins LB $18.89 (978-0-06-021586-6); paper $6.95 (978-0-06-440021-3). The storks are brought back to their island by the schoolchildren in a Dutch village. Newbery Medal 1955.

4398 Dent, Grace. *Diary of a Chav* (8–11). 2008, Little, Brown $16.99 (978-031603483-8). Fifteen-year-old Shiraz is already a bit of a trouble-maker when things go awry both at home and with her friends. ⓔ Lexile 1090L (Rev: BLO 3/16/09; SLJ 12/08; VOYA 12/08)

4399 Dhami, Narinder. *Bhangra Babes* (5–8). Series: Babes. 2006, Delacorte $14.95 (978-0-385-73318-2). Their troublesome auntie's marriage plans go awry in this funny, engaging third volume of the trilogy about the Bindi sisters who are adapting their Indian heritage to life in England. (Rev: BL 4/15/06; SLJ 6/06)

4400 Dickinson, Peter. *Shadow of a Hero* (7–12). 1995, Doubleday $20.95 (978-0-385-30976-9). Letta's grandfather fights for the freedom of Varina, her family's Eastern European homeland. Living in England, she becomes interested in Varina's struggle. (Rev: BL 9/15/94*; SLJ 11/94; VOYA 10/94)

4401 Doherty, Berlie. *Street Child* (5–7). 1994, Orchard LB $18.99 (978-0-531-08714-5). The story of a street urchin in Victorian London who is forced to work on a river barge until he escapes. (Rev: BCCB 11/94; BL 9/1/94; SLJ 10/94)

4402 Doherty, Berlie. *Treason* (8–12). 2012, IPG/Andersen paper $9.99 (978-18493912-1-4). William, a Catholic, is appointed a page to Henry VIII's son Edward and must hide his faith as he tries to save his father from execution. Lexile 760L (Rev: BLO 3/15/12; SLJ 3/12*)

4403 Dowd, Siobhan. *Bog Child* (8–11). 2008, Random House $16.99 (978-0-385-75169-8). Set in 1981 in politically troubled Northern Ireland, this richly told story weaves together two historical eras through 18-year-old Fergus, who finds the body of a girl in the peat bogs — apparently murdered perhaps 2000 years before — and begins to dream of her past. (Rev: BL 8/08; SLJ 8/08)

4404 Dowswell, Paul. *Battle Fleet* (5–8). 2008, Bloomsbury $16.95 (978-1-59990-080-3). Young Sam is again on the high seas, this time on Lord Nelson's ship for the battle of Trafalgar. A follow-up to *Powder Monkey* and *Prison Ship*. (Rev: BL 4/15/08; SLJ 9/08)

4405 Dowswell, Paul. *Powder Monkey: Adventures of a Young Sailor* (5–9). 2005, Bloomsbury $16.95 (978-1-58234-675-5). In this stirring historical novel set in the opening years of the 19th century, 13-year-old Sam Witchall begins his career at sea as a "powder monkey," assisting the gun crews on a warship. (Rev: SLJ 11/05; VOYA 10/05)

4406 Dowswell, Paul. *Prison Ship: Adventures of a Young Sailor* (5–9). 2006, Bloomsbury $16.95 (978-1-58234-676-2). In this action-packed sequel to *Powder Monkey* set at the beginning of the 19th century, 13-year-old English sailor Sam Witchall is falsely convicted of theft and sent off to prison in Australia, where he escapes into the Outback. (Rev: SLJ 12/06)

4407 Dunlap, Susanne. *Anastasia's Secret* (8–11). 2010, Bloomsbury $16.99 (978-1-59990-420-7). The Russian Revolution is on the horizon as young Anastasia falls in love with one of the royal guards; historical details add to this story of doomed romance. (Rev: BL 2/1/10; LMC 3–4/10; SLJ 3/10)

4408 Dunlap, Susanne. *The Musician's Daughter* (8–11). 2009, Bloomsbury $16.99 (978-159990332-3). Fifteen-year-old viola virtuoso Theresa Maria gets a boost from her godfather — who conveniently turns out to be composer Franz Joseph Haydn — as she struggles to support her family after her father's murder. ⓔ Lexile 950L (Rev: BL 11/1/08*; LMC 5–6/09; SLJ 5/1/09; VOYA 2/09)

4409 Dunlop, Eileen. *Tales of St. Patrick* (6–9). 1996, Holiday $15.95 (978-0-8234-1218-1). Using original sources when possible, the author has fashioned a fictionalized biography of Saint Patrick that focuses on his return to Ireland as a bishop and his efforts to convert the Irish. (Rev: BL 4/15/96; VOYA 8/96)

4410 Eisner, Will. *The Last Knight: An Introduction to Don Quixote by Miguel de Cervantes* (4–8). 2000, NBM $15.95 (978-1-56163-251-0). Using an engaging text and a comic book format, this is a fine retelling of Cervantes' classic. (Rev: BL 6/1–15/00; HBG 10/00; SLJ 7/00)

4411 Elliott, Patricia. *The Pale Assassin* (7–10). 2009, Holiday House $17.95 (978-0-8234-2250-0). Pampered aristocrat Eugénie, 15, must leave behind her posh lifestyle to flee an arranged marriage and the turmoil of the French Revolution in this historical adventure full of political intrigue. Lexile 840L (Rev: BL 10/1/09*; SLJ 12/09)

4412 Ellis, Deborah. *A Company of Fools* (5–8). 2002, Fitzhenry & Whiteside $15.95 (978-1-55041-719-7). Quiet Henri and free-spirited Micah try to cheer the people of a France devastated by the Black Death of 1348 by singing. (Rev: BCCB 1/03; BL 1/1–15/03; HB 1–2/03; HBG 3/03; VOYA 2/03)

4413 Flegg, Aubrey. *Katie's War* (5–8). 2000, O'Brien paper $7.95 (978-0-86278-525-3). Set during Ireland's fight for independence from England, this story shows a girl torn between two sides when her father wants peace and her brother is preparing to use force. (Rev: BL 12/1/00)

4414 Fletcher, Susan. *Alphabet of Dreams* (6–9). 2006, Simon & Schuster $16.95 (978-0-689-85042-4). Mitra and her brother Babak, who can see the future in his dreams, go from being Persian royalty to beggars on the street after their father's death; they join Melchior and two other magi when Babak dreams of a bright star. ∩ (Rev: BL 9/1/06; SLJ 11/06)

4415 Forsyth, Kate. *The Gypsy Crown* (6–9). 2008, Hyperion $16.99 (978-1-4231-0494-0). Set in England in the 17th century, this story of Emilia and Luka tells of the Puritan persecution of Gypsies during that time. (Rev: BL 4/15/08)

4416 French, Jackie. *Rover* (5–8). 2007, HarperCollins $17.99 (978-0-06-085078-4). When Vikings raid Hekja's Scottish village, she and her puppy are taken to Greenland, where she's enslaved to Freydis, Leif Erikson's sister; Hekja's dog can spot icebergs, and the two accompany Freydis on her voyage to North America in this compelling, historically accurate story. (Rev: BL 1/1–15/07; SLJ 6/07)

4417 Frost, Helen. *The Braid* (7–10). 2006, Farrar $16.00 (978-0-374-30962-6). Set in 1850, this moving tale of two Scottish sisters who become separated — Jeannie moving to Canada with her parents and younger siblings and Sarah staying behind with their grandmother — is told in narrative poems in alternating voices. (Rev: BL 6/1–15/06; HB 11–12/06; LMC 3/07; SLJ 10/06*)

4418 Gilman, Laura Anne. *Grail Quest: The Camelot Spell* (5–8). Series: Grail Quest. 2006, HarperCollins LB $14.89 (978-0-06-077280-2). On the eve of King Arthur's quest for the Holy Grail, three young teens of different backgrounds — Gerard, Newt, and Ailias — must reverse a spell crippling all adults. (Rev: BL 2/1/06; SLJ 6/06)

4419 Gilson, Jamie. *Stink Alley* (4–7). 2002, HarperCollins LB $15.89 (978-0-06-029217-1). Twelve-year-old orphan Lizzy Tinker, a Separatist who fled England with her family for Holland in 1608, is befriended by the boy who would one day be known as Rembrandt. (Rev: BCCB 9/02; BL 4/15/02; HB 9–10/02; HBG 3/03; SLJ 7/02)

4420 Golding, Julia. *Den of Thieves* (7–9). Series: Cat Royal Adventure. 2009, Roaring Brook $16.95 (978-159643444-8). In this installment in the series, Cat is homeless and disguised as a ballerina when she is caught up in the French Revolution. Lexile 760L (Rev: BL 4/1/09; HB 7–8/09; SLJ 6/1/09)

4421 Gonzalez, Christina Diaz. *A Thunderous Whisper* (5–8). 2012, Knopf $16.99 (978-037586929-7); LB $19.99 (978-037596929-4). During the Spanish Civil War 12-year-old Ani and Mathias, a 14-year-old German Jew, become friends and work for the rebels resisting Franco in the weeks before the bombing of Guernica. **e** Lexile 660L (Rev: BL 12/15/12; LMC 1–2/13; SLJ 1/13)

4422 Gould, Sasha. *Cross My Heart* (8–12). 2012, Delacorte $17.99 (978-038574150-7); LB $20.99 (978-037599007-6). Laura gives up her studies at the convent to determine what really happened to her drowned sister in this story set in 16th-century Venice. Lexile HL700L (Rev: BL 4/15/12; LMC 8–9/12; SLJ 4/12; VOYA 2/12)

4423 Graber, Janet. *The White Witch* (5–8). 2009, Roaring Brook $16.95 (978-1-59643-337-3). Set in 17th-century England, and with period prose that some may find challenging, this is a suspenseful story about 14-year-old Gwendoline's trials when the Great Plague breaks out. (Rev: BL 4/15/09; LMC 10/09; SLJ 7/09; VOYA 6/09)

4424 Grant, K. M. *How the Hangman Lost His Heart* (7–12). 2007, Walker $16.95 (978-0-8027-9672-1). Alice is on a mission — to bury the head of her Uncle Frank, who was executed and beheaded for treason — and danger and romance won't stop her in this funny, action-packed tale set in England in 1746 and inspired by the fate of one of the author's ancestors. (Rev: BL 11/15/07; SLJ 12/07)

4425 Gray, Keith. *Ostrich Boys* (8–12). 2010, Random House LB $20.99 (978-0-375-95843-4). When Ross, 15, dies in an accident, his three best friends decide to take his ashes from England to the village of Ross in Scotland for the burial he would have wanted, encountering many challenges along the way. ∩ Lexile HL630L (Rev: BL 2/1/10; LMC 5–6/10; SLJ 2/10)

4426 Gregory, Kristiana. *Catherine: The Great Journey* (4–7). Series: Royal Diaries. 2005, Scholastic $10.99 (978-0-439-25385-7). The imagined diary of Catherine the Great's teenage years and her engagement to the Grand Duke of Russia; plenty of historical background gives readers a sense of Catherine's times. (Rev: SLJ 5/06)

4427 Harris, Robert J., and Jane Yolen. *Prince Across the Water* (6–10). 2004, Penguin $18.99 (978-0-399-23897-0). Thirteen-year-old Duncan shares his countrymen's pride at Bonnie Prince Charlie's struggle to reclaim the crown of England and Scotland from German-born George II, but when the boy runs away from home to join the battle, he discovers the true horrors of war. (Rev: BL 11/15/04; SLJ 12/04; VOYA 10/04)

4428 Harrison, Cora. *The Famine Secret* (5–7). Illus. by Orla Roche. Series: Drumshee Timeline. 1998, Irish American paper $6.95 (978-0-86327-649-1). In 1847 the four McMahon children are orphaned and sent to an Irish workhouse, but their determination prevails and they are soon plotting to regain their home. (Rev: SLJ 12/98)

4429 Harrison, Cora. *The Secret of Drumshee Castle* (5–7). Illus. by Orla Roche. Series: Drumshee Timeline. 1998, Irish American paper $6.95 (978-0-86327-632-3). Grace Barry, the orphaned heiress to a castle in Ireland during Elizabethan times, flees to England to escape threats by her acquisitive guardians. (Rev: SLJ 12/98)

4430 Harrison, Cora. *The Secret of the Seven Crosses* (4–7). 1998, Wolfhound paper $6.95 (978-0-86327-616-3). In medieval Ireland, three youngsters hope to find hidden treasure by examining sources in their monastery library. Preceded by *Nauala and Her Secret Wolf* and followed by *The Secret of Drumshee Castle*. (Rev: BL 12/15/98)

4431 Hartnett, Sonya. *The Midnight Zoo* (5–8). Illus. by Andrea Offermann. 2011, Candlewick $16.99 (978-0-7636-5339-2). Caged animals share their horrors with Romany brothers Andrej, 12, and Tomas, 9, who are fleeing a German attack in World War II. ♫ ℮ Lexile 940L (Rev: BL 8/11; HB 9–10/11; LMC 11–12/11; SLJ 9/1/11; VOYA 10/11)

4432 Hassinger, Peter W. *Shakespeare's Daughter* (7–12). 2004, HarperCollins $15.99 (978-0-06-028467-1). An assortment of historical figures make appearances, including papa, in this story about the 14-year-old daughter of William Shakespeare. (Rev: BL 3/1/04; SLJ 4/04)

4433 Havill, Juanita. *Eyes Like Willy's* (6–9). Illus. by David Johnson. 2004, HarperCollins LB $16.89 (978-0-688-13673-4). Guy, who lives in Paris, and Willy, an Austrian, have been friends since they met in the summer of 1906; now they may face each other across the trenches of World War I. (Rev: BCCB 9/04; BL 3/1/04*; SLJ 7/04)

4434 Hawes, Louise. *The Vanishing Point* (8–10). 2004, Houghton Mifflin $17.00 (978-0-618-43423-7). In this appealing historical novel that imagines the adolescence of Italian Renaissance artist Lavinia Fontana, young Vini resorts to subterfuge to get her father to let her paint in his studio. (Rev: BL 11/1/04; SLJ 12/04; VOYA 12/04)

4435 Hearn, Julie. *Ivy* (8–10). 2008, Atheneum $17.99 (978-1-4169-2506-4). In 19th-century London, Ivy struggles with addiction to laudanum as she earns a living as a model for a pre-Raphaelite painter. (Rev: BL 6/1–15/08; SLJ 7/08)

4436 Hemphill, Stephanie. *Sisters of Glass* (6–10). 2012, Knopf $16.99 (978-037586109-3); LB $19.99 (978-037596109-0). In 14th-century Murano, Italy, two daughters of a glassmaker grow apart after the death of their father and his request that the younger marry a nobleman; a romantic tale written in verse. (Rev: BL 4/15/12*; HB 3–4/13; LMC 10/12; SLJ 5/1/12; VOYA 4/12)

4437 Hendry, Frances Mary. *Quest for a Maid* (8–10). 1992, Farrar paper $6.95 (978-0-374-46155-3). The story of an 8-year-old princess and her maid who travel to Britain during the 13th century. (Rev: BL 7/90)

4438 Heneghan, James. *Safe House* (5–8). 2006, Orca paper $7.95 (978-1-55143-640-1). Twelve-year-old Liam Fogarty is forced to go on the run after he sees the face of one of the gunmen who killed his mother and father in their Belfast home. (Rev: BL 11/1/06; SLJ 1/07)

4439 Hinton, Nigel. *The Road from Home* (6–10). 2009, Sourcebooks paper $13.99 (978-1-4022-2461-4). Eleven-year-old Leo leaves his native Poland in 1870 and sets out for America, encountering many adventures on the way. (Rev: BLO 12/1/09; LMC 1–2/10; SLJ 11/09)

4440 Hoffman, Mary. *The Falconer's Knot* (8–11). 2007, Bloomsbury $16.95 (978-1-59990-056-8). Silvano, 16, is suspected of murder when Angelica's husband is stabbed in this multilayered mystery set in Renaissance Italy. (Rev: BCCB 6/07; BL 3/15/07; LMC 8–9/07; SLJ 4/07)

4441 Holmes, Victoria. *The Horse from the Sea* (5–8). 2005, HarperCollins LB $16.89 (978-0-06-052029-8). In 1588, Nora, an Irish girl, defies the English and helps a young Spanish sailor and a beautiful stallion, survivors of a shipwreck. (Rev: BL 5/15/05; SLJ 8/05)

4442 Holub, Josef. *An Innocent Soldier* (8–11). Trans. by Michael Gofmann. 2005, Scholastic $16.99 (978-0-439-62771-9). Pressed into Napoleon's army for the ill-fated Russian campaign, Adam, a teenage farmhand, is selected as a personal servant by Konrad, an officer from a wealthy family, and the two develop a strong friendship. Batchelder Award, 2006. (Rev: BL 11/15/05; SLJ 12/05; VOYA 2/06)

4443 Holub, Josef. *The Robber and Me* (5–8). Trans. from German by Elizabeth D. Crawford. 1997, Henry Holt $16.95 (978-0-8050-5591-7). On his way to live with his uncle, an orphan is helped by a mysterious stranger and he must later make a decision about whether to stand up to his uncle and the town authorities to clear the name of this man in this novel set in 19th-century Germany. (Rev: SLJ 12/97*)

4444 Hooper, Mary. *At the Sign of the Sugared Plum* (5–8). 2003, Bloomsbury $16.95 (978-1-58234-849-0). The horrors of the bubonic plague and the squalor of 17th-century London are brought to life in this story of Hannah and her sister Sarah, owner of a sweetmeats shop. (Rev: BL 9/15/03; HBG 4/04; SLJ 8/03; VOYA 10/03)

4445 Hooper, Mary. *Velvet* (6–10). 2012, Bloomsbury $16.99 (978-159990912-7). In Victorian London, Velvet Groves, a 16-year-old orphan, is thrilled to find an alternative to the steam laundry where she has been toiling but does not realize that her new position assisting a famous spiritualist also has pitfalls. ♫ ℮ Lexile 1000L

(Rev: BL 11/15/12; LMC 1–2/13*; SLJ 1/13; VOYA 8/12)

4446 Hopkins, Cathy. *The Princess of Pop* (6–8). Series: Truth or Dare. 2004, Simon & Schuster paper $5.99 (978-0-689-87002-6). On a dare, Becca competes in the British version of "American Idol." (Rev: SLJ 7/04)

4447 Hunter, Mollie. *The King's Swift Rider* (7–12). 1998, HarperCollins $16.95 (978-0-06-027186-2). A fast-paced historical novel about a young Scot, Martin Crawford, who became Robert the Bruce's page, confidante, and spy. (Rev: BL 9/15/98; HB 1–2/99; HBG 3/99; SLJ 12/98)

4448 Hunter, Mollie. *You Never Knew Her as I Did!* (7–10). 1981, HarperCollins $13.95 (978-0-06-022678-7). A historical novel about a plan to help the imprisoned Mary, Queen of Scots, to escape from prison.

4449 Ibbotson, Eva. *The Star of Kazan* (4–8). Illus. by Kevin Hawkes. 2004, Dutton $16.99 (978-0-525-47347-3). Set in the Austro-Hungarian empire, this richly detailed and very readable novel tells the story of 12-year-old Annika, who gets a rude awakening when her aristocratic mother whisks her away from her adoptive family. (Rev: BL 10/15/04*; SLJ 10/04*)

4450 Jennings, Patrick. *The Wolving Time* (6–8). 2003, Scholastic $15.95 (978-0-439-39555-7). Fantasy and historical fiction are interwoven in this tale, set in 16th-century France, of two werewolves and their son. (Rev: BL 9/15/03; SLJ 1/04)

4451 Jocelyn, Marthe. *Folly* (8–12). 2010, Random House $15.99 (978-0-385-73846-0). In alternating sequences set in late-19th-century London, this book tells the stories of homeless, unmarried Mary Finn and of the son she must send to the Foundling Hospital so that he will have a chance for a decent future. Lexile 850L (Rev: BL 4/15/10; HB 5–6/10; LMC 8–9/10; SLJ 7/10)

4452 Jones, Terry. *The Lady and the Squire* (5–7). 2001, Pavilion $22.95 (978-1-86205-417-2). A beautiful aristocrat joins Tom and Ann as they make their way through a war-torn countryside to the papal court at Avignon. (Rev: BL 2/15/01; SLJ 3/01)

4453 Juster, Norton. *Alberic the Wise* (4–8). Illus. by Leonard Baskin. 1992, Picture Book $16.95 (978-0-88708-243-6). In this picture book set in the Renaissance, Alberic becomes an apprentice to a stained-glass maker. (Rev: BCCB 2/93; BL 1/15/93; SLJ 3/93)

4454 Kanefield, Teri. *Rivka's Way* (4–8). 2001, Front St $15.95 (978-0-8126-2870-8). Daily life inside and outside the Prague ghetto in 1778 is explored in this novel about an unconventional Jewish girl, 15-year-old Rivka Liebermann. (Rev: BCCB 3/02; BL 4/1/01; HBG 10/01; SLJ 3/01; VOYA 10/01)

4455 Karr, Kathleen. *The 7th Knot* (6–9). 2003, Marshall Cavendish $15.95 (978-0-7614-5135-8). Brothers Wick, 15, and Miles, 12, romp through a series of adventures involving art and politics when they set off across Europe in pursuit of their uncle's kidnapped valet in the late 19th century. (Rev: BL 7/03; HBG 10/03; SLJ 8/03)

4456 Kelley, Ann. *Inchworm* (5–8). 2009, Luath paper $12.95 (978-1-906307-62-2). Recovering from a heart and lung transplant, 12-year-old Gussie is living in London and missing Cornwall, worrying about her parents' divorce, and hoping to live to the age of 22. (Rev: SLJ 4/09; VOYA 4/09)

4457 Kelly, Eric P. *The Trumpeter of Krakow* (5–9). Illus. by Janina Domanska. 1966, Macmillan $17.95 (978-0-02-750140-7); paper $4.99 (978-0-689-71571-6). Mystery surrounds a precious jewel and the youthful patriot who stands watch over it in a church tower in this novel of 15th-century Poland. Newbery Medal 1929.

4458 Kent, Trilby. *Medina Hill* (6–9). 2009, Tundra $19.95 (978-0-88776-888-0). In 1935 England 11-year-old Dominic has been mute for years but a holiday in Cornwall relieves his stress, and in the face of discrimination he finds the courage to speak. Lexile 790L (Rev: BL 1/1/10*; SLJ 3/10)

4459 Kirwan, Anna. *Victoria: May Blossom of Britannia* (5–8). Series: Royal Diaries. 2001, Scholastic paper $10.95 (978-0-439-21598-5). Young Victoria's fictional diary describes her over-regimented life at the ages of 10 and 11; background material adds some historical context to this account of the girl who grew up to rule England. (Rev: BL 12/1/01; HBG 10/02; SLJ 1/02; VOYA 2/02)

4460 Klein, Lisa. *Lady Macbeth's Daughter* (7–12). 2009, Bloomsbury $16.99 (978-1-59990-347-7). This re-imagining of Shakespeare's *Macbeth* is delivered in alternating chapters by Lady Macbeth and Albia, Macbeth's banished daughter. ℮ Lexile 730L (Rev: BL 8/09; LMC 11–12/09; SLJ 12/09; VOYA 2/10)

4461 Kolosov, Jacqueline. *A Sweet Disorder* (7–12). 2009, Hyperion $16.99 (978-1-4231-1245-7). Sixteen-year-old seamstress Miranda hopes to avoid an unfavorable arranged marriage by winning the favor of Queen Elizabeth I. Lexile 1080L (Rev: SLJ 12/09; VOYA 12/09)

4462 Konigsburg, E. L. *A Proud Taste for Scarlet and Miniver* (7–9). 1973, Macmillan $18.95 (978-0-689-30111-7). Eleanor of Aquitaine tells her story in heaven while awaiting her second husband, Henry II.

4463 Kujer, Guus. *The Book of Everything* (8–11). 2006, Scholastic $16.99 (978-0-439-74918-3). Thomas, a 9-year-old living in Amsterdam in 1951, strives to be happy in spite of his difficult, deeply religious father in this compelling and often humorous novel. (Rev: BCCB 5/06; BL 6/1–15/06; HB 7–8/06; LMC 10/06; SLJ 7/06)

4464 Laird, Elizabeth. *The Betrayal of Maggie Blair* (8–11). 2011, Houghton $16.99 (978-0-547-34126-2).

In 17th-century Scotland, Maggie, 16, escapes being executed for witchcraft but must still deal with danger amid the political and religious turmoil of the time. **e** Lexile 840L (Rev: BL 4/15/11; HB 9–10/11; SLJ 4/11*; VOYA 4/11)

4465 Lasky, Kathryn. *Ashes* (6–12). 2010, Viking $16.99 (978-0-670-01157-5). In 1932 Berlin, Gabriella, 13, watches as Hitler's rise affects society, she is pressured to join the Hitler Youth, her sister dates a Nazi, and her astrophysicist father helps his friend Einstein. **e** Lexile 770L (Rev: BL 1/1/10*; HB 3–4/10; SLJ 2/10; VOYA 4/10)

4466 Lasky, Kathryn. *Broken Song* (5–8). 2005, Viking $15.99 (978-0-670-05931-7). Reuven Bloom, a 15-year-old Jew and promising violinist, escapes from late 19th-century Russia with his baby sister, the only surviving member of his family. (Rev: BL 1/1–15/05; SLJ 3/05)

4467 Lasky, Kathryn. *Dancing Through Fire* (4–7). Series: Portraits. 2005, Scholastic paper $9.99 (978-0-439-71009-1). The Franco-Prussian War interrupts the dreams of 13-year-old Sylvie, a student at the Paris Opera Ballet in the 1870s. (Rev: BCCB 1/06; BL 12/1/05; SLJ 11/05)

4468 Lasky, Kathryn. *Elizabeth I: Red Rose of the House of Tudor* (4–7). Series: Royal Diaries. 1999, Scholastic paper $10.95 (978-0-590-68484-2). Told in diary form, this is a fictionalized account of Elizabeth I's childhood after her mother was killed and she lived with her father, Henry VIII, and Catherine Parr. (Rev: BCCB 12/99; BL 9/15/99; HBG 3/00; SLJ 10/99)

4469 Lasky, Kathryn. *Marie Antoinette: Princess of Versailles* (5–8). Series: Royal Diaries. 2000, Scholastic paper $10.95 (978-0-439-07666-1). This fictional diary covers two years in the life of Marie Antoinette, beginning in 1769 when the 13-year-old was preparing for her fateful marriage. (Rev: BL 4/15/00; HBG 10/00; SLJ 5/00; VOYA 6/00)

4470 Lasky, Kathryn. *Mary, Queen of Scots: Queen Without a Country* (5–8). Series: Royal Diaries. 2002, Scholastic paper $10.95 (978-0-439-19404-4). Part of the Royal Diary series, this is a fictional diary of the year 1553, when Mary was betrothed to the son of King Henry II of France. (Rev: BL 5/15/02; HBG 10/02; SLJ 6/02)

4471 Lawlor, Laurie. *The Two Loves of Will Shakespeare* (8–11). 2006, Holiday $16.95 (978-0-8234-1901-2). This well-written story imagines the wild love life of young William Shakespeare, based on historical records. (Rev: BL 4/15/06; SLJ 6/06)

4472 Lawrence, Iain. *The Smugglers* (5–8). 1999, Delacorte $15.95 (978-0-385-32663-6). In this continuation of *The Wreckers*, 16-year-old John Spencer faces more adventures aboard the *Dragon*, where he faces powerful enemies and must bring the ship safely to port. (Rev:

BCCB 7–8/99; BL 4/1/99*; HB 5–6/99; HBG 10/99; SLJ 6/99)

4473 Lawrence, Iain. *The Wreckers* (5–8). 1998, Bantam paper $5.50 (978-0-440-41545-9). In this historical novel, young John Spencer narrowly escapes with his life after the ship on which he is traveling is wrecked off the Cornish coast, lured to its destruction by a gang seeking to plunder its cargo. (Rev: BCCB 6/98; BL 6/1–15/98; HB 7–8/98*; HBG 10/98; SLJ 6/98; VOYA 2/99)

4474 Leeds, Constance. *The Unfortunate Son* (5–8). 2012, Viking $16.99 (978-0-670-01398-2). Born in 15th-century France, Luc, who is highly intelligent but has only one ear, is captured and sold into slavery but manages still to lead a lucky — and perhaps romantically succcessful — life. **e** Lexile 690L (Rev: BL 7/12; SLJ 9/12*)

4475 Levine, Anna. *Freefall* (7–12). 2008, Greenwillow $16.99 (978-006157654-6); LB $17.89 (978-006157656-0). Eighteen-year-old Aggie is determined to do her compulsory service in the Israeli army as a soldier, not stuck in an office job, in this apolitical story with a touch of romance. Sydney Taylor Book Honor 2009. **e** Lexile HL600L (Rev: BL 10/15/08; HB 1–2/09; SLJ 1/1/09)

4476 Libby, Alisa M. *The King's Rose* (8–11). 2009, Dutton $17.99 (978-052547970-3). A well-written account of the tragic life of Catherine Howard, the doomed fifth wife of King Henry VIII, full of court intrigue. **e** Lexile HL810L (Rev: BL 3/1/09; LMC 5–6/09; SLJ 5/1/09; VOYA 6/09)

4477 Lisson, Deborah. *Red Hugh* (6–12). 2001, O'Brien paper $7.95 (978-0-86278-604-5). A exciting tale of 16th-century Ireland's Hugh Roe O'Donnell, a teen whose life is endangered when he is caught up in clan violence. (Rev: BL 12/1/01; SLJ 12/01)

4478 McCaughrean, Geraldine. *Cyrano* (7–10). 2006, Harcourt $16.00 (978-0-15-205805-0). McCaughrean retells the classic tale of Cyrano de Bergerac, a famous swordsman and romantic poet with a very large nose, who lets a fellow French soldier use his poems and letters to win the love of Roxanne, the woman he secretly loves. (Rev: BL 9/15/06; SLJ 10/06)

4479 MacColl, Michaela. *Prisoners in the Palace: How Princess Victoria Became Queen with the Help of Her Maid, a Reporter, and a Scoundrel* (7–12). 2010, Chronicle $16.99 (978-0-8118-7300-0). Liza Hastings, a 17-year-old orphan, finds work as a lady's maid to 16-year-old Princess Victoria in 1835, the year before Victoria becomes queen, and helps her employer navigate the ins and outs of court life. (Rev: BL 8/10; LMC 1/2/11; SLJ 12/1/10*)

4480 MacKall, Dandi Daley. *Eva Underground* (8–11). 2006, Harcourt $17.00 (978-0-15-205462-5). In 1978, Eva Lott's father moves her from her high school life in Chicago to Communist Poland, where she initially rebels but later meets a young political activist named Tomek and develops a strong affection for him and an understanding of the oppression he is fighting. (Rev: BL 3/1/06; SLJ 6/06)

4481 McKenzie, Nancy. *Guinevere's Gift* (5–8). 2008, Knopf $15.99 (978-0-375-84345-7). As a young orphan, the plucky Guinevere lives with her aunt, Queen Alyse, and involves herself in castle intrigue, coming to realize that her destiny may be closer to prophecy than she thought. (Rev: BL 6/1–15/08; SLJ 4/08)

4482 Magorian, Michelle. *Back Home* (7–9). 1992, HarperCollins paper $6.95 (978-0-06-440411-2). A young English girl who returns to Britain after World War II wants to go back to her second home in the United States.

4483 Mankell, Henning. *When the Snow Fell* (5–8). Trans. from Swedish by Laurie Thompson. 2009, Delacorte $15.99 (978-0-385-73497-4); LB $18.99 (978-0-385-90491-9). Now almost 14, Joel becomes a hero when he rescues an old man from freezing to death in this third volume about the appealing young Swede. (Rev: BL 10/1/09*; SLJ 12/09)

4484 Marsden, Carolyn. *My Own Revolution* (5–8). 2012, Candlewick $16.99 (978-0-7636-5395-8). In 1960s Czechoslovakia, 14-year-old Patrik rebels against the regime and his family decides to flee to Italy. (Rev: BL 10/15/12; SLJ 10/12)

4485 Marsden, Carolyn. *Take Me with You* (4–7). 2010, Candlewick $14.99 (978-0-7636-3739-2). In Italy after World War II best friends Pina and Susanna, both 11, are still at the orphanage and hoping for eventual adoption even if it means separation. (Rev: BL 1/1/10*; LMC 5–6/10; SLJ 3/10)

4486 Marsh, Katherine. *Jepp, Who Defied the Stars* (8–10). 2012, Hyperion $16.99 (978-1-4231-3500-5). Jepp, a 15-year-old dwarf in 16th-century Europe, struggles to find a life that rewards his intelligence and longing for love. ∩ **e** Lexile 1010L (Rev: BL 11/15/12; LMC 3–4/13; SLJ 12/12*; VOYA 4/13)

4487 Marston, Elsa. *Figs and Fate: Stories About Growing Up in the Arab World Today* (6–9). 2005, George Braziller $22.50 (978-0-8076-1551-5); paper $15.95 (978-0-8076-1554-6). A revealing collection of stories portraying contemporary Arab teens living in Egypt, Iraq, Lebanon, Palestine, and Syria. (Rev: BL 2/15/05; HB 5–6/05; SLJ 3/05; VOYA 10/05)

4488 Masson, Sophie. *The Madman of Venice* (7–10). 2010, Delacorte $17.99 (978-0-385-73843-9). In the early 17th century young Ned travels to Venice with his employer and his daughter Celia; there they investigate piracy and a disappearance as the two young people fall for each other. Lexile 740L (Rev: BLO 7/10; LMC 11–12/10; SLJ 8/10; VOYA 12/10)

4489 Meyer, Carolyn. *Anastasia: The Last Grand Duchess, Russia, 1914* (4–8). Series: Royal Diaries. 2000, Scholastic paper $10.95 (978-0-439-12908-4). Anastasia's fictional diary begins when she is 12 in 1914 and ends with her captivity in 1918. (Rev: HBG 10/01; SLJ 10/00; VOYA 4/01)

4490 Meyer, Carolyn. *In Mozart's Shadow* (7–12). 2008, Harcourt $17.00 (978-0-15-205594-3). The fictionalized story of Wolfgang's older sister, Nannerl, who was also a talented musician but remains virtually unknown. (Rev: BL 4/15/08; SLJ 6/08; VOYA 4/08)

4491 Meyer, Carolyn. *Loving Will Shakespeare* (8–11). 2006, Harcourt $17.00 (978-0-15-205451-9). Follows Anne Hathaway's difficult life until her marriage to William Shakespeare. (Rev: BL 9/15/06; LMC 3/07; SLJ 10/06; VOYA)

4492 Meyer, Carolyn. *Marie, Dancing* (6–9). 2005, Harcourt $17.00 (978-0-15-205116-7). Marie van Goethem, the girl who posed for Degas' famous *Little Dancer, Aged Fourteen* sculpture, is at the center of this moving novel about the lives of three sisters struggling to make their way in the artistic world of 19th-century Paris. (Rev: BCCB 1/06; BL 11/1/05; SLJ 11/05)

4493 Meyer, Carolyn. *Patience, Princess Catherine* (6–9). 2004, Harcourt $17.00 (978-0-15-216544-4). This appealing historical novel recounts the confusion surrounding the future of 15-year-old Catherine of Aragon, alone in England when she is widowed only six months after her marriage to Prince Arthur, heir to the British throne. (Rev: BL 3/15/04; SLJ 7/04)

4494 Meyer, Carolyn. *The Wild Queen: The Days and Nights of Mary, Queen of Scots* (6–9). Series: Young Royals. 2012, Harcourt $16.99 (978-015206188-3). Awaiting her execution in 1587, condemned by her cousin Queen Elizabeth I, Mary recounts the intrigues of her life. **e** Lexile 1000L (Rev: BLO 4/1/12; SLJ 6/12)

4495 Meyer, Susan Lynn. *Black Radishes* (4–7). 2010, Delacorte $16.99 (978-0-385-73881-1); LB $19.99 (978-0-385-90748-4). In World War II France, young Gustave, a Jew, takes personal risks to help the Resistance. Sydney Taylor Book Honor 2011. (Rev: BL 12/15/10; SLJ 1/1/11)

4496 Molloy, Michael. *Peter Raven Under Fire* (6–9). 2005, Scholastic $17.95 (978-0-439-72454-8). A fast-paced multilayered story featuring midshipman Peter Raven, 13, who becomes embroiled in international politics during the Napoleonic Wars. (Rev: BL 8/05; SLJ 10/05; VOYA 10/05)

4497 Morgan, Nicola. *The Highwayman's Footsteps* (7–9). 2007, Candlewick $16.99 (978-0-7636-3472-8). Based on the poem by Alfred Noyes, this thrilling novel set in 18th-century England centers on Bess, the highwayman's daughter, and Will, a runaway who becomes

Bess's friend and confidant. (Rev: BL 11/15/07; HB 1–2/08; LMC 2/08; SLJ 12/07)

4498 Morris, Gerald. *The Lioness and Her Knight* (6–9). 2005, Houghton Mifflin $16.00 (978-0-618-50772-6). Lady Luneta, 16 and headstrong, travels to Camelot with her cousin Ywain and a fool named Rhience and finds adventure and romance. (Rev: BL 9/15/05; SLJ 9/05; VOYA 12/05)

4499 Morris, Gerald. *The Quest of the Fair Unknown* (5–8). 2006, Houghton Mifflin $16.00 (978-0-618-63152-0). To fulfill the deathbed plea of his mother, Beaufils sets off to find his long-absent father, a knight in the court of King Arthur. (Rev: BL 10/15/06; SLJ 11/06)

4500 Napoli, Donna Jo. *Breath* (8–12). 2003, Simon & Schuster $16.95 (978-0-689-86174-1). Salz, a sickly youth, seems to be immune to the sufferings of the people of Hameln in this reinterpretation of the Pied Piper story that conveys much of the atmosphere of 13th-century Europe. (Rev: BL 9/15/03; HBG 4/04; SLJ 11/03; VOYA 12/03)

4501 Nelson, Mary Elizabeth. *Catla and the Vikings* (5–8). 2012, Orca paper $9.95 (978-14598005-7-1). In northern England in 1066, 13-year-old Catla survives a Viking attack and journeys to a neighboring town to warn the citizens, facing her fears as she goes. **e** Lexile 640L (Rev: BL 4/15/12; LMC 10/12; SLJ 6/12)

4502 Newbery, Linda. *At the Firefly Gate* (5–8). 2007, Random House $15.99 (978-0-385-75113-1). Henry befriends a neighbor who was once engaged to another Henry, a Royal Air Force pilot who failed to return from a mission in World War II. When Henry begins to see a mysterious figure at his gate and reenacts the pilot's final flight on a simulator, the war seems not so long ago. (Rev: BCCB 4/07; BL 2/15/07; HB 3–4/07; SLJ 3/07)

4503 Orgad, Dorit. *The Boy from Seville* (6–8). 2007, Kar-Ben $16.95 (978-1-58013-253-4). Readers will learn what life was like for Jews in Spain during the Inquisition through the story of Manuel and his family, who risk being burned at the stake if they are found out. (Rev: BL 10/1/07; LMC 1/08; SLJ 11/07)

4504 Orlev, Uri. *The Lady with the Hat* (7–10). Trans. by Hillel Halkin. 1995, Houghton Mifflin $16.00 (978-0-395-69957-7). Yulek, a concentration camp survivor, encounters anti-Semitism on her return to Poland, while another Jewish girl, hidden from the Nazis, wants to be a nun. (Rev: BL 3/15/95; SLJ 5/95)

4505 Ortiz, Michael J. *Swan Town: The Secret Journal of Susanna Shakespeare* (7–10). 2006, HarperCollins LB $16.89 (978-0-06-058127-5). Shakespeare's teenage daughter Susanna writes in her diary about her current circumstances and her literary and acting ambitions, revealing much about Elizabethan life. (Rev: BL 2/15/06; SLJ 3/06; VOYA 2/06)

4506 Parkinson, Siobhan. *Long Story Short* (6–9). 2011, Roaring Brook $16.99 (978-1-59643-647-3). Jono, 14,

and his 8-year-old sister take to the streets when their mother's drinking becomes intolerable; on their own, they find things more grim and harsh than expected. Set in Galway, Ireland, this novel's Irish vernacular may challenge some readers. **e** Lexile 760L (Rev: BL 5/1/11; HB 7–8/11; LMC 11–12/11; SLJ 6/11; VOYA 8/11)

4507 Parry, Rosanne. *Second Fiddle* (5–8). 2011, Random House $16.99 (978-0-375-86196-3); LB $19.99 (978-0-375-96196-0). In 1990 Berlin, three 8th-grade American girls rescue a soldier beaten by Soviet officers and plot to get him safely to Paris. ∩ **e** Lexile 810L (Rev: BL 4/15/11; SLJ 3/1/11)

4508 Pennington, Kate. *Brief Candle* (6–9). 2005, Hodder paper $12.50 (978-0-340-87370-0). Fourteen-year-old Emily Brontë helps two hapless lovers in this novel set in Yorkshire and featuring the whole Brontë family. (Rev: BL 12/1/05; SLJ 11/05)

4509 Perera, Anna. *The Glass Collector* (8–12). 2012, Albert Whitman $17.99 (978-080752948-5). A Zabbaleen (garbage collectors and recyclers) living on the outskirts of Cairo, 15-year-old Aaron is a glass collector until he is caught stealing and is shunned by his family and villagers, leaving him with difficult options for survival. Lexile 990L (Rev: BL 2/15/12; LMC 8–9/12; SLJ 3/12; VOYA 2/12)

4510 Pignat, Caroline. *Greener Grass* (7–10). 2009, Red Deer paper $12.95 (978-088995402-1). In 1847, 14-year-old Kit's family is threatened by the Irish potato famine. When she loses her job as a kitchen maid, escaping to Canada may be her only hope. Canada Council for the Arts Governor General's Literary Award 2009. Lexile 650L (Rev: BL 4/15/09*; LMC 5–6/09; VOYA 6/09)

4511 Pratchett, Terry. *Dodger* (8–12). 2012, HarperCollins $17.99 (978-0-06-200949-4); LB $18.89 (978-006200950-0). Street urchin Dodger, 17, meets a mysterious girl, gets to know Charles Dickens, and thwarts the barbaric barber Sweeny Todd in this caper set in an alternative Victorian London. Printz Honor 2013. ∩ **e** Lexile 1210L (Rev: BL 10/15/12*; HB 11–12/12; LMC 3–4/13; SLJ 11/12*)

4512 Priestley, Chris. *Redwulf's Curse* (6–9). Series: Tom Marlowe Adventure. 2005, Doubleday $16.99 (978-0-385-60695-0). When the elderly Dr. Harker and 18-year-old Tom Marlowe travel from London to the English countryside in the early 18th century, they become swept up in intrigues surrounding the looting of the grave of Redwulf, a 7th-century East Anglian king. (Rev: BL 11/1/05; SLJ 12/05)

4513 Priestley, Chris. *The White Rider* (5–8). 2005, Corgi paper $8.99 (978-0-440-86608-4). In this riveting sequel to *Death and the Arrow*, 16-year-old Tom Marlowe is swept up in a series of intrigues in early 18th-century London. (Rev: BL 10/15/05)

4514 Pyron, Bobbie. *The Dogs of Winter* (5–9). 2012, Scholastic $16.99 (978-0-545-39930-2). In 1990s Russia a 5-year-old boy living on the streets joins a pack of street dogs and scavenges with them. **e** Lexile HL610L (Rev: BL 12/15/12*; HB 1–2/13; SLJ 12/12)

4515 Quick, Barbara. *A Golden Web* (7–10). 2010, HarperCollins $16.99 (978-0-06-144887-4). In 14th-century Italy, 15-year-old Alessandra rebels against the arranged marriage that awaits her and, disguised as a boy, studies anatomy at the university. **e** (Rev: BL 4/15/10; LMC 5–6/10; SLJ 5/10)

4516 Rees, Celia. *The Fool's Girl* (8–11). 2010, Bloomsbury $16.99 (978-1-59990-486-3). Violetta and Feste go to London to retrieve from Malvolio a stolen holy relic; they meet William Shakespeare, who joins the quest and includes elements of *Twelfth Night*. **e** Lexile HL780L (Rev: BL 4/15/10; LMC 10/10; SLJ 8/10; VOYA 10/10)

4517 Rees, Celia. *Sovay* (7–10). 2008, Bloomsbury $16.99 (978-159990203-6). In this fictional tale rooted in history, beautiful 17-year-old Sovay abandons her pastime as a highwayman and becomes caught up in the danger and intrigue surrounding the French Revolution as she endeavors to clear her father's name. ∩ **e** Lexile 810L (Rev: BLO 11/6/08; LMC 1–2/09; SLJ 10/1/08; VOYA 8/08)

4518 Rees, Elizabeth M. *The Wedding: An Encounter with Jan van Eyck* (8–11). Series: Art Encounters. 2005, Watson-Guptill $15.95 (978-0-8230-0407-2). In this novel set in 15th-century Bruges and channeling Jan van Eyck's *The Arnolfini Portrait*, 14-year-old Giovanna falls in love with a troubador called Angelo even as her father plans her marriage to a wealthy man. (Rev: BL 9/15/05; SLJ 9/05)

4519 Richter, Jutta. *The Summer of the Pike* (4–7). Trans. by Anna Brailovsky. Illus. by Quint Buchholz. 2006, Milkweed $16.95 (978-1-57131-671-4); paper $6.95 (978-1-57131-672-1). Anna, Daniel, and Lucas, who live on the grounds of a German manor, spend a difficult summer as Anna wishes for a closer relationship with her mother and the boys' mother is slowly dying of cancer; translated from German. (Rev: BL 1/1–15/07; SLJ 12/06)

4520 Rinaldi, Ann. *Nine Days a Queen: The Short Life and Reign of Lady Jane Grey* (6–8). 2005, HarperCollins $16.89 (978-0-06-054924-4). This fictionalized first-person account of the tragically brief life of Lady Jane Grey relates the complex palace intrigues that brought the 16-year-old Jane to the throne of England for nine days. (Rev: BL 12/1/04; SLJ 3/05; VOYA 2/05)

4521 Rinaldi, Ann. *The Redheaded Princess* (6–9). 2008, HarperCollins $15.99 (978-0-06-073374-2). An enjoyable novel about the dangerous and intrigue-filled life of Elizabeth I from her childhood until she became queen. (Rev: BL 10/15/07; SLJ 3/08)

4522 Robert, Na'ima B. *From Somalia, with Love* (7–10). 2009, Frances Lincoln $15.95 (978-184507831-7); paper $7.95 (978-184507832-4). Safia, a 14-year-old Muslim girl, has grown up in East London and finds her whole life changing when her father arrives from Somalia after a 12-year absence with different expectations. (Rev: BL 7/09; SLJ 7/1/09)

4523 Roy, Jennifer. *Yellow Star* (5–8). 2006, Marshall Cavendish $16.95 (978-0-7614-5277-5). The fictionalized story, told in first-person free-verse chapters introduced by historical notes, of the author's aunt Syvia, a Holocaust survivor who spent much of her childhood in the grim Lodz ghetto. ∩ (Rev: BL 4/15/06; SLJ 7/06*; VOYA 6/06)

4524 Rushton, Rosie. *The Dashwood Sisters' Secrets of Love* (6–9). 2005, Hyperion $15.99 (978-0-7868-5136-2). In the wake of their father's remarriage and sudden death, the three Dashwood sisters experience a humbling reversal of fortunes. (Rev: BCCB 3/05; BL 3/1/05; SLJ 4/05; VOYA 6/05)

4525 Schlitz, Laura Amy. *Splendors and Glooms* (4–8). 2012, Candlewick $17.99 (978-076365380-4). When Clara vanishes on her 12th birthday, suspicion falls on the puppeteer who entertained her and his two young orphan assistants in this novel set in 1860 Britain with elements of fantasy, a witch, and three children facing danger. Newbery Honor Book 2013. ∩ **e** Lexile 670L (Rev: BL 6/12*; HB 9–10/12; LMC 3–4/13; SLJ 8/1/12*; VOYA 10/12)

4526 Schmidt, Gary D. *Anson's Way* (5–9). 1999, Houghton Mifflin $16.00 (978-0-395-91529-5). During the reign of George II, Anson begins his proud career in the British army as part of the forces occupying Ireland, then becomes disillusioned as he develops a growing respect and concern for the Irish. (Rev: BL 4/1/99*; HBG 10/99; SLJ 4/99; VOYA 8/99)

4527 Scott, Elaine. *Secrets of the Cirque Medrano* (5–8). 2008, Charlesbridge $15.95 (978-1-57091-712-7). In Montmartre, Paris, in 1904, 14-year-old Brigitte works in her aunt's cafe and meets the young artist Pablo Picasso and the circus performers who posed for his painting *Family of Saltambiques*. (Rev: BL 1/1–15/08; LMC 10/08; SLJ 3/08)

4528 *Sir Gawain and the Green Knight* (4–7). Retold by Michael Morpurgo. Illus. by Michael Foreman. 2005, Candlewick $18.99 (978-0-7636-2519-1). Morpurgo retells in contemporary prose the story of the Green Knight's challenge to the court of King Arthur. (Rev: BL 11/1/04*; SLJ 10/04)

4529 Smith, Jenny. *Diary of a Parent Trainer* (5–8). 2012, Random House $12.99 (978-0-385-74198-9); LB $15.99 (978-0-375-99035-9). In her journal, 13-year-old Katie explains how to deal with adult relatives, but her mother's relationship with boyfriend Stuart poses particular problems; a humorous novel set in Great Britain. **e** Lexile 860L (Rev: LMC 10/12; SLJ 7/12)

258

4530 Strauss, Victoria. *Passion Blue* (7–10). 2012, Amazon Children's $18.99 (978-0-7614-6230-9). Giulia, 17, the illegitimate daughter of a count in 15th-century Italy, learns how to mix paints and create art, discovering to her surprise that she enjoys the creative life possible inside the convent where she has been sent. **℮** (Rev: BL 12/1/12; SLJ 11/12; VOYA 12/12)

4531 Sturtevant, Katherine. *A True and Faithful Narrative* (6–9). 2006, Farrar $17.00 (978-0-374-37809-7). In 17th-century London, 16-year-old Meg has abandoned some of her early dreams but still hopes to be a writer and not just a wife in this sequel to *At the Sign of the Star* (2000). (Rev: BL 3/1/06*; SLJ 5/06*)

4532 Sutcliff, Rosemary. *The Shining Company* (7–12). 1990, Farrar paper $6.95 (978-0-374-46616-9). A novel set in early Britain about a young man who with his friends confronts the enemy Saxons. (Rev: BL 6/15/90; SLJ 7/90)

4533 Swindells, Robert. *Shrapnel* (6–9). 2010, Corgi paper $9.95 (978-0-552-55930-0). Gullible young Gordon is envious of his older brother, and bored with his life of constant air raids, rations, and shelter drills in this novel set in World War II England. ∩ (Rev: BLO 12/1/09; SLJ 3/10)

4534 Szablya, Helen M., and Peggy K. Anderson. *The Fall of the Red Star* (7–9). 1996, Boyds Mills paper $9.95 (978-1-56397-977-4). A novel, partially based on fact, about a 14-year-old Hungarian boy who becomes a freedom fighter during the rebellion against the Soviets in 1956. (Rev: BL 2/1/96; SLJ 2/96; VOYA 6/96)

4535 Thomas, Jane Resh. *The Counterfeit Princess* (5–8). 2005, Clarion $15.00 (978-0-395-93870-6). Iris, a young English girl with an uncanny resemblance to Princess Elizabeth (soon to be Elizabeth I), finds herself embroiled in intrigue in this novel set in the 16th century. (Rev: BL 11/15/05; SLJ 10/05)

4536 Thompson, Kate. *Highway Robbery* (4–7). Illus. by Robert Dress. 2009, HarperCollins $15.99 (978-0-06-173034-4). A young boy suffers through a long cold night looking after a stranger's horse only to learn that the stranger might have been Dick Turpin and the horse his famous Black Bess. (Rev: BCCB 7–8/09; BL 6/1–15/09; HB 7/09; SLJ 6/09)

4537 Thomson, Sarah L. *The Secret of the Rose* (6–9). 2006, Greenwillow $16.99 (978-0-06-087250-2). In Elizabethan England, 14-year-old Rosalind must protect herself by hiding the fact that she's a Catholic and a female; however, she stumbles on more danger when she becomes servant to playwright Christopher Marlowe, who has his own secrets to hide. (Rev: BL 5/1/06; HB 7–8/06; SLJ 9/06)

4538 Town, Florida Ann. *With a Silent Companion* (7–12). 2000, Red Deer paper $7.95 (978-0-88995-211-9). Beginning in 1806, this novel based on fact tells how a young Irish girl hides her identity and becomes a "man"

to pursue a medical career. (Rev: BL 4/15/00; VOYA 6/00)

4539 Updale, Eleanor. *Montmorency* (6–9). 2004, Scholastic $16.95 (978-0-439-58035-9). After surviving a near-fatal accident, a petty thief in Victorian London creates a double life and in the process becomes a criminal mastermind. (Rev: BCCB 4/04; BL 5/1/04; HB 3–4/04; SLJ 4/04; VOYA 6/05)

4540 Van Rijckeghem, Jean-Claude, and Pat Van Beirs. *A Sword in Her Hand* (7–10). Trans. by John Nieuwenhuizen. 2011, Annick $21.95 (978-1-55451-291-1); paper $12.95 (978-1-55451-291-1). The Count of Flanders is disappointed when his child turns out to be a girl, and Marguerite must endure his disdain while trying to make a good life for herself; full of details of the Middle Ages, this novel is based on the real Marguerite (1348–1405). **℮** Lexile 550L (Rev: BL 6/1/11; LMC 11–12/11; SLJ 11/1/11)

4541 Vande Velde, Vivian. *The Book of Mordred* (8–11). 2005, Houghton Mifflin $18.00 (978-0-618-50754-2). A multilayered account of Mordred's acts, seen through the eyes of three women who know him well. (Rev: BL 9/15/05; SLJ 10/05; VOYA 10/05)

4542 Vogiel, Eva. *Friend or Foe?* (5–8). 2001, Judaica $19.95 (978-1-880582-66-4). In this novel set in London during 1948, the girls of the Migdal Binoh School for Orthodox Jewish girls notice strange happenings when the Campbell family moves next door. (Rev: BL 4/1/01)

4543 Wallace, Karen. *The Unrivalled Spangles* (7–10). 2006, Simon & Schuster $16.95 (978-1-4169-1503-4). Ellen and Lucy Spangle, teenaged circus performers in 19th-century England, long to live new lives outside of the three rings. (Rev: BL 12/1/06; SLJ 12/06)

4544 Weatherly, Lee. *Breakfast at Sadie's* (6–9). 2006, Random House $15.95 (978-0-385-75094-3). When her mother becomes very ill and her aunt skips town, Sadie is left to run her family's bed-and-breakfast all on her own in this upbeat story set in Wales. (Rev: SLJ 9/06)

4545 Weyn, Suzanne. *Distant Waves: A Novel of the Titanic* (8–11). 2009, Scholastic $17.99 (978-054508572-4). Spiritualism and science intersect in this novel featuring Jane, 16-year-old daughter of a spirit medium, and inventor Nikola Tesla, who are traveling aboard the *Titanic*. Lexile 790L (Rev: BL 4/15/09*; LMC 10/09; SLJ 9/09)

4546 Wheeler, Thomas Gerald. *All Men Tall* (7–9). 1969, Phillips $26.95 (978-0-87599-157-3). An adventure tale set in early England about a 15-year-old boy's search for security.

4547 Wheeler, Thomas Gerald. *A Fanfare for the Stalwart* (7–9). 1967, Phillips $26.95 (978-0-87599-139-9). An injured Frenchman is left behind when Napoleon retreats from Russia.

4548 Whelan, Gerard. *The Guns of Easter* (6–10). 2000, O'Brien paper $7.95 (978-0-86278-449-2). Twelve-year-old Jimmy Conway grapples with the reasons for, and impact of, the violence erupting in Ireland in the early 20th century. (Rev: BL 3/1/01)

4549 Whelan, Gerard. *A Winter of Spies* (6–10). 2002, O'Brien paper $6.95 (978-0-86278-566-6). The story of the Conway family, begun in *The Guns of Easter* (2000), continues in this novel as 11-year-old Sarah sees spies and counterspies all around her in 1920 Dublin. (Rev: BL 6/1–15/02)

4550 Whelan, Gloria. *After the Train* (6–9). 2009, HarperCollins $15.99 (978-006029596-7); LB $16.89 (978-006029597-4). Eighth-grader Peter learns he was adopted by his Catholic parents but was born to a Jewish mother who was killed in a concentration camp, and sets out to discover his roots in this novel set in 1955 Germany. e Lexile 860L (Rev: BL 12/1/08; LMC 8–9/09; SLJ 3/1/09)

4551 Whelan, Gloria. *Parade of Shadows* (7–10). 2007, HarperCollins $15.99 (978-0-06-089028-5). Julia learns about the harsh realities of 1907 Turkish-occupied Syria while traveling across the country with her British father. (Rev: BL 11/15/07; SLJ 10/07)

4552 Whitehouse, Howard. *The Strictest School in the World: Being the Tale of a Clever Girl, a Rubber Boy and a Collection of Flying Machines, Mostly Broken* (5–8). Illus. by Bill Slavin. 2006, Kids Can $16.95 (978-1-55337-882-2); paper $6.95 (978-1-55337-883-9). Raised in India where her father is a British colonial official, Emmaline Cayley is upset when her parents send her to a strict school in England, so she hatches a plan to escape; an appealing blend of humor, fantasy, and Gothic atmosphere. (Rev: SLJ 11/06)

4553 Williams, Laura E. *The Spider's Web* (5–7). 1999, Milkweed paper $6.95 (978-1-57131-622-6). Lexi, a modern German girl, joins a racist skinhead organization and discovers the consequences of irrational hatred — from her own actions and from speaking with an older woman who was once a member of Hitler's Youth. (Rev: BL 6/1–15/99; HBG 10/99)

4554 Wilson, John. *Lost Cause* (6–9). 2012, Orca paper $9.95 (978-15546994-4-5). His grandfather's will asks Steve to travel to Barcelona, Spain, where he learns of his grandfather's experiences in the Spanish Civil War. e Lexile 850L (Rev: BLO 10/15/12; SLJ 2/13)

4555 Wiseman, Eva. *The Last Song* (8–12). 2012, Tundra $17.95 (978-088776979-5). In the late 15th century 14-year-old Isabel faces family and romantic dilemmas during the Spanish Inquisition. e (Rev: BL 4/15/12; SLJ 4/12)

4556 Wiseman, Eva. *Puppet* (7–12). 2009, Tundra $17.95 (978-088776828-6). A Jewish boy is forced into giving false witness in this story based on an actual case

of anti-Semitic violence in Hungary in 1883. e Lexile HL660L (Rev: BL 2/15/09; SLJ 3/1/09)

4557 Woelfle, Gretchen. *All the World's a Stage: A Novel in Five Acts* (4–7). Illus. by Thomas Cox. 2011, Holiday House $16.95 (978-0-8234-2281-4). When he is caught picking pockets, 12-year-old Kit is offered a chance to redeem himself by working as a stage hand, and participates in the construction of the Globe Theatre in this atmospheric story set in Elizabethan England. (Rev: BL 4/15/11; HB 5–6/11; LMC 10/11; SLJ 5/11)

4558 Woodruff, Elvira. *Fearless* (5–8). 2008, Scholastic $16.99 (978-0-439-67703-5). Young brothers Digory and Cubby are befriended by Henry Winstanley, the builder of a unusual lighthouse on the Cornish coast, in this intriguing and action-packed story, set in 1703, about bravery and sacrifice. (Rev: BL 5/1/08; LMC 4–5/08; SLJ 4/08)

4559 Woodruff, Elvira. *The Ravenmaster's Secret* (4–7). 2003, Scholastic $15.95 (978-0-439-28133-1). Eleven-year-old Forrest becomes embroiled in dangerous intrigue in this story set inside the Tower of London in the early 18th century, with a glossary and historical notes appended. (Rev: BL 1/1–15/04; SLJ 1/04; VOYA 4/04)

4560 Wulf, Linda Press. *The Night of the Burning: Devorah's Story* (7–10). 2006, Farrar $16.00 (978-0-374-36419-9). Devorah and her younger sister Nechama are the only survivors left in their Polish town after a pogrom but are rescued and taken to a safe community in South Africa. They begin to build a new life and find happiness when they are adopted by families there. (Rev: BL 8/06; SLJ 1/07)

4561 Yelchin, Eugene. *Breaking Stalin's Nose* (6–9). Illus. by author. 2011, Henry Holt $15.99 (978-0-8050-9216-5). Proud of his father and faithful to his party, 10-year-old Sasha grapples with internal conflicts when his secret policeman father is arrested in this novel set in the Stalinist Soviet Union. Newbery Medal 2012. ⌒ e Lexile 670L (Rev: BL 10/15/11; HB 9–10/11; SLJ 8/11)

Latin America and Canada

4562 Belpre, Pura. *Firefly Summer* (5–8). 1996, Piñata paper $9.95 (978-1-55885-180-1). This gentle novel depicts family and community life in rural Puerto Rico at the turn of the 20th century as experienced by young Teresa Rodrigo, who has just completed 7th grade. (Rev: SLJ 2/97; VOYA 4/97)

4563 Brandis, Marianne. *The Quarter-Pie Window* (6–8). 2003, Tundra paper $9.95 (978-0-88776-624-4). Fourteen-year-old Emma and her younger brother, recently orphaned, go to live with their aunt and soon discover that the aunt is exploiting them in this novel set in 1830 Canada. (Rev: BL 7/03; VOYA 8/03)

4564 Brooks, Martha. *Queen of Hearts* (7–10). 2011, Farrar $16.99 (978-0-374-34229-6). In early 1940s Canada, tuberculosis hits a family and the three children are sent to a sanitarium, where young Marie-Claire experiences first love. ALA Notable Books 2012. **e** Lexile HL710L (Rev: BL 6/1/11; HB 7–8/11; LMC 11–12/11; SLJ 7/11*; VOYA 2/11)

4565 Cardenas, Teresa. *Old Dog* (7–12). Trans. by David Unger. 2007, Groundwood $16.95 (978-0-88899-757-9); paper $8.95 (978-0-88899-836-1). Seventy-year-old Cuban slave Perro Viejo helps to shelter 10-year-old runaway slave Aisa on the sugar plantation where Perro has lived a difficult life since childhood. (Rev: BL 12/15/07)

4566 Caswell, Maryanne. *Pioneer Girl* (5–8). Illus. by Lindsay Grater. 2001, Tundra $16.95 (978-0-88776-550-6). In letters to her grandmother, a 14-year-old girl describes the hardships and interesting experiences of her journey from Ontario to the prairies in the late 1880s. (Rev: HBG 10/01; SLJ 10/01)

4567 Clark, Ann Nolan. *Secret of the Andes* (6–8). 1970, Penguin paper $5.99 (978-0-14-030926-3). In this Newbery Medal winner (1953), a young Inca boy searches for his birthright and his identity.

4568 Collison, Linda. *Star-Crossed* (7–10). 2006, Knopf $16.95 (978-0-375-83363-2). After her father's death in 1760, Patricia stows away on a ship bound for Barbados to claim his estate; there she finds romance and learns a valuable trade. (Rev: BL 9/15/06; SLJ 12/06)

4569 Crook, Connie Brummel. *The Hungry Year* (5–8). 2001, Stoddart paper $7.95 (978-0-7737-6206-0). Twelve-year-old Kate must care for her brothers and handle the household chores during a severe Canadian winter in the late 1700s. (Rev: BL 1/1–15/02; SLJ 11/01)

4570 Crook, Connie Brummel. *The Perilous Year* (5–7). 2003, Fitzhenry & Whiteside paper $8.95 (978-1-55041-818-7). In this fast-paced sequel to *The Hungry Year* (2001), 11-year-old twins Alex and Ryan face constant challenges and adventures — including more encounters with pirates — in 18th-century Canada. (Rev: SLJ 3/04)

4571 Curtis, Christopher Paul. *Elijah of Buxton* (6–8). 2007, Scholastic $16.99 (978-0-439-02344-3). Eleven-year-old Elijah, the first child born in the Buxton Settlement for former slaves in Ontario, describes his life and those of the residents and newcomers to the settlement. Coretta Scott King Author Award, 2008; Newbery Honor Book, 2008. (Rev: BL 9/1/07; SLJ 10/07)

4572 Danticat, Edwidge. *Anacaona, Golden Flower: Haiti, 1490* (5–8). Series: Royal Diaries. 2005, Scholastic $10.95 (978-0-439-49906-4). In 15th-century Haiti, Anacaona, a girl of royal heritage, records her people's struggles against the Spanish explorers. (Rev: BL 5/15/05)

4573 Downie, Mary Alice, and John Downie. *Danger in Disguise* (5–8). Series: On Time's Wing. 2001, Roussan paper $6.95 (978-1-896184-72-2). Young Jamie, a Scot raised in Normandy in secrecy, is scooped up to serve in the British navy and sent to Quebec to fight the French in this complex tale of adventure and intrigue set in the mid-18th century. (Rev: SLJ 5/01)

4574 Eboch, Chris. *The Well of Sacrifice* (5–8). 1999, Houghton Mifflin $16.00 (978-0-395-90374-2). In this novel set during Mayan times, Eveningstar Macaw sets out to avenge the death of her older brother, Smoke Shell. (Rev: BL 4/1/99; HBG 10/99; SLJ 5/99; VOYA 2/00)

4575 Ellis, Deborah. *I Am a Taxi* (6–9). 2006, Groundwood $16.95 (978-0-88899-735-7). Twelve-year-old Diego lives in a Bolivian prison with his parents, who were wrongfully accused of drug smuggling, and runs errands for prisoners but his life is forever changed when he's lured into working for an illegal cocaine operation deep in the jungle. (Rev: BL 11/15/06; HB 1–2/07; LMC 4–5/07; SLJ 12/06)

4576 Ellis, Deborah. *Sacred Leaf: The Cocalero Novels* (5–8). Series: The Cocalera Novels. 2007, Groundwood $16.95 (978-0-88899-751-7). Twelve-year-old Diego is living with a family of poor Bolivian coca farmers when their crop is destroyed by soldiers and they join a national protest. (Rev: BL 1/1–15/08; SLJ 12/07)

4577 Engle, Margarita. *The Lightning Dreamer* (7–12). 2013, Harcourt $16.99 (978-054780743-0). This novel in free verse tells the story of 19th-century Cuban abolitionist poet Gertrudis Gómez de Avellaneda, known as Tula, describing her teen years and her hatred of injustice. **e** (Rev: BL 2/15/13*; HB 5–6/13; SLJ 6/13; VOYA 4/13)

4578 Engle, Margarita. *Wild Book* (5–8). Illus. 2012, Harcourt $16.99 (978-054758131-6). Dyslexic Josefa comes to understand the freeing power of words in this story set in 1912 Cuba; based on the life of the author's grandmother. **e** (Rev: BL 3/1/12; LMC 11–12/12; SLJ 3/12)

4579 Finn, Daniel. *She Thief* (6–9). 2010, Feiwel & Friends $16.99 (978-0-312-56330-1). In a Latin American city, street kids Baz and Demi find their lives turned upside down when Demi steals a valuable ring and the repercussions reverberate throughout the barrio. **e** (Rev: BL 2/15/10; LMC 5–6/10; SLJ 5/10)

4580 Gantos, Jack. *Jack's New Power: Stories from a Caribbean Year* (5–8). 1995, Farrar $16.00 (978-0-374-33657-8); paper $5.95 (978-0-374-43715-2). Eight stories about the interesting people Jack meets when his family moves to the Caribbean. A sequel to *Heads or Tails* (1994). (Rev: BCCB 12/95; BL 12/1/95; SLJ 11/95*)

4581 Harrison, Troon. *A Bushel of Light* (5–8). 2001, Stoddart paper $7.95 (978-0-7737-6140-7). Fourteen-year-old orphan Maggie juggles her need to search for her twin sister and her responsibilities for 4-year-old Lizzy, in this novel set in Canada in the early 1900s. (Rev: SLJ 10/01)

4582 Haworth-Attard, Barbara. *Home Child* (5–8). 1996, Roussan paper $6.95 (978-1-896184-18-0). Set in Canada during the early 1900s, this is the story of 13-year-old Arthur Fellowes, a London orphan who is treated like an outcast when he joins the Wilson family as a home child (that is, a cheap farm laborer). (Rev: VOYA 8/97)

4583 Holeman, Linda. *Promise Song* (5–8). 1997, Tundra paper $6.95 (978-0-88776-387-8). In 1900, Rosetta, an English orphan who has been sent to Canada, becomes an indentured servant. (Rev: BL 6/1–15/97; SLJ 10/97)

4584 Ibbotson, Eva. *Journey to the River Sea* (5–8). 2002, Dutton $17.99 (978-0-525-46739-7). Orphaned Maia journeys from 1910 London to live with relatives in Brazil in this complex story that involves an unwelcoming family, a beloved governess, a child actor, a runaway, and the wonders of Brazil, all presented with a mix of drama and humor. (Rev: BCCB 4/02; BL 12/15/01; HB 1–2/02; HBG 10/02; SLJ 1/02*; VOYA 12/01)

4585 Jefferson, Joanne K. *Lightning and Blackberries* (7–10). 2008, Nimbus paper $10.95 (978-155109654-4). In 1774 Nova Scotia 17-year-old Elizabeth longs for independence but knows she must settle for marriage and domesticity until she meets an Acadian woman who widens her horizons. **e** (Rev: BLO 11/11/08; VOYA 10/08)

4586 Jocelyn, Marthe. *Mable Riley: A Reliable Record of Humdrum, Peril, and Romance* (5–10). 2004, Candlewick $15.99 (978-0-7636-2120-9). This is a charming, humorous diary set in 1901 by a 14-year-old girl who accompanies her sister when she becomes a teacher in Stratford, Ontario. (Rev: BL 3/1/04; HB 5–6/04; SLJ 3/04; VOYA 6/04)

4587 Kerz, Anna. *The Gnome's Eye* (4–7). 2010, Orca paper $9.95 (978-1-55469-195-1). Theresa, 10, describes her Yugoslav family's journey from an Austrian refugee camp to Toronto, Canada, where Theresa struggles to make the transition to a new language, a new school, and a new culture in the early 1950s. **e** Lexile 650L (Rev: BL 5/15/10; LMC 11–12/10; SLJ 8/10)

4588 Kositsky, Lynne. *Claire by Moonlight* (7–10). 2005, Tundra paper $9.95 (978-0-88776-659-6). History and romance are interwoven in this story of 15-year-old Claire's struggle to return to Acadia with her brother and sister after their deportation in the 1750s. (Rev: BL 7/05; SLJ 10/05)

4589 Lawson, Julie. *Goldstone* (5–8). 1998, Stoddart paper $7.95 (978-0-7737-5891-9). Karin, a 13-year-old Swedish Canadian girl, lives with her family in a mountainous town in British Columbia in 1910 when heavy winter snows bring avalanches that cause death and destruction. (Rev: BL 7/97; SLJ 5/98)

4590 Limón, Graciela. *Song of the Hummingbird* (6–10). 1996, Arte Publico paper $12.95 (978-1-55885-091-0). The conquest of the Aztec Empire by Cortes is told through the experiences of Huizitzilin (Hummingbird), a descendent of Mexican kings. (Rev: VOYA 8/97)

4591 Lowery, Linda. *Truth and Salsa* (4–7). 2006, Peachtree $14.95 (978-1-59145-366-6). Staying with her grandmother in Mexico after her parents separate, Haley makes a new friend and learns about people living on the edge of poverty. (Rev: SLJ 7/06)

4592 Major, Kevin. *Ann and Seamus* (5–9). Illus. by David Blackwood. 2003, Groundwood $16.95 (978-0-88899-561-2). Based on an early 19th-century shipwreck off the coast of Newfoundland, this historical novel in verse chronicles the romance that develops between 17-year-old Ann Harvey and the Irish teenager she rescues from the ship. (Rev: BL 3/1/04; HB 3–4/04; SLJ 2/04; VOYA 4/04)

4593 Mikaelsen, Ben. *Tree Girl* (7–12). 2004, HarperTempest $16.99 (978-0-06-009004-3). Through the first-person narrative of Mayan teenager Gabriela Flores, the reader experiences the civil war in Guatemala. (Rev: BL 2/15/04; SLJ 4/04; VOYA 6/04)

4594 Mordecai, Martin. *Blue Mountain Trouble* (5–8). 2009, Scholastic $16.99 (978-0-545-04156-0). A strange goat appears to 11-year-old twins Pollyread and Jackson, who live high in the Blue Mountains of Jamaica, and coincidentally there is a series of strange events. (Rev: BL 4/15/09; HB 5/09; SLJ 7/09)

4595 Noël, Michel. *Good for Nothing* (8–11). 2004, Douglas & McIntyre $18.95 (978-0-88899-478-3). In this powerful coming-of-age novel set in northern Quebec in the late 1950s and early 1960s, 15-year-old Nipishish, part Algonquin and part white, struggles to find his own identity. (Rev: BL 1/1–15/05; SLJ 1/05; VOYA 2/05)

4596 O'Dell, Scott. *The Captive* (7–9). 1979, Houghton Mifflin $17.00 (978-0-395-27811-6). During a voyage in the 1500s, a young Jesuit seminarian discovers that the crew of his ship plans to enslave a colony of Mayans. A sequel is *The Feathered Serpent* (1981).

4597 O'Dell, Scott. *The King's Fifth* (7–10). 1966, Houghton Mifflin $17.00 (978-0-395-06963-9). In a story told in flashbacks, Esteban explains why he is in jail in the Mexico of the Conquistadors. Also use *The Hawk That Dare Not Hunt by Day* (1975).

4598 Porter, Pamela. *The Crazy Man* (6–8). 2005, Douglas & McIntyre $15.95 (978-0-88899-694-7). In appealing free verse, this novel set in 1960s Saskatchewan tells the story of young Emaline, who has been crippled in a farm accident and who befriends Angus, a mental patient who's been hired to help out around the farm. (Rev: BL 11/1/05; SLJ 12/05; VOYA 2/06)

4599 Porter, Pamela. *I'll Be Watching* (7–12). 2011, Groundwood $18.95 (978-1-55498-095-6); paper $12.95 (978-15549809-6-3). Four orphans struggle to make their own way in 1941 Saskatchewan in this inspiring story told in verse. ❸ (Rev: BL 10/1/11; HB 11–12/11; LMC 1–2/12; SLJ 9/1/11)

4600 Resau, Laura, and Maria Virginia Farinango. *The Queen of Water* (8–12). 2011, Delacorte $16.99 (978-0-385-73897-2); LB $19.99 (978-038590761-3). Virginia, 7, is sent by her poor Quechua Indian family to be an indentured servant to a mestizo family; there she learns some skills and puts up with a certain amount of abuse, but can she ever go back home? (Rev: BL 2/15/11*; HB 7–8/11; SLJ 6/11*)

4601 Ryan, Pam Muñoz. *The Dreamer* (4–8). Illus. by Peter Sís. 2010, Scholastic $17.99 (978-0-439-26970-4). Ryan imagines the young life of the poet Pablo Neruda, who was shy, afraid of his demanding father, and interested in nature and the lives of the indigenous Indians of Chile. Belpré Medal 2011; ALA Notable Books 2011; Boston Globe–Horn Book Honor 2010. ♫ Lexile 650L (Rev: BL 2/1/10*; HB 3–4/10; LMC 3–4/10; SLJ 4/10)

4602 Schwartz, Virginia Frances. *Messenger* (5–9). 2002, Holiday $17.95 (978-0-8234-1716-2). This story of the hardships and joys of a Croatian family living in Ontario's mining towns in the 1920s and 1930s is based on the lives of the author's mother and grandmother. (Rev: HBG 3/03; SLJ 11/02; VOYA 12/02)

4603 Slaughter, Charles H. *The Dirty War* (6–9). 1994, Walker $15.95 (978-0-8027-8312-7). Arte, 14, lives in Buenos Aires, Argentina. When his father is taken prisoner by the government, his grandmother stages public protests. (Rev: BL 11/1/94; SLJ 12/94; VOYA 2/95)

4604 Stenhouse, Ted. *Across the Steel River* (6–8). 2001, Kids Can $16.95 (978-1-55074-891-8). In 1952, a Canadian boy and his Indian friend find the badly beaten body of an Indian man and, in the process of investigating his death, reassess their own relationship. (Rev: BCCB 1/02; BL 1/1–15/02; HBG 3/02; SLJ 10/01; VOYA 2/02)

4605 Stenhouse, Ted. *A Dirty Deed* (6–8). 2003, Kids Can $16.95 (978-1-55337-360-5). In this sequel to *Across the Steel River* (2001), friends Will Samson and Arthur, a Blackfoot Indian, have exciting adventures as they struggle to return a deed to its rightful owners. (Rev: BL 3/15/03; HBG 10/03; SLJ 5/03; VOYA 10/03)

4606 Taylor, Joanne. *There You Are: A Novel* (4–7). 2004, Tundra paper $8.95 (978-0-88776-658-9). On post-World War II Cape Breton Island, 12-year-old Jeannie lives in a remote community and longs for a friend. (Rev: SLJ 11/04)

4607 Temple, Frances. *Taste of Salt: A Story of Modern Haiti* (7–12). 1992, Orchard LB $17.99 (978-0-531-08609-4). A first novel simply told in the voices of two Haitian teenagers who find political commitment and love. (Rev: BL 8/92; SLJ 9/92*)

4608 Trottier, Maxine. *A Circle of Silver* (5–8). 2000, Stoddart paper $7.95 (978-0-7737-6055-4). Set in the 1760s, this is the story of 13-year-old John MacNeil who is sent to Canada by his father to toughen him up. (Rev: SLJ 9/00)

4609 Trottier, Maxine. *Sister to the Wolf* (6–9). 2004, Kids Can $16.95 (978-1-55337-519-7). In this engaging historical novel, which begins in Quebec in the early 18th century, Cecile, the teenage daughter of a fur trader, buys an Indian slave to save him from further abuse. (Rev: BL 1/1–15/05; SLJ 12/04)

4610 Trueman, Terry. *Hurricane* (5–7). 2008, HarperCollins $15.99 (978-0-06-000018-9). José is 13 when Hurricane Mitch hits his village in Honduras and he must deal with the death and destruction left behind. (Rev: BL 12/1/07; SLJ 3/08)

4611 Weber, Lori. *If You Live Like Me* (7–10). 2009, Lobster $14.95 (978-189755012-0). After a series of moves, Cheryl learns to love Newfoundland and her new neighbor, Jim, only to learn that she can finally return to Montreal. (Rev: BL 4/15/09; SLJ 6/1/09)

4612 Weir, Joan. *The Brideship* (7–9). 1999, Stoddart paper $5.95 (978-0-7736-7474-5). Three plucky British teens journey to British Columbia as mail-order brides in the 1860s. (Rev: SLJ 10/99)

4613 Whelan, Gloria. *The Disappeared* (8–12). 2008, Dial $16.99 (978-0-8037-3275-9). Silvia tries to save her brother Eduardo when he is imprisoned for protesting against the government in Argentina in the 1970s. (Rev: BL 4/15/08; LMC 10/08*; SLJ 7/08)

United States

NATIVE AMERICANS

4614 Armstrong, Nancy M. *Navajo Long Walk* (4–7). 1994, Roberts Rinehart $8.95 (978-1-879373-56-3). The story of the Long Walk of the Navajo in 1864 and their confinement in an internment camp are vividly told. (Rev: BL 10/1/94; SLJ 1/95)

4615 Bruchac, Joseph. *A Boy Called Slow: The True Story of Sitting Bull* (5–8). Illus. by Rocco Baviera. 1995, Putnam $17.99 (978-0-399-22692-2). The story of the boyhood of Sitting Bull, who, because of his sluggishness, had been called Slow. (Rev: BCCB 4/95; BL 3/15/95; HB 9–10/95; SLJ 10/95)

4616 Bruchac, Joseph. *Geronimo* (7–10). 2006, Scholastic $16.99 (978-0-439-35360-1). Geronimo's fictional adopted grandson narrates the tragic story of Geronimo's final surrender and the subsequent treatment of his people in this well-researched novel. (Rev: BL 3/15/06; SLJ 4/06)

4617 Bruchac, Joseph. *The Journal of Jesse Smoke: The Trail of Tears, 1838* (5–8). Series: My Name Is America. 2001, Scholastic paper $10.95 (978-0-439-12197-2). Jesse, a 16-year-old Cherokee, chronicles in his diary the tribe's forced journey to Oklahoma and tries to understand the reasons behind this cruel action. (Rev: BL 7/01; HBG 10/01; SLJ 7/01; VOYA 8/01)

4618 Burks, Brian. *Runs with Horses* (5–9). 1995, Harcourt paper $6.00 (978-0-15-200994-6). An adventure story set in 1886 in which 16-year-old Runs with Horses completes his Apache warrior training by performing feats of endurance, survival, and daring, and partly as a result of information he gathers during raids, his tribe realizes that they can no longer continue to resist the white man. (Rev: BL 11/1/95; SLJ 11/95; VOYA 2/96)

4619 Carvell, Marlene. *Sweetgrass Basket* (7–10). 2005, Dutton $16.99 (978-0-525-47547-7). Mohawk sisters Mattie and Sarah describe the abuse they endure at the Carlisle Indian Industrial School at the turn of the 20th century. (Rev: BL 8/05*; SLJ 12/05)

4620 Creel, Ann Howard. *Under a Stand Still Moon* (6–10). 2005, Brown Barn paper $8.95 (978-0-9746481-8-7). In this captivating story set among the ancient Anasazi of the American Southwest, a young girl uses her magical powers to preserve her people's way of life. (Rev: SLJ 11/05)

4621 Doughty, Wayne Dyre. *Crimson Moccasins* (7–9). 1980, HarperCollins paper $2.95 (978-0-06-440015-2). During the Revolutionary War a white boy is raised as the son of an Indian chief.

4622 Driving Hawk Sneve, Virginia. *Lana's Lakota Moons* (5–8). 2008, Univ. of Nebraska paper $12.95 (978-0-8032-6028-3). Lori and Lana, Lakotas whose lives are a combination of Native American tradition and modern American culture, have disturbing premonitions about the future that sadly come true in this thoughtful, moving story. (Rev: BL 5/1/08)

4623 Edwardson, Debby Dahl. *Blessing's Bead* (5–8). 2009, Farrar $16.99 (978-0-374-30805-6). Two narratives — the first set in 1917 and the second in 1989 — tell the stories of Inupiaq Eskimo teenagers and the quite different challenges they face. (Rev: BL 10/15/09*; LMC 11–12/09; SLJ 11/09)

4624 Erdrich, Louise. *Chickadee* (4–7). Series: Birchbark House. 2012, HarperCollins $15.99 (978-0-06-057790-2). In 1866 Omakayas's son Chickadee, 8, is kidnapped and the family sets out to find him despite the winter cold. (Rev: BL 8/12; HB 9–10/12; SLJ 9/12*)

4625 Erdrich, Louise. *The Game of Silence* (5–8). 2005, HarperCollins LB $16.89 (978-0-06-029790-9). As 9-year-old Omakayas is coming of age, the intrusion of the European settlers increasingly impacts the Ojibwe

lifestyle in this sequel to *The Birchbark House* (1999). (Rev: BL 5/15/05*; SLJ 7/05)

4626 Erdrich, Louise. *The Porcupine Year* (4–7). Illus. by author. 2008, HarperCollins $15.99 (978-0-06-029787-9). In this sequel to *The Birchbark House* (1999) and *The Game of Silence* (2005), Omakayas is now 12 and the family is traveling north, looking for a new home far from the intruding white settlers. (Rev: BL 6/1–15/08; SLJ 9/08)

4627 Gall, Grant. *Apache: The Long Ride Home* (7–10). 1988, Sunstone paper $9.95 (978-0-86534-105-0). Pedro was only nine when Apache raiders kidnapped him and renamed him Cuchillo. (Rev: BL 9/15/87)

4628 Gregory, Kristiana. *The Legend of Jimmy Spoon* (6–8). 1990, Harcourt $15.95 (978-0-15-200506-1). The story of a 12-year-old white boy who is adopted by the Shoshoni in 1855. (Rev: BL 7/90)

4629 Grutman, Jewel, and Gay Matthaei. *The Ledgerbook of Thomas Blue Eagle* (4–8). Illus. by Adam Cvijanovic. 1994, Thomasson-Grant $17.95 (978-1-56566-063-2). A young Native American boy attends a white man's school but tries to retain his own identity and culture in this story that takes place in the West 100 years ago. (Rev: SLJ 12/94)

4630 Hausman, Gerald. *The Coyote Bead* (7–12). 1999, Hampton Roads paper $11.95 (978-1-57174-145-5). With the help of his grandfather and Indian magic, a young Navajo boy evades the American soldiers who killed his parents. (Rev: SLJ 1/00; VOYA 4/00)

4631 Highwater, Jamake. *Legend Days* (7–10). Series: Ghost Horse. 1984, HarperCollins $12.95 (978-0-06-022303-8). This story about a young Indian girl begins a moving trilogy about three generations of Native Americans and their fate in a white man's world. Followed by *The Ceremony of Innocence* and *I Wear the Morning Star*.

4632 Homstad, Daniel W. *Horse Dreamer* (7–12). 2001, PublishAmerica paper $27.95 (978-1-58851-042-6). A historical adventure in which 16-year-old Zakarias, son of a white father and a Dakota mother, serves as a scout for the army in the early 1860s until he is captured by renegade Dakotas and decides to join their cause. (Rev: VOYA 4/02)

4633 Hudson, Jan. *Sweetgrass* (5–8). 1989, Scholastic paper $3.99 (978-0-590-43486-7). A description of the culture of the Dakota Indians in the 1830s. (Rev: BCCB 4/89; BL 4/1/89; SLJ 4/89)

4634 Landman, Tanya. *I Am Apache* (8–12). 2008, Candlewick $17.99 (978-076363664-7). When 14-year-old Apache Siki witnesses her brother's death at the hands of brutal Mexican raiders in the late 19th century, she vows to avenge him by earning her stripes as a daring, if unlikely, warrior. Lexile 860L (Rev: BL 10/1/08; LMC 3–4/09; SLJ 8/08; VOYA 12/08)

4635 Matthaei, Gay, and Jewel Grutman. *The Sketchbook of Thomas Blue Eagle* (4–7). 2001, Chronicle $16.95 (978-0-88182-908-2). Through drawings and narration, the Lakota artist Thomas Blue Eagle tells how he joined Buffalo Bill's show, traveled to Europe, and made enough money to marry. (Rev: BCCB 5/01; BL 4/1/01)

4636 O'Dell, Scott. *Sing Down the Moon* (6–9). 1970, Houghton Mifflin $18.00 (978-0-395-10919-9); paper $5.99 (978-0-440-97975-3). A young Navajo girl sees her culture destroyed by Spanish slavers and white soldiers. (Rev: BL 11/1/87)

4637 O'Dell, Scott, and Elizabeth Hall. *Thunder Rolling in the Mountains* (5–9). 1992, Dell paper $5.50 (978-0-440-40879-6). From the viewpoint of Chief Joseph's daughter, this historical novel concerns the forced removal of the Nez Perce from their homeland in 1877. (Rev: BL 6/15/92*; SLJ 8/92)

4638 Patent, Dorothy Hinshaw. *The Buffalo and the Indians: A Shared Destiny* (4–8). Illus. by William Muñoz. 2006, Clarion $18.00 (978-0-618-48570-3). This beautifully illustrated title explores the unique bonds — both spiritual and economic — between Native Americans and the American bison. (Rev: BL 6/1/06*; HBG 4/07; LMC 2/07; SLJ 8/06*) [978.004]

4639 Rees, Celia. *Sorceress* (7–11). 2002, Candlewick $15.99 (978-0-7636-1847-6). Agnes, a Native American who is beginning college, researches Mary Newbury, first seen in *Witch Child* (2001), and discovers a connection that results in a vision quest. (Rev: BL 1/1–15/03; HB 1–2/03; HBG 3/03; SLJ 12/02; VOYA 4/03)

4640 Sandoz, Mari. *The Horsecatcher* (7–9). 1957, Univ. of Nebraska paper $13.95 (978-0-8032-9160-7). A Cheyenne youth gains stature with his tribe and earns the name of Horsecatcher. (Rev: BL 11/1/87)

4641 Schwartz, Virginia Frances. *Initiation* (5–8). 2003, Fitzhenry & Whiteside $15.95 (978-1-55005-053-0). Kwakiuti Indian twins Nana and Nanolatch prepare to face the responsibilities of adulthood in this story set on the West Coast of North America in the 15th century. (Rev: SLJ 3/04) [813]

4642 Shefelman, Janice. *Comanche Song* (6–9). 2000, Eakin $17.95 (978-1-57168-397-7). Tsena, 16, is imprisoned with other Comanches after peace talks falter and 12 Indian chiefs are killed in this story based on a real event in 1840. (Rev: BL 2/15/01; HBG 10/01; SLJ 10/00)

4643 Smith, Patricia Clark. *Weetamoo: Heart of the Pocassets, Massachusetts — Rhode Island, 1653* (5–8). Series: Royal Diaries. 2003, Scholastic $10.95 (978-0-439-12910-7). Weetamoo prepares to succeed her father as leader of the tribe and describes relationships with the European settlers and how daily life changes with the seasons. (Rev: BL 12/15/03; HBG 4/04; SLJ 1/04)

4644 Spooner, Michael. *Last Child* (8–11). 2005, Henry Holt $16.95 (978-0-8050-7739-1). Rosalie, who is part Mandan and part Scottish American, is caught up in the conflicts between the Native Americans and the whites in 1837 North Dakota. (Rev: BL 9/1/05; SLJ 11/05; VOYA 8/05)

4645 Vick, Helen H. *Shadow* (5–7). Series: Courage of the Stone. 1998, Roberts Rinehart $15.95 (978-1-57098-218-7); paper $9.95 (978-1-57098-195-1). Shadow, an independent Pueblo Indian girl in pre-Columbian Arizona, leaves her home to rescue her father. (Rev: SLJ 10/98)

4646 Wyss, Thelma Hatch. *Bear Dancer: The Story of a Ute Girl* (4–7). 2005, Simon & Schuster $15.95 (978-1-4169-0285-0). In this fact-based historical novel, life is turned upside down for Elk Girl, a member of the Tabaguache Ute, when she is kidnapped by a rival tribe. (Rev: BL 10/15/05; SLJ 10/05)

DISCOVERY AND EXPLORATION

4647 Carbone, Elisa. *Blood on the River: James Town, 1607* (5–8). 2006, Viking $16.99 (978-0-670-06060-3). As a page for Captain John Smith in the Jamestown Colony, 11-year-old Samuel Collier experiences firsthand the hardships and adventures that confront the settlers; a powerful, historically detailed novel. (Rev: BL 4/15/06; LMC 1/07; SLJ 7/06*)

4648 Duble, Kathleen Benner. *Quest* (5–8). 2008, Simon & Schuster $16.99 (978-1-4169-3386-1). Through the thoughts of four characters, two of them on Henry Hudson's ship *Discovery*, readers will learn of the significance of the voyage to find the Northwest Passage and why it failed. (Rev: BL 4/15/08; SLJ 8/08)

4649 Howard, Ellen. *The Crimson Cap* (5–8). 2009, Holiday House $16.95 (978-0-8234-2152-7). Eleven-year-old Pierre Talon finds himself living with the Hasinai Indians after setting out on an ill-fated mission with explorer La Salle. Lexile 720L (Rev: BLO 12/1/09; LMC 1–2/10; SLJ 11/09)

4650 Kudlinski, Kathleen. *My Lady Pocahontas* (7–10). 2006, Marshall Cavendish $16.95 (978-0-7614-5293-5). This fictional account of the life of Pocahontas from the time of the Jamestown settlement until her death focuses on her strength and inner conflicts. (Rev: BL 5/1/06; LMC 11–12/06; SLJ 12/06)

COLONIAL PERIOD AND FRENCH AND INDIAN WARS

4651 Avi. *Night Journeys* (6–9). 1994, Morrow paper $4.95 (978-0-688-13628-4). In the Pennsylvania of 1767, a 12-year-old orphan boy joins a hunt for escaped bondsmen. Another novel set at the same time by this author is *Encounter at Easton* (1994).

4652 Bruchac, Joseph. *Pocahontas* (6–12). 2003, Harcourt $17.00 (978-0-15-216737-0). Pocahontas and John Smith take turns describing the relationship between the Jamestown colonists and the Powhatan Indians. (Rev: BL 9/15/03; HBG 4/04; SLJ 5/04; VOYA 4/04)

4653 Bruchac, Joseph. *The Winter People* (6–10). 2002, Dial $18.99 (978-0-8037-2694-9). A 14-year-old Abenaki boy searches for his mother and sisters after they are kidnapped by English soldiers in the French and Indian War. (Rev: BL 10/1/02*; HBG 3/03; SLJ 11/02*)

4654 Butler, Amy. *Virginia Bound* (4–7). 2003, Clarion $15.00 (978-0-618-24752-3). Thirteen-year-old Rob is kidnapped in London and shipped to Virginia as an indentured servant to work on a tobacco farm in 1627. (Rev: BL 3/1/03; HBG 10/03; SLJ 6/03)

4655 Collier, James Lincoln. *The Corn Raid: A Story of the Jamestown Settlement* (5–9). 2000, Jamestown paper $5.95 (978-0-8092-0619-3). History and fiction mix in this adventure tale set in the Jamestown settlement and featuring a 12-year-old indentured servant and his cruel master. (Rev: SLJ 4/00)

4656 Coombs, Karen M. *Sarah on Her Own* (6–10). 1996, Avon paper $3.99 (978-0-380-78275-8). Through the eyes of a sensitive English teenager who voyaged to America in 1620, the reader relives the harsh realities and joys of life in an early Virginia settlement. (Rev: SLJ 9/96)

4657 Duble, Kathleen Benner. *The Sacrifice* (6–9). 2005, Simon & Schuster $15.95 (978-0-689-87650-9). Strong-minded Abigail, 10, and her older sister are accused of witchcraft in 1692 Massachusetts in this compelling novel full of social history. (Rev: BL 9/15/05*; SLJ 12/05)

4658 Durrant, Lynda. *The Beaded Moccasins: The Story of Mary Campbell* (5–9). 1998, Clarion $15.00 (978-0-395-85398-6). Told in the first person, this is a fictionalized account of the true story of 12-year-old Mary Campbell who was captured by the Delaware Indians in 1759. (Rev: BCCB 5/98; BL 3/15/98; HBG 10/98; SLJ 6/98; VOYA 12/98)

4659 Edmonds, Walter D. *The Matchlock Gun* (5–7). Illus. by Paul Lantz. 1941, Putnam $16.99 (978-0-399-21911-5). Exciting, true story of a courageous boy who protected his mother and sister from the Indians of the Hudson Valley. Newbery Medal 1942.

4660 Field, Rachel. *Calico Bush* (5–7). Illus. by Allen Louis. 1987, Macmillan $17.95 (978-0-02-734610-7). This 1932 Newbery Honor Book is an adventure story of a French girl "loaned" to a family of American pioneers in Maine in the 1740s.

4661 Greene, Jacqueline D. *Out of Many Waters* (6–8). 1988, Walker $16.95 (978-0-8027-6811-7). A historical novel that begins in Brazil and ends with a group of Jewish settlers who, after landing in New Amsterdam, began the first synagogue in America. (Rev: BL 1/15/89; SLJ 10/88; VOYA 12/88)

4662 Grote, JoAnn A. *Queen Anne's War* (5–8). Series: The American Adventure. 1998, Chelsea LB $15.95 (978-0-7910-5045-3). During Queen Anne's War in 1710, Will Smith's family becomes involved in the attempt to drive the French out of New England, but 11-year-old Will is preoccupied with a jealous classmate. (Rev: HBG 3/99; SLJ 1/99)

4663 Hemphill, Stephanie. *Wicked Girls: A Novel of the Salem Witch Trials* (7–12). 2010, HarperCollins LB $16.99 (978-0-06-185328-9). Three of the Salem accusers relate the story of the false testimony and resulting deaths in alternate verse voices. e Lexile 700L (Rev: BL 6/10*; HB 7–8/10; LMC 10/10; SLJ 8/10; VOYA 10/10)

4664 Hermes, Patricia. *Salem Witch* (5–8). Series: My Side of the Story. 2006, Kingfisher paper $7.95 (978-0-7534-5991-1). Two teenage friends develop different views during the witch trials in 17th-century Salem, and readers can flip the book to read each person's opinion. (Rev: SLJ 2/07)

4665 Hurst, Carol Otis, and Rebecca Otis. *A Killing in Plymouth Colony* (5–7). 2003, Houghton Mifflin $15.00 (978-0-618-27597-7). John Bradford, the son of the governor of Plymouth Colony, has always struggled to gain his father's approval and feels an affinity toward an outcast who is accused of murder. (Rev: BL 12/1/03; HBG 4/04; SLJ 10/03)

4666 Karr, Kathleen. *Worlds Apart* (4–7). 2005, Marshall Cavendish $15.95 (978-0-7614-5195-2). In 1670 South Carolina, Christopher — a teenage settler — and Sewee Indian Asha-po become friends. (Rev: BCCB 5/05; SLJ 5/05)

4667 Karwoski, Gail Langer. *Surviving Jamestown: The Adventures of Young Sam Collier* (5–7). Illus. by Paul Casale. 2001, Peachtree $14.95 (978-1-56145-239-2); paper $8.95 (978-1-56145-245-3). Full of facts, this novel tells the story of a 12-year-old English boy who sails in 1606 for the colony of Virginia, with details of the struggles the colonists faced. (Rev: HBG 10/01; SLJ 8/01; VOYA 8/01)

4668 Keehn, Sally M. *Moon of Two Dark Horses* (6–9). 1995, Puffin paper $6.99 (978-0-698-11949-9). A sensitively drawn friendship between a Native American boy and a white settler. (Rev: BL 11/15/95*; SLJ 11/95; VOYA 12/95)

4669 Ketchum, Liza. *Where the Great Hawk Flies* (4–7). 2005, Clarion $16.00 (978-0-618-40085-0). The Coombs family and the Tuckers have trouble getting along — even the young boys — because Mrs. Tucker is a Pequot Indian and the Coombs suffered mightily during an Indian raid seven years before. (Rev: BCCB 12/05; BL 9/15/05*; HB 1–2/06; LMC 1/06; SLJ 1/06; VOYA 4/06)

4670 Laird, Marnie. *Water Rat* (7–9). 1998, Winslow $15.95 (978-1-890817-08-4). An action-filled adventure story set in colonial times about Matt, a 14-year-old orphan, and his struggle to survive and prove his worth. (Rev: SLJ 1/99; VOYA 2/99)

4671 Lasky, Kathryn. *Beyond the Burning Time* (7–12). 1994, Scholastic paper $14.95 (978-0-590-47331-6). In this docunovel that captures the ignorance, violence, and hysteria of the Salem witch trials, Mary, 12, tries to save her mother, accused of witchcraft. (Rev: BL 10/15/94; SLJ 1/95; VOYA 12/94)

4672 Lasky, Kathryn. *A Journey to the New World: The Diary of Remember Patience Whipple* (4–7). Series: Dear America. 1996, Scholastic paper $10.95 (978-0-590-50214-6). Using diary entries as a format, this is the story of 12-year-old Mem Whipple, her journey on the *Mayflower*, and her first year in the New World. (Rev: BCCB 10/96; HB 9–10/96; SLJ 8/96; VOYA 10/96)

4673 Moore, Robin. *The Man with the Silver Oar* (6–12). 2002, HarperCollins LB $15.89 (978-0-06-000048-6). Daniel, a Quaker 15-year-old, stows away on a ship hunting pirates in this fine adventure story set in 1718. (Rev: BL 6/1–15/02; HBG 10/02; SLJ 7/02; VOYA 8/02)

4674 Ovecka, Janice. *Cave of Falling Water* (4–8). Illus. by David K. Fadden. 1992, New England paper $10.95 (978-0-933050-98-3). A cave in the hills of Vermont plays a part in the lives of three girls, one an Indian and one white, both from colonial times, and the last, a contemporary adolescent. (Rev: BL 5/1/93)

4675 Rinaldi, Ann. *The Journal of Jasper Jonathan Pierce: A Pilgrim Boy, Plymouth, 1620* (4–8). 2000, Scholastic paper $10.95 (978-0-590-51078-3). This fictionalized account of the Pilgrims in journal format follows the adventures of a 14-year-old indentured servant aboard the *Mayflower* and during his first year in the New World. (Rev: BL 2/15/00; HBG 10/00; SLJ 7/00)

4676 Rinaldi, Ann. *Or Give Me Death: A Novel of Patrick Henry's Family* (7–9). 2003, Harcourt $17.00 (978-0-15-216687-8). The treatment of the mentally ill in the colonial era is shown in this novel narrated by the daughters of an insane mother. (Rev: BL 5/15/03; SLJ 7/03; VOYA 8/03)

4677 Rinaldi, Ann. *A Stitch in Time* (7–10). Series: Quilt Trilogy. 1994, Scholastic paper $13.95 (978-0-590-46055-2). This historical novel set in 18th-century Salem, Massachusetts, concerns the tribulations of a 16-year-old girl and her family. (Rev: BL 3/1/94; SLJ 5/94; VOYA 4/94)

4678 Schwabach, Karen. *A Pickpocket's Tale* (5–8). 2006, Random House LB $17.99 (978-0-375-93379-0). After being caught picking pockets on the streets of London in 1730, 10-year-old orphan Molly is exiled to America where she learns many new things from the Jewish family to which she is indentured. (Rev: BL 11/15/06; SLJ 11/06)

4679 Speare, Elizabeth George. *The Sign of the Beaver* (6–9). 1983, Houghton Mifflin $16.00 (978-0-395-33890-2); paper $5.99 (978-0-440-47900-0). In Maine in 1768, Matt, though only 12, is struggling to survive on his own until the Indians help him. (Rev: BL 3/1/88)

4680 Speare, Elizabeth George. *The Witch of Blackbird Pond* (6–9). 1958, Houghton Mifflin $16.00 (978-0-395-07114-4); paper $5.99 (978-0-440-99577-7). Historical romance set in Puritan Connecticut with the theme of witchcraft. Newbery Medal 1959. (Rev: BL 7/88)

4681 Stainer, M. L. *The Lyon's Cub* (5–9). 1998, Chicken Soup LB $9.95 (978-0-9646904-5-5); paper $6.95 (978-0-9646904-6-2). This novel, a continuation of *The Lyon's Roar* (1997), tells what happened to the settlers of the lost colony of Roanoke and their life with peaceful Indian tribes. Continued in *The Lyon's Pride* (1998). (Rev: SLJ 8/98)

4682 Steinmetz, Karen. *The Mourning Wars* (7–10). 2010, Roaring Brook $18.99 (978-1-59643-290-1). In 1704 young Eunice Williams is seized by Mohawk Indians and adopted by Atironta and Kenniontie, whose daughter has died; she soon adjusts to her new life and must make a difficult choice when her father finally comes looking for her. Based on a true story. e Lexile 910L (Rev: BL 6/10; LMC 11–12/10; SLJ 11/1/10; VOYA 10/10)

4683 Strickland, Brad. *The Guns of Tortuga* (5–8). 2003, Simon & Schuster paper $4.99 (978-0-689-85297-8). Young Davy helps the crew of the *Aurora* defeat a band of pirates in this sequel to *Mutiny!* (Rev: BL 2/1/03; SLJ 3/03)

4684 Wisler, G. Clifton. *This New Land* (5–9). 1987, Walker LB $14.85 (978-0-8027-6727-1). Twelve-year-old Richard and his family begin a new life in Plymouth, Massachusetts, in 1620. (Rev: BL 3/15/88; SLJ 11/87)

REVOLUTIONARY PERIOD AND THE YOUNG NATION (1775–1809)

4685 Alsheimer, Jeanette E., and Patricia J. Friedle. *The Trouble with Tea* (5–8). 2002, Pentland $15.95 (978-1-57197-299-6). When Patience visits her friend Anne in Boston in 1773, she witnesses many of the events that led to the American Revolution. (Rev: BL 6/1–15/02)

4686 Amateau, Gigi. *Come August, Come Freedom: The Bellows, the Gallows, and the Black General Gabriel* (8–12). 2012, Candlewick $16.99 (978-0-7636-4792-6). A fictionalized biography of the brave blacksmith who inspired rebellion in post-Revolution Richmond, Virginia. e Lexile 900L (Rev: BL 10/1/12; SLJ 11/12)

4687 Anderson, Joan. *1787* (7–10). 1987, Harcourt $14.95 (978-0-15-200582-5). The story of a teenager who became James Madison's aide during the 1787 Constitutional Convention in Philadelphia. (Rev: BL 5/87; VOYA 12/87)

4688 Anderson, Laurie Halse. *Chains* (7–10). 2008, Simon & Schuster $16.99 (978-141690585-1). Hoping to gain her freedom — and learn the whereabouts of her missing sister — slave Isabel decides to spy for the rebels in American Revolution-era New York City. ALA Notable Books 2009. ◯ ℮ Lexile 780L (Rev: BL 11/1/08*; HB 11–12/09; LMC 1–2/09; SLJ 10/1/08; VOYA 10/08)

4689 Anderson, Laurie Halse. *Fever 1793* (6–10). 2000, Simon & Schuster $16.00 (978-0-689-83858-3). Matilda must find the strength to go on when her family is killed by yellow fever in a 1793 outbreak in Philadelphia. Margaret A. Edwards Award 2009. (Rev: BCCB 10/00; BL 10/1/00; HB 9–10/00; HBG 3/01; SLJ 8/00*)

4690 Anderson, Laurie Halse. *Forge* (5–8). 2010, Simon & Schuster $16.99 (978-1-4169-6144-4). In this sequel to 2008's *Chains*, recently freed slave Curzon, 15, is on the run during the time of the American Revolution, eventually joining the army to battle the British at Saratoga. ◯ ℮ Lexile 820L (Rev: BL 9/15/10; HB 11–12/10; LMC 1–2/11; SLJ 10/1/10)

4691 Armstrong, Jennifer. *Thomas Jefferson: Letters from a Philadelphia Bookworm* (5–8). Series: Dear Mr. President. 2001, Winslow $8.95 (978-1-890817-30-5). Twelve-year-old Amelia and President Jefferson discuss the events of the times in a continuing exchange of letters. (Rev: BL 5/15/01; HBG 10/01; SLJ 6/01; VOYA 8/01)

4692 Avi. *The Fighting Ground* (5–9). Illus. by Ellen Thompson. 1984, HarperCollins LB $16.89 (978-0-397-32074-5); paper $5.99 (978-0-06-440185-2). Thirteen-year-old Jonathan marches off to fight the British. (Rev: BL 4/87)

4693 Avi. *Sophia's War: A Tale of the Revolution* (6–8). 2012, Simon & Schuster $16.99 (978-1-4424-1441-9). Despite the risks, Sophia, 12, becomes involved in espionage when her brother dies on a crowded British prison ship in this story set during the American Revolution and featuring Benedict Arnold. ℮ Lexile 730L (Rev: BL 8/12*; HB 11–12/12; LMC 3–4/13; SLJ 10/12*)

4694 Bradley, Kimberly Brubaker. *Jefferson's Sons* (7–10). 2011, Dial $17.99 (978-0-8037-3499-9). Tells the story of the children Thomas Jefferson fathered with Sally Hemings and their aspirations for freedom. ALA Notable Books 2012. ◯ ℮ Lexile 600L (Rev: BL 9/15/11; HB 1–2/12; LMC 1–2/12; SLJ 10/1/11*)

4695 Bruchac, Joseph. *The Arrow over the Door* (4–7). 1998, Dial $15.99 (978-0-8037-2078-7). Two boys, one a Quaker and the other a Native American, share the narration of this story that takes place immediately before the Battle of Saratoga in 1777. (Rev: BCCB 4/98; BL 2/15/98; HBG 10/98; SLJ 4/98)

4696 Calkhoven, Laurie. *Daniel at the Siege of Boston, 1776* (4–7). Series: Boys of Wartime. 2010, Dutton $16.99 (978-052542144-3). Twelve-year-old Daniel finds the courage to reveal a traitor to General Washington in this coming-of-age story set in Revolutionary War-era America. Lexile 710L (Rev: BL 2/1/10; LMC 5–6/10)

4697 Collier, James Lincoln, and Christopher Collier. *My Brother Sam Is Dead* (6–9). 1984, Simon & Schuster $17.95 (978-0-02-722980-6); paper $5.99 (978-0-590-42792-0). The story, based partially on fact, of a Connecticut family divided in loyalties during the Revolutionary War.

4698 Cooper, Afua. *My Name Is Phillis Wheatley: A Story of Slavery and Freedom* (5–8). 2009, Kids Can $16.95 (978-1-55337-812-9). Set in Senegal, Boston, and London, this first-person account tells the fictionalized true story of Phillis Wheatley, the 18th-century slave who became a renowned poet. Lexile 790L (Rev: BL 9/1/09; SLJ 10/09)

4699 Demas, Corinne. *If Ever I Return Again* (5–8). 2000, HarperCollins LB $15.89 (978-0-06-028718-4). Twelve-year-old Celia describes life aboard a whaling ship in letters home to her cousin. (Rev: BCCB 6/00; BL 4/1/00; HBG 10/00; SLJ 8/00)

4700 Durrant, Lynda. *Betsy Zane, the Rose of Fort Henry* (5–8). 2000, Clarion $15.00 (978-0-395-97899-3). Toward the end of the Revolutionary War, Betsy sets out alone from Philadelphia to rejoin her five brothers in western Virginia. (Rev: BCCB 10/00; BL 9/15/00; HBG 3/01; SLJ 4/01)

4701 Elliott, L. M. *Give Me Liberty* (5–8). 2006, HarperCollins $16.99 (978-0-06-074421-2). Nathaniel Dunn, a 13-year-old indentured servant in colonial Virginia, is taken under the wing of an elderly schoolmaster and watches as the revolutionary movement grows and affects his own behavior. (Rev: BL 10/1/06; SLJ 9/06)

4702 Fleischman, Paul. *Path of the Pale Horse* (7–9). 1992, HarperCollins paper $3.95 (978-0-06-440442-6). Dr. Peale and his apprentice help fight a yellow fever epidemic in 1793 Philadelphia.

4703 Forbes, Esther. *Johnny Tremain: A Novel for Old and Young* (6–9). Illus. by Lynd Ward. 1943, Houghton Mifflin $17.00 (978-0-395-06766-6); paper $6.50 (978-0-440-94250-4). The story of a young silversmith's apprentice who plays an important part in the American Revolution. Newbery Medal 1944. (Rev: BL 1/1/90)

4704 Giff, Patricia Reilly. *Storyteller* (4–7). 2010, Random House $15.99 (978-0-375-83888-0); LB $18.99 (978-0-375-93888-7). While staying with an aunt, Elizabeth uncovers the story of an 18th-century ancestor whose dramatic Revolutionary War experiences culminated in the Battle of Oriskany. **℮** Lexile HL610L (Rev: BL 9/15/10; LMC 1–2/11; SLJ 11/1/10)

4705 Goodman, Joan Elizabeth. *Hope's Crossing* (5–8). 1998, Houghton Mifflin $16.00 (978-0-395-86195-0). Kidnapped by British loyalists during the Revolution, Hope must try to escape and find her way home. (Rev: BCCB 7–8/98; BL 6/1–15/98; HBG 10/98; SLJ 5/98; VOYA 8/98)

4706 Gregory, Kristiana. *Cannons at Dawn: The Second Diary of Abigail Jane Stewart* (4–8). Series: Dear America. 2011, Scholastic $12.99 (978-0-545-21319-6); LB $16.99 (978-0-545-28088-4). Abigail and her family follow the Continental Army after their Valley Forge home burns down and the 13-year-old matures as the war progresses. **℮** (Rev: SLJ 7/11)

4707 Guzman, Lila, and Rick Guzman. *Lorenzo's Revolutionary Quest* (6–9). 2003, Piñata paper $9.95 (978-1-55885-392-8). In this sequel to *Lorenzo's Secret Mission* (2001), Lorenzo has exciting adventures when he is charged with buying 500 head of cattle for the Revolutionary Army. (Rev: SLJ 5/03)

4708 Guzman, Lila, and Rick Guzman. *Lorenzo's Secret Mission* (6–9). 2001, Piñata paper $9.95 (978-1-55885-341-6). In 1776, 15-year-old Lorenzo Bannister leaves Texas in search of his Virginia grandfather he has never known, and finds himself working on behalf of the American rebels. (Rev: SLJ 12/01)

4709 Hughes, Pat. *Five 4ths of July* (8–10). 2011, Viking $16.99 (978-0-670-01207-7). Relates the experiences of 14-year-old Jake from 1777 to 1781 as war affects all aspects of his life. Lexile 710L (Rev: BL 5/1/11; LMC 11–12/11; SLJ 6/11; VOYA 8/11)

4710 Klass, Sheila Solomon. *Soldier's Secret: The Story of Deborah Sampson* (6–9). 2009, Henry Holt $17.95 (978-080508200-5). A fictionalized account of a young woman who disguised herself as a man and fought in the Revolutionary War. Lexile 790L (Rev: BL 2/15/09; LMC 10/09; SLJ 4/1/09)

4711 Moore, Ruth Nulton. *Distant Thunder* (5–8). Illus. by Allan Eitzen. 1991, Herald paper $6.99 (978-0-8361-3557-2). During the Revolution, when wounded Americans are sent to Pennsylvania to recover, young Kate experiences the horrors of war. (Rev: BCCB 1/92; SLJ 1/92)

4712 Nordan, Robert. *The Secret Road* (5–9). 2001, Holiday $16.95 (978-0-8234-1543-4). Young Laura helps an escaped slave on a long and suspenseful journey to freedom by posing as her sister. (Rev: BL 9/15/01; HBG 3/02; SLJ 10/01; VOYA 12/01)

4713 O'Dell, Scott. *Sarah Bishop* (6–9). 1980, Scholastic paper $5.99 (978-0-590-44651-8). A first-person narrative of a girl who lives through the American Revolution and its toll of suffering and misery. (Rev: BL 3/1/88)

4714 Paulsen, Gary. *Woods Runner* (6–9). 2010, Random House LB $18.99 (978-0-385-90751-4). Samuel, 13, braves dangers as he searches for his parents after they are taken prisoner by British soldiers in rural Pennsylvania during the American Revolution. ⋒ **℮** Lexile 870L (Rev: BL 1/1/10; HB 3–4/10; LMC 5–6/10; SLJ 2/10)

4715 Pryor, Bonnie. *Captain Hannah Pritchard: The Hunt for Pirate Gold* (5–8). Series: Historical Fiction Adventures. 2011, Enslow LB $27.93 (978-0-7660-3817-2). Still disguised as Jack, Hannah Pritchard leads her crew on missions for the Continental navy while searching for lost pirate treasure in this final installment in the trilogy set during the American Revolution. (Rev: BLO 10/15/11; SLJ 2/12; VOYA 12/11)

4716 Reit, Seymour. *Guns for General Washington: A Story of the American Revolution* (6–8). 1992, Harcourt paper $6.00 (978-0-15-232695-1). The true account of Colonel Henry Knox's attempt to bring cannons and artillery to the Continental Army during the blockade of 1775-1776. (Rev: BL 1/1/91; SLJ 1/91)

4717 Rinaldi, Ann. *Taking Liberty: The Story of Oney Judge, George Washington's Runaway Slave* (7–12). 2002, Simon & Schuster $16.95 (978-0-689-85187-2). An elderly Oney looks back on her life as Martha's personal slave, her initial acceptance of her lot, and her final decision to trade comfort for freedom. (Rev: HBG 3/03; SLJ 1/03; VOYA 2/03)

4718 Rinaldi, Ann. *Wolf by the Ears* (8–12). 1991, Scholastic $13.95 (978-0-590-43413-3). Harriet Hemings — the alleged daughter of Thomas Jefferson and his slave mistress — faces moral dilemmas in regard to freedom, equal rights, and her future. (Rev: BL 2/1/91; SLJ 4/91)

4719 Roop, Peter, and Connie Roop. *An Eye for an Eye: A Story of the Revolutionary War* (5–9). 2000, Jamestown paper $5.95 (978-0-8092-0628-5). During the Revolutionary War, Samantha, disguised as boy, sets out to save her brother who is being held prisoner on a British ship. (Rev: BCCB 7–8/00; SLJ 4/00)

4720 Rosenburg, John. *First in War: George Washington in the American Revolution* (7–10). 1998, Millbrook LB $25.90 (978-0-7613-0311-4). This second part of the fictionalized biography of George Washington covers his career from 1775, when he was elected commander-in-chief, to the end of 1783, when he resigned from his military duties. (Rev: HBG 9/98; SLJ 7/98; VOYA 4/99)

4721 Schwartz, Virginia Frances. *Send One Angel Down* (5–8). 2000, Holiday $16.95 (978-0-8234-1484-0). This is the story of a young slave girl, Eliza, the skills she learns on the plantation, and how this knowledge helps her when she gains freedom. (Rev: BL 6/1–15/00; HB 7–8/00; HBG 10/00; SLJ 8/00)

4722 Thomas, Velma M. *Lest We Forget: The Passage from Africa to Slavery and Emancipation* (5–8). 1997,

Crown $29.95 (978-0-609-60030-6). An interactive book about slavery based on material from the Black Holocaust Museum. (Rev: BL 12/15/97) [973.6]

4723 Wait, Lea. *Seaward Born* (4–7). 2003, Simon & Schuster $16.95 (978-0-689-84719-6). Michael, a young slave, makes a dangerous journey to Canada and freedom in this dramatic historical novel. (Rev: BL 2/15/03; HBG 10/03; SLJ 1/03)

NINETEENTH CENTURY TO THE CIVIL WAR (1809–1861)

4724 Armstrong, Jennifer. *Steal Away* (6–9). 1993, Scholastic paper $4.50 (978-0-590-46921-0). Two unhappy 13-year-old girls — one a slave, the other a white orphan — disguise themselves as boys and run away. (Rev: BL 2/1/92; SLJ 2/92)

4725 Avi. *Beyond the Western Sea: Book Two: Lord Kirkle's Money* (6–9). 1996, Orchard LB $19.99 (978-0-531-08870-8). In this sequel to *Beyond the Western Sea: The Escape from Home* (1996), Patrick and Maura O'Connell and their two friends arrive in America, end up in the mill town of Lowell, Massachusetts, and encounter the villains that pursued them in the first book. (Rev: SLJ 10/96; VOYA 12/96)

4726 Avi. *The True Confessions of Charlotte Doyle* (6–9). 1990, Watts LB $17.99 (978-0-531-08493-9). An adventure story set in the 1850s about a 13-year-old girl and her voyage to America on a ship with a murderous crew. (Rev: BL 9/1/90; SLJ 9/90)

4727 Barker, M. P. *A Difficult Boy* (5–9). 2008, Holiday $16.95 (978-0-8234-2086-5). Indentured to a shopkeeper against his will, Ethan befriends young Daniel, a young Irishman, and the two find friendship and a joint love of horses in this story set in 1839 Massachusetts. (Rev: BL 4/15/08; SLJ 5/08)

4728 Blos, Joan W. *A Gathering of Days: A New England Girl's Journal, 1830–32* (6–8). 1979, Macmillan $16.00 (978-0-684-16340-6); paper $4.99 (978-0-689-71419-1). A fictional diary kept by 13-year-old Catherine Cabot, who is growing up in the town of Meredith, New Hampshire. Newbery Medal 1980.

4729 Blos, Joan W. *Letters from the Corrugated Castle: A Novel of Gold Rush California, 1850–1852* (4–8). 2007, Simon & Schuster $17.99 (978-0-689-87077-4). Reunited with a mother long believed to be dead, 13-year-old Eldora must learn to adjust to living a life of comfort in San Francisco; newspaper articles and her correspondence with Luke, who hopes to find a fortune, reveal much about life during the Gold Rush. (Rev: BL 4/15/07; SLJ 6/07)

4730 Bryant, Louella. *The Black Bonnet* (6–9). 1996, New England paper $12.95 (978-1-881535-22-5). An exciting story of two young escaped slaves, Charity and her older sister Bea, and their last stop on the Underground Railroad in Burlington, Vermont, which they find is crawling with slave hunters. (Rev: BL 2/1/97; SLJ 2/97)

4731 Bryant, Louella. *Father by Blood* (6–9). 1999, New England paper $12.95 (978-1-881535-33-1). The story of John Brown and his raid on Harper's Ferry as seen through the eyes of his daughter Annie. (Rev: SLJ 9/99)

4732 Charbonneau, Eileen. *Honor to the Hills* (8–10). 1996, Tor $18.95 (978-0-312-86094-3). Returning to her home in the Catskill Mountains in 1851, 15-year-old Lily Woods finds that her family is involved in the Underground Railroad. (Rev: VOYA 6/96)

4733 Cooper, Afua. *My Name Is Henry Bibb: A Story of Slavery and Freedom* (5–8). 2009, Kids Can $16.95 (978-1-55337-813-6). Based on a true story, this gritty first-person account of Henry Bibb, the son of a black woman and a white plantation owner in 19th-century Kentucky, depicts the cruelty, humiliation, and yearning for freedom that was part of a slave's daily experience. Lexile 800L (Rev: BL 8/09; LMC 11–12/09; SLJ 10/09)

4734 Dahlberg, Maurine F. *The Story of Jonas* (4–7). 2007, Farrar $16.00 (978-0-374-37264-4). In the mid-1800s, Jonas, a 13-year-old slave, is sent on an expedition to find gold in the Kansas Territory and realizes that freedom is not beyond his grasp. (Rev: BL 4/07; SLJ 4/07)

4735 Donaldson, Joan. *A Pebble and a Pen* (5–8). 2000, Holiday $15.95 (978-0-8234-1500-7). In 1853, to avoid an arranged marriage, 14-year-old Matty runs away to study penmanship at Mr. Spencer's famous Ohio school. (Rev: BCCB 12/00; BL 1/1–15/01; HBG 10/01; SLJ 12/00; VOYA 2/01)

4736 Duble, Kathleen Benner. *Hearts of Iron* (5–8). 2006, Simon & Schuster $15.95 (978-1-4169-0850-0). In a Connecticut iron-working community in the early 19th century, two young lovers rebel against their families' plans for their future. (Rev: BL 9/15/06; SLJ 11/06)

4737 Duey, Kathleen, and Karen A. Bale. *Hurricane: Open Seas, 1844* (5–7). Series: Survival! 1999, Simon & Schuster paper $4.50 (978-0-689-82544-6). This exciting sea story, set in 1844, tells of two youngsters who are on a whaler when a killer hurricane strikes. (Rev: SLJ 8/99)

4738 Ferris, Jean. *Underground* (6–9). 2007, Farrar $16.00 (978-0-374-37243-9). Charlotte, a 16-year-old slave, is sold to the owner of a hotel near Kentucky's Mammoth Cave and soon discovers that the cave is part of the Underground Railroad. (Rev: BL 11/15/07; SLJ 12/07)

4739 Garland, Sherry. *In the Shadow of the Alamo* (5–8). Series: Great Episodes. 2001, Harcourt $17.00 (978-0-15-201744-6). Fifteen-year-old Lorenzo Bonifacio, a conscript in the Mexican army of Santa Ana, describes the harsh life of the soldiers and the family members who follow them on the trek to Texas and the battle of the Alamo. (Rev: BCCB 1/02; BL 10/15/01; HB 11–12/01; HBG 3/02; SLJ 12/01; VOYA 10/01)

4740 Guccione, Leslie D. *Come Morning* (4–7). 1995, Carolrhoda LB $19.15 (978-0-87614-892-1). A young boy takes over his father's duties as a conductor on the Underground Railroad. (Rev: BCCB 1/96; HB 11–12/95; SLJ 11/95)

4741 Helgerson, Joseph. *Crows and Cards* (4–7). Illus. by Peter De Seve. 2009, Houghton $16.00 (978-0-618-88395-0). In the mid-19th century, 12-year-old Zeb is sent off to become a tanner but on the riverboat to St. Louis meets a gambler who offers a more enticing life. (Rev: BL 4/15/09; HB 5/09; LMC 10/09; SLJ 8/09)

4742 Hill, Donna. *Shipwreck Season* (5–8). 1998, Clarion $16.00 (978-0-395-86614-6). In the 1800s, 16-year-old Daniel joins a crew of seamen who patrol America's eastern coastline, rescuing people and cargo from shipwrecks. (Rev: BCCB 7–8/98; BL 6/1–15/98; HBG 3/99; SLJ 6/98)

4743 Hilts, Len. *Timmy O'Dowd and the Big Ditch: A Story of the Glory Days on the Old Erie Canal* (5–7). 1988, Harcourt $13.95 (978-0-15-200606-8). Timmy and his cousin Dennis don't get along, but when the canals threaten to flood, they realize each other's strengths and stamina. (Rev: BCCB 12/88; BL 10/1/88; SLJ 12/88)

4744 Houston, Gloria. *Bright Freedom's Song: A Story of the Underground Railroad* (4–7). 1998, Harcourt $17.00 (978-0-15-201812-2). A tense, dramatic story about a girl who helps her parents operate a North Carolina station on the Underground Railroad. (Rev: BCCB 1/99; BL 11/1/98; HBG 3/99; SLJ 12/98; VOYA 2/99)

4745 Hurst, Carol Otis. *Through the Lock* (5–8). 2001, Houghton Mifflin $15.00 (978-0-618-03036-1). In this novel set in Connecticut in the first half of the 19th century, a young orphan named Etta shares many adventures with a boy who lives in an abandoned cabin by a canal. (Rev: BCCB 3/01; BL 4/1/01; HB 3–4/01; HBG 10/01; SLJ 3/01; VOYA 4/01)

4746 Ketchum, Liza. *Orphan Journey Home* (5–7). 2000, Avon $15.99 (978-0-380-97811-3). When their parents die in southern Illinois in 1828, Jesse and her three siblings must find their way to their grandmother in eastern Kentucky. (Rev: BCCB 6/00; BL 6/1–15/00; HBG 10/00; SLJ 8/00)

4747 Krisher, Trudy. *Uncommon Faith* (7–10). 2003, Holiday $17.95 (978-0-8234-1791-9). The year 1837-1838 is a time of change in Millbrook, Massachusetts, and 10 of the residents narrate their experiences in a collage that connects the reader to the townspeople and to the history. (Rev: BL 10/15/03; HBG 4/04; SLJ 10/03*; VOYA 10/03)

4748 Lester, Julius. *Day of Tears: A Novel in Dialogue* (6–9). 2005, Hyperion $15.99 (978-0-7868-0490-0). In this heart-rending novel based on a real event and told mostly in present-tense dialogue, a slave named Emma is torn from the life she knows when her master puts her up for sale at the biggest slave auction in American history. Coretta Scott King Author Award, 2006. (Rev: BCCB 7–8/05; BL 2/1/05*; HB 7–8/05; SLJ 3/05; VOYA 6/05)

4749 Lester, Julius. *The Old African* (4–7). Illus. by Jerry Pinkney. 2005, Dial $19.99 (978-0-8037-2564-5). An elderly slave who never speaks uses his acute mental powers to relieve the pain of his people on a Georgia plantation. (Rev: BL 7/05*; SLJ 9/05; VOYA 12/05)

4750 Lyons, Mary E. *Letters from a Slave Boy: The Story of Joseph Jacobs* (6–9). 2007, Simon & Schuster $15.99 (978-0-689-87867-1). Joseph's story, told through letters as he learns to read and write, describes events in the life of the actual slave who was the son of Harriet Jacobs, the subject of *Letters from a Slave Girl: The Story of Harriet Jacobs* (1992). (Rev: BCCB 5/07; BL 1/1–15/07; HB 3–4/07; LMC 4–5/07; SLJ 2/07)

4751 McGill, Alice. *Miles' Song* (6–9). 2000, Houghton Mifflin $15.00 (978-0-395-97938-9). The story of a slave, Miles, who secretly learns to read and write and later plans a daring escape. (Rev: BL 4/1/00; HBG 9/00; SLJ 4/00; VOYA 6/00)

4752 McKissack, Patricia C., and Fredrick McKissack. *Let My People Go* (5–8). 1998, Simon & Schuster $20.00 (978-0-689-80856-2). This novel set in the early 19th century combines Bible stories and the hardships endured by slaves as told by Price Jefferson, a former slave who is now an abolitionist living in South Carolina. (Rev: BCCB 12/98; BL 10/1/98; HBG 3/99; SLJ 11/98)

4753 Moses, Shelia P. *I, Dred Scott* (8–11). Illus. by Bonnie Christensen. 2005, Simon & Schuster $16.95 (978-0-689-85975-5). In this fictionalized account, Dred Scott, born a slave, chronicles the ultimately unsuccessful 11-year legal battle to win his freedom. (Rev: BCCB 4/05; BL 3/15/05; SLJ 2/05; VOYA 4/05)

4754 Murphy, Jim. *Desperate Journey* (6–9). 2006, Scholastic $16.99 (978-0-439-07806-1). On the Erie Canal in 1848, 12-year-old Maggie Haggerty faces huge challenges when her father and uncle are arrested, her mother falls ill, and Maggie must save the family's barge by delivering a shipment to Buffalo on time. (Rev: BL 10/15/06; LMC 3/07; SLJ 11/06)

4755 Myers, Anna. *The Grave Robber's Secret* (4–7). 2011, Walker $16.99 (978-0-8027-2183-9). In 19th-century Philadelphia, 12-year-old Robby Hare has helped his father to rob graves, but he suspects that actual murder may be afoot when a boarder called Mr. Burke moves in; loosely based on the murders that took place in Edinburgh, Scotland, in the early 1800s. **e** Lexile 650L (Rev: BL 4/15/11; LMC 3–4/11; SLJ 3/1/11)

4756 Nolen, Jerdine. *Eliza's Freedom Road: An Underground Railroad Diary* (4–7). 2011, Simon & Schuster $14.99 (978-1-4169-5814-7). House slave Eliza, 12, describes in her diary her escape from a cruel master with the help of the Underground Railroad, and records some of the stories she has heard and read; set in 1855. e Lexile 670L (Rev: BLO 1/1–15/11; SLJ 2/1/11)

4757 Olson, Tod. *How to Get Rich in the California Gold Rush: An Adventurer's Guide to the Fabulous Riches Discovered in 1848* (4–8). Illus. by Scott Allred. 2008, National Geographic $16.95 (978-142630315-9); LB $25.90 (978-142630316-6). In this fictional story set in factual historical context, three young men head west to become gold barons and reach the conclusion that they're better off seeking their fortune in other ways. Lexile NC990L (Rev: BL 10/15/08; SLJ 12/08*; VOYA 2/09)

4758 Paterson, Katherine. *Jip: His Story* (5–9). 1998, Puffin paper $6.99 (978-0-14-038674-5). Jip, a foundling boy in Vermont of the 1850s, wonders about his origins, particularly after he finds he is being watched by a mysterious stranger. (Rev: BCCB 12/96; BL 9/1/96*; HB 11–12/96; SLJ 10/96*; VOYA 4/97)

4759 Paulsen, Gary. *Nightjohn* (6–12). 1993, Delacorte $15.95 (978-0-385-30838-0). Told in the voice of Sarny, 12, Paulsen exposes the myths that African American slaves were content, well cared for, ignorant, and childlike, and that brave, resourceful slaves easily escaped. (Rev: BL 12/15/92)

4760 Platt, Kin. *A Mystery for Thoreau* (5–8). 2008, Farrar $16 (978-037435337-7). In mid-19th-century Concord, Massachusetts, teen journalist Oliver Puckle investigates a murder near Thoreau's cabin at Walden Pond; both humorous and melodramatic, this novel conveys much about the time and place. (Rev: BL 11/1/08; SLJ 12/08; VOYA 12/08)

4761 Preus, Margi. *Heart of a Samurai: Based on the True Story of Nakahama Manjiro* (7–11). Illus. 2010, Abrams $15.95 (978-0-8109-8981-8). This is a fictionalized version of the true story of Manjiro, the 14-year-old Japanese boy rescued from the sea by an American whaling ship in 1841; he becomes known as the first Japanese to set foot in the United States and must make many adjustments. Newbery Honor 2011; ALA Notable Books 2011. (Rev: BL 7/10*; HB 9–10/10; LMC 1–2/11; SLJ 9/1/10*)

4762 Prince, Bryan. *I Came as a Stranger: The Underground Railroad* (7–12). 2004, Tundra paper $15.95 (978-0-88776-667-1). This account tells what happened after the runaway slaves reached Canada and contains material both about famous leaders and about ordinary people involved in the Underground Railroad. (Rev: BL 5/1/04; SLJ 6/04) [971.1]

4763 Rinaldi, Ann. *The Blue Door* (5–8). Series: Quilt. 1996, Scholastic paper $15.95 (978-0-590-46051-4). In this final volume of the Quilt trilogy — following

A Stitch in Time (1994) and *Broken Days* — Amanda is forced to take a mill job in Lowell, Massachusetts, after an adventurous trip north from her South Carolina home. (Rev: BL 11/1/96; VOYA 2/97)

4764 Rinaldi, Ann. *Broken Days* (6–10). Series: Quilt. 1995, Scholastic $14.95 (978-0-590-46053-8). When her cousin steals the piece of quilt that will establish her identity, Walking Breeze, who has come to live with her white family in Massachusetts at the age of 14 after being raised by Shawnees, is demoted to servant status in this story that takes place during the War of 1812. The second part of the Quilt trilogy. (Rev: VOYA 4/96)

4765 Rinaldi, Ann. *The Ever-After Bird* (5–8). 2007, Harcourt $17.00 (978-0-15-202620-2). CeCe travels with her uncle, an abolitionist and ornithologist, to Georgia to search for a rare bird and help slaves get to the Underground Railroad. (Rev: BL 11/1/07; LMC 1/08; SLJ 12/07)

4766 Rinaldi, Ann. *Mine Eyes Have Seen* (8–12). 1998, Scholastic paper $16.95 (978-0-590-54318-7). The story of the raid at Harper's Ferry is retold through the eyes of John Brown's daughter Annie. (Rev: BL 2/15/98; HBG 9/98; SLJ 2/98; VOYA 4/98)

4767 Salerni, Dianne K. *We Hear the Dead* (8–11). 2010, Sourcebooks paper $12.99 (978-1-4022-3092-9). Explorer Elisha Kane falls in love with beautiful "spiritualist" Maggie Fox in this story based on actual events in the mid-19th century. e Lexile 1070L (Rev: BL 4/15/10; LMC 8–9/10; SLJ 6/10)

4768 Sanchez, Anita. *The Invasion of Sandy Bay* (5–8). 2008, Boyds Mills $16.95 (978-1-59078-560-7). Twelve-year-old Lemuel attempts to save his little fishing village during the War of 1812 when he spots a British warship in the harbor; with extensive historical endnotes. (Rev: BL 10/1/08; LMC 1/02; VOYA 10/08)

4769 Schneider, Mical. *Annie Quinn in America* (5–9). 2001, Carolrhoda LB $15.95 (978-1-57505-510-7). In 1847, young Annie and her brother travel from Ireland, a land ravaged by the potato famine, to America, a land fraught with dangers of its own. (Rev: BL 11/15/01; HBG 3/02; SLJ 9/01)

4770 Schwartz, Virginia Frances. *If I Just Had Two Wings* (6–10). 2001, Stoddart $15.95 (978-0-7737-3302-2). Accompanied by a friend and her two children, a young slave named Phoebe makes a daring escape to Canada and freedom via the Underground Railroad. (Rev: BL 12/1/01; SLJ 12/01; VOYA 12/01)

4771 Siegelson, Kim L. *Honey Bea* (7–10). 2006, Hyperion $15.99 (978-0-7868-0853-3). Beatrice, a young slave in Louisiana, relies on the magic of bees as her work in the master's house leads to discoveries about her past. (Rev: BL 4/15/06)

4772 Stiles, Martha Bennett. *Sailing to Freedom* (4–8). 2012, Henry Holt $16.99 (978-0-8050-9238-7). Ray, 12, joins his uncle's ship as a cook's helper in the mid-

19th century and discovers that they are transporting an escaping slave to safety in the north. **e** Lexile 890L (Rev: LMC 1–2/13; SLJ 8/1/12)

4773 Stowe, Cynthia M. *The Second Escape of Arthur Cooper* (5–7). 2000, Marshall Cavendish LB $14.95 (978-0-7614-5069-6). Based on a true story, this novel tells of Arthur Cooper, an escaped slave, and the Quakers on Nantucket Island who saved him from slave catchers in 1822. (Rev: BL 8/00; HBG 3/01; SLJ 10/00)

4774 Torrey, Michele. *Voyage of Midnight* (8–11). 2006, Knopf $15.95 (978-0-375-82382-4). In the early 19th century, orphan Philip joins his uncle's crew and is shocked to find that his uncle is a slave trader; when the crew and slaves are blinded by a disease, Philip takes matters into his own hands and steers the ship back to Africa. (Rev: BL 12/15/06; SLJ 1/07)

4775 Trottier, Maxine. *Under a Shooting Star* (5–8). Series: The Circle of Silver Chronicles. 2002, Stoddart paper $7.95 (978-0-7737-6228-2). During the War of 1812, a 15-year-old boy who is half English and half Oneida Indian struggles with conflicting loyalties as he tries to protect the two American girls he is escorting. (Rev: SLJ 5/02)

4776 Turner, Glennette Tilley. *Running for Our Lives* (5–7). 1994, Holiday $16.95 (978-0-8234-1121-4). A thoroughly researched novel about a boy and his family who escape slavery in the 1850s and traveled on the Underground Railroad to Canada. (Rev: BCCB 6/94; BL 6/1–15/94; SLJ 4/94)

4777 Wait, Lea. *Finest Kind* (4–7). 2006, Simon & Schuster $16.95 (978-1-4169-0952-1). When his family falls on hard times and is forced to move from Boston to Maine in the 1830s, 12-year-old Jake Webber finds himself shouldering new responsibilities, including looking after his disabled younger brother. (Rev: BL 10/15/06; SLJ 11/06)

4778 Wall, Bill. *The Cove of Cork* (5–9). 1999, Irish American paper $7.95 (978-0-85635-225-6). In this novel, the third in a trilogy revolving around the War of 1812, an Irish lad, the first mate of the American schooner *Shenandoah*, sees action in a battle against a British vessel and eventually wins the hand of the granddaughter of a shipbuilding magnate. (Rev: SLJ 7/99)

4779 Wanttaja, Ronald. *The Key to Honor* (5–9). 1996, Fireworks paper $9.99 (978-0-88092-270-8). During the War of 1812, midshipman Nate Lawton has doubts about his courage in battle and worries about his father, who has been taken prisoner by the British. (Rev: VOYA 8/96)

4780 Whelan, Gloria. *Farewell to the Island* (5–8). 1998, HarperCollins $16.95 (978-0-06-027751-2). In this sequel to *Once on This Island,* Mary leaves her Michigan home after the War of 1812 and travels to England where she falls in love with Lord Lindsay. (Rev: BL 12/1/98; HBG 3/99; SLJ 1/99)

4781 Whelan, Gloria. *Once on This Island* (4–7). 1995, HarperCollins LB $14.89 (978-0-06-026249-5). In 1812, Mary and her older brother and sister must tend the family farm on Mackinac Island when their father goes off to war. (Rev: BCCB 11/95; BL 10/1/95; SLJ 11/95; VOYA 2/96)

4782 Wiley, Melissa. *On Tide Mill Lane* (4–8). 2001, HarperCollins $16.95 (978-0-06-027013-1). Charlotte experiences a number of household crises in Roxbury, Massachusetts, where she lives with her blacksmith father at the time of the War of 1812. (Rev: BL 2/15/01; HBG 10/01)

4783 Wilson, Diane Lee. *Black Storm Comin'* (7–10). 2005, Simon & Schuster $16.95 (978-0-689-87137-5). Son of a white father and a freed-slave mother, 12-year-old Colton Westcott joins the Pony Express in an effort to make sure his mother and siblings finally make it to the West Coast. (Rev: BL 8/05*; SLJ 7/05; VOYA 10/05)

4784 Woods, Brenda. *My Name Is Sally Little Song* (4–7). 2006, Putnam $15.99 (978-0-399-24312-7). Eleven-year-old Sally, a slave on a Georgia plantation at the beginning of the 19th century, escapes with her family and heads south to seek refuge with the Seminole Indians. (Rev: BCCB 11/06; BL 8/06; HBG 4/07; SLJ 9/06)

THE CIVIL WAR (1861–1865)

4785 Avi. *Iron Thunder* (5–8). 2007, Hyperion $14.99 (978-1-4231-0446-9). Tom, a 13-year-old naval yard worker and later crew member, describes the construction of the *Monitor,* the perilous voyage to the Union blockade, and the ensuing battle with the *Merrimac*; period photographs and newspaper headlines add historic context. (Rev: BL 8/07; LMC 11/07; SLJ 9/07)

4786 Beatty, Patricia. *Jayhawker* (6–9). 1995, Morrow paper $6.99 (978-0-688-14422-7). The story of 12-year-old Elijah, son of a Kansas abolitionist, who becomes a spy and infiltrates Charles Quantrill's infamous Bushwhacker network. (Rev: BL 9/1/91*; SLJ 9/91*)

4787 Brill, Marlene Targ. *Diary of a Drummer Boy* (4–7). 1998, Millbrook LB $23.90 (978-0-7613-0118-9). Using a diary format, this novel tells of a 12-year-old's experiences as a drummer in the Union Army during the Civil War. (Rev: BL 3/1/98; HBG 10/98; SLJ 5/98)

4788 Bruchac, Joseph. *March Toward the Thunder* (7–10). 2008, Dial $16.99 (978-0-8037-3188-2). In this story of a Canadian Indian who enters the Civil War with the Irish Brigade, readers are introduced to many important figures, issues, and lessons of the war. (Rev: BL 4/15/08; SLJ 7/08)

4789 Calkhoven, Laurie. *Will at the Battle of Gettysburg, 1863* (4–7). Series: Boys of Wartime. 2011, Dutton $16.99 (978-0-525-42145-0). Twelve-year-old Will lives in Gettysburg and dreams of being a drummer boy in the Union Army until the war comes right to his doorstep. ℮ (Rev: SLJ 3/1/11)

4790 Collier, James Lincoln, and Christopher Collier. *With Every Drop of Blood: A Novel of the Civil War* (6–10). 1994, Dell paper $5.99 (978-0-440-21983-5). A Civil War docunovel about Johnny, a young Confederate soldier, and Cush, a black Union soldier who captures him. Together, the two experience the horrors of war and bigotry. (Rev: BL 7/94; SLJ 8/94; VOYA 12/94)

4791 Crist-Evans, Craig. *Moon over Tennessee: A Boy's Civil War Journal* (4–7). 1999, Houghton Mifflin $15.00 (978-0-395-91208-9). In free-verse diary entries, 13-year-old Crist-Evans reports on the Civil War from his vantage point in a camp behind the front lines. (Rev: BCCB 6/99; BL 5/15/99; HBG 10/99; SLJ 8/99; VOYA 10/99)

4792 Donahue, John. *An Island Far from Home* (4–7). 1994, Carolrhoda LB $15.95 (978-0-87614-859-4). Joshua, a Union supporter, forms an unusual friendship through corresponding with a young Southern soldier who is a prisoner of war. (Rev: BCCB 2/95; BL 2/15/95; SLJ 2/95)

4793 Durrant, Lynda. *My Last Skirt* (5–8). 2006, Clarion $16.00 (978-0-618-57490-2). After migrating from Ireland to America, Jennie Hodgers, who prefers wearing pants to skirts, adopts the persona of Albert Cashier and joins the Union army in this novel based on a true story. (Rev: BL 2/15/06; SLJ 4/06*)

4794 Elliott, L. M. *Annie, Between the States* (7–11). 2004, HarperCollins LB $16.99 (978-0-06-001211-3). As the Civil War rages around her northern Virginia home, 15-year-old Annie finds her feelings about the North-South conflict evolving. (Rev: BL 12/1/04; SLJ 11/04)

4795 Ernst, Kathleen. *The Bravest Girl in Sharpsburg* (6–9). 1998, White Mane paper $8.95 (978-1-57249-083-3). Told from the viewpoint of three girls in Maryland during the Civil War, this is the story of friendships that are tested when the the girls support different sides and what happens when the Confederate Army marches through their town, thrusting the community into the middle of the war. (Rev: SLJ 9/98)

4796 Ernst, Kathleen. *Ghosts of Vicksburg* (6–10). 2003, White Mane paper $8.95 (978-1-57249-322-3). Jamie and Elisha, 15-year-old Union Army soldiers from Wisconsin, experience the horrors of war as their forces march to Mississippi. (Rev: SLJ 12/03)

4797 Ernst, Kathleen. *Hearts of Stone* (5–8). 2006, Dutton $16.99 (978-0-525-47686-3). Fifteen-year-old Hannah and her three younger siblings struggle to survive after they're orphaned in Civil War Tennessee. (Rev: BL 11/1/06; SLJ 12/06)

4798 Ernst, Kathleen. *The Night Riders of Harper's Ferry* (6–8). 1996, White Mane paper $7.95 (978-1-57249-013-0). Told from the standpoint of 17-year-old Solomon, this is a story of romance, divided families, and dangerous secrets, set on the border between North and South during the Civil War. (Rev: BL 1/1–15/97; SLJ 5/97)

4799 Ernst, Kathleen. *Retreat from Gettysburg* (5–8). 2000, White Mane LB $17.95 (978-1-57249-187-8). When a doctor orders 14-year-old Chig and his mother to care for a wounded Confederate soldier, the boy finds it hard to be kind to a man who belongs to the side that killed his father and brothers. (Rev: BL 9/15/00; HBG 10/01; SLJ 12/00)

4800 Fleischner, Jennifer. *Nobody's Boy* (5–8). 2006, Missouri Historical Society $12.95 (978-1-883982-58-4). George's mother buys freedom for herself and her son; she goes on to work for Mrs. Lincoln in the White House while George chooses the more dangerous avenue of helping slaves find freedom. (Rev: BL 2/1/07)

4801 Garrity, Jennifer Johnson. *The Bushwhacker: A Civil War Adventure* (5–8). Illus. by Paul Bachem. 1999, Peachtree paper $8.95 (978-1-56145-201-9). The clash of divided loyalties is the main conflict in this story of a boy torn between his Unionist feelings and the friendship he feels towards his protector, a Confederate sympathizer. (Rev: SLJ 4/00)

4802 Greenberg, Martin H., and Charles G. Waugh, eds. *Civil War Women II: Stories by Women About Women* (7–10). 1997, August House paper $9.95 (978-0-87483-487-1). A collection of short stories by such female writers as Louisa May Alcott and Edith Wharton that deal with women's lives during the Civil War. (Rev: SLJ 8/97)

4803 Hahn, Mary Downing. *Hear the Wind Blow: A Novel of the Civil War* (6–9). 2003, Clarion $16.00 (978-0-618-18190-2). A moving novel of the Civil War in which 13-year-old Haswell searches for his wounded older brother after his mother is killed and his farm destroyed. (Rev: BCCB 7–8/03; BL 5/15/03; HB 5–6/03; HBG 5–6/03; SLJ 5/03; VOYA 10/03)

4804 Hart, Alison. *Fires of Jubilee* (5–7). 2003, Simon & Schuster paper $4.99 (978-0-689-85528-3). Abby, 13, is suddenly a free person when the Civil War ends and finally able to search for her mother, who left long before. (Rev: BL 11/1/03; SLJ 3/04)

4805 Hart, Alison. *Gabriel's Horses* (6–9). 2007, Peachtree $14.95 (978-1-56145-398-6). Twelve-year-old Gabriel, a slave during the Civil War, cares for the racehorses on his master's plantation and dreams of becoming a jockey in this exciting story based on fact. (Rev: BL 5/15/07; LMC 10/07; SLJ 6/07)

4806 Hart, Alison. *Gabriel's Triumph* (6–9). Series: Racing to Freedom. 2007, Peachtree $14.95 (978-1-56145-410-5). Young freed slave Gabriel (first seen in *Gabriel's Horses* (2007) gets a chance to race a horse at

274

Saratoga and is surprised by the racial climate he meets in the North. (Rev: BL 12/1/07; SLJ 1/08)

4807 Hill, Pamela S. *A Voice from the Border* (6–8). 1998, Holiday $16.95 (978-0-8234-1356-0). Set in Missouri, a border state during the Civil War, this novel introduces 15-year-old Reeves, whose family owns slaves and whose house is commandeered by Union forces after Reeves' father dies in battle. (Rev: BCCB 9/98; HBG 3/99; SLJ 9/98)

4808 Hughes, Pat. *Guerrilla Season* (7–12). 2003, Farrar $18.00 (978-0-374-32811-5). This multilayered novel clearly conveys the confusion that Matt, 15, feels in the face of the approaching violence of the Civil War. **e** (Rev: BL 8/03; HBG 4/04; SLJ 11/03; VOYA 12/03)

4809 Hurst, Carol Otis. *Torchlight* (4–7). 2006, Houghton Mifflin $16.00 (978-0-618-27601-1). As tension mounts between the Yankee and Irish immigrant settlers in a Massachusetts town in 1864, Charlotte and Maggie struggle to maintain their friendship. (Rev: BL 12/1/06; SLJ 1/07)

4810 Johnson, Nancy. *My Brother's Keeper: A Civil War Story* (6–10). 1997, Down East $14.95 (978-0-89272-414-7). Two orphaned brothers from upstate New York, ages 15 and 13, join the Union Army, one as a soldier, the other as a drummer boy, and soon find themselves surrounded by the blood and tragedy of battle in this story based on the experiences of the author's great-great-uncles. (Rev: HBG 9/98; SLJ 1/98)

4811 Joslyn, Mauriel Phillips. *Shenandoah Autumn: Courage Under Fire* (6–10). 1999, White Mane paper $8.95 (978-1-57249-137-3). During the Civil War, young Mattie and her mother, though afraid of the Union troops around their Virginia home, save a wounded Confederate soldier and return him to his companions. (Rev: BL 5/1/99)

4812 Keehn, Sally M. *Anna Sunday* (4–8). 2002, Putnam $18.99 (978-0-399-23875-8). In 1863, 12-year-old Anna travels with her younger brother from Pennsylvania to Virginia to find her wounded father. (Rev: BCCB 9/02; BL 6/1–15/02; HBG 10/02; SLJ 6/02; VOYA 8/02)

4813 Keith, Harold. *Rifles for Watie* (6–9). 1957, HarperCollins paper $6.99 (978-0-06-447030-8). Jeff, a Union soldier, learns about the realities of war when he becomes a spy. Newbery Medal 1958.

4814 Klein, Lisa. *Two Girls of Gettysburg* (7–10). 2008, Bloomsbury $16.99 (978-159990105-3). The voices of two young women — quiet, dutiful Lizzie and frivolous Rosanna — are woven together to tell the story of the Battle of Gettysburg. Lexile 830L (Rev: BL 9/1/08; SLJ 11/1/08; VOYA 12/08)

4815 Kluger, Jeffrey. *Freedom Stone* (5–7). 2011, Philomel $16.99 (978-0-399-25214-3). Young slave Lillie struggles to clear her father's name and gain freedom for herself, her brother, and her mother with the

help of a magical stone from Africa. **e** Lexile 1030L (Rev: BL 2/1/11*; LMC 5–6/11; SLJ 6/11)

4816 Love, D. Anne. *Three Against the Tide* (5–8). 1998, Holiday $15.95 (978-0-8234-1400-0). In this Civil War novel, 12-year-old Confederate Susanna Simons must care for her two younger brothers when Yankee troops invade South Carolina. (Rev: BL 12/1/98; HBG 10/99; SLJ 1/99)

4817 Lyons, Mary E, and Muriel M. Branch. *Dear Ellen Bee: A Civil War Scrapbook of Two Union Spies* (5–8). 2000, Atheneum $17.00 (978-0-689-82379-4). Set in Richmond, Virginia, before and during the Civil War, this novel, based on fact, tells how a strong-willed lady and her emancipated slave get involved in a spying adventure. (Rev: BCCB 10/00; BL 11/1/00; HBG 3/01; SLJ 10/00; VOYA 2/01)

4818 McGowen, Tom. *Jesse Bowman: A Union Boy's War Story* (5–8). Series: Historical Fiction Adventure. 2008, Enslow LB $20.95 (978-0-7660-2929-3). The story of a young soldier who is horrified by the brutality of the Civil War. (Rev: BL 4/15/08; SLJ 7/08)

4819 McMullan, Margaret. *How I Found the Strong: A Civil War Story* (5–9). 2004, Houghton Mifflin $15.00 (978-0-618-35008-7). The Civil War changes the way a boy looks at life when it takes away his father and brother and comes close to his Mississippi home. (Rev: BL 2/15/04; SLJ 4/04; VOYA 6/04)

4820 Moss, Marissa. *A Soldier's Secret: The Incredible True Story of Sarah Edmonds, a Civil War Hero* (7–12). Illus. 2012, Abrams $16.95 (978-1-4197-0427-7). This novel drawing on her own journals and correspondence tells the story of the woman who served in various capacities for the Union Army in the Civil War using the name of Frank Thompson. **e** Lexile 860L (Rev: BL 11/15/12; LMC 3–4/13; SLJ 11/12)

4821 Myers, Anna. *Assassin* (7–12). 2005, Walker $16.95 (978-0-8027-8989-1). The events surrounding the assassination of Abraham Lincoln are explored in this fictionalized account, narrated in alternating chapters by a teenage White House seamstress and assassin John Wilkes Booth. (Rev: BL 10/1/05; SLJ 12/05; VOYA 10/05)

4822 Myers, Walter Dean. *Riot* (7–12). 2009, Egmont $16.99 (978-1-60684-000-9); LB $19.99 (978-1-60684-042-9). Set in New York City in the summer of 1863, this story presented in screenplay format follows Claire, a biracial teen who lives amidst the chaos, ethnic tension, and anxiety of the Civil War and the riots that took place when Irish immigrants protested the draft. ∩ **e** (Rev: BL 8/09*; LMC 11–12/09; SLJ 9/09; VOYA 12/09)

4823 Nixon, Joan Lowery. *A Dangerous Promise* (6–8). Series: Orphan Train Adventures. 1996, Bantam paper $4.99 (978-0-440-21965-1). Mike Kelly, 12, and his friend Todd Blakely run away to help the Union forces in the Civil War and experience the terrors of war. (Rev: BL 9/1/94; SLJ 11/94; VOYA 10/94)

4824 Paulsen, Gary. *Soldier's Heart* (5–8). 1998, Delacorte $15.95 (978-0-385-32498-4). A powerful novel about the agony of the Civil War, based on the real-life experiences of a Union soldier who was only 15 when he went to war. (Rev: BCCB 9/98; BL 6/1–15/98*; HB 11–12/98; HBG 3/99; SLJ 9/98; VOYA 10/98)

4825 Peck, Richard. *The River Between Us* (7–12). 2003, Dial $16.99 (978-0-8037-2735-9). In 1861 Illinois, Tilly's family makes room for two young women of different complexions from the South. (Rev: BL 9/15/03*; HB 9–10/03; HBG 4/04; SLJ 9/03; VOYA 10/03)

4826 Philbrick, Rodman. *The Mostly True Adventures of Homer P. Figg* (4–7). 2009, Scholastic $16.99 (978-0-439-66818-7). There's comedy in the midst of war and innocence in the midst of knavery as Homer runs away from from his evil uncle and has many adventures while seeking to save the brother forced to join the Union Army. Newbery Honor 2010; ALA Notable Books 2010. ⌂ (Rev: BCCB 1/09; BL 1/1–15/09; HB 1/09; SLJ 1/09)

4827 Pinkney, Andrea Davis. *Abraham Lincoln: Letters from a Slave Girl* (4–7). Series: Dear Mr. President. 2001, Winslow $8.95 (978-1-890817-60-2). Twelve-year-old Lettie Tucker, a slave, exchanges thought-provoking letters with President Abraham Lincoln in this story set in the 1860s packed with interesting illustrations. (Rev: BCCB 2/02; BL 9/1/01; HBG 3/02; SLJ 9/01)

4828 Reeder, Carolyn. *Before the Creeks Ran Red* (6–9). 2003, HarperCollins $16.99 (978-0-06-623615-5). Three stories examine the impact of the Civil War on three young men, who all come to reassess their perspectives on war, valor, and duty. (Rev: BCCB 3/03; BL 2/15/03; HBG 10/03; SLJ 2/03)

4829 Reeder, Carolyn. *Captain Kate* (6–8). 1999, Avon $15.00 (978-0-380-97628-7). This is an unusual Civil War story about 12-year-old Kate, her stepbrother Seth, and their dangerous trip down the C&O Canal on the family's coal boat. (Rev: BL 1/1–15/99; HBG 10/99; SLJ 1/99)

4830 Richardson, George C. *Drummer* (6–9). 2001, Writer's Showcase paper $9.95 (978-0-595-15359-6). A young slave survives a dangerous journey north and joins a Colored Infantry unit in Philadelphia, becoming a drummer boy. (Rev: SLJ 12/01)

4831 Rinaldi, Ann. *Come Juneteenth* (8–11). 2007, Harcourt $17.00 (978-0-15-205947-7). The news of emancipation was slow to arrive to parts of Texas, and when it did, not everyone believed it, as readers will learn from this story of young slaves Luli and Sis Goose. (Rev: BCCB 9/07; BL 2/15/07; LMC 8–9/07; SLJ 5/07)

4832 Rinaldi, Ann. *In My Father's House* (7–10). 1993, Scholastic paper $14.95 (978-0-590-44730-0). A coming-of-age novel set during the Civil War about 7-year-old Oscie. (Rev: BL 2/15/93)

4833 Rinaldi, Ann. *Juliet's Moon* (5–8). Series: Great Episodes. 2008, Harcourt paper $17.00 (978-0-15-206170-8). Juliet's home and family are destroyed by the Civil War, and she and her brother, Seth, must fight and even kill to survive in this novel, which is loosely based on actual events. (Rev: BL 4/15/08)

4834 Rinaldi, Ann. *Leigh Ann's Civil War* (6–8). 2009, Harcourt $17 (978-0-15-206513-3). In Civil War Georgia, young Leigh Ann is dealing with family difficulties even before the Yankees arrive and she is arrested as a traitor. ℮ Lexile 620L (Rev: BL 9/15/09; SLJ 9/09; VOYA 2/10)

4835 Rinaldi, Ann. *My Vicksburg* (5–8). 2009, Harcourt $16.00 (978-0-15-206624-6). In 1863 Vicksburg, Mississippi, families choose to live in caves for safety and 13-year-old Claire Louise worries about the members of her family serving on different sides of the war. (Rev: BL 4/15/09; SLJ 7/09; VOYA 8/09)

4836 Rinaldi, Ann. *Sarah's Ground* (6–9). 2004, Simon & Schuster $15.95 (978-0-689-85924-3). In this appealing Civil War novel based on a true story, 18-year-old Sarah leaves her New York home in 1861 to take a job as a caretaker at Mount Vernon, but as the war intensifies, Sarah and the rest of the staff face mounting challenges to ensure the plantation's security and neutrality. (Rev: BL 2/1/04; SLJ 5/04; VOYA 4/04)

4837 Sappey, Maureen Stack. *Letters from Vinnie* (7–10). 1999, Front St $16.95 (978-1-886910-31-7). A novel that mixes fact and fiction to tell the story of the tiny woman who sculpted the large statue of Abraham Lincoln found in the Capitol Building in Washington. (Rev: BL 9/15/99; HBG 4/00; SLJ 11/99; VOYA 2/00)

4838 Schwabach, Karen. *The Storm Before Atlanta* (5–8). 2010, Random House $16.99 (978-0-375-85866-6); LB $19.99 (978-0-375-95866-3). Jeremy dreams of glory when he joins the Union Army, but as the war progresses and he meets an escaped slave, Dulcie, and a Confederate soldier named Charlie, reality sets in. ℮ (Rev: BL 1/1–15/11; SLJ 2/1/11)

4839 Severance, John B. *Braving the Fire* (7–12). 2002, Clarion $15.00 (978-0-618-22999-4). Jem finds war is far from the "glory" described by others in this coming-of-age story set in the realistic horrors of the Civil War. (Rev: BL 10/1/02; HBG 10/03; SLJ 11/02)

4840 Spain, Susan Rosson. *The Deep Cut* (5–8). 2006, Marshall Cavendish $16.99 (978-0-7614-5316-1). Thirteen-year-old Lonzo, often considered "slow," finally gains the respect of his father for his actions during the hostilities. (Rev: BL 12/1/06*; SLJ 12/06)

4841 Thomas, Carroll. *Blue Creek Farm* (4–8). 2001, Smith & Kraus paper $9.95 (978-1-57525-243-8). In

Kansas of the 1860s, Matty Trescott and her father manage a farm and feel the effects of the Civil War. (Rev: BL 4/1/01; VOYA 6/01)

4842 Wells, Rosemary. *Red Moon at Sharpsburg* (6–9). 2007, Viking $16.99 (978-0-670-03638-7). Young India Moody hopes to attend college one day even though this is virtually unheard-of, but her goal must be put on hold when the Civil War breaks out and its bloody and frightening realities alter her world. ALA Notable Books 2008. (Rev: BCCB 7–8/07; BL 4/15/07; HB 5–6/07; SLJ 3/07*)

4843 Williams, Jeanne. *The Confederate Fiddle* (6–9). 1997, Hendrick-Long $16.95 (978-1-885777-04-1). On his wagon train taking cotton to Mexico in 1862, 17-year-old Vin Clayburn is torn between fulfilling his duty to his family and joining his brother fighting for the South in the Civil War. (Rev: BL 3/15/98; HBG 9/98)

4844 Wilson, John. *Death on the River* (8–10). 2009, Orca paper $12.95 (978-1-55469-111-1). Jake, a young Union soldier, survives the horrors of Andersonville prison but then worries about the support he gets from a fellow prisoner. ℮ Lexile 890 (Rev: BL 10/15/09; LMC 1–2/10; SLJ 11/09)

4845 Wisler, G. Clifton. *Red Cap* (6–8). 1991, Penguin paper $5.99 (978-0-14-036936-6). An adolescent boy lies about his age to join the Union Army and ends up as a prisoner of war in the infamous Andersonville camp. (Rev: BL 8/91; SLJ 8/91)

WESTWARD EXPANSION AND PIONEER LIFE

4846 Altsheler, Joseph A. *Kentucky Frontiersman: The Adventures of Henry Ware, Hunter and Border Fighter* (6–10). 1988, Voyageur $16.95 (978-0-929146-01-0). A reissue of a fine frontier adventure story featuring young Henry Ware who is captured by an Indian hunting party. (Rev: SLJ 3/89)

4847 Applegate, Stan. *The Devil's Highway* (5–8). Illus. by James Watling. 1998, Peachtree paper $8.95 (978-1-56145-184-5). In this adventure novel set in the early 1800s, 14-year-old Zeb and his horse, Christmas, set out on the bandit-infested Natchez Trail to search for the boy's grandfather. (Rev: SLJ 2/99)

4848 Bauer, Marion Dane. *Land of the Buffalo Bones: The Diary of Mary Elizabeth Rodgers, an English Girl in Minnesota* (4–8). Series: Dear America. 2003, Scholastic $12.95 (978-0-439-22027-9). Based on real-life events, Polly Rodgers's diary reveals the hardships endured by a group of English settlers who arrived in Minnesota in 1873. (Rev: BL 5/15/03; HBG 10/03; SLJ 9/01)

4849 Benchley, Nathaniel. *Gone and Back* (7–9). 1971, HarperCollins paper $1.95 (978-0-06-440016-9). Obed's family moves west to take advantage of the Homestead Act, and he soon finds he must assume new family responsibilities.

4850 Benner, J. A. *Uncle Comanche* (5–8). 1996, Texas Christian Univ. paper $12.95 (978-0-87565-152-1). Based on fact, this is the story of the adventures of 12-year-old Sul Ross, who runs away from home in pre-Civil War Texas and is pursued by a family friend nicknamed Uncle Comanche. (Rev: VOYA 10/96)

4851 Blakeslee, Ann R. *A Different Kind of Hero* (5–7). 1997, Marshall Cavendish $14.95 (978-0-7614-5000-9). In 1881 Colorado, Renny is criticized for befriending and helping a Chinese boy new to town. (Rev: BL 9/1/97; HBG 3/98; SLJ 1/98)

4852 Bowers, Terrell L. *Ride Against the Wind* (7–10). 1996, Walker $21.95 (978-0-8027-4156-1). Set in Eden, Kansas, in the late 1800s, this sequel to *The Secret of Snake Canyon* (1993) involves Jerrod Danmyer and his attachment to Marion Gates, daughter of his family's sworn enemies. (Rev: BL 12/15/96; VOYA 8/97)

4853 Bruchac, Joseph. *Sacajawea: The Story of Bird Woman and the Lewis and Clark Expedition* (7–10). 2000, Harcourt $17.00 (978-0-15-202234-1). Told in alternating chapters by Sacajawea and William Clark, this novel re-creates the famous cross-country journey of Lewis and Clark. (Rev: BL 4/1/00; HBG 9/00; SLJ 5/00)

4854 Burks, Brian. *Soldier Boy* (6–9). 1997, Harcourt paper $6.00 (978-0-15-201219-9). To escape a crooked boxing ring in 1870s Chicago, Johnny joins the army to fight Indians and eventually finds himself at Little Big Horn with Custer. (Rev: BL 5/15/97; SLJ 5/97; VOYA 8/97)

4855 Collier, James Lincoln. *Me and Billy* (6–9). 2004, Marshall Cavendish $15.95 (978-0-7614-5174-7). In the Old West, Billy and Possum, best friends who grew up together in the same orphanage, escape and head for a legendary lake full of gold. (Rev: BL 9/15/04; SLJ 1/05)

4856 Collier, James Lincoln. *Wild Boy* (5–8). 2002, Marshall Cavendish $15.95 (978-0-7614-5126-6). After knocking his father out during an argument, 12-year-old Jesse runs away from his frontier home to live in the mountains, where he has many adventures, learns many skills, and reflects on his own characteristics before finally deciding to return home in this story that appears to be set in the 19th century. (Rev: BL 11/1/02; HBG 10/03; SLJ 11/02)

4857 Couloumbis, Audrey. *The Misadventures of Maude March, or, Trouble Rides a Fast Horse* (5–8). 2005, Random House LB $17.99 (978-0-375-93245-8). When their aunt and sole guardian is killed, Maude and Sallie March rebel against their new foster family and set off on their own in this rollicking tale of the Old West. (Rev: SLJ 9/05)

4858 Cullen, Lynn. *Nelly in the Wilderness* (5–8). 2002, HarperCollins LB $15.89 (978-0-06-029134-1). Set in the Indiana frontier of 1821, 12-year-old Nelly and her brother, Cornelius, must adjust to a new stepmother after their beloved Ma dies. (Rev: BCCB 5/02; BL 4/1/02; HB 7–8/02; HBG 10/02; SLJ 2/02)

4859 Cushman, Karen. *The Ballad of Lucy Whipple* (5–8). 1996, Clarion $16.00 (978-0-395-72806-2). Lucy hates being stuck in the California wilderness with an overbearing mother who runs a boarding house. (Rev: BCCB 9/96; BL 8/96*; HB 9–10/96; SLJ 8/96*; VOYA 12/96)

4860 Dallas, Sandra. *The Quilt Walk* (4–7). 2012, Sleeping Bear $18.95 (978-158536800-6). Traveling west to Colorado in 1864, 10-year-old Emmy learns to make quilts — and friends — while facing many challenges. (Rev: BLO 10/15/12; SLJ 1/13)

4861 Donahue, Marilyn Cram. *The Valley in Between* (6–9). 1987, Walker LB $15.85 (978-0-8027-6733-2). In a story that spans a four-year period, a young girl comes of age in California of the 1850s. (Rev: BL 11/1/87; SLJ 11/87; VOYA 12/87)

4862 Durrant, Lynda. *The Sun, the Rain, and the Apple Seed: A Novel of Johnny Appleseed's Life* (5–8). 2003, Clarion $15.00 (978-0-618-23487-5). This fictionalized biography of John Chapman's life focuses on his eccentricities. (Rev: BL 5/15/03; HBG 10/03; SLJ 5/03)

4863 Ferris, Jean. *Much Ado About Grubstake* (5–8). 2006, Harcourt $17.00 (978-0-15-205706-0). Sixteen-year-old Arley, owner of her family's mine and boarding house in 1888 Grubstake, Colorado, becomes suspicious when a stranger takes an unusual interest in the rundown mining town; adventure, romance, and humor are combined in this mystery. (Rev: BL 8/06; SLJ 11/06)

4864 Finley, Mary Peace. *Meadow Lark* (5–8). Series: Santa Fe Trail trilogy. 2003, Filter $15.95 (978-0-86541-070-1). In this sequel to *Soaring Eagle* (1993) and *White Grizzly* (2000) set in 1845, Teresita Montoya, 13, has various adventures on the Santa Fe Trail as she searches for her older brother and for a new life for herself. (Rev: BL 12/1/03; HBG 4/04; SLJ 2/04)

4865 Finley, Mary Peace. *White Grizzly* (5–9). 2000, Filter $15.95 (978-0-86541-053-4); paper $8.95 (978-0-86541-058-9). Fifteen-year-old Julio sets out on an arduous journey along the Santa Fe Trail to discover his true identity. (Rev: BL 12/1/00; HBG 10/01; SLJ 1/01; VOYA 2/01)

4866 Fleischman, Paul. *The Borning Room* (5–8). 1991, HarperCollins paper $4.99 (978-0-06-447099-5). Georgina remembers important turning points in her life and the role played by the room set aside for giving birth and dying in her grandfather's house in 19th-century rural Ohio. (Rev: BCCB 9/91; BL 10/1/91*; HB 11–12/91*; SLJ 9/91*)

4867 Garland, Sherry. *Valley of the Moon: The Diary of Rosalia de Milagros* (5–8). 2001, Scholastic paper $10.95 (978-0-439-08820-6). Rosalia, a 13-year-old orphan, keeps a diary about working on a California ranch in 1846. (Rev: BL 4/1/01; HBG 3/02; SLJ 4/01; VOYA 8/01)

4868 Gray, Dianne E. *Tomorrow, the River* (6–9). 2006, Houghton Mifflin $16.00 (978-0-618-56329-6). Life on a Mississippi steamboat in 1896 is rough and dirty, but young Megan finds romance and other rewards among the hard work. (Rev: BL 12/1/06; HB 1–2/07; SLJ 12/06)

4869 Gregory, Kristiana. *Across the Wide and Lonesome Prairie: The Oregon Trail Diary of Hattie Campbell* (4–7). Series: Dear America. 1997, Scholastic paper $10.95 (978-0-590-22651-6). In a diary format, this novel chronicles the hardships that pioneers endured during a trip west on the Oregon Trail. (Rev: SLJ 3/97)

4870 Gregory, Kristiana. *Jimmy Spoon and the Pony Express* (6–8). 1997, Scholastic paper $4.50 (978-0-590-46578-6). Jimmy answers an ad for Pony Express riders, but he's haunted by his previous life with the Shoshoni (see *The Legend of Jimmy Spoon*, Harcourt, 1991), especially the beautiful Nahanee. (Rev: BL 11/15/94; SLJ 11/94; VOYA 4/95)

4871 Gregory, Kristiana. *My Darlin' Clementine* (4–7). 2009, Holiday $16.95 (978-0-8234-2198-5). Based on the traditional folk song, this is the story of 16-year-old Clementine, who in Idaho Territory in the late 1860s has to deal with family problems including her father's gambling and drinking while still hoping to become a doctor. (Rev: BL 4/15/09; SLJ 5/09; VOYA 6/09)

4872 Gregory, Kristiana. *Seeds of Hope: The Gold Rush Diary of Susanna Fairchild* (4–8). 2001, Scholastic paper $10.95 (978-0-590-51157-5). After Susanna's mother dies in 1849, the 14-year-old takes over her journal and describes the hardships she and her sisters face when their father decides to move the family to California in search of gold. (Rev: BL 9/1/01; HBG 10/01; SLJ 7/01; VOYA 10/01)

4873 Hahn, Mary Downing. *The Gentleman Outlaw and Me — Eli: A Story of the Old West* (5–8). 1996, Clarion $16.00 (978-0-395-73083-6). In frontier days, Eliza, masquerading as a boy, travels west in search of her father. (Rev: BCCB 4/96; BL 4/1/96; HB 9–10/96; SLJ 5/96; VOYA 6/96)

4874 Heisel, Sharon E. *Precious Gold, Precious Jade* (5–8). 2000, Holiday $16.95 (978-0-8234-1432-1). At the end of the Gold Rush in southern Oregon, two sisters create hostilities when they befriend a Chinese family that has moved to town. (Rev: BCCB 4/00; HBG 10/00; SLJ 4/00)

4875 Hemphill, Helen. *The Adventurous Deeds of Deadwood Jones* (7–12). 2008, Front St $16.95 (978-159078637-6). Inspired by the true story of an African

American cowboy, this book tells the story of Prometheus Jones, who rides a raffle-won horse away from racist-riddled Tennessee to adventure in the Wild West. **e** Lexile 720L (Rev: BL 10/1/08; HB 1–2/09; LMC 1–2/09; SLJ 12/08)

4876 Hill, Pamela S. *Ghost Horses* (6–9). 1996, Holiday $15.95 (978-0-8234-1229-7). In this novel set in the late 19th century, Tabitha rebels at her preacher father's old-fashioned ideas and, disguised as a boy, joins an expedition digging for dinosaur bones in the American West. (Rev: BL 4/15/96; SLJ 3/96)

4877 Holland, Isabelle. *The Promised Land* (5–8). 1996, Scholastic paper $15.95 (978-0-590-47176-3). Orphaned Maggie and Annie, who have been happily living with the Russell family on the Kansas frontier for three years, are visited by an uncle who wants them to come home with him to Catholicism and their Irish heritage in New York City. A sequel to *The Journey Home*. (Rev: BL 4/15/96; SLJ 8/96; VOYA 6/96)

4878 Holling, Holling C. *Tree in the Trail* (4–7). Illus. by author. 1942, Houghton Mifflin $20.00 (978-0-395-18228-4); paper $11.95 (978-0-395-54534-8). The history of the Santa Fe Trail, described through the life of a cottonwood tree, a 200-year-old landmark to travelers and a symbol of peace to the Indians.

4879 Holm, Jennifer L. *Boston Jane: An Adventure* (5–8). 2001, HarperCollins LB $17.89 (978-0-06-028739-9). A well-bred young woman faces hardships as she searches the 19th-century Washington Territory for her lost fiancé. (Rev: BL 9/1/01; HB 9–10/01; HBG 3/02; SLJ 8/01)

4880 Holm, Jennifer L. *Boston Jane: The Claim* (5–8). 2004, HarperCollins $15.99 (978-0-06-029045-0). In the third installment in Jane's story, an old rival named Sally and a former suitor cause difficulties for Jane. (Rev: BL 3/1/04; SLJ 5/04; VOYA 4/04)

4881 Holm, Jennifer L. *Boston Jane: Wilderness Days* (5–8). 2002, HarperCollins LB $18.89 (978-0-06-029044-3). Jane's continued adventures in 1854 Washington Territory include helping to stop a murderer and adjusting to the hardships of pioneer life. (Rev: BL 9/1/02; HB 9–10/02; HBG 3/03; SLJ 10/02)

4882 Holmas, Stig. *Apache Pass* (6–8). Trans. from Norwegian by Anne Born. Series: Chiricahua Apache. 1996, Harbinger $15.95 (978-1-57140-010-9); paper $9.95 (978-1-57140-011-6). The kidnapping of a white boy by Indians leads to confrontations and killings in this novel set in what is now New Mexico. (Rev: SLJ 1/97; VOYA 4/97)

4883 Holt, Kimberly Willis. *The Water Seeker* (7–12). 2010, Henry Holt $16.99 (978-0-8050-8020-9). Young Amos travels the Oregon Trail with his father and takes on adult responsibilities out of necessity. Lexile 730L (Rev: BL 4/15/10; LMC 8–9/10; SLJ 7/10)

4884 Karr, Kathleen. *Exiled: Memoirs of a Camel* (4–8). 2004, Marshall Cavendish $15.95 (978-0-7614-5164-8). This fascinating story of the U.S. Camel Corps is told from the viewpoint of Ali, an Egyptian camel drafted for service in this shortlived branch of the United States Army. (Rev: BL 5/1/04; SLJ 5/04)

4885 Karr, Kathleen. *Oregon Sweet Oregon* (5–8). Series: Petticoat Party. 1997, HarperCollins LB $14.89 (978-0-06-027234-0). This novel, set in Oregon City, Oregon, from 1846 through 1848, recounts the adventures of 13-year-old Phoebe Brown and her family when they stake a land claim along the Willamette River. (Rev: BL 7/97; SLJ 7/98)

4886 Karwoski, Gail L. *Seaman: The Dog Who Explored the West with Lewis and Clark* (4–8). 1999, Peachtree paper $8.95 (978-1-56145-190-6). This historical novel dramatizes the story of Seaman, the Newfoundland dog that accompanied Lewis and Clark on their expedition. (Rev: BL 8/99; HBG 10/03; SLJ 10/99)

4887 Kerr, Rita. *Texas Footprints* (4–7). 1988, Eakin $13.95 (978-0-89015-676-6). A tale of the author's great-great-grandparents who went to Texas in 1823. (Rev: BL 3/1/89)

4888 Ketchum, Liza. *Newsgirl* (4–7). 2009, Viking $16.99 (978-0-670-01119-3). Set in 1851 San Francisco, this is the story of 12-year-old Amelia, who dresses as a boy to sell newspapers and eventually becomes a news item herself. Lexile 640L (Rev: BL 9/15/09; SLJ 9/09)

4889 Kirkpatrick, Katherine. *The Voyage of the Continental* (6–9). 2002, Holiday $16.95 (978-0-8234-1580-9). A 17-year-old girl relates in her diary the events of her journey by ship from New England to Seattle in 1866, which involve her in adventure, mystery, and romance. (Rev: BL 12/15/02; HBG 3/03; SLJ 11/02; VOYA 12/02)

4890 Laxalt, Robert. *Dust Devils* (6–10). 1997, Univ. of Nevada paper $16.00 (978-0-87417-300-0). A Native American teenager named Ira sets out to retrieve his prize-winning horse that has been stolen by a rustler named Hawkeye. (Rev: BL 10/15/97; VOYA 12/98)

4891 Levine, Ellen. *The Journal of Jedediah Barstow: An Emigrant on the Oregon Trail* (4–7). Series: My Name Is America. 2002, Scholastic $10.95 (978-0-439-06310-4). Jedediah continues his mother's journal about their experiences on the Oregon Trail after she and the rest of his family are drowned while crossing a river. (Rev: BL 2/15/03; HBG 10/03; SLJ 11/02)

4892 Levitin, Sonia. *Clem's Chances* (4–7). 2001, Scholastic paper $17.95 (978-0-439-29314-3). Fourteen-year-old Clem becomes acquainted with the hardships and rewards of frontier life when he travels to California to find his father in 1860. (Rev: BL 9/15/01; HB 11–12/01; HBG 3/02; SLJ 10/01)

4893 Luger, Harriett. *The Last Stronghold: A Story of the Modoc Indian War, 1872-1873* (5–8). 1995, Linnet paper $17.50 (978-0-208-02403-9). The Modoc Indian War of 1872-1873 is re-created in this story involving three young people: Charka, a Modoc youth; Ned, a frontier boy; and Yankel, a Russian Jew who has been tricked into joining the army. (Rev: VOYA 6/96)

4894 McArthur, Debra. *A Voice for Kanzas* (6–9). 2012, Kane/Miller $15.99 (978-161067044-9). In 1855 Lucy, 13, and her family move to Kansas, where the young girl quickly learns about the antislavery efforts and helps slaves escape to safety. (Rev: BL 4/1/12; LMC 11–12/12; SLJ 6/12)

4895 MacBride, Roger L. *New Dawn on Rocky Ridge* (4–7). Series: Rocky Ridge. 1997, HarperCollins paper $7.99 (978-0-06-440581-2). This part of the Wilder family story covers 1900-1903 and focuses on Rose's difficult early teen years. (Rev: BL 11/1/97; HBG 3/98; SLJ 2/98)

4896 McClain, Margaret S. *Bellboy: A Mule Train Journey* (6–10). 1989, New Mexico $17.95 (978-0-9622468-1-4). Set in California in the 1870s, this is the story of a 12-year-old boy and his first job on a mule train. (Rev: BL 3/1/90; SLJ 3/90)

4897 McDonald, Brix. *Riding on the Wind* (5–10). 1998, Avenue paper $5.95 (978-0-9661306-0-7). In frontier Wyoming during the early 1860s, 15-year-old Carrie Sutton is determined to become a rider in the Pony Express after her family's ranch has been chosen as a relay station. (Rev: SLJ 1/99)

4898 McKernan, Victoria. *The Devil's Paintbox* (8–12). 2009, Knopf $16.99 (978-037583750-0). Orphans Aiden, 15, and his younger sister Maddy face disease, death, and disasters as they travel with a wagon train from Kansas to Oregon in 1866. **e** Lexile 740L (Rev: BL 1/1–15/09; LMC 5–6/09; SLJ 2/1/09*; VOYA 4/09)

4899 McKissack, Patricia C. *Run Away Home* (4–7). 1997, Scholastic paper $14.95 (978-0-590-46751-3). In 1888 rural Alabama, a young African American girl helps shelter a fugitive Apache boy. (Rev: BL 10/1/97; HB 11–12/97; HBG 3/98; SLJ 11/97)

4900 Meyer, Carolyn. *Where the Broken Heart Still Beats: The Story of Cynthia Ann Parker* (7–12). 1992, Harcourt paper $7.00 (978-0-15-295602-8). A fictional retelling of the abduction of Cynthia Parker, who was stolen by Comanches as a child and lived with them for 24 years, first as a slave, then as a chief's wife. (Rev: BL 12/1/92; SLJ 9/92)

4901 Milligan, Bryce. *With the Wind, Kevin Dolan: A Novel of Ireland and Texas* (5–7). 1987, Corona paper $7.95 (978-0-931722-45-5). The story of Kevin and Tom, brothers who leave the famine in Ireland in the 1830s and head for America. (Rev: BL 8/87; SLJ 9/87)

4902 Mitchell, Saundra. *The Springsweet* (7–10). 2012, Harcourt $16.99 (978-054760842-6). Tells the story of

17-year-old Zora's move from Baltimore to Oklahoma Territory in the late 1800s, and her adjustment to the hard life there — and to the knowledge that she has the power to find water underground. **e** (Rev: BLO 4/1/12; SLJ 4/12)

4903 Moeri, Louise. *Save Queen of Sheba* (5–7). 1990, Avon paper $3.50 (978-0-380-71154-3). Young David survives a wagon train massacre and must take care of his young sister.

4904 Moore, Robin. *The Bread Sister of Sinking Creek* (7–10). 1990, HarperCollins LB $14.89 (978-0-397-32419-4). An orphaned 14-year-old girl becomes a servant in Pennsylvania during pioneer days. (Rev: BL 7/90; SLJ 4/90; VOYA 8/90)

4905 Nixon, Joan Lowery. *In the Face of Danger* (5–8). 1996, Bantam paper $4.99 (978-0-440-22705-2). Megan fears she will bring bad luck to her adoptive family in this story set in the prairies of Kansas. This is the third part of the Orphan Train Quartet. (Rev: SLJ 12/88; VOYA 12/88)

4906 Oatman, Eric. *Cowboys on the Western Trail: The Cattle Drive Adventures of Josh McNabb and Davy Bartlett* (4–7). Series: I Am America. 2004, National Geographic paper $6.99 (978-0-7922-6553-5). The excitement of a cattle drive is shown in the journals and letters of two young teen boys in this blend of fact and fiction set in 1887 and presented in an appealing magazine format. (Rev: BL 5/15/04)

4907 O'Dell, Scott. *Streams to the River, River to the Sea: A Novel of Sacagawea* (5–9). 1986, Houghton Mifflin $16.00 (978-0-395-40430-0). A fictionalized portrait of the real-life Indian woman who traveled west with Lewis and Clark on their famous journey. (Rev: BL 3/15/86; HB 9–10/86; SLJ 5/86; VOYA 6/86)

4908 Olson, Tod. *How to Get Rich on the Oregon Trail: My Adventures Among Cows, Crooks, and Heroes on the Road to Fame and Fortune* (4–8). Illus. by Scott Allred. 2009, National Geographic $16.95 (978-1-4263-0412-5). In his journal, 15-year-old Will Reed records the events of his family's 1852 journey to Oregon. (Rev: BCCB 5/09; BL 3/1/09; LMC 10/09; SLJ 5/09)

4909 Patrick, Denise Lewis. *The Longest Ride* (6–9). 1999, Henry Holt $15.95 (978-0-8050-4715-8). This sequel to *The Adventures of Midnight Son* explores slavery and Indian-black relations when escaped Texas slave Midnight Sun becomes lost during a long cattle drive and is rescued by some Arapahos at the time of the Civil War. (Rev: BL 6/1–15/99; HBG 3/00; SLJ 12/99; VOYA 2/00)

4910 Patron, Susan. *Behind the Masks: The Diary of Angeline Reddy* (4–8). Series: Dear America. 2012, Scholastic $12.99 (978-054530437-5). In California in 1880, 14-year-old Angeline investigates her father's disappearance and meets a variety of obstacles, including a ghost and a gang of vigilantes. (Rev: BL 12/15/11; SLJ 1/12; VOYA 12/11)

4911 Paulsen, Gary. *The Legend of Bass Reeves* (5–8). 2006, Random House $15.95 (978-0-385-74661-8). This fictionalized biography profiles the little-known life and career of Bass Reeves, the former slave who became one of the West's most effective lawmen. (Rev: BCCB 10/06; BL 6/1–15/06; HBG 10/07; SLJ 8/06)

4912 Philbrick, Rodman. *The Journal of Douglas Allen Deeds: The Donner Party Expedition* (5–7). Series: My Name Is America. 2001, Scholastic paper $10.95 (978-0-439-21600-5). A fictional account of the Donner Party's hardships as written in a 15-year-old orphaned boy's journal. (Rev: BL 1/1–15/02; HBG 3/02; SLJ 12/01)

4913 Rinaldi, Ann. *The Second Bend in the River* (5–9). 1997, Scholastic paper $15.95 (978-0-590-74258-0). In Ohio in 1798, 7-year-old Rebecca begins a long-lasting friendship with the Shawnee chief Tecumseh that eventually leads to a marriage proposal. (Rev: BCCB 3/97; BL 2/15/97; HBG 3/98; SLJ 6/97)

4914 Rose, Caroline. *May B* (3–7). 2012, Random House $15.99 (978-158246393-3); LB $18.99 (978-158246412-1). May, 11, a housemaid to a young family in a Kansas sod house in the late 1870s, struggles to survive when the husband and wife leave her alone to care for the house. ALA Notable Books 2013. **e** Lexile 680L (Rev: BL 1/1/12; HB 1–2/12; LMC 3–4/12)

4915 Schultz, Jan Neubert. *Battle Cry* (5–9). 2006, Carolrhoda LB $15.95 (978-1-57505-928-0). Native American Chaska and white settler Johnny are drawn into the bloody 1862 Dakota Conflict in this dramatic tale. (Rev: SLJ 7/06)

4916 Schultz, Jan Neubert. *Horse Sense* (5–7). 2001, Carolrhoda LB $15.95 (978-1-57505-998-3); paper $6.95 (978-1-57505-999-0). Fourteen-year-old Will and his father do not get along, but they join a posse tracking dangerous outlaws in this adventure based on a true story. (Rev: BL 8/01; HBG 3/02; VOYA 12/01)

4917 Seeley, Debra. *Grasslands* (5–8). 2002, Holiday $16.95 (978-0-8234-1731-5). The hard life on the prairie disappoints a 13-year-old newcomer from Virginia until he has the chance to ride as a cowboy in this novel set in the late 19th century. (Rev: BL 11/1/02; HBG 3/03; SLJ 1/03*; VOYA 12/02)

4918 Sommerdorf, Norma. *Red River Girl* (4–7). 2006, Holiday $16.95 (978-0-8234-1903-6). In 1846 after her Ojibwa mother dies, 12-year-old Metis girl Josette starts a journal that documents her family's journey by wagon train from Canada to St. Paul, Minnesota, where they settle and she becomes a teacher. (Rev: BL 11/15/06; SLJ 12/06)

4919 Taylor, Theodore. *Billy the Kid* (6–9). 2005, Harcourt $17.00 (978-0-15-204930-0). In this fictionalized account, author Theodore Taylor provides a different

twist on the story of Old West outlaw Billy the Kid. (Rev: BCCB 9/05; BL 5/15/05; SLJ 7/05; VOYA 4/06)

4920 Vick, Helen H. *Charlotte* (6–8). Series: Courage of the Stone. 1999, Roberts Rinehart $15.95 (978-1-57098-278-1); paper $9.95 (978-1-57098-282-8). After her parents are killed by Apache warriors in frontier Arizona Territory, 13-year-old Charlotte learns the ways of survival from an elderly Native American woman. (Rev: HBG 9/99; SLJ 7/99)

4921 Wallace, Bill. *Buffalo Gal* (6–8). 1992, Holiday $16.95 (978-0-8234-0943-3). Amanda's plans for an elegant 16th birthday party evaporate when her mother drags her to the wilds of Texas to search for buffalo with cowboys. (Rev: BL 6/15/92; SLJ 5/92)

4922 Whelan, Gloria. *Miranda's Last Stand* (4–7). 1999, HarperCollins LB $14.89 (978-0-06-028252-3). After her husband was killed at Little Big Horn, Miranda's mother can't bear to be around Indians, including Sitting Bull, who works with her at Buffalo Bill's Wild West Show. (Rev: BL 11/1/99; HBG 3/00; SLJ 11/99)

4923 Whelan, Gloria. *Return to the Island* (4–7). 2000, HarperCollins LB $15.89 (978-0-06-028254-7). In the early 19th century on Mackinac Island, Mary must decide between two men who love her: White Hawk, an orphan raised by a white family, and James, an English painter. (Rev: BL 1/1–15/01; HBG 3/01; SLJ 12/00)

4924 Wilder, Laura Ingalls. *The Long Winter* (5–8). 1953, HarperCollins LB $17.89 (978-0-06-026461-1). Number six in the Little House books. In this one, the Ingalls face a terrible winter with only seed grain for food.

4925 Wisler, G. Clifton. *All for Texas: A Story of Texas Liberation* (4–8). 2000, Jamestown paper $5.95 (978-0-8092-0629-2). A thirteen-year-old boy tells about moving west with his family in 1838 to Texas, where his father has been promised land if he will fight against Mexico. (Rev: BCCB 7–8/00; SLJ 8/00)

4926 Wolf, Allan. *New Found Land: Lewis and Clark's Voyage of Discovery* (7–12). 2004, Candlewick $18.99 (978-0-7636-2113-1). Seaman the dog, here called Oolum, is the primary narrator of this verse account of the famous expedition that draws heavily on such primary source documents as letters and journals. (Rev: BL 9/04; SLJ 9/04)

4927 Yep, Laurence. *Dragon's Gate* (6–9). 1993, HarperCollins $17.99 (978-0-06-022971-9). The adventures of a privileged Chinese teenager who travels to California in 1865 to join his father and uncle working on the transcontinental railroad. (Rev: BL 1/1/94; SLJ 1/94; VOYA 12/93)

4928 Yep, Laurence. *The Journal of Wong Ming-Chung* (4–7). 2000, Scholastic paper $10.95 (978-0-590-38607-4). Told in diary format beginning in October 1851, this is the story of a Chinese boy nicknamed Runt who travels from his native country to join an uncle in the gold mining fields of America. (Rev: BL 4/1/00; HBG 10/00; SLJ 4/00; VOYA 6/00)

RECONSTRUCTION TO WORLD WAR I (1865–1918)

4929 Alter, Judith. *Luke and the Van Zandt County War* (5–9). 1984, Texas Christian Univ $14.95 (978-0-912646-88-6). Life in Reconstruction Texas as seen through the eyes of two 14-year-olds. (Rev: SLJ 3/85)

4930 Arato, Rona. *Ice Cream Town* (5–8). 2007, Fitzhenry & Whiteside paper $11.95 (978-1-55041-591-9). Ten-year-old Sammy Levin, a recent Jewish immigrant from Poland, finds it tough to adjust to his new life on the streets of New York City's Lower East Side in the early 1900s. (Rev: BL 4/1/07; SLJ 6/07)

4931 Avi. *City of Orphans* (5–8). Illus. by Greg Ruth. 2011, Simon & Schuster $16.99 (978-1-4169-7102-3). Newsboy Maks, 13, contends with filthy living conditions, poverty, and the predicament of his sister, who's been falsely accused of stealing a watch from the Waldorf Hotel in this tense story set in 1893 New York City. ⌂ e Lexile HL570L (Rev: BL 8/11*; HB 9–10/11; LMC 11–12/11; SLJ 8/11)

4932 Bass, Ruth. *Sarah's Daughter* (8–10). 2007, Gadd $14.95 (978-0-9774053-4-3). When 14-year-old Rose's mother dies, she must look after her family and the farm while her father goes out carousing in this novel set in the 1800s. (Rev: BL 7/07)

4933 Bolden, Tonya. *Finding Family* (4–7). 2010, Bloomsbury $15.99 (978-1-59990-318-7). In Charleston, West Virginia, at the turn of the 20th century, 12-year-old African American Delana learns that many of the stories she was told about her family were pure fiction. (Rev: BL 9/1/10*; LMC 10/10; SLJ 9/1/10)

4934 Boling, Katharine. *1/1/1905* (4–7). 2004, Harcourt $16.00 (978-0-15-205119-8). In alternating voices, 11-year-old mill worker Pauline and her deformed, stay-at-home twin sister Arlene describe the harsh circumstances of their early 20th-century life. (Rev: BL 5/15/04; HB 7–8/04; SLJ 7/04)

4935 Bond, Victoria, and T. R. Simon. *Zora and Me* (5–8). 2010, Candlewick $16.99 (978-0-7636-4300-3). The fictionalized story of Zora Neale Hurston's childhood is told by her best friend Carrie, 10, as they play together and overhear adult secrets in Eatonville, Florida. ⌂ e Lexile 860L (Rev: BL 10/15/10*; LMC 11–12/10; SLJ 11/1/10)

4936 Bourke, Pat. *Yesterday's Dead* (5–8). 2012, Second Story paper $11.95 (978-19269203-2-0). In the face of the 1918 flu epidemic, doctor's aide Meredith, 13, must find a way to stay healthy as one adult after another contracts the flu. (Rev: BLO 3/15/12; SLJ 4/12; VOYA 6/12)

4937 Brown, Don. *The Notorious Izzy Fink* (6–9). 2006, Roaring Brook $16.95 (978-1-59643-139-3). On the Lower East Side of New York in the 1890s, 13-year-old Sam, half Irish and half Jewish, struggles to make ends meet and to avoid the racism and violence that are rampant. (Rev: BL 11/15/06; LMC 2/07; SLJ 9/06)

4938 Brown, Irene Bennett. *Before the Lark* (5–9). 2011, Texas Tech Univ. paper $18.95 (978-08967272-7-4). Cleft-lip sufferer Jocey, 12, contends with bullying and poverty, eventually discovering the empowerment that comes with self-sufficiency in this story set in 19th-century Missouri; a new edition of an award-winning book first published in 1981. (Rev: BLO 10/15/11)

4939 Burleigh, Robert. *Into the Air: The Story of the Wright Brothers' First Flight* (5–8). Illus. by Bill Wylie. Series: American Heroes. 2002, Harcourt paper $6.00 (978-0-15-216803-2). A high-interest, comic-book presentation of the first flight with fictionalized dialogue. (Rev: HBG 3/03; SLJ 9/02)

4940 Byars, Betsy. *Keeper of the Doves* (5–8). 2002, Viking $14.99 (978-0-670-03576-2). Young Amie McBee is a thoughtful child who loves to write and — unlike her older twin sisters — has the sensitivity to see the softer side of the mysterious Polish immigrant who lives on their estate and keeps doves in this story set at the turn of the 20th century and presented in 26 short, alphabetical chapters. (Rev: BCCB 1/03; BL 10/1/02*; HB 9–10/02*; HBG 3/03; SLJ 10/02)

4941 Carter, Alden R. *Crescent Moon* (5–8). 1999, Holiday $16.95 (978-0-8234-1521-2). In the early part of the 20th century, Jeremy joins Great-Uncle Mac on a log drive where they become friends with a Native American and his daughter and, through them, experience the shame of racial prejudice. (Rev: BCCB 1/00; BL 2/15/00; HB 3–4/00; HBG 10/00; SLJ 3/00; VOYA 6/00)

4942 Cindrich, Lisa. *In the Shadow of the Pali: A Story of the Hawaiian Leper Colony* (6–9). 2002, Putnam $18.99 (978-0-399-23855-0). Liliha is only 12 when she is sent in the mid-19th century to the leper colony on the island of Molokai and must deal with the lawless thugs who live there. (Rev: BCCB 10/02; HBG 10/02; SLJ 6/02; VOYA 8/02)

4943 Clark, Clara Gillow. *Hattie on Her Way* (4–7). Series: Hattie. 2005, Candlewick $15.99 (978-0-7636-2286-2). The sequel to *Hill Hawk Hattie* (2003) finds Hattie living with her grandmother after her mother's death and seeking to solve a family mystery. (Rev: BL 3/1/05; SLJ 3/05)

4944 Cross, Gillian. *The Great American Elephant Chase* (5–8). 1993, Holiday $17.95 (978-0-8234-1016-3). In 1881, Tad, 15, and young friend Cissie attempt to get to Nebraska with her showman father's elephant, pursued by two unsavory characters who claim they have bought the animal. (Rev: BCCB 6/93; BL 3/15/93*; SLJ 5/93*; VOYA 10/93)

4945 Crowley, James. *Starfish* (4–8). 2010, Hyperion $16.99 (978-1-4231-2588-4). Beatrice and Lionel, young Blackfoot Nation children, run away from their boarding school in the early 1900s and hide in the Montana mountains. ℮ (Rev: BL 6/10; LMC 11–12/10; VOYA 12/10)

4946 Cushman, Karen. *Rodzina* (5–9). 2003, Clarion $16.00 (978-0-618-13351-2). On an orphan train going from Chicago to California in 1881, plucky Rodzina worries about her fate and aims to find a better life than some of the other children on the train. (Rev: BCCB 3/03; BL 3/1/03*; HB 5–6/03; HBG 10/03; SLJ 4/03*)

4947 Davies, Jacqueline. *Lost* (7–10). 2009, Marshall Cavendish $16.99 (978-076145535-6). Sixteen-year-old Essie, who works in the Triangle Shirtwaist Factory in the early 1900s, must come to terms with losses in her life in this multilayered story. Lexile 680L (Rev: BL 3/15/09; LMC 8–9/09; SLJ 4/1/09; VOYA 8/09)

4948 Donaldson, Joan. *On Viney's Mountain* (6–9). 2009, Holiday House $16.95 (978-0-8234-2129-9). In 1870s rural Tennessee, 16-year-old Viney is distressed when she learns that Englishmen plan to build a utopian community on her precious mountain and ruin the woodlands that inspire her weaving designs; based on the true story of the ill-fated Rugby colony. Lexile 670L (Rev: BL 9/15/09; SLJ 12/09)

4949 Easton, Richard. *A Real American* (4–7). 2002, Clarion $15.00 (978-0-618-03339-3). Against his father's wishes, 11-year-old Nathan befriends Arturo, the son of Italian immigrants newly arrived in a Pennsylvania coal-mining town. (Rev: BCCB 9/02; BL 5/15/02; SLJ 3/02)

4950 Feldman, Ruth Tenzer. *Blue Thread* (6–9). 2012, Ooligan paper $12.95 (978-19320104-1-1). In 1912 Oregon 16-year-old Miriam, daughter of strict Jewish Americans, yearns to work and to support women's suffrage, while her parents make plans for marriage to a suitable husband; then Miriam is transported back to biblical times and her support of women grows. (Rev: BLO 2/15/12; SLJ 3/12)

4951 Giff, Patricia Reilly. *Water Street* (5–8). 2006, Random House $15.95 (978-0-385-73068-6). In this poignant sequel to *Nory Ryan's Song* (2000) and *Maggie's Door* (2003), set in late 19th-century Brooklyn and told from alternating points of view, 13-year-old Bird Ryan and her new upstairs neighbor Thomas develop a close friendship. ♩ (Rev: BCCB 1/07; BL 8/06; HB 9–10/06; HBG 4/07; LMC 2/07; SLJ 9/06)

4952 Gray, Dianne E. *Together Apart* (5–9). 2002, Houghton Mifflin $16.00 (978-0-618-18721-8). After surviving the blizzard of 1888, Isaac and Hannah discover their love for each other while working for feminist publisher Eliza Moore. (Rev: BCCB 11/02; BL 9/15/02; HB 11–12/02; HBG 3/03; SLJ 12/02; VOYA 2/03)

4953 Greenwood, Barbara. *Factory Girl* (5–8). 2007, Kids Can $18.95 (978-1-55337-648-4); paper $12.95 (978-1-55337-649-1). A story about 12-year-old Emily, who in the early 20th century must take a job in a sweatshop and suffer intolerable conditions, is accompanied by historic photographs of children at work and details of key events on the road to reform. (Rev: BL 2/15/07; LMC 8–9/07; SLJ 5/07)

4954 Gregory, Kristiana. *Earthquake at Dawn* (5–9). Series: Great Episodes. 2003, Harcourt paper $6.99 (978-0-15-204681-1). Based on actual letters and photographs, this historical novel depicts the devastating 1906 San Francisco earthquake. (Rev: BL 4/15/92; SLJ 8/92)

4955 Gregory, Kristiana. *Orphan Runaways* (5–7). 1998, Scholastic paper $15.95 (978-0-590-60366-9). Two brothers run away from a San Francisco orphanage in 1879 to look for an uncle in the gold fields. (Rev: BCCB 3/98; BL 2/15/98; HBG 10/98; SLJ 3/98)

4956 Gundisch, Karin. *How I Became an American* (4–8). Trans. by James Skofield. 2001, Cricket $15.95 (978-0-8126-4875-1). This is the story of Johann, a young German immigrant, who arrives in an Ohio steel town in the early 20th century. (Rev: BL 11/15/01; HBG 3/02; SLJ 12/01; VOYA 4/02)

4957 Gutman, Dan. *Race for the Sky: The Kitty Hawk Diaries of Johnny Moore* (4–7). 2003, Simon & Schuster $15.95 (978-0-689-84554-3). Fact and fiction are interwoven in this diary by 14-year-old John Moore, recording his firsthand observations of the Wright brothers' progress. (Rev: BL 1/1–15/04; SLJ 1/04)

4958 Haas, Jessie. *Chase* (5–9). 2007, HarperCollins $16.99 (978-0-06-112850-9). In mid-19th-century Pennsylvania, Phin Chase witnesses a murder and flees, pursued by a stranger and a horse that seems to have tracking abilities. (Rev: BL 2/1/07; SLJ 4/07)

4959 Haas, Jessie. *Westminster West* (6–9). 1997, Greenwillow $15.00 (978-0-688-14883-6). This novel, set in 1884 Vermont, features two very different sisters and their struggle for position and control within their farming family. (Rev: BL 4/15/97; SLJ 5/97)

4960 Haddix, Margaret Peterson. *Uprising* (5–8). 2007, Simon & Schuster $16.99 (978-1-4169-1171-5). Three very different young girls — 15-year-old Italian immigrant Bella, Russian Jewish immigrant Yetta, and privileged Jane — give their perspective of the strike that occurred 13 months before the Triangle Shirtwaist Fire in 1911, protesting working conditions in the garment industry. (Rev: BL 9/15/07; SLJ 9/07)

4961 Hale, Marian. *Dark Water Rising* (6–8). 2006, Henry Holt $16.95 (978-0-8050-7585-4). Seth, 17, lives in Galveston, TX, in the year 1900 and dreams of being a carpenter although his parents want him to be a doctor; when the deadly hurricane hits, Seth struggles to help where he can. ♩ (Rev: BL 10/15/06; SLJ 10/06)

4962 Hale, Marian. *The Goodbye Season* (7–10). 2009, Henry Holt $16.99 (978-080508855-7). Sixteen-year-old Mercy Kaplan, daughter of a Texas sharecropper, struggles to make her way after her family dies in the 1918 flu epidemic. (Rev: BL 7/09; SLJ 10/09)

4963 Hansen, Joyce. *The Heart Calls Home* (6–9). 1999, Walker $16.95 (978-0-8027-8636-4). In this, the third story about Obi and Easter, the two black lovers have survived the Civil War and are trying to build a new life in Reconstruction America. (Rev: BL 12/1/99; HBG 4/00)

4964 Hansen, Joyce. *I Thought My Soul Would Rise and Fly: The Diary of Patsy, a Freed Girl* (4–8). Series: Dear America. 1997, Scholastic paper $10.95 (978-0-590-84913-5). In this novel in the form of a diary, a freed slave girl wonders what to do with her life after leaving the plantation. (Rev: BL 12/15/97; HBG 3/98; SLJ 11/97)

4965 Harlow, Joan Hiatt. *Firestorm!* (4–7). 2010, Simon & Schuster $16.99 (978-141698485-6). Poppy, a 12-year-old pickpocket, and Justin, 13-year-old son of a wealthy jeweler, become unlikely friends and manage a daring escape from the Great Chicago Fire of 1871; an Afterword distinguishes between fiction and fact. Lexile 660L (Rev: BL 11/15/10; SLJ 2/1/11)

4966 Harris, Carol Flynn. *A Place for Joey* (4–8). 2001, Boyds Mills $15.95 (978-1-56397-108-2). Twelve-year-old Joey, an Italian immigrant living in Boston in the early 20th century, learns an important lesson through a heroic act. (Rev: BL 9/1/01; HBG 3/02; SLJ 9/01; VOYA 10/01)

4967 Hesse, Karen. *Brooklyn Bridge* (7–12). 2008, Feiwel & Friends $17.95 (978-0-312-37886-8). Set in 1903 Brooklyn, this story alternates chapters about 14-year-old Joe, whose immigrant family manufactures America's first teddy bears, and abandoned children fending for themselves in the shadow of the Brooklyn Bridge; includes interesting final notes about the history of teddy bears. Sidney Taylor Book Award 2009. ∩ (Rev: BL 8/08; SLJ 9/08)

4968 Hill, Kirkpatrick. *Dancing at the Odinochka* (4–7). 2005, Simon & Schuster $15.95 (978-0-689-87388-1). An atmospheric life of Erinia — daughter of a Russian father and Athabascan mother — growing up in the 1860s in what is now Alaska. (Rev: BL 8/05; SLJ 8/05)

4969 Hurwitz, Johanna. *Faraway Summer* (5–7). Illus. by Mary Azarian. 1998, Morrow $14.95 (978-0-688-15334-2). In 1910, a Jewish orphan who lives in a tenement in New York City is thrilled at the thought of spending two weeks on a farm in Vermont, thanks to the Fresh Air Fund. (Rev: BL 3/1/98; HB 7–8/98; HBG 10/98; SLJ 5/98)

4970 Hurwitz, Johanna. *The Unsigned Valentine: And Other Events in the Life of Emma Meade* (6–9). Illus. by Mary Azarian. 2006, HarperCollins LB $16.89 (978-0-

06-056054-6). Emma, 15, has left school to work on her family's Vermont farm in 1911 and is dismayed when her father won't allow handsome Cole Berry to court her. (Rev: BL 3/1/06; SLJ 1/06)

4971 Jocelyn, Marthe. *Earthly Astonishments* (4–8). 2000, Tundra paper $7.95 (978-0-88776-628-2). The setting is New York City in the 1880s and the novel involves a girl who is only 22 inches tall and her career in a glorified freak show. (Rev: BCCB 2/00; HBG 10/00; SLJ 4/00)

4972 Kelly, Jacqueline. *The Evolution of Calpurnia Tate* (4–7). 2009, Holt $16.95 (978-0-8050-8841-0). In Texas at the turn of the 20th century, 11-year-old Calpurnia, the only daughter among seven children, has an independent streak and an interest in natural science that she shares with her grandfather. Newbery Honor 2010; ALA Notable Books 2010. ∩ Lexile 830L (Rev: BL 5/1/09*; HB 9/09; LMC 10/09; SLJ 5/09*; VOYA 4/09)

4973 Kephart, Beth. *Dangerous Neighbors* (8–12). 2010, Egmont $16.99 (978-1-60684-080-1); LB $19.99 (978-1-60684-106-8). In 1876 during the Philadelphia Centennial Exhibition 17-year-old Katherine is contemplating suicide in her grief over her twin sister's death, but the celebration itself serves to bring her out of her despondency. e Lexile 930L (Rev: BL 9/1/10; LMC 1–2/11; SLJ 10/1/10)

4974 Klass, Sheila Solomon. *A Shooting Star: A Novel About Annie Oakley* (4–8). 1996, Holiday $15.95 (978-0-8234-1279-2). A fictionalized biography of the woman who rose from poverty to become a famous show-business sharpshooter. (Rev: BL 12/15/96; SLJ 5/97)

4975 Korman, Gordon. *Unsinkable* (5–8). Series: Titanic. 2011, Scholastic paper $5.99 (978-0-545-12-331-0). A young Irish pickpocket named Paddy finds himself aboard the *Titanic* in this tense historical adventure, the first installment in a series. The second volume is *Collision Course* (2011). Also use *S.O.S.* (2011). ∩ e Lexile 820L (Rev: BLO 8/11; SLJ 9/1/11)

4976 LaFaye, A. *The Keening* (7–10). 2010, Milkweed $17 (978-1-57131-692-9). When 14-year-old Lyza's mother dies in the flu epidemic of 1918, her father begins acting strangely and Lyza learns that both she and her father can communicate with the dead. (Rev: BL 4/15/10; LMC 8–9/10; SLJ 6/10)

4977 Lasky, Kathryn. *Dreams in the Golden Country: The Diary of Zipporah Feldman, a Jewish Immigrant Girl* (4–8). 1998, Scholastic paper $10.95 (978-0-590-02973-5). Twelve-year-old Zipporah Feldman, a Jewish immigrant from Russia, keeps a diary about her life with her family on New York's Lower East Side around 1910. (Rev: BL 4/1/98; HBG 9/98; SLJ 5/98)

4978 Lerangis, Peter. *Smiler's Bones* (7–10). 2005, Scholastic $16.95 (978-0-439-34485-2). Lerangis brings alive the sad story, based on truth, of an Inuit boy named Minik, who, with his father and four others, was brought to New York City in the late 19th century by explorer Robert Peary. (Rev: BCCB 6/05; BL 4/1/05; SLJ 6/05; VOYA 8/05)

4979 Levine, Kristin. *The Best Bad Luck I Ever Had* (5–8). 2009, Putnam $16.99 (978-0-399-25090-3). In early-20th-century small-town Alabama, 12-year-old Dit is surprised that the new postmaster is African American and disappointed that his daughter is unskilled in baseball, hunting, and fishing; as Emma and Dit become friends they have to deal with racism and injustice. YALSA Amazing Audiobooks Top Ten 2011. ∩ (Rev: BCCB 4/09; BL 11/15/08; HB 5/09; LMC 3/09; SLJ 1/09)

4980 Lowry, Lois. *Like the Willow Tree: The Diary of Lydia Amelia Pierce* (4–7). Illus. Series: Dear America. 2011, Scholastic $12.99 (978-0-545-14469-8); LB $16.99 (978-0-545-26556-0). Eleven-year-old Lydia and her brother are sent to live with the Shakers at Sabbathday Lake, Maine, when their parents die in the influenza epidemic of 1918. Lexile 830L (Rev: BL 12/1/10; SLJ 2/1/11)

4981 Lowry, Lois. *The Silent Boy* (6–10). 2003, Houghton Mifflin $15.00 (978-0-618-28231-9). Young Katy, who has a comfortable existence as a doctor's daughter in early-20th-century New England, makes friends with a mentally backward boy and learns that there are tragedies in life. (Rev: BL 4/15/03; HB 5–6/03; HBG 10/03; SLJ 4/03)

4982 McCaughrean, Geraldine. *The Glorious Adventures of the Sunshine Queen* (5–8). 2011, HarperCollins $16.99 (978-0-06-200806-0). In the 1890s, 12-year-old Cissy and two friends have great adventures on a Missouri River paddle steamer when they are pulled out of school because of a diphtheria outbreak. ∩ Lexile 950L (Rev: BL 4/1/11; HB 5–6/11; SLJ 7/11; VOYA 6/11)

4983 McMullan, Margaret. *When I Crossed No-Bob* (5–8). 2007, Houghton Mifflin $16.00 (978-0-618-71715-6). Addy O'Donnell, 12, manages to separate herself from her violent and racist family in this novel about post-Civil War Mississippi and the beginnings of the Ku Klux Klan. (Rev: BL 10/1/07; HB 1–2/08; SLJ 11/07)

4984 Marshall, Catherine. *Christy* (8–12). 1976, Avon paper $7.99 (978-0-380-00141-5). This story set in Appalachia in 1912 tells about a spunky young girl who goes there to teach. (Rev: BL 5/1/89)

4985 Massie, Elizabeth. *1870: Not with Our Blood* (6–9). Series: Young Founders. 2000, Tor paper $4.99 (978-0-312-59092-5). After his father dies in the Civil War, Patrick and his family seek mill work, which is so discouraging that Patrick considers turning to burglary. (Rev: BL 4/1/00; SLJ 6/00)

4986 Mattern, Joanne. *Coming to America: The Story of Immigration* (4–8). Illus. by Margaret Sanfilippo. 2000, Perfection Learning $17.95 (978-0-7807-9715-4); paper $8.95 (978-0-7891-2851-5). A fictional presenta-

tion centering on the Martini family and their journey from Italy at the turn of the 20th century to find a new home in America. (Rev: HBG 3/01; SLJ 2/01)

4987 Moss, Jenny. *Winnie's War* (5–8). 2009, Walker $16.99 (978-0-8027-9819-0). In 1918 Texas Winnie, 12, must deal with her difficult grandmother, her troubled mother, her overworked father, her two little sisters, and now an epidemic of flu. (Rev: BCCB 2/09; BLO 12/9/08)

4988 Myers, Anna. *Hoggee* (5–7). 2004, Walker $16.95 (978-0-8027-8926-6). Despite all his own problems, 14-year-old mule driver Howard decides to do what he can to help a deaf mute girl in this novel set in 19th-century New York State. (Rev: SLJ 11/04)

4989 Napoli, Donna Jo. *Alligator Bayou* (7–10). 2009, Random House $16.99 (978-038574654-0). Based on a true event — a lynching of Sicilian immigrants in Louisiana in 1899 — this novel follows young Calogero, who is shut out of both black and white society. YALSA Top Ten 2010. Lexile HL430L (Rev: BL 2/15/09; LMC 8–9/09; SLJ 5/1/09; VOYA 4/09)

4990 Napoli, Donna Jo. *The King of Mulberry Street* (6–9). 2005, Random House LB $17.99 (978-0-385-90890-0). In the 1890s, 9-year-old Italian Jew Beniamino travels alone by ship from Naples to New York, where he assumes the name of Dom and tries to make his way while longing for his home. Sidney Taylor Book Honor 2006. (Rev: BL 8/05; SLJ 10/05; VOYA 12/05)

4991 Nixon, Joan Lowery. *Land of Hope* (6–9). Series: Ellis Island. 1993, Dell paper $4.99 (978-0-440-21597-4). Rebekah, 15, and her family escape persecution in Russia in the early 1900s and flee to New York City, where life is harsh but hopeful. (Rev: BL 12/15/92; SLJ 10/92)

4992 Paterson, Katherine. *Bread and Roses, Too* (5–8). 2006, Clarion $16.00 (978-0-618-65479-6). Jake and Rosa, children from different backgrounds, suffer from the effects of the textile workers' strike in early 20th-century Massachusetts. ∩ (Rev: BCCB 3/07; BL 8/06; HB 9–10/06; HBG 4/07; LMC 2/07; SLJ 9/06; VOYA 12/06)

4993 Paterson, Katherine. *Preacher's Boy* (5–8). 1999, Clarion $15.00 (978-0-395-83897-6). In small-town Vermont in 1899, a time of new ideas and technological change, Robbie, the restless, imaginative, questioning son of a preacher, causes unforeseen trouble when he plans his own kidnapping for profit. (Rev: BCCB 10/99; BL 8/99; HB 9–10/99; HBG 3/00; SLJ 8/99)

4994 Peck, Richard. *Here Lies the Librarian* (5–8). 2006, Dial $16.99 (978-0-8037-3080-9). Four young female librarians arrive in a small town in Indiana in 1914 and inspire 14-year-old Peewee McGrath to consider her future in different ways. (Rev: BL 3/1/06; SLJ 4/06*; VOYA 2/06)

4995 Porter, Tracey. *Billy Creekmore* (5–7). 2007, HarperCollins $16.99 (978-0-06-077570-4). From a grim orphanage to the mines of West Virginia and on to a life in the circus, 10-year-old Billy describes in picaresque style the difficult life of the young and poor in the early 20th century. (Rev: BL 4/15/07; SLJ 7/07)

4996 Raphael, Marie. *A Boy from Ireland* (6–9). 2007, Persea $19.95 (978-0-89255-331-0). Liam, son of an Englishman, has grown up in Ireland and learned to face prejudice over his heritage; moving to New York City in 1901, he finds himself in a similar situation. (Rev: BL 1/15/08; SLJ 2/08)

4997 Raphael, Marie. *Streets of Gold* (7–9). 1998, TreeHouse paper $7.95 (978-1-883088-05-7). After fleeing Poland and conscription in the Russian czar's army, Stefan and his sister Marisia begin a new life in America on the Lower East Side of New York City at the turn of the 20th century. (Rev: SLJ 12/98)

4998 Reich, Susanna. *Penelope Bailey Takes the Stage* (4–7). 2006, Marshall Cavendish $16.95 (978-0-7614-5287-4). A frustrated Penny takes a role in the school play against the wishes of her aunt in this novel set in Victorian San Francisco. (Rev: BL 5/15/06; SLJ 5/06)

4999 Richards, Jame. *Three Rivers Rising* (7–11). 2010, Knopf $16.99 (978-0-375-85885-7). Three characters caught up in the disaster tell their stories of survival following the 1889 Johnstown Flood. ☊ Lexile HL780L (Rev: BL 4/15/10; LMC 8–9/10; SLJ 4/10)

5000 Robinet, Harriette G. *Forty Acres and Maybe a Mule* (4–7). 1998, Simon & Schuster $16.00 (978-0-689-82078-6). After the Civil War, Gideon and other freed slaves begin working the 40 acres of land each has been promised in spite of the opposition of white settlers. (Rev: BL 1/1–15/99; HBG 3/99; SLJ 11/98)

5001 Rogers, Lisa Waller. *Get Along, Little Dogies: The Chisholm Trail Diary of Hallie Lou Wells: South Texas, 1878* (4–7). 2001, Texas Tech Univ. $14.50 (978-0-89672-446-4); paper $8.95 (978-0-89672-448-8). Feisty 14-year-old Hallie Lou records in her diary the details and dangers of a cattle drive from Texas to Kansas. (Rev: HBG 10/01; SLJ 7/01)

5002 Schlitz, Laura Amy. *A Drowned Maiden's Hair* (6–9). 2006, Candlewick $15.99 (978-0-7636-2930-4). Orphan Maud is happy to be adopted by the spinster Hawthorne sisters, until she discovers their plan to use her to trick trusting people out of their money in this novel set in Victorian times. (Rev: BL 12/15/06; HB 11–12/06; LMC 2/07; SLJ 10/06)

5003 Schmidt, Gary D. *Lizzie Bright and the Buckminster Boy* (7–12). 2004, Clarion $15.00 (978-0-618-43929-4). When Turner, son of a rigid minister, moves with his family to a small town in Maine during 1912, he doesn't fit in. Newbery Honor 2005; Printz Honor 2005. (Rev: BL 5/15/04*; SLJ 5/04)

5004 Sherman, Eileen B. *Independence Avenue* (5–9). 1990, Jewish Publication Society $14.95 (978-0-8276-0367-7). This story of Russian Jews who immigrate to Texas in 1907 has a resourceful, engaging hero, an unusual setting, and plenty of action. (Rev: BL 2/15/91; SLJ 1/91)

5005 Stewart, Elizabeth. *The Lynching of Louie Sam* (7–12). 2012, Annick $21.95 (978-1-55451-439-7); paper $12.95 (978-1-55451-438-0). In 1884, 15-year-old George Gillies witnesses a lynching and later worries that the young Native American was in fact innocent. ☻ Lexile 840L (Rev: BL 12/15/12; LMC 3–4/13; SLJ 9/12)

5006 Swain, Gwenyth. *Hope and Tears: Ellis Island Voices* (5–8). Illus. 2012, Boyds Mills $17.95 (978-159078765-6). Fictionalized personal histories in the form of letters, diary entries, poems, and monologues and dialogues — accompanied by a factual commentary — provide lots of information about the experiences of immigrants arriving at Ellis Island. (Rev: BL 4/15/12; HB 5–6/12; SLJ 5/1/12)

5007 Tal, Eve. *Double Crossing: A Jewish Immigration Story* (7–10). 2005, Cinco Puntos $16.95 (978-0-938317-94-4). At the beginning of the 20th century, young Raizel and her Orthodox Jewish grandfather travel from Europe to New York only to find they are rejected by immigration officials. (Rev: BL 8/05*; SLJ 10/05; VOYA 4/06)

5008 Tall, Eve. *Cursing Columbus* (7–10). 2009, Cinco Puntos $16.95 (978-1-933693-59-0). In this sequel to *Double Crossing* (2005), 14-year-old Raizel and her younger brother Lemmel react in opposite ways to the challenges of being Ukrainian Jewish immigrants on the Lower East Side of Manhattan in 1908. ☻ Lexile 500L (Rev: BL 10/15/09; LMC 5–6/10; SLJ 1/10)

5009 Taylor, Kim. *Bowery Girl* (8–11). 2006, Viking $16.99 (978-0-670-05966-9). A realistic story about orphaned teen girls who resort to picking pockets and prostitution to survive in late-19th-century New York City. (Rev: BL 3/1/06; SLJ 3/06; VOYA 4/06)

5010 Taylor, Mildred D. *The Land* (7–12). 2001, Penguin $17.99 (978-0-8037-1950-7). In this prequel to *Roll of Thunder, Hear My Cry* (1976), Taylor weaves her own family history into a moving story of a young man of mixed parentage facing prejudice, cruelty, and betrayal during the time of Reconstruction. (Rev: BCCB 10/01; BL 8/01; HB 9–10/01; HBG 3/02; SLJ 8/01; VOYA 10/01)

5011 Tubb, Kristin O' Donnell. *Selling Hope* (5–8). 2010, Feiwel & Friends $16.99 (978-031261122-4). As Halley's Comet approaches in 1910, imaginative 13-year-old Hope sells "anti-comet" pills with the help of a young Buster Keaton. (Rev: BL 11/15/10*; SLJ 12/1/10)

5012 Tucker, Terry Ward. *Moonlight and Mill Whistles* (5–7). 1998, Summerhouse $15.00 (978-1-887714-32-7). Thirteen-year-old Tommy is unaware how his life will change after he meets a gypsy girl named Rhona in this novel set in an early 1900s South Carolina cotton mill town. (Rev: BL 3/1/99; SLJ 5/99)

5013 Twomey, Cathleen. *Charlotte's Choice* (6–8). 2001, Boyds Mills $15.95 (978-1-56397-938-5). In 1905 Missouri, 13-year-old Charlotte must decide whether to betray her friend Jesse's trust and reveal why Jesse has committed murder. (Rev: BL 1/1–15/02; HBG 3/02; SLJ 12/01; VOYA 2/02)

5014 Warner, Sally. *Finding Hattie* (5–8). 2001, HarperCollins $15.95 (978-0-06-028464-0). Hattie Knowlton's 1882 journal describes Miss Bulkey's school in Tarrytown, New York, and the people she meets there, including her sophisticated, shallow but popular cousin Sophie. (Rev: BCCB 6/01; BL 2/1/01; HB 5–6/01; HBG 10/01; SLJ 2/01; VOYA 8/01)

5015 Watts, Irene N. *No Moon* (6–8). 2010, Tundra paper $12.95 (978-0-88776-971-9). Afraid of the water since her baby brother drowned, 14-year-old nursery maid Louisa nevertheless agrees to accompany a wealthy family on their voyage to New York aboard the *Titanic*. (Rev: BL 4/15/10*; SLJ 8/10)

5016 Welsh, T. K. *The Unresolved* (7–12). 2006, Dutton $15.99 (978-0-525-47731-0). The story of the *General Slocum* steamship disaster of 1904, told from the point of view of Mallory, the ghost of one of the victims. (Rev: SLJ 9/06)

5017 Wemmlinger, Raymond. *Booth's Daughter* (8–11). 2007, Boyds Mills $17.95 (978-1-932425-86-4). The niece of John Wilkes Booth, who assassinated Lincoln, and the daughter of famous actor Edwin Booth, Edwina must find an identity apart from her famous family in this novel set in the Gilded Age. (Rev: BCCB 6/07; BL 2/15/07; LMC 10/07; SLJ 9/07)

5018 Wilson, Diane Lee. *Firehorse* (7–10). 2006, Simon & Schuster $16.95 (978-1-4169-1551-5). Rachel, 15, living in 1872 Boston, loves horses and dreams of becoming a veterinarian, despite what her family and society thinks; when she saves a fire-station horse that has been severely burned, opportunities appear to open. (Rev: BL 10/15/06; LMC 4–5/07; SLJ 1/07)

5019 Winthrop, Elizabeth. *Counting on Grace* (6–9). 2006, Random House LB $18.99 (978-0-385-90878-8). In the early 20th century, 12-year-old Grace chafes against her long hours working in the textile mill and longs to go back to school in this story based on a 1910 photograph by Lewis Hines. (Rev: BL 2/15/06; SLJ 3/06*; VOYA 4/06)

BETWEEN THE WARS AND THE GREAT DEPRESSION (1919–1941)

5020 Barnaby, Hannah. *Wonder Show* (7–10). 2012, Houghton Mifflin $16.99 (978-054759980-9). In Depression-era America Portia escapes from a Home for Wayward Girls and joins a traveling circus. Lexile 830L (Rev: BLO 4/15/12; HB 7–8/12; SLJ 8/12)

5021 Beard, Darleen Bailey. *The Babbs Switch Story* (5–8). 2002, Farrar $16.00 (978-0-374-30475-1). A young girl saves her sister from a fire on Christmas Eve in 1924 in this fictional account of a real event. (Rev: BL 3/15/02; HBG 10/02; SLJ 3/02; VOYA 4/02)

5022 Blackwood, Gary. *Moonshine* (5–8). 1999, Marshall Cavendish $14.95 (978-0-7614-5056-6). Thirteen-year-old Thad, growing up with his mother in rural Mississippi during the Depression, makes a little extra money by running an illegal still that produces moonshine for the locals. (Rev: BCCB 11/99; BL 9/1/99; HBG 3/00; SLJ 10/99)

5023 Blakeslee, Ann R. *Summer Battles* (5–8). 2000, Marshall Cavendish $14.95 (978-0-7614-5064-1). The story of Kath, age 11, growing up in a small town in Indiana in 1926 and of her father, a preacher, who is attacked for opposing the Ku Klux Klan. (Rev: BCCB 3/00; BL 4/1/00; HBG 10/00; SLJ 4/00)

5024 Bornstein, Ruth Lercher. *Butterflies and Lizards, Beryl and Me* (5–7). 2002, Marshall Cavendish LB $14.95 (978-0-7614-5118-1). Eleven-year-old Charley befriends an odd woman named Beryl while her mother works hard to make it through the Great Depression. (Rev: BL 5/15/02; HBG 10/02; SLJ 5/02)

5025 Brown, Don. *The Train Jumper* (6–9). 2007, Roaring Brook $16.95 (978-1-59643-218-5). During the Depression, 14-year-old Collie sets out to find his troubled older brother and encounters both danger and friendship on his journey. (Rev: BL 8/07; LMC 11/07)

5026 Bryant, Jen. *Ringside, 1925: Views from the Scopes Trial* (6–10). 2008, Knopf $15.99 (978-037584047-0); LB $18.99 (978-037594047-7). A series of first-person free-verse poems brings to life the events of the Scopes Monkey Trial and the divisive, circus-like atmosphere it brought to town as citizens debated the teaching of evolution. (Rev: BLO 10/30/08; HB 5–6/08; LMC 4–5/08; SLJ 3/08; VOYA 6/08)

5027 Burandt, Harriet, and Shelley Dale. *Tales from the Homeplace: Adventures of a Texas Farm Girl* (4–8). 1997, Henry Holt $15.95 (978-0-8050-5075-2). A family story that takes place on a Texas cotton farm during the Depression and features spunky 12-year-old heroine Irene and her six brothers and sisters. (Rev: BCCB 7–8/97; HB 5–6/97; SLJ 4/97*; VOYA 12/97)

5028 Choldenko, Gennifer. *Al Capone Shines My Shoes* (5–8). 2009, Dial $17.99 (978-0-8037-3460-9). In *Al*

Capone Does My Shirts (2004), 12-year-old Moose benefited from his acquaintance with the famous gangster; now Capone is demanding help in return. ◯ ℮ Lexile 620L (Rev: BL 9/1/09; HB 9–10/09; SLJ 9/09; VOYA 10/09)

5029 Cummings, Priscilla. *Saving Grace* (4–7). 2003, Dutton $17.99 (978-0-525-47123-3). Eleven-year-old Grace faces a tough dilemma when a wealthy family offers to adopt her while her own family is suffering grinding poverty and illness during the Depression. (Rev: BCCB 9/03; BL 5/15/03; HBG 10/03; SLJ 6/03; VOYA 10/03)

5030 Currier, Katrina Saltonstall. *Kai's Journey to Gold Mountain* (4–7). Illus. by Gabhor Utomo. 2005, Angel Island $16.95 (978-0-9667352-7-7); paper $10.95 (978-0-9667352-4-6). Based on the experiences of a Chinese immigrant to the United States in the 1930s, this troubling tale describes the internment of 12-year-old Kai on Angel Island in San Francisco Bay. (Rev: BL 2/15/05*)

5031 Dotty, Kathryn Adams. *Wild Orphan* (5–8). 2006, Edinborough $14.95 (978-1-889020-20-4). In the Midwest in the 1920s, Lizbeth's friendship with an independent-minded orphan named Georgiana gives her courage. (Rev: BL 6/1–15/06)

5032 Dudley, David L. *The Bicycle Man* (5–8). 2005, Clarion $16.00 (978-0-618-54233-8). In this poignant portrait of African American life in the rural South during the late 1920s, 12-year-old Carissa develops a mutually beneficial relationship with Bailey, an elderly jack-of-all-trades to whom she and her mother offer a home. (Rev: BL 11/15/05; SLJ 11/05)

5033 Easton, Kelly. *Walking on Air* (6–8). 2004, Simon & Schuster $16.95 (978-0-689-84875-9). Traveling the 1930s revival circuit and performing as an aerialist to draw people into her father's tent shows, unhappy 12-year-old June makes some important discoveries about her birth and faith. (Rev: BCCB 7–8/04; BL 4/1/04; SLJ 7/04; VOYA 6/04)

5034 Erickson, John R. *Moonshiner's Gold* (5–9). 2001, Viking $15.99 (978-0-670-03502-1). Fourteen-year-old Riley becomes embroiled in exciting intrigue involving moonshiners and corruption in this novel set in Texas in the 1920s. (Rev: HBG 3/02; SLJ 8/01; VOYA 10/01)

5035 Fisher, Leonard Everett. *The Jetty Chronicles* (5–9). 1997, Marshall Cavendish $15.95 (978-0-7614-5017-7). A series of vignettes based on fact about the unusual people the author met while growing up in Sea Gate, New York, at a time when the United States was drifting into World War II. (Rev: BL 10/15/97; HBG 3/98; SLJ 12/97; VOYA 2/98)

5036 Flood, Nancy Bo. *No-Name Baby* (6–10). 2012, Namelos $18.95 (978-160898117-5). Fourteen-year-old Sophie blames herself when her little brother is born prematurely in this taut family drama set in the

Midwest after World War I. ℮ (Rev: BL 5/1/12; SLJ 3/12)

5037 Franklin, Kristine L. *Grape Thief* (5–9). 2003, Candlewick $16.99 (978-0-7636-1325-9). In 1925 Washington State, a boy of Croatian heritage tries to find a way to stay in school even though his family is in financial difficulty. (Rev: BL 10/1/03; SLJ 9/03)

5038 Fuqua, Jonathon. *Darby* (4–7). 2002, Candlewick $15.99 (978-0-7636-1417-1). A 9-year-old white girl, Darby, and her family become the target of KKK violence after she protests the killing of a black sharecropper's son in 1926 South Carolina. (Rev: BCCB 7–8/02; BL 3/15/02; HB 3–4/02; HBG 10/02; SLJ 3/02; VOYA 4/02)

5039 Fusco, Kimberly Newton. *The Wonder of Charlie Anne* (5–8). 2010, Knopf $16.99 (978-0-375-86104-8). When Charlie Anne's mother dies in the Depression era, cousin Mirabel comes to live with the family and life becomes even tougher; however, a friendship with an African American neighbor — despite the disapproval of bigoted neighbors — brings her comfort. ◯ Lexile 970L (Rev: BL 9/1/10; LMC 11–12/10; SLJ 10/1/10*)

5040 Giff, Patricia Reilly. *R My Name Is Rachel* (4–7). 2011, Random House $15.99 (978-0-375-83889-7); LB $18.99 (978-0-375-93889-4). Three formerly city children are left to fend for themselves on an isolated farm in upstate New York when their father must leave to work near Canada during the Great Depression; Rachel, 12, takes solace in her correspondence with an old neighbor. ◯ ℮ Lexile 550L (Rev: BLO 1/12; HB 11–12/11; LMC 5–6/12; SLJ 11/1/11)

5041 Griffin, Molly Beth. *Silhouette of a Sparrow* (7–12). 2012, Milkweed $16.95 (978-157131701-8). In Minnesota for the summer of 1926, 16-year-old Garnet shocks her wealthy relatives by taking a job in a milliner's shop, where she meets and and falls in love with Isabella. ℮ (Rev: BL 9/15/12; VOYA 8/12)

5042 Hesse, Karen. *Letters from Rifka* (4–8). 1992, Henry Holt $16.95 (978-0-8050-1964-3). In letters back to Russia, Rifka, 12, recounts her long journey to the United States in 1919, starting with the dangerous escape over the border. (Rev: BCCB 10/92; BL 7/92; HB 9–10/92*; SLJ 8/92*)

5043 Hesse, Karen. *Out of the Dust* (6–12). 1997, Scholastic $16.95 (978-0-590-36080-7). In free verse, 15-year-old Billie Jo describes the tragedies that befall her family during the Dust Bowl years in Oklahoma. Newbery Medal, 1998. (Rev: HBG 3/98)

5044 Hesse, Karen. *A Time of Angels* (5–8). 1995, Hyperion LB $16.49 (978-0-7868-2072-6). As influenza sweeps her city in 1918, killing thousands, Hannah tries to escape its ravages by moving to Vermont, where an old farmer helps her. (Rev: BCCB 1/96; BL 12/1/95; SLJ 12/95)

5045 Hesse, Karen. *Witness* (7–12). 2001, Scholastic paper $16.95 (978-0-439-27199-8). Hesse uses fictional first-person accounts in free verse to describe Ku Klux Klan activity in a 1924 Vermont town. (Rev: BCCB 11/01; BL 9/1/01; HB 11–12/01; HBG 3/02; SLJ 9/01*; VOYA 10/01)

5046 Honeyman, Kay. *The Fire Horse Girl* (8–12). 2013, Scholastic $17.99 (978-054540310-8). Born under the ominous sign of the Fire Horse in 1906, Jade Moon leaves China for America carrying false papers, and disguises herself as a boy while finding work in San Francisco's Chinatown. ❂ Lexile 660L (Rev: BL 1/13*; LMC 8–9/12; SLJ 1/13; VOYA 2/13)

5047 Hunt, Irene. *No Promises in the Wind* (6–8). 1987, Berkley paper $4.99 (978-0-425-09969-8). During the Great Depression, Josh must assume responsibilities far beyond his years. A reissue.

5048 Ingold, Jeanette. *Hitch* (8–11). 2005, Harcourt $17.00 (978-0-13-204747-0). When he loses his job during the Great Depression, 17-year-old Moss Trawnley leaves home in search of his father and ends up in an interesting job with the Civilian Conservation Corps. (Rev: BCCB 9/05; BL 5/15/05; SLJ 8/05)

5049 Jackson, Alison. *Rainmaker* (5–8). 2005, Boyds Mills $16.95 (978-1-59078-309-2). The farmers in Pidge Martin's town hire a rainmaker in the hopes that she will save their crops in this story set in 1939 Florida. (Rev: BL 3/15/05; SLJ 4/05)

5050 Jocelyn, Marthe. *How It Happened in Peach Hill* (5–9). 2007, Random House $15.99 (978-0-375-83701-2). Fifteen-year-old Annie, who does research for her "clairvoyant" mother mainly by pretending she is stupid, longs for a normal life in this compelling novel set in the 1920s. (Rev: BL 1/1–15/07; SLJ 4/07*)

5051 Kidd, Ronald. *Monkey Town: The Summer of the Scopes Trial* (6–9). 2006, Simon & Schuster $15.95 (978-1-4169-0572-1). This fictionalized account of the 1925 Scopes Monkey Trial in Dayton, Tennessee, is narrated by the perceptive 15-year-old Frances Robinson, daughter of the man primarily responsible for taking the evolution test case to the courts. (Rev: BL 12/15/05; SLJ 2/06*; VOYA 2/06)

5052 Koller, Jackie F. *Nothing to Fear* (5–7). 1991, Harcourt $14.95 (978-0-15-200544-3); paper $8.00 (978-0-15-257582-3). Danny Garvey is a first-generation Catholic Irish American growing up in New York City in the 1930s. (Rev: BCCB 3/91; BL 3/1/91; SLJ 5/91)

5053 Kudlinski, Kathleen. *The Spirit Catchers: An Encounter with Georgia O'Keeffe* (6–9). Series: Art Encounters. 2004, Watson-Guptill $16.95 (978-0-8230-0408-9); paper $6.99 (978-0-8230-0412-6). Fact and fiction are mixed in this story of 15-year-old Parker, a Dust Bowl refugee who finds himself on Georgia O'Keeffe's New Mexico ranch and becomes her assistant. (Rev: SLJ 10/04)

5054 Laskas, Gretchen Moran. *The Miner's Daughter* (6–9). 2007, Simon & Schuster $15.99 (978-1-4169-1262-0). Willa, 16, must disguise herself as a boy to get work when her father loses his mining job during the Depression. (Rev: BCCB 5/07; BL 2/15/07; LMC 8–9/07; SLJ 2/07)

5055 Latham, Irene. *Leaving Gee's Bend* (5–8). 2010, Putnam $16.99 (978-0-399-25179-5). Ten-year-old African American Ludelphia sets out on a dangerous journey to get help for her ailing mother in 1932. Lexile 700L (Rev: BL 2/1/10; LMC 1–2/10; SLJ 1/10; VOYA 2/10)

5056 Laxalt, Robert. *Time of the Rabies* (7–12). 2000, Univ. of Nevada $16.00 (978-0-87417-350-5). Set in 1920s Nevada, this novella recalls a harrowing fight against a rabies epidemic. (Rev: VOYA 4/01)

5057 Lottridge, Celia Barker. *The Listening Tree* (4–8). 2011, Fitzhenry & Whiteside paper $11.95 (978-1-55455-052-4). Nine-year-old Ellen, new to city life, gains the courage to talk to strangers when she overhears plans to evict her neighbors in this Depression story set in Canada. Lexile 1240 (Rev: BL 4/15/11; SLJ 5/11; VOYA 4/11)

5058 Luper, Eric. *Bug Boy* (8–12). 2009, Farrar $16.99 (978-0-374-31000-4). Set at the Saratoga Race Track during the Depression, this is the story of 15-year-old Jack, an apprentice jockey whose dreams of racing are almost sidetracked by shady characters and his own father's betrayal. ❂ (Rev: BL 9/1/09; SLJ 9/09)

5059 Meltzer, Milton. *Tough Times* (5–8). 2007, Clarion $16.00 (978-0-618-87445-3). With detailed historical background, this novel describes the struggles and despair experienced by high school senior Joey Singer and his family as the Depression deepens. (Rev: BL 9/1/07; SLJ 12/07)

5060 Mills, Claudia. *What About Annie?* (6–8). 1985, Walker $9.95 (978-0-8027-6573-4). A harrowing story of a family in Baltimore living through the Depression as seen through the eyes of a young teenage girl. (Rev: BL 9/1/85)

5061 Myers, Anna. *Tulsa Burning* (8–10). 2002, Walker $16.95 (978-0-8027-8829-0). In 1921 Oklahoma, a 15-year-old boy helps an African American man who is injured during race riots. (Rev: BCCB 12/02; BL 10/1/02*; HBG 3/03; SLJ 9/02; VOYA 12/02)

5062 Myers, Walter Dean. *Harlem Summer* (7–10). 2007, Scholastic $16.99 (978-0-439-36843-8). The atmosphere of 1925 Harlem is strongly evoked in this story of 16-year-old Mark Purvis, an aspiring jazz saxophonist, who takes a job at the NAACP magazine *The Crisis* but soon becomes involved with mobsters. (Rev: BCCB 4/07; BL 2/1/07; HB 5–6/07; LMC 8–9/07; SLJ 3/07)

5063 Naylor, Phyllis Reynolds. *Blizzard's Wake* (7–12). 2002, Simon & Schuster $16.95 (978-0-689-85220-6).

In a blizzard in 1941, 15-year-old Kate comes face to face with the man who caused her mother's death. (Rev: BCCB 1/03; BL 10/15/02; HBG 3/03; SLJ 12/02)

5064 O'Sullivan, Mark. *Wash-Basin Street Blues* (7–10). 1996, Wolfhound paper $6.95 (978-0-86327-467-1). In 1920s New York City, 16-year-old Nora is reunited with her two younger brothers but the reunion causes unforeseen problems. A sequel to *Melody for Nora* (1994). (Rev: BL 6/1–15/96)

5065 Peck, Robert Newton. *Arly* (5–8). 1989, Walker $16.95 (978-0-8027-6856-8). A teacher changes the life of a young boy in a migrant camp in Florida in 1927. (Rev: BL 7/89; VOYA 8/89)

5066 Pinkney, Andrea Davis. *Bird in a Box* (4–7). 2011, Little, Brown $16.99 (978-0-316-07403-2). Three young boxing fans facing personal challenges come together at the Mercy Home for Negro Orphans and are inspired by the great Joe Louis's victories during the Great Depression. ⌒ **e** (Rev: BL 4/15/11; HB 5–6/11; LMC 10/11; SLJ 3/1/11)

5067 Porter, Tracey. *Treasures in the Dust* (5–7). 1997, HarperCollins LB $14.89 (978-0-06-027564-8). With alternating points of view, two girls from poor families in Oklahoma's Dust Bowl tell their stories. (Rev: BL 8/97; HB 9–10/97; HBG 3/98; SLJ 12/97*; VOYA 10/98)

5068 Rabe, Berniece. *Hiding Mr. McMulty* (5–8). 1997, Harcourt $18.00 (978-0-15-201330-1). This novel, set in southeast Missouri in 1937, tells a story of race and class conflicts as experienced by 11-year-old Rass. (Rev: BL 10/15/97; HBG 3/98; SLJ 12/97; VOYA 2/98)

5069 Ray, Delia. *Ghost Girl: A Blue Ridge Mountain Story* (5–8). 2003, Clarion $16.00 (978-0-618-33377-6). In rural Virginia during the Depression, young April longs to go to the new school built by President Hoover and learn to read, but her family circumstances do not make this easy. (Rev: BCCB 11/03; BL 11/15/03; HB 1–2/04*; HBG 4/04; SLJ 11/03*)

5070 Rostkowski, Margaret I. *After the Dancing Days* (6–9). 1986, HarperCollins paper $5.99 (978-0-06-440248-4). Annie encounters the realities of war when she helps care for wounded soldiers after World War I. (Rev: BL 10/15/86; SLJ 12/86; VOYA 4/87)

5071 Ryan, Pam Muñoz. *Esperanza Rising* (5–8). 2000, Scholastic paper $17.99 (978-0-439-12041-8). During the Great Depression, poverty forces Esperanza and her mother to leave Mexico and seek work in an agricultural labor camp in California. (Rev: BCCB 12/00; BL 12/1/00; HB 1–2/01; HBG 3/01; SLJ 10/00; VOYA 12/00)

5072 Snyder, Zilpha Keatley. *William S. and the Great Escape* (5–7). 2009, Simon & Schuster $16.99 (978-1-4169-6763-7). In a small California town during the Great Depression, the four youngest Baggett siblings flee their coarse, abusive family for their aunt's house

after sister Janey's guinea pig is flushed down the toilet. A sequel is *William's Midsummer Dreams* (2011), in which William is living with his Aunt Fiona and playing the role of Puck. ⌒ **e** Lexile 980L (Rev: BL 7/09; LMC 11–12/09; SLJ 10/09)

5073 Sternberg, Libby. *The Case Against My Brother* (6–9). 2007, Bancroft $19.95 (978-1-890862-51-0). Carl Matuski, 15 and from a Polish Catholic family, sets out to solve a mystery and encounters prejudice and ethnic hatred in this story set in Oregon in 1922. (Rev: BL 11/15/07; SLJ 1/08)

5074 Stolz, Mary. *Ivy Larkin* (7–9). 1986, Harcourt $13.95 (978-0-15-239366-3). During the Depression in New York City, 15-year-old Ivy's father loses his job and the family moves to the Lower East Side. (Rev: BL 11/1/86; SLJ 12/86)

5075 Stuber, Barbara. *Crossing the Tracks* (7–12). 2010, Simon & Schuster $16.99 (978-1-4169-9703-0). In 1930s Missouri, 15-year-old Iris is sent to be a caregiver to an elderly woman and despite initial trepidation finds herself making a happy new home. **e** Lexile 680L (Rev: BL 7/10; LMC 10/10; SLJ 8/10; VOYA 10/10)

5076 Tarshis, Lauren. *I Survived the Shark Attacks of 1916* (3–7). Illus. by Scott Dawson. Series: I Survived. 2010, Scholastic $16.99 (978-0-545-20688-4). Based on the New Jersey shark attacks of 1916, this story follows of group of boys who play pranks on each other, doubting the existence of the shark — until they see it for themselves. Lexile 610L (Rev: SLJ 12/1/10)

5077 Tate, Eleanora E. *Celeste's Harlem Renaissance* (4–7). 2007, Little, Brown $15.99 (978-0-316-52394-3). In the early 1920s Celeste arrives in New York from North Carolina and discovers that her aunt is not the famous singer and dancer she was told but that the lively spirit of the Harlem Renaissance brings her rewards. (Rev: BL 2/1/07; SLJ 5/07)

5078 Taylor, Kim. *Cissy Funk* (6–9). 2001, HarperCollins LB $15.89 (978-0-06-029042-9). Cissy is neglected and abused until her Aunt Vera arrives in this novel of complex family relationships that evokes the privations of the Depression years in Colorado. (Rev: BCCB 5/01; BL 8/01; HBG 10/01; SLJ 5/01; VOYA 8/01)

5079 Taylor, Sarah Stewart. *Amelia Earhart: This Broad Ocean* (4–7). Illus. by Ben Towle. 2010, Hyperion $17.99 (978-1-4231-1337-9). Young Grace, who wants to be a reporter one day, is entranced by Earhart and her bravery in this graphic novel presentation of a portion of Earhart's life. (Rev: BL 3/15/10*; LMC 8–9/10; SLJ 5/10)

5080 Vanderpool, Clare. *Moon Over Manifest* (5–8). 2010, Delacorte $16.99 (978-0-385-73883-5); LB $19.99 (978-0-385-90750-7). Twelve-year-old Abilene arrives in Manifest in 1936 hoping to learn more about her father, and a box of mementos sets her and her new friends on a journey of discovery. Newbery

Medal 2011; ALA Notable Book 2011. ∩ ℮ (Rev: BL 10/15/10*; LMC 5–6/11; SLJ 11/1/10)

5081 Vernick, Shirley Reva. *The Blood Lie* (7–10). 2011, Cinco Puntos $15.95 (978-1-933693-84-2). In upstate New York in 1928 a Jewish teen named Jack is accused of killing a little girl as part of a blood sacrifice; based on a true story. Sydney Taylor Book Honor 2012. ℮ Lexile 740L (Rev: BL 11/15/11; LMC 5–6/12; SLJ 11/1/11)

5082 Weatherford, Carole Boston. *Becoming Billie Holiday* (6–9). Illus. by Floyd Cooper. 2008, Boyds Mills $19.95 (978-159078507-2). Weatherford gives fictionalized, poetic voice to Billie Holiday as she climbs up out of her troubled youth to become a celebrated figure in American culture. Coretta Scott King Author Honor Book 2009. (Rev: BL 10/1/08; LMC 3–4/09; SLJ 10/1/08*; VOYA 12/08)

5083 Winthrop, Elizabeth. *Franklin Delano Roosevelt: Letters from a Mill Town Girl* (5–7). Series: Dear Mr. President. 2001, Winslow $9.95 (978-1-890817-61-9). Fictional letters between Franklin Delano Roosevelt and a 12-year-old girl illustrate living conditions and government policy during the Depression. (Rev: BL 2/1/02; HBG 3/02; SLJ 12/01)

5084 Wolfert, Adrienne. *Making Tracks* (5–7). Series: Adventures in America. 2000, Silver Moon LB $14.95 (978-1-893110-16-8). In this novel set in the Depression, young Henry leaves his foster home to ride the rails to Chicago to find his father. (Rev: BL 7/00; HBG 3/01; SLJ 11/00)

5085 Wyatt, Leslie J. *Poor Is Just a Starting Place* (5–8). 2005, Holiday $16.95 (978-0-8234-1884-8). In rural Kentucky during the Great Depression, 12-year-old Artie longs for a different life. (Rev: BL 6/1–15/05; SLJ 7/05)

POST WORLD WAR II UNITED STATES (1945–)

5086 Abbott, Tony. *Lunch-Box Dream* (5–8). 2011, Farrar $16.99 (978-0-374-34673-7). Two families — one white and one black — traveling through the South in 1959 are brought together by unlikely circumstances in this tense story. (Rev: BL 7/11; SLJ 9/1/11)

5087 Armistead, John. *The Return of Gabriel* (6–9). 2002, Milkweed $17.95 (978-1-57131-637-0); paper $6.95 (978-1-57131-638-7). Friendships and family loyalties are tested when the civil rights movement comes to Mississippi and parents take sides in this story set in 1964. (Rev: BL 12/15/02; HBG 3/03; SLJ 12/02)

5088 Armstrong, Alan. *Racing the Moon* (5–8). Illus. by Tim Jessell. 2012, Random House $16.99 (978-0-375-85889-5); LB $19.99 (978-0-375-95889-2). In 1947 Alex, 11, and her older brother are excited when they meet a real scientist who shares their passion for space. ℮ Lexile 780L (Rev: BL 6/12; LMC 10/12; SLJ 8/1/12)

5089 Baker, Julie. *Up Molasses Mountain* (6–9). 2002, Random House LB $17.99 (978-0-385-90048-5). Clarence and Elizabeth find themselves on opposite sides of a labor dispute involving their coal-mining fathers in this multilayered novel set in 1953 West Virginia. (Rev: BL 5/15/02; HBG 10/02; SLJ 7/02; VOYA 8/02)

5090 Banks, Steven. *King of the Creeps* (6–9). 2006, Knopf $15.95 (978-0-375-83291-8). Set in 1963, this is the story of 17-year-old Tom, a geeky teen who discovers he can attract girls — and attention — by playing guitar and playing up his resemblance to folk star Bob Dylan. (Rev: BL 5/1/06; LMC 10/06; SLJ 6/06)

5091 Bauer, Marion Dane. *Killing Miss Kitty and Other Sins* (8–11). 2007, Clarion $16.00 (978-0-618-69000-8). Five interconnected stories about Claire, a girl growing up in the 1950s and exploring life and sexuality. (Rev: BCCB 9/07; BL 2/15/07; LMC 8–9/07; SLJ 5/07)

5092 Blundell, Judy. *What I Saw and How I Lied* (8–12). 2008, Scholastic $16.99 (978-043990346-2). Fifteen-year-old Evie uncovers unsettling truths about her family while on vacation in Palm Beach in 1947. ∩ ℮ Lexile HL620L (Rev: BL 11/1/08*; SLJ 12/08; VOYA 2/09)

5093 Brandeis, Gayle. *My Life with the Lincolns* (5–7). 2010, Henry Holt $16.99 (978-0-8050-9013-0). In the summer of 1966, intelligent 12-year-old Mina Edelmann believes that she is the reincarnation of one of Abraham Lincoln's sons as she learns about racism and watches the civil rights movement. ∩ ℮ Lexile 840L (Rev: BL 2/15/10; LMC 5–6/10; SLJ 3/10)

5094 Brown, Chris Carlton. *Hoppergrass* (7–10). 2009, Henry Holt $17.95 (978-080508879-3). This dark novel about 15-year-old Bowser's experiences in an institution for delinquent teens is set in 1969 Virginia. Lexile 850L (Rev: BL 4/15/09; SLJ 7/1/09)

5095 Bryant, Jen. *Kaleidoscope Eyes* (5–7). 2009, Knopf $15.99 (978-0-375-84048-7). In 1968 New Jersey, 13-year-old Lyza and her friends search for buried treasure; a compelling free-verse novel that conveys the tensions of the time. (Rev: BL 4/15/09; LMC 8/09; SLJ 6/09; VOYA 6/09)

5096 Burg, Shana. *A Thousand Never Evers* (7–12). 2008, Delacorte $15.99 (978-0-385-73470-7). African American Addie finds all aspects of life in her Mississippi town are affected by the civil rights movement of the 1960s. ∩ (Rev: BL 4/15/08; LMC 4–5/08*; SLJ 7/08)

5097 Cheng, Andrea. *Eclipse* (5–8). 2006, Front St $16.95 (978-1-932425-21-5). In 1952 Cincinnati, 8-year-old immigrant Peti is disappointed when his relatives arrive to live with them; his cousin is a bully and his mother still worries about her father, who cannot get out of Hungary. (Rev: BL 11/1/06)

291

5098 Coleman, Evelyn. *Freedom Train* (5–8). 2008, Simon & Schuster $15.99 (978-1-4169-5211-4). Clyde, who comes from a poor white family, stands up for himself by refusing to join his father in harassing a black family in this story set in 1947 Atlanta. (Rev: BL 2/1/08)

5099 Crowe, Chris. *Mississippi Trial, 1955* (7–12). 2002, Penguin $17.99 (978-0-8037-2745-8). The story of the racist murder in 1955 of a 14-year-old black boy called Emmett Till is told through the eyes of Hiram, a white teenager. (Rev: BCCB 4/02; BL 2/15/02; HBG 10/02; SLJ 5/02; VOYA 4/02)

5100 Crum, Shutta. *Spitting Image* (5–8). 2003, Clarion $15.00 (978-0-618-23477-6). Jessie has a busy summer in 1967 in her Kentucky hometown, tackling family problems and dealing with well-meaning volunteers and reporters who view them as "rural poor." (Rev: BL 3/1/03; HBG 10/03; SLJ 4/03*)

5101 Cushman, Karen. *The Loud Silence of Francine Green* (6–9). 2006, Clarion $16.00 (978-0-618-50455-8). Francine, an 8th-grader in a Catholic girls school in Los Angeles, befriends a headstrong, opinionated girl whose father is suspected of being a Communist in this McCarthy-era novel. ◯ (Rev: BL 7/06; HB 9–10/06; LMC 11–12/06; SLJ 8/06*)

5102 Edwardson, Debby Dahl. *My Name Is Not Easy* (7–10). 2011, Marshall Cavendish $17.99 (978-0-7614-5980-4). Inupiaq Luke and his fellow students relate their difficult experiences adapting when they submit to cultural reeducation at a Catholic boarding school in the early 1960s. ◯ e Lexile 830L (Rev: BL 9/15/11; SLJ 11/1/11*)

5103 Fawcett, Katie Pickard. *To Come and Go Like Magic* (5–8). 2010, Knopf $15.99 (978-0-375-85846-8); LB $18.99 (978-0-375-95846-5). A new teacher nurtures 12-year-old Chili Sue Mahoney's desire to leave the depressed town of Mercy Hill, in the Appalachian hills of Kentucky; set in the 1970s. e (Rev: BL 3/1/10; SLJ 2/10; VOYA 4/10)

5104 Fixmer, Elizabeth. *Saint Training* (5–7). 2010, Zondervan $14.99 (978-0-310-72018-8). In the turbulent 1960s, 6th-grader Mary Clare is the oldest in a large Catholic family and decides that sainthood will be her — and her family's — salvation. e (Rev: BL 11/15/10; SLJ 11/1/10)

5105 Flores-Galbis, Enrique. *90 Miles to Havana* (5–8). 2010, Roaring Brook $16.99 (978-1-59643-168-3). A fictionalized account of the author's experience of coming to America from Cuba in the 1960s, when he was separated from his parents and placed in a camp in Miami. Belpré Honor 2011; ALA Notable Books 2011. Lexile 790L (Rev: BL 5/1/10; LMC 8–9/10; SLJ 8/10; VOYA 12/10)

5106 Gantos, Jack. *Dead End in Norvelt* (5–8). 2011, Farrar $15.99 (978-0-374-37993-3). Grounded for the entire summer, spirited Jack, 11, finds himself helping to write obituaries and coping with small-town life full of eccentric people in this funny and thoughtful story set in 1962. Newbery Medal 2012; ALA Notable Books 2012. ◯ e Lexile 920L (Rev: BL 8/11; HB 9–10/11; LMC 11–12/11; SLJ 9/1/11)

5107 Harrar, George. *The Wonder Kid* (4–7). Illus. by Anthony Winiarski. 2006, Houghton Mifflin $16.00 (978-0-618-56317-3). As a kid growing up in the 1950s, Jesse contracts polio and with the encouragement of a friend passes the time creating a comic strip hero called the Wonder Kid. (Rev: SLJ 3/07)

5108 Hayles, Marsha. *Breathing Room* (5–9). Illus. 2012, Henry Holt $16.99 (978-0-8050-8961-5). Tuberculosis-stricken Evvy is sent to live at a remote sanatorium in this story set in 1940 against the background of war; there, she gains confidence and makes friends. e Lexile 800L (Rev: BLO 8/12; HB 7–8/12; LMC 11–12/12; SLJ 9/12)

5109 Hegedus, Bethany. *Between Us Baxters* (7–10). 2009, WestSide $17.95 (978-193481302-7). In late 1950s Georgia, 12-year-old Polly, from a struggling white family, and black 14-year-old Timbre Ann find their friendship threatened by the turmoil around them. Lexile 610L (Rev: BL 3/15/09; SLJ 5/1/09; VOYA 10/09)

5110 Hemingway, Edith M. *Road to Tater Hill* (5–8). 2009, Delacorte $16.99 (978-0-385-73677-0). In the mountains of North Carolina in 1963, 10-year-old Annie must deal with her baby sister's death, her mother who is silent and absent with grief, and her father who is overseas. (Rev: BCCB 10/09; BL 7/09; SLJ 12/09)

5111 Hemphill, Helen. *Long Gone Daddy* (8–11). 2006, Front St $16.95 (978-1-932425-38-3). Set in the late 1960s, this is the story of Harlan, a 14-year-old funeral home worker who reconciles with his hard-line-preacher father when the two take a road trip to Las Vegas to transport Harlan's grandfather's body and collect their inheritance. (Rev: BL 5/1/06; HB 11–12/06; SLJ 7/06)

5112 Hemphill, Helen. *Runaround* (5–8). 2007, Front St $16.95 (978-1-932425-83-3). In 1960s Kentucky, motherless 11-year-old Sassy needs more information about love but has trouble finding a source as her Dad is busy with other things, her housekeeper wants her just to act like a young lady, and her sister may be involved with the same handsome neighbor. (Rev: BL 3/1/07*; SLJ 4/07)

5113 Hilmo, Tess. *With a Name Like Love* (6–9). 2011, Farrar $16.99 (978-0-374-38465-4). Itinerant preacher's daughter Olivene, 13, becomes embroiled in a murder investigation in Arkansas in 1957 when she meets a poor boy whose mother is in jail. e Lexile 710L (Rev: BL 11/15/11*; HB 11–12/11; LMC 11–12/11; SLJ 10/1/11*; VOYA 10/11)

5114 Holm, Jennifer L. *Penny from Heaven* (5–8). 2006, Random House $15.95 (978-0-375-83687-9). Set in 1953, this is the story of how 12-year-old Penny gets to know her late father's lively Italian American family and comes to understand the circumstances surrounding her father's death. Newbery Honor 2007. (Rev: BL 4/15/06; HB 3–4/07; SLJ 7/06)

5115 Hostetter, Joyce Moyer. *Comfort* (6–10). 2009, Boyds Mills $17.95 (978-159078606-2). Ann Fay, although reluctant to leave her troubled family, goes to Warm Springs in Georgia to receive therapy for her polio. Lexile 680L (Rev: BLO 3/15/09; LMC 10/09; SLJ 5/1/09)

5116 Houston, Julian. *New Boy* (8–11). 2005, Houghton Mifflin $16.00 (978-0-618-43253-0). In the late 1950s, Rob Garrett, an African American teen from Virginia, is the first black student at a tony Connecticut prep school, where he learns about different forms of prejudice and watches civil rights developments in the South. (Rev: BL 11/15/05*; SLJ 3/06; VOYA 2/06)

5117 Jones, Traci L. *Finding My Place* (5–8). 2010, Farrar $16.99 (978-0-374-33573-1). In mid-1970s Denver, Tiphanie starts her freshman year as the only black girl in her school and discovers that there are other outsiders. ℮ Lexile 750L (Rev: BL 4/15/10; LMC 8–9/10; SLJ 6/10)

5118 Kadohata, Cynthia. *Kira-Kira* (6–12). 2004, Simon & Schuster $15.95 (978-0-689-85639-6). Poverty, exploitation, and racial prejudice form a backdrop to this moving story of two Japanese American sisters growing up in a small Georgia town in the late 1950s and facing the older sister's death from lymphoma. Newbery Medal, 2005. (Rev: BCCB 1/04; BL 1/1–15/04; HB 3–4/04; SLJ 3/04; VOYA 8/04)

5119 Klages, Ellen. *White Sands, Red Menace* (5–8). 2008, Viking $16.99 (978-0-670-06235-5). In this riveting sequel to *The Green Glass Sea* (2006), Dewey's father has died and she is living near Los Alamos with her friend Suze, whose father is working on a new rocket for the space race. (Rev: BL 8/08)

5120 Krisher, Trudy. *Fallout* (7–10). 2006, Holiday $17.95 (978-0-8234-2035-3). Growing up during the Cold War in a very conservative coastal town in North Carolina, Genevieve is struck by the ideas introduced by the outspoken Brenda Womper, a new student who has arrived from California. (Rev: BL 11/15/06; SLJ 11/06)

5121 Lasky, Kathryn. *Chasing Orion* (6–9). 2010, Candlewick $17.99 (978-0-7636-3982-2). In 1952 Indiana, 11-year-old Georgie comes to mistrust the affection between her older brother Emmett and their neighbor Phyllis, who has polio and is in an iron lung. Lexile 700L (Rev: BL 4/15/10; HB 7–8/10; LMC 5–6/10; SLJ 6/10)

5122 Lawrence, Iain. *Gemini Summer* (4–7). 2006, Delacorte $15.95 (978-0-385-73089-1). In the mid-1960s, soon after Danny's brother Beau dies in an accident, a stray dog appears and adopts Danny; Danny becomes devoted to the dog and, because he sees much of Beau in Rocket, he and Rocket set off for Cape Canaveral to realize Beau's dream of seeing the Gemini mission. (Rev: BL 12/15/06; SLJ 11/06)

5123 Lemna, Don. *Out in Left Field* (4–7). Illus. by Matt Collins. 2012, Holiday House $16.95 (978-082342313-2). Eleven-year-old Donald has a miserable time in 1947 and into 1948, starting with a humiliating flop in baseball and continuing through other misadventures in this funny sequel to *When the Sergeant Came Marching Home* (2008). (Rev: BL 4/1/12; SLJ 6/12)

5124 Lemna, Don. *When the Sergeant Came Marching Home* (4–7). Illus. by Matt Colins. 2008, Holiday $16.95 (978-0-8234-2083-4). Set in the 1940s, this novel of a family that moves to a farm in Montana paints a realistic picture of the hardships and joys of rural life at that time. (Rev: BL 4/15/08; SLJ 7/08)

5125 Levine, Ellen. *Catch a Tiger by the Toe* (5–8). 2005, Viking $15.99 (978-0-670-88461-2). Jamie's world is turned upside down when her father is put in jail for refusing to reveal the names of other Communists to the House Un-American Activities Committee. (Rev: BL 3/15/05*; SLJ 6/05)

5126 Levine, Ellen. *In Trouble* (8–12). 2011, Carolrhoda $17.95 (978-0-7613-6558-7). In 1950s New York two teens cope with pregnancies even as they deal with other difficulties including Jamie's father's imprisonment for refusing to name Communists. ℮ Lexile HL510L (Rev: BL 8/11; LMC 1–2/12; SLJ 8/11)

5127 Levine, Kristin. *The Lions of Little Rock* (5–8). 2012, Putnam $16.99 (978-039925644-8). In 1958 Little Rock, Arkansas, 13-year-old Marlee, who is already struggling with acute shyness, must deal with the fact that her best friend is thrown out of school because she is a light-skinned black. ∩ (Rev: BL 1/1/12; SLJ 1/12)

5128 Lurie, April. *Brothers, Boyfriends and Other Criminal Minds* (7–10). 2007, Delacorte $15.99 (978-0-385-73124-9). April is growing up in Brooklyn in the 1970s, and makes accommodations with the local Mafia partly to support her older brother. (Rev: BL 7/07; SLJ 10/07)

5129 McDowell, Marilyn Taylor. *Carolina Harmony* (4–7). 2009, Delacorte $16.99 (978-0-385-73590-2). In 1964 in the Blue Ridge Mountains 10-year-old runaway orphan Carolina begins to recover from the traumas she has experienced. (Rev: BL 2/1/09; SLJ 8/09)

5130 McGuigan, Mary Ann. *Morning in a Different Place* (8–11). 2009, Front St $17.95 (978-159078551-5). Friendship between white Fiona and black Yolanda causes problems in 1963 New York. Lexile HL710L (Rev: BL 2/1/09; LMC 8–9/09; SLJ 3/1/09; VOYA 8/09)

5131 McMullan, Margaret. *Sources of Light* (5–8). 2010, Houghton Mifflin $16 (978-054707659-1). A young African American girl copes with racial tensions when her mother moves the family from Pennsylvania to Jackson, Mississippi, after her father's death in Vietnam in 1962. **e** Lexile 840L (Rev: BL 4/15/10; HB 5–6/10; SLJ 5/10; VOYA 8/10)

5132 Madden, Kerry. *Gentle's Holler* (5–8). Series: Maggie Valley. 2005, Viking $16.99 (978-0-670-05998-0). Livy Two, part of a large, poor family living in the North Carolina mountains, learns a lesson when her father is injured. (Rev: BL 3/1/05; SLJ 6/05)

5133 Madden, Kerry. *Jessie's Mountain* (5–8). Series: Maggie Valley. 2008, Viking $16.99 (978-0-670-06154-9). Livy Two and her family are still struggling to make it in this final installment in the series, but they start to turn things around using their love of music. (Rev: BL 2/8/08; SLJ 3/08)

5134 Madden, Kerry. *Louisiana's Song* (5–8). Series: Maggie Valley. 2007, Viking $16.99 (978-0-670-06153-2). Their father is home from the hospital but cannot work, so Livy Two and her nine siblings do everything they can to support their family in this sequel to *Gentle's Holler* (2005) set in North Carolina in 1963. (Rev: BL 6/1–15/07; SLJ 8/07)

5135 Magoon, Kekla. *The Rock and the River* (6–10). 2009, Aladdin $15.99 (978-141697582-3). Fourteen-year-old Sam considers turning to violence and the Black Panthers when peaceful attempts to gain civil rights seem to fail in this novel set in 1968 Chicago. Coretta Scott King/John Steptoe New Talent Author Award Winner 2010; ALA Notable Books 2010; YALSA Amazing Audiobooks Top Ten 2011. ⌒ Lexile HL550L (Rev: BL 2/1/09*; LMC 8–9/09; SLJ 2/1/09)

5136 Manzano, Sonia. *The Revolution of Evelyn Serrano* (6–9). 2012, Scholastic $17.99 (978-0-545-32505-9). Puerto Rican Evelyn, 14, finds herself caught up in family drama surrounding the Spanish Harlem protests of 1969. Belpré Honor 2013; ALA Notable Books 2013. **e** Lexile 720L (Rev: BL 10/15/12*; HB 11–12/12; LMC 3–4/13; SLJ 11/12)

5137 Matthews, Kezi. *Scorpio's Child* (7–10). 2001, Cricket $15.95 (978-0-8126-2890-6). In South Carolina in 1947, 14-year-old Afton has difficulty welcoming a taciturn, previously unknown uncle into her home despite her mother's pleas for compassion. (Rev: BCCB 10/01; BL 9/15/01; HB 1–2/02; HBG 3/02; SLJ 10/01; VOYA 4/02)

5138 Moranville, Sharelle Byars. *A Higher Geometry* (8–11). 2006, Henry Holt $16.95 (978-0-8050-7470-3). Fifteen-year-old Anna's love for mathematics sets her apart from her peers in this thoughtful novel about romance and identity in the rural Midwest of 1959. (Rev: BL 4/15/06; SLJ 6/06)

5139 Moses, Shelia P. *The Baptism* (6–9). 2007, Simon & Schuster $15.99 (978-1-4169-0671-1). Leon and Luke must cope with the hardships that are part of being black in South Carolina in the 1940s in this companion to the author's two Buddy Bush novels. (Rev: BCCB 5/07; BL 2/1/07; LMC 10/07; SLJ 3/07)

5140 Moses, Shelia P. *The Legend of Buddy Bush* (6–9). 2004, Simon & Schuster $15.95 (978-0-689-85839-0). In this poignant, fact-based novel, 12-year-old Pattie Mae Sheals faces many challenges when her beloved Uncle Buddy is accused of the attempted rape of a white woman in 1940s North Carolina. (Rev: BCCB 4/04; BL 3/1/04; SLJ 2/04; VOYA 2/04)

5141 Nelson, Vaunda Micheaux. *No Crystal Stair* (8–12). Illus. by R. Gregory Christie. 2012, Carolrhoda $17.95 (978-076136169-5). Nelson presents the fictionalized story of her great-uncle Lewis Michaux, a hugely influential Harlem bookseller during the mid-1930s. Boston Globe–Hornbook Fiction Award Winner 2012; Coretta Scott King Author Honor Book 2013. **e** Lexile 850L (Rev: BL 2/1/12; HB 3–4/12*; LMC 5–6/12; SLJ 2/12*; VOYA 6/12)

5142 Nemeth, Sally. *The Heights, the Depths, and Everything in Between* (5–8). 2006, Knopf LB $17.99 (978-0-375-93458-2). Jake Little, a dwarf, and Lucy Small, who despite her name is unusually tall, become friends and navigate the rough waters of middle school and dealing with parents in this story set in the 1970s. (Rev: BL 7/06)

5143 Neri, G. *Yummy: The Last Days of a Southside Shorty* (8–12). Illus. by Randy DuBurke. 2010, Lee Low paper $16.95 (978-158430267-4). Yummy, an 11-year-old African American with a sweet tooth, was a gang member in Chicago in the 1990s; this graphic novel based on documented sources describes his life on the streets, his shooting of a young girl, and his death at the hands of his own gang. Coretta Scott King Author Honor 2011; ALA Notable Books 2011; YALSA Great Graphic Novels Top Ten 2011; YALSA Quick Picks for Reluctant Young Adult Readers 2011. (Rev: BL 8/10*; HB 11–12/10; SLJ 9/10; VOYA 10/10)

5144 Nolan, Han. *A Summer of Kings* (6–9). 2006, Harcourt $17.00 (978-0-15-205108-2). When her family takes in an African American man fleeing the South in the summer of 1963, 14-year-old Esther questions her own feelings and beliefs. (Rev: BL 4/15/06; SLJ 4/06*)

5145 Noonan, Brandon. *Plenty Porter* (7–10). 2006, Abrams $16.95 (978-0-8109-5996-5). Set in 1950s Illinois, this is the story of 12-year-old Plenty, the 11th child of a sharecropper, who struggles to find a sense of belonging within her family and the secretive rural community in which they live. (Rev: BL 4/15/06; LMC 11–12/06; SLJ 8/06)

5146 O'Connor, Sheila. *Keeping Safe the Stars* (5–7). 2012, Putnam $16.99 (978-0-399-25459-8). In rural Minnesota in 1974, 13-year-old Pride must look after her younger sister and brother when their grandfather is hospitalized. **e** Lexile HL650L (Rev: BL 10/15/12; LMC 3–4/13; SLJ 12/12)

5147 Paratore, Coleen Murtagh. *Dreamsleeves* (7–9). 2012, Scholastic $16.99 (978-054531020-8). In this story set in the 1960s, Aislinn, 12, nurtures her dreams of family stability (her father is an alcoholic) and greater freedom for herself and her siblings. **e** (Rev: BL 4/1/12; LMC 8–9/12; SLJ 5/1/12; VOYA 4/12)

5148 Peck, Richard. *A Season of Gifts* (5–8). 2009, Dial $16.99 (978-0-8037-3082-3). Spunky, rifle-toting Grandma Dowdel, last seen in *A Long Way from Chicago* (1998) and *A Year Down Yonder* (2000), intervenes in the life of a weak-kneed preacher's son in this tale of neighborly kindness set in 1958 small-town Illinois. ∩ Lexile 690L (Rev: BL 8/09*; HB 9–10/09; SLJ 10/09; VOYA 12/09)

5149 Pérez, L. King. *Remember as You Pass Me By* (5–8). 2007, Milkweed $16.95 (978-1-57131-677-6); paper $6.95 (978-1-57131-678-3). In 1950s Texas racial tensions come between 12-year-old Silvy Lane and her black friend Mabelee. (Rev: LMC 2/08; SLJ 11/07)

5150 Pinkney, Andrea Davis. *With the Might of Angels: The Diary of Dawnie Rae Johnson, Hadley, Virginia, 1954* (5–8). Illus. Series: Dear America. 2011, Scholastic $12.99 (978-0-545-29705-9). Dawnie Rae chronicles her life in her diary: she's 12 and has been chosen to integrate an all-white school in her town in 1954 while also facing difficulties at home. ∩ **e** (Rev: BL 9/1/11; SLJ 9/1/11)

5151 Raschke, Erik. *The Book of Samuel* (6–9). 2009, St. Martin's paper $14.99 (978-0-312-37969-8). In the early 1980s, 12-year-old Samuel tries to navigate middle school and domestic life with his religious father, feminist mother, and racist grandmother. (Rev: BL 11/15/09; SLJ 12/09)

5152 Ray, Delia. *Singing Hands* (4–7). 2006, Clarion $16.00 (978-0-618-65762-9). Gussie's parents are deaf, which means she can be even more mischievous than the average child in this book set in the 1940s American South. (Rev: BL 5/1/06; SLJ 7/06)

5153 Rodman, Mary Ann. *Yankee Girl* (4–8). 2004, Farrar $17.00 (978-0-374-38661-0). In 1964, Alice's family moves from Chicago to Mississippi and 6th-grader Alice must cope not only with the stress of a new school but also with her ambivalence about the only black girl in her class; newspaper headlines introducing each chapter keep the racial violence of the time in the reader's mind. (Rev: BL 3/1/04; SLJ 4/04)

5154 Rogers, Kenny, and Donald Davenport. *Christmas in Canaan* (5–8). 2002, HarperCollins $15.99 (978-0-06-000746-1). In 1960s Texas, after a black boy and a white boy fight on the school bus, the adults decree that the two boys must spend time together, and a difficult start ends in the boys becoming fast friends when they

help a wounded dog. (Rev: BL 11/1/02; HBG 3/03; SLJ 10/02; VOYA 4/03)

5155 Rubin, Sarah. *Someday Dancer* (6–9). 2012, Scholastic $16.99 (978-0-545-39378-2). Casey's drive to study ballet leads her to New York City and the Martha Graham School in this personal growth story set in 1959. **e** Lexile 730L (Rev: BLO 10/15/12; LMC 1–2/13; SLJ 9/12; VOYA 10/12)

5156 Schmidt, Gary D. *Okay for Now* (6–9). Illus. 2011, Clarion $16.99 (978-0-547-15260-8). In this companion to the award-winning *The Wednesday Wars* (2007), Doug Swieteck's family moves to Marysville, NY, where the 8th-grader must cope with a new school, his brother Doug's nefarious activities, his father's drunkenness, and an injured brother returning from Vietnam — but a teacher and a library and Broadway (!) offer him some hope. ALA Notable Books 2012; Odyssey Honor Recording 2012. ∩ **e** Lexile 850L (Rev: BL 4/15/11; HB 5–6/11; LMC 8–9/11; SLJ 4/11*; VOYA 6/11)

5157 Schmidt, Gary D. *The Wednesday Wars* (6–9). 2007, Clarion $16.00 (978-0-618-72483-3). In suburban Long Island during the late 1960s, Presbyterian 7th-grader Holling Hoodhood must spend Wednesday afternoons alone with his teacher while his Jewish and Catholic classmates attend religious instruction, and she teaches him about Shakespeare, life, and stretching beyond his limits. Newbery Honor 2008; ALA Notable Books 2008. (Rev: BL 6/1–15/07; HB 7–8/07)

5158 Shank, Marilyn Sue. *Child of the Mountains* (4–7). 2012, Delacorte $16.99 (978-038574079-1); LB $19.99 (978-037598969-8). In rural Appalachia in 1953, Lydia, 11, confides in her diary as she struggles to come to terms with her brother's death from cystic fibrosis and her mother's stint in jail. **e** (Rev: BL 4/15/12; LMC 8–9/12; SLJ 5/1/12)

5159 Sharenow, Robert. *My Mother the Cheerleader* (7–10). 2007, HarperCollins $16.99 (978-0-06-114896-5). Louise's mother pulls her out of school when young African American Ruby Bridges enrolls in their New Orleans school district in 1960. (Rev: BCCB 9/07; BL 7/07; LMC 10/07; SLJ 7/07)

5160 Shimko, Bonnie. *The Private Thoughts of Amelia E. Rye* (5–8). 2010, Farrar $16.99 (978-0-374-36131-0). Abandoned by her father before birth and feeling unloved by her mother, Amelia finds a friend in Fancy Nelson, a feisty girl who is the first African American in Amelia's class; set in upstate New York in the 1960s. **e** Lexile 790L (Rev: BL 4/15/10*; LMC 5–6/10; SLJ 4/10)

5161 Slayton, Fran Cannon. *When the Whistle Blows* (6–9). 2009, Philomel $16.99 (978-039925189-4). Looking at Halloween over a period of seven years, this novel follows the life and development of young Jimmy Cannon, growing up in a railroad town in West Virginia in the 1940s. ⌒ **e** (Rev: BL 7/09; SLJ 6/1/09*; VOYA 10/09)

5162 Smiley, Jane. *The Georges and the Jewels* (4–8). Illus. by Elaine Clayton. 2009, Knopf $16.99 (978-0-375-86227-4); LB $19.99 (978-0-375-96227-1). Twelve-year-old Abby cares for her family's horses as a way of escaping isolation, family drama, and her father's strict religious views in 1960s California. **e** Lexile 970L (Rev: BL 9/15/09; HB 11–12/09; SLJ 10/09)

5163 Smith, D. James. *The Boys of San Joaquin* (5–8). 2005, Simon & Schuster $15.95 (978-0-689-87606-6). An episodic tale set in the 1950s, in which 12-year-old Paolo describes events of his life and a mystery involving a half-eaten $20 bill. (Rev: BL 3/1/05; SLJ 1/05)

5164 Smith, D. James. *Probably the World's Best Story About a Dog and the Girl Who Loved Me* (5–8). 2006, Simon & Schuster $15.95 (978-1-4169-0542-4). In 1951 California, 12-year-old Paolo's beloved dog Rufus is dognapped and he enlists the help of his younger brother and a deaf cousin to unravel the mystery while also coping with a new paper route and a budding romance; this sequel to *The Boys of San Joaquin* (2004) introduces a sign language word with each chapter. (Rev: BL 9/1/06; SLJ 8/06)

5165 Sullivan, Jacqueline Levering. *Annie's War* (4–7). 2007, Eerdmans $15.00 (978-0-8028-5325-7). In 1946, 10-year-old Annie is having a hard time coping with her father's MIA status and her 19-year-old uncle's emotional problems, and she finds some comfort in imagined conversations with President Truman. (Rev: BL 8/07; SLJ 9/07)

5166 Vanderpool, Clare. *Navigating Early* (5–8). 2013, Delacorte $16.99 (978-038574209-2); LB $19.99 (978-037599040-3). Sent from Kansas to a boarding school in Maine after his mother's death, Jack has trouble adjusting and joins a strange boy named Early in an eventful trek along the Appalachian Trail tracking a bear. ⌒ **e** Lexile 790L (Rev: BL 12/15/12*; HB 3–4/13; SLJ 3/13*)

5167 Wallace, Rich. *War and Watermelon* (5–8). 2011, Viking $15.99 (978-0-670-01152-0). In 1969, 12-year-old Brody longs to make the football team, goes to Woodstock, and mediates between his older brother and his father on the subject of Vietnam; presented in a first-person, diary format. **e** Lexile 630L (Rev: BL 7/11; LMC 11–12/11; SLJ 7/11)

5168 Watkins, Steve. *Down Sand Mountain* (7–12). 2008, Candlewick $16.99 (978-0-7636-3839-9). A loss-of-innocence story set in 1966, simply yet beautifully told, in which a 12-year-old boy discovers the cruelty of racism in his small Florida hometown. (Rev: BL 8/08)

5169 White, Ruth. *Little Audrey* (5–8). 2008, Farrar $16.00 (978-0-374-34580-8). Using the voice of her older sister, the author describes their family life in the late 1940s; 11-year-old Audrey must cope with her own physical problems, her father's drinking, her mother's emotional absence, and her three needy little sisters. (Rev: BL 9/1/08*; SLJ 9/08*; VOYA 8/08)

5170 White, Ruth. *Way Down Deep* (4–7). 2007, Farrar $16.00 (978-0-374-38251-3). In 1944 West Virginia, the arrival of a new family in a town called Way Down Deep suddenly raises questions about the origins of Ruby June, a foundling who has lived there for 10 years. (Rev: BL 3/1/07; SLJ 4/07)

5171 Whittenberg, Allison. *Hollywood and Maine* (5–8). 2009, Delacorte $15.99 (978-0-385-73671-8). When her jailbird uncle shows up to displace her from her attic bedroom, 14-year-old Maine Upshaw puts her energy into winning a beauty contest and steps on a lot of toes in this sequel to *Sweet Thang* (2006) set in the 1970s. (Rev: BCCB 3/09; BL 2/1/09; SLJ 2/09)

5172 Wiles, Deborah. *Countdown* (5–7). Series: Sixties Trilogy. 2010, Scholastic $17.99 (978-0-545-10605-4). In October 1962 life is tense for 11-year-old Franny, whose father is a fighter pilot, as relations between the United States and the Soviet Union become increasingly strained; extracts from songs and speeches, plus black-and-white photographs, add to readers' understanding. ALA Notable Books 2011. ⌒ Lexile 800L (Rev: BL 5/1/10*; HB 5–6/10; LMC 10/10; SLJ 7/10)

5173 Williams Garcia, Rita. *One Crazy Summer* (4–7). 2010, Amistad $15.99 (978-0-06-076088-5); LB $16.89 (978-0-06-076089-2). African American Delphine, 11, and her younger sisters are sent from Brooklyn to visit the mother who abandoned them and moved to California; there they find little welcome and spend time at a community center run by the Black Panthers. Newbery Honor 2011; Scott O'Dell Award for Historical Fiction; Coretta Scott King Award; ALA Notable Books 2011; YALSA Amazing Audiobooks Top Ten 2011. ⌒ **e** Lexile 750L (Rev: BL 2/1/10*; HB 3–4/10; LMC 3–4/10; SLJ 3/10)

5174 Wittlinger, Ellen. *This Means War!* (5–8). 2010, Simon & Schuster $16.99 (978-1-4169-7101-6). After her best friend Lowell abandons her for the company of boys, 10-year-old Juliet befriends Polly, and the girls become intent on challenging the boys to increasingly risky and dangerous tests of will in this story set during the Cold War. Lexile 740L (Rev: BL 2/1/10; HB 5–6/10; SLJ 4/10)

5175 Wolf, Elaine. *Camp* (7–10). 2012, Sky Pony $16.95 (978-161608657-2). In the early 1960s, 14-year-old Amy suffers bullying at Camp Takawanda for Girls but decides not to report this to her troubled home. ⌒ **e** (Rev: BLO 9/15/12; LMC 1–2/13; SLJ 1/13; VOYA 12/12)

5176 Woods, Brenda. *The Red Rose Box* (5–8). 2002, Putnam $16.99 (978-0-399-23702-7). In 1953, Leah, a southern black girl, and her family travel to Los Angeles where they find a different culture and more progressive attitudes. (Rev: BCCB 7–8/02; BL 6/1–15/02; HBG 10/02; SLJ 6/02; VOYA 6/02)

Twentieth-Century Wars

WORLD WAR I

5177 Frost, Helen. *Crossing Stones* (7–12). 2009, Farrar $16.99 (978-0-374-31653-2). Siblings Muriel and Ollie and their friends Emma and Frank describe in heartfelt, evocative verse their experiences as the young men leave for World War I and Muriel and Emma take separate paths toward womanhood. ♫ (Rev: BL 10/1/09*; HB 11–12/09; LMC 11–12/09; SLJ 10/09; VOYA 10/09)

5178 Hamley, Dennis. *Without Warning: Ellen's Story, 1914-1918* (7–12). 2007, Candlewick $17.99 (978-0-7636-3338-7). World War I hits close to home for Ellen, whose brother is wounded and boyfriend is killed in the fighting; she later works as a nurse on the front, ministering to English soldiers and even a German prisoner of war. Although long, this first-person narrative is very readable. (Rev: BL 10/1/07; SLJ 2/08)

5179 Hartnett, Sonya. *The Silver Donkey* (5–8). Illus. by Don Powers. 2006, Candlewick $15.99 (978-0-7636-2937-3). Two young French children find and help a wounded World War I soldier in the woods near their home, and as he heals he tells them stories about the tiny silver donkey he carries with him. (Rev: BL 11/15/06; SLJ 12/06)

5180 Jorgensen, Norman. *In Flanders Fields* (4–7). Illus. by Brian Harrison Lever. 2002, Fremantle Arts Centre $22.95 (978-1-86368-369-2). During a Christmas Day ceasefire in the World War I trenches, a soldier rescues a trapped robin. (Rev: SLJ 2/03)

5181 Lottridge, Celia Barker. *Home Is Beyond the Mountains* (7–10). 2010, Groundwood $16.95 (978-0-88899-932-0). A moving story, based on the experiences of the author's aunt, about Assyrian children who become orphaned refugees during World War I. Lexile 680L (Rev: BL 4/15/10; LMC 8–9/10; SLJ 4/10)

5182 McKay, Sharon E. *Charlie Wilcox* (5–8). 2000, Stoddart paper $7.95 (978-0-7737-6093-6). This is the story of a 14-year-old Canadian boy who becomes involved in the trench warfare in France during World War I. (Rev: SLJ 11/00)

5183 Magorian, Michelle. *Good Night, Mr. Tom* (7–9). 1981, HarperCollins paper $7.99 (978-0-06-440174-6). A quiet recluse takes in an abused 8-year-old who has been evacuated from World War II London.

5184 Morpurgo, Michael. *Private Peaceful* (7–12). 2004, Scholastic $16.95 (978-0-439-63648-3). Fifteen-year-old Thomas, who lied about his age to follow his beloved older brother into combat in World War I, reflects on the life he left behind in England and the hor-

rors of life on the front lines. (Rev: BL 10/1/04*; SLJ 11/04; VOYA 12/04)

5185 Morpurgo, Michael. *War Horse* (5–8). 2007, Scholastic $16.99 (978-0-439-79663-7). This gripping tale of World War I and all its horrors is told from the point of view of Joey, an English farm horse that's been drafted for service on the battlefront. (Rev: BL 4/1/07)

5186 Schroder, Monika. *My Brother's Shadow* (7–12). 2011, Farrar $16.99 (978-0-374-35122-9). In 1918 Berlin 16-year-old Moritz struggles to feed and care for his family even as he worries about their conflicting political views. **e** (Rev: BL 10/1/11; LMC 11–12/11*; SLJ 11/1/11)

5187 Sedgwick, Marcus. *The Foreshadowing* (8–11). 2006, Random House LB $18.99 (978-0-385-90881-8). Plagued by premonitions about her brother, 17-year-old Sasha signs up as a nurse so that she can look for him on the grim battlefields of World War I France. (Rev: BL 4/1/06*; SLJ 7/06)

5188 Slade, Arthur. *Megiddo's Shadow* (8–11). 2006, Random House $15.95 (978-0-385-74701-1). Edward, a 16-year-old Canadian, enlists in the army to avenge his brother's death and ends up fighting in a bloody battle against the Turks in this World War I novel. (Rev: BL 12/15/06; HB 11–12/06; SLJ 12/06*)

5189 Spillebeen, Geert. *Kipling's Choice* (7–10). Trans. by Terese Edelstein. 2005, Houghton Mifflin $16.00 (978-0-618-43124-3). In this fictionalized biography of John Kipling, the son of the world-famous British author uses his father's influence to get into the army despite his poor eyesight, giving the teen a chance to do battle with the "barbaric Huns" in World War I. (Rev: BCCB 6/05; BL 5/15/05; SLJ 6/05; VOYA 12/05)

5190 Wilson, John. *And in the Morning* (8–12). 2003, Kids Can $16.95 (978-1-55337-400-8). This absorbing story of fighting in the trenches of World War I, told in diary form by a teenage boy, is enhanced by newspaper headlines and clippings. (Rev: BL 3/15/03; HBG 10/03; SLJ 6/03)

WORLD WAR II AND THE HOLOCAUST

5191 Adler, David A. *Don't Talk to Me About the War* (4–7). 2008, Viking $15.99 (978-0-670-06307-9). Tommy tries hard to ignore the problems overseas and at home in this novel set in the Bronx in 1940. (Rev: BL 4/15/08; SLJ 3/08)

5192 Atlema, Martha. *A Time to Choose* (8–12). 1995, Orca paper $7.95 (978-1-55143-045-4). While growing up in Holland under the Nazi occupation, 16-year-old Johannes tries to separate himself from his father, who is considered a collaborator. (Rev: VOYA 10/97)

5193 Avi. *Who Was That Masked Man, Anyway?* (5–7). 1992, Orchard LB $17.99 (978-0-531-08607-0). In a story told through dialogue, 6th-grader Frankie lives through World War II by immersing himself in his beloved radio serials. (Rev: BCCB 10/92*; BL 8/92*; HB 3–4/93; SLJ 10/92*)

5194 Barrow, Randi. *Saving Zasha* (4–7). 2011, Scholastic $16.99 (978-0-545-20632-7). In Russia at the end of World War II, a young boy finds a beautiful German shepherd in the woods, and becomes determined to shield the dog from the anti-German sentiment that is running rampant. ⌒ (Rev: BL 2/1/11; SLJ 4/11)

5195 Bartoletti, Susan Campbell. *The Boy Who Dared* (6–12). 2008, Scholastic $16.99 (978-0-439-68013-4). This compelling story of a German teenager who was executed for resisting the Nazis is based on a true story. (Rev: BL 2/15/08; SLJ 5/08)

5196 Bawden, Nina. *Carrie's War* (6–9). 1973, HarperCollins LB $14.89 (978-0-397-31450-8). Carrie relives her days during World War II when she and her brothers were evacuated to Wales. (Rev: BL 3/1/88)

5197 Benchley, Nathaniel. *Bright Candles: A Novel of the Danish Resistance* (6–9). 1974, HarperCollins $13.95 (978-0-06-020461-7). The Danish underground during World War II. (Rev: BL 7/88)

5198 Bloor, Edward. *London Calling* (6–9). 2006, Knopf $16.95 (978-0-375-83635-0). Seventh-grader Martin Conway travels back to World War II-era London and uncovers hidden truths about the past while at the same time dealing in the present with problems plaguing his father; this is a multilayered novel combining magical realism and history. (Rev: BL 7/06; LMC 1/07; SLJ 9/06)

5199 Boyne, John. *The Boy in the Striped Pajamas: A Fable* (7–10). 2006, Random House $15.95 (978-0-385-75106-3). The 9-year old son of a Nazi commandant befriends a Jewish boy he meets through the fence of a concentration camp. (Rev: BL 7/06; HB 9–10/06; LMC 1/07; SLJ 9/06)

5200 Bruchac, Joseph. *Code Talker* (6–9). 2005, Dial $16.99 (978-0-8037-2921-6). This inspiring novel chronicles the experiences of one of the Navajo code talkers who played a crucial role in the American victory in World War II. (Rev: BCCB 2/05; BL 2/15/05*; SLJ 5/05; VOYA 4/05)

5201 Buckvar, Felice. *Dangerous Dream* (6–9). 1998, Fireworks paper $9.99 (978-0-88092-277-7). In postwar Germany, 13-year-old Hella, a concentration camp survivor, mistakenly believes that a new arrival in the infirmary is her father. (Rev: SLJ 4/99; VOYA 8/99)

5202 Bunting, Eve. *Spying on Miss Miller* (6–8). 1995, Clarion $15.00 (978-0-395-69172-4). During World War II in Belfast, Jessie, 13, believes her half-German teacher is a spy. (Rev: BL 3/15/95*; SLJ 5/95)

5203 Calkhoven, Laurie. *Michael at the Invasion of France, 1943* (4–7). 2012, Dial $16.99 (978-080373724-2). Michael, 13, finds ways to contribute to the Resistance in Nazi-occupied France. ℮ Lexile 660L (Rev: BL 2/1/12; SLJ 3/12)

5204 Casanova, Mary. *The Klipfish Code* (4–7). 2007, Houghton Mifflin $16.00 (978-0-618-88393-6). Marit and her brother Lars struggle under the restrictions of Nazi-occupied Norway in this action- and suspense-filled novel. (Rev: BL 10/15/07; SLJ 10/07)

5205 Chan, Gillian. *A Foreign Field* (7–10). 2002, Kids Can $16.95 (978-1-55337-349-0). Friendship develops into love for 14-year-old Ellen and a young British pilot who is training at an air base near her home in Canada. (Rev: BCCB 12/02; BL 9/15/02; HBG 3/03; SLJ 11/02; VOYA 2/03)

5206 Chapman, Fern Schumer. *Is It Night or Day?* (6–10). 2010, Farrar $17.99 (978-0-374-17744-7). In 1938, 12-year-old Edith's German Jewish parents send her to Chicago where she leads a miserable, anxious life apart from her fondness for baseball; this story is based on the life of the author's mother. ℮ (Rev: BL 2/1/10*; LMC 5–6/10; SLJ 5/10)

5207 Cheng, Andrea. *Marika* (7–12). 2002, Front St $16.95 (978-1-886910-78-2). Marika's earlier preoccupations disappear when the arrival of Nazis in 1944 Budapest changes her life. (Rev: BL 11/15/02; HB 11–12/02; HBG 3/03; SLJ 12/02; VOYA 2/03)

5208 Chotjewitz, David. *Daniel, Half Human: And the Good Nazi* (7–12). Trans. by Doris Orgel. 2004, Simon & Schuster $17.95 (978-0-689-85747-8). Daniel and Armin, best friends in Germany in the early 1930s, both admire Hitler, but their friendship is tested when Daniel learns that he is half-Jewish. Sidney Taylor Book Honor 2004. (Rev: BL 9/15/04; SLJ 12/04)

5209 Clark, Kathy. *Guardian Angel House* (5–8). Series: Holocaust Remembrance. 2009, Second Story paper $14.95 (978-1-897187-58-6). Two Jewish sisters — 12-year-old Susan and 6-year-old Vera — find a safe haven from the Nazis in the Guardian Angel House, a Catholic convent in Budapest; based on the experiences of the author's aunt. (Rev: SLJ 2/10; VOYA 2/10)

5210 Coerr, Eleanor. *Mieko and the Fifth Treasure* (4–7). 2003, Puffin paper $5.99 (978-0-698-11990-1). A Japanese girl believes that she will never draw again after she is injured during the atomic bomb attack on Nagasaki. (Rev: BCCB 4/93; BL 4/1/93*; SLJ 7/93)

5211 Copeland, Cynthia. *Elin's Island* (5–7). 2003, Millbrook LB $22.90 (978-0-7613-2522-2). Raised since infancy by lighthouse keepers, 13-year-old Elin is left on her own to tend the house and light on an eventful night in 1941. (Rev: BL 3/15/03; HBG 10/03; SLJ 7/03)

5212 Couloumbis, Audrey, and Akila Couloumbis. *War Games: A Novel Based on a True Story* (4–7). 2009, Random House $16.99 (978-0-375-85628-0); LB $19.99 (978-0-375-95628-7). In Greece in 1941, adventuresome Petros and his family must hide their ties to America when a Nazi commandant comes to live at their house. **e** Lexile 710L (Rev: BL 10/1/09; HB 11–12/09; LMC 11–12/09; SLJ 10/09)

5213 Davies, Jacqueline. *Where the Ground Meets the Sky* (6–9). 2002, Marshall Cavendish $14.95 (978-0-7614-5105-1). During World War II, 12-year-old Hazel lives a lonely life in a compound in the New Mexico desert while her father works on a top secret project, until she makes a friend and uncovers a secret. (Rev: BL 9/1/02; HBG 10/02; SLJ 4/02)

5214 DeJong, Meindert. *The House of Sixty Fathers* (6–9). Illus. by Maurice Sendak. 1956, HarperCollins LB $17.89 (978-0-06-021481-4); paper $5.95 (978-0-06-440200-2). In war-torn China, a young boy searches for his family as the Japanese invade his country.

5215 Dowswell, Paul. *The Auslander* (7–10). 2011, Bloomsbury $16.99 (978-1-59990-633-1). Thirteen-year-old Peter's Aryan features make him an attractive adoptee but when he settles into his new home in Berlin and membership in the Hitler Youth, he discovers his distaste for the Nazi party and, with his friend Anna, works against them. **e** Lexile 760L (Rev: BL 5/1/11; HB 9–10/11; LMC 8–9/11*; SLJ 9/1/11)

5216 Drucker, Malka, and Michael Halperin. *Jacob's Rescue: A Holocaust Story* (6–10). 1993, Dell paper $4.99 (978-0-440-40965-6). The fictionalized true story of two Jewish children saved from the Holocaust in Poland by "righteous Gentiles." (Rev: BL 2/15/93; SLJ 5/93)

5217 Dudley, David L. *Caleb's Wars* (8–12). 2011, Clarion $16.99 (978-0-547-23997-2). In 1944 rural Georgia 15-year-old African American Caleb forms a friendship with a young German P.O.W. **e** Lexile HL600L (Rev: BL 10/1/11; SLJ 11/1/11; VOYA 10/11)

5218 Durbin, William. *The Winter War* (6–9). 2008, Random House $15.99 (978-0-385-74652-6). When Russia invades Finland during World War II, Marko — who is an excellent skier despite his crippled leg — enlists in the Junior Civil Guard and endures unspeakable horrors in the winter of 1939-1940. (Rev: BL 11/15/07; LMC 4–5/08; SLJ 3/08)

5219 Elmer, Robert. *Into the Flames* (5–7). Series: Young Underground. 1995, Bethany paper $5.99 (978-1-55661-376-0). Danish twins are captured by the Gestapo while trying to rescue their uncle during World War II. (Rev: BL 5/15/95; SLJ 8/95)

5220 Engle, Margarita. *Tropical Secrets: Holocaust Refugees in Cuba* (7–11). 2009, Henry Holt $16.95 (978-080508936-3). Paloma, a Cuban girl, and Daniel, a German Jew who fled to Cuba to escape the Nazis, become friends in this story told in verse. Sydney Taylor Book Award 2010. ⌒ **e** Lexile 1170L (Rev: BL 1/1–15/09; LMC 10/09; SLJ 6/1/09*; VOYA 4/09)

5221 Fitzmaurice, Kathryn. *A Diamond in the Desert* (5–8). 2012, Viking $16.99 (978-067001292-3). A young boy at a Japanese internment camp in 1942 gets so caught up in building a baseball diamond that he abandons his younger sister, which has serious consequences. (Rev: BL 3/15/12; LMC 8–9/12; SLJ 2/12)

5222 Flood, Nancy Bo. *Warriors in the Crossfire* (6–9). 2010, Front St $17.95 (978-1-59078-661-1). On the island of Saipan toward the end of World War II, 13-year-old Joseph and his cousin Kento find themselves caught between Japanese and American forces. **e** Lexile HL560L (Rev: BL 4/15/10*; LMC 10/10; SLJ 5/10)

5223 Fox, Robert Barlow. *To Be a Warrior* (6–9). 1997, Sunstone paper $12.95 (978-0-86534-253-8). A Navajo boy joins the marines after the bombing of Pearl Harbor and becomes one of the celebrated "code talkers." (Rev: BL 9/1/97)

5224 Friedman, D. Dina. *Escaping into the Night* (7–10). 2006, Simon & Schuster $14.95 (978-1-4169-0258-4). Based on true events, this is the story of Halina Rudowski's escape into the forest during a Nazi roundup of Jews, and her subsequent efforts to survive. (Rev: BL 1/1–15/06; SLJ 3/06; VOYA 4/06)

5225 Giff, Patricia Reilly. *Lily's Crossing* (5–8). 1997, Delacorte $15.95 (978-0-385-32142-6). During World War II, motherless Lily loses her father when he is sent to fight in France but becomes friendly with Albert, an orphaned Hungarian refugee. (Rev: BCCB 4/97; BL 2/1/97; HB 3–4/97; SLJ 2/97)

5226 Glatshteyn, Yankev. *Emil and Karl* (5–8). Ed. by Jeffrey Shandler. 2006, Roaring Brook $16.95 (978-1-59643-119-5). Two 9-year-old friends — one Jewish, one Aryan — try to elude the Nazis on the streets of Vienna shortly after Germany's invasion; a fast-paced, moving story initially published in 1940. (Rev: BL 4/15/06; SLJ 6/06*; VOYA 4/06)

5227 Gleitzman, Morris. *Once* (7–10). 2010, Henry Holt $16.99 (978-0-8050-9026-0). After living in a Catholic orphanage for four years, young Felix, a Polish Jew, runs away to find his parents and experiences directly the horrors of the Holocaust. Sydney Taylor Book Honor 2011. ⌒ **e** (Rev: BL 2/15/10; HB 3–4/10; SLJ 4/10)

5228 Gleitzman, Morris. *Then* (7–10). 2011, Henry Holt $16.99 (978-0-8050-9027-7). In 1942 Poland Felix, 10, and Zelda, 6, struggle to survive in the countryside after escaping from a train headed to a death camp; the sequel to *Once* (2010). Sydney Taylor Book Honor 2012. ⌒ **e** (Rev: BL 4/15/11; HB 5–6/11; SLJ 6/11*)

5229 Graber, Janet. *Resistance* (7–10). 2005, Marshall Cavendish $15.95 (978-0-7614-5214-0). In this suspenseful World War II novel, 15-year-old Marianne reluctantly joins her mother and brother in fighting for the French Resistance despite her fears that they will be found out by the German soldier billeted in their home. (Rev: BCCB 6/05; BL 5/15/05; SLJ 8/05)

5230 Graff, Nancy Price. *Taking Wing* (5–8). 2005, Clarion $15.00 (978-0-618-53591-0). A multilayered story set in 1942 Vermont and featuring 13-year-old Gus, who, over the course of the book, learns about prejudice, and about killing and death. (Rev: BL 5/15/05*; SLJ 5/05)

5231 Griffis, Molly Levite. *The Feester Filibuster* (4–8). 2002, Eakin $17.95 (978-1-57168-541-4); paper $8.95 (978-1-57168-694-7). John Allen Feester is determined to show he's not a spy in this sequel to *The Rachel Resistance* (2001). (Rev: BL 11/1/02; HBG 10/01)

5232 Gwaltney, Doris. *Homefront* (5–8). 2006, Simon & Schuster $15.95 (978-0-689-86842-9). A young girl must cope with the diverse effects of World War II on her Virginia farming family. (Rev: BCCB 10/06; BL 7/06; SLJ 7/06*)

5233 Hahn, Mary Downing. *Stepping on the Cracks* (5–8). 1991, Houghton Mifflin $16.00 (978-0-395-58507-8); paper $5.99 (978-0-380-71900-6). The compelling story of a 6th-grade girl during World War II and her difficult decision whether to help a pacifist deserter. (Rev: BCCB 12/91*; BL 10/15/91*; HB 11–12/91; SLJ 12/91*)

5234 Harlow, Joan Hiatt. *Shadows on the Sea* (7–10). 2003, Simon & Schuster $16.95 (978-0-689-84926-8). Fourteen-year-old Jill, staying with her grandmother in Maine in 1942, finds a pigeon carrying a message in German and suspects U-boats may be close. (Rev: BL 9/15/03; HBG 4/04; SLJ 9/03)

5235 Hertenstein, Jane. *Beyond Paradise* (6–10). 1999, Morrow $16.00 (978-0-688-16381-5). This historical novel recounts the horrors of life in Japanese internment camps in the Pacific during World War II as seen through the eyes of a missionary's daughter. (Rev: BCCB 9/99; BL 8/99; HBG 4/00; SLJ 9/99)

5236 Hinton, Nigel. *Time Bomb* (5–8). 2006, Tricycle $15.95 (978-1-58246-186-1). Coming of age in post-World War II London, four 12-year-old friends who have lost their trust in adults discover an unexploded German bomb and set in motion a chain of events. (Rev: SLJ 12/06)

5237 Hostetter, Joyce Moyer. *Blue* (4–7). 2006, Boyds Mills $16.95 (978-1-59078-389-4). When her father leaves for World War II, Ann Fay, the oldest of four children, struggles to keep up with the chores in their North Carolina home until polio strikes the community. (Rev: BL 2/15/06; SLJ 6/06)

5238 Hughes, Dean. *Missing in Action* (6–9). 2010, Simon & Schuster $16.99 (978-1-4169-1502-7). Jay, a part-Navajo 12-year-old who has experienced prejudice himself yet maintains some of his own, makes many mental adjustments when his father goes missing in World War II, and Jay befriends Ken, an interned Japanese American boy. Lexile HL620L (Rev: BL 2/15/10; LMC 5–6/10; SLJ 3/10)

5239 Hughes, Dean. *Soldier Boys* (7–9). 2001, Simon & Schuster $16.00 (978-0-689-81748-9). Parallel stories follow two teenage boys — one American, one German — through the horrors of World War II and the Battle of the Bulge. (Rev: BCCB 3/02; HB 1–2/02; HBG 3/02; SLJ 11/01; VOYA 2/02)

5240 Hull, Nancy L. *On Rough Seas* (6–9). 2008, Clarion $16.00 (978-0-618-89743-8). Alec becomes a galley boy on the *Britannia* to prove himself to his father and ends up helping in the evacuation at Dunkirk early in World War II. (Rev: BL 4/15/08; SLJ 5/08)

5241 Hunter, Bernice Thurman. *The Girls They Left Behind* (7–10). 2005, Fitzhenry & Whiteside paper $9.95 (978-1-55041-927-6). This coming-of-age novel, set in Toronto against the backdrop of World War II, paints a vivid portrait of what life was like for the teenage girls left behind on the home front. (Rev: BCCB 7–8/05; BL 5/15/05; SLJ 8/05; VOYA 8/05)

5242 Kacer, Kathy. *The Night Spies* (4–7). 2003, Second Story paper $5.95 (978-1-896764-70-2). Hiding from the Nazis, Gabi and her family can leave their cramped quarters only at night, but Gabi and her cousin Max manage to help the partisans. (Rev: BL 1/1–15/04; SLJ 3/04)

5243 Kadohata, Cynthia. *Weedflower* (5–8). 2006, Simon & Schuster $16.95 (978-0-689-86574-9). Sumiko and her Japanese American family are moved from their California flower farm to an internment camp in Arizona after the attack on Pearl Harbor; there she grows a garden and befriends a local Mojave boy. ∩ (Rev: BL 4/15/06*; HB 7–8/06; SLJ 7/06*)

5244 Klages, Ellen. *The Green Glass Sea* (4–7). 2006, Viking $16.99 (978-0-670-06134-1). In 1943, talented 10-year-old Dewey goes to live with her father at the Los Alamos compound, a tense place where she initially has trouble making friends. ∩ (Rev: BL 11/15/06; SLJ 11/06)

5245 Kositsky, Lynne. *The Thought of High Windows* (8–12). 2004, Kids Can $16.95 (978-1-55337-621-7). A Jewish refugee named Esther describes her experiences in France during World War II — lice and other discomforts, loneliness, longing for her family, her differences from the other refugees — and her involvement in the Resistance in this affecting novel based on true events. (Rev: HB 5–6/04; SLJ 5/04)

5246 Larson, Kirby. *The Fences Between Us: The Diary of Piper Davis* (4–7). Series: Dear America. 2010, Scholastic $12.99 (978-0-545-22418-5); LB $16.99 (978-0-545-26232-3). Thirteen-year-old Piper describes in her diary the many changes that take place in her life starting in December 1941. (Rev: BL 7/10; SLJ 12/1/10; VOYA 10/10)

5247 Levitin, Sonia. *Journey to America* (5–8). Illus. by Charles Robinson. 1970, Macmillan paper $4.99 (978-0-689-71130-5). A Jewish mother and her three daughters flee Nazi Germany in 1938 and undertake a long and difficult journey to join their father in America. (Rev: BL 9/1/93)

5248 LeZotte, Ann Clare. *T4* (6–9). 2008, Houghton Mifflin $14.00 (978-054704684-6). When Paula, a deaf 13-year-old, learns of Hitler's decree that all disabled people must be euthanized, she goes into hiding; this short read is told in spare free verse. ℮ (Rev: BL 11/15/08; SLJ 9/1/08)

5249 Lowry, Lois. *Number the Stars* (5–7). 1989, Houghton Mifflin $16.00 (978-0-395-51060-5); paper $5.99 (978-0-440-40327-2). The story of war-torn Denmark and best friends Annemarie Johansen and Ellen Rosen. Newbery Medal 1990. (Rev: BCCB 3/89; BL 3/1/89; SLJ 3/89)

5250 McRobbie, David. *Vinnie's War* (5–8). Illus. 2012, IPG/Allen & Unwin paper $14.99 (978-17423757-6-2). Vinnie, 13, has trouble adjusting when he is evacuated from London to the country in World War II, but his music and some new friends bring him comfort. ℮ (Rev: BLO 8/12; SLJ 1/13)

5251 McSwigan, Marie. *Snow Treasure* (4–7). Illus. by Andre Le Blanc. 1986, Scholastic paper $4.99 (978-0-590-42537-7). Children smuggle gold out of occupied Norway on their sleds.

5252 Manley, Joan B. *She Flew No Flags* (7–10). 1995, Houghton Mifflin $16.00 (978-0-395-71130-9). A strongly autobiographical World War II novel about a 10-year-old's voyage from India to her new home in the United States and the people she meets on the ship. (Rev: BL 3/15/95; SLJ 4/95; VOYA 5/95)

5253 Matas, Carol. *Daniel's Story* (6–9). 1994, Scholastic paper $6.99 (978-0-590-46588-5). In this companion to an exhibit at the U.S. Holocaust Memorial Museum, Daniel symbolizes the millions of young people who suffered or died under Hitler's regime. (Rev: BL 5/15/93)

5254 Matas, Carol. *The Whirlwind* (6–9). 2007, Orca paper $8.95 (978-1-55143-703-3). Ben, a young German Jew, survives World War II and arrives in Seattle only to be faced with discrimination and hardship there. (Rev: BCCB 7–8/07; BL 3/1/07; SLJ 5/07)

5255 Mazer, Harry. *A Boy at War: A Novel of Pearl Harbor* (7–9). 2001, Simon & Schuster $15.00 (978-0-689-84161-3). Young Adam Pelko, new to Honolulu, is pressed into action on the morning of the attack on Pearl Harbor while trying to find his father, in this absorbing novel that also looks at relations with Japanese Americans. (Rev: BL 4/1/01; HB 5–6/01; HBG 10/01; SLJ 5/01; VOYA 6/01)

5256 Mazer, Harry. *A Boy No More* (7–9). 2004, Simon & Schuster $15.95 (978-0-689-85533-7). In this poignant sequel to *A Boy at War*, Adam Pelko, who lost his father in the Japanese bombing of Pearl Harbor, moves with his mother and sister from Hawaii to California

where a Japanese American friend's request presents Adam with a moral dilemma. (Rev: BL 9/1/04; SLJ 9/04)

5257 Mazer, Harry. *Heroes Don't Run: A Novel of the Pacific War* (7–10). 2005, Simon & Schuster $15.95 (978-0-689-85534-4). In this gripping sequel to *A Boy at War* (2001) and *A Boy No More* (2004), 17-year-old Adam Pelko lies about his age to join the U.S. Marines and fights in a climactic battle with the Japanese on Okinawa. (Rev: BL 5/15/05; SLJ 8/05; VOYA 8/05)

5258 Mazer, Harry. *The Last Mission* (7–10). 1981, Dell paper $5.50 (978-0-440-94797-4). An underage Jewish American boy joins the Air Corps and is taken prisoner by the Germans. (Rev: BL 5/1/88)

5259 Melnikoff, Pamela. *Prisoner in Time: A Child of the Holocaust* (6–10). 2001, Jewish Publication Soc. paper $9.95 (978-0-8276-0735-4). Melnikoff combines history, fantasy, and Jewish legend in this story of 12-year-old Jan, in hiding from the Nazis in 1942 Czechoslovakia. (Rev: BL 10/1/01; SLJ 12/01)

5260 Morpurgo, Michael. *The Amazing Story of Adolphus Tips* (4–7). 2006, Scholastic $16.99 (978-0-439-79661-3). This is the story of Lily, a 12-year-old British girl who struggles with anger as her father is sent to war in 1943 and her family is relocated to make room for Allied rehearsals of the Normandy invasion. (Rev: BL 4/15/06; SLJ 8/06)

5261 Morpurgo, Michael. *An Elephant in the Garden* (4–8). 2011, Feiwel & Friends $16.99 (978-0-312-59369-8). On the eve of the Allied bombing of Dresden in 1945, Lizzie and her family rescue a zoo elephant named Marlene and together they flee toward the west. (Rev: BL 10/1/11; SLJ 9/1/11)

5262 Morpurgo, Michael. *The Mozart Question* (6–9). Illus. by Michael Foreman. 2008, Candlewick $15.99 (978-0-7636-3552-7). A famous violinist reveals the horrifying reason why he never plays Mozart, dating back to the Holocaust and his father's experiences in the death camps. (Rev: BL 3/15/08; SLJ 5/08)

5263 Myers, Walter Dean. *The Journal of Scott Pendleton Collins: A World War II Soldier* (5–9). Series: My Name Is America. 1999, Scholastic paper $10.95 (978-0-439-05013-5). Through a series of letters, readers get to know 17-year-old Collins, an American soldier who participates in the D-Day invasion of Europe. (Rev: BL 6/1–15/99; HBG 10/99; SLJ 7/99)

5264 Napoli, Donna Jo. *Fire in the Hills* (5–8). 2006, Dutton $16.99 (978-0-525-47751-8). In this fact-based sequel to *Stones in Water* (1997), 14-year-old Roberto returns to Italy after escaping from a Nazi prison camp and joins the resistance movement. (Rev: BL 9/1/06; SLJ 9/06)

5265 Orlev, Uri. *The Island on Bird Street* (7–9). 1984, Houghton Mifflin $16.00 (978-0-395-33887-2); paper $6.95 (978-0-395-61623-9). A young Jewish boy struggles to survive inside the Warsaw ghetto during World War II. (Rev: BL 11/1/88)

5266 Orlev, Uri. *The Man from the Other Side* (6–10). Trans. by Hillel Halkin. 1991, Houghton Mifflin $16.00 (978-0-395-53808-1). The story of a teenager in Nazi-occupied Warsaw who helps desperate Jews despite his dislike of them. (Rev: BL 6/15/91*; SLJ 9/91*)

5267 Orlev, Uri. *Run, Boy, Run* (7–12). 2003, Houghton Mifflin $15.00 (978-0-618-16465-3). A Polish boy survives the Holocaust by pretending to be a Catholic in this harrowing book full of historical detail. (Rev: BCCB 12/03; BL 10/15/03*; HB 11–12/03; HBG 4/04; SLJ 11/03; VOYA 12/03)

5268 Parker, Marjorie Hodgson. *David and the Mighty Eighth* (4–7). Illus. by Mark Postlethwaite. 2007, Bright Sky $17.95 (978-1-931721-93-6). David is sent to stay on his grandparents' farm in rural England and there befriends an American soldier stationed with the U.S. Eighth Air Force in this novel set in 1944. (Rev: BL 12/15/07)

5269 Parkinson, Curtis. *Domenic's War: A Story of the Battle of Monte Cassino* (6–9). 2006, Tundra paper $9.95 (978-0-88776-751-7). Domenic and his family are caught up in one of the most heartbreaking battles of World War II as Allied Forces and Germans fight at Monte Cassino in Italy, destroying the Benedictine monastery that was supposed to be a safe haven for Italian civilians. (Rev: SLJ 8/06)

5270 Patneaude, David. *Thin Wood Walls* (6–10). 2004, Houghton Mifflin $16.00 (978-0-618-34290-7). In this poignant tale set against the backdrop of an America reeling from the Japanese attack on Pearl Harbor, Joe Hanada and his Japanese American family feel the rising tide of prejudice and are eventually sent to an internment camp in California. (Rev: BL 9/15/04; SLJ 10/04; VOYA 12/04)

5271 Patt, Beverly. *Best Friends Forever: A World War II Scrapbook* (6–9). Illus. by Shula Klinger. 2010, Marshall Cavendish $17.99 (978-0-7614-5577-6). This fictional diary tells the story of 14-year-old Louise and her unhappiness when she is separated from her best friend Dottie, who is relocated with her Japanese American family after Pearl Harbor; artifacts of the time add to the impact. Lexile 770L (Rev: BL 4/15/10; LMC 8–9/10; SLJ 4/10)

5272 Pausewang, Gudrun. *Dark Hours* (5–8). Trans. from German by John Brownjohn. 2006, Annick $21.95 (978-1-55451-042-9). In Germany during the closing days of World War II, Gisela and her younger siblings become trapped in an air raid shelter after being separated from their mother and grandmother. (Rev: BL 11/1/06; SLJ 2/07)

5273 Pausewang, Gudrun. *Traitor* (7–10). 2006, Carolrhoda $16.95 (978-0-8225-6195-8). Young Anna, a German girl whose family is involved in the Nazi move-

ment, shelters a Russian soldier at great risk to herself in this novel set in 1944. (Rev: BL 12/1/06; SLJ 11/06)

5274 Pearsall, Shelley. *Jump into the Sky* (5–8). 2012, Knopf $16.99 (978-0-375-83699-2); LB $19.99 (978-037593699-9). Levi, a 13-year-old African American, leaves Chicago to join his father in North Carolina in 1945, only to find that his paratrooper father has just shipped out and Levi must face southern bigotry alone. ☊ ⓔ Lexile 940L (Rev: BL 9/15/12*; LMC 1–2/13*; SLJ 9/12; VOYA 10/12)

5275 Peet, Mal. *Tamar* (8–12). 2007, Candlewick paper $8.99 (978-076364063-7). With parallel narratives set in Nazi-occupied Holland and 1995 England, this award-winning novel is about resistance fighters in World War II and the curiosity of a granddaughter on inheriting a box of memorabilia. ⓔ (Rev: BL 2/1/07*; SLJ 4/07*)

5276 Polak, Monique. *What World Is Left* (7–12). 2008, Orca $12.95 (978-155143847-4). When 14-year-old Anneke and her Jewish family are taken from Holland to Theresienstadt, she suffers filthy, overcrowded conditions and the terror of the gas chambers while her artist father is charged with painting scenery that will make the town look hospitable to Red Cross inspectors, in this powerful book written in memoir format. (Rev: BL 12/15/08; LMC 5–6/09; SLJ 4/1/09)

5277 Pressler, Mirjam. *Malka* (6–10). Trans. by Brian Murdoch. 2003, Putnam $18.99 (978-0-399-23984-7). Escaping from the Nazis in Poland, a mother is forced to leave one daughter behind in this story based on truth that alternates between the difficult experiences of the anguished mother and the abandoned child. (Rev: BL 4/1/03; HB 5–6/03*; HBG 10/03; SLJ 5/03; VOYA 10/03)

5278 Preus, Margi. *Shadow on the Mountain* (6–9). 2012, Abrams/Amulet $16.95 (978-1-4197-0424-6). In Nazi-occupied Germany, 14-year-old Espen becomes a courier for the resistance in this exciting novel inspired by a true story. ☊ ⓔ (Rev: BL 9/1/12; HB 7–8/13; LMC 3–4/13; SLJ 10/12*)

5279 Ray, Karen. *To Cross a Line* (7–10). 1994, Orchard LB $16.99 (978-0-531-08681-0). The story of a 17-year-old Jewish boy who is pursued by the Gestapo and encounters barriers in his desperate attempts to escape Nazi Germany. (Rev: BL 2/15/94; SLJ 6/94; VOYA 6/94)

5280 Richter, Hans Peter. *Friedrich* (7–9). Trans. by Edite Kroll. 1987, Penguin $5.99 (978-0-14-032205-7). The story of a Jewish boy and his family caught in the horror of the rise of the Nazi party and the Holocaust. (Rev: BL 4/1/90)

5281 Rodman, Mary Ann. *Jimmy's Stars* (5–8). 2008, Farrar $16.95 (978-0-374-33703-2). Ellie's beloved brother Jimmy's deferments run out and he is sent off to fight in World War II; when news arrives that he has been killed, Ellie finds it almost impossible to believe. (Rev: BL 4/1/08; SLJ 6/08)

5282 Ruby, Lois. *Shanghai Shadows* (7–10). 2006, Holiday $16.95 (978-0-8234-1960-9). Ilse and her Jewish family flee Vienna during the Nazi regime and settle in Japanese-occupied Shanghai, where they face many hardships and fears. (Rev: BL 11/1/06; SLJ 9/07)

5283 Salisbury, Graham. *House of the Red Fish* (5–8). 2006, Random House $16.95 (978-0-385-73121-8). After his father is sent to an internment camp, Japanese American teen Tomi rallies the community to help raise his father's sunken fishing boat in this inspiring sequel to *Under the Blood-Red Sun* (2005). (Rev: BL 4/15/06; LMC 10/06; SLJ 8/06)

5284 Saroyan, William. *The Human Comedy* (7–12). 1973, Dell paper $6.50 (978-0-440-33933-5). Homer Macauley is growing up during World War II in America, part of the everyday life that is the human comedy.

5285 Say, Allen. *Music for Alice* (4–7). 2004, Houghton Mifflin $17.00 (978-0-618-31118-7). Based on a real story, this is the moving portrait of a Japanese American couple who make the best of the challenges forced upon them during World War II. (Rev: BL 2/1/04; HB 5–6/04; SLJ 4/04)

5286 Schröder, Monika. *The Dog in the Wood* (6–9). 2009, Front St $17.95 (978-1-59078-701-4). Ten-year-old Fritz's life is turned upside down when the Russians approach his home in eastern Germany near the end of World War II. e Lexile 710L (Rev: BL 10/15/09; LMC 1–2/10; SLJ 1/10)

5287 Serraillier, Ian. *The Silver Sword* (6–8). Illus. by C. Walter Hodges. 1959, Phillips $32.95 (978-0-87599-104-7). A World War II story of Polish children who are separated from their parents and finally reunited.

5288 Sharenow, Robert. *The Berlin Boxing Club* (7–10). Illus. by author. 2011, HarperCollins $17.99 (978-0-06-157968-4). In 1936 Berlin 14-year-old Karl, from a nonobservant Jewish family, enjoys learning to box from the famous Max Schmeling even as he grapples with the horrors of Nazi oppression. YALSA Best Fiction for Young Adults; Sydney Taylor Award. Lexile 880L (Rev: BL 4/15/11; HB 5–6/11; SLJ 6/11*; VOYA 8/11)

5289 Smith, Roland. *Elephant Run* (5–8). 2007, Hyperion $15.99 (978-1-4231-0402-5). During World War II, 14-year-old Nick is sent to his father's plantation in Burma to escape the London Blitz but ends up running from cruel Japanese occupiers in this suspenseful historical novel. (Rev: BL 2/15/08; SLJ 1/08)

5290 Smith, Sherri L. *Flygirl* (7–10). 2009, Putnam $16.99 (978-039924709-5). Even though she is black, Ida Mae manages to become a pilot in the WASP (Women Airforce Service Program) during World War II. e Lexile 680L (Rev: BL 1/1–15/09*; HB 5–6/09; LMC 5–6/09; SLJ 2/1/09; VOYA 2/09)

5291 Spinelli, Jerry. *Milkweed* (6–10). 2003, Knopf LB $17.99 (978-0-375-91374-7). A boy who is uncertain of his ethnic background and adopts the name of Misha struggles to survive in the Warsaw ghetto and is befriended by a generous family. (Rev: BCCB 11/03; BL 10/15/03*; HB 11–12/03; HBG 4/04; SLJ 11/03)

5292 Stone, Phoebe. *The Romeo and Juliet Code* (5–8). 2011, Scholastic $16.99 (978-0-545-21511-4). Eleven-year-old Felicity is sent from London to relatives in Maine to protect her from bombardment by the Germans; she becomes friends with adoptee Derek and together they solve a family mystery. (Rev: BL 1/1–15/11; HB 3–4/11; LMC 5–6/11; SLJ 2/1/11)

5293 Tak, Bibi Dumon. *Soldier Bear* (4–8). Trans. by Laura Watkinson. Illus. by Philip Hopman. 2011, Eerdmans $13 (978-0-8028-5375-2). Based on a true story, this engaging novel is about a bear called Voytek that served in the Polish army in World War II and boosts morale while also carrying live ammunition. Batchelder Award 2012; ALA Notable Books 2012. e Lexile 780L (Rev: BL 10/15/11; HB 11–12/11; LMC 1–2/12; SLJ 11/1/11)

5294 Tamar, Erika. *Good-bye, Glamour Girl* (7–10). 1984, HarperCollins LB $12.89 (978-0-397-32088-2). Liesl and her family flee from Hitler's Europe and Liesl must now become Americanized. (Rev: BL 1/1/85)

5295 Taylor, Marilyn. *Faraway Home* (5–8). 2000, O'Brien paper $7.95 (978-0-86278-643-4). Taken from his Austrian homeland by the Kindertransport, 13-year-old Karl is sent to County Down in Ireland where he endures the hardship of country life and the hostility of the locals. (Rev: BL 3/1/01)

5296 Thesman, Jean. *Molly Donnelly* (6–9). 1993, Houghton Mifflin $16.00 (978-0-395-64348-8); paper $4.50 (978-0-380-72252-5). The saga of a young girl growing up in Seattle during World War II and coping not only with the changes wrought by war but also with typical adolescent concerns. (Rev: BL 4/1/93; SLJ 5/93; VOYA 8/93)

5297 Toksvig, Sandi. *Hitler's Canary* (5–8). 2007, Roaring Brook $16.95 (978-1-59643-247-5). A Danish family decides to risk everything in order to help Jews escape the Nazis. (Rev: BL 1/1–15/07; SLJ 4/07)

5298 Tunnell, Michael O. *Brothers in Valor: A Story of Resistance* (6–10). 2001, Holiday $16.95 (978-0-8234-1541-0). Tunnell interweaves history and fiction in this account of three young Germans, members of the Mormon Church, who protest Hitler's actions and put their own lives at risk. (Rev: BL 5/1/01; HBG 3/02; SLJ 6/01; VOYA 8/01)

5299 Twomey, Cathleen. *Beachmont Letters* (8–12). 2003, Boyds Mills $16.95 (978-1-59078-050-3). During World War II, 17-year-old Eleanor reaches out to a soldier through the letters that she writes him although she holds back those that deal with her own pain and suffering. (Rev: BL 3/1/03; HBG 10/03; SLJ 3/03)

5300 Van Dijk, Lutz. *Damned Strong Love: The True Story of Willi G. and Stefan K.* (8–12). Trans. by Elizabeth D. Crawford. 1995, Henry Holt $15.95 (978-0-8050-3770-8). Nazi persecution of homosexuals, based on the life of Stefan K., a Polish teenager. (Rev: BL 5/15/95; SLJ 8/95)

5301 Van Steenwyk, Elizabeth. *A Traitor Among Us* (6–9). 1998, Eerdmans $15.00 (978-0-8028-5150-5). Set in Nazi-occupied Holland in 1944, this thriller describes the resistance activities of 13-year-old Pieter including his hiding of a wounded American soldier. (Rev: BL 8/98; HBG 9/98; SLJ 8/98)

5302 Vander Els, Betty. *The Bombers' Moon* (5–7). 1992, Farrar paper $4.50 (978-0-374-30877-3). Missionary children Ruth and Simeon are evacuated to escape the Japanese invasion of China; they will not see their parents for four years. A sequel is *Leaving Point* (1987). (Rev: BCCB 9/85; BL 11/1/85; HB 9–10/85)

5303 Voorhoeve, Anne C. *My Family for the War* (7–12). Trans. by Tammi Reichel. Illus. 2012, Dial $17.99 (978-080373360-2). Ziska Mangold, 10, is rescued from Nazi Germany by a Jewish family in London, where she endures bullying and hardships and worries about the family she left behind. Batchelder Award 2013; ALA Notable Books 2013. **e** Lexile 900L (Rev: BL 4/15/12*; LMC 9–10/12; SLJ 5/1/12*)

5304 Waters, Zack C. *Blood Moon Rider* (5–8). 2006, Pineapple $13.95 (978-1-56164-350-9). Abandoned by his stepmother after his father is killed in World War II, 14-year-old Harley Wallace survives an eventful journey to the home of a grandfather he's never met and there finds more excitement waiting. (Rev: SLJ 8/06)

5305 Watts, Irene N. *Finding Sophie: A Search for Belonging in Postwar Britain* (5–8). 2002, Tundra paper $6.95 (978-0-88776-613-8). In this sequel to *Remember Me* (2000), World War II has ended and 13-year-old Sophie waits anxiously to hear news of her Jewish family in Germany, at the same time hoping she will not have to leave her happy life in London. (Rev: BL 1/1–15/03; SLJ 3/03; VOYA 8/03)

5306 Watts, Irene N. *Remember Me: A Search for Refuge in Wartime Britain* (5–8). 2000, Tundra paper $7.95 (978-0-88776-519-3). A heart-tugging story of an 11-year-old Jewish girl who, at the beginning of World War II, is transported from her home in Berlin to live in a Welsh mining town where she knows no one and speaks no English. (Rev: BL 12/1/00; SLJ 1/01; VOYA 2/01)

5307 Weston, Elise. *The Coastwatcher* (5–8). 2005, Peachtree $14.95 (978-1-56145-350-4). Vacationing on the South Carolina coast with his family in 1943, 11-year-old Hugh sees some signs that Germans are nearby and is determined to convince the doubting adults that he is right. (Rev: BL 11/1/05; SLJ 3/06)

5308 Whelan, Gloria. *Summer of the War* (6–9). 2006, HarperCollins $15.99 (978-0-06-008072-3). In the summer of 1942 a relaxing vacation in Michigan becomes stressful for 14-year-old Belle and her family when her snobby cousin comes to visit. (Rev: BL 4/15/06; SLJ 8/06)

5309 Whitney, Kim Ablon. *The Other Half of Life* (7–10). 2009, Knopf $16.99 (978-037585219-0); LB $19.99 (978-037595219-7). This moving story of Jewish refugees in 1939 is based on the true-life experiences of those aboard the MS *St. Louis,* which was denied entry to Cuba and the United States. Lexile HL730L (Rev: BL 4/15/09; LMC 10/09; SLJ 7/1/09; VOYA 6/09)

5310 Williams, Laura E. *Behind the Bedroom Wall* (5–8). 1996, Milkweed paper $6.95 (978-1-57131-606-6). Korinna, a young Nazi, discovers that her parents are hiding a Jewish couple in wartime Germany. (Rev: BL 8/96; SLJ 9/96)

5311 Wilson, John. *Flames of the Tiger* (5–8). 2003, Kids Can $16.95 (978-1-55337-618-7). The horrors of World War II are seen through the eyes of 17-year-old Dieter, who with his younger sister is fleeing his native Germany as the war nears an end. (Rev: SLJ 1/04; VOYA 6/04) [813]

5312 Wilson, John. *Four Steps to Death* (7–9). 2005, Kids Can $16.95 (978-1-55337-704-7); paper $6.95 (978-1-55337-705-4). The horrors of war are plain in this story of the Battle of Stalingrad in 1942, featuring 17-year-old Vasily, a Russian defending his soil; 18-year-old Conrad, a committed German tank officer; and 8-year-old Sergei, who is simply trying to survive. (Rev: SLJ 2/06; VOYA 2/06)

5313 Wiseman, Eva. *Kanada* (7–10). 2006, Tundra paper $9.95 (978-0-88776-729-6). Jutka, a young Hungarian Jew, loses her family at Auschwitz and barely survives herself; after she is released, she must decide whether to settle in Israel with a young man with whom she has fallen in love or to join relatives in Canada. (Rev: BL 2/15/07)

5314 Wiseman, Eva. *My Canary Yellow Star* (8–12). 2002, Tundra paper $7.95 (978-0-88776-533-9). Marta Weisz's privileged life as the daughter of a wealthy Jewish surgeon comes to an abrupt end when Hitler invades Hungary, but her life is spared through the efforts of Raoul Wallenberg. (Rev: BL 1/1–15/02; SLJ 6/02)

5315 Wolf, Joan M. *Someone Named Eva* (6–9). 2007, Clarion $16.00 (978-0-618-53579-8). At the age of 11, Milada, a blonde and blue-eyed Czechoslovakian girl, is seized by the Nazis and renamed Eva. (Rev: BL 9/15/07; SLJ 9/07)

5316 Wulffson, Don. *Soldier X* (8–12). 2001, Viking $16.99 (978-0-670-88863-4). After a battle in World

War II, a 16-year-old German boy switches uniforms with a dead Russian in a desperate effort to survive. (Rev: BCCB 3/01; BL 5/1/01; HB 7–8/01; HBG 10/01; SLJ 3/01; VOYA 4/01)

5317 Yep, Laurence. *Hiroshima* (4–7). 1995, Scholastic paper $9.95 (978-0-590-20832-1). A powerful work of fiction that explores the bombing of Hiroshima in 1945 and its aftermath. (Rev: BCCB 6/95; BL 3/15/95*; HB 9–10/95; SLJ 5/95)

5318 Yolen, Jane. *The Devil's Arithmetic* (7–12). 1988, Puffin paper $6.99 (978-0-14-034535-3). This time-warp story transports a young Jewish girl back to Poland in the 1940s, conveying the horrors of the Holocaust. (Rev: BL 9/1/88; SLJ 11/88)

5319 Zeinert, Karen. *To Touch the Stars: A Story of World War II* (5–8). Series: Jamestown's American Portraits. 2000, Jamestown paper $5.95 (978-0-8092-0630-8). Eighteen-year-old Liz Erickson, who loves to fly airplanes, longs for independence while she investigates possible sabotage in the Women's Airforce Service pilots program. (Rev: SLJ 9/00)

5320 Zucker, Jonny. *The Bombed House* (5–8). Illus. by Paul Savage. Series: Keystone Books. 2006, Stone Arch LB $21.26 (978-1-59889-092-1). This fast-paced story, which will attract reluctant readers, features brothers Ned and Harry Jennings, who find a German soldier hiding in London during World War II. (Rev: SLJ 1/07)

KOREAN, VIETNAM, AND OTHER WARS

5321 Brown, Don. *Our Time on the River* (7–10). 2003, Houghton Mifflin $15.00 (978-0-618-31116-3). Two brothers learn more about each other on a canoe trip that precedes the older brother's departure to fight in Vietnam. (Rev: BL 4/1/03; HBG 10/03; SLJ 4/03)

5322 Burg, Ann. *All the Broken Pieces* (6–10). 2009, Scholastic $16.99 (978-054508092-7). Told in free verse, this is the story of a boy adopted from Vietnam in the 1970s and his conflicting emotions. ∩ Lexile HL680L (Rev: BL 2/15/09; HB 5–6/09; LMC 5–6/09; SLJ 5/1/09)

5323 Crist-Evans, Craig. *Amaryllis* (7–12). 2003, Candlewick paper $7.99 (978-0-7636-2990-8). Jimmy— who is facing problems at home including his alcoholic father's behavior—learns that his older brother Frank, off fighting in Vietnam, has become depressed and drug-addicted as a result of the war. (Rev: BCCB 1/04; BL 4/15/06; LMC 1/04; SLJ 4/05)

5324 Dorros, Arthur. *Under the Sun* (6–9). 2004, Abrams $16.95 (978-0-8109-4933-1). Thirteen-year-old Ehmet and his mother flee war-torn Sarajevo in search of refuge in Croatia; after soldiers kill his mother, the boy struggles on alone until he reaches a multiethnic orphan community. (Rev: BL 9/15/04; SLJ 12/04; VOYA 12/04)

5325 Dowell, Frances O'Roark. *Shooting the Moon* (4–8). 2008, Atheneum $16.99 (978-1-4169-2690-0). Jamie is surprised when her military father is not pleased about her big brother volunteering to go to Vietnam, until TJ sends home increasingly disturbing photographs of the war. Boston Globe–Horn Book Honor 2008. (Rev: BL 3/15/08; SLJ 5/08)

5326 Hughes, Dean. *Search and Destroy* (7–10). 2006, Simon & Schuster $16.95 (978-0-689-87023-1). Rick Ward, who joined the army during the Vietnam War to escape his home life, returns from a tour of duty unable to adjust to normal life. (Rev: BL 2/1/06; SLJ 1/06; VOYA 2/06)

5327 Kadohata, Cynthia. *Cracker!* (6–9). 2007, Simon & Schuster $16.99 (978-1-4169-0637-7). Cracker is trained to be part of a military canine unit and becomes 17-year-old handler Rick's lifeline on the front lines of the Vietnam War. ∩ (Rev: BL 2/15/07; HB 3–4/07; LMC 4–5/07; SLJ 2/07)

5328 Lynch, Chris. *I Pledge Allegiance* (8–11). Series: Vietnam. 2011, Scholastic $16.99 (978-054527029-8). Four friends make a pact to look out for each other at the start of the Vietnam War; this first volume in a series follows Morris, who joins the Navy. YALSA Quick Picks for Reluctant Young Adult Readers 2013. **e** Lexile 860L (Rev: BL 10/15/11; LMC 11–12/11; SLJ 1/12; VOYA 2/12)

5329 Lynch, Chris. *Sharpshooter* (8–11). Series: Vietnam. 2012, Scholastic $16.99 (978-054527026-7). Ivan becomes a sharpshooter for the United States Army and works to halt the shipment of weapons from the north of Vietnam to the south. YALSA Quick Picks for Reluctant Young Adult Readers 2013. **e** Lexile 850L (Rev: BL 3/1/12; SLJ 6/12; VOYA 8/12)

5330 Mead, Alice. *Dawn and Dusk* (6–9). 2007, Farrar $16.00 (978-0-374-31708-9). Azad's Iranian Kurdish family is torn apart during the Iran-Iraq war when his father becomes an informer for Iran's secret police, and Saddam Hussein's gas attack prompts the 13-year-old to flee to Turkey. (Rev: BCCB 5/07; BL 2/15/07; LMC 10/07; SLJ 4/07)

5331 Myers, Walter Dean. *Patrol: An American Soldier in Vietnam* (4–8). Illus. by Ann Grifalconi. 2002, HarperCollins LB $17.89 (978-0-06-028364-3). A penetrating picture book for older readers told in narrative verse from the perspective of a teenage soldier in Vietnam. (Rev: BL 3/15/02; HB 7–8/02; HBG 10/02; SLJ 5/02)

5332 Nelson, Theresa. *And One for All* (7–12). 1989, Scholastic paper $16.95 (978-0-531-05804-6). Wing faces the disapproval of his best friend, a pacifist, when he decides to sign up to fight in Vietnam. (Rev: BL 4/15/06; SLJ 9/97)

5333 Paterson, Katherine. *The Day of the Pelican* (6–9). 2009, Clarion $16 (978-0-547-18188-2). Told from the point of view of a 13-year-old girl, this is the compelling story of an Albanian Muslim family fleeing oppression and hatred in the 1990s, ultimately escaping to the United States. ∩ e Lexile 770L (Rev: BL 9/15/09; HB 11–12/09; LMC 1–2/10; SLJ 10/09)

5334 Rostkowski, Margaret I. *The Best of Friends* (7–12). 1989, HarperCollins $12.95 (978-0-06-025104-8). Three Utah teenagers have a growing interest in the Vietnam War and how it affects each of them. (Rev: BL 9/1/89; SLJ 9/89; VOYA 12/89)

5335 Sherlock, Patti. *Letters from Wolfie* (6–9). 2004, Penguin $16.99 (978-0-670-03694-3). In a moment of patriotic fervor, 13-year-old Mark lends his beloved dog Wolfie to the U.S. Army for use in its scout program in Vietnam; Mark's struggles to get his dog back play out against the backdrop of family disagreements about the war. (Rev: BL 7/04; SLJ 6/04; VOYA 8/04)

5336 White, Ellen Emerson. *The Journal of Patrick Seamus Flaherty: United States Marine Corps* (6–9). Series: Dear America. 2002, Scholastic $10.95 (978-0-439-14890-0). White uses Patrick's journal to portray the life of a soldier in Vietnam, describing the horrors of war and the questions surrounding American involvement in the conflict. (Rev: BL 7/02; HBG 10/02; SLJ 10/02)

5337 White, Ellen Emerson. *The Road Home* (8–12). 1995, Scholastic paper $15.95 (978-0-590-46737-7). This story re-creates a Vietnam War medical base in claustrophobic and horrific detail, and features army nurse Rebecca Phillips, from the Echo Company book series. (Rev: BL 1/15/95; SLJ 4/95; VOYA 4/95)

5338 White, Ellen Emerson. *Where Have All the Flowers Gone? The Diary of Molly Mackenzie Flaherty* (7–10). 2002, Scholastic paper $10.95 (978-0-439-14889-4). Molly, whose brother Patrick is off fighting in the Vietnam War, sees firsthand the casualties of the conflict while working in a Boston hospital. This book is a companion to the story of her brother, *The Journal of Patrick Seamus Flaherty, United States Marine Corps, Khe Sanh, Vietnam, 1968* (2002). (Rev: BL 4/15/06)

5339 Woodworth, Chris. *Georgie's Moon* (5–8). 2006, Farrar $16.00 (978-0-374-33306-5). Seventh-grader Georgie Collins lives her life waiting for her father to return from Vietnam, and is unable to accept his death at first. (Rev: BL 3/1/06; SLJ 4/06)

TWENTY-FIRST CENTURY CONFLICTS

5340 Myers, Walter Dean. *Sunrise over Fallujah* (8–11). 2008, Scholastic $17.99 (978-0-439-91624-0). Robin — nephew of Richie, the young black Vietnam War soldier in 1988's *Fallen Angels* — is serving in Operation Iraqi Freedom and now understands his uncle's reluctance to talk about his experiences. ∩ (Rev: BL 2/15/08; SLJ 4/08)

Horror Stories and the Supernatural

5341 Abbott, Tony. *City of the Dead* (5–8). Series: The Haunting of Derek Stone. 2009, Scholastic paper $4.99 (978-0-545-03429-6). Derek Stone's normal life ends when his father and brother Ronny are supposedly killed in a train accident; but Ronny then turns up — a changed person — and Derek learns about a similar accident many years before that has sinister overtones. (Rev: BCCB 1/09; BL 1/1–15/09; LMC 5/09)

5342 Alender, Katie. *Bad Girls Don't Die* (7–10). 2009, Hyperion $15.99 (978-142310876-4). Alexis must determine why her little sister is possessed by the spirit of a child who died long ago. Lexile HL670L (Rev: BL 4/1/09; SLJ 8/09)

5343 Alender, Katie. *From Bad to Cursed* (7–9). 2011, Hyperion $16.99 (978-1-4231-3471-8). Alexis is worried about her younger sister Kasey, 14, who is home from mental hospital but seems to have joined a strange club that brings popularity to its members — but at what cost? e Lexile HL620L (Rev: BL 6/1/11; SLJ 6/11)

5344 Alphin, Elaine Marie. *Ghost Soldier* (5–7). 2001, Henry Holt $16.95 (978-0-8050-6158-1). Alex, who has special powers, meets a Civil War ghost and helps him discover what happened to his family. (Rev: BCCB 7–8/01; BL 8/01; HBG 10/02; SLJ 8/01; VOYA 8/01)

5345 Alter, Stephen. *The Phantom Isles* (4–7). 2007, Bloomsbury $16.95 (978-1-58234-738-7). Sixth-graders Courtney, Orion, and Ming join with the librarian of their Massachusetts town in an effort to free ghosts that have become trapped in books. (Rev: BL 2/1/07; SLJ 3/07)

5346 Anderson, Jodi Lynn. *May Bird Among the Stars* (4–7). 2006, Simon & Schuster $16.95 (978-0-689-86924-2). In this sequel to *May Bird and the Ever After*, 10-year-old May Bird and her cat Somber Kitty remain trapped in the Afterlife torn between finding a way home and helping to save Ever After from the villainous Bo Cleevil. (Rev: BL 12/1/06; SLJ 11/06)

5347 Anderson, M. T. *The Game of Sunken Places* (5–8). 2004, Scholastic $16.95 (978-0-439-41660-3). Brian and Gregory, both 13, find themselves embroiled in a dangerous and suspenseful game during a stay at the spooky mansion of Gregory's eccentric Uncle Max. (Rev: BL 4/15/04*; SLJ 9/04; VOYA 6/04)

5348 Arthur, Artist. *Manifest* (7–11). Series: Mystyx. 2010, Kimani/Tru paper $9.99 (978-03738319-6-8). After her parents' divorce and her move to Connecticut, unhappy African American 15-year-old Krystal eventually finds two friends who also have supernatural powers and can help her in her quest to save an unhappy teen ghost. (Rev: BL 10/1/10; SLJ 9/1/10)

5349 Asimov, Isaac, ed. *Young Witches and Warlocks* (6–9). 1987, HarperCollins $12.95 (978-0-06-020183-

8). A collection of 10 stories, most of them scary, about witches. (Rev: BL 7/87; SLJ 1/88)

5350 Atwater-Rhodes, Amelia. *Persistence of Memory* (7–10). 2008, Delacorte $15.99 (978-038573437-0); LB $18.99 (978-038590443-8). Sixteen-year-old Erin has been treated for schizophrenia for most of her life, but after a two-year hiatus from her alter-ego Shevaun, she discovers she isn't mentally ill at all, but entwined with the soul of a 500-year-old vampire. **e** Lexile 860L (Rev: BL 12/1/08; LMC 5–6/09; SLJ 2/1/09)

5351 Atwater-Rhodes, Amelia. *Token of Darkness* (6–10). 2010, Delacorte $16.99 (978-0-385-73750-0). A strange spectral girl named Samantha has remained at Cooper's side since his car accident, but who is she and how can he help her in her quest for a physical presence? **e** Lexile 900L (Rev: BLO 11/19/10; LMC 5–6/10; SLJ 1/10)

5352 Atwood, Megan. *The Haunting of Apartment 101* (6–9). Series: The Paranormalists. 2012, Darby Creek LB $27.93 (978-0-7613-8332-1); paper $7.95 (978-0-8225-9077-4). Paranormal investigators Jinx and Jackson look into a haunting at classmate Emily's apartment in this first installment in the series. **e** (Rev: LMC 5–6/13; SLJ 10/12)

5353 Avi. *Devil's Race* (7–9). 1984, Avon paper $3.50 (978-0-380-70406-4). John Proud is in constant battle with a demon who has the same name and was hanged in 1854.

5354 Avi. *The Seer of Shadows* (4–7). 2008, HarperCollins $16.99 (978-0-06-000015-8). Horace, a photographer's apprentice in 1872, is told by his boss to fake photographs of ghosts, but discovers that he has the ability to conjure actual ghosts with his camera. ♫ (Rev: BL 2/15/08; SLJ 2/08)

5355 Avi. *Something Upstairs: A Tale of Ghosts* (5–7). 1988, Orchard LB $16.99 (978-0-531-08382-6); paper $5.99 (978-0-380-70853-6). Kenny moves into a house in Rhode Island that is haunted by the ghost of a slave who was murdered in 1800. (Rev: BCCB 9/88; BL 11/1/88; SLJ 10/88)

5356 Baer, Marianna. *Frost* (8–11). 2011, HarperCollins $17.99 (978-0-06-179949-5). The arrival of an eccentric classmate named Celeste disrupts Leena's plans for a perfect senior year in this suspenseful modern gothic novel set in a boarding school. **e** (Rev: BL 9/1/11; SLJ 9/1/11; VOYA 10/11)

5357 Barnes, Jennifer Lynn. *Every Other Day* (7–10). 2011, Egmont $17.99 (978-160684169-3). Sixteen-year-old Kali is an ordinary high school student who is transformed every other day into an efficient demon hunter. **e** (Rev: BL 1/1/12; LMC 3–4/12; SLJ 1/12)

5358 Barnes, Jennifer Lynn, and Sarah Rees Brennan, et al. *Enthralled: Paranormal Diversions* (8–11). Ed. by Melissa Marr and Kelley Armstrong. 2011, HarperCollins $17.99 (978-0-06-201579-2). Sixteen paranormal

short stories include some unexpected and novel twists in this intriguing collection. **e** (Rev: BL 10/1/11; SLJ 10/1/11; VOYA 10/11)

5359 Barraclough, Lindsey. *Long Lankin* (8–11). 2012, Candlewick $16.99 (978-076365808-3). Cora and her younger sister go to live with their Aunt Ida in a remote English village in 1958 and find they are in danger from an ancient evil. ♫ **e** Lexile 890L (Rev: BL 4/15/12; HB 7–8/12; LMC 10/12; SLJ 8/12; VOYA 6/12)

5360 Barrett, Tracy. *Cold in Summer* (4–7). 2003, Henry Holt $16.95 (978-0-8050-7052-1). An enjoyable story about a lonely girl who slowly comes to realize that her new friend is a ghost. (Rev: BL 4/1/03; HB 5–6/03; HBG 10/03; SLJ 7/03; VOYA 6/03)

5361 Bawden, Nina. *Devil by the Sea* (6–8). 1976, HarperCollins $12.95 (978-0-397-31683-0). Is the strange old man Hilary sees at the beach really the devil?

5362 Beaudoin, Sean. *The Infects* (8–11). 2012, Candlewick $16.99 (978-0-7636-5947-9). Nero, 17, is distressed to find himself on a wilderness trek with other juvenile delinquents, but his predicament worsens when the counselors turn into aggressive zombies. ♫ **e** (Rev: BL 7/12; HB 9–10/12; LMC 3–4/13; SLJ 11/12; VOYA 8/12)

5363 Becker, Tom. *Lifeblood* (5–8). Series: Darkside. 2008, Scholastic $16.99 (978-0-545-03742-6). In this second action-packed installment in the series, Jonathan, born of a Darkside mother and Lightside father, travels between these contemporary and fantasy worlds as he tries to solve a series of murders. (Rev: LMC 3/08; SLJ 3/09)

5364 Belkom, Edo Van, ed. *Be Afraid! Tales of Horror* (8–12). 2000, Tundra $6.95 (978-0-88776-496-7). Fifteen horror stories for and about teens feature sinister twists, hauntings, and violence. (Rev: BL 2/1/01; SLJ 3/01; VOYA 2/01)

5365 Bial, Raymond. *The Fresh Grave: And Other Ghostly Stories* (5–7). 1997, Midwest Traditions paper $13.95 (978-1-883953-22-5). A series of ten short, humorous ghost stories featuring two teenage heroes and their escapades in a small midwestern town. (Rev: SLJ 12/97)

5366 Bial, Raymond. *The Ghost of Honeymoon Creek* (5–8). 1999, Midwest Traditions paper $13.95 (978-1-883953-27-0). While investigating a strange light in a neighboring farm, 15-year-old Hank encounters a ghost. (Rev: BL 9/1/00; HBG 3/01; SLJ 1/01)

5367 Bick, Ilsa J. *Ashes* (7–10). 2011, Egmont $17.99 (978-1-60684-175-4). After electromagnetic pulses turn much of the surviving population into zombies, 17-year-old Alex and her companions find new threats to their survival. ♫ **e** Lexile HL730L (Rev: BL 9/15/11; HB 9–10/12; LMC 1–2/12*; SLJ 10/1/11)

5368 Bick, Ilsa J. *Shadows* (7–10). 2012, Egmont $17.99 (978-160684176-1). In this sequel to *Ashes* (2011), 17-year-old Alex discovers that the town of Rule is not the haven she thought and is populated by a variety of horrors. ⌒ **e** Lexile HL730L (Rev: BLO 10/1/12; HB 9–10/12; SLJ 1/13)

5369 Black, Bekka. *iDrakula* (7–10). 2010, Sourcebooks paper $9.99 (978-14022446-5-0). This modern retelling of Dracula captures all the original's shock and drama via text messages, emails, and screenshots. **e** Lexile HL660L (Rev: BL 10/15/10; VOYA 12/10)

5370 Black, Yelena. *Dance of Shadows* (7–10). 2013, Bloomsbury $17.99 (978-159990940-0). Vanessa, 15, attends New York Ballet Academy and enjoys the dance while also seeking clues to the disappearance of her older sister, who was also a student there. **e** (Rev: BL 11/1/12; SLJ 1/13; VOYA 12/12)

5371 Blake, Kendare. *Girl of Nightmares* (8–12). 2012, Tor Teen $17.99 (978-0-7653-2866-3). In this sequel to 2011's *Anna Dressed in Blood*, ghost hunter Cas decides he must rescue Anna from the tortures she is suffering in hell on his account. ⌒ **e** (Rev: BL 10/1/12; SLJ 11/12)

5372 Bradbury, Ray. *The Halloween Tree* (7–12). 1972, Knopf $19.95 (978-0-394-82409-3). Nine boys discover the true meaning — and horror — of Halloween.

5373 Bradman, Tony. *Voodoo Child* (4–7). Illus. by Martin Chatterton. Series: Tales of Terror. 2005, Egmont paper $7.50 (978-1-4052-1126-0). Megan hopes a voodoo doll will get rid of her father's girlfriend. Other scary titles in this series are *Deadly Game* and *Final Cut* (both 2005). (Rev: SLJ 6/05)

5374 Bray, Libba, et al. *Vacations from Hell* (8–11). 2009, HarperTeen $16.99 (978-0-06-168873-7); paper $9.99 (978-0-06-168872-0). A collection of stories by well-known authors about teens whose vacations take scary turns. (Rev: BL 8/09; SLJ 8/09; VOYA 10/09)

5375 Brennan, Sarah Rees. *Unspoken* (7–12). Series: Lynburn Legacy. 2012, Random House $18.99 (978-0-375-87041-5); LB $21.99 (978-037597041-2). Kami recognizes that things are not quite as they seem in her English village when the boy she has talked to in her head for years turns up; the first volume in a paranormal romance. **e** (Rev: BL 8/12; HB 9–10/12; LMC 1–2/13; SLJ 10/12; VOYA 10/12)

5376 Brewer, Heather. *Tenth Grade Bleeds* (6–10). Series: The Chronicles of Vladimir Tod. 2009, Dutton $16.99 (978-0-525-42135-1). Half-vampire Vlad, now in 10th grade in the third volume in the series, is grappling with teen angst while at the same time fighting the supernatural forces seeking to destroy him. ⌒ **e** Lexile 820L (Rev: SLJ 9/09; VOYA 6/09)

5377 Brown, Roberta Simpson. *The Queen of the Cold-Blooded Tales* (6–9). 1993, August House $19.95 (978-0-87483-332-4). A collection of 23 contemporary horror stories. (Rev: BL 9/1/93; VOYA 4/94)

5378 Bruchac, Joseph. *Whisper in the Dark* (5–8). 2005, HarperCollins $16.99 (978-0-06-058087-2). A frightening Native American legend seems to be coming true for 13-year-old Maddie, descended from a Narragansett chief. (Rev: BL 9/1/05; SLJ 8/05)

5379 Buckingham, Royce. *The Dead Boys* (5–8). 2010, Putnam $16.99 (978-0-399-25222-8). Arriving in a Washington town where his mother will work at a nuclear plant, 12-year-old Teddy finds that his new friends are all dead and there is a menacing sycamore tree next door. **e** Lexile 850L (Rev: SLJ 11/1/10)

5380 Buckingham, Royce. *Demonkeeper* (4–7). 2007, Putnam $15.99 (978-0-399-24649-4). Nat lives in Seattle and looks after mostly harmless demons in his creaky old house — until the day when the scary Beast gets loose and Nat must try to retrieve this orphan-eating demon; this fast-paced romp will please reluctant readers. (Rev: SLJ 9/07)

5381 Buffie, Margaret. *The Dark Garden* (6–10). 1997, Kids Can $16.95 (978-1-55074-288-6). Thea, who suffers from amnesia after an accident, begins hearing voices, one of which belongs to a young woman who died tragically years before. (Rev: BL 10/15/97; HBG 3/98; SLJ 10/97)

5382 Bunting, Eve. *The Presence: A Ghost Story* (6–10). 2003, Clarion $16.00 (978-0-618-26919-8). Catherine, 17, who is still grieving over the death of a friend, finds solace in a handsome young man but at the same time senses that something isn't quite right. (Rev: BL 10/15/03; HBG 4/04; SLJ 10/03; VOYA 2/04)

5383 Byng, Georgia. *Molly Moon Stops the World* (5–8). 2004, HarperCollins LB $18.89 (978-0-06-051413-6). Molly Moon, a girl of unusual hypnotic powers, is dispatched to California to foil a power-mad hypnotist called Primo Cell. (Rev: BL 5/1/04; SLJ 5/04)

5384 Cabot, Meg. *Twilight* (7–10). Series: The Mediator. 2005, HarperCollins LB $16.89 (978-0-06-072468-9). Suze, deeply in love with a ghost named Jesse, faces a real dilemma when she discovers a way to give Jesse back his life that would mean losing him as a boyfriend; the sixth installment in the series. (Rev: SLJ 2/05)

5385 Cameron, Eleanor. *The Court of the Stone Children* (5–7). 1990, Puffin paper $6.99 (978-0-14-034289-5). Nina's move with her family to San Francisco is a disaster until she encounters a young ghost in a small museum.

5386 Cargill, Linda. *The Surfer* (6–9). 1995, Scholastic paper $3.99 (978-0-590-22215-0). After Nick meets Marina, a strange but beautiful surfer, he realizes that she is an immortal who has plotted against male members of his family for generations. (Rev: SLJ 1/96)

5387 Carter, Dean Vincent. *The Hand of the Devil* (8–11). 2006, Delacorte LB $9.99 (978-0-385-90386-8); paper $7.95 (978-0-385-73371-7). Young journalist Ashley Reeves travels to an island in Britain's Lake District to investigate an unusual mosquito and finds himself in dire straits. (Rev: BL 10/1/06; LMC 2/07; SLJ 1/07)

5388 Carus, Marianne, ed. *That's Ghosts for You: 13 Scary Stories* (4–7). Illus. by YongSheng Xuan. 2000, Front St $15.95 (978-0-8126-2675-9). A fine collection of 13 chilling stories set in locations around the world, each with a supernatural twist. (Rev: BL 12/1/00; HBG 3/01; SLJ 12/00)

5389 Chadda, Sarwat. *Devil's Kiss* (7–10). 2009, Hyperion $17.99 (978-1-4231-1999-9). Fifteen-year-old Billi SanGreal is secretly a Templar Knight in training in this complex and compelling novel that features the Angel of Death on a rampage. ∩ Lexile HL620L (Rev: BL 10/15/09; LMC 1–2/10; SLJ 11/09)

5390 Chadda, Sarwat. *The Savage Fortress* (8–12). 2012, Scholastic $16.99 (978-0-545-38516-9). When Ash Mistry visits India he finds himself dragged into a battle with *rakshasas* (demons) from which he tries to save his uncle, his aunt, and finally his sister and all of mankind. ∩ **e** Lexile 660L (Rev: SLJ 1/13*)

5391 Citra, Becky. *Never to Be Told* (6–12). 2006, Orca paper $7.95 (978-1-55143-567-1). A ghost story set in a small town called Cold Creek and featuring a 12-year-old girl named Asia who faces upheavals in her life. (Rev: SLJ 12/06)

5392 Clarke, Judith. *Starry Nights* (5–9). 2003, Front St $15.95 (978-1-886910-82-9). When Jess's family moves to a new house, a ghost seems to be involved in the family's emotional upheavals. (Rev: BL 6/1–15/03; HB 9–10/03; HBG 4/04)

5393 Cochran, Molly. *Legacy* (7–11). 2011, Simon & Schuster $17.99 (978-1-4424-1739-7). At a new school in Massachusetts, not far from Salem, 16-year-old half-witch and outsider Katy discovers that her family has a history here and that her powers may help save the town. **e** Lexile HL690L (Rev: BL 12/15/11; SLJ 12/1/11)

5394 Cody, Matthew. *The Dead Gentleman* (5–8). 2011, Knopf $15.99 (978-037585596-2); LB $18.99 (978-037595596-9). A time-traveling device enables Tommy, a 1901 street urchin, to contact modern-day teen Jezebel; the two unite their strengths to save the world from zombies. **e** (Rev: BL 2/1/12; SLJ 3/12)

5395 Cole, Steve. *Z. Rex* (5–8). Series: The Hunting. 2009, Philomel $16.99 (978-0-399-25253-2). Scottish teenager Adam has to rely on himself when his dad leaves for a business trip and all manner of scary thugs — including a man-eating dinosaur — show up at his house. (Rev: BL 8/09; LMC 11–12/09; SLJ 10/09)

5396 Colfer, Eoin. *The Wish List* (6–9). 2003, Hyperion $16.95 (978-0-7868-1863-1). Meg's mix of good and bad deeds leaves her poised between Heaven and Hell, and she is sent on a mission that will tip the balance one way or the other. (Rev: BL 10/1/03; SLJ 12/03*)

5397 Cooney, Caroline B. *Night School* (7–10). 1995, Scholastic paper $3.50 (978-0-590-47878-6). Four California teens enroll in a mysterious night school course and encounter an evil instructor and their own worst character defects. (Rev: BL 5/1/95)

5398 Coville, Bruce. *Oddly Enough* (6–9). 1994, Harcourt $15.95 (978-0-15-200093-6). Nine short horror stories involving blood drinking, elves, unicorns, ghosts, werewolves, and executioners. (Rev: BL 10/1/94; SLJ 12/94; VOYA 2/95)

5399 Cowing, Sue. *You Will Call Me Drog* (5–8). 2011, Carolrhoda $16.95 (978-076136076-6). A possessed puppet that won't come off a boy's hand turns out to be a good thing, helping him to stick up for himself. (Rev: BL 9/15/11; LMC 1–2/12; SLJ 2/12)

5400 Cray, Jordan. *Gemini 7* (6–10). 1997, Simon & Schuster paper $4.50 (978-0-689-81432-7). In this horror story, Jonah Lanier begins to realize that his new friend, Nicole, might be responsible for the mysterious disasters that are befalling his family and other friends. (Rev: SLJ 1/98)

5401 Creedon, Catherine. *Blue Wolf* (4–8). 2003, HarperCollins LB $16.89 (978-0-06-050869-2). Fantasy lurks around each corner of this story of Jamie, a 14-year-old for whom running is a retreat from life and who sometimes feels that wolves are right at his heels. (Rev: BCCB 1/04; BL 11/15/03; SLJ 10/03)

5402 Crewe, Megan. *Give Up the Ghost* (7–9). 2009, Henry Holt $17.99 (978-080508930-1). Cass has few friends except the ghosts she talks to, until Tim asks her to contact his dead mother. Lexile HL660L (Rev: BLO 5/27/09; SLJ 10/09)

5403 Crowley, Bridget. *Step into the Dark* (5–7). 2003, Hodder & Stoughton paper $8.95 (978-0-340-84416-8). This ghost story is set in a theater and conveys the attraction of the stage. (Rev: BL 12/1/03)

5404 Cusick, Richie Tankersley. *The House Next Door* (6–12). 2002, Simon & Schuster paper $4.99 (978-0-7434-1838-6). Emma dares to spend a night in a haunted house and becomes caught up in a struggle to free a spirit from the past in this tale of supernatural suspense. (Rev: BL 1/1–15/02; SLJ 2/02; VOYA 6/02)

5405 Damico, Gina. *Scorch* (8–12). 2012, Houghton Mifflin $8.99 (978-054762457-0). Neophyte grim reaper Lex, 16, works to earn her stripes in this darkly comic sequel to *Croak* (2012). ∩ **e** (Rev: BLO 10/1/12; SLJ 4/13; VOYA 12/12)

5406 Davis, Heather. *Never Cry Werewolf* (7–10). 2009, HarperTeen $16.99 (978-006134923-2). At a "brat camp," willful 16-year-old Shelby meets an attractive young werewolf named Austin Bridges III. (Rev: BL 7/09; SLJ 12/09)

5407 de Lint, Charles. *The Blue Girl* (8–11). 2004, Penguin $17.99 (978-0-670-05924-9). Imogene, determined to turn over a new leaf at her new high school, strikes up an alliance with loner Maxine and meets the ghost of a former pupil, foreshadowing a struggle between an evil underworld and an inhospitable reality. (Rev: BL 11/15/04; SLJ 11/04; VOYA 12/04)

5408 Del Negro, Janice M. *Passion and Poison: Tales of Shape-Shifters, Ghosts, and Spirited Women* (5–8). Illus. by Vince Natale. 2007, Marshall Cavendish $16.99 (978-0-7614-5361-1). A collection of seven creepy supernatural tales, each featuring females who face peril and challenges. (Rev: BL 9/1/07; SLJ 12/07)

5409 Delaney, Joseph. *Curse of the Bane* (6–9). Illus. by Patrick Arrasmith. Series: The Last Apprentice. 2006, Greenwillow $16.99 (978-0-06-076621-4). On their second adventure Tom and the Spook encounter the Bane and also fall afoul of the Quisitor; when the Spook gets arrested, it's up to Tom and his friend Alice, to save him. (Rev: BL 8/06; SLJ 11/06)

5410 Delaney, Joseph. *Night of the Soul Stealer* (6–9). Series: Last Apprentice. 2007, Greenwillow $16.99 (978-0-06-076624-5). Tom Ward, the 13-year-old apprentice to Mr. Gregory (a Spook who rids the country of ghosts, witches, and boggarts) must decide what to do when the former apprentice, Morgan, tortures his deceased father from beyond the grave. ⌒ (Rev: BL 8/07; SLJ 2/08)

5411 Delaney, Joseph. *Revenge of the Witch* (5–8). Illus. by Patrick Arrasmith. Series: The Last Apprentice. 2005, Greenwillow LB $17.89 (978-0-06-076619-1). A scary story in which young Tom, seventh son of a seventh son, becomes an apprentice spook and must protect the people from ghouls, boggarts, and beasties. (Rev: BCCB 10/05; BL 8/05*; HB 11–12/05; HBG 4/06; LMC 3/06; SLJ 11/05; VOYA 8/06)

5412 Dennard, Susan. *Something Strange and Deadly* (8–12). 2012, HarperCollins $17.99 (978-0-06-208326-5). In a 19th-century Philadelphia troubled by walking dead, gutsy 16-year-old Eleanor is determined to find her missing brother. e (Rev: SLJ 9/12; VOYA 4/12)

5413 Diver, Lucienne. *Fangtastic* (8–12). Series: Vamped. 2012, Flux paper $9.95 (978-07387303-9-4). Gina, an undercover vampire federal agent, and her boyfriend Bobby investigate murders committed by a group of humans acting like vampires. e Lexile 760L (Rev: BLO 2/15/12; SLJ 1/12; VOYA 2/12)

5414 Drago, Ty. *Queen of the Dead* (4–7). 2012, Sourcebooks paper $7.99 (978-1-4022-7-557-9). Will Ritter and his Undertaker friends continue their efforts against the zombies even as a new leader, the Queen of the Dead, enters the picture; a sequel to *Rise of the Corpses*

(2011). e Lexile 660L (Rev: BL 11/1/12; LMC 5–6/13; SLJ 12/12)

5415 Duncan, Lois. *Gallows Hill* (6–9). 1997, Bantam paper $4.99 (978-0-440-22725-0). Sarah is alarmed when her harmless "future telling" turns out to be true and she begins dreaming of the Salem witch trials. (Rev: BL 4/15/97; HBG 3/98; SLJ 5/97; VOYA 4/97)

5416 Duncan, Lois. *Locked in Time* (7–10). 1985, Dell paper $4.99 (978-0-440-94942-8). Nore's father marries into a family that somehow never seems to age. (Rev: BL 7/85; SLJ 11/85)

5417 Duncan, Lois. *Stranger with My Face* (7–10). 1984, Dell paper $5.50 (978-0-440-98356-9). A girl encounters her evil twin, who wishes to take her place.

5418 Duncan, Lois. *Summer of Fear* (7–10). 1976, Dell paper $5.50 (978-0-440-98324-8). An orphaned cousin who comes to live with Rachel's family is really a witch.

5419 Dunkle, Clare B. *By These Ten Bones* (6–9). 2005, Henry Holt $16.95 (978-0-8050-7496-3). Maddie, the weaver's daughter in a medieval Scottish village, finds herself drawn to a mysterious young wood carver who has newly arrived in her town only to discover that he is in fact a werewolf. (Rev: BCCB 5/05; BL 5/1/05; SLJ 6/05; VOYA 6/05)

5420 Dunkle, Clare B. *The House of Dead Maids* (7–10). 2010, Henry Holt $15.99 (978-0-8050-9116-8). In this prequel to *Wuthering Heights,* 11-year-old Tabby arrives at the spooky Seldon House to be a nursemaid to the young Heathcliff (here called Himself) and learns about many previous housemaids who did not survive. ⌒ e (Rev: BL 8/10; HB 11–12/10; LMC 11–12/10; SLJ 11/1/10; VOYA 12/10)

5421 Durst, Sarah Beth. *Drink, Slay, Love* (7–10). 2011, Simon & Schuster $16.99 (978-1-4424-2373-2). After a unicorn attack, teen vampire Pearl develops an uneasy amount of empathy for her victims. ⌒ e (Rev: BL 9/15/11; SLJ 10/1/11)

5422 Enthoven, Sam. *The Black Tattoo* (5–8). 2006, Penguin $19.99 (978-1-59514-114-9). In this action-packed fantasy epic set in London and Hell, three teenage friends — Esme, Charlie, and Jack — work together to defeat a demonic entity that has taken possession of Charlie. ⌒ (Rev: BL 9/1/06; SLJ 1/07)

5423 Fahy, Thomas. *Sleepless* (8–11). 2009, Simon & Schuster $15.99 (978-141695901-4). Emma and her friends are sleepwalking and having horrible nightmares. Could they be responsible for the deaths of some of their classmates? Lexile 710L (Rev: BLO 5/27/09; SLJ 12/09)

5424 Fahy, Thomas. *The Unspoken* (8–12). 2008, Simon & Schuster $15.99 (978-1-4169-4007-4). Allison escaped from a deadly cult years ago, but today she and other teenage survivors are facing mysterious and gory deaths. (Rev: BL 1/1–15/08; LMC 4–5/08; SLJ 4/08)

5425 Falcone, L. M. *Walking with the Dead* (5–8). 2005, Kids Can $16.95 (978-1-55337-708-5). Alex finds himself entangled in the world of Greek mythology when a mummy in his father's museum awakens to take care of some unfinished business in the underworld. (Rev: BL 3/15/05; SLJ 6/05)

5426 Fleischman, Sid. *The Entertainer and the Dybbuk* (6–9). 2007, Greenwillow $16.99 (978-0-06-134445-9). In postwar Europe, Freddie, an ex-GI who's a struggling ventriloquist, meets the ghost of a Jewish child killed in the Holocaust and agrees to help him find the SS officer who murdered him in exchange for help with his act. Sydney Taylor Book Award 2008. (Rev: BL 9/1/07; SLJ 8/07)

5427 Fleming, Candace. *On the Day I Died: Stories from the Grave* (7–10). 2012, Random House $16.99 (978-0-375-86781-1); LB $19.99 (978-0-375-96781-8). Teenage ghosts who died over the decades tell their stories to Mike Kowalski, who has strayed into a Chicago cemetery. ⌒ e Lexile 720L (Rev: BL 5/15/12; LMC 11–12/12; SLJ 10/12)

5428 Ford, Michael. *The Poisoned House* (6–9). 2011, Albert Whitman $16.99 (978-0-8075-6589-6). Abigail, a 14-year-old orphan working as a serving girl in a mansion in Victorian London, discovers dark secrets in this suspenseful novel with a ghostly presence. Lexile HL710L (Rev: BL 8/11; LMC 11–12/11; SLJ 8/11*)

5429 Gabhart, Ann H. *Wish Come True* (7–10). 1988, Avon paper $2.50 (978-0-380-75653-7). Lyssie receives as a gift a mirror that grants her wishes. (Rev: VOYA 6/89)

5430 Garretson, Jerri. *The Secret of Whispering Springs* (7–12). 2002, Ravenstone paper $6.99 (978-0-9659712-4-9). A ghost and a mysterious stranger alert Cassie to potential danger, and a potential fortune, in this suspenseful adventure. (Rev: BL 8/02; SLJ 8/02)

5431 Gibson, Marley. *The Awakening* (7–10). Series: Ghost Huntress. 2009, Harcourt paper $8.99 (978-054715093-2). Newly moved from Chicago to a tiny town in Georgia, 16-year-old Kendall finds herself part of a ghost-hunting team that seeks to free Kendall's father of a troublesome spirit. (Rev: BL 5/15/09; LMC 10/09; SLJ 6/1/09)

5432 Gidwitz, Adam. *A Tale Dark and Grimm* (4–7). 2010, Dutton $16.99 (978-0-525-42334-8). Capitalizing on the gruesome nature of many of the Grimm tales, Gidwitz puts long-suffering Hansel and Gretel through a series of torturous scenarios en route to their happy ending. ALA Notable Books 2011. (Rev: BL 11/15/10; HB 1–2/11; LMC 1–2/11; SLJ 11/1/10*)

5433 Gifaldi, David. *Yours Till Forever* (7–10). 1989, HarperCollins LB $13.89 (978-0-397-32356-2). In this easily read novel, a high school senior sees disturbing

similarities between his friends and his dead parents. (Rev: BL 10/1/89; SLJ 11/89; VOYA 2/90)

5434 Gill, David Macinnis. *Soul Enchilada* (7–10). 2009, Greenwillow $16.99 (978-006167301-6); LB $17.89 (978-006167302-3). A quirky story in which 18-year-old Bug Smoot, whose prize possession is a 1958 Cadillac Biarritz, discovers that the car — and her soul — are part of a deal with the Devil made years before by her grandfather. Best Books for Young Adults 2010. (Rev: BL 11/15/08; SLJ 4/1/09)

5435 Gonick, Larry. *Attack of the Smart Pies* (4–7). Illus. by author. 2005, Cricket $15.95 (978-0-8126-2740-4). This complex novel with graphic elements blends fantasy, horror, mystery, and humor in the story of Emma, a 12-year-old orphan who flees from her threatening foster father and finds herself in Kokonino County, land of the New Muses. (Rev: SLJ 6/05)

5436 Gorog, Judith. *Please Do Not Touch* (6–12). 1995, Scholastic paper $3.50 (978-0-590-46683-7). The reader enters a different fantasy for each of the 11 horror stories. (Rev: BL 9/1/93; VOYA 12/93)

5437 Gorog, Judith. *When Nobody's Home* (6–12). 1996, Scholastic paper $15.95 (978-0-590-46862-6). A collection of 15 terrifying (supposedly true) tales on the theme of baby-sitting. (Rev: BL 5/1/96; SLJ 4/96; VOYA 12/96)

5438 Grabenstein, Chris. *The Black Heart Crypt* (5–8). Series: Haunted Mystery. 2011, Random House $16.99 (978-037586900-6); LB $19.99 (978-037596900-3). Thirteen-year-old Zack and his friends face vengeful ghosts on Halloween in this scary fourth book in the series. e (Rev: BL 8/11; SLJ 2/12)

5439 Grabenstein, Chris. *The Crossroads* (5–8). 2008, Random House $16.99 (978-0-375-84697-7). Zack sees creepy faces in trees in this ghost story full of action, suspense, and likable characters. (Rev: BL 5/1/08)

5440 Gray, Claudia. *Balthazar* (8–11). Series: Evernight. 2012, HarperTeen $17.99 (978-006196118-2). Rogue vampire Balthazar helps psychic Skye, who attended Evernight Academy, when she is threatened by vampire master Redgrave. (Rev: BL 3/1/12; SLJ 3/12; VOYA 2/12)

5441 Griffin, Adele. *Vampire Island* (4–7). 2007, Putnam $14.99 (978-0-399-23785-0). Three Manhattan youngsters — vegetarian vampire siblings Lexington, Madison, and Hudson — try to behave like normal people but their respective vampire traits keep getting in the way in this lighthearted, action-packed story. (Rev: BL 8/07; LMC 11–12/08; SLJ 8/07)

5442 Hahn, Mary Downing. *All the Lovely Bad Ones* (4–7). 2008, Clarion $16.00 (978-0-618-85467-7). Travis and Corey encounter ghosts at their grandmother's bed-and-breakfast, which was a poor house long ago. (Rev: BL 5/1/08; SLJ 5/08)

5443 Hahn, Mary Downing. *Deep and Dark and Dangerous* (5–8). 2007, Clarion $16.00 (978-0-618-66545-7). While spending the summer at her aunt's cottage in Maine, 13-year-old Ali meets a mysterious girl named Sissie who seems to know a great deal about a tragic accident that occurred three decades earlier. (Rev: BL 3/15/07; SLJ 5/07)

5444 Hahn, Mary Downing. *Look for Me by Moonlight* (7–10). 1995, Clarion $16.00 (978-0-395-69843-3). A 16-year-old girl seeking friendship meets a boy whose attention has dangerous strings attached. (Rev: BL 3/15/95; SLJ 5/95)

5445 Hahn, Mary Downing. *Wait Till Helen Comes: A Ghost Story* (5–7). 1986, Houghton Mifflin $15.00 (978-0-89919-453-0); paper $5.99 (978-0-380-70442-2). Things go from bad to worse for Molly and Michael and their stepsister Heather when Heather becomes involved in a frightening relationship with the ghost of a dead child. (Rev: BCCB 10/86; BL 9/1/86; SLJ 10/86)

5446 Hahn, Mary Downing. *Witch Catcher* (4–7). 2006, Clarion $16.00 (978-0-618-50457-2). When Jen and her widowed father move into a rambling old mansion, the 12-year-old girl disregards warnings and investigates an old stone tower behind the house. (Rev: BL 6/1–15/06; SLJ 8/06)

5447 Hamilton, Virginia. *Sweet Whispers, Brother Rush* (7–10). 1982, Putnam $21.99 (978-0-399-20894-2). A 14-year-old girl who cares for her older retarded brother meets a charming ghost who reveals secrets of her past.

5448 Harper, Suzanne. *The Secret Life of Sparrow Delaney* (7–10). 2007, Greenwillow $16.99 (978-0-06-113158-5). Sparrow is a reluctant psychic who must face up to her abilities when she begins seeing a ghost named Luke, the dead brother of a friend at school, who needs help. (Rev: BCCB 9/07; BL 7/07; SLJ 11/07)

5449 Harrison, Kim. *Once Dead, Twice Shy* (8–11). Series: Madison Avery. 2009, HarperTeen $16.99 (978-006171816-8). Madison joins angels, "timekeepers," and other supernatural beings when her soul hovers between life and death following a car crash. ℮ (Rev: BL 2/1/09; SLJ 7/1/09; VOYA 8/09)

5450 Harvey, Alyxandra. *Hearts at Stake* (8–10). Series: Drake Chronicles. 2010, Walker $16.99 (978-0-8027-9840-4). This funny, coming-of-age vampire story — involving 15-year-old Solange (vampire queen to be), her seven protective older brothers, and her feisty mortal friend Lucy — is the first in a series. ℮ Lexile HL660L (Rev: BL 12/1/09; LMC 3–4/10; SLJ 3/10)

5451 Hawes, Jason, and Grant Wilson. *Ghost Hunt: Chilling Tales of the Unknown* (4–8). 2010, Little, Brown $16.99 (978-0-316-09959-2). Stories of ghost investigations by the Atlantic Paranormal Society are paired with discussion of the techniques used. Also use *Ghost Hunt 2: More Chilling Tales of the Unknown* (2011). ℮ (Rev: SLJ 11/1/10; VOYA 12/10)

5452 Hawes, Louise. *Rosey in the Present Tense* (8–12). 1999, Walker $15.95 (978-0-8027-8685-2). After the death of his girlfriend, Rosey, 17-year-old Franklin can't stop living in the past until the ghost of Rosey and his family and friends help him accept his loss and begin to think of the present. (Rev: BL 4/1/99; HBG 9/99; SLJ 5/99; VOYA 10/99)

5453 Hawkins, Rachel. *Demonglass* (7–11). Series: Hex Hall. 2011, Disney/Hyperion $16.99 (978-1-4231-2131-2). Young demon Sophie must decide whether to live out her family legacy or have her magical powers removed. ⌾ ℮ (Rev: BL 2/15/11; SLJ 7/11; VOYA 12/10)

5454 Hawkins, Rachel. *Hex Hall* (8–11). 2010, Hyperion $16.99 (978-142312130-5). When an attempt at casting a spell is unsuccessful, 16-year-old part-warlock Sophie is shipped off to a school for unruly supernaturally talented beings; a humorous and clever series starter. ⌾ ℮ Lexile 790L (Rev: BL 3/15/10; VOYA 6/10)

5455 Henderson, Jason. *Vampire Rising* (5–8). Series: Alex Van Helsing. 2010, HarperTeen $16.99 (978-006195099-5). When he is sent to school in Switzerland, 14-year-old Alex Van Helsing learns that vampires are real and that his family has been participating in a vampire-hunting agency called the Polidorium since 1821. ℮ Lexile HL780L (Rev: BL 3/1/10; SLJ 5/10; VOYA 6/10)

5456 Henderson, Jason. *Voice of the Undead* (5–8). Series: Alex Van Helsing. 2011, HarperTeen $16.99 (978-0-06-195101-5). Vampire hunter Alex Van Helsing has another exciting adventure, this time involving Ultravox, a vampire with special vocal gifts. (Rev: BL 5/1/11; SLJ 9/1/11)

5457 Hightman, J. P. *Spirit* (6–10). 2008, HarperTeen $16.99 (978-006085063-0); LB $17.89 (978-006085064-7). Depraved, ghostly Old Widow Malgore haunts 1892 Blackthorne, Massachusetts, and newlyweds Tess and Tobias have their share of gruesome, eerie encounters as they explore the abandoned town and try to wrest Blackthorn's secret from its keeper. ℮ Lexile NC800L (Rev: BL 8/08; SLJ 9/1/08; VOYA 12/08)

5458 Hodges, Margaret, ed. *Hauntings: Ghosts and Ghouls from Around the World* (5–8). Illus. by David Wenzel. 1991, Little, Brown $16.95 (978-0-316-36796-7). A diverse collection of 16 familiar and lesser-known tales about the supernatural. (Rev: BL 11/15/91; HB 11–12/91; SLJ 11/91) [398.2]

5459 Hoffman, Nina Kiriki. *Spirits That Walk in Shadow* (8–11). 2006, Viking $17.99 (978-0-670-06071-9). In alternating narratives, roommates Kim and Jaimie describe their story; Jaimie, blessed with unusual powers, is determined to rid Kim of a tiresome "viri." (Rev: BL 11/1/06; SLJ 1/07)

5460 Holder, Nancy, and Debbie Viguié. *Crusade* (7–11). 2010, Simon & Schuster $16.99 (978-1-4169-

9802-0). Jenn has trained at Spain's Salamanca Academy for vampire hunters and is now part of a teenage team battling power-hungry vampires. **e** (Rev: BL 9/15/10; SLJ 12/1/10)

5461 Holt, Simon. *Soulstice* (8–12). Series: The Devouring. 2009, Little, Brown $16.99 (978-0-316-03571-2). In this sequel to 2008's *The Devouring,* the evil Vours return, and Reggie — who can access the "fearscape" and retrieve human spirits — faces more demons in order to protect those she holds dear. **e** Lexile HL750L (Rev: SLJ 1/10; VOYA 2/10)

5462 Horowitz, Anthony. *Horowitz Horror: Stories You'll Wish You'd Never Read* (6–9). 2006, Philomel $9.99 (978-0-399-24489-6). A collection of nine creepy tales — about a camera that kills its subjects, a haunted bathtub that drips blood, and more; also use *More Horowitz Horror* (2007). (Rev: BL 9/1/06; SLJ 10/06)

5463 Horowitz, Anthony. *Raven's Gate* (5–8). Series: The Gatekeepers. 2005, Scholastic $17.95 (978-0-439-67995-4). Faced with a choice between jail and life in a remote Yorkshire village, 14-year-old Matt chooses the latter, unaware that he's about to enter a world of frightening evil. (Rev: BL 7/05*; SLJ 7/05; VOYA 10/05)

5464 Ita, Sam. *Frankenstein: A Pop-Up Book* (4–7). Illus. by author. 2010, Sterling $26.95 (978-1-4027-5865-2). With pop-up features, this abridged graphic novel version is effectively scary. (Rev: BL 12/15/10; SLJ 9/1/10)

5465 Jacobs, Deborah Lynn. *Powers* (7–10). 2006, Roaring Brook $16.95 (978-1-59643-112-6). When Gwen meets Adrian they feel a powerful connection between themselves, and their powers — hers to see future tragedies and his to read others' minds — are increased; but can they learn to trust each other and work together? (Rev: BL 8/06; LMC 2/07; SLJ 10/06; VOYA)

5466 Jacques, Brian. *Seven Strange and Ghostly Tales* (4–7). 1991, Avon paper $3.99 (978-0-380-71906-8). Seven genuinely scary stories with touches of humor. (Rev: BCCB 12/91; BL 1/1/91*; HB 5–6/92; SLJ 12/91)

5467 Jarvis, Robin. *Thomas: Book Three of the Deptford Histories* (5–8). 2006, Chronicle $17.95 (978-0-8118-5412-2). This prequel to the Deptford Mice trilogy, written as the memoirs of an old sea mouse, contains plenty of battles, storms and heroic deeds and can be read as a stand-alone novel. (Rev: BL 1/1–15/07)

5468 Jennings, Patrick. *Wish Riders* (5–8). 2006, Hyperion $15.99 (978-1-4231-0010-2). Combining historical fiction and fantasy, this tale of transformation focuses on Edith, 15, who slaves with four other foster children, cooking and cleaning in a Depression-era logging camp until a mysterious seed pod grows into five horses that spirit the children away to forest adventures. (Rev: BL 1/1–15/07)

5469 Jobling, Curtis. *Shadow of the Hawk* (5–7). Series: Wereworld. 2012, Viking $16.99 (978-067078455-4). Young werewolf Drew fights for his life while enslaved on the isle of Scoria; the third volume in the series. **e** Lexile 910L (Rev: BL 10/1/12; SLJ 9/12)

5470 Johnson, Charles. *Pieces of Eight* (5–7). Illus. by Jennie Anne Nelson. 1989, Discovery $9.95 (978-0-944770-00-9). David and Mitchell rouse a sea captain's ghost and get to meet Blackbeard the pirate. (Rev: BL 3/15/89)

5471 Johnson, Maureen. *Devilish* (8–11). 2006, Penguin $16.99 (978-1-59514-060-9). Jane, a high school senior, finds out that her best friend Ally has sold her soul to a demon in exchange for popularity; Jane's efforts to help lead her into real danger. (Rev: BL 10/15/06; HB 11–12/06; SLJ 10/06)

5472 Johnson, Maureen. *The Name of the Star* (8–11). 2011, Putnam $16.99 (978-0-399-25660-8). A paranormal mystery/romance in which 18-year-old Rory arrives in London from Louisiana and discovers that she can see ghosts that may be involved in a series of horrific murders mirroring Jack the Ripper's 1888 killings. YALSA Popular Paperbacks for Young Adults Top Ten 2013. ∩ **e** Lexile HL710L (Rev: BL 9/1/11; HB 11–12/11; LMC 1–2/12; SLJ 9/1/11)

5473 Jones, Claudia. *Riding Out the Storm* (6–8). 2006, Llewellyn paper $8.95 (978-0-7387-0867-6). Thirteen-year-old Emily attends therapy after a near-drowning incident gives her constant nightmares; here she uncovers that she is the reincarnation of a man who died in a boating accident and goes on a search for more information on her past life. (Rev: SLJ 5/06)

5474 Jones, Diana Wynne. *The Game* (5–8). 2007, Penguin $11.99 (978-0-14-240718-9). Hayley, an orphan who has been raised by her difficult grandparents, now finds herself amid a large, happy family in Ireland with cousins who love to play in the mythosphere, a land of stories where secrets about her past reside. (Rev: BL 12/1/06; SLJ 3/07)

5475 Kade, Stacey. *Queen of the Dead* (8–12). 2011, Hyperion $16.99 (978-1-4231-3467-1). Ghost Alona is shocked to find that her parents are recovering from her death, while Will is becoming involved with a group of ghost-talkers; a sequel to *The Ghost and the Goth* (2010). **e** Lexile 810L (Rev: BL 7/11; SLJ 11/1/11)

5476 Kagawa, Julie. *The Immortal Rules* (7–10). Series: Blood of Eden. 2012, HarlequinTeen $18.99 (978-0-373-21051-0). Desperate to survive in the new world with few humans, Allison chooses to become a vampire but then must face the rabids. ∩ **e** (Rev: BL 4/15/12; LMC 10/12; SLJ 10/12)

5477 Kaye, Marilyn. *Better Late Than Never* (6–9). Series: Gifted. 2009, Kingfisher paper $6.99 (978-8-7534-6300-0). An ability to read minds has made strong, savvy Jenna unwilling to trust others — until she meets a man who claims to be her father. Lexile HL680L (Rev: LMC 10/09; SLJ 6/1/09)

5478 Keehn, Sally M. *Gnat Stokes and the Foggy Bottom Swamp Queen* (5–8). 2005, Putnam $16.99 (978-0-399-24287-8). This fantasy, set in the Appalachian mountains, features a 12-year-old girl named Gnat who faces swamp creatures and spells in her quest to rescue Goodlow Pryce. (Rev: BL 3/1/05; SLJ 4/05)

5479 Kehret, Peg. *Ghost's Grave* (5–8). 2005, Dutton $16.99 (978-0-525-46162-3). Josh expects to be bored when he stays in his aunt's old house, but the ghost of a coal miner who died in 1903 livens things up. (Rev: BL 5/15/05; SLJ 10/05)

5480 Kelleher, Victor. *Del-Del* (7–12). 1992, Walker $17.95 (978-0-8027-8154-3). A family believes its son is possessed by an evil alien. (Rev: BL 3/1/92; SLJ 6/92)

5481 Kennedy, Kim. *Misty Gordon and the Mystery of the Ghost Pirates* (4–7). Illus. by Greg Call. 2010, Abrams $15.95 (978-0-8109-9357-0). Eleven-year-old Misty finds an old diary that draws her into secrets of the past in this mystery involving ghosts and pirates. e Lexile 780L (Rev: BL 9/1/10; LMC 1–2/11; SLJ 10/1/10)

5482 Klause, Annette Curtis. *The Silver Kiss* (8–12). 1992, Bantam paper $5.50 (978-0-440-21346-8). A teenage girl, beset with personal problems, meets a silver-haired boy who is a vampire in this suspenseful, sometimes gory, novel. (Rev: BL 10/15/90; SLJ 9/90)

5483 Knight, Karsten. *Wildfire* (8–10). 2011, Simon & Schuster $16.99 (978-1-4424-2117-2). Ashline contends with life in a new boarding school, and the sudden realization that she's descended from Polynesian fire goddess Pele. e Lexile 970L (Rev: BL 7/11; SLJ 12/1/11; VOYA 8/11)

5484 Koontz, Dean. *Life Expectancy* (8–12). 2004, Bantam $27.00 (978-0-553-80414-0). Jimmy is stalked by a mad clown from the moment of his birth in this novel that spoofs cinematic and literary conventions. (Rev: BL 11/1/04)

5485 Krovatin, Christopher. *Gravediggers: Mountain of Bones* (6–9). 2012, HarperCollins $16.99 (978-006207740-0). Three 11-year-olds — athletic Ian, brainy Kendra, and thoughtful PJ — find themselves dealing with zombies in the mountains of Montana. ∩ e (Rev: BL 9/15/12; SLJ 2/13; VOYA 6/12)

5486 Lackey, Mercedes, and Rosemary Edghill. *Dead Reckoning* (7–10). 2012, Bloomsbury $16.99 (978-1-59990-684-3). In 1867 Texas 17-year-old Jeff Gallatin, a girl posing as a boy as she searches for her twin brother, joins up with a motley crew — including an independent-minded scientist inventor named Honoria Gibbons — to determine the source of a scourge of zombies. e Lexile 960L (Rev: BL 8/12; LMC 10/12; SLJ 7/12; VOYA 4/12)

5487 Langrish, Katherine. *Troll Fell* (5–7). 2004, HarperCollins $16.99 (978-0-06-058304-0). Sent to live with his evil twin uncles after his father's death, 12-year-old Peer Ulfsson seeks a way to foil their plan to sell children to the trolls. (Rev: BL 4/15/04*; SLJ 7/04; VOYA 6/04)

5488 Langston, Laura. *Exit Point* (8–12). 2006, Orca $14.95 (978-1-55143-525-1); paper $7.95 (978-1-55143-505-3). When Logan wakes up dead, he watches over his family in spirit form, and commits himself to saving his younger sister from abuse before he moves on forever; for reluctant readers. (Rev: SLJ 8/06)

5489 Lindsey, Mary. *Shattered Souls* (8–12). 2011, Philomel $16.99 (978-039925622-6). After she starts hearing voices, high school student Lenzi discovers she is a "Speaker" and can help the dead with unresolved issues. e (Rev: BL 12/15/11; SLJ 1/12)

5490 Lubar, David. *Beware the Ninja Weenies and Other Warped and Creepy Tales* (4–7). 2012, Starscape $15.99 (978-076533213-4). Horror and humor are combined in 33 varied short stories. e (Rev: BL 8/12; LMC 1–2/13)

5491 Lubar, David. *The Curse of the Campfire Weenies: And Other Warped and Creepy Tales* (5–7). 2007, Tor $15.95 (978-0-7653-1807-7). Thirty-five creepy stories combine scariness and dark humor in a way that will attract reluctant readers. (Rev: SLJ 12/07)

5492 Lubar, David. *True Talents* (5–8). 2007, Tor $17.95 (978-0-7653-0977-8). In this sequel to *Hidden Talents* (1999), the paranormally gifted student friends from Edgeview Alternative School flex their extraordinary powers in a series of interconnected adventures; memos, e-mails, and illustrations add to the action-packed narrative. (Rev: BL 3/15/07; SLJ 4/07)

5493 MacDonald, Caroline. *Hostilities: Nine Bizarre Stories* (7–10). 1994, Scholastic paper $13.95 (978-0-590-46063-7). A collection of nine tales with strange, unsettling themes and Australian locales. (Rev: BL 1/15/94; SLJ 3/94; VOYA 10/94)

5494 MacHale, D. J. *The Light* (6–10). Series: Morpheus Road. 2010, Aladdin $17.99 (978-1-4169-6516-9). A fast-paced fantasy thriller in which Marshall has frightening visions and is pursued by a figure called Gravedigger while he searches for his missing friend Coop. ∩ e (Rev: BLO 4/15/10; LMC 8–9/10; SLJ 5/10)

5495 McKay, Kristy. *Undead* (7–10). 2012, Scholastic $17.99 (978-0-545-38188-8). On a school trip to Scotland, four teens deal with various challenges after their companions turn into zombies. ∩ e Lexile HL630L (Rev: BL 10/15/12; LMC 1–2/13; SLJ 10/12)

5496 McKissack, Patricia C. *The Dark-Thirty: Southern Tales of the Supernatural* (5–8). 1992, Knopf $17.99 (978-0-679-91863-9). Ten original stories, rooted in African American history and the oral-storytelling tradition, deal with such subjects as slavery, belief in "the sight," and the Montgomery bus boycott. (Rev: BCCB 12/92; BL 12/15/92; HB 3–4/93; SLJ 12/92*)

5497 McNamee, Graham. *Beyond* (7–10). 2012, Random House $15.99 (978-0-385-73775-3); LB $18.99 (978-0-385-90687-6). Jane, 17, is accused of attempting suicide when really her shadow is trying to kill her. **e** Lexile HL600L (Rev: BL 9/15/12; HB 11–12/12; SLJ 10/12; VOYA 12/12)

5498 McNeil, Gretchen. *Possess* (7–10). 2011, HarperCollins $17.99 (978-006206071-6). Fifteen-year-old exorcist Bridget must cope with many demonic challenges in this entertaining tale of possession. **e** (Rev: BL 9/15/11; LMC 1–2/12; SLJ 3/12; VOYA 10/12)

5499 McNeil, Gretchen. *Ten* (8–11). 2012, HarperCollins $17.99 (978-0-06-211878-3). A teen house party on a remote island turns lethal and young Meg and Minnie must deal with the nightmare. YALSA Quick Picks for Reluctant Young Adult Readers 2013. **e** (Rev: BL 10/1/12; SLJ 10/12; VOYA 8/12)

5500 Mahy, Margaret, and Susan Cooper. *Don't Read This! And Other Tales of the Unnatural* (7–10). 1998, Front St $15.95 (978-1-886910-22-5). Great stories of ghosts and the supernatural are included in this international collection that represents some of the top writers of scary fiction at work today. (Rev: BL 4/1/99; HBG 9/99; SLJ 7/99; VOYA 6/99)

5501 Maguire, Eden. *Jonas* (6–9). Series: Beautiful Dead. 2010, Sourcebooks paper $8.99 (978-1-4022-3944-1). The "Beautiful Dead" are four teens from her high school who recently died, and Darina agrees to help them resolve the mysteries of their deaths in exchange for time with her late boyfriend, Phoenix. Lexile HL700L (Rev: BLO 2/15/10; LMC 5–6/10; SLJ 3/10)

5502 Matthews, L. S. *The Outcasts* (7–10). 2007, Delacorte $15.99 (978-0-385-73367-0). Five misfit students wonder why they have been chosen for a field trip to a mysterious estate — until they discover that they must endure surreal trials to make it back alive. (Rev: BL 11/15/07; SLJ 1/08)

5503 Medearis, Angela Shelf. *Haunts: Five Hair-Raising Tales* (4–7). Illus. by Trina Schart Hyman. 1996, Holiday $15.95 (978-0-8234-1280-8). Five stories that contain elements of horror and the supernatural. (Rev: BL 2/1/97; SLJ 4/97)

5504 Meyer, Stephenie. *Eclipse* (8–11). Series: Twilight. 2007, Little, Brown $18.99 (978-0-316-16020-9). Human teen Bella and vampire Edward continue their relationship in the face of opposition from werewolf Jacob (who's in love with Bella too) while Bella also faces decisions about college and her future. ∩ (Rev: BL 9/15/07; SLJ 10/07)

5505 Meyer, Stephenie. *New Moon* (8–11). Series: Twilight. 2006, Little, Brown $17.99 (978-0-316-16019-3). In this sequel to *Twilight* (2005), Bella laments boy-friend Edward's departure and engages in dangerous behavior. ∩ (Rev: BL 7/06; SLJ 8/06)

5506 Moloney, James. *Trapped* (4–8). Illus. by Shaun Tan. 2008, Stone Arch LB $16.95 (978-1-59889-863-7). David, a skateboarder, can't resist exploring a huge drainpipe even though he knows that two boys once died there in this illustrated book that will appeal to reluctant readers. (Rev: BL 12/15/07; SLJ 2/08)

5507 Montes, Marisa. *A Circle of Time* (6–8). 2002, Harcourt $17.00 (978-0-15-202626-4). In a coma after an accident, 14-year-old Allison Blair travels back in time to 1906 California to help two young people in trouble there. (Rev: BL 5/1/02; HBG 10/02; SLJ 8/02; VOYA 6/02)

5508 Moore, Peter. *Red Moon Rising* (7–10). 2011, Disney/Hyperion $16.99 (978-1-4231-1665-3). Dante "Danny" Gray is part vamp and part wulf, not a good combination in his world where vampyres are top, humans are in the middle, and werewolves are the lowest; now his wulf side seems to be coming to the fore . . . **e** Lexile HL580L (Rev: BL 6/1/11; SLJ 11/1/11)

5509 Morpurgo, Michael, ed. *Ghostly Haunts* (6–9). 1997, Trafalgar paper $16.95 (978-1-85793-833-3). Some of Britain's best writers for young people, including Dick King-Smith and Joan Aiken, have contributed to this collection of supernatural stories. (Rev: BL 3/15/97)

5510 Morton-Shaw, Christine. *The Hunt for the Seventh* (5–8). 2008, HarperCollins $16.99 (978-0-06-072822-9). Recently moved with his family to the stately Minerva Hall, young Jim finds himself haunted by the ghosts of children who have died in strange accidents. (Rev: BL 1/1–15/09; LMC 3/09; SLJ 5/09)

5511 Moskowitz, Hannah. *Zombie Tag* (5–8). 2011, Roaring Brook $15.99 (978-1-59643-720-3). Zombie tag is just a game until 12-year-old Will's older brother Graham suddenly comes back to life. (Rev: BL 12/15/11; SLJ 12/1/11)

5512 Myracle, Lauren. *Rhymes with Witches* (8–11). 2005, Abrams $16.95 (978-0-8109-5859-3). Invited to join a super-popular clique at her high school, Jane is at first flattered but soon discovers that she's involved in something sinister. (Rev: BCCB 5/05; BL 3/15/05; SLJ 4/05)

5513 Nance, Andrew. *Daemon Hall* (7–10). Illus. by Coleman Polhemus. 2007, Henry Holt $16.95 (978-0-8050-8171-8). Three teenaged writers win a night at a haunted mansion with a horror writer, and each contestant must tell a spooky story by candlelight. Will all the contestants survive? (Rev: BCCB 6/07; BL 7/07; SLJ 12/07)

5514 Nance, Andrew. *Return to Daemon Hall: Evil Roots* (7–10). Illus. by Coleman Polhemus. 2011, Henry Holt $16.99 (978-0-8050-8748-2). In this follow-up to *Daemon Hall* (2007), author Tremblin holds another

315

horror writing contest, this time in a supposedly safer location. **e** Lexile HL690L (Rev: BLO 8/11; SLJ 8/11)

5515 Nayeri, Daniel, and Dina Nayeri. *Another Faust* (8–10). 2009, Candlewick $16.99 (978-0-7636-3707-1). In this well-written, Faustian tale, a wicked governess leads five siblings to exchange their souls for supernatural gifts. ∩ **e** Lexile 740L (Rev: BL 9/15/09; LMC 10/09; SLJ 9/09; VOYA 8/09)

5516 Nayeri, Daniel, and Dina Nayeri. *Another Jekyll, Another Hyde* (7–10). 2012, Candlewick $17.99 (978-076365261-6). Wealthy teen Thomas Goodman-Brown is in danger of losing his mind and soul through his evil stepmother's machinations; the sequel to *Another Faust* (2009) and *Another Pan* (2010). **e** (Rev: BL 2/1/12; SLJ 3/12; VOYA 4/12)

5517 Naylor, Phyllis Reynolds. *Jade Green: A Ghost Story* (5–8). 2000, Simon & Schuster $16.00 (978-0-689-82005-2). Set in South Carolina about 100 years ago, this ghost story involves Judith Sparrow, age 15, and the mystery surrounding the gruesome death of a girl named Jade Green. (Rev: BL 12/15/99; HBG 10/00; SLJ 2/00; VOYA 6/00)

5518 Nelson, Marilyn, and Tonya C. Hegamin. *Pemba's Song: A Ghost Story* (7–10). 2008, Scholastic $16.99 (978-054502076-3). African American 14-year-old Pemba is aghast when her family relocates from Brooklyn to rural Connecticut, and unsettled when she starts having dreams about an 18th-century slave girl. Lexile 730L (Rev: BL 11/1/08; LMC 3–4/09; SLJ 12/08)

5519 Newbery, Linda. *Lost Boy* (5–8). 2008, Random House $15.99 (978-0-375-84574-1). New to the town of Hay-on-Wye in Wales, Matt feels the presence of a boy who died there several years before. (Rev: BCCB 3/08; BL 4/1/08; LMC 4–5/08; SLJ 3/08)

5520 Nixon, Joan Lowery. *Whispers from the Dead* (7–12). 1991, Bantam paper $4.99 (978-0-440-20809-9). After being saved from drowning, Sarah is able to communicate with dead spirits. (Rev: BL 9/15/89; SLJ 9/89; VOYA 12/89)

5521 Noël, Alyson. *Radiance* (5–8). Series: Riley Bloom. 2010, Square Fish paper $7.99 (978-0-312-62917-5). When Riley crosses over into the afterlife, she must adapt to her surroundings by relying on Bodhi, her well-intentioned guide. ∩ **e** Lexile 1120L (Rev: LMC 3–4/11; SLJ 9/1/10)

5522 Noël, Alyson. *Shimmer* (5–8). Series: Riley Bloom. 2011, Square Fish paper $7.99 (978-0-312-64-825-1). Riley, a dead 12-year-old who is now a Soul Catcher, works with her mentor Bodhi to control the antics of vengeful Rebecca, who died during a slave revolt in 1733. (Rev: BL 5/1/11; SLJ 4/11)

5523 Norton, Andre, and Phyllis Miller. *House of Shadows* (7–9). 1984, Tor paper $2.95 (978-0-8125-4743-6). While staying with a great-aunt, three children learn about the family curse.

5524 Noyes, Deborah. *Gothic! Ten Original Dark Tales* (7–10). 2005, Candlewick $15.99 (978-0-7636-2243-5). Ten Gothic tales by contemporary authors embody the dark fantasy and the fairy tale aspects of the genre as well as offering supernatural horror plus humor. (Rev: BL 10/15/04; SLJ 1/05)

5525 Noyes, Deborah, ed. *The Restless Dead: Ten Original Stories of the Supernatural* (8–12). 2007, Candlewick $16.99 (978-0-7636-2906-9). Vampires, corpses, ghosts, and more appear in these scary stories by well-known YA authors. (Rev: BL 5/15/07; HB 9–10/07; LMC 11/07; SLJ 9/07)

5526 Olson, Arielle North, and Howard Schwartz. *More Bones: Scary Stories from Around the World* (4–7). Illus. by E. M. Gist. 2008, Viking $15.99 (978-0-670-06339-0). This collection of 22 retellings of scary stories from around the world features witches and wizards, corpses and ghosts, and lots of unexpected twists. (Rev: BL 10/1/08; SLJ 9/08)

5527 Olson, Arielle North, and Howard Schwartz, eds. *Ask the Bones: Scary Stories from Around the World* (5–9). 1999, Viking $16.99 (978-0-670-87581-8). A collection of 22 scary stories about subjects ranging from ghosts to witches and voodoo spells, accompanied by spooky illustrations. (Rev: BCCB 4/99; BL 5/1/99; HB 5–6/99; HBG 10/99; SLJ 4/99)

5528 Oppel, Kenneth. *This Dark Endeavor: The Apprenticeship of Victor Frankenstein* (8–12). 2011, Simon & Schuster $17.99 (978-1-4424-0315-4). In this first installment in a series set in the independent republic of Geneva in the 18th century, young Victor seeks a cure for his deathly ill twin brother, enlisting the help of an alchemist. ∩ **e** Lexile 690L (Rev: BL 6/1/11; HB 7–8/11; SLJ 10/1/11; VOYA 10/11)

5529 Patten, E. J. *Return to Exile* (5–8). Illus. by John Rocco. Series: Hunter Chronicles. 2011, Simon & Schuster $16.99 (978-1-4424-2032-8). Twelve-year-old Sky and his family have moved back to the small town of Exile, Sky's Uncle Phineas has disappeared, and Sky appears to be being targeted by monsters. **e** Lexile 800L (Rev: BL 10/15/11; LMC 5–6/12; SLJ 12/1/11)

5530 Pearce, Jackson. *Sisters Red* (8–12). 2010, Little, Brown $16.99 (978-0-316-06868-0). Sisters Scarlett and Rosie set out for revenge when a werewolf kills their grandmother and injures Scarlett; a retelling of the Little Red Riding Hood story with a twist that will appeal to fans of werewolves and vampires. (Rev: BL 4/15/10; HB 9–10/10; LMC 8–9/10; SLJ 5/10)

5531 Peck, Richard. *The Ghost Belonged to Me* (5–8). 1997, Viking paper $5.99 (978-0-14-038671-4). Richard unwillingly receives the aid of his nemesis, Blossom Culp, in trying to solve the mystery behind the ghost of a young girl. Two sequels are *Ghosts I Have Been* (1977); *The Dreadful Future of Blossom Culp* (1983).

5532 Peck, Richard. *Three Quarters Dead* (6–9). 2010, Dial $16.99 (978-0-8037-3454-8). When the three mean-spirited but popular girls who briefly adopted underdog Kerry as one of their own die in a car accident, Kerry is startled to receive a text message from them — from beyond the grave. ⌒ **℮** Lexile HL550L (Rev: BL 10/15/10; HB 9–10/10; LMC 1–2/11; SLJ 10/1/10)

5533 Pendleton, Thomas. *Mason* (8–10). 2008, Harper-Collins paper $8.99 (978-0-06-117736-1). Cruel and violent Gene terrorizes his brother Mason, as well as Mason's friends, until Mason begins to use his mind to retaliate. (Rev: BL 5/15/08)

5534 Perez, Marlene. *Dead Is a Battlefield* (7–9). Series: Nightshade. 2012, Houghton Mifflin paper $7.99 (978-05476073-4-4). Ninth-grader Jessica Walsh discovers she is a Virago — a woman warrior — but is she ready to protect the city of Nightshade from vampires and zombies? **℮** Lexile HL580L (Rev: BL 2/1/12)

5535 Perez, Marlene. *Dead Is a State of Mind* (7–10). Series: Nightshade. 2009, Graphia paper $7.99 (978-015206210-1). In this sequel to *Dead Is the New Black* (2008), 17-year-old Daisy and other residents of Night-shade, California — some of them with supernatural abilities — are shaken when a teacher at the high school is murdered. An entertaining combination of romance, mystery, and the paranormal. **℮** Lexile HL620L (Rev: BLO 1/7/09; SLJ 2/1/09)

5536 Perez, Marlene. *Dead Is Not an Option* (7–9). Series: Nightshade. 2011, Houghton Mifflin paper $7.99 (978-05473459-3-2). Senior Daisy copes with typical high school social woes along with worrying about college acceptance and the vampires and werewolves threatening the prom. ⌒ **℮** Lexile HL630L (Rev: BL 5/1/11; VOYA 10/11)

5537 Perez, Marlene. *Dead Is the New Black* (7–9). Series: Nightshade. 2008, Harcourt paper $7.95 (978-015206408-2). Daisy suspects that popular cheerleader Samantha isn't just trying to look undead, she really is, in this fun, fast-paced book that is part mystery, part romance, and part supernatural thriller. **℮** Lexile 640L (Rev: BLO 12/8/08; SLJ 11/1/08)

5538 Peterson, Will. *Triskellion* (5–9). Series: Triskellion. 2008, Candlewick $16.99 (978-0-7636-3971-6). Telepathic twins Adam and Rachel, 14, are spending the summer in an ancient English village and find themselves swept into an adventure involving archaeology, folklore, and an ancient artifact; the first volume in a series. (Rev: BCCB 9/08; LMC 10/08; SLJ 11/08; VOYA 8-08)

5539 Pines, T., ed. *Thirteen: 13 Tales of Horror by 13 Masters of Horror* (8–12). 1991, Scholastic paper $6.99 (978-0-590-45256-4). Popular horror writers' stories of revenge, lust, and betrayal. (Rev: BL 3/1/92)

5540 Pipe, Jim. *The Werewolf* (4–7). Series: In the Foot-steps Of. 1996, Millbrook LB $24.90 (978-0-7613-0450-0). A horror story in which Bernard, a werewolf, commits terrible acts under the influence of a full moon. (Rev: SLJ 7/96)

5541 Poblocki, Dan. *The Nightmarys* (6–10). 2010, Random House $16.99 (978-0-375-84256-6). In this scary mystery story 7th-grader Timothy and his new classmate Abigail try to undo the curse on Abigail's family that is having an impact on them all. **℮** Lexile 680L (Rev: BL 8/10; LMC 11–12/10; SLJ 12/1/10)

5542 Poe, Edgar Allan. *The Cask of Amontillado* (8–12). Illus. by Gary Kelley. Series: Creative Short Stories. 2008, Creative Education LB $19.95 (978-1-58341-580-1). This chilling short story of revenge is accompanied by illustrations and brief biographical information about the author. (Rev: BL 4/30/08; SLJ 8/08)

5543 Potter, Ellen. *Olivia Kidney and the Exit Academy* (4–7). Illus. by Peter H. Reynolds. Series: Olivia Kidney. 2005, Putnam $15.99 (978-0-399-24162-8). After her brother's death, Olivia and her father move into a creepy apartment building where, she discovers, people go to rehearse their deaths. (Rev: BL 3/15/05; SLJ 5/05)

5544 Potter, Ellen. *Olivia Kidney and the Secret Beneath the City* (5–7). Series: Olivia Kidney. 2007, Philomel $16.99 (978-0-399-24701-9). Twelve-year-old Olivia is starting 7th grade at a new arts school and also dealing with other problems real and surreal in this third book in the series. (Rev: BL 5/1/07; SLJ 6/07)

5545 Pratchett, Terry. *Johnny and the Dead* (5–8). Series: Johnny Maxwell. 2006, HarperCollins LB $16.89 (978-0-06-054189-7). In the funny second volume of this trilogy, ghosts of the "post-senior citizens" buried in a local cemetery ask the title character to help block plans to bulldoze their final resting place. (Rev: BL 12/15/05; HB 1–2/06; SLJ 12/05; VOYA 2/06)

5546 Preussler, Otfried. *The Satanic Mill* (7–10). 1987, Peter Smith $31.50 (978-0-8446-6196-4). A young apprentice outwits a strange magician in this fantasy first published in 1972. (Rev: BL 6/1–15/98)

5547 Primavera, Elise. *The Secret Order of the Gumm Street Girls* (4–7). 2006, HarperCollins $16.99 (978-0-06-056946-4). Four girls who live on Gumm Street have little in common until a series of incidents appear to threaten their picturesque town of Sherbet and Franny, Pru, Cat, and Ivy find themselves on a very Oz-like adventure. (Rev: BL 12/15/06; SLJ 12/06)

5548 Prose, Francine. *The Turning* (8–12). 2012, HarperTeen $17.99 (978-0-06-199966-6). In this gripping modern twist on *The Turn of the Screw,* Jackson finds himself looking after two children on a remote island where there are strange events. **℮** (Rev: BL 8/12; SLJ 10/12; VOYA 8/12)

5549 Radford, Michelle. *Totally Fabulous* (7–10). 2009, HarperTeen paper $8.99 (978-006128531-8). British 14-year-old Fiona travels to New Jersey to spend time with her long-lost father and attend an ESP boot camp to hone her psychic powers. (Rev: BL 7/09)

5550 Rees, Celia. *The Soul Taker* (5–8). 2004, Hodder paper $7.95 (978-0-340-87817-0). Lewis, overweight and lacking confidence, finds himself in thrall to a sinister toy maker. (Rev: BL 1/1–15/04)

5551 Rees, Douglas. *Vampire High* (6–9). 2003, Delacorte $15.95 (978-0-385-73117-1). A flunking Cody is sent to Vlad Dracul Magnet School where he finds his classmates very strange, but he soon adapts to their vampire nature. (Rev: BCCB 11/03; BL 8/03; HB 9–10/03; SLJ 11/03)

5552 Reiss, Kathryn. *Sweet Miss Honeywell's Revenge* (4–7). 2004, Harcourt $17.00 (978-0-15-216574-1). A haunted dollhouse, a parallel story about the original owner of the antique, and the problems of blended family life are intertwined in this story about 12-year-old Zibby Thorne. (Rev: BL 5/1/04; SLJ 8/04)

5553 Rich, Susan, ed. *Half-Minute Horrors* (5–8). 2009, HarperCollins $12.99 (978-0-06-183379-3). A collection of varied short horror stories by more than 70 authors. Lexile 720L (Rev: BL 9/15/09; HB 1–2/10; SLJ 1/10)

5554 Richards, Justin. *The Parliament of Blood* (6–9). 2008, Bloomsbury $16.99 (978-159990140-4). Set in Victorian England, this book oozes zombies, vampires, and outright gore as three teens endeavor to halt a plot to bring down the queen; a sequel to 2006's *The Death Collector.* Lexile HL670L (Rev: BL 11/15/08; SLJ 1/1/09; VOYA 2/09)

5555 Richardson, E. E. *Devil's Footsteps* (8–11). 2005, Delacorte LB $17.99 (978-0-385-90279-3). Still troubled by his brother's disappearance at the hands of the Dark Man five years earlier, 15-year-old Bryan meets two other teens struggling with the effects of similar attacks. (Rev: BCCB 10/05; BL 5/1/05; SLJ 1/06)

5556 Richardson, E. E. *The Intruders* (6–9). 2006, Delacorte $15.95 (978-0-385-73264-2). Joel and his new stepfamily move into a spooky old mansion filled with mysterious spirits in this suspenseful tale. (Rev: BL 6/1–15/06; SLJ 9/06)

5557 Roach, Marilynne K. *Encounters with the Invisible World* (5–9). Illus. by author. 1977, Amereon $18.95 (978-0-89190-874-6). Spooky stories about witches, demons, spells, and ghosts in New England.

5558 Rodriguez, Pedro. *Chilling Tales of Horror: Dark Graphic Short Stories* (7–10). Illus. by author. 2012, Enslow LB $30.60 (978-076604085-4). Seven classic horror stories including Maupassant's "The Hand" and Robert Louis Stevenson's "The Body Snatcher" are given graphic-novel treatment here. (Rev: BL 8/12; SLJ 7/1/12)

5559 Rosati, Gina. *Auracle* (7–10). 2012, Roaring Brook $16.99 (978-1-59643-710-4). Her power to project as-

trally puts 17-year-old Anna in danger in this novel combining romance, suspense, and paranormal activity. ℮ Lexile 890L (Rev: BL 9/15/12; HB 9–10/12; SLJ 12/12; VOYA 10/12)

5560 Ruby, Lois. *The Secret of Laurel Oaks* (7–10). 2008, Tor $16.95 (978-076531366-9). Siblings Lila and Gabe set out to solve the puzzle of who really poisoned the owner of Laurel Oaks Plantation in 1839; the narration alternates between Lila and Gabe and Daphne, the slave girl wrongly blamed for the murder. ℮ Lexile 850L (Rev: BLO 10/30/08; LMC 5–6/09; SLJ 11/1/08; VOYA 12/08)

5561 Rupp, Rebecca. *Journey to the Blue Moon: In Which Time Is Lost and Then Found Again* (5–8). 2006, Candlewick $15.99 (978-0-7636-2544-3). A multilayered story in which Alex loses his grandfather's pocket watch and takes a trip to the blue moon, where all things lost go; there he finds other searchers and a group that threatens his chances of returning home. (Rev: BL 12/1/06; SLJ 10/06)

5562 Sage, Angie. *Book One: Magyk* (5–8). Illus. by Mark Zug. 2005, HarperCollins LB $18.89 (978-0-06-057732-2). A fantasy of magic, spells, and evil forces, focusing on young Jenna, who was raised by Septimus Heap's family and who now must flee the evil Supreme Custodian. (Rev: BL 3/15/05; SLJ 4/05)

5563 St. Crow, Lili. *Strange Angels* (8–11). Series: Strange Angels. 2009, Penguin paper $9.99 (978-159514251-1). Dru's mother is dead and she was forced to kill her father, who was turned into a zombie, in this first book in the series populated by vampires, werewolves, and demons. ℮ Lexile HL810L (Rev: BL 5/15/09; SLJ 7/1/09)

5564 San Souci, Robert D. *Dare to Be Scared: Thirteen Stories to Chill and Thrill* (4–8). Illus. by David Ouimet. 2003, Cricket $15.95 (978-0-8126-2688-9). A baker's dozen of spooky stories suitable for this age group that feature diverse characters. (Rev: BL 10/1/03; HBG 10/03; SLJ 9/03)

5565 San Souci, Robert D. *Triple-Dare to Be Scared: Thirteen Further Freaky Tales* (6–9). Illus. by David Ouimet. 2007, Cricket $16.95 (978-0-8126-2749-7). Well-written and illustrated, this third book of stories by San Souci in which the protagonists don't always escape will give readers the creeps. (Rev: SLJ 6/07)

5566 *Scary Stories* (6–9). Illus. by Barry Moser. 2006, Chronicle $16.95 (978-0-8118-5414-6). A collection of twenty classic creepy stories — many by well-known authors — accompanied by stark black-and-white illustrations. (Rev: BL 12/1/06; SLJ 1/07)

5567 Schreiber, Ellen. *Vampireville* (7–10). 2006, HarperCollins $15.99 (978-0-06-077625-1). Raven and her vampire boyfriend Alexander must get rid of the bad vampire twins Luna and Jagger before they sink their fangs into soccer star Trevor and try and take over the town of Dullsville. (Rev: BL 8/06; SLJ 11/06)

5568 Schwartz, Alvin. *Scary Stories 3: More Tales to Chill Your Bones* (4–7). Illus. by Stephen Gammell. 1991, HarperCollins LB $17.89 (978-0-06-021795-2); paper $5.99 (978-0-06-440418-1). A modernized version of spooky tales handed down through the years. (Rev: BL 8/91; HB 11–12/91; SLJ 11/91)

5569 Seabrooke, Brenda. *The Vampire in My Bathtub* (4–7). 1999, Holiday $16.95 (978-0-8234-1505-2). After 13-year-old Jeff moves to a new home with his mother, he finds a friendly vampire hidden inside an old trunk. (Rev: BL 1/1–15/00; HBG 3/00; SLJ 12/99)

5570 Sedgwick, Marcus. *White Crow* (8–12). 2011, Roaring Brook $15.99 (978-1-59643-594-0). Rebecca and her policeman father arrive in Winterfold, a town with disturbingly deep secrets, and begin to learn the scary truth. ∩ e Lexile 810L (Rev: BL 5/1/11; HB 7–8/11; LMC 8–9/12; SLJ 8/11*)

5571 Shan, Darren. *Blood Beast, Book 5* (7–10). Series: Demonata. 2007, Little, Brown $16.99 (978-0-316-00377-3). Grubbs worries that he too will become a werewolf in this gripping fifth installment in the series. (Rev: SLJ 2/08)

5572 Shan, Darren. *Demon Thief* (7–12). Series: Demonata. 2006, Little, Brown $15.99 (978-0-316-01237-9). An inventive horror story in which a boy who is able to construct windows from light discovers that demons live behind them. (Rev: SLJ 9/06)

5573 Shan, Darren. *A Living Nightmare* (5–8). Series: Cirque du Freak. 2001, Little, Brown $15.95 (978-0-316-60340-9). A supernatural story about a young boy who visits the Cirque Du Freak and is turned into a vampire. (Rev: BL 4/15/01; HBG 10/01; SLJ 5/01; VOYA 4/01)

5574 Shan, Darren. *Tunnels of Blood* (5–8). Series: Cirque du Freak. 2002, Little, Brown $15.95 (978-0-316-60763-6). Darren Shan, teenage half-vampire, sets out to investigate a spate of recent killings for which he believes his vampire master might be responsible. (Rev: BL 8/02; HBG 10/02; SLJ 5/02; VOYA 6/02)

5575 Shan, Darren. *Vampire Mountain* (5–8). Series: Cirque du Freak. 2002, Little, Brown $15.95 (978-0-316-60806-0). Darren Shan, teenage half-vampire, and his mentor travel to Vampire Mountain. The fifth, sixth, and seventh installments in the series are *Trials of Death*, *The Vampire Prince* (both 2003), and *Hunters of the Dusk* (2004). (Rev: BL 8/02; HBG 3/03; SLJ 9/02; VOYA 12/02)

5576 Shan, Darren. *The Vampire's Assistant* (5–8). Series: Cirque du Freak. 2001, Little, Brown $15.95 (978-0-316-60610-3). The creepy, suspenseful second installment about a boy who is "half vampire" and his efforts to adjust to the world of a traveling freak show. (Rev: BL 10/15/01; HBG 3/02; SLJ 8/01; VOYA 10/01)

5577 Shreve, Susan. *Ghost Cats* (4–7). 1999, Scholastic paper $14.95 (978-0-590-37131-5). A boy, who is trying to adjust to a new family home and the loss of his five cats, is helped when the cats return as ghosts. (Rev: BCCB 12/99; BL 9/1/99; HBG 3/00; SLJ 11/99; VOYA 6/00)

5578 Shusterman, Neal. *Bruiser* (8–12). 2010, HarperCollins $16.99 (978-0-06-113408-1). When Bronte, 16, starts dating the seemingly inappropriate Bruiser and her twin brother Tennyson comes to accept this, they are amazed to find that Bruiser absorbs all their physical and emotional pains; told from four perspectives. ∩ e Lexile 820L (Rev: BL 5/1/10; LMC 10/10; SLJ 8/10; VOYA 8/10)

5579 Shusterman, Neal. *Darkness Creeping: Twenty Twisted Tales* (5–8). 2007, Penguin paper $6.99 (978-0-14-240721-9). Four of these creepy stories were written for this collection; others have been published before but are not easily found. (Rev: BL 5/15/07; SLJ 7/07)

5580 Shusterman, Neal. *Everfound* (7–10). Series: Skinjacker. 2011, Simon & Schuster $17.99 (978-1-4169-9049-9). An action-packed epic conclusion to the trilogy in which the fates of Everlost and the real world hang in the balance. ∩ e Lexile 910L (Rev: BL 5/1/11; HB 7–8/11; SLJ 6/11; VOYA 6/11)

5581 Shusterman, Neal. *Everlost* (7–10). Series: Skinjacker Trilogy. 2006, Simon & Schuster $16.95 (978-0-689-87237-2). Nick and Allie are killed in an automobile accident and end up in Everlost, a world for lost souls, where they must learn to survive. Nick accepts the situation but Allie will do anything to escape. (Rev: BL 9/15/06; SLJ 10/06*)

5582 Shusterman, Neal. *Full Tilt* (6–10). 2003, Simon & Schuster $16.95 (978-0-689-80374-1). A suspenseful drama in which 16-year-old Blake must tackle frightening rides at a mysterious carnival and face his own worst fears in order to save his daredevil older brother Quinn. (Rev: BCCB 9/03; BL 5/15/03; HB 7–8/03; HBG 10/03; SLJ 6/03; VOYA 10/03)

5583 Sierra, Judy. *The Gruesome Guide to World Monsters* (5–8). Illus. by Henrik Drescher. 2005, Candlewick $17.99 (978-0-7636-1727-1). A wonderfully ghoulish field guide to more than 60 monsters from world folklore, complete with Gruesomeness Ratings and Survival Tips if appropriate. (Rev: BCCB 9/05; BL 9/15/05*; HBG 4/06; LMC 2/06; SLJ 9/05)

5584 Singer, Nicky. *The Innocent's Story* (7–10). 2007, Holiday $16.95 (978-0-8234-2082-7). After dying in a suicide bomb attack, 13-year-old Cassina becomes a vapor and enters into the mind and hearts of living characters including her parents and the terrorists responsible for her death. (Rev: BL 5/15/07; SLJ 9/07)

5585 Sinykin, Sheri. *Giving Up the Ghost* (5–8). 2007, Peachtree $15.95 (978-1-56145-423-5). Davia is only 13, has asthma, is worried about her mother's cancer, and afraid of various things; now her dying Aunt Mari wants Davi to help Emilie, a young Creole ghost, to find peace. (Rev: LMC 2/08; SLJ 2/08)

5586 Skovron, Jon. *Misfit* (8–11). 2011, Abrams $16.95 (978-1-4197-0021-7). Demon half-breed Jael discovers the truth about her identity when she receives a necklace that was her deceased mother's prized possession. e Lexile 660L (Rev: BLO 9/1/11; LMC 3–4/12; SLJ 10/1/11*; VOYA 10/11)

5587 Slater, Adam. *Skinned* (6–10). Series: The Shadowing. 2012, Egmont $16.99 (978-160684262-1). A tense story in which young Callum is pitted against a flesh-eating monster named Black Annis. e (Rev: BLO 10/1/12; SLJ 2/13)

5588 Sleator, William. *Hell Phone* (5–8). 2006, Abrams $16.95 (978-0-8109-5479-3). In this dark, suspenseful novel, 17-year-old Nick discovers that the cell phone he bought at a bargain price constantly rings with frightening requests. (Rev: BL 10/1/06; SLJ 11/06)

5589 Snyder, Zilpha Keatley. *The Headless Cupid* (4–7). 1971, Dell paper $4.99 (978-0-440-43507-5). Amanda, a student of the occult, upsets her new family. A sequel is *The Famous Stanley Kidnapping Case* (1985).

5590 Somper, Justin. *Demons of the Ocean* (6–9). Series: Vampirates. 2006, Little, Brown $15.99 (978-0-316-01373-4). Young twins Connor and Grace, attracted to the sea by stories they heard as children, decide to make it their life when their father dies; early on they are separated in a storm and find themselves on very different ships. (Rev: SLJ 11/06)

5591 Somper, Justin. *Tide of Terror* (6–9). Series: Vampirates. 2007, Little, Brown $15.99 (978-0-316-01374-1). Grace and Connor Tempest, 14-year-old orphan twins, leave their dangerous life aboard the pirate ship *Diablo* and spend time at the elite Pirate Academy; but Grace yearns to go back to the vampirate way of life. (Rev: BL 5/1/07; SLJ 8/07)

5592 Soto, Gary. *The Afterlife* (7–10). 2003, Harcourt $16.00 (978-0-15-204774-0). After he is stabbed to death, 17-year-old Chuy lingers long enough to watch the reactions of family and friends while getting to know some other ghosts. (Rev: BL 8/03*; HB 11–12/03; HBG 4/04; SLJ 11/03; VOYA 2/04)

5593 Springer, Nancy. *Sky Rider* (5–8). 2000, HarperCollins paper $4.95 (978-0-380-79565-9). In this contemporary supernatural mystery, Dusty's beloved horse Tazz is cured by a visitor who turns out to be the angry ghost of a teenage boy recently killed on her father's property. (Rev: BCCB 10/99; HBG 3/00; SLJ 8/99)

5594 Stahler, David, Jr. *A Gathering of Shades* (7–10). 2005, HarperCollins LB $16.89 (978-0-06-052295-7). Sixteen-year-old Aidan, who moves to rural Vermont with his mother after his father's death, discovers that his grandmother is secretly feeding ghosts with a mix-

ture of her own blood and spring water. (Rev: BCCB 5/05; BL 5/1/05; SLJ 8/05)

5595 Starkey, Dinah, ed. *Ghosts and Bogles* (5–10). 1987, David & Charles $17.95 (978-0-434-96440-6). A collection of 16 British ghost stories, each nicely presented with illustrations. (Rev: SLJ 9/87)

5596 Staub, Wendy Corsi. *Lily Dale: Awakening* (7–10). 2007, Walker $15.95 (978-0-8027-9654-7). At the age of 17, following her mother's accidental death and on a visit to the spiritualist community of Lily Dale, Calla discovers her psychic abilities. (Rev: BL 11/1/07; LMC 1/08; SLJ 11/07)

5597 Staub, Wendy Corsi. *Lily Dale: Connecting* (7–10). 2008, Walker $16.99 (978-0-8027-9785-8). Still in the spiritualist community of Lily Dale, Calla is preoccupied with romance and friendship even as she investigates her mother's death with the aid of the Internet and spirit guides; the third book in the series. e Lexile 1230 (Rev: BL 2/1/09; SLJ 2/1/09)

5598 Stewart, Trenton Lee. *The Mysterious Benedict Society* (4–7). Illus. by Carson Ellis. Series: The Mysterious Benedict Society. 2007, Little, Brown $16.99 (978-0-316-05777-6). Orphan Reynie Muldoon is one of a number of gifted children selected to take part in an effort to infiltrate the Learning Institute for the Very Enlightened; a complex story of mystery and adventure. (Rev: BL 1/1–15/07; SLJ 3/07*)

5599 Stine, R. L. *The Haunting Hour: Chill in the Dead of Night* (5–8). 2001, HarperCollins $14.89 (978-0-06-623605-6). Ten chilling short stories, each with an introduction by the author. (Rev: BCCB 11/01; BL 1/1–15/02; HBG 3/02)

5600 Stine, R. L. *Nightmare Hour* (4–7). 1999, HarperCollins $16.99 (978-0-06-028688-0). Ten scary stories by a master of mystery, with characters that include aliens, sorcerers, werewolves, witches, and ghosts. (Rev: BL 10/15/99; HBG 3/00; SLJ 12/99)

5601 Stolarz, Laurie Faria. *Project 17* (7–10). 2007, Hyperion $15.99 (978-0-7868-3856-1). Five teenagers spend a spooky night at the ghost-filled Danvers State Insane Asylum. (Rev: BL 11/15/07; LMC 1/08; SLJ 12/07)

5602 Storrie, Paul D. *Nightmare on Zombie Island* (4–8). Illus. by David Witt. Series: Twisted Journeys. 2008, Lerner LB $27.93 (978-0-8225-6198-9); paper $7.95 (978-0-8225-6200-9). Readers can choose which way the plot will go in this horror story. (Rev: SLJ 5/08)

5603 Strand, Jeff. *A Bad Day for Voodoo* (7–10). 2012, Sourcebooks paper $8.99 (978-140226680-5). An annoying teacher whose leg is severed after Tyler, 16, pricks his voodoo doll is just the beginning of a funny action-packed adventure. e Lexile HL730L (Rev: BLO 6/12; SLJ 6/12; VOYA 8/12)

5604 Strasser, Todd. *Hey Dad, Get a Life!* (5–8). 1996, Holiday $15.95 (978-0-8234-1278-5). Twelve-year-old Kelly and her younger sister use the ghost of their dead father to accomplish their everyday chores and finally let their mother know about their secret helper. (Rev: BCCB 3/97; BL 2/15/97; SLJ 3/97)

5605 Strickland, Brad. *The Whistle, the Grave, and the Ghost* (5–8). Series: Lewis Barnevalt. 2003, Dial $16.99 (978-0-8037-2622-2). A silver whistle frees a woman vampire, drawing Lewis Barnevalt and his friends into suspenseful adventures battling an ancient threat. (Rev: BL 8/03; HBG 4/04; SLJ 8/03)

5606 Taylor, Laini. *Lips Touch Three Times* (8–12). Illus. by Jim Di Bartolo. 2009, Scholastic $16.99 (978-0-545-05585-7). Three supernatural short stories feature kisses that change lives. YALSA Top Ten 2010. 🎧 🅴 Lexile 990L (Rev: BL 10/1/09*; SLJ 11/09)

5607 Teitelbaum, Michael. *The Scary States of America* (5–8). 2007, Delacorte LB $12.99 (978-0-385-90348-6); paper $7.99 (978-0-385-73331-1). A collection of short stories about paranormal events that take place in each of the 50 states. (Rev: BL 6/1–15/07; SLJ 8/07)

5608 Thornton, Duncan. *Shadow-Town* (6–9). Series: Vastlands. 2008, Annick $19.95 (978-155451163-1); paper $9.95 (978-155451162-4). Jack, Rose, and Tam venture into the forbidden territory of Shadow-Town, where they are nearly captured by the Whisperers; the first volume in a complex and spooky quartet. (Rev: BLO 1/13/09; SLJ 1/1/09)

5609 Tolan, Stephanie S. *The Face in the Mirror* (6–9). 1998, Morrow $15.00 (978-0-688-15394-6). When Jared goes to live with his father, a theater director, he isn't prepared for the malicious pranks of his stepbrother or the encounters with George Marsden, a sympathetic ghost. (Rev: BCCB 9/98; BL 9/1/98; HBG 3/99; SLJ 11/98; VOYA 4/99)

5610 Tolan, Stephanie S. *Who's There?* (5–8). 1994, Morrow $15.00 (978-0-688-04611-8); paper $4.95 (978-0-688-15289-5). Fourteen-year-old Drew is convinced that there is a ghost in her crusty grandfather's house, where she and her brother Evan, who has been mute since their parents' deaths, are currently living. (Rev: BCCB 12/94; BL 9/1/94; SLJ 10/94)

5611 Tunnell, Michael O. *School Spirits* (5–8). 1997, Holiday $15.95 (978-0-8234-1310-2). Three students at creepy Craven Hill School, including the son of the new principal, discover a ghost and solve a decades-old murder mystery involving an 8-year-old boy. (Rev: BCCB 3/98; BL 2/15/98; HBG 3/98; SLJ 3/98; VOYA 8/98)

5612 Van Tol, Alex. *Shallow Grave* (4–7). Series: Orca Soundings. 2012, Orca LB $16.95 (978-145980203-2); paper $9.95 (978-145980202-5). For reluctant readers, this is a ghost story involving a murdered girl with

a mission for Elliot and Shannon. 🅴 Lexile HL460L (Rev: BL 10/15/12; LMC 5–6/13; SLJ 4/13)

5613 Vande Velde, Vivian. *All Hallows' Eve: 13 Stories* (7–10). 2006, Harcourt $17.00 (978-0-15-205576-9). Thirteen chilling horror stories that take place on Halloween night feature teens and their encounters with vampires, killers, ghosts, and more. (Rev: BL 10/1/06; HB 9–10/06; LMC 4–5/07; SLJ 11/06)

5614 Viehl, Lynn. *Dead of Night* (8–11). Series: Youngbloods. 2012, Flux paper $9.95 (978-07387264-6-5). Catlyn Youngblood and her vampire boyfriend Jesse investigate a string of scary disappearances. 🅴 (Rev: BLO 8/12; SLJ 8/12)

5615 Wade, Rebecca. *The Theft and the Miracle* (5–8). 2007, HarperCollins $16.99 (978-0-06-077493-6). Mystery and supernatural are combined in this story of Hannah, a plain, overweight 12-year-old with artistic abilities, who — with her friend Sam — finds herself on a hunt for a missing religious statue. (Rev: BL 11/15/06; SLJ 1/07)

5616 Watts, Leander. *Beautiful City of the Dead* (8–11). 2006, Houghton Mifflin $16.00 (978-0-618-59443-6). Zee and her fellow heavy metal bandmates discover they have unsuspected powers and must battle the evil forces around them that want to take these powers away. (Rev: BL 9/15/06)

5617 Welch, R. C. *Scary Stories for Stormy Nights* (5–7). 1995, Lowell House paper $5.95 (978-1-56565-262-0). Ten contemporary horror stories that involve such characters as a werewolf and some pirates. (Rev: BL 5/1/95)

5618 Welvaert, Scott R. *The Curse of the Wendigo: An Agate and Buck Adventure* (5–9). Illus. by Brann Garvey. 2006, Stone Arch LB $23.93 (978-1-59889-066-2). Searching for their parents in the vast Canadian wilderness in the late 19th century, 16-year-old Buck and his younger sister Agate find themselves being pursued by the mythical Wendigo; suitable for reluctant readers. (Rev: SLJ 1/07)

5619 Westall, Robert. *Ghost Abbey* (5–9). 1990, Scholastic paper $3.25 (978-0-590-41693-1). Maggi realizes that the abbey her father is restoring seems to have a life of its own. (Rev: BCCB 2/89; BL 2/1/89; SLJ 3/89; VOYA 6/89)

5620 Westall, Robert. *Shades of Darkness: More of the Ghostly Best Stories of Robert Westall* (7–12). 1994, Macmillan paper $11.95 (978-0-330-35318-2). Eleven eerie tales, not the guts-and-gore variety of supernatural fiction but haunting and insightful stories. (Rev: BL 4/15/94; SLJ 5/94; VOYA 8/94)

5621 Westerfeld, Scott. *Blue Noon* (6–12). Series: Midnighters. 2006, HarperCollins $15.99 (978-0-06-051957-5). In this action-packed third volume in the series, the darklings have found a way to expand their time, threatening all human beings. (Rev: SLJ 7/06)

5622 Westerfeld, Scott. *The Secret Hour* (6–10). Series: Midnighters. 2004, HarperCollins LB $17.89 (978-0-06-051952-0). In this exciting first volume, 15-year-old Jessica Day discovers that — like several others — she has special abilities to battle supernatural creatures. (Rev: SLJ 6/04; VOYA 4/04)

5623 Westerfeld, Scott. *Touching Darkness* (6–10). Series: Midnighters. 2005, HarperCollins LB $16.89 (978-0-06-051955-1). In volume two of the Midnighters series, five teens born at the stroke of midnight learn about the hidden past of their Oklahoma hometown and a frightening conspiracy that threatens them all. (Rev: SLJ 3/05)

5624 Westwood, Chris. *Calling All Monsters* (7–12). 1993, HarperCollins LB $14.89 (978-0-06-022462-2). Joanne is a huge fan of a horror writer, so when she starts seeing nightmare creatures from his books, she recognizes them. (Rev: BL 6/1–15/93; SLJ 7/93; VOYA 12/93)

5625 Westwood, Chris. *He Came from the Shadows* (5–8). 1991, HarperCollins LB $14.89 (978-0-06-021659-7). In a cautionary tale about the dangers of wishing for too much, odd things start to happen after a stranger comes to town. (Rev: BL 4/1/91; SLJ 6/91)

5626 Whelan, Gerard. *Dream Invader* (5–7). 2002, O'Brien paper $7.95 (978-0-86278-516-1). Only Simon's grandmother can break the spell behind the bad dreams he's been having in this supernatural tale set in Ireland. (Rev: BL 9/1/02)

5627 Whinnem, Reade Scott. *The Pricker Boy* (6–9). 2009, Random House $16.99 (978-0-375-85719-5); LB $19.99 (978-0-375-95719-2). Something strange is going on, and 14-year-old Stucks and his friends begin to wonder about their years-long fear of going into the woods past the hawthorns. (Rev: BL 8/09; SLJ 12/09)

5628 Whitten, A. J. *The Well* (6–9). 2009, Graphia paper $8.99 (978-0-547-23229-4). High school freshman Cooper Warner faces many challenges including an angry stepfather, an English-teacher father, and a homicidal mother who shoves him into a well that is home to a monster. e (Rev: BL 8/09; LMC 1–2/10; SLJ 12/09)

5629 Wiggins, Bethany. *Shifting* (7–10). 2011, Walker $16.99 (978-0-8027-2280-5). Troubled teen and shapeshifter Maggie Mae, who has been in numerous foster homes and has been arrested frequently for indecent exposure, starts at a new school in a new town — with perhaps a new romance — only to find herself threatened by malevolent Skinwalkers. e Lexile 720L (Rev: BL 10/15/11; LMC 1–2/12; SLJ 12/1/11; VOYA 10/11)

5630 Wild, Margaret. *Woolvs in the Sitee* (6–9). Illus. by Anne Spudvilas. 2007, Front St $17.95 (978-1-59078-500-3). A strange and disturbing picture book, in which a boy living in a post-apocalyptic world writes in scrawled, desperate-looking handwriting about terrifying "woolvs" that the reader never sees. (Rev: BL 11/15/07; HB 11–12/07; SLJ 9/07)

5631 Willis, Alette J. *How to Make a Golem and Terrify People* (5–8). 2012, Floris paper $9.95 (978-08631584-0-7). After her home in Edinburgh is broken into, 13-year-old Edda accepts a boy named Michael's help with making a golem to protect her — but things go awry. e (Rev: BLO 4/1/12; LMC 11–12/12; SLJ 6/12)

5632 Winnacker, Susanne. *The Other Life. Bk. 1* (7–10). Series: The Weepers. 2012, Marshall Cavendish $17.99 (978-0-7614-6275-0). In postapocalyptic Los Angeles more than three years after a rabies outbreak that drove survivors into underground bunkers, 15-year-old Sherry and 17-year-old Joshua rescue her family and find refuge from the Weepers (part humans, part animals) in Safe Haven. e Lexile 570L (Rev: BLO 5/16/12; LMC 1–2/13*; SLJ 7/12; VOYA 10/12)

5633 Wright, Betty R. *Crandalls' Castle* (4–7). 2003, Holiday $16.95 (978-0-8234-1726-1). This gripping suspense story combines supernatural elements with a look at teen girls' yearning to belong. (Rev: BL 4/1/03; HBG 10/03; SLJ 5/03)

5634 Wright, Betty R. *A Ghost in the House* (5–7). 1991, Scholastic paper $13.95 (978-0-590-43606-9). Bizarre happenings take place when Sarah's elderly aunt moves in. (Rev: BCCB 11/91; BL 1/1/91; SLJ 11/91)

5635 Wright, Nina. *Sensitive* (8–10). 2007, Flux paper $9.95 (978-0-7387-1170-6). Cal and Easter, who have supernatural abilities, make contact with the dead and, more romantically, with each other in this novel set in ghost-filled St. Augustine, Florida; the sequel to *Homefree* (2006). (Rev: BL 11/1/07; SLJ 3/08)

5636 Yashinsky, Dan, ed. *Ghostwise: A Book of Midnight Stories* (7–12). 1997, August House $11.95 (978-0-87483-499-4). A collection of 35 short but chilling stories of the supernatural and ghosts. (Rev: BCCB 3/98; VOYA 2/98)

5637 Yee, Paul. *The Bone Collector's Son* (6–9). 2005, Marshall Cavendish $15.95 (978-0-7614-5242-3). In early 20th-century Vancouver, Bing is ashamed of his father's occupation as shipper of bones back to China for burial in this novel that interweaves the real and supernatural worlds. (Rev: BCCB 11/05; BL 12/1/05; HB 11–12/05; VOYA 12/05)

5638 Yolen, Jane, and Martin H. Greenberg, eds. *Werewolves: A Collection of Original Stories* (6–9). 1988, HarperCollins $13.95 (978-0-06-026798-8). Fifteen mostly scary stories about all kinds of werewolves. (Rev: BL 7/88; SLJ 9/88; VOYA 8/88)

5639 Young, Richard, and Judy Dockery Young. *Ozark Ghost Stories* (6–12). 1995, August House paper $12.95 (978-0-87483-410-9). Spooky Ozark stories are the focus of this horror anthology, including old favorites and less-well-known jokes and tales. (Rev: BL 6/1–15/95)

5640 Young, Richard, and Judy Dockery Young. *The Scary Story Reader* (6–9). 1993, August House $19.00 (978-0-87483-271-6). Forty-one scary urban legends are presented, including traditional tales of horror as well as less-well-known stories from Alaska and Hawaii. (Rev: BL 11/15/93; SLJ 5/94)

5641 Zafon, Carlos Ruiz. *The Watcher in the Shadows* (8–11). Trans. by Lucia Graves. 2013, Little, Brown $17.99 (978-031604476-9). After her family moves to an estate in Normandy owned by a toymaker, 15-year-old Irene starts to sense that all is not right. (Rev: BL 12/1/12; HB 5–6/13; LMC 8–9/12*)

5642 Zindel, Paul. *Loch* (7–10). 1994, HarperCollins LB $15.89 (978-0-06-024543-6). Lovable, though human-eating, creatures trapped in a Vermont lake become prey for a ruthless man. (Rev: BL 11/15/94; SLJ 1/95; VOYA 4/95)

Humor

5643 Acampora, Paul. *Defining Dulcie* (7–10). 2006, Dial $16.99 (978-0-8037-3046-5). Dulcie may only be 16 but she knows her own mind, and when her mother moves her to California following her janitor father's death, Dulcie drives home to Connecticut and lives with her janitor grandfather. (Rev: BL 4/1/06*; SLJ 4/06*; VOYA 4/06)

5644 Anderson, M. T. *Agent Q, or the Smell of Danger!* (4–7). Illus. by Kurt Cyrus. Series: Pals in Peril. 2010, Simon & Schuster $16.99 (978-1-4169-8640-9). Crime-fighting teens Lily, Jasper, and Katie are trying to get home to New Jersey after their adventures in Delaware, but the evil Autarch has other things in mind. (Rev: BL 9/15/10*; SLJ 11/1/10)

5645 Anderson, M. T. *Jasper Dash and the Flame-Pits of Delaware* (4–7). 2009, Simon & Schuster $16.99 (978-1-4169-8639-3). Jasper Dash, Boy Technonaut, and his sidekicks Lily and Katie delve into an alternate Delaware, find art thieves, and battle strange enemies; a funny parody. ⌂ (Rev: BL 7/09; HB 9/09; SLJ 9/09)

5646 Anderson, M. T. *Zombie Mommy* (5–8). Illus. by Kurt Cyrus. Series: Pals in Peril. 2011, Simon & Schuster $16.99 (978-144243068-6). Lily, Katie, Drgnan, and Jasper Dash, Boy Technonaut must save Lily's mother, who has been possessed by a zombie with ambitions. Lexile 710L (Rev: BL 10/15/11; HB 11–12/11)

5647 Angleberger, Tom. *Fake Mustache: How Jodie O'Rodeo and Her Wonder Horse (and Some Nerdy Kid) Saved the U.S. Presidential Election from a Mad Genius Criminal Mastermind* (4–7). Illus. by Jen Wang. 2012, Abrams Amulet $13.95 (978-1-4197-0194-8). In the small town of Hairsprinkle a fake mustache sparks hilarious chaos as 7th-grader Casper takes to robbing banks, hypnotizing residents, becoming mayor . . . and

then governor . . . and then president? ⌂ ℮ Lexile 710L (Rev: BL 5/15/12; HB 5–6/12; LMC 11–12/12; SLJ 6/12)

5648 Ardagh, Philip. *Dreadful Acts* (4–7). Illus. by David Roberts. Series: Eddie Dickens. 2003, Henry Holt $14.95 (978-0-8050-7155-9). This zany sequel to *A House Called Awful End* (2002) throws more wild adventures at 12-year-old Eddie Dickens. (Rev: BL 4/15/03; HBG 10/03; SLJ 5/03)

5649 Ardagh, Philip. *Terrible Times* (4–7). Illus. by David Roberts. 2003, Henry Holt $12.95 (978-0-8050-7156-6). Young Eddie Dickens sails for America and encounters all sorts of zany situations in this last installment in the trilogy set in Victorian England. (Rev: BL 2/1/04; SLJ 12/03)

5650 Avi. *Punch with Judy* (6–8). 1993, Bradbury LB $14.95 (978-0-02-707755-1). The orphan boy Punch encounters tragedy and comedy in his attempt to keep a medicine show alive with the help of the owner's daughter. (Rev: BL 3/15/93; SLJ 6/93; VOYA 8/93)

5651 Avi. *Romeo and Juliet: Together (and Alive) at Last!* (6–8). 1987, Watts LB $16.99 (978-0-531-08321-5); paper $5.99 (978-0-380-70525-2). Ed Sitrow decides to help true love along by casting his friends as Romeo and Juliet in a school play. Sitrow is also the "genius" behind the soccer escapades in *S.O.R. Losers*. (Rev: BL 8/87; SLJ 10/87)

5652 Baker, Kim. *Pickle: The (Formerly) Anonymous Prank Club of Fountain Point Middle School* (4–7). Illus. by Tim Probert. 2012, Roaring Brook $15.99 (978-1-59643-765-4). Calling themselves the League of Picklemakers, 6th-graders Ben Diaz and friends engage in a series of escalating pranks. ℮ (Rev: BL 11/1/12; HB 11–12/12; LMC 3–4/13; SLJ 11/12)

5653 Barry, Dave, and Ridley Pearson. *Science Fair: A Story of Mystery, Danger, International Suspense, and a Very Nervous Frog* (5–8). 2008, Hyperion $18.99 (978-1-4231-1324-9). Inept secret agents from Krpshtskan plan to use American middle-school students to build secret weapons in their science fair projects. ⌂ (Rev: BL 12/15/08; SLJ 3/09; VOYA 12/08)

5654 Bath, K. P. *Escape from Castle Cant* (6–9). Illus. by Leah Palmer Preiss. 2006, Little, Brown $16.99 (978-0-316-10857-7). A civil war over chewing gum has Pauline and her half-sister Lucy on the run in this sequel to *The Secret of Castle Cant* (2006). (Rev: SLJ 10/06)

5655 Binder, Mark. *The Brothers Schlemiel* (6–9). Illus. by Zevi Blum. 2008, Jewish Publication Soc $19.95 (978-0-8276-0865-8). Identical twin brothers Abraham and Adam grow up in the town of Chelm, Poland, where their pranks and pratfalls keep everyone laughing; full-color illustrations add to the fun. (Rev: BL 3/1/08)

5656 Blume, Judy. *Starring Sally J. Freedman as Herself* (4–7). 1977, Dell paper $5.99 (978-0-440-48253-6). A story of a 5th-grader's adventures in New Jersey and Florida in the late 1940s.

5657 Bradley, Alex. *24 Girls in 7 Days* (8–11). 2005, Dutton $15.99 (978-0-525-47369-5). Dateless only two weeks before the senior prom, Jack is desperate, so desperate that two of his friends run a personal ad in the school paper in an effort to get Jack a date. (Rev: BL 1/1–15/05; SLJ 3/05; VOYA 2/05)

5658 Brett, Cathy. *Scarlett Dedd: It's a Grave Situation* (6–9). 2012, Delacorte $14.99 (978-0-385-74175-0); LB $17.99 (978-0-375-99022-9). Dark humor abounds in this story of Scarlett who, after accidentally killing herself and her family, seeks creative ways to deal with her boring ghostly existence. Lexile 850L (Rev: BLO 9/1/12; SLJ 10/12; VOYA 6/12)

5659 Brockmeier, Kevin. *Grooves: A Kind of Mystery* (4–7). 2006, HarperCollins LB $17.89 (978-0-06-073692-7). In this funny mystery with science fiction overtones, unprepossessing 7th-grader Dwayne Ruggles finds out that the sounds coming from his blue jeans are really cries for help from imprisoned factory workers. (Rev: BL 2/1/06; SLJ 3/06)

5660 Brooke, William J. *A Is for AARRGH!* (5–8). 1999, HarperCollins LB $14.89 (978-0-06-023394-5). A humorous story about a prehistoric boy, Mog, and his amazing discoveries about language and communication. (Rev: BCCB 11/99; BL 10/15/99; HB 9–10/99; HBG 3/00; SLJ 9/99)

5661 Burnham, Niki. *Royally Jacked* (8–10). 2004, Simon & Schuster paper $5.99 (978-0-689-86668-5). Valerie, a 15-year-old product of divorce accompanies her father to live in a castle in Europe in this lively, humorous story. (Rev: BL 3/1/04; SLJ 2/04)

5662 Burnham, Niki. *Spin Control* (8–10). 2005, Simon & Schuster paper $5.99 (978-0-689-86669-2). Valerie is desperately unhappy when she's forced to leave Schwerinborg and her prince boyfriend and return to Virginia, but a reunion with an old boyfriend soon eases her pain in this sequel to *Royally Jacked* (2004). (Rev: SLJ 2/05)

5663 Byars, Betsy. *Bingo Brown's Guide to Romance* (5–8). 2000, Puffin paper $5.99 (978-0-14-036080-6). Romance, confusion, and comedy occur when Bingo Brown meets his true love in the produce section of the grocery store. (Rev: BL 4/1/92; SLJ 4/92)

5664 Byars, Betsy. *The Burning Questions of Bingo Brown* (6–8). 1990, Puffin paper $6.99 (978-0-14-032479-2). During Bingo's 6th-grade year, he falls in love three times for starters. (Rev: BCCB 4/88; BL 4/15/88; SLJ 5/88)

5665 Cabot, Meg. *Airhead* (7–10). 2008, Scholastic $16.99 (978-0-545-04052-5). Feminist loner Em's brain is transplanted into the body of a famous model, allowing her to experience life as one of the beautiful people. (Rev: BL 4/15/08; SLJ 8/08)

5666 Cabot, Meg. *The Princess Diaries* (7–10). Series: Princess Diaries. 2000, HarperCollins LB $17.89 (978-0-06-029210-2). Fourteen-year-old Mia's diary reveals a fairly interesting life even before she learns that she is actually a royal princess, heir to the throne of Genovia. (Rev: BCCB 12/00; BL 9/15/00; HBG 3/01; SLJ 10/00; VOYA 4/01)

5667 Cabot, Meg. *Princess in Love: The Princess Diaries, Vol. 3* (6–9). Series: The Princess Diaries. 2002, HarperCollins $16.99 (978-0-06-029467-0). This action-packed installment follows Mia's life from Thanksgiving through her December departure for Genovia, with details of typical teen life and of her efforts to learn about her new country. (Rev: BCCB 5/02; BL 7/02; HBG 10/02; SLJ 10/02; VOYA 6/02)

5668 Cabot, Meg. *Princess in Pink* (7–10). Series: Princess Diaries. 2004, HarperCollins $15.99 (978-0-06-009610-6). In this, the fifth volume of the Princess Diaries series, Mia celebrates her 15th birthday and her pregnant mom is about to give birth. (Rev: BL 4/15/04; SLJ 8/04)

5669 Cabot, Meg. *Princess in Training* (7–10). Series: Princess Diaries. 2005, HarperCollins $16.99 (978-0-06-009613-7). Princess Mia's current worries range from English and geometry, running for student council president, and her college boyfriend's expectations, to her new baby brother and the ecology of the Bay of Genovia. (Rev: BL 8/05; SLJ 6/05; VOYA 8/05)

5670 Cabot, Meg. *Princess in Waiting* (5–7). Series: Princess Diaries. 2003, HarperCollins $16.99 (978-0-06-009607-6). Princess Mia gets in a royal mess when her duties interfere with her love life. (Rev: BL 5/15/03; HBG 10/03; SLJ 5/03; VOYA 6/03)

5671 Cabot, Meg. *Princess on the Brink* (8–11). Series: Princess Diaries. 2007, HarperCollins $16.99 (978-0-06-072456-6). Princess Mia contemplates the pros and cons of having sex with her boyfriend in this continuation of the series. ⌒ (Rev: BL 12/15/06)

5672 Carvell, Tim. *Planet Tad* (5–8). Illus. by Doug Holgate. 2012, HarperCollins $12.99 (978-006193436-0). Twelve-year-old Tad's blog recounts everything he goes through — girl problems, school problems, awful summer job — in the year he's in 7th and 8th grades. Lexile 940L (Rev: BL 4/15/12; SLJ 6/12)

5673 Castle, M. E. *Popular Clone* (4–7). 2012, Egmont $15.99 (978-160684232-4). Socially inept and bullied scientific genius Fisher is frustrated when he clones himself so he can stay home and play video games while his clone attends school, and it turns out that Fisher Two becomes popular. ⌒ ℮ (Rev: BL 1/1/12)

5674 Cheshire, Simon. *The Prince and the Snowgirl* (6–9). 2007, Delacorte LB $12.99 (978-0-385-90359-2); paper $8.99 (978-0-385-73342-7). Tom has been earning money impersonating Prince George (heir to the British throne) and hoping at the same time to impress the lovely Louise, but fate intervenes at a skiing championship and Tom must make a quick decision. (Rev: BCCB 3/07; SLJ 5/07)

5675 Collins, Ross. *Medusa Jones* (4–7). Illus. by author. 2008, Scholastic $16.99 (978-0-439-90100-0). Yes, Medusa does have snakes for hair, and her friend Mino is half bull; they are part of the outcast group at school, where Theseus and his friends push them around. A trip to Mount Olympus changes all that, since the students must pull together. (Rev: BL 12/1/07; LMC 3/08; SLJ 1/08)

5676 Conford, Ellen. *The Alfred G. Graebner Memorial High School Handbook of Rules and Regulations* (6–9). 1976, Little, Brown $14.95 (978-0-316-15293-8). The trials and tribulations of student life in a typical high school. (Rev: BL 7/88)

5677 Conford, Ellen. *Dear Lovey Hart, I Am Desperate* (6–7). 1975, Little, Brown $14.95 (978-0-316-15306-5). Freshman reporter Carrie Wasserman gets into trouble with her advice column in the school newspaper. (Rev: BL 10/15/87)

5678 Conford, Ellen. *Seven Days to Be a Brand-New Me* (6–9). 1990, Scholastic paper $3.50 (978-0-590-43824-7). Maddy knows she will become a teenage vamp after following Dr. Dudley's program.

5679 Conford, Ellen. *Why Me?* (6–9). 1985, Little, Brown $14.95 (978-0-316-15326-3). G.G. Graffman has a crush on Hobie, who only has eyes for Darlene, who is ga-ga over Warren. (Rev: BL 10/15/85; SLJ 11/85; VOYA 2/86)

5680 Crawford, Brent. *Carter Finally Gets It* (7–10). 2009, Hyperion $15.99 (978-142311246-4). Clumsy freshman Will, who has ADD, attempts to talk to girls, cope with humiliation, and survive sports in this funny, believable account of high school from a hormone-crazed boy's perspective. ∩ e Lexile HL760L (Rev: BL 11/15/08; SLJ 3/1/09; VOYA 4/09)

5681 Daneshvari, Gitty. *Class Is Not Dismissed!* (4–7). Series: School of Fear. 2010, Little, Brown $16.99 (978-0-316-03328-2). In this lighthearted followup to 2009's *School of Fear*, the four phobia-ridden students return to take another stab at curing their unreasonable and paralyzing fears and together investigate who is stealing from their school. (Rev: BL 10/1/10; SLJ 9/1/10)

5682 Dent, Grace. *LBD: Friends Forever!* (7–10). Series: LBD. 2006, Putnam $16.99 (978-0-399-24189-5). Claude enters a modeling contest while the girls are working and vacationing at Destiny Bay in the latest installment of the LBD (Les Bambinos Dangereuses) series. (Rev: SLJ 10/06)

5683 Devillers, Julia, and Jennifer Roy. *Trading Faces* (4–7). 2008, Simon & Schuster $16.99 (978-1-4169-7531-1). Middle school twins Emma and Payton have very different social lives — one is popular while the other is brainy — and switch places with interesting results. e Lexile HL460L (Rev: SLJ 5/1/09)

5684 Feiffer, Jules. *The Man in the Ceiling* (5–7). 1993, HarperCollins paper $9.99 (978-0-06-205907-9). Jimmy turns to cartooning in an effort to gain some recognition in a family that is intent on ignoring him. (Rev: BCCB 12/93; BL 11/15/93; SLJ 2/94*)

5685 Ferraiolo, Jack D. *The Big Splash* (5–7). 2008, Abrams $15.95 (978-0-8109-7067-0). Matt Stevens, an average middle-schooler with a glib tongue and a knack for solving crimes, uncovers a mystery while working with "the organization," a mafia-like syndicate run by 7th-grader Vincent "Mr. Biggs" Biggio, and specializing in forged hall passes, test-copying rings, black market candy selling, and so forth. ∩ (Rev: BCCB 11/08; BLO 10/7/08; LMC 3/09; SLJ 11/08; VOYA 10/08)

5686 Fleischman, Sid. *Chancy and the Grand Rascal* (5–7). Illus. by Eric Von Schmidt. 1966, Little, Brown $14.95 (978-0-316-28575-9); paper $4.95 (978-0-316-26012-1). The boy and his uncle, the grand rascal, combine hard work and quick wits to outsmart a scoundrel, hoodwink a miser, and capture a band of outlaws.

5687 Foley, June. *Susanna Siegelbaum Gives Up Guys* (5–8). 1992, Scholastic paper $3.25 (978-0-590-43700-4). Susanna, a flirt, makes a bet that she can give up guys for three months. (Rev: SLJ 8/91)

5688 Foley, Lizzie K. *Remarkable* (3–7). 2012, Dial $16.99 (978-080373706-8). Ordinary enough to be unsuitable for the town of Remarkable's School for the Remarkably Gifted, 10-year-old Jane Doe is the only student in the public school until the trouble-making Grimlet twins and a pirate captain arrive and lead her in a series of adventures. (Rev: BL 3/15/12*; HB 3–4/12; LMC 10/12; SLJ 4/12)

5689 Gidwitz, Adam. *In a Glass Grimmly* (5–12). 2012, Dutton $16.99 (978-0-525-42581-6). Jack and Jill — and a lonely frog — brave many scary situations in this gory yet humorous fairy-tale companion to *A Tale Dark and Grimm* (2010). ALA Notable Books 2013. ∩ e Lexile 630L (Rev: HB 11–12/12; LMC 5–6/13*; SLJ 10/12*; VOYA 12/12)

5690 Giff, Patricia Reilly. *Hunter Moran Saves the Universe* (4–7). 2012, Holiday House $16.95 (978-0-8234-1949-4). Imaginative 5th-grade twins Hunter and Zack investigate a dentist they believe is planning mayhem. e Lexile 550L (Rev: BL 11/1/12; SLJ 11/12)

5691 Gonzalez, Julie. *Imaginary Enemy* (6–10). 2008, Delacorte $15.99 (978-0-385-73552-0). Jane, 16, is shocked when her imaginary enemy, Bubba (whom she has blamed for any misbehavior since second grade), responds to one of her letters; a rich and funny novel. (Rev: BL 3/15/08)

5692 Gorman, Carol. *Lizard Flanagan, Supermodel??* (4–7). 1998, HarperCollins $14.95 (978-0-06-024868-

0). Sixth-grader Lizard Flanagan will do anything to make enough money to go by bus from her home in Iowa to a game in Wrigley Field, but is entering a local fashion show for teens going too far? (Rev: BL 11/15/98; HBG 3/99; SLJ 10/98)

5693 Gosselink, John. *The Defense of Thaddeus A. Ledbetter* (4–7). 2010, Abrams $14.95 (978-0-8109-8977-1). Mastermind and social misfit Thaddeus, 12, spends his time writing a "Prison Diary" and campaigning for his release from unfair In-school Suspension. Lexile 970L (Rev: BL 11/1/10; LMC 1–2/11; SLJ 11/1/10; VOYA 12/10)

5694 Greenwald, Tommy. *Charlie Joe Jackson's Guide to Extra Credit* (4–7). Illus. by J. P. Coovert. 2012, Roaring Brook $14.99 (978-1-59643-692-3). Desperate to boost his grades and avoid the dreaded Camp Rituhbukkee (Reading Camp), Charlie Joe signs up for the school play and agrees to be a model in art class; a sequel to 2011's *Charlie Joe Jackson's Guide to Not Reading*. ⌒ (Rev: BL 10/1/12; SLJ 11/12)

5695 Greenwald, Tommy. *Charlie Joe Jackson's Guide to Not Reading* (4–7). Illus. by J. P. Coovert. 2011, Roaring Brook $14.99 (978-1-59643-691-6). Middle-schooler Charlie Joe goes to great lengths to avoid reading, although he is partial to some kinds of books — checkbooks, comic books, and Facebook. (Rev: BL 5/1/11; SLJ 8/11)

5696 Griffiths, Andy. *Killer Koalas from Outer Space: And Lots of Other Very Bad Stuff That Will Make Your Brain Explode* (4–7). Illus. by Terry Denton. 2011, Feiwel & Friends $12.99 (978-0-312-36789-3). Often gross and silly, this collection of short stories, verse, and cartoons featuring "Very Bad" characters — everything from zombie kittens, killer koalas, and inadequate adults — will captivate its intended audience. (Rev: BL 11/1/11; SLJ 10/1/11)

5697 Griggs, Terry. *Cat's Eye Corner* (6–8). 2003, Raincoast paper $7.95 (978-1-55192-350-5). Wordplay stars in this entertaining novel full of eccentric characters whom Olivier finds on a scavenger hunt through his grandfather's old mansion; a sequel is *Invisible Ink* (2006). (Rev: BL 6/1–15/03; SLJ 8/03)

5698 Harmel, Kristin. *When You Wish* (7–10). 2008, Delacorte $15.99 (978-0-385-73475-2). Beck is tired of being a pop star and rebels against her manager mother by disguising herself and hopping on a bus to Florida. (Rev: BL 4/1/08; SLJ 5/08)

5699 Hautman, Pete. *Godless* (7–10). 2004, Simon & Schuster $15.95 (978-0-689-86278-6). Rebelling against his devoutly Catholic father, 16-year-old Jason Block and his best friend Shin create a religion of their own with the town's water tower as the deity. (Rev: BL 6/1–15/04*; HB 7–8/04; SLJ 8/04; VOYA 10/04)

5700 Hayes, Daniel. *Eye of the Beholder* (5–8). 1992, Fawcett paper $6.99 (978-0-449-00235-3). Tyler and Lymie are in trouble again when they fake some works of a famous sculptor. (Rev: BL 2/1/93; SLJ 12/92)

5701 Henry, Chad. *DogBreath Victorious* (6–10). 1999, Holiday $16.95 (978-0-8234-1458-1). Tim's rock band, DogBreath, ends up competing against his mom's group, the Angry Housewives, in this entertaining story. (Rev: HBG 9/00; SLJ 2/00; VOYA 6/00)

5702 Hite, Sid. *Those Darn Dithers* (5–8). 1996, Henry Holt $15.95 (978-0-8050-3838-5). A humorous novel about the dithering Dithers with adventures involving Porcellina the dancing pig and an eccentric who drifts out to sea on a rubber raft. (Rev: BL 12/15/96; SLJ 12/96; VOYA 10/97)

5703 Horvath, Polly. *When the Circus Came to Town* (5–8). 1996, Farrar paper $5.95 (978-0-374-48367-8). Opinion is sharply divided in Ivy's town when a circus troupe decides to relocate there. (Rev: BCCB 12/96; BL 11/15/96; SLJ 12/96*)

5704 Howe, James. *Bunnicula Meets Edgar Allan Crow* (4–7). Illus. by Eric Fortune. 2006, Simon & Schuster $15.95 (978-1-4169-1458-7). When world-famous author M. T. Graves and his pet, Edgar Allan Crow, come to stay with the Monroe family, Bunnicula the vampire bunny suspects that the household guests are up to no good. (Rev: BL 1/1–15/07; SLJ 2/07)

5705 Howe, James. *The New Nick Kramer or My Life as a Baby-Sitter* (5–9). 1995, Hyperion LB $14.49 (978-0-7868-2053-5). Nick and rival Mitch make an unusual bet on who will win the affections of newcomer Jennifer. (Rev: BL 12/15/95; SLJ 1/96)

5706 Ives, David. *Monsieur Eek* (4–7). 2001, HarperCollins LB $15.89 (978-0-06-029530-1). Thirteen-year-old Emmaline defends a monkey against criminal charges in the not-quite-right town of MacOongafoondsen, population 21. (Rev: BL 6/1–15/01; HBG 3/02; SLJ 6/01)

5707 Ives, David. *Scrib* (6–9). 2005, HarperCollins LB $17.89 (978-0-06-059842-6). His spelling and grammar may leave a lot to be desired, but 16-year-old Billy Christmas enjoys an adventure-filled life as he travels the Old West writing and delivering letters. (Rev: BCCB 4/05; BL 3/1/05; SLJ 2/05; VOYA 6/05)

5708 Ives, David. *Voss: How I Come to America and Am Hero, Mostly* (7–10). 2008, Putnam $17.99 (978-039924722-4). The hilarious misadventures of Voss, a 15-year-old immigrant, are populated with larger-than-life characters including gangsters, socialites, and crazy relatives, and are told in broken English through letters to a friend back home in Slobovia. (Rev: BL 12/1/08; LMC 1–2/09; SLJ 12/08)

5709 Jennings, Richard W. *Ferret Island* (5–7). 2007, Houghton Mifflin $16.00 (978-0-618-80632-4). Will and a huge, friendly ferret named Jim are on the run from a ferret gang that has been trained to attack McDonald's restaurants. (Rev: BCCB 5/07; BL 7/07; HB 5–6/07; SLJ 5/07)

5710 Jennings, Richard W. *My Life of Crime* (4–8). 2002, Houghton Mifflin $15.00 (978-0-618-21433-4). Nothing goes right when 6th-grader Fowler decides to "rescue" a caged parrot. (Rev: BL 1/1–15/03; HBG 3/03; VOYA 2/03)

5711 Juby, Susan. *Miss Smithers* (7–12). 2004, Harper-Collins LB $16.89 (978-0-06-051547-8). Told through journal articles and a zine, this is the story of Alice of *Alice, I Think* (2003) and how she enters a beauty contest in spite of her mother's opposition. (Rev: BL 5/1/04; HB 7–8/04; SLJ 10/04)

5712 Kidd, Ronald. *Sammy Carducci's Guide to Women* (5–7). 1995, Dramatic Publg $6.25 (978-0-87129-522-4). A somewhat sexist 6th grader discovers that, where women are concerned, perhaps he is not as irresistible as he thinks he is. (Rev: BCCB 1/92; BL 1/1/92; SLJ 1/92)

5713 Kiesel, Stanley. *The War Between the Pitiful Teachers and the Splendid Kids* (7–9). 1980, Avon paper $3.50 (978-0-380-57802-3). A humorous fantasy about schoolchildren who decide to wage war on their teachers.

5714 Kimmel, Elizabeth Cody. *The Reinvention of Moxie Roosevelt* (5–7). 2010, Dial $16.99 (978-0-8037-3303-9). Thirteen-year-old Moxie decides to reinvent herself when she heads off to boarding school, eventually realizing that it's easiest to just be herself. Lexile 780L (Rev: BL 6/10; LMC 1–2/11; SLJ 7/10)

5715 Kinard, Kami. *The Boy Project (Notes and Observations of Kara McAllister)* (5–8). Illus. by author. 2012, Scholastic $12.99 (978-054534515-6). Kara employs scientific method to help figure out the best way to land a date, documenting her progress on note cards. e (Rev: BL 3/1/12; SLJ 2/12)

5716 Kinney, Jeff. *Cabin Fever* (5–8). Illus. by author. Series: Diary of a Wimpy Kid. 2011, Abrams $12.95 (978-141970223-5). It's the month between Thanksgiving and Christmas, and Greg is tired of having to behave for Santa, especially when the adults in his life are so unreasonable. YALSA Amazing Audiobooks Top Ten 2013. (Rev: BLO 11/1/11)

5717 Kinney, Jeff. *The Last Straw* (5–8). Illus. by author. 2009, Abrams $12.95 (978-0-8109-7068-7). Middle school non-jock Greg Heffley keeps a diary in which he details his angst about his troublesome brothers, his demanding father, and other aspects of life. ∩ (Rev: BL 2/1/09; SLJ 4/09)

5718 Kinney, Jeff. *Rodrick Rules* (5–8). Illus. by author. Series: Diary of a Wimpy Kid. 2008, Abrams $12.95 (978-0-8109-9473-7). Twelve-year-old Greg Heffley of *Diary of a Wimpy Kid* (2007) will make readers laugh again with this diary that recounts his struggles at home and at school, particularly those involving his annoying older brother Rodrick. (Rev: BL 2/1/08; SLJ 3/08)

5719 Kinney, Jeff. *The Third Wheel* (5–8). Illus. by author. Series: Diary of a Wimpy Kid. 2012, Abrams $13.95 (978-141970584-7). To his surprise, Greg has a date for the Valentine's Day dance and must leave best friend Rowley to fend for himself; the 7th volume in the series. e Lexile 1060L (Rev: BLO 11/15/12)

5720 Kinney, Jeff. *The Ugly Truth* (5–8). Illus. by author. Series: Diary of a Wimpy Kid. 2010, Abrams $13.95 (978-081098491-2). Charging headlong toward puberty, Greg Heffley suffers a series of mortifying tween social gaffes. Lexile 1000L (Rev: BLO 11/1/10; SLJ 5/11)

5721 Kline, Suzy. *Orp Goes to the Hoop* (5–7). 1993, Avon paper $3.50 (978-0-380-71829-0). Seventh-grader Orp gets a chance to play a big part in the basketball team's big game. (Rev: BCCB 7–8/91; BL 7/91; SLJ 7/91)

5722 Korman, Gordon. *Don't Care High* (7–10). 1986, Scholastic paper $2.50 (978-0-590-40251-4). A new student in a high school where apathy is so rife it's nicknamed Don't Care High decides to infuse some school spirit into the student body. (Rev: BL 10/15/85)

5723 Korman, Gordon. *Losing Joe's Place* (7–10). 1991, Scholastic paper $5.99 (978-0-590-42769-2). Three teenage boys take over an apartment for the summer with hilarious results. (Rev: BL 3/1/90; SLJ 5/90; VOYA 6/90)

5724 Lawson, Robert. *Ben and Me* (5–8). Illus. by author. 1939, Little, Brown $16.95 (978-0-316-51732-4); paper $5.99 (978-0-316-51730-0). The events of Benjamin Franklin's life, as told by his good mouse Amos, who lived in his old fur cap.

5725 Lawson, Robert. *Mr. Revere and I* (5–8). Illus. by author. 1953, Little, Brown paper $6.99 (978-0-316-51729-4). A delightful account of certain episodes in Revere's life, as revealed by his horse Scheherazade. (Rev: SLJ 1/05)

5726 Limb, Sue. *Girl, Barely 15: Flirting for England* (7–10). Series: Jess Jordan. 2008, Delacorte $15.99 (978-0-385-73538-4). Jess's class welcomes a group of French exchange students, and romance and hijinks ensue on a combined camping trip in this funny British import. (Rev: BL 1/1–15/08; SLJ 4/08)

5727 Limb, Sue. *Girl, Going on 17: Pants on Fire* (7–10). Series: Jess Jordan. 2006, Delacorte $15.95 (978-0-385-73218-5). Jess copes with love and school difficulties with her usual humor and fortitude. (Rev: BL 7/06; SLJ 9/06)

5728 Lockhart, E. *Fly on the Wall: How One Girl Saw Everything* (7–10). 2006, Delacorte LB $17.99 (978-0-385-90299-1). Gretchen Yee's wish to be a fly on the wall of the boys' locker room comes true and in the process she gains confidence and learns a lot about boys and friendship. (Rev: BCCB 4/06; BL 7/06; HB 3–4/06; SLJ 3/06)

5729 Lowry, Brigid. *Follow the Blue* (8–12). 2004, Holiday $16.95 (978-0-8234-1827-5). A delightful novel from Australia about 15-year-old Bec, who, with her two younger siblings, is left in the care of a dowdy housekeeper while her parents are away. (Rev: BL 5/1/04*; HB 7–8/04; SLJ 5/04)

5730 Lowry, Lois. *Anastasia at This Address* (5–9). 1991, Houghton Mifflin $16.00 (978-0-395-56263-5); paper $4.50 (978-0-440-40652-5). The irrepressible Anastasia answers a personal ad, using her mother's picture instead of her own, with typically hilarious results. (Rev: BCCB 3/91; BL 4/1/91; SLJ 8/91)

5731 Lowry, Lois. *Anastasia on Her Own* (5–7). 1985, Houghton Mifflin $16.00 (978-0-395-38133-5); paper $4.50 (978-0-440-40291-6). Seventh-grader Anastasia Krupnik must face both domestic crisis and romance. Another chapter in Anastasia's busy life is recounted in *Anastasia Has the Answers* (1986). (Rev: BL 5/15/85; HB 9–10/85; SLJ 8/85)

5732 Lowry, Lois. *Anastasia's Chosen Career* (5–7). 1987, Houghton Mifflin $16.00 (978-0-395-42506-0); paper $4.50 (978-0-440-40100-1). Thirteen-year-old Anastasia gets some surprises when she begs to go to charm school to change her freaky looks. Anastasia's baby brother is featured in *All About Sam* (1988). (Rev: BCCB 9/87; BL 9/1/87; SLJ 9/87)

5733 Lowry, Lois. *Switcharound* (5–7). 1985, Houghton Mifflin $16.00 (978-0-395-39536-3). Caroline and her nemesis brother J.P. must spend the summer with their divorced father's new family in Des Moines. A sequel to *The One Hundredth Thing About Caroline* (1983). (Rev: BCCB 1/86; BL 10/1/85; HB 1–2/86)

5734 Lowry, Lois. *Your Move, J.P.!* (6–8). 1990, Houghton Mifflin $16.00 (978-0-395-53639-1). J. P. Tate, a 7th grader, is hopelessly in love with Angela. (Rev: BL 3/1/90; SLJ 5/90; VOYA 4/90)

5735 Lubar, David. *Punished!* (4–7). 2006, Darby Creek $15.95 (978-1-58196-042-6). Thanks to a curse, Logan becomes a non-stop punster and must uncover oxymorons, anagrams, and palindromes to break the spell. (Rev: BL 5/1/06; SLJ 5/06*)

5736 MacDonald, Amy. *No More Nice* (4–7). 1996, Orchard LB $15.99 (978-0-531-08892-0). A humorous story about a spring vacation spent by a boy with his eccentric great-aunt and -uncle. (Rev: BCCB 10/96; BL 9/1/96; SLJ 9/96)

5737 McFann, Jane. *Deathtrap and Dinosaur* (7–12). 1989, Avon paper $2.75 (978-0-380-75624-7). An unlikely pair works to force the departure of a disliked history teacher. (Rev: SLJ 10/89; VOYA 10/89)

5738 McGowan, Anthony. *Jack Tumor* (7–10). 2009, Farrar $17.95 (978-037432955-6). Funny and vulgar, this British novel features a teen boy named Hector and his brain tumor, Jack; Jack and Hector face an uncertain future and an interesting present as Jack tries to improve Hector's social life. (Rev: BL 6/1–15/09; SLJ 6/1/09)

5739 Mackay, Claire, sel. *Laughs* (5–8). 1997, Tundra paper $6.95 (978-0-88776-393-9). An anthology of humorous stories (and some poems) by several well-known Canadian writers. (Rev: SLJ 9/97)

5740 McKenna, Colleen O'Shaughnessy. *Mother Murphy* (5–7). 1993, Scholastic paper $2.95 (978-0-590-44856-7). With her mother confined to bed, 12-year-old Collette volunteers as mother-for-a-day with disastrous and funny results. (Rev: BCCB 2/92; BL 2/1/92; SLJ 2/92)

5741 MacLeod, Doug. *I'm Being Stalked by a Moon Shadow* (7–10). 2007, Front St $16.95 (978-1-59078-501-0). Seth, the son of hippies, falls in love with tough-girl Miranda, the daughter of an uptight neighbor in this funny Australian novel. (Rev: BL 10/1/07; SLJ 1/08)

5742 McManus, Patrick F. *Never Cry "Arp!" and Other Great Adventures* (6–9). 1996, Henry Holt $16.95 (978-0-8050-4662-5). Based on fact, the 12 stories in this collection deal humorously with the problems of growing up in the mountains of Idaho. (Rev: BL 8/96; SLJ 7/96)

5743 Maguire, Gregory. *One Final Firecracker* (4–7). Illus. by Elaine Clayton. Series: The Hamlet Chronicles. 2005, Clarion $17.00 (978-0-618-27480-2). In the final pun-filled installment in the series, the rival Tattletales and Copycats must cooperate to defend the class and the soon-to-be-wed Miss Earth from myriad threats. (Rev: SLJ 5/05)

5744 Manes, Stephen. *Comedy High* (7–10). 1992, Scholastic paper $13.95 (978-0-590-44436-1). A comic story of a new high school designed to graduate jocks, performers, gambling experts, and hotel workers. (Rev: BL 12/1/92; SLJ 11/92)

5745 Many, Paul. *These Are the Rules* (7–10). 1997, Walker $15.95 (978-0-8027-8619-7). In this hilarious first-person narrative, Colm tries to figure out the rules of dating, driving, girls, and getting some direction in his life. (Rev: BL 5/1/97; HBG 3/98; SLJ 5/97)

5746 Maxwell, Katie. *They Wear What Under Their Kilts?* (8–11). 2004, Dorchester paper $5.99 (978-0-8439-5258-2). Emily Williams, the 16-year-old American introduced in the riotous *The Year My Life Went Down the Loo*, is off to a Scottish sheep farm on a month-long work-study program. (Rev: BL 1/1–15/04)

5747 Meacham, Margaret. *A Fairy's Guide to Understanding Humans* (5–8). 2007, Holiday $16.95 (978-0-8234-2078-0). Morgan's unreliable fairy godmother tries to improve 14-year-old Morgan's life after her move to a new house and new school in this sequel to *A Mid-Semester Night's Dream* (2004). (Rev: BL 2/1/08; SLJ 2/08)

5748 Meehl, Brian. *Suck It Up* (8–11). 2008, Delacorte $15.99 (978-0-385-73300-7). Sixteen-year-old Morning is an unlikely vampire — he drinks only blood substitute and is something of a nerd — but he is chosen to be the first of his kind to reveal his true nature to humans; romance and humor add to the appeal. (Rev: BL 3/1/08)

5749 Merrill, Jean. *The Pushcart War* (6–9). Illus. by Ronni Solbert. 1987, Dell paper $5.50 (978-0-440-47147-9). Mack, driving a Mighty Mammoth, runs down a pushcart belonging to Morris the Florist and starts a most unusual war that is humorous and also reveals many human foibles. (Rev: BL 4/87)

5750 Mills, Claudia. *Alex Ryan, Stop That!* (4–7). Series: West Creek Middle School. 2003, Farrar $16.00 (978-0-374-34655-3). All Alex's efforts to attract classmate Marcia go awry in this humorous account of 7th-grade and son-father relations. (Rev: BL 4/1/03; HBG 10/03; SLJ 4/03)

5751 Mlynowski, Sarah. *Frogs and French Kisses* (7–10). 2006, Delacorte $15.95 (978-0-385-73182-9). This funny, cleverly written sequel to *Bras and Broomsticks* (2005) features Rachel's efforts to control her family members' overuse of magic while she copes with the consequences. (Rev: BL 7/06; SLJ 9/06)

5752 Mlynowski, Sarah. *Parties and Potions* (6–9). Series: Magic in Manhattan. 2008, Delacorte $16.99 (978-038573645-9); LB $19.99 (978-038573645-9). In this fourth installment in the series about teenage witch sisters Miri and Rachel, the girls meet a community of witches and at the same time worry about being revealed to friends and family. 🎧 ℮ (Rev: BL 11/15/08; VOYA 2/09)

5753 Mlynowski, Sarah. *Spells and Sleeping Bags* (6–9). 2007, Delacorte $16.99 (978-0-385-73387-8). In this third book about witch sisters Rachel and Miri, the girls go to a summer camp in the Adirondacks and Rachel tries to keep her powers under cover. (Rev: SLJ 8/07)

5754 Montgomery, Claire, and Monte Montgomery. *Hubert Invents the Wheel* (4–7). Illus. by Jeff Shelly. 2005, Walker $16.95 (978-0-8027-8990-7). Hubert, a struggling 15-year-old inventor in ancient Sumeria, finally finds success when he invents the wheel, but things quickly spin out of control. (Rev: SLJ 11/05)

5755 Mulford, Philippa Greene. *Making Room for Katherine* (5–9). 1994, Macmillan $14.95 (978-0-02-767652-5). A 16-year-old is recovering from her father's death when a 13-year-old cousin arrives from Paris to visit for the summer. (Rev: BL 4/15/94; SLJ 5/94; VOYA 8/94)

5756 Naylor, Phyllis Reynolds. *Alice Alone* (6–10). 2001, Simon & Schuster $15.00 (978-0-689-82634-4). Alice's story continues as she starts high school and deals with the misery of breaking up with her boyfriend. (Rev: BCCB 5/01; BL 5/15/01; HB 7–8/01; HBG 10/01; SLJ 6/01; VOYA 8/01)

5757 Naylor, Phyllis Reynolds. *Alice in April* (5–8). 1993, Dell paper $4.50 (978-0-440-91032-9). Alice is back, this time caught between her desire to be a perfect housekeeper and her fascination with her developing body. (Rev: BL 3/1/93; SLJ 6/93)

5758 Naylor, Phyllis Reynolds. *Alice in Lace* (6–8). 1996, Simon & Schuster $17.00 (978-0-689-80358-1). Alice, in her usual bumbling, endearing way, confronts society's greatest problems when her health class does a unit on "Critical Choices." (Rev: BL 3/1/96; SLJ 4/96; VOYA 8/96)

5759 Naylor, Phyllis Reynolds. *Alice the Brave* (5–7). 1995, Simon & Schuster paper $4.99 (978-0-689-80598-1). Alice conquers her fear of deep water and also feels the pangs of growing up in this amusing continuation of a popular series. (Rev: BCCB 4/95; BL 5/1/95; HB 7–8/95; SLJ 5/95)

5760 Naylor, Phyllis Reynolds. *The Grooming of Alice* (6–9). 2000, Simon & Schuster $16.00 (978-0-689-82633-7). In this, the twelfth Alice story, our heroine discovers what is meant by "normal" for girls and also helps a friend who is having trouble at home. (Rev: BL 6/1–15/00; HB 7–8/00; HBG 9/00; SLJ 5/00)

5761 Naylor, Phyllis Reynolds. *Including Alice* (6–9). 2004, Simon & Schuster $15.95 (978-0-689-82637-5). Alice has trouble adjusting to life with her new stepmother as well as the usual problems of a sophomore. (Rev: HB 7–8/04; SLJ 5/04; VOYA 8/04)

5762 Naylor, Phyllis Reynolds. *Outrageously Alice* (6–8). 1997, Simon & Schuster $15.95 (978-0-689-80354-3); paper $4.99 (978-0-689-80596-7). Thirteen-year-old Alice, now in the 8th grade, decides that she is too ordinary and wants to do something about it. (Rev: BCCB 7–8/97; BL 5/15/97; HB 7–8/98; SLJ 6/97; VOYA 10/97)

5763 Naylor, Phyllis Reynolds. *Patiently Alice* (6–9). 2003, Simon & Schuster $15.95 (978-0-689-82636-8). Alice spends summer as a camp counselor and despite a lack of romance has lots of fun (including talk of sex) and learns about her disadvantaged charges. (Rev: BL 8/03; HB 7–8/03; HBG 10/03; SLJ 5/03; VOYA 8/03)

5764 Naylor, Phyllis Reynolds. *Reluctantly Alice* (5–8). 1991, Macmillan $16.00 (978-0-689-31681-4). Alice's life in the 7th grade seems full of embarrassment. (Rev: BCCB 4/91*; BL 2/1/91; HB 7–8/91; SLJ 3/91*)

5765 Naylor, Phyllis Reynolds. *Simply Alice* (6–9). 2002, Simon & Schuster $16.00 (978-0-689-82635-1). Now 14, Alice is in 9th grade and living a full life while learning to deal with family, friendships, and embarrassing situations. (Rev: BCCB 6/02; BL 6/1–15/02; HB 7–8/02; HBG 10/02; SLJ 5/02; VOYA 6/02)

5766 Naylor, Phyllis Reynolds. *Who Won the War?* (4–7). 2006, Delacorte LB $17.99 (978-0-385-90172-7). In the last weeks before they return to Ohio (and the last volume in the series), the Malloy sisters mount a last-ditch campaign to prove their superiority over the Hatford boys. (Rev: BL 11/1/06; SLJ 9/06)

5767 Nesbo, Jo. *Doctor Proctor's Fart Powder* (4–7). Illus. by Mike Lowery. 2010, Simon & Schuster $14.99 (978-1-4169-7972-2). Dr. Proctor's loud but non-smelly invention launches Nilly into outer space at the beginning of this humorous, action-packed story in which bad people try to steal this wondrous product; set in Norway. ∩ Lexile 830L (Rev: BL 1/1/10; SLJ 2/10)

5768 Nesbo, Jo. *Who Cut the Cheese?* (4–7). Trans. by Tara F. Chance. Illus. by Mike Lowery. Series: Doctor Proctor's Fart Powder. 2012, Aladdin $15.99 (978-144243307-6). In this sequel to *Doctor Proctor's Fart Powder* (2010), Nilly, Lisa, and Dr. Procter apply their zany inventions to the burgeoning crises threatening Norway. **e** Lexile 770L (Rev: BL 1/1/12; LMC 5–6/12; SLJ 6/12)

5769 Park, Barbara. *Buddies* (5–8). 1986, Avon paper $2.95 (978-0-380-69992-6). Dinah's dreams of being popular at camp are dashed in this humorous novel because she is forever being accompanied by Fern, the camp nerd. (Rev: BCCB 5/85; BL 4/15/85; SLJ 5/85)

5770 Pastis, Stephan. *Timmy Failure: Mistakes Were Made* (4–7). Illus. by author. 2013, Candlewick $14.99 (978-076366050-5). This illustrated comic novel presents 11-year-old Timmy Failure, detective par excellence, and his sidekick, a giant polar bear named Total. **e** Lexile 520L (Rev: BL 12/1/12; SLJ 5/13)

5771 Patterson, James, and Chris Grabenstein. *I Funny* (4–7). Illus. by Laura Park. 2012, Little, Brown $15.99 (978-0-316-20693-8). Aspiring middle school comedian Jamie Grimm uses humor to cope with the fact that he's confined to a wheelchair. ∩ **e** Lexile 610L (Rev: BL 10/15/12; LMC 3–4/13; SLJ 12/12; VOYA 12/12)

5772 Paulsen, Gary. *Harris and Me: A Summer Remembered* (6–10). 1993, Harcourt $16.00 (978-0-15-292877-3). A humorous story in which the 11-year-old narrator often gets the blame for mischief caused by troublemaker Harris. (Rev: BL 12/1/93*; SLJ 2/00; VOYA 2/94)

5773 Paulsen, Gary. *Lawn Boy* (5–8). 2007, Random House $12.99 (978-0-385-74686-1). Given his late grandfather's somewhat battered riding mower as a gift, a 12-year-old entrepreneur launches a phenomenally successful lawn care business in this zany, tongue-in-cheek story. (Rev: BL 4/15/07; HB 7–8/07; SLJ 6/07)

5774 Paulsen, Gary. *Lawn Boy Returns* (5–8). Series: Lawn Boy. 2010, Random House $12.99 (978-0-385-74662-5); LB $15.99 (978-0-385-90899-3). The enterprising 12-year-old's lawn business grows into a monster and his hippie stockbroker gets him involved in

risky high finance — and then there's the sponsorship of a boxer — when all he really wants is to play with the other kids. ∩ **e** Lexile 920L (Rev: BLO 6/16/10; HB 7–8/10; SLJ 6/10)

5775 Peck, Richard. *A Long Way from Chicago* (6–10). 1998, Dial $16.99 (978-0-8037-2290-3). Seven stories are included in this book, each representing a different summer from 1929 to 1935 that Joey spent visiting in Illinois with his lying, cheating, conniving, and thoroughly charming grandmother. (Rev: BCCB 10/98; BL 9/1/98; HB 11–12/98; HBG 3/99; SLJ 10/98*; VOYA 12/98)

5776 Peck, Richard. *A Year Down Yonder* (6–10). 2000, Dial $16.99 (978-0-8037-2518-8). In this 2001 Newbery Medal winner, 15-year-old Mary Alice visits her feisty, independent, but lovable Grandma Dowdel in rural Illinois during the Great Depression. A sequel to *A Long Way from Chicago* (1998). (Rev: BCCB 1/01; BL 10/15/00*; HB 11–12/00; HBG 3/01; SLJ 9/00; VOYA 12/00)

5777 Peck, Robert Newton. *Higbee's Halloween* (5–7). 1990, Walker LB $14.85 (978-0-8027-6969-5). Higbee decides something must be done about the unruly Striker children. (Rev: SLJ 10/90)

5778 Petty, J. T. *The Squampkin Patch: A Nasselrogt Adventure* (4–7). Illus. by David Michael Friend. 2006, Simon & Schuster $15.95 (978-1-4169-0274-4). A funny, far-fetched fantasy about two children who escape hard labor at the zipper factory/orphanage (their parents are tied up in tanning beds) and find themselves pursued by squampkins — pumpkin-like creatures — that are out for blood. (Rev: SLJ 7/06)

5779 Pinder, Margaret. *But I Don't Want to Be a Movie Star* (6–9). 2006, Dutton $15.99 (978-0-525-47634-4). This is the wildly funny story of Kat, a 15-year-old English girl who visits her Oscar-winning grandmother in California and, after the grandmother breaks an ankle, decides to impersonate her. (Rev: BL 4/15/06; SLJ 4/06)

5780 Pinkwater, Daniel. *Adventures of a Cat-Whiskered Girl* (5–8). 2010, Houghton Mifflin $16 (978-0-547-22324-7). Fourteen-year-old Audrey, who resembles a cat, has a series of chaotic and wacky adventures around the Hudson river town of Poughkeepsie, encountering characters from other realms, dimensions, and places. (Rev: BL 5/15/10; HB 5–6/10; SLJ 8/10)

5781 Pinkwater, Daniel. *Bushman Lives!* (6–9). Illus. by Calef Brown. 2012, Houghton Mifflin $16.99 (978-0-547-38539-6). In 1960s Chicago young Harold Knishke meets and enjoys a number of surreal characters and situations. **e** Lexile 910L (Rev: BL 10/15/12; LMC 3–4/13; SLJ 11/12)

5782 Pinkwater, Daniel. *The Neddiad: How Neddie Took the Train, Went to Hollywood, and Saved Civilization* (6–9). 2007, Houghton Mifflin $16.00 (978-0-618-

59444-3). A sacred stone turtle, ghosts, movie stars, and woolly mammoths are some of the characters that enter into this story of Neddie Wentworthstein and his travels with his family across 1940s America on the way to have dinner in Los Angeles. ♩ (Rev: BL 2/1/07; HB 5–6/07; SLJ 4/07)

5783 Pratchett, Terry. *Going Postal* (8–12). Series: Discworld. 2004, HarperCollins $24.95 (978-0-06-001313-4). In this humorous and inventive 29th Discworld novel, career criminal Moist von Lipwig escapes hanging by accepting the job of postmaster for Ankh-Morpork, a job he intends to leave far behind as soon as he can. Margaret A. Edwards Award 2011. (Rev: BL 9/1/04; SLJ 2/05)

5784 Raschka, Chris. *Seriously, Norman!* (5–8). Illus. by author. 2011, Scholastic $17.95 (978-0-545-29877-3). Twelve-year-old Norman's tutor Balthazar Birdsong assigns him, along with kite flying, to read the dictionary, inspiring some interesting vocabulary in this quirkily amusing book. (Rev: BL 9/15/11; SLJ 11/1/11)

5785 Rennison, Louise. *Angus, Thongs and Full-Frontal Snogging: Confessions of Georgia Nicolson* (6–9). 2000, HarperCollins $16.99 (978-0-06-028814-3). In her diary, 14-year-old Georgia Nicolson writes with humor and charm of her latest crush, learning to kiss, hunting for her cat, and other teen concerns. (Rev: BL 7/00; HB 5–6/00; HBG 9/00; SLJ 7/00; VOYA 6/00)

5786 Rennison, Louise. *A Midsummer Tights Dream* (7–10). Series: (Mis)adventures of Tallulah Casey. 2012, HarperCollins $17.99 (978-0-06-179936-5). In this sequel to *Withering Tights*, Tallulah begins a new school year full of hope and anticipation about dancing, boys, and saving her school's performing arts program. Lexile 660L (Rev: HB 9–10/12; SLJ 10/12; VOYA 12/12)

5787 Rennison, Louise. *Startled by His Furry Shorts: Confessions of Georgia Nicolson* (7–10). 2006, HarperTempest $16.99 (978-0-06-085384-6). Georgia, a British teenager, gives her hilarious views about dealing with boys, her family, having fun with friends, and getting stuck with a part in her school's play. ♩ (Rev: BL 10/15/06; SLJ 7/06)

5788 Rennison, Louise. *Then He Ate My Boy Entrancers: More Mad, Marvy Confessions of Georgia Nicolson* (7–10). 2005, HarperCollins $15.99 (978-0-06-058937-0). In her sixth volume of diaries, Georgia travels to and critiques the United States as well as cataloging her usual problems at home with friends, boyfriends, siblings, and cats. (Rev: BL 8/05; SLJ 8/05; VOYA 10/05)

5789 Rennison, Louise. *Withering Tights* (7–10). 2011, HarperTeen $16.99 (978-0-06-179931-0). Georgia Nicolson's British cousin Tallulah, 14, navigates a summer at performing arts camp where she worries about her ugly knees, makes new friends, and meets some interesting boys. ♩ ℮ Lexile HL620L (Rev: BL 7/11; HB 9–10/11; SLJ 7/11; VOYA 8/11)

5790 Riggs, Bob. *My Best Defense* (6–10). 1996, Ward Hill paper $5.95 (978-1-886747-01-2). Sarcasm is the best defense of the narrator in this humorous story of a family and the unusual characters they attract. (Rev: SLJ 8/96; VOYA 10/96)

5791 Robertson, Keith. *Henry Reed, Inc.* (5–7). Illus. by Robert McCloskey. 1989, Puffin paper $6.99 (978-0-14-034144-7). Told deadpan in diary form, this story of Henry's enterprising summer in New Jersey presents one of the most amusing boys since Tom and Huck. Others in the series *Henry Reed's Journey* (1963); *Henry Reed's Baby-Sitting Service* (1966); *Henry Reed's Big Show* (1970).

5792 Rodgers, Mary. *Freaky Friday* (4–7). 1972, HarperCollins LB $16.89 (978-0-06-025049-2); paper $5.99 (978-0-06-440046-6). Thirteen-year-old Annabel learns some valuable lessons during the day she becomes her mother. Two sequels are *A Billion for Boris* (1974) and *Summer Switch* (1982). (Rev: BL 4/15/89)

5793 Ryan, Mary C. *Who Says I Can't?* (7–10). 1988, Little, Brown $12.95 (978-0-316-76374-5). Tessa decides to get revenge on a boy who shows too much ardor in his romancing. (Rev: SLJ 11/88)

5794 Rylander, Chris. *The Fourth Stall, Part II* (4–7). 2012, HarperCollins $15.99 (978-006199630-6). Expert problem-solvers Mac and Vince continue to build their advice business (conducted from the washroom) even as their classmates' dilemmas get more and more complex. (Rev: BL 3/1/12; VOYA 12/11)

5795 Sachar, Louis. *Sideways Arithmetic from Wayside School* (4–8). Series: Wayside School. 1992, Scholastic paper $4.99 (978-0-590-45726-2). Sue learns a new kind of math and encounters some humorous brainteasers when she transfers to Wayside School. (Rev: BL 12/15/89)

5796 Scieszka, Jon, ed. *Guys Read: Funny Business* (4–7). Illus. by Adam Rex. 2010, HarperCollins $16.99 (978-0-06-196374-2); paper $5.99 (978-0-06-196373-5). A collection of humorous stories by well-known writers that will appeal to boys. ℮ (Rev: BL 10/1/10*; SLJ 10/1/10; VOYA 2/11)

5797 Scrimger, Richard. *Noses Are Red* (4–7). 2002, Tundra paper $7.95 (978-0-88776-590-2). Norbert, the alien who likes to live in Alan's nose, works to Alan's benefit once again when Alan and a friend meet a variety of perils on a camping trip. (Rev: BL 1/1–15/03; HBG 3/03; SLJ 12/02; VOYA 2/03)

5798 Seegert, Scott. *How to Grow Up and Rule the World* (5–8). Illus. by John Martin. Series: Vordak the Incomprehensible. 2010, Egmont $13.99 (978-1-60684-013-9). The comically sinister Vordak provides dazzling insights into the mind of an evil genius in this giggle-worthy personal development book, featuring tips on wardrobe, social behavior, housing, and death traps. Lexile NC1140L (Rev: BL 9/1/10; SLJ 12/1/10)

5799 Selzer, Adam. *Pirates of the Retail Wasteland* (6–9). 2008, Delacorte $15.99 (978-0-385-73482-0). Leon, an inventive 14-year-old, and a group of friends in his gifted class decide to stage a protest against the big-business coffee shop that is threatening their downtown favorite. (Rev: BL 3/15/08; SLJ 7/08)

5800 Sheldon, Dyan. *Confessions of a Hollywood Star* (7–10). 2006, Candlewick $208.00 (978-0-7636-3075-1). In this funny follow-up to *Confessions of a Teenage Drama Queen* (1999), Lola schemes to get a part in a Hollywood movie being filmed in her suburban New Jersey hometown. (Rev: BL 6/1–15/06; HB 7–8/06; LMC 11–12/06; SLJ 10/06)

5801 Sherman, Deborah. *The BEDMAS Conspiracy* (5–7). 2011, Fitzhenry & Whiteside paper $9.95 (978-1-55455-181-1). Cousins Adam and Daniela are determined to win the middle school talent show with their rock band despite their respective deficiencies. Lexile 660L (Rev: LMC 3–4/12; SLJ 12/1/11)

5802 Shields, Gillian. *The Actual Real Reality of Jennifer James* (7–10). 2006, HarperCollins $16.99 (978-0-06-082240-8). Unpopular British high school student Jennifer James becomes a contestant on a TV reality show in this funny story told through diary entries (with helpful definitions of British slang). (Rev: BL 5/15/06; SLJ 6/06)

5803 Shipton, Paul. *The Pig Scrolls* (6–9). 2005, Candlewick $15.99 (978-0-7636-2702-7). Shipton turns ancient Greek history and mythology on its ear to create this rollicking tale of Gryllus, who is transformed into a talking pig by Circe and goes on to save the world. (Rev: BL 10/15/05; SLJ 12/05)

5804 Shipton, Paul. *The Pig Who Saved the World: By Gryllus the Pig* (5–8). 2007, Candlewick $15.99 (978-0-7636-3446-9). In this sequel to *The Pig Scrolls* (2005), Gryllus the pig and his mythological friends — including the young poet Homer — are searching for Circe, the sorceress who can make Gryllus human again. (Rev: BL 10/1/07; SLJ 11/07)

5805 Shusterman, Neal. *Antsy Does Time* (6–9). 2008, Dutton $16.99 (978-0-525-47825-6). Fourteen-year-old Antsy, last seen in *The Schwa Was Here* (2004), is back in this quirky, funny novel in which he donates a month of his life to a dying friend and starts a trend that has unexpected consequences. (Rev: BL 9/1/08; LMC 1–2/09; SLJ 9/1/08*)

5806 Shusterman, Neal. *The Schwa Was Here* (6–9). 2004, Penguin $16.99 (978-0-525-47182-0). The virtual invisibility of 8th-grader Calvin Schwa proves profitable for newfound friend Anthony Bonano, who takes wagers on how much his new pal can get away with. (Rev: BL 12/1/04; SLJ 10/04; VOYA 10/04)

5807 Sitomer, Alan Lawrence. *A Catastrophe of Nerdish Proportions* (5–8). Series: Nerd Girls. 2012, Hyperion/Disney $16.99 (978-1-4231-3997-3). Warring groups

the Nerd Girls and the ThreePees (Pretty, Popular, Perfect) are sentenced to compete together in the Academic Septathlon. ⌒ ⅇ Lexile HL720L (Rev: BLO 9/15/12; SLJ 8/1/12)

5808 Skye, Obert. *Wonkenstein: The Creature from My Closet* (4–7). Illus. by author. 2011, Henry Holt $12.99 (978-0-8050-9268-4). Twelve-year-old Rob is uninterested in books and they pile up in his closet — until the day a strange being emerges from the heap, appearing to be a combination of Willy Wonka and Frankenstein, complicating Rob's all-too-average life. Lexile 860L (Rev: BL 10/15/11; SLJ 9/1/11)

5809 Sleator, William. *Oddballs* (8–12). 1995, Penguin paper $5.99 (978-0-14-037438-4). A collection of stories based on experiences from the author's youth and peopled with an unusual assortment of family and friends.

5810 Smith, Edwin R. *Blue Star Highway: A Tale of Redemption from North Florida, Vol. 1* (7–12). 1997, Mile Marker Twelve Publg. paper $9.95 (978-0-9659054-0-4). In this humorous novel, 14-year-old Marty Crane tells of the events in his life leading up to being sentenced to a detention home in 1962. (Rev: BL 2/15/99)

5811 Snicket, Lemony. *The Bad Beginning* (4–7). Series: A Series of Unfortunate Events. 1999, HarperCollins $12.99 (978-0-06-440766-3). A humorous story about the ill-fated Beaudelaire orphans and the creepy, wicked villains they never seem to avoid. (Rev: BL 12/1/99; HBG 3/00; SLJ 11/99)

5812 Snicket, Lemony. *The Carnivorous Carnival* (4–8). Illus. by Brett Helquist. Series: A Series of Unfortunate Events. 2002, HarperCollins LB $15.89 (978-0-06-029640-7). The Baudelaire orphans pose as carnival freaks in the ninth volume of this unhappily-ever-after series. (Rev: BL 12/15/02; HBG 3/03; SLJ 1/03)

5813 Snicket, Lemony. *The End* (5–8). Illus. by Brett Helquist. Series: A Series of Unfortunate Events. 2006, HarperCollins $12.99 (978-0-06-441016-8). The Baudelaire orphans find themselves stranded on an island with none other than the villainous Count Olaf; will this be the last installment in the series? (Rev: BL 10/15/06)

5814 Snicket, Lemony. *The Wide Window* (4–7). Series: A Series of Unfortunate Events. 2000, HarperCollins LB $15.89 (978-0-06-028314-8). The three Baudelaire children have a new guardian, timid cousin Josephine, but they are pursued by former keeper Count Olaf. (Rev: BL 2/1/00; HBG 10/00; SLJ 1/00)

5815 Soto, Gary. *Summer on Wheels* (5–8). 1995, Scholastic paper $13.95 (978-0-590-48365-0). In this sequel to *Crazy Weekend* (1994), Hector and Mando take a bike ride from their barrio home in Los Angeles to Santa Monica. (Rev: BL 1/15/95; SLJ 4/95; VOYA 4/95)

5816 Spinelli, Jerry. *The Library Card* (4–8). 1997, Scholastic paper $15.95 (978-0-590-46731-5). Four humorous, poignant stories about how books changed the lives of several youngsters. (Rev: BCCB 3/97; BL 2/1/97; HB 3–4/97; SLJ 3/97; VOYA 10/97)

5817 Standiford, Natalie. *Blonde at Heart* (5–8). Series: Elle Woods. 2006, Hyperion $4.99 (978-0-7868-3843-1). How Elle Woods, the central character of the 2001 movie *Legally Blonde*, became a blond bombshell in her effort to attract the attention of her crush. (Rev: BL 7/06; SLJ 5/06)

5818 Stanley, George E. *Hershell Cobwell and the Miraculous Tattoo* (4–8). 1991, Avon paper $2.95 (978-0-380-75897-5). A junior high boy decides to gain popularity by getting a tattoo. (Rev: BL 3/15/91)

5819 Taha, Karen T. *Marshmallow Muscles, Banana Brainstorms* (6–8). 1988, Harcourt $13.95 (978-0-15-200525-2). A puny youngster tries a regime of body development through the help of his dream girl. (Rev: BL 1/1/89)

5820 Trahey, Jane. *The Clovis Caper* (5–8). 1990, Avon paper $2.95 (978-0-380-75914-9). Martin is so upset at leaving his dog, Clovis, when going to England that Aunt Hortense plots to smuggle the dog out of the country. (Rev: BL 7/90)

5821 Trembath, Don. *A Fly Named Alfred* (7–10). 1997, Orca paper $6.95 (978-1-55143-083-6). In this sequel to *The Tuesday Cafe*, Harper Winslow gets into more trouble when he write an anonymous column in the school newspaper that enrages the school bully. (Rev: BL 8/97; SLJ 9/96)

5822 Tulloch, Richard. *Weird Stuff* (5–8). Illus. by Shane Nagle. 2006, Walker $16.95 (978-0-8027-8058-4). A borrowed pen gives school soccer star Brian Hobble amazing new writing abilities, but they're limited to a single genre — romantic fiction. (Rev: SLJ 8/06)

5823 Uderzo, Albert. *Asterix and Son* (4–8). Trans. by Anthea Bell and Derek Hockridge. 2002, Orion paper $9.95 (978-0-7528-4775-7). In comic-book format, this is the entertaining story of French heroes Asterix and Obelix and how they became guardians of a kidnapped baby. Also use *Asterix and the Black Gold* (2002) and *Asterix and the Great Divide* (2002). (Rev: BL 4/15/02)

5824 Venuti, Kristin Clark. *The Butler Gets a Break* (4–7). Series: Bellweather Tales. 2010, Egmont $15.99 (978-1-60684-087-0). Hospitalized with a broken leg, Benway the butler hears about the escapades of the Bellweathers and worries that he may lose his job; a sequel to *Leaving the Bellweathers* (2009). (Rev: BL 11/1/10; SLJ 11/1/10)

5825 Venuti, Kristin Clark. *Leaving the Bellweathers* (4–7). Series: Bellweather Tales. 2009, Egmont $15.99 (978-160684006-1). Butler Tristan Benway is looking forward to ending his tenure with the eccentric Bellweathers and starts a memoir about their outrageous behaviors. ⌒ (Rev: BL 9/15/09; HB 11–12/09; SLJ 9/09)

5826 Ware, Cheryl. *Venola in Love* (4–7). Illus. by Kristin Sorra. 2000, Orchard LB $16.99 (978-0-531-33306-8). Told through diary entries, e-mail messages, and class notes, this humorous novel tells how 7th-grader Venola discovers the problems of falling in love. (Rev: BCCB 10/00; HBG 10/01; SLJ 10/00)

5827 Weiner, Ellis. *The Templeton Twins Have an Idea, Bk. 1* (4–7). Illus. by Jeremy Holmes. Series: The Templeton Twins. 2012, Chronicle $16.99 (978-0-8118-6679-8). Resourceful twins Abigail and John, 12, along with their dog, are kidnapped by one of their father's former students and his twin brother. ℮ Lexile 850L (Rev: BL 9/1/12; HB 9–10/12; LMC 8–9/12; SLJ 7/12; VOYA 10/12)

5828 Wersba, Barbara. *You'll Never Guess the End* (7–12). 1992, HarperCollins $14.00 (978-0-06-020448-8). A send-up of the New York City literary scene, rich dilettantes, and scientology. (Rev: BL 11/15/92; SLJ 9/92)

5829 Weyn, Suzanne. *The Makeover Club* (7–9). 1986, Avon paper $2.50 (978-0-380-75007-8). Three girls decide they are going to be glamorous by forming the Makeover Club. (Rev: SLJ 1/87; VOYA 12/86)

5830 Whitehouse, Howard. *The Island of Mad Scientists: Being an Excursion to the Wilds of Scotland, Involving Many Marvels of Experimental Invention, Pirates, a Heroic Cat, a Mechanical Man and a Monkey* (4–7). Illus. by Bill Slavin. Series: The Mad Misadventures of Emmaline and Rubberbones. 2008, Kids Can $17.95 (978-1-55453-236-0); paper $7.95 (978-1-55453-237-7). The third and final installment in this fast-paced series involves more running from villains, crazy characters, and many comic moments as the group tries to reach Urrgghh. (Rev: SLJ 2/09)

5831 Whytock, Cherry. *My Scrumptious Scottish Dumplings: The Life of Angelica Cookson Potts* (6–9). 2004, Simon & Schuster $14.95 (978-0-689-86549-7). In this rollicking sequel to *My Cup Runneth Over* (2003), poor privileged — and unsylphlike — Angel finds herself barred from the Harrods' food halls after her Scottish-born father stages a protest against the quality of the big store's haggis. (Rev: BL 1/1–15/05; SLJ 1/05)

5832 Wibberley, Leonard. *The Mouse That Roared* (7–12). 1992, Buccaneer LB $27.95 (978-0-89966-887-1). To get foreign aid, the tiny Duchy of Grand Fenwick declares war on the United States.

5833 Wood, Maryrose. *Sex Kittens and Horn Dawgs Fall in Love* (7–10). 2006, Delacorte LB $17.99 (978-0-385-90296-0). To get closer to Matthew, the object of her affection, 14-year-old Felicia suggests that the two of them work together on a science fair project investigating the workings of love's "X-factor." (Rev: BL 11/15/05; SLJ 2/06)

5834 Yee, Lisa. *So Totally Emily Ebers* (5–8). 2007, Scholastic $16.99 (978-0-439-83847-4). In this companion to *Millicent Min, Girl Genius* (2003) and *Stanford Wong Flunks Big-Time* (2005), Emily writes a series of letters to her absent father, telling him about her friends Millicent and Stanford and their tutoring arrangement. (Rev: BL 3/15/07; SLJ 4/07)

5835 Yee, Lisa. *Stanford Wong Flunks Big-Time* (4–7). 2005, Scholastic $16.99 (978-0-439-62247-9). In this rollicking sequel to *Millicent Minn, Girl Genius*, Stanford Wong is upset when his parents hire Millicent, his arch-nemesis, to tutor him in English. (Rev: BL 11/15/05; SLJ 12/05)

5836 Zeitlin, Meredith. *Freshman Year and Other Unnatural Disasters* (8–11). 2012, Putnam $16.99 (978-039925423-9). Kelsey, 14, navigates a perilous freshman year at a new school in Manhattan; this humorous story is full of social and romantic missteps. **e** (Rev: BL 4/15/12; SLJ 3/12; VOYA 4/12)

5837 Ziegler, Jennifer. *Alpha Dog* (8–11). 2006, Delacorte paper $7.99 (978-0-385-73285-7). When Katie learns to be alpha dog and control her adopted mutt, she also learns to assert herself with her mother and friends in this funny novel. (Rev: BL 7/06; LMC 10/06)

5838 Ziegler, Jennifer. *How Not to Be Popular* (7–10). 2008, Delacorte $15.99 (978-0-385-73465-3). When her family moves yet again, Sugar Magnolia (Maggie) ditches her usual effort to make friends and instead decides to become an outsider at school. (Rev: BL 4/1/08; SLJ 3/08)

Mysteries, Thrillers, and Spy Stories

5839 Abbott, Tony. *The Postcard* (6–9). 2008, Little, Brown $15.99 (978-0-316-01172-3). When Jason discovers an old postcard that belonged to his recently deceased grandmother, he is drawn into a mystery that mirrors a story in an old magazine. (Rev: BL 5/1/08; SLJ 4/08)

5840 Abrahams, Peter. *Down the Rabbit Hole* (7–10). Series: Echo Falls. 2005, HarperCollins LB $17.89 (978-0-06-073702-3). Thirteen-year-old Ingrid Levin-Hill takes a page from her idol Sherlock Holmes and sets out to track down the murderer of an eccentric townswoman. (Rev: BCCB 4/05; BL 5/1/05*; SLJ 5/05; VOYA 6/05)

5841 Abrahams, Peter. *Into the Dark* (5–12). Series: Echo Falls. 2008, HarperCollins $15.99 (978-0-06-073708-5). Ingrid's grandfather, a World War II veteran, is a suspect in a murder committed using a World War II-era rifle. Can Ingrid solve the mystery and clear her grandfather's name? (Rev: BL 5/1/08; SLJ 3/08)

5842 Abrahams, Peter. *Reality Check* (8–11). 2009, HarperTeen $16.99 (978-006122766-0); LB $17.89 (978-006122767-7). Cody Laredo is already facing difficulties — a knee injury keeps him off the football team and ruins his chances of a college scholarship — when his rich girlfriend Clea disappears from her boarding school in Vermont and he sets off from Colorado to find her. ⋒ **e** (Rev: BL 7/09; SLJ 5/1/09; VOYA 4/09*)

5843 Adam, Paul. *Max Cassidy: Escape from Shadow Island* (5–9). 2009, HarperCollins $16.99 (978-0-06-186323-3). Max Cassidy, a British 14-year-old escape artist who still performs despite the fact that his mother is accused of murdering his father; sets out to prove her innocence in this fast-paced novel full of tension. (Rev: SLJ 4/10; VOYA 4/10)

5844 Aguiar, Nadia. *Secrets of Tamarind* (5–8). 2011, Feiwel & Friends $16.99 (978-0-312-38030-4). The Nelson children first seen in *The Lost Island of Tamarind* (2008) return to the magical island to save it from environmental disaster in this blend of adventure and fantasy. **e** Lexile 860L (Rev: BL 7/11; SLJ 9/1/11)

5845 Aiken, Joan. *The Teeth of the Gale* (7–9). 1988, HarperCollins $14.95 (978-0-06-020044-2). Eighteen-year-old Felix tries to rescue three children who have been kidnapped. A sequel to *Go Saddle the Sea* and *Bridle the Wind*. (Rev: BL 9/15/88; SLJ 11/88; VOYA 12/88)

5846 Allison, Jennifer. *The Bones of the Holy* (5–8). Series: Gilda Joyce Psychic Investigator. 2011, Dutton $16.99 (978-052542212-9). Teen sleuth Gilda uses her perceptive powers to investigate a spooky and sinister past her mother's prospective new husband seems to be hiding. ⋒ (Rev: BL 5/1/11; SLJ 6/12)

5847 Allison, Jennifer. *The Dead Drop* (6–9). Series: Gilda Joyce. 2009, Dutton $16.99 (978-052547980-2). In this installment, Gilda is a 14-year-old summer intern at the International Spy Museum in Washington, D.C., where her psychic abilities serve her well. ⋒ Lexile 960L (Rev: BL 5/1/09; SLJ 6/1/09; VOYA 8/09)

5848 Allison, Jennifer. *Gilda Joyce: Psychic Investigator* (5–7). 2005, Dutton $13.99 (978-0-525-47375-6). Thirteen-year-old Gilda Joyce and a new friend, Juliet, look into the suicide of Juliet's aunt in this richly layered mystery. (Rev: BL 5/1/05*; SLJ 7/05*)

5849 Allison, Jennifer. *Gilda Joyce: The Ghost Sonata* (5–8). 2007, Dutton $15.99 (978-0-525-47808-9). Gilda's psychic abilities come in handy as she accompanies her friend Wendy to a piano competition in England and discovers that Wendy is being haunted. ⋒ (Rev: SLJ 8/07)

5850 Allison, Jennifer. *Gilda Joyce: The Ladies of the Lake* (5–8). 2006, Dutton $16.99 (978-0-525-47693-1). Thirteen-year-old Gilda Joyce — introduced in *Gilda Joyce: Psychic Investigator* (2005) — uses all her psychic abilities to unravel the mystery surrounding a drowning death at her school. (Rev: BL 10/15/06; HBG 4/07; SLJ 9/06)

5851 Alphin, Elaine Marie. *The Perfect Shot* (8–12). 2005, Carolrhoda LB $16.95 (978-1-57505-862-7). Brian, a high school basketball star, learns important lessons about justice, racial prejudice, and civic responsibility when his girlfriend's father is charged with the murder of his wife and two daughters and an African American teammate is arrested on trumped-up charges. (Rev: SLJ 10/05*; VOYA 12/05)

5852 Anastasio, Dina. *The Case of the Glacier Park Swallow* (4–7). 1994, Roberts Rinehart paper $6.95 (978-1-879373-85-3). Juliet, who wants to be a veterinarian, stumbles upon a drug-smuggling ring in this tightly knit mystery. (Rev: BL 12/1/94; SLJ 10/94)

5853 Anastasio, Dina. *The Case of the Grand Canyon Eagle* (5–8). Series: Juliet Stone Environmental Mystery. 1994, Roberts Rinehart paper $6.95 (978-1-879373-84-6). In this ecological mystery, 17-year-old Juliet Stone investigates the disappearance of eagle eggs. (Rev: SLJ 10/94)

5854 Anderson, M. T. *The Clue of the Linoleum Lederhosen: M. T. Anderson's Thrilling Tales* (4–7). Illus. by Kurt Cyrus. 2006, Harcourt $15.00 (978-0-15-205352-9). Jasper Dash, Boy Technonaut, Katie, and Lily are caught up in an exciting mystery at Moose Tongue Lodge in this zany sequel to *Whales on Stilts* (2005). ⌒ (Rev: BCCB 7–8/06; BL 5/1/06*; HB 5–6/06; HBG 10/06; SLJ 6/06; VOYA 6/06)

5855 Apone, Claudio. *My Grandfather, Jack the Ripper* (6–12). 2000, Herodias $19.00 (978-1-928746-16-4). Thirteen-year-old Andy Dobson, a clairvoyant Londoner, travels back in time — with the help of hallucinogenic drugs — to discover the true identity of the legendary murderer. (Rev: HBG 10/01; SLJ 6/01; VOYA 6/01)

5856 Arnold, Tedd. *Rat Life: A Mystery* (7–10). 2007, Dial $16.99 (978-0-8037-3020-5). Todd, 14, loves to write funny, crude stories to entertain his classmates until he befriends a Vietnam veteran named Rat; his writing takes on a new perspective while he also begins to uncover clues to an unsolved murder. (Rev: BL 5/1/07; SLJ 5/07)

5857 Avi. *Murder at Midnight* (5–8). 2009, Scholastic $17.99 (978-0-545-08090-3). In this compelling companion to *Midnight Magic* (2009) set in Italy in 1490, Mangus the magician and his young servant Fabrizio race against the clock as they strive to uncover a traitor. ⌒ (Rev: BL 8/09; LMC 1–2/10; SLJ 10/09)

5858 Balliett, Blue. *Chasing Vermeer* (5–8). Illus. by Brett Helquist. 2004, Scholastic $16.95 (978-0-439-37294-7). Petra and Calder, brainy 12-year-old classmates at the University of Chicago Lab School, join forces to find out what happened to a missing Vermeer painting. (Rev: BL 4/1/04*; HB 7–8/04; SLJ 7/04)

5859 Balliett, Blue. *The Danger Box* (5–7). 2010, Scholastic $16.99 (978-0-439-85209-8). When isolated,

myopic Zoomy, 12, receives a mysterious box of "treasures" from his alcoholic father, curious things begin to happen. ⌒ **e** Lexile 750L (Rev: BL 10/1/10; LMC 3–4/11; SLJ 9/1/10*)

5860 Balliett, Blue. *Hold Fast* (4–7). 2013, Scholastic $17.99 (978-054529988-6). When her father disappears, 11-year-old Early, her mother, and her younger brother can no longer afford their South Side Chicago one-room apartment and must move to a homeless shelter while Early investigates the mystery. ⌒ **e** Lexile 780L (Rev: BL 1/13*; SLJ 4/13)

5861 Bauer, Joan. *Peeled* (6–9). 2008, Putnam $16.99 (978-0-399-23475-0). Hildy and her friends start up an underground newspaper when the principal shuts down the school paper following inflammatory articles about mysterious happenings around town. (Rev: BL 4/15/08; SLJ 4/08)

5862 Beaufrand, Mary Jane. *The River* (8–12). 2010, Little, Brown $16.99 (978-0-316-04168-3). Ronnie, unhappy following her family's move from Portland to rural Oregon, is overwhelmed when the 10-year-old girl she has been babysitting drowns; suspicious about the circumstances, she sets out to discover what happened. Lexile HL730L (Rev: BL 12/15/09; HB 5–6/10; SLJ 2/10; VOYA 4/10)

5863 Beil, Michael D. *The Mistaken Masterpiece* (5–8). Series: The Red Blazer Girls. 2011, Knopf $16.99 (978-0-375-86740-8); LB $19.99 (978-0-375-96740-5). The Red Blazer Girls are asked to investigate the ownership of a family heirloom, and discover more than they bargained for. ⌒ **e** (Rev: BL 5/1/11; SLJ 8/11)

5864 Beil, Michael D. *The Red Blazer Girls: The Ring of Rocamadour* (5–8). 2009, Knopf $15.99 (978-0-375-84814-8). In this snappy title, a quirky bunch of schoolgirls from St. Veronica's in Manhattan attempt to solve a mystery while also dealing with almost-boyfriends and other daily challenges. (Rev: BL 1/1–15/09*; SLJ 6/09)

5865 Beil, Michael D. *The Vanishing Violin* (5–8). Series: The Red Blazer Girls. 2010, Knopf $16.99 (978-0-375-86103-1); LB $19.99 (978-0-375-96103-8). The four Red Blazer Girls — Sophie, Margaret, Becca, and Leigh Ann — must solve various violin-related mysteries at St. Veronica's School. ⌒ **e** (Rev: BL 7/10; SLJ 8/10)

5866 Bell, Hilari. *Rogue's Home* (7–10). Series: Knight and Rogue. 2008, Eos $17.99 (978-0-06-082506-5). The second adventure in the series, this buddy story has the "knight" Mike and his sidekick squire Fisk returning to Fisk's hometown to investigate blackmail and arson. (Rev: BL 8/08; SLJ 9/08)

5867 Bennett, Jay. *Coverup* (8–10). 1992, Fawcett paper $5.99 (978-0-449-70409-7). Realizing his friend has killed a pedestrian on a deserted road after a party, Brad returns to the accident scene and meets a girl searching for her homeless father. (Rev: BL 11/1/91)

5868 Berlin, Eric. *The Potato Chip Puzzles* (4–7). Series: The Puzzling World of Winston Breen. 2009, Putnam $16.99 (978-0-399-25198-6). Winston and his friends compete to win $50,000 for their school by solving puzzles. Brainteasers throughout the story will entertain readers. (Rev: BL 5/1/09; SLJ 8/09)

5869 Birch, Beverley. *Rift* (6–9). Illus. 2008, Egmont paper $9.95 (978-140521589-3). Three teens and a journalist disappear from their archaeological camp in remote Africa in this tense, exciting story that is part adventure story, part mystery. Lexile 780L (Rev: BL 10/15/08; SLJ 2/1/09; VOYA 12/08)

5870 Bloor, Edward. *Taken* (5–8). 2007, Knopf $16.99 (978-0-375-83636-7). In Florida in the year 2035, where kidnapping has become a common crime with recognized procedures, 13-year-old Charity must find a way to escape and survive when her wealthy family's payoff to the kidnappers goes wrong. (Rev: BL 9/1/07; SLJ 12/07)

5871 Boie, Kirsten. *The Princess Plot* (4–8). 2009, Scholastic $17.99 (978-0-545-03220-9). Fourteen-year-old Jenna soon realizes her "acting test" assignment — impersonating the princess of a government in dangerous turmoil — involves more than she was told. ⌂ (Rev: BCCB 9/09; BLO 5/28/09; SLJ 10/09; VOYA 10/09)

5872 Bonk, John J. *Madhattan Mystery* (5–8). 2012, Walker $16.99 (978-080272349-9). Twelve-year-old Lexi and her younger brother Kevin overhear details about stolen jewels while staying in New York City with their aunt; a wild chase through subway tunnels and parks ensues. ℮ Lexile 790L (Rev: BL 5/1/12*; LMC 10/12; SLJ 5/1/12)

5873 Bosch, Pseudonymous. *The Name of This Book Is Secret* (4–7). 2007, Little, Brown $16.99 (978-0-316-11366-3). What's inside this book is secret, too, and only after much cautioning does the narrator begin to tell the story of a group trying to discover the key to immortality. ⌂ (Rev: BL 7/07; SLJ 1/08)

5874 Bossley, Michele Martin. *Swiped* (6–8). Series: Orca Currents. 2006, Orca paper $8.95 (978-1-55143-646-3). Even though their efforts meet with suspicion and disapproval, middle-schoolers Trevor, Nick, and Robyn investigate mysteries — missing sandwiches, stolen books — with gusto; for reluctant and challenged readers. (Rev: SLJ 3/07)

5875 Bowler, Tim. *Frozen Fire* (7–10). 2008, Philomel $17.99 (978-0-399-25053-8). Set in a wintry England, this is a disquieting and complex story of a ghostlike boy whom Dusty suspects knows the whereabouts of her missing brother. (Rev: BL 5/15/08; SLJ 7/08)

5876 Bowler, Tim. *Storm Catchers* (6–10). 2003, Simon & Schuster $16.95 (978-0-689-84573-4). A multilayered, suspenseful story of the kidnapping of a 13-year-old girl on the Cornwall coast, her brother's agonized guilt, and the discovery of a dark family secret. (Rev: BL 9/1/03; HBG 4/04; SLJ 5/03; VOYA 8/03)

5877 Bracegirdle, P. J. *Fiendish Deeds* (5–7). Series: The Joy of Spooking. 2008, Simon & Schuster $15.99 (978-1-4169-3416-5). When 11-year-old Joy learns that there are plans to build a water park on Spooking's bog — where she believes a monster resides — the young fan of horror stories sets out to stop this; the spooky setting and dark humor add to the appeal. (Rev: LMC 3/09; SLJ 3/09)

5878 Bradbury, Jennifer. *Shift* (7–12). 2008, Atheneum $16.99 (978-1-4169-6219-9). Friends Chris and Win take a cross-country bike trip the summer after high school; but Win disappears in Montana and Chris becomes the focus of an FBI investigation. (Rev: BL 3/1/08)

5879 Brennan, Herbie. *The Secret Prophecy* (6–9). 2012, HarperCollins $16.99 (978-006207180-4). Edward Michael ("Em") Goverton finds himself embroiled in international intrigue after his father dies unexpectedly and his mother is committed to a mental facility. ℮ Lexile 730L (Rev: BL 11/1/12; SLJ 1/13; VOYA 8/12)

5880 Broach, Elise. *Shakespeare's Secret* (6–9). 2005, Henry Holt $16.95 (978-0-8050-7387-4). Hero, a 6th-grade misfit named for a character in a Shakespeare play, embarks on a search for a diamond with links to the Elizabethan era. (Rev: BCCB 6/05; BL 5/1/05; SLJ 6/05; VOYA 8/05)

5881 Bruchac, Joseph. *Night Wings* (5–8). Illus. by Sally Wern Comport. 2009, HarperCollins $15.99 (978-0-06-112318-4). Indian lore gives this thriller an additional layer of meaning. (Rev: BL 6/1–15/09; SLJ 7/09)

5882 Bunting, Eve. *The Haunting of Safe Keep* (7–10). 1985, HarperCollins LB $12.89 (978-0-397-32113-1). In this romantic mystery, two college friends work out their family problems while investigating strange occurrences where they work. (Rev: BL 4/15/85; SLJ 5/85; VOYA 8/85)

5883 Burgess, Melvin. *Sara's Face* (8–12). 2007, Simon & Schuster $16.99 (978-1-4169-3295-6). Wealthy rock star Jonathan Heat, whose obsession with plastic surgery has left him without a face, offers to pay for surgery for pretty teen Sara; could his motives be less than generous? (Rev: BL 5/15/07; SLJ 6/07)

5884 Butcher, A. J. *Spy High: Mission One* (7–10). 2004, Little, Brown paper $6.99 (978-0-316-73760-9). This thriller is set in the year 2060 and deals with a group of students at a school known as Spy High who are training to become secret agents. (Rev: BL 5/1/04; SLJ 7/04)

5885 Butler, Dori Hillestad. *Do You Know the Monkey Man?* (5–7). 2005, Peachtree $14.95 (978-1-56145-340-5). After a psychic says that her twin sister — believed drowned 10 years before — is not dead at all,

13-year-old Samantha sets off with a friend to investigate. (Rev: BL 5/1/05; SLJ 6/05)

5886 Cadnum, Michael. *Seize the Storm* (7–10). 2012, Farrar $17.99 (978-037436705-3). On a yacht in the Pacific, Susannah and her family find a boat carrying two dead bodies and a large amount of cash, putting them directly in the sights of some very bad people. Lexile 980L (Rev: BL 6/12; HB 7–8/12; LMC 11–12/12; SLJ 8/1/12; VOYA 6/12)

5887 Cantor, Jillian. *The September Sisters* (7–12). 2009, HarperCollins $16.99 (978-006168648-1); LB $17.89 (978-006168649-8). Abigail's sister, missing for two years, is found dead in this story about grief, anger, suspicion, and loneliness. Lexile 850L (Rev: BL 2/1/09; SLJ 6/1/09; VOYA 6/09)

5888 Carey, Benedict. *The Unknowns* (6–10). 2009, Abrams $16.95 (978-081097991-8). A group of preteens sets out to solve a mystery on their island, home to a nuclear power plant. Their math teacher has left behind clues in the form of equations and geometry puzzles. Lexile 760L (Rev: BL 5/1/09; LMC 10/09; SLJ 10/09)

5889 Cargill, Linda. *Pool Party* (7–10). 1996, Scholastic paper $3.99 (978-0-590-58111-0). Sharon's beach party at a resort with a reputation for being haunted ends in murder. (Rev: SLJ 1/97)

5890 Carman, Patrick. *Dark Eden* (7–10). 2011, HarperCollins $17.99 (978-0-06-200970-8). A suspenseful story in which teenager Will learns unsettling secrets about a phobia-treatment center called Fort Eden. ∩ e (Rev: BL 11/15/11; LMC 11–12/11; SLJ 10/1/11; VOYA 8/11)

5891 Carman, Patrick. *Skeleton Creek* (5–8). 2009, Scholastic $14.99 (978-0-545-07566-4). Sidelined by a broken leg, teenage Ryan nevertheless keeps in touch with his friend Sarah as she continues to investigate a mystery and documents her adventures on film; readers can view the videos on an accompanying Web site. (Rev: BL 12/1/08; LMC 5/09; SLJ 3/09)

5892 Carman, Patrick. *Thirteen Days to Midnight* (7–10). 2010, Little, Brown $16.99 (978-0-316-00403-9). When his foster father dies in an accident, Jacob discovers that he has a unique power to ward off death but that this power is not without pitfalls; a suspenseful read. ∩ Lexile 1010L (Rev: BL 5/1/10; LMC 8–9/10; SLJ 5/10)

5893 Carman, Patrick. *Trackers: Book One* (6–9). 2010, Scholastic $14.99 (978-0-545-16500-6). This exciting adventure about 15-year-old Adam Henderson and his team of trackers, who pursue hackers, has an accompanying Web site that enhances the story with puzzles and videos. Lexile 810L (Rev: BL 7/10; LMC 10/10; SLJ 7/10)

5894 Carter, Ally. *Cross My Heart and Hope to Spy* (6–9). 2007, Hyperion $13.55 (978-1-4231-0005-8).

Espionage and intrigue are interwoven with romance in this second (after 2006's *I'd Tell You I Love You, But Then I'd Have to Kill You*) story about Cammie Morgan and the other students at the Gallagher spy camp. (Rev: SLJ 10/07)

5895 Cassidy, Anne. *Dead Time* (7–10). Series: Murder Notebooks. 2012, Walker $16.99 (978-080272351-2). Five years ago Rose's mother and Joshua's father disappeared and now the two step-siblings are investigating this and two potentially linked murders. e Lexile 630L (Rev: BL 5/1/12; LMC 10/12; SLJ 5/1/12; VOYA 6/12)

5896 Cassidy, Anne. *Killing Rachel* (8–11). Series: Murder Notebooks. 2013, Walker $16.99 (978-080273416-7). Rose investigates the death of Rachel, a former classmate, even as she and Joshua continue the search for their missing parents. e (Rev: BL 12/15/12; LMC 5–6/13; SLJ 4/13; VOYA 12/12)

5897 Chandler, Elizabeth. *Dark Secrets: Legacy of Lies* (6–12). Series: Dark Secrets. 2000, Pocket paper $4.99 (978-0-7434-0028-2). Megan, 16, has finally met her grandmother, but she still feels like an outsider and her frightening dreams become more and more intense. (Rev: BCCB 2/01; BL 2/1/01; SLJ 1/01; VOYA 12/00)

5898 Chari, Sheela. *Vanished* (4–7). 2011, Hyperion/Disney $16.99 (978-1-4231-3163-2). East Indian American Neela, 11, gets embroiled in a mystery when her grandmother's prized veena (a traditional Indian instrument) is stolen. (Rev: BL 9/1/11; SLJ 12/1/11)

5899 Cheshire, Simon. *Treasure of Dead Man's Lane and Other Case Files* (4–7). Illus. by R. W. Alley. Series: Saxby Smart, Private Detective. 2010, Roaring Brook $16.99 (978-159643475-2). Schoolboy sleuth Saxby solves three challenging mysteries with the help of his sidekicks in this book that underlines the clues. e (Rev: BL 5/15/10*; SLJ 7/10)

5900 Child, Lauren. *Ruby Redfort: Look into My Eyes* (5–8). Illus. 2012, Candlewick $16.99 (978-076365120-6). Brilliant 13-year-old Ruby is hired to crack codes for a secret crime-fighting organization in this multilayered, fast-paced novel. ∩ e Lexile 800L (Rev: BL 2/15/12; LMC 8–9/12; SLJ 4/12; VOYA 4/12)

5901 Clark, Mary Higgins, ed. *The International Association of Crime Writers Presents Bad Behavior* (8–12). 1995, Harcourt $20.00 (978-0-15-200179-7). Features many stories with young characters and less overt violence than adult fare. Includes works by Sara Paretsky, P. D. James, Lawrence Block, and Liza Cody. (Rev: BL 7/95)

5902 Coben, Harlan. *Seconds Away* (8–11). Series: Mickey Bolitar. 2012, Putnam $18.99 (978-0-399-25651-6). In this sequel to 2011's *Shelter*, Mickey and friends Spoon and Ema must resolve two parallel mysteries, one involving the death of Mickey's father and the other the shooting of a classmate's mother. (Rev: BL 10/1/12; SLJ 11/12)

5903 Coben, Harlan. *Shelter* (8–12). 2011, Putnam $18.99 (978-0-399-25650-9). Myron Bolitar's nephew Mickey comes to live with him and finds himself embroiled in strange events relating to his father and to a classmate named Ashley. ⌒ ℮ Lexile HL530L (Rev: BL 9/15/11; LMC 1–2/12*; SLJ 9/1/11)

5904 Coburn, Ann. *Glint* (6–9). 2007, HarperCollins LB $17.89 (978-0-06-084724-1). Ellie's younger brother is kidnapped and Ellie sets out to find him, inspired by a story the two siblings had read years before. (Rev: BL 1/1–15/07; SLJ 6/07)

5905 Collard, Sneed B. *Double Eagle* (5–8). 2009, Peachtree $15.95 (978-1-56145-480-8). In 1973, 13-year-old Mike and a friend find a rare coin and rush to see if there are more before an approaching hurricane arrives. (Rev: BL 5/1/09; SLJ 12/09)

5906 Collard, Sneed B. *The Governor's Dog Is Missing!* (4–7). Series: Slate Stephens Mysteries. 2011, Bucking Horse $16 (978-0-9844460-1-8). Slate and Daphne, both 12, investigate the disappearance of Cat, the governor of Minnesota's dog. (Rev: BL 5/1/11; SLJ 6/11)

5907 Collard, Sneed B. *Hangman's Gold* (4–7). Series: Slate Stephens Mysteries. 2011, Bucking Horse $16 (978-098444602-5). Crime-solving duo Slate and Daphne return with a Wild West mystery involving cowboy art and missing gold. (Rev: BL 1/1/12; SLJ 1/12)

5908 Collier, James Lincoln. *The Dreadful Revenge of Ernest Gallen* (5–8). 2008, Bloomsbury $16.95 (978-1-59990-220-3). Gene, the main character in this Depression-era mystery, is haunted by a ghost looking for revenge and searches for the role his family and neighbors played in a horrible crime. (Rev: BL 8/08; SLJ 9/08)

5909 Collins, Brandilyn, and Amberly Collins. *Final Touch* (8–12). Series: The Rayne Tour. 2010, Zondervan paper $9.99 (978-0-310-71933-5). On the very day her mother, rock star Rayne O'Connor, is to get remarried, teenage Shaley is abducted by a stalker. (Rev: BL 9/1/10; SLJ 12/1/10)

5910 Comino, Sandra. *The Little Blue House* (4–7). 2003, Douglas & McIntyre $15.95 (978-0-88899-504-9). Young Cintia and her friend Bruno investigate why an abandoned house in their small town in Argentina turns blue for one day each year in this suspenseful novel that contains some violence. (Rev: BL 2/15/04)

5911 Conly, Jane Leslie. *In the Night, on Lanvale Street* (6–8). 2005, Henry Holt $16.95 (978-0-8050-7464-2). When their next-door neighbor is murdered, 13-year-old Charlie and her younger brother are swept up in a mystery that envelops the whole community. (Rev: SLJ 6/05)

5912 Conrad, Hy. *Kids' Whodunits 2: Crack the Cases!* (4–7). Illus. by Sue Blanchard. 2009, Sterling paper $6.95 (978-1-4027-5398-5). Twelve-year-old Jonah

Bixby, who has learned much at the Fifth Precinct, solves 20 varied cases while giving readers plenty of clues. (Rev: BL 5/1/09)

5913 Constable, Kate. *Crow Country* (6–9). 2012, IPG/ Allen & Unwin paper $13.99 (978-1-74237-395-9). Sadie discovers some unsettling secrets when she moves to a rural Australian town and meets Aboriginal Walter. (Rev: BL 8/12; SLJ 7/12)

5914 Cooney, Caroline B. *If the Witness Lied* (7–10). 2009, Delacorte $16.99 (978-0-385-73448-6); LB $19.99 (978-0-385-90451-3). After their mother's death from cancer and their father's demise in an accident, siblings Smithy, Madison, and Jack must act to keep their toddler brother safe from their evil aunt and the threat of a reality TV show about their grief. ℮ Lexile HL670L (Rev: BL 5/1/09; HB 5–6/09; LMC 8–9/09; SLJ 5/1/09; VOYA 6/09)

5915 Cooney, Caroline B. *They Never Came Back* (6–9). 2010, Delacorte $16.99 (978-0-385-73808-8); LB $19.99 (978-0-385-90709-5). A suspenseful story in which 15-year-old Cathy is (correctly) suspected of being the daughter of a couple who fled the country after stealing millions. ℮ Lexile 660L (Rev: BL 11/15/09; LMC 11–12/09; SLJ 1/10)

5916 Copeland, Mark. *The Bundle at Blackthorpe Heath* (4–7). 2006, Houghton Mifflin $15.00 (978-0-618-56302-9). With the help of a spyglass he receives as a birthday present, 12-year-old Arthur Piper uncovers a conspiracy to undermine his grandfather's traveling insect circus. (Rev: BL 6/1–15/06; SLJ 7/06)

5917 Corriveau, Art. *Thirteen Hangmen* (5–7). 2012, Abrams $16.95 (978-1-4197-0159-7). Transported during the night on his 13th birthday, Tony finds himself in the company of 13-year-old boys from throughout Boston's history, tasked with solving a dynamic mystery. (Rev: BL 5/1/12; LMC 11–12/12; SLJ 9/12)

5918 Cox, Judy. *The Case of the Purloined Professor* (4–7). Illus. by Omar Rayyan. 2009, Marshall Cavendish $16.99 (978-076145544-8). Rat brothers Ishbu and Frederick team up to find a missing scientist in this adventure-filled story. Lexile 710L (Rev: BL 9/15/09; LMC 11–12/09; SLJ 11/09)

5919 Cox, Suzy. *The Dead Girls Detective Agency* (8–12). 2012, HarperTeen paper $8.99 (978-0-06-202-064-2). Charlotte, 16, wakes up in the Hotel Attlesa to find that she was murdered on the New York subway and must find the perpetrator before she can pass to the Other Side. ℮ (Rev: BL 10/1/12; SLJ 12/12; VOYA 6/12)

5920 Cray, Jordan. *Dead Man's Hand* (5–9). Series: danger.com. 1998, Simon & Schuster paper $3.99 (978-0-689-82383-1). In this light read, Nick Annunciato and his stepsister, Annie Hanley, use their brains and a computer to solve a murder and escape a biological-weapons smuggling ring. (Rev: SLJ 2/99)

5921 Cray, Jordan. *Shiver* (5–8). Series: danger.com. 1998, Simon & Schuster paper $3.99 (978-0-689-82384-8). Six drama students are spending a weekend in the Green Mountains of Vermont, when one of the group is murdered. (Rev: SLJ 2/99)

5922 Cross, Gillian. *Phoning a Dead Man* (6–10). 2002, Holiday $16.95 (978-0-8234-1685-1). This suspenseful novel set in Russia alternates between the story of John, an amnesiac who is fleeing danger, and that of his sister and wheelchair-bound fiancee who are searching for him. (Rev: BCCB 5/02; BL 5/1/02; HB 7–8/02; HBG 10/02; SLJ 5/02; VOYA 6/02)

5923 Crossman, David A. *The Mystery of the Black Moriah* (5–8). Series: A Bean and Ab Mystery. 2002, Down East $16.95 (978-0-89272-536-6). The ever-curious Bean and Ab become caught up in a mystery adventure involving pirates, kidnappers, and a legendary ghost. (Rev: HBG 3/03; SLJ 12/02)

5924 Crossman, David A. *The Secret of the Missing Grave* (5–8). Series: A Bean and Ab Mystery. 1999, Down East $16.95 (978-0-89272-456-7). Two girls investigate a haunted house and become involved in a mystery concerning a missing treasure and stolen paintings in this fast-paced novel set in Maine. (Rev: HBG 3/00; SLJ 1/00)

5925 Davidson, Nicole. *Dying to Dance* (8–12). 1996, Avon paper $3.99 (978-0-380-78152-2). Carrie, a competitor on the ballroom-dance circuit, is suspected of murdering her archrival. (Rev: SLJ 7/96)

5926 Dean, Claire. *Girlwood* (6–9). 2008, Houghton Mifflin $16.00 (978-0-618-88390-5). Mystery, New Age mysticism, environmentalism, and magic are intertwined in this story of 12-year-old Polly and her older sister, Bree, who has run away and may be living in a forest threatened by developers. (Rev: BL 2/15/08; SLJ 6/08)

5927 DeFelice, Cynthia. *The Missing Manatee* (5–8). 2005, Farrar $16.00 (978-0-374-31257-2). Skeet Waters sets out to solve the mystery of a murdered manatee he finds near his Florida home. (Rev: BL 3/1/05; SLJ 6/05)

5928 Delaney, Mark. *Of Heroes and Villains* (7–10). 1999, Peachtree paper $5.95 (978-1-56145-178-4). Using the world of comic books as a backdrop, this mystery features four teen sleuths known as the Misfits and the puzzle of a stolen film starring comic book hero Hyperman. (Rev: BL 7/99)

5929 Delaney, Mark. *The Protester's Song* (5–9). Series: Misfits, Inc. 2001, Peachtree paper $5.95 (978-1-56145-244-6). Four teens keep themselves busy investigating an incident that occurred during riots in Ohio in 1970 and, in a subplot, try to stop the new principal from removing books from the library. (Rev: SLJ 8/01)

5930 Delaney, Mark. *The Vanishing Chip* (5–8). Series: Misfits, Inc. 1998, Peachtree paper $5.95 (978-1-56145-176-0). Four teens who don't fit in at school investigate the disappearance of the world's most powerful computer chip. (Rev: BL 12/15/98; SLJ 2/99)

5931 Denman, K. L. *Agent Angus* (6–9). Series: Orca Currents. 2012, Orca $16.95 (978-145980104-2); paper $9.95 (978-14598010-3-5). Hoping to impress Ella, Angus pretends to have special abilities that will help him solve the mystery of her missing sketchbook; suitable for reluctant readers. (Rev: BL 5/1/12; SLJ 3/13)

5932 Derting, Kimberly. *The Body Finder* (7–12). 2010, HarperCollins $16.99 (978-0-06-177981-7). Violet's ability to sense the bodies of murdered people brings her anxious moments even as she is absorbed in her growing fascination with her best friend Jay; this suspenseful thriller, with a dollop of romance, contains language and sexual content that may limit the grade range. ❤ Lexile 940L (Rev: BL 10/15/09; LMC 3–4/10; SLJ 5/10)

5933 Doctorow, Cory. *Homeland* (8–12). 2013, Tor Teen $17.99 (978-076533369-8). In this sequel to *Little Brother* (2008), Marcus is at a Burning Man festival when he receives a USB drive holding the key to many documents revealing government treachery; can he pass on this information and retain his own job and security? ❤ Lexile 1060L (Rev: BL 1/13*; HB 5–6/13; SLJ 3/13)

5934 Doctorow, Cory. *Little Brother* (8–12). 2008, Tor $17.95 (978-0-7653-1985-2). A terrorist attack on the San Francisco of the not-too-distant future results in Marcus being detained by the Department of Homeland Security and organizing a group of hackers to fight the powers that be. (Rev: BL 4/1/08; SLJ 5/08)

5935 Doder, Joshua. *Operation Tortoise* (5–8). Series: The Grk Books. 2009, Random $15.99 (978-0-385-73362-5). Tim, 12, and his dog Grk are in the Seychelles and find themselves investigating a sinister laboratory in this fast-paced suspense story. (Rev: BL 3/1/09)

5936 Dowd, Siobhan. *The London Eye Mystery* (5–8). 2008, Random House $15.99 (978-0-375-84976-3). Ted and Kat's cousin Salim disappears after entering a ride called the London Eye, and Ted relies on his unusual intellectual abilities to try to find him. (Rev: BL 1/1–15/08; HB 5–6/08; LMC 3/08; SLJ 2/08)

5937 Downham, Jenny. *You Against Me* (8–12). 2011, Random House $16.99 (978-0-385-75160-5); LB $19.99 (978-038575161-2). Meeting — and liking — the sister of the young man who raped his younger sister Ellie complicates 18-year-old Mikey's life and his investigation of the crime. ❤ Lexile HL630L (Rev: BL 8/11*; HB 11–12/11; SLJ 11/1/11*; VOYA 10/11)

5938 Draanen, Wendelin Van. *Sammy Keyes and the Skeleton Man* (5–8). 1998, Knopf paper $4.99 (978-0-375-80054-2). Sammy, the youthful sleuth, is challenged when she tries to solve the mystery of a man dressed in a skeleton costume. (Rev: BL 9/1/98; HBG 3/99; SLJ 9/98)

5939 Duncan, Lois. *Daughters of Eve* (7–10). 1979, Dell paper $4.99 (978-0-440-91864-6). A group of girls comes under the evil influence of the faculty sponsor of their club.

5940 Duncan, Lois. *Down a Dark Hall* (7–10). 1974, Little, Brown paper $5.50 (978-0-440-91805-9). From the moment of arrival, Kit feels uneasy at her new boarding school.

5941 Duncan, Lois. *Killing Mr. Griffin* (7–10). 1978, Dell paper $5.50 (978-0-440-94515-4). A kidnapping plot involving a disliked English teacher leads to murder. (Rev: BL 10/15/88)

5942 Duncan, Lois. *The Third Eye* (7–10). 1984, Little, Brown $15.95 (978-0-316-19553-9); paper $5.50 (978-0-440-98720-8). Karen learns that she has mental powers that enable her to locate missing children. (Rev: BL 7/87)

5943 Duncan, Lois. *The Twisted Window* (7–10). 1987, Dell paper $5.50 (978-0-440-20184-7). Tracy grows to regret the fact that she has helped a young man kidnap his 2-year-old half-sister. (Rev: BL 9/1/87; SLJ 9/87; VOYA 11/87)

5944 Eden, Alexandra. *Holy Smoke: A Bones and Duchess Mystery* (5–7). 2004, Alien A. Knoll $16.00 (978-1-888310-46-7). Ex-cop Bones Fatzinger and Verity Buscador, a 12-year-old girl with Asperger's syndrome, work together to track down the person responsible for setting fire to a local church. (Rev: BL 5/1/04)

5945 Ehrenhaft, Daniel. *Dirty Laundry* (8–11). 2009, HarperTeen $16.99 (978-006113103-5). A playful mystery about a teen actress who goes undercover at a New England boarding school in order to research a part, but becomes embroiled in the mystery of a missing student. e Lexile HL630L (Rev: BL 12/15/08; SLJ 3/1/09)

5946 Ehrenhaft, Daniel. *Drawing a Blank: or, How I Tried to Solve a Mystery, End a Feud, and Land the Girl of My Dreams* (8–11). Illus. by Trevor Ristow. 2006, HarperCollins $15.99 (978-0-06-075252-1). In this clever novel, with the narrative switching from first person to comic book panels, boarding school student Carlton travels to Scotland to solve a mystery and find his kidnapped father; footnotes are both informative and amusing. (Rev: BL 5/1/06; SLJ 6/06*)

5947 Ellis, Deborah. *True Blue* (5–8). 2012, Pajama $19.95 (978-098694953-1). When her friend Casey is arrested for the murder of an 8-year-old girl, 17-year-old Jess finds it hard to support her in the face of widespread suspicion from the people of their town. Lexile 710L (Rev: BL 5/1/12; LMC 11–12/12; SLJ 5/1/12)

5948 Elmer, Robert. *Far from the Storm* (4–7). Series: Young Underground. 1995, Bethany paper $5.99 (978-0-556-61377-0). At the end of World War II, Danish twins Peter and Elise set out to find the culprit who set their uncle's boat on fire. (Rev: BL 2/15/96)

5949 Emerson, Kathy L. *The Mystery of the Missing Bagpipes* (5–7). 1991, Avon paper $2.95 (978-0-380-76138-8). Kim tries to find the real culprit when a young boy is wrongfully accused of stealing a set of ancient bagpipes and some precious daggers. (Rev: BL 9/15/91)

5950 Emerson, Scott. *The Case of the Cat with the Missing Ear: From the Notebooks of Edward R. Smithfield, D.V.M.* (5–7). 2003, Simon & Schuster LB $15.95 (978-0-689-85861-1). This canine takeoff of the Sherlock Holmes format features Yorkshire terrier Samuel Blackthorne and his sidekick and chronicler Dr. Edward Smithfield, who investigate mysteries with humor and deductive prowess. (Rev: BCCB 10/02; BL 12/1/03; HBG 4/04; SLJ 3/04)

5951 Erickson, John R. *Discovery at Flint Springs* (5–8). 2004, Viking $16.99 (978-0-670-05946-1). In 1927, 14-year-old Riley and his younger brother Coy join in an exciting search for archaeological sites on their Texas ranch. (Rev: BL 2/1/05; SLJ 12/04)

5952 Ernst, Kathleen. *Secrets in the Hills: A Josefina Mystery* (4–7). Series: American Girl Mystery. 2006, Pleasant paper $6.95 (978-1-59369-097-7). In 1820s New Mexico, Josefina decides to investigate the possibility that there is treasure buried near her home. (Rev: BL 5/15/06; SLJ 4/06)

5953 Evans, Lissa. *Horten's Miraculous Mechanisms* (4–7). 2012, Sterling $14.95 (978-140279806-1). Diminutive 10-year-old Stuart Horten has moved with his family to his father's hometown, and soon discovers mysterious old coins that offer clues to the disappearance long ago of his great-uncle Tony, a magician. (Rev: BL 4/1/12; SLJ 5/1/12)

5954 Evarts, Hal G. *Jay-Jay and the Peking Monster* (7–9). 1984, Peter Smith $15.75 (978-0-8446-6166-7). Two teenagers discover the bones of a prehistoric man, and then the criminals move in.

5955 Falcone, L. M. *The Mysterious Mummer* (5–7). 2003, Kids Can $16.95 (978-1-55337-376-6). When Joey, 13, arrives in Newfoundland to spend Christmas with his aunt, he finds some very mysterious goings-on. (Rev: HBG 4/04; SLJ 10/03)

5956 Feder, Harriet K. *Death on Sacred Ground* (6–10). Series: Vivi Hartman. 2001, Lerner $14.95 (978-0-8225-0741-3). Teen sleuth Vivi Hartman encounters a mystery at the funeral of an Orthodox Jewish girl who died on sacred Indian ground. (Rev: BCCB 3/01; BL 11/15/01; HBG 10/01; SLJ 3/01)

5957 Feder, Harriet K. *Mystery of the Kaifeng Scroll* (6–9). 1995, Lerner LB $14.95 (978-0-8225-0739-0). In this sequel to *Mystery in Miami Beach*, Vivi Hartman, 15, must use her wits and knowledge of the Torah to save her mother from Palestinian terrorists. (Rev: BL 6/1–15/95)

5958 Feiffer, Kate. *Signed by Zelda* (5–7). 2012, Simon & Schuster $16.99 (978-1-4424-3331-1). When Nicky's grandmother Zelda goes missing, the boy sets out to find her with the help of his friend Lucy, who analyzes handwriting, and a talking pigeon. **e** Lexile 750L (Rev: HB 7–8/12; LMC 11–12/12; SLJ 5/1/12)

5959 Feinstein, John. *Change-Up: Mystery at the World Series* (5–8). 2009, Knopf $16.99 (978-0-375-85636-5); LB $19.99 (978-0-375-95636-2). What is Nationals pitcher Norbert Doyle hiding? Teen sports reporters Stevie and Susan Carol investigate. ∩ Lexile 770L (Rev: BL 9/1/09; SLJ 9/09; VOYA 6/09)

5960 Feinstein, John. *Cover-Up: Mystery at the Super Bowl* (6–9). 2007, Knopf $16.99 (978-0-375-84247-4). After being fired from Kid Sports, teen reporter Steve meets up with his former co-host Susan Carol at the Super Bowl, where they uncover another sports scandal. ∩ (Rev: BL 9/1/07; SLJ 12/07)

5961 Feinstein, John. *Rush for the Gold: Mystery at the Olympics* (6–9). 2012, Knopf $16.99 (978-037586963-1); LB $19.99 (978-037596963-8). Teen journalists Susan Carol and Stevie, who are also dating, investigate a match-fixing scheme at the 2012 Olympics even as Susan Carol competes for a swimming place on the U.S. team. ∩ **e** Lexile 820L (Rev: BL 5/1/12; LMC 9–10/12; SLJ 6/12)

5962 Feinstein, John. *Vanishing Act* (6–9). 2006, Knopf LB $18.99 (978-0-375-83592-6). Susan Carol Anderson and Stevie Thomas, 13-year-old sports reporters, are covering the U.S. Open tennis championships when one of the star players is kidnapped. (Rev: BL 9/1/06; SLJ 10/06)

5963 Ferguson, Alane. *The Christopher Killer* (7–10). Series: Forensic Mystery. 2006, Viking $15.99 (978-0-670-06008-5). In this CSI-like story, a serial killer is on the loose and 17-year-old Cameryn, an aspiring forensic pathologist, helps her coroner father investigate. (Rev: BL 7/06; LMC 10/06; SLJ 8/06)

5964 Ferguson, Alane. *Overkill* (7–10). 1992, Avon paper $3.99 (978-0-380-72167-2). Lacey is seeing a therapist about nightmares in which she stabs her friend Celeste; when Celeste is found dead, Lacey is falsely arrested for the crime. (Rev: BL 1/1/93; SLJ 1/93)

5965 Ferguson, Alane. *Show Me the Evidence* (7–12). 1989, Avon paper $3.99 (978-0-380-70962-5). In this mystery story, a 17-year-old girl is fearful that her best friend might be involved in the mysterious deaths of several children. (Rev: BL 4/1/89; SLJ 3/89; VOYA 6/89)

5966 Fields, Terri. *Holdup* (6–10). 2007, Roaring Brook $16.95 (978-1-59643-219-2). Nine teen characters give their first-person accounts of the evening of a holdup of a fast-food restaurant. (Rev: BL 5/1/07; LMC 8–9/07; SLJ 4/07)

5967 Finney, Patricia. *Feud* (4–7). Series: Lady Grace Mysteries. 2006, Delacorte $7.95 (978-0-385-73323-6); paper $9.99 (978-0-385-90342-4). Lady Grace, maid of honor to Queen Elizabeth I, attempts to unravel the mystery surrounding the poisoning of another maid of honor. (Rev: BL 10/15/06)

5968 Fox, Janet. *Forgiven* (7–10). 2011, Penguin paper $8.99 (978-0-14-241-414-9). In San Francisco on a mission to clear her father's name, Kula is introduced into society, meets interesting men, uncovers current and past secrets, and experiences the 1906 earthquake. Lexile HL710L (Rev: BL 8/11; SLJ 9/1/11)

5969 Foyt, Victoria. *The Virtual Life of Lexie Diamond* (6–8). 2007, HarperCollins $16.99 (978-0-06-082563-8). Lexie's recently deceased mother appears on Lexie's computer screen and reveals that she was murdered, and Lexie sets out to find out who killed her. (Rev: BCCB 6/07; BL 4/1/07; SLJ 5/07)

5970 Frazier, Angie. *The Mastermind Plot* (4–7). 2012, Scholastic $16.99 (978-054520864-2). Zanna hopes to get closer to her detective uncle while in Boston, and fulfill her dream of becoming a real sleuth in this mystery set in 1904; a sequel to *The Midnight Tunnel* (2011). (Rev: BL 5/1/12; SLJ 2/12)

5971 Frazier, Angie. *The Midnight Tunnel* (4–7). 2011, Scholastic $16.99 (978-0-545-20862-8). In New Brunswick at the turn of the 20th century, 11-year-old Suzanna (Zanna) Snow prefers sleuthing to working at her family's inn; however, her famous detective uncle's efforts to solve a mysterious disappearance disappoint her. **e** Lexile 800L (Rev: BL 2/1/11; LMC 5–6/11; SLJ 4/11)

5972 Fredericks, Mariah. *The Girl in the Park* (8–12). 2012, Random House $16.99 (978-037586843-6); LB $19.99 (978-037589907-2). When the only person who believed in her is murdered, Rain, an outcast with a cleft palate, struggles to speak up for truth and justice. Lexile HL510L (Rev: BL 4/1/12; LMC 3–4/12; SLJ 5/1/12; VOYA 2/12)

5973 Fusilli, Jim. *Marley Z. and the Bloodstained Violin* (5–8). 2008, Dutton $16.99 (978-0-525-47907-9). Marley's musician friend Marisol is accused of stealing a valuable violin, and Marley is determined to prove her innocence in this mystery set in New York City. (Rev: BL 5/1/08; SLJ 9/08)

5974 Garretson, Dee. *Wildfire Run* (4–7). Series: Danger's Edge. 2010, HarperCollins $16.99 (978-006195347-7). In this action-packed story, the president's son and two friends are marooned at Camp David when a series of natural disasters overwhelms the security system. (Rev: BL 10/15/10; SLJ 9/1/10)

5975 Gavin, Jamila. *See No Evil* (7–10). 2009, Farrar $16.95 (978-037436333-8). Nettie, 12, searches her family's London mansion for the secrets to her father's vast wealth after her tutor mysteriously disappears. (Rev: BL 5/1/09; SLJ 7/1/09; VOYA 2/09)

5976 George, Elizabeth. *The Edge of Nowhere* (8–12). 2012, Viking $18.99 (978-0-670-01296-1). Becca, a psychic 14-year-old who is on the run from her stepfather, must make her way by herself on a remote island near Seattle, where she meets a Ugandan orphan with a secret. ⌒ ℮ Lexile HL800L (Rev: BL 7/12; LMC 3–4/13; SLJ 10/12; VOYA 10/12)

5977 Gerber, Linda. *Death by Bikini* (7–10). 2008, Penguin paper $7.99 (978-0-14-241117-9). A murder mystery complicates the romance between Aphra and Adam, a guest at the resort that Aphra's father runs. (Rev: BL 5/1/08; SLJ 8/08)

5978 Gerber, Linda. *Death by Denim* (7–10). Series: Death By. 2009, Penguin paper $7.99 (978-014241119-3). Sixteen-year-old Aphra and her mother, a CIA agent, race through Europe to escape the Mole and save Aphra's boyfriend, Seth. The third book after *Death by Bikini* and *Death by Latte* (both 2008). Lexile HL740L (Rev: BL 5/1/09; SLJ 6/1/09)

5979 Gerson, Corrine. *My Grandfather the Spy* (5–7). 1990, Walker $14.95 (978-0-8027-6955-8). When a man arrives on the family farm in Vermont with a briefcase full of money, Danny suspects his grandfather is a spy. (Rev: BL 6/15/90; SLJ 8/90)

5980 Gibbs, Stuart. *Belly Up* (5–7). 2010, Simon & Schuster $15.99 (978-1-4169-8731-4). Who is responsible for the death of the zoo's star hippo? Twelve-year-old Teddy and Summer, daughter of the zoo owner, investigate in this fast-paced story full of humor and animal facts. ℮ Lexile 820L (Rev: BL 5/1/10; LMC 10/10; SLJ 5/10)

5981 Gibbs, Stuart. *Spy School* (4–7). 2012, Simon & Schuster $15.99 (978-144242182-0). Twelve-year-old Ben achieves his lifelong wish when he leaves his middle school for the CIA's secretive Academy of Espionage — only to find that a life of spying isn't all it's cracked up to be. (Rev: BL 3/15/12; SLJ 2/12)

5982 Giles, Gail. *Dead Girls Don't Write Letters* (6–9). 2003, Millbrook $15.95 (978-0-7613-1727-2). Sunny, a 9th grader, is dealing with the aftermath of her 18-year-old sister Jazz's death in an apartment fire — until one day, a mysterious new Jazz appears. (Rev: BCCB 3/03; BL 3/15/03; HBG 10/03; SLJ 5/03; VOYA 6/03)

5983 Giles, Gail. *What Happened to Cass McBride?* (8–11). 2006, Little, Brown $16.99 (978-0-316-16638-6). When a cruel note from Cass pushes classmate David over the edge to suicide, David's older brother Kyle takes Cass captive in this suspenseful novel. (Rev: BCCB 12/06; BL 1/1–15/07; LMC 4–5/07; SLJ 2/07)

5984 Giles, Stephen M. *The Body Thief* (5–7). Series: The Death (and Further Adventures) of Silas Winterbottom. 2010, Sourcebooks $12.99 (978-1-4022-4090-4). When rich, elderly Uncle Silas invites three 12-year-old prospective heirs to his estate, the three very different cousins — Adele, Milo, and Isabella — become closer as they recognize that his intentions are far from benign. ℮ Lexile 830L (Rev: BL 9/15/10; LMC 11–12/10)

5985 Godwin, Jane. *Falling from Grace* (6–9). 2007, Holiday $16.95 (978-0-8234-2105-3). Thirteen-year-old Grace disappears into the surf off an Australian beach at the same moment a boy is rescued from drowning in this suspenseful thriller. (Rev: BL 10/1/07; LMC 1/08; SLJ 11/07)

5986 Golden, Christopher, and Rick Hautala. *Throat Culture* (8–11). Series: Body of Evidence. 2005, Simon & Schuster paper $5.99 (978-0-689-86527-5). College sophomore Jenna Blake investigates the mysterious illness that has stricken her father's new bride. (Rev: BL 5/1/05; SLJ 7/05)

5987 Golding, Julia. *Cat Among the Pigeons* (6–9). 2008, Roaring Brook $16.95 (978-159643352-6). In this followup to 2008's *The Diamond of Drury Lane* set in 1790s London, young Cat tries to protect Pedro — a talented young actor — from being sent back to slavery in the West Indies. ℮ Lexile 740L (Rev: BL 11/1/08; SLJ 12/08; VOYA 12/08)

5988 Golding, Julia. *The Diamond of Drury Lane* (7–10). Series: Cat Royal Adventures. 2008, Roaring Brook $12.50 (978-1-59643-351-9). Catherine Royal, called Cat, lives with danger and intrigue in the Drury Lane theater in London in 1790. Her life is further complicated when she learns that a diamond is hidden somewhere in the theater. (Rev: BL 4/15/08; SLJ 6/08)

5989 Gordon, Amy. *Twenty Gold Falcons* (4–7). 2010, Holiday House $16.95 (978-0-8234-2252-4). Aiden's finding it hard to adjust to her new life in the city of Gloria until she learns about 20 missing gold coins and sets out to find them with some newly made friends. Lexile 710L (Rev: BL 5/1/10; LMC 11–12/10; SLJ 8/10)

5990 Gordon, Lawrence. *Haunted High* (6–9). Series: Ghost Chronicles. 2000, Karmichael paper $11.95 (978-0-9653966-1-5). Eddie discovers he is receiving messages on his computer from long-dead high school students. (Rev: SLJ 7/00; VOYA 4/00)

5991 Grabenstein, Chris. *The Smoky Corridor* (5–8). Series: Haunted Places Mystery. 2010, Random House $16.99 (978-0-375-86511-4); LB $19.99 (978-0-375-96511-1). Zach Jennings, the boy who can communicate with ghosts, starts 6th grade at a new school and discovers that its many challenges include a brain-eating zombie and a host of ghosts guarding a cemetery. ℮ Lexile 690L (Rev: BLO 12/1/10; SLJ 7/10)

5992 Grant, Vicki. *Quid Pro Quo* (7–10). 2005, Orca $16.95 (978-1-55143-394-3); paper $7.95 (978-1-55143-370-7). When his mother — newly graduated from law school — suddenly disappears, 13-year-old

Cyril Floyd MacIntyre tries to unravel the mystery surrounding her disappearance. (Rev: SLJ 6/05)

5993 Graves, Keith. *The Orphan of Awkward Falls* (5–8). Illus. by author. 2011, Chronicle $16.99 (978-0-8118-7814-2). When 12-year-old Josephine Cravitz and her family move to Awkward Falls, she becomes the target of a mad cannibal escaped from the town's Asylum for the Dangerously Insane; a complex, suspenseful story with light humor and horror. (Rev: BLO 11/15/11; LMC 1–2/12; SLJ 10/1/11)

5994 Green, Timothy. *Twilight Boy* (7–10). 1998, Northland LB $12.95 (978-0-87358-670-2); paper $6.95 (978-0-87358-640-5). Navajo folkways form the background of this gripping mystery about a boy who is haunted by the memory of his dead brother and an evil that is preying on his Navajo community. (Rev: BL 4/15/98; HBG 9/98; VOYA 8/98)

5995 Greene, Michele Dominguez. *Chasing the Jaguar* (7–10). 2006, HarperCollins $15.99 (978-0-06-076353-4). Strange dreams lead Martika, a Mexican American teenager living in Los Angeles, to discover she is descended from Mayan healers and has psychic powers that may help her solve a kidnapping. (Rev: BL 5/1/06; LMC 2/07; SLJ 7/06)

5996 Griffin, Adele, and Lisa Brown. *Picture the Dead* (6–9). Illus. by Lisa Brown. 2010, Sourcebooks $17.99 (978-1-4022-3712-6). A Civil War mystery story that incorporates supernatural overtones and scrapbook entries including newspaper clippings. Lexile 800L (Rev: BL 5/1/10; LMC 8–9/10; SLJ 10/1/10)

5997 Griffin, Paul. *Burning Blue* (8–12). 2012, Dial $17.99 (978-0-8037-3815-7). Jay Nazarro, a reclusive hacker since having a very public seizure, is determined to find out who threw acid in the face of popular, beautiful classmate Nicole in this compelling story. e Lexile HL660L (Rev: BLO 1/13; HB 9–10/12; LMC 3–4/13*; SLJ 10/12; VOYA 8/12)

5998 Grisham, John. *Theodore Boone: Kid Lawyer* (6–8). 2010, Dutton $16.99 (978-0-525-42384-3). Theo, the 13-year-old son of two lawyers, helps to gather important evidence in a murder case in this story by the famous author of adult legal thrillers. ∩ Lexile 790L (Rev: BL 6/10; HB 9–10/10; LMC 8–9/10; SLJ 6/10)

5999 Grisham, John. *Theodore Boone: The Abduction* (6–8). 2011, Dutton $16.99 (978-052542557-1). Theodore Boone, 13, investigates the disappearance of his best friend, April, in this sequel to *Theodore Boone: Kid Lawyer* (2010). ∩ e Lexile 830L (Rev: BLO 6/9/11; SLJ 11/11)

6000 Gutman, Dan. *Shoeless Joe and Me* (4–7). Series: Baseball Card Adventure. 2002, HarperCollins LB $17.89 (978-0-06-029254-6). Thirteen-year-old Joe travels back in time to remedy the 1919 Black Sox scandal and save Shoeless Joe's reputation. (Rev: BL 1/1–15/02; HBG 10/02; SLJ 3/02)

6001 Hahn, Mary Downing. *Closed for the Season: A Mystery Story* (5–8). 2009, Clarion $16 (978-0-547-08451-0). Thirteen-year-old Logan's search for a murderer leads him and his new friend Arthur to an eerie, abandoned amusement park in this well-executed mystery. ∩ e Lexile 670L (Rev: LMC 10/09; SLJ 9/09; VOYA 10/09)

6002 Hahn, Mary Downing. *The Dead Man in Indian Creek* (6–8). 1990, Clarion $15.00 (978-0-395-52397-1). On a harmless camping trip, Matt and friend Parker find a body floating in Indian Creek. (Rev: BL 2/15/90; SLJ 4/90)

6003 Hahn, Mary Downing. *The Ghost of Crutchfield Hall* (4–7). 2010, Clarion $17 (978-0-547-38560-0). Florence goes to live at her great-aunt's house, realizing too late that the house is haunted by the malicious ghost of her cousin Sophia, who died suspiciously. ∩ e Lexile 680L (Rev: BL 10/1/10; LMC 1–2/11; SLJ 8/10)

6004 Hahn, Mary Downing. *Mister Death's Blue-Eyed Girls* (8–11). 2012, Clarion $16.99 (978-0-547-76062-9). This scary story told from several perspectives describes the 1956 murder of two teenage girls in suburban Baltimore and the desperate rush to identify the perpetrator. ∩ e Lexile HL700L (Rev: BL 5/1/12; HB 7–8/12; SLJ 7/12; VOYA 10/12)

6005 Haines, Kathryn Miller. *The Girl Is Murder* (7–10). 2011, Roaring Brook $16.99 (978-1-59643-609-1). Still grieving for her mother, who committed suicide, 15-year-old Iris copes with moving from a life of luxury to an apartment and public school, and helps her detective father who lost a leg at Pearl Harbor; set in 1940s New York City. ∩ e Lexile HL700L (Rev: BL 5/1/11; LMC 10/11*; SLJ 8/11*)

6006 Hall, Lynn. *A Killing Freeze* (6–10). 1990, Avon paper $2.95 (978-0-380-75491-5). A loner endangers her own life to find a murderer. (Rev: BL 8/88; SLJ 9/88; VOYA 12/88)

6007 Hall, Lynn. *Ride a Dark Horse* (7–10). 1987, Avon paper $2.95 (978-0-380-75370-3). A teenage girl is fired from her job on a horse-breeding farm because she is getting too close to solving a mystery. (Rev: BL 9/15/87; SLJ 12/87; VOYA 10/87)

6008 Hamilton, Virginia. *The House of Dies Drear* (6–9). 1968, Macmillan paper $5.99 (978-0-02-043520-4). First-rate suspense as history professor Small and his young son Thomas investigate their rented house, formerly a station on the Underground Railroad, unlocking the secrets and dangers from attitudes dating back to the Civil War. (Rev: BL 10/15/87)

6009 Harrington, Kim. *Partners in Crime* (4–7). Series: Sleuth or Dare. 2012, Scholastic paper $5.99 (978-05453896-4-8). Best friend 7th-graders Darcy and Norah create a detective website for a school project and uncover a real mystery in this light story. e Lexile 580L (Rev: BL 5/1/12; LMC 8–9/12)

6010 Harrington, Kim. *Perception* (8–12). 2012, Scholastic $16.99 (978-054523053-7). Clare, the psychically gifted high schooler introduced in 2011's *Clarity*, investigates a classmate's disappearance and tries to choose between tall, dark Justin and Gabriel, attractive son of the new police detective. **e** Lexile HL600L (Rev: BL 2/15/12; SLJ 3/12)

6011 Harvey, Alyxandra. *Haunting Violet* (7–10). 2011, Walker $16.99 (978-0-8027-9839-8). Violet, 16, is used to fraudulent seances conducted by her mother, but is startled when she actually starts seeing ghosts herself; set in Victorian England. **e** Lexile HL710L (Rev: BL 5/1/11; LMC 8–9/11; SLJ 11/1/11; VOYA 8/11)

6012 Hautman, Pete, and Mary Logue. *Doppelganger* (6–9). Series: Bloodwater Mysteries. 2008, Putnam $16.99 (978-0-399-24379-0). Could Roni's private-eye partner, Brian, have been kidnapped as a child? Roni sets out to find the truth about Brian's past as an orphan adopted from Korea in this fast-paced adventure. (Rev: BL 5/1/08; SLJ 7/08)

6013 Hautman, Pete, and Mary Logue. *Skullduggery* (6–9). Series: Bloodwater Mysteries. 2007, Putnam $16.99 (978-0-399-24378-3). Young sleuths Roni and Brian — first seen in *Snatched* (2006) — investigate a local land development scheme after they find an archaeologist lying injured in a cave. (Rev: BL 5/1/07; SLJ 6/07)

6014 Hautman, Pete, and Mary Logue. *Snatched* (7–10). Series: Bloodwater Mysteries. 2006, Philomel $15.99 (978-0-399-24377-6). High school students Roni and Brian investigate the mystery of the missing Alicia in this suspenseful novel that holds readers' interest. (Rev: BL 5/1/06; HB 7–8/06; SLJ 6/06)

6015 Haven, Paul. *The Seven Keys of Balabad* (5–8). Illus. by Mark Zug. 2009, Random $16.99 (978-0-375-83350-2). Twelve-year-old Oliver, whose father is a foreign correspondent assigned to Balabad, finds himself pulled out of Manhattan and into the middle of an exotic and dangerous mystery surrounding a 500-year-old sacred carpet. (Rev: BCCB 2/09; BL 1/1–15/09; SLJ 4/09)

6016 Hayes, Daniel. *The Trouble with Lemons* (5–8). 1991, Random House paper $5.99 (978-0-449-70416-5). Tyler, 14, has all kinds of problems — allergies, asthma, and nightmares — and then he finds a dead body. (Rev: BL 5/1/91; SLJ 6/91)

6017 Henry, April. *Girl, Stolen!* (7–10). 2010, Henry Holt $16.99 (978-0-8050-9005-5). Things go from bad to worse when a young carjacker steals Cheyenne's mother's car — not realizing the blind, pneumonia-stricken teen is in the back seat. **e** Lexile HL700L (Rev: BL 9/15/10; SLJ 10/1/10)

6018 Henry, April. *The Night She Disappeared* (7–10). 2012, Henry Holt $16.99 (978-080509262-2). When Kayla disappears while delivering a pizza, Gabie realizes she was the intended victim and determines to uncover the truth. YALSA Quick Picks for Reluctant Young Adult Readers 2013. ∩ **e** Lexile HL680L (Rev: BL 5/1/12; LMC 1–2/13*; SLJ 4/12)

6019 Heyes, Eileen. *O'Dwyer and Grady Starring in Tough Act to Follow* (4–7). Illus. by Eric Bowman. Series: O'Dwyer and Grady. 2003, Simon & Schuster paper $4.99 (978-0-689-84920-6). Young actors Billy and Virginia stumble into a mystery while searching for props for a show in this action-packed story set in the 1930s. (Rev: BL 5/15/03; SLJ 7/03)

6020 Hiaasen, Carl. *Scat* (5–8). 2009, Knopf $16.99 (978-037583486-8); LB $19.99 (978-037593486-5). Nick and Marta team up to solve the real cause of their high school biology teacher's disappearance in this well-paced, conservation-themed read set in the Florida Everglades. ∩ Lexile 810L (Rev: BL 11/1/08; HB 1–2/09; SLJ 1/1/09*)

6021 Hill, William. *The Vampire Hunters* (7–12). 1998, Otter Creek $19.95 (978-1-890611-05-7); paper $12.95 (978-1-890611-02-6). Members of a gang called the Graveyard Armadillos are convinced that Marcus Chandler is a vampire, and 15-year-old Scooter Keyshaw is determined to find the truth. (Rev: BL 10/15/98; SLJ 2/99)

6022 Hogan, Edward. *Daylight Saving* (7–10). 2012, Candlewick $16.99 (978-0-7636-5913-4). On a reluctant vacation at Leisure World, unhappy Daniel meets a strange girl called Lexi who has wounds that keep getting worse and a watch that runs backward. **e** (Rev: BL 11/1/12; HB 9–10/12; LMC 3–4/13; SLJ 11/12; VOYA 10/12)

6023 Holm, Jennifer L. *The Creek* (6–8). 2003, HarperCollins $15.99 (978-0-06-000133-9). When local bad boy Caleb Devlin returns to town, he quickly gains 12-year-old Penny's fascinated attention, but his return coincides with a series of increasingly alarming events. (Rev: BCCB 7–8/03; BL 8/03; HBG 10/03; SLJ 7/03; VOYA 10/03)

6024 Hopper, Nancy J. *Ape Ears and Beaky* (4–7). 1987, Avon paper $2.50 (978-0-380-70270-1). Scott and Beaky solve the mystery of the robberies in a condominium.

6025 Horowitz, Anthony. *Alex Rider: The Gadgets* (5–8). Illus. by John Lawson. 2006, Philomel $15.99 (978-0-399-24486-5). A look at all the gadgets used in the first five Alex Rider mysteries — including such wonders as a radio mouth brace, exploding ear stud, and pizza delivery assassin kit — with diagrams and details of how they were used. (Rev: BL 4/1/06; SLJ 4/06)

6026 Horowitz, Anthony. *Ark Angel* (6–9). Series: Alex Rider. 2006, Philomel $17.99 (978-0-399-24152-9). Alex Rider battles "eco warriors" and becomes involved in the projected first hotel in space in this action- and gadget-packed sixth installment in the series. (Rev: BL 4/15/06; SLJ 4/06)

6027 Horowitz, Anthony. *Crocodile Tears* (6–9). Series: Alex Rider. 2009, Philomel $17.99 (978-0-399-25056-9). In this exciting installment, the teenage British intelligence agent is nearly fed to crocodiles when he tries to expose a fake philanthropist. ∩ **e** Lexile 740L (Rev: BL 1/1/10; SLJ 1/10; VOYA 2/10)

6028 Horowitz, Anthony. *Eagle Strike* (7–12). Series: Alex Rider Adventure. 2004, Putnam $17.99 (978-0-399-23979-3). Alex Rider, the hero of many adventures, recognizes a famous Russian assassin while Alex is vacationing in France, and a new thriller begins. (Rev: BL 5/1/04; SLJ 3/04; VOYA 4/04)

6029 Horowitz, Anthony. *The Greek Who Stole Christmas* (4–7). Series: A Diamond Brothers Mystery. 2008, Penguin paper $7.99 (978-01424037-5-4). Amid the Christmas noise and bustle, Diamond brothers Nick and Tim bumble their way through protecting a dazzling young pop star who has received death threats. **e** Lexile 630L (Rev: BL 11/1/08; SLJ 8/09)

6030 Horowitz, Anthony. *Point Blank* (6–10). Series: Alex Rider Adventure. 2002, Putnam $17.99 (978-0-399-23621-1). Alex, the young British spy, infiltrates an exclusive Swiss boarding school in this action-filled adventure. (Rev: BL 4/1/02; HBG 10/02; SLJ 3/02; VOYA 2/02)

6031 Horowitz, Anthony. *Scorpia* (8–11). Series: Alex Rider Adventure. 2005, Penguin $17.99 (978-0-399-24151-2). Teenage spy Alex Rider infiltrates a terrorist organization called Scorpia. (Rev: BL 2/1/05; SLJ 3/05; VOYA 4/05)

6032 Horowitz, Anthony. *Skeleton Key* (6–9). Series: Alex Rider. 2003, Philomel $17.99 (978-0-399-23777-5). Alex confronts and confounds a former Russian commander who intends to resurrect the Soviet Union in this action-packed novel a la James Bond. (Rev: BL 5/15/03; HBG 10/03; SLJ 5/03; VOYA 6/03)

6033 Horowitz, Anthony. *South by Southeast* (4–7). Series: Diamond Brothers. 2005, Philomel $16.99 (978-0-399-24155-0); paper $5.99 (978-0-14-240374-7). Hapless private eye Tim Diamond and his brother Nick find themselves drawn into a labyrinthine mystery after a visit from a stranger. (Rev: BL 12/1/05; SLJ 12/05)

6034 Horowitz, Anthony. *Stormbreaker* (5–9). Series: Alex Rider. 2001, Philomel $17.99 (978-0-399-23620-4). Fourteen-year-old Alex becomes embroiled in dangerous undercover exploits when his MI6 uncle is murdered. (Rev: BCCB 9/01; BL 9/1/01; HBG 10/01; SLJ 6/01; VOYA 8/01)

6035 Horowitz, Anthony. *Three of Diamonds* (5–8). Series: Diamond Brothers. 2005, Philomel $16.99 (978-0-399-24157-4). Tim and Nick succeed in solving crimes despite Tim's blunderings in these three fast-paced and entertaining mystery stories full of wordplay. (Rev: BL 5/15/05; SLJ 5/05)

6036 Hrdlitschka, Shelley. *Tangled Web* (6–12). 2000, Orca paper $6.95 (978-1-55143-178-9). Telepathic twins Alex and Tanner again tangle with their former kidnapper in this fast-paced sequel to *Disconnected* (1999). (Rev: BL 10/15/00; SLJ 10/00; VOYA 12/00)

6037 Jackson, Melanie. *The Big Dip* (4–7). 2009, Orca paper $9.95 (978-1-55469-178-4). Fifteen-year-old Joe's little sister is kidnapped soon after Joe witnessed a man shot to death at an amusement park; Joe investigates in this suspenseful novel suitable for reluctant readers. (Rev: BL 2/1/10; LMC 5–6/10; SLJ 11/09)

6038 Jennings, Richard W. *Mystery in Mt. Mole* (6–9). 2003, Houghton Mifflin $15.00 (978-0-618-28478-8). The assistant principal has disappeared but nobody seems to care much except 13-year-old Andy. (Rev: BL 9/15/03*; SLJ 12/03)

6039 Johns, Linda. *Hannah West in Deep Water* (5–8). Series: Hannah West. 2006, Puffin paper $5.99 (978-0-14-240700-4). Hannah investigates environmental shenanigans while she and her mother are house-sitting a houseboat and a dog. (Rev: BL 12/15/06)

6040 Johns, Linda. *Hannah West in the Belltown Towers: A Mystery* (5–8). Series: Hannah West. 2006, Sleuth paper $5.99 (978-0-14-240637-3). Hannah, an adopted Chinese girl with lots of nerve and curiosity, moves with her mother to Seattle and soon finds herself embroiled in an art theft. (Rev: BL 5/1/06)

6041 Johns, Linda. *Hannah West on Millionaire's Row* (5–8). Series: Hannah West. 2007, Puffin paper $5.99 (978-0-14-240824-7). Girl sleuth Hannah West, who was adopted from China, solves a mystery involving feng shui, antiques, and old mansions in this fourth installment in the series. (Rev: BL 10/1/07)

6042 Johnson, Henry, and Paul Hoppe. *Travis and Freddy's Adventures in Vegas* (5–8). 2006, Dutton $15.99 (978-0-525-47646-7). A lighthearted, fast-paced adventure in which preteens Travis and Freddy head to Las Vegas to win enough money to save Travis's home; there they win big but soon find they have the mob at their heels. (Rev: BL 2/15/06; SLJ 4/06; VOYA 4/06)

6043 Johnson, Rodney. *The Secret of Dead Man's Mine* (5–7). Illus. by Jill Thompson. Series: Rinnah Two Feathers Mystery. 2001, Uglytown paper $12.00 (978-0-9663473-3-3). Rinnah Two Feathers and two friends set out to solve the mystery of a suspicious stranger and find themselves in danger. (Rev: SLJ 9/01)

6044 Jorgensen, Christine T. *Death of a Dustbunny: A Stella the Stargazer Mystery* (8–12). 1998, Walker $22.95 (978-0-8027-3315-3). An uncomplicated mystery in which sleuth Stella the Stargazer, who writes a combination astrology and advice-to-the-lovelorn column for a local newspaper, investigates the disappearance of her friend Elena Ruiz, an employee of the Dustbunnies housekeeping and nanny agency. (Rev: BL 4/15/98; VOYA 8/98)

6045 Jubert, Hervé. *Devil's Tango* (8–11). 2006, Harper-Collins $16.99 (978-0-06-077720-3). Crime is virtually impossible in the futuristic city of Basle, Switzerland, thanks to tracers that monitor all parts of the city, but when a serial killer called the Baron of the Mists goes on a killing spree and can't be detected it's up to detective Roberta Morgenstern and her partner Clement to track him; this is a complex novel of suspense with elements of fantasy, science fiction, and romance. (Rev: BL 10/1/06; SLJ 2/07)

6046 Karas, Phyllis. *The Hate Crime* (7–10). 1995, Avon paper $3.99 (978-0-380-78214-7). A docunovel/whodunit about a teen who scrawls the names of seven concentration camps on a Jewish temple. (Rev: BL 12/1/95; VOYA 2/96)

6047 Karbo, Karen. *Minerva Clark Gets a Clue* (6–9). 2005, Bloomsbury $16.95 (978-1-58234-677-9). An electric shock changes 7th-grader Minerva from a self-concious but humorous worrier into a self-confident solver of mysteries. (Rev: BL 9/15/05; SLJ 10/05)

6048 Karbo, Karen. *Minerva Clark Gives Up the Ghost* (6–8). Series: Minerva Clark Mysteries. 2007, Bloomsbury $16.95 (978-1-58234-679-3). This time, Minerva is tackling a mystery in a haunted grocery store — and dealing with the return of her long-lost, newly remarried mother. (Rev: BL 11/15/07; SLJ 6/08)

6049 Keaney, Brian. *The Haunting of Nathaniel Wolfe* (4–7). 2012, IPG/Hodder paper $8.99 (978-18461652-0-7). Scam medium's son Nathaniel discovers an unexpected entrance into the spirit world, where he and a friend are tasked with solving a spine-chilling murder in this mystery set in Victorian-era London. ℮ (Rev: BL 5/1/12)

6050 Keene, Carolyn. *Where's Nancy?* (4–7). Series: Nancy Drew Super Mystery. 2005, Simon & Schuster paper $4.99 (978-0-416-90034-7). Nancy herself is missing in this first installment of a new series. (Rev: BL 5/1/05)

6051 Kehret, Peg. *Stolen Children* (4–7). 2008, Dutton $16.99 (978-0-525-47835-5). Fourteen-year-old Amy is babysitting for a wealthy family when she and 3-year-old Kendra are kidnapped in this fast-paced, dramatic story. (Rev: BL 12/15/08; SLJ 12/08)

6052 Kennedy, Emma. *The Case of the Fatal Phantom* (5–8). 2012, Dial $16.99 (978-080373542-2). In this third installment in the humorous mystery series with complex plots, Wilma and her beagle look for a treasure supposedly guarded by a dangerous ghost. ℮ (Rev: BLO 7/12)

6053 Kennedy, Emma. *The Case of the Frozen Hearts* (4–7). Series: Wilma Tenderfoot. 2011, Dial $16.99 (978-0-8037-3540-8). Wilma Tenderfoot, a 10-year-old orphan servant, finally gets the chance to try her sleuthing skills when she meets a famous detective. ℮ (Rev: BL 11/15/11; LMC 1–2/12; SLJ 10/1/11)

6054 Kephart, Beth. *Nothing but Ghosts* (8–11). 2009, HarperCollins $17.95 (978-006166796-1); LB $18.89 (978-006166797-8). Katie, 16, in an effort to recover from her mother's death, works on the construction of a gazebo at a nearby estate and stumbles on a mystery that she investigates with some help from her art restorer father and fellow worker Danny. (Rev: BL 4/1/09; LMC 1–2/10; SLJ 7/1/09; VOYA 8/09)

6055 Kerr, M. E. *Fell* (8–12). 1987, HarperCollins paper $4.95 (978-0-06-447031-5). In a bizarre identity switch, a teenager from a middle-class background enters a posh prep school. Followed by *Fell Back* and *Fell Down*. (Rev: BL 6/1/87; SLJ 8/87; VOYA 10/87)

6056 Kerr, M. E. *Fell Down* (7–12). 1991, HarperCollins $15.00 (978-0-06-021763-1). Fell has dropped out of prep school but is haunted by the death of his best friend there, so he returns, to find kidnapping, murder, and obsession. (Rev: BL 9/15/91*; SLJ 10/91)

6057 Kidd, Ronald. *The Year of the Bomb* (4–7). 2009, Simon & Schuster $15.99 (978-1-4169-5892-5). In 1955 California as *Invasion of the Body Snatchers* is being filmed, four 7th-grade boys face danger as they learn about Cold War tensions and spies. (Rev: BL 5/1/09; LMC 10/09; SLJ 7/09; VOYA 10/09)

6058 Klise, Kate. *Trial by Jury Journal* (5–8). Illus. by M. Sarah Klise. 2001, HarperCollins LB $16.89 (978-0-06-029541-7). When she is given the opportunity to serve as her state's first juvenile juror, 12-year-old Lily's sleuthing skills solve a murder mystery and save the day. (Rev: BCCB 4/01; BL 9/1/01; HB 5–6/01; HBG 10/01; SLJ 6/01)

6059 Konigsburg, E. L. *Silent to the Bone* (5–9). 2000, Simon & Schuster $16.00 (978-0-689-83601-5). A mystery story filled with suspense about a baby who's been dropped and a 13-year-old suspect who has lost his ability to speak. (Rev: BL 8/00*; HB 11–12/00; HBG 3/01; SLJ 9/00; VOYA 12/00)

6060 Korman, Gordon. *Framed* (5–7). 2010, Scholastic $16.99 (978-0-545-17849-5). A Super Bowl ring has gone missing and Griffin's retainer is found in its place. He and his friends try to clear his name in this follow-up to *Swindle* (2008) and *Zoobreak* (2009). ∩ Lexile 730L (Rev: LMC 11–12/10; SLJ 9/1/10)

6061 Korman, Gordon. *One False Note* (4–8). Series: The 39 Clues. 2008, Scholastic $12.99 (978-0-545-06042-4). Amy and Dan Cahill's arguments continue as they race to stay ahead of their cousins in hunting down the next clue that will solve their family mystery; a sequel to Rick Riordan's *The Maze of Bones* (2008). ∩ (Rev: BL 2/1/09; SLJ 7/09; VOYA 4/09)

6062 Kotzwinkle, William. *Trouble in Bugland: A Collection of Inspector Mantis Mysteries* (6–8). Illus. by Joe Servello. 1996, Godine paper $14.95 (978-1-56792-070-3). An all-insect cast in a takeoff on Sherlock Holmes mysteries.

6063 Kress, Adrienne. *The Friday Society* (7–12). 2012, Dial $17.99 (978-080373761-7). In Edwardian England three talented teenage women meet by chance and join forces to solve a mystery. ℮ Lexile HL710L (Rev: BL 12/15/12; LMC 3–4/13; SLJ 2/13; VOYA 11–12/12)

6064 Krieg, Jim. *Griff Carver, Hallway Patrol* (4–7). 2010, Penguin $15.99 (978-1-59514-276-4). Thirteen-year-old Griff Carver fights crime as part of the Safety Patrol at Rampart Middle School, disciplining everyone from the principal on down in this humorous spoof of a police procedural that includes a hall-pass counterfeiting ring. ☊ ℮ Lexile 710L (Rev: BL 5/1/10*; HB 5–6/10; LMC 3–4/10; SLJ 3/10)

6065 L'Engle, Madeleine. *Troubling a Star* (7–10). 1994, Farrar $19.00 (978-0-374-37783-0). Vicki Austin, 16, travels to Antarctica and meets a Baltic prince looking for romance, and the two try to solve a mystery involving nuclear waste. (Rev: BL 8/94; SLJ 10/94; VOYA 12/94)

6066 Lacey, Josh. *Island of Thieves* (4–7). 2012, Houghton Mifflin $15.99 (978-054776327-9). Tom and his shifty Uncle Harvey hunt for lost treasure in Peru and find themselves almost immediately in danger in this exciting, fast-paced story. ☊ ℮ Lexile 640L (Rev: BL 5/1/12*; LMC 8–9/12; SLJ 6/12)

6067 Lachtman, Ofelia Dumas. *Looking for La Única* (6–9). 2004, Arte Publico paper $9.95 (978-1-55885-412-3). In the summer before her senior year at high school, Monica gets swept into a series of adventures after a treasured guitar disappears from a shop owned by family friends in this sequel to *The Summer of El Pintor* (2001). (Rev: BL 1/1–15/05)

6068 Lachtman, Ofelia Dumas. *The Summer of El Pintor* (7–10). 2001, Arte Publico paper $9.95 (978-1-55885-327-0). Sixteen-year-old Monica's father loses his job and the two move from their wealthy neighborhood to the barrio house in which her dead mother grew up, where Monica searches for a missing neighbor and discovers the truth of her past. (Rev: BL 8/01; SLJ 7/01; VOYA 12/01)

6069 Lachtman, Ofelia Dumas. *The Truth About Las Mariposas* (7–10). 2007, Arte Publico paper $9.95 (978-1-55885-494-9). While Caroline (called Caro) is spending the summer with Tía Matilde, helping her run her bed-and-breakfast in the tiny town of Two Sands, she stumbles on a mystery that could affect her aunt's livelihood. (Rev: BL 12/15/07)

6070 LaFevers, R. L. *Theodosia and the Eyes of Horus* (5–8). Illus. by Yoko Tanaka. Series: Theodosia. 2010, Houghton Mifflin $16 (978-0-547-22592-0). Supernaturally talented Theodosia, 11, copes with her difficult family while using her knowledge of Egyptian lore to stymie the evil powers of the Arcane Order of the Black Sun. (Rev: BLO 2/1/10; SLJ 7/10)

6071 LaFevers, R. L. *Theodosia and the Last Pharaoh* (5–8). Illus. by Yoko Tanaka. Series: Theodosia. 2011, Houghton Mifflin $16.99 (978-054739018-5). Endeavoring to return a priceless Egyptian artifact, 11-year-old Theodosia and her cat Isis arouse interest as soon as they arrive in Cairo. (Rev: BL 5/1/11)

6072 Lafevers, R. L. *Theodosia and the Serpents of Chaos* (5–8). Illus. by Yoko Tanaka. 2007, Houghton Mifflin $16.00 (978-0-618-75638-4). In the early 20th century, precocious 11-year-old Theodosia finds herself embroiled in a supernatural mystery involving Egyptian artifacts. (Rev: BL 5/1/07*; SLJ 4/07)

6073 Lalicki, Tom. *Shots at Sea: A Houdini and Nate Mystery* (4–7). Series: Houdini and Nate. 2007, Farrar $15.95 (978-0-374-31679-2). In the second book in the series, Nate, 13, is aboard the *Lusitania* and finds among his fellow-passengers both Harry Houdini and Teddy Roosevelt; Nate and the former rescue the latter from an assassination attempt. (Rev: BL 1/1–15/08; SLJ 11/07)

6074 Lane, Andrew. *Rebel Fire* (7–10). Series: Sherlock Holmes: The Legend Begins. 2012, Farrar $16.99 (978-037438768-6). A teenaged Sherlock Holmes discovers that John Wilkes Booth is alive and living in England in this action-packed tale that takes the young sleuth to the United States. ☊ ℮ Lexile 920L (Rev: BL 5/1/12; HB 5–6/12; SLJ 4/12; VOYA 4/12)

6075 Lawrence, Iain. *The Séance* (5–7). 2008, Delacorte $15.99 (978-0-385-73375-5). Scooter, whose spiritualist mother performs fake séances, is caught up in a murder mystery involving his idol, Houdini, in this novel that captures the tone of 1920s New York City. (Rev: BL 5/1/08; SLJ 8/08)

6076 Lee, Y. S. *The Body at the Tower* (8–12). Series: Agency. 2010, Candlewick $16.99 (978-076364968-5). Mary Quinn resorts to disguising herself as a boy to solve a murder in this second book in the series set in Victorian England. ☊ ℮ (Rev: BL 12/15/10; SLJ 9/1/10; VOYA 10/10)

6077 Lee, Y. S. *A Spy in the House* (8–12). Series: Mary Quinn Mysteries. 2010, Candlewick $16.99 (978-0-7636-4067-5); paper $11.20 (978-1-4063-1516-5). Saved from hanging in 1850s London five years earlier, Mary Quinn, now 17, is part of an all-female detective agency and charged with tracing some missing cargo ships; this first installment in a series is full of Victorian details. ☊ ℮ (Rev: BL 1/1–15/10; LMC 5–6/10; SLJ 4/10)

6078 Leonard, Julia Platt. *Cold Case* (6–8). 2011, Aladdin $15.99 (978-1-4424-2009-0). Thirteen-year-old Oz finds himself in the midst of a gruesome murder investigation that may involve both his older brother Dave and his deceased father, who was accused of espionage. ℮ (Rev: BL 5/1/11; LMC 8–9/11; SLJ 9/1/11)

6079 Levithan, David. *Every You, Every Me* (8–12). Illus. 2011, Knopf $16.99 (978-0-375-86098-0); LB $19.99 (978-037596098-7). Using a journal format including color photographs, this novel describes 16-year-old Evan's distress about the loss of his friend Ariel and his reactions when photographs of her start appearing in his locker and on his way home. **e** Lexile HL440L (Rev: BL 10/15/11; SLJ 10/1/11; VOYA 10/11)

6080 Lewman, David. *The Case of the Mystery Meat Loaf* (4–7). Series: Club CSI. 2012, Simon & Schuster $15.99 (978-144244646-5); paper $5.99 (978-14424339-4-6). When the whole school swim team comes down with food poisoning, three middle-grade sleuths kick into action to figure out the cause and the culprit. **e** (Rev: BLO 4/1/12; SLJ 4/12)

6081 Lisle, Janet Taylor. *Black Duck* (7–10). 2006, Philomel $15.99 (978-0-399-23963-2). In hopes of getting his story published, a teen boy interviews his elderly neighbor about the days of Prohibition and learns of lawlessness and mysterious events occurring in their Rhode Island town. ᶯ (Rev: BL 5/1/06; HB 7–8/06; LMC 1/07; SLJ 5/06*)

6082 Littke, Lael. *Lake of Secrets* (7–10). 2002, Henry Holt $16.95 (978-0-8050-6730-9). Carlene experiences strong and puzzling feelings of deja vu when she and her mother go to the town where Carlene's brother died 18 years earlier, before Carlene's birth. (Rev: BCCB 4/02; BL 3/1/02; HB 5–6/02; HBG 10/02; SLJ 3/02; VOYA 6/02)

6083 Logsted, Greg. *Alibi Junior High* (6–9). 2009, Simon & Schuster $15.99 (978-1-4169-7959-3). Gifted in martial arts, Cody, the 13-year-old son of an undercover agent, adjusts to living with his aunt and attending a new junior high in all the wrong ways — by crushing the school bullies, and correcting his teachers — in this fast-paced and humorous novel. **e** Lexile HL570L (Rev: BL 8/09; SLJ 6/1/09)

6084 Low, Dene. *The Entomological Tales of Augustus T. Percival: Petronella Saves Nearly Everyone* (5–8). Illus. by Jen Corace. 2009, Houghton $16.00 (978-0-547-15250-9). In Victorian London, 16-year-old Petronella must deal with her embarrassing, bug-eating uncle and save an international dignitary who has been kidnapped. (Rev: BL 7/09; SLJ 10/09)

6085 Lucashenko, Melissa. *Killing Darcy* (8–10). 1998, Univ. of Queensland paper $13.95 (978-0-7022-3041-7). In this complex supernatural murder mystery set in New South Wales, 16-year-old Filomena uncovers a family murder, discovers a camera that can take pictures of the past, and is helped by a gay Aboriginal boy to solve the mystery. (Rev: SLJ 2/99)

6086 McClintock, Norah. *Dooley Takes the Fall* (8–12). 2008, Red Deer $12.95 (978-0-88995-403-8). Ryan Dooley, a 17-year-old with a record, is a suspect in two deaths and, to complicate matters, is attracted to the sis-

ter of one of the victims; eventually it seems that only he can clear himself. (Rev: BLO 6/17/08)

6087 McClintock, Norah. *Last Chance* (6–9). Series: Robyn Hunter Mysteries. 2012, Lerner/Darby Creek LB $27.93 (978-076138311-6); paper $8.95 (9780761385295). Reluctantly volunteering at an animal shelter (she is afraid of dogs) as part of a community service sentence, 15-year-old Robyn recognizes that her co-offender Nick may be innocent and sets out to prove this. **e** Lexile 640L (Rev: BLO 4/15/12; LMC 5–6/12; SLJ 5/1/12)

6088 McClintock, Norah. *Victim Rights* (7–12). Series: Ryan Dooley Mystery. 2011, Red Deer paper $12.95 (978-0-88995-447-2). In this third volume in the series, Ryan's girlfriend accuses wealthy Parker Albright of rape and Ryan falls under suspicion when Parker is found dead. (Rev: BL 5/1/11; SLJ 5/11)

6089 MacDonald, Bailey. *The Secret of the Sealed Room: A Mystery of Young Benjamin Franklin* (5–8). 2010, Simon & Schuster $16.99 (978-1-4169-9760-3). A young Benjamin Franklin helps 14-year-old Patience, a runaway indentured servant who is suspected of murder. **e** Lexile 1050L (Rev: BL 12/1/10; SLJ 1/1/11)

6090 MacDonald, Bailey. *Wicked Will: A Mystery of Young William Shakespeare* (4–7). 2009, Aladdin $16.99 (978-1-4169-8660-7). In Stratford in the 16th century, Viola, an actress disguised as a boy, meets 12-year-old Will Shakespeare and together they try to trap a murderer. (Rev: BL 5/1/09; LMC 10/09; SLJ 8/09)

6091 McDonnell, Margot. *Torn to Pieces* (8–11). 2008, Delacorte $15.99 (978-038573559-9); LB $18.99 (978-038590542-8). Anne, 17, discovers the horrifying truth about her mother's past in this occasionally violent teen thriller. **e** Lexile NC510L (Rev: BL 11/1/08; SLJ 1/1/09)

6092 Machado, Ana Maria. *From Another World* (4–7). Illus. by Lucia Brandao. 2005, Douglas & McIntyre $15.95 (978-0-88899-597-1). Spending a night in an outbuilding of an old farmhouse, Mariano and his three friends meet the ghost of a 19th-century slave girl and promise to help in this story set in Brazil. (Rev: BL 5/1/05; SLJ 6/05)

6093 Mack, Tracy, and Michael Citrin. *The Fall of the Amazing Zalindas* (4–7). Illus. by Greg Ruth. Series: Sherlock Holmes and the Baker Street Irregulars. 2006, Scholastic $16.99 (978-0-439-82836-9). Sherlock Holmes calls on a gang of street children to help him investigate the mysterious deaths of a family of trapeze artists. (Rev: BL 11/1/06; SLJ 1/07)

6094 Mack, Tracy, and Michael Citrin. *The Mystery of the Conjured Man* (5–7). Series: Sherlock Holmes and the Baker Street Irregulars. 2009, Scholastic paper $6.99 (978-0-439-83667-8). This second fast-paced installment in the series contains séances, death, hidden passages, fraud, and a twist at the end. (Rev: BLO 6/16/09; SLJ 6/09)

6095 Mackall, Dandi Daley. *The Silence of Murder* (8–12). 2011, Knopf $16.99 (978-0-375-86896-2); LB $19.99 (978-037596896-9). Hope defends her autistic brother when he is accused of murdering the baseball coach, and sets out to find the perpetrator. ∩ e (Rev: BL 10/1/11; SLJ 11/1/11)

6096 McLoughlin, Jane. *At Yellow Lake* (7–10). 2012, Frances Lincoln paper $8.99 (978-18478028-7-3). Three troubled teens' story lines converge on a remote lake where they become the targets of kidnappers. e (Rev: BLO 8/12; LMC 3–4/13)

6097 McNab, Andy, and Robert Rigby. *Avenger* (7–12). 2007, Putnam $16.99 (978-0-399-24685-2). In this sequel to *Traitor* (2005) and *Payback* (2006), Danny, his grandfather Fergus, and his friend Elena pit their skills under Black Star, an evil computer expert. (Rev: SLJ 12/07; VOYA date)

6098 McNab, Andy, and Robert Rigby. *Meltdown* (8–11). 2008, Putnam $16.99 (978-0-399-24686-9). Danny and his secret agent grandfather Fergus investigate a new — and fatal — designer drug called Meltdown in this action-packed British story. (Rev: BL 7/08; SLJ 1/1/09)

6099 McNamee, Graham. *Bonechiller* (7–10). 2008, Random House $15.99 (978-038574658-8); LB $18.99 (978-038590895-5). High-schoolers Danny and Howie grapple with a merciless, bloodthirsty beast in this supernatural thriller set in the Canadian tundra. Lexile 580L (Rev: BL 11/1/08*; LMC 11–12/08; SLJ 1/1/09)

6100 Madison, Bennett. *Lulu Dark and the Summer of the Fox* (8–12). 2006, Sleuth paper $10.99 (978-0-595-14086-2). Lulu Dark's summer plans are ruined when she investigates the disappearances of her boyfriend and two actresses working on a movie in town — could her mother be involved? (Rev: BL 5/1/06; LMC 8–9/06; SLJ 8/06)

6101 Madormo, John. *The Homemade Stuffing Caper: Charlie Collier, Snoop for Hire* (4–7). 2012, Philomel $15.99 (978-039925543-4). An exciting mystery in which Charlie and his friend Henry investigate missing pet birds. e (Rev: BL 5/1/12; LMC 11–12/12; SLJ 6/12)

6102 Margolin, Phillip, and Ami Margolin Rome. *Vanishing Acts* (4–7). 2011, HarperCollins $16.99 (978-006188556-3). Nancy Drew protégée Madison Kincaid, 12, solves two missing-person cases — one in collaboration with her attorney father — while coping with junior high in Portland, Oregon. (Rev: BL 5/1/11; SLJ 2/12)

6103 Margolis, Leslie. *Girl's Best Friend: A Maggie Brooklyn Mystery* (5–8). 2010, Bloomsbury $14.99 (978-1-59990-525-9). Twelve-year-old Maggie, a Nancy Drew fan, solves the mystery of disappearing dogs in

Park Slope, Brooklyn, and then tackles missing money in this lighthearted novel. e Lexile 620L (Rev: HB 9–10/10; LMC 10/10; SLJ 12/1/10)

6104 Marks, Graham. *Omega Place* (8–11). 2007, Bloomsbury $16.95 (978-1-59990-127-5). Paul, 17, runs away from home and joins a resistance group in London—Omega Place—that is bent on destroying the ubiquitous closed-circuit cameras that keep tabs on the nation's citizens. (Rev: BL 10/15/07; LMC 1/08; SLJ 4/08)

6105 Marks, Graham. *Zoo* (8–11). 2005, Bloomsbury paper $8.95 (978-1-58234-991-6). A complex and suspenseful adventure story in which 17-year-old Cam escapes from kidnappers only to find that he has a mysterious chip in his arm and his parents may have been involved in his capture. (Rev: BL 9/15/05; SLJ 10/05; VOYA 8/05)

6106 Marrone, Amanda. *Devoured* (8–12). 2009, Simon & Schuster paper $9.99 (978-1-4169-7890-9). In this fast-paced murder mystery, 17-year-old Megan grapples with volatile politics at her summer job, her distant mother, and her dead twin sister's increasingly foreboding ghost. e (Rev: BLO 8/20/09; SLJ 10/09)

6107 Martin, Terri. *A Family Trait* (5–7). 1999, Holiday $15.95 (978-0-8234-1467-3). In this fast-paced story, Iris, 11 years old and incurably curious, has a number of mysteries to solve while trying to finish a book report. (Rev: BL 10/1/99; HBG 3/00; SLJ 10/99)

6108 Michaels, Rune. *Genesis Alpha* (7–10). 2007, Atheneum $15.99 (978-1-4169-1886-8). Josh was a designer baby whose stem cells saved his older brother Max from cancer; now Max is accused of murder — is Josh in some way guilty too? (Rev: BCCB 9/07; BL 5/1/07; LMC 8–9/07; SLJ 7/07)

6109 Miller, Ashley Edward, and Zack Stentz. *Colin Fischer* (5–8). 2012, Penguin $17.99 (978-159514578-9). Colin, a 14-year-old with Asperger's and few friends, is nonetheless a good observer and sets out to solve a shooting and absolve the bully who is initially presumed to be responsible. e Lexile 870L (Rev: BL 11/1/12; HB 1–2/13; LMC 5–6/13*; SLJ 1/13)

6110 Miller, Kirsten. *Kiki Strike: The Empress's Tomb* (5–8). 2007, Bloomsbury $16.95 (978-1-59990-047-6). Kiki and the Irregulars tackle assorted bad guys in this sequel to *Kiki Strike: Inside the Shadow City*, again set in the world under New York City. (Rev: SLJ 12/07)

6111 Milway, Alex. *The Mousehunter* (4–7). Illus. by author. 2009, Little, Brown $15.99 (978-0-316-02454-9). Twelve-year-old Emiline is a mousekeeper in a world where many breeds of mice are prized, and she bravely sets out to defeat a pirate named Mousebeard. (Rev: BL 12/15/08; SLJ 3/09)

6112 Mitchard, Jacquelyn. *The Midnight Twins* (6–12). 2008, Penguin $16.99 (978-159514160-6). Identical twins Meredith and Mallory's eerie ability to communicate with each other forms the heart of this thrilling series starter. **e** (Rev: BL 7/08; LMC 11–12/08; SLJ 10/1/08)

6113 Mitchard, Jacquelyn. *Now You See Her* (8–11). 2007, HarperTempest $15.99 (978-0-06-111683-4). Is 15-year-old Hope telling the truth about her affair with the leading man in the school play? Was she truly abducted? Readers will have a hard time separating Hope's truth from the lies in this suspenseful psychological thriller. (Rev: BCCB 4/07; BL 2/15/07; SLJ 3/07)

6114 Mitchard, Jacquelyn. *What We Saw at Night* (8–12). 2013, Soho $17.99 (978-161695141-2). Three teens — Allie, Rob, and Juliet — are confined during the day because of a rare sensitivity to sunlight, and react by enjoying parkour at night — which leads them to witness a murder. ♩ **e** (Rev: BL 12/15/12; SLJ 2/13)

6115 Mitchell, Marianne. *Finding Zola* (5–8). 2003, Boyds Mills $16.95 (978-1-59078-070-1). A 13-year-old girl in a wheelchair investigates the disappearance of an elderly woman who has been staying with her. (Rev: BL 5/15/03; HBG 10/03; SLJ 2/03; VOYA 10/03)

6116 Mitchell, Marianne. *Firebug* (5–8). 2004, Boyds Mills $16.95 (978-1-59078-170-8). Twelve-year-old Haley investigates a suspicious fire at her Uncle Jake's Arizona ranch. (Rev: BL 3/15/04; SLJ 2/04)

6117 Mitchell, Saundra. *Shadowed Summer* (8–12). 2009, Delacorte $15.99 (978-038573571-1); LB $18.99 (978-038590560-2). Iris, 14, accidentally contacts a ghost who pressures her to solve the mystery of his long-ago murder; her investigation uncovers unpleasant secrets about her Louisiana town. **e** Lexile 760L (Rev: BL 2/15/09; SLJ 4/1/09)

6118 Moloney, James. *Black Taxi* (8–11). 2005, HarperCollins LB $16.89 (978-0-06-055938-0). When her grandfather is sent to jail for six months, 16-year-old Rosie Sinclair is appointed caretaker of his eye-catching black Mercedes; she enlists the help of her friends — one an attractive young man — when she starts getting threatening phone calls. (Rev: BCCB 5/05; BL 3/1/05; SLJ 3/05; VOYA 8/05)

6119 Monaghan, Annabel. *A Girl Named Digit* (7–9). 2012, Houghton Mifflin $16.99 (978-054766852-9). Math whiz Digit, 17, uncovers a terrorist plot and is given protection by a handsome young FBI agent in this suspenseful romance. **e** (Rev: BLO 6/12; LMC 1–2/13; SLJ 6/12)

6120 Mundis, Hester. *My Chimp Friday* (4–7). 2002, Simon & Schuster $16.00 (978-0-689-83837-8). Rachel and her family grow to love their new pet, a chimp named Friday, but when kidnappers try to steal Friday, Rachel realizes he is not an ordinary chimp. (Rev: BL 6/1–15/02; HBG 10/02; SLJ 6/02)

6121 Murphy, T. M. *The Secrets of Code Z* (4–8). Series: A Belltown Mystery. 2001, J. N. Townsend paper $9.95 (978-1-880158-33-3). Orville Jacques becomes embroiled in a fast-paced mystery involving CIA cover-ups, a death powder, and an evil Russian. (Rev: BL 5/15/01; SLJ 7/01)

6122 Murray, Susan, and Robert Davies. *Panic in Puerto Vallarta* (7–9). Series: K. C. Flanagan, Girl Detective. 1998, Robert Davies Multimedia paper $8.99 (978-1-55207-015-4). After witnessing a murder in Puerto Vallarta, young K. C. Flanagan finds that the killers are out to get her. (Rev: SLJ 12/98)

6123 Myers, Kate Kae. *The Vanishing Game* (8–12). 2012, Bloomsbury $16.99 (978-159990694-2). Is her twin brother still alive? Jocelyn, 17, is receiving mysterious communications, and she sets out with Jack's friend Noah to investigate. **e** (Rev: BL 5/1/12; LMC 3–4/12; SLJ 3/12)

6124 Naylor, Phyllis Reynolds. *Bernie Magruder and the Bats in the Belfry* (4–7). 2003, Simon & Schuster $16.95 (978-0-689-85066-0). Bernie is investigating a bat with a fatal bite; could it be connected to the fact that the bells in the belfry are annoyingly stuck on the same tune? (Rev: BL 1/1–15/03; HBG 10/03; SLJ 4/03)

6125 Nickerson, Sara. *How to Disappear Completely and Never Be Found* (4–8). Illus. by Sally Wern Comport. 2002, HarperCollins LB $17.89 (978-0-06-029772-5). Two youngsters with problems, 12-year-old Margaret and her friend Boyd, explore a deserted mansion and solve the mystery of the supernatural terrors it supposedly contains. (Rev: BCCB 5/02; BL 4/1/02; HB 7–8/02; HBG 10/02; SLJ 4/02)

6126 Nixon, Joan Lowery. *A Candidate for Murder* (6–12). 1991, Dell paper $4.99 (978-0-440-21212-6). While Cary's father enters the political limelight, his daughter becomes embroiled in a series of strange events. (Rev: BL 3/1/91)

6127 Nixon, Joan Lowery. *The Dark and Deadly Pool* (7–12). 1989, Bantam paper $4.99 (978-0-440-20348-3). Mary Elizabeth becomes aware of strange happenings at the health club where she works. (Rev: BL 11/1/87; SLJ 2/88; VOYA 12/87)

6128 Nixon, Joan Lowery. *The Ghosts of Now* (7–10). 1984, Dell paper $4.99 (978-0-440-93115-7). Angie investigates a hit-and-run accident that has left her brother in a coma.

6129 Nixon, Joan Lowery. *Murdered, My Sweet* (6–9). 1997, Delacorte $15.95 (978-0-385-32245-4). The son of a millionaire is murdered and young Jenny and her mystery-writer mother try to solve the case. (Rev: BL 9/1/97; HBG 3/98; SLJ 9/97; VOYA 2/98)

6130 Nixon, Joan Lowery. *The Name of the Game Was Murder* (6–8). 1994, Dell paper $4.99 (978-0-440-21916-3). Teenager Samantha must work with her uncle's houseguests to find a damning manuscript and uncover the murderer of its author. (Rev: BL 3/1/93)

6131 Nixon, Joan Lowery. *Nightmare* (6–10). 2003, Delacorte LB $17.99 (978-0-385-90151-2). This suspenseful mystery features 10th-grader Emily, who has suffered a recurring nightmare since childhood and now finds herself facing a killer at her summer camp. (Rev: BL 10/15/03; HBG 4/04; SLJ 10/03; VOYA 10/03)

6132 Nixon, Joan Lowery. *The Other Side of Dark* (7–10). 1986, Dell paper $4.99 (978-0-440-96638-8). After waking from a four-year coma, Stacy is now the target of the man who wounded her and killed her mother. (Rev: BL 9/15/86; SLJ 9/86; VOYA 12/86)

6133 Nixon, Joan Lowery. *Shadowmaker* (7–9). 1995, Dell paper $4.99 (978-0-440-21942-2). When Katie's mother, an investigative journalist, probes evidence of toxic-waste dumping, Katie discovers that events at her school are related. (Rev: BL 3/1/94; SLJ 5/94; VOYA 8/94)

6134 Nixon, Joan Lowery. *The Weekend Was Murder!* (6–10). 1992, Dell paper $4.99 (978-0-440-21901-9). A teen sleuth and her boyfriend attend a murder mystery enactment weekend and discover a real murder. (Rev: BL 2/15/92; SLJ 3/92)

6135 Odyssey, Shawn Thomas. *The Wizard of Dark Street* (4–7). 2011, Egmont $16.99 (978-1-60684-143-3). Blending fantasy and mystery, this book set in 1877 New York City follows 12-year-old Oona, who has decided to become a detective rather than follow in her wizard family's footsteps — until her wizard uncle is attacked. Lexile 890L (Rev: BL 7/11; SLJ 9/1/11)

6136 Oliver, Andrew. *If Photos Could Talk* (4–7). Series: A Sam and Stephanie Mystery. 2005, Adams-Pomeroy paper $12.95 (978-0-9661009-6-9). Twelve-year-olds Sam and Stephanie investigate the disappearance of an elderly man in their small Wisconsin town in this well-plotted novel. (Rev: SLJ 1/06)

6137 Orenstein, Denise Gosliner. *The Secret Twin* (7–10). 2007, HarperCollins $16.99 (978-0-06-078564-2). Skinny, sickly Noah, whose twin died at birth, is thrown for a loop when hearty Grace comes to take care of him after his grandmother's facelift in this suspenseful and complex novel. (Rev: BL 12/15/06; SLJ 3/07)

6138 Parker, Robert B. *Chasing the Bear: A Young Spenser Novel* (7–10). 2009, Philomel $17.99 (978-039924776-7). An adult Spenser tells his girlfriend the story of being brought up by his rough-and-tumble father and uncles. ∩ e Lexile HL500L (Rev: BL 5/1/09; SLJ 8/09; VOYA 8/09)

6139 Parkinson, Curtis. *Death in Kingsport* (6–8). 2007, Tundra paper $11.95 (978-0-88776-827-9). This fast-paced mystery set in Canada in 1941 starts with 15-year-old Neil hearing thumping sounds from his uncle's coffin. (Rev: SLJ 12/07)

6140 Pascal, Francine. *Fearless FBI: Kill Game* (8–11). Series: Fearless FBI. 2005, Simon & Schuster paper $7.99 (978-0-689-87821-3). Despite her unreliability, the FBI invites intrepid Gaia — of the earlier Fearless series — to try their boot camp training program. (Rev: BL 8/05; SLJ 6/05)

6141 Patrick, Cat. *Forgotten* (7–11). 2011, Little, Brown $17.99 (978-0-316-09461-0). London, 16, has memory problems caused by a traumatic event in her past — she "remembers" into the future and forgets everything each night until, with the help of her boyfriend she unravels the causes behind her problems. ∩ e Lexile HL720L (Rev: BL 4/1/11; LMC 10/11; SLJ 7/11)

6142 Patrick, Cat. *Revived* (7–11). 2012, Little, Brown $17.99 (978-0-316-09462-7). Daisy faces difficult decisions when she meets Audrey and Matt and starts to question the government's Revive program, which has brought her back from death repeatedly. ∩ e Lexile HL690L (Rev: BL 5/1/12; HB 5–6/12; LMC 8–9/12; SLJ 7/12; VOYA 4/12)

6143 Peacock, Shane. *Eye of the Crow* (7–10). Series: The Boy Sherlock Holmes. 2007, Tundra $19.95 (978-0-88776-850-7). Named one of the *Booklist* Top Ten in Young Mysteries, this first book in the series begins in 1867, when Sherlock is 13 and accused of murder, launching his career of detective work. (Rev: BL 11/1/07; SLJ 11/07)

6144 Peacock, Shane. *Vanishing Girl* (7–10). Series: The Boy Sherlock Holmes. 2009, Tundra $19.95 (978-0-88776-852-1). The young daughter of a government official disappears, a ransom note arrives, and young Sherlock investigates in this fast-paced mystery full of Victorian atmosphere. e Lexile 810L (Rev: BLO 11/20/09; SLJ 2/10)

6145 Pearson, Ridley. *The Challenge* (5–8). 2008, Disney $16.99 (978-1-4231-0640-1). Steve is caught up in a terrorist kidnapping plot when he looks inside an abandoned briefcase in this fast-paced adventure. (Rev: BL 1/1–15/08; LMC 4–5/08)

6146 Peloquin, Lili. *The Innocents* (8–10). 2012, Penguin $17.99 (978-159514582-6). When their mother remarries, sisters Alice and Charlie have different reactions to their new, wealthy surroundings and the secrets they uncover there. e (Rev: BL 10/15/12; LMC 1–2/13; SLJ 3/13)

6147 Penn, Audrey. *Mystery at Blackbeard's Cove* (5–8). Illus. by Joshua Miller. 2004, Tanglewood $14.95 (978-0-9749303-1-2). The death of Mrs. McNemmish, a descendant of Blackbeard the pirate, sets in motion a series of adventures for four young residents of Okracoke Island. (Rev: BL 1/1–15/05)

6148 Peterson, Lois. *Beyond Repair* (6–9). Series: Orca Currents. 2011, Orca LB $16.95 (978-155469817-2); paper $9.95 (9781554698165). Teenager Cam has been the "man of the house" since his father's death in a car accident and is unnerved when the man who killed him keeps turning up. e Lexile HL480L (Rev: BL 5/1/11; LMC 10/11)

6149 Petrucha, Stefan. *Ripper* (8–10). 2012, Philomel $17.99 (978-039925524-3). In this exciting adventure set in 1895 New York, 14-year-old Carver is adopted by a detective who turns out to be a serial killer. **e** Lexile 710L (Rev: BL 3/1/12; HB 3–4/12; LMC 5–6/12; SLJ 3/12; VOYA 2/12)

6150 Phillips, Helen. *Here Where the Sunbeams Are Green* (4–7). 2012, Delacorte $17.99 (978-038574236-8); LB $20.99 (978-037599056-4). Sisters Madeline and Ruby travel to a Central American jungle to join their father, an ornithologist, only to find themselves embroiled in ecological intrigue. **e** Lexile 940L (Rev: BLO 12/15/12; LMC 3–4/13; SLJ 1/13)

6151 Phillips, Suzanne Marie. *Lindsey Lost* (7–10). 2012, Viking $16.99 (978-0-670-78460-8). Athletic Micah struggles to piece together what happened to his sister Lindsey, whose even greater athletic prowess may have made her a target for a murderer. **e** (Rev: BL 9/15/12; LMC 3–4/13; SLJ 10/12; VOYA 10/12)

6152 Pike, Christopher. *Gimme a Kiss* (7–12). 1991, Pocket paper $4.50 (978-0-671-63682-1). A girl fakes her own death in a wild plot to get revenge. (Rev: BL 10/15/88; VOYA 4/89)

6153 Pike, Christopher. *Slumber Party* (7–10). 1985, Scholastic paper $5.99 (978-0-590-43014-2). Six teenage girls stranded in a winter vacation home experience mysterious occurrences that bring terror into their lives. (Rev: SLJ 12/86)

6154 Plum-Ucci, Carol. *The Body of Christopher Creed* (8–12). 2000, Harcourt $17.00 (978-0-15-202388-1). Torey and his friends are implicated in the disappearance of his classmate Chris, causing Torey to examine his life while trying to find Chris. (Rev: HBG 9/00; SLJ 7/00)

6155 Plum-Ucci, Carol. *Following Christopher Creed* (8–12). 2011, Harcourt $16.99 (978-0-15-204759-7). College student Mike begins researching the fate of Christopher Creed, uncovering one eerie similarity after another in this light, fast-paced read. A sequel to the award-winning *The Body of Christopher Creed* (2007). Ω **e** (Rev: BL 9/15/11; SLJ 9/1/11; VOYA 8/11)

6156 Plum-Ucci, Carol. *The She* (8–12). 2003, Harcourt $17.00 (978-0-15-216819-3). Evan, his brother, and a friend set out to find the truth behind the disappearance of Evan's parents years before. (Rev: BL 9/15/03*; SLJ 10/03; VOYA 12/03)

6157 Plum-Ucci, Carol. *Streams of Babel* (8–11). 2008, Harcourt $17.00 (978-0-15-216556-7). A Palestinian teenager working for the U.S. government uncovers a terrorist plot to poison drinking water that has already sickened and killed two people in New York. (Rev: BL 4/15/08; SLJ 7/08)

6158 Plummer, Louise. *Finding Daddy* (6–9). 2007, Delacorte $15.99 (978-0-385-73092-1). Nearly 16, Mira decides to track down her long-absent father, but soon after she finds him on the Internet things begin to happen; someone seems to be watching — and threatening — her and her family. (Rev: BL 12/1/07; SLJ 12/07)

6159 Pow, Tom. *Captives* (6–9). 2007, Roaring Brook $17.95 (978-1-59643-201-7). The story of a deadly kidnapping of American tourists by Caribbean guerrillas is told by one of the fathers and amplified by 16-year-old Martin, whose perspective is quite different. (Rev: BCCB 9/07; BL 5/15/07; SLJ 5/07)

6160 Priestley, Chris. *The Dead of Winter* (7–10). 2012, Bloomsbury $16.99 (978-159990745-1). Michael finds himself in the midst of a spooky murder mystery unfolding in an isolated mansion in the middle of winter. (Rev: BL 3/1/12; LMC 3–4/12; SLJ 2/12; VOYA 2/12)

6161 Promitzer, Rebecca. *The Pickle King* (5–8). 2010, Scholastic $17.99 (978-0-545-17087-1). A complex, multilayered novel in which 11-year-old Bea and her friends investigate a mystery involving a ghost. Ω Lexile 880L (Rev: BL 2/1/10; LMC 3–4/10; SLJ 6/10)

6162 Quimby, Laura. *The Icarus Project* (4–7). 2012, Abrams $16.95 (978-1-4197-0402-4). On an expedition to the Arctic with her father, 13-year-old Maya discovers a strange creature preserved in ice. **e** (Rev: BL 12/1/12; SLJ 12/12)

6163 Raskin, Ellen. *The Westing Game* (6–9). 1978, Avon paper $3.50 (978-0-380-67991-1). Sixteen possible heirs try to decipher an enigmatic will. Newbery Medal, 1979.

6164 Ravel, Edeet. *Held* (8–11). 2011, Annick $21.95 (978-155451283-6); paper $12.95 (978-15545128-2-9). Chloe, 17, is kidnapped on a vacation in Greece and held hostage by a kind abductor who makes her life quite comfortable — to the point that she finds herself attracted to him. **e** (Rev: BL 6/1/11; LMC 11–12/11)

6165 Reaver, Chap. *A Little Bit Dead* (8–12). 1992, Delacorte $15.00 (978-0-385-30801-4). When Reece saves an Indian boy from lynching by U.S. marshals, lawmen claim that Reece murdered one of the marshals and he must clear himself. (Rev: BL 9/1/92; SLJ 9/92)

6166 Reger, Rob, and Jessica Gruner. *The Lost Days* (7–10). Illus. by author. Series: Emily the Strange. 2009, HarperCollins $16.99 (978-006145229-1); LB $17.89 (978-006145230-7). Emily (first featured in graphic-novel form) has amnesia and uses her diary to sort out who she is. Lexile 870L (Rev: BL 5/1/09; SLJ 6/1/09)

6167 Reger, Rob, and Jessica Gruner. *Stranger and Stranger* (7–10). Illus. by author and Buzz Parker. Series: Emily the Strange. 2010, HarperTeen $16.99 (978-0-06-145232-1); LB $17.89 (978-0-06-145233-8). In a series of diary entries with manga-style cartoons, this quirky story follows Emily through a confusing cloning experience full of dark humor; a sequel to 2009's *The Lost Days*. Lexile 900L (Rev: BL 1/1–15/10; SLJ 1/10; VOYA 8/10)

6168 Reid, Kimberly. *Creeping with the Enemy* (8–12). Series: Langdon Prep. 2012, Kensington paper $9.95 (978-07582674-1-2). Chanti, 15, uses sleuthing skills she inherited from her undercover cop mom to investigate the disappearance of her friend Bethanie. (Rev: BL 5/1/12; SLJ 6/12)

6169 Reiss, Kathryn. *A Bundle of Trouble* (4–7). Illus. by Sergio Giovine. 2011, American Girl $10.95 (978-159369753-2); paper $6.95 (978-15936975-4-9). In early 20th-century New York during a rash of kidnappings, Rebecca becomes suspicious of some of the people she meets in her neighborhood. (Rev: BL 5/1/11)

6170 Renn, Diana. *Tokyo Heist* (7–10). 2012, Viking $17.99 (978-067001332-6). Aspiring manga artist Violet, 16, travels to Japan with her father to search for some missing Van Goghs. (Rev: BL 5/1/12; LMC 11–12/12; SLJ 6/12; VOYA 8/12)

6171 Richards, Justin. *The Death Collector* (6–9). 2006, Bloomsbury $16.95 (978-1-58234-721-9). In this creepy, page-turner mystery set in Victorian Britain, three teenagers try to prevent a monster-creating villain from taking over the world. (Rev: BL 5/15/06; LMC 10/06; SLJ 7/06)

6172 Richardson, Nigel. *The Wrong Hands* (8–11). 2006, Knopf $15.95 (978-0-375-83459-2). Fourteen-year-old Graham has large, strange hands and an even bigger secret — with these hands, he can fly; when he rescues a baby and is considered a hero, this ability becomes harder for the British boy to conceal. ∩ (Rev: BL 8/06; SLJ 10/06)

6173 Ripslinger, Jon. *Last Kiss* (8–12). 2007, Flux paper $9.95 (978-0-7387-1072-3). Billy, a simple farm boy, is the prime suspect when his girlfriend — from a wealthy and prominent family — is found murdered. (Rev: BL 11/1/07; SLJ 2/08)

6174 Roberts, Willo Davis. *Baby-Sitting Is a Dangerous Job* (5–7). 1987, Fawcett paper $6.50 (978-0-449-70177-5). Darcy tries to cope with three bratty children, but a kidnapping puts her and her charges in the hands of three dangerous men. (Rev: BCCB 3/85; BL 5/1/85; SLJ 5/85)

6175 Roberts, Willo Davis. *The One Left Behind* (4–7). 2006, Simon & Schuster $16.95 (978-0-689-85075-2). Mandy, an 11-year-old mourning her dead twin sister, is accidentally left home alone for the weekend and pluckily investigates when there's a break-in downstairs. (Rev: BL 4/1/06; SLJ 5/06)

6176 Roberts, Willo Davis. *Undercurrents* (7–10). 2002, Simon & Schuster $16.00 (978-0-689-81671-0). Fourteen-year-old Nikki is troubled when her father remarries only months after her mother's death and his new wife seems to be hiding facts about her unhappy past. (Rev: BCCB 4/02; BL 2/15/02; HBG 10/02; SLJ 2/02; VOYA 2/02)

6177 Roberts, Willo Davis. *The View from the Cherry Tree* (7–9). 1994, Simon & Schuster paper $4.99 (978-0-689-71784-0). A boy who witnesses a murder becomes targeted as the next victim.

6178 Rodman, Sean. *Dead Run* (6–9). Series: Orca Soundings. 2012, Orca LB $16.95 (978-145980245-2); paper $9.95 (9781459802445). Aspiring bicycle road racer Sam finds himself working as a courier delivering mysterious packages in this fast-paced novel suitable for reluctant readers. ℮ Lexile HL530L (Rev: BL 11/1/12; LMC 5–6/13; SLJ 4/13)

6179 Roecker, Lisa, and Laura Roecker. *The Lies That Bind* (7–10). Series: The Liar Society. 2012, Sourcebooks paper $9.99 (978-14022702-4-6). Despite her dislike of secret societies, Kate becomes involved with the Sisterhood as part of her effort to solve the mystery of her friend Grace's death. ℮ Lexile 840L (Rev: BL 12/15/12)

6180 Rose, Malcolm. *Blood Brother* (4–7). Series: Traces. 2008, Kingfisher paper $5.95 (978-0-7534-6170-9). Luke and his robot sidekick are investigating 26 mysterious deaths at York Hospital; could Luke's doctor father, the principal investigator on a clinical trial at the hospital, somehow be responsible? (Rev: BL 11/15/07)

6181 Rose, Malcolm. *Final Lap* (8–12). 2007, Kingfisher paper $5.95 (978-0-7534-6005-4). Luke and his robot use their forensic skills in investigating sabotage at the Youth International Games. (Rev: SLJ 3/07)

6182 Rose, Malcolm. *Lost Bullet* (6–9). Series: Traces. 2005, Kingfisher paper $5.95 (978-0-7534-5830-3). In a futuristic London, forensic investigator Luke Harding and his robotic sidekick try to find out who's responsible for the murder of a doctor and find themselves facing a cult. (Rev: BL 6/1–15/05; SLJ 7/05)

6183 Ross, Jeff. *Dawn Patrol* (5–12). Series: Orca Sports. 2012, Orca paper $9.95 (978-1-4598-0062-5). Luca and Esme travel to Panama in search of their missing friend Kevin in this story for reluctant readers that features surfing and mystery. ℮ Lexile HL530L (Rev: LMC 11–12/12; SLJ 6/12)

6184 Runholt, Susan. *Adventure at Simba Hill* (5–8). 2011, Viking $16.99 (978-0-670-01201-5). Fourteen-year-old friends Kari and Lucas accompany Kari's archaeologist uncle to Kenya, where they solve a mystery involving disappearing artifacts. ℮ Lexile 870L (Rev: BL 5/1/11; SLJ 7/11)

6185 Runholt, Susan. *The Mystery of the Third Lucretia* (7–10). 2008, Viking $16.99 (978-0-670-06252-2). Two young artists are caught up in an international mystery when they pursue a painter who has forged a Rembrandt work; set in Minneapolis, London, and Amsterdam, this mystery combines art history with intrigue. (Rev: BL 5/1/08; SLJ 3/08)

6186 Runholt, Susan. *Rescuing Seneca Crane* (5–8). 2009, Viking $16.99 (978-0-670-06291-1). While in

Edinburgh with Kari's mother, 14-year-old friends Kari and Lucas help to save a kidnapped piano prodigy. ∩ (Rev: BLO 4/15/09; SLJ 8/09; VOYA 12/09)

6187 Scheier, Leah. *Secret Letters* (7–11). 2012, Disney/Hyperion $16.99 (978-142312405-4). Dora, 16, goes to London to seek the help of Sherlock Holmes, who may be her biological father, in recovering her cousin's stolen letters; she arrives in London to find that Holmes has died, but fortunately there is a handsome young detective who is willing to help. **e** Lexile 880L (Rev: BL 5/1/12; LMC 10/12; SLJ 6/12; VOYA 6/12)

6188 Schmidt, Gary D. *First Boy* (7–10). 2005, Henry Holt $16.95 (978-0-8050-7859-6). With the help of kind neighbors, 14-year-old Cooper hopes to be able to live alone on his grandparents' farm, but questions about his missing parents seem linked to politics and the presidential elections. (Rev: BCCB 2/06; BL 9/15/05; HB 9–10/05; SLJ 10/05; VOYA 4/06)

6189 Schreiber, Joe. *Au Revoir, Crazy European Chick* (8–10). 2011, Houghton Mifflin $16.99 (978-0-547-57738-8). Perry's ho-hum night at the prom takes a turn when his frumpy exchange-student date turns out to be an undercover international assassin. ∩ **e** Lexile 800L (Rev: BL 10/15/11*; HB 11–12/11; SLJ 8/11; VOYA 10/11)

6190 Schreiber, Joe. *Perry's Killer Playlist* (8–10). 2012, Houghton Mifflin $16.99 (978-0-547-60117-5). Touring Italy with his rock band, 18-year-old Perry finds himself embroiled in dangerous adventures in this action-packed sequel to *Au Revoir, Crazy European Chick* (2011). ∩ **e** Lexile 850L (Rev: BLO 12/15/12; LMC 1–2/13; SLJ 12/12; VOYA 8/12)

6191 Scrimger, Richard. *From Charlie's Point of View* (7–10). 2005, Dutton $10.99 (978-0-525-47374-9). Fourteen-year-old Charlie is blind, but best friend Bernadette acts as his eyes, and together they set out to prove that Charlie's dad had nothing to do with a series of neighborhood ATM thefts. (Rev: BCCB 9/05; BL 5/1/05; SLJ 8/05)

6192 Sedgwick, Marcus. *Revolver* (7–10). 2010, Roaring Brook $16.99 (978-1-59643-592-6). In the early 20th century above the Arctic Circle, young Sig's father has been found frozen to death; Sig's sister and stepmother go for help and Sig is alone when a stranger bearing a Colt revolver arrives demanding gold he is owed. Printz Honor 2011; YALSA Top Ten Best Fiction for Young Adults 2011. ∩ **e** Lexile 890L (Rev: BL 5/1/10; HB 3–4/10; LMC 5–6/10; SLJ 4/10)

6193 Selfors, Suzanne. *Smells Like Treasure* (4–7). 2011, Little, Brown $15.99 (978-0-316-04399-1). Homer Winslow Pudding, 12, faces a challenger for his uncle's place in the society of Legends, Objects, Secrets, and Treasures (LOST) and hopes his basset hound, Dog, will help him prevail. A sequel to *Smells Like Dog* (2010). (Rev: BL 5/1/11; SLJ 9/1/11*)

6194 Selzer, Adam. *I Put a Spell on You: From the Files of Chrissie Woodward, Spelling Bee Detective* (5–7). 2008, Delacorte $15.99 (978-0-385-73504-9). Ambitious adults may be planning to fix the spelling bee at the Gordon Liddy Community School, and sleuth Chrissie Woodward is determined to find out what's going on. (Rev: BCCB 9/08; HB 9/08; SLJ 11/08)

6195 Selznick, Brian. *The Invention of Hugo Cabret* (4–9). Illus. by author. 2007, Scholastic $22.99 (978-0-439-81378-5). In 1930s Paris a young apprentice clock keeper, an orphan who struggles to make his way in life, finds himself drawn into a complex mystery that threatens the anonymity he treasures; part graphic novel, part flip book, the design is as compelling as the story. Caldecott Medal 2008; ALA Notable Books 2008. (Rev: BL 1/1–15/07; SLJ 3/07*)

6196 Shaw, Diana. *Lessons in Fear* (6–9). 1987, Little, Brown $12.95 (978-0-316-78341-5). An unpopular teacher has a series of mysterious accidents and one of her students, Carter Colborn, decides she must investigate them. (Rev: BL 4/15/88; SLJ 10/87)

6197 Shearer, Alex. *Canned* (6–9). 2008, Scholastic $16.99 (978-0-439-90309-7). Fergal finds a finger in an old can, and Charlotte finds a ring in another — a grisly opening to a mystery story full of black humor. (Rev: BL 2/15/08; SLJ 2/08)

6198 Sherry, Maureen. *Walls Within Walls* (4–7). Illus. by Adam Stower. 2010, HarperCollins $16.99 (978-0-06-176700-5). When three young siblings move into a luxurious Manhattan apartment, they discover that their new home is full of clues that may reveal a treasure. **e** Lexile 770L (Rev: BL 9/15/10; LMC 3–4/11; SLJ 10/1/10)

6199 Shoemaker, Tim. *Code of Silence: Living a Lie Comes with a Price* (7–10). 2012, Zonderkidz $14.99 (978-031072653-1). Three 13-year-old witnesses to a violent crime must choose between remaining silent and coming forward to clear an innocent man. **e** (Rev: BL 5/1/12*; SLJ 8/12)

6200 Simmons, Michael. *Finding Lubchenko* (7–10). 2005, Penguin paper $16.99 (978-1-59514-021-0). Evan Macalister, a 16-year-old slacker, steals high-value computer equipment from his father's business and sells it for spending cash, but he faces a moral dilemma when he discovers evidence that could clear his father of murder charges on a laptop he's stolen; a funny, offbeat novel. (Rev: BCCB 7–8/05; SLJ 6/05; VOYA 12/04)

6201 Simmons, Michael. *The Rise of Lubchenko* (8–11). 2006, Penguin $16.99 (978-1-59514-061-6). in this sequel to *Finding Lubchenko* (2005), wealthy Evan Macalister is informed that his father's business partner is planning to smuggle a live smallpox virus into Europe. (Rev: BL 9/1/06; SLJ 9/06)

6202 Singleton, Linda Joy. *Buried* (8–12). Series: Goth Girl Mysteries. 2012, Flux paper $9.95 (978-0-7387-1958-0). Thorn, a Goth high school student who has the ability to "find" lost objects, is newly living in Nevada when she becomes embroiled in a mystery involving a dead child; this paranormal mystery is a quick read. ℮ (Rev: SLJ 5/1/12; VOYA 2/12)

6203 Skurzynski, Gloria, and Alane Ferguson. *Buried Alive* (4–7). Series: Mysteries in Our National Parks. 2003, National Geographic $15.95 (978-0-7922-6966-3). A hit man and an avalanche are only two of the challenges Jack and Ashley face while on vacation with their parents in Denali National Park. (Rev: HBG 10/03; SLJ 12/03)

6204 Skurzynski, Gloria, and Alane Ferguson. *Deadly Waters* (4–7). Series: Mysteries in Our National Parks. 1999, National Geographic $15.95 (978-0-7922-7037-9). The Landon kids — Jack, Ashley, and foster brother, Bridger — travel to the Florida Everglades where their parents are investigating the mysterious deaths of some manatees. (Rev: BL 10/15/99; HBG 3/00; SLJ 10/99)

6205 Skurzynski, Gloria, and Alane Ferguson. *The Hunted* (5–8). Series: Mysteries in Our National Parks. 2000, National Geographic $15.95 (978-0-7922-7053-9). The Landon family sets out to discover why young grizzly bears are disappearing from Glacier National Park. (Rev: BL 6/1–15/00; HBG 10/00; SLJ 8/00)

6206 Skurzynski, Gloria, and Alane Ferguson. *Wolf Stalker* (5–8). Series: Mysteries in Our National Parks. 1997, National Geographic $15.00 (978-0-7922-7034-8). Three youngsters solve the mystery of who is killing the wolves of Yellowstone Park. (Rev: HBG 3/98; SLJ 1/98)

6207 Smith, Roland. *I, Q* (5–8). Series: I, Q. 2008, Sleeping Bear paper $8.95 (978-15853632-5-4). Q and Angela's musician parents have recently married, sentencing the two teens to a yearlong band tour enlivened by mysterious stalkers who may be related to Angela's dead mother, who worked for the Secret Service. Lexile HL660L (Rev: BL 10/15/08; SLJ 12/08)

6208 Smith, Roland. *Jack's Run* (5–8). 2005, Hyperion $15.99 (978-0-7868-5592-6). Last seen adapting to being in the witness protection program in *Zach's Lie* (2001), Jack and Joanne are now in danger after Joanne has blown their cover in this fast-paced, suspenseful story. (Rev: BL 8/05; SLJ 12/05; VOYA 10/05)

6209 Snicket, Lemony. *Who Could That Be at This Hour?* (4–7). Illus. by Seth. Series: All the Wrong Questions. 2012, Little, Brown $15.99 (978-0-316-12308-2). Thirteen-year-old Lemony Snicket, an apprentice to S. Theodora Markson, helps investigate the theft of a statue in this fast-paced "autobiographical" romp. ☊ ℮ Lexile 870L (Rev: BL 9/15/12; SLJ 12/12*)

6210 Sniegoski, Tom. *Sleeper Code* (8–12). Series: Sleeper Conspiracy. 2006, Penguin paper $6.99 (978-1-

59514-052-4). In this suspenseful adventure, Tom discovers that his narcolepsy is the result of government intervention and realizes he cannot trust anyone. (Rev: SLJ 8/06)

6211 Sorrells, Walter. *Club Dread* (8–11). 2006, Dutton paper $10.99 (978-0-525-47618-4). In this thrilling, action-packed sequel to *Fake I.D.* (2004), 16-year-old Chass has formed a band in San Francisco but witnesses a murder and becomes drawn into the investigation. (Rev: BL 1/1–15/06; SLJ 3/06)

6212 Sorrells, Walter. *Fake I.D.* (8–11). 2005, Dutton $12.99 (978-0-525-47514-9). On the run with her mother since she was a baby, 16-year-old Chastity Pureheart has only six days to find out what happened to her mother or face placement in foster care. (Rev: BL 5/1/05*; SLJ 6/05)

6213 Sorrells, Walter. *First Shot* (7–12). 2007, Dutton $16.99 (978-0-525-47801-0). In this taut teen thriller set at a New England boarding school, a young man named David Crandall is beset with problems: his own feelings of inadequacy; his mother's murder, his father's emotional and physical abuse, and above all the suspicion that his father is the murderer. (Rev: BL 9/15/07; SLJ 3/08)

6214 Sorrells, Walter. *The Silent Room* (8–11). 2006, Dutton $16.99 (978-0-525-47697-9). Oz is wrongly sent to an institution for wayward boys in a remote Florida swamp and hatches a desperate plot to escape after learning that he and his roommates are in danger. (Rev: BL 5/1/06; SLJ 7/06)

6215 Sorrells, Walter. *Whiteout* (7–12). Series: Hunted. 2009, Dutton $15.99 (978-0-525-42141-2). Sixteen-year-old Chass is determined to work out who's stalking herself and her mother rather than relocate yet again in this third installment in the series. ℮ Lexile HL530L (Rev: BLO 8/20/09; SLJ 1/10; VOYA 10/09)

6216 Spirn, Michele. *The Bridges in London: Going to London* (5–7). Series: Going To. 2000, Four Corners paper $7.95 (978-1-893577-00-8). When two sisters fly to London with their parents, they become involved in a mystery when they find a suitcase full of knives. (Rev: SLJ 3/00)

6217 Spizman, Robyn Freedman, and Mark Johnston. *The Secret Agents Strike Back* (5–8). 2007, Simon & Schuster $16.99 (978-1-4169-0086-3). Information about a possible cure for cancer is stolen and Kyle and his friends chase clues all over New York City in this entertaining mystery. (Rev: SLJ 6/07)

6218 Spradlin, Michael P. *To Hawaii, with Love* (7–10). Series: Spy Goddess. 2006, HarperCollins $15.99 (978-0-06-059410-7). This latest action-filled thriller has 15-year-old Rachel racing to recover an ancient Hawaiian artifact before it is seized by an evil foe. (Rev: BL 5/1/06)

355

6219 Springer, Nancy. *The Case of the Bizarre Bouquets* (6–9). Series: Enola Holmes. 2008, Philomel $14.99 (978-0-399-24518-3). Enola Holmes uses her knowledge of the Victorian language of flowers to solve the case of the missing Dr. Watson. (Rev: BL 2/1/08; SLJ 1/08)

6220 Springer, Nancy. *The Case of the Cryptic Crinoline* (5–8). Series: Enola Holmes Mystery. 2009, Philomel $14.99 (978-0-399-24781-1). Florence Nightingale may be able to help Sherlock's younger sister Enola Holmes as she investigates the disappearance of her landlady. (Rev: BLO 4/23/09; SLJ 7/09)

6221 Springer, Nancy. *The Case of the Left-Handed Lady* (6–9). Series: Enola Holmes. 2007, Philomel $12.99 (978-0-399-24517-6). Enola Holmes, Sherlock's younger sister, disguises herself to find a missing person in this story set in 19th-century London. (Rev: BL 3/15/07; SLJ 3/07)

6222 Springer, Nancy. *The Case of the Missing Marquess: An Enola Holmes Mystery* (5–8). Series: Enola Holmes. 2006, Philomel paper $10.99 (978-0-399-24304-2). Enola Holmes, the much younger sister of Sherlock and Mycroft, embarks on a search for her mother, who disappears on Enola's 14th birthday. (Rev: BCCB 2/06; BL 12/1/05*; HBG 10/06; SLJ 2/06*)

6223 Springer, Nancy. *The Case of the Peculiar Pink Fan* (6–9). Series: Enola Holmes Mystery. 2008, Philomel $14.99 (978-039924780-4). Young Enola seeks to save her friend from an arranged marriage — evading detection by her older brother Sherlock, who's concerned about her lack of etiquette all the while. **e** Lexile 1100L (Rev: BL 10/15/08; SLJ 11/1/08)

6224 Springer, Nancy. *My Sister's Stalker* (5–8). 2012, Holiday House $16.95 (978-082342358-3). Rig, 16, discovers his college-age sister is being stalked and pursues him with the help of his father in this taut novel that will appeal to reluctant readers. ∩ Lexile 770L (Rev: BL 5/1/12; SLJ 5/1/12)

6225 Standiford, Natalie. *The Secret Tree* (4–7). 2012, Scholastic $16.99 (978-0-545-33479-2). Minty discovers a tree with a hole in its trunk where people have placed notes about their aspirations and secrets; she and her new friend Raymond start spying on the neighbors to match them with the notes. **e** Lexile 510L (Rev: BL 5/1/12; LMC 8–9/12; SLJ 7/12)

6226 Stanley, Diane. *The Mysterious Case of the Allbright Academy* (4–7). 2008, HarperCollins $15.99 (978-0-06-085817-9). What's going on at Allbright Academy? Frannie suspects that her "perfect" classmates are being brainwashed and placed into positions of authority in the U.S. government, and she sets out to foil the plot. (Rev: BL 11/15/07; SLJ 3/08)

6227 Steiner, Barbara. *Dreamstalker* (8–12). 1992, Avon paper $3.50 (978-0-380-76611-6). A girl wonders if she's psychic when her terrifying nightmares start coming true. (Rev: BL 3/15/92)

6228 Steiner, Barbara. *Spring Break* (7–10). 1996, Scholastic paper $3.99 (978-0-590-54419-1). Five high schoolers rent a haunted house where they contend with odd appearances and disappearances, arson, and a skeleton. (Rev: SLJ 12/96)

6229 Stengel, Joyce A. *Mystery of the Island Jewels* (5–8). 2002, Simon & Schuster paper $4.99 (978-0-689-85049-3). On a cruise to Martinique with her father and new stepfamily, 14-year-old Cassie and new friend Charles uncover a mystery. (Rev: SLJ 6/02)

6230 Sternberg, Libby. *Finding the Forger* (6–9). 2004, Bancroft $19.95 (978-1-890862-32-9); paper $14.95 (978-1-890862-37-4). Bianca Balducci, 15-year-old wannabe detective, gets caught up in the investigation of an art forgery at the local museum while at the same time worrying in humorous first-person narrative about friends, boyfriends, and family. (Rev: BL 2/1/05; SLJ 4/05; VOYA 8/05)

6231 Sternberg, Libby. *Uncovering Sadie's Secrets: A Bianca Balducci Mystery* (6–9). Series: Bianca Balducci Mystery. 2003, Bancroft $16.95 (978-1-890862-23-7). Bianca Balducci is a sophomore in high school with all of the everyday teen anxieties as well as an interest in the mysterious circumstances surrounding her new friend, Sadie. (Rev: BL 1/1–15/03; SLJ 3/03; VOYA 4/03)

6232 Stine, R. L. *The Wrong Number* (5–9). 1990, Pocket paper $4.99 (978-0-671-69411-1). While making a crank telephone call, a teenager hears a murder being committed. (Rev: SLJ 6/90)

6233 Strasser, Todd. *Wish You Were Dead* (8–12). 2009, Egmont $16.99 (978-1-60684-007-8); LB $19.99 (978-1-60684-049-8). In this technology-filled thriller, Madison seeks the identity of a local killer — and her own cyberstalker — by unraveling clues in blog posts and Facebook conversations. ∩ **e** Lexile HL650L (Rev: BL 10/1/09; LMC 11–12/09; SLJ 10/09; VOYA 12/09)

6234 Sturman, Jennifer. *And Then Everything Unraveled* (7–10). 2009, Scholastic $16.99 (978-054508722-3). Delia Truesdale investigates her mother's disappearance at the same time as she tries to adapt to her new life in Manhattan with two very different aunts. **e** (Rev: BL 7/09; SLJ 8/09)

6235 Sukach, Jim. *Clever Quicksolve Whodunit Puzzles* (4–7). Illus. by Lucy Corvino. Series: Mini-Mysteries for You to Solve. 1999, Sterling $14.95 (978-0-8069-6569-7). Thirty-five mini-mysteries are presented with answers appended. (Rev: SLJ 1/00)

6236 Suma, Nova Ren. *Dani Noir* (5–8). 2009, Simon & Schuster $15.99 (978-1-4169-7564-9). Thirteen-year-old Dani's main enjoyment is watching noir films at the local art theater, and these fuel her imagination to the point that she suspects an older teen, Jackson, of two-timing his girlfriend. Her resulting investigation teachers her about life and herself. (Rev: BL 11/1/09; LMC 11–12/09; SLJ 12/09)

6237 Sylvester, Kevin. *Neil Flambé and the Marco Polo Murders* (4–8). Illus. by author. 2012, Simon & Schuster $12.99 (978-144244604-5). Fourteen-year-old Neil Flambé's ultrasensitive nose serves him well in the kitchen but also while investigating crimes, in this case the murders of chefs that are somehow linked to exotic spices; first published in Canada in 2010. (Rev: BL 4/15/12; LMC 10/12; SLJ 4/10)

6238 Taylor, Cora. *Murder in Mexico* (4–7). Series: The Spy Who Wasn't There. 2007, Coteau paper $7.95 (978-1-55050-353-1). In this second, fast-paced installment in the mystery series, twins Jennifer and Maggie are visiting ruins in the Yucatan when Jennifer must use her ability to become invisible to solve a crime. (Rev: SLJ 4/07)

6239 Taylor, G. P. *Mariah Mundi: The Midas Box* (6–9). Series: Mariah Mundi. 2008, Putnam $17.99 (978-0-399-24347-9). In Victorian England, Mariah finds himself working at a creepy hotel where something very odd is going on. (Rev: BL 5/1/08; SLJ 8/08)

6240 Thesman, Jean. *Rachel Chance* (6–9). 1990, Houghton Mifflin $16.00 (978-0-395-50934-0). Rachel's young brother has been kidnapped, but no one seems to be taking any action. (Rev: BL 5/1/90; SLJ 4/90)

6241 Thurlo, David, and Aimée Thurlo. *The Spirit Line* (6–10). 2004, Viking $16.99 (978-0-670-03645-5). Fifteen-year-old Crystal Manyfeathers solves a theft and in so doing begins to question her Navajo beliefs. (Rev: BL 5/1/04; SLJ 6/04; VOYA 6/04)

6242 Timberlake, Amy. *One Came Home* (6–9). 2013, Knopf $16.99 (978-037586925-9); LB $19.99 (978-037596925-6). In 1871 incredibly capable 13-year-old Georgia sets out to investigate the presumed death of her sister Agatha. ℮ Lexile 690L (Rev: BL 12/15/12; HB 1–2/13; LMC 5–6/13; SLJ 1/13*; VOYA 12/12)

6243 Trembath, Don. *Emville Confidential* (5–8). 2007, Orca paper $8.95 (978-1-55143-671-5). A tongue-in-cheek hard-boiled detective novel featuring 7th-graders Baron, Myles, and Rebecca. (Rev: BL 11/1/07; SLJ 2/08)

6244 Trout, Richard E. *Czar of Alaska: The Cross of Charlemagne* (5–8). Series: MacGregor Family Adventure. 2005, Pelican $15.95 (978-1-58980-328-2). In volume four of the series, the five MacGregors travel to Alaska to assess the environmental impact of drilling for oil and become entangled with ecoterrorists and priests seeking an ancient cross. (Rev: SLJ 12/05)

6245 Twain, Mark. *The Stolen White Elephant* (4–8). 1882, Ayer $19.95 (978-0-8369-3486-1). The tale of the elephant's guardian who naively is impressed by a corrupt police detective. (Rev: BL 5/1/88; SLJ 2/88)

6246 Updale, Eleanor. *Montmorency and the Assassins* (7–10). 2006, Scholastic $16.99 (978-0-439-68343-2). Montmorency and Lord George Fox-Selwyn, plus some teen helpers, investigate bomb-planting anarchists in this Victorian mystery that ranges from London to Florence to New Jersey. (Rev: BL 3/15/06; SLJ 5/06; VOYA 2/06)

6247 Updale, Eleanor. *Montmorency on the Rocks: Doctor, Aristocrat, Murderer?* (6–9). 2005, Scholastic $16.95 (978-0-439-60676-9). Montmorency, recovering from opium addiction, and sidekicks Lord George Fox-Selwyn and Dr. Fawcett must unravel a London bomb plot and mysterious deaths in Scotland. (Rev: BL 5/15/05; SLJ 4/05)

6248 Updale, Eleanor. *Montmorency's Revenge* (7–10). Series: Montmorency. 2007, Scholastic $16.99 (978-0-439-81373-0). Lord George Fox-Selwyn has been murdered, and this leads to the pursuit of revenge by his powerful group of friends in this fourth installment in the action-packed series. (Rev: BCCB 5/07; BL 7/07; HB 7–8/07; SLJ 8/07)

6249 Van Draanen, Wendelin. *Sammy Keyes and the Art of Deception* (5–8). Series: Sammy Keyes. 2003, Knopf $15.95 (978-0-375-81176-0). Sammy (with some help from Grams) solves a mystery involving an art thief. (Rev: BL 2/1/03; HBG 10/03; SLJ 3/03; VOYA 8/03)

6250 Van Draanen, Wendelin. *Sammy Keyes and the Cold Hard Cash* (6–9). 2008, Knopf $15.99 (978-037583526-1); LB $18.99 (978-037593526-8). Sneaking up the fire escape in her Gram's seniors-only apartment complex, Sammy startles an elderly man — who promptly suffers a heart attack — and gets tied up in a web of deceit, secrecy, and moral quandary. ⌒ ℮ Lexile 740L (Rev: BL 10/1/08*; SLJ 12/08)

6251 Van Draanen, Wendelin. *Sammy Keyes and the Dead Giveaway* (5–8). 2005, Knopf LB $17.99 (978-0-375-92350-0). Seventh-grade sleuth Sammy tackles personal problems — should she make a confession that would exonerate her archenemy? — and community ones as she investigates abuse of eminent domain. (Rev: BL 9/1/05; SLJ 11/05)

6252 Van Draanen, Wendelin. *Sammy Keyes and the Night of Skulls* (5–8). 2011, Knopf $15.99 (978-037586108-6); LB $18.99 (978-037596108-3). Junior high sleuth Sammy and her friends find themselves in the midst of a mystery in a graveyard on Halloween night. (Rev: BL 10/1/11)

6253 Van Draanen, Wendelin. *Sammy Keyes and the Power of Justice Jack* (5–8). 2012, Knopf $16.99 (978-037587052-1); LB $19.99 (978-037597052-8). Sammy contends with a growing tangle of complications: a new superhero wannabe in town, her friend Billy angling to be the guy's sidekick, a missing woman, and a City Hall statue that has disappeared. ℮ (Rev: BL 5/1/12)

6254 Van Draanen, Wendelin. *Sammy Keyes and the Wedding Crasher* (5–8). 2010, Knopf $16.99 (978-037586107-9); LB $19.99 (978-037596107-6). Starting 8th grade Sammy is shocked to find herself suspected of making threats against her history teacher; she also must cope with her nemesis Heather and her duties as a reluctant bridesmaid. ⌒ ℮ Lexile 750L (Rev: BL 12/15/10; VOYA 2/11)

6255 Van Draanen, Wendelin. *Sammy Keyes and the Wild Things* (6–9). Series: Sammy Keyes. 2007, Knopf $18.99 (978-0-375-93525-1). While on a Girl Scout camping trip, Sammy does some detective work to help save an endangered condor. (Rev: BL 5/1/07; SLJ 6/07)

6256 Varrato, Tony. *Fakie* (7–10). 2008, Lobster paper $7.95 (978-1-897073-79-7). Danny and his mother, in the Witness Protection Program since Danny's father's murder, stay one step ahead of the bad guys in this suspenseful story. (Rev: BL 4/1/08)

6257 Voigt, Cynthia. *The Vandemark Mummy* (6–9). 1991, Atheneum $18.95 (978-0-689-31476-6). This story involves a break-in at a museum of Egyptian antiquities and two teenage siblings who attempt to solve the mystery. (Rev: BL 9/1/91; SLJ 9/91)

6258 Vrettos, Adrienne Maria. *Sight* (8–10). 2007, Simon & Schuster $16.99 (978-1-4169-0657-5). Dylan, 16, is able to picture the details of the murders that took place in her town years before; when the killing begins again she must try to use her talent to bring the murderer to justice before the town splits apart. (Rev: BL 1/1–15/08; SLJ 3/08)

6259 Wade, Rebecca. *The Whispering House* (5–8). 2012, HarperCollins $16.99 (978-006077497-4). When 14-year-old Hannah's family moves into Cowleigh Lodge, she discovers that a young girl was probably murdered there in 1877; a sequel to *The Theft and the Miracle* (2007). ℮ Lexile 830L (Rev: BL 5/1/12; SLJ 6/12)

6260 Wahl, Mats. *The Invisible* (8–11). Trans. by Katarina E. Tucker. 2007, Farrar $17.00 (978-0-374-33609-7). A teenage Swedish boy named Hilmer is thought to be missing but has merely become invisible. Could neo-Nazis be responsible? (Rev: BCCB 4/07; BL 3/15/07; SLJ 4/07)

6261 Walden, Mark. *Dreadnought* (5–8). Series: H.I.V.E. 2011, Simon & Schuster $16.99 (978-144242186-8). When an especially villainous classmate hijacks the villain school's airborne defense platform, Otto and his friends come to the rescue. ℮ Lexile 1000L (Rev: BL 4/15/11)

6262 Walden, Mark. *Escape Velocity* (5–8). Series: H.I.V.E. 2011, Simon & Schuster $16.99 (978-144242185-1). Otto, who is still learning to use his newfound abilities, must break into MI6 in order to rescue Dr. Nero from H.O.P.E. — the Hostile Opera-tive Prosecution Executive. Also use *Rogue* (2011). ℮ Lexile 990L (Rev: BL 6/1/11)

6263 Walden, Mark. *H.I.V.E: The Higher Institute of Villainous Education* (5–8). Series: H.I.V.E. 2007, Simon & Schuster $15.99 (978-1-4169-3571-1). Kidnapped along with three of his friends and enrolled in an academy that grooms students in the villainous arts, 13-year-old brilliant orphan Otto maps a plan to escape, a feat never before accomplished. (Rev: BL 4/1/07; SLJ 6/07)

6264 Walden, Mark. *The Overlord Protocol* (5–8). Series: H.I.V.E. 2008, Simon & Schuster $15.99 (978-1-4169-6016-4). Wing and Otto, students at the Higher Institute of Villainous Education (H.I.V.E.), travel to Japan for Wing's father's funeral and realize they have fallen into an evil trap. (Rev: BL 3/1/08)

6265 Wasserman, Robin. *The Book of Blood and Shadow* (8–12). 2012, Knopf $17.99 (978-037586876-4); LB $20.99 (978-037596876-1). High school senior Nora's boyfriend is implicated in the murder of her best friend in this drama; a subplot involving a search for a mysterious divine communication device adds intrigue to this multilayered novel. ⌒ ℮ Lexile 900L (Rev: BL 2/1/12; HB 3–4/12; LMC 5–6/12; SLJ 2/12)

6266 Watson, Geoff. *Edison's Gold* (4–7). 2010, Egmont $15.99 (978-160684094-8). Tom Edison IV, the great-great-grandson of the esteemed inventor, hatches a plan to restore his family's fortune by creating gold in this action-filled mystery involving a secret society and a descendant of Nikola Tesla. Lexile 880L (Rev: BL 11/1/10; LMC 1–2/11; SLJ 1/1/11)

6267 Weir, Joan. *The Mysterious Visitor* (5–7). Series: Lion and Bobbi. 2002, Raincoast paper $6.99 (978-1-55192-404-5). Two Canadian youngsters, Lion and sister Bobbi, try to solve the mystery of strange events occurring on a friend's land. (Rev: BL 5/1/02)

6268 Weltman, June. *Mystery of the Missing Candlestick* (5–8). 2004, Mayhaven $23.95 (978-1-878044-98-3). Miranda, 17, and her friends Leila and Rebecca join forces to solve the mystery of a valuable antique candlestick that has been stolen from Rebecca's grandfather. (Rev: BL 5/1/04)

6269 Werlin, Nancy. *Black Mirror* (7–12). 2001, Dial $16.99 (978-0-8037-2605-5). Lonely Frances, 16, struggles with her Jewish-Japanese heritage and with her guilt and puzzlement over her brother's suicide in this intriguing and suspenseful novel set in a private boarding school. (Rev: BCCB 10/01; BL 9/15/01; HB 9–10/01; HBG 3/02; SLJ 9/01*; VOYA 10/01)

6270 Westerfeld, Scott. *So Yesterday* (7–12). 2004, Penguin $16.99 (978-1-59514-000-5). Two teenagers who help big companies identify coming trends in the consumer marketplace find themselves caught up in a mystery when their boss disappears. (Rev: BL 9/15/04; SLJ 10/04; VOYA 10/04)

358

6271 White, Ruth. *The Search for Belle Prater* (4–7). 2005, Farrar $16.00 (978-0-374-30853-7). In this sequel to *Belle Prater's Boy*, 13-year-old Woodrow and his cousin Gypsy continue to search for Woodrow's missing mother against the backdrop of mid-1950s segregation. (Rev: BL 2/15/05*; SLJ 4/05)

6272 Whitehouse, Howard. *The Faceless Fiend: Being the Tale of a Criminal Mastermind, His Masked Minions and a Princess with a Butter Knife, Involving Explosives and a Certain Amount of Pushing and Shoving* (4–7). Illus. by Bill Slavin. 2007, Kids Can $16.95 (978-1-55453-130-1); paper $7.95 (978-1-55453-180-6). In this sequel to *The Strictest School in the World* (2006), Emmaline and her friend Princess Purnah escape from St. Grimelda's School for Young Ladies and — with a motley crew of supporters and many comical mishaps along the way — manage to foil a kidnapping. (Rev: LMC 1/08; SLJ 11/07)

6273 Whyman, Matt. *Goldstrike* (6–9). 2010, Simon & Schuster $16.99 (978-1-4169-9510-4). Hacker Carl Hobbes, 18, is pursued by the CIA and Al-Qaeda in this exciting sequel to *Icecore* (2007). Lexile 850L (Rev: BLO 12/1/09; LMC 5–6/10; SLJ 4/10)

6274 Whyman, Matt. *Icecore: A Carl Hobbes Thriller* (8–12). 2007, Simon & Schuster $16.99 (978-1-4169-4907-7). British Carl Hobbes, 17, hacks into the security system at Fort Knox — just to prove he can do it — and soon finds himself a prisoner at a maximum-security American site above the Arctic Circle — and that's just the beginning of the plot-driven adventure. (Rev: BCCB 2/08; SLJ 1/08)

6275 Wildavsky, Rachel. *The Secret of Rover* (4–7). 2011, Abrams $16.95 (978-0-8109-9710-3). Katie and David, 12-year-old twins whose parents invented a secret spying device, find themselves embroiled in political intrigue. (Rev: BL 5/1/11; SLJ 4/11*)

6276 Willey, Margaret. *Four Secrets* (7–10). Illus. by Bill Hauser. 2012, Carolrhoda $17.95 (978-0-7613-8535-6). Three teens accused of kidnapping a boy who was bullying them tell their story through journal entries. e Lexile 850L (Rev: BL 10/1/12*; HB 11–12/12; LMC 5–6/13; SLJ 12/12; VOYA 12/12)

6277 Williams, Carol Lynch. *The Chosen One* (7–10). 2009, St. Martin's $16.95 (978-031255511-5). In this compelling novel, 13-year-old Kyra is commanded to marry her uncle and plans a daring escape from the polygamous sect in which she has been raised. ♫ Lexile HL480L (Rev: BL 2/15/09; HB 5–6/09; LMC 10/09; SLJ 7/1/09)

6278 Williams, Katie. *The Space Between Trees* (8–12). 2010, Chronicle $16.99 (978-0-8118-7175-4). Sixteen-year-old Evie, a loner given to making up stories, must grow up when the body of a classmate is found and she is drawn into the investigation. e Lexile 850L (Rev: BLO 4/1/10; LMC 8–9/10; SLJ 5/10)

6279 Wilson, Eric. *Code Red at the Supermall* (6–8). Illus. by Richard Row. Series: A Tom and Liz Austen Mystery. 2000, Orca paper $4.99 (978-1-55143-172-7). The intrepid Tom and Liz Austen investigate criminal activities at the Edmonton supermall. Also recommended in this series is *Disneyland Hostage* (2000). (Rev: SLJ 6/00)

6280 Wilson, Eric. *Murder on the Canadian: A Tom Austen Mystery* (4–8). Illus. by Richard Row. 2000, Orca paper $4.99 (978-1-55143-151-2). A fast-moving mystery starring an intrepid hero who is also featured in *Vancouver Nightmare: A Tom Austen Mystery* (2000). (Rev: SLJ 1/01)

6281 Wilson, F. Paul. *Jack: Secret Circles* (6–9). Series: Young Repairman Jack. 2010, Tor $15.99 (978-0-7653-1855-8). In this followup to 2008's *Jack: Secret Histories,* Jack and his friend Weezy discover a mysterious pyramid-shaped cage in the New Jersey Pine Barrens, alongside a scary, foul-smelling creature that could be the Jersey Devil. (Rev: BL 2/1/10; SLJ 3/10)

6282 Wilson, F. Paul. *Jack: Secret Histories* (6–9). 2008, Tor $15.95 (978-0-7653-1854-1). When members of a mysterious cult in Jack's town are found dead, he and his friends find a strange box that may hold the answer. (Rev: BL 5/1/08)

6283 Winters, Ben H. *The Mystery of the Missing Everything* (5–8). 2011, HarperCollins $16.99 (978-0-06-196544-9). Eighth-grader Bethesda Fielding investigates a missing sports trophy in this sequel to *The Secret Life of Ms. Finkleman* (2010). (Rev: BL 10/1/11; SLJ 10/1/11)

6284 Wolf, Jennifer Shaw. *Breaking Beautiful* (8–11). 2012, Walker $16.99 (978-080272352-9). Allie, 18, survived the accident that killed her boyfriend Trip, but she doesn't remember anything about it; however, she does know that Trip was not as perfect as he seemed. e (Rev: BLO 4/15/12; LMC 3–4/12; SLJ 3/12; VOYA 2/12)

6285 Wright, Betty R. *The Dollhouse Murders* (4–7). 1983, Holiday $16.95 (978-0-8234-0497-1). Dolls in a dollhouse come to life in this mystery about long-ago murders.

6286 Yep, Laurence. *The Case of the Firecrackers* (4–7). 1999, HarperCollins LB $15.89 (978-0-06-024452-1). In this Chinatown mystery, Tiger Lil and her great-niece Lily are on the trail of the murderer who killed the star of the television show in which they were extras. (Rev: BL 9/15/99; HBG 3/00; SLJ 9/99)

6287 Young, E. L. *The Infinity Code* (5–8). 2008, Dial $16.99 (978-0-8037-3265-0). Young computer whizzes Andrew, Will, Gaia, and Caspian make up the group STORM ("Science and Technology to Over-Rule Misery") and find themselves in a tech-driven battle against a group that has kidnapped Caspian's father. (Rev: BL 3/1/08; SLJ 5/08)

6288 Zambreno, Mary F. *Journeyman Wizard* (4–7). 1994, Harcourt $16.95 (978-0-15-200022-6). Student wizard Jeremy is studying the casting of spells with Lady Allons when an unfortunate death occurs and he is accused of murder. (Rev: BL 5/1/94; SLJ 6/94)

Romances

6289 Anderson, Katie D. *Kiss and Make Up* (7–10). 2012, Amazon Children's $16.99 (978-0-761-46316-0). Sixteen-year-old Emerson can read people's minds through a kiss and sets out to rescue her academic career using this strategy, in the process finding a neat guy called Edwin. ⌂ e (Rev: BL 11/15/12; SLJ 11/12; VOYA 12/12)

6290 Applegate, Katherine. *See You in September* (7–9). 1995, Avon paper $3.99 (978-0-380-78088-4). Four chaste and charming short stories by four popular YA romance authors. (Rev: BL 1/1–15/96; SLJ 3/96)

6291 Baratz-Logsted, Lauren. *Crazy Beautiful* (7–10). 2009, Houghton Mifflin $16 (978-0-547-22307-0). This high school romance chronicles the unlikely attraction between the beautiful and popular Aurora and Lucius, the alienated loner who sports steel hooks after accidentally blowing his hands off in a mysterious accident. e Lexile 910L (Rev: BLO 8/20/09; SLJ 12/09; VOYA 12/09)

6292 Bat-Ami, Miriam. *Two Suns in the Sky* (8–12). 1999, Front St $15.95 (978-0-8126-2900-2). A docu-novel set in upstate New York during 1944 about the love between a Catholic teenage girl and a Jewish Holocaust survivor from Yugoslavia who is living in a refugee camp. (Rev: BL 4/15/99; HB 7–8/99; HBG 9/99; SLJ 7/99; VOYA 10/99)

6293 Bernardo, Anilú. *Loves Me, Loves Me Not* (7–10). 1998, Arte Publico $16.95 (978-1-55885-258-7). A teen romance that involves Cuban American Maggie, a basketball player named Zach, newcomer Justin, and Maggie's friend, Susie. (Rev: BL 1/1–15/99)

6294 Bertrand, Diane Gonzales. *Lessons of the Game* (7–10). 1998, Arte Publico paper $9.95 (978-1-55885-245-7). Student teacher Kaylene Morales is attracted to the freshman football coach but wonders if romance and her school assignments will mix. (Rev: BL 1/1–15/99; VOYA 10/99)

6295 Blumenthal, Deborah. *The Lifeguard* (8–12). 2012, Albert Whitman $16.99 (978-080754535-5). A paranormal romance featuring 16-year-old Sirena, who is spending the summer at her aunt's beach house while her parents divorce, and a handsome but mysterious lifeguard named Pilot. e Lexile 670L (Rev: BL 3/15/12; SLJ 4/12; VOYA 4/12)

6296 Brooks, Martha. *Two Moons in August* (7–12). 1992, Little, Brown $15.95 (978-0-316-10979-6). A midsummer romance in the 1950s between a newcomer to a small Canadian community and a 16-year-old girl who is mourning her mother's death. (Rev: BL 11/15/91*; SLJ 3/92*)

6297 Burnham, Niki. *Fireworks: Four Summer Stories* (7–12). 2007, Scholastic paper $8.99 (978-0-439-90300-4). Well-written with believable characters, these stories of summer romances occur in varied locales and are sure to please a wide spectrum of readers. (Rev: SLJ 7/07)

6298 Caletti, Deb. *The Six Rules of Maybe* (8–12). 2010, Simon & Schuster $16.99 (978-1-4169-7969-2). When Scarlet's beautiful older sister returns home with doting new husband Hayden in tow and a baby on the way, Scarlet finds herself increasingly drawn to Hayden. ⌂ e Lexile 820L (Rev: BL 2/15/10; HB 5–6/10; SLJ 3/10)

6299 Caletti, Deb. *The Story of Us* (8–12). 2012, Simon & Schuster $16.99 (978-144242346-6). Teenage Cricket contends with the crises that seem to be converging in her personal life just before her mother's third attempt at marriage. e Lexile HL660L (Rev: BL 1/1/12*; HB 5–6/12; LMC 8–9/12; SLJ 3/12; VOYA 2/12)

6300 Cann, Kate. *Grecian Holiday: Or, How I Turned Down the Best Possible Thing Only to Have the Time of My Life* (7–12). 2002, Avon paper $5.99 (978-0-06-447302-6). In addition to the beach, the food, and the drink, Kelly's vacation in Greece is a time of learning about herself, friendship, romance, and sex; for mature teens. (Rev: VOYA 2/03)

6301 Cann, Kate. *Ready? Love Trilogy #1* (8–12). 2001, HarperCollins paper $6.95 (978-0-06-440869-1). In the first book of a British romantic trilogy, 16-year-old Collette falls for Art, who is both rich and handsome, but she is troubled by his unrelenting pressure for physical intimacy. The sequels are *Sex* (2001) and *Go!* (2001). (Rev: HBG 10/02; SLJ 8/01; VOYA 10/01)

6302 Cleary, Beverly. *Fifteen* (7–9). 1956, Avon paper $6.99 (978-0-380-72804-6). A young adolescent discovers that having a boyfriend isn't the answer to all her social problems.

6303 Cleary, Beverly. *The Luckiest Girl* (7–9). 1958, Avon paper $6.99 (978-0-380-72806-0). New social opportunities arise when a young girl spends her senior year at a school in California.

6304 Coffey, Jan. *Tropical Kiss* (8–11). 2005, HarperCollins paper $5.99 (978-0-06-076003-8). Morgan's summer on Aruba with her father turns out to be more fun than she expected, but the discovery that her dad may be in trouble casts a cloud over her enjoyment of a new friend and boyfriend. (Rev: SLJ 8/05)

6305 Colasanti, Susane. *Waiting for You* (7–10). 2009, Viking $17.99 (978-067001130-8). Marisa learns about heartbreak when her handsome boyfriend's eye begins to wander and her parents' marriage falls apart. Lexile HL570L (Rev: BLO 3/24/09; SLJ 8/09; VOYA 8/09)

6306 Cooney, Caroline B. *Both Sides of Time* (6–10). 1997, Delacorte paper $4.99 (978-0-440-21932-3). Annie Lockwood, who has been yearning for love, suddenly finds herself in the 1890s, in a much more appealing era; however, traveling through time can lack romance. (Rev: BL 9/15/95; HB 11/95; HBG 3/02; SLJ 7/95)

6307 Crowley, Cath. *Graffiti Moon* (7–10). 2012, Knopf $16.99 (978-037586953-2); LB $19.99 (978-037596953-9). Obsessed with a graffiti artist named Shadow, Lucy fails to realize that Ed, a young man she disdains, is in fact the artist himself; set in Australia, this novel is told in alternating voices and includes poems by Ed's friend Leo, aka Poet. ◗ e Lexile HL630L (Rev: BL 3/1/12; LMC 3–4/12; SLJ 2/12; VOYA 2/12)

6308 Daly, Maureen. *Seventeenth Summer* (6–8). 1981, Harmony LB $19.95 (978-0-89967-029-4); paper $5.99 (978-0-671-61931-2). Angie experiences an idyllic summer after she meets Jack in this classic 1942 novel.

6309 Davis, Leila. *Lover Boy* (7–12). 1989, Avon paper $2.95 (978-0-380-75722-0). Ryan finds that his racy reputation is keeping him from the girl he really loves. (Rev: SLJ 10/89; VOYA 8/89)

6310 Delsol, Wendy. *Stork* (7–11). 2010, Candlewick $15.99 (978-0-7636-4844-2). Romance and Norse mythology blend in this story of 16-year-old Kat, who returns to a Minnesota town and discovers some startling facts about herself while falling for the young man, Jack, who rescued her from a long-ago accident. A sequel is *Frost* (2011). e Lexile 680L (Rev: BL 10/15/10; LMC 11–12/10; SLJ 1/1/11; VOYA 12/10)

6311 Dessen, Sarah. *This Lullaby* (8–12). 2002, Viking $16.99 (978-0-670-03530-4). Eighteen-year-old Remy's complex family life leads her to avoid deep romantic attachments until she meets Dexter. (Rev: BCCB 5/02; BL 4/1/02; HB 7–8/02; HBG 10/02; SLJ 4/02; VOYA 6/02)

6312 Doyle, Marissa. *Courtship and Curses* (8–12). 2012, Henry Holt $17.99 (978-0-8050-9187-8). Magic, history, and romance are combined in this story about 18-year-old Sophie and her debut into society in Napoleonic Europe. e Lexile 820L (Rev: BL 9/15/12; LMC 11–12/12; SLJ 9/12; VOYA 12/12)

6313 DuJardin, Rosamond. *Boy Trouble* (7–9). 1988, HarperCollins LB $12.89 (978-0-397-32263-3). A harmless romance first published in the 1960s and now back in print. (Rev: SLJ 2/88)

6314 Dyan, Sheldon. *The Crazy Things Girls Do for Love* (7–10). 2011, Candlewick $15.99 (978-076365018-6). Environmental concerns, humor, and romance intersect in this story about the arrival of gorgeous Cody — an advocate of vegan food, hemp clothing, and so forth —

and the interest he arouses among the in-crowd (and all the other) girls. ◗ e (Rev: BL 10/1/11; SLJ 1/12)

6315 Echols, Jennifer. *Major Crush* (8–12). 2006, Simon & Schuster paper $5.99 (978-1-4169-1830-1). Virginia wants to become the drum major in her high school band but finds she has competition in the form of the exasperating but very cute Drew. (Rev: SLJ 9/06)

6316 Eulberg, Elizabeth. *The Lonely Hearts Club* (7–10). 2010, Scholastic $17.99 (978-0-545-14031-7). Disillusioned with high school boys, Penny Lane Bloom starts a no-dating Lonely Hearts Club that proves very successful until a nice guy enters Penny's life and club rules are amended. Lexile HL640L (Rev: BL 1/1–15/10; SLJ 2/10)

6317 Fallon, Leigh. *The Carrier of the Mark* (8–12). 2011, HarperTeen paper $8.99 (978-00620278-7-0). An American student living in Ireland, Megan is drawn to a boy in her class and discovers that they share supernatural powers. ◗ e (Rev: BL 9/15/11; SLJ 2/12; VOYA 10/12)

6318 Fiedler, Lisa. *Romeo's Ex: Rosaline's Story* (8–11). 2006, Henry Holt $16.95 (978-0-8050-7500-7). A retelling of *Romeo and Juliet* from the point of view of Rosaline, Juliet's cousin and Romeo's first love. (Rev: BL 9/15/06; SLJ 11/06)

6319 Filichia, Peter. *Not Just Another Pretty Face* (7–10). 1988, Avon paper $2.50 (978-0-380-75244-7). A high school story in which the course of true love does not run smoothly for Bill Richards. (Rev: BL 3/1/88; SLJ 5/88)

6320 Frank, Lucy. *Will You Be My Brussels Sprout?* (7–10). 1996, Holiday $15.95 (978-0-8234-1220-4). In this continuation of *I Am an Artichoke*, Emily, now 16, studies the cello at a New York music conservatory and falls in love for the first time. (Rev: BL 4/15/96; SLJ 4/96; VOYA 10/96)

6321 Fredericks, Mariah. *In the Cards: Love* (5–8). 2007, Simon & Schuster $15.99 (978-0-689-87654-7). Three eighth-grade girls in Manhattan use tarot cards to discover whether Anna will succeed in turning her crush on Declan into a romance; likable, believable characters populate this funny novel. (Rev: BL 1/1–15/07; SLJ 4/07)

6322 Freitas, Donna. *The Survival Kit* (7–10). 2011, Farrar $16.99 (978-0-374-39917-7). Rose's mother recently died of cancer and the girl finds comfort in the "survival kit" her mother left behind, which leads her to a new romance. e Lexile 850L (Rev: BL 10/1/11; HB 1–2/12; LMC 1–2/12; SLJ 11/1/11)

6323 Friedman, Aimee. *A Novel Idea* (7–11). 2006, Simon & Schuster paper $5.99 (978-1-4169-0785-5). A light romantic comedy in which Norah's focus switches from her college resumé to the attractive James. (Rev: SLJ 2/06)

6324 Friedman, Aimee. *Sea Change* (6–9). 2009, Scholastic $16.99 (978-043992228-9). Sixteen-year-old Miranda visits an island off Georgia for the summer and falls in love with Leo, whom she soon suspects may be a member of a race of sea creatures. Lexile 840L (Rev: BLO 5/15/09; SLJ 6/1/09; VOYA 6/09)

6325 Garvey, Amy. *Cold Kiss* (7–10). 2011, HarperTeen $17.99 (978-0-06-199622-1). When her boyfriend is killed in a car accident, Wren uses her supernatural abilities to bring him back to life, but things don't quite work out. ℮ (Rev: BLO 9/1/11; HB 1–2/12; SLJ 11/1/11; VOYA 10/11)

6326 Geras, Adele. *Pictures of the Night* (7–12). 1993, Harcourt $16.95 (978-0-15-261588-8). A modern version of *Snow White,* with the heroine an 18-year-old singer in London and Paris. (Rev: BL 3/1/93; SLJ 6/93)

6327 Geras, Adele. *The Tower Room* (7–12). 1992, Harcourt $15.95 (978-0-15-289627-0). The fairy tale *Rapunzel* is updated and set in an English girls' boarding school in the 1960s. (Rev: BL 2/15/92; SLJ 5/92)

6328 Goldblatt, Stacey. *Girl to the Core* (7–10). 2009, Delacorte $16.99 (978-0-385-73609-1); LB $19.99 (978-0-385-90587-9). Molly grows more self-confident over the course of this book as the motherless 15-year-old learns valuable lessons about friendship and dating, partly through her exposure to the younger girls in the Girl Corps. (Rev: BL 9/15/09; SLJ 9/09)

6329 Greenwald, Lisa. *Sweet Treats and Secret Crushes* (5–8). 2010, Abrams $16.95 (978-0-8109-8990-0). It's Valentine's Day, and a snowstorm promises to ruin the romantic plans of 13-year-old BFFs Olivia, Kate, and Georgia, but distributing fortune cookies to neighbors in the Brooklyn, New York, apartment building brings unexpected benefits. (Rev: BL 9/15/10; SLJ 12/1/10)

6330 Gunn, Robin Jones. *I Promise* (6–12). Series: Christy and Todd, The College Years. 2001, Bethany $10.99 (978-0-7642-2274-0). Christy and Todd are finally engaged, but the complicated wedding plans and accompanying turmoil threaten to derail their happiness. (Rev: BL 1/1–15/02; VOYA 12/01)

6331 Hahn, Mary Downing. *The Wind Blows Backward* (8–12). 1993, Clarion $16.00 (978-0-395-62975-8). Spencer's downward emotional spiral and Lauren's deep commitment evoke a fantasy love gone awry. (Rev: BL 5/1/93; SLJ 5/93)

6332 Han, Jenny. *The Summer I Turned Pretty* (7–10). 2009, Simon & Schuster $16.99 (978-141696823-8). The summer she is 15, Belly is finally noticed by two boys she's known all her life and finds that other boys are starting to appreciate her too. ⋒ Lexile HL600L (Rev: BLO 5/28/09; SLJ 4/1/09*; VOYA 8/09)

6333 Hart, Bruce, and Carole Hart. *Sooner or Later* (8–12). 1978, Avon paper $2.95 (978-0-380-42978-3). In order to fool her 17-year-old boyfriend into thinking she is older than 13, Jessie begins an intricate pattern of lies.

6334 Hart, Bruce, and Carole Hart. *Waiting Games* (7–10). 1981, Avon paper $3.50 (978-0-380-79012-8). Jessie and Michael are in love and must make difficult decisions about sex.

6335 Hepler, Heather. *Love? Maybe* (6–9). 2012, Dial $16.99 (978-080373721-1). Romance-averse from watching her mother's experiences, Piper nonetheless cooperates with her friends' plans for Valentine's Day. ℮ Lexile HL670L (Rev: BL 1/1/12; SLJ 1/12; VOYA 12/11)

6336 Herbsman, Cheryl Renee. *Breathing* (7–10). 2009, Viking $16.99 (978-067001123-0). Fifteen-year-old Savannah's asthma begins to ease when she meets gorgeous Jackson Channing in this romance set on the Carolina coast and using local dialect. (Rev: BL 4/1/09; SLJ 6/1/09; VOYA 8/09)

6337 Hobbs, Valerie. *Anything but Ordinary* (8–12). 2007, Farrar $16.00 (978-0-374-30374-7). High school sweethearts Bernie and Winifred are separated when Winifred goes off to college and Bernie stays behind; the distance between them increases when Winifred is "madeover" at school. (Rev: BCCB 5/07; BL 4/15/07; SLJ 3/07)

6338 Jabaley, Jennifer. *Crush Control* (8–10). 2011, Penguin paper $9.99 (978-1-59514-424-9). Seventeen-year-old Willow, daughter of a "hip hypnotist," decides to borrow her mother's technique in an effort to make Max jealous, but things get complicated. ℮ (Rev: SLJ 12/1/11; VOYA 8/11)

6339 Jacobs, Holly. *Pickup Lines* (8–12). 2005, Avalon $21.95 (978-0-8034-9704-7). A comic romance in which teacher Mary Rosenthal and businessman Ethan Westbrook vie to win a pickup truck. (Rev: BL 4/1/05)

6340 Johnson, Kathleen Jeffrie. *Dumb Love* (8–11). 2005, Roaring Brook $16.95 (978-1-59643-062-4). A funny romance in which high school student Carlotta aspires both to win the heart of Pete and to write a novel. (Rev: BL 9/15/05; SLJ 11/05)

6341 Jones, Jenny B. *There You'll Find Me* (7–10). 2011, Thomas Nelson paper $12.99 (978-1-59554-540-4). Eighteen-year-old Finley's quest for answers about faith and quiet time for practicing violin is interrupted by romance when she spends a summer in Ireland. ⋒ ℮ Lexile HL560L (Rev: BL 11/15/11; SLJ 12/1/11)

6342 Kantor, Melissa. *Confessions of a Not It Girl* (7–12). 2004, Hyperion $15.99 (978-0-7868-1837-2). Jan Miller has high hopes that love will come her way during her senior year in high school, but it's soon obvious that it won't be easy in this entertaining, true-to-life romantic comedy. (Rev: BL 6/1–15/04; HB 7–8/04; SLJ 4/04; VOYA 6/04)

6343 Kantor, Melissa. *The Darlings in Love* (7–10). 2012, Hyperion $16.99 (978-142312369-9). The three Darlings, 14-year-old best friends each in their first year of high school, share the triumphs and trials of first love; a sequel to *The Darlings Are Forever* (2011). ℮ Lexile 810L (Rev: BL 1/1/12; SLJ 2/12)

6344 Kaplow, Robert. *Alessandra in Love* (8–10). 1989, HarperCollins LB $12.89 (978-0-397-32282-4). Alessandra's boyfriend turns out to be a self-centered disappointment. (Rev: BL 4/15/89; SLJ 4/89; VOYA 8/89)

6345 Kenneally, Miranda. *Stealing Parker* (8–12). 2012, Sourcebooks paper $8.99 (978-1-4022-7-187-8). Parker's happy life and balanced social relationships are turned upside down when her mother leaves her father for a woman in this multilayered novel. ℮ (Rev: BL 9/15/12; LMC 5–6/13; SLJ 10/12; VOYA 12/12)

6346 Kerr, M. E. *Someone Like Summer* (7–12). 2007, HarperTempest $15.99 (978-0-06-114100-3). Annabel, 17, falls in love with Esteban, an illegal alien working for her father, in this novel set in the Hamptons. (Rev: BCCB 9/07; BL 4/1/07; SLJ 11/07)

6347 Kindl, Patrice. *Keeping the Castle* (7–11). 2012, Viking $16.99 (978-067001438-5). Seventeen-year-old Althea must marry well to support her extended family and hold onto their rundown castle — but how to find a suitable suitor? Set in 19th-century Yorkshire, this is a humorous take on classic Regency romances. ℮ (Rev: BL 4/15/12*; HB 9–10/12; LMC 11–12/12; SLJ 6/12)

6348 Klass, David. *Screen Test* (7–9). 1997, Scholastic paper $16.95 (978-0-590-48592-0). Sixteen-year-old Liz Weaton is whisked off to Hollywood, where she almost falls in love with her costar. (Rev: BL 12/1/97; HBG 3/98; SLJ 10/97)

6349 Klein, Lisa. *Cate of the Lost Colony* (7–10). 2010, Bloomsbury $16.99 (978-1-59990-507-5). Lady Catherine (Cate), 14, is banished to Roanoke, Virginia, when she and Sir Walter Ralegh form an attachment; there, however, she meets a handsome Croatoan Indian named Manteo. (Rev: BL 9/15/10; LMC 10/10; SLJ 1/1/11; VOYA 12/10)

6350 Knudson, R. R. *Just Another Love Story* (7–10). 1983, Avon paper $2.50 (978-0-380-65532-8). Dusty takes up body building to help forget the girlfriend who has spurned him.

6351 Koertge, Ron. *Now Playing: Stoner and Spaz II* (8–12). 2011, Candlewick $16.99 (978-0-7636-5081-0). Cerebral palsy sufferer Ben struggles to wield a positive influence on his beautiful friend Colleen, who's battling drug addiction, even as he becomes reacquainted with his mother, enjoys his documentary film success, and spends time with fellow filmmaker AJ. A sequel to *Stoner and Spaz* (2002) ⌒ ℮ Lexile HL580L (Rev: BL 8/11*; HB 9–10/11; SLJ 9/1/11; VOYA 8/11)

6352 Lachtman, Ofelia Dumas. *The Girl from Playa Bianca* (7–12). 1995, Arte Publico paper $9.95 (978-1-55885-149-8). A gothic romance in which a Mexican teenager and her young brother travel to Los Angeles in search of their father. (Rev: BL 11/15/95; SLJ 10/95; VOYA 12/95)

6353 Lenhard, Elizabeth. *Knit Two Together* (6–9). Series: Chicks with Sticks. 2006, Dutton $16.99 (978-0-525-47764-8). The knitting foursome is back, and this time boys and romance take up as many pages as knitting and chatting. (Rev: BL 12/15/06; SLJ 2/07)

6354 Lon, Kiki. *Enter the Parrot* (8–12). Series: Got Kung Fu? 2009, Wild Rose paper $12.99 (978-160154459-9). Romance and mystery feature in this novel about 16-year-old Jade who is learning Cantonese and martial arts while hunting for her grandfather's missing parrot. (Rev: BL 7/09)

6355 Long, Ruth Frances. *The Treachery of Beautiful Things* (7–12). 2012, Dial $17.99 (978-0-8037-3580-4). Visiting the site where she saw her brother swallowed up by trees, 17-year-old Jenny is transported into the fairy realm where she finds danger and romance. ℮ Lexile HL690L (Rev: BL 9/15/12*; SLJ 10/12; VOYA 8/12)

6356 McClymer, Kelly. *Getting to Third Date* (8–11). 2006, Simon & Schuster paper $5.99 (978-1-4169-1479-2). College advice columnist Katelyn is forced to take a dose of her own medicine and give her ex-boyfriends another chance. (Rev: BL 4/15/06)

6357 McClymer, Kelly. *Must Love Black* (6–9). 2008, Simon & Schuster paper $8.99 (978-141696994-5). All-black wardrobe devotee Pippa gains confidence, identity — and a touch of romance — when she takes a summer job as a nanny for 10-year-old twins at an isolated mansion. ℮ (Rev: BL 10/15/08; SLJ 12/08)

6358 McDaniel, Lurlene. *Don't Die, My Love* (7–12). 1995, Bantam paper $4.99 (978-0-553-56715-1). A young couple, Julie and Luke, "engaged" since 6th grade, discover that Luke has Hodgkin's lymphoma. (Rev: BL 9/15/95; SLJ 10/95; VOYA 12/95)

6359 McFann, Jane. *Maybe by Then I'll Understand* (7–9). 1987, Avon paper $2.50 (978-0-380-75221-8). Cath and Tony become a pair but Tony demands more attention and loyalty than she can give. (Rev: BL 11/15/87; SLJ 1/88; VOYA 12/87)

6360 McLaughlin, Emma, and Nicola Kraus. *Over You* (8–12). 2012, HarperTeen $17.99 (978-0-06-172043-7). Max, 17, runs a business helping dumped girls get over their exes but she suffers an attack of jitters when her own ex comes to town, prompting her to question her whole program. ℮ Lexile 740L (Rev: BL 7/12; SLJ 12/12; VOYA 8/12)

6361 MacLean, Sarah. *The Season* (7–10). 2009, Orchard $16.99 (978-054504886-6). Lady Alexandra Stafford falls in love while solving a murder mystery in this traditional romance set in 1815 but featuring a feisty and independent heroine. Lexile 900L (Rev: BL 2/15/09; LMC 5–6/09; SLJ 6/1/09)

6362 Malcolm, Jahnna N. *Mixed Messages* (6–9). Series: Love Letters. 2005, Simon & Schuster paper $5.99 (978-0-689-87222-8). Jade, a high school senior, has had a crush on Zephyr Strauss for years, but when she finally writes him a love letter, it ends up in the wrong hands. (Rev: SLJ 1/05)

6363 Malcolm, Jahnna N. *Perfect Strangers* (6–9). Series: Love Letters. 2005, Simon & Schuster paper $5.99 (978-0-689-87221-1). There's no love lost between high school juniors Madison and Jeremy, who are running against each other for class president, until they're secretly paired up in their school's Heart-2-Heart e-mail-pal program. (Rev: SLJ 1/05)

6364 Martin, Ann M. *Just a Summer Romance* (6–8). 1987, Holiday $13.95 (978-0-8234-0649-4). While spending a summer on Fire Island, 14-year-old Melanie becomes attracted to Justin. (Rev: BL 4/1/87; SLJ 6/87; VOYA 10/87)

6365 Matthews, Phoebe. *The Boy on the Cover* (6–8). 1988, Avon paper $2.75 (978-0-380-75407-6). Cyndi falls in love with a boy whose picture is on the cover of a book she owns. (Rev: VOYA 2/89)

6366 Mauser, Pat Rhoads. *Love Is for the Dogs* (7–10). 1989, Avon paper $2.50 (978-0-380-75723-7). Janna realizes that Brian, the boy next door, can be very desirable. (Rev: BL 4/15/89; SLJ 4/89)

6367 Mills, Tricia. *Heartbreak River* (8–12). 2009, Penguin paper $8.99 (978-159514256-6). After her father's death in a whitewater rafting accident, 16-year-old Alex works through her grief and her fear of the water during a difficult summer in which she also struggles with her love for Sean. **e** (Rev: BL 3/1/09; SLJ 4/1/09)

6368 Mines, Jeanette. *Risking It* (7–9). 1988, Avon paper $2.75 (978-0-380-75401-4). Jeannie is attracted to Trent Justin, who has joined her senior class. (Rev: BL 9/1/88; SLJ 1/89; VOYA 6/88)

6369 *Mistletoe: Four Holiday Stories* (7–10). 2006, Scholastic paper $8.99 (978-0-439-86368-1). A collection of four different winter holiday stories about love by YA authors. (Rev: BL 11/1/06; SLJ 10/06)

6370 Morrill, Lauren. *Meant to Be* (7–12). 2012, Delacorte $17.99 (978-038574177-4); LB $20.99 (978-037599023-6). On a class trip to London, high school junior Julia finds herself spending unexpected time with class clown Jason; light mystery is combined with romance. ∩ **e** (Rev: BL 11/1/12; SLJ 1/13; VOYA 2/13)

6371 Murdock, Catherine Gilbert. *Wisdom's Kiss: A Thrilling and Romantic Adventure, Incorporating Magic, Villainy, and a Cat* (7–10). 2011, Houghton Mifflin $16.99 (978-0-547-56687-0). The rebellious Princess Wisdom, a circus performer named Tips who attracts her attention, and other colorful characters star in this tongue-in-cheek romantic fantasy set in the kingdom of Montagne. ∩ **e** Lexile 1280L (Rev: BL 8/11*; HB 9–10/11; SLJ 10/1/11*; VOYA 10/11)

6372 Myers, Walter Dean. *Amiri and Odette* (4–8). Illus. by Javaka Steptoe. 2009, Scholastic $17.99 (978-059068041-7). Overtones of urban youth, hip-hop, and Shakespeare abound in this colorfully illustrated, modern-day version in verse of the ballet Swan Lake. (Rev: BL 12/1/08; LMC 5–6/09; SLJ 1/1/09; VOYA 10/09)

6373 Napoli, Donna Jo. *The Smile* (8–11). 2008, Dutton $17.99 (978-052547999-4). In this story about the mysterious woman behind daVinci's Mona Lisa, we follow Monna Elisabetta through her tumultuous Italian youth and young womanhood, and her propitious meeting with the artist. Lexile 580L (Rev: BL 10/1/08; HB 11–12/08; LMC 1–2/09; SLJ 11/1/08; VOYA 12/08)

6374 Nicholson, William. *Rich and Mad* (8–12). 2010, Egmont $17.99 (978-1-60684-120-4). Seventeen-year-olds Maddy Fisher and Rich Ross yearn for love, and after their first attempts at relationships go awry, they find one another and form a deep bond that can only be expressed one way. (Rev: BLO 8/10; SLJ 12/1/10)

6375 O'Connell, Tyne. *True Love, the Sphinx and Other Unsolvable Riddles* (7–10). 2007, Bloomsbury $16.95 (978-1-59990-050-6). A ritzy school trip to Egypt brings together students from an American boys' school and an English girls' school in this romance that offers humor and informative travelogue. (Rev: BL 11/1/07; SLJ 3/08)

6376 Osterlund, Anne. *Aurelia* (7–12). 2008, Penguin paper $8.99 (978-0-14-240579-6). Princess Aurelia's life is in danger and she faces a marriage arranged by her father; can her childhood friend Robert save her? (Rev: BL 5/1/08)

6377 Pearson, Joanna. *Rites and Wrongs of Janice Wills* (7–10). Illus. 2011, Scholastic $16.99 (978-0-545-19773-1). Intellectually inclined 16-year-old Janice is persuaded to compete in the local beauty pageant, and learns about social relationships of all kinds. ∩ **e** Lexile 810L (Rev: BL 9/15/11; LMC 11–12/11; SLJ 7/11; VOYA 12/11)

6378 Perkins, Stephanie. *Lola and the Boy Next Door* (8–12). 2011, Dutton $16.99 (978-0-525-42328-7). Lola, 17, who lives with her two fathers in San Francisco, finds herself torn between current boyfriend Max and former crush Cricket. ∩ **e** Lexile HL570L (Rev: BL 9/15/11; SLJ 10/1/11)

6379 Picoult, Jodi, and Samantha van Leer. *Between the Lines* (7–10). Illus. by Yvonne Gilbert. 2012, Simon & Schuster $19.99 (978-145163575-1). Delilah, 15, is delighted to discover the handsome fairy tale prince Oliver is an actual person who can communicate with her. ∩ **e** (Rev: BL 5/1/12; SLJ 8/1/12)

6380 Plummer, Louise. *The Unlikely Romance of Kate Bjorkman* (7–10). 1997, Bantam paper $4.50 (978-

0-440-22704-5). A brainy teen foils a beautiful, evil temptress and gets the man of her dreams. (Rev: SLJ 10/95; VOYA 12/95)

6381 Rallison, Janette. *It's a Mall World After All* (8–11). 2006, Walker $16.95 (978-0-8027-8853-5). Charlotte is so busy trying to catch Bryant cheating on her friend that she doesn't notice what a nice guy Bryant's best friend Colton is. (Rev: BL 1/1–15/07; SLJ 12/06)

6382 Rallison, Janette. *Just One Wish* (7–11). 2009, Putnam $15.99 (978-039924618-0). Annika, 17, gets more than she bargained for (including romance) when she tries to get Steve Raleigh, a teen TV star, to visit her sick little brother. Lexile HL730L (Rev: BL 2/1/09; SLJ 5/1/09)

6383 Reinhardt, Dana. *How to Build a House* (8–12). 2008, Random House $15.99 (978-0-375-84453-9). Harper sends a summer helping to build houses in Tennessee and learns that happiness is always possible. ∩ (Rev: BL 4/15/08; HB 7–8/08; SLJ 6/08—)

6384 Resau, Laura. *The Ruby Notebook* (7–11). 2010, Delacorte $16.99 (978-0-385-90615-9); LB $19.99 (978-0-385-73653-4). Recently arrived in France, 16-year-old Zeeta's relationship with her American boyfriend gets complicated when she's enchanted by gorgeous, mysterious Jean-Claude in this sequel to *The Indigo Notebook* (2009). e Lexile HL750L (Rev: BLO 8/10; SLJ 10/1/10; VOYA 12/10)

6385 Rothenberg, Jess. *The Catastrophic History of You and Me* (8–11). 2012, Dial $17.99 (978-080373720-4). Brie, 16, dies of a broken heart when Jacob tells her he does not love her; in the afterlife she passes through the stages of grief, watches the actions of her family and friends, and eventually finds love and hope; humor blends with romance. ∩ e (Rev: BL 2/15/12; SLJ 2/12; VOYA 4/12)

6386 Ryan, Mary C. *Frankie's Run* (6–8). 1987, Little, Brown $12.95 (978-0-316-76370-7). In this teen novel, Mary Frances falls for the new boy in town but also organizes a run to aid her local library. (Rev: BL 8/87; SLJ 5/87)

6387 Schreiber, Ellen. *Teenage Mermaid* (6–8). 2003, HarperCollins LB $16.89 (978-0-06-008205-5). Romance and entertainment abound in this story of a teen mermaid who rescues a young surfer. (Rev: BL 7/03; HBG 10/03; SLJ 8/03; VOYA 8/03)

6388 Schroeder, Lisa. *Chasing Brooklyn* (8–12). 2010, Simon & Schuster $15.99 (978-1-4169-9168-7). A year after Lucca died, his girlfriend — Brooklyn — and his brother Nico are still grappling with grief; when Gabe, who was driving that night, dies of an overdose, Brooklyn and Nico experience strange dreams and draw closer together; a moving novel told in verse. e Lexile HL510L (Rev: BLO 11/17/09; SLJ 2/10; VOYA 4/10)

6389 Shinn, Sharon. *General Winston's Daughter* (7–10). 2007, Viking $16.99 (978-0-670-06248-5). Averie,

whose father is a general in the Aebrian military, goes to visit a colonized land named Chiarrin and as she learns more about its culture, finds her views of many things in life — love, politics, even her father — are changing. (Rev: BL 8/07; SLJ 1/08)

6390 Sierra, Patricia. *One-Way Romance* (7–10). 1986, Avon paper $2.50 (978-0-380-75107-5). A talented girl who does well with carpentry and track seems to be losing out with her boyfriend. (Rev: BL 8/86; SLJ 11/86; VOYA 12/86)

6391 Smith, Emily Wing. *Back When You Were Easier to Love* (7–10). 2011, Dutton $16.99 (978-0-525-42199-3). When her boyfriend Zan leaves their Mormon community in Utah to attend college in California, a miserable Joy drives with Zan's best friend Noah to visit him, slowly shifting her affections along the way. e (Rev: BL 4/1/11; SLJ 7/11; VOYA 6/11)

6392 Sones, Sonya. *What My Girlfriend Doesn't Know* (7–10). 2007, Simon & Schuster paper $7.99 (978-0-689-87603-5). Popular Sophie falls for geeky Robin despite disapproval and disbelief from their friends in this stand-alone follow-up to *What My Mother Doesn't Know* (2001), narrated by Robin in first-person free verse. (Rev: BL 4/1/07*; SLJ 6/07)

6393 Springer, Kristina. *The Espressologist* (7–10). 2009, Farrar $16.99 (978-0-374-32228-1). High school senior Jane's amazing ability to make matches among her coffeehouse customers doesn't extend to herself, but in the end . . . . e Lexile HL640L (Rev: BL 10/15/09; SLJ 9/09)

6394 Stacey, Cherylyn. *Gone to Maui* (7–9). 1996, Roussan paper $8.95 (978-1-896184-14-2). In this novel, teenage Becky accompanies her mother on a trip to Maui, and there finds romance. (Rev: VOYA 4/97)

6395 Stanek, Lou W. *Katy Did* (8–12). 1992, Avon paper $2.99 (978-0-380-76170-8). A shy country girl and popular city boy fall in love, with tragic consequences. (Rev: BL 3/15/92)

6396 Strohm, Stephanie Kate. *Pilgrims Don't Wear Pink* (7–10). 2012, Houghton paper $8.99 (978-054756459-3). History buff and fashionista Libby spends the summer working at a living history camp, where she meets a handsome, Shakespeare-quoting young man. e Lexile HL720L (Rev: BL 7/12; SLJ 5/1/12; VOYA 2/12)

6397 Sunshine, Tina. *An X-Rated Romance* (7–9). 1982, Avon paper $2.50 (978-0-380-79905-3). Two 13-year-old girls have a crush on their English teacher. A reissue.

6398 Tayleur, Karen. *Chasing Boys* (8–11). 2009, Walker $16.99 (978-080279830-5). El starts at a new school and finds that the boy of her dreams is already taken — by a "perfect" girl named Angelique. e Lexile 690L (Rev: BL 2/15/09; SLJ 6/1/09)

6399 Thesman, Jean. *Who Said Life Is Fair?* (7–9). 1987, Avon paper $3.50 (978-0-380-75088-7). Teddy is trying to cope with work on the school newspaper while keeping her love life in order. (Rev: BL 5/87; VOYA 8/87)

6400 Thompson, Alicia. *Psych Major Syndrome* (8–10). 2009, Hyperion $16.99 (978-1-4231-1457-4). Leigh, a serious-minded college freshman in California, wrestles with her relationships with friends and the opposite sex. (Rev: BL 10/15/09; SLJ 9/09)

6401 Tracy, Kristen. *Sharks and Boys* (7–12). 2011, Disney/Hyperion $16.99 (978-1-4231-4354-3). Worried that her boyfriend Wick is becoming involved with someone else, 15-year-old Enid sneaks onto a yacht he is sharing with a group of twins; a storm later sets them adrift and they must struggle to survive. e Lexile HL510L (Rev: BL 6/1/11; SLJ 6/11; VOYA 8/11)

6402 Trembath, Don. *A Beautiful Place on Yonge Street* (8–10). 1999, Orca paper $6.95 (978-1-55143-121-5). Budding writer Harper Winslow falls in love with Sunny Taylor when he attends a summer writing camp, and experiences all the angst that goes with it. (Rev: BL 3/1/99; SLJ 7/99; VOYA 6/99)

6403 Weyn, Suzanne. *The Makeover Summer* (6–8). 1988, Avon paper $2.95 (978-0-380-75521-9). An exchange student who needs help joins the three girls of the Makeover Club. (Rev: BL 2/15/89)

6404 Williams, Kathryn. *Pizza, Love, and Other Stuff That Made Me Famous* (8–10). 2012, Henry Holt $16.99 (978-080509285-1). Sophie, 16, works hard to parlay her experiences in her Italian-Greek family's restaurant into success in a reality TV show while at the same time nurturing a crush for an adorable French chef. e Lexile 780L (Rev: BL 9/15/12; SLJ 8/1/12)

6405 Wittlinger, Ellen. *Lombardo's Law* (7–10). 1993, Morrow paper $4.95 (978-0-688-05294-2). The conventions of romance are thrown aside when sophomore Justine and 8th-grader Mike find themselves attracted to each other, despite obstacles. (Rev: BL 9/15/93; VOYA 12/93)

6406 Woodson, Jacqueline. *If You Come Softly* (7–10). 1998, Putnam $17.99 (978-0-399-23112-4). The story of the love between a black boy and a white girl, their families, and the prejudice they encounter. (Rev: BL 10/1/98; HBG 9/99; SLJ 12/98; VOYA 12/98)

6407 Zeises, Lara M. *The Sweet Life of Stella Madison* (8–11). 2009, Delacorte $16.99 (978-0-385-73146-1); LB $19.99 (978-0-385-90178-9). Stella, 17, becomes an intern for Baltimore's *Daily Journal* and, perhaps because of her foodie parents, is assigned to restaurant reviews; she is grateful for the help of the gorgeous Jeremy while fretting about her feelings toward her boyfriend Max. (Rev: BL 9/1/09; SLJ 7/1/09; VOYA 10/09)

6408 Ziegler, Jennifer. *Sass and Serendipity* (8–10). 2011, Delacorte $15.99 (978-0-385-73898-9); LB $18.99 (978-038590762-0). Gabby Rivera is sensible and down-to-earth whereas her sister Daphne is romantic and dreamy, and their views about their parents and about boys are equally different. e Lexile 710L (Rev: BL 7/11; SLJ 8/11)

Science Fiction

6409 Adams, John Joseph, ed. *Under the Moons of Mars: New Adventures on Barsoom* (7–12). Illus. 2012, Simon & Schuster $16.99 (978-144242029-8). An anthology of original stories featuring John Carter, the Earthman in Edgar Rice Burroughs's Barsoom series, by such authors as Tobias S. Buckell, David Barr Kirtley, and Garth Nix. e Lexile 1050L (Rev: BL 2/1/12; SLJ 5/1/12)

6410 Allen, Roger MacBride. *David Brin's Out of Time: The Game of Worlds* (7–12). Series: David Brin's Out of Time. 1999, Avon paper $4.99 (978-0-380-79969-5). Adam O'Connor, a mischievous high school student in the late 20th century, finds himself facing a whole new set of problems when he's yanked 350 years into the future. (Rev: VOYA 4/00)

6411 Anastasiu, Heather. *Glitch* (7–12). 2012, St. Martin's paper $9.99 (978-1-250-00-299-0). Zoe discovers a way to disconnect from her dystopia's mind-control software, and is suddenly forced to contend with emotions — which include love. (Rev: BL 8/12; SLJ 11/12; VOYA 10/12)

6412 Anderson, Kevin J., ed. *War of the Worlds: Global Dispatches* (7–12). 1996, Bantam $22.95 (978-0-553-10352-6). This tribute to H. G. Wells's *War of the Worlds* features stories of Martian invasions that are either take-offs on the writing styles of such famous authors as Conrad, London, Verne, and Kipling, or the experiences of famous individuals, such as Teddy Roosevelt and Pablo Picasso, during a Martian invasion. (Rev: VOYA 10/96)

6413 Anthony, Joelle. *Restoring Harmony* (6–9). 2010, Putnam $17.99 (978-0-399-25281-5). It's 2041, oil is scarce, travel is dangerous, and her grandmother in Oregon is ill, so brave 16-year-old Molly McClure sets out from British Columbia to bring her home, with only her fiddle to support her on this risky journey. Lexile 750L (Rev: BL 5/15/10; LMC 10/10; SLJ 8/10)

6414 Applegate, K. A. *Animorphs #1: The Invasion* (5–8). 1996, Scholastic paper $4.99 (978-0-590-62977-5). Jake, an average suburban kid, is confronted one night by a creature from space who teaches him how to morph into the forms of other creatures. (Rev: VOYA 12/96)

6415 Armstrong, Jennifer, and Nancy Butcher. *The Kindling* (7–10). Series: Fire-Us. 2002, HarperCollins LB $16.89 (978-0-06-029411-3). In 2007, after a virus has killed the adults, a small band of children join together in a Florida town and try to carry on with life. (Rev: BCCB 6/02; BL 4/15/02; HBG 10/02; SLJ 10/02)

6416 Arntson, Steven. *The Wikkeling* (5–8). Illus. by Daniela Jaglenka Terrazzini. 2011, Running Press $18 (978-0-7624-3903-4). In the dystopian city of the Addition, Henrietta and her friends Gary and Rose are being menaced by a yellow creature called the Wikkeling that gives them headaches. (Rev: BL 5/1/11; SLJ 5/11)

6417 Asimov, Isaac. *Caves of Steel* (7–12). 1955, Spectra paper $6.99 (978-0-553-29034-9). A human and a robot combine forces in this science fiction classic to work together to help mankind. Part of Asimov's well-written Robot series. (Rev: BL BL 5/1/00)

6418 Asimov, Isaac. *Fantastic Voyage: A Novel* (8–12). 1966, Houghton Mifflin paper $6.99 (978-0-553-27572-8). Five people are miniaturized to enter the body of a sick man and save his life.

6419 Asimov, Isaac, ed. *Young Extraterrestrials* (7–9). 1984, HarperCollins paper $7.95 (978-0-06-020167-8). Eleven stories by well-known authors about youngsters who are aliens from space.

6420 Asimov, Janet. *Norby and the Terrified Taxi* (4–8). 1997, Walker $15.95 (978-0-8027-8642-5). Norby, the bungling robot, is kidnapped, and while trying to find him, Jeff and his friends stumble on a plot by Garc the Great to take over the Federation. This is one of a large series of Norby books suitable for middle school readers. (Rev: BL 1/1–15/98; SLJ 12/97)

6421 Asimov, Janet. *The Package in Hyperspace* (5–7). 1988, Walker LB $14.85 (978-0-8027-6823-0). Two space-wrecked children must fend for themselves as they try to reach Merkina. (Rev: BL 1/1/89; SLJ 11/88)

6422 Asimov, Janet, and Isaac Asimov. *Norby and the Invaders* (5–8). 1985, Walker LB $10.85 (978-0-8027-6607-6). Jeff and his unusual robot Norby travel to a planet to help one of Norby's ancestors. Part of a series that includes *Norby's Other Secret*. (Rev: BL 3/1/86; SLJ 2/86)

6423 Asimov, Janet, and Isaac Asimov. *Norby and Yobo's Great Adventure* (5–8). 1989, Walker LB $13.85 (978-0-8027-6894-0). Norby the robot time-travels to help Admiral Yobo of Mars to trace his family roots. Part of a series that also includes *Norby Down to Earth*. (Rev: BL 10/15/89)

6424 Asimov, Janet, and Isaac Asimov. *Norby Finds a Villain* (4–8). 1987, Walker LB $13.85 (978-0-8027-6711-0). Norby the robot and his human friends set out to free Pera, who has been robot-napped by the traitor Ing, in this sixth book of the Norby series. Also use *Norby and the Queen's Necklace* (1986). (Rev: BL 1/1/88; SLJ 11/87)

6425 Bacigalupi, Paolo. *Ship Breaker* (8–12). 2010, Little, Brown $17.99 (978-0-316-05621-2). In a future, chaotic Accelerated Age Nailer and his friend Pima come across a wealthy girl as they scavenge among wrecks on the beach; can they help her and keep her safe from her enemies? Printz Winner 2011; ALA Notable Books 2011; YALSA Top Ten Best Fiction for Young Adults 2011. ☊ Lexile HL690L (Rev: BL 5/15/10*; HB 7–8/10; LMC 8–9/10; SLJ 6/10)

6426 Ball, Justin, and Evan Croker. *Space Dogs* (4–7). 2006, Knopf $15.95 (978-0-375-83256-7). When a powerful force threatens to destroy Gersbach, the planet's inhabitants dispatch dog-shaped vehicles to Earth in a desperate attempt to head off disaster; they end up battling in the front yard of Amy and Lucy Buckley in this humorous, action-packed story. (Rev: BL 6/1–15/06; SLJ 8/06)

6427 Ball, Margaret. *Lost in Translation* (8–12). 1995, Baen $5.99 (978-0-671-87638-8). American teenager Allie flies to France to attend a university but lands in a fantasy world filled with spells of every kind, where people communicate through voice-bubbles and a group of terrifying monsters controls an important subterranean substance called landvirtue. (Rev: VOYA 4/96)

6428 Bawden, Nina. *Off the Road* (5–9). 1998, Clarion $16.00 (978-0-395-91321-5). In this science fiction novel set in a time when the elderly are exterminated, 11-year-old Tom follows his grandfather to the "savage jungle" Outside the Wall, where the old man hopes to escape his fate, and discovers a different kind of society. (Rev: BCCB 10/98; BL 9/15/98; HBG 10/99; SLJ 11/98)

6429 Beaudoin, Sean. *Fade to Blue* (8–11). Illus. by author. 2009, Little, Brown $16.99 (978-031601417-5). Goth girl Sophie Blue's father disappears on her 17th birthday and she and her hunk friend Kenny Fade share a feeling they may be losing their minds in this quirky, dark yet funny novel that incorporates a comic book and involves a lab that may be infecting young people with software code. (Rev: BL 6/1–15/09; SLJ 10/09)

6430 Bechard, Margaret. *Spacer and Rat* (6–9). 2005, Roaring Brook $16.95 (978-1-59643-058-7). Space resident Jack revises his views about Earth "rats" when he meets Kit and her highly intelligent bot Waldo in this novel full of references to classic works and entertaining jargon. (Rev: BL 9/1/05; SLJ 11/05; VOYA 10/05)

6431 Beck, Ian. *Pastworld: A Mystery of the Near Future* (7–10). 2009, Bloomsbury $16.99 (978-1-59990-040-7). The year is 2050 and London has been turned into a Victorian theme park complete with a series of gruesome murders. ℮ Lexile 880L (Rev: BL 11/15/09; LMC 11–12/09; SLJ 12/09)

6432 Belden, Wilanne Schneider. *Mind-Find* (6–9). 1988, Harcourt $14.95 (978-0-15-254270-2). A 13-year-old girl adjusts with difficulty to her amazing powers of ESP. (Rev: BL 2/15/88; SLJ 8/88)

6433 Boulle, Pierre. *Planet of the Apes* (7–12). 2001, Random House paper $6.99 (978-0-345-44798-2).

Stranded on the planet Soror, Ulysse Merou discovers a civilization ruled by apes.

6434 Boyce, Frank Cottrell. *Cosmic* (4–7). 2010, HarperCollins $16.99 (978-0-06-183683-1). Twelve-year-old Liam is so big that he's often mistaken for an adult, and he decides to capitalize on this and enter the Greatest Dad Ever Contest to win a flight into space. ∩ ℮ Lexile 670L (Rev: BL 11/15/09*; HB 3–4/10; LMC 3–4/10; SLJ 2/10)

6435 Bracken, Alexandra. *The Darkest Minds* (8–12). 2012, Disney/Hyperion $17.99 (978-142315737-3). In a dystopian future where the few children who have survived are classified by their psychic abilities, 16-year-old Ruby escapes from a camp and faces many difficult choices. ∩ ℮ Lexile 870L (Rev: BL 12/1/12; LMC 3–4/13; SLJ 3/13)

6436 Bradbury, Ray. *Fahrenheit 451* (7–12). 1953, Ballantine paper $6.99 (978-0-345-34296-6). In this futuristic novel, book reading has become a crime.

6437 Bradbury, Ray. *The October Country* (7–12). 1999, Avon $15.95 (978-0-380-97387-3). Ordinary people are caught up in unreal situations in these 19 strange stories.

6438 Brennan, Herbie. *The Doomsday Box* (6–9). Series: Shadow Project. 2011, HarperCollins $16.99 (978-0-06-175647-4). Sent back to 1962 Moscow the British teens from *The Shadow Project* (2009) struggle to avert an outbreak of the plague. ℮ Lexile HL780L (Rev: BL 2/15/11; SLJ 4/11)

6439 Brennan, Herbie. *The Shadow Project* (6–9). 2010, HarperCollins $16.99 (978-0-06-175642-9). Three new terrorist-fighting teen recruits navigate the love triangle that's formed between them as they battle the world's deadliest terror organization in this sci-fi fantasy thriller. Lexile HL730L (Rev: BL 12/1/09; SLJ 3/10; VOYA 4/10)

6440 Brindley, John. *The Rule of Claw* (7–10). 2009, Carolrhoda $18.95 (978-158013608-2). In a land and time where mutants run wild, 15-year-old Ash is kidnapped by the Raptors and caught up in a war between two genetically altered races. Lexile HL740L (Rev: BLO 2/9/09; SLJ 5/1/09)

6441 Buckley-Archer, Linda. *Gideon the Cutpurse* (6–9). 2006, Simon & Schuster $17.95 (978-1-4169-1525-6). Two 12-year-olds named Kate and Peter find themselves transported back to 1763 London where the only person to offer them help is a cutpurse named Gideon. (Rev: BL 8/06; SLJ 7/06*)

6442 Bunting, Eve. *The Cloverdale Switch* (7–9). 1979, HarperCollins LB $12.89 (978-0-397-31867-4). John and Cindy encounter unusual changes in their world and find a mysterious black box.

6443 Butts, Nancy. *The Door in the Lake* (5–8). 1997, Front St $17.95 (978-1-886910-27-0). Twenty-seven

months after being abducted by aliens, Joey returns home to find that everything has changed while he has remained the same. (Rev: BCCB 7–8/98; BL 5/15/98; HBG 10/98; SLJ 6/98; VOYA 10/98)

6444 Card, Orson Scott. *First Meetings: In the Enderverse* (6–12). 2003, Tor $17.95 (978-0-7653-0873-3). Contains the novella "Ender's Game," first published in 1977, and three other stories, one previously unpublished. (Rev: SLJ 1/04)

6445 Card, Orson Scott. *Pathfinder* (8–12). 2010, Simon & Schuster $18.99 (978-1-4169-9176-2). Thirteen-year-old Rigg can see the paths of others' pasts, and revelations after his father's death set him on a dangerous quest accompanied by friends who can bend time. ℮ (Rev: BL 11/1/10*; SLJ 12/1/10)

6446 Carman, Patrick. *Atherton: The House of Power* (5–8). 2007, Little, Brown $16.99 (978-0-316-16670-6). Atherton is a socially divided world under threat and 12-year-old Edgar has a book that contains key secrets. ∩ (Rev: BL 5/15/07; LMC 11/07; SLJ 6/07)

6447 Carman, Patrick. *The Dark Planet* (5–8). Illus. by Squire Broel. Series: Atherton. 2009, Little, Brown $16.99 (978-0-316-16674-4). In the action-driven conclusion to this trilogy, Edgar seeks answers about himself as he desperately works to save the homeland of his friend, Dr. Harding. ∩ (Rev: SLJ 10/09; VOYA 10/09)

6448 Carman, Patrick. *Pulse* (7–12). 2013, HarperCollins $17.99 (978-006208576-4). In 2051 the United States is divided in two but a small group lives in the middle zone, including Faith and Dylan — who have the Pulse — and the brilliant Hawk. Can these three teens save the world from impending doom? ℮ Lexile HL820L (Rev: BL 12/15/12; SLJ 3/13; VOYA 12/12)

6449 Carmichael, Claire. *Leaving Simplicity* (6–9). 2007, Annick $21.95 (978-1-55451-090-0); paper $10.95 (978-1-55451-089-4). In a future where advertising and marketing are king, teenagers Taylor and Barrett find themselves in danger when they decide to resist. (Rev: BL 12/15/07)

6450 Carroll, Michael. *Super Human* (5–8). 2010, Philomel $16.99 (978-0-399-25297-6). Four teens with superpowers challenge the Helotry's plans to resurrect an ancient warrior. YALSA Popular Paperbacks for Young Adults Top Ten 2012. ℮ Lexile 690L (Rev: BL 5/1/10; LMC 10/10; SLJ 7/10; VOYA 8/10)

6451 Cart, Michael, ed. *Tomorrowland: 10 Stories About the Future* (7–10). 1999, Scholastic paper $15.95 (978-0-590-37678-5). Ten writers, including Ron Koertge, Lois Lowry, and Katherine Paterson, have contributed original stories to this anthology that reflect their concepts of the future. (Rev: BCCB 12/99; BL 8/99; HBG 4/00; SLJ 9/99; VOYA 12/99)

6452 Cass, Kiera. *The Selection* (7–10). 2012, HarperCollins $17.99 (978-006205993-2). In a dystopian future America with strict social structures America

Singer is one of 35 young women competing to win the heart of Prince Maxon even though she is already in love with Aspen. ℮ Lexile HL680L (Rev: BL 5/1/12; SLJ 6/12)

6453 Castellucci, Cecil. *First Day on Earth* (7–10). 2011, Scholastic $17.99 (978-054506082-0). A brief, absorbing novel in which Mal, who has contended with an absent father and alcoholic mother, also believes he has been temporarily abducted by aliens and then returned to an uncertain Earth. ℮ Lexile HL540L (Rev: BL 10/1/11; HB 11–12/11; LMC 1–2/12*)

6454 Castro, Adam-Troy. *Spider-Man: Secret of the Sinister Six* (7–12). Illus. by Mike Zeck. 2002, BP $24.95 (978-0-7434-4464-4). Six supervillains attack New York City and Spider-Man comes to the rescue in this humorous and action-packed final installment in a trilogy. (Rev: SLJ 7/02)

6455 Cheva, Cherry. *DupliKate* (7–10). 2009, HarperTeen $16.99 (978-0-06-128854-8). When 17-year-old Kate's online gaming avatar comes to life, the overbooked teen welcomes the extra set of hands — until her duplicate's wild nature and separate agenda begin to come through. ℮ (Rev: BL 12/1/09; SLJ 10/09)

6456 Clancy, Tom, and Steve Pieczenik. *Virtual Vandals* (7–12). Series: Net Force. 1999, Berkley paper $4.99 (978-0-425-16173-9). In 2025, after Matt Hunter and his computer friends attend an all-star virtual reality baseball game where terrorists shoot wildly at the stands, our hero and his pals set out to catch the culprits. Followed by *The Deadliest Game*. (Rev: BL 3/15/99)

6457 Clarke, Arthur C. *Childhood's End* (7–12). 1963, Ballantine paper $6.99 (978-0-345-34795-4). The overlords' arrival on Earth marks the beginning of the end for humankind.

6458 Clayton, Emma. *The Roar* (5–8). 2009, Scholastic $17.99 (978-0-439-92593-8). This fast-paced science fiction novel revolves around twins from a society ruined by plagues and chemicals and under the control of an evil government bent on selecting (through arcade games) and training unsuspecting youth for an army. ∩ (Rev: BCCB 5/09; LMC 5/09; SLJ 5/09)

6459 Clements, Andrew. *Things Not Seen* (7–10). 2002, Putnam $16.99 (978-0-399-23626-6). Bobby, 15, suddenly becomes invisible and must deal with all the problems his "disappearance" causes. (Rev: BCCB 6/02; BL 4/15/02; HB 3–4/02; HBG 10/02; SLJ 3/02; VOYA 2/02)

6460 Colfer, Eoin. *The Supernaturalist* (6–9). 2004, Hyperion $16.95 (978-0-7868-5148-5). In this action-packed futuristic novel, 14-year-old Cosmo Hill escapes from an orphanage and is befriended by an unlikely trio known as the Supernaturalists, who draft the teen to join them in their campaign against the invisible but deadly Parasites. (Rev: BCCB 9/04; BL 8/04; SLJ 7/04; VOYA 8/04)

6461 Collins, Paul. *The Skyborn* (8–11). 2005, Tor $17.95 (978-0-7653-1273-0). Accepted by the Earthborn after his ship *Colony* crashed on post-holocaust Earth, 14-year-old Welkin, born a Skyborn, learns the Earthborn are in danger from the Skyborn; a sequel to *The Earthborn* (2003). (Rev: BL 2/15/06)

6462 Collins, Suzanne. *The Hunger Games* (7–12). 2008, Scholastic $17.99 (978-0-439-02348-1). A tense survival story set in a future dystopian North America, in which 16-year-old Kat is thrust into a fight to the death on live TV. ALA Notable Books 2009. ∩ (Rev: BL 9/1/08*; HB 7–8/08; LMC 11–12/08*; SLJ 9/1/08*; VOYA 4/08)

6463 Cooper, Clare. *Ashar of Qarius* (5–8). 1990, Harcourt $14.95 (978-0-15-200409-5). A teenage girl, two children, and their pets are left alone in a space dome and must find a way to survive. (Rev: BL 5/15/90; SLJ 7/90)

6464 Cowley, Joy. *Starbright and the Dream Eater* (5–8). 2000, HarperCollins LB $14.89 (978-0-06-028420-6). A child born to a mentally disabled teenage mother and named Starbright is destined to save the earth from the Dream Eater. (Rev: BCCB 7–8/00; BL 4/15/00; HBG 10/00; SLJ 6/00)

6465 Craig, Joe. *Jimmy Coates: Assassin?* (4–7). 2005, HarperCollins LB $16.89 (978-0-06-077264-2). Thirty-five percent human and 65 percent technologically engineered assassin, 11-year-old Jimmy Coates faces external dangers and internal struggles, all with action, suspense, and humor. (Rev: BL 5/1/05; SLJ 6/05)

6466 Craig, Joe. *Jimmy Coates: Target* (5–8). 2007, HarperCollins $16.99 (978-0-06-077266-6). Jimmy Coates, mostly robot but part human, chooses his human side and ends up on the run from the government that wants him assassinated. (Rev: BL 6/1–15/07)

6467 Crockett, S. D. *After the Snow* (8–12). 2012, Feiwel & Friends $16.99 (978-031264169-6). In a new Ice Age 15-year-old Willo's family disappears and he sets off in the cold to find them, meeting a young girl called Mary and facing many dangers; in this postapocalyptic world with little government Willo speaks a fractured English. ℮ Lexile HL700L (Rev: BL 3/1/12; HB 3–4/12; LMC 8–9/12; SLJ 3/12*)

6468 Czerneda, Julie E. *In the Company of Others* (7–12). 2001, DAW paper $7.99 (978-0-88677-999-3). Biologist Gail Smith embarks on the space ship Seeker to track down Aaron Pardell, whose help she needs in her mission to find and destroy a deadly life form called the Quill. (Rev: VOYA 2/02)

6469 Daley, Michael J. *Shanghaied to the Moon* (5–8). 2007, Putnam $16.99 (978-0-399-24619-7). In the year 2165, 13-year-old Stewart Hale wants above all to become a space pilot like his mother was before she died in a crash; when his father refuses to help him, he runs away and finds himself on a secret mission to the moon. (Rev: BL 5/1/07; SLJ 5/07)

6470 Diamand, Emily. *Flood and Fire* (4–7). 2011, Scholastic $17.99 (978-0-545-24268-4). In this sequel to *Raiders' Ransom* set in a troubled 23rd-century England, Lilly struggles to protect Lexy and their game-playing computer while grappling with tense problems that arise in their dystopian world. ℮ Lexile 700L (Rev: BL 7/11; SLJ 7/11)

6471 Dick, Philip K. *Nick and the Glimmung* (7–10). 2008, Subterranean $35.00 (978-159606168-2). Die-hard science fiction fans will enjoy this complex story in which Dick travels from Earth to a more animal-friendly planet. (Rev: BL 3/1/09)

6472 Dickinson, Peter. *Eva* (8–12). 1990, Dell paper $5.50 (978-0-440-20766-5). When Eva wakes up after an accident she finds that she has retained her memory but been given the body of a chimpanzee. (Rev: HB 7/89; SLJ 4/89)

6473 Dicks, Terrance. *Doctor Who and the Genesis of the Daleks* (7–9). 1979, Amereon $18.95 (978-0-8488-0151-9). Based on the TV series, this is the story of an unusual Time Lord and his adventures in space.

6474 DiTerlizzi, Tony. *The Search for Wondla* (5–8). 2010, Simon & Schuster $17.99 (978-1-4169-8310-1). Eva Nine, 12, who has been raised by a robot in an underground home, finally gets to see the real world and finds it a dangerous place full of bizarre creatures; features many rich illustrations and, using a Webcam, readers can access additional information on Eva Nine's world. ∩ Lexile 760L (Rev: BL 9/1/10; LMC 11–12/10; SLJ 8/10)

6475 Doyle, Debra, and James D. MacDonald. *Groogleman* (5–8). 1996, Harcourt $15.00 (978-0-15-200235-0). In this novel set in the future, 13-year-old Dan is immune to the plague that is devastating the countryside and sets out with friend Leesie to help tend the sick. (Rev: BCCB 12/96; SLJ 12/96; VOYA 6/97)

6476 Dunkle, Clare B. *The Sky Inside* (4–8). 2008, Atheneum $16.99 (978-1-4169-2422-7). Martin discovers the terrible truth about his flawless, enclosed suburb when he gathers the courage to venture outside it. (Rev: BL 5/15/08; SLJ 5/08)

6477 Dunkle, Clare B. *The Walls Have Eyes* (5–8). 2009, Atheneum $16.99 (978-1-4169-5379-1). Martin continues his life-threatening adventures as he faces the controlling forces of his society in this sci-fi sequel to *The Sky Inside* (2008). (Rev: BL 7/09)

6478 Dunn, Mark. *The Age of Altertron* (4–7). Series: The Calamitous Adventures of Rodney and Wayne, Cosmic Repairboys. 2009, McAdam/Cage paper $12.95 (978-0-59692-345-4). In an alternate 1956 the town of Pitcherville is facing numerous strange calamities that 13-year-old twins Rodney and Wayne attempt to resolve with the aid of a physics teacher; the first

installment in a zany series. (Rev: LMC 3–4/10; SLJ 2/10)

6479 Emerson, Kevin. *The Lost Code. Bk. 1* (8–10). Series: Atlanteans. 2012, HarperCollins $17.99 (978-0-06-206279-6). At a summer camp under a giant dome that allows survival in a world ravaged by environmental problems, Owen learns that he may be the descendant of an ancient race and may hold the key to Earth's salvation. ℮ Lexile HL730L (Rev: SLJ 7/12)

6480 Enthoven, Sam. *Tim, Defender of the Earth* (5–8). 2008, Penguin $19.99 (978-1-59514-184-2). Tim, a huge, T. rex-type fighting monster, breaks out of his underground lab to save London and the world from a crazy scientist — with the help of 14-year-old Anna and her friend Chris. (Rev: BL 1/1–15/08; SLJ 3/08)

6481 Evans, Richard Paul. *Michael Vey: The Prisoner of Cell 25* (7–10). 2011, Simon & Schuster $17.99 (978-1-4516-6183-5). Michael, 14, has the power to produce electric shocks and is surprised to find that a lovely girl in his new school has similar powers — and then the two discover there is a deeper force at work. ∩ ℮ (Rev: BLO 9/1/11; LMC 1–2/12; SLJ 11/1/11)

6482 Fagan, Deva. *Circus Galacticus* (4–7). 2011, Harcourt $16.99 (978-054758136-1). Frustrated orphan Trix joins a circus that tours the universe in a spaceship and learns to navigate new relationships and explore her past. (Rev: BL 11/15/11; SLJ 1/12; VOYA 12/11)

6483 Falkner, Brian. *The Assault* (7–12). 2012, Random House $17.99 (978-0-375-86946-4); LB $20.99 (978-0-375-96946-1). In 2030 a Recon Team Angel consisting of six teens modified to look like the aliens that are close to controlling the Earth infiltrates the enemy lines and discovers shocking secrets. ℮ (Rev: LMC 1–2/13; SLJ 1/13; VOYA 10/12)

6484 Falls, Kat. *Dark Life* (6–9). 2010, Scholastic $16.99 (978-0-545-17814-3). From an undersea community that supplies food to the "Topsiders" in the mostly destroyed Earth above, 16-year-old Ty works with his new friend Gemma to catch pirates. ∩ Lexile 690L (Rev: BL 5/15/10; LMC 10/10; SLJ 6/10; VOYA 4/10)

6485 Farmer, Nancy. *The Ear, the Eye and the Arm* (7–10). 1994, Orchard LB $19.99 (978-0-531-08679-7). In Zimbabwe in 2194, the military ruler's son, 13, and his younger siblings leave their technologically overcontrolled home and embark on a series of perilous adventures. (Rev: BL 4/1/94; SLJ 6/94; VOYA 6/94)

6486 Farmer, Nancy. *House of the Scorpion* (7–10). 2002, Simon & Schuster $17.95 (978-0-689-85222-0). Young Matt, who has spent his childhood in cruel circumstances, discovers he is in fact a clone of the 142-year-old ruler of Opium, a land south of the U.S. border. (Rev: BL 9/15/02; HB 11–12/02; HBG 3/03; SLJ 9/02)

6487 Fergus, Maureen. *Ortega* (5–8). 2010, Kids Can $16.95 (978-1-55453-474-6). A gorilla named Ortega has been raised in a laboratory and given the ability to speak, but when he is asked to attend middle school, things go awry. Lexile 1040L (Rev: LMC 10/10; SLJ 7/10)

6488 Fisher, Catherine. *Corbenic* (8–11). 2006, Greenwillow $16.99 (978-0-06-072470-2). Cal leaves his alcoholic mother to live with his uncle but on the train ride there is transported to a mythical place called Corbenic, where the fate of the Fisher King lies in his hands. (Rev: BL 8/06; HB 9–10/06; SLJ 11/06)

6489 Follett, Ken. *The Power Twins* (4–8). 1991, Scholastic paper $2.75 (978-0-590-42507-0). Three youngsters travel to a planet where large, gentle worms live. (Rev: SLJ 1/91)

6490 Foster, Alan Dean. *The Hand of Dinotopia* (6–10). Series: Dinotopia. 1999, HarperCollins $22.99 (978-0-06-028005-5). In this adventure involving dinosaurs, our heroes journey through the Great Desert and Outer Island to find the key to a sea route that will link Dinotopia to the rest of the world. (Rev: BL 5/1/99; HBG 10/99; SLJ 4/99)

6491 Foster, Alan Dean. *Splinter of the Mind's Eye* (8–12). 1978, Ballantine paper $6.99 (978-0-345-32023-0). A novel about Luke Skywalker and Princess Leia of *Star Wars* fame and their battle against the Empire.

6492 Fukui, Isamu. *Truancy* (8–12). 2008, Tor $17.95 (978-0-7653-1767-4). Fifteen-year-old Tack joins a children's resistance movement called the Truancy that is bent on violently overthrowing the establishment. (Rev: BL 4/15/08; LMC 4–5/08; SLJ 6/08)

6493 Gaiman, Neil, and Michael Reaves. *InterWorld* (5–8). 2007, Eos $16.99 (978-0-06-123896-3). Joey, 16, discovers that he can walk into alternate dimensions where he finds other versions of himself and is recruited into an army of Joeys that battles Lord Dogknife and Lady Indigo, two evil magicians. ⌂ (Rev: BL 9/1/07; SLJ 11/07)

6494 Gerrold, David. *Blood and Fire* (8–12). 2004, BenBella paper $14.95 (978-1-932100-11-2). In this story that is a metaphor for the AIDS problem, a starship happens on another one, adrift in space, that contains blood worms, a deadly parasite. (Rev: BL 1/1–15/04)

6495 Gerrold, David. *Chess with a Dragon* (8–12). 1988, Avon paper $3.50 (978-0-380-70662-4). The entire human race becomes slaves of giant slugs and Yake must save them. (Rev: BL 6/15/87; SLJ 9/87)

6496 Ghislain, Gary. *How I Stole Johnny Depp's Alien Girlfriend* (8–11). 2011, Chronicle $16.99 (978-0-8118-7460-1). Fourteen-year-old David, son of a French psychologist, falls for Zelda, a beautiful patient who believes she is an alien and who is devoted to Johnny Depp. ℮ Lexile HL570L (Rev: BL 6/1/11; LMC 8–9/11; SLJ 7/11; VOYA 6/11)

6497 Gideon, Melanie. *Pucker* (8–11). 2006, Penguin $16.99 (978-1-59514-055-5). Nicknamed "Pucker" by his classmates for the horrible burn scars on his face, 17-year-old Thomas Quicksilver has even larger issues to confront as he returns to his home world of Isaura on a mission to save his mother's life. (Rev: BL 4/15/06; SLJ 5/06)

6498 Gilden, Mel. *Outer Space and All That Junk* (5–7). 1989, HarperCollins LB $12.89 (978-0-397-32307-4). Myron's uncle is collecting junk, which he believes will help aliens return to their home in outer space. (Rev: BL 12/1/89; SLJ 12/89)

6499 Gill, David Macinnis. *Black Hole Sun* (8–11). 2010, Greenwillow $16.99 (978-0-06-167304-7). In this action-packed novel set on a dystopian Mars, 16-year-old Durango and other mercenaries fight to protect mines at the South Pole. (Rev: BL 6/10*; SLJ 11/1/10)

6500 Gill, David Macinnis. *Invisible Sun* (8–11). 2012, Greenwillow $16.99 (978-006207332-7). Teens Durango and Vienne, mercenary soldiers, continue their adventures on Mars as they investigate his past in this action-packed stand-alone companion to *Black Hole Sun* (2010). ℮ (Rev: BL 4/1/12; SLJ 5/1/12; VOYA 2/12)

6501 Gilmore, Kate. *The Exchange Student* (6–9). 1999, Houghton Mifflin $15.00 (978-0-395-57511-6). Set in the year 2094, this novel describes the problems faced by a group of exchange students from the planet Chela who are studying on Earth. (Rev: BL 9/15/99; HB 9–10/99; HBG 4/00; SLJ 10/99)

6502 Grant, Michael. *Fear* (7–10). Series: Gone. 2012, HarperCollins $17.99 (978-006144915-4). This fifth installment in the series finds the young people of Perdido Beach threatened by the Darkness, heightening their ever-present fear. ℮ Lexile HL610L (Rev: BL 2/1/12)

6503 Grant, Michael. *Gone* (6–9). 2008, HarperTeen $17.99 (978-0-06-144876-8). When everyone older than 13 simply vanishes one day, the children are left to fend for themselves and realize that strange things are happening to the humans and animals left behind. (Rev: BL 5/15/08*; SLJ 8/08)

6504 Grant, Michael. *Hunger: A Gone Novel* (6–9). Series: Gone. 2009, HarperTeen $17.99 (978-0-06-144906-2); LB $18.89 (978-0-06-144907-9). Three months after the events of *Gone* (2008), the young adults who survived the catastrophe are running out of food and dividing into groups according to their abilities even as they face a new, mind-manipulating danger. ℮ Lexile HL570L (Rev: BL 8/09; SLJ 7/1/09; VOYA 4/10)

6505 Grant, Michael, and Katherine Applegate. *Eve and Adam* (7–10). 2012, Feiwel & Friends $17.99 (978-0-312-58351-4). After having her leg reattached following a car accident, Evening, daughter of a genetic engineering specialist, meets a boy named Solo and makes alarming discoveries. ∩ Lexile HL560L (Rev: BL 9/15/12; HB 1–2/13; LMC 3–4/13; SLJ 11/12; VOYA 10/12)

6506 Grant, Sara. *Dark Parties* (8–12). 2011, Little, Brown $17.99 (978-0-316-08594-6). Neva, 16, and her friend Sanna begin to question the need for their people to live enclosed in the Protectosphere that has covered the Homeland since the "Terror." **e** Lexile HL560L (Rev: BL 5/1/11; LMC 10/11; SLJ 12/1/11; VOYA 8/11)

6507 Guibert, Emmanuel, and Joann Sfar. *Sardine in Outer Space 3* (5–8). Trans. by Elisabeth Brizzi. 2007, Roaring Brook paper $12.95 (978-1-59643-128-7). Sardine and her space-pirate friends tackle Supermuscleman among others in this series of zany adventures. (Rev: BL 3/15/07; SLJ 7/07)

6508 Gutman, Dan. *Cyberkid* (4–8). 1998, Hyperion LB $14.49 (978-0-7868-2344-4). Yip, a computer-savvy 12-year-old, and his sister, Paige, create a "virtual actor," or "vactor," who breaks out of cyberspace and reveals a serious flaw: his database does not include a conscience. (Rev: BL 6/1–15/98; SLJ 8/98)

6509 Haarsma, P. J. *Betrayal on Orbis 2* (5–8). Series: The Softwire. 2008, Candlewick $16.99 (978-0-7636-2710-2). This sequel to *Virus on Orbis 1* finds JT and his friends enslaved to aquatic aliens called Samirans on a wormhole ring. (Rev: BL 5/15/08; SLJ 7/08)

6510 Haarsma, P. J. *Virus on Orbis 1* (6–9). 2006, Candlewick $15.99 (978-0-7636-2709-6). Johnny, 12, and his sister have spent their lives traveling with other children on a spaceship to Orbis, where Johnny learns that he has the ability to communicate telepathically with computers, an ability that puts him in danger. (Rev: BL 11/15/06; LMC 2/07; SLJ 12/06)

6511 Haarsma, P. J. *Wormhole Pirates on Orbis 3* (6–9). Series: The Softwire. 2009, Candlewick $16.99 (978-076362711-9). On Orbis 3, J. T. and his friends face hostile wormhole pirates and a challenging and dangerous game. **e** (Rev: BLO 6/16/09)

6512 Haddix, Margaret Peterson. *The Always War* (6–8). 2011, Simon & Schuster $16.99 (978-1-4169-9526-5). The war has lasted more than 75 years when 15-year-old Tessa and her friends Gideon and Dek begin to discover the truth behind its cause. **e** Lexile 700L (Rev: SLJ 12/1/11)

6513 Haddix, Margaret Peterson. *Among the Barons* (5–8). 2003, Simon & Schuster $16.95 (978-0-689-83906-1). Luke, a third child who has been living underground in this two-child society, comes close to exposure in this exciting installment in the series that began with *Among the Hidden* (1998). (Rev: BL 5/15/03; HBG 10/03; SLJ 6/03; VOYA 8/03)

6514 Haddix, Margaret Peterson. *Among the Betrayed* (5–9). 2002, Simon & Schuster $16.95 (978-0-689-

83905-4). In this third novel in the series that started with *Among the Hidden* (1998), illegal third child Nina faces danger and difficult decisions. (Rev: BCCB 10/02; HBG 10/02; SLJ 6/02; VOYA 6/02)

6515 Haddix, Margaret Peterson. *Among the Brave* (4–7). Series: Shadow Children. 2004, Simon & Schuster $15.95 (978-0-689-85794-2). This sequel to *Among the Barons* (2003) features Trey's efforts to rescue Luke and other third-born children. (Rev: BL 5/15/04; SLJ 6/04)

6516 Haddix, Margaret Peterson. *Among the Enemy* (5–8). Series: Shadow Children. 2005, Simon & Schuster $15.95 (978-0-689-85796-6). Matthias, one of the third children illegal in his society, is mistakenly welcomed into the Population Police; there he is confused by divided loyalties. (Rev: BL 6/1–15/05; SLJ 6/05)

6517 Haddix, Margaret Peterson. *Among the Free* (5–8). Series: Shadow Children. 2006, Simon & Schuster $16.95 (978-0-689-85798-0). Illegal third child Luke inadvertently sets off an uprising that leads to the overthrow of his country's oppressive government. (Rev: BL 6/1–15/06; SLJ 8/06)

6518 Haddix, Margaret Peterson. *Among the Hidden* (5–8). 1998, Simon & Schuster $16.95 (978-0-689-81700-7). In a society where only two children are allowed per family, Luke, the third, endures a secret life hidden from authorities. (Rev: HBG 3/99; SLJ 9/98; VOYA 10/98)

6519 Haddix, Margaret Peterson. *Among the Impostors* (5–7). 2001, Simon & Schuster $16.00 (978-0-689-83904-7). As a third child in a society that allows only two per family, Luke has assumed a new identity and at age 12 enrolls in a nightmarish boarding school. (Rev: BCCB 9/01; BL 4/15/01; HBG 10/01; SLJ 7/01; VOYA 8/01)

6520 Haddix, Margaret Peterson. *Caught* (5–8). Series: Missing. 2012, Simon & Schuster $16.99 (978-141698982-0). Jonah and Katherine travel to 1903 Switzerland and Serbia to return Albert Einstein's daughter Lieserl to history, but his wife Mileva, who seems to understand a lot about time travel, is unwilling to let her daughter go. ∩ **e** Lexile 730L (Rev: BL 8/12; SLJ 3/13)

6521 Haddix, Margaret Peterson. *Double Identity* (5–8). 2005, Simon & Schuster $15.95 (978-0-689-87374-4). In this science fiction page-turner, 12-year-old Bethany Cole, left with her aunt after her mother suffers a nervous breakdown, uncovers some shocking family secrets. (Rev: BL 10/1/05; SLJ 11/05; VOYA 10/05)

6522 Haddix, Margaret Peterson. *Found* (6–12). Series: The Missing. 2008, Simon & Schuster $15.99 (978-1-4169-6227-4). Thirteen-year-old Jonah, who was adopted, receives strange notes referring to his past and discovers that, as babies, he and 35 other children traveled through time and arrived on an unpiloted airplane. ∩ (Rev: BL 5/1/08; LMC 4–5/08; SLJ 5/08)

6523 Haddix, Margaret Peterson. *Sabotaged* (5–8). Series: The Missing. 2010, Simon & Schuster $16.99 (978-141695424-8). Siblings Jonah and Katherine are sent back in time to help a missing child in the mysterious Roanoke Colony, but things do not go as planned. ∩ ℯ (Rev: BL 10/1/10; SLJ 7/10)

6524 Haddix, Margaret Peterson. *Sent* (5–8). Series: The Missing. 2009, Simon & Schuster $15.99 (978-1-4169-5422-4). In this suspenseful sequel to 2008's *Found*, Chip, Jonah, Katherine, and Alex arrive in 15th-century England through the magic of time travel, and struggle to save Princes Edward and Richard from their fates while watching history unfold. (Rev: BL 8/09; SLJ 10/09)

6525 Hall, Teri. *Away* (5–8). 2011, Dial $16.99 (978-0-8037-3502-6). In this sequel to *The Line* (2010), Rachel is struggling to adapt to living among the Others and continues to search for father, who she now learns is still alive. (Rev: BLO 9/15/11; SLJ 12/1/11)

6526 Hall, Teri. *The Line* (5–8). 2010, Dial $16.99 (978-0-803-73466-1). Rachel lives with her mother on an estate close to the Line, which separates the Unified States from the territory called Away; when she hears a plaintive recording from Away, Rachel feels compelled to act. ℯ Lexile 760L (Rev: BL 2/1/10; LMC 3–4/10; SLJ 4/10)

6527 Harland, Richard. *Liberator* (6–9). 2012, Simon & Schuster $17.99 (978-144242333-6). The Swanks and the Filthies remain in conflict as Col and Riff attempt to build a new society aboard the *Liberator* in this steampunk sequel to *Worldshaker* (2010). ∩ ℯ Lexile 680L (Rev: BLO 4/1/12; SLJ 6/12; VOYA 4/12)

6528 Hauge, Lesley. *Nomansland* (8–11). 2010, Henry Holt $16.99 (978-0-8050-9064-2). In a future dystopian world, members of a society of women discover a trove of fashion magazines , with unsettling results. ∩ (Rev: BL 5/15/10; HB 7–8/10; LMC 8–9/10; SLJ 8/10)

6529 Hautman, Pete. *The Obsidian Blade* (8–12). 2012, Candlewick $16.99 (978-076365403-0). After 13-year-old Tucker's parents disappear, he investigates the strange disks that hover in the air and is transported through time, visiting many civilizations. ∩ ℯ Lexile 740L (Rev: BL 2/15/12*; HB 5–6/12; LMC 10/12; SLJ 6/12; VOYA 4/12)

6530 Hayden, Patrick Nielsen, ed. *New Skies: An Anthology of Today's Science Fiction* (7–12). 2003, Tor $19.95 (978-0-7653-0010-2). Short stories that were originally published in science fiction magazines include pieces by Orson Scott Card, Philip K. Dick, and Connie Willis. (Rev: BL 1/1–15/04)

6531 Heath, Jack. *The Lab* (5–8). 2008, Scholastic $17.99 (978-0-545-06860-4). This action-packed thriller features a teen known as Agent Six of Hearts who

was created in a lab using a variety of genes and works for an underground organization called The Deck. (Rev: BCCB 12/08; BL 12/1/08; LMC 1/09; SLJ 2/09)

6532 Heath, Jack. *Remote Control* (5–8). 2010, Scholastic $17.99 (978-0-545-07591-6). Genetically engineered teen agent Six of Hearts faces a crime lord and the ChaosSonic corporation as he battles to rescue his kidnapped clone-brother Kyntak; a sequel to *The Lab* (2008). ℯ Lexile 840L (Rev: BL 4/15/10; SLJ 4/10)

6533 Heinlein, Robert A. *The Star Beast* (7–10). 1977, Macmillan $15.00 (978-0-684-15329-2). A pet smuggled to Earth never seems to stop growing.

6534 Heintze, Ty. *Valley of the Eels* (5–8). 1993, Eakin $15.95 (978-0-89015-904-0). A dolphin leads two boys to an underwater station where friendly aliens are cultivating trees to replant on their own planet. (Rev: BL 3/1/94)

6535 Henderson, J. A. *Bunker 10* (6–9). 2007, Harcourt $17.00 (978-0-15-206240-8). To survive the coming destruction of their military installation, a group of techno-genius teens must use all their skills — in both reality and virtual reality. (Rev: BL 10/1/07; LMC 1/08; SLJ 1/08)

6536 Hickam, Homer. *Crater* (6–12). Series: Helium-3. 2012, Thomas Nelson $14.99 (978-1-595-54664-7). After a daring rescue, 16-year-old Crater Trueblood who has been a mine worker on the moon, is sent on a dangerous quest; set in the 22nd century. ∩ ℯ Lexile 910L (Rev: SLJ 5/1/12*)

6537 Hill, William. *The Magic Bicycle* (5–8). 1998, Otter Creek paper $13.95 (978-1-890611-00-2). For helping an alien escape, Danny receives a magical bicycle that is capable of transporting him through time and space. (Rev: BL 1/1–15/98; SLJ 3/98)

6538 Hirsch, Jeff. *The Eleventh Plague* (7–10). 2011, Scholastic $17.99 (978-054529014-2). In the aftermath of the Collapse, 15-year-old Stephen warily enters a community that tries to emulate the pre-apocalyptic world. ∩ ℯ Lexile 790L (Rev: BL 9/1/11; LMC 1–2/12; SLJ 2/12)

6539 Hobbs, Will. *Go Big or Go Home* (5–8). 2008, HarperCollins $15.99 (978-0-06-074141-9). A meteorite crashes into Brady's bedroom in South Dakota, and Brady soon finds that something in the space debris has changed him. (Rev: BL 4/1/08; HB 5–6/08; SLJ 4/08)

6540 Holt, K. A. *Mike Stellar: Nerves of Steel* (4–7). 2009, Random $15.99 (978-0-375-84556-7). Mike's world is turned upside down when his parents make him move to Mars, and he discovers that they are part of a secret plot. (Rev: BLO 7/6/09)

6541 Hughes, Monica. *Invitation to the Game* (7–10). 1991, Simon & Schuster paper $4.99 (978-0-671-86692-1). In 2154, a high school graduate and her friends face life on welfare in a highly robotic society and are invited to participate in a sinister government "game." (Rev: BL 9/15/91)

6542 Hughes, Monica. *The Keeper of the Isis Light* (7–9). 2008, Atheneum paper $11.99 (978-1-4169-8963-9). A 16-year-old girl's lonely existence on planet Isis comes to an end when settlers arrive; first published in 1981.

6543 Hulme, John, and Michael Wexler. *The Split Second* (5–8). Series: The Seems. 2008, Bloomsbury $16.99 (978-159990130-5). In this followup to 2007's *The Glitch in Sleep,* 13-year-old Becker Drane sets about using his talents to save a fantastical world beset by horrifying storms. ⌒ ℮ Lexile 1030L (Rev: BL 10/15/08; SLJ 1/1/09; VOYA 2/09)

6544 James, Nick. *Skyship Academy: The Pearl Wars* (7–10). 2011, Flux paper $9.95 (978-07387234-1-9). In 2095, when people either live in the Chosen Cities or the Fringe Towns, young Jesse and Cassius meet while searching for prized energy-full Pearls and wonder about the past. ⌒ ℮ Lexile HL650L (Rev: BL 10/15/11; LMC 11–12/11; VOYA 10/11)

6545 Jeapes, Ben. *The Xenocide Mission* (7–10). 2002, Viking $15.95 (978-0-385-75007-3). A complex and exciting adventure set in the distant future in which humans and their quadruped companions must fight against ferocious aliens known as the Kin. (Rev: BCCB 6/02; BL 4/15/02; HBG 3/03; SLJ 6/02; VOYA 8/02)

6546 Jeter, K. W. *The Mandalorian Armor* (7–9). Series: The Bounty Hunter Wars. 1998, Bantam paper $6.99 (978-0-553-57885-0). This first installment in a trilogy involves Boba Fett, the bounty hunter who captured Han Solo in *The Empire Strikes Back.* (Rev: VOYA 2/99)

6547 Jinks, Catherine. *Living Hell* (7–10). 2010, Houghton Mifflin $17 (978-0-15-206193-7). On a spaceship on a long journey to find a habitable planet, 17-year-old Cheney finds the peaceful routine turned on its head when they pass through a radiation field. ℮ Lexile 600L (Rev: BL 2/15/10; HB 3–4/10; SLJ 4/10; VOYA 6/10)

6548 Johansen, K. V. *The Cassandra Virus* (5–8). 2006, Orca paper $7.95 (978-1-55143-497-1). Computer geek Jordan designs a powerful computer program that takes on a life of its own, spreading via the Internet to other computers and taking control of their operations. (Rev: SLJ 11/06; VOYA 8/06)

6549 John, Antony. *Elemental* (7–10). 2012, Dial $17.99 (978-080373682-5). Thomas, 16, copes with his seemingly powerless condition in a dystopia where everyone else represents either wind, water, fire, or earth. ℮ Lexile HL580L (Rev: BL 11/15/12; LMC 1–2/13; SLJ 1/13)

6550 Jones, Diana Wynne. *Hexwood* (8–12). 1994, Greenwillow $16.00 (978-0-688-12488-5). A complex science fiction story about virtual realism, time manipulation, and a young girl who investigates the disappear-

ance of guests at Hexwood Farm. (Rev: BL 6/1–15/94; SLJ 3/94; VOYA 10/94)

6551 Kacvinsky, Katie. *Awaken* (8–11). 2011, Houghton Mifflin $16.99 (978-0-547-37148-1). In 2060 Americans rarely leave their homes and everything takes place online; but 17-year-old Maddie finds herself targeted by a group, including the handsome Justin, that advocates disconnecting from the virtual world. ℮ Lexile HL700L (Rev: BL 4/1/11; LMC 10/11; SLJ 11/1/11; VOYA 4/11)

6552 Kacvinsky, Katie. *Middle Ground* (8–12). 2012, Houghton Mifflin $16.99 (978-054786336-8). In 2060 Los Angeles 17-year-old Maddie is sent to a detention center and must struggle to resist the reprogramming done there; a sequel to *Awaken* (2011). (Rev: BLO 11/1/12; SLJ 3/13; VOYA 10/12)

6553 Keaney, Brian. *The Hollow People* (6–9). Illus. by Nicoletta Ceccoli. Series: The Promises of Dr. Sigmundus. 2007, Knopf $16.99 (978-0-375-84332-7). Dante and Beatrice, both 13, attempt to escape from Tarnegar island, where dreams and subversive thoughts are controlled by medication under the supervision of Dr. Sigmundus. (Rev: BL 11/1/07; SLJ 1/08)

6554 Key, Alexander. *The Forgotten Door* (5–7). 1986, Scholastic paper $4.99 (978-0-590-43130-9). When little Jon falls to earth from another planet, he encounters suspicion and hostility as well as sympathy. A reissue.

6555 Khoury, Jessica. *Origin* (7–10). 2012, Penguin $17.99 (978-1-59514-595-6). Created by scientists striving to create a new immortal race, 17-year-old Pia escapes from her compound in the Amazon and meets Eio, from an indigenous tribe; as she falls in love with him she must take risks and make difficult choices. ℮ Lexile HL740L (Rev: BL 8/12; LMC 3–4/13; SLJ 10/12; VOYA 10/12)

6556 Kiesel, Stanley. *Skinny Malinky Leads the War for Kidness* (6–8). 1984, Avon paper $2.50 (978-0-380-69875-2). Skinny is about to be captured by a powerful mutant red ant.

6557 Kilworth, Garry. *The Electric Kid* (6–9). 1995, Orchard LB $15.99 (978-0-531-08786-2). Two homeless young people struggle for survival in a large city's oppressive underworld in this bleak novel set in the horrifying world of 2061. (Rev: BL 1/1–15/96; SLJ 10/95; VOYA 12/95)

6558 Kincaid, S. J. *Insignia* (8–12). 2012, HarperCollins $17.99 (978-0-06-209299-1). Virtual reality gamer Tom, 14, must submit to having a computer implanted in his brain when he becomes a pilot of drones fighting around the solar system. ℮ Lexile HL750L (Rev: BL 7/12; SLJ 7/12*; VOYA 12/12)

6559 Klass, David. *Firestorm* (8–11). 2006, Farrar $17.00 (978-0-374-32307-3). A thrilling adventure about Jack who learns that he has special powers and was sent back from the future to save the dying planet. (Rev: BL 9/15/06; SLJ 9/06)

6560 Klass, David. *Stuck on Earth* (6–9). 2010, Farrar $16.99 (978-0-374-39951-1). In this funny and thought-provoking novel, the inhabitants of Earth are under evaluation, and Ketchvar takes over the brain of 14-year-old Tom, experiencing school and family life in suburban New Jersey. ℮ Lexile 740L (Rev: BL 12/15/09; HB 3–4/10; LMC 3–4/10; SLJ 2/1/11*)

6561 Krokos, Dan. *False Memory* (8–11). 2012, Hyperion $17.99 (978-1-4231-4976-7). Miranda, 17, wakes up to find she has lost her memory — and that she can emit a strange energy that causes terror and suicide in those around her. ℮ (Rev: BL 8/12; HB 9–10/12; LMC 1–2/13; SLJ 10/12; VOYA 8/12)

6562 Krumwiede, Lana. *Freaking* (5–8). 2012, Candlewick $15.99 (978-076365937-0). When Taemon, 12, loses his psychic abilities, he is cast out from Deliverance to find a mysterious new world where people enjoy using their hands. ⌂ ℮ Lexile HL600L (Rev: BL 10/15/12; SLJ 1/13; VOYA 10/12)

6563 L'Engle, Madeleine. *Many Waters* (7–10). 1986, Farrar $18.00 (978-0-374-34796-3). The Murry twins, from the author's Wrinkle in Time trilogy, time-travel to the Holy Land prior to the Great Flood. (Rev: BL 8/86; SLJ 11/86; VOYA 12/86)

6564 L'Engle, Madeleine. *A Wrinkle in Time* (6–9). 1962, Farrar $17.00 (978-0-374-38613-9). Meg and Charles Wallace Murry, with the help of Calvin O'Keefe, set out in space to find their scientist father. Newbery Medal 1963. Followed by *A Wind in the Door* (1973), *A Swiftly Tilting Planet* (1978), and *A Ring of Endless Light* (1981).

6565 Lancaster, Mike A. *The Future We Left Behind* (7–10). 2012, Egmont $16.99 (978-160684410-6). Long after the release of the Straker Tapes, Peter and Alpha learn that humans were indeed "upgraded" by aliens and that a new upgrade may be on the horizon. ℮ (Rev: BL 11/1/12*; LMC 3–4/13; SLJ 3/13)

6566 Lancaster, Mike A. *Human.4* (7–10). 2011, Egmont $16.99 (978-160684099-3). Kyle, 15, was under hypnosis when humanity was upgraded, and he and his fellow three volunteers are invisible to the larger population. ℮ Lexile 770L (Rev: BL 5/1/11)

6567 Landon, Kristen. *The Limit* (8–11). 2010, Simon & Schuster $15.99 (978-1-4424-0271-3). When his family goes over its spending limit, 13-year-old Matt is sent to the Federal Debt Rehabilitation Agency, where his own living conditions are tolerable, but he recognizes that others are suffering and must be rescued. ℮ (Rev: BL 10/1/10; SLJ 12/1/10)

6568 Lassiter, Rhiannon. *Shadows* (7–10). 2002, Simon & Schuster paper $4.99 (978-0-7434-2212-3). Raven, the superhacker introduced in *Hex*, faces new dangers as the government seeks to destroy her and her fellow mutants. The last volume in the trilogy is *Ghosts* (2002). (Rev: BL 4/15/02; SLJ 4/02)

6569 Lawrence, Louise. *Andra* (6–10). 1991, HarperCollins $14.95 (978-0-06-023685-4). This novel is set 2,000 years in the future, when humanity, having destroyed Earth's environment, lives in rigidly governed, sealed underground cities. (Rev: BL 5/1/91; SLJ 5/91)

6570 Lawrence, Theo. *Mystic City* (7–11). 2012, Delacorte $17.99 (978-038574160-6); LB $20.99 (978-037599013-7). In a dystopian Manhattan submerged by global warming, 18-year-old Aria Rose has lost her memory but is told that she is engaged to Thomas Foster, whose family has been engaged in a long-standing feud with her own. ⌂ ℮ (Rev: BLO 10/15/12; LMC 5–6/13; SLJ 1/13; VOYA 12/12)

6571 Layne, Steven L. *This Side of Paradise* (7–10). 2001, North Star $15.99 (978-0-9712336-9-0). Jack, a junior in high school, soon questions his father's motives for moving the family into a town called Paradise, where things are definitely not what they seem. (Rev: BL 2/1/02; SLJ 1/02; VOYA 2/02)

6572 Le Guin, Ursula K. *The Left Hand of Darkness* (7–12). 1969, Ace paper $7.99 (978-0-441-47812-5). An envoy is sent to the ice-covered planet Gethen where people can be either male or female at will.

6573 Lee, Tanith. *Indigara* (4–7). 2007, Penguin $11.99 (978-0-14-240922-0). Jet and her dog Otis encounter mindless celebrities in the underworld of Planet Obelisk in this humorous meeting of science fiction and pop culture. (Rev: BL 12/15/07; SLJ 12/07)

6574 Lennon, Joan. *Questors* (5–8). 2007, Simon & Schuster $16.99 (978-1-4169-3658-9). When an energy leak threatens the existence of three separate worlds, three youthful half siblings — Bryn, Madlen, and Cam — find they bear a heavy responsibility. (Rev: BL 8/07; HB 1–2/08; LMC 1/08; SLJ 12/07)

6575 Lewis, Jon S. *Invasion* (7–10). Series: C.H.A.O.S. 2011, Thomas Nelson $14.99 (978-159554753-8). After his parents die in a car crash, 16-year-old Colt is recruited by a secret organization that battles aliens. ⌂ ℮ Lexile HL760L (Rev: BL 5/1/11; VOYA 2/11)

6576 Lipsyte, Robert. *The Twinning Project* (5–8). 2012, Clarion $16.99 (978-0-547-64571-1). When Tom discovers that his imaginary friend Eddie is not only real but also his twin living on an another Earth 50 years apart, the brothers both become involved in a struggle to save both planets. ℮ Lexile HL570L (Rev: LMC 3–4/13; SLJ 10/12)

6577 Lo, Malinda. *Adaptation* (8–11). 2012, Little, Brown $17.99 (978-0-316-19796-0). Teens Reese and David are treated at a mysterious facility following a series of bizarre events and begin to realize they've been genetically altered in this science fiction thriller. ℮ (Rev: BL 10/1/12; HB 11–12/12; LMC 3–4/13; SLJ 9/12)

6578 Lore, Pittacus. *The Power of Six* (8–11). Series: Lorien Legacies. 2011, HarperCollins $17.99 (978-0-06-197455-7). In this sequel to *I Am Number Four* (2010) aliens John and Six, with human Sam, are on the run from authorities who think John is a terrorist while Marina, 17, who is in a Spanish convent and is in fact Number Seven, hopes to join them. ∩ ℮ Lexile 840L (Rev: BL 7/11; SLJ 11/1/11)

6579 Lowenstein, Sallie. *Evan's Voice* (5–8). 1998, Lion Stone paper $15.00 (978-0-9658486-1-9). Teenager Jake cares for his catatonic younger brother while seeking civilization's last chance for survival in an area known as the Dead Zone. (Rev: BL 3/1/99; VOYA 6/99)

6580 Lowenstein, Sallie. *Focus* (5–9). 2001, Lion Stone paper $15.00 (978-0-9658486-3-3). The Haldrans leave their planet and relocate to Miners World, where humans live, in order to save their son from discrimination because of his creative intelligence. (Rev: BL 4/15/01; SLJ 8/01; VOYA 8/01)

6581 Lowry, Lois. *Son* (7–10). 2012, Houghton Mifflin $17.99 (978-0-547-88720-3). Set in the same world as *The Giver* (1993), this final volume in the quartet centers on 14-year-old Claire, who gives birth as a Birthmother and then is not given the pills that suppress emotion, leaving her missing her son. ∩ ℮ Lexile 720L (Rev: BL 6/12*; HB 9–10/12; LMC 1–2/13; SLJ 9/12*)

6582 Lu, Marie. *Prodigy* (8–12). 2013, Putnam $17.99 (978-039925676-9). In this sequel to 2011's *Legend*, June and Day travel to Las Vegas and get involved in an assassination plot. ∩ ℮ Lexile 780L (Rev: BL 12/15/12; HB 3–4/13; SLJ 2/13; VOYA 4/13)

6583 Lyga, Barry. *Archvillain* (4–7). 2010, Scholastic $16.99 (978-0-545-19649-9). A plasma storm brings 6th-grader Kyle, already confident and smart, additional strength and intellect, plus the ability to fly; however, to Kyle's dismay, the storm also produces an annoying rival — superpower-endowed Mighty Mike. Lexile 740L (Rev: BL 9/15/10; LMC 11–12/10; SLJ 10/1/10)

6584 Lyga, Barry. *The Mad Mask* (4–7). 2012, Scholastic $17.99 (978-054519651-2). Determined to prove that his rival Might Mike is an alien with sinister designs on the world, 12-year-old Kyle (aka the Azure Avenger) teams up with Mad Mask in this fast-paced superhero spoof; a sequel to *Archvillain* (2010). Lexile 810L (Rev: BL 1/1/12; SLJ 3/12)

6585 McCaffrey, Anne, and Todd McCaffrey. *Dragon's Fire* (7–12). Series: Dragonriders of Pern. 2006, Del Rey $24.95 (978-0-345-48028-6). The series continues as the MacCaffreys return to Pern and as the colonists prepare for a phenomenon known as the Thread that follows the Red Star every 50 years and falls onto the planet killing all organic material that it touches; this preparation proves dangerous for the miners of explosive firestone and for the dragons who must chew it to burn the Thread from the sky. (Rev: BL 6/1–15/06; SLJ 8/06)

6586 McDonald, Ian. *Planesrunner* (8–11). Series: Everness. 2011, Prometheus $16.95 (978-161614541-5). When his physicist father is kidnapped, 14-year-old Everett finds a mysterious app on his computer that plunges him into a steampunk parallel world and threatening dark powers; the first book in the series. ℮ (Rev: BL 2/1/12)

6587 Mackel, Kathy. *Alien in a Bottle* (4–8). 2004, HarperCollins LB $16.89 (978-0-06-029282-9). An entertaining and action-packed novel in which 8th-grader Sean Winger, an aspiring glassblower, mistakes an alien space ship for an ornate glass bottle and becomes swept up in intergalactic intrigue. (Rev: BL 5/1/04; SLJ 4/04)

6588 McKinty, Adrian. *The Lighthouse Land* (5–8). 2006, Abrams $16.95 (978-0-8109-5480-9). In this first installment in an action-packed science fiction series, Jamie (a 13-year-old who is mute after losing his left arm to bone cancer) and his mother move to an Irish island, where he and a new friend discover an artifact that transports them to a far-off planet in time to help a girl named Wishaway. (Rev: BL 11/15/06; SLJ 1/07)

6589 McKissack, Patricia C., et al. *Clone Codes* (4–7). 2010, Scholastic $16.99 (978-0-439-92983-7). In 2170, 13-year-old Leanna learns about slaves in the Civil War and realizes that her own life is similar; she is not a human being but an enslaved clone. Lexile 680L (Rev: BL 1/1/10; LMC 3–4/10; SLJ 2/10)

6590 McNamee, Eoin. *The Frost Child* (5–8). Illus. by Jon Goodell. Series: The Navigator. 2009, Random $15.99 (978-0-385-73563-6). In this action-packed concluding volume to the trilogy the Navigator must once again rally the Resistors to battle against the Harsh. (Rev: BLO 4/24/09; SLJ 10/09)

6591 McNamee, Eoin. *The Navigator: Chosen to Save the World* (5–8). 2007, Random House $15.99 (978-0-375-83910-8). Owen finds himself suddenly in a different world where he and a girl named Cati must battle the Harsh, evil beings who freeze all that they touch and have set time running backward. (Rev: BL 12/1/06; SLJ 3/07)

6592 Marino, Andy. *Unison Spark* (7–10). 2011, Henry Holt $16.99 (978-080509293-6). Living in a sub-canopy slum city, feisty 15-year-old Mistletoe meets Ambrose, 16-year-old heir to the Unison empire, and they discover strange similarities; together they investigate their pasts and realize they may play a key role in the future territory of Unison 3.0. ℮ Lexile 810L (Rev: BL 10/15/11; LMC 3–4/12; SLJ 3/12; VOYA 12/11)

6593 Mariz, Rae. *The Unidentified* (7–11). 2010, HarperCollins $16.99 (978-0-06-180208-9). Kid rejects the corporate, technology-based education system in which students learn by playing games in malls, and is drawn toward the underground activists called the Unidentified. **e** Lexile HL740L (Rev: BL 9/15/10; SLJ 10/1/10; VOYA 12/10)

6594 Marley, Louise. *The Glass Harmonica* (7–12). 2000, Ace paper $16.00 (978-0-441-00729-5). In an appealing blend of science fiction, mystery, romance, and historical fiction, two related stories — one from the 18th century and the other from the not-so-distant future — feature young girls and a glass harmonica. (Rev: VOYA 2/01)

6595 Matas, Carol. *The Edge of When* (5–8). 2012, Fitzhenry & Whiteside paper $12.95 (978-15545519-8-9). In three separate but linked stories first published 30 years ago and now updated, 12-year-old Rebecca is transported into the future, at one point to 2050 where a postapocalyptic society is kidnapping healthy children from the past. (Rev: BL 3/15/12)

6596 Messner, Kate. *Eye of the Storm* (5–8). 2012, Walker $16.99 (978-0-8027-2313-0). In a 2050 world under a constant threat of tornadoes, 13-year-old Jaden starts to suspect that her scientist father has something to do with the ferocious weather. **e** Lexile 740L (Rev: SLJ 3/12)

6597 Meyer, Marissa. *Cinder* (7–10). Series: Lunar Chronicles. 2012, Feiwel & Friends $17.99 (978-031264189-4). In a future New Beijing in a world ravaged by plague, a cyborg named Cinder, shunned because of her low status, attracts the attention of the handsome Prince Kai. ∩ **e** Lexile 790L (Rev: BL 10/15/11; HB 1–2/12; LMC 3–4/12; SLJ 1/12; VOYA 12/11)

6598 Meyer, Marissa. *Scarlet* (7–10). Series: The Lunar Chronicles. 2013, Feiwel & Friends $17.99 (978-031264296-9). The lives of Scarlet and Cinder as Scarlet searches for her missing grandmother and Cinder escapes from jail, both of them wary of the wicked Lunar Queen Levana. ∩ **e** Lexile 810L (Rev: BL 1/13*; HB 3–4/13; LMC 8–9/13*; SLJ 2/13; VOYA 6/13)

6599 Michaels, Rune. *The Reminder* (6–9). 2008, Simon & Schuster $16.99 (978-141694131-6). When Daze's mother dies from cancer, her father creates a robotic replica of her head that allows Daze a chance to grieve and accept her loss. **e** Lexile 630L (Rev: BL 10/15/08; LMC 11–12/08; SLJ 11/1/08; VOYA 12/08)

6600 Mullin, Mike. *Ashen Winter* (8–12). 2012, Tanglewood $17.95 (978-1-933718-75-0). More than six months after the volcano erupted in *Ashfall* (2011), Alex and Darla search for his parents amid the dangerous and dystopian wintry world. **e** Lexile 730L (Rev: BL 8/12; LMC 1–2/13; SLJ 10/12; VOYA 10/12)

6601 Myklusch, Matt. *Jack Blank and the Imagine Nation* (4–7). 2010, Aladdin $16.99 (978-1-4169-9561-6). Jack Blank fits right in at St. Barnaby's Home for the Hopeless, Abandoned, Forgotten, and Lost until he destroys a zombie robot and is taken to the Imagine

Nation to hone his superpowers and save the world. ∩ Lexile 780L (Rev: BL 7/10; LMC 10/10; SLJ 9/1/10)

6602 Myklusch, Matt. *The Secret War* (5–8). Series: Jack Blank Adventures. 2011, Aladdin $16.99 (978-1-4169-9564-7). In this second complex volume in the series, Jack must deal with a dangerous computer virus while battling the spyware parasite in his own body. (Rev: BLO 9/15/11; LMC 11–12/11; SLJ 11/1/11; VOYA 12/11)

6603 Nelson, O. T. *The Girl Who Owned a City* (7–9). 1977, Dell paper $4.99 (978-0-440-92893-5). A mysterious virus kills off Earth's population except for children under the age of 13.

6604 Ness, Patrick. *The Knife of Never Letting Go* (8–12). Series: Chaos Walking. 2008, Candlewick $18.99 (978-076363931-0). Young Todd Hewitt realizes that there is a hole in the Noise — which makes the thoughts of men and animals audible — and sets off with his talking dog Viola to seek answers; the opening volume in a trilogy. Odyssey Award 2011; YALSA Top Ten Amazing Audiobooks for Young Adults. ∩ **e** Lexile 860L (Rev: BL 9/1/08*; HB 11–12/08; LMC 3–4/09; SLJ 11/1/08; VOYA 10/08)

6605 Nix, Garth. *A Confusion of Princes* (8–11). 2012, HarperCollins $17.99 (978-006009694-6). Khemri realizes that he must battle many other princes before he can gain stature, even as he meets Raine, a young woman who expands his horizons; a space opera with lots of fascinating details. ∩ **e** Lexile 1070L (Rev: BL 2/15/12; HB 5–6/12*; SLJ 6/12)

6606 Nix, Garth. *Shade's Children* (7–12). 1997, HarperCollins LB $15.89 (978-0-06-027325-5). In this science fiction novel, when a person reaches age 16, he or she is sent to the Meat Factory, where body parts are turned into hideous creatures. (Rev: BL 10/1/97; SLJ 8/97; VOYA 6/98)

6607 Norton, Andre. *Key Out of Time* (7–12). 1978, Ultramarine $25.00 (978-0-89366-186-1). Two Time Agents re-create the conflict that destroyed life on the planet Hawaika.

6608 Norton, Andre. *Time Traders II* (8–12). Series: Time Traders. 2001, Baen $24.00 (978-0-671-31968-7). This single volume contains two of Norton's Time Traders novellas: *Key Out of Time* and *The Defiant Agents.* (Rev: BL 2/1/01)

6609 Nylund, Eric. *The Resisters* (5–8). 2011, Random House $16.99 (978-0-375-86856-6); LB $19.99 (978-0-375-96856-3). Twelve-year-old Ethan learns that his understanding of the world has been false and that adults are all subject to mind control; only prepubescent children are safe and can resist. ∩ **e** Lexile 720L (Rev: BL 3/15/11; LMC 10/11; SLJ 7/11)

6610 Oldham, June. *Found* (7–12). 1996, Orchard LB $17.99 (978-0-531-08893-7). In this novel set in the

21st century, Ren becomes lost in a bleak countryside, gets involved with three other misfits, and finds an abandoned baby. (Rev: BL 9/15/96; SLJ 10/96; VOYA 2/97)

6611 Oppel, Kenneth. *Skybreaker* (6–9). 2005, Harper-Collins LB $17.89 (978-0-06-053228-4). In this action-packed sequel to *Airborn* (2003), Matt Cruse, now an officer trainee at Airship Academy, races to locate the long-lost *Hyperion* before pirates can loot the ghost ship. (Rev: BCCB 2/06; BL 11/15/05; HB 1–2/06; SLJ 12/05; VOYA 12/05)

6612 Osterlund, Anne. *Academy 7* (8–12). 2009, Penguin paper $8.99 (978-014241437-8). Aerin and Dane both attend the elite Academy 7 but come from very different worlds. They find themselves attracted to each other as they navigate the demands of school and political intrigue. Lexile 760L (Rev: BL 5/15/09; SLJ 9/09; VOYA 4/10)

6613 Patterson, James. *Maximum Ride: Saving the World and Other Extreme Sports* (6–9). Series: Maximum Ride. 2007, Little, Brown $16.99 (978-0-316-15560-1). This third installment in the series follows Max and her winged mutant flock as they run from the scientists who created and now want to exterminate them, while they also try to stop the Itex Corporation's evil plot. (Rev: BL 8/07; SLJ 7/07)

6614 Pearson, Mary E. *The Adoration of Jenna Fox* (8–12). 2008, Henry Holt $16.95 (978-0-8050-7668-4). Jenna, 17, awakens from a coma to find her brain has been altered in this first-person narrative set in a not-too-distant future in which bioengineering has made great strides. ∩ (Rev: BL 3/1/08; SLJ 5/08)

6615 Pearson, Mary E. *The Fox Inheritance* (8–12). 2011, Henry Holt $16.99 (978-0-8050-8829-8). Two hundred and sixty years after their deaths, Locke and Kara are brought back to life in new bio-engineered bodies and set out to find their friend Jenna; a sequel to *The Adoration of Jenna Fox* (2008). ∩ ℮ Lexile 660L (Rev: BLO 9/15/11; HB 9–10/11; SLJ 9/1/11; VOYA 10/11)

6616 Peel, John. *The Zanti Misfits* (6–10). 1997, Tor paper $3.99 (978-0-8125-9063-0). This quick read, a product of *The Outer Limits* television show, tells how the planet Zanti sent to Earth a shipload of its worst criminals and how three teenagers wander into the landing area. Also use *The Choice* and *The Time Shifter* (both 1997). (Rev: VOYA 4/98)

6617 Peterfreund, Diana. *For Darkness Shows the Stars* (7–12). 2012, HarperCollins $17.99 (978-006200614-1). This postapocalyptic retelling of Jane Austen's *Persuasion* features 18-year-old Elliot, a wealthy Luddite who looks after her family's threatened estate and takes care of their Reduced laborers while she longs for Kai, a Reduced whose love she once rejected. ℮ Lexile HL770L (Rev: BLO 6/12; HB 5–6/12; SLJ 6/12; VOYA 4/12)

6618 Pfeffer, Susan Beth. *Life as We Knew It* (7–10). 2006, Harcourt $17.00 (978-0-15-205826-5). Miranda, 16, describes the drastic changes in her life after a meteor hits the moon and causes major weather and other catastrophes on Earth. (Rev: BL 9/1/06; SLJ 10/06)

6619 Pierce, Tamora. *Street Magic* (5–9). Series: The Circle Opens. 2001, Scholastic paper $16.95 (978-0-590-39628-8). Briar, a 14-year-old former gang member, finds he is again caught between warring gangs when he helps a female street urchin in this futuristic novel. (Rev: BL 4/15/01; HB 3–4/01; HBG 10/01; SLJ 7/01; VOYA 4/01)

6620 Pow, Tom. *The Pack* (6–9). 2006, Roaring Brook $16.95 (978-1-59643-159-1). After the collapse of civilization as we know it, three children — Bradley, Victor, and Floris —and three dogs struggle to survive in the dangerous and chaotic world of the near-future, watched over by an Old Woman whose stories may bring salvation. (Rev: BL 5/15/06; SLJ 9/06)

6621 Powell, J. *Big Brother at School* (5–8). Illus. by Paul Savage. Series: Keystone Books. 2006, Stone Arch LB $21.26 (978-1-59889-091-4). At a school where cameras watch students' every move, Lee becomes convinced that the principal and a visiting doctor are aliens and takes step to save his fellow students from abduction. (Rev: SLJ 1/07)

6622 Pratchett, Terry. *Only You Can Save Mankind* (5–8). 2005, HarperCollins LB $17.89 (978-0-06-054186-6). It's up to Johnny to save the aliens in a new computer game, and the situation forces him to do some thinking about the very nature of war. (Rev: BL 4/15/05*; SLJ 10/05)

6623 Price, Lissa. *Starters* (7–10). 2012, Delacorte $17.99 (978-0-385-74237-5); LB $20.99 (978-037599060-1). Callie, 16, hires out her body for old people to experience youth again in this dystopian story fringed with dark consequences. ∩ ℮ (Rev: BL 3/15/12; LMC 10/12; SLJ 7/12; VOYA 12/12)

6624 Price, Susan. *The Sterkarm Handshake* (7–10). 2000, HarperCollins LB $18.89 (978-0-06-029392-5). Violent confrontations result when a 21st-century corporation makes inroads into the 16th-century Scottish Borders. (Rev: BL 10/1/00; HBG 3/01; SLJ 12/00)

6625 Read Magazine, ed. *Read into the Millennium: Tales of the Future* (6–8). 1999, Millbrook LB $24.90 (978-0-7613-0962-8). This collection of 10 science fiction stories includes works by Robert Lipsyte, Kurt Vonnegut, and Lois Lowry, plus adaptations of Wells's *The Time Machine* and Shelley's *Frankenstein*. (Rev: BL 5/15/99; HBG 9/99; SLJ 6/99)

6626 Reese, Jenn. *Above World* (5–8). 2012, Candlewick $16.99 (978-076365417-7). When her undersea-dwelling people's breathing apparatuses begin to fail, Aluna, 13, sets out for dry land with her friend Hoku, and there they find another society. ⌂ e Lexile 710L (Rev: BL 2/15/12; LMC 8–9/12; SLJ 4/12; VOYA 4/12)

6627 Reeve, Philip. *Fever Crumb* (6–9). 2010, Scholastic $17.99 (978-0-545-20719-5). In an era before Reeve's steampunk Hungry City Chronicles, young Fever Crumb, an orphan adopted by a member of the Order of Engineers, slowly learns about her past as she faces new dangers. ALA Notable Books 2011; YALSA Amazing Audiobooks Top Ten 2012. ⌂ Lexile 1000L (Rev: BL 1/1/10*; LMC 3–4/10; SLJ 4/10)

6628 Reeve, Philip. *Infernal Devices* (7–10). Series: Hungry City Chronicles. 2006, HarperCollins $16.99 (978-0-06-082635-2). In this gripping third book of the post-apocalyptic series that started with *Mortal Engines*, adventure-seeking 15-year-old Wren is kidnapped and her parents must come to her rescue. (Rev: BL 5/15/06; HB 7–8/06; SLJ 6/06)

6629 Reeve, Philip. *Larklight, or, The Revenge of the White Spiders!, or, To Saturn's Rings and Back!* (5–8). Illus. by David Wyatt. 2006, Bloomsbury $16.95 (978-1-59990-020-9). Art and Myrtle Mumby, who live with their father in a Victorian mansion orbiting the earth, become embroiled in a plot to destroy the solar system; a science fiction romp with a touch of romance and a dollop of Victorian manners. (Rev: BCCB 2/07; BL 10/1/06; HB 11–12/06; HBG 4/07; LMC 2/07; SLJ 11/06*; VOYA 12/06)

6630 Reeve, Philip. *Mothstorm* (5–8). Illus. by David Wyatt. 2008, Bloomsbury $16.99 (978-1-59990-303-3). All is calm and all is bright as the Mumbys gather to celebrate Christmas but new threats soon arise, involving a cloud of giant moths and an evil Shaper. (Rev: BLO 4/9/09; HB 1/09; SLJ 12/08)

6631 Reeve, Philip. *Starcross* (5–8). Illus. by David Wyatt. 2007, Bloomsbury $16.95 (978-1-59990-121-3). Starcross is the name of the asteroid belt hotel where Art, Myrtle, and their mother go for a holiday that turns into a strange journey through time; the sequel to *Larklight* (2006). (Rev: BL 11/1/07; HB 1–2/08; SLJ 12/07)

6632 Reeve, Philip. *A Web of Air* (6–9). 2011, Scholastic $17.99 (978-0-545-22216-7). In the postapocalyptic city of Mayda, Fever (of 2010's *Fever Crumb*) finds her engineering abilities in demand although this makes her a target of powerful enemies. ⌂ e Lexile 1000L (Rev: BL 10/15/11; HB 9–10/11; SLJ 9/1/11)

6633 Regan, Dian C. *Princess Nevermore* (5–7). 1995, Scholastic $14.95 (978-0-590-47582-2). A princess from another world gets her wish to visit Earth, where she is befriended by two teenagers, Sarah and Adam. (Rev: BCCB 11/95; SLJ 9/95)

6634 Reichs, Kathy. *Virals* (6–9). 2010, Penguin $17.99 (978-1-59514-342-6). On an island off the South Carolina coast, Tony Brennan and her science nerd friends uncover a disease that will affect them all. ⌂ (Rev: BL 10/1/10; SLJ 12/1/10*)

6635 Reisman, Michael. *Simon Bloom, the Gravity Keeper* (4–7). 2008, Dutton $15.99 (978-0-525-47922-2). When a book teaches 11-year-old Simon how to control gravity, velocity, friction, and other physical properties; magic, adventure, and suspense ensue. (Rev: BL 3/1/08; SLJ 4/08)

6636 Rex, Adam. *The True Meaning of Smekday* (5–8). 2007, Hyperion $16.99 (978-0-7868-4900-0). Gratuity (called Tip) resents having to write an essay about the day aliens took over America in this funny and visually engaging story. (Rev: BL 10/1/07; HB 11–12/07; LMC 1/08; SLJ 11/07)

6637 Rosenblum, Gregg. *Revolution 19* (7–10). 2013, HarperTeen $17.99 (978-006212595-8). In 2051, after the robots took over, siblings Nick, Kevin, and Cass leave their wilderness community and try to rescue their parents from the bot-controlled city. e (Rev: BL 11/15/12; SLJ 5/13)

6638 Rossi, Veronica. *Under the Never Sky* (8–11). 2012, HarperCollins $17.99 (978-006207203-0). Aria, from a privileged community, and Peregrine, from a wasteland, must work together despite their differences if they are to survive; but the longer they know each other the closer they become. ⌂ e Lexile HL580L (Rev: BL 2/15/12; HB 3–4/12; SLJ 3/12*; VOYA 12/11)

6639 Rubenstein, Gillian. *Galax-Arena* (7–10). 1995, Simon & Schuster paper $15.00 (978-0-689-80136-5). A 13-year-old girl and 20 other children from Earth are removed to another planet and trained to perform dangerous acrobatic tricks. (Rev: BL 10/15/95*; SLJ 10/95)

6640 Russell, David O., and Andrew Auseon. *Alienated* (5–8). 2009, Simon & Schuster $16.99 (978-1-4169-8298-2). Best friends Gene and Vince have fun publishing a tabloid focusing on extraterrestrials until things turn serious and they find themselves embroiled in an intergalactic war. e Lexile 780L (Rev: BL 11/15/09; SLJ 1/10)

6641 Ryan, Amy Kathleen. *Glow* (7–11). Series: Sky Chasers. 2011, St. Martin's $17.99 (978-0-312-59056-7). War breaks out between two pioneer spaceships over the issue of human reproduction. ⌂ e Lexile 750L (Rev: BL 9/1/11; SLJ 9/1/11*; VOYA 10/11)

6642 Ryan, Amy Kathleen. *Spark* (7–11). 2012, St. Martin's/Griffin $17.99 (978-0-312-62135-3). Waverly's former fiance tries to belittle her contributions to the spaceship crew's safety in this sequel to *Glow* (2011). ⌂ e (Rev: BLO 7/12; SLJ 11/12)

6643 Sampson, Jeff. *Havoc* (8–12). Series: Deviants. 2012, HarperCollins $17.99 (978-0-06-199278-0). Transformed into werewolves by a genetic experiment, Emily, 16, and her friends struggle to control their new powers and investigate the reason behind this change. e (Rev: SLJ 5/1/12; VOYA 12/11)

6644 Sargent, Pamela. *Alien Child* (8–12). 1988, HarperCollins $13.95 (978-0-06-025202-1). A teenage girl raised in an alien world discovers there is another human living in her complex. (Rev: BL 2/1/88; SLJ 4/88; VOYA 8/88)

6645 Schmid, Susan Maupin. *Lost Time* (5–8). 2008, Philomel $16.99 (978-0-399-24460-5). On the sparsely populated planet Lindos, Violynne searches for her lost parents while living with her aunt Madelyn. (Rev: BL 5/15/08; SLJ 9/08)

6646 Scrimger, Richard. *The Nose from Jupiter* (5–8). 2004, Tundra paper $5.95 (978-0-88776-428-8). Alan doesn't mind that Norbert, an alien from Jupiter, is living in his nose, but Norbert's outspoken remarks often get Alan into trouble. Also use *The Boy from Earth* (2004). (Rev: BL 7/98)

6647 Sheehan, Anna. *A Long, Long Sleep* (8–12). 2011, Candlewick $16.99 (978-0-7636-5260-9). After 60 years in stasis, Rosalinda, still 16 years old, is awakened by a kiss to discover that she is in danger from a robot assassin. ⌒ e Lexile HL670L (Rev: LMC 1–2/12; SLJ 12/1/11)

6648 Shusterman, Neal. *UnWholly* (7–10). Series: Unwind Trilogy. 2012, Simon & Schuster $17.99 (978-1-4424-2366-4). The practice of harvesting organs from "troubled" teens continues in this thought-provoking second installment as Cam, totally constructed from grafted parts, begins to question the nature of humanity. ⌒ e Lexile 860L (Rev: BL 7/12; HB 9–10/12; LMC 3–4/13; SLJ 9/12)

6649 Simmons, Michael. *Alien Feast* (5–8). Illus. by George O'Connor. Series: Chronicles of the First Invasion. 2009, Roaring Brook $15.95 (978-1-59643-281-9). Aliens have invaded Earth in 2017 and 12-year-old William, who has already faced many adversities in his life, joins up with his friend Sophie and Uncle Maynard to try to rescue Sophie's parents; humor, action, and science fiction conventions add to the drama. (Rev: BCCB 7–8/08; BL 5/15/09; HB 5/09; LMC 5/08; SLJ 8/08)

6650 Simons, Jamie, and E. W. Scollon. *Goners: The Hunt Is On* (4–7). 1998, Avon paper $3.99 (978-0-380-79730-1). Four alien teens from the planet Roma time-travel to Monticello to fetch Thomas Jefferson. (Rev: BL 5/15/98)

6651 Skurzynski, Gloria. *The Choice* (5–8). Series: The Virtual War Chronologs. 2006, Simon & Schuster $16.95 (978-0-689-84267-2). In the fast-paced concluding installment in the series, 16-year-old Corgan has a final confrontation with the murderous Brigand. (Rev: SLJ 10/06)

6652 Skurzynski, Gloria. *The Clones* (6–9). Series: The Virtual War Chronologs. 2002, Simon & Schuster $16.00 (978-0-689-84463-8). In this sequel to *Virtual War* (1997), in which Corgan successfully defended the Western Hemisphere Federation, Corgan's peaceful life is disturbed by the arrival of a pair of surprisingly different clones. (Rev: BL 4/15/02; VOYA 8/02)

6653 Skurzynski, Gloria. *The Revolt* (8–12). Series: The Virtual War Chronologs. 2005, Simon & Schuster $16.95 (978-0-689-84265-8). In this action-packed third volume in the series, Corgan flees to Florida to put an end to his battle with Brigand but is soon followed there by his violent enemy. (Rev: SLJ 7/05)

6654 Sleator, William. *The Boy Who Reversed Himself* (8–12). 1998, Puffin paper $5.99 (978-0-14-038965-4). Laura travels into the fourth dimension with her gifted neighbor and literally everything in her life becomes upside-down. (Rev: BL 10/15/86; SLJ 11/86; VOYA 6/87)

6655 Sleator, William. *House of Stairs* (7–10). 1991, Puffin paper $5.99 (978-0-14-034580-3). Five teenage orphans are kidnapped to become part of an experiment on aggression.

6656 Sleator, William. *Interstellar Pig* (7–10). 1996, Peter Smith $22.25 (978-0-8446-6898-7); paper $6.99 (978-0-14-037595-4). Barney plays an odd board game with strangers who are actually aliens from space.

6657 Sleator, William. *The Last Universe* (6–9). 2005, Abrams $16.95 (978-0-8109-5858-6). Quantum mechanics plays a key role in the tension in this story of 14-year-old Susan who must care for her 16-year-old, wheelchair-bound brother Gary; they spend a lot of time in a maze that seems to allow travel to other dimensions. (Rev: BCCB 4/05; BL 4/15/05; SLJ 7/05; VOYA 4/05)

6658 Sleator, William. *Parasite Pig* (7–10). 2002, Dutton $15.99 (978-0-525-46918-6). Barney and Katie continue playing the board game they began in *Interstellar Pig* and wind up on a planet called J'koot, threatened by crablike aliens with cannibal tendencies. (Rev: BCCB 2/03; BL 11/15/02; HB 11–12/02*; HBG 3/03; SLJ 10/02; VOYA 12/02)

6659 Sleator, William. *Singularity* (7–12). 1995, Puffin paper $6.99 (978-0-14-037598-5). Twin boys discover a playhouse on the property they have inherited that contains a mystery involving monsters from space and a new dimension in time. (Rev: BL 4/1/85; SLJ 8/85)

6660 Slote, Alfred. *My Robot Buddy* (5–8). 1986, HarperCollins $12.95 (978-0-397-31641-0). An easily read novel about Danny and the robot that is created for him. (Rev: BL 11/1/87)

6661 Smibert, Angie. *Memento Nora* (8–11). 2011, Marshall Cavendish $16.99 (978-0-7614-5829-6). In a future where people are given pills that wipe out unpleasant memories, Nora and her friends create an underground comic that will allow them to save their experiences. ⌒ e Lexile 670L (Rev: BL 6/1/11; HB 7–8/11; LMC 8–9/11; SLJ 4/11)

6662 Smith, Alexander Gordon. *Death Sentence* (6–9). Series: Escape from Furnace. 2011, Farrar $15.99 (978-037432494-0). Readers of earlier books in the series will enjoy this bloodthirsty third volume. ⌒ ℮ (Rev: BLO 9/15/11; VOYA 8/11)

6663 Smith, Alexander Gordon. *Execution* (6–9). Series: Escape from Furnace. 2012, Farrar $16.99 (978-037436224-9). In this final volume in this dark saga Alex must face the evil Alfred Furnace. Will he be executed or executioner? ℮ Lexile 910L (Rev: BLO 12/15/12)

6664 Smith, Alexander Gordon. *Lockdown: Escape from Furnace* (6–9). Series: Escape from Furnace. 2009, Farrar $14.99 (978-0-374-32491-9). Framed for a murder he did not commit, 14-year-old Alex finds himself in a brutal prison in which inmates disappear and return altered; it is patrolled by furless dogs but escape may just be possible. ℮ Lexile 1010L (Rev: BL 2/1/10; SLJ 2/10; VOYA 2/10)

6665 Smith, Sherri L. *Orleans* (8–12). 2013, Putnam $17.99 (978-039925294-5). A dark multilayered tale set on the Gulf Coast, separated from the United States after the appearance of a deadly plague in the wake of ever-stronger hurricanes. ℮ Lexile HL750L (Rev: BL 2/1/13*; HB 3–4/13; SLJ 4/13; VOYA 2/13)

6666 Souders, J. A. *Renegade* (8–11). Series: The Elysium Chronicles. 2012, Tor Teen $17.99 (978-076533245-5). In the underwater utopia of Elysium 16-year-old Evelyn, Daughter of the People, is quite content until a surface dweller, Gavin, appears on the scene and turns her world upside down. ℮ Lexile HL690L (Rev: BL 12/15/12; SLJ 1/13)

6667 Stackpole, Michael A. *I, Jedi* (8–12). 1998, Random House paper $6.99 (978-0-553-57873-7). In order to find his wife, Corran must take a quick course at the Jedi Academy founded by Luke Skywalker and learn to use his hidden powers. (Rev: VOYA 12/98)

6668 Stahler, David, Jr. *The Seer* (5–7). Series: The Truesight Trilogy. 2007, HarperCollins $16.99 (978-0-06-052288-9). Jacob, 13, leaves the colony of Harmony, where he is the only person who can see, and seeks both a new life and his childhood friend Delaney, who is a talented musician. (Rev: BCCB 5/07; SLJ 8/07)

6669 Stahler, David, Jr. *Truesight* (5–7). Series: The Truesight Trilogy. 2004, HarperCollins LB $16.89 (978-0-06-052286-5). A race of blind people living in a colony on a distant planet includes one teenager who discovers he can see, and he sees all sorts of flaws in the people of his community. (Rev: SLJ 3/04; VOYA 4/04)

6670 Starmer, Aaron. *The Only Ones* (6–8). 2011, Delacorte $17.99 (978-0-385-74043-2); LB $20.99 (978-038590839-9). After the strange disappearance of most inhabitants of the world, Martin finds his way to a town full of eccentric young teenagers and starts to build a machine he believes will help them. ℮ Lexile 700L

(Rev: BLO 10/15/11; HB 11–12/11; SLJ 8/11; VOYA 10/11)

6671 Sutherland, Tui T. *So This Is How It Ends* (8–11). Series: Avatars. 2006, HarperCollins $16.99 (978-0-06-075024-4). Five teenagers are the only young people left in a future world, and their special powers will help them survive among crystal monsters and old, confused humans. (Rev: BCCB 2/07; BL 1/1–15/07; SLJ 11/06)

6672 Teague, Mark. *The Doom Machine* (4–7). 2009, Scholastic $17.99 (978-0-545-15142-9). Set in the 1950s, this zany science fiction yarn follows town troublemaker Jack on an intergalactic journey of discovery to save his uncle's invention from the grips of aliens. Lexile 610L (Rev: BL 10/15/09; HB 1–2/10; LMC 11–12/09; SLJ 10/09; VOYA 10/09)

6673 Testa, Dom. *The Cassini Code* (7–10). Series: Galahad. 2010, Tor paper $8.99 (978-07653607-9-3). The teens aboard starship *Galahad* must decide between returning to Earth and continuing on their mission even as they enter a deadly asteroid field. (Rev: BL 2/1/11)

6674 Testa, Dom. *The Comet's Curse* (7–10). Series: Galahad. 2009, Tor $16.95 (978-076532107-7). The first book in a six-part series, this sci-fi drama starts when a comet spews deadly dust, killing the adults on Earth and forcing 250 teens into space to colonize a safer planet. ℮ Lexile 840L (Rev: BL 12/15/08; LMC 8–9/09; SLJ 3/1/09; VOYA 4/09)

6675 Testa, Dom. *The Galahad Legacy* (7–10). Series: Galahad. 2012, Tor $16.99 (978-076532112-1). A rousing conclusion to the story of 251 teens venturing into space, in which they must make a difficult choice in the face of an alien race's offer. ℮ (Rev: BL 12/15/11*)

6676 Testa, Dom. *The Web of Titan* (7–10). Series: Galahad. 2010, Tor $16.99 (978-076532108-4). As they approach Saturn, the 251 teens aboard the *Galahad* contend with a mysterious illness and technological problems; the sequel to *The Comet's Curse* (2009). ℮ (Rev: BLO 5/15/10)

6677 Thompson, Kate. *Fourth World* (5–8). Series: Missing Link. 2005, Bloomsbury $16.95 (978-1-58234-650-2). Christie and his older stepbrother Danny go from Ireland to Scotland, where they discover strange developments at Fourth World, the compound where Danny's scientist mother lives and works, in this first volume of a trilogy. (Rev: BL 5/15/05; SLJ 10/05)

6678 Tolan, Stephanie S. *Welcome to the Ark* (7–10). 1996, Morrow $15.00 (978-0-688-13724-3). Science fiction and adventure combine in the story of four young people who are able to act for good or evil through telecommunications. (Rev: BL 10/15/96; SLJ 10/96; VOYA 4/97)

6679 Townsend, John Rowe. *The Creatures* (7–10). 1980, HarperCollins $12.95 (978-0-397-31864-3). Earth is dominated by creatures from another planet who believe in mind over emotion.

6680 Treggiari, Jo. *Ashes, Ashes* (7–10). 2011, Scholastic $17.99 (978-0-545-25563-9). In a postapocalyptic Manhattan, 16-year-old Lucy learns that her blood is of value to the dreaded Sweepers. ⌒ e Lexile 810L (Rev: BLO 8/11; SLJ 8/11)

6681 Ungar, Richard. *Time Snatchers* (6–9). 2012, Putnam $16.99 (978-039925485-7). Time-traveling orphan Caleb, 13, is used to his life stealing valuable artifacts for his ruthless uncle but finds himself longing for more. e Lexile 710L (Rev: BL 4/1/12*; LMC 8–9/12; SLJ 4/12)

6682 Ure, Jean. *Plague* (7–12). 1991, Harcourt $16.95 (978-0-15-262429-3). Three teenagers must band together to survive in a hostile, nearly deserted London after a catastrophe has killed almost everyone. (Rev: BL 11/15/91*; SLJ 10/91)

6683 van Eekhout, Greg. *The Boy at the End of the World* (5–8). 2011, Bloomsbury $16.99 (978-1-59990-524-2). The only human survivor of a Life Ark in this post-apocalyptic story, Fisher has instinctive knowledge of many things and sets out to explore his environment in the company of a robot he calls Click. (Rev: BL 5/1/11; SLJ 9/1/11)

6684 Vande Velde, Vivian. *Heir Apparent* (6–9). 2002, Harcourt $17.00 (978-0-15-204560-9). When Giannine, 14, enters a virtual reality game set in medieval times, she doesn't expect the game to be damaged or her playing skill to become a matter of life and death. (Rev: BCCB 12/02; BL 2/1/03; HB 11–12/02; HBG 3/03; SLJ 10/02; VOYA 12/02)

6685 Verne, Jules. *Around the Moon* (8–12). 1968, Airmont paper $1.50 (978-0-8049-0182-6). An early science fiction relic about a trip to the moon. Also use *From the Earth to the Moon* (1984).

6686 Voake, Steve. *The Web of Fire* (5–8). Illus. by Mark Watkinson. 2007, Bloomsbury $17.95 (978-1-58234-737-0). Sam and Skipper are back with new adventures and gadgetry in this fast-paced sequel to *The Dreamwalker's Child* (2006). (Rev: SLJ 6/07)

6687 Wallenfels, Stephen. *POD* (8–11). 2010, Namelos $18.95 (978-160898011-6); paper $9.95 (978-16089801-0-9). Told in alternate chapters, this is the story of two young people — 15-year-old Josh and 12-year-old Megs — who have different experiences in different cities when aliens attack the earth. e Lexile HL650L (Rev: BL 5/15/10; HB 7–8/10)

6688 Walsh, Jill Paton. *The Green Book* (4–7). Illus. by Lloyd Bloom. 1982, Farrar paper $4.95 (978-0-374-42802-0). The exodus of a group of Britons from dying Earth to another planet.

6689 Weaver, Will. *The Survivors* (7–10). 2012, HarperTeen $17.99 (978-006009476-8). In a cabin in the Minnesota woods, 16-year-old Miles and his younger sister Sarah are struggling to survive after the volcanic eruptions disrupted society in *Memory Boy* (2001); Sarah's

goat and Miles's memory prove invaluable until Miles's abilities are threatened. e (Rev: BL 2/15/12; SLJ 2/12)

6690 Weber, David. *A Beautiful Friendship* (6–9). 2011, Baen $18.99 (978-145163747-2). On the planet of Sphinx a six-legged treecat risks his life to save Stephanie, a genetically enhanced 12-year-old, and the two bond as they face various challenges. ⌒ e (Rev: BL 7/11; SLJ 2/12)

6691 Wells, Dan. *Partials* (8–12). 2012, HarperCollins $17.99 (978-006207104-0). The future of the human race rests in the hands of 16-year-old medical intern Kira in this post-apocalyptic thriller. ⌒ e (Rev: BL 1/1/12; SLJ 4/12; VOYA 2/12)

6692 Wells, H. G. *First Men in the Moon* (7–12). 1993, Tuttle paper $7.95 (978-0-460-87304-8). The first men on the moon discover strange creatures living there.

6693 Wells, H. G. *The Invisible Man* (8–12). 1987, Buccaneer LB $21.95 (978-0-89966-377-7); paper $4.95 (978-0-553-21353-9). Two editions of many available of the story of a scientist who finds a way to make himself invisible.

6694 Wells, H. G. *The Time Machine* (7–12). 1984, Bantam paper $4.95 (978-0-553-21351-5). This is one of the earliest novels to use traveling through time as its subject.

6695 Wells, H. G. *The War of the Worlds* (7–12). 1988, Bantam paper $4.95 (978-0-553-21338-6). In this early science fiction novel, first published in 1898, strange creatures from Mars invade England.

6696 Wells, Robison. *Variant* (8–11). 2011, HarperTeen $17.99 (978-006202608-8). Benson, 17, is initially happy to have left a series of foster homes for Maxfield Academy but soon discovers that the school is a prison, the students are split into warring factions, and nothing is what it seems. A sequel is *Feedback* (2012). ⌒ e Lexile HL640L (Rev: BL 10/15/11; LMC 3–4/12)

6697 Westerfeld, Scott. *Extras* (7–10). Series: The Uglies. 2007, Simon & Schuster $16.99 (978-1-4169-5117-9). In the future world in which human worth is now based on celebrity, Aya, an Ugly and now an Extra, discovers the underside to her city while she chases popularity. (Rev: BL 1/1–15/08; HB 11–12/07; SLJ 1/08)

6698 Westerfeld, Scott. *Goliath* (7–10). Illus. by Keith Thompson. 2011, Simon & Schuster $19.99 (978-1-4169-7177-1). This finale to the steampunk trilogy that began with *Leviathan* (2009) centers on a Nikola Tesla invention, a weapon that could end World War I and bring Alek and Deryn together. ⌒ Lexile 790L (Rev: BL 8/11; HB 11–12/11; LMC 11–12/11; SLJ 9/1/11)

6699 Westerfeld, Scott. *Pretties* (8–11). Series: The Uglies. 2005, Simon & Schuster paper $6.99 (978-0-689-86539-8). In the sequel to *Uglies* (2005), Tally enjoys her transformation into a Pretty and the accompanying hedonistic lifestyle until she is reminded of her underlying purpose and faces real danger. (Rev: BL 9/15/05; SLJ 12/05; VOYA 10/05)

6700 Westerfeld, Scott. *Specials* (7–10). Series: The Uglies. 2006, Simon & Schuster $15.95 (978-1-4169-2165-3). Sixteen-year-old Tally (of *Uglies* and *Pretties,* 2004 and 2005 respectively) transforms yet again, this time becoming a Special, part of her government's high-powered commando unit that enforces adherence to the norms. ∩ (Rev: BL 5/15/06; HB 9–10/06)

6701 Westerfeld, Scott. *Uglies* (7–10). Series: The Uglies. 2005, Simon & Schuster paper $6.99 (978-0-689-86538-1). In a futuristic dystopia, 15-year-old Tally is counting the days until she turns 16 and is transformed from ugly to pretty but events threaten this happening on schedule; a thought-provoking novel about the importance of image and ethics. (Rev: BCCB 2/05; BL 3/15/05*; SLJ 3/05; VOYA 6/05)

6702 White, Andrea. *No Child's Game: Reality TV 2083* (7–10). 2005, HarperCollins LB $16.89 (978-0-06-055455-2). In this chilling look at a future in which television is used to distract the populace from grim reality, five teens will live or die while reenacting a historic Antarctic expedition for the entertainment of the viewing audience. (Rev: BL 4/15/05; SLJ 7/05)

6703 Wismer, Donald. *Starluck* (6–8). 1982, Ultramarine $20.00 (978-0-89366-255-4). A boy with unusual powers tries to overthrow a wicked emperor.

6704 Wooding, Chris. *Storm Thief* (6–9). 2006, Scholastic $16.99 (978-0-439-86513-5). Rail and Moa are two thieves trying to live in the city of Orokos, which is plagued with probability storms; they will need the help of a golem named Vago to survive and unlock the secrets of the city and its tempests. (Rev: BL 9/1/06; SLJ 10/06)

6705 Yolen, Jane, ed. *Spaceships and Spells* (5–9). 1987, HarperCollins $12.95 (978-0-06-026796-4). A collection of 13 original tales, mostly science fiction but also some fantasy. (Rev: BL 1/15/88; SLJ 11/87)

6706 Zakour, John. *Baxter Moon: Galactic Scout* (4–7). 2008, Brown Barn paper $8.95 (978-0-9768126-9-2). Baxter and his crew travel through space to rescue an Aquarian ship from robotic aliens in this entertaining romp. (Rev: BL 5/15/08; SLJ 6/08)

Sports

6707 Altman, Millys N. *Racing in Her Blood* (7–12). 1980, HarperCollins LB $12.89 (978-0-397-31895-7). A junior novel about a young girl who wants to succeed in the world of automobile racing.

6708 Aronson, Sarah. *Beyond Lucky* (4–7). 2011, Dial $16.99 (978-0-8037-3520-0). Soccer looms more important on Ari's radar than his forthcoming bar mitzvah, and he is convinced that the trading card he has found will bring him luck. (Rev: BL 9/1/11; SLJ 8/11)

6709 Barber, Tiki, and Paul Mantell. *Goal Line* (4–7). Illus. 2011, Simon & Schuster $15.99 (978-141699095-6). Ronde Barber copes with a case of sibling envy after his twin brother's summer growth spurt in this football-fueled family story. *e* Lexile 760L (Rev: BLO 8/11)

6710 Barber, Tiki, and Ronde Barber. *End Zone* (4–7). 2012, Simon & Schuster $15.99 (978-141699097-0). Tiki and Ronde's high school football team contends with a variety of setbacks on the road to the state finals. *e* Lexile 830L (Rev: BLO 8/12)

6711 Barber, Tiki, and Ronde Barber, et al. *Red Zone* (4–7). 2010, Simon & Schuster $15.99 (978-141696860-3). The Eagles junior-high football team manages to make it to the state championship despite an outbreak of chicken pox. *e* Lexile 790L (Rev: BL 9/1/10)

6712 Barwin, Steven. *Icebreaker* (4–8). Series: Sports Stories. 2007, Lorimer paper $7.95 (978-1-55028-950-3). Hockey fans will love this book featuring Greg, a junior high school hockey player whose year gets complicated when his stepsister tries out for the team. (Rev: SLJ 7/07)

6713 Barwin, Steven, and Gabriel David Tick. *Slam Dunk* (5–7). Series: Sports Stories. 1999, Orca paper $5.50 (978-1-55028-598-7). An easy read about a junior high basketball team in Canada that goes coed and the problems that result. (Rev: SLJ 1/00)

6714 Baskin, Nora Raleigh. *Basketball (or Something Like It)* (6–9). 2005, HarperCollins LB $16.89 (978-0-06-059611-8). In alternating chapters, three 6th-grade basketball players — and the basketball-loving sister of one team member — tell stories of parental interference or indifference and how these have taken away some of the fun of the game. (Rev: BCCB 3/05; BL 2/1/05; SLJ 2/05; VOYA 6/05)

6715 Bledsoe, Lucy Jane. *Hoop Girlz* (5–7). 2002, Holiday $16.95 (978-0-8234-1691-2). When 11-year-old River is denied a place on the girls' basketball team, she forms her own team, with her brother as the coach. (Rev: BL 9/1/02; HBG 10/03; SLJ 12/02)

6716 Bo, Ben. *The Edge* (5–8). 1999, Lerner LB $14.95 (978-0-8225-3307-8). Conflicted Declan is sent to a rehabilitation program in Canada's Glacier National Park, where he learns to snowboard and is drawn into a duel with the local champion. (Rev: BCCB 1/00; BL 10/15/99; HBG 3/00; SLJ 1/00; VOYA 4/00)

6717 Bo, Ben. *Skullcrack* (7–12). 2000, Lerner LB $14.95 (978-0-8225-3308-5). Jonah, an avid surfer, travels with his father to Florida to be united with his twin sister who was put up for adoption at birth. (Rev: BL 6/1–15/00; HBG 9/00; SLJ 6/00)

6718 Bowen, Fred. *The Final Cut* (4–7). Illus. by Ann Barrow. Series: AllStar Sport Story. 1999, Peachtree paper $4.95 (978-1-56145-192-0). A fast-paced novel about four friends and their efforts to make the junior high school basketball team. (Rev: SLJ 7/99)

6719 Bowen, Fred. *Hardcourt Comeback* (4–7). Series: Fred Bowen Sports Story. 2010, Peachtree paper $5.95 (978-15614551-6-4). Basketball star Brett's confidence is shaken when he misses an easy shot and his uneasiness spreads to other areas. (Rev: BL 4/15/10; SLJ 5/10)

6720 Bowen, Fred. *On the Line* (4–7). Illus. by Ann Barrow. 1999, Peachtree paper $4.95 (978-1-56145-199-9). A young boy learns about self-image and open-mindedness while trying to improve his foul shots in this novel about an 8th grader and his basketball skills. (Rev: SLJ 4/00)

6721 Brooks, Bruce. *Dooby* (5–8). Series: Wolfbay Wings. 1998, HarperCollins LB $14.89 (978-0-06-027898-4); paper $4.50 (978-0-06-440708-3). Dooby sulks when he is not made captain of his Peewee hockey team, but is completely humiliated to learn he has lost out to a girl. Also recommended in this series is *Reed* (1998). (Rev: HBG 3/99; SLJ 2/99)

6722 Brooks, Bruce. *The Moves Make the Man* (7–9). 1984, HarperCollins paper $6.99 (978-0-06-447022-3). Jerome, the only African American student in his high school and a star basketball player, forms an unusual friendship with Bix. (Rev: BL 3/87)

6723 Brooks, Bruce. *Prince* (5–8). Series: Wolfbay Wings. 1998, HarperCollins paper $4.50 (978-0-06-440600-0). Prince, the only African American boy on the Wolfbay Wings hockey team, is pressured by his middle school coach to switch to basketball. (Rev: HBG 10/98; SLJ 6/98)

6724 Brooks, Bruce. *Reed* (5–8). Series: Wolfbay Wings. 1998, HarperCollins LB $14.89 (978-0-06-028055-0). Reed, a member of the Wolfbay Wings hockey team, is considered a "puck-hog" and must learn to be more of a team player. (Rev: HBG 3/99; SLJ 2/99)

6725 Brooks, Bruce. *Shark* (5–8). Series: Wolfbay Wings. 1998, HarperCollins LB $14.89 (978-0-06-027570-9); paper $4.50 (978-0-06-440681-9). In spite of being fat, slow, and confused, Shark becomes a valuable player on the Wolfbay Wings hockey team. (Rev: HBG 10/98; SLJ 6/98)

6726 Bruchac, Joseph. *The Warriors* (5–8). 2003, Darby Creek $15.95 (978-1-58196-002-0). Jake Forrest, a Native American teenager and lacrosse whiz, leaves the reservation to attend a private school and encounters many new situations, including a different attitude toward sports. (Rev: BL 12/1/03; HBG 10/01; SLJ 10/03)

6727 Butcher, Kristin. *Cairo Kelly and the Man* (4–8). 2002, Orca paper $6.95 (978-1-55143-211-3). When Midge discovers that his baseball team's umpire, Hal Mann, is illiterate, Midge and his friend Kelly set out to solve the problem. (Rev: BL 9/1/02; VOYA 4/03)

6728 Butler, Dori Hillestad. *Sliding into Home* (5–8). 2003, Peachtree $14.95 (978-1-56145-222-4). Joelle, 13, refuses to accept a ban on girls playing baseball when she moves to a small town in Iowa. (Rev: BL 5/1/03; HBG 10/03; SLJ 1/04)

6729 Carter, Alden R. *Bull Catcher* (7–10). 1997, Scholastic paper $15.95 (978-0-590-50958-9). High school friends Bull and Jeff seem to live for baseball and plan their futures around the sport, but one of them begins to move in a different direction. (Rev: BL 4/15/97; SLJ 5/97; VOYA 10/97)

6730 Carter, Alden R. *Love, Football, and Other Contact Sports* (8–11). 2006, Holiday House $16.95 (978-0-8234-1975-3). The football team at Argyle West High School is at the center of these entertaining short stories. (Rev: BL 3/15/06*; SLJ 6/06)

6731 Choat, Beth. *Soccerland* (5–8). Series: The International Sports Academy. 2010, Marshall Cavendish $16.99 (978-0-7614-5724-4). Soccer phenom Flora struggles to adjust when she goes from her tiny Maine town to a prestigious soccer camp where her talents aren't as exceptional and the culture is cutthroat. (Rev: BLO 8/10; SLJ 11/1/10)

6732 Christopher, Matt. *Mountain Bike Mania* (5–7). 1998, Little, Brown paper $4.50 (978-0-316-14292-2). Will is at loose ends with no after-school activities until he becomes involved in a mountain bike club. (Rev: BL 2/1/99; HBG 10/99; SLJ 3/99)

6733 Christopher, Matt. *Prime-Time Pitcher* (4–7). 1998, Little, Brown paper $4.50 (978-0-316-14213-7). Koby Caplin becomes arrogant about his winning streak on the baseball team and soon loses games because of his lack of teamwork. (Rev: HBG 3/99; SLJ 12/98)

6734 Christopher, Matt. *Return of the Home Run Kid* (4–7). Illus. by Paul Casale. 1994, Little, Brown paper $4.50 (978-0-316-14273-1). In this sequel to *The Kid Who Only Hit Homers* (1972), Sylvester learns to be more aggressive on the field but gets criticism from his friends. (Rev: BL 4/15/92; SLJ 5/92)

6735 Christopher, Matt. *Snowboard Maverick* (4–7). 1997, Little, Brown paper $4.50 (978-0-316-14203-8). Dennis overcomes his fears and begins snowboarding. (Rev: BL 4/1/98; HBG 3/98; SLJ 3/98)

6736 Clare, Cassandra. *Toby Wheeler: Eighth-Grade Bench Warmer* (5–8). 2007, Delacorte $14.99 (978-0-385-73390-8). Toby, an 8th-grader, joins the basketball team to be closer to his best friend but find himself stuck on the bench, the 12th man. (Rev: BL 9/1/07; SLJ 9/07)

6737 Clippinger, Carol. *Open Court* (5–8). 2007, Knopf $15.99 (978-0-375-84049-4). Thirteen-year-old Holloway ("Hall") is only 13 but must deal with the pressures of competitive tennis as well as everyday stresses of being a teenager. (Rev: SLJ 7/07)

6738 Corbett, Sue. *Free Baseball* (4–7). 2006, Dutton $15.99 (978-0-525-47120-2). An endearing 11-year-old called Felix, who loves baseball and is annoyed that his mother won't tell him more about his Cuban outfielder father, is thrilled when he gets the chance to be batboy for a minor league Florida team. (Rev: BCCB 2/06; SLJ 2/06; VOYA 4/06)

6739 Coy, John. *Box Out* (7–9). 2008, Scholastic $16.99 (978-043987032-0). Level-headed Liam is disturbed when he is promoted to the varsity basketball team and witnesses the coach's prayer sessions along with rampant discrimination and rule-breaking. **e** (Rev: BL 9/1/08*; SLJ 9/1/08)

6740 Coy, John. *Crackback* (8–11). 2005, Scholastic $16.99 (978-0-439-69733-0). High school football player Miles Manning faces many challenges including difficult relationships with his father and his coach, girl problems, and whether to join his teammates in using steroids. (Rev: BL 9/1/05*; SLJ 12/05; VOYA 12/05)

6741 Crutcher, Chris. *The Crazy Horse Electric Game* (7–12). 1987, Greenwillow $16.99 (978-0-688-06683-3). A motorboat accident ends the comfortable life and budding baseball career of a teenage boy. (Rev: BL 4/15/87; SLJ 5/87; VOYA 6/87)

6742 Crutcher, Chris. *Ironman* (8–12). 1995, Greenwillow $17.99 (978-0-688-13503-4). A psychological sports novel in which a 17-year-old carries an attitude that fuels the plot. (Rev: BL 3/1/95*; SLJ 3/95; VOYA 5/95)

6743 Crutcher, Chris. *Running Loose* (7–10). 1983, Greenwillow $18.99 (978-0-688-02002-6). A senior in high school faces problems when he opposes the decisions of a football coach. (Rev: BL 3/87)

6744 Crutcher, Chris. *Stotan!* (8–12). 2008, Harper-Tempest paper $7.99 (978-0-06-009492-8). A group of boys from different backgrounds but all close friends sign up for a brutally taxing physical program run by their school coach; first published in 1986. (Rev: BL 3/15/86; SLJ 5/86; VOYA 4/86)

6745 Crutcher, Chris. *Whale Talk* (8–12). 2001, Harper-Teen $15.95 (978-0-688-18019-5). Well-adjusted and academically able, T. J. is not into sports, which goes against the grain at his high school; he eventually is persuaded to form a swimming team and deliberately picks members from who buck the sports formula. ⌒ (Rev: BL 4/1/01; HB 5–6/01; SLJ 4/01)

6746 Day, Karen. *No Cream Puffs* (6–9). 2008, Random House $15.99 (978-0-375-83775-3). Talented player Madison becomes the first girl to play on a boys' Little League baseball team in this story set in Michigan in 1980. (Rev: BL 5/15/08; SLJ 7/08)

6747 Deuker, Carl. *Gym Candy* (8–11). 2007, Houghton Mifflin $16.00 (978-0-618-77713-6). To improve his high school football performance, Mick begins using steroids ("gym candy") and suffers physical and emotional consequences. (Rev: BL 9/1/07; SLJ 10/07)

6748 Deuker, Carl. *Night Hoops* (7–11). 2000, Houghton Mifflin $15.00 (978-0-395-97936-5). When older brother Scott gives up basketball for music, Nick develops his own presence on the court. (Rev: BL 5/1/00; HB 5–6/00; HBG 9/00; SLJ 5/00)

6749 Deuker, Carl. *On the Devil's Court* (8–12). 1991, Avon paper $5.99 (978-0-380-70879-6). In this variation on the Faust legend, a senior high basketball star believes he has sold his soul to have a perfect season. (Rev: BL 12/15/88; SLJ 1/89; VOYA 4/89)

6750 Deuker, Carl. *Payback Time* (7–10). 2010, Houghton Mifflin $16 (978-0-547-27981-7). Student reporter Mitch finds himself in a tough situation as he investigates a potential football cheating scandal. **e** (Rev: BL 9/1/10*; HB 11–12/10; SLJ 9/1/10; VOYA 12/10)

6751 Drumtra, Stacy. *Face-Off* (4–8). 1992, Avon paper $3.50 (978-0-380-76863-9). T.J. and his twin Brad become rivals for friends and for status on the hockey team. (Rev: BL 4/1/93; SLJ 1/05; VOYA 8/93)

6752 Durant, Alan, sel. *Sports Stories* (5–9). Illus. by David Kearney. Series: Story Library. 2000, Kingfisher $14.95 (978-0-7534-5322-3). A collection of 21 previously published short stories by well-known authors dealing with a variety of sports. (Rev: HBG 10/01; SLJ 11/00)

6753 Dygard, Thomas J. *Second Stringer* (6–12). 1998, Morrow $15.99 (978-0-688-15981-8). A star quarterback's knee injury gives second-stringer Kevin Taylor the opportunity of a lifetime during his senior year in high school. (Rev: BL 9/1/98; HBG 3/99; SLJ 12/98; VOYA 2/99)

6754 Eskilsen, Erik E. *Offsides* (6–10). 2004, Houghton Mifflin $15.00 (978-0-618-46284-1). Tom Gray, a top-notch soccer player, is proud of his Mohawk heritage and when he moves to a new town where the school's mascot is an Indian, he refuses to play. (Rev: BL 9/1/04; SLJ 1/05; VOYA 12/04)

6755 Eskilsen, Erik E. *The Outside Groove* (7–10). 2006, Houghton Mifflin $16.00 (978-0-618-66854-0). Casey's family only cares about her brother and his stock-car racing career, ignoring all of her accomplishments, so she decides to start racing, finding out a lot of family secrets in the process. (Rev: BL 9/15/06)

6756 Evans, Zoe. *Confessions of a Wannabe Cheerleader* (6–9). Illus. by Brigette Barrager. Series: Cheer! 2011, Simon & Schuster paper $6.99 (978-14424224-1-4). Madison is disappointed when she makes the B-squad Grizzlies cheerleading squad. **e** (Rev: BLO 7/11)

6757 Fehler, Gene. *Beanball* (7–9). 2008, Clarion $16.00 (978-0-618-84348-0). In free verse, witnesses to a baseball accident describe what happened (a popular, talented player is blinded in one eye) and how it affected them. (Rev: BL 2/15/08; SLJ 5/08)

6758 Fink, Mark. *Stepping Up* (6–9). 2009, WestSide $16.95 (978-1-934813-03-4). Clumsy but likable underdog Ernie, 14, is upset when his best friend joins the "in crowd" at basketball camp but gains confidence when a scary near-tragedy delivers him instant hero status in this fast-paced sports novel. Lexile 730L (Rev: BL 8/09; SLJ 6/1/09)

6759 Fitzgerald, Dawn. *Getting in the Game* (4–7). 2005, Roaring Brook $15.95 (978-1-59643-044-0). In first-person narrative, Joanna Giordano describes her difficult experiences as the only girl on a 7th-grade ice hockey team that doesn't want her, plus her problems with peers, parents, and ailing grandfather. (Rev: BCCB 9/05; BL 3/1/05; SLJ 7/05; VOYA 6/05)

6760 Fitzgerald, Dawn. *Soccer Chick Rules* (5–8). 2006, Roaring Brook $16.95 (978-1-59643-137-9). When her school's sports program is threatened, Tess Munro, a talented 13-year-old soccer player, joins the campaign to win approval for the school levy. (Rev: BL 9/1/06; SLJ 10/06)

6761 Flynn, Pat. *Alex Jackson: SWA* (6–10). 2002, Univ. of Queensland paper $13.50 (978-0-7022-3307-4). Alex flirts with physical danger and trouble with the police when he joins up with Skateboarders with Attitude. (Rev: SLJ 1/03)

6762 Freitas, Donna. *Gold Medal Summer* (5–8). 2012, Scholastic $16.99 (978-054532788-6). Joey, 14, is torn between her gymnastic ambitions and the desire to live a normal life. ℮ Lexile 790L (Rev: BL 6/12; LMC 8–9/12; SLJ 6/12)

6763 Godfrey, Martyn. *Ice Hawk* (7–12). 1986, EMC paper $13.50 (978-0-8219-0235-6). An easy-to-read story about a young minor league hockey player who balks at unnecessary use of violence. (Rev: BL 2/1/87)

6764 Gratz, Alan. *The Brooklyn Nine* (5–8). 2009, Dial $16.99 (978-0-8037-3224-7). This saga, told in nine stories or "innings," follows nine generations of a German immigrant family with links to both baseball and Brooklyn. (Rev: BCCB 4/09; BL 2/1/09; HB 3/09; LMC 5/09; SLJ 3/09)

6765 Green, Tim. *Baseball Great* (6–8). 2009, HarperCollins $16.99 (978-006162686-9); LB $17.89 (978-006162687-6). Josh, 12, blows the whistle on his steroid-dealing baseball coach and is rewarded for his good deed. ℮ Lexile 840L (Rev: BL 3/15/09; SLJ 4/1/09; VOYA 6/09)

6766 Green, Tim. *Best of the Best* (6–8). Series: Baseball Great Novels. 2011, HarperCollins $16.99 (978-0-06-168622-1). Josh, a 12-year-old baseball star and Little League team leader, works to succeed even as he is dis-

tracted by his parents' forthcoming divorce. ∩ ℮ (Rev: BL 4/1/11; SLJ 4/11; VOYA 4/11)

6767 Green, Tim. *Football Champ* (4–8). 2009, HarperCollins $16.99 (978-0-06-162689-0). Twelve-year-old Troy, who has an amazing ability to predict football plays, is accused of cheating in this exciting sequel to *Football Genius* (2007). (Rev: BL 9/15/09; SLJ 7/09)

6768 Green, Tim. *Football Genius* (5–8). 2007, HarperCollins $16.99 (978-0-06-112270-5). Troy's football skills are ignored until a linebacker for the Atlanta Falcons sees his ability to predict upcoming plays and uses him as the team's secret weapon. (Rev: BL 5/1/07; SLJ 7/07)

6769 Guest, Jacqueline. *Racing Fear* (7–10). Series: SideStreets. 2004, Lorimer paper $4.99 (978-1-55028-838-4). Trent and Adam are best friends and car racing buddies until an accident puts a strain on their friendship; suitable for reluctant readers. (Rev: SLJ 1/05)

6770 Gutman, Dan. *Ted and Me* (5–8). 2012, HarperCollins $15.99 (978-006123487-3). Charged with going back in time to warn FDR of the impending attack of Pearl Harbor, Stosh meets Ted Williams and gets some solid baseball advice. ∩ ℮ Lexile 630L (Rev: BLO 4/1/12)

6771 Hale, Daniel J., and Matthew LaBrot. *Red Card* (4–7). Series: Zeke Armstrong Mystery. 2002, Top paper $8.95 (978-1-929976-15-7). Someone is trying to kill the soccer coach, and young Zeke sets out to discover who and why. (Rev: SLJ 12/02; VOYA 12/02)

6772 Halpin, Brendan. *Shutout* (8–10). 2010, Farrar $16.99 (978-0-374-36899-9). Amanda and Lena's long-standing friendship begins to fray when they enter high school and Lena makes the varsity soccer team while Amanda's sore heel disqualifies her. (Rev: BL 9/1/10*; SLJ 8/10)

6773 Hampshire, Anthony. *Fast Track* (6–12). Series: Redline Racing. 2006, Fitzhenry & Whiteside paper $6.95 (978-1-55041-570-4). For reluctant readers, this is an action-packed story with good car racing scenes. Also use *Full Throttle* and *On the Limit* (both 2006). (Rev: SLJ 2/07; VOYA)

6774 Harkrader, L. D. *Airball: My Life in Briefs* (4–7). 2005, Roaring Brook $15.95 (978-1-59643-060-0). Kirby's middle school basketball team begins to improve when their coach — whom Kirby secretly believes is his father — insists the boys practice in their underwear. (Rev: BL 9/1/05; SLJ 11/05; VOYA 10/05)

6775 Haven, Paul. *Two Hot Dogs with Everything* (4–7). Illus. by Tim Jessell. 2006, Random House LB $17.99 (978-0-375-93350-9). Danny, 11, follows many superstitious rituals each time the Sluggers play, but his efforts seem to have no effect until he chews some 108-year-old gum that belonged to the team's founder. (Rev: BL 4/1/06)

6776 Hirschfeld, Robert. *Goalkeeper in Charge* (5–7). Series: Christopher Sports. 2002, Little, Brown paper $4.50 (978-0-316-07548-0). Seventh-grader Tina works to overcome her shyness on and off the soccer field. (Rev: BL 9/1/02; HBG 3/03)

6777 Holohan, Maureen. *Catch Shorty by Rosie* (4–8). Series: The Broadway Ballplayers. 1999, Broadway Ballplayers paper $6.95 (978-0-9659091-6-7). Sixth-grader Rosie Jones devotes her time to organizing an all-girls football league while coping with a series of minor personal problems at home and school. (Rev: SLJ 3/00)

6778 Johnson, Scott. *Safe at Second* (5–8). 2001, Penguin paper $7.99 (978-0-698-11877-5). The story of the friendship between Paulie and Todd, their love of baseball, and what happens after Todd is hit during a game and loses an eye. (Rev: BL 6/1–15/99; SLJ 7/99; VOYA 8/99)

6779 Kew, Trevor. *Sidelined* (5–8). Series: Sports Stories. 2011, Orca $9.95 (978-155277550-9); LB $16.95 (978-155277551-6). Marjan copes with competitive jealousy when her talented friend Vicky lands a spot on an elite soccer team in this story set in Vancouver. (Rev: BLO 8/11)

6780 King, Donna. *Double Twist* (5–8). 2007, Kingfisher paper $5.95 (978-0-7534-6023-8). When her ice-dancing partner injures his knee, 12-year-old Laura Lee scrambles to replace him just one month before the Junior Grand Prix. (Rev: BL 1/1–15/07)

6781 Klass, David. *Danger Zone* (7–12). 1996, Scholastic paper $16.95 (978-0-590-48590-6). Jimmy Doyle, a young basketball star, tries to prove to himself as well as to his mostly African American teammates that he deserves a place on the American High School Dream Team. (Rev: BL 4/1/96; SLJ 3/96; VOYA 4/96)

6782 Knudson, R. R. *Fox Running* (7–9). 1977, Avon paper $2.50 (978-0-380-00930-5). Kathy and an Apache Indian girl find friendship and inspiration in their mutual love of running.

6783 Korman, Gordon. *The Zucchini Warriors* (6–8). 1991, Scholastic paper $4.50 (978-0-590-44174-2). Hank, a former football player, promises to build Bruno and Boots's school a recreation hall if their team has a winning season. (Rev: VOYA 10/88)

6784 Levy, Elizabeth. *Tackling Dad* (5–8). 2005, HarperCollins LB $16.89 (978-0-06-000050-9). Cassie, 13, has won a place on the football team but her father won't sign the consent form. (Rev: BL 9/1/05; SLJ 8/05)

6785 Levy, Marilyn. *Run for Your Life* (7–9). 1997, Penguin paper $6.99 (978-0-698-11608-5). Thirteen-year-old Kisha tries to escape the Oakland projects and her parents' crumbling marriage by joining a track team that has been started by a new community center direc-tor. (Rev: BL 4/1/96; BR 9–10/96; SLJ 3/96; VOYA 6/96)

6786 Lipsyte, Robert. *Yellow Flag* (8–11). 2007, HarperTeen $16.99 (978-0-06-055707-2). When his brother, a NASCAR driver, is injured, Kyle takes his place and does so well that he must decide whether to continue racing or instead pursue his love of music. (Rev: BL 9/1/07; SLJ 9/07)

6787 Lupica, Mike. *The Batboy* (5–8). 2010, Philomel $17.99 (978-0-399-25000-2). Fourteen-year-old Brian gets permission to become a bat boy for the Detroit Tigers despite his mother's misgivings. (Rev: BL 1/1/10; SLJ 4/10)

6788 Lupica, Mike. *The Big Field* (5–8). 2008, Philomel $17.99 (978-0-399-24625-8). Fourteen-year-old Hutch and his team are going to the Florida State finals, but Hutch's happiness is marred by troubled relationships with his father and a new, difficult teammate. (Rev: BL 12/1/07; SLJ 2/08)

6789 Lupica, Mike. *Heat* (6–9). 2006, Philomel $16.99 (978-0-399-24301-1). Cuban American Michael Arroyo, who has been hiding his father's death to avoid the attention of the social services, finds his Little League pitching career in jeopardy when he can't produce a birth certificate. (Rev: BL 4/1/06*; SLJ 4/06; VOYA 4/06)

6790 Lupica, Mike. *Million-Dollar Throw* (5–8). 2009, Philomel $17.99 (978-0-399-24626-5). Thirteen-year-old Nate Brodie, star quarterback of the school football team, gets a chance to solve his family's money problems when he is selected for the million-dollar football toss during halftime at a pro football game. ∩ ℮ Lexile 960L (Rev: BL 9/1/09; SLJ 12/09; VOYA 12/09)

6791 Lupica, Mike. *Summer Ball* (5–8). 2007, Philomel $17.99 (978-0-399-24487-2). Even though his coach offers little encouragement, Danny Walker's determination helps him lead his summer basketball team to victory. (Rev: BL 4/15/07; SLJ 6/07)

6792 Lupica, Mike. *Travel Team* (6–8). 2004, Penguin $16.99 (978-0-399-24150-5). Twelve-year-old Danny Walker, cut from the 7th-grade basketball travel team, fights back with a team of his own. (Rev: BL 9/1/04; SLJ 11/04; VOYA 12/04)

6793 Lupica, Mike. *The Underdogs* (5–8). 2011, Philomel $17.99 (978-039925001-9). When his economically depressed town cuts funding for his football program, 12-year-old Will Tyler swings into action and revives the team. (Rev: BL 9/1/11)

6794 McGinley, Jerry. *Joaquin Strikes Back* (6–9). 1998, Tudor $18.95 (978-0-936389-58-5). Joaquin forms a soccer team in his new school that eventually plays the team from his former school. (Rev: BL 3/15/98; SLJ 3/99)

6795 Mackel, Kathy. *MadCat* (5–8). 2005, HarperCollins LB $16.89 (978-0-06-054870-4). Madelyn Catherine (aka MadCat), catcher on her local girls' fast-pitch softball team, is at the center of this story about sports, team play, and family involvement. (Rev: BL 2/15/05; SLJ 3/05)

6796 Maddox, Jake. *Diving Off the Edge* (4–7). Illus. by Sean Tiffany. Series: Jake Maddox Sports Fiction. 2009, Stone Arch $17.99 (978-1-4342-1205-4). A fast-paced story about swimming, peer pressure, and friendship. (Rev: BLO 3/19/09)

6797 Maddox, Jake. *Full Court Dreams* (4–7). Illus. by Tuesday Mourning. Series: Impact. 2008, Stone Arch LB $16.95 (978-1-4342-0469-1). Megan is determined to make the basketball team this year and gives the tryouts her all; for reluctant readers. (Rev: BL 4/1/08)

6798 Maddox, Jake, and Eric Stevens. *Karate Countdown* (4–7). Illus. by Sean Tiffany. Series: Jake Maddox Sports Fiction. 2009, Stone Arch $17.99 (978-1-4342-1200-9). Karate helps Kenny to defuse his anger over his mother's death. (Rev: BLO 3/19/09)

6799 Martino, Alfred C. *Over the End Line* (7–10). 2009, Harcourt $17 (978-0-15-206121-0). Jonny Fehey enjoys his celebrity when he scores a winning soccer goal during his senior year at high school, but the pleasure is brief when he realizes that the exchange student he has been seeing has been raped. ℰ Lexile HL660L (Rev: BL 9/15/09; SLJ 9/09; VOYA 10/09)

6800 Mercado, Nancy E., ed. *Baseball Crazy: Ten Short Stories That Cover All the Bases* (6–9). 2008, Dial $16.99 (978-0-8037-3162-2). An eclectic mix of baseball-related stories (plus a play) by writers including Ron Koertge and Joseph Bruchac, some of which range far from the sport itself. (Rev: BL 1/1–15/08; LMC 11–12/08; SLJ 5/08)

6801 Messner, Kate. *The Brilliant Fall of Gianna Z* (4–7). 2009, Bloomsbury $16.99 (978-0-8027-9842-8). Seventh-grader Gianna must complete a science assignment in order to compete in the cross-country running sectionals but life keeps interfering. (Rev: BL 8/09; SLJ 12/09)

6802 Messner, Kate. *Sugar and Ice* (5–7). 2010, Walker $16.99 (978-0-8027-2081-8). When Russian skating coach Andrei Grosheva offers 12-year-old farm girl Claire a scholarship to train with the elite in Lake Placid, she encounters a world of mean girls on ice, where competition is everything. (Rev: BL 9/1/10; SLJ 12/1/10)

6803 Myers, Walter Dean. *Game* (8–12). 2008, HarperTeen $16.99 (978-0-06-058294-4). Harlem born and bred, Drew hopes to become an NBA star, but the appearance of a talented white player on his team threatens his future. ⌂ (Rev: BL 2/1/08; SLJ 2/08)

6804 Myers, Walter Dean. *Hoops* (7–10). 1981, Dell paper $5.50 (978-0-440-93884-2). Lonnie plays basket-ball in spite of his coach, a has-been named Cal. Followed by *The Outside Shot* (1987).

6805 Myers, Walter Dean. *Me, Mop, and the Moondance Kid* (5–7). 1988, Dell paper $4.99 (978-0-440-40396-8). The efforts of T.J. and Moondance to get their friend Mop adopted. (Rev: BCCB 12/88; BL 2/1/89; SLJ 1/88)

6806 Nicholson, Lorna Schultz. *Roughing* (5–8). 2005, Lorimer paper $5.50 (978-1-55028-858-2). This story set in a hockey camp in Calgary, Alberta, features Josh, a boy with type 1 diabetes; Peter, a native Canadian; and Peter, a bully who plans to teach Peter a lesson. (Rev: BL 5/15/05; SLJ 9/05)

6807 Nicholson, Lorna Schultz. *Too Many Men* (4–8). Series: Sports Stories. 2007, Lorimer paper $7.95 (978-1-55028-948-0). Hockey player Sam juggles his busy home life with hockey practice as starting goalie. (Rev: SLJ 7/07)

6808 Nitz, Kristin Wolden. *Defending Irene* (5–7). 2004, Peachtree $14.95 (978-1-56145-309-2). When her family moves to Italy for a year, 13-year-old Irene is determined to continue playing soccer, even if it's on the boys' team. (Rev: SLJ 9/04)

6809 Norman, Rick. *Cross Body Block* (8–10). 1996, Colonial paper $9.95 (978-1-56883-060-5). An anguished story about a middle-aged football coach and his personal family tragedies, including the brutal death of a son. (Rev: VOYA 8/96)

6810 Northrop, Michael. *Plunked* (5–8). 2012, Scholastic $16.99 (978-054529714-1). Formerly bold and brassy 6th-grader Jack struggles to recover his pluck after being struck in the head by a baseball. ℰ Lexile 640L (Rev: BL 3/1/12; LMC 8–9/12; SLJ 4/12; VOYA 6/12)

6811 Park, Linda Sue. *Keeping Score* (4–7). 2008, Clarion $16.00 (978-0-618-92799-9). In 1951 fireman Jim teaches Brooklyn Dodgers fan Maggie, 9, how to score a game and the two remain friends even when Jim is sent to Korea; when Jim is horribly injured, Maggie is determined to help. (Rev: BL 2/1/08; SLJ 3/08)

6812 Parker, Robert B. *Edenville Owls* (6–9). 2007, Philomel $17.99 (978-0-399-24656-2). Eighth-grader Bobby tries to help an abused teacher and solve the mystery of her past while also starting a basketball team with his friends and dreaming of winning a local tournament. (Rev: BL 5/1/07; HB 7–8/07; SLJ 7/07)

6813 Patneaude, David. *Haunting at Home Plate* (4–7). 2000, Albert Whitman LB $15.99 (978-0-8075-3181-5). Twelve-year-old Nelson is amazed when mysterious instructions are left on the playing field in this baseball novel about a losing team that suddenly seems to be getting help from a ghost. (Rev: BCCB 11/00; BL 9/1/00; HBG 3/01; SLJ 9/00)

6814 Peers, Judi. *Shark Attack* (5–7). Series: Sports Stories. 1999, Orca paper $6.50 (978-1-55028-620-5). An easily read story set in Canada, in which a young baseball player wants to impress his father but doesn't think he can ever reach his older brother's record. (Rev: SLJ 1/00)

6815 Platt, Kin. *Brogg's Brain* (6–9). 1981, HarperCollins LB $11.89 (978-0-397-31946-6). Monty is a runner who is pushed by his father and his coach to win.

6816 Powell, Randy. *Dean Duffy* (8–12). 1995, Farrar paper $5.95 (978-0-374-41698-0). A Little League baseball great has problems with his pitching arm and sees his career collapse. (Rev: BL 4/15/95; SLJ 5/95)

6817 Powell, Randy. *The Whistling Toilets* (7–10). 1996, Farrar paper $5.95 (978-0-374-48369-2). When Stan tries to help his friend Ginny with her tennis game, he finds that something strange is troubling the rising young tennis star. (Rev: BL 9/15/96; SLJ 10/96; VOYA 12/96)

6818 Preller, James. *Six Innings* (5–8). 2008, Feiwel & Friends $16.95 (978-0-312-36763-3). Six innings of a Little League game reveal much about the game's young players and about the young announcer, a player side-lined by cancer. ALA Notable Books 2009. (Rev: BL 4/1/08; SLJ 4/08)

6819 Priebe, Val. *Running Rivals* (4–8). Illus. by Tuesday Mourning. Series: Impact Books: A Jake Maddox Sports Story. 2008, Stone Arch LB $17.95 (978-1-4342-0874-3); paper $5.99 (978-1-4342-0778-4). Amy, an African American girl who lives for her running, suffers an injury and faces two months without practice. (Rev: SLJ 3/09)

6820 Pyron, Bobbie. *The Ring* (6–9). 2009, WestSide $15.95 (978-1-934813-09-6). Boxing proves to be a salvation for troubled 15-year-old Mardie who has been drinking, shoplifting, and experimenting with drugs and boys. Lexile HL570L (Rev: BL 10/15/09; LMC 11–12/09; SLJ 1/10)

6821 Ripken, Cal, Jr. *Hothead* (5–8). 2011, Hyperion/Disney $16.99 (978-1-4231-4000-9). Gifted — and frustrated by family woes — 7th-grade shortstop Connor finally learns to control his temper when it threatens to derail his sports career. ⌒ e Lexile 810L (Rev: BL 2/15/11; SLJ 4/11)

6822 Ripken, Cal, Jr., and Kevin Cowherd. *Super-Sized Slugger* (4–7). Series: Cal Ripken, Jr.'s All-Stars. 2012, Hyperion/Disney $16.99 (978-1-4231-4001-6). Eighth-grader Cody must deal with teasing about his weight and now a series of mysterious thefts; can his baseball skills compensate? ⌒ e Lexile 810L (Rev: SLJ 8/1/12)

6823 Ritter, John H. *The Boy Who Saved Baseball* (5–7). 2003, Putnam $17.99 (978-0-399-23622-8). A small town depends on its baseball team to rescue it from big developers. (Rev: BL 5/1/03*; HBG 4/04; SLJ 6/03; VOYA 8/03)

6824 Ritter, John H. *Choosing Up Sides* (5–9). 1998, Putnam $18.99 (978-0-399-23185-8). Jake is a great southpaw in baseball, but his preacher father forbids the boy to use his left hand for pitching as it is the instrument of Satan. (Rev: BCCB 6/98; BL 5/1/98; HBG 10/98; SLJ 6/98; VOYA 12/98)

6825 Ritter, John H. *The Desperado Who Stole Baseball* (5–8). 2009, Philomel $17.99 (978-0-399-24664-7). In the 1880s, 12-year-old Jack Dillon — self-proclaimed baseball whiz — and outlaw Billy the Kid play in a key game in which a California mining town competes against the Chicago White Stockings; a rollicking prequel to *The Boy Who Saved Baseball* (2003). ⌒ Lexile 750L (Rev: BL 2/15/09; SLJ 4/1/09)

6826 Ritter, John H. *Fenway Fever!* (5–8). 2012, Philomel $16.99 (978-0-399-24665-4). Twelve-year-old "Stats" Pagano's devotion to baseball and the Red Sox is at the center of this story about a family's declining hot dog business and a pitcher's theory about the curse on the Fenway Park team. e (Rev: BLO 4/15/12; LMC 11–12/12; SLJ 9/12)

6827 Roberts, Kristi. *My Thirteenth Season* (5–8). 2005, Henry Holt $15.95 (978-0-8050-7495-6). When Fran, whose mother has recently died, tries to play baseball for the boys' team in her new town, she is in for a world of trouble. (Rev: BL 3/15/05*; SLJ 3/05)

6828 Romain, Joseph. *The Mystery of the Wagner Whacker* (7–12). 1997, Warwick paper $8.95 (978-1-895629-94-1). Matt, a baseball enthusiast, is upset at moving to a small Canadian town where the sport is all but unknown, but an accidental travel in time to 1928 changes the situation. (Rev: BL 7/98; SLJ 7/98)

6829 Ross, Jeff. *The Drop* (4–7). Series: Orca Sports. 2011, Orca paper $9.95 (978-1-55469-392-4). For reluctant readers, this is an exciting snowboarding adventure story set in the mountains of British Columbia. (Rev: BL 7/11; SLJ 8/11)

6830 Rottman, S. L. *Slalom* (6–8). 2004, Penguin $16.99 (978-0-670-05913-3). Seventeen-year-old Sandro, raised in the shadow of a posh ski resort by his single mother, is shaken when the handsome Italian skier who is his father turns up and reunites with his mother. (Rev: BL 9/1/04; SLJ 11/04; VOYA 10/04)

6831 Rud, Jeff. *In the Paint* (5–8). 2005, Orca paper $7.95 (978-1-55143-337-0). Matt is glad to make the basketball team but soon finds there are pressures he would prefer to avoid. (Rev: BL 7/05)

6832 Scaletta, Kurtis. *Mudville* (4–8). 2009, Knopf $15.99 (978-0-375-85579-5). It has been raining in Moundville (aka Mudville) for 22 years, but with the arrival of a foster child named Sturgis the sun suddenly reappears and allows baseball and the interrupted game against Sinister Bend to resume. (Rev: BL 3/1/09; SLJ 3/09)

6833 Sherman, M. Zachary. *Impulse* (5–8). Illus. by Caio Majado. Series: Tony Hawk's 900 Revolution. 2011, Capstone LB $25.32 (978-1-4342-3203-8); paper $6.95 (978-1-4342-3452-0). Fourteen-year-old foster child Dylan, aka Slider, contends with the mysterious disappearance of his admired older brother in this skateboard-fueled thriller with magical elements; this series appeals to reluctant readers. Lexile 660L (Rev: BLO 8/11; LMC 1–2/12; SLJ 12/1/11; VOYA 10/11)

6834 Smith, Charles R. *Winning Words: Sports Stories and Photographs* (5–8). Illus. by author. 2008, Candlewick $17.99 (978-076361445-4). This short story collection from sportswriter Smith interprets some of sport's best themes, including confidence, determination, and motivation, and includes photographs that add interest. Lexile 620L (Rev: BL 9/1/08; SLJ 8/08)

6835 Spring, Debbie. *Breathing Soccer* (5–8). 2008, Thistledown $10.95 (978-189723542-3). Asthmatic soccer buff Lisa, 12, gains inspiration from stories of athletes overcoming physical struggles in this believable, happy-ending tale. (Rev: BLO 8/08; SLJ 1/1/09)

6836 Stoudemire, Amar'e. *Home Court* (4–7). Illus. by Tim Jessell. Series: STAT "Standing Tall and Talented". 2012, Scholastic $17.99 (978-054543169-9); paper $5.99 (978-054538759-0). In this semiautobiographical tale 11-year-old Amar'e works hard at school and enjoys skateboarding — and is ready, with his friends, to take on a trio of older bullies trying to invade their basketball court. e Lexile 650L (Rev: BL 6/12)

6837 Strasser, Todd. *Cut Back* (7–12). Series: Impact Zone. 2004, Simon & Schuster paper $5.99 (978-0-689-87030-9). In this action-packed series installment, 15-year-old Kai faces off against his nemesis, Lucas Frank, in a surfing competition; a sequel is *Take Off* (2004). (Rev: BL 7/04; SLJ 8/04)

6838 Swan, Bill. *The Enforcer* (5–8). Series: Canadian Sports Stories. 2008, James Lorimer $8.95 (978-1-55028-981-7); paper $8.95 (978-1-55028-979-4). Hockey is the focus in this book about Jake, a boy with three grandfathers who all intrude into his life in different ways. (Rev: BL 6/1–15/08)

6839 Sweeney, Joyce. *Players* (6–12). 2000, Winslow $16.95 (978-1-890817-54-1). Corey, leader of the basketball team, is determined to find out who is sabotaging its chances of success. (Rev: BL 10/1/00; HBG 10/01; SLJ 9/00; VOYA 12/00)

6840 Tharp, Tim. *Knights of the Hill Country* (8–11). 2006, Knopf $16.95 (978-0-375-83653-4). In his senior year, Hampton, the star linebacker in a school and town that live for football, begins to deal with his uncertainties and realize that he is more than just an athlete. (Rev: BL 10/1/06; LMC 1/07; SLJ 9/06)

6841 Tocher, Timothy. *Bill Pennant, Babe Ruth, and Me* (5–9). 2009, Cricket $16.95 (978-0-8126-2755-8). In 1920, 16-year-old Hank Cobb is put in charge of the Giants' mascot, a Mexican wildcat, and then must keep an eye on the Yankees' new player called Babe Ruth. (Rev: LMC 8/09; SLJ 6/09)

6842 Tocher, Timothy. *Chief Sunrise, John McGraw, and Me* (6–9). 2004, Cricket $15.95 (978-0-8126-2711-4). In this appealing baseball tale set in 1919, 15-year-old Hank Cobb escapes from an abusive father, joins forces with a 19-year-old baseball hopeful who claims to be a Seminole, and travels to New York in search of a career playing ball. (Rev: BCCB 7–8/04; BL 5/15/04; SLJ 9/04)

6843 Tooke, Wes. *King of the Mound: My Summer with Satchel Paige* (5–7). 2012, Simon & Schuster $15.99 (978-144243346-5). Recovering from a bout with polio that has left him with a leg brace, 12-year-old Nick is happy to help with odd jobs at the North Dakota stadium where his father is catcher, and to meet the great Satchel Paige. (Rev: BL 2/15/12; SLJ 2/12)

6844 Trembath, Don. *Frog Face and the Three Boys* (4–7). Series: Black Belt. 2001, Orca paper $6.95 (978-1-55143-165-9). Three very different 7th-graders are enrolled in a karate class to teach them discipline. (Rev: BL 3/1/01; SLJ 9/01; VOYA 8/02)

6845 Tunis, John R. *The Kid from Tomkinsville* (6–9). 1990, Harcourt $14.95 (978-0-15-242568-5). This novel, first published in 1940, introduces Roy Tucker and his remarkable pitching arm. It is continued in *The Kid Comes Back* (1946). Also use *Rookie of the Year* (1944). (Rev: BL 8/87)

6846 Wallace, Bill. *Never Say Quit* (5–7). 1993, Holiday $16.95 (978-0-8234-1013-2). A group of misfits who don't make the soccer team decide to form one of their own. (Rev: BL 4/15/93)

6847 Walters, Eric. *Juice* (6–9). 2005, Orca paper $7.95 (978-1-55143-351-6). Moose gets caught up in his high school football team's doping scandal in this novel for reluctant readers. (Rev: BL 9/1/05; VOYA 8/05)

6848 Weaver, Will. *Hard Ball* (7–12). 1998, HarperCollins LB $15.89 (978-0-06-027122-0). Billy Baggs discovers that his rival for the star position on the freshman baseball team is also his rival for the attention of the girl he is attracted to. (Rev: BL 1/1–15/98; HBG 9/98; SLJ 4/98; VOYA 6/98)

6849 Weaver, Will. *Saturday Night Dirt* (8–11). Series: Motor. 2008, Farrar $14.95 (978-0-374-35060-4). A racetrack in rural Minnesota is the setting for this story about a group of people who share a love of racing. (Rev: BL 3/1/08; SLJ 4/08)

6850 Weaver, Will. *Striking Out* (8–12). 1993, HarperCollins paper $7.99 (978-0-06-447113-8). When Minnesota farmboy Billy Baggs picks up a stray baseball and fires it back to the pitcher, his baseball career begins, but his family isn't enthusiastic. (Rev: BL 11/1/93; SLJ 10/93; VOYA 12/93)

6851 Weaver, Will. *Super Stock Rookie* (8–11). Series: Motor Novels. 2009, Farrar $14.95 (978-037435061-1). High-schooler Trace wins a corporate sponsorship, giving him the chance to compete on the stock-car circuit, but is suspicious about the motives of Team Blu. Lexile HL720L (Rev: BL 2/15/09; SLJ 3/1/09; VOYA 6/09)

6852 Webster-Doyle, Terrence. *Breaking the Chains of the Ancient Warrior: Tests of Wisdom for Young Martial Artists* (5–8). 1995, Martial Arts for Peace paper $14.95 (978-0-942941-32-6). A collection of inspirational stories, karate parables, and tests that promote ethical behavior, with accompanying follow-up questions and a message for adult readers. (Rev: SLJ 1/96)

6853 Withers, Pam. *Skater Stuntboys* (6–9). Series: Take It to the Xtreme. 2005, Walrus paper $6.95 (978-1-55285-647-5). An action-filled novel about 15-year-olds Jake and Peter, who take jobs as skateboarding stunt doubles on the set of an extreme-sports film and find they're in the middle of a mystery. (Rev: SLJ 11/05)

6854 Wolff, Virginia Euwer. *Bat 6* (5–9). 1998, Scholastic paper $16.95 (978-0-590-89799-0). In this novel narrated by the members of the opposing teams, a Japanese American girl just out of an internment camp meets a bitter girl whose father was killed at Pearl Harbor, and the two become rivals in baseball. (Rev: BCCB 6/98; BL 5/1/98*; HBG 10/98; SLJ 5/98; VOYA 6/98)

6855 Wooldridge, Frosty. *Strike Three! Take Your Base* (5–9). Illus. by Pietri Freeman. 2001, Brookfield Reader $16.95 (978-1-930093-01-0); paper $6.95 (978-1-930093-07-2). Baseball provides the setting as two brothers deal individually with the sudden death of their umpire father. (Rev: SLJ 3/02)

6856 Wunderli, Stephen. *The Heartbeat of Halftime* (6–9). 1996, Henry Holt $14.95 (978-0-8050-4713-4). Wing tries to forget his father's declining health by becoming totally absorbed in football. (Rev: BL 10/1/96; SLJ 11/96; VOYA 10/96)

6857 Zadoff, Allen. *Food, Girls, and Other Things I Can't Have* (8–10). 2009, Egmont $16.99 (978-1-60684-004-7); LB $19.99 (978-1-60684-051-1). Overweight high school sophomore Andy Zansky finds his popularity soaring when he joins the football team but soon discovers that many pitfalls await him. ℮ Lexile HL520L (Rev: BL 10/15/09; HB 11–12/09; LMC 11–12/09; SLJ 9/09; VOYA 10/09)

6858 Zirpoli, Jane. *Roots in the Outfield* (5–7). 1988, Houghton Mifflin $16.00 (978-0-395-45184-7). Josh spends a summer with his newly married father in Wisconsin and discovers some baseball memorabilia that help him overcome his own fears and ineptness in right field. (Rev: BL 4/1/88; SLJ 5/88)

6859 Zusak, Markus. *Fighting Ruben Wolfe* (8–12). 2001, Scholastic $15.95 (978-0-439-24188-5). Two brothers, Ruben and Cameron, try to assist their struggling family by boxing under the direction of an unethical promoter. (Rev: BL 2/15/01; HB 3–4/01; HBG 10/01; SLJ 3/01; VOYA 4/01)

Short Stories and General Anthologies

6860 Abrahams, Peter. *Up All Night: A Short Story Collection* (7–12). 2008, HarperCollins $16.99 (978-0-06-137076-2). "What keeps you up all night?" Popular YA authors — including Libba Bray, David Levithan, and Patricia McCormick — contribute quite different answers to the question. (Rev: BL 4/1/08; SLJ 4/08)

6861 Asher, Sandy, and David L. Harrison, eds. *Dude! Stories and Stuff for Boys* (4–7). 2006, Dutton $17.99 (978-0-525-47684-9). Selections for boys — poems, short stories, and other works — offer diverse experiences; authors include Sneed B. Collard III, Clyde Robert Bulla, Jane Yolen, and Ron Koertge. (Rev: BL 7/06; HBG 4/07; LMC 1/07; SLJ 8/06; VOYA 12/06)

6862 Avi, sel. *Best Shorts: Favorite Short Stories for Sharing* (5–9). Ed. by Carolyn Shute. Illus. by Chris Raschka. 2006, Houghton Mifflin $16.95 (978-0-618-47603-9). The 24 short stories in this anthology provide a sampling of some of the best writing in a wide variety of genres. (Rev: SLJ 10/06)

6863 Bauer, Marion Dane, ed. *Am I Blue?* (8–12). 1995, HarperCollins paper $7.99 (978-0-06-440587-4). Sixteen short stories from well-known YA writers who have something meaningful to share about gay awareness and want to present positive, credible gay role models. (Rev: BL 5/1/94*; SLJ 6/94; VOYA 8/94)

6864 Belleza, Rhoda, ed. *Cornered: 14 Stories of Bullying and Defiance* (8–11). 2012, Running Press paper $9.95 (978-0-7624-4-515-8). Fourteen stories explore the experience of being bullied from a variety of perspectives. (Rev: BL 8/12; LMC 1–2/13; SLJ 11/12)

6865 *The Big Book of Horror: 21 Tales to Make You Tremble* (5–7). Illus. by Pedro Rodriguez. 2007, Sterling $12.95 (978-1-4027-3860-9). This collection of 21 horror tales includes stories by Edgar Allan Poe, Charles Dickens, Robert Louis Stevenson, and H. P. Lovecraft. (Rev: BL 3/15/07; SLJ 7/07)

6866 Black, Holly, and Cecil Castellucci, eds. *Geektastic: Stories from the Nerd Herd* (8–12). 2009, Little, Brown $16.99 (978-0-316-00809-9). A collection of short stories that will please fans of everything from Star Trek to Dungeon Maters, underlining some of the difficult sides of geekiness. YALSA Popular Paperbacks for Young Adults Top Ten 2012. ℮ (Rev: BL 9/09; HB 9–10/09; LMC 1–2/10; SLJ 8/09)

6867 Book Wish Foundation. *What You Wish For: A Book for Darfur* (5–8). 2011, Putnam $17.99 (978-0399-25454-3). With a foreword by Mia Farrow and contributions by authors including Alexander McCall Smith, Jane Yolen, Naomi Shihab Nye, and Cynthia Voigt, this is a collection of stories and poems that focus on young people's aspirations, created to benefit the refugees of Darfur. ℮ (Rev: BL 10/1/11*; LMC 1–2/12; SLJ 11/1/11; VOYA 2/12)

6868 Bradman, Tony, ed. *My Dad's a Punk: 12 Stories about Boys and Their Fathers* (7–10). 2006, Kingfisher paper $7.95 (978-0-7534-5870-9). The complexities of father/son relationships are explored in this collection of 12 short stories by writers including Ron Koertge and Tim Wynne-Jones. (Rev: BL 5/1/06; HB 7–8/06; SLJ 8/06)

6869 Bradman, Tony, ed. *Under the Weather: Stories About Climate Change* (4–7). 2010, Frances Lincoln $16.95 (978-1-84507-930-7). This multicultural selection of short stories examines how climate change is affecting people in different parts of the world. (Rev: BL 1/1–15/11; SLJ 1/1/11) [808.83936]

6870 Brooks, Bruce. *All That Remains* (7–12). 2001, Simon & Schuster $16.00 (978-0-689-83351-9). Three darkly entertaining novellas tackle the topic of death and how young people cope with it. (Rev: BCCB 6/01; BL 5/1/01; HB 7–8/01; HBG 10/01; SLJ 5/01; VOYA 6/01)

6871 Busby, Cylin, ed. *First Kiss (Then Tell): A Collection of True Lip-Locked Moments* (7–10). 2008, Bloomsbury $15.95 (978-1-59990-199-2); paper $8.95 (978-1-59990-241-8). Popular YA authors including Jon Scieszka, David Levithan, Deb Caletti, and Justine Larbalestier describe their first kisses — some romantic, some sloppy, some embarrassing, some clumsy. (Rev: BL 2/1/08; SLJ 2/08)

6872 Canfield, Jack, ed. *Chicken Soup for the Kid's Soul: 101 Stories of Courage, Hope and Laughter* (4–7). 1998, Health Communications paper $14.95 (978-1-55874-609-1). A collection of inspiring true stories, some by well-known people, but mostly by children who sent them to the editors. (Rev: BL 9/1/98; HBG 3/99) [158.1]

6873 Canfield, Jack, ed. *Chicken Soup for the Preteen Soul: 101 Stories of Changes, Choices and Growing Up for Kids Ages 9-13* (5–7). 2000, Health Communications $24.00 (978-1-55874-801-9); paper $14.95 (978-1-55874-800-2). The usual mix of verse and prose written by and for preteens, with the aim of offering inspiration, comfort, and practical advice. (Rev: HBG 10/01; SLJ 4/01) [158.1]

6874 Carter, Anne Laurel. *No Missing Parts and Other Stories About Real Princesses* (7–12). 2003, Red Deer paper $9.95 (978-0-88995-253-9). Ten thoughtful stories from Canada portray young women who rely on their own resources in difficult situations. (Rev: BL 5/1/03; SLJ 5/03; VOYA 10/03)

6875 Carver, Peter, ed. *Close-Ups: Best Stories for Teens* (6–8). 2000, Red Deer paper $9.95 (978-0-88995-200-3). Self-image, sexuality, and a variety of other teen topics are presented in this collection of stories by Canadian authors. (Rev: BL 2/15/01; VOYA 4/01)

6876 Compestine, Ying Chang. *A Banquet for Hungry Ghosts* (6–8). Illus. by Coleman Polhemus. 2009, Henry Holt $16.99 (978-0-8050-8208-1). Organized to resemble a Chinese banquet, this collection of chilling and gory ghost stories serves up frights and Chinese culture in equal helpings. ℮ Lexile 880L (Rev: BL 11/15/09; HB 11–12/09; SLJ 12/09)

6877 *Cowboy Stories* (7–12). Illus. by Barry Moser. 2007, Chronicle $16.95 (978-0-8118-5418-4). A collection of traditional western stories featuring cowboys, gunslingers, and lawmen by famous authors including Louis L'Amour and Elmer Kelton. (Rev: BL 9/15/07; SLJ 9/07)

6878 Crebbin, June, ed. *Horse Tales* (4–7). Illus. by Inga Moore. 2005, Candlewick $18.99 (978-0-7636-2657-0). Diverse short stories about horses, with color illustrations. (Rev: BL 9/1/05; SLJ 8/05)

6879 Dahl, Roald. *Skin and Other Stories* (7–12). 2000, Viking $15.99 (978-0-670-89184-9). Selected from the author's short stories for adults, these 13 bizarre tales will also delight younger readers. (Rev: BL 10/1/00; HBG 3/01; VOYA 12/00)

6880 Datlow, Ellen, and Terri Windling, eds. *The Green Man: Tales from the Mythic Forest* (7–12). 2002, Viking $18.99 (978-0-670-03526-7). Mythical beings with special relevance to the natural world are portrayed in a collection of stories and poems. (Rev: BL 4/15/02; HBG 10/02; SLJ 7/02; VOYA 6/02)

6881 Davis, Donald. *Mama Learns to Drive and Other Stories: Stories of Love, Humor, and Wisdom* (4–7). 2005, August House $17.95 (978-0-87483-745-2). Brief, slow-paced short stories based on his mother, who grew up in the Smoky Mountains in the 1930s, are mixed with tales about the author's own youth in the 1950s. (Rev: BL 8/05; SLJ 10/05)

6882 Editors of McSweeney's. *Noisy Outlaws, Unfriendly Blobs, and Some Other Things* (4–7). 2005, McSweeney's $22.00 (978-1-932416-35-0). Kid-friendly stories by well-known authors including Nick Hornby, Neil Gaiman, and Jon Scieskza. (Rev: BL 9/1/05)

6883 Ellis, Deborah. *Lunch with Lenin and Other Stories* (7–12). 2008, Fitzhenry & Whiteside $14.95 (978-155455105-7). This collection of uneven but nonetheless worthy short stories centers around the theme of drugs and drug addiction in different countries around the world. (Rev: BL 12/1/08; SLJ 2/1/09; VOYA 2/09)

6884 Estevis, Anne. *Down Garrapata Road* (6–12). 2003, Arte Publico paper $12.95 (978-1-55885-397-3). In this collection of closely linked short stories, Estevis paints an appealing portrait of life in a small Mexican American community in South Texas during the 1930s and 1940s. (Rev: BL 1/1–15/04)

6885 Fleischman, Paul. *Graven Images: Three Stories* (7–9). 1982, HarperCollins paper $4.95 (978-0-06-440186-9). Three stories that explore various aspects of human nature.

6886 Fox, Carol. *In Times of War: An Anthology of War and Peace in Children's Literature* (6–12). 2001, Pavilion $24.95 (978-1-86205-446-2). Educators in the United Kingdom, Belgium, and Portugal worked together on this anthology of fiction, memoirs, and poetry — most of which deals with World Wars I and II in Europe — that is presented in thematic groupings. (Rev: BL 4/15/01; SLJ 6/01)

6887 Gac-Artigas, Alejandro. *Off to Catch the Sun* (5–8). 2001, Espacio paper $11.95 (978-1-930879-28-7). Thirteen-year-old author Gac-Artigas explores serious issues through poetry, essays, and short stories. (Rev: BL 1/1–15/02)

6888 Gallo, Donald R., ed. *What Are You Afraid Of? Stories About Phobias* (7–10). 2006, Candlewick $15.99 (978-0-7636-2654-9). This is a collection of short stories (by well-known authors) about a variety of phobias, how their victims' day-to-day lives are affected, and how they cope with their fears. (Rev: BL 9/1/06; SLJ 9/06)

6889 Gratz, Alan. *Fantasy Baseball* (5–8). 2011, Dial $16.99 (978-0-8037-3463-0). Twelve-year-old Alex finds himself joining an odd baseball league populated by characters from classic children's literature and fairy tales in this multilayered fantastical story. e Lexile 730L (Rev: BLO 1/1–15/11; SLJ 4/11)

6890 Hearne, Betsy. *Hauntings and Other Tales of Danger, Love, and Sometimes Loss* (5–8). 2007, Greenwillow $15.99 (978-0-06-123910-6). A collection of 15 eerie stories set in the past (mostly in Ireland), in the present (mostly America), and in the hereafter (mostly Heaven and Hell). (Rev: BL 8/07; LMC 9–10/07; SLJ 11/07)

6891 Hollander, John, ed. *O. Henry* (5–8). Illus. by Miles Hyman. 2006, Sterling $14.95 (978-1-4027-0988-3). A collection of seven O. Henry short stories, including "The Gift of the Magi," with helpful introductions before each story. (Rev: BL 4/15/06; SLJ 5/06)

6892 Holt, Kimberly Willis. *Part of Me: Stories of a Louisiana Family* (5–8). 2006, Henry Holt $16.95 (978-0-8050-6360-8). Reading is the thread that links this collection of short stories that spans four generations of a Louisiana family, from 1939 to the early 21st century. (Rev: BL 9/1/06; SLJ 9/06)

6893 Hopkins, Ellen, et al. *Does This Book Make Me Look Fat?: Stories About Loving — and Loathing — Your Body* (7–12). Ed. by Marissa Walsh. 2008, Clarion $16.00 (978-054701496-8). A primarily fiction-based collection of essays and short stories by multiple YA authors that focus on various aspects of body image. (Rev: BL 12/15/08; LMC 3–4/09; SLJ 1/1/09; VOYA 2/09)

6894 Howe, James, ed. *13: Thirteen Stories That Capture the Agony and Ecstasy of Being Thirteen* (6–9). 2003, Simon & Schuster $16.95 (978-0-689-82863-8). This collection of short stories by such popular authors as Ann Martin, Alex Sanchez, and Ellen Wittlinger beautifully captures what it means to be 13 years old. (Rev: BCCB 1/04; BL 1/1–15/04; SLJ 10/03; VOYA 12/03)

6895 Hudson, Wade, and Cheryl W. Hudson, eds. *In Praise of Our Fathers and Our Mothers* (6–12). 1997, Just Us Bks $29.95 (978-0-940975-59-0); paper $17.95 (978-0-940975-60-6). Nearly 50 well-known African American writers, among them Walter Dean Myers, Virginia Hamilton, and Brian Pinkney, recall their family life in this anthology of poetry, essays, paintings, and interviews. (Rev: BL 4/1/97; HB 3–4/97; SLJ 6/97) [920]

6896 Jocelyn, Marthe, sel. *Secrets* (5–8). 2005, Tundra paper $8.95 (978-0-88776-723-4). A collection of 12 short stories that reveal the importance of secrets. (Rev: SLJ 2/06)

6897 Kibuishi, Kazu, ed. *Explorer: The Mystery Boxes* (4–8). Illus. 2012, Abrams $19.95 (978-141970010-1); paper $10.95 (978-14197000-9-5). An anthology of short graphic works all centering on the theme of a mysterious box and its contents. (Rev: BL 2/15/12; HB 5–6/12; LMC 8–8/12; SLJ 3/1/12*; VOYA 4/12)

6898 Kulpa, Kathryn, ed. *Something Like a Hero* (6–10). 1995, Merlyn's Pen paper $9.95 (978-1-886427-03-7). A collection of 11 short stories from different genres, reprinted from the national magazine of student writing *Merlyn's Pen*. (Rev: VOYA 2/96)

6899 Lanagan, Margo. *White Time* (8–11). 2006, HarperCollins $15.99 (978-0-06-074393-2). From the author of Black Juice comes a thought-provoking collection of 10 short stories with topics on death, love, and more set in alternate realities. (Rev: BL 8/06; SLJ 11/06)

6900 Levithan, David, ed. *Where We Are, What We See: Poems, Stories, Essays, and Art from the Best Young Writers and Artists in America* (8–11). 2005, Scholastic paper $7.99 (978-0-439-73646-6). Winning entries in the Scholastic Art and Writing Awards program. (Rev: BL 9/15/05; SLJ 1/06) [810]

6901 London, Jack. *The Portable Jack London* (8–12). Ed. by Earle Labor. 1994, Penguin paper $18.00 (978-0-14-017969-9). As well as several short stories and the full text of *The Call of the Wild*, this anthology contains some letters and general nonfiction. [818]

6902 Lord, Christine, ed. *Eighth Grade: Stories of Friendship, Passage and Discovery by Eighth Grade Writers* (6–12). Series: American Teen Writer. 1996, Merlyn's Pen paper $9.95 (978-1-886427-08-2). This is a group of short stories collected by *Merlyn's Pen* magazine that were written by 8th-graders. Also in this series are *Freshman: Fiction, Fantasy, and Humor by Ninth Grade Writers* and *Sophomores: Tales of Reality, Conflict, and the Road,* plus eight other volumes (all 1996). Each is accompanied by an audiotape. (Rev: VOYA 6/98)

6903 Loughead, Deb, and Jocelyn Shipley, eds. *Cleavage: Breakaway Fiction for Real Girls* (8–12). 2009, Sumach paper $12.95 (978-1-894549-76-9). Fifteen diverse stories by Canadian writers explore the relationship between teen girls and their mothers, many with a focus on different perspectives of body image. (Rev: SLJ 2/1/09; VOYA 2/09)

6904 Lubar, David. *The Battle of the Red Hot Pepper Weenies and Other Warped and Creepy Tales* (4–7). 2009, Tor $15.95 (978-0-7653-2099-5). A collection of 35 varied short stories with something for everyone — humor, horror, science fiction, suspense. (Rev: BLO 3/5/09; SLJ 5/09)

6905 Lubar, David. *Invasion of the Road Weenies and Other Warped and Creepy Tales* (4–7). 2005, Tor $16.95 (978-0-7653-1447-5). Entertaining stories about how things don't always work out how you hope or expect; suitable for reluctant readers. (Rev: BL 8/05; SLJ 9/05; VOYA 10/05)

6906 McKinley, Robin, and Peter Dickinson. *Water: Tales of Elemental Spirits* (7–12). 2002, Putnam $18.99 (978-0-399-23796-6). Six captivating and imaginative stories feature magical sea-beings and the humans who love or fight them. (Rev: BL 4/15/02; HB 7–8/02; HBG 10/02; SLJ 6/02*; VOYA 6/02)

6907 Macy, Sue, ed. *Girls Got Game: Sports Stories and Poems* (6–9). 2001, Henry Holt $15.95 (978-0-8050-6568-8). A collection of original stories and poems about girls playing sports that range from team games to individual pursuits. (Rev: BL 6/1–15/01; HB 7–8/01; HBG 10/01; SLJ 7/01; VOYA 8/01)

6908 Mazer, Anne, ed. *America Street: A Multicultural Anthology of Stories* (5–8). 1993, Persea paper $7.95 (978-0-89255-191-0). Fourteen short stories about growing up in America's diverse society by Robert Cormier, Langston Hughes, Grace Paley, Gary Soto, and others. (Rev: BCCB 11/93; BL 9/1/93; SLJ 11/93; VOYA 12/93)

6909 Miller-Lachmann, Lyn, ed. *Once Upon a Cuento* (6–9). 2003, Curbstone paper $15.95 (978-1-880684-99-3). A diverse collection of short stories by Hispanic American authors, each preceded by editor's comments that add context. (Rev: SLJ 1/04; VOYA 12/04)

6910 Mooney, Ben, ed. *You Never Did Learn to Knock: 14 Stories about Girls and Their Mothers* (7–10). 2006, Kingfisher paper $7.95 (978-0-7534-5877-8). Fourteen enjoyable stories about all types of mothers and the relationships — be they strained, loving, or complicated — they have with their daughters. (Rev: BL 4/15/06; LMC 8–9/06; SLJ 6/06)

6911 Morpurgo, Michael, comp. *The Kingfisher Book of Great Boy Stories: A Treasury of Classics from Children's Literature* (4–8). 2000, Kingfisher $19.95 (978-0-7534-5320-9). An attractively illustrated collection of stories from authors including Carlo Collodi, Roald Dahl, Ted Hughes, C. S. Lewis, A. A. Milne, Donald Sobol, and Mark Twain. (Rev: HBG 10/01; SLJ 4/01)

6912 Myers, Walter Dean. *What They Found: Love on 145th Street* (7–11). 2007, Random House $15.99 (978-0-385-32138-9). A collection of 15 interrelated stories about love of family among African Americans, many dealing with poverty, drug addiction, incarceration, and other hardships. (Rev: BCCB 11/07; BL 7/07; SLJ 8/07)

6913 Naidoo, Beverley. *Out of Bounds: Seven Stories of Conflict and Hope* (6–10). 2003, HarperCollins LB $17.89 (978-0-06-050800-5). The seven stories in this book, with a foreword by Archbishop Desmond Tutu, look at the racism, apartheid, discrimination, and progress in South Africa from the 1950s to the present. (Rev: BL 2/15/03; HB 3–4/03*; HBG 10/03; SLJ 1/03; VOYA 6/03)

6914 Nix, Garth. *Across the Wall: A Tale of the Abhorsen and Other Stories* (7–10). 2005, HarperCollins LB $17.89 (978-0-06-074714-5). In this collection of short stories, Garth offers an eclectic mix of genres and settings — only the first is related to Abhorsen — suitable for a range of readers. (Rev: BL 6/1–15/05; SLJ 11/05; VOYA 10/05)

6915 November, Sharyn, ed. *Firebirds* (7–12). 2003, Putnam $19.99 (978-0-14-250142-9). An excellent collection of stories by authors who publish with the Firebird imprint, including Michael Cadnum, Garth Nix, and Meredith Ann Pierce. (Rev: BL 10/15/03; HBG 4/04; VOYA 12/03)

6916 November, Sharyn, ed. *Firebirds Rising: An Anthology of Original Science Fiction and Fantasy* (7–10). 2006, Penguin $19.99 (978-0-14-240549-9). Contributors to this anthology of 16 original stories include Tamora Pierce, Charles de Lint, Patricia A. McKillip, Kara Dalkey, and Tanith Lee. (Rev: BL 4/1/06; SLJ 4/06; VOYA 4/06)

6917 November, Sharyn, ed. *Firebirds Soaring: An Anthology of Original Speculative Fiction* (7–12). Illus. by Mike Dringenberg. Series: Firebirds. 2008, Penguin $19.99 (978-014240552-9). Nancy Springer, Nancy Farmer, Jane Yolen, Carol Emshwiller, and Kara Dalkey are among the authors of the 19 short stories included in this volume, diverse tales that reflect a number of genres. Lexile 820L (Rev: BL 1/1–15/09; LMC 5–6/09; SLJ 12/08)

6918 Oldfield, Jenny, comp. *The Kingfisher Book of Horse and Pony Stories* (4–7). 2005, Kingfisher $16.95 (978-0-7534-5850-1). The special relationship between horses and humans is celebrated in this collection of 12 contemporary, fantasy, and historical short stories. (Rev: SLJ 12/05)

6919 Paulsen, Gary, ed. *Shelf Life: Stories by the Book* (4–7). 2003, Simon & Schuster $16.95 (978-0-689-84180-4). Books are the stars of these 10 stories by well-known authors that show that reading can change lives. (Rev: BL 8/03; HBG 4/04; SLJ 8/03; VOYA 8/03)

6920 Peck, Richard. *Past Perfect, Present Tense* (5–12). 2004, Dial $16.99 (978-0-8037-2998-8). This anthology includes 11 previously published stories and two new ones, with comments on each story's inspiration and tips on writing fiction. (Rev: BL 4/1/04; HB 3–4/04; SLJ 4/04; VOYA 6/04)

6921 Pullman, Philip, sel. *Whodunit? Detective Stories* (6–12). 2007, Kingfisher paper $6.95 (978-0-7534-6142-6). Pullman introduces this collection of stories — by the likes of Arthur Conan Doyle, Agatha Christie, Isaac Asimov, and Damon Runyon — with a history of the genre. (Rev: SLJ 11/07)

6922 Rosen, Roger, and Patra M. Sevastiades, eds. *On Heroes and the Heroic: In Search of Good Deeds* (7–12). Series: Icarus World Issues. 1993, Rosen LB $21.95 (978-0-8239-1384-8); paper $11.95 (978-0-8239-1385-5). Nine fiction and nonfiction pieces explore the concepts of heroes and antiheroes. (Rev: BL 9/15/93; SLJ 1/94; VOYA 12/93)

6923 Salisbury, Graham. *Blue Skin of the Sea* (8–12). 1992, Delacorte $15.95 (978-0-385-30596-9). These 11 stories contain a strong sense of time and place, fully realized characters, stylish prose, and universal themes. (Rev: BL 6/15/92*; SLJ 6/92*)

6924 Sherman, Josepha, ed. *Orphans of the Night* (6–10). 1995, Walker $16.95 (978-0-8027-8368-4). Brings together 11 short stories and two poems about creatures from folklore, most with teen protagonists. (Rev: BL 6/1–15/95; SLJ 6/95; VOYA 12/95)

6925 *Shining On: 11 Star Authors' Illuminating Stories* (7–10). 2007, Delacorte LB $11.99 (978-0-385-90470-4); paper $8.99 (978-0-385-73472-1). A collection of 11 short stories by well-known British and American authors — Lois Lowry, Celia Rees, and Meg Cabot, among them — with the theme of growing up and dealing with problems. (Rev: BL 6/1–15/07; LMC 10/07; SLJ 4/07)

6926 Singer, Isaac Bashevis. *Stories for Children* (7–9). 1984, Farrar paper $14.00 (978-0-374-46489-9). This collection includes 36 stories, most of which are fantasies about Jewish life in old Europe.

6927 Singer, Marilyn. *Make Me Over: 11 Original Stories About Transforming Ourselves* (7–10). 2005, Dutton $17.99 (978-0-525-47480-7). Teenage transformations and the importance of relationships are themes of these stories by writers including Joseph Bruchac, Margaret Peterson Haddix, and Joyce Sweeney. (Rev: BL 9/15/05; SLJ 2/06)

6928 Singer, Marilyn, comp. *I Believe in Water: Twelve Brushes with Religion* (7–10). 2000, HarperCollins LB $15.89 (978-0-06-028398-8). Short stories by writers including Virginia Euwer Wolff and M. E. Kerr look at religion from varied viewpoints. (Rev: BL 10/1/00; HBG 3/01; SLJ 11/00; VOYA 4/01)

6929 Soto, Gary. *Help Wanted* (7–10). 2005, Harcourt $17.00 (978-0-15-205201-0). In this collection of ten short stories, Soto explores the dreams and struggles of Mexican American teens living in central California. (Rev: BCCB 5/05; BL 5/1/05; HB 5–6/05; SLJ 5/05)

6930 Spiegelman, Art, and Francoise Mouly, eds. *Little Lit: Strange Stories for Strange Kids* (4–9). 2001, HarperCollins paper $19.95 (978-0-06-028626-2). This collection of offbeat, imaginative, graphic stories includes something for everyone, from humor to fantasy to horror, from Maurice Sendak to David Sedaris. (Rev: BL 12/15/01; HB 1–2/02; HBG 3/02; SLJ 3/02)

6931 *Sports Shorts* (4–7). 2005, Darby Creek $15.99 (978-1-58196-040-2). Eight writers contribute "semi-autobiographical" tales about their sporting achievements at school, many humorously revealing failings rather than triumphs. (Rev: BL 9/1/05; SLJ 11/05)

6932 Thompson, Holly, ed. *Tomo: Friendship Through Fiction — An Anthology of Japan Teen Stories* (7–10). 2012, Stone Bridge $14.95 (978-161172006-8). Thirty-six diverse stories — in prose, verse, and graphic art — were created by artists and writers who have a connection to Japan and published to benefit teens affected by the 2011 tsunami. (Rev: BL 4/15/12; LMC 1–2/13*; SLJ 5/1/12; VOYA 4/12)

6933 *Twice Told: Original Stories Inspired by Original Artwork* (7–10). Illus. by Scott Hunt. 2006, Dutton $19.99 (978-0-525-46818-9). Nine charcoal drawings by Scott Hunt were provided as inspiration to pairs of popular YA writers; the resulting short stories cover a wide range of styles and themes. (Rev: BL 2/15/06*; SLJ 4/06)

6934 Van Allsburg, Chris, ed. *The Chronicles of Harris Burdick: 14 Amazing Authors Tell the Tales* (3–7). Illus. by editor. 2011, Houghton Mifflin $24.99 (978-0-547-54810-4). Well-known authors present stories inspired by the illustrations in Van Allsburg's *The Mysteries of Harris Burdick*. YALSA Best Fiction for Young Adults 2012. ℮ Lexile 840L (Rev: BL 9/1/11; HB 9–10/11; SLJ 8/11; VOYA 10/11)

6935 Weiss, M. Jerry, and Helen S. Weiss, eds. *Big City Cool: Short Stories About Urban Youth* (7–12). 2002,

Persea paper $8.95 (978-0-89255-278-8). A variety of urban settings and cultural and racial experiences are portrayed in these 14 stories, half of which have previously appeared in print. (Rev: BL 10/15/02; SLJ 11/02; VOYA 12/02)

6936 Weiss, M. Jerry, and Helen S. Weiss, eds. *This Family Is Driving Me Crazy: Ten Stories About Surviving Your Family* (5–8). 2009, Putnam $17.99 (978-0-399-25040-8). Gordon Korman, Jack Gantos, Walter Dean Myers, and Nancy Springer are among the authors represented in this collection of varied stories with themes including forgiveness, self-discovery, and compassion in the face of adversity. Lexile 830L (Rev: BL 10/1/09; LMC 11/09; SLJ 10/09; VOYA 2/10)

6937 White, Trudy. *Table of Everything* (7–12). 2001, Allen & Unwin paper $16.95 (978-1-86508-135-9). Australian writer White captivates readers with this collection of offbeat short stories. (Rev: VOYA 8/02)

6938 Yee, Paul. *Dead Man's Gold and Other Stories* (6–12). Illus. by Harvey Chan. 2002, Groundwood $16.95 (978-0-88899-475-2). A collection of disturbing ghost stories featuring Chinese immigrants to America and Canada. (Rev: BL 11/1/02; HB 1–2/03*; HBG 3/03; SLJ 1/03)

6939 Yee, Paul. *What Happened This Summer* (7–10). 2006, Tradewind $10.95 (978-1-896580-88-3). A collection of nine short stories about Chinese Canadian teens and the particular tensions they face. (Rev: BL 11/1/06; LMC 4–5/07; SLJ 2/07)

Plays

General and Miscellaneous Collections

6940 Bansavage, Lisa, and L. E. McCullough, eds. *111 Shakespeare Monologues for Teens: The Ultimate Audition Book for Teens, Vol. V* (7–12). Series: Young Actors. 2003, Smith & Kraus paper $11.95 (978-1-57525-356-5). Monologues ranging from 15 seconds to 2 minutes and chosen for the youthful speakers or topics of interest to young people are arranged in three sections: for female actors, for male actors, and for male or female; an introduction explains Shakespeare's language and rhythms. (Rev: SLJ 7/04) [808.82]

6941 Bert, Norman A., and Deb Bert. *Play It Again! More One-Act Plays for Acting Students* (8–12). 1993, Meriwether paper $14.95 (978-0-916260-97-2). This is a collection of 21 one-act plays and monologs for young actors. [812.008]

6942 Dabrowski, Kristen. *Teens Speak, Boys Ages 16 to 18: Sixty Original Character Monologues* (7–12). Series: Kids Speak. 2005, Smith & Kraus paper $11.95 (978-1-57525-415-9). A collection of brief, varied monologues for teenage boys from 16 to 18. Also in the series are *Teens Speak, Boys Ages 13 to 15: Sixty Original Character Monologues*, *Teens Speak, Girls Ages 16 to 18: Sixty Original Character Monologues*, and *Teens Speak, Girls Ages 13 to 15: Sixty Original Character Monologues* (all 2005). (Rev: SLJ 7/05) [808.82]

6943 Ellis, Roger, ed. *Audition Monologs for Student Actors II: Selections from Contemporary Plays* (8–12). 2001, Meriwether paper $15.95 (978-1-56608-073-6). Fifty monologues for both sexes from ages 10 to mid-20s are accompanied by scene-setting notes and acting tips. (Rev: SLJ 4/02)

6944 Ellis, Roger, ed. *International Plays for Young Audiences: Contemporary Works from Leading Play-*

wrights (7–12). 2000, Meriwether paper $16.95 (978-1-56608-065-1). The 12 short plays in this collection come from varied cultures and deal with situations of interest to young people. (Rev: SLJ 2/01)

6945 Fairbanks, Stephanie S. *Spotlight: Solo Scenes for Student Actors* (7–12). 1996, Meriwether paper $14.95 (978-1-56608-020-0). This book contains 55 excellent one- to three-page monologues, some specifically for girls, others for boys, and others nonspecific. (Rev: BL 12/1/96; SLJ 5/97) [812]

6946 Fredericks, Anthony D. *Tadpole Tales and Other Totally Terrific Treats for Readers Theatre* (4–8). 1997, Libraries Unlimited paper $23.00 (978-1-56308-547-5). A delightful collection of scripts for young performers that are spin-offs from folktales, fables, and nursery rhymes. (Rev: BL 3/1/98) [372.67]

6947 Gallo, Donald R., ed. *Center Stage: One-Act Plays for Teenage Readers and Actors* (7–12). 1990, HarperCollins $17.00 (978-0-06-022170-6); paper $8.99 (978-0-06-447078-0). A collection of 10 one-act plays especially written for this collection by such authors as Walter Dean Myers and Ouida Sebestyen. (Rev: BL 12/1/90; SLJ 9/90) [812]

6948 *Great Scenes for Young Actors* (7–12). Series: Young Actors. 1997, Smith & Kraus paper $14.95 (978-1-57525-107-3). A variety of scenes representing different forms of drama are reprinted from such playwrights as Arthur Miller, George S. Kaufman, Horton Foote, and Paul Zindel. (Rev: BL 3/1/99; SLJ 6/99) [808.82]

6949 Hamlett, Christina. *Humorous Plays for Teen-Agers* (7–10). 1987, Plays paper $12.95 (978-0-8238-0276-0). Easily read one-act plays for beginners in acting. (Rev: BL 5/1/87; SLJ 11/87) [812]

6950 Henderson, Heather H. *The Flip Side II: 60 More Point-of-View Monologs for Teens* (6–9). 2001, Meriwether paper $15.95 (978-1-56608-074-3). A second collection of paired monologues that present two sides of a variety of situations. (Rev: SLJ 7/02) [812]

6951 Jennings, Coleman A., and Aurand Harris, eds. *A Treasury of Contemporary and Classic Plays for Children: Plays Children Love, Vol. II* (5–8). Illus. by Susan Swan. 1988, St. Martin's $19.95 (978-0-312-01490-2). A group of 20 plays requiring royalties based on such stories as Charlotte's Web, The Wizard of Oz, and The Wind in the Willows. [812.00809282]

6952 Kamerman, Sylvia, ed. *The Big Book of Large-Cast Plays: 27 One-Act Plays for Young Actors* (5–10). 1994, Plays $12.95 (978-0-8238-0302-6). Thirty short plays on varied subjects, arranged according to audience appeal. (Rev: BL 3/15/95) [812]

6953 Lamedman, Debbie. *The Ultimate Audition Book for Teens: 111 One-Minute Monologues, Vol. 4* (7–12). Series: Young Actors. 2003, Smith & Kraus paper $11.95 (978-1-57525-353-4). Monologues for both girls and boys give young actors ample opportunity to display their talent in a range of selections. (Rev: SLJ 4/03) [812]

6954 Latrobe, Kathy Howard, and Mildred Knight Laughlin. *Readers Theatre for Young Adults: Scripts and Script Development* (7–12). 1989, Libraries Unlimited paper $22.00 (978-0-87287-743-6). A collection of short scripts based on literary classics, plus tips on how to do one's own adaptations. (Rev: BL 1/1/90) [808.5]

6955 Nolan, Paul T. *Folk Tale Plays Round the World: A Collection of Royalty-Free, One-Act Plays About Lands Far and Near* (4–7). 1982, Plays paper $15.00 (978-0-8238-0253-1). Johnny Appleseed and Robin Hood are heroes featured in two of the 17 plays in this collection.

6956 Ratliff, Gerald L., and Theodore O. Zapel, eds. *Playing Contemporary Scenes: 31 Famous Scenes and How to Play Them* (8–12). 1996, Meriwether paper $16.95 (978-1-56608-025-5). A selection of scenes by contemporary playwrights, arranged according to age and gender. (Rev: VOYA 6/97) [812]

6957 Ratliff, Gerald L., ed. *Millennium Monologs: 95 Contemporary Characterizations for Young Actors* (8–12). 2002, Meriwether paper $15.95 (978-1-56608-082-8). High school thespians will appreciate this collection of monologues, which are arranged by theme, as well as the advice on auditions. (Rev: BL 3/15/03; SLJ 5/03) [792]

6958 Slaight, Craig, and Jack Sharrar, eds. *Great Scenes and Monologues for Children* (5–8). Series: Young Actors. 1993, Smith & Kraus paper $12.95 (978-1-880399-15-6). Includes selections from children's novels and fairy tales, as well as adult drama and short stories. (Rev: BL 10/1/93; SLJ 11/93) [808.82]

6959 Slaight, Craig, and Jack Sharrar, eds. *Short Plays for Young Actors* (8–12). 1996, Smith & Kraus paper $16.95 (978-1-880399-74-3). An impressive collection of short plays in a variety of genres, plus material on how to approach acting as a serious pursuit. (Rev: BL 9/15/96) [812]

6960 Stevens, Chambers. *Magnificent Monologues for Kids* (4–8). Ed. by Renee Rolle Whatley. 1999, Sandcastle paper $13.95 (978-1-883995-08-9). A collection of 51 monologues — some best for girls, others for boys — representing different situations and emotions. (Rev: BL 4/1/99; SLJ 8/99) [808.82]

6961 Surface, Mary Hall. *Short Scenes and Monologues for Middle School Actors* (6–9). 2000, Smith & Kraus paper $11.95 (978-1-57525-179-0). This is an excellent collection of monologues and scenes for two actors on a variety of subjects and settings that are suitable for 12- to14-year-old actors. (Rev: BL 2/15/00; SLJ 7/00; VOYA 6/00) [812.5408.]

6962 Vigil, Angel. *¡Teatro! Hispanic Plays for Young People* (4–8). 1996, Teacher Ideas paper $25.00 (978-1-56308-371-6). This collection contains 14 English-language scripts that integrate elements of the Hispanic traditions of the Southwest. (Rev: BL 3/1/97; VOYA 6/97) [812]

Geographical Regions

Europe

GREAT BRITAIN AND IRELAND

6963 Birch, Beverley. *Shakespeare's Stories: Histories* (5–8). 1988, Bedrick paper $6.95 (978-0-87226-226-3). Retelling the classic stories of Shakespeare. (Rev: BL 2/15/89; SLJ 2/89) [813.54]

6964 Birch, Beverley. *Shakespeare's Stories: Tragedies* (5–8). 1988, Bedrick paper $6.95 (978-0-87226-227-0). Retelling the great tragedies. (Rev: BL 2/15/89; SLJ 2/89) [813.54]

6965 Birch, Beverley. *Shakespeare's Tales* (5–8). Illus. by Stephen Lambert. 2002, Hodder $22.95 (978-0-340-79725-9). This appealing and accessible large-format book introduces modern teens to the plots and language of four Shakespeare plays — Hamlet, Othello, Antony and Cleopatra, and The Tempest. (Rev: BL 1/1–15/03; SLJ 4/03) [823.914]

6966 Coville, Bruce. *William Shakespeare's Hamlet* (4–8). Illus. by Leonid Gore. 2004, Dial $18.99 (978-0-8037-2708-3). This masterful prose retelling makes the famous play accessible to young people. (Rev: BL 5/15/04; SLJ 2/04) [822.3]

6967 Coville, Bruce. *William Shakespeare's Macbeth* (4–8). 1997, Dial $18.99 (978-0-8037-1899-9). Using a picture-book format, the story of Macbeth is retold with emphasis on the supernatural aspects. (Rev: BL 11/1/97; HBG 3/98; SLJ 12/97) [822.3]

6968 Coville, Bruce. *William Shakespeare's The Winter's Tale* (4–7). Illus. by LeUyen Pham. 2007, Dial $16.99 (978-0-8037-2709-0). An illustrated prose retelling of the classic tale of jealousy and renewal. (Rev: BL 11/1/07; SLJ 12/07) [822.3]

6969 Kahle, Peter V. T. *Shakespeare's The Tempest: A Prose Narrative* (5–8). Illus. by Barbara Nickerson. 1999, Seventy Fourth Street $22.95 (978-0-9655702-2-0). An illustrated retelling of Shakespeare's play that uses much of its dialogue. (Rev: SLJ 1/00) [822.3]

6970 Kindermann, Barbara. *William Shakespeare's Romeo and Juliet* (4–7). Trans. by J. Alison James. Illus. by Christa Unzner. 2006, North-South $17.95 (978-0-7358-2090-6). This well-phrased prose retelling of the ill-fated romance is enhanced by the Renaissance-style illustrations. (Rev: BL 8/06; SLJ 12/06)

6971 Lamb, Charles, and Mary Lamb. *Tales from Shakespeare* (7–9). 1993, Buccaneer LB $24.95 (978-1-56849-117-2). The famous retelling of 20 of Shakespeare's plays in a version first published in 1807. [822.3]

6972 McKeown, Adam. *Julius Caesar* (5–8). Illus. by Janet Hamlin. Series: Young Reader's Shakespeare. 2008, Sterling $14.95 (978-1-4027-3579-0). An accessible retelling to assist students of the play, with engaging illustrations and a tone that is respectful to the original. (Rev: BL 5/15/08; SLJ 6/08) [813.6]

6973 McKeown, Adam. *Romeo and Juliet: Young Reader's Shakespeare* (5–10). Illus. by Peter Fiore. 2004, Sterling $14.95 (978-1-4027-0004-0). Faithful to the original, this retelling uses finely crafted prose and interweaves many of the best-known poetic stanzas. (Rev: BL 8/04; SLJ 10/04) [822.3]

6974 McKeown, Adam, retel. *Macbeth* (5–10). Retold by Adam McKeown. Illus. by Lynne Cannoy. Series: The Young Reader's Shakespeare. 2005, Sterling $14.95 (978-1-4027-1116-9). This conversational prose retelling includes an introduction to the play and incorporates many of the important poetic passages. (Rev: BL 3/1/05; SLJ 5/05) [822.3]

6975 Miles, Bernard. *Favorite Tales from Shakespeare* (7–10). 1993, Checkerboard $14.95 (978-1-56288-257-0). Shakespeare's most famous plays in a modern retelling. [822.3]

6976 Rosen, Michael. *Shakespeare's Romeo and Juliet* (7–10). Illus. by lane Ray. 2004, Candlewick $17.99 (978-0-7636-2258-9). Vivid, evocative illustrations and a conversational narrative accompany passages of Shakespeare in an appealing retelling of the popular story that includes references and glossaries. (Rev: BL 12/1/03; SLJ 2/04) [823]

6977 Schlitz, Laura Amy. *Good Masters! Sweet Ladies!* (5–8). Illus. by Robert Byrd. 2007, Candlewick $19.99 (978-0-7636-1578-9). Providing a glimpse into medieval life, a series of interconnected monologues and dialogues feature 23 young people in medieval England and convey information about society at the time. Newbery Medal 2008; ALA Notable Books 2008. ☊ (Rev: BL 8/07*; HB 11–12/07; LMC 11/07; SLJ 8/07) [812.6]

6978 Shakespeare, William. *William Shakespeare* (5–7). Ed. by David Scott Kastan and Marina Kastan. Series: Poetry for Young People. 2000, Sterling $14.95 (978-0-8069-4344-2). In a large format illustrated by paintings, this volume contains three sonnets and 23 short excerpts from the plays of William Shakespeare. (Rev: BL 1/1–15/01; HBG 3/01; SLJ 1/01) [821]

Other Countries

6979 Goodrich, Frances. *The Diary of Anne Frank* (7–12). 1958, Dramatists Play Service paper $6.50 (978-0-8222-0307-0). This is the prize-winning play based on the diary. [812]

6980 Perry, Mark. *A Dress for Mona* (7–12). 2002, Fifth Epoch $10.00 (978-1-931492-02-7). Iranian persecution of people of the Baha'i faith is illustrated in this moving play that features Mona, a 16-year-old who will die for her beliefs; staging advice and a pronunciation guide are among the aids provided. (Rev: VOYA 6/03)

6981 Wasserman, Dale. *Man of La Mancha* (7–12). 1966, Random House paper $9.95 (978-0-394-40619-0). Based loosely on Cervantes's novel, this is a musical play of the adventures of Don Quixote and his servant Sancho Panza. [812]

United States

6982 Chanda, Justin, ed. *Acting Out* (4–8). 2008, Atheneum $16.99 (978-1-4169-6213-7). Young people challenge authority in these one-act plays written by six Newbery Medal winners. (Rev: BL 6/1–15/08) [812]

6983 Kamerman, Sylvia, ed. *The Big Book of Holiday Plays* (6–9). 1990, Plays $16.95 (978-0-8238-0291-3). An assortment of one-act plays and adaptations, both dramas and comedies, related to 14 holidays. (Rev: BL 2/1/91; SLJ 1/91) [812]

6984 Kamerman, Sylvia, ed. *Great American Events on Stage: 15 Plays to Celebrate America's Past* (5–8). 1996, Plays paper $15.95 (978-0-8238-0305-7). A collection of short plays, each of which revolves around a single incident or individual important in U.S. history. (Rev: SLJ 5/97) [812]

6985 Kamerman, Sylvia, ed. *Plays of Black Americans: The Black Experience in America, Dramatized for Young People* (7–12). 1994, Plays paper $13.95 (978-0-8238-0301-9). Eleven dramas focus on the history of African Americans. (Rev: BL 5/15/95; SLJ 2/95) [812]

6986 McCullough, L. E. *Plays of America from American Folklore for Young Actors* (7–12). Series: Young Actors. 1996, Smith & Kraus paper $14.95 (978-1-57525-040-3). Ten original short plays based on folk traditions are included, along with suggestions for staging and costumes. (Rev: BL 8/96; SLJ 8/96) [812]

6987 Mason, Timothy. *The Children's Theatre Company of Minneapolis: 10 Plays for Young Audiences* (6–9). Series: Young Actors. 1997, Smith & Kraus paper $19.95 (978-1-57525-120-2). This is a collection of 10 plays, each about an hour long, adapted from such classics as *Pinocchio, Aladdin,* and *Huckleberry Finn.* (Rev: SLJ 8/98) [812]

6988 Smith, Marisa, ed. *Seattle Children's Theatre: Six Plays for Young Audiences* (7–12). 1996, Smith & Kraus $21.95 (978-1-57525-008-3). A collection of six plays commissioned and performed by the Seattle Children's Theatre that explore adolescence, its problems and concerns. (Rev: BL 6/1–15/97; SLJ 6/97) [812]

6989 Smith, Ronn. *Nothing but the Truth* (7–10). 1997, Avon paper $4.99 (978-0-380-78715-9). This is a play version of Avi's novel about a 9th-grader whose suspension from school becomes a national issue. (Rev: VOYA 8/97) [812]

6990 Soto, Gary. *Nerdlandia: A Play* (8–12). 1999, Penguin paper $5.99 (978-0-698-11784-6). Young love causes transformations in nerdy Martin and cool Ceci in this hip play full of Spanish dialogue. (Rev: BL 10/1/99) [812.4]

6991 Thoms, Annie, ed. *With Their Eyes: September 11th: The View from a High School at Ground Zero* (7–12). Photos by Ethan Moses. 2002, HarperCollins paper $7.99 (978-0-06-051718-2). A collection of moving and dramatic monologues created after students at a high school near Ground Zero interviewed fellow students, faculty, and others about their experiences that day. (Rev: BL 9/1/02; SLJ 1/03) [812]

Poetry

General and Miscellaneous Collections

6992 Adoff, Arnold. *Roots and Blues: A Celebration* (4–8). Illus. by R. Gregory Christie. 2011, Clarion $17.99 (978-054723554-7). In prose and poetry, Adoff explores the history of the blues from the days of slavery to the present. (Rev: BL 2/15/11*; LMC 1–2/11; SLJ 2/1/11*) [811]

6993 Alexander, Kwame. *Crush: Love Poems* (8–12). 2007, Word of Mouth paper $10.00 (978-1-888018-40-0). An anthology of varied poems about love. (Rev: SLJ 10/07) [811]

6994 Anaya, Rudolfo. *Elegy on the Death of Cesar Chavez* (4–7). 2000, Cinco Puntos $16.95 (978-0-938317-51-7). This is an elegiac poem that celebrates the life, work, and struggle of the respected labor leader. (Rev: BL 12/15/00; HBG 3/01; SLJ 1/01) [811]

6995 Appelt, Kathi. *Poems from Homeroom: A Writer's Place to Start* (7–12). 2002, Henry Holt $16.95 (978-0-8050-6978-5). Poems that speak to the adolescent experience are accompanied by encouraging writing tips from the poet. (Rev: BL 11/15/02; SLJ 9/02) [811]

6996 Argueta, Jorge. *A Movie in My Pillow / Una Pelicula en Mi Almohada* (4–8). Illus. by Elizabeth Gomez. 2001, Children's $15.95 (978-0-89239-165-3). The author remembers in poetry his family's immigration to the United States from El Salvador, with each poem accompanied by the translation and rich illustrations. (Rev: BL 10/1/01; HBG 10/01; SLJ 5/01*) [861]

6997 Atkins, Jeannine. *Borrowed Names: Poems About Laura Ingalls Wilder, Madame C J Walker, Marie Curie, and Their Daughters* (6–9). 2010, Henry Holt $16.99 (978-0-8050-8934-9). Vivid free-verse poems recount the lives of three successful women who were born in 1867, and describe their relationships with their children. (Rev: BL 2/1/10*; HB 5–6/10; LMC 1–2/10; SLJ 2/10) [811]

6998 Berry, James, ed. *Classic Poems to Read Aloud* (4–8). 1995, Kingfisher $18.95 (978-1-85697-987-0). Jamaican writer Berry has collected old favorites, mostly British, along with new voices usually excluded from the literary canon. (Rev: BL 5/1/95; SLJ 5/95) [811]

6999 Bloom, Harold, ed. *Poets of World War I: Wilfred Owen and Isaac Rosenberg* (7–12). Series: Bloom's Major Poets. 2002, Chelsea LB $31.95 (978-0-7910-5932-6). This introduction to the work of these two poets includes four poems by each, with analysis. (Rev: SLJ 7/02) [821]

7000 Brewton, Sara, ed. *My Tang's Tungled and Other Ridiculous Situations* (6–9). 1973, HarperCollins $12.95 (978-0-690-57223-0). A wonderful collection of humorous verse. [811]

7001 Brewton, Sara, ed. *Of Quarks, Quasars and Other Quirks: Quizzical Poems for the Supersonic Age* (5–8). Illus. by Quentin Blake. 1977, HarperCollins LB $13.89 (978-0-690-04885-8). Contemporary poems that poke fun at such modern innovations as transplants and water beds.

7002 Bulion, Leslie. *At the Sea Floor Café: Odd Ocean Critter Poems* (5–8). Illus. by Leslie Evans. 2011, Peachtree $14.95 (978-1-56145-565-2). Eighteen poems provide compelling glimpses into the lives of some of the more interesting and bizarre marine creatures. (Rev: LMC 11–12/11; SLJ 4/11) [811]

7003 Donegan, Patricia. *Haiku: Asian Arts and Crafts for Creative Kids* (4–8). 2004, Tuttle $14.95 (978-0-8048-3501-5). Haiku advice and exercises follow an introduction to the verse form. (Rev: BL 3/15/04; SLJ 8/04) [372.6]

7004 Dunning, Stephen, ed. *Reflections on a Gift of Watermelon Pickle and Other Modern Verse* (6–8). 1967, Lothrop $19.99 (978-0-688-41231-9). An attractive volume of 114 expressive poems by recognized modern poets, illustrated with striking photographs.

7005 Fleischman, Paul. *Big Talk: Poems for Four Voices* (4–7). 2000, Candlewick $17.99 (978-0-7636-0636-7). This collection of spirited, evocative poems for four voices to read aloud covers a variety of topics. (Rev: BCCB 4/00; BL 6/1–15/00; HB 5–6/00; HBG 10/00; SLJ 6/00) [811]

7006 Fletcher, Ralph. *Have You Been to the Beach Lately? Poems* (4–7). Photos by Andrea Sperling. 2001, Scholastic paper $15.95 (978-0-531-30330-6). More than 30 chatty poems, illustrated with black-and-white photographs, are written from the perspective of a smart and funny 11-year-old. (Rev: HBG 10/01; SLJ 8/01) [811]

7007 Fletcher, Ralph. *Relatively Speaking: Poems About Family* (5–7). 1999, Orchard LB $15.99 (978-0-531-33141-5). From an 11-year-old boy's point of view, these original poems explore relationships as family members go through periods of change. (Rev: BCCB 5/99; BL 7/99; HBG 10/99; SLJ 4/99) [811]

7008 Frost, Helen. *Spinning Through the Universe: A Novel in Poems from Room 214* (5–7). 2004, Farrar $16.00 (978-0-374-37159-3). A variety of poetic forms — including haiku, tercelle, sonnet, pantoun, and tanka — are used in these diverse and compelling poems about the lives of a fifth-grade teacher and her students. (Rev: BL 4/1/04; SLJ 4/04) [811]

7009 George, Kristine O'Connell. *Swimming Upstream: Middle School Poems* (5–8). Illus. by Debbie Tilley. 2002, Clarion $14.00 (978-0-618-15250-6). Brief poems describe how one girl navigates the rapids of middle school, discussing everything from school lunches and lockers to making friends and relationships with boys. (Rev: BL 1/1–15/03; HB 1–2/03; HBG 3/03; SLJ 9/02) [811]

7010 Gillooly, Eileen, ed. *Rudyard Kipling* (4–8). Illus. by Jim Sharpe. 2000, Sterling $14.95 (978-0-8069-4484-5). This book contains complete poems or excerpts from 28 poems by this well-liked writer including "If" and "The Ballad of East and West." (Rev: HBG 3/01; SLJ 5/00) [821]

7011 Gordon, Ruth, ed. *Peeling the Onion* (8–12). 1993, HarperCollins $15.89 (978-0-06-021728-0). A collection of 66 poems with multilayered meanings by world-famous contemporary poets. (Rev: BL 6/1–15/93*; SLJ 7/93; VOYA 8/93) [808.81]

7012 Gordon, Ruth, sel. *Under All Silences: Shades of Love* (8–12). 1987, HarperCollins $13.00 (978-0-06-022154-6). Sixty-six love poems, dating from ancient Egypt to modern days. (Rev: BL 9/15/87; SLJ 10/87; VOYA 4/88) [808.1]

7013 Grandits, John. *Blue Lipstick: Concrete Poems* (5–9). Illus. by author. 2007, Clarion $15.00 (978-0-618-56860-4); paper $5.95 (978-0-618-85132-4). A visually entertaining collection of poems about Jessie, a 9th-grader whose main concerns are clothes, friends, and conflicts with her parents. ALA Notable Books 2008. (Rev: SLJ 7/07) [811]

7014 Greenberg, Jan, ed. *Heart to Heart: New Poems Inspired by Twentieth-Century American Art* (5–10). 2001, Abrams $19.95 (978-0-8109-4386-5). This book contains specially commissioned poems from well-known writers to accompany some of the finest artworks of the 20th century. (Rev: BL 3/15/01*; HBG 10/01; SLJ 4/01*; VOYA 8/01) [811]

7015 Greenberg, Jan, ed. *Side by Side: New Poems Inspired by Art from Around the World* (8–12). 2008, Abrams $19.95 (978-0-8109-9471-3). Poems in many languages (with English translations) and inspired by art of all kinds are featured in this book that includes maps pinpointing each poet's country. (Rev: BL 5/1/08; SLJ 7/08) [811]

7016 Grimes, Nikki. *At Jerusalem's Gate: Poems of Easter* (5–8). Illus. by David Frampton. 2005, Eerdmans $20.00 (978-0-8028-5183-3). More than 20 poems are introduced by thoughtful paragraphs and enhanced by handsome illustrations. (Rev: BL 2/15/05; SLJ 3/05) [232.96]

7017 Grimes, Nikki. *Tai Chi Morning: Snapshots of China* (4–8). Illus. by Ed Young. 2004, Cricket $15.95 (978-0-8126-2707-7). Grimes's journal in verse describes her impressions on a tour of China. (Rev: BL 3/1/04; SLJ 5/04) [811]

7018 Grimes, Nikki. *What Is Goodbye?* (4–8). Illus. by Raul Colon. 2004, Hyperion $15.99 (978-0-7868-0778-9). A brother and sister mourn the death of their older brother in poems in alternating voices. (Rev: BL 5/1/04; SLJ 6/04) [811]

7019 Hall, Donald. *The Man Who Lived Alone* (4–7). 1998, Godine paper $11.95 (978-1-56792-050-5). A narrative poem concerning a man who ran away from abuse to see the world and returns in later life.

7020 Harrison, Michael, and Christopher Stuart-Clark, comps. *The Oxford Treasury of Time Poems* (4–9). 1999, Oxford LB $25.00 (978-0192761750). From John Milton and William Blake to W. H. Auden and Sylvia Plath, this anthology contains poetry and thoughts about time. (Rev: SLJ 7/99) [811]

7021 Hoberman, Mary Ann. *The Tree That Time Built: A Celebration of Nature, Science, and Imagination* (3–7). 2009, Sourcebooks $19.99 (978-1-4022-2517-8). A well-chosen selection of classic and contemporary poems that contemplate various aspects of the natural world. (Rev: BL 12/15/09; LMC 1–2/10; SLJ 1/10) [811]

7022 Hollander, John, ed. *Animal Poems* (5–7). Illus. by Simona Mulazzani. Series: Poetry for Young People. 2005, Sterling $14.95 (978-1-4027-0926-5). A collection of classic poems (by such poets as Blake, Frost, Melville, and Yeats) accompanied by artwork and explanatory notes. (Rev: BL 4/1/05; SLJ 3/05) [808.81]

7023 Hollyer, Belinda, sel. *She's All That! Poems About Girls* (4–7). Illus. by Susan Hellard. 2006, Kingfisher $14.95 (978-0-7534-5852-5). Poems celebrate today's diverse girls and their interests and concerns, with breezy, hip illustrations. (Rev: SLJ 7/06) [811]

7024 Hopkins, Lee Bennett, ed. *America at War: Poems Selected by Lee Bennett Hopkins* (5–8). Illus. by Stephen Alcorn. 2008, Simon & Schuster $21.99 (978-1-4169-1832-5). A collection of 50-plus poems about American wars from the Revolutionary War to the conflict in Iraq, many centered on the pain felt by soldiers and their families. (Rev: BL 3/1/08; SLJ 3/08) [811]

7025 Hopkins, Lee Bennett, ed. *Days to Celebrate: A Full Year of Poetry, People, Holidays, History, Fascinating Facts, and More* (4–7). Illus. by Stephen Alcorn. 2005, Greenwillow LB $19.89 (978-0-06-000766-9). A wide-ranging collection organized by month, each introduced by a calendar page that highlights important dates. (Rev: BL 1/1–15/05; SLJ 1/05) [811]

7026 Hopkins, Lee Bennett, ed. *Got Geography!* (4–7). Illus. by Philip Stanton. 2006, Greenwillow LB $17.89 (978-0-06-055602-0). Poems celebrate the joys of travel and the maps that guide the way. (Rev: BL 2/1/06; SLJ 5/06) [811]

7027 Janeczko, Paul B. *The Place My Words Are Looking For: What Poets Say About and Through Their Work* (4–9). 1990, Macmillan $17.95 (978-0-02-747671-2). A collection of works by some of the best contemporary poets. (Rev: BCCB 7–8/90; BL 5/1/90; HB 5–6/90*; SLJ 5/90; VOYA 6/90) [811]

7028 Janeczko, Paul B, sel. *A Foot in the Mouth: Poems to Speak, Sing, and Shout* (4–7). Illus. by Chris Raschka. 2009, Candlewick $17.99 (978-0-7636-0663-3). Appealing poems ranging from evocative to nonsensical are chosen for their suitability to be read aloud and organized into useful categories. (Rev: BL 2/15/09*; HB 3–4/09; SLJ 3/1/09*; VOYA 2/10) [811]

7029 Janeczko, Paul B., ed. *Stone Bench in an Empty Park* (5–12). 2000, Orchard LB $16.99 (978-0-531-33259-7). An inspired collection of haiku from a variety of poets, illustrated with stunning black-and-white photographs. (Rev: BCCB 6/00; BL 3/15/00*; HB 3–4/00; HBG 10/00; SLJ 3/00) [811]

7030 Janeczko, Paul B., ed. *Wherever Home Begins: 100 Contemporary Poems* (8–12). 1995, Orchard LB $17.99 (978-0-531-08781-7). One hundred poems that express various approaches to a sense of place. (Rev: BL 10/1/95; SLJ 11/95; VOYA 12/95) [811]

7031 Kennedy, Caroline, ed. *A Family of Poems: My Favorite Poetry for Children* (4–7). Illus. by Jon J Muth. 2005, Hyperion $19.95 (978-0-7868-5111-9). This collection of poems for children includes a number of Kennedy family favorites. (Rev: BL 10/15/05; SLJ 12/05*) [811]

7032 Lawson, JonArno. *Black Stars in a White Night Sky* (4–7). Illus. by Sherwin Tjia. 2008, Boyds Mills $16.95 (978-1-59078-521-8). An eclectic collection of poems — some silly, some serious, and all full of unusual turns of phrase and wordplay. (Rev: BL 2/15/08; SLJ 4/08) [811]

7033 Lawson, JonArno. *Think Again* (5–8). Illus. by Julie Morstad. 2010, Kids Can $16.95 (978-1-55453-423-4). Forty-eight poems look at the uncertainty and poignancy of first love. (Rev: BL 3/15/10; LMC 8–9/10) [811]

7034 Lewis, J. Patrick. *Heroes and She-roes: Poems of Amazing and Everyday Heroes* (4–7). Illus. by Jim Cooke. 2005, Dial $16.99 (978-0-8037-2925-4). Helen Keller, Rosa Parks, and Gandhi are among the courageous individuals featured in this collection of poems. (Rev: BL 1/1–15/05; SLJ 3/05) [811]

7035 Lewis, J. Patrick. *The House* (4–7). Illus. by Roberto Innocenti. 2009, Creative Education $19.95 (978-1-56846-201-1). This unusual picture book for older children uses poetry and arresting images to present the passing of time from the perspective of a house. (Rev: BL 12/15/09; LMC 3–4/10; SLJ 1/10) [811]

7036 Lewis, J. Patrick. *Skywriting: Poems to Fly* (4–7). Illus. by Laslo Kubinyi. 2010, Creative Editions $17.95 (978-156846203-5). This anthology of poems celebrates the adventure of flight, examining scenes in history from the myth of Icarus to the modern day. (Rev: BL 11/15/10; LMC 1–2/11; SLJ 11/1/10) [811.54]

7037 Lewis, J. Patrick. *Vherses: A Celebration of Outstanding Women* (4–7). Illus. by Mark Summers. 2005, Creative $18.95 (978-1-56846-185-4). The accomplishments of 14 notable and diverse women — including Emily Dickinson, Georgia O'Keeffe, and Venus and Serena Williams — are celebrated in an appealing blend of poetry and art. (Rev: BL 12/15/05) [811]

7038 Lewis, J. Patrick, and Rebecca Kai Dotlich. *Castles: Old Stone Poems* (4–7). Illus. by Dan Burr. 2006, Boyds Mills $18.95 (978-1-59078-380-1). The poems in this attractive collection celebrate castles of past and present. (Rev: BL 10/1/06; SLJ 10/06) [811]

7039 Little, Jean. *I Gave My Mom a Castle* (4–7). Illus. by Kady MacDonald Denton. 2004, Orca paper $7.95 (978-1-55143-253-3). Gifts — expected and unexpected, rewarding and trying — are the theme of this diverse collection of prose poems. (Rev: BL 3/1/04; SLJ 4/04) [811]

7040 McCord, David. *All Day Long: Fifty Rhymes of the Never Was and Always Is* (4–7). Illus. by Henry

B. Kane. 1975, Little, Brown paper $6.95 (978-0-316-55532-6). A collection of poems on a variety of subjects, chiefly times that are important in childhood.

7041 McCullough, Frances, ed. *Love Is Like a Lion's Tooth: An Anthology of Love Poems* (7–12). 1984, HarperCollins $12.95 (978-0-06-024138-4). A collection of love poems that span time from ancient days to the 20th century. [808.81]

7042 McGough, Roger, ed. *Wicked Poems* (4–8). Illus. by Neal Layton. 2005, Bloomsbury paper $15.00 (978-0-7475-6195-8). Misbehavior of varying degrees is displayed in this varied collection of poems accompanied by cartoons. (Rev: SLJ 1/05) [811]

7043 McGough, Roger, sel. *The Kingfisher Book of Funny Poems* (4–7). Illus. by Caroline Holden. 2002, Kingfisher $19.00 (978-0-7534-5480-0). An anthology of poems arranged by theme that includes many by familiar names such as Ogden Nash, Lewis Carroll, and Shel Silverstein. (Rev: SLJ 6/02) [811]

7044 Maddox, Marjorie. *Rules of the Game: Baseball Poems* (5–8). Illus. by John Sandford. 2009, Boyds Mills $16.95 (978-1-59078-603-1). Maddox celebrates the game of baseball in this collection of more than 40 brief poems with titles such as "View from the Dugout" and "Sacrifice Bunt." (Rev: BL 4/15/09; SLJ 5/09) [811]

7045 Mark, Jan, ed. *A Jetblack Sunrise: Poems About War and Conflict* (7–10). Illus. by John Yates. 2005, Hodder paper $8.99 (978-0-340-89379-1). This anthology of poems explores not only the barbarity and savagery of war but also the courage, selflessness, and valor that sometimes shine through. (Rev: BL 9/1/05) [808.9]

7046 Miller, Kate. *Poems in Black and White* (4–7). 2007, Boyds Mills $17.95 (978-1-59078-412-9). The poems and striking artwork in this slim volume explore images in black and white. (Rev: BL 4/1/07; SLJ 5/07) [811]

7047 Mora, Pat. *Dizzy in Your Eyes: Poems About Love* (7–10). 2010, Knopf $15.99 (978-0-375-84375-4). Typical teen experiences with young love are covered in a collection of poems written in a wide variety of formats. e (Rev: BL 11/15/09; LMC 1–2/10; SLJ 1/10) [811]

7048 Morgenstern, Constance. *Waking Day* (4–7). 2006, North Word $17.95 (978-1-55971-919-3). In a picture book for older readers, Morgenstern melds Impressionist works with lines from her own poetry. (Rev: BL 2/15/06) [811]

7049 Morris, Jackie, comp. *The Barefoot Book of Classic Poems* (3–9). Illus. by Jackie Morris. 2006, Barefoot Books $19.99 (978-1-905236-56-5). A handsomely illustrated anthology of nearly 75 classic poems, with works by such well-known writers as Robert Frost,

John Donne, Robert Louis Stevenson, and William Wordsworth. (Rev: SLJ 1/07) [811]

7050 Morrison, Lillian. *Way to Go! Sports Poems* (4–8). Illus. by Susan Spellman. 2001, Boyds Mills $16.95 (978-1-56397-961-3). Sport lovers will appreciate this collection of poems full of rhythm and life, with vibrant illustrations. (Rev: HBG 3/02; SLJ 10/01) [811]

7051 Myers, Walter Dean. *Blues Journey* (5–8). Illus. by Christopher Myers. 2003, Holiday $18.95 (978-0-8234-1613-4). Poems reflecting the soulfulness of blues music, accompanied by illustrations. (Rev: BL 2/15/03; HB 5–6/03; HBG 10/03; SLJ 4/03*; VOYA 4/03) [811]

7052 New, William. *The Year I Was Grounded* (4–7). Illus. by Robert Kakegamic. 2009, Tradewind paper $12.95 (978-1-896580-35-7). Stuck at home, Geordie finds plenty of time to write in his journal, recording events and thoughts in a variety of poetic forms. (Rev: BL 5/1/09; SLJ 7/09) [811]

7053 Nye, Naomi Shihab. *Honeybee: Poems and Short Prose* (7–12). 2008, Greenwillow $16.99 (978-0-06-085390-5). A collection of poems and short pieces of prose that use honeybee imagery as a metaphor for human experiences and resilience. (Rev: BL 8/08; SLJ 3/08) [811]

7054 Nye, Naomi Shihab, sel. *Time You Let Me In: 25 Poets Under 25* (7–12). 2010, Greenwillow $16.99 (978-0-06-189637-8); LB $17.89 (978-0-06-189638-5). Diverse poems by young writers deal with contemporary themes both personal and political. (Rev: BL 1/1–15/10; SLJ 2/10) [811]

7055 *Once Upon a Poem: Favorite Poems That Tell Stories* (4–7). 2004, Scholastic $18.95 (978-0-439-65108-0). This appealing collection of 15 narrative poems includes offerings from Lewis Carroll, Longfellow, C. S. Lewis, Roald Dahl, Edward Lear, and Robert Service. (Rev: BL 1/1–15/05; SLJ 1/05) [811]

7056 Philip, Neil, ed. *War and the Pity of War* (6–12). 1998, Clarion $20.00 (978-0-395-84982-8). An outstanding collection of poetry from different times and cultures that explores the cruelty, bravery, and tragedy of war. (Rev: BL 9/15/98; HBG 10/99; SLJ 9/98; VOYA 2/99) [808.81]

7057 Prelutsky, Jack. *Nightmares: Poems to Trouble Your Sleep* (5–8). Illus. by Arnold Lobel. 1976, Greenwillow LB $17.89 (978-0-688-84053-2). Shuddery, macabre poems that will frighten but amuse a young audience. A sequel is *The Headless Horseman Rides Tonight: More Poems to Trouble Your Sleep* (1980).

7058 Prelutsky, Jack, ed. *The Random House Book of Poetry for Children* (6–9). 1983, Random House LB $21.99 (978-0-394-95010-5). A selection of verse suitable for children that concentrates on light verse written recently. [821.08]

7059 Rogasky, Barbara, ed. *Leaf by Leaf: Autumn Poems* (5–8). Illus. by Marc Tauss. 2001, Scholastic paper $16.95 (978-0-590-25347-5). Verses by poets including Shelley, Yeats, and Whitman accompany stunning autumnal photographs. (Rev: BL 7/01; HBG 3/02; SLJ 9/01*) [811.008]

7060 Rosen, Michael, ed. *Classic Poetry: An Illustrated Collection* (6–8). 1998, Candlewick $21.99 (978-1-56402-890-7). A fine selection of poems by major writers, supplying a brief biography of each, plus one or two poems or excerpts from poems, and an illustration that evokes the poet's times or the mood of the poems. (Rev: BL 1/1–15/99; HBG 3/99; SLJ 5/99) [821.008]

7061 Rosenberg, Liz, ed. *Light-Gathering Poems* (6–12). 2000, Henry Holt $15.95 (978-0-8050-6223-6). An excellent anthology of high-quality poems, mainly from classic writers such as Byron and Frost but also from some newer voices. (Rev: BL 3/15/00; HB 5–6/00; HBG 9/00; SLJ 6/00; VOYA 6/00) [808.81]

7062 Rowden, Justine. *Paint Me a Poem: Poems Inspired by Masterpieces of Art* (4–7). 2005, Boyds Mills $16.95 (978-1-59078-289-7). Each of the 14 poems in this collection is inspired by a famous painting from the National Gallery of Art. (Rev: BL 11/1/05; SLJ 10/05) [811.54]

7063 Shange, Ntozake. *We Troubled the Waters* (4–8). Illus. by Rod Brown. 2009, Amistad $16.99 (978-0-06-133735-2); LB $17.89 (978-0-06-133737-6). This is a moving collection of unflinching poems portraying the brutality of racism, with stark artwork. (Rev: BL 10/1/09*; SLJ 12/09) [811]

7064 Sidman, Joyce. *This Is Just to Say: Poems of Apology and Forgiveness* (4–7). Illus. by Pamela Zagarenski. 2007, Houghton Mifflin $16.00 (978-0-618-61680-0). Poems of all kinds written by a fictional 6th-grade class to say "sorry" are paired with responses from the recipients. (Rev: BL 5/15/07; SLJ 5/07) [811]

7065 Simon, Seymour, ed. *Star Walk* (4–8). 1995, Morrow LB $14.93 (978-0-688-11887-7). Simple poems and outstanding photographs create an impressive introduction to stars and outer space. (Rev: BL 3/1/95; SLJ 4/95) [811]

7066 Smith, Charles R. *Hoop Kings* (4–7). 2004, Candlewick $14.99 (978-0-7636-1423-2). This celebration of basketball, presented in a blend of rap-style poetry with eye-catching photographs, focuses on 12 of the biggest stars. (Rev: BL 2/15/04; SLJ 3/04) [811]

7067 Smith, Hope Anita. *Keeping the Night Watch* (5–8). Illus. by E. B. Lewis. 2008, Henry Holt $18.95 (978-0-8050-7202-0). In this equally poetic and well-illustrated sequel to *The Way a Door Closes* (2003), 13-year-old C.J.'s father is back home but the family's foundation remains shaky at first. Coretta Scott King Author Honor Book, 2009. (Rev: BL 3/15/08; SLJ 6/08) [811]

7068 Soto, Gary. *Partly Cloudy: Poems of Love and Longing* (6–9). 2009, Houghton Mifflin $16.00 (978-015206301-6). Brief free verse poems about young love appear in two sections: "A Girl's Tears, Her Songs" and "A Boy's Body, His Words." (Rev: BL 2/15/09; LMC 8–9/09; SLJ 3/1/09) [811]

7069 Strand, Mark, ed. *100 Great Poems of the Twentieth Century* (8–12). 2005, Norton $24.95 (978-0-393-05894-9). Pulitzer Prize-winning poet Strand offers his selection of the 100 best poems of the 20th century. (Rev: BL 5/15/05) [821]

7070 Swenson, May. *The Complete Poems to Solve* (5–8). Illus. by Christy Hale. 1993, Macmillan $13.95 (978-0-02-788725-9). From simple riddles to more complex questions, each of these poems contains a puzzle. (Rev: HB 3–4/93; SLJ 5/93) [811]

7071 Thomas, Joyce Carol. *A Mother's Heart, A Daughter's Love* (6–12). 2001, HarperCollins LB $14.89 (978-0-06-029650-6). Two poetic voices — a mother's and a daughter's — describe their life together from the birth of the daughter through the death of the mother. (Rev: BL 3/15/01; HBG 10/01; SLJ 9/01) [811]

7072 Vecchione, Patrice, ed. *Faith and Doubt: An Anthology of Poems* (8–12). 2007, Henry Holt $16.95 (978-0-8050-8213-5). Poems by authors of many faiths both challenge and embrace traditional religion; prayers, reflections, and supplications will appeal to readers with all sorts of spiritual lives. (Rev: BL 4/1/07; LMC 10/07; SLJ 6/07) [808.81]

7073 Vecchione, Patrice, ed. *Revenge and Forgiveness: An Anthology of Poems* (8–12). 2004, Henry Holt $16.95 (978-0-8050-7376-8). This anthology on war, violence, and the search for peace contains poems from many lands and times. (Rev: BL 3/15/04; HB 3–4/04; SLJ 7/04; VOYA 6/04) [808.81]

7074 Viorst, Judith. *If I Were in Charge of the World and Other Worries: Poems for Children and Their Parents* (5–8). 1984, Macmillan paper $5.99 (978-0-689-70770-4). Easily read poems focus on topics familiar to young people. [811]

7075 Wallace, Daisy, ed. *Ghost Poems* (4–7). Illus. by Tomie dePaola. 1979, Holiday paper $4.95 (978-0-8234-0849-8). New and old poems to delight and frighten young readers.

7076 Waters, Fiona, comp. *Dark as a Midnight Dream: Poetry Collection 2* (5–8). Illus. by Zara Slattery. 1999, Evans Brothers $24.95 (978-0-237-51845-5). An extensive anthology of poetry arranged by subjects such as "Mythical Creatures" and "City Life" that features such writers as Robert Browning, William Shakespeare, William Butler Yeats, William Wordsworth, Langston Hughes, and Carl Sandburg. (Rev: SLJ 11/99) [811]

7077 Watson, Esther Pearl, and Mark Todd, sels. *The Pain Tree: And Other Teenage Angst-Ridden Poetry* (7–12). Illus. by Esther Pearl Watson and Mark Todd.

405

2000, Houghton Mifflin paper $6.95 (978-0-618-04758-1). Poems collected from teen Web sites and magazines and illustrated with paintings express a wide range of emotions. (Rev: HBG 9/00; SLJ 9/00; VOYA 6/00) [811]

7078 Willard, Nancy, ed. *Step Lightly: Poems for the Journey* (7–12). 1998, Harcourt paper $12.00 (978-0-15-202052-1). These works from the pens of about 40 poets represent the poems that the editor particularly loves. (Rev: BL 10/1/98; HBG 3/99; SLJ 11/98; VOYA 4/99) [811:008]

7079 Worth, Valerie. *Animal Poems* (4–7). 2007, Farrar $17.00 (978-0-374-38057-1). A diverse, sometimes challenging collection of poems highlighting animals' individual characteristics. (Rev: BL 4/1/07; SLJ 4/07*) [811]

7080 Worthen, Tom, ed. *Broken Hearts . . . Healing: Young Poets Speak Out on Divorce* (5–9). Illus. by Kyle Hernandez. Series: Young Poets Speak Out. 2001, Poet Tree $26.95 (978-1-58876-150-7); paper $14.95 (978-1-58876-151-4). This large selection of poems written by their peers about divorce, family breakups, and blended families will resonate with young readers. (Rev: SLJ 9/01; VOYA 10/01) [811]

7081 Yolen, Jane. *Sacred Places* (5–9). 1996, Harcourt $16.00 (978-0-15-269953-6). An international collection of informational poems about the places sacred to various faiths. (Rev: BCCB 12/00; BL 10/1/96; SLJ 3/96) [811]

7082 Zimmer, Tracie Vaughn. *Steady Hands: Poems About Work* (4–7). Illus. by Megan Halsey. 2009, Clarion $16.00 (978-0-618-90351-1). Short poems celebrate a variety of contemporary occupations from bakers to surgeons to dog walkers. (Rev: BL 1/1–15/09; SLJ 4/09) [811]

Geographical Regions

Europe

GREAT BRITAIN AND IRELAND

7083 Chaucer, Geoffrey. *The Canterbury Tales* (5–9). 1985, Checkerboard $14.95 (978-1-56288-259-4). An adaptation for young readers of 13 tales that still keep the flavor and spirit of the originals. (Rev: SLJ 2/86) [826]

7084 Coleridge, Samuel Taylor. *Samuel Taylor Coleridge* (6–10). Ed. by James Engell. Illus. by Harvey Chan. Series: Poetry for Young People. 2003, Sterling $14.95 (978-0-8069-6951-0). Biographical information introduces a sampling of Coleridge's most famous poems, which are accompanied by editorial notes and full-color illustrations. Also use *William Wordsworth* and *William*

Butler Yeats (both 2003). (Rev: BL 4/1/03; HBG 4/04; SLJ 9/03) [821]

7085 Corrin, Sara, and Stephen Corrin. *The Pied Piper of Hamelin* (6–9). 1989, Harcourt $14.95 (978-0-15-261596-3). A fine edition of the Browning poem with stunning illustrations by Errol Le Cain. (Rev: BL 4/1/89) [398.2]

7086 Dahl, Roald. *Vile Verses* (5–8). 2005, Viking $25.00 (978-0-670-06042-9). New illustrations adorn the poems in this aptly titled collection. (Rev: BL 11/1/05; SLJ 11/05*) [811]

7087 Gillooly, Eileen, ed. *Robert Browning* (7–12). Illus. by Joel Spector. Series: Poetry for Young People. 2001, Sterling $14.95 (978-0-8069-5543-8). A fine, well-illustrated introduction to the works of the English poet that gives historical context, references, and explanations of terms. (Rev: HBG 10/01; SLJ 10/01) [811]

7088 Hughes, Ted. *Collected Poems for Children* (4–8). Illus. by Raymond Briggs. 2007, Farrar $18.00 (978-0-374-31429-3). A nicely illustrated collection of 250 British-flavored children's poems by the late Hughes, some funny, some serious, some even scary. (Rev: BL 2/15/07; HB 7–8/07; LMC 11–12/07; SLJ 3/07) [811]

7089 Lear, Edward. *The Owl and the Pussycat* (5–10). Illus. by Stephane Jorisch. Series: Visions in Poetry. 2007, Kids Can $16.95 (978-1-55337-828-0); paper $9.95 (978-1-55453-232-2). A charmingly illustrated version of Lear's classic poem using watercolor and ink. (Rev: SLJ 1/08)

7090 Livingston, Myra Cohn, comp. *Poems of Lewis Carroll* (7–9). 1986, HarperCollins LB $11.89 (978-0-690-04540-6). A complete collection of rhymes, poems, and riddles from the creator of Alice. (Rev: SLJ 8/86) [821]

7091 Maynard, John, ed. *Alfred, Lord Tennyson* (5–8). Illus. by Allen Garns. Series: Poetry for Young People. 2004, Sterling $14.95 (978-0-8069-6612-0). This large-format introduction to Tennyson's works includes an informative profile of the poet, selections accompanied by notes, and rich illustrations. (Rev: BL 2/15/04) [821]

7092 Noyes, Alfred. *The Highwayman* (7–10). Illus. by Murray Kimber. Series: Visions in Poetry. 2005, Kids Can $16.95 (978-1-55337-425-1). In this beautifully illustrated Art Deco version of Noyes's immortal poem, the title character is transformed into a motorcycle-riding thief who roams the streets of New York City, while his beloved Bess is now a voluptuous glamour girl. (Rev: BL 5/1/05; SLJ 8/05; VOYA 10/05) [821]

7093 Opie, Iona, and Peter Opie. *I Saw Esau: The Schoolchild's Pocket Book* (7–12). 1992, Candlewick $19.99 (978-1-56402-046-8). Traces schoolyard folk rhymes to their roots. (Rev: BL 4/15/92*; SLJ 6/92) [821]

7094 Tennyson, Alfred Lord. *The Lady of Shalott* (5–7). Illus. by Genevieve Cote. 2005, Kids Can $16.95 (978-1-55337-874-7). The setting of Tennyson's "The Lady of Shalott" is moved from the England of King Arthur to the streets of an early 20th-century city in this beautifully illustrated adaptation. (Rev: BL 10/1/05; SLJ 12/05) [821]

7095 Thomas, Dylan. *A Child's Christmas in Wales* (5–8). Illus. by Trina Schart Hyman. 1985, Holiday $16.95 (978-0-8234-0565-7). A prose poem about the poet's childhood in a small Welsh village. [821.912]

OTHER COUNTRIES

7096 Levy, Debbie. *The Year of Goodbyes: A True Story of Friendship, Family, and Farewells* (5–8). Illus. 2010, Hyperion $16.99 (978-142312901-1). Based on a poetry album created by the author's mother in 1938 as the Jewish family waited for U.S. visas while their German friends disappeared around them. Lexile 910L (Rev: BL 2/15/10; SLJ 5/10) [811]

United States

7097 Alexander, Elizabeth, and Marilyn Nelson. *Miss Crandall's School for Young Ladies and Little Misses of Color* (6–10). Illus. by Floyd Cooper. 2007, Boyds Mills $17.95 (978-1-59078-456-3). Told in poetry, this is the true story of a Connecticut teacher who founded a school for black girls in 1833 and faced cruel opposition. ALA Notable Books 2008. (Rev: BCCB 11/07; BL 10/1/07; HB 9–10/07; LMC 11–12/07; SLJ 9/07) [811]

7098 Carlson, Lori Marie, ed. *Red Hot Salsa: Bilingual Poems on Being Young and Latino in the United States* (8–11). 2005, Henry Holt $14.95 (978-0-8050-7616-5). Poems in Spanish and English voice issues important to teens and the joys and sorrows of straddling two cultures. (Rev: BL 8/05; SLJ 8/05*) [811]

7099 Clinton, Catherine, ed. *I, Too, Sing America: Three Centuries of African American Poetry* (6–10). 1998, Houghton Mifflin $22.00 (978-0-395-89599-3). This heavily illustrated volume of 36 poems by 25 authors traces the history of African American poetry, from Phillis Wheatley to Rita Dove. (Rev: BL 11/15/98; HBG 3/99; SLJ 11/98; VOYA 8/99) [712.2]

7100 Clinton, Catherine, ed. *A Poem of Her Own: Voices of American Women Yesterday and Today* (6–9). Illus. by Stephen Alcorn. 2003, Abrams $17.95 (978-0-8109-4240-0). Biographical profiles enhance this collection of poems by 25 women in U.S. history. (Rev: BL 4/1/03*; HBG 10/03; SLJ 5/03; VOYA 8/03) [811.008]

7101 DeDonato, Collete. *City of One: Young Writers Speak to the World* (7–12). 2004, Aunt Lute paper $10.95 (978-1-879960-69-5). In this moving collection of poetry from San Francisco-based WritersCorps, scores of young people give voice to their feelings about peace and violence. (Rev: BL 8/04; SLJ 8/04; VOYA 10/04) [810.8]

7102 Dickinson, Emily. *I'm Nobody! Who Are You?* (6–9). 1978, Stemmer $21.95 (978-0-916144-21-0); paper $19.75 (978-0-916144-22-7). A well-illustrated edition of poems that young people can appreciate. [811]

7103 Dunbar, Paul Laurence. *The Complete Poems of Paul Laurence Dunbar* (7–12). 1980, Dodd paper $10.95 (978-0-396-07895-1). The definitive collection, first published in 1913, of this African American poet's work. [811]

7104 Fleischman, Paul. *I Am Phoenix: Poems for Two Voices* (4–9). 1985, HarperCollins paper $5.99 (978-0-06-446092-7). A group of love poems about birds that are designed to be read by two voices or groups of voices. (Rev: BL 12/1/85) [811]

7105 Fletcher, Ralph. *Buried Alive: The Elements of Love* (5–8). 1996, Simon & Schuster $14.00 (978-0-689-80593-6). A series of free-verse poems that explore various aspects of love — puppy and otherwise. (Rev: BCCB 6/96; BL 5/1/96; SLJ 5/96; VOYA 10/96) [811]

7106 Frost, Robert. *A Swinger of Birches* (6–9). 1982, Stemmer $21.95 (978-0-916144-92-0); paper $19.75 (978-0-916144-93-7). A collection of Frost's poems suitable for young readers in a well-illustrated edition. [811]

7107 Gardner, Joann, ed. *Runaway with Words: Poems from Florida's Youth Shelters* (6–12). 1996, Anhinga paper $14.95 (978-0-938078-47-0). Joy, anger, confusion, and fear are some of the emotions expressed in this collection of poems culled from writing workshops for teens in Florida's shelters. (Rev: BL 6/1–15/97) [811]

7108 Glenn, Mel. *Jump Ball: A Basketball Season in Poems* (6–12). 1997, Dutton $15.99 (978-0-525-67554-9). In a series of poems, people involved in an inner-city high school are introduced, including basketball players, parents, teachers, and friends. (Rev: BL 10/15/97; SLJ 11/97*; VOYA 12/97) [811]

7109 Grady, Cynthia. *I Lay My Stitches Down* (4–7). Illus. by Michele Wood. 2012, Eerdmans $17 (978-080285386-8). Drawing from the structures and discipline of a quilt, these free-verse poems — each consisting of 10 lines of 10 syllables — explore various aspects of the African American experience. (Rev: BL 2/1/12; HB 1–2/12; LMC 5–6/12; SLJ 1/12) [1.3.2.2]

7110 Grimes, Nikki. *A Dime a Dozen* (5–8). 1998, Dial $17.99 (978-0-8037-2227-9). Through a series of original poems, the writer explores her childhood: its happy moments, its painful memories — including divorce, foster homes, and parents with drinking and gambling problems — and her search for herself as a teenager. (Rev: BL 12/1/98; HBG 3/99; SLJ 11/98; VOYA 4/99) [811]

7111 Grimes, Nikki. *Stepping Out with Grandma Mac* (4–7). 2001, Orchard paper $16.95 (978-0-531-30320-7). A loving 10-year-old girl describes a very independent grandmother. (Rev: BL 5/15/01*; HBG 10/01; SLJ 7/01) [811.54]

7112 Hayford, James. *Knee-Deep in Blazing Snow: Growing Up in Vermont* (4–7). Illus. by Michael McCurdy. 2005, Boyds Mills $17.95 (978-1-59078-338-2). Hayford's simple, quiet poems evoke a simpler country life. (Rev: BL 1/1–15/06; SLJ 11/05) [811]

7113 Herrera, Juan Felipe. *Laughing Out Loud, I Fly (A Caracajadas Yo Vuelo): Poems in English and Spanish* (6–10). 1998, HarperCollins $16.99 (978-0-06-027604-1). In this series of poems in both languages, the poet celebrates incidents in his childhood. Belpré Honor 2000. (Rev: SLJ 5/98; VOYA 6/99) [811]

7114 Holbrook, Sara. *Walking on the Boundaries of Change: Poems of Transition* (8–12). 1998, Boyds Mills paper $9.95 (978-1-56397-737-4). In this collection of 53 poems, the author explores the problems of being a teen with amazing insight into concerns and decisions. (Rev: VOYA 2/99) [811]

7115 Hollander, John, ed. *American Poetry* (4–10). Illus. by Sally Wern Comport. Series: Poetry for Young People. 2004, Sterling $14.95 (978-1-4027-0517-5). A colorful celebration of American life, containing 26 poems by well-known poets including Robert Frost, Walt Whitman, Maya Angelou, and Langston Hughes. (Rev: SLJ 8/04) [811]

7116 Hopkins, Lee Bennett, ed. *Hand in Hand* (5–8). 1994, Simon & Schuster $21.95 (978-0-671-73315-5). An overview of the history of American poetry, with an interesting selection of poems arranged chronologically. (Rev: BCCB 1/95; BL 1/1/95; SLJ 12/94; VOYA 4/95) [811]

7117 Hudson, Wade, ed. *Poetry from the Masters: The Pioneers* (6–12). Illus. by Stephan J. Hudson. 2003, Just Us Bks. paper $9.95 (978-0-940975-96-5). Two-page biographical profiles introduce 11 African Americans and their works; among them are Phillis Wheatley, Paul Laurence Dunbar, Countee Cullen, Langston Hughes, and Gwendolyn Brooks. (Rev: SLJ 2/04) [811]

7118 Hughes, Langston. *The Dream Keeper and Other Poems* (6–12). 1994, Knopf LB $14.99 (978-0-679-94421-8). A classic collection by the renowned African American poet, originally published in 1932, is presented in an updated, illustrated edition. (Rev: BL 3/15/94; VOYA 6/94) [811]

7119 Johnson, Angela. *The Other Side: Shorter Poems* (6–12). 1998, Orchard LB $16.99 (978-0-531-33114-9). This African American poet gives us glimpses of her childhood in Alabama, her family life, and her views on such issues as the Vietnam War, racism, and the Black Panthers. (Rev: BL 11/15/98; HB 11–12/98; HBG 3/99; SLJ 9/98; VOYA 2/99) [811]

7120 Johnson, Dave, ed. *Movin': Teen Poets Take Voice* (5–10). Illus. by Chris Raschka. 2000, Orchard $15.95 (978-0-531-30258-3); paper $6.95 (978-0-531-07171-7). An anthology of poems by teens who participated in New York Public Library workshops or submitted their work via the Web. (Rev: BL 3/15/00; HBG 10/00; SLJ 5/00; VOYA 6/00) [811]

7121 Knudson, R. R., and May Swenson, eds. *American Sports Poems* (7–12). 1988, Watts LB $19.99 (978-0-531-08353-6). An excellent collection that concentrates on such popular sports as baseball, football, and swimming. (Rev: BL 8/88; SLJ 11/88; VOYA 10/88) [811]

7122 Levin, Jonathan, ed. *Walt Whitman: Poetry for Young People* (5–9). 1997, Sterling $14.95 (978-0-8069-9530-4). After a brief biographical sketch, this volume contains 26 poems and excerpts from longer poems, each introduced with an analysis. (Rev: HBG 3/98; SLJ 11/97) [811]

7123 Lewis, J. Patrick. *The Brothers' War: Civil War Voices in Verse* (6–9). 2007, National Geographic $17.95 (978-1-4263-0036-3). Eleven powerful poems about the pain and tragedy of the Civil War; reproductions of photographs from the war add to the poignancy. (Rev: BL 12/15/07; HB 1–2/08; LMC 2/08; SLJ 1/08) [811]

7124 Lewis, J. Patrick. *Freedom Like Sunlight: Praisesongs for Black Americans* (5–12). 2000, Creative $17.95 (978-1-56846-163-2). This collection of original poems pays tribute to such important African Americans as Sojourner Truth, Arthur Ashe, Rosa Parks, Marian Anderson, Malcolm X, and Langston Hughes. (Rev: BL 9/15/00*; HBG 3/01; SLJ 12/00) [811]

7125 Loewen, Nancy, ed. *Walt Whitman* (7–12). 1994, Creative Editions LB $23.95 (978-0-88682-608-6). A dozen selections from *Leaves of Grass* are juxtaposed with biographical vignettes and sepia photographs. (Rev: SLJ 7/94*) [811]

7126 Longfellow, Henry Wadsworth. *The Children's Own Longfellow* (5–8). 1908, Houghton Mifflin $20.00 (978-0-395-06889-2). Eight selections from the best-known and best-loved of Longfellow's poems. (Rev: BL 2/15/04*; SLJ 3/04)

7127 Longfellow, Henry Wadsworth. *Hiawatha and Megissogwon* (4–7). Illus. by Jeffrey Thompson. 2001, National Geographic $16.95 (978-0-7922-6676-1). Artwork with an authentic Native American feel illustrates Hiawatha's exciting adventures in the "Pearl-Feather" section of Longfellow's epic poem. (Rev: BCCB 3/02; BL 11/15/01; HBG 3/02; SLJ 9/01) [811]

7128 McLaughlin, Timothy P., ed. *Walking on Earth and Touching the Sky: Poetry and Prose by Lakota Youth at Red Cloud Indian School* (7–12). Illus. by S. D. Nelson. 2012, Abrams $19.95 (978-141970179-5). Poems and poetic prose by Lakota students are divided into such chapters as "Natural World," "Native Thoughts," and

"Family, Youth, and Dreams" and accompanied by rich paintings. (Rev: BL 5/1/12*; LMC 11–12/12*) [811]

7129 Meltzer, Milton, ed. *Hour of Freedom: American History in Poetry* (6–12). Illus. by Marc Nadel. 2003, Boyds Mills $16.95 (978-1-59078-021-3). Brief histories introduce many classic and some less-familiar poems — plus lyrics and speeches — that are grouped in chronological chapters, ranging from the colonial period to the 20th century. (Rev: BL 9/1/03; HBG 4/04; SLJ 7/03; VOYA 2/04) [811.54]

7130 Millay, Edna St. Vincent. *Edna St. Vincent Millay's Poems Selected for Young People* (7–10). 1979, Harper-Collins $14.00 (978-0-06-024218-3). A fine selection of the poet's work, illustrated with woodcuts. [811]

7131 Mora, Pat. *My Own True Name: New and Selected Poems for Young Adults, 1984-1999* (6–12). 2000, Arte Publico paper $11.95 (978-1-55885-292-1). The Mexican American poet looks at her bilingual heritage, the beauty of the desert country in which she was raised, her love of language, and racial discrimination. (Rev: SLJ 7/00; VOYA 12/00) [811]

7132 Mullins, Tom, ed. *Running Lightly . . . : Poems for Young People* (4–9). 1998, Mercier paper $12.95 (978-1-85342-193-8). A charming collection of old songs and ballads, nonsense rhymes, and lyrics. (Rev: BL 5/15/98; SLJ 7/98) [811]

7133 Myers, Walter Dean. *Angel to Angel: A Mother's Gift of Love* (4–8). 1998, HarperCollins LB $15.89 (978-0-06-027722-2). A photo/poetry montage with 10 distinctly styled poems and photographs focusing on African American mothers and children, and reflecting the relationship between words and pictures. (Rev: BL 2/15/98; HBG 10/98; SLJ 6/98) [811]

7134 Myers, Walter Dean. *Voices from Harlem: Poems in Many Voices* (7–10). 2004, Holiday House $16.95 (978-0-8234-1853-4). In this appealing collection of 54 poems, modeled on Edgar Lee Masters's *Spoon River Anthology*, Myers speaks in the diverse voices of imagined Harlem residents from many walks of life. (Rev: BCCB 12/04; BL 11/1/04*; HB 1–2/05; SLJ 12/04; VOYA 2/05) [811]

7135 Myers, Walter Dean, and Christopher Myers. *We Are America: A Tribute from the Heart* (4–8). 2011, HarperCollins $16.99 (978-0-06-052308-4). Fourteen short, free-verse poems explore key events and figures in American history ranging from Tecumseh and Abraham Lincoln to Jimi Hendrix and Barbara Jordan. (Rev: BL 5/1/11; SLJ 5/11) [811]

7136 Nelson, Marilyn. *Fortune's Bones: The Manumission Requiem* (7–12). 2005, Front St $16.95 (978-1-932425-12-3). Six poems celebrate the life of Fortune, a slave who died in 1798 but continued to serve his master, who rendered his bones and used Fortune's skeleton to teach anatomy. (Rev: BCCB 2/05; BL 11/15/04; HB 1–2/05; SLJ 12/04) [811]

7137 Nelson, Marilyn. *Sweethearts of Rhythm: The Story of the Greatest All-Girl Swing Band in the World* (5–8). Illus. by Jerry Pinkney. 2009, Dial $21.99 (978-0-8037-3187-5). Nelson offers up accessible, rhythmic poems that pay homage to an all-female New Orleans jazz band — the Sweethearts of Rhythm — from the 1940s in this lively, beautifully illustrated book. (Rev: BL 10/15/09; HB 11–12/09; LMC 11–12/09; SLJ 10/09; VOYA 12/09) [811]

7138 Paschen, Elise. *Poetry Speaks Who I Am* (6–9). 2010, Sourcebooks $19.99 (978-1-40221074-7). Langston Hughes, Sherman Alexie, Robert Frost, and Gwendolyn Brooks are among the poets represented in this collection of classic and contemporary works that speak in different ways to middle school students; an accompanying CD features many of the poets reading. (Rev: BL 6/10; LMC 8–9/10; SLJ 6/10) [811]

7139 Poe, Edgar Allan. *Complete Poems* (8–12). Ed. by Thomas Ollive Mabbott. 2000, Univ. of Illinois paper $25.00 (978-0-252-06921-5). This is an exhaustive collection of Poe's poems, totaling 101 works. [811]

7140 Poe, Edgar Allan. *The Raven* (6–9). Illus. by Ryan Price. 2006, Kids Can $16.95 (978-1-55337-473-2). Edgar Allen Poe's famous poem is accompanied by the dry point printmaking art of Ryan Price in this new edition. (Rev: BL 9/1/06; SLJ 12/06) [811]

7141 Roessel, David, and Arnold Rampersad, eds. *Poetry for Young People: Langston Hughes* (7–10). Illus. by Benny Andrews. 2006, Sterling $14.95 (978-1-4027-1845-8). An illustrated picture-book-format collection of 26 poems with a useful introduction, a biography, and notes. Coretta Scott King Illustrator Honor Award, 2007. (Rev: BL 2/1/06*; SLJ 5/06) [811]

7142 Rosenberg, Liz, ed. *The Invisible Ladder: An Anthology of Contemporary American Poems for Young Readers* (6–10). 1996, Henry Holt $19.95 (978-0-8050-3836-1). As well as an excellent anthology of modern American poetry, this volume provides commentary by the poets, photographs of them, and suggestions for using each of the poems. (Rev: BL 9/15/96; SLJ 2/97; VOYA 2/97) [811]

7143 Rylant, Cynthia. *Boris* (7–10). 2005, Harcourt $16.00 (978-0-15-205412-0). This collection of free-verse poems celebrates the life and times of Boris, a big, gray cat adopted from a humane shelter. (Rev: BCCB 4/05; BL 2/15/05; HB 5–6/05; SLJ 4/05; VOYA 4/05) [811]

7144 Rylant, Cynthia. *Soda Jerk* (7–12). 1990, Watts LB $16.99 (978-0-531-08464-9). A group of poems about the inhabitants of a small town, written from the viewpoint of a teenage soda jerk. (Rev: BL 2/15/90; SLJ 4/90; VOYA 6/90) [811]

7145 Rylant, Cynthia. *Something Permanent* (7–12). 1994, Harcourt $18.00 (978-0-15-277090-7). Combines Rylant's poetry with Walker Evans's photographs to evoke strong emotions of southern life during the Depression. (Rev: BL 7/94*; SLJ 8/94; VOYA 12/94) [811]

7146 Schmidt, Gary D., ed. *Robert Frost* (5–7). Illus. by Henri Sorensen. Series: Poetry for Young People. 1994, Sterling $14.95 (978-0-8069-0633-1). An anthology of 25 poems suitable for young people, with watercolor illustrations that picture the New England landscape that Frost loved. (Rev: BL 12/1/94; SLJ 2/95) [811]

7147 Schoonmaker, Frances, ed. *Henry Wadsworth Longfellow* (4–8). Series: Poetry for Young People. 1999, Sterling $14.95 (978-0-8069-9417-8). A generous, carefully selected presentation of Longfellow's poetry illustrated by full-color paintings and accompanied by biographical notes. (Rev: BL 3/15/99; HBG 9/99; SLJ 3/99) [811]

7148 Shange, Ntozake. *Freedom's a-Callin Me* (4–7). Illus. by Rod Brown. 2012, HarperCollins $16.99 (978-0-06-133741-3). Poems and paintings capture the danger, strife, and hope experienced by those who strove to escape from slavery via the Underground Railroad. (Rev: BL 2/1/12; HB 1–2/12; SLJ 12/1/11) [811]

7149 Shields, Carol Diggory. *BrainJuice: American History Fresh Squeezed!* (4–8). Illus. by Richard Thompson. 2002, Handprint $14.95 (978-1-929766-62-8). A timeline runs across the tops of these pages of poems about events in American history. (Rev: HBG 3/03; SLJ 1/03) [811]

7150 Siebert, Diane. *Tour America: A Journey Through Poems and Art* (4–7). 2006, Chronicle $17.95 (978-0-8118-5056-8). Natural and manmade sights across America are celebrated in this appealing collection of poetry and art. (Rev: BL 6/1–15/06; SLJ 6/06*) [811]

7151 Silverstein, Shel. *A Light in the Attic* (6–9). 1981, HarperCollins LB $19.89 (978-0-06-025674-6). More than 100 humorous poems that deal with children's interests and need for fun. Also use the author's earlier *Where the Sidewalk Ends* (1974). [811]

7152 Smith, Hope Anita. *Mother Poems* (4–7). Illus. by author. 2009, Henry Holt $16.95 (978-0-8050-8231-9). In simple free-verse poems, a young African American girl expresses her love for her mother, and the loss she feels upon her death. ALA Notable Books 2010. (Rev: BL 2/15/09; SLJ 4/1/09) [811]

7153 Smith, Hope Anita. *The Way a Door Closes* (5–8). Illus. by Shane W. Evans. 2003, Henry Holt $18.95 (978-0-8050-6477-3). A series of poems convey the feelings of a 13-year-old African American boy whose warm, loving home is destroyed when his father loses his job. (Rev: BL 5/1/03; HBG 10/03; SLJ 5/03*) [811]

7154 Soto, Gary. *A Fire in My Hands. Rev. ed.* (6–9). 2006, Harcourt $16.00 (978-0-15-205564-6). The joys and agonies of everyday life are captured in these poems, half of them new to this edition. (Rev: BL 4/1/06; SLJ 5/06) [811]

7155 Spires, Elizabeth. *I Heard God Talking to Me: William Edmondson and His Stone Carvings* (6–12). Illus. 2009, Farrar $17.95 (978-037433528-1). Poems celebrate the art of African American sculptor William Edmondson, who started carving tombstones in 1931 when he was in his 50s; with photographs of the artist and his works. (Rev: BL 2/1/09; SLJ 3/1/09*) [811]

7156 Stavans, Ilan, ed. *Wachale! Poetry and Prose About Growing Up Latino in America* (5–8). 2001, Cricket $16.95 (978-0-8126-4750-1). A bilingual anthology about Latino experiences, both in the past and in the present. (Rev: BCCB 2/02; BL 2/1/02; HBG 10/02; SLJ 2/02; VOYA 6/02) [810.8]

7157 Steig, Jeanne. *Alpha Beta Chowder* (5–8). 1992, HarperCollins LB $14.89 (978-0-06-205007-6). A collection of nonsense verses celebrating the joy of words — their sound and meaning — with each verse playing with a letter of the alphabet. (Rev: BL 11/15/92; SLJ 12/92) [811]

7158 Stepanek, Mattie J. T. *Hope Through Heartsongs* (6–12). 2002, Hyperion $14.95 (978-0-7868-6944-2). Hope and courage are central to this third collection of poems by Mattie Stepanek, who died of muscular dystrophy in June 2004, less than a month before his 14th birthday. (Rev: SLJ 8/02; VOYA 8/02) [811]

7159 Strickland, Michael R., ed. *My Own Song: And Other Poems to Groove To* (6–12). 1997, Boyds Mills $14.95 (978-1-56397-686-5). A collection of poems about music and its relationship to such subjects as love, cities, and birds. (Rev: BL 10/15/97; HBG 3/98; SLJ 12/97) [811]

7160 *Tell the World: Teen Poems from Writerscorps* (7–12). 2008, HarperTeen $16.99 (978-0-06-134505-0). Brief poems by teen participants in WritersCorps workshops are organized in chapters titled "Who We Are," "Where We're From," "What We Love," "What We Think," "How It Feels," and "Why We Hope." (Rev: SLJ 1/1/09) [811]

7161 Thayer, Ernest L. *Casey at the Bat* (5–10). Illus. by Joe Morse. Series: Visions in Poetry. 2006, Kids Can $16.95 (978-1-55337-827-3). The famous poem is reimagined in a contemporary setting, with a multicultural crowd and modern technology grounding the poem in the here-and-now. (Rev: SLJ 6/06) [811]

7162 Thayer, Ernest L. *Casey at the Bat: A Ballad of the Republic Sung in the Year 1888* (4–8). Illus. by C. F. Payne. 2003, Simon & Schuster $16.95 (978-0-689-85494-1). An impossibly muscular Casey is the star of this version of the classic baseball poem. (Rev: BCCB 1/01*; BL 2/1/03; HBG 10/03; SLJ 3/03*) [811]

7163 Turner, Ann W. *Grass Songs: Poems* (7–12). 1993, Harcourt $16.95 (978-0-15-136788-7). Dramatic monologues in poetic form that express courage and despair, passion and loneliness, and the struggle to find a home in the wilderness. (Rev: BL 6/1–15/93; VOYA 8/93) [811]

7164 Turner, Ann W. *A Lion's Hunger: Poems of First Love* (8–12). 1999, Marshall Cavendish $15.95 (978-0-7614-5035-1). Written from a young woman's point of view, this is a collection of poems by the author chronicling the joys and sorrows of first love. (Rev: BL 3/1/99; HBG 3/99; SLJ 1/99; VOYA 2/99) [811]

7165 Weatherford, Carole Boston. *Remember the Bridge: Poems of a People* (7–12). 2002, Putnam $17.99 (978-0-399-23726-3). This collection of poems celebrates African Americans from the era of slavery through today, with accompanying archival images. (Rev: BL 2/15/02; HBG 10/02; SLJ 1/02; VOYA 8/02) [811]

7166 Whitman, Walt. *Voyages: Poems by Walt Whitman* (7–12). 1988, Harcourt $15.95 (978-0-15-294495-7). An introductory biographical sketch is followed by 53 representative poems selected by Lee Bennett Hopkins. (Rev: BL 11/15/88; SLJ 12/88; VOYA 1/89) [811.3]

7167 Wong, Janet S. *Behind the Wheel* (7–12). 1999, Simon & Schuster $15.00 (978-0-689-82531-6). In a series of free-verse poems, the author explores individuals and their relationships within families. (Rev: BL 1/1–15/00*; HB 11–12/99; HBG 4/00; VOYA 2/00) [811]

7168 Yolen, Jane, sel. *Once Upon Ice: And Other Frozen Poems* (4–8). 1997, Boyds Mills $19.95 (978-1-56397-408-3). A collection of 17 poems inspired by photographs of ice formations, which are also included. (Rev: BL 2/1/97; SLJ 3/97) [811]

Other Regions

7169 Agard, John. *Half-Caste and Other Poems* (4–7). 2005, Hodder $16.99 (978-0-340-89382-1). Guyana-born Agard offers a collection of his saucy, Caribbean-flavored poetry dealing with topics such as tolerance and diversity that young people will recognize. (Rev: BL 10/15/05; HB 1–2/06; HBG 4/06; SLJ 1/06; VOYA 2/06) [811]

7170 Brand, Dionne. *Earth Magic* (4–7). Illus. by Eugenie Fernandes. 2006, Kids Can $14.95 (978-1-55337-706-1). In her first collection of poetry for young people, Brand writes about life in Trinidad, the island of her birth. (Rev: BL 4/1/06; SLJ 7/06) [811]

7171 Caduto, Michael J. *Earth Tales from Around the World* (5–8). 1997, Fulcrum paper $17.95 (978-1-55591-968-9). This collection of 48 folktales from around the world emphasizes respect for the natural world. (Rev: BL 4/1/98; SLJ 5/98; VOYA 4/98) [398.27]

7172 Cole, Joanna, ed. *Best-Loved Folktales of the World* (7–12). 1982, Doubleday paper $17.00 (978-0-385-

18949-1). A collection of 200 tales from around the globe, arranged geographically. [398.2]

7173 Coombs, Kate. *The Runaway Princess* (4–7). 2006, Farrar $17.00 (978-0-374-35546-3). In this entertaining takeoff on traditional fairy tales, 15-year-old Princess Meg, angry over being sequestered while princes from far and wide compete for her hand in marriage, escapes and takes matters into her own hands. (Rev: BL 9/1/06; SLJ 9/06) [398.2]

7174 Dokey, Cameron. *Before Midnight: A Retelling of "Cinderella"* (6–10). Series: Once upon a Time. 2007, Simon & Schuster paper $5.99 (978-1-4169-3471-4). Dokey adds details to the Cinderella tale, explaining that the girl's father left her in his grief over his wife's death in childbirth. (Rev: SLJ 4/07)

7175 Dokey, Cameron. *Golden* (6–10). 2006, Simon & Schuster paper $5.99 (978-1-4169-0580-6). Obviously based on the Rapunzel fairy tale, but with several interesting twists on the original, this story tells of a bald Rapunzel whom her mother gave up to sorceress Melisande, who raised her as her own, having lost her own daughter Rue to a wizard who cursed her and imprisoned her in a magic tower. Rapunzel — in the midst of feelings of jealousy — leads the effort to save Rue before it is too late. (Rev: SLJ 8/06*)

7176 Dokey, Cameron. *Sunlight and Shadow* (6–10). Series: Once upon a Time. 2004, Simon & Schuster paper $5.99 (978-0-689-86999-0). Mina — daughter of Pamina, the Queen of the Night, and of Sarastro, the Mage of the Day — falls in love with a prince called Tern and together the two face obstacles in this reworking of "The Magic Flute." (Rev: SLJ 11/04; VOYA 12/04)

7177 Engle, Margarita. *The Firefly Letters: A Suffragette's Journey to Cuba* (6–12). 2010, Henry Holt $16.99 (978-0-8050-9082-6). In alternating free-verse narratives Swedish suffragist Frederika Bremer, her teenage slave Cecilia, and a privileged 12-year-old daughter of a planter describe their lives and quite different experiences. Belpré Honor 2011; ALA Notable Books 2011. **e** Lexile NC1230L (Rev: BL 12/15/09; HB 3–4/10; LMC 11–12/09; SLJ 2/10) [813]

7178 Engle, Margarita. *The Surrender Tree: Poems of Cuba's Struggle for Freedom* (6–12). 2008, Henry Holt $16.95 (978-0-8050-8674-4). In free verse Engle describes the lives of residents of Cuba in the mid- to late-19th century who fought for freedom. Belpré Medal 2009; Newbery Honor 2009; ALA Notable Books 2009. (Rev: BL 3/15/08*; LMC 11–12/08) [811]

7179 Ferris, Jean. *Once Upon a Marigold* (5–8). 2002, Harcourt $17.00 (978-0-15-216791-2). Christian falls in love with Princess Marigold and wins her heart through his bravery in this fairy tale full of fun. (Rev: BCCB 2/03; BL 9/15/02; HB 9–10/02; HBG 3/03; SLJ 11/02; VOYA 12/02)

411

7180 Ferris, Jean. *Twice Upon a Marigold: Part Comedy, Part Tragedy, Part Two* (5–8). 2008, Harcourt $17.00 (978-0-15-206382-5). Queen Marigold and King Christian, introduced in *Once upon a Marigold*, are now married and Queen Olympia, who fell into a river at the end of the first book, is now dried off and back to her wicked ways. (Rev: BL 4/15/08; SLJ 6/08)

7181 Forest, Heather. *Wisdom Tales from Around the World* (4–7). 1996, August House $27.95 (978-0-87483-478-9); paper $19.95 (978-0-87483-479-6). Fifty fables, folktales, and myths from around the world. (Rev: BCCB 2/97; BL 3/1/97; SLJ 4/97) [398.2]

7182 Hamilton, Martha, and Mitch Weiss. *How and Why Stories: World Tales Kids Can Read and Tell* (5–10). 1999, August House $21.95 (978-0-87483-562-5); paper $12.95 (978-0-87483-561-8). This excellent collection of 25 pourquoi (how and why) stories from around the world also contains a useful introduction on folklore, plus tips on delivering each of the tales. (Rev: BL 5/15/00; HBG 3/00; SLJ 1/00) [398.2]

7183 Harley, Avis. *African Acrostics: A Word in Edgewise* (4–7). Illus. by Deborah Noyes. 2009, Candlewick $17.99 (978-0-7636-3621-0). Poems featuring acrostic puzzles are paired with photographs of animals in Africa. (Rev: BL 7/09; SLJ 6/09*) [811.6]

7184 Jaffe, Nina, and Steve Zeitlin. *The Cow of No Color: Riddle Stories and Justice Tales from Around the World* (5–8). 1998, Henry Holt $17.00 (978-0-8050-3736-4). A collection of folktales from around the world that deal with the theme of justice. (Rev: BCCB 12/98; BL 11/1/98; HBG 3/99; SLJ 12/98) [398.2]

7185 Johnston, Tony. *The Ancestors Are Singing* (4–8). Illus. by Karen Barbour. 2003, Farrar $16.00 (978-0-374-30347-1). Mexico's geography, history, and culture are portrayed in poems full of vivid images. (Rev: BL 4/1/03; HBG 10/03; SLJ 4/03; VOYA 10/03) [811]

7186 Liu, Siyu, and Orel Protopopescu. *A Thousand Peaks: Poems from China* (6–10). Illus. by Siyu Liu. 2002, Pacific View $19.95 (978-1-881896-24-1). Thirty-five translations of Chinese poems are accompanied by information giving historical and cultural context, the original in Chinese characters and pinyin transliteration, a literal translation, and black-and-white drawings. (Rev: BL 3/15/02; SLJ 2/02*) [895.1]

7187 Lupton, Hugh, ed. *The Songs of Birds: Stories and Poems from Many Cultures* (4–7). 2000, Barefoot Bks $19.95 (978-1-84148-045-9). A beautifully illustrated collection of stories (mostly creation myths) and poems about birds culled from a wide range of cultures. (Rev: BL 3/15/00; SLJ 9/00) [808.819]

7188 MacDonald, Margaret Read. *Peace Tales: World Folktales to Talk About* (5–7). 1992, Shoe String LB $25.00 (978-0-208-02328-5); paper $17.50 (978-0-208-02329-2). Stories and proverbs directed toward

achieving world peace. (Rev: BL 6/15/92; SLJ 10/92) [398.2]

7189 MacDonald, Margaret Read. *Three Minute Tales: Stories from Around the World to Tell or Read When Time Is Short* (8–12). 2004, August House $24.95 (978-0-87483-728-5); paper $17.95 (978-0-87483-729-2). Brief tales that are easy to learn come with notes about sources and tips about effective telling. (Rev: BL 9/15/04; SLJ 10/04) [398.2]

7190 Matthews, John. *The Barefoot Book of Knights* (4–7). Illus. by Giovanni Manna. 2002, Barefoot Bks $19.99 (978-1-84148-064-0). This book contains retellings of seven tales of knights and chivalry from countries around the world. (Rev: BCCB 9/02; BL 4/15/02; HBG 10/02; SLJ 6/02) [398.2]

7191 Mutén, Burleigh. *Grandfather Mountain: Stories of Gods and Heroes from Many Cultures* (4–7). Retold by Burleigh Muten. Illus. by Siân Bailey. 2004, Barefoot Bks $19.99 (978-1-84148-789-2). Strong male protagonists are featured in folktales from England, Greece, Ireland, Japan, Mexico, New Zealand, Nigeria, and the Seneca Indians. (Rev: BL 11/15/04; SLJ 1/05) [398.2]

7192 Nye, Naomi Shihab, ed. *The Space Between Our Footsteps: Poems and Paintings from the Middle East* (8–12). 1998, Simon & Schuster $21.95 (978-0-689-81233-0). More than 100 poets and artists from 19 countries in the Middle East are featured in this handsome volume of verse about families, friends, and everyday events. (Rev: BCCB 5/98; BL 3/1/98; HB 3–4/98; SLJ 5/98; VOYA 10/98) [808.81]

7193 Oberman, Sheldon. *Solomon and the Ant* (5–8). 2006, Boyds Mills $19.95 (978-1-59078-307-8). Nearly 50 traditional Jewish stories are arranged chronologically and accompanied by notes and commentary. (Rev: BL 2/1/06; SLJ 3/06) [398.2]

7194 Opie, Iona, and Peter Opie, eds. *The Classic Fairy Tales* (6–12). 1987, Oxford paper $19.99 (978-0-19-520219-9). The definitive retelling of 24 of the most popular fairy tales of all time. [398.2]

7195 Pearson, Maggie. *The Headless Horseman and Other Ghoulish Tales* (4–7). 2001, Interlink $18.95 (978-1-56656-377-2). From Bluebeard to Baba Yaga and Ichabod Crane, this is a collection of 14 tales about eerie beings. (Rev: BL 3/1/01; HBG 10/01; SLJ 1/01) [398.2]

7196 Rosen, Michael J. *How the Animals Got Their Colors* (5–8). Illus. by John Clementson. 1992, Harcourt $14.95 (978-0-15-236783-1). Tales from around the world that explain such things as a leopard's spots and the green on a frog's back. (Rev: BCCB 7–8/92; BL 6/15/92; SLJ 9/91) [398.2]

7197 Rossel, Seymour. *Sefer Ha-Aggadah: The Book of Legends for Young Readers* (4–7). Illus. by Judy Dick. 1996, UAHC paper $14.00 (978-0-8074-0603-8). A collection of legends based on stories about the Jewish people from the Old Testament. (Rev: SLJ 3/97) [398.2]

7198 Sherman, Josepha. *Merlin's Kin: World Tales of the Heroic Magician* (5–8). 1998, August House paper $11.95 (978-0-87483-519-9). A splendid international collection of folktales that feature magicians, sorcerers, shamans, healers, and wizards. (Rev: BL 4/15/99; SLJ 3/99; VOYA 12/98) [398.21]

7199 Tadjo, Veronique. *Talking Drums: A Selection of Poems from Africa South of the Sahara* (4–8). Illus. by author. 2004, Bloomsbury $15.95 (978-1-58234-813-1). Arranged by theme, these 75 poems — traditional and contemporary — cover a broad range of topics. (Rev: BL 3/1/04; SLJ 4/04; VOYA 4/04) [811]

7200 Thompson, Stith, ed. *One Hundred Favorite Folktales* (5–8). Illus. by Franz Altschuler. 1968, Indiana Univ $39.95 (978-0-253-15940-3); paper $19.95 (978-0-253-20172-0). A selection from an international store of folktales. [398.2]

7201 Yolen, Jane, and Shulamith Oppenheim. *The Fish Prince and Other Stories* (7–12). Illus. by Paul Hoffman. 2001, Interlink $29.95 (978-1-56656-389-5); paper $15.00 (978-1-56656-390-1). An absorbing and informative collection of stories of mermaids and mermen from around the world, accompanied by black-and-white illustrations. (Rev: BL 11/15/01) [398.21]

7202 Yolen, Jane, ed. *Mightier than the Sword: World Folktales for Strong Boys* (4–8). Illus. by Raul Colon. 2003, Harcourt $20.00 (978-0-15-216391-4). Yolen has collected stories from countries including Afghanistan, Angola, and China that portray intelligence as an invaluable asset. (Rev: BL 4/1/03; HB 5–6/03; HBG 10/03; SLJ 5/03) [398.2]

7203 Young, Richard, and Judy Dockery Young, eds. *Stories from the Days of Christopher Columbus: A Multicultural Collection for Young Readers* (5–9). 1992, August House paper $8.95 (978-0-87483-198-6). An anthology of stories translated from a variety of languages, including Italian, Spanish, Portuguese, and Aztec. (Rev: BL 9/15/92; SLJ 7/92) [398.2]

413

Folklore and Fairy Tales

General and Miscellaneous

7204 Lairamore, Dawn. *Ivy and the Meanstalk* (5–8). 2011, Holiday House $16.95 (978-0-8234-2392-7). Princess Ivy and her dragon friend Elridge struggle to set things right by returning a magical harp to the giant's widow in this fractured take on Jack and the Beanstalk. (Rev: BL 10/1/11; LMC 1–2/12; SLJ 9/1/11)

7205 Vande Velde, Vivian. *Cloaked in Red* (7–10). 2010, Marshall Cavendish $15.99 (978-0-7614-5793-0). A collection of eight diverse stories that give new twists to the well-known tale. Lexile 920L (Rev: BL 9/15/10; LMC 11–12/10; SLJ 12/1/10; VOYA 10/10)

7206 Zahler, Diane. *Princess of the Wild Swans* (4–7). Illus. by Yvonne Gilbert. 2012, HarperCollins $16.99 (978-006200492-5). When tasked with making shirts from stinging nettles for each of her five brothers to free them from a curse, 12-year-old Princess Meriel rues her distaste for sewing; based on Grimm's "The Six Swans." (Rev: BL 3/1/12; SLJ 3/12)

Geographical Regions

Africa

7207 Abrahams, Roger D., ed. *African Folktales: Traditional Stories of the Black World* (7–12). 1983, Pantheon paper $18.00 (978-0-394-72117-0). A collection of about 100 tales from south of the Sahara. [398.2]

7208 Arkhurst, Joyce Cooper. *The Adventures of Spider: West African Folktales* (4–7). Illus. by Jerry Pinkney. 1992, Little, Brown paper $8.99 (978-0-316-05107-1). Six humorous stories featuring the crafty spider. [398.2]

7209 Ashabranner, Brent, and Russell Davis. *The Lion's Whiskers and Other Ethiopian Tales* (4–7). 1997, Linnet LB $19.95 (978-0-208-02429-9). A classic collection of 16 Ethiopian folktales originally published in 1995. (Rev: BL 10/1/97; SLJ 5/97*) [398.2]

7210 Eisner, Will. *Sundiata: A Legend of Africa* (5–8). 2003, NBM $15.95 (978-1-56163-332-6). A retelling, in comic book style, of an African folktale about a lame prince who conquers an evil king. (Rev: BL 2/1/03; HBG 10/03; SLJ 2/03) [398.2]

7211 Giles, Bridget. *Myths of West Africa* (6–10). Series: Mythic World. 2002, Gale LB $27.12 (978-0-7398-4976-7). A general introduction to this area of Africa through text and pictures is followed by retellings of important myths and relevant background information. (Rev: BL 7/02; HBG 10/02; SLJ 5/02) [398.2]

7212 Greaves, Nick. *When Hippo Was Hairy: And Other Tales from Africa* (4–8). 1988, Barron's paper $11.95 (978-0-8120-4548-2). Thirty-one traditional African tales, a combination of folklore and fact. (Rev: BL 2/15/89; SLJ 2/89) [398.2]

7213 Green, Roger L. *Tales of Ancient Egypt* (5–9). 1972, Penguin paper $4.99 (978-0-14-036716-4). A collection of folktales from ancient Egypt including one about the source of the Nile. [398]

7214 Kituku, Vincent Muli Wa, retel. *East African Folktales: From the Voice of Mukamba* (6–9). Retold by Vincent Muli Wa Kituku. 1997, August House $9.95 (978-0-87483-489-5). This bilingual book contains 18 folktales in English and Kikamba, the language of the Kamba community in Kenya. (Rev: SLJ 8/97) [398.2]

7215 McCall Smith, Alexander. *The Girl Who Married a Lion and Other Tales from Africa* (8–12). 2004, Pantheon $20.00 (978-0-375-42312-3). Traditional tales feature characterful animals and humans. (Rev: BL 11/1/04) [398.2]

7216 McIntosh, Gavin. *Hausaland Tales from the Nigerian Marketplace* (4–9). 2002, Linnet $22.50 (978-0-208-02523-4). This collection of 12 Nigerian folktales skillfully interweaves details of contemporary Hausa society. (Rev: HBG 3/03; SLJ 11/02) [398.2]

7217 Mama, Raouf, retel. *Why Goats Smell Bad and Other Stories from Benin* (4–8). Retold by Raouf Mama. 1998, Linnet LB $21.50 (978-0-208-02469-5). A delightful collection of 20 folktales from the Fon culture of Benin, handsomely illustrated with woodcuts. (Rev: BCCB 5/98; BL 2/15/98; HBG 9/98; SLJ 4/98) [398.2]

7218 *Nelson Mandela's Favorite African Folktales* (6–12). 2002, Norton $24.95 (978-0-393-05212-1). Thirty-two folktales from the African continent are complemented by artwork as diverse as the stories. (Rev: BL 12/1/02; HBG 10/03; SLJ 2/03) [398.2]

7219 Tchana, Katrin Hyman. *The Serpent Slayer and Other Stories of Strong Women* (4–7). Illus. by Trina Schart Hyman. 2000, Little, Brown $21.95 (978-0-316-38701-9). A collection of 18 folktales from around the world featuring brave, creative, and strong women and girls. (Rev: BCCB 11/00*; BL 12/15/00; HB 11–12/00; HBG 3/01; SLJ 11/00) [398.2]

Asia and the Middle East

7220 Bedard, Michael, ed. *The Painted Wall and Other Strange Tales* (4–7). 2003, Tundra $16.95 (978-0-88776-652-7). Chinese folktales collected centuries ago are full of action and the supernatural. (Rev: BL 1/1–15/04; SLJ 1/04) [398.2]

7221 Carpenter, F. R. *Tales of a Chinese Grandmother* (5–7). Illus. by Malthe Hasselriis. 1973, Amereon LB $24.95 (978-0-89190-481-6); paper $8.95 (978-0-8048-1042-5). A boy and a girl listen to 30 classic Chinese tales. [398.2]

7222 Chin, Yin-lien C., ed. *Traditional Chinese Folktales* (5–8). Illus. by Lu Wang. 1989, East Gate $44.95 (978-0-87332-507-3). This is a collection of 12 Chinese folktales that express a variety of themes and genres from faithful lovers to trickster tales. (Rev: SLJ 8/89) [398.2]

7223 Conover, Sarah, ed. *Kindness: A Treasury of Buddhist Wisdom for Children and Parents* (4–7). 2001, Eastern Washington Univ. paper $19.95 (978-0-910055-67-3). Thirty-one stories related to Buddhism, including Jataka tales about the Buddha's incarnations, have been effectively translated and adapted for this anthology. (Rev: BL 2/15/01; SLJ 3/01) [294.3]

7224 Fu, Shelley. *Ho Yi the Archer and Other Classic Chinese Tales* (6–9). 2001, Linnet LB $22.50 (978-0-208-02487-9). This collection of folktales and myths, some of which may be familiar, is introduced by a look at Chinese folklore and the influence of Taoism and

Buddhism and includes a pronunciation guide, and list of characters. (Rev: BL 7/01; HB 9–10/01; HBG 3/02; SLJ 7/01) [398.2]

7225 Jaffrey, Madhur. *Seasons of Splendor: Tales, Myths, and Legends from India* (5–8). Illus. by Michael Foreman. 1985, Puffin paper $7.95 (978-0-317-62172-3). Folktales and family stories as well as accounts of Rama and Krishna. (Rev: BCCB 1/86; BL 1/15/86) [398.2]

7226 Kendall, Carol, retel. *Haunting Tales from Japan* (6–9). Retold by Carol Kendall. 1985, Spencer Museum Publns. paper $6.00 (978-0-913689-22-6). A retelling of six Japanese folktales, some of which deal with murder and suicide. (Rev: SLJ 2/86) [398]

7227 Krishnaswami, Uma, retel. *Shower of Gold: Girls and Women in the Stories of India* (6–10). Retold by Uma Krishnaswami. 1999, Linnet LB $21.50 (978-0-208-02484-8). All of the enchanting tales in this fine collection of Indian folklore feature wise and powerful women. (Rev: BCCB 5/99; BL 3/15/99; HBG 3/00; SLJ 8/99) [891]

7228 Lang, Andrew. *The Arabian Nights Entertainments* (5–9). 1969, Dover paper $12.95 (978-0-486-22289-9). Aladdin and Sinbad are only two of the characters in these 26 tales of Arabia and the East. (Rev: BL 9/1/89) [398.2]

7229 Lee, Jeanne M. *The Song of Mu Lan* (5–8). 1995, Front St $17.95 (978-1-886910-00-3). Mu Lan disguises herself as a boy and joins the emperor's army in this traditional Chinese tale. (Rev: BL 11/15/95; SLJ 12/95) [398.2]

7230 Lee, Jeanne M, retel. *Toad Is the Uncle of Heaven: A Vietnamese Folk Tale* (4–7). Retold by Jeanne M. Lee. Illus. by Jeanne M. Lee. 1985, Henry Holt paper $6.95 (978-0-8050-1147-0). This book tells the story of Toad who collects companions on his way to see the King of Heaven, who makes rain. (Rev: BL 11/1/85; HB 3–4/86) [398.2]

7231 McCaughrean, Geraldine. *Gilgamesh the Hero* (6–9). Illus. by David Parkins. 2003, Eerdmans $20.00 (978-0-8028-5262-5). McCaughrean retells the ancient epic story of Gilgamesh, a Sumerian king around 3000 B.C.E., in this volume illustrated with evocative paintings. (Rev: BL 9/1/03*; HB 9–10/03; SLJ 12/03*) [398.]

7232 Meeker, Clare Hodgson. *A Tale of Two Rice Birds: A Folktale from Thailand* (4–8). Illus. by Christine Lamb. 1994, Sasquatch $14.95 (978-1-57061-008-0). Two rice birds are reincarnated as a princess and a farmer's son in this Thai folktale. (Rev: BL 1/15/95; SLJ 11/94) [398.2]

7233 Merrill, Jean. *The Girl Who Loved Caterpillars: A Twelfth-Century Tale from Japan* (5–8). Illus. by Floyd Cooper. 1992, Putnam $16.99 (978-0-399-21871-2). The story of a young Izumi who has no interest in lute playing or writing poetry but is fascinated with "creepy crawlies" instead. (Rev: BCCB 11/92; BL 9/1/92*; SLJ 9/92) [398.2]

7234 Napoli, Donna Jo. *Bound* (7–12). 2004, Simon & Schuster $16.95 (978-0-689-86175-8). In this multilayered and thought-provoking Cinderella tale that draws on traditional Chinese elements, Xing Xing is mistreated by her stepmother and stepsister after the death of the girl's beloved father, but she escapes the cruel foot binding inflicted on her stepsister. (Rev: BL 12/1/04*; SLJ 11/04; VOYA 2/05)

7235 Riordan, James. *Tales from the Arabian Nights* (7–9). 1985, Checkerboard $14.95 (978-1-56288-258-7). Among the 10 stories retold are those of Sinbad, Ali Baba, and Aladdin. (Rev: SLJ 3/86) [398.2]

7236 Tarnowska, Wafa'. *The Arabian Nights* (4–8). Illus. by Carole Hénaff. 2010, Barefoot $24.99 (978-1-84686-122-2). Eight of Scheherazade's tales — including Aladdin but also ones that will not be familiar to most children — are presented with evocative illustrations. (Rev: BL 1/1–15/11; SLJ 2/1/11*) [398.2]

7237 Vuong, Lynette Dyer. *The Brocaded Slipper and Other Vietnamese Tales* (5–7). Illus. by Vo-Dinh Mai. 1982, HarperCollins paper $4.95 (978-0-06-440440-2). Five Vietnamese fairy tales, some of which are similar to our own. [398.2]

7238 Williams, Marcia. *The Elephant's Friend and Other Tales from Ancient India* (3–7). Illus. by author. 2012, Candlewick $16.99 (978-076365916-5). Eight Indian animal folktales are retold here and accompanied by colorful comic book illustrations. (Rev: BL 10/1/12; HB 11–12/12; LMC 3–4/13; SLJ 7/12) [398.2]

7239 Yep, Laurence. *The Rainbow People* (7–10). 1989, HarperCollins $16.00 (978-0-06-026760-5); paper $6.99 (978-0-06-440441-9). The retelling of 20 Chinese folktales with illustrations by David Wiesner. (Rev: BL 4/1/89; SLJ 5/89) [398.2]

Australia and the Pacific Islands

7240 Flood, Bo, and Beret E. Strong. *Pacific Island Legends: Tales from Micronesia, Melanesia, Polynesia, and Australia* (6–12). Illus. by Connie J. Adams. 1999, Bess $22.95 (978-1-57306-084-4); paper $14.95 (978-1-57306-078-3). The ocean's impact on island life is a theme that runs through many of these tales, which are organized in geographical groupings with introductions on each area's culture and history. (Rev: HBG 4/00; SLJ 10/99) [398.2]

7241 Oodgeroo. *Dreamtime: Aboriginal Stories* (6–10). 1994, Lothrop $16.00 (978-0-688-13296-5). Traditional and autobiographical stories of aboriginal culture and its roots. Also examines current aboriginal life alongside white civilization. (Rev: BCCB 1/99; BL 10/1/94; SLJ 10/94) [398.2]

7242 Te Kanawa, Kiri. *Land of the Long White Cloud: Maori Myths, Tales and Legends* (7–12). 1997, Pavilion paper $17.95 (978-1-86205-075-4). A group of magical Maori folktales about sea gods, fairies, monsters, and fantastic voyages, retold by the famous opera singer from New Zealand. (Rev: BL 9/1/97) [398.2]

Europe

7243 Afanasév, Aleksandr. *Russian Fairy Tales* (7–12). 1976, Pantheon paper $18.00 (978-0-394-73090-5). This is a standard collection of traditional Russian tales. [398]

7244 Collodi, Carlo. *The Adventures of Pinocchio* (5–7). Illus. by Iassen Ghiuselev. 2002, Simply Read $29.95 (978-0-9688768-0-0). The full text of the original is used here with effective black-and-white illustrations and several full-page watercolors. (Rev: BL 4/1/02)

7245 Delamare, David. *Cinderella* (7–12). 1993, Simon & Schuster paper $15.00 (978-0-671-76944-4). The familiar story is set in a locale much like Venice and enhanced by Delamare's paintings, both realistic and surreal. (Rev: BCCB 11/00; BL 9/15/93; SLJ 12/93) [398.2]

7246 Green, Roger L. *Adventures of Robin Hood* (5–9). 1994, Knopf $15.00 (978-0-679-43636-2); paper $4.99 (978-0-14-036700-3). The exploits of this folk hero are retold in this reissue of a classic version. [398]

7247 Grimm Brothers. *Household Stories of the Brothers Grimm* (4–7). Illus. by Walter Crane. 1963, Dover paper $9.95 (978-0-486-21080-3). First published in the United States in 1883. [398.2]

7248 Grimm Brothers. *The Three Feathers* (5–8). Illus. by Eleonore Schmid. 1984, Creative Editions LB $13.95 (978-0-87191-941-0). A version for older readers that is faithful to the original. [398.2]

7249 Kilgannon, Eily. *Folktales of the Yeats Country* (5–8). 1990, Mercier paper $10.95 (978-0-85342-861-9). Seventeen folktales that originate in County Sligo in Ireland. (Rev: BL 8/90; SLJ 2/91) [398.2]

7250 Krull, Kathleen, ed. *A Pot o' Gold: A Treasury of Irish Stories, Poetry, Folklore and (of Course) Blarney* (4–8). Illus. by David McPhail. 2004, Hyperion $16.99 (978-0-7868-0625-6). This is a comprehensive collection — including riddles, blessing, and battle cries — with attractive and appropriate illustrations. (Rev: BL 2/15/04; SLJ 3/04) [820.8]

7251 Leavy, Una. *Irish Fairy Tales and Legends* (4–8). 1997, Roberts Rinehart $18.95 (978-1-57098-177-7). An attractive book that contains 10 Irish legends, some going back 2,000 years. (Rev: BL 2/1/98; HBG 10/98; SLJ 2/98) [398.2]

7252 Levine, Gail Carson. *Ella Enchanted* (5–8). 1997, HarperCollins LB $17.89 (978-0-06-027511-2). A spirited, cleverly plotted retelling of the Cinderella story in which Ella is finally paired with the Prince Charmant. (Rev: BCCB 5/97; BL 4/15/97*; HB 5–6/97; SLJ 4/97*; VOYA 8/97)

7253 Matthews, John. *Arthur of Albion* (4–8). Illus. by Pavel Tatarnikov. 2008, Barefoot $24.99 (978-184686049-2). This compendium includes ten Arthurian legends ranging from familiar to obscure and interspersed with background information. (Rev: BLO 10/15/08) [398.2]

7254 Miles, Bernard. *Robin Hood: His Life and Legend* (7–9). 1979, Checkerboard $12.95 (978-1-56288-412-3). A collection of tales about this English folk hero and his merry men. [398.2]

7255 Molnar, Irma. *One-Time Dog Market at Buda and Other Hungarian Folktales* (5–8). Illus. by Georgeta-Elena Enesel. 2001, Linnet $25.00 (978-0-208-02505-0). A collection of 23 clever, thought-provoking Hungarian folktales for older readers. (Rev: BL 1/1–15/02; HBG 3/02; SLJ 2/02) [398.2]

7256 Morpurgo, Michael. *Beowulf* (7–10). Illus. by Michael Foreman. 2006, Candlewick $17.99 (978-0-7636-3206-9). A retelling of the ancient story that does not leave out any gory details and that captures the atmosphere of the original through both prose and illustrations. (Rev: BL 3/1/07; LMC 4–5/07; SLJ 12/06) [398.2]

7257 Nye, Robert. *Beowulf: A New Telling* (7–9). 1982, Dell paper $4.99 (978-0-440-90560-8). A retelling in modern English of the monster Grendel and the hero Beowulf. [398.2]

7258 Prokofiev, Sergei. *Peter and the Wolf* (4–8). Adapted by Miguelanxo Prado. Illus. by author. 1998, NBM $15.95 (978-1-56163-200-8). A somber version of the Russian folktale filled with menacing situations and scary settings. (Rev: HBG 10/98; SLJ 6/98) [398.2]

7259 Pyle, Howard. *The Merry Adventures of Robin Hood of Great Renown in Nottinghamshire* (7–9). Series: Illustrated Classics. 1968, Peter Smith $29.25 (978-0-8446-2765-6); paper $10.95 (978-0-486-22043-7). The classic (first published in 1883) retelling of 22 of the most famous stories. e [398.2]

7260 Pyle, Howard. *The Story of King Arthur and His Knights* (8–12). 1973, Peter Smith $25.75 (978-0-8446-2766-3); paper $12.95 (978-0-486-21445-0). A retelling that has been in print since its first publication in 1903. [398.2]

7261 Pyle, Howard. *The Story of Sir Launcelot and His Companions* (7–12). 1991, Dover paper $13.95 (978-0-486-26701-2). This book of episodes in the Arthurian legend is noteworthy because of the illustrations of Howard Pyle. [398.2]

7262 Pyle, Howard. *The Story of the Grail and the Passing of Arthur* (5–8). Illus. by author. 1985, Macmillan

paper $12.95 (978-0-486-27361-7). The last title of a four-volume King Arthur series, first published in 1910. (Rev: BL 12/15/85) [398.2]

7263 Radunsky, Vladimir. *The Mighty Asparagus* (4–7). 2004, Harcourt $16.00 (978-0-15-216743-1). In this entertaining version of the Russian folktale "The Enormous Turnip" with eye-catching illustrations full of artistic allusions, a gigantic stalk of asparagus sprouts in the courtyard of an Italian king. (Rev: BL 5/15/04; SLJ 7/04) [398.2]

7264 Raven, Nicky. *Beowulf: A Tale of Blood, Heat, and Ashes* (6–12). Illus. by John Howe. 2007, Candlewick $18.99 (978-0-7636-3647-0). This is a beautifully illustrated retelling of the epic story. (Rev: BL 11/15/07; SLJ 2/08) [398.2]

7265 Rumford, James. *Beowulf: A Hero's Tale Retold* (5–8). Illus. by reteller. 2007, Houghton Mifflin $17.00 (978-0-618-75637-7). Beautifully illustrated, this is a simplified retelling of the ancient tale about the warrior who defeats the monster Grendel. (Rev: BCCB 11/07; BL 8/07; HB 7–8/07; SLJ 8/07) [398.2]

7266 Sauvant, Henriette. *Rapunzel and Other Magic Fairy Tales* (4–7). Trans. by Anthea Bell. Illus. by author. 2008, Egmont $15.95 (978-1-4052-2702-5). Retellings of fourteen fairy tales, many of them by the Grimm brothers, and some of them grim or even grisly, accompanied by lush illustrations. (Rev: BL 5/1/08; SLJ 7/08) [398.2]

7267 Spariosu, Mihai I., and Dezso Benedek. *Ghosts, Vampires, and Werewolves: Eerie Tales from Transylvania* (6–10). 1994, Orchard LB $19.99 (978-0-531-08710-7). An anthology of horror tales by two authors who heard the stories as children living in the Transylvanian Alps. (Rev: BL 10/15/94; SLJ 10/94) [398.2]

7268 Sutcliff, Rosemary, retel. *Beowulf* (5–8). Retold by Rosemary Sutcliff. Illus. by Charles Keeping. 1984, Smith $24.50 (978-0-8446-6165-0). This is a reissue of the Anglo-Saxon tale published originally in 1962. Also use the King Arthur story, *The Sword and the Circle* (1981, Dutton). [398.2]

7269 Talbott, Hudson. *Lancelot* (5–7). 1999, Morrow LB $15.89 (978-0-688-14833-1). A retelling of the life of Lancelot, from his rescue as a child by the Lady of the Lake to his love for Guinevere, marriage to Elaine, and fathering of Galahad. (Rev: BL 9/1/99; HBG 3/00; SLJ 10/99) [398.2]

7270 Vivian, E. Charles. *The Adventures of Robin Hood* (6–9). n.d., Airmont paper $1.75 (978-0-8049-0067-6). The principal stories about Robin Hood and his men are retold in this inexpensive edition. [398]

7271 Walker, Barbara K., ed. *A Treasury of Turkish Folktales for Children* (4–7). 1988, Shoe String LB $25.00 (978-0-208-02206-6). A witty collection interspersed with riddles. (Rev: BL 10/15/88; SLJ 10/88) [398.2]

7272 Whipple, Laura. *If the Shoe Fits* (5–8). Illus. by Laura Beingessner. 2002, Simon & Schuster $17.95 (978-0-689-84070-8). A handsome retelling of the Cinderella story using blank verse. (Rev: BCCB 3/02; BL 5/1/02; HBG 10/02; SLJ 8/02) [398.2]

7273 Wolfson, Evelyn. *King Arthur and His Knights in Mythology* (6–9). Series: Mythology. 2002, Enslow LB $26.60 (978-0-7660-1914-0). The myths and legends surrounding King Arthur are retold with valuable historical background material. (Rev: BL 12/15/02; HBG 3/03) [398]

7274 Wyly, Michael. *King Arthur* (7–10). Series: Mystery Library. 2001, Lucent LB $27.45 (978-1-56006-771-9). An engrossing account that explores the fact and fiction surrounding this legendary king and his knights. (Rev: BL 9/15/01) [942]

North America

GENERAL AND MISCELLANEOUS

7275 Currie, Stephen. *African American Folklore* (7–12). Series: Lucent Library of Black History. 2008, Gale/Lucent $32.45 (978-1-4205-0082-0). In chapters on folk stories, folk songs, jokes and rhymes, and roots and influences, Currie explores the genre. (Rev: SLJ 2/1/09) [398.08996]

7276 Gerson, Mary-Joan. *Fiesta Feminina: Celebrating Women in Mexican Folktales* (4–8). 2001, Barefoot Bks $19.99 (978-1-84148-365-8). This volume includes eight tales from Mexican folklore about strong and magical women, presented with bold illustrations, a pronunciation guide, and a glossary. (Rev: BL 9/15/01; HBG 3/02; SLJ 10/01) [398.2]

7277 Kirwan, Anna. *Lady of Palenque: Flower of Bacal, Mesoamerica, c.e. 749* (6–9). 2004, Scholastic $10.95 (978-0-439-40971-1). In this gripping adventure, ShahnaK'in Yaxchel Pacal, a 13-year-old Maya princess, embarks on a dangerous journey to meet her future husband. (Rev: BL 5/15/04; SLJ 7/04)

7278 McManus, Kay. *Land of the Five Suns* (6–8). Series: Looking at Myths and Legends. 1997, NTC $12.95 (978-0-8442-4762-5). Classic Aztec myths, including creation stories and tales of Aztec gods, are retold in novelized format. (Rev: SLJ 4/98) [398.2]

7279 Madrigal, Antonio H. *The Eagle and the Rainbow: Timeless Tales from México* (4–7). Illus. by Tomie dePaola. 1997, Fulcrum $15.95 (978-1-55591-317-5). A collection of wise, wonderful, but little-known folktales from Mexico. (Rev: BL 7/97; HBG 4/04) [398.2]

7280 Montejo, Victor, retel. *Popol Vuh: A Sacred Book of the Maya* (5–8). Trans. by David Under. Retold by Victor Montejo. Illus. by Luis Garay. 1999, Groundwood $19.95 (978-0-88899-334-2). A creation story from the Mayans in a beautifully designed book that features

gods, giants, mortals, and animals. (Rev: HBG 3/00; SLJ 12/99) [398.2]

7281 Philip, Neil, ed. *Horse Hooves and Chicken Feet: Mexican Folktales* (4–8). Illus. by Jacqueline Main. 2003, Clarion $19.00 (978-0-618-19463-6). Bright folk-art illustrations accompany 14 stories that feature humor and the importance of the Catholic church. (Rev: BL 10/15/03; HBG 4/04; SLJ 9/03) [398.2]

7282 Turenne Des Pres, Francois. *Children of Yayoute: Folktales of Haiti* (6–9). 1994, Universe $19.95 (978-0-87663-791-3). Traditional folktales that depict Haitian history and customs. Includes paintings that illustrate island life. (Rev: BL 10/1/94; SLJ 1/95) [398.2]

NATIVE AMERICANS

7283 Bierhorst, John. *The Way of the Earth: Native America and the Environment* (7–12). 1994, Morrow $15.00 (978-0-688-11560-9). Explores the mythologic and folkloric patterns of Native American belief systems. (Rev: BL 5/15/94; SLJ 5/94; VOYA 10/94) [179]

7284 Bruchac, Joseph. *Native American Animal Stories* (5–8). 1992, Fulcrum paper $12.95 (978-1-55591-127-0). Animal stories from various Native American tribes, for reading aloud and storytelling. (Rev: BL 9/1/92; SLJ 11/92) [398.2]

7285 Bruchac, Joseph. *Native Plant Stories* (4–8). 1995, Fulcrum paper $12.95 (978-1-55591-212-3). A collection of stories about plants that come from various Native American cultures in North and Central America. (Rev: BL 9/1/95) [398.24]

7286 Connolly, James E. *Why the Possum's Tail Is Bare: And Other North American Indian Nature Tales* (4–7). 1992, Stemmer $15.95 (978-0-88045-069-0); paper $7.95 (978-0-88045-107-9). Nature and folklore are combined in 13 Native American animal tales. (Rev: BL 9/1/85; SLJ 10/85) [398.2]

7287 Goble, Paul. *The Legend of the White Buffalo Woman* (4–8). 1998, National Geographic $16.95 (978-0-7922-7074-4). In this picture book for older readers recounting a Lakata Indian tale, an earth woman and an eagle mate after a great flood to produce a new people. (Rev: BL 3/15/98; HBG 10/98; SLJ 5/98) [398.2]

7288 Highwater, Jamake. *Anpao: An American Indian Odyssey* (5–8). Illus. by Fritz Scholder. 1993, HarperCollins paper $8.99 (978-0-06-440437-2). A young hero encounters great danger on his way to meet his father, the Sun, in this dramatic American Indian folktale. [398.2]

7289 Hillerman, Tony, ed. *The Boy Who Made Dragonfly: A Zuni Myth* (5–7). Illus. by Laszlo Kubinyi. 1986, Univ. of New Mexico paper $11.95 (978-0-8263-0910-5). A Zuni boy and his little sister are left behind by their tribe and survive hunger and deprivation through the intervention of the Cornstalk Being. [398.2]

7290 Martin, Rafe. *The World Before This One* (5–8). Illus. by Calvin Nichols. 2002, Scholastic paper $16.95 (978-0-590-37976-2). Crow, a Seneca Indian, comes upon a storytelling stone that tells him about the origins of the earth in this series of stories. (Rev: BL 2/15/03; HBG 3/03; SLJ 12/02; VOYA 2/03) [398.2]

7291 Mayo, Gretchen Will. *Star Tales: North American Indian Stories About the Stars* (4–7). Illus. by author. 1987, Walker LB $13.85 (978-0-8027-6673-1). Fourteen tales, each introduced by a one-page commentary on a constellation. (Rev: BL 6/15/87; SLJ 5/87) [398.2]

7292 Philip, Neil, ed. *The Great Mystery: Myths of Native America* (8–12). 2001, Clarion $25.00 (978-0-395-98405-5). A collection of creation and other stories from many Native American tribes, organized by region. (Rev: BL 11/15/01; HBG 10/02; SLJ 11/01) [398.2]

7293 Pijoan, Teresa. *White Wolf Woman: Native American Transformation Myths* (7–12). 1992, August House paper $11.95 (978-0-87483-200-6). Drawn from a wide range of Indian tribes, a collection of 37 stories about animal and human transformations and connections. (Rev: BL 10/1/92) [398.2]

7294 Shenandoah, Joanne, and Douglas M. George-Kanentiio. *Skywoman: Legends of the Iroquois* (4–8). 1998, Clear Light $14.95 (978-0-940666-99-3). Good writing and effective artwork are combined in this retelling of nine traditional Iroquois tales, including a series of creation stories. (Rev: HBG 10/99; SLJ 2/99) [398.2]

7295 Tingle, Tim. *Spirits Dark and Light: Supernatural Tales from the Five Civilized Tribes* (6–9). 2006, August House $15.95 (978-0-87483-778-0). A collection of 25 Native American folk tales from the southeastern United States that involve supernatural creatures and themes. (Rev: BL 11/1/06; LMC 2/07; SLJ 1/07) [398.2]

7296 Tingle, Tim. *Walking the Choctaw Road* (6–12). 2003, Cinco Puntos $16.95 (978-0-938317-74-6). A collection of stories that convey Choctaw traditions and culture, including experiences on the Trail of Tears. (Rev: BL 6/1–15/03; HBG 4/04; VOYA 2/04) [398.2]

7297 Van Etten, Teresa. *Ways of Indian Magic* (7–12). 1985, Sunstone paper $8.95 (978-0-86534-061-9). A fine retelling of six legends of the Pueblo Indians. [398.2]

7298 Van Etten, Teresa. *Ways of Indian Wisdom* (7–10). 1987, Sunstone paper $10.95 (978-0-86534-090-9). A collection of 20 Pueblo tales that reflect the Southeastern Indians' culture and customs. [398.2]

7299 Webster, M. L, retel. *On the Trail Made of Dawn: Native American Creation Stories* (4–9). Retold by M. L. Webster. 2001, Linnet LB $19.50 (978-0-208-02497-8). The author retells 13 creation stories and places

them in cultural context. (Rev: HBG 3/02; SLJ 12/01) [398.2]

7300 Wolfson, Evelyn. *Inuit Mythology* (5–9). Illus. by William Sauts Bock. Series: Mythology. 2001, Enslow LB $26.60 (978-0-7660-1559-3). Seven tales from Inuit folklore are accompanied by information on the history and culture of the Inuit peoples. (Rev: BL 4/15/02; HBG 3/02; SLJ 3/02) [398.2]

UNITED STATES

7301 Anaya, Rudolfo. *My Land Sings: Stories from the Rio Grande* (5–9). 1999, Morrow $17.00 (978-0-688-15078-5). A magical collection of 10 stories, set mostly in New Mexico, that deal with Mexican and Native American folklore. (Rev: BL 8/99; HBG 10/00; SLJ 9/99) [398.2]

7302 Avila, Kat, ed. *Mexican Ghost Tales of the Southwest* (7–9). 1994, Arte Publico paper $9.95 (978-1-55885-107-8). A collection of Mexican tales of ghosts and the spirit world from the Southwest. (Rev: BL 10/1/94; SLJ 9/94; VOYA 4/95) [398.25]

7303 Brown, Marcia. *Backbone of the King: The Story of Paka'a and His Son Ku* (5–7). Illus. by author. 1984, Univ. of Hawaii $19.00 (978-0-8248-0963-8). A reissue of the book based on a Hawaiian legend of a boy who wants to help his exiled father. [398.2]

7304 Cohen, Daniel. *Southern Fried Rat and Other Gruesome Tales* (6–10). 1989, Avon paper $3.50 (978-0-380-70655-6). A collection of stories — some funny, some grisly — about people living in urban areas today. [398.2]

7305 Hamilton, Virginia. *Her Stories: African American Folktales, Fairy Tales, and True Tales* (5–8). 1995, Scholastic paper $22.95 (978-0-590-47370-5). Nineteen tales about African American females are retold in the wonderful style of Virginia Hamilton. (Rev: BL 11/1/95*; SLJ 11/95*) [398.2]

7306 Hamilton, Virginia. *The People Could Fly: American Black Folk Tales* (4–9). Illus. by Leo Dillon and Diane Dillon. 1985, Knopf LB $18.99 (978-0-394-96925-1); paper $13.00 (978-0-679-84336-8). A retelling of 24 folktales — some little known, others familiar, such as Tar Baby. (Rev: BCCB 7/85; BL 7/85; SLJ 11/85) [398.2]

7307 Jacobs, Jimmy. *Moonlight Through the Pines: Tales from Georgia Evenings* (5–7). 2000, Franklin-Sarrett paper $11.95 (978-0-9637477-3-0). A collection of humorous reminiscences, family stories, tall tales, and other examples of folklore, all from the South. (Rev: BL 8/00) [398.2]

7308 Reneaux, J. J. *Cajun Folktales* (6–8). 1992, August House $19.95 (978-0-87483-283-9); paper $11.95 (978-0-87483-282-2). An assortment of Cajun folktales divided into broad groups: animal tales, fairy tales, funny folk tales, and ghost stories. (Rev: BL 9/15/92) [398.2]

7309 Reneaux, J. J. *Haunted Bayou: And Other Cajun Ghost Stories* (4–8). 1994, August House paper $9.95 (978-0-87483-385-0). Thirteen scary, entertaining folktales from Cajun country are retold effectively. (Rev: SLJ 12/94) [398.2]

7310 Rhyne, Nancy. *More Tales of the South Carolina Low Country* (7–9). 1984, Blair paper $9.95 (978-0-89587-042-1). A collection of eerie and unusual folktales. [398.2]

7311 Rounds, Glen. *Ol' Paul, the Mighty Logger* (6–8). 1976, Holiday paper $5.95 (978-0-8234-0713-2). The colorful saga of the great tall-tale hero of American folklore. [398.2]

7312 Schwartz, Alvin. *More Scary Stories to Tell in the Dark* (4–7). Illus. by Stephen Gammell. 1984, Harper-Collins LB $16.89 (978-0-397-32082-0); paper $5.99 (978-0-06-440177-7). Brief tales from folk stories and hearsay with a scary bent. [398.2]

7313 Schwartz, Alvin. *Scary Stories to Tell in the Dark* (6–9). 1981, HarperCollins LB $16.89 (978-0-397-31927-5). Stories about ghosts and witches that are mostly scary but often also humorous. Continued in *More Scary Stories to Tell in the Dark* (1984). [398.2]

7314 Shepherd, Esther. *Paul Bunyan* (7–10). 1941, Harcourt paper $6.95 (978-0-15-259755-9). The tall-tale lumberjack is brought to life by the text and the stunning illustrations by Rockwell Kent. [398.2]

South and Central America

7315 Aldana, Patricia, ed. *Jade and Iron: Latin American Tales from Two Cultures* (5–8). Trans. by Hugh Hazelton. 1996, Douglas & McIntyre $18.95 (978-0-88899-256-7). Fourteen folktales on a variety of subjects and from many regions in Latin America are retold in this large-format picture book. (Rev: BCCB 1/97; BL 12/1/96) [398.2]

7316 Delacre, Lulu, retel. *Golden Tales: Myths, Legends, and Folktales from Latin America* (4–8). Retold by Lulu Delacre. 1996, Scholastic paper $18.95 (978-0-590-48186-1). Twelve important Latin American folktales from before and after the time of Columbus are featured. (Rev: BL 12/15/96; SLJ 9/96) [398.2]

7317 Dorson, Mercedes, and Jeanne Wilmot. *Tales from the Rain Forest: Myths and Legends from the Amazonian Indians of Brazil* (5–8). 1997, Ecco $18.00 (978-0-88001-567-7). Ten entertaining folktales from the Amazonian Indians of Brazil. (Rev: BL 2/15/98; HB 3–4/98; HBG 10/98) [398.2]

7318 Ehlert, Lois. *Moon Rope: A Peruvian Folktale* (4–8). 1992, Harcourt $17.00 (978-0-15-255343-2). In both English and Spanish, this is the story of Fox, who wants to go to the moon and persuades his friend Mole to go along. (Rev: BCCB 12/92; BL 10/15/92*; HB 11–12/92; SLJ 10/92*) [398.2]

7319 Kimmel, Eric A. *The Witch's Face: A Mexican Tale* (7–12). 1993, Holiday $15.95 (978-0-8234-1038-5). Kimmel uses a picture book format for this Mexican tale of a man who rescues his love from becoming a witch, only to lose her to his own doubt. (Rev: BL 11/15/93; SLJ 2/94) [398.22]

7320 Munduruku, Daniel. *Tales of the Amazon: How the Munduruku Indians Live* (5–8). Trans. by Jane Springer. Illus. by Laurabeatriz. 2000, Groundwood $18.95 (978-0-88899-392-2). This is an interesting view of the life of the human inhabitants of the Amazon rain forest with material on lifestyles, houses, languages, myths, and marriage. (Rev: BL 9/1/03; HBG 3/01; SLJ 9/00) [981]

7321 Schuman, Michael A. *Mayan and Aztec Mythology* (6–9). Series: Mythology. 2002, Enslow LB $26.60 (978-0-7660-1409-1). As well as retelling famous myths from the Aztec and Mayan cultures, this account gives good historical background information. (Rev: BL 4/15/02; HBG 10/02) [398.2]

Mythology

General and Miscellaneous

7322 Berk, Ari. *The Runes of Elfland* (7–12). Illus. by Brian Froud. 2003, Abrams $25.00 (978-0-8109-4612-5). Brief stories and wonderful art highlighting the rune's significance and associations accompany each of 24 runes. (Rev: SLJ 5/04; VOYA 2/04) [398.2]

7323 Bingham, Ann. *South and Meso-American Mythology A to Z* (6–12). Series: Mythology A to Z. 2004, Facts on File $40.00 (978-0-8160-4889-2). A handsome and thorough guide to the legends and folklore of early civilizations in Central and South America. (Rev: BL 10/1/04; SLJ 2/05) [398.2]

7324 Bini, Renata. *A World Treasury of Myths, Legends, and Folktales: Stories from Six Continents* (6–9). 2000, Abrams $24.95 (978-0-8109-4554-8). Stories from around the world are organized geographically in this handsome, large-format volume full of rich illustrations. (Rev: BL 1/1–15/01; HBG 3/01; SLJ 12/00) [291.1]

7325 Boughn, Michael. *Into the World of the Dead: Astonishing Adventures in the Underworld* (5–8). 2006, Annick LB $24.95 (978-1-55037-959-4); paper $12.95 (978-1-55037-958-7). This illustrated collection of myths and legends from diverse cultures includes a variety of gods, monsters, and heroes who survived travels to the Underworld. (Rev: SLJ 1/07) [398.2]

7326 Dalal, Anita. *Myths of Oceania* (5–8). Series: Mythic World. 2002, Raintree LB $27.12 (978-0-7398-4978-1). Information about Oceania and its people is included as well as 10 myths about the sea, fishing, and other unique aspects of island living. (Rev: BL 7/02; HBG 10/02) [398.3]

7327 Dalal, Anita. *Myths of Russia and the Slavs* (5–8). Series: Mythic World. 2002, Raintree LB $27.12 (978-0-7398-4979-8). This lavishly illustrated, oversize vol-

ume contains 10 myths from Eastern Europe as well as material on the society that created them. (Rev: BL 7/02; HBG 10/02; SLJ 5/02) [398.2]

7328 Echlin, Kim. *Inanna: From the Myths of Ancient Sumer* (7–12). Illus. by Linda Wolfsgruber. 2003, Groundwood $19.95 (978-0-88899-496-7). The stories of the powerful goddess Inanna and her adventures in love and war, based on 4,000-year-old sources. (Rev: BL 3/1/04; HBG 4/04; SLJ 3/04; VOYA 12/03) [398.2]

7329 Evslin, Bernard. *Pig's Ploughman* (7–12). 1990, Chelsea LB $19.95 (978-1-55546-256-7). In Celtic mythology, Pig's Ploughman is the huge hog who fights Finn McCool. (Rev: BL 8/90; SLJ 3/91) [398.2]

7330 Fisher, Leonard Everett. *Gods and Goddesses of the Ancient Maya* (4–7). 1999, Holiday $16.95 (978-0-8234-1427-7). This book provides a fascinating introduction to Mayan mythology by describing 10 gods and two goddesses. (Rev: BL 2/1/00; HBG 3/00; SLJ 12/99) [299]

7331 Green, Jen. *Myths of China and Japan* (5–8). Series: Mythic World. 2002, Raintree LB $27.12 (978-0-7398-4977-4). This handsome, oversize book explores the ancient mythology of China and Japan and, in addition to the retelling of 10 myths, contains information on the societies that created them. (Rev: BL 7/02; HBG 10/02) [398.2]

7332 Hamilton, Dorothy. *Mythology* (8–12). 1942, Little, Brown $27.95 (978-0-316-34114-1). An introduction to the mythology of Greece and Scandinavia, plus a retelling of the principal myths. [292]

7333 Harpur, James. *Celtic Myth: A Treasury of Legends, Art, and History* (8–12). Series: World Mythology. 2007, M.E. Sharpe LB $35.95 (978-0-7656-8102-7). A collection of artifacts of ancient Celtic culture, including myths (some violent), weapons, and artwork. (Rev: BL 12/15/07; LMC 2/08; SLJ 4/08) [299]

7334 Harris, Geraldine. *Gods and Pharaohs from Egyptian Mythology* (5–8). Illus. by David O'Connor and John Sibbick. 1992, Bedrick LB $24.95 (978-0-87226-907-1). A collection of myths and legends from ancient Egypt. [398.2]

7335 January, Brendan. *The New York Public Library Amazing Mythology: A Book of Answers for Kids* (5–8). 2000, Wiley paper $14.95 (978-0-471-33205-3). This compendium of information covers Middle Eastern, African, Mediterranean, Asian, Pacific, Northern European, and North and Central American mythology. (Rev: BL 11/1/00; SLJ 9/00) [291.1]

7336 Lynch, Patricia Ann. *Native American Mythology A to Z* (6–12). Series: Mythology A to Z. 2004, Facts on File $40.00 (978-0-8160-4891-5). A handsome and thorough guide to Native American legends and folklore. (Rev: BL 10/1/04; SLJ 2/05) [398.2]

7337 Malam, John. *Dragons* (4–7). Series: Mythologies. 2010, Black Rabbit LB $28.50 (978-1-59566-982-7). Malam looks at dragons, with and without wings, in legends around the world; with color illustrations and many sidebars, this book is aimed at reluctant readers. Also use *Fairies, Giants,* and *Monsters.* (Rev: LMC 10/10; SLJ 4/1/10) [398.24]

7338 Mutén, Burleigh, retel. *The Lady of Ten Thousand Names: Goddess Stories from Many Cultures* (4–7). Retold by Burleigh Mutén. Illus. by Helen Cann. 2001, Barefoot $19.99 (978-1-84148-048-0). Eight myths that feature goddesses from cultures around the world are retold in this appealing volume. (Rev: HBG 3/02; SLJ 11/01) [291.2]

7339 Nardo, Don. *Egyptian Mythology* (6–12). Series: Mythology. 2001, Enslow $26.60 (978-0-7660-1407-7). Eight Egyptian myths are related here, with background historical and cultural information, question-and-answer sections, and commentary from scholars. (Rev: BL 5/15/01; SLJ 5/01) [299]

7340 Ollhoff, Jim. *Indian Mythology* (4–7). Series: The World of Mythology. 2011, ABDO LB $27.07 (978-1-61714-722-7). With chapters on Brahma, Vishnu, Shiva, and Kali, this is a clear introduction to Hindu gods and goddesses. (Rev: BL 2/1/12; SLJ 12/1/11) [398.20954]

7341 Ollhoff, Jim. *Japanese Mythology* (4–7). Series: The World of Mythology. 2011, ABDO LB $27.07 (978-1-61714-723-4). With chapters on Amaterasu, O-Kuni-Nushi, and Jimmu, this is a clear introduction to Japanese gods and goddesses. (Rev: BL 2/1/12; SLJ 12/1/11) [398.20952]

7342 Ollhoff, Jim. *Mayan and Aztec Mythology* (4–7). Series: The World of Mythology. 2011, ABDO LB $27.07 (978-1-61714-724-1). This appealing introduction to the mythology and legends of the Mayan and Aztec cultures features concise text and eye-catching illustrations and reproductions. (Rev: BL 2/1/12; SLJ 12/1/11) [972.81]

7343 Ollhoff, Jim. *Middle Eastern Mythology* (4–7). Series: The World of Mythology. 2011, ABDO LB $27.07 (978-1-61714-725-8). This appealing introduction to the mythology and legends of the Middle East provides information on various Mesopotamian and Canaanite gods and goddesses. (Rev: BL 2/1/12; SLJ 12/1/11) [398.20939]

7344 Philip, Neil. *The Illustrated Book of Myths: Tales and Legends of the World* (5–8). Illus. by Nilesh Mistry. 1995, DK paper $19.99 (978-0-7894-0202-8). Ancient myths from both the Old World and the New World have been collected under such headings as creation, destruction, and fertility. (Rev: BL 12/1/95; SLJ 12/95; VOYA 4/96) [291.1]

7345 Philip, Neil. *Mythology of the World* (8–12). 2004, Houghton Mifflin $24.95 (978-0-7534-5779-5). An excellent and thorough overview of world mythology, introducing readers to the plots and characters of myth and legend and examining the historical, cultural, and spiritual aspects of mythology. (Rev: BL 12/1/04; SLJ 10/04) [398.2]

7346 Roberts, Jeremy. *Japanese Mythology A to Z* (6–12). Series: Mythology A to Z. 2003, Facts on File $40.00 (978-0-8160-4871-7). An easy-to-use alphabetically arranged volume introducing important places, practices and rituals, people, creatures, and so forth, with guidance on pronunciation. (Rev: SLJ 4/04) [299]

7347 Ross, Anne. *Druids, Gods and Heroes of Celtic Mythology* (6–10). 1994, Bedrick LB $24.95 (978-0-87226-918-7); paper $14.95 (978-0-87226-919-4). An oversized book that gives detailed information on Irish and Welsh Celtic mythology as well as material on King Arthur. (Rev: SLJ 2/87) [291.1]

7348 Schomp, Virginia. *The Ancient Egyptians* (5–7). Series: Myths of the World. 2007, Marshall Cavendish LB $22.95 (978-0-7614-2549-6). Schomp provides background information on the myths of ancient Egypt and retells several of the best-known ones; full-color illustrations add to the appeal. (Rev: LMC 3/08; SLJ 1/08)

7349 Schomp, Virginia. *The Native Americans* (5–7). Series: Myths of the World. 2007, Marshall Cavendish LB $22.95 (978-0-7614-2550-2). Schomp provides background information on the myths of the Native Americans and retells several of the best-known ones; full-color illustrations add to the appeal. (Rev: LMC 3/08; SLJ 1/08)

7350 Tchana, Katrin Hyman. *Changing Woman and Her Sisters* (5–8). Illus. by Trina Schart Hyman. 2006, Holiday $18.95 (978-0-8234-1999-9). An illustrated collection of traditional stories about ten goddesses from a variety of lesser-known cultures, including Celtic, ancient Mayan, Shinto, Buddhist, and Navajo. (Rev:

BCCB 9/06; BL 6/1–15/06; HB 7–8/06; HBG 10/06; LMC 1/07; SLJ 8/06) [398.2]

7351 Tomlinson, Theresa. *The Moon Riders* (6–9). 2006, HarperCollins $16.99 (978-0-06-084736-4). Myrina, 13, a member of the Moon Riders (a group of warrior women better known as the Amazons), tells about the Trojan War and the role the Moon Riders play as allies to the Trojans. (Rev: BL 11/1/06; SLJ 12/06)

7352 Welsh, M. L. *Mistress of the Storm: A Verity Gallant Tale* (4–8). 2011, Random House $16.99 (978-0-385-75244-2); LB $19.99 (978-0-385-75245-9). Twelve-year-old Verity's life takes a turn for the eventful when she uncovers family secrets that lead to a confrontation with a powerful witch. The second installment in the series is *Heart of Stone* (2012). **e** Lexile 750L (Rev: LMC 11–12/11; SLJ 10/1/11*; VOYA 6/11)

Classical

7353 Aesop. *Aesop's Fables* (7–12). 1988, Scholastic paper $4.50 (978-0-590-43880-3). This is one of many editions of the short moral tales from ancient Greece. (Rev: BCCB 12/00) [398.2]

7354 Bryant, Megan E. *Oh My Gods! A Look-It-Up Guide to the Gods of Mythology* (4–7). Series: Mythlopedia. 2010, Franklin Watts LB $39 (978-1-6063-1026-7). An irreverent, highly graphic volume that succeeds in conveying lots of information in an entertaining manner; with a useful map of ancient Greece, pronunciation guides, and a list of top 10 things to know about each divine being. Companion volumes are *All in the Family! A Look-It-Up Guide to the In-Laws, Outlaws, and Offspring of Mythology* (2009), *She's All That! A Look-It-Up Guide to the Goddesses of Mythology* and *What a Beast! A Look-It-Up Guide to the Monsters and Mutants of Mythology* (both 2010). (Rev: BL 10/1/09; LMC 3–4/10) [398.2]

7355 Cadnum, Michael. *Nightsong: The Legend of Orpheus and Eurydice* (7–10). 2006, Scholastic $16.99 (978-0-439-54535-8). The story of Orpheus traveling to the underworld to bring back his bride, Eurydice, only to lose her is retold as a novel. (Rev: BL 12/15/06; LMC 3/07; SLJ 4/07)

7356 Catran, Ken. *Voyage with Jason* (5–8). 2003, Lothian paper $10.95 (978-0-7344-0151-9). A new twist on the story of Jason and the Argonauts, narrated by a youth who is part of the eventful three-year quest for the Golden Fleece and concentrating on character as well as adventure. (Rev: SLJ 4/04) [398.2]

7357 Curlee, Lynn. *Mythological Creatures: A Classical Bestiary* (4–8). Illus. by author. 2008, Atheneum $17.99 (978-1-4169-1453-2). A beautiful book with dreamy color illustrations of creatures that roam through classical mythology, such as gryphons, the Minotaur, Cer-

berus, and centaurs; each illustration is accompanied by comments about the creature's part in mythology. (Rev: BL 4/1/08; SLJ 5/08) [292.2]

7358 Daly, Kathleen N. *Greek and Roman Mythology A to Z. Rev. ed.* (6–12). Series: Mythology A to Z. 2003, Facts on File $40.00 (978-0-8160-5155-7). A newly updated, easy-to-use volume containing more than 500 entries of differing lengths covering places, practices and rituals, people, creatures, and so forth. (Rev: BL 3/1/04; SLJ 4/04; VOYA 6/04) [292]

7359 DiPrimio, Pete. *The Sphinx* (4–7). Illus. Series: Monsters in Myth. 2010, Mitchell Lane LB $21.50 (978-158415931-5). This volume explores the role of the Sphinx in Greek and Egyptian mythology. (Rev: BL 6/1/11) [398.2209182]

7360 Evslin, Bernard. *The Adventures of Ulysses: The Odyssey of Homer* (8–12). 1989, Scholastic paper $5.99 (978-0-590-42599-5). A modern retelling of the adventures of Ulysses during the 10 years he wandered after the Trojan War. [292]

7361 Evslin, Bernard. *Anteus* (6–9). 1988, Chelsea LB $19.95 (978-1-55546-241-3). A retelling of the story of Hercules and his battle against the horrible giant Anteus. Also use by the same author *Hecate* (1988). (Rev: BL 9/1/88) [292]

7362 Evslin, Bernard. *Cerberus* (6–12). 1987, Chelsea LB $19.95 (978-1-55546-243-7). The story of the three-headed dog in Greek mythology that guards the gates of Hell. Also in this series are *The Dragons of Boeotia* and *Geryon* (both 1987). (Rev: BL 11/15/87; SLJ 1/88) [398.2]

7363 Evslin, Bernard. *The Chimaera* (6–10). 1987, Chelsea LB $19.95 (978-1-55546-244-4). This ugly, dangerous creature is composed of equal parts lion, goat, and reptile. Another in the series is *The Sirens* (1987). (Rev: BL 3/1/88) [398.2]

7364 Evslin, Bernard. *The Cyclopes* (6–12). 1987, Chelsea LB $19.95 (978-1-55546-236-9). The story of the ferocious one-eyed monster and how he was blinded by Ulysses. Others in this series about mythical monsters are *Medusa, The Minotaur,* and *Procrustes* (all 1987). (Rev: BL 6/15/87; SLJ 8/87) [398.2]

7365 Evslin, Bernard. *The Furies* (7–12). 1989, Chelsea LB $19.95 (978-1-55546-249-9). In Greek mythology the Furies were three witches. This retelling also includes the story of Circe, the famous sorceress. (Rev: BL 12/15/89; SLJ 4/90) [398.21]

7366 Evslin, Bernard. *Heroes, Gods and Monsters of Greek Myths* (8–12). 1984, Bantam paper $5.99 (978-0-553-25920-9). The most popular Greek myths are retold in modern language. (Rev: SLJ 2/06) [292]

7367 Evslin, Bernard. *Ladon* (7–12). 1990, Chelsea LB $19.95 (978-1-55546-254-3). A splendid retelling of the Greek myth about the sea serpent called up by Hera to fight Hercules. (Rev: BL 8/90) [398.24]

7368 Evslin, Bernard. *The Trojan War: The Iliad of Homer* (8–12). 1988, Scholastic paper $2.95 (978-0-590-41626-9). The story of the 10-year war between the Greeks and the Trojans is retold for the modern reader. [292]

7369 Graves, Robert. *Greek Gods and Heroes* (6–8). 1973, Dell paper $5.50 (978-0-440-93221-5). Tales of 12 of the most important figures in Greek mythology in 27 short chapters. (Rev: SLJ 2/06) [292]

7370 Green, Jen. *Myths of Ancient Greece* (5–8). Series: Mythic World. 2001, Raintree LB $27.12 (978-0-7398-3191-5). This volume for older readers separates myth from reality about ancient Greece. (Rev: BL 3/1/02; HBG 3/02; SLJ 12/01) [398.2]

7371 Harris, John. *Strong Stuff: Herakles and His Labors* (4–7). Illus. by Gary Baseman. 2005, Getty $16.95 (978-0-89236-784-9). A lively, tongue-in-cheek account of the 12 labors of ancient Greece's mythical strongman, Herakles (known to the ancient Romans as Hercules). (Rev: BL 11/15/05; SLJ 11/05) [398.2]

7372 Hawthorne, Nathaniel. *Wonder Book and Tanglewood Tales* (5–7). 1972, Ohio State Univ. $72.95 (978-0-8142-0158-9). This is a highly original retelling of the Greek myths, originally published in 1853. (Rev: BL 2/15/04; SLJ 4/04) [398.2]

7373 Kelly, Sophia. *What a Beast: A Look-It-Up Guide to the Monsters and Mutants of Mythology* (4–7). Illus. Series: Mythlopedia. 2009, Scholastic LB $39 (978-160631028-1); paper $13.95 (978-160631060-1). Greek and Roman mythology is given a fresh, modern spin in this irreverent guide to the multi-dimensional beasts of legend. (Rev: BL 3/1/10; LMC 3–4/10*) [398.2]

7374 Kindl, Patrice. *Lost in the Labyrinth* (6–10). 2002, Houghton Mifflin $16.00 (978-0-618-16684-8). Told by Xenodice, a 14-year-old princess and the younger sister of Ariadne, this is an expanded version of the legend of Theseus and the Minotaur. (Rev: BCCB 11/02; BL 1/1–15/03; HB 11–12/02; HBG 3/03; SLJ 11/02; VOYA 2/03)

7375 McCarty, Nick, retel. *The Iliad* (4–8). Retold by Nick McCarty. Illus. by Victor G. Ambrus. 2000, Kingfisher paper $15.95 (978-0-7534-5321-6). This account of the Trojan War uses an exciting text and action-packed illustrations. (Rev: SLJ 1/01) [398.2]

7376 Napoli, Donna Jo. *Treasury of Greek Mythology: Classic Stories of Gods, Goddesses, Heroes and Monsters* (4–7). Illus. by Christina Balit. 2011, National Geographic $24.95 (978-1-4263-0844-4); LB $33.90 (978-1-4263-0845-1). This large, eye-catching volume introduces 25 major characters in Greek mythology, outlining each one's origins, realm of power, and legendary story lines; the lyrical text is enhanced by humor

and helpful back matter. ALA Notable Books 2012. (Rev: BL 12/1/11; SLJ 10/1/11*) [398.2]

7377 *Odysseus* (4–8). Retold by Geraldine McCaughrean. 2004, Cricket $15.95 (978-0-8126-2721-3). Homer's dramatic story is retold in rhythmic prose. (Rev: BL 12/15/04; SLJ 12/04)

7378 *The Odyssey* (4–7). Retold by Gillian Cross. Illus. by Neil Packer. 2012, Candlewick $19.99 (978-076364791-9). A handsome retelling with compelling text and rich, varied illustrations. (Rev: BL 12/1/12; LMC 5–6/13; SLJ 1/13)

7379 Orr, Tamra. *The Sirens* (4–7). Illus. 2010, Mitchell Lane LB $21.50 (978-158415930-8). This volume explores the importance of the sirens in mythologies around the Mediterranean. (Rev: BL 6/1/11) [398.20938]

7380 Pickels, Dwayne E. *Roman Myths, Heroes, and Legends* (5–8). Series: Costume, Tradition, and Culture: Reflecting on the Past. 1998, Chelsea $28.00 (978-0-7910-5164-1). Using double-page spreads and old collectors' cards as illustrations, this work retells the major Roman myths and introduces their important characters. (Rev: BL 3/15/99; HBG 10/99) [398.2]

7381 Rylant, Cynthia. *The Beautiful Stories of Life: Six Greek Myths, Retold* (6–9). Illus. by Carson Ellis. 2009, Harcourt $16 (978-0-15-206184-5). The stories of Pandora, Persephone, Orpheus, Pygmalion, Narcissus, and Psyche are retold here, accompanied by black-and-white illustrations. ⌂ (Rev: HB 5–6/09; SLJ 5/1/09) [398.2]

7382 Schomp, Virginia. *The Ancient Greeks* (5–7). Series: Myths of the World. 2007, Marshall Cavendish LB $22.95 (978-0-7614-2547-2). Schomp provides background information on the myths of ancient Greece and retells several of the best-known ones; full-color illustrations add to the appeal. (Rev: LMC 3/08; SLJ 1/08)

7383 Spies, Karen Bornemann. *Heroes in Greek Mythology* (6–9). Series: Mythology. 2002, Enslow LB $26.60 (978-0-7660-1560-9). Through an introduction to the heroes in Greek mythology, many of the most famous myths are retold. (Rev: BL 4/15/02; HBG 10/02) [292]

7384 Spies, Karen Bornemann. *The Iliad and the Odyssey in Greek Mythology* (6–9). Series: Mythology. 2002, Enslow LB $26.60 (978-0-7660-1561-6). The two great epics of Homer are retold with many original illustrations and with useful historical background material. (Rev: BL 12/15/02; HBG 3/03; VOYA 8/03) [292]

7385 Spinner, Stephanie. *Quicksilver* (8–11). 2005, Knopf LB $17.99 (978-0-375-92638-9). Hermes, son of Zeus and quite a character in this incarnation, describes his participation in various well-known myths. (Rev: BCCB 4/05; BL 4/15/05; HB 3–4/05; SLJ 9/05; VOYA 4/05)

7386 Spinner, Stephanie. *Quiver* (7–12). 2002, Knopf LB $17.99 (978-0-375-91489-8). A deft retelling of the Greek myth of Atalanta, who will marry only a man who can outrun her. (Rev: BCCB 2/03; BL 1/1–15/03*; HB 1–2/03; HBG 3/03; SLJ 10/02; VOYA 12/02)

7387 Tracy, Kathleen. *Cerberus* (4–7). Illus. Series: Monsters in Myth. 2010, Mitchell Lane LB $21.50 (978-158415924-7). This volume explores the mythological importance of the three-headed dog. (Rev: BL 6/1/11) [398.20938]

7388 Usher, Kerry. *Heroes, Gods and Emperors from Roman Mythology* (8–12). 1992, NTC LB $24.95 (978-0-87226-909-5). The origins of Roman mythology are given, accompanying retellings of famous myths. [292]

7389 Woff, Richard. *A Pocket Dictionary of Greek and Roman Gods and Goddesses* (4–8). 2003, Getty $9.95 (978-0-89236-706-1). Varied reproductions from the British Museum add visual appeal to this brief who's who. (Rev: SLJ 2/04) [292.2]

7390 Wolfson, Evelyn. *Roman Mythology* (6–9). Series: Mythology. 2002, Enslow LB $26.60 (978-0-7660-1558-6). This is a general introduction to Roman mythology with a retelling of the major stories and an introduction to important characters. (Rev: BL 12/15/02; HBG 3/03) [398]

Scandinavian

7391 Coville, Bruce. *Thor's Wedding Day* (4–7). 2005, Harcourt $15.00 (978-0-15-201455-1). A hilarious retelling of an ancient Norse poem, in which Thor's goat boy describes how he helped Thor to retrieve his stolen magic hammer. (Rev: BL 8/05) [398.2]

7392 Daly, Kathleen N. *Norse Mythology A to Z. Rev. ed.* (6–12). Series: Mythology A to Z. 2003, Facts on File $40.00 (978-0-8160-5156-4). A newly updated, easy-to-use volume containing approximately 400 entries covering places, practices and rituals, people, creatures, and so forth. (Rev: BL 3/1/04; SLJ 4/04; VOYA 6/04) [292.1]

7393 Schomp, Virginia. *The Norsemen* (5–7). Series: Myths of the World. 2007, Marshall Cavendish LB $22.95 (978-0-7614-2548-9). Schomp provides background information on the myths of Scandinavia and retells several of the best-known ones; full-color illustrations add to the appeal. (Rev: LMC 3/08; SLJ 1/08)

Humor and Satire

7394 Mash, Robert. *How to Keep Dinosaurs. Rev. ed.* (7–12). 2003, Weidenfeld & Nicolson $14.99 (978-0-297-84347-4). A tongue-in-cheek cleverly illustrated guide to the selection and care of your own pet prehistoric animal. (Rev: SLJ 4/04; VOYA 8/04)

7395 Sedaris, David. *Dress Your Family in Corduroy and Denim* (8–12). 2004, Little, Brown $24.95 (978-0-316-14346-2). In this collection of 27 essays, David Sedaris mines humor from a series of incidents in his personal life, some of which were not at all funny when they happened. (Rev: SLJ 1/05) [813]

Speeches, Essays, and General Literary Works

7396 Davis, Jill, ed. *Open Your Eyes: Extraordinary Experiences in Faraway Places* (8–12). 2003, Viking $16.99 (978-0-670-03616-5). Ten writers, among them Lois Lowry and Harry Mazer, tell stories about how travel changed their lives. (Rev: BL 1/1–15/04; HBG 4/04; SLJ 1/04; VOYA 4/04) [910.4]

7397 Halliburton, Warren J., ed. *Historic Speeches of African Americans* (7–12). Series: African American Experience. 1993, Watts LB $24.00 (978-0-531-11034-8). Chronologically organized speeches by such leaders as Sojourner Truth, Frederick Douglass, Marcus Garvey, James Baldwin, Angela Davis, and Jesse Jackson. (Rev: BL 4/15/93; SLJ 7/93) [815]

7398 *Lines in the Sand: New Writing on War and Peace* (6–10). 2003, Disinformation paper $7.95 (978-0-9729529-1-0). More than 150 children from around the world have written essays, stories, and memoirs or drawn pictures calling for peace. (Rev: BL 2/1/04) [808.803]

7399 McIntire, Suzanne, ed. *The American Heritage Book of Great American Speeches for Young People* (7–12). 2001, Wiley paper $14.95 (978-0-471-38942-2). More than 100 key speeches by individuals ranging from politicians to athletes are provided in this single volume. (Rev: SLJ 12/01) [815.008]

7400 *Merlyn's Pen: Fiction, Essays, and Poems by American Teens* (6–12). 2001, Merlyn's Pen paper $15.95 (978-1-886427-50-1). This annual anthology of teen writings offers selected poetry, fiction, and essays written by students in middle school and high school. (Rev: VOYA 8/01)

7401 Meyer, Stephanie H., and John Meyer, eds. *Friends and Family* (6–12). Series: Teen Ink. 2001, Health Communications paper $12.95 (978-1-55874-931-3). This collection of fiction, poetry, and essays written by young people that appeared in *Teen Ink* magazine is organized by themes such as "Snapshots: Friends and Family" and "Out of Focus: Facing Challenges." (Rev: BL 1/1–15/02; SLJ 12/01) [810.8]

7402 Meyer, Stephanie H., and John Meyer, eds. *Love and Relationships* (6–12). Series: Teen Ink. 2002, Health Communications paper $12.95 (978-1-55874-969-6). In this collection of poems, essays, and photographs, teens give voice to their thoughts about love in all its many forms. e (Rev: SLJ 8/02; VOYA 8/02) [810.8]

7403 Meyer, Stephanie H., and John Meyer, eds. *Teen Ink 2: More Voices, More Visions* (6–12). Series: Teen Ink. 2001, Health Communications paper $12.95 (978-1-55874-913-9). This collection of teen creativity includes poems, essays, short stories, and photographs that reflect their views on such themes as Family, Love, Friends, Challenges, Imagination, Fitting In, Memories, and School Days. e (Rev: SLJ 8/01; VOYA 12/01)

7404 Rosen, Roger, and Patra McSharry, eds. *East-West: The Landscape Within* (7–12). Series: World Issues. 1992, Rosen LB $21.95 (978-0-8239-1375-6); paper $11.95 (978-0-8239-1376-3). Short stories and nonfiction selections by diverse authors of varied nationalities on their cultures' beliefs and values, among them the Dalai Lama, Joseph Campbell, Lydia Minatoya, and Aung Aung Taik. (Rev: BL 12/15/92; SLJ 2/93) [909]

7405 Stone, Miriam. *At the End of Words: A Daughter's Memoir* (6–12). 2003, Candlewick $14.00 (978-0-7636-1854-4). Moving poetry and narrative describe the author's grief and emotional upheaval over her mother's death from cancer. (Rev: BL 4/15/03; HBG 10/03; SLJ 5/03; VOYA 12/03) [362.1]

7406 WritersCorps Youth. *Smart Mouth: Poetry and Prose by WritersCorps Youth* (7–12). 2000, San Francisco WritersCorps paper $12.95 (978-1-888048-05-6). This anthology offers multiple selections of both prose and poetry written by students who participated in the WritersCorps program. (Rev: VOYA 6/01)

Literary History and Criticism

General and Miscellaneous

7407 Alexander, Carol. *How to Tell a Folktale* (3–8). Series: Text Styles. 2012, Crabtree LB $26.60 (978-0-7787-1631-0); paper $8.95 (978-0-7787-1636-5). This volume explains how to identify folktales, looking at dialogue, setting, plot, theme, characters, and so forth, and gives tips on creative writing. Lexile IG530L (Rev: SLJ 5/1/12) [398.2]

7408 Currie, Stephen. *African American Literature* (7–10). Illus. Series: Lucent Library of Black History. 2011, Gale/Lucent LB $33.45 (978-142050383-8). Useful for researchers, this is a review of African American literature from the 1600s forward. (Rev: BL 2/1/12; SLJ 2/12) [810.9]

7409 Hahn, Daniel, and Leonie Flynn, eds. *The Ultimate Teen Book Guide* (7–12). 2008, Walker paper $16.95 (978-0-8027-9731-5). This well-organized guide contains more than 700 well-written reviews of teen fiction, nonfiction, classics and graphic novels. (Rev: SLJ 3/08)

7410 Rosen, Suri. *How to Tell a Fable* (3–8). Series: Text Styles. 2012, Crabtree LB $26.60 (978-0-7787-1630-3); paper $8.95 (978-0-7787-1635-8). This volume explains how to identify fables, looking at dialogue, setting, plot, theme, characters, and so forth, and gives tips on creative writing. (Rev: SLJ 5/1/12)

Fiction

General and Miscellaneous

7411 Barlowe, Wayne Douglas, and Neil Duskis. *Barlowe's Guide to Fantasy* (7–12). 1996, HarperCollins paper $19.95 (978-0-06-100817-7). Using double-page spreads, this handsome book covers the history of fantasy literature from ancient times to the present by highlighting 50 examples, among them *Beowulf*, *Wind in the Willows*, and *Mists of Avalon*. (Rev: VOYA 10/97)

7412 Reid, Suzanne Elizabeth. *Presenting Young Adult Science Fiction* (7–12). Series: Twayne's United States Authors. 1998, Twayne $35.00 (978-0-8057-1653-5). This comprehensive introduction to science fiction describes the history of the genre, profiles such classical masters as Asimov, Bradbury, Heinlein, and Le Guin, and presents members of the new generation, among them Orson Scott Card, Pamela Service, Piers Anthony, and Douglas Adams. (Rev: SLJ 6/99) [808.3]

Europe

Great Britain and Ireland

7413 Brontë, Charlotte. *Jane Eyre* (8–12). Ed. by Beth Newman. Series: Case Studies in Contemporary Criticism. 1964, St. Martin's paper $18.74 (978-031209545-1). An author biography is accompanied by brief critical comments, plot and theme analysis, and a list of characters.

7414 Brown, Alan. *The Story Behind George Orwell's Animal Farm* (6–9). Series: History in Literature. 2006, Heinemann LB $32.86 (978-1-4034-8203-7). Brown introduces readers to Orwell's life, times, and influences. (Rev: SLJ 2/07)

United States

7415 Cart, Michael. *Presenting Robert Lipsyte* (8–12). 1995, Twayne $29.00 (978-0-8057-4151-3). A probing look at Lipsyte's life and work. (Rev: BL 6/1–15/95; VOYA 6/96) [813]

7416 Crowe, Chris. *Presenting Mildred D. Taylor* (6–12). Series: United States Authors. 1999, Twayne $39.00 (978-0-8057-1687-0). As well as some biographical material, this book gives an analysis of Taylor's works, their historical context, and a history of racism and the civil rights movement in Mississippi. (Rev: BL 2/15/00; VOYA 6/00) [813]

7417 Curry, Barbara K., and James Michael Brodie. *Sweet Words So Brave: The Story of African American Literature* (5–8). 1996, Zino $24.95 (978-1-55933-179-1). An outline of African American literature, from slave narratives to the great writers of today, such as Nikki Giovanni and Toni Morrison. (Rev: BL 2/15/97*; SLJ 4/97) [810.9]

7418 Glenn, Wendy J. *Laurie Halse Anderson: Speaking in Tongues* (7–12). Illus. Series: Scarecrow Studies in Young Adult Literature. 2010, Scarecrow $40 (978-081087281-3). This well-researched volume analyzes the works of YA author Laurie Halse Anderson and includes excerpts from interviews, blog posts, and essays by the author. (Rev: BLO 1/1–15/10; VOYA 4/10) [813]

7419 Johnson-Feelings, Dianne. *Presenting Laurence Yep* (8–12). 1995, Twayne $35.00 (978-0-8057-8201-1). A biocritical study that uses material from the Chinese American's autobiography, *The Lost Garden*. (Rev: BL 12/15/95) [813]

7420 MacRae, Cathi Dunn. *Presenting Young Adult Fantasy Fiction* (7–12). 1998, Twayne $35.00 (978-0-8057-8220-2). An excellent survey of current writers of fantasy plus in-depth interviews with Terry Brooks,

Barbara Hambly, Jane Yolen, and Meredith Ann Pierce. (Rev: BL 1/1–15/99; VOYA 8/98) [813]

7421 Pingelton, Timothy J. *A Student's Guide to Ernest Hemingway* (7–12). Series: Understanding Literature. 2005, Enslow LB $27.93 (978-0-7660-2431-1). Introduces Hemingway's life and works, with analysis of some of his best-known writings. (Rev: SLJ 10/05) [813]

7422 *A Student's Guide to Jack London* (7–12). Series: Understanding Literature. 2007, Enslow LB $20.95 (978-0-7660-2707-7). Provides summaries and critical analysis of London's most famous books as well as

information on his life and beliefs. (Rev: BL 9/1/07) [813]

7423 Vickers, Rebecca. *The Story Behind Mark Twain's The Adventures of Huckleberry Finn* (6–9). Series: History in Literature. 2006, Heinemann LB $32.86 (978-1-4034-8206-8). Vickers introduces readers to Twain's life, times, and influences. (Rev: SLJ 2/07)

7424 Williams, Brian. *The Story Behind John Steinbeck's Of Mice and Men* (6–9). Series: History in Literature. 2006, Heinemann LB $32.86 (978-1-4034-8207-5). Williams introduces readers to Steinbeck's life, times, and influences. (Rev: SLJ 2/07)

Plays and Poetry

General and Miscellaneous

7425 Deutsch, Babette. *Poetry Handbook: A Dictionary of Terms. 4th ed.* (7–12). 1981, Barnes & Noble paper $14.00 (978-0-06-463548-6). The standard introduction to the technical aspects of poetry through definitions of terms with examples. [808.1]

7426 Lewis, J. Patrick. *When Thunder Comes: Poems for Civil Rights Leaders* (4–7). Illus. by Jim Burke. 2013, Chronicle $16.99 (978-145210119-4). With rich and diverse images this collection of poems introduces 17 civil rights leaders from countries around the world. (Rev: BL 2/15/13*; SLJ 4/13) [811]

7427 Lithgow, John, ed. *The Poet's Corner: The One-and-Only Poetry Book for the Whole Family* (7–12). 2007, Grand Central $24.99 (978-0-446-58002-1). Well-known poems by English and American poets are accompanied by conversational commentary, quotations, and other items of interest. ☊ (Rev: BL 10/15/07) [821.008]

7428 Vecchione, Patrice, ed. *The Body Eclectic: An Anthology of Poems* (8–12). 2002, Henry Holt $16.95 (978-0-8050-6935-8). A collection of poems, both contemporary and classic, that look at parts of the body from serious, comic, tragic, reflective, and romantic points of view. (Rev: BL 7/02; HB 7–8/02; HBG 10/02; SLJ 8/02; VOYA 8/02) [808.81]

Europe

Shakespeare

7429 Greenhill, Wendy, and Paul Wignall. *Macbeth. Rev. ed.* (6–9). Series: Shakespeare Library. 2006, Heinemann LB $29.29 (978-1-4034-8606-6). Information on *Macbeth* is abundant in this slim book, covering the plot, characters, historical background, actors' viewpoints, themes, and past productions; it also includes illustrations and photographs of recent plays. Also use *Romeo and Juliet* and *A Midsummer Night's Dream* (both 2006). (Rev: SLJ 8/06)

7430 Olster, Fredi, and Rick Hamilton. *A Midsummer Night's Dream: A Workbook for Students* (8–12). Series: Discovering Shakespeare. 1996, Smith & Kraus paper $19.95 (978-1-57525-042-7). The text of the play is presented in a double-page, four-column format that provides stage directions, scene description, and the original text, plus a version in the vernacular. Supplemental background material is also appended. (Rev: BL 1/1–15/97; SLJ 12/96; VOYA 2/97) [822.3]

7431 Olster, Fredi, and Rick Hamilton. *Romeo and Juliet: A Workbook for Students* (8–12). Series: Discovering Shakespeare. 1996, Smith & Kraus paper $19.95 (978-1-57525-044-1). This Shakespearean tragedy is presented in a four-column format that gives the original text, stage directions, scene descriptions, and a reworking into modern English. (Rev: BL 1/1–15/97; VOYA 2/97) [822.3]

7432 Olster, Fredi, and Rick Hamilton. *The Taming of the Shrew* (7–12). Series: Discovering Shakespeare. 1997, Smith & Kraus paper $19.95 (978-1-57525-046-5). This guide to Shakespeare's comedy uses a paraphrased text opposite the original script with details on stage directions. (Rev: BL 2/15/97; SLJ 6/97; VOYA 2/97) [822.3]

7433 Page, Philip, and Marilyn Pettit, eds. *Romeo and Juliet* (8–11). Series: Picture This! Shakespeare. 2005, Barron's paper $7.99 (978-0-7641-3144-8). This attractive title uses both straight text and cartoon characters to present not only the full text of Shakespeare's tragic romance but also notes on devices and related information. (Rev: BL 3/15/05; SLJ 9/05) [745.1]

United States

7434 Borus, Audrey. *A Student's Guide to Emily Dickinson* (7–12). Series: Understanding Literature. 2005, Enslow LB $27.93 (978-0-7660-2285-0). Introduces Dickinson's life and poetry, with discussion of key themes, how to analyze the poems, and a glossary of terms. (Rev: SLJ 10/05) [813]

7435 Dunkleberger, Amy. *A Student's Guide to Arthur Miller* (7–12). Series: Understanding Literature. 2005, Enslow LB $27.93 (978-0-7660-2432-8). Combines biographical information and discussion of Miller's key works. (Rev: SLJ 10/05) [813]

7436 MacGowan, Christopher, ed. *Poetry for Young People: William Carlos Williams* (6–12). Illus. by Robert Crockett. 2004, Sterling $14.95 (978-1-4027-0006-4). Thirty-one poems by Williams plus biographical and critical material are included in this excellent collection. (Rev: BL 3/1/04) [811]

7437 Silverstein, Shel. *Every Thing On It* (2–7). Illus. by author. 2011, HarperCollins $19.99 (978-0-06-199816-4). This posthumous Silverstein collection features drawings and poems taken from the author's personal archive and never previously published. (Rev: BL 9/1/11; SLJ 9/1/11*) [811]

Language and Communication

Signs and Symbols

7438 Ferry, Joseph. *The American Flag* (5–7). Series: American Symbols and Their Meanings. 2002, Mason Crest LB $18.95 (978-1-59084-026-9). Designs that preceded the familiar flag accompany material on Betsy Ross and Francis Scott Key, illustrations of important flag raisings, and discussion of proper use and treatment of the flag, all in a package that will appeal to reluctant readers. (Rev: SLJ 4/02) [929.9]

7439 Radlauer, Ruth. *Honor the Flag: A Guide to Its Care and Display* (4–7). Illus. by J. J. Smith Moore. 1992, Forest LB $14.95 (978-1-878363-61-9). Lots of information about the American flag and its care. (Rev: BL 10/15/92) [929.92]

7440 Williams, Earl P. *What You Should Know About the American Flag* (4–8). 1989, Thomas paper $5.95 (978-0-939631-10-0). A comprehensive guide to facts and legends, history and traditions concerning the U.S. flag. (Rev: BL 11/15/87) [929.9]

7441 Woods, Mary B., and Michael Woods. *Ancient Communication: From Grunts to Graffiti* (5–8). Series: Ancient Technologies. 2000, Runestone LB $25.26 (978-0-8225-2996-5). Beginning with cave paintings and hieroglyphics and ending with modern alphabets and universal languages, this account of the history of communication emphasizes ancient cultures. (Rev: BL 9/15/00; HBG 3/01; SLJ 1/01) [652]

Words and Languages

7442 *The Art of Reading: Forty Illustrators Celebrate RIF's 40th Anniversary* (7–10). 2005, Dutton $19.99 (978-0-525-47484-5). To mark Reading Is Fundamental's 40th birthday, 40 illustrators choose a favorite children's book, talk about its importance, and create an image that captures the spirit of the book; a large, attractive volume. (Rev: BL 7/05; SLJ 8/05*) [745.6]

7443 Bailey, LaWanda. *Miss Myrtle Frag, the Grammar Nag* (5–9). Illus. by Brian Strassburg. 2000, Absey paper $13.95 (978-1-888842-19-7). A clever book that explains key grammar rules through a series of witty letters from Miss Myrtle Frag. (Rev: SLJ 2/01) [415]

7444 Baker, Rosalie. *In a Word: 750 Words and Their Fascinating Stories and Origins* (4–8). Illus. by Tom Lopes. 2003, Cobblestone $17.95 (978-0-8126-2710-7). Useful for reference, this guide to the origins and meanings of words and phrases is drawn from a monthly column in *Cobblestone*. (Rev: BL 2/15/04; SLJ 4/04) [422]

7445 Bell-Rehwoldt, Sheri. *Speaking Secret Codes* (4–7). Series: Edge Books: Making and Breaking Codes. 2010, Capstone LB $26.65 (978-1-4296-4569-0). Readers learn about spoken codes and how to work with codes, with activities and photographs. Lexile 770L (Rev: SLJ 1/1/11) [302.2]

7446 Casagrande, June. *Grammar Snobs Are Great Big Meanies: A Guide to Language for Fun and Spite* (8–12). 2006, Penguin paper $14.00 (978-0-14-303683-8). A lighthearted review of the rules of grammar, from prepositions and split infinitives to new conventions for e-mail and text messaging. (Rev: BL 4/1/06) [428]

7447 Cooper, Kay. *Why Do You Speak as You Do? A Guide to World Languages* (5–8). Illus. by Brandon Kruse. 1992, Children's Press LB $14.85 (978-0-8027-8165-9). A simple yet lively presentation of linguistics. (Rev: BCCB 2/93; BL 1/15/93) [400]

7448 Dubosarsky, Ursula. *The Word Snoop* (5–8). Illus. by Tohby Riddle. 2009, Dial $16.99 (978-0-8037-3406-7). The character Word Snoop introduces readers to many aspects, old and new, some amazing, of the English language and includes puzzles, secret codes, and humor. (Rev: BLO 6/23/09; HB 9/09; SLJ 9/09) [400]

7449 Edwards, Wallace. *The Cat's Pajamas* (4–7). Illus. by author. 2010, Kids Can $18.95 (978-1-55453-308-4). Rich illustrations depicting animals acting out idioms make clear that these 26 figures of speech cannot be taken literally. Lexile AD820L (Rev: SLJ 2/1/11) [428]

7450 Edwards, Wallace. *Monkey Business* (4–8). 2004, Kids Can $16.95 (978-1-55337-462-6). Whimsical artwork introduces such common idioms as "opening a can of worms" and "a bull in a china shop"; readers will also enjoy looking for hidden monkeys. (Rev: BL 11/1/04; SLJ 9/04*) [423]

7451 Espinasse, Kristin. *Words in a French Life: Lessons in Love and Language from the South of France* (7–12). 2006, Simon & Schuster $18.00 (978-0-7432-8728-9). Beef up French vocabulary with this collection of amusing stories by an American living in France combined with useful lists of words and phrases. (Rev: BL 4/15/06) [305.81]

7452 Gorrell, Gena K. *Say What? The Weird and Mysterious Journey of the English Language* (7–12). 2009, Tundra paper $10.95 (978-0-88776-878-1). A clever and often amusing history of the English language that emphasizes external influences and language's ability to change with the times, with word exercises and guessing games. (Rev: SLJ 1/10; VOYA 2/10) [420.9]

7453 Gregory, Jillian. *Breaking Secret Codes* (4–7). Series: Edge Books: Making and Breaking Codes. 2010, Capstone LB $26.65 (978-1-4296-4568-3). Gregory looks at various kinds of codes and the methods used to break them. Also use *Making Secret Codes* (2010). Lexile 830L (Rev: SLJ 1/1/11) [652]

7454 Johnson, Stephen T. *Alphabet City* (4–7). 1995, Viking $16.99 (978-0-670-85631-2). A sophisticated alphabet book that consists of a series of paintings, each of which represents a letter. (Rev: BCCB 11/95; BL 1/1–15/96; HB 11–12/95; SLJ 1/96*) [421]

7455 Lederer, Richard. *The Circus of Words: Acrobatic Anagrams, Parading Palindromes, Wonderful Words on a Wire, and More Lively Letter Play* (5–8). Illus. by Dave Morice. 2001, Chicago Review paper $12.95 (978-1-55652-380-9). Lovers of words will find lots of entertainment in this selection of challenging exercises. (Rev: SLJ 8/01) [428.1]

7456 Preciado, Tony. *Super Grammar* (4–7). Illus. by Rhode Montijo. 2012, Scholastic paper $8.99 (978-0-545-42-515-5). In comic book style, superheroes introduce the basics of sentences, parts of speech, punctuation marks and so forth. Lexile 970L (Rev: BL 12/1/12; SLJ 12/12) [428]

7457 Shields, Carol Diggory. *English, Fresh Squeezed! 40 Thirst-for-Knowledge-Quenching Poems* (4–7). Illus. by Tony Ross. Series: BrainJuice. 2005, Handprint $14.95 (978-1-59354-053-1). A humorous, rhyming look at annoying grammatical and other rules of language, with appealing illustrations and useful mnemonic devices. (Rev: BL 2/15/04; HB 5–6/04; SLJ 5/05)

7458 Terban, Marvin. *The Dove Dove: Funny Homograph Riddles* (4–7). Illus. by Tom Huffman. 1988, Houghton Mifflin paper $7.95 (978-0-89919-810-1). Making homographs less puzzling. Also use *Mad As a Wet Hen! and Other Funny Idioms* (1987). (Rev: BL 1/1/89) [818.5402]

7459 Warner, Penny. *Signing Fun: American Sign Language Vocabulary, Phrases, Games and Activities* (4–8). Illus. by Paula Gray. 2006, Gallaudet Univ. paper $19.95 (978-1-56368-292-6). This fun-filled introduction to American Sign Language introduces the basic vocabulary of ASL and offers a wide selection of related games and puzzles. (Rev: SLJ 12/06) [419]

7460 Wilbur, Richard. *Opposites* (5–7). Illus. by author. 1991, Harcourt $11.95 (978-0-15-258720-8). Through verses and cartoonlike illustrations, antonyms are given for a series of words. [811.52]

Writing and the Media

General and Miscellaneous

7461 Bauer, Marion Dane. *Our Stories: A Fiction Workshop for Young Authors* (6–10). 1996, Clarion paper $6.95 (978-0-395-81599-1). Using critiques of 30 selections by students, the author explores such writing techniques as character development, dialogue, and point of view. (Rev: BL 10/15/96; SLJ 12/96; VOYA 12/96) [808.3]

7462 Bush, Valerie Chow, ed. *Jump: Poetry and Prose by WritersCorps Youth* (6–12). 2001, WritersCorps $12.95 (978-1-888048-06-3). This collection of prose and poetry showcases the creativity of teenage members of the San Francisco-based WritersCorps youth writing program. (Rev: VOYA 6/02)

7463 Currie, Stephen, ed. *Terrorism* (7–10). Series: Writing the Critical Essay. 2005, Gale LB $29.95 (978-0-7377-3206-1). Opposing viewpoints on terrorism are combined with tips for writing a succinct essay on the subject. (Rev: BL 3/1/06) [363.32]

7464 Donoughue, Carol. *The Story of Writing* (4–7). Illus. 2007, Firefly $19.95 (978-1-55407-306-1). From early alphabets through tablets and scrolls, illuminated manuscripts, and the printing press, this is an appealing introduction to the development of writing. (Rev: BL 1/1–15/08)

7465 Francis, Barbara. *Other People's Words: What Plagiarism Is and How to Avoid It* (6–12). Series: Issues in Focus Today. 2005, Enslow LB $31.93 (978-0-7660-2525-7). Practical suggestions about avoiding plagiarism are accompanied by examples of plagiarism through history and current instances of "borrowing" ideas and words. (Rev: SLJ 12/05)

7466 Jean, Georges. *Writing: The Story of Alphabets and Scripts* (7–12). Series: Discoveries. 1992, Abrams paper $12.95 (978-0-8109-2893-0). Traces the beginnings of writing from the development of alphabets to printing and bookmaking, emphasizing the technological rather than intellectual aspects of the process. (Rev: BL 7/92) [652.1]

7467 Jones, Diana Wynne. *Reflections: On the Magic of Writing* (8–12). 2012, Greenwillow $24.99 (978-006221989-3). This collection of 28 essays about Jones's life and works was compiled before the author's death and will be of interest to her fans, young and old; includes a foreword by Neil Gaiman. (Rev: BL 11/1/12; HB 1–2/13; SLJ 1/13) [823]

7468 Levine, Gail Carson. *Writing Magic: Creating Stories That Fly* (5–10). 2006, HarperCollins $16.99 (978-0-06-051961-2); paper $5.99 (978-0-06-051960-5). Well-known author Levine provides upbeat, practical tips on such topics as finding story ideas, character and plot development, and investigating the possibility of publication. (Rev: BL 12/15/06; SLJ 2/07*)

7469 Litwin, Laura Baskes. *Write Horror Fiction in 5 Simple Steps* (5–8). 2012, Enslow LB $23.93 (978-076603836-3). Basic tips on planning and research, organization, and publication accompany advice on writing, examples of the genre, and creepy ideas. (Rev: BL 10/1/12; LMC 5–6/13*) [808.3]

7470 Otfinoski, Steven. *Extraordinary Short Story Writing* (5–8). Illus. by Kevin Pope. Series: F. W. Prep. 2005, Watts LB $31.00 (978-0-531-16760-1). Tips and activities reinforce the information on writing different types of stories, choosing ideas, and using available resources effectively; a sample short story offers step-by-step guidance. (Rev: SLJ 2/06) [808]

7471 Rivera, Shelia. *The Media War* (5–8). Series: World in Conflict. 2004, ABDO LB $25.65 (978-1-59197-418-5). A brief overview of American journalism's impact on war from the Civil War to the U.S. invasion of Afghanistan. (Rev: BL 4/1/04) [070.1]

7472 Roy, Jennifer Rozines. *You Can Write a Story or Narrative* (4–8). Series: You Can Write! 2003, Enslow LB $22.60 (978-0-7660-2085-6). Sound advice for plotting and writing a wide array of different narratives, including adventure, history, fantasy, and folklore. (Rev: SLJ 1/04; VOYA 4/04) [808]

7473 Senn, Joyce. *The Young People's Book of Quotations* (5–10). 1999, Millbrook LB $39.90 (978-0-7613-0267-4). Beginning with "accomplishment" and ending with "zoos," this is a collection of 2,000 quotations of special interest to young people, arranged by topic. (Rev: BL 3/1/99*; SLJ 4/99) [082]

7474 Van Allsburg, Chris. *The Mysteries of Harris Burdick* (7–9). 1984, Houghton Mifflin LB $18.95 (978-0-395-35393-6). Fourteen drawings and captions invite the reader to write stories that explain them. (Rev: BL 9/86) [808]

7475 Wolf, Allan. *Immersed in Verse: An Informative, Slightly Irreverent and Totally Tremendous Guide to Living the Poet's Life* (6–12). Illus. by Tuesday Mourning. 2006, Sterling LB $14.95 (978-1-57990-628-3). A humorous and inspirational guide for young people interested in writing poetry, this is full of helpful tips and ends with useful appendixes. (Rev: SLJ 6/06*)

Books and Publishing

7476 *Dear Author: Students Write About the Books That Changed Their Lives* (5–9). 1995, Conari paper $9.95 (978-1-57324-003-1). A collection of young adults' letters to authors, both dead and alive, expressing, with wit and honesty, how the authors' books have affected them. (Rev: BL 1/1–15/96; SLJ 11/95) [028.5]

7477 Garcia, John. *The Success of Hispanic Magazine* (7–10). Series: Success. 1996, Walker LB $16.85 (978-0-8027-8310-3). A behind-the-scenes look at the magazine business, from starting out to marketing research, staffing, sales, circulation, and distribution. Traces an article from initial conception to final version and publication. (Rev: BL 5/15/96; SLJ 4/96) [051]

7478 Hamilton, John. *You Write It! Horror* (4–7). Illus. Series: You Write It! 2009, ABDO LB $17.95 (978-1-60453-506-8). Tips for budding horror writers cover inspiration, good work habits, effective plots, and how to get published. (Rev: BL 4/1/09) [808.3]

7479 Harper, Timothy, and Elizabeth Harper. *Your Name in Print: A Teen's Guide to Publishing for Fun, Profit and Academic Success* (8–12). 2005, St. Martin's paper $13.95 (978-0-312-33759-9). The Harpers (father and daughter) offer alternating how-to advice on writing and getting published in a variety of formats. (Rev: BL 9/1/05; SLJ 11/05; VOYA 8/05) [808]

7480 Myron, Vicki, and Bret Witter. *Dewey the Library Cat: A True Story* (4–8). 2010, Little, Brown $15.99 (978-0-316-06871-0). A kindhearted librarian takes pity when she finds a freezing kitten in the library's book return in this children's adaptation that focuses on Dewey's everyday adventures. (Rev: BL 5/15/10; LMC 8–9/10; SLJ 6/10) [636.80092]

7481 Rosinsky, Natalie M. *Graphic Content! The Culture of Comic Books* (6–10). Illus. Series: Pop Culture Revolutions. 2010, Compass Point LB $31.99 (978-0-7565-4241-2). The history of comics from Captain America to the modern world of Web comics is captured in this guide, which spotlights the medium's role in pop culture. (Rev: BL 4/1/10; SLJ 5/10) [780.9]

7482 Rosinsky, Natalie M. *Write Your Own Graphic Novel* (4–8). 2008, Compass Point LB $24.95 (978-075653856-9). Rosinsky introduces such helpful concepts as storyboarding, editing, and peer collaboration while providing photos of young writers at work and referencing familiar graphic novels. Lexile 1010L (Rev: BL 11/1/08; SLJ 3/1/09) [741.5]

7483 Slate, Barbara. *You Can Do a Graphic Novel* (7–12). Illus. 2010, Penguin paper $19.95 (978-1-59257-955-6). In addition to advice on drawing, writing, and layout, this volume discusses the creative process, creative block, and creating characters and includes a chapter of students' work. (Rev: SLJ 5/10) [741.5]

Print and Other Media

7484 Bausum, Ann. *Muckrakers: How Ida Tarbell, Upton Sinclair, and Lincoln Steffens Helped Expose Scandal, Inspire Reform, and Invent Investigative Journalism* (6–9). 2007, National Geographic $21.95 (978-1-4263-0137-7). An inspiring introduction to the work of writers who exposed scandals including conditions in the meatpacking industry and immoral practices by Standard Oil. ALA Notable Books 2008. (Rev: BL 11/1/07; LMC 4–5/08; SLJ 11/07) [070.4]

7485 Botzakis, Stergios. *Pretty in Print: Questioning Magazines* (4–7). Series: Fact Finders. Media Literacy. 2006, Capstone LB $22.60 (978-0-7368-6764-1). This book explores how magazines capture readers' attention, why they need to do so, and the influences they may have on society; it includes colorful graphics and interesting sidebars. (Rev: SLJ 6/07) [050]

7486 Bowers, Rick. *Superman versus the Ku Klux Klan: The True Story of How the Iconic Superhero Battled the Men of Hate* (6–10). Illus. 2012, National Geographic $16.95 (978-142630915-1); LB $25.90 (978-142630917-5). Tells the story of the creation of the Superman comics alongside the evolution of the Klan, emphasizing Superman's fight against prejudice and other evils. ℮ (Rev: BL 2/15/12; HB 3–4/12; SLJ 3/12*; VOYA 4/12) [741.5]

7487 Cohen, Daniel. *Yellow Journalism: Scandal, Sensationalism, and Gossip in the Media* (6–12). 2000, Twenty-First Century LB $22.90 (978-0-7613-1502-5). The history of tabloid journalism and sensation-driven media is the focus of this fascinating book that uses many modern cases as examples. (Rev: BL 5/15/00; SLJ 8/00) [302.23]

7488 Crewe, Sabrina. *War Correspondents* (4–7). Illus. Series: World's Most Dangerous Jobs. 2012, Crabtree LB $24.83 (978-077875103-8). A frank look at the dangers journalists face when they cover wars, with color photographs and quotations from primary sources. (Rev: BL 10/15/12) [070.4]

7489 Day, Nancy. *Sensational TV: Trash or Journalism?* (7–10). Series: Issues in Focus. 1996, Enslow LB $26.60 (978-0-89490-733-3). A history of tabloid journalism both in print and on TV, plus a discussion of present-day controversies surrounding it. (Rev: BL 4/1/96; SLJ 4/96; VOYA 6/96) [791.45]

7490 DeFalco, Tom. *Hulk: The Incredible Guide* (6–12). 2003, DK $24.99 (978-0-7894-9771-0). Full-color illustrations spanning 40 years of comics portray the Hulk's life and escapades in this oversize volume. Also use *X-Men: The Ultimate Guide* (2003). (Rev: BL 5/1/03) [741.5]

7491 Elish, Dan. *Screenplays* (6–10). Illus. Series: Craft of Writing. 2011, Marshall Cavendish LB $34.21 (978-160870501-6). This book made for aspiring filmmakers includes a brief history of film before delving deeper into the actual craft of creating a screenplay. (Rev: BL 10/1/11; VOYA 2/12) [808.2]

7492 Gourley, Catherine. *War, Women, and the News: How Female Journalists Won the Battle to Cover World War II* (6–9). 2007, Simon & Schuster $19.99 (978-0-689-87752-0). Readers will be fascinated by the obstacles that women journalists had to overcome to become war correspondents; photographs add interest. (Rev: BCCB 5/07; BL 1/1–15/07; LMC 8–9/07; SLJ 2/07) [070]

7493 Ketcham, Hank. *Hank Ketcham's Complete Dennis the Menace: 1955-1956* (7–12). 2006, Fantagraphics $24.95 (978-1-56097-770-4). A collection of the funny cartoons about Dennis and his antics. (Rev: BL 1/1–15/07) [741.5]

7494 Krensky, Stephen. *Comic Book Century: The History of American Comic Books* (5–8). Illus. Series: People's History. 2007, Lerner LB $30.60 (978-0-8225-6654-0). The history of comics is presented as a part of America's history in this illustration- and photo-filled volume. (Rev: BL 10/1/07; LMC 1/08; SLJ 11/07) [741.5]

7495 Marcovitz, Hal. *Bias in the Media* (5–8). Series: Hot Topics. 2010, Gale/Lucent LB $32.45 (978-1-4205-0224-4). With chapters titled "Why Are the Media Biased?," "The Cable Wars," "Citizens as Journalists: Bias in the Blogosphere," "Pockets of Bias," and "Are There Unbiased Media?," this is a useful introduction to assessing the media. (Rev: SLJ 2/1/11) [302.23097]

7496 Rollins, Prentis. *The Making of a Graphic Novel* (7–12). Illus. by author. 2006, Watson-Guptill paper $19.95 (978-0-8230-3053-8). One side of this "double-sided flip book" contains the text of a graphic novel called *The Resonator*; the other side holds a detailed account of the construction of this novel and the inspirations for the designs. (Rev: SLJ 3/06) [741.5]

7497 Schulz, Charles M. *The Complete Peanuts: 1950 to 1952* (7–12). Ed. by Gary Groth. Series: Peanuts. 2004, Fantagraphics paper $28.95 (978-1-56097-589-2). The first volume in a series collecting the entire 50 years of this classic comic strip. (Rev: BL 4/1/04) [741.5]

7498 Segar, E. C. *I Yam What I Yam!: E.C. Segar's Popeye, Vol. 1* (7–12). 2006, Fantagraphics $29.95 (978-1-56097-779-7). An oversize volume collecting the first two years of the Popeye comic strip. (Rev: BL 1/1–15/07) [741.5]

7499 Streissguth, Thomas. *Media Bias* (8–12). Series: Open for Debate. 2006, Benchmark LB $27.95 (978-0-7614-2296-9). After a discussion of media bias in America (from the first newspaper in 1690), Streissguth illustrates how public opinion can be swayed. (Rev: SLJ 4/07) [302.23]

7500 Sullivan, George. *Journalists at Risk: Reporting America's Wars* (6–9). Series: People's History. 2005, Twenty-First Century LB $29.27 (978-0-7613-2745-5). A look at the historical role of journalists in reporting on U.S. wars in far-flung corners of the globe, including information on the embedded journalists covering the war in Iraq. (Rev: BL 10/15/05; SLJ 12/05; VOYA 2/06)

Biography, Memoirs, Etc.

General and Miscellaneous

7501 Berson, Robin Kadison. *Young Heroes in World History* (7–12). 1999, Greenwood $57.95 (978-0-313-30257-2). Real people — of both sexes and many nationalities — who achieved amazing things before the age of 25 are profiled, with quotations and black-and-white illustrations. (Rev: SLJ 1/00; VOYA 4/00) [920.02]

7502 Gifford, Clive. *1000 Years of Famous People* (6–10). 2002, Kingfisher $24.95 (978-0-7534-5540-1). Brief descriptions of famous men and women in sports, medicine, politics, the arts, and other fields are included in this large-format book that is organized by subject and provides historical overviews of each discipline. (Rev: BL 12/1/02; HBG 3/03; SLJ 2/03; VOYA 6/03) [920.02]

7503 Hatch, Robert, and William Hatch. *The Hero Project: How We Met Our Greatest Heroes and What We Learned from Them* (8–12). 2005, McGraw-Hill paper $16.95 (978-0-07-144904-5). Fascinating interviews with such luminaries as Jackie Chan, Lance Armstrong, Orson Scott Card, Yo-Yo Ma, and Jimmy Carter result from the Hatch brothers' "hero project," which started when William was only 11 years old. (Rev: BL 9/15/05; SLJ 1/06) [920]

7504 Hazell, Rebecca. *Heroes: Great Men Through the Ages* (5–8). 1997, Abbeville $19.95 (978-0-7892-0289-5). A collection of 12 biographies, from Socrates to Martin Luther King, Jr., and including Shakespeare, Mohandas Gandhi, Leonardo da Vinci, and Jorge Louis Borges. (Rev: SLJ 6/97) [920]

Adventurers and Explorers

Collective

7505 Bledsoe, Karen E. *Daredevils of the Air: Thrilling Tales of Pioneer Aviators* (7–12). Series: Avisson Young Adult. 2003, Avisson paper $19.95 (978-1-888105-58-2). The Wright brothers, Eddie Rickenbacker, Bessie Coleman, and Beryl Markham are among the early flyers profiled in stories of exciting aerial exploits. (Rev: SLJ 1/04) [920]

7506 Colman, Penny. *Adventurous Women: Eight True Stories About Women Who Made a Difference* (6–9). 2006, Henry Holt $17.95 (978-0-8050-7744-5). Letters and other primary sources add to these accessible profiles of women adventurers, many of whom are not well-known. (Rev: BL 2/15/06; SLJ 3/06) [920.72]

7507 Cummins, Julie. *Women Explorers: Perils, Pistols, and Petticoats* (4–7). Illus. by Cheryl Harness. 2012, Dial $17.99 (978-080373713-6). This tribute to female explorers focuses on 10 fearless and brilliant adventurers virtually unheard of in the history books. (Rev: BL 3/1/12; SLJ 3/12) [920]

7508 Doherty, Kieran. *Ranchers, Homesteaders, and Traders: Frontiersmen of the South-Central States* (6–10). 2001, Oliver LB $22.95 (978-1-881508-53-3). Seven important settlers — including Sam Houston, Daniel Boone, and Eli Thayer — are introduced with plenty of historical and geographical background material. (Rev: BL 5/1/02; HBG 10/02; SLJ 1/02) [976]

7509 Gifford, Clive. *10 Explorers Who Changed the World* (5–8). Illus. by David Cousens. 2008, Kingfisher $14.95 (978-0-7534-6103-7). Marco Polo, Magellan, and Roald Amundsen are among the explorers briefly profiled in this bright volume with cartoon illustrations and a strong sense of adventure. (Rev: BL 12/1/08; SLJ 2/09) [920]

7510 Gueldenpfennig, Sonia. *Women in Space Who Changed the World* (8–10). Illus. Series: Great Women of Achievement. 2012, Rosen LB $33.25 (978-144885998-6). Caroline Herschel, Valentina Tereshkova, and Sally Ride are among the 11 women — representing several nationalities — profiled in this collective biography. (Rev: BL 6/12) [920]

7511 Hagglund, Betty. *Epic Treks* (5–9). Illus. by Peter Bull. Series: Epic Adventure. 2011, Kingfisher $19.99 (978-0-7534-6668-1). An exciting account of explorers' expeditions — including those of Lewis and Clark, Stanley and Livingstone, and Amundsen and Scott, and the less-known Burke and Wills — with many graphics and technical details. (Rev: BL 11/1/11; SLJ 11/1/11) [920]

7512 Jones, Charlotte Foltz. *Westward Ho! Explorers of the American West* (5–8). 2005, Holiday $22.95 (978-0-8234-1586-1). Intriguing narrative describes the lives and adventures of 11 explorers, including Zebulon Pike and John Wesley Powell. (Rev: BL 5/1/05; SLJ 8/05) [920]

7513 Kimmel, Elizabeth Cody. *The Look-It-Up Book of Explorers* (5–9). 2004, Random House LB $17.99 (978-0-375-92478-1); paper $10.99 (978-0-375-82478-4). Chronologically arranged spreads introduce explorers from Leif Eriksson to Robert Ballard, with maps, illustrations, and historical context. (Rev: SLJ 1/05) [920]

7514 McLean, Jacqueline. *Women of Adventure* (5–9). Series: Profiles. 2003, Oliver LB $19.95 (978-1-881508-73-1). Seven 19th- and 20th-century women with diverse interests who broke social barriers by exploring far from home are profiled here, with biographical information, photographs, and maps. (Rev: BCCB 5/03; HBG 10/03; SLJ 7/03; VOYA 8/03) [910]

7515 Miller, Brandon Marie. *Women of the Frontier: 16 Tales of Trailblazing Homesteaders, Entrepreneurs, and*

Rabble-Rousers (6–10). Illus. Series: Women of Action. 2013, Chicago Review $19.95 (978-188305297-3). Tells the stories of 16 western women and their often grueling experiences. **e** Lexile 1160L (Rev: BL 12/1/12; SLJ 2/13) [920]

7516 Mooney, Carla. *Explorers of the New World: Discover the Golden Age of Exploration* (3–7). Illus. by Tom Casteel. Series: Build It Yourself. 2011, Nomad paper $15.95 (978-1-936313-44-0). With chapters focusing on Columbus, Cabot, Magellan, and the Spanish conquistadors, this volume gives an overview of the men who discovered and later explored the New World. (Rev: SLJ 9/1/11) [910.9]

7517 Mundy, Robyn, and Nigel Rigby. *Epic Voyages* (5–9). Illus. Series: Epic Adventure. 2011, Kingfisher $19.99 (978-0-7534-6574-5). Magellan, Cook, Shackleton, Heyerdahl, and the more recent Chichester are the focus of this large-format volume full of gripping accounts and color photographs. (Rev: BL 11/1/11; SLJ 5/11) [910.4]

7518 Murphy, Claire Rudolf, and Jane G. Haigh. *Gold Rush Women* (7–12). 1997, Alaska Northwest paper $16.95 (978-0-88240-484-4). A collective biography of several women in the late 19th century who went to the Yukon and Alaska, where they panned for gold, ran boarding houses, and worked as dance hall girls and prostitutes. (Rev: BL 8/97; SLJ 11/97*) [920]

7519 Phelan, Matt. *Around the World* (4–7). Illus. by author. 2011, Candlewick $24.99 (978-076363619-7). In graphic novel form, Phelan tells the story of three 19th-century adventurers inspired by Verne's *Around the World in Eighty Days*: Thomas Stevens, a bicyclist; reporter Nellie Bly; and retired sea captain Joshua Slocum. (Rev: BL 9/15/11*; HB 11–12/11; LMC 1–2/12; SLJ 9/1/11) [920]

7520 Richie, Jason. *Spectacular Space Travelers* (6–10). Series: Profiles. 2001, Oliver LB $19.95 (978-1-881508-71-7). Three Soviet cosmonauts and four American astronauts are profiled in this volume that provides a brief history of the space race. (Rev: HBG 10/02; SLJ 4/02) [629.45]

7521 Rooney, Frances. *Extraordinary Women Explorers* (5–8). Series: Women's Hall of Fame. 2005, Second Story paper $7.95 (978-1-896764-98-6). Women endowed with curiosity and courage are celebrated in this text-dense volume. (Rev: BL 3/1/06; SLJ 12/05) [910]

7522 Stone, Tanya Lee. *Almost Astronauts: 13 Women Who Dared to Dream* (5–8). 2009, Candlewick $24.99 (978-0-7636-3611-1). The story of the 13 women who fought to prove they were just as qualified, intelligent, and brave as the men who were training as astronauts in the early 1960s. Sibert Medal 2010; Boston Globe–Horn Book nonfiction Honor 2009; ALA Notable Books 2010. ⌒ (Rev: BL 2/15/09; HB 3–4/09; LMC 8–9/09; SLJ 3/1/09*; VOYA 2/09) [920]

7523 Weatherly, Myra. *Women Pirates: Eight Stories of Adventure* (4–7). 1998, Morgan Reynolds LB $21.95 (978-1-883846-24-4). These stories of eight women pirates from the 17th and 18th centuries — including Grace O'Malley, Maria Cobham, and Rachel Wall — are enlivened by period prints and portraits and good maps. (Rev: BCCB 4/98; BL 4/15/98; HBG 3/99; SLJ 7/98; VOYA 10/98) [920]

7524 Yolen, Jane. *Sea Queens: Women Pirates around the World* (4–7). Illus. by Christine Joy Pratt. 2008, Charlesbridge $18.95 (978-1-58089-131-8). Yolen introduces 12 women pirates — from Artemisia in the 5th century B.C. to Madame Ching in the 19th century and including the well-known Anne Bonny. (Rev: BL 6/1–15/08; SLJ 7/08) [920]

Individual

ANZA, JUAN BAUTISTA DE

7525 Bankston, John. *Juan Bautista de Anza* (5–7). Series: Latinos in American History. 2003, Mitchell Lane LB $29.95 (978-1-58415-196-8). The biography of the Spanish explorer of the American Southwest who was a governor of New Mexico in the late 18th century. (Rev: BL 1/1–15/04) [921]

BURTON, RICHARD FRANCIS

7526 Young, Serinity. *Richard Francis Burton: Explorer, Scholar, Spy* (5–9). Series: Great Explorations. 2006, Benchmark LB $32.79 (978-0-7614-2222-8). This biography chronicles the English adventurer's explorations in Africa, the Middle East, South Asia, and South America and looks at his interest in the cultures of the people he encountered there. (Rev: SLJ 1/07) [921]

BYRD, ADMIRAL RICHARD EVELYN

7527 Burleigh, Robert. *Black Whiteness: Admiral Byrd Alone in the Antarctic* (4–8). Illus. by Walter L. Krudop. 1998, Simon & Schuster $16.95 (978-0-689-81299-6). An outstanding picture biography, with generous quotations from Byrd's diary that describe his great endurance and his lonely vigil in a small underground structure in the Antarctic. (Rev: BL 1/1–15/98*; HB 3–4/98; HBG 10/98; SLJ 3/98) [921]

CABEZA DE VACA, ALVAR NUNEZ

7528 Menard, Valerie. *Alvar Nunez Cabeza de Vaca* (5–7). Series: Latinos in American History. 2002, Mitchell Lane LB $29.95 (978-1-58415-153-1). A biography of the 16th-century Spanish nobleman who lived with Native Americans for eight years and who claimed Florida, Louisiana, and Texas for Spain. (Rev: BL 2/15/03; HBG 10/03) [921]

CHAMPLAIN, SAMUEL DE

7529 Faber, Harold. *Samuel de Champlain: Explorer of Canada* (5–8). Series: Great Explorations. 2004, Benchmark LB $29.93 (978-0-7614-1608-1). Drawing on Champlain's own accounts, this well-illustrated volume examines his voyages to Canada and achievements as governor of New France. (Rev: SLJ 3/05) [921]

7530 Sherman, Josepha. *Samuel de Champlain: Explorer of the Great Lakes Region and Founder of Quebec* (4–7). Series: The Library of Explorers and Exploration. 2003, Rosen LB $33.25 (978-0-8239-3629-8). In addition to covering Champlain's life, this volume places his explorations in historical context and gives interesting information on the fur trade and relations with Native Americans. (Rev: SLJ 9/03) [971.01]

COCHRAN, JACQUELINE

7531 Smith, Elizabeth Simpson. *Coming Out Right: The Story of Jacqueline Cochran, the First Woman Aviator to Break the Sound Barrier* (5–8). 1991, Walker LB $15.85 (978-0-8027-6989-3). From her impoverished childhood to her triumphs in the air and later, this is the story of a female aviation pioneer. (Rev: BL 4/15/91; SLJ 5/91) [921]

COLEMAN, BESSIE

7532 Fisher, Lillian M. *Brave Bessie: Flying Free* (4–7). 1995, Hendrick-Long $16.95 (978-0-937460-94-8). This biography tells of the struggles of Bessie Coleman, who became the first African American aviatrix in the United States. (Rev: BL 2/15/96; SLJ 2/96) [921]

COLUMBUS, CHRISTOPHER

7533 Clare, John D., ed. *The Voyages of Christopher Columbus* (5–8). Series: Living History. 1992, Harcourt $16.95 (978-0-15-200507-8). Using actors and backdrops of the period, this account reconstructs each of Columbus's New World voyages. (Rev: SLJ 11/92) [921]

COOK, CAPTAIN JAMES

7534 Lawlor, Laurie. *Magnificent Voyage: An American Adventurer on Captain James Cook's Final Expedition* (7–12). 2002, Holiday $22.95 (978-0-8234-1575-5). This absorbing account of Captain Cook's ill-fated efforts to locate the Northwest Passage gives details of the various difficulties encountered and of Cook's violent death. (Rev: BL 1/1–15/03; HBG 10/03; SLJ 2/03; VOYA 4/03) [910]

DA GAMA, VASCO

7535 Calvert, Patricia. *Vasco da Gama: So Strong a Spirit* (5–8). Series: Great Explorations. 2004, Benchmark LB $29.93 (978-0-7614-1611-1). After material on da Gama's early life, Calvert looks at the 15th-century Portuguese explorer's voyages. (Rev: SLJ 3/05) [921]

7536 Kratoville, Betty Lou. *Vasco da Gama* (4–7). Series: Trade Route Explorers. 2000, High Noon paper $17.00 (978-1-57128-168-5). The story of the famous explorer who rounded the Cape of Good Hope and visited India, told in a simple, interesting account. (Rev: SLJ 3/01) [921]

DE SOTO, HERNANDO

7537 Whiting, Jim. *Hernando de Soto* (5–7). Series: Latinos in American History. 2002, Mitchell Lane LB $29.95 (978-1-58415-147-0). A simple biography of the Spanish explorer who discovered the Mississippi River in the 16th century while traveling through what is now the southern United States. (Rev: BL 2/15/03; HBG 10/03; SLJ 6/03) [921]

DRAKE, SIR FRANCIS

7538 Whitfield, Peter. *Sir Francis Drake* (8–12). Series: British Library Historic Lives. 2004, New York Univ. $25.00 (978-0-8147-9403-6). Drake's great naval accomplishments are balanced against less admirable activities. (Rev: BL 10/15/04) [942.05]

EARHART, AMELIA

7539 Fleming, Candace. *Amelia Lost: The Life and Disappearance of Amelia Earhart* (4–7). Illus. 2011, Random House $18.99 (978-0-375-84198-9); LB $21.99 (978-0-375-94598-4). Fleming uses twin narratives — one a biographical overview of Earhart's life and the other the drama of her final flight — to create a compelling and suspenseful account. ALA Notable Books 2012. Lexile 930L (Rev: BL 12/1/10; HB 3–4/11; LMC 8–9/11*; SLJ 3/1/11*) [921]

7540 Lauber, Patricia. *Lost Star: The Story of Amelia Earhart* (5–7). 1988, Scholastic paper $4.50 (978-0-590-41159-2). A candid biography of the famed lost aviator. (Rev: BL 10/1/88; SLJ 12/88) [921]

7541 Micklos, John, Jr. *Unsolved: What Really Happened to Amelia Earhart?* (4–8). 2006, Enslow LB $31.93 (978-0-7660-2365-9). The mystery of Earhart's last flight makes this a compelling read, even for researchers, and it provides what they need in terms of information about her childhood and motivations, photographs, maps, and so forth. (Rev: SLJ 7/07)

7542 Sloate, Susan. *Amelia Earhart: Challenging the Skies* (5–8). 1990, Fawcett paper $6.99 (978-0-449-90396-4). The aviator's life story is told along with an examination of all the theories concerning her disappearance. (Rev: SLJ 6/90) [921]

GRAHAM, ROBIN LEE

7543 Graham, Robin Lee, and Derek Gill. *Dove* (7–12). 1991, HarperCollins paper $13.00 (978-0-06-092047-0). A five-year solo voyage around the world and a tender romance with a girl the author met in Fiji. [921]

HENSON, MATTHEW

7544 Hoena, B. A. *Matthew Henson: Arctic Adventurer* (4–7). Illus. by Phil Miller. Series: Graphic Biographies. 2005, Capstone LB $26.60 (978-0-7368-4634-9). The life of the African American explorer is presented in speedy, user-friendly, classic comic book format. (Rev: BL 11/1/05) [910]

7545 Johnson, Dolores. *Onward: A Photobiography of African-American Polar Explorer Matthew Henson* (5–8). Series: National Geographic Photobiography. 2005, National Geographic LB $27.90 (978-0-7922-7915-0). The extraordinary life and achievements of African American explorer Matthew Henson are beautifully documented in this volume that also discusses the racism that Henson faced. (Rev: BCCB 5/06; BL 12/15/05*; HB 5–6/06; HBG 10/06; LMC 8–9/06; SLJ 3/06*; VOYA 6/06) [910]

7546 Olmstead, Kathleen. *Matthew Henson: The Quest for the North Pole* (7–9). Series: Sterling Biographies. 2008, Sterling paper $5.95 (978-1-4027-4441-9). Olmstead describes Henson's life and career from his early days as a cabin boy to becoming the first African American to explore the North Pole. (Rev: BL 2/1/09; SLJ 1/1/09) [921]

HILLARY, SIR EDMUND

7547 Coburn, Broughton. *Triumph on Everest: A Photobiography of Sir Edmund Hillary* (5–8). 2000, National Geographic $17.95 (978-0-7922-7114-7). Using many quotations and excellent photographs, this work records the lifetime accomplishments of one of the first men to reach the top of Mount Everest. (Rev: BCCB 9/00; HBG 3/01; SLJ 10/00) [921]

7548 Crompton, Samuel Willard. *Sir Edmund Hillary* (6–12). Series: Great Explorers. 2009, Chelsea House $30 (978-1-60413-420-9). With photographs and journal excerpts, this biography gives an overview of the life of the mountaineer, his celebrated expeditions, his relationship with the Sherpa people, and other exploration taking place at that time. (Rev: LMC 3–4/10) [921]

7549 Elish, Dan. *Edmund Hillary: First to the Top* (5–9). Series: Great Explorations. 2006, Benchmark LB $32.79 (978-0-7614-2224-2). This biography focuses on the New Zealand mountain climber's 1953 conquest of Mount Everest and includes coverage of Sherpa Tenzing Norgay. (Rev: SLJ 1/07) [921]

7550 Stewart, Whitney. *Sir Edmund Hillary: To Everest and Beyond* (5–8). Photos by Anne B. Keiser. Series: Newsmakers. 1996, Lerner LB $30.35 (978-0-8225-4927-7). The life of this famous mountain climber is presented with interesting details about his other interests, including bee keeping, conservation, and helping the Sherpa people. (Rev: SLJ 9/96) [921]

JOHNSON, OSA

7551 Arruda, Suzanne Middendorf. *From Kansas to Cannibals: The Story of Osa Johnson* (6–8). Series: Avisson Young Adult. 2001, Avisson paper $19.95 (978-1-888105-50-6). This is the biography of an intrepid woman who, with her husband, traveled to remote areas of Africa and the South Pacific from the 1920s to the 1940s, coming across wild beasts and cannibal headhunters. (Rev: SLJ 11/01) [910]

LEWIS AND CLARK

7552 Crompton, Samuel Willard. *Lewis and Clark* (6–12). Series: Great Explorers. 2009, Chelsea House $30 (978-1-60413-418-6). With photographs and journal excerpts, this biography gives an overview of the lives of these two explorers, their celebrated expedition, their treatment of the native peoples, and other exploration taking place at that time. e (Rev: LMC 3–4/10) [920]

LINDBERGH, ANNE MORROW

7553 Gherman, Beverly. *Anne Morrow Lindbergh: Between the Sea and the Stars* (6–9). 2007, Lerner LB $27.93 (978-0-8225-5970-2). Gherman looks at Lindbergh's character and emotions as well as her youth, marriage, the murder of her son, and her accomplishments as a pilot and writer. (Rev: BL 9/1/07) [921]

LINDBERGH, CHARLES

7554 Denenberg, Barry. *An American Hero: The True Story of Charles A. Lindbergh* (8–12). 1996, Scholastic paper $16.95 (978-0-590-46923-4). Beginning with Lindbergh's transatlantic flight, this fascinating biography then recounts the story of his early years followed by details about his multifaceted life. (Rev: BL 3/15/96*; SLJ 7/96; VOYA 6/96) [921]

7555 Giblin, James Cross. *Charles A. Lindbergh: A Human Hero* (6–12). 1997, Clarion $22.00 (978-0-395-63389-2). A book about the public and private life of one of America's heroes that deals with his pro-Nazi sympathies and anti-Semitism, the adoration he received for his transatlantic flight, and pity the public felt for the kidnapping and murder of his child. (Rev: BL 9/15/97; HBG 3/98; SLJ 11/97*; VOYA 6/98) [921]

LIVINGSTONE, DAVID

7556 Otfinoski, Steven. *David Livingstone: Deep in the Heart of Africa* (5–9). Series: Great Explorations. 2006, Benchmark LB $32.79 (978-0-7614-2226-6). This biography focuses on the three decades during which the Scottish-born adventurer explored central Africa. (Rev: SLJ 1/07) [921]

MACMILLAN, DONALD BAXTER

7557 Cowan, Mary Morton. *Captain Mac* (6–9). 2010, Boyds Mills $17.95 (978-1-59078-709-0). Subtitled *The Life of Donald Baxter MacMillan, Arctic Explorer,* this book chronicles the life of the man who participated in many expeditions to the Arctic and left numerous films and photographs. Lexile 930L (Rev: BLO 5/15/10; LMC 10/10; SLJ 7/10) [921]

MAGELLAN, FERDINAND

7558 Burnett, Betty. *Ferdinand Magellan: The First Voyage Around the World* (4–7). Series: The Library of Explorers and Exploration. 2003, Rosen LB $33.25 (978-0-8239-3617-5). In addition to covering Magellan's life, this volume places his 16th-century voyage in historical context and gives interesting information on the funding of such expeditions and life at sea. (Rev: SLJ 9/03) [910]

7559 Levinson, Nancy Smiler. *Magellan and the First Voyage Around the World* (5–8). 2001, Clarion $19.00 (978-0-395-98773-5). A straightforward biography of Magellan, with information on his times and insightful analysis of his character. (Rev: BCCB 2/02; BL 2/1/02; HB 1–2/02; HBG 3/02; SLJ 1/02) [910.92]

7560 Stefoff, Rebecca. *Ferdinand Magellan and the Discovery of the World Ocean* (7–12). 1990, Chelsea LB $32.00 (978-0-7910-1291-8). Using many quotations from original sources, this is an engrossing account of the explorer and his voyage. (Rev: BL 6/15/90) [921]

7561 Waldman, Stuart. *Magellan's World* (4–7). Illus. by Gregory Manchess. Series: Great Explorers. 2007, Mikaya $22.95 (978-1-931414-19-7). "Magellan was driven to ever-greater extremes of brilliance, courage, brutality and madness as he sailed around the world," states this book, which offers an unvarnished portrait of the explorer as well as beautiful illustrations and maps. (Rev: BL 11/1/07)

MALLORY, GEORGE

7562 Salkeld, Audrey. *Mystery on Everest: A Photobiography of George Mallory* (5–8). Series: Photobiography. 2000, National Geographic $17.95 (978-0-7922-7222-9). The life of the famous English mountain climber George Mallory, who died in 1924 in a climbing accident on Mount Everest, written by a member of the team that discovered his body in 1999. (Rev: BCCB 9/00; BL 11/1/00; HBG 3/01; SLJ 11/00) [921]

MARKHAM, BERYL

7563 Gourley, Catherine. *Beryl Markham: Never Turn Back* (6–10). Series: Bernard Biography. 1997, Conari paper $11.95 (978-1-57324-073-4). An exciting biography of the unconventional Englishwoman who was the first person to fly the Atlantic from east to west. (Rev: BL 3/15/97; SLJ 5/97; VOYA 12/97) [921]

OCHOA, ELLEN

7564 Iverson, Teresa. *Ellen Ochoa* (4–8). Series: Hispanic-American Biographies. 2005, Raintree LB $32.86 (978-1-4109-1299-2). The personal and profes-

sional life of the first Hispanic American woman astronaut. (Rev: SLJ 1/06) [921]

PEARY, ROBERT E.

7565 Dwyer, Christopher. *Robert Peary and the Quest for the North Pole* (6–9). Series: World Explorers. 1992, Chelsea LB $14.95 (978-0-7910-1316-8). Courage and endurance are highlighted in this account of Peary's expeditions to reach the South Pole. (Rev: BL 2/1/93) [921]

POLO, MARCO

7566 Demi. *Marco Polo* (4–7). Illus. by author. 2008, Marshall Cavendish $19.99 (978-0-7614-5433-5). A visually impressive picture-book biography of the explorer who made an incredible journey from Europe to China taking nearly a quarter of a century; with a double-page map. (Rev: BL 10/1/08; LMC 3/09*; SLJ 9/08*) [910.4]

7567 Freedman, Russell. *The Adventures of Marco Polo* (7–10). Illus. by Bagram Ibatoulline. 2006, Scholastic $17.99 (978-0-439-52394-3). Vivid illustrations accompany the descriptions of Marco Polo's exciting journey to Kublai Khan's court. (Rev: BL 10/15/06; HB 11–12/06; SLJ 11/06*) [910.4]

PONCE DE LEON, JUAN

7568 Whiting, Jim. *Juan Ponce de Leon* (5–7). Series: Latinos in American History. 2002, Mitchell Lane LB $29.95 (978-1-58415-149-4). This is the story of the man who is credited with discovering Florida in 1513 while searching for the fountain of youth. (Rev: BL 2/15/03; HBG 10/03; SLJ 6/03) [921]

RALEIGH, SIR WALTER

7569 Aronson, Marc. *Sir Walter Ralegh and the Quest for El Dorado* (7–10). 2000, Clarion $20.00 (978-0-395-84827-2). The fascinating life and times of the colorful Elizabethan explorer, with illustrations, maps, and quotations from Sir Walter himself. (Rev: BL 8/00; HB 9–10/00; HBG 9/00; SLJ 7/00*) [942.05]

RAMON, ILAN

7570 Sofer, Barbara. *Ilan Ramon: Israel's Space Hero* (4–8). 2004, Lerner LB $16.95 (978-1-58013-115-5); paper $6.95 (978-1-58013-116-2). The story of the first Israeli astronaut, from his early life and schooling to his selection for the crew of the ill-fated Columbia space shuttle that broke apart on re-entry in 2003. (Rev: SLJ 6/04) [921]

RIDE, SALLY

7571 Camp, Carole Ann. *Sally Ride: First American Woman in Space* (6–10). Series: People to Know. 1997, Enslow LB $20.95 (978-0-89490-829-3). A lively account of Sally Ride's work as an astronaut and astrophysicist, with material on her training, shuttle flight, and life in microgravity. (Rev: BL 1/1–15/98; HBG 3/98; SLJ 12/97) [921]

7572 Hurwitz, Jane, and Sue Hurwitz. *Sally Ride: Shooting for the Stars* (5–8). 1989, Ballantine paper $6.99 (978-0-449-90394-0). An interestingly written account in paperback format of the female space pioneer. (Rev: BL 12/15/89; SLJ 2/90; VOYA 2/90) [921]

7573 Riddolls, Tom. *Sally Ride: The First American Woman in Space* (5–8). Illus. 2010, Crabtree LB $31.93 (978-077872541-1). Chronicling her life from youth to adulthood, this biography presents a straightforward and clearly written portrait of astronaut Sally Ride. (Rev: BL 1/1–15/11) [911]

SELKIRK, ALEXANDER

7574 Kraske, Robert. *Marooned: The Strange but True Adventures of Alexander Selkirk, the Real Robinson Crusoe* (5–8). Illus. by Robert Andrew Parker. 2005, Clarion $15.00 (978-0-618-56843-7). The adventurous life of Alexander Selkirk, the Scottish navigator who served as the model for Daniel Defoe's *Robinson Crusoe*. (Rev: BL 11/15/05; SLJ 12/05) [996.1]

SERRA, JUNÍPERO

7575 Whiting, Jim. *Junípero José Serra* (5–7). Series: Latinos in American History. 2003, Mitchell Lane LB $29.95 (978-1-58415-187-6). Profiles the monk who was responsible for founding nine California missions and converting thousands of Native Americans to Christianity. (Rev: BL 1/1–15/04; SLJ 3/00) [921]

SHACKLETON, SIR ERNEST

7576 Johnson, Rebecca L. *Ernest Shackleton: Gripped by the Antarctic* (6–10). Series: Trailblazer Biogra-

phies. 2003, Carolrhoda LB $30.60 (978-0-87614-920-1). Photographs, anecdotes, and quotations are sprinkled throughout this exciting account of Shackleton's youth and famous expeditions. (Rev: BL 6/1–15/03; HBG 10/03; SLJ 8/03; VOYA 8/03) [919.8]

7577 Kostyal, K. M. *Trial by Ice: A Photobiography of Sir Ernest Shackleton* (4–8). 1999, National Geographic $17.95 (978-0-7922-7393-6). A biography that details the life of Sir Ernest Shackleton, his 1915 Antarctic expedition, and the survival of the explorers aboard the *Endurance*. (Rev: BCCB 12/99; BL 12/1/99; HBG 3/00; SLJ 3/00) [921]

7578 Riffenburgh, Beau. *Shackleton's Forgotten Expedition: The Voyage of the Nimrod* (8–12). 2004, Bloomsbury $25.95 (978-1-58234-488-1). This story of Shackleton's first expedition to the Antarctic aboard the *Nimrod* underlines its significant scientific and exploratory achievements. (Rev: BL 10/15/04) [919.8]

SMITH, JOHN

7579 Doherty, Kieran. *To Conquer Is to Live: The Life of Captain John Smith of Jamestown* (6–8). 2001, Twenty-First Century LB $23.90 (978-0-7613-1820-0). A compelling biography that includes details of Smith's adventures before coming to the New World. (Rev: HBG 3/02; SLJ 12/01) [973.2]

WHITMAN, NARCISSA

7580 Harness, Cheryl. *The Tragic Tale of Narcissa Whitman and a Faithful History of the Oregon Trail* (4–7). Illus. 2006, National Geographic $16.95 (978-0-7922-5920-6). A biography of Narcissa Whitman, the first woman to cross the Rockies on the perilous Oregon Trail in order to bring her Christian beliefs to the Indians of that area. (Rev: BL 12/1/06)

Artists, Authors, Composers, and Entertainers

Collective

7581 Amend, Allison. *Hispanic-American Writers* (8–12). Series: Multicultural Voices. 2010, Chelsea House $35 (978-1-60413-312-7). Rudolfo Anaya, Julia Alvarez, and Sandra Cisneros are among the eight writers introduced in this volume that places them in historical and cultural context and examines major themes in their work. ℮ (Rev: LMC 10/10; SLJ 9/1/10) [920]

7582 Ball, Heather. *Magnificent Women in Music* (4–7). Series: The Women's Hall of Fame. 2006, Second Story paper $7.95 (978-1-897187-02-9). Ten women from different times and with different musical gifts are profiled here, including Clara Schumann, Marian Anderson, and k.d. lang. (Rev: SLJ 7/06)

7583 Barnes, Rachel. *Abstract Expressionists* (6–8). Series: Artists in Profile. 2003, Heinemann LB $28.50 (978-1-58810-644-5). An introduction to the art and artists of this period, with profiles of major artists and examples of their works. Also use *Harlem Renaissance Artists* (2003). (Rev: HBG 10/03; LMC 10/03; SLJ 7/03) [759.13]

7584 Bostrom, Kathleen Long. *Winning Authors: Profiles of the Newbery Medalists* (5–10). Series: Popular Authors. 2003, Libraries Unlimited $52.00 (978-1-56308-877-3). Report writers will find useful information on the authors who won this prestigious award, including quotations and material on experiences that relate to the winning books. (Rev: SLJ 6/04; VOYA 6/04) [920]

7585 Bredeson, Carmen. *American Writers of the 20th Century* (5–8). 1996, Enslow LB $20.95 (978-0-89490-704-3). Ten writers for adults, including Toni Morrison and F. Scott Fitzgerald, are introduced in brief profiles. (Rev: BL 6/1–15/96; SLJ 9/96) [920]

7586 Britton, Felicity. *The Glee Cast: Inspiring Gleek Mania* (6–9). Illus. Series: Lifeline Biographies. 2012, Lerner/Twenty-First Century LB $34.60 (978-076138639-1). An attractive and accessible collective biography full of photographs. ℮ (Rev: BL 10/15/12) [920]

7587 Cotter, Charis. *Born to Write: The Remarkable Lives of Six Famous Authors* (4–8). 2009, Annick $24.95 (978-1-55451-192-1); paper $14.95 (978-1-55451-191-4). E. B. White, C. S. Lewis, and Madeleine L'Engle are among the authors featured in this interesting volume that discusses the writers that inspired them. (Rev: BL 12/15/09; SLJ 12/09) [920]

7588 Datnow, Claire. *American Science Fiction and Fantasy Writers* (5–8). Series: Collective Biographies. 1999, Enslow LB $26.60 (978-0-7660-1090-1). Science fiction and fantasy writers profiled in this book include Asimov, Heinlein, Bradbury, Anderson, Norton, L'Engle, and Le Guin. (Rev: BL 4/15/99; VOYA 6/99) [920]

7589 Davidson, Sue. *Getting the Real Story: Nellie Bly and Ida B. Wells* (6–10). 1992, Seal paper $8.95 (978-1-878067-16-6). A dual biography of two women who broke down barriers in journalism and how their different races shaped their individual stories. (Rev: BL 3/1/92; SLJ 7/92) [920]

7590 De Angelis, Gina. *Motion Pictures: Making Cinema Magic* (6–10). Series: Innovators. 2004, Oliver LB $21.95 (978-1-881508-78-6). Profiles eight inventors of motion picture technology, including Auguste and Louis Lumière, Lee de Forest, and Mike Todd. (Rev: BCCB 5/04; SLJ 9/04) [920]

7591 Earls, Irene. *Young Musicians in World History* (7–12). 2002, Greenwood $51.95 (978-0-313-31442-1). Thirteen musicians whose skills were recognized before the age of 25 are profiled, ranging from Bach and

Beethoven to Louis Armstrong, Bob Dylan, and John Lennon. (Rev: LMC 2/03; SLJ 1/03) [780]

7592 Gourse, Leslie. *Sophisticated Ladies: The Great Women of Jazz* (5–8). Illus. by Martin French. 2007, Dutton $19.99 (978-0-525-47198-1). Profiles 14 female jazz singers, with full-color portraits, biographical details, and comments on vocal style and importance. (Rev: BL 12/15/06; SLJ 5/07)

7593 Govenar, Alan. *Extraordinary Ordinary People: Five American Masters of Traditional Arts* (5–8). 2006, Candlewick $19.99 (978-0-7636-2047-9). Five American artists, recipients of National Endowment for the Arts fellowships, who practice unique — but traditional — art forms are profiled here. (Rev: BL 9/1/06; SLJ 8/06*)

7594 Hill, Anne E. *Broadcasting and Journalism* (6–9). Series: Female Firsts in Their Fields. 1999, Chelsea $28.00 (978-0-7910-5139-9). The biographies of six pioneering women in the mass media and how their work became an inspiration for other women. (Rev: BL 5/15/99; HBG 9/99) [920]

7595 Hill, Christine M. *Ten Terrific Authors for Teens* (5–7). Series: Collective Biographies. 2000, Enslow LB $26.60 (978-0-7660-1380-3). Among the authors profiled are Judy Blume, Virginia Hamilton, Julius Lester, Lois Lowry, Katherine Paterson, Gary Soto, and Lawrence Yep. (Rev: BL 9/15/00; HBG 10/01; SLJ 12/00; VOYA 8/01) [920]

7596 Holme, Merilyn, and Bridget McKenzie. *Expressionists* (5–9). Series: Artists in Profile. 2002, Heinemann LB $28.50 (978-1-58810-647-6). Introduces the movement and gives biographical information on the major artists and their key works, with reproductions and photographs. Also use *Impressionists* and *Pop Artists* (both 2002). (Rev: HBG 3/03; SLJ 3/03) [759.06]

7597 Koopmans, Andy. *Filmmakers* (7–10). Series: History Makers. 2005, Gale LB $29.95 (978-1-59018-598-8). Profiles five of the world's most influential filmmakers — Alfred Hitchcock, Stanley Kubrick, Francis Ford Coppola, Spike Lee, and Peter Jackson. (Rev: BL 6/1–15/05) [920]

7598 Krull, Kathleen. *Lives of the Musicians: Good Times, Bad Times (And What the Neighbors Thought)* (5–8). 1993, Harcourt $20.00 (978-0-15-248010-3). Biographies of 16 musical giants, from Vivaldi, Mozart, and Beethoven to Gershwin, Joplin, and Woody Guthrie. (Rev: BL 4/1/93*; SLJ 5/93*) [920]

7599 Marcus, Leonard S. *A Caldecott Celebration: Seven Artists and Their Paths to the Caldecott Medal* (3–8). Illus. 2008, Walker $19.95 (978-0-8027-9703-2). An updated version of the 1998 edition, this volume features seven Caldecott-winning artists (one for each decade of the award), introducing their prize-winning books and supplying background information on each. The artists are Sendak, McCloskey, Marcia Brown,

Steig, Van Allsburg, Wiesner, and now Gerstein. (Rev: HB 11/08; LMC 5/08; SLJ 4/08) [920]

7600 Marcus, Leonard S. *Pass It Down: Five Picture-Book Families Make Their Mark* (5–8). 2007, Walker $19.95 (978-0-8027-9600-4). Multigenerational families of picture book authors/illustrators are featured here: Donald Crews, Ann Jonas, and Nina Crews; Clement, Edith, and Thacher Hurd; Walter Dean and Christopher Myers; Jerry and Brian Pinkney; and Harlow, Anne, and Lizzy Rockwell. (Rev: BL 12/15/06; SLJ 1/07)

7601 Marcus, Leonard S., ed. *The Wand in the Word: Conversations with Writers of Fantasy* (6–9). 2006, Candlewick $19.99 (978-0-7636-2625-9). This is a collection of interviews with 13 top authors of fantasy fiction (including Susan Cooper, Tamora Pierce, Philip Pullman, and Madeleine l'Engle), with profiles of the writers, discussion of their inspiration, and advice for young writers. (Rev: BL 5/15/06; HB 7–8/06; LMC 2/07; SLJ 5/06*) [813.009]

7602 Mazer, Anne, ed. *Going Where I'm Coming From: Memoirs of American Youth* (8–12). 1995, Persea paper $7.95 (978-0-89255-206-1). Writers from different cultures talk about growing up and the incidents in their lives that helped to establish their identities. (Rev: BL 1/15/95; VOYA 5/95) [818]

7603 Nathan, Amy. *Meet the Dancers: From Ballet, Broadway, and Beyond* (6–12). 2008, Henry Holt $19.95 (978-0-8050-8071-1). Sixteen very different dancers describe their training and their careers, which run the gamut from Broadway to MTV. (Rev: BL 5/1/08; SLJ 4/08) [792.802]

7604 Raczka, Bob. *Before They Were Famous: How Seven Artists Got Their Start* (4–7). Illus. 2010, Millbrook LB $25.26 (978-0-7613-6077-3). Durer, Michelangelo, Gentileschi, Sargent, Paul Klee, Picasso, and Salvador Dali are the artists featured here, each with a page devoted to their childhood plus early artwork and several other works including a self-portrait. (Rev: BL 11/1/10; LMC 3–4/11; SLJ 1/1/11) [920]

7605 Satter, James. *Journalists Who Made History* (7–12). Series: Profiles. 1998, Oliver LB $19.95 (978-1-881508-39-7). Ten journalists famous for their fearless reporting are profiled, including Horace Greeley, Ida Tarbell, Carl Bernstein and Bob Woodward, William Randolph Hearst, and Edward R. Murrow. (Rev: BL 10/15/98; SLJ 11/98) [920]

7606 Scieszka, Jon, ed. *Guys Write for Guys Read: Favorite Authors Write About Being Boys* (6–9). 2005, Viking $16.99 (978-0-670-06007-8). Well-known male authors and illustrators share boyhood memories in this delightful collection of stories, anecdotes, poems, drawings, and comics. (Rev: BL 4/15/05; SLJ 4/05) [810.8]

7607 Sigafus, Kim, and Lyle Ernst. *Native Writers: Voices of Power* (8–12). Illus. Series: Native Trailblazers. 2012, 7th Generation paper $9.95 (978-0-977918-3-8-6). This collective biography includes profiles of contemporary Native American writers such as Sherman Alexie, Joseph Bruchac, and Louise Erdrich. (Rev: BL 11/1/12; SLJ 11/12) [920]

7608 Tate, Eleanora E. *African American Musicians* (4–7). Series: Black Stars. 2000, Wiley $24.95 (978-0-471-25356-3). This collective biography highlights both past and present contributions to different kinds of music by several African Americans. (Rev: BL 7/00; HBG 3/01; SLJ 7/00) [920]

7609 Wilds, Mary. *Raggin' the Blues: Legendary Country Blues and Ragtime Musicians* (6–9). 2001, Avisson paper $19.95 (978-1-888105-47-6). Although many readers will not be familiar with these musicians — including Lightnin' Hopkins, Skip James, Libba Cotton, and Blind Willie Johnson — they will appreciate their contributions to the foundations of modern blues, jazz, and improvisational music. (Rev: BL 2/15/03) [781]

7610 Woog, Adam. *Rock and Roll Legends* (6–9). Series: History Makers. 2001, Lucent $24.95 (978-1-56606-741-6). Included in this book of short profiles are Elvis Presley, John Lennon, Janis Joplin, Jimi Hendrix, Bruce Springsteen, and Kurt Cobain. (Rev: BL 8/1/01) [920]

Artists and Architects

ABBOTT, BERENICE

7611 Sullivan, George. *Berenice Abbott, Photographer: An Independent Vision* (6–9). 2006, Clarion $20.00 (978-0-618-44026-9). A comprehensive look at the life and work of Abbott, an accomplished 20th-century photographer, with excellent reproductions. (Rev: BL 6/1–15/06; SLJ 8/06) [921]

ADAMS, ANSEL

7612 Strangis, Joel. *Ansel Adams: American Artist with a Camera* (6–8). Series: People to Know. 2003, Enslow LB $26.60 (978-0-7660-1847-1). The life of the famous American photographer of landscapes who died in 1984. (Rev: BL 6/1–15/03; HBG 10/03) [921]

AUDUBON, JOHN JAMES

7613 Roop, Peter, and Connie Roop, eds. *Capturing Nature* (5–7). Illus. by Rick Farley. 1993, Walker LB $17.85 (978-0-8027-8205-2). Audubon's prints and original paintings and excerpts from his journals are combined to produce a stunning biography. (Rev: BCCB 12/93; BL 12/15/93; SLJ 1/94) [921]

BAMA, JAMES

7614 Kane, Brian M. *James Bama: American Realist* (8–12). 2006, Flesk $34.95 (978-0-9723758-8-7). This is a tribute to James Bama, a triumphantly successful illustrator who did hundreds of paperback covers during the 1960s and 1970s as well as artwork for magazines, advertising, military, and sports publications. (Rev: BL 11/1/06) [759.13]

BOTTICELLI, SANDRO

7615 Connolly, Sean. *Botticelli* (4–8). Series: Lives of the Artists. 2005, World Almanac LB $31.00 (978-0-8368-5648-4). A tall, slender volume full of facts about Botticelli's life and times, with many color reproductions. (Rev: BL 6/1–15/04; SLJ 3/05) [921]

BOURGEOIS, LOUISE

7616 Greenberg, Jan, and Sandra Jordan. *Runaway Girl: The Artist Louise Bourgeois* (8–12). 2003, Abrams $19.95 (978-0-8109-4237-0). The life of the famous sculptor, with details of her youth and her difficult relations with her parents, is accompanied by many black-and-white and color photographs. (Rev: BL 4/15/03*; HB 7–8/03; HBG 10/03; SLJ 5/03*; VOYA 8/03) [730]

BOURKE-WHITE, MARGARET

7617 Rubin, Susan Goldman. *Margaret Bourke-White: Her Pictures Were Her Life* (6–12). 1999, Abrams $19.95 (978-0-8109-4381-0). An excellent biography of a courageous, highly disciplined photographer whose work remains a hallmark of quality in the field. (Rev: BL 11/1/99* ; HBG 4/00) [770]

BRADY, MATHEW

7618 Murray, Stuart A. P. *Mathew Brady: Photographer of Our Nation* (6–9). Series: Show Me America. 2008, Sharpe Focus LB $32.95 (978-0-7656-8151-5). Excellent illustrations and succinct text give an overview of the celebrated photographer's life and work and explain the historical context. (Rev: SLJ 5/1/09) [921]

BRYAN, ASHLEY

7619 Bryan, Ashley. *Words to My Life's Song* (3–7). Illus. by author. 2009, Atheneum $18.99 (978-1-4169-0541-7). Full of art, this autobiography chronicles Bryan's rich life and the ever-present importance of drawing and painting, even during war. ALA Notable Books 2010. (Rev: BCCB 1/09; BL 12/15/08*; HB 1–2/09; LMC 8–9/09; SLJ 2/09*) [921]

CALDECOTT, RANDOLPH

7620 Hegel, Claudette. *Randolph Caldecott: An Illustrated Life* (5–9). Series: Avisson Young Adult. 2004, Avisson $27.50 (978-1-888105-60-5). Many of Caldecott's drawings are included in this account of the artist's life and work, with coverage of the children's award named in his honor. (Rev: BL 10/1/04; SLJ 11/04) [741.6]

CALDER, ALEXANDER

7621 Lipman, Jean, and Margaret Aspinwall. *Alexander Calder and His Magical Mobiles* (6–9). 1981, Hudson Hills $19.95 (978-0-933920-17-0). A biography of the noted sculptor with many interesting incidents from his childhood. [921]

CANALETTO

7622 Rice, Earle, Jr. *Canaletto* (7–12). Series: Art Profiles for Kids. 2007, Mitchell Lane LB $29.95 (978-1-58415-561-4). Report writers will appreciate this thorough introduction to the artist's life and work, with interesting "FYI" sections and small color reproductions. (Rev: SLJ 1/08)

CARLE, ERIC

7623 Carle, Eric. *Flora and Tiger: 19 Very Short Stories from My Life* (4–8). 1997, Putnam $17.99 (978-0-399-23203-9). An autobiography of the famous picture-book artist who was born in Germany but who has lived in the United States since 1952. (Rev: BL 12/15/97; HBG 3/98; SLJ 2/98) [921]

CARR, EMILY

7624 Bogart, Jo Ellen. *Emily Carr: At the Edge of the World* (4–8). Illus. by Maxwell Newhouse. 2003, Tundra $18.95 (978-0-88776-640-4). This picture book for older readers presents the life and work of the Canadian artist and writer who became famous for her depictions of the native peoples of the Pacific Coast. (Rev: BL 11/1/03; HBG 4/04; SLJ 12/03) [759.11]

7625 Debon, Nicolas. *Four Pictures by Emily Carr* (5–9). 2003, Douglas & McIntyre $15.95 (978-0-88899-532-2). This small comic-book biography uses four of Carr's paintings to introduce chapters that trace the Canadian artist's life and interest in Native Americans. (Rev: BL 12/1/03; HB 1–2/04; HBG 3/02; SLJ 11/03) [759.11]

CASSATT, MARY

7626 Ferrara, Cos. *Mary Cassatt: The Life and Art of a Genteel Rebel* (5–8). Series: Girls Explore, Reach for the Stars. 2005, Girls Explore $20.00 (978-0-9749456-3-7). Cassatt's art, shown in small full-color reproductions, is introduced in this biography that also discusses her independence and feminist views. (Rev: BL 2/15/05) [921]

7627 Streissguth, Thomas. *Mary Cassatt* (4–8). Series: Trailblazers. 1999, Lerner LB $27.93 (978-1-57505-291-5). Full-color illustrations enhance this biography of the American painter who was associated with the Impressionists and spent most of her adult life in France. (Rev: BL 5/1/99; HBG 10/99; SLJ 9/99) [921]

CATLIN, GEORGE

7628 Reich, Susanna. *Painting the Wild Frontier: The Art and Adventures of George Catlin* (7–12). 2008, Clarion $21.00 (978-0-618-71470-4). This excellent introduction to the artwork and life of George Catlin, a 19th-century painter of Native Americans, includes prints and photographs of his work and extensive back matter. (Rev: BL 6/1–15/08; SLJ 8/08) [921]

CÉZANNE, PAUL

7629 Burleigh, Robert. *Paul Cézanne: A Painter's Journey* (4–7). Illus. 2006, Abrams $17.95 (978-0-8109-5784-8). A lavishly illustrated and thoughtfully written profile of Cézanne's life and art. (Rev: BL 2/15/06; SLJ 3/06)

7630 Tracy, Kathleen. *Paul Cézanne* (4–7). Series: Art Profiles for Kids. 2007, Mitchell Lane LB $29.95 (978-1-58415-565-2). Suitable for both research and browsing, this examination of the artist's life and times includes many reproductions and interesting sidebars. (Rev: LMC 2/08; SLJ 12/07) [921]

CHAGALL, MARC

7631 Lewis, J. Patrick, and Jane Yolen. *Self-Portrait with Seven Fingers: The Life of Marc Chagall in Verse* (5–8). Illus. by Marc Chagall. 2011, Creative Editions $18.99 (978-156846211-0). Poems by writers including Yolen and Lewis accompany reproductions of Chagall's works in this elegant large-format book. (Rev: BL 12/15/11; SLJ 1/12) [921]

7632 Mason, Antony. *Marc Chagall* (4–8). Series: Lives of the Artists. 2005, World Almanac LB $31.00 (978-0-8368-5649-1). A tall, slender volume full of facts about Chagall's life and times, with many color reproductions. (Rev: BL 6/1–15/04; SLJ 3/05) [921]

CHONG, GORDON H.

7633 *The Success of Gordon H. Chong and Associates: An Architecture Success Story* (7–10). Series: Success. 1996, Walker $15.95 (978-0-8027-8307-3). The amazing rise of the contemporary American architect, with examples of his work. (Rev: BL 5/15/96; SLJ 9/96) [921]

CHRISTO AND JEANNE-CLAUDE

7634 Greenberg, Jan, and Sandra Jordan. *Christo and Jeanne-Claude: Through the Gates and Beyond* (6–9). Illus. 2008, Flash Point $19.95 (978-159643071-6). The life and work of husband-wife art duo Christo and Jeanne-Claude is brought to life in this beautifully photographed book that shows examples of their outdoor installations and examines the underlying motivations. ALA Notable Books 2009. (Rev: BL 11/1/08*; HB 1–2/09; SLJ 12/08) [921]

CLOSE, CHUCK

7635 Close, Chuck. *Face Book* (5–8). Illus. 2012, Abrams $18.95 (978-141970163-4). Portrait artist Chuck Close offers insight into his creative process and how he has dealt with disability; with 14 beautifully reproduced works that can be mixed and matched. (Rev: BL 3/15/12; HB 5–6/12; SLJ 6/12) [921]

DA VINCI, LEONARDO

7636 Augarde, Steve. *Leonardo da Vinci* (4–8). Illus. by Leo Brown. Series: Lifelines. 2009, Kingfisher $16.99 (978-0-7534-6174-7). This book opens with an illustrated, diary-style narrative in which a fictional 10-year-old apprentice to Leonardo da Vinci reveals glimpses into the artist's personality, process, and intellect; the second half of the book looks at everyday life in the Renaissance and details of da Vinci's work. (Rev: BL 11/1/09; SLJ 1/10) [921]

7637 Herbert, Janis. *Leonardo da Vinci for Kids: His Life and Ideas* (4–8). 1998, Chicago Review paper $16.95 (978-1-55652-298-7). This biography of Leonardo da Vinci contains background information on history, art techniques, science, and philosophy. (Rev: BL 3/1/99; SLJ 4/99) [921]

7638 Krull, Kathleen. *Leonardo da Vinci* (5–8). Illus. by Boris Kulikov. Series: Giants of Science. 2005, Viking $15.99 (978-0-670-05920-1). The less attractive features of da Vinci's times are covered here, along with the artist's childhood and adolescence and his development into both an artist and a scientist, drawing connections between the two disciplines and incorporating much from da Vinci's notebooks. (Rev: BL 9/1/05; SLJ 10/05*) [921]

7639 Kuhne, Heinz. *Leonardo da Vinci: Dreams, Schemes, and Flying Machines* (4–8). Series: Adventures in Art. 2000, Prestel $14.95 (978-3-7913-2166-0). This well-illustrated biography covers da Vinci's accomplishments as a scientist, engineer, inventor, and artist. (Rev: BL 7/00) [921]

7640 Mason, Antony. *Leonardo da Vinci* (4–8). 1994, Barron's paper $8.99 (978-0-8120-1997-1). A brief biography that chronicles the achievements of this multifaceted genius and supplies pictures of some of his great triumphs. (Rev: BL 12/1/94) [921]

7641 O'Connor, Barbara. *Leonardo da Vinci: Renaissance Genius* (5–8). Series: Trailblazer Biographies. 2002, Carolrhoda LB $27.93 (978-0-87614-467-1). An excellent biography that details Leonardo's life from childhood, discusses some of his famous paintings, and looks at his inventions and experiments. (Rev: BL 3/15/03; HBG 3/03; SLJ 11/02; VOYA 8/03) [921]

7642 Reed, Jennifer. *Leonardo da Vinci: Genius of Art and Science* (4–7). Series: Great Minds of Science. 2005, Enslow LB $26.60 (978-0-7660-2500-4). Reed describes da Vinci's wide-ranging achievements —

showing, for example, his urban planning ideas, his design for a flying machine, and his anatomical drawings — and emphasizes his originality and creativity. (Rev: SLJ 6/05) [921]

DESJARLAIT, PATRICK

7643 Williams, Neva. *Patrick DesJarlait: Conversations with a Native American Artist* (5–7). 1994, Lerner LB $22.60 (978-0-8225-3151-7). A beautifully illustrated biography of the Native American artist who worked at the Red Lake Indian Reservation in Minnesota. (Rev: BL 1/1/95; SLJ 1/95) [921]

DISNEY, WALT

7644 Ford, Barbara. *Walt Disney* (4–8). 1989, Walker LB $17.00 (978-0-8027-6865-0). The story of Disney's youth and his struggle to fulfill his dreams. (Rev: BL 5/15/89) [791.430924]

ELLABBAD, MOHIEDDIN

7645 Ellabbad, Mohieddin. *The Illustrator's Notebook* (5–10). Trans. from French by Sarah Quinn. Illus. by author. 2006, Groundwood $16.95 (978-0-88899-700-5). In this fascinating journal printed from right to left, Egyptian-born illustrator Ellabbad reflects on the influences that led him to a life in art and offers valuable insights into Arabic cultural sensibilities. (Rev: SLJ 8/06)

EVANS, WALKER

7646 Nau, Thomas. *Walker Evans: Photographer of America* (6–9). 2007, Roaring Brook $19.95 (978-1-59643-225-3). A profile of Evans is accompanied by reproductions of many of his photographs, arranged to show how his work changed and progressed during his career. (Rev: BL 3/1/07; HB 5–6/07; LMC 8–9/07; SLJ 3/07) [921]

GEHRY, FRANK

7647 Lazo, Caroline Evensen. *Frank Gehry* (7–10). Series: A&E Biography. 2005, Twenty-First Century LB $29.27 (978-0-8225-2649-0); paper $7.95 (978-0-8225-3388-7). Introduces the architect and his most famous structures, with full-color photos and reproductions. (Rev: SLJ 2/06) [921]

GORMAN, R. C.

7648 Hermann, Spring. *R. C. Gorman: Navajo Artist* (4–8). Series: Multicultural Junior Biographies. 1995, Enslow LB $20.95 (978-0-89490-638-1). The story of this contemporary Native American artist, who reflects his heritage in his work. (Rev: BL 2/15/96; SLJ 3/96) [921]

HINE, LEWIS

7649 Worth, Richard. *Lewis Hine: Photographer of Americans at Work* (6–9). Series: Show Me America.

2008, Sharpe Focus LB $32.95 (978-0-7656-8153-9). Excellent illustrations and succinct text give an overview of the celebrated photographer's life and work and explain the historical context. (Rev: SLJ 5/1/09) [921]

HOPPER, EDWARD

7650 Lyons, Deborah. *Edward Hopper: Summer at the Seaside* (4–8). Series: Adventures in Art. 2003, Prestel $14.95 (978-3-7913-2737-2). The story of the American painter who died in 1967, with a good analysis of many of his important works. (Rev: BL 11/15/03; SLJ 9/03) [921]

7651 Rubin, Susan Goldman. *Edward Hopper: Painter of Light and Shadow* (5–8). Illus. 2007, Abrams $18.95 (978-0-8109-9347-1). Along with a life of the painter, Rubin provides good reproductions of his work plus discussion of his themes, images, and technique. (Rev: BL 9/1/07; SLJ 10/07)

HUNTER, CLEMENTINE

7652 Lyons, Mary E. *Talking with Tebe: Clementine Hunter, Memory Artist* (7–12). 1998, Houghton Mifflin $17.00 (978-0-395-72031-8). This richly illustrated book, which quotes extensively from taped interviews and is as much about social history as about painting, tells the story of the first illiterate, self-taught African American folk artist to receive national attention for her work. (Rev: BCCB 1/99; BL 8/98; HB 9–10/98; HBG 3/99; SLJ 9/98) [921]

KAHLO, FRIDA

7653 Bernier-Grand, Carmen T. *Frida: Viva la vida! Long Live Life!* (7–12). Illus. by Frida Kahlo. 2007, Marshall Cavendish $18.99 (978-0-7614-5336-9). Free-verse poems about the art and life of Frida Kahlo accompany reproductions of her artwork and photographs of the artist and her family; some poems deal with adult subjects such as a troubled marriage and a pregnancy loss. (Rev: BL 11/1/07; SLJ 12/07) [921]

7654 Holzhey, Magdalena. *Frida Kahlo: The Artist in the Blue House* (4–8). Series: Adventures in Art. 2003, Prestel $14.95 (978-3-7913-2863-8). A colorful introduction to this Mexican painter with an interesting analysis of individual paintings. (Rev: BL 11/15/03; SLJ 9/03) [921]

KIRBY, JACK

7655 Hamilton, Sue. *Jack Kirby* (4–8). Series: Comic Book Creators. 2007, ABDO LB $16.95 (978-1-59928-298-5). A biography of comic book legend Kirby, with information on his childhood, early career, and work on comics such as the *Incredible Hulk* and *Captain America*. (Rev: BL 5/1/07) [921]

LANGE, DOROTHEA

7656 King, David C. *Dorothea Lange: Photographer of the People* (6–9). Series: Show Me America. 2008, Sharpe Focus LB $32.95 (978-0-7656-8154-6). Excellent illustrations and succinct text give an overview of this influential photojournalist's life and work. (Rev: SLJ 5/1/09) [921]

LAWRENCE, JACOB

7657 Duggleby, John. *Story Painter: The Life of Jacob Lawrence* (5–8). 1998, Chronicle $16.95 (978-0-8118-2082-0). Using 50 color reproductions, this biography of the great African American illustrator and painter tells how he moved to Harlem in the 1930s and developed his own techniques and style. (Rev: BCCB 1/99; BL 10/15/98; HB 3–4/99; HBG 3/99; SLJ 12/98) [921]

LEE, STAN

7658 Miller, Raymond H. *Stan Lee: Creator of Spider-Man* (4–8). Series: Inventors and Creators. 2006, Gale LB $26.20 (978-0-7377-3447-8). Superhero fans will enjoy this biography of the man behind Spider-Man and other comic-book characters. (Rev: SLJ 6/06) [921]

LICHTENSTEIN, ROY

7659 Rubin, Susan Goldman. *Whaam! The Art and Life of Roy Lichtenstein* (4–7). Illus. 2008, Abrams $18.95 (978-081099492-8). With many reproductions of his works and thoughtful, engaging text, this eye-catching book offers a portrait of Roy Lichtenstein and his diverse artistic achievements. Lexile 1030L (Rev: BL 11/1/08; HB 1–2/09; SLJ 10/1/08) [921]

LIN, MAYA

7660 Lashnits, Tom. *Maya Lin* (6–10). Series: Asian Americans of Achievement. 2007, Chelsea House LB $30.00 (978-0-7910-9268-2). This is an attractive biography of the designer of the Vietnam Veterans Memorial in Washington, D.C. (Rev: SLJ 8/07) [921]

MATISSE, HENRI

7661 Hollein, Max, and Nina Hollein. *Matisse: Cut-Out Fun with Matisse* (4–8). Series: Adventures in Art. 2003, Prestel $14.95 (978-3-7913-2858-4). This large-formatted book that originated in Germany, successfully introduces the life and work of the great French master. (Rev: BL 11/15/03; HBG 3/02; SLJ 8/01) [921]

MICHELANGELO

7662 Connolly, Sean. *Michelangelo* (5–8). Series: The Lives of the Artists. 2004, World Almanac LB $31.00 (978-0-8368-5600-2). A tall, slender volume full of facts about Michelangelo's life and times, with many color reproductions. (Rev: SLJ 8/04) [921]

7663 Somervill, Barbara A. *Michelangelo: Sculptor and Painter* (6–9). Series: Signature Lives. 2005, Compass Point LB $34.60 (978-0-7565-0814-2). Michelangelo comes to life in this readable biography that includes color images. (Rev: BL 8/05) [709]

7664 Whiting, Jim. *Michelangelo* (4–7). Series: Art Profiles for Kids. 2007, Mitchell Lane LB $29.95 (978-1-58415-562-1). Suitable for both research and browsing, this examination of the artist's life and times includes many reproductions and interesting sidebars. (Rev: LMC 2/08; SLJ 12/07) [921]

MONET, CLAUDE

7665 Connolly, Sean. *Claude Monet* (4–8). Series: Lives of the Artists. 2005, World Almanac LB $31.00 (978-0-8368-5650-7). A tall, slender volume full of facts about Monet's life and times, with many color reproductions. (Rev: BL 6/1–15/04; SLJ 3/05) [921]

7666 Kallen, Stuart A. *Claude Monet* (7–10). Series: Eye on Art. 2008, Gale/Lucent $32.45 (978-1-4205-0074-5). This attractive Monet biography offers a compelling glimpse at the man behind the famed artwork, including his personal struggles, flaws, and volatile genius. (Rev: SLJ 6/1/09) [921]

7667 Whiting, Jim. *Claude Monet* (4–7). Series: Art Profiles for Kids. 2007, Mitchell Lane LB $29.95 (978-1-58415-563-8). Suitable for both research and browsing, this examination of the artist's life and times includes many reproductions and interesting sidebars. (Rev: LMC 2/08; SLJ 12/07) [921]

MOUNT, WILLIAM SIDNEY

7668 Howard, Nancy S. *William Sidney Mount: Painter of Rural America* (4–7). 1994, Sterling $14.95 (978-1-871922-75-2). An interactive book that explores the work and paintings of the 19th-century American painter William Sidney Mount. (Rev: BL 1/15/95) [921]

MUNCH, EDVARD

7669 Whiting, Jim. *Edvard Munch* (6–9). Series: Art Profiles for Kids. 2008, Mitchell Lane LB $20.95 (978-1-58415-712-0). Whiting recounts Munch's often difficult life, provides color reproductions and interesting sidebars on related people and events, and discusses the theft of his most famous work, *The Scream*. (Rev: SLJ 3/1/09) [921]

NOGUCHI, ISAMU

7670 Tiger, Caroline. *Isamu Noguchi* (6–12). Series: Asian Americans of Achievement. 2007, Chelsea House LB $30.00 (978-0-7910-9276-7). This is the fascinating story of Noguchi's search for an identity and a place to call home as well as his development into an internationally renowned sculptor. (Rev: SLJ 10/07) [921]

PEI, I. M.

7671 Rubalcaba, Jill. *I. M. Pei: Architect of Time, Place, and Purpose* (7–10). Illus. 2011, Marshall Cavendish $23.99 (978-0-7614-5973-6). Rubalcaba gives an interesting and well-designed overview of Pei's life and works, including reproductions of sketches and plans as well as photographs of buildings, with in-depth discussion of seven projects. (Rev: BL 11/1/11*; LMC 3–4/12; SLJ 10/1/11) [921]

PICASSO, PABLO

7672 Bernier-Grand, Carmen T. *Picasso: I the King, Yo el rey* (6–12). Illus. by David Diaz. 2012, Amazon Children's $19.99 (978-076146177-7). In free-style verse and dramatic images, Bernier-Grand profiles the famous artist. (Rev: BL 11/1/12; SLJ 1/13) [921]

7673 Jacobson, Rick. *Picasso: Soul on Fire* (4–7). Illus. by Rick Jacobson and Laura Fernandez. 2004, Tundra $15.95 (978-0-88776-599-5). Oil paintings of the Spanish-born artist, along with reproductions of some of his best-known pieces, introduce his work and brief facts about his life. (Rev: BL 11/1/04) [921]

POLITI, LEO

7674 Stalcup, Ann. *Leo Politi: Artist of the Angels* (4–9). Illus. by Leo Politi. 2004, Silver Moon $24.95 (978-1-893110-38-0). The life of the American-born man who spent his formative years in Italy and returned as an adult to make his home in Los Angeles and protray the ethnic communities there in his books for children. (Rev: SLJ 4/05) [921]

REMBERT, WINFRED

7675 Rembert, Winfred. *Don't Hold Me Back: My Life and Art* (4–7). 2003, Cricket $19.95 (978-0-8126-2703-9). Rembert reflects on his life in the South as a sharecropper's son — picking cotton, dealing with racism, the civil rights movement — and displays his evocative works of art with comments on their creation. (Rev: BL 11/1/03*; HBG 4/04; SLJ 12/03*) [759.1]

REMBRANDT VAN RIJN

7676 Mason, Antony. *Rembrandt* (4–8). Series: Lives of the Artists. 2005, World Almanac LB $31.00 (978-0-8368-5651-4). A tall, slender volume full of facts about Rembrandt's life and times, with many color reproductions. (Rev: BL 6/1–15/04; SLJ 3/05) [921]

7677 Roberts, Russell. *Rembrandt* (6–9). Series: Art Profiles for Kids. 2008, Mitchell Lane LB $20.95 (978-1-58415-710-6). Roberts documents Rembrandt's often tragic life and includes color reproductions of his best-known works and sidebar information on related people and events. (Rev: SLJ 3/1/09) [921]

7678 Schwartz, Gary. *Rembrandt* (7–12). Series: First Impressions. 1992, Abrams $19.95 (978-0-8109-3760-

4). This jargon-free, accessible biography presents Rembrandt with all his flaws and quirks. (Rev: BL 5/1/92; SLJ 6/92*) [921]

RENOIR, PIERRE-AUGUSTE

7679 Somervill, Barbara A. *Pierre-Auguste Renoir* (5–8). Series: Art Profiles for Kids. 2007, Mitchell Lane LB $29.95 (978-1-58415-566-9). A brief introduction to the artist's life and work and the times in which he lived, with reproductions of his art. (Rev: BL 1/1–15/08; LMC 2/08; SLJ 12/07) [921]

RIVERA, DIEGO

7680 Bankston, John. *Diego Rivera* (5–7). Series: Latinos in American History. 2003, Mitchell Lane LB $29.95 (978-1-58415-208-8). A biography of the famous 20th-century Mexican artist who is best known for his murals with political overtones. (Rev: BL 1/1–15/04; HBG 4/04; SLJ 2/04) [921]

7681 Bernier-Grand, Carmen T. *Diego: Bigger Than Life* (7–10). Illus. by David Diaz. 2009, Marshall Cavendish $18.99 (978-076145383-3). The story of artist Diego Rivera's life is told using first-person free-verse poems; fact and fiction are defined in the informative back matter. Belpré Honor 2010; ALA Notable Books 2010. (Rev: BL 2/15/09; HB 5–6/09; LMC 8–9/09; SLJ 4/1/09) [921]

7682 Litwin, Laura Baskes. *Diego Rivera: Legendary Mexican Painter* (7–10). Series: Latino Biography. 2005, Enslow LB $31.93 (978-0-7660-2486-1). The life, art, and controversial politics of Mexican artist Diego Rivera are explored in this attractive and readable title. (Rev: BL 11/1/05; SLJ 4/06) [759.972]

7683 Rubin, Susan Goldman. *Diego Rivera: An Artist for the People* (6–10). Illus. 2013, Abrams $21.95 (978-081098411-0). With many examples of Rivera's paintings, drawings, and murals, this is an honest and accessible portrait of the Mexican artist. (Rev: BL 2/15/13*; SLJ 5/13*) [921]

ROCKWELL, NORMAN

7684 Gherman, Beverly. *Norman Rockwell: Storyteller with a Brush* (4–7). 2000, Simon & Schuster $19.95 (978-0-689-82001-4). An appealing biography of this New England artist who reflected mid-20th-century American life and values in his many paintings. (Rev: BCCB 7–8/00; BL 2/15/00; HB 3–4/00; HBG 10/00; SLJ 2/00) [921]

SAY, ALLEN

7685 Say, Allen. *Drawing from Memory* (4–7). Illus. by author. 2011, Scholastic $17.99 (978-0-545-17686-6). Say tells the story of his creative awakening in words and illustrations, beginning with his childhood in World War II Japan. Sibert Honor 2012; ALA Notable Books 2012. Lexile HL560L (Rev: BL 8/11*; SLJ 9/1/11*) [921]

SCHULKE, FLIP

7686 Schulke, Flip. *Witness to Our Times: My Life as a Photojournalist* (6–12). 2003, Cricket $19.95 (978-0-8126-2682-7). In this volume full of examples of his work, Schulke describes his early life and his career covering events of the 20th century including the space program and the civil rights movement. (Rev: BL 4/15/03; HBG 10/03; SLJ 6/03; VOYA 2/04) [070.4]

SCHULZ, CHARLES

7687 Gherman, Beverly. *Sparky: The Life and Art of Charles Schulz* (4–8). Illus. 2010, Chronicle $16.99 (978-0-8118-6790-0). A graphic-format biography of the creator of *Peanuts,* with many excerpts from the comic strip. (Rev: BL 6/10; SLJ 8/10; VOYA 6/10) [921]

7688 Marvis, Barbara. *Charles Schulz: The Story of the Peanuts Gang* (4–8). Series: Robbie Reader. 2004, Mitchell Lane LB $25.70 (978-1-58415-289-7). This photo-filled biography traces Schulz's life and his love of cartoons; it is especially suitable for reluctant readers. (Rev: BL 9/1/05)

SIMMONS, PHILIP

7689 Lyons, Mary E. *Catching the Fire: Philip Simmons, Blacksmith* (4–8). 1997, Houghton Mifflin $17.00 (978-0-395-72033-2). A biography of the contemporary African American craftsman and artist from Charleston, South Carolina, with extensive quotations from personal interviews. (Rev: BL 9/1/97; HBG 3/98; SLJ 9/97) [921]

THIEBAUD, WAYNE

7690 Rubin, Susan Goldman. *Delicious: The Life and Art of Wayne Thiebaud* (5–8). Illus. 2007, Chronicle $15.95 (978-0-8118-5168-8). Paintings (by Thiebaud, of course) of gum balls and cupcakes on the cover of this nicely designed volume draw readers in to the story of a man who paints "happy pictures." (Rev: BL 2/15/08; SLJ 3/08)

TRUMBULL, JOHN

7691 Murray, Stuart A. P. *John Trumbull: Painter of the Revolutionary War* (6–9). Series: Show Me America. 2008, Sharpe Focus LB $32.95 (978-0-7656-8150-8). Excellent illustrations and succinct text give an overview of the celebrated photographer's life and work and explain the historical context. (Rev: SLJ 5/1/09) [921]

VAN GOGH, VINCENT

7692 Bonafoux, Pascal. *Van Gogh: The Passionate Eye* (7–12). Series: Discoveries. 1992, Abrams paper $12.95

(978-0-8109-2828-2). An overview of the life and work of this disturbed Dutch painter. (Rev: BL 7/92) [921]

7693 Crispino, Enrica. *Van Gogh* (6–10). Illus. Series: Art Masters. 2008, Oliver LB $27.95 (978-193454505-8). This insightful look at Van Gogh's work focuses more on the painter in the context of his times rather than providing a chronology of personal events. (Rev: BL 12/15/08; LMC 11–12/08) [921]

7694 Whiting, Jim. *Vincent Van Gogh* (7–12). Series: Art Profiles for Kids. 2007, Mitchell Lane LB $29.95 (978-1-58415-564-5). Report writers will appreciate this thorough introduction to the artist's life and work, with interesting "FYI" sections and small color reproductions. (Rev: SLJ 1/08)

WALDMAN, NEIL

7695 Waldman, Neil. *Out of the Shadows: An Artist's Journey* (5–8). Illus. 2006, Boyds Mills $21.95 (978-1-59078-411-2). In this candid memoir, Waldman describes how his challenging childhood experiences influenced him as an artist. (Rev: BL 4/15/06; SLJ 5/06)

WANG YANI

7696 Zhensun, Zheng, and Alice Low. *A Young Painter: The Life and Paintings of Wang Yani — China's Extraordinary Young Artist* (5–8). 1991, Scholastic paper $17.95 (978-0-590-44906-9). The story of a self-taught prodigy whose paintings are highly regarded in China. Includes many examples of her unique work, based on the traditional Chinese style. (Rev: BCCB 9/91; BL 10/1/91*; SLJ 8/91) [921]

WARHOL, ANDY

7697 Greenberg, Jan, and Sandra Jordan. *Andy Warhol, Prince of Pop* (8–12). 2004, Random House LB $18.99 (978-0-385-73056-3). Warhol had a successful career in commercial art before rising to fame as a pop icon; this volume covers his youth, early career, love of celebrity, and early death as well as his art and its lasting influence. (Rev: BCCB 12/04; BL 6/1–15/04*; HB 1–2/05; SLJ 11/04; VOYA 10/04) [709]

7698 Rubin, Susan Goldman. *Andy Warhol: Pop Art Painter* (4–7). Illus. 2006, Abrams $18.95 (978-0-8109-5477-9). This picture-book biography chronicles Warhol's life and career, focusing in particular on his art and his childhood in Pittsburgh; there are many reproductions plus a timeline and a glossary. (Rev: BL 11/1/06; SLJ 11/06)

WILHEIM, LILY RENEE

7699 Robbins, Trina. *Lily Renee, Escape Artist: From Holocaust Survivor to Comic Book Pioneer* (4–7). Illus. by Anne Timmons. 2011, Lerner LB $29.27 (978-

076136010-0); paper $7.95 (978-076138114-3). With helpful back matter that provides historical context, this is the story of a Jewish girl who escapes from Germany in 1939 and goes on to become a cartoonist in America. Sydney Taylor Book Honor 2012. **e** Lexile GN510L (Rev: BL 10/15/11; LMC 3–4/12; SLJ 11/1/11; VOYA 12/11) [921]

WOOD, GRANT

7700 Duggleby, John. *Artist in Overalls: The Life of Grant Wood* (4–8). 1996, Chronicle $15.95 (978-0-8118-1242-9). The life of this American artist tells of his difficult struggle with poverty and his great attachment to the Midwest. (Rev: BCCB 6/96; BL 4/15/96; HB 7–8/96; SLJ 5/96) [921]

WOOD, MICHELE

7701 Igus, Toyomi. *Going Back Home: An Artist Returns to the South* (4–8). 1996, Children's $16.95 (978-0-89239-137-0). The author re-creates the family history and life of the African American illustrator Michele Wood. (Rev: BCCB 12/96; BL 9/15/96; SLJ 7/97) [921]

WRIGHT, FRANK LLOYD

7702 Adkins, Jan. *Frank Lloyd Wright* (7–12). Series: Up Close. 2007, Viking $16.99 (978-0-670-06138-9). The biographer does not gloss over the architect's infamously prickly nature but also emphasizes Wright's talent and his influence on building design. (Rev: BL 11/1/07; SLJ 11/07) [921]

7703 Fandel, Jennifer. *Frank Lloyd Wright* (7–12). Series: Xtraordinary Artists. 2005, Creative Education LB $21.95 (978-1-58341-378-4). This well-illustrated life of the visionary architect draws on comments from his students, contemporaries, and admirers. (Rev: SLJ 12/05) [921]

7704 Mayo, Gretchen Will. *Frank Lloyd Wright* (5–8). Series: Trailblazers of the Modern World. 2004, World Almanac LB $31.00 (978-0-8368-5101-4). Report writers will find useful information on Wright's life, achievements, and lasting contributions. (Rev: SLJ 7/04) [921]

ZHANG, ANGE

7705 Zhang, Ange. *Red Land, Yellow River: A Story from the Cultural Revolution* (5–8). 2004, Groundwood $16.95 (978-0-88899-489-9). In this compelling autobiography, artist Ange Zhang tells how he came of age during one of the most turbulent periods in modern Chinese history — the Cultural Revolution of the late 1960s. (Rev: BL 12/1/04*; SLJ 12/04) [921]

Authors

ALLENDE, ISABEL

7706 Main, Mary. *Isabel Allende: Award-Winning Latin American Author* (6–9). Series: Latino Biography Library. 2005, Enslow LB $31.93 (978-0-7660-2488-5). An engaging life of the writer that gives readers a perspective on life in Chile and on the world affairs that have impacted Allende. (Rev: SLJ 1/06) [921]

ALVAREZ, JULIA

7707 Aykroyd, Clarissa. *Julia Alvarez: Novelist and Poet* (7–10). Series: Twentieth Century's Most Influential Hispanics. 2007, Gale LB $32.45 (978-1-4205-0022-6). The poet's life and work, with many quotations from Alvarez and excerpts from her poems. (Rev: BL 2/15/08) [921]

ANDERSEN, HANS CHRISTIAN

7708 Varmer, Hjordis. *Hans Christian Andersen: His Fairy Tale Life* (4–7). Trans. by Tina Nunnally. Illus. by Lilian Bregger. 2005, Groundwood $19.95 (978-0-88899-670-1). This large-format, lively biography presents the Danish storyteller's single-minded struggle to rise above adversity. (Rev: BL 11/1/05; SLJ 6/06) [839.81]

ANGELOU, MAYA

7709 Shapiro, Miles. *Maya Angelou* (7–10). Series: Black Americans of Achievement. 1994, Chelsea LB $21.95 (978-0-7910-1862-0). A chronological narrative of the life of this amazing African American writer that describes her hardships and triumphs. (Rev: BL 6/1–15/94; SLJ 6/94) [921]

AUSTEN, JANE

7710 Locke, Juliane. *England's Jane: The Story of Jane Austen* (8–11). 2006, Morgan Reynolds LB $26.95 (978-1-931798-82-2). The parallels between Austen's life and novels are evident in this appealing biography. (Rev: BL 2/15/06; SLJ 2/06) [823]

7711 Wagner, Heather Lehr. *Jane Austen* (7–10). Series: Who Wrote That? 2003, Chelsea House LB $30.00 (978-0-7910-7623-1). Details of Austen's family life and education and of the mores of the time give insight into her humorous attitude toward society and romance. (Rev: SLJ 6/04) [921]

AVI

7712 Markham, Lois. *Avi* (5–8). 1996, Learning Works paper $7.99 (978-0-88160-280-7). This profile of the gifted writer recounts his triumph over dysgraphia, a learning disability that makes writing difficult, and explores his creative process and the major themes of his work. (Rev: BL 4/1/96; SLJ 8/96) [921]

7713 Mercier, Cathryn M., and Susan P. Bloom. *Presenting Avi* (6–10). Series: Twayne's United States Authors. 1997, Macmillan $35 (978-0-8057-4569-6). This biography of the noted writer of books for children and young adults is divided into chapters based on roles he has assumed as a writer, including storyteller, stylist, magician, and historian, and explores his many beliefs about the significance of literature. (Rev: SLJ 6/98) [921]

7714 Sommers, Michael A. *Avi* (5–8). Series: The Library of Author Biographies. 2004, Rosen LB $27.95 (978-0-8239-4522-1). Covers Avi's life and career as a YA author, with analysis of his work, an interview, and lists of works and awards. (Rev: SLJ 1/05) [921]

BARRIE, J. M.

7715 Aller, Susan Bivin. *J. M. Barrie: The Magic Behind Peter Pan* (6–8). 1994, Lerner LB $25.26 (978-0-8225-4918-5). This biography of the author reveals Barrie's similarities to his character Peter Pan and also gives details of his failed marriages. (Rev: BL 11/1/94; SLJ 12/94) [921]

BRADBURY, RAY

7716 Bankston, John. *Ray Bradbury* (6–9). Illus. Series: Who Wrote That? 2011, Chelsea House LB $35 (978-160413778-1). Describes the personal life and the works of the well-known science fiction writer. (Rev: BL 10/15/11; SLJ 5/1/12) [921]

BRONTË FAMILY

7717 Kenyon, Karen Smith. *The Brontë Family: Passionate Literary Geniuses* (5–9). Series: Lerner Biographies. 2002, Lerner LB $30.35 (978-0-8225-0071-1). An absorbing introduction to the individual members of this literary family, with many illustrations and quotations from letters. (Rev: HBG 3/03; SLJ 1/03; VOYA 2/03) [921]

7718 Reef, Catherine. *The Bronte Sisters: The Brief Lives of Charlotte, Emily, and Anne* (5–9). Illus. 2012, Clarion $18.99 (978-0-547-57966-5). A balanced, well-researched, and very readable biography of the three sisters who wrote poetry and novels under men's names. (Rev: BL 6/12*; LMC 1–2/13; SLJ 9/12) [921]

BROOKS, GWENDOLYN

7719 Hill, Christine M. *Gwendolyn Brooks: "Poetry Is Life Distilled"* (7–10). Series: African-American Biography Library. 2005, Enslow LB $31.93 (978-0-7660-

2292-8). Poet Gwendolyn Brooks, the first African American to win the Pulitzer Prize, is profiled in accessible text with lots of photos and background information. (Rev: BL 11/1/05; SLJ 11/05) [811]

BYARS, BETSY

7720 Byars, Betsy. *The Moon and I* (4–7). 1996, Morrow paper $5.99 (978-0-688-13704-5). A memoir from this well-known children's author, which gives her the opportunity to tell how she likes both writing and snakes. (Rev: BCCB 3/92*; BL 5/15/92; SLJ 4/92) [921]

7721 Cammarano, Rita. *Betsy Byars* (4–7). Series: Who Wrote That? 2002, Chelsea $30.00 (978-0-7910-6720-8). A profile in text and pictures of one of America's best-loved authors and winner of the Newbery and other prizes. (Rev: BL 10/15/02; HBG 3/03) [921]

CARD, ORSON SCOTT

7722 Willett, Edward. *Orson Scott Card: Architect of Alternate Worlds* (7–9). Series: Authors Teens Love. 2006, Enslow LB $31.93 (978-0-7660-2354-3). A thorough profile of the creator of the "Enderverse." (Rev: SLJ 1/07) [921]

CARROLL, LEWIS

7723 Carpenter, Angelica Shirley. *Lewis Carroll: Through the Looking Glass* (6–9). Series: Lerner Biographies. 2002, Lerner LB $27.93 (978-0-8225-0073-5). The mathematician and author who created Alice is introduced through a look at his youth, education, university career, and Oxford friendships. (Rev: BCCB 1/03; HBG 3/03; SLJ 3/03; VOYA 8/03) [828]

CATHER, WILLA

7724 Meltzer, Milton. *Willa Cather* (7–12). Series: Literary Greats. 2008, Lerner LB $33.26 (978-0-8225-7604-4). An easy-to-understand profile that describes Cather's upbringing on the plains and provides historical context. (Rev: BL 4/15/08; SLJ 6/08) [921]

CHAUCER, GEOFFREY

7725 Hubbard-Brown, Janet. *Chaucer: Celebrated Poet and Author* (6–9). Series: Makers of the Middle Ages and Renaissance. 2005, Chelsea House LB $30 (978-0-7910-8635-3). A biography of the famous medieval writer, with information on his childhood, background, influences, career, and works. (Rev: SLJ 5/06) [921]

CHRISTIE, AGATHA

7726 Dommermuth-Costa, Carol. *Agatha Christie: Writer of Mystery* (5–9). Series: Biographies. 1997, Lerner LB $30.35 (978-0-8225-4954-3). A biography of the "First Lady of Crime," with material on her personal life, including her two marriages. (Rev: SLJ 8/97; VOYA 4/98)

CISNEROS, SANDRA

7727 Mirriam-Goldberg, Caryn. *Sandra Cisneros: Latina Writer and Activist* (5–8). Series: Hispanic Biographies. 1998, Enslow LB $19.95 (978-0-7760-1045-8). A biography, enlivened with many quotations, of the woman who received Cs and Ds in school and later became a first-rate author and leading Hispanic American activist. (Rev: BL 1/1–15/99; VOYA 10/99) [921]

7728 Warrick, Karen Clemens. *Sandra Cisneros: Inspiring Latina Author* (5–8). Series: Latino Biography Library. 2009, Enslow $31.93 (978-0-7660-3162-3). The story of the Mexican American author, the challenges she faced growing up, and how her books reflect her life. (Rev: SLJ 4/10) [921]

COLLINS, SUZANNE

7729 Bailey, Diane. *Suzanne Collins* (6–9). Illus. Series: All About the Author. 2012, Rosen LB $34.60 (978-144886938-1). An interesting biography of the author of the Hunger Games series. (Rev: BL 10/1/12; VOYA 2/13) [921]

7730 Sapet, Kerrily. *Suzanne Collins* (7–10). Illus. Series: World Writers. 2012, Morgan Reynolds LB $28.95 (978-159935346-3). Sapet traces Suzanne Collins's life and work, discussing the plots and characters of the popular *Hunger Games*. (Rev: BL 11/1/12; SLJ 11/12; VOYA 12/12) [921]

COURLANDER, HAROLD

7731 Jaffe, Nina. *A Voice for the People: The Life and Work of Harold Courlander* (7–10). 1997, Henry Holt $16.95 (978-0-8050-3444-8). A biography of the famous collector of folktales from minority groups who was also a noted writer and storyteller. (Rev: BL 11/1/97; HBG 3/98; SLJ 12/97) [921]

COVILLE, BRUCE

7732 Marcovitz, Hal. *Bruce Coville* (6–9). Series: Who Wrote That? 2005, Chelsea House LB $30 (978-0-7910-8656-8). A biography of author Bruce Coville, covering his childhood, life experiences, career, how books and reading affected his life, and his inspirations. (Rev: SLJ 5/06) [921]

CRANE, STEPHEN

7733 Kepnes, Caroline. *Stephen Crane* (5–8). Series: Classic Storytellers. 2004, Mitchell Lane LB $29.95 (978-1-58415-272-9). An introduction to Crane's life, work, and legacy, with background information on relevant historical, cultural, and economic factors. (Rev: BL 1/05; SLJ 1/05) [921]

CRUTCHER, CHRIS

7734 Davis, Terry. *Presenting Chris Crutcher* (6–10). 1997, Macmillan $29 (978-0-8057-8223-3). A warm biography of this important young adult author who combines sports stories with important themes such as tolerance and the meaning of friendship. (Rev: SLJ 6/98; VOYA 6/98) [921]

7735 Summers, Michael A. *Chris Crutcher* (5–8). Series: The Library of Author Biographies. 2005, Rosen LB $27.95 (978-1-4042-0325-9). An interview with Crutcher is an interesting addition to this description of the author's life — including his experiences as a novelist, educator, therapist, and child protection advocate — and his works for children. (Rev: SLJ 9/05) [921]

CUMMINGS, E. E.

7736 Reef, Catherine. *E. E. Cummings: A Poet's Life* (8–11). 2006, Clarion $21.00 (978-0-618-56849-9). In addition to Cummings's poetry, Reef looks at his difficult teen years and romantic relationships and at the culture of the time. (Rev: BL 11/15/06; HB 11–12/06; SLJ 3/07*) [921]

D'ANGELO, PASCAL

7737 Murphy, Jim. *Pick and Shovel Poet: The Journeys of Pascal D'Angelo* (6–12). 2000, Clarion $20.00 (978-0-395-77610-0). The story of the short, hard life of the Italian American poet who wrote an important autobiography about coming to the New World. (Rev: BCCB 12/00; BL 3/1/01; HB 1–2/01; HBG 3/01; SLJ 1/01; VOYA 2/02) [973.04]

DAHL, ROALD

7738 Cooling, Wendy. *D Is for Dahl: A Gloriumptious A-Z Guide to the World of Roald Dahl* (5–8). Illus. by Quentin Blake. 2005, Viking $15.99 (978-0-670-06023-8). For Dahl fans, this is an alphabetically arranged collection of trivia about his life and writings. (Rev: BL 8/05; SLJ 10/05) [823]

7739 Dahl, Roald. *Boy: Tales of Childhood* (7–12). 1984, Farrar $17.00 (978-0-374-37374-0). The famous author's autobiography — sometimes humorous, sometimes touching — of growing up in Wales and spending summers in Norway. (Rev: BL 6/87) [921]

7740 Dahl, Roald. *More About Boy: Roald Dahl's Tales from Childhood* (6–12). Illus. by Quentin Blake. 2009, Farrar $24.99 (978-0-374-35055-0). This updated and expanded scrapbook-style version of Dahl's original autobiography *Boy* (1984) includes personal artifacts (report cards, photographs, letters, and so forth) as well as new anecdotes and a quiz. (Rev: HB 11–12/09; LMC 3–4/10; SLJ 1/10) [921]

7741 Gelletly, LeeAnne. *Gift of Imagination: The Story of Roald Dahl* (7–10). 2006, Morgan Reynolds $26.95 (978-1-59935-026-4). Dahl's early life and career are detailed in this profile that includes many photographs, a timeline, and a bibliography of the author's works. (Rev: BL 11/1/06; SLJ 12/06) [823]

7742 Houle, Michelle M. *Roald Dahl: Author of Charlie and the Chocolate Factory* (6–9). Series: Authors Teens Love. 2006, Enslow LB $23.95 (978-0-7660-2353-6). Covers Dahl's life and work, with glossary, chapter notes, and bibliography. (Rev: BL 7/06; SLJ 7/06) [921]

DANTE ALIGHIERI

7743 Davenport, John C. *Dante: Poet, Author, and Proud Florentine* (6–9). Series: Makers of the Middle Ages and Renaissance. 2005, Chelsea House LB $30 (978-0-7910-8634-6). Describes the childhood, background, influences, career, and works of the Italian author. (Rev: SLJ 5/06) [921]

DANZIGER, PAULA

7744 Krull, Kathleen. *Presenting Paula Danziger* (6–12). Series: United States Authors. 1995, Twayne $35.00 (978-0-8057-4153-7). Examines writer Danziger's personal problems, humorous teaching experiences, and group discussions of her books in six thematic chapters. (Rev: BL 9/1/95; VOYA 2/96) [921]

7745 Reed, Jennifer. *Paula Danziger: Voice of Teen Troubles* (5–8). Series: Authors Teens Love. 2006, Enslow LB $31.93 (978-0-7660-2444-1). This profile of the popular author includes interviews in which she discusses her dysfunctional family and her struggles with depression and bulimia. (Rev: BL 9/15/06) [921]

DEPAOLA, TOMIE

7746 dePaola, Tomie. *Christmas Remembered* (5–8). 2006, Putnam $19.99 (978-0-399-24622-7). Folk artist dePaola recalls some of the most memorable Christmases from his past. (Rev: BL 10/1/06; SLJ 10/06)

DIAKITE, BABA WAGUE

7747 Diakité, Baba Wagué. *A Gift from Childhood: Memories of an African Boyhood* (6–10). 2010, Groundwood $18.95 (978-0-88899-931-3). The author relates his childhood living with his grandparents in a village in Mali and recalls the wisdom and folklore he learned there along with many practical lessons. (Rev: BL 4/15/10; HB 7–8/10; LMC 8–9/10; SLJ 5/10) [921]

DICKENS, CHARLES

7748 Caravantes, Peggy. *Best of Times: The Story of Charles Dickens* (7–10). Series: Writers of Imagination. 2005, Morgan Reynolds LB $26.95 (978-1-931798-68-6). Examines the events in the author's life that led to his literary preoccupation with social injustices. (Rev: BL 8/05; SLJ 12/05) [823]

7749 Rosen, Michael. *Dickens: His Work and His World* (4–7). Illus. by Robert Ingpen. 2005, Candlewick $19.99 (978-0-7636-2752-2). Before reviewing Dickens's major works, Rosen discusses the author's difficult childhood and the social conditions of his times.

(Rev: BCCB 3/06; BL 9/15/05*; HBG 4/06; LMC 3/06; SLJ 11/05*) [921]

7750 Wells-Cole, Catherine. *Charles Dickens: England's Most Captivating Storyteller* (4–7). Illus. Series: Historical Notebook. 2011, Candlewick $19.99 (978-0-7636-5567-9). A visually appealing introduction to Dickens and his world, using a scrapbook format with double-page spreads covering various aspects of his life and work. (Rev: BLO 11/15/11; LMC 3–4/12; SLJ 11/1/11; VOYA 4/12) [921]

DICKINSON, EMILY

7751 Meltzer, Milton. *Emily Dickinson* (8–11). Series: American Literary Greats. 2006, Lerner LB $31.93 (978-0-7613-2949-7). Dickinson's life story is interwoven with quotes from her poetry and excerpts from primary sources including letters. (Rev: BL 2/15/06; SLJ 6/06; VOYA 4/06) [811]

DINESEN, ISAK

7752 Leslie, Roger. *Isak Dinesen: Gothic Storyteller* (8–12). 2004, Morgan Reynolds LB $23.95 (978-1-931798-17-4). Danish-born author Isak Dinesen, best known for *Out of Africa*, a memoir of her years spent in Kenya, is profiled in this engaging volume that emphasizes her battle with syphilis. (Rev: BL 4/1/04; SLJ 5/04) [921]

DOYLE, SIR ARTHUR CONAN

7753 Pascal, Janet B. *Arthur Conan Doyle: Beyond Baker Street* (7–12). 2000, Oxford $32.95 (978-0-19-512262-6). This biography of the creator of Sherlock Holmes tells how he was also a defender of those unjustly accused of crimes, a spiritualist, and a prolific author in various genres. (Rev: BL 2/15/00; HBG 9/00; SLJ 6/00) [921]

EMERSON, RALPH WALDO

7754 Caravantes, Peggy. *Self-Reliance: The Story of Ralph Waldo Emerson* (7–10). Illus. Series: World Writers. 2010, Morgan Reynolds LB $28.95 (978-159935124-7). This chronological biography captures Emerson's life and work, and reveals his lack of self-esteem as a young adult. (Rev: BL 8/10; VOYA 10/10) [921]

FITZGERALD, F. SCOTT

7755 Bankston, John. *F. Scott Fitzgerald* (5–8). Series: Classic Storytellers. 2004, Mitchell Lane LB $29.95 (978-1-58415-249-1). An introduction to Fitzgerald's life, work, and legacy, with background information on relevant historical, cultural, and economic factors. (Rev: BL 1/05; SLJ 1/05) [921]

7756 Boon, Kevin Alexander. *F. Scott Fitzgerald* (7–10). Series: Writers and Their Works. 2005, Benchmark LB $25.95 (978-0-7614-1947-1). *The Great Gatsby* is dis-

cussed in some detail in this overview of Fitzgerald's life and works. (Rev: SLJ 3/06) [921]

7757 Lazo, Caroline Evensen. *F. Scott Fitzgerald: Voice of the Jazz Age* (6–9). Series: Lerner Biographies. 2002, Lerner LB $27.93 (978-0-8225-0074-2). Fitzgerald's life from childhood, marriage, and work are covered in this interesting account that includes many black-and-white photographs. (Rev: HBG 3/03; SLJ 12/02; VOYA 2/03) [813]

FLEISCHMAN, SID

7758 Fleischman, Sid. *The Abracadabra Kid: A Writer's Life* (6–12). 1996, Greenwillow $16.99 (978-0-688-14859-1). The exciting autobiography of the famous author who was also a magician, gold miner, and World War II sailor. (Rev: BL 9/1/96*; SLJ 8/96*; VOYA 4/97) [921]

FOX, PAULA

7759 Daniel, Susanna. *Paula Fox* (5–8). Series: The Library of Author Biographies. 2004, Rosen LB $27.95 (978-0-8239-4525-2). Covers Fox's life and career, with analysis of her work and its themes, an interview, and lists of works and awards. (Rev: SLJ 1/05) [921]

FRITZ, JEAN

7760 Fritz, Jean. *Homesick: My Own Story* (7–12). Illus. by Margot Tomes. 1982, Putnam $17.99 (978-0-399-20933-8). Growing up in the troubled China of the 1920s. (Rev: BL 2/1/89) [921]

FROST, ROBERT

7761 Caravantes, Peggy. *Deep Woods: The Story of Robert Frost* (7–10). 2006, Morgan Reynolds LB $26.95 (978-1-931798-92-1). An introduction to the poet's life and successful career. (Rev: BL 9/15/06; SLJ 6/06) [921]

7762 Wooten, Sara McIntosh. *Robert Frost: The Life of America's Poet* (5–8). Series: People to Know Today. 2006, Enslow LB $31.93 (978-0-7660-2627-8). A fine introduction to the New England poet whose poetry is loved by young people and adults, with information on his difficult childhood and continuing struggles with depression and financial woes. (Rev: SLJ 1/07) [921]

GANTOS, JACK

7763 Gantos, Jack. *Hole in My Life* (8–12). 2002, Farrar $16.00 (978-0-374-39988-7). The gritty story of the author's experiences in prison after being convicted for drug smuggling — and his successful efforts to live a better life. (Rev: BCCB 5/02; BL 4/1/02; HB 5–6/02*; HBG 10/02; SLJ 5/02*; VOYA 6/02) [813.54]

GEISEL, THEODOR SEUSS

7764 Cohen, Charles D. *The Seuss, the Whole Seuss, and Nothing but the Seuss* (8–12). 2004, Random House $35.00 (978-0-375-82248-3). This oversize, abundantly illustrated book gives a profile of the great author/illustrator and an analysis of his ideas and work. (Rev: BL 3/15/04; SLJ 6/04) [921]

GIFF, PATRICIA REILLY

7765 Giff, Patricia Reilly. *Don't Tell the Girls: A Family Memoir* (4–7). 2005, Holiday $16.95 (978-0-8234-1813-8). The author tells of the search for her family's roots that led her to Ireland. (Rev: BL 3/1/05; SLJ 7/05) [813]

GRIMM BROTHERS

7766 Hettinga, Donald R. *The Brothers Grimm: Two Lives, One Legacy* (5–8). 2001, Clarion $22.00 (978-0-618-05599-9). An interesting biography that places the brothers' lives in the context of their time and discusses their skills as lexicographers and scholars. (Rev: BL 7/01; HB 1–2/02; HBG 3/02; SLJ 10/01) [430]

HALEY, ALEX

7767 Shirley, David. *Alex Haley* (7–10). Series: Black Americans of Achievement. 1993, Chelsea LB $30.00 (978-0-7910-1979-5); paper $8.95 (978-0-7910-1980-1). The story of the African American writer who gave us the family saga *Roots*. (Rev: BL 2/15/94) [921]

HAMILTON, VIRGINIA

7768 Adoff, Arnold, and Kacy Cook, eds. *Virginia Hamilton: Speeches, Essays, and Conversations* (8–12). 2010, Scholastic $29.99 (978-043927193-6). This collection, edited by her husband and Kacy Cook, gives insight into the life and work of the popular, award-winning author of children's books. (Rev: BL 3/1/10; LMC 8–9/10; SLJ 3/10*; VOYA 4/10) [921]

HANSBERRY, LORRAINE

7769 Sinnott, Susan. *Lorraine Hansberry: Award-Winning Playwright and Civil Rights Activist* (7–12). 1998, Conari paper $11.95 (978-1-57324-093-2). This story of the great African American playwright who grew up with a passion for theater and politics conveys a sense of the politics from the 1930s to the 1960s and the pressures of fame on an artist. (Rev: BL 2/15/99) [921]

HAWTHORNE, NATHANIEL

7770 Meltzer, Milton. *Nathaniel Hawthorne: A Biography* (6–12). 2006, Twenty-First Century LB $31.93 (978-0-7613-3459-0). Hawthorne had an event-filled life according to this biography that covers both triumphs and blemishes and puts the whole in historical context. (Rev: SLJ 11/06)

HEMINGWAY, ERNEST

7771 Reef, Catherine. *Ernest Hemingway: A Writer's Life* (8–12). Illus. 2009, Clarion $20.00 (978-061898705-4). With many quotations from Hemingway's contemporaries, Reef creates a vivid and balanced portrait of the author's complex life. ∩ (Rev: BL 6/1–15/09; SLJ 8/09) [921]

7772 Whiting, Jim. *Ernest Hemingway* (6–8). Series: Classic Storytellers. 2005, Mitchell Lane LB $29.95 (978-1-58415-376-4). A concise and readable introduction to the author's life and works. (Rev: SLJ 12/05) [921]

HENRY, MARGUERITE

7773 Collins, David R. *Write a Book for Me: The Story of Marguerite Henry* (7–10). Series: World Writers. 1999, Morgan Reynolds LB $23.95 (978-1-883846-39-8). A short, simple biography of the writer of such memorable books for young people as *King of the Wind*. (Rev: BL 3/15/99; SLJ 9/99; VOYA 10/99) [921]

HINTON, S. E.

7774 Kjelle, Marylou Morano. *S. E. Hinton: Author of The Outsiders* (5–8). Series: Authors Teens Love. 2007, Enslow LB $31.93 (978-0-7660-2720-6). A life of the author of the well-known novel, with an "In Her Own Words" section that researchers will find useful. (Rev: SLJ 11/07) [921]

HOMER

7775 Tracy, Kathleen. *The Life and Times of Homer* (5–8). Series: Biography from Ancient Civilizations: Legends, Folklore, and Stories of Ancient Worlds. 2004, Mitchell Lane LB $29.95 (978-1-58415-260-6). Drawing on ancient legends, this is a profile of ancient Greek poet and storyteller Homer. (Rev: BL 10/15/04; SLJ 12/04)

HOROWITZ, ANTHONY

7776 Abrams, Dennis. *Anthony Horowitz* (6–9). Series: Who Wrote That? 2006, Chelsea House LB $30.00 (978-0-7910-8968-2). This biography of British horror and spy fiction author Horowitz explores how his unhappy childhood experiences influenced his books. (Rev: BL 6/1–15/06) [921]

HUGHES, LANGSTON

7777 Rummel, Jack. *Langston Hughes: Poet.* Rev. ed. (7–12). Series: Black Americans of Achievement. 2005, Chelsea House LB $30.00 (978-0-7910-8250-8). A revised edition of the highly readable and well illustrated biography of the African American poet and fiction writer, containing excerpts from his writings. (Rev: SLJ 11/05) [921]

7778 Wallace, Maurice. *Langston Hughes: The Harlem Renaissance* (8–12). Series: Writers and Their Works. 2007, Marshall Cavendish LB $27.95 (978-0-7614-2591-5). Accessible analysis of Hughes's works is combined with information about his life and the environment in which he worked. (Rev: BL 2/1/08; SLJ 2/08) [921]

HURSTON, ZORA NEALE

7779 Litwin, Laura Baskes. *Zora Neale Hurston: "I Have Been in Sorrow's Kitchen"* (7–10). 2007, Enslow LB $23.95 (978-0-7660-2536-3). Presents the life of legendary author and folklorist Zora Neale Hurston, including her childhood, her influences, and her remarkable career. (Rev: BL 6/1–15/07; SLJ 7/07) [921]

7780 Porter, A. P. *Jump at de Sun: The Story of Zora Neale Hurston* (7–12). 1992, Carolrhoda paper $8.95 (978-0-87614-546-3). A brief, easy-to-read biography that places Hurston within the context of the racism of her era. (Rev: BL 12/15/92; SLJ 1/93*) [921]

7781 Sapet, Kerrily. *Rhythm and Folklore: The Story of Zora Neale Hurston* (7–12). 2008, Morgan Reynolds LB $27.95 (978-1-59935-067-7). This vibrant biography of the author of *Their Eyes Were Watching God* contains plenty of personal quotes, full-page photographs, and complete back matter. (Rev: BL 6/1–15/08; SLJ 8/08) [921]

IRVING, WASHINGTON

7782 Collins, David R. *Washington Irving: Storyteller for a New Nation* (4–8). Series: World Writers. 2000, Morgan Reynolds LB $23.95 (978-1-883846-50-3). This biography introduces the globetrotting American writer and gives details of his work and personality. (Rev: BL 4/1/00; HBG 3/00; SLJ 5/00; VOYA 6/01) [921]

KERR, M. E.

7783 Nilsen, Alleen P. *Presenting M. E. Kerr. Rev. ed.* (8–12). Series: Twayne's United States Authors. 1997, Twayne $35.00 (978-0-8057-9248-5). A biography of this popular young adult writer that also discusses her works, with a detailed analysis of her five most popular books. (Rev: SLJ 4/98; VOYA 4/98) [810]

KING, STEPHEN

7784 Whitelaw, Nancy. *Dark Dreams: The Story of Stephen King* (7–10). Series: World Writers. 2005, Morgan Reynolds $26.95 (978-1-931798-77-8). An inviting introduction to King and to his writing, with lots of interesting anecdotes and snippets of his work. (Rev: BL 11/15/05; VOYA 2/06) [813]

L'ENGLE, MADELEINE

7785 McClellan, Marilyn. *Madeleine L'Engle: Banned, Challenged, and Censored* (8–12). Series: Authors of Banned Books. 2008, Enslow LB $25.95 (978-0-7660-2708-4). Why do some groups question if the author's *A Wrinkle in Time* is appropriate for young readers? This book examines the objections and the author's defense of her award-winning book. (Rev: BL 4/1/08) [921]

LEE, HARPER

7786 Don, Katherine. *Real Courage: The Story of Harper Lee* (7–10). Illus. Series: World Writers. 2012, Morgan Reynolds LB $28.95 (978-159935348-7). An interesting life of the woman who wrote only one novel, but an enduring classic. (Rev: BL 11/1/12; SLJ 12/12; VOYA 12/12) [921]

7787 Madden, Kerry. *Harper Lee* (7–12). Illus. Series: Up Close. 2009, Viking $16.99 (978-067001095-0). An introduction to the life and work of the reclusive author of *To Kill a Mockingbird*. Lexile 1210 (Rev: BL 4/15/09; HB 3–4/09; SLJ 6/1/09) [921]

LEWIS, C. S.

7788 Parker, Vic. *C. S. Lewis* (4–7). Series: Writers Uncovered. 2006, Heinemann LB $23.00 (978-1-4034-7336-3). In addition to providing biographical information on Lewis, Parker looks at his books, especially the Narnia series, giving plot outlines and discussing the stories and themes. (Rev: BL 8/06) [921]

LONDON, JACK

7789 Bankston, John. *Jack London* (4–7). Series: Classic Storytellers. 2005, Mitchell Lane LB $29.95 (978-1-58415-263-7). An introduction to London's life, work, and legacy, with background information on relevant historical, cultural, and economic factors. (Rev: BL 1/05) [921]

7790 Stefoff, Rebecca. *Jack London: An American Original* (7–10). Series: Oxford Portraits. 2002, Oxford LB $32.95 (978-0-19-512223-7). A profile of this American original, his life, his work, and his lasting importance. (Rev: BL 7/02; HBG 10/02; SLJ 8/02) [921]

LOVECRAFT, H. P.

7791 Schoell, William. *H. P. Lovecraft: Master of Weird Fiction* (5–8). 2003, Morgan Reynolds LB $23.95 (978-1-931798-15-0). Lovecraft, known for his stories of horror and the supernatural, was born into privilege that ended with his parents' early deaths; his works only received real acclaim after his death. (Rev: BL 9/15/03; HBG 4/04; SLJ 12/03) [813]

LOWRY, LOIS

7792 Bankston, John. *Lois Lowry* (6–9). Illus. Series: Who Wrote That? 2009, Chelsea House LB $30.00 (978-160413335-6). An interesting profile of the Newbery Medal-winning author and the factors that influenced her work, with discussion of the reasons for censorship challenges to her books. (Rev: BLO 6/17/09) [921]

7793 Lowry, Lois. *Looking Back: A Book of Memories* (4–8). 1998, Houghton Mifflin $17.00 (978-0-395-89543-6). This autobiographical work centers around a series of photographs and the author's comments on each. (Rev: BL 11/1/98; HB 1–2/99; HBG 3/99; SLJ 9/98; VOYA 4/99) [921]

7794 Markham, Lois. *Lois Lowry* (5–8). Series: Meet the Author. 1995, Learning Works paper $7.99 (978-0-88160-278-4). This biography of the Newbery Medal-winning author tells how she became a writer and looks at the personal experiences that are reflected in her books. (Rev: SLJ 1/96) [921]

MAGEE, JOHN

7795 Granfield, Linda. *High Flight: A Story of World War II* (5–7). 1999, Tundra $15.95 (978-0-88776-469-1). The moving story of John Magee, a young Canadian Air Force pilot who was killed in World War II and who is best known for writing the poem "High Flight." (Rev: BCCB 12/99; BL 1/1–15/00; HBG 3/00; SLJ 2/00) [921]

MANZANO, JUAN FRANCISCO

7796 Engle, Margarita. *The Poet Slave of Cuba: A Biography of Juan Francisco Manzano* (7–10). Illus. by Sean Quails. 2006, Henry Holt $16.95 (978-0-8050-7706-3). This lyrical free-verse biography tells the story of the poet born into slavery in Cuba in 1797, describing his early talent with languages and how it helped him survived amazing brutality. Belpré Medal 2008; ALA Notable Books 2008. (Rev: BL 2/15/06*; SLJ 4/06*) [811]

MELVILLE, HERMAN

7797 Meltzer, Milton. *Herman Melville: A Biography* (8–12). Series: American Literary Greats. 2005, Twenty-First Century LB $31.93 (978-0-7613-2749-3). Traces the writer's difficult life and links his struggles to passages from his works, in particular *Moby Dick*. (Rev: SLJ 1/06) [921]

MEYER, STEPHENIE

7798 Krohn, Katherine. *Stephenie Meyer: Dreaming of Twilight* (6–12). Illus. Series: Lifeline Biographies. 2010, Lerner LB $33.26 (978-076135220-4). This attractive biography draws on the archives of *USA Today* to describe the author's life and publishing career. (Rev: BL 9/1/10*) [921]

MILLER, ARTHUR

7799 Andersen, Richard. *Arthur Miller* (7–10). Series: Writers and Their Works. 2005, Benchmark LB $25.95 (978-0-7614-1946-4). *The Crucible* and *Death of a*

Salesman are discussed in some detail in this overview of Miller's life and works. (Rev: SLJ 3/06) [921]

MOEYAERT, BART

7800 Moeyaert, Bart. *Brothers: The Oldest, the Quietest, the Realest, the Farthest, the Nicest, the Fastest, and I* (7–9). Trans. from Flemish by Wanda J. Boeke. Illus. by Cercla Dendooven. 2005, Front St. $16.95 (978-1-932425-18-5). The Belgian author offers candid and often wistful vignettes of growing up the youngest of seven brothers and the incidents that seemed of utmost importance to him. (Rev: SLJ 1/06; VOYA 4/06) [921]

MONTGOMERY, L. M.

7801 Kjelle, Marylou Morano. *L. M. Montgomery* (6–9). Series: Who Wrote That? 2005, Chelsea House LB $30.00 (978-0-7910-8234-8). This interesting profile shows the parallels between Montgomery and her most famous character, Anne of Green Gables. (Rev: BL 11/1/05) [813]

MORRISON, TONI

7802 Andersen, Richard. *Toni Morrison* (7–10). Series: Writers and Their Works. 2005, Benchmark LB $25.95 (978-0-7614-1945-7). *Sula* and *The Bluest Eye* are discussed in some detail in this overview of Morrison's life and works. (Rev: SLJ 3/06) [921]

7803 Haskins, Jim. *Toni Morrison: Telling a Tale Untold* (7–12). 2002, Millbrook LB $26.90 (978-0-7613-1852-1). Haskins adds discussion of each of Morrison's books to this account of her life and literary career. (Rev: BL 10/1/02; HBG 3/03; VOYA 12/02) [813]

NAYLOR, PHYLLIS REYNOLDS

7804 Naylor, Phyllis Reynolds. *How I Came to Be a Writer. Rev. ed.* (4–9). 2001, Simon & Schuster paper $4.99 (978-0-689-83887-3). Naylor describes the joys and difficulties of life as a writer and includes excerpts of her work in this autobiographical account. (Rev: SLJ 5/01) [921]

NIXON, JOAN LOWERY

7805 Wade, Mary Dodson. *Joan Lowery Nixon: Masterful Mystery Writer* (5–8). Series: Authors Teens Love. 2004, Enslow LB $26.60 (978-0-7660-2194-5). Examines Nixon's life, writings, and her focus on girls of character and strength. (Rev: SLJ 11/04) [921]

O'BRIEN, SOLEDAD

7806 Robson, David. *Soledad O'Brien* (6–9). Series: Transcending Race in America. 2010, Mason Crest $22.95 (978-1-4222-1617-0). This biography is part of a series that looks at famous biracial achievers in America and considers this aspect of the journalist's life. (Rev: LMC 3–4/10) [921]

ORWELL, GEORGE

7807 Agathocleous, Tanya. *George Orwell: Battling Big Brother* (8–12). Series: Oxford Portraits. 2000, Oxford $32.95 (978-0-19-512185-8). A concise, well-written life of this fascinating English writer and his contributions to world literature. (Rev: BL 10/1/00; HBG 10/01) [921]

PAREDES, AMERICO

7808 Murcia, Rebecca Thatcher. *Americo Paredes* (5–7). Series: Latinos in American History. 2003, Mitchell Lane LB $29.95 (978-1-58415-207-1). The story of the Mexican American author, folklorist, and professor at the University of Texas in Austin who is also famous for establishing a center for intercultural studies. (Rev: BL 1/1–15/04) [921]

PATERSON, KATHERINE

7809 Kjelle, Marylou Morano. *Katherine Paterson* (4–7). Series: Classic Storytellers. 2004, Mitchell Lane LB $29.95 (978-1-58415-268-2). Examines the life and times of the award-winning children's author, including her work as a missionary in Japan and how religious faith informs her writing. (Rev: BL 1/1–15/05; SLJ 3/05) [921]

7810 McGinty, Alice B. *Katherine Paterson* (5–8). Series: The Library of Author Biographies. 2005, Rosen LB $27.95 (978-1-4042-0328-0). An interview with Paterson is an interesting addition to this description of the author's life and works for children. (Rev: SLJ 9/05) [921]

PAULSEN, GARY

7811 Paterra, Elizabeth. *Gary Paulsen* (4–7). Series: Who Wrote That? 2002, Chelsea $30.00 (978-0-7910-6723-9). A profile of the prolific author (of almost 200 books) who is best known for his young adult outdoor survival stories. (Rev: BL 10/15/02; HBG 3/03) [921]

7812 Paulsen, Gary. *Caught by the Sea* (5–8). 2001, Delacorte $15.95 (978-0-385-32645-2). The author describes his ongoing love of the sea and the adventures he's had, some funny, some scary. (Rev: BL 9/15/01; HBG 3/02; SLJ 10/01; VOYA 12/01) [818]

7813 Peters, Stephanie True. *Gary Paulsen* (4–8). 1999, Learning Works paper $7.99 (978-0-88160-324-8). A straightforward biography of the outdoorsman and author that tells about his books, his interests, his alcoholism, and his continuing health problems. (Rev: BL 6/1–15/99; SLJ 6/99) [921]

POE, EDGAR ALLAN

7814 Frisch, Aaron. *Edgar Allan Poe* (5–9). Illus. by Gary Kelley. Photos by Tina Mucci. Series: Voices in Poetry. 2005, Creative Education LB $31.35 (978-1-58341-344-9). A brief biography that adds atmospheric

paintings and photographs to a chronological narrative and excerpts from Poe's works. (Rev: SLJ 3/06) [921]

7815 Lange, Karen E. *Nevermore: A Photobiography of Edgar Allan Poe* (5–8). Illus. 2009, National Geographic $17.95 (978-1-4263-0398-2). This readable photobiography offers an overview of the writer's work and life starting with his difficult childhood and covering his struggles as an adult. (Rev: BCCB 5/09; BL 4/1/09; LMC 10/09; SLJ 4/09*) [921]

7816 Meltzer, Milton. *Edgar Allan Poe* (6–12). 2003, Millbrook LB $31.90 (978-0-7613-2910-7). Poe's difficult life and literary accomplishments are described within the larger context of early 19th-century society in this well-illustrated and well-documented biography. (Rev: BL 11/15/03; HBG 4/04; VOYA 2/04) [818]

7817 Peltak, Jennifer. *Edgar Allan Poe* (6–8). Series: Who Wrote That? 2003, Chelsea House LB $30.00 (978-0-7910-7622-4). The dark details of Poe's personal life provide insight into the themes of his stories and poems; a well-written and attractive volume. (Rev: SLJ 6/04; VOYA 6/04) [921]

PULLMAN, PHILIP

7818 Yuan, Margaret Speaker. *Philip Pullman* (7–10). Series: Who Wrote That? 2005, Chelsea House LB $30.00 (978-0-7910-8658-2). In addition to profiling this author of award-winning books, this biography describes his writing methods. (Rev: BL 3/15/06; SLJ 5/06) [823]

RIIS, JACOB

7819 Pascal, Janet B. *Jacob Riis: Reporter and Reformer* (8–11). Series: Oxford Portraits. 2006, Oxford LB $28.00 (978-0-19-514527-4). Riis's groundbreaking photography and journalism exposing 19th-century living and working conditions is explored in this well-balanced biography of the Danish American. (Rev: BL 6/1–15/06; SLJ 7/06) [921]

RIORDAN, RICK

7820 Sparks, Barry. *Rick Riordan* (7–10). Illus. Series: World Writers. 2012, Morgan Reynolds LB $28.95 (978-159935350-0). Sparks traces Riordan's life and work, discussing the plots and characters of popular works including the Percy Jackson series. (Rev: BL 11/1/12; SLJ 11/12) [921]

ROWLING, J. K.

7821 Harmin, Karen Leigh. *J. K. Rowling: Author of Harry Potter* (4–7). Series: People to Know Today. 2006, Enslow LB $31.93 (978-0-7660-1850-1). An attractive and accessible biography of the creator of the wildly popular series, with details of her youth, career, and the impact success has had on her life; plus information on aspects of British life that will interest young readers. (Rev: BL 11/1/06) [921]

7822 Peterson-Hilleque, Victoria. *J. K. Rowling: Extraordinary Author* (5–8). Series: Essential Lives. 2010, ABDO LB $32.79 (978-1-61613-517-1). This volume describes Rowling's youth and personal life as well as her career, giving information on her efforts to get Harry Potter published, her success, and some of the key characters. (Rev: SLJ 3/1/11) [921]

RUMI

7823 Demi. *Rumi: Whirling Dervish* (5–8). Illus. by author. 2009, Marshall Cavendish $19.99 (978-0-7614-5527-1). This picture-book profile of the 13th-century Persian mystical poet is enhanced by the rich illustrations. (Rev: BL 4/15/09; LMC 10/09; SLJ 6/09) [921]

SANDBURG, CARL

7824 Meltzer, Milton. *Carl Sandburg: A Biography* (5–10). 1999, Millbrook LB $31.90 (978-0-7613-1364-9). The story of a literary giant who, in addition to his poetry, is noted for nonfiction works including a biography of Abraham Lincoln. (Rev: BL 12/15/99; HBG 10/00; VOYA 6/00) [921]

SCIESZKA, JON

7825 Scieszka, Jon. *Knucklehead: Tall Tales and Mostly True Stories of Growing Up Scieszka* (4–7). 2008, Viking $16.99 (978-0-670-01106-3). Scieszka's entertaining autobiography tells a story of growing up one of six irreverent brothers in Flint, Michigan. ALA Notable Books 2009. ∩ (Rev: BL 9/1/08; HB 11–12/08; LMC 1–2/09; SLJ 10/1/08*; VOYA 12/08) [921]

SEBESTYEN, OUIDA

7826 Monseau, Virginia R. *Presenting Ouida Sebestyen* (6–12). Series: United States Authors. 1995, Twayne $28.00 (978-0-8057-8224-0). Sebestyen's unorthodox writing habits enliven this text, with biographical information and detailed analysis of six novels. (Rev: BL 9/1/95) [921]

SENDAK, MAURICE

7827 Marcovitz, Hal. *Maurice Sendak* (6–9). 2006, Chelsea House LB $30.00 (978-0-7910-8796-1). A look at the life of Maurice Sendak, with information on his childhood, his art and stories, and his concern with the Holocaust. (Rev: BL 9/1/06) [921]

SHAKESPEARE, WILLIAM

7828 Aliki. *William Shakespeare and the Globe* (4–7). 1999, HarperCollins LB $18.89 (978-0-06-027821-2). Shakespeare and Elizabethan England come to life in this detailed picture book that uses many quotations from his plays and also tells of the recent rebuilding of the Globe theater. (Rev: BCCB 4/99; BL 6/1–15/99*; HB 5–6/99; HBG 10/99; SLJ 5/99) [921]

7829 Berk, Ari, and Kristen McDermott. *William Shakespeare: His Life and Times, in His Own Words* (6–9). 2010, Candlewick $19.99 (978-0-7636-4794-0). In the form of a scrapbook that Shakespeare compiled for his daughter, this detail-filled volume includes inventive first-person narrative and real drawings, paintings, and other items from museums. (Rev: LMC 11–12/10; SLJ 9/1/10) [921]

7830 Bryson, Bill. *Shakespeare: The World as Stage* (8–12). 2007, HarperCollins $19.95 (978-0-06-074022-1). Bryson has created an unusual and enjoyable survey of Shakespeare's life and times, explaining his research as he goes and disproving earlier claims. ∩ (Rev: BL 10/15/07) [921]

7831 Hilliam, David. *William Shakespeare: England's Greatest Playwright and Poet* (5–8). Series: Rulers, Scholars, and Artists of the Renaissance. 2005, Rosen LB $33.25 (978-1-4042-0318-1). Information on Shakespeare's life and on the theater scene in 16th-century London is interwoven with quotes from the plays and poems. (Rev: BL 8/05) [822.3]

7832 Nettleton, Pamela Hill. *William Shakespeare: Playwright and Poet* (5–9). Series: Signature Lives. 2005, Compass Point $34.60 (978-0-7565-0816-6). Nettleton places facts about Shakespeare's life within the context of everyday life of the time, with details about the theater and publishing. (Rev: SLJ 6/05) [921]

SHELLEY, MARY WOLLSTONECRAFT

7833 Miller, Calvin Craig. *Spirit Like a Storm: The Story of Mary Shelley* (7–10). 1996, Morgan Reynolds LB $21.95 (978-1-883846-13-8). The life story of the fascinating, talented creator of *Frankenstein,* who was also the wife of poet Percy Bysshe Shelley. (Rev: BL 2/15/96; SLJ 3/96; VOYA 6/96) [921]

SINGER, ISAAC BASHEVIS

7834 Singer, Isaac Bashevis. *A Day of Pleasure: Stories of a Boy Growing Up in Warsaw* (6–8). Illus. by Roman Vishniac. 1969, Farrar paper $8.95 (978-0-374-41696-6). A Hasidic Jew's fond remembrances of the world in which he grew up. [921]

SÍS, PETER

7835 Sís, Peter. *The Wall: Growing Up Behind the Iron Curtain* (7–10). Illus. by author. 2007, Farrar $18.00 (978-0-374-34701-7). This autobiographical picture book portrays Sis's childhood in Czechoslovakia and the impact of Soviet rule on life in the nation. Sibert Medal 2008; Boston Globe–Horn Book Honor 2008; Caldecott Honor 2008; ALA Notable Books 2008. (Rev: BL 9/1/07; SLJ 8/07) [943.7]

SPINELLI, JERRY

7836 Spinelli, Jerry. *Knots in My Yo-Yo String: The Autobiography of a Kid* (5–8). 1998, Knopf paper $10.95

(978-0-679-88791-1). A frank, delightful memoir of growing up in Norristown, Pennsylvania, during the 1950s by the renowned Newbery Medal-winning writer of fiction for young people. (Rev: BCCB 7–8/98; BL 5/1/98; HBG 10/98; SLJ 6/98; VOYA 12/98) [921]

STEINBECK, JOHN

7837 Meltzer, Milton. *John Steinbeck* (6–9). Series: Up Close. 2008, Viking $16.99 (978-0-670-06139-6). Meltzer provides good background information on the time and society in which Steinbeck lived. (Rev: BL 3/15/08; SLJ 1/08) [921]

7838 Reef, Catherine. *John Steinbeck* (7–12). 1996, Clarion $17.95 (978-0-395-71278-8). A handsome photobiography that not only covers salient aspects of Steinbeck's life but also explores the themes and locales of his work. (Rev: BL 5/1/96; SLJ 3/96; VOYA 8/96) [921]

7839 Tracy, Kathleen. *John Steinbeck* (5–8). Series: Classic Storytellers. 2004, Mitchell Lane LB $29.95 (978-1-58415-271-2). An introduction to Steinbeck's life, work, and legacy, with background information on relevant historical, cultural, and economic factors. (Rev: BL 1/05; SLJ 1/05) [921]

STINE, R. L.

7840 Parker-Rock, Michelle. *R. L. Stine: Creator of Creepy and Spooky Stories* (5–8). Series: Authors Teens Love. 2005, Enslow LB $26.60 (978-0-7660-2445-8). Stine's writing career is the main focus of this biography that includes an interview. (Rev: SLJ 1/06) [921]

STOWE, HARRIET BEECHER

7841 Griskey, Michèle. *Harriet Beecher Stowe* (5–7). Series: Classic Storytellers. 2005, Mitchell Lane LB $29.95 (978-1-58415-375-7). Good historical and social context makes clear the importance of Stowe's achievements. (Rev: SLJ 11/05) [921]

7842 Sonneborn, Liz. *Harriet Beecher Stowe* (5–8). Series: Leaders of the Civil War Era. 2009, Chelsea House $30 (978-1-60413-302-8). Enhanced by a mix of illustrations, period documents, photographs, and concise sidebars, this book provides a balanced look at the author who inspired many to support abolitionism. (Rev: LMC 10/09) [921]

TAYLOR, MILDRED

7843 Houghton, Gillian. *Mildred Taylor* (5–8). Series: The Library of Author Biographies. 2005, Rosen LB $27.95 (978-1-4042-0330-3). An interview with Taylor is an interesting addition to this description of the African American author's life and writings. (Rev: SLJ 9/05) [921]

THOREAU, HENRY DAVID

7844 Hausman, Gerald, and Loretta Hausman. *A Mind with Wings: The Story of Henry David Thoreau* (6–9). 2006, Shambhala $15.95 (978-1-59030-228-6). Told in a series of anecdotes, this is a lively portrayal of Thoreau's life that uses dialogue based on his own statements. (Rev: BL 3/1/06; SLJ 9/06) [921]

7845 Meltzer, Milton. *Henry David Thoreau* (8–11). Series: American Literary Greats. 2007, Lerner LB $31.93 (978-0-8225-5893-4). A clear examination of Thoreau's life and work, exploring his philosophy and wit and their continuing relevance today. (Rev: BL 6/1–15/07; SLJ 5/07) [818]

7846 Thoreau, Henry David. *Thoreau at Walden* (8–12). Illus. by John Porcellino. Series: Center for Cartoon Studies. 2008, Hyperion $16.99 (978-1-4231-0038-6); paper $9.99 (978-1-4231-0039-3). Using Thoreau's words and spare, clean illustrations, this is a graphic novel-style introduction to the philosopher's beliefs about leading a simple life. (Rev: BL 3/15/08; SLJ 3/08) [921]

TOLKIEN, J. R. R.

7847 Willett, Edward. *J. R. R. Tolkien: Master of Imaginary Worlds* (6–9). Series: Authors Teens Love. 2004, Enslow LB $26.60 (978-0-7660-2246-1). Tolkien's interesting life will grab readers' attention, as will the quotations in the "In His Own Words" section. (Rev: BCCB 9/04; BL 11/1/04; SLJ 12/04) [921]

TWAIN, MARK

7848 Caravantes, Peggy. *A Great and Sublime Fool: The Story of Mark Twain* (7–10). Illus. Series: World Writers. 2009, Morgan Reynolds LB $28.95 (978-159935088-2). Well-chosen illustrations add to this informative survey of Twain's life and work. (Rev: BL 6/1–15/09; SLJ 7/1/09) [921]

7849 Fleischman, Sid. *The Trouble Begins at 8: A Life of Mark Twain in the Wild, Wild West* (5–8). 2008, Greenwillow $18.99 (978-0-06-134431-2). This is a spirited account of Twain's adventurous early years and how they formed the foundation for his writing. (Rev: BL 6/1–15/08; SLJ 7/08) [921]

7850 Howard, Todd, ed. *Mark Twain* (7–12). Series: People Who Made History. 2002, Gale paper $36.20 (978-0-7377-0897-4). Detailed essays that explore various aspects of Twain's life and writing are preceded by a general introductory that gives an overview of his life and times. (Rev: BL 4/1/02) [921]

7851 Lasky, Kathryn. *A Brilliant Streak: The Making of Mark Twain* (4–7). Illus. by Barry Moser. 1998, Harcourt $18.00 (978-0-15-252110-3). Using many quotations and anecdotes from the author's work, this nicely illustrated biography of Mark Twain concentrates on his first 30 years when he was a steamboat pilot, prospector, reporter, and budding writer. (Rev: BCCB 7–8/98; BL 4/1/98; HB 5–6/98; HBG 10/98; SLJ 4/98) [921]

7852 Rasmussen, R. Kent. *Mark Twain for Kids: His Life and Times, 21 Activities* (4–7). Series: For Kids. 2004, Chicago Review paper $14.95 (978-1-55652-527-8). An engaging biography that reveals interesting details of Twain's life and shows how many of the episodes in his books were based on his own experiences. (Rev: BL 9/15/04; SLJ 9/04) [921]

7853 Ward, Geoffrey C. *Mark Twain* (8–12). 2001, Knopf $40.00 (978-0-375-40561-7). As well as a good text, this biography contains a treasure trove of photographs and other illustrations that depict the life and times of Mark Twain. (Rev: BL 10/15/01; SLJ 6/02) [921]

VERNE, JULES

7854 Schoell, William. *Remarkable Journeys: The Story of Jules Verne* (4–8). Series: World Writers. 2002, Morgan Reynolds LB $23.95 (978-1-883846-92-3). Writing was not Verne's first love, as Schoell explains in this accessible biography. (Rev: BL 6/1–15/02; HBG 10/02; SLJ 9/02) [843.8]

7855 Teeters, Peggy. *Jules Verne: The Man Who Invented Tomorrow* (5–7). 1993, Walker LB $14.85 (978-0-8027-8191-8). The life of the famous writer of science fiction, including his childhood in France. (Rev: BL 3/15/93; SLJ 5/93) [921]

WELLS, H. G.

7856 Abrams, Dennis. *H. G. Wells* (6–9). Illus. Series: Who Wrote That? 2011, Chelsea House LB $35 (978-160413770-5). A well-written profile of the famous science fiction writer, with descriptions of the plots and characters of his key works. (Rev: BL 10/15/11; SLJ 5/1/12) [921]

WHARTON, EDITH

7857 Wooldridge, Connie Nordhielm. *The Brave Escape of Edith Wharton: A Biography* (7–10). 2010, Clarion $20 (978-0-547-23630-8). Explaining the social structure of the Gilded Age, this biography reveals Wharton's own rebellion against conventions and shows how her experiences are reflected in those of her literary characters. (Rev: BL 10/1/10*; LMC 3–4/11; SLJ 9/1/10; VOYA 12/10) [921]

WHEATLEY, PHILLIS

7858 Kent, Deborah. *Phillis Wheatley: First Published African-American Poet* (4–7). Series: Our People. 2003, Child's World LB $27.07 (978-1-59296-009-5). The life of the 18th-century poet is outlined in this well-illustrated work that features large type and includes historical background. (Rev: SLJ 4/04) [921]

7859 McLendon, Jacquelyn. *Phillis Wheatley: A Revolutionary Poet* (4–7). Series: Library of American Lives and Times. 2003, Rosen LB $34.60 (978-0-8239-5750-7). Kidnapped into slavery from Senegal, Phillis Wheatley became a major voice in the American literary scene. (Rev: BL 6/1–15/03; SLJ 5/03) [921]

WHITE, E. B.

7860 Bernard, Catherine. *E. B. White: Spinner of Webs and Tales* (5–8). Series: Authors Teens Love. 2005, Enslow LB $26.60 (978-0-7660-2350-5). An introductory chapter that gives a good overview of White's life is followed by chapters that delve into more detail plus a timeline and an excerpt from a 1969 interview that adds a more personal dimension. (Rev: BCCB 12/05; SLJ 10/05) [921]

7861 Murcia, Rebecca Thatcher. *E. B. White* (5–8). Series: Classic Storytellers. 2004, Mitchell Lane LB $29.95 (978-1-58415-273-6). An introduction to White's life, work, and legacy, with background information on relevant historical, cultural, and economic factors. (Rev: BL 1/05; SLJ 1/05) [921]

WHITMAN, WALT

7862 Kerley, Barbara. *Walt Whitman: Words for America* (4–8). Illus. by Brian Selznick. 2004, Scholastic $16.95 (978-0-439-35791-3). Whitman's experiences during the Civil War, including his service as a nurse to injured and dying soldiers, are highlighted in this picture-book biography. (Rev: BL 11/15/04; SLJ 11/04) [811]

7863 Meltzer, Milton. *Walt Whitman: A Biography* (6–12). 2002, Millbrook LB $31.90 (978-0-7613-2272-6). This life story of the American poet emphasizes his place in the country's history. (Rev: BL 4/1/02; HB 9–10/02; HBG 3/03; SLJ 3/02; VOYA 6/03) [921]

7864 Reef, Catherine. *Walt Whitman* (7–12). 1995, Clarion $16.95 (978-0-395-68705-5). A biography of the 19th-century poet who sang of America and the self. (Rev: BL 5/1/95; SLJ 5/95) [921]

WILDER, LAURA INGALLS

7865 Berne, Emma Carlson. *Laura Ingalls Wilder* (5–8). Series: Essential Lives. 2007, ABDO LB $22.95 (978-1-59928-843-7). The life of the author of the beloved Little House books, with an emphasis on the hard realities that she faced both as a pioneer child and as an adult during the Great Depression. (Rev: BL 2/1/08; SLJ 3/08) [813]

7866 Wadsworth, Ginger. *Laura Ingalls Wilder: Storyteller of the Prairie* (5–8). Series: Biography. 1997, Lerner LB $27.93 (978-0-8225-4950-5). A solid, readable biography of this author that clarifies the chronology in the Little House books. (Rev: BL 3/1/97; SLJ 4/97) [921]

473

7867 Wilder, Laura Ingalls. *A Little House Traveler: Writings from Laura Ingalls Wilder's Journeys Across America* (5–8). 2006, HarperCollins $16.99 (978-0-06-072491-7). Three of Wilder's diaries — one never before published — chronicle the Little House author's travels with her husband Almanzo and daughter Rose. (Rev: BL 12/15/05; VOYA 4/06)

WILSON, JACQUELINE

7868 Bankston, John. *Jacqueline Wilson* (6–9). Illus. Series: Who Wrote That? 2011, Chelsea House LB $35 (978-160413773-6). A well-written profile that discusses Wilson's evolution from crime novelist to writer of children's books. (Rev: BL 10/15/11; SLJ 10/1/11) [921]

WOODSON, JACQUELINE

7869 Hinton, KaaVonia. *Jacqueline Woodson* (5–8). Series: Classic Storytellers. 2008, Mitchell Lane LB $20.95 (978-1-58415-533-1). The story of Woodson's life, from her childhood in the 1960s to her adulthood — including her lesbian relationship — with photographs and discussions of her work. (Rev: BL 3/3/08; SLJ 8/08) [921]

WOOLF, VIRGINIA

7870 Brackett, Virginia. *Restless Genius: The Story of Virginia Woolf* (7–12). Series: Writers of Imagination. 2004, Morgan Reynolds LB $23.95 (978-1-931798-37-2). Woolf's personal life — her relationship with Vita Sackville-West is touched on — and mental stability are the main focus of this brief, interesting biography that also discusses her writing and its influence. (Rev: BCCB 11/04; BL 10/1/04; SLJ 11/04) [921]

WRIGHT, RICHARD

7871 Hart, Joyce. *Native Son: The Story of Richard Wright* (6–10). Series: World Writers. 2002, Morgan Reynolds LB $23.95 (978-1-931798-06-8). This biography describes best-selling African American author Richard Wright's controversial works and his development as a writer. (Rev: BL 2/15/03; HBG 3/03; SLJ 4/03) [921]

7872 Levy, Debbie. *Richard Wright* (7–12). Series: Literary Greats. 2007, Lerner LB $33.26 (978-0-8225-6793-6). The life and times of the author of *Native Son* and *Black Boy,* with photographs and a timeline. (Rev: BL 12/1/07; SLJ 12/07) [921]

7873 Wright, Richard. *Black Boy: A Record of Childhood and Youth* (8–12). 1998, HarperCollins paper $13.95 (978-0-06-092978-7). The tortured boyhood of the great black writer growing up in the South. This autobiography is continued in *American Hunger* (1977). [921]

YEATS, WILLIAM BUTLER

7874 Allison, Jonathan, ed. *William Butler Yeats* (6–12). Illus. by Glenn Harrington. Series: Poetry for Young People. 2003, Sterling $14.95 (978-0-8069-6615-1). A handsomely illustrated collection of Yeats's poems, each introduced with commentary and followed by explanations of any challenging vocabulary. (Rev: BL 4/1/03; HBG 10/03; SLJ 2/03) [921]

ZINDEL, PAUL

7875 Daniel, Susanna. *Paul Zindel* (5–8). Series: The Library of Author Biographies. 2004, Rosen LB $27.95 (978-0-8239-4524-5). Covers Zindel's career as a YA author, with analysis of his work, an interview, and lists of works and awards. (Rev: SLJ 1/05) [921]

Composers

BACH, JOHANN SEBASTIAN

7876 Getzinger, Donna, and Daniel Felsenfeld. *Johann Sebastian Bach and the Art of Baroque Music* (6–12). Series: Classical Composers. 2004, Morgan Reynolds LB $26.95 (978-1-931798-22-8). This biography reviews Bach's life and times, emphasizing in particular his musical education and commitment and his love for this family. (Rev: BL 6/1–15/04; SLJ 8/04) [780]

BEETHOVEN, LUDWIG VAN

7877 Viegas, Jennifer. *Beethoven's World* (5–8). Series: Music Throughout History. 2007, Rosen LB $29.25 (978-1-4042-0724-0). Six biographical chapters cover the composer's early life, family, personal life, musical training, compositions, and influences, with photographs of key people and places. (Rev: SLJ 1/08)

BERLIN, IRVING

7878 Furstinger, Nancy. *Say It with Music: The Story of Irving Berlin* (5–9). Series: Masters of Music. 2003, Morgan Reynolds LB $23.95 (978-1-931798-12-9). Well-researched and very readable, this account traces Berlin's life from Russia to the United States and his popular and lasting success as a songwriter. (Rev: BL 6/1–15/03; HBG 4/04; SLJ 10/03) [780.92]

BERLIOZ, HECTOR

7879 Whiting, Jim. *The Life and Times of Hector Berlioz* (5–7). Series: Masters of Music: The World's Greatest Composers. 2004, Mitchell Lane LB $20.95 (978-1-58415-259-0). A brief biography of the talented and troubled creator of the *Symphonie fantastique.* (Rev: SLJ 2/05) [921]

BERNSTEIN, LEONARD

7880 Blashfield, Jean F. *Leonard Bernstein: Composer and Conductor* (4–7). Series: Ferguson Career Biographies. 2001, Ferguson LB $25.00 (978-0-89434-337-7). Numerous black-and-white photographs accompany the easily read text in this interesting account of Bernstein's life and career. (Rev: SLJ 7/01) [780]

7881 Lazo, Caroline Evensen. *Leonard Bernstein: In Love with Music* (7–12). 2002, Lerner LB $27.93 (978-0-8225-0072-8). This detailed portrait of Bernstein's life and musical accomplishments includes many black-and-white photographs. (Rev: BL 10/15/02; HBG 3/03; VOYA 12/02) [780]

7882 Rubin, Susan Goldman. *Music Was It: Young Leonard Bernstein* (5–10). Illus. 2011, Charlesbridge $19.95 (978-1-58089-344-2). A compelling account of the composer/conductor's youth through the age of 25 and his determination to succeed in music despite his father's resistance to the idea. ALA Notable Children's Book; Sydney Taylor Award. (Rev: BL 2/15/11*; HB 5–6/11; LMC 8–9/11; SLJ 3/1/11)

CHOPIN, FREDERIC

7883 Malaspina, Ann. *Chopin's World* (5–8). Series: Music Throughout History. 2007, Rosen LB $29.25 (978-1-4042-0723-3). Six biographical chapters cover the composer's early life, family, personal life, musical training, compositions, and influences, with photographs of key people and places. (Rev: SLJ 1/08)

DVORAK, ANTONIN

7884 Horowitz, Joseph. *Dvorak in America* (6–12). 2003, Cricket $17.95 (978-0-8126-2481-6). Dvorak's life in the United States (he arrived from Prague in the 1890s) is the focus of this narrative, which also covers the composition of the New World symphony. (Rev: BL 6/1–15/03) [780]

GERSHWIN, GEORGE

7885 Reef, Catherine. *George Gershwin: American Composer* (5–8). Series: Masters of Music. 2000, Morgan Reynolds LB $23.95 (978-1-883846-58-9). This biography traces the life one of America's great composers, giving insight into his personality, family, and times. (Rev: BL 2/15/00; HBG 10/00; SLJ 3/00) [921]

GUTHRIE, WOODY

7886 Partridge, Elizabeth. *This Land Was Made for You and Me: The Life and Songs of Woodie Guthrie* (6–12). 2002, Viking $21.99 (978-0-670-03535-9). The life, work, and times of the folk singer, from his childhood in the Dust Bowl to his death from Huntington's Disease. (Rev: BL 4/1/02; HB 3–4/02*; HBG 10/02; SLJ 4/02; VOYA 8/02) [782.42162]

7887 Yates, Janelle. *Woody Guthrie: American Balladeer* (6–10). 1995, Ward Hill LB $14.95 (978-0-9623380-0-7); paper $10.95 (978-0-9623380-5-2). Describes Guthrie's creative life and provides important historical information, including the many tragedies suffered by his family and his friendly relationship with labor, members of the Communist Party, and other musicians. (Rev: BL 2/1/95; SLJ 3/95) [921]

HANDEL, GEORGE FRIDERIC

7888 Getzinger, Donna, and Daniel Felsenfeld. *George Frideric Handel and Music for Voices* (6–10). Series: Classical Composers. 2004, Morgan Reynolds LB $26.95 (978-1-931798-23-5). Handel's life and career are placed in historical context. (Rev: SLJ 11/04) [921]

7889 Lee, Lavina. *Handel's World* (5–8). Series: Music Throughout History. 2007, Rosen LB $29.25 (978-1-4042-0726-4). Six biographical chapters cover the composer's early life, family, personal life, musical training, compositions, and influences, with photographs of key people and places. (Rev: LMC 1/08; SLJ 1/08)

HAYDN, FRANZ JOSEPH

7890 Norton, James R. *Haydn's World* (5–8). Series: Music Throughout History. 2007, Rosen LB $29.25 (978-1-4042-0727-1). Six biographical chapters cover the composer's early life, family, personal life, musical training, compositions, and influences, with photographs of key people and places. (Rev: SLJ 1/08)

JOPLIN, SCOTT

7891 Bankston, John. *The Life and Times of Scott Joplin* (5–7). Series: Masters of Music: The World's Greatest Composers. 2004, Mitchell Lane LB $20.95 (978-1-58415-270-5). Joplin's career as a ragtime piano player and composer is documented, with coverage of his African American heritage. (Rev: SLJ 2/05) [921]

MENDELSSOHN, FANNY

7892 Shichtman, Sandra H., and Dorothy Indenbaum. *Gifted Sister: The Story of Fanny Mendelssohn* (8–11). 2007, Morgan Reynolds LB $27.95 (978-1-59935-038-7). Fanny, the sister of the noted musician, was very talented herself and composed throughout her life; this biography shows how her life evolved under the social constraints of the early 1800s. (Rev: BL 9/15/07; SLJ 9/07) [921]

MESSIAEN, OLIVIER

7893 Bryant, Jen. *Music for the End of Time* (4–7). Illus. by Beth Peck. 2005, Eerdmans $17.00 (978-0-8028-5229-8). This fictionalized picture-book biography tells how French soldier Olivier Messiaen composed and performed music while in a German prison camp during World War II. (Rev: BL 9/1/05; SLJ 12/05) [921]

MOZART, WOLFGANG AMADEUS

7894 Weeks, Marcus. *Mozart: The Boy Who Changed the World with His Music* (5–8). Series: World History Biographies. 2007, National Geographic $17.95 (978-1-4263-0002-8). An attractive, well-organized life of the young composer, with details of his music lessons and instruments, his first job, and his later financial worries. (Rev: SLJ 6/07)

VIVALDI, ANTONIO

7895 Getzinger, Donna, and Daniel Felsenfeld. *Antonio Vivaldi and the Baroque Tradition* (6–10). Series: Classical Composers. 2004, Morgan Reynolds LB $26.95 (978-1-931798-20-4). The story of the rise and fall of this prolific composer as well as of his music world and the importance of Venice in this sphere. (Rev: BL 4/15/04; SLJ 6/04) [921]

Performers and Media Personalities

ABDUL, PAULA

7896 Zannos, Susan. *Paula Abdul* (4–8). Series: Real-Life Reader Biographies. 1999, Mitchell Lane LB $15.95 (978-1-883845-74-2). A brief biography of this choreographer and recording artist that recounts her many problems, including a struggle with bulimia and a series of failed marriages. (Rev: BL 6/1–15/99) [921]

ALI, RUBINA

7897 Ali, Rubina, et al. *Slumgirl Dreaming: Rubina's Journey to the Stars* (6–9). 2009, Delacorte paper $9.99 (978-0-385-73908-5). Ali, 9, describes her life in the slums of Mumbai before she was chosen to appear in *Slumdog Millionaire*, as well as how her circumstances have changed since. e Lexile 780L (Rev: BLO 10/1/09; SLJ 2/10) [921]

ALLEN, TIM

7898 Wukovits, John F. *Tim Allen* (6–9). Series: Overcoming Adversity. 1998, Chelsea paper $9.95 (978-0-7910-4697-5). A sympathetic portrait of the show business star who once went to jail for selling cocaine and rebounded to gain success on TV's *Home Improvement*. (Rev: HBG 3/99; SLJ 11/98) [921]

ALONSO, ALICIA

7899 Arnold, Sandra M. *Alicia Alonso: First Lady of the Ballet* (6–10). 1993, Walker LB $15.85 (978-0-8027-8243-4). Overcoming the lack of dance schools in her native Cuba and going blind in her 20s, Alicia Alonso became a prima ballerina and went on to teach, study, and perform in Cuba. (Rev: BL 12/15/93; SLJ 11/93; VOYA 2/94) [921]

7900 Bernier-Grand, Carmen T. *Alicia Alonso: Prima Ballerina* (5–8). Illus. by Raúl Colón. 2011, Marshall Cavendish $19.99 (978-0-7614-5562-2). Cuban ballerina Alicia Alonso's success in overcoming personal disability is chronicled in this free-verse biography. (Rev: BL 9/1/11*; SLJ 9/1/11) [921]

ANDERSON, MARIAN

7901 Freedman, Russell. *The Voice That Challenged a Nation: Marian Anderson and the Struggle for Equal Rights* (4–8). 2004, Houghton Mifflin $18.00 (978-0-618-15976-5). Beautifully illustrated with period photographs, this picture-book biography of the African American vocalist describes her life and the events leading up to her historic concert at the Lincoln Memorial. (Rev: BL 6/1–15/04; HB 5–6/04; SLJ 7/04) [921]

7902 Jones, Victoria Garrett. *Marian Anderson: A Voice Uplifted* (6–9). Series: Sterling Biographies. 2008, Sterling $12.95 (978-1-4027-5802-7); paper $5.95 (978-1-4027-4239-2). The inspiring story of the African American singer is presented in historical context. (Rev: BL 2/1/08; SLJ 8/08) [921]

BALANCHINE, GEORGE

7903 Gottlieb, Robert. *George Balanchine: The Ballet Maker* (8–12). 2004, HarperCollins $19.95 (978-0-06-075070-1). Balanchine's ballet talent was recognized at a young age; this biography follows his progress from St. Petersburg to New York and worldwide fame. (Rev: BL 11/1/04) [792.8]

7904 Seibert, Brian. *George Balanchine* (6–9). Series: Library of American Choreographers. 2005, Rosen LB $23.95 (978-0-404-20447-1). The life and career of the Russian-born ballet choreographer; there are no source notes. (Rev: BL 11/1/05) [792.8]

BEATLES (MUSICAL GROUP)

7905 Sawyers, June S., ed. *Read the Beatles: Classic and New Writings on the Beatles, Their Legacy, and Why They Still Matter* (8–12). 2006, Penguin paper $16.00 (978-0-14-303732-3). A compilation of articles and essays about the Beatles, by writers including Gloria Steinem, Allen Ginsberg, and Philip Glass. (Rev: BL 11/1/06) [920]

7906 Spitz, Bob. *Yeah! Yeah! Yeah!* (7–10). 2007, Little, Brown $18.99 (978-0-316-11555-1). A fluent history of the Beatles, with information on the group's beginnings, influences, growth, and worldwide legacy, enhanced by black-and-white photographs; from the author of the adult book *The Beatles* (2005). (Rev: BL 11/1/07; SLJ 12/07) [782.421]

BERRY, HALLE

7907 Sapet, Kerrily. *Halle Berry* (6–9). Series: Transcending Race in America. 2010, Mason Crest $22.95 (978-1-4222-1612-5). This biography is part of a series that looks at famous biracial achievers in America and considers the racism Berry faced while growing up. (Rev: LMC 3–4/10; SLJ 1/10) [921]

BEYONCÉ

7908 Bednar, Chuck. *Beyoncé* (5–8). Series: Transcending Race in America. 2010, Mason Crest $22.95 (978-1-4222-1607-1). Beyoncé Knowles is of African American and Creole descent, and this biography explains how she feels her background has influenced her life. Lexile 1180L (Rev: LMC 3–4/10; SLJ 1/10) [921]

BIEBER, JUSTIN

7909 Bieber, Justin. *Justin Bieber: First Step 2 Forever: My Story* (4–8). 2010, HarperCollins $21.99 (978-0-06-203974-3). Bieber tells the story of his rise to stardom and includes many photographs of himself. ℮ (Rev: SLJ 1/1/11; VOYA 2/11) [921]

BOONE, JOHN WILLIAM

7910 Harrah, Madge. *Blind Boone* (5–8). 2003, Carolrhoda LB $30.60 (978-1-57505-057-7). The son of a runaway slave, Boone became blind as an infant but soon revealed a musical talent and went on to become a composer and concert pianist. (Rev: BL 12/1/03; HBG 3/02; SLJ 10/01) [781.64]

CASH, JOHNNY

7911 Neimark, Anne E. *Johnny Cash* (6–9). Series: Up Close. 2007, Viking $15.99 (978-0-670-06215-7). This account of the complicated and difficult life of the famous musician discusses Cash's admirable traits (such as musical talent and compassion for the downtrodden) as well as his less-admirable (such as drug use and a quick temper). (Rev: BL 2/1/07; HB 3–4/07; SLJ 4/07) [921]

CHAPLIN, CHARLIE

7912 Fleischman, Sid. *Sir Charlie: Chaplin, The Funniest Man in the World* (6–10). 2010, Greenwillow $19.99 (978-0-06-189640-8). This engaging profile covers Chaplin's life from his start in the slums of London through a Vaudeville career, success in Hollywood, and eventual move to Switzerland and relative obscurity. (Rev: BL 6/10*; LMC 11–12/10; SLJ 6/10; VOYA 6/10) [921]

CHARLES, RAY

7913 Duggleby, John. *Uh Huh! The Story of Ray Charles* (6–12). 2005, Morgan Reynolds LB $26.95 (978-1-931798-65-5). In addition to an account of Ray Charles's life and music, this volume reveals much about the social context of his times. (Rev: BL 6/1–15/05; SLJ 10/05) [921]

7914 Woog, Adam. *Ray Charles and the Birth of Soul* (7–12). 2006, Gale LB $28.70 (978-1-59018-844-6).

Covering Charles's life from a child of poverty in Florida to the legendary soul musician, Woog touches on his mother's influence and chronicles the development of his talents and innovations despite his blindness. (Rev: SLJ 6/06)

CHO, MARGARET

7915 Tiger, Caroline. *Margaret Cho* (7–12). Series: Asian Americans of Achievement. 2007, Chelsea House LB $30.00 (978-0-7910-9275-0). This biography of the edgy Asian American comedian will appeal to all teenagers who feel marginalized or who simply appreciate Cho's brand of angry but hilarious humor. (Rev: BL 4/15/07) [921]

COBAIN, KURT

7916 Burlingame, Jeff. *Kurt Cobain: "Oh Well, Whatever, Nevermind"* (8–11). Series: American Rebels. 2006, Enslow $20.95 (978-0-7660-2426-7). The author has the inside scoop on the rocker's adolescence, and he delves into what influenced Cobain's troubled youth and sad death. (Rev: BL 1/1–15/07) [921]

7917 McDougall, Chros. *Kurt Cobain: Alternative Rock Innovator* (7–10). Illus. Series: Lives Cut Short. 2012, ABDO LB $23.95 (978-161783480-6). This profile includes first-person quotes, comments from insiders and critics, interesting sidebars, and relevant photographs. (Rev: BL 12/1/12) [921]

COLTRANE, JOHN

7918 Golio, Gary. *Spirit Seeker: John Coltrane's Musical Journey* (4–7). Illus. by Rudy Gutierrez. 2012, Clarion $17.99 (978-0-547-23994-1). With vibrant illustrations, this is a compelling biography of the jazz musician and his challenges. (Rev: BL 11/1/12; HB 11–12/12; LMC 11–12/12; SLJ 12/12*) [921]

COSBY, BILL

7919 Haskins, Jim. *Bill Cosby: America's Most Famous Father* (5–7). 1988, Walker LB $17.00 (978-0-8027-6786-8). The childhood and career of this famous entertainer. (Rev: BL 6/1/88) [921]

DAMON, MATT

7920 Greene, Meg. *Matt Damon* (5–8). Series: Galaxy of Superstars. 2000, Chelsea $25.00 (978-0-7910-5779-7). An entertaining biography of the actor who gained star status as the cowriter and lead actor in *Good Will Hunting*. (Rev: BL 12/15/00; HBG 10/01) [921]

DAVIS, MILES

7921 Dell, Pamela. *Miles Davis: Jazz Master* (5–8). Series: Journey to Freedom. 2005, Child's World LB $28.50 (978-1-59296-232-7). An easy-to-read biography that deals frankly with the trumpeter's addiction to heroin and his difficult personality. (Rev: SLJ 8/05) [921]

DEGENERES, ELLEN

7922 Paprocki, Sherry Beck. *Ellen DeGeneres: Entertainer* (6–10). Series: Women of Achievement. 2009, Chelsea House $30 (978-1-60413-082-9). This is a balanced profile of the popular TV host and her impact on pop culture. (Rev: SLJ 5/1/09) [921]

DICAPRIO, LEONARDO

7923 Stauffer, Stacey. *Leonardo DiCaprio* (5–8). Series: Galaxy of Superstars. 1999, Chelsea $25.00 (978-0-7910-5151-1); paper $25.00 (978-0-7910-5326-3). The story of this young actor's life, with special attention to his role in *Titanic*. (Rev: BL 4/15/99; HBG 10/99; SLJ 5/99) [921]

DOWD, OLYMPIA

7924 Dowd, Olympia. *A Young Dancer's Apprenticeship: On Tour with the Moscow City Ballet* (6–9). 2003, Twenty-First Century LB $24.90 (978-0-7613-2917-6). Dowd tells the story of how, at the age of only 14, she was offered the opportunity to dance with the Moscow City Ballet. (Rev: HBG 10/03; SLJ 5/03; VOYA 10/03) [792.8]

DYLAN, BOB

7925 Roberts, Jeremy. *Bob Dylan: Voice of a Generation* (8–11). Series: Lerner Biographies. 2005, Lerner LB $27.93 (978-0-8225-1368-1). This evenhanded biography chronicles the folk singer's transformation from Bobby Zimmerman in small-town Minnesota to cultural icon. (Rev: BL 6/1–15/05) [921]

ELLINGTON, DUKE

7926 Crease, Stephanie Stein. *Duke Ellington: His Life in Jazz with 21 Activities* (6–9). Illus. 2009, Chicago Review paper $16.95 (978-155652724-1). A large-format profile of the jazz musician and composer, with many illustrations and sidebars as well as a timeline and activities relating to his life, times, and compositions. (Rev: BL 2/1/09; SLJ 3/1/09) [921]

FERRERA, AMERICA

7927 Anderson, Sheila. *America Ferrera: Latina Superstar* (5–8). Illus. Series: Hot Celebrity Biographies. 2009, Enslow LB $23.93 (978-0-7660-3210-1). A celebrity biography of a Latina role model. (Rev: BL 6/1–15/09) [921]

FITZGERALD, ELLA

7928 Stone, Tanya Lee. *Ella Fitzgerald* (7–10). Series: Up Close. 2008, Viking $16.99 (978-0-670-06149-5). The singer's hard work and exceptional voice are the main focus of this biography. (Rev: BL 2/1/08; SLJ 2/08) [782.421]

FREEMAN, MORGAN

7929 De Angelis, Gina. *Morgan Freeman* (7–12). Series: Black Americans of Achievement. 1999, Chelsea LB $30.00 (978-0-7910-4963-1). The life and career of the African American actor who has starred on Broadway, on television, and in movies. (Rev: HBG 4/00; SLJ 1/00) [791.43]

GOH, CHAN HON

7930 Goh, Chan Hon, and Cary Fagan. *Beyond the Dance: A Ballerina's Life* (6–12). 2002, Tundra LB $15.95 (978-0-88776-596-4). A readable account of Goh's childhood in Vancouver and rapid rise as a ballet dancer to become a prima ballerina with the National Ballet of Canada. (Rev: HBG 10/03; SLJ 4/03; VOYA 4/03) [921]

GOLDBERG, WHOOPI

7931 Blue, Rose, and Corinne J. Naden. *Whoopi Goldberg* (7–10). Series: Black Americans of Achievement. 1995, Chelsea LB $30.00 (978-0-7910-2152-1); paper $8.95 (978-0-7910-2153-8). A biography that tells how, in spite of great odds, this unusual comedian and actress rose to the top. (Rev: BL 3/15/95) [921]

7932 Caper, William. *Whoopi Goldberg: Comedian and Movie Star* (6–9). 1999, Enslow LB $26.60 (978-0-7660-1205-9). Goldberg's journey from the New York housing projects to Hollywood is detailed here with black-and-white photographs and a chronology and filmography. (Rev: BL 10/1/99) [791.43]

GRAHAM, MARTHA

7933 Freedman, Russell. *Martha Graham: A Dancer's Life* (4–8). 1998, Clarion $19.00 (978-0-395-74655-4). Martha Graham's amazing talents, driving force, and complex personality are well depicted in this handsomely illustrated biography. (Rev: BCCB 6/98; BL 4/1/98; SLJ 5/98; VOYA 8/98) [921]

HANSON (MUSICAL GROUP)

7934 Powell, Phelan. *Hanson* (5–8). Series: Galaxy of Superstars. 1999, Chelsea $25.00 (978-0-7910-5148-1); paper $25.00 (978-0-7910-5325-6). An attractive volume with information on the three-brother singing group that hails from Tulsa, Oklahoma. (Rev: BL 4/15/98; HBG 10/99) [921]

HENDRIX, JIMI

7935 Willett, Edward. *Jimi Hendrix: "Kiss the Sky"* (7–10). Series: American Rebels. 2006, Enslow LB $20.95 (978-0-7660-2449-6). From the musician's childhood to his death at the age of 27, this biography does not shy away from describing Hendrix's destructive behavior, including the use of alcohol and drugs. (Rev: BL 2/1/07) [921]

HENSON, JIM

7936 Krull, Kathleen. *Jim Henson: The Guy Who Played with Puppets* (4–7). Illus. by Steve Johnson. 2011, Random House $16.99 (978-0-375-85721-8); LB $19.99 (978-0-375-95721-5). A portrait of the creator of the Muppets, with details of his first job on TV at the age of 16. (Rev: BL 11/1/11; SLJ 10/1/11) [921]

HITCHCOCK, ALFRED

7937 Adair, Gene. *Alfred Hitchcock: Filming Our Fears* (7–10). Series: Oxford Portraits. 2002, Oxford LB $32.95 (978-0-19-511967-1). Hitchcock's youth in England is covered in addition to chronological details of his career from the silent movies through his classic creations. (Rev: HBG 3/03; SLJ 11/02) [921]

HOUDINI, HARRY

7938 Carlson, Laurie. *Harry Houdini for Kids: His Life and Adventures with 21 Magic Tricks and Illusions* (4–8). Illus. 2009, Chicago Review paper $16.95 (978-1-55652-782-1). This attractive biography full of illustrations and sidebars also includes 21 simple tricks. **e** (Rev: BL 2/15/09; SLJ 4/1/09) [921]

7939 Fleischman, Sid. *Escape! The Story of the Great Houdini* (4–8). 2006, HarperCollins $18.99 (978-0-06-085694-6). A lively and entertaining biography by a great writer and professional magician, who reveals just enough of the magic behind the tricks; includes many photographs. Boston Globe–Horn Book Honor 2007. (Rev: SLJ 8/06*; VOYA 6/06)

7940 Weaver, Janice. *Harry Houdini: The Legend of the World's Greatest Escape Artist* (4–7). Illus. by Chris Lane. 2011, Abrams $18.95 (978-1-4197-0014-9). Covers Houdini's life and career as well as his interest in exposing fake mediums; historical sidebars add interest. (Rev: BL 12/1/11; LMC 3–4/12; SLJ 11/1/11*) [921]

HOUSTON, WHITNEY

7941 Heppermann, Christine. *Whitney Houston: Recording Artist and Actress* (7–10). Illus. Series: Lives Cut Short. 2012, ABDO LB $34.22 (978-161783544-5). This profile includes first-person quotes, comments from insiders and critics, interesting sidebars, and relevant photographs. (Rev: BL 12/1/12; SLJ 12/12) [921]

HUDSON, JENNIFER

7942 Cartlidge, Cherese. *Jennifer Hudson* (6–9). Illus. Series: People in the News. 2012, Gale/Lucent LB $33.45 (978-142050607-5). With well-chosen photographs and accessible text, this is an interesting profile of the singer and actor. (Rev: BL 4/15/12) [921]

JACKSON, MICHAEL

7943 Collins, Terry. *King of Pop: The Story of Michael Jackson* (4–7). Illus. by Michael Byers. 2012, Capstone LB $29.99 (978-142966015-0); paper $7.95 (978-142967994-7). Though it omits the more controversial aspects of Jackson's life, this biography does include information about Jackson's turbulent early life. (Rev: BL 3/15/12) [921]

7944 Pratt, Mary K. *Michael Jackson: King of Pop* (5–8). Series: Lives Cut Short. 2009, ABDO LB $32.79 (978-1-60453-788-8). From his childhood through performing in the Jackson 5, then going solo, and the various controversies of his later life, this is a balanced profile of the performer who died at the age of 50. (Rev: BL 2/1/10; SLJ 3/10) [921]

JAY-Z

7945 Gunderson, Jessica. *Jay-Z: Hip-Hop Icon* (5–7). Illus. by Pat Kinsella. Series: American Graphic. 2012, Capstone LB $29.99 (978-142966017-4); paper $7.95 (978-142967993-0). This evenhanded graphic-novel biography of Jay-Z focuses on the less glamorous aspects of stardom, showing readers the hard work and shrewd decision making it takes to succeed. (Rev: BL 3/15/12) [921]

7946 Heos, Bridget. *Jay-Z* (5–8). Illus. Series: Library of Hip-Hop Biographies. 2009, Rosen LB $26.50 (978-1-4358-5052-1). From his childhood rhymes to his adolescent drug dealing, his first hit single, and his marriage to Beyoncé, this is a frank and arresting profile. (Rev: BL 6/1–15/09) [921]

7947 Spilsbury, Richard. *Jay-Z* (5–7). Illus. Series: Titans of Business. 2012, Capstone $32 (978-143296430-6); paper $8.99 (978-14329643-7-5). Spilsbury introduces Jay-Z's role as a music industry entrepreneur, as well as covering his hip-hop career. (Rev: BL 11/1/12) [921]

JOHANSSON, SCARLETT

7948 Schuman, Michael. *Scarlett Johansson: Hollywood Superstar* (6–9). Illus. Series: People to Know Today. 2011, Enslow $31.93 (978-076603556-0). With information on her family and childhood followed by descriptions of her work and the benefits and hardships of her stardom, this is an appealing biography with color photographs, quotations, and a filmography. **e** (Rev: BL 6/1/11) [921]

JOHNSON, ROBERT

7949 Lewis, J. Patrick. *Black Cat Bone* (7–12). Illus. by Gary Kelley. 2006, Creative LB $19.95 (978-1-56846-194-6). A picture book for big kids, this story in poetry of blues musician Robert Johnson alludes to the legend that he sold his soul to the devil in exchange for some wicked skills on the guitar. (Rev: BL 1/1–15/07; LMC 8–9/07; SLJ 12/06*) [921]

479

JOLIE, ANGELINA

7950 La Bella, Laura. *Angelina Jolie: Goodwill Ambassador for the United Nations* (6–8). Illus. Series: Celebrity Activists. 2008, Rosen LB $24.95 (978-140421762-1). The popular movie star's work as an ambassador has brought increased public attention to humanitarian issues. (Rev: BL 1/1–15/09) [921]

JONAS BROTHERS

7951 Janic, Susan. *Jonas Brothers Forever: The Unofficial Story of Kevin, Joe and Nick* (5–8). Illus. 2009, ECW paper $14.95 (978-1-55022-851-9). A well-designed profile of the popular trio, with plenty of photographs. (Rev: BLO 3/24/09) [782.42166092]

KELLAR, HARRY

7952 Jarrow, Gail. *The Amazing Harry Kellar: Great American Magician* (5–8). Illus. 2012, Boyds Mills $17.95 (978-159078865-3). Introduces the magician who performed around the world at the turn of the 20th century. Lexile 910L (Rev: BL 6/12; LMC 1–2/13*; SLJ 6/12) [921]

KELLY, EMMETT, SR.

7953 Wilkerson, J. L. *Sad-Face Clown: Emmett Kelly* (5–8). Series: The Great Heartlanders. 2004, Acorn paper $9.95 (978-0-9664470-9-5). The story of Emmett Kelly, Sr., who — as Weary Willie — became possibly the world's most famous circus clown. (Rev: SLJ 4/04) [791.3]

KEYS, ALICIA

7954 Roberts, Russell. *Alicia Keys* (6–9). Series: Transcending Race in America. 2010, Mason Crest $22.95 (978-1-4222-1606-4). This biography is part of a series that looks at famous biracial achievers in America and considers this aspect of the musician in a chapter titled "A Child of Several Cultures." (Rev: LMC 3–4/10) [921]

KISS (ROCK GROUP)

7955 Weintraub, Aileen. *KISS: I Wanna Rock and Roll All Night* (5–8). Illus. Series: Rebels of Rock. 2009, Enslow LB $23.95 (978-0-7660-3027-5). An accessible account of the flamboyant rock group's ascent to stardom and subsequent revivals. (Rev: BL 4/1/09) [921]

LADY GAGA

7956 Heos, Bridget. *Lady Gaga* (5–8). Illus. 2011, Rosen LB $26.50 (978-143583574-0). This biography chronicles Gaga's fairly conventional childhood growing up in Manhattan and documents her fast rise to fame. (Rev: BL 4/1/11) [921]

LANG, LANG

7957 Lang, Lang, and Michael French. *Lang Lang: Playing with Flying Keys* (7–10). 2008, Delacorte $16.99 (978-0-385-73578-0). The internationally respected pianist recalls the stresses of his childhood, his unending training schedule, and his triumphs. (Rev: BL 6/1–15/08; SLJ 9/08) [921]

LATIFAH, QUEEN

7958 Allen, Amy Ruth. *Queen Latifah: From Jersey Girl to Superstar* (6–10). Illus. Series: Lifeline Biographies. 2012, Lerner/Twenty-First Century LB $34.60 (978-076134234-2). An attractive profile of the rap star with many quotations, photographs, and sidebars from *USA Today*. (Rev: BL 6/12; VOYA 6/12) [921]

LAWRENCE, JENNIFER

7959 Krohn, Katherine. *Jennifer Lawrence: Star of The Hunger Games* (4–7). Illus. 2012, Lerner LB $26.60 (978-076138642-1); paper $8.95 (978-076138665-0). Hunger Games star Jennifer Lawrence's meteoric rise to fame is captured in this colorful biography that looks at her life chronologically and includes many quotations and photographs. e Lexile 900L (Rev: BL 2/1/12; SLJ 1/12) [921]

LED ZEPPELIN (MUSICAL GROUP)

7960 Hoskyns, Barney. *Led Zeppelin IV* (8–12). 2006, Rodale $16.95 (978-1-59486-370-7). This profile of the rock band looks behind the scenes, especially at the making of its classic fourth album. (Rev: BL 11/15/06) [921]

LEDGER, HEATH

7961 Watson, Stephanie. *Heath Ledger: Talented Actor* (5–8). Series: Lives Cut Short. 2009, ABDO LB $32.79 (978-1-60453-789-5). The brief life story of the Australian actor who died at the age of 28. (Rev: SLJ 3/10) [921]

LEE, BRUCE

7962 Little, John, ed. *Bruce Lee: The Celebrated Life of the Golden Dragon* (6–12). 2000, Tuttle $24.95 (978-0-8048-3230-4). Stunning photographs and excerpts from Lee's own writings paint an absorbing portrait of the late martial arts film star. (Rev: VOYA 8/01) [921]

LEE, SPIKE

7963 Haskins, Jim. *Spike Lee: By Any Means Necessary* (6–10). 1997, Walker LB $16.85 (978-0-8027-8496-4). Compiling previously published biographical material, the author has produced an interesting profile of this important African American filmmaker, including a behind-the-cameras view of each of Lee's 10 films. (Rev: BL 5/1/97; SLJ 6/97; VOYA 10/97) [921]

LENNON, JOHN

7964 Behnke, Alison. *Death of a Dreamer: The Assassination of John Lennon* (6–9). Illus. 2012, Knopf LB $33.26 (978-0-8225-9036-1). This account of Lennon's life and career is interwoven with details of his assassin's life. **e** (Rev: BL 6/12; LMC 10/12; SLJ 7/12; VOYA 6/12) [921]

LI, ZHONGMEI

7965 Bernstein, Richard. *A Girl Named Faithful Plum: The Story of a Dancer from China and How She Achieved Her Dream* (6–9). 2011, Knopf $15.99 (978-0-375-86960-0); LB $18.99 (978-037596960-7). Chinese dancer Zhongmei Li's determination in the face of great challenges adds inspiration to this accessible biography full of cultural information. **e** Lexile 1080L (Rev: BL 10/15/11; SLJ 11/1/11) [921]

LIL WAYNE

7966 Earl, C. F. *Lil Wayne* (5–8). Illus. Series: Superstars of Hip-Hop. 2012, Mason Crest LB $19.95 (978-142222532-5). This is an appealing profile of the rapper and his adventures and accomplishments. (Rev: BL 10/1/12) [921]

LOPEZ, JENNIFER

7967 Hill, Anne E. *Jennifer Lopez* (5–8). Series: Galaxy of Superstars. 2000, Chelsea $25.00 (978-0-7910-5775-9). This book chronicles the career of the young Latina star who is a fine singer and actress. (Rev: BL 10/15/00; HBG 10/01) [921]

M.I.A.

7968 Peppas, Lynn. *M. I. A.* (5–8). Illus. Series: Superstars! 2010, Crabtree LB $26.60 (978-077877249-1). An interesting profile of the British rap star who came to prominence with the soundtrack of *Slumdog Millionaire*. (Rev: BL 6/1/11) [921]

MA, YO-YO

7969 Worth, Richard. *Yo-Yo Ma* (6–10). Series: Asian Americans of Achievement. 2007, Chelsea House LB $30.00 (978-0-7910-9270-5). This attractive profile recounts the highlights of Ma's personal life and covers his career as a cellist and his work with young people. (Rev: SLJ 8/07) [921]

MADONNA

7970 Gnojewski, Carol. *Madonna: "Express Yourself"* (8–11). 2007, Enslow LB $25.95 (978-0-7660-2442-7). Covers the life and career of musical icon Madonna from childhood. (Rev: BL 8/07) [921]

MARLEY, BOB

7971 Medina, Tony. *I and I: Bob Marley* (4–8). Illus. by Jesse Joshua Watson. 2009, Lee & Low $19.95 (978-1-60060-257-3). This picture-book biography in verse profiles the musician who put reggae into the spotlight. (Rev: BL 6/1–15/09*; LMC 10/09; SLJ 6/09) [782]

7972 Miller, Calvin Craig. *Reggae Poet: The Story of Bob Marley* (7–10). 2007, Morgan Reynolds LB $27.95 (978-1-59935-071-4). A look at the good and the bad about the late reggae musician, including his influential style, his drug use, and his difficult childhood; with photographs. (Rev: BL 11/15/07; SLJ 2/08) [921]

MCCARTNEY, PAUL

7973 Sounes, Howard. *Fab: The Life of Paul McCartney* (10–12). Illus. 2010, Da Capo $27.50 (978-030681783-0). Sounes's meticulously researched and impartial biography covers every aspect of McCartney's life from his start with the Beatles through his failed marriage to Heather Mills. (Rev: BL 10/1–15/10*) [921]

MILLER, NORMA

7974 Govenar, Alan, ed. *Stompin' at the Savoy: The Story of Norma Miller* (5–8). Illus. by Martin French. 2006, Candlewick $16.99 (978-0-7636-2244-2). The energy of Norma Miller, who was still going strong in her early 80s, infuses the pages of this brief biography, made up largely of excerpts from interviews with the legendary African American swing dancer. (Rev: BL 2/1/06; SLJ 3/06)

MONROE, MARILYN

7975 Krohn, Katherine E. *Marilyn Monroe: Norma Jeane's Dream* (6–9). Series: Newsmakers Biographies. 1997, Lerner LB $30.35 (978-0-8225-4930-7). A well-illustrated biography that gives a good overview of the actress's life without probing into the mystery surrounding her death. (Rev: SLJ 7/97) [921]

7976 Lefkowitz, Frances. *Marilyn Monroe* (7–12). Series: Pop Culture Legends. 1995, Chelsea LB $21.95 (978-0-7910-2342-6); paper $8.95 (978-0-7910-2367-9). The story of the Hollywood star who, despite immense popularity, had a tragic life. (Rev: BL 8/95) [921]

7977 Owings, Lisa. *Marilyn Monroe: Hollywood Icon* (7–10). Illus. Series: Lives Cut Short. 2012, ABDO LB $34.22 (978-161783481-3). This profile includes first-person quotes, comments from insiders and critics, interesting sidebars, and relevant photographs. (Rev: BL 12/1/12; SLJ 12/12) [921]

NUREYEV, RUDOLF

7978 Maybarduk, Linda. *The Dancer Who Flew: A Memoir of Rudolf Nureyev* (5–9). 1999, Tundra $18.95 (978-0-88776-415-8). The author, a friend and colleague of Nureyev, not only gives a straightforward biography of the dancer but also tells many backstage stories and introduces his most important roles. (Rev: BL 1/1–15/00; HBG 3/00; SLJ 2/00; VOYA 4/00) [921]

OAKLEY, ANNIE

7979 Macy, Sue. *Bull's-Eye: A Photobiography of Annie Oakley* (5–8). 2001, National Geographic $17.95 (978-0-7922-7008-9). This book separates fact from fiction in the life of Phoebe Ann Moses Butler, who came to be known as Annie Oakley. (Rev: BL 11/15/01; HBG 3/02; SLJ 10/01; VOYA 4/02) [799.3]

PRESLEY, ELVIS

7980 Brown, Adele Q. *Elvis Presley* (6–9). Series: Trailblazers of the Modern World. 2003, World Almanac paper $11.95 (978-0-8368-5245-5). A biography of the international pop music star who reigned as king for many years. (Rev: BL 6/1–15/03) [921]

7981 Hampton, Wilborn. *Elvis Presley* (6–9). Series: Up Close. 2007, Viking $15.99 (978-0-670-06166-2). Hampton covers Elvis's rise to fame, his personal life and drug-related downfall, and his influence on music and culture. (Rev: BL 5/1/07; HB 7–8/07; SLJ 6/07) [921]

PRINCE (ROCK STAR)

7982 Robson, David. *Prince: Singer-Songwriter, Musician, and Record Producer* (6–9). Series: Transcending Race in America. 2010, Mason Crest $22.95 (978-1-4222-1614-9). This biography is part of a series that looks at famous biracial achievers in America and considers this aspect of the musician's life. (Rev: LMC 3–4/10; SLJ 2/10) [921]

PUENTE, TITO

7983 Olmstead, Mary. *Tito Puente* (4–7). Series: Hispanic-American Biographies. 2004, Raintree LB $32.86 (978-1-4109-0713-4). A concise account of the life and career of Tito Puente, the popular American bandleader and percussionist who in the 1950s was nicknamed the Mambo King. (Rev: BL 2/1/05; SLJ 8/05) [784.4]

QUINN, ANTHONY

7984 Amdur, Melissa. *Anthony Quinn* (5–9). Series: Hispanics of Achievement. 1993, Chelsea LB $19.95 (978-0-7910-1251-2). The life of this Mexican American actor is told with many interesting asides concerning his career and black-and-white stills from his movies. (Rev: BL 9/15/93) [921]

REEVE, CHRISTOPHER

7985 Finn, Margaret L. *Christopher Reeve: Actor and Activist* (6–10). 1997, Chelsea LB $32.00 (978-0-7910-4446-9); paper $8.95 (978-0-7910-4447-6). The story of the gallant film actor, his tragic accident, and the causes he champions. (Rev: HBG 3/98; VOYA 2/98) [921]

RIHANNA

7986 Schuman, Michael A. *Rihanna: Music Megastar* (5–8). Illus. Series: Hot Celebrity Biographies. 2012, Enslow LB $23.93 (978-076603871-4). Five short chapters with full-color photographs make this balanced profile appealing to reluctant readers as well as to report writers seeking basic information. (Rev: BL 6/12; SLJ 1/12) [921]

ROCK, CHRIS

7987 Blue, Rose, and Corinne J. Naden. *Chris Rock* (4–7). Series: Black Americans of Achievement. 2000, Chelsea $30.00 (978-0-7910-5277-8). The story of the comedian and actor who began his career on *Saturday Night Live* and is noted for his acerbic wit. (Rev: BL 6/1–15/00; HBG 10/00) [921]

RODRIGUEZ, ROBERT

7988 Marvis, Barbara. *Robert Rodriguez* (5–10). Series: A Real-Life Reader Biography. 1997, Mitchell Lane LB $15.95 (978-1-883845-48-3). This simple, attractive biography of the successful movie maker focuses on his problems growing up in a large family and clinging to his career dreams. (Rev: BL 6/1–15/98; HBG 3/98; SLJ 2/98) [921]

ROGERS, WILL

7989 Donovan, Sandy. *Will Rogers: Cowboy, Comedian, and Commentator* (4–8). Series: Signature Lives. 2007, Compass Point LB $31.93 (978-0-7565-2542-9). This detailed biography of Will Rogers will be useful for report writers. (Rev: SLJ 6/07) [921]

SCHUMANN, CLARA

7990 Allman, Barbara. *Her Piano Sang: A Story About Clara Schumann* (4–7). 1996, Carolrhoda LB $25.55 (978-1-57505-012-6). The story of this groundbreaking composer and pianist who also championed her husband's music. (Rev: BL 1/1–15/97; SLJ 1/97) [921]

7991 Reich, Susanna. *Clara Schumann: Piano Virtuoso* (5–8). 1999, Houghton Mifflin $18.00 (978-0-395-89119-3). A thorough, well-researched biography of this amazing pianist and composer that describes her life as a child prodigy, her marriage to Robert Schumann, and her life promoting his music after his death. (Rev: BL 8/99; HB 3–4/99; HBG 10/99; SLJ 4/99*; VOYA 4/00) [921]

SHAKUR, TUPAC

7992 Golus, Carrie. *Tupac Shakur: Hip-Hop Idol* (6–12). Illus. Series: Lifeline Biographies. 2010, Lerner LB $33.26 (978-076135473-4). This attractive biography draws on the archives of *USA Today* to give an unvarnished account of the rap star's life. (Rev: BL 9/1/10*) [921]

7993 Harris, Ashley Rae. *Tupac Shakur: Multi-Platinum Rapper* (5–8). Series: Lives Cut Short. 2009, ABDO LB $32.79 (978-1-60453-791-8). Focusing on the achievements of a life tragically cut short, this appealing book reveals that Shakur was a gifted student in high school. (Rev: SLJ 3/10) [921]

SIEGEL, SIENA CHERSON

7994 Siegel, Siena Cherson. *To Dance: A Ballerina's Graphic Novel* (5–8). Illus. by Mark Siegel. 2006, Simon & Schuster $17.95 (978-0-689-86747-7). In graphic novel format, Siegel tells the story of her dance career, from her introduction to ballet at the age of 6 to her stage debut with the New York City Ballet. Sibert Honor 2007. (Rev: BCCB 1/07; BL 9/1/06; LMC 1/07; SLJ 11/06*; VOYA 4/07)

SPIELBERG, STEVEN

7995 Edge, Laura B. *Steven Spielberg: Director of Blockbuster Films* (5–8). Series: People to Know Today. 2008, Enslow LB $23.95 (978-0-7660-2888-3). With many photographs and lists of print and Web resources, this profile provides up-to-date information on the filmmaker's career, personal life, work ethic, and storytelling skills. (Rev: BL 6/1–15/08) [921]

7996 Schoell, William. *Magic Man: The Life and Films of Steven Spielberg* (4–7). 1998, Tudor $18.95 (978-0-936389-57-8). This biography of Spielberg concentrates on how he produces the astonishing special effects for his movies. (Rev: BL 5/15/98; SLJ 2/99) [921]

SUPREMES (MUSICAL GROUP)

7997 Rivera, Ursula. *The Supremes* (4–8). Series: Rock and Roll Hall of Famers. 2002, Rosen LB $29.25 (978-0-8239-3527-7). The Supremes' rise to stardom — and eventual fall from fame without leader Diana Ross — is chronicled here with photographs, glossary, discography, and bibliography. (Rev: BL 10/1/02; SLJ 5/02) [782.421644]

THUMB, TOM

7998 Sullivan, George. *Tom Thumb: The Remarkable True Story of a Man in Miniature* (6–8). Illus. 2011, Clarion $20 (978-054718203-2). Tom Thumb, who never grew above 3 feet tall, became a star at the age of 4 and lived a long and successful life touring the world. (Rev: BL 1/1/11*; HB 3–4/11; LMC 1–2/11; SLJ 2/1/11) [921]

TWAIN, SHANIA

7999 Gallagher, Jim. *Shania Twain: Grammy Award-Winning Singer* (4–7). Series: Real-Life Reader Biographies. 1999, Mitchell Lane LB $15.95 (978-1-58415-000-8). The story of the entertainer who was adopted into the Ojibwa tribe, began singing in bars at age eight, and went on to marry producer Mutt Lange. (Rev: SLJ 1/00) [921]

WINFREY, OPRAH

8000 Cooper, Ilene. *Up Close: Oprah Winfrey* (7–12). Series: Up Close. 2007, Viking $15.99 (978-0-670-06162-4). Cooper focuses on Winfrey's unhappy childhood and her philanthropic work when she became successful. (Rev: SLJ 5/07) [921]

8001 Krohn, Katherine. *Oprah Winfrey* (6–9). Series: Just the Facts Biographies. 2005, Lerner LB $27.93 (978-0-8225-2472-4). Simple text and clear definitions make this biography suitable for reluctant and ESL readers. (Rev: BL 4/1/05) [794.4502]

8002 Stone, Tanya Lee. *Oprah Winfrey: Success with an Open Heart* (4–7). Series: Gateway Biographies. 2001, Millbrook LB $23.90 (978-0-7613-1814-9). Oprah's story, with concise text and excellent photographs, will attract and inspire young readers. (Rev: BL 6/1–15/01; HBG 10/01) [791.45]

8003 Westen, Robin. *Oprah Winfrey: "I Don't Believe in Failure"* (5–8). Series: African-American Biography Library. 2005, Enslow LB $31.93 (978-0-7660-2462-5). Winfrey's phenomenal rise to success in the worlds of business and entertainment is placed in social context. (Rev: SLJ 11/05; VOYA 6/06) [921]

Miscellaneous Artists

BARNUM, P. T.

8004 Barnum, P. T. *Barnum's Own Story* (7–12). 1962, Peter Smith $20.50 (978-0-8446-4001-3). The autobiography of the showman who could fool people like no one else. [921]

8005 Fleming, Alice. *P. T. Barnum: The World's Greatest Showman* (5–8). 1993, Walker LB $15.85 (978-0-8027-8235-9). A look at the circus owner's childhood and various successful entrepreneurial ventures. (Rev: BL 1/15/94; SLJ 12/93; VOYA 2/94) [921]

8006 Fleming, Candace. *The Great and Only Barnum: The Tremendous, Stupendous Life of Showman P. T. Barnum* (4–8). Illus. by Ray Fenwick. 2009, Random $18.99 (978-0-375-84197-2). The story of Barnum's rags-to-success life providing entertainment to the public, with frank discussion of some of his methods and personality defects. ALA Notable Books 2010. (Rev: BL 6/1–15/09*; HB 9/09; LMC 10/09; SLJ 9/09*) [921]

FINGER, BILL

8007 Nobleman, Marc Tyler. *Bill the Boy Wonder: The Secret Co-Creator of Batman* (4–7). Illus. by Ty Templeton. 2012, Charlesbridge $17.95 (978-158089289-6). Bill Finger, the overlooked co-creator of Batman comics, gets his due in this interesting biography. Lexile GN970L (Rev: BL 8/12; LMC 3–4/13; SLJ 8/12) [921]

LANTZ, WALTER

8008 Lenburg, Jeff. *Walter Lantz* (7–10). Illus. Series: Legends of Animation. 2012, Chelsea House LB $34.95 (978-160413839-9). Profiles the man whose studio produced more than 800 cartoons, notably those featuring Woody Woodpecker. (Rev: BL 11/1/12) [921]

LASSETER, JOHN

8009 Lenburg, Jeff. *John Lasseter* (7–10). Illus. Series: Legends of Animation. 2012, Chelsea House LB $34.95 (978-160413840-5). Traces Lasseter's life and progress as an animator, from Disney to Pixar and *Toy Story*. (Rev: BL 11/1/12) [921]

Contemporary and Historical Americans

Collective

8010 Alegre, Cèsar. *Extraordinary Hispanic Americans* (6–9). Series: Extraordinary People. 2006, Children's Pr. LB $40.00 (978-0-516-25343-5). More than 200 Hispanic Americans are introduced in brief profiles with black-and-white photographs. (Rev: BL 3/1/07; SLJ 5/07) [920]

8011 Bailey Hutchinson, Kay. *Leading Ladies: American Trailblazers* (7–12). 2007, HarperCollins $25.95 (978-0-06-113824-9). Pioneering American women in all walks of lives are celebrated in this collective biography that includes wives of presidents, activists, scientists, doctors, and journalists. (Rev: BL 12/1/07) [920]

8012 Barber, James, and Amy Pastan. *Presidents and First Ladies* (4–8). 2002, DK paper $12.99 (978-0-7894-8453-6). For each president and his First Lady, there are biographies, a list of key events, and a box highlighting an important event during that administration, plus plenty of color illustrations. (Rev: BL 4/1/02; HBG 10/02; SLJ 5/02) [920]

8013 Bausum, Ann. *Our Country's First Ladies* (4–8). 2007, National Geographic $19.95 (978-1-4263-0006-6). These profiles of America's first ladies provide material for report writers and enough interest for browsers. (Rev: SLJ 1/07)

8014 Blassingame, Wyatt. *The Look-It-Up Book of Presidents* (6–9). 1990, Random House paper $9.95 (978-0-679-80358-4). The author devotes two to six pages to each president and covers all the salient facts about each. (Rev: HBG 10/01; SLJ 5/90) [920]

8015 Bruning, John Robert. *Elusive Glory: African-American Heroes of World War II* (5–8). Series: Avisson Young Adult. 2001, Avisson paper $19.95 (978-1-888105-48-3). The true stories of African American servicemen, including six Tuskegee Airmen, who

served the United States during World War II. (Rev: BL 1/1–15/02; SLJ 4/02) [940.54]

8016 Buller, Jon. *Smart About the Presidents* (4–7). Illus. by authors. Series: Smart About History. 2004, Penguin paper $5.99 (978-0-448-43372-1). Pertinent facts about each president are conveyed in an informative, accessible style. (Rev: BL 9/1/04; SLJ 4/05) [920]

8017 Colman, Penny. *Elizabeth Cady Stanton and Susan B. Anthony: A Friendship That Changed the World* (7–10). Illus. 2011, Henry Holt $18.99 (978-0-8050-8293-7). Tells the story of the friendship between a married mother of five (Stanton) and an unmarried career woman (Anthony) and the impact they were to make on human rights in America. **e** Lexile 1180L (Rev: BL 6/1/11; LMC 10/11*; SLJ 5/11; VOYA 6/11) [920]

8018 Delano, Marfé Ferguson. *American Heroes* (5–8). 2005, National Geographic LB $45.90 (978-0-7922-7215-1). Fifty men and women whose heroism has helped to shape America are profiled in this attractive large-format volume. (Rev: BL 12/1/05; SLJ 2/06) [920.073]

8019 Doherty, Kieran. *Explorers, Missionaries, and Trappers: Trailblazers of the West* (5–8). Series: Shaping America. 2000, Oliver LB $22.95 (978-1-881508-52-6). Nine important pioneers of the American West are profiled including a Spanish conquistador, two Spanish priests, John Sutter, Marcus and Narcissa Whitman, and Brigham Young. (Rev: HBG 10/00; SLJ 5/00) [920]

8020 Doherty, Kieran. *Voyageurs, Lumberjacks, and Farmers: Pioneers of the Midwest* (5–8). Series: Shaping America. 2004, Oliver LB $22.95 (978-1-881508-54-0). The lives and accomplishments of eight individuals — including Antoine Cadillac, Jean du Sable, and Josiah and Abigail Snelling — who played key roles in the settlement of the Midwest are placed in historical context, with discussion of the plight of Native Americans in the region. (Rev: SLJ 9/04) [920]

8021 Fradin, Dennis Brindell. *The Founders: The 39 Stories Behind the U.S. Constitution* (4–7). Illus. by Michael McCurdy. 2005, Walker $22.95 (978-0-8027-8972-3). The 39 men who signed the Constitution are profiled in brief chapters that include information on their home states. (Rev: BL 10/15/05; SLJ 9/05) [973.3]

8022 Freedman, Russell. *Abraham Lincoln and Frederick Douglass: The Story Behind an American Friendship* (5–9). Illus. 2012, Clarion $18.99 (978-054738562-4). This attractive title offers a glimpse into the respectful friendship that grew between Frederick Douglass and Abraham Lincoln after Emancipation. ALA Notable Books 2013. (Rev: BL 2/1/12*; HB 5–6/12; SLJ 5/1/12*; VOYA 4/12) [920]

8023 Freedman, Russell. *Indian Chiefs* (6–9). 1987, Holiday $22.95 (978-0-8234-0625-8). Brief biographies of six Indian chiefs including Red Cloud, Sitting Bull, and Joseph of the Nez Perce. (Rev: BL 5/1/87; SLJ 5/87; VOYA 8/87) [920]

8024 George-Warren, Holly. *The Cowgirl Way: Hats Off to America's Women of the West* (5–8). Illus. 2010, Houghton Mifflin $18 (978-0-618-73738-3). With many photographs, posters, quotes, and other elements, this is a comprehensive account of the activities of cowgirls on the western frontier. e Lexile 1180L (Rev: BL 8/10; HB 7–8/10; SLJ 7/10; VOYA 6/10) [920]

8025 Hacker, Carlotta. *Great African Americans in History* (5–8). Series: Outstanding African Americans. 1997, Crabtree LB $22.60 (978-0-86505-805-7); paper $8.95 (978-0-86505-819-4). There are profiles of 13 great African Americans in American history, including Frederick Douglass, Harriet Tubman, W. E. B. Du Bois, Mary McLeod Bethune, and George Washington Carver. (Rev: BL 9/15/97; SLJ 1/98) [920]

8026 Hancock, Sibyl. *Famous Firsts of Black Americans* (7–12). 1983, Pelican $14.95 (978-0-88289-240-5). Biographies of 20 famous African Americans who have contributed in a unique way to our culture. [920]

8027 Haskins, Jim, and Kathleen Benson. *African-American Religious Leaders* (7–10). Series: Black Stars. 2008, Wiley LB $24.95 (978-0-471-73632-5). Leaders of the black church in America since the days of slavery are profiled in this book that is organized in five chronological sections. (Rev: BL 2/1/08; SLJ 7/08) [277.3]

8028 Hoose, Phillip. *We Were There, Too! Young People in U.S. History* (5–8). 2001, Farrar $28.00 (978-0-374-38252-0). Hoose tells the stories of dozens of young people who contributed to the making of America — some famous but many who will be new to readers. (Rev: BCCB 10/01; BL 8/01; HB 9–10/01*; HBG 3/02; SLJ 8/01*) [973]

8029 Hudson, Wade, and Valerie Wesley Wilson. *Afro-Bets Book of Black Heroes from A to Z: An Introduction to Important Black Achievers* (4–7). 1988, Just Us Bks. paper $7.95 (978-0-940975-02-6). Forty-nine African American men and women of outstanding accomplishment. (Rev: BL 1/1/89; SLJ 12/88) [920]

8030 Hughes, Chris. *The Constitutional Convention* (5–9). Series: People at the Center Of. 2005, Gale LB $24.95 (978-1-56711-918-3). After an overview of the convention, this volume provides biographical information on key figures including George Washington, Benjamin Franklin, James Madison, and Alexander Hamilton. (Rev: SLJ 6/05) [920]

8031 Kallen, Stuart A. *Women of the Civil Rights Movement* (7–12). Series: Women in History. 2005, Gale LB $32.45 (978-1-59018-569-8). Women who made important contributions to the U.S. civil rights movement are celebrated in chapters devoted to organizations, protests, education, voting rights, radicals, and so forth. (Rev: SLJ 11/05) [920]

8032 Katz, William L. *Black People Who Made the Old West* (6–9). 1992, Africa World $35.00 (978-0-86543-363-2); paper $14.95 (978-0-86543-364-9). Sketches of 35 black explorers, pioneers, etc., who helped open up the West. [920]

8033 Kennedy, John F. *Profiles in Courage. Memorial Ed. (* (7–12). 1964, Perennial paper $7.00 (978-0-06-080698-9). Sketches of several famous Americans who took unpopular stands during their lives. (Rev: BL 4/87) [920]

8034 Kimmel, Elizabeth Cody. *Ladies First: 40 Daring American Women Who Were Second to None* (4–7). 2006, National Geographic $18.95 (978-0-7922-5393-8). From well-known women such as Sacagawea and Helen Keller to racing driver Shirley Muldowney and rabbi Sally Priesand, this is a well-written and informative resource. (Rev: SLJ 10/06; VOYA 8/06)

8035 Krull, Kathleen. *Lives of the Presidents: Fame, Shame (and What the Neighbors Thought)* (4–8). Illus. by Kathryn Hewitt. 1998, Harcourt $20.00 (978-0-15-200808-6). An entertaining collective biography that stresses the human side of U.S. presidents, with interesting, insightful tidbits and details that bring the presidents to life. (Rev: BL 8/98; HB 11–12/98; HBG 3/99; SLJ 9/98) [920]

8036 Langley, Wanda. *Women of the Wind: Early Women Aviators* (6–9). 2006, Morgan Reynolds LB $26.95 (978-1-931798-81-5). From childhood through achievements in the air, this attractive collective biography covers nine American women flyers. (Rev: BL 2/15/06; SLJ 2/06) [629.13]

8037 Lindop, Edmund. *Dwight D. Eisenhower, John F. Kennedy, Lyndon B. Johnson* (4–7). Series: Presidents Who Dared. 1996, Twenty-First Century LB $23.90 (978-0-8050-3404-2). The highlights of these three administrations are presented, preceded by an introduction to the American presidency. (Rev: BL 4/15/96; SLJ 6/96) [920]

8038 Lindop, Edmund. *George Washington, Thomas Jefferson, Andrew Jackson* (4–7). Series: Presidents Who Dared. 1995, Twenty-First Century LB $23.90 (978-0-8050-3401-1). After a general introduction on the duties of the president, brief biographies of three are given, with emphasis on their accomplishments in office. (Rev: BL 1/1–15/96; SLJ 11/95) [920]

8039 Lindop, Edmund. *James K. Polk, Abraham Lincoln, Theodore Roosevelt* (4–7). Series: Presidents Who Dared. 1995, Twenty-First Century LB $23.90 (978-0-8050-3402-8). Highlights and evaluations of the presidencies of Polk, Lincoln, and Theodore Roosevelt. (Rev: BL 1/1–15/96; SLJ 11/95) [920]

8040 Lindop, Edmund. *Richard M. Nixon, Jimmy Carter, Ronald Reagan* (4–8). Series: Presidents Who Dared. 1996, Twenty-First Century LB $23.90 (978-0-8050-3405-9). This account traces salient events in each of these presidents' terms, for example: Nixon and Watergate and relations with China; Carter and ending the war between Egypt and Israel; and Reagan and his arms agreement with the Soviet Union. (Rev: BL 4/15/96; SLJ 6/96) [920]

8041 Lindop, Edmund. *Woodrow Wilson, Franklin D. Roosevelt, Harry S. Truman* (5–8). Series: Presidents Who Dared. 1995, Twenty-First Century LB $23.90 (978-0-8050-3403-5). After an overview of the presidency and brief profiles of these men, this account looks at daring decisions they made as presidents. (Rev: BL 1/1–15/96; SLJ 11/95; VOYA 6/96) [920]

8042 Lynne, Douglas. *Contemporary United States: 1968 to the Present* (5–8). Illus. Series: Presidents of the United States. 2007, Weigl LB $20.35 (978-1-59036-753-7). The lives and times of recent U.S. presidents — from Nixon to George W. Bush — are covered in this eighth volume in the series. (Rev: BL 10/15/07) [973.92092]

8043 McCullough, Noah. *The Essential Book of Presidential Trivia* (7–12). 2006, Random House paper $9.95 (978-1-4000-6482-3). Written by a 10-year-old presidential hopeful and historian, this book gives a short presidential biography per chapter, a "Did You Know?" section of trivia, and a black-and-white drawing for each. (Rev: SLJ 6/06)

8044 McLean, Jacqueline. *Women with Wings* (4–7). Series: Profiles. 2001, Oliver $19.95 (978-1-881508-70-0). An absorbing account of the achievements of women pilots, including Bessie Coleman, Amelia Earhart, and Anne Morrow Lindbergh. (Rev: BL 5/15/01; HBG 10/01; SLJ 10/01) [629.13]

8045 Marvis, Barbara. *Famous People of Asian Ancestry, Vol. 4* (4–7). Series: Contemporary American Success Stories. 1994, Mitchell Lane paper $10.95 (978-1-

883845-09-4). A collective biography of Asian Americans, including actor Dustin Nguyen, novelist Amy Tan, and businessman Rocky Aoki. Also use volumes 1 through 3 (2nd ed., 1997). (Rev: BL 10/1/94; SLJ 11/94) [920]

8046 Marvis, Barbara. *Famous People of Hispanic Heritage, Vol. 4* (5–9). 1996, Mitchell Lane paper $12.95 (978-1-883845-29-2). The lives of two Hispanic men and two women who have succeeded in their careers are presented in an easy-to-read style. Other volumes in this series by the same author are available. (Rev: BL 12/15/96; SLJ 1/97; VOYA 2/97) [920]

8047 Masters, Nancy Robinson. *Extraordinary Patriots of the United States of America: Colonial Times to Pre-Civil War* (5–8). Series: Extraordinary People. 2005, Children's Pr. LB $40.00 (978-0-516-24404-4). Interesting 3- to 5-page profiles are arranged chronologically by year of birth. (Rev: SLJ 2/06) [920]

8048 Morey, Janet Nomura, and Wendy Dunn. *Famous Hispanic Americans* (7–10). 1996, Dutton $16.99 (978-0-525-65190-1). Fourteen men and women of Hispanic heritage from science, sports, the arts, and other professions are featured in this collective biography. (Rev: BL 2/15/96; SLJ 2/96; VOYA 8/96) [920]

8049 Morin, Isobel V. *Women Chosen for Public Office* (5–7). 1995, Oliver LB $19.95 (978-1-881508-20-5). Nine biographies of women who are involved in the federal government from the superintendent of army nurses to Supreme Court Justice Ruth Bader Ginsburg. (Rev: BL 5/1/95; SLJ 6/95) [920]

8050 Morin, Isobel V. *Women of the U.S. Congress* (6–10). 1994, Oliver LB $19.95 (978-1-881508-12-0). Lists all the women who have served in Congress as of 1994 and provides political biographies of seven of them, citing their accomplishments and their different backgrounds and views. (Rev: BL 7/94; SLJ 5/94; VOYA 6/94) [920]

8051 Morin, Isobel V. *Women Who Reformed Politics* (7–12). 1994, Oliver LB $19.95 (978-1-881508-16-8). Describes the political activism of eight American women, including Abby Foster's abolition fight, Carrie Catt's suffrage battle, and Gloria Steinem's feminist crusade. (Rev: BL 10/15/94; SLJ 11/94; VOYA 2/95) [920]

8052 Morris, Juddi. *At Home with the Presidents* (4–8). 1999, Wiley paper $13.95 (978-0-471-25300-6). In three to five pages each, this account profiles the presidents of the United States from Washington through Clinton. (Rev: SLJ 3/00) [920]

8053 Morrison, Jessica. *Military* (4–7). Illus. Series: Great African Americans. 2011, Weigl LB $20.99 (978-161690661-0); paper $14.95 (978-161690665-8). African Americans who played pivotal roles in America's wars, from the Revolution to Iraq and Afghanistan are portrayed in this inspiring title. (Rev: BL 2/1/12) [920]

8054 Munson, Sammye. *Today's Tejano Heroes* (5–8). 2000, Eakin $13.95 (978-1-57168-328-1). In alphabetical order, this volume introduces 16 important 20th-century Mexican Americans who have contributed to the history and culture of Texas, including Vikki Carr, Attorney General Dan Morales, and federal judge Hilda Tagle. (Rev: BL 2/1/01) [920]

8055 O'Connor, Jane. *If the Walls Could Talk: Family Life at the White House* (4–7). Illus. by Gary Hovland. 2004, Simon & Schuster $16.95 (978-0-689-86863-4). This inside view of family life within the White House — with caricatures and interesting trivia — is similar to Judith St. George's *So You Want to Be President* (Putnam, 2000). (Rev: BL 8/04; SLJ 9/04)

8056 Pinkney, Andrea Davis. *Let It Shine: Stories of Black Women Freedom Fighters* (5–8). 2000, Harcourt $20.00 (978-0-15-201005-8). This work contains chatty profiles of 10 important African American women, including Sojourner Truth, Rosa Parks, and Shirley Chisholm. (Rev: BCCB 11/00; BL 11/15/00; HB 11–12/00; HBG 3/01; SLJ 10/00; VOYA 12/00) [921]

8057 Rappaport, Doreen. *In the Promised Land: Lives of Jewish Americans* (4–7). Illus. by Cornelius Van Wright. 2005, HarperCollins LB $16.89 (978-0-06-059395-7). A look at the lives and diverse accomplishments of 13 notable Jewish Americans, including Asser Levy, Harry Houdini, Jonas Salk, and Steven Spielberg. (Rev: BL 1/1–15/05; SLJ 5/05) [920]

8058 Rodriguez, Robert, and Tamra Orr. *Great Hispanic-Americans* (6–12). 2005, Publications Int'l LB $15.98 (978-1-4127-1148-7). More than 50 Hispanic Americans from different walks of life are profiled in accessible text. (Rev: SLJ 1/06) [920]

8059 St. George, Judith. *The Duel: The Parallel Lives of Alexander Hamilton and Aaron Burr* (6–9). Illus. 2009, Viking $16.99 (978-067001124-7). St. George emphasizes the similarity of the lives of Hamilton and Burr as she chronicles the various stages on their journey to the famous duel. (Rev: BL 6/1/09; LMC 10/09; SLJ 7/1/09*) [920]

8060 Streissguth, Thomas. *Legendary Labor Leaders* (7–12). Series: Profiles. 1998, Oliver LB $19.95 (978-1-881508-44-1). The eight labor leaders profiled in this collective biography are Samuel Gompers, Cesar Chavez, A. Philip Randolph, Jimmy Hoffa, Eugene Debs, William Haywood, Mother Jones, and John L. Lewis. (Rev: BL 10/15/98; SLJ 1/99) [920]

8061 Sullivan, Otha Richard. *African American Millionaires* (5–10). Series: Black Stars. 2004, Wiley $24.95 (978-0-471-46928-5). Tyra Banks and Oprah Winfrey are included here, but so are many names that may be unfamiliar to readers, such as William Alexander Leidesdorff and Annie Turnbo Malone. (Rev: SLJ 5/05) [920]

8062 Taylor, Kimberly H. *Black Abolitionists and Freedom Fighters* (6–10). 1996, Oliver LB $19.95 (978-1-881508-30-4). Profiles are given for eight African Americans who fought to end slavery, some well-known (including Nat Turner and Harriet Tubman) and others less familiar, such as Richard Allen and Mary Terrell. (Rev: SLJ 10/96) [920]

8063 Taylor, Kimberly H. *Black Civil Rights Champions* (6–12). 1995, Oliver LB $19.95 (978-1-881508-22-9). In separate chapters, seven civil rights leaders, including W. E. B. Du Bois, James Farmer, Ella Baker, and Malcolm X, are profiled, with a final chapter that gives thumbnail sketches of many more. (Rev: BL 1/1–15/96; SLJ 3/96; VOYA 6/96) [920]

8064 Thimmesh, Catherine. *Madam President: The Extraordinary, True (and Evolving) Story of Women in Politics. Rev. ed.* (4–7). Illus. by Douglas B. Jones. 2008, Houghton Mifflin $17.00 (978-0-618-39666-5); paper $8.95 (978-0-618-97143-5). This update includes profiles of more than 20 women who have been influential in the political arena, including Margaret Chase Smith, Sirimavo Bandaranaike, Margaret Thatcher, Nancy Pelosi, Hillary Clinton, and Condoleezza Rice. (Rev: BL 10/1/04; SLJ 5/08) [920]

8065 Thro, Ellen. *Twentieth-Century Women Politicians* (7–12). Series: American Profiles. 1998, Facts on File $25.00 (978-0-8160-3758-2). Beginning in the mid-20th century, this work features 10 women who were elected to important public offices, including Margaret Chase Smith, Geraldine Ferraro, Dianne Feinstein, Christine Todd Whitman, and Ann Richards. (Rev: BL 12/15/98) [920]

8066 Ungar, Harlow G. *Teachers and Educators* (7–10). Series: American Profiles. 1994, Facts on File $25.00 (978-0-8160-2990-7). This book profiles eight great American educators of the past, including John Dewey, Horace Mann, Emma Willard, Booker T. Washington, and Henry Barnard. (Rev: BL 7/95; VOYA 5/95) [920]

8067 Wheeler, Jill C. *America's Leaders* (4–7). Series: War on Terrorism. 2002, ABDO LB $25.65 (978-1-57765-661-6). This book contains brief profiles of important American figures in the war against terrorism such as President Bush, Colin Powell, John Ashcroft, and Rudy Giuliani. (Rev: BL 5/15/02; HBG 10/02) [920]

8068 Young, Jeff C. *Inspiring African-American Inventors: Nine Extraordinary Lives* (5–8). Illus. Series: Great Scientists and Famous Inventors. 2009, Enslow LB $33.27 (978-159845080-4). Nine African American inventors are profiled here, with details of their inventions and links to relevant Web sites. (Rev: BL 2/1/10; VOYA 4/10) [920]

8069 Zimmerman, Dwight Jon. *First Command: Paths to Leadership* (7–12). 2005, Vandamere $22.95 (978-0-918339-62-1). A collective biography of 23 American soldiers and marines who went on to become generals, focusing on their early commands and the leadership qualities that helped them advance. (Rev: SLJ 5/06)

Civil and Human Rights Leaders

ADDAMS, JANE

8070 Caravantes, Peggy. *Waging Peace: The Story of Jane Addams* (5–8). 2004, Morgan Reynolds LB $23.95 (978-1-931798-40-2). Covers Addams's life and achievements, with good material on her youth and the lessons she learned from her Quaker father. (Rev: SLJ 2/05) [921]

8071 Fradin, Judith Bloom, and Dennis Brindell Fradin. *Jane Addams: Champion of Democracy* (6–9). 2006, Clarion $21.00 (978-0-618-50436-7). This account of the fascinating life of Jane Addams, social activist and Nobel Peace Prize winner, provides lots of historical context and clearly shows her legacy today. (Rev: BL 10/15/06; HB 11–12/06; LMC 3/07; SLJ 11/06*) [361.2]

ANTHONY, SUSAN B.

8072 Orr, Tamra. *The Life and Times of Susan B. Anthony* (5–8). Series: Profiles in American History. 2007, Mitchell Lane LB $19.95 (978-1-58415-445-7). This biography of Anthony traces her life and work in the women's rights movement and contains supplemental facts that will interest readers. (Rev: SLJ 7/07) [921]

8073 Todd, Anne M. *Susan B. Anthony: Activist* (6–10). Series: Women of Achievement. 2009, Chelsea House $30 (978-1-60413-087-4). This concise and balanced profile is a good starting place for anyone researching the famous suffragette and her legacy. (Rev: SLJ 5/1/09) [921]

BAKER, ELLA

8074 Bohannon, Lisa Frederiksen. *Freedom Cannot Rest: Ella Baker and the Civil Rights Movement* (7–12). Series: Civil Rights Leaders. 2005, Morgan Reynolds LB $26.95 (978-1-931798-71-6). A well-illustrated and evenhanded introduction to the life and accomplishments of Ella Baker, a major — but often overlooked — player in the U.S. civil rights movement. (Rev: SLJ 12/05) [921]

BATES, DAISY

8075 Fradin, Judith Bloom, and Dennis Brindell Fradin. *The Power of One: Daisy Bates and the Little Rock Nine* (8–11). 2004, Clarion $19.00 (978-0-618-31556-7). A detailed profile of Daisy Bates, who as president of the Arkansas chapter of the NAACP played a pivotal role in the 1957 integration of Central High School in Little Rock. (Rev: BL 2/1/05; SLJ 4/05) [323]

BETHUNE, MARY MCLEOD

8076 Somervill, Barbara A. *Mary McLeod Bethune: African-American Educator* (4–7). Series: Our People. 2003, Child's World LB $27.07 (978-1-59296-008-8). A profile of the African American educator and leader, with sidebars that add historical context. (Rev: SLJ 4/04) [921]

BROWN, JOHN

8077 Hendrix, John. *John Brown: His Fight for Freedom* (5–8). 2009, Abrams $18.95 (978-0-8109-3798-7). Bold illustrations enhance this picture book for older readers that covers the famed abolitionist's life, ideals, and sometimes questionable actions. (Rev: BL 10/15/09*; LMC 3–4/10; SLJ 11/09) [921]

8078 Reynolds, David S. *John Brown, Abolitionist: The Man Who Killed Slavery, Sparked the Civil War, and Seeded Civil Rights* (8–12). 2005, Knopf $30.00 (978-0-375-41188-5). This insightful biography adds fuel to the continuing debate over what motivated the fiery abolitionist. (Rev: BL 2/1/05) [973.7]

CHAPMAN, OSCAR

8079 Hopkinson, Deborah. *Sweet Land of Liberty* (3–7). Illus. by Leonard Jenkins. 2007, Peachtree $16.95 (978-1-56145-395-5). With bold illustrations, this volume traces the life of Oscar Chapman, a white government official who spent much of his life fighting injustice, most notably finding a public venue for singer Marian Anderson after she was denied the right to perform in Constitution Hall. (Rev: BL 4/15/07)

CHAVEZ, CESAR

8080 Brown, Jonatha A. *Cesar Chavez* (5–8). Series: Trailblazers of the Modern World. 2004, World Almanac LB $31.00 (978-0-8368-5097-0). Report writers will find lots of suitable information in this work that covers Chavez's life and accomplishments. (Rev: SLJ 7/04) [921]

8081 Tracy, Kathleen. *Cesar Chavez* (5–7). Series: Latinos in American History. 2003, Mitchell Lane LB $29.95 (978-1-58415-224-8). This biography covers the life and accomplishments of the Mexican American labor leader who founded the United Farm Workers. (Rev: BL 1/1–15/04) [921]

8082 Young, Jeff C. *Cesar Chavez* (7–10). Series: American Workers. 2007, Morgan Reynolds $27.95 (978-1-59935-036-3). The activist's early life and inspirations as well as his influence on labor practices are well presented in this easy-to-read biography. (Rev: BL 3/15/07; SLJ 4/07) [331.88]

CHILD, LYDIA MARIA

8083 Kenschaft, Lori. *Lydia Maria Child: The Quest for Racial Justice* (6–10). Series: Oxford Portraits. 2002,

489

Oxford LB $32.95 (978-0-19-513257-1). Lydia Maria Child, an activist for civil rights in the early and middle 1800s, is also known for her literary career. (Rev: BL 3/1/03; HBG 3/03; SLJ 1/03) [303.48]

DOUGLASS, FREDERICK

8084 Adler, David A. *Frederick Douglass: A Noble Life* (6–10). 2010, Holiday House $18.95 (978-0-8234-2056-8). With many quotations from Douglass's own writings, this generally admiring profile tells the story of his life and considerable achievements. (Rev: BL 6/10*; LMC 1–2/11; SLJ 9/1/10*) [921]

8085 Meltzer, Milton, ed. *Frederick Douglass: In His Own Words* (8–12). 1995, Harcourt $22.00 (978-0-15-229492-2). An introduction to the articles and speeches of the great 19th-century abolitionist leader, arranged chronologically. (Rev: BL 12/15/94; SLJ 2/95) [305.8]

8086 Sanders, Nancy I. *Frederick Douglass for Kids: His Life and Times, with 21 Activities* (4–7). Illus. 2012, Chicago Review $16.95 (978-156976717-7). Activities ranging from making a hat and a cravat to making a paste to keep flies away extend the scope of this informative profile of the orator and abolitionist. **e** (Rev: BL 6/12; SLJ 7/12) [921]

8087 Schuman, Michael A. *Frederick Douglass: "Truth Is of No Color"* (4–8). Illus. 2009, Enslow LB $23.95 (978-0-7660-3025-1). This biography tracks the famous abolitionist's life from his childhood escape from slavery into his adult years. (Rev: BL 6/1/09; LMC 11–12/09; SLJ 9/09) [921]

8088 Sterngass, John. *Frederick Douglass* (5–8). Series: Leaders of the Civil War Era. 2009, Chelsea House $30 (978-1-60413-306-6). Enhanced by a mix of illustrations, period documents, photographs, and concise sidebars, this book provides a balanced look at the eloquent man who galvanized many in the fight against slavery. (Rev: LMC 10/09) [921]

DU BOIS, W. E. B.

8089 Bolden, Tonya. *W. E. B. Du Bois: A Twentieth-Century Life* (7–10). Illus. Series: Up Close. 2008, Viking $16.99 (978-067006302-4). A look at the life of the complex African American leader, this will be helpful to report writers and others interested in important civil rights figures. (Rev: BL 2/1/09; HB 3–4/09; SLJ 1/1/09) [921]

8090 Whiting, Jim. *W. E. B. DuBois: Civil Rights Activist, Author, and Historian* (6–9). Series: Transcending Race in America. 2010, Mason Crest $22.95 (978-1-4222-1618-7). This biography is part of a series that looks at famous biracial achievers in America and considers this aspect of Du Bois's life. (Rev: BL 2/1/10; LMC 3–4/10; SLJ 2/10) [921]

FARRAKHAN, LOUIS

8091 Haskins, Jim. *Louis Farrakhan and the Nation of Islam* (7–12). 1996, Walker LB $16.85 (978-0-8027-8423-0). Beginning with a history of African American nationalism and the Nation of Islam, this biography places the life of Farrakhan within the movement for black solidarity. (Rev: BL 10/1/96; SLJ 1/97) [921]

FREEMAN, ELIZABETH

8092 Wilds, Mary. *MumBet: The Life and Times of Elizabeth Freeman: The True Story of a Slave Who Won Her Freedom* (7–12). 1999, Avisson LB $19.95 (978-1-888105-40-7). The story of MumBet (Elizabeth Freeman), a slave who sued for her freedom in Massachusetts in 1781 after hearing a reading of the Declaration of Independence and won, helping to set the legal precedents that ended slavery in New England. (Rev: BL 6/1–15/99; SLJ 6/99; VOYA 2/00) [921]

GARVEY, MARCUS

8093 Caravantes, Peggy. *Marcus Garvey: Black Nationalist* (6–10). Series: Twentieth Century Leaders. 2004, Morgan Reynolds LB $23.95 (978-1-931798-14-3). A biography of this black nationalist, Pan-Africanist, and exponent of black civil rights. (Rev: BL 2/15/04; HBG 4/04; SLJ 11/03; VOYA 6/04) [921]

8094 Kallen, Stuart A. *Marcus Garvey and the Back to Africa Movement* (7–12). 2006, Gale LB $28.70 (978-1-59018-838-5). An excellent account of Garvey's contributions to the black pride and power movements, touching on his charisma but also on his deficiencies. (Rev: SLJ 8/06)

GONZALEZ, HENRY B.

8095 Haugen, Brenda. *Henry B. Gonzalez: Congressman of the People* (6–9). 2005, Compass Point LB $30.60 (978-0-7565-0996-5). In his 37 years as a representative in the U.S. Congress, Henry Gonzalez (a Democrat from Texas) fought for racial equality, civil rights, and efforts to end poverty. (Rev: SLJ 8/06) [921]

HAMER, FANNIE LOU

8096 Fiorelli, June Estep. *Fannie Lou Hamer: A Voice for Freedom* (5–10). Series: Avisson Young Adult. 2005, Avisson paper $19.95 (978-1-888105-62-9). Hamer's life, including her youth, are described and placed in the context of events in the United States at the time. (Rev: SLJ 2/06) [921]

HAYDEN, LEWIS

8097 Strangis, Joel. *Lewis Hayden and the War Against Slavery* (7–12). 1998, Shoe String LB $25.00 (978-0-208-02430-5). The dramatic story of the former slave who became an active abolitionist and a stationmaster on the Underground Railroad. (Rev: BL 2/15/99; HBG 9/99; SLJ 5/99; VOYA 10/99) [921]

HESCHEL, ABRAHAM JOSHUA

8098 Rose, Or. *Abraham Joshua Heschel* (4–8). 2003, Jewish Publication Soc. paper $9.95 (978-0-8276-0758-3). A portrait of the rabbi and teacher who was born in Poland, emigrated to the United States, and became a leader in the civil rights movement. (Rev: BL 6/1–15/03; HBG 10/01) [921]

HUERTA, DOLORES

8099 Murcia, Rebecca Thatcher. *Dolores Huerta* (5–7). Series: Latinos in American History. 2002, Mitchell Lane LB $29.95 (978-1-58415-155-5). The story of the gallant woman who worked along with Cesar Chavez to protect the rights of farm workers. (Rev: BL 2/15/03; HBG 10/03) [921]

8100 Van Tol, Alex. *Dolores Huerta: Voice for the Working Poor* (5–8). Illus. Series: Crabtree Groundbreakers Biographies. 2010, Crabtree LB $31.93 (978-077872536-7). Dolores Huerta's lifetime of advocacy for farm safety and environmental conscience is portrayed here in clear language and many black-and-white photographs. (Rev: BL 1/1–15/11; VOYA 12/10) [921]

IDAR, JOVITA

8101 Gibson, Karen Bush. *Jovita Idar* (5–7). Series: Latinos in American History. 2002, Mitchell Lane LB $29.95 (978-1-58415-151-7). The inspiring story of the Latin American woman who started San Antonio's first free kindergarten and who founded the League of Mexican American women in 1911 to educate poor children. (Rev: BL 2/15/03; HBG 10/03) [921]

JACOBS, HARRIET A.

8102 Fleischner, Jennifer. *I Was Born a Slave: The Story of Harriet Jacobs* (4–8). 1997, Millbrook LB $26.90 (978-0-7613-0111-0). The turbulent life of Harriet Jacobs, who was born into slavery and lived for many years as a fugitive before winning her freedom and becoming an abolitionist. (Rev: BL 9/15/97; HBG 3/98; SLJ 1/98) [921]

KING, CORETTA SCOTT

8103 Bankston, John. *Coretta Scott King and the Story Behind the Coretta Scott King Award* (4–8). Series: Great Achievement Awards. 2003, Mitchell Lane LB $29.95 (978-1-58415-202-6). The story of the widow of Martin Luther King, Jr., her continuing fight for civil rights, and the children's book prize named after her are covered in this biography. (Rev: BL 10/15/03; SLJ 10/03) [921]

8104 Rhodes, Lisa Renee. *Coretta Scott King: Civil Rights Activist* (7–12). Series: Black Americans of Achievement. 2005, Chelsea House LB $30.00 (978-0-7910-8251-5). This revised edition of King's life adds new photographs and information boxes to the description of her childhood, education, marriage, participa-

tion in the civil rights movement, and work after her husband's assassination. (Rev: SLJ 11/05) [921]

KING, MARTIN LUTHER, JR.

8105 Bolden, Tonya. *M. L. K: Journey of a King* (7–10). 2007, Abrams $19.95 (978-0-8109-5476-2). An inspiring biography of the civil rights leader that emphasizes his influences and legacy. (Rev: BCCB 3/07; BL 2/1/07; LMC 8–9/07; SLJ 2/07*) [921]

8106 Darby, Jean. *Martin Luther King, Jr.* (4–8). Series: Lerner Biographies. 1990, Lerner LB $27.93 (978-0-8225-4902-4). An in-depth look at King's life and the civil rights movement. (Rev: BL 7/90; SLJ 11/90) [921]

LOCKWOOD, BELVA

8107 Norgren, Jill. *Belva Lockwood: Equal Rights Pioneer* (5–8). Illus. Series: Trailblazer Biographies. 2008, Twenty-First Century $31.93 (978-0-8225-9068-2). Norgren introduces the 19th-century woman who worked for the rights of Native Americans and for equal voting rights for all. (Rev: BL 1/1–15/09; SLJ 11/08) [921]

LYON, MARITCHA REYMOND

8108 Bolden, Tonya. *Maritcha: A Nineteenth-Century American Girl* (4–7). 2005, Abrams $17.95 (978-0-8109-5045-0). Drawing on primary sources, Bolden tells the story of Maritcha Remond Lyon, a free black girl who succeeded in her fight to attend an all-white high school in Rhode Island in the mid-19th century. Coretta Scott King Illustrator Award and Author Honor Book 2006. (Rev: BL 2/1/05*; SLJ 2/05) [921]

MALCOLM X

8109 Malcolm X, and Alex Haley. *The Autobiography of Malcolm X* (7–12). 1999, Ballantine $20.00 (978-0-345-91536-8); paper $12.00 (978-0-345-91503-0). The story of the man who turned from Harlem drug pusher into a charismatic leader of his people. [921]

8110 Sharp, Anne Wallace. *Malcolm X and Black Pride* (6–9). Illus. Series: Lucent Library of Black History. 2010, Gale/Lucent LB $32.45 (978-142050123-0). This straightforward biography of civil rights activist Malcolm X is enhanced by frequent photographs, extensive back matter, and a balanced approach. (Rev: BL 2/1/11) [921]

PARKS, ROSA

8111 Davis, Kenneth C. *Don't Know Much About Rosa Parks* (4–7). Illus. by Sergio Martinez. Series: Don't Know Much About. 2005, HarperCollins paper $4.99 (978-0-06-442126-3). A question-and-answer format, interesting sidebars, and news photographs enliven this profile of Parks, which emphasizes her long-term commitment to civil rights. (Rev: BL 2/1/05) [323]

8112 Parks, Rosa, and Jim Haskins. *Rosa Parks: My Story* (6–10). 1992, Dial $17.99 (978-0-8037-0673-6). This autobiography of the civil rights hero becomes an oral history of the movement, including her recollections of Martin Luther King, Jr., Roy Wilkins, and others. (Rev: BL 12/15/91; SLJ 2/92) [921]

8113 Schraff, Anne. *Rosa Parks: "Tired of Giving In"* (4–8). Series: African-American Biography Library. 2005, Enslow LB $31.93 (978-0-7660-2463-2). An accessible profile of Parks and her importance. (Rev: SLJ 10/05) [921]

RANDOLPH, A. PHILIP

8114 Miller, Calvin Craig. *A. Philip Randolph and the African-American Labor Movement* (7–10). Series: Civil Rights Leaders. 2005, Morgan Reynolds $26.95 (978-1-931798-50-1). The life and achievements of the founding president of the Brotherhood of Sleeping Car Porters. (Rev: BL 2/15/05; SLJ 5/05) [323]

RUSTIN, BAYARD

8115 Brimner, Larry Dane. *We Are One: The Story of Bayard Rustin* (5–8). Illus. 2007, Boyds Mills $17.95 (978-1-59078-498-3). With lively text, photographs, quotations, and song lyrics, Brimner explains Bayard Rustin's importance in the struggle for civil rights. (Rev: BL 9/1/07; SLJ 11/07)

8116 Miller, Calvin Craig. *No Easy Answers: Bayard Rustin and the Civil Rights Movement* (7–10). Series: Civil Rights Leaders. 2005, Morgan Reynolds LB $26.95 (978-1-931798-43-3). Rustin's significant achievements in the field of civil rights are discussed along with his homosexuality, which was a large factor in his relative obscurity. (Rev: BL 2/1/05; SLJ 6/05; VOYA 8/05) [323]

STANTON, ELIZABETH CADY

8117 Sigerman, Harriet. *Elizabeth Cady Stanton: The Right Is Ours* (6–10). Series: Oxford Portraits. 2001, Oxford $32.95 (978-0-19-511969-5). The life of the pioneering suffragist, accompanied by photographs and historic documents such as newspaper articles and cartoons. (Rev: BL 12/15/01; HBG 3/02; SLJ 11/01; VOYA 2/02) [921]

STEINEM, GLORIA

8118 Lazo, Caroline Evensen. *Gloria Steinem: Feminist Extraordinaire* (5–7). Series: Lerner Biographies. 1998, Lerner LB $27.93 (978-0-8225-4934-5). The story of Steinem, who overcame a troubled childhood to become a great humanitarian, writer, and leader of the feminist movement. (Rev: BL 7/98; SLJ 7/98) [921]

TERRELL, MARY CHURCH

8119 Fradin, Dennis Brindell, and Judith Bloom Fradin. *Fight On! Mary Church Terrell's Battle for Integra-*tion (5–9). 2003, Clarion $18.00 (978-0-618-13349-9). Terrell's efforts to end discrimination are detailed in a readable, large-format biography that includes primary sources and lots of illustrations. (Rev: BL 6/1–15/03; HB 7–8/03; HBG 10/03; SLJ 5/03*; VOYA 6/03) [323]

TRUTH, SOJOURNER

8120 Brezina, Corona. *Sojourner Truth's "Ain't I a Woman?" Speech: A Primary Source Investigation* (6–9). Series: Great Historic Debates and Speeches. 2005, Rosen LB $29.25 (978-1-4042-0154-5). A fascinating account of Truth's historic 1851 speech to the Women's Convention in Akron, Ohio; the primary sources offer insight into the words of a woman who could neither read nor write. (Rev: BL 2/15/05; SLJ 5/05) [306.3]

8121 Butler, Mary G. *Sojourner Truth: From Slave to Activist for Freedom* (4–8). Series: Library of American Lives and Times. 2003, Rosen LB $34.60 (978-0-8239-5736-1). A forerunner of the modern civil rights movement, Sojourner Truth rose from slavery to become a crusader for good race relations and women's rights. (Rev: BL 6/1–15/03; SLJ 5/03; VOYA 6/03) [921]

8122 Horn, Geoffrey M. *Sojourner Truth: Speaking Up for Freedom* (4–7). Illus. Series: Voices for Freedom: Abolitionist Views. 2009, Crabtree LB $30.60 (978-077874824-3). With many images and clear text, this is an attractive profile of the woman who fought for the rights of her people. (Rev: BL 2/1/10) [921]

8123 Rockwell, Anne. *Only Passing Through* (4–8). 2000, Knopf $16.95 (978-0-679-89186-4). A moving picture-book biography of Sojourner Truth, who was a pioneer in the struggle for racial equality and devoted her life to the abolitionist movement. (Rev: BCCB 1/01; BL 11/15/00; HB 11–12/00; HBG 3/01; SLJ 12/00) [921]

TUBMAN, HARRIET

8124 Adler, David A. *Harriet Tubman and the Underground Railroad* (5–8). Illus. 2013, Holiday $18.95 (978-082342365-1). This thorough introduction to Tubman's life and achievements provides clear historical context and details her relationships with key figures of the time. (Rev: BL 2/1/13*; SLJ 2/13; VOYA 6/13) [921]

8125 Malaspina, Ann. *Harriet Tubman* (5–8). Series: Leaders of the Civil War Era. 2009, Chelsea House $30 (978-1-60413-303-5). Enhanced by a mix of illustrations, period documents, photographs, and concise sidebars, this book provides a balanced look at the courageous woman who led so many to freedom. (Rev: LMC 10/09) [921]

8126 Sawyer, Kem Knapp. *Harriet Tubman* (5–9). Series: DK Biography. 2010, DK $14.99 (978-0-7566-5807-6); paper $5.99 (978-0-7566-5806-9). A well-written and illustrated biography of the famous abolitionist, with a useful timeline and chapter notes. (Rev: BL 4/1/10; SLJ 5/10) [921]

TURNER, NAT

8127 Bisson, Terry. *Nat Turner: Slave Revolt Leader* (6–9). Series: Black Americans of Achievement. 2004, Chelsea House LB $30.00 (978-0-7910-8167-9). New illustrations, essays on related figures, and a list of Web sites enhance this new edition of a profile of Nat Turner, who led a bloody Virginia slave uprising in 1831. (Rev: BL 2/1/05) [975.5]

WASHINGTON, BOOKER T.

8128 Washington, Booker T. *Up from Slavery: An Autobiography by Booker T. Washington* (7–12). 1963, Airmont paper $3.95 (978-0-8049-0157-4). The story of the slave who later organized the Tuskegee Institute. [921]

8129 Whiting, Jim. *Booker T. Washington: Educator, Author, and Civil Rights Leader* (6–9). Series: Transcending Race in America. 2010, Mason Crest $22.95 (978-1-4222-1608-8). This biography is part of a series that looks at famous biracial achievers in America and considers this aspect of Washington's life. (Rev: LMC 3–4/10; SLJ 1/10) [921]

WELLS, IDA B.

8130 Fradin, Dennis Brindell, and Judith Bloom Fradin. *Ida B. Wells: Mother of the Civil Rights Movement* (5–10). 2000, Clarion $19.00 (978-0-395-89898-7). An inspiring biography of the African American who was born a slave and went on to become a school teacher, journalist, and an activist who fought for black women's right to vote and helped found the NAACP. (Rev: BL 2/15/00; HB 5–6/00; HBG 10/00; SLJ 4/00*) [921]

8131 Schraff, Anne. *Ida B. Wells-Barnett: "Strike a Blow against a Glaring Evil"* (6–9). Series: African-American Biography Library. 2008, Enslow LB $23.95 (978-0-7660-2704-6). This book about the journalist and activist will give readers a glimpse into the days before civil rights were granted to all and what it took to achieve those rights. (Rev: BL 2/1/08) [921]

8132 Welch, Catherine A. *Ida B. Wells-Barnett: Powerhouse with a Pen* (5–8). Series: Trailblazer Biographies. 2000, Carolrhoda LB $30.35 (978-1-57505-352-3). This book introduces Wells-Barnett, who was born a slave and became a powerful journalist and activist as well as a spokesperson for all African Americans. (Rev: BL 6/1–15/00; HBG 10/00; SLJ 7/00; VOYA 2/01) [921]

WOODHULL, VICTORIA

8133 Brody, Miriam. *Victoria Woodhull: Free Spirit for Women's Rights* (7–12). Series: Oxford Portraits. 2004, Oxford LB $32.95 (978-0-19-514367-6). Presenting historical and social context, this biography covers the

American reformer's difficult childhood and complex adult life. (Rev: SLJ 2/05) [921]

8134 Havelin, Kate. *Victoria Woodhull: Fearless Feminist* (7–10). Series: Trailblazer Biographies. 2006, Twenty-First Century LB $30.60 (978-0-8225-5986-3). A concise, well-researched biography of the ardent suffragist who ran for U.S. president in 1872. (Rev: SLJ 11/06) [921]

Presidents and Their Families

ADAMS, ABIGAIL

8135 McCarthy, Pat. *Abigail Adams: First Lady and Patriot* (5–8). Series: Historical American Biographies. 2002, Enslow LB $26.60 (978-0-7660-1618-7). The life story of the prolific letter-writer who was wife of the second president of the United States, John Adams. (Rev: BCCB 4/01; BL 4/1/02; HBG 10/02; SLJ 7/02) [921]

ADAMS, JOHN

8136 Lukes, Bonnie L. *John Adams: Public Servant* (8–12). Series: Notable Americans. 2000, Morgan Reynolds LB $23.95 (978-1-883846-80-0). An excellent biography of the second president of the United States that reveals both his virtues and his flaws. (Rev: BL 12/1/00; HBG 3/01; SLJ 2/01) [921]

8137 Yoder, Carolyn P., ed. *John Adams The Writer: A Treasury of Letters, Diaries, and Public Documents* (7–10). 2007, Boyds Mills $16.95 (978-1-59078-247-7). Selected writings of the second president of the United States are drawn from speeches, diaries, letters, and other sources, providing a full picture of this important figure from his own words. (Rev: BL 12/1/07; LMC 1/08; SLJ 4/08) [793.4]

ADAMS, JOHN AND ABIGAIL

8138 Ashby, Ruth. *John and Abigail Adams* (5–8). Series: Presidents and First Ladies. 2005, Gareth Stevens LB $31.00 (978-0-8368-5755-9). An accessible, balanced, and attractive discussion of the Adamses and the contributions each made to their joint lives. (Rev: BL 3/1/05) [921]

BUSH, GEORGE H. W.

8139 Anderson, Ken. *George Bush: A Lifetime of Service* (6–12). 2003, Eakin $16.95 (978-1-57168-663-3); paper $12.95 (978-1-57168-600-8). George Herbert Walker Bush, the 41st president, is profiled in this biography that gives insights into his relationship with his son, George W. Bush. (Rev: BL 1/1–15/03; HBG 10/03; SLJ 2/03) [921]

BUSH, GEORGE W.

8140 Burgan, Michael. *George W. Bush* (5–8). Illus. Series: Presidents and Their Times. 2012, Marshall Cavendish LB $34.21 (978-160870184-1). An appealing, chronological profile that gives an evenhanded account of Bush's life and administrations. (Rev: BL 6/12) [921]

8141 Jones, Veda Boyd. *George W. Bush* (5–8). Illus. Series: Modern World Leaders. 2006, Chelsea House $30.00 (978-0-7910-9217-0). This biography traces Bush's life and political career from his 1946 birth in New Haven, Connecticut, through the first five years of his presidency. (Rev: BL 10/15/06)

8142 Marquez, Heron. *George W. Bush* (5–8). Series: Presidential Leaders. 2006, Lerner LB $29.27 (978-0-8225-1507-4). A balanced profile that examines Bush's childhood and adolescence as well as his accomplishments and the controversies surrounding some of his decisions. (Rev: BL 10/15/06) [921]

8143 Thompson, Bill, and Dorcas Thompson. *George W. Bush* (4–8). Series: Childhoods of the Presidents. 2003, Mason Crest $17.95 (978-1-59084-281-2). Bush's privileged childhood and education, his role as eldest son, and the death of his sister from leukemia are covered in an interesting narrative that highlights his character. (Rev: BL 6/1–15/03; SLJ 2/03) [973.931]

8144 Wheeler, Jill C. *George W. Bush* (4–7). Series: War on Terrorism. 2002, ABDO LB $25.65 (978-1-57765-662-3). A brief profile of President Bush with particular emphasis on his war on terrorism. (Rev: BL 5/15/02; HBG 10/02) [921]

BUSH, LAURA WELCH

8145 Gormley, Beatrice. *Laura Bush: America's First Lady* (5–8). 2003, Simon & Schuster paper $4.99 (978-0-689-85366-1). A chronological account of Laura Bush's life, with information on her childhood as well as her later public life. (Rev: BL 3/1/03; HBG 10/03; SLJ 5/03) [973.931]

CARTER, JIMMY

8146 Kent, Deborah. *Jimmy Carter* (4–7). Series: Encyclopedia of Presidents — Second Series. 2005, Children's Pr. LB $34.00 (978-0-516-22975-1). Updated from the 1989 volume, this new, redesigned edition covers the former president's life and career and adds information about his recent work. (Rev: BL 6/1–15/05) [973.926]

8147 Santella, Andrew. *James Earl Carter Jr.* (4–7). Series: Profiles of the Presidents. 2002, Compass Point LB $26.60 (978-0-7565-0283-6). A straightforward profile that touches on Carter's southern roots, his successes and failures as president, and his subsequent work in the fields of human rights and democracy. (Rev: SLJ 1/03) [921]

8148 Smith, Betsy. *Jimmy Carter, President* (5–7). 1986, Walker LB $13.85 (978-0-8027-6652-6). A profile of Jimmy Carter and his one-term presidency. (Rev: BL 2/15/87; SLJ 12/86) [921]

CLEVELAND, GROVER

8149 Collins, David R. *Grover Cleveland: 22nd and 24th President of the United States* (7–9). 1988, Garrett LB $21.27 (978-0-944483-01-5). A fine introduction to this president and his career, with interesting sidebar features. (Rev: SLJ 9/88) [921]

CLINTON, BILL

8150 Cwiklik, Robert. *Bill Clinton: President of the 90's. Rev. ed.* (4–8). Series: Gateway Biographies. 1997, Millbrook $22.90 (978-0-7613-0129-5); paper $8.95 (978-0-7613-0146-2). A readable biography that concentrates on Clinton's career as governor of Arkansas and his early years as president. (Rev: BL 9/15/97; SLJ 7/97) [921]

8151 Heinrichs, Ann. *William Jefferson Clinton* (4–8). Series: Profiles of the Presidents. 2002, Compass Point LB $26.60 (978-0-7565-0207-2). This absorbing account of Clinton's life and career covers both the good and bad sides of his presidency and includes a discussion of Hillary's role. (Rev: SLJ 6/02) [921]

8152 Marcovitz, Hal. *Bill Clinton* (4–8). Series: Childhoods of the Presidents. 2003, Mason Crest LB $17.95 (978-1-59084-273-7). This brief, well-illustrated overview of Clinton's childhood and adolescence looks in particular at his relationships with family members, his support for civil rights, and his popularity. (Rev: BL 6/1–15/03; SLJ 2/03) [973.929]

EISENHOWER, DWIGHT D.

8153 Darby, Jean. *Dwight D. Eisenhower: A Man Called Ike* (6–9). Series: Lerner Biographies. 1989, Lerner LB $30.35 (978-0-8225-4900-0). An easily read account of the highlights in the life of this general and president. (Rev: BL 11/15/89; SLJ 9/89) [921]

8154 Deitch, Kenneth, and Joanne B. Weisman. *Dwight D. Eisenhower: Man of Many Hats* (5–7). Illus. by Jay Connolly. 1990, Discovery LB $14.95 (978-1-878668-02-8). Each stage of Eisenhower's multifaceted career is represented. (Rev: SLJ 2/91) [921]

8155 Raatma, Lucia. *Dwight D. Eisenhower* (4–7). Series: Profiles of the Presidents. 2002, Compass Point LB $26.60 (978-0-7565-0279-9). A straightforward account that focuses on Eisenhower's military career and successes in World War II. (Rev: SLJ 1/03) [921]

8156 Van Steenwyk, Elizabeth. *Dwight David Eisenhower, President* (5–8). 1987, Walker LB $13.85 (978-0-8027-6671-7). The focus is on the career of this war-hero president. (Rev: BL 5/15/87) [921]

8157 Young, Jeff C. *Dwight D. Eisenhower: Soldier and President* (6–12). 2001, Morgan Reynolds LB $23.95 (978-1-883846-76-3). This well-written and interesting biography of the 34th president covers his life from boyhood, his career, and his personality. (Rev: BL 11/15/01; HBG 3/02; SLJ 2/02) [921]

FILLMORE, MILLARD

8158 Gottfried, Ted. *Millard Fillmore* (4–7). Series: Presidents and Their Times. 2007, Marshall Cavendish LB $22.95 (978-0-7614-2431-4). A clear and thorough life of the president, describing his early years, presidential career, and later life, with discussion of important events that took place during his life. (Rev: SLJ 1/08)

GARFIELD, JAMES A.

8159 Kingsbury, Robert. *The Assassination of James A. Garfield* (6–9). Series: The Library of Political Assassinations. 2002, Rosen LB $27.95 (978-0-8239-3540-6). The life and death of this lesser-known President are examined with material on the strange life of the assassin, Charles Guiteau. (Rev: BL 8/02) [921]

GRANT, ULYSSES S.

8160 Crompton, Samuel Willard. *Ulysses S. Grant* (5–8). Series: Leaders of the Civil War Era. 2009, Chelsea House $30 (978-1-60413-301-1). Enhanced by a mix of illustrations, period documents, photographs, and concise sidebars, this book provides a balanced look at the most successful leader of the Union Army and president of the United States. (Rev: LMC 10/09) [921]

8161 Rice, Earle, Jr. *Ulysses S. Grant: Defender of the Union* (8–11). Series: Civil War Leaders. 2005, Morgan Reynolds LB $26.95 (978-1-931798-48-8). A vivid portrait of Grant, who rose from humble beginnings in his native Ohio to achieve acclaim as a military leader and ascend to the highest office in the land. (Rev: BL 3/15/05; SLJ 11/05) [973.8]

8162 Sapp, Richard. *Ulysses S. Grant and the Road to Appomattox* (5–8). Series: In the Footsteps of American Heroes. 2006, World Almanac LB $34.00 (978-0-8368-6431-1). This life of Grant includes information on historical sites in sidebar features. (Rev: SLJ 9/06) [921]

JACKSON, ANDREW

8163 Behrman, Carol H. *Andrew Jackson* (5–8). Series: Presidential Leaders. 2002, Lerner LB $29.27 (978-0-8225-0093-3). Jackson's life and character are brought to life in this narrative that points out his failings as well as his achievements. (Rev: HBG 3/03; SLJ 1/03) [921]

8164 Whitelaw, Nancy. *Andrew Jackson: Frontier President* (7–10). Series: Notable Americans. 2000, Morgan Reynolds LB $23.95 (978-1-883846-67-1). A fine biography of an interesting, multifaceted man who over-

came many obstacles to achieve prominence. (Rev: BL 11/1/00; HBG 3/01; SLJ 2/01) [921]

JEFFERSON, THOMAS

8165 Davis, Kenneth C. *Don't Know Much About Thomas Jefferson* (4–7). Illus. by Rob Shepperson. Series: Don't Know Much About. 2005, HarperTrophy paper $4.99 (978-0-06-442128-7). Jefferson's many accomplishments and contributions are presented in a question-and-answer format amplified by sidebar features, maps, and quotations that add context. (Rev: BL 2/1/05; SLJ 5/05) [921]

8166 Ferris, Jeri. *Thomas Jefferson: Father of Liberty* (5–8). 1998, Lerner LB $30.35 (978-1-57505-009-6). This readable biography covers both the public and the private sides of Jefferson's life, with details on his personality and his family. (Rev: BL 3/1/99; HBG 3/99; SLJ 12/98) [921]

8167 Harness, Cheryl. *Thomas Jefferson* (4–7). 2004, National Geographic $17.95 (978-0-7922-6496-5). Harness paints a personal portrait of Jefferson and his various roles in this picture book, enhanced by maps and eye-catching illustrations. (Rev: BL 2/1/04; SLJ 2/04) [973.4]

8168 Miller, Brandon Marie. *Thomas Jefferson for Kids: His Life and Times with 21 Activities* (5–8). Illus. 2011, Chicago Review paper $16.95 (978-1-56976-348-3). Age-appropriate activities (dancing a reel, making a simple microscope) extend this balanced biography that covers personal and political aspects of Jefferson. (Rev: BLO 9/15/11; SLJ 10/1/11) [921]

8169 Mullin, Rita Thievon. *Thomas Jefferson: Architect of Freedom* (7–10). Series: Sterling Biographies. 2007, Sterling paper $5.95 (978-1-4027-3397-0). Report writers will find a wealth of information on the president's prolific and remarkable life, as well as drawings and photographs to enhance the text. (Rev: BL 4/1/07; SLJ 5/07) [973.4]

8170 Severance, John B. *Thomas Jefferson: Architect of Democracy* (7–12). 1998, Clarion $18.00 (978-0-395-84513-4). A thoughtful, well-rounded biography that focuses on Jefferson's accomplishments and his beliefs, with many quotations from his writings. (Rev: BL 9/1/98; HBG 3/99; SLJ 12/98; VOYA 4/99) [921]

8171 Whitelaw, Nancy. *Thomas Jefferson: Philosopher and President* (7–10). 2001, Morgan Reynolds LB $23.95 (978-1-883846-81-7). This concise and thorough biography, which covers Jefferson's strengths and weaknesses, will be useful for report writers. (Rev: HBG 3/02; SLJ 3/02) [921]

JOHNSON, ANDREW

8172 Stevens, Rita. *Andrew Johnson: 17th President of the United States* (5–7). 1989, Garrett LB $21.27 (978-0-944483-16-9). Story of the man who became president on Lincoln's assassination. (Rev: BL 5/1/89) [973.810924]

KENNEDY, JOHN F.

8173 Anderson, Catherine Corley. *John F. Kennedy* (5–8). Series: Presidential Leaders. 2004, Lerner LB $29.27 (978-0-8225-0812-0). Quotations, photographs, and informative sidebars add to the engaging text about Kennedy's life and times. (Rev: SLJ 1/05) [921]

8174 Hodge, Marie. *John F. Kennedy: Voice of Hope* (5–8). Series: Sterling Biographies. 2007, Sterling $12.95 (978-1-4027-4749-6); paper $5.95 (978-1-4027-3232-4). This generally admiring, well-illustrated profile covers Kennedy's life from childhood. (Rev: SLJ 5/07)

8175 Kaplan, Howard S. *John F. Kennedy* (5–10). Series: DK Biography. 2004, DK paper $4.99 (978-0-7566-0340-3). A heavily illustrated, attractive biography of Kennedy that offers broad historical background. (Rev: BL 6/1–15/04) [921]

8176 Spencer, Lauren. *The Assassination of John F. Kennedy* (6–10). Series: Library of Political Assassinations. 2001, Rosen LB $27.95 (978-0-8239-3541-3). This is a highly readable account of the assassination, its political buildup, and the social fallout. (Rev: BL 3/15/02; SLJ 6/02) [921]

LINCOLN, ABRAHAM

8177 Barter, James. *Abraham Lincoln* (7–12). Series: The Importance Of. 2003, Gale LB $32.45 (978-1-56006-965-2). This biography of Lincoln uses ample quotations from important sources and tries to evaluate Lincoln's importance by present-day standards. (Rev: BL 3/15/03) [921]

8178 Freedman, Russell. *Lincoln: A Photobiography* (4–8). 1987, Houghton Mifflin $20.00 (978-0-89919-380-9); paper $9.95 (978-0-395-51848-9). A no-nonsense, unromanticized look at this beloved president. Newbery Medal 1988. (Rev: BL 12/15/87; SLJ 12/87) [921]

8179 Herbert, Janis. *Abraham Lincoln for Kids: His Life and Times with 21 Activities* (4–8). Illus. 2007, Chicago Review paper $14.95 (978-1-55652-656-5). With many quotations, illustrations, and sidebars, this volume covers Lincoln's life, beliefs, and contributions and includes activities (such as drawing a cartoon and learning Morse code). (Rev: SLJ 10/07) [921]

8180 Holzer, Harold. *Abraham Lincoln: The Writer* (6–10). 2000, Boyds Mills $16.95 (978-1-56397-772-5). Following a brief biography, this resource contains letters, excerpts from speeches, notes, debates, and inaugural addresses, each with explanatory introductions that connect the snippet to his life. (Rev: BL 5/1/00; HBG 9/00; SLJ 6/00) [921]

8181 Holzer, Harold. *The President Is Shot! The Assassination of Abraham Lincoln* (5–8). 2004, Boyds Mills $17.95 (978-1-56397-985-9). A riveting account of

Lincoln's assassination, with archival illustrations and historical context. (Rev: BL 3/1/04*; SLJ 2/04) [973.7]

8182 Sandburg, Carl. *Abe Lincoln Grows Up* (6–9). 1975, Harcourt paper $6.99 (978-0-15-602615-4). From the pen of one of America's great poets, this is an account of the boyhood of his great hero. [921]

8183 Sandler, Martin W. *Lincoln Through the Lens: How Photography Revealed and Shaped an Extraordinary Life* (7–9). 2008, Walker LB $20.89 (978-0-8027-9667-7). Full of fascinating images, this book presents the life of Lincoln and the story of his presidency, the first ever to be photographed. (Rev: BL 9/15/08*; LMC 1–2/09*; SLJ 10/1/08*) [921]

8184 Sloate, Susan. *Abraham Lincoln: The Freedom President* (5–8). 1989, Ballantine paper $15.00 (978-0-449-90375-9). An accessible account of the president who led his country through division back to unity. (Rev: BL 12/15/89) [921]

8185 Stone, Tanya Lee. *Abraham Lincoln* (5–10). Series: DK Biography. 2005, DK $14.99 (978-0-7566-0833-0); paper $4.99 (978-0-7566-0834-7). A heavily illustrated, attractive biography of Lincoln that offers broad historical background. (Rev: BL 6/1–15/04) [921]

8186 Sullivan, George. *Picturing Lincoln: Famous Photographs That Popularized the President* (5–8). 2000, Clarion $16.00 (978-0-395-91682-7). Using five images of Lincoln taken between 1846 and 1864, this book gives historical and biographical information on each and tells how they have been used for posters, button, ribbons, postage stamps, and currency. (Rev: BL 2/1/01; HB 3–4/01; HBG 10/01; SLJ 3/01) [921]

8187 Swanson, James L. *Bloody Times: The Funeral of Abraham Lincoln and the Manhunt for Jefferson Davis* (6–9). Illus. 2011, HarperCollins $16.99 (978-0-06-156089-7). Swanson offers a riveting account of Lincoln's death and funeral and the simultaneous manhunt for the Confederate president who is suspected of being involved in an assassination conspiracy. e (Rev: BL 3/15/11*; SLJ 4/11*; VOYA 6/11) [921]

8188 Waldman, Neil. *Voyages: Reminiscences of Young Abe Lincoln* (5–8). Illus. by author. 2009, Boyds Mills $16.95 (978-1-59078-471-6). Blending fiction and nonfiction, these anecdotes about the life of the young Lincoln include direct quotations in a contrasting color. (Rev: BL 3/15/09; SLJ 4/09) [921]

LINCOLN, ABRAHAM AND MARY TODD

8189 Fleming, Candace. *The Lincolns: A Scrapbook Look at Abraham and Mary* (7–12). 2008, Random House LB $28.99 (978-0-375-93618-0). With a pleasing mix of narrative, documents, paintings and etchings, and political cartoons, this attractive volume provides a detailed life of both Abraham and Mary. Boston Globe–Horn Book Award 2009; ALA Notable Books

2009. (Rev: BL 9/15/08; LMC 1–2/09; SLJ 10/1/08*) [921]

MADISON, DOLLEY

8190 Weatherly, Myra. *Dolley Madison: America's First Lady* (5–8). Series: Founders of the Republic. 2002, Morgan Reynolds LB $23.95 (978-1-883846-95-4). This portrait of Dolley Madison conveys her popularity and courage, with reproductions of period paintings, prints, and maps. (Rev: BL 11/1/02; HBG 3/03; SLJ 3/03) [973.5]

MADISON, JAMES

8191 Elish, Dan. *James Madison* (4–7). Series: Presidents and Their Times. 2007, Marshall Cavendish LB $22.95 (978-0-7614-2432-1). A clear and thorough profile of the president, describing his early years, presidential career, and later life, with discussion of important events that took place during his life. (Rev: LMC 5/08; SLJ 1/08)

MADISON, JAMES AND DOLLEY

8192 Ashby, Ruth. *James and Dolley Madison* (5–8). Series: Presidents and First Ladies. 2005, Gareth Stevens LB $31.00 (978-0-8368-5757-3). An accessible, balanced, and attractive discussion of the Madisons and the contributions each made to their joint lives. (Rev: BL 3/1/05; SLJ 8/05) [921]

MCKINLEY, WILLIAM

8193 Wilson, Antoine. *The Assassination of William McKinley* (6–9). Series: The Library of Political Assassinations. 2002, Rosen LB $27.95 (978-0-8239-3546-8). The life of this President is re-created with emphasis on details leading up to the crime and the characters involved. (Rev: BL 8/02) [921]

NIXON, RICHARD M.

8194 Aronson, Billy. *Richard M. Nixon* (5–8). Illus. Series: Presidents and Their Times. 2007, Marshall Cavendish LB $22.95 (978-0-7614-2428-4). This biography of the 37th president covers his childhood, his candidacy, and his accomplishments in office, as well as his downfall and impeachment. (Rev: BL 10/15/07; SLJ 1/08) [921]

8195 Randolph, Sallie. *Richard M. Nixon, President* (6–9). 1989, Walker LB $14.85 (978-0-8027-6849-0). A straightforward account using many original sources that doesn't skirt the controversial issues. (Rev: BL 1/15/90; SLJ 12/90; VOYA 2/90) [921]

OBAMA, BARACK

8196 Abramson, Jill. *Obama: The Historic Journey* (4–7). Illus. 2009, The New York Times $24.95 (978-0-670-01208-4). Striking photographs, informative text drawing on reports from the *New York Times*, and careful explanation of political terms combine to make this a useful and educational biography of the president. (Rev: SLJ 8/09; VOYA 6/09) [921]

8197 Brill, Marlene Targ. *Barack Obama: Working to Make a Difference* (5–8). Series: Gateway Biography. 2006, Lerner LB $23.93 (978-0-8225-3417-4). Obama, the U.S. senator from Illinois, is profiled with details of his family life, education, and entrance to politics. (Rev: BL 3/15/06; SLJ 8/06) [328.73]

8198 Burgan, Michael. *Barack Obama* (6–9). Series: Front-Page Lives. 2010, Heinemann-Raintree $38.93 (978-1-4329-3218-3). Using a headlines format that highlights events, Burgan covers Obama's life from childhood and includes a timeline, glossary, and other useful back matter. (Rev: LMC 3–4/10) [921]

8199 Davis, William Michael. *Barack Obama: The Politics of Hope* (6–9). Series: Shapers of America. 2007, OTTN $25.95 (978-1-59556-024-7); paper $16.99 (978-1-59556-032-2). Published before Obama was elected to the office of president in 2008, this biography looks at the former senator's early life, service, and writings, as well as his motivations and inspirations. (Rev: BL 2/1/08; SLJ 6/08) [921]

8200 Krensky, Stephen. *Barack Obama* (5–9). Illus. 2009, DK $14.99 (978-0-7566-5804-5); paper $5.99 (978-0-7566-5-805-2). With the usual DK visual format, this is an attractive portrait of Obama's life, placing his background and experience in historical context. (Rev: BL 4/1/10; SLJ 4/10) [921]

8201 Robinson, Tom. *Barack Obama: 44th U.S. President* (6–9). Illus. Series: Essential Lives. 2009, ABDO LB $22.95 (978-160453527-3). An engaging biography with plenty of additional resources and facts for report writers. (Rev: BLO 3/17/09) [921]

8202 Schuman, Michael A. *Barack Obama: "We Are One People"* (5–8). Series: African-American Biography Library. 2008, Enslow LB $23.95 (978-0-7660-2891-3). Opening with Obama's speech at the 2004 Democratic Convention, this biography goes on to cover his life chronologically from childhood through running for president. (Rev: BL 6/1–15/08) [328.730]

OBAMA, MICHELLE

8203 Brophy, David Bergen. *Michelle Obama: Meet the First Lady* (4–8). 2008, Collins $16.99 (978-0-06-177991-6); HarperCollins paper $6.99 (978-0-06-177990-9). A chronological look at Obama's life from childhood, incorporating many quotations but few photographs. (Rev: BL 3/1/09) [921]

8204 Colbert, David. *Michelle Obama: An American Story* (5–8). Illus. 2009, Houghton $16.00 (978-0-547-24941-4); paper $6.99 (978-0-547-24770-0). This profile looks mainly at Obama's ancestry and her childhood and early married life. (Rev: BL 3/1/09) [921]

PIERCE, FRANKLIN

8205 Brown, Fern G. *Franklin Pierce* (5–8). Series: Presidents of the United States. 1989, GEC LB $21.27 (978-0-944483-25-1). The story of Pierce, his political life and presidency, plus material on his personal life. (Rev: SLJ 9/89) [921]

REAGAN, RONALD

8206 Burgan, Michael. *Ronald Reagan: A Photographic Story of a Life* (5–8). Illus. Series: DK Biography. 2011, DK $14.99 (978-0-7566-7075-7); paper $5.99 (978-0-7566-7-074-0). A visual introduction to the life of the actor who became president. **e** (Rev: BL 6/1/11; SLJ 11/1/11) [921]

8207 Sutherland, James. *Ronald Reagan* (6–9). Series: Up Close. 2008, Viking $16.99 (978-0-670-06345-1). A thought-provoking character portrait as well an account of the president's life and career. (Rev: BL 6/1–15/08) [921]

8208 Young, Jeff C. *Great Communicator: The Story of Ronald Reagan* (6–10). Series: Twentieth-Century Leaders. 2003, Morgan Reynolds LB $23.95 (978-1-931798-10-5). Reagan's career is the main focus of this biography that includes many quotations and black-and-white photographs and deals objectively with the former president's strengths and weaknesses. (Rev: BL 6/1–15/03; HBG 10/03; SLJ 10/03; VOYA 12/03) [921]

ROOSEVELT, ELEANOR

8209 Fleming, Candace. *Our Eleanor: A Scrapbook Look at Eleanor Roosevelt's Remarkable Life* (6–9). 2005, Simon & Schuster $19.95 (978-0-689-86544-2). Archival photos, first-person accounts, direct quotes, and informative sidebars document Roosevelt's life and cover her character and questions about her sexuality. (Rev: BL 9/1/05; SLJ 11/05*; VOYA 10/05) [973.917]

8210 Freedman, Russell. *Eleanor Roosevelt: A Life of Discovery* (5–9). 1993, Clarion $17.95 (978-0-89919-862-0). This admiring photobiography captures Roosevelt's public role and personal sadness. (Rev: BL 7/93*; SLJ 8/93*; VOYA 2/94) [921]

8211 Hubbard-Brown, Janet. *Eleanor Roosevelt: First Lady* (6–10). Series: Women of Achievement. 2009, Chelsea House $30 (978-1-60413-076-8). This volume is a good source of basic information on former First Lady Eleanor Roosevelt and her influence on American culture. (Rev: SLJ 5/1/09) [921]

8212 Jones, Victoria Garrett. *Eleanor Roosevelt: A Courageous Spirit* (5–8). Series: Sterling Biographies. 2007, Sterling $12.95 (978-1-4027-4746-5); paper $5.95 (978-1-4027-3371-0). This well-illustrated profile covers Eleanor Roosevelt's life from childhood and discusses her contributions as First Lady, a position she transformed. (Rev: SLJ 5/07)

8213 Koestler-Grack, Rachel A. *The Story of Eleanor Roosevelt* (4–7). Series: Breakthrough Biographies. 2004, Chelsea House LB $23.00 (978-0-7910-7313-1). This brief biography covers Roosevelt's early years as well as her later contributions to her country and to the world. (Rev: BL 3/1/04) [973917]

8214 Lassieur, Allison. *Eleanor Roosevelt: Activist for Social Change* (5–8). Series: Great Life Stories. 2006, Watts LB $30.50 (978-0-531-13871-7). This biography of Eleanor Roosevelt focuses on the first lady's personal life and on her social activism while in the White House and later as an envoy to the United Nations. (Rev: SLJ 2/07) [921]

8215 Somervill, Barbara A. *Eleanor Roosevelt: First Lady of the World* (5–8). Series: Signature Lives: Modern America. 2005, Compass Point $34.60 (978-0-7565-0992-7). An appealing biography that traces the First Lady's life and focuses on her tireless efforts to make life better for America's disadvantaged minorities. (Rev: BL 10/15/05) [973.917]

8216 Westervelt, Virginia Veeder. *Here Comes Eleanor: A New Biography of Eleanor Roosevelt for Young People* (5–8). Series: Avisson Young Adult. 1999, Avisson paper $16.00 (978-1-888105-33-9). A clear account of the life of Eleanor Roosevelt that gives a fine assessment of her many contributions to humankind. (Rev: BL 2/15/99; SLJ 7/99; VOYA 10/99) [921]

ROOSEVELT, FRANKLIN D.

8217 Bardhan-Quallen, Sudipta. *Franklin Delano Roosevelt: A National Hero* (5–8). Series: Sterling Biographies. 2007, Sterling $12.95 (978-1-4027-4747-2); paper $5.95 (978-1-4027-3545-5). The author emphasizes the contrast between Roosevelt's privileged background and his concern about social injustice. (Rev: SLJ 5/07)

8218 Burgan, Michael. *Franklin D. Roosevelt* (4–8). Series: Profiles of the Presidents. 2002, Compass Point LB $26.60 (978-0-7565-0203-4). An absorbing introduction to Roosevelt's life and career, with details of his youth and education and the role that his illness played in shaping his character. (Rev: SLJ 6/02) [973.917092]

8219 Devaney, John. *Franklin Delano Roosevelt, President* (6–10). 1987, Walker $12.95 (978-0-8027-6713-4). A detailed account of Roosevelt's personality and career. (Rev: SLJ 1/88; VOYA 12/87) [921]

8220 Freedman, Russell. *Franklin Delano Roosevelt* (5–8). 1990, Houghton Mifflin $20.00 (978-0-89919-379-3). A carefully researched and well-illustrated account of the man and the times. (Rev: HB 3–4/90; SLJ 12/90*) [921]

8221 Haugen, Brenda. *Franklin Delano Roosevelt: The New Deal President* (4–8). Series: Signature Lives. 2006, Compass Point LB $34.60 (978-0-7565-1586-7). Slim but fact-filled, this is a useful biography for report writers, with excerpts from speeches and writings and full discussion of key events in Roosevelt's life. (Rev: SLJ 9/06) [921]

8222 Nardo, Don. *Franklin D. Roosevelt: U.S. President* (7–10). Series: Great Achievers: Lives of the Physically Challenged. 1995, Chelsea LB $14.95 (978-0-7910-2406-5). This biography stresses the physical challenges Roosevelt faced and the strong personality that allowed him to achieve great success. (Rev: SLJ 1/96) [921]

8223 Panchyk, Richard. *Franklin Delano Roosevelt for Kids: His Life and Times with 21 Activities* (6–9). 2007, Chicago Review paper $14.95 (978-1-55652-657-2). In addition to an informative biography that places FDR's life in historical context, this volume includes such activities as giving a "fireside chat," collecting stamps, and researching genealogy. (Rev: BL 11/15/07; SLJ 10/07) [921]

ROOSEVELT, FRANKLIN D. AND ELEANOR

8224 Ashby, Ruth. *Franklin and Eleanor Roosevelt* (5–8). Series: Presidents and First Ladies. 2005, Gareth Stevens LB $31.00 (978-0-8368-5758-0). An accessible, balanced, and attractive discussion of the Roosevelts and the contributions each made to their joint lives. (Rev: BL 3/1/05) [921]

ROOSEVELT, THEODORE

8225 Cooper, Michael L. *Theodore Roosevelt* (6–9). Illus. Series: Up Close. 2009, Viking $16.99 (978-067001134-6). A slim and accessible profile of the sickly child who grew to be a robust president. (Rev: BL 7/09; HB 9–10/09; SLJ 9/09) [921]

8226 Donnelly, Matt. *Theodore Roosevelt: Larger Than Life* (6–9). 2003, Linnet $27.50 (978-0-208-02510-4). Information about the presidency of Theodore Roosevelt is presented along with coverage of his childhood and early experiences in the West and as a public servant. (Rev: BL 1/1–15/03; HB 3–4/03; HBG 10/03; SLJ 3/03; VOYA 10/03) [973.91]

8227 Elish, Dan. *Theodore Roosevelt* (4–7). Series: Presidents and Their Times. 2007, Marshall Cavendish LB $22.95 (978-0-7614-2429-1). A clear and thorough profile of the president, describing his early years, presidential career, and later life, with discussion of important events that took place during his life. (Rev: SLJ 1/08)

8228 Kelley, Alison Turnbull. *Theodore Roosevelt* (5–7). Series: Great American Presidents. 2003, Chelsea House LB $30.00 (978-0-7910-7606-4). An illustrated profile of the 26th president, from his childhood through his public life and legacy. (Rev: SLJ 4/04) [921]

8229 Kraft, Betsy Harvey. *Theodore Roosevelt: Champion of the American Spirit* (5–9). 2003, Clarion $19.00 (978-0-618-14264-4). The determination that carried Roosevelt through a difficult childhood and drove his

successful career is emphasized in this engrossing biography of his life and survey of his diverse accomplishments. (Rev: BL 10/15/03; HB 11–12/03; HBG 4/04; SLJ 12/03*; VOYA 10/03) [973.9]

8230 Marrin, Albert. *The Great Adventure: Theodore Roosevelt and the Rise of Modern America* (8–11). 2007, Dutton $30.00 (978-0-525-47659-7). Marrin provides excellent, balanced information on Roosevelt's life and political career, giving good background on the social and political mores of the time and covering the president's achievements and peculiarities. (Rev: BL 9/1/07; SLJ 12/07) [973.91]

8231 Whitelaw, Nancy. *Theodore Roosevelt Takes Charge* (6–9). 1992, Albert Whitman LB $16.99 (978-0-8075-7849-0). A clear, credible biography of a larger-than-life American hero who was full of contradictions. (Rev: BL 6/1/92*; SLJ 7/92*) [921]

TAYLOR, ZACHARY

8232 Collins, David R. *Zachary Taylor: 12th President of the United States* (5–7). 1989, Garrett LB $21.27 (978-0-944483-17-6). Tells the life story of a military man elected president in 1848. (Rev: BL 5/1/89) [921]

TRUMAN, HARRY S

8233 Fleming, Thomas. *Harry S Truman, President* (6–12). 1993, Walker LB $15.85 (978-0-8027-8269-4). The author of this uncritical biography of the former president had access to family photographs and documents. (Rev: BL 1/1/94; SLJ 12/93; VOYA 2/94) [921]

VAN BUREN, MARTIN

8234 Doak, Robin. *Martin Van Buren* (4–7). 2003, Compass Point LB $26.60 (978-0-7565-0256-0). Van Buren's strengths and weakness receive equal weight in this balanced and readable biography that covers his life from a young age. (Rev: SLJ 11/03) [973.5]

8235 Ellis, Rafaela. *Martin Van Buren: 8th President of the United States* (5–7). 1989, Garrett LB $21.27 (978-0-944483-12-1). The story of a New York governor who became president. (Rev: BL 5/1/89) [921]

WASHINGTON, GEORGE

8236 Adler, David A. *George Washington: An Illustrated Biography* (5–7). 2004, Holiday House $24.95 (978-0-8234-1838-1). Adler presents a balanced and well-researched biography of Washington, giving details of his character as well as information on key events of his time. (Rev: BL 9/15/04; SLJ 12/04) [973.4]

8237 Earl, Sari. *George Washington: Revolutionary Leader and Founding Father* (6–9). Series: Military Heroes. 2010, ABDO LB $32.79 (978-1-60453-967-7). A well-written and richly illustrated account of the life of Washington, covering his childhood, education, military career, and role as a statesman. (Rev: LMC 10/10; SLJ 4/10) [921]

8238 Hilton, Suzanne. *The World of Young George Washington* (5–8). 1987, Walker $12.95 (978-0-8027-6657-1). Washington as a youth plus detailed information on life in pre-Revolutionary America. (Rev: SLJ 4/87) [921]

8239 Hort, Lenny. *George Washington* (5–10). Series: DK Biography. 2005, DK $14.99 (978-0-7566-0832-3); paper $4.99 (978-0-7566-0835-4). A heavily illustrated, attractive biography of the man born in Virginia. (Rev: BL 6/1–15/04) [921]

8240 McClafferty, Carla Killough. *The Many Faces of George Washington: Remaking a Presidential Icon* (7–9). Illus. 2011, Carolrhoda $20.95 (978-0-7613-5608-0). A fascinating look at Washington's life through the various images that have portrayed him. (Rev: BL 5/1/11; SLJ 5/11*) [921]

8241 McClung, Robert M. *Young George Washington and the French and Indian War: 1753-1758* (6–9). 2002, Linnet $22.50 (978-0-208-02509-8). A portrait of Washington as a military leader who matures from youthful impetuosity to a more thoughtful outlook on life. (Rev: BL 8/02; HBG 3/03; SLJ 10/02) [973.2]

8242 McNeese, Tim. *George Washington: America's Leader in War and Peace* (4–8). Series: Leaders of the American Revolution. 2005, Chelsea House LB $30.00 (978-0-7910-8619-3). An even-handed introduction to Washington's life and contributions, presented chronologically with occasional factboxes; suitable for report writers. (Rev: SLJ 1/06) [921]

8243 Roberts, Jeremy. *George Washington* (5–7). Series: Presidential Leaders. 2003, Lerner LB $29.27 (978-0-8225-0818-2). This engaging biography chronicles the life and achievements of America's first president and dispels some widely believed myths. (Rev: SLJ 2/04) [921]

8244 Rosenburg, John. *First in Peace: George Washington, the Constitution, and the Presidency* (7–10). 1998, Millbrook LB $25.90 (978-0-7613-0422-7). The last of a trilogy about Washington, this installment describes the emergence of the new nation and the role played by the first president. (Rev: HBG 3/99; SLJ 1/99) [921]

8245 Yoder, Carolyn P., ed. *George Washington: The Writer: A Treasury of Letters, Diaries, and Public Documents* (7–10). 2003, Boyds Mills $16.95 (978-1-56397-199-0). Washington's speeches, letters, will, and other documents — many excerpted — reveal much about his life and career. (Rev: BL 3/15/03; HBG 10/03; SLJ 2/03; VOYA 12/03) [921]

WILSON, WOODROW

8246 Lukes, Bonnie L. *Woodrow Wilson and the Progressive Era* (6–10). Series: World Leaders. 2005, Morgan Reynolds LB $26.95 (978-1-931798-79-2).

A chronological survey of Wilson's life from birth in 1856 through his death in 1924, with discussion of his achievements in light of the global events of the time. (Rev: SLJ 2/06) [921]

8247 Randolph, Sallie. *Woodrow Wilson, President* (5–9). Series: Presidential Biography. 1992, Walker LB $15.85 (978-0-8027-8144-4). Offers a concise overview of Wilson's tragic personal and political struggles, his achievements, and his place in history. (Rev: BL 12/15/91; SLJ 3/92) [921]

WILSON, WOODROW AND EDITH

8248 Ashby, Ruth. *Woodrow and Edith Wilson* (5–8). Series: Presidents and First Ladies. 2005, Gareth Stevens LB $31.00 (978-0-8368-5759-7). An accessible, balanced, and attractive discussion of the Wilsons and the contributions each made to their joint lives. (Rev: BL 3/1/05; SLJ 8/05) [921]

Other Government and Public Figures

ADAMS, SAMUEL

8249 Burgan, Michael. *Samuel Adams: Patriot and Statesman* (4–7). Series: Signature Lives (Revolutionary War Era). 2005, Compass Point LB $34.60 (978-0-7565-0823-4). Profiles the man who played a key role in the tax rebellion and Boston Tea Party. (Rev: BL 4/1/05) [921]

8250 Fradin, Dennis Brindell. *Samuel Adams: The Father of American Independence* (5–9). 1998, Houghton Mifflin $20.00 (978-0-395-82510-5). An attractive biography of the amazing Sam Adams, whom Jefferson called "the Man of the Revolution." (Rev: BCCB 7–8/98; BL 7/98; SLJ 7/98; VOYA 2/99) [921]

ALBRIGHT, MADELEINE

8251 Byman, Jeremy. *Madam Secretary: The Story of Madeleine Albright* (5–9). Series: Notable Americans. 1997, Morgan Reynolds LB $21.95 (978-1-883846-23-7). The emphasis in this biography is on Albright's public life, first as adviser to various political figures, then as ambassador to the United Nations, and finally as secretary of state. (Rev: BL 12/15/97; SLJ 4/98; VOYA 6/98) [921]

ALLEN, ETHAN

8252 Haugen, Brenda. *Ethan Allen: Green Mountain Rebel* (4–7). Series: Signature Lives (Revolutionary War Era). 2005, Compass Point LB $34.60 (978-0-7565-0824-1). Traces the life of the man who, along with Benedict Arnold, led the Green Mountain Boys in capturing Fort Ticonderoga from the British. (Rev: BL 4/1/05; SLJ 8/05) [921]

ARNOLD, BENEDICT

8253 Dell, Pamela. *Benedict Arnold: From Patriot to Traitor* (4–7). Series: Signature Lives (Revolutionary War Era). 2005, Compass Point LB $34.60 (978-0-7565-0825-8). A well-designed and informative profile of the man who betrayed his country. (Rev: BL 4/1/05) [921]

8254 Murphy, Jim. *The Real Benedict Arnold* (7–10). 2007, Clarion $20.00 (978-0-395-77609-4). An examination of Arnold's character reveals what may have led him to become a traitor. (Rev: BL 10/1/07; HB 1–2/08; LMC 2/08; SLJ 12/07) [921]

8255 Powell, Walter L. *Benedict Arnold: Revolutionary War Hero and Traitor* (5–8). Series: Library of American Lives and Times. 2004, Rosen LB $34.60 (978-0-8239-6627-1). The life of Benedict Arnold, the American patriot who switched his allegiance to the British cause. (Rev: SLJ 7/04) [921]

8256 Sonneborn, Liz. *Benedict Arnold: Hero and Traitor* (4–8). Series: Leaders of the American Revolution. 2005, Chelsea House LB $30.00 (978-0-7910-8617-9). An even-handed introduction to Arnold's life, presented chronologically with occasional factboxes; suitable for report writers. (Rev: SLJ 1/06) [921]

AUSTIN, STEPHEN F.

8257 Haley, James L. *Stephen F. Austin and the Founding of Texas* (5–8). Series: The Library of American Lives and Times. 2003, Rosen LB $34.60 (978-0-8239-5738-5). A concise biography of the pioneer who became one of the founders of Texas. (Rev: SLJ 5/03) [976.4]

BIDEN, JOE

8258 Young, Jeff C. *Joe Biden* (6–9). Illus. Series: Political Profiles. 2009, Morgan Reynolds LB $28.95 (978-159935131-5). The highs and lows of Vice President Biden's life — including his election to the Senate at the age of only 30 and the death of his wife and daughter in a car accident just months later — are described in this engaging profile. (Rev: BL 3/15/10*) [921]

BLOOMBERG, MICHAEL

8259 Shichtman, Sandra H. *Michael Bloomberg* (6–8). Illus. Series: Political Profiles. 2011, Morgan Reynolds LB $28.95 (978-159935135-3). This biography suitable both for research and browsing discusses Bloomberg's life from childhood and looks at his business and mayoral successes. (Rev: BL 4/1/11) [921]

BRADFORD, WILLIAM

8260 Doherty, Kieran. *William Bradford: Rock of Plymouth* (5–9). 1999, Twenty-First Century LB $24.90 (978-0-7613-1304-5). Using Bradford's own writings and other contemporary accounts as sources, this is an objective biography of the man who was the governor of the Plymouth Plantation. (Rev: BL 12/1/99; HBG 3/00; SLJ 1/00) [921]

BRADLEY, BILL

8261 Buckley, James, Jr. *Bill Bradley* (5–8). Series: Basketball Hall of Famers. 2002, Rosen LB $29.25 (978-0-8239-3479-9). An easy-to-read, detailed biography of the former athlete, with plenty of photographs. (Rev: BL 9/1/02) [921]

8262 Jaspersohn, William. *Senator: A Profile of Bill Bradley in the U.S. Senate* (6–10). 1992, Harcourt $19.95 (978-0-15-272880-9). An in-depth photoessay about Congress in general and Senator Bradley of New Jersey in particular, showing how his sports career led to the Senate. (Rev: BL 7/92; SLJ 10/92) [921]

CAMPBELL, BEN NIGHTHORSE

8263 Henry, Christopher. *Ben Nighthorse Campbell: Cheyenne Chief and U.S. Senator* (5–8). Series: North American Indians of Achievement. 1994, Chelsea $19.95 (978-0-7919-2046-6). The story of the Cheyenne leader who gained prominence not only among his own people but also in the U.S. Congress. (Rev: BL 6/1–15/93) [921]

CLINTON, HILLARY RODHAM

8264 Abrams, Dennis. *Hillary Rodham Clinton: Politician* (6–10). Series: Women of Achievement. 2009, Chelsea House $30 (978-1-60413-077-5). Covering her youth, her university career, her marriage and political life with Bill Clinton, and her election to the Senate and run for the White House, this volume provides a balanced account. (Rev: LMC 10/09; SLJ 5/1/09) [921]

8265 Burgan, Michael. *Hillary Rodham Clinton: First Lady and Senator* (6–9). Series: Modern America: Signature Lives. 2008, Compass Point LB $25.95 (978-0-7565-1588-1). Clinton's childhood, early political activity, and time as First Lady are covered (including a mention of the Lewinsky scandal); the book ends with her attempt to become a presidential candidate in 2008. An appealing design makes this a friendly choice for researchers. (Rev: BL 4/15/08) [921]

8266 Guernsey, JoAnn Bren. *Hillary Rodham Clinton* (5–8). 2005, Lerner LB $29.27 (978-0-8225-2372-7); paper $7.95 (978-0-8225-9613-4). Traces Clinton's life from childhood, and covers the trials of her husband's second term in office in some detail. (Rev: BL 6/1–15/05; SLJ 7/05) [921]

8267 Wells, Catherine. *Hillary Clinton* (5–8). Series: Political Profiles. 2007, Morgan Reynolds LB $27.95 (978-1-59935-047-9). Readers will learn of the former First Lady and presidential hopeful's life and achievements from this positive portrait. (Rev: BL 11/15/07) [921]

CRAZY HORSE (SIOUX CHIEF)

8268 Freedman, Russell. *The Life and Death of Crazy Horse* (6–12). 1996, Holiday $24.95 (978-0-8234-1219-8). This biography of Crazy Horse tells an uncompromising story of bloody wars, terrible grief, tragedy, and the Sioux's losing battle to preserve their independence and their land. (Rev: BL 6/1–15/96*; SLJ 6/96*; VOYA 10/96) [921]

8269 Haugen, Brenda. *Crazy Horse: Sioux Warrior* (5–8). Series: Signature Lives. 2005, Compass Point LB $34.60 (978-0-7565-0999-6). Crazy Horse's life and efforts to save his native lands and way of life are documented here. (Rev: SLJ 2/06) [921]

CROW, JOSEPH MEDICINE

8270 Medicine Crow, Joseph. *Counting Coup: Becoming a Crow Chief on the Reservation and Beyond* (5–8). Illus. 2006, National Geographic LB $23.90 (978-0-7922-8328-7); paper $6.95 (978-0-7922-7297-7). The memoirs of a Crow chief who was educated in mission and boarding schools and went on to fight in World War II. (Rev: BCCB 5/06; BL 4/15/06; LMC 11/06; SLJ 7/06)

CUSTER, GEORGE ARMSTRONG

8271 Anderson, Paul Christopher. *George Armstrong Custer: The Indian Wars and the Battle of the Little Big Horn* (4–8). Series: The Library of American Lives and Times. 2004, Rosen LB $34.60 (978-0-8239-6631-8). The importance of understanding history is emphasized in this balanced and well-illustrated look at Custer's life and stance at Little Big Horn. (Rev: SLJ 7/04) [920]

DAVIS, JEFFERSON

8272 Aretha, David. *Jefferson Davis* (5–8). Series: Leaders of the Civil War Era. 2009, Chelsea House $30 (978-1-60413-297-7). Enhanced by a mix of illustrations, period documents, photographs, and concise sidebars, this book provides a balanced look at the leader of the Confederacy. (Rev: LMC 10/09) [921]

DE ZAVALA, LORENZO

8273 Tracy, Kathleen. *Lorenzo de Zavala* (5–7). Series: Latinos in American History. 2002, Mitchell Lane LB $29.95 (978-1-58415-154-8). The biography of the 19th-century Mexican who became vice president of the Republic of Texas and was one of the signers of its constitution. (Rev: BL 2/15/03; HBG 10/03) [921]

FRANKLIN, BENJAMIN

8274 Adler, David A. *B. Franklin, Printer* (4–8). 2001, Holiday $19.95 (978-0-8234-1675-2). Quotations, anecdotes, and wonderful illustrations round out this ex-

cellent volume about the life and accomplishments of Benjamin Franklin. (Rev: BCCB 2/02; BL 1/1–15/02; HBG 10/02; SLJ 2/02*; VOYA 4/02) [973.3]

8275 Cousins, Margaret. *Ben Franklin of Old Philadelphia* (6–8). 1963, Random House paper $5.99 (978-0-394-84928-7). A well-rounded portrait of this major figure in American history. [921]

8276 Dash, Joan. *A Dangerous Engine: Benjamin Franklin, from Scientist to Diplomat* (6–10). Illus. by Dusan Petricic. 2006, Farrar $17.00 (978-0-374-30669-4). Franklin's keen interest in science and the development of new technology is emphasized in this lively biography illustrated with pen-and-ink drawings. (Rev: BCCB 1/06; BL 3/1/06; HB 3–4/06; SLJ 2/06) [921]

8277 Fleming, Candace. *Ben Franklin's Almanac: Being a True Account of the Gentleman's Life* (6–9). 2003, Simon & Schuster $19.95 (978-0-689-83549-0). Compiled in scrapbook style, this is an appealing biography full of anecdotes and graphic elements and covering Franklin's family life and scientific, literary, and political achievements. (Rev: BL 8/03; HB 9–10/03; SLJ 9/03*) [973.3]

8278 Gaustad, Edwin S. *Benjamin Franklin: Inventing America* (7–10). Series: Oxford Portraits. 2004, Oxford LB $32.95 (978-0-19-515732-1). The life and achievements of Benjamin Franklin are described using many quotations from Franklin's autobiography. (Rev: SLJ 2/05) [921]

8279 Lee, Tanja, ed. *Benjamin Franklin* (7–12). Series: People Who Made History. 2002, Gale LB $24.95 (978-0-7377-0898-1); paper $36.20 (978-0-7377-0899-8). After a general introduction to Franklin, his life, and his times, essays explore his talents, contributions, accomplishments, and his place in world history. (Rev: BL 4/1/02) [921]

8280 Miller, Brandon Marie. *Benjamin Franklin, American Genius: His Life and Ideas with 21 Activities* (7–12). Illus. 2009, Chicago Review paper $16.95 (978-1-55652-757-9). The life and times of Benjamin Franklin — inventor, publisher, scientist, founding father — are presented clearly and engagingly in this illustrated, large-format biography. (Rev: BL 12/15/09; SLJ 10/09) [921]

8281 Van Vleet, Carmella. *Amazing Ben Franklin Inventions You Can Build Yourself* (4–8). 2007, Nomad paper $14.95 (978-0-9771294-7-8). Activities — making invisible ink, wave bottles, kites, and so forth — and the accompanying narrative bring Franklin's inquisitive nature to light. (Rev: LMC 2/08; SLJ 11/07) [921]

GERONIMO

8282 Haugen, Brenda. *Geronimo: Apache Warrior* (5–8). Series: Signature Lives. 2005, Compass Point LB $34.60 (978-0-7565-1002-2). Geronimo's unsuccessful efforts to secure freedom for his people are documented in this attractive book. (Rev: SLJ 2/06) [921]

GIULIANI, RUDOLPH W.

8283 Sharp, Anna Layton. *Rudy Giuliani* (6–9). Series: Political Profiles. 2007, Morgan Reynolds LB $27.95 (978-1-59935-048-6). An evenhanded look at the former mayor of New York City, with details about his shortcomings as well as his successes. (Rev: BL 1/1–15/08; SLJ 1/08) [921]

GREENE, NATHANAEL

8284 Mierka, Gregg A. *Nathanael Greene: The General Who Saved the Revolution* (5–8). Illus. Series: Forgotten Heroes of the American Revolution. 2006, OTTN LB $23.95 (978-1-59556-012-4). Employing primary and previously unpublished sources, Mierka's lively text examines Greene's pivotal role as quartermaster general and southern commander in Washington's Revolutionary army. (Rev: BL 1/1–15/07) [973.3]

HALE, NATHAN

8285 Tracy, Kathleen. *The Life and Times of Nathan Hale* (5–8). Series: Profiles in American History. 2007, Mitchell Lane LB $19.95 (978-1-58415-447-1). This is an appealing life of Nathan Hale, from his childhood through his execution by the British. (Rev: SLJ 7/07) [921]

HAMILTON, ALEXANDER

8286 DeCarolis, Lisa. *Alexander Hamilton: Federalist and Founding Father* (4–7). Series: Library of American Lives and Times. 2003, Rosen LB $31.95 (978-0-8239-5735-4). The story of the military hero of the American Revolution who was the first secretary of the treasury and helped write the Federalist Papers. (Rev: BL 6/1–15/03; SLJ 4/03) [921]

8287 Haugen, Brenda. *Alexander Hamilton: Founding Father and Statesman* (4–7). Series: Signature Lives (Revolutionary War Era). 2005, Compass Point LB $34.60 (978-0-7565-0827-2). Traces the life of the man who became the first secretary of the treasury. (Rev: BL 4/1/05; SLJ 8/05) [921]

HANCOCK, JOHN

8288 Kjelle, Marylou Morano. *The Life and Times of John Hancock* (5–8). Illus. Series: Profiles in American History. 2007, Mitchell Lane LB $19.95 (978-1-58415-443-3). Little-known facts about John Hancock's life make this well-organized biography an interesting read. (Rev: SLJ 7/07) [921]

8289 Raatma, Lucia. *A Signer for Independence: John Hancock* (5–8). Series: We the People. 2009, Compass Point LB $26.65 (978-0-7565-4122-4). Accessible and well-illustrated, with a useful timeline, this book provides a balanced look at John Hancock. (Rev: LMC 10/09) [921]

HOOVER, J. EDGAR

8290 Cunningham, Kevin. *J. Edgar Hoover: Controversial FBI Director* (5–8). Series: Signature Lives. 2005, Compass Point LB $34.60 (978-0-7565-0997-2). This introduction to Hoover's career provides limited personal details, concentrating instead on his political ambitions and tendency to ignore ethical standards. (Rev: SLJ 1/06) [921]

HOUSTON, SAM

8291 Caravantes, Peggy. *An American in Texas: The Story of Sam Houston* (5–8). Series: Founders of the Republic. 2003, Morgan Reynolds LB $23.95 (978-1-931798-19-8). A portrait of the colorful general who became the first president of the Republic of Texas. (Rev: SLJ 5/04) [921]

8292 Woodward, Walter M. *Sam Houston: For Texas and the Union* (5–8). Series: The Library of American Lives and Times. 2003, Rosen LB $34.60 (978-0-8239-5739-2). A concise biography of the man credited with gaining Texas's independence. (Rev: SLJ 5/03) [976.4]

INOUYE, DANIEL K.

8293 Slavicek, Louise Chipley. *Daniel Inouye* (6–10). Series: Asian Americans of Achievement. 2007, Chelsea House LB $30.00 (978-0-7910-9271-2). A useful profile of the first Japanese American elected to the U.S. Congress, with information on his family's arrival in Hawaii and Inouye's experiences in World War II. (Rev: SLJ 8/07) [921]

JACKSON, STONEWALL

8294 Brager, Bruce L. *There He Stands: The Story of Stonewall Jackson* (8–10). Series: Civil War Leaders. 2005, Morgan Reynolds LB $26.95 (978-1-931798-44-0). The life and military career of Stonewall Jackson, one of the Civil War's most skilled tacticians; photographs, reproductions, and maps complement the well-written text. (Rev: SLJ 11/05) [921]

8295 Doak, Robin. *Confederate General: Stonewall Jackson* (4–8). Series: We the People. 2009, Compass Point LB $26.65 (978-0-7565-4110-1). Doak provides a balanced overview of the life and career of the enigmatic general, with a timeline and well-chosen illustrations. (Rev: LMC 10/09) [921]

8296 Koestler-Grack, Rachel A. *Stonewall Jackson* (5–8). Series: Leaders of the Civil War Era. 2009, Chelsea House $30 (978-1-60413-299-1). Enhanced by a mix of illustrations, period documents, photographs, and concise sidebars, this book provides an even-handed profile of the general responsible for some significant military victories. (Rev: LMC 10/09) [921]

JONES, JOHN PAUL

8297 Bradford, James C. *John Paul Jones and the American Navy* (4–7). Series: Library of American Lives and Times. 2001, Rosen $34.60 (978-0-8239-5726-2). This attractively designed volume combines the life story of the naval hero of the American Revolution with a history of the birth and growth of the American navy. (Rev: BL 10/15/01) [921]

8298 Brager, Bruce L. *John Paul Jones: America's Sailor* (7–10). 2006, Morgan Reynolds LB $26.95 (978-1-931798-84-6). The naval commander's life (flaws and attributes) and times are covered in well-organized text plus maps, timeline, sources, and a bibliography. (Rev: BL 7/06; SLJ 5/06) [921]

8299 Cooper, Michael L. *Hero of the High Seas: John Paul Jones* (4–7). 2006, National Geographic $21.95 (978-0-7922-5547-5). This biography focuses on the Scottish immigrant's naval heroics during the American Revolution and includes a detailed timeline and a useful listing of "Words and Expressions from the Days of Sailing Ships." (Rev: BL 6/1–15/06; SLJ 9/06)

JOSEPH (NEZ PERCE CHIEF)

8300 Biskup, Agnieszka. *Thunder Rolling Down the Mountain: The Story of Chief Joseph and the Nez Perce* (4–7). Illus. by Rusty Zimmerman. Series: American Graphic. 2011, Capstone LB $29.32 (978-142965472-2). A graphic novel account of the life of the Nez Perce leader and his efforts on behalf of his people. (Rev: BL 6/1/11) [921]

8301 Yates, Diana. *Chief Joseph: Thunder Rolling from the Mountains* (7–12). 1992, Ward Hill LB $14.95 (978-0-9623380-9-0); paper $10.95 (978-0-9623380-8-3). A sensitive distillation of the life and times of Chief Joseph of the Nez Perce. (Rev: BL 12/15/92; SLJ 12/92) [921]

KENNEDY, EDWARD M.

8302 McElroy, Lisa Tucker. *Ted Kennedy: A Remarkable Life in the Senate* (4–7). Series: Gateway Biographies. 2009, Lerner LB $25.26 (978-0-7613-4457-5). A useful resource for report writers, this biography has all the facts about the late senator's life and political service. (Rev: SLJ 8/09) [921]

8303 Sapet, Kerrily. *Ted Kennedy* (6–9). Illus. Series: Political Profiles. 2009, Morgan Reynolds LB $28.95 (978-159935089-9). This somewhat admiring portrait covers Kennedy's youth and family life, the many tragedies and difficulties he faced, and his achievements as a senator; includes a timeline and appealing photographs. (Rev: BL 6/1–15/09; LMC 8–9/09; SLJ 7/1/09) [921]

KENNEDY, ROBERT F.

8304 Aronson, Marc. *Robert F. Kennedy* (8–11). Series: Up Close. 2007, Viking $15.99 (978-0-670-06066-5). True to the series' title, this book looks at Robert F. Kennedy up close, examining his personal life more than his public achievements. (Rev: BCCB 6/07; BL 3/1/07; HB 3–4/07; SLJ 5/07) [921]

8305 Koestler-Grack, Rachel A. *The Assassination of Robert F. Kennedy* (5–8). Series: American Moments. 2005, ABDO LB $25.65 (978-1-59197-931-9). Kennedy's assassination is placed in historical context, with a brief biography and discussion of the aftermath of this tragedy. (Rev: SLJ 11/05) [921]

KERRY, JOHN

8306 Brager, Bruce L. *John Kerry: Senator from Massachusetts* (6–10). 2005, Morgan Reynolds LB $23.95 (978-1-931798-64-8). Kerry's life and military service are presented along with his career in politics and unsuccessful bid for the presidency in 2004. (Rev: SLJ 8/05) [921]

LEE, ROBERT E.

8307 Anderson, Paul Christopher. *Robert E. Lee: Legendary Commander of the Confederacy* (4–7). Series: Library of American Lives and Times. 2003, Rosen LB $34.60 (978-0-8239-5748-4). Extensive original sources are used to re-create the life of this Confederate general and the times in which he lived. (Rev: BL 6/1–15/03) [921]

8308 Rice, Earle, Jr. *Robert E. Lee: First Soldier of the Confederacy* (8–10). Series: Civil War Leaders. 2005, Morgan Reynolds LB $26.95 (978-1-931798-47-1). Lee's childhood, adult life, and military career are covered; photographs, reproductions, and maps complement the well-written text. (Rev: SLJ 11/05) [921]

8309 Robertson, James I. *Robert E. Lee: Virginian Soldier, American Citizen* (7–10). 2005, Simon & Schuster $21.95 (978-0-689-85731-7). A rich and even-handed portrait of Robert E. Lee, including a number of excerpts from such primary sources as letters and diaries. (Rev: BL 11/15/05; SLJ 1/06; VOYA 10/05) [973.7]

LEWIS, JOHN

8310 Sapet, Kerrily. *John Lewis* (6–9). Illus. Series: Political Profiles. 2009, Morgan Reynolds LB $28.95 (978-159935130-8). The highs and lows of the life of the sharecropper's son who became a Freedom Rider in 1961, was arrested many times, and has served as a representative from Georgia for more than 20 years are described in this engaging profile. (Rev: BL 3/15/10*) [921]

MACARTHUR, DOUGLAS

8311 Haugen, Brenda. *Douglas MacArthur: America's General* (5–8). Series: Signature Lives. 2005, Compass Point LB $34.60 (978-0-7565-0994-1). This introduction to MacArthur's career provides limited personal details but concentrates instead on his leadership abilities and military achievements. (Rev: SLJ 1/06) [921]

MARSHALL, THURGOOD

8312 Crowe, Chris. *Thurgood Marshall* (6–12). Series: Up Close. 2008, Viking $16.99 (978-0-670-06228-7). Using many quotations, Crowe covers Marshall's life, work as an NAACP lawyer, civil rights activism, and career on the Supreme Court. (Rev: BL 6/1–15/08) [921]

MCCAIN, JOHN

8313 Feinberg, Barbara S. *John McCain: Serving His Country* (4–7). Series: Gateway. 2000, Millbrook LB $23.90 (978-0-7613-1974-0). A biography of the senator that tells about his youth and later political career but concentrates on his stint in the navy and his imprisonment during the Vietnam War. (Rev: BL 3/1/01; HBG 10/01) [921]

8314 Kozar, Richard. *John McCain* (8–12). Series: Overcoming Adversity. 2002, Chelsea LB $30.00 (978-0-7910-6299-9). The story of the prominent U.S. politician and how he survived the ordeal of a POW camp in Vietnam. (Rev: BL 4/15/02; HBG 10/02) [921]

8315 Robinson, Tom. *John McCain: POW and Statesman* (6–9). Series: Military Heroes. 2010, ABDO LB $32.79 (978-1-60453-963-9). A well-written and richly illustrated account of the life of the politician who comes from a military family, was a prisoner of war in Vietnam, and went on to run for president. (Rev: LMC 10/10; SLJ 4/10) [921]

8316 Wells, Catherine. *John McCain* (5–8). Series: Political Profiles. 2008, Morgan Reynolds LB $27.95 (978-1-59935-046-2). Beginning with his early years and ending just before his nomination as a presidential candidate, this book examines McCain's life as well as his public and military service. (Rev: BL 5/15/08; SLJ 1/08) [921]

MCCARTHY, JOSEPH

8317 Giblin, James Cross. *The Rise and Fall of Senator Joe McCarthy* (8–12). 2010, Clarion $22 (978-0-618-61058-7). This well-researched biography of McCarthy includes photographs, quotes, and little-known facts to provide a complete portrait of the man and his life. Lexile 1400 (Rev: BL 10/15/09; HB 11–12/09; LMC 1–2/10; SLJ 12/09) [921]

NADER, RALPH

8318 Graham, Kevin. *Ralph Nader: Battling for Democracy* (6–12). 2000, Windom paper $9.95 (978-0-9700323-0-0). A readable biography of the man who has devoted his life to fighting for liberty and justice for all. (Rev: BL 12/1/00; SLJ 11/00) [921]

O'CONNOR, SANDRA DAY

8319 Herda, D. J. *Sandra Day O'Connor: Independent Thinker* (6–10). Series: Justices of the Supreme Court. 1995, Enslow LB $17.95 (978-0-89480-558-5). The story of the first female Supreme Court justice, including her personal life and some key decisions since becoming a Supreme Court member in 1981. (Rev: BL 2/15/96) [921]

PAINE, THOMAS

8320 Burgan, Michael. *Thomas Paine: Great Writer of the Revolution* (4–7). Series: Signature Lives (Revolutionary War Era). 2005, Compass Point LB $34.60 (978-0-7565-0830-2). A well designed profile of the revolutionary thinker. (Rev: BL 4/1/05) [921]

8321 Kaye, Harvey J. *Thomas Paine: Firebrand of the Revolution* (6–10). 2000, Oxford LB $32.95 (978-0-19-511627-4). A readable, well-illustrated biography on the career, accomplishments, and lasting importance of this Revolutionary War personality, with material on the social and political conditions of the period. (Rev: BL 3/1/00; HBG 9/00; SLJ 4/00) [921]

8322 McCartin, Brian. *Thomas Paine: Common Sense and Revolutionary Pamphleteering* (4–7). Series: Library of American Lives and Times. 2001, Rosen $34.60 (978-0-8239-5729-3). The story of the British-born colonialist who heard the cries for liberty around him and whose writings set the stage for the Declaration of Independence. (Rev: BL 10/15/01) [921]

PALIN, SARAH

8323 Petrillo, Lisa. *Sarah Palin* (6–9). Illus. Series: Political Profiles. 2009, Morgan Reynolds LB $28.95 (978-159935133-9). With lots of information on Palin's childhood, this is an interesting and balanced profile of the former governor of Alaska. (Rev: BL 3/15/10*; SLJ 7/10)

PATTON, GEORGE S.

8324 Gitlin, Martin. *George S. Patton: World War II General and Military Innovator* (7–10). Series: Military Heroes. 2010, ABDO LB $32.79 (978-1-60453-964-6). A well-written and richly illustrated account of the life of the World War II commander, covering his childhood, education, military career, and his strengths and weaknesses. (Rev: BL 4/1/10; LMC 10/10; SLJ 4/10) [921]

PELOSI, NANCY

8325 Marcovitz, Hal. *Nancy Pelosi* (6–9). Illus. Series: Women in Politics. 2009, Chelsea House LB $30.00 (978-160413075-1). For report writers, this is a useful biography of the first woman to hold the position of Speaker of the United States House of Representatives. (Rev: BLO 5/15/09; SLJ 5/1/09) [921]

8326 Shichtman, Sandra H. *Nancy Pelosi* (5–8). Series: Political Profiles. 2007, Morgan Reynolds LB $27.95 (978-1-59935-049-3). An admiring portrait of this important political figure, with photographs. (Rev: BL 11/15/07; SLJ 1/08) [328.7]

PENN, WILLIAM

8327 Somervill, Barbara A. *William Penn: Founder of Pennsylvania* (7–9). 2006, Compass Point LB $30.60 (978-0-7565-1598-0). A straightforward profile of the colonial figure, covering his childhood, his reasons for leaving England, and his commitment to religious freedom. (Rev: SLJ 7/06) [921]

PERKINS, FRANCES

8328 Keller, Emily. *Frances Perkins: First Woman Cabinet Member* (8–12). 2006, Morgan Reynolds LB $27.95 (978-1-931798-91-4). Perkins, a social reformer, served as Secretary of Labor under Franklin D. Roosevelt; this thorough biography documents her achievements and covers her personal life. (Rev: SLJ 5/07) [921]

POWELL, COLIN

8329 Blue, Rose, and Corinne J. Naden. *Colin Powell: Straight to the Top. Rev. ed.* (4–8). Series: Gateway Biographies. 1997, Millbrook LB $23.90 (978-0-7613-0256-8); paper $9.95 (978-0-7613-0242-1). A balanced biography of Colin Powell that focuses on his adult life and his stint as chairman of the Joint Chiefs of Staff. (Rev: BL 9/15/97; SLJ 1/98) [921]

8330 Brown, Warren. *Colin Powell* (7–10). Series: Black Americans of Achievement. 1992, Chelsea LB $30.00 (978-0-7910-1647-3). A nicely illustrated account of the African American general who distinguished himself during the Persian Gulf War. (Rev: BL 8/92) [921]

8331 Senna, Carl. *Colin Powell: A Man of War and Peace* (4–8). 1992, Walker LB $16.85 (978-0-8027-8181-9). The life of the general who became the first African American chairman of the Joint Chiefs of Staff. (Rev: BL 3/15/93) [921]

8332 Shichtman, Sandra H. *Colin Powell: "Have a Vision. Be Demanding."* (5–8). Series: African-American Biography Library. 2005, Enslow LB $31.93 (978-0-7660-2464-9). Sandra H. Shichtman profiles former Secretary of State Colin Powell in this title from the African-American Biography Library series. (Rev: SLJ 11/05) [921]

8333 Vander Hook, Sue. *Colin Powell: General and Statesman* (7–9). Series: Military Heroes. 2010, ABDO LB $32.79 (978-1-60453-965-3). A well-written and richly illustrated account of the life of the African American general who went on to become chairman of the joint chiefs of staff and then secretary of state. (Rev: LMC 10/10; SLJ 4/10) [921]

RANKIN, JEANNETTE

8334 Woelfle, Gretchen. *Jeannette Rankin: Political Pioneer* (6–9). 2007, Boyds Mills $18.95 (978-1-59078-437-2). Jeannette Rankin became Montana's representative in Congress in 1916 and went on to advocate for women's rights; this is an informative and interesting profile. (Rev: BL 2/15/07) [921]

RICE, CONDOLEEZZA

8335 Cunningham, Kevin. *Condoleezza Rice* (4–8). Series: Journey to Freedom. 2009, Child's World LB $28.50 (978-1-60253-120-8). Providing a compelling, inspiring overview of the achievements of Condoleezza Rice, this book includes a timeline. (Rev: BL 3/15/09; LMC 10/09)

8336 Ditchfield, Christin. *Condoleezza Rice: America's Leading Stateswoman. Rev. ed.* (5–8). Series: Great Life Stories. 2006, Watts LB $30.50 (978-0-531-13874-8). An updated version of the 2003 biography, adding information on Rice's role as secretary of state and the continuing events in Iraq. (Rev: SLJ 2/07) [921]

SCHWARZKOPF, NORMAN

8337 McNeese, Tim. *H. Norman Schwarzkopf* (6–9). Series: Great Military Leaders of the Twentieth Century. 2003, Chelsea House LB $30.00 (978-0-7910-7406-0). Schwarzkopf's personal life and military career are explored in this admiring biography of the Persian Gulf War general. (Rev: SLJ 2/04) [921]

SEQUOYAH (CHEROKEE CHIEF)

8338 Basel, Roberta. *Sequoyah: Inventor of Written Cherokee* (5–8). Series: Signature Lives. 2007, Compass Point LB $31.93 (978-0-7565-1887-5). A life of the Cherokee leader whose efforts to transcribe spoken Cherokee into a written language were not greatly appreciated; this volume will be useful for report writers. (Rev: SLJ 7/07) [921]

8339 Klausner, Janet. *Sequoyah's Gift: A Portrait of the Cherokee Leader* (4–7). 1993, HarperCollins LB $16.89 (978-0-06-021236-0). The life of this Cherokee leader is retold, with material on his invention of a written alphabet and his behavior during the Trail of Tears journey. (Rev: BL 9/1/93; HB 9–10/93; SLJ 11/93) [921]

SHARPTON, AL

8340 Mallin, Jay. *Al Sharpton: Community Activist* (6–12). Series: Great Life Stories. 2006, Watts LB $30.50 (978-0-531-13872-4). Mallin looks at Sharpton's personal and professional life from childhood to his bid for the presidency. (Rev: SLJ 3/07) [921]

SITTING BULL

8341 Schleichert, Elizabeth. *Sitting Bull: Sioux Leader* (6–9). Series: Native American Biographies. 1997, Enslow LB $26.60 (978-0-89490-868-2). A well-documented account of this important Sioux leader, including his reasons for participating in Buffalo Bill's Wild West Show. (Rev: BL 4/15/97; SLJ 6/97) [921]

SOTOMAYOR, SONIA

8342 Gitlin, Martin. *Sonia Sotomayor: Supreme Court Justice* (5–8). Series: Essential Lives. 2010, ABDO LB $32.79 (978-1-61613-518-8). After covering Sotomayor's youth and education, this volume looks at her legal career and explains some of the legal issues in sidebars. (Rev: SLJ 3/1/11) [921]

8343 McElroy, Lisa Tucker. *Sonia Sotomayor: First Hispanic U.S. Supreme Court Justice* (5–8). Illus. Series: Gateway Biographies. 2010, Lerner LB $26.60 (978-0-7613-5861-9). This concise, straightforward biography provides an introduction to the first Hispanic Supreme Court justice. Lexile 940L (Rev: BL 6/10; SLJ 5/10) [921]

VALLEJO, MARIANO GUADALUPE

8344 Tracy, Kathleen. *Mariano Guadalupe Vallejo* (5–7). Series: Latinos in American History. 2002, Mitchell Lane LB $29.95 (978-1-58415-152-4). The story of the 19th-century military man who supported the U.S. annexation of California and later served in the state's first Senate. (Rev: BL 2/15/03; HBG 10/03) [921]

WARD, NANCY

8345 Furbee, Mary R. *Wild Rose: Nancy Ward and the Cherokee Nation* (6–9). Series: Women of the Frontier. 2001, Morgan Reynolds LB $23.95 (978-1-883846-71-8). This is the absorbing story of the Cherokee woman who became a much-respected leader and advocate for peaceful coexistence with the white settlers. (Rev: HBG 3/02; SLJ 9/01; VOYA 6/02) [975]

WARREN, EARL

8346 Compston, Christine L. *Earl Warren: Justice for All* (7–10). Series: Oxford Portraits. 2002, Oxford $32.95 (978-0-19-513001-0). In addition to Warren's family life and career, this portrait presents his belief in the rule of law and his dealings with successive presidents. (Rev: BL 4/15/02; HBG 10/02; SLJ 6/02) [921]

WILLIAMS, ROGER

8347 Burgan, Michael. *Roger Williams: Founder of Rhode Island* (7–9). 2006, Compass Point LB $30.60 (978-0-7565-1596-6). A straightforward profile of the colonial figure, covering his childhood, his reasons for leaving England, and his belief in separation of church and state. (Rev: SLJ 7/06) [921]

WINTHROP, JOHN

8348 Burgan, Michael. *John Winthrop: Colonial Governor of Massachusetts* (7–9). 2006, Compass Point LB $30.60 (978-0-7565-1591-1). A straightforward profile of the governor, covering his childhood, his reasons for leaving England, and his Puritan beliefs. (Rev: SLJ 7/06) [921]

Miscellaneous Persons

BARTON, CLARA

8349 Hamen, Susan E. *Clara Barton: Civil War Hero and American Red Cross Founder* (7–9). Series: Military Heroes. 2010, ABDO LB $32.79 (978-1-60453-960-8). A well-written and richly illustrated account of the life of the woman best known for creating the American Red Cross. (Rev: LMC 10/10; SLJ 4/10) [921]

8350 Hamilton, Leni. *Clara Barton* (5–10). 1987, Chelsea LB $19.95 (978-1-55546-641-1). The story of the Civil War nurse and how she prepared for the founding of the American Red Cross. (Rev: BL 11/1/87) [921]

8351 Krensky, Stephen. *Clara Barton* (5–7). Illus. Series: DK Biography. 2011, DK $14.99 (978-0-7566-7279-9); paper $5.99 (978-0-7566-7-278-2). A life of the woman who nursed the wounded on the battlefields of the Civil War and founded the American Red Cross. **e** (Rev: BLO 7/11; SLJ 9/1/11) [921]

8352 Somervill, Barbara A. *Clara Barton: Founder of the American Red Cross* (5–8). Series: Signature Lives: Civil War Era. 2007, Compass Point LB $23.95 (978-0-7565-1888-2). Chronicles the life of Clara Barton and provides information on the time in which she worked. (Rev: BL 6/1–15/07) [921]

BECK, GLENN

8353 Novak, Amy. *Glenn Beck* (6–9). Illus. Series: People in the News. 2011, Gale/Lucent LB $33.45 (978-142050605-1). With well-chosen photographs and accessible text, this is an interesting profile of the conservative TV and radio personality. (Rev: BL 4/15/12) [921]

BECKWOURTH, JAMES

8354 Gregson, Susan R. *James Beckwourth: Mountaineer, Scout, and Pioneer* (5–8). Series: Signature Lives. 2005, Compass Point LB $34.60 (978-0-7565-1000-8). Beckwourth was one of the first African Americans to play a role in the exploration of the West. (Rev: SLJ 2/06) [921]

BILLY THE KID

8355 Cline, Don. *Alias Billy the Kid, the Man Behind the Legend* (8–12). 1986, Sunstone paper $12.95 (978-0-86534-080-0). The real story of Billy the Kid, clearing up many misconceptions. [921]

BLACK ELK

8356 Nelson, S. D. *Black Elk's Vision: A Lakota Story* (5–8). 2010, Abrams $19.95 (978-0-8109-8399-1). A look at the life of the Lakota medicine man who fought in the Battle of Little Bighorn and later traveled with Buffalo Bill's Wild West show before being injured at the massacre at Wounded Knee. ALA Notable Books 2011. (Rev: BL 3/15/10*; SLJ 4/10) [921]

BLY, NELLIE

8357 Bankston, John. *Nellie Bly: Journalist* (7–10). Illus. Series: Women of Achievement. 2012, Chelsea House LB $35 (978-160413908-2). A balanced and thorough life of the reporter known for her investigative flair and round-the-world journey. (Rev: BL 6/12) [921]

8358 Fredeen, Charles. *Nellie Bly: Daredevil Reporter* (5–9). Series: Lerner Biographies. 2000, Lerner LB $25.26 (978-0-8225-4956-7). The story of the daring reporter who traveled around the world in 72 days and was a champion of the women's suffrage movement. (Rev: HBG 10/00; SLJ 3/00) [921]

8359 Macy, Sue. *Bylines: A Photobiography of Nellie Bly* (5–7). 2009, National Geographic $19.95 (978-1-4263-0513-9); LB $28.90 (978-1-4263-0514-6). This well-researched photobiography of reporter Nellie Bly weaves together maps, period photographs, artifacts, and illuminating captions to paint a memorable portrait. (Rev: BL 8/09; SLJ 10/09) [921]

8360 Peck, Ira, and Nellie Bly. *Nellie Bly's Book: Around the World in 72 Days* (6–8). 1998, Twenty-First Century LB $27.90 (978-0-7613-0971-0). An abridged version of the account written by the famous muckraking journalist about her trip around the world in which she beat Phileas Fogg's record by six days. (Rev: BL 2/15/99; HBG 10/99; SLJ 4/99) [921]

BOONE, DANIEL

8361 Faragher, John Mack. *Daniel Boone: The Life and Legend of an American Pioneer* (7–12). 1992, Henry Holt paper $18.00 (978-0-8050-3007-5). A biography

of the complex frontier pioneer/politician/maverick. (Rev: BL 11/1/92*; SLJ 5/93*) [921]

BOOTH, EDWIN AND JOHN WILKES

8362 Giblin, James Cross. *Good Brother, Bad Brother: The Story of Edwin Booth and John Wilkes Booth* (5–8). 2005, Clarion $22.00 (978-0-618-09642-8). In a compelling and highly readable narrative, Giblin reveals the alcoholism and depression that plagued the theatrical Booth family, the disagreement between the two brothers over the Civil War, and the effects of the assassination on Edwin's later life. (Rev: BL 5/1/05*; SLJ 5/05) [921]

BOOTH, JOHN WILKES

8363 Swanson, James L. *Chasing Lincoln's Killer: The Search for John Wilkes Booth* (7–12). Illus. 2009, Scholastic $16.99 (978-043990354-7). This engaging account of the hunt for John Wilkes Booth in the 12 days following Lincoln's assassination is adapted from the author's 2006 adult book, "Manhunt," but lacks source notes and bibliography. ⌒ Lexile 980L (Rev: BL 12/1/08; LMC 5–6/09; SLJ 1/1/09*; VOYA 12/08) [921]

BRIDGMAN, LAURA

8364 Alexander, Sally Hobart, and Robert Alexander. *She Touched the World: Laura Bridgman, Deaf-Blind Pioneer* (5–8). 2008, Clarion $18.00 (978-0-618-85299-4). A little-known pioneer in the education of the deaf-blind, Bridgman (two generations older than Helen Keller) is an important figure, and this book ably introduces her to young readers. (Rev: BL 3/1/08; SLJ 3/08) [921]

BROADWICK, GEORGIA "TINY"

8365 Roberson, Elizabeth Whitley. *Tiny Broadwick: The First Lady of Parachuting* (4–8). 2001, Pelican paper $9.95 (978-1-56554-780-3). Less than 5 feet tall, "Tiny" Broadwick joined a hot-air balloon act as a teenager and became the first woman to jump with a parachute. (Rev: BL 7/01) [797.5]

CHIPETA

8366 Krudwig, Vickie Leigh. *Searching for Chipeta: The Story of a Ute and Her People* (4–7). 2004, Fulcrum paper $12.95 (978-1-55591-466-0). In the second half of the 19th century, Chipeta and her Ute husband worked tirelessly — but ultimately unsuccessfully — to forge an agreement with the U.S. government that would allow the tribe to remain in its traditional homeland. (Rev: BL 9/1/04) [921]

COLVIN, CLAUDETTE

8367 Hoose, Phillip. *Claudette Colvin: Twice Toward Justice* (7–12). Illus. 2009, Farrar $19.95 (978-

037431322-7). Readers will be inspired by the story of teenager Claudette Colvin, who was arrested when she refused to give up her seat on a bus months before Rosa Parks made her famous stand; with photographs and background information about the civil rights movement. Newbery Honor 2010; Sibert Honor 2010; ALA Notable Books 2010. Lexile 1000L (Rev: BL 2/1/09; LMC 8–9/09; SLJ 2/1/09*) [921]

CRANDALL, PRUDENCE

8368 Jurmain, Suzanne. *The Forbidden Schoolhouse: The True and Dramatic Story of Prudence Crandall and Her Students* (5–8). 2005, Houghton Mifflin $19.00 (978-0-618-47302-1). The inspiring story of Prudence Crandall, who in the 1830s risked ostracism — and worse — from the townspeople of Canterbury, Connecticut, when she opens her academy to young African American women. (Rev: BCCB 11/05; BL 10/1/05*; HB 11–12/05; HBG 4/06; LMC 8–9/05; SLJ 11/05) [370]

DAVE THE POTTER

8369 Cheng, Andrea. *Etched in Clay: The Life of Dave, Enslaved Potter and Poet* (5–8). Illus. by author. 2013, Lee & Low $17.95 (978-160060451-5). This portrait in verse focuses on the life of a slave who took many risks as he created his pots, jugs, and jars and not only signed them but added simple verses. Lexile 790L (Rev: BL 2/1/13; HB 1–2/13; LMC 8–9/13*; SLJ 2/13*) [738.092]

DAVIS, BENJAMIN O., JR.

8370 Earl, Sari. *Benjamin O. Davis, Jr.: Air Force General and Tuskegee Airmen Leader* (6–9). Series: Military Heroes. 2010, ABDO LB $32.79 (978-1-60453-961-5). A well-written and richly illustrated account of the life of the African American military leader and the challenges he faced. (Rev: BL 2/1/11*; LMC 10/10) [921]

EDMONDS, EMMA

8371 Reit, Seymour. *Behind Rebel Lines: The Incredible Story of Emma Edmonds, Civil War Spy* (5–8). 1988, Harcourt $12.95 (978-0-15-200416-3); paper $6.00 (978-0-15-200424-8). The remarkable Canadian-born spy who helped to defend the Union in the Civil War. (Rev: BL 3/1/88; SLJ 3/88) [973.785]

FRY, VARIAN

8372 McClafferty, Carla Killough. *In Defiance of Hitler: The Secret Mission of Varian Fry* (7–12). 2008, Farrar $19.95 (978-0-374-38204-9). This is the amazing story of a New York journalist who helped to save more than 2,000 — Jews and non-Jews — from Nazi-occupied France. (Rev: BL 6/1–15/08; SLJ 9/08) [921]

GRANDIN, TEMPLE

8373 Montgomery, Sy. *Temple Grandin: How the Girl Who Loved Cows Embraced Autism and Changed the World* (4–8). Illus. 2012, Houghton Mifflin $17.99 (978-054744315-7). A fascinating account of how Temple Grandin's autism has allowed her to design facilities that are substantially less threatening to livestock. ALA Notable Books 2013. (Rev: BL 3/15/12; SLJ 4/12*) [921]

HALE, SARAH JOSEPHA BUELL

8374 Dubois, Muriel L. *To My Countrywomen: The Life of Sarah Josepha Hale* (6–9). 2006, Apprentice Shop Books $15.00 (978-0-9723410-1-1). This is the story of Sarah Hale, who successfully used her skills as a writer after her husband died in 1822, leaving her to raise their small children on her own. (Rev: BL 9/15/06) [921]

HAYSLIP, LE LY

8375 Englar, Mary. *Le Ly Hayslip* (5–8). Series: Asian-American Biographies. 2005, Raintree LB $23.00 (978-1-4109-1055-4). An interesting profile of the Vietnamese-born woman who started the East Meets West Foundation. (Rev: SLJ 3/06) [921]

HEARST, WILLIAM RANDOLPH

8376 Whitelaw, Nancy. *William Randolph Hearst and the American Century* (6–12). 1999, Morgan Reynolds $21.95 (978-1-883846-46-6). Hearst's eccentricities and lively, thrusting approach to life are well portrayed in this vivid biography. (Rev: BL 10/1/99; HBG 4/00; VOYA 6/00) [921]

JACOBS, JANE

8377 Lang, Glenna, and Marjory Wunsch. *Genius of Common Sense: Jane Jacobs and the Story of the Death and Life of Great American Cities* (7–12). 2009, Godine $17.95 (978-1-56792-384-1). Jane Jacobs fought against urban renewal projects she feared would do more harm to New York City than good, changing the way Americans view cities and city life. (Rev: BL 9/1/09; HB 7–8/09; SLJ 4/1/09) [921]

JOHN HENRY (LEGENDARY CHARACTER)

8378 Nelson, Scott Reynolds, and Marc Aronson. *Ain't Nothing But a Man: My Quest to Find the Real John Henry* (6–9). 2008, National Geographic $18.95 (978-1-4263-0000-4). This first-person narrative combines biographical information about the real John Henry with details of the research Nelson conducted and how setbacks and disappointments sometimes led to breakthroughs. (Rev: BL 2/1/08; SLJ 12/07) [921]

KANDER, LIZZIE

8379 Kann, Bob. *A Recipe for Success: Lizzie Kander and Her Cookbook* (5–8). Illus. Series: Badger Biographies. 2006, Wisconsin Historical Soc. paper $12.95 (978-0-87020-373-2). Lizzie Kander was a social reformer in the mid-19th century, responsible among other things for a successful cookbook that benefited the Milwaukee Settlement House; in addition to a profile of Kander, this volume offers interesting information on the time she lived in. (Rev: BL 2/15/07) [921]

KELLER, HELEN

8380 Garrett, Leslie. *Helen Keller: Biography* (5–10). Series: DK Biography. 2004, DK paper $5.99 (978-0-7566-0339-7). Keller's struggles to conquer her physical disabilities and her worldwide recognition as a political activist and public speaker are covered in the usual rich DK format. (Rev: BL 6/1–15/04) [921]

8381 Keller, Helen. *The Story of My Life: The Restored Classic, Complete and Unabridged, Centennial Edition* (8–12). 2003, Norton $21.95 (978-0-393-05744-7). The autobiography of the blind and deaf women who overcame her handicaps through the help of a devoted teacher, Anne Sullivan. Originally published in 1903. [921]

8382 Lambert, Joseph. *Annie Sullivan and the Trials of Helen Keller* (6–12). Illus. by author. 2012, Disney/Hyperion $17.99 (978-142311336-2). Informative and poignant, this graphic-novel format biography uses words and images to show the relationship between Helen Keller and her teacher. YALSA Great Graphic Novels Top Ten 2013. (Rev: BL 3/15/12*; HB 5–6/12; LMC 10/12*; SLJ 5/1/12) [921]

8383 Lawlor, Laurie. *Helen Keller: Rebellious Spirit* (4–8). 2001, Holiday $22.95 (978-0-8234-1588-5). This account puts Keller's life in the context of her time and looks at the opinions and beliefs that made her a "rebellious spirit," with photographs, quotations, a bibliography, and the manual alphabet. (Rev: BL 9/1/01; HB 9–10/01; HBG 3/02; SLJ 9/01*; VOYA 2/02) [362.4]

KLECKLEY, ELIZABETH

8384 Rutberg, Becky. *Mary Lincoln's Dressmaker: Elizabeth Kleckley's Remarkable Rise from Slave to White House Confidante* (6–10). 1995, Walker $15.95 (978-0-8027-8224-3). The story of a slave, a fine seamstress, who was freed and became Mary Todd Lincoln's dressmaker. (Rev: BL 10/15/95; SLJ 12/95; VOYA 12/95) [921]

LOVE, NAT

8385 Bloom, Barbara Lee. *Nat Love* (6–9). Series: Legends of the Wild West. 2010, Chelsea House $30 (978-1-60413-599-2). The story of the black cowboy who was born a slave and went on to become a Pullman porter and write an interesting autobiography, with sidebars and illustrations that add historical context. (Rev: BL 6/10; LMC 8–9/10) [921]

8386 McKissack, Patricia C., and Fredrick McKissack, Jr. *Best Shot in the West: The Adventures of Nat Love* (6–9). Illus. by Randy DuBurke. 2012, Chronicle $16.99 (978-081185749-9). Using a graphic-novel format, the McKissacks tell the story of Nat Love, crack shot of the Wild West born into slavery in 1854. Lexile GN650L (Rev: BL 3/15/12; HB 3–4/12; LMC 8–9/12; SLJ 5/1/12*; VOYA 4/12) [921]

LOW, JULIETTE GORDON

8387 Wadsworth, Ginger. *First Girl Scout: The Life of Juliette Gordon Low* (4–7). Illus. 2011, Clarion $17.99 (978-0-547-24394-8). An appealing account of the life of the woman known as Daisy who came from a privileged background, was partially deaf, and founded the Girl Scout movement in the United States. **e** (Rev: BL 12/1/11; HB 11–12/11; SLJ 10/1/11) [921]

NEWTON, JOHN

8388 Granfield, Linda. *Amazing Grace: The Story of the Hymn* (4–8). 1997, Tundra $15.95 (978-0-88776-389-2). The life story of John Newton, a sea captain in the slave trade who later rejected slavery, became a minister, and wrote several hymns, including "Amazing Grace." (Rev: SLJ 8/97) [921]

NORTHUP, SOLOMON

8389 Fradin, Judith Bloom, and Dennis Brindell Fradin. *Stolen into Slavery: The True Story of Solomon Northup, Free Black Man* (5–8). Illus. 2012, National Geographic $18.95 (978-142630937-3); LB $27.90 (978-142630938-0). Drawing on his memoir, this dramatic story tells of free black man Northup's ordeal after he was kidnapped and sold into slavery in 1841. **e** (Rev: BL 2/1/12; SLJ 4/12) [921]

POKIAK-FENTON, MARGARET

8390 Jordan-Fenton, Christy, and Margaret Pokiak-Fenton. *Fatty Legs* (4–8). Illus. by Liz Amini-Holmes. 2010, Annick $21.95 (978-1-55451-247-8); paper $12.95 (978-1-55451-246-1). This autobiography tells the moving story of a young Inuvialuit girl whose desire to learn to read led her to spend two years in a church-run school that tried to erase the students' identities; set in the 1940s. (Rev: SLJ 12/1/10) [921]

PRINTZ, MICHAEL

8391 Bankston, John. *Michael L. Printz and the Story of the Michael L. Printz Award* (4–8). Series: Great Achievement Awards. 2003, Mitchell Lane LB $19.95 (978-1-58415-182-1). Printz's career as a high school librarian is highlighted in this account of his establishment of the well-known award for YA literature, which includes a list of prize winners. (Rev: BL 10/15/03; SLJ 10/03) [020]

510

REVERE, PAUL

8392 Giblin, James Cross. *The Many Rides of Paul Revere* (4–7). Illus. 2007, Scholastic $17.99 (978-0-439-57290-3). This well-illustrated, large-format book provides lots of often overlooked information on Paul Revere, covering his childhood, training, career, and role in the American Revolution. (Rev: BL 9/1/07; SLJ 11/07)

ROGERS, ROBERT

8393 Quasha, Jennifer. *Robert Rogers: Rogers' Rangers and the French and Indian War* (4–7). Series: Library of American Lives and Times. 2001, Rosen $34.60 (978-0-8239-5731-6). A beautifully illustrated biography of Major Robert Rogers, who recruited companies of soldiers known as Rogers' Rangers to fight for the British in the French and Indian War. (Rev: BL 10/15/01) [921]

ROSS, BETSY

8394 Harkins, Susan Sales, and William H. Harkins. *The Life and Times of Betsy Ross* (5–8). 2007, Mitchell Lane LB $19.95 (978-1-58415-446-4). This profile provides a balanced account of what is known about the life of Betsy Ross and her role, if any, in creating the American flag. (Rev: SLJ 7/07) [921]

8395 Randolph, Ryan P. *Betsy Ross: The American Flag and Life in a Young America* (4–7). Series: Library of American Lives and Times. 2001, Rosen $34.60 (978-0-8239-5730-9). This contemporary of George Washington was supposedly the seamstress of the American flag. (Rev: BL 1/1–15/02) [921]

STANDISH, MYLES

8396 Harness, Cheryl. *The Adventurous Life of Myles Standish and the Amazing-but-True Survival Story of Plymouth Colony* (6–9). Series: Cheryl Harness Histories. 2006, National Geographic $16.95 (978-0-7922-5918-3). A reader-friendly, well-illustrated account of how the Pilgrims (just barely) survived in the New World with Standish's guidance. (Rev: BL 12/15/06; SLJ 1/07) [921]

STEWART, BRIDGETT

8397 Stewart, Bridgett, and Franklin White. *No Matter What* (7–12). 2002, Blue/Black $12.99 (978-0-9652827-1-0). In diary form, Stewart relates the hardships of growing up poor in a shack in Georgia and the uphill battle she faced in her effort to get a full education. (Rev: BL 7/02) [921]

STUYVESANT, PETER

8398 Krizner, L. J., and Lisa Sita. *Peter Stuyvesant: New Amsterdam, and the Origins of New York* (4–7). Series: Library of American Lives and Times. 2001, Rosen LB $34.60 (978-0-8239-5732-3). The story of New

Amsterdam's best-known leader and how the Dutch presence in America influenced our culture for years to come. (Rev: BL 10/15/01; SLJ 7/01*) [921]

SULLIVAN, ANNIE

8399 Delano, Marfé Ferguson. *Helen's Eyes: A Photobiography of Annie Sullivan, Helen Keller's Teacher* (4–7). 2008, National Geographic $17.95 (978-1-4263-0209-1). Full of photographs, this attractive, oversize book tells the story of Sullivan's often-sad life. (Rev: BL 6/1–15/08; SLJ 9/08) [921]

TILL, EMMETT

8400 Wright, Simeon, and Herb Boyd. *Simeon's Story: An Eyewitness Account of the Kidnapping of Emmett Till* (6–10). 2010, Chicago Review $19.95 (978-1-55652-783-8). Author Wright was just 12 years old when his cousin Till came from the North to visit relatives in Mississippi, and he gives real insight into the murder of the 14-year-old African American and the events that followed. (Rev: BL 2/1/10; SLJ 2/10; VOYA 12/09) [921]

TILLAGE, LEON

8401 Tillage, Leon W. *Leon's Story* (4–9). 1997, Farrar $15.00 (978-0-374-34379-8). An autobiographical account of growing up African American and poor in the segregated South and of participating in the civil rights movement. (Rev: BL 10/1/97*; HB 11–12/97; HBG 3/98; SLJ 12/97) [975.6]

VAN LEW, ELIZABETH

8402 Vander Hook, Sue. *Civil War Spy: Elizabeth Van Lew* (5–8). Series: We the People. 2009, Compass Point LB $26.65 (978-0-7565-4104-0). Accessible and well-illustrated, with a useful timeline, this book provides a balanced look at the canny female spy who provided the Union with key information during the Civil War. (Rev: LMC 10/09) [921]

WALKER, MARY EDWARDS

8403 Goldsmith, Bonnie Z. *Dr. Mary Edwards Walker: Civil War Surgeon and Medal of Honor Recipient* (7–9). Series: Military Heroes. 2010, ABDO LB $32.79 (978-1-60453-966-0). A well-written and richly illustrated account of the life of the woman who played many roles, covering her childhood, education, marriage, service in World War II, and Medal of Honor. (Rev: LMC 10/10; SLJ 4/10) [921]

WEBER, EDNAH NEW RIDER

8404 Weber, EdNah New Rider. *Rattlesnake Mesa: Stories from a Native American Childhood* (4–8). 2004, Lee & Low $18.95 (978-1-58430-231-5). In this poignant memoir, Weber tells of her life as a student at a government-run boarding school for Native Americans during the 1920s. (Rev: BL 12/15/04; SLJ 12/04) [921]

WEBSTER, NOAH

8405 Shea, Pegi Deitz. *Noah Webster: Weaver of Words* (4–7). Illus. by Monica Vachula. 2009, Boyds Mills $18.95 (978-1-59078-441-9). This is a large-format, illustrated biography of Webster (1758–1843), who was a man of many interests but is best known for his dictionary of the American language. Lexile 1000L (Rev: BL 11/15/09; LMC 5–6/10; SLJ 11/09) [921]

WILSON, BILL

8406 White, Tom. *Bill W., a Different Kind of Hero* (4–7). 2003, Boyds Mills $16.95 (978-1-59078-067-1). The founder of Alcoholics Anonymous is the subject of this biography that describes his long battle with addiction. (Rev: BL 4/15/03; HBG 10/03; SLJ 2/03) [362.292]

WINNEMUCCA, SARAH

8407 Ray, Deborah Kogan. *Paiute Princess: The Story of Sarah Winnemucca* (4–7). Illus. by author. 2012, Farrar $17.99 (978-037439897-2). Ray tells the story of the Native American woman born in 1844, whose talent with languages allowed her to bridge two worlds and defend her people in the face of oppression. ⌒ e Lexile 1010L (Rev: BL 6/12; HB 5–6/12; LMC 10/12*; SLJ 7/12*) [921]

YOUNG, BRIGHAM

8408 Sanford, William R., and Carl R. Green. *Brigham Young: Courageous Mormon Leader* (5–8). Illus. Series: Courageous Heroes of the American West. 2012, Enslow LB $21.26 (978-076604004-5). An interesting profile of the religious leader and his challenge-filled westward trek. (Rev: BL 10/1/12; LMC 5–6/13) [921]

Science, Medicine, Industry, and Business Figures

Collective

8409 Aaseng, Nathan. *Business Builders in Broadcasting* (7–10). Series: Business Builders. 2005, Oliver LB $24.95 (978-1-881508-83-0). From Morse and Marconi to Sarnoff and Rupert Murdoch, this is a useful overview of key figures in broadcasting. (Rev: SLJ 3/06) [920]

8410 Aaseng, Nathan. *Business Builders in Computers* (5–8). Series: Business Builders. 2000, Oliver LB $22.95 (978-1-881508-57-1). Bill Gates, Steve Jobs of Apple, and Steve Case of AOL are among the individuals profiled in this interesting volume on the growth of the computer industry. (Rev: BL 2/1/01; HBG 10/01; SLJ 5/01) [338.4]

8411 Aaseng, Nathan. *Business Builders in Fast Food* (5–8). Series: Business Builders. 2001, Oliver $22.95 (978-1-881508-58-8). An interesting look at the creators of fast food empires such as McDonald's and Wendy's. (Rev: BL 9/15/01; HBG 10/01; SLJ 9/01) [381]

8412 Aaseng, Nathan. *Business Builders in Oil* (5–8). Series: Business Builders. 2000, Oliver LB $22.95 (978-1-881508-56-4). This lively introduction to the oil industry provides profiles of key individuals such as John D. Rockefeller, Andrew Mellon, and J. Paul Getty. (Rev: BL 2/1/01; HBG 10/01; SLJ 5/01) [338.2]

8413 Aaseng, Nathan. *Construction: Building the Impossible* (5–9). 2000, Oliver LB $21.95 (978-1-881508-59-5). This book profiles eight famous builders — from Imhotep, who built the first stone pyramids in Egypt, to Frank Crowe, the visionary behind the Hoover Dam. (Rev: BL 5/1/00; HBG 10/00; SLJ 10/00) [920]

8414 Armstrong, Mabel. *Women Astronomers: Reaching for the Stars* (7–10). Series: Discovering Women in Science. 2008, Stone Pine paper $16.95 (978-0-9728929-

5-7). Readers may be surprised to learn that women have been studying the skies since 2350 b.c. and that many of them made important discoveries; this volume has a browser-friendly format. (Rev: BL 4/1/08; SLJ 1/08) [508.2]

8415 Balchin, Jon. *Science: 100 Scientists Who Changed the World* (6–12). 2003, Enchanted Lion $18.95 (978-1-59270-017-2). Two-page chapters introduce 100 scientists and their accomplishments, grouped by century. (Rev: SLJ 1/04) [920]

8416 Bankston, John. *Francis Crick and James Watson: Pioneers in DNA Research* (5–7). Series: Unlocking the Secrets of Science. 2002, Mitchell Lane LB $17.95 (978-1-58415-122-7). An accessible account of the discovery of the structure of DNA and the lives of the two scientists involved. (Rev: HBG 10/03; SLJ 1/03) [576.5]

8417 Bradley, Michael J. *The Birth of Mathematics: Ancient Times to 1300* (6–9). Series: Pioneers in Mathematics. 2006, Ferguson $29.95 (978-0-8160-5423-7). Covers the contributions and discoveries of 10 important early mathematicians (such as Archimedes, Euclid, Hypatia of Alexandria, and Fibonacci). (Rev: BL 10/15/06; SLJ 5/07) [510.9]

8418 Bussing-Burks, Marie. *Influential Economists* (7–12). 2003, Oliver $19.95 (978-1-881508-72-4). The historical perspective of this book provides insights into economic theories and introduces some of the key people — including John Maynard Keynes and Milton Friedman — who have shaped the world's economy. (Rev: BL 3/1/03; HBG 10/03; SLJ 12/03) [920]

8419 Byrnes, Patricia. *Environmental Pioneers* (6–10). 1998, Oliver LB $19.95 (978-1-881508-45-8). This collective biography of early environmentalists includes profiles of John Muir, David Brower, Rachel Carson, Jay Darling, Rosalie Edge, Aldo Leopold, and Gaylord Nelson. (Rev: BL 9/15/98; SLJ 11/98) [920]

8420 Cooney, Miriam P. *Celebrating Women in Mathematics and Science* (6–10). 1996, National Council of Teachers of Math paper $26.95 (978-0-87353-425-3). Covering ancient times to the present, this collective biography highlights the struggles and triumphs of women in the fields of mathematics and sciences. (Rev: SLJ 10/96) [920]

8421 Cox, Clinton. *African American Healers* (4–7). Series: Black Stars. 1999, Wiley $24.95 (978-0-471-24650-3). Using entries of two to three pages each, this work profiles more than 20 African Americans who have achieved prominence in medicine and related areas. (Rev: BL 2/15/00; HBG 10/00; SLJ 2/00) [910]

8422 Cullen, Katherine. *Science, Technology, and Society: The People Behind the Science* (8–11). Series: Pioneers in Science. 2006, Chelsea House $29.95 (978-0-8160-5468-8). Pioneers whose biographies appear in this volume include Marie Curie, Louis Pasteur, Guglielmo Marconi, Rachel Carson, and J. Robert Oppenheimer. Also use *Earth Science: The People Behind the Science* and *Marine Science: The People Behind the Science* (both 2006). (Rev: BL 4/1/06) [509]

8423 De Angelis, Gina, and David J. Bianco. *Computers: Processing the Data* (7–10). Series: Innovators. 2005, Oliver LB $24.95 (978-1-881508-87-8). Profiles of computer pioneers including Charles Babbage, Steve Wozniak, and Tim Berners-Lee are accompanied by explanations of the technology involved. (Rev: BL 12/1/05; SLJ 1/06) [004]

8424 Di Domenico, Kelly. *Super Women in Science* (6–8). 2002, Second Story paper $10.95 (978-1-896764-66-5). Ten women are featured for their contributions to the scientific community, among them environmentalist Rachel Carson, physicist Chien-Shiung Wu, researcher Rosalind Franklin, and astronaut Mae Jemison. (Rev: BL 3/1/03) [509]

8425 Evans, Harold. *They Made America: From the Steam Engine to the Search Engine: Two Centuries of Innovators* (8–12). 2004, Little, Brown $40.00 (978-0-316-27766-2). For both browsing and research, this is an interesting and information-packed celebration of American inventiveness, focusing as much on the entrepreneurs as on the products. (Rev: BL 10/1/04) [609.2]

8426 Evernden, Margery. *The Experimenters: Twelve Great Chemists* (6–8). 2001, Avisson paper $19.95 (978-1-888105-49-0). The lives and research of 12 chemists are introduced in this accessible volume that is suitable for report writers. (Rev: BL 1/1–15/01) [540]

8427 Fortey, Jacqueline. *Great Scientists* (5–8). Illus. Series: Eyewitness. 2007, DK $15.99 (978-0-7566-2974-8). From Aristotle to Stephen Hawking, this volume offers brief introductions to 30 great scientists, discussing their accomplishments and providing personal information, a timeline, and a few photographs with captions adding historical details. (Rev: BL 9/1/07)

8428 Hall, Derek, ed. *Philosophy, Invention, and Engineering* (8–11). Illus. Series: Facts at Your Fingertips: Great Scientists. 2009, Brown Bear LB $24.95 (978-193383448-1). Aristotle, Thomas Edison, Alan Turing, and Jonas Salk are among the scientists profiled in this attractive and informative volume. (Rev: BL 10/1/09*; LMC 5–6/10) [920]

8429 Hansen, Ole Steen. *The Wright Brothers and Other Pioneers of Flight* (4–7). Series: The Story of Flight. 2003, Crabtree $25.27 (978-0-7787-1200-8). In text and pictures, this book introduces the pioneers of flight, with a concentration on the Wright brothers. (Rev: BL 10/15/03) [921]

8430 Harris, Laurie Lanzen, ed. *Biography Today: Profiles of People of Interest to Young Readers* (4–7). Series: Scientists and Inventors. 1996, Omnigraphics LB $39.00 (978-0-7808-0068-7). Profiles of 14 important contemporaries including Carl Sagan and Jane Goodall are accompanied by those of some lesser-known figures, such as geneticist and AIDS fighter Mathilde Krim. (Rev: SLJ 2/97) [920]

8431 Haskins, Jim. *Outward Dreams: Black Inventors and Their Inventions* (7–12). 1991, Walker LB $14.85 (978-0-8027-6994-7). Examines the lives and inventions of African American men and women did not receive recognition for their contributions until after the Civil War. (Rev: BL 5/15/91) [920]

8432 Henderson, Harry. *Larry Page and Sergey Brin: Information at Your Fingertips* (7–10). Illus. Series: Trailblazers in Science and Technology. 2012, Chelsea House LB $35 (978-160413676-0). Combining biography and science, this informative volume explores the lives and contributions of the Google founders. (Rev: BL 12/15/12) [920]

8433 Hudson, Wade. *Book of Black Heroes: Scientists, Healers and Inventors* (5–8). 2002, Just Us Bks $9.95 (978-0-940975-97-2). One historic or present-day African American figure is presented on each page of this collective biography of doctors, engineers, and inventors. (Rev: BL 2/15/03) [925]

8434 Kent, Jacqueline C. *Business Builders in Cosmetics* (6–9). Series: Business Builders. 2004, Oliver LB $22.95 (978-1-881508-82-3). Entrepreneurs including Elizabeth Arden, Max Factor, and Anita Roddick are profiled here, with a history of cosmetics dating back to Queen Nefertiti and sidebars on companies such as Clinique and Gillette. (Rev: SLJ 9/04) [920]

8435 Kent, Jacqueline C. *Business Builders in Fashion* (6–9). Series: Business Builders. 2003, Oliver LB $22.95 (978-1-881508-80-9). Chanel, Dior, Worth, Mary Quant, and Ralph Lauren are among the designers introduced. (Rev: BL 5/1/03; HBG 10/03; SLJ 6/03) [746.9]

8436 Kimmel, Elizabeth Cody. *Dinosaur Bone War: Cope and Marsh's Fossil Feud* (4–7). Illus. 2006, Random $11.99 (978-0-375-91349-5); paper $5.99 (978-0-375-81349-8). The story of American fossil hunters Edward Cope and Othniel Charles Marsh and the bitter rivalry that led to many dinosaur fossil discoveries and spurred the development of paleontology as a science. (Rev: BL 12/1/06)

8437 Kirsh, Shannon, and Florence Kirsh. *Fabulous Female Physicians* (4–8). 2002, Second Story paper $7.95 (978-1-896764-43-6). Using short chapters and black-and-white photographs, this account profiles 10 mostly unknown female doctors and their accomplishments. (Rev: BL 6/1–15/02; VOYA 8/02) [921]

8438 Lomask, Milton. *Great Lives: Invention and Technology* (5–8). Series: Invention and Technology. 1991, Scribner $23.00 (978-0-684-19106-5). Profiles of great names in invention and technology around the world. (Rev: BL 11/1/91; SLJ 1/92) [920]

8439 McClafferty, Carla Killough. *Tech Titans: One Frontier, Six Bios* (5–7). Illus. 2012, Scholastic paper $6.99 (978-05453657-7-2). Bill Gates, Steve Jobs, Mark Zuckerberg, Larry Page, Sergey Brin, and Jeff Bezos — the men behind Windows, Apple, Facebook, Google, and Amazon — are profiled here. Lexile 1010L (Rev: BL 4/15/12; LMC 10/12) [920]

8440 Mayberry, Jodine. *Business Leaders Who Built Financial Empires* (5–8). Series: 20 Events. 1995, Raintree LB $27.12 (978-0-8114-4934-2). The biographies of 19 financial wizards and entrepreneurs, beginning with Levi Strauss and Andrew Carnegie and ending with Steven Jobs and Anita Roddick. (Rev: SLJ 7/95) [920]

8441 Mulcahy, Robert. *Medical Technology: Inventing the Instruments* (5–8). Series: Innovators. 1997, Oliver LB $21.95 (978-1-881508-34-2). Seven short biographies of scientists who were responsible for such inventions as the X-ray, stethoscope, thermometer, and electrocardiograph. (Rev: BCCB 7–8/97; SLJ 7/97) [920]

8442 Pile, Robert B. *Top Entrepreneurs and Their Business* (6–12). 1993, Oliver LB $19.95 (978-1-881508-04-5). The rags-to-riches stories of nine entrepreneurs, among them L. L. Bean, Walt Disney, and Sam Walton. With photographs. (Rev: BL 11/15/93; SLJ 1/94) [920]

8443 Polking, Kirk. *Oceanographers and Explorers of the Sea* (5–9). Series: Collective Biographies. 1999, Enslow LB $20.95 (978-0-7660-1113-7). Profiles 10 scientists and adventurers who have devoted their lives to the oceans, marine life, and ocean-related pursuits, including Maurice Ewing, who mapped the ocean floor, and Robert Ballard, discoverer of the *Titanic*. (Rev: BL 8/99; SLJ 9/99) [920]

8444 Richie, Jason. *Space Flight: Crossing the Last Frontier* (5–9). Series: Innovators. 2002, Oliver LB $21.95 (978-1-881508-77-9). Biographies of seven men who were instrumental in the development of space flight — including Robert Goddard, Wernher von Braun, and Sergei Korolev — are arranged in chronological order. (Rev: HBG 3/03; LMC 4–5/03; SLJ 4/03) [629.4]

8445 Rohmer, Harriet. *Heroes of the Environment: True Stories of People Who Are Helping to Protect Our Planet* (6–10). Illus. by Julie McLaughlin. 2009, Chronicle $16.99 (978-0-8118-6779-5). This book highlights 12 environmental crusaders — many of them teens or young adults — and their work to end pollution and industrial development from Appalachia to Alaska. (Rev: BLO 11/1/09; SLJ 1/10; VOYA 12/09) [920]

8446 Sapet, Kerrily. *Google Founders: Larry Page and Sergey Brin* (7–12). Illus. Series: Business Leaders. 2011, Morgan Reynolds LB $28.95 (978-159935177-3). This biography combines information about the founders of Google with details of the creation, amazing growth, and importance of its browser and related technology. (Rev: BL 11/15/11) [920]

8447 Shell, Barry. *Sensational Scientists: The Journeys and Discoveries of 24 Men and Women of Science* (8–11). 2006, Raincoast paper $15.95 (978-1-55192-727-5). Profiles of 24 scientists associated with Canada cover a wide range of interests. (Rev: BL 2/15/06) [509]

8448 Sherman, Josepha. *Jerry Yang and David Filo: Chief Yahoos of Yahoo* (5–8). Series: Techies. 2001, Millbrook LB $23.90 (978-0-7613-1961-0). This is the story of the creators of Yahoo!, the world's most heavily trafficked Web site. (Rev: BL 4/1/02; HBG 3/02; SLJ 12/01) [921]

8449 Skurzynski, Gloria. *This Is Rocket Science: True Stories of the Risk-Taking Scientists Who Figure Out Ways to Explore Beyond Earth* (6–9). 2010, National Geographic $18.95 (978-1-4263-0597-9). From the earliest Chinese gunpowder and fireworks to the space shuttle and today's commercial rocket enterprises and new technologies, this volume full of photographs and illustrations explains the basic technology and introduces key figures. (Rev: BLO 11/5/09; LMC 3–4/10; SLJ 4/10) [920]

8450 Smith, Chris, and Marci McGrath. *Twitter: Jack Dorsey, Biz Stone and Evan Williams* (7–12). Illus. Series: Business Leaders. 2011, Morgan Reynolds LB $28.95 (978-159935179-7). Describes the founders of Twitter and the impact of this technology. (Rev: BL 11/15/11; VOYA 4/12) [920]

8451 Thimmesh, Catherine. *The Sky's the Limit: Stories of Discovery by Women and Girls* (5–7). Illus. by Melissa Sweet. 2002, Houghton Mifflin $16.00 (978-0-618-07698-7). Details discoveries in the sciences, all made by women and girls. A sequel to *Girls Think of Everything* (2000). (Rev: BL 3/1/02; HB 5–6/02; HBG 10/02; SLJ 5/02; VOYA 6/02) [500]

8452 VanCleave, Janice. *Janice VanCleave's Scientists Through the Ages* (4–7). 2003, Wiley paper $12.95 (978-0-471-25222-1). A collective biography profiling

515

25 scientists, with explanations of each one's important work and a relevant experiment for the reader to perform. (Rev: BL 12/1/03) [509]

8453 White, Casey. *Sergey Brin and Larry Page: The Founders of Google* (5–9). Series: Internet Career Biographies. 2006, Rosen LB $31.95 (978-1-4042-0716-5). The interesting story of the two Stanford graduates who created a company that added a new word to our vocabulary. (Rev: LMC 8–9/07; SLJ 5/07) [920]

8454 Yount, Lisa. *Edward Pickering and His Women "Computers": Analyzing the Stars* (7–10). Illus. Series: Trailblazers in Science and Technology. 2012, Chelsea House LB $35 (978-160413664-7). Combining biography and science, this informative volume explores the lives and contributions of the talented women who helped Harvard astronomer Pickering. (Rev: BL 12/15/12) [920]

8455 Zach, Kim K. *Hidden from History: The Lives of Eight American Women Scientists* (6–12). 2002, Avisson paper $19.95 (978-1-888105-54-4). The important achievements of eight women who made often unacknowledged contributions to the sciences are accompanied by some personal details. (Rev: BL 12/1/02; SLJ 4/03; VOYA 12/03) [920]

Individual

AL-HAYTHAM, IBN

8456 Steffens, Bradley. *Ibn Al-Haytham: First Scientist* (8–11). Series: Profiles in Science. 2007, Morgan Reynolds $27.95 (978-1-59935-024-0). A Muslim who was born in A.D. 965 in the Middle East, Ibn al-Haytham made important contributions to science. (Rev: BL 12/1/06; SLJ 7/07) [921]

ALVAREZ, LUIS

8457 Allison, Amy. *Luis Alvarez and the Development of the Bubble Chamber* (5–8). Series: Unlocking the Secrets of Science. 2002, Mitchell Lane LB $25.70 (978-1-58415-140-1). Alvarez was a scientist of wide-ranging interests who won a Nobel Prize for developing a bubble chamber to track atomic particles. (Rev: HBG 3/03; SLJ 2/03; VOYA 6/03) [921]

ANDREESSEN, MARC

8458 Ehrenhaft, Daniel. *Marc Andreessen: Web Warrior* (5–8). Series: The Techies. 2001, Twenty-First Century LB $23.90 (978-0-7613-1964-1). This biography introduces Marc Andreessen, who coauthored the Web-browsing software Mosaic, cofounded the firm Netscape, and was a multimillionaire at age 24. (Rev: BL 3/15/01; HBG 10/01; SLJ 7/01; VOYA 8/01) [921]

ANDREWS, ROY CHAPMAN

8459 Bausum, Ann. *Dragon Bones and Dinosaur Eggs: A Photobiography of Explorer Roy Chapman Andrews* (5–8). 2000, National Geographic $17.95 (978-0-7922-7123-9). A biography of the famous paleontologist who made several important dinosaur discoveries in central Asia and later became director of the American Museum of Natural History in New York City. (Rev: BCCB 5/00*; BL 3/15/00; HBG 10/00; SLJ 3/00) [921]

ARCHIMEDES

8460 Gow, Mary. *Archimedes: Mathematical Genius of the Ancient World* (5–8). Series: Great Minds of Science. 2005, Enslow LB $26.60 (978-0-7660-2502-8). Archimedes' mathematical discoveries are explained and placed in social, scientific, and cultural context. (Rev: SLJ 12/05) [921]

8461 Hasan, Heather. *Archimedes: The Father of Mathematics* (6–10). Series: The Library of Greek Philosophers. 2006, Rosen LB $33.25 (978-1-4042-0774-5). The importance of this ancient thinker is explained, and readers learn of his times and his influence. (Rev: SLJ 9/06)

AVERY, OSWALD

8462 Severs, Vesta-Nadine, and Jim Whiting. *Oswald Avery and the Story of DNA* (4–7). Series: Unlocking the Secrets of Science. 2002, Mitchell Lane LB $25.70 (978-1-58415-110-4). The importance of Avery's early research is reinforced by a description of DNA evidence being used to free wrongly accused prisoners. (Rev: HBG 10/02; SLJ 6/02) [579.3092]

BELL, ALEXANDER GRAHAM

8463 Bankston, John. *Alexander Graham Bell and the Story of the Telephone* (5–8). Series: Uncharted, Unexplored, and Unexplained. 2004, Mitchell Lane LB $29.95 (978-1-58415-243-9). As a teacher of the deaf and son of a deaf mother, Bell had a special interest in finding new and better ways to communicate. (Rev: BL 10/15/04) [921]

8464 Carson, Mary Kay. *Alexander Graham Bell: Giving Voice to the World* (5–8). Series: Sterling Biographies. 2007, Sterling LB $12.95 (978-1-4027-4951-3); paper $5.95 (978-1-4027-3230-0). Covers Bell's childhood and his lifelong commitment to improving communication. (Rev: SLJ 10/07)

8465 Pasachoff, Naomi. *Alexander Graham Bell: Making Connections* (6–9). Series: Oxford Portraits in Science. 1996, Oxford $32.95 (978-0-19-509908-9). A fine biography that focuses on Bell's work as a teacher of the deaf and his career as an inventor. (Rev: SLJ 2/97*) [921]

8466 Shulman, Seth. *The Telephone Gambit: Chasing Alexander Graham Bell's Secret* (8–12). 2008, Norton

$24.95 (978-0-393-06206-9). Did Bell really invent the telephone? History and science students will find this well-written investigation riveting. (Rev: BL 12/1/07) [921]

BENZ, KARL

8467 Bankston, John. *Karl Benz and the Single Cylinder Engine* (5–8). Series: Uncharted, Unexplored, and Unexplained. 2004, Mitchell Lane LB $29.95 (978-1-58415-244-6). The first person to build a three-wheeled automobile, Benz went on to design many more-sophisticated cars. (Rev: BL 10/15/04) [921]

BERNERS-LEE, TIM

8468 Gaines, Ann. *Tim Berners-Lee and the Development of the World Wide Web* (4–7). Series: Unlocking the Secrets of Science. 2001, Mitchell Lane LB $25.70 (978-1-58415-096-1). A profile of the man who created the user-friendly way of accessing much of the information on the Internet. (Rev: HBG 10/02; SLJ 2/02) [921]

BEZOS, JEFF

8469 Garty, Judy. *Jeff Bezos* (5–8). Series: Internet Biographies. 2003, Enslow LB $23.93 (978-0-7660-1972-0). A reader-friendly biography of the creator of Amazon.com, with plenty of information on his youth. (Rev: BL 3/15/03; HBG 10/03) [380.1]

8470 Robinson, Tom. *Jeff Bezos: Amazon.com Architect* (5–8). Illus. Series: Publishing Pioneers. 2009, ABDO LB $22.95 (978-160453759-8). This positive, informative biography of Amazon founder Jeff Bezos focuses on business innovation. (Rev: BL 12/1/09) [921]

8471 Scally, Robert D. *Jeff Bezos: Founder of Amazon and the Kindle* (7–12). Illus. Series: Business Leaders. 2011, Morgan Reynolds LB $28.95 (978-159935178-0). This biography combines information about Bezos with details of the creation, growth, and influence of Amazon and its e-books. (Rev: BL 11/15/11) [921]

8472 Sherman, Josepha. *Jeff Bezos: King of Amazon* (5–8). 2001, Twenty-First Century LB $23.90 (978-0-7613-1963-4). Jeff Bezos, the genius behind Amazon.com, is introduced along with information on his struggle to found a book company on the Web. (Rev: BL 3/15/01; HBG 10/01; SLJ 7/01; VOYA 8/01) [921]

BLACKWELL, ELIZABETH

8473 Kline, Nancy. *Elizabeth Blackwell: A Doctor's Triumph* (5–9). Series: Barnard Biography. 1997, Conari paper $11.95 (978-1-57324-057-4). The story of the first woman doctor in America, with generous excerpts from her journal and letters. (Rev: BL 2/15/97; SLJ 6/97; VOYA 12/97) [921]

BOYLE, ROBERT

8474 Baxter, Roberta. *Skeptical Chemist: The Story of Robert Boyle* (8–11). 2006, Morgan Reynolds $26.95 (978-1-59935-025-7). Boyle's natural curiosity led to his developing an important methodology for scientific experimentation, and his biography will inspire students interested in both science and history. (Rev: BL 12/1/06; SLJ 1/07) [921]

8475 Gow, Mary. *Robert Boyle: Pioneer of Experimental Chemistry* (6–9). Series: Great Minds of Science. 2005, Enslow LB $26.60 (978-0-7660-2501-1). Pioneering 17th-century chemist Robert Boyle is profiled in this volume that will be useful for report writers. (Rev: BL 3/15/05; SLJ 6/05) [530]

BRAHE, TYCHO

8476 Boerst, William J. *Tycho Brahe: Mapping the Heavens* (6–9). 2003, Morgan Reynolds LB $26.95 (978-1-883846-97-8). A concise biography with many illustrations of the man whose research on astronomy in the 1500s provided the foundation for future scientific inquiry. (Rev: BL 3/15/03; HBG 10/03; SLJ 8/03) [520]

8477 Nardo, Don. *Tycho Brahe: Pioneer of Astronomy* (5–8). Illus. Series: Signature Lives: Scientific Revolution. 2007, Compass Point LB $23.95 (978-0-7565-3309-0). In addition to this Danish scientist's career and discoveries, this well-designed volume explores the basics of scientific investigation and the nature of his breakthroughs. (Rev: BL 12/1/07; SLJ 1/08) [921]

BRANSON, RICHARD

8478 Redmond, Shirley Raye. *Richard Branson: Virgin Megabrand Mogul* (5–8). Illus. Series: Innovators. 2011, Gale/KidHaven LB $28.75 (978-073775536-7). Tells the success story of the creator of the Virgin Group, offering records and transportation from trains to planes to spaceships. (Rev: BL 12/15/11) [921]

BREAZEAL, CYNTHIA

8479 Brown, Jordan D. *Robo World: The Story of Robot Designer Cynthia Breazeal* (6–10). Series: Women's Adventures in Science. 2005, Watts LB $31.50 (978-0-531-16782-3). An interesting biography that blends personal information with scientific facts. (Rev: SLJ 2/06) [921]

BROWN, HELEN GURLEY

8480 Falkof, Lucille. *Helen Gurley Brown: The Queen of Cosmopolitan* (5–8). Series: Wizards of Business. 1992, Garrett LB $17.26 (978-1-56074-013-1). An interesting, accessible, and inspiring biography of the magazine magnate. (Rev: BL 6/15/92; SLJ 7/92) [921]

BUFFETT, WARREN

8481 Johnson, Anne Janette. *Warren Buffett* (7–12). Series: Business Leaders. 2008, Morgan Reynolds LB $27.95 (978-1-59935-080-6). This biography of Buffett covers both the personal and professional milestones of his life in clear, accessible prose. (Rev: SLJ 10/1/08) [921]

BURROUGHS, JOHN

8482 Wadsworth, Ginger. *John Burroughs: The Sage of Slabsides* (5–8). 1997, Clarion $16.95 (978-0-395-77830-2). A biography of the American naturalist and essayist who lived in a cabin in the Catskill Mountains and wrote about his observations. (Rev: BCCB 5/97; BL 3/15/97; HB 7–8/97; SLJ 5/97) [508.73]

CARNEGIE, ANDREW

8483 Edge, Laura B. *Andrew Carnegie: Industrial Philanthropist* (7–10). Series: Lerner Biography. 2004, Lerner LB $27.93 (978-0-8225-4965-9). The fascinating story of Carnegie's progress from poor Scottish immigrant to wealthy industrialist and generous philanthropist. (Rev: BL 6/1–15/04; SLJ 2/04) [936.2]

CARSON, RACHEL

8484 Levine, Ellen. *Rachel Carson* (7–10). Series: Up Close. 2007, Viking $15.99 (978-0-670-06220-1). A well-documented biography of the groundbreaking environmentalist that provides details of her personal life as well as her career and of the obstacles she faced. (Rev: BL 2/15/07; HB 3–4/07; SLJ 4/07*) [921]

8485 Scherer, Glenn, and Marty Fletcher. *Who on Earth Is Rachel Carson? Mother of the Environmental Movement* (4–7). Series: Scientists Saving the Earth. 2009, Enslow LB $31.93 (978-1-59845-116-0). Readers gain insight into the environmental climate of the 1970s, and the importance of Carson, who strove to raise awareness and end pesticide-related threats to wildlife. (Rev: SLJ 1/10; VOYA 2/10) [921]

8486 Wadsworth, Ginger. *Rachel Carson: Voice for the Earth* (5–7). Series: Lerner Biographies. 1992, Lerner LB $27.93 (978-0-8225-4907-9). The life and work of the conservationist and author, best known for *Silent Spring*. (Rev: BL 6/1/92; HB 7–8/92; SLJ 7/92) [921]

CARVER, GEORGE WASHINGTON

8487 MacLeod, Elizabeth. *George Washington Carver: An Innovative Life* (4–7). Illus. 2007, Kids Can $14.95 (978-1-55337-906-5); paper $6.95 (978-1-55337-907-2). Well-organized with attractive graphics, this biography of Carver provides interesting details about his life as well as his major accomplishments. (Rev: SLJ 6/07)

CASE, STEVE

8488 Ashby, Ruth. *Steve Case: America Online Pioneer* (5–8). Series: Techies. 2002, Millbrook LB $23.90 (978-0-7613-2655-7). The story of the Honolulu native who was a leader of AOL and the driving force behind its merger with Time-Warner. (Rev: BL 4/1/02; HBG 10/02) [921]

CHIEN-SHIUNG WU

8489 Cooperman, Stephanie H. *Chien-Shiung Wu: Pioneering Physicist and Atomic Researcher* (5–8). Series: Women Hall of Famers in Mathematics and Science. 2004, Rosen LB $29.25 (978-0-8239-3875-9). This biography describes Wu's life and achievements, explaining how she found a flaw in a widely held assumption about atoms. (Rev: BL 3/1/04; SLJ 9/04) [921]

CHOO, JIMMY

8490 Sapet, Kerrily. *Jimmy Choo* (7–10). Illus. Series: Profiles in Fashion. 2010, Morgan Reynolds LB $28.95 (978-159935151-3). This intriguing biography chronicles the success of Malaysian-born footwear pioneer Jimmy Choo. (Rev: BL 10/1/10) [921]

COPERNICUS, NICOLAUS

8491 Andronik, Catherine M. *Copernicus: Founder of Modern Astronomy* (4–8). Series: Great Minds of Science. 2002, Enslow LB $26.60 (978-0-7660-1755-9). This absorbing biography that covers Copernicus's youth and succeeds in explaining necessary scientific concepts also includes activities that reinforce this understanding. (Rev: HBG 10/02; SLJ 6/02) [520.92]

COUSTEAU, JACQUES

8492 Olmstead, Kathleen. *Jacques Cousteau: A Life Under the Sea* (7–9). Series: Sterling Biographies. 2008, Sterling paper $5.95 (978-1-4027-4440-4). Olmstead examines the life and accomplishments of the scientist, explorer, filmmaker and inventor, mentioning his secret second family . (Rev: SLJ 1/1/09) [921]

CURIE FAMILY

8493 Henderson, Harry. *The Curie Family: Exploring Radioactivity* (7–10). Illus. Series: Trailblazers in Science and Technology. 2012, Chelsea House LB $35 (978-160413675-3). Combining biography and science, this informative volume explores the lives of Marie and Pierre Curie — and of their daughter Irene and her husband — and their important contributions in the study of radioactivity. (Rev: BL 12/15/12) [920]

CURIE, MARIE

8494 Birch, Beverley. *Marie Curie, Spanish and English* (5–8). Series: Giants of Science Bilingual. 2005, Gale LB $28.70 (978-1-4103-0505-3). English and Spanish versions of this life of Curie are presented side by side, and the timeline, glossary, and index are also bilingual. (Rev: SLJ 2/06) [921]

8495 Healy, Nick. *Marie Curie* (6–9). Series: Genius. 2005, Creative Education LB $21.95 (978-1-58341-332-6). This attractive picture-book biography will interest readers but report writers will want more documentation. (Rev: BL 2/15/06) [540]

8496 Koestler-Grack, Rachel A. *Marie Curie: Scientist* (6–10). Series: Women of Achievement. 2009, Chelsea House $30 (978-1-60413-086-7). This is a balanced profile that provides good basic information on Curie and her impact on the world of science. (Rev: SLJ 5/1/09) [921]

8497 Krull, Kathleen. *Marie Curie* (5–8). Illus. by Boris Kulikov. Series: Giants of Science. 2007, Viking $15.99 (978-0-670-05894-5). This biography of the Nobel Prize-winning scientist supplies plenty of information about her family life and personality as well as her discoveries and her legacy. ALA Notable Books 2008. (Rev: BL 12/15/07; HB 11/07; SLJ 12/07)

8498 McClafferty, Carla Killough. *Something Out of Nothing: Marie Curie and Radium* (7–10). 2006, Farrar $18.00 (978-0-374-38036-6). This readable biography examines Curie's personal life and her valuable contributions to scientific knowledge. (Rev: BL 3/1/06; SLJ 5/06*) [540]

8499 Poynter, Margaret. *Marie Curie: Discoverer of Radium. Rev. ed.* (4–7). Illus. Series: Great Minds of Science. 2007, Enslow LB $31.93 (978-0-89490-477-6). The life and significance of this discoverer of radium are covered, with a chapter of suggested activities. (Rev: BL 1/1/95; SLJ 10/94)

8500 Yannuzzi, Della A. *New Elements: The Story of Marie Curie* (5–10). Illus. Series: Profiles in Science. 2006, Morgan Reynolds $26.95 (978-1-59935-023-3). More about the scientist's life than about the significance of her research, this introduction will be helpful to report writers. (Rev: BL 12/1/06; SLJ 1/07)

DAMADIAN, RAYMOND

8501 Kjelle, Marylou Morano. *Raymond Damadian and the Development of MRI* (5–7). Series: Unlocking the Secrets of Science. 2002, Mitchell Lane LB $25.70 (978-1-58415-141-8). This account focuses on Damadian's scientific accomplishments. (Rev: HBG 10/03; SLJ 1/03) [921]

DARWIN, CHARLES

8502 Anderson, Margaret J. *Charles Darwin: Naturalist* (4–7). Series: Great Minds of Science. 1994, Enslow LB $26.60 (978-0-89490-476-9). In addition to a biography of this controversial naturalist, there is a chapter on activities for the reader. (Rev: BL 1/1/95; SLJ 10/94) [921]

8503 Ashby, Ruth. *Young Charles Darwin and the Voyage of the Beagle* (4–7). Illus. by Suzanne Duranceau. 2009, Peachtree $12.95 (978-1-56145-478-5). Focusing on Darwin's five-year voyage on the *Beagle*, this interesting biography includes many direct quotations. (Rev: BL 3/15/09; SLJ 3/09) [921]

8504 Eldredge, Niles, and Susan Pearson. *Charles Darwin and the Mystery of Mysteries* (7–10). 2010, Flash Point LB $19.99 (978-1-59643-374-8). This engaging biography gives lots of information on Darwin's youth and private life as well as his research and the voyages of the *Beagle*. (Rev: BL 7/10; LMC 5–6/10; SLJ 6/10) [921]

8505 Greenberger, Robert. *Darwin and the Theory of Evolution* (5–8). Series: Primary Sources of Revolutionary Scientific Discoveries and Theories. 2005, Rosen LB $29.25 (978-1-4042-0306-8). Profiles English naturalist Charles Darwin and the events that led up to his groundbreaking theory of evolution; useful for brief reports. (Rev: SLJ 11/05) [921]

8506 Krull, Kathleen. *Charles Darwin* (5–8). Illus. by Boris Kulikov. Series: Giants of Science. 2010, Viking $15.99 (978-0-670-06335-2). An engaging profile of the famous scientist, covering his life from childhood and explaining his theories. (Rev: BL 12/1/10*; HB 1–2/11; SLJ 3/1/11) [921]

8507 Lawson, Kristan. *Darwin and Evolution for Kids: His Life and Ideas with 21 Activities* (5–9). 2003, Chicago Review paper $16.95 (978-1-55652-502-5). The naturalist's life and work are examined in clear, interesting text, with thorough coverage of his five-year research voyage on *H.M.S. Beagle* and the continuing controversy over his theories. (Rev: SLJ 4/04) [921]

8508 Leone, Bruno. *Origin: The Story of Charles Darwin* (6–9). Illus. Series: Profiles in Science. 2009, Morgan Reynolds $28.95 (978-159935110-0). Leone provides a thorough introduction to the life and work of Darwin, with attention to his student years and his mentors. (Rev: BL 3/15/09; SLJ 4/1/09) [921]

8509 Sís, Peter. *The Tree of Life: Charles Darwin* (4–7). 2003, Farrar $18.00 (978-0-374-45628-3). Highly illustrated, this imaginative and visual biography traces Darwin's life and development as a naturalist, with a focus on his voyages on the *Beagle*. (Rev: BL 10/15/03; HB 11–12/03*; HBG 4/04; SLJ 10/03*) [576.8]

8510 Wood, A. J. *Charles Darwin and the Beagle Adventure* (5–8). 2009, Candlewick $19.99 (978-0-7636-4538-0). Creatively designed to look like Charles Darwin's journal, this book shares a wealth of information about Darwin's journey on the *HMS Beagle* . (Rev: LMC 1–2/10; SLJ 10/09*) [921]

DARWIN, CHARLES AND EMMA

8511 Heiligman, Deborah. *Charles and Emma: The Darwins' Leap of Faith* (8–12). 2009, Henry Holt $18.95

(978-080508721-5). The story of Charles Darwin and his relationship with his wife (and cousin) Emma; family letters and other primary sources document a loving marriage between two very different people. National Book Award Finalist, YALSA Nonfiction Winner 2010, Printz Honor 2010. ∩ e Lexile 1020L (Rev: BL 1/1–15/09*; HB 1–2/09; LMC 8–9/09; SLJ 1/1/09*; VOYA 12/08) [920]

DE LA RENTA, OSCAR

8512 Darraj, Susan Muaddi. *Oscar de la Renta* (6–9). Illus. Series: Great Hispanic Heritage. 2010, Chelsea House LB $30 (978-160413733-0). An admiring biography of the fashion designer, with emphasis on Hispanic themes. (Rev: BL 2/1/11) [921]

DYSON, ESTHER

8513 Jablonski, Carla. *Esther Dyson: Web Guru* (5–8). Series: Techies. 2002, Millbrook LB $23.90 (978-0-7613-2657-1). A leading light in the computer world, Dyson is the owner of EDventure Holdings, and is an active developer of emerging technologies and companies. (Rev: BL 4/1/02; HBG 10/02) [921]

EARLE, SYLVIA

8514 Baker, Beth. *Sylvia Earle: Guardian of the Sea* (4–7). Series: Lerner Biographies. 2000, Lerner LB $27.93 (978-0-8225-4961-1). This is a thrilling biography of the famous underwater explorer and marine scientist who was one of the first humans to swim with whales. (Rev: BL 10/15/00; HBG 3/01; SLJ 11/00) [921]

8515 Reichard, Susan E. *Who on Earth Is Sylvia Earle? Undersea Explorer of the Ocean* (4–7). Series: Scientists Saving the Earth. 2009, Enslow LB $31.93 (978-1-59845-118-4). An interesting biography of the scientist devoted to underwater exploration and the protection of this environment from threats including oil pollution. (Rev: SLJ 1/10; VOYA 2/10) [921]

EDISON, THOMAS ALVA

8516 Baxter, Roberta. *Illuminated Progress: The Story of Thomas Edison* (6–9). Illus. Series: Profiles in Science. 2008, Morgan Reynolds LB $27.95 (978-159935085-1). A chronological overview of the inventions and collaborations of Thomas Edison, including his financial failures and disputes with other inventors, and his lesser-known projects. (Rev: BL 12/1/08; LMC 1–2/09; SLJ 12/08) [921]

8517 Carlson, Laurie. *Thomas Edison for Kids: His Life and Ideas: 21 Activities* (4–7). Illus. 2006, Chicago Review paper $14.95 (978-1-55652-584-1). Activities allow readers to try some of the inventor's experiments; the biography section covers Edison's personal life as well as his achievements and introduces some of his contemporaries. (Rev: BL 2/15/06; SLJ 6/06) [621.3]

8518 Graham, Amy. *Thomas Edison: Wizard of Light and Sound* (5–8). Illus. Series: Inventors Who Changed the World. 2007, Enslow LB $24.95 (978-1-59845-052-1). The text of this profile of Edison and his achievements is augmented by links to carefully evaluated Web sites. (Rev: SLJ 11/07) [921]

8519 Tagliaferro, Linda. *Thomas Edison: Inventor of the Age of Electricity* (6–9). 2003, Lerner LB $27.93 (978-0-8225-4689-4). Clear, lively language is used to give details of Edison's youth and trace his interest in science and invention throughout his life. (Rev: HBG 10/03; SLJ 7/03) [621.3]

8520 Woodside, Martin. *Thomas A. Edison: The Man Who Lit Up the World* (5–8). Series: Sterling Biographies. 2007, Sterling LB $12.95 (978-1-4027-4955-1); paper $5.95 (978-1-4027-3229-4). A concise account of Edison's life from childhood and his many achievements in varied fields. (Rev: SLJ 10/07)

EINSTEIN, ALBERT

8521 Bankston, John. *Albert Einstein and the Theory of Relativity* (5–8). Series: Unlocking the Secrets of Science. 2002, Mitchell Lane LB $25.70 (978-1-58415-137-1). Einstein's accomplishments and the many challenges he faced are explored in concise text with many black-and-white photographs. (Rev: SLJ 2/03) [921]

8522 Delano, Marfé Ferguson. *Genius: A Photobiography of Albert Einstein* (5–8). 2005, National Geographic $17.95 (978-0-7922-9544-0). Photographs of the scientist's life, as well as brief explanations of his work, help to make the man and his theories more accessible to young readers; an oversized and engaging volume. (Rev: BL 4/1/05*; SLJ 5/05) [921]

8523 Krull, Kathleen. *Albert Einstein* (6–9). Illus. by Boris Kulikov. Series: Giants of Science. 2009, Viking $15.99 (978-0-670-06332-1). Krull provides an accessible, at times funny, account of the life and times of the illustrious physicist. (Rev: BL 9/1/09; HB 11–12/09; LMC 11–12/09; SLJ 10/09) [921]

8524 Lassieur, Allison. *Albert Einstein: Genius of the Twentieth Century* (5–8). Series: Great Life Stories. 2005, Watts LB $30.50 (978-0-531-12401-7). In addition to placing Einstein's life (including his childhood) and contributions in historical and social context, Lassieur explains his theories and their application. (Rev: SLJ 9/05) [921]

8525 McPherson, Stephanie Sammartino. *Ordinary Genius: The Story of Albert Einstein* (4–7). 1995, Carolrhoda LB $27.93 (978-0-87614-788-7). Good historical background information is given on the life of Einstein plus a clear explanation of his discoveries. (Rev: BL 6/1–15/95; SLJ 9/95) [921]

8526 Severance, John B. *Einstein: Visionary Scientist* (7–12). 1999, Clarion $18.00 (978-0-395-93100-4). This book covers Einstein's academic theories as well as his private life and his celebrity. (Rev: BCCB 9/99; BL 9/1/99; HB 9–10/99; HBG 4/00; SLJ 9/99) [921]

8527 Speregen, Devra Newberger. *Albert Einstein: The Jewish Man Behind the Theory* (6–9). 2006, Jewish Publication Society $12.95 (978-0-8276-0824-5). This book explores the development of Einstein's sense of identity as a Jew as he became aware of Nazi anti-Semitism. (Rev: BL 6/1–15/06) [921]

8528 Yeatts, Tabatha. *Albert Einstein: The Miracle Mind* (7–12). Series: Sterling Biography. 2007, Sterling LB $12.95 (978-1-4027-4950-6); paper $5.95 (978-1-4027-3228-7). Covers the life and scientific accomplishments of Albert Einstein, as well as his stand against racism and nuclear war. (Rev: BL 9/1/07) [921]

ELION, GERTRUDE

8529 MacBain, Jennifer. *Gertrude Elion: Nobel Prize Winner in Physiology and Medicine* (5–8). Series: Women Hall of Famers in Mathematics and Science. 2004, Rosen LB $29.25 (978-0-8239-3876-6). Elion, a biochemist and pharmacologist who never earned a doctorate, won a Nobel Prize for her advances in the field of chemotherapy. (Rev: BL 3/1/04; SLJ 9/04) [615]

ELLISON, LARRY

8530 Ehrenhaft, Daniel. *Larry Ellison: Sheer Nerve* (5–8). Series: Techies. 2001, Millbrook LB $23.90 (978-0-7613-1962-7). The life story of one of the world's richest men and co-founder of Oracle, the world's leading supplier of software for information management. (Rev: BL 4/1/02; HBG 3/02; SLJ 12/01) [921]

EUCLID

8531 Hayhurst, Chris. *Euclid: The Great Geometer* (6–10). 2006, Rosen LB $33.25 (978-1-4042-0497-3). The importance of this ancient thinker (who is called the father of geometry) is explained, and readers learn of his times and his influence. (Rev: SLJ 9/06) [921]

FANNING, SHAWN

8532 Mitten, Christopher. *Shawn Fanning: Napster and the Music Revolution* (5–8). Series: Techies. 2002, Millbrook LB $23.90 (978-0-7613-2656-4). Using many photographs and an interesting text, this is the biography of the creator of Napster, a software package for downloading music from computers. (Rev: BL 4/1/02; HBG 10/02; SLJ 6/02) [921]

FARADAY, MICHAEL

8533 Russell, Colin A. *Michael Faraday: Physics and Faith* (8–12). Series: Oxford Portraits in Science. 2001, Oxford LB $32.95 (978-0-19-511763-9). The story of the inventor of the electric transformer and the dynamo is placed in interesting historical context. (Rev: HBG 10/01; SLJ 3/01) [921]

FARNSWORTH, PHILO

8534 McPherson, Stephanie Sammartino. *TV's Forgotten Hero: The Story of Philo Farnsworth* (4–7). 1996, Carolrhoda LB $27.93 (978-1-57505-017-1). The biography of the genius who invented electronic television when he was only 14. (Rev: BL 2/1/97; SLJ 2/97) [921]

FERMI, ENRICO

8535 Cooper, Dan. *Enrico Fermi: And the Revolutions of Modern Physics* (8–12). Series: Oxford Portraits in Science. 1999, Oxford $32.95 (978-0-19-511762-2). A readable biography of the Italian scientist who immigrated to the United States in 1939 and worked on the first atomic bomb. Some of the coverage of quantum and nuclear physics is challenging. (Rev: SLJ 6/99) [921]

FEYNMAN, RICHARD

8536 Henderson, Harry. *Richard Feynman: Quarks, Bombs, and Bongos* (7–10). Illus. Series: Makers of Modern Science. 2010, Chelsea House $35 (978-081606176-1). Feynman is known for his brilliance in the fields of particle physics and quantum mechanics, but this biography also tells readers about his personal life — and his love of bongo drums. (Rev: BL 6/1/11) [921]

8537 Levine, Harry, III. *The Great Explainer: The Story of Richard Feynman* (6–9). Series: Profiles in Science. 2009, Morgan Reynolds LB $28.95 (978-1-59935-113-1). Nobel laureate physicist Feynman is known for his role in the investigation into the crash of the shuttle *Challenger*, as well his work on developing the atomic bomb. (Rev: BL 12/1/09; SLJ 1/10) [921]

FLEMING, ALEXANDER

8538 Bankston, John. *Alexander Fleming and the Story of Penicillin* (5–8). Series: Unlocking the Secrets of Science. 2001, Mitchell Lane LB $25.70 (978-1-58415-106-7). This absorbing biography of the Scottish Nobel Prize winner covers his personal life as well as his scientific career. (Rev: HBG 3/02; SLJ 1/02) [616.014092]

FORD, HENRY

8539 Mitchell, Don. *Driven: A Photobiography of Henry Ford* (4–7). 2010, National Geographic $18.95 (978-1-4263-0155-1); LB $27.90 (978-1-4263-0156-8). With many photographs and quotations, this is a fine portrait of the founder of the automobile company, frankly discussing his social views, ideals, and character flaws. (Rev: BL 6/10; HB 5–6/10; SLJ 4/10; VOYA 6/10) [338.7]

FOSSEY, DIAN

8540 Gogerly, Liz. *Dian Fossey* (5–8). Series: Scientists Who Made History. 2003, Raintree LB $27.12 (978-0-7368-5225-8). A riveting profile of the woman who became an expert on gorillas and the militant stance that may have led to her murder. (Rev: BL 3/1/03) [599.884]

8541 Kushner, Jill Menkes. *Who on Earth Is Dian Fossey?: Defender of the Mountain Gorillas* (4–7). Series: Scientists Saving the Earth. 2009, Enslow LB $31.93 (978-1-59845-117-7). Readers gain insight into threats facing gorillas and learn about the committed work of Fossey, who strove to save and understand them. (Rev: BL 2/15/10; SLJ 1/10; VOYA 2/10) [921]

FRANCE, DIANE

8542 Hopping, Lorraine Jean. *Bone Detective: The Story of Forensic Anthropologist Diane France* (7–10). Series: Women's Adventures in Science. 2005, Watts LB $31.50 (978-0-531-16776-2). Part of the Women's Adventures in Science series, this compelling biography of Diane France traces the forensic anthropologist's life from her childhood in Colorado to her role in identifying victims of the 9/11 terrorist attacks. (Rev: BL 10/15/05; SLJ 2/06) [363.25]

FRANKLIN, ROSALIND

8543 Polcovar, Jane. *Rosalind Franklin and the Structure of Life* (8–11). Series: Profiles in Science. 2006, Morgan Reynolds LB $26.95 (978-1-59935-022-6). Franklin had a small part in the discovery of DNA — she took the image that set Watson and Crick on the path to found the field of genetics; this profile looks at her advancement in a profession generally closed to women and at the competitive nature of the search for the double helix. (Rev: BL 12/1/06; SLJ 3/07) [921]

FREUD, SIGMUND

8544 Krull, Kathleen. *Sigmund Freud* (6–9). Illus. by Boris Kulikov. Series: Giants of Science. 2006, Viking $15.99 (978-0-670-05892-1). This book examines the complex life of the father of psychoanalysis — his flaws as well as his virtues — and the enormous influence his theories have had on modern life. (Rev: BL 12/1/06; HB 9–10/06; SLJ 12/06) [921]

8545 Reef, Catherine. *Sigmund Freud: Pioneer of the Mind* (7–12). 2001, Clarion $19.00 (978-0-618-01762-1). Reef looks at Freud's life and career, showing the ways in which his ideas evolved over time and the initial rejection of many of his revolutionary thoughts. Sidney Taylor Book Award 2001. (Rev: BL 7/01; HB 7–8/01*; HBG 10/01; SLJ 8/01; VOYA 10/01) [921]

FULTON, ROBERT

8546 Pierce, Morris A. *Robert Fulton and the Development of the Steamboat* (4–8). Series: Library of American Lives and Times. 2003, Rosen LB $34.60 (978-0-8239-5737-8). The inventor of the steamboat was a man of determination and wide interests who also worked on naval weapons. (Rev: BL 6/1–15/03; SLJ 4/03) [921]

FUNG, INEZ

8547 Skelton, Renee. *Forecast Earth: The Story of Climate Scientist Inez Fung* (6–10). Series: Women's Adventures in Science. 2005, Watts LB $31.50 (978-0-531-16777-9). An interesting biography that blends personal information with scientific facts. (Rev: SLJ 2/06) [921]

GALILEO

8548 Boerst, William J. *Galileo Galilei and the Science of Motion* (6–10). Series: Great Scientists. 2003, Morgan Reynolds LB $26.95 (978-1-931798-00-6). Galileo's early insistence on adherence to scientific verification is emphasized in this detailed yet accessible biography that includes color period reproductions and a timeline. (Rev: BL 11/1/03; HBG 4/04; SLJ 12/03) [921]

8549 Hightower, Paul. *Galileo: Astronomer and Physicist* (4–7). Series: Great Minds of Science. 1997, Enslow LB $26.60 (978-0-89490-787-6). This biography not only includes material on the life and accomplishments of this courageous scientist but also contains several activities that give an understanding of his work. (Rev: BL 6/1–15/97) [921]

8550 Hilliam, Rachel. *Galileo Galilei: Father of Modern Science* (5–8). Series: Rulers, Scholars, and Artists of the Renaissance. 2005, Rosen LB $33.25 (978-1-4042-0314-3). Ford places Galileo's life and accomplishments in the context of culture and politics of the time. (Rev: SLJ 10/05) [921]

8551 Panchyk, Richard. *Galileo for Kids: His Life and Ideas* (5–9). 2005, Chicago Review paper $16.95 (978-1-55652-566-7). A clearly written and well-illustrated overview of Galileo's life and scientific achievements, with excerpts from Galileo's writings and suggested activities. (Rev: SLJ 9/05) [921]

GATES, BILL

8552 Aronson, Marc. *Bill Gates* (6–10). Illus. Series: Up Close. 2008, Viking $16.99 (978-067006348-2). This book provides an insightful and evenhanded glimpse into Bill Gates's world, from his ultra-competitive childhood to his business practices and philanthropic works. (Rev: BL 12/1/08) [921]

8553 Lockwood, Brad. *Bill Gates: Profile of a Digital Entrepreneur* (5–8). 2007, Rosen LB $31.95 (978-1-4042-1906-9). Well-written and updated, this volume on Gates focuses on his career. (Rev: LMC 1/08; SLJ 3/08)

GATES, BILL AND MELINDA

8554 Isaacs, Sally. *Bill and Melinda Gates* (6–10). Series: Front-Page Lives. 2010, Heinemann-Raintree $38.93 (978-1-4329-3220-6). Using a headlines format that highlights events, Isaacs covers the Gates's lives from childhood and includes a timeline, glossary, and other useful back matter. (Rev: LMC 3–4/10) [921]

8555 Schuman, Michael A. *Bill Gates: Computer Mogul and Philanthropist* (5–8). 2007, Enslow LB $31.93 (978-0-7660-2693-3). Gates and his wife Melinda and their far-reaching philanthropic efforts are covered in this clearly written volume. (Rev: SLJ 3/08) [921]

GODDARD, ROBERT

8556 Bankston, John. *Robert Goddard and the Liquid Rocket Engine* (4–7). Series: Unlocking the Secrets of Science. 2001, Mitchell Lane LB $17.95 (978-1-58415-107-4). Bankston combines an introduction to Goddard's commitment to rocketry and his difficulty finding funding with an understandable explanation of the scientific challenges. (Rev: HBG 3/02; SLJ 2/02) [621.43]

GOODALL, JANE

8557 Bardhan-Quallen, Sudipta. *Jane Goodall: Primatologist* (6–9). Series: Up Close. 2008, Viking $16.99 (978-0-670-06263-8). This sometimes very detailed profile that covers Goodall's life from childhood will be useful for report writers. (Rev: BL 6/1–15/08; SLJ 9/08) [921]

8558 Kozleski, Lisa. *Jane Goodall: Primatologist/Naturalist* (7–12). Series: Women in Science. 2003, Chelsea LB $30.00 (978-0-7910-6905-9). An absorbing biography that discusses the primatologist's personal life as well as her dedicated work with chimpanzees in Tanzania. (Rev: LMC 11–12/03; SLJ 7/03) [921]

GUTENBERG, JOHANNES

8559 Feinstein, Stephen. *Johannes Gutenberg: The Printer Who Gave Words to the World* (5–8). Illus. 2008, Enslow LB $33.27 (978-1-59845-077-4). A history of printing from the ancient civilizations to the Renaissance is included in this book about Gutenberg's contribution of a movable metal type and printing press. (Rev: SLJ 2/09) [921]

HALLEY, EDMOND

8560 Fox, Mary Virginia. *Scheduling the Heavens: The Story of Edmond Halley* (6–9). 2007, Morgan Reynolds LB $27.95 (978-1-59935-021-9). Details the life, career, and achievements of the scientist best known for calculating the orbit and accurately predicting the return of the eponymous comet. (Rev: BL 6/1–15/07; SLJ 4/07) [921]

HAMMEL, HEIDI

8561 Bortz, Fred. *Beyond Jupiter: The Story of Planetary Astronomer Heidi Hammel* (6–10). Series: Women's Adventures in Science. 2005, Watts LB $31.50 (978-0-531-16775-5). An interesting biography that

blends personal information with scientific facts. (Rev: SLJ 2/06) [921]

HARVEY, WILLIAM

8562 Yount, Lisa. *William Harvey: Discoverer of How Blood Circulates* (4–8). Series: Great Minds of Science. 1994, Enslow LB $26.60 (978-0-89490-481-3). A biography of the 17th-century scientist that describes early theories about the blood system and the importance of Harvey's discoveries. (Rev: SLJ 2/95) [921]

HAWKING, STEPHEN

8563 Bankston, John. *Stephen Hawking: Breaking the Boundaries of Time and Space* (6–9). Series: Great Minds of Science. 2005, Enslow LB $26.60 (978-0-7660-2281-2). The life and scientific career of British physicist Stephen Hawking are presented in clear and simple text. (Rev: SLJ 6/05) [921]

HEWLETT, WILLIAM

8564 Tracy, Kathleen. *William Hewlett: Pioneer of the Computer Age* (5–7). Series: Unlocking the Secrets of Science. 2002, Mitchell Lane LB $25.70 (978-1-58415-142-5). This accessible account focuses on Hewlett's scientific accomplishments and career in business. (Rev: SLJ 1/03) [921]

HOOKE, ROBERT

8565 Gow, Mary. *Robert Hooke: Creative Genius, Scientist, Inventor* (5–9). Series: Great Minds of Science. 2006, Enslow LB $31.93 (978-0-7660-2547-9). A biography of the 17th-century man of science and arts who made discoveries in many fields and also helped to redesign London after the fire of 1666. (Rev: SLJ 6/07) [921]

HUBBLE, EDWIN

8566 Datnow, Claire. *Edwin Hubble: Discoverer of Galaxies* (4–8). Series: Great Minds of Science. 1997, Enslow LB $26.60 (978-0-89490-934-4). A portrait of the great astronomer, noted for his amazing scientific abilities and quirky pretentions. (Rev: BL 12/1/97; HBG 3/98; SLJ 3/98; VOYA 12/97) [921]

8567 Kupperberg, Paul. *Hubble and the Big Bang* (6–9). Series: Primary Sources of Revolutionary Scientific Discoveries and Theories. 2005, Rosen LB $29.25 (978-1-4042-0307-5). A profile of American astronomer Edwin Hubble with an easy-to-understand explanation of his theory of the expanding universe and reproductions of newspaper and journal articles. (Rev: BL 9/1/05; SLJ 11/05; VOYA 12/05) [921]

IVE, JONATHAN

8568 Hirschmann, Kris. *Jonathan Ive: Designer of the iPod* (5–8). Illus. Series: Innovators. 2007, Gale LB $27.45 (978-0-7377-3533-8). Introduces the man behind this popular gadget; the inside info on Apple is also fascinating. (Rev: BL 12/15/07) [745.2092]

JACKSON, SHIRLEY ANN

8569 O'Connell, Diane. *Strong Force: The Story of Physicist Shirley Ann Jackson* (5–8). Series: Women's Adventures in Science. 2005, Watts LB $31.50 (978-0-531-16784-7). The life and scientific career of Jackson, physicist and former chairman of the U.S. Nuclear Regulatory Commission. (Rev: SLJ 12/05) [921]

JEMISON, MAE

8570 Jemison, Mae. *Find Where the Wind Goes* (7–12). 2001, Scholastic $16.95 (978-0-439-13195-7). The fascinating autobiography of the first African American woman in space. (Rev: BL 11/1/01; HBG 10/01; SLJ 4/01; VOYA 8/01) [629.45]

JOBS, STEVE

8571 Blumenthal, Karen. *Steve Jobs: The Man Who Thought Different* (7–10). Illus. 2012, Feiwel & Friends $16.99 (978-125001557-0); paper $8.99 (978-12500144-5-0). Chronicles the life and career of the Apple founder, with details of his childhood, college days, work, faith, friendships, and death from pancreatic cancer. ALA Notable Books 2013. (Rev: BL 2/15/12*; HB 5–6/12; VOYA 6/12) [921]

8572 Corrigan, Jim. *Steve Jobs* (6–9). Series: Business Builders. 2008, Morgan Reynolds $27.95 (978-1-59935-076-9). A somewhat critical look at the founder of Apple, focusing on his career and management approach. (Rev: BL 6/1–15/08; SLJ 8/08) [338.7]

8573 Doeden, Matt. *Steve Jobs: Technology Innovator and Apple Genius* (4–7). Illus. Series: Gateway Biographies. 2012, Lerner LB $26.60 (978-146770215-7). Tells the story of the creation of Apple and the factors underlying its success. **e** (Rev: BL 6/12; SLJ 4/12) [921]

8574 Goldsworthy, Steve. *Steve Jobs* (4–7). Illus. Series: Remarkable People. 2011, Weigl LB $27.13 (978-161690670-2); paper $12.95 (9781616906757). A generally admiring life of the Apple CEO. (Rev: BL 9/15/11) [921]

8575 Imbimbo, Anthony. *Steve Jobs: The Brilliant Mind Behind Apple* (7–10). Illus. Series: Life Portraits. 2009, Gareth Stevens LB $34.00 (978-143390060-0). Photographs and anecdotes add interest to this profile of the inventive computer engineer. Lexile 980L (Rev: BL 4/1/09; LMC 8–9/09) [921]

JONES, CAROLINE

8576 Fleming, Robert. *The Success of Caroline Jones Advertising, Inc.* (7–10). Series: Success. 1996, Walker LB $16.85 (978-0-8027-8354-7). The story of Jones's

rapid rise in the world of advertising. (Rev: BL 1/1–15/96; SLJ 4/96) [921]

KEPLER, JOHANNES

8577 Boerst, William J. *Johannes Kepler: Discovering the Laws of Celestial Motion* (6–9). Series: Renaissance Scientists. 2003, Morgan Reynolds LB $26.95 (978-1-883846-98-5). Astronomer and mathematician Kepler's life and achievements are placed in historical context, with details of the religious tensions of the time and the uncertainty of a scientific career. (Rev: BL 6/1–15/03; HBG 10/03; SLJ 8/03) [520]

KOEHL, MIMI

8578 Parks, Deborah. *Nature's Machines: The Story of Biomechanist Mimi Koehl* (6–10). Series: Women's Adventures in Science. 2005, Watts LB $31.50 (978-0-531-16780-9). An interesting biography that blends personal information with scientific facts. (Rev: SLJ 2/06) [921]

KOLFF, WILLEM

8579 Tracy, Kathleen. *Willem Kolff and the Invention of the Dialysis Machine* (5–8). Series: Unlocking the Secrets of Science. 2002, Mitchell Lane LB $25.70 (978-1-58415-135-7). Kolff invented the dialysis machine in 1942 in the Nazi-occupied Netherlands. (Rev: HBG 3/03; SLJ 12/02) [617.461059092]

LAUREN, RALPH

8580 Weatherly, Myra. *Business Leaders: Ralph Lauren* (7–12). 2008, Morgan Reynolds LB $27.95 (978-1-59935-084-4). This volume covers Lauren's successful career in the fashion industry. (Rev: SLJ 10/1/08) [921]

LAVOISIER, ANTOINE

8581 Yount, Lisa. *Antoine Lavoisier: Founder of Modern Chemistry* (4–7). Series: Great Minds of Science. 1997, Enslow LB $26.60 (978-0-89490-785-2). In addition to providing an assessment of the life and works of Lavoisier, called the Father of Chemistry, this book includes several hands-on activities that depend on an understanding of his work. (Rev: BL 6/1–15/97) [921]

LEAKEY FAMILY

8582 Henderson, Harry. *The Leakey Family: Unearthing Human Ancestors* (7–10). Illus. Series: Trailblazers in Science and Technology. 2012, Chelsea House LB $35 (978-160413674-6). Combining biography and science, this informative volume explores the lives and contributions of these anthropologists. (Rev: BL 12/15/12) [920]

LEEUWENHOEK, ANTONI VAN

8583 Yount, Lisa. *Antoni van Leeuwenhoek: First to See Microscopic Life* (4–8). Series: Great Minds of Science.

1996, Enslow LB $26.60 (978-0-89490-680-0). A brief biography of the Dutch maker of microscopes, who was also the first to examine closely bacteria and blood cells. (Rev: BL 10/15/96; SLJ 12/96) [921]

LEOPOLD, ALDO

8584 Lorbiecki, Marybeth. *Of Things Natural, Wild, and Free: A Story About Aldo Leopold* (4–7). 1993, Carolrhoda LB $15.95 (978-0-87614-797-9). The story of a man who was a great hunter until he realized the importance of the balance in nature, and then turned a tract of farmland into a nature refuge. (Rev: BL 11/1/93; SLJ 11/93) [921]

LINNAEUS, CARL

8585 Anderson, Margaret J. *Carl Linnaeus: Father of Classification* (4–8). Series: Great Minds of Science. 1997, Enslow LB $26.60 (978-0-89490-786-9). This biography discusses the personal life of Linnaeus, including his explorations in Lapland, but the focus is on the development of his important biological classification system. (Rev: BL 12/1/97; HBG 3/98; SLJ 9/97) [921]

MALONE, ANNIE TURNBO

8586 Wilkerson, J. L. *Story of Pride, Power and Uplift: Annie T. Malone* (4–8). 2003, Acorn $9.95 (978-0-9664470-8-8). Malone, a child of slaves, created beauty products for African American women at the turn of the 20th century and became a wealthy woman and philanthropist. (Rev: BL 3/1/03; SLJ 7/03) [646.7]

MASON, ANDREW

8587 Wolny, Philip. *Andrew Mason and Groupon* (6–9). Illus. Series: Internet Biographies. 2012, Rosen LB $34.60 (978-144886916-9). A portrait of the founder of Groupon and of the company itself, its growth, and its innovations. (Rev: BL 10/1/12) [921]

MAYER, MARIA GOEPPERT

8588 Ferry, Joseph. *Maria Goeppert Mayer: Physicist* (6–12). Series: Women in Science. 2003, Chelsea LB $30.00 (978-0-7910-7247-9). Ferry explores the life and achievements of Mayer, who won a Nobel Prize in 1963 for research into the atomic nucleus. (Rev: HBG 10/03; SLJ 10/03) [921]

MCCLINTOCK, BARBARA

8589 Cullen, J. Heather. *Barbara McClintock: Geneticist* (6–12). Series: Women in Science. 2003, Chelsea LB $30.00 (978-0-7910-7248-6). Cullen explores the life and achievements of McClintock, who won a Nobel Prize in 1983 for research in genetics that she conducted decades earlier. (Rev: HBG 10/03; SLJ 10/03) [921]

8590 Spangenburg, Ray, and Diane Kit Moser. *Barbara McClintock: Pioneering Geneticist* (8–11). Series:

Makers of Modern Science. 2008, Chelsea House LB $29.95 (978-0-8160-6172-3). A biography of the 1983 winner of a Nobel Prize for her work on the genetics of maize. (Rev: BL 4/15/08) [576.5092]

8591 Tracy, Kathleen. *Barbara McClintock: Pioneering Geneticist* (4–7). Series: Unlocking the Secrets of Science. 2001, Mitchell Lane LB $25.70 (978-1-58415-111-1). An absorbing look at the life and research of this Nobel Prize winner. (Rev: HBG 3/02; SLJ 2/02) [921]

MEAD, MARGARET

8592 Horn, Geoffrey M. *Margaret Mead* (5–8). Series: Trailblazers of the Modern World. 2004, World Almanac LB $31.00 (978-0-8368-5099-4). Report writers will find useful information on Mead's life, achievements, and lasting contributions. (Rev: SLJ 7/04) [921]

8593 Mark, Joan. *Margaret Mead: Coming of Age in America* (6–10). Series: Oxford Portraits in Science. 1999, Oxford $32.95 (978-0-19-511679-3). An introduction to the life and work of the pioneering anthropologist and her research with the peoples of the South Seas, particularly in Samoa. (Rev: BL 4/1/99; SLJ 3/99) [921]

MENDEL, GREGOR

8594 Bankston, John. *Gregor Mendel and the Discovery of the Gene* (5–8). Series: Uncharted, Unexplored, and Unexplained. 2004, Mitchell Lane LB $29.95 (978-1-58415-266-8). Profiles the 19th-century Austrian monk who discovered the laws of genetics. (Rev: BL 10/15/04; SLJ 12/04) [921]

8595 Edelson, Edward. *Gregor Mendel: And the Roots of Genetics* (7–10). Series: Oxford Portraits in Science. 1999, Oxford $34.99 (978-0-19-512226-8). Describes Mendel's life and his work on plant heredity and the study of genetics in the context of the social, scientific, and political events of his time. (Rev: SLJ 7/99) [921]

MENDELEYEV, DMITRI

8596 Zannos, Susan. *Dmitri Mendeleyev and the Periodic Table* (5–8). Series: Uncharted, Unexplored, and Unexplained. 2004, Mitchell Lane LB $29.95 (978-1-58415-267-5). This brief biography looks at the life of the inventor of the periodic table, focusing initially on his childhood and offering political context. (Rev: BL 10/15/04) [540]

MERCATOR, GERARDUS

8597 Heinrichs, Ann. *Gerardus Mercator: Father of Modern Mapmaking* (5–12). Series: Signature Lives. 2007, Compass Point LB $31.93 (978-0-7565-3312-0). Scientific concepts are presented clearly in this profile that covers Mercator's life, with excerpts from his writing and a timeline that adds historical context. (Rev: SLJ 1/08)

MEXIA, YNES

8598 Anema, Durlynn. *Ynes Mexia: Botanist and Adventurer* (6–9). 2005, Morgan Reynolds $26.95 (978-1-931798-67-9). Mexia is known for her adventurous spirit and her important collections of plants from North and South America, which she started in her mid-50s. (Rev: SLJ 1/06) [921]

MONTAGNIER, LUC

8599 Yount, Lisa. *Luc Montagnier: Identifying the AIDS Virus* (7–10). Illus. Series: Trailblazers in Science and Technology. 2011, Chelsea House $35 (978-160413661-6). Yount provides a life of the famous French virologist and background information on the virus that came to light in the United States in the 1980s. (Rev: BLO 3/15/12) [921]

MUIR, JOHN

8600 Wadsworth, Ginger. *John Muir: Wilderness Protector* (6–12). 1992, Lerner LB $18.95 (978-0-8225-4912-3). Original photographs and Muir's letters, journals, and writings provide an overview of the conservationist's personal life, achievements, and contributions to the environmental movement. (Rev: BL 8/92) [921]

MURRAY, JOSEPH E.

8601 Mattern, Joanne. *Joseph E. Murray and the Story of the First Human Kidney Transplant* (5–8). Series: Unlocking the Secrets of Science. 2002, Mitchell Lane LB $25.70 (978-1-58415-136-4). A look at the work of the surgeon who performed the first successful kidney transplant. (Rev: SLJ 12/02; VOYA 6/03) [617.95092]

NEWTON, SIR ISAAC

8602 Boerst, William J. *Isaac Newton: Organizing the Universe* (6–10). Series: Renaissance Scientists. 2004, Morgan Reynolds LB $26.95 (978-1-931798-01-3). A fine biography of Newton that includes good explanations of the laws of motion and excellent color reproductions of period paintings. (Rev: BL 2/1/04; SLJ 4/04) [921]

8603 Christianson, Gale E. *Isaac Newton and the Scientific Revolution* (8–12). Series: Oxford Portraits in Science. 1996, Oxford $32.95 (978-0-19-509224-0). A challenging biography that gives the scientist's life history plus detailed explanations of theories of gravity, relativity, and calculus. (Rev: BL 12/1/96; SLJ 1/97; VOYA 2/97) [921]

8604 Hollihan, Kerrie Logan. *Isaac Newton and Physics for Kids: His Life and Ideas with 21 Activities* (4–8). Illus. 2009, Chicago Review $16.95 (978-1-55652-778-4). This well-balanced story offers a picture of the physicist's work and personal life. (Rev: BL 6/1–15/09; LMC 1–2/10; SLJ 8/09) [530.092]

8605 Krull, Kathleen. *Isaac Newton* (5–8). Illus. by Boris Kulikov. Series: Giants of Science. 2006, Viking $15.99 (978-0-670-05921-8). Newton's childhood and adult personality are highlighted in this readable biography that gives good explanations of his scientific theories. (Rev: BL 4/1/06; SLJ 3/06*; VOYA 6/06)

8606 Steele, Philip. *Isaac Newton: The Scientist Who Changed Everything* (4–7). Illus. Series: National Geographic World History Biographies. 2007, National Geographic $17.95 (978-1-4263-0114-8). A colorful, well-designed survey of Newton's life and legacy. (Rev: BL 12/1/07; SLJ 6/07)

OMIDYAR, PIERRE

8607 Viegas, Jennifer. *Pierre Omidyar: The Founder of eBay* (5–8). Illus. Series: Internet Career Biographies. 2006, Rosen LB $31.95 (978-1-4042-0715-8). A look at the successful founder of eBay and his hopes for the future. (Rev: BL 10/15/06; SLJ 5/07) [921]

OPPENHEIMER, J. ROBERT

8608 Allman, Toney. *J. Robert Oppenheimer: Father of the Atomic Bomb* (5–9). Series: Giants of Science. 2005, Gale $26.20 (978-1-56711-889-6). Controversial physicist Oppenheimer, who played a key role in the development of the atomic bomb, is profiled in readable text with lots of details for report writers. (Rev: SLJ 7/05) [921]

8609 Scherer, Glenn, and Marty Fletcher. *J. Robert Oppenheimer: The Brain Behind the Bomb* (6–10). Series: Inventors Who Changed the World. 2007, Enslow LB $33.27 (978-1-59845-050-7). The story of the physicist who shepherded the Manhattan Project, with discussion of the science involved and the key political and social factors. (Rev: BL 7/07; SLJ 11/07) [921]

PASTEUR, LOUIS

8610 Ackerman, Jane. *Louis Pasteur and the Founding of Microbiology* (7–12). Series: Great Scientists. 2004, Morgan Reynolds $26.95 (978-1-931798-13-6). Using his microscope, Pasteur developed the fields of immunology and microbiology and invented the pasteurization of milk. (Rev: BL 2/1/04; SLJ 4/04) [921]

8611 Robbins, Louise E. *Louis Pasteur and the Hidden World of Microbes* (8–12). Series: Oxford Portraits in Science. 2001, Oxford $34.99 (978-0-19-512227-5). A look at the life of the famous scientist, with glimpses of his personality as well as his research and discoveries. (Rev: BL 12/1/01; HBG 3/02; SLJ 12/01) [921]

8612 Smith, Linda W. *Louis Pasteur: Disease Fighter. Rev. ed.* (4–8). Illus. Series: Great Minds of Science. 2007, Enslow LB $31.93 (978-0-89490-790-6). The story of the "father of microbiology," who discovered pasteurization while working on a wine problem for Napoleon. (Rev: BL 12/1/97; HBG 3/98; SLJ 12/97) [921]

PAVLOV, IVAN

8613 Saunders, Barbara R. *Ivan Pavlov: Exploring the Mysteries of Behavior.* Rev. ed. (5–9). Series: Great Minds of Science. 2006, Enslow LB $31.93 (978-0-7660-2506-6). This well-written profile chronicles Pavlov's famous experiments and discoveries and shows how his work influenced other branches of science. (Rev: SLJ 6/07) [921]

PRIESTLEY, JOSEPH

8614 Conley, Kate A. *Joseph Priestley and the Discovery of Oxygen* (6–8). Series: Uncharted, Unexplored, and Unexplained: Scientific Advancements of the 19th Century. 2005, Mitchell Lane LB $19.95 (978-1-58415-367-2). An introduction to the scientist Joseph Priestley, including his childhood in England, setting his life and discoveries in historical context. (Rev: SLJ 5/06) [921]

PULITZER, JOSEPH

8615 Zannos, Susan. *Joseph Pulitzer and the Story Behind the Pulitzer Prize* (4–8). Series: Great Achievement Awards. 2003, Mitchell Lane LB $29.95 (978-1-58415-179-1). Pulitzer's difficulty personality and passion for journalism are highlighted in this account of his establishment of the well-known awards. (Rev: BL 10/15/03; SLJ 9/03) [070.9]

QUADRINO, JAMES

8616 Pearce, Q. L. *James Quadrino: Wildlife Protector* (4–7). Series: Young Heroes. 2006, Gale LB $23.70 (978-0-7377-3612-0). At age 13, James Quadrino took it upon himself to save a fire-ravaged bird sanctuary by building nesting boxes. (Rev: SLJ 6/07) [921]

RAY, RACHAEL

8617 Abrams, Dennis. *Rachael Ray: Food Entrepreneur* (6–10). Illus. Series: Women of Achievement. 2009, Chelsea House LB $30.00 (978-160413078-2). The popular TV personality and cookbook author is profiled here in appealing text with many interesting quotations. (Rev: BL 4/1/09; SLJ 5/1/09) [921]

RINGLING BROTHERS

8618 Apps, Jerry. *Tents, Tigers, and the Ringling Brothers* (3–7). Illus. Series: Badger Biographies. 2006, Wisconsin Historical Soc. paper $12.95 (978-0-87020-374-9). The true story of how the seven Ringling Brothers followed their dreams and began their own circus, describing their day-to-day struggles to keep the business successful. (Rev: BL 2/15/07)

ROBERTS, EDWARD

8619 Zannos, Susan. *Edward Roberts and the Story of the Personal Computer* (5–7). Series: Unlocking the Secrets of Science. 2002, Mitchell Lane LB $25.70 (978-1-58415-118-0). This accessible account focuses on

Roberts's accomplishments as an electronic engineer. (Rev: HBG 10/03; SLJ 1/03) [921]

ROCKEFELLER, JOHN D.

8620 Laughlin, Rosemary. *John D. Rockefeller: Oil Baron and Philanthropist* (5–8). Series: American Business Leaders. 2001, Morgan Reynolds LB $21.95 (978-1-883846-59-6). A biography of the determined and skilled businessman who made Standard Oil the dominant company in the oil industry and who was later noted for his philanthropy. (Rev: BL 3/1/01; HBG 10/01; SLJ 7/01) [921]

RUTHERFORD, ERNEST

8621 Pasachoff, Naomi. *Ernest Rutherford: Father of Nuclear Science* (6–12). Series: Great Minds of Science. 2005, Enslow LB $26.60 (978-0-7660-2441-0). The life and scientific career of the New Zealand-born physicist who helped to pave the way for the development of nuclear physics. (Rev: SLJ 8/05) [921]

SALK, JONAS

8622 McPherson, Stephanie Sammartino. *Jonas Salk: Conquering Polio* (5–8). Series: Lerner Biographies. 2001, Lerner LB $27.93 (978-0-8225-4964-2). An absorbing account of Salk's life and contributions to medicine that discusses his confrontation with Sabin and the early failures of Salk's vaccine. (Rev: HBG 3/02; SLJ 4/02) [921]

SCHALLER, GEORGE

8623 Turner, Pamela S. *A Life in the Wild: George Schaller's Struggle to Save the Last Great Beasts* (5–8). Illus. 2008, Farrar $21.95 (978-0-374-34578-5). Turner traces the environmentalist's work to save gorillas, tigers, lions, snow leopards, and other large endangered animals. (Rev: BCCB 11/08; BL 12/1/08; SLJ 11/08) [590.92]

STEWART, MARTHA

8624 Paprocki, Sherry Beck. *Martha Stewart: Lifestyle Entrepreneur* (6–10). Series: Women of Achievement. 2009, Chelsea House $30 (978-1-60413-083-6). Paprocki does not shy away from controversy in this evenhanded profile of the business and lifestyle maven and her impact on American culture. (Rev: SLJ 5/1/09) [921]

STRAUSS, LEVI

8625 Van Steenwyk, Elizabeth. *Levi Strauss: The Blue Jeans Man* (5–9). 1988, Walker LB $14.85 (978-0-8027-6796-7). A biography of the Bavarian immigrant, Levi Strauss, who became the blue jeans king of the western world. (Rev: BL 6/15/88; SLJ 10/88; VOYA 8/88) [921]

SUI, ANNA

8626 Darraj, Susan Muaddi. *Anna Sui* (7–10). Series: Asian Americans of Achievement. 2009, Chelsea House $30 (978-1-60413-570-1). Sui's devotion to fashion — and her success at creating an international company with interests in fragrance, cosmetics, and even cell phones — are documented here, with interesting sidebars on culture and business. (Rev: BL 5/15/10; SLJ 2/10) [921]

TAJIRI, SATOSHI

8627 Mortensen, Lori. *Satoshi Tajiri: Pokémon Creator* (4–7). Illus. 2009, Gale LB $27.45 (978-0-7377-4269-5). A brief biography of the Japanese designer known for creating Pokemon and other Nintendo games, with information on his diagnosis with Asperger's syndrome. (Rev: BLO 5/28/09; SLJ 8/09) [921]

TESLA, NIKOLA

8628 Aldrich, Lisa J. *Nikola Tesla and the Taming of Electricity* (8–11). Series: Modern Scientists. 2005, Morgan Reynolds LB $26.95 (978-1-931798-46-4). The life and many inventions — including radio — of the Croatian-born electrical engineer. (Rev: BL 5/1/05; SLJ 10/05; VOYA 10/05) [621.3]

8629 Dommermuth-Costa, Carol. *Nikola Tesla: A Spark of Genius* (5–9). 1994, Lerner LB $27.93 (978-0-8225-4920-8). Traces the life and career of this pioneer in the field of electricity. (Rev: BL 12/15/94; SLJ 2/95) [921]

TIENDA, MARTA

8630 O'Connell, Diane. *People Person: The Story of Sociologist Marta Tienda* (5–8). Series: Women's Adventures in Science. 2005, Watts LB $31.50 (978-0-531-16781-6). An informative and accessible profile of sociologist Marta Tienda and her work to create opportunities for people around the world. (Rev: SLJ 12/05) [921]

TORVALDS, LINUS

8631 Brashares, Ann. *Linus Torvalds: Software Rebel* (5–8). Series: Techies. 2001, Millbrook LB $23.90 (978-0-7613-1960-3). The story of the computer genius who created the Linux operating system. (Rev: BL 4/1/02; HBG 3/02; SLJ 12/01) [921]

TURING, ALAN

8632 Corrigan, Jim. *Alan Turing* (7–10). 2008, Morgan Reynolds LB $27.95 (978-1-59935-064-6). This biography of "the father of computer science" goes beyond his work in mathematics into his private life, discussing how his homosexuality affected his career. (Rev: BL 6/1–15/08) [921]

8633 Henderson, Harry. *Alan Turing: Computing Genius and Wartime Code Breaker* (7–10). Illus. Series: Makers of Modern Science. 2011, Chelsea House $35 (978-081606175-4). A fascinating, detailed life of the man whose childhood was lonely, whose education was difficult, and who went on to make amazing contributions to mathematics and science, especially in the area of computers; includes discussion of his homosexuality and his early death. (Rev: BL 6/1/11) [921]

VEDDER, AMY

8634 Ebersole, Rene. *Gorilla Mountain: The Story of Wildlife Biologist Amy Vedder* (5–8). Series: Women's Adventures in Science. 2005, Watts LB $31.50 (978-0-531-16779-3). An informative and accessible account of Vedder's efforts to protect the endangered mountain gorillas of Rwanda. (Rev: SLJ 12/05)

WAKSMAN, SELMAN

8635 Gordon, Karen. *Selman Waksman and the Discovery of Streptomycin* (5–7). Series: Unlocking the Secrets of Science. 2002, Mitchell Lane LB $25.70 (978-1-58415-138-8). An accessible account of Waksman's life and scientific research. (Rev: HBG 10/03; SLJ 1/03) [921]

WALKER, MADAM C. J.

8636 Bundles, A'Lelia. *Madam C. J. Walker: Entrepreneur* (7–12). Illus. Series: Black Americans of Achievement. 2008, Chelsea House $30.00 (978-160413072-0). The story of the successful African American businesswoman, complete with photographs and background information. (Rev: BLO 1/13/09) [921]

WALKER, MARY

8637 Joinson, Carla. *Civil War Doctor: The Story of Mary Walker* (8–11). 2007, Morgan Reynolds LB $27.95 (978-1-59935-028-8). Walker studied medicine at a time when this was very unusual for a woman; she later served as a surgeon in the Union Army and in 1865 was the first woman to be awarded the Congressional Medal of Honor. (Rev: BL 1/1–15/07) [921]

WALTON, SAM

8638 Blumenthal, Karen. *Mr. Sam: How Sam Walton Built Wal-Mart and Became America's Richest Man* (5–8). Illus. 2011, Viking $17.99 (978-0-670-01177-3). A frank profile of the Oklahoma-born man who had a profound influence on the retail face of America — and beyond. e (Rev: BL 6/1/11; HB 7–8/11; LMC 11–12/11; SLJ 7/11) [381]

WANG, VERA

8639 Dakers, Diane. *Vera Wang: A Passion for Bridal and Lifestyle Design* (5–8). Illus. Series: Crabtree Groundbreakers Biographies. 2010, Crabtree LB $31.93 (978-077872535-0). Chronicling life from youth to adulthood, this biography presents a straightforward and clearly written portrait of fashion great Vera Wang. Lexile NC1210L (Rev: BL 1/1–15/11) [921]

8640 Todd, Anne M. *Vera Wang* (6–10). Series: Asian Americans of Achievement. 2007, Chelsea House LB $30.00 (978-0-7910-9272-9). This attractive profile recounts the highlights of Wang's personal life and covers her work for *Vogue* and Ralph Lauren before starting her own business. (Rev: SLJ 8/07) [921]

WEINBERG, ROBERT A.

8641 Gaines, Ann, and Jim Whiting. *Robert A. Weinberg and the Search for the Cause of Cancer* (4–7). Series: Unlocking the Secrets of Science. 2002, Mitchell Lane LB $25.70 (978-1-58415-095-4). The life and achievements of the scientist who specializes in the genetic causes of disease. (Rev: HBG 10/02; SLJ 6/02) [616.9940092]

WEXLER, NANCY

8642 Glimm, Adele. *Gene Hunter: The Story of Neuropsychologist Nancy Wexler* (6–10). Series: Women's Adventures in Science. 2005, Watts LB $31.50 (978-0-531-16778-6). An interesting biography that blends personal information with scientific facts. (Rev: SLJ 2/06) [921]

WHITNEY, ELI

8643 Gibson, Karen Bush. *The Life and Times of Eli Whitney* (5–8). Illus. Series: Profiles in American History. 2006, Mitchell Lane LB $20.95 (978-1-58415-434-1). An interesting profile of the cotton gin inventor, with period reproductions and relevant sidebar features. (Rev: BL 10/15/06) [609.2]

WOZNIAK, STEPHEN

8644 Riddle, John, and Jim Whiting. *Stephen Wozniak and the Story of Apple Computer* (4–7). Series: Unlocking the Secrets of Science. 2001, Mitchell Lane LB $17.95 (978-1-58415-109-8). A profile of the life and achievements of the co-founder of Apple, who is known for his philanthropy and teaching in elementary schools. (Rev: HBG 10/02; SLJ 2/02) [921]

WRIGHT, WILBUR AND ORVILLE

8645 Collins, Mary. *Airborne: A Photobiography of Wilbur and Orville Wright* (4–8). 2003, National Geographic $18.95 (978-0-7922-6957-1). Sixty photographs are only the beginning of this intriguing book packed with information about the brothers and their famous flight. (Rev: BL 2/1/03*; HB 3–4/03; HBG 10/03; SLJ 3/03) [629.13]

8646 Crompton, Samuel Willard. *The Wright Brothers: First in Flight* (6–12). Series: Milestones in American History. 2007, Chelsea House LB $35.00 (978-0-7910-9356-6). An accessible account of the lives of the two brothers and their contributions to aviation. (Rev: LMC 1/08; SLJ 10/07) [921]

8647 Dixon-Engel, Tara, and Mike Jackson. *The Wright Brothers: First in Flight* (5–8). Series: Sterling Biographies. 2007, Sterling LB $12.95 (978-1-4027-4954-4); paper $5.95 (978-1-4027-3231-7). The brothers' early life, inspiration, and eventual success are all covered here. (Rev: SLJ 10/07)

8648 McPherson, Stephanie Sammartino, and Joseph Sammartino Gardner. *Wilbur and Orville Wright: Taking Flight* (4–7). Series: Trailblazer Biographies. 2003, Carolrhoda LB $30.60 (978-1-57505-443-8). A well-written, detailed account of the Wright brothers' landmark experiments, enlivened with period photographs and other illustrations. (Rev: SLJ 4/04) [921]

8649 Martin, Michael J. *The Wright Brothers* (7–12). Series: The Importance Of. 2003, Gale LB $32.45 (978-1-56006-847-1). With lengthy quotations from primary and secondary sources, this is a lively biography of Wilbur and Orville Wright and how they changed history at Kitty Hawk. (Rev: BL 6/1–15/03) [921]

8650 Reynolds, Quentin. *The Wright Brothers* (5–8). 1963, Random House paper $5.99 (978-0-394-84700-9). An easily read account of the two young men and their dream of flight. [921]

ZUCKERBERG, MARK

8651 Hasday, Judy L. *Facebook and Mark Zuckerberg* (7–12). Illus. Series: Business Leaders. 2011, Morgan Reynolds LB $28.95 (978-159935176-6). This biography profiles Facebook founder Mark Zuckerberg, emphasizing his youth and entrepreneurial spirit. (Rev: BL 11/15/11; VOYA 8/12) [921]

Sports Figures

Collective

8652 Berman, Len. *The Twenty-five Greatest Baseball Players of All Time* (5–8). Illus. 2010, Sourcebooks $16.99 (978-140223886-4). Twenty-five of baseball's greatest are profiled in short chapters emphasizing career statistics and triumphs over challenges. (Rev: BL 9/1/10; SLJ 1/1/11; VOYA 12/10) [920]

8653 Bryant, Jill. *Amazing Women Athletes* (4–8). Series: Women's Hall of Fame. 2002, Second Story paper $7.95 (978-1-896764-44-3). This book contains profiles of 10 distinguished women athletes including mountain climber Annie Smith Peck and tennis stars Venus and Serena Williams. (Rev: BL 6/1–15/02; SLJ 8/02) [920]

8654 Christopher, Andre. *Top 10 Men's Tennis Players* (4–7). Series: Sports Top 10. 1998, Enslow LB $17.95 (978-0-7600-1009-9). Brief biographies of past and present tennis greats, with fact boxes, career statistics, and chapter notes. (Rev: BL 3/15/98) [920]

8655 Deane, Bill. *Top 10 Men's Baseball Hitters* (4–7). Series: Sports Top 10. 1998, Enslow LB $17.95 (978-0-7600-1007-5). Brief biographies of great past and present baseball hitters, with fact boxes, career statistics, and chapter notes. (Rev: BL 3/15/98) [920]

8656 Gaines, Ann. *Sports and Activities* (6–9). Series: Female Firsts in Their Fields. 1999, Chelsea $12.95 (978-0-7910-5144-3). A collection of six biographies of outstanding female trail blazers in athletics, focusing on how each achieved firsts for their sex. (Rev: BL 5/15/99; HBG 9/99) [920]

8657 Halberstam, David. *The Teammates* (8–12). 2003, Hyperion $22.95 (978-1-4013-0057-9). The story of the lives and friendships of four Boston Red Sox players: Ted Williams, Dominic DiMaggio, Johnny Pesky, and Bobby Doerr. [920]

8658 Hasday, Judy L. *Extraordinary Women Athletes* (6–12). Series: Extraordinary People. 2000, Children's Press LB $16.95 (978-0-516-27039-5). A collective biography of 45 women who have gained recognition in a wide variety of sports. (Rev: BL 10/1/00; VOYA 2/01) [920]

8659 Hotchkiss, Ron. *The Matchless Six: The Story of Canada's First Women's Olympic Team* (5–8). Illus. 2006, Tundra $16.95 (978-0-88776-738-8). Profiles the individual athletes and achievements of Canada's groundbreaking women's Olympic team of 1928. (Rev: BL 3/15/06; SLJ 6/06)

8660 Kaminsky, Marty. *Uncommon Champions: Fifteen Athletes Who Battled Back* (5–8). 2000, Boyds Mills $14.95 (978-1-56397-787-9). Profiles of 15 athletes in several different sports who have conquered such mental and physical problems as blindness and drug addiction to achieve their goals. (Rev: BCCB 1/01; BL 11/1/00; HBG 3/01; SLJ 10/00; VOYA 12/00) [921]

8661 Krull, Kathleen. *Lives of the Athletes* (4–7). Illus. by Kathryn Hewitt. 1997, Harcourt $20.00 (978-0-15-200806-2). A collective biography that describes the public and private lives of 20 famous athletes, including Johnny Weissmuller, Red Grange, Babe Didrikson Zaharias, Sonja Henie, and Bruce Lee. (Rev: BCCB 6/97; BL 3/15/97; HB 5–6/97; SLJ 5/97) [920]

8662 Lipsyte, Robert. *Heroes of Baseball: The Men Who Made It America's Favorite Game* (4–7). Illus. 2006, Simon & Schuster $19.95 (978-0-689-86741-5). As well as introducing key players of the game, this volume presents a concise history of the sport itself. (Rev: BL 2/15/06; SLJ 4/06)

8663 Rappoport, Ken. *Guts and Glory: Making It in the NBA* (4–8). 1997, Walker LB $16.85 (978-0-8027-8431-5). The 10 basketball players profiled in this book had to overcome obstacles to get to the top. (Rev: BL 8/97; SLJ 7/97) [920]

8664 Rappoport, Ken. *Ladies First: Women Athletes Who Made a Difference* (5–8). 2005, Peachtree $14.95 (978-1-56145-338-2). Gymnast Nadia Comaneci and dogsled racer Susan Butcher are only two of the many women in diverse sports featured in this collective biography that also gives a brief history of women's participation in sports. (Rev: BL 5/1/05; SLJ 6/05) [920]

8665 Rappoport, Ken. *Profiles in Sports Courage* (4–7). 2006, Peachtree $15.95 (978-1-56145-368-9). Twelve stories of bravery on and off the playing field (or court, ring, or track) by men and women from all types of sport and from all around the world. (Rev: BL 7/06; SLJ 6/06)

8666 Rutledge, Rachel. *The Best of the Best in Figure Skating* (4–7). Series: Women of Sports. 1998, Millbrook LB $24.90 (978-0-7613-1302-1). After a brief history of figure skating and mention of its women pioneers, this book devotes separate chapters to the sport's present-day female leaders. (Rev: BL 2/15/99; HBG 10/99) [920]

8667 Rutledge, Rachel. *The Best of the Best in Gymnastics* (5–8). Series: Women of Sports. 1999, Millbrook LB $24.90 (978-0-7613-1321-2); paper $7.95 (978-0-7613-0784-6). After an overview of the sport and its history, the author profiles eight important contemporary female gymnasts, five of whom are American. (Rev: HBG 10/99; SLJ 7/99; VOYA 2/00) [920]

8668 Staples, Bill, and Rich Herschlag. *Before the Glory: 20 Baseball Heroes Talk About Growing Up and Turning Hard Times into Home Runs* (8–12). 2007, Health Communications paper $14.95 (978-0-7573-0626-6). Twenty major-league players talk about their childhoods and relate anecdotes that influenced their future careers. (Rev: BLO 5/22/07) [796.357]

8669 Stout, Glenn. *Yes, She Can! Women's Sports Pioneers* (4–7). 2011, Houghton Mifflin paper $5.99 (978-0-547-41-725-7). Profiles women from different backgrounds and eras who made their name in various sports, from Gertrude Eberle through Julie Krone and Danica Patrick. e (Rev: BL 5/1/11; SLJ 7/11) [920]

Automobile Racing

EARNHARDT, DALE, JR.

8670 Stewart, Mark. *Dale Earnhardt Jr.: Driven by Destiny* (5–8). Series: Auto Racing's New Wave. 2003, Millbrook LB $22.90 (978-0-7613-2908-4). An exciting biography of the NASCAR driver who was voted the most popular driver of 2003. (Rev: BL 6/1–15/03; HBG 10/03; SLJ 10/03) [796.72]

GORDON, JEFF

8671 Gitlin, Martin. *Jeff Gordon: Racing's Brightest Star* (5–8). Series: Heroes of Racing. 2008, Enslow LB $23.95 (978-0-7660-2997-2). For NASCAR fans, a biography that concentrates on Gordon's victories and charisma. (Rev: BL 4/1/08) [796.72]

LABONTE, TERRY AND BOBBY

8672 Hubbard-Brown, Janet. *The Labonte Brothers* (4–8). Series: Race Car Legends: Collector's Edition. 2005, Chelsea House LB $25.00 (978-0-7910-8767-1). The famous brothers Terry and Bobby Labonte and their racing rivalry and successes are the focus of this readable, photo-filled volume. (Rev: SLJ 5/06) [921]

PATRICK, DANICA

8673 Mello, Tara Baukus. *Danica Patrick* (5–8). Series: Race Car Legends Collector's Edition. 2008, Chelsea House LB $25.00 (978-0-7910-9126-5). An attractive portrait of this history-making race car driver. (Rev: BL 4/15/08) [921]

8674 Sirvaitis, Karen. *Danica Patrick: Racing's Trailblazer* (6–10). Illus. 2010, Lerner/Twenty-First Century LB $33.26 (978-076135222-8). Visually appealing graphics, excerpts from news stories, and back matter add heft to this well-written biography of racing icon Danica Patrick. (Rev: BL 9/1/10*) [921]

STEWART, TONY

8675 Leebrick, Kristal. *Tony Stewart* (4–7). Series: NASCAR Racing. 2004, Capstone LB $23.93 (978-0-7368-2425-5). This profile of auto racing star Tony Stewart chronicles his meteoric rise from go-karts and midget racers to the top ranks of NASCAR. (Rev: BL 4/1/04) [790.72]

UNSER FAMILY

8676 Bentley, Karen. *The Unsers* (4–8). Series: Race Car Legends: Collector's Edition. 2005, Chelsea House LB $25.00 (978-0-7910-8764-0). The famous Unser automobile racing family is the focus of this book that describes their rivalries with the Andretti family and their victories at important races including the Indianapolis 500. (Rev: SLJ 5/06) [921]

Baseball

AARON, HANK

8677 Morrison, Jessica. *Hank Aaron: Home Run Hero* (5–8). Illus. Series: Crabtree Groundbreakers Biographies. 2010, Crabtree LB $31.93 (978-077872538-1). Morrison covers Hammerin' Hank's life from childhood and his move from the Negro Leagues to major-league baseball. Lexile 1080L (Rev: BL 1/1–15/11) [921]

8678 Spencer, Lauren. *Hank Aaron* (4–7). Series: Baseball Hall of Famers. 2003, Rosen LB $29.25 (978-0-8239-3600-7). In 1974, Hank Aaron, an African American, was crowned home run king, taking the title away from Babe Ruth. This is his story. (Rev: BL 6/1–15/03; SLJ 6/03) [921]

ALOMAR, ROBERTO

8679 Macht, Norman L. *Roberto Alomar* (6–10). Series: Latinos in Baseball. 1999, Mitchell Lane LB $18.95 (978-1-883845-84-1). Using extensive interviews with Alomar, his family, friends, and colleagues, this profile of the famous Puerto Rican baseball player shows his strong self-discipline, work ethic, and close family ties. (Rev: BL 4/15/99; HBG 10/99; SLJ 5/99) [921]

BELL, COOL PAPA

8680 McCormack, Shaun. *Cool Papa Bell* (4–7). Series: Baseball Hall of Famers of the Negro Leagues. 2002, Rosen LB $29.25 (978-0-8239-3474-4). A biography of James Thomas "Cool Papa" Bell of Negro League baseball, who is said to have stolen 175 bases in one season. (Rev: BL 7/02) [921]

BONILLA, BOBBY

8681 Rappoport, Ken. *Bobby Bonilla* (5–9). 1993, Walker LB $15.85 (978-0-8027-8256-4). A biography of the baseball player who rose from poverty in the South Bronx to superstardom and multimillionaire status. (Rev: BL 5/15/93; SLJ 5/93; VOYA 8/93) [921]

CLEMENTE, ROBERTO

8682 Marquez, Heron. *Roberto Clemente: Baseball's Humanitarian Hero* (4–7). 2005, Carolrhoda LB $30.60 (978-1-57505-767-5). The story of the ballplayer, from his birth in Puerto Rico to his death in a plane crash, with photographs. (Rev: BL 3/15/05; SLJ 5/05) [796.357]

8683 Walker, Paul R. *Pride of Puerto Rico: The Life of Roberto Clemente* (4–7). 1988, Harcourt paper $6.00 (978-0-15-263420-9). The life of a baseball star and hero who died trying to help others. (Rev: BL 10/1/88; HB 9–10/88; SLJ 1/89) [921]

GEHRIG, LOU

8684 Buckley, James, Jr. *Lou Gehrig: Iron Horse of Baseball* (5–8). Series: Sterling Biographies. 2010, Sterling $12.95 (978-1-4027-7151-4). Details of Gehrig's life and personality are placed in historical context and enhanced by an appealing layout, plentiful images, and first-person accounts. (Rev: BL 5/1/10; LMC 8–9/10) [921]

8685 Viola, Kevin. *Lou Gehrig* (4–7). Series: Sports Heroes and Legends. 2004, Lerner LB $8.95 (978-0-8225-5311-3). Starting with Gehrig's sad retirement and his "Luckiest Man" speech, this well-written and informative biography goes back to look at his life and successful career. (Rev: BL 9/1/04) [921]

GIBSON, JOSH

8686 Twemlow, Nick. *Josh Gibson* (4–7). Series: Baseball Hall of Famers of the Negro Leagues. 2002, Rosen LB $29.25 (978-0-8239-3475-1). In addition to racial prejudice in the world of baseball, Josh Gibson suffered many personal misfortunes as this life story recounts. (Rev: BL 7/02) [921]

GREENBERG, HANK

8687 Sommer, Shelley. *Hammerin' Hank Greenberg: Baseball Pioneer* (4–7). 2011, Calkins Creek $17.95 (978-1-59078-452-5). Pioneering Jewish baseball player Hank Greenberg overcame considerable prejudice in his time on the diamond during the 1930s and 1940s. Sydney Taylor Book Honor 2012. (Rev: BL 3/1/11; SLJ 4/11; VOYA 8/11) [921]

HERSHISER, OREL

8688 Knapp, Ron. *Orel Hershiser* (5–8). Series: Sports Greats. 1993, Enslow LB $17.95 (978-0-89490-389-2). An easily read sports biography that re-creates the great moments in this baseball star's career up to 1993. (Rev: BL 4/1/93) [921]

IRVIN, MONTE

8689 Haegele, Katie. *Monte Irvin* (4–7). Series: Baseball Hall of Famers of the Negro Leagues. 2002, Rosen LB $29.25 (978-0-8239-3477-5). Though recruited into the Negro leagues when he was 17, Irvin, a very talented player, was past his prime when he finally became a major leaguer. (Rev: BL 7/02) [921]

JETER, DEREK

8690 Robinson, Tom. *Derek Jeter: Captain On and Off the Field* (5–8). Series: Sports Stars with Heart. 2006, Enslow LB $31.93 (978-0-7660-2819-7). This biography focuses primarily on Jeter's career in baseball and his work with the philanthropic Turn 2 Foundation. (Rev: BL 9/1/06) [921]

JOHNSON, JUDY

8691 Billus, Kathleen. *Judy Johnson* (4–7). Series: Baseball Hall of Famers of the Negro Leagues. 2002, Rosen LB $29.25 (978-0-8239-3476-8). A biography of Johnson covering his years as player, coach, manager, and scout, with black-and-white photographs, glossary, timeline, and lists of additional resources. (Rev: BL 7/02) [796.357]

LEONARD, BUCK

8692 Payment, Simone. *Buck Leonard* (4–7). Series: Baseball Hall of Famers of the Negro Leagues. 2002, Rosen LB $29.25 (978-0-8239-3473-7). The story of one of the greatest baseball players of all time, who missed worldwide fame because of his color. (Rev: BL 7/02) [921]

MANTLE, MICKEY

8693 Marlin, John. *Mickey Mantle* (4–7). Series: Sports Heroes and Legends. 2004, Lerner LB $27.93 (978-0-8225-1796-2). A concise, well-written biography that focuses on Mantle's illustrious career. (Rev: BL 9/1/04; SLJ 11/04) [921]

MARTINEZ, PEDRO

8694 Lashnits, Tom. *Pedro Martinez* (6–10). Series: Great Hispanic Heritage. 2006, Chelsea House LB $30 (978-0-7910-8840-1). Baseball fans will enjoy this account of the Red Sox player's life and career. (Rev: SLJ 9/06) [921]

MATSUI, HIDEKI

8695 Beach, Jerry. *Godzilla Takes the Bronx: The Inside Story of Hideki Matsui* (8–12). 2004, Taylor $24.95 (978-1-58979-113-8). A biography of the Japanese baseball player who joined the Yankees. (Rev: BL 3/15/04) [921]

PUJOLS, ALBERT

8696 Buckingham, Mark. *Albert Pujols: MVP On and Off the Field* (4–7). Illus. 2007, Enslow LB $23.95 (978-0-7660-2866-1). Presents facts on the life of the baseball legend, including his childhood in the Dominican Republic, his move to the United States, his career and accomplishments with the St. Louis Cardinals, and his family. (Rev: BL 9/1/07) [921]

ROBINSON, JACKIE

8697 Teitelbaum, Michael. *Jackie Robinson: Champion for Equality* (5–8). Series: Sterling Biographies. 2010, Sterling $12.95 (978-1-4027-7148-4). Details of Robinson's life and personality are placed in historical context and enhanced by an appealing layout, plentiful images, and first-person accounts. (Rev: LMC 8–9/10) [921]

8698 Weidhorn, Manfred. *Jackie Robinson* (6–12). 1993, Atheneum LB $15.95 (978-0-689-31644-9). This biography of the African American legend who integrated baseball in 1947 focuses on the personal qualities of the boy, the man, and the athlete. (Rev: BL 3/15/94; SLJ 2/94; VOYA 4/94) [921]

8699 Wukovits, John F. *Jackie Robinson and the Integration of Baseball* (5–8). Series: Lucent Library of Black History. 2006, Gale LB $32.45 (978-1-59018-913-9).

The social background to Robinson's achievements is well laid out in this biography suitable for report writers. (Rev: SLJ 3/07) [921]

RUTH, BABE

8700 Fischer, David. *Babe Ruth: Legendary Slugger* (5–8). Series: Sterling Biographies. 2010, Sterling $12.95 (978-1-4027-7147-7). Details of Ruth's life and personality are placed in historical context and enhanced by an appealing layout, plentiful images, and first-person accounts. Lexile 1080L (Rev: LMC 8–9/10) [921]

8701 Hampton, Wilborn. *Babe Ruth* (6–9). Illus. Series: Up Close. 2009, Viking $16.99 (978-067006305-5). Hampton covers Ruth's difficult childhood, his fascinating career, and his personal life in this balanced, well-written biography. **e** Lexile 1120L (Rev: BL 3/1/09; HB 5–6/09; SLJ 6/1/09) [921]

8702 Nicholson, Lois. *Babe Ruth: Sultan of Swat* (5–8). 1995, Goodwood $17.95 (978-0-9625427-1-8). This well-written account of the famous slugger explains his lasting influence on baseball. (Rev: SLJ 7/95) [921]

SOSA, SAMMY

8703 Muskat, Carrie. *Sammy Sosa* (6–10). Series: Latinos in Baseball. 1999, Mitchell Lane LB $18.95 (978-1-883845-92-6). This account of Sosa's life tells of his beginning as a poor shoeshine boy in the Dominican Republic and his rise in baseball to his record-setting home run at age 29. (Rev: BL 4/15/99; HBG 10/99; SLJ 5/99) [921]

SUZUKI, ICHIRO

8704 Levin, Judith. *Ichiro Suzuki* (5–8). Illus. Series: Baseball Superstars. 2007, Chelsea House LB $30.00 (978-0-7910-9440-2). A biography of the record-setting, award-winning Seattle Mariners player from Japan. (Rev: BL 3/18/08) [921]

8705 Stewart, Mark. *Ichiro Suzuki: Best in the West* (4–7). Series: Sports New Wave. 2002, Millbrook LB $22.90 (978-0-7613-2616-8). A well-constructed biography of the famous Japanese Seattle Mariners player that offers information on the game itself as well as statistics, color photographs, and quotations that illustrate his achievements. (Rev: BL 9/1/02; HBG 3/03) [796.357]

Basketball

BRYANT, KOBE

8706 Savage, Jeff. *Kobe Bryant: Basketball Big Shot* (4–7). Series: Sports Biography. 2000, Lerner LB $22.60 (978-0-8225-3680-2). A very readable, attractive biography of the new NBA sensation that ends with the

1999–2000 season. (Rev: BL 1/1–15/01; HBG 10/01) [921]

DUNCAN, TIM

8707 Adams, Sean. *Tim Duncan* (4–7). Series: Sports Heroes and Legends. 2004, Lerner LB $27.93 (978-0-8225-1793-1). A balanced, well-crafted life of the basketball star. (Rev: BL 9/1/04) [921]

8708 Stewart, Mark. *Tim Duncan: Tower of Power* (4–8). Series: Basketball's New Wave. 1999, Millbrook LB $22.90 (978-0-7613-1513-1). Although this biography of basketball's rising star is brief, the information is ample and important topics are all covered. (Rev: HBG 10/00; SLJ 7/00) [921]

GARNETT, KEVIN

8709 Stewart, Mark. *Kevin Garnett: Shake Up the Game* (4–7). Series: Sports New Wave. 2002, Millbrook LB $22.90 (978-0-7613-2615-1). A short biography that chronicles the career of the new star of the Minnesota Timberwolves. (Rev: BL 9/1/02; HBG 10/02) [921]

HILL, GRANT

8710 Rappoport, Ken. *Grant Hill* (6–9). 1996, Walker LB $16.85 (978-0-8027-8456-8). The story of the basketball star, from the AAU National Basketball Championship at age 13 through high school, where he played on the varsity team as a freshman, and his college years playing at Duke, to the Detroit Pistons, where he was the NBA Rookie of the Year. (Rev: BL 1/1–15/97; SLJ 1/97; VOYA 8/97) [796.323]

JAMES, LEBRON

8711 Morgan, David Lee, Jr. *LeBron James* (7–12). 2003, Gray & Company paper $14.95 (978-1-886228-74-0). The biography of the African American basketball superstar who came from a culture of poverty and drugs to reach the peak of the sports world. (Rev: BL 2/15/04; SLJ 6/04) [921]

JORDAN, MICHAEL

8712 Aaseng, Nathan. *Michael Jordan* (5–8). Series: Sports Greats. 1992, Enslow LB $17.95 (978-0-89490-370-0). Michael Jordan's life, his successes as guard of the Chicago Bulls, and his commercials for TV are discussed in this easily read book. (Rev: BL 10/15/92) [921]

8713 Berger, Phil, and John Rolfe. *Michael Jordan* (4–7). 1990, Little, Brown paper $4.95 (978-0-316-09229-6). This account covers Jordan's childhood and his career development. (Rev: BL 12/15/90; SLJ 4/91) [921]

8714 Lovitt, Chip. *Michael Jordan* (6–10). 1998, Scholastic paper $4.50 (978-0-590-59644-2). This quick read, an update of the 1993 edition, traces Jordan's

remarkable career from a young age to the end of the Chicago Bulls' 1998 season. (Rev: VOYA 4/99) [921]

KIDD, JASON

8715 Gray, Valerie A. *Jason Kidd: Star Guard* (5–8). Series: Sports Reports. 2000, Enslow LB $20.95 (978-0-7660-1333-9). The story of the basketball superstar with behind-the-scenes reporting on his life and career. (Rev: BL 10/15/00; HBG 10/00) [921]

LIEBERMAN-CLINE, NANCY

8716 Greenberg, Doreen, and Michael Greenberg. *A Drive to Win: The Story of Nancy Lieberman-Cline* (4–8). Illus. by Phil Velikan. Series: Anything You Can Do — New Sports Heroes for Girls. 2000, Wish paper $9.95 (978-1-930546-40-0). Based on personal interviews, this is an informative biography of the basketball star Lieberman-Cline. (Rev: SLJ 3/01; VOYA 2/01) [921]

MING, YAO

8717 Clark, Travis. *Yao Ming* (5–8). Series: Modern Role Models. 2008, Mason Crest LB $22.95 (978-1-4222-0484-9). Yao Ming's great basketball career, his generous charitable works, and his influences are examined in this book, part of a high-interest biography series that includes a section with information on awards, events, and organizations. (Rev: SLJ 2/09) [921]

8718 Krawiec, Richard. *Yao Ming: Gentle Giant of Basketball* (6–8). 2004, Avisson paper $19.95 (978-1-888105-63-6). This story of the Chinese basketball player's path to stardom brings up interesting questions about the business and patriotic aspects of professional sports. (Rev: BL 2/15/04; SLJ 3/04) [790.323]

8719 Ming, Yao, and Ric Bucher. *Yao: A Life in Two Worlds* (8–12). 2004, Miramax $22.95 (978-1-4013-5214-1). Yao Ming writes of his success in the NBA and also of the sharp contrast between the culture of his native China and that of the United States. (Rev: BL 9/1/04) [796.323]

MULLIN, CHRIS

8720 Morgan, Terri, and Shmuel Thaler. *Chris Mullin: Sure Shot* (4–8). Series: Sports Achievers. 1994, Lerner LB $10.13 (978-0-8225-2887-6). The story of this amazing basketball star who overcame many obstacles, including alcoholism. (Rev: BL 1/1/95; SLJ 1/95) [921]

NUNEZ, TOMMY

8721 Marvis, Barbara. *Tommy Nunez, NBA Referee: Taking My Best Shot* (6–10). 1996, Mitchell Lane paper $12.95 (978-1-883845-28-5). The story of the youngster who grew up in the poverty of Phoenix's barrio to become the first Mexican American referee in the NBA. (Rev: BL 5/15/96; SLJ 3/96; VOYA 6/96) [921]

O'NEAL, SHAQUILLE

8722 Sullivan, Michael J. *Shaquille O'Neal* (5–8). Series: Sports Greats. 1998, Enslow LB $22.60 (978-0-7660-1003-1). The life and career of this well-known basketball star are covered in this easily read biography containing career statistics and many illustrations. (Rev: BL 2/15/99; HBG 10/99) [921]

WEST, JERRY

8723 Ramen, Fred. *Jerry West* (5–8). Series: Basketball Hall of Famers. 2002, Rosen LB $29.25 (978-0-8239-3482-9). Facts, stories, and full-color photographs are used to bring alive the story of this basketball great, with material on his NBA career and beyond. (Rev: BL 9/1/02) [921]

Boxing

ALI, MUHAMMAD

8724 *Muhammad Ali* (6–10). 1997, Random House $20.00 (978-0-517-20080-3). Using plenty of sidebars, quotations from his poetry, and photographs, this excellent biography, based on A&E cable TV's *Biography* show, traces the boxer's life from his days as a scrawny kid named Cassius Clay, Jr. to his becoming "the greatest," ending with the 1996 lighting of the Olympic torch in Atlanta. (Rev: VOYA 8/98) [921]

8725 Smith, Charles R. *Twelve Rounds to Glory: The Story of Muhammad Ali* (5–8). Illus. by Bryan Collier. 2007, Candlewick $19.99 (978-0-7636-1692-2). Twelve poems and dynamic mixed-media pictures illustrate the drama of Ali's victories and his life's struggles. Coretta Scott King Author Honor Book, 2008. (Rev: BL 2/1/08; SLJ 12/07)

8726 Timblin, Stephen. *Muhammad Ali: King of the Ring* (5–8). Series: Sterling Biographies. 2010, Sterling $12.95 (978-1-4027-7152-1). Details of Ali's life and personality are placed in historical context and enhanced by an appealing layout, plentiful images, and first-person accounts. (Rev: BL 5/1/10; LMC 8–9/10) [921]

HAWKINS, DWIGHT

8727 Hawkins, Dwight, and Morrie Greenberg. *Survival in the Square* (7–10). 1989, Richards paper $5.95 (978-0-9622652-0-4). The story of an African American who overcame a physical handicap and became a boxing champion. (Rev: BL 11/15/89; VOYA 12/89) [921]

LOUIS, JOE

8728 Sullivan, George. *Knockout! A Photobiography of Boxer Joe Louis* (6–9). Illus. 2008, National Geographic $17.95 (978-142630328-9); LB $27.90 (978-142630329-6). The dramatic story of the African American boxer who fought against racism and poverty—as well as German boxer Max Schmeling—in the years leading up to World War II. Lexile 830L (Rev: BL 1/1–15/09; LMC 5–6/09; SLJ 2/1/09; VOYA 10/09) [921]

Football

8729 Stewart, Mark. *Randy Moss: First in Flight* (4–8). Series: Football's New Wave. 2000, Millbrook LB $22.90 (978-0-7613-1518-6). The story of the footballer who came from a poor, segregated West Virginia town, was arrested as a young man, but went on to attend college and play professional football. (Rev: HBG 10/00; SLJ 1/01) [921]

BETTIS, JEROME

8730 Majewski, Stephen. *Jerome Bettis* (5–8). Series: Sports Greats. 1997, Enslow LB $17.95 (978-0-89490-872-9). The great football hero Jerome Bettis and his amazing career are highlighted in this easily read biography. (Rev: BL 2/15/97; VOYA 6/97) [921]

CULPEPPER, DAUNTE

8731 Stewart, Mark. *Daunte Culpepper: Command and Control* (4–7). Series: Sports New Wave. 2002, Millbrook LB $22.90 (978-0-7613-2613-7). This brief biography celebrates the career of the young African American footballer and his achievements as quarterback of the Minnesota Vikings. (Rev: BL 9/1/02; HBG 10/02) [921]

DAVIS, TERRELL

8732 Stewart, Mark. *Terrell Davis: Toughing It Out* (4–8). Series: Football's New Wave. 1999, Millbrook LB $22.90 (978-0-7613-1514-8). A brief biography of this football hero that uses color photographs and many fact boxes. (Rev: HBG 10/00; SLJ 7/00) [921]

JACKSON, BO

8733 Devaney, John. *Bo Jackson: A Star for All Seasons* (5–7). 1992, Walker LB $15.85 (978-0-8027-8179-6). Biography of the Kansas City Royals baseball star, who also played pro football for the Los Angeles Raiders. (Rev: BL 2/15/89; SLJ 1/89) [921]

MANNING, PEYTON

8734 Crompton, Samuel Willard. *Peyton Manning* (7–10). Illus. Series: Football Superstars. 2008, Chelsea House LB $30 (978-079109605-5). Star quarterback Peyton Manning's childhood, school years, and early career are documented in this well-organized book with a chronology, statistics, and play-by-plays. (Rev: BLO 8/08) [921]

RICE, JERRY

8735 Dickey, Glenn. *Jerry Rice* (5–8). Series: Sports Greats. 1993, Enslow LB $17.95 (978-0-89490-419-6). A brief biography of the star football player who gained fame with the San Francisco 49ers. (Rev: BL 9/15/93) [921]

SANDERS, BARRY

8736 Knapp, Ron. *Barry Sanders* (5–8). Series: Sports Greats. 1993, Enslow LB $17.95 (978-0-89490-418-9). This brief biography of the star football player contains many action photographs and a separate section on his career statistics. (Rev: BL 9/15/93) [921]

Gymnastics

DAWES, DOMINIQUE

8737 Washburn, Kim. *Heart of a Champion: The Dominique Dawes Story* (5–8). Series: Zonderkidz Biography. 2012, Zonderkidz paper $6.99 (978-0-310-72268-7). A profile of the African American Olympic gymnast, emphasizing her ability to bounce back from disappointments, her religious faith, and her later career as a spokesperson. (Rev: BL 6/12; SLJ 8/1/12) [921]

Ice Skating and Hockey

BOITANO, BRIAN

8738 Boitano, Brian, and Suzanne Harper. *Boitano's Edge: Inside the Real World of Figure Skating* (4–8). 1997, Simon & Schuster $25.00 (978-0-689-81915-5). In this autobiography, Boitano tells about his life, the 1988 Olympics, his training programs, touring, and preparing for competitions. (Rev: BCCB 3/98; BL 2/15/98; SLJ 4/98; VOYA 4/98) [921]

FORREST, ALBERT

8739 McFarlane, Brian. *The Youngest Goalie* (6–9). 1997, Warwick paper $8.95 (978-1-895629-95-8). This is an exciting, fictionalized biography of Albert Forrest, who was born in 1887 and became the youngest goalie to play in a Stanley Cup final. (Rev: VOYA 2/99) [921]

KWAN, MICHELLE

8740 Koestler-Grack, Rachel A. *Michelle Kwan* (7–10). 2007, Chelsea House LB $30.00 (978-0-7910-9273-6). Details the accomplishments of figure skater Kwan and provides information about her training, competition, and her life off the ice. (Rev: BL 9/1/07) [920]

LEMIEUX, MARIO

8741 Stewart, Mark. *Mario Lemieux: Own the Ice* (5–8). 2002, Millbrook LB $24.90 (978-0-7613-2555-0); paper $8.95 (978-0-7613-1687-9). A readable biography of the ice hockey star, with photographs, statistics, and information about the athlete's personal life and work ethic. (Rev: BL 9/15/02; HBG 3/03) [796.962]

OHNO, APOLO ANTON

8742 Aldridge, Rebecca. *Apolo Anton Ohno* (7–10). Series: Asian Americans of Achievement. 2009, Chelsea House $30 (978-1-60413-565-7). Son of a Japanese father, Ohno has won medals as a speed skater at the Olympics. (Rev: SLJ 2/10) [921]

8743 Robison, Ken. *Apolo Ohno* (6–9). Illus. Series: Xtreme Athletes. 2011, Morgan Reynolds LB $28.95 (978-159935186-5). An appealing profile of the short track speed skaters who has won many Olympic medals and a *Dancing with the Stars* championship. (Rev: BL 2/1/12) [921]

8744 Uschan, Michael V. *Apolo Anton Ohno* (6–9). Illus. Series: People in the News. 2011, Gale/Lucent LB $33.45 (978-142050603-7). With well-chosen photographs and accessible text, this is an interesting profile of the champion speed skater. (Rev: BL 4/15/12) [921]

WICKENHEISER, HAYLEY

8745 Etue, Elizabeth. *Hayley Wickenheiser: Born to Play* (4–7). 2005, Kids Can paper $6.95 (978-1-55337-791-7). The story of Canadian-born Wickenheiser, a member of Canada's gold medal-winning women's ice hockey team at the Salt Lake City Olympics, who went on to become the first woman to play professional hockey. (Rev: BL 9/1/05) [921]

Tennis

AGASSI, ANDRE

8746 Savage, Jeff. *Andre Agassi: Reaching the Top — Again* (4–8). Series: Sports Achievers. 1997, Lerner paper $9.55 (978-0-8225-9750-6). A short, easily read biography of this volatile tennis star. (Rev: BL 1/1–15/98; HBG 3/98) [921]

ASHE, ARTHUR

8747 Cunningham, Kevin. *Arthur Ashe: Athlete and Activist* (5–8). Series: Journey to Freedom: The African American Library. 2005, Child's World LB $28.50 (978-1-59296-228-0). Chronicles the Virginia-born athlete's rise to tennis stardom and his involvement in the fight against apartheid. (Rev: BL 2/1/05) [921]

8748 Lazo, Caroline Evensen. *Arthur Ashe* (4–7). Series: A&E Biography. 1999, Lerner $25.26 (978-0-8225-1932-4). The inspiring story of this great African American tennis star and humanitarian is told in a clear, well-organized text with several black-and-white photographs. (Rev: BL 3/15/00) [921]

WILLIAMS, VENUS AND SERENA

8749 Bailey, Diane. *Venus and Serena Williams: Tennis Champions* (5–8). Illus. Series: Sports Families. 2010, Rosen LB $26.50 (978-143583552-8). Bailey tells the story of the sisters' childhood in California and their famous rivalry on the courts. (Rev: BL 9/1/10) [921]

Track and Field

BOLT, USAIN

8750 Cantor, George. *Usain Bolt* (6–9). Illus. Series: People in the News. 2011, Gale/Lucent LB $33.45 (978-142050341-8). With well-chosen photographs and accessible text, this is a straightforward profile of the Jamaican runner. (Rev: BL 4/15/12) [921]

JOYNER-KERSEE, JACKIE

8751 Harrington, Geri. *Jackie Joyner-Kersee: Champion Athlete* (6–10). 1995, Chelsea LB $21.95 (978-0-7910-2085-2). Describes Joyner-Kersee's four Olympic championships, despite asthma attacks. (Rev: BL 10/1/95) [921]

LEWIS, RAY

8752 Cooper, John. *Rapid Ray: The Story of Ray Lewis* (5–9). 2002, Tundra paper $8.95 (978-0-88776-612-1). An absorbing profile of the Canadian-born black athlete (and train porter) who won a bronze medal in the 1932 Olympics and the racial hurdles he had to overcome. (Rev: SLJ 6/03) [796.42]

LONGBOAT, TOM

8753 Batten, Jack. *The Man Who Ran Faster Than Everyone: The Story of Tom Longboat* (7–12). 2002, Tundra paper $12.95 (978-0-88776-507-0). A straightforward biography of the Onondaga Indian distance runner who won fame in the early 20th century. (Rev: BL 4/1/02; SLJ 6/02) [796.42]

OWENS, JESSE

8754 Burlingame, Jeff. *Jesse Owens: "I Always Loved Running"* (6–8). Illus. Series: African-American Biography Library. 2011, Enslow LB $31.93 (978-076603497-6). Covers Owens's life from his sickly childhood to his Olympic success. (Rev: BL 2/1/11) [921]

8755 Gigliotti, Jim. *Jesse Owens: Gold Medal Hero* (5–8). Series: Sterling Biographies. 2010, Sterling $12.95 (978-1-4027-7149-1). Details of Owens's life and personality are placed in historical context and enhanced by an appealing layout, plentiful images, and first-person accounts. Lexile 1040L (Rev: LMC 8–9/10) [921]

THORPE, JIM

8756 Bruchac, Joseph. *Jim Thorpe: Original All-American* (5–8). 2006, Dial $16.99 (978-0-8037-3118-9). Using the first person, this biography chronicles the Native American's youth, his amazing sporting abilities, and his quiet determination to overcome barriers. (Rev: BL 6/1–15/06; SLJ 8/06)

8757 Crawford, Bill. *All American: The Rise and Fall of Jim Thorpe* (8–12). 2004, Wiley $32.50 (978-0-471-55732-6). An in-depth look at the tumultuous life of the Native American athlete who triumphed on the world's playing fields but ultimately died in relative obscurity. (Rev: BL 11/15/04) [796]

8758 Labrecque, Ellen. *Jim Thorpe: An Athlete for the Ages* (5–8). Series: Sterling Biographies. 2010, Sterling $12.95 (978-1-4027-7150-7). Details of Thorpe's life and personality are placed in historical context and enhanced by an appealing layout, plentiful images, and first-person accounts. (Rev: BL 5/1/10; LMC 8–9/10) [921]

8759 Schuman, Michael A. *Jim Thorpe: "There's No Such Thing as 'Can't'"* (5–8). Series: Americans — The Spirit of a Nation. 2009, Enslow LB $31.93 (978-0-7660-3021-3). A dramatic introduction draws readers into this informative and accessible account of Thorpe's life and achievements. (Rev: LMC 11–12/09; SLJ 9/09) [921]

Miscellaneous Sports

ARMSTRONG, LANCE

8760 Benson, Michael. *Lance Armstrong: Cyclist* (5–8). Series: Ferguson Career Biographies. 2003, Ferguson LB $25.00 (978-0-8160-5479-4). Traces the inspiring life of the great bicycle-racer through his fifth Tour de France win, with an emphasis on his perseverance and optimism. (Rev: SLJ 5/04) [796.6]

8761 Coyle, Daniel. *Lance Armstrong's War: One Man's Battle Against Fate, Fame, Love, Death, Scandal, and a Few Other Rivals on the Road to the Tour de France* (8–12). 2005, HarperCollins $25.95 (978-0-06-073794-8). Traces Armstrong's winning 2004 season and reviews the daunting challenges the cyclist has had to overcome in his life. (Rev: BL 6/1–15/05) [796.6]

BASS, TOM

8762 Wilkerson, J. L. *From Slave to World-Class Horseman: Tom Bass* (4–8). 2000, Acorn paper $9.95 (978-0-9664470-3-3). A fast-paced narrative about the man who was born a slave and later became such a renowned horseman that he performed for Queen Victoria. (Rev: SLJ 4/00) [921]

CENA, JOHN

8763 Sandler, Michael. *John Cena* (4–7). Illus. Series: Wrestling's Tough Guys. 2012, Bearport LB $23.93 (978-161772573-9). Sandler tells the story of the bullied youngster who grew up to be a wrestling champ. (Rev: BL 10/1/12) [921]

HAMILTON, BETHANY

8764 Hamilton, Bethany. *Soul Surfer: A True Story of Faith, Family, and Fighting to Get Back on the Board* (6–9). 2004, Pocket $18.00 (978-0-7434-9922-4). Bethany Hamilton, the teenage surfer who lost an arm in a shark attack off Kauai in 2003, tells how her family and faith helped to sustain her and give her the courage to return to surfing. (Rev: BL 1/1–15/05) [797.1]

HAWK, TONY

8765 Hawk, Tony, and Sean Mortimer. *Hawk: Occupation, Skateboarder* (8–12). 2000, Regan paper $15.00 (978-0-06-095831-2). The biography of a man who, during a rebellious youth, discovered skateboarding and was determined to excel at it. [921]

8766 Peterson, Todd. *Tony Hawk: Skateboarder and Businessman* (8–11). Series: Ferguson Career Biographies. 2005, Ferguson LB $25.00 (978-0-8160-5893-8). Skateboarder Tony Hawk's childhood, skating career, and business achievements are all covered in this readable volume. (Rev: BL 9/1/05) [796.22]

KAHANAMOKU, DUKE

8767 Crowe, Ellie. *Surfer of the Century: The Life of Duke Kahanamoku* (4–7). Illus. by Richard Waldrep. 2007, Lee & Low $18.95 (978-1-58430-276-6). A wonderfully illustrated picture-book biography of Duke Kahanamoku, an Olympic Gold Medal swimmer and well-known surfer from Hawaii who was born in 1890. (Rev: BL 9/1/07; SLJ 10/07)

LESNAR, BROCK

8768 Savage, Jeff. *Brock Lesnar* (6–9). Illus. Series: Xtreme Athletes. 2011, Morgan Reynolds LB $28.95 (978-159935185-8). An appealing profile of the wrestler who found success as both an amateur and professional. (Rev: BL 2/1/12; VOYA 10/12) [921]

LOPEZ, NANCY

8769 Sharp, Anne Wallace. *Nancy Lopez: Golf Hall of Famer* (6–10). Illus. Series: 20th Century's Most Influential Hispanics. 2008, Gale/Lucent LB $32.45 (978-142050060-8). Sharp highlights the various obstacles Lopez faced as she rose to prominence in a male-dominated sport in this appealing profile. (Rev: BL 9/1/08) [921]

MONPLAISIR, SHARON

8770 Greenberg, Doreen, and Michael Greenberg. *Sword of a Champion: The Story of Sharon Monplaisir* (4–8). Illus. by Phil Velikan. Series: Anything You Can Do — New Sports Heroes for Girls. 2000, Wish paper $9.95 (978-1-930546-39-4). The life story of the timid, shy high schooler who found her place in fencing via a coach who encouraged her to develop her natural talents. (Rev: SLJ 3/01; VOYA 2/01) [796.8]

PAK, SE RI

8771 Stewart, Mark. *Se Ri Pak: Driven to Win* (4–8). Series: Golf's New Wave. 2000, Millbrook LB $22.90 (978-0-7613-1519-3). The story of the South Korean who won the Ladies Professional Golf Association Championship in 1998. (Rev: HBG 10/00; SLJ 8/00) [921]

PELE (SOCCER PLAYER)

8772 Buckley, James. *Pele* (6–9). Series: DK Biographies. 2007, DK $14.99 (978-0-7566-2996-0); paper $4.99 (978-0-7566-2987-8). Profiles the childhood, life, and extraordinary career of the Brazilian soccer legend. (Rev: BL 9/1/07) [921]

REECE, GABRIELLE

8773 Morgan, Terri. *Gabrielle Reece: Volleyball's Model Athlete* (4–7). Series: Sports Achievers. 1999, Lerner LB $22.60 (978-0-8225-3667-3). An accessible biography of the woman who is not only a volleyball champ but also a fashion model and TV personality. (Rev: BL 10/15/99; HBG 3/00) [921]

ROSENFELD, FANNY BOBBIE

8774 Dublin, Anne. *Bobbie Rosenfeld: The Olympian Who Could Do Everything* (5–8). 2004, Second Story paper $11.95 (978-1-896764-82-5). Fanny Bobbie Rosenfeld migrated from the Ukraine to Canada in 1905, became an outstanding athlete excelling in many sports, and led the Canadian women's relay team to an Olympic gold in 1928. Sidney Taylor Book Honor 2004. (Rev: BL 9/1/04) [921]

TAYLOR, MARSHALL B.

8775 Brill, Marlene Targ. *Marshall "Major" Taylor: World Champion Bicyclist, 1899–1901* (5–8). Series: Trailblazer Biographies. 2007, Lerner LB $31.93 (978-

0-8225-6610-6). An inspiring profile of the first African American world cycling champion and his struggles with racism. (Rev: BL 9/1/07) [921]

WHITE, SHAUN

8776 Schweitzer, Karen. *Shaun White* (5–8). Series: Modern Role Models. 2008, Mason Crest LB $22.95 (978-1-4222-0493-1). Shaun White's story of how he became the best snowboarder and skateboarder is detailed in this book, a high-interest biography that includes information on awards, events, and organizations. (Rev: SLJ 2/09; VOYA 8/09) [921]

WHITFIELD, SIMON

8777 Whitfield, Simon, and Cleve Dheensaw. *Simon Says Gold: Simon Whitfield's Pursuit of Athletic Excellence* (7–12). 2009, Orca paper $14 (978-1-55469-141-8). In this illustrated biography, Whitfield chronicles his successes, failures, and eventual rise to Olympic stardom. (Rev: BLO 11/20/09; SLJ 1/10; VOYA 6/10) [921]

WIE, MICHELLE

8778 Young, Jeff C. *Michelle Wie* (6–9). Illus. Series: Xtreme Athletes. 2011, Morgan Reynolds LB $28.95 (978-159935187-2). A profile of the Korean American (born in Hawaii) champion golfer. (Rev: BL 2/1/12; VOYA 10/12) [921]

WOODS, TIGER

8779 Collins, David R. *Tiger Woods, Golfing Champion* (5–8). Illus. by Larry Nolte. 1999, Pelican $14.95 (978-1-56554-322-5). A chronologically arranged book end-ing in 1999 that reveals Tiger Woods's determination and love of the game. (Rev: SLJ 1/00) [921]

8780 Roberts, Jeremy. *Tiger Woods: Golf's Master* (5–8). Illus. Series: USA Today Lifeline Biographies. 2008, Lerner LB $33.26 (978-158013569-6). Newsy sidebars, photographs, personal stories, and historical context enrich this well-designed biography that also provides thorough descriptions of golf and its gear. (Rev: BL 9/1/08; LMC 3–4/09; SLJ 11/1/08) [921]

ZAHARIAS, BABE DIDRIKSON

8781 Cayleff, Susan E. *Babe Didrikson: The Greatest All-Sport Athlete of All Time* (7–12). 2000, Conari paper $8.95 (978-1-57324-194-6). A candid, honest look at the life of this difficult, brash, competitive golf legend. (Rev: BL 10/1/00; VOYA 8/01) [921]

8782 Freedman, Russell. *Babe Didrikson Zaharias: The Making of a Champion* (6–12). 1999, Clarion $19.00 (978-0-395-63367-0). Although she was known to most for her golf career, this entertaining biography points out that Babe Didrikson Zaharias was also an Olympic athlete, a track star, leader of a women's amateur basketball team, and an entrepreneur. (Rev: BCCB 10/99; BL 7/99; HB 9–10/99; HBG 3/00; SLJ 7/99; VOYA 12/00) [921]

8783 Wakeman, Nancy. *Babe Didrikson Zaharias: Driven to Win* (4–7). Series: Biography. 2000, Lerner LB $27.93 (978-0-8225-4917-8). The account focuses on this sportswoman's professional career and her strong personality plus her accomplishments in track and field, basketball, and baseball. (Rev: BL 6/1–15/00; HBG 10/00; SLJ 7/00; VOYA 12/00) [921]

World Figures

Collective

8784 Aaseng, Nathan. *The Peace Seekers: The Nobel Peace Prize* (5–8). 1987, Lerner paper $7.95 (978-0-8225-9604-2). Martin Luther King, Jr., and Lech Walesa are among those whose lives and works are introduced. (Rev: BL 2/1/88) [327.1720922]

8785 Axelrod-Contrada, Joan. *Women Who Led Nations* (7–10). Series: Profiles. 1999, Oliver LB $19.95 (978-1-881508-48-9). Corazon Aquino, Benazir Bhutto, and Golda Meir are among the seven women profiled in detail in this collective biography. (Rev: HBG 4/00; SLJ 10/99) [920]

8786 Baker, Rosalie F., and Charles F. Baker. *Ancient Egyptians: People of the Pyramids* (6–12). Series: Oxford Profiles. 2001, Oxford $55.00 (978-0-19-512221-3). Detailed biographies of key figures such as Nefertiti, Hatshepsut, Tutankhamen, and Ramses give plenty of background social and cultural information and are accompanied by sidebar features and black-and-white photographs. (Rev: BL 9/15/01; HBG 10/02; SLJ 11/01) [920.032]

8787 Bardhan-Quallen, Sudipta. *The Mexican-American War* (5–9). Series: People at the Center Of. 2005, Gale LB $24.95 (978-1-56711-927-5). After an overview of the war, this volume provides biographical information on key figures including James K. Polk, Abraham Lincoln, Santa Anna, and Zachary Taylor. (Rev: SLJ 6/05) [920]

8788 Benjamin, Michelle, and Maggie Mooney. *Nobel's Women of Peace* (6–9). Illus. Series: Women's Hall of Fame. 2008, Second Story paper $10.95 (978-189718738-8). The inspiring stories of 12 female Nobel laureates from around the world. (Rev: BL 1/1–15/09; VOYA 2/09) [920]

8789 Benson, Sonia G. *Korean War: Biographies* (6–10). 2001, Gale LB $70.00 (978-0-7876-5692-8). A collection of 25 biographies of individuals — Koreans, Americans, and other nationalities — who participated in or affected the course of the Korean War. (Rev: BL 3/15/02; SLJ 5/02) [920]

8790 Blue, Rose, and Corinne J. Naden. *People of Peace* (4–7). 1994, Millbrook LB $26.90 (978-1-56294-409-4). Brief biographies of 10 people in modern history who have made great sacrifices for world peace, including Mohandas Gandhi and Desmond Tutu. (Rev: BL 12/15/94; SLJ 2/95) [920]

8791 Butts, Ed. *She Dared: True Stories of Heroines, Scoundrels, and Renegades* (6–9). Illus. by Heather Collins. 2005, Tundra paper $8.95 (978-0-88776-718-0). Engaging profiles of 15 diverse women who defied social norms. (Rev: BL 12/1/05; SLJ 12/05) [920.72]

8792 Chin-Lee, Cynthia. *Amelia to Zora: Twenty-Six Women Who Changed the World* (4–7). 2005, Charlesbridge $15.95 (978-1-57091-522-2). Brief information on 26 remarkable and varied women (scientists, artists, athletes, inventors) along with beautiful artwork and quotations from the subjects. (Rev: BL 4/1/05*; SLJ 4/05) [920.72]

8793 Cotter, Charis. *Kids Who Rule: The Remarkable Lives of Five Child Monarchs* (5–8). Illus. 2007, Annick $24.95 (978-1-55451-062-7); paper $14.95 (978-1-55451-061-0). King Tutankhamen, Mary Queen of Scots, Queen Christina of Sweden, Emperor Puyi of China, and the fourteenth Dalai Lama are the young rulers included in this interesting book that provides historical context. (Rev: BL 12/15/07)

8794 Gifford, Clive. *10 Kings and Queens Who Changed the World* (4–8). Illus. by David Cousens. 2009, Kingfisher $14.99 (978-0-7534-6252-2). With compelling, graphic-novel style artwork, Gifford presents ten of the most notable and influential royal leaders — from

Hatshepsut to Elizabeth I — through clear, concise paragraphs in this snazzy research guide. (Rev: BL 6/1–15/09; SLJ 7/09) [929.7]

8795 Haskins, Jim. *African Heroes* (5–8). Series: Black Stars. 2005, Wiley $24.95 (978-0-471-46672-7). Profiles 27 important Africans, both contemporary and from the past, in entries of varying length. (Rev: SLJ 7/05) [920]

8796 Hazell, Rebecca. *Heroines: Great Women Through the Ages* (5–8). 1996, Abbeville $19.95 (978-0-7892-0210-9). This is a collective biography of 12 great women spanning the period from ancient Greece to modern times, including Sacagawea, Madame Sun Yat-Sen, Frido Kahlo, Joan of Arc, Harriet Tubman, and Marie Curie. (Rev: SLJ 12/96) [920]

8797 Humphrey, Sandra McLeod. *Dare to Dream! 25 Extraordinary Lives* (4–7). 2005, Prometheus paper $15.98 (978-1-59102-280-0). Twenty-five individuals — including artists, athletes, politicians, and scientists — who overcame obstacles to achieve greatness are profiled, with information on childhood and adult life. (Rev: BL 3/1/05; SLJ 6/05) [920]

8798 Hunter, Ryan Ann. *In Disguise: Stories of Real Women Spies* (5–8). 2004, Beyond Words paper $9.95 (978-1-58270-095-3). Profiles 26 women who risked their lives to spy for causes in which they believed, from 1640 to the Cold War. (Rev: SLJ 8/04) [920]

8799 Krull, Kathleen. *Lives of Extraordinary Women: Rulers, Rebels (and What the Neighbors Thought)* (5–8). Series: Extraordinary Lives. 2000, Harcourt $20.00 (978-0-15-200807-9). Short biographies of women who affected the course of history, from Cleopatra to contemporary Burma's Aung San Suu Kyi. (Rev: BCCB 9/00; BL 9/1/00; HB 11–12/00; HBG 3/01; SLJ 9/00; VOYA 6/01) [920]

8800 Leon, Vicki. *Outrageous Women of the Middle Ages* (4–7). 1998, Wiley paper $12.95 (978-0-471-17004-4). Using a witty writing style and modern comparisons, this fascinating book profiles a diverse group of amazing women who lived from the 6th through the 14th centuries in Europe, Asia, and Africa. (Rev: BL 4/15/98; SLJ 8/98) [920]

8801 Meltzer, Milton. *Ten Kings and the Worlds They Ruled* (5–8). Illus. by Bethanne Andersen. 2002, Scholastic paper $21.95 (978-0-439-31293-6). Ten kings from around the world and across the ages are discussed in this attractive book that includes impressive portraits and other illustrations. Also use *Ten Queens* (1998). (Rev: BCCB 9/02; BL 7/02; HBG 10/02; SLJ 10/02*) [920.02]

8802 Phibbs, Cheryl Fisher, ed. *Pioneers of Human Rights* (8–11). Series: Profiles in History. 2005, Gale LB $36.20 (978-0-7377-2146-1). Among the figures profiled in this volume are Mohandas Gandhi, Freder-

ick Douglass, Nelson Mandela, and Eleanor Roosevelt. (Rev: BL 7/05) [323]

8803 Pouy, Jean-Bernard. *The Big Book of Dummies, Rebels and Other Geniuses* (7–10). Illus. by Serge Bloch. 2008, Enchanted Lion $19.95 (978-159270103-2). This often funny, irreverently illustrated book showcases the unlikely, often chaotic beginnings of 26 prominent figures in art, science, literature, and history, from Charlemagne and Dumas to Pablo Picasso and Agatha Christie. (Rev: BLO 10/7/08; SLJ 9/1/08; VOYA 8/08) [920]

8804 Price-Groff, Claire. *Twentieth-Century Women Political Leaders* (7–10). Series: Global Profiles. 1998, Facts on File LB $25.00 (978-0-8160-3672-1). A look at 12 women political leaders in the second half of the 20th century: Golda Meir, Indira Gandhi, Eva Peron, Margaret Thatcher, Corazon Aquino, Winnie Mandela, Barbara Jordan, Violeta Chamorro, Wilma Mankiller, Gro Harlem Brundtland, Aung San Suu Kyi, and Benazir Bhutto. (Rev: SLJ 1/99) [920]

8805 Sanderson, Ruth. *More Saints: Lives and Illuminations* (4–7). Illus. 2007, Eerdmans $20.00 (978-0-8028-5272-4). A sequel to *Saints: Lives and Illuminations* (2003), this volume adds profiles of 36 saints, this time of the second millennium. (Rev: BL 2/1/07)

8806 Scandiffio, Laura. *Evil Masters: The Frightening World of Tyrants* (7–10). 2005, Annick $24.95 (978-1-55037-895-5); paper $12.95 (978-1-55037-894-8). Nero, Ivan the Terrible, Hitler, Stalin, and Saddam Hussein are five of the seven rulers profiled; an introduction discusses personality traits and the reasons why such men are able to assume power. (Rev: SLJ 1/06) [920]

8807 Scandiffio, Laura. *People Who Said No: Courage Against Oppression* (8–11). Illus. 2012, Annick $24.95 (978-1-55451-383-3); paper $14.95 (978-1-55451-382-6). Rosa Parks, Andrei Sakharov, and Aung San Suu Kyi are among the seven individuals profiled here, with historical sidebars and well-chosen photographs. (Rev: BL 11/15/12; SLJ 9/12)

8808 Shaw, Maura D. *Ten Amazing People: And How They Changed the World* (4–7). 2002, SkyLight Paths $17.95 (978-1-893361-47-8). Shaw presents 10 well-illustrated biographies of 20th-century religious figures, each with timelines, a quotation, a glossary, and an emphasis on the individual's beliefs. (Rev: BL 10/1/02; HBG 3/03; SLJ 12/02) [200]

8809 Traub, Carol G. *Philanthropists and Their Legacies* (7–12). Series: Profiles. 1997, Oliver LB $19.95 (978-1-881508-42-7). Profiles — warts and all — of nine of the world's greatest benefactors, including Alfred Nobel, Andrew Carnegie, Cecil Rhodes, George Eastman, and Will Kellogg. (Rev: BL 2/15/98; SLJ 2/98) [920]

8810 Weatherly, Myra. *Women of the Sea: Ten Pirate Stories* (6–9). 2006, Morgan Reynolds LB $26.95 (978-1-931798-80-8). This revised edition of a 1998 publication (*Women Pirates: Eight Stories of Adventure*) adds information on two women pirates plus source notes and additional resources. (Rev: BL 12/15/05; SLJ 4/06) [910.4]

8811 Zalben, Jane Breskin. *Paths to Peace: People Who Changed the World* (4–7). Illus. 2006, Dutton $18.99 (978-0-525-47734-1). Zalben profiles 16 individuals who have devoted much of their lives to the goal of making peace a reality. (Rev: BL 1/1–15/06; SLJ 2/06)

Africa

CLEOPATRA

8812 Blackaby, Susan. *Cleopatra: Egypt's Last and Greatest Queen* (5–8). Series: Sterling Biographies. 2009, Sterling $12.95 (978-1-4027-6540-7); paper $5.95 (978-1-4027-5710-5). A useful and engaging biography for report writers or anyone interested in the renowned queen and her times. (Rev: SLJ 8/09) [921]

8813 Nardo, Don. *Cleopatra: Egypt's Last Pharaoh* (6–10). Series: The Lucent Library of Historical Eras. 2005, Gale LB $32.45 (978-1-59018-660-2). Presenting many quotations from ancient writings about Cleopatra, Nardo discusses their biases plus the importance of the Egyptian leader's relationships with Julius Caesar and Marc Antony. (Rev: SLJ 11/05) [921]

8814 Sapet, Kerrily. *Cleopatra: Ruler of Egypt* (8–12). 2007, Morgan Reynolds LB $27.95 (978-1-59935-035-6). Presents the fascinating details of the life of the Egyptian queen, with descriptions of the cultural wealth of the ancient world, the role of women, and life along the Nile. (Rev: BL 6/1–15/07; SLJ 7/07) [921]

8815 Shecter, Vicky Alvear. *Cleopatra Rules! The Amazing Life of the Original Teen Queen* (4–7). 2010, Boyds Mills $17.95 (978-1-59078-718-2). Using irreverent teenspeak that will not appeal to all readers, Schecter presents detailed information in a layout full of sidebars and illustrations. Lexile 880L (Rev: BL 10/1/10; LMC 11–12/10; SLJ 10/1/10; VOYA 12/10) [921]

HANNIBAL

8816 Mills, Clifford W. *Hannibal* (6–10). Series: Ancient World Leaders. 2008, Chelsea House LB $30 (978-0-7910-9580-5). Mills covers the founding of Carthage and Hannibal's famous journey through the Alps and campaign against Rome. (Rev: SLJ 1/1/09) [921]

8817 Warrick, Karen Clemens. *Hannibal: Great General of the Ancient World* (5–8). Series: Rulers of the Ancient World. 2006, Enslow LB $27.93 (978-0-7660-2564-6). The story of Hannibal's life and successes against the Romans are placed in historical context, with details of important battles as well as insight into his character. (Rev: SLJ 6/06) [921]

HATSHEPSUT

8818 Dell, Pamela. *Hatshepsut: Egypt's First Female Pharaoh* (6–8). Series: Signature Lives. 2008, Compass Point LB $34.60 (978-0-7565-3835-4). The life of Egypt's first female pharaoh is placed in historical context, with descriptions of daily life at the time and the role of women. Lexile 1060L (Rev: SLJ 1/1/09) [921]

MANDELA, NELSON

8819 Catel, Patrick. *Nelson Mandela* (6–9). Series: Front-Page Lives. 2010, Heinemann-Raintree $38.93 (978-1-4329-3219-0). Using a headlines format that highlights events, Catel covers Mandela's life from childhood and includes a timeline, glossary, and other useful back matter. (Rev: LMC 3–4/10) [921]

8820 Keller, Bill. *Tree Shaker: The Story of Nelson Mandela* (6–12). 2008, Kingfisher $16.95 (978-0-7534-5992-8). The accomplishments of the South African leader are related by a former *New York Times* Johannesburg bureau chief. An explanation of the history of apartheid helps readers to understand what Mandela was fighting for. (Rev: BL 11/1/07; SLJ 8/08) [921]

8821 Sawyer, Kem Knapp. *Nelson Mandela* (7–12). Illus. Series: Champion of Freedom. 2012, Morgan Reynolds LB $28.95 (978-159935167-4). A fascinating and detailed life of the South African leader who did so much to end apartheid. (Rev: BL 3/15/12; LMC 10/12; SLJ 5/1/12) [921]

MUBARAK, HOSNI

8822 Darraj, Susan Muaddi. *Hosni Mubarak* (8–12). Series: Modern World Leaders. 2007, Chelsea House LB $30.00 (978-0-7910-9280-4). Events in Egypt during Mubarak's presidency are the main focus of this profile. (Rev: SLJ 10/07) [921]

NEFERTITI

8823 Lange, Brenda. *Nefertiti* (6–12). Series: Ancient World Leaders. 2008, Chelsea House $30 (978-0-7910-9581-2). Full of illustrations that complement the text, this volume describes everyday life in ancient Egypt and the importance of religion and royalty as well as documenting what we know about the queen's life. (Rev: SLJ 3/1/09) [921]

RAMSES II

8824 Fitzgerald, Stephanie. *Ramses II: Egyptian Pharaoh, Warrior, and Builder* (6–8). Series: Signature Lives. 2008, Compass Point LB $34.60 (978-0-7565-3836-1). The life of the pharaoh is placed in historical context, with descriptions of daily life and a detailed timeline. Lexile 1060L (Rev: SLJ 1/1/09) [921]

TUTANKHAMEN, KING

8825 Hawass, Zahi. *Tutankhamun: The Mystery of the Boy King* (4–7). 2005, National Geographic $17.95 (978-0-7922-8354-6). The director of excavations at key Egyptian archaeological sites offers a fascinating account of the life, death, and burial of King Tut and of new revelations about his fate. (Rev: BL 11/1/05; SLJ 10/05*) [932]

Asia and the Middle East

AHMADINEJAD, MAHMOUD

8826 Broyles, Matthew. *Mahmoud Ahmadinejad: President of Iran* (8–12). Series: Newsmakers. 2007, Rosen LB $31.95 (978-1-4042-1900-7). Readers are introduced to the president of Iran, whose provocative and challenging statements have enraged many and impressed others; Iran's current political climate and its history are covered as well. (Rev: BL 10/15/07) [955.05]

ARAFAT, YASIR

8827 Ferber, Elizabeth. *Yasir Arafat: The Battle for Peace in Palestine* (7–12). 1995, Millbrook $23.90 (978-1-56294-585-5). A balanced presentation of Arafat's political career. (Rev: BL 10/1/95; SLJ 12/95) [921]

ATTILA THE HUN

8828 Price, Sean Stewart. *Attila the Hun: Leader of the Barbarian Hordes* (5–8). Illus. Series: Wicked History. 2009, Scholastic LB $30.00 (978-0-531-21801-3); paper $5.95 (978-0-531-20737-6). This compelling, well-designed biography provides lots of historical context. (Rev: BL 4/15/09; VOYA 6/09) [936]

AUNG SAN SUU KYI

8829 O'Keefe, Sherry. *Aung San Suu Kyi* (7–12). Illus. Series: Champion of Freedom. 2012, Morgan Reynolds LB $28.95 (978-159935168-1). A fascinating and detailed life of the daughter of the assassinated leader of Burma (Myanmar) and her commitment to human rights. (Rev: BL 3/15/12*; LMC 10/12; SLJ 6/12) [921]

8830 Rose, Simon. *Aung San Suu Kyi* (4–7). Illus. Series: Remarkable People. 2011, Weigl LB $27.13 (978-161690833-1); paper $12.95 (978-161690834-8). An admiring, informative profile of the Myanmar activist who won the Nobel Prize. (Rev: BL 9/15/11) [921]

BHATT, ELA

8831 Sreenivasan, Jyotsna. *Ela Bhatt: Uniting Women in India* (5–8). Series: Women Changing the World. 2000, Feminist $19.95 (978-1-55861-229-7). Inspired by Gandhi, this Indian lawyer founded an organization to help and protect the lives of her country's poorest women and organized a labor union for them. (Rev: BL 9/15/00; HBG 3/01; SLJ 12/00) [921]

BHUTTO, BENAZIR

8832 Price, Sean Stewart. *Benazir Bhutto* (6–9). Series: Front-Page Lives. 2010, Heinemann-Raintree $38.93 (978-1-4329-3222-0). Using a headlines format that highlights events, Price covers Bhutto's life from childhood and includes a timeline, glossary, and other useful back matter. (Rev: BL 10/1/09*; LMC 3–4/10) [921]

BIN LADEN, OSAMA

8833 Louis, Nancy. *Osama bin Laden* (4–7). Series: War on Terrorism. 2002, ABDO LB $25.65 (978-1-57765-663-0). A brief biography of the terrorist leader told through a matter-of-fact text and many color photographs. (Rev: BL 5/15/02; HBG 10/02) [921]

8834 Price, Sean Stewart. *Osama Bin Laden* (6–9). Series: Front-Page Lives. 2010, Heinemann-Raintree $38.93 (978-1-4329-3221-3). Using a headlines format that highlights events, Price covers Bin Laden's life from childhood and includes a timeline, glossary, and other useful back matter. (Rev: LMC 3–4/10) [921]

BUDDHA

8835 Gedney, Mona. *The Life and Times of Buddha* (5–7). Series: Biography from Ancient Civilizations: Legends, Folklore, and Stories of Ancient Worlds. 2005, Mitchell Lane LB $29.95 (978-1-58415-342-9). Gedney recounts what is known of the life of Siddartha Gautama, whose search for a better way of living led to the founding of Buddhism. (Rev: SLJ 9/05) [921]

DALAI LAMA

8836 Kimmel, Elizabeth Cody. *Boy on the Lion Throne: The Childhood of the 14th Dalai Lama* (5–8). 2009, Roaring Brook $18.95 (978-1-59643-394-6). The compelling and wide-ranging story of the childhood of the current Dalai Lama, who was born Lhamo Thondup in 1935. (Rev: BCCB 6/09; SLJ 6/09) [921]

GANDHI, INDIRA

8837 Dommermuth-Costa, Carol. *Indira Gandhi: Daughter of India* (7–12). Series: Lerner Biographies. 2001, Lerner LB $6.95 (978-0-8225-4963-5). A thorough profile that places Gandhi's life in historical context and provides a good history of modern India. (Rev: HBG 3/02; SLJ 3/02) [921]

GANDHI, MAHATMA

8838 Sawyer, Kem Knapp. *Mohandas Gandhi* (6–9). Illus. Series: Champion of Freedom. 2011, Morgan Reynolds LB $28.95 (978-159935166-7). This straightforward profile places Gandhi's life in clear historical context. (Rev: BL 10/1/11; SLJ 10/1/11; VOYA 10/11) [921]

8839 Severance, John B. *Gandhi, Great Soul* (6–9). 1997, Clarion $19.00 (978-0-395-77179-2). The life and times of Gandhi are covered in this attractive, informative book, which explains Gandhi's philosophy of peaceful resistance and describes the evolution of his beliefs. (Rev: BL 2/15/97; SLJ 4/97*) [921]

8840 Wilkinson, Philip. *Gandhi: The Young Protestor Who Founded a Nation* (4–7). Series: World History Biographies. 2005, National Geographic LB $27.90 (978-0-7922-3648-1). Gandhi's character shines through the straightforward text and interesting anecdotes in this biography that gives historical context plus maps and photographs. (Rev: BL 6/1–15/05) [954.03]

GENGHIS KHAN

8841 Goldberg, Enid A., and Norman Itzkowitz. *Genghis Khan: 13th-Century Mongolian Tyrant* (5–7). Illus. Series: Wicked History. 2007, Scholastic LB $30.00 (978-0-531-12596-0). The bloody deeds of the tyrant are emphasized (this is the Wicked History series, after all), but readers will also learn about ancient Mongolia and its people as well as the few positive results of Genghis Khan's rule. (Rev: BL 12/15/07; LMC 2/08; SLJ 1/08) [921]

8842 Nardo, Don. *Genghis Khan and the Mongol Empire* (5–9). Series: World History. 2011, Gale/Lucent $33.45 (978-1-4205-0326-5). An accessible portrait of Genghis Khan, his military reforms, his conquests in western Asia, and his legacy. e (Rev: SLJ 7/11) [921]

8843 Rice, Earle, Jr. *Empire in the East: The Story of Genghis Khan* (7–11). Series: World Leaders. 2005, Morgan Reynolds LB $26.95 (978-1-931798-62-4). A life of Genghis Khan, who rose from obscurity to become leader of the Great Mongol Nation and ruler of vast territories that stretched from the Adriatic to the Pacific. (Rev: BL 8/05; SLJ 8/05) [950]

HUSSEIN, SADDAM

8844 Shields, Charles J. *Saddam Hussein* (5–8). Series: Major World Leaders. 2002, Chelsea $30.00 (978-0-7910-6943-1). An account of the Iraqi leader's regime, with information on the Iran-Iraq and Persian Gulf wars and on United Nations sanctions and weapons inspections. (Rev: BL 2/1/03; HBG 3/03; SLJ 4/03) [956.7044]

8845 Stewart, Gail B. *Saddam Hussein* (8–12). Series: Heroes and Villains. 2004, Gale LB $29.95 (978-1-59018-350-2). Ending before Saddam Hussein's capture by U.S. forces, this is a portrait of a ruthless dictator and his ascent to and maintenance of power. (Rev: SLJ 4/04) [921]

KARZAI, HAMID

8846 Abrams, Dennis. *Hamid Karzai* (8–12). Series: Modern World Leaders. 2007, Chelsea House LB $30.00 (978-0-7910-9267-5). Karzai was sworn in as the first democratically elected president of Afghanistan in 2004, and since then has faced many challenges in the struggle to rebuild the war-torn country. (Rev: SLJ 10/07) [921]

KHAMENEI, ALI

8847 Murphy, John. *Ali Khamenei* (8–12). Series: Modern World Leaders. 2007, Chelsea House LB $30.00 (978-0-7910-9517-1). A look at the rise to power of Ali Khamenei, who became the Grand Ayatollah of Iran upon Khomeini's death. (Rev: BL 4/10/08) [955.05]

KIM JONG IL

8848 Behnke, Alison. *Kim Jong Il's North Korea* (7–12). 2007, Lerner LB $38.60 (978-0-8225-7282-4). Extensive background about North Korea gives the reader a foundation for understanding Kim Jong Il's dictatorship. (Rev: BL 10/15/07; SLJ 11/07) [921]

8849 Wyborny, Sheila. *Kim Jong Il* (6–9). Illus. Series: People in the News. 2009, Gale/Lucent LB $32.45 (978-142050091-2). This is an interesting introduction to the man who has led North Korea since the death of his father, Kim Il Sung, in the mid-1990s. (Rev: BLO 5/15/09) [921]

KOLLEK, TEDDY

8850 Rabinovich, Abraham. *Teddy Kollek: Builder of Jerusalem* (5–8). 1996, Jewish Publication Society $14.95 (978-0-8276-0559-6); paper $9.95 (978-0-8276-0561-9). The story of the former mayor of Jerusalem, who supervised the city's unification after the Six Days War in 1967. (Rev: BL 5/15/96) [921]

LAO TZU

8851 Demi. *The Legend of Lao Tzu and the Tao Te Ching* (4–7). Illus. by author. 2007, Simon & Schuster $21.99 (978-1-4169-1206-4). A well-designed introduction to the legendary Chinese religious figure Lao Tzu, with 20 verses from the book of wisdom associated with him. (Rev: BL 5/15/07; HB 7/07; LMC 11/07; SLJ 5/07)

MUHAMMAD

8852 Demi. *Muhammad* (4–7). 2003, Simon & Schuster $19.95 (978-0-689-85264-0). This readable account of the life of the founding prophet of Islam is accompanied by quotations from the Koran and intricate illustrations. (Rev: BL 6/1–15/03*; HB 7–8/03; HBG 4/04; SLJ 8/03) [297.6]

NOOR, QUEEN

8853 Raatma, Lucia. *Queen Noor: American-Born Queen of Jordan* (6–9). Series: Signature Lives. 2006, Compass Point LB $34.60 (978-0-7565-1595-9). The life of the American-born woman who became the queen of Jordan. (Rev: BL 4/1/06; SLJ 6/06) [956.9504]

RIZAL, JOSE

8854 Arruda, Suzanne Middendorf. *Freedom's Martyr: The Story of José Rizal, National Hero of the Philippines* (6–12). Series: Avisson Young Adult. 2003, Avisson paper $19.95 (978-1-888105-55-1). A patriot and activist on behalf of the native peoples of the Philippines, Rizal was executed by the Spanish for treason in 1896 and remains the country's national hero. (Rev: SLJ 5/04) [921]

SHEBA, QUEEN OF

8855 Lucks, Naomi. *Queen of Sheba* (6–12). Series: Ancient World Leaders. 2008, Chelsea House $30 (978-0-7910-9579-9). Lucks provides a glimpse into the past with this well-illustrated volume that documents what we know about the Queen of Sheba. (Rev: SLJ 3/1/09) [921]

TERESA, MOTHER

8856 Morgan, Nina. *Mother Teresa: Saint of the Poor* (4–7). 1998, Raintree paper $7.95 (978-0-8172-7848-9). A biography of the nun whose work with the poor of India made her an international celebrity and earned her a Nobel Peace Prize. (Rev: BL 7/98; HBG 10/98; SLJ 7/98) [921]

8857 Slavicek, Louise Chipley. *Mother Teresa: Caring for the World's Poor* (8–12). Series: Modern Peacemakers. 2007, Chelsea House LB $30.00 (978-0-7910-9433-4). An evenhanded profile of the Nobel Peace Prize winner, including the text of her acceptance speech. (Rev: SLJ 8/07) [921]

XIAOPING, DENG

8858 Stewart, Whitney. *Deng Xiaoping: Leader in a Changing China* (4–7). Series: Lerner Biographies. 2001, Lerner LB $30.35 (978-0-8225-4962-8). An accessible biography of the most powerful man in China from the 1970s until his death, with details of how his reputation was tarnished by the Tiananmen Square massacre. (Rev: BL 9/15/01; HBG 10/01; SLJ 7/01) [921]

ZEDONG, MAO

8859 Slavicek, Louise Chipley. *Mao Zedong* (6–9). Series: Great Military Leaders of the Twentieth Century. 2003, Chelsea House LB $30.00 (978-0-7910-7407-7). Mao's beliefs, personal life, and political career are clearly described, with maps, photographs, and reproductions. (Rev: SLJ 3/04) [921]

Europe

ALEXANDER THE GREAT

8860 Adams, Simon. *Alexander: The Boy Soldier Who Conquered the World* (5–7). Series: National Geographic World History Biographies. 2005, National Geographic LB $27.90 (978-0-7922-3661-0). An attractive, well-illustrated account of Alexander's life and accomplishments, with references to his less-appealing characteristics. (Rev: HBG 4/06; SLJ 9/05) [921]

8861 Behnke, Alison. *The Conquests of Alexander the Great* (6–12). Series: Pivotal Moments in History. 2007, Twenty-First Century LB $38.60 (978-0-8225-5920-7). A thorough biography of Alexander's life and achievements, with background information on the time as well as details of battles, maps, a timeline, and key figures. (Rev: SLJ 9/07) [921]

8862 Demi. *Alexander the Great* (4–7). Illus. by author. 2010, Marshall Cavendish $19.99 (978-0-7614-5700-8). The story of the infamous Macedonian conquerer is presented in this concise, beautifully illustrated book. e (Rev: BL 9/15/10; LMC 1–2/11; SLJ 10/1/10) [921]

8863 Greenblatt, Miriam. *Alexander the Great and Ancient Greece* (5–8). Series: Rulers and Their Times. 1999, Marshall Cavendish LB $29.93 (978-0-7614-0913-7). The first part of this biography introduces Alexander the Great and his accomplishments and the second tells about daily life in ancient Greece. (Rev: BL 1/1–15/00; HBG 10/00; SLJ 2/00) [921]

8864 McGowen, Tom. *Alexander the Great: Conqueror of the Ancient World* (5–8). Series: Rulers of the Ancient World. 2006, Enslow LB $27.93 (978-0-7660-2560-8). Excellent for report writers, this biography covers Alexander the Great's life and distinguishes between fact and legend. (Rev: BL 6/1–15/06; SLJ 6/06) [921]

8865 Marsico, Katie. *Alexander the Great* (6–9). Illus. Series: Essential Lives. 2009, ABDO LB $22.95 (978-160453520-4). An engaging biography with quotations from primary sources, illustrations, and plenty of additional resources and facts for report writers. (Rev: BLO 3/17/09) [921]

8866 Saunders, Nicholas. *The Life of Alexander the Great* (5–8). Illus. Series: Stories from History. 2006, School Specialty $9.95 (978-0-7696-4713-5); paper $6.95 (978-0-7696-4694-7). Full-color illustrations and graphic-novel format make this engaging biography — which covers the bond between Alexander and his horse as well as his relationship with Hephaestion — attractive to reluctant readers. (Rev: SLJ 1/07)

8867 Shecter, Vicky Alvear. *Alexander the Great Rocks the World* (5–8). Illus. by Terry Naughton. 2006, Darby Creek $18.95 (978-1-58196-045-7). Shecter employs an irreverent, kid-appealing tone to accurately present

Alexander's amazing travels; cartoons, historical depictions, detailed notes, and resources round out the volume. (Rev: BL 1/1–15/07; SLJ 12/06)

ANIELEWICZ, MORDECHAI

8868 Callahan, Kerry P. *Mordechai Anielewicz: Hero of the Warsaw Uprising* (5–8). Series: Holocaust Biographies. 2001, Rosen LB $31.95 (978-0-8239-3377-8). The story of Anielewicz and other members of the Jewish resistance in the Warsaw ghetto is told in gripping text accompanied by black-and-white photographs. (Rev: BL 10/15/01) [921]

BLAIR, TONY

8869 Hinman, Bonnie. *Tony Blair. Rev. ed.* (7–10). Series: Major World Leaders. 2006, Chelsea House $30.00 (978-0-7910-9216-3). An updated profile (to 2006, before his resignation) of the leader of the British Labour Party who in 1997 became the youngest prime minister in nearly 200 years. (Rev: BL 1/1–15/07) [921]

BRAILLE, LOUIS

8870 Freedman, Russell. *Out of Darkness: The Story of Louis Braille* (4–8). 1997, Clarion $16.00 (978-0-395-77516-5). The story of the blind Frenchman who, more than 170 years ago, invented a system of reading using raised dots. (Rev: BCCB 5/97; BL 3/1/97; HB 5–6/97; SLJ 3/97*) [686.2]

CAESAR, JULIUS

8871 Galford, Ellen. *Julius Caesar: The Boy Who Conquered an Empire* (5–8). Series: World History Biographies. 2007, National Geographic $17.95 (978-1-4263-0064-6). A brief but well-organized biography of Caesar, covering his childhood, adolescence, marriage, military career, rise to power, and murder, and offering pertinent historical context. (Rev: SLJ 6/07)

8872 Kent, Zachary. *Julius Caesar: Ruler of the Roman World* (6–9). 2006, Enslow LB $20.95 (978-0-7660-2563-9). Using both modern and ancient sources, Kent introduces one of the most powerful leaders in the history of Western civilization. (Rev: SLJ 8/06) [921]

8873 Saunders, Nicholas. *The Life of Julius Caesar* (5–8). Illus. Series: Stories from History. 2006, School Specialty $9.95 (978-0-7696-4717-3); paper $6.95 (978-0-7696-4697-8). Full-color illustrations and graphic-novel format make this engaging biography attractive to reluctant readers. (Rev: SLJ 1/07)

CATHERINE THE GREAT

8874 Vincent, Zu. *Catherine the Great: Empress of Russia* (6–9). Illus. Series: Wicked History. 2009, LB $30.00 (978-053121802-0); paper $5.95 (978-053120738-3). An appealing profile of the Russian ruler, with information on her youth and personality. Lexile 890L (Rev: BL 4/15/09) [921]

8875 Whitelaw, Nancy. *Catherine the Great and the Enlightenment in Russia* (8–12). Series: European Queens. 2004, Morgan Reynolds LB $26.95 (978-1-931798-27-3). The colorful life of the Russian empress from childhood in her native Germany to her pivotal role in leading her adopted country into full participation in the cultural and political life of Europe. (Rev: BL 12/15/04; SLJ 12/04) [921]

CAVELL, EDITH

8876 Batten, Jack. *Silent in an Evil Time: The Brave War of Edith Cavell* (6–9). 2007, Tundra paper $16.95 (978-0-88776-737-1). Cavell, a British nurse who was executed by the Germans in World War I for her resistance activities, is remembered in this biography that explains the tenor of the times in which she lived and worked. (Rev: BL 11/1/07; SLJ 11/07) [921]

CHARLEMAGNE

8877 Westwood, Jennifer. *Stories of Charlemagne* (7–9). 1976, Phillips $26.95 (978-0-87599-213-6). A biography of the famous emperor of the Holy Roman Empire, who was one of the most influential men of the Middle Ages. [921]

CHURCHILL, SIR WINSTON

8878 Ashworth, Leon. *Winston Churchill* (5–8). Series: British History Makers. 2002, Cherrytree $17.95 (978-1-84234-072-1). A balanced look at the life and career of the British statesman, with a useful timeline and excellent illustrations. (Rev: SLJ 8/02) [941.082092]

8879 Haugen, Brenda. *Winston Churchill: British Soldier, Writer, Statesman* (4–8). 2006, Compass Point LB $34.60 (978-0-7565-1582-9). Slim but fact-filled, this is a useful biography for report writers, with excerpts from speeches and writings and full discussion of key events in Churchill's life. (Rev: SLJ 9/06) [921]

8880 Severance, John B. *Winston Churchill: Soldier, Statesman, Artist* (5–8). 1996, Clarion $19.00 (978-0-395-69853-2). A well-organized, clearly written account of the life and works of Britain's great statesman. (Rev: BL 4/15/96; HB 7–8/96; SLJ 4/96*; VOYA 6/96) [941.084]

CLEISTHENES

8881 Parton, Sarah. *Cleisthenes: Founder of Athenian Democracy* (7–10). Series: Leaders of Ancient Greece. 2004, Rosen LB $33.25 (978-0-8239-3826-1). Information about Cleisthenes and his times is carefully couched in discussion of the sources used and the ways in which this material has been gathered and analyzed. (Rev: SLJ 9/04) [921]

CONSTANTINE I, EMPEROR

8882 Morgan, Julian. *Constantine: Ruler of Christian Rome* (6–9). Series: Leaders of Ancient Rome. 2003,

Rosen LB $33.25 (978-0-8239-3592-5). The story of the 4th-century emperor who was the first Roman ruler to convert to Christianity. (Rev: SLJ 6/03) [937]

DIANA, PRINCESS OF WALES

8883 Owings, Lisa. *Diana: The People's Princess* (7–10). Illus. Series: Lives Cut Short. 2012, ABDO LB $34.22 (978-161783545-2). This profile includes first-person quotes, comments from insiders and critics, interesting sidebars, and relevant photographs. (Rev: BL 12/1/12) [921]

ELEANOR OF AQUITAINE

8884 Hilliam, David. *Eleanor of Aquitaine: The Richest Queen in Medieval Europe* (6–9). Series: Leaders of the Middle Ages. 2005, Rosen LB $33.25 (978-1-4042-0162-0). A readable life of the wealthy monarch, underlining her unusual accomplishments. (Rev: BL 4/1/05; SLJ 6/05) [942.03]

8885 Sapet, Kerrily. *Eleanor of Aquitaine: Medieval Queen* (8–11). 2006, Morgan Reynolds $26.95 (978-1-931798-90-7). A look at the rise and fall of Eleanor of Aquitaine, who was Queen of France and then Queen of England during the Middle Ages. (Rev: BL 8/06; SLJ 8/06) [921]

ELIZABETH I

8886 Hollihan, Kerrie Logan. *Elizabeth I, the People's Queen: Her Life and Times: 21 Activities* (4–8). Illus. 2011, Chicago Review paper $16.95 (978-1-56976-349-0). The life and times of England's Queen Elizabeth I are given plenty of historical and political context in this well-organized book that includes 21 activities. (Rev: LMC 10/11; SLJ 5/11) [921]

8887 Thomas, Jane Resh. *Behind the Mask: The Life of Queen Elizabeth I* (5–8). 1998, Clarion $20.00 (978-0-395-69120-5). A behind-the-scenes look at the long-lived queen, discussing her childhood, how she overcame opposition to become queen, and her subsequent manipulation of people, the court, and foreigners to attain greatness. (Rev: BL 12/15/98; HB 1–2/99; HBG 3/99; SLJ 12/98*; VOYA 4/99) [921]

8888 Weatherly, Myra. *Elizabeth I: Queen of Tudor England* (6–8). Series: Signature Lives. 2005, Compass Point LB $34.60 (978-0-7565-0988-0). A clearly written and well illustrated life of the fascinating queen. (Rev: SLJ 1/06) [921]

FRANK FAMILY

8889 Denenberg, Barry. *Shadow Life: A Portrait of Anne Frank and Her Family* (6–10). 2005, Scholastic $16.95 (978-0-439-41678-8). In this engaging title from the Shadow Life series, author Barry Denenberg tells the complete story of Anne Frank and her family from their earlier life in Frankfurt to their eventual transport to Nazi concentration camps. (Rev: BL 2/1/05*; SLJ 4/05; VOYA 4/05) [940.53]

FRANK, ANNE

8890 Colbert, David. *Anne Frank* (5–8). Illus. Series: 10 Days That Shook Your World. 2008, Aladdin paper $6.99 (978-1-4169-6445-2). Interweaving fact and fiction, Colbert describes 10 important days in Anne Frank's life — from the Netherlands' surrender to the Nazis to March 1945, when Anne is moved to a new camp full of disease. (Rev: BLO 12/8/08) [921]

8891 Frank, Anne. *Anne Frank: The Diary of a Young Girl* (5–8). 1967, Pocket paper $3.95 (978-0-685-05466-6). The moving diary of a young Jewish girl hiding from the Nazis in World War II Amsterdam. [921]

8892 Frank, Anne. *The Diary of a Young Girl: The Definitive Edition* (7–12). Trans. by Susan Massotty. 1995, Doubleday $27.50 (978-0-385-47378-1). This edition contains all of the writings of Anne Frank, including some short passages in the diary that had been formerly suppressed. (Rev: BL 4/15/95) [921]

8893 Gold, Alison L. *Memories of Anne Frank: Reflections of a Childhood Friend* (4–8). 1997, Scholastic paper $16.95 (978-0-590-90722-4). Anne Frank's story as told through recollections of her best friend in Amsterdam, Hannah Goslar, a survivor of the Holocaust. (Rev: BL 9/1/97; HBG 3/98; SLJ 11/97) [921]

8894 Hermann, Spring. *Anne Frank: Hope in the Shadows of the Holocaust* (5–7). Series: Holocaust Heroes and Nazi Criminals. 2005, Enslow LB $27.93 (978-0-7660-2531-8). The story of Anne Frank before, during, and after the two years she and her family hid from the Nazis. (Rev: SLJ 11/05) [921]

8895 Hurwitz, Johanna. *Anne Frank: Life in Hiding* (4–7). Illus. by Vera Rosenberry. 1989, Jewish Publication Society $13.95 (978-0-8276-0311-0). This biography describes Anne's life in hiding. (Rev: BL 4/15/89) [921]

8896 Lee, Carol Ann. *Anne Frank and the Children of the Holocaust* (7–10). 2006, Viking $16.99 (978-0-670-06107-5). Lee describes Anne Frank's life before she went into hiding, providing historical context and stories of other children who suffered. (Rev: BL 10/1/06; HB 3–4/05; LMC 4–5/07; SLJ 12/06) [940.53]

8897 Lindwer, Willy. *The Last Seven Months of Anne Frank* (8–12). 1992, Doubleday paper $12.95 (978-0-385-42360-1). Moving testimony from six women interned in a concentration camp with Anne Frank tells of the tragic conclusion of the young diarist's life. (Rev: BL 3/15/91) [921]

8898 Metselaar, Menno, and Ruud van der Rol. *Anne Frank: Her Life in Words and Pictures* (6–12). Trans. by Arnold J. Pomerans. 2009, Flash Point $19.99 (978-1-59643-546-9); paper $12.99 (978-1-59643-547-6). Short excerpts from Anne Frank's diary are interspersed with news photos, scrapbook pages, and family history to paint a rich and harrowing picture of Nazism, World War II, and the Frank family's place in history. Sydney Taylor Book Honor 2010; ALA Notable Books 2010; Boston Globe–Horn Book nonfiction Honor 2010. (Rev: BL 11/1/09*; HB 1–2/11; LMC 11/09; SLJ 10/09) [921]

GROSS, ELLY BERKOVITS

8899 Gross, Elly Berkovits. *Elly: My True Story of the Holocaust* (4–7). Illus. 2009, Scholastic $14.99 (978-0-545-07494-0). A memoir of a woman recalling her experiences as a teenager in a concentration camp and later as a factory slave laborer. (Rev: BL 6/1–15/09; SLJ 9/09) [940.53]

HAVEL, VACLAV

8900 Duberstein, John. *A Velvet Revolution: Vaclav Havel and the Fall of Communism* (8–11). 2006, Morgan Reynolds $26.95 (978-1-931798-85-3). This profile of the magnetic Czech leader cleverly interweaves history with biographical information (includes photos and resource lists). (Rev: BL 7/06; SLJ 9/06) [921]

HIMMLER, HEINRICH

8901 Worth, Richard. *Heinrich Himmler: Murderous Architect of the Holocaust* (8–11). Series: Holocaust Heroes and Nazi Criminals. 2005, Enslow LB $27.93 (978-0-7660-2532-5). A profile of the career of the architect of Nazi Germany's lethally effective campaign against the Jews and other victims of the Holocaust. (Rev: BL 10/15/05; SLJ 1/06) [940.53]

HITLER, ADOLF

8902 Giblin, James Cross. *The Life and Death of Adolf Hitler* (7–9). 2002, Clarion $21.00 (978-0-395-90371-1). This absorbing biography examines the forces that shaped Hitler's personality and philosophy and rise to power, covers Hitler's behavior during the war, and looks at today's neo-Nazis. (Rev: BL 4/1/02; HB 5–6/02; HBG 10/02; SLJ 5/02*; VOYA 6/02) [943.086]

8903 Rice, Earle, Jr. *Adolf Hitler and Nazi Germany* (6–9). Series: World Leaders. 2005, Morgan Reynolds LB $26.95 (978-1-931798-78-5). This accessible biography traces Hitler's progress from a modest childhood and uncertain adolescence through his army career, rise to power, and crafting of the German war machine. (Rev: BL 1/1–15/06; SLJ 1/06) [921]

JOAN OF ARC

8904 Lee, William W. *Joan of Arc and the Hundred Years' War in World History* (5–9). Series: In World History. 2003, Enslow LB $26.60 (978-0-7660-1938-6). This combination of biography and history tells the story of Joan of Arc and gives details on the long conflict between France and England. (Rev: BL 6/1–15/03; HBG 10/03; SLJ 9/03) [921]

8905 Yeatts, Tabatha. *Joan of Arc: Heavenly Warrior* (4–7). Illus. Series: Sterling Biographies. 2009, Sterling $12.95 (978-1-4027-6542-1); paper $5.95 (978-1-4027-5662-7). An accessible biography with many illustrations, maps, a timeline, and useful sources. (Rev: BL 2/1/09; SLJ 8/09) [921]

JOHN PAUL II, POPE

8906 Behnke, Alison. *Pope John Paul II* (7–10). Series: A&E Biography. 2005, Lerner paper $7.95 (978-0-8225-3387-0). This very human portrait of Pope John Paul II traces his life and presents the views of his critics as well as his supporters. (Rev: BL 10/1/05; SLJ 9/05) [282]

8907 Mainardi, Alessandro. *The Life of Pope John Paul II . . . in Comics!* (7–10). Illus. by Werner Maresta. 2006, Papercutz $16.95 (978-1-59707-039-3); paper $9.95 (978-1-59707-057-7). A biography of the life of Pope John Paul II, told in graphic-novel format, covering his childhood, journey into priesthood, his accomplishments, and leadership as the Pope. (Rev: BL 10/1/06; LMC 4–5/07; SLJ 1/07) [921]

8908 Sullivan, George. *Pope John Paul II: The People's Pope* (7–9). 1984, Walker $11.95 (978-0-8027-6523-9). A very readable biography of this beloved pope and his activities for world peace. [921]

LENIN, VLADIMIR ILICH

8909 Naden, Corinne J., and Rose Blue. *Lenin* (6–10). Series: Importance Of. 2005, Gale $32.45 (978-1-59018-233-8). The life and political career of Vladimir Lenin, founder of the Russian Communist Party. (Rev: BL 6/1–15/04) [921]

MACHIAVELLI, NICCOLÒ

8910 Ford, Nick. *Niccolò Machiavelli: Florentine Statesman, Playwright, and Poet* (5–8). Series: Rulers, Scholars, and Artists of the Renaissance. 2005, Rosen LB $33.25 (978-1-4042-0316-7). Ford places Machiavelli's life and accomplishments in the context of culture and politics of the time. (Rev: SLJ 10/05) [921]

MARY, QUEEN OF SCOTS

8911 Lotz, Nancy, and Carlene Phillips. *Mary Queen of Scots* (7–10). Series: European Queens. 2007, Morgan Reynolds LB $27.95 (978-1-59935-040-0). Chronicling the life of Mary Queen of Scots and her involvement in politics, conspiracies, and religious conflict, this volume will be helpful for report writers. (Rev: BL 6/1–15/07; SLJ 9/07) [921]

MEDICI, LORENZO DE

8912 Hancock, Lee. *Lorenzo De' Medici: Florence's Great Leader and Patron of the Arts* (5–8). Series: Rulers, Scholars, and Artists of the Renaissance. 2005, Rosen LB $33.25 (978-1-4042-0315-0). Ford places de Medici's life and accomplishments in the context of culture and politics of the time. (Rev: SLJ 10/05) [921]

NAPOLEON I

8913 Burleigh, Robert. *Napoleon: The Story of the Little Corporal* (5–8). Illus. 2007, Abrams $18.95 (978-0-8109-1378-3). This informative and attractive biography of Napoleon from his childhood through his final defeat and exile uses an accessible, conversational style. (Rev: BL 6/1–15/07; SLJ 7/07)

8914 Landau, Elaine. *Napoleon Bonaparte* (7–10). 2006, Twenty-First Century LB $27.93 (978-0-8225-3420-4). This biography of Bonaparte chronicles his most important milestones with the help of a timeline, map, quotations, and black-and-white photographs. (Rev: SLJ 6/06) [921]

PULASKI, CASIMIR

8915 Collins, David R. *Casimir Pulaski: Soldier on Horseback* (4–8). 1995, Pelican $14.95 (978-1-56554-082-8). A smoothly written biography of the Polish patriot who, though he could scarcely speak English, became an important figure helping the colonists during the Revolutionary War. (Rev: BL 2/15/96) [921]

PUTIN, VLADIMIR

8916 Streissguth, Thomas. *Vladimir Putin* (7–10). Series: A&E Biography. 2005, Lerner LB $29.27 (978-0-8225-2374-1); paper $7.95 (978-0-8225-9630-1). Putin's professional and political life take center stage in this biography that will be useful for report writers. (Rev: BL 9/1/05) [947.086]

RASPUTIN, GRIGORY

8917 Goldberg, Enid A., and Norman Itzkowitz. *Grigory Rasputin: Holy Man or Mad Monk?* (6–8). 2007, Watts LB $30.00 (978-0-531-12594-6). This biography of Rasputin provides a full account of his background and rise to power, and leads readers to ponder his true nature. (Rev: SLJ 3/08) [921]

RINGELBLUM, EMMANUEL

8918 Beyer, Mark. *Emmanuel Ringelblum: Historian of the Warsaw Ghetto* (5–8). Series: Holocaust Biographies. 2001, Rosen LB $31.95 (978-0-8239-3375-4). This true story of a man who recorded events in the Warsaw Ghetto during the Holocaust includes black-and-white photographs. (Rev: BL 10/15/01) [940.53]

ROBINSON, MARY

8919 Friedman, Lita. *Mary Robinson: Fighter for Human Rights* (6–9). Series: Avisson Young Adult. 2004, Avisson paper $19.95 (978-1-888105-65-0). In 1990 Robinson became the first female president of Ireland; subsequently she served as the United Nations High Commissioner for Human Rights. (Rev: SLJ 10/04) [921]

SARKOZY, NICOLAS

8920 Abrams, Dennis. *Nicolas Sarkozy* (7–10). Illus. Series: Modern World Leaders. 2009, Chelsea House $30.00 (978-160413081-2). With many quotations from Sarkozy and others, Abrams covers the French president's private life and public achievements. (Rev: BL 6/1–15/09) [921]

SCHOLL, HANS AND SOPHIE

8921 Axelrod, Toby. *Hans and Sophie Scholl: German Resisters of the White Rose* (7–12). Series: Holocaust Biographies. 2001, Rosen LB $31.95 (978-0-8239-3316-7). The Scholls, brother and sister, were arrested and executed for their role in organizing the group known as the White Rose, which worked to expose the Nazis' atrocities. (Rev: SLJ 6/01) [921]

SENDLER, IRENA

8922 Vaughan, Marcia. *Irena's Jars of Secrets* (4–7). Illus. by Ron Mazellan. 2011, Lee & Low $18.95 (978-1-60060-439-3). A picture-book profile of Irena Sendler, a Polish Catholic social worker who helped save nearly 2,500 children in the Warsaw Ghetto from deportation to the death camps in the early 1940s. Sydney Taylor Book Honor 2012. Lexile 1040L (Rev: BL 12/1/11; LMC 5–6/12; SLJ 11/1/11) [921]

SOCRATES

8923 Dell, Pamela. *Socrates: Ancient Greek in Search of Truth* (5–8). Illus. Series: Signature Lives. 2006, Compass Point LB $34.60 (978-0-7565-1874-5). A solid profile of the Greek philosopher that underlines his importance and provides insight into life in ancient Athens. (Rev: BL 10/15/06) [183]

SOLON

8924 Randall, Bernard. *Solon: The Lawmaker of Athens* (7–10). Series: Leaders of Ancient Greece. 2004, Rosen LB $33.25 (978-0-8239-3829-2). Information about Solon and his times is carefully introduced with discussion of the sources used and the ways in which this material has been gathered and analyzed. (Rev: SLJ 9/04) [921]

THEMISTOCLES

8925 Morris, Ian Macgregor. *Themistocles: Defender of Greece* (7–10). Series: Leaders of Ancient Greece.

2004, Rosen LB $33.25 (978-0-8239-3830-8). Information about Themistocles and his times is carefully couched in discussion of the sources used and the ways in which this material has been gathered and analyzed. (Rev: SLJ 9/04) [921]

VAN BEEK, CATO BONTJES

8926 Friedman, Ina R. *Flying Against the Wind: The Story of a Young Woman Who Defied the Nazis* (6–10). 1995, Lodgepole paper $11.95 (978-1-886721-00-5). The story of Cato Bontjes van Beek, who grew up in a progressive German household and was executed by the Nazis with her boyfriend for joining an underground movement. (Rev: BL 7/95; VOYA 4/96) [921]

WALLENBERG, RAOUL

8927 Borden, Louise W. *His Name Was Raoul Wallenberg: Courage, Rescue, and Mystery During World War II* (7–12). Illus. 2012, Houghton Mifflin $18.99 (978-061850755-9). A free-verse portrait of Wallenberg's life, his courageous efforts to save tens of thousands of Jews, and his mysterious disappearance in the hands of the Soviets; the many photographs, documents, and profiles will appeal to reluctant readers. Sydney Taylor Book Award 2013. Lexile 1080L (Rev: BL 9/15/11; HB 1–2/12; LMC 8–9/12*; SLJ 1/12; VOYA 2/12)

8928 Linnea, Sharon. *Raoul Wallenberg: The Man Who Stopped Death* (5–7). 1993, Jewish Publication Soc. paper $9.95 (978-0-8276-0448-3). This Swedish architect saved thousands of Jews in Hungary from the Nazi Holocaust. (Rev: BL 6/1–15/93) [940]

8929 McArthur, Debra. *Raoul Wallenberg: Rescuing Thousands from the Nazis' Grasp* (5–7). Series: Holocaust Heroes and Nazi Criminals. 2005, Enslow LB $27.93 (978-0-7660-2530-1). A well-documented profile of the courageous Swedish diplomat who saved thousands of Hungarian Jews and disappeared after the end of the war. (Rev: SLJ 11/05) [921]

WIESENTHAL, SIMON

8930 Rubin, Susan Goldman. *The Anne Frank Case: Simon Wiesenthal's Search for the Truth* (4–7). Illus. by Bill Farnsworth. 2009, Holiday $18.95 (978-0-8234-2109-1). This profile of the Nazi hunter and his career starts with an account of Holocaust deniers prompting Wiesenthal to search for the Gestapo officer who arrested Anne Frank's family. (Rev: BCCB 4/09; BL 3/1/09*; SLJ 3/09) [921]

WILLIAM, PRINCE, AND MIDDLETON, KATE

8931 Doeden, Matt. *Prince William and Kate: A Royal Romance* (5–8). Illus. 2011, Lerner LB $26.60 (978-076138029-0). Tells the story of Kate and William's individual lives and their relationship, ending with their wedding day; with many photographs and a timeline. (Rev: BL 11/1/11) [921]

South and Central America, Canada, and Mexico

BOLIVAR, SIMON

8932 Reis, Ronald A. *Simon Bolivar* (6–9). Illus. Series: Great Hispanic Heritage. 2010, Chelsea House LB $30 (978-160413731-6). Venezuelan military strategist Simon Bolivar was determined to create independent Latin American states; this well-organized biography includes ample back matter. (Rev: BL 2/1/11) [921]

CALCINES, EDUARDO F.

8933 Calcines, Eduardo F. *Leaving Glorytown: One Boy's Struggle Under Castro* (7–10). 2009, Farrar $16.95 (978-037434394-1). The author writes of his childhood in Communist Cuba in the 1960s, the hardships that Castro's regime brought to Cuba, and how they affected one close family. ⌒ Lexile 800L (Rev: BL 4/1/09; SLJ 6/1/09*; VOYA 4/09) [921]

CASTRO, FIDEL

8934 Marsico, Katie. *Fidel Castro: Cuban President and Revolutionary* (6–9). Illus. Series: Essential Lives. 2009, ABDO LB $22.95 (978-160453522-8). An engaging biography that describes Castro's life until he stepped down from ruling Cuba, with plenty of additional resources and facts for report writers. (Rev: BLO 3/17/09) [921]

CHAVEZ, HUGO

8935 Young, Jeff C. *Hugo Chavez: Leader of Venezuela* (6–12). 2007, Morgan Reynolds LB $27.95 (978-1-59935-068-4). Covers the life of Venezuela's leader from his childhood to the present, as well as his military career, brief imprisonment, presidency, and attitude toward the United States. (Rev: BL 8/07) [921]

CRUZ, CELIA

8936 Cartlidge, Cherese. *Celia Cruz* (6–9). Illus. Series: Great Hispanic Heritage. 2010, Chelsea House LB $30 (978-160413771-2). Cuban singer-songwriter Celia Cruz rejected Castro's policies and immigrated to the United States; this well-organized biography includes interesting sidebars and ample back matter. (Rev: BL 2/1/11) [921]

DE PORTOLA, GASPAR

8937 Whiting, Jim. *Gaspar de Portola* (5–7). Series: Latinos in American History. 2002, Mitchell Lane LB $29.95 (978-1-58415-148-7). The story of the Latino governor of "Las Californias" from 1768 to 1770 who was responsible for expelling Jesuits from the area. (Rev: BL 2/15/03; HBG 10/03) [921]

FOX, VICENTE

8938 Paprocki, Sherry Beck. *Vicente Fox* (5–8). Series: Major World Leaders. 2002, Chelsea $30.00 (978-0-7910-6944-8). The story of the man who became president of Mexico in July 2000, the first opposition candidate to gain presidential office in more than 70 years. (Rev: BL 1/1–15/03) [921]

GUEVARA, CHE

8939 Abrams, Dennis. *Ernesto "Che" Guevara* (6–9). Illus. Series: Great Hispanic Heritage. 2010, Chelsea House LB $30 (978-160413732-3). Argentinean revolutionary Che Guevara grew up the son of aristocrats; this well-organized biography covers his life from a young age and his cultural heritage. (Rev: BL 2/1/11; LMC 5–6/11) [921]

8940 Havelin, Kate. *Che Guevara* (7–12). Series: Biography. 2006, Twenty-First Century LB $27.93 (978-0-8225-5951-1). This is a brief but thorough profile of the revolutionary who had so much impact in his short life. (Rev: SLJ 3/07) [921]

8941 Kallen, Stuart A. *Che Guevara: You Win or You Die* (7–10). Illus. 2012, Lerner/Twenty-First Century LB $33.27 (978-082259035-4). A clear profile of Guevara's revolutionary ideals and activities. (Rev: BL 11/1/12; SLJ 10/12) [921]

8942 Miller, Calvin Craig. *Che Guevara: In Search of the Revolution* (7–10). 2006, Morgan Reynolds LB $26.95 (978-1-931798-93-8). A captivating biography of Che Guevara, with details on his personal life, his role as a revolutionary leader in Cuba, and the time he spent working with Castro. (Rev: BL 8/06; SLJ 3/07) [921]

8943 Uschan, Michael V. *Che Guevara, Revolutionary* (8–11). Series: The Twentieth Century's Most Influential Hispanics. 2006, Gale LB $31.20 (978-1-59018-970-2). A balanced profile of the socialist rebel who has become a popular icon. (Rev: BL 4/1/07) [921]

MENCHU, RIGOBERTA

8944 Kallen, Stuart A. *Rigoberta Menchú: Indian Rights Activist* (6–12). Series: The Twentieth Century's Most Influential Hispanics. 2006, Gale LB $32.45 (978-1-59018-975-7). A life of the Nobel laureate and advocate for human rights. (Rev: SLJ 9/07) [921]

8945 Menchú, Rigoberta, and Dante Liano. *The Girl from Chimel* (4–7). Trans. by David Unger. Illus. by Domi. 2005, Groundwood $16.95 (978-0-88899-666-4). Rigoberta Menchu, winner of the 1992 Nobel Peace Prize and Maya activist, tells about growing up in the Guatemalan Indian village of Chimel. (Rev: BL 11/1/05; SLJ 2/06) [868]

8946 Schulze, Julie. *Rigoberta Menchú Túm: Champion of Human Rights* (8–12). Series: Contemporary Profile and Policy. 1998, John Gordon Burke $20.00 (978-0-934272-42-1); paper $12.95 (978-0-934272-43-8). This biography combines the life story of Nobel Peace Prize-winner Rigoberta Menchu Tum with the story of the struggle of the Mayan people for equality in Guatemala and throughout Central America. (Rev: BL 4/1/98) [921]

8947 Wagner, Heather Lehr. *Rigoberta Menchú Tum: Activist for Indigenous Rights in Guatemala* (8–12). 2007, Chelsea House LB $30.00 (978-0-7910-8998-9). An introduction to the life of the 1992 Nobel Peace Prize winner, from her impoverished childhood in a Mayan-K'iche community, through the murder of her activist parents and siblings, to her fight for the rights of indigenous people. (Rev: BL 6/1–15/07) [921]

NEZAHUALCOYOTL

8948 Serrano, Francisco. *The Poet King of Tezcoco: A Great Leader of Ancient Mexico* (5–8). Trans. by Trudy Balch. Illus. by Pablo Serrano. 2007, Groundwood $18.95 (978-0-88899-787-6). This picture book for older readers introduces the life of Nezahualcoyotl, a 15th-century Toltec royal and poet who brought much advancement to his kingdom. (Rev: BL 6/1–15/07; SLJ 12/07)

SANTA ANNA, ANTONIO LOPEZ DE

8949 Bankston, John. *Antonio López de Santa Anna* (5–7). Series: Latinos in American History. 2003, Mitchell Lane LB $29.95 (978-1-58415-209-5). A biography of the Mexican general, president, and statesman who is best known for his part in the Battle of the Alamo. (Rev: BL 1/1–15/04; HBG 4/04; SLJ 2/04) [921]

SILVA, MARINA

8950 Hildebrant, Ziporah. *Marina Silva: Defending Rainforest Communities in Brazil* (5–8). Series: Women Changing the World. 2001, Feminist $19.95 (978-1-55861-292-1). Though battling a serious illness, this gallant women, once a leader of the native Amazonians, has become a leading figure in protecting the forests of Brazil. (Rev: BL 12/15/01) [921]

TOUSSAINT L'OUVERTURE, FRANÇOIS-DOMINIQUE

8951 Rockwell, Anne. *Open the Door to Liberty: A Biography of Toussaint L'Ouverture* (5–8). Illus. by R. Gregory Christie. 2009, Houghton $18.00 (978-0-618-60570-5). A well-written and well-researched biography of the freed slave who led a rebellion against the French in 1793 on what is now known as Haiti. (Rev: BL 2/1/09; LMC 10/09; SLJ 3/09) [921]

Miscellaneous Interesting Lives

Collective

8952 Cox, Clinton. *African American Teachers* (4–7). Series: Black Stars. 2000, Wiley $22.95 (978-0-471-24649-7). A collection of short profiles of important African American teachers who have inspired their students and championed the cause of education. (Rev: BL 7/00; HBG 3/01; SLJ 7/00) [920]

8953 Fleischman, John. *Black and White Airmen: Their True History* (5–8). Illus. 2007, Houghton $20.00 (978-0-618-56297-8). At a reunion decades later, white bomber pilot Herb Heilbrun and Tuskegee Airman John Leahr discover how much of World War II they shared although separated by segregation. (Rev: BL 2/1/07)

8954 Gilbreth, Frank B., and Ernestine Gilbreth Carey. *Cheaper by the Dozen. Rev. ed.* (8–12). 1963, Crowell paper $11.95 (978-0-06-008460-8). A biographical account of the Gilbreth family, whose 12 children were reared by a father who believed in time and efficiency applications even in the home. [920]

8955 Warren, Andrea. *We Rode the Orphan Trains* (4–8). 2001, Houghton Mifflin $18.00 (978-0-618-11712-3). Eight moving biographical accounts of men and women, now in their 80s and 90s, who traveled to the Midwest to find new homes and families. (Rev: BCCB 11/01; BL 11/1/01; HBG 3/02; SLJ 11/01; VOYA 12/01) [362.73]

8956 Yolen, Jane, and Heidi E. Y. Stemple. *Bad Girls: Sirens, Jezebels, Murderesses, Thieves and Other Female Villains* (7–10). Illus. by Rebecca Guay. 2013, Charlesbridge $18.95 (978-158089185-1). Twenty-six notorious women ranging from Delilah, Cleopatra, and Queen Mary to Calamity Jane, Bonnie Parker, and Typhoid Mary are introduced in an attractive combination of text and portraits. (Rev: BL 2/15/13*; SLJ 4/13) [920]

Individual

APPELT, KATHI

8957 Appelt, Kathi. *My Father's Summers: A Daughter's Memoir* (6–12). 2004, Henry Holt $15.95 (978-0-8050-7362-1). In a series of prose poems, Appelt paints a poignant portrait of her life growing up in Houston and the pain caused by the extended absences of her father. (Rev: BCCB 7–8/04; BL 6/1–15/04; SLJ 6/04; VOYA 6/04) [813]

BARAKAT, IBTISAM

8958 Barakat, Ibtisam. *Tasting the Sky: A Palestinian Childhood* (7–10). 2007, Farrar $16.00 (978-0-374-35733-7). A memoir of the author's war-torn youth, which included running from bomb attacks, living at detention centers, and uneven schooling. ALA Notable Books 2008. (Rev: BL 3/15/07; LMC 10/07; SLJ 5/07*) [921]

BLOOMER, ELIZABETH

8959 Reed, Jennifer. *Elizabeth Bloomer: Child Labor Activist* (4–8). Series: Young Heroes. 2006, Gale LB $23.70 (978-0-7377-3615-1). Bloomer became an activist against child labor when she was in middle school and learned about Iqbal Masih, a Pakistani boy sold into slavery. (Rev: SLJ 5/07) [921]

BONETTA, SARAH FORBES

8960 Myers, Walter Dean. *At Her Majesty's Request: An African Princess in Victorian England* (5–8). 1999, Scholastic paper $17.95 (978-0-590-48669-9). The intriguing story of the African princess who at age 7 was saved from becoming a sacrifice and sent her to England, where she became the ward of Queen Victoria.

(Rev: BCCB 2/99; BL 4/1/99; HBG 10/99; SLJ 1/99; VOYA 4/99) [921]

BONHOEFFER, DIETRICH

8961 Martin, Michael J. *Dietrich Bonhoeffer* (7–12). Illus. Series: Champion of Freedom. 2012, Morgan Reynolds LB $28.95 (978-159935169-8). Tells the story of the German theologian who opposed Nazi activities, conspired in a plot to assassinate Hitler, and died in a concentration camp in 1945. **e** (Rev: BL 3/15/12*; LMC 10/12; SLJ 6/12) [921]

CANADA, GEOFFREY

8962 Canada, Geoffrey, and Jamar Nicholas. *Fist Stick Knife Gun: A Personal History of Violence* (7–12). Illus. by Jamar Nicholas. 2010, Beacon paper $14 (978-08070444-9-0). Using graphic novel format, the author presents 10 vignettes from his gritty urban childhood that are designed to show readers coping mechanisms for violence and instability. (Rev: BL 11/15/10; VOYA 12/10) [921]

CHILD, JULIA

8963 Abrams, Dennis. *Julia Child: Chef* (6–9). Illus. Series: Women of Achievement. 2011, Chelsea House LB $35 (978-160413912-9). An appealing biography of the chef who introduced French cooking to America. (Rev: BL 12/1/11) [921]

DEMALLIE, HOWARD R.

8964 DeMallie, Howard R. *Behind Enemy Lines: A Young Pilot's Story* (7–9). 2007, Sterling paper $6.95 (978-1-4027-4137-1). DeMallie tells the true story of his capture and imprisonment by the Nazis in occupied Holland after his B-17 ran into trouble in 1944. (Rev: BL 6/1–15/07; SLJ 8/07) [921]

FRIEDMAN, CORY

8965 Patterson, James, and Hal Friedman. *Med Head: My Knock-Down, Drag-Out, Drugged-Up Battle with My Brain* (7–10). Illus. 2010, Little, Brown paper $8.99 (978-03160761-7-3). With an introduction, photographs, and question-and-answer sessions, this version of *Against Medical Advice,* intended for youth readers, tells the story of Cory Friedman's struggle to find a resolution to the obsessive-compulsive disorder and Tourette's syndrome making his young life so difficult. **e** (Rev: BLO 3/1/10; VOYA 6/10) [921]

GAC-ARTIGAS, ALEJANDRO

8966 Gac-Artigas, Alejandro. *Yo, Alejandro* (5–7). 2000, Espacio paper $11.95 (978-1-930879-21-8). This is a collection of personal essays written by the author before his 12th birthday about his life in Puerto Rico, the state of Georgia, and later New York City. (Rev: BL 3/1/01) [921]

GARNER, ELEANOR

8967 Garner, Eleanor Ramrath. *Eleanor's Story: An American Girl in Hitler's Germany* (7–12). 1999, Peachtree $15.95 (978-1-56145-193-7). The author recounts her family's struggle to survive in Germany during World War II. (Rev: BL 10/1/99*; HBG 4/00; SLJ 3/00) [940.54]

GREITENS, ERIC

8968 Greitens, Eric. *The Warrior's Heart: Becoming a Man of Compassion and Courage* (8–12). 2012, Houghton Harcourt $16.99 (978-0-547-86852-3). In this thought-provoking adaptation of the adult title *The Heart and the Fist* (2011), Greitens describes his adventures in various countries around the world and the circumstances that led him to become a Navy SEAL. **e** (Rev: SLJ 9/12) [921]

GRIMBERG, TINA

8969 Grimberg, Tina. *Out of Line: Growing Up Soviet* (8–12). 2007, Tundra $22.95 (978-0-88776-803-3). Grimberg, now a rabbi in Canada, recalls her life as a girl in a Jewish family in the Soviet Union in the 1960s and 1970s. (Rev: BL 12/1/07; SLJ 1/08) [305.2]

HALILBEGOVICH, NADJA

8970 Halilbegovich, Nadja. *My Childhood Under Fire: A Sarajevo Diary* (4–7). 2006, Kids Can $14.95 (978-1-55337-797-9). As a 12-year-old, Halilbegovich kept a diary that reveals the frightening details of her life during the Balkans war. (Rev: BL 5/15/06; SLJ 6/06)

HAUTZIG, ESTHER

8971 Hautzig, Esther. *The Endless Steppe: Growing Up in Siberia* (7–12). 1968, HarperCollins paper $5.99 (978-0-06-447027-8). The autobiography of a Polish girl who, with her family, was exiled to Siberia during World War II. [921]

JACOBSEN, RUTH

8972 Jacobsen, Ruth. *Rescued Images: Memories of a Childhood in Hiding* (6–12). 2001, Mikaya $19.95 (978-1-931414-00-5). The author, who was 8 years old when her family fled the Nazis and went into hiding in the Netherlands, relates memories evoked by family photographs, which are also included. (Rev: BCCB 2/02; BL 1/1–15/02; HBG 3/02; SLJ 1/02; VOYA 2/02) [921]

JENKINS, MISSY

8973 Jenkins, Missy, and William Croyle. *I Choose to Be Happy: A School Shooting Survivor's Triumph Over Tragedy* (6–12). 2008, LangMarc paper $16.95 (978-1-880292-31-0). School shooting survivor Missy Jenkins documents the horrific events of December 1, 1997, in West Paducah, Kentucky, and the long road to hope and forgiveness. (Rev: SLJ 3/1/09; VOYA 6/09) [921]

JIANG, JI-LI

8974 Jiang, Ji-li. *Red Scarf Girl: A Memoir of the Cultural Revolution* (6–10). 1997, HarperCollins $17.99 (978-0-06-027585-3). An engrossing memoir of a Chinese girl, her family, and how their lives became a nightmare during Chairman Mao's Cultural Revolution of the late 1960s. (Rev: BL 10/1/97; SLJ 12/97; VOYA 6/98) [921]

KEAT, NAWUTH

8975 Keat, Nawuth, and Martha Kendall. *Alive in the Killing Fields: The True Story of Nawuth Keat, a Khmer Rouge Survivor* (7–12). 2009, National Geographic $15.95 (978-1-4263-0515-3); LB $23.90 (978-1-4263-0516-0). In this stirring memoir, Cambodian Nawuth Keat provides a graphic, wrenching picture of the life of a young refugee and his struggle toward freedom. (Rev: BL 8/09; LMC 11–12/09; SLJ 10/09) [921]

KHERDIAN, JERON

8976 Kherdian, Jeron. *The Road from Home: The Story of an Armenian Girl* (6–8). 1979, Morrow paper $6.99 (978-0-688-14425-8). A portrait of the youth of the author's mother, an Armenian girl who suffered many hardships and finally arrived in America as a mail-order bride. [921]

KOR, EVA MOZES

8977 Kor, Eva Mozes, and Lisa Rojany Buccieri. *Surviving the Angel of Death: The Story of a Mengele Twin in Auschwitz* (6–10). 2009, Tanglewood $14.95 (978-1-933718-28-6). Kor tells the horrifying story of her treatment — with her twin sister — at the hands of Mengele in Auschwitz. (Rev: LMC 5–6/10; SLJ 5/10) [921]

KORCZAK, JANUSZ

8978 Bogacki, Tomek. *The Champion of Children: The Story of Janusz Korczak* (4–7). Illus. by author. 2009, Farrar $17.99 (978-0-374-34136-7). A brave doctor who gave up his medical practice to found a Jewish orphanage in Poland during World War II and to accompany the children to Treblinka is profiled in this stark but inspiring story. (Rev: BL 10/1/09; LMC 11–12/09; SLJ 12/09) [921]

KOSSMAN, NINA

8979 Kossman, Nina. *Behind the Border* (5–7). 1994, Lothrop $14.00 (978-0-688-13494-5). This book contains 12 episodes about the author's childhood in Communist Russia before emigrating to the United States. (Rev: BCCB 10/94; BL 8/94; SLJ 10/94) [921]

LAFAYETTE, MARQUIS DE

8980 Freedman, Russell. *Lafayette and the American Revolution* (6–9). Illus. 2010, Holiday House $24.95 (978-0-8234-2182-4). Freedman provides a fascinating account of Lafayette's life and importance in the Revo-lutionary War. Sibert Honor 2011; ALA Notable Books 2011. (Rev: BL 8/10*; HB 11–12/10; LMC 3–4/11; SLJ 9/1/10) [921]

LAGASSE, EMERIL

8981 Albright, Sawyer. *Emeril Lagasse* (4–8). Series: Top Chefs. 2012, Eldorado Ink LB $29.95 (978-1-61900-016-2); paper $16.95 (978-1-61900-017-9). Describes the chef's childhood, culinary achievements, and philanthropic work. (Rev: SLJ 7/12) [921]

LAMBKE, BRYAN

8982 Lambke, Bryan, and Tom Lambke. *I Just Am: A Story of Down Syndrome Awareness and Tolerance* (4–10). 2006, Five Star $14.99 (978-1-58985-020-0). In this compelling photoessay, a young adult with Down syndrome — with some help from his father — explains what it's like to live with this disability. (Rev: SLJ 10/06)

LEKUTON, JOSEPH LEMASOLAI

8983 Lekuton, Joseph Lemasolai. *Facing the Lion: Growing Up Maasai on the African Savanna* (5–12). 2003, National Geographic $15.95 (978-0-7922-5125-5). Lekuton, a member of a nomadic Masai tribe and now a teacher in Virginia, remembers his youth in Kenya. (Rev: BCCB 5/06; BL 9/15/03; HBG 4/04; LMC 11–12/06; SLJ 10/03*) [967.62]

LI, MOYING

8984 Li, Moying. *Snow Falling in Spring: Coming of Age in China During the Cultural Revolution* (7–12). 2008, Farrar $16.00 (978-0-374-39922-1). Moying Li tells the story of her childhood during the Great Leap Forward, followed by the shock of the Cultural Revolution, during which her mother was sent to the countryside and her father to a labor camp; Li's remarkable grandmother and Li's own love of literature nurtured her through this difficult time. (Rev: BL 2/15/08; SLJ 4/08) [951.05]

MACDONALD, WARREN

8985 MacDonald, Warren. *A Test of Will: One Man's Extraordinary Story of Survival* (8–12). 2004, Douglas & McIntyre paper $14.95 (978-1-55365-064-5). The riveting story of Macdonald's survival after his legs were pinned under a massive rock on an island off Australia. (Rev: BL 9/15/04) [790.5]

MILLMAN, ISAAC

8986 Millman, Isaac. *Hidden Child* (4–7). 2005, Farrar $18.00 (978-0-374-33071-2). The author relates his experiences as a child in World War II, when he was hidden in various homes in France to save him from the Nazis. (Rev: BL 6/1–15/05*; SLJ 9/05) [921]

MOHAPATRA, JYOTIRMAYEE

8987 Woog, Adam. *Jyotirmayee Mohapatra: Advocate for India's Young Women* (4–8). Illus. Series: Young Heroes. 2006, Gale LB $27.45 (978-0-7377-3611-3). From a village in rural India, Mohapatra became worried at a young age about the challenges facing girls and young women; she went on to found the network of Meena Clubs for which she received the prestigious Youth Action Network award. (Rev: BL 1/1–15/07; SLJ 4/07)

MOLNAR, HAYA LEAH

8988 Molnar, Haya Leah. *Under a Red Sky: Memoir of a Childhood in Communist Romania* (6–9). Illus. 2010, Farrar $17.99 (978-037431840-6). Molnar remembers the rigors of growing up under communism in Eastern Europe, and her surprise at finding out that she was Jewish and would emigrate to Israel. (Rev: BL 2/15/10; SLJ 5/10; VOYA 6/10) [921]

MONAQUE, MATHILDE

8989 Monaque, Mathilde. *Trouble in My Head: A Young Girl's Fight with Depression* (7–12). Trans. by Lorenza Garcia. 2009, Trafalgar paper $15.95 (978-009191723-4). A memoir of a French teen's struggle to overcome depression. (Rev: BL 4/1/09; SLJ 9/09) [921]

MOORE, WES

8990 Moore, Wes. *Discovering Wes Moore* (7–12). Illus. 2012, Delacorte $15.99 (978-038574167-5); LB $18.99 (978-037599018-2). A memoir about two Wes Moores, one a Rhodes scholar and combat veteran and the other serving a life sentence for murder, who came from very similar backgrounds. ⌒ ℮ (Rev: BL 10/1/12; SLJ 3/13; VOYA 10/12)

NORTH, STERLING

8991 North, Sterling. *Rascal: A Memoir of a Better Era* (7–12). 1963, Dutton $16.99 (978-0-525-18839-1). Remembrances of growing up in Wisconsin in 1918 and of the joys and problems of owning a pet raccoon. Newbery Honor. (Rev: BL 9/1/89) [599.74]

PAYNE, LUCILLE M. W.

8992 Rice, Dorothy M., and Lucille Payne. *The Seventeenth Child* (7–12). 1998, Linnet LB $18.50 (978-0-208-02414-5). The story of an African American woman growing up in rural Virginia during the 1930s and 1940s, as recorded and edited by her daughter. (Rev: HBG 3/99; SLJ 1/99; VOYA 6/99) [921]

PEARY, MARIE AHNIGHITO

8993 Kirkpatrick, Katherine. *The Snow Baby: The Arctic Childhood of Robert E. Peary's Daring Daughter* (5–8). Illus. 2007, Holiday $16.95 (978-0-8234-1973-9). This engaging account of a child growing up partly among the Inuit and partly in her mother's nice home in the United States is based on the autobiography, published in 1934, of Marie Ahnighito Peary, daughter of explorer Robert E. Peary, who was born north of the Arctic Circle in 1893. (Rev: BL 4/15/07; SLJ 3/07)

RAMSAY, GORDON

8994 Galioto, Annette. *Gordon Ramsay* (7–9). Illus. Series: Top Chefs. 2012, Eldorado Ink LB $36.95 (978-161900022-3). Tells the interesting story of the mercurial chef and how he came to success on television. (Rev: BL 4/1/12; SLJ 7/12) [921]

REISS, JOHANNA

8995 Reiss, Johanna. *The Upstairs Room* (7–10). 1972, HarperCollins $19.99 (978-0-690-85127-4); paper $6.99 (978-0-06-447043-8). The author's story of her years spent hiding from the Nazis in occupied Holland. Followed by *The Journey Back* (1976). (Rev: BL 3/1/88) [921]

RHODES-COURTER, ASHLEY

8996 Rhodes-Courter, Ashley. *Three Little Words* (8–12). 2008, Atheneum $17.99 (978-1-4169-4806-3). A product of the U.S. foster care system describes her childhood with foster parents, some who were kind, others who were abusive; a disturbing story, explicitly told. (Rev: BL 1/1–15/08; LMC 2/08; SLJ 1/08) [362.73]

RODRIGUEZ, GABY

8997 Rodriguez, Gaby, and Jenna Glatzer. *The Pregnancy Project* (8–11). 2012, Simon & Schuster $17.99 (978-144244622-9). From a family with a history of teen mothers, 17-year-old Gaby decided to make her senior project a fake pregnancy, recording the reactions of students, teachers, family, and friends; her story became a sensation. YALSA Quick Picks for Reluctant Young Adult Readers 2013. ℮ Lexile 970L (Rev: BL 2/15/12; SLJ 4/12; VOYA 2/12) [306.874]

RUNYAN, BRENT

8998 Runyon, Brent. *The Burn Journals* (8–12). 2004, Random House LB $19.99 (978-0-375-82621-4). In this powerful memoir, Runyon recounts his journey to recovery from life-threatening burns suffered in a teenage suicide attempt. (Rev: BL 6/1–15/04; SLJ 11/04) [362.28]

SIEGAL, ARANKA

8999 Siegal, Aranka. *Memories of Babi* (4–7). 2008, Farrar $16.00 (978-0-374-39978-8). The author recalls her pleasant, simple life as a child in Hungary and her closeness to her Jewish grandmother in the years preceding those covered in *Upon the Head of a Goat* (1981). Sidney Taylor Book Honor 2009. (Rev: BL 12/15/07; HB 9–10/08) [947.7]

SIMMONS, RUSSELL

9000 Lommel, Cookie. *Russell Simmons* (7–10). Series: Hip-Hop Stars. 2007, Chelsea House LB $30.00 (978-0-7910-9467-9). Lommel includes lots of hip-hop history in this profile of the founder of Def Jam records. (Rev: BL 3/1/08) [921]

SON THI ANH, TUYET

9001 Skrypuch, Marsha Forchuk. *Last Airlift: A Vietnamese Orphan's Rescue from War* (4–8). Illus. 2012, Pajama $17.95 (978-098694954-8). Tells the story of 8-year-old Son Thi Anh Tuyet, a Vietnamese orphan whose suffering had included polio, who was on the last Canadian flight out of Saigon in 1975. Lexile 670L (Rev: BL 4/15/12; HB 9–10/12; SLJ 4/12) [921]

9002 Skrypuch, Marsha Forchuk. *One Step at a Time: A Vietnamese Child Finds Her Way* (4–8). Illus. 2012, Pajama $17.95 (978-192748501-9). This sequel to *Last Airlift* (2012) continues Tuyet's story as she adjusts to her new Toronto family and undergoes surgery for the deformities caused by polio. (Rev: BL 12/1/12; HB 3–4/13; SLJ 2/13) [921]

STEINER, MATTHEW

9003 Warren, Andrea. *Escape from Saigon: How a Vietnam War Orphan Became an American Boy* (5–12). 2004, Farrar $17.00 (978-0-374-32224-3). An inspiring account of a young Amerasian war orphan's long journey from Vietnam to a new and successful life in the United States; Long was part of the 1975 Operation Babylift and took the name of Matt Steiner when he was adopted by an American family. (Rev: BL 6/1–15/04*; SLJ 10/04) [959.704]

STEVE AND BINDI IRWIN

9004 Breguet, Amy E. *Steve and Bindi Irwin* (5–8). Illus. Series: Conservation Heroes. 2011, Chelsea House LB $35 (978-160413957-0). This book describes the conservation efforts of Steve Irwin, who appeared in the *Crocodile Hunter* TV show until his death — and his daughter Bindi's following in his footsteps. (Rev: BL 4/1/11) [921]

SWADOS, ELIZABETH

9005 Swados, Elizabeth. *My Depression: A Picture Book* (8–12). 2005, Hyperion $16.95 (978-1-4013-0789-9). In a candid yet entertaining cartoon picture-book format, Swados reveals her struggles with severe depression. (Rev: BL 3/15/05) [818]

TAMANG, JHALAK MAN

9006 Miller, Raymond H. *Jhalak Man Tamang: Slave Labor Whistleblower* (4–7). Series: Young Heroes. 2006, Gale LB $23.70 (978-0-7377-3616-8). This biography chronicles the life of Tamang, who was able to escape a life as a child weaving carpets in Nepal and bring to light the abuses of the industry. (Rev: SLJ 6/07) [921]

VINCENT, ERIN

9007 Vincent, Erin. *Grief Girl* (8–11). 2007, Delacorte $15.99 (978-0-385-73353-3). An account of how the author, then 14, and her siblings coped with the deaths of their parents in a car crash in 1983. (Rev: BCCB 4/07; BL 2/1/07; LMC 8–9/07; SLJ 2/07) [155.9]

WEINSTEIN, LAUREN

9008 Weinstein, Lauren. *Girl Stories* (7–10). 2006, Henry Holt paper $16.95 (978-0-8050-7863-3). Episodic graphic novel-format vignettes paint a vivid portrait of the author's 8th- and 9th-grade years. (Rev: BL 3/15/06; SLJ 7/06; VOYA 4/06) [741.5]

WONG, LI KENG

9009 Wong, Li Keng. *Good Fortune: My Journey to Gold Mountain* (4–7). 2006, Peachtree $14.95 (978-1-56145-367-2). Wong, who migrated to the United States from China with her mother and sister in 1933, writes about the challenges of adjusting to a new culture. (Rev: BL 3/1/06; SLJ 7/06)

YEBOAH, EMMANUEL OFOSU

9010 Currie-McGhee, Leanne K. *Emmanuel Ofosu Yeboah: Champion for Ghana's Disabled* (4–7). Series: Young Heroes. 2006, Gale LB $23.70 (978-0-7377-3614-4). The inspiring story of a disabled Ghanaian who fought for equal rights in a culture that discriminated against the physically challenged. (Rev: SLJ 6/07)

YU, CHUN

9011 Yu, Chun. *Little Green: Growing Up During the Chinese Cultural Revolution* (7–10). 2005, Simon & Schuster $15.95 (978-0-689-86943-3). Chun Yu, who was born the year that China's Cultural Revolution began, recounts in poetry what life was like during one of the most tumultuous periods in Chinese history. (Rev: BL 1/1–15/05; SLJ 3/05; VOYA 10/05) [951.05]

ZENATTI, VALÉRIE

9012 Zenatti, Valérie. *When I Was a Soldier* (8–11). Trans. by Adriana Hunter. 2005, Bloomsbury $16.95 (978-1-58234-978-7). In this compelling memoir, Valérie Zenatti, an immigrant to Israel from France, chronicles her two years of compulsory service in the Israeli army. (Rev: BCCB 7–8/05; BL 5/1/05*; SLJ 5/05) [921]

The Arts and Entertainment

General and Miscellaneous

9013 Bingham, Jane. *Science and Technology* (4–7). Series: Through Artists' Eyes. 2006, Raintree LB $32.86 (978-1-4109-2241-0). A brief but interesting exploration of the ways in which artists have documented the progress of science and technology over the years. Also use *Landscape and the Environment* and *Society and Class* (both 2006). (Rev: SLJ 1/07)

9014 Chapman, Caroline. *Battles and Weapons: Exploring History Through Art* (4–9). Series: Picture That! 2007, Two-Can $19.95 (978-1-58728-588-2). A look at how weapons and war have been depicted in artwork beginning in ancient times and ending in the 1950s. (Rev: SLJ 8/07)

9015 Flatt, Lizann. *Arts and Culture in the Early Islamic World* (5–7). Illus. Series: Life in the Early Islamic World. 2012, Crabtree LB $30.60 (978-077872167-3). With excellent illustrations, this attractive volume provides a solid introduction to Islamic calligraphy, architecture, and decorative arts and their importance to the overall culture of the time. (Rev: BL 8/12*; SLJ 8/12) [700.917]

9016 Marcovitz, Hal. *Anime* (6–9). Series: Eye on Art. 2007, Gale LB $32.45 (978-1-59018-995-5). Fans of Japanese comics will enjoy this history of the genre. (Rev: BL 2/15/08) [791.43]

9017 O'Kane, Bernard. *Treasures of Islam: Artistic Glories of the Muslim World* (8–12). 2007, Sterling $35.00 (978-1-84483-483-9). With about 170 color photographs, this handsome volume traces Islamic art and architecture from the 7th to 19th centuries and discusses political and religious aspects throughout. (Rev: BL 10/1/07) [709]

9018 Raczka, Bob. *Where in the World? Around the Globe in 13 Works of Art* (5–8). Illus. Series: Art Adventures. 2007, Lerner LB $23.93 (978-0-8225-6371-6). Full-page reproductions and lively text introduce 13 famous works of art, with information on the artist. (Rev: BL 6/1–15/07; SLJ 8/07)

9019 Robson, David. *The Black Arts Movement* (7–12). Series: Lucent Library of Black History. 2008, Gale/Lucent $32.45 (978-1-4205-0053-0). Black nationalism, cultural influences, identity, and assimilation are all considered as factors in this overview of the movement that has had an impact in literature, music, and art. (Rev: SLJ 2/1/09) [700.89]

9020 Tan, Shaun. *The Bird King: An Artist's Notebook* (7–12). Illus. by author. 2013, Scholastic $19.99 (978-054546513-7). A collection of fascinating sketches that show how an expert artist records his ideas. (Rev: BL 11/1/12*; SLJ 3/13; VOYA 4/13) [741.6]

9021 Tomecek, Stephen M. *Art and Architecture* (4–7). Illus. Series: Experimenting with Everyday Science. 2010, Chelsea House LB $35 (978-1-60413-168-0). Twenty-five accessible experiments illustrate important concepts in art or architecture ranging from the practical — testing stress on metal, how an arch supports a load — to the more artistic — mixing pigments, how image depth affects perspective. (Rev: SLJ 11/1/10) [701.03]

Architecture and Building

General and Miscellaneous

9022 Arbogast, Joan Marie. *Buildings in Disguise: Architecture That Looks Like Animals, Food, and Other Things* (4–7). 2004, Boyds Mills $16.95 (978-1-59078-099-2). Buildings in the shapes of milk bottles, elephants, wigwams, and baskets are among the wonders shown in many period and contemporary photographs. (Rev: BL 11/1/04; SLJ 1/05) [720]

9023 Bos, Samone. *Super Structures* (5–8). Illus. by Alessandro Rabatti. 2008, DK $19.99 (978-0-7566-4088-0). Captivating photographs, illustrations, and diagrams enhance the text in this fascinating survey of buildings and structures across history. (Rev: BL 12/1/08; SLJ 3/09) [720]

9024 Curlee, Lynn. *Skyscraper* (4–7). Illus. 2007, Simon & Schuster $17.99 (978-0-689-84489-8). Accompanied by striking acrylic paintings, Curlee's detailed narrative explores the architectural history and engineering of skyscrapers. (Rev: BL 1/1–15/07; SLJ 3/07)

9025 Glenn, Patricia Brown. *Under Every Roof: A Kid's Style and Field Guide to the Architecture of American Houses* (5–8). 1993, Preservation $16.95 (978-0-89133-214-5). An introduction to the history and styles of architecture of American homes, with a look at more than 70 houses. (Rev: BL 7/94; SLJ 6/94) [728]

9026 Hosack, Karen. *Buildings* (4–8). Illus. Series: What Is Art? 2008, Raintree LB $27.50 (978-1-4109-3165-8). Hosack introduces a number of kinds of buildings — public spaces, private residences, memorials, and so forth — and discusses their function and form; a bright layout and well-chosen illustrations add appeal. (Rev: SLJ 3/1/09) [720]

9027 Laroche, Giles. *What's Inside? Fascinating Structures Around the World* (4–8). Illus. by author. 2009,

Houghton Mifflin $17 (978-0-618-86247-4). This handsome, fact-filled volume looks at both the exteriors and interiors (with people going about activities) of 14 structures ranging from tombs, temples, and castles to skyscrapers and the Sydney Opera House. (Rev: BL 2/15/09; SLJ 5/1/09) [720]

9028 Phillips, Cynthia, and Shana Priwer. *Ancient Monuments* (7–10). Illus. Series: Frameworks. 2008, Sharpe Focus LB $43.95 (978-076568123-2). A look at monuments in ancient Greece, Rome, China, Europe, and other regions, with discussion of the engineering feats involved as well as their beauty and significance. (Rev: BL 4/1/09; SLJ 9/09) [732]

History of Architecture

9029 Curlee, Lynn. *Parthenon* (5–8). Illus. by author. 2004, Simon & Schuster $17.95 (978-0-689-84490-4). A beautifully composed overview of the construction and history of the temple built by the ancient Greeks to honor the goddess Athena. (Rev: BL 9/15/04*; HB 7–8/04; SLJ 6/04) [726]

9030 De Medeiros, James. *Parthenon* (6–9). Series: Structural Wonders. 2007, Weigl LB $26.00 (978-1-59036-727-8); paper $7.95 (978-1-59036-728-5). This interesting account of the construction of the Parthenon also discusses its current status and includes excellent full-color photographs. (Rev: SLJ 12/07) [726]

9031 Forward, Toby. *Shakespeare's Globe: An Interactive Pop-up Theatre* (5–8). Illus. by Juan Wijngaard. 2005, Candlewick $19.99 (978-0-7636-2694-5). A large-format pop-up model of the Globe Theatre, with narrative by a Shakespeare colleague and scenes from Shakespeare's plays. (Rev: BL 5/1/05; SLJ 11/05) [792]

9032 George, Charles. *Pyramids* (5–9). Series: Mysterious and Unknown. 2007, Reference Point LB $24.95 (978-1-60152-027-2). Pyramids around the world are addressed in this well-written text with color photographs; useful for reports. (Rev: SLJ 2/08)

9033 Macaulay, David. *Building the Book Cathedral* (5–9). 1999, Houghton Mifflin $29.95 (978-0-395-92147-0). The author retells the fascinating story behind the creation of the original *Cathedral* book 25 years ago and adds numerous changes as he leads a tour of the cathedral, such as alterations in scale and page placement. (Rev: BCCB 12/99; BL 11/15/99; HB 9–10/99; SLJ 9/99) [726]

9034 Macaulay, David. *Castle* (5–8). Illus. by author. 1977, Houghton Mifflin $20.00 (978-0-395-25784-5); paper $9.95 (978-0-395-32920-7). Another of the author's brilliant, detailed works, this one on the planning and building of a Welsh castle. [940.1]

9035 Macaulay, David. *Cathedral: The Story of Its Construction* (6–8). Illus. by author. 1973, Houghton Mifflin $18.00 (978-0-395-17513-2). Gothic architecture as seen through a detailed examination of the construction of an imaginary cathedral. [726]

9036 Macaulay, David. *Mill* (5–8). Illus. by author. 1983, Houghton Mifflin $19.00 (978-0-395-34830-7); paper $9.95 (978-0-395-52019-2). Rhode Island textile mills of the 19th century are described in text and excellent drawings. [690]

9037 Macaulay, David. *Mosque* (6–12). 2003, Houghton Mifflin $18.00 (978-0-618-24034-0). Macaulay follows a 16th-century mosque through initial design and planning, construction, and the uses of the finished structure and all its associated support buildings. (Rev: BL 10/1/03*; HB 11–12/03; SLJ 11/03*) [726]

9038 Macaulay, David. *Pyramid* (7–12). 1975, Houghton Mifflin $20.00 (978-0-395-21407-7); paper $9.95 (978-0-395-32121-8). In beautiful line drawings, the author describes how an ancient Egyptian pyramid was constructed. [726]

9039 Mann, Elizabeth. *The Parthenon: The Height of Greek Civilization* (4–7). Illus. by Yuan Lee. 2006, Mikaya $22.95 (978-1-931414-15-9). The engineering feats involved in the construction of the Parthenon are placed in historical and cultural context; includes a foldout spread, a useful map, and many illustrations. (Rev: BL 12/1/06; SLJ 3/07)

9040 Nardo, Don. *Artistry in Stone: Great Structures of Ancient Egypt* (6–10). Series: The Lucent Library of Historical Eras. 2005, Gale LB $32.45 (978-1-59018-661-9). Photographs, reproductions, and film and documentary stills illustrate this well-documented examination of massive ancient Egyptian structures such as the pyramids and the Sphinx. (Rev: SLJ 11/05) [932]

9041 Weaver, Janice. *Building America* (5–8). Illus. by Bonnie Shemie. 2002, Tundra $17.95 (978-0-88776-606-0). This brief history of architecture in America, from the 17th century to today, features detailed renderings, an illustrated timeline, and a useful glossary. (Rev: HBG 3/03; SLJ 5/03) [721]

9042 Webster, Christine. *Great Wall of China* (6–9). Series: Structural Wonders. 2007, Weigl LB $26.00 (978-1-59036-723-0); paper $7.95 (978-1-59036-724-7). This interesting account of the construction of the Great Wall also discusses its current status and includes excellent full-color photographs. (Rev: SLJ 12/07) [623]

Painting, Sculpture, and Photography

General and Miscellaneous

9043 Albert, Michael. *An Artist's America* (3–8). 2008, Holt $17.95 (978-0-8050-7857-2). Pop artist Albert uses recycled materials to create collages interpreting a number of historic events and trends. (Rev: SLJ 4/08) [709.2]

9044 Aldana, Patricia, ed. *Under the Spell of the Moon: Art for Children from the World's Great Illustrators* (6–12). Trans. by Stan Dragland. 2004, Groundwood $25.00 (978-0-88899-559-9). Artwork by children's book illustrators from around the world celebrates children's literature and the work of the International Board on Books for Young People. (Rev: BL 12/15/04; SLJ 1/05) [741.6]

9045 *Artist to Artist: 23 Major Illustrators Talk to Children About Their Art* (5–8). Illus. 2007, Philomel $30.00 (978-0-399-24600-5). More than 20 children's book illustrators (including Quentin Blake, Leo Lionni, and Tomie dePaola) contribute creative self-portraits and insightful thoughts to this beautiful gatefolded book. (Rev: BL 11/1/07; SLJ 10/07)

9046 Barber, Nicola. *Islamic Art and Culture* (5–8). Series: World Art and Culture. 2005, Raintree LB $32.86 (978-1-4109-1105-6). High-quality color photographs document the architecture, sculpture, painting, pottery, music, dance, and other art forms found in the Islamic world from early times to the present. (Rev: BL 4/1/04)

9047 Bingham, Jane. *Graffiti* (5–7). Illus. Series: Culture in Action. 2009, Raintree LB $28.21 (978-1-4109-3401-7); paper $7.99 (978-1-4109-3418-5). Bingham traces the history of graffiti back to cave walls and describes (with examples) modern forms and the pitfalls of indulging in this activity. (Rev: LMC 3–4/10; SLJ 2/10) [751.7]

9048 *Children's Book of Art: An Introduction to the World's Most Amazing Paintings and Sculptures* (5–8). Illus. 2009, DK $24.99 (978-0-7566-5511-2). This well-designed, large-format volume includes everything from artist profiles to style analysis to how-to instructions. (Rev: BLO 10/1/09; LMC 11–12/09; SLJ 10/09) [700]

9049 Coyne, Jennifer Tarr. *Come Look with Me: Discovering Women Artists for Children* (4–7). Series: Come Look with Me. 2005, Lickle $15.95 (978-1-890674-08-3). Beautifully reproduced examples of works by women artists are paired with brief biographical information and questions that direct the reader's attention to different aspects of art. (Rev: BL 5/1/05; SLJ 6/05) [709]

9050 de Rynck, Patrick, ed. *How to Read a Painting: Lessons from the Old Masters* (8–12). 2004, Abrams $35.00 (978-0-8109-5576-9). Introduces readers to the symbols, themes, and motifs that aid understanding of the great masters' art; two-page spreads display 150 paintings and frescoes. (Rev: BL 12/15/04) [753]

9051 Delafosse, Claude. *Landscapes* (4–7). Series: First Discovery Art. 1996, Scholastic $11.95 (978-0-590-50216-0). The art and techniques of landscape painting are introduced, with many examples from the masters in various historical periods. (Rev: BL 6/1–15/96; SLJ 7/96) [750]

9052 Delafosse, Claude. *Paintings* (4–7). Series: First Discovery Art. 1996, Scholastic $11.95 (978-0-590-55201-1). A general introduction to painting, with many reproductions and lessons in art appreciation. (Rev: BL 6/1–15/96; SLJ 7/96) [750]

9053 Fillion, Susan. *Miss Etta and Dr. Claribel: Bringing Matisse to America* (8–12). Illus. 2011, Godine $18.95 (978-1-56792-434-3). Tells the story of two art-loving sisters responsible for introducing America to Picasso, Matisse, and many other artists from Europe, Asia, and Africa in the early 20th century; this well-designed book includes many illustrations and reproductions. (Rev: BL 10/1/11; HB 9–10/11; SLJ 9/1/11*) [709.2]

9054 Fritz, Jean. *Leonardo's Horse* (4–7). Illus. by Hudson Talbott. 2001, Putnam $18.99 (978-0-399-23576-4). The story of a Leonardo da Vinci sculpture that was begun in 1493 and finally completed — thanks to the efforts of Charles Dent — in 1999, along with biographical information about da Vinci and examples of his work. (Rev: BCCB 10/01; BL 10/15/01; HB 9–10/01; HBG 3/02; SLJ 9/01) [730]

9055 Ganz, Nicholas. *Graffiti World: Street Art from Five Continents* (8–12). Ed. by Tristan Manco. 2004, Abrams $35.00 (978-0-8109-4979-9). Graffiti from around the world is organized by continent and then by artist, with more than 2,000 color photos showing the common themes and wonderful inventiveness of these artists. (Rev: BL 1/1–15/05; SLJ 5/05) [751.7]

9056 Gunderson, Jessica. *Impressionism* (6–9). Illus. Series: Movements in Art. 2008, Creative Education $32.80 (978-158341611-2). An accessible overview of the art movement, the principal artists, and their subjects and techniques, with high-quality reproductions and discussion of background context. (Rev: BL 11/1/08; SLJ 12/08; VOYA 6/09) [709.03]

9057 Hand, John Oliver. *National Gallery of Art: Master Paintings from the Collection* (8–12). 2004, Abrams $60.00 (978-0-8109-5619-3). Four hundred paintings from the National Gallery serve as the base for a satisfying review of European and American art. (Rev: BL 11/15/04) [750]

9058 Hosack, Karen. *Drawings and Cartoons* (4–8). Illus. Series: What Is Art? 2008, Raintree LB $27.50 (978-1-4109-3163-4). Drawings from Michelangelo to modern-day are on display here, accompanied by a paragraph disclosing their purpose and posing questions about their style. (Rev: SLJ 3/1/09) [741]

9059 Kallen, Stuart A. *Photography* (7–12). Series: Eye on Art. 2007, Gale LB $32.45 (978-1-59018-986-3). Tracing the history of the camera and of photography as an art form, this volume includes plenty of photographs that illustrate concepts and styles. (Rev: BL 11/1/07; LMC 2/08; SLJ 12/07) [770]

9060 *Life: The Platinum Anniversary Collection* (7–12). 2006, Time-Life $29.95 (978-1-933405-17-9). This is a showcase of the best of 70 years of *Life* photography. (Rev: BL 11/15/06) [070.4]

9061 Nilsen, Anna. *Art Auction Mystery* (5–8). 2005, Kingfisher $16.95 (978-0-7534-5842-6). Wannabe art sleuths are challenged to find forgeries hidden in a selection of world-famous paintings. (Rev: BL 11/1/05; SLJ 1/06; VOYA 12/05) [759]

9062 Nilsen, Anna. *The Great Art Scandal: Solve the Crime, Save the Show!* (4–9). 2003, Kingfisher $16.95 (978-0-7534-5587-6). Readers must solve a mystery involving an art exhibition in this comic-book-format work that introduces many famous paintings and artists. (Rev: SLJ 3/04) [759.06]

9063 Ogier, Susan. *Objects and Meanings* (5–8). Series: Step-Up Art and Design. 2010, Cherrytree LB $27.10 (978-1-84234-573-3). With plenty of photographs, this volume looks at the artistic techniques involved in everything from still life and trompe l'oeil to folk art and using found objects. Also use *People in Action, A Sense of Place,* and *Talking Textiles* (all 2010). (Rev: LMC 10/10; SLJ 5/10) [700]

9064 Raczka, Bob. *Unlikely Pairs: Fun with Famous Works of Art* (4–10). 2005, Millbrook LB $23.93 (978-0-7613-2936-7); paper $9.95 (978-0-7613-2378-5). Raczka pairs famous works from different eras and styles (Rodin's "The Thinker" appears to be considering a move on Klee's chessboard, for example); a closing catalog offers factual information. (Rev: SLJ 12/05) [750]

9065 Sousa, Jean. *Faces, Places, and Inner Spaces* (5–8). Illus. 2006, Abrams $18.95 (978-0-8109-5966-8). The director of interpretive exhibitions and family programs at the Art Institute of Chicago introduces a variety of works — portraits, landscapes, and abstract pieces — and asks questions that stimulate analysis. (Rev: BL 5/15/06; SLJ 7/06)

9066 Wenzel, Angela. *Thirteen Art Mysteries Children Should Know* (5–7). Illus. 2011, Prestel $14.95 (978-3-7913-7044-6). In chronological order, this volume presents 13 mysteries of the art world, including questions about the Mona Lisa, a Raphael painting, van Gogh's ear, and the identity of graffiti artist Banksy. (Rev: BL 11/1/11; SLJ 10/1/11) [759]

9067 White, Matt. *Cameras on the Battlefield: Photos of War* (5–7). Series: High Five Reading. 2002, Capstone LB $23.93 (978-0-7368-4004-0). For reluctant readers, this is an appealing look at photographs of war, both those that celebrate war and those that document its horrors. (Rev: SLJ 8/02) [779.9355]

History of Art

9068 Baskett, John. *The Horse in Art* (8–12). 2006, Yale $45.00 (978-0-300-11740-0). Representations of horses in both two- and three-dimensional art are presented here, from ancient Greek and Roman battle scenes to medieval, Renaissance, Baroque, 19th-century, and modern-day works, including pieces by Stubbs, Rubens, and Remington. (Rev: BL 11/1/06) [704.94]

9069 Belloli, Andrea. *Exploring World Art* (7–12). 1999, Getty Museum $27.50 (978-0-89236-510-4). Using examples from world art and artifacts, this work introduces a variety of media and images under such chapter headings as "Daily Life" and "History and Myth." (Rev: BL 1/1–15/00; HBG 4/00; SLJ 4/00) [709]

9070 D'Harcourt, Claire. *Masterpieces Up Close: Western Painting from the 14th to 20th Centuries* (4–8). Trans. from French by Shoshanna Kirk. Series: Up Close. 2006, Chronicle $22.95 (978-0-8118-5403-0). An oversize volume that challenges readers to analyze major works of Western art. (Rev: SLJ 7/06)

9071 Demilly, Christian. *Pop Art* (6–9). Series: Adventures in Art. 2007, Prestel $14.95 (978-3-7913-3894-1). Beautiful reproductions of many of the most important and most memorable works of Pop Art will draw readers in to this book, which traces the early-20th-century movement from its origins to its influence. (Rev: BL 11/1/07; SLJ 4/08) [709]

9072 Khalili, Nasser D. *Islamic Art and Culture: A Visual History* (8–12). 2006, Overlook $60.00 (978-1-58567-839-6). This is a large and varied collection of examples of Islamic art, ranging from carpets and textiles, paintings, jewelry, and lacquer to calligraphy, metal work, scientific instruments, and weapons; a good introduction to the culture of Islam. (Rev: BL 11/1/06) [709]

9073 Knapp, Ruthie, and Janice Lehmberg. *Impressionist Art* (5–9). Series: Off the Wall Museum Guides for Kids. 1999, Davis paper $9.95 (978-0-87192-385-1). This pocket-size guide supplies an overview of Impressionism and brief introductions to major artists, including Sisley and Monet. (Rev: BL 1/1–15/99) [709.03]

9074 Knapp, Ruthie, and Janice Lehmberg. *Modern Art* (5–9). Series: Off the Wall Museum Guides for Kids. 2001, Davis paper $9.95 (978-0-87192-458-2). A lively and colorful survey of 20th-century art including examples from expressionists, cubists, surrealists, and pop artists. (Rev: BL 8/1/01) [709]

9075 Langley, Andrew. *Ancient Greece* (4–8). Series: History in Art. 2004, Raintree LB $29.93 (978-1-4109-0517-8). A look at what art can reveal about the culture and technology of a society. (Rev: SLJ 4/05) [709]

9076 Mason, Antony. *A History of Western Art: From Prehistory to the 20th Century* (7–10). 2007, Abrams $22.50 (978-0-8109-9421-8). A sweeping overview of important sculpture, architecture, painting, and other works from Western culture from the ancient to the postmodern, presented in a pleasing, uncrowded design. (Rev: BL 2/1/08; SLJ 4/08) [709]

9077 Mason, Antony. *In the Time of Michelangelo: The Renaissance Period* (7–10). Series: Art Around the World. 2001, Millbrook LB $23.90 (978-0-7613-2455-3). Full of full-color reproductions, this volume not only looks at the work of major artists of the Renaissance but also profiles artists in other parts of the world during the 15th and 16th centuries. Also use *In the Time of Renoir: The Impressionist Era* (2001). (Rev: HBG 10/02; SLJ 3/02) [709]

9078 Opie, Mary-Jane. *Sculpture* (7–12). Series: Eyewitness Art. 1994, DK $16.95 (978-1-56458-613-1). A handsome book filled with color illustrations introducing the world of sculpture, its history, and its various forms and materials. (Rev: BL 12/1/94; SLJ 6/95; VOYA 5/95) [730]

9079 Robinson, Shannon. *Cubism* (6–12). Series: Movements in Art. 2005, Creative Education LB $31.35 (978-1-58341-347-0). A review of cubism from the works of Picasso and Braque through the movement's influence on sculpture and architecture, with large, clear reproductions. (Rev: SLJ 2/06)

9080 Sabbeth, Carol. *Monet and the Impressionists for Kids* (6–9). 2002, Chicago Review paper $17.95 (978-1-55652-397-7). Sabbeth introduces the life and work of seven impressionist artists — Monet, Renoir, Degas, Cassatt, Cezanne, Gauguin, and Seurat — and provides 21 related activities. (Rev: BL 7/02; SLJ 6/02) [759.05]

9081 Sabbeth, Carol. *Van Gogh and the Post-Impressionists for Kids: Their Lives and Ideas, 21 Activities* (6–9). Illus. 2011, Chicago Review paper $17.95 (978-1-56976-275-2). This appealing volume covers van Gogh's life from childhood, explores the lives of other artists of his time, and presents many reproductions as well as activities such as a Starry Night Peep Box and a Pointillist Sailboat. e (Rev: BL 6/1/11; SLJ 5/11) [709.03]

9082 Salvi, Francesco. *The Impressionists. Rev. ed.* (5–8). Illus. by L. R. Galante. Series: Art Masters. 2008, Oliver LB $24.95 (978-1-934545-03-4). A look at the work of the main artists contributing to this movement: Manet, Monet, Renoir, Degas, Cezanne, Pissaro, Sisley, Morisot, Cassatt, Guillaumin, and Caillebotte; the appealing design will please report writers. (Rev: BL 4/15/08) [759.054]

9083 Sandler, Martin W. *Photography: An Illustrated History* (6–12). 2002, Oxford $39.99 (978-0-19-512608-2). An overview of photography's major figures and developments, from its invention to new technologies, featuring many photographs. (Rev: BL 4/15/02; HBG 3/03; SLJ 6/02; VOYA 4/02) [770.9]

9084 *30,000 Years of Art: The Story of Human Creativity across Time and Space* (7–12). 2007, Phaidon $49.95 (978-0-7148-4789-4). Arranged chronologically, 1,000 beautifully reproduced pieces of art illustrate the evolution of creativity around the world. (Rev: BL 11/1/07) [700]

9085 Zuffi, Stefano. *The Cat in Art* (8–12). Trans. by Simon Jones. 2007, Abrams $35.00 (978-0-8109-9328-0). A survey of art featuring cats serves to introduce a wide variety of artists — from Raphael and Rembrandt to Picasso and Warhol — and art forms. (Rev: BL 5/1/07) [704.9]

Regions

Asia and the Middle East

9086 Hibbert, Clare. *Chinese Art and Culture* (5–8). Series: World Art and Culture. 2005, Raintree LB $29.99 (978-1-4109-1107-0). High-quality color photographs document the architecture, sculpture, painting, pottery, music, dance, and other art forms found in China from early times to the present. (Rev: BL 4/1/04)

9087 Khanduri, Kamini. *Japanese Art and Culture* (5–8). Series: World Art and Culture. 2004, Raintree LB $29.99 (978-0-7398-6609-2). High-quality color photographs document the architecture, sculpture, painting, pottery, music, dance, and other art forms found in Japan from early times to the present. (Rev: BL 4/1/04)

9088 Lane, Kimberly. *Come Look with Me: Asian Art* (3–7). Illus. by author. 2008, Charlesbridge $15.95 (978-1-890674-19-9). Lane introduces readers to a wide variety of Asian works of art, prefacing each with pertinent questions. (Rev: BLO 6/17/08; SLJ 8/08) [709.5]

Europe

9089 Etienne, Vincent. *Vermeer's Secret World* (6–8). Trans. by Sarah Kane. Illus. Series: Adventures in Art. 2008, Prestel $14.95 (978-379133987-0). Readers are encouraged to examine Vermeer's works closely and to analyze the emotions they convey. (Rev: BLO 10/7/08)

9090 Gunderson, Jessica. *Gothic Art* (5–10). Series: Movements in Art. 2008, Creative Education $32.80 (978-1-58341-610-5). With good reproductions and clear historical context, Gunderson looks at the era of Gothic art. Also use *Realism* and *Romanticism* (both 2008). (Rev: SLJ 12/08) [709.02]

9091 Impelluso, Lucia. *Nature and Its Symbols* (8–12). Trans. by Stephen Sartarelli. 2004, Getty Museum paper $24.95 (978-0-89236-772-6). A helpful guide to the symbols found in European painters' depictions of the natural world from the 14th through the 17th centuries. (Rev: BL 12/15/04) [704.9]

9092 Raczka, Bob. *The Vermeer Interviews: Conversations with Seven Works of Art* (3–7). 2009, Millbrook LB $25.26 (978-0-8225-9402-4). Raczka uses an interview format here, talking directly to the subjects of seven important Vermeer works and learning about their lives and times. (Rev: LMC 8/09; SLJ 5/09; VOYA 4/09) [759.9492]

9093 Rebman, Renee C. *The Sistine Chapel* (7–10). Series: Building History. 2000, Lucent LB $28.70 (978-1-56006-640-8). This account includes material on Michelangelo's original creation, his conflicts with the Pope, and the recent restorations of the ceiling. (Rev: BL 9/15/00; HBG 3/01) [945]

9094 Serres, Alain. *And Picasso Painted Guernica* (4–8). Trans. by Rosalind Price. 2011, Allen & Unwin $24.99 (978-1-74175-994-5). This handsome volume explores Picasso's major mural documenting the destruction of Guernica during the Spanish Civil War, and illustrates the evolution of his art. Lexile 900L (Rev: SLJ 1/1/11*)

9095 Wenzel, Angela. *Rene Magritte: Now You See It — Now You Don't* (4–7). Series: Adventures in Art. 1998, Prestel $14.95 (978-3-7913-1873-8). An examination of some of the works of Belgian surrealist Rene Magritte. (Rev: BL 8/98; SLJ 8/98) [759.949]

United States

9096 Amaki, Amalia K., ed. *A Century of African American Art: The Paul R. Jones Collection* (8–12). 2004, Rutgers paper $29.95 (978-0-8135-3457-2). The work of 66 African American artists is showcased in this attractive volume that includes profiles and commentary. (Rev: BL 2/1/05) [704.03]

9097 Butler, Jerry. *A Drawing in the Sand: A Story of African American Art* (4–7). 1999, Zino $24.95 (978-1-55933-216-3). This oversize book contains two narratives; the first is a history of African American art and artists, the second, an autobiography of Jerry Butler, the African American artist. (Rev: BL 2/15/99*) [704.03]

9098 Clee, Paul. *Photography and the Making of the American West* (6–9). 2003, Linnet LB $27.50 (978-0-208-02512-8). Clee explores the photographs that documented the exploration of the West and the impact they had on Americans' perceptions. (Rev: SLJ 1/04; VOYA 4/04) [770]

9099 Cummings, Pat. *Talking with Artists, Vol. 3* (4–8). Series: Talking with Artists. 1999, Clarion $22.00 (978-0-395-89132-2). This is the third volume of interviews with children's artists and includes Peter Sis, Betsy Lewin, and Paul O. Zelinsky, with examples of their works. (Rev: BCCB 4/99; BL 3/15/99; HB 5–6/99; HBG 10/99; SLJ 4/99) [741.6]

9100 Curtis, Edward S., and Christopher Cardozo. *Edward S. Curtis: The Women* (8–12). 2005, Bulfinch $35.00 (978-0-8212-2895-1). This stunning volume showcases 100 of photographer Edward S. Curtis's portraits of Native American women. (Rev: BL 4/1/05) [779]

9101 January, Brendan. *Native American Art and Culture* (5–8). Series: World Art and Culture. 2005, Raintree LB $32.86 (978-1-4109-1108-7). Pottery, textiles, carving, painting, textiles, and architecture are all discussed, along with body art, ceremonies, songs, and dances; many color photographs are included and a list of museums is appended. (Rev: BL 4/1/04; SLJ 6/05)

9102 Knapp, Ruthie, and Janice Lehmberg. *American Art* (5–9). Series: Off the Wall Museum Guides for Kids. 1999, Davis paper $9.95 (978-0-87192-386-8). An informal pocket-size art appreciation book that features portraits from several centuries of American art, plus various artifacts and furniture. (Rev: BL 1/1–15/99) [709.73]

9103 Panchyk, Richard. *American Folk Art for Kids: With 21 Activities* (6–12). 2004, Chicago Review paper $16.95 (978-1-55652-499-8). This historical survey of American folk art is supplemented by detailed instructions for projects that readers can make for themselves. (Rev: BL 11/1/04; SLJ 11/04) [745]

9104 Sandler, Martin W. *America Through the Lens: Photographers Who Changed the Nation* (6–9). 2005, Henry Holt $18.95 (978-0-8050-7367-6). Profiles 11 American photographers whose inspiring works may have influenced how America perceives itself and its actions. (Rev: BL 9/1/05; SLJ 11/05; VOYA 8/05) [770]

9105 Slowik, Theresa J. *America's Art: Smithsonian American Art Museum* (8–12). 2006, Abrams $65.00 (978-0-8109-5532-5). An oversize volume showcasing some of the best-known works in the collection of the Smithsonian American Art Museum. (Rev: BL 3/15/06) [709]

South and Central America

9106 Lane, Kimberly. *Come Look with Me: Latin American Art* (4–8). Illus. Series: Come Look with Me. 2007, Charlesbridge $15.95 (978-1-890674-20-5). An oversize introduction to Latin American art over the last two centuries, with color reproductions and information on the artists' lives and techniques. (Rev: BL 8/07; LMC 1/08; SLJ 8/07)

9107 Presilla, Maricel E. *Mola: Cuna Life Stories and Art* (5–7). 1996, Henry Holt $17.95 (978-0-8050-3801-9). An examination of the life and art of the Cuna Indians, who live on islands off the coast of Panama. (Rev: BCCB 1/97; BL 10/1/96; SLJ 10/96) [305.48]

Decorative Arts

9108 Emert, Phyllis Raybin. *Art in Glass* (7–12). Series: Eye on Art. 2007, Gale LB $32.45 (978-1-59018-983-2). This book reviews the history of glassmaking from ancient times through Venetian glass to art nouveau and art deco to contemporary styles and techniques. (Rev: LMC 2/08; SLJ 12/07) [748]

Music

General and Miscellaneous

9109 Crossingham, John. *Learn to Speak Music: A Guide to Creating, Performing, and Promoting Your Songs* (5–8). Illus. by Jeff Kulak. 2009, Owlkids paper $17.95 (978-1-897349-65-6). An attractive overview of the basics of music with advice on writing music, forming a band, dealing with stage fright, and so forth. (Rev: BL 11/1/09; LMC 1–2/10; SLJ 11/09) [782.42]

9110 Evans, Roger. *How to Read Music: For Singing, Guitar, Piano, Organ, and Most Instruments* (8–12). 1979, Crown paper $10.00 (978-0-517-88438-6). An easily understood introduction to music notation and score reading for the beginner. [781.4]

9111 Garty, Judy. *Marching Band Competition* (6–9). Series: Let's Go Team. 2003, Mason Crest LB $19.95 (978-1-59084-539-4). Students considering joining a marching band will learn about the kinds of competitions that take place and the planning and rehearsing necessary. Also use *Techniques of Marching Bands* (2003). (Rev: SLJ 11/03) [784.8]

9112 Igus, Toyomi. *I See the Rhythm* (5–8). 1998, Children's $15.95 (978-0-89239-151-6). Using a timeline to set the social context, this title traces African American contributions to such musical forms as the blues, big band, jazz, bebop, gospel, and rock. (Rev: BCCB 7–8/98; BL 2/15/98; SLJ 6/98) [780]

History of Music

9113 Cornish, Melanie J. *The History of Hip Hop* (4–7). Illus. 2009, Crabtree LB $19.95 (978-0-7787-3820-6); paper $8.95 (978-0-7787-3841-1). A single house party

in 1973 started hip-hop and it bopped on from there. (Rev: BL 6/1–15/09) [782.42164909]

9114 Gilbert, Sara. *Play It Loud! The Rebellious History of Music* (6–10). Illus. Series: Pop Culture Revolutions. 2010, Compass Point LB $31.99 (978-0-7565-4243-6). This title discusses the history of music with a counterculture message, and profiles artists ranging from J. S. Bach to Tupac Shakur. (Rev: SLJ 5/10) [780.9]

9115 Handyside, Christopher. *Folk* (5–9). 2006, Heinemann LB $31.43 (978-1-4034-8150-4). This attractive volume traces the evolution of American folk music from its post-Civil War roots to its influence on the contemporary music scene and introduces some of its most influential figures, including Leadbelly, Woody Guthrie, Joan Baez, and Bob Dylan. (Rev: SLJ 9/06)

9116 Kallen, Stuart A. *The History of Classical Music* (6–10). Series: Music Library. 2002, Gale LB $32.45 (978-1-59018-123-2). This overview covers classical music and composers starting with the Middle Ages, providing interesting excerpts from primary documents. Also use *The History of Jazz* (2002). (Rev: BL 11/1/02) [781.6]

Jazz and Popular Music (Country, Rap, Rock, etc.)

9117 Aquila, Richard. *That Old Time Rock and Roll: A Chronicle of an Era, 1954-1963* (8–12). 1989, Schirmer $25.00 (978-0-02-870082-3). A history complete with important biographies from the first decade of rock. (Rev: BL 9/15/89) [784.5]

9118 Bertholf, Bret. *The Long Gone Lonesome History of Country Music* (5–8). Illus. 2007, Little, Brown $18.99 (978-0-316-52393-6). A chatty survey of country music, discussing its roots and early instruments, tracing the evolution to today's sounds, and introducing some of its greatest performers. (Rev: BL 4/1/07; SLJ 4/07*)

9119 Bolden, Tonya. *Take-Off: American All-Girl Bands during WWII* (6–9). 2007, Knopf $18.99 (978-0-375-82797-6). Women on the homefront during World War II stepped in and formed their own bands when male swing musicians went off to fight. This book and music CD celebrates their sound; photographs, newspaper accounts, and other elements add interest. (Rev: BL 2/15/07; SLJ 6/07) [784.4]

9120 Delancey, Morgan. *Dave Matthews Band: Step Into the Light. Rev. 2nd ed.* (7–12). 2001, ECW paper $16.95 (978-1-55022-443-6). In addition to a detailed history of the band, this revised edition includes interviews with band members. (Rev: VOYA 8/02) [782.42]

9121 George-Warren, Holly. *Shake, Rattle and Roll: The Founders of Rock and Roll* (4–7). 2001, Houghton Mifflin $16.00 (978-0-618-05540-1). After an informative introduction on the history of rock and roll, there is a series of one-page biographies of famous personalities. (Rev: BL 3/1/01; HBG 10/01; SLJ 5/01*) [781.66]

9122 Handyside, Christopher. *Country* (5–9). Series: A History of American Music. 2006, Heinemann LB $31.43 (978-1-4034-8151-1). This history of country music traces the genre from its hillbilly roots to the present and introduces some of its most influential figures, including the Carter family, Johnny Cash, Loretta Lynn, and John Denver. (Rev: SLJ 9/06) [781.642]

9123 Hasan, Heather. *How to Produce, Release, and Market Your Music* (5–8). Illus. Series: Garage Bands. 2012, Rosen LB $12.95 (978-144885658-9). Everything you need to know about making it in the music world, from initial recording through booking shows, establishing copyright, marketing strategies, and use of social media. (Rev: BL 4/1/12) [780.23]

9124 Kallen, Stuart A. *The History of Rock and Roll* (6–10). Series: Music Library. 2002, Gale LB $32.45 (978-1-59018-126-3). Beginning in the early 1950s, this account traces the history of rock and roll, profiles many musicians involved, and describes the unique characteristics of this form of music. (Rev: BL 3/15/03) [781.66]

9125 Marsalis, Wynton. *Jazz A B Z: An A to Z Collection of Jazz Portraits* (7–12). Illus. by Paul Rogers. 2005, Candlewick $24.99 (978-0-7636-2135-3). Arranged in alphabet-book format, this strikingly illustrated volume celebrates jazz and its best-known practitioners. (Rev: BL 1/1–15/06; SLJ 1/06*) [811]

9126 Mendelson, Aaron A. *American R and B: Gospel Grooves, Funky Drummers, and Soul Power* (6–9). Illus. Series: American Music Milestones. 2012, Lerner/Twenty-First Century LB $30.60 (978-076134501-5). With photographs, a timeline, mini-biographies, and recommended songs and albums, this is a history of rhythm and blues that covers doo-wop, girl groups,

Motown, soul, funk, disco, and hip-hop. **e** (Rev: BL 10/1/12*; LMC 5–6/13) [781.644]

9127 Nichols, Travis. *Punk Rock Etiquette: The Ultimate How-To Guide for DIY, Punk, Indie and Underground Bands* (7–10). Illus. by author. 2008, Flash Point $10.95 (978-159643415-8). This irreverent guide delivers lots of laughs as well as some practical, sage advice. **e** (Rev: BL 9/1/08; SLJ 12/08; VOYA 10/08) [781.6]

9128 Raymer, Miles. *How to Analyze the Music of Paul McCartney* (8–12). Illus. Series: Essential Critiques. 2010, ABDO LB $22.95 (978-161613531-7). After an overview of McCartney himself and the Beatles' music, this book explains how to apply biographical and historical criticism to his music over the decades, with a particular focus on gender and historical themes. (Rev: BL 12/15/10) [782.42]

9129 Reisfeld, Randi. *This Is the Sound: The Best of Alternative Rock* (7–9). 1996, Simon & Schuster paper $7.99 (978-0-689-80670-4). Although it is now somewhat dated, this is a rundown on the hottest alternative rock bands as of 1996. (Rev: BL 6/1–15/96; SLJ 7/96; VOYA 12/96) [791.66]

Opera and Musicals

9130 Gatti, Anne, retel. *The Magic Flute* (4–8). Retold by Anne Gatti. Illus. by Peter Malone. 1997, Chronicle $17.95 (978-0-8118-1003-6). An elegant retelling of the Mozart opera, with each scene given a full-color painting and a page of text. The accompanying CD has 16 selections coded to each page. (Rev: SLJ 1/98*) [782.1]

Orchestra and Musical Instruments

9131 Evans, Roger. *How to Play Guitar: A New Book for Everyone Interested in Guitar* (8–12). 1980, St. Martin's paper $9.95 (978-0-312-36609-4). An easily followed basic guidebook on how to play the guitar with information on such topics as buying equipment and reading music. [787.6]

9132 Helsby, Genevieve. *Those Amazing Musical Instruments!* (4–9). Illus. 2007, Sourcebooks $19.95 (978-1-4022-0825-6). A CD-ROM is included with this engaging and comprehensive guide to orchestral instruments. (Rev: SLJ 3/08)

9133 Levine, Robert. *The Story of the Orchestra* (5–7). Illus. by Meredith Hamilton. 2001, Black Dog & Leventhal $19.98 (978-1-57912-148-8). Orchestra Bob introduces young readers to orchestra history, famous conductors and their eras, and instruments, in a guided tour that includes amusing cartoons, illustrations, and links to selections on the accompanying CD. (Rev: BL 12/15/01; SLJ 9/01) [784.2]

9134 VanHecke, Susan. *Raggin', Jazzin', Rockin': A History of American Musical Instrument Makers* (7–9). Illus. 2011, Boyds Mills $17.95 (978-1-59078-574-4). A fascinating overview of eight American instrument makers including Steinway, Fender, and Moog. ALA Notable Books 2012. (Rev: BL 5/1/11; LMC 9–10/11; SLJ 5/11; VOYA 4/11) [784.19092]

Songs and Folk Songs

9135 Berger, Melvin. *The Story of Folk Music* (6–9). 1976, Phillips LB $29.95 (978-0-87599-215-0). The story of the origins and characteristics of American folk music, with biographical information on singers from Woody Guthrie to John Denver. [781.7]

9136 Cooper, Michael L. *Slave Spirituals and the Jubilee Singers* (6–9). 2001, Clarion $16.00 (978-0-395-97829-0). All about the songs of American slavery and the Fisk University Jubilee Singers, who kept the songs alive after slavery ended. With photographs and sheet music. (Rev: BL 12/1/01; HB 1–2/02; HBG 3/02; SLJ 12/01; VOYA 2/02) [782.42162]

9137 McGill, Alice. *In the Hollow of Your Hand: Slave Lullabies* (5–7). 2000, Houghton Mifflin $18.00 (978-0-395-85755-7). Family life in the days of slavery is revealed in this moving collection of 13 folk lullabies; a CD of the songs is also included. (Rev: BCCB 1/01; BL 11/15/00; HBG 3/01; SLJ 12/00) [811.008]

9138 McNeil, Keith, and Rusty McNeil. *Colonial and Revolution Songbook: With Historical Commentary* (4–7). 1996, WEM Records paper $11.95 (978-1-878360-08-3). This songbook contains 39 traditional songs from the 17th century through the War of 1812, with brief historical comments for each. (Rev: SLJ 12/96) [973]

9139 McNeil, Keith, and Rusty McNeil. *Moving West Songbook: With Historical Commentary* (7–10). 2003, $15.95 (978-1-878360-30-4). Historical information, anecdotes, illustrations, and guitar chords accompany

this large-format selection of about 50 songs of the early to mid-19th century. (Rev: BL 7/03; SLJ 11/03) [782.42]

9140 McNeil, Keith, and Rusty McNeil, eds. *California Songbook with Historical Commentary* (6–10). 2001, WEM Records $15.95 (978-1-878360-27-4). Music, chords, lyrics, and background information are given for a large selection of songs that originated in California. (Rev: BL 8/01) [782.42]

9141 Sandburg, Carl. *The American Songbag* (7–12). 1970, Harcourt paper $35.00 (978-0-15-605650-2). A fine collection of all kinds of American folk songs with music and background notes from Mr. Sandburg. [784.7]

9142 Sieling, Peter. *Folk Music* (6–9). Series: North American Folklore. 2003, Mason Crest LB $22.95 (978-1-59084-342-0). Sieling defines the essence of folk music, looks at the instruments used, and explores its roots in the Old World, and the ways in which it has evolved in the New World. Also use *Folk Songs* (2003), which has a chapter on children's songs. (Rev: SLJ 6/03) [781.62]

9143 Stotts, Stuart. *We Shall Overcome: The Song That Changed the World* (5–8). Illus. by Terrance Cummings. 2010, Houghton Mifflin LB $18 (978-0-547-18210-0). Stotts reviews the history of the song that inspired, encouraged, and comforted those involved in the U.S. civil rights movement; includes a CD with a Pete Seeger recording. Lexile 1080L (Rev: BL 11/1/09; LMC 1–2/10; SLJ 2/10) [782.42162]

9144 Turck, Mary C. *Freedom Song: Young Voices and the Struggle for Civil Rights* (6–9). Illus. 2008, Chicago Review paper $18.95 (978-155652773-9). A look at the inspirational songs sung during the civil rights movement and their roots in folk tunes, African music, and spirituals; with photographs and a CD. (Rev: BL 2/1/09; LMC 5–6/09; SLJ 1/1/09*) [323.0973]

9145 Yolen, Jane. *Apple for the Teacher: Thirty Songs for Singing While You Work* (4–7). 2005, Abrams $24.95 (978-0-8109-4825-9). This collection of work songs, compiled by Yolen and featuring music arrangements by her son Adam Stemple, celebrates 30 diverse occupations from astronaut to weaver. (Rev: BL 10/1/05; SLJ 10/05) [782.42]

Theater, Dance, and Other Performing Arts

General and Miscellaneous

9146 Amendola, Dana. *A Day at the New Amsterdam Theatre* (4–9). Photos by Gino Domenico. 2004, Disney $24.95 (978-0-7868-5438-7). A behind-the-scenes look at a production of a musical in the renovated theater in New York City, introducing the wide variety of individuals involved. (Rev: SLJ 1/05) [792]

Dance (Ballet, Modern, etc.)

9147 Ancona, George. *¡Olé! Flamenco* (5–8). Photos by author. 2010, Lee & Low $19.95 (978-1-60060-361-7). A photo-essay about the Spanish art form that incorporates dance, music, and song, explaining its history and traditions and following a group of young people who are studying flamenco in Santa Fe, New Mexico. Belpré Honor 2011; ALA Notable Books 2011. (Rev: BL 12/1/10; HB 1–2/11; LMC 5–6/11; SLJ 1/1/11) [793.3]

9148 Anderson, Janet. *Modern Dance* (7–12). Series: World of Dance. 2003, Chelsea House LB $30.00 (978-0-7910-7644-6). Traces the history of modern dance, describing key personalities and innovations and looking at a modern dance class. (Rev: SLJ 3/04; VOYA 8/04) [792.8]

9149 Balanchine, George, and Francis Mason. *101 Stories of the Great Ballets* (7–12). 1975, Doubleday paper $16.00 (978-0-385-03398-5). Both the classics and newer ballets are introduced plus general background material such as a brief history of ballet. [792.8]

9150 Berger, Melvin. *The World of Dance* (6–8). 1978, Phillips $29.95 (978-0-87599-221-1). An overview of the subject that begins in prehistoric times and ends with today's social dancing and ballet. [792]

9151 Bingham, Jane. *Ballet* (4–8). Series: Dance. 2009, Heinemann LB $31.43 (978-1-4329-1374-8). A colorful overview of the origins and evolution of ballet, with discussion of the various skills required, the rigorous training, and the complexities of staging a ballet. (Rev: LMC 3–4/09)

9152 Dillman, Lisa. *Ballet* (4–7). Series: Get Going! Hobbies. 2005, Heinemann LB $27.79 (978-1-4034-6115-5). A photo-filled introduction to ballet, with historical information plus basic positions and steps and exercises to help would-be dancers get in shape; also use *Tap* (2005). (Rev: BL 11/1/05; SLJ 3/06) [792.8]

9153 Haskins, Jim. *Black Dance in America: A History Through Its People* (7–12). 1990, HarperCollins LB $14.89 (978-0-690-04659-5). Beginning with the dances brought from Africa by the slaves, this history moves to the present with the contributions of such people as Gregory Hines and Alvin Ailey. (Rev: BL 8/90; SLJ 6/90; VOYA 6/90) [792.8]

9154 Kuklin, Susan. *Reaching for Dreams: A Ballet from Rehearsal to Opening Night* (7–12). 2001, iUniverse paper $13.95 (978-0-595-17081-4). Using the introduction of a new ballet into the Alvin Ailey dance company's repetoire as a springboard, this is the account of the pangs of creation in the ballet world; first published in 1987. (Rev: BL 3/1/87; BR 11–12/87; SLJ 5/87; VOYA 12/87) [792.8]

9155 Rinaldi, Robin. *Ballet* (7–12). Series: World of Dance. 2003, Chelsea House LB $30.00 (978-0-7910-7640-8). Traces the history of ballet, describing key personalities and innovations and looking at a modern ballet class. (Rev: SLJ 3/04; VOYA 8/04) [792.8]

9156 Schorer, Suki, and School of American Ballet. *Put Your Best Foot Forward: A Young Dancer's Guide to Life* (4–8). Illus. by Donna Ingemanson. Photos by Chris Carroll. 2005, Workman $9.95 (978-0-7611-3795-5). Practical tips are combined with artistic advice in this helpful guide for young ballet dancers, written by a former principal dancer. (Rev: SLJ 3/06) [792.8]

9157 Williams, Ann-Marie. *Learn to Speak Dance: A Guide to Creating, Performing and Promoting Your Moves* (5–8). Illus. by Jeff Kulak. 2011, OwlKids $22.95 (978-1-926818-88-7); paper $14.95 (978-1-926818-89-4). A large-format introduction to styles of dance — ballet, ballroom, flamenco, and so forth — with discussion of choreography, preparing for performances, stage fright, and other aspects. (Rev: BL 11/1/11; SLJ 7/11) [792.8]

Motion Pictures

9158 Brackett, Leigh, and Lawrence Kasdan. *The Empire Strikes Back: The Illustrated Screenplay* (8–12). 1998, Ballantine paper $12.00 (978-0-345-42070-1). The shooting script for the second of the original *Star Wars* trilogy, with action direction and drawings of action scenes, preceded by an introduction that includes background and thoughts about the movie trilogy from the perspectives of people who were involved with the first release of the films. (Rev: SLJ 12/98) [791.43]

9159 Burtt, Ben. *Star Wars Galactic Phrase Book and Travel Guide: Beeps, Bleats, and Other Common Intergalactic Verbiage* (7–12). 2001, Ballantine $8.00 (978-0-345-44074-7). A small-format, travel guide/phrase book that will fascinate devotees of Star Wars. (Rev: SLJ 12/01; VOYA 6/02) [791.43]

9160 Clee, Paul. *Before Hollywood: From Shadow Play to the Silver Screen* (7–12). 2005, Clarion $22.00 (978-0-618-44533-2). Early technologies and the reactions of early audiences are the focus of this fascinating account. (Rev: BCCB 7–8/05; HB 9–10/05; SLJ 7/05) [791.43]

9161 Hamen, Susan E. *How to Analyze the Films of the Coen Brothers* (8–11). Illus. Series: Essential Critiques. 2012, ABDO LB $34.22 (978-161783454-7). Biographical information on the brothers is followed by analysis of films including *O Brother, Where Art Thou?* and *Fargo.* (Rev: BL 11/1/12) [791.4302]

9162 Jones, Sarah. *Film* (7–10). Series: MediaWise. 2003, Smart Apple LB $28.50 (978-1-58340-256-6). The world of film making is clearly explained, with information on everything from initial concept to financing to the mechanics of production. (Rev: BL 10/15/03; SLJ 11/03) [791.43]

9163 Lace, William W. *Blacks in Film* (7–10). Illus. Series: Lucent Library of Black History. 2008, Gale/Greenhaven LB $32.45 (978-142050084-4). From the earliest appearances of African Americans in silent films through their roles in today's movies, this book covers how blacks have been depicted in the cinema; photographs add to the presentation. (Rev: BL 2/1/09; SLJ 2/1/09) [791.43089]

9164 McCaig, Iain. *Star Wars Visionaries* (7–10). 2005, Dark Horse paper $17.95 (978-1-59307-311-4). Artists who worked on *The Revenge of the Sith* showcase their individual artistic styles in this gallery of Star Wars scenarios. (Rev: BL 5/15/05; SLJ 11/05) [741.5]

9165 Miller, Ron. *Special Effects: An Introduction to Movie Magic* (7–10). 2006, Lerner LB $26.60 (978-0-7613-2918-3). Covers both the history of special effects and the techniques used today; boxed features discuss key figures and offer career advice. (Rev: BL 3/15/06; SLJ 6/06) [778.5]

9166 Osborne, Robert A. *75 Years of the Oscar: The Official History of the Academy Awards* (8–12). 2003, Abbeville $75.00 (978-0-7892-0787-6). A history of the Oscars through 2003, with asides about the ceremonies, winners, nominees, and the Academy of Motion Picture Arts and Sciences. [791.43]

9167 Reynolds, David West. *Star Wars: Incredible Cross-Sections* (4–8). 1998, DK $19.95 (978-1-78943-480-4). This large-format book includes cross-sections of the TIE fighter, the X-wing fighter, the AT-AT, the Millennium Falcon, Jabba's sail barge, and the Death Star. (Rev: BL 12/15/98) [791.43]

9168 Reynolds, David West. *Star Wars: The Visual Dictionary* (4–8). 1998, DK $19.99 (978-0-7894-3481-4). Using a large-format dictionary approach, the people, creatures, and droids of the *Star Wars* saga are presented, with large photographs of the characters and many stills from the movies. (Rev: BL 12/15/98; HBG 3/99; SLJ 2/99) [791.43]

9169 Reynolds, Mike. *How to Analyze the Films of Spike Lee* (8–12). Illus. Series: Essential Critiques. 2010, ABDO LB $32.79 (978-161613530-0). Spike Lee's best-known films are deconstructed with an eye toward racial and identity issues. (Rev: BL 12/15/10) [791.43]

9170 Richards, Andrea. *Girl Director: A How-to Guide for the First-Time Flat-Broke Film Maker (and Video Maker)* (7–12). Illus. by Elizabeth McCallie. 2001, Alloy $17.95 (978-1-931497-00-8). Technical tips, inspiration, and instruction for would-be directors, with plenty of illustrations and other graphic elements. (Rev: BL 11/1/01; VOYA 6/01) [791.43]

9171 Salisbury, Mark. *Planet of the Apes: Re-Imagined by Tim Burton* (6–12). 2001, Newmarket $32.95 (978-1-55704-487-7); paper $22.95 (978-1-55704-486-0). A richly illustrated look behind the scenes at film director Tim Burton's recent remake of *The Planet of the Apes.* (Rev: VOYA 2/02)

9172 Vaz, Mark Cotta. *The Art of The Incredibles* (8–12). 2004, Chronicle $40.00 (978-0-8118-4433-8). Many illustrations enhance this look at the making of the popular animated motion picture. (Rev: BL 10/15/04) [791.43]

9173 Wallace, Daniel. *Star Wars: The Essential Guide to Planets and Moons* (6–12). 1998, Del Rey paper $19.95 (978-0-345-42068-8). This volume provides fascinating information on 110 different planets and moons in the *Star Wars* universe, arranged alphabetically from Abregado-rae, a popular stop for smugglers, to Zhar, a gas-filled giant, covering each world's inhabitants, climate, language, points of interest, and history. (Rev: VOYA 6/99) [791.45]

Radio, Television, and Video

9174 Killick, Jane. *Babylon 5: The Coming of Shadows* (7–12). 1998, Ballantine paper $11.00 (978-0-345-42448-8). This is the second of a five-volume guide to this popular television series. (Rev: VOYA 12/98) [791.45]

9175 Schieffer, Bob. *Face the Nation: My Favorite Stories from the First 50 Years of the Award-Winning News Broadcast* (8–12). 2004, Simon & Schuster $26.95 (978-0-7432-6585-0). Highlights from the first 50 years of CBS's popular *Face the Nation*. (Rev: BL 9/1/04) [791.45]

9176 Wan, Guofang. *TV Takeover: Questioning Television* (4–7). Illus. Series: Fact Finders. Media Literacy. 2006, Capstone LB $22.60 (978-0-7368-6763-4). In alerting readers to the motivations behind those who produce television shows, this book fosters critical thinking about the mass media. (Rev: SLJ 6/07) [384.55]

Theater and Other Dramatic Forms

9177 Caruso, Sandra, and Susan Kosoff. *The Young Actor's Book of Improvisation: Dramatic Situations from Shakespeare to Spielberg: Ages 12-16* (6–12). 1998, Heinemann paper $22.95 (978-0-325-00049-7). This work supplies hundreds of situations suitable for improvisation culled from all forms of literature, plays, and movie scripts, arranged by themes such as confrontation and relationships. (Rev: BL 9/15/98; SLJ 1/99) [793]

9178 Haskins, Jim, and Kathleen Benson. *Conjure Times: Black Magicians in America* (6–12). 2001, Walker LB $17.85 (978-0-8027-8763-7). The authors explore the substantial contributions of black performers to the early theater in America. (Rev: BL 7/01; HBG 3/02; SLJ 11/01; VOYA 4/02) [793.8]

9179 Kipnis, Claude. *The Mime Book* (7–12). 1988, Meriwether paper $16.95 (978-0-916260-55-2). One of the world's greatest mimes explains what it is and how it is done. [792.3]

9180 Lee, Robert L. *Everything About Theatre! The Guidebook of Theatre Fundamentals* (7–12). 1996, Meriwether paper $19.95 (978-1-56608-019-4). This excellent introduction to the backstage world includes material ranging from theater history to stagecraft, acting, and play production. (Rev: BL 12/1/96; SLJ 2/97) [792]

9181 Stevens, Chambers. *Sensational Scenes for Teens: The Scene Studyguide for Teen Actors!* (7–10). Series: Hollywood 101. 2001, Sandcastle paper $14.95 (978-1-883995-10-2). Acting coach Stevens includes more than 30 scenes — both comedy and drama — suitable for two teen actors, with choices for boy-girl, boy-boy, and girl-girl combinations. (Rev: BL 5/15/01; SLJ 4/01) [812.6]

History and Geography

General History and Geography

Atlases, Maps, and Mapmaking

9182 Bramwell, Martyn. *How Maps Are Made* (5–8). Series: Maps and Mapmakers. 1998, Lerner LB $22.60 (978-0-8225-2920-0). The difficulties in representing the globe on a flat surface are explored, plus details on how maps are made — both by hand and by computer — and on the use of aerial photography in mapmaking. (Rev: BL 3/15/99; HBG 3/99; SLJ 2/99) [526]

9183 Jouris, David. *All Over the Map: An Extraordinary Atlas of the United States* (8–10). 1994, Ten Speed paper $11.95 (978-0-89815-649-2). A U.S. atlas that explores the history of the names of towns and cities, including such places as Peculiar, Ding Dong, Vendor, and Joy. (Rev: BL 7/94) [910]

9184 Ross, Val. *The Road to There: Mapmakers and Their Stories* (7–10). 2003, Tundra $19.95 (978-0-88776-621-3). Mapmakers of different eras and nationalities, well-known figures such as Henry the Navigator and less familiar individuals, and the charts they created are featured in this interesting volume with period illustrations and many maps. (Rev: BCCB 1/04; BL 12/15/03; HBG 4/04; SLJ 12/03*) [912]

9185 Wilkinson, Philip. *The Kingfisher Student Atlas* (5–8). 2003, Kingfisher $24.95 (978-0-7534-5589-0). An atlas of the earth, with detail on each area's physical characteristics and political boundaries and material on such problems as pollution and deforestation. An accompanying CD offers printable maps. (Rev: SLJ 4/04)

Paleontology

9186 Aaseng, Nathan. *American Dinosaur Hunters* (6–9). 1996, Enslow LB $26.60 (978-0-89490-710-4). A history of paleontology, the story of major discoveries, and brief biographies of such scientists as Edward Hitchcock and Roy Chapman Andrews. (Rev: BL 11/15/96; SLJ 12/96) [560]

9187 Bardoe, Cheryl. *Mammoths and Mastodons: Titans of the Ice Age* (4–7). Illus. 2010, Abrams $18.95 (978-0-8109-8413-4). Two boys discover a perfectly preserved frozen baby mammoth in this story, which offers a glimpse into the lives of these Ice Age giants as well as an introduction to the science of paleontology. Orbis Pictus Honor Award for Outstanding Nonfiction for Children 2011. (Rev: BL 3/15/10; SLJ 4/10) [569]

9188 Barrett, Paul. *National Geographic Dinosaurs* (6–10). 2001, National Geographic $29.95 (978-0-7922-8224-2). This comprehensive and attractive guide provides a wealth of information about dinosaurs, their timeframe and evolution, individual species, and eventual extinction, with maps, fact boxes, and graphics. (Rev: BL 7/01; SLJ 10/01) [567.9]

9189 Bonner, Hannah. *When Dinos Dawned, Mammals Got Munched, and Pterosaurs Took Flight: A Cartoon Prehistory of Life in the Triassic* (4–7). Illus. by author. 2012, National Geographic $17.95 (978-142630862-8); LB $25.90 (978-142630863-5). An appealing tour of the Triassic era, focusing on everything from insects to dinosaurs as well as plants, geography, and geology, with eye-catching illustrations, humor, and informative text. (Rev: BL 7/12; LMC 11–12/12) [567.9]

9190 Bradley, Timothy J. *Paleo Bugs: Survival of the Creepiest* (5–8). Illus. by author. 2008, Chronicle $15.99 (978-0-8118-6022-2). The author provides information about prehistoric bugs alongside his own illustrations imagining what they might have looked like in those long-ago days. A companion to *Paleo Sharks*. (Rev: BL 5/15/08; SLJ 7/08) [565]

9191 Bradley, Timothy J. *Paleo Sharks: Survival of the Strangest* (4–7). Illus. 2007, Chronicle $15.95 (978-0-8118-4878-7). Well-arranged double-page spreads introduce sharks of prehistoric times and examine how they compare to their modern descendants. (Rev: BL 4/1/07; SLJ 6/07)

9192 Christian, Spencer, and Antonia Felix. *Is There a Dinosaur in Your Backyard? The World's Most Fascinating Fossils, Rocks, and Minerals* (5–8). Series: Spencer Christian's World of Wonders. 1998, Wiley paper $12.95 (978-0-471-19616-7). In addition to discussing dinosaurs, this fascinating book introduces earth science, with interesting details about rocks, minerals, and fossils. (Rev: BL 9/1/98; SLJ 10/98) [552]

9193 Cooley, Brian, and Mary Ann Wilson. *Make-a-Saurus: My Life with Raptors and Other Dinosaurs* (4–8). Photos by Gary Campbell. 2000, Annick paper $14.95 (978-1-55037-644-9). A two-part book giving a step-by step description of how museum-quality models of dinosaurs are made using the latest discoveries in paleontology, followed by an exploration of how these techniques can be adapted so the reader can make models at home. (Rev: HBG 3/01; SLJ 9/00) [567.9]

9194 Currie, Philip J., and Colleayn O. Mastin. *The Newest and Coolest Dinosaurs* (4–8). 1998, Grasshopper $18.95 (978-1-895910-41-4). Using double-page spreads, this useful volume introduces 15 of the most recent finds in the world of dinosaurs. (Rev: SLJ 1/99) [560]

9195 Currie, Philip J., and Kevin Padian, eds. *Encyclopedia of Dinosaurs* (8–12). 1997, Academic $148.00 (978-0-12-226810-6). An adult reference book, written by scientists, with interesting, alphabetically arranged articles on dinosaurs, digs, and sites. (Rev: BL 11/1/97; SLJ 5/98) [567.9]

9196 Cutchins, Judy, and Ginny Johnston. *Giant Predators of the Ancient Seas* (4–7). Series: Southern Fossil Discoveries. 2001, Pineapple $14.95 (978-1-56164-237-3). A look at the reptiles, fish, whales, sharks, and sea snakes that were found in the seas that once covered much of North America, as well as a discussion of the methods scientists used to reconstruct them. (Rev: HBG 3/02; SLJ 12/01) [566]

9197 Dingus, Lowell. *Dinosaur Eggs Discovered!* (6–9). 2007, Lerner LB $30.60 (978-0-8225-6791-2). Describes the discovery of Titanosaur fossils and what the evidence has revealed about the huge prehistoric creatures. (Rev: BL 9/1/07; SLJ 10/07) [567.909]

9198 Dixon, Dougal. *Amazing Dinosaurs: More Feathers, More Claws, Big Horns, Wide Jaws! 2nd ed.* (5–7). 2007, Boyds Mills $19.95 (978-1-59078-537-9). This carefully updated edition provides new illustrations and text reflecting recent discoveries about dinosaurs. (Rev: SLJ 3/08) [567.9]

9199 Holmes, Thom, and Laurie Holmes. *Feathered Dinosaurs: The Origin of Birds* (6–10). Illus. by Michael William Skrepnick. Series: Dinosaur Library. 2002, Enslow LB $26.60 (978-0-7660-1454-1). A well-organized introduction to these dinosaurs and their relationship to today's birds, with illustrations, graphic elements, a timeline of scientific discoveries, and a glossary. (Rev: BL 8/02; HBG 10/02; SLJ 10/02) [567.9]

9200 Holtz, Thomas R., Jr. *Dinosaurs: The Most Complete, Up-to-Date Encyclopedia for Dinosaur Lovers of All Ages* (5–12). Illus. by Luis V. Rey. 2007, Random $34.99 (978-0-375-82419-7). Paleontologist Holtz offers a well-organized overview of dinosaurs and everything dinosaur-related in a well-illustrated volume that will be appreciated by users of many ages (those not interested in cladistics, for example, may find just the information they need on dinosaur eggs). (Rev: HB 1/08; SLJ 12/07)

9201 Larson, Peter, and Kristin Donnan. *Bones Rock! Everything You Need to Know to Be a Paleontologist* (5–9). 2004, Invisible Cities paper $19.95 (978-1-931229-35-7). A comprehensive, accessible guide to paleontology, describing how to dig for fossils, clean them, keep records, and develop and test theories, with interesting accounts of the authors' experiences. (Rev: SLJ 11/04) [560]

9202 Lessem, Don. *Dinosaur Worlds: New Dinosaurs, New Discoveries* (5–8). 1996, Boyds Mills $19.95 (978-1-56397-597-4). The reader visits various dinosaur digs worldwide in a review of what we know about these amazing creatures. (Rev: BL 11/15/96; SLJ 12/96*) [567.9]

9203 Malam, John. *Dinosaur* (5–8). Illus. 2006, DK $15.99 (978-0-7566-1412-6). Tyrannosaurus rex is the star of this attractive book that covers the dinosaur's

anatomy, life cycle, and hunting techniques plus archaeological findings and the science that has allowed us to reconstruct the animal from what we know today. (Rev: SLJ 4/07)

9204 Manning, Phillip Lars. *Dinomummy: The Life, Death, and Discovery of Dakota, a Dinosaur from Hell Creek* (5–8). Illus. 2007, Kingfisher $18.95 (978-0-7534-6047-4). The 2006 discovery of a hadrosaur fossil — so complete its skin was still intact — is the subject of this dramatically designed book that takes readers into the world of paleontology. (Rev: BL 3/3/08)

9205 Naish, Darren. *Dinosaurs Life Size* (5–7). Illus. 2010, Barron's $14.99 (978-0-7641-6378-4). A large-format eye-catching book full of dinosaur facts and pictures of life-size dinosaur parts — jaws, eyes, and claws and so forth — plus fold-out pages including a timeline. (Rev: LMC 3–4/11; SLJ 12/1/10) [567.9]

9206 Sloan, Christopher. *Baby Mammoth Mummy: Frozen in Time: A Prehistoric Animal's Journey into the 21st Century* (5–8). Illus. 2011, National Geographic $17.95 (978-1-4263-0865-9); LB $26.90 (978-1-4263-0866-6). Tells the story of the discovery in Siberia of the baby mammoth called Lyuba, and discusses what scientists have learned about her world. (Rev: BL 11/15/11; SLJ 12/1/11) [569]

9207 Sloan, Christopher. *Supercroc and the Origin of Crocodiles* (5–8). 2002, National Geographic $18.95 (978-0-7922-6691-4). A fascinating account of the discovery in Africa of the fossil *Sarcosuchus*, or Supercroc, with additional information on paleontology and crocodile evolution. (Rev: BCCB 5/02; BL 9/15/02; HBG 10/02; SLJ 7/02*) [567.9]

9208 Thompson, Ida. *The Audubon Society Field Guide to North American Fossils* (7–12). 1982, Knopf $19.95 (978-0-394-52412-2). An illustrated guide to the identification of North American fossils plus some background information on their formation. [560]

9209 Thompson, Sharon E. *Death Trap: The Story of the La Brea Tar Pits* (4–8). 1995, Lerner LB $28.75 (978-0-8225-2851-7). A history of the 40,000-year-old tar pits in Los Angeles and of the many species of prehistoric animals that were trapped in them, with color photographs. (Rev: BL 6/1–15/95; SLJ 5/95) [560]

9210 VanCleave, Janice. *Dinosaurs for Every Kid: Easy Activities That Make Learning Science Fun* (4–7). Series: Science for Every Kid. 1994, Wiley paper $12.95 (978-0-471-30812-6). With accompanying activities, this book explores the world of dinosaurs and how paleontology has discovered, through fossils, how they lived. (Rev: BL 4/1/94; SLJ 7/94) [567.9]

9211 Walker, Sally M., and Douglas W. Owsley. *Their Skeletons Speak: Kennewick Man and the Paleoamerican World* (6–9). Illus. 2012, Carolrhoda $22.95 (978-

0-7613-7457-2). Detailed but compelling, this volume discusses the discovery of the Kennewick Man and what scientists learned about the early peoples of North America from the 9,400-year-old skeleton. Lexile 1140L (Rev: BL 12/1/12; HB 11–12/12; SLJ 10/12*) [970.01]

9212 Williams, Judith. *The Discovery and Mystery of a Dinosaur Named Jane* (5–7). Illus. 2007, Enslow LB $23.93 (978-0-7660-2730-5); paper $13.26 (978-0-7660-2709-1). A straightforward account of the discovery, excavation and installation of this important fossil find. (Rev: SLJ 7/07)

Anthropology and Evolution

9213 Batten, Mary. *Anthropologist: Scientist of the People* (4–7). Series: Scientists in the Field. 2001, Houghton Mifflin $16.00 (978-0-618-08368-8). Striking photographs of a Paraguayan tribe of huntergatherers serve as a powerful backdrop to this explanation of the work of anthropologists. (Rev: BL 8/01; HB 1–2/02*; HBG 3/02; SLJ 9/01) [627]

9214 Corbishley, Mike. *What Do We Know About Prehistoric People?* (4–7). Series: What Do We Know About. 1996, Bedrick LB $18.95 (978-0-87226-383-3). Using double-page spreads, this book explores the known facts about human prehistoric life around the world. (Rev: BL 6/1–15/96) [930.1]

9215 Crump, Donald J., ed. *Giants from the Past: The Age of Mammals* (7–10). 1983, National Geographic LB $12.50 (978-0-87044-429-6). A description of early animals, such as the mastodon, and how they evolved during the Ice Age. [569]

9216 Deem, James M. *Faces from the Past: Forgotten People of North America* (6–10). Illus. 2012, Houghton Mifflin $18.99 (978-0-547-37024-8). A look at the human remains found in North America dating as far back as 10,500 years and moving forward to include a Mexican soldier killed in 1836, providing a fascinating mix of history and science. Lexile 1190L (Rev: BL 11/15/12*; HB 11–12/12; SLJ 12/12*) [599.9]

9217 Gibson, Phil, and Terri R. Gibson. *Natural Selection* (6–12). Series: Science Foundations. 2009, Chelsea House $35 (978-0-7910-9784-7). Following a review of Darwin and Mendel's importance in this field, this volume looks at artificial selection, natural selection, and sexual selection, and discusses objections to Darwin's theory. (Rev: LMC 11–12/09) [576.8]

9218 Goldenberg, Linda. *Little People and a Lost World: An Anthropological Mystery* (5–8). 2006, Twenty-First Century LB $29.27 (978-0-8225-5983-2). In 2003, a team of archaeologists and anthropologists discovered the skeleton of what's believed to be a small human being who lived more than 12,000 years ago on Flores Island in Indonesia; this book looks at the controversy over the discovery and the insights it has given into early human life. (Rev: BL 12/1/06; SLJ 4/07) [569.9]

9219 Gordon, Sherri Mabry. *The Evolution Debate: Darwinism vs. Intelligent Design* (8–12). Series: Issues in Focus Today. 2009, Enslow LB $31.93 (978-0-7660-2911-8). Gordon provides an unbiased look at the debate over the teaching of Darwinism and intelligent design in American schools. (Rev: SLJ 4/1/09) [576.8]

9220 Lauber, Patricia. *Who Came First? New Clues to Prehistoric Americans* (5–10). 2003, National Geographic $18.95 (978-0-7922-8228-0). An attractive, oversized volume that encompasses anthropology, archaeology, genetics, and linguistics in its discussion of the provenance of the peoples of the Americas. (Rev: BL 7/03*; HB 7–8/03; HBG 10/03; SLJ 8/03*) [970.01]

9221 Loxton, Daniel. *Evolution: How We and All Living Things Came to Be* (3–8). Illus. by author and Jim W. W. Smith. 2010, Kids Can $18.95 (978-1-55453-430-2). Helpful images and question-and-answer sections enhance this accessible presentation of the theory of evolution and the evidence that supports it. (Rev: BLO 2/15/10; LMC 8–9/10; SLJ 5/10) [576.8]

9222 McGowen, Tom. *Giant Stones and Earth Mounds* (4–8). 2000, Millbrook LB $25.90 (978-0-7613-1372-4). A history of the New Stone Age of about 9,000 years ago and the constructions that still exist in the United States today from that period. (Rev: BL 10/1/00; HBG 10/01; SLJ 10/00) [930.1]

9223 Naff, Clay Farris, ed. *Evolution* (7–12). Series: Exploring Science and Medical Discoveries. 2005, Gale LB $34.95 (978-0-7377-2823-1). This collection of writings documents the history of theories about human origins from ancient Greece to the 20th century. (Rev: SLJ 12/05)

9224 Pickering, Robert. *The People* (5–8). Series: Prehistoric North America. 1996, Millbrook LB $22.90 (978-1-56294-550-3). An account of the development of the prehistoric North American tribes that may have crossed the land bridge from Asia to the Americas. (Rev: SLJ 4/96) [973.01]

9225 Pringle, Laurence. *Billions of Years, Amazing Changes: The Story of Evolution* (5–8). Illus. by Steve Jenkins. 2011, Boyds Mills $17.95 (978-1-59078-723-6). A fascinating, colorful presentation of man's discoveries over time about evolution, with clear explanation of the four core principles plus examples of natural selection and many images. ALA Notable Books 2012. Lexile 1000L (Rev: BL 12/1/11; HB 1–2/12; LMC 1–2/12*; SLJ 12/1/11*) [596.8]

9226 Robertshaw, Peter, and Jill Rubalcaba. *The Early Human World* (8–12). Series: The World in Ancient Times. 2005, Oxford LB $32.95 (978-0-19-516157-1). Using primary sources and good illustrations, this volume looks at the world's earliest hominids and the evidence that they evolved from more primitive primates. (Rev: SLJ 6/05; VOYA 8/04) [599]

9227 Sloan, Christopher. *Bury the Dead: Tombs, Corpses, Mummies, Skeletons, and Rituals* (5–9). 2002, National Geographic $18.95 (978-0-7922-7192-5). Young readers will be fascinated by this serious account of burial practices throughout the ages, with timelines, color photographs, diagrams, and clear descriptions of rites around the world. (Rev: BL 12/1/02; HBG 3/03; SLJ 10/02*) [393]

9228 Stefoff, Rebecca. *First Humans* (6–9). Series: Humans: An Evolutionary History. 2010, Marshall Cavendish LB $37.07 (978-0-7614-4184-7). This attractive and well-illustrated volume is part of a series that presents human evolutionary information in an appealing yet detailed format. Other volumes are *Origins, Ice Age Neanderthals,* and *Modern Humans* (all 2010). **e** (Rev: LMC 3–4/10; SLJ 3/10) [569.9]

9229 Thimmesh, Catherine. *Lucy Long Ago: Uncovering the Mystery of Where We Came From* (5–7). Illus. 2009, Houghton $18.00 (978-0-547-05199-4). The story behind Lucy, a skeleton found in Ethiopia in 1974, that made science rethink how humans evolved. (Rev: BCCB 7–8/09; BL 6/1–15/09; HB 7/09; SLJ 7/09*) [569.9]

9230 Thorndike, Jonathan L. *Epperson v. Arkansas: The Evolution-Creationism Debate* (6–10). Series: Landmark Supreme Court Cases. 1999, Enslow LB $20.95 (978-0-7660-1084-0). This book examines the issues involved in this case of evolution versus creationism, traces the case from lower courts to the Supreme Court, and discusses the present-day impact of the court's decision. (Rev: BL 3/15/99) [116]

9231 Walker, Sally M. *Written in Bone: Buried Lives of Jamestown and Colonial Maryland* (7–11). Illus. 2009, Carolrhoda $22.95 (978-082257135-3). Walker explores how forensic anthropology has helped researchers to learn more about the hard realities of life in colonial America. ALA Notable Books 2010. Lexile NC1140L (Rev: BL 2/1/09; HB 5–6/09; LMC 10/09; SLJ 2/1/09*) [614]

9232 Westrup, Hugh. *The Mammals* (5–8). Series: Prehistoric North America. 1996, Millbrook LB $22.90 (978-1-56294-546-6). The woolly mammoth and saber-toothed tiger are two of the prehistoric mammals described in words and pictures. (Rev: BL 5/15/96; SLJ 4/96) [569]

9233 Winston, Robert. *Evolution Revolution* (5–8). Illus. 2009, DK $16.99 (978-0-7566-4524-3). This attractive and accessible large-format picture book looks first at creation stories and Darwin's theories before progressing to modern understanding of genetics, evolutionary biology, and the role of DNA. (Rev: BL 3/15/09; SLJ 2/09) [576.82]

Archaeology

9234 Arnold, Caroline. *Stone Age Farmers Beside the Sea: Scotland's Prehistoric Village of Skara Brae.* (5–8). 1997, Clarion $16.00 (978-0-395-77601-8). A stunning volume that tells the story of the Stone Age village of Skara Brae, dating to about 3000 B.C., that was unearthed in the Orkney Islands in 1850. (Rev: BCCB 4/97; BL 4/15/97; SLJ 7/97) [930]

9235 Buell, Janet. *Greenland Mummies* (5–8). Series: Time Travelers. 1998, Twenty-First Century LB $25.90 (978-0-7613-3004-2). By examining mummified human corpses found in Greenland, archaeologists have been able to reconstruct the life and culture of Inuits who lived 500 years ago. (Rev: SLJ 10/98) [930]

9236 Buell, Janet. *Ice Maiden of the Andes* (5–8). Series: Time Travelers. 1997, Twenty-First Century paper $25.90 (978-0-8050-5185-8). The story of the discovery of the frozen body of a young Inca girl who died 500 years ago and of how forensic methods such as DNA testing have revealed insights into Inca society, its religion, and gender roles. (Rev: BL 2/1/98; SLJ 3/98) [985]

9237 Capek, Michael. *Easter Island* (5–8). Series: Unearthing Ancient Worlds. 2008, Lerner LB $30.60 (978-0-8225-7583-2). This volume focuses on the statues of Easter Island, exploring their discovery and significance. (Rev: SLJ 10/1/08)

9238 Compoint, Stephane. *Buried Treasures: Uncovering Secrets of the Past* (5–8). Illus. 2011, Abrams $19.95 (978-0-8109-9781-3). Suitable mainly for browsing, this volume features eye-catching photographs of discoveries around the world and shots of scientists at work. (Rev: BL 6/1/11; SLJ 7/11) [930.1]

9239 Dean, Arlan. *Terra-Cotta Soldiers: Army of Stone* (4–7). Series: High Interest Books: Digging Up the Past. 2005, Children's Pr. LB $24.50 (978-0-516-25124-0); paper $6.95 (978-0-516-25093-9). For reluctant readers, this is a useful introduction to one of the world's most extraordinary archaeological finds: the 8,000 terracotta warriors of China. (Rev: BL 10/15/05; SLJ 2/06) [931]

9240 Deem, James M. *Bodies from the Ice: Melting Glaciers and the Recovery of the Past* (4–7). Illus. 2008, Houghton $17.00 (978-0-618-80045-2). Deem explores what researchers are learning about history and culture as melting glaciers reveal the remains of previously hidden bodies. Sibert Honor 2009; ALA Notable Books 2009. (Rev: BCCB 12/08; BL 12/1/08; HB 1/09; SLJ 12/08*) [599.9]

9241 Echo-Hawk, Roger C., and Walter R. Echo-Hawk. *Battlefields and Burial Grounds: The Indian Struggle to Protect Ancestral Graves in the United States* (7–10). 1994, Lerner LB $22.60 (978-0-8225-2663-6); paper $8.95 (978-0-8225-9722-3). A solid discussion of the conflict over Indian graves that have been plundered in the name of scientific research. (Rev: BL 5/15/94; SLJ 7/94*) [393]

9242 Funston, Sylvia. *Mummies* (5–7). Illus. by Joe Weissmann. Series: Strange Science. 2000, Owl $19.95 (978-1-894379-03-8); paper $9.95 (978-1-894379-04-5). All kinds of mummified human remains are discussed, from those in ancient Egypt to the 1999 discovery of George Mallory's body on Mount Everest. (Rev: HBG 3/01; SLJ 11/00) [909]

9243 Greene, Meg. *Buttons, Bones, and the Organ-Grinder's Monkey: Tales of Historical Archaeology* (5–8). 2001, Linnet LB $25.00 (978-0-208-02498-5). This introduction to historical archaeology looks at finds at five different sites in the United States. (Rev: BL 10/1/01; HBG 10/02; SLJ 1/02; VOYA 4/02) [973]

9244 Guiberson, Brenda Z. *Mummy Mysteries: Tales from North America* (4–7). Illus. by author. Series: A Redfeather Chapter Book. 1998, Henry Holt $15.95 (978-0-8050-5369-2). Reading like a mystery story, this book focuses on mummies found in North America, how and where they were found, and the information they reveal. (Rev: BCCB 2/99; HBG 3/99; SLJ 12/98) [937]

9245 Harris, Nathaniel. *Ancient Maya: Archaeology Unlocks the Secrets of the Maya's Past* (5–8). Series: National Geographic Investigates. 2008, National Geographic $17.95 (978-1-4263-0227-5). With photographs, illustrations, and maps, this book shows how archaeology has uncovered information about the Maya and their culture. (Rev: BL 3/3/08) [972.8]

9246 Huey, Lois Miner. *American Archaeology Uncovers the Dutch Colonies* (5–8). Series: American Archaeology. 2009, Marshall Cavendish LB $21.95 (978-0-7614-4263-9). Fascinating artifacts and field research bring the Dutch colonies to life in this visually appealing book that includes dig techniques and glimpses at excavation sites. Other recommended titles in this series include *American Archaeology Uncovers the Vikings, American Archaeology Uncovers the Earliest English Colonies, American Archaeology Uncovers the Westward Movement,* and *American Archaeology Uncovers the Underground Railroad* (all 2009). ℮ (Rev: BL 10/1/09; LMC 3–4/10; SLJ 2/1/10) [974.7]

9247 Jameson, W. C. *Buried Treasures of the Atlantic Coast: Legends of Sunken Pirate Treasures, Mysterious Caches, and Jinxed Ships — From Maine to Florida* (4–8). Series: Buried Treasure. 1997, August House $11.95 (978-0-87483-484-0). An account of how buried treasures were acquired and lost and the modern efforts to locate and retrieve them. Also use *Buried Treasures of New England* (1997). (Rev: SLJ 10/97) [910.4]

9248 Kops, Deborah. *Palenque* (5–8). Series: Unearthing Ancient Worlds. 2008, Twenty-First Century LB $30.60 (978-0-8225-7504-7). With many large photographs and interesting text, this volume traces the discovery of the ruins at Palenque in the mid-19th century and the work that has been done since then on this Mayan site. (Rev: LMC 11–12/08; SLJ 2/08)

9249 Lourie, Peter. *The Mystery of the Maya: Uncovering the Lost City of Palenque* (5–8). 2001, Boyds Mills $19.95 (978-1-56397-839-5). The author relates his interesting and often exciting experiences at a dig in Mexico and describes the work of the archaeologists and the history of the site. (Rev: BL 9/15/01; HBG 3/02; SLJ 11/01) [972.75]

9250 Malam, John. *Mummies* (5–8). Series: Kingfisher Knowledge. 2003, Kingfisher $11.95 (978-0-7534-5623-1). A highly illustrated, readable exploration of preserved bodies of all eras and areas of the world. (Rev: HBG 4/04; SLJ 12/03) [393]

9251 Panchyk, Richard. *Archaeology for Kids: Uncovering the Mysteries of Our Past with 25 Activities* (5–8). 2001, Chicago Review paper $14.95 (978-1-55652-395-3). An introduction for older readers to the history and scientific method of archaeology, full of illustrations and with interesting activities. (Rev: BL 1/1–15/02; SLJ 12/01) [930.1]

9252 Rubalcaba, Jill, and Peter Robertshaw. *Every Bone Tells a Story: Hominin Discoveries, Deductions, and Debates* (8–12). 2010, Charlesbridge $18.95 (978-1-58089-164-6). Rubalcaba and Robertshaw tell a compelling version of human prehistory by focusing on four landmark discoveries, and the questions they raised and answered. (Rev: BL 2/15/10; SLJ 3/10) [930.1]

9253 Scheller, William. *Amazing Archaeologists and Their Finds* (6–10). 1994, Oliver LB $19.95 (978-1-881508-17-5). This work presents eight archaeologists' discoveries, including the walls of Troy, the tomb of King Tut, Jericho, and Incan ruins. (Rev: BL 11/1/94; SLJ 2/95; VOYA 2/95) [930.1]

9254 Sonneborn, Liz. *Pompeii* (5–8). Series: Unearthing Ancient Worlds. 2008, Lerner LB $30.60 (978-0-8225-7505-4). Concentrating on the original excavation of Pompeii in the 18th century, this book explains how early archaeological digs were conducted. (Rev: BL 4/1/08; SLJ 2/08) [937]

9255 Tanaka, Shelley. *Mummies: The Newest, Coolest and Creepiest from Around the World* (4–7). 2005, Abrams $16.95 (978-0-8109-5797-8). Mummies from across history and around the world are on display in the colorful — and often graphic — pages of this fascinating book. (Rev: BL 12/1/05*; HBG 4/06; LMC 4–5/06; SLJ 12/05*) [393]

9256 Wheatley, Abigail, and Struan Reid. *The Usborne Introduction to Archaeology: Internet-Linked* (6–9). Series: Archaeology. 2005, EDC $19.95 (978-0-7945-0806-7). This excellent, large-format introduction to archaeology explores the discipline itself, the various techniques used to date and preserve artifacts, and significant discoveries around the world. (Rev: BL 4/1/05) [930.1]

World History and Geography

General

9257 Aaseng, Nathan. *You Are the Explorer* (4–8). Series: Great Decisions. 2000, Oliver LB $19.95 (978-1-881508-55-7). In this interactive book about famous explorers, the reader is asked to make decisions similar to those made by real explorers such as Columbus, Cortes, Champlain, and Robert Scott. (Rev: BL 5/1/00; HBG 10/00; SLJ 9/00) [910]

9258 Aaseng, Nathan. *You Are the General II: 1800-1899* (6–9). Series: Great Decisions. 1995, Oliver LB $19.95 (978-1-881508-25-0). In this account of famous battles such as Waterloo, Gettysburg, and Little Bighorn, the reader is asked to become a field marshal and interact with history. (Rev: SLJ 2/96) [900]

9259 Albee, Sarah. *Poop Happened! A History of the World from the Bottom Up* (4–8). 2010, Walker LB $20.89 (978-0-8027-9825-1). Albee recounts the story of public health and sanitation with flair and interesting detail. (Rev: BL 2/15/10; LMC 8–9/10; SLJ 5/10) [363.72]

9260 Andryszewski, Tricia. *Walking the Earth: The History of Human Migration* (5–9). 2006, Twenty-First Century LB $27.93 (978-0-7613-3458-3). A thorough introduction to the movements of human population across more than 150,000 years, with many illustrations, maps, and charts. (Rev: HBG 4/07; LMC 3/07; SLJ 1/07; VOYA 12/06) [304.8]

9261 Arnold, Caroline. *The Geography Book: Activities for Exploring, Mapping, and Enjoying Your World* (4–7). Illus. by Tina Cash Walsh. 2001, Wiley paper $14.95 (978-0-471-41236-6). An organized introduction to several geography concepts along with step-by-step instructions for projects and experiments. (Rev: BL 2/15/02; SLJ 3/02) [910]

9262 Arthus-Bertrand, Yann. *Our Living Earth: A Story of People, Ecology, and Preservation* (6–12). Illus. by David Giraudon. 2008, Abrams $24.95 (978-081097132-5). Eye-catching aerial photographs of locations around the world reveal how people live, work, and relate to nature; statistics on sustainability and disparities will open readers' eyes to issues that affect the lives of millions on Earth. Lexile 1060L (Rev: BL 2/15/09; SLJ 1/1/09*; VOYA 12/08) [779]

9263 Badcott, Nicholas. *Pocket Timeline of Islamic Civilizations* (7–12). 2009, Interlink $13.95 (978-1-56656-758-9). An informative, eye-catching guide to the various achievements of Islamic civilizations from the 7th to the 20th century; includes color photographs and a detachable timeline. (Rev: LMC 3–4/10; SLJ 9/09)

9264 Barnard, Bryn. *The Genius of Islam: How Muslims Made the Modern World* (6–9). Illus. by author. 2011, Knopf $17.99 (978-0-375-84072-2). A richly illustrated introduction to the Muslim world and its contributions to such varied fields as architecture, mathematics, agriculture, and music. (Rev: BL 5/1/11; SLJ 6/11) [297.2]

9265 Beccia, Carlyn. *The Raucous Royals: Test Your Royal Wits: Crack Codes, Solve Mysteries, and Deduce Which Royal Rumors Are True* (4–7). Illus. by author. 2008, Houghton Mifflin $17 (978-061889130-6). Beccia encourages critical thinking in this book that examines the rumors and mystery surrounding eleven royal figure including Richard II, Catherine the Great, Prince Dracula, and Marie Antoinette. (Rev: BL 10/15/08; SLJ 12/08) [929.7]

9266 Beller, Susan Provost. *The History Puzzle: How We Know What We Know about the Past* (8–11). 2006, Lerner LB $26.60 (978-0-7613-2877-3). This concise overview of how archaeology and other methods allow historians to piece together the past includes sepia photographs, illustrations, and paintings. (Rev: BL 4/15/06; LMC 11–12/06; SLJ 5/06) [901]

9267 Beyer, Rick. *The Greatest Stories Never Told: 100 Tales from History to Astonish, Bewilder, and Stupefy* (6–12). 2003, HarperCollins $18.95 (978-0-06-001401-8). Browsers will enjoy this well-illustrated and well-researched chronological overview of historical tidbits. (Rev: VOYA 10/03)

9268 Blackwood, Gary. *Enigmatic Events* (5–8). Series: Unsolved History. 2005, Marshall Cavendish LB $20.95 (978-0-7614-1889-4). Explores some of history's most enduring mysteries — the disappearance of the dinosaurs and of the *Mary Celeste*, to name only two. (Rev: BL 3/1/06; SLJ 3/06) [904]

9269 Blackwood, Gary. *Mysterious Messages: A History of Codes and Ciphers* (5–8). 2009, Dutton $16.99 (978-0-525-47960-4). This well-written history clearly explains the ins and outs of codes and ciphers and includes many interesting examples and stories. (Rev: BL 10/15/09; LMC 11–12/09; SLJ 12/09) [652]

9270 Burgan, Michael. *The Spanish Conquest of America: Prehistory to 1775* (5–8). Series: Latino-American History. 2006, Chelsea House LB $35.00 (978-0-8160-6440-3). A thorough and clear account of Spain's influence on the Americas, with discussion of individual explorers as well as the impact on native peoples and the conflicts with other colonial powers. (Rev: BL 3/15/07) [979]

9271 Butts, Ed. *Bodyguards! From Gladiators to the Secret Service* (3–7). Illus. by Scott Plumbe. 2012, Annick $24.95 (978-155451437-3); paper $14.95 (978-1-55451-436-6). From samurai to gladiators to bodyguards of Al Capone and Indira Gandhi, this is an entertaining overview of the profession and the tasks these men (and women) perform. (Rev: BL 11/15/12; SLJ 12/12) [363.28]

9272 Butts, Ed. *SOS: Stories of Survival* (6–9). 2007, Tundra paper $12.95 (978-0-88776-786-9). Thirteen historic and modern-day disasters, both acts of God (such as the 2004 tsunami) and acts of man (such as the Triangle Shirtwaist factory fire), are included in this book that emphasizes brave acts and survivors. (Rev: BL 7/07; SLJ 8/07) [363.34]

9273 Cawthorne, Nigel. *Military Commanders: The 100 Greatest Throughout History* (6–12). 2004, Enchanted Lion $18.95 (978-1-59270-029-5). This chronology identifies the greatest military battles in world history and the men who led their forces to victory in those battles. (Rev: BL 6/1–15/04; SLJ 4/04) [355]

9274 Christie, Peter. *The Curse of Akkad: Climate Upheavals That Rocked Human History* (5–8). 2008, Annick $19.95 (978-1-55451-119-8); paper $11.95 (978-1-55451-118-1). The effects of climate change through history are described in segments of one to three pages, making this a good choice for reluctant readers. (Rev: BL 8/08) [551.609]

9275 Connolly, Sean. *Gender Equality* (5–8). Series: Campaigns for Change. 2005, Smart Apple Media LB $29.95 (978-1-58340-515-4). An exploration of women's status and struggles to improve it throughout history; also use *The Right to Vote* (2005). (Rev: SLJ 5/06) [305.42]

9276 De Porti, Andrea. *Explorers: The Most Exciting Voyages of Discovery — from the African Expeditions to the Lunar Landing* (8–12). 2005, Firefly $49.95 (978-1-55407-101-2). Rare archival photos document the history of exploration over the past 150 years, telling 53 stories of discovery — some well-known and others more obscure. (Rev: BL 12/1/05) [910.92]

9277 Deary, Terry. *The Wicked History of the World: History with the Nasty Bits Left In!* (4–7). Illus. by Martin Brown. 2006, Scholastic $10.99 (978-0-439-87786-2). This pun-filled survey of world history, with its emphasis on the shadier side, will attract reluctant readers with sections on "Beastly Barbarians," "Rotten Rules," and "Vicious Villains." (Rev: SLJ 12/06)

9278 Defries, Cheryl L. *Seven Natural Wonders of the United States and Canada* (4–7). Series: Seven Wonders of the World. 2005, Enslow LB $25.26 (978-0-7660-5291-8). This tour of seven of North America's natural wonders, including the Grand Canyon, Everglades, and Niagara Falls, is extended by constantly updated links to Web sites. (Rev: SLJ 11/05) [557]

9279 Eamer, Claire. *Traitors' Gate: And Other Doorways to the Past* (6–9). Illus. 2008, Annick $24.95 (978-155451145-7); paper $12.95 (978-155451144-0). This introduction to the history of eight UNESCO World Heritage Sites, including a slave-trader's gate in Ghana and a 12-story-high structure carved into cliffs in Jordan, is written in clear, concise language, and accompanied by excellent photographs. (Rev: BL 12/15/08; SLJ 2/1/09) [909]

9280 Everett, J. H., and Marilyn Scott Waters. *Haunted Histories: Creepy Castles, Dark Dungeons, and Powerful Palaces* (4–7). 2012, Henry Holt $14.99 (978-0-8050-8971-4). Virgil Dante, Ghostarian, shows readers around places (Krak des Chevaliers and the Tower of London, for example), describes life in various dungeons and jails (Newgate Prison, Castle Neuschwanstein, the Bastille), and moves on to ancient palaces and graveyards; includes stories of ghosts and gruesome tortures. **e** (Rev: LMC 1–2/13; SLJ 7/12) [133.1]

9281 Gelber, Carol. *Masks Tell Stories* (5–7). Series: Beyond Museum Walls. 1993, Millbrook LB $24.90 (978-1-56294-224-3). Explores the nature, meaning, and uses of masks in different cultures at various times. (Rev: BL 8/93) [391]

9282 Gilkerson, William. *A Thousand Years of Pirates* (6–10). Illus. by author. 2009, Tundra $32.95 (978-0-88776-924-5). With interesting biographical sketches, maps, and beautiful illustrations, this is a sweeping survey of piratical activity across time and geography. (Rev: BL 12/15/09; SLJ 2/10; VOYA 2/10) [910.4]

9283 Gilpin, Daniel. *Food and Clothing* (6–9). Series: History of Invention. 2004, Facts on File $35.00 (978-0-8160-5441-1). A slim introductory overview of advances in food and clothing from prehistoric times to today, with maps, illustrations, and profiles of key figures. (Rev: SLJ 12/04) [973]

9284 Gold, Susan Dudley. *Governments of the Western Hemisphere* (5–8). Series: Comparing Continents. 1997, Twenty-First Century LB $24.90 (978-0-8050-5602-0). This book examines the struggles for independence in the United States, Canada, Mexico, Central America, and South America and the different directions taken by each once independence was achieved, highlighting the diversity across the nations. (Rev: BL 2/1/98; SLJ 3/98) [320.3]

9285 Graham, Amy. *Seven Wonders of the Natural World* (4–7). Series: Seven Wonders of the World. 2005, Enslow LB $25.26 (978-0-7660-5290-1). A tour of seven of the world's natural wonders, including Mount Everest, the Great Barrier Reef, and the Grand Canyon; the text is extended by constantly updated links to Web sites. (Rev: SLJ 11/05)

9286 Guiberson, Brenda Z. *Disasters: Natural and Man-Made Catastrophes Through the Centuries* (5–8). 2010, Henry Holt $18.99 (978-0-8050-8170-1). Guiberson presents compelling accounts of 10 well-known disasters including the sinking of the *Titanic*, the Great Chicago Fire, the 1918 flu pandemic, and Hurricane Katrina. (Rev: BL 5/15/10; HB 7–8/10; LMC 8–9/10; SLJ 6/10) [904]

9287 Hannigan, Des. *One People: Many Journeys* (8–12). 2005, Lonely Planet $40.00 (978-1-74104-600-7). Striking photographs from around the world capture the universality of the human experience and demonstrate the wide diversity of resources. (Rev: BL 1/1–15/06) [910]

9288 Huff, Toby. *An Age of Science and Revolutions: 1600–1800* (7–10). Series: Medieval and Early Modern World. 2005, Oxford $32.95 (978-0-19-517724-4). A sweeping overview of history in both the East and West from the beginning of the 17th century through the end of the 18th century, with color photographs, maps, profiles of key figures, and so forth. (Rev: BL 10/15/05; SLJ 7/06) [909]

9289 Jenkins, Martin. *The Time Book: A Brief History from Lunar Calendars to Atomic Clocks* (4–7). Illus. by Richard Holland. 2009, Candlewick $18.99 (978-0-7636-4112-2). A clearly written history of how humans have measured the passage of time from ancient calendars through Einstein's theory of relativity. Lexile NC1200L (Rev: BL 5/1/09; LMC 10/09; SLJ 9/09) [529]

9290 Kachur, Matthew. *The Slave Trade* (6–9). Series: Slavery in the Americas. 2006, Chelsea House $35.00 (978-0-8160-6134-1). Provides a broad overview of the transatlantic slave trade and how it affected both Africa and the Americas, with discussion of the Middle Passage, sugar production, and other related issues. (Rev: BL 7/06) [306.3]

9291 Kyi, Tanya Lloyd. *Fires!* (6–9). Series: True Stories from the Edge. 2004, Annick $18.95 (978-1-55037-877-1); paper $8.95 (978-1-55037-876-4). The stories behind ten of history's most horrific fires — including the Great Fire of London in 1666 and the Chernobyl nuclear plant explosion in 1986 — are recounted in this compelling title. (Rev: BL 1/1–15/05; VOYA 6/05) [363.37]

9292 Langley, Andrew. *Ancient Medicine* (6–8). Illus. Series: Medicine Through the Ages. 2012, Raintree $33.99 (978-141094642-3). Egypt and the Middle East, India, China, Greece, and Rome are covered in this survey of ancient medical practices. (Rev: BL 10/1/12) [910.9]

9293 Lassieur, Allison. *Trade and Commerce in the Early Islamic World* (5–7). Illus. Series: Life in the Early Islamic World. 2012, Crabtree LB $30.60 (978-077872172-7). With excellent illustrations, this attractive volume provides a solid introduction to early Islamic trade and commerce and how these activities affected social and cultural life. (Rev: BL 8/12*; SLJ 8/12) [381.0956]

9294 Llewellyn, Claire. *Great Discoveries and Amazing Adventures: The Stories of Hidden Marvels and Lost Treasures* (4–7). 2004, Kingfisher $18.95 (978-0-7534-5783-2). Important discoveries — and hoaxes — are described in inviting text, plus many illustrations, factoids, and a foreword by Robert Ballard. (Rev: SLJ 1/05) [509]

9295 MacDonald, Fiona. *Top 10 Worst Ruthless Warriors You Wouldn't Want to Know!* (4–7). Illus. by David Antram. 2012, Gareth Stevens LB $26.60 (978-143396685-9). The exploits of Genghis Khan, Alexander the Great, and Japanese warrior Yoshitsune, among others, are portrayed in this lively and irreverent history that is not for the faint-hearted. Also use *Top 10 Worst Wicked Rulers You Wouldn't Want to Know!* — which introduces Robespierre, Ivan the Terrible, and others. (Rev: BL 4/15/12; SLJ 6/12) [920]

9296 Markle, Sandra. *Rescues!* (4–7). Illus. 2006, Lerner LB $25.26 (978-0-8225-3413-6). Markle covers rescue efforts in 11 recent disasters (2004 to 2005), giving details of technology used and providing accounts by victims, rescuers, and eyewitnesses. (Rev: BL 4/1/06*; HBG 10/06; LMC 11–12/06; SLJ 8/06; VOYA 6/06) [363.34]

9297 Mason, Antony. *People Around the World* (5–7). 2002, Kingfisher $24.95 (978-0-7534-5497-8). An oversize guide to people of different cultures around the world, organized by continent, featuring hundreds of full-color photographs and illustrations, and detailing such topics as diet, language, employment, and leisure of urban and rural dwellers. (Rev: BL 5/1/03; HBG 10/03; SLJ 4/03; VOYA 6/03) [305.8]

9298 Millard, Anne. *A Street Through Time* (4–8). 1998, DK $17.99 (978-0-7894-3426-5). Western European history is traced in this oversize book that contains 14 views of the same riverside location at various times in history, including the Stone Age, Viking times, the Roman period, the Middle Ages, and modern times. (Rev: BL 1/1–15/99; HB 1–2/99; HBG 3/99; SLJ 12/98) [936]

9299 Mooney, Carla. *The Industrial Revolution: Investigate How Science and Technology Changed the World with 25 Projects* (4–7). Illus. by Jen Vaughn. Series: Build It Yourself. 2011, Nomad $21.95 (978-1-936313-81-5); paper $15.95 (978-1-936313-80-8). This illustrated title introduces the great minds that gave rise to the Industrial Revolution and showcases their innovations; includes 25 very varied projects. (Rev: BL 12/1/11; SLJ 1/12) [338.0973]

9300 Moore, Christopher. *From Then to Now: A Short History of the World* (5–8). Illus. by Andrej Krystoforski. 2011, Tundra $25.95 (978-0-88776-540-7). Moore offers a broad and fascinating overview of developments in human history from hunter-gatherers to industrialization and the modern, interconnected world. (Rev: BL 5/1/11; SLJ 5/11) [909]

9301 Murrell, Deborah. *Gladiator* (4–7). Series: Qeb Warriors. 2010, Black Rabbit LB $28.50 (978-1-59566-736-6). This volume gives arresting descriptions of the lives, battle tactics, and weapons of Roman centurions and Greek hoplites, with maps and eye-catching illustrations. (Rev: LMC 1–2/10)

9302 O'Brien, Patrick. *Mutiny on the Bounty* (4–7). Illus. 2007, Walker $17.95 (978-0-8027-9587-8). Clear, balanced narrative and vivid illustrations tell both sides of the story of the famous mutiny and its aftermath. (Rev: BL 1/1–15/07; SLJ 3/07)

9303 Phillips, Dee. *People of the World* (4–7). Series: Just the Facts. 2006, School Specialty paper $9.95 (978-0-7696-4257-4). Statistics and fast facts on the countries and peoples of the world are presented on double-page spreads. (Rev: BL 4/1/06) [305.8]

9304 Platt, Richard. *The Scoop on Poop* (4–7). Illus. by John Kelly. 2012, Kingfisher paper $7.99 (978-07534692-3-1). An informative and entertaining survey of waste material and its treatment through the ages. (Rev: BL 12/1/12) [392.3]

9305 Prentzas, G. S. *The Marshall Plan* (8–12). Illus. Series: Milestones in Modern World History. 2011, Chelsea House LB $35 (978-160413460-5). With photographs, timelines, and maps, this volume explains the aid that the United States gave to Europe in the aftermath of World War II. **e** (Rev: BL 2/15/12) [338.91]

9306 Romanek, Trudee. *Science, Medicine, and Math in the Early Islamic World* (5–7). Illus. Series: Life in the Early Islamic World. 2012, Crabtree LB $30.60 (978-077872170-3). With excellent illustrations, this attractive volume provides a solid introduction to science, medicine, and math in the early Islamic world and emphasizes how advanced these fields were. (Rev: BL 8/12*; SLJ 8/12) [509.56]

9307 Roop, Peter, and Connie Roop. *Tales of Famous Animals* (4–8). Illus. by Zachary Pullen. 2012, Scholastic $17.99 (978-054543029-6). Roop recounts the achievements of 17 famous animals ranging from Bucephalus to Balto, Seabiscuit, and Punxsutawney Phil. (Rev: BL 12/1/12; SLJ 12/12) [591]

9308 Ross, Stewart. *Conquerors and Explorers* (5–7). Series: Fact or Fiction? 1996, Millbrook LB $26.90 (978-0-7613-0532-3). The subtitle of this work is "The Greed, Cunning, and Bravery of the Travelers and Plunderers Who Opened Up the World." (Rev: BL 10/15/96; SLJ 4/97) [910]

9309 Ross, Stewart. *Into the Unknown: How Great Explorers Found Their Way by Land, Sea, and Air* (4–8). Illus. by Stephen Biesty. 2011, Candlewick $19.99 (978-0-7636-4948-7). A handsome and informative overview of 14 important journeys of exploration, starting in 340 B.C. with Pytheas the Greek's voyage to the Arctic Circle and ending in 1969 with Neil Armstrong and Buzz Aldrin's landing on the moon. Boston Globe–Horn Book Honor 2011; ALA Notable Books 2012. (Rev: BL 7/11; HB 5–6/11; LMC 10/11; SLJ 5/11*) [910.9]

9310 Sanna, Ellyn. *Nature's Wrath: Survivors of Natural Disasters* (6–12). Series: Survivors — Ordinary People, Extraordinary Circumstances. 2009, Mason Crest LB $24.95 (978-1-4222-0454-2). Sanna discusses our relationship with our planet and describes the experiences of survivors of tsunamis, hurricanes, and volcanoes. (Rev: SLJ 9/09)

9311 Scandiffio, Laura. *Escapes!* (5–9). Illus. by Stephen MacEachern. Series: True Stories from the Edge. 2004, Annick $18.95 (978-1-55037-823-8); paper $7.95 (978-1-55037-822-1). Ten stories of great escapes and escape attempts, from the first century B.C. to the late 1970s, with a concentration on resourcefulness and bravery. (Rev: SLJ 6/04) [904]

9312 Shapiro, Stephen. *Battle Stations! Fortifications Through the Ages* (5–8). 2005, Annick LB $19.95 (978-1-55037-889-4); paper $7.95 (978-1-55037-888-7). A tall, slim, and very visual overview of fortifications around the world and throughout history. (Rev: BL 9/15/05) [355.7]

9313 Sharp, S. Pearl, and Virginia Schomp. *The Slave Trade and the Middle Passage* (5–8). Series: Drama of African-American History. 2006, Benchmark LB $23.95 (978-0-7614-2176-4). A brief overview of the triangular trade between Africa, the American colonies, and Europe, looking at conditions aboard the slave ships. (Rev: SLJ 5/07)

9314 Sloan, Christopher. *Mummies: Dried, Tanned, Sealed, Drained, Frozen, Embalmed, Stuffed, Wrapped, and Smoked . . . and We're Dead Serious* (4–7). Illus. 2010, National Geographic $17.95 (978-1-4263-0695-2); LB $26.90 (978-1-4263-0696-9). Mummies from around the world are profiled in this fascinating book featuring plenty of close-up photographs. (Rev: BLO 10/15/10; LMC 3–4/11; SLJ 12/1/10) [393]

9315 Smith, Bonnie G. *Imperialism: A History in Documents* (6–12). Series: Pages from History. 2000, Oxford $39.95 (978-0-19-510801-9). This detailed account of how powerful nations spread their influence around the globe draws on many primary sources and includes eye-catching photographs and a useful timeline. (Rev: BL 11/15/00; HBG 10/01; SLJ 4/01) [325]

9316 Stewart, Robert. *Mysteries of History* (7–12). 2003, National Geographic $29.95 (978-0-7922-6232-9). Such controversial topics as Stonehenge, Napoleon's death, and Custer's Last Stand are presented with 16 others in this well-illustrated book. (Rev: BL 2/1/04; HBG 4/04) [902]

9317 Swanson, Diane. *Tunnels!* (5–8). Series: True Stories from the Edge. 2003, Annick $18.95 (978-1-55037-781-1); paper $6.95 (978-1-55037-780-4). Ten thrilling stories of tunnel escapes and escapades are accompanied by maps. (Rev: BL 4/15/03; SLJ 5/03) [624.1]

9318 Wiesner-Hanks, Merry E. *An Age of Voyages, 1350–1600* (7–12). 2006, Oxford LB $32.95 (978-0-19-517672-8). Exploration from Europe to Asia, Africa, the Middle East, and the Americas is examined with many illustrations and extracts from primary sources, including letters and diaries, and text that discusses the accompanying discoveries, inventions, and social changes. (Rev: LMC 11–12/06; SLJ 7/06)

9319 Wojtanik, Andrew. *Afghanistan to Zimbabwe: Country Facts That Helped Me Win the National Geographic Bee* (5–12). 2005, National Geographic paper $12.95 (978-0-7922-7981-5). Facts and figures about the world's 192 independent countries are organized into three categories: Physical, Political, and Environmental/Economic. (Rev: SLJ 10/05; VOYA 8/05) [910]

9320 Worth, Richard. *New France 1534–1763: Featuring the Region That Now Includes All or Parts of Michigan, Minnesota, Wisconsin, Illinois, Indiana, Ohio, Pennsylvania, Vermont, Maine, and Canada from Manitoba to Newfoundland* (6–9). Series: Voices from Colonial America. 2007, National Geographic $21.95 (978-1-4263-0147-6). As the title indicates, a huge part of North America was once the colony of New France; this book uses quotations from colony residents as well as other primary and secondary sources to introduce the territory. (Rev: BL 2/15/08) [971.01]

Ancient History

General and Miscellaneous

9321 Allan, Tony. *Exploring the Life, Myth, and Art of Ancient Vikings* (8–11). Series: Civilizations of the World. 2011, Rosen LB $39.95 (978-144884833-1). A handsome, well-written survey of Viking history, mythology, and arts, with maps and color illustrations. ℮ (Rev: BL 2/15/12; LMC 5–6/12) [948]

9322 Ball, Jacqueline, and Richard H. Levey. *Ancient China: Archaeology Unlocks the Secrets of China's Past* (5–8). Illus. Series: National Geographic Investigates. 2006, National Geographic $17.95 (978-0-7922-7783-5). After an introduction to China and its history, this volume looks at individual archaeological finds and at the lives revealed; vivid illustrations and good descriptions of archaeological techniques add to the value. (Rev: BL 10/15/06)

9323 Barter, James. *The Ancient Persians* (5–8). Series: Lost Civilizations. 2005, Gale LB $29.95 (978-1-59018-621-3). The lost civilization of the ancient Persians, with information about the society's people, customs, monetary system, and military, with maps and illustrations. (Rev: SLJ 6/06) [935]

9324 Bingham, Jane. *The Ancient World* (5–8). Series: A History of Fashion and Costume. 2005, Facts on File $35.00 (978-0-8160-5944-7). A broad overview of the clothing and personal adornment worn during ancient times, with many visual aids. (Rev: SLJ 5/06) [391]

9325 Calvert, Patricia. *The Ancient Celts* (5–8). Series: People of the Ancient World. 2005, Watts LB $30.50 (978-0-531-12359-1); paper $9.95 (978-0-531-16845-5). Introduces readers to the arts, religious beliefs, and society of the ancient Celts, with discussion of individual occupations and of the discoveries by archaeologists and anthropologists. (Rev: SLJ 9/05) [973]

9326 Caselli, Giovanni. *The First Civilizations* (6–8). 1985, Bedrick $18.95 (978-0-911745-59-7). This account traces the early history of man, from the first toolmakers to the civilizations of Egypt and Greece, through the objects that were made and used. (Rev: BL 11/15/85; SLJ 1/87) [930]

9327 Croy, Anita, ed. *Ancient Aztec and Maya* (5–9). Series: Facts at Your Fingertips. 2010, Black Rabbit LB $35.65 (978-1-933834-58-0). After presenting historical facts about the Aztec and Mayan civilizations, this volume goes on to look at specific sites and the cultures of these peoples. (Rev: LMC 3–4/10) [972]

9328 Fagan, Brian M., ed. *The Seventy Great Inventions of the Ancient World* (7–12). 2004, Thames & Hudson $40.00 (978-0-500-05130-6). This photo-filled volume explores inventions in categories ranging from hunting and farming to artwork and communications. (Rev: BL 12/1/04) [609]

9329 Galloway, Priscilla, and Dawn Hunter. *Adventures on the Ancient Silk Road* (5–8). 2009, Annick $24.95 (978-1-55451-198-3); paper $14.95 (978-1-55451-197-6). The ancient trade route is brought to life in accounts of three travelers many years apart: the monk Xuanzang, the conqueror Genghis Khan, and the merchant Marco Polo. (Rev: BL 1/1/10; SLJ 12/09) [950]

9330 George, Charles, and Linda George. *Maya Civilization* (7–10). Illus. Series: World History. 2010, Gale/Lucent LB $33.45 (978-142050240-4). With a timeline, photographs, illustrations, and quotations, this survey of the Maya civilization is useful for report writers. (Rev: BL 2/1/11; LMC 5–6/11) [305.897]

9331 Gruber, Beth. *Ancient Inca: Archaeology Unlocks the Secrets of Inca's Past* (3–7). Series: National Geographic Investigates. 2006, National Geographic $17.95 (978-0-7922-7827-6). This well-illustrated title examines how archaeologists gain knowledge about the ancient Inca civilization of pre-Columbian America, including information on pottery, textiles, and mummies. (Rev: SLJ 2/07)

9332 Haywood, John. *The Encyclopedia of Ancient Civilizations of the Near East and the Mediterranean* (8–12). 1997, M.E. Sharpe $95.00 (978-1-56324-799-6). Divided into three parts — ancient Near East and Egypt, the Greek world, and the Roman world — this adult narrative presents basic history and, through the use of sidebars, provides material on important places, cultural advances, scientific progress, religious practices, and military advances. (Rev: SLJ 8/98) [909]

9333 Hinds, Kathryn. *Ancient Celts* (6–8). Series: Barbarians! 2010, Marshall Cavendish LB $35.64 (978-0-7614-4062-8). An overview of the history of the Celts and the reasons for their success and eventual failure, with attractive features showing various aspects of Celtic culture. Also recommended in this series are *Early Germans, Huns, Vikings,* and *Goths* (all 2010). (Rev: LMC 3–4/10; SLJ 3/10) [936.4]

9334 Laughton, Timothy. *Exploring the Life, Myth, and Art of the Maya* (8–11). Illus. Series: Civilizations of the World. 2011, Rosen LB $39.95 (978-144884832-4). A handsome, well-written survey of the Mayans' history, mythology, society, and arts, with maps and color illustrations. e (Rev: BL 2/15/12; LMC 5–6/12) [972.8]

9335 Lourie, Peter. *Hidden World of the Aztec* (5–8). Illus. 2006, Boyds Mills $17.95 (978-1-59078-069-5). This lavishly illustrated title uses modern archaeological projects to introduce the history and culture of the ancient Aztec civilization. (Rev: BL 10/15/06; SLJ 10/06)

9336 Mellor, Ronald, and Amanda H. Podany. *The World in Ancient Times: Primary Sources and Reference Volume* (6–12). Series: The World in Ancient Times. 2006, Oxford LB $32.95 (978-0-19-522220-3). More than 75 selections from poems, letters, inscriptions, and other accounts introduce civilizations and everyday life in ancient times. (Rev: SLJ 5/06) [930]

9337 Miller, Reagan. *Communication in the Ancient World* (5–7). Illus. Series: Life in the Ancient World. 2011, Crabtree LB $19.95 (978-077871733-1); paper $8.95 (978-077871740-9). This accessible book explores the development of writing, counting, and calendars in various cultures — Rome, South America, Egypt, Japan — around the ancient world. (Rev: BL 10/1/11; LMC 9–10/12) [302.2]

9338 Nardo, Don. *Aztec Civilization* (6–9). Illus. Series: World History. 2010, Gale/Lucent LB $32.45 (978-142050242-8). With a timeline, photographs, illustrations, and quotations, this survey of the Aztec civilization is useful for report writers. (Rev: BL 2/1/11) [972]

9339 Nardo, Don. *The Vikings* (6–9). Illus. Series: World History. 2010, Gale/Lucent LB $33.45 (978-142050316-6). With a timeline, photographs, illustrations, and quotations, this survey of the Viking civilization is useful for report writers. (Rev: BL 2/1/11) [948]

9340 Perl, Lila. *The Ancient Maya* (5–8). Series: People of the Ancient World. 2005, Watts LB $30.50 (978-0-531-12381-2); paper $9.95 (978-0-531-16848-6). Introduces readers to the arts, religious beliefs, and society of the Maya, with discussion of individual occupations and of the discoveries by archaeologists and anthropologists. (Rev: SLJ 9/05) [973]

9341 Raum, Elizabeth. *What Did the Vikings Do for Me?* (4–7). Illus. Series: Linking Past to Present. 2010, Heinemann LB $29 (978-143293745-4). This intriguing overview of Viking history and culture also explains their legacy in aspects including language, justice, and the role of women. (Rev: BL 10/1/10; LMC 1–2/11) [948]

9342 Richardson, Hazel. *Life in Ancient Africa* (4–7). Series: Peoples of the Ancient World. 2005, Crabtree LB $26.60 (978-0-7787-2043-0); paper $8.95 (978-0-7787-2073-7). Introduces the early civilizations of Africa, examining their arts, spiritual beliefs, government, language, and technology; color photographs, sidebars, and timelines add information and appeal. (Rev: SLJ 11/05) [973]

9343 Richardson, Hazel. *Life in Ancient Japan* (4–7). Series: Peoples of the Ancient World. 2005, Crabtree LB $26.60 (978-0-7787-2041-6); paper $8.95 (978-0-7787-2071-3). Introduces ancient Japan's arts, spiritual beliefs, government, language, and technology; color photographs, sidebars, and timelines add information and appeal. (Rev: SLJ 11/05) [952]

9344 Richardson, Hazel. *Life in the Ancient Indus River Valley* (4–7). Series: Peoples of the Ancient World. 2005, Crabtree LB $26.60 (978-0-7787-2040-9); paper $8.95 (978-0-7787-2070-6). Introduces life in the earliest urban civilization on the Indian subcontinent, examining the arts, spiritual beliefs, government, language, and technology; color photographs, sidebars, and timelines add information and appeal. (Rev: SLJ 11/05) [973]

9345 Richardson, Hazel. *Life of the Ancient Celts* (4–7). Series: Peoples of the Ancient World. 2005, Crabtree LB $26.60 (978-0-7787-2045-4); paper $8.95 (978-0-7787-2075-1). Introduces the early Celtic civilization, examining arts, spiritual beliefs, government, language, and technology; color photographs, sidebars, and timelines add information and appeal. (Rev: SLJ 11/05) [973]

9346 Schomp, Virginia. *Ancient India* (6–8). Series: People of the Ancient World. 2005, Watts LB $30.50 (978-0-531-12379-9). Readable text and attractive illustrations introduce readers to ancient India and its art, culture, religion, government, agriculture, and societal levels. (Rev: SLJ 6/05) [954]

9347 Schomp, Virginia. *The Vikings* (6–8). Series: People of the Ancient World. 2005, Watts LB $30.50 (978-0-531-12382-9). The culture, literature, arts, religious beliefs, and government of the Vikings are explored in readable text and attractive illustrations. (Rev: SLJ 6/05) [948]

9348 Service, Pamela F. *300 B.C.* (5–8). Series: Around the World In. 2002, Benchmark $29.93 (978-0-7614-1080-5). The author explores what was going on in Europe, Africa, Asia, and the Americas in the year 300 B.C. Also use *1200* (2002). (Rev: HBG 3/03; SLJ 2/03) [930]

9349 Sonneborn, Liz. *The Ancient Aztecs* (6–8). Series: People of the Ancient World. 2005, Watts LB $30.50 (978-0-531-12362-1). The culture, arts, literature, religious beliefs, and government of the Aztecs are explored in readable text accompanied by attractive illustrations. (Rev: SLJ 6/05) [972]

9350 Sonneborn, Liz. *The Ancient Kushites* (5–8). Series: People of the Ancient World. 2005, Watts LB $30.50 (978-0-531-12380-5). Explores the arts, religious beliefs, and culture of Africa's ancient Kushites, who were also known as Nubians. (Rev: SLJ 9/05) [973]

9351 Stefoff, Rebecca. *The Ancient Mediterranean* (5–8). Series: World Historical Atlases. 2004, Benchmark LB $27.07 (978-0-7614-1641-8). Maps, text, and illustrations give a broad overview of the cultures found in the ancient Mediterranean. Also use *The Ancient Near East* and *The Asian Empires* (both 2004). (Rev: SLJ 2/05) [930]

9352 Strapp, James. *Science and Technology* (7–10). Illus. Series: Inside Ancient China. 2009, Sharpe Focus LB $31.45 (978-076568169-0). Strapp looks at ancient Chinese inventions and innovations ranging from gunpowder and the compass to *feng shui*; includes

maps, photographs, timelines, and drawings. (Rev: BL 2/15/09; SLJ 6/1/09) [609.31]

Egypt and Mesopotamia

9353 Berger, Melvin, and Gilda Berger. *Mummies of the Pharaohs: Exploring the Valley of the Kings* (4–7). 2001, National Geographic $17.95 (978-0-7922-7223-6). Beginning with King Tut's tomb and continuing through other sites, this book uses stunning photographs and a clear text to describe workings of archaeological digs that are studying Egypt's past. (Rev: BL 2/1/01) [932]

9354 Broida, Marian. *Ancient Egyptians and Their Neighbors: An Activity Guide* (4–8). 1999, Chicago Review paper $16.95 (978-1-55652-360-1). The lives and times of the ancient Egyptians, Nubians, Hittites, and Mesopotamians are examined using text and a series of 40 fascinating projects. (Rev: BL 3/15/00; SLJ 2/00) [939]

9355 Chrisp, Peter. *Mesopotamia: Iraq in Ancient Times* (4–7). Series: Picturing the Past. 2004, Enchanted Lion $15.95 (978-1-59270-024-0). History and archaeology are the highlights of this nicely illustrated overview of Mesopotamian civilization. (Rev: BL 10/15/04; SLJ 11/04) [935]

9356 Chrisp, Peter. *Pyramid* (4–8). Illus. Series: DK Experience. 2006, DK $15.99 (978-0-7566-1410-2). Full-color illustrations, 3-D diagrams, and CT scans make this survey of the construction and importance of the Great Pyramid of Giza informative and attractive. (Rev: SLJ 11/06)

9357 Cline, Eric H., and Jill Rubalcaba. *The Ancient Egyptian World* (5–10). Series: The World in Ancient Times. 2005, Oxford LB $32.95 (978-0-19-517391-8). An overview of ancient Egyptian history and culture, with chronologically arranged chapters covering religion, medicine, clothing, arts, and so forth and introducing key figures such as Hatshepsut, Tutankhamen, and Cleopatra. (Rev: SLJ 1/06) [932]

9358 Croy, Anita, ed. *Ancient Egypt* (5–9). Series: Facts at Your Fingertips. 2010, Black Rabbit LB $35.65 (978-1-933834-54-2). After presenting historical facts about ancient Egypt before and after the pharaohs, this volume goes on to look at specific sites of importance — Abu Simbel, Thebes, Memphis, and so forth. Also use *Ancient Mesopotamia* (2010). (Rev: LMC 3–4/10) [932.222]

9359 Day, Nancy. *Your Travel Guide to Ancient Egypt* (4–8). Series: Passport to History. 2000, Runestone LB $26.50 (978-0-8225-3075-6). Written in the style of a modern-day travel guide, this book on ancient Egypt covers such subjects as sites to see, food, clothing, religious beliefs, politics, and daily life. (Rev: BL 11/15/00; HBG 3/01; SLJ 5/01; VOYA 8/01) [932]

591

9360 England, Victoria. *Top 10 Worst Things About Ancient Egypt You Wouldn't Want to Know* (4–7). Illus. by David Antram. 2012, Gareth Stevens LB $26.60 (978-143396688-0). Starvation, irascible pharaohs, and drudging stone cutting and hauling work are a few of the things ancient Egyptians had to endure; this lively and irreverent history book will appeal to browsers and reluctant readers. (Rev: BL 4/15/12; SLJ 6/12) [932]

9361 Filer, Joyce. *Pyramids* (3–8). Illus. 2006, Oxford Univ. $19.99 (978-0-19-530521-0). A detailed introduction to the pyramids of ancient Egypt and their design, their builders, their construction, and their contents; there is also information on pyramids outside Egypt. (Rev: SLJ 7/06)

9362 Fletcher, Joann. *Exploring the Life, Myth, and Art of Ancient Egypt* (7–12). Series: Civilizations of the World. 2010, Rosen LB $39.95 (978-1-4358-5616-5). Daily life, mythology, arts, religion, and various aspects of preparing for the afterlife are covered in this well-designed book that includes illustrations and a list of Web sites. (Rev: BL 10/1/09; LMC 1–2/10)

9363 Giblin, James Cross. *Secrets of the Sphinx* (7–12). Illus. by Bagram Ibatoulline. 2004, Scholastic LB $17.95 (978-0-590-09847-2). Full of interesting facts and details of archaeological discoveries, this is a handsome, well-illustrated picture-book-format account of the mysteries that still surround the Sphinx and the facts that are known. (Rev: BL 9/15/04; HB 11–12/04; SLJ 11/04) [932]

9364 Hawass, Zahi. *Tutankhamun and the Golden Age of the Pharaohs* (8–12). 2005, National Geographic $35.00 (978-0-7922-3873-7). Companion to a traveling exhibit, this volume highlights the importance of items retrieved from Tutankhamen's tomb. (Rev: BL 6/1–15/05) [932]

9365 Hinds, Kathryn. *The City* (6–9). Series: Life in Ancient Egypt. 2006, Benchmark LB $22.95 (978-0-7614-2184-9). This handsome, well-illustrated volume describes city life in Egypt's New Kingdom (from 1550 B.C. to 1070 B.C.) from numerous perspectives and includes interesting in-depth sidebar features; also recommended in this series are *The Countryside, The Pharaoh's Court,* and *Religion* (all 2006). (Rev: SLJ 5/07) [932]

9366 Hollar, Sherman. *Ancient Egypt* (5–8). Series: Ancient Civilizations. 2011, Britannica Educational LB $31.70 (978-1-61530-523-0). This slim volume offers an accessible introduction to the culture, religion, architecture, and inventions of ancient Egypt. ℮ (Rev: SLJ 12/1/11) [932]

9367 Hynson, Colin. *The Building of the Great Pyramid* (5–8). Illus. Series: Stories from History. 2006, School Specialty $9.95 (978-0-7696-4708-1); paper $6.95 (978-0-7696-4692-3). Full-color illustrations and graphic novel format make this survey of the ancient engineering feat attractive to reluctant readers. (Rev: SLJ 1/07)

9368 Kallen, Stuart A. *Ancient Egypt* (7–12). Illus. Series: Understanding World History. 2011, ReferencePoint LB $27.95 (978-160152152-1). With information on the pyramids and the mysteries that surround their construction, this is a thorough overview of the culture of ancient Egypt and its legacy on art, medicine, religion, and so forth. (Rev: BL 10/1/11; LMC 9–10/12) [932.01]

9369 Kaplan, Sarah Pitt. *The Great Pyramid at Giza: Tomb of Wonders* (5–8). Series: Digging Up the Past. 2005, Children's Pr. LB $24.50 (978-0-516-25131-8); paper $6.95 (978-0-516-25095-3). A richly illustrated survey of the important pyramid and the reasons for its creation; suitable for reluctant readers. (Rev: SLJ 2/06) [932]

9370 Kennett, David. *Pharaoh: Life and Afterlife of a God* (4–7). Illus. by author. 2008, Walker $18.95 (978-0-8027-9567-0). This attractive book introduces readers to the elaborate burial of Seti I and in doing so also explains many aspects of life in ancient Egypt, for royalty as well as common people. (Rev: BL 5/1/08; SLJ 2/08) [932]

9371 Lace, William W. *The Curse of King Tut* (5–8). Illus. Series: Mysterious & Unknown. 2007, Reference Point LB $24.95 (978-1-60152-024-1). Readers will learn factual information about the discovery of King Tutankhamen's tomb while searching for the truth about his "curse." (Rev: BL 10/15/07; LMC 2/08; SLJ 2/08) [932]

9372 Lace, William W. *King Tut's Curse* (6–9). Illus. Series: Ancient Egyptian Wonders. 2012, ReferencePoint LB $27.95 (978-160152250-4). An engaging exploration of the reasons underlying the supposed curse, with details on the life of Tutankhamen and the discovery of his tomb. (Rev: BL 10/1/12; LMC 5–6/13*) [932]

9373 McNeill, Sarah. *Ancient Egyptian People* (4–8). Series: People and Places. 1997, Millbrook LB $21.90 (978-0-7613-0056-4). This basic introduction to the people of ancient Egypt and how they lived consists of several attractive double-page spreads and a brief text. (Rev: BL 2/15/97; SLJ 3/97) [932]

9374 McNeill, Sarah. *Ancient Egyptian Places* (4–8). Series: People and Places. 1997, Millbrook LB $21.90 (978-0-7613-0057-1). Some of the great constructions of ancient Egypt are pictured in a series of elegant double-page spreads with a simple text. (Rev: BL 2/15/97; SLJ 3/97) [932]

9375 Malam, John. *Ancient Egypt* (5–8). Series: Remains to Be Seen. 1998, Evans Brothers $19.95 (978-0-237-51839-4). This introduction to ancient Egypt's culture and history is organized in double-page spreads and is noteworthy for its many sidebars, charts, and illustrations. (Rev: SLJ 9/98) [932]

9376 Mann, Elizabeth. *The Great Pyramid* (4–7). Series: Wonders of the World. 1996, Mikaya $19.95 (978-0-9650493-1-3). The building of this architectural marvel is told graphically, with details on the society of ancient Egypt. (Rev: BL 2/1/97; SLJ 6/97*) [932]

9377 Matthews, Sheelagh. *Pyramids of Giza* (6–9). Series: Structural Wonders. 2007, Weigl LB $26.00 (978-1-59036-725-4); paper $7.95 (978-1-59036-726-1). This interesting account of the construction of the pyramids at Giza also discusses their current status and includes excellent full-color photographs. (Rev: SLJ 12/07) [932]

9378 Morgan, Julian. *Cleopatra: Ruling in the Shadow of Rome* (6–8). Series: Leaders of Ancient Egypt. 2003, Rosen LB $33.25 (978-0-8239-3591-8). Cleopatra's relations with Julius Caesar and Mark Anthony are central to this account that homes in on their individual characteristics and provides ample historical context. (Rev: SLJ 9/03) [921]

9379 Nardo, Don. *Ancient Alexandria* (6–10). Series: A Travel Guide To. 2003, Gale LB $29.95 (978-1-59018-142-3). Readers are treated to a guidebook-style survey of ancient Alexandria's attractions, with a focus on weather, transport, hotels, shopping, festivals and sporting events, institutions, and people. (Rev: SLJ 6/03) [962]

9380 Nardo, Don. *Arts, Leisure, and Sport in Ancient Egypt* (6–10). Series: The Lucent Library of Historical Eras. 2005, Gale LB $32.45 (978-1-59018-706-7). Photographs, reproductions, and film and documentary stills illustrate this well-documented examination of the art and leisure activities of ancient Egyptians, from music and dance to hunting and fishing. Also use *Mummies, Myth, and Magic: Religion in Ancient Egypt* (2005). (Rev: SLJ 11/05) [932]

9381 Nardo, Don. *Peoples and Empires of Ancient Mesopotamia* (8–12). Series: Lucent Library of Historical Eras. 2008, Gale/Lucent $32.45 (978-1-4205-0101-8). This informative, well-illustrated volume describes ancient Mesopotamian society and politics, looking at urban and rural life, early systems of writing, and the successive empires of the region. Also use *Arts and Literature in Ancient Mesopotamia, Life and Worship in Ancient Mesopotamia,* and *Science, Technology, and Warfare of Ancient Mesopotamia* (all 2009). (Rev: SLJ 5/1/09)

9382 Orr, Tamra. *How'd They Do That in Ancient Egypt?* (5–8). Series: How'd They Do That? 2010, Mitchell Lane LB $24.50 (978-1-58415-821-9). Covers aspects of life in ancient Egypt, from slaves to pharaohs, ranging from work and play, to hieroglyphs, architecture, religion, and mummies, providing FYInfo sections and a craft (making a reed boat). (Rev: BL 4/1/10; LMC 5–6/10; SLJ 5/10) [932]

9383 Payne, Elizabeth. *The Pharaohs of Ancient Egypt* (6–8). 1981, Random House paper $5.99 (978-0-394-

84699-6). A fascinating study of this important period in Egyptian history. [932]

9384 Podany, Amanda H., and Marni McGee. *The Ancient Near Eastern World* (8–12). Series: The World in Ancient Times. 2005, Oxford LB $32.95 (978-0-19-516159-5). Using primary sources and useful illustrations, this volume explores the ancient civilizations that flourished in the Fertile Crescent until the region was conquered by Alexander the Great in the 4th century B.C. (Rev: SLJ 6/05; VOYA 10/04) [935]

9385 Rubalcaba, Jill. *Ancient Egypt: Archaeology Unlocks the Secrets of Egypt's Past* (3–7). 2006, National Geographic $17.95 (978-0-7922-7784-2). This well-illustrated overview of what archaeologists have uncovered about life in ancient Egypt highlights two related events: the 1922 discovery of King Tutankhamen's tomb and the 2005 CT scan of the boy king's mummy. (Rev: SLJ 2/07)

9386 Tyldesley, Joyce. *Egypt* (5–8). Illus. Series: Insiders. 2007, Simon & Schuster $16.99 (978-1-4169-3858-3). An introduction to ancient Egypt — the pyramids, mummies, Abu Simbel, transportation, arts and crafts, and so forth — with eye-catching illustrations. (Rev: LMC 10/07; SLJ 12/07)

9387 Woods, Geraldine. *Science in Ancient Egypt* (4–8). Series: Science of the Past. 1998, Watts paper $8.95 (978-0-531-15915-6). The many contributions to science by the ancient Egyptians, including architecture, astronomy, and mathematics, are outlined in this richly illustrated volume. (Rev: BL 6/1–15/98; HBG 10/98; SLJ 6/98) [932]

Greece

9388 Anderson, Michael, ed. *Ancient Greece* (5–8). Series: Ancient Civilizations. 2011, Britannica Educational LB $31.70 (978-1-61530-513-1). This slim volume offers an accessible introduction to the culture, religion, architecture, and inventions of ancient Greece. **e** (Rev: SLJ 12/1/11) [938]

9389 Croy, Anita, ed. *Ancient Greece* (5–9). Series: Facts at Your Fingertips. 2010, Black Rabbit LB $35.65 (978-1-933834-55-9). Crete, Mycenai, Sparta, Olympia, and Athens are among the sites described in this overview of the history and culture of ancient Greece. (Rev: LMC 3–4/10) [938]

9390 Day, Nancy. *Your Travel Guide to Ancient Greece* (4–8). Series: Passport to History. 2000, Runestone LB $26.50 (978-0-8225-3076-3). An outstanding introduction to ancient Greece arranged in the format of a guided tour and covering topics including geography, history, customs, and places to visit in an exciting, interesting way. (Rev: BL 10/15/00*; HBG 3/01; SLJ 2/01) [938]

9391 Jovinelly, Joann, and Jason Netelkos. *The Crafts and Culture of the Ancient Greeks* (5–8). Series: Crafts of the Ancient World. 2002, Rosen LB $29.25 (978-0-8239-3510-9). As well as basic information on ancient Greece, this book outlines many craft projects. (Rev: BL 5/15/02) [938]

9392 McGee, Marni. *Ancient Greece: Archaeology Unlocks the Secrets of Greece's Past* (3–7). Series: National Geographic Investigates. 2006, National Geographic $17.95 (978-0-7922-7826-9). This well-illustrated title looks at archaeologists' efforts over the years to uncover — on land and under the sea — information about life in ancient Greece. (Rev: SLJ 2/07)

9393 Malam, John. *Ancient Greece* (4–7). Series: Picturing the Past. 2004, Enchanted Lion $15.95 (978-1-59270-022-6). This photo-filled volume uses images of ancient Greek artifacts and structures to introduce the civilization's governmental organization, religion, mythology, recreation, and theater. (Rev: BL 10/15/04; SLJ 11/04) [938]

9394 Malam, John. *Exploring Ancient Greece* (5–8). Series: Remains to Be Seen. 1999, Evans Brothers $19.95 (978-0-237-51994-0). Particularly noteworthy in this basic account of the history of ancient Greece are the stunning photographs of temples, theaters, artifacts, and landscapes. (Rev: SLJ 1/00) [938]

9395 Martell, Hazel Mary, and Cleo Kuhtz. *Ancient Greek Civilization* (5–8). Series: Ancient Civilizations and Their Myths and Legends. 2010, Rosen LB $26.50 (978-1-4042-8033-5). This volume introduces daily life in ancient Greece and describes religion, agriculture, government, trade, clothing, entertainment, and so forth, at the same time retelling some of the best-known myths. (Rev: LMC 1–2/10) [292.13]

9396 Nardo, Don. *Women of Ancient Greece* (7–10). Series: World History. 2000, Lucent LB $32.45 (978-1-56006-646-0). The story of the place of women in ancient Greek society, how they lacked political rights and lived sheltered lives yet performed many important duties. (Rev: BL 6/1–15/00; HBG 3/01) [938]

9397 Roberts, Jennifer T., and Tracy Barrett. *The Ancient Greek World* (7–10). Series: The World in Ancient Times. 2004, Oxford LB $32.95 (978-0-19-515696-6). The authors take a lively and humorous approach to their carefully researched account of political and cultural life in ancient Greece. (Rev: SLJ 8/04) [938]

9398 Robinson, C. E. *Everyday Life in Ancient Greece* (7–12). 1933, AMS $45.00 (978-0-404-14592-7). The classic account, first published in 1933, of how people lived during various periods in ancient Greek history. [938]

9399 Stafford, Emma J. *Exploring the Life, Myth, and Art of Ancient Greece* (8–11). Illus. Series: Civilizations of the World. 2011, Rosen LB $39.95 (978-144884830-0). A handsome, well-written survey of

ancient Greece's history, mythology, society, and arts, with maps and color illustrations. e (Rev: BL 2/15/12; LMC 5–6/12) [938]

9400 Woodford, Susan. *The Parthenon* (6–10). 1983, Cambridge Univ. paper $19.00 (978-0-521-22629-5). A history of the famous temple in Athens and of the religion of ancient Greece. [938]

9401 Wright, Anne. *Art and Architecture* (7–10). Series: Inside Ancient Greece. 2007, M.E. Sharpe LB $31.45 (978-0-7656-8130-0). Focusing on practical and decorative art and architecture in ancient Greece, this volume describes in detail how art was produced during this time. (Rev: BL 10/15/07; LMC 2/08; SLJ 12/07) [709.38]

Middle East

9402 Broida, Marian. *Ancient Israelites and Their Neighbors: An Activity Guide* (4–7). 2003, Chicago Review paper $16.95 (978-1-55652-457-8). Readers will find out what life was like for the ancient Israelis, Phoenicians, and Philistines through the information and activities in this attractive book. Sidney Taylor Book Honor 2003. (Rev: BL 5/15/03; SLJ 8/03) [933]

9403 Price, Massoume. *Ancient Iran* (4–8). Illus. Series: Culture of Iran Youth Series. 2008, Anahita $19.95 (978-0-9809714-0-8). After a brief discussion of Iran today, this well-illustrated volume gives a chronological overview of the peoples and culture of ancient Iran. (Rev: SLJ 3/1/09) [935]

9404 Trumble, Kelly. *The Library of Alexandria* (5–7). Illus. by Robina MacIntyre Marshall. 2003, Clarion $17.00 (978-0-395-75832-8). An introduction to the famous library, its collection, its scholars, and its destruction by fire. (Rev: BCCB 1/04; BL 11/15/03; HBG 4/04; SLJ 1/04) [027.032]

9405 Zeinert, Karen. *The Persian Empire* (7–10). Series: Cultures of the Past. 1996, Benchmark LB $29.93 (978-0-7614-0089-9). A brief history of the Persian Empire, with material on the kings Cyrus, Darius, and Xerxes, is followed by chapters on daily life, culture, religion, and lasting contributions the empire made to human achievement. (Rev: SLJ 3/97) [935]

Rome

9406 Allan, Tony. *Exploring the Life, Myth, and Art of Ancient Rome* (8–11). Illus. Series: Civilizations of the World. 2011, Rosen LB $39.95 (978-144884831-7). A handsome, well-written survey of ancient Rome's history, mythology, society, and arts, with maps and color illustrations. e (Rev: BL 2/15/12; LMC 5–6/12) [937]

9407 Anderson, Michael, ed. *Ancient Rome* (5–8). Series: Ancient Civilizations. 2011, Britannica Educational LB $31.70 (978-1-61530-522-3). This slim volume offers an accessible introduction to the culture, religion, architecture, and inventions of ancient Rome. ℮ (Rev: SLJ 12/1/11) [937]

9408 Beller, Susan Provost. *Roman Legions on the March: Soldiering in the Ancient Roman Army* (5–8). 2007, Twenty-First Century LB $33.26 (978-0-8225-6781-3). After background information on the Roman army, this volume examines the life of the soldiers and provides interesting sidebar features and photographs. (Rev: SLJ 1/08)

9409 Croy, Anita, ed. *Ancient Rome* (5–9). Series: Facts at Your Fingertips. 2010, Black Rabbit LB $35.65 (978-1-933834-56-6). From the birth of Rome through the peak of imperial power to the later empire, this well-illustrated volume provides easy access to facts and looks at different areas of the Roman Empire in some detail. (Rev: LMC 3–4/10) [937]

9410 Deem, James M. *Bodies from the Ash: Life and Death in Ancient Pompeii* (5–8). 2005, Houghton Mifflin $17.00 (978-0-618-47308-3). This photoessay full of vivid illustrations outlines what archaeologists have uncovered about the destruction of Pompeii when Mount Vesuvius erupted nearly 2,000 years ago. (Rev: BL 11/1/05; SLJ 12/05*) [937]

9411 DuTemple, Lesley A. *The Colosseum* (4–7). Series: Great Building Feats. 2003, Lerner LB $27.93 (978-0-8225-4693-1). Using many colorful diagrams and illustrations, this is the story of the construction of the famous colosseum in Rome. (Rev: BL 11/15/03; HBG 4/04) [937]

9412 Hanel, Rachael. *Gladiators* (5–8). Series: Fearsome Fighters. 2007, Creative Education LB $31.35 (978-1-58341-535-1). Weapons, armor, fighting techniques, and motivation are all discussed in this description of gladiators in ancient Rome and the kinds of people who were tempted to this career. (Rev: SLJ 1/08)

9413 Hinds, Kathryn. *Everyday Life in the Roman Empire* (7–10). 2009, Marshall Cavendish $29.95 (978-0-7614-4484-8). Hinds looks at society across the Roman Empire, examining in turn the court, the city, the countryside, and the church. (Rev: BL 4/1/10*; LMC 5–6/10; SLJ 12/09) [937]

9414 Jovinelly, Joann, and Jason Netelkos. *The Crafts and Culture of the Romans* (5–8). Series: Crafts of the Ancient World. 2002, Rosen LB $29.25 (978-0-8239-3513-0). The daily life and contributions of the ancient Romans are covered, as well as such craft projects as designing a toga. (Rev: BL 5/15/02; SLJ 6/02) [937]

9415 Macaulay, David. *City: A Story of Roman Planning and Construction* (6–10). 1974, Houghton Mifflin $18.00 (978-0-395-19492-8); paper $9.95 (978-0-395-34922-9). In text and detailed drawing, the artist explores an imaginary Roman city over approximately 125 years. [711]

9416 Mann, Elizabeth. *The Roman Colosseum* (4–7). Series: Wonders of the World. 1998, Mikaya $19.95 (978-0-9650493-3-7). An oversize book that is crammed with factual material on the Colosseum in Rome. (Rev: BL 12/15/98; SLJ 2/99) [937]

9417 Mellor, Ronald, and Marni McGee. *The Ancient Roman World* (7–10). Series: The World in Ancient Times. 2004, Oxford LB $32.95 (978-0-19-515380-4). This attractive and accessible volume introduces readers to the history, people, and culture of ancient Rome, using many quotations and illustrations. (Rev: BL 4/1/04; SLJ 7/04) [937]

9418 Nardo, Don. *A Roman Senator* (6–9). Series: Working Life. 2004, Gale LB $29.95 (978-1-59018-481-3). Black-and-white illustrations add to this account of the evolution of the Roman senate over almost 12 centuries. (Rev: BL 2/1/05) [328]

9419 Solway, Andrew. *Rome: In Spectacular Cross-Section* (4–7). Illus. by Stephen Biesty. 2003, Scholastic paper $18.95 (978-0-439-45546-6). An inside look at life in ancient Rome, with views of a private home, the Colosseum, the docks, and a bustling festival. (Rev: BL 2/15/03; HBG 10/03; SLJ 7/03) [937]

9420 Stroud, Jonathan. *Ancient Rome: A Guide to the Glory of Imperial Rome* (4–7). Series: Sightseers. 2000, Kingfisher $8.95 (978-0-7534-5235-6). This book on ancient Rome is presented like a handbook for tourists, with material on such topics as accommodations, shopping, key sites, etc. (Rev: HBG 3/01; SLJ 9/00) [937]

Middle Ages Through the Renaissance (500–1700)

9421 Allen, Kathy. *The Horrible, Miserable Middle Ages: The Disgusting Details About Life During Medieval Times* (4–8). Series: Fact Finders: Disgusting History. 2010, Capstone LB $25.32 (978-1-4296-3958-3). Allen concentrates on the grosser side of medieval life, describing poor sanitation, rotten food, bugs, medical horrors, and so forth. Lexile 850L (Rev: LMC 11–12/10) [940.1]

9422 Aronson, Marc. *John Winthrop, Oliver Cromwell, and the Land of Promise* (7–10). 2004, Houghton Mifflin $20.00 (978-0-618-18177-3). In this fascinating historical study, Aronson explores the interrelationship between John Winthrop, 17th-century governor of the Massachusetts Bay Colony, and Oliver Cromwell, who led the successful Puritan revolt against Britain's King Charles I. (Rev: BL 6/1–15/04; HB 7–8/04; SLJ 9/04) [974.4]

9423 Barter, James. *A Medieval Knight* (6–9). Series: Working Life. 2005, Gale LB $29.95 (978-1-59018-580-3). A medieval knight's life involves training, tournaments, fighting, and administration and legal duties as laid out in this thorough overview that includes relevant images and excerpts from primary sources. (Rev: SLJ 11/05) [940]

9424 Claybourne, Anna. *The Renaissance* (5–9). Series: Time Travel Guides. 2007, Raintree LB $34.29 (978-1-4109-2910-5); paper $9.99 (978-1-4109-2916-7). With chapter headings like "Facts," "Everyday Life," and "Things to See and Do," this volume takes an effective travel-guide approach to the Renaissance, incorporating many visual elements. (Rev: SLJ 1/08)

9425 Crompton, Samuel Willard. *The Third Crusade: Richard the Lionhearted vs. Saladin* (7–12). Series: Great Battles Through the Ages. 2003, Chelsea House LB $30.00 (978-0-7910-7437-4). A useful survey of the First and Second Crusades is followed by details of the third campaign and portrayals of Richard and Saladin. (Rev: SLJ 5/04) [909.07]

9426 Currie, Stephen. *Miracles, Saints, and Superstition: The Medieval Mind* (5–9). 2006, Gale LB $32.45 (978-1-59018-861-3). Describes the Middle Ages and the role of Christianity at that time. (Rev: SLJ 3/07*) [940.1]

9427 Davenport, John. *The Age of Feudalism* (8–11). Series: World History. 2007, Gale LB $32.45 (978-1-59018-649-7). A look at the feudal social and economic system in Europe, which lasted from the 5th century until the rise of nation-states. (Rev: BL 2/1/08) [940.1]

9428 Day, Nancy. *Your Travel Guide to Renaissance Europe* (4–8). Series: Passport to History. 2000, Lerner LB $26.50 (978-0-8225-3080-0). This book uses a travel guide format to introduce the reader to the life and people of Europe from 1350 to 1550 with coverage of culture, style, inventions, religious beliefs, and scientific discoveries. (Rev: BL 3/1/01; HBG 10/01) [940.2]

9429 Elgin, Kathy. *Elizabethan England* (6–12). Series: Costume and Fashion Source Books. 2009, Chelsea House $35 (978-1-60413-379-0). This volume looks at fashion and clothing in the Elizabethan area, describing the garb of men and women at court, the middle classes and professions, urban and rural residents, soldiers and sailors, and children. (Rev: LMC 11–12/09; SLJ 10-09) [391]

9430 Elgin, Kathy. *The Medieval World* (6–12). Series: Costume and Fashion Source Books. 2009, Chelsea House $35 (978-1-60413-378-3). This volume looks at the attire of men and women of various different walks of life in the Middle Ages. (Rev: LMC 11–12/09; SLJ 10/09) [391]

9431 Ford, Nick. *Jerusalem Under Muslim Rule in the Eleventh Century: Christian Pilgrims Under Islamic Government* (5–9). Series: The Library of the Middle Ages. 2004, Rosen LB $29.25 (978-0-8239-4216-9). Useful for report writers, this volume looks at life in

Jerusalem for people of all religions, providing details from primary sources. (Rev: SLJ 8/04) [956.94]

9432 Hanawalt, Barbara. *The Middle Ages: An Illustrated History* (8–12). 1999, Oxford $37.99 (978-0-19-510359-5). A carefully researched account of the Roman Empire and its gradual fall, the rise of the church, its use of power, and feudal society, including such topics as castles, the Crusades, the Black Death, the rise of guilds and universities, and the growth of the middle class. (Rev: BL 3/1/99; HBG 3/99; SLJ 4/99) [909.07]

9433 Hanel, Rachael. *Knights* (5–8). Series: Fearsome Fighters. 2007, Creative Education LB $31.35 (978-1-58341-536-8). Weapons, armor, fighting techniques, and motivation are all discussed in this description of the knights of the Middle Ages and the kinds of people who were tempted to this career. (Rev: SLJ 1/08)

9434 Haywood, John. *Medieval Europe* (5–9). Series: Time Travel Guides. 2007, Raintree LB $34.29 (978-1-4109-2909-9); paper $9.99 (978-1-4109-2915-0). With chapter headings like "Facts," "Everyday Life," and "Things to See and Do," this volume takes an effective travel-guide approach to the Middle Ages, incorporating many visual elements. (Rev: SLJ 1/08)

9435 Helget, Nicole. *Barbarians* (5–8). Illus. Series: Fearsome Fighters. 2012, Creative Education $24.95 (978-160818182-7). With many illustrations, maps, and primary documents, this volume looks at such groups as the Celts, Franks, Goths, and Huns that were regarded by the Greeks and Romans as "barbarians," discussing their social mores, weapons, fighting techniques, key figures, and so forth. (Rev: BL 11/1/12; LMC 5–6/13; SLJ 12/12) [940.1]

9436 Hinds, Kathryn. *The City* (6–8). Series: Life in Elizabethan England. 2007, Marshall Cavendish LB $22.95 (978-0-7614-2544-1). Details of city life in Elizabethan England, including living conditions, food and sanitation, are discussed in this well-illustrated volume. (Rev: LMC 4/08; SLJ 3/08)

9437 Hinds, Kathryn. *The Countryside* (6–8). Series: Life in Elizabethan England. 2007, Marshall Cavendish LB $22.95 (978-0-7614-2543-4). A handsome representation of country life in Elizabethan England. (Rev: LMC 4/08; SLJ 3/08)

9438 Hinds, Kathryn. *Elizabeth and Her Court* (6–8). Series: Life in Elizabethan England. 2007, Marshall Cavendish LB $22.95 (978-0-7614-2542-7). A look at the queen and royal court in Elizabethan times. (Rev: SLJ 3/08)

9439 Hinds, Kathryn. *Everyday Life in Medieval Europe* (6–9). 2009, Marshall Cavendish LB $42.79 (978-0-7614-3927-1). Neatly divided into castle, city, countryside, and church, this book provides a compelling, illustrated glimpse into the day-to-day goings-on in medieval Europe. (Rev: LMC 10/09) [940]

9440 Hinds, Kathryn. *Everyday Life in the Renaissance* (7–10). 2010, Marshall Cavendish LB $42.79 (978-0-7614-4483-1). Hinds looks at society in the Renaissance, examining in turn the court, the city, the countryside, and the church. (Rev: LMC 5–6/10; SLJ 12/09) [940.21]

9441 Kallen, Stuart A. *A Medieval Merchant* (6–9). Series: The Working Life. 2005, Gale LB $29.95 (978-1-59018-581-0). Trade routes, guilds, training, fairs, and the banking system are all covered in this thorough overview that includes relevant images and excerpts from primary sources. (Rev: SLJ 11/05) [909]

9442 Knight, Judson. *Middle Ages: Almanac* (6–10). Series: UXL Middle Ages Reference Library. 2000, Gale LB $70.00 (978-0-7876-4856-5). A comprehensive review of events around the world during the Middle Ages, with material on Africa and Asia as well as on Europe and the Middle East. Also use *Middle Ages: Biographies* and *Middle Ages: Primary Sources* (both 2000). (Rev: BL 4/1/01; SLJ 5/01) [940.1]

9443 Knight, Judson. *Middle Ages: Primary Sources* (8–12). 2000, U.X.L $70.00 (978-0-7876-4860-2). This book includes 19 entire or excerpted documents from the Middle Ages by such authors as Dante and Marco Polo. (Rev: BL 4/1/01; SLJ 5/01) [909.07]

9444 Lace, William W. *Elizabethan England* (8–12). 2005, Gale LB $31.20 (978-1-59018-655-8). The major issues and figures important in Queen Elizabeth I's reign — as well as the social, scientific, and geographic developments of the 1500s — are described in this book, with lots of color reproductions, a timeline, sidebars, and a further reading section. (Rev: SLJ 6/06)

9445 MacDonald, Fiona. *Knights, Castles, and Warfare in the Middle Ages* (5–8). Series: World Almanac Library of the Middle Ages. 2005, World Almanac LB $31.00 (978-0-8368-5895-2). Describes the role of knights, the equipment they used, and their lives and homes. Also use *The Plague and Medicine in the Middle Ages* (2005). (Rev: SLJ 1/06) [940.1]

9446 Martin, Alex. *Knights and Castles: Exploring History Through Art* (5–8). Series: Picture That! 2004, Two-Can $19.95 (978-1-58728-441-0). Paintings serve as the vehicle to draw students into the discussion of life in Europe during the late medieval period. (Rev: BL 11/1/04; SLJ 2/05) [940.1]

9447 Morgan, Gwyneth. *Life in a Medieval Village* (5–7). Illus. by author. 1991, HarperCollins paper $14.95 (978-0-06-092046-3). A story of activities in a medieval village and of the church's importance in life in the Middle Ages. [306.094265]

9448 Nardo, Don. *Lords, Ladies, Peasants, and Knights: Class in the Middle Ages* (7–10). Series: The Lucent Library of Historical Eras — Middle Ages. 2006, Gale LB $28.70 (978-1-59018-928-3). Nardo describes the social classes of medieval Europe — from kings and popes down through knights and clergy to the peasants and serfs. (Rev: SLJ 4/07)

9449 Padrino, Mercedes. *Cities and Towns in the Middle Ages* (5–8). Series: World Almanac Library of the Middle Ages. 2005, World Almanac LB $31.00 (978-0-8368-5893-8). A look at medieval urban living — social structure, government structure, employment, education, religion, food and clothing, and so forth. Also use *Feudalism and Village Life in the Middle Ages* (2005). (Rev: SLJ 1/06) [940.1]

9450 Prum, Deborah Mazzotta. *Rats, Bulls, and Flying Machines: A History of Renaissance and Reformation* (4–8). Series: Core Chronicles. 1999, Core Knowledge $21.95 (978-1-890517-19-9); paper $11.95 (978-1-890517-18-2). A handsome volume that gives a basic history of the Renaissance and Reformation and highlights the accomplishments of people such as the Medici family, Machiavelli, Michelangelo, Cervantes, Shakespeare, and Gutenberg. (Rev: BL 12/15/99) [909.08]

9451 Ross, Stewart. *Monarchs* (5–8). Series: Medieval Realms. 2004, Gale $29.95 (978-1-59018-535-3). This colorfully illustrated, oversize volume explores the structure of European governments during the Middle Ages and such topics as the birth of new nations, wars, and the Crusades. (Rev: BL 10/15/04) [940.1]

9452 Senker, Cath. *The Black Death 1347–1350: The Plague Spreads Across Europe* (4–7). Series: When Disaster Struck. 2006, Raintree LB $32.86 (978-1-4109-2278-6). Documents the widespread devastation caused by the plague that spread across Europe in the mid-14th century causing an estimated 20 million deaths and discusses current medical understanding and practices. (Rev: SLJ 1/07) [614.5732]

9453 Steele, Philip. *Castles* (5–7). 1995, Kingfisher $16.95 (978-1-85697-547-6). In this oversized, well-designed book, castles, jousting, armor, and feast days are described. (Rev: BL 8/95; SLJ 4/95) [940.1]

9454 Steele, Philip. *The Medieval World* (5–8). Series: A History of Fashion and Costume. 2005, Facts on File $35.00 (978-0-8160-5945-4). A broad overview of the clothing and personal adornment worn during this time period, with many visual aids. (Rev: SLJ 5/06) [391]

9455 White, Pamela. *Exploration in the World of the Middle Ages, 500-1500* (6–12). Series: Discovery and Exploration. 2005, Facts on File $40.00 (978-0-8160-5264-6). The expeditions of Marco Polo, the Vikings, and other explorers of the Middle Ages are chronicled in clear, informative text plus maps, illustrations, and excerpts from primary sources. (Rev: SLJ 8/05) [973]

9456 Woolf, Alex. *Education* (5–8). Series: Medieval Realms. 2004, Gale LB $29.95 (978-1-59018-532-2). Discusses the forms of education available during the Middle Ages — including apprenticeships, song schools, monastic schools, universities — and who was able to enjoy them and what they learned, ending with material on the rise of humanism. (Rev: SLJ 3/05) [370]

9457 Zahler, Diane. *The Black Death* (8–12). Series: Pivotal Moments in History. 2009, Lerner LB $38.60 (978-0-8225-9076-7). Full-color illustrations and first-person accounts punctuate this well-written history of the 14th-century pandemic that killed nearly half of Europe's population. (Rev: SLJ 5/1/09) [614.5]

Eighteenth Through Nineteenth Centuries (1700–1900)

9458 Allport, Alan. *The Congress of Vienna* (8–12). Illus. Series: Milestones in Modern World History. 2011, Chelsea House LB $35 (978-160413497-1). Allport introduces the events that took place after the defeat of Napoleon and includes photographs and a timeline. (Rev: BL 2/15/12) [940.2]

9459 Hicks, Peter. *Documenting the Industrial Revolution* (6–10). Series: Documenting History. 2010, Rosen LB $26.50 (978-1-4358-9670-3). Following an overview of Britain's position as the first industrial nation, this slim volume looks in turn at steam, coal, and iron; the factory system; the transport revolution and the importance of steam; urbanization; and the problems involved in such rapid progress; a rich variety of primary source materials add interest. **e** (Rev: LMC 11–12/10) [330.941]

9460 Sommerville, Donald. *Revolutionary and Napoleonic Wars* (8–10). Series: History of Warfare. 1998, Raintree LB $29.97 (978-0-8172-5446-9). This well-illustrated book looks at the wars fought from the late-18th through mid-19th centuries, focusing primarily on the Americans and the French and their wars of independence and subsequent battles with other enemies. (Rev: HBG 3/99; SLJ 1/99) [909]

Twentieth Century

General and Miscellaneous

9461 Corrigan, Jim. *The 1900s Decade in Photos: A Decade of Discovery* (4–9). Series: Amazing Decades in Photos. 2010, Enslow LB $27.93 (978-0-7660-3129-6). With many color photographs and illustrations and simple text, this volume covers events around the world in the first decade of the 20th century. Other titles in this series include *The 1910s Decade in Photos: A Decade That Shook the World, The 1920s Decade in Photos:*

The Roaring Twenties, and *The 1930s Decade in Photos: Depression and Hope.* and continue on through the beginning of the 21st century. (Rev: LMC 3–4/10) [973.911]

9462 Crew, David F. *Hitler and the Nazis: A History in Documents* (8–12). 2006, Oxford $36.95 (978-0-19-515285-2). Government documents, propaganda, letters, articles, personal memoirs, and trial testimony reveal much about the growth, success, and eventual defeat of the Nazis. (Rev: SLJ 6/06)

9463 Jedicke, Peter. *Great Inventions of the 20th Century* (5–8). Series: Scientific American. 2007, Chelsea House LB $30.00 (978-0-7910-9048-0). With plenty of photographs and clear text, this volume — produced in association with *Scientific American* — presents inventions of the 20th century including cellophane and the microwave in chapters such as "On the Road," "At Home," and "In the Air." (Rev: SLJ 2/08)

9464 Kaufman, Michael T. *1968* (7–12). Illus. 2009, Flash Point $22.95 (978-159643428-8). Drawing on *New York Times* articles, Kaufman chronicles the events of the tumultuous year that saw the escalation of the Vietnam War, assassinations in the United States, uprisings in Europe, and first pictures of Earth from space. Lexile NC1310L (Rev: BL 11/15/08; HB 1–2/09; LMC 3–4/09; SLJ 12/08; VOYA 10/08) [909.82]

9465 McEvoy, Anne. *The 1920s and 1930s* (6–12). Series: Costume and Fashion Source Books. 2009, Chelsea House $35 (978-1-60413-383-7). This volume looks at the attire of men and women of various different walks of life in the 1920s and 1930s, examining in particular the casual wear and sportswear. (Rev: LMC 11–12/09; SLJ 10/09) [391]

9466 Rooney, Anne. *The 1950s and 1960s* (6–12). Series: Costume and Fashion Source Books. 2009, Chelsea House $35 (978-1-60413-385-1). This volume looks at the attire of men and women of various different walks of life in the 1950s and 1960s, covering formal evening wear, leisure wear, work wear and uniforms, and accessories. (Rev: LMC 11–12/09; SLJ 10/09) [391]

9467 Steere, Deirdre Clancy. *The 1980s and 1990s* (6–12). Series: Costume and Fashion Source Books. 2009, Chelsea House $35 (978-1-60413-686-8). This volume looks at the attire of men and women of various different walks of life in the 1980s and 1990s, covering the new fashion trends, the clothing of average people, and the extreme fashions and celebrity culture. (Rev: LMC 11–12/09; SLJ 10/09) [391]

9468 Wilson, Janet. *Imagine That!* (4–8). Illus. by author. 2000, Stoddart $14.95 (978-0-7737-3221-6). In the form of a reminiscence by 100-year-old Auntie Violet, this is a brief history of the past century, with major events highlighted. (Rev: SLJ 11/00) [909]

World War I

9469 Freedman, Russell. *The War to End All Wars: World War I* (6–10). 2010, Clarion $22 (978-0-547-02686-2). Freedman's photo-essay combines analysis of the key events and personalities of World War I with maps and personal stories drawn from letters and diaries. ⌒ ℮ Lexile 1220L (Rev: BL 3/1/10*; HB 7–8/10; LMC 10/10; SLJ 6/10) [940.3]

9470 Granfield, Linda. *Where Poppies Grow: A World War I Companion* (4–7). 2002, Stoddart $16.95 (978-0-7737-3319-0). The horrors of war in the trenches are portrayed in this scrapbook full of photographs, propaganda, and ephemera that includes accounts of two Canadian soldiers. (Rev: BL 6/1–15/02; HBG 10/02; SLJ 7/02) [940.3]

9471 Hamilton, John. *Aircraft of World War I* (5–8). Series: World War I. 2003, ABDO LB $24.21 (978-1-57765-912-9). How aircraft became a valuable military tool for the first time in World War I, and how some of the pilots became internationally famous. (Rev: SLJ 6/04) [940.4]

9472 Hamilton, John. *Battles of World War I* (5–8). Series: World War I. 2003, ABDO LB $24.21 (978-1-57765-913-6). A review of key battles that took place during the three years before the United States entered the conflict in 1917, with information on key figures. (Rev: SLJ 6/04) [940.4]

9473 Hamilton, John. *Events Leading to World War I* (5–8). Series: World War I. 2003, ABDO LB $24.21 (978-1-57765-914-3). An evenhanded description of events and circumstances during the years leading up to World War I in each of the countries that became involved in the conflict. (Rev: SLJ 6/04) [940.3]

9474 Hansen, Ole Steen. *Military Aircraft of WWI* (4–7). Series: The Story of Flight. 2003, Crabtree $25.27 (978-0-7787-1201-5). This book introduces in text and pictures the aircraft used by the allies and enemies during World War I. (Rev: BL 10/15/03) [940.3]

9475 Murphy, Jim. *Truce: The Day the Soldiers Stopped Fighting* (5–8). 2009, Scholastic $19.99 (978-0-545-13049-3). The famous Christmas Truce on the western front in December 1914 is explained in this well-written book that features sepia illustrations and discussion of changing attitudes throughout this long war. (Rev: BL 10/15/09*; HB 11–12/09; LMC 1–2/10; SLJ 11/09) [940.4]

9476 Myers, Walter Dean, and Bill Miles. *The Harlem Hellfighters: When Pride Met Courage* (5–8). Illus. 2006, HarperCollins LB $18.89 (978-0-06-001137-6). A tribute to the World War I heroism of the 369th Infantry Regiment, which was made up entirely of African Americans. (Rev: BL 2/1/06; SLJ 4/06) [940.4]

9477 Steele, Philip. *Documenting World War I* (6–10). Series: Documenting History. 2010, Rosen LB $26.50 (978-1-4358-9673-4). With many interesting primary source materials — posters, postage stamps, photographs, cartoons, quotations — this slim volume looks at the causes of the war, the strategies, the social impact, and the eventual peace. (Rev: LMC 11–12/10) [940.3]

9478 Vander Hook, Sue. *The United States Enters World War I* (6–8). Series: Essential Events. 2010, ABDO LB $32.79 (978-1-60453-947-9). From the sinking of the *Lusitania* to the horrors of war in the trenches, this volume covers the U.S. decision to become involved in the war in Europe. (Rev: LMC 10/10; SLJ 5/10) [940.373]

World War II and the Holocaust

9479 Adler, David A. *We Remember the Holocaust* (4–7). 1995, Henry Holt paper $14.95 (978-0-8050-3715-9). Through interview excerpts, the terrible days of the Holocaust are remembered. (Rev: SLJ 12/89) [940.54]

9480 Allen, Thomas B. *Remember Pearl Harbor: American and Japanese Survivors Tell Their Stories* (5–9). 2001, National Geographic $17.95 (978-0-7922-6690-7). First-person accounts by Japanese and American men and women give readers a close-up view of the 1941 Japanese attack on Pearl Harbor, with maps and photographs. (Rev: BL 9/1/01; HBG 3/02; SLJ 9/01*; VOYA 10/01) [940.54]

9481 Allport, Allan. *The Battle of Britain* (8–11). Illus. Series: Milestones in Modern World History. 2012, Chelsea House LB $35 (978-160413920-4). With many eye-catching photographs this volume tells the story of the air battle between the German Luftwaffe and Britain's Royal Air Force in 1940. (Rev: BL 2/15/13) [940.54]

9482 Altman, Linda J. *Hidden Teens, Hidden Lives: Primary Sources from the Holocaust* (8–12). Series: True Stories of Teens in the Holocaust. 2010, Enslow LB $31.93 (978-076603271-2). In chapters such as "Plans and Preparations," "Secret Places," and "Hiding in Plain Sight," this is a fascinating collection of stories about teens who hid from the Nazis, their strategies, and their protectors; with photographs and news pictures. (Rev: BL 4/1/10) [940.53]

9483 Altshuler, David A. *Hitler's War Against the Jews: A Young Reader's Version of The War Against the Jews, 1933-1945, by Lucy S. Dawidowicz* (7–10). 1995, Behrman paper $14.95 (978-0-87441-298-7). The tragic story of Hitler's Final Solution and its aftermath. [940.54]

9484 Ambrose, Stephen E. *The Good Fight: How World War II Was Won* (7–12). 2001, Simon & Schuster $19.95 (978-0-689-84361-7). Historian Ambrose presents an appealing and well-written overview of World War II, from its origins through the Marshall Plan, with many photographs, fact boxes, and maps. (Rev: BL 7/01; HBG 10/01; SLJ 5/01; VOYA 6/01) [940.53]

9485 Auerbacher, Inge. *I Am a Star: Child of the Holocaust* (5–7). 1993, Puffin paper $5.99 (978-0-14-036401-9). The memoirs of a former child survivor of the Terezin concentration camp in Czechoslovakia. (Rev: BCCB 7–8/87; BL 6/1/87; SLJ 4/87) [940.5]

9486 Bard, Mitchell G., ed. *The Holocaust* (7–12). Series: Turning Points in World History. 2001, Greenhaven LB $37.45 (978-0-7377-0576-8); paper $24.95 (978-0-7377-0575-1). The Jewish genocide in Nazi Germany is explored in an anthology of essays, each of which examines a different aspect of this terrible period in history. (Rev: BL 6/1–15/01) [940.54]

9487 Beller, Susan Provost. *Battling in the Pacific: Soldiering in World War II* (5–8). 2007, Twenty-First Century LB $33.26 (978-0-8225-6381-5). After background information on the war, this volume examines the life of soldiers in the Pacific and provides interesting sidebar features and photographs. (Rev: SLJ 1/08)

9488 Bodden, Valerie. *The Bombing of Hiroshima and Nagasaki* (5–9). Illus. Series: Days of Change. 2007, Creative Education LB $21.95 (978-1-58341-545-0). Survivors of the bombings in both cities recall the horrors of the attacks; a brief background on World War II will help readers to place the bombings in context. (Rev: BL 12/15/07; SLJ 3/08) [940.54]

9489 Boraks-Nemetz, Lillian, and Irene N. Watts, eds. *Tapestry of Hope: Holocaust Writing for Young People* (6–12). 2003, Tundra $24.99 (978-0-88776-638-1). Two Holocaust survivors have collected fiction, poetry, drama, and nonfiction excerpts that detail the experiences of those who went into hiding, were sent to the camps, joined the resistance movement, and made their way to other countries. (Rev: BL 6/1–15/03; HBG 10/03; SLJ 8/03; VOYA 10/03) [810.8]

9490 Burgan, Michael. *Hiroshima: Birth of the Nuclear Age* (8–12). Series: Perspectives On. 2010, Marshall Cavendish LB $39.93 (978-0-7614-4023-9). Burgan provides a concise account of the developments that led up to the destruction of Hiroshima, and of the long aftermath; sidebars, photographs, and illustrations enhance the well-written text. (Rev: LMC 3–4/10; SLJ 2/10)

9491 Burgan, Michael. *Refusing to Crumble: The Danish Resistance in World War II* (5–8). Series: Taking a Stand. 2010, Compass Point LB $31.99 (978-0-7565-4298-6). An introduction to the Danish response to the Nazi invasion in 1940, giving the reasons for surrender and highlighting the actions of the underground resistance, brave Danes who worked to save Jews and sabotage the Germans. Lexile 970L (Rev: LMC 11–12/10; VOYA 8/10)

9492 Byers, Ann. *The Holocaust Camps* (8–12). Series: Holocaust Remembered. 1998, Enslow LB $18.95 (978-0894909955). This work traces the evolution of political prison camps to labor camps and eventually to death camps during the Nazi regime. (Rev: SLJ 12/98; VOYA 8/98) [940.54]

9493 Clive, A. Lawton. *Hiroshima* (6–12). 2004, Candlewick $18.99 (978-0-7636-2271-8). This powerful photoessay presents the history of the development and dropping of the first atom bomb, documenting with many quotations the misgivings of some of the key figures. (Rev: BL 7/04; SLJ 11/04) [940.54]

9494 Cox, Jeromy. *Holocaust: The Events and Their Impact on Real People* (6–12). 2007, DK $29.99 (978-0-7566-2535-1). Using DK's usual layout and accompanying DVD with narratives by Holocaust survivors and eyewitnesses, this volume provides a well-rounded overview of anti-Semitism in world history and of the events of the Holocaust itself. (Rev: BL 9/1/07; SLJ 8/07) [940.53]

9495 Cretzmeyer, Stacy. *Your Name Is Renée: Ruth Kapp Hartz's Story as a Hidden Child in Nazi-Occupied France* (5–8). 2003, Bt. Bound $22.20 (978-0-613-56879-1). The story of a German Jewish family living in France during the Holocaust, how they survived, and how young Ruth hid in an orphanage run by Catholic nuns. (Rev: BCCB 7–8/99; SLJ 8/99) [940.54]

9496 Deem, James M. *Kristallnacht: The Nazi Terror That Began the Holocaust* (8–12). Illus. Series: The Holocaust Through Primary Sources. 2011, Enslow LB $31.93 (978-076603324-5). Eyewitness accounts from Jews, Nazis, and others — old and young — tell the story of the atrocity that took place in 1938. (Rev: BL 10/1/11) [940.53]

9497 DeSaix, Deborah Durland, and Karen Gray Ruelle. *Hidden on the Mountain: Stories of Children Sheltered from the Nazis in Le Chambon* (6–9). 2007, Holiday $24.95 (978-0-8234-1928-9). First-person accounts by the former children and profiles of their rescuers give a compelling portrait of the courage of the residents of this small French town and the resilience of the children. (Rev: BCCB 9/07; BL 3/15/07; SLJ 5/07) [940.53]

9498 Devaney, John. *America Fights the Tide: 1942* (6–10). 1991, Walker $17.95 (978-0-8027-6997-8). Using a diary format and anecdotal accounts, this volume focuses on the United States' entry into World War II in both the European and the Pacific theaters. (Rev: BL 10/15/91; SLJ 10/91) [940.54]

9499 Devaney, John. *America Goes to War: 1941* (5–8). 1991, Walker LB $17.85 (978-0-8027-6980-0). An illustrated, datelined, day-by-day account that covers personal and public events of America's first year of World War II. (Rev: BL 10/1/91; SLJ 8/91) [940.53]

9500 Devaney, John. *America on the Attack: 1943* (6–10). Series: Walker's World War II. 1992, Walker LB $18.85 (978-0-8027-8195-6). This well-illustrated account describes America's active participation in World War II once the war effort got under way. (Rev: BL 12/1/92) [940.53]

9501 Downing, David. *The Origins of the Holocaust* (7–10). Series: World Almanac Library of the Holocaust. 2005, World Almanac LB $31.00 (978-0-8368-5943-0). Downing looks at the roots of anti-Semitism and the continuing persecution of the Jews over the centuries, connecting this history with the rise of the Nazi Party. (Rev: BL 10/15/05; SLJ 3/06) [940.53]

9502 Drez, Ronald J. *Remember D-Day: The Plan, the Invasion, Survivor Stories* (4–8). 2004, National Geographic $17.95 (978-0-7922-6666-2). Filled with period photographs and personal stories, this large-format survey of the Allied invasion of Normandy focuses on the military operation and on the strategic planning that preceded it. (Rev: BL 7/04; SLJ 7/04) [940.54]

9503 Drucker, Olga L. *Kindertransport* (5–8). 1995, Henry Holt paper $8.95 (978-0-8050-4251-1). A true account of a Jewish girl sent from Germany to live in England until she could join her parents in New York City in 1945. (Rev: BCCB 1/93; SLJ 11/92) [940.54]

9504 Dvorson, Alexa. *The Hitler Youth: Marching Toward Madness* (5–9). Series: Teen Witnesses to the Holocaust. 1999, Rosen LB $27.95 (978-0-8239-2783-8). This volume describes how thousands of German boys and girls joined the Hitler Youth, why they were seduced into obeying the Nazis, and how their dreams were eventually shattered. (Rev: BL 4/15/99) [943.086]

9505 Fisch, Robert O. *Light from the Yellow Star: A Lesson of Love from the Holocaust* (7–12). 1996, Univ. of Minnesota $14.95 (978-1-885116-00-0); paper $9.95 (978-0-9644896-0-8). A biographical account that uses the author's abstract paintings to tell about his childhood in Budapest and his death camp experiences. (Rev: BL 4/15/96) [940.53]

9506 Fox, Anne L., and Eva Abraham- Podietz. *Ten Thousand Children: True Stories Told by Children Who Escaped the Holocaust on the Kindertransport* (5–8). 1998, Behrman paper $12.95 (978-0-87441-648-0). The moving stories of 21 survivors who were part of the rescue operation known as the Kindertransport that took 10,000 Jewish children from Nazi-occupied Europe to freedom during late 1938 and 1939. (Rev: BL 1/1–15/99) [940.53]

9507 Friedman, Ina R. *The Other Victims: First-Person Stories of Non-Jews Persecuted by the Nazis* (7–12). 1995, Houghton Mifflin paper $7.99 (978-0-395-74515-1). This account deals with the other victims of the Holocaust — including Gypsies, homosexuals, dissenters, and some religious minorities. (Rev: BL 6/15/90; SLJ 4/90; VOYA 6/90) [940.53]

9508 Fuller, William, and Jack James. *Reckless Courage: The True Story of a Norwegian Boy Under Nazi Rule* (8–11). 2005, Taber Hall paper $13.95 (978-0-9769252-0-0). The true story of a Norwegian boy's participation in the resistance against his country's Nazi occupiers. (Rev: BL 9/15/05) [940.53]

9509 Galloway, Priscilla, ed. *Too Young to Fight: Memories from Our Youth During World War II* (6–12). 2000, Stoddart $22.95 (978-0-7737-3190-5). Eleven Canadian authors of books for young people describe what it was like growing up on the home front during World War II. (Rev: BL 5/1/00; SLJ 7/00) [940.53]

9510 Gies, Miep, and Alison L. Gold. *Anne Frank Remembered: The Story of Miep Gies, Who Helped to Hide the Frank Family* (8–12). 1987, Simon & Schuster paper $14.00 (978-0-671-66234-9). The story of the woman who helped the Frank family during World War II and of the Resistance movement in the Netherlands. (Rev: BL 4/1/87; SLJ 11/87; VOYA 12/87) [940.53]

9511 Gonzales, Doreen. *The Secret of the Manhattan Project* (5–8). Illus. Series: Stories in American History. 2012, Enslow LB $31.93 (978-076603954-4). Placing events in clear historical context, this is a compelling account of the development and deployment of the atomic bomb. (Rev: BL 4/1/12*; SLJ 4/12) [355.8]

9512 Gottfried, Ted. *Displaced Persons: The Liberation and Abuse of Holocaust Survivors* (6–12). 2001, Twenty-First Century LB $29.90 (978-0-7613-1924-5). Survivors of the Holocaust went on to suffer many indignities and rejections, as Gottfried shows in this account of continued racism, displaced persons camps, and denial of shelter by countries including the United States. (Rev: BL 9/1/01; HBG 3/02) [940]

9513 Graham, Ian. *You Wouldn't Want to Be a World War II Pilot! Air Battles You Might Not Survive* (4–8). Illus. by David Antram. Series: You Wouldn't Want to Be. 2009, Franklin Watts LB $29 (978-0-531-21326-1). This appealing volume provides facts and examples of the dangers of flying in World War II. Lexile IG910L (Rev: LMC 1–2/10)

9514 Hama, Larry, and Anthony Williams. *The Battle of Iwo Jima: Guerrilla Warfare in the Pacific* (5–8). Illus. Series: Graphic Battles of World War II. 2007, Rosen LB $29.25 (978-1-4042-0781-3). After background text to provide context, this graphic novel account of the battle of Iwo Jima takes readers behind the lines on both sides of the bloody conflict. (Rev: BL 4/1/07; SLJ 7/07) [940.54]

9515 Heyes, Eileen. *Children of the Swastika: The Hitler Youth* (7–12). 1993, Millbrook LB $22.40 (978-1-56294-237-3). A study of the Hitler Youth's structure, purpose, impact on the war effort, and effects on the youth. (Rev: BL 2/15/93) [324.243]

9516 Hill, Jeff, ed. *The Holocaust* (7–12). 2006, Omnigraphics LB $65 (978-0-7808-0935-2). Provides primary sources that will help students researching the various stages of the Holocaust from its roots through the camps for displaced persons and the aftermath of the war. (Rev: SLJ 1/07)

9517 Hillman, Laura. *I Will Plant You a Lilac Tree: A Memoir of a Schindler's List Survivor* (8–11). 2005, Simon & Schuster $16.95 (978-0-689-86980-8). In this inspiring true story of Holocaust survival, Hannelore escapes the Nazi gas chambers when her name is added to Schindler's list. (Rev: BCCB 7–8/05; BL 5/1/05*; HB 7–8/05; SLJ 9/05; VOYA 8/05) [940.5]

9518 Hipperson, Carol Edgemon. *The Belly Gunner* (6–9). 2001, Twenty-First Century LB $27.90 (978-0-7613-1873-6). This is the absorbing story, told in the first person and enhanced by informative side notes, of one man's experiences in World War II as a B-17 gunner and in a German prison camp. (Rev: HBG 3/02; SLJ 8/01) [940.54]

9519 Hodge, Deborah. *Rescuing the Children: The Story of the Kindertransport* (5–12). Illus. 2012, Tundra $17.95 (978-1-77049-256-1). Using first-person accounts, accessible text, and effective illustrations, this book tells the story of the 10,000 Jewish children rescued from the Nazis in 1939. (Rev: BL 12/1/12*; SLJ 11/12) [940.53]

9520 Jones, Steven L. *The Red Tails: World War II's Tuskegee Airmen* (4–8). Series: Cover-to-Cover. 2002, Perfection Learning $17.95 (978-0-7569-0251-3); paper $8.95 (978-0-7891-5487-3). The story of the heroic African American squadron of World War II fighter pilots, their successful missions, and the prejudices they faced. (Rev: BL 5/1/02) [940.5404]

9521 Kacer, Kathy. *Hiding Edith: A Holocaust Remembrance Book for Young Readers* (4–7). Illus. 2006, Second Story $10.95 (978-1-897187-06-7). Focusing on a young Jewish girl named Edith Schwalb, this is the story of a French couple who hid 100 Jewish refugee children during World War II with the help of their town. (Rev: BL 12/1/06; SLJ 12/06)

9522 Kacer, Kathy. *The Underground Reporters: A True Story* (5–8). 2005, Second Story $11.95 (978-1-896764-85-6). Based on real events, this inspiring story tells how a newspaper, published by a group of Jewish teenagers in Budejovice, Czechoslovakia, helped to lift the spirits of the Jewish community during the years of Nazi occupation. (Rev: BL 2/15/05; SLJ 8/05) [940.53]

9523 Kodama, Tatsuharu. *Shin's Tricycle* (5–8). Trans. by Kazuko Hokumen Jones. Illus. by Noriyuki Ando. 1995, Walker LB $16.85 (978-0-8027-8376-9). A father recalls the life of his young son, who was killed in the bombing of Hiroshima. (Rev: BCCB 12/95; BL 9/1/95*; SLJ 12/95) [940.54]

9524 Kramer, Ann. *Women and War* (5–8). Illus. Series: World War II. 2009, Sea-to-Sea LB $18.95 (978-1-59771-142-5). Double-page spreads look at the situa-

tion of women during World War II, whether volunteering, serving in the military, working in factories or on farms, or coping with shortages. (Rev: BL 4/1/09; LMC 10/09) [940.53]

9525 Krinitz, Esther Nisenthal, and Bernice Steinhardt. *Memories of Survival* (6–9). 2005, Hyperion $15.99 (978-0-7868-5126-3). Steinhardt adds commentary to her mother's affecting hand-embroidered panels depicting her experiences during the Holocaust. Sidney Taylor Book Honor 2006. (Rev: BL 10/15/05*; SLJ 11/05*) [910]

9526 Kuhn, Betsy. *Angels of Mercy* (5–8). 1999, Simon & Schuster $18.00 (978-0-689-82044-1). A series of narratives on courage and bravery gives us a fascinating look at the contributions of nurses in World War II. (Rev: BCCB 12/99; BL 10/15/99; HBG 3/00; SLJ 11/99; VOYA 4/00) [940.54]

9527 Levine, Karen. *Hana's Suitcase* (5–8). 2002, Albert Whitman $15.95 (978-0-8075-3148-8). A Japanese curator of a Holocaust exhibit traces the owner of a suitcase and learns the story of young Hana, who died in Auschwitz. Sidney Taylor Book Award 2002. (Rev: BL 3/15/03; HB 5–6/03; HBG 10/03) [940.53]

9528 McGowen, Tom. *Germany's Lightning War: Panzer Divisions of World War II* (5–8). Series: Military Might. 1999, Twenty-First Century LB $26.90 (978-0-7613-1511-7). After a general history of tank warfare, this account focuses on the Germans' Panzer tank divisions and the part they played in World War II. (Rev: HBG 3/00; SLJ 9/99) [940.54]

9529 McGowen, Tom. *Sink the Bismarck: Germany's Super-Battleship of World War II* (5–8). Series: Military Might. 1999, Twenty-First Century LB $26.90 (978-0-7613-1510-0). A history of German sea power during World War II and the many (eventually successful) British efforts to sink the *Bismarck*. (Rev: HBG 3/00; SLJ 9/99) [940.54]

9530 McKissack, Patricia C., and Fredrick McKissack. *Red-Tail Angels: The Story of the Tuskegee Airmen of World War II* (6–8). 1995, Walker LB $20.85 (978-0-8027-8293-9). A carefully researched account of the formation and training of the 332nd Fighter Group of African American aviators and their exploits during World War II in the North African and European theaters of war. (Rev: BL 2/15/96*; SLJ 2/96; VOYA 4/96) [940.54]

9531 Madison, James H. *World War II: A History in Documents* (7–12). Illus. Series: Pages from History. 2010, Oxford LB $39.95 (978-019516176-2). This volume provides a generous mix of primary sources from many countries — letters, speeches, posters, maps, songs, and so forth. (Rev: BL 9/15/10; SLJ 6/10) [940.5373]

9532 Mara, Wil. *Kristallnacht: Nazi Persecution of the Jews in Europe* (8–12). Series: Perspectives On. 2010, Marshall Cavendish LB $39.93 (978-0-7614-4026-0).

Mara provides a concise account of the developments that led up to Kristallnacht and the long and terrible events that ensued; sidebars, photographs, and illustrations enhance the well-written text. (Rev: LMC 3–4/10; SLJ 2/10) [940.531]

9533 Maruki, Toshi. *Hiroshima No Pika* (7–10). 1982, Lothrop $17.99 (978-0-688-01297-7). One family's experiences during the day the bomb dropped on Hiroshima, told in text and moving illustrations by the author. (Rev: BL 3/87) [940.54]

9534 Marx, Trish. *Echoes of World War II* (5–8). 1994, Lerner LB $14.95 (978-0-8225-4898-0). The true stories of six children around the world whose lives were changed dramatically by World War II. (Rev: BCCB 5/94; BL 9/15/94; SLJ 5/94) [940.53]

9535 Meltzer, Milton. *Rescue: The Story of How Gentiles Saved Jews in the Holocaust* (6–9). 1988, HarperCollins paper $9.99 (978-0-06-446117-7). The uplifting story of those courageous few who helped save Jews from Nazi death camps. (Rev: BL 10/1/88; SLJ 8/88; VOYA 8/88) [940.53]

9536 Meserole, Mike. *The Great Escape: Tunnel to Freedom* (6–8). Illus. 2008, Sterling paper $6.95 (978-1-4027-5705-1). In World War II a group of British and American POWs worked together to dig a 30-foot-deep tunnel out of their camp; Meserole tells the story in a suspenseful narrative enhanced by photographs and blueprints. (Rev: SLJ 3/1/09) [940.54]

9537 Miller, Donald L. *D-Days in the Pacific* (8–12). 2005, Simon & Schuster paper $16.00 (978-0-7432-6929-2). The Allied military offensives that finally brought an end to World War II in the Pacific are described in readable text with excellent illustrations. (Rev: BL 3/15/05) [940.54]

9538 Milman, Barbara. *Light in the Shadows* (5–9). 1997, Jonathan David paper $14.95 (978-0-8246-0401-1). Illustrated with powerful woodcut prints, this book tells the story of five Holocaust survivors. (Rev: BL 11/15/97) [940.53]

9539 Nathan, Amy. *Yankee Doodle Gals: Women Pilots of World War II* (6–9). 2001, National Geographic $21.00 (978-0-7922-8216-7). The fascinating story of the Women's Airforce Service Pilots (WASPs) of World War II, with photographs and biographical information on individuals. (Rev: BL 12/15/01; VOYA 8/02) [940.54]

9540 Nicholson, Dorinda Makanaonalani. *Remember World War II: Kids Who Survived Tell Their Stories* (5–8). Series: Remember. 2005, National Geographic LB $27.90 (978-0-7922-7191-8). First-person accounts of World War II are given historical context plus illustrations, maps, and so forth; Madeleine Albright contributes an effective introduction. (Rev: BL 7/05; SLJ 8/05) [940.53]

9541 Nobleman, Marc Tyler. *The Sinking of the USS Indianapolis* (4–7). Series: We the People. 2006, Compass Point LB $26.60 (978-0-7565-2031-1). The story of the sinking of the USS Indianapolis, two weeks before the end of World War II, is told in straightforward text, with photographs and useful "Did You Know?" features. (Rev: SLJ 1/07)

9542 Panchyk, Richard. *World War II for Kids: A History with 21 Activities* (5–7). 2002, Chicago Review paper $14.95 (978-1-55652-455-4). Features on such topics as living on rations for a day, growing a victory garden, and tracking a ship's movements depict conditions in America and Europe during the war. (Rev: SLJ 12/02) [940.53]

9543 Perl, Lila, and Marion B. Lazan. *Four Perfect Pebbles: A Holocaust Story* (5–9). 1996, Greenwillow $16.99 (978-0-688-14294-0). A memoir of the horror and incredible tribulations suffered by the author's family in the detention camps and later death camps during the Holocaust. (Rev: BL 4/1/96; SLJ 5/96) [940.53]

9544 Rappaport, Doreen. *Beyond Courage: The Untold Story of Jewish Resistance During the Holocaust* (7–12). Illus. 2012, Candlewick $22.99 (978-076362976-2). Tells moving and unsettling stories of the ways in which Jews saved themselves and others, fighting back in Nazi-occupied Europe. Sidney Taylor Book Honor 2013. ⌒ Lexile 1030L (Rev: BL 7/12*; HB 11–12/12; LMC 1–2/13; SLJ 8/1/12*; VOYA 8/12) [940.53]

9545 Rice, Earle, Jr. *Blitzkrieg! Hitler's Lightning War* (5–8). Series: Monumental Milestones: Great Events of Modern Times. 2008, Mitchell Lane LB $20.95 (978-1-58415-542-3). The joint air-and-ground attacks that brought Hitler great success at the outset of World War II are the focus of this book that will interest reluctant readers. (Rev: BL 2/15/08) [940.54]

9546 Rogow, Sally M. *Faces of Courage: Young Heroes of World War II* (5–9). 2003, Granville Island $12.95 (978-1-894694-20-9). Based on true stories, this volume presents 12 fictionalized accounts of heroic actions by teenagers under Nazi rule in Europe. (Rev: BL 10/15/03) [940.53]

9547 Rubin, Susan Goldman. *Fireflies in the Dark: The Story of Friedl Dicker-Brandeis and the Children of Terezin* (5–10). 2000, Holiday $18.95 (978-0-8234-1461-1). A heartbreaking picture book that reproduces some of the artwork and writings of the children imprisoned at the Terezin concentration camp, where only 100 of 15,000 children survived. Sidney Taylor Book Honor 2000. (Rev: BCCB 11/00; BL 7/00*; HB 9–10/00; HBG 10/00; SLJ 8/00) [940.53]

9548 Rubin, Susan Goldman. *Searching for Anne Frank: Letters from Amsterdam to Iowa* (5–12). 2003, Abrams $19.95 (978-0-8109-4514-2). A brief penpal exchange between two sisters in Iowa and Anne Frank and her sister serves as the basis for a comparison between life in America and life for Jews in Europe. (Rev: BL

11/1/03; HB 11–12/03; HBG 4/04; SLJ 11/03; VOYA 10/03) [940.5]

9549 Samuels, Charlie. *Propaganda* (7–9). Illus. Series: World War II Sourcebook. 2012, Black Rabbit LB $34.25 (978-193633323-3). A large-format review of the propaganda issued by all sides in World War II, with relevant background information. (Rev: BLO 3/1/12; LMC 10/12) [940.54]

9550 Seiple, Samantha. *Ghosts in the Fog: The Untold Story of Alaska's WWII Invasion* (5–8). Illus. 2011, Scholastic $16.99 (978-0-545-29654-0). Seiple gives us a fascinating and well-researched account of the Japanese invasion and occupation of Alaska in June 1942, including information about the detention of Native Americans. (Rev: BL 12/1/11; LMC 1–2/12; SLJ 11/1/11; VOYA 10/11) [940.54]

9551 Shapiro, Stephen, and Tina Forrester. *Hoodwinked: Deception and Resistance* (7–10). Illus. by David Craig. Series: Outwitting the Enemy: Stories from World War II. 2004, Annick paper $14.95 (978-1-55037-832-0). This compelling title explores some of the inventive deceptive strategies that Allied forces employed against the Axis powers. (Rev: BL 1/1–15/05; SLJ 1/05) [940.54]

9552 Shapiro, Stephen, and Tina Forrester. *Ultra Hush-Hush: Espionage and Special Missions* (5–8). Illus. by David Craig. Series: Outwitting the Enemy. 2003, Annick LB $29.95 (978-1-55037-779-8); paper $14.95 (978-1-55037-778-1). Undercover activities during World War II are the focus of this volume that covers such groups and missions as the Navajo Code Talkers and Britain's double agents. (Rev: BL 8/03; SLJ 5/04) [940.54]

9553 Soumerai, Eve Nussbaum, and Carol D. Schulz. *A Voice from the Holocaust* (6–9). Series: Voices of Twentieth-Century Conflict. 2003, Greenwood $41.95 (978-0-313-32358-4). Photographs and diary entries help to tell the story of Soumerai's childhood as a privileged Jewish girl in Nazi Berlin, her years as a refugee, and her later experiences, all introduced with background information and a timeline of Nazi history. (Rev: SLJ 4/04) [940.53]

9554 Stalcup, Ann. *On the Home Front: Growing up in Wartime England* (6–10). 1998, Shoe String LB $19.50 (978-0-208-02482-4). A vivid first-person account about growing up in a small town in Shropshire during World War II. (Rev: BCCB 9/98; BL 10/15/98; HBG 9/98; SLJ 7/98) [940.54]

9555 Taylor, Theodore. *Air Raid — Pearl Harbor: The Story of December 7, 1941* (5–8). 1991, Harcourt paper $6.00 (978-0-15-201655-5). A fine account of why the attack occurred and the effects that were felt around the world. A revised edition. (Rev: SLJ 12/91) [940.54]

9556 Torres, John A. *The Battle of Midway* (6–9). Illus. Series: Technologies and Strategies in Battle. 2011,

Mitchell Lane LB $29.95 (978-161228078-3). A detailed look at the 1942 battle, focusing on the weapon technologies and strategies used and how they fared in combat. (Rev: BL 10/1/11) [940.54]

9557 Tregaskis, Richard. *Guadalcanal Diary* (6–9). 1993, Buccaneer LB $25.95 (978-1-56849-231-5). This is a simplified version of the adult book that tells of the Marine landing at Guadalcanal in 1942. [940.54]

9558 van Maarsen, Jacqueline, and Carol Ann Lee. *A Friend Called Anne: One Girl's Story of War, Peace, and a Unique Friendship with Anne Frank* (5–8). 2005, Viking $15.99 (978-0-670-05958-4). Anne Frank's ordinary life before the war, and how things changed once the Nazis arrived, told by Anne's childhood friend. (Rev: BL 4/1/05; SLJ 4/05) [940.53]

9559 White, Steve. *The Battle of Midway: The Destruction of the Japanese Fleet* (5–9). Illus. by Richard Elson. Series: Graphic Battles of World War II. 2007, Rosen LB $29.25 (978-1-4042-0783-7). Historically accurate and detailed, this graphic account will engage readers in the story of an important World War II battle. (Rev: SLJ 7/07) [940.54265933]

9560 Whiteman, Dorit Bader. *Lonek's Journey: The True Story of a Boy's Escape to Freedom* (5–8). 2005, Star Bright $15.95 (978-1-59572-021-4). In this gripping true story that starts in 1939, a young Jew named Lonek survives the Nazis' arrival in Poland, a slave labor camp in Siberia, and the long, perilous journey to Palestine. (Rev: BL 11/15/05*; HBG 4/06; LMC 4–5/06; SLJ 1/06) [940.53]

9561 Whiting, Jim. *The Story of the Holocaust* (5–7). Series: Monumental Milestones: Great Events of Modern Times. 2006, Mitchell Lane LB $29.95 (978-1-58415-400-6). Although slim, this volume conveys a lot of information about the roots and atrocities of the Holocaust. (Rev: SLJ 5/06) [940.53]

9562 Whitman, Sylvia. *Uncle Sam Wants You!* (5–7). 1993, Lerner LB $30.35 (978-0-8225-1728-3). This work describes the experiences of the many men and women who served in the various armed forces during World War II. (Rev: BL 5/1/93) [940.54]

9563 Wood, Douglas. *Franklin and Winston: A Christmas That Changed the World* (5–8). Illus. by Barry Moser. 2011, Candlewick $16.99 (978-076363383-7). In December 1941, Churchill and FDR met and became friends during a tense time, discussing strategies that would have lasting consequences. (Rev: BL 9/15/11*; SLJ 10/1/11) [940.53]

Modern World History (1945–)

9564 Benson, Sonia G. *Korean War: Almanac and Primary Sources* (6–10). 2001, Gale LB $70.00 (978-0-7876-5691-1). After an almanac section that traces the progress of the war, a selection of primary materials — speeches, memoirs, government documents, and so forth — are presented with introductions that place them in historical context. (Rev: SLJ 5/02) [951.904]

9565 Burgan, Michael. *The Berlin Airlift* (4–7). Series: We the People. 2006, Compass Point LB $26.60 (978-0-7565-2024-3). The story of the Berlin Airlift is told in straightforward text, with photographs and useful "Did You Know?" features. (Rev: SLJ 1/07) [943]

9566 Burgan, Michael. *The My Lai Massacre* (5–8). Series: We the People. 2008, Compass Point LB $26.60 (978-0-7565-3849-1). A simple account of the massacre with large photographs, useful for young researchers and reluctant readers. (Rev: SLJ 12/08) [959.704]

9567 Carlisle, Rodney P. *Iraq War* (6–12). Series: America at War. 2007, Facts on File LB $35.00 (978-0-8160-7129-6). An update of a 2004 title, this straightforward volume covers developments in the war from 2003 to 2006. (Rev: BL 11/1/07) [946.002]

9568 Englar, Mary. *The Tet Offensive* (5–8). Series: We the People. 2008, Compass Point LB $26.60 (978-0-7565-3844-6). A simple account of the offensive with discussion of its importance and large photographs, useful for young researchers and reluctant readers. (Rev: SLJ 12/08) [959.704]

9569 Gallagher, Jim. *Causes of the Iraq War* (5–8). Series: Road to War. 2005, OTTN LB $22.95 (978-1-59556-009-4). Explores the case put forward for the recent Iraq War, along with the views of those who oppose the conflict with good illustrations and appended material. (Rev: BL 10/15/05) [956.7044]

9570 Gay, Kathlyn, and Martin Gay. *Korean War* (6–8). Series: Voices from the Past. 1996, Twenty-First Century LB $25.90 (978-0-8050-4100-2). A discussion of the often forgotten Korean War — its causes, its battles, and the people involved. (Rev: BL 11/15/96; SLJ 12/96; VOYA 4/97) [951.904]

9571 Gay, Kathlyn, and Martin Gay. *Vietnam War* (6–8). Series: Voices from the Past. 1996, Twenty-First Century LB $25.90 (978-0-8050-4101-9). An objective overview of the Vietnam War, illustrated with black-and-white photographs. (Rev: BL 11/15/96; SLJ 12/96; VOYA 2/97) [959.704]

9572 Gerdes, Louise I., ed. *The Cold War* (6–12). Series: Great Speeches in History. 2003, Gale LB $36.20 (978-0-7377-0869-1); paper $24.95 (978-0-7377-0868-4). Winston Churchill and Che Guevara are among the world leaders whose words are given in this collection that examines the confrontation between East and West. (Rev: BL 5/1/03; SLJ 9/03) [909.82]

9573 Gunderson, Cory. *The Need for Oil* (5–8). Series: World in Conflict. 2004, ABDO LB $25.65 (978-1-59197-417-8). This history of conflicts over oil includes useful statistics and will be helpful to students seeking

information for reports or background context before the recent Iraq war. (Rev: BL 4/1/04; SLJ 3/04) [338.2]

9574 Hillstrom, Kevin, and Laurie Collier Hillstrom. *Vietnam War: Almanac* (7–12). Series: UXL Vietnam War Reference Library. 2000, Gale LB $70.00 (978-0-7876-4883-1). An absorbing and comprehensive overview of the causes, conduct, and aftermath of the war that includes interesting sidebars and black-and-white photographs. Also use *Vietnam War: Biographies* and *Vietnam War: Primary Sources* (both 2000). (Rev: BL 3/15/01; SLJ 5/01) [959.704]

9575 Langley, Andrew. *The Collapse of the Soviet Union: The End of an Empire* (7–12). Series: Snapshots in History. 2006, Compass Point LB $31.93 (978-0-7565-2009-0). This is an informative survey of the events that led to the disintegration of the Soviet empire. (Rev: SLJ 2/07)

9576 Levy, Pat, and Sean Sheehan. *From Punk Rock to Perestroika: The Mid 1970s to the Mid 1980s* (6–9). Series: Modern Eras Uncovered. 2005, Raintree LB $32.86 (978-1-4109-1789-8). Focuses on the mid-1970s through mid-1980s, presenting the major social, political, economic, and technological changes as well as fashion and pop culture. Also use *From Compact Discs to the Gulf War: The Mid 1980s to the Early 1990s* and *From the World Wide Web to September 11: The Early 1990s to 2001* (2005). (Rev: SLJ 5/06)

9577 Murdico, Suzanne J. *The Gulf War* (5–9). Series: War and Conflict in the Middle East. 2004, Rosen LB $27.95 (978-0-8239-4551-1). Examines the 1991 war between Iraq and a coalition of nations. (Rev: BL 11/1/04) [956.7]

9578 Nakaya, Andrea C., ed. *Iraq* (8–12). Series: Current Controversies. 2004, Gale LB $36.20 (978-0-7377-2210-9); paper $24.95 (978-0-7377-2211-6). Statements by key U.S. figures including President Bush and Colin Powell are included in this survey of opinions about the Iraq war. (Rev: SLJ 12/04; VOYA 6/05) [956]

9579 Santella, Andrew. *The Korean War* (4–7). Series: We the People. 2006, Compass Point LB $26.60 (978-0-7565-2027-4). A brief overview of the roots and progress of the conflict between the two parts of a divided nation. (Rev: SLJ 1/07) [951.904]

9580 Smith-Llera, Danielle. *Vietnam War POWs* (5–8). Series: We the People. 2008, Compass Point LB $26.60 (978-0-7565-3846-0). A simple discussion of the plight of prisoners of war with large photographs, useful for young researchers and reluctant readers. (Rev: SLJ 12/08) [959.704]

9581 Stanley, George E. *America and the Cold War (1949–1969)* (5–8). Series: A Primary Source History of the United States. 2005, World Almanac LB $31.00 (978-0-8368-5830-3). A simple narrative links well-chosen primary sources documenting the key events of the Cold War. Also use *America in Today's World (1969–2004)* (2005). (Rev: BL 4/1/05)

9582 Sutherland, James. *The Ten-Year Century: Explaining the First Decade of the New Millennium* (7–10). 2010, Viking $18.99 (978-0-670-01223-7). An engaging overview of key events of the first decade of the 21st century, a time of great innovation and political change. ℮ (Rev: BL 11/15/10; HB 11–12/10; LMC 11–12/10; SLJ 5/11; VOYA 10/10) [973.93]

9583 Young, Marilyn B., and John J. Fitzgerald. *The Vietnam War: A History in Documents* (6–12). Series: Pages from History. 2002, Oxford $39.95 (978-0-19-512278-7). Primary sources cover the conflict in Vietnam from French involvement through the U.S. withdrawal and include everything from official documents, speeches, and transcripts of White House tapes to North Vietnamese political cartoons and U.S. anti-war posters. (Rev: BCCB 9/02; BL 6/1–15/02; HBG 10/02; SLJ 9/02) [959.704]

Geographical Regions

Africa

General and Miscellaneous

9584 Baroin, Catherine. *Tubu: The Teda and the Daza* (7–12). Series: Heritage Library of African Peoples. 1997, Rosen LB $29.25 (978-0-8239-2000-6). The history and contemporary life of these peoples of Chad, Libya, Niger, and the Sudan are presented in easy-reading text. (Rev: BL 4/15/97) [967.43]

9585 Beckwith, Carol, and Angela Fisher. *Faces of Africa: Thirty Years of Photography* (8–12). 2004, National Geographic $35.00 (978-0-7922-6830-7). Eye-catching photographs document the traditional life of diverse African peoples. (Rev: BL 9/1/04) [305.896]

9586 Bowden, Rob. *Africa* (5–8). Series: Continents of the World. 2006, World Almanac LB $34.00 (978-0-8368-5910-2). Factboxes and "In Focus" articles add to this overview of the history, geography, people, culture, and so forth of the continent of Africa. (Rev: SLJ 2/06)

9587 Croze, Harvey. *Africa for Kids: Exploring a Vibrant Continent* (4–7). Illus. 2006, Chicago Review paper $17.95 (978-1-55652-598-8). Africa's diversity is highlighted in this accessible volume that covers history, nature, key individuals, and contemporary problems such as poverty, war, AIDS, and the environment; there are 19 activities. (Rev: BL 8/06) [916.22]

9588 Habeeb, Mark W. *Africa: Facts and Figures* (7–10). Series: Continent in the Balance: Africa. 2005, Mason Crest LB $21.95 (978-1-59084-817-3). An excellent overview of the continent, including its natural features, climate, cultural diversity, history, and economy. (Rev: BL 4/1/05*) [960]

9589 Hall, Linley Erin. *Starvation in Africa* (6–9). Series: In the News. 2007, Rosen LB $27.95 (978-1-4042-0976-3). For reluctant readers, this is a good introduc-tion to the continent of Africa and the reasons why starvation is so prevalent there; wars and internal unrest are underlined as aggravating factors. (Rev: SLJ 8/07) [363.8096]

9590 Nardo, Don. *The European Colonization of Africa* (7–12). Illus. Series: World History. 2010, Morgan Reynolds LB $28.95 (978-159935142-1). This detailed history of imperialism in Africa covers successive European arrivals and their impact on the continent, the slave trade, missionaries, and independence. (Rev: BL 10/1/10)

9591 Reader, John. *Africa* (8–12). Illus. by Michael Lewis. 2001, National Geographic $50.00 (978-0-7922-7681-4). A lavishly illustrated overview of Africa with sections on each of the many ecological divisions, such as savanna, desert, mountains, and coast. (Rev: BL 8/01) [960]

9592 Woods, Michael, and Mary B. Woods. *Seven Natural Wonders of Africa* (5–8). Series: Seven Natural Wonders. 2009, Twenty-First Century LB $33.26 (978-0-8225-9071-2). The Nile, Victoria Falls, Sahara Desert, Mount Kilimanjaro, Seychelles Islands, Serengeti Plain, and mountain gorillas are the seven wonders featured in this attractive volume. (Rev: BL 4/1/09; LMC 10/09*; SLJ 5/09) [508.6]

Central and Eastern Africa

9593 Ayodo, Awuor. *Luo* (4–7). Series: Heritage Library of African Peoples. 1995, Rosen LB $29.25 (978-0-8239-1758-7). A portrait of the culture, history, and society of the Luo people, who lived on the shores of Lake Victoria in Kenya. (Rev: BL 3/1/96) [967.8]

9594 Bangura, Abdul Karim. *Kipsigis* (5–8). Series: Heritage Library of African Peoples. 1994, Rosen LB $29.25 (978-0-8239-1765-5). An attractive title that deals with the history and present status of the Kipsigis people of Kenya. (Rev: SLJ 5/95) [967.62]

9595 Beard, Peter. *Zara's Tales: Perilous Escapades in Equatorial Africa* (8–12). 2004, Knopf $26.95 (978-0-679-42659-2). In this compelling memoir, Beard talks about his many encounters — some life-threatening — with the animals of East Africa. (Rev: BL 10/15/04) [967.70]

9596 Bessire, Aimee, and Mark Bessire. *Sukuma* (5–8). Series: Heritage Library of African Peoples. 1997, Rosen LB $29.25 (978-0-8239-1992-5). Describes the history, culture, leaders, customs, and present situation of the Sukuma people of Tanzania. (Rev: BL 9/15/97; VOYA 12/97) [967.6]

9597 Bojang, Ali Brownlie. *Sudan in Our World* (5–8). Series: Countries in Our World. 2010, Smart Apple $28.50 (978-1-59920-434-5). Bojang covers Sudan's geography, people, culture, economy, government, and future, with frank discussion of the poverty and fighting that have plagued the country. (Rev: SLJ 12/1/10) [962.4]

9598 Bowden, Rob. *Kenya* (6–10). Series: Countries of the World. 2003, Facts on File $30.00 (978-0-8160-5384-1). This profile of an impoverished nation gives material on physical geography, resources, population, tourism, commerce, and geography. (Rev: BL 2/1/04) [967.62]

9599 Broberg, Catherine. *Kenya in Pictures* (6–10). Series: Visual Geography. 2002, Lerner LB $27.93 (978-0-8225-1957-7). Information on all aspects of life in this African country, including extensive coverage of its history, is accompanied by plenty of photographs and a Web site that offers up-to-date links. (Rev: BL 10/15/02; HBG 3/03; SLJ 12/02) [967]

9600 Burnham, Philip. *Gbaya* (7–12). Series: Heritage Library of African Peoples. 1997, Rosen LB $29.25 (978-0-8239-1995-6). These African people who live in Cameroon, Central African Republic, Congo, and Zaire, are introduced through illustrations and simple text. (Rev: BL 4/15/97) [967]

9601 Corona, Laurel. *Ethiopia* (5–8). Series: Modern Nations of the World. 2000, Lucent LB $29.95 (978-1-56006-823-5). An attractive, well-organized introduction to Ethiopia that gives its history, geography, and culture plus national statistics, a chronology, and bibliographies. (Rev: BL 3/1/01) [963]

9602 DiPiazza, Francesca Davis. *Sudan in Pictures* (5–8). Illus. Series: Visual Geography. 2006, Twenty-First Century LB $27.93 (978-082252678-0). An updated overview of history, culture, geography, economy, education, and health in this African nation. (Rev: BL 2/1/89)

9603 *Ethiopia in Pictures* (5–8). Series: Visual Geography. 1994, Lerner LB $21.27 (978-0-8225-1836-5).

Land, history and government, culture, education, religion, and health are covered. (Rev: BL 2/1/89) [963]

9604 Gaertner, Ursula. *Elmolo* (7–10). Series: Heritage Library of African Peoples. 1995, Rosen LB $29.25 (978-0-8239-1764-8). Looks at the customs, daily life, and values of the Elmolo tribe in Kenya. (Rev: BL 7/95; SLJ 5/95) [967.62]

9605 Hall, Martin, and Rebecca Stefoff. *Great Zimbabwe: Digging for the Past* (7–10). Series: Digging for the Past. 2006, Oxford $21.95 (978-0-19-515773-4). Traces our knowledge of the ancient city-state that lies in present-day Mozambique, with an emphasis on the archaeological discoveries and discussion of racial preconceptions that blurred understanding. (Rev: BL 6/1–15/06; SLJ 11/06) [968.91]

9606 Holtzman, Jon. *Samburu* (7–10). Series: Heritage Library of African Peoples. 1995, Rosen LB $29.25 (978-0-8239-1759-4). Discusses in detailed but simple text the culture and lifestyle of the Samburu people of Kenya. (Rev: BL 7/95; SLJ 5/95) [967]

9607 Hussein, Ikram. *Teenage Refugees from Somalia Speak Out* (7–12). Series: Teenage Refugees Speak Out. 1997, Rosen LB $27.95 (978-0-8239-2444-8). Teenage refugees from Somalia recount the violent anarchy and acute famine in their country and their journey from Africa to the United States. (Rev: BL 12/15/97; SLJ 12/97) [967]

9608 Ifemesia, Chieka. *Turkana* (7–10). Series: Heritage Library of African Peoples. 1996, Rosen LB $29.25 (978-0-8239-1761-7). Using a simple text and color photographs, this account describes the past and present of the Turkana people, who now live in Ethiopia, Kenya, Sudan, and Uganda. (Rev: BL 2/15/95) [960]

9609 Jansen, Hanna. *Over a Thousand Hills I Walk with You* (7–10). Trans. by Elizabeth D. Crawford. 2006, Carolrhoda $16.95 (978-1-57505-927-3). The heartbreaking story of 8-year-old Jeanne, the only member of her family to survive the Rwandan genocide of 1994, is told by the girl's adoptive mother. (Rev: BL 4/1/06*; SLJ 6/06*) [833]

9610 Kabira, Wanjiku M. *Agikuyu* (7–10). Series: Heritage Library of African Peoples. 1995, Rosen LB $29.25 (978-0-8239-1762-4). Presents social and cultural aspects of the Agikuyu community of Kenya in ways that make them accessible to Western readers. (Rev: BL 7/95; SLJ 6/95) [967]

9611 Koopmans, Andy. *Rwanda* (7–10). Series: Africa. 2005, Mason Crest LB $21.95 (978-1-59084-812-8). Covers the geography, history, politics, government, economy, people, and culture of Rwanda, providing a map, flag, recipes, glossary, timeline, and colorful photographs. (Rev: SLJ 3/05) [967.571]

9612 MacDonald, Joan Vos. *Tanzania* (7–10). Series: Africa. 2005, Mason Crest LB $21.95 (978-1-59084-813-5). Covers the geography, history, politics, government, economy, people, and culture of Tanzania, providing a map, flag, recipes, glossary, timeline, and colorful photographs. (Rev: SLJ 3/05; VOYA 8/04) [967.8]

9613 *Malawi in Pictures* (5–8). Series: Visual Geography. 1989, Lerner LB $25.55 (978-0-8225-1842-6). An overview of climate, history, geography, culture, education, and other aspects of life. (Rev: BL 2/1/89) [968.97]

9614 NgCheong-Lum, Roseline. *Eritrea* (6–9). Illus. Series: Cultures of the World. 2011, Marshall Cavendish LB $29.95 (978-160870454-5). A revised edition of this volume covering Eritrea's geography, history, political system, economy, environment, people, and culture. (Rev: BL 6/1/11) [963.5]

9615 Nwaezeigwe, Nwankwo T. *Ngoni* (7–12). Series: Heritage Library of African Peoples. 1997, Rosen LB $29.25 (978-0-8239-2006-8). The history, traditions, and struggle for freedom of this African group in Malawi are laid out in accessible text. (Rev: BL 4/15/97) [968.97]

9616 Ojo, Onukaba A. *Mbuti* (7–10). Series: Heritage Library of African Peoples. 1996, Rosen LB $29.25 (978-0-8239-1998-7). The Mbuti people of Zaire are introduced with details on their environment, history, customs, and present situation. (Rev: BL 2/15/96; SLJ 7/96) [305.896]

9617 Okeke, Chika. *Kongo* (7–12). Series: Heritage Library of African Peoples. 1997, Rosen LB $29.25 (978-0-8239-2001-3). The Kongo people of Angola, Congo, and Zaire in Central Africa are featured in easy-reading text with material on their land, kingdoms, political life, and culture. (Rev: BL 4/15/97) [967]

9618 Parris, Ronald. *Rendille* (5–8). Series: Heritage Library of African Peoples. 1994, Rosen LB $29.25 (978-0-8239-1763-1). With extensive use of black-and-white and color photographs, introduces the history and customs of the Rendille people of Kenya. (Rev: SLJ 5/95) [967.62]

9619 Pateman, Robert. *Kenya* (4–7). Series: Cultures of the World. 1993, Marshall Cavendish LB $35.64 (978-1-85435-572-0). The background story of Kenya is revealed through color photographs and a text that also covers present concerns. (Rev: BL 8/93) [967.62]

9620 *Peoples of East Africa* (6–12). Series: Peoples of Africa. 1997, Facts on File $28.00 (978-0-8160-3484-0). This book gives a concise overview of 15 ethnic groups of eastern Africa, with details on history, language, way of life, society, religion, and culture. Included are Falasha, Ganda, Hutus and Tutsis, Masai, Nyoro, Somalis, and Swahili. (Rev: SLJ 10/97) [967]

9621 Pritchett, Bev. *Tanzania in Pictures* (5–8). Illus. Series: Visual Geography. 2007, Lerner LB $31.93 (978-0-8225-1838-9). This revised edition contains information on history, geography, economy, religion, and culture. (Rev: BL 2/1/89)

9622 Roberts, Mary N., and Allen F. Roberts. *Luba* (6–10). Series: Heritage Library of African Peoples. 1997, Rosen LB $29.25 (978-0-8239-2002-0). The Luba people of Zaire are introduced with material on their history, present conditions, and cultural resources. (Rev: BL 9/15/97) [967]

9623 Roth, Susan L., and Cindy Trumbore. *The Mangrove Tree: Planting Trees to Feed Families* (3–7). Illus. by author. 2011, Lee & Low $19.95 (978-1-60060-459-1). In simple cumulative verse, this picture book tells the story of Japanese American biologist Gordon Sato's project to plant mangrove trees in Eritrea and help the surrounding community. ALA Notable Books 2012. (Rev: BL 5/1/11; SLJ 5/1/11*) [577.69]

9624 Schnapper, LaDena. *Teenage Refugees from Ethiopia Speak Out* (5–10). Series: Teenage Refugees Speak Out. 1997, Rosen LB $27.95 (978-0-8239-2438-7). Ethiopian teens now living in America tell of the violence, famine, and civil war that drove them from their country and of their reception in America. (Rev: SLJ 2/98) [963]

9625 *Sudan in Pictures* (5–8). Series: Visual Geography. 1990, Lerner LB $25.55 (978-0-8225-1839-6). An overview of history, culture, geography, economy, education, and health. (Rev: BL 2/1/89) [962.4]

9626 Swinimer, Ciarunji C. *Pokot* (5–8). Series: Heritage Library of African Peoples. 1994, Rosen LB $29.25 (978-0-8239-1756-3). Using a good balance of text and visuals, this account describes the history, culture, and present status of the Pokot people of Kenya. (Rev: SLJ 5/95) [967.62]

9627 Tanguay, Bridget. *Kenya* (4–7). Illus. Series: Countries of the World. 2006, National Geographic $19.95 (978-0-7922-7628-9). An overview of Kenya with information on the country's history, land, people, government, economy and present issues; excellent color photographs and maps are included. (Rev: SLJ 3/07)

9628 Twagilimana, Aimable. *Hutu and Tutsi* (5–9). Series: The Heritage Library of African Peoples. 1997, Rosen LB $29.25 (978-0-8239-1999-4). A large section of this book is devoted to the current struggle between the Hutu and Tutsi people of central Africa, along with chapters on art and religion. (Rev: SLJ 3/98) [967]

9629 Twagilimana, Aimable. *Teenage Refugees from Rwanda Speak Out* (5–10). Series: Teenage Refugees Speak Out. 1997, Rosen LB $27.95 (978-0-8239-2443-1). Teenage refugees from Rwanda describe the warfare between Tutsi and Hutu peoples, the terrible living conditions that forced them to leave their country, and the challenges and difficulties they have experienced in the United States. (Rev: SLJ 2/98) [967]

9630 Wangari, Esther. *Ameru* (7–10). Series: Heritage Library of African Peoples. 1995, Rosen LB $29.25 (978-0-8239-1766-2). An introduction to the history, traditions, and culture of the Ameru people of Kenya in easy-reading text. (Rev: BL 9/15/95; SLJ 11/95) [967.6]

9631 Zeleza, Tiyambe. *Akamba* (7–10). Series: Heritage Library of African Peoples. 1995, Rosen LB $29.25 (978-0-8239-1768-6). The history, traditions, and fight for freedom of the Akamba people of Kenya are covered in this book with many color illustrations. (Rev: BL 7/95; SLJ 6/95) [960]

9632 Zeleza, Tiyambe. *Maasai* (5–8). Series: Heritage Library of African Peoples. 1994, Rosen LB $29.25 (978-0-8239-1757-0). An introduction to these people of Kenya and Tanzania, their culture, customs, and history. (Rev: SLJ 5/95) [967.62]

9633 Zeleza, Tiyambe. *Mijikenda* (7–10). Series: Heritage Library of African Peoples. 1995, Rosen LB $29.25 (978-0-8239-1767-9). Combines history and anthropology to provide an easy-to-read portrait of the Mijikenda people. (Rev: BL 9/15/95; SLJ 11/95) [967]

North Africa

9634 Azuonye, Chukwuma. *Dogon* (7–10). Series: Heritage Library of African Peoples. 1995, Rosen LB $29.25 (978-0-8239-1976-5). Provides information on the history, culture, and lifestyles of the Dogon people of Mali. (Rev: BL 2/15/96) [966.23]

9635 Malcolm, Peter. *Libya* (4–7). 1993, Marshall Cavendish LB $35.64 (978-1-85435-573-7). Well-chosen photographs and readable text give good background information as well as material on present problems. (Rev: BL 8/93) [961.2]

Southern Africa

9636 Beecroft, Simon. *The Release of Nelson Mandela* (6–12). Series: Days that Changed the World. 2004, World Almanac LB $31.00 (978-0-8368-5571-5). The significance of Mandela's release after 27 years of imprisonment is made clear through the explanation of the struggle against apartheid, with discussion of the progress South Africa has made since then. (Rev: BL 4/1/04; SLJ 7/04) [618.1]

9637 Blauer, Ettagale, and Jason Lauré. *South Africa.* Rev. ed. (6–9). 2006, Children's Pr. LB $25.20 (978-0-516-24853-0). A clear view of modern South Africa — including geography, history, economy, religion, and current challenges — is presented along with maps, photographs, and a timeline. (Rev: BL 7/06; SLJ 8/06) [968]

9638 Bojang, Ali Brownlie. *South Africa in Our World* (5–8). Series: Countries in Our World. 2010, Smart Apple $28.50 (978-1-59920-444-4). Bojang covers South Africa's geography, people, culture, economy, government, and future, with frank discussion of such topics as apartheid and AIDS. (Rev: SLJ 12/1/10) [968.06]

9639 Bolaane, Maitseo, and Part T. Mgadla. *Batswana* (6–10). Series: Heritage Library of African Peoples. 1997, Rosen LB $29.25 (978-0-8239-2008-2). This work discusses the history, culture, and present status of the Batswana people of southern Africa. (Rev: BL 1/1–15/98) [968]

9640 Green, Rebecca L. *Merina* (7–12). Series: Heritage Library of African Peoples. 1997, Rosen LB $29.25 (978-0-8239-1991-8). The history and culture of the Merina people of Madagascar are covered in simple text and many illustrations. (Rev: BL 4/15/97; VOYA 6/97) [969.1]

9641 Harrison, Peter, ed. *History of Southern Africa* (7–12). Series: History of Africa. 2003, Facts on File $30.00 (978-0-8160-5065-9). From prehistory to today, this volume covers in detail the history of southern Africa, detailing in particular European settlement, independence, and apartheid. (Rev: BL 9/15/03; SLJ 5/04) [968]

9642 Langley, Andrew. *Cape Town* (4–7). Series: Great Cities of the World. 2005, World Almanac LB $31.00 (978-0-8368-5045-1). An informative and appealing overview of this major city, with material on its history, its economy, and what it's like to live there. (Rev: BL 4/15/04)

9643 Mitchell, Peter, ed. *Southern Africa* (8–11). Series: Peoples and Cultures of Africa. 2006, Chelsea House LB $39.00 (978-0-8160-6265-2). A detailed look at the nations of southern Africa (including Madagascar), discussing their culture, history, ethnic groups, religions, languages, and arts and architecture. (Rev: BL 10/15/06) [900]

9644 Njoku, Onwuka N. *Mbundu* (7–12). Series: Heritage Library of African Peoples. 1997, Rosen LB $29.25 (978-0-8239-2004-4). An easy-to-read introduction to the history and contemporary culture of this people of Angola. (Rev: BL 4/15/97) [967.3]

9645 Oluikpe, Benson O. *Swazi* (7–12). Series: Heritage Library of African Peoples. 1997, Rosen LB $29.25 (978-0-8239-2012-9). This accessible book describes the history, traditions, and struggles for freedom of the Swazi people of Swaziland and South Africa. (Rev: BL 4/15/97; SLJ 12/97) [968]

9646 Rosemarin, Ike. *South Africa* (4–7). Series: Cultures of the World. 1993, Marshall Cavendish LB $35.64 (978-1-85435-575-1). Historical and modern concerns are covered in this look at South Africa. (Rev: BL 8/93) [968]

9647 Schneider, Elizabeth Ann. *Ndebele* (7–12). Series: Heritage Library of African Peoples. 1997, Rosen LB $29.25 (978-0-8239-2009-9). Topics covered about the Ndebele people of South Africa include environment, history, religion, social organization, politics, and customs. (Rev: BL 4/15/97) [968]

610

9648 *South Africa in Pictures* (5–8). Series: Visual Geography. 1996, Lerner LB $25.55 (978-0-8225-1835-8). Focusing on climate, geography, wildlife, and the history of this troubled country. (Rev: BL 8/88) [968.06]

9649 Udechukwu, Ada. *Herero* (7–10). Series: Heritage Library of African Peoples. 1996, Rosen LB $29.25 (978-0-8239-2003-7). In simple text, this book introduces the three Herero subgroups that share a similar language and culture in today's Botswana, Angola, and Namibia, with an emphasis on their political history. (Rev: BL 3/15/96; SLJ 6/96) [968]

9650 Van Wyk, Gary N. *Basotho* (5–7). Series: Heritage Library of African Peoples. 1996, Rosen LB $29.25 (978-0-8239-2005-1). Describes the Basotho people, who live in Lesotho and South Africa, with simple text on their history, religion, social organization, and customs. (Rev: BL 11/15/96; SLJ 3/97) [968]

9651 Van Wyk, Gary N., and Robert Johnson. *Shona* (5–7). Series: Heritage Library of African Peoples. 1997, Rosen LB $29.25 (978-0-8239-2011-2). The Shona people of Zimbabwe are presented in outstanding photographs, with a text that covers their past, their culture, and their present living conditions and problems. (Rev: BL 1/1–15/98) [968]

9652 *Zimbabwe in Pictures* (5–8). Series: Visual Geography. 1997, Lerner LB $25.55 (978-0-8225-1825-9). Many photographs highlight this overview of Zimbabwe's history, climate, wildlife, and culture. (Rev: BL 4/15/88) [968]

West Africa

9653 Adeleke, Tunde. *Songhay* (5–7). Series: Heritage Library of African Peoples. 1996, Rosen LB $29.25 (978-0-8239-1986-4). Both historical information and material on contemporary life are given in this account of the African people who live chiefly in Mali, Niger, and Benin. (Rev: BL 11/15/96) [960]

9654 Azuonye, Chukwuma. *Edo: The Bini People of the Benin Kingdom* (7–10). Series: Heritage Library of African Peoples. 1996, Rosen LB $29.25 (978-0-8239-1985-7). A review of the history, culture, society, and the struggle for freedom of the Bini people, whose empire was part of present-day Nigeria. (Rev: BL 3/15/96) [966.9]

9655 Boateng, Faustine Ama. *Asante* (5–7). Series: Heritage Library of African Peoples. 1996, Rosen LB $29.25 (978-0-8239-1975-8). This African people living in present-day Ghana is described, with information on history, traditions, and lifestyle. (Rev: BL 11/15/96; SLJ 3/97) [966.7]

9656 Brook, Larry. *Daily Life in Ancient and Modern Timbuktu* (5–7). 1999, Lerner LB $25.26 (978-0-8225-3215-6). A fascinating look at this ancient West African city that was once a center of commerce and learning. (Rev: BL 9/1/99; HBG 10/99; SLJ 7/99) [966.23]

9657 Harmon, Daniel E. *Nigeria: 1880 to the Present: The Struggle, the Tragedy, the Promise* (6–12). 2000, Chelsea LB $35.00 (978-0-7910-5452-9). This survey of Nigerian history is careful to highlight changes and achievements that did not involve European influence; it includes many Royal Geographic Society black-and-white photographs. (Rev: HBG 3/01; SLJ 2/01) [966.9]

9658 *Liberia in Pictures* (5–8). Series: Visual Geography. 1996, Lerner LB $25.55 (978-0-8225-1837-2). Covers climate, geography, wildlife, vegetation, and natural resources. (Rev: BL 8/88) [966.62]

9659 Ndukwe, Pat I. *Fulani* (7–10). Series: Heritage Library of African Peoples. 1995, Rosen LB $29.25 (978-0-8239-1982-6). A description of the history, surroundings, politics, customs, and current conditions of the Fulani people, who live in Cameroon, Mali, and Nigeria. (Rev: BL 2/15/96; SLJ 7/96) [966]

9660 *Nigeria in Pictures* (5–8). Series: Visual Geography. 1995, Lerner LB $25.55 (978-0-8225-1826-6). A visual focus on this African land. (Rev: BL 8/88) [966.9]

9661 Nwanunobi, C. O. *Malinke* (5–7). Series: Heritage Library of African Peoples. 1996, Rosen LB $29.25 (978-0-8239-1979-6). Features the culture, history, and contemporary lifeways of the Malinke people, now living along the western coast of Africa. (Rev: BL 11/15/96) [966.23]

9662 Nwanunobi, C. O. *Soninke* (5–7). Series: Heritage Library of African Peoples. 1996, Rosen LB $29.25 (978-0-8239-1978-9). A discussion of the African people found in such countries as Ghana, Mali, Nigeria, and Senegal, with material on history, customs, and present living conditions. (Rev: BL 11/15/96) [966]

9663 Ogbaa, Kalu. *Igbo* (7–10). Series: Heritage Library of African Peoples. 1995, Rosen LB $29.25 (978-0-8239-1977-2). An introduction to the Igbo people, one of the three most important ethnic groups in Nigeria. (Rev: BL 9/15/95; SLJ 11/95) [966.9]

9664 Parris, Ronald. *Hausa* (5–7). Series: Heritage Library of African Peoples. 1996, Rosen LB $29.25 (978-0-8239-1983-3). A look at the Hausa people of Niger and Nigeria, with material on history and contemporary life. (Rev: BL 11/15/96) [966]

9665 Reef, Catherine. *This Our Dark Country: The American Settlers of Liberia* (7–12). 2002, Clarion $17.00 (978-0-618-14785-4). This chronological account of Liberia's history makes good use of excerpts from letters and diaries. (Rev: BL 11/15/02; HBG 3/03; SLJ 12/02; VOYA 6/03) [966.62]

9666 Sallah, Tijan M. *Wolof* (7–12). Series: Heritage Library of African Peoples. 1996, Rosen LB $29.25 (978-0-8239-1987-1). Using maps, many color illustrations, and simple text, this book introduces the Wolof people of Senegal and their history, social and political life, customs, religious beliefs, and relations with other peoples in their region. (Rev: BL 3/15/96; SLJ 7/96) [966.3]

9667 Taylor, Dereen. *Nigeria* (4–7). Illus. Series: A World of Food. 2010, Oliver LB $24.95 (978-193454514-0). This book presents an overview of Nigeria's cuisine, complete with simple recipes, colorful illustrations, and plenty of cultural context. (Rev: BL 4/1/10; LMC 10/10) [394.1]

9668 Walker, Ida. *Nigeria* (7–10). Series: Africa. 2005, Mason Crest LB $21.95 (978-1-59084-811-1). Covers the geography, history, politics, government, economy, people, and culture of Nigeria, providing a map, flag, recipes, glossary, timeline, and colorful photographs. (Rev: SLJ 3/05) [966.9]

Asia

General and Miscellaneous

9669 Bowden, Rob. *Asia* (5–8). Series: Continents of the World. 2006, World Almanac LB $34.00 (978-0-8368-5911-9). Factboxes and "In Focus" articles add to this overview of the history, geography, people, culture, and so forth of the continent of Asia. (Rev: SLJ 2/06) [915]

9670 Des Forges, Roger V., and John S. Major. *The Asian World, 600–1500* (7–12). 2006, Oxford LB $32.95 (978-0-19-517843-2). The authors explore the contributions, culture, empires, and conflicts of China, Japan, India, and Korea over nine centuries, with color photographs, artwork, maps, and quotations. (Rev: SLJ 7/06)

9671 Helget, Nicole. *Mongols* (5–8). Illus. Series: Fearsome Fighters. 2012, Creative Education $24.95 (978-160818184-1). With many illustrations, maps, and primary documents, this volume looks at the Mongols and their society, weapons, fighting techniques, key figures, and so forth. (Rev: BL 11/1/12; LMC 5–6/13; SLJ 12/12)

9672 Kort, Michael. *Central Asian Republics* (7–12). Series: Nations in Transition. 2003, Facts on File $40.00 (978-0-8160-5074-1). After a history of the region, each of the independent republics is introduced with discussion of the current challenges it faces; these include border disputes, poor environment, poor health care and quality of life, and government corruption. (Rev: SLJ 4/04)

9673 Major, John S., and Betty J. Belanus. *Caravan to America: Living Arts of the Silk Road* (5–8). 2002, Cricket $24.95 (978-0-8126-2666-7); paper $15.95 (978-0-8126-2677-3). The traditions and skills emanating from the ancient trade routes are shown as surviv-

ing today in the work of a rug restorer in New York, an artist-monk in Los Angeles, a cook from Iran, and other examples in this fascinating approach to an interesting subject. (Rev: BL 11/1/02; HB 1–2/03; HBG 3/03; SLJ 2/03; VOYA 6/03) [745]

9674 Pascoe, Elaine. *The Pacific Rim: East Asia at the Dawn of a New Century* (7–12). 1999, Twenty-First Century LB $25.90 (978-0-7613-3015-8). Brief historical information and current economic figures are given for Japan, China, Taiwan, the Koreas, Indonesia, Singapore, Malaysia, and the Philippines. (Rev: BL 7/99; SLJ 9/99) [950.4]

China

9675 Baldwin, Robert F. *Daily Life in Ancient and Modern Beijing* (4–7). Illus. by Ray Webb. Series: Cities Through Time. 1999, Runestone LB $25.26 (978-0-8225-3214-9). Topics introduced in this contrast between Beijing past and present include the arts, religion, school, history, and daily life. (Rev: HBG 10/99; SLJ 7/99) [951]

9676 Barber, Nicola. *Beijing* (4–7). Series: Great Cities of the World. 2004, World Almanac LB $31.00 (978-0-8368-5028-4). In addition to the usual information on history and people, this attractive volume describes living conditions and leisure time and provides maps and sidebars about contemporary environmental and political issues. (Rev: BL 4/15/04; SLJ 6/04) [951]

9677 Ferroa, Peggy. *China* (4–7). Series: Cultures of the World. 1991, Marshall Cavendish LB $35.64 (978-1-85435-399-3). Unusual facts highlight this look at China, with emphasis on culture. (Rev: BL 2/15/92; SLJ 3/92) [951]

9678 Gay, Kathlyn. *The Aftermath of the Chinese Nationalist Revolution* (7–10). Illus. 2008, Lerner LB $38.60 (978-082257601-3). A well-researched exploration of the Chinese civil turmoil — and eventual transition to communism — after the 1911 Wuchang Rebellion led by Sun Yat-sen. (Rev: BL 10/15/08; LMC 3–4/09; SLJ 3/1/09) [951.04]

9679 Haugen, David M., ed. *China* (8–12). 2006, Gale LB $34.95 (978-0-7377-3389-1); paper $23.70 (978-0-7377-3390-7). China's economic growth, steps toward democracy, military threat, and other important aspects are discussed in this collection of brief articles that present different perspectives. (Rev: SLJ 8/06)

9680 Kagda, Falaq. *Hong Kong* (5–8). Series: Cultures of the World. 1998, Marshall Cavendish LB $37.07 (978-0-7614-0692-1). An attractive book that introduces us to Hong Kong's history and geography, its people, and their culture and lifestyles. (Rev: HBG 3/98; SLJ 6/98) [951]

9681 Langley, Andrew. *The Cultural Revolution: Years of Chaos in China* (6–10). Series: Snapshots in History.

2008, Compass Point LB $24.95 (978-0-7565-3483-7). A look at the events leading up to the violence in China in the 1960s begins this book, which then delves into what happened during the Cultural Revolution and why. (Rev: BL 3/3/08; SLJ 7/08) [951.05]

9682 Mah, Adeline Yen. *China: Land of Dragons and Emperors* (6–12). 2009, Delacorte $17.99 (978-0-385-73748-7); LB $20.99 (978-0-385-90669-2). An engaging history of China from ancient times to the present, with insight into the land's people, traditions, beliefs, and cultures. (Rev: LMC 10/09; SLJ 8/09) [951]

9683 Mann, Elizabeth. *The Great Wall: The Story of Thousands of Miles of Earth and Stone* (4–8). Series: Wonders of the World. 1997, Mikaya $19.95 (978-0-9650493-2-0). The story behind the building of this massive structure, which began as far back as 200 B.C. and involves historical battles for land and power between the Chinese and the nomadic Mongols. (Rev: BL 1/1–15/98; SLJ 12/97) [951]

9684 Marx, Trish. *Elephants and Golden Thrones: Inside China's Forbidden City* (4–7). Illus. by Ellen B. Senisi. 2008, Abrams $18.95 (978-0-8109-9485-0). Full of photographs, this is an inside look at the sights and history of the huge palace complex. (Rev: BL 6/1–15/08; SLJ 7/08) [951]

9685 Pellegrini, Nancy. *Beijing* (4–8). Photos by Adrian Cooper. Series: Global Cities. 2007, Chelsea House LB $30.00 (978-0-7910-8848-7). With plenty of photographs and maps, this volume introduces the history of Beijing as well as its geography, people, environment, transportation, and so forth. (Rev: SLJ 7/07)

9686 Pilon, Pascal, and Elizabeth Thomas. *We Live in China* (4–7). Illus. Series: Kids Around the World. 2006, Abrams $15.95 (978-0-8109-5735-0). Four children from different areas of China introduce their region and everyday life; the lack of an index and photo captions limit the book's usefulness for reports, but it will nevertheless serve as an attractive introduction. (Rev: BL 10/15/06; SLJ 2/07)

9687 Qing, Zheng. *China* (4–7). Illus. by Tim Hutchinson. Series: Find Out About. 2007, Barron's $12.99 (978-0-7641-5952-7). This well-organized, attractively illustrated guide looks at China's history and contemporary life, and introduces basic phrases in Mandarin. (Rev: BL 4/1/07; SLJ 2/07)

9688 Shuter, Jane. *Ancient China* (5–8). Series: Time Travel Guides. 2007, Raintree LB $34.29 (978-1-4109-2729-3). An attractive trip back in time to ancient China, providing details about daily life there — accommodation, food, shopping, and so forth — and suggesting sights to see. (Rev: SLJ 9/07) [931]

9689 Slavicek, Louise Chipley. *The Chinese Cultural Revolution* (7–10). Series: Milestones in Modern World History. 2010, Chelsea House $35 (978-1-60413-278-6). With first-person narratives, excerpts from primary

documents, and a timeline, this volume tells the story of the political and social upheaval in China from the mid-1960s to the mid-1970s. **e** (Rev: BL 5/15/10; LMC 8–9/10; SLJ 5/10) [951.05]

9690 Tsiang, Sarah. *Warriors and Wailers: One Hundred Ancient Chinese Jobs You Might Have Relished or Reviled* (4–8). Illus. by Martha Newbigging. Series: Jobs in History. 2012, Annick $25.95 (978-155451391-8); paper $16.95 (978-1-55451-390-1). Tsiang surveys the social structure of ancient China and the benefits and disadvantages of ranks ranging from highest to lowest. (Rev: BLO 11/1/12; LMC 3–4/13*; SLJ 7/12) [331.700951]

9691 Walker, Kathryn. *Shanghai* (4–7). Series: Great Cities of the World. 2005, World Almanac LB $31.00 (978-0-8368-5046-8). An informative and appealing overview of this important Chinese city, with material on its history, its economy, and what it's like to live there. (Rev: BL 4/15/04)

India, Pakistan, and Bangladesh

9692 Arnold, Caroline, and Madeleine Comora. *Taj Mahal* (4–7). Illus. by Rahul Bhushan. 2007, Carolrhoda LB $17.95 (978-0-7613-2609-9). A beautifully designed, oversized picture book, this volume on the Taj Mahal and the story behind its construction includes detailed paintings and a fictionalized narrative about the Mogul prince who built it in memory of his wife. (Rev: BL 6/1–15/07; SLJ 7/07)

9693 Crompton, Samuel Willard. *Pakistan* (7–12). Series: Modern World Nations. 2002, Chelsea LB $30.00 (978-0-7910-7098-7). An overview of the history, geography, people, politics, and religion of Pakistan, with discussion of current difficulties such as ethnic strife, population problems, and disputes with India. (Rev: SLJ 2/03) [954.91]

9694 Darraj, Susan Muaddi. *The Indian Independence Act of 1947* (8–12). Illus. Series: Milestones in Modern World History. 2011, Chelsea House LB $35 (978-160413496-4). With photographs, timelines, and maps, this volume explains the granting of independence to India and the partitioning of India and Pakistan. **e** (Rev: BL 2/15/12) [954.03]

9695 DuTemple, Lesley A. *The Taj Mahal* (4–7). Series: Great Building Feats. 2003, Lerner LB $27.93 (978-0-8225-4694-8). Using many illustrations, this account traces the building of the magnificent tomb that was inspired by one man's love for his wife. (Rev: BL 11/15/03) [954]

9696 Ejaz, Khadija. *Recipe and Craft Guide to India* (4–7). Illus. 2010, Mitchell Lane LB $24.50 (978-158415938-4). Cultural and culinary projects introduce readers to many aspects of India. (Rev: BL 1/1–15/11; LMC 1–2/11*) [641.5954]

9697 Goodwin, William. *Pakistan* (6–12). Series: Modern Nations of the World. 2002, Gale LB $29.95 (978-1-59018-218-5). An overview of Pakistan's geography, history, culture, and society, with biographical information on key individuals. (Rev: BL 11/15/02; SLJ 1/03) [954.91]

9698 Green, Jen. *Mumbai* (4–8). Photos by Chris Fairclough. Series: Global Cities. 2007, Chelsea House LB $30.00 (978-0-7910-8851-7). With plenty of photographs and maps, this overview of the city of Mumbai (formerly Bombay) provides concise information on its history, geography, people, environment, transportation, and so forth. (Rev: SLJ 7/07)

9699 Guile, Melanie. *Culture in India* (4–7). Series: Culture In. 2005, Raintree LB $25.70 (978-1-4109-1134-6). Customs, holidays, clothing, food, and arts and crafts are well covered in this volume that also provides basic information needed for reports and interesting sidebar features on such topics as ancestor worship and celebrities. (Rev: BL 2/15/04; SLJ 5/05) [954]

9700 Hinman, Bonnie. *We Visit Pakistan* (4–8). Illus. Series: Your Land and My Land: The Middle East. 2011, Mitchell Lane LB $33.95 (978-158415960-5). With illustrations, photographs, maps, reproductions, a recipe, a craft project, and a timeline, this is a useful overview of the history and geography of Pakistan. (Rev: BL 2/1/12) [954.91]

9701 Orr, Tamra. *Bangladesh* (5–9). Series: Enchantment of the World Second Series. 2007, Children's Pr. LB $36.00 (978-0-516-25012-0). Features information on the Asian nation of Bangladesh, including its culture, religion, family life, arts, and sports and looks in particular at the country's struggles with pollution, poor living and working conditions, and political instability. (Rev: BL 8/07) [954.92]

9702 Rowe, Percy, and Patience Coster. *Delhi* (4–7). Series: Great Cities of the World. 2005, World Almanac LB $31.00 (978-0-8368-5037-6). An informative and appealing overview of this major Indian city, with material on its history, its economy, and what it's like to live there. (Rev: BL 4/15/04)

9703 Sonneborn, Liz. *Pakistan* (6–9). Illus. Series: Enchantment of the World. 2012, Scholastic LB $40 (978-053127544-3). An attractive revision of the guide to the land and people of Pakistan. (Rev: BL 12/1/12)

9704 Valliant, Doris. *Bangladesh* (8–12). Series: The Growth and Influence of Islam in the Nations of Asia and Central Asia. 2005, Mason Crest LB $25.95 (978-1-59084-879-1). A well-illustrated look at Bangladesh and the importance of Islam in the country's history, politics, economy, and foreign relations. (Rev: SLJ 9/05) [954.9]

9705 Viswanath, R. *Teenage Refugees and Immigrants from India Speak Out* (7–12). Series: Teenage Refugees Speak Out. 1997, Rosen LB $27.95 (978-0-8239-2440-

0). A description of the ethnic and religious conflicts and economic conditions that have caused the displacement of tens of thousands of Indians, plus the stories of those who came to the United States, told in first-person teenage accounts. (Rev: BL 12/15/97; SLJ 4/98) [954]

9706 Whyte, Mariam. *Bangladesh* (5–9). Series: Cultures of the World. 1998, Marshall Cavendish LB $37.07 (978-0-7614-0869-7). A sympathetic look at the history and geography of Bangladesh, with details of the country's rich background and current problems. (Rev: HBG 10/99; SLJ 6/99) [954.9]

Japan

9707 Blumberg, Rhoda. *Commodore Perry in the Land of the Shogun* (5–8). 1985, Lothrop $21.99 (978-0-688-03723-9). Japan was a mysterious country when Perry arrived in 1853 to open its harbors to American ships. (Rev: BL 11/1/85; SLJ 10/85) [952.025]

9708 Case, Robert. *Japan* (6–10). Series: Countries of the World. 2003, Facts on File $30.00 (978-0-8160-5381-0). An attractive introduction to Japan that includes material on history, geography, economy, people, and culture. (Rev: BL 1/1–15/04) [952]

9709 Donovan, Sandy. *Teens in Japan* (6–9). Series: Global Connections. 2007, Compass Point LB $23.95 (978-0-7565-2444-9). This volume covers many aspects of Japanese culture and traditions practiced by people of all ages, focusing in particular on everyday life for teens and the stresses they suffer. (Rev: BL 4/1/07) [305.2350]

9710 Hanel, Rachael. *Samurai* (5–8). Series: Fearsome Fighters. 2007, Creative Education LB $31.35 (978-1-58341-538-2). Weapons, armor, fighting techniques, and motivation are all discussed in this description of the Japanese feudal warriors and the kinds of people who were tempted to this career. (Rev: SLJ 1/08)

9711 Kallen, Stuart A. *Life in Tokyo* (6–10). Series: The Way People Live. 2001, Lucent LB $29.95 (978-1-56006-797-9). After a brief historical introduction, life in present-day Tokyo is featured with material on such topics as daily life, education, entertainment, jobs, food, and culture. (Rev: BL 6/1–15/01; SLJ 6/01) [952]

9712 Mofford, Juliet Haines. *Recipe and Craft Guide to Japan* (4–7). Illus. 2010, Mitchell Lane LB $24.50 (978-158415933-9). Cultural and culinary projects introduce readers to many aspects of Japan. (Rev: BL 1/1–15/11; LMC 1–2/11*) [641.5952]

9713 Shelley, Rex, and Teo Chuu Yong. *Japan. 2nd ed.* (5–8). Series: Cultures of the World. 2001, Benchmark LB $37.07 (978-0-7614-1356-1). An updated edition of the 1996 title, covering the history, geography, politics, people, arts, culture, and environmental concerns of Japan. (Rev: HBG 3/02; SLJ 3/02) [952]

Other Asian Countries

9714 *Afghanistan in Pictures* (5–8). Series: Visual Geography. 1997, Lerner LB $25.55 (978-0-8225-1849-5). Includes sections on vegetation and wildlife, minerals, cities, history, and government. (Rev: BL 5/1/89) [958.1]

9715 Ali, Sharifah Enayat. *Afghanistan* (4–7). Series: Cultures of the World. 1995, Marshall Cavendish LB $37.07 (978-0-7614-0177-3). After general background information, this account focuses on the arts, leisure activities, and festivals of the people of Afghanistan. (Rev: BL 1/1–15/96; SLJ 4/96) [958.1]

9716 Ali, Sharifah Enayat. *Afghanistan. 2nd ed.* (5–9). Series: Cultures of the World. 2006, Benchmark LB $27.95 (978-0-7614-2064-4). A revised and updated edition of the guide to Afghanistan and its history, geography, culture, and government including maps and color photographs. (Rev: SLJ 3/07) [958.1]

9717 Barber, Nicola. *Singapore* (4–7). Series: Great Cities of the World. 2005, World Almanac LB $31.00 (978-0-8368-5047-5). An informative and appealing overview of one of the world's most famous cities, with material on its history, its economy, and what it's like to live there. (Rev: BL 4/15/04)

9718 Behnke, Alison. *Angkor Wat* (5–8). Series: Unearthing Ancient Worlds. 2008, Lerner LB $30.60 (978-0-8225-7585-6). This volume focuses on the ruins of Angkor Wat, thoroughly explaining the archaeological science that fueled the discoveries and providing color maps, illustrations, and photos. (Rev: SLJ 10/1/08)

9719 Burbank, Jon. *Nepal* (4–7). Series: Cultures of the World. 1991, Marshall Cavendish LB $35.64 (978-1-85435-401-3). The emphasis is on culture as well as the basics of geography, history, government, and people. (Rev: BL 2/15/92) [954.96]

9720 Corona, Laurel. *Afghanistan* (6–12). Series: Modern Nations of the World. 2002, Gale LB $29.95 (978-1-59018-217-8). This book covers cultural, geographical, religious, and other aspects of Afghanistan, with discussion of the Taliban and the role of women. (Rev: BL 11/15/02; SLJ 12/02) [958.1]

9721 Cottrell, Robert C. *Vietnam: 17th Parallel* (7–9). Series: Arbitrary Borders. 2004, Chelsea House LB $35.00 (978-0-7910-7834-1). This series discusses the importance of borders in the stability (or instability) of a country; this volume looks at Vietnam and the lengthy conflict over the arbitrary division of the nation. (Rev: BL 8/04; SLJ 7/04) [959.70]

9722 Gogol, Sara. *A Mien Family* (4–7). Series: Journey Between Two Worlds. 1996, Lerner LB $22.60 (978-0-8225-3407-5); paper $8.95 (978-0-8225-9745-2). The story of a refugee family from the mountainous area of Laos and their journey to the United States. (Rev: BL 11/15/96; SLJ 1/97) [306.85]

9723 Goodman, Jim. *Thailand* (5–9). Series: Cultures of the World. 1991, Marshall Cavendish LB $35.64 (978-1-85435-402-0). Thailand's history, land, and culture. (Rev: BL 3/15/92) [959.3]

9724 Gritzner, Jeffrey A. *Afghanistan* (7–12). Series: Modern World Nations. 2002, Chelsea LB $30.00 (978-0-7910-6774-1). An overview of the history, geography, people, politics, and religion of Afghanistan, with discussion of the current antiterrorist and rebuilding efforts. (Rev: SLJ 2/03) [958.1]

9725 Guile, Melanie. *Culture in Malaysia* (4–7). Series: Culture In. 2005, Raintree LB $25.70 (978-1-4109-1133-9). Customs, holidays, clothing, food, and arts and crafts are well covered in this volume that also provides basic information needed for reports and interesting sidebar features. (Rev: SLJ 5/05)

9726 Hanson, Jennifer L. *Mongolia* (7–10). Series: Nations in Transition. 2003, Facts on File $40.00 (978-0-8160-5221-9). A thorough review of Mongolia's history, geography, and culture, detailing the difficulties involved in making a transition to democracy. (Rev: SLJ 5/04; VOYA 6/04) [951]

9727 Kizilos, Peter. *Tibet: Disputed Land* (7–10). Series: World in Conflict. 2000, Lerner LB $25.26 (978-0-8225-3563-8). The history of Tibet and its present political divisions are covered in this well-illustrated account. (Rev: BL 10/15/2000; HBG 3/01) [951.1]

9728 Kummer, Patricia K. *North Korea* (7–12). Illus. Series: Enchantment of the World. 2008, Children's Press LB $37.00 (978-0-531-18485-1). Geography, history, economy, religion, sports, and education are all discussed here, along with government oppression, censorship, and the nuclear weapons program; includes numerous maps and photographs. (Rev: BL 8/08) [951.93]

9729 Layton, Lesley. *Singapore* (5–8). Series: Cultures of the World. 1990, Marshall Cavendish LB $35.64 (978-1-85435-295-8). As well as history and economy, this introduction to Singapore includes coverage of lifestyles and current problems. (Rev: BL 3/1/91; SLJ 6/91) [959.57]

9730 Levy, Patricia. *Tibet* (4–7). Series: Cultures of the World. 1996, Marshall Cavendish LB $37.07 (978-0-7614-0277-0). Tibet is introduced with general background information, followed by material on its people and their culture, festivals, and food. (Rev: BL 8/96; SLJ 9/96) [951.1]

9731 Miller, Raymond H. *The War in Afghanistan* (6–8). Series: American War Library: The War on Terrorism. 2004, Gale LB $29.95 (978-1-59018-331-1). An account of the U.S.-led campaign to force the Taliban and al-Qaeda out of Afghanistan, the difficulties the military faced, and the resulting political reforms and efforts to rebuild the country and deal with problems such as remaining land mines. (Rev: BL 8/04) [958.10]

9732 Mortenson, Greg, and David Oliver Relin. *Three Cups of Tea: One Man's Journey to Change the World . . . One Child at a Time* (4–8). Illus. 2009, Dial $16.99 (978-0-8037-3392-3). Focusing mainly on the young people, this simplified version of Mortenson's bestseller for adults describes his successes building schools in Pakistan and Afghanistan. (Rev: BL 2/1/09; SLJ 2/09) [371]

9733 Munan, Heidi. *Malaysia* (5–8). Series: Cultures of the World. 1990, Marshall Cavendish LB $35.64 (978-1-85435-296-5). Cultural diversity and lifestyles of the people are two topics covered in this introduction to Malaysia. (Rev: BL 3/1/91) [959.5]

9734 O'Brien, Tony. *Afghan Dreams: Young Voices of Afghanistan* (4–9). Photos by Tony O'Brien. 2008, Bloomsbury $18.99 (978-1-59990-287-6). This photo-essay featuring more than 30 young Afghans illustrates their poignant situation and provides background information. ALA Notable Books 2009. (Rev: BCCB 12/08; SLJ 12/08; VOYA 12/08) [305.235092]

9735 Otfinoski, Steven. *Afghanistan* (7–12). Series: Nations in Transition. 2003, Facts on File $40.00 (978-0-8160-5056-7). A thorough overview of Afghanistan presenting the current political and security problems — including healthcare needs, opium trade, and reliance on foreign funding — as well as material on the country's history, geography, people, culture, and so forth. (Rev: SLJ 4/04; VOYA 6/04) [958.1]

9736 Pang, Guek-Cheng. *Mongolia* (5–8). Series: Cultures of the World. 1999, Marshall Cavendish LB $37.07 (978-0-7614-0954-0). A clear, well-illustrated introduction to this remote land that includes good background information as well as coverage of modern life. (Rev: HBG 10/99; SLJ 10/99) [957]

9737 Salter, Christopher. *North Korea* (6–12). 2003, Chelsea LB $30.00 (978-0-7910-7233-2). A thorough and concise overview of North Korea's geography, history, government, politics, economics, language, peoples, and religion, with maps, photographs, and a look at the future. (Rev: BL 9/15/03; HBG 10/03) [951.93]

9738 Sheehan, Sean. *Cambodia* (4–7). Series: Cultures of the World. 1996, Marshall Cavendish LB $37.07 (978-0-7614-0281-7). The troubled land of Cambodia is introduced, with emphasis on its people, their lifestyles, and culture. (Rev: BL 8/96; SLJ 9/96) [959]

9739 Sheehan, Sean, and Shahrezad Samiuddin. *Pakistan* (5–9). Series: Cultures of the World. 2004, Benchmark LB $37.07 (978-0-7614-1787-3). Pakistan's geography, history, economy, and people are all examined, with discussion of interesting aspects of Pakistani culture. (Rev: SLJ 2/05) [954.9]

9740 Sís, Peter. *Tibet: Through the Red Box* (7–12). 1998, Farrar $25.00 (978-0-374-37552-2). Using a journal kept by the author's filmmaker father when he journeyed to Tibet long ago, old tales, and pictures of landscapes and intriguing illustrations inspired by the Tibetan wheel of life, the author writes about the past and present of this land, its culture, and its religion. (Rev: BCCB 12/98; BL 9/15/98; HB 11–12/98; HBG 3/99; SLJ 10/98) [954.96]

9741 Sonneborn, Liz. *The Khmer Rouge* (7–10). Illus. Series: Great Escapes. 2011, Marshall Cavendish LB $34.21 (978-160870474-3). The experiences of journalist Dith Pran introduce this account of the genocide that occurred under the rule of the Khmer Rouge in Cambodia. e (Rev: BLO 3/1/12; LMC 8–9/12) [959.604]

9742 *South Korea in Pictures* (5–7). Series: Visual Geography. 1997, Lerner LB $25.55 (978-0-8225-1868-6). An introduction to South Korea that focuses on its politics and economy. (Rev: SLJ 5/90) [951.9]

9743 Taus-Bolstad, Stacy. *Pakistan in Pictures. Rev. ed.* (5–9). Series: Visual Geography. 2003, Lerner LB $27.93 (978-0-8225-4682-5). This substantially revised volume covers Pakistan's history, geography, culture, and lifestyle. (Rev: SLJ 7/03) [954.9]

9744 *Vietnam in Pictures* (5–8). Series: Visual Geography. 1994, Lerner LB $25.55 (978-0-8225-1909-6). This well-illustrated account of Vietnam covers its history, geography, people, government, and economy. (Rev: BL 11/1/94) [915.97]

9745 Wanasundera, Nanda P. *Sri Lanka* (4–7). Series: Cultures of the World. 1991, Marshall Cavendish LB $213.86 (978-1-85435-397-9). The history, geography, and culture of Sri Lanka are introduced with an emphasis on contemporary problems. (Rev: BL 2/15/92) [954.93]

9746 Whitehead, Kim. *Afghanistan* (8–12). Series: The Growth and Influence of Islam in the Nations of Asia and Central Asia. 2005, Mason Crest LB $25.95 (978-1-59084-833-3). A well-illustrated look at Afghanistan and the importance of Islam in the country's history, politics, economy, and foreign relations. (Rev: SLJ 9/05) [958.104]

9747 Withington, William A. *Southeast Asia* (5–8). 1988, Gateway $16.95 (978-0-934291-32-3). Sections on lifestyle, land and climate, history and government, festivals, sports, arts, and crafts. (Rev: BL 12/1/88)

9748 Yin, Saw Myat. *Myanmar. Rev. ed.* (4–8). Series: Cultures of the World. 2001, Benchmark LB $37.07 (978-0-7614-1353-0). An introduction to every aspect of Myanmar with useful information on daily life and phonetic pronunciations of many foreign words. Also use *Indonesia* (2001). (Rev: HBG 3/02; SLJ 4/02) [959.1]

9749 Zwier, Lawrence J. *Sri Lanka: War Torn Island* (8–12). Series: World in Conflict. 1998, Lerner LB $25.26 (978-0-8225-3550-8). The author describes the long political struggle in Sri Lanka. (Rev: BL 4/15/98) [305.8]

Australia and the Pacific Islands

9750 Arnold, Caroline. *Easter Island: Giant Stone Statues Tell of a Rich and Tragic Past* (4–7). 2000, Clarion LB $15.00 (978-0-395-87609-1). This chronological history of Easter Island tells how the stone statues got there and what they mean. (Rev: BCCB 4/00; BL 3/15/00; HB 5–6/00; HBG 10/00; SLJ 4/00) [996.1]

9751 Arnold, Caroline. *Uluru: Australia's Aboriginal Heart* (4–8). Illus. by Arthur Arnold. 2003, Clarion $16.00 (978-0-618-18181-0). Uluru, formerly known as Ayers Rock, is a giant sandstone monolith that changes color in the setting sun and is a spiritual landmark for the native people of the central Australian desert. (Rev: BCCB 12/03; BL 12/15/03; HB 11–12/03; HBG 11–12/03; SLJ 1/04) [994.01]

9752 Darian-Smith, Kate. *Australia, Antarctica, and the Pacific* (5–8). Series: Continents of the World. 2006, World Almanac LB $34.00 (978-0-8368-5912-6). Factboxes and "In Focus" articles add to this overview of the history, geography, people, culture, and so forth of the continents of Australia, Antarctica, and island of the Pacific. (Rev: SLJ 2/06)

9753 Jackson, Barbara. *New Zealand* (4–8). Series: Countries of the World. 2008, National Geographic LB $27.90 (978-1-4263-0301-2). With lots of color images, this thorough volume looks at the geography, nature, history, culture, government, and economy of New Zealand, with interesting sidebars on customs, celebrations, and so forth. (Rev: SLJ 3/09) [992]

9754 Mason, Paul. *Sydney* (4–8). Photos by Rob Bowden. Series: Global Cities. 2007, Chelsea House LB $30.00 (978-0-7910-8849-4). With plenty of photographs and maps, this volume introduces the history of Sydney, Australia, as well as its geography, people, environment, transportation, and so forth. (Rev: SLJ 7/07)

9755 Pelta, Kathy. *Rediscovering Easter Island* (5–9). Series: How History Is Invented. 2001, Lerner LB $28.75 (978-0-8225-4890-4). An assortment of illustrations, maps, and inserts add to this exploration of the mysteries of Easter Island. (Rev: BCCB 7–8/01; HBG 10/01; SLJ 2/02) [996.18]

9756 Rajendra, Vijeya, and Sundran Rajendra. *Australia* (4–7). Series: Cultures of the World. 1991, Marshall Cavendish LB $35.64 (978-1-85435-400-6). Beyond the basics, this volume highlights contemporary problems and concerns in the Land Down Under. (Rev: BL 2/15/92; SLJ 3/92) [994]

9757 Turner, Kate. *Australia* (5–8). Series: Countries of the World. 2007, National Geographic LB $27.90 (978-1-4263-0055-4). Excellent photographs and maps make this an appealing introduction to the country's history, geography, government, economy, people, culture, and nature. (Rev: SLJ 10/07) [994]

9758 Vail, Martha. *Exploring the Pacific. Rev. ed.* (6–9). Series: Discovery and Exploration. 2010, Chelsea House LB $35 (978-1-60413-197-0). This updated volume covers exploration in the Pacific from the early Polynesians onward and includes such figures as Magellan and Cook, with clear, informative text plus maps, illustrations, and excerpts from primary sources (Rev: LMC 8–9/10) [551.46]

9759 Vail, Martha, and John S. Bowman, eds. *Exploring the Pacific* (6–12). Series: Discovery and Exploration. 2005, Facts on File $40.00 (978-0-8160-5258-5). Exploration in the Pacific, from early Polynesians onward and including such figures as Magellan and Cook, is the focus of this volume that contains clear, informative text plus maps, illustrations, and excerpts from primary sources. (Rev: SLJ 8/05) [973]

Europe

General and Miscellaneous

9760 Bowden, Rob. *Istanbul* (4–8). Photos by Edward Parker. Series: Global Cities. 2007, Chelsea House LB $30.00 (978-0-7910-8850-0). With plenty of photographs and maps, this volume introduces the history of Istanbul as well as its geography, people, environment, transportation, and so forth. (Rev: SLJ 7/07)

9761 *Cyprus in Pictures* (5–8). Series: Visual Geography. 1992, Lerner LB $25.55 (978-0-8225-1910-2). The divided island of Cyprus is introduced, with good background information and material on the standoff between Greece and Turkey up to 1992. (Rev: BL 2/1/93) [956.45]

9762 Feinstein, Steve. *Turkey in Pictures* (5–8). 1989, Lerner LB $25.55 (978-0-8225-1831-0). An overview of Turkey and its people that includes lots of images. (Rev: BL 8/88) [956.1]

9763 Flint, David. *Europe* (5–8). Series: Continents of the World. 2006, World Almanac LB $34.00 (978-0-8368-5913-3). Factboxes and "In Focus" articles add to this overview of the history, geography, people, culture, and so forth of the continent of Europe. (Rev: SLJ 2/06) [940]

9764 Sheehan, Sean. *Malta* (5–9). Series: Cultures of the World. 2000, Marshall Cavendish LB $37.07 (978-0-7614-0993-9). This work covers the culture, geography, and history of Malta with material on such subjects as government, economy, people, lifestyles, and leisure. (Rev: HBG 10/00; SLJ 11/00) [945]

9765 Sheehan, Sean. *Turkey* (4–7). Series: Cultures of the World. 1993, Marshall Cavendish LB $35.64 (978-1-85435-576-8). This introduction to Turkey covers history, culture, economics, and present-day concerns. (Rev: BL 8/93) [956.1]

9766 Stafford, James. *The European Union: Facts and Figures* (8–11). Series: European Union. 2006, Mason Crest LB $21.95 (978-1-4222-0045-2). A useful, information-packed guide to the European Union and its origins and goals. (Rev: BL 4/1/06) [641.242]

Eastern Europe and the Balkans

9767 Bultje, Jan Willem. *Looking at the Czech Republic* (6–9). Series: Looking at Europe. 2006, Oliver LB $22.95 (978-1-881508-29-8). Numerous color photographs enhance the text that covers many aspects — history, geography, culture, economy, and so forth — of this eastern European land. (Rev: BL 10/15/06; SLJ 12/06) [943.71]

9768 Cooper, Robert, and Michael Spilling. *Croatia* (6–9). Illus. Series: Cultures of the World. 2011, Marshall Cavendish LB $29.95 (978-160870215-2). A revised edition of this volume covering Croatia's geography, history, political system, economy, environment, people, and culture from prehistoric man through today. (Rev: BL 6/1/11) [949.72]

9769 Fireside, Harvey, and Bryna J. Fireside. *Young People From Bosnia Talk About War* (6–9). Series: Issues in Focus. 1996, Enslow LB $20.95 (978-0-89490-730-2). Several students from Bosnia who have been brought to this country to study by the Bosnian Student Project tell about the effects of the war on them, their families, and their country. (Rev: BL 10/15/96; SLJ 10/96; VOYA 2/97) [949.702]

9770 Ganeri, Anita. *Focus on Turkey* (6–9). Series: World in Focus. 2007, World Almanac LB $33.27 (978-0-8368-6753-4); paper $11.95 (978-0-8368-6760-2). Turkey's history, geography, economy, culture, and handicrafts are all covered in this survey. (Rev: SLJ 2/08)

9771 *Hungary in Pictures* (5–8). Series: Visual Geography. 1993, Lerner LB $25.55 (978-0-8225-1883-9). Concise text and extensive photographs introduce the land, history, and people of Hungary. (Rev: BL 12/1/93; SLJ 12/93) [943.9]

9772 King, David C. *Bosnia and Herzegovina* (7–10). Series: Cultures of the World. 2005, Benchmark LB $37.07 (978-0-7614-1853-5). Explores the geography, history, people, culture, and lifestyles of Bosnia and Herzegovina. (Rev: SLJ 7/05) [949.7]

9773 Nichols, Jeremy, and Emilia Trembicka- Nichols. *Poland* (7–10). Series: Countries of the World. 2005, Facts on File LB $30.00 (978-0-8160-6005-4). History, geography, culture, government, and economy are all covered in this attractive overview of Poland. (Rev: SLJ 1/06) [9.4.3]

9774 Otfinoski, Steven. *The Czech Republic* (7–12). Series: Nations in Transition. 2004, Facts on File $40.00 (978-0-8160-5083-3). An updated edition that adds more recent events to the 1997 text about the history, people, culture, and government of the Czech Republic. (Rev: BL 12/1/04) [943.7105]

9775 Ricchiardi, Sherry. *Bosnia: The Struggle for Peace* (5–8). 1996, Millbrook LB $25.90 (978-0-7613-0031-1). An account that gives background information but concentrates on the recent (through 1995) history of Bosnia. (Rev: BL 7/96; SLJ 7/96) [949.702]

9776 Rollyson, Carl S. *Teenage Refugees from Eastern Europe Speak Out* (7–12). Series: Teenage Refugees Speak Out. 1997, Rosen LB $27.95 (978-0-8239-2437-0). Young refugees from Slovakia, Bulgaria, Hungary, Romania, Poland, Yugoslavia, and the former East Germany tell about conditions in their homelands and their receptions in the United States. (Rev: BL 12/15/97) [947]

France

9777 Corona, Laurel. *France* (5–8). Series: Modern Nations of the World. 2002, Gale LB $29.95 (978-1-56006-760-3). A comprehensive introduction to the land and people of France with material on history, geography, culture, and lifestyles. (Rev: BL 12/15/02) [944]

9778 Egendorf, Laura K., ed. *The French Revolution* (7–12). Series: Opposing Viewpoints: World History. 2004, Gale LB $37.45 (978-0-7377-1815-7). Questions about the French Revolution, such as the justification for the many executions, are explored in this collection of different points of view about this turning point in French history. (Rev: BL 2/15/04; SLJ 5/04) [944]

9779 Gofen, Ethel C. *France* (4–7). Series: Cultures of the World. 1992, Marshall Cavendish LB $35.64 (978-1-85435-449-5). This account provides information on the history, culture, and people of France and discusses the current problems and concerns. (Rev: BL 10/15/92) [944]

9780 Hoban, Sarah. *Daily Life in Ancient and Modern Paris* (4–7). 2000, Runestone LB $25.26 (978-0-8225-3222-4). This well-illustrated history of Paris is divided chronologically into seven sections, beginning with early Paris and working through the Middle Ages to World War II and the Paris of today. (Rev: BL 2/1/01; HBG 3/01; SLJ 2/01) [944]

9781 Kranz, Nickie. *Teens in France* (7–12). Series: Global Connections. 2006, Compass Point LB $31.93 (978-0-7565-2062-5). Introduces French teens and their schools, family life, hobbies, sports, and so forth, covering both traditional aspects and those that have arrived with new technology and new immigration. (Rev: SLJ 5/07) [305.235]

9782 LaRoche, Amelia. *Recipe and Craft Guide to France* (4–7). Illus. Series: World Crafts and Recipes. 2010, Mitchell Lane LB $24.50 (978-158415936-0).

Cultural and culinary projects introduce readers to many aspects of France. (Rev: BL 1/1–15/11; LMC 1–2/11*) [641.5941]

9783 Plain, Nancy. *Louis XVI, Marie-Antoinette and the French Revolution* (5–8). Series: Rulers and Their Times. 2001, Marshall Cavendish LB $29.93 (978-0-7614-1029-4). In three well-illustrated parts, this book offers a biography of Marie Antoinette, a history of France and its people during the French Revolution, and a generous selection of original documents of the period. (Rev: BL 1/1–15/02; HBG 3/02; SLJ 3/02) [944]

9784 Prosser, Robert. *France* (6–10). Series: Countries of the World. 2003, Facts on File $30.00 (978-0-8160-5380-3). This basic introduction to the land and people of France includes material on economy, culture, and present-day problems. (Rev: BL 1/1–15/04) [944]

9785 Stacey, Gill. *Paris* (4–7). 2004, World Almanac LB $31.00 (978-0-8368-5030-7). This attractive introduction to Paris covers the French capital's history and examines some of its modern-day problems. (Rev: BL 4/15/04; SLJ 6/04) [944]

Germany, Austria, and Switzerland

9786 Barber, Nicola. *Berlin* (4–7). Series: Great Cities of the World. 2005, World Almanac LB $31.00 (978-0-8368-5043-7). An informative and appealing overview of one of the world's most famous cities, with material on its history, its economy, and what it's like to live there. (Rev: BL 4/15/04)

9787 Bartoletti, Susan Campbell. *Hitler Youth: Growing Up in Hitler's Shadow* (7–10). 2005, Scholastic $19.95 (978-0-439-35379-3). This chilling look at the Hitler Youth movement, which at its peak boasted a membership of roughly 3.5 million boys and girls, includes excerpts from diaries, letters, oral histories, and the author's interviews with former members and resisters. Newbery Honor Book, 2006. (Rev: BL 4/15/05*; SLJ 6/05; VOYA 8/05) [943.086]

9788 Fuller, Barbara. *Germany* (4–7). Series: Cultures of the World. 1992, Marshall Cavendish LB $35.64 (978-1-85435-530-0). In addition to the usual information on the history and geography of Germany, this account stresses how the people live and their traditions. (Rev: BL 1/1/93) [943]

9789 *Germany in Pictures* (5–8). Series: Visual Geography. 1994, Lerner LB $21.27 (978-0-8225-1873-0). The new united Germany is introduced with a basic text and copious illustrations, including maps, charts, and attractive photographs. (Rev: BL 1/15/95) [943]

9790 Halleck, Elaine, ed. *Living in Nazi Germany* (8–12). Series: Exploring Cultural History. 2004, Gale LB $24.95 (978-0-7377-1732-7). First-person accounts excerpted from other works offer insight into life in Ger-

many under the Nazis, from the point of view of those brutalized and of those who took part in the regime. (Rev: BL 8/04) [943.086]

9791 Russell, Henry. *Germany* (5–8). Series: Countries of the World. 2007, National Geographic LB $27.90 (978-1-4263-0059-2). Excellent photographs and maps make this an appealing introduction to the country's history, geography, government, economy, people, culture, and nature. (Rev: SLJ 10/07) [943]

9792 Sheehan, Sean. *Austria* (4–7). Series: Cultures of the World. 1992, Marshall Cavendish LB $35.64 (978-1-85435-454-9). This introduction to Austria covers its history, lifestyles of the people, and contemporary problems. (Rev: BL 10/15/92) [943.6]

9793 *Switzerland in Pictures* (5–8). Series: Visual Geography. 1996, Lerner LB $25.55 (978-0-8225-1895-2). With a generous number of color pictures, this account traces the history and geography of Switzerland, with emphasis on the modern nation and its people. (Rev: BL 9/15/96; SLJ 8/98) [949.4]

Great Britain and Ireland

9794 Bean, Rachel. *United Kingdom* (4–8). Illus. Series: Countries of the World. 2007, National Geographic LB $27.90 (978-1-4263-0126-1). This attractive volume full of photographs covers the United Kingdom's geography, history, economy, people, and so forth. (Rev: SLJ 2/08)

9795 Bowden, Rob. *United Kingdom* (6–10). Series: Countries of the World. 2003, Facts on File $30.00 (978-0-8160-5383-4). An attractive volume that presents basic material about Great Britain including history, geography, and present social conditions. (Rev: BL 1/1–15/04) [941]

9796 Childress, Diana. *Chaucer's England* (7–12). 2000, Linnet LB $25.00 (978-0-208-02489-3). A fascinating glimpse into the social life, community structure, landscape, and economy of 14th-century England. (Rev: BL 9/15/00; HBG 10/01; SLJ 10/00; VOYA 4/01) [942.03]

9797 Elgin, Kathy. *Elizabethan England, Vol. 3* (5–8). Series: A History of Fashion and Costume. 2005, Facts on File $35.00 (978-0-8160-5946-1). A broad overview of the clothing and personal adornment worn during this time period, with many visual aids. (Rev: SLJ 5/06) [391]

9798 Hamilton, Janice. *The Norman Conquest of England* (7–9). Series: Pivotal Moments in History. 2007, Twenty-First Century LB $38.60 (978-0-8225-5902-3). An attractive and interesting account of the Norman invasion of 1066 with maps, photographs, and reproductions of manuscripts. (Rev: SLJ 1/08)

619

9799 Hestler, Anna, and Jo-Ann Spilling. *Wales* (6–9). Illus. Series: Cultures of the World. 2011, Marshall Cavendish LB $29.95 (978-160870457-6). A revised edition of this volume covering the geography, history, political system, economy, environment, people, and culture of Wales. (Rev: BL 6/1/11) [942.9]

9800 Hinds, Kathryn. *The Church* (6–8). Series: Life in Elizabethan England. 2007, Marshall Cavendish LB $22.95 (978-0-7614-2545-8). This visually appealing volume discusses the church during the Elizabethan era. (Rev: SLJ 3/08; VOYA 4/08)

9801 Hynson, Colin. *Elizabeth I and the Spanish Armada* (5–8). Illus. Series: Stories from History. 2006, School Specialty $9.95 (978-0-7696-4703-6); paper $6.95 (978-0-7696-4629-9). A graphic novel presentation of the confrontation between England's Queen Elizabeth I and the Spanish empire, climaxing in the defeat of the Spanish Armada by the English; full-color depictions of battles, fast facts, and maps aid comprehension. (Rev: BL 10/15/06; SLJ 1/07)

9802 *Ireland in Pictures* (5–8). Series: Visual Geography. 1997, Lerner LB $25.55 (978-0-8225-1878-5). Contemporary Ireland is highlighted in this illustrated account. (Rev: BL 12/1/90) [941.5]

9803 Jocelyn, Marthe. *A Home for Foundlings* (7–10). Series: Lord Museum. 2005, Tundra paper $15.95 (978-0-88776-709-8). A fascinating history of London's Foundling Hospital, which was opened in the 18th century to provide a home for babies whose mothers were unable to care for them and did not close until 1953. (Rev: BL 3/1/05; SLJ 6/05) [362.7]

9804 Jones, Becky, and Clare Lewis. *The Bumper Book of London: Fun Facts for All the Family* (5–12). Series: Adventure Walks. 2012, Frances Lincoln paper $19.95 (978-0-7112-3145-0). This attractive volume provides facts and trivia about London's development since Roman times, highlighting notable sites and interesting details about everyday life throughout the ages. (Rev: SLJ 5/1/12) [942.1]

9805 Levy, Debbie. *The Signing of the Magna Carta* (7–9). Series: Pivotal Moments in History. 2007, Twenty-First Century LB $38.60 (978-0-8225-5917-7). An attractive and interesting account of the creation and signing of this important document with maps, photographs, and reproductions of manuscripts. (Rev: SLJ 1/08)

9806 Levy, Patricia. *Ireland* (4–7). Series: Cultures of the World. 1993, Marshall Cavendish LB $25.95 (978-1-85435-580-5). An account that traces the role of women in Irish history to the present day. (Rev: SLJ 2/94) [941]

9807 Losure, Mary. *The Fairy Ring; or, Elsie and Frances Fool the World* (5–8). Illus. 2012, Candlewick $16.99 (978-076365670-6). Losure tells the story of two cousins who as girls in early-20th-century England

posed with paintings of fairies and convinced many, including Arthur Conan Doyle, that they were real. ∩ ℮ Lexile 940L (Rev: BL 3/1/12*; HB 3–4/12*; SLJ 5/1/12*; VOYA 2/12) [398]

9808 Lyons, Mary E., ed. *Feed the Children First: Irish Memories of the Great Hunger* (4–8). 2002, Simon & Schuster $17.00 (978-0-689-84226-9). Text, full-color reproductions, and occasional photographs clearly document the suffering of ordinary people during the Irish potato famine. (Rev: BL 12/15/01; HB 3–4/02; HBG 10/02; SLJ 3/02*) [941.5081]

9809 McQuinn, Anna, and Colm McQuinn. *Ireland* (4–8). Series: Countries of the World. 2008, National Geographic LB $27.90 (978-1-4263-0299-2). With lots of color images, this thorough volume looks at the geography, nature, history, culture, government, and economy of Ireland, with interesting sidebars on customs, celebrations, and so forth. (Rev: SLJ 3/09) [941.5]

9810 *Northern Ireland in Pictures* (5–8). Series: Visual Geography. 1991, Lerner LB $25.55 (978-0-8225-1898-3). This beautiful but troubled land is introduced in text and pictures. (Rev: BL 2/15/92) [941.6]

9811 Shields, Charles J. *The Great Plague and Fire of London* (6–8). Series: Great Disasters. 2001, Chelsea LB $21.95 (978-0-7910-6324-8). This is the story of the plague that ravished England in 1665 and of the fire the following year that nearly destroyed the entire city of London. (Rev: BL 6/1–15/02; SLJ 6/02) [941]

9812 Stacey, Gill. *London* (4–8). Series: Great Cities of the World. 2003, World Almanac LB $31.00 (978-0-8368-5022-2). In an appealing blend of text, photographs, quotations, and sidebar features, this volume introduces readers to some of London's history and attractions. (Rev: SLJ 1/04) [942.1]

9813 Swisher, Clarice. *Victorian England* (7–10). Series: World History. 2000, Lucent LB $32.45 (978-1-56006-323-0). Quotations and period reproductions enhance this interesting survey of the long and eventful reign of Queen Victoria, a time of technological and social innovation and of growing power for Great Britain. (Rev: BL 12/15/00; SLJ 3/01) [942]

9814 Toht, Betony, and David Toht. *Daily Life in Ancient and Modern London* (6–9). Series: Cities Through Time. 2001, Lerner LB $25.26 (978-0-8225-3223-1). London's evolution from earliest times to today is presented in double-page spreads, with information on political, social, and religious life. (Rev: BL 4/15/01; HBG 10/01; SLJ 7/01) [942]

9815 Warren, Andrea. *Charles Dickens and the Street Children of London* (6–9). Illus. 2011, Houghton Mifflin $18.99 (978-0-547-39574-6). This informative book that includes many portraits and photographs blends details of Dickens's life and works with a look at the plight of the street children of London in this era and their limited choices in the workhouses, the slums, and the schools. **e** (Rev: BL 6/1/11; HB 9–10/11; SLJ 8/11*) [823]

Greece

9816 Dubois, Jill, and Xenia Skoura. *Greece. 2nd ed.* (5–8). Series: Cultures of the World. 2003, Benchmark LB $37.07 (978-0-7614-1499-5). In addition to coverage of the geography, history, and economics of Greece, this volume looks at the people and the culture of this Mediterranean nation and provides recipes. (Rev: HBG 10/03; SLJ 8/03) [949.5]

9817 Heinrichs, Ann. *Greece* (6–9). Illus. Series: Enchantment of the World. 2012, Scholastic LB $40 (978-053127543-6). An attractive revision of the guide to the land and people of Greece. (Rev: BL 12/1/12; SLJ 4/13) [949.5]

9818 Kotapish, Dawn. *Daily Life in Ancient and Modern Athens* (5–8). Illus. by Bob Moulder. Series: Cities Through Time. 2000, Runestone LB $25.26 (978-0-8225-3216-3). Kotapish explores everyday life, government, and culture in Athens through the ages. (Rev: HBG 3/01; SLJ 5/01) [949.5]

Italy

9819 Barber, Nicola. *Rome* (4–7). Series: Great Cities of the World. 2005, World Almanac LB $31.00 (978-0-8368-5040-6). An informative and appealing overview of one of the world's most famous cities, with material on its history, its economy, and what it's like to live there. (Rev: BL 4/15/04)

9820 Grodin, Elissa D., and Mario M. Cuomo. *C Is for Ciao: An Italy Alphabet* (7–10). Illus. by Marco Ventura. 2009, Sleeping Bear $17.95 (978-158536361-2). Many areas of Italy's culture, history, and language are explored in this alphabet book for older readers. (Rev: BLO 2/9/09) [945]

9821 Hinds, Kathryn. *Venice and Its Merchant Empire* (5–8). Series: Cultures of the Past. 2001, Marshall Cavendish LB $29.93 (978-0-7614-0305-0). A well-illustrated overview of the history of Venice with a focus on the city's glory during the Renaissance. (Rev: BL 2/15/02; HBG 3/02) [945]

9822 Lamprell, Klay. *Not-for-Parents Rome: Everything You Ever Wanted to Know* (4–7). Illus. 2011, Lonely Planet paper $14.99 (978-17422081-8-3). More a source of trivia and amusement than a guidebook, this is nonetheless informative and directed at young visitors to the city; includes many photographs, maps, and images. (Rev: BL 12/1/11) [914.5632]

9823 Macaulay, David. *Rome Antics* (5–8). 1997, Houghton Mifflin $18.00 (978-0-395-82279-1). The reader gets a pigeon-eye view of vistas and buildings as the bird flies over Rome. (Rev: BL 9/15/97; SLJ 11/97*) [945]

9824 Parker, Vic. *Pompeii AD 79: A City Buried by a Volcanic Eruption* (4–7). Series: When Disaster Struck. 2006, Raintree LB $32.86 (978-1-4109-2276-2). Parker looks at Pompeii both before and after its destruction by the eruption of Mount Vesuvius, discussing the nature (and likelihood) of volcanic eruptions and what archaeologists have learned from their excavations. (Rev: SLJ 1/07) [937.7]

Russia and Other Former Soviet Republics

9825 Aizpuriete, Amanda. *Latvia* (5–8). Trans. by Katarina Hartgers. Photos by Jan Willem Bultje. Series: Looking at Europe. 2006, Oliver $22.95 (978-1-881508-37-3). This colorful volume with excellent photographs introduces readers to Latvia's geography, history, people, culture, economy, and lifestyle. (Rev: LMC 3/07; SLJ 1/07)

9826 Bassis, Volodymyr. *Ukraine* (4–7). Series: Cultures of the World. 1997, Marshall Cavendish LB $37.07 (978-0-7614-0684-6). An introduction to this former Soviet state, with emphasis on current history and culture. (Rev: BL 8/97; SLJ 10/97) [947.7]

9827 Batalden, Stephen K., and Sandra L. Batalden. *The Newly Independent States of Eurasia: Handbook of Former Soviet Republics. 2nd ed.* (7–12). 1997, Oryx paper $59.95 (978-0-89774-940-4). Arranged by geographical region, this volume examines each of the newly formed republics created from the former USSR, with details on their past, their culture, and key problems facing each today. (Rev: SLJ 11/97) [947]

9828 Bultje, Jan Willem. *Lithuania* (5–8). Trans. by Wilma Hoving. Photos by author. Series: Looking at Europe. 2006, Oliver $22.95 (978-1-881508-43-4). This colorful volume with excellent photographs introduces readers to Lithuania's geography, history, people, culture, economy, and lifestyle. (Rev: SLJ 1/07)

9829 Carrion, Esther. *The Empire of the Czars* (4–7). Series: World Heritage. 1994, Children's Press LB $15.00 (978-0-516-08319-3). An overview of Russian history from early times to the breakup of the Soviet Union, with special material on Russia's famous sights, such as Red Square, the Kremlin, and St. Petersburg. (Rev: SLJ 5/95) [947.07]

9830 Cartlidge, Cherese. *The Central Asian States* (6–12). Series: Modern Nations of the World: Former Soviet Republics. 2001, Lucent LB $29.95 (978-1-56006-735-1). This well-illustrated introduction to the former Soviet republics of Kazakhstan, Turkmenistan, Uzbekistan, Kyrgyzstan, and Tajikistan presents material on physical features, people, culture, economy, history, and efforts to enter the global market. (Rev: BL 8/01; SLJ 9/01) [958]

621

9831 Corona, Laurel. *Ukraine* (5–8). Series: Modern Nations of the World. 2001, Lucent LB $29.95 (978-1-56006-737-5). This well-illustrated introduction to the former Soviet republic presents material on the people, culture, economy, history, and physical features. (Rev: BL 6/1–15/01) [947]

9832 Corrigan, Jim. *Kazakhstan* (8–12). Series: The Growth and Influence of Islam in the Nations of Asia and Central Asia. 2005, Mason Crest LB $25.95 (978-1-59084-882-1). A well-illustrated look at Kazakhstan and the importance of Islam in the country's history, politics, economy, and foreign relations. (Rev: SLJ 9/05) [958]

9833 Gay, Kathlyn. *The Aftermath of the Russian Revolution* (8–12). Series: Aftermath of History. 2009, Lerner LB $38.60 (978-0-8225-9092-7). Gay outlines how the Bolshevik revolution and the establishment of communism in Russia would shape the future not only of that country's people, but of world politics as well. (Rev: SLJ 4/1/09)

9834 Gottfried, Ted. *The Road to Communism* (8–12). Illus. by Melanie Reim. 2002, Millbrook LB $28.90 (978-0-7613-2557-4). This first volume on the rise and fall of the Soviet Union traces in depth the developments that led to the establishment of a communist state. The second volume is titled *Stalinist Empire*. (Rev: BL 10/15/02; HBG 3/03; SLJ 11/02) [957]

9835 Harmon, Daniel E. *Kyrgyzstan* (8–12). Series: The Growth and Influence of Islam in the Nations of Asia and Central Asia. 2005, Mason Crest LB $25.95 (978-1-59084-883-8). A well-illustrated look at Kyrgyzstan and the importance of Islam in the country's history, politics, economy, and foreign relations. (Rev: SLJ 9/05)

9836 Kagda, Sakina. *Lithuania* (4–7). Series: Cultures of the World. 1997, Marshall Cavendish LB $37.07 (978-0-7614-0681-5). An introduction to Lithuania, with material on geography, history, government, culture, daily life, and festivals. (Rev: BL 8/97; SLJ 10/97) [947.93]

9837 Kollár, Daniel. *Slovakia* (4–7). Series: Looking at Europe. 2006, Oliver $22.95 (978-1-881508-49-6). This photo-filled introduction to Slovakia explores its geography, history, people, culture, cuisine, economy, transportation, tourism, and natural resources. (Rev: SLJ 12/06)

9838 Lugovskaya, Nina. *I Want to Live: The Diary of a Young Girl in Stalin's Russia* (8–11). Trans. by Andrew Bromfeld. 2007, Houghton Mifflin $17.00 (978-0-618-60575-0). This diary of a teenage girl living in a Soviet gulag is remarkable for its passages (in bold type) that were censored by police who seized it, and also for the fact that its author survived. (Rev: BL 4/15/07; SLJ 8/07) [946.0842]

9839 McCray, Thomas. *Russia and the Former Soviet Republics* (7–10). 2006, Chelsea House LB $30.00 (978-0-7910-8144-0). Examines many aspects of Russia including its geography, economy, history, politics, people, and culture with additional information on some of the surrounding countries that also belonged to the former Soviet Union. (Rev: BL 9/1/06; SLJ 9/06) [947]

9840 O'Neill, Joseph R. *The Bolshevik Revolution* (6–9). Series: Essential Events. 2009, ABDO LB $32.79 (978-1-60453-511-2). O'Neill examines the causes, key events, and aftermath of the Russian Revolution. (Rev: SLJ 6/1/09) [947]

9841 Otfinoski, Steven. *The Baltic Republics* (7–10). Series: Nations in Transition. 2004, Facts on File LB $40.00 (978-0-8160-5117-5). Introduces the Baltic republics of Estonia, Latvia, and Lithuania, and the geography, history, people, culture, religious beliefs, and economy of each. (Rev: SLJ 1/05) [947]

9842 Pang, Guek-Cheng. *Kazakhstan* (6–9). Illus. Series: Cultures of the World. 2011, Marshall Cavendish LB $29.95 (978-160870455-2). A revised edition of this volume covering Kazakhstan's geography, history, political system, economy, environment, people, and culture. (Rev: BL 6/1/11) [958.45]

9843 Pavlenkov, Victor, and Peter Pappas, eds. *Russia: Yesterday, Today, Tomorrow: Voice of the Young Generation* (8–12). 1997, FC-Izdat paper $12.95 (978-0-9637035-5-2). This is a collection of essays written by Russian high school students who reflect on the past, present, and future of their country. (Rev: BL 2/15/97) [947.08]

9844 Robbins, Gerald. *Azerbaijan* (8–12). Series: The Growth and Influence of Islam in the Nations of Asia and Central Asia. 2005, Mason Crest LB $25.95 (978-1-59084-878-4). A well-illustrated look at Azerbaijan and the importance of Islam in the country's history, politics, economy, and foreign relations. (Rev: SLJ 9/05) [947]

9845 Schemann, Serge. *When the Wall Came Down* (6–9). 2006, Kingfisher $15.95 (978-0-7534-5994-2). Primary sources, personal insights, and edited *New York Times* columns make this a useful account of the fall of the Berlin Wall and its impact on the whole Eastern Bloc. (Rev: BL 2/15/06; SLJ 7/06) [943]

9846 Sheehan, Patricia. *Moldova* (5–9). Series: Cultures of the World. 2000, Marshall Cavendish LB $37.07 (978-0-7614-0997-7). This book on the former Soviet republic that borders on the Ukraine covers such topics as culture, land, people, history, resources, and government. (Rev: HBG 10/00; SLJ 11/00) [947]

9847 Spilling, Michael. *Estonia* (7–10). Series: Cultures of the World. 1999, Marshall Cavendish LB $37.07 (978-0-7614-0951-9). An overview of this Baltic land that covers basic information and contemporary life and culture. (Rev: HBG 9/99; SLJ 7/99) [947]

9848 Streissguth, Thomas. *Life in Communist Russia* (6–10). Series: The Way People Live. 2001, Lucent LB $29.95 (978-1-56006-378-0). From the 1917 revolution through the collapse of the regime in the 1980s, the history of Communist Russia is told with emphasis on social and economic conditions and everyday life. (Rev: BL 6/1–15/01; SLJ 7/01) [947]

9849 Streissguth, Thomas, ed. *The Rise of the Soviet Union* (7–12). Series: Turning Points in World History. 2002, Gale LB $24.95 (978-0-7377-0928-5). Following an overview of Russian and Soviet history, each of the essays in this anthology explores a different aspect of the rise of Communism and the creation of the Soviet Union. (Rev: BL 6/1–15/02; SLJ 6/02) [947]

9850 Taylor, Peter Lane, and Christos Nicola. *The Secret of Priest's Grotto* (7–10). 2007, Kar-Ben $18.95 (978-1-58013-260-2); paper $8.95 (978-1-58013-261-9). The true story of how 38 members of three Ukrainian Jewish families survived nearly a year hiding from the Nazis in a cave; photographs add impact. Sidney Taylor Book Honor 2008. (Rev: BL 3/1/07; HB 7–8/07; LMC 10/07; SLJ 4/07) [940.53]

9851 Veceric, Danica. *Slovenia* (4–7). Series: Looking at Europe. 2006, Oliver $22.95 (978-1-881508-74-8). A tour of Slovenia, examining the country's geography, history, people, culture, cuisine, economy, transportation, tourism, and natural resources. (Rev: SLJ 12/06)

9852 Yomtov, Nel. *Russia* (6–9). Illus. Series: Enchantment of the World. 2012, Scholastic LB $40 (978-053127545-0). An attractive revision of the guide to the land and people of Russia. (Rev: BL 12/1/12; SLJ 4/13) [947]

Scandinavia, Iceland, and Greenland

9853 Berger, Melvin, and Gilda Berger. *The Real Vikings: Craftsmen, Traders, and Fearsome Raiders* (4–8). 2003, National Geographic $18.95 (978-0-7922-5132-3). A highly illustrated introduction to the Vikings and their world, with information on their political and social ideals — including democracy — as well as their more fearsome and acquisitive traits. (Rev: BL 12/1/03; HBG 4/04; SLJ 1/04) [948]

9854 Corona, Laurel. *Norway* (5–8). Series: Modern Nations of the World. 2000, Lucent LB $29.95 (978-1-56006-647-7). Norway is introduced with coverage of history, geography, and culture plus material on everyday modern life. (Rev: BL 3/1/01) [948.1]

9855 *Denmark in Pictures* (5–8). Series: Visual Geography. 1997, Lerner LB $25.55 (978-0-8225-1880-8). In photographs, maps, charts, and concise text, the land of Denmark and its people are introduced. (Rev: BL 4/1/91; SLJ 7/91) [948]

9856 Gan, Delice. *Sweden* (4–7). Series: Cultures of the World. 1992, Marshall Cavendish LB $35.64 (978-1-85435-452-5). This introduction to Sweden gives special coverage of the people and their lifestyles. (Rev: BL 10/15/92) [948.5]

9857 Gunderson, Jessica. *Vikings* (5–8). Illus. Series: Fearsome Fighters. 2012, Creative Education $24.95 (978-160818185-8). With many illustrations, maps, and primary documents, this volume looks at the Vikings and their society, weapons, fighting techniques, key figures, and so forth. (Rev: BL 11/1/12; LMC 5–6/13; SLJ 12/12) [948]

9858 *Iceland in Pictures* (5–8). Series: Visual Geography. 1996, Lerner LB $25.55 (978-0-8225-1892-1). The history, government, people, and economy of the northern republic of Iceland are covered in words and pictures. (Rev: BL 8/91) [949.12]

9859 Lassieur, Allison. *The Vikings* (6–9). Series: Lost Civilizations. 2001, Lucent LB $29.95 (978-1-56006-816-7). Using archaeological evidence, this account recreates the history and culture of the Vikings from their glory days to their ultimate demise. (Rev: BL 8/1/01) [948]

9860 Lee, Tan Chung. *Finland* (4–7). Series: Cultures of the World. 1996, Marshall Cavendish LB $37.07 (978-0-7614-0280-0). The small country of Finland with its thousands of lakes is introduced, with emphasis on the people and how they live. (Rev: BL 8/96; SLJ 7/96) [984.97]

9861 Schaffer, David. *Viking Conquests* (7–10). Series: World History. 2002, Gale LB $32.45 (978-1-56006-322-3). Though the Vikings were known mainly for their raids and pillaging, this account also gives details of their lasting contributions to the world. (Rev: BL 8/02) [948]

9862 *Sweden in Pictures* (5–8). Series: Visual Geography. 1993, Lerner LB $21.27 (978-0-8225-1872-3). Gives the background geography and history of Sweden, along with contemporary material. (Rev: BL 12/1/90) [948.5]

9863 Wilcox, Jonathan. *Iceland* (4–7). Series: Cultures of the World. 1996, Marshall Cavendish LB $37.07 (978-0-7614-0279-4). The history, geography, people, and culture of this remote island republic are introduced, with many color photographs. (Rev: SLJ 7/96) [949.12]

Spain and Portugal

9864 Anderson, Wayne. *The ETA: Spain's Basque Terrorists* (4–8). Series: Inside the World's Most Infamous Terrorist Organizations. 2003, Rosen LB $27.95 (978-0-8239-3818-6). This is the history and present status of the violent organization committed to creating an ethnic homeland separate from Spain. (Rev: BL 10/15/03; SLJ 9/03) [946]

9865 Croy, Anita. *Spain* (4–8). Series: Countries of the World. 2010, National Geographic LB $27.90 (978-1-4263-0633-4). In addition to giving an overview of the country's geography, people, culture, history, government, economy, and climate, this volume includes special features such as "The Wild West — in Spain!" and "The Real El Cid." (Rev: BL 4/1/10; SLJ 4/10) [946]

9866 Heale, Jay. *Portugal* (5–8). Series: Cultures of the World. 1995, Marshall Cavendish LB $37.07 (978-0-7614-0169-8). Present-day conditions in Portugal are emphasized in this account, which also covers history, geography, and culture. (Rev: SLJ 11/95) [914.9]

9867 Kohen, Elizabeth. *Spain* (4–7). Series: Cultures of the World. 1992, Marshall Cavendish LB $35.64 (978-1-85435-451-8). With text, photographs, maps, and fact sheets, the land and people of Spain are introduced. (Rev: BL 10/15/92) [946]

9868 Melchiore, Susan McCarthy. *The Spanish Inquisition* (6–8). Series: Great Disasters. 2001, Chelsea LB $32.00 (978-0-7910-6327-9). The story of this institution established by Spanish monarchs in 1478, and its ruthless treatment of Jews and Muslims as well as Christians suspected of heresy. (Rev: BL 6/1–15/02; HBG 10/02; SLJ 6/02) [946]

9869 *Portugal in Pictures* (5–8). Series: Visual Geography. 1996, Lerner LB $25.55 (978-0-8225-1886-0). Current conditions and problems in Portugal are introduced along with the standard material on history, geography, and social conditions. (Rev: BL 12/15/91) [946.9]

9870 Skog, Jason. *Teens in Spain* (7–12). Series: Global Connections. 2006, Compass Point LB $31.93 (978-0-7565-2446-3). Introduces Spanish teens and their schools, family life, hobbies, sports, and so forth, covering both traditional aspects and those that have arrived with new technology and new immigration. (Rev: SLJ 5/07) [305.235]

Middle East

General and Miscellaneous

9871 Broyles, Matthew. *The Six-Day War* (5–9). Series: War and Conflict in the Middle East. 2004, Rosen LB $27.95 (978-0-8239-4549-8). A well-organized, balanced account of the 1973 war between Israel and its Arab neighbors Egypt, Jordan, and Syria. (Rev: BL 11/1/04; SLJ 1/05)

9872 Einfeld, Jann, ed. *Can Democracy Succeed in the Middle East?* (6–12). Series: At Issue. 2006, Gale LB $28.70 (978-0-7377-3393-8). The title question and many others (can democracy be imposed?) are addressed in this collection of 12 essays. (Rev: SLJ 3/07)

9873 Fiscus, James W. *The Suez Crisis* (5–9). Series: War and Conflict in the Middle East. 2004, Rosen LB $27.95 (978-0-8239-4550-4). Examines the 1956 conflict over control of the canal, involving Egypt, Israel, Britain, and France. (Rev: BL 11/1/04)

9874 Hampton, Wilborn. *War in the Middle East: A Reporter's Story: Black September and the Yom Kippur War* (6–9). 2007, Candlewick $19.99 (978-0-7636-2493-4). Reporter Hampton describes the events of the 1970 Jordanian "Black September" civil conflict and of the 1973 Yom Kippur War, giving a personal perspective that will interest students of journalism in particular. (Rev: BL 8/07; LMC 1/08; SLJ 8/07) [956.04]

9875 January, Brendan. *The Arab Conquests of the Middle East* (8–11). Series: Pivotal Moments in History. 2009, Lerner LB $38.60 (978-0-8225-8744-6). This volume traces the history of the Arab conquest of the Middle East and parts of Europe, and how the new religion of Islam impacted society in the region. (Rev: SLJ 4/1/09) [956.013]

9876 Senker, Cath. *The Arab-Israeli Conflict* (5–8). Series: Questioning History. 2004, Smart Apple Media LB $28.50 (978-1-58340-441-6). A clear and balanced discussion of the history and current status of relations between Arabs and Israelis, with a timeline, glossary, and detailed index. (Rev: SLJ 2/05) [956.04]

9877 Steele, Philip. *Middle East* (4–7). Series: Kingfisher Knowledge. 2006, Kingfisher LB $12.95 (978-0-7534-5984-3). Traces the history of the region — extending from Eastern Mediterranean countries into Iraq, Iran, and Afghanistan — as well as its geography, peoples, cultures, religions, economies, and politics. (Rev: SLJ 12/06) [956]

9878 Worth, Richard. *The Arab-Israeli Conflict* (7–12). Series: Open for Debate. 2006, Benchmark LB $27.95 (978-0-7614-2295-2). Worth gives a balanced overview of this long-running conflict, with historical information, accounts of the key areas of dispute, and explanations of each side's beliefs and goals. (Rev: SLJ 2/07)

Egypt

9879 Barghusen, Joan. *Daily Life in Ancient and Modern Cairo* (6–9). Series: Cities Through Time. 2001, Lerner LB $25.26 (978-0-8225-3221-7). Cairo's evolution from earliest times to today is presented in richly illustrated double-page spreads with information on political, social, and religious life as well as women's issues, with a timeline and quotations. (Rev: BL 4/15/01; HBG 10/01; SLJ 7/01) [962.16]

9880 Bowden, Rob, and Roy Maconachie. *Cairo* (4–7). Series: Great Cities of the World. 2005, World Almanac LB $31.00 (978-0-8368-5035-2). An informative and appealing overview of one of the world's most famous cities, with material on its history, its economy, and what it's like to live there. (Rev: BL 4/15/04)

9881 Orr, Tamra. *Egyptian Islamic Jihad* (4–8). Series: Inside the World's Most Infamous Terrorist Organizations. 2003, Rosen LB $27.95 (978-0-8239-3819-3). Dedicated to the overthrow of the secular Egyptian government, this terrorist organization has links to the Al Qaeda terrorist network. (Rev: BL 10/15/03) [962]

9882 Weitzman, David. *Pharaoh's Boat* (4–7). Illus. by author. 2009, Houghton $17.00 (978-0-547-05341-7). Weitzman recounts the fascinating discovery in 1954 of a boat in the Great Pyramid of Giza, explains its origins (it was built as a vehicle to take the Pharaoh Cheops to the afterlife), and details its restoration. ALA Notable Books 2010. (Rev: BCCB 9/09; BL 5/15/09*; HB 5/09; SLJ 4/09*) [932]

9883 Zuehlke, Jeffrey. *Egypt in Pictures. Rev. ed.* (4–8). Series: Visual Geography. 2002, Lerner LB $27.93 (978-0-8225-0367-5). Covers Egypt's geography, history, people, economy, and culture with maps, photographs, and illustrations. (Rev: SLJ 3/03) [962]

Israel and Palestine

9884 Corona, Laurel. *Israel* (6–9). Series: Modern Nations of the World. 2003, Gale $29.95 (978-1-59018-115-7). A thorough overview of the geography, history, and people of the land of Israel, with informative and interesting sidebars on historical and contemporary topics. (Rev: BL 4/15/03; SLJ 8/03) [956.94]

9885 Feinstein, Steve. *Israel in Pictures* (5–8). 1992, Lerner LB $25.55 (978-0-8225-1833-4). An overview of geography, climate, wildlife, and vegetation with photographs, maps, and charts. (Rev: BL 8/88) [956.9405]

9886 Frank, Mitch. *Understanding the Holy Land: Answering Questions About the Israeli-Palestinian Conflict* (6–9). 2005, Viking $17.99 (978-0-670-06032-0). In easy-to-read question-and-answer format, author Mitch Frank provides an excellent introduction to the history of the Holy Land and the diverse factors involved in the continuing conflict between Israelis and Palestinians. (Rev: BL 3/1/05*; SLJ 3/05; VOYA 4/05) [956.9405]

9887 Goodman, Michael E. *The Mossad and Other Israeli Spies* (6–9). Illus. Series: Spies Around the World. 2012, Creative Education $24.95 (978-160818228-2). Explores the activities of the Mossad, founded in 1951, and other Israeli spies, with information about training, equipment, and accomplishments. (Rev: BL 10/1/12*; LMC 5–6/13) [327.125694]

9888 Greenfeld, Howard. *A Promise Fulfilled: Theodor Herzl, Chaim Weizmann, David Ben-Gurion, and the Creation of the State of Israel* (7–10). 2005, Greenwillow LB $19.89 (978-0-06-051505-8). This story of the creation of the state of Israel focuses on the contributions of three remarkable and very different men. (Rev: BL 4/15/05; SLJ 7/05) [320.54]

9889 Hayhurst, Chris. *Israel's War of Independence* (5–9). Series: War and Conflict in the Middle East. 2004, Rosen LB $27.95 (978-0-8239-4548-1). An even-handed overview of Israel's struggle for independence and the ensuing years of violence, with statistics, maps, photographs, and profiles of leaders. (Rev: BL 11/1/04; SLJ 1/05) [956.04]

9890 Katz, Samuel M. *Jerusalem or Death: Palestinian Terrorism* (7–12). Series: Terrorist Dossiers. 2003, Lerner LB $26.60 (978-0-8225-4033-5). This book focuses on the terrorist groups that have been active in Israel and the West Bank. (Rev: BL 3/15/04; HBG 4/04; SLJ 3/04; VOYA 4/04) [956.9]

9891 Marshood, Nabil. *Palestinian Teenage Refugees and Immigrants Speak Out* (7–12). Series: Teenage Refugees Speak Out. 1997, Rosen LB $27.95 (978-0-8239-2442-4). The exodus of Palestinians, many to the United States, and their reasons for leaving their homes are shown through the stories of several teenage immigrants. (Rev: BL 12/15/97) [956.04]

9892 Saul, Laya. *We Visit Israel* (4–8). Illus. Series: Your Land and My Land: The Middle East. 2011, Mitchell Lane LB $33.95 (978-158415957-5). With illustrations, photographs, maps, reproductions, a recipe, a craft project, and a timeline, this is a useful overview of the history and geography of Israel. (Rev: BL 2/1/12) [956.94]

9893 Scharfstein, Sol. *Understanding Israel* (5–7). 1994, KTAV paper $14.95 (978-0-88125-428-0). A heavily illustrated introduction to Israel that covers history, religion, government, culture, and current concerns. (Rev: SLJ 10/94) [956.94]

9894 Silverman, Maida. *Israel: The Founding of a Modern Nation* (4–7). 1998, Dial LB $15.00 (978-0-8034-2136-3). This account covers 3,000 years of Jewish history, with emphasis on recent centuries, and includes a timeline showing Israel's history from 1948 to 1998. (Rev: BL 5/1/98) [956.94]

9895 Slavicek, Louise Chipley. *The Establishment of the State of Israel* (8–12). Illus. 2011, Chelsea House LB $35 (978-160413917-4). With photographs, timelines, and maps, this volume explains why and how the state of Israel was established. **e** (Rev: BL 2/15/12) [956.74]

9896 Slavik, Diane. *Daily Life in Ancient and Modern Jerusalem* (6–9). Series: Cities Through Time. 2000, Lerner $25.26 (978-0-8225-3218-7). Slavik traces the history of Jerusalem from the earliest times, exploring what life was like for the inhabitants of each period. (Rev: BL 3/1/01; HBG 10/01; SLJ 9/01) [956.94]

9897 Wingate, Katherine. *The Intifadas* (5–9). Series: War and Conflict in the Middle East. 2004, Rosen LB $27.95 (978-0-8239-4546-7). An even-handed overview of the events leading up to the Palestinian uprisings, with statistics, maps, photographs, and profiles of leaders. (Rev: BL 11/1/04) [956.95]

Other Middle East Countries

9898 Augustin, Byron, and Jake Kubena. *Iraq* (5–8). Illus. Series: Enchantment of the World. 2006, Children's Pr. LB $37.00 (978-0-516-24852-3). An updated version of a 1998 book on the country, with additional information on ethnic groups, the environment, and continuing violence. (Rev: SLJ 7/06)

9899 Bodnarchuk, Kari. *Kurdistan: Region Under Siege* (7–10). Series: World in Conflict. 2000, Lerner LB $25.26 (978-0-8225-3556-0). This work gives an unbiased historical picture of this mountainous region of the Middle East and tells of the frequent upheavals that mark its past and present. (Rev: BL 6/1–15/00; HBG 3/01; SLJ 12/00) [955]

9900 Boueri, Marijean, and Jill Boutros. *Lebanon A to Z: A Middle Eastern Mosaic* (4–8). Illus. by Tatiana Sabbagh. 2006, Publishing Works $25.00 (978-0-9744803-4-3). Eleven-year-old Kareem takes readers on a tour through the country's present and past, with an emphasis on cultural traditions and Lebanon's people. (Rev: SLJ 7/06)

9901 Broberg, Catherine. *Saudi Arabia in Pictures* (6–10). Series: Visual Geography. 2002, Lerner LB $27.93 (978-0-8225-1958-4). Full-color photographs complement information on the country's geography, history, government, economy, people, and culture. (Rev: BL 10/15/02; HBG 3/03) [953.8]

9902 Byers, Ann. *Lebanon's Hezbollah* (4–8). Series: Inside the World's Most Infamous Terrorist Organizations. 2003, Rosen LB $27.95 (978-0-8239-3821-6). This is the story of the Lebanese terrorist organization dedicated to installing a conservative Islamic government in Lebanon and to the destruction of Israel. (Rev: BL 10/15/03; SLJ 9/03) [956.92]

9903 Cartlidge, Cherese. *Iran* (5–8). Series: Modern Nations of the World. 2002, Gale LB $29.95 (978-1-56006-971-3). This colorful account gives a comprehensive overview of Iran, including history, geography, and culture. (Rev: BL 12/15/02; SLJ 1/03) [955]

9904 Clark, Charles. *Iran* (7–12). Series: Nations in Transition. 2002, Gale LB $32.45 (978-0-7377-1096-0). Iran's internal political upheavals and difficult relationship with the rest of the world are the focus of this thorough and concise volume that includes biographical and cultural features. (Rev: SLJ 1/03) [955]

9905 Eboch, Chris. *Turkey* (5–9). Series: Modern Nations of the World. 2003, Gale LB $29.95 (978-1-59018-122-5). This account presents a broad spectrum of material about Turkey including history, geography, and culture. (Rev: BL 11/15/03; SLJ 6/03) [961]

9906 Gibson, Karen Bush. *Ancient Babylon* (5–8). Illus. Series: Explore Ancient Worlds. 2012, Mitchell Lane LB $29.95 (978-161228278-7). A description of our knowledge of the ancient city, its hanging gardens,

systems of writing and justice, with information on Alexander the Great and two crafts (making a sundial and barley bread). (Rev: BL 10/1/12) [935]

9907 Goodwin, William. *Saudi Arabia* (5–8). Series: Modern Nations of the World. 2001, Lucent LB $29.95 (978-1-56006-763-4). The land ruled by the Saud dynasty is presented with details on history, government, geography, resources, and world importance. (Rev: BL 6/1–15/01) [953.8]

9908 Graham, Amy. *Iran in the News: Past, Present, and Future* (5–8). Illus. Series: Middle East Nations in the News. 2006, Enslow LB $33.27 (978-1-59845-022-4). History, culture, people, and current political issues are all covered in this readable overview of Iran that includes links to Web sites that extend the text. (Rev: BL 4/1/06; SLJ 5/06) [955]

9909 Gray, Leon. *Iran* (4–8). Series: Countries of the World. 2008, National Geographic LB $27.90 (978-1-4263-0200-8). Useful for researchers, this book provides basic information about the country as well as data and additional facts presented in sidebars and other features. (Rev: BL 4/15/08) [955.22]

9910 Hassig, Susan M. *Iraq* (4–7). Series: Cultures of the World. 1992, Marshall Cavendish LB $35.64 (978-1-85435-533-1). This introduction stresses the lifestyles of the people, their religion, and culture. (Rev: BL 1/1/93) [956.7]

9911 Hestler, Anna. *Yemen* (5–8). Series: Cultures of the World. 1999, Marshall Cavendish LB $37.07 (978-0-7614-0956-4). A fine introduction to this country on the Gulf of Aden with good background information and an overview of modern life. (Rev: HBG 10/99; SLJ 10/99) [956]

9912 *Iran in Pictures* (5–8). Series: Visual Geography. 1992, Lerner LB $21.27 (978-0-8225-1848-8). Basic coverage on this Middle Eastern land and its people. (Rev: BL 5/1/89) [955]

9913 Isiorho, Solomon A. *Kuwait* (7–12). Series: Modern World Nations. 2002, Chelsea LB $30.00 (978-0-7910-6781-9). An overview of the history, geography, people, politics, and religion of Kuwait, with discussion of the importance of Islam. Also use *Bahrain* (2002). (Rev: SLJ 2/03) [953.67]

9914 Janin, Hunt. *Saudi Arabia* (4–7). Series: Cultures of the World. 1992, Marshall Cavendish LB $35.64 (978-1-85435-532-4). The history, geography, economy, language, and people are discussed in this book about Saudi Arabia. (Rev: BL 1/1/93) [953.8]

9915 *Jordan in Pictures* (5–8). 1992, Lerner LB $25.55 (978-0-8225-1834-1). Young readers learn what life is like in this Middle East land. (Rev: BL 2/1/89; SLJ 2/89) [956.9504]

9916 LaRoche, Amelia. *We Visit Turkey* (4–8). Illus. Series: Your Land and My Land: The Middle East. 2011,

Mitchell Lane LB $33.95 (978-158415956-8). With illustrations, photographs, maps, reproductions, a recipe, a craft project, and a timeline, this is a useful overview of the history and geography of Turkey. (Rev: BL 2/1/12) [956.1]

9917 *Lebanon in Pictures* (5–8). Series: Visual Geography. 1992, Lerner LB $25.55 (978-0-8225-1832-7). A country torn apart by strife is the focus of this edition. (Rev: BL 2/1/89) [956.9204]

9918 Levy, Janey. *Iran and the Shia* (8–12). Series: Understanding Iran. 2010, Rosen LB $30.60 (978-1-4358-5282-2). Levy discusses the history of the Shia community in Iran and its current importance in the political and daily life of the nation. (Rev: LMC 1–2/10; SLJ 12/09) [955.05]

9919 Marcovitz, Hal. *Jordan* (7–12). Series: Creation of the Modern Middle East. 2002, Chelsea LB $35.00 (978-0-7910-6507-5). This volume on the history of Jordan, its importance in the Middle East, and its relations with the United States will be useful for report writers. Also use *Syria*, *Oman*, and *The Kurds* (all 2002). (Rev: LMC 4–5/03; SLJ 2/03) [956.9504]

9920 Miller, Debra A. *Iraq* (6–12). Series: The World's Hot Spots. 2004, Gale LB $31.20 (978-0-7377-1813-3); paper $23.70 (978-0-7377-1814-0). Reprinted essays, speeches, and news articles provide a fascinating overview of Iraq's history and the factors that precipitated the American-led invasion in 2003. (Rev: BL 6/1–15/04; SLJ 8/04) [956.704]

9921 Rajendra, Vijeya, and Gisela Kaplan. *Iran* (4–7). Series: Cultures of the World. 1992, Marshall Cavendish LB $35.64 (978-1-85435-534-8). As well as standard introductory information about Iran, this book tells about how the people live and what the country's present problems are. (Rev: BL 1/1/93) [955]

9922 Riverbend. *Baghdad Burning II: More Girl Blog from Iraq* (8–12). 2006, Feminist paper $14.95 (978-1-55861-529-8). This second volume of compiled blogs describes the continuing shortages of water, power, and food; religious and political violence at the hands of Iraqi security forces; repression; and the general chaos that has reigned during the U.S. occupation. (Rev: BL 11/1/06) [956.7044]

9923 Riverbend. *Baghdad Burning: Girl Blog from Iraq* (8–12). 2005, Feminist paper $14.95 (978-1-55861-489-5). A young Iraqi blogger paints a grim picture of life in her country after the 2003 invasion of U.S. and allied forces. (Rev: BL 4/1/05) [956.7]

9924 Sheehan, Sean. *Lebanon* (5–10). Series: Cultures of the World. 1996, Marshall Cavendish LB $37.07 (978-0-7614-0283-1). A lively, well-written introduction to this war-ravaged country with details on history, economy, culture, religion and foods, including a recipe for a typical dish. (Rev: SLJ 6/97) [569.2]

9925 South, Coleman. *Jordan* (5–10). Series: Cultures of the World. 1996, Marshall Cavendish LB $37.07 (978-0-7614-0287-9). Everyday life in Jordan is the focus of this book that also covers history, religion, culture, geography, festivals, and foods; a single recipe is included. (Rev: SLJ 6/97) [569.5]

9926 Spencer, William. *Iraq: Old Land, New Nation in Conflict* (7–12). 2000, Twenty-First Century LB $23.90 (978-0-7613-1356-4). This account traces the history of Iraq from its Mesopotamian origins to Saddam Hussein's rule prior to the American invasion. (Rev: BL 11/15/00; HBG 3/01; SLJ 12/00) [956.7]

9927 Wilkes, Sybella. *Out of Iraq: Refugees' Stories in Words, Paintings and Music* (5–9). Illus. 2010, Evans Brothers $17.99 (978-0-237-53930-6). A variety of compelling interviews conducted with artists, journalists, teachers, children, and young adults show a moving picture of the humanitarian implications of the 2003 invasion of Iraq. (Rev: BL 10/15/10; SLJ 11/1/10) [305.9]

9928 Wills, Karen. *Jordan* (5–8). Series: Modern Nations of the World. 2001, Lucent LB $29.95 (978-1-56006-822-8). A good profile of Jordan is presented, with basic background material and information on present conditions and the people today. (Rev: BL 6/1–15/01) [956.95]

9929 *Yemen in Pictures* (5–8). Series: Visual Geography. 1993, Lerner LB $25.55 (978-0-8225-1911-9). In introduction to this Muslim republic on the Gulf of Aden, with material on its economic and social conditions. (Rev: BL 12/1/93; SLJ 12/93) [953.3]

North and South America (excluding the United States)

General and Miscellaneous

9930 Aronson, Marc, and John W. Glenn. *The World Made New: Why the Age of Exploration Happened and How It Changed the World* (5–8). 2007, National Geographic $17.95 (978-0-7922-6454-5). This is an enlightening and well-illustrated survey of world exploration — in particular of European expeditions to the Western Hemisphere in the 15th and 16th centuries — looking at key figures and at the lasting consequences for the people, plants, and animals. (Rev: BL 9/15/07; SLJ 8/07)

9931 Gunderson, Jessica. *Conquistadors* (5–8). Illus. Series: Fearsome Fighters. 2012, Creative Education $24.95 (978-160818183-4). With many illustrations, maps, and primary documents, this volume looks at the Spanish colonists who invaded the Americas and their society, weapons, fighting techniques, key figures, and so forth. (Rev: BL 11/1/12; LMC 5–6/13; SLJ 12/12) [970.01]

9932 Haas, Robert B. *Through the Eyes of the Condor: An Aerial Vision of Latin America* (8–12). 2007, National Geographic $50.00 (978-1-4262-0132-5). Haas's camera takes a bird's-eye view of Central and South America, showing the diversity of the landscape in vast panoramas. (Rev: BL 9/15/07) [779.36098]

9933 Long, Cathryn J. *Ancient America* (7–10). Series: World History. 2002, Gale LB $32.45 (978-1-56006-889-1). The story of the hunter-gatherers, agriculturalists, and city dwellers of North and South America from the arrival of the first humans in America to Columbus. (Rev: BL 8/02) [970]

9934 Mann, Charles C. *Before Columbus: The Americas of 1491* (5–8). 2009, Simon & Schuster $24.99 (978-1-4169-4900-8). This clearly written and designed history of pre-Columbian America includes brightly colored illustrations and sidebars that illuminate what for many is a misunderstood period of history. (Rev: BL 9/1/09*; LMC 11–12/09; SLJ 9/09*) [970.01]

9935 Murphy, Jim. *Gone a-Whaling: The Lure of the Sea and the Hunt for the Great Whale* (7–12). 1998, Clarion $18.00 (978-0-395-69847-1). Diary entries are used to describe American whale hunting and life aboard whaling vessels from the 19th century to the present. (Rev: BCCB 4/98; BL 3/15/98; HB 5–6/98; SLJ 5/98; VOYA 12/98) [306.3]

9936 O'Neill, Thomas. *Lakes, Peaks, and Prairies: Discovering the United States-Canadian Border* (7–12). 1984, National Geographic LB $12.95 (978-0-87044-483-8). A trip across the continent that reveals much about the diversity of these regions. [973]

9937 Patent, Dorothy Hinshaw. *Treasures of the Spanish Main* (6–10). Series: Frozen in Time. 1999, Marshall Cavendish LB $28.50 (978-0-7614-0786-7). This lavishly illustrated book describes the sinking of Spanish galleons near the Florida Keys in the 1600s and how their excavation has brought us amazing information about life and culture in the New World at that time. (Rev: BL 2/15/00; HBG 10/00; SLJ 3/00) [930]

9938 Smith, Tom. *Discovery of the Americas 1492–1800. Rev. ed.* (6–9). Series: Discovery and Exploration. 2010, Chelsea House LB $35 (978-1-60413-195-6). This updated volume covers European exploration of the New World with clear, informative text plus maps, illustrations, and excerpts from primary sources. (Rev: LMC 8–9/10) [973]

9939 Smith, Tom. *Discovery of the Americas, 1492-1800* (6–12). Series: Discovery and Exploration. 2005, Facts on File $40.00 (978-0-8160-5262-2). European exploration of the New World is the focus of this volume that contains clear, informative text plus maps, illustrations, and excerpts from primary sources. (Rev: SLJ 8/05) [973]

9940 Woods, Michael, and Mary B. Woods. *Seven Natural Wonders of Central and South America* (5–8). Illus. 2009, Twenty-First Century LB $33.26 (978-0-8225-9070-5). Angel Falls, the Amazon River, the Atacama Desert, the Galápagos Islands, the Montecristo Cloud Forest, Poás Volcano, and the Andes Mountains are the seven wonders featured in this attractive volume. (Rev: BL 4/1/09; LMC 10/09*; SLJ 5/09) [508.8]

9941 Wyatt, Valerie. *Who Discovered America?* (4–7). Illus. by Howie Woo. 2008, Kids Can $17.95 (978-1-55453-128-8); paper $8.95 (978-1-55453-129-5). This large-format book examines who arrived on this continent first, introducing the possible candidates and providing lots of interesting information on archaeological finds and how researchers approach this question. (Rev: BL 10/1/08; SLJ 2/09) [970.01]

North America

GENERAL AND MISCELLANEOUS

9942 Woods, Michael, and Mary B. Woods. *Seven Natural Wonders of North America* (5–8). Illus. 2009, Twenty-First Century LB $33.26 (978-0-8225-9069-9). Dinosaur Provincial Park, Pacific Rim National Park, the redwood forests, Niagara Falls, the Grand Canyon, Yellowstone National Park, and the Paricutín Volcano are the seven wonders featured in this attractive volume. (Rev: BL 4/1/09; LMC 10/09*; SLJ 5/09) [917]

CANADA

9943 Beattie, Owen, and John Geiger. *Buried in Ice: The Mystery of a Lost Arctic Expedition* (4–7). Illus. by Janet Wilson. Series: Time Quest. 1993, Scholastic paper $6.95 (978-0-590-43849-0). The story of Sir John Franklin's unsuccessful 1845 expedition from England to find the Northwest Passage. (Rev: BCCB 3/92; BL 4/1/92; SLJ 4/92*) [919.804]

9944 Braun, Eric. *Canada in Pictures. Rev. ed.* (5–9). Series: Visual Geography. 2003, Lerner LB $27.93 (978-0-8225-4679-5). An informative and interesting overview of Canada's history, geography, government, economy, and people suitable for both research and browsing. (Rev: HBG 10/03; SLJ 7/03) [971.064]

9945 Campbell, Marjorie Wilkins. *The Nor'westers: The Fight for the Fur Trade* (6–12). 2003, Fitzhenry & Whiteside paper $12.95 (978-1-894004-97-8). An absorbing account of the Canadian fur trade in the 19th century, with details of company politics and relations between traders and Native Americans. (Rev: BL 4/1/03) [380.1]

9946 Cooper, John. *Season of Rage: Racial Conflict in a Small Town* (6–9). 2005, Tundra paper $9.95 (978-0-88776-700-5). The arresting story of the fight to win equal treatment for blacks in the small town of Dresden, Ontario, in the 1950s. (Rev: BL 2/1/05; SLJ 7/05; VOYA 4/06) [323.1196]

9947 Cooper, Michael L. *Klondike Fever: The Famous Gold Rush of 1898* (5–8). 1990, Houghton Mifflin paper $6.95 (978-0-395-54784-7). The events that turned a remote part of the Yukon into a three-ring circus of gold-hungry prospectors. (Rev: BCCB 1/90; BL 11/15/89; HB 1–2/90) [971.9]

9948 *Destination Vancouver* (6–9). Series: Port Cities of North America. 1998, Lerner LB $23.93 (978-0-8225-2787-9). A small volume that is full of information about Vancouver, its history, economy, and details about materials and goods that are shipped in and out of this port city. (Rev: HBG 9/98; SLJ 8/98) [971]

9949 Garrington, Sally. *Canada* (7–10). Series: Countries of the World. 2005, Facts on File LB $30.00 (978-0-8160-6009-2). History, geography, culture, government, and economy are all covered in this attractive overview of Canada. (Rev: SLJ 1/06) [971]

9950 Hughes, Susan. *Coming to Canada: Building a Life in a New Land* (6–9). Series: Wow Canada! 2005, Maple Tree $18.95 (978-1-897066-46-1). From the first arrivals thousands of years ago to today's diverse immigrants, this is a fascinating overview of Canadian history that does not whitewash unhappy episodes. (Rev: BL 8/05; SLJ 11/05*) [971.004]

9951 Kizilos, Peter. *Quebec: Province Divided* (7–10). Series: World in Conflict. 2000, Lerner LB $25.26 (978-0-8225-3562-1). The history of the French Canadian province and the separatist movement there. (Rev: BL 10/15/2000; HBG 4/00; VOYA 8/01) [971]

9952 Pang, Guek-Cheng. *Canada. 2nd ed.* (5–9). Series: Cultures of the World. 2004, Benchmark LB $37.07 (978-0-7614-1788-0). History, geography, and culture are all covered in this useful volume that attempts to impart a comprehensive understanding of life in all parts of Canada. (Rev: SLJ 2/05) [971]

9953 Renaud, Anne. *Pier 21: Stories from Near and Far* (4–7). Illus. by Aries Cheung. Series: Canadian Immigration. 2008, Lobster $16.95 (978-1-897073-70-4). This book is a collection of documents, memories, photographs, and illustrations relating to the site on Halifax Harbor where thousands of immigrants to Canada (in the years 1928 to 1971) started their new lives. (Rev: BL 4/15/08) [325.71]

9954 Walker, Sally M. *Blizzard of Glass: The Halifax Explosion of 1917* (5–8). Illus. 2011, Henry Holt $18.99 (978-0-8050-8945-5). With many archival photographs and compelling narrative, this book tells the story of the explosion of a munitions ship in Halifax harbor in Canada in 1917 following a collision with another vessel; almost 2,000 people were killed. ALA Notable Books 2012. (Rev: BL 11/1/11; SLJ 10/1/11) [971.6]

CENTRAL AMERICA

9955 Freedman, Russell. *In the Days of the Vaqueros: America's First True Cowboys* (5–9). 2001, Clarion $18.00 (978-0-395-96788-1). Vivid artwork complements this history of the earliest cowboys, the Central American vaqueros who first rode the range in the late 15th century. (Rev: BL 11/15/01*; HB 1–2/02; HBG 3/02; SLJ 9/01) [636.2]

9956 Haverstock, Nathan A. *Nicaragua in Pictures* (5–8). 1993, Lerner LB $25.55 (978-0-8225-1817-4). A visit to this controversial country is highlighted by color photographs and clear text. (Rev: BL 10/15/87) [972.85]

9957 *Honduras in Pictures* (4–7). Series: Visual Geography. 1994, Lerner LB $25.55 (978-0-8225-1804-4). Chapters focus on history, culture, education, people, geography, and lifestyles. (Rev: BL 8/87)

9958 Kallen, Stuart A. *The Aftermath of the Sandinista Revolution* (8–12). Series: Aftermath of History. 2009, Lerner LB $38.60 (978-0-8225-9091-0). Kallen outlines how the overthrow of the Nicaraguan government by the Sandinistas in 1979 had an international impact as well as a domestic one, spreading new fears about Communism. (Rev: SLJ 4/1/09) [972.8]

9959 McGaffey, Leta. *Honduras* (5–9). Series: Cultures of the World. 1999, Marshall Cavendish LB $37.07 (978-0-7614-0955-7). After background material on the history and geography of Honduras, this book focuses on modern times and such topics as the economy, population, religion, holidays, and recreation. (Rev: HBG 10/99; SLJ 11/99) [972.8]

9960 Mann, Elizabeth. *Tikal: The Center of the Maya World* (4–8). Illus. by Tom McNeely. Series: Wonders of the World. 2002, Mikaya $19.95 (978-1-931414-05-0). Mann provides an overview for older readers of the Mayan city of Tikal, covering the location, the people, the architecture, the culture, and their sometimes blood-thirsty customs. (Rev: BL 12/15/02; HBG 3/03; SLJ 1/03) [972.81]

9961 Markun, Patricia M. *It's Panama's Canal!* (5–9). 1999, Linnet LB $22.50 (978-0-208-02499-2). This account gives a good background history of the canal plus current information on Panama's control of the zone and its plans for successful management. (Rev: BL 1/1–15/00; HBG 3/00) [972.87]

9962 Netzley, Patricia D. *Maya Civilization* (6–9). 2002, Gale LB $32.45 (978-1-56006-806-8). Primary and secondary sources are incorporated into the text of this introduction to the Mayans and their culture that emphasizes the role of historians. (Rev: SLJ 12/02) [972]

9963 Sheehan, Sean. *Guatemala* (6–10). Series: Cultures of the World. 1998, Marshall Cavendish LB $37.07 (978-0-7614-0812-3). A solid introduction to Guatemala's geography, politics, and culture. (Rev: HBG 9/98; SLJ 2/99) [972.8]

9964 Silverstone, Michael. *Rigoberta Menchu: Defending Human Rights in Guatemala* (5–8). 1999, Feminist paper $9.95 (978-1-55861-199-3). In addition to a biography of Nobel Peace Prize winner Rigoberta Menchu, this account presents Guatemala, its civil war, and the efforts to end it. (Rev: BL 3/15/00) [972.81]

MEXICO

9965 Bingham, Jane. *The Aztec Empire* (5–8). Series: Time Travel Guides. 2007, Raintree LB $34.29 (978-1-4109-2730-9). An attractive trip back in time to the Aztec Empire, providing details about daily life there — accommodation, food, shopping, and so forth — as well as the calendar and festivals. (Rev: LMC 11–12/07; SLJ 9/07) [972]

9966 Burr, Claudia. *Broken Shields* (4–8). 1997, Douglas & McIntyre paper $6.95 (978-0-88899-304-5). From firsthand eyewitness accounts, this is the story of the betrayal of Montezuma at the hands of the Spanish conqueror Cortez. (Rev: BL 12/1/97; HB 11–12/97; HBG 3/98; SLJ 1/98) [972]

9967 Gruber, Beth. *Mexico* (4–8). Series: Countries of the World. 2006, National Geographic $19.95 (978-0-7922-7629-6). This book covers the geography, people, language, customs, and natural resources of Mexico, with plenty of graphics to add interest to the presentation. (Rev: BL 2/15/07; LMC 5/07)

9968 Hadden, Gerry. *Teenage Refugees from Mexico Speak Out* (7–12). Series: Teenage Refugees Speak Out. 1997, Rosen LB $27.95 (978-0-8239-2441-7). Teens who have left Mexico and come to the U.S. to escape economic conditions and political instability tell about their experiences. (Rev: BL 10/15/97; SLJ 1/98) [972]

9969 Hamilton, Janice. *Mexico in Pictures. Rev. ed.* (4–8). Series: Visual Geography. 2002, Lerner LB $27.93 (978-0-8225-1960-7). An excellent introduction to Mexico that includes material on geography, history, people, economy, and culture with maps, photographs, and illustrations. (Rev: HBG 3/03; SLJ 3/03) [972]

9970 Jovinelly, Joann, and Jason Netelkos. *The Crafts and Culture of the Aztecs* (5–8). Series: Crafts of the Ancient World. 2002, Rosen LB $29.25 (978-0-8239-3512-3). The culture of the Aztecs is covered through a discussion of their crafts and a variety of easily accomplished projects related to them. (Rev: BL 4/1/02; VOYA 6/02) [972]

9971 Libura, Krystyna. *What the Aztecs Told Me* (4–8). 1997, Douglas & McIntyre paper $6.95 (978-0-88899-306-9). Based on an original 12-volume work written in the 16th century, this book describes the Aztec people from observation and eyewitness accounts. (Rev: BL 12/1/97; HB 11–12/97; HBG 3/98; SLJ 12/97) [972]

9972 Reilly, Mary J. *Mexico* (5–8). Series: Cultures of the World. 1991, Marshall Cavendish LB $35.64 (978-

1-85435-385-6). This account emphasizes the geography, history, economy, and lifestyles of the Mexican people. (Rev: BL 4/1/91) [972]

9973 Rosenblum, Morris. *Heroes of Mexico* (5–8). 1972, Fleet $9.50 (978-0-8303-0082-2). A collected group of profiles of people important in the history of Mexico. (Rev: BL 6/87) [972]

9974 Stein, R. Conrad. *The Mexican Revolution* (6–12). 2007, Morgan Reynolds LB $27.95 (978-1-59935-051-6). This comprehensive, well-written book covers the Mexican Revolution in detail and does not gloss over the more violent aspects of the conflict (includes maps, photos, reproductions, bibliography, chronology, index, notes and Web sites). (Rev: SLJ 3/08)

9975 Stein, R. Conrad. *The Mexican War of Independence* (6–12). 2007, Morgan Reynolds LB $27.95 (978-1-59935-054-7). Lively text and illustrations will appeal to readers of this volume, which covers three centuries of Spanish rule of Mexico, from 1521-1855 (includes maps, photos, reproductions, bibliography, chronology, index, notes and Web sites). (Rev: SLJ 3/08)

PUERTO RICO, CUBA, AND OTHER CARIBBEAN ISLANDS

9976 Carey, Charles W., Jr, ed. *Castro's Cuba* (7–12). Series: History Firsthand. 2004, Gale LB $36.20 (978-0-7377-1654-2); paper $24.95 (978-0-7377-1655-9). Historical documents, interviews, and newspaper and magazine articles are used in this account of Castro's takeover in Cuba and developments since then. (Rev: SLJ 11/04) [972]

9977 Fernandez, Ronald M. *Puerto Rico Past and Present: An Encyclopedia* (8–12). 1998, Greenwood $86.95 (978-0-313-29822-6). A browsable book that contains biographies of famous Puerto Ricans as well as political terms and groups, buildings, important court decisions, and other information on the island's cultural and historical developments. (Rev: BL 7/97; VOYA 10/98) [972.95]

9978 Fisanick, Christina. *The Bay of Pigs* (6–12). Series: At Issue in History. 2004, Gale paper $23.70 (978-0-7377-1990-1). The failed Bay of Pigs invasion is described in an introductory overview followed by a collection of essays, speeches, and editorials that provide diverse views about the event. (Rev: BL 9/1/04) [972.910]

9979 Haverstock, Nathan A. *Cuba in Pictures* (5–8). Series: Visual Geography. 1997, Lerner LB $25.55 (978-0-8225-1811-2). A look at America's island neighbor, with color photographs. Also use *Dominican Republic in Pictures* (1997). (Rev: BL 10/15/87) [972.91064]

9980 Hintz, Martin. *The Bahamas* (6–9). Illus. Series: Enchantment of the World. 2012, Scholastic LB $40 (978-053127541-2). An attractive revision of the guide to the land and people of the Bahamas. (Rev: BL 12/1/12) [972.96]

9981 McCarthy, Pat. *The Dominican Republic* (5–8). Series: Top Ten Countries of Recent Immigrants. 2004, Enslow LB $25.26 (978-0-7660-5179-9). Information on the Dominican Republic — culture, history, climate, and people — accompanies an explanation of the reasons for migration to the United States and discussion of the contributions of this community; supported by Web links. (Rev: SLJ 3/05) [304]

9982 Sheehan, Sean, and Leslie Jermyn. *Cuba* (7–10). Series: Cultures of the World: Second Edition. 2005, Marshall Cavendish LB $25.95 (978-0-7614-1964-8). A frank, balanced, and readable overview of Cuba's history, geography, economy, culture, and people. (Rev: BL 2/15/06) [972.91]

9983 Tuck, Jay, and Norma C. Vergara. *Heroes of Puerto Rico* (5–8). 1969, Fleet $9.50 (978-0-8303-0070-9). A series of profiles of famous Puerto Ricans. (Rev: BL 6/87) [972.9]

9984 Will, Emily Wade. *Haiti* (5–8). Series: Modern Nations of the World. 2001, Lucent LB $29.95 (978-1-56006-761-0). The history, geography, and culture of this island country are presented with colorful prose and pictures plus unusual facts contained in sidebars. (Rev: BL 6/1–15/01) [972.94]

9985 Worth, Richard. *Puerto Rico in American History* (7–12). Series: From Many Cultures, One History. 2008, Enslow LB $23.95 (978-0-7660-2836-4). An interesting overview of an often-overlooked part of the United States, with an attractive layout. (Rev: BL 4/1/08) [972.95]

South America

9986 *Argentina in Pictures* (5–8). Series: Visual Geography. 1994, Lerner LB $25.55 (978-0-8225-1807-5). An overview of climate, wildlife, cities, vegetation, and mineral resources. (Rev: BL 4/15/88; SLJ 5/88) [982]

9987 Aronson, Marc. *Trapped: How the World Rescued 33 Miners from 2,000 Feet Below the Chilean Desert* (4–8). Illus. 2011, Atheneum $16.99 (978-1-4169-1397-9). A gripping story of the mine disaster in 2010 and the massive effort to rescue the survivors, with information on geology and mining techniques. (Rev: BL 9/1/11*; SLJ 8/11*) [363.11]

9988 Bingham, Jane. *The Inca Empire* (5–8). Series: Time Travel Guides. 2007, Raintree LB $34.29 (978-1-4109-2731-6). An attractive trip back in time to the Inca Empire, providing details about daily life there — accommodation, food, shopping, and so forth. (Rev: SLJ 9/07) [985]

9989 *Colombia in Pictures* (5–8). Series: Visual Geography. 1996, Lerner LB $25.55 (978-0-8225-1810-5).

Many photographs highlight this visit to a South American nation. (Rev: BL 10/15/87) [986.1]

9990 Deckker, Zilah. *Brazil* (4–8). Series: Countries of the World. 2008, National Geographic LB $27.90 (978-1-4263-0298-5). With lots of color images, this thorough volume looks at the geography, nature, history, culture, government, and economy of Brazil, with interesting sidebars on customs, celebrations, and so forth. (Rev: SLJ 3/09) [981]

9991 Dicks, Brian. *Brazil* (6–10). Series: Countries of the World. 2003, Facts on File $30.00 (978-0-8160-5382-7). A well-illustrated account that covers all important topics including present-day racial friction and economic inequality. (Rev: BL 2/1/04) [949.12]

9992 Dubois, Jill. *Colombia* (5–8). Series: Cultures of the World. 1991, Marshall Cavendish LB $35.64 (978-1-85435-384-9). Background information on Colombia is given as well as coverage of contemporary concerns. (Rev: BL 4/1/91) [986.1]

9993 Falconer, Kieran. *Peru* (4–7). Series: Cultures of the World. 1995, Marshall Cavendish LB $37.07 (978-0-7614-0179-7). The focus of this book is on the people of Peru, their lifestyles, artistic endeavors, religion, and leisure activities. (Rev: BL 1/1–15/96; SLJ 4/96) [985]

9994 Fearns, Les, and Daisy Fearns. *Argentina* (7–10). Series: Countries of the World. 2005, Facts on File LB $30.00 (978-0-8160-6008-5). History, geography, culture, government, and economy are all covered in this attractive overview of Argentina. (Rev: SLJ 1/06) [982]

9995 Foley, Erin. *Ecuador* (5–8). Series: Cultures of the World. 1995, Marshall Cavendish LB $37.07 (978-0-7614-0173-5). This book supplies good background material on Ecuador but is strongest in describing contemporary conditions. (Rev: SLJ 11/95) [980]

9996 Gofen, Ethel C. *Cultures of the World: Argentina* (5–8). Series: Cultures of the World. 1991, Marshall Cavendish LB $213.86 (978-1-85435-380-1). This book provides standard information on history and geography and tells about the contemporary lifestyles of the people. (Rev: BL 4/1/91) [962]

9997 Gorrell, Gena K. *In the Land of the Jaguar: South America and Its People* (6–10). Illus. by Andrej Krystoforski. 2007, Tundra $22.95 (978-0-88776-756-2). A beautiful and informative book that covers all the countries of South America, discussing their geography, animals, and natural resources as well as their people and their customs. (Rev: BL 10/1/07; SLJ 11/07) [980]

9998 *Guyana in Pictures* (5–8). Series: Visual Geography. 1997, Lerner LB $25.55 (978-0-8225-1815-0). History, climate, wildlife, and major cities are covered in this overview. (Rev: BL 4/15/88) [988.1]

9999 Haverstock, Nathan A. *Paraguay in Pictures* (5–8). Series: Visual Geography. 1995, Lerner LB $25.55 (978-0-8225-1819-8). This overview of Paraguay includes its history to 1987 and possible future developments. (Rev: BL 4/15/88) [989.2]

10000 Jermyn, Leslie. *Paraguay* (5–8). 1999, Marshall Cavendish LB $37.07 (978-0-7614-0979-3). This book about Paraguay covers history, geography, government, and economy as well as such social and cultural topics as religion, the arts, food, and recreation. (Rev: HBG 10/00; SLJ 4/00) [989]

10001 Jermyn, Leslie. *Uruguay* (7–10). Series: Cultures of the World. 1998, Marshall Cavendish LB $37.07 (978-0-7614-0873-4). An attractive book that covers all the basic topics relating to Uruguay, plus material on leisure activities, festivals, and food. (Rev: HBG 9/99; SLJ 6/99) [980]

10002 Litteral, Linda L. *Boobies, Iguanas, and Other Critters: Nature's Story in the Galapagos* (6–10). 1994, American Kestrel $23.00 (978-1-883966-01-0). After a historical overview of the Galapagos Islands, this richly illustrated book covers the islands' animals, plants, and geology. (Rev: BL 6/1–15/94; SLJ 9/94) [508.866]

10003 Lourie, Peter. *Lost Treasure of the Inca* (4–7). 1999, Boyds Mills $18.95 (978-1-56397-743-5). A thrilling narrative of a modern search for the gold supposedly hidden by the Incas in the Ecuadorian mountains. (Rev: BCCB 11/99; BL 10/15/99; HBG 3/00; SLJ 11/99) [986.6]

10004 Pateman, Robert. *Bolivia* (4–7). Series: Cultures of the World. 1995, Marshall Cavendish LB $37.07 (978-0-7614-0178-0). The people of Bolivia, how they live, and their traditions are some of the topics covered in this general introduction. (Rev: BL 1/1–15/96; SLJ 4/96) [984]

10005 Peck, Robert McCracken. *Headhunters and Hummingbirds: An Expedition into Ecuador* (7–10). 1987, Walker LB $14.85 (978-0-8027-6646-5). An account of an ill-fated scientific expedition into the land of the Jívaro Indians in Ecuador. (Rev: SLJ 6/87; VOYA 8/87) [986]

10006 *Peru in Pictures* (5–8). Series: Visual Geography. 1997, Lerner LB $25.55 (978-0-8225-1820-4). An introduction to this South American land, highlighted by color photographs. (Rev: BL 10/15/87) [985]

10007 Rice, Earle, Jr. *A Brief Political and Geographic History of Latin America: Where Are Gran Colombia, La Plata, and Dutch Guiana?* (6–9). Series: Places in Time. 2007, Mitchell Lane LB $24.95 (978-1-58415-626-0). The history of the region (beginning in the 16th century) as well as information about Latin America's culture, geography, natural resources, and important people, in an attractive format. (Rev: BL 10/15/07; SLJ 8/08) [980]

10008 *Venezuela in Pictures* (4–7). Series: Visual Geography. 1993, Lerner LB $21.27 (978-0-8225-1824-2). The land, people, and government of this oil-rich coun-

try are explored in maps, text, and photographs. (Rev: BL 1/1/88) [987]

10009 Winter, Jane K. *Chile* (5–8). Series: Cultures of the World. 1991, Marshall Cavendish LB $35.64 (978-1-85435-383-2). The geography, history, government, and economy of Chile are some of the topics covered in this fine introduction. (Rev: BL 4/1/91) [983]

10010 Winter, Jane K. *Venezuela* (5–8). Series: Cultures of the World. 1991, Marshall Cavendish LB $35.64 (978-1-85435-386-3). In detailed text and color photographs, the land, people, and contemporary problems and concerns of Venezuela are introduced. (Rev: BL 4/1/91) [987]

Polar Regions

10011 Anderson, Harry S. *Exploring the Polar Regions. Rev. ed.* (8–11). Series: Discovery and Exploration. 2010, Chelsea House LB $35 (978-1-60413-190-1). An updated edition of Anderson's analytical history of polar exploration that looks at the motivations behind the expeditions as well as the specifics of early and modern ventures into new terrain. (Rev: LMC 8–9/10) [910]

10012 Bledsoe, Lucy Jane. *How to Survive in Antarctica* (5–8). 2006, Holiday $16.95 (978-0-8234-1890-9). An account of the author's trips to Antarctica, filled with interesting facts about the frigid land — from wildlife notes to survival tips — plus photographs by the author. (Rev: BCCB 10/06; BL 7/06; HBG 4/07; SLJ 8/06; VOYA 8/06)

10013 Bocknek, Jonathan. *Antarctica: The Last Wilderness* (5–8). Series: Understanding Global Issues. 2003, Smart Apple $19.95 (978-1-58340-356-3). This nicely illustrated book introduces Antarctica with material on climate, animals, exploration, and possible future developments. (Rev: BL 11/15/03; HB 9–10/01; HBG 3/02; SLJ 12/03) [998.9]

10014 Bredeson, Carmen. *After the Last Dog Died: The True-Life, Hair-Raising Adventures of Douglas Mawson and his 1911-1914 Antarctic Expedition* (5–8). 2003, National Geographic $18.95 (978-0-7922-6140-7). This enthralling story of courage in the face of starvation and harsh conditions draws on primary materials including the writings of expedition leader Mawson himself. (Rev: BL 11/1/03; HBG 4/04; SLJ 1/04*) [919.8]

10015 Fiennes, Ranulph. *Race to the Pole: Tragedy, Heroism, and Scott's Antarctic Quest* (8–12). 2004, Hyperion $27.95 (978-1-4013-0047-0). Fiennes, a polar explorer himself, offers an in-depth account of Captain Robert Scott's ill-fated 1911-1912 expedition to the South Pole. (Rev: BL 9/15/04) [919.8]

10016 Henderson, Bruce. *True North: Peary, Cook, and the Race to the Pole* (8–12). 2005, Norton $24.95 (978-0-393-05791-1). Who got to the North Pole first? Henderson offers evidence for the reader to mull over. (Rev: BL 1/1–15/05) [910]

10017 Hooper, Meredith. *Antarctic Journal: The Hidden Worlds of Antarctica's Animals* (5–7). Illus. by Lucia deLeiris. 2001, National Geographic $16.95 (978-0-7922-7188-8). An exciting account of a summer the author spent at Palmer Station in the Antarctic and the wildlife there. (Rev: BL 6/1–15/01; HBG 10/01; SLJ 3/01) [988]

10018 Kimmel, Elizabeth Cody. *Ice Story: Shackleton's Lost Expedition* (4–7). 1999, Clarion $19.00 (978-0-395-91524-0). A fine, accurate, and engrossing description of Shackleton's Imperial Transatlantic Expedition to the Antarctic — one of the great survival stories of all time. (Rev: BL 4/1/99; HBG 10/99; SLJ 4/99) [910.9]

10019 Lynch, Wayne. *The Arctic* (5–9). Series: Our Wild World Ecosystems. 2007, NorthWord $16.95 (978-1-55971-960-5); paper $8.95 (978-1-55971-961-2). Lynch introduces the flora and fauna of the Arctic with interesting anecdotes about his own experiences, color photographs, sidebar features, and eco-fact boxes. (Rev: SLJ 5/07) [577.0911]

10020 Markle, Sandra. *Animals Robert Scott Saw: An Adventure in Antarctica* (4–7). Illus. by Phil. Series: Explorers. 2008, Chronicle LB $16.99 (978-0-8118-4918-0). As the title indicates, this book focuses on the animals that explorer Scott took with him to the South Pole in 1912 and those he observed on the way. (Rev: BL 4/1/08) [919.8]

10021 Sandler, Martin W. *Trapped in Ice! An Amazing True Whaling Adventure* (5–8). Illus. 2006, Scholastic $16.99 (978-0-439-74363-1). A gripping account of 1,219 people forced to abandon ship after their whaling vessels became imprisoned in Arctic ice during the early winter of 1871; includes maps, photographs, and journal accounts. (Rev: BL 4/15/06; SLJ 6/06)

10022 Senungetuk, Vivian, and Paul Tiulana. *A Place for Winter: Paul Tiulana's Story* (7–12). 1988, CIRI Foundation $17.95 (978-0-938227-02-1). The story of a King Island Eskimo boy, his childhood, and his people. (Rev: BL 5/15/88) [917.98]

10023 Sommers, Michael A. *Antarctic Melting: The Disappearing Antarctic Ice Cap* (4–8). Series: Extreme Environmental Threats. 2006, Rosen LB $27.95 (978-1-4042-0741-7). An examination of the impact that global warming has had on Antarctica since 1995, with discussion of the research that takes place on the continent and the work of glaciologists. (Rev: LMC 8–9/07; SLJ 8/07) [363.738]

10024 Steger, Will, and Jon Bowermaster. *Over the Top of the World: Explorer Will Steger's Trek Across the Arctic* (4–7). 1997, Scholastic paper $17.95 (978-0-590-84860-2). Describes the grueling, dangerous adventures involved in a journey across the Arctic Ocean. (Rev: BCCB 2/97; BL 4/15/97; SLJ 4/97*) [919.804]

10025 Tulloch, Coral. *Antarctica: The Heart of the World* (6–9). Illus. by author. 2006, Enchanted Lion $17.95 (978-1-59270-054-7). A continent visited by a tiny percentage of humans is described in this informative, illustrated book that covers historical and contemporary aspects. (Rev: SLJ 8/06) [919.89]

10026 Wade, Rosalyn. *Polar Worlds* (4–7). Illus. Series: Insiders. 2011, Simon & Schuster $16.99 (978-144243275-8). Three-D illustrations draw readers into this overview of the Arctic and Antarctic regions and their topography and flora and fauna, with discussion of exploration, survival measures, and environmental threats. (Rev: BL 12/1/11) [919]

10027 Walker, Sally M. *Frozen Secrets: Antarctica Revealed* (6–9). 2010, Carolrhoda LB $20.95 (978-1-5801-3607-5). History, geology, archaeology, climate science, and technology are all covered in this informative and accessible book that ends with a look at the future. (Rev: BL 12/1/10; HB 11–12/10; LMC 11–12/10; SLJ 11/1/10) [919.8]

10028 Winner, Cherie. *Life in the Tundra* (5–8). Series: Ecosystems in Action. 2003, Lerner LB $26.60 (978-0-8225-4686-3). In text and pictures, the Arctic tundra is presented with material on the organisms that live there and how human life has changed this ecosystem. (Rev: BL 9/15/03; HBG 10/03) [551.4]

10029 Wu, Norbert, and Jim Mastro. *Under Antarctic Ice: The Photographs of Norbert Wu* (8–12). 2004, Univ. of California $45.00 (978-0-520-23504-5). Life beneath the ice of Antarctica is brilliantly captured in the photographs of Norbert Wu; with a useful introduction. (Rev: BL 10/15/04) [779]

10030 Yue, Charlotte, and David Yue. *The Igloo* (6–8). 1988, Houghton Mifflin $16.00 (978-0-395-44613-3). This account describes the geography of the Arctic and the life led by the native Inuit. (Rev: BL 9/1/88; SLJ 12/88) [970.004]

United States

General History and Geography

10031 Andryszewski, Tricia. *Step by Step Along the Appalachian Trail* (4–8). 1998, Twenty-First Century LB $24.90 (978-0-7613-0273-5). A state-by-state tour of the Appalachian Trail, with material on the terrain, elevations, landmarks, and sites along the way. (Rev: BL 3/1/99; HBG 9/99; SLJ 4/99) [973]

10032 Armstrong, Jennifer. *The American Story: 100 True Tales from American History* (4–7). Illus. by

Roger Roth. 2006, Knopf $34.95 (978-0-375-81256-9). The 100 stories in this large-format collection bring American history to life and include such diverse events as Paul Revere's midnight ride, the first flight of the Wright brothers, the eruption of Mount St. Helens, and the Supreme Court decision resolving the disputed 2000 presidential election. (Rev: BCCB 10/06; BL 8/06; HBG 4/07; SLJ 8/06*)

10033 Baker, Patricia. *The 1950s* (7–10). Series: Fashions of a Decade. 2007, Chelsea House $35.00 (978-0-8160-6721-3). Pictures and discussion of the fashions of this decade are accompanied by information about the trends and events of the times and how they affected what Americans wore. Also use *The 1940s* (2007). (Rev: BL 4/15/07) [391]

10034 Bockenhauer, Mark H., and Stephen F. Cunha. *Our Fifty States* (4–10). 2004, National Geographic LB $45.90 (978-0-7922-6992-2). Maps of the states are accompanied by basic facts, photographs, and archival reproductions of key historical events; also includes the U.S. territories. (Rev: SLJ 1/05) [973]

10035 Bolden, Tonya, ed. *33 Things Every Girl Should Know About Women's History: From Suffragettes to Skirt Lengths to the E. R. A.* (6–9). 2002, Random House paper $12.95 (978-0-375-81122-7). This well-designed follow-up to *33 Things Every Girl Should Know* (1998) is an appealing compilation of articles, fiction, poetry, diary entries, charts, and a timeline that reveal much about women's roles in America — from the struggle for equal rights to fashion and 1960s singing groups. (Rev: BL 3/1/02; HB 7–8/02; HBG 10/02; SLJ 4/02; VOYA 12/02) [305.4]

10036 Brexel, Bernadette. *The Knights of Labor and the Haymarket Riot: The Fight for an Eight-Hour Workday* (5–8). Series: America's Industrial Society in the 19th Century. 2004, Rosen LB $22.50 (978-0-8239-4028-8). For reluctant readers, this overview of the struggle to improve working conditions features large print and short chapters. Also use *The Populist Party: A Voice for the Farmers in an Industrial Society* (2004). (Rev: BL 4/1/04)

10037 Buckley, Susan, and Elspeth Leacock. *Journeys for Freedom: A New Look at America's Story* (4–7). Illus. by Rodica Prato. 2006, Houghton $17.00 (978-0-618-22323-7). Twenty stories of personal struggles for freedom — ranging from the early 17th century to the late 20th century — feature quotations from primary sources. (Rev: BL 11/15/06; SLJ 1/07)

10038 Buckley, Susan, and Elspeth Leacock. *Kids Make History: A New Look at America's Story* (4–8). Illus. by Randy Jones. 2006, Houghton $17.00 (978-0-618-22329-9). Twenty stories of young people who experienced milestone events in American history — from Pocahontas in 1607 to a high school senior on 9/11 — are told in text, quotations, fictionalized dialogue, and illustrations. (Rev: SLJ 1/07)

10039 Colman, Penny. *Girls: A History of Growing Up Female in America* (5–8). 2000, Scholastic paper $18.95 (978-0-590-37129-2). Using diaries, memoirs, letters, magazine articles, and other sources, the author presents a history of girls in America from the first females to cross the Bering Strait to the present day. (Rev: BCCB 2/00; BL 2/1/00; HBG 10/00; SLJ 3/00) [305.23]

10040 Cooper, Jason. *Árboles / Trees* (4–8). Trans. by Blanca Rey. Series: La Guía de Rourke Para los Símbolos de los Estados/Rourke's Guide to State Symbols. 2002, Rourke LB $20.95 (978-1-58952-399-9). The 50 state trees are introduced in bilingual text and illustrations. Also use *Aves / Birds, Banderas / Flags*, and *Flores / Flowers*. (Rev: SLJ 3/03) [582]

10041 Coster, Patience. *A New Deal for Women, 1938–1960: The Expanding Roles of Women* (6–12). Illus. Series: Cultural History of Women in America. 2011, Chelsea House LB $35 (978-160413934-1). This attractive, accessible volume describes the new opportunities available for women during and after World War II. (Rev: BL 10/1/11; SLJ 10/1/11) [305.40973]

10042 Croy, Elden. *United States* (4–8). Series: Countries of the World. 2010, National Geographic LB $27.90 (978-1-4263-0632-7). In addition to giving an overview of the country's geography, people, culture, history, government, economy, and climate, this volume includes special features such as "Mississippi Flyway" and "Go West, Young Man!" (Rev: BL 4/1/10; SLJ 4/10) [973]

10043 DiPiazza, Francesca Davis. *Friend Me! 600 Years of Social Networking in America* (5–8). Illus. 2012, Lerner/Twenty-First Century $33.26 (978-076135869-5). From wampum beads and quilting bees to Facebook and Twitter, this is an interesting survey of modes of communication over the centuries. Lexile 1040L (Rev: BL 4/1/12; LMC 10/12; SLJ 4/12; VOYA 6/12) [302.3]

10044 Ehlert, Willis J. *America's Heritage: Capitols of the United States* (6–12). 1993, State House paper $10.95 (978-0-9634908-3-4). Provides data on state capitals and capitol buildings, descriptions of architectural details, brief state histories, state symbols, and an extensive bibliography. (Rev: BL 4/15/93) [725]

10045 Feinstein, Stephen. *The 1960s: From the Vietnam War to Flower Power* (4–7). Series: Decades of the Twentieth Century. 2000, Enslow LB $22.60 (978-0-7660-1426-8). An account of America's turbulent 1960s that includes lifestyles, politics, fashion, fads, and entertainment. (Rev: BL 10/15/00; HBG 3/01; SLJ 12/00) [973.92]

10046 Feinstein, Stephen. *The 1990s: Fom the Persian Gulf War to Y2K* (5–8). Series: Decades of the Twentieth Century. 2001, Enslow LB $22.60 (978-0-7660-1613-2). The events of the 1990s are covered in chapters on lifestyle and fashion; arts and entertainment;

sports; politics; and science, technology, and medicine. (Rev: HBG 10/02; SLJ 2/02) [973.9]

10047 Foster, Genevieve, and Joanna Foster. *George Washington's World. Rev. ed.* (5–8). 1997, Beautiful Feet paper $15.95 (978-0-9643803-4-9). A new edition of this 50-year-old book that re-creates what was happening in the world during Washington's life, now with expanded coverage on minorities. (Rev: SLJ 3/98) [909]

10048 Foster, Mark. *Whale Port: A History of Tuckanucket* (4–7). Illus. by Gerald Foster. 2007, Houghton $18.00 (978-0-618-54722-7). The life and times of a fictitious New England town from 1683 to today reveal how changes in population, technology, commerce, and society all affect a town's growth; detailed illustrations. (Rev: BL 12/1/07; SLJ 11/07)

10049 Garrington, Sally. *The United States* (6–10). Series: Countries of the World. 2003, Facts on File $30.00 (978-0-8160-5385-8). This basic work supplies an overview of information on the United States with emphasis on present conditions. (Rev: BL 1/1–15/04) [973]

10050 Gay, Kathlyn, and Martin Gay. *After the Shooting Stops: The Aftermath of War* (7–12). 1998, Millbrook LB $24.90 (978-0-7613-3006-6). A look at the political, economic, and social changes that have followed U.S. involvement in various wars. (Rev: BL 8/98; HBG 3/99; SLJ 9/98) [355.00973]

10051 Gourley, Catherine. *Gibson Girls and Suffragists: Perceptions of Women from 1900 to 1918, Vol. 1* (7–12). Series: Images and Issues of Women in the Twentieth Century. 2007, Twenty-First Century LB $38.60 (978-0-8225-7150-6). With many photographs and reproductions, this volume looks at images and issues relating to women's roles in the early 20th century. Also use *Rosie and Mrs. America: Perceptions of Women in the 1930s and 1940s* (2007). (Rev: SLJ 11/07) [305.4]

10052 Haban, Rita D. *How Proudly They Wave: Flags of the Fifty States* (4–9). 1989, Lerner LB $23.93 (978-0-8225-1799-3). Pictures of the state flags are accompanied by background information. (Rev: BL 12/15/89; SLJ 3/90) [929.9]

10053 Haskins, James, and Kathleen Benson. *Africa: A Look Back* (5–8). Series: Drama of African-American History. 2006, Benchmark LB $23.95 (978-0-7614-2148-1). Slave narratives form a substantial portion of this survey of African American culture, tracing its roots back to the western part of Africa. (Rev: SLJ 5/07) [967]

10054 Head, Judith. *America's Daughters: 400 Years of American Women* (6–12). 1999, Perspectives paper $16.95 (978-0-9622036-8-8). This overview of the part played by women in American history highlights the work of many who have been unjustly ignored. (Rev: BL 1/1–15/00; SLJ 3/00) [305.4]

10055 Heinemann, Sue. *The New York Public Library Amazing Women in History* (6–10). 1998, Wiley paper $14.95 (978-0-471-19216-9). Using a question-and-answer format, this work supplies hundreds of facts about women in American history, arranged by topics that include activism, sports, recreation, and racial and ethnic groups. (Rev: BL 4/15/98; SLJ 8/98) [973]

10056 Hemming, Heidi, and Julie Hemming Savage. *Women Making America* (6–12). 2009, Clotho $45.95 (978-0-9821271-1-7); paper $28.95 (978-0-9821271-0-0). Women's roles — domestic and professional — throughout American history are the focus of this well-laid out book, which employs numerous biographical sketches, period photographs, and compelling vignettes to engage readers. (Rev: BLO 7/09; SLJ 6/1/09) [900]

10057 Hopkinson, Deborah. *Up Before Daybreak: Cotton and People in America* (5–8). Illus. 2006, Scholastic $18.99 (978-0-439-63901-9). A concise, readable history of the American cotton industry with a focus on laborers, especially children; contains archival photographs, reading list, and bibliography. (Rev: BL 4/15/06*; HB 5/06; LMC 11/06; SLJ 6/06*)

10058 Johnston, Robert D. *The Making of America* (5–8). 2002, National Geographic $29.95 (978-0-7922-6944-1). An informative and balanced overview of American history, this appealing volume divides American history into eight periods; in addition to the narrative, each period includes profiles of two major figures and examines important issues of the time. (Rev: BL 1/1–15/03; HBG 3/03; SLJ 12/02*) [973]

10059 Jordan, Anne Devereaux, and Virginia Schomp. *Slavery and Resistance* (5–8). Illus. 2006, Marshall Cavendish LB $34.21 (978-0-7614-2178-8). A well-illustrated, well-organized history of slavery in America from the first colony in Jamestown up until the Civil War. (Rev: BL 2/1/07; SLJ 5/07)

10060 King, David C. *World Wars and the Modern Age* (5–8). Series: American Heritage, American Voices. 2004, Wiley paper $12.95 (978-0-471-44392-6). A concise overview of the profound changes seen in the United States during the decades from 1870 to 1950, with excerpts from primary sources. (Rev: BL 2/1/05; SLJ 5/05) [973]

10061 McKendry, Joe. *One Times Square: A Century of Change at the Crossroads of the World* (5–8). Illus. by author. 2012, Godine $19.95 (978-156792364-3). A fascinating and very visual history of Times Square, New York City. (Rev: BL 9/15/12; SLJ 8/1/12) [974.7]

10062 McNeese, Tim. *Early National America: 1790–1850* (5–8). Illus. Series: Discovering U.S. History. 2010, Chelsea House $35 (978-1-60413-351-6). A satisfying survey of social and political developments in the early years of the United States, with illustrations, maps, photographs, and interesting sidebar feature **e** (Rev: LMC 11–12/10; SLJ 8/10) [973]

10063 Masoff, Joy. *We Are All Americans: Understanding Diversity* (4–7). 2006, Five Ponds $26.50 (978-0-9727156-2-1). This celebration of immigration to America — full of photographs, maps, and diagrams — looks at the reasons for migration, the problems involved, and the contributions made by immigrants in all aspects of American life, including music, sports, games, celebrations, literature, food, and art. (Rev: SLJ 1/07)

10064 Miller, Marilyn. *Words That Built a Nation: A Young Person's Collection of Historic American Documents* (4–8). 1999, Scholastic paper $18.95 (978-0-590-29881-0). A collection of 37 documents important in American history — from the Mayflower Compact and the Declaration of Independence to Hillary Rodham Clinton's address to the United Nations Conference on Women and Malcolm X's "The Ballot or the Bullet" speech. (Rev: BL 10/15/99; HBG 3/00; SLJ 2/00) [973]

10065 Miller, Page Putnam. *Landmarks of American Women's History* (5–8). 2004, Oxford LB $32.95 (978-0-19-514501-4). Landmarks — all on the National Register of Historic Places — highlighted for their importance in women's history include Taos Pueblo, New Mexico, chosen for the strong Native American women who lived there; the Wesleyan Chapel at Seneca Falls, where the first women's rights conference was held; and the Boardinghouse at Boott Cotton Mill in Lowell, Massachusetts, home to many young women who worked in the textile industry. (Rev: SLJ 9/04) [973]

10066 Nathan, Amy. *Count on Us: American Women in the Military* (6–9). 2004, National Geographic $21.95 (978-0-7922-6330-2). Nathan celebrates women's diverse contributions to the United States' military causes — from women who disguised themselves as men in the Revolutionary War to World War I nurses to women flying Black Hawk missions today. (Rev: BL 2/15/04; SLJ 3/04) [355]

10067 Panchyk, Richard. *Keys to American History: Understanding Our Most Important Historic Documents* (6–12). Illus. 2009, Chicago Review $24.95 (978-155652716-6); paper $19.95 (978-155652804-0). An anthology of 72 important documents in the history of the United States, from the Mayflower Compact to the Patriot Act. With explanatory notes, facsimiles, and maps. (Rev: BL 5/1/09; SLJ 2/1/09) [973]

10068 Peterson, Cris. *Birchbark Brigade: A Fur Trade History* (6–9). 2009, Boyds Mills $18.95 (978-1-59078-426-6). The history of fur trading in North America from the 16th to the 19th century is artfully interwoven with historical events and personalities. Lexile NC1250L (Rev: BL 12/15/09; LMC 1–2/10; SLJ 11/09) [970.01]

10069 Rydell, Robert W. *Fair America: World's Fairs in the United States* (8–12). 2000, Smithsonian $29.95 (978-1-56098-968-4); paper $15.95 (978-1-56098-384-2). This book examines world's fairs held in the United States from 1853 to 1984. [907]

10070 Sills, Leslie. *From Rags to Riches: A History of Girls' Clothing in America* (4–7). 2005, Holiday $16.95 (978-0-8234-1708-7). Changes in clothing over the centuries are linked to the social mores of the time in this appealing volume. (Rev: BL 5/1/05; SLJ 8/05) [391]

10071 Stanley, George E. *The New Republic (1763–1815)* (5–8). Series: A Primary Source History of the United States. 2005, World Almanac LB $31.00 (978-0-8368-5825-9). A simple narrative links well-chosen primary sources documenting the key events of the revolutionary period. (Rev: BL 4/1/05; SLJ 7/05)

10072 Streissguth, Thomas. *Utopian Visionaries* (7–12). 1999, Oliver LB $19.95 (978-1-881508-47-2). This account presents material on attempts to build utopian communities in the U.S. during the 18th and 19th centuries by such visionaries as Ann Lee, a Shaker, and John Humphrey Noyes, who created the Oneida community. (Rev: BL 12/15/99; HBG 4/00; SLJ 11/99) [321]

10073 Tarrant-Reid, Linda. *Discovering Black America* (7–12). Illus. 2012, Abrams $29.95 (978-0-8109-7098-4). A handsome and thorough overview of more than 400 years of African American history, drawing on diaries, autobiographies, written oral accounts, and interviews. Lexile 1370L (Rev: BL 9/1/12; LMC 3–4/13; SLJ 10/12) [973]

10074 *United States in Pictures* (5–8). Series: Visual Geography. 1995, Lerner LB $25.55 (978-0-8225-1896-9). An attractive basic introduction to the geography, history, and people of the United States. (Rev: BL 8/95) [973]

10075 Uschan, Michael V. *Lynching and Murder in the Deep South* (8–12). Series: Lucent Library of Black History. 2006, Gale LB $28.70 (978-1-59018-845-3). This is a frank discussion of the lynchings and other violence that took place in the South from Reconstruction right up to the 1950s. (Rev: SLJ 4/07) [364.1]

10076 Uschan, Michael V. *The 1940s* (5–10). Series: Cultural History of the United States. 1998, Lucent LB $28.70 (978-1-56510-554-6). Life at home and abroad during World War II dominate this book, which also discusses the Great Depression, the New Deal, events leading up to U.S. participation in the war, the beginnings of the Cold War, the growth of suburban living, and the rise of television, with sidebars on such topics as the Holocaust, the influences of radio, movies, and comics, 1940s slang, and the first computers. (Rev: SLJ 1/99) [973.9]

10077 Uschan, Michael V. *Protests and Riots* (5–8). Series: American History. 2010, Gale/Lucent LB $33.45 (978-1-4205-0278-7). Primary source quotes and period photographs enhance this overview of key protests throughout American history. (Rev: SLJ 4/11) [973]

10078 Wacker, Grant. *Religion in Nineteenth Century America* (5–8). Series: Religion in American Life. 2000, Oxford $32.95 (978-0-19-511021-0). This is the story of how religion in America affected such 19th-century events as the westward movement, the Civil War, and immigration, with additional coverage of the careers of such people as Sojourner Truth and Mary Baker Eddy. (Rev: BL 6/1–15/00; HBG 10/00; SLJ 8/00) [973]

10079 Wormser, Richard. *American Childhoods: Three Centuries of Youth at Risk* (7–12). 1996, Walker LB $17.85 (978-0-8027-8427-8). A graphic, realistic picture of childhood and growing up in America from the repressive Puritans to the present day with chapters on work, crime, disease, education, sex, and related topics. (Rev: BL 9/15/96; SLJ 9/96; VOYA 12/96) [305.23]

10080 Wormser, Richard. *Hoboes: Wandering in America, 1870-1940* (6–12). 1994, Walker $17.95 (978-0-8027-8279-3). This account covers the history, rules, literature, songs, and customs of those who rode the rails from the end of the Civil War to the outbreak of World War II. (Rev: BL 6/1–15/94; SLJ 7/94) [305.5]

10081 Worth, Richard. *The Slave Trade in America: Cruel Commerce* (6–12). Series: Slavery in American History. 2004, Enslow LB $26.60 (978-0-7660-2151-8). The slave trade is traced back to its origins in the days of early Romans before a more detailed survey of the American slave trade in the 17th and 18th centuries, with attention to the social and economic aspects. (Rev: SLJ 8/04) [382]

10082 Yorinks, Adrienne. *Quilt of States: Piecing Together America* (5–8). 2005, National Geographic LB $29.90 (978-0-7922-7286-1). With contributions from librarians from all 50 states, this beautifully illustrated volume offers a brief story of each state's accession to the Union, along with other pertinent facts and figures. (Rev: BL 10/1/05; SLJ 12/05) [973]

Historical Periods

NATIVE AMERICANS

10083 Anderson, Dale. *The Anasazi Culture at Mesa Verde* (5–8). Series: Landmark Events in American History. 2003, World Almanac LB $31.00 (978-0-8368-5371-1). The story of the native people from the region around the Four Corners and of their many cultural accomplishment including basketry, pottery, and urban architecture. (Rev: BL 10/15/03) [973]

10084 Ayer, Eleanor H. *The Anasazi* (6–9). 1993, Walker LB $15.85 (978-0-8027-8185-7). An in-depth look at the Anasazi Indians of the Southwest, who came to this country about 2,000 years ago. (Rev: BL 3/1/93; SLJ 11/93) [979]

10085 Bial, Raymond. *The Delaware* (5–9). Series: Lifeways. 2005, Benchmark LB $23.95 (978-0-7614-

1904-4). The history, culture, traditions, and present-day life of the Native American tribe, with photographs and other visuals. (Rev: SLJ 6/06) [974.004]

10086 Bial, Raymond. *The Menominee* (5–9). Series: Lifeways. 2005, Benchmark LB $23.95 (978-0-7614-1903-7). The history, culture, traditions and present-day life of the Native American tribe, with photographs and other visuals. (Rev: SLJ 6/06) [977.4004]

10087 Bjornlund, Lydia. *The Trail of Tears: The Relocation of the Cherokee Nation* (5–8). Series: American History. 2010, Gale/Lucent LB $33.45 (978-1-4205-0211-4). Primary source quotations and period photographs enhance this account of the tragic journey of the Cherokee away from their homeland. (Rev: SLJ 4/11) [975.004]

10088 Bond, Fred G. *Flatboating on the Yellowstone, 1877* (7–12). 1998, Ward Hill $19.95 (978-1-886747-03-6). A first-person account of the relocation in 1877 of Chief Joseph and other Nez Perce Indians from Oregon to Oklahoma by raft down the Yellowstone and Missouri Rivers, written by their pilot, who documented the trip for the New York Public Library in 1925. (Rev: BL 12/15/98) [973]

10089 Bruchac, Joseph. *Navajo Long Walk: The Tragic Story of a Proud People's Forced March from Their Homeland* (4–8). Illus. by Shonto Begay. 2002, National Geographic $18.95 (978-0-7922-7058-4). Using revealing words and pictures, this large picture book for older readers re-creates the shameful story of the deadly marches of the Navajo in the 1860s. (Rev: BL 5/1/02; HBG 10/02; SLJ 7/02) [979.1]

10090 Cooper, Michael L. *Indian School: Teaching the White Man's Way* (5–10). 1999, Clarion $18.00 (978-0-395-92084-8). A moving photoessay about Native American children and how they were removed from their homes and uprooted from their culture to attend Indian boarding schools in an effort to "civilize" them. (Rev: BL 12/1/99; HBG 3/00; SLJ 2/00; VOYA 4/00) [370]

10091 Cornell, George L., and Gordon Henry. *Ojibwa* (8–12). Series: North American Indians Today. 2003, Mason Crest LB $22.95 (978-1-59084-673-5). The contemporary status of Ojibwa Indians is emphasized in this volume that covers religion, government, and the arts. (Rev: SLJ 5/04) [973]

10092 Cory, Steven. *Pueblo Indian* (5–8). Series: American Pastfinder. 1996, Lerner LB $21.27 (978-0-8225-2976-7). Color illustrations and maps accompany this account of the Pueblo Indians and the incredible cities they built. (Rev: BL 7/96) [973]

10093 Denny, Sidney G., and Ernest L. Schusky. *The Ancient Splendor of Prehistoric Cahokia* (4–8). 1997, Ozark paper $3.95 (978-1-56763-272-9). Using the findings at the Cahokia Mounds in southern Illinois as a beginning, the author re-creates the life and culture of these prehistoric American Indians. (Rev: BL 5/1/97) [977.3]

10094 *Do All Indians Live in Tipis? Questions and Answers from the National Museum of the American Indian* (8–12). 2007, Smithsonian paper $14.95 (978-0-06-115301-3). With answers to questions posed by the general public, this book aims to set the facts straight about Native American cultures. (Rev: SLJ 3/08)

10095 Durrett, Deanne. *Healers* (8–12). Series: American Indian Lives. 1997, Facts on File $17.95 (978-0-8160-3460-4). This work profiles 12 Native American healers, ranging from the traditional medicine man to modern physicians and nurses. (Rev: VOYA 8/97) [973]

10096 Fowler, Verna. *The Menominee* (4–7). Series: Indian Nations. 2000, Raintree LB $25.69 (978-0-8172-5458-2). Opening with a folk tale, this book describes the Menominee Indians, their life and culture, and how they were overrun in the 19th century and pushed onto a reservation in northern Wisconsin. (Rev: BL 3/15/01; HBG 10/01) [973]

10097 Freedman, Russell. *An Indian Winter* (6–9). 1992, Holiday $24.95 (978-0-8234-0930-3); paper $12.95 (978-0-8234-1158-0). A German naturalist/explorer and a Swiss artist recorded in words and pictures their 1832 observations of Mandan and Hidatsa Indian tribes in North Dakota. (Rev: BL 6/1/92*; HB 7–8/92; SLJ 6/92*) [917.804]

10098 Gibson, Karen Bush. *Native American History for Kids* (6–10). Illus. 2010, Chicago Review paper $16.95 (978-15697628-0-6). With profiles of key individuals and 21 hands-on activities, this is an attractive and accessible survey of Native American life through the centuries. (Rev: BL 7/10; SLJ 2/11) [970.004]

10099 Gold, Susan Dudley. *Indian Treaties* (5–8). Series: Pacts and Treaties. 1997, Twenty-First Century LB $24.90 (978-0-8050-4813-1). A history of the successive treaties under which the Native Americans gradually lost their homes and livelihood. (Rev: BL 5/15/97; SLJ 6/97) [323.1]

10100 Gorsline, Marie, and Douglas Gorsline. *North American Indians* (5–8). Illus. by Douglas Gorsline. 1978, Random House paper $3.25 (978-0-394-83702-4). Major tribes are identified and briefly described. [973]

10101 Holm, Tom. *Code Talkers and Warriors: Native Americans and World War II* (5–9). Series: Landmark Events in Native American History. 2007, Chelsea House LB $35.00 (978-0-7910-9340-5). How Native Americans have aided their country in wars (many more than WWII are discussed), with an emphasis on Navajo and Comanche code talk. (Rev: BL 12/15/07) [940.54]

10102 Katz, Jane B., ed. *We Rode the Wind: Recollections of Native American Life. Rev. ed.* (6–10). 1995,

Lerner LB $22.60 (978-0-8225-3154-8). A collection of the autobiographical writings of eight notable Native Americans, among them Charles Eastman and Black Elk, who grew up on the Great Plains. (Rev: BL 2/1/96; SLJ 12/95) [978]

10103 Keoke, Emory Dean, and Kay Marie Porterfield. *Trade, Transportation, and Warfare* (7–10). Series: American Indian Contributions to the World. 2005, Facts on File $35.00 (978-0-8160-5395-7). Native American accomplishments in both North and South America in the realms of transportation, trade, sports, governance, and military strategy are among the aspects highlighted here. (Rev: BL 4/1/05; SLJ 6/05) [970.004]

10104 McIntosh, Kenneth. *Apache* (8–12). Series: North American Indians Today. 2003, Mason Crest LB $22.95 (978-1-59084-664-3). The contemporary status of Apache Indians is emphasized in this volume that covers religion, government, and the arts. (Rev: SLJ 5/04) [973]

10105 McIntosh, Kenneth. *Navajo* (6–9). Series: North American Indians Today. 2003, Mason Crest LB $22.95 (978-1-59084-672-8). This portrait of the Navajo people offers a brief history of the tribe but focuses primarily on their present-day culture and government. (Rev: BL 4/1/04; SLJ 5/04) [979.1]

10106 McIntosh, Kenneth, and Marsha McIntosh. *Cheyenne* (8–12). Series: North American Indians Today. 2003, Mason Crest LB $22.95 (978-1-59084-666-7). The contemporary status of Cheyenne Indians is emphasized in this volume that covers religion, government, and the arts. Also use *Iroquois* (2003). (Rev: SLJ 5/04) [973]

10107 Margolin, Malcolm, and Yolanda Montijo, eds. *Native Ways: California Indian Stories and Memories* (5–8). 1996, Heyday paper $8.95 (978-0-930588-73-1). Reminiscences and stories reflect California Indian culture, both past and present. (Rev: BL 7/96) [979.4]

10108 Marsico, Katie. *The Trail of Tears: The Tragedy of the American Indians* (8–10). Series: Perspectives on. 2009, Marshall Cavendish LB $27.95 (978-0-7614-4029-1). Marsico examines the historical context, heartbreak, and aftermath of the American Cherokee relocation program and provides photographs, illustrations, and engaging sidebars. (Rev: LMC 3–4/10; SLJ 1/10) [973.04]

10109 Mayfield, Thomas Jefferson. *Adopted by Indians: A True Story* (5–8). Ed. by Malcolm Margolin. 1997, Heyday paper $10.95 (978-0-930588-93-9). This is an adaption of the memoirs of a white man who lived with the Choinumne Indians in California for 10 years, beginning in 1850 when he was 8 years old. (Rev: BL 3/1/98) [979.4]

10110 Meyers, Madeleine, ed. *Cherokee Nation: Life Before the Tears* (4–8). Series: Perspectives on History. 1994, Discovery paper $6.95 (978-1-878668-26-4). A history of the Cherokees that emphasizes the leadership of Sequoyah and the life of the tribe before their forced displacement. (Rev: BL 8/94) [970.3]

10111 Nies, Judith. *Native American History: A Chronology of a Culture's Vast Achievements and Their Links to World Events* (6–12). 1997, Ballantine paper $15.00 (978-0-345-39350-0). This chronology of Native North American history and culture from 28,000 B.C. through 1996, using a split-page format to juxtapose simultaneous political, social, religious, and military developments occurring in North America and in other parts of the world. (Rev: SLJ 5/97) [970.003]

10112 Patent, Dorothy Hinshaw. *The Horse and the Plains Indians: A Powerful Partnership* (5–8). Illus. by William Muñoz. 2012, Clarion $17.99 (978-054712551-0). The changes horses brought to Plains Indian culture are described in this companion to *The Buffalo and the Indians: A Shared Destiny* (2006). (Rev: BL 8/12; SLJ 5/1/12*) [978.004]

10113 Philip, Neil. *The Great Circle: A History of the First Nations* (6–9). 2006, Clarion $20.00 (978-0-618-15941-3). An excellent history of Native American tribes — their leaders, beliefs, traditions — and, in particular, their interactions with white settlers. (Rev: BL 10/1/06; SLJ 11/06*) [973.04]

10114 Philip, Neil, ed. *A Braid of Lives: Native American Childhood* (4–8). 2000, Clarion $20.00 (978-0-395-64528-4). Twenty vignettes of one or two pages in length give a many-faceted picture of growing up Native American in different parts of the county. (Rev: BL 10/1/00; HBG 10/01; SLJ 6/01; VOYA 4/01) [973]

10115 Philip, Neil, ed. *In a Sacred Manner I Live: Native American Wisdom* (4–8). 1997, Clarion $20.00 (978-0-395-84981-1). More than 30 Native American leaders — including Geronimo and Cochise — are quoted on topics relating to the conduct of life and their beliefs. (Rev: BL 7/97; HBG 3/98; SLJ 12/97) [973]

10116 Seymour, Tryntje Van Ness. *The Gift of Changing Woman* (5–8). 1993, Henry Holt $16.95 (978-0-8050-2577-4). A description of the Apache initiation rite for young women in picture-book format, illustrated by Apache artists. (Rev: BL 11/15/93; SLJ 3/94) [299]

10117 Siegel, Beatrice. *Indians of the Northeast Woodlands* (4–8). Illus. by William Sauts Bock. 1991, Walker LB $14.85 (978-0-8027-8157-4). In question-and-answer format — following the original 1972 edition — this volume contains much information on Native Americans in New England. (Rev: BL 11/15/92) [973]

10118 Sonneborn, Liz. *The New York Public Library Amazing Native American History: A Book of Answers for Kids* (5–8). 1999, Wiley paper $16.95 (978-0-471-33204-6). Organized by regions and using a question-and-answer approach, this is a fine overview of the history of Native Americans, ending with a chapter on

contemporary conditions. (Rev: BL 5/1/00; SLJ 7/00) [970.004]

10119 Stewart, Mark, ed. *The Indian Removal Act: Forced Relocation* (6–8). 2007, Compass Point LB $23.95 (978-0-7565-2452-4). Presents historical information on the issues and events leading up to the Indian Removal Act of 1830 and the many deaths along the Trail of Tears. (Rev: BL 5/15/07) [973.04]

10120 Stone, Amy M. *Creek* (4–8). Series: Native American Peoples. 2004, Gareth Stevens LB $26.00 (978-0-8368-4217-3). History, tradition, and contemporary life are described with photographs, timeline, fact boxes, and activities. (Rev: SLJ 1/05) [973]

10121 Stout, Mary. *Blackfoot* (4–8). Series: Native American Peoples. 2004, Gareth Stevens LB $26.00 (978-0-8368-4216-6). History, tradition, and contemporary life are described with photographs, timeline, fact boxes, and activities. (Rev: SLJ 1/05) [973]

10122 Taylor, C. J. *Peace Walker: The Legend of Hiawatha and Tekanawita* (6–9). 2004, Tundra $15.95 (978-0-88776-547-6). In rhythmic prose and full-page paintings, Taylor retells the story of Hiawatha and places it in cultural context. (Rev: BL 2/15/05; SLJ 4/05) [398.2]

10123 Tehanetorens. *Roots of the Iroquois* (7–10). 2000, Native Voices paper $9.95 (978-1-57067-097-8). A lively, detailed look at the history of the Iroquois Confederation before and after the arrival of European settlers. (Rev: BL 11/15/00) [974.004]

10124 Thompson, Linda. *The California People* (4–7). Series: Native People, Native Lands. 2003, Rourke LB $29.93 (978-1-58952-753-9). One of a well-illustrated series on individual groups of native Americans, with attention to the negative impact of the arrival of European settlers. Other titles in the series include *People of the Northwest and Subarctic*, *People of the Great Basin*, *People of the Northeast Woodlands*, and *People of the Plains and Prairies* (all 2003). (Rev: SLJ 4/04) [979.4]

10125 Vander Hook, Sue. *Trail of Tears* (6–8). Series: Essential Events. 2010, ABDO LB $32.79 (978-1-60453-946-2). This book describes the forced removal of the Cherokee from their homeland, the events leading up to this evacuation, and the aftermath — including the tribe's situation today. (Rev: BL 5/1/10; LMC 10/10; SLJ 6/10) [975.004]

10126 Young, Robert. *A Personal Tour of Mesa Verde* (4–7). Series: How It Was. 1999, Lerner LB $30.35 (978-0-8225-3577-5). This book gives a special glimpse into the lives of the Native Americans known as the Puebloans, how they lived, and the culture they developed. (Rev: BL 6/1–15/99; HBG 10/99; SLJ 7/99) [978.8]

10127 Yue, Charlotte, and David Yue. *The Wigwam and the Longhouse* (4–9). Illus. by authors. 2000, Houghton Mifflin $15.00 (978-0-395-84169-3). A well-balanced account that describes the life and history of several tribes of Native Americans from the eastern woodlands. (Rev: HB 7–8/00; HBG 10/00; SLJ 10/00; VOYA 12/00) [973]

10128 Zimmerman, Dwight Jon. *Saga of the Sioux: An Adaptation of Dee Brown's Bury My Heart at Wounded Knee* (5–8). Illus. 2011, Henry Holt $18.99 (978-0-8050-9364-3). This adaptation of Dee Brown's classic work provides a short history of the Sioux tribe and examines the events leading up to the Wounded Knee massacre. (Rev: BL 10/1/11; LMC 11–12/11; SLJ 9/1/11; VOYA 8/11) [978]

DISCOVERY AND EXPLORATION

10129 Arenstam, Peter. *Mayflower 1620: A New Look at a Pilgrim Voyage* (5–9). 2003, National Geographic $17.95 (978-0-7922-6142-1). A large-format photoessay of a voyage of the *Mayflower II* — re-creating the original journey — is the backdrop for detail about the 1620 passengers, supplies, navigation techniques, and the new country they arrived in. (Rev: BL 11/1/03; HBG 4/04; SLJ 11/03) [974.4]

10130 Cox, Caroline, and Ken Albala. *Opening Up North America, 1497–1800* (6–12). Series: Discovery and Exploration. 2005, Facts on File $40.00 (978-0-8160-5261-5). Chronicles the arrival of Europeans in North America and their progression across the continent, with maps, illustrations, and excerpts from primary sources. (Rev: SLJ 8/05) [973]

10131 Freedman, Russell. *Who Was First? Discovering the Americas* (6–9). 2007, Clarion $19.00 (978-0-618-66391-0). Freedman explores various claims to the discovery of the Americas, providing lots of reader-friendly information plus a good grounding in the purpose of studying history. (Rev: BL 10/1/07; SLJ 11/07) [970.01]

10132 Lepore, Jill. *Encounters in the New World: A History in Documents* (7–12). Series: Pages from History. 1999, Oxford LB $39.95 (978-0-19-510513-1). Documents including letters, journals, and advertisements make relations between Native Americans and European arrivals more real to readers. (Rev: HBG 9/00; SLJ 3/00) [970]

10133 Patent, Dorothy Hinshaw. *Animals on the Trail with Lewis and Clark* (4–8). Illus. by William Muñoz. 2002, Clarion $18.00 (978-0-395-91415-1). A handsome account of the Lewis and Clark expedition with emphasis on the animals that were discovered during the journey. (Rev: BCCB 5/02; BL 4/15/02*; HB 5–6/02; HBG 10/02; SLJ 4/02) [917.804]

10134 Perritano, John. *Spanish Missions* (3–7). Series: A True Book. 2010, Children's Press LB $26 (978-0-531-20575-4). A look at Spanish mission buildings, with beautiful color photographs and discussion of their history and the impact of the missions on the Na-

tive Americans. Lexile 950L (Rev: BL 11/15/10; LMC 8–9/10) [266.27]

10135 Roberts, Russell. *Pedro Menendez de Aviles* (5–7). Series: Latinos in American History. 2002, Mitchell Lane LB $29.95 (978-1-58415-150-0). This account of explorer Pedro Menendez de Aviles's efforts to procure Florida for Spain uses some fictionalized narrative to illustrate the times. (Rev: BL 10/15/02; HBG 3/03; SLJ 10/02) [975.9]

10136 Roop, Peter, and Connie Roop. *River Roads West* (5–8). 2007, Boyds Mills $19.95 (978-1-59078-430-3). The Hudson, Ohio, and Mississippi rivers and the Erie Canal are among the American waterways introduced in this large-format book that discusses the Native American peoples who lived along them and the impact of European exploration and settlement. (Rev: BL 9/15/07; SLJ 9/07) [917]

10137 Whiting, Jim. *Francisco Vasquez de Coronado* (5–7). Series: Latinos in American History. 2002, Mitchell Lane LB $29.95 (978-1-58415-146-3). This account of Francisco Vasquez de Coronado's search for the lost cities of gold, and his subsequent trial for cruelty to Native Americans, uses some fictionalized narrative. (Rev: BL 10/15/02; HBG 3/03; SLJ 10/02; VOYA 6/03) [979]

10138 Yero, Judith Lloyd. *The Mayflower Compact* (4–7). Series: American Documents. 2006, National Geographic $15.95 (978-0-7922-5891-9). Yero distinguishes fact from myth in this examination of the *Mayflower*'s voyage, the colony the Separatists create, and the document they drafted as their governing compact. (Rev: BL 9/15/06; SLJ 10/06)

COLONIAL PERIOD AND FRENCH AND INDIAN WARS

10139 Altman, Linda J. *Trade and Commerce* (5–9). Series: Colonial Life. 2007, Sharpe Focus $37.95 (978-0-7656-8111-9). With color illustrations and interesting sidebars, this volume looks at trade and commerce in the colonies. (Rev: SLJ 1/08)

10140 Brown, Gene. *Discovery and Settlement: Europe Meets the New World (1490-1700)* (5–7). Series: First Person America. 1993, Twenty-First Century LB $20.90 (978-0-8050-2574-3). Using excerpts from original documents, this book covers the exploration of the United States, the Puritans, and the role of Native Americans, African Americans, and women in early colonial days. (Rev: SLJ 3/94) [973.2]

10141 Butler, Jon. *Religion in Colonial America* (5–8). Series: Religion in American Life. 2000, Oxford $32.95 (978-0-19-511998-5). This book describes the mix of Catholics, Jews, Africans, Native Americans, Puritans, and various Protestant faiths that coexisted during colonial times. (Rev: BL 6/1–15/00; HBG 10/00) [973.2]

10142 Cooper, Michael L. *Jamestown 1607* (6–9). 2007, Holiday $18.95 (978-0-8234-1948-7). The story of the Jamestown colony is told in concise text with excellent illustrations, quotations from primary sources, and background context. (Rev: BCCB 6/07; BL 4/15/07; SLJ 4/07) [973.2]

10143 Daugherty, James. *The Landing of the Pilgrims* (5–7). Illus. by author. 1981, Random House paper $5.99 (978-0-394-84697-2). Based on his own writings, this is the story of the Pilgrims from the standpoint of William Bradford. [974.4]

10144 Doherty, Kieran. *Puritans, Pilgrims, and Merchants: Founders of the Northeastern Colonies* (4–8). 1999, Oliver LB $22.95 (978-1-881508-50-2). A history of each of the northeastern colonies is supplemented with brief biographies of such people as William Bradford, John Winthrop, Peter Stuyvesant, Anne Hutchinson, and William Penn. (Rev: BL 8/99; HBG 3/00; SLJ 1/00) [974]

10145 Doherty, Kieran. *Soldiers, Cavaliers, and Planters: Settlers of the Southeastern Colonies* (4–8). 1999, Oliver LB $22.95 (978-1-881508-51-9). This book focuses on the early southern colonies and their founders and leaders, among them Captain John Smith, Sir Walter Raleigh, and Pedro Menendez de Aviles. (Rev: BL 8/99; HBG 3/00; SLJ 10/99) [975]

10146 Harkins, Susan Sales, and William H. Harkins. *Georgia: The Debtors Colony* (4–7). Series: Building America. 2006, Mitchell Lane LB $29.95 (978-1-58415-465-5). A look at Georgia's early history — including climate, early industry, and population — with information on James Oglethorpe, a key figure who aimed to provide a haven in America for debtors imprisoned in England. (Rev: SLJ 2/07) [975.8]

10147 Hinds, Kathryn. *Daily Living* (5–9). Series: Colonial Life. 2007, Sharpe Focus $37.95 (978-0-7656-8110-2). With color illustrations and interesting sidebars, this volume looks at social life in the colonies, exploring food, family life, and so forth. (Rev: SLJ 1/08)

10148 Hinman, Bonnie. *Pennsylvania: William Penn and the City of Brotherly Love* (4–7). Series: Building America. 2006, Mitchell Lane LB $29.95 (978-1-58415-463-1). This history of colonial Pennsylvania explores the reasons why William Penn established the colony in the late 17th century. (Rev: SLJ 2/07) [974.8]

10149 Hossell, Karen. *Delaware 1638–1776* (5–8). Series: Voices from Colonial America. 2006, National Geographic $21.95 (978-0-7922-6408-8). This well-illustrated title traces the history of Delaware from the 17th-century massacre of Dutch settlers by Native Americans to the eve of the American Revolution; maps and a timeline make this useful for research. (Rev: SLJ 1/07)

10150 Howarth, Sarah. *Colonial Places* (4–8). Series: People and Places. 1994, Millbrook LB $22.90 (978-1-56294-513-8). Highlights various places of importance in everyday colonial life, such as the meetinghouse and the church. (Rev: BL 5/15/95; SLJ 3/95) [973]

10151 Jackson, Shirley. *The Witchcraft of Salem Village* (4–7). 1963, Random House paper $5.99 (978-0-394-89176-7). An account of the witch-hunting hysteria that hit Salem Village. [133.43097445]

10152 Kelly, Martin, and Melissa Kelly. *Government* (5–9). Series: Colonial Life. 2007, Sharpe Focus $37.95 (978-0-7656-8112-6). With color illustrations and interesting sidebars, this volume looks at government in the colonies, exploring the Native American tribal organization as well as the colonial structure. (Rev: SLJ 1/08)

10153 Kent, Deborah. *In Colonial New England* (4–8). Series: How We Lived. 1999, Benchmark LB $28.50 (978-0-7614-0905-2). Topics such as home life, childhood, religion, problems, and amusements are covered for the colonial period in New England. Companion volumes are *In the Middle Colonies* and *In the Southern Colonies* (1999). (Rev: HBG 10/00; SLJ 2/00) [973.2]

10154 McKissack, Patricia C., and Fredrick McKissack, Jr. *Hard Labor: The First African Americans, 1619* (5–8). Illus. by Joseph Fiedler. Series: Milestone Books. 2004, Simon & Schuster paper $3.99 (978-0-689-86149-9). Drawing on the meager evidence available, the authors reconstruct the story of the first Africans brought to America. (Rev: BL 2/15/04; SLJ 3/04) [306.3]

10155 McNeese, Tim. *Colonial America 1543–1763* (5–8). Series: Discovering U.S. History. 2010, Chelsea House $35 (978-1-60413-349-3). McNeese provides a succinct overview of the key events and issues of Colonial America, with a chronology and timeline plus illustrations and primary sources. e (Rev: LMC 11–12/10; SLJ 8/10) [973.2]

10156 McNeese, Tim. *Jamestown* (5–8). Illus. Series: Colonial Settlements in America. 2007, Chelsea House $30 (978-0-7910-9335-1). This overview of the settlement of the colony will be helpful to report writers and includes maps and other graphics. (Rev: BL 7/07; LMC 11/07; SLJ 7/07)

10157 Marrin, Albert. *Struggle for a Continent: The French and Indian Wars, 1690-1760* (6–9). 1987, Macmillan LB $15.95 (978-0-689-31313-4). A vivid recreation of the events and personalities of these wars and how they helped lead to the Revolution. (Rev: BL 1/15/88; SLJ 12/87; VOYA 10/87) [973.2]

10158 Miller, Brandon Marie. *Good Women of a Well-Blessed Land: Women's Lives in Colonial America* (5–8). Series: People's History. 2003, Lerner LB $29.27 (978-0-8225-0032-2). The lives and roles of women from all layers of early American society are presented in this well-written account that includes many quotations, maps, and period reproductions. (Rev: BL 5/15/03; HBG 10/03; SLJ 7/03) [305.4]

10159 Miller, Brandon Marie. *Growing Up in a New World* (5–8). Series: Our America. 2002, Lerner LB $26.60 (978-0-8225-0658-4). The thrill of landing in the New World for the first time is re-created through true-life adventures of young people. (Rev: BL 2/15/03; HBG 3/03; SLJ 7/03) [973.2]

10160 Miller, Lee. *Roanoke: The Mystery of the Lost Colony* (4–7). 2007, Scholastic $18.99 (978-0-439-71266-8). Author Miller presents her theory that the colony at Roanoke was sabotaged. (Rev: BL 6/1–15/07; LMC 10/07) [975.6]

10161 Roop, Connie, and Peter Roop, eds. *Pilgrim Voices: Our First Year in the New World* (4–7). 1995, Walker LB $17.85 (978-0-8027-8315-8). Using first-person sources, the experiences of the Pilgrims from their sea journey to the first Thanksgiving are re-created. (Rev: BL 2/1/96; SLJ 1/96) [974.4]

10162 Schanzer, Rosalyn. *Witches!: The Absolutely True Tale of Disaster in Salem* (5–8). Illus. by author. 2011, National Geographic $16.95 (978-1-4263-0869-7); LB $27.90 (978-1-4263-0870-3). With arresting illustrations this is a compelling account of how the illness afflicting two young girls leads to accusations of witchcraft. Sibert Honor 2012; ALA Notable Books 2012. ⌒ **e** (Rev: BL 11/1/11; SLJ 12/1/11*; VOYA 12/11) [133.4]

10163 Sherrow, Victoria. *Huskings, Quiltings, and Barn Raisings: Work-Play Parties in Early America* (4–7). Illus. by Laura LoTurco. 1992, Walker LB $14.85 (978-0-8027-8188-8). How people in early America helped each other with difficult tasks, such as clearing land and raising barns. (Rev: BL 1/15/93) [973.2]

10164 Smith, Carter, ed. *The Arts and Sciences: A Sourcebook on Colonial America* (5–8). Series: American Albums. 1991, Millbrook $25.90 (978-1-56294-037-9). Through many well-captioned illustrations and brief text, this sourcebook traces cultural and scientific life during the U.S. colonial period. (Rev: BL 1/1/92) [973.2]

10165 Steere, Deirdre Clancy, and Amela Baksic. *Colonial America* (6–12). Series: Costume and Fashion Source Books. 2009, Chelsea House $35 (978-1-60413-380-6). This volume looks at the attire of men and women from various different walks of life in Colonial America. (Rev: LMC 11–12/09; SLJ 10/09) [391]

10166 Stefoff, Rebecca. *Cities and Towns* (5–9). Series: Colonial Life. 2007, Sharpe Focus $37.95 (978-0-7656-8109-6). With color illustrations and interesting sidebars, this volume looks at the development of cities and towns from the earlier forts and fishing camps. (Rev: SLJ 1/08)

10167 Stefoff, Rebecca. *Exploration and Settlement* (5–9). Series: Colonial Life. 2007, Sharpe Focus $37.95

(978-0-7656-8108-9). With color illustrations and interesting sidebars, this volume looks at the progress of exploration in the 15th and 16th centuries and includes profiles of key explorers. (Rev: SLJ 1/08)

10168 Turner, Glennette Tilley. *Fort Mose: And the Story of the Man Who Built the First Free Black Settlement in Colonial America* (7–10). 2010, Abrams $18.95 (978-0-8109-4056-7). Documenting the first free black settlement in North America and the key role of a slave called Francisco Menendez, Turner provides a thorough look at the culture of the place, which blended African, Native American, and Spanish elements. (Rev: BL 10/15/10*; LMC 1–2/11; SLJ 10/1/10) [975.9]

10169 Winters, Kay. *Colonial Voices: Hear Them Speak* (4–7). Illus. by Larry Day. 2008, Dutton $17.99 (978-0-525-47872-0). Fictional residents of colonial Boston offer their opinions on independence and revolution in this illustrated book by the author of *Voices of Egypt*. (Rev: BL 5/15/08; LMC 11–12/08; SLJ 6/08*) [973.3]

10170 Worth, Richard. *Colonial America: Building Toward Independence* (5–8). Series: The American Saga. 2006, Enslow LB $31.93 (978-0-7660-2569-1). Tracing the history of the original 13 colonies from the earliest English settlements through the ratification of the Constitution, this volume will be useful for report writers seeking information on politics, government, economy, and culture. (Rev: SLJ 12/06) [973.2]

REVOLUTIONARY PERIOD AND THE YOUNG NATION (1775–1809)

10171 Allen, Thomas B. *George Washington, Spymaster: How the Americans Outspied the British and Won the Revolutionary War* (6–8). 2004, National Geographic $16.95 (978-0-7922-5126-2). This interesting volume focuses on the general's strategic use of espionage to win America's freedom from the British, providing details about invisible ink, codes and ciphers, and secret messages. (Rev: BL 4/15/04*; SLJ 5/04) [973.3]

10172 Allen, Thomas B. *Remember Valley Forge: Patriots, Tories, and Redcoats Tell Their Stories* (6–9). 2007, National Geographic $17.95 (978-1-4263-0149-0). All sorts of facts about what went on at Valley Forge, many drawn from the writings of eyewitnesses; maps, photographs, important documents, and other visuals add interest and information. (Rev: BL 12/15/07; SLJ 2/08) [973.3]

10173 Allison, Robert J., ed. *American Eras: The Revolutionary Era (1754–1783)* (7–12). 1998, Gale $140.00 (978-0-7876-1480-5). A good reference source that opens with an overview of world events during the Revolutionary period, followed by chapters on specific topics such as the arts; business and the economy; law and justice; lifestyles, social trends, and fashions; religion; and sports and recreation. (Rev: BL 3/15/99; SLJ 2/99) [973.3]

10174 Anderson, Dale. *The American Colonies Declare Independence* (5–8). Series: World Almanac Library of the American Revolution. 2005, World Almanac LB $31.00 (978-0-8368-5926-3). Excerpts from primary sources bolster the informative, clearly written text, which is sprinkled with biographical sidebars. Also use *The Causes of the American Revolution, The Patriots Win the American Revolution*, and *Forming a New American Government* (all 2005). (Rev: SLJ 1/06) [973.3]

10175 Beller, Susan Provost. *Yankee Doodle and the Redcoats: Soldiering in the Revolutionary War* (5–8). Illus. by Larry Day. 2003, Millbrook LB $26.90 (978-0-7613-2612-0). This attractive book covers the plight of the Revolutionary War soldier, with artwork as well as soldiers' letters and other documents adding to the presentation. (Rev: BL 5/15/03; HBG 10/03; SLJ 9/01) [973.3]

10176 Blair, Margaret Whitman. *Liberty or Death: The Surprising Story of Runaway Slaves Who Sided with the British During the American Revolution* (5–8). 2010, National Geographic $18.95 (978-1-4263-0590-0); LB $27.90 (978-1-4263-0591-7). Using personal quotes and anecdotes, Blair tells the unhappy story of the runaway slaves who were promised freedom if they fought for the British during the Revolution. Lexile 1160L (Rev: BL 1/1/10*; LMC 5–6/10; SLJ 3/10) [973.3]

10177 Bliven, Bruce, Jr. *The American Revolution, 1760–1783* (6–9). 1958, Random House paper $5.99 (978-0-394-84696-5). A concise account of the causes, battles, and results of the Revolution. [973.3]

10178 Bobrick, Benson. *Fight for Freedom: The American Revolutionary War* (5–8). 2004, Simon & Schuster $22.95 (978-0-689-86422-3). Full-page illustrations face text and "Quick Facts" about topics ranging from the origins and progress of the war to the Continental Congresses, with profiles of key figures and maps. (Rev: BL 11/15/04; SLJ 11/04) [973.3]

10179 Brenner, Barbara. *If You Were There in 1776* (4–8). 1994, Bradbury $17.95 (978-0-02-712322-7). The year 1776 is explored, with particular emphasis on the everyday life of young people in the colonies. (Rev: BCCB 6/94; BL 5/15/94; SLJ 6/94) [973.3]

10180 Castrovilla, Selene. *Upon Secrecy* (4–7). Illus. by Jeff Crosby and Shelley Ann Jackson. 2009, Boyds Mills $17.95 (978-1-59078-573-7). This illustrated book provides a well-written, slightly fictionalized history of the Culper Spy Ring, a New York City organization instrumental in Washington's ultimate defeat of the British. (Rev: LMC 11–12/09; SLJ 10/09) [973.3]

10181 Chase, John Churchill. *Louisiana Purchase: An American Story. Rev. ed.* (5–8). 2002, Pelican paper $12.95 (978-1-58980-084-7). The story of the Louisiana Purchase, engagingly told in comic-strip format. (Rev: BL 2/1/03) [973.4]

10182 Deem, James M. *Primary Source Accounts of the Revolutionary War* (5–8). Series: America's Wars Through Primary Sources. 2006, Enslow LB $33.27 (978-1-59845-004-0). Soldiers' journal entries, letters from home, personal recollections, songs and poetry, and newspaper articles are among the primary sources included in this general history of the war. (Rev: SLJ 4/07) [973.3]

10183 Delano, Marfé Ferguson. *Master George's People: George Washington, His Slaves, and His Revolutionary Transformation* (5–8). Illus. 2013, National Geographic $18.95 (978-142630759-1); LB $27.90 (978-142630760-7). Delano explores Washington's ownership of slaves and his gradually evolving attitude during the Revolutionary War, leading to his slaves being freed in his will; the book includes many color illustrations and interesting vignettes drawn from primary sources. (Rev: BL 2/1/13*; SLJ 2/13) [973.4]

10184 Diouf, Sylviane A. *Growing Up in Slavery* (6–12). 2001, Millbrook LB $25.90 (978-0-7613-1763-0). A compelling account that dispels any myths about happy slave children and describes the hard life on the plantation as well as the atrocious conditions on slave ships. (Rev: BL 3/1/01; HBG 10/01; SLJ 6/01) [380.1]

10185 Fleming, Thomas. *Everybody's Revolution* (4–7). Illus. 2006, Scholastic $19.99 (978-0-439-63404-5). A fascinating introduction to the diverse heroes and heroines of many nationalities who contributed to the success of the American Revolution. (Rev: BL 10/15/06; SLJ 11/06)

10186 Freedman, Russell. *Give Me Liberty! The Story of the Declaration of Independence* (4–7). 2000, Holiday $24.95 (978-0-8234-1448-2). Beginning with the Boston Tea Party, this stirring account introduces characters including Patrick Henry and Paul Revere, events such as the battles at Lexington and Concord, and ends with the Continental Congress and the drawing up of the Declaration of Independence. (Rev: BCCB 10/00; BL 10/1/00*; HB 1–2/01; HBG 3/01; SLJ 10/00) [973.3]

10187 Freedman, Russell. *Washington at Valley Forge* (6–9). Illus. 2008, Holiday House $24.95 (978-082342069-8). This vivid account — bolstered by stunning full-color reproductions — of Washington's encampment at Valley Forge during the winter of 1777 shows exactly why he was considered such a remarkable leader. ALA Notable Books 2009. Lexile 1210L (Rev: BL 12/1/08; HB 1–2/09; SLJ 12/08; VOYA 12/08) [973.3]

10188 Gaines, Ann Graham. *The Louisiana Purchase in American History* (7–10). Series: In American History. 2000, Enslow LB $26.60 (978-0-7660-1301-8). A well-documented and illustrated account of the 1803 purchase of southern land from the French government. (Rev: BL 1/1–15/00; HBG 9/00) [973.5]

10189 Herbert, Janis. *The American Revolution for Kids* (5–8). 2002, Chicago Review paper $14.95 (978-1-

55652-456-1). A comprehensive look at the American Revolution from its causes through the early 18th century, with biographical information and interesting features. (Rev: BL 10/1/02; SLJ 11/02) [973.3]

10190 Karapalides, Harry J. *Dates of the American Revolution: Who, What, and Where in the War for Independence* (7–12). 1998, Burd Street paper $19.95 (978-1-57249-106-9). A chronological record tracing the American Revolution from 1760, when King George II inherited the British throne, to George Washington's death in 1799, with an emphasis on military action and commanders. (Rev: SLJ 2/99) [973.3]

10191 King, David C. *Saratoga* (5–8). Series: Battlefields Across America. 1998, Twenty-First Century LB $26.90 (978-0-7613-3011-0). The significance of the battle at Saratoga in 1777, in which General Burgoyne's British army was defeated, and where and how the history of this battle is preserved today. (Rev: HBG 9/98; SLJ 8/98) [973.3]

10192 McCullough, David. *1776* (8–12). 2005, Simon & Schuster $32.00 (978-0-7432-2671-4). McCullough brings to life the key events of the year 1776 for George Washington and the new young nation. (Rev: SLJ 10/05) [973]

10193 McNeese, Tim. *Revolutionary America 1764–1789* (5–8). Series: Discovering U.S. History. 2010, Chelsea House $35 (978-1-60413-350-9). McNeese provides a succinct overview of the key events and issues of this period of turmoil, with a chronology and timeline plus illustrations and primary sources. (Rev: LMC 11–12/10) [973.3]

10194 Miller, Brandon Marie. *Declaring Independence: Life During the American Revolution* (5–8). Series: People's History. 2005, Lerner LB $29.27 (978-0-8225-1275-2). A thorough look at what life was like during the American Revolution, using primary sources. (Rev: SLJ 9/05; VOYA 6/05) [973.3]

10195 Morton, Joseph C. *The American Revolution* (7–12). Series: Greenwood Guides to Historic Events, 1500-1900. 2003, Greenwood $51.95 (978-0-313-31792-7). A thorough, text-dense overview of the events leading up to the war, the war itself, and its aftermath, with profiles of key individuals. (Rev: SLJ 7/04) [973.3]

10196 Murphy, Jim. *An American Plague: The True and Terrifying Story of the Yellow Fever Epidemic of 1793* (6–12). 2003, Clarion $18.00 (978-0-395-77608-7). Narrative, newspaper articles, and archival prints and photographs combine to tell the dramatic story of the epidemic that hit Philadelphia in the late 18th century. Margaret A. Edwards Award 2010. (Rev: BL 6/1–15/03; HB 7–8/03; HBG 10/03; SLJ 6/03*; VOYA 12/03) [614.5]

10197 Murphy, Jim. *The Crossing: How George Washington Saved the American Revolution* (5–8). 2010,

Scholastic $21.99 (978-0-439-69186-4). With many quotations, illustrations, maps, and reproductions, plus clear text, this is an appealing account of Washington's efforts to whip a ragtag army into shape and his various triumphs and failures. (Rev: BL 11/15/10*; SLJ 12/1/10*) [973.3]

10198 Murphy, Jim. *A Young Patriot: The American Revolution as Experienced by One Boy* (5–8). 1996, Clarion $16.00 (978-0-395-60523-3). The American Revolution as seen through the eyes of a 15-year-old volunteer. Margaret A. Edwards Award 2010. (Rev: BCCB 6/96; BL 6/1–15/96*; HB 9–10/96; SLJ 6/96*) [973.3]

10199 Sanders, Nancy I. *America's Black Founders: Revolutionary Heroes and Early Leaders with 21 Activities* (6–10). Series: For Kids. 2010, Chicago Review paper $16.95 (978-15565281-1-8). With activities such as filling a straw mattress, making a stamp, and drawing a political cartoon, this is a lively introduction to the role of African Americans in the early days of the nation, covering well-known figures and ordinary people. (Rev: BL 2/1/10; LMC 3–4/10; SLJ 1/10) [973]

10200 Schanzer, Rosalyn. *George vs. George: The Revolutionary War as Seen by Both Sides* (5–7). 2004, National Geographic $16.95 (978-0-7922-7349-3). The two sides' differences — and commonalities — are portrayed in an appealing combination of well-written text, colorful art, and speech balloons; sensationalist aspects detract from the overall value. (Rev: BL 11/15/04; SLJ 10/04*) [973.3]

10201 Sheinkin, Steve. *King George: What Was His Problem? Everything Your Schoolbooks Didn't Tell You About the American Revolution* (4–7). Illus. by Tim Robinson. 2008, Roaring Brook $19.95 (978-1-59643-319-9). First published as *The American Revolution* (2005), this is a breezy and often funny collection of stories that history students will remember. (Rev: BL 8/08) [973.3]

10202 Smith, Carter, ed. *The Revolutionary War: A Sourcebook on Colonial America* (5–8). Series: American Albums. 1991, Millbrook $25.90 (978-1-56294-039-3). This volume illustrates the major events leading up to the Revolution and the battles and personalities involved. (Rev: BL 1/1/92) [973.38]

10203 Weber, Michael. *Yorktown* (4–7). Series: Battlefields Across America. 1997, Twenty-First Century LB $26.90 (978-0-8050-5226-8). Background material on the Revolutionary War is given, along with details of the battle and the present-day condition of its site. (Rev: SLJ 1/98) [973.3]

NINETEENTH CENTURY TO THE CIVIL WAR
(1809–1861)

10204 Bial, Raymond. *The Strength of These Arms: Life in the Slave Quarters* (5–8). 1997, Houghton Mifflin

$16.00 (978-0-395-77394-9). This photoessay re-creates daily life in the slave quarters on large plantations, contrasts it with the luxurious lifestyles of the slave holders, and documents how slaves tried to preserve their heritage, dignity, and hope. (Rev: BL 9/15/97; HBG 3/98; SLJ 11/97) [975]

10205 Bozonelis, Helen Koutras. *Primary Source Accounts of the War of 1812* (5–8). Illus. Series: America's Wars Through Primary Sources. 2006, Enslow LB $33.27 (978-1-59845-006-4). Soldiers' journal entries, letters from the homefront, personal recollections, songs and poetry, and newspaper articles are among the primary sources included in this general history of the war. (Rev: SLJ 4/07) [973.5]

10206 Carson, Mary Kay. *The Underground Railroad for Kids: From Slavery to Freedom* (6–9). Series: For Kids. 2005, Chicago Review paper $14.95 (978-1-55652-554-4). With an engaging blend of first-person accounts and brief profiles, this is an easy-to-understand history of the Underground Railroad and the men and women who used it to escape from slavery. (Rev: BL 2/1/05; SLJ 3/05) [973.7]

10207 Cloud Tapper, Suzanne. *The Abolition of Slavery: Fighting for a Free America* (7–12). Series: The American Saga. 2006, Enslow LB $31.93 (978-0-7660-2605-6). The history of the abolitionist movement is chronicled in this well-organized book that includes primary source material, photographs, and maps. (Rev: SLJ 7/07) [973.7]

10208 Coleman, Wim, and Pat Perrin. *The Amazing Erie Canal and How a Big Ditch Opened Up the West* (4–7). Illus. Series: Wild History of the American West. 2006, Enslow LB $33.27 (978-1-59845-017-0). Why was the Erie Canal built? What was its impact on American commerce and history? This richly illustrated profile answers those questions and offers a general overview of canals; 30 Internet links are provided for further research. (Rev: BL 10/15/06) [386]

10209 DeFord, Deborah H. *Life Under Slavery* (6–12). Series: Slavery in the Americas. 2006, Chelsea House $35 (978-0-8160-6135-8). Middle schoolers studying slavery in the United States will be interested to learn how African blacks adapted their culture and traditions in an effort to survive life as captives. (Rev: SLJ 9/06)

10210 Fradin, Dennis Brindell. *Bound for the North Star: True Stories of Fugitive Slaves* (8–12). 2000, Clarion $21.00 (978-0-395-97017-1). Personal experiences form the basis of these moving profiles that spare no details of the horrors suffered by escaping slaves and the courage of their helpers. (Rev: BL 1/1–15/01*; HB 1–2/01; HBG 3/01; SLJ 11/00*; VOYA 10/01) [973.7]

10211 Gay, Kathlyn, and Martin Gay. *War of 1812* (5–8). Series: Voices of the Past. 1995, Twenty-First Century LB $25.90 (978-0-8050-2846-1). Excerpts from letters, memoirs, and official reports highlight this well-illus-

trated history of the War of 1812 and its consequences. (Rev: BL 12/15/95; SLJ 3/96) [973.5]

10212 Hansen, Joyce, and Gary McGowan. *Freedom Roads: Searching for the Underground Railroad* (5–8). Illus. by James Ransome. 2003, Cricket $18.95 (978-0-8126-2673-5). This look at the history of the Underground Railroad emphasizes how much of our knowledge consists of speculation and anecdotal material rather than hard evidence. (Rev: BL 5/1/03; HB 7–8/03; HBG 10/03; SLJ 9/03*) [973.7]

10213 Heidler, David S., and Jeanne T. Heidler. *The War of 1812* (8–12). Series: Greenwood Guides to Historic Events, 1500-1900. 2002, Greenwood $51.95 (978-0-313-31687-6). This thorough and detailed description of the causes, events, and key figures of the War of 1812 will be useful for report writers. (Rev: BL 10/15/02; SLJ 10/02) [973.5]

10214 King, David C. *New Orleans* (5–8). Series: Battlefields Across America. 1998, Twenty-First Century LB $26.90 (978-0-7613-3010-3). The story of the famous 1815 battle in New Orleans in which the British were decisively defeated, including the background of the War of 1812, the role of Andrew Jackson, and the significance of this defeat to the British. (Rev: HBG 9/98; SLJ 8/98) [973.6]

10215 Landau, Elaine. *Fleeing to Freedom on the Underground Railroad: The Courageous Slaves, Agents, and Conductors* (6–9). Series: People's History. 2006, Lerner LB $29.27 (978-0-8225-3490-7). Anecdotes about individual contributions and quotations from primary sources add to this account of the Underground Railroad and those who created and used it; excerpts from key legislation round out this useful volume. (Rev: BL 2/1/06; SLJ 5/06) [973.7]

10216 McKissack, Patricia C., and Fredrick McKissack. *Rebels Against Slavery: American Slave Revolts* (5–8). 1996, Scholastic paper $15.95 (978-0-590-45735-4). A fascinating account of the men and women who led revolts against slavery, including Toussaint L'Ouverture, Cinque, Harriet Tubman, and Nat Turner. (Rev: BCCB 6/96; BL 2/15/96; SLJ 3/96; VOYA 4/96) [970]

10217 McNeese, Tim. *The Abolitionist Movement: Ending Slavery* (8–12). Series: Reform Movements in American History. 2007, Chelsea House LB $30.00 (978-0-7910-9502-7). An informative survey of the movement and its leaders. (Rev: BL 11/15/07; LMC 4–5/08) [973.7114]

10218 Mancall, Peter C., ed. *American Eras: Westward Expansion (1800–1860)* (8–12). 1999, Gale $140.00 (978-0-7876-1483-6). The period of growth and change in America from the early 19th century up to the Civil War is examined. (Rev: BL 3/15/99; SLJ 8/99) [973.6]

10219 Marquette, Scott. *War of 1812* (4–7). Series: America at War. 2002, Rourke LB $20.95 (978-1-58952-389-0). This book for middle-graders studies the war itself and the events that led up to it. (Rev: BL 10/15/02) [973.5]

10220 Morrison, Taylor. *Coast Mappers* (4–8). 2004, Houghton Mifflin $16.00 (978-0-618-25408-8). Science and biography are interwoven in this examination of the mid-19th-century mapping of the U.S. Pacific coastline. (Rev: BL 3/15/04; SLJ 5/04) [623.89]

10221 Paulson, Timothy J. *Days of Sorrow, Years of Glory, 1831–1850: From the Nat Turner Revolt to the Fugitive Slave Law* (5–9). Series: Milestones in Black American History. 1994, Chelsea paper $14.93 (978-0-7910-2552-9). An examination of the Underground Railroad, slave resistance, the Seminole Wars, and the abolition movement. (Rev: BL 11/1/94; SLJ 4/95; VOYA 12/94) [973]

10222 Stewart, Mark. *The Alamo, February 23–March 6, 1836* (5–7). Series: American Battlefields. 2004, Enchanted Lion $14.95 (978-1-59270-026-4). This overview of the Battle of the Alamo offers a clear account of the conflict and an examination of the developments leading up to it; sidebars, illustrations, a timeline, and other features add to the narrative. (Rev: BL 11/1/04) [976.4]

10223 Swain, Gwenyth. *Dred and Harriet Scott: A Family's Struggle for Freedom* (6–9). 2004, Borealis paper $12.95 (978-0-87351-483-5). The story of the Scotts' desire that their young daughters should not have to live as slaves and the lengthy court battle that they ultimately lost, a battle that brought the Civil War a step closer. (Rev: SLJ 7/04) [973.7]

10224 Turner, Glennette Tilley. *The Underground Railroad in Illinois* (5–8). 2001, Newman Educational paper $16.95 (978-0-938990-05-5). Using a question-and-answer format, this book focuses on the Underground Railroad in Illinois, the historical period, the problems, people who worked on the effort, and the many heroic deeds. (Rev: BL 2/15/01) [973.7]

10225 Walker, Paul R. *Remember the Alamo: Texians, Tejanos, and Mexicans Tell Their Stories* (5–8). Illus. 2007, National Geographic $17.95 (978-1-4263-0010-3). A detailed account of the siege of the Alamo, with explanation of the events leading up to the crisis and with many firsthand descriptions. (Rev: BL 5/15/07; SLJ 8/07)

10226 Zeinert, Karen. *The Amistad Slave Revolt and American Abolition* (7–10). 1997, Shoe String LB $21.50 (978-0-208-02438-1); paper $12.95 (978-0-208-02439-8). The dramatic story of Cinque and 52 other slaves onboard the Spanish ship *Amistad* in 1839 and of their historic mutiny and subsequent trial. (Rev: BL 7/97; SLJ 6/97) [326]

10227 Zeinert, Karen. *Tragic Prelude: Bleeding Kansas* (6–10). 2001, Linnet $25.00 (978-0-208-02446-6). An accessible account of the conflict that erupted in Kansas over the question of slavery, with information on

individuals including John Brown and Hannah Ropes, a timeline, extracts from primary documents, photographs, and references. (Rev: BL 6/1–15/01; HBG 10/01; SLJ 6/01; VOYA 2/02) [978.1]

CIVIL WAR (1861–1865)

10228 Allen, Thomas B. *Harriet Tubman, Secret Agent: How Daring Slaves and Free Blacks Spied for the Union During the Civil War* (5–8). Illus. by Carla Bauer. 2006, National Geographic $16.95 (978-0-7922-7889-4). The efforts of Tubman and other slaves to gather important information and pass it to the Union forces is the focus of this volume that includes examples of a code sometimes used. (Rev: BCCB 1/07; BL 12/1/06; HBG 4/07; LMC 5/07; SLJ 2/07*)

10229 Allen, Thomas B., and Roger MacBride Allen. *Mr. Lincoln's High-Tech War: How the North Used the Telegraph, Railroads, Surveillance Balloons, Ironclads, High-Powered Weapons, and More to Win the Civil War* (6–10). Illus. 2008, National Geographic $18.95 (978-1-4263-0379-1); LB $25.90 (978-1-4263-0380-7). The authors argue that Lincoln's enthusiasm for technology contributed directly to the Union's success in the Civil War. ALA Notable Books 2010. Lexile 1180L (Rev: BL 12/15/08*; LMC 5–6/09; SLJ 2/1/09*; VOYA 2/09) [973.7]

10230 Armstrong, Jennifer. *Photo by Brady: A Picture of the Civil War* (6–9). 2005, Simon & Schuster $18.95 (978-0-689-85785-0). This photoessay artfully uses the photographs of Mathew Brady to document Civil War history from the inauguration of Abraham Lincoln to his assassination, only days after the end of hostilities. (Rev: BL 3/15/05; SLJ 3/05; VOYA 4/05) [973.7]

10231 Arnold, James R., and Roberta Wiener. *Divided in Two: The Road to Civil War* (4–7). Series: The Civil War. 2002, Lerner LB $25.26 (978-0-8225-2312-3). A well-designed oversize book that describes the events of 1861 that led to the outbreak of the Civil War. (Rev: BL 10/15/02; HBG 10/02; SLJ 7/02) [973.7]

10232 Arnold, James R., and Roberta Wiener. *Life Goes On: The Civil War at Home* (4–7). Series: The Civil War. 2002, Lerner LB $25.26 (978-0-8225-2315-4). Many easy-to-follow maps and illustrations are used with a simple text to describe life on the home front in both South and North during the Civil War. (Rev: BL 10/15/02; HBG 10/02; SLJ 7/02) [973.7]

10233 Arnold, James R., and Roberta Wiener. *Lost Cause: The End of the Civil War* (4–7). Series: The Civil War. 2002, Lerner LB $25.26 (978-0-8225-2317-8). Beginning with the campaign of 1864, this well-illustrated account traces the Civil War to Appomattox and beyond. (Rev: BL 10/15/02; HBG 10/02; SLJ 6/02) [973.7]

10234 Arnold, James R., and Roberta Wiener. *On to Richmond: The Civil War in the East, 1861-1862* (4–7).

Series: Civil War. 2002, Lerner LB $25.26 (978-0-8225-2313-0). Early battles in the Civil War are the subject of this volume for older readers that includes timelines, notes, and lists of Web sites and battlefields to visit. (Rev: BL 10/15/02; HBG 10/02; SLJ 6/02; VOYA 6/03) [973.7]

10235 Arnold, James R., and Roberta Wiener. *River to Victory: The Civil War in the West* (4–7). Series: The Civil War. 2002, Lerner LB $25.26 (978-0-8225-2314-7). The Civil War in the West from 1861 through 1863 is re-created in text and illustrations with many maps and sidebars on personalities and events. (Rev: BL 10/15/02; HBG 10/02; SLJ 6/02; VOYA 6/03) [973.7]

10236 Arnold, James R., and Roberta Wiener. *This Unhappy Country: The Turn of the Civil War* (4–7). Series: Civil War. 2002, Lerner LB $25.26 (978-0-8225-2316-1). Maps and other period illustrations flesh out the events of 1863, a pivotal year in the Civil War, in this volume for older readers. (Rev: BL 10/15/02; HBG 10/02; SLJ 7/02) [973.7]

10237 Bailey, Ronald H. *The Bloodiest Day: The Battle of Antietam* (7–12). 1984, Silver Burdett LB $25.93 (978-0-8094-4741-1). The story of Lee's defeat in the battle that caused terrible losses on both sides. [973.7]

10238 Barney, William L. *The Civil War and Reconstruction: A Student Companion* (7–12). Series: Oxford Student Companions to American History. 2001, Oxford LB $65.00 (978-0-19-511559-8). An alphabetically arranged series of articles covering all aspects of the Civil War and Reconstruction, illustrated with photographs, maps, and reproductions. (Rev: BL 9/15/01; SLJ 6/01) [973.7]

10239 Beller, Susan Provost. *Billy Yank and Johnny Reb: Soldiering in the Civil War* (5–8). 2000, Twenty-First Century LB $26.90 (978-0-7613-1869-9). Solid, interesting information is provided in this illustrated account that describes the everyday life of soldiers on both sides of the Civil War. (Rev: BL 10/15/00; HBG 3/01; SLJ 12/00; VOYA 2/01) [973.7]

10240 Bolden, Tonya. *Emancipation Proclamation: Lincoln and the Dawn of Liberty* (6–10). Illus. 2013, Abrams $24.95 (978-141970390-4). Drawing extensively on primary sources, archival photographs, posters and letters, and so forth, this accessible and attractive volume offers well-written text and detailed captions. (Rev: BL 2/1/13*; HB 7–8/13; SLJ 1/13*) [973.714]

10241 Butzer, C. M. *Gettysburg: The Graphic Novel* (4–8). Illus. by author. 2009, HarperCollins $16.99 (978-0-06-156176-4); paper $9.99 (978-0-06-156175-7). After a brief section on the Battle of Gettysburg, Butzer moves on to present Lincoln's famous address; the graphic novel format works well and he integrates words from primary sources including letters and diaries. (Rev: BL 12/1/08; LMC 10/09; SLJ 11/08) [973.7]

10242 *Chancellorsville* (7–12). Series: Voices of the Civil War. 1996, Time-Life $24.95 (978-0-7853-4708-8). A handsome description of this key Civil War battle, featuring regimental histories, letters, diaries, and memoirs. (Rev: BL 1/1–15/97) [973.7]

10243 Clinton, Catherine. *Scholastic Encyclopedia of the Civil War* (4–7). 1999, Scholastic paper $18.95 (978-0-590-37227-5). Using many black-and-white illustrations, this narrative gives a good chronological introduction to the Civil War, with interesting supplementary information. (Rev: BL 1/1–15/00; HBG 3/00; SLJ 5/00) [973.7]

10244 Colbert, Nancy. *The Firing on Fort Sumter: A Splintered Nation Goes to War* (6–12). 2000, Morgan Reynolds LB $23.95 (978-1-883846-51-0). An intriguing, detailed account, told in lively prose and many photographs, of the incident that began the Civil War. (Rev: BL 10/1/00; HBG 3/01; VOYA 6/01) [973.7]

10245 Damon, Duane. *Growing Up In the Civil War: 1861 to 1865* (5–8). Series: Our America. 2002, Lerner LB $26.60 (978-0-8225-0656-0). The lives of children in this period are described with many quotations and excerpts from diaries, letters, and memoirs. (Rev: BL 2/15/03; HBG 3/03; SLJ 2/03) [973.7]

10246 DeFord, Deborah H. *African Americans during the Civil War* (6–12). Series: Slavery in the Americas. 2006, Chelsea House $35 (978-0-8160-6138-9). The importance of blacks in America during the Civil War — as slaves, civilians, and soldiers — is covered, as is the "National Convention of Colored Men" and the effects that the war had on African Americans' rights. (Rev: SLJ 9/06)

10247 Dolan, Edward F. *The American Civil War: A House Divided* (5–8). 1997, Millbrook LB $29.90 (978-0-7613-0255-1). A chronologically arranged, well-organized account of the Civil War, beginning with the shots fired at Fort Sumter. (Rev: BL 3/1/98; HBG 3/98; SLJ 3/98) [973.7]

10248 Egger-Bovet, Howard, and Marlene Smith-Baranzini. *Book of the American Civil War* (5–7). Illus. by D. J. Simison. Series: Brown Paper School. 1998, Little, Brown paper $12.95 (978-0-316-22243-3). Facts, photographs, illustrations, stories and appealing activities are combined in this overview of the Civil War. (Rev: SLJ 12/98) [973.7]

10249 Heinrichs, Ann. *The Emancipation Proclamation* (5–8). Series: We the People. 2002, Compass Point LB $26.60 (978-0-7565-0209-6). An accessible examination of the proclamation's creation that reveals Lincoln's careful attention to detail. (Rev: SLJ 7/02) [973.7]

10250 Herbert, Janis. *The Civil War for Kids: A History with 21 Activities* (4–8). 1999, Chicago Review paper $14.95 (978-1-55652-355-7). As well as supplying information about leaders, battles, daily life, and the contributions of women and African Americans, this book on the Civil War includes activities such as reenactments of battles, most of which are geared toward groups. (Rev: SLJ 12/99) [973.7]

10251 Hughes, Christopher. *Antietam* (5–8). Series: Battlefields Across America. 1998, Millbrook LB $26.90 (978-0-7613-3009-7). This book describes the battle at Antietam in detail, discusses its impact on the outcome of the war and on the future of the United States, profiles the major people involved, and provides information on where the history of this battle is preserved. (Rev: HBG 9/98; SLJ 8/98) [973.7]

10252 January, Brendan. *Gettysburg, July 1–3, 1863* (5–7). Series: American Battlefields. 2004, Enchanted Lion $14.95 (978-1-59270-025-7). This overview of the Battle of Gettysburg offers a clear account of the bloody conflict and an examination of the developments leading up to it; sidebars, illustrations, a timeline, and other features add to the narrative. (Rev: BL 11/1/04) [973]

10253 Jarrow, Gail. *Lincoln's Flying Spies* (7–10). Illus. 2010, Boyds Mills $18.95 (978-159078719-9). This volume tells the story of the Union Army's Aeronautics Corps and its fleet of hot-air balloons that helped to spy on the Confederate Army, focusing in particular on the aeronaut Thaddeus Lowe and his contributions. Lexile 1060L (Rev: BL 10/15/10; LMC 1–2/11; SLJ 11/10) [973.7]

10254 Jones, Lynda. *Mrs. Lincoln's Dressmaker: The Unlikely Friendship of Elizabeth Keckley and Mary Todd Lincoln* (6–9). Illus. 2008, National Geographic $18.95 (978-142630377-7); LB $27.90 (978-142630378-4). Readers will gain insight into the life and times of both Mary Todd Lincoln and her dressmaker, a former slave; primary sources and duotone illustrations add to the account's authenticity. Lexile 960L (Rev: BL 1/1–15/09; LMC 5–6/09; SLJ 1/1/09) [973.7092]

10255 Kantor, MacKinlay. *Gettysburg* (6–9). 1952, Random House paper $5.99 (978-0-394-89181-1). The story of the crucial battle of the Civil War that could have meant a total victory for the Confederacy. [973.7]

10256 McComb, Marianne. *The Emancipation Proclamation* (4–7). Illus. Series: American Documents. 2006, National Geographic LB $23.90 (978-0-7922-7936-5). The background, nature, and impact of this important document are explained clearly, with photos and illustrations plus full texts of the Emancipation Proclamation, the Fugitive Slave Law of 1850, and Constitutional Amendments XIII through XV. (Rev: BL 2/1/06; SLJ 2/06; VOYA 8/06) [973.7]

10257 McNeese, Tim. *Civil War Battles* (6–12). Series: Civil War: A Nation Divided. 2009, Chelsea House $35 (978-1-60413-034-8). Bull Run, Shiloh, Antietam, Fredericksburg, Chancellorsville, and Gettysburg are among the battles covered in this volume that looks at

real-life stories and the cost of war. (Rev: LMC 11–12/09) [973.73]

10258 McNeese, Tim. *The Civil War Era 1851–1865* (5–8). Series: Discovering U.S. History. 2010, Chelsea House $35 (978-1-60413-352-3). McNeese provides a succinct overview of the key events and issues of the Civil War, with a chronology and timeline plus illustrations and primary sources. (Rev: LMC 11–12/10) [973.7]

10259 McPherson, James M. *Fields of Fury: The American Civil War* (6–8). 2002, Simon & Schuster $22.95 (978-0-689-84833-9). Packed with interesting illustrations and sidebars, this large-format book gives an overview of the Civil War that will attract both report writers and casual browsers. (Rev: BL 11/15/02; HBG 3/03; SLJ 10/02*) [973.7]

10260 Marinelli, Deborah A. *The Assassination of Abraham Lincoln* (6–9). Series: The Library of Political Assassinations. 2002, Rosen LB $27.95 (978-0-8239-3539-0). In addition to describing the assassination itself, Marinelli covers the Civil War and Lincoln's legacy. (Rev: BL 8/02; SLJ 8/02) [976]

10261 Mountjoy, Shane. *Causes of the Civil War: The Differences Between the North and South* (5–8). Series: The Civil War: A Nation Divided. 2009, Chelsea House $35 (978-1-60413-036-2). This volume looks at the political scene in the early 19th century and the rivalries that led to the outbreak of war. (Rev: SLJ 10/09) [973.711]

10262 Mountjoy, Shane. *Technology and the Civil War* (5–8). Series: The Civil War: A Nation Divided. 2009, Chelsea House $35 (978-1-60413-037-9). In chapters covering railroads and the telegraph, weapons, ironclads, submarines, medicine, and photography, this volume documents the advances made during the war. (Rev: SLJ 8/09) [973.7301]

10263 Murphy, Jim. *The Long Road to Gettysburg* (6–9). 1992, Clarion $18.00 (978-0-395-55965-9). An account of the Civil War from both the Union and Confederate perspectives. Margaret A. Edwards Award 2010. (Rev: BL 5/15/92*; SLJ 6/92*) [973.7]

10264 Murphy, Jim. *A Savage Thunder: Antietam and the Bloody Road to Freedom* (6–10). 2009, Simon & Schuster $17.99 (978-0-689-87633-2). The terrible battle of Antietam is chronicled here, with maps, firsthand accounts, and discussion of its importance to the overall war. ∩ (Rev: BL 8/09*; HB 9–10/09; LMC 10/09; SLJ 8/09) [973.7]

10265 O'Reilly, Bill, and Dwight Jon Zimmerman. *Lincoln's Last Days: The Shocking Assassination That Changed America* (6–9). Illus. 2012, Henry Holt $19.99 (978-0-8050-9675-0). This adaptation of *Killing Lincoln* (2011) describes for younger readers the events surrounding Lincoln's assassination. ∩ e Lexile 1020L (Rev: BL 10/1/12; SLJ 12/12) [973.7092]

10266 Reis, Ronald A. *African Americans and the Civil War* (6–12). Series: Civil War: A Nation Divided. 2009, Chelsea House $35 (978-1-60413-038-6). Free blacks and ex-slaves fought in more than 400 battles but faced prejudice and were underpaid despite their contributions. (Rev: LMC 11–12/09) [973.73]

10267 Schomp, Virginia. *The Civil War* (5–8). Series: Letters from the Homefront. 2001, Marshall Cavendish LB $29.93 (978-0-7614-1095-9). After placing the conflict in historical context, Schomp uses excerpts from letters and other accounts that bring the period to life. (Rev: BL 10/15/01; HBG 3/02; SLJ 3/02) [973.7]

10268 Sheinkin, Steve. *Two Miserable Presidents: Everything Your Schoolbooks Didn't Tell You About the Civil War* (4–8). Illus. by Tim Robinson. 2008, Roaring Brook $19.95 (978-1-59643-320-5). This unusual take on the war and its leaders will attract reluctant history students. It focuses on the personalities but does not leave out the larger issues that led to the war and affected its outcome. (Rev: BL 4/15/08) [973.7]

10269 Silvey, Anita. *I'll Pass for Your Comrade: Women Soldiers in the Civil War* (6–9). Illus. 2008, Clarion $17.00 (978-061857491-9). Silvey weaves together the lives of women who fought as soldiers in the Civil War, exploring such topics as how they concealed their identities in hospitals and how they coped with so little privacy at camp. Lexile 1130L (Rev: BL 11/15/08; HB 1–2/09; LMC 3–4/09; SLJ 12/08; VOYA 2/09) [973.7]

10270 Slavicek, Louise Chipley. *Women and the Civil War* (5–8). Series: The Civil War: A Nation Divided. 2009, Chelsea House $35 (978-1-60413-040-9). Chapters cover women's roles as nurses, spies, soldiers, and scouts, and look at their work in the camps and on the home front in both North and South; there is also discussion of the situation of African American women. (Rev: SLJ 8/09) [973.7301]

10271 Smith, Carter, ed. *The Road to Appomattox: A Sourcebook on the Civil War* (5–8). Series: American Albums. 1993, Millbrook $25.90 (978-1-56294-264-9). The last battles of the Civil War are covered in this album that uses period illustrations and excerpts from first-person accounts. (Rev: BL 3/1/93) [973.7]

10272 Stanley, George E. *The Crisis of the Union (1815–1865)* (5–8). Series: A Primary Source History of the United States. 2005, World Almanac LB $31.00 (978-0-8368-5826-6). A simple narrative links well-chosen primary sources documenting the key events of the Civil War. (Rev: BL 4/1/05)

10273 Tackach, James, ed. *The Battle of Gettysburg* (8–12). Series: At Issue in History. 2002, Greenhaven paper $18.70 (978-0-7377-0826-4). Excerpts from historical documents and contemporary writings portray events at Gettysburg from both Union and Confederate points of view, with maps, photographs, and other illustrations. (Rev: BL 5/1/02; SLJ 4/02) [973.7]

10274 Taschek, Karen. *The Civil War* (6–12). Series: Costume and Fashion Source Books. 2009, Chelsea House $35 (978-1-60413-381-3). This volume looks at the attire of men and women from various different walks of life in the years before and during the Civil War, including the uniforms of North and South. (Rev: LMC 11–12/09; SLJ 10/09) [391]

10275 Wagner, Heather Lehr. *Spies in the Civil War* (6–12). Series: Civil War: A Nation Divided. 2009, Chelsea House $35 (978-1-60413-039-3). Wagner tells the stories of the men and women who served as spies during the Civil War, examining their motivations and diverse backgrounds. (Rev: LMC 11–12/09) [973.73]

10276 Warren, Andrea. *Under Siege: Three Children at the Civil War Battle for Vicksburg* (5–8). Illus. 2009, Farrar $17.95 (978-0-374-31255-8). Using the reminiscences of three children between the ages of 10 and 12 (including General Grant's son), this is an interesting account of the battle and of the plight of the city's residents who retreated to caves. (Rev: BL 4/15/09*; HB 5/09; SLJ 5/09) [973.7]

10277 Zeinert, Karen. *The Lincoln Murder Plot* (6–12). 1999, Shoe String LB $22.50 (978-0-208-02451-0). A detailed, well-documented retelling of the first assassination of a U.S. president and its world-shaking results. (Rev: BL 3/1/99; HB 7–8/99; SLJ 5/99; VOYA 4/99) [973.7]

WESTWARD EXPANSION AND PIONEER LIFE

10278 Calabro, Marian. *The Perilous Journey of the Donner Party* (5–8). 1999, Houghton Mifflin $20.00 (978-0-395-86610-8). The story of the ill-fated Donner Party, as seen through the eyes of 12-year-old Virginia Reed. (Rev: BL 4/1/99*; HB 5–6/99; SLJ 5/99; VOYA 2/00) [979.4]

10279 Coleman, Wim, and Pat Perrin. *What Made the Wild West Wild* (4–8). Illus. Series: The Wild History of the American West. 2006, Enslow LB $33.27 (978-1-59845-016-3). The myths and legends of the Wild West are debunked in this expansive overview of media portrayals and reality. (Rev: SLJ 1/07) [978]

10280 Dary, David. *The Oregon Trail: An American Saga* (8–12). 2004, Knopf $35.00 (978-0-375-41399-5). A sweeping and very readable history of the Oregon Trail, from its early-19th-century origins through a period of obscurity to its present importance. (Rev: BL 10/15/04) [978]

10281 Freedman, Russell. *Children of the Wild West* (5–9). 1983, Clarion $18.00 (978-0-89919-143-0). A look at the life of the children of pioneers. (Rev: BL 1/1/90) [978]

10282 Freedman, Russell. *Cowboys of the Wild West* (5–8). 1990, Houghton Mifflin paper $9.95 (978-0-395-54800-4). Text and excellent historical photographs describe these romantic figures. (Rev: BCCB 12/85; HB 3–4/86) [978.02]

10283 Galford, Ellen. *The Trail West: Exploring History Through Art* (5–8). Series: Picture That! 2004, Two-Can $19.95 (978-1-58728-442-7). Paintings serve as the vehicle to draw students into the story of westward expansion. (Rev: BL 11/1/04; SLJ 2/05) [978]

10284 Hirschfelder, Arlene B. *Photo Odyssey: Solomon Cavalho's Remarkable Western Adventure, 1853-54* (6–10). 2000, Clarion $18.00 (978-0-395-89123-0). The story of the last westward journey of John C. Fremont as seen through the eyes of a painter/photographer who was a member of the expedition. (Rev: BCCB 9/00; BL 7/00; HBG 9/00; SLJ 8/00*; VOYA 12/00) [917.8]

10285 Isserman, Maurice. *Exploring North America, 1800-1900* (6–12). Series: Discovery and Exploration. 2005, Facts on File $40.00 (978-0-8160-5263-9). Clear text and primary sources explain the 19th-century explorations of North America by John Fremont, John Wesley Powell, and others, and put them in historical and social context. (Rev: SLJ 8/05) [973]

10286 January, Brendan. *Little Bighorn: June 25, 1876* (5–7). Series: American Battlefields. 2004, Enchanted Lion $14.95 (978-1-59270-028-8). This overview of the Battle of Little Bighorn offers a clear-cut account of the bloody conflict and an examination of the developments leading up to it; sidebars, illustrations, a timeline, and other features add to the narrative. (Rev: BL 11/1/04) [973]

10287 Katz, William L. *Black Pioneers: An Untold Story* (7–12). 1999, Simon & Schuster $17.00 (978-0-689-81410-5). The stories of the many determined African Americans who defied prejudice, slavery, and severe legal restrictions such as the Northwest Territory's "Black Laws" to make a new life for themselves in the frontier of pre-Civil War days. (Rev: BL 7/99; HB 7–8/99; HBG 9/99; SLJ 9/99; VOYA 8/99) [977]

10288 Katz, William L. *Black Women of the Old West* (6–9). 1995, Atheneum $19.95 (978-0-689-31944-0). The role black women played in the settlement of the West — a topic virtually ignored in history books. (Rev: BL 12/15/95; SLJ 12/95; VOYA 4/96) [978]

10289 Kimball, Violet T. *Stories of Young Pioneers: In Their Own Words* (6–9). 2000, Mountain Press paper $14.00 (978-0-87842-423-8). Using diaries and memoirs as sources, the editor brings to life the experiences of youngsters who traveled westward in the mid-19th century. (Rev: BL 12/15/00; VOYA 4/01) [978]

10290 Klausmeier, Robert. *Cowboy* (4–7). Series: American Pastfinder. 1996, Lerner LB $21.27 (978-0-8225-2975-0). This account focuses on the huge cattle drives and the men who led them in the years following the Civil War. (Rev: BL 3/1/96; SLJ 3/96) [636.2]

10291 Landau, Elaine. *The Transcontinental Railroad* (5–8). Series: Watts Library: American West. 2005, Watts LB $25.50 (978-0-531-12326-3). The story behind the building of the Transcontinental Railroad, with illustrations, maps, a timeline, and sidebar features. (Rev: SLJ 12/05)

10292 McEvoy, Anne. *The American West* (6–12). Series: Costume and Fashion Source Books. 2009, Chelsea House $35 (978-1-60413-382-0). This volume looks at the attire of men and women of various different walks of life in the American West, covering explorers, settlers, Native Americans, soldiers, cowboys, and outlaws and lawmen. (Rev: LMC 11–12/09; SLJ 10/09) [391]

10293 McNeese, Tim. *The Donner Party: A Doomed Journey* (8–10). Series: Milestones in American History. 2009, Chelsea House $35 (978-1-60413-025-6). The author does not shy away from describing exactly what happened to the Donner Party on its trek to California, and places the events in historical context, aiding in understanding of the journey. (Rev: SLJ 8/09) [979.4]

10294 Miller, Brandon Marie. *Buffalo Gals: Women of the Old West* (4–7). 1995, Lerner LB $30.35 (978-0-8225-1730-6). A realistic portrait of the hardships faced by women pioneers during the 19th century on the western frontier. (Rev: BCCB 7–8/95; BL 5/1/95; SLJ 6/95*) [978]

10295 Morris, Juddi. *The Harvey Girls: The Women Who Civilized the West* (6–9). 1994, Walker $15.95 (978-0-8027-8302-8). The story of the waitresses at Fred Harvey's restaurants along the Santa Fe railroad, and how they left their homes in the East in search of adventure and independence. (Rev: BL 6/1–15/94; SLJ 7/94) [979]

10296 Peavy, Linda, and Ursula Smith. *Frontier Children* (6–12). 1999, Univ. of Oklahoma $24.95 (978-0-8061-3161-0). This richly illustrated volume full of excerpts from primary sources looks at the lives of children on America's frontier during the 19th century. (Rev: BL 10/1/99; VOYA 12/00) [978]

10297 Rau, Margaret. *The Mail Must Go Through: The Story of the Pony Express* (7–10). Series: America's Moving Frontier. 2005, Morgan Reynolds LB $26.95 (978-1-931798-63-1). A lively account of the exciting — but brief — history of the Pony Express. (Rev: BL 6/1–15/05; SLJ 10/05) [383]

10298 Reinfeld, Fred. *Pony Express* (7–12). 1973, Univ. of Nebraska paper $11.95 (978-0-8032-5786-3). A history of the communication system that linked the East and West and the courageous riders who manned it. [383]

10299 Richards, Colin. *Sheriff Pat Garrett's Last Days* (8–12). 1986, Sunstone paper $8.95 (978-0-86534-079-4). A history of the Wild West drawn into focus by the death of the man who shot Billy the Kid. [978]

10300 Ross, Stewart. *Cowboys* (5–7). Series: Fact or Fiction? 1995, Millbrook LB $26.90 (978-1-56294-

618-0). The life of cowboys during the late 1800s is covered, with information that tries to separate fact from fable. (Rev: BL 7/95; SLJ 5/95) [978.02]

10301 Savage, Candace. *Born to Be a Cowgirl: A Spirited Ride Through the Old West* (6–9). 2001, Tricycle $15.95 (978-1-58246-019-2); paper $10.95 (978-1-58246-020-8). An appealing package of fascinating text, excerpts from letters and journals, and period illustrations that introduces female cowhands and their lifestyle. (Rev: BL 5/15/01; HB 7–8/01; HBG 10/01; SLJ 6/01; VOYA 12/01) [978]

10302 Schaffer, David. *The Louisiana Purchase: The Deal of the Century That Doubled the Nation* (5–8). Illus. Series: The Wild History of the American West. 2006, Enslow LB $33.27 (978-1-59845-018-7). Tells the story behind America's negotiations to buy the vast Louisiana Territory for $15 million, or less than 3 cents an acre; includes a list of carefully selected Web sites that offer additional information. (Rev: SLJ 12/06) [973.4]

10303 Schlaepfer, Gloria G. *The Louisiana Purchase* (5–8). Series: Watts Library: American West. 2005, Watts LB $25.50 (978-0-531-12300-3). The story behind the Louisiana Purchase and its role in America's westward expansion, with illustrations, maps, a timeline, and sidebar features. (Rev: SLJ 12/05)

10304 Schwartz, Heather E. *Foul, Filthy American Frontier: The Disgusting Details About the Journey Out West* (4–8). Series: Fact Finders: Disgusting History. 2010, Capstone LB $25.32 (978-1-4296-3957-6). Allen concentrates on the grosser side of life on the American frontier, describing poor sanitation, rotten food, bugs, medical horrors, and so forth. (Rev: LMC 11–12/10)

10305 Sheinkin, Steve. *Which Way to the Wild West?* (5–9). Illus. by Tim Robinson. 2009, Flash Point $19.95 (978-1-59643-321-2). Useful for both researchers and browsers, this is a fact-filled but lively history of just what went on in the West. Lexile 940L (Rev: HB 9–10/09; LMC 10/09; SLJ 9/09)

10306 Sonneborn, Liz. *The Mormon Trail* (5–8). Series: Watts Library: American West. 2005, Watts LB $25.50 (978-0-531-12317-1). The story behind the westward trek of thousands of Mormons during the middle of the 19th century, with illustrations, maps, a timeline, and sidebar features. (Rev: SLJ 12/05)

10307 Sonneborn, Liz. *Women of the American West* (4–7). Series: Watts Library: American West. 2005, Watts LB $25.50 (978-0-531-12318-8). Excerpts from first-person accounts offer a glimpse into what life was like for the women who helped to open the American West. (Rev: BL 10/15/05) [978]

10308 Stein, R. Conrad. *On the Old Western Frontier* (4–8). Series: How We Lived. 1999, Benchmark LB $28.50 (978-0-7614-0909-0). An interesting book that gives an overview of the history and living conditions

on the American frontier with material on everyday life, farming and ranching, social life, religion, Native Americans, and slaves. (Rev: HBG 10/00; SLJ 3/00) [978]

10309 Swanson, Wayne. *Why the West Was Wild* (5–8). 2004, Annick $12.95 (978-1-55037-837-5); paper $12.95 (978-1-55037-836-8). The excitement of the Old West is captured in this lavishly illustrated survey of the region's history during the second half of the 19th century. (Rev: BL 8/04; SLJ 6/04) [978]

10310 Torr, James D., ed. *The American Frontier* (7–12). Series: Turning Points in World History. 2001, Greenhaven LB $24.95 (978-0-7377-0785-4); paper $37.45 (978-0-7377-0786-1). A collection of essays that explores the opening up of the West, the nature of the pioneer spirit, and the changes this development brought to our history. (Rev: BL 3/15/02) [973.7]

10311 Tunis, Edwin. *Frontier Living* (7–12). 1976, Crowell paper $18.95 (978-1-58574-137-3). Using more than 200 original drawings and a fine text, the author portrays the life, artifacts, and customs of the American frontier. [978]

10312 Uschan, Michael V. *The Transcontinental Railroad* (4–7). Series: Landmark Events in American History. 2003, World Almanac LB $31.00 (978-0-8368-5382-7). In accessible language and with plenty of illustrations, this is the story of the railroad that spanned the nation. (Rev: SLJ 6/04) [385]

10313 Wadsworth, Ginger. *Words West: Voices of Young Pioneers* (5–8). 2003, Clarion $18.00 (978-0-618-23475-2). Excerpts from journals and other documents give a clear picture of the experiences of young people traveling west between 1840 and 1870. (Rev: HBG 4/04; SLJ 12/03) [917.804]

10314 Waldman, Stuart. *The Last River: John Wesley Powell and the Colorado River Exploring Expedition* (4–7). Illus. by Gregory Manchess. 2005, Mikaya $19.95 (978-1-931414-09-8). This is the exciting story of the three-month exploration of the Colorado River led by the one-armed John Wesley Powell in 1869; excerpts from journals and letters reveal details of the dangers faced. (Rev: BL 12/15/05; SLJ 2/06) [550.92]

RECONSTRUCTION TO WORLD WAR I
(1865–1914)

10315 Baker, Julie. *The Bread and Roses Strike of 1912* (6–10). 2007, Morgan Reynolds LB $27.95 (978-1-59935-044-8). Tells the story of the largest textile labor strike in American history, which occurred in Massachusetts in 1912, with profiles of union leaders, photographs of suffering families, and details of the employees' (including children) horrific living and working conditions. (Rev: BL 5/15/07; SLJ 7/07)

10316 Bartoletti, Susan Campbell. *Growing Up in Coal Country* (5–8). 1996, Houghton Mifflin $17.00 (978-

0-395-77847-0). The life of child laborers in the coal mines of Pennsylvania 100 years ago is covered in this brilliant photoessay. (Rev: BCCB 2/97; BL 12/1/96*; SLJ 2/97*) [331.3]

10317 Bartoletti, Susan Campbell. *Kids on Strike!* (5–8). 1999, Houghton Mifflin $20.00 (978-0-395-88892-6). This book chronicles the history of child labor in America during the 19th and early 20th centuries and features such personalities as William Randolph Hearst, Pauline Newman, and Mother Jones. (Rev: BCCB 12/99; BL 12/1/99; HBG 3/00; SLJ 12/99*; VOYA 2/00) [973.8]

10318 Brezina, Corona. *America's Political Scandals in the late 1800s: Boss Tweed and Tammany Hall* (5–8). Series: America's Industrial Society in the 19th Century. 2004, Rosen LB $22.50 (978-0-8239-4021-9). For reluctant readers, this overview of the political scandals of the late 19th century features large print and short chapters. (Rev: BL 4/1/04)

10319 Burgan, Michael. *Breaker Boys: How A Photograph Helped End Child Labor* (6–9). Illus. Series: Captured History. 2011, Capstone LB $33.99 (978-075654439-3); paper $8.95 (9780756545109). Uses an iconic photograph by Lewis Hine to introduce the shocking conditions faced by children working in mines and other industries in the early 1900s. Lexile 1020L (Rev: BL 11/1/11*) [331.3]

10320 Currie, Stephen. *We Have Marched Together: The Working Children's Crusade* (7–12). Series: People's History. 1996, Lerner LB $30.35 (978-0-8225-1733-7). The focus of this book is on child labor in the United States and the protest march from Philadelphia to New York led by Mother Jones in 1903. (Rev: BL 5/1/97; SLJ 7/97) [331.3]

10321 Ferrell, Claudine L. *Reconstruction* (5–10). Series: Greenwood Guides to Historic Events, 1500-1900. 2003, Greenwood $51.95 (978-0-313-32062-0). Covers key individuals involved in Reconstruction and the speeches, proclamations, and other primary documents that cast light on the events of the time. (Rev: SLJ 6/04) [973.8]

10322 Gourley, Catherine. *Good Girl Work: Factories, Sweatshops, and How Women Changed Their Role in the American Workforce* (7–10). 1999, Millbrook LB $26.90 (978-0-7613-0951-2). This history of the exploitation of female children around the turn of the 20th century includes dramatic, in-depth personal testimonies and first-person accounts from letters, diaries, memoirs, and newspaper interviews. (Rev: BL 5/1/99; SLJ 8/99) [331.3]

10323 Greene, Meg. *Into the Land of Freedom: African Americans in Reconstruction* (5–8). Series: People's History. 2004, Lerner LB $29.27 (978-0-8225-4690-0). Sepia-toned photographs and historical documents and interviews add to this portrait of the situation of African Americans during Reconstruction. (Rev: BL 2/15/04*; SLJ 5/04) [973]

10324 Greenwood, Janette Thomas. *The Gilded Age: A History in Documents* (6–12). 2000, Oxford LB $39.95 (978-0-19-510523-0). Documents of all kinds are used to show readers the many changes that took place in American society in the last years of the 19th century. (Rev: BL 10/1/00; HBG 3/01; SLJ 10/00) [973.8]

10325 Haskins, Jim. *Geography of Hope: Black Exodus from the South After Reconstruction* (7–12). 1999, Twenty-First Century LB $31.90 (978-0-7613-0323-7). After information on slavery and the Reconstruction, the author describes the migrations of African Americans to the North, their leaders, and the politics that made life in the South intolerable. (Rev: BL 10/15/99; HBG 4/00; SLJ 11/99; VOYA 6/00) [973]

10326 Josephson, Judith Pinkerton. *Growing Up in a New Century* (5–8). Series: Our America. 2002, Lerner LB $26.60 (978-0-8225-0657-7). A look at the lives of American children of different backgrounds and situations at the dawn of the 20th century. (Rev: BL 2/1/03; HBG 3/03; SLJ 7/03) [973.91]

10327 McNeese, Tim. *The Gilded Age and Progressivism 1891–1913* (5–8). Series: Discovering U.S. History. 2010, Chelsea House $35 (978-1-60413-355-4). McNeese provides a succinct overview of the key events and issues of this period of industrial progress and expanded immigration, with a chronology and timeline plus illustrations and primary sources. (Rev: LMC 11–12/10; SLJ 8/10)

10328 Marrin, Albert. *Flesh and Blood So Cheap: The Triangle Fire and Its Legacy* (7–10). Illus. 2011, Knopf $19.99 (978-0-375-86889-4). This is a compelling account of the 1911 fire in which 146 workers died, documenting the horrible working conditions in the factory, the fact that the victims were mostly poor Jewish and Italian immigrants, and the fire's legacy in improving workplace safety regulations — in the United States if not around the world. ⌖ ℮ (Rev: BL 4/1/11; LMC 10/11*; SLJ 5/11*) [974.7]

10329 Marsico, Katie. *The Triangle Shirtwaist Factory Fire: Its Legacy of Labor Rights* (7–12). Series: Perspectives On. 2009, Marshall Cavendish LB $27.95 (978-0-7614-4027-7). With direct quotations and historical background, this volume offers different perspectives on the 1911 disaster and its causes and consequences. (Rev: LMC 3–4/10; SLJ 2/10) [974.7]

10330 Osborne, Linda Barrett. *Traveling the Freedom Road: From Slavery and the Civil War Through Reconstruction* (6–9). Illus. 2009, Abrams $24.95 (978-081098338-0). A sweeping overview of a fascinating and troubled period in American history. Historical documents and firsthand accounts by slaves, abolitionists, and others will capture readers' attention. Lexile 1120L (Rev: BL 2/1/09; LMC 8–9/09; SLJ 5/1/09*; VOYA 6/09) [973.7]

10331 Porterfield, Jason. *Problems and Progress in American Politics: The Growth of the Democratic Party* *in the Late 1800s* (5–8). Series: America's Industrial Society in the 19th Century. 2004, Rosen LB $22.50 (978-0-8239-4026-4). For reluctant readers, this overview of the growth of the Democratic Party features large print and short chapters. (Rev: BL 4/1/04)

10332 Ruggiero, Adriane. *American Voices from Reconstruction* (8–11). Series: American Voices. 2006, Marshall Cavendish LB $25.95 (978-0-7614-2168-9). This volume effectively uses primary sources — newspaper accounts, speeches, letters and diary entries, songs, and so forth — to tell the story of Reconstruction, presenting the points of view of key politicians as well as former slaves and slave owners. (Rev: BL 2/1/07) [973.8]

10333 Sandler, Martin W. *The Impossible Rescue: The True Story of an Amazing Arctic Adventure* (5–8). Illus. 2012, Candlewick $22.99 (978-0-7636-5080-3). The death-defying 1897–1898 rescue of nearly 300 sailors trapped in winter ice on Alaska's Point Barrow is described in this dramatic tale. (Rev: BL 5/15/12*; HB 9–10/12; LMC 1–2/13; SLJ 9/12*; VOYA 8/12) [979.803]

10334 Sandler, Martin W. *Island of Hope: The Story of Ellis Island and the Journey to America* (5–7). 2004, Scholastic $19.99 (978-0-439-53082-8). Drawing heavily on first-hand accounts, Sandler traces immigrants' progress through the processing at Ellis Island and on into the cities and farms of their new country. (Rev: BL 4/15/04; SLJ 6/04) [304.8]

10335 Schwartz, Eric. *Crossing the Seas: Americans Form an Empire 1890–1899* (5–8). Series: How America Became America. 2005, Mason Crest LB $22.95 (978-1-59084-910-1). Schwartz explores America's turn to imperialism in the final decade of the 19th century. Also use *Super Power: Americans Today* (2005). (Rev: SLJ 11/05) [973]

10336 Stanley, George E. *An Emerging World Power (1900–1929)* (5–8). Series: A Primary Source History of the United States. 2005, World Almanac LB $31.00 (978-0-8368-5828-0). A simple narrative links well-chosen primary sources documenting the key events of the early 20th century. Also use *The Era of Reconstruction and Expansion (1865–1900)* and *The Great Depression and World War II (1929–1949)* (both 2005). (Rev: BL 4/1/05; SLJ 7/05)

10337 Stites, Bill. *The Republican Party in the Late 1800s: A Changing Role for American Government* (5–8). Series: America's Industrial Society in the 19th Century. 2004, Rosen LB $22.50 (978-0-8239-4030-1). For reluctant readers, this overview of the growth of the Republican Party features large print and short chapters. (Rev: BL 4/1/04)

10338 Stroud, Bettye, and Virginia Schomp. *The Reconstruction Era* (5–8). Series: Drama of African-American History. 2006, Benchmark LB $23.95 (978-0-7614-2181-8). This volume traces the history of Reconstruction and the tensions remaining between

the many factions after the Civil War. (Rev: SLJ 5/07) [973.8]

10339 Wilder, Laura Ingalls. *West from Home: Letters of Laura Ingalls Wilder, San Francisco 1915* (7–9). 1974, HarperCollins paper $5.99 (978-0-06-440081-7). The author describes her trip from Missouri to San Francisco in 1915. [973.9]

WORLD WAR I

10340 Bausum, Ann. *Unraveling Freedom: The Battle for Democracy on the Home Front During World War I* (8–11). 2010, National Geographic $19.95 (978-1-4263-0702-7); LB $34 (978-1-4263-0703-4). Bausum provides a riveting overview of life in the United States from the sinking of the *Lusitania* to the end of the war, covering the public outrage, the restrictions imposed on free speech and German Americans, the spying, and so forth. (Rev: BL 12/15/10*; SLJ 12/1/10*) [940.3]

10341 Ruggiero, Adriane. *World War I* (6–9). Series: American Voices From. 2002, Benchmark LB $34.21 (978-0-7614-1203-8). Excerpts from primary documents including letters, newspaper articles, speeches, and journals present a variety of different experiences of those who lived through World War I. (Rev: HBG 10/03; SLJ 3/03) [940.3]

BETWEEN THE WARS AND THE GREAT DEPRESSION (1918–1941)

10342 Blumenthal, Karen. *Six Days in October: The Stock Market Crash of 1929* (7–12). 2002, Simon & Schuster $17.95 (978-0-689-84276-4). An absorbing look at the factors that led to the infamous crash and the fortunes that were lost, with clear definitions of economic concepts and interesting illustrations. (Rev: BL 11/1/02; HB 1–2/03; HBG 3/03; SLJ 10/02; VOYA 12/02) [332.64]

10343 Bolden, Tonya. *FDR's Alphabet Soup: New Deal America, 1932–1939* (5–8). 2010, Knopf LB $22.99 (978-0-375-95214-2). A lively review of FDR's presidency and in particular of the provisions of the New Deal and the impact it had on the American people. (Rev: BL 12/1/09; LMC 1–2/10; SLJ 1/10) [900]

10344 Bragg, Rick. *Ava's Man* (7–12). 2001, Knopf $25.00 (978-0-375-41062-8). Bragg paints a loving portrait of his maternal grandfather, Charlie Bundrum, a simple backwoods man who, with his wife Ava, struggled to raise seven children to adulthood during the lean years of the Great Depression. (Rev: BL 6/1–15/01*; VOYA 4/02) [975]

10345 Callan, Jim. *America in the 1930s* (7–10). Series: Decades of American History. 2005, Facts on File $35.00 (978-0-8160-5638-5). Excellent information — especially for report writers — is hampered by poor design. (Rev: BL 1/1–15/06) [973.917]

10346 Carter, Ron. *The Youngest Drover* (5–9). 1995, Harbour $19.95 (978-0-9643672-1-0); paper $14.95 (978-0-9643672-0-3). In 1923, when he was 15, the author's father participated in an exciting cattle drive from Alberta to Montana. (Rev: BL 1/1–15/96) [978]

10347 Cooper, Michael L. *Dust to Eat: Drought and Depression in the 1930s* (5–8). 2004, Clarion $17.00 (978-0-618-15449-4). First-person accounts and period photographs convey the hopelessness of those who were caught in the grip of the Depression and the drought in the Midwest. (Rev: BL 7/04; SLJ 9/04) [973.917]

10348 Costantino, Maria. *Fashions of a Decade: The 1930s* (5–10). 2007, Chelsea House LB $35 (978-0-8160-6719-0). With illustrations, photographs, and a helpful chronology of trends and events, this book captures the fashions of the 1930s and relates them to the conditions of the times. (Rev: SLJ 7/07)

10349 Cryan-Hicks, Kathryn, ed. *Pride and Promise: The Harlem Renaisssance* (4–8). Series: Perspectives on History. 1994, Enterprises paper $6.95 (978-1-878668-30-1). The story of the great artistic awakening in New York's Harlem and of its many leaders, including Langston Hughes. (Rev: BL 8/94) [305.896]

10350 Davis, Barbara J. *The Teapot Dome Scandal: Corruption Rocks 1920s America* (5–8). Series: Snapshots in History. 2007, Compass Point LB $31.93 (978-0-7565-3336-6). Davis traces the corruption in the Harding administration and the scandal that erupted over oil leasing without competitive bidding. (Rev: SLJ 1/08)

10351 Doak, Robin. *Struggling to Become American: 1899–1940* (5–10). Series: Latino-American History. 2007, Chelsea House LB $35.00 (978-0-8160-6443-4). Doak looks at Latino immigration — especially from Puerto Rico, Cuba, and Mexico — and at the conditions of Hispanic laborers in the United States during World War I and the Great Depression; includes photographs, sidebars, political cartoons, maps, and so forth. (Rev: SLJ 7/07)

10352 Freedman, Russell. *Children of the Great Depression* (5–8). 2005, Clarion $20.00 (978-0-618-44630-8). The works of such notable photographers as Dorothea Lange and Walker Evans, moving quotations, and the accessible text of Freedman make this a memorable photoessay. (Rev: BCCB 12/05; BL 12/15/05*; HBG 4/05; LMC 3/06; SLJ 12/05*; VOYA 6/06) [305.23]

10353 Garland, Sherry. *Voices of the Dust Bowl* (4–7). Illus. by Judith Hierstein. Series: Voices of History. 2012, Pelican $16.99 (978-1-58980-964-2). Sixteen moving first-person narratives convey how the drought and dust storms of the 1930s affected people in all walks of lives — even Bonnie and Clyde. (Rev: BL 5/15/12; LMC 10/12; SLJ 7/12) [973.917]

10354 Herald, Jacqueline. *Fashions of a Decade: The 1920s* (5–10). 2007, Chelsea House LB $35.00 (978-0-8160-6718-3). Photographs, illustrations, and timelines accompany text that relates the fashion of the 1920s to events and the culture of the times. (Rev: SLJ 7/07)

10355 Hintz, Martin. *Farewell, John Barleycorn: Prohibition in the United States* (6–10). Series: People's History. 1996, Lerner LB $25.26 (978-0-8225-1734-4). A well-organized, readable account that traces the history of alcohol use in the United States, covers the 18th Amendment and its effects, and ends with repeal of Prohibition. (Rev: BL 8/96; SLJ 10/96) [363.4]

10356 Hoffman, Nancy. *Eleanor Roosevelt and the Arthurdale Experiment* (5–8). 2001, Linnet LB $22.50 (978-0-208-02504-3). Hoffman includes quotations and black-and-white photographs in her account of the story of Arthurdale, a government-planned community of the 1930s. (Rev: BL 10/15/01; HBG 3/02; SLJ 12/01) [975.4]

10357 Marrin, Albert. *Years of Dust: The Story of the Dust Bowl* (5–8). 2009, Dutton $22.99 (978-0-525-42077-4). This is a moving explanation of the nature of the Dust Bowl and its impact on agriculture and the population that lived there; personal accounts add depth, as do numerous sidebars and a warning about future events like this. ALA Notable Books 2010. (Rev: BL 8/09*; LMC 10/09; SLJ 8/09) [978]

10358 Nardo, Don. *Migrant Mother: How a Photograph Defined the Great Depression* (5–8). Illus. Series: Captured History. 2011, Compass Point $33.99 (978-075654397-6). Dorothea Lange's photograph of a Depression-era farm worker serves as the anchor for a discussion of the Great Depression and Lange's contributions. (Rev: BL 4/1/11; LMC 10/11) [973.917]

10359 Rice, Earle, Jr. *FDR and the New Deal* (6–9). Series: Monumental Milestones. 2009, Mitchell Lane LB $21.50 (978-1-58415-828-8). Useful for research, this slim volume provides facts and biographical sketches key to Roosevelt's administration and the New Deal, and supplies the necessary background to fully understand the issues involved — also drawing parallels to problems we face today. (Rev: LMC 5–6/10; SLJ 1/10) [973.917]

10360 Sandler, Martin W. *The Dust Bowl Through the Lens: How Photography Revealed and Helped Remedy a National Disaster* (5–9). 2009, Walker $19.99 (978-0-8027-9547-2). Sandler tells the devastating story of the American Dust Bowl through a series of photo-essays including period quotations and concise, engaging captions. (Rev: BL 11/1/09; HB 1–2/10; LMC 10/09; SLJ 10/09; VOYA 8/09) [973.917022]

10361 Swisher, Clarice. *Women of the Roaring Twenties* (6–10). Series: Women in History. 2005, Gale LB $22.96 (978-1-59017-363-3). Using primary sources, this readable volume looks at life for women from diverse backgrounds during the turbulent 1920s. (Rev: BL 2/15/06) [305.4]

10362 Worth, Richard. *The Harlem Renaissance: An Explosion of African-American Culture* (5–8). Illus. 2008, Enslow LB $23.95 (978-0-7660-2907-1). This attractive overview of the Harlem Renaissance traces the origins and spirit of the movement and profiles many of its writers, artists, musicians, and thinkers. (Rev: BL 2/1/09; LMC 11/08) [700.89]

WORLD WAR II

10363 Brinkley, Douglas, ed. *The World War II Memorial: A Grateful Nation Remembers* (8–12). 2004, Smithsonian $39.95 (978-1-58834-210-2). Published in conjunction with the dedication of the World War II Memorial in Washington, D.C., this striking coffee table book is loaded with photos and remembrances of the war and its lasting impact on America. (Rev: BL 9/1/04) [940.54]

10364 Cooper, Michael L. *Fighting for Honor: Japanese Americans and World War II* (6–12). 2000, Clarion $18.00 (978-0-395-91375-8). The experiences of Japanese Americans who were sent to internment camps or faced anti-Asian attacks in their communities are well-documented here. (Rev: BCCB 2/01; BL 1/1–15/01; HB 3–4/01; HBG 10/01; SLJ 3/01) [940.53]

10365 Cooper, Michael L. *Remembering Manzanar: Life in a Japanese Relocation Camp* (4–8). 2002, Clarion $15.00 (978-0-618-06778-7). This evocative account of life in a Japanese American World War II internment center tells its tale through personal accounts of survivors, quotations from the camp newspaper, and revealing photographs. (Rev: BL 1/1–15/03; HBG 10/03; SLJ 2/03) [940.54]

10366 Gorman, Jacqueline Laks. *Pearl Harbor: A Primary Source History* (5–8). Illus. Series: In Their Own Words. 2009, Gareth Stevens $27.00 (978-1-4339-0047-1). With excerpts from primary sources, narrative text, and many photographs, this is an overview of events leading up to the attack on Pearl Harbor, the attack itself, the aftermath, and its importance today, with profiles of key figures. (Rev: BL 4/1/09) [940.54]

10367 Hillstrom, Laurie Collier. *The Attack on Pearl Harbor* (7–12). Series: Defining Moments. 2009, Omnigraphics $49 (978-0-7808-1069-3). Readers learn why the Japanese attack on Pearl Harbor triggered the U.S. entry into the Second World War; primary documents and biographical information on key figures are included. (Rev: SLJ 8/09; VOYA 10/09) [940.5426]

10368 Komatsu, Kimberly, and Kaleigh Komatsu. *In America's Shadow* (5–8). 2003, Thomas George $35.00 (978-0-9709829-0-2). This account of the internment of Japanese Americans during World War II draws on the memories and archives of the authors' family. (Rev: BL 4/1/03) [940.531]

10369 Nicholson, Dorinda Makanaonalani. *Pearl Harbor Child: A Child's View of Pearl Harbor — from At-* tack to Peace (5–8). 1998, Woodson House paper $9.95 (978-1-892858-00-9). This photoessay describes a child's experience during the bombing of Pearl Harbor, the temporary evacuation, and everyday life growing up in Hawaii during World War II. (Rev: BL 1/1–15/99) [996.9]

10370 Sheinkin, Steve. *Bomb: The Race to Build — and Steal — the World's Most Dangerous Weapon* (5–10). 2012, Roaring Brook/Flash Point $19.99 (978-1-59643-487-5). A compelling account of the race to build the atom bomb, full of espionage, heroism, and eccentric but brilliant characters. Robert F. Sibert Informational Book Award; Newbery Honor Book; Notable Children's Book; YALSA Award for Excellence in Nonfiction for Young Adults. ∩ ℮ Lexile 920L (Rev: BL 9/1/12; HB 11–12/12; SLJ 10/12*; VOYA 10/12) [623.4]

10371 Stone, Tanya Lee. *Courage Has No Color: The True Story of the Triple Nickles, America's First Black Paratroopers* (5–9). Illus. 2013, Candlewick $24.99 (978-076365117-6). A moving, large-format introduction to activities of the 555th Parachute Infantry Battalion, the results of a long effort to increase racial integration in U.S. military forces. ∩ ℮ Lexile 1090L (Rev: BL 2/1/13*; HB 1–2/13; LMC 8–9/13; SLJ 1/13*) [940.5403]

POST WORLD WAR II UNITED STATES
(1945–)

10372 Aretha, David. *Freedom Summer* (7–12). Series: The Civil Rights Movement. 2007, Morgan Reynolds LB $27.95 (978-1-59935-059-2). The summer of 1964, when white college students traveled to Mississippi to help blacks register to vote, is the focus of this volume in the Civil Rights Movement series. (Rev: BL 2/1/08; SLJ 3/08) [323.1196]

10373 Aretha, David. *Sit-Ins and Freedom Rides* (5–8). Series: Civil Rights Movement. 2009, Morgan Reynolds LB $28.95 (978-1-59935-098-1). Aretha offers a detailed, well-illustrated look at the grassroots efforts of the early 1960s, with personal anecdotes, a helpful timeline, and lists of additional resources. (Rev: BL 2/1/10; SLJ 9/09) [323.1196]

10374 Bausum, Ann. *Marching to the Mountaintop: How Poverty, Labor Fights, and Civil Rights Set the Stage for Martin Luther King, Jr.'s Final Hours* (5–8). Illus. 2012, National Geographic $19.95 (978-142630939-7); LB $28.90 (978-142630940-3). With succinct text, use of primary resources, gripping photographs, and attractive design, this is a compelling account — suitable for research and for browsing — of the 1968 Memphis sanitation workers strike and the death of Martin Luther King, Jr. ℮ (Rev: BL 2/1/12; LMC 8–9/12; SLJ 3/12) [323.092]

10375 Bowers, Rick. *Spies of Mississippi: The True Story of the State-Run Spy Network That Tried to Destroy* *the Civil Rights Movement* (7–10). 2010, National Geographic LB $26.96 (978-1-4263-0596-2). The alarming story of a spy network established in Mississippi in the mid-1950s to support segregation and work against civil rights. ⌂ e (Rev: BL 2/1/10*; HB 3–4/10; LMC 3–4/10; SLJ 2/10) [323.1196]

10376 Brown, Gene. *The Nation in Turmoil: Civil Rights and the Vietnam War (1960-1973)* (5–8). Series: First Person America. 1994, Twenty-First Century LB $20.90 (978-0-8050-2588-0). An overview of the civil rights movement and the Vietnam War, highlighting excerpts from letters, diaries, and speeches. (Rev: BL 5/15/94) [973.92]

10377 Ching, Juliet. *The Assassination of Robert F. Kennedy* (6–10). Series: The Library of Political Assassinations. 2002, Rosen LB $27.95 (978-0-8239-3545-1). In addition to discussing the assassination and the events preceding it, the author looks at the rumors of a conspiracy and allegations of incompetence on the part of the Los Angeles police force. (Rev: BL 8/02; SLJ 8/02) [976]

10378 Draper, Allison Stark. *The Assassination of Malcolm X* (6–10). Series: The Library of Political Assassinations. 2002, Rosen LB $27.95 (978-0-8239-3542-0). A description of the assassination and its aftermath is followed by information on Malcolm X's life and beliefs. (Rev: BL 2/15/02; SLJ 7/02) [976.2]

10379 Epstein, Dan. *The 80s: The Decade of Plenty* (7–10). Series: Twentieth Century Pop Culture. 2000, Chelsea LB $22.95 (978-0-7910-6088-9). A mix of popular entertainment and fashion with key news events, all arranged chronologically and accompanied by lots of color photographs. Other books in the series include *The 50s: America Tunes In* and *The 60s: A Decade of Change: The Flintstones to Woodstock.* (Rev: SLJ 6/01) [973.9]

10380 Feinstein, Stephen. *The 1950s: From the Korean War to Elvis* (6–9). Series: Decades of the Twentieth Century in Color. 2006, Enslow LB $27.93 (978-0-7660-2635-3). Ample illustrations and a useful timeline make this an appealing reference to the events — cultural, scientific, and sporting — of the 1950s. (Rev: BL 4/1/06) [973.92]

10381 Fitzgerald, Brian. *McCarthyism: The Red Scare* (7–12). Series: Snapshots in History. 2006, Compass Point LB $31.93 (978-0-7565-2007-6). This is a clear account of the period of anti-Communism in the United States stirred up by Senator Joseph McCarthy, including the impact on the lives of individuals around the country plus quotations from the Army-McCarthy hearings. (Rev: SLJ 2/07)

10382 Gard, Carolyn. *The Attack on the Pentagon on September 11, 2001* (4–8). Series: Terrorist Attacks. 2003, Rosen LB $27.95 (978-0-8239-3858-2). In addition to describing the attack itself, Gard looks at the organization of Al-Qaeda. (Rev: SLJ 2/04) [975.5]

10383 Hampton, Wilborn. *Kennedy Assassinated! The World Mourns* (5–8). 1997, Candlewick $17.99 (978-1-56402-811-2). A gripping first-person account of John Kennedy's assassination by a veteran newspaper reporter who was in Dallas that day. (Rev: BL 9/15/97; HBG 3/98; SLJ 10/97) [364.1]

10384 McNeese, Tim. *Modern America: 1964–Present* (5–8). Illus. Series: Discovering U.S. History. 2010, Chelsea House $35 (978-1-60413-361-5). Covering American history from LBJ through Obama, this is a satisfying survey of social and political developments with illustrations, maps, photographs, and interesting sidebar features. e (Rev: SLJ 8/10) [973.92]

10385 Mara, Wil. *Civil Unrest in the 1960s: Riots and Their Aftermath* (8–12). Series: Perspectives On. 2009, Marshall Cavendish LB $27.95 (978-0-7614-4025-3). With excerpts from primary sources and many pertinent sidebars and images, this is a useful survey of the causes, key events, and significance of the civil unrest of the 1960s. (Rev: LMC 3–4/10; SLJ 2/10) [303.6]

10386 Maus, Derek C., ed. *Living Through the Red Scare* (8–12). Series: Living Through the Cold War. 2005, Gale LB $32.45 (978-0-7377-2615-2). This fascinating collection of readings revisits the fear of communism that was rampant in the United States at the beginning of the Cold War. (Rev: SLJ 6/06)

10387 Maus, Derek C., ed. *Living Under the Threat of Nuclear War* (7–10). Series: Living Through the Cold War. 2005, Gale LB $33.70 (978-0-7377-2130-0). This title examines how Americans coped with the ever-present threat of nuclear war during the half-century-long Cold War. (Rev: SLJ 10/05) [973]

10388 Niven, Felicia Lowenstein. *Fabulous Fashions of the 1970s* (4–7). Illus. Series: Fabulous Fashions of the Decades. 2011, Enslow LB $23.93 (978-076603826-4). Looks at all aspects of fashion in the 1970s, from men's and women's clothing to hairstyles, accessories, and pop culture. (Rev: BL 4/1/12; VOYA 10/10) [746.9]

10389 Steins, Richard. *The Postwar Years: The Cold War and the Atomic Age (1950-1959)* (5–8). Series: First Person America. 1994, Twenty-First Century LB $20.90 (978-0-8050-2587-3). Coverage of the 1950s includes first-person material on the Cold War and the Korean conflict. (Rev: BL 5/15/94; SLJ 12/94) [973.92]

10390 Tougas, Shelley. *Little Rock Girl 1957: How a Photograph Changed the Fight for Integration* (6–9). Illus. Series: Captured History. 2011, Capstone LB $33.99 (978-075654440-9); paper $8.95 (9780756545123). Uses an iconic photograph to introduce the events in Little Rock in 1957 and the importance of the struggle for school integration. Lexile 1010L (Rev: BL 11/1/11*; SLJ 1/12) [379.2]

10391 Tracy, Kathleen. *The McCarthy Era* (7–10). Series: Monumental Milestones. 2009, Mitchell Lane LB $29.95 (978-1-58415-694-9). Historic and political factors pertaining to McCarthy's persecution of innocent Americans are the focus of this interesting and informative book. (Rev: SLJ 6/1/09) [973.91]

10392 Tracy, Kathleen. *The Watergate Scandal* (6–9). Series: Monumental Milestones: Great Events of Modern Times. 2006, Mitchell Lane LB $19.95 (978-1-58415-470-9). The complexity of the Watergate affair will restrict this account to the strongest readers. (Rev: SLJ 11/06)

KOREAN, VIETNAM, AND GULF WARS

10393 Al-Windawi, Thura. *Thura's Diary: My Life in Wartime Iraq* (6–12). 2004, Viking $15.99 (978-0-670-05886-0). This diary was kept by a 19-year-old girl in Baghdad from the first bombings to the first days of the occupation by American forces. (Rev: BL 5/15/04; HB 7–8/04; SLJ 7/04) [956]

10394 Canwell, Diane, and Jon Sutherland. *African Americans in the Vietnam War* (5–8). Series: American Experience in Vietnam. 2005, World Almanac LB $31.00 (978-0-8368-5772-6). Personal stories and full-color photographs add to the information on black Americans' contributions to the conflict and the military's efforts toward integration. Also use *American Women in the Vietnam War* (2005). (Rev: BL 2/1/05) [959.705]

10395 Caputo, Philip. *10,000 Days of Thunder: A History of the Vietnam War* (7–10). 2005, Simon & Schuster $22.95 (978-0-689-86231-1). In this sweeping overview of the Vietnam War, Caputo traces the fractured country's history from the beginnings of resistance to French colonial rule to the fall of Saigon and also assesses the conflict's enduring impact on Americans. (Rev: BL 10/1/05; SLJ 11/05*; VOYA 10/05) [959.704]

10396 Galt, Margot Fortunato. *Stop This War! American Protest of the Conflict in Vietnam* (8–12). Series: People's History. 2000, Lerner LB $26.60 (978-0-8225-1740-5). The author cites her husband, a conscientious objector, among those who protested the war from the early 1960s until its end, and details key events and student and other groups. (Rev: BL 7/00; HBG 9/00; SLJ 8/00) [959.704]

10397 Gitlin, Martin. *U.S. Involvement in Vietnam* (6–8). Series: Essential Events. 2010, ABDO LB $32.79 (978-1-60453-949-3). An attractive and informative overview of the progression from initial involvement through full-scale deployment of troops and the final pull-out, with discussion of the aftermath. (Rev: LMC 10/10; SLJ 5/10) [959.704]

10398 Granfield, Linda. *I Remember Korea: Veterans Tell Their Stories of the Korean War, 1950-53* (6–12). 2003, Clarion $16.00 (978-0-618-17740-0). First-person accounts by American combatants that reveal a wide variety of experiences are accompanied by brief introductory notes, photographs, and a short account of

the war itself. (Rev: BCCB 2/04; BL 12/15/03; HBG 4/04; SLJ 2/04) [951.904]

10399 Koestler-Grack, Rachel A. *The Kent State Tragedy* (4–7). Series: American Moments. 2005, ABDO LB $25.65 (978-1-59197-934-0). A concise overview of the deadly 1970 clash between National Guard troops and war protesters on the campus of Ohio's Kent State University. (Rev: BL 9/1/05; SLJ 11/05) [378.771]

10400 McCloud, Bill. *What Should We Tell Our Children About Vietnam?* (7–12). 1989, Univ. of Oklahoma paper $16.95 (978-0-8061-3240-2). More than 120 individuals, including the first President Bush and Gary Trudeau, tell what they think young people should know about the war. (Rev: BL 9/15/89) [959.704]

10401 Mason, Andrew. *The Vietnam War: A Primary Source History* (5–8). Series: In Their Own Words. 2005, Gareth Stevens LB $27.00 (978-0-8368-5981-2). Primary sources — including letters, articles, speeches, and songs — deliver the views of combatants in Vietnam and people on the home front in this well-illustrated volume. (Rev: BL 10/15/05) [959.704]

10402 Murray, Stuart. *Vietnam War* (6–9). Series: Eyewitness Books. 2005, DK LB $19.99 (978-0-7566-1165-1). This photo-filled volume introduces the key events, figures, armaments, and political and social issues of the Vietnam War. (Rev: BL 9/1/05) [959.704]

10403 O'Connell, Kim A. *Primary Source Accounts of the Vietnam War* (6–9). Series: America's Wars Through Primary Sources. 2006, Enslow LB $24.95 (978-1-59845-001-9). Learn about the Vietnam War from the perspective of soldiers (American and Vietnamese), nurses, and Vietnamese civilians through diaries, letters, songs, and other documents. (Rev: BL 10/15/06) [959.704]

10404 Pendergast, Tom. *The Vietnam War* (7–10). Series: Defining Moments. 2006, Omnigraphics LB $44.00 (978-0-7808-0954-3). Ten years of the conflict's history are covered in detail and copious background information is provided to help report writers. (Rev: BL 3/15/07) [959.704]

10405 Richie, Jason. *Iraq and the Fall of Saddam Hussein.* Rev. ed. (8–10). 2004, Oliver LB $24.95 (978-1-881508-63-2). This account traces the story of the invasion of Iraq and ends with the capture of Saddam Hussein in December 2003. (Rev: BL 5/1/04; HBG 4/04; SLJ 1/04) [956.7]

10406 Zeinert, Karen. *The Valiant Women of the Vietnam War* (5–8). 2000, Millbrook LB $29.90 (978-0-7613-1268-0). Provides a good overview of the Vietnam War and highlights the contributions of women at home and abroad during this conflict. (Rev: BL 4/1/00; HBG 10/00; SLJ 5/00) [959.704]

Regions

MIDWEST

10407 Baldwin, Guy. *Oklahoma* (4–8). Series: Celebrate the States. 2000, Marshall Cavendish LB $148.29 (978-0-7614-1061-4). The beauties and hidden treasures of Oklahoma are covered in this colorful introduction to the state, its past, its present, and its people. (Rev: BL 12/15/00) [976.6]

10408 Bennett, Michelle. *Missouri* (4–8). Series: Celebrate the States. 2001, Benchmark LB $37.07 (978-0-7614-1063-8). A logically organized, thorough introduction to Missouri with material on such topics as history, people, landmarks, and famous natives. (Rev: BL 9/15/01; HBG 10/01) [977.8]

10409 Bial, Raymond. *Nauvoo: Mormon City on the Mississippi River* (4–7). Illus. 2006, Houghton $17.00 (978-0-618-39685-6). This richly illustrated title profiles the Illinois city of Nauvoo and the important role it played in the history of the Church of Jesus Christ of Latter-day Saints. (Rev: BL 11/1/06; SLJ 12/06)

10410 Bjorklund, Ruth. *Kansas* (4–8). Series: Celebrate the States. 2000, Marshall Cavendish LB $37.07 (978-0-7614-0646-4). A broad introduction to Kansas — its geography and history, its government and people, its songs and folktales, and a few of its recipes. (Rev: BL 6/1–15/00; HBG 10/00) [978.1]

10411 Brill, Marlene Targ. *Illinois* (4–7). Series: Celebrate the States. 2005, Benchmark LB $37.07 (978-0-7614-1735-4). A revised edition of this introduction to the state — including its history, culture, famous sites, and important individuals — with updated illustrations. (Rev: SLJ 5/06) [913.73]

10412 Burgan, Michael. *Illinois* (5–8). Illus. Series: America the Beautiful: Third Series. 2007, Children's Press LB $38.00 (978-0-531-18559-9). This new edition of the classic series entry about the state features a new design and layout, definitions of difficult words in the margins, more history and mini biographies, and project ideas in writing, art, and science. (Rev: BL 2/1/08) [8. 977.3]

10413 Edge, Laura B. *A Personal Tour of Hull-House* (4–7). Series: How It Was. 2001, Lerner LB $25.26 (978-0-8225-3583-6). A firsthand account of the settlement house founded in Chicago by Jane Addams. (Rev: BL 8/1/01) [977.3]

10414 Jameson, W. C. *Buried Treasures of the Great Plains* (5–8). Series: Buried Treasure. 1997, August House $11.95 (978-0-87483-486-4). Stories of buried treasure are organized by the individual states of the Great Plains region. (Rev: SLJ 7/97) [977]

10415 Martin, Michael A. *Ohio: The Buckeye State* (4–7). Series: World Almanac Library of the States. 2002, World Almanac LB $31.00 (978-0-8368-5124-

3). Facts, statistics, a pleasing layout, and color photographs make this a useful choice for report writers. Also use *Oklahoma: The Sooner State* (2002). (Rev: SLJ 9/02) [977.1]

10416 Murphy, Jim. *The Great Fire* (5–9). 1995, Scholastic paper $18.95 (978-0-590-47267-8). A dramatic re-creation of the great Chicago fire that combines documents, personal accounts, illustrations, photographs, and street maps to give an in-depth view of the disaster. Margaret A. Edwards Award 2010. (Rev: BCCB 5/95; BL 6/1–15/95; HB 5–6/95, 9–10/95; SLJ 7/95) [977.3]

10417 Peterson, Sheryl. *Wisconsin* (3–8). Series: This Land Called America. 2010, Creative Education $28.50 (978-1-58341-802-4). History, culture, and geography are all covered in this attractive slim volume that provides the vital facts report writers need. (Rev: LMC 8–9/10) [977.5]

10418 Schwabacher, Martin. *Minnesota* (4–7). Series: Celebrate the States. 1999, Benchmark LB $37.07 (978-0-7614-0658-7). Minnesota is introduced in six chapters that cover history, geography, government and economy, people, achievements, and landmarks. (Rev: HBG 10/99; SLJ 10/99) [977.6]

10419 Wills, Charles A. *A Historical Album of Michigan* (4–7). Series: Historical Albums. 1996, Millbrook LB $24.40 (978-0-7613-0036-6). Using many archival prints, drawings, photographs, and ample text, the history of Michigan is told. (Rev: BL 10/15/96) [977]

MOUNTAIN AND PLAINS STATES

10420 Aretha, David. *Yellowstone National Park* (6–9). Illus. Series: America's National Parks. 2008, Enslow LB $24.95 (978-159845087-3). Yellowstone's history, topography, ecology, and flora and fauna are described in this volume that includes the park's major attractions and Web sites that extend research. (Rev: BL 10/15/08) [978.7]

10421 Lynch, Wayne, and Aubrey Lang. *Rocky Mountains* (4–7). Illus. by Wayne Lynch. Series: Our Wild World. 2006, NorthWord $16.95 (978-1-55971-948-3); paper $8.95 (978-1-55971-949-0). An appealing introduction to the geography, animals, and plants of the region, with full-color photographs and first-person anecdotes. (Rev: BL 10/15/06; SLJ 1/07*)

10422 McDaniel, Melissa. *Arizona* (4–8). Series: Celebrate the States. 2000, Marshall Cavendish LB $37.07 (978-0-7614-0647-1). This introduction to Arizona discusses its land, history, economy, festivals, cultural diversity, and landmarks. (Rev: BL 6/1–15/00; HBG 10/00; SLJ 9/00) [979.1]

10423 Stefoff, Rebecca. *Idaho* (4–8). Series: Celebrate the States. 2000, Benchmark LB $37.07 (978-0-7614-0663-1). Interesting charts, graphs, and maps are used to illustrate such topics as the people, land, history, and culture of Idaho. (Rev: BL 1/1–15/00; HBG 10/00) [978.8]

10424 Stefoff, Rebecca. *Nevada* (4–8). Series: Celebrate the States. 2001, Benchmark LB $37.07 (978-0-7614-1073-7). This well-organized introduction to Nevada gives general information followed by a timeline and special material on tourist attractions, famous natives of Nevada, and local festivals. (Rev: BL 9/15/01; HBG 10/01) [979.3]

NORTHEASTERN AND MID-ATLANTIC STATES

10425 Aaseng, Nathan. *The White House* (7–10). Series: Building History. 2000, Lucent LB $32.45 (978-1-56006-708-5). The history of this Washington landmark is given plus material on the presidents and architects who shaped this building through the years. (Rev: BL 9/15/00) [975.3]

10426 Allen, Thomas B. *The Washington Monument: It Stands for All* (8–12). 2000, Discovery $29.95 (978-1-56331-921-1). Full of photographs and drawings plus an interesting text that supplies good background material, this is a handsome guide to one of the capital's most famous landmarks. (Rev: BL 6/1–15/00) [975.3]

10427 Ashabranner, Brent. *A Date with Destiny: The Women in Military Service for America Memorial* (5–8). 2000, Twenty-First Century LB $25.90 (978-0-7613-1472-1). This book tells the story of the memorial outside Arlington National Cemetery that honors American women in the military and retells some of the stories of these servicewomen. (Rev: BL 2/1/00; HBG 10/00; SLJ 4/00) [355.1]

10428 Attie, Alice. *Harlem on the Verge* (8–12). 2003, Quantuck Lane $35.00 (978-0-9714548-7-3). After an introductory essay, this book consists of unforgettable color photographs that depict life in Manhattan's Harlem and Spanish Harlem. (Rev: BL 2/15/04*) [974.7]

10429 Avakian, Monique. *A Historical Album of Massachusetts* (4–8). Series: Historical Albums. 1994, Millbrook LB $24.40 (978-1-56294-481-0). A history of Massachusetts that begins with the Native American culture and ends with the 1900s, including basic material on major events and personalities. (Rev: SLJ 2/95) [974.4]

10430 Barenblat, Rachel. *Massachusetts: The Bay State* (4–7). Series: World Almanac Library of the States. 2002, World Almanac LB $31.00 (978-0-8368-5123-6). History, politics, government, culture, and state symbols are all covered, with charts, maps, photographs, biographical sketches, and a list of important events and attractions. (Rev: SLJ 6/02) [974.4]

10431 Belanger, Jeff. *Who's Haunting the White House?* (4–7). Illus. by Rick Powell. 2008, Sterling $14.95 (978-1-4027-3822-7). A history of the White House and paranormal incidents there, with period illustrations,

paintings, drawings, and prints. (Rev: BL 12/15/08; SLJ 12/08) [133.1]

10432 Bial, Raymond. *Tenement: Immigrant Life on the Lower East Side* (5–8). 2002, Houghton Mifflin $16.00 (978-0-618-13849-4). Historic photographs complement the simple, descriptive text about life in New York City tenement housing in the late 1800s and early 1900s. (Rev: BL 10/15/02; HB 11–12/02; HBG 3/03; SLJ 9/02) [307.76]

10433 Conway, Lorie. *Forgotten Ellis Island: The Extraordinary Story of America's Immigrant Hospital* (7–12). Photos by Chris Barnes. 2007, Smithsonian $26.95 (978-0-06-124196-3). The story of the construction and use of the Ellis Island hospital facilities is enhanced by archival photographs and many quotations from doctors and immigrants. (Rev: SLJ 10/07) [362.1109747]

10434 Cytron, Barry. *Fire! The Library Is Burning* (4–7). 1988, Lerner LB $15.93 (978-0-8225-0525-9). How workers and volunteers helped to restore the Jewish Theological Seminary in New York City when it was nearly destroyed by fire. (Rev: BL 7/88; SLJ 9/88) [027.63]

10435 Doak, Robin. *New Jersey* (5–8). Series: Voices from Colonial America. 2005, National Geographic LB $32.90 (978-0-7922-6680-8). A compelling account of life in early New Jersey, from its initial settlement by the Dutch through the adoption of the Constitution. (Rev: BL 6/1–15/05; SLJ 1/06) [974.9]

10436 Doherty, Craig A., and Katherine M. Doherty. *Pennsylvania* (5–9). Series: The Thirteen Colonies. 2005, Facts on File LB $35.00 (978-0-8160-5413-8). Traces the history of Pennsylvania from the early settlers through 1787, with discussion of the Native American culture and the Quakers, and with excerpts from primary documents, maps, and profiles of key individuals. (Rev: SLJ 8/05) [973]

10437 Doherty, Craig A., and Katherine M. Doherty. *Rhode Island* (5–9). Series: The Thirteen Colonies. 2005, Facts on File LB $35.00 (978-0-8160-5415-2). Traces the history of Rhode Island from the early settlers through 1787, with discussion of the Native American culture and with excerpts from primary documents, maps, and profiles of key individuals. (Rev: SLJ 8/05) [973]

10438 Elish, Dan. *Vermont* (6–9). Series: Celebrate the States. 2006, Marshall Cavendish $25.95 (978-0-7614-2018-7). This revised edition contains more on Vermont's political, economic and social issues as well as its history and traditions. (Rev: BL 6/1–15/06) [974.3]

10439 Elish, Dan. *Washington, D.C.* (5–8). Series: Celebrate the States. 1998, Benchmark LB $37.07 (978-0-7614-0423-1). An attractive introduction to the people and government of the U.S. capital with material on parks, landmarks, history, economics, and racial problems. (Rev: HBG 10/98; SLJ 1/99) [975.3]

10440 Hempstead, Anne. *The Statue of Liberty* (4–7). Series: Land of the Free. 2006, Heinemann LB $28.21 (978-1-4034-7004-1). With many illustrations and interesting sidebars, this history of the Statue of Liberty details key events and examines its significance as an American symbol. (Rev: SLJ 10/06) [974.7]

10441 Hempstead, Anne. *The Supreme Court* (4–7). Series: Land of the Free. 2006, Heinemann LB $28.21 (978-1-4034-7001-0). With many illustrations and interesting sidebars, this history of the U.S. Supreme Court details key events and examines its significance as an American symbol. Also use *The U.S. Capitol* and *The White House* (both 2006). (Rev: SLJ 10/06) [347]

10442 Herda, D. J. *Environmental America: The Northeastern States* (4–7). Series: American Scene. 1991, Millbrook LB $22.40 (978-1-878841-06-3). This volume discusses the condition of the environment and presents information on such topics as water and land pollution in the northeastern states. (Rev: BL 8/91; SLJ 7/91) [639.9]

10443 Ingram, Scott. *Pennsylvania: The Keystone State* (4–7). Series: World Almanac Library of the States. 2002, World Almanac LB $31.00 (978-0-8368-5120-5). Facts, statistics, a pleasing layout, and color photographs make this a useful choice for report writers. (Rev: SLJ 9/02) [974.8]

10444 Jameson, W. C. *Buried Treasures of New England: Legends of Hidden Riches, Forgotten War Loots, and Lost Ship Treasures* (4–8). Series: Buried Treasure. 1997, August House $11.95 (978-0-87483-485-7). This account describes how these treasures were amassed and lost, and furnishes maps to indicate their general location. (Rev: SLJ 10/97) [910.4]

10445 Locker, Thomas. *In Blue Mountains: An Artist's Return to America's First Wilderness* (6–12). 2000, Bell Pond $18.00 (978-0-88010-471-5). This picture book is a tribute to nature, chronicling the author-artist's return to Kaaterskill Cove in New York State to find inspiration. (Rev: BL 7/00; SLJ 11/00) [974.7]

10446 Louis, Nancy. *Ground Zero* (4–7). Series: War on Terrorism. 2002, ABDO LB $16.95 (978-1-57765-675-3). This heavily illustrated, factually accurate account describes the search, recovery, and cleanup that took place after September 11, 2001, in New York City. (Rev: BL 5/15/02) [974.7]

10447 Lourie, Peter. *Erie Canal: Canoeing America's Great Waterway* (5–8). 1997, Boyds Mills $17.95 (978-1-56397-669-8). This colorful book about a journey along the Erie Canal also supplies historical facts about its construction and uses. (Rev: BL 7/97; HBG 3/98; SLJ 9/97) [974.7]

10448 McCurdy, Michael. *Walden Then and Now: An Alphabetical Tour of Henry Thoreau's Pond* (5–8). Illus. by author. 2010, Charlesbridge $16.95 (978-158089253-7). "C is for the cabin Henry built with

his own hands." This handsome book explores Walden Pond in Thoreau's time and today. (Rev: BL 9/1/10; LMC 1–2/11; SLJ 9/1/10) [818]

10449 Morgane, Wendy. *New Jersey* (4–8). Series: Celebrate the States. 2000, Benchmark LB $37.07 (978-0-7614-0673-0). This excellent introduction to New Jersey covers its history, land, government, economy, unique characteristics, and famous residents. (Rev: BL 1/1–15/00; HBG 10/00) [974.9]

10450 Myers, Walter Dean. *Harlem* (6–12). 1997, Scholastic paper $16.95 (978-0-590-54340-8). This book is an impressionistic appreciation of Harlem and its culture as seen through the eyes of author Walter Dean Myers and his artist son, Christopher. (Rev: BL 2/15/97; SLJ 2/97; VOYA 10/97) [811]

10451 *Our White House: Looking In, Looking Out* (5–8). 2008, Candlewick $29.99 (978-0-7636-2067-7). Essays, historical fiction, and poetry from contemporary children's writers are combined with firsthand accounts from former presidents, their family members, and White House visitors to create this attractive, large-format look at the White House and its place in America's history. (Rev: BL 8/08; SLJ 9/08) [975.3]

10452 Pascoe, Elaine. *History Around You: A Unique Look at the Past, People, and Places of New York* (4–7). 2004, Gale LB $27.45 (978-1-4103-0490-2). Using a news-style format with maps, charts, and illustrations, Pascoe details the history of New York State and profiles famous individuals. (Rev: SLJ 3/05) [974.7]

10453 Raabe, Emily. *Uniquely Vermont* (4–7). Series: Heinemann State Studies. 2005, Heinemann LB $31.36 (978-1-4034-4664-0). In addition to providing the facts necessary for report writers, this volume emphasizes the features that distinguish Vermont from its neighbors. (Rev: BL 10/15/03)

10454 Rock, Howard B., and Deborah Moore. *Cityscapes: A History of New York in Images* (8–12). 2001, Columbia $80.50 (978-0-231-10624-5). Using fine prints and photographs, this account traces the evolution of Manhattan from a Dutch settlement to the great modern city of massive towers that it is today. (Rev: BL 12/1/01) [974.7]

10455 Schnurnberger, Lynn. *Kids Love New York! The A-to-Z Resource Book* (4–8). 1990, Congdon & Weed paper $133.65 (978-0-312-92415-7). A group of suggestions for various activities in New York City.

10456 Schomp, Virginia. *New York* (4–7). Series: Celebrate the States. 2005, Benchmark LB $37.07 (978-0-7614-1738-5). A revised edition of this introduction to the Empire State — including its history, culture, famous sites, and distinguished New Yorkers — with updated illustrations. (Rev: SLJ 5/06) [917.47]

10457 Schuman, Michael. *Delaware* (4–8). Series: Celebrate the States. 2000, Marshall Cavendish LB $37.07 (978-0-7614-0645-7). Beginning with quotations about

Delaware and its people, this account covers the basic topics plus information on folklore, food, and festivals. (Rev: BL 6/1–15/00; HBG 10/00) [975.1]

10458 Tagliaferro, Linda. *Destination New York* (4–8). Series: Port Cities of North America. 1998, Lerner LB $23.93 (978-0-8225-2793-0). Written with a focus on New York's economic life and its handling of goods moving in and out of the port, this book also gives information on the city's history, geography, and daily life. (Rev: HBG 3/99; SLJ 1/99) [974.7]

10459 Talbott, Hudson. *River of Dreams: The Story of the Hudson River* (4–7). Illus. by author. 2009, Putnam $17.99 (978-0-399-24521-3). An engaging history of the river, covering its role in early settlements, shipping and the Erie Canal, the pollution that afflicted the ecosystem and efforts to clean it up, and the river's influence on art. ALA Notable Books 2010. (Rev: BL 12/15/08; HB 3/09; SLJ 3/09) [974.7]

10460 Tougas, Joe. *New York* (3–8). Series: This Land Called America. 2010, Creative Education $28.50 (978-1-58341-785-0). History, culture, and geography are all covered in this attractive slim volume that provides the vital facts report writers need. (Rev: LMC 8–9/10) [974.7]

10461 Warrick, Karen Clemens. *Independence National Historical Park* (5–8). Series: Virtual Field Trips. 2005, Enslow LB $25.26 (978-0-7660-5224-6). A visit to Independence Park, using both print and related Web sites, that covers its historical importance, including Independence Hall and the Liberty Bell. (Rev: SLJ 5/05)

10462 Wills, Charles A. *A Historical Album of Pennsylvania* (4–8). Series: Historical Albums. 1996, Millbrook LB $24.40 (978-1-56294-595-4). Beginning with its Native American origins and settlement by Europeans and the Quakers, this book traces the history of Pennsylvania from the First Continental Congress and the ratification of the United States Constitution, through the Battle of Gettysburg and President Lincoln's famous Gettysburg Address, and up to today. (Rev: BL 7/96; SLJ 7/96) [974.8]

PACIFIC STATES

10463 Altman, Linda J. *California* (5–8). Series: Celebrate the States. 2005, Benchmark LB $37.07 (978-0-7614-1737-8). This revised edition updates facts and adds information on the government and economy plus new, full-color photographs. (Rev: SLJ 3/06) [979.4]

10464 Ansary, Mir Tamim. *People of California* (4–7). Series: Heinemann State Studies. 2003, Heinemann LB $27.07 (978-1-4034-0342-1). Ansary looks at groups of people who have settled in California and offers brief biographies of individuals who have contributed to all fields of endeavor, with many color photographs. (Rev: BL 10/15/03; HBG 4/04; SLJ 11/03) [305.8]

10465 Bowermaster, Jon. *Aleutian Adventure* (6–12). 2001, National Geographic $17.95 (978-0-7922-7999-0). Beautifully illustrated, this book chronicles a harrowing but ultimately successful kayak expedition among the rugged islands of the Aleutian chain. (Rev: VOYA 8/01) [797.1]

10466 Corral, Kimberly. *A Child's Glacier Bay* (4–8). 1998, Graphic Arts Center $15.95 (978-0-88240-503-2). A photoessay chronicling a three-week kayak trip in Alaska's Glacier Bay, told from the perspective of a 13-year-old girl. (Rev: BL 7/98; HBG 10/98; SLJ 8/98) [978.652]

10467 Doak, Robin. *California 1542–1850* (5–8). Series: Voices from Colonial America. 2006, National Geographic $21.95 (978-0-7922-6391-3). This well-illustrated title traces the history of California from its 1542 "discovery" by Juan Rodriguez Cabrillo to the frenzied Gold Rush years of the mid-19th century; maps and a timeline make this useful for research. (Rev: SLJ 1/07)

10468 Feinstein, Stephen. *Hawai'i Volcanoes National Park* (4–8). Illus. Series: America's National Parks: Adventure, Explore, Discover. 2009, Enslow LB $33.27 (978-1-59845-094-1). Links to Web sites add to the information provided here on the Hawaiian park and its geology and ecology, as well as its history and myths associated with it. Lexile 870 (Rev: SLJ 9/09)

10469 Gendell, Megan. *The Spanish Missions of California* (3–7). Series: A True Book. 2010, Children's Press LB $26 (978-0-531-20577-8). An interesting survey of the history and structure of the Spanish mission buildings and their importance to society 500 years ago. (Rev: LMC 8–9/10) [979.4]

10470 Gill, Shelley. *Hawai'i* (5–8). Illus. by Scott Goto. 2006, Charlesbridge paper $6.95 (978-0-88106-297-7). A boy and his father tour the state of Hawaii by kayak; as they pass each island the father tells his son a little about its history, geography, people, culture, and economy. (Rev: SLJ 8/06) [996.9]

10471 Gish, Melissa. *Washington* (3–8). Series: This Land Called America. 2010, Creative Education $28.50 (978-1-58341-800-0). History, culture, and geography are all covered in this attractive slim volume that provides the vital facts report writers need. (Rev: LMC 8–9/10) [979.7]

10472 Goldberg, Jake. *Hawaii* (5–8). Series: Celebrate the States. 1998, Benchmark LB $37.07 (978-0-7614-0203-9). Using fine illustrations, fact boxes, graphs, and maps, this attractive book gives an excellent introduction to Hawaii, with the added bonus of a recipe and two songs. (Rev: HBG 10/98; SLJ 1/99) [996.9]

10473 Graf, Mike. *My Yosemite: A Guide for Young Adventurers* (6–9). Illus. by Annette Filice. 2012, Yosemite Conservancy paper $12.95 (978-193023830-5). Rather than a travel book, this is a handsome introduction to the history, geography, and attractions of the national park and includes interviews with rangers and visitors. (Rev: BLO 7/12; LMC 1–2/13) [979.4]

10474 Henry, Judy. *Uniquely Alaska* (4–7). Series: Heinemann State Studies. 2005, Heinemann LB $31.36 (978-1-4034-4642-8). In addition to providing the facts necessary for report writers, this volume emphasizes the features that make Alaska unique. (Rev: BL 10/15/03)

10475 Murphy, Claire Rudolf. *Children of Alcatraz: Growing Up on the Rock* (4–7). Illus. 2006, Walker $17.95 (978-0-8027-9577-9). This is the story of the children who have grown up on Alcatraz Island over time — early Native American children, children of lighthouse keepers, children of prison authorities, and so forth — with archival photographs and a timeline. (Rev: BL 12/15/06; SLJ 11/06)

10476 Orr, Tamra. *California* (5–8). Illus. Series: America the Beautiful: Third Series. 2007, Children's Press LB $38.00 (978-0-531-18557-5). This new edition of the classic series entry about the state features a new design and layout, definitions of difficult words in the margins, more history and mini biographies, and project ideas in writing, art, and science. (Rev: BL 2/1/08) [979.4]

10477 Pratt, Helen Jay. *The Hawaiians: An Island People* (6–8). 1991, Tuttle paper $9.95 (978-0-8048-1709-7). An account of early Hawaii and its inhabitants, with emphasis on folk customs.

10478 Rice, Oliver D. *Lone Woman of Ghalas-Hat* (5–7). Illus. by Charles Zafuto. 1993, California Weekly LB $13.00 (978-0-936778-52-5); paper $6.00 (978-0-936778-51-8). The true story of the Indian woman who lived alone on a California island for 18 years. This was the basis of *Island of the Blue Dolphins*. A reissue. [979.7]

10479 Ruth, Maria Mudd. *The Pacific Coast* (7–12). Series: Ecosystems of North America. 2000, Benchmark LB $28.50 (978-0-7614-0935-9). A detailed look at the tides, plants, animals, and ecosystems found along the Pacific Coast from Alaska south to Mexico. (Rev: HBG 3/01; SLJ 4/01) [577.5]

10480 Seibold, J. Otto, and Vivian Walsh. *Going to the Getty: A Book About the Getty Center in Los Angeles* (4–7). 1997, Getty Museum $17.50 (978-0-89236-493-0). This introduction to the Getty Museum in Los Angeles is a patchwork of impressions, photographs, drawings, and reproductions of artworks. (Rev: BL 2/15/98; HBG 10/98) [708]

10481 Stepanchuk, Carol. *Exploring Chinatown* (4–8). Illus. by Leland Wong. 2002, Pacific View LB $22.95 (978-1-881896-25-8). This "walk" through San Francisco's Chinatown explores the Chinese culture and customs, and offers historical facts as well as a few hands-on projects. (Rev: BL 8/02; SLJ 9/02) [305.8951073]

10482 Uschan, Michael V. *The California Gold Rush* (5–8). Series: Landmark Events in American History. 2003, World Almanac LB $31.00 (978-0-8368-5374-2). An attractive account of the California gold rush, famous people involved, and its consequences. (Rev: BL 10/15/03) [979.4]

10483 Wills, Charles A. *A Historical Album of California* (4–8). Series: Historical Albums. 1994, Millbrook LB $24.40 (978-1-56294-479-7). A slim volume that covers the basic history of California, with material on major events and important personalities. (Rev: SLJ 3/95) [979.4]

10484 Young, Robert. *A Personal Tour of La Purisima* (4–7). Series: How It Was. 1999, Lerner LB $30.35 (978-0-8225-3576-8). A you-are-there visit to La Purisima — one of the 21 missions built by the Spanish in California — in which the reader experiences life in the mission as it was in 1820. (Rev: BL 6/1–15/99; HBG 10/99) [979.4]

SOUTH

10485 Altman, Linda J. *Arkansas* (4–8). Series: Celebrate the States. 2000, Benchmark LB $37.07 (978-0-7614-0672-3). An broad introduction to the culture, land, government, history, and unique characteristics of Arkansas, with emphasis on its inhabitants. (Rev: BL 1/1–15/00; HBG 10/00) [976.7]

10486 Barrett, Tracy. *Virginia* (4–7). Series: Celebrate the States. 2005, Benchmark LB $37.07 (978-0-7614-1734-7). A revised edition of this introduction to the state — including its history, culture, famous sites, and important Virginians — with updated illustrations. (Rev: SLJ 5/06) [975.5]

10487 Bredeson, Carmen, and Mary Dodson Wade. *Texas* (5–8). Series: Celebrate the States. 2005, Benchmark LB $37.07 (978-0-7614-1736-1). This revised edition updates facts and adds information on the government and economy plus new, full-color photographs. (Rev: SLJ 3/06) [976.4]

10488 Cocke, William. *A Historical Album of Virginia* (4–8). Series: Historical Albums. 1995, Millbrook paper $6.95 (978-1-56294-856-6). A broad overview of Virginia's history, using many period prints and paintings, with equal space given to past and current events, and including general information on the state. (Rev: SLJ 1/96) [975.5]

10489 Coleman, Wim, and Pat Perrin. *Colonial Williamsburg* (5–8). Series: Virtual Field Trips. 2005, Enslow LB $25.26 (978-0-7660-5220-8). A visit to Williamsburg, using both print and related Web sites, that covers its historical importance and its portrayal of colonial life. (Rev: SLJ 5/05)

10490 Cribben, Patrick. *Uniquely West Virginia* (4–7). Series: Heinemann State Studies. 2005, Heinemann LB $31.36 (978-1-4034-4665-7). In addition to providing the facts necessary for report writers, this volume emphasizes the features that distinguish West Virginia from its neighbors. (Rev: BL 10/15/03)

10491 Doherty, Craig A., and Katherine M. Doherty. *North Carolina* (5–9). Series: The Thirteen Colonies. 2005, Facts on File LB $35.00 (978-0-8160-5412-1). Traces the history of North Carolina from the early settlers through 1787, with discussion of the Native American culture and with excerpts from primary documents, maps, and profiles of key individuals. (Rev: SLJ 8/05) [973]

10492 Herda, D. J. *Environmental America: The South Central States* (4–7). Series: American Scene. 1991, Millbrook LB $22.40 (978-1-878841-09-4). This account discusses the general state of the environment and presents information on animal species, pollution, waste, and urban sprawl for 10 states, including Georgia, Kansas, Missouri, and Texas. (Rev: BL 8/91; SLJ 7/91) [639.9]

10493 Hoffman, Nancy. *South Carolina* (4–8). Series: Celebrate the States. 2000, Marshall Cavendish LB $37.07 (978-0-7614-1065-2). An interesting introduction to South Carolina, with material on its land and waterways, history, government, economy, landmarks, and success stories. (Rev: BL 12/15/00; HBG 3/01) [975.7]

10494 Kostyal, K. M. *1776: A New Look at Revolutionary Williamsburg* (4–8). 2009, National Geographic $27.90 (978-1-4263-0517-7). The history of Williamsburg, Virginia, is told from the perspectives of a variety of period characters, who focus on everything from food and dress to slavery. (Rev: BL 10/15/09; LMC 11–12/09; SLJ 11/1/09) [973.3]

10495 Lynch, Wayne. *The Everglades* (4–7). Illus. Series: Our Wild World. 2007, NorthWord $16.95 (978-1-55971-970-4); paper $8.95 (978-1-55971-971-1). With eye-catching color photographs and conversational narrative, Lynch introduces the flora and fauna of the Everglades and highlights the threats to this ecosystem. (Rev: BL 9/1/07; SLJ 11/07)

10496 Martin, Michael A. *Alabama: The Heart of Dixie* (4–7). Series: World Almanac Library of the States. 2002, World Almanac LB $31.00 (978-0-8368-5127-4). Full-color photographs and graphic elements enhance this informative introduction to the state. Also use *Arizona: The Grand Canyon State* (2002). (Rev: SLJ 2/03) [976.1]

10497 Odinoski, Steve. *Georgia* (4–8). Series: Celebrate the States. 2000, Marshall Cavendish LB $37.07 (978-0-7614-1062-1). An informative, attractive introduction to Georgia with material on its land, history, people, social issues, and hidden treasures. (Rev: BL 12/15/00; HBG 3/01; SLJ 2/01) [975.8]

10498 Pobst, Sandy. *Virginia, 1607–1776* (5–8). Series: Voices from Colonial America. 2005, National Geographic LB $32.90 (978-0-7922-6771-3). A thorough

political and social history of early Virginia, with excellent illustrations. (Rev: BL 10/15/05; SLJ 11/05) [975.5]

10499 Rauth, Leslie. *Maryland* (5–9). Series: Celebrate the States. 1999, Benchmark LB $37.07 (978-0-7614-0671-6). This book explores Maryland with material on topics including land and waterways, government, economy, festivals, and people. (Rev: BL 1/1–15/00; HBG 10/00; SLJ 5/00) [975.2]

10500 Sherrow, Victoria. *Uniquely South Carolina* (4–7). Series: Heinemann State Studies. 2005, Heinemann LB $31.36 (978-1-4034-4661-9). In addition to providing the facts necessary for report writers, this volume emphasizes the features that distinguish South Carolina from its neighbors. (Rev: BL 10/15/03)

10501 Shirley, David. *North Carolina* (4–8). Series: Celebrate the States. 2001, Benchmark LB $37.07 (978-0-7614-1072-0). A fine introduction to the land, history, economy, and people of North Carolina. (Rev: BL 9/15/01; HBG 10/01) [975.6]

10502 Stout, Mary. *Atlanta* (4–7). Series: Great Cities of the World. 2005, World Almanac LB $31.00 (978-0-8368-5042-0). Report writers will find useful information on Atlanta's history, culture, lifestyle, and current problems. (Rev: BL 4/15/04)

10503 Suben, Eric. *The Spanish Missions of Florida* (3–7). Series: A True Book. 2010, Children's Press LB $26 (978-0-531-20578-9). A look at Spanish mission buildings in Florida, with beautiful color photographs and discussion of their history and the impact of the missions on the Native Americans. Lexile 910L (Rev: LMC 8–9/10) [975.9]

10504 Weatherford, Carole Boston. *Sink or Swim: African-American Lifesavers of the Outer Banks* (4–8). 1999, Coastal Carolina $15.95 (978-1-928556-01-5); paper $12.95 (978-1-928556-03-9). A history of the African Americans who participated in lifesaving efforts on the Outer Banks of North Carolina, known as "the graveyard of the Atlantic." (Rev: BL 12/15/99) [363.28]

SOUTHWEST

10505 Coleman, Wim, and Pat Perrin. *The Alamo* (6–9). Series: Virtual Field Trips. 2005, Enslow LB $25.26 (978-0-7660-5221-5). An attractive overview of the events that make the Alamo an important historical landmark, with Web links for further research. (Rev: BL 8/05; SLJ 5/05) [976.4]

10506 Gendell, Megan. *The Spanish Misssions of Texas* (3–7). Series: A True Book. 2010, Children's Press LB $26 (978-0-531-20580-8). A look at the Spanish mission buildings of Texas, with beautiful color photographs and discussion of their history and their impact of the missions on the Native Americans. Lexile 940L (Rev: LMC 8–9/10) [976.4]

10507 Herda, D. J. *Environmental America: The South-western States* (4–7). Series: American Scene. 1991, Millbrook LB $22.40 (978-1-878841-11-7). This account, which discusses the state of the environment and how it can be changed for the better, covers Arizona, California, Colorado, Nevada, New Mexico, and Utah. (Rev: BL 8/91; SLJ 7/91) [639.9]

10508 Lourie, Peter. *The Lost World of the Anasazi: Exploring the Mysteries of Chaco Canyon* (5–8). 2003, Boyds Mills $19.95 (978-1-56397-972-9). With many full-color photographs, the author describes his trip to the ruins of Chaco Canyon and discusses the mysterious disappearance of its Anasazi residents. (Rev: BL 9/1/03; HBG 4/04; SLJ 1/04) [978.9]

10509 Lynch, Wayne, and Aubrey Lang. *Sonoran Desert* (5–8). Series: Our Wild World Ecosystems. 2009, NorthWord $16.95 (978-1-58979-389-7). The fascinating flora, fauna, topography, and climate of America's Sonoran Desert are described in chatty, well-written text and an abundance of eye-catching illustrations and color photographs. (Rev: SLJ 10/09) [77.5409791]

10510 Lyon, Robin. *The Spanish Missions of Arizona* (3–7). Series: A True Book. 2010, Children's Press LB $26 (978-0-531-20576-1). A look at the Spanish mis-sion buildings of Arizona, with beautiful color photographs and discussion of their history and the impact of the missions on the Native Americans. Also use *The Spanish Missions of New Mexico* (2010). Lexile 930L (Rev: LMC 8–9/10) [979.1]

10511 McCarry, Charles. *The Great Southwest* (7–12). 1980, National Geographic LB $12.95 (978-0-87044-288-9). In pictures and text, descriptions are given of such states as New Mexico, Colorado, and Arizona. [979.1]

10512 Marcovitz, Hal. *The Alamo* (4–8). Series: American Symbols and Their Meanings. 2002, Mason Crest LB $18.95 (978-1-59084-037-5). A basic and readable introduction to the history of the Alamo and its importance to Americans, with illuminating illustrations and inset features. (Rev: SLJ 9/02) [976]

10513 Tweit, Susan J. *Meet the Wild Southwest: Land of Hoodoos and Gila Monsters* (4–8). 1996, Alaska Northwest paper $14.95 (978-0-88240-468-4). An impressive collection of facts and curiosities about the natural history of the Southwest, with many appendixes that supply more-traditional information. (Rev: BL 3/1/96) [508.79]

Philosophy and Religion

Philosophy

10514 Law, Stephen. *Really, Really Big Questions About the Weird, the Wonderful, and Everything Else* (5–8). Illus. by Nishant Choksi. 2009, Kingfisher $16.99 (978-0-75346-309-3). What is nothing? Is my mind my brain? How important is happiness? Is time travel possible? These are only a few of the questions posed here as Law tackles some weighty problems in an accessible manner. (Rev: BL 12/15/09; LMC 1–2/10; SLJ 1/10) [100]

World Religions and Holidays

General and Miscellaneous

10515 Batmanglij, Najmieh. *Happy Nowruz: Cooking with Children to Celebrate the Persian New Year* (4–8). 2008, Mage $40.00 (978-1-933823-16-4). This attractive spiral-bound book combines the history and customs of the Persian New Year with recipes. (Rev: BL 6/1–15/08) [641.59]

10516 Blackwell, Amy Hackney. *Lent, Yom Kippur, and Other Atonement Days* (5–8). Series: Holidays and Celebrations. 2010, Knopf $19.99 (978-1-60413-100-0). The customs of Lent, Yom Kippur, and the Buddhist holiday Rains Retreat are detailed and given historical context in this illustrated book. (Rev: BL 11/15/09; SLJ 1/10) [202]

10517 Braude, Ann. *Women and American Religion* (8–12). Series: Religion in America. 2000, Oxford LB $32.95 (978-0-19-510676-3). Beginning with Native American and Puritan women and continuing to the present, this account traces the many contributions women have made to religion in America. (Rev: BL 3/15/00; HBG 3/01; SLJ 5/00) [200]

10518 Breuilly, Elizabeth. *Religions of the World: The Illustrated Guide to Origins, Beliefs, Traditions and Festivals* (7–12). 1997, Facts on File $29.95 (978-0-8160-3723-0). This well-illustrated work defines religion generally, discusses each of the world's major religions, points out similarities, and links each religion to current events and international politics. (Rev: BL 10/1/97; HBG 3/98; SLJ 2/98) [291]

10519 Brown, Alan, and Andrew Langley. *What I Believe: A Young Person's Guide to the Religions of the World* (4–7). 1999, Millbrook LB $24.90 (978-0-7613-1501-8). Young people of eight major faiths explain their religion's principal tenets, rituals, holy days, and celebrations. (Rev: BL 10/1/99; HBG 3/00; SLJ 2/00) [291]

10520 Brunelli, Roberto. *A Family Treasury of Bible Stories: One for Each Week of the Year* (4–8). 1997, Abrams $24.95 (978-0-8109-1248-9). A collection of 52 short stories from the Old and New Testaments. (Rev: BL 10/1/97; SLJ 2/98) [220.9]

10521 Chaikin, Miriam. *Angels Sweep the Desert Floor: Bible Legends About Moses in the Wilderness* (4–7). Illus. by Alexander Koshkin. 2002, Clarion $19.00 (978-0-395-97825-2). This collection of stories mixes religious history and rabbinic literature to tell the story of the Israelites' 40 years in the wilderness. (Rev: BL 10/1/02; HB 11–12/02; HBG 3/03; SLJ 9/02) [296.1]

10522 Cotner, June, ed. *Teen Sunshine Reflections: Words for the Heart and Soul* (6–12). 2002, HarperCollins $15.95 (978-0-06-000525-2); paper $9.95 (978-0-06-000527-6). This anthology of poems and quotations that celebrate spiritual beliefs and appreciation of the world about us includes the works of the well-known (such as Saint Francis, Gandhi, and Anne Frank) and the unknown. (Rev: BL 7/02; HBG 10/02; SLJ 8/02; VOYA 8/02) [082]

10523 Dillon, Leo, and Diane Dillon. *To Every Thing There Is a Season: Verses from Ecclesiastes* (4–7). 1998, Scholastic paper $16.95 (978-0-590-47887-8). Using verses from Ecclesiastes such as "A time to be born and a time to die," the artists have created a stunning picture book on the cycle of life. (Rev: BCCB 11/98; BL 10/1/98*; HB 9–10/98; HBG 3/99; SLJ 9/98) [223]

10524 Fischer, Chuck, and Curtis Flowers. *In the Beginning: The Art of Genesis* (5–8). Illus. by Bruce Foster. 2008, Little, Brown $35.00 (978-0-316-11842-2). This artful pop-up book highlights stories from the Book of Genesis, including the Garden of Eden, Noah's Ark, the

Tower of Babel, and Jacob's Ladder. (Rev: BL 2/1/09*) [222]

10525 Gaskins, Pearl Fuyo. *I Believe In . . .: Christian, Jewish, and Muslim Young People Speak About Their Faiths* (7–10). 2004, Cricket $18.95 (978-0-8126-2713-8). Suitable for browsing, this is a collection of interviews with about 100 young adults from diverse religious backgrounds in the Chicago area. (Rev: BCCB 9/04; BL 10/1/04; HB 7–8/04) [200]

10526 Hartz, Paula. *Baha'i Faith* (6–10). Series: World Religions. 2002, Facts on File $30.00 (978-0-8160-4729-1). A look at the history and beliefs of the Baha'i Faith and its spread from Persia to the rest of the world. (Rev: HBG 3/03; SLJ 12/02) [297.9]

10527 Hartz, Paula R. *Taoism* (6–9). Series: World Religions. 1993, Facts on File $30.00 (978-0-8160-2448-3). A clear, objective explanation of the Chinese religion Taoism, with details on its metamorphosis from mysticism to a more secular form. (Rev: BL 7/93) [299]

10528 Hoffman, Nancy. *Sikhism* (6–9). Series: Religions of the World. 2005, Gale LB $29.95 (978-1-59018-453-0). A basic introduction to the beliefs and practices of Sikhism, with a chronology of important events. (Rev: SLJ 2/06) [294.6]

10529 Hoobler, Thomas, and Dorothy Hoobler. *Confucianism* (6–9). Series: World Religions. 1993, Facts on File $30.00 (978-0-8160-2445-2). Describes how the teachings of Confucius evolved from a social order to a religion, permeating all phases of Chinese life for 2,000 years. (Rev: BL 3/1/93) [299]

10530 Ikeda, Daisaku. *The Way of Youth* (6–12). 2000, Middleway paper $14.95 (978-0-9674697-0-6). The great questions of human behavior — such as the nature of love, friendship, and compassion — are discussed from a Buddhist perspective. (Rev: BL 12/1/00) [294.3]

10531 Krishnaswami, Uma. *The Broken Tusk: Stories of the Hindu God Ganesha* (4–8). 1996, Linnet $19.95 (978-0-208-02242-4). A collection of tales about the elephant-headed Hindu god Ganesha, the god of good beginnings. (Rev: SLJ 7/97) [294.5]

10532 Lester, Julius. *When the Beginning Began: Stories About God, the Creatures, and Us* (4–8). 1999, Harcourt $17.00 (978-0-15-201138-3). Using parts of Genesis and creation stories from Jewish legends, this wondrous retelling adds thought-provoking human interest to the stories that end with Adam and Eve. (Rev: BL 4/15/99*; SLJ 5/99) [296.1]

10533 Lincoln, Frances. *A Family Treasury of Prayers* (4–8). 1996, Simon & Schuster $16.00 (978-0-689-80956-9). Classic art works illustrate this lovely collection of prayers from famous sources. (Rev: BL 10/1/96; SLJ 10/96; VOYA 6/97) [242]

10534 Lottridge, Celia B. *Stories from Adam and Eve to Ezekiel: Retold from the Bible* (4–7). Illus. by Gary

Clement. 2004, Groundwood $24.95 (978-0-88899-490-5). Some of the best-loved stories from the Hebrew Bible are engagingly adapted in this attractively illustrated volume. (Rev: BL 10/1/04; SLJ 4/05) [220]

10535 Lugira, Aloysius. *African Religion* (7–10). Series: World Religions. 1999, Facts on File $30.00 (978-0-8160-3876-3). The author gives a fine overview of the major religious beliefs of the different ethnic groups in Africa plus material on organized religion, witchcraft, and the influence of Western religions on the area. (Rev: BL 1/1–15/00; HBG 4/00; SLJ 1/00) [299]

10536 Mann, Gruinder Singh. *Buddhists, Hindus, and Sikhs in America* (6–12). Series: Religion in American Life. 2002, Oxford $32.95 (978-0-19-512442-2). Photographs, anecdotes, and excerpts from primary sources add appeal to this survey of how three major religions have affected, and been affected by, life in America. (Rev: BL 1/1–15/02; HBG 10/02; SLJ 1/02; VOYA 4/02) [294]

10537 Marcovitz, Hal. *Religious Fundamentalism* (6–9). Series: Compact Research. 2009, ReferencePoint LB $25.95 (978-1-60152-082-1). After a definition of fundamentalism, this thorough volume looks at its prevalence and the threats it may pose, with facts, statistics, and quotations. (Rev: BL 11/15/09; SLJ 12/09) [200.9.]

10538 Martin, Joel W. *Native American Religion* (7–12). 1999, Oxford LB $32.95 (978-0-19-511035-7). An overview of historical and contemporary Native American religious beliefs and practices, their importance in daily life, and the conflicts introduced by the Europeans. (Rev: HBG 4/00; SLJ 9/99; VOYA 10/99) [299]

10539 Mayer, Marianna. *Remembering the Prophets of Sacred Scripture* (6–10). 2003, Penguin $16.99 (978-0-8034-2727-3). Old Testament prophets — from Daniel and Moses to Amos and Obadiah — are introduced in this handsome picture book for older readers. (Rev: BL 7/03; SLJ 8/03) [224]

10540 Metcalf, Franz. *Buddha in Your Backpack: Everyday Buddhism for Teens* (7–12). 2002, Ulysses paper $12.95 (978-1-56975-321-7). This humorous and informative guide will satisfy young adults' interest in the spiritual world of Buddhism. (Rev: BL 1/1–15/03; SLJ 2/03; VOYA 2/04) [294.3]

10541 Murphy, Claire Rudolf. *Daughters of the Desert: Stories of Remarkable Women from Christian, Jewish, and Muslim Traditions* (7–10). 2003, SkyLight Paths $19.95 (978-1-893361-72-0). Five authors contributed to these 18 stories, based on the Bible and Koran, of the lives of women including Eve, Esther, Mary Magdalene, Sarah, and Khadiji, the wife of Mohammed. (Rev: BL 10/15/03) [220.9]

10542 Philip, Neil. *In the House of Happiness: A Book of Prayer and Praise* (6–9). Illus. by Isabelle Brent. 2003, Clarion $17.00 (978-0-618-23481-3). Reflective verses are accompanied by images of nature in this book of inspirational messages. (Rev: BL 2/1/03; HBG 10/03; SLJ 7/03) [291.4]

10543 Simpson, Nancy. *Face-to-Face with Women of the Bible* (6–8). 1996, Chariot-Victor $16.99 (978-0-7814-0251-4). Both well-known and obscure women from the Bible are introduced in two or three pages per subject. (Rev: BL 10/15/96) [220.92]

10544 Singh, Nikky-Guninder Kaur. *Sikhism* (6–9). Series: World Religions. 1993, Facts on File $30.00 (978-0-8160-2446-9). Describes the development of Sikhism an outgrowth of Hinduism and discusses its traditions, customs, and beliefs. (Rev: BL 7/93) [294.6]

10545 Stein, Stephen J. *Alternative American Religions* (8–12). Series: Religion in American Life. 2000, Oxford LB $32.95 (978-0-19-511196-5). From Puritan dissenters to cults like Heaven's Gate, this is a look at the alternative religions that have attracted followers in the Americas. (Rev: HBG 9/00; SLJ 4/00; VOYA 12/00) [291.9]

10546 Sweeney, Jon M., ed. *God Within: Our Spiritual Future — As Told by Today's New Adults* (8–12). 2001, SkyLight Paths paper $14.95 (978-1-893361-15-7). Writers in their teens and 20s, who reflect a wide variety of beliefs, present very personal essays on their faiths and their paths to spirituality. (Rev: BL 1/1–15/02) [200]

10547 Thompson, Jan. *Islam* (5–8). Series: World Religions. 2005, Walrus paper $12.95 (978-1-55285-654-3). Using a question-and-answer format, this attractive introduction explores the history and beliefs of Islam; a first-person account by a 15-year-old Muslim boy in London starts the book. (Rev: BL 10/15/05) [297]

10548 Waldman, Neil. *The Promised Land: The Birth of the Jewish People* (4–7). 2002, Boyds Mills $21.95 (978-1-56397-332-1). Waldman interweaves information on religious tradition and the experiences of the Jewish people over time in this handsome volume. (Rev: BL 10/1/02; HBG 3/03; SLJ 9/02) [909]

10549 Wangu, Madhu Bazaz. *Buddhism* (6–9). Series: World Religions. 1993, Facts on File $30.00 (978-0-8160-2442-1). Describes Buddha's life, the spread of Buddhism, and its existence today. (Rev: BL 3/1/93; SLJ 6/93) [294.3]

10550 Ward, Elaine. *Old Testament Women* (5–10). Series: Art Revelations. 2004, Enchanted Lion $18.95 (978-1-59270-011-0). Paintings by masters accompany stories about 18 women including Rachel, Ruth, and Bathsheba. (Rev: SLJ 8/04) [224]

10551 *What Do You Believe? Religion and Faith in the World Today* (5–8). Illus. 2011, DK $16.99 (978-0-7566-7228-7). The major world religions are introduced here — along with minor religions, spiritual movements, and atheism — with discussion of religious practices, morality, science and Creationism, and other related aspects. (Rev: BL 6/1/11; SLJ 6/11) [200]

10552 Winston, Diana. *Wide Awake: A Buddhist Guide for Teens* (6–10). 2003, Putnam paper $14.95 (978-0-399-52897-2). In a conversational style, the author introduces the tenets of Buddhism, explains her own beliefs and how she arrived at them, and looks at ways teens can apply Buddhist teachings to their own experiences. (Rev: BL 10/1/03) [294]

10553 Zarin, Cynthia. *Saints Among the Animals* (5–8). Illus. by Leonid Gore. 2006, Atheneum $17.95 (978-0-689-85031-8). An attractive collection of ten stories about saints interacting with animals; brief biographies of the saints are appended. (Rev: BL 12/1/06; SLJ 1/07)

Christianity

10554 Bolick, Nancy O., and Sallie Randolph. *Shaker Inventions* (6–8). 1990, Walker LB $13.85 (978-0-8027-6934-3). This book describes the Shaker religion and explores the many contributions of the Shakers to American life, such as the clothespin and washing machine. (Rev: BL 8/90) [289]

10555 Capek, Michael. *A Personal Tour of a Shaker Village* (4–7). Series: How It Was. 2001, Lerner LB $30.35 (978-0-8225-3584-3). An account of life in a Shaker village, seen through the eyes of people who lived there. (Rev: BL 8/1/01; HBG 10/01; SLJ 8/01) [289.8]

10556 *Christmas in Colonial and Early America* (4–7). 1996, World Book $19.00 (978-0-7166-0875-2). The evolution of Christmas celebrations is traced through more than 100 years of American history to the end of the 19th century. (Rev: BL 11/1/96) [394.26]

10557 *Christmas in Greece* (5–10). Series: Christmas Around the World. 2000, World Book $19.00 (978-0-7166-0859-2). This account focuses on the religious practices of the Greek Orthodox Church at Christmastime, which begins with a long fasting period. (Rev: BL 9/1/00) [398.2]

10558 Connolly, Sean. *New Testament Miracles* (5–10). Series: Art Revelations. 2004, Enchanted Lion $18.95 (978-1-59270-012-7). Presents brief retellings of 12 miracles performed by Jesus Christ, each illustrated by a well-known painting by an eminent artist, such as Rembrandt, El Greco, and Tintoretto. (Rev: SLJ 8/04) [226.7]

10559 Demi. *Mary* (4–7). 2006, Simon & Schuster $19.95 (978-0-689-87692-9). Traces the story of the mother of Jesus from the days preceding her birth through her ascension into heaven. (Rev: BL 10/1/06; SLJ 11/06) [232.91]

10560 John Paul II, Pope. *Every Child a Light: The Pope's Message to Young People* (4–7). Ed. by Jerome M. Vereb. 2002, Boyds Mills $16.95 (978-1-56397-090-0). Using photographs and snippets from Pope

John Paul II's writings for children and teens, this is an inspirational book of comments and advice for youngsters. (Rev: BL 6/1–15/02; HBG 10/02; SLJ 5/02) [248.8]

10561 Lottridge, Celia B. *Stories from the Life of Jesus* (5–7). Illus. by Linda Wolfsgruber. 2004, Douglas & McIntyre $24.95 (978-0-88899-497-4). Lottridge draws on the first four books of the New Testament for this illustrated collection of stories. (Rev: BL 5/1/04; HB 7–8/04; SLJ 11/04) [232.9]

10562 Noll, Mark. *Protestants in America* (7–12). Series: Religion in America. 2000, Oxford $32.95 (978-0-19-511034-0). From the arrival of the Puritans to today, this is a well-organized overview of Protestantism and how it has evolved, changed, and splintered in America. (Rev: BL 10/1/00; HBG 3/01; SLJ 2/01) [280]

10563 Schmidt, Gary D., retel. *The Blessing of the Lord: Stories from the Old and New Testaments* (5–8). 1997, Eerdmans $20.00 (978-0-8028-3789-9). Using 25 Old and New Testament stories as a focus, these insightful accounts describe how biblical personalities react to such events as Daniel's struggle with the lions and Jesus causing nets to be filled with fish. (Rev: BL 11/1/97; HBG 3/98; SLJ 10/97) [222]

10564 Self, David. *Christianity* (5–8). Series: Religions of the World. 2005, World Almanac LB $31.00 (978-0-8368-5866-2). A basic introduction to the beliefs and practices of Christianity, with a chronology of important events. (Rev: SLJ 2/06)

10565 Visconte, Guido. *Clare and Francis* (4–7). Illus. by Bimba Landmann. 2004, Eerdmans $20.00 (978-0-8028-5269-4). Eye-catching artwork highlights the inspiring stories of saints Clare and Francis in this picture book for older readers. (Rev: BL 2/1/04*; SLJ 6/04) [270]

Islam

10566 Ali-Karamali, Sumbul. *Growing Up Muslim: Understanding Islamic Beliefs and Practices* (5–8). Illus. 2012, Delacorte $16.99 (978-0-385-74095-1); LB $19.99 (978-0-375-98977-3). The Muslim author, who grew up in California, explains Muslim beliefs and customs — holidays, diet, clothing, praying, and so forth — and provides brief details on the history of Islam and the differences between the various sects. ⌒ ℮ (Rev: BL 11/15/12; HB 9–10/12; LMC 11–12/12; SLJ 9/12; VOYA 6/12) [297]

10567 Barnes, Trevor. *Islam* (5–8). Series: World Faiths. 2005, Kingfisher paper $6.95 (978-0-7534-5882-2). Originally published in 1999 as part of *The Kingfisher Book of Religions: Festivals, Ceremonies, and Beliefs from Around the World*, this 40-page expanded volume provides a wide-ranging overview of Islam and its fol-

lowers. (Rev: BL 10/1/05; SLJ 10/05; VOYA 6/06) [297]

10568 Clark, Charles. *Islam* (6–9). Series: Religions of the World. 2002, Gale LB $29.95 (978-1-56006-986-7). Clark explains the history and practice of Islam and discusses the challenges facing this religion today, with interesting sidebars on topics including dietary laws and dress for women. (Rev: BL 8/02; SLJ 7/02) [297]

10569 Conover, Sarah, and Freda Crane. *Beautiful Signs/Ayat Jamilah: A Treasury of Islamic Wisdom for Children and Parents* (5–7). Illus. by Valerie Wahl. Series: Little Light of Mine. 2004, Eastern Washington Univ. paper $19.95 (978-0-910055-94-9). Muslim folktales, fables, stories from the Koran, and historic tales originate from countries around the world. (Rev: BL 10/15/04; SLJ 8/04) [297.1]

10570 Egendorf, Laura K., ed. *Islam in America* (7–12). Series: At Issue. 2005, Gale LB $29.95 (978-0-7377-2727-2). Essays cover topics including discrimination against Muslims, the growing popularity of the religion among Hispanic Americans, and the degree of support of terrorism. (Rev: SLJ 2/06) [297]

10571 Einfeld, Jann, ed. *Is Islam a Religion of War or Peace?* (7–9). Series: At Issue. 2005, Gale LB $28.70 (978-0-7377-3100-2). Opposing perspectives on Islam's attitude toward violence are examined in this thought-provoking collection of essays, many of which quote from the Koran in support of their assertions. (Rev: SLJ 11/05) [297]

10572 Gordon, Matthew S. *Islam. 3rd ed.* (7–10). 2006, Facts on File $30.00 (978-0-8160-6612-4). An overview of the history of Islam, its branches, the Koran, and Islam's place in the modern world. (Rev: SLJ 3/07) [297]

10573 Hafiz, Dilara, et al. *The American Muslim Teenager's Handbook* (7–12). Illus. 2009, Simon & Schuster paper $11.99 (978-141698578-5). Friendly tips for young Muslim Americans on how to stand up to stereotypes and how to discuss their faith are accompanied by facts about the religion that will be useful for all readers. Lexile 1260 (Rev: BL 4/1/09; LMC 10/09; SLJ 4/08) [297.5]

10574 Jeffrey, Laura S. *Celebrate Ramadan* (5–8). Illus. Series: Celebrate Holidays. 2007, Enslow LB $23.95 (978-0-7660-2774-9). Report writers and others wanting to know about this Muslim holiday will find the facts they need here, as well as more general information about Islam in America. (Rev: BL 10/1/07; SLJ 11/07) [297.3]

10575 O'Connor, Frances. *The History of Islam* (5–8). Series: Understanding Islam. 2009, Rosen LB $29.25 (978-1-4358-5064-4). After looking at the origins of Islam, this volume distinguishes between Sunnis and Shiites, discusses the Koran, describes Islam's spread through the world, and gives an overview of the practice of Islam today. (Rev: LMC 10/09*) [297.09]

10576 Siddiqui, Haroon. *Being Muslim* (8–12). Series: Groundwork Guide. 2006, Groundwood $15.95 (978-0-88899-785-2). This is an objective introduction to the Muslim faith and to related topics of current interest including women's rights and terrorist elements. (Rev: BL 12/15/06; LMC 4–5/07; SLJ 2/07) [297]

10577 Whiting, Jim. *The Role of Religion in the Early Islamic World* (5–7). Illus. Series: Life in the Early Islamic World. 2012, Crabtree LB $30.60 (978-077872169-7). With excellent illustrations, this attractive volume provides a solid introduction to Islam and its importance to the overall culture of the time. (Rev: BL 8/12*; SLJ 8/12) [297.09]

10578 Wormser, Richard. *American Islam: Growing Up Muslim in America* (7–12). 1994, Walker $16.85 (978-0-8027-8344-8). A portrait of Muslim American youth and their faith. (Rev: BL 12/15/94; SLJ 3/95; VOYA 2/95) [297]

Judaism

10579 Abrams, Judith Z. *The Secret World of Kabbalah* (5–9). Illus. 2006, Lerner paper $9.95 (978-1-58013-224-4). This interesting introduction to Kabbalah defines this form of Jewish mysticism as "the journey to come as closely in touch with God as you can." (Rev: SLJ 12/06)

10580 Burstein, Chaya M. *The Jewish Kids Catalog* (7–9). 1983, Jewish Publication Soc. paper $15.95 (978-0-8276-0215-1). All sorts of information is given on Jewish culture and history including holidays, folktales, and even some recipes. [296]

10581 Chaikin, Miriam. *Menorahs, Mezuzas, and Other Jewish Symbols* (5–9). 1990, Clarion $17.00 (978-0-89919-856-9). A Jewish historian explains some of the symbols of the faith. (Rev: BL 1/15/91; HB 5–6/91; SLJ 1/91) [296.4]

10582 Corona, Laurel. *Judaism* (6–9). Series: Religions of the World. 2003, Gale LB $29.95 (978-1-56006-987-4). The history, teachings, and contemporary customs of Judaism are clearly presented, with information on some famous Jews. (Rev: BL 11/15/03; SLJ 11/03) [296]

10583 David, Jo, and Daniel B. Syme. *The Book of the Jewish Life* (5–8). 1997, UAHC paper $13.95 (978-0-8074-0628-1). This book explores common Jewish traditions in such areas as birth and naming, religious schools, bar/bat mitzvahs, confirmation, marriage, and mourning. (Rev: SLJ 9/98) [296]

10584 Feinstein, Edward. *Tough Questions Jews Ask: A Young Adult's Guide to Building a Jewish Life* (5–7). 2003, Jewish Lights $14.99 (978-1-58023-139-8). Rabbi Feinstein effectively answers hypothetical questions posed by an imagined class of thoughtful young students. Sidney Taylor Book Honor 2003. (Rev: BL 4/1/03) [296.7]

10585 Isaacs, Ron. *Ask the Rabbi: The Who, What, Where, Why, and How of Being Jewish* (7–12). 2003, Jossey-Bass paper $22.95 (978-0-7879-6784-0). Questions and answers are divided into thematic chapters and provide information on practices in different denominations. (Rev: BL 10/15/03) [296]

10586 Keene, Michael. *Judaism* (5–8). Series: Religions of the World. 2005, World Almanac LB $31.00 (978-0-8368-5869-3). A basic introduction to the beliefs and practices of Judaism around the world, with a chronology of important events. (Rev: SLJ 2/06) [296]

10587 Kimmel, Eric A. *Wonders and Miracles: A Passover Companion* (4–8). 2004, Scholastic $18.95 (978-0-439-07175-8). In addition to a description of the holiday and its rituals, Kimmel provides stories, songs, prayers, poems, and recipes. Sidney Taylor Book Honor 2004. (Rev: BL 2/15/04*; SLJ 2/04) [296.4]

10588 Metter, Bert. *Bar Mitzvah, Bat Mitzvah: The Ceremony, the Party, and How the Day Came to Be* (4–7). Illus. by Joan Reilly. 2007, Clarion $15.00 (978-0-618-76772-4); paper $5.95 (978-0-618-76773-1). This book about the coming-of-age ceremony for Jewish children (and now adults) covers its history but does not leave out the fun part — the party — and even includes details about the parties of some celebrities. (Rev: BL 7/07; SLJ 11/07)

10589 Scharfstein, Sol. *Understanding Jewish History I* (6–9). 1996, KTAV paper $15.95 (978-0-88125-545-4). Using many colorful illustrations, this work traces Jewish history from biblical times to the expulsion of the Jews from Spain in the 15th century. (Rev: BL 10/1/96; SLJ 1/97) [909]

Religious Cults

10590 Cohen, Daniel. *Cults* (7–10). 1994, Millbrook LB $23.40 (978-1-56294-324-0). This work describes cults throughout American history, including Pilgrims, Quakers, Moonies, and Satanists, and examines their recruiting methods. (Rev: BL 11/1/94; SLJ 2/95; VOYA 2/95) [291.9]

10591 Streissguth, Thomas. *Charismatic Cult Leaders* (7–12). 1995, Oliver LB $19.95 (978-1-881508-18-2). A balanced presentation of a potentially sensational topic. Includes biblical references where appropriate in the discussion of various cults and their leaders. (Rev: BL 8/95; SLJ 5/95) [291]

Society and the Individual

Government and Political Science

General and Miscellaneous

10592 Connolly, Sean. *Theocracy* (5–8). Illus. Series: Systems of Government. 2012, Black Rabbit LB $35.65 (978-159920806-0). Tackling such questions as "Is a Pure Theocracy Possible?" and "In God We Trust?," this is an interesting survey of religion's role in governments around the world. Also in this series: *Dictatorship, Democracy,* and *Communism* (all 2012). (Rev: BL 11/15/12*) [321]

10593 Laxer, James. *Democracy* (7–12). Series: Groundwork Guide. 2009, Groundwood $18.95 (978-088899912-2); paper $11.00 (978-088899913-9). Laxer discusses the history, present status, and future of democracy in this clearly written volume. (Rev: BL 7/09; VOYA 2/10) [321.8]

United Nations and Other International Organizations

10594 Darraj, Susan Muaddi. *The Universal Declaration of Human Rights* (8–12). Illus. Series: Milestones in Modern World History. 2010, Chelsea House LB $35 (978-160413494-0). An accessible account of the creation of this important document, highlighting the role of Eleanor Roosevelt and introducing other key individuals, as well as the continuing relevance of these rights today. (Rev: BL 5/15/10) [341.4]

10595 Ring, Susan. *Greenpeace* (4–8). Series: International Organizations. 2003, Weigl LB $16.95 (978-1-59036-020-0). An introduction to the goals, structure, members, and volunteers who work with this international organization. Also use *Peace Corps* (2003). (Rev: HBG 3/03; SLJ 4/03) [333.72]

10596 Smith, David J. *This Child, Every Child: A Book About the World's Children* (4–7). Illus. by Shelagh Armstrong. Series: CitizenKid. 2011, Kids Can $18.95 (978-1-55453-466-1). The impact of the 1989 United Nations Convention on the Rights of the Child is outlined in this accessible, well-researched and thought-provoking volume. Lexile 1020L (Rev: BL 4/15/11; LMC 10/11; SLJ 5/1/11) [305.23]

International Relations, Peace, and War

10597 Barker, Geoff. *War* (7–9). Series: Voices. 2010, Smart Apple Media LB $34.25 (978-1-59920-278-5). In chapters titled with questions such as "Can war be justified?," "Is it right to fight for religion?," and "What is the future of war?," this title explores causes and solutions and includes various perspectives. (Rev: LMC 5–6/10; SLJ 11/1/09) [355.02]

10598 Bixler, Mark. *The Lost Boys of Sudan: An American Story of the Refugee Experience* (8–12). 2005, Univ. of Georgia $24.95 (978-0-8203-2499-9). Journalist Bixler tracks the progress of four young men — refugees who were part of the so-called Lost Boys of Sudan — as they adjust to their new lives in America. (Rev: BL 2/1/05) [962.404]

10599 Bradbury, Adrian, and Eric Walters. *When Elephants Fight: The Lives of Children in Conflict in Afghanistan, Bosnia, Sri Lanka, Sudan and Uganda* (6–12). Illus. 2008, Orca $19.95 (978-155143900-6). Each of five chapters provides a haunting, unflinching glimpse into the experience of one child in war — whether as target, child soldier, or collateral damage. ℮ (Rev: BL 10/15/08; LMC 3–4/09; VOYA 4/09) [305.230]

675

10600 Bradman, Tony, ed. *Give Me Shelter: Stories About Children Who Seek Asylum* (5–8). 2007, Frances Lincoln $16.95 (978-1-84507-522-4). These gripping stories of real children seeking refuge from countries torn apart by war or strife will capture readers' hearts. (Rev: SLJ 3/08)

10601 Dalton, David. *Living in a Refugee Camp: Carbino's Story* (6–9). Series: Children in Crisis. 2005, World Almanac LB $31.00 (978-0-8368-5960-7). A Sudanese native tells the story of his 14-year exile from his country; background information and photographs add context. (Rev: SLJ 11/05)

10602 Dalton, David. *Refugees and Asylum Seekers* (7–10). Series: People on the Move. 2005, Heinemann LB $31.36 (978-1-4034-6961-8). A look at the plight of civilians who have been forced from their native lands by war or ethnic cleansing; a poor layout is offset by the personal stories. (Rev: BL 8/05; SLJ 12/05) [305.9]

10603 Dunson, Donald H. *Child, Victim, Soldier: The Loss of Innocence in Uganda* (8–12). Illus. 2008, Orbis paper $16.00 (978-157075799-0). The author, a Christian missionary in Uganda, describes the horrors of war and child abuse in that country. (Rev: BL 1/1–15/09) [261.8]

10604 Earnest, Peter, and Suzanne Harper. *The Real Spy's Guide to Becoming a Spy* (4–8). Illus. by Bret Bertholf. 2009, Abrams $16.95 (978-0-8109-8329-8). This guide to spying covers skills and training, tactics, jargon, and true-life stories. (Rev: SLJ 10/09; VOYA 12/09) [27.1200]

10605 Ellis, Deborah. *Children of War: Voices of Iraqi Refugees* (7–12). Illus. 2009, Groundwood $15.95 (978-088899907-8). Interviews with children who have fled Iraq bring to life the harsh realities of war. Lexile 860L (Rev: BL 3/1/09*; LMC 8–9/09; SLJ 4/1/09; VOYA 6/09) [305.23086]

10606 Ellis, Deborah. *Off to War: Voices of Soldiers' Children* (6–12). Illus. 2008, Groundwood $15.95 (978-088899894-1). Interviews with about 40 children of Canadian and American soldiers deployed in Afghanistan and Iraq reveal pride, anger, and frustration, and a desire for a "normal" life. (Rev: BL 10/15/08; HB 11–12/08; LMC 1–2/09; SLJ 10/1/08; VOYA 12/08) [303.6]

10607 Friedman, Lauri S., ed. *Torture* (7–10). Illus. Series: Introducing Issues with Opposing Viewpoints. 2011, Greenhaven LB $36.82 (978-073775203-8). Presents pro and con arguments on such topics as whether torture is ever justified, what constitutes torture, and what the U.S. position on torture should be. (Rev: BL 12/1/11) [364.6]

10608 Gerdes, Louise I., ed. *Rogue Nations* (6–12). Series: Opposing Viewpoints. 2006, Gale LB $34.95 (978-0-7377-3421-8). What is a "rogue" nation? Iran, North Korea, Pakistan, and the United States are among those mentioned in this provocative pro/con discussion. (Rev: SLJ 3/07) [355]

10609 Gold, Susan Dudley. *Arms Control* (6–9). Series: Pacts and Treaties. 1997, Twenty-First Century LB $24.90 (978-0-8050-4812-4). Beginning with the 1868 Declaration of St. Petersburg calling for a ban on the use of explosive projectiles, the author tells of the many subsequent attempts by world leaders to limit the sale and use of arms. (Rev: BL 9/1/97; SLJ 12/97) [327.1]

10610 Gottfried, Ted. *The Fight for Peace: A History of Antiwar Movements in America* (8–11). Series: People's History. 2005, Twenty-First Century LB $29.90 (978-0-7613-2932-9). Chronicles the history of American protest movements from the Civil War to the present. (Rev: BL 10/1/05; SLJ 11/05) [303.6]

10611 Head, Honor. *Famous Spies* (5–8). Series: Spies and Spying. 2010, Smart Apple $28.50 (978-1-59920-358-4). Different types of espionage are explored in readable, eye-catching profiles with sidebars covering technology and codes. (Rev: LMC 1–2/10)

10612 Janeczko, Paul B. *The Dark Game: True Spy Stories* (6–10). 2010, Candlewick $16.99 (978-0-7636-2915-1). Famous spies from the Revolutionary War through the cold war are the focus of this volume that also looks at modern techniques including cryptology and at organizations like the CIA and FBI. (Rev: BL 9/15/10; LMC 11–12/10; SLJ 8/10; VOYA 10/10) [327.73]

10613 Landau, Elaine. *Big Brother Is Watching: Secret Police and Intelligence Services* (7–12). 1992, Walker LB $15.85 (978-0-8027-8161-1). Describes the activities and methods of intelligence and police services in several Western and former Eastern-bloc nations, including the KGB, the Mossad, the CIA, and Honduran death squads. (Rev: BL 6/1/92; SLJ 8/92) [363.2]

10614 *Making It Home: Real Life Stories from Children Forced to Flee* (5–8). Illus. 2006, Dial $17.99 (978-0-8037-3083-0); paper $6.99 (978-0-14-240455-3). The horrific impact of war on children is documented in these first-person accounts, with many photographs, from children who were displaced from their homes in Afghanistan, Bosnia, Burundi, Congo, Iraq, Kosovo, Liberia, and Sudan. (Rev: BL 12/1/05; SLJ 2/06)

10615 Ousseimi, Maria. *Caught in the Crossfire: Growing Up in a War Zone* (6–10). 1995, Walker LB $20.85 (978-0-8027-8364-6). Examines the effects of violence on children and how violence changes children's perception of the world. (Rev: BL 9/1/95; SLJ 9/95; VOYA 12/95) [305.23]

10616 Perl, Lila. *Torture* (7–10). Illus. Series: Controversy! 2011, Marshall Cavendish LB $25.95 (978-160870495-8). With a history of torture and examples of contemporary instances in Abu Ghraib and Guantanamo, this volume gives teens material for reports and food for thought. (Rev: BL 5/1/12; SLJ 2/12) [364.6]

10617 Stewart, Sheila, and Joyce Zoldak. *In Defense of Our Country: Survivors of Military Conflict* (6–12). Illus. Series: Survivors — Ordinary People, Extraordinary Circumstances. 2009, Mason Crest LB $24.95 (978-1-4222-0452-8). Wars in Eastern Europe, the Middle East, Africa, and Asia are the focus of this volume that features first-person accounts as well as sidebars with interesting information on nonmilitary aspects of warfare. (Rev: SLJ 9/09) [362.87]

10618 Suvanjieff, Ivan, and Dawn Gifford Engle. *Peace-Jam: A Billion Simple Acts of Peace* (5–10). 2008, Puffin paper $16.99 (978-0-14-241234-3). This volume introduces the Nobel Peace laureates who are active in the work of the PeaceJam Foundation and describes their activism along with efforts by young people to support their causes. (Rev: SLJ 5/1/09; VOYA 12/08) [303.6]

10619 Winckelmann, Thom. *Genocide* (7–12). Series: Man's Inhumanities. 2008, Erickson LB $23.95 (978-160217975-2). For reluctant and struggling readers, this is a simple overview of recent genocides with discussion of the social implications. (Rev: BL 10/15/08; LMC 8–9/09) [364.15]

10620 Woog, Adam. *Military Might and Global Intervention* (7–10). Illus. Series: Controversy! 2011, Marshall Cavendish LB $25.95 (978-160870492-7). This balanced volume gives readers straightforward information on armed and nonmilitary interventions and the pros and cons of such actions. (Rev: BL 5/1/12; SLJ 2/12) [327.1]

United States Government and Institutions

General and Miscellaneous

10621 Anderson, Jodi Lynn, and Daniel Ehrenhaft, et al. *Americapedia: Taking the Dumb out of Freedom* (7–12). Illus. 2011, Walker $24.99 (978-0-8027-9792-6); paper $16.99 (978-0-8027-9-793-3). A breezy, sometimes irreverent and often amusing survey of American government and history that will prompt discussion. (Rev: BL 7/11; LMC 8–9/11; SLJ 8/11; VOYA 4/11) [320.60973]

10622 McIntosh, Kenneth, and Marsha McIntosh. *When Religion and Politics Mix: How Matters of Faith Influence Political Policies* (7–10). Series: Religion and Modern Culture. 2006, Mason Crest LB $22.95 (978-1-59084-971-2). Statistics from the 2004 election provide a basis for this overview of Americans' views on religion and politics. (Rev: BL 4/1/06) [201]

The Constitution

10623 Baer, Nadja. *The United States Constitution: A Round Table Comic* (5–8). Illus. by Nathan Lueth. 2012, Round Table Comics paper $12.95 (978-161066025-9). This fresh offering presents a graphic-novel take on the creation of the U.S. Constitution, and includes little-known facts and trivia. (Rev: BL 5/15/12; LMC 1–2/13*) [342.7302]

10624 Boaz, John, ed. *Free Speech* (7–12). Series: Current Controversies. 2006, Gale LB $34.95 (978-0-7377-2204-8); paper $23.70 (978-0-7377-2205-5). Previously published articles involving free speech answer four main questions: "Should Free Speech Be Limited? Is Free Speech Threatened? Does the War on Terror Threaten Free Speech?" and "How Should the Right to Free Speech Apply to Corporations?" (Rev: SLJ 6/06)

10625 Carson, Brian, and Catherine Ramen. *Understanding Your Right to Freedom from Searches* (6–9). Illus. Series: Personal Freedom and Civic Duty. 2011, Rosen LB $33.25 (978-144884670-2). With a good history of the 4th Amendment, this balanced volume also discusses current topics of interest such as car searches, body searches, wiretapping, and so forth. (Rev: BL 10/1/11) [323.44]

10626 Conway, John Richard. *A Look at the 13th and 14th Amendments: Slavery Abolished, Equal Protection Established* (6–9). Illus. Series: Constitution of the United States. 2008, Enslow LB $24.95 (978-159845070-5). Packed with information and web links, this is a well-organized resource that will help report writers. (Rev: BLO 1/13/09) [342.7308]

10627 Eck, Kristin. *Drafting the Constitution: Weighing the Evidence to Draw Sound Conclusions* (5–8). Series: Critical Thinking in American History. 2005, Rosen LB $26.50 (978-1-4042-0412-6). This slim volume offers a review of the issues debated at the Constitutional Convention, plus study questions, a reading list, and a Web site with links to related online resources. (Rev: BL 10/15/05) [342.7302]

10628 Feinberg, Barbara S. *The Articles of Confederation: The First Constitution of the United States* (7–10). 2002, Twenty-First Century LB $24.90 (978-0-7613-2114-9). Feinberg presents the history and text of the constitution that was in force from 1776 to 1787, along with a list of the signers, a timeline, and source notes. (Rev: BL 2/1/02; HBG 10/02; SLJ 3/02) [342.73]

10629 Feinberg, Barbara S. *Constitutional Amendments* (5–8). Series: Inside Government. 1996, Twenty-First Century LB $22.40 (978-0-8050-4619-9). After presenting a brief history of the Constitution, this work examines the Bill of Rights and then covers the remaining amendments in chapters arranged by topic. (Rev: SLJ 12/96) [342.73]

10630 Finkelman, Paul. *The Constitution* (4–8). Series: American Documents. 2006, National Geographic LB $23.90 (978-0-7922-7975-4). An unusually attractive introduction to the Constitution, with reproductions, photographs, and profiles of key individuals. (Rev: SLJ 2/06; VOYA 8/06) [342.73]

10631 Friedman, Ian C. *Freedom of Speech and the Press* (7–12). Series: American Rights. 2005, Facts on File $35.00 (978-0-8160-5662-0). Issues relating to the freedoms of speech and the press — in the past, present, and future — are explored in this title. (Rev: SLJ 12/05)

10632 Gerber, Larry. *The Second Amendment: The Right to Bear Arms* (5–8). Illus. Series: Amendments to the United States Constitution: The Bill of Rights. 2011, Rosen $29.95 (978-144881253-0). This thorough, unbiased offering discusses the historical roots, political implications, and court cases pertaining to the Second Amendment. (Rev: BL 4/1/11) [344.7305]

10633 Gerberg, Mort. *The U.S. Constitution for Everyone* (8–12). 1987, Putnam paper $7.95 (978-0-399-51305-3). The text of the Constitution and amendments is analyzed with many interesting asides and background information. (Rev: BL 5/1/87) [342.73]

10634 Gonzales, Doreen. *A Look at the Second Amendment: To Keep and Bear Arms* (4–7). Illus. Series: MyReportLinks.com. 2007, Enslow LB $24.95 (978-1-59845-061-3). Links to relevant Web sites enhance the text introducing students to the content and intent of the Second Amendment to the United States Constitution. (Rev: BL 10/15/07; LMC 11/07; SLJ 1/08) [344.7305]

10635 Graham, Amy. *A Look at the 18th and 21st Amendments: The Prohibition and Sale of Intoxicating Liquors* (5–8). Illus. Series: The Constitution of the United States. 2007, Enslow LB $33.27 (978-1-59845-063-7). A clear overview of these two amendments with links to Web sites that offer additional information. (Rev: SLJ 1/08)

10636 Haesly, Richard, ed. *The Constitutional Convention* (6–9). Series: History Firsthand. 2001, Gale LB $36.20 (978-0-7377-1072-4). Excerpts from personal accounts bring to life the events and key characters surrounding the writing of the U.S. Constitution. (Rev: SLJ 2/02) [342.73]

10637 Haynes, Charles C., and Sam Chaltain. *First Freedoms: A Documentary History of the First Amendment Rights in America* (7–12). 2006, Oxford $40.00 (978-0-19-515750-5). A look at the key figures in the struggle for First Amendment rights — John Locke, Thomas Jefferson, Elizabeth Cady Stanton, and John Scopes, among them — and at the topics that raised people's ire. (Rev: SLJ 11/06*)

10638 Head, Tom. *Freedom of Religion* (7–10). Series: American Rights. 2005, Facts on File $35.00 (978-0-8160-5664-4). Examines the significance of freedom of religion as guaranteed by the First Amendment to the Constitution and provides an overview of the role played by religion in America's early history, the Scopes trial, and questions surrounding school prayer. (Rev: BL 10/15/05) [323.44]

10639 Hubbard-Brown, Janet. *How the Constitution Was Created* (5–8). Series: The U.S. Government: How It Works. 2007, Chelsea House LB $30.00 (978-0-7910-9420-4). This is a thorough introduction to the Constitution, with interesting text and accompanying historical and biographical sidebars. (Rev: SLJ 1/08)

10640 Johnson, Terry. *Legal Rights* (7–12). Series: American Rights. 2005, Facts on File $35.00 (978-0-8160-5665-1). A look at the controversial issue of legal rights under the U.S. Constitution, with discussion of government initiatives since September 11, 2001. (Rev: SLJ 12/05)

10641 Krull, Kathleen. *A Kids' Guide to America's Bill of Rights: Curfews, Censorship, and the 100-Pound Giant* (5–8). 1999, Avon $16.99 (978-0-380-97497-9). After a description of the first 10 amendments, this book details famous court cases and what each amendment means to young people. (Rev: BL 12/1/99; HBG 3/00; VOYA 4/00) [342.73]

10642 Richie, Donald A. *Our Constitution* (7–12). 2006, Oxford $40 (978-0-19-522385-9). From the reasons for having a constitution to the amendments and their relevance to well-known cases, this is a well-presented overview. (Rev: SLJ 12/06)

The Presidency

10643 Aaseng, Nathan. *You Are the President* (7–10). 1994, Oliver LB $19.95 (978-1-881508-10-6). Devotes one chapter each to a crisis faced by eight presidents in the 20th century, among them Theodore Roosevelt, Eisenhower, and Nixon. (Rev: BL 4/1/94; SLJ 7/94; VOYA 8/94) [973.9]

10644 Aaseng, Nathan. *You Are the President II: 1800–1899* (7–10). Series: Great Decisions. 1994, Oliver LB $19.95 (978-1-881508-15-1). This work discusses the powers of the presidency during the 19th century and the major decisions made by presidents during that time. (Rev: BL 11/15/94; SLJ 12/94) [973.5]

10645 Bausum, Ann. *Our Country's Presidents* (5–8). 2005, National Geographic LB $45.90 (978-0-7922-9330-9). Full of interesting facts, quotations, and illustrations, this new edition has been extended with information on vice presidents, the Electoral College, and presidential security. (Rev: BL 5/15/05; SLJ 4/05) [973]

10646 Bernstein, Richard B., and Jerome Agel. *The Presidency* (8–12). 1989, Walker LB $13.85 (978-0-8027-6831-5). A basic history of this institution with some biographical information and a final section that explores the advisability of concentrating such power in one office. (Rev: BL 5/1/89; SLJ 1/89; VOYA 4/89) [353.03]

10647 Horn, Geoffrey M. *The Presidency* (5–8). Series: World Almanac Library of American Government.

2003, World Almanac LB $31.00 (978-0-8368-5458-9). Information on the first lady, the White House, and key presidents add to the coverage here, which includes primary sources as well as many photographs and statistics. (Rev: SLJ 1/04) [973]

10648 Price, Sean Stewart. *U.S. Presidents* (3–8). Illus. by Eldon Doty. Series: Truth and Rumors. 2010, Capstone LB $25.32 (978-1-4296-3952-1). Did John Quincy Adams give an interview while naked? Was Jimmy Carter attacked by a rabbit? Price answers these and other questions and ends with a final chapter on how to tell the difference between fact and fiction. (Rev: LMC 11–12/10) [923.173]

10649 Rubel, David. *Scholastic Encyclopedia of the Presidents and Their Times. Rev. ed.* (4–8). 1997, Scholastic paper $18.95 (978-0-590-49366-6). This fine reference book introduces each of the presidents and his administration and supplies material on related historical events, movements, and personalities. (Rev: HBG 10/01; SLJ 5/97) [920]

10650 Schlesinger, Arthur M., Jr, ed. *The Election of 2000 and the Administration of George W. Bush* (8–12). Series: Major Presidential Elections and the Administrations That Followed. 2003, Mason Crest LB $24.95 (978-1-59084-365-9). The circumstances of Bush's election and the major events of his administration through 2002 are presented with reference to many primary sources; brief biographical facts about the president and his cabinet are also included. (Rev: HBG 4/04; SLJ 10/03) [324.973]

10651 Smith, Carter, ed. *Presidents of a Divided Nation: A Sourcebook on the U.S. Presidency* (5–8). Series: American Albums. 1993, Millbrook $25.90 (978-1-56294-360-8). A visual sourcebook about the presidents during the Civil War and immediately after, from the Library of Congress collection on U.S. presidents. Also use *Presidents of a Growing Country.* (Rev: BL 12/1/93) [973.8]

10652 Smith, Carter, ed. *Presidents of a Growing Country: A Sourcebook on the U.S. Presidency* (5–8). Series: American Albums. 1993, Millbrook $25.90 (978-1-56294-358-5). Through extensive use of pictorials, a thorough timeline, and concise text, this attractive book traces the presidency from Hayes through McKinley. (Rev: BL 12/1/93; SLJ 4/94) [973.8]

10653 Smith, Carter, ed. *Presidents of a Young Republic: A Sourcebook on the U.S. Presidency* (5–8). Series: American Albums. 1993, Millbrook $25.90 (978-1-56294-359-2). A well-illustrated account that traces U.S. history from the presidency of John Quincy Adams through James Buchanan. (Rev: BL 12/1/93; SLJ 4/94) [973.5]

10654 Waldman, Michael, comp. *My Fellow Americans: The Most Important Speeches of American Presidents from George Washington to George W. Bush* (7–12). 2003, Sourcebooks paper $45.00 (978-1-4022-0027-4).

A collection of more than 40 speeches by 17 presidents, some of which are shown with early drafts; two accompanying CDs contain all the speeches, with the actual voices of presidents starting with Teddy Roosevelt. (Rev: BL 10/15/03; SLJ 10/03*) [352.23]

Federal Government, Its Agencies, and Public Administration

10655 Aaseng, Nathan. *You Are the Senator* (7–10). Series: Great Decisions. 1997, Oliver LB $19.95 (978-1-881508-36-6). This book describes the duties and responsibilities of a U.S. senator and the nature of the decisions that senators make. (Rev: BL 4/15/97; SLJ 8/97; VOYA 8/97) [328.73]

10656 Anderson, Dale. *The FBI Files: Successful Investigations* (5–8). Series: The FBI Story. 2009, Mason Crest LB $22.95 (978-1-4222-0561-7). Anderson reviews several FBI success stories using accessible text full of illustrations. Also use *The FBI and White-Collar Crime, The FBI and Organized Crime,* and *The FBI and Civil Rights* (all 2009). (Rev: LMC 5–6/10) [363.25]

10657 Bernstein, Richard B., and Jerome Agel. *The Congress* (7–12). 1989, Walker LB $13.85 (978-0-8027-6833-9). An introduction to this branch of the government with material arranged chronologically and including some coverage of scandals and decline in prestige. (Rev: BL 5/1/89; SLJ 1/89; VOYA 4/89) [328.73]

10658 Burlingame, Jeff. *Government Entitlements* (7–10). Illus. Series: Controversy! 2011, Marshall Cavendish LB $25.95 (978-160870491-0). Discusses controversial topics such as social security, welfare, workers' compensation, and veterans' benefits. (Rev: BL 5/1/12; VOYA 10/12) [361.60973]

10659 Crewe, Sabrina. *A History of the FBI* (5–8). Series: The FBI Story. 2009, Mason Crest LB $22.95 (978-1-4222-0563-1). A succinct, highly illustrated account of the FBI's creation and significant achievements over the years. Also use *The FBI and Crimes Against Children* (2009) and other volumes in this series. (Rev: LMC 5–6/10; SLJ 4/10) [363.25]

10660 Emert, Phyllis Raybin. *Attorneys General: Enforcing the Law* (6–9). 2005, Oliver LB $24.95 (978-1-881508-66-3). An introduction to the responsibilities of the attorney general and to eight key individuals who have held the position. (Rev: SLJ 6/06)

10661 Esherick, Joan. *The FDA and Psychiatric Drugs: How a Drug Is Approved* (6–10). Series: Psychiatric Disorders: Drugs and Psychology for the Mind and Body. 2003, Mason Crest LB $24.95 (978-1-59084-578-3). As well as a clear explanation of the drug approval process, this volume contains information on alternative medicines and an interesting look at how treatment of schizophrenia has advanced over time. (Rev: SLJ 5/04)

10662 Harmon, Daniel E. *The FBI* (7–10). Series: Crime, Justice, and Punishment. 2001, Chelsea LB $30.00 (978-0-7910-4289-2). The highest branch of criminal investigation in the United States is discussed with material on powers, methods, and personnel. (Rev: BL 6/1–15/01; HBG 10/01) [363.2]

10663 Newton, Michael. *Bomb Squad* (6–9). Illus. Series: Law Enforcement Agencies. 2011, Chelsea House LB $35 (978-160413624-1). Explains the history of bomb squads and the techniques they use to find and disarm explosives. (Rev: BL 4/1/11) [363.17]

10664 Ricciuti, Edward R. *Federal Bureau of Investigation* (6–9). Illus. Series: Law Enforcement Agencies. 2011, Chelsea House LB $35 (978-160413636-4). Traces the history of the FBI and its battles against crime and espionage over the decades, explains its role in protecting civil rights and stopping terrorism, and looks at some real-life cases. (Rev: BL 4/1/11) [363.250973]

10665 Richie, Jason. *Secretaries of State: Making Foreign Policy* (7–10). Series: Cabinet. 2002, Oliver LB $22.95 (978-1-881508-65-6). Succinct profiles of eight secretaries of state, ranging chronologically from John Quincy Adams to James Baker, look at their beliefs and how they influenced the nation's foreign policy. Also recommended in this series is *Secretaries of War, Navy, and Defense: Ensuring National Security* (2002). (Rev: BL 10/15/02; HBG 3/03; SLJ 4/03) [327.73]

10666 Thomas, William David. *How to Become an FBI Agent* (5–8). Series: The FBI Story. 2009, Mason Crest LB $22.95 (978-1-4222-0571-6). Readers learn about the process of applying to the FBI and the training that successful applicants receive. (Rev: LMC 5–6/10) [363.25]

10667 Wagner, Heather Lehr. *The Central Intelligence Agency* (5–8). Illus. Series: The U.S. Government: How It Works. 2007, Chelsea House LB $30.00 (978-0-7910-9282-8). Provides information on the Central Intelligence Agency; its history, how it influences government policies, and the kinds of jobs available there. (Rev: BL 8/07) [327]

10668 Weir, William. *Border Patrol* (6–9). Illus. Series: Law Enforcement Agencies. 2011, Chelsea House LB $35 (978-160413635-7). Traces the history of the U.S. Border Patrol and how it has evolved since 1904, discussing technology and equipment used as well as the hot issues of today: drugs, smuggling of goods and people, bandits, and immigration. (Rev: BL 4/1/11) [363.28]

State and Municipal Governments and Agencies

10669 Gorrell, Gena K. *Catching Fire: The Story of Firefighting* (7–10). 1999, Tundra paper $16.95 (978-0-88776-430-1). This is a history of firefighting, from the bucket brigades of the past to the sophisticated equipment of today, with related information on how fires burn, important fires in history, equipment, firefighting tactics, forms of arson, wildfires, and more. (Rev: BCCB 5/99; BL 6/1–15/99; SLJ 6/99) [363.3]

10670 Newton, Michael. *The Texas Rangers* (6–9). Illus. Series: Law Enforcement Agencies. 2011, Chelsea House LB $35 (978-160413626-5). Explains the role of the Texas Rangers, traces their history since their establishment in 1823, and looks at developments into modern times, with profiles of some famous Ranger heroes. (Rev: BL 4/1/11) [976.4]

10671 Ryan, Bernard, Jr. *Serving with Police, Fire, and EMS* (7–12). Series: Community Service for Teens. 1998, Ferguson LB $19.95 (978-0-89434-232-5). This work explains how teens can play an active and productive role in police, fire, and allied community agencies. (Rev: BL 9/15/98; SLJ 2/99) [361.8]

The Law and the Courts

10672 Aaseng, Nathan. *The O. J. Simpson Trial: What It Shows Us About Our Legal System* (6–9). 1996, Walker LB $16.85 (978-0-8027-8405-6). The author uses the Simpson trial to explain such aspects of the American judicial system as investigative techniques, the grand jury, defense, prosecution, the media's role, and emerging technologies. (Rev: BL 5/1/96; SLJ 4/96) [345.73]

10673 Aaseng, Nathan. *You Are the Juror* (6–10). 1997, Oliver LB $19.95 (978-1-881508-40-3). The author recreates eight famous criminal trials of the 20th century, including the Lindbergh kidnapping case, the Patty Hearst and O. J. Simpson trials, and the Ford Pinto case, and asks the reader to become a jury member and make a decision. (Rev: SLJ 1/98) [347.73]

10674 Aaseng, Nathan. *You Are the Supreme Court Justice* (7–10). Series: Great Decisions. 1994, Oliver LB $19.95 (978-1-881508-14-4). A description of how the Supreme Court works and the decisions and responsibilities involved in being a Justice. (Rev: BL 11/15/94; SLJ 12/94) [347.73]

10675 Anderson, Wayne. *Brown v. Board of Education: The Case Against School Segregation* (5–8). Series: Supreme Court Cases Through Primary Sources. 2004, Rosen LB $29.25 (978-0-8239-4009-7). Primary sources — photographs, police records, newspaper clippings, and court documents — provide details of the case and the narrative discusses the historical and social context. Also use *Plessy v. Ferguson: Legalizing Segregation* (2004). (Rev: SLJ 6/04) [345.73]

10676 Anderson, Wayne. *The Chicago Black Sox Trial: A Primary Source Account* (5–8). Series: Great Trials of the Twentieth Century. 2003, Rosen LB $29.25 (978-0-8239-3969-5). This is a detailed, readable account of the 1919 Chicago Black Sox scandal and the plot to fix the World Series. (Rev: BL 4/1/04; SLJ 6/04; VOYA 4/04) [796.357]

10677 Aretha, David. *The Trial of the Scottsboro Boys* (7–12). Series: Civil Rights. 2007, Morgan Reynolds $27.95 (978-1-59935-058-5). A compelling account of what happened to nine young black men in 1930s Alabama. (Rev: BL 11/1/07; SLJ 12/07) [345.761]

10678 Berger, Leslie. *The Grand Jury* (7–12). Series: Crime, Justice, and Punishment. 2000, Chelsea $30.00 (978-0-7910-4290-8). This work traces the history of the grand jury system, outlines procedures at the local and national level, and cites famous grand jury hearings including the Monica Lewinsky case. (Rev: BL 8/00) [345.73]

10679 Bernstein, Richard B., and Jerome Agel. *The Supreme Court* (8–12). 1989, Walker LB $13.85 (978-0-8027-6835-3). An account that gives a history of the Supreme Court, details on landmark cases, and an outline of how it operates today. (Rev: BL 5/1/89; SLJ 1/89; VOYA 4/89) [347]

10680 Burnett, Betty. *The Trial of Julius and Ethel Rosenberg: A Primary Source Account* (5–8). Series: Great Trials of the Twentieth Century. 2004, Rosen LB $29.25 (978-0-8239-3976-3). Primary sources — photographs, original transcripts, quotations, and so forth — give depth to this compelling account of the complex trial. (Rev: BL 4/1/04; SLJ 10/04)

10681 Campbell, Andrew. *Rights of the Accused* (7–10). Series: Crime, Justice, and Punishment. 2001, Chelsea LB $30.00 (978-0-7910-4303-5). A cleverly written, informative exploration of how and why the judicial system tries to safeguard the rights of accused criminals. (Rev: BL 6/1–15/01; HBG 3/01; SLJ 2/01; VOYA 12/01) [345]

10682 Carrel, Annette. *It's the Law! A Young Person's Guide to Our Legal System* (8–12). 1994, Volcano paper $12.95 (978-1-884244-01-8). The book's goal is voter responsibility through understanding of the laws, how they developed, and how they can be changed. (Rev: BL 2/15/95; VOYA 12/95) [349.73]

10683 Carroll, Jamuna, ed. *Civil Liberties and War* (7–12). Series: Issues on Trial. 2006, Gale LB $34.95 (978-0-7377-2503-2). Jamuna examines the United States' history of restriction of civil liberties during wartime, looking in depth at four instances in the 20th and 21st centuries. (Rev: SLJ 8/06)

10684 Crewe, Sabrina, and Michael V. Uschan. *The Scottsboro Case* (4–7). Series: Events That Shaped America. 2005, Gareth Stevens LB $26.00 (978-0-8368-3407-9). A thorough and thought-provoking look at the infamous Scottsboro case in which nine young African Americans were accused of raping two white women. (Rev: BL 1/1–15/05; SLJ 3/05) [345.73]

10685 Donnelly, Karen. *Cruzan v. Missouri: The Right to Die* (5–7). Series: Supreme Court Cases Through Primary Sources. 2004, Rosen LB $29.25 (978-0-8239-4014-1). The lengthy legal battle for a patient's right to die is chronicled in this account of the Supreme Court's decision in Cruzan v. Missouri. (Rev: BL 6/1–15/04; SLJ 6/04) [344.73]

10686 Dudley, Mark E. *Engel v. Vitale (1962): Religion and the Schools* (5–9). Series: Supreme Court Decisions. 1995, Twenty-First Century LB $25.90 (978-0-8050-3916-0). The story of the Supreme Court case on school prayer that originated with two Jewish youngsters who objected to being forced to pray every morning in a New York City school. (Rev: BL 11/15/95; SLJ 1/96; VOYA 4/96) [347]

10687 Dudley, Mark E. *Gideon v. Wainright (1963): Right to Counsel* (6–10). Series: Supreme Court Decisions. 1995, Twenty-First Century LB $25.90 (978-0-8050-3914-6). Reviews how the case was built, argued, and decided, and discusses its impact. (Rev: BL 6/1–15/95; SLJ 8/95) [347.3]

10688 Dudley, Mark E. *United States v. Nixon (1974)* (6–10). Series: Supreme Court Decisions. 1994, Twenty-First Century LB $25.90 (978-0-8050-3658-9). This landmark Supreme Court case concerning the definition of presidential powers is reported on in a step-by-step analysis of the arguments in the Watergate case. (Rev: BL 12/15/94; SLJ 2/95) [342.73]

10689 Egendorf, Laura K., ed. *The Death Penalty* (7–12). Series: Examining Issues Through Political Cartoons. 2002, Gale paper $21.20 (978-0-7377-1101-1). Egendorf uses cartoons focusing on the death penalty as the basis for a discussion of the controversies surrounding this practice. Also recommended in this series is *Euthanasia* (2002). (Rev: BL 8/02) [364.44]

10690 Gold, Susan Dudley. *Brown v. Board of Education: Separate But Equal?* (7–12). Series: Supreme Court Milestones. 2004, Benchmark LB $37.07 (978-0-7614-1842-9). An overview of the groundbreaking decision, with information on the key individuals involved and on the legal process itself plus human-interest stories that add depth. (Rev: SLJ 1/05) [344.73]

10691 Gold, Susan Dudley. *The Pentagon Papers: National Security or the Right to Know* (7–12). Series: Supreme Court Milestones. 2004, Benchmark LB $37.07 (978-0-7614-1843-6). An easily understood account of the events surrounding the Pentagon Papers case and the high court's decision that blocked the Nixon administration's efforts to keep the papers secret. (Rev: SLJ 1/05) [342.73]

10692 Gottfried, Ted. *The Death Penalty: Justice or Legalized Murder?* (7–12). 2002, Twenty-First Century LB $24.90 (978-0-7613-2155-2). Gottfried presents an absorbing and balanced examination of the arguments for and against the death penalty, with historical information and details of specific cases. (Rev: BL 3/15/02; HBG 10/02; SLJ 3/02) [364.66]

10693 Gottfried, Ted. *Police Under Fire* (7–12). 1999, Twenty-First Century LB $24.90 (978-0-7613-1313-7). A well-balanced account that gives a history of policing, police culture, pressures on police personnel, corruption, and cases of police brutality. (Rev: BL 12/15/99; HBG 4/00; SLJ 1/00) [363.2]

10694 Harmon, Daniel E. *Defense Lawyers* (7–10). Series: Crime, Justice, and Punishment. 2001, Chelsea LB $30.00 (978-0-7910-4284-7). This introduction to the roles of defense attorney and public defender provides brief profiles of figures including Clarence Darrow and Alan Dershowitz. (Rev: HBG 10/02; SLJ 4/02) [345.73]

10695 Henningfeld, Diane Andrews, ed. *The Death Penalty* (7–12). Series: Opposing Viewpoints. 2006, Gale LB $34.95 (978-0-7377-2929-0); paper $23.70 (978-0-7377-2930-6). A thought-provoking collection of essays providing many points of view on the use of the death penalty. (Rev: SLJ 9/06)

10696 Herda, D. J. *Furman v. Georgia: The Death Penalty Case* (6–10). Series: Landmark Supreme Court Cases. 1994, Enslow LB $26.60 (978-0-89490-489-9). Summarizes the historical background of this case, the case itself, and its impact. (Rev: BL 11/15/94; SLJ 11/94) [345.73]

10697 Himton, Kerry. *The Trial of Sacco and Vanzetti: A Primary Source Account* (5–8). Series: Great Trials of the Twentieth Century. 2004, Rosen LB $29.25 (978-0-8239-3973-2). Primary sources — photographs, original transcripts, quotations, and so forth — give depth to this compelling account of the complex trial. (Rev: BL 4/1/04; SLJ 6/04)

10698 Hinton, KaaVonia. *Brown v. Board of Education of Topeka, Kansas, 1954* (5–8). Series: Monumental Milestones: Great Events of Modern Times. 2010, Mitchell Lane LB $29.95 (978-1-58415-738-0). Useful for research, this slim volume provides facts and biographical sketches key to this important ruling and supplies the necessary background to fully understand the issues involved. (Rev: BL 2/1/10; LMC 5–6/10; SLJ 1/10)

10699 Horn, Geoffrey M. *The Supreme Court* (5–8). Series: World Almanac Library of American Government. 2003, World Almanac LB $31.00 (978-0-8368-5459-6). An excellent introduction to the U.S. Supreme Court and the important role it plays in interpreting the laws of the land. (Rev: SLJ 1/04)

10700 Jacobs, Thomas A. *Teens on Trial: Young People Who Challenged the Law — and Changed Your Life* (8–12). 2000, Free Spirit paper $14.95 (978-1-57542-081-3). Student rights and responsibilities are explored through this examination of 21 cases in which teens participated in the legal process. (Rev: BL 1/1–15/01; SLJ 1/01; VOYA 4/01) [346.7301]

10701 Jacobs, Thomas A. *They Broke the Law, You Be the Judge: True Cases of Teen Crime* (7–12). 2003, Free Spirit paper $15.95 (978-1-57542-134-6). A former juvenile court judge presents 21 real-life cases involving juveniles, gives the reader the sentencing options, and reveals the actual outcome of each case. (Rev: BL 2/1/04; SLJ 1/04) [345.73]

10702 Jarrow, Gail. *The Printer's Trial: The Case of John Peter Zenger and the Fight for a Free Press* (7–10). 2006, Boyds Mills $18.95 (978-1-59078-432-7). Covers the events leading up to and the 1735 trial of John Peter Zenger, a printer from New York who was found not guilty of seditious libel against the British government, establishing freedom of the press. (Rev: BL 10/1/06; LMC 2/07; SLJ 11/06) [345.73]

10703 Koopmans, Andy. *Leopold and Loeb: Teen Killers* (7–12). Series: Famous Trials. 2004, Gale LB $29.95 (978-1-59018-227-7). The story of the famous trial of two privileged boys for the murder of a third, with details of Clarence Darrow's innovative defense strategy. (Rev: SLJ 6/04) [345.73]

10704 Kowalski, Kathiann M. *Lemon v. Kurtzman and the Separation of Church and State Debate* (8–12). Series: Debating Supreme Court Decisions. 2005, Enslow LB $26.60 (978-0-7660-2391-8). This well-documented title examines the Supreme Court's decision in Lemon v. Kurtzman and reviews its impact on the doctrine of separation of church and state. (Rev: SLJ 12/05)

10705 Krygier, Leora. *Juvenile Court: A Judge's Guide for Young Adults and Their Parents* (7–12). 2009, Scarecrow $29.95 (978-081086127-5). Written by a judge in the Los Angeles Superior Court, this book arms teens with advice and practical information about what goes on in juvenile court. **e** (Rev: BL 3/15/09; SLJ 3/1/09; VOYA 2/09) [345.73]

10706 McNeese, Tim. *Dred Scott v. Sandford* (7–10). Series: Great Supreme Court Decisions. 2006, Chelsea House LB $30.00 (978-0-7910-9236-1). Illustrations and graphics add interest to this account of the Dred Scott court case and its significance in the nation's division over slavery. (Rev: BL 2/1/07) [342]

10707 Madani, Hamed. *The Supreme Court and the Judicial Branch: How the Federal Courts Interpret Our Laws* (6–9). Illus. Series: Constitution and the United States Government. 2012, Enslow LB $31.93 (978-076604065-6). Introduces the organization and responsibilities of the Supreme Court, with a review of its history and profiles of the current justices. (Rev: BL 10/1/12; LMC 5–6/13; SLJ 11/12) [347.73]

10708 Margulies, Phillip, and Maxine Rosaler. *The Devil on Trial: Witches, Anarchists, Atheists, Communists, and Terrorists in America's Courtrooms* (8–12). Illus. 2008, Houghton Mifflin $22.00 (978-061871717-0). The authors examine five key trials in American history: the Salem witch trials, the Haymarket bomb trial, the Scopes monkey trial, the trials of Alger Hiss, and the trials of Zacarias Moussaoui. (Rev: BL 11/15/08; SLJ 9/1/08; VOYA 8/08) [345.73]

10709 Mountjoy, Shane. *Engel v. Vitale: School Prayer and the Establishment Clause* (7–12). Series: Great Supreme Court Decisions. 2006, Chelsea House LB $30.00 (978-0-7910-9241-5). An accessible overview of the ongoing debate about school prayer in the United States. (Rev: SLJ 7/07) [344.73]

10710 Naden, Corinne J., and Rose Blue. *Dred Scott: Person or Property?* (5–8). Series: Supreme Court Milestones. 2005, Benchmark LB $37.07 (978-0-7614-1841-2). The Supreme Court's 1857 Dred Scott decision, arguably the high court's most misguided ruling ever, is examined in detail. (Rev: BL 2/1/05) [342.7]

10711 Nakaya, Andrea, ed. *The Environment* (7–12). Series: Issues on Trial. 2006, Gale LB $34.95 (978-0-7377-2797-5). Four benchmark court cases illustrate how environmental laws can become forces for social change. (Rev: SLJ 7/06)

10712 Olson, Steven P. *The Trial of John T. Scopes: A Primary Source Account* (5–8). Series: Great Trials of the Twentieth Century. 2004, Rosen LB $29.25 (978-0-8239-3974-9). Primary sources — photographs, original transcripts, quotations, and so forth — give depth to this compelling account of the complex trial. (Rev: BL 4/1/04; SLJ 8/04) [344.73]

10713 Owens, L. L. *American Justice: Seven Famous Trials of the 20th Century* (6–8). Series: Cover-to-Cover. 2000, Perfection Learning $17.95 (978-0-7807-7831-3); paper $8.95 (978-0-7891-2869-0). Kidnappings, murder, and a classic civil rights case are among the trials presented here. (Rev: BL 1/1–15/01) [345.73]

10714 Paddock, Lisa. *Facts About the Supreme Court of the United States* (8–12). 1996, H.W. Wilson $105.00 (978-0-8242-0896-7). A one-stop reference source for information about the Supreme Court, from individual justices to the court's history and important cases. (Rev: VOYA 12/96) [347]

10715 Panchyk, Richard. *Our Supreme Court: A History with 14 Activities* (7–10). 2006, Chicago Review paper $17.95 (978-1-55652-607-7). Focusing on the history and development of the Supreme Court and landmark cases handled, this large-format book with effective illustrations includes interviews with attorneys, politicians, and other related figures as well as a variety of activities, a glossary, and useful facts. (Rev: BL 11/1/06; SLJ 3/07) [347.73]

10716 Payment, Simone. *The Trial of Leopold and Loeb: A Primary Source Account* (5–8). Series: Great Trials of the Twentieth Century. 2004, Rosen LB $29.25 (978-0-8239-3970-1). Primary sources — photographs, original transcripts, quotations, and so forth — give depth to this compelling account of the complex trial. (Rev: BL 4/1/04; SLJ 6/04; VOYA 4/04)

10717 Persico, Deborah A. *New Jersey v. T.L.O.: Drug Searches in Schools* (7–12). Series: Landmark Supreme Court Cases. 1998, Enslow LB $20.95 (978-0-89490-969-6). This Supreme Court case lasted five years and explored the rights of a student, identified as T.L.O., whose handbag was searched by a school administrator who found marijuana and articles that indicated the student was selling drugs. (Rev: BL 8/98; HBG 9/98; SLJ 8/98; VOYA 2/99) [345.73]

10718 Roensch, Greg. *The Lindbergh Baby Kidnapping Trial: A Primary Source Account* (5–8). Series: Great Trials of the Twentieth Century. 2004, Rosen LB $29.25 (978-0-8239-3971-8). Primary sources — photographs, original transcripts, handwriting samples, and so forth — give depth to this account of this controversial trial. (Rev: BL 4/1/04; SLJ 8/04) [345.73]

10719 Scheppler, Bill. *The Mississippi Burning Trial: A Primary Source Account* (5–8). Series: Great Trials of the Twentieth Century. 2004, Rosen LB $29.25 (978-0-8239-3972-5). Primary sources — photographs, original transcripts, quotations, and so forth — give depth to this compelling account of the complex trial. (Rev: BL 4/1/04; SLJ 10/04)

10720 Sorensen, Lita. *The Scottsboro Boys Trial: A Primary Source Account* (5–8). 2003, Rosen LB $29.25 (978-0-8239-3975-6). Sorensen dissects the sensational Scottsboro Boys rape case in Alabama that attracted media attention from around the globe. (Rev: BL 4/1/04) [345.761]

10721 Steffens, Bradley. *Furman v. Georgia: Fairness and the Death Penalty* (6–9). Series: Famous Trials. 2001, Lucent LB $29.95 (978-1-56006-470-1). The Supreme Court case of 1972 that stuck down the death penalty as cruel and unusual punishment is investigated with good background material and information about this case's significance. (Rev: BL 12/15/01) [345]

10722 Telgen, Diane. *Brown v. Board of Education* (8–12). Series: Defining Moments. 2005, Omnigraphics LB $49.00 (978-0-7808-0775-4). An accessible examination of the landmark Supreme Court decision on school segregation, including many interesting sidebar features and chronicling events before and after the ruling, up to the present day. (Rev: SLJ 12/05*)

Politics

GENERAL AND MISCELLANEOUS

10723 Anderson, Dale. *The Democratic Party: America's Oldest Party* (5–8). Series: Snapshots in History. 2007, Compass Point LB $31.93 (978-0-7565-2450-0). This well-designed book provides a thorough, unbiased history of the Democratic Party and includes sidebars, charts, photographs, maps, and Web sites. (Rev: SLJ 7/07) [324.2736]

10724 Anderson, Dale. *The Republican Party: The Story of the Grand Old Party* (5–8). Series: Snapshots in History. 2007, Compass Point LB $31.93 (978-0-7565-2449-4). This history of the Republican Party presents a balanced view of the how the party formed, its values, and its highs and lows since its formation. (Rev: SLJ 7/07) [324.273]

10725 Boyers, Sara Jane. *Teen Power Politics: Make Yourself Heard* (7–12). 2000, Twenty-First Century LB $24.90 (978-0-7613-1307-6); paper $9.95 (978-0-7613-1391-5). An in-depth and inspiring look at the ways in which teens too young to vote can nonetheless exert their influence. (Rev: BL 11/15/00; HBG 3/01; SLJ 1/01; VOYA 4/01) [323]

10726 Cox, Vicki. *The History of Third Parties* (7–10). Series: The U.S. Government: How It Works. 2007, Chelsea House LB $30.00 (978-0-7910-9421-1). Third parties have not seen success in the United States; this volume explores the history of third parties and looks at the reasons why they have had trouble attracting voters. (Rev: BL 2/15/08) [324.273]

10727 Lindop, Edmund. *Political Parties* (5–8). Series: Inside Government. 1996, Twenty-First Century LB $24.90 (978-0-8050-4618-2). This work traces the origins of political parties and the role they play in presidential elections. (Rev: BL 9/15/96; SLJ 12/96) [324.273]

10728 Morin, Isobel V. *Politics, American Style: Political Parties in American History* (6–12). 1999, Twenty-First Century $24.90 (978-0-7613-1267-3). An engaging account of the history of American political parties, accompanied by political cartoons. (Rev: BL 11/15/99; HBG 4/00; SLJ 1/00) [324.273]

10729 Staton, Hilarie. *The Progressive Party: The Success of a Failed Party* (5–8). Series: Snapshots in History. 2007, Compass Point LB $31.93 (978-0-7565-2451-7). This history of the Progressives is well-organized and shows how the party's agenda moved forward even though the party itself didn't survive. (Rev: SLJ 7/07) [324.2732]

ELECTIONS

10730 Goldman, David J. *Presidential Losers* (6–9). 2004, Lerner LB $25.26 (978-0-8225-0100-8). From Aaron Burr to Al Gore, this account profiles unsuccessful presidential candidates across two centuries of American history. (Rev: BL 4/1/04) [973]

10731 Horn, Geoffrey M. *Political Parties, Interest Groups, and the Media* (5–8). Series: World Almanac Library of American Government. 2004, World Almanac LB $31.00 (978-0-8368-5478-7). An engaging introduction to the world of politics, the importance of money and lobbying, and the role of the press. (Rev: SLJ 9/04) [324]

10732 Israel, Fred L. *Student's Atlas of American Presidential Elections 1789 to 1996* (7–12). 1997, Congressional Quarterly $45.00 (978-1-56802-377-9). Each of the 53 presidential elections in U.S. history is described on a page or two, accompanied by maps to illustrate election results. (Rev: BL 11/15/97; SLJ 11/97) [973]

10733 Lansford, Tom, ed. *Voting Rights* (7–12). Series: Opposing Viewpoints. 2008, Gale/Greenhaven $36.20 (978-073774014-1); paper $24.95 (978-073774015-8). Essays by experts address issues relating to voting in the United States and other countries. (Rev: BL 1/1–15/09) [324.6]

10734 Morris-Lipsman, Arlene. *Presidential Races: The Battle for Power in the United States* (5–8). Illus. Series: People's History. 2007, Lerner LB $30.60 (978-0-8225-6783-7). Political cartoons, photographs, and other memorabilia add to the text of this guide to the growth in importance of presidential election campaigns; the author gives pertinent background information on each election and provides a useful chart of election results. (Rev: BL 9/15/07; SLJ 10/07) [324.973]

10735 Tracy, Kathleen. *The Historic Fight for the 2008 Democratic Presidential Nomination: The Clinton View* (5–8). Series: Monumental Milestones. 2009, Mitchell Lane LB $29.95 (978-1-58415-731-1). A brief biography of Hillary Clinton accompanies a detailed account of the campaign to win the Democratic presidential nomination. (Rev: BL 4/1/09; SLJ 4/1/09) [973.931092]

10736 Wagner, Heather Lehr. *How the President Is Elected* (5–8). Series: The U.S. Government: How It Works. 2007, Chelsea House LB $30.00 (978-0-7910-9418-1). This is a thorough introduction to the presidential election process (using the drama of the 2000 election to draw readers in), with interesting text and accompanying historical and biographical sidebars. (Rev: SLJ 1/08)

The Armed Forces

10737 Aaseng, Nathan. *You Are the General* (7–12). Series: Great Decisions. 1994, Oliver $19.95 (978-1-881508-11-3). This book deals with decisions that have to be made by members of the military, with many examples. (Rev: BL 6/1–15/94) [355]

10738 Benson, Michael. *The U.S. Marine Corps* (4–7). Series: U.S. Armed Forces. 2004, Lerner LB $26.60 (978-0-8225-1648-4). Introduces the history of the Marine Corps, followed by information on recruitment, training, and daily life. (Rev: BL 1/05; SLJ 3/05) [359.6]

10739 Earl, C. F., and Gabrielle Vanderhoof. *Army Rangers* (6–9). Illus. Series: Special Forces. 2010, Mason Crest LB $22.95 (978-142221838-9). A well-designed overview of extensive training involved in becoming an Army Ranger. (Rev: BL 7/11) [356]

10740 Goldish, Meish. *Coast Guard: Civilian to Guardian* (4–7). Illus. Series: Becoming a Soldier. 2010, Bearport LB $22.61 (978-193608812-6). Recent recruits' journeys from enlistment through placement, conditioning, training, and graduation are presented in this true-to-life book that doesn't gloss over the rigors of military life. (Rev: BL 10/1/10) [363.28]

10741 McNab, Chris. *Protecting the Nation with the U.S. Army* (6–10). Series: Rescue and Prevention: Defending Our Nation. 2003, Mason Crest LB $22.95 (978-1-59084-414-4). This series about the specific roles the various services play in defending U.S. interests at home and abroad also discusses each service's history, structure, equipment, and recent operations. Also use *Protecting the Nation with the U.S. Air Force* and *Protecting the Nation with the U.S. Navy* (2003). (Rev: HBG 4/04; SLJ 7/03) [355]

10742 Montana, Jack. *Elite Forces Selection* (6–9). Illus. Series: Special Forces. 2010, Mason Crest LB $22.95 (978-142221839-6). A well-designed overview of the elite groups in the U.S. armed forces, with information on qualifications and training. (Rev: BL 7/11) [356.16]

10743 Montana, Jack. *Navy SEALs* (6–9). Illus. Series: Special Forces. 2010, Mason Crest LB $22.95 (978-142221843-3). A well-designed overview of the elite groups in the Navy, some of their accomplishments, and how these people are chosen. (Rev: BL 7/11) [359.9]

10744 Nardo, Don. *Special Operations: Paratroopers* (5–8). Illus. Series: Military Experience. 2012, Morgan Reynolds LB $27.45 (978-159935360-9). Readers learn about the demanding training and dramatic combat adventures of special ops paratroopers. (Rev: BL 10/1/12)

10745 Pelta, Kathy. *The U.S. Navy* (5–7). 1990, Lerner LB $23.93 (978-0-8225-1435-0). A look at the history and present status and activities of the U.S. Navy. (Rev: BL 12/1/90) [359]

10746 Schwartz, Heather E. *Women of the U.S. Air Force: Aiming High* (3–7). Series: Snap: Women in the U.S. Armed Forces. 2011, Capstone LB $26.65 (978-1-4296-5449-4). A real-life story of a female Air Force recruit adds personal appeal to this title that explores women's history and growing presence and importance in the U.S. Air Force. Also use *Women of the U.S. Navy: Making Waves* (2011). (Rev: SLJ 6/11) [358.4]

10747 Stremlow, Mary V. *Coping with Sexism in the Military* (7–12). 1990, Rosen LB $21.95 (978-0-8239-1025-0). An analysis of the military from the perspective of the female recruit that reflects conditions in the late 1980s. (Rev: BL 2/15/91) [355]

10748 Vanderhoof, Gabrielle. *Air Force* (6–9). Illus. Series: Special Forces. 2010, Mason Crest LB $22.95 (978-142221837-2). A well-designed overview of the elite groups in the Air Force, some of their accomplishments, and how these people are chosen. (Rev: BL 7/11) [358.4]

10749 Zeinert, Karen, and Mary Miller. *The Brave Women of the Gulf Wars: Operation Desert Storm and Operation Iraqi Freedom* (5–8). Series: Women at War. 2005, Twenty-First Century LB $30.60 (978-0-7613-2705-9). Highlights women's roles in the Persian Gulf military campaigns. (Rev: BL 10/1/05; SLJ 11/05) [956.7]

Citizenship and Civil Rights

General and Miscellaneous

10750 Andryszewski, Tricia. *Same-Sex Marriage: Moral Wrong or Civil Right?* (7–12). 2008, Lerner LB $38.60 (978-0-8225-7176-6). A balanced look at many aspects of this issue in the United States. The author's discussion is enhanced by quotations from people of all opinions on gay marriage. (Rev: BL 5/1/08; SLJ 6/08) [306.84]

10751 Ellis, Richard J. *To the Flag: The Unlikely History of the Pledge of Allegiance* (7–12). 2005, Univ. Press of Kansas $29.95 (978-0-7006-1372-4). Traces the history of the Pledge of Allegiance and the flap over two words — "under God" — that were inserted into the pledge nearly 60 years after it was written. (Rev: BL 3/1/05) [323.6]

10752 Grodin, Elissa D. *D Is for Democracy: A Citizen's Alphabet* (5–8). Illus. by Victor Juhasz. 2004, Sleeping Bear $16.95 (978-1-58536-234-9). From "Amendment" to "Zeitgeist," this is an exploration of key concepts, people, places, and things, with the emphasis on the United States. (Rev: BL 1/1–15/05; SLJ 10/04) [320.973]

10753 Hollihan, Kerrie Logan. *Rightfully Ours: How Women Won the Vote* (5–8). Illus. 2012, Chicago Review Press paper $16.95 (978-1-883052-89-8). After profiles of Lucy Stone, Elizabeth Cady Stanton, and Susan B. Anthony, Hollihan describes the long road to women's suffrage and offers activities, archival photographs, and sidebar features. e Lexile 1020L (Rev: BLO 8/29/12; LMC 5–6/13; SLJ 9/12) [324.6]

10754 Luthringer, Chelsea. *So What Is Citizenship Anyway?* (5–8). Series: A Student's Guide to American Civics. 1999, Rosen LB $23.95 (978-0-8239-3097-5). Describes and defines the roles and responsibilities of citizens in a democracy and encourages young people to become active in political and social affairs and issues. (Rev: HBG 10/00; SLJ 3/00; VOYA 4/00) [323.6]

Civil and Human Rights

10755 Anderson, Judith. *Education for All* (4–7). Series: Working for Our Future. 2010, Black Rabbit LB $28.50 (978-1-59771-193-7). This volume explains why the United Nations chose education for all as one of its eight Millennium Development goals and looks at the various reasons why children do not go to school. (Rev: BL 6/10; LMC 10/10; SLJ 4/10) [370]

10756 Anderson, Judith. *An Equal Chance for Girls and Women* (4–7). Series: Working for Our Future. 2010, Black Rabbit LB $28.50 (978-1-59771-196-8). This volume explains why the United Nations chose equal opportunity for girls and women as one of its eight Millennium Development goals and looks at the various reasons why girls are deprived of opportunity and what can be done to improve the situation. (Rev: BL 6/10; LMC 10/10; SLJ 4/10) [323.3]

10757 Aretha, David. *Montgomery Bus Boycott* (7–10). Illus. Series: Civil Rights Movement. 2008, Morgan Reynolds $28.95 (978-159935020-2). An examination of an important event in the civil rights movement, with letters, photographs, and personal accounts that add impact. (Rev: BL 2/1/09; LMC 5–6/09; SLJ 2/1/09) [323.1196]

10758 Aretha, David. *The Murder of Emmett Till* (7–12). Series: Civil Rights Movement. 2007, Morgan Reynolds LB $27.95 (978-1-59935-057-8). This book explains how the shocking death of Emmett Till sparked outrage around the country and was one factor leading to the civil rights movement. (Rev: BL 12/1/07; SLJ 1/08) [364.1]

10759 Aretha, David. *Selma and the Voting Rights Act* (7–12). Series: Civil Rights. 2007, Morgan Reynolds LB $27.95 (978-1-59935-056-1). This book explains how events in Alabama in the 1960s led to the 1965 Voting Rights Act. (Rev: BL 12/15/07; SLJ 1/08) [324.6]

10760 Bausum, Ann. *Freedom Riders: John Lewis and Jim Zwerg on the Front Lines of the Civil Rights Movement* (6–9). 2005, National Geographic LB $28.90 (978-0-7922-4174-4). The passion of those involved in the 1961 Freedom Rides is captured in these profiles of two young men — John Lewis and Jim Zwerg — who played key roles in the protests. Sibert Honor 2007. (Rev: BL 2/1/06*; SLJ 5/06*) [323]

10761 Bausum, Ann. *With Courage and Cloth: Winning the Fight for a Woman's Right to Vote* (6–12). 2004, National Geographic $32.90 (978-0-7922-6996-0). A lively, well-illustrated text chronicles the history of the women's suffrage movement in America, focusing in particular on the period between 1913 and 1920 when the more militant National Women's Party, led by Alice Paul, stepped up pressure for women's right to vote. (Rev: BCCB 1/05; BL 10/15/04; SLJ 9/04) [324.6]

10762 Bickerstaff, Linda. *Modern Day Slavery* (6–9). Series: In the News. 2010, Rosen LB $29.95 (978-1-4358-5274-7). The plight of today's slaves — children in sweatshops, migrant workers, sex slaves, and so forth — is examined in this well-organized volume. (Rev: LMC 1–2/10)

10763 Boerst, William J. *Marching in Birmingham* (7–12). Series: Civil Rights. 2008, Morgan Reynolds LB $27.95 (978-1-59935-055-4). This well-designed volume with firsthand accounts discusses the various efforts to achieve civil rights in Alabama. (Rev: SLJ 3/08)

10764 Bradley, David, and Shelley Fisher Fishkin, eds. *The Encyclopedia of Civil Rights in America* (5–10). 1997, Sharpe Reference $299.00 (978-0-7656-8000-6). This three-volume set contains 683 alphabetically arranged articles that explore the history, meaning, and application of civil rights issues in the United States. (Rev: BL 2/15/98; SLJ 5/98) [323]

10765 Brimner, Larry Dane. *Birmingham Sunday* (5–8). 2010, Boyds Mills LB $17.95 (978-1-59078-613-0). This highly illustrated and moving account of the bombing in 1963 Alabama that killed four young girls places the tragedy in context of the civil rights turmoil of the time. Lexile NC1190L (Rev: BL 2/1/10; LMC 8–9/10; SLJ 4/10) [323.1196]

10766 Brimner, Larry Dane. *Black and White: The Confrontation Between Reverend Fred L. Shuttlesworth and Eugene "Bull" Connor* (7–12). Illus. 2011, Boyds Mills $16.95 (978-1-59078-766-3). Brimner tells the fascinating story of the tension between two key individuals on opposite sides of the struggle for integration in Birmingham, Alabama. Sibert Honor 2012; ALA Notable

Books 2012. (Rev: BL 10/15/11*; LMC 1–2/12; SLJ 11/1/11) [323.1196]

10767 Ching, Jacqueline, and Juliet Ching. *Women's Rights* (7–9). Series: Individual Rights and Civic Responsibility. 2001, Rosen LB $31.95 (978-0-8239-3233-7). A concise account of the struggle for women's rights in America. (Rev: BL 12/1/01) [305.42]

10768 Crowe, Chris. *Getting Away with Murder: The True Story of the Emmett Till Case* (7–12). 2003, Penguin $18.99 (978-0-8037-2804-2). A gripping and detailed account of the brutal murder of 14-year-old Emmett Till, an African American boy from Chicago who was visiting relatives in Mississippi in 1954, with discussion of the impact of his death and the ensuing trial on the civil rights movement. (Rev: BL 2/15/03; HB 7–8/03; HBG 10/03; SLJ 5/03*) [364.15]

10769 Deutsch, Stacia, and Rhody Cohon. *Hot Pursuit: Murder in Mississippi* (5–8). Illus. by Craig Orback. 2010, Kar-Ben $17.95 (978-0-7613-3955-7). A dramatic fictional story about civil rights activists who were murdered in Mississippi in 1964 is intertwined with informational chapters providing background context. (Rev: BL 4/1/10; LMC 8–9/10) [323.092]

10770 Englebert, Phillis, and Beth Des Chenes, eds. *American Civil Rights: Primary Sources* (7–12). 1999, U.X.L $70.00 (978-0-7876-3170-3). This is a collection of 15 documents relating to the civil rights movement in America, such as speeches, proclamations, and autobiographical texts. (Rev: BL 1/1–15/00; SLJ 5/00; VOYA 4/00) [323.1]

10771 *Every Human Has Rights: A Photographic Declaration for Kids* (4–8). Illus. 2009, National Geographic $17.95 (978-1-4263-0510-8). Compelling photographs, accompanied by poems, illustrate the 30 rights covered in the Universal Declaration of Human Rights. (Rev: BL 12/15/08; SLJ 3/09) [300]

10772 Farrell, Courtney. *Children's Rights* (7–10). Series: Essential Issues. 2010, ABDO LB $32.79 (978-1-60453-952-3). Child labor, child trafficking, child sexual abuse, and child soldiers are all discussed in this volume that also looks specifically at the rights of children in the United States. (Rev: LMC 10/10; SLJ 4/1/10) [305.23086]

10773 Finkelstein, Norman H. *Heeding the Call: Jewish Voices in the Civil Rights Struggle* (6–9). 1997, Jewish Publication Society $14.95 (978-0-8276-0590-9). Beginning with the 1600s when both Africans and Jews first came to first country, this book traces the bond between these groups as they fought for civil rights. (Rev: BL 2/15/98) [323.1]

10774 Fireside, Harvey. *New York Times v. Sullivan: Affirming Freedom of the Press* (6–10). Series: Landmark Supreme Court Cases. 1999, Enslow LB $26.60 (978-0-7660-1085-7). The limits to freedom of the press was the subject of this Supreme Court case that had far-reaching results in the world of journalism. (Rev: BL 8/99) [347.3]

10775 Freedman, Jeri. *America Debates Civil Liberties and Terrorism* (5–8). Series: America Debates. 2007, Rosen LB $29.25 (978-1-4042-1927-4). Presents facts and opinions on both sides of issues including governmental surveillance and homeland security. (Rev: LMC 2/08; SLJ 11/07) [323.4]

10776 Freedman, Jeri. *America Debates Privacy Versus Security* (5–8). Series: America Debates. 2007, Rosen LB $29.25 (978-1-4042-1929-8). Presents facts and opinions on both sides of issues including profiling and the right to privacy. (Rev: LMC 2/08; SLJ 11/07) [323.44]

10777 Freedman, Jeri. *Women in the Workplace: Wages, Respect, and Equal Rights* (7–12). Series: A Young Woman's Guide to Contemporary Issues. 2010, Rosen LB $31.95 (978-1-4358-3541-2). A conversational discussion of the history of women in the workplace, the need for equal opportunity and pay, and the protections available to women today, with chapters on sexual harassment and women in the military. (Rev: LMC 10/10; SLJ 4/1/10) [331.4]

10778 Freedman, Russell. *Freedom Walkers: The Story of the Montgomery Bus Boycott* (4–7). 2006, Holiday $18.95 (978-0-8234-2031-5). First-person accounts enliven this history of the 381-day Montgomery Bus Boycott of the mid-1950s, which ended segregation on the buses. (Rev: BCCB 12/06; BL 9/15/06; HBG 4/07; LMC 3/07; SLJ 11/06*; VOYA 10/06)

10779 Gay, Kathlyn. *Cultural Diversity: Conflicts and Challenges: The Ultimate Teen Guide* (7–12). Series: It Happened to Me. 2003, Scarecrow paper $25.95 (978-0-8108-4805-4). Prejudice, stereotypes, and intolerance are among the topics discussed in this overview of the challenges faced and the possible solutions; teens' personal stories add immediacy. (Rev: SLJ 5/04; VOYA 4/04) [305.8]

10780 George, Charles, ed. *Living through the Civil Rights Movement* (7–12). Series: Living Through the Cold War. 2006, Gale LB $32.45 (978-0-7377-2919-1). Speeches and essays by those who experienced the civil rights movement firsthand lend depth to this overview. (Rev: SLJ 6/07) [323.1196]

10781 Gifford, Clive. *Child Labor* (7–9). Series: Voices. 2010, Smart Apple Media LB $34.25 (978-1-59920-279-2). In chapters titled with questions such as "Is child labor a problem in wealthy countries?," "Are multinationals to blame?," and "Can individuals make a difference?," this title explores causes and solutions and includes various perspectives. (Rev: LMC 5–6/10; SLJ 11/1/09) [331.31]

10782 Gottfried, Ted. *Homeland Security Versus Constitutional Rights* (8–12). 2003, Millbrook LB $24.90 (978-0-7613-2862-9). Gottfried addresses important

questions, both historical and contemporary, in the balancing of safety versus civil liberties. (Rev: BL 11/15/03; HBG 4/04; SLJ 12/03; VOYA 2/04) [303.3]

10783 Gottfried, Ted. *Privacy: Individual Rights v. Social Needs* (8–12). 1994, Millbrook LB $25.90 (978-1-56294-403-2). Discusses debates on privacy in relation to law enforcement, surveillance, abortion, AIDS, and the media. (Rev: BL 9/15/94; SLJ 10/94; VOYA 2/95) [342.73]

10784 Grant, Reg. *Slavery: Real People and Their Stories of Enslavement* (4–7). 2009, DK $24.99 (978-0-7566-5169-5). The history of slavery around the world and information about its continued practice today is accompanied by firsthand accounts of people involved in slavery. (Rev: BL 7/09; LMC 11–12/09; SLJ 8/09) [306.362]

10785 Greenberg, Keith Elliot. *Adolescent Rights: Are Young People Equal Under the Law?* (5–8). Series: Issues of Our Time. 1995, Twenty-First Century LB $22.90 (978-0-8050-3877-4). This unbiased account of the controversial subject encourages readers to form their own conclusions. (Rev: SLJ 9/95) [323]

10786 Guernsey, JoAnn Bren. *Voices of Feminism: Past, Present, and Future* (7–10). Series: Frontline. 1996, Lerner LB $19.95 (978-0-8225-2626-1). After a 150-year history of feminism, this account covers the complicated issues and concerns surrounding this subject and discusses past and present leaders in the movement. (Rev: BL 9/15/96; SLJ 7/97; VOYA 4/97) [305.42]

10787 Hudson, David L., Jr. *Gay Rights* (8–12). Series: Point/Counterpoint. 2004, Chelsea House LB $32.95 (978-0-7910-8094-8). Both sides of the heated debate over gay rights are addressed, including the peripheral issues of military service, rights in the workplace, gay marriage, and adoption rights. (Rev: SLJ 4/05) [305.9]

10788 Jacobs, Thomas A. *What Are My Rights? 95 Questions and Answers About Teens and the Law* (7–12). 1997, Free Spirit paper $14.95 (978-1-57542-028-8). Using a question-and-answer format, this topically arranged manual describes in simple terms concerns relating to teens' rights within the family, at school, and on the job. (Rev: BL 4/1/98; SLJ 4/98; VOYA 6/98) [346.7301]

10789 Kafka, Tina. *Gay Rights* (8–11). 2006, Gale $28.70 (978-1-59018-637-4). A look at the issue of gay rights, with information on historical and contemporary controversies. (Rev: BL 9/15/06; SLJ 1/07) [323.3]

10790 King, Casey. *Oh, Freedom! Kids Talk About the Civil Rights Movement with the People Who Made It Happen* (5–9). 1997, Random House paper $12.95 (978-0-679-89005-8). In 31 interviews, children ask family members, neighbors, and friends about the part they played in the civil rights movement. (Rev: BL 4/1/97; SLJ 6/97*) [973]

10791 King, David C. *Freedom of Assembly* (4–8). Series: Land of the Free. 1997, Millbrook LB $22.90 (978-0-7613-0064-9). This book covers this basic civil right with examples throughout U.S. history and landmark court cases that helped define its limits. (Rev: BL 5/15/97; SLJ 10/97) [342.73]

10792 Kowalski, Kathiann M. *Affirmative Action* (6–9). Series: Open for Debate. 2006, Benchmark LB $27.95 (978-0-7614-2300-3). Kowalski gives a balanced overview of the policy that favors preferential treatment for women and minority groups in employment and education, presenting various opinions for and against that will be useful for research. (Rev: SLJ 2/07)

10793 Kramer, Ann. *Human Rights: Who Decides?* (5–8). Series: Behind the News. 2006, Heinemann LB $32.86 (978-1-4034-8832-9). With photographs and examples of news stories, this volume offers various viewpoints on the information we receive on human rights and asks readers how they will make up their minds. (Rev: SLJ 4/07) [323]

10794 Landau, Elaine. *Your Legal Rights: From Custody Battles to School Searches, the Headline-Making Cases That Affect Your Life* (6–10). 1995, Walker LB $14.85 (978-0-8027-8360-8). A review of advances in protection of the legal rights of children and teenagers. (Rev: BL 5/15/95; SLJ 8/95) [346.7301]

10795 Levinson, Cynthia Y. *We've Got a Job: The 1963 Birmingham Children's March* (6–12). Illus. 2012, Peachtree $19.95 (978-156145627-7). This compelling photo-essay account of the May 1963 march by 4,000 African American students features large black-and-white photographs and draws extensively on primary sources. ALA Notable Books 2013. ∩ Lexile 1020L (Rev: BL 2/1/12*; HB 5–6/12; LMC 8–9/12*; SLJ 5/1/12*) [323.1196]

10796 Lucas, Eileen. *Civil Rights: The Long Struggle* (6–10). Series: Issues in Focus. 1996, Enslow LB $20.95 (978-0-89490-729-6). After a discussion of the first 10 amendments to the U.S. Constitution, this account focuses on the civil rights struggles of African Americans. (Rev: BL 9/15/96; SLJ 12/96) [323]

10797 McKissack, Patricia C., and Fredrick McKissack. *Days of Jubilee: The End of Slavery in the United States* (5–8). 2003, Scholastic $19.99 (978-0-590-10764-8). A combination of clear, interesting narrative, relevant quotations from primary sources, thorough historical approach, and well-chosen illustrations make this a worthwhile volume on the gradual end of slavery. (Rev: BCCB 4/03; BL 5/15/03; HBG 10/03; LMC 8–9/03; SLJ 5/03; VOYA 4/03) [973.7]

10798 McWhorter, Diane. *Dream of Freedom: The Civil Rights Movement from 1954-1968* (6–8). 2004, Scholastic $19.99 (978-0-439-57678-9). A sweeping, chronological survey of the modern civil rights movement, with personal commentary and many photographs. (Rev: BL 11/15/04*; SLJ 12/04; VOYA 4/05) [323.1]

10799 Marsico, Katie. *Racism* (4–8). Series: Global Perspectives. 2008, Cherry Lake LB $27.07 (978-1-60279-134-3). An accessible look at racism and its causes, history, and ways to alleviate this problem. (Rev: SLJ 11/08) [305.8]

10800 Mayer, Robert H. *The Civil Rights Act of 1964* (6–12). Series: At Issue in History. 2004, Gale LB $33.70 (978-0-7377-2304-5); paper $23.70 (978-0-7377-2305-2). The landmark act is described in an introductory overview followed by a collection of essays, speeches, and editorials that provide diverse views about the legislation and its impact on race relations in the United States. (Rev: BL 9/1/04; SLJ 9/04) [342.73]

10801 Mayer, Robert H. *When the Children Marched: The Birmingham Civil Rights Movement* (6–12). 2008, Enslow LB $25.95 (978-0-7660-2930-9). A moving account of the role young people played in Birmingham, Alabama, during the violent events of the civil rights movement, with photographs, news reports, quotations, a timeline, and so forth. (Rev: BL 6/1–15/08) [323.1196]

10802 Meany, John. *Has the Civil Rights Movement Been Successful?* (7–12). Series: What Do You Think? 2008, Heinemann LB $32.86 (978-1-4329-1675-6). After a history of the civil rights movement, this volume looks at legal reform, discrimination in popular culture, stereotyping, and national security, with a chapter discussing the circumstances revealed by Hurricane Katrina. (Rev: SLJ 1/1/09) [323.0973]

10803 Meyers, Madeleine, ed. *Forward into Light: The Struggle for Woman's Suffrage* (4–8). Series: Perspectives on History. 1994, Discovery paper $6.95 (978-1-878668-25-7). The story of the long struggle for women's right to vote, including the contributions of Elizabeth Cady Stanton, Susan B. Anthony, Sojourner Truth, and other leaders. (Rev: BL 8/94) [324.6]

10804 Miller, Calvin Craig. *Backlash: Race Riots in the Jim Crow Era* (8–11). Illus. Series: Civil Rights Movement. 2012, Morgan Reynolds LB $28.95 (978-159935183-4). A survey of the horrific racial violence during the Jim Crow era, with a focus on riots in cities. (Rev: BL 2/1/12; SLJ 6/12) [305.800973]

10805 Monroe, Judy. *The Susan B. Anthony Women's Voting Rights Trial* (6–10). Series: Headline Court Cases. 2002, Enslow LB $26.60 (978-0-7660-1759-7). Monroe explores the fight for women's suffrage and the trial of Susan B. Anthony for voting illegally in the 1872 election. (Rev: BL 3/15/03; HBG 3/03; SLJ 12/02) [324.6]

10806 Morrison, Toni. *Remember: The Journey to School Integration* (5–12). 2004, Houghton Mifflin $18.00 (978-0-618-39740-2). With striking archival photographs and a fictionalized narrative based on historical fact, this fascinating book explores the impact of the American struggle for civil rights on the children who were often at its center. (Rev: BL 4/15/04; SLJ 6/04) [379.2]

10807 Nakaya, Andrea C., ed. *Censorship* (7–12). Series: Opposing Viewpoints. 2005, Gale LB $36.20 (978-0-7377-2925-2); paper $24.95 (978-0-7377-2926-9). This new edition adds thoughtful essays on censorship and free speech as they relate to the press, telemarketing, electronic filtering, spam, and other issues. (Rev: SLJ 9/05) [363.3]

10808 Nakaya, Andrea C., ed. *Civil Liberties* (8–12). Series: Introducing Issues with Opposing Viewpoints. 2005, Gale LB $32.45 (978-0-7377-3387-7). A collection of articles and essays by various authors, all debating issues of civil liberties including the Patriot Act. (Rev: SLJ 5/06) [342.7308]

10809 Nakaya, Andrea C., ed. *Civil Liberties and War* (8–11). Series: Examining Issues Through Political Cartoons. 2005, Gale LB $29.95 (978-0-7377-2517-9). A current hot-button issue — the suspension of civil liberties during wartime — is put into historical perspective in this volume with cartoons dating from the wars as far back as the Civil War. (Rev: BL 2/1/06; SLJ 7/06) [323]

10810 Parks, Rosa, and Gregory J. Reed. *Dear Mrs. Parks: A Dialogue with Today's Youth* (5–8). 1996, Lee & Low $16.95 (978-1-880000-45-8). This book contains a sampling of the thousands of letters sent to civil rights leader Rosa Parks and her replies. (Rev: BL 12/1/96; SLJ 12/96) [323]

10811 Partridge, Elizabeth. *Marching for Freedom: Walk Together, Children, and Don't You Grow Weary* (6–12). 2009, Viking $19.99 (978-0-670-01189-6). Children and young adults' role in the civil rights movement is the focus of this moving photo-essay that features quotes from personal interviews and detailed photographs. Boston Globe–Horn Book nonfiction winner 2010; ALA Notable Books 2010. ∩ (Rev: BL 8/09*; HB 11–12/09; LMC 11/09; SLJ 10/09; VOYA 10/09) [323.1196]

10812 Rappaport, Doreen. *Nobody Gonna Turn Me 'Round* (4–7). Illus. by Shane W. Evans. 2006, Candlewick $19.99 (978-0-7636-1927-5). This concluding volume of a trilogy documenting the black experience in America focuses on the stormy decade between the Montgomery bus boycott and the signing of the Voting Rights Act in August 1965, providing profiles of key figures. (Rev: BL 8/06; SLJ 10/06)

10813 Robinson, J. Dennis. *Striking Back: The Fight to End Child Labor Exploitation* (5–8). Series: Taking a Stand. 2010, Compass Point LB $31.99 (978-0-7565-4297-9). After an overview of child labor, this volume describes some of the dangers children faced and the movement to stop this exploitation, highlighting Mother Jones and others who had the courage to fight. Lexile 1000L (Rev: LMC 11–12/10; VOYA 8/10) [331.3]

10814 Robson, David. *The Murder of Emmett Till* (6–9). Series: Crime Scene Investigations. 2010, Gale/Lucent LB $33.45 (978-1-4205-0213-8). With a focus on how the crime scene was handled, this volume tells the story of the 1955 murder and the impact it had on the public attitude toward segregation and hate crimes. (Rev: LMC 11–12/10; VOYA 6/10) [364.1]

10815 Sawvel, Patty Jo, ed. *Student Drug Testing* (7–12). Series: Issues That Concern You. 2006, Gale LB $32.45 (978-0-7377-2424-0). Students, educators, journalists, government officials, and a selection of experts present their opinions on the efficacy and ethics of student drug testing. (Rev: SLJ 2/07)

10816 Serres, Alain. *I Have the Right to Be a Child* (4–8). Trans. by Helen Mixter. Illus. by Aurelia Fronty. 2012, Groundwood $18.95 (978-155498149-6). This colorful book encourages readers to think about the United Nations Convention on the Rights of the Child through simple text and eye-catching illustrations. (Rev: BL 7/12; LMC 1–2/13) [323.352]

10817 *Stand Up, Speak Out: A Book About Children's Rights* (6–8). 2002, Two-Can $14.95 (978-1-58728-540-0); paper $9.95 (978-1-58728-541-7). Children's artwork and writings address children's rights issues around the world, with information on the U.N.'s Convention on the Rights of the Child, UNICEF, and other aid organizations. (Rev: BL 4/15/02; HBG 10/02; SLJ 6/02) [323]

10818 Steele, Philip. *Documenting Slavery and Civil Rights* (6–10). Series: Documenting History. 2010, Rosen LB $26.50 (978-1-4358-9671-0). With many interesting primary source materials — posters, postage stamps, photographs, cartoons, quotations — this slim volume discusses slavery from ancient times and the struggle to achieve civil rights. (Rev: LMC 11–12/10) [306.3]

10819 Stokes, John A., and Lois Wolfe. *Students on Strike: Jim Crow, Civil Rights, Brown, and Me* (5–8). 2008, National Geographic $15.95 (978-1-4263-0153-7). The author recounts his days on strike to protest the conditions at a black high school in Virginia in 1951 and explains how this strike helped lead to school desegregation in the 1960s. (Rev: BL 3/15/08; SLJ 4/08) [371.829]

10820 Torr, James D. *The Patriot Act* (7–12). Series: The Lucent Terrorism Library. 2005, Gale LB $29.95 (978-1-59018-774-6). Torr explores the provisions of this controversial piece of legislation and looks at the ongoing criticisms about its threats to privacy and the Fourth Amendment. (Rev: SLJ 3/06) [345.73]

10821 Turck, Mary C. *The Civil Rights Movement for Kids: A History with 21 Activities* (4–8). 2000, Chicago Review paper $14.95 (978-1-55652-370-0). The story of the civil rights movement with coverage of key events and personalities plus a number of related activities. (Rev: SLJ 10/00) [973.9]

10822 Turner, Chérie. *Everything You Need to Know About the Riot Grrrl Movement: The Feminism of a New Generation* (6–10). Series: Need to Know Library. 2001, Rosen LB $27.95 (978-0-8239-3400-3). A look at the movement that evolved from a 1970s aggressive punk attitude to a 1990s emphasis on equality and self-esteem. (Rev: SLJ 12/01) [781.66]

10823 Walker, Paul R. *Remember Little Rock: The Time, the People, the Stories* (4–7). Illus. 2008, National Geographic $17.95 (978-1-4263-0402-6). This title offers a dramatic and solidly researched account of the attempt to integrate an all-white school in Little Rock, Arkansas, in September 1957, with eyewitness accounts and news photography. (Rev: BL 2/1/09; SLJ 3/09*) [379.2]

10824 Williams, Mary E., ed. *Civil Rights* (7–12). Series: Examining Issues Through Political Cartoons. 2002, Gale LB $29.95 (978-0-7377-1100-4). This limited but unusual approach to exploration of the civil rights movement looks at political cartoons in four thematic chapters. (Rev: SLJ 10/02) [323.1]

10825 Wilson, Reginald. *Our Rights: Civil Liberties and the U.S.* (7–12). 1988, Walker $14.85 (978-0-8027-6751-6). A book that explains what civil rights are, how we have these freedoms, and how to protect them. (Rev: SLJ 8/88; VOYA 8/88) [323.4]

10826 Wilson, Reginald. *Think About Our Rights: Civil Liberties and the United States* (5–8). 1991, Walker LB $15.85 (978-0-8027-8127-7); paper $9.95 (978-0-8027-7371-5). The focus is on such civil rights questions as integration, affirmative action, and women's rights. (Rev: SLJ 1/92) [323.4]

Immigration

10827 Ambrosek, Renee. *America Debates United States Policy on Immigration* (6–9). Series: America Debates. 2007, Rosen LB $21.95 (978-1-4042-1924-3). A thorough and attractive introduction to the issues surrounding immigration into the United States. (Rev: BL 11/15/07; SLJ 11/07) [325.73]

10828 Andryszewski, Tricia. *Immigration: Newcomers and Their Impact on the U.S.* (7–9). 1995, Millbrook $24.90 (978-1-56294-499-5). A detailed study of immigration as it pertains to the United States. (Rev: BL 1/15/95; SLJ 5/95) [304.8]

10829 Aykroyd, Clarissa. *Refugees* (8–12). Series: The Changing Face of North America: Immigration Since 1965. 2004, Mason Crest LB $24.95 (978-1-59084-692-6). An overview of the origins of refugees to the United States and Canada, the reasons for their flight from their home countries, and the process they must undergo on arrival. (Rev: SLJ 11/04)

10830 Barbour, Scott. *Does Illegal Immigration Harm Society?* (8–12). Series: In Controversy. 2009, ReferencePoint LB $25.95 (978-1-60152-085-2). A timely discussion of immigration issues, answering questions such as "Does Illegal Immigration Harm the American Economy?" and "Does Illegal Immigration Lead to Increased Crime and Terrorism?" (Rev: BL 10/1/09; LMC 1–2/10)

10831 Bausum, Ann. *Denied, Detained, Deported: Stories from the Dark Side of American Immigration* (6–12). Illus. 2009, National Geographic $21.95 (978-142630332-6); LB $32.90 (978-142630333-3). The author discusses cases in which immigrants (Jews, Mexicans, Japanese, and others) have been mistreated by the U.S. government in the past; she also looks at some of today's issues surrounding immigration. Lexile 1170L (Rev: BL 4/15/09; SLJ 5/1/09*) [325.73]

10832 Berg, Lois Anne. *An Eritrean Family* (4–7). Series: Journey Between Two Worlds. 1997, Lerner LB $22.60 (978-0-8225-3405-1); paper $8.95 (978-0-8225-9755-1). The story of the Kiklu family, which fled Eritrea in eastern Africa in 1978, spent 10 years in a refugee camp, and resettled in Minnesota. (Rev: BL 6/1–15/97; SLJ 8/97) [304.895]

10833 Daniels, Roger. *American Immigration: A Student Companion* (6–12). Series: Oxford Student Companions to American History. 2001, Oxford LB $65.00 (978-0-19-511316-7). An alphabetically arranged series of articles covering all aspects of immigration to the United States and the various ethnic groups that have made the journey, illustrated with photographs, maps, and reproductions. (Rev: BL 10/15/01; SLJ 6/01) [304.8]

10834 Emsden, Katharine, ed. *Coming to America: A New Life in a New Land* (4–8). Series: Perspectives on History. 1993, Discovery paper $6.95 (978-1-878668-23-3). Diaries, journals, and letters of immigrants from many countries are used to provide insights into their lives. (Rev: BL 11/15/93) [325.73]

10835 Haerens, Margaret, ed. *Illegal Immigration* (7–12). Series: Opposing Viewpoints. 2006, Gale LB $34.95 (978-0-7377-3356-3); paper $23.70 (978-0-7377-3357-0). This collection of essays on illegal immigration captures all sides of the issue, allowing readers to form their own opinions. (Rev: SLJ 10/06)

10836 Hauser, Pierre. *Illegal Aliens* (5–8). Series: Immigrant Experience. 1996, Chelsea LB $14.95 (978-0-7910-3363-0). A history of attitudes toward immigration is followed by a discussion of illegal immigrants, where they come from, why they came, and the government's policy toward them. (Rev: SLJ 2/97) [932]

10837 Hay, Jeff, ed. *Immigration* (7–12). Series: Turning Points in World History. 2001, Greenhaven paper $24.95 (978-0-7377-0638-3). In a series of engaging essays, the phenomenon of immigration is explored and how shifting populations have changing world history. (Rev: BL 3/15/02) [325]

10838 Hopkinson, Deborah. *Shutting Out the Sky* (5–12). 2003, Scholastic $17.95 (978-0-439-37590-0). Five personal stories of young immigrants, striking photographs, and excerpts from primary documents form the backbone of this history of immigration to New York City in the late 19th century. (Rev: BL 11/1/03*; HBG 4/04; SLJ 12/03*; VOYA 6/04) [307.76]

10839 Keedle, Jayne. *Americans from the Caribbean and Central America* (4–8). Series: New Americans. 2010, Marshall Cavendish LB $35.64 (978-0-7614-4302-5). Part of a series that looks at the experiences of recent immigrants, this book discusses the challenges that new arrivals face and the impact they have on society; the citizenship process is explained and personal accounts add impact. Also use by this author *Mexican Americans* and *West African Americans* (2010). (Rev: LMC 3–4/10; SLJ 2/10)

10840 Knight, Margy B. *Who Belongs Here? An American Story* (4–7). Illus. by Anne S. O'Brien. 1993, Tilbury House $16.95 (978-0-88448-110-2). The story of ten-year-old Nari, who survived the killing fields of Cambodia and found a new life in the United States. (Rev: BL 3/1/94; SLJ 10/93) [305.895]

10841 Meltzer, Milton. *Bound for America: The Story of the European Immigrants* (6–10). Series: Great Journeys. 2001, Benchmark LB $32.79 (978-0-7614-1227-4). An absorbing examination of the reasons for migration within and from Europe in the 19th and early 20th centuries, and of the hardships these travelers suffered. (Rev: BCCB 3/99; HBG 10/02; SLJ 3/02) [325.73]

10842 Miller, Debra A. *Illegal Immigration* (8–12). Series: Compact Research: Current Issues. 2007, Reference Point LB $24.95 (978-1-60152-009-8). Will a guest-worker program work? Do illegal aliens strain social services in the United States? All sides of these questions and many more are examined in this overview. (Rev: BL 4/1/07; LMC 10/07; SLJ 5/07) [304.8]

10843 Miller, Debra A., ed. *Illegal Immigration* (6–9). Series: Current Controversies. 2007, Gale LB $36.20 (978-0-7377-3723-3); paper $24.95 (978-0-7377-3724-0). A collection of writings presenting various points of view about the issues that surround illegal immigration. (Rev: BL 2/1/08) [325.73]

10844 Miller, Karen, ed. *Immigration* (8–12). Series: Social Issues Firsthand. 2006, Gale LB $28.70 (978-0-7377-2893-4). This compilation of 14 previously published essays gives insight into the experiences of varied immigrants to the United States — from Cuba, Vietnam, Bosnia, and Ethiopia, to name just a few nations — and looks at the difficulties they met in their new country. (Rev: SLJ 6/07) [304.8]

10845 Orr, Tamra. *The Korean Americans* (5–8). Illus. Series: Major American Immigration. 2009, Mason

Crest LB $22.95 (978-1-4222-0612-6). Orr provides a thorough overview of migration from Korea to the United States, with information on the history of Korea, the reasons for leaving the country, and the "picture brides" who arrived here in the early 20th century, plus profiles of key figures. (Rev: BL 5/15/09) [973]

10846 Outman, James L., and Lawrence W. Baker. *U.S. Immigration and Migration Primary Sources* (7–10). Series: Immigration and Migration Reference Library. 2004, Gale $70.00 (978-0-7876-7669-8). Primary source documents — including articles, letters, and Supreme Court rulings — chronicle the history of immigration to and migration within America. (Rev: SLJ 2/05) [304.8]

10847 Rangaswamy, Padma. *Indian Americans* (8–12). Series: The New Immigrants. 2006, Chelsea House $27.95 (978-0-7910-8786-2). This volume traces the history of immigration from India to the United States — and of Indians who have been living in Africa, Europe, and the Caribbean. (Rev: LMC 8–9/07; SLJ 3/07) [977.3]

10848 Santos, Edward J. *Everything You Need to Know If You and Your Parents Are New Americans* (7–12). Series: Need to Know Library. 2002, Rosen LB $27.95 (978-0-8239-3547-5). A useful and attractive guide for immigrant teens that gives practical advice on dealing with various facets of American life and emphasizes the possibility of retaining one's heritage while fitting in to a new culture. (Rev: BL 6/1–15/02; SLJ 4/02; VOYA 2/03) [304.8]

10849 Schroeder, Michael J. *Mexican Americans* (6–10). Series: The New Immigrants. 2007, Chelsea House LB $27.95 (978-0-7910-8785-5). A look at the political and social issues surrounding immigrants to the United States from Mexico, with graphics that will improve readers' understanding. (Rev: BL 7/07) [973]

10850 Senker, Cath. *Immigrants and Refugees* (6–9). Illus. Series: Mapping Global Issues. 2012, Black Rabbit LB $35.65 (978-159920509-0). A survey of voluntary and involuntary migrations, both within and between countries. (Rev: BL 10/1/12) [304.8]

10851 Sherman, Augustus F. *Augustus F. Sherman: Ellis Island Portraits, 1905–1920* (8–12). 2005, Aperture $40.00 (978-1-931788-60-1). Moving photographs taken by an Ellis Island immigration clerk spotlight would-be immigrants — many of them young people — who were held for further interrogation. (Rev: BL 5/15/05) [779.9]

10852 Solway, Andrew. *Graphing Immigration* (4–8). Illus. Series: Real World Data. 2010, Raintree LB $28.21 (978-143292617-5); paper $7.99 (978-143292626-7). Solway uses charts, graphs, and tables — as well as interesting sidebars and photographs — to present trends in immigration and associated problems. (Rev: BL 2/1/10; SLJ 6/10) [304.802]

10853 Teichmann, Iris. *Immigration and the Law* (5–8). Series: Understanding Immigration. 2006, Smart Apple LB $31.35 (978-1-58340-970-1). Covers all aspects of immigration including the laws granting admission, visas, and how to gain citizenship. (Rev: SLJ 3/07)

Ethnic Groups and Prejudice

General and Miscellaneous

10854 Bartoletti, Susan Campbell. *They Called Themselves the K.K.K.: The Birth of an American Terrorist Group* (7–12). 2010, Houghton Mifflin $19 (978-0-618-44033-7). Today's young readers will be fascinated by this account of the rise of the Ku Klux Klan at the end of the Civil War and its continuing presence through much of the 20th century. ALA Notable Books 2011. ∩ (Rev: BL 8/10*; SLJ 8/10) [322.4]

10855 Birdseye, Debbie H., and Tom Birdseye. *Under Our Skin: Kids Talk About Race* (4–8). 1997, Holiday $15.95 (978-0-8234-1325-6). In separate chapters, six 8th-grade students in Oregon from different racial and ethnic backgrounds talk about race and what racism means to them. (Rev: HBG 3/98; SLJ 4/98) [572.973]

10856 Cole, Carolyn Kozo, and Kathy Kobayashi. *Shades of L.A.: Pictures from Ethnic Family Albums* (7–12). 1996, New Press paper $20.00 (978-1-56584-313-4). A collection of photographs of African American, Mexican American, Asian American, and Native American family life in Los Angeles' ethnic and racial neighborhoods prior to 1965. (Rev: BL 8/96; VOYA 2/97) [979.4]

10857 Gaskins, Pearl Fuyo, ed. *What Are You? Voices of Mixed-Race Young People* (7–12). 1999, Henry Holt $18.95 (978-0-8050-5968-7). In essays, interviews, and poetry, 45 mixed-race young people ages 14 to 26 talk about themselves and growing up. (Rev: BL 5/15/99; HB 7–8/99; SLJ 7/99; VOYA 10/99) [973]

10858 Haugen, David M., ed. *Interracial Relationships* (7–12). Series: At Issue. 2006, Gale LB $28.70 (978-0-7377-2390-8); paper $19.95 (978-0-7377-2391-5). Pro and con articles present viewpoints on the degree of acceptance of interracial relationships in various sectors of society. (Rev: SLJ 8/07) [306.84]

10859 Kassam, Nadya, ed. *Telling It Like It Is: Young Asian Women Talk* (7–12). 1998, Livewire paper $11.95 (978-0-7043-4941-4). These 22 short, informal essays reveal various attitudes toward sexism and racism as experienced by Hindu and Moslem girls living in Britain whose families are from the Indian subcontinent. (Rev: BL 9/15/98; SLJ 8/98) [305.8914]

10860 Kops, Deborah. *Racial Profiling* (6–9). Series: Open for Debate. 2006, Benchmark LB $27.95 (978-0-7614-2298-3). Kops gives a balanced overview of racial profiling, presenting various opinions for and against that will be useful for research. (Rev: SLJ 2/07)

10861 O'Hearn, Claudine Chiawei, ed. *Half and Half: Writers on Growing Up Biracial and Bicultural* (7–12). 1998, Pantheon paper $13.00 (978-0-375-70011-8). This work contains 18 personal essays by people who live and work in the U.S., but who, because they are biracial and bicultural, are not sure where they belong. (Rev: BL 9/1/98) [306.84]

10862 St. Stephen's Community House. *It's Not All Black and White: Multiracial Youth Speak Out* (7–12). Illus. 2012, Annick paper $12.95 (978-15545138-0-2). In poems, interviews, essays, and artwork, multiracial young people in Canada discuss racial identity, family ties, stereotypes, assimilation, and so forth. (Rev: BL 12/15/12; LMC 5–6/13; SLJ 3/13) [305.800971]

10863 Stanford, Eleanor, ed. *Interracial America* (7–12). Series: Opposing Viewpoints. 2006, Gale LB $34.95 (978-0-7377-2943-6); paper $23.70 (978-0-7377-2944-3). A useful compilation of essays and excerpts on racial issues such as equal opportunity, interracial families, immigration, and profiling; each chapter includes a bibliography of related articles. (Rev: SLJ 8/06)

10864 Williams, Mary E., ed. *The White Separatist Movement* (8–12). Series: American Social Movements. 2002, Gale LB $36.20 (978-0-7377-1054-0); paper $24.95 (978-0-7377-1053-3). This collection of essays, speeches, book excerpts, and personal observations looks at groups ranging from the Ku Klux Klan to neo-Nazi skinheads and discusses the reasons why people are attracted to such organizations. (Rev: BL 9/15/02) [305.8]

10865 Young, Mitchell, ed. *Racial Discrimination* (7–12). Series: Issues on Trial. 2006, Gale LB $34.95 (978-0-7377-2787-6). Young has compiled a useful volume of opinions on cases brought before the Supreme Court that involved racial discrimination. (Rev: SLJ 1/07)

African Americans

10866 Bolden, Tonya. *Tell All the Children Our Story: Memories and Mementos of Being Young and Black in America* (4–8). 2002, Abrams $24.95 (978-0-8109-4496-1). From the first recorded birth of a black child in the United States to the Million Man March, this book describes the African American experience through both personal and historical accounts, using a scrapbook format. (Rev: BL 2/15/02; HB 3–4/02; HBG 10/02; SLJ 3/02*; VOYA 4/02) [973]

10867 Clinton, Catherine. *The Black Soldier: 1492 to the Present* (5–8). 2000, Houghton Mifflin $17.00 (978-0-395-67722-3). This history of African Americans in the army begins with colonial slaves who were given muskets to fight the Indians and continues through each of America's wars to the present with emphasis on the slow progress toward equality in the ranks. (Rev:

BCCB 10/00; BL 9/15/00; HBG 3/01; SLJ 10/00; VOYA 2/01) [355]

10868 Cole, Harriette, and John Pinderhuges. *Coming Together: Celebrations for African American Families* (4–12). 2003, Hyperion $22.99 (978-0-7868-0753-6). Traditions surrounding celebrations including Christmas, Kwanzaa, and naming ceremonies are covered here, with accompanying crafts, menu suggestions, and activities. (Rev: BL 12/15/03; HBG 4/04; VOYA 2/04) [306.8]

10869 Ebony, ed. *Ebony Pictorial History of Black America* (7–12). 1971, Johnson $54.95 (978-0-87485-049-9). These three volumes trace African American history from slavery to today's fight for integration and equality. [305.8]

10870 Feelings, Tom. *Tommy Traveler in the World of Black History* (5–8). 1991, Black Butterfly $13.95 (978-0-86316-202-2). A history of African Americans seen through the eyes of a boy who imagines himself participating in the important events. (Rev: BL 9/15/91; SLJ 2/92) [973]

10871 Fradin, Judith Bloom, and Dennis Brindell Fradin. *5,000 Miles to Freedom: Ellen and William Craft's Flight from Slavery* (6–9). 2005, National Geographic LB $29.90 (978-0-7922-7886-3). Ellen and William Craft, a married couple, escaped slavery in Georgia only to find they were in danger again in Boston; this appealing volume documents their adventures, including their flight to England. (Rev: BL 3/15/06; SLJ 5/06*) [326.0]

10872 Garrison, Mary. *Slaves Who Dared: The Stories of Ten African-American Heroes* (7–12). 2002, White Mane LB $19.95 (978-1-57249-272-1). Historical prints and quotations from original texts lend authenticity to these moving accounts of famous and less-well-known men and women who escaped from slavery. (Rev: BL 9/1/02; HBG 3/03; SLJ 7/02) [973]

10873 Greenfield, Eloise, and Lessie Jones Little. *Childtimes: A Three-Generation Memoir* (5–8). Illus. by Jerry Pinkney. 1979, HarperCollins LB $16.89 (978-0-690-03875-0); paper $9.99 (978-0-06-446134-4). The childhoods of three generations of African American women.

10874 Haley, James, ed. *Reparations for American Slavery* (6–12). Series: At Issue. 2004, Gale LB $29.95 (978-0-7377-1340-4). The arguments for and against the payments or other compensation for the years of slavery to present-day African Americans are the subject of this collection of writings. (Rev: BL 2/15/04) [326]

10875 Hansen, Joyce, and Gary McGowan. *Breaking Ground, Breaking Silence: The Story of New York's African Burial Ground* (8–12). 1998, Henry Holt $19.95 (978-0-8050-5012-7). The graphic story of the finding, in 1991, of the mid-18th-century African Burial

Ground in Manhattan and what it reveals about the lives of slaves in New York. (Rev: BL 5/15/98; HBG 10/98; SLJ 5/98; VOYA 8/98) [974.7]

10876 Harris, Laurie Lanzen. *The Great Migration North, 1910–1970* (7–12). Illus. Series: Defining Moments. 2011, Omnigraphics LB $55 (978-078081186-7). This is a detailed yet readable account of the migration of approximately 6 million African Americans to the cities of the North in the 20th century. **e** (Rev: BL 3/15/12*; SLJ 6/12) [307.2]

10877 Holliday, Laurel, ed. *Dreaming in Color, Living in Black and White: Our Own Stories of Growing Up Black in America* (8–12). 2000, Pocket paper $4.99 (978-0-671-04127-4). This is a moving collection of first-person accounts by African Americans who tell of the racism they faced while growing up. (Rev: BL 2/15/00; SLJ 4/00; VOYA 4/00) [305.896]

10878 Horton, James Oliver. *Landmarks of African American History* (8–12). Series: American Landmarks. 2005, Oxford LB $32.95 (978-0-19-514118-4). A tour of 13 historic sites that played a significant role in African American history, with good illustrations and maps. (Rev: SLJ 8/05) [973]

10879 Jacob, Iris. *My Sisters' Voices: Teenage Girls of Color Speak Out* (7–12). 2002, Henry Holt paper $13.00 (978-0-8050-6821-4). Teen girls of color describe their feelings, aspirations, and disappointments in prose and poetry. (Rev: BL 3/1/02; SLJ 10/02; VOYA 12/02) [305.235]

10880 McKissack, Patricia C., and Fredrick McKissack. *Black Hands, White Sails: The Story of African-American Whalers* (6–10). 1999, Scholastic paper $17.95 (978-0-590-48313-1). This account of African American involvement in the whaling industry from colonial times through the 19th century also touches on the abolitionist movement, the Underground Railroad, and the Civil War. (Rev: BCCB 11/99; BL 9/1/99; HB 11–12/99; HBG 4/00; VOYA 2/00) [639.2]

10881 Meltzer, Milton. *The Black Americans: A History in Their Own Words, 1619-1983* (7–10). 1984, Crowell paper $12.99 (978-0-06-446055-2). As told through letters, speeches, articles, and other original sources, this is a history of black people in America. [305.8]

10882 Nelson, Kadir. *Heart and Soul: The Story of America and African Americans* (3–7). Illus. by author. 2011, HarperCollins $19.99 (978-0-06-173074-0). An elderly African American woman narrates the story of her people's struggle to be accepted and free in America in this compelling portrait with evocative full-page paintings. Coretta Scott King Author Winner 2012; ALA Notable Books 2012. **e** Lexile 1050L (Rev: BL 8/11*; HB 11–12/11; SLJ 9/1/11*) [973]

10883 Osborne, Linda Barrett. *Miles to Go for Freedom: Segregation and Civil Rights in the Jim Crow Years* (6–10). Illus. 2012, Abrams $24.95 (978-141970020-0).

Drawing on first-person accounts and including many photographs, this companion to *Traveling the Freedom Road* (2009) looks at racial segregation and early civil rights efforts from the 1890s to mid-1950s. (Rev: BL 5/15/12*; LMC 8–9/12; SLJ 1/12) [305.896]

10884 Schomp, Virginia. *Marching Toward Freedom* (6–10). Series: Drama of African-American History. 2008, Marshall Cavendish LB $23.95 (978-0-7614-2643-1). With lots of primary source material, this volume provides a good overview of the struggle for equal rights between the years 1929 and 1954, with profiles of key figures and stories about individuals. (Rev: BLO 6/17/08) [305.896]

10885 Sharp, Anne Wallace. *A Dream Deferred: The Jim Crow Era* (7–10). Series: Lucent Library of Black History. 2005, Gale LB $32.45 (978-1-59018-700-5). An overview of the impact of the Jim Crow laws that stretched from Reconstruction to the Supreme Court's decision in *Brown v. Board of Education* (1954). (Rev: BL 10/15/05) [323.1196]

10886 Sharp, Anne Wallace. *Separate but Equal: The Desegregation of America's Schools* (7–12). Series: Lucent Library of Black History. 2006, Gale LB $28.70 (978-1-59018-953-5). A thorough history of the education of African Americans, complete with interviews of those who experienced first hand the desegregation battles of the 1950s and 1960s. (Rev: SLJ 6/07) [379.2]

10887 Straub, Deborah G., ed. *African American Voices* (5–8). 1996, Gale $126.00 (978-0-8103-9497-1). This is a collection of excerpts from important speeches delivered by a vast array of African Americans, past and present. (Rev: SLJ 2/97) [973]

10888 Summers, Barbara, ed. *Open the Unusual Door: True Life Stories of Challenge, Adventure, and Success by Black Americans* (8–11). 2005, Houghton Mifflin paper $7.99 (978-0-618-58531-1). Sixteen successful African Americans write about choices they made that changed the direction of their lives. (Rev: BL 1/1–15/06; SLJ 12/05) [920]

10889 Van Peebles, Mario. *Panther: A Pictorial History of the Black Panthers and the Story Behind the Film* (8–12). 1995, Newmarket paper $16.95 (978-1-55704-227-9). The first part of this heavily illustrated book recounts the beginnings of the Black Panther Party and its eventual collapse; the second half describes the making of the movie about the party. (Rev: VOYA 2/96) [973]

10890 Wallenfeldt, Jeff, ed. *The Black Experience in America: From Civil Rights to the Present* (8–12). Illus. Series: African American History and Culture. 2010, Rosen LB $45 (978-161530146-1). With a useful timeline and interesting sidebars, this is a broad and informative overview of black influence on American life in the years involved, with profiles of key figures. ℮ (Rev: BL 2/1/11; LMC 5–6/11) [323.1196]

Asian Americans

10891 Coleman, Lori. *Vietnamese in America* (4–8). Series: In America. 2004, Lerner LB $27.93 (978-0-8225-3951-3). The reasons for Vietnamese migration to the United States and the life the newcomers find when they arrive are discussed in engaging narrative, with personal stories, notes on key figures, illustrations, and a timeline. Also use *Koreans in America* (2004). (Rev: BL 11/15/04; SLJ 3/05) [973]

10892 Goldstein, Margaret J. *Japanese in America* (4–7). Series: In America. 2006, Lerner LB $27.93 (978-0-8225-3952-0). The author discusses the history of U.S.-Japan relations and the course of Japanese immigration to America from the 1800s to today, including the internments during World War II; profiles of famous Japanese Americans are appended. (Rev: SLJ 5/06) [973.0495]

10893 Nam, Vickie, ed. *Yell-Oh Girls! Emerging Voices Explore Culture, Identity, and Growing up Asian American* (8–12). 2001, HarperCollins $13.00 (978-0-06-095944-9). An anthology of fiction and poetry written by Asian American high school and college students, revealing their feelings about topics including heritage, stereotypes, adoption, and interracial dating. (Rev: BL 7/01; SLJ 10/01; VOYA 2/02) [305.235]

10894 Omoto, Susan. *Hmong Milestones in America: Citizens in a New World* (5–8). 2003, John Gordon Burke $27.00 (978-0-934272-57-5); paper $15.00 (978-0-934272-56-8). The author introduces the Hmong people's history and traditions and traces the steps of Hmong refugees who migrated to the United States, profiling five individuals who have found success in their new country. (Rev: BL 4/15/03) [973]

10895 Oppenheim, Joanne. *Dear Miss Breed: True Stories of the Japanese American Incarceration During World War II and a Librarian Who Made a Difference* (7–10). 2006, Scholastic $22.99 (978-0-439-56992-7). An affecting portrait of a World War II children's librarian and the incarcerated young Japanese Americans who benefited from her commitment to her profession. (Rev: BL 1/1–15/06*; SLJ 3/06; VOYA 2/06) [940.53]

10896 She, Colleen. *Teenage Refugees from China Speak Out* (7–12). Series: In Their Own Voices. 1995, Rosen LB $27.95 (978-0-8239-1847-8). Interviews with native Chinese teenagers who are now living in the United States. (Rev: BL 6/1–15/95; SLJ 5/95) [305.23]

10897 Teitelbaum, Michael. *Chinese Immigrants* (5–8). Series: Immigration to the United States. 2004, Facts on File $35.00 (978-0-8160-5687-3). After an overview of the reasons underlying immigration in general, this illustrated volume looks at the circumstances of migrants from China, the group's history in the United States, and the contemporary situation, with sidebar features, a timeline, and a glossary. (Rev: SLJ 4/05)

Hispanic Americans

10898 Behnke, Alison. *Mexicans in America* (4–8). Series: In America. 2004, Lerner LB $27.93 (978-0-8225-3955-1). The reasons for Mexican migration to the United States and the life the newcomers find when they arrive are discussed in engaging narrative, with personal stories, notes on key figures, illustrations, and a timeline. (Rev: SLJ 3/05) [304.8]

10899 Catalano, Julie. *The Mexican Americans* (5–8). Series: Immigrant Experience. 1995, Chelsea LB $14.95 (978-0-7910-3359-3); paper $9.95 (978-0-7910-3381-4). This book traces the reasons for leaving Mexico, the immigrants' reception in the United States, and their contributions and achievements. (Rev: BL 11/15/95; SLJ 1/96) [973]

10900 Cerar, K. Melissa. *Teenage Refugees from Nicaragua Speak Out* (7–12). Series: In Their Own Voices. 1995, Rosen LB $27.95 (978-0-8239-1849-2). The horror of the contra war, after the corrupt rule of the Somoza family was ended by the Sandinistas, is recalled by Nicaraguan teens who fled their country, leaving their families, to seek refuge in the United States. (Rev: BL 6/1–15/95) [973]

10901 Cofer, Judith Ortiz, ed. *Riding Low on the Streets of Gold* (6–12). 2003, Arte Publico $14.95 (978-1-55885-380-5). Latino writers consider issues close to teen hearts in this collection of fiction, poetry, and memoirs. (Rev: BL 12/1/03; SLJ 6/04) [810]

10902 Cole, Melanie. *Famous People of Hispanic Heritage* (4–7). Series: Contemporary American Success Stories. 1997, Mitchell Lane LB $21.95 (978-1-883845-44-5); paper $12.95 (978-1-883845-43-8). This useful series, now in nine volumes, profiles famous Hispanics, past and present, from around the world. (Rev: BL 3/15/98; HBG 3/98) [920]

10903 Doak, Robin. *Struggling to Become American: 1899-1940* (5–10). Series: Latino-American History. 2007, Chelsea House LB $35.00 (978-0-8160-6443-4). Doak looks at Latino immigration — especially from Puerto Rico, Cuba, and Mexico — and at the conditions of Hispanic laborers in the United States during World War I and the Great Depression; includes photographs, sidebars, political cartoons, maps, and so forth. (Rev: SLJ 7/07)

10904 Gay, Kathlyn. *Leaving Cuba: From Operation Pedro Pan to Elian* (6–12). 2000, Twenty-First Century LB $22.90 (978-0-7613-1466-0). The plight of young Elian Gonzalez brought attention to Cubans' efforts to escape their oppressive regime and the uncertain welcome they face in the United States. (Rev: BL 3/1/01; HBG 3/01; SLJ 1/01; VOYA 6/01) [362.87]

10905 Ochoa, George. *The New York Public Library Amazing Hispanic American History: A Book of Answers for Kids* (4–9). 1998, Wiley paper $12.95 (978-0-471-19204-6). Using a question-and-answer format, this work explores such topics as Hispanic American identity and history, cultural groups, accomplishments, and immigrant experiences. (Rev: BL 12/1/98; SLJ 11/98) [973]

10906 Petrillo, Valerie. *A Kid's Guide to Latino History: More Than 50 Activities* (4–8). Illus. 2009, Chicago Review paper $14.95 (978-1-55652-771-5). This is a sweeping introduction to the history of Hispanic Americans in the United States, covering the countries they came from, the reasons they left, and their reception and contributions here, with profiles of key figures and discussion of such issues as bilingual education; activities include crafts, dancing, writing stories, and so forth. (Rev: BL 6/1–15/09; SLJ 8/09) [973]

10907 Worth, Richard. *Mexican Immigrants* (5–8). Series: Immigration to the United States. 2004, Facts on File $35.00 (978-0-8160-5690-3). After an overview of the reasons underlying immigration in general, this illustrated volume looks at the circumstances of migrants from Mexico, the group's history in the United States, and the contemporary situation, with sidebar features, a timeline, and a glossary. Also use *Jewish Immigrants* and *Africans in America* (both 2004). (Rev: SLJ 4/05) [304.8]

Jewish Americans

10908 Finkelstein, Norman H. *Forged in Freedom: Shaping the Jewish-American Experience* (6–12). 2002, Jewish Publication Society $19.95 (978-0-8276-0748-4). Text and photographs present an overview of Jews' contributions to the United States, their influence on the culture, and the problems they have faced. (Rev: BL 8/02; HBG 3/03) [973.04]

10909 Horton, Casey. *The Jews* (4–8). Series: We Came to North America. 2000, Crabtree LB $25.27 (978-0-7787-0187-3); paper $8.95 (978-0-7787-0201-6). As well as discussing the reasons why Jews left Europe, this account describes the trip across the Atlantic, reception in America, and the many contributions to the United States. (Rev: SLJ 10/00) [973]

10910 Rubin, Susan Goldman. *L'Chaim! to Jewish Life in America! Celebrating from 1654 Until Today* (7–9). 2004, Abrams $24.95 (978-0-8109-5035-1). This beautifully illustrated volume chronicles the history of Jews in America with many quotations and personal stories. (Rev: BL 11/1/04; SLJ 1/05; VOYA 2/05) [973]

10911 Schleifer, Jay. *A Student's Guide to Jewish American Genealogy* (7–12). Series: American Family Tree. 1996, Oryx $36.95 (978-0-89774-977-0). An in-depth survey of Jewish history serves as a framework for realistic genealogical information, with plenty of valuable sources cited. (Rev: SLJ 1/97) [973]

Native Americans

10912 Adare, Sierra. *Mohawk* (4–8). 2003, Gareth Stevens LB $26.00 (978-0-8368-3665-3). An introduction to the history, culture, and current status of the Mohawk people, with photographs, maps, and interesting sidebar features that will be useful for reports. Also use *Apache* and *Nez Perce* (both 2003). (Rev: HBG 10/03; SLJ 9/03) [974.7004]

10913 Secakuku, Susan. *Meet Mindy: A Native Girl from the Southwest* (5–8). Photos by John Harrington. Series: My World: Young Native Americans Today. 2003, Beyond Words paper $15.95 (978-1-58270-091-5). A Hopi teen named Mindy talks about her life and heritage in this full-color photoessay. (Rev: BL 4/1/03; SLJ 3/03) [979.1004]

10914 Weitzman, David. *Skywalkers: Mohawk Ironworkers Build the City* (7–10). 2010, Flash Point $19.99 (978-1-59643-162-1). With a dramatic account of a bridge collapse in Quebec in 1907, this volume describes the central role Mohawk men have played in ironwork and bridge and skyscraper construction, discussing the hazards they faced and including primary sources. Lexile 1150L (Rev: BL 10/15/10*; HB 11–12/10; LMC 11–12/10; SLJ 10/1/10; VOYA 8/10) [690.092]

Other Ethnic Groups

10915 Brockman, Terra Castiglia. *A Student's Guide to Italian American Genealogy* (7–12). Series: American Family Tree. 1996, Oryx $35.00 (978-0-89774-973-2). This book, a guide to searching for Italian American ancestors, contains Web sites, computer programs, addresses, and other sources of information. (Rev: SLJ 10/96) [929]

10916 Burgan, Michael. *Italian Immigrants* (5–8). Series: Immigration to the United States. 2004, Facts on File $35.00 (978-0-8160-5681-1). After an overview of the reasons underlying immigration in general, this illustrated volume looks at the circumstances of migrants from Italy, the group's history in the United States, and the contemporary situation, with sidebar features, a timeline, and a glossary. (Rev: SLJ 4/05)

10917 Cavan, Seamus. *The Irish-American Experience* (5–7). Series: Coming to America. 1993, Millbrook LB $23.40 (978-1-56294-218-2). Beginning with the potato famine that forced millions of Irish to come to America, this is the story of the rise of Irish Americans to positions of prominence. (Rev: BCCB 4/93; BL 6/1–15/93) [973]

10918 Di Franco, J. Philip. *The Italian Americans* (5–8). 1995, Chelsea LB $14.95 (978-0-7910-3353-1); paper $9.95 (978-0-7910-3375-3). A heavily illustrated discussion of the culture that Italian immigrants left behind and their contributions to American life. (Rev: BL 1/1/88) [973.0451]

10919 Goldstein, Margaret J. *Irish in America* (5–8). Series: In America. 2004, Lerner LB $27.93 (978-0-8225-3950-6). This overview of Irish migration to the United States looks at the underlying reasons for the exodus and explores the lives of the new arrivals and the traditions they maintained. (Rev: BL 11/15/04) [973]

10920 Hossell, Karen Price. *The Irish Americans* (6–12). Series: Immigrants in America. 2003, Gale LB $29.95 (978-1-56006-752-8). The story of the thousands of Irish people who migrated to America, where they faced discrimination before being assimilated into society and being accepted as true Americans. (Rev: BL 11/15/03) [973]

10921 Howard, Helen. *Living as a Refugee in America: Mohammed's Story* (6–9). Series: Children in Crisis. 2005, World Almanac $31.00 (978-0-8368-5959-1). This accessible story about Mohammed, an Afghan teenager who fled the Taliban with his family and eventually made his way to the United States, incorporates historical and cultural information plus discussion of such topics as discrimination. (Rev: BL 12/1/05*; SLJ 11/05) [973.086]

10922 Hunter, David. *Teen Life Among the Amish and Other Alternative Communities: Choosing a Lifestyle* (5–8). Series: Youth in Rural North America. 2007, Mason Crest LB $22.95 (978-1-4222-0017-9). Hunter introduces readers to the traditions and beliefs of Amish and other alternative communities found around the United States and Canada (including monasteries and kibbutzim), emphasizing how teens in these groupings cope with their different lifestyles; includes many photographs. (Rev: LMC 3/08; SLJ 2/08)

10923 Ingram, W. Scott. *Greek Immigrants* (5–8). Series: Immigration to the United States. 2004, Facts on File $35.00 (978-0-8160-5689-7). After an overview of the reasons underlying immigration in general, this illustrated volume looks at the circumstances of migrants from Greece, the group's history in the United States, and the contemporary situation, with sidebar features, a timeline, and a glossary. Also use *Japanese Immigrants* and *Polish Immigrants* (both 2004). (Rev: BL 4/1/04; HB 3–4/04; SLJ 4/05)

10924 Katz, William L. *Black Indians: A Hidden Heritage* (7–10). 1986, Macmillan $17.95 (978-0-689-31196-3). A history of the group that represented a mixture of the Indian and black races and its role in opening up the West. (Rev: BL 6/15/86; SLJ 8/86) [970]

10925 Kuropas, Myron B. *Ukrainians in America* (5–7). Series: In America. 1996, Lerner LB $19.93 (978-0-8225-1043-7). The story of Ukrainian immigrants to the United States, their cultural traditions, and their contributions to American life. (Rev: BL 3/15/96; SLJ 3/96) [973]

SOCIETY AND THE INDIVIDUAL

10926 Paddock, Lisa, and Carl S. Rollyson. *A Student's Guide to Scandinavian American Genealogy* (7–12). Series: American Family Tree. 1996, Oryx $36.95 (978-0-89774-978-7). An introduction to the Scandinavian countries, people, and emigration to America, and information on how to research specific nationalities. (Rev: SLJ 10/96) [929]

10927 Paulson, Timothy J. *Irish Immigrants* (5–8). Series: Immigration to the United States. 2004, Facts on File $35.00 (978-0-8160-5682-8). After an overview of the reasons underlying immigration in general, this illustrated volume looks at the circumstances of migrants from Ireland, the group's history in the United States, and the contemporary situation, with sidebar features, a timeline, and a glossary. (Rev: SLJ 4/05)

10928 Sawyers, June S. *Famous Firsts of Scottish-Americans* (4–8). 1996, Pelican $13.95 (978-1-56554-122-1). Brief biographies of 30 Americans of Scottish descent, including Neil Armstrong, Alexander Calder, Herman Melville, and Patrick Henry. (Rev: BL 6/1–15/97) [920]

10929 Schouweiler, Thomas. *Germans in America* (5–7). Series: In America. 1994, Lerner LB $19.93 (978-0-8225-0245-6). The causes and results of German immigration to the United States are outlined, with good coverage of their contributions and important figures. (Rev: BL 1/15/95; SLJ 12/94) [973]

10930 Schur, Joan Brodsky. *The Arabs* (8–11). Series: Coming to America. 2005, Gale LB $34.95 (978-0-7377-2148-5). With profiles of several famous Arab Americans (including Ralph Nader and Naomi Shihab Nye), this title uses primary and secondary sources to present an overview of Arab Americans, their reasons for migrating, their social mores, and their adaptation to their new country. (Rev: BL 3/15/05; SLJ 3/05) [973]

10931 Silverman, Robin L. *A Bosnian Family* (4–7). Series: Journey Between Two Worlds. 1997, Lerner LB $27.15 (978-0-8225-3404-4); paper $8.95 (978-0-8225-9754-4). The story of Velma Dusper, her homeland of Bosnia, and her journey with her family to freedom and a new home in North Dakota. (Rev: BL 6/1–15/97; SLJ 7/97) [304.8]

10932 Testa, Maria. *Something About America* (6–9). 2005, Candlewick $14.99 (978-0-7636-2528-3). In free verse, Testa recounts the poignant story of a young immigrant from Kosovo who was badly burned as she and her family fled their war-torn homeland. (Rev: BL 8/05; SLJ 9/05; VOYA 2/06) [811]

10933 Trumbauer, Lisa. *German Immigrants* (5–8). Series: Immigration to the United States. 2004, Facts on File $35.00 (978-0-8160-5683-5). After an overview of the reasons underlying immigration in general, this illustrated volume looks at the circumstances of migrants from Germany, the group's history in the United States, and the contemporary situation, with sidebar features, a timeline, and a glossary. Also use *Russian Immigrants* (2004). (Rev: SLJ 4/05)

10934 Weiss, Gail Garfinkel. *Americans from Russia and Eastern Europe* (5–8). Series: New Americans. 2009, Marshall Cavendish LB $24.95 (978-0-7614-4310-0). This volume provides an overview of immigration past and present from these regions, providing census data and population maps and charts as well as discussing these immigrants' contributions to American culture. (Rev: LMC 3–4/10; SLJ 2/10) [305.8991]

Forms of Dissent

10935 Williams, Mary E., ed. *Is It Unpatriotic to Criticize One's Country?* (7–9). Series: At Issue. 2005, Gale LB $29.95 (978-0-7377-2396-0); paper $21.20 (978-0-7377-2397-7). Previously published articles offer diverse views on whether criticism of one's country is unpatriotic. (Rev: SLJ 7/05) [323.6]

698

Social Concerns and Problems

General and Miscellaneous

10936 Andryszewski, Tricia. *The Militia Movement in America: Before and After Oklahoma City* (7–12). 1997, Millbrook LB $24.90 (978-0-7613-0119-6). This work traces the roots of the anti-government militia movement in the United States from the late 1800s to the present, with coverage of events in Ruby Ridge, Waco, Oklahoma City, and elsewhere. (Rev: BL 2/15/97; SLJ 3/97; VOYA 2/98) [320.4]

10937 Atkin, S. Beth. *Gunstories: Life-Changing Experiences with Guns* (7–10). 2006, HarperCollins LB $17.89 (978-0-06-052660-3). In first-person accounts, teenagers write about their very varied experiences with guns. (Rev: BL 1/1–15/06; SLJ 1/06) [363.33]

10938 Desetta, Al, and Sybil Wolin, eds. *The Struggle to Be Strong: True Stories by Teens About Overcoming Tough Times* (6–12). 2000, Free Spirit paper $14.95 (978-1-57542-079-0). Teens talk about problems such as addicted and abusive parents, AIDS, drugs and alcohol, school, health, and so forth. (Rev: SLJ 8/00)

10939 Donald, Rhonda Lucas. *Animal Rights: How You Can Make a Difference* (4–7). Series: Take Action. 2009, Capstone LB $25.32 (978-1-4296-2796-2). Step-by-step instructions guide readers through formulating a plan of action, and profiles of activist teens describe their goals and strategies. (Rev: SLJ 5/1/09) [179.3]

10940 Gifford, Clive. *Violence on the Screen* (7–10). Series: Voices. 2006, Black Rabbit LB $21.95 (978-1-58340-985-5). Readers are presented with facts, statistics, and opinions about the possible effects of violence in movies and video games and on TV. (Rev: BL 12/15/06) [303.6]

10941 Ginn, Janel, ed. *Do Religious Groups in America Experience Discrimination?* (7–12). Series: At Issue. 2007, Gale LB $28.70 (978-0-7377-3399-0). Many interesting questions are addressed in the articles collected here, including whether feminists discriminate against Islamic women and whether the Episcopal Church discriminates against homosexuals. (Rev: BL 10/1/07) [305.609]

10942 Gleason, Carrie. *Animal Rights Activist* (5–8). Series: Get Involved! 2009, Crabtree LB $26.60 (978-0-7787-4693-5); paper $8.95 (978-0-7787-4705-5). Gleason explains animal rights and the nature of activism before discussing vegetarianism, animal testing, factory farming, and so forth, and giving tips on what young people can do to protect animals. (Rev: SLJ 2/10) [179]

10943 Gourley, Catherine. *Media Wizards: A Behind-the-Scenes Look at Media Manipulations* (5–9). 1999, Twenty-First Century LB $26.90 (978-0-7613-0967-3). An informative account of how the media can manipulate the truth. (Rev: HBG 3/00; SLJ 2/00; VOYA 4/00) [380.3]

10944 Griffin, Starla. *Girl, 13: A Global Snapshot of Generation e* (6–12). 2005, Hylas paper $22.95 (978-1-59258-112-2). Thirteen-year-olds around the world contributed to this volume, answering questions about their views of the world and writing essays about their lives and aspirations. (Rev: SLJ 2/06)

10945 Haddock, Patricia. *Teens and Gambling: Who Wins?* (7–12). Series: Issues in Focus. 1996, Enslow LB $20.95 (978-0-89490-719-7). The controversial subject of gambling is introduced — its lure, addiction, and problems, particularly as related to teenagers. (Rev: BL 8/96; SLJ 8/96; VOYA 10/96) [363.4]

10946 Herumin, Wendy. *Child Labor Today: A Human Rights Issue* (7–12). Series: Issues in Focus Today. 2007, Enslow LB $23.95 (978-0-7660-2682-7). A look at the often-deplorable working conditions of children around the world, with many photographs and personal stories. (Rev: BL 11/15/07) [331.3]

10947 Hyde, Margaret O. *Gambling: Winners and Losers* (6–10). 1995, Millbrook LB $23.40 (978-1-56294-532-9). A timely subject gets rather dry treatment in this book that tells of the history, types, and psychology of gambling, with quotations from many case studies. (Rev: BL 12/15/95; SLJ 3/96) [363.4]

10948 Judson, Karen. *Animal Testing* (7–12). 2005, Benchmark LB $25.95 (978-0-7614-1882-5). Covers the history, science, ethics, and new laws relating to experimentation using animals, with sidebars, quotations, and color and black-and-white photographs. (Rev: SLJ 7/06)

10949 Kuhn, Betsy. *Prying Eyes: Privacy in the Twenty-first Century* (5–8). 2008, Lerner LB $38.60 (978-0-8225-7179-7). From video cameras that can track our every move to personal data stored on computers, this book looks at security/privacy issues and court cases related to them to provide an overview of the important issues in this arena. (Rev: BL 1/1–15/08; LMC 10/08; SLJ 5/08) [323.44]

10950 Milite, George A. *Gun Control* (8–12). Series: Compact Research. 2007, Reference Point LB $24.95 (978-1-60152-010-4). This compact volume provides lots of information for report writers, with illustrations, quotations from primary sources, lists of facts, statistical charts, and brief timelines. (Rev: SLJ 5/07) [363.3]

10951 Pringle, Laurence. *The Animal Rights Controversy* (7–12). 1989, Harcourt $16.95 (978-0-15-203559-4). A book about the way animals are abused and misused that covers topics such as factory farming, experimentation, and zoos. (Rev: BL 1/15/90; SLJ 5/90; VOYA 4/90) [197]

10952 Senker, Cath. *Privacy and Surveillance* (8–11). Illus. Series: Ethical Debates. 2012, Rosen LB $27.95 (978-144886022-7). This volume takes a balanced look at contemporary surveillance techniques, the reasons for increases in surveillance, and the importance of maintaining individuals' right to privacy. (Rev: BL 5/1/12; SLJ 6/12) [323.44]

10953 Sherman, Aliza. *Working Together Against Violence Against Women* (6–10). Series: Library of Social Activism. 1996, Rosen LB $27.95 (978-0-8239-2258-1). An examination of violence against women, including date rape, stranger rape, assault, and domestic violence, and of the actions being taken by both government and private agencies; advice on how teenagers can help themselves, a friend, and their communities is also offered. (Rev: SLJ 2/97; VOYA 6/97) [303.6]

10954 Spilsbury, Louise. *Same-Sex Marriage* (8–11). Illus. Series: Ethical Debates. 2012, Rosen LB $27.95 (978-144886020-3). A balanced discussion of the controversies surrounding same-sex marriage, with details of solutions adopted in various places. **e** (Rev: BL 5/1/12; SLJ 6/12) [306.84]

10955 Streissguth, Thomas. *Hatemongers and Demagogues* (6–9). 1995, Oliver LB $19.95 (978-1-881508-23-6). A survey of American leaders who have used hate and inflammatory language to incite violence, along with an examination of the conditions that led people to support these demagogues, from the individuals who provoked the Salem witch hunts to Louis Farrakhan. (Rev: BL 12/15/95; SLJ 2/96; VOYA 6/96) [305.8]

10956 Watkins, Christine. *Child Labor and Sweatshops* (8–12). Series: At Issue. 2010, Greenhaven $31.80 (978-073774874-1); paper $22.50 (978-07377487-5-8). Does child labor harm girls more than boys? This and many other controversies are discussed in this volume that presents opposing viewpoints. (Rev: BL 4/1/11) [331.3]

10957 Wiloch, Tom. *Everything You Need to Know About Protecting Yourself and Others from Abduction* (6–9). Series: Need to Know Library. 1998, Rosen LB $27.95 (978-0-8239-2553-7). This book describes the dangers of abduction and its frequency in America and provides safety tips for home, at school, while babysitting, jogging, and bicycling, and using the Internet. (Rev: SLJ 9/98) [364]

Environmental Issues

General and Miscellaneous

10958 Adair, Rick, ed. *Critical Perspectives on Politics and the Environment* (8–11). Series: Critical Anthologies on Environment and Climate. 2006, Rosen LB $31.95 (978-1-4042-0823-0). A compilation of 16 articles from *Scientific American* that focus on the tension between environmental and political issues, looking in turn at international treaties, domestic regulation, free trade, and current and future problems. (Rev: BL 11/1/06) [333.7]

10959 Anderson, Judith. *Sustaining the Environment* (4–7). Series: Working for Our Future. 2010, Black Rabbit LB $28.50 (978-1-59771-198-2). This volume explains why the United Nations chose sustaining the environment as one of its eight Millennium Development goals and looks at the various obstacles challenging this mission. (Rev: BL 6/1/10; LMC 10/10; SLJ 4/10)

10960 Anderson, Michael. *The Politics of Saving the Environment* (7–10). Illus. Series: Environment: Ours to Save. 2011, Britannica LB $31.70 (978-161530505-6). This volume provides a history of the environmental movement, discussion of environmental laws, and information on endangered species. (Rev: BL 2/15/12; VOYA 12/11) [337.72]

10961 Andryszewski, Tricia. *The Environment and the Economy: Planting the Seeds for Tomorrow's Growth* (7–12). 1995, Millbrook LB $24.90 (978-1-56294-524-

4). Traces the emergence of environment-versus-economy issues. (Rev: BL 12/1/95; SLJ 11/95) [363.7]

10962 Apte, Sunita. *Eating Green* (4–7). Series: Going Green. 2010, Bearport LB $25.27 (978-1-59716-965-3). Things people can do to lessen damage to the environment are discussed in this book series, which is supported with a Web site featuring additional information and activities. (Rev: LMC 1–2/10)

10963 Arnold, Caroline. *A Warmer World: From Polar Bears to Butterflies, How Climate Change Affects Wildlife* (3–7). Illus. by Jamie Hogan. 2012, Charlesbridge $16.95 (978-158089266-7); paper $7.95 (978-15808926-7-4). Global warming's challenges to the animal kingdom are the focus of this cautionary book. **e** (Rev: BL 2/15/12; LMC 11–12/12; SLJ 4/1/12) [363.738]

10964 Ballard, Carol. *The Search for Better Conservation* (4–7). Series: Science Quest. 2005, Gareth Stevens LB $26.00 (978-0-8368-4553-2). A look at how lack of conservation affects us, and what scientists are doing to tackle this problem. (Rev: BL 4/1/05)

10965 Ballesta, Laurent, and Pierre Descamp. *Planet Ocean: Voyage to the Heart of the Marine Realm* (8–12). 2007, National Geographic $40.00 (978-1-4262-0186-8). Full of eye-catching photographs, this ecology-focused volume visits various undersea environments to show just what we may lose to pollution, overfishing, and other threats. (Rev: BLO 11/19/07) [577.7]

10966 Begley, Ed. *Living Like Ed* (8–12). 2008, Clarkson Potter paper $18.00 (978-0-307-39643-3). Begley offers practical tips on adopting a greener way of living, categorizing the changes as "easy," "not-so-big," and "big" and looking separately at the home, transportation, recycling, energy, the garden and kitchen, clothing, and personal care. (Rev: BL 12/1/07) [333.72]

10967 Bellamy, Rufus. *Tourism* (4–7). Illus. Series: Sustaining Our Environment. 2010, Amicus LB $31.35 (978-160753138-8). Takes a look at tourism's impact on the environment and the emergence of ecotourism, "slow travel," and other new trends. (Rev: BLO 2/14/11; LMC 8–9/11) [363.738]

10968 Berne, Emma Carlson. *Global Warming and Climate Change* (8–12). Series: Compact Research. 2007, Reference Point LB $24.95 (978-1-60152-019-7). What are the consequences of global warming? What are the controversies surrounding global warming? These and other questions are discussed from various points of view, with facts, profiles, and illustrations. (Rev: SLJ 1/08)

10969 Bily, Cynthia A. *Global Warming* (8–12). 2006, Gale LB $34.95 (978-0-7377-2935-1); paper $23.70 (978-0-7377-2936-8). Pro and con essays provide diverse viewpoints on the threat of global warming, its

causes and effects, and the measures to be taken to combat it. (Rev: SLJ 7/06)

10970 Blatt, Harvey. *America's Environmental Report Card: Are We Making the Grade?* (8–12). 2004, MIT $35.00 (978-0-262-02572-0). From global warming to water pollution, this volume looks at today's burning environmental issues and potential solutions. (Rev: BL 11/1/04) [363.7]

10971 Bowden, Rob. *Building Homes for Tomorrow* (8–12). Series: Development Without Damage. 2010, Smart Apple Media LB $34.25 (978-1-59920-252-5). This is an informative and accessible introduction to the global housing crisis and solutions including sustainable housing, improved energy conservation, and new strategies in urban planning. A companion title explores *Food and Water* (2010). (Rev: LMC 5–6/10; SLJ 11/09) [728.047]

10972 Bowden, Rob. *Earth's Water Crisis* (7–12). Series: What If We Do Nothing? 2007, World Almanac LB $30.60 (978-0-8368-7754-0). Bowden underlines the importance of water in key areas of our lives, presents future scenarios, and asks readers what they would do. (Rev: LMC 11–12/07; SLJ 5/07) [333.91]

10973 Burnie, David. *Endangered Planet* (4–8). Series: Kingfisher Knowledge. 2004, Kingfisher $11.95 (978-0-7534-5776-4). This volume looks at how human requirements threaten the flora, fauna, and resources of our planet. (Rev: BL 9/1/04; SLJ 1/05) [333.95]

10974 Caduto, Michael J. *Catch the Wind, Harness the Sun: 22 Super-Charged Science Projects for Kids* (5–8). Illus. 2011, Storey $26.95 (978-1-60342-971-9); paper $16.95 (978-1-60342-794-4). Focusing on energy conservation and global warming, this book collects 22 empowering projects that can be undertaken by young people concerned about the environment. **e** (Rev: BL 5/1/11; SLJ 7/11*) [333.79]

10975 Calhoun, Yael. *The Environment in the News* (8–12). Series: Science News Flash. 2007, Chelsea House LB $31.95 (978-0-7910-9253-8). Serious researchers will find this slim volume a useful starting place — it covers various viewpoints on many issues and provides graphs, illustrations, photographs, and resources for further information. (Rev: SLJ 8/07)

10976 Chandler, Gary, and Kevin Graham. *Environmental Causes* (5–10). Series: Celebrity Activists. 1997, Twenty-First Century LB $25.90 (978-0-8050-5232-9). This book discusses how entertainers including Robert Redford, Sting, and Chevy Chase and other celebrities such as Al Gore, Ted Turner, and Jerry Greenfield support environmental causes. (Rev: SLJ 1/98) [363.7]

10977 Cherry, Lynne. *How We Know What We Know about Our Changing Climate: Scientists and Kids Explore Global Warming* (4–7). Illus. by Gary Braasch. 2008, Dawn $17.95 (978-1-58469-103-7). Children are called to be "citizen scientists" as they learn about the scientific evidence for global warming and are armed with specific strategies to help turn things around. (Rev: BL 2/15/08; SLJ 6/08) [551.6]

10978 Coley, Mary McIntyre. *Environmentalism: How You Can Make a Difference* (4–7). Series: Take Action. 2009, Capstone LB $25.32 (978-1-4296-2797-9). This title provides directions for correctly researching an environmental problem, making a plan, and dealing with the rejection that sometimes accompanies speaking out. (Rev: SLJ 5/09) [333.72]

10979 Collard, Sneed B. *Global Warming: A Personal Guide to Causes and Solutions* (6–9). Illus. 2011, Lifelong Learning $18 (978-0-9785367-7-0). An appealing and informative discussion of the ways in which individuals can contribute to reducing the impact of global warming. (Rev: BLO 9/15/11; SLJ 12/1/11) [363.738]

10980 David, Laurie, and Cambria Gordon. *The Down-to-Earth Guide to Global Warming* (4–7). Illus. 2007, Scholastic paper $15.99 (978-0-439-02494-5). The authors balance alarming information on climate change and its impact with practical ways in which readers can reduce their carbon footprint and details of new technologies that may help. (Rev: BL 9/15/07; SLJ 11/07) [363.738]

10981 Farrell, Courtney. *Keeping Water Clean* (3–7). Series: Language Arts Explorer: Save the Planet. 2010, Cherry Lake LB $27.07 (978-1-60279-659-1). Students are given a mission at the beginning of the book and must use creative thinking and problem solving to gather facts as they travel on a virtual trip researching water conservation. (Rev: LMC 8–9/10; SLJ 4/10) [363.7394]

10982 Flannery, Tim. *We Are the Weather Makers: The History of Climate Change* (7–12). Adapted by Sally M. Walker. 2009, Candlewick $17.99 (978-0-7636-3656-2). This succinct overview of the perils of global warming provides explanations of our scientific understanding of the problem as well as examples of steps we each can take to reduce carbon emissions. (Rev: BL 12/1/09; LMC 11–12/09; SLJ 12/09) [363.73874]

10983 Gore, Al. *Our Choice: How We Can Solve the Climate Crisis* (6–9). Adapted by Richie Chevat. Illus. 2009, Viking $24.99 (978-0-670-01248-0). Gore emphasizes that it's up to the residents of our planet — and to a great extent the young people who will face the consequences — to tackle the climate crisis. (Rev: BL 2/15/10; SLJ 2/10) [363.738]

10984 Gore, Al, and Jane O'Connor. *An Inconvenient Truth* (6–12). 2007, Viking $23.00 (978-0-670-06271-3). The adult companion to the award-winning documentary, adapted for middle- and high-schoolers, will alarm readers and compel them to act. ALA Notable Books 2008. (Rev: BL 4/15/07; HB 5–6/07; SLJ 3/07*) [363.73874]

10985 Gutman, Dan, ed. *Recycle This Book: 100 Top Children's Book Authors Tell You How to Go Green*

(5–9). 2009, Random House paper $5.99 (978-0-385-73721-0). In brief essays (and a poem) Laurie Halse Anderson, Lois Lowry, Rick Riordan, and 97 other authors children will recognize describe what they do to help the earth; some serious, some lighthearted, these pieces are grouped by location (home, school, community, and so forth) and usually include a practical suggestion. (Rev: LMC 5–6/09; SLJ 8/09) [640]

10986 Haddock, Patricia. *Environmental Time Bomb: Our Threatened Planet* (6–12). Series: Issues in Focus. 2000, Enslow LB $26.60 (978-0-7660-1229-5). Up-to-date information is given on current dangers to our environment. (Rev: BL 9/15/00; HBG 3/01; SLJ 12/00) [363.7]

10987 Hanel, Rachael. *Climate Fever: Stopping Global Warming* (5–8). Series: Green Generation. 2010, Compass Point LB $31.99 (978-0-7565-4246-7). Well organized and clearly written, this book is part of a series explaining about steps people can take to adjust their consumption and ease environmental impact, encouraging readers to spur change in their own communities. (Rev: LMC 1–2/10)

10988 Hirsch, Rebecca. *Protecting Our Natural Resources* (3–7). Series: Language Arts Explorer: Save the Planet. 2010, Cherry Lake LB $27.07 (978-1-60279-661-4). Students are given a mission at the beginning of the book and must use creative thinking and problem solving to gather facts as they travel on a virtual trip through the various ways to protect natural resources. (Rev: LMC 8–9/10; SLJ 4/10) [333.72]

10989 Ingram, W. Scott. *The Chernobyl Nuclear Disaster* (5–8). Series: Environmental Disasters. 2005, Facts on File $35.00 (978-0-8160-5755-9). Ingram assesses the continuing environmental fallout from the 1986 Chernobyl nuclear disaster. (Rev: SLJ 11/05) [333.79]

10990 Jakab, Cheryl. *Global Warming* (4–7). Series: Global Issues. 2009, Smart Apple Media LB $28.50 (978-1-59920-451-2). Offering a global perspective, this volume covers warmer temperatures, declining ice cover, changing seasons and rainfall patterns, and the migration that will be caused by all these changes. (Rev: SLJ 2/10) [363.738]

10991 Jakab, Cheryl. *Sustainable Cities* (4–7). Series: Global Issues. 2009, Smart Apple Media LB $28.50 (978-1-59920-454-3). This volume discusses the factors that lead to unsustainable urban growth and the transportation and construction changes that could improve the situation. (Rev: SLJ 2/10) [307.76]

10992 Johnson, Rebecca L. *Investigating Climate Change: Scientists' Search for Answers in a Warming World* (6–10). Illus. Series: Discovery! 2008, Lerner LB $30.60 (978-082256792-9). A compelling historical overview of climate change and its causes is presented in this book full of data, diagrams, photographs, charts, and maps. (Rev: BL 9/1/08; SLJ 1/1/09; VOYA 12/08) [551.6]

10993 Kaye, Cathryn Berger. *Going Blue: A Teen Guide to Saving Our Oceans, Lakes, Rivers, and Wetlands* (6–10). 2010, Free Spirit paper $14.99 (978-1-57542-348-7). Readers learn about the need to protect Earth's water supply in this volume that provides practical tips on water preservation and activism. (Rev: BL 12/1/10; SLJ 12/1/10*) [333.91]

10994 Kirk, Ellen. *Human Footprint* (3–7). Illus. 2011, National Geographic paper $6.95 (978-1-4263-0-767-6). Based on a National Geographic documentary and subtitled "Everything You Will Eat, Use, Wear, Buy, and Throw Out in your Lifetime," this attractive book looks at the average American's consumption. (Rev: BL 7/11; SLJ 6/11) [304.2]

10995 Kusky, Timothy. *Climate Change: Shifting Glaciers, Deserts, and Climate Belts* (8–12). Series: The Hazardous Earth. 2009, Facts on File $39.50 (978-0-8160-6466-3). The many factors contributing to global warming — both natural and the result of human activities — are covered in this wide-ranging volume. (Rev: SLJ 3/1/09) [551.6]

10996 Langley, Andrew. *Avoiding Hunger and Finding Water* (5–8). Illus. Series: The Environment Challenge. 2011, Raintree LB $32 (978-141094298-2). Famine and drought are the main focuses of this effective volume that also covers population growth, climate change, pollution, and so forth. (Rev: BL 2/15/12) [363.8]

10997 Lishak, Antony. *Global Warming* (4–7). Illus. Series: What's That Got to Do with Me? 2007, Smart Apple Media LB $18.95 (978-1-59920-037-8). People from around the world who have been affected by climate change — and those who fear they may be — are interviewed to demonstrate various aspects of global warming. (Rev: BL 10/15/07; LMC 2/08) [363.738]

10998 Marcovitz, Hal. *How Serious a Threat Is Climate Change?* (8–11). Illus. Series: In Controversy. 2011, ReferencePoint LB $26.95 (978-1-60152-142-2). What are the potential economic impacts of climate change? How has the world responded to climate change? This volume offers opposing points of view on these and other questions. (Rev: BL 6/1/11; SLJ 9/1/11) [363.738]

10999 Marcovitz, Hal. *Is Offshore Oil Drilling Worth the Risks?* (8–11). Illus. Series: In Controversy. 2011, ReferencePoint LB $26.65 (978-1-60152-143-9). Is America's energy security dependent on offshore oil? Can offshore drilling be made safer? This volume offers opposing points of view on these and other questions. (Rev: BL 6/1/11; SLJ 9/1/11) [363.738]

11000 Mason, Paul. *How Big Is Your Clothing Footprint?* (5–9). Series: Environmental Footprints. 2010, Marshall Cavendish LB $28.50 (978-0-7614-4410-7). Fibers (natural and artificial), cleaning techniques, fashion, shipping, and other aspects of the clothes we wear are discussed in this useful title. Other volumes in the series include *How Big Is Your Energy Footprint?*, *How Big Is Your Food Footprint?*, and *How Big Is Your*

Water Footprint? (all 2010). (Rev: LMC 5–6/10; SLJ 11/1/09) [391]

11001 Minden, Cecilia. *Reduce, Reuse, and Recycle* (3–7). Series: Language Arts Explorer: Save the Planet. 2010, Cherry Lake LB $27.07 (978-1-60279-662-1). Students are given a mission at the beginning of the book and must use creative thinking and problem solving to gather facts as they travel on a virtual trip through the various ways to minimize waste. (Rev: LMC 8–9/10; SLJ 4/10) [363.72]

11002 Morris, Neil. *Global Warming* (7–12). Series: What If We Do Nothing? 2007, World Almanac LB $30.60 (978-0-8368-7755-7). Morris looks at how we measure climate change, the human and natural causes of these changes, and what we can do to prevent the situation from deteriorating further. (Rev: LMC 11–12/07; SLJ 5/07) [363.738]

11003 Nakaya, Andrea, ed. *The Environment* (5–9). Series: Introducing Issues with Opposing Viewpoints. 2006, Gale LB $33.70 (978-0-7377-3459-1). This thought-provoking study examines the delicate balance between the preservation of our natural environment and the need for energy to fuel economic growth. (Rev: SLJ 8/06)

11004 Parker, Janice, ed. *The Disappearing Forests* (5–8). Series: Understanding Global Issues. 2002, Smart Apple Media LB $19.95 (978-1-58340-168-2). A great deal of information about forest use, abuse, and conservation is packed into double-paged spreads with color illustrations. (Rev: BL 10/15/02; HBG 3/03; SLJ 12/02) [634.9]

11005 Parks, Peggy J. *Ecotourism* (5–8). Series: Our Environment. 2005, Gale LB $26.20 (978-0-7377-3048-7). All about how ecologically sensitive areas can be protected while being explored, with explanations of the advantages and disadvantages of this type of travel. (Rev: SLJ 5/06) [338.4]

11006 Parks, Peggy J. *Global Warming* (5–8). Series: Lucent Library of Science and Technology. 2004, Gale LB $29.95 (978-1-59018-319-9). Explores the controversies surrounding the theory of global warming and the potential consequences of the Earth's rising temperature. (Rev: BL 1/05)

11007 Parks, Peggy J. *Global Warming* (5–8). Series: Our Environment. 2004, Gale LB $26.20 (978-0-7377-1822-5). Answers such questions as "Caused by humans or caused by nature?" and "What can be done?" in four chapters that feature many illustrations and large type. (Rev: SLJ 4/05) [363.738]

11008 Parry, Ann. *Greenpeace* (5–8). Series: Humanitarian Organizations. 2005, Chelsea House LB $25.00 (978-0-7910-8815-9). Maps, timelines, factboxes, and color photographs add to this account of Greenpeace's history and mission. (Rev: SLJ 12/05)

11009 Petrikin, Jonathan S., ed. *Environmental Justice* (8–12). Series: At Issue. 1995, Greenhaven LB $19.95 (978-0-565-10264-7). A collection of essays exploring whether the wealthy and powerful are risking the health and living conditions of others while protecting their own resources. (Rev: BL 3/15/95) [363.7]

11010 Pringle, Laurence. *The Environmental Movement: From Its Roots to the Challenges of a New Century* (5–8). 2000, HarperCollins $16.95 (978-0-688-15626-8). This is a fine history of environmentalism in America, beginning with the conflicts between Native Americans and early settlers concerning natural resources and ending with current issues. (Rev: BL 4/1/00; HBG 10/00; SLJ 6/00) [363.7]

11011 Pringle, Laurence. *Global Warming: The Threat of Earth's Changing Climate* (4–8). 2001, North-South $16.95 (978-1-58717-009-6). A straightforward account that covers topics including the causes of global warming, the signs that it is occurring, and possible solutions. (Rev: BL 4/1/01; HBG 10/01; SLJ 6/01) [363.738]

11012 Rae, Alison. *Oil, Plastics, and Power* (8–12). Series: Development Without Damage. 2010, Smart Apple Media LB $34.25 (978-1-59920-251-8). Oil, gas, nuclear, and alternative sources of power are all covered in this introduction to the environmental damage caused. (Rev: LMC 5–6/10; SLJ 11/09) [333.82]

11013 Rae, Alison. *Trees and Timber Products* (8–12). Series: Development Without Damage. 2010, Smart Apple Media LB $34.25 (978-1-59920-247-1). This is an informative and accessible introduction to the timber industry around the world, discussing deforestation, soil erosion, and pollution as well as opportunities for agroforestry. (Rev: LMC 5–6/10; SLJ 11/09)

11014 Reilly, Kathleen M. *Planet Earth: 25 Environmental Projects You Can Build Yourself* (4–7). Series: Projects You Can Build Yourself. 2008, Nomad $21.95 (978-1-934670-05-7); paper $14.95 (978-1-934670-04-0). A worm composting castle and a wind-powered bubble machine are just two of the projects in this book that teaches about the environment and important environmental issues. (Rev: BL 5/1/08) [507.8]

11015 Revkin, Andrew C. *The North Pole Was Here: Puzzles and Perils at the Top of the World* (6–9). 2006, Kingfisher $15.99 (978-0-7534-5993-5). Revkin, an environmental reporter for the *New York Times*, describes his journey to the North Pole with researchers and explores current thinking (in 2006) about the connection between the melting ice cap and global warming. (Rev: BL 5/1/06; SLJ 6/06*) [910]

11016 Robbins, Ocean, and Sol Solomon. *Choices for Our Future* (7–12). 1994, Book Publg. paper $9.95 (978-1-57067-002-2). The founders of Youth for Environmental Sanity believe that young people can convince other young people to adopt more ecologically

responsible lifestyles. This book explains how we can all help. (Rev: BL 3/15/95) [363.7]

11017 Rockliff, Mara. *Get Real: What Kind of World Are You Buying?* (6–9). Illus. 2010, Running Press paper $10.95 (978-07624374-5-0). This is a practical, sensible guide to how purchasing decisions in all areas of life affect the environment and the lives of workers around the world. (Rev: BL 8/10; LMC 1–2/11; SLJ 10/10) [333]

11018 Rooney, Anne. *Is Our Climate Changing?* (4–8). Illus. Series: Global Questions. 2008, Arcturus LB $22.95 (978-1-84837-011-1). What is climate change? Has the climate changed in the past? This brief title answers these and other questions in clear text and color photographs, with a final chapter that looks at the future. (Rev: BL 12/1/08; LMC 5/09) [551.6]

11019 Royston, Angela. *Sustainable Cities* (6–8). Series: How Can We Save Our World? 2010, Black Rabbit LB $32.80 (978-1-84837-288-7). How can we make cities more sustainable? This interesting volume provides a history of city growth and explains how various environmental and transportation strategies would improve the situation; with worldwide examples, graphics, and easy-to-understand fact sections. Also by this author is *Sustainable Energy* (2010). (Rev: LMC 3–4/10) [307.76]

11020 Rutter, John. *Mining, Minerals, and Metals* (8–12). Series: Development Without Damage. 2010, Smart Apple Media LB $34.25 (978-1-59920-249-5). Rutter reviews how we use coal, iron, and other ores, metals, and minerals and the impact on the environment, before exploring ways to mitigate this. (Rev: LMC 5–6/10; SLJ 11/09) [622.028]

11021 Ryan, Bernard, Jr. *Protecting the Environment* (7–12). Series: Community Service for Teens. 1998, Ferguson LB $19.95 (978-0-89434-228-8). After a general introduction on volunteerism, the author describes how teens can become involved in existing conservation projects and begin their own. (Rev: BL 9/15/98; SLJ 2/99; VOYA 8/99) [363.7]

11022 Senker, Cath. *Sustainable Transportation* (6–8). Series: How Can We Save Our World? 2010, Black Rabbit LB $32.80 (978-1-84837-287-0). Senker looks at transportation on the road, by rail, by water, by plane, and by bike and on foot, pointing out ways in which we can reduce the environmental impact. (Rev: LMC 3–4/10) [388]

11023 Sivertsen, Linda, and Tosh Sivertsen. *Generation Green: The Ultimate Teen Guide to Living an Eco-Friendly Life* (7–12). 2008, Simon & Schuster paper $9.99 (978-141697242-6). Sivertsen and her 18-year-old son Tosh explore various aspects of green living in this very accessible yet solidly informative guide. (Rev: BLO 10/30/08; SLJ 8/08) [363.73874]

11024 Solway, Andrew. *Biofuels* (5–8). Illus. Series: Energy for the Future and Global Warming. 2007, Gareth Stevens LB $26.60 (978-0-8368-8398-5); paper $9.95 (978-0-8368-8407-4). A brief introduction to the use of alternatives to fossil fuels — ethanol, biogas, and so forth — with an explanation of how these could benefit the environment. (Rev: BL 10/15/07)

11025 Spilsbury, Louise, and Richard Spilsbury. *Water* (5–8). Series: Planet Under Pressure. 2006, Heinemann LB $31.43 (978-1-4034-8214-3). Discusses the demand for water, its sources, and what's being done to conserve it. (Rev: SLJ 3/07)

11026 Spilsbury, Richard. *Climate Change Catastrophe* (4–8). Series: Can the Earth Survive? 2010, Rosen LB $26.50 (978-1-4358-5354-6). With case studies and suggested strategies for the future, this volume looks at global warming problems around the world and the impact on everyday life. Additional titles in this series by this author are *Deforestation Crisis* and *Threats to Our Water Supply* (both 2010). (Rev: LMC 3–4/10; SLJ 1/10) [363.738]

11027 Stenstrup, Allen. *Forests* (7–12). Illus. Series: Diminishing Resources. 2009, Morgan Reynolds LB $28.95 (978-159935116-2). Direct quotes and hard-hitting facts add drama and appeal to this title discussing the rapid decline of the world's forests, focusing in particular on U.S. forests, deforestation in the Amazon basin, and the disappearing mangroves. (Rev: BL 1/1–15/10) [333.75]

11028 Stille, Darlene R. *Nature Interrupted: The Science of Environmental Chain Reactions* (5–7). Series: Headline Science. 2008, Compass Point LB $27.93 (978-0-7565-3949-8). Through understandable text and helpful charts, this title clearly explains the fragile and important links between all things in the environment and how breaks in the chain can have detrimental, widespread results. (Rev: SLJ 2/09) [577.27]

11029 Suzuki, David, and Kathy Vanderlinden. *Eco-Fun* (5–8). 2001, Douglas & McIntyre paper $10.95 (978-1-55054-823-5). The activities in this collection reinforce some basic scientific concepts about air, water, earth, and fire, and encourage young readers to think about environmental issues and avoid pollution. (Rev: BL 6/1–15/01; SLJ 8/01) [577]

11030 Suzuki, David, and Kathy Vanderlinden. *You Are the Earth: Know Your World So You Can Help Make It Better* (4–8). Illus. by Wallace Edwards. 2011, Greystone paper $16.95 (978-1-55365-476-6). This wide-ranging survey discusses the importance of clean air, water, and soil and the interrelatedness of the sun's energy and plant, animal, and human life, with information on creation myths plus activities and experiments. (Rev: BL 3/1/11; SLJ 3/1/11*) [577]

11031 Tanaka, Shelley. *Climate Change* (7–10). Series: Groundwood Guide. 2006, Groundwood $15.95 (978-0-88899-783-8). An introduction to the topic for the middle grades that presents possible solutions to the growing problem. (Rev: BL 12/1/06; SLJ 12/06) [363.738]

11032 Taudte, Jeca. *MySpace/OurPlanet* (8–11). Illus. 2008, HarperTeen paper $12.99 (978-00615620-4-4). This engaging guide to eco-savvy, online environmental community OurPlanet provides tips on such compelling, relevant topics as "eco-dating" and green room makeovers via posts from online forums. (Rev: BL 8/08) [363.73874]

11033 Thomas, Keltie. *Animals That Changed the World* (4–8). Illus. 2010, Annick $21.95 (978-1-55451-243-0); paper $12.95 (978-1-55451-242-3). A fascinating look at the ways in which animals impact life on earth and human history; the cat, dog, beaver, pigeon, and horse are profiled, and expressions involving animals are explained. (Rev: LMC 5–6/11; SLJ 1/1/11) [590]

11034 VanCleave, Janice. *Janice VanCleave's Ecology for Every Kid* (4–7). 1996, Wiley paper $12.95 (978-0-471-10086-7). Clear instructions and many diagrams introduce a series of experiments that highlight environmental issues. (Rev: BL 3/1/96; SLJ 4/96) [574.5]

11035 Welsbacher, Anne. *Earth-Friendly Design* (4–8). Illus. Series: Saving Our Living Earth. 2008, Lerner LB $30.60 (978-082257564-1). A straightforward look at the life cycle of the products we use daily (including vehicles and houses), examining how innovative thinking can lead to greener solutions. (Rev: BL 12/1/08; LMC 3–4/09; VOYA 12/08) [745.2]

11036 Whitman, Sylvia. *This Land Is Your Land: The American Conservation Movement* (5–7). 1994, Lerner LB $30.35 (978-0-8225-1729-0). A history of the conservation movement from its beginnings in 1870 when there were efforts to save Yellowstone and ending with today's major problems such as oil spills and trash disposal. (Rev: BL 12/15/94; HB 3–4/94; SLJ 12/94) [363.7]

11037 Woods, Michael, and Mary B. Woods. *Environmental Disasters* (4–7). Series: Disasters Up Close. 2008, Lerner LB $27.93 (978-0-8225-6774-5). Love Canal, Bhopal, the *Exxon Valdez* — these are only three of the disasters covered in this well-illustrated account of disasters that could have been avoided. (Rev: BL 2/15/08; SLJ 8/08) [363.7]

11038 Woodward, John, and Jennifer Skancke, eds. *Conserving the Environment* (7–12). Series: Current Controversies. 2006, Gale LB $34.95 (978-0-7377-2476-9); paper $23.70 (978-0-7377-2477-6). Including a review of relevant acts and discussion of various environmentally friendly options (renewable energy, organic farming, fuel-efficient vehicles), this volume explores the seriousness of the problem and what should be done at this point in time. (Rev: SLJ 2/07)

11039 Workman, James G. *Water* (7–12). Illus. Series: Diminishing Resources. 2009, Morgan Reynolds LB

$28.95 (978-159935115-5). Discusses everything from the demand for water and regulations that could even out the supply to drought, the benefits and problems associated with water, and the price and availability of bottled water. (Rev: BL 1/1–15/10) [363.6]

Pollution

11040 Bang, Molly. *Nobody Particular: One Woman's Fight to Save the Bays* (6–12). 2001, Henry Holt $18.00 (978-0-8050-5396-8). Teens will connect to this appealingly presented account about Diane Wilson, who became an environmental activist working to restore the ecology of the bays around her Texas home. (Rev: BCCB 2/01; BL 2/1/01; HB 1–2/01; HBG 10/01; SLJ 1/01; VOYA 4/02) [363.738]

11041 Bridges, Andrew. *Clean Air* (5–8). Series: Sally Ride Science. 2009, Roaring Brook paper $6.99 (978-1-59643-576-6). A look at the importance of clean air and the ways in which it is threatened by human activity. Lexile 740 (Rev: SLJ 9/09) [363.739]

11042 Coad, John. *Reducing Pollution* (4–9). Series: Why Science Matters. 2009, Heinemann-Raintree $32.86 (978-1-4329-2483-6). Illustrating science's role in everyday life, this volume offers a comprehensive overview of the causes and consequences of pollution, and what we can do to reduce it. (Rev: LMC 11–12/09) [363.73]

11043 Geiger, Beth. *Clean Water* (5–8). Series: Sally Ride Science. 2009, Roaring Brook paper $6.99 (978-1-59643-577-3). A look at the importance of clean water and the ways in which it is threatened by human activity. Lexile 740 (Rev: SLJ 9/09)

11044 Gifford, Clive. *Pollution* (4–7). Illus. Series: Planet Under Pressure. 2006, Heinemann LB $31.43 (978-1-4034-7742-2). An overview of the various types of pollution, their sources and impact, and possible future remedies. (Rev: SLJ 6/06)

11045 Leacock, Elspeth. *The Exxon Valdez Oil Spill* (5–8). Series: Environmental Disasters. 2005, Facts on File $35.00 (978-0-8160-5754-2). A look at the environmental impact of the 1989 *Exxon Valdez* oil spill in Alaska's Prince William Sound. (Rev: SLJ 11/05) [363.7]

11046 Reed, Jennifer. *Love Canal* (6–12). Series: Great Disasters: Reforms and Ramifications. 2002, Chelsea LB $30.00 (978-0-7910-6742-0). The story of the town that had to be evacuated in the 1970s when hazardous wastes leaked from a disposal site. (Rev: HBG 3/03; SLJ 12/02) [363.738]

11047 Sanna, Emily. *Air Pollution and Health* (7–10). Illus. Series: Health and the Environment. 2008, Alpha-House LB $29.95 (978-193497035-5). This thought-provoking look at the impact of air pollution on human health discusses such topics as ozone depletion,

smog, and acid rain. (Rev: BLO 2/2/09; LMC 3–4/09) [363.739]

Recycling

11048 Dorion, Christiane. *Earth's Garbage Crisis* (7–12). Series: What If We Do Nothing? 2007, World Almanac LB $30.60 (978-0-8368-7753-3). Dorion discusses how and why we create so much garbage and the measures we need to take before this problem swamps us. (Rev: LMC 11–12/07; SLJ 5/07) [363.728]

11049 Hall, Eleanor J. *Recycling* (5–8). Series: Our Environment. 2004, Gale LB $26.20 (978-0-7377-1517-0). Answers such questions as "What is recycling?" and "What does the future hold?" in four chapters that feature many illustrations and large type. (Rev: SLJ 4/05) [363.72]

11050 Miller, Debra A. *Garbage and Recycling* (6–9). Illus. Series: Hot Topics. 2010, Gale LB $32.45 (978-142050147-6). Well-organized back matter adds value to this research-ready overview of the planet's growing waste problem. **e** (Rev: BL 2/15/10) [363.72]

11051 Spilsbury, Richard. *Waste and Recycling Challenges* (4–8). Series: Can the Earth Survive? 2010, Rosen LB $26.50 (978-1-4358-5355-3). With case studies and suggested strategies for the future, this volume looks at waste disposal problems around the world and the impact on everyday life. (Rev: LMC 3–4/10; SLJ 1/10) [363.72]

Population Issues

General and Miscellaneous

11052 Barber, Nicola. *Coping with Population Growth* (5–8). Illus. Series: Environment Challenge. 2011, Raintree LB $32 (978-141094296-8); paper $8.99 (978-141094303-3). This book looks at the importance of population growth to our world and at the relationship between population and food supply, poverty, pollution, education, and so forth. (Rev: BL 2/15/12) [304.6]

11053 Lankford, Ronnie D., Jr., ed. *Are America's Wealthy Too Powerful?* (8–12). Series: At Issue. 2010, Greenhaven $31.80 (978-073775087-4); paper $22.50 (978-07377508-8-1). This volume presents pro and con viewpoints on the question of wealth and power in America, looking at Wall Street, the tax system, the roles of celebrities and corporations, philanthropy, and so forth. (Rev: BL 4/1/11) [305.5]

11054 Lorinc, John. *Cities* (7–12). Series: Groundwork Guides. 2008, Groundwood $18.95 (978-088899820-0). A fast-paced, detailed look at urban history and the issues cities face, such as poverty, overcrowding, and transportation. (Rev: BL 12/1/08) [307.76]

11055 McLeish, Ewan. *Overcrowded World* (5–8). Illus. Series: What If We Do Nothing? 2009, Gareth Stevens LB $31.00 (978-1-4339-0088-4). Overpopulation and the associated problems of famine, water shortages, poverty, and homelessness are addressed in this volume that looks at the past, the current status, and the future outlook. (Rev: BL 4/15/09; SLJ 6/09; VOYA 10/09) [363.9]

11056 McLeish, Ewan. *Population Explosion* (4–8). Series: Can the Earth Survive? 2010, Rosen LB $26.50 (978-1-4358-5356-0). With case studies and suggested strategies for the future, this volume looks at population problems around the world and the impact on everyday life. (Rev: LMC 3–4/10; SLJ 1/10) [363.9]

11057 Mason, Paul. *Population* (4–7). Series: Planet Under Pressure. 2006, Heinemann LB $31.43 (978-1-4034-7741-5). The problems created by overpopulation are the focus of this book that also explores the underlying reasons and possible solutions. (Rev: SLJ 6/06)

11058 Proulx, Brenda, ed. *The Courage to Change: A Teen Survival Guide* (7–12). 2002, Second Story paper $16.95 (978-1-896764-41-2). A thought-provoking compilation of personal stories, poems, and photographs created by teens who participate in Canada's L.O.V.E. (Leave Out ViolencE) program. (Rev: BL 9/1/02; SLJ 7/02; VOYA 8/02) [364.4]

11059 Reef, Catherine. *Alone in the World: Orphans and Orphanages in America* (8–11). 2005, Clarion $18.00 (978-0-618-35670-6). A history of orphanages in America from the early years of the 18th century through their decline in the early 1900s. (Rev: BL 4/1/05; SLJ 6/05; VOYA 10/05) [362.73]

Aging, Death, and Burial Practices

11060 Gignoux, Jane Hughes. *Some Folk Say: Stories of Life, Death, and Beyond* (6–12). 1998, Foulketale $29.95 (978-0-9667168-0-1). A collection of 38 literary selections on various aspects of death and how people adjust to it, taken from world folklore and such writers as Shakespeare and Walt Whitman. (Rev: BL 2/15/99) [398.27]

11061 Orr, Tamra. *Ways to Help the Elderly* (5–8). Series: How to Help: A Guide to Giving Back. 2010, Mitchell Lane LB $21.50 (978-1-58415-915-5). Using real-life examples, this thoughtful book suggests many ways in which children can help elderly people. (Rev: SLJ 12/1/10) [305.26]

Crime, Gangs, and Prisons

11062 Aaseng, Nathan. *Treacherous Traitors* (5–9). Series: Profiles. 1997, Oliver LB $19.95 (978-1-881508-

38-0). This book profiles 12 Americans who were tried for treason, including Benedict Arnold, John Brown, Alger Hiss, Julius and Ethel Rosenberg, and Aldrich Ames. (Rev: SLJ 2/98) [355.3]

11063 Allman, Toney. *The Medical Examiner* (7–10). Series: Crime Scene Investigations. 2006, Gale LB $31.20 (978-1-59018-912-2). A look at the responsibilities, tools, methods, and training of a medical examiner. (Rev: SLJ 9/06)

11064 Barbour, Scott, ed. *Gangs* (8–12). Series: Introducing Issues with Opposing Viewpoints. 2005, Gale LB $33.70 (978-0-7377-3221-4). Diverse opinions are presented on topics including the reasons why young people join gangs and measures that can be taken to reduce the violence. (Rev: SLJ 1/06) [364.1]

11065 Barton, Chris. *Can I See Your I.D.? True Stories of False Identities* (7–10). Illus. by Paul Hoppe. 2011, Dial $16.99 (978-0-8037-3310-7). With graphic panels and second-person presentations, this volume presents gripping stories of daring impostors throughout history. (Rev: BL 4/15/11; LMC 10/11; SLJ 5/11; VOYA 6/11) [001.9]

11066 Bell, Suzanne. *Fakes and Forgeries* (7–12). Illus. Series: Essentials of Forensic Science. 2008, Facts on File $35.00 (978-081605514-2). Covering examples of forgery dating from Mesopotamia to the present day, Bell provides a compelling, accessible portrait of the crime, discussing techniques used and methods of detection. (Rev: BL 10/15/08) [363.25]

11067 Beres, D. B. *Dusted and Busted! The Science of Fingerprinting* (4–8). Illus. Series: 24/7: Science Behind the Scenes: Forensic Files. 2007, Watts LB $25.00 (978-0-531-11822-1); paper $7.95 (978-0-531-15457-1). Introduces the scientific process of fingerprinting through easy-to-read text, illustrations, and real-life examples. (Rev: SLJ 7/07)

11068 Burnscott, Leela. *Big Bangs: Looking at Explosions and Crashes* (6–8). Series: Forensic Investigations. 2010, Smart Apple Media LB $28.50 (978-1-59920-457-4). This eye-catching, highly readable series volume introduces readers to the science of gathering and examining crime evidence relating to fires, explosions, crashes, and use of firearms. (Rev: LMC 1–2/10)

11069 Butterfield, Moira. *Pirates and Smugglers* (5–7). Series: Kingfisher Knowledge. 2005, Kingfisher paper $12.95 (978-0-7534-5864-8). A broad historical survey of outlaws on the high seas, from early smugglers to today's dealers in drugs and exotic animals. (Rev: SLJ 12/05)

11070 Coleman, Janet Wyman. *Secrets, Lies, Gizmos, and Spies: A History of Spies and Espionage* (6–9). 2006, Abrams $24.95 (978-0-8109-5756-5). Readers learn all about the secrets of espionage, its history, famous spies and agencies, missions, and the weapons, tools, and gadgets used. (Rev: BL 10/1/06; LMC 2/07; SLJ 2/07) [327.12009]

11071 Coppin, Cheryl Branch. *Everything You Need to Know About Healing from Rape Trauma* (7–12). Series: Need to Know Library. 2000, Rosen $27.95 (978-0-8239-3122-4). Emphasizing that rape is about power not sex and that the victim is blameless, the author looks in particular at prevention and recovery. (Rev: SLJ 9/00) [362.883]

11072 Denega, Danielle. *Have You Seen This Face? The Work of Forensic Artists* (4–8). Illus. Series: 24/7: Science Behind the Scenes: Forensic Files. 2007, Watts LB $25.00 (978-0-531-11823-8); paper $7.95 (978-0-531-15458-8). Introduces the work of forensic artists through easy-to-read text, illustrations, and real-life examples. (Rev: SLJ 7/07)

11073 Dudley, William, and Louise I. Gerdes, eds. *Gangs* (8–12). Series: Opposing Viewpoints. 2005, Gale LB $36.20 (978-0-7377-2234-5); paper $24.95 (978-0-7377-2235-2). A look at the causes of gang behavior and what can be done to combat the alarming increase in violence. (Rev: SLJ 8/05) [364.1]

11074 Evans, Colin. *Evidence* (6–9). Series: Criminal Justice. 2010, Chelsea House $35 (978-1-60413-615-9). After a history of evidence, this well-written text explains direct and circumstantial evidence and how they are collected; Evans also discusses false confessions, expert testimony, and the use of new technology. **e** (Rev: BL 4/1/10; LMC 11–12/10) [363]

11075 Farman, John. *The Short and Bloody History of Spies* (5–8). 2002, Lerner LB $19.93 (978-0-8225-0845-8); paper $5.95 (978-0-8225-0846-5). A witty and fascinating account of the intriguing lives of spies, with descriptions of spying techniques and gadgets. (Rev: BL 1/1–15/03; HBG 3/03) [327.12]

11076 Fridell, Ron. *Forensic Science* (4–7). Series: Cool Science. 2006, Lerner LB $25.25 (978-0-8225-5935-1). The history of forensic science from 1910 to today is accompanied by information on the professionals involved (medical examiners, forensic entomologists) and the equipment used; effective photographs add to the appeal. (Rev: SLJ 4/07) [363.25]

11077 Fridell, Ron. *Spy Technology* (4–7). Series: Cool Science. 2006, Lerner LB $26.60 (978-0-8225-5934-4). A review of the kinds of technology available in the past and today — including gadgets used by the CIA and KGB and spy satellites — is followed by accounts of dangerous missions and discussion of future technologies. (Rev: SLJ 4/07) [623]

11078 Fridell, Ron. *Spying: The Modern World of Espionage* (7–12). 2002, Millbrook LB $24.90 (978-0-7613-1662-6). What spies do, the technology they use, and the politics of espionage are all covered in this concise volume. (Rev: BL 5/1/02; HBG 10/02; SLJ 4/02; VOYA 12/02) [327.1]

11079 Gardner, Robert. *Who Forged This Document? Crime-Solving Science Project* (4–7). 2010, Enslow LB $23.93 (978-0-7660-3246-0). After a review of the scientific method, this volume explores methods of analyzing handwriting, identifying types of paper, exposing counterfeit money, and so forth, with suggestions for science fair projects. (Rev: LMC 3–4/10; SLJ 7/10) [363.25]

11080 Gifford, Clive. *Spies* (5–9). Series: Kingfisher Knowledge. 2004, Kingfisher LB $11.95 (978-0-7534-5777-1). Stories of notable espionage achievements are included along with brisk facts, plenty of high-interest illustrations, a history of spying, and discussion of the future of this field. (Rev: BL 9/1/04; SLJ 5/05)

11081 Gimpel, Diane Marczely. *The Columbine Shootings* (6–10). Illus. Series: Essential Events. 2012, ABDO LB $23.95 (978-161783308-3). Introduces the perpetrators and victims of this 1999 attack and explores the potential causes and ways to prevent future incidents. (Rev: BL 7/12) [373.17]

11082 Gordon, Olivia. *Cold Case File: Murder in the Mountains* (5–8). Series: Crime Solvers. 2007, Bearport LB $25.27 (978-1-59716-547-1). After a description of the crime, the victim (a photographer who disappeared in the Rockies in the 1970s), and the accused, Gordon recounts the steps taken in the nearly 20-year effort to find the body and solve the crime. "Crime Solving Up Close" looks at forensic terminology. (Rev: LMC 1/08; SLJ 11/07)

11083 Graham, Ian. *Forensic Technology* (4–7). Illus. Series: New Technology. 2011, Black Rabbit LB $34.25 (978-159920532-8). Describes the technology being used in investigating, deaths, fires and explosions, fakes and forgeries, and computer crimes, as well as the importance of print evidence and DNA profiling. (Rev: BL 10/15/11) [363.25]

11084 Hanrahan, Clare, ed. *America's Prisons* (7–12). Series: Opposing Viewpoints. 2006, Gale LB $34.95 (978-0-7377-3344-0); paper $23.70 (978-0-7377-3345-7). This thought-provoking title tackles the thorny issues surrounding America's penal system through a selection of pro and con essays. (Rev: SLJ 9/06)

11085 Harris, Elizabeth Snoke. *Crime Scene Science Fair Projects* (6–10). 2007, Sterling LB $19.95 (978-1-57990-765-5). After an introduction to forensic science and its application, Harris provides projects that teach about fingerprints, lie detection, and so forth. (Rev: SLJ 2/07)

11086 Hasday, Judy L. *Forty-Nine Minutes of Madness: The Columbine High School Shooting* (5–8). Illus. Series: Disasters: People in Peril. 2012, Enslow LB $23.93 (978-076604013-7). Hasday examines the circumstances that led to the 1999 massacre, the event itself, the impact on the community, and related events. (Rev: BL 10/1/12; SLJ 12/12) [373.17]

11087 Haugen, Brenda. *The Zodiac Killer: Terror and Mystery* (6–9). Illus. 2010, Compass Point LB $33.99 (978-075654357-0). Reading like a thriller, this is the story of the serial killer who terrorized California in the late 1960s and early 1970s and kept journalists and investigators on their toes. YALSA Quick Picks for Reluctant Young Adult Readers 2012. Lexile 900L (Rev: BL 10/1/10*) [364.152]

11088 Haugen, David M., and Susan Musser, eds. *Media Violence* (7–12). Series: Opposing Viewpoints. 2008, Gale/Greenhaven $37.40 (978-073774218-3); paper $25.95 (978-073774219-0). Readers explore many aspects of the debate over whether violence in the media encourages violence in society. (Rev: BL 4/1/09) [363.3]

11089 Innes, Brian. *Fingerprints and Impressions* (7–12). Series: Forensic Evidence. 2007, Sharpe Focus $39.95 (978-0-7656-8114-0). Readers learn about DNA fingerprinting and will gain an understanding of the work of forensic scientists. (Rev: LMC 2/08; SLJ 1/08)

11090 Innes, Brian. *Forensic Science* (8–12). 2003, Mason Crest LB $22.95 (978-1-59084-373-4). A well-illustrated exploration of historic and international crime investigations, with a look at evolving techniques and the importance of evidence in court cases. (Rev: SLJ 6/03) [363.25]

11091 Joyce, Jaime. *Bullet Proof! The Evidence That Guns Leave Behind* (5–10). Series: 24/7: Science Behind the Scenes. 2007, Watts LB $25.00 (978-0-531-11820-7); paper $7.95 (978-0-531-15455-7). Joyce uses three real cases to illustrate how ballistics experts can help to solve crimes; reluctant readers will enjoy this. (Rev: SLJ 8/07)

11092 Lewis, Brenda Ralph. *Hostage Rescue with the FBI* (6–10). Series: Rescue and Prevention: Defending Our Nation. 2003, Mason Crest LB $22.95 (978-1-59084-403-8). Famous hostage situations such as the *Achille Lauro* incident are mentioned in this well-illustrated survey of the process of rescuing hostages, negotiating with their takers, and the use of snipers. Also use *Police Crime Prevention* (2003). (Rev: SLJ 7/03) [364.15]

11093 Marcovitz, Hal. *Gangs* (7–10). Series: Essential Issues. 2010, ABDO LB $32.79 (978-1-60453-954-7). "Why do young people join gangs?" "How do communities respond to gangs?" "Is there life after gangs?" These and other questions are answered in this well-organized volume. (Rev: LMC 10/10; SLJ 4/1/10) [364.106]

11094 Mason, Paul. *Frauds and Counterfeits* (6–12). Series: Solve It with Science. 2010, Smart Apple Media LB $34.25 (978-1-59920-329-4). The books in this series explore different ways to catch criminals using crime scene clues. (Rev: LMC 1–2/10)

11095 Nakaya, Andrea C., ed. *Juvenile Crime* (8–12). Series: Opposing Viewpoints. 2005, Gale LB $36.20 (978-0-7377-2945-0); paper $24.95 (978-0-7377-2946-7). A collection of diverse opinions on the causes of juvenile crime and on ways to prevent it, to punish or treat offenders, and to improve the juvenile justice system. (Rev: SLJ 1/06) [364.9]

11096 Newton, Michael. *Crime Fighting and Crime Prevention* (6–9). Series: Criminal Justice. 2010, Chelsea House $35 (978-1-60413-629-6). After a history of crime, this U.S.-focused volume looks at the roles of local, state, and federal police and at crime committed outside the country, with further discussion of community efforts to battle crime and the media's portrayals of crimes. ❤ (Rev: LMC 11–12/10) [363]

11097 Owen, David. *Police Lab: How Forensic Science Tracks Down and Convicts Criminals* (6–12). 2002, Firefly $19.95 (978-1-55297-620-3); paper $9.95 (978-1-55297-619-7). The nitty-gritty of forensic science is covered here, with information about the investigations of some well-known crimes and criminals and attention-grabbing photographs, some of them grisly. (Rev: BL 12/15/02; HBG 3/03; SLJ 5/03) [363.25]

11098 Owens, Lois Smith, and Vivian Verdell Gordon. *Think About Prisons and the Criminal Justice System* (6–10). Series: Think. 1991, Walker LB $15.85 (978-0-8027-8121-5); paper $9.95 (978-0-8027-7370-8). Basic information on incarceration, crime and its consequences, the criminal justice system, and the basis for laws. (Rev: BL 6/1/92; SLJ 2/92) [364.973]

11099 Parks, Peggy J. *Gangs* (7–10). Illus. Series: Compact Research: Current Issues. 2010, ReferencePoint LB $26.95 (978-160152114-9). Presents opposing points of view on the nature of gangs, why young people join them, whether they are free to leave gang life, and whether gang violence can be stopped; includes primary source quotes and facts and illustrations plus extensive back matter. (Rev: BL 4/1/11) [364.1]

11100 Parks, Peggy J. *School Violence* (6–9). Illus. Series: Compact Research. 2008, ReferencePoint LB $25.95 (978-1-60152-057-9). Parks examines the prevalence of school violence, its causes and results, and strategies to prevent it, providing varying perspectives, data, and pages of quotations. (Rev: SLJ 1/1/09) [371.7]

11101 Platt, Richard. *Forensics* (5–10). Series: Kingfisher Knowledge. 2005, Kingfisher paper $12.95 (978-0-7534-5862-4). This introduction to the use of the forensic sciences in crime investigation is presented in short blocks of text that will make it appealing to reluctant readers. (Rev: SLJ 11/05) [363.2]

11102 Powell, Phelan. *Major Unsolved Crimes* (6–9). Series: Crime, Justice, and Punishment. 1999, Chelsea $30.00 (978-0-7910-4277-9). Such crimes as the riddle of Jack the Ripper, the Zodiac killer, the Tylenol murders, and the Kennedy assassination are discussed in this fascinating volume. (Rev: BL 12/15/99; HBG 4/00) [364.15]

11103 Prokos, Anna. *Guilty by a Hair! Real-Life DNA Matches!* (4–8). Illus. Series: 24/7: Science Behind the Scenes: Forensic Files. 2007, Watts LB $25.00 (978-0-531-11821-4); paper $7.95 (978-0-531-18733-3). In clear, engaging prose with illustrations and real-life examples, this volume discusses the science behind DNA analysis used in crime investigations. (Rev: SLJ 7/07)

11104 Prokos, Anna. *Killer Wallpaper: True Cases of Deadly Poisonings* (5–10). Series: 24/7: Science Behind the Scenes. 2007, Watts LB $25.00 (978-0-531-12061-3); paper $7.95 (978-0-531-15459-5). Prokos uses three real cases to illustrate the work of forensic toxicologists; reluctant readers will enjoy this. (Rev: SLJ 8/07)

11105 Rainis, Kenneth G. *Crime-Solving Science Projects: Forensic Science Experiments* (5–9). 2000, Enslow LB $26.60 (978-0-7660-1289-9). After defining forensic science, this book contains experiments and projects involving such areas as fingerprints, inks, writing samples, fibers, forgeries, and blood evidence. (Rev: HBG 10/01; SLJ 2/01) [363.2]

11106 Rainis, Kenneth G. *Fingerprints: Crime-Solving Science Experiments* (7–12). Series: Forensic Science Projects. 2006, Enslow LB $31.93 (978-0-7660-1960-7). Projects and experiments teach students about collecting evidence, taking notes, and reporting findings as well as the basics of fingerprinting; also use *Hair, Clothing, and Tire Track Evidence* (2006). (Rev: SLJ 7/07) [363.2]

11107 Rainis, Kenneth G. *Forgery: Crime-Solving Science Experiments* (4–8). Series: Forensic Science Projects. 2006, Enslow LB $31.93 (978-0-7660-1961-4). Rainis explores how forensic scientists identify forgeries, with 10 interesting case studies. (Rev: SLJ 5/07) [363.25]

11108 Roleff, Tamara L., ed. *Police Corruption* (6–12). Series: At Issue. 2003, Gale $29.95 (978-0-7377-1172-1); paper $21.20 (978-0-7377-1171-4). This is a thought-provoking exploration of the reasons why corruption can flourish within the law enforcement community. (Rev: BL 4/15/03) [353.4]

11109 Rollins, Barbara B., and Michael Dahl. *Blood Evidence* (4–8). Series: Forensic Crime Solvers. 2004, Capstone LB $23.93 (978-0-7368-2418-7). Reluctant readers will be attracted to the gruesome nature of the subject matter and the often lurid presentation of facts. (Rev: BL 5/1/04; SLJ 8/04) [363.25]

11110 Rollins, Barbara B., and Michael Dahl. *Cause of Death* (4–8). Series: Forensic Crime Solvers. 2004, Capstone LB $23.93 (978-0-7368-2420-0). This look at how crime scene technicians and medical examiners determine cause of death will draw in reluctant readers. (Rev: BL 5/1/04; SLJ 8/04) [614]

11111 Rollins, Barbara B., and Michael Dahl. *Fingerprint Evidence* (4–7). Series: Edge Books, Forensic Crime Solvers. 2004, Capstone LB $23.93 (978-0-7368-2419-4). After a story that draws the readers in, the authors describe the features of fingerprints and discusses their use in solving crimes. (Rev: BL 5/1/04; SLJ 8/04) [363.25]

11112 Ross, Stewart. *Spies and Traitors* (5–8). Series: Fact or Fiction? 1995, Millbrook LB $26.90 (978-1-56294-648-7). A history of the people who have placed themselves above their country in the dangerous game of espionage and betrayal. (Rev: BL 11/15/95; SLJ 3/96) [355.3]

11113 Schroeder, Andreas. *Robbers! True Stories of the World's Most Notorious Thieves* (4–8). Illus. by Remy Simard. 2012, Annick $21.95 (978-155451441-0); paper $12.95 (978-15545144-0-3). Schroeder offers eight well-written accounts of criminal masterminds and their bank robberies, art thefts, and other heists. (Rev: BL 11/15/12; SLJ 2/13) [364.15]

11114 Schroeder, Andreas. *Scams!* (5–8). Series: True Stories from the Edge. 2004, Annick $18.95 (978-1-55037-853-5); paper $7.95 (978-1-55037-852-8). Ten stories reveal daring trickery, con jobs, and scams, including the 1938 radio broadcast of *War of the Worlds* that terrified millions of Americans and the baseless claim that a tribe of cavemen had been found living in a remote corner of the Philippines. (Rev: SLJ 8/04) [364.16]

11115 Schroeder, Andreas. *Thieves!* (5–10). Series: True Stories from the Edge. 2005, Annick $18.95 (978-1-55037-933-4); paper $8.95 (978-1-55037-932-7). Ten world-class crimes are described in compelling detail. (Rev: SLJ 3/06) [364]

11116 Senker, Cath. *Violence* (7–9). Series: Voices. 2010, Smart Apple Media LB $34.25 (978-1-59920-280-8). In chapters titled with questions such as "Is mankind naturally violent?," "Do drugs and alcohol cause violence?," and "Should we ban guns?," this title explores causes and solutions and includes various perspectives. (Rev: LMC 5–6/10; SLJ 11/1/09) [303.6]

11117 Silverstein, Herma. *Threads of Evidence: Using Forensic Science to Solve Crimes* (7–12). 1996, Twenty-First Century LB $26.90 (978-0-8050-4370-9). A discussion of the new forensic technology now available to criminologists, such as the use of DNA, blood splatters, fibers, and shell casings, and the role this science has played in solving famous cases. (Rev: BL 12/1/96; SLJ 2/97; VOYA 6/97) [363.2]

11118 Spilsbury, Richard. *Bones Speak! Solving Crimes from the Past* (5–9). 2009, Enslow $23.93 (978-0-7660-3377-1). Spilsbury provides a thorough overview of all things forensic, covering everything from insect evidence to careers in this field. (Rev: LMC 11–12/09; SLJ 11/1/09) [363.2]

11119 Stefoff, Rebecca. *Criminal Profiling* (7–10). Series: Forensic Science Investigated. 2010, Marshall Cavendish $23.95 (978-076144141-0). After introducing the history and basic principles of forensic sciences, this volume goes on to look at the work of profilers and the kinds of criminals they investigate. (Rev: BL 11/15/10) [363.25]

11120 Stiefel, Chana. *Fingerprints: Dead People Do Tell Tales* (5–7). Illus. Series: True Forensic Crime Stories. 2011, Enslow LB $31.93 (978-076603689-5). Looking at what makes fingerprints unique, how they are located, and the ways in which criminals try to hide their fingerprints, this is a useful volume for young researchers. (Rev: BL 10/1/11) [363.25]

11121 Swift, Richard. *Gangs* (8–12). Series: Groundwork Guides. 2011, Groundwood $18.95 (978-0-88899-979-5); paper $11 (978-0-88899-978-8). A compact but informative discussion of the forces that motivate young people to join gangs, the prevalence of gangs around the world, and the possibilities for reform. ℯ (Rev: BL 5/1/11; LMC 10/11; SLJ 6/11; VOYA 6/11) [364.106]

11122 Townsend, John. *Breakouts and Blunders* (5–8). Series: True Crime. 2005, Raintree LB $31.43 (978-1-4109-1427-9). Attempted and successful escapes through history are the subject of this book in the True Crime series, which features a scrapbook format with engaging photographs and graphics. Also use *Fakes and Forgeries* and *Kidnappers and Assassins* (both 2005). (Rev: SLJ 6/06) [365.641]

11123 Townsend, John. *Famous Forensic Cases* (5–7). Illus. Series: Amazing Crime Scene Science. 2011, Amicus LB $19.95 (978-160753169-2). A chronological look at forensic science from early fingerprinting through DNA developments with case studies of particular interest. (Rev: BL 12/1/11) [363.25]

11124 Webber, Diane. *Do You Read Me? Famous Cases Solved by Handwriting Analysis!* (5–10). Series: 24/7: Science Behind the Scenes. 2007, Watts LB $25.00 (978-0-531-12066-8); paper $7.95 (978-0-531-15456-4). Webber uses three real cases to illustrate ways in which the study of handwriting can help to solve crimes; reluctant readers will enjoy this. (Rev: SLJ 8/07)

11125 West, David. *Detective Work with Ballistics* (4–7). Illus. by Emanuele Boccanfuso. Series: Graphic Forensic Science. 2008, Rosen LB $21.95 (978-1-4042-1434-7). Graphic-novel-like depictions of actual cases in which ballistic evidence pointed to the culprit make this an interesting introduction to this forensic specialty. (Rev: BL 3/15/08) [363.25]

11126 Wiese, Jim. *Detective Science: 40 Crime-Solving, Case-Breaking, Crook-Catching Activities for Kids* (4–7). 1996, Wiley paper $12.95 (978-0-471-11980-7). Presents 40 experiments and activities that illustrate techniques in forensic science related to observing, collecting, and analyzing evidence. (Rev: BL 4/15/96; SLJ 6/96) [363.2]

11127 Willis, Laurie, ed. *Hate Crimes* (7–12). Series: Social Issues Firsthand. 2007, Gale LB $28.70 (978-0-7377-2889-7). Hate crimes of various kinds are discussed in the articles and interview excerpts collected here. (Rev: BL 11/1/07) [364.15]

11128 Winchester, Elizabeth Siris. *The Right Bite: Dentists as Detectives* (4–8). Series: Digital and Information Literacy. 2007, Scholastic LB $26.00 (978-0-531-12062-0); paper $7.95 (978-0-531-18734-0). Conversational text focuses on the work of forensic dentists and offers multiple (sometimes gruesome) examples of cases in which their findings identified victims and perpetrators; factual inserts add interest and a final section discusses the equipment used. (Rev: BL 4/1/07; SLJ 6/07) [001.4]

11129 Wright, Cynthia. *Everything You Need to Know About Dealing with Stalking* (7–12). Series: Need to Know Library. 2000, Rosen LB $27.95 (978-0-8239-2841-5). What to do if you're being stalked, as well as where to get help. (Rev: HBG 9/00; SLJ 3/00) [362.88]

11130 Wright, John D. *Fire and Explosives* (7–12). Series: Forensic Evidence. 2007, Sharpe Focus $39.95 (978-0-7656-8117-1). Readers learn about arson and explosives investigation and will gain an understanding of the work of forensic scientists. (Rev: LMC 2/08; SLJ 1/08)

11131 Yancey, Diane. *Murder* (7–10). Series: Inside the Crime Lab. 2006, Gale LB $32.45 (978-1-59018-619-0). Readers learn how clues found at a murder scene are analyzed and interpreted to reconstruct what happened; there are references to famous cases, and sidebar features and photographs add interest. (Rev: BL 4/1/06; SLJ 9/06) [363.25]

11132 Yeatts, Tabatha. *Forensics: Solving the Crime* (6–9). Series: Innovators. 2001, Oliver LB $21.95 (978-1-881508-75-5). An absorbing exploration of the development of forensics and the contributions of individual scientists, with clear explanations of some new technologies. (Rev: BCCB 2/02; HBG 10/02; SLJ 4/02) [363.25]

Poverty, Homelessness, and Hunger

11133 Anderson, Judith. *Ending Poverty and Hunger* (4–7). Series: Working for Our Future. 2010, Black Rabbit LB $28.50 (978-1-59771-195-1). This volume explains why the United Nations chose eliminating poverty and hunger as one of its eight Millennium Development goals and looks at the various reasons why children are deprived of these basics and what can be done to improve the situation. (Rev: BL 6/1/10; LMC 10/10; SLJ 4/10)

11134 Barker, Geoff. *Hunger* (7–9). Series: Voices. 2010, Smart Apple Media LB $34.25 (978-1-59920-281-5). In chapters titled with questions such as "How aware are we of the hungry?," "Does hunger affect only poor countries?," and "Should we feel guilty about wasting food?," this title explores causes and solutions and includes various perspectives. (Rev: LMC 5–6/10; SLJ 11/1/09) [363.8]

11135 Erlbach, Arlene. *Everything You Need to Know If Your Family Is on Welfare* (6–10). Series: Need to Know Library. 1997, Rosen LB $27.95 (978-0-8239-2433-2). This book explains the welfare system and details recipients' rights as well as offering tips on how to cope with being on welfare and the social stigma often associated with it. (Rev: SLJ 4/98) [362.5]

11136 Flood, Nancy Bohac. *Working Together Against World Hunger* (7–12). Series: Library of Social Activism. 1995, Rosen LB $27.95 (978-0-8239-1773-0). A rundown on world hunger, the conditions that cause it, and ways of becoming active in fighting it. (Rev: BL 4/15/95) [363.8]

11137 Gifford, Clive. *Poverty* (7–9). Series: Voices. 2010, Smart Apple Media LB $34.25 (978-1-59920-277-8). "Is bad government to blame?," "Shouldn't we help those at home rather than abroad?," and "Could rich people do more?," are among the chapters in this title that explores causes and solutions and includes various perspectives. (Rev: LMC 5–6/10; SLJ 11/1/09) [362.55]

11138 Green, Robert. *Poverty* (4–8). Series: Global Perspectives. 2008, Cherry Lake LB $27.07 (978-1-60279-126-8). An accessible look at poverty, how we measure it, its effects, and what can be done to curb this problem. (Rev: LMC 10/08; SLJ 11/08) [362.5]

11139 Haugen, David M., and Matthew J. Box, eds. *Poverty* (8–11). Series: Social Issues Firsthand. 2005, Gale LB $29.95 (978-0-7377-2899-6). Wide-ranging essays present the plight of those living in poverty as well as the thoughts of those who are determined to do something about the problem. (Rev: BL 10/15/05) [362.5]

11140 Lusted, Marcia Amidon. *Poverty* (7–10). Series: Essential Issues. 2010, ABDO LB $32.79 (978-1-60453-957-8). The causes, impact, and stigma of poverty are examined in this volume that also looks at effects including homelessness, lack of education, and lack of health care and at various efforts to alleviate poverty. (Rev: LMC 10/10; SLJ 4/1/10) [363]

11141 Mason, Paul. *Poverty* (4–7). Illus. Series: Planet Under Pressure. 2006, Heinemann LB $31.43 (978-1-4034-7743-9). A clear presentation of how poverty affects people around the world, with charts, photographs, and profiles. (Rev: BL 4/1/06; SLJ 6/06) [362.5]

11142 Parker, Julie. *Everything You Need to Know About Living in a Shelter* (8–12). 1995, Rosen LB $27.95 (978-0-8239-1874-4). A straightforward account that describes life for teens living in shelters, with material on what they can do to control at least some aspects of their lives. (Rev: SLJ 12/95; VOYA 2/96) [362.5]

11143 Roleff, Tamara L., ed. *Inner-City Poverty* (8–12). Series: Contemporary Issues Companion. 2003, Gale LB $36.20 (978-0-7377-0841-7); paper $24.95 (978-0-7377-0840-0). This examination of theories about the causes of urban poverty, the resulting crime and drug use, the impact of the welfare system, and the potential for effective reform provides lots of material for students doing research. (Rev: LMC 4–5/03; SLJ 2/03) [362.5]

11144 Stavsky, Lois, and I. E. Mozeson. *The Place I Call Home: Faces and Voices of Homeless Teens* (8–12). 1990, Shapolsky $14.95 (978-0-944007-81-5). A series of interviews with homeless teens reveals lives of violence, poverty, and drugs. (Rev: BL 11/15/90; SLJ 2/91) [362.7]

11145 Wagner, Viqi, ed. *Poverty* (7–12). Series: Opposing Viewpoints. 2008, Gale/Greenhaven $36.20 (978-0-7377-3747-9); paper $24.95 (978-0-7377-3748-6). This anthology describes the causes of poverty in America and around the world and debates the possible solutions, ranging from migration to government intervention; a revision of the 2003 edition. (Rev: SLJ 2/1/09) [362.5]

11146 Wolny, Philip. *Food Supply Collapse* (7–10). Series: Doomsday Scenarios: Separating Fact from Fiction. 2010, Rosen LB $29.25 (978-1-4358-3563-4). Are we facing food supply doomsday? This volume describes the current situation and the threats that face nations around the world. (Rev: LMC 11–12/10) [363.8]

Public Morals

11147 Berne, Emma Carlson. *Online Pornography* (8–12). Series: Opposing Viewpoints. 2007, Gale LB $36.20 (978-0-7377-3657-1); paper $23.70 (978-0-7377-3658-8). Is online pornography harmful to society? Is online pornography a form of free speech? Questions like these are discussed from different points of view. (Rev: SLJ 1/08)

11148 Burns, Kate, ed. *Censorship* (7–12). Series: History of Issues. 2006, Gale LB $34.95 (978-0-7377-2009-9). Primary documents help to illustrate the issues discussed in this pro and con review of censorship throughout American history. (Rev: SLJ 6/07)

11149 Day, Nancy. *Censorship or Freedom of Expression?* (7–12). Series: Pro/Con Issues. 2000, Lerner LB

$25.26 (978-0-8225-2628-5). A look at censorship in areas including schools and the arts and entertainment, with discussion of age appropriateness and use of the Internet. (Rev: HBG 3/01; SLJ 1/01) [363.3]

11150 Gold, John C. *Board of Education v. Pico (1982)* (6–10). Series: Supreme Court Decisions. 1994, Twenty-First Century LB $25.90 (978-0-8050-3660-2). A thorough analysis of the Supreme Court case that began in a Long Island school and involved censoring library materials. (Rev: BL 11/15/94; SLJ 1/95) [344.73]

11151 Ross, Val. *You Can't Read This: Forbidden Books, Lost Writing, Mistranslations and Codes* (7–10). 2006, Tundra $19.95 (978-0-88776-732-6). A survey of censorship of the written word throughout history. (Rev: BL 5/15/06) [028]

Sex Roles

11152 Chipman, Dawn. *Cool Women: The Reference* (6–9). 1998, Girl paper $19.95 (978-0-9659754-0-7). This work spotlights an eclectic variety of heroines, past and present, real and fictional, from around the world, ranging from athletes and spies to Amazons and comic book queens, chosen for their uniqueness, strength, tenacity, contributions, and ability to blaze new trails for women. (Rev: VOYA 2/99) [305.4]

11153 Gourley, Catherine. *Flappers and the New American Woman: Perceptions of Women from 1918 through the 1920s* (7–12). Series: Images and Issues of Women in the Twentieth Century. 2007, Lerner LB $38.60 (978-0-8225-6060-9). An interesting chronological examination of the roles women played in this period and how they were portrayed in various media. (Rev: BL 1/1–15/08; LMC 2/08; SLJ 11/07) [305.40973]

11154 Levithan, David, and Billy Merrell, eds. *The Full Spectrum: A New Generation of Writing about Gay, Lesbian, Bisexual, Transgender, Questioning, and Other Identities* (8–11). 2006, Knopf LB $17.99 (978-0-375-93290-8); paper $9.95 (978-0-375-83290-1). Forty essays and other contributions by young people under age 23 reveal their own real-life experiences questioning or establishing their sexual identities. (Rev: BL 5/15/06; HB 7–8/06; SLJ 7/06) [306.76]

11155 Mills, J. Elizabeth. *Expectations for Women: Confronting Stereotypes* (7–12). Series: A Young Woman's Guide to Contemporary Issues. 2010, Rosen LB $31.95 (978-1-4358-3543-6). Growing up too fast, body image, plastic surgery, the need to balance home and work, and aging gracefully are all explored in an easy, conversational manner. (Rev: LMC 10/10; SLJ 4/1/10; VOYA 8/10) [305.235]

Social Action, Social Change, and Futurism

11156 Alsenas, Linas. *Gay America: Struggle for Equality* (7–12). Illus. 2008, Abrams $24.95 (978-081099487-4). Personal accounts of gays and lesbians are interspersed with historical information about their struggles for acceptance in the United States since the Victorian period. Stonewall Honor 2010. Lexile 1340L (Rev: BL 2/1/09; LMC 1–2/09; SLJ 7/08) [306.76]

11157 Coon, Nora E., ed. *It's Your Rite: Girls' Coming-of-Age Stories* (6–12). 2003, Beyond Words paper $9.95 (978-1-58270-074-8). Young authors from around the world describe practical and ceremonial milestones that mark their coming of age, and the associated worries and joys. (Rev: SLJ 10/03) [305.235]

11158 Fleming, Robert. *Rescuing a Neighborhood: The Bedford-Stuyvesant Volunteer Ambulance Corps* (4–8). 1995, Walker LB $16.85 (978-0-8027-8330-1). The story of how two determined, dedicated men organized emergency response services in their inner-city neighborhood. (Rev: BL 5/1/95; SLJ 9/95) [362]

11159 Gay, Kathlyn. *Volunteering: The Ultimate Teen Guide* (8–12). Series: It Happened to Me. 2004, Scarecrow $32.50 (978-0-8108-4922-8). This guide examines a wide range of volunteering opportunities for teenagers, from working with the elderly or the homeless to tutoring to building houses; real-life stories add interest. (Rev: SLJ 4/05; VOYA 4/05) [361.8]

11160 Halpin, Mikki. *It's Your World — If You Don't Like It, Change It: Activism for Teenagers* (7–12). 2004, Simon & Schuster paper $8.99 (978-0-689-87448-2). Covering activism on a wide range of topics — the environment, war, gay rights, women's rights, and so forth — this is a useful guide, providing practical ideas and sensible cautions. (Rev: BL 12/15/04; SLJ 12/04) [305.23]

11161 Hovanec, Erin M. *Get Involved! A Girl's Guide to Volunteering* (5–8). Series: Girls' Guides. 1999, Rosen LB $27.95 (978-0-8239-2985-6). Two case studies of successful volunteers are given in this account that explains where to volunteer, how to approach organizations, and how to determine one's interests. (Rev: HBG 10/00; SLJ 1/00; VOYA 2/00) [361]

11162 Karnes, Frances A., and Kristen R. Stephens. *Empowered Girls: A Girl's Guide to Positive Activism, Volunteering, and Philanthropy* (6–12). 2005, Prufrock paper $14.95 (978-1-59363-163-5). A helpful, information-packed guide that will motivate young people to volunteer. (Rev: SLJ 2/06; VOYA 4/06) [361.8]

11163 Kurian, George Thomas, and Graham T. T. Molitor, eds. *The 21st Century* (8–12). 1999, Macmillan

713

$130.00 (978-0-02-864977-1). This book makes predictions for future developments in such areas as abortion, artificial intelligence, crime, extinction, household appliances, sexual behavior, and utopias. (Rev: BL 4/1/99; SLJ 8/99) [133.3]

11164 Lesko, Wendy Schaetzel. *Youth: The 26% Solution* (7–12). 2000, Information U.S.A. paper $14.95 (978-1-878346-47-6). A community action handbook for teens prepared by Project 2000 that provides basic, workable advice, based on the premise that the 26 percent of the population of the United States under the age of 18 can make a difference. (Rev: BL 11/1/98; VOYA 12/98) [361.8]

11165 Lewis, Barbara A. *The Kid's Guide to Social Action: How to Solve the Social Problems You Choose — and Turn Creative Thinking into Positive Action. Rev. ed.* (4–8). 1998, Free Spirit paper $18.95 (978-1-57542-038-7). An inspirational guide that shows how young people can make a difference by becoming involved in social action, such as instigating a cleanup of toxic waste, lobbying, or youth rights campaigns. (Rev: SLJ 1/99) [361.6]

11166 Marcovitz, Hal. *Teens and Volunteerism* (7–10). Series: The Gallup Youth Survey, Major Issues and Trends. 2005, Mason Crest LB $22.95 (978-1-59084-877-7). An attractive volume documenting Gallup findings on teens' attitudes toward various forms of volunteerism including community service, military service, and activism. (Rev: SLJ 1/06) [361.8]

11167 O'Brien, Anne Sibley, and Perry Edmond O'Brien. *After Gandhi* (4–7). Illus. by author. 2009, Charlesbridge $15.95 (978-1-58089-129-5). Subtitled *One Hundred Years of Nonviolent Resistance,* this volume looks at Gandhi's legacy through the work of activists such as Martin Luther King, Jr., Nelson Mandela, and Cesar Chavez. (Rev: BL 2/15/09; SLJ 2/1/09)

11168 Rubel, David. *If I Had a Hammer: Building Homes and Hope with Habitat for Humanity* (6–12). 2009, Candlewick $19.99 (978-0-7636-4701-8). With a foreword by Jimmy Carter, this account of the work of Habitat for Humanity covers everything from the organization's Christian foundation to how it chooses partner families and the various tools and techniques the volunteers use. ∩ Lexile 1150L (Rev: BL 12/1/09; LMC 1–2/10; SLJ 11/09) [363.5]

11169 Ryan, Bernard, Jr. *Expanding Education and Literacy* (7–12). Series: Community Service for Teens. 1998, Ferguson LB $19.95 (978-0-89434-231-8). This book describes literacy and reading programs in the United States and how teens can participate in them. (Rev: BL 9/15/98; SLJ 11/98) [361.3]

11170 Ryan, Bernard, Jr. *Participating in Government: Opportunities to Volunteer* (7–12). Series: Community Service for Teens. 1998, Ferguson LB $19.95 (978-0-89434-230-1). An upbeat guide that advises teens about how they can volunteer in the areas of government and

politics and become involved in their community. Also use *Promoting the Arts and Sciences: Opportunities to Volunteer* (1998). (Rev: SLJ 2/99) [302.14]

11171 Ryan, Bernard, Jr. *Promoting the Arts and Sciences* (7–12). Series: Community Service for Teens. 1998, Ferguson LB $19.95 (978-0-89434-234-9). This work tells how teens can become involved in local agencies that promote the arts and sciences and how their services can make a difference both to the community and to themselves. (Rev: BL 9/15/98; SLJ 2/99) [361.8]

11172 Sanders, Lynn Bogen. *Social Justice: How You Can Make a Difference* (4–7). Series: Take Action. 2009, Capstone LB $25.32 (978-1-4296-2798-6). Step-by-step instructions guide readers through formulating a plan of action, and profiles of activist teens describe their goals and strategies. (Rev: SLJ 5/1/09) [303.372]

11173 Schwartz, Heather E. *Political Activism: How You Can Make a Difference* (4–7). Series: Take Action. 2009, Capstone LB $25.32 (978-1-4296-2799-3). Personal profiles and practical advice are the hallmarks of books in this appealing series. (Rev: BL 4/1/09; SLJ 5/1/09) [322.40973]

11174 Senker, Cath. *Poverty* (7–12). Series: What If We Do Nothing? 2007, Gareth Stevens LB $22.95 (978-0-8368-7757-1). Individuals can make a difference in fighting poverty, this title suggests, even as it lists discouraging statistics on the pervasiveness of poverty around the globe. (Rev: BL 4/1/07) [363]

11175 Shostak, Arthur B., ed. *Futuristics: Looking Ahead* (6–9). Series: Tackling Tomorrow Today. 2005, Chelsea House LB $35.00 (978-0-7910-8401-4). A collection of thought-provoking essays about the field of futuristics. (Rev: BL 4/1/05) [303.49]

11176 Wilson, Janet. *One Peace: True Stories of Young Activists* (4–7). Illus. by author. 2008, Orca $19.95 (978-1-55143-892-4). In double-page spreads featuring children's poems, artwork, photos, and quotations, this picture book for older readers tells the stories of activists ages 8 to 15, who have often experienced atrocities. (Rev: BL 1/1/09; SLJ 2/1/09) [327.1]

Social Customs and Holidays

11177 Breuilly, Elizabeth, and Joanne O'Brien. *Festivals of the World: The Illustrated Guide to Celebrations, Customs, Events and Holidays* (6–12). 2002, Checkmark $29.95 (978-0-8160-4481-8). Festivals around the world are organized by religion, with maps, photographs, and interesting sidebar features. (Rev: SLJ 4/03) [394.2]

11178 Bruchac, Joseph. *Squanto's Journey: The Story of the First Thanksgiving* (4–8). Illus. by Greg Shed. 2000, Harcourt $17.00 (978-0-15-201817-7). A picture book for older readers about the Pilgrims, the first Thanksgiving, and the important role played by the Paluxet Indian Squanto in helping the colony survive. (Rev: BL 9/1/00; HBG 3/01; SLJ 11/00) [394.2]

11179 Colman, Penny. *Thanksgiving: The True Story* (5–8). Illus. 2008, Henry Holt $18.95 (978-080508229-6). Colman presents a fascinating look at the origins, customs, and foods of America's Thanksgiving, drawing on survey responses as well as historical research. (Rev: BL 9/1/08; HB 11–12/08; SLJ 11/1/08; VOYA 8/08) [394.2649]

11180 Gelber, Carol. *Love and Marriage Around the World* (5–7). 1998, Millbrook LB $23.90 (978-0-7613-0102-8). From courtship to the wedding, this book introduces marriage customs from around the world and among different ethnic groups. (Rev: BCCB 7–8/98; HBG 10/98; SLJ 6/98) [392]

11181 Greene, Meg. *Rest in Peace: A History of American Cemeteries* (8–11). Series: People's History. 2008, Lerner LB $30.60 (978-0-8225-3414-3). American burial traditions are constantly evolving, and this volume looks at everything from early Native American practices to gigantic modern cemeteries, with mentions of ethnic communities and environmentally conscious options along the way. (Rev: BL 3/15/08; SLJ 6/08) [393.09]

11182 Harris, Zoe, and Suzanne Williams. *Pinatas and Smiling Skeletons* (4–8). 1998, Pacific View LB $19.95 (978-1-881896-19-7). This book introduces six festivals celebrated in Mexico: the Feast of the Virgin of Guadalupe, Christmas, Carnaval, Corpus Christi, Independence Day, and the Day of the Dead. (Rev: BL 3/15/99; HBG 3/99; SLJ 3/99) [394.26972]

11183 Karenga, Maulana. *Kwanzaa: A Celebration of Family, Community and Culture, Special Commemorative Edition* (6–12). 1997, Univ. of Sankore $24.95 (978-0-943412-21-4). This complete book on Kwanzaa explains its African and African American origins, devotes a chapter to each of its seven principles, suggests activities, and gives answers to the most frequently asked questions about this holiday. (Rev: SLJ 10/98) [394.2]

11184 Lopez, Adriana, ed. *Fifteen Candles: 15 Tales of Taffeta, Hairspray, Drunk Uncles, and Other Quinceanera Stories* (8–12). 2007, HarperCollins paper $14.95 (978-0-06-124192-5). Fifteen contributions — some fiction, some nonfiction — describe varied quinceañera experiences. (Rev: BL 6/1–15/07; SLJ 10/07) [395.2]

11185 Perl, Lila. *Pinatas and Paper Flowers: Holidays of the Americas in English and Spanish* (6–9). 1983, HarperCollins paper $7.95 (978-0-89919-155-3). The origins and customs of eight holidays celebrated in the Americas are outlined in a bilingual text. [394.2]

11186 Taylor, Charles A. *Juneteenth: A Celebration of Freedom* (5–8). Illus. by author. 2002, Open Hand $19.95 (978-0-940880-68-9). A well-organized account of this holiday, which celebrates emancipation, with a discussion of the history of slavery. (Rev: SLJ 11/02) [394.2]

Terrorism

11187 Abbott, David. *The Twin Towers* (7–10). Illus. Series: A Place in History. 2011, Black Rabbit LB $34.25 (978-184837677-9). Discusses the events of September 11, 2001, exploring the motivation for the attack and the resulting "War on Terror." (Rev: BL 4/1/11) [973.931]

11188 Anderson, Judith. *Terrorism* (6–9). Series: World Today. 2010, Black Rabbit LB $34.25 (978-1-59771-201-9). In attractively laid-out pages with brief paragraphs of text per spread, Anderson presents a balanced definition of terrorism and descriptions of various terrorist groups and their actions. (Rev: LMC 10/10; SLJ 6/09)

11189 Balkin, Karen F., ed. *The War on Terrorism* (7–12). Series: Opposing Viewpoints. 2004, Gale LB $36.20 (978-0-7377-2336-6); paper $24.95 (978-0-7377-2337-3). The 28 essays in this collection present both sides of the ongoing debate over the Bush administration's measures to combat terrorism. (Rev: SLJ 3/05) [973.9]

11190 Burgan, Michael. *Terrorist Groups* (5–7). Series: Terrorism. 2010, Compass Point LB $27.99 (978-0-7565-4311-2). After providing a definition of terrorism, Burgan looks at various terrorist groups past and present: the IRA, Irgun, Fatah, ETA, Farc, Tamil Tigers, Hezbollah, Aum Shinrikyo, Hamas, and al-Qaeda. Lexile 990L (Rev: LMC 11–12/10) [363.325]

11191 Campbell, Geoffrey. *A Vulnerable America* (7–12). Series: Library of Homeland Security. 2004, Gale LB $29.95 (978-1-59018-383-0). This book discusses national security, how the government dealt with terrorist attacks in the past, and how 9/11/01 changed intelligence activities. (Rev: BL 4/15/04; SLJ 5/04) [363.3]

11192 Cart, Michael, ed. *911: The Book of Help* (8–12). 2002, Cricket $17.95 (978-0-8126-2659-9); paper $9.95 (978-0-8126-2676-6). A collection of essays, stories, and poems by well-known writers presented in sections titled "Healing," "Searching for History," "Asking Why? Why? Why?," and "Reacting and Recovering." (Rev: BL 7/02; HB 9–10/02; HBG 3/03; SLJ 9/02*) [818]

11193 Ching, Jacqueline. *Cyberterrorism* (5–8). Series: Doomsday Scenarios: Separating Fact from Fiction. 2010, Rosen LB $29.25 (978-1-4358-3565-8). After describing cyberterrorists and their techniques, this volume describes some worst-case scenarios, assesses the scope of the threat, and looks at ways of fighting back. (Rev: LMC 11–12/10) [363.325]

11194 Farrell, Courtney. *Terror at the Munich Olympics* (6–8). Series: Essential Events. 2010, ABDO LB $32.79 (978-1-60453-945-5). Farrell describes the murder of the Israeli athletes and places the tragedy in historical context, concluding with discussion of peace efforts since then. (Rev: BL 5/1/10; LMC 10/10; SLJ 5/10) [796.48]

11195 Friedman, Lauri S. *Terrorist Attacks* (7–12). Series: Compact Research. 2007, Reference Point LB $24.95 (978-1-60152-022-7). Why do people commit terrorist attacks? How can terrorist attacks be prevented? These and other questions are discussed from various points of view, with facts, profiles, and illustrations. (Rev: SLJ 1/08)

11196 Friedman, Lauri S., ed. *How Should the United States Treat Prisoners in the War on Terror?* (7–9). Series: At Issue. 2005, Gale LB $29.95 (978-0-7377-3113-2); paper $21.20 (978-0-7377-3114-9). Previously published articles examine questions surrounding the Geneva Convention and treatment of detainees in America's war on terror. (Rev: SLJ 7/05)

11197 Gaines, Ann. *Terrorism* (7–12). Series: Crime, Justice, and Punishment. 1998, Chelsea LB $30.00 (978-0-7910-4596-1). Beginning with the bombing of Pan Am flight 103 over Lockerbie, Scotland, in 1988, this thorough account discusses terrorism around the world and the groups that are responsible. (Rev: BL 12/15/98; SLJ 3/99) [364.1]

11198 Goodman, Robin, and Andrea Henderson Fahnestock. *The Day Our World Changed: Children's Art of 9/11* (7–12). 2002, Abrams $19.95 (978-0-8109-3544-0). Children's words and art are the main focus of this handsome volume. (Rev: BL 9/15/02) [700]

11199 Gow, Mary. *Attack on America: The Day the Twin Towers Collapsed* (8–12). Series: American Disasters. 2002, Enslow LB $23.93 (978-0-7660-2118-1). This dramatic account of the events of September 11, 2001, includes many survivor and eyewitness accounts. (Rev: BL 9/1/02; HBG 3/03; SLJ 1/03) [973.931]

11200 Gupta, Dipak K. *Who Are the Terrorists?* (8–11). Series: Roots of Terrorism. 2006, Chelsea House $35.00 (978-0-7910-8306-2). This book describes more than 30 terrorist organizations deemed dangerous by the U.S.State Department, providing a balanced account with regard to Islam and looking at the activities of three Nobel Peace Prize winners who were once thought to be terrorists. (Rev: BL 7/06) [303.6]

11201 Hamilton, John. *Operation Enduring Freedom* (4–7). Series: War on Terrorism. 2002, ABDO LB $25.65 (978-1-57765-665-4). Using many color photographs and a matter-of-fact text, this book covers various aspects of the U.S. war against terrorism. (Rev: BL 5/15/02; HBG 10/02) [973.9]

11202 Hamilton, John. *Operation Noble Eagle* (4–7). Series: War on Terrorism. 2002, ABDO LB $25.65

(978-1-57765-664-7). A look at U.S. efforts to police and defend its borders as part of the war on terrorism. (Rev: BL 5/15/02; HBG 10/02) [973.9]

11203 Hampton, Wilborn. *September 11, 2001: Attack on New York City* (6–9). 2003, Candlewick $17.99 (978-0-7636-1949-7). Personal stories give depth to a description of the tragedy in New York City and speculation about the motivation of the perpetrators. (Rev: BL 7/03; HB 9–10/03; SLJ 7/03) [974.7]

11204 Haugen, David M., and Susan Musser, eds. *Can the War on Terrorism Be Won?* (6–9). Series: At Issue: National Security. 2007, Gale LB $29.95 (978-0-7377-1973-4); paper $21.20 (978-0-7377-1974-1). A collection of articles and speeches that express diverse views on the conduct of the "War on Terror." (Rev: BL 1/1–15/08) [973.931]

11205 Kallen, Stuart A. *National Security* (7–12). Series: Compact Research. 2007, Reference Point LB $24.95 (978-1-60152-020-3). How serious a threat to national security is terrorism? How is the government protecting national security? These and other questions are discussed from various points of view, with facts, profiles, and illustrations. (Rev: SLJ 1/08)

11206 Katz, Samuel M. *Against All Odds: Counterterrorist Hostage Rescues* (6–12). Series: Terrorist Dossiers. 2004, Lerner LB $26.60 (978-0-8225-1567-8). The notable hostage rescues by antiterrorist groups around the world covered here go back to the early 19th century. (Rev: SLJ 4/05; VOYA 6/05) [364.15]

11207 Katz, Samuel M. *At Any Cost: National Liberation Terrorism* (7–12). Series: Terrorist Dossiers. 2004, Lerner LB $26.60 (978-0-8225-0949-3). This is an excellent introduction to the terrorist groups active today whose cause is the liberation of their homelands. (Rev: BL 3/15/04; HBG 4/04; SLJ 3/04; VOYA 4/04) [363.2]

11208 Katz, Samuel M. *Jihad: Islamic Fundamentalist Terrorism* (7–12). Series: Terrorist Dossiers. 2003, Lerner LB $26.60 (978-0-8225-4031-1). A look at Middle East-based terrorist groups, their histories, and present-day activities. (Rev: BL 3/15/04; HBG 4/04; SLJ 5/04) [303.6]

11209 Katz, Samuel M. *Raging Within: Ideological Terrorism* (7–12). Series: Terrorist Dossiers. 2004, Lerner LB $26.60 (978-0-8225-4032-8). This book examines terrorists whose motivation is based on ideologies and religion. (Rev: BL 3/15/04; HBG 4/04; SLJ 5/04) [363.2]

11210 Landau, Elaine. *Suicide Bombers: Foot Soldiers of the Terrorist Movement* (8–11). 2006, Lerner LB $31.93 (978-0-7613-3470-5). Examines suicide bombers, their motivation and reasoning, and how terrorist groups recruit and train them. (Rev: BL 11/1/06; LMC 3/07) [363.325]

11211 Louis, Nancy. *Heroes of the Day* (4–7). Series: War on Terrorism. 2002, ABDO LB $25.65 (978-1-

57765-658-6). This account of September 11, 2001, describes through pictures and case studies the gallant feats of firefighters, police, and those who fought back on Flight 93. (Rev: BL 5/15/02; HBG 10/02; SLJ 6/02) [973.9]

11212 Louis, Nancy. *United We Stand* (4–7). Series: War on Terrorism. 2002, ABDO LB $25.65 (978-1-57765-660-9). In text and pictures, this account describes the support offered to the victims of the terrorist attacks of September 11, 2001, and their families. (Rev: BL 5/15/02; HBG 10/02) [909.9]

11213 Margulies, Phillip. *Al-Qaeda: Osama Bin Laden's Army of Terrorists* (5–7). Series: Inside the World's Most Infamous Terrorist Organizations. 2003, Rosen LB $27.95 (978-0-8239-3817-9). Al-Qaeda's history, missions, methods, and structure are described, with a detailed profile of Osama Bin Laden. (Rev: BL 10/15/03) [973.93]

11214 Nardo, Don. *The History of Terrorism* (5–7). Series: Terrorism. 2010, Compass Point LB $27.99 (978-0-7565-4310-5). A broad, well-illustrated survey of terrorism through time, looking at the governments, groups, and individuals that have sought to achieve their goals through violence and the various strategies they have used. (Rev: LMC 11–12/10) [363.3]

11215 Roleff, Tamara L., ed. *America Under Attack: Primary Sources* (6–12). Series: Lucent Terrorism Library. 2002, Gale LB $29.95 (978-1-59018-216-1). Interviews, speeches, articles, and other items relating to the terrorist attacks of September 11, 2001, are collected in a volume that researchers will find useful. (Rev: BL 11/1/02; SLJ 9/02) [973.931]

11216 Ruschmann, Paul. *The War on Terror* (7–10). Series: Point/Counterpoint. 2005, Chelsea House LB $32.95 (978-0-7910-8091-7). Offers opposing views on terrorism-related topics, including preemptive wars,

the suspension of human rights, and anti-terror laws. (Rev: SLJ 9/05)

11217 Streissguth, Thomas. *Combating the Global Terrorist Threat* (6–8). Series: American War Library: The War on Terrorism. 2004, Gale LB $29.95 (978-1-59018-327-4). An overview of efforts to combat terrorism in Afghanistan, Iraq, Pakistan, the Philippines, and Saudi Arabia. (Rev: BL 8/04) [973.93]

11218 Streissguth, Thomas. *International Terrorists* (6–10). Series: Profiles. 1993, Oliver LB $19.95 (978-1-881508-07-6). This book describes the causes of international terrorism, the responsible organizations, and famous incidents. (Rev: BL 10/15/93; SLJ 1/94; VOYA 2/94) [909.82]

11219 Taylor, Robert. *The History of Terrorism* (6–12). Series: Lucent Terrorism Library. 2002, Gale LB $29.95 (978-1-59018-206-2). A chronological look at the history of terrorism around the globe, with discussion of the reasons it has been so widespread and of terrorists' motivation. Also use *Terrorists and Terrorist Groups* (2002). (Rev: BL 11/1/02; SLJ 11/02) [303.6]

11220 Uschan, Michael V. *The Beslan School Siege and Separatist Terrorism* (5–8). Series: Terrorism in Today's World. 2005, World Almanac LB $186.00 (978-0-8368-6555-4). The deadly 2004 attack on a Russian school by Chechen Muslim terrorists is only the first of several attacks described in this volume on independence movements that use violence. (Rev: BL 4/1/06) [947.5]

11221 Wachtel, Alan. *September 11: A Primary Source History* (5–8). Illus. Series: In Their Own Words. 2009, Gareth Stevens LB $27.00 (978-1-4339-0048-8). With narrative text and numerous photographs, plus excerpts from primary sources — including transcripts of phone conversations aboard the planes and firsthand accounts from responders and eyewitnesses — this volume covers the attack itself and the aftermath. (Rev: BL 4/1/09) [973.931]

Economics and Business

General and Miscellaneous

11222 Aaseng, Nathan. *Business Builders in Sweets and Treats* (5–8). Series: Business Builders. 2005, Oliver LB $24.95 (978-1-881508-84-7). This attractive title examines food companies that succeed through satisfying America's sweet tooth. (Rev: BL 12/1/05; HBG 4/06) [338.7]

11223 Bailey, Diane. *How Markets Work* (7–11). Illus. Series: Real World Economics. 2012, Rosen LB $31.95 (978-144885564-3). This visually appealing offering presents clearly focused, well-written information about how people exchange money, goods, and resources. (Rev: BL 7/12; SLJ 5/1/12) [381]

11224 Furgang, Kathy. *Understanding Economics Indicators: Predicting Future Trends in the Economy* (7–11). Illus. Series: Real World Economics. 2012, Rosen LB $31.95 (978-144885571-1). This visually appealing offering presents clearly focused, well-written information about economists' analysis of key indicators. Also use *Understanding Budget Deficits and the National Debt* (2012). (Rev: BL 7/12) [330.01]

11225 Gilbert, Sara. *The Story of Apple* (6–9). Illus. Series: Built for Success. 2011, Creative Education LB $23.95 (978-160818061-5). This appealing business profile emphasizes the ingenuity and perseverance necessary to Apple's success. (Rev: BL 10/15/11*) [338.7]

11226 Gilbert, Sara. *The Story of CNN* (5–8). Illus. Series: Built for Success. 2012, Creative Education $24.95 (978-160818175-9). Tells the story of the creation of the first 24-hour all-news cable network, its success, and some of the events it has covered. Also in this series: *The Story of Amazon.com, The Story of Facebook,* and *The Story of Fedex* (all 2012). Lexile NC1330L (Rev: BL 9/15/12; LMC 5–6/13) [070.4]

11227 Gilbert, Sara. *The Story of eBay* (6–9). Illus. Series: Built for Success. 2011, Creative Education LB $23.95 (978-160818062-2). Tells the story of the creations of the successful online auction Web site. (Rev: BL 10/15/11*) [381]

11228 Gilbert, Sara. *The Story of the NFL* (6–9). Illus. Series: Built for Success. 2011, Creative Education LB $23.95 (978-160818063-9). This volume explains the history of this football league and how it has become the success it is today, with details of negotiations with players. (Rev: BL 10/15/11*) [796.332]

11229 Gilbert, Sara. *The Story of Wal-Mart* (6–9). Illus. Series: Built for Success. 2011, Creative Education LB $23.95 (978-160818064-6). Tells the story of Wal-Mart's relatively modest beginnings and growth into the international success it is today. (Rev: BL 10/15/11*) [381]

11230 Hamen, Susan E. *Google: The Company and Its Founders* (5–8). Illus. Series: Technology Pioneers. 2011, ABDO LB $34.22 (978-161714808-8). Google's cofounders Sergey Brin and Larry Page transformed a friendship into a thriving business; this profile of the company and its key players includes dynamic photographs and thorough back matter. (Rev: BL 4/1/11) [338.7]

11231 Harman, Hollis Page. *Money $ense for Kids! 2nd ed.* (4–7). 2004, Barron's paper $14.99 (978-0-7641-2894-3). Explains the basics of money and currency and of earning, saving, and investing, with exercises at the end of each chapter and a "Money Games" section. (Rev: SLJ 11/04) [332.024]

11232 Heinrichs, Ann. *The Great Recession* (4–7). Series: Cornerstones of Freedom. 2011, Scholastic LB $30 (978-053125035-8); paper $8.95 (978-053126560-4). This visually appealing volume offers straightforward, age-appropriate information on the economic crisis of the first decade of the 21st century and its causes and impact on U.S. residents. (Rev: BL 10/1/11) [330.973]

11233 Kamberg, Mary-Lane. *How Business Decisions Are Made* (7–10). Illus. 2012, Rosen LB $31.95 (978-144885565-0). Explores the need for wise decision-making and how such decisions are reached. (Rev: BL 7/12) [658.4]

11234 Linecker, Adelia Cellini. *What Color Is Your Piggy Bank? Entrepreneurial Ideas for Self-Starting Kids* (6–8). 2004, Lobster paper $10.95 (978-1-894222-82-2). Suggestions for making money are presented in concise chapters on topics including brainstorming, creating a business plan, advertising, and opening a bank account; tip sheets are provided for common activities such as baby sitting and dog walking. (Rev: BL 6/1–15/04; SLJ 9/04) [650.1]

11235 Oleksy, Walter. *Business and Industry* (6–12). Series: Information Revolution. 1996, Facts on File $25.00 (978-0-8160-3075-0). This book describes how companies use Powerbook computers, supercomputers, modems, and videophones to distribute information, increase productivity, and make better business decisions. (Rev: BL 2/15/96; VOYA 6/96) [650]

11236 Wilson, Antoine. *The Young Zillionaire's Guide to Distributing Goods and Services* (5–7). Series: Be a Zillionaire. 2000, Rosen LB $26.50 (978-0-8239-3259-7). This book explains how goods and services are distributed, the importance of retailing and wholesaling, how transportation affects prices and availability, and how the Internet might change these conditions. (Rev: SLJ 2/01) [330]

Economic Systems and Institutions

General and Miscellaneous

11237 Aaseng, Nathan. *You Are the Corporate Executive* (7–10). Series: Great Decisions. 1997, Oliver LB $19.95 (978-1-881508-35-9). This book describes the work of a company's CEO and the nature and consequences of the decisions that CEOs have to make. (Rev: BL 6/1–15/97; SLJ 6/97) [658.4]

11238 Brezina, Corona. *Understanding the Federal Reserve and Monetary Policy* (7–10). Series: Real World Economics. 2012, Rosen LB $31.95 (978-1-4488-5567-4). This volume looks at the history and activities of the Federal Reserve, emphasizing its role during the great recession and the outlook for the future. ℮ (Rev: SLJ 5/1/12) [332.1]

11239 Trahant, LeNora B. *The Success of the Navajo Arts and Crafts Enterprise* (7–10). Series: Success. 1996, Walker LB $16.85 (978-0-8027-8337-0). After a brief history of the Navajo Nation, the author describes how the arts and crafts of the Navajos have prospered under a manufacturing and marketing cooperative. (Rev: BL 5/15/96; SLJ 7/96) [381]

Stock Exchanges

11240 Brennan, Kristine. *The Stock Market Crash of 1929* (8–12). Series: Great Disasters: Reforms and Ramifications. 2000, Chelsea LB $21.95 (978-0-7910-5268-6). This account of the crash and its causes and aftermath looks carefully at the economy of the time and discusses the changes of a similar crash happening today. (Rev: HBG 3/01; SLJ 12/00) [338.5]

11241 Caes, Charles J. *The Young Zillionaire's Guide to the Stock Market* (5–8). Series: Be a Zillionaire. 2000, Rosen LB $26.50 (978-0-8239-3265-8). Basic information on the inner workings of the stock market is presented with many examples from the corporate world. (Rev: HBG 10/01; SLJ 3/01) [332.6]

Employment and Jobs

11242 Ching, Jacqueline. *Outsourcing U.S. Jobs* (7–10). Illus. Series: In the News. 2009, Rosen LB $21.95 (978-143585039-2). A helpful resource for students exploring the effects of the global economy on U.S. and foreign workers; includes photographs and diagrams. (Rev: BL 4/15/09) [331.13]

Labor Unions and Labor Problems

11243 Laughlin, Rosemary. *The Pullman Strike of 1894. Rev. ed.* (7–12). 2006, Morgan Reynolds LB $26.95 (978-1-931798-89-1). A revised edition of this engrossing account of the bitter railroad strike, with good background material on the railroad industry, the planned city of Pullman, the depression of 1893, and the personalities involved, including Eugene Debs; additions include primary source excerpts and recommended Web sites. (Rev: SLJ 5/06)

11244 McKissack, Patricia C., and Fredrick McKissack. *A Long Hard Journey* (5–9). 1989, Walker LB $18.85 (978-0-8027-6885-8). A 150-year saga of the organization of porters into the first black American union, the Brotherhood of Sleeping Car Porters. (Rev: BL 9/15/89; SLJ 1/90; VOYA 12/89) [331]

11245 Skurzynski, Gloria. *Sweat and Blood: A History of U.S. Labor Unions* (7–10). Illus. Series: People's History. 2008, Lerner LB $31.93 (978-082257594-8).

Charting the course of workers' rights from Jamestown through industrialization to the present day, Skurzynski provides a detailed, historically grounded survey of the rights, rules, and governance of labor unions in America. (Rev: BL 10/1/08; SLJ 11/1/08) [331.880]

with real-life examples and discussion of labor laws. (Rev: BL 10/1/09; LMC 1–2/10) [381.3]

Money and Trade

11246 January, Brendan. *Globalize It!* (8–12). 2003, Millbrook LB $26.90 (978-0-7613-2417-1). The continuing advance of globalization and arguments for and against this phenomenon are thoughtfully examined in this accessible overview. (Rev: BL 1/1–15/04; SLJ 5/04) [337]

11247 Johanson, Paula. *Making Good Choices About Fair Trade* (5–8). Series: Green Matters. 2010, Rosen LB $29.95 (978-1-4358-5315-7). A thought-provoking introduction to international trade and the ways in which consumers can encourage fair trade practices,

Marketing and Advertising

11248 Graydon, Shari. *Made You Look: How Advertising Works and Why You Should Know* (5–9). Illus. by Warren Clark. 2003, Annick $24.95 (978-1-55037-815-3); paper $14.95 (978-1-55037-814-6). The 8- to 14-year-old age group is an advertising target, and this title teaches readers to recognize the various techniques used and to assess products' value. (Rev: BL 12/1/03*; SLJ 12/03) [659.1]

11249 Green, Jen. *Advertising* (8–11). Illus. Series: Ethical Debates. 2012, Rosen LB $27.95 (978-144886018-0). This volume takes a balanced look at the business of advertising in general with a focus on how ads work, the impact on society, and the various checks and controls that are in place. (Rev: BL 5/1/12) [659.1]

Guidance and Personal Development

Education and Schools

General and Miscellaneous

11250 Armstrong, Thomas. *You're Smarter Than You Think: A Kid's Guide to Multiple Intelligences* (5–8). 2003, Free Spirit paper $15.95 (978-1-57542-113-1). Eight different intelligences are defined in understandable terms, with quizzes that help readers investigate their own strengths. (Rev: BL 4/15/03; SLJ 6/03; VOYA 6/03) [153.9]

11251 Bluestein, Jane, and Eric D. Katz. *High School's Not Forever* (8–12). 2005, Health Communications paper $12.95 (978-0-7573-0256-5). High school students talk about their experiences in high school, covering a range of typical problems plus some of the joys of those years. (Rev: SLJ 1/06) [373.18]

11252 Farrell, Juliana, and Beth Mayall. *Middle School: The Real Deal* (5–7). 2001, HarperCollins paper $7.99 (978-0-380-81313-1). Advice on coping with school work, teachers, and social life is presented in an appealing format. (Rev: BL 6/1–15/01; VOYA 8/01) [373.18]

11253 Greene, Rebecca. *The Teenagers' Guide to School Outside the Box* (8–12). 2000, Free Spirit paper $15.95 (978-1-57542-087-5). Many learning opportunities are available to teens, including travel, volunteer work, serving as an intern or apprentice, mentoring, and job shadowing. (Rev: BL 2/15/01; SLJ 3/01; VOYA 4/01) [373.2]

11254 Hughes, Susan. *Off to Class: Incredible and Unusual Schools Around the World* (3–7). Illus. 2011, OwlKids $12.95 (978-1-926818-85-6). A fascinating look at schools ranging from tent schools in Haiti to schools in caves in China, boat schools, e-mail schools, and more. (Rev: BL 11/1/11; SLJ 9/1/11) [371]

11255 Hurwitz, Sue. *High Performance Through Effective Scheduling* (8–12). Series: Learning-a-Living Library. 1996, Rosen LB $27.95 (978-0-8239-2204-8). This book discusses the basic skill of scheduling time and how it helps students at school, in extracurricular activities, and on the job. (Rev: BL 8/96; SLJ 12/96; VOYA 2/97) [640]

11256 Schneider, Meg. *Help! My Teacher Hates Me* (5–8). 1994, Workman paper $7.95 (978-1-56305-492-1). Helpful hints for developing a positive attitude in school. (Rev: BL 3/15/95) [371.8]

11257 Williams, Heidi. *Homeschooling* (7–10). Series: At Issue: Education. 2007, Gale LB $29.95 (978-0-7377-3685-4); paper $21.20 (978-0-7377-3686-1). The controversial practice of homeschooling is examined in 13 articles that look at both sides of such questions as academic worth and the possibility of government involvement. (Rev: BL 3/3/08) [370.04]

Development of Academic Skills

Study Skills

11258 Greenberg, Michael. *Painless Study Techniques* (6–12). Illus. by Michele Earle-Bridges. 2009, Barron's paper $9.99 (978-0-7641-4059-4). Pop culture references will draw students into this guide that teaches skills in all aspects of study organization, including note taking, creating outlines, time management, and effective studying (includes charts and lists of Web sites). (Rev: SLJ 9/09)

Tests and Test Taking

11259 Kern, Roy, and Richard Smith. *The Grade Booster Guide for Kids* (7–9). 1987, Thomas paper $7.95 (978-0-944162-00-2). This book covers the proper strategies and techniques to use for successful test-taking. [371.3]

Writing and Speaking Skills

11260 Asher, Sandy. *Where Do You Get Your Ideas? Helping Young Writers Begin* (5–7). 1987, Walker LB $13.85 (978-0-8027-6691-5). Keeping a journal and other interesting ideas for would-be journalists. (Rev: BCCB 12/87; BL 9/15/87; SLJ 9/87) [808.02]

11261 Bauer, Marion Dane. *What's Your Story? A Young Person's Guide to Writing Fiction* (5–10). 1992, Clarion paper $7.95 (978-0-395-57780-6). An award-winning writer gives advice to young authors, including suggestions for planning, writing, and revising. (Rev: BL 4/15/92; SLJ 6/92*) [808.3]

11262 Bauer, Marion Dane. *A Writer's Story from Life to Fiction* (5–8). 1995, Clarion $14.95 (978-0-395-72094-3); paper $6.95 (978-0-395-75053-7). Readers and aspiring writers will enjoy this famous author's explanations of how she draws on her own experiences to develop her works. (Rev: BL 9/15/95; SLJ 10/95; VOYA 2/96) [813]

11263 Bentley, Nancy, and Donna Guthrie. *Writing Mysteries, Movies, Monster Stories, and More* (5–8). 2001, Millbrook LB $24.90 (978-0-7613-1452-3). This book gives solid information on all kinds of fictional writing, including novels, short stories, fantasy, science fiction, humor, and even movie scripts. (Rev: BL 3/15/01; HBG 10/01; SLJ 4/01; VOYA 8/01) [808]

11264 Betz, Adrienne, comp. *Scholastic Treasury of Quotations for Children* (4–8). 1998, Scholastic paper $16.95 (978-0-590-27146-2). From Socrates to Bill Clinton, this is a useful compendium of quotations arranged under 75 subjects. (Rev: SLJ 2/99) [080]

11265 Block, Francesca Lia, and Hillary Carlip. *Zine Scene: The Do-It-Yourself Guide to Zines* (8–12). 1998, Girl paper $14.95 (978-0-9659754-3-8). This is a step-by-step guide to producing one's own magazine, from getting started and writing to layout, production, and marketing. (Rev: VOYA 8/99) [808]

11266 Bodart, Joni Richards. *The World's Best Thin Books: What to Read When Your Book Report Is Due Tomorrow* (6–12). 2000, Scarecrow paper $16.95 (978-1-57886-007-4). For each of the books listed, the author provides background material, themes, characters, and possible book talk or book report ideas. (Rev: BL 1/1–15/00) [028.1]

11267 Cibula, Matt. *How to Be the Greatest Writer in the World* (4–8). Illus. by Brian Strassburg. 1999, Zino $11.95 (978-1-55933-276-7). A spiral-bound book that presents 88 interesting and engaging exercises to help youngsters who feel they have nothing to write about. (Rev: SLJ 2/00) [808]

11268 Craig, Steve. *Sports Writing: A Beginner's Guide* (6–12). 2002, Discover Writing paper $15.00 (978-0-9656574-9-5). A fine introduction to writing news and features about sports, to conducting good interviews, and to the training of journalists. (Rev: BL 9/1/02; VOYA 4/03) [070.449]

11269 Detz, Joan. *You Mean I Have to Stand Up and Say Something?* (7–12). 1986, Macmillan LB $13.95 (978-0-689-31221-2). An entertaining guide to effective speaking and overcoming the fear of facing an audience. (Rev: BCCB 2/87; BL 2/87; SLJ 3/87) [808.5]

11270 Dubrovin, Vivian. *Storytelling Adventures: Stories Kids Can Tell* (4–7). Illus. by Bobbi Shupe. 1997, Storycraft paper $14.95 (978-0-9638339-2-1). This book not only includes a selection of stories to tell but also suggests appropriate props to use, with directions on how to make them. (Rev: SLJ 5/97) [808.5]

11271 Dubrovin, Vivian. *Storytelling for the Fun of It* (4–8). Illus. by Bobbi Shupe. 1994, Storycraft paper $16.95 (978-0-9638339-0-7). This useful guide is divided into three parts that give general information, where and what kinds of stories to tell, and how to learn and perform them. (Rev: SLJ 4/94) [808.5]

11272 Estepa, Andrea, and Philip Kay, eds. *Starting with "I": Personal Essays by Teenagers* (7–12). 1997, Persea paper $13.95 (978-0-89255-228-3). This is a collection of 35 brief essays written by teenagers about their families, neighborhoods, race, and culture. (Rev: BL 9/15/97; SLJ 10/97; VOYA 10/97) [305.235]

11273 Fletcher, Ralph. *How to Write Your Life Story* (5–8). 2007, HarperCollins $15.99 (978-0-06-050770-1); paper $5.99 (978-0-06-050769-5). Writing exercises and examples will help readers to get started on autobiographies or memoirs. (Rev: BL 10/1/07; SLJ 11/07)

11274 Fletcher, Ralph. *How Writers Work: Finding a Process That Works for You* (4–8). 2000, HarperTrophy paper $4.99 (978-0-380-79702-8). Using a conversational style, the author explains the process of writing with material on brainstorming, rough drafts, revising, proofreading, and publishing. (Rev: SLJ 12/00) [808]

11275 Fletcher, Ralph. *Poetry Matters: Writing a Poem from the Inside Out* (4–7). 2002, HarperTrophy paper $5.99 (978-0-380-79703-5). A how-to book for young poets, with ideas on how to make images and "music" with words. (Rev: BL 5/15/02; HBG 10/02; SLJ 2/02*) [808.1]

11276 Fogarty, Mignon. *Grammar Girl Presents the Ultimate Writing Guide for Students* (7–10). Illus. by Erwin Haya. 2011, Henry Holt $19.99 (978-0-8050-8943-1); paper $12.99 (978-0-8050-8-944-8). Covering parts of speech, sentence structure, punctuation, usage, and improving writing in general, this appealing guide includes mnemonics, pop quizzes, and cartoon illustrations. **e** Lexile 960L (Rev: BL 7/11; LMC 10/11; SLJ 6/11) [428.2]

11277 Friedman, Lauri S. *Self-Mutilation* (7–10). Illus. Series: Writing the Critical Essay: An Opposing Viewpoints Guide. 2008, Gale/Greenhaven $29.95 (978-073774266-4). After presenting six perspectives on various forms of self-mutilation (including plastic surgery and body art), this volume provides sample essays and exercises that help the student to create thoughtful, well-researched theses. (Rev: BLO 2/17/09) [616.85]

11278 Friedman, Lauri S., ed. *Racism* (7–12). Series: Writing the Critical Essay. 2006, Gale LB $26.20 (978-0-7377-3464-5). Essays on racism that originally appeared in an Opposing Viewpoints volume help students research, draft, and edit effective papers on this topic. (Rev: SLJ 9/06)

11279 Gaines, Ann Graham. *Don't Steal Copyrighted Stuff!* (5–10). 2008, Enslow LB $28.95 (978-0-7660-2861-6). Students who don't see the harm in cutting and pasting from the Internet will discover that plagiarism can ruin reputations and careers; the story of a writer who got caught brings this truth home, and there are plenty of practical tips on keeping one's work original. (Rev: BL 4/1/08; LMC 3/08) [808]

11280 Graham, Paula W. *Speaking of Journals: Children's Book Writers Talk About Their Diaries, Notebooks and Sketchbooks* (5–8). 1999, Boyds Mills paper $14.95 (978-1-56397-741-1). A book that discusses the how-tos and the rewards of keeping a personal journal, and features interviews with 27 writers including Jim Arnosky, Pam Conrad, and Jean George. (Rev: BL 3/1/99; SLJ 5/99; VOYA 2/00) [818]

11281 Hambleton, Vicki, and Cathleen Greenwood. *So, You Wanna Be a Writer? How to Write, Get Published, and Maybe Even Make It Big!* (5–9). Illus. by Laura Eldridge and Corey Mistretta. Series: So, You Wanna Be. 2001, Beyond Words paper $8.95 (978-1-58270-043-4). Practical advice is offered in straightforward text with lots of examples, sample letters, interviews with published writers, details of writing contests, and lists of magazines that accept submissions from young writers. (Rev: SLJ 10/01; VOYA 2/02) [808]

11282 Hamilton, Fran Santoro. *Hands-On English* (4–8). 1998, Portico paper $9.95 (978-0-9664867-0-4). A user-friendly volume that takes a visual approach to illustrate sentence patterns, such as using icons to represent the eight parts of speech, with clear, interesting explanations. Also included are irregular verbs, using modifiers, spelling rules, punctuation and capitalization, homonyms, and how to make outlines. (Rev: SLJ 2/99; VOYA 4/99) [415]

11283 Hamilton, Martha, and Mitch Weiss. *Stories in My Pocket: Tales Kids Can Tell* (4–7). 1997, Fulcrum paper $15.95 (978-1-55591-957-3). This handbook of storytelling for young storytellers includes 30 tales to begin with. (Rev: BL 1/1–15/97) [372.6]

11284 Hamlett, Christina. *Screenwriting for Teens: The 100 Principles of Screenwriting Every Budding Writer Must Know* (8–12). 2006, Michael Wiese paper $18.95 (978-1-932907-18-6). Practical, friendly advice for screenwriting wannabes. (Rev: SLJ 2/07)

11285 James, Elizabeth, and Carol Barkin. *How to Write a Term Paper* (7–12). 1980, Lothrop paper $3.95 (978-0-688-45025-0). A practical step-by-step approach to report writing that uses many examples. [808]

11286 Janeczko, Paul B, comp. *Poetry from A to Z: A Guide for Young Writers* (4–8). Series: NetGuide. 1994, Simon & Schuster $16.95 (978-0-02-747672-9). This book of 72 poems, alphabetized by topic, gives examples to get young writers started, and the 23 poets represented give advice on how to become a better poet. (Rev: BCCB 3/95; BL 12/15/94; VOYA 5/95) [808.1]

11287 Janeczko, Paul B., ed. *Seeing the Blue Between: Advice and Inspiration for Young Poets* (7–10). 2002, Candlewick $17.99 (978-0-7636-0881-1). More than 30 poets who write for young people give advice on writing, reading, and simply enjoying poetry, with selected poems and biographical information. (Rev: BL 3/15/02; HB 7–8/02; HBG 10/02; SLJ 5/02; VOYA 6/02) [811]

11288 Mlynowski, Sarah, and Farrin Jacobs. *See Jane Write: A Girl's Guide to Writing Chick Lit* (8–12). Illus. by Chuck Gonzalez. 2006, Quirk paper $14.95 (978-1-59474-115-9). Girls who love "chick lit" and who want to take advantage of its popularity will enjoy this practical and readable guide. (Rev: SLJ 9/06)

11289 Myers, Walter Dean. *Just Write: Here's How* (8–12). 2012, HarperCollins $17.99 (978-0-06-220389-2); paper $7.99 (978-0-06-220-390-8). With examples from his own work, Myers offers practical advice on writing both fiction and nonfiction. e (Rev: BL 6/12; SLJ 7/12) [808.02]

11290 Nobleman, Marc Tyler. *Extraordinary E-Mails, Letters, and Resumes* (5–8). Illus. by Kevin Pope. Series: F. W. Prep. 2005, Watts LB $31.00 (978-0-531-16759-5). Advice for students who want to write effective e-mails, letters, and resumés, with an explanation of the importance of communicating clearly. (Rev: SLJ 1/06) [808]

11291 Otfinoski, Steven. *Speaking Up, Speaking Out: A Kid's Guide to Making Speeches, Oral Reports, and Conversation* (5–8). 1996, Millbrook LB $24.90 (978-1-56294-345-5). All kinds of public-speaking situations are introduced, with suggestions on how to be a success at each. (Rev: BL 1/1–15/97; SLJ 1/97) [808.5]

11292 Rosinsky, Natalie M. *Write Your Own Biography* (4–8). Series: Write Your Own. 2007, Compass Point LB $31.93 (978-0-7565-3366-3). A helpful guide to writing a biography with excerpts from published works and writing exercises. (Rev: SLJ 12/07) [808]

11293 Sullivan, Helen, and Linda Sernoff. *Research Reports: A Guide for Middle and High School Students* (6–10). 1996, Millbrook LB $24.90 (978-1-56294-694-4). A well-organized, concise book on writing reports that covers each step from selecting a topic to compiling the final bibliography. (Rev: SLJ 9/96) [372.6]

11294 Veljkovic, Peggy, and Arthur Schwartz, eds. *Writing from the Heart: Young People Share Their Wisdom* (5–9). 2001, Templeton Foundation paper $12.95 (978-1-890151-48-5). A collection of the best essays by young people that have been submitted to the Laws of Life program since it began in 1987. (Rev: SLJ 6/01) [170]

11295 Vinton, Ken. *Alphabet Antics: Hundreds of Activities to Challenge and Enrich Letter Learners of All Ages* (5–8). Illus. by author. 1996, Free Spirit paper $19.95 (978-0-915793-98-3). For each letter of the alphabet, there is a history, how it appears in different alphabets, important words that begin with that letter, a quotation from someone whose name starts with it, and a number of interesting related projects. (Rev: SLJ 1/97) [411]

11296 Waldo, Dixie. *Persuasive Speaking* (6–10). 2007, Rosen LB $19.95 (978-1-4042-1028-8). Tips for debaters will also be helpful to teams and individuals who speak in front of groups. (Rev: BL 4/1/07) [808.5]

11297 Williams, Heidi, ed. *Plagiarism* (8–12). Series: Issues That Concern You. 2008, Gale/Greenhaven $33.70 (978-0-7377-4072-1). Twelve essays address the problem of plagiarism from various perspectives, discussing in particular the temptations of new technology and the services available to prevent plagiarism. (Rev: SLJ 2/1/09) [808]

11298 Williams, Mary E. *Global Warming* (7–12). Series: Writing the Critical Essay. 2006, Gale LB $26.20 (978-0-7377-3210-8). Essays on global warming are presented along with questions to encourage students to evaluate their effectiveness; instructions for researching and editing a persuasive essay are included too. (Rev: SLJ 10/06)

11299 Wooldridge, Susan Goldsmith. *Poemcrazy: Freeing Your Life with Words* (6–12). 1996, Clarkson Potter paper $13.00 (978-0-609-80098-0). The author tries to show young people how to free their minds and spirits to write poetry and shares her own poetic experiences and inspirations as well as those of other poets. (Rev: VOYA 12/97) [811]

11300 Young, Sue. *Writing with Style* (5–8). Series: Scholastic Guides. 1997, Scholastic $12.95 (978-0-590-50977-0). A guide for the novice writer, with chapters on planning, presenting, and publishing one's work. (Rev: BL 3/1/97; SLJ 5/97) [372.6]

Academic Guidance

General and Miscellaneous

11301 Lieberman, Susan A. *The Real High School Handbook: How to Survive, Thrive, and Prepare for What's Next* (8–12). 1997, Houghton Mifflin paper $13.00 (978-0-395-79760-0). A book of tips about prospering in high school and making it enjoyable, with material on topics including grade points, testing, course selection, and getting into a college. (Rev: BL 10/15/97) [373.18]

Colleges and Universities

11302 Funk, Gary. *A Balancing Act: Sports and Education* (5–8). Series: Sports Issues. 1995, Lerner LB $28.75 (978-0-8225-3301-6). A frank, thorough discussion of the many issues involved in sports and their place in educational institutions. (Rev: BL 1/1–15/96; SLJ 9/95) [796.04]

Scholarships and Financial Aid

11303 Karnes, Frances A., and Tracy L. Riley. *Competitions for Talented Kids: Win Scholarships, Big Prize Money, and Recognition* (7–10). 2005, Prufrock paper $17.95 (978-1-59363-156-7). More than 140 competitions covering a number of academic subjects, the performing arts, and leadership are listed alphabetically, with brief advice on entering these contests. (Rev: BL 12/1/05) [371.95]

11304 Minnis, Whitney. *How to Get an Athletic Scholarship: A Student-Athlete's Guide to Collegiate Athletics* (6–12). 1995, ASI paper $12.95 (978-0-9645153-0-7). Basic information on athletic scholarships and the recruitment process, plus tips on training and academic considerations. (Rev: BL 2/1/96) [796]

Careers and Occupational Guidance

General and Miscellaneous

11305 McGlothlin, Bruce. *High Performance Through Understanding Systems* (7–10). Series: Learning-a-Living Library. 1996, Rosen LB $27.95 (978-0-8239-2210-9). Aimed primarily at youths preparing to enter the world of work directly after graduation, this book explains systems ("any combination of elements that operate together and form a whole") in the family, at school, and at work, and tells how individuals can diagnose problems, predict outcomes, and improve the systems. (Rev: SLJ 3/97) [001.6]

11306 Reber, Deborah. *In Their Shoes: Extraordinary Women Describe Their Amazing Careers* (8–12). Series: The Real Deal. 2007, Simon & Schuster paper $12.99 (978-1-4169-2578-1). Girls will be inspired to pursue any career they want to after reading these accounts of women and the jobs they love, from sheriff to librarian, and their daily tasks. (Rev: BL 4/1/07; LMC 8–9/07; SLJ 5/07*) [331.4092]

11307 Strazzabosco, Jeanne M. *High Performance Through Dealing with Diversity* (8–12). Series: Learning-a-Living Library. 1996, Rosen LB $27.95 (978-0-8239-2202-4). Through applying attitudes of tolerance and positive feelings, this book prepares students to work with diverse populations in a multicultural workplace. (Rev: BL 8/96) [650.1]

Careers

General and Miscellaneous

11308 *Activism* (7–12). Illus. Series: Careers in Focus. 2011, Ferguson LB $32.95 (978-081608029-8). From environmental activists to lobbyists and elder law at-

torneys, this is a useful guide to careers in this field and the education and training required. (Rev: BL 12/15/11) [322.4023]

11309 Alagna, Magdalena. *War Correspondents: Life Under Fire* (5–10). Series: Extreme Careers. 2003, Rosen LB $26.50 (978-0-8239-3798-1). The dangers of wartime assignments are emphasized in this volume that also stresses job requirements that include a good education and broad knowledge of world events. (Rev: BL 9/15/03; SLJ 11/03) [808]

11310 *Archaeology* (7–10). Illus. Series: Careers in Focus. 2010, Ferguson $32.95 (978-081608022-9). Covering 19 professions — from anthropologists, historians, and museum curators to underwater archaeologists and writers and editors — this is a thorough survey of job opportunities in this diverse field. (Rev: BL 4/15/11) [930.1023]

11311 Brezina, Corona. *Jobs in Sustainable Energy* (7–10). Series: Green Careers. 2010, Rosen LB $30.60 (978-1-4358-3569-6). Following an overview of the field, this well-organized book looks at jobs in various sectors (solar, wind, geothermal, and so forth) and explains the necessary education and training and the job prospects and salaries. (Rev: LMC 10/10; SLJ 8/10) [621.042]

11312 *Broadcasting. 2nd ed.* (7–12). Series: Careers in Focus. 2002, Ferguson LB $22.95 (978-0-89434-440-4). Careers in animation, lighting, reporting, editing, and weather forecasting are just a few of those covered in this concise introduction to the world of broadcasting and its educational requirements, employment outlook, and potential salaries. Also use *Fashion* (2002). (Rev: SLJ 7/01) [384.54]

11313 Burns, Monique. *Cool Careers Without College for People Who Love to Make Things Grow* (6–9). Series: Cool Careers Without College. 2004, Rosen LB $33.25 (978-0-8239-3789-9). Explores careers such as landscaper and soil conservationist that do not require college degrees, with application advice and information about activities on the job. (Rev: SLJ 10/04)

11314 Byers, Ann. *Jobs as Green Builders and Planners* (7–10). Series: Green Careers. 2010, Rosen LB $30.60 (978-1-4358-3566-5). This well-organized book looks at the kinds of jobs available and explains the necessary education and training and the job prospects and salaries. Part of a series that covers other "green" careers in law, tourism, and cleanup of hazardous spills. (Rev: LMC 10/10; SLJ 8/10) [690.023]

11315 Camelo, Wilson. *The U.S. Air Force and Military Careers* (7–10). Series: U.S. Armed Forces and Military Careers. 2006, Enslow LB $23.95 (978-0-7660-2524-0). Traces the history of the U.S. Air Force, its structure, its contributions to U.S. defense and major wars, recent operations, and the various career opportunities within the organization. (Rev: BL 10/15/06) [358.400973]

11316 Coon, Nora E. *Teen Dream Jobs: How to Find the Job You Really Want Now!* (8–12). 2004, Beyond Words paper $9.95 (978-1-58270-093-9). Written by a teen, this is a reader-friendly guide that refers teens to online career-choice quizzes, gives advice on job-finding activities, and suggests possible careers and ways to enter them. (Rev: SLJ 6/04)

11317 Devantier, Alecia T., and Carol A. Turkington. *Extraordinary Jobs for Adventurers* (8–12). 2006, Ferguson $35 (978-0-8160-5852-5). Careers for the adventurous are found in fields including logging, vulcanology, and white-water rafting, according to this guide that gives worker profiles. Also use *Extraordinary Jobs for Creative People* and *Extraordinary Jobs in Agriculture and Nature* (both 2006). (Rev: SLJ 1/07)

11318 Dolan, Edward F. *Careers in the U.S. Air Force* (5–8). Series: Military Service. 2009, Marshall Cavendish $24.95 (978-0-7614-4205-9). This straightforward guide to the U.S. Air Force covers everything from training to joining requirements to salary; part of a recommended series that covers other branches of service. (Rev: BL 10/1/09; SLJ 3/10) [358.40023]

11319 *Fashion* (5–10). Illus. Series: Discovering Careers. 2011, Ferguson LB $24.95 (978-081608056-4). With information on education and training, earnings potential, and so forth, this volume explores the work of everyone from fashion models and writers to retail sales workers and merchandise displayers. (Rev: BL 5/1/12) [746.9]

11320 Flath, Camden. *Freelance and Technical Writers: Words for Sale* (7–10). Illus. Series: The New Careers for the 21st Century: Find Your Role in the Global Renewal. 2010, Mason Crest $22.95 (978-142222035-1); paper $9.95 (978-14222181-4-3). The ins and outs of being a freelance writer are described in this straightforward guide for students thinking about their place in the future workplace. (Rev: BL 10/1/10) [808]

11321 *Food* (5–10). Illus. Series: Discovering Careers. 2012, Ferguson LB $30 (978-081608057-1). With information on education and training, earnings potential, and so forth, this volume explores the work of everyone involved in the field, from farmers to chefs. (Rev: BL 5/1/12) [647.95023]

11322 Frydenborg, Kay. *They Dreamed of Horses: Careers for Horse Lovers* (6–9). 1994, Walker LB $16.85 (978-0-8027-8284-7). Suggests career possibilities that involve working with horses, telling the stories of 13 women who love and work with them. (Rev: BL 7/94; SLJ 7/94; VOYA 8/94) [636.1]

11323 Giacobello, John. *Careers in the Fashion Industry* (7–12). Series: Exploring Careers. 1999, Rosen LB $18.95 (978-0-8239-2890-3). This book explains what it takes to get started in a variety of fashion-related careers, and includes tips on writing résumés, interviewing, and so forth. (Rev: SLJ 2/00) [746.9]

11324 Hayhurst, Chris. *Cool Careers Without College for Animal Lovers* (7–12). Series: Cool Careers Without College. 2002, Rosen LB $33.25 (978-0-8239-3500-0). Veterinary technician, groomer, and pet photographer are some of the options explored in this book that gives information on training and on-the-job activities. (Rev: BL 5/15/02; SLJ 7/02) [636]

11325 Heos, Bridget. *A Career as a Hairstylist* (7–12). Illus. Series: Essential Careers. 2010, Rosen LB $30.60 (978-143589474-7). This comprehensive guide to becoming a hairstylist covers everything from training and business plans to ethics and the history of the trade. (Rev: BL 10/1/10; VOYA 2/11) [646.7]

11326 Jackson, Donna M. *ER Vets: Life in an Animal Emergency Room* (5–8). 2005, Houghton Mifflin $17.00 (978-0-618-43663-7). With many photos, this is a behind-the-scenes look at life in a veterinary emergency clinic and the frustrations and joys to be found working there. (Rev: BL 11/1/05; SLJ 1/06*) [636.089]

11327 Lee, Barbara. *Working with Animals* (4–8). Series: Exploring Careers. 1996, Lerner LB $23.93 (978-0-8225-1759-7). Profiles of 12 careers involving animals, such as veterinarian, animal shelter worker, or pet sitter. (Rev: BL 2/15/97) [591]

11328 McAlpine, Margaret. *Working in the Fashion Industry* (6–12). Series: My Future Career. 2005, Gareth Stevens LB $27.00 (978-0-8368-4774-1). Seven careers in the field of fashion are highlighted with plenty of good photographs, explanations of a typical day's activities, and "Good Points and Bad Points." (Rev: SLJ 1/06)

11329 McAlpine, Margaret. *Working in the Food Industry* (6–12). Series: My Future Career. 2005, Gareth Stevens LB $27.00 (978-0-8368-4776-5). Seven careers in the food industry are highlighted with plenty of good photographs, explanations of a typical day's activities, and "Good Points and Bad Points." (Rev: SLJ 1/06)

11330 McAlpine, Margaret. *Working with Animals* (6–10). Series: My Future Career. 2005, Gareth Stevens LB $27.00 (978-0-8368-4240-1). In addition to describing various jobs working with animals, McAlpine discusses the best personality type for each task and provides a detailed breakdown of a typical day. (Rev: SLJ 3/05) [636]

11331 McAlpine, Margaret. *Working with Children* (6–10). Series: My Future Career. 2005, Gareth Stevens LB $27.00 (978-0-8368-4241-8). In addition to describing various jobs working with children, McAlpine discusses the best personality type for each one and provides a detailed breakdown of a typical day. (Rev: SLJ 3/05) [362.7]

11332 Nelson, Corinna. *Working in the Environment* (6–8). Series: Exploring Careers. 1999, Lerner LB $23.93 (978-0-8225-1763-4). A recycling manager, a fisheries technician, and a nonprofit organization director are among the 12 people profiled in this title that describes the wide range of jobs related to the environment. (Rev: BL 7/99; SLJ 10/99) [363.7]

11333 Ollhoff, Jim. *Hazmat* (5–8). Illus. Series: Emergency Workers. 2012, ABDO LB $27.07 (978-161783514-8). Describes the nine classes of hazardous materials and the training and equipment of the technicians who work to clean them up; includes an interview with a hazmat technician and a glossary. (Rev: BL 10/1/12) [363.17]

11334 *Organization Skills* (8–12). Series: Career Skills Library. 2009, Ferguson $25.95 (978-0-8160-7774-8). Time management, avoiding procrastination, and organization of materials and schedules are emphasized in this easy-to-read book that includes quizzes and exercises. (Rev: LMC 3–4/10) [650.1]

11335 Owen, Ruth. *Building Green Places: Careers in Planning, Designing, and Building* (5–8). Illus. Series: Green-Collar Careers. 2011, Crabtree LB $31.93 (978-077874852-6). Looks at careers that involve designing and constructing eco-friendly buildings, cities, and parks. (Rev: BL 2/15/12) [720]

11336 Pasternak, Ceel. *Cool Careers for Girls with Animals* (5–8). Series: Cool Careers for Girls. 1998, Impact $19.95 (978-1-57023-108-7); paper $12.95 (978-1-57023-105-6). Veterinarian, pet sitter, bird handler, animal trainer, and horse-farm owner are among the careers covered, supplemented by interviews with women who work in each field. (Rev: SLJ 4/99; VOYA 8/99) [371.7]

11337 Pasternak, Ceel, and Linda Thornburg. *Cool Careers for Girls in Air and Space* (6–12). Series: Cool Careers for Girls. 2001, Impact LB $12.95 (978-1-57023-147-6); paper $12.95 (978-1-57023-146-9). This account discusses various careers open to women in the aircraft and space industries with information on qualifications, working conditions, and compensation. (Rev: BL 4/15/01; SLJ 4/01) [629]

11338 Pasternak, Ceel, and Linda Thornburg. *Cool Careers for Girls in Food* (5–10). Series: Cool Careers for Girls. 2000, Impact $19.95 (978-1-57023-127-8); paper $12.95 (978-1-57023-120-9). The 11 women featured in this book are involved in various aspects of the food industry such as cheese making, baking, wine making, selling health food, and cooking for the military. (Rev: SLJ 2/00) [641]

11339 *Publishing* (5–9). Series: Discovering Careers for Your Future. 2005, Ferguson LB $21.95 (978-0-8160-5845-7). Education and training, salaries, and outlook for the field are all covered here along with a description of the kinds of daily activities found in various positions. (Rev: SLJ 1/06)

11340 Rauf, Don, and Monique Vescia. *Computer Game Designer* (6–9). Series: Virtual Apprentice. 2008, Ferguson LB $29.95 (978-0-8160-6754-1). Is it possible to make a living playing games? Yes, if you are a computer game designer. This book describes what game creators do and how they got where they are. (Rev: BL 4/1/08) [794.8]

11341 Reeves, Diane Lindsey. *Career Ideas for Kids Who Like Art* (5–9). Series: Career Ideas for Kids Who Like. 1998, Facts on File $23.00 (978-0-8160-3681-3). An upbeat book that explores a variety of art-related careers, including many peripheral ones such as chef, animator, and photojournalist, with suggestions on how to test one's suitability for each area and reports from people working in the field. (Rev: SLJ 10/98; VOYA 8/98) [791]

11342 Reeves, Diane Lindsey. *Career Ideas for Kids Who Like Talking* (5–9). Illus. by Nancy Bond. Series: Career Ideas for Kids. 1998, Facts on File $23.00 (978-0-8160-3683-7); paper $12.95 (978-0-8160-3689-9). This is a guide to careers in communications, from hotel manager to publicist to broadcaster, with reports from people in the field, tests to check one's aptitude, and lists of resources. (Rev: SLJ 10/98) [331.7]

11343 Reeves, Diane Lindsey, and Gail Karlitz. *Career Ideas for Teens in Architecture and Construction* (8–12). Series: Career Ideas for Teens. 2005, Ferguson $40.00 (978-0-8160-5289-9). In addition to details of education requirements, salaries, and so forth, this attractive guide offers interview tips, advice from "real people," and questionnaires. (Rev: SLJ 2/06)

11344 Reeves, Diane Lindsey, and Gayle Bryan. *Career Ideas for Kids Who Like Travel* (6–10). Series: Career Ideas for Kids. 2001, Checkmark $23.00 (978-0-8160-4325-5); paper $12.95 (978-0-8160-4326-2). A number of careers in the travel industry are presented with coverage of qualifications, training, rewards, and working conditions. (Rev: BL 3/15/02; HBG 10/02) [331.7]

11345 Rosenberg, Aaron. *Cryptologists: Life Making and Breaking Codes* (5–10). Series: Extreme Careers. 2004, Rosen LB $26.50 (978-0-8239-3965-7). After some background material on the history of codes, this volume discusses career opportunities as a cryptologist. (Rev: BL 5/15/04; SLJ 5/90) [410]

11346 Scott, Jennifer Power. *Green Career$: You Can Make Money and Save the Planet* (8–12). 2010, Lobster paper $16.95 (978-1-897550-18-2). Students whose interests range from farming to architecture will find that they can use their talents in environmentally friendly ways. (Rev: BL 2/15/10; LMC 8–9/10; SLJ 4/10) [333.72]

11347 *Teamwork Skills* (7–12). Series: Career Skills Library. 2009, Ferguson $25.95 (978-0-8160-7771-7). The importance of working as a team and solving conflicts are emphasized in this easy-to-read book that includes quizzes and exercises. (Rev: LMC 3–4/10) [658.4022]

11348 *The Teen Vogue Handbook: An Insider's Guide to Careers in Fashion* (7–12). 2009, Penguin paper $24.95 (978-1-59514-261-0). Full of profiles and advice from top fashion-industry movers and shakers, this book provides a practical, authoritative guide to breaking into a career in fashion. (Rev: SLJ 1/10; VOYA 12/09) [746.9]

11349 Thompson, Lisa. *Creating Cuisine: Have You Got What It Takes to Be a Chef?* (5–8). Series: On the Job. 2008, Compass Point LB $19.95 (978-0-7565-3625-1). An inside look at professional kitchens and the training to become a restaurant cook. (Rev: BL 4/1/08) [641.5092]

11350 Turner, Chérie. *Adventure Tour Guides: Life on Extreme Outdoor Adventures* (5–10). Series: Extreme Careers. 2003, Rosen LB $26.50 (978-0-8239-3793-6). A look at the profession of tour guiding on excursions such as white-water rafting and mountain climbing, with material on qualifications and future possibilities. (Rev: BL 9/15/03) [908]

11351 Vogt, Peter. *Career Opportunities in the Fashion Industry* (7–12). 2002, Facts on File $49.50 (978-0-8160-4616-4). More than 60 jobs in the fashion industry are described with details of daily activities, salary potential, necessary training, and future outlook. (Rev: SLJ 2/03) [746.9]

11352 Weiss, Ann E. *The Glass Ceiling: A Look at Women in the Workforce* (8–12). 1999, Twenty-First Century LB $23.90 (978-0-7613-1365-6). After a brief history of women's place in the world of work, this book focuses on recent changes and new opportunities (and dangers) for women in the workforce. (Rev: BL 6/1–15/99; SLJ 9/99) [331.4]

11353 Whynott, Douglas. *A Country Practice: Scenes from the Veterinary Life* (7–10). 2004, Farrar $24.00 (978-0-86547-647-9). Covering all aspects of veterinary practice — including finances, staff, and bedside manner — this is an intriguing account of a year in the life of a veterinarian who treats both domestic pets and farm animals. (Rev: BL 11/1/04) [636.089]

11354 Willett, Edward. *Careers in Outer Space: New Business Opportunities* (4–9). Series: The Career Resource Library. 2002, Rosen LB $31.95 (978-0-8239-3358-7). An interesting look at opportunities in the fields of science, math, engineering, technology, communication, and, of course, aeronautics, with information on required skills and training and on the pros and cons of working in the public and private sectors. (Rev: SLJ 6/02) [629.4]

11355 Wilson, Wayne. *Careers in Publishing and Communications* (8–12). Series: Latinos at Work. 2001, Mitchell Lane LB $22.95 (978-1-58415-088-6). This career guide for Latinos explores job opportunities for authors, copy editors, disc jockeys, artists, and agents, and includes personal interviews with successful Hispanic Americans in these fields. (Rev: BL 10/15/01; HBG 3/02) [808]

11356 Zannos, Susan. *Careers in Science and Medicine* (8–12). Series: Latinos at Work. 2001, Mitchell Lane LB $22.95 (978-1-58415-084-8). Descriptions of careers in these fields are accompanied by information on salary and qualifications as well as profiles of Latino men and women who have found success in a variety of career positions. (Rev: BL 10/15/01; HBG 3/02; SLJ 11/01) [502]

11357 Zannos, Susan. *Latino Entrepreneurs* (8–12). Series: Latinos at Work. 2001, Mitchell Lane LB $32.75 (978-1-58415-089-3). This book looks at the many possibilities for self-employment for Hispanics with personal interviews of successful Latinos in a variety of fields. (Rev: BL 3/15/02; HBG 10/02; SLJ 3/02) [650.1]

Arts, Entertainment, and Sports

11358 Amara, Philip. *So, You Wanna Be a Comic Book Artist?* (5–8). Illus. by Pop Mhan. 2001, Beyond Words paper $9.95 (978-1-58270-058-8). A comprehensive, engaging look at the world of comic-book illustration, with tips on everything from buying supplies to submitting work to publishers. (Rev: BL 1/1–15/02; SLJ 4/02) [808]

11359 Amara, Philip. *So, You Want to Be a Comic Book Artist? The Ultimate Guide on How to Break into Comics!* (6–9). Illus. 2012, Aladdin $16.99 (978-158270358-9). Provides advice on starting a studio, illustrating and creating characters, writing scripts, and submitting finished comics to publishers. (Rev: BL 11/1/12; LMC 1–2/13) [741.5]

11360 Apel, Melanie Ann. *Cool Careers Without College for Film and Television Buffs* (6–9). Series: Cool Careers Without College. 2002, Rosen LB $33.25 (978-0-8239-3501-7). A variety of options are presented for students interested in jobs in this sector, from actor and agent to grip, gaffer, makeup artist, animator, and puppeteer. (Rev: SLJ 7/02; VOYA 2/03) [331.7]

11361 *Art* (5–10). Illus. Series: Discovering Careers. 2011, Ferguson LB $24.95 (978-081608055-7). With information on education and training, earnings potential, this volume explores the work of everyone involved in the field, from art dealers, teachers, and curators to artists, cartoonists, graphic designers, and so forth. Also use *Movies* (2011). (Rev: BL 5/1/12) [700.23]

11362 *Art* (4–8). Series: Discovering Careers for Your Future. 2001, Ferguson LB $21.95 (978-0-89434-388-9). A useful introduction to career opportunities in art, with information on the skills required, potential earnings, and job outlook. (Rev: SLJ 11/01) [702.373]

11363 Croce, Nicholas. *Cool Careers without College for People Who Love Video Games* (6–12). Series: Cool Careers Without College. 2007, Rosen LB $33.25 (978-1-4042-0747-9). This is a well-organized book with detailed information about the careers available in the field of video games (writing, producing, marketing, for example). (Rev: SLJ 6/07)

11364 *Design. 2nd ed.* (7–12). Series: Careers in Focus. 2005, Ferguson $22.95 (978-0-8160-5865-5). Describes careers in the broad field of design — Including architects, fashion designers, exhibit designers, industrial designers, and toy and game designers. (Rev: SLJ 12/05)

11365 Hambleton, Vicki, and Cathleen Greenwood. *So, You Want to Be a Writer? How to Write, Get Published, and Maybe Even Make It Big!* (5–8). 2012, Beyond Words $17.99 (978-158270359-6); paper $9.99 (978-15827035-3-4). From "What's It Like to Be a Writer" to "How to Get Published: Creating a Proposal" and "Writing as a Career: You Mean I Can Get Paid for That?," this is a thorough overview of the writing process, covering all formats and genres and providing many examples. (Rev: BL 4/1/12; LMC 8–9/12) [808]

11366 Hofstetter, Adam B. *Cool Careers without College for People Who Love Sports* (6–12). Series: Cool Careers Without College. 2007, Rosen LB $33.25 (978-1-4042-0749-3). Scout, groundskeeper, official scorer, Zamboni driver — these are only a few of the sports careers detailed in this well-organized book. (Rev: SLJ 6/07) [796.023]

11367 Jay, Annie, and Luanne Feik. *Stars in Your Eyes . . . Feet on the Ground: A Practical Guide for Teenage Actors (and Their Parents!)* (7–12). 1999, Theatre Directories paper $16.95 (978-0-933919-42-6). A young actress gives practical advice on how to break into show business, including information on publicity photographs, auditions, managers, agents, publicity packages, résumés, and casting calls. (Rev: BL 6/1–15/99) [792.02]

11368 Johnson, Marlys H. *Careers in the Movies* (5–9). Series: Career Resource Library. 2001, Rosen LB $31.95 (978-0-8239-3186-6). Job descriptions and qualifications are clearly laid out in this guide for aspiring filmmakers that also discusses the history of the industry and the basic steps in film production. (Rev: SLJ 8/01) [791.43]

11369 Lee, Barbara. *Working in Sports and Recreation* (5–9). Series: Exploring Careers. 1996, Lerner LB $23.93 (978-0-8225-1762-7). Twelve people involved in careers related to sports and recreation talk candidly about their professions. (Rev: BL 2/15/97) [796]

11370 McAlpine, Margaret. *Working in Film and Television* (6–10). Series: My Future Career. 2005, Gareth Stevens LB $27.00 (978-0-8368-4237-1). In addition to describing various jobs in the film and television world, McAlpine discusses the best personality type for each one and provides a detailed breakdown of a typical day. (Rev: SLJ 3/05) [791.43]

11371 McAlpine, Margaret. *Working in Music and Dance* (6–12). Series: My Future Career. 2005, Gareth Stevens LB $27.00 (978-0-8368-4777-2). Seven careers in the fields of music and dance are highlighted with plenty of good photographs, explanations of a typical day's activities, and "Good Points and Bad Points." (Rev: SLJ 1/06)

11372 McLaglen, Mary. *You Can Be a Woman Movie Maker* (4–8). Series: You Can Be a Woman. 2003, Cascade Pass $19.95 (978-1-880599-64-8); paper $14.95 (978-1-880599-63-1). Three women — a producer, an independent filmmaker, and an executive producer — talk about their jobs, how they got into the movie industry, and what a day on the job is like. Interviews and film clips are on an accompanying DVD. (Rev: SLJ 4/04) [791.43]

11373 Marsico, Katie. *Choreographer* (4–7). Illus. Series: Cool Arts Careers. 2011, Cherry Lake $18.95 (978-161080136-2). Bright photos add appeal to this career guide, which gives readers a sense of what's required to be a professional choreographer. (Rev: BL 10/1/11) [792.82]

11374 Michael, Ted. *So You Wanna Be a Superstar? The Ultimate Audition Guide* (4–8). 2012, Running Press paper $10.95 (978-07624461-0-0). With personality quizzes, dance terms, and audition tips, this is a useful guide to breaking into the entertainment industry. (Rev: BL 12/1/12; SLJ 2/13) [808.8245]

11375 Nagle, Jeanne. *Careers in Coaching* (7–12). Series: Careers Library. 2000, Rosen LB $31.95 (978-0-8239-2966-5). This guide to how to become a successful coach covers all aspects of the job. (Rev: SLJ 7/00) [796]

11376 Nathan, Amy. *Meet the Musicians: From Prodigy (or Not) to Pro* (5–8). Illus. 2006, Henry Holt $17.95 (978-0-8050-7743-8). Profiles of members of the New York Philharmonic give readers a good understanding of the different roles of various instruments and the careers of professional musicians. (Rev: BL 3/15/06; SLJ 5/06; VOYA 6/06) [750.92]

11377 Nathan, Amy. *The Young Musician's Survival Guide: Tips from Teens and Pros* (5–8). 2000, Oxford $21.99 (978-0-19-512611-2). A thorough study of how to break into the music world, with information on working with music teachers, conductors, and peers, and tips on practicing, choosing an instrument, and handling fears and frustrations. (Rev: BL 4/1/00; HBG 10/00; SLJ 6/00) [780]

11378 Parks, Peggy J. *Musician* (4–7). Series: Exploring Careers. 2004, Gale LB $26.20 (978-0-7377-2067-9). In addition to a description of the work that musicians (including DJs) do, there is a frank assessment of the opportunities available. (Rev: BL 3/15/04) [780]

11379 Parks, Peggy J. *Writer* (4–7). Series: Exploring Careers. 2004, Gale LB $26.20 (978-0-7377-2069-3). The ups and downs of a career in writing are frankly discussed in this slim guide. (Rev: BL 3/15/04) [808]

11380 Pasternak, Ceel, and Linda Thornburg. *Cool Careers for Girls in Sports* (5–10). Series: Cool Careers for Girls. 1999, Impact $19.95 (978-1-57023-107-0); paper $12.95 (978-1-57023-104-9). A golf pro, basketball player, ski instructor, sports broadcaster, trainer, sports psychologist, and athletic director are among the 10 women profiled in this overview of careers for women in sports. (Rev: SLJ 7/99; VOYA 8/99) [796]

11381 *Radio and Television* (5–9). Series: Discovering Careers for Your Future. 2005, Ferguson LB $21.95 (978-0-8160-5846-4). Education and training, salaries, and outlook for the field are all covered here along with a description of the kinds of daily activities found in various positions. (Rev: SLJ 1/06)

11382 Sommers, Michael A. *Wildlife Photographers: Life Through a Lens* (5–10). Series: Extreme Careers. 2003, Rosen LB $26.50 (978-0-8239-3638-0). A concise explanation of the work of wildlife photographers, the attributes needed, and the training and tenacity required to enter this field. (Rev: BL 9/15/03; SLJ 5/03) [771]

11383 Svitil, Torene. *So You Want to Work in Animation and Special Effects?* (6–9). Series: Careers in Film and Television. 2007, Enslow LB $23.95 (978-0-7660-2737-4). A look at how special effects and animation are rendered today in comparison with days past (1933's *King Kong* is used as an example) is followed by information on the training required for this field. (Rev: BL 4/1/07; SLJ 8/07) [778.5]

11384 Sylvester, Kevin. *Game Day: Meet the People Who Make It Happen* (5–8). 2010, Annick $21.95 (978-1-55451-251-5); paper $12.95 (978-1-55451-250-8). Sylvester looks beyond the athletes to explore the roles of people behind the scenes of professional sports — a mechanic, a game scheduler, an umpire, a Zamboni driver, and so forth. **e** (Rev: BL 2/1/11; SLJ 1/1/11; VOYA 12/10) [796]

11385 Torres, John A., and Susan Zannos. *Careers in the Music Industry* (8–12). Series: Latinos at Work. 2001, Mitchell Lane LB $32.75 (978-1-58415-085-5). Along with personal interviews with Hispanics who did well in the music world, there are descriptions of such related careers as singers, songwriters, managers, and agents. (Rev: BL 3/15/02; HBG 10/02) [780]

11386 Weigant, Chris. *Careers as a Disc Jockey* (8–12). Series: Careers. 1997, Rosen LB $16.95 (978-0-8239-2528-5). This informative book gives many practical tips on how to get started and be successful in radio, with material on making demo tapes, applying for jobs and internships, and working oneself up. There are interviews with eight DJs. Careers in management, sales, technical areas, talk shows, and others are included. (Rev: SLJ 12/97; VOYA 2/98) [384.54]

11387 Wilson, Wayne. *Careers in Entertainment* (8–12). Series: Latinos at Work. 2001, Mitchell Lane LB $32.75 (978-1-58415-083-1). With an emphasis on Hispanic American success stories, this book features careers in film, television, and theater. (Rev: BL 10/15/01; HBG 3/02) [791]

Business

11388 *Advertising and Marketing* (5–9). Series: Discovering Careers for Your Future. 2005, Ferguson $21.95 (978-0-8160-5847-1). Education and training, salaries, and outlook for the field are all covered here along with a description of the kinds of daily activities found in various positions. (Rev: SLJ 1/06)

11389 Giles, M. J. *Young Adult's Guide to a Business Career* (8–12). 2004, Business Bks $14.95 (978-0-9723714-3-8). Full of useful tips, this guide describes more than 25 occupations in business and finance, giving details of benefits and drawbacks, salaries, educational requirements, and so forth. (Rev: SLJ 7/04) [331.7]

11390 Thomason-Carroll, Kristi L. *Young Adult's Guide to Business Communications* (8–12). 2004, Business Bks $14.95 (978-0-9723714-4-5). Full of useful tips, this guide describes the basics required for a job in the business world, including telephone skills, the ability to communicate clearly by letter and e-mail, and proper behavior during meetings. (Rev: SLJ 7/04) [651.7]

Construction and Mechanical Trades

11391 Paige, Joy. *Cool Careers Without College for People Who Love to Build Things* (7–12). Series: Cool Careers Without College. 2002, Rosen LB $33.25 (978-0-8239-3506-2). Twenty careers in construction are outlined with useful information about salary, future prospects, and training. (Rev: BL 1/1–15/03; SLJ 7/02) [690]

Education and Librarianship

11392 Reeves, Diane Lindsey, and Gail Karlitz. *Career Ideas for Teens in Education and Training* (8–12). Series: Career Ideas for Teens. 2005, Ferguson $40.00 (978-0-8160-5295-0). In addition to details of education requirements, salaries, and so forth, this attractive guide offers interview tips, advice from "real people," and questionnaires. (Rev: SLJ 2/06)

11393 Zannos, Susan. *Careers in Education* (8–12). Series: Latinos at Work. 2001, Mitchell Lane LB $22.95 (978-1-58415-081-7). Descriptions of careers in this field are accompanied by information on salary and qualifications as well as profiles of Latino men and women who have found success in a variety of career positions. (Rev: BL 10/15/01; HBG 3/02; SLJ 11/01; VOYA 6/02) [370]

Law, Police, and Other Society-Oriented Careers

11394 Bankston, John. *Careers in Community Service* (8–12). Series: Latinos at Work. 2001, Mitchell Lane LB $32.75 (978-1-58415-082-4). Aimed at Latino youths, this career guide features a multitude of jobs in non-profit agencies, including legal and medical fields, with accompanying stories of success. (Rev: BL 10/15/01; HBG 3/02; SLJ 1/02) [353.001]

11395 Binney, Greg A. *Careers in the Federal Emergency Management Agency's Search and Rescue Unit* (5–9). Series: Careers in Search and Rescue Operations. 2003, Rosen LB $26.50 (978-0-8239-3832-2). Starting with September 11, 2001, this volume explores the work of the teams that specialize in search and rescue after disasters such as tornadoes, hazardous materials spills, and building collapses, with material on the training required. (Rev: BL 10/15/03) [363.3]

11396 Croce, Nicholas. *Detectives: Life Investigating Crimes* (5–10). Series: Extreme Careers. 2003, Rosen LB $26.50 (978-0-8239-3796-7). As well as exploring the exciting side of detective work, this account explains the qualifications and training needed and the techniques that help do this job well. (Rev: BL 9/15/03) [340]

11397 Down, Susan Brophy. *Legally Green: Careers in Environmental Law* (5–8). Illus. Series: Green-Collar Careers. 2011, Crabtree LB $31.93 (978-077874857-1). An accessible, well-illustrated guide to the options available in the field of environmental law, with profiles of lawyers and their work. (Rev: BL 2/15/12) [344.7304]

11398 Freedman, Jeri. *Careers in Emergency Medical Response Team's Search and Rescue Unit* (5–9). Series: Careers in Search and Rescue Operations. 2003, Rosen LB $26.50 (978-0-8239-3831-5). Starting with September 11, 2001, this volume explores the various

roles played by emergency response teams, the use of equipment including helicopters and ambulances, and the training required. (Rev: BL 10/15/03) [616.0]

11399 Giacobello, John. *Bodyguards: Life Protecting Others* (5–10). Series: Extreme Careers. 2003, Rosen LB $26.50 (978-0-8239-3795-0). This book explores the duties and responsibilities of a bodyguard and includes information how to stay safe on the job and get ahead in this profession. (Rev: BL 9/15/03; SLJ 11/03) [340]

11400 Greene, Meg. *Careers in the National Guards' Search and Rescue Unit* (5–9). Series: Careers in Search and Rescue Operations. 2003, Rosen LB $26.50 (978-0-8239-3836-0). This account describes the vital role that citizen-soldiers play in the line of defense and tells of the their search and rescue activities during the terrorist attacks of September 11, 2001. (Rev: BL 10/15/03; SLJ 4/04) [335]

11401 Hopping, Lorraine Jean. *Investigating a Crime Scene* (7–10). Series: Crime Scene Science. 2007, World Almanac LB $22.95 (978-0-8368-7709-0). A matter-of-fact look at what it is like to examine crime scenes, this should appeal to teens interested in forensic work as a career and to those who just want more of what they see on TV. (Rev: BL 3/15/07) [614]

11402 Horn, Geoffrey M. *FBI Agent* (4–8). Illus. Series: Cool Careers: Helping Careers. 2008, Gareth Stevens LB $24 (978-083689193-5). What *do* FBI agents do? This book answers the question with facts about the training and responsibilities plus information on key cases. Lexile 760L (Rev: BL 10/15/08) [363.250973]

11403 Kiland, Taylor Baldwin. *The U.S. Navy and Military Careers* (5–8). Series: U.S. Armed Forces and Military Careers. 2006, Enslow LB $31.93 (978-0-7660-2523-3). Straightforward and informative, this title provides a history of the Navy, looks at its role in the nation's defense, and details various jobs within this branch of the armed forces. (Rev: SLJ 6/07)

11404 Murdico, Suzanne J. *Bomb Squad Experts: Life Defusing Explosive Devices* (5–10). Series: Extreme Careers. 2004, Rosen LB $26.50 (978-0-8239-3968-8). A look at the career opportunities in bomb squads, with material on training, salaries, and working conditions. (Rev: BL 5/15/04) [363]

11405 Pasternak, Ceel, and Linda Thornburg. *Cool Careers for Girls in Law* (6–12). Series: Cool Careers for Girls. 2001, Impact LB $19.95 (978-1-57023-160-5); paper $12.95 (978-1-57023-157-5). Ten women who have succeeded in various areas of the legal profession are highlighted, with material on qualifications, salaries, and working conditions. (Rev: BL 4/15/01; SLJ 7/01) [340]

11406 Payment, Simone. *Frontline Marines: Fighting in the Marine Combat Arms Units* (5–8). Series: Extreme Careers. 2007, Rosen LB $26.50 (978-1-4042-0946-

6). Students looking for exciting careers may want to look into the combat arms units of the U.S. Marines, suggests this book, which tells readers what these units do and explains the training involved. (Rev: BL 7/07) [359.9]

11407 Stein, R. Conrad. *The U.S. Marine Corps and Military Careers* (5–8). Series: U.S. Armed Forces and Military Careers. 2006, Enslow LB $31.93 (978-0-7660-2521-9). This overview of careers in the U.S. Marine Corps discusses expectations, duties, and pay scales as well as the Marines' role in national defense. (Rev: SLJ 6/07)

11408 Wade, Linda R. *Careers in Law and Politics* (8–12). Series: Latinos at Work. 2001, Mitchell Lane LB $22.95 (978-1-58415-080-0). Along with interviews of successful Hispanic Americans in the fields of law and politics, this book describes such careers as lawyer, law professor, judge, police officer, and state representative. (Rev: BL 3/15/02; HBG 10/02; SLJ 3/02) [340]

11409 Wirths, Claudine G. *Choosing a Career in Law Enforcement* (6–10). Series: World of Work. 1996, Rosen LB $17.95 (978-0-8239-2274-1). Careers in law enforcement, such as police officer, security guard, and private investigator, are explored. (Rev: SLJ 3/97) [363]

Medicine and Health

11410 Asher, Dana. *Epidemiologists: Life Tracking Deadly Diseases* (5–10). Series: Extreme Careers. 2003, Rosen LB $26.50 (978-0-8239-3633-5). A concise explanation of the work of epidemiologists, the history of this discipline, and the training required to enter this field, with a case study. (Rev: BL 5/15/03; SLJ 5/03) [614.4]

11411 Field, Shelly. *Career Opportunities in Health Care. 2nd ed.* (7–12). 2002, Facts on File $49.50 (978-0-8160-4816-8). Information on 80 or so careers is organized in 16 categories, and includes a job profile, salary outlook, and details of necessary education and skills. (Rev: BL 11/1/02; SLJ 1/03) [610.69]

11412 *Health Care* (7–12). Series: What Can I Do Now? 2007, Ferguson $29.95 (978-0-8160-6031-3). Following a general introduction to the health care industry, this book describes jobs in the field, education and skill requirements, and salary ranges, and tells students what they can do now, emphasizing volunteer opportunities and internships. (Rev: SLJ 11/07) [610.69]

11413 Pasternak, Ceel, and Linda Thornburg. *Cool Careers for Girls in Health* (5–9). Series: Cool Careers for Girls. 1999, Impact $19.95 (978-1-57023-125-4); paper $12.95 (978-1-57023-118-6). This book describes health-related careers for girls — as doctors, nurses, dentists, personal trainers, medical technologists, physical therapists, and dietitians. (Rev: SLJ 10/99) [610]

11414 Reeves, Diane Lindsey, and Gail Karlitz. *Career Ideas for Teens in Health Science* (7–12). Series: Career Ideas for Teens. 2005, Ferguson $40.00 (978-0-8160-5290-5). In addition to details of education requirements, salaries, and so forth, this attractive guide offers interview tips, advice from "real people," and questionnaires. (Rev: SLJ 2/06) [610.69]

Science and Engineering

11415 Burnett, Betty. *Math and Science Wizards* (7–12). Series: Cool Careers Without College. 2002, Rosen $33.25 (978-0-8239-3502-4). Jobs in medicine and science that do not require college degrees, such as chemical lab workers, miners, and doctors' helpers, are described with information on salaries, duties, training, and future outlooks. (Rev: BL 5/15/02; SLJ 7/02) [520]

11416 Gaffney, Timothy R. *Storm Scientist: Careers Chasing Severe Weather* (4–8). Series: Wild Science Careers. 2009, Enslow LB $31.93 (978-0-7660-3050-3). Full of tales of hard work and engaging action, this book presents an in-depth look at the real life, skills, and even salary expectations of scientists studying severe weather. (Rev: SLJ 10/09) [551.5023]

11417 Jackson, Donna M. *Extreme Scientists: Exploring Nature's Mysteries from Perilous Places* (4–8). Illus. Series: Scientists in the Field. 2009, Houghton $18.00 (978-0-618-77706-8). Jackson shows the work of scientists who face danger in the field — a meteorologist who flies into hurricanes, a biologist who goes deep into caves, an ecologist who climbs high into tall redwoods — and discusses their motivations. (Rev: BCCB 6/09; BL 5/15/09*; HB 7/09; SLJ 7/09) [509.2]

11418 Latta, Sara L. *Ice Scientist: Careers in the Frozen Antarctic* (6–9). Series: Wild Science Careers. 2009, Enslow LB $31.93 (978-0-7660-3048-0). With colorful photographs and firsthand accounts, this interesting volume provides information on becoming a paleontologist, geologist, ecologist, glaciologist, astrophysicist, marine biologist, or oceanographer. (Rev: LMC 5–6/09; SLJ 8/09) [559.8]

11419 Latta, Sara L. *Lava Scientist: Careers on the Edge of Volcanoes* (6–9). Series: Wild Science Careers. 2009, Enslow LB $31.93 (978-0-7660-3049-7). With colorful photographs and firsthand accounts, this volume will interest all readers in addition to those seeking information on volcanology. (Rev: LMC 5/09; SLJ 8/09) [559.8]

11420 *Meteorology* (7–12). Illus. Series: Careers in Focus. 2011, Ferguson LB $32.95 (978-081608033-5). Careers covered in this useful volume range from broadcast meteorologist to aviation meteorologist, with information about education, opportunities, and salaries. (Rev: BL 12/15/11) [551.5023]

11421 Reeves, Diane Lindsey. *Career Ideas for Kids Who Like Science* (5–9). Illus. by Nancy Bond. Series:

Career Ideas for Kids. 1998, Facts on File $23.00 (978-0-8160-3680-6); paper $12.95 (978-0-8060-3686-1). An upbeat, breezy introduction to 15 careers, providing aptitude tests and information on educational requirements, working conditions, activities, etc. (Rev: SLJ 9/98) [500]

11422 Swinburne, Stephen R. *The Woods Scientist* (4–8). Photos by Susan C. Morse. Series: Scientists in the Field. 2003, Houghton Mifflin $16.00 (978-0-618-04602-7). Swinburne describes his fascinating expeditions in the company of a conservationist and ecologist in the woods of Vermont, and provides lots of information on risks to wildlife. (Rev: BCCB 3/03; BL 3/15/03; HBG 10/03; SLJ 4/03) [591.73]

11423 Willett, Edward. *Disease-Hunting Scientist: Careers Hunting Deadly Diseases* (4–8). Series: Wild Science Careers. 2009, Enslow LB $31.93 (978-0-7660-3052-7). Full of real-life tales of hard work and engaging action, this book presents an in-depth look at the everyday activities, skills, and even salary expectations of scientists studying deadly epidemics. (Rev: SLJ 10/09) [614.4023]

Technical and Industrial Careers

11424 Apel, Melanie Ann. *Careers in Information Technology* (6–12). Series: Exploring Careers. 2000, Rosen LB $18.95 (978-0-8239-2892-7). Testimonials from working professionals add to this survey of opportunities in information technology that gives details on skills required and employment outlook. (Rev: BL 3/15/01; HBG 10/01; SLJ 2/01) [004]

11425 Brown, Marty. *Webmaster* (4–8). Series: Coolcareers.com. 2000, Rosen LB $23.95 (978-0-8239-3111-8). This volume describes a Web page, types of networks, servers, browsers, and protocols and introduces some careers in Web-related areas. (Rev: SLJ 6/00) [004]

11426 *Computer and Video Game Design* (7–12). Series: Careers in Focus. 2005, Ferguson $22.95 (978-0-8160-5850-1). Describes the tasks of artists and animators, game designers, packaging designers, technical support specialists, and video game testers. (Rev: SLJ 12/05)

11427 *Computers* (4–8). Series: Discovering Careers for Your Future. 2001, Ferguson LB $21.95 (978-0-89434-389-6). A useful introduction to the career opportunities in this field, with information on the skills required, potential earnings, and job outlook. (Rev: SLJ 11/01) [004.02373]

11428 Fulton, Michael T. *Exploring Careers in Cyberspace* (7–12). Series: Careers. 1997, Rosen LB $31.95 (978-0-8239-2633-6). A worthwhile source of information on how to prepare oneself to work in cyberspace, the types of jobs available, and the way to make a solid impression. (Rev: BL 6/1–15/98; SLJ 7/98) [004.67802373]

11429 Garcia, Kimberly. *Careers in Technology* (8–12). Series: Latinos at Work. 2001, Mitchell Lane LB $32.75 (978-1-58415-087-9). An easy-to-read guide to careers in computer technology such as Web designers, programmers, and Internet marketing, with particular emphasis on Hispanic success stories in these fields. (Rev: BL 10/15/01; HBG 3/02; SLJ 1/02) [004.6]

11430 Gerardi, Dave, and Peter Suciu. *Careers in the Computer Game Industry* (6–12). Series: Careers in the New Economy. 2005, Rosen LB $31.95 (978-1-4042-0252-8). The authors review a wide array of job opportunities in the computer game industry, including designers, testers, graphic artists, animators, and programmers. (Rev: SLJ 10/05) [331.7]

11431 Hovanec, Erin M. *Careers as a Content Provider for the Web* (5–8). Series: The Library of E-Commerce and Internet Careers. 2001, Rosen LB $26.50 (978-0-8239-3418-8). A basic guide to career opportunities in the high-tech sector, with personal stories, information on skills needed and how to get started, and lists of recommended resources, many of which are on the Web. Also use *E-Tailing: Careers Selling Over the Web* (2001). (Rev: SLJ 4/02) [004]

11432 McAlpine, Margaret. *Working with Computers* (6–10). Series: My Future Career. 2005, Gareth Stevens LB $27.00 (978-0-8368-4242-5). In addition to describing various jobs working with computers, McAlpine discusses the best personality type for each one and provides a detailed breakdown of a typical day. (Rev: SLJ 3/05) [004]

11433 McGinty, Alice B. *Software Designer* (4–8). Series: Coolcareers.com. 2000, Rosen LB $23.95 (978-0-8239-3149-1). This book explains what a software engineer does, the skills required, education needed, and future prospects. (Rev: SLJ 6/00) [004]

11434 Mazor, Barry. *Multimedia and New Media Developer* (4–8). Series: Coolcareers.com. 2000, Rosen LB $26.50 (978-0-8239-3102-6). This work explains the nature of multimedia careers, the training and skills necessary, and the job opportunities. (Rev: SLJ 6/00) [004]

11435 Pasternak, Ceel, and Linda Thornburg. *Cool Careers for Girls in Computers* (7–12). 1999, Impact paper $12.95 (978-1-57023-103-2). This career book for girls features interviews with 10 women in computer-related fields, including a software engineer, sales executive, online specialist, technology trainer, and network administrator. (Rev: SLJ 4/00; VOYA 8/99) [004.6]

11436 Reeves, Diane Lindsey, and Peter Kent. *Career Ideas for Kids Who Like Computers* (5–9). Illus. by Nancy Bond. Series: Career Ideas for Kids. 1998, Facts on File $23.00 (978-0-8160-3682-0). An upbeat, breezy introduction to careers related to computers, providing aptitude tests and information on educational requirements, working conditions, activities, etc. (Rev: SLJ 6/99) [004]

736

11437 Sawyer, Sarah. *Career Building through Podcasting* (7–10). Series: Digital Career Building. 2007, Rosen LB $21.95 (978-1-4042-1944-1). Readers looking into tech careers will enjoy this exploration into how one can make a living podcasting. (Rev: BL 10/15/07; LMC 2/08) [070.5]

11438 Thornburg, Linda. *Cool Careers for Girls in Cybersecurity and National Safety* (8–11). Series: Cool Careers for Girls. 2004, Impact $21.95 (978-1-57023-209-1). This volume contains 10 case studies of women who have launched careers dealing with the protection of computer networks and the Internet as well as other high-tech areas. (Rev: BL 3/1/04; SLJ 10/04) [331.7]

Personal Finances

Money-Making Ideas

General and Miscellaneous

11439 Bernstein, Daryl. *Better Than a Lemonade Stand! Small Business Ideas for Kids* (5–8). 1992, Beyond Words paper $9.95 (978-0-941831-75-8). The author, a 15-year-old entrepreneur, provides ideas for starting 51 different small businesses and offers advice on start-up costs, billing, and customer relations. (Rev: BL 10/1/92; SLJ 1/93) [650.1]

11440 Bielagus, Peter G. *Quick Cash for Teens: Be Your Own Boss and Make Big Bucks* (7–12). Illus. 2009, Sterling paper $12.95 (978-140276038-9). Bielagus recommends 101 businesses suited for teens and provides step-by-step strategies for success with interesting anecdotes and sample worksheets. (Rev: BL 6/1–15/09) [658.1]

11441 Drew, Bonnie, and Noel Drew. *Fast Cash for Kids* (4–7). 1995, Career Pr. paper $13.99 (978-1-56414-154-5). The authors present a variety of possible ways to make money. (Rev: BL 6/15/87) [658.041]

11442 Kravetz, Stacy. *Girl Boss: Running the Show Like the Big Chicks* (7–10). 1999, Girl paper $19.95 (978-0-9659754-2-1). This book gives practical advice and tips for teenage girls who want to start a business of their own. (Rev: VOYA 8/99) [658.1]

Baby-sitting

11443 Barkin, Carol, and Elizabeth James. *The New Complete Babysitter's Handbook* (5–7). 1995, Clarion paper $7.95 (978-0-395-66558-9). A fine manual that covers such topics as first aid, ways to amuse children, and how to get jobs baby sitting. (Rev: BL 5/1/95; SLJ 6/95) [649.1]

11444 Bondy, Halley. *Don't Sit on the Baby! The Ultimate Guide to Sane, Skilled, and Safe Babysitting* (6–12). Illus. 2012, Zest paper $12.99 (978-098273223-6). A lighthearted guide full of practical advice, playtime ideas, real-life anecdotes, and tips on getting, keeping, and quitting jobs. (Rev: BL 7/12; LMC 11–12/12; SLJ 2/13) [649]

11445 Buckley, Annie. *Be a Better Babysitter* (5–6). Series: Girls Rock! 2006, The Child's World LB $25.64 (978-1-59296-740-7). This introductory guide to babysitting explains the nature of the job, looks at its pros and cons and safety issues, and offers advice on doing a good job. (Rev: SLJ 2/07)

11446 Chassé, Jill D. *The Babysitter's Survival Guide: Fun Games, Cool Crafts, and How to Be the Best Babysitter in Town* (5–10). Illus. by Jessica Secheret. 2010, Sterling $12.95 (978-1-40274-654-3). With information on how to assess job opportunities, this helpful guide offers plenty of activity ideas, advice for coping with difficult behaviors, and general tips on running a business. (Rev: SLJ 9/1/10) [649]

11447 Weintraub, Aileen. *Everything You Need to Know About Being a Baby-Sitter: A Teen's Guide to Responsible Child Care* (5–8). 2000, Rosen LB $25.25 (978-0-8239-3085-2). This book covers all facets of babysitting from preparation, responsibilities, and safety precautions to employment opportunities. (Rev: SLJ 7/00) [649]

Managing Money

11448 Bostick, Nan, and Susan M. Freese. *Managing Money* (8–12). Illus. Series: Life Skills Handbooks. 2011, Saddleback Educational paper $16.95 (978-16165165-9-8). Covering spending, banking, credit, and budgeting, this is a useful and practical guide. (Rev: BL 3/1/12) [332.024]

11449 Byers, Ann. *First Apartment Smarts* (8–12). Series: Get Smart With Your Money. 2010, Rosen LB $29.95 (978-1-4358-5272-3). Clearly written and practical, this volume covers planning, budgeting, apartment searching, and moving in, and living smart, asking readers to assess their preparedness frankly. (Rev: BL 10/1/09; LMC 1–2/10)

11450 Cipriano, Jeri. *How Do Mortgages, Loans, and Credit Work?* (5–8). Illus. Series: Economics in Action. 2010, Crabtree LB $26.60 (978-077874445-0); paper $8.95 (978-077874456-6). Covers interest rates and borrowing and lending in general, with particular attention to credit cards. (Rev: BLO 8/10) [332.7]

11451 Fisanick, Christina, ed. *Debt* (8–12). Illus. Series: Opposing Viewpoints. 2010, Gale/Greenhaven LB $38.50 (978-073774202-2); paper $26.75 (9780737742039). A collection of essays and article excerpts explore the reasons underlying individual and government debt from various perspectives. (Rev: BL 5/1/10) [332.024]

11452 Guthrie, Donna, and Jan Stiles. *Real World Math: Money, Credit, and Other Numbers in Your Life* (6–9).

1998, Millbrook $26.90 (978-0-7613-0251-3). A practical and entertaining guide that shows how math is used in everyday situations including shopping, managing money, buying a car, and using credit wisely. (Rev: BL 6/1–15/98; HBG 9/98; SLJ 6/98; VOYA 8/98) [332.024]

11453 Holyoke, Nancy. *A Smart Girl's Guide to Money: How to Make It, Save It, and Spend It* (4–7). Illus. by Ali Douglass. Series: A Smart Girl's Guide. 2006, Pleasant paper $9.95 (978-1-59369-103-5). Shopping and investing are only two of the topics covered in this user-friendly guide. (Rev: BL 5/15/06; SLJ 5/06)

11454 Silver, Don. *The Generation Y Money Book: 99 Smart Ways to Handle Money* (7–12). 2000, Adams-Hall paper $15.95 (978-0-944708-64-4). Sound advice about money management, credit card use, planning for college, savings, and investment. (Rev: VOYA 6/01) [332.024]

11455 Vermond, Kira. *The Secret Life of Money: A Kid's Guide to Cash* (7–10). Illus. by Clayton Hanmer. 2012, Owl $19.95 (978-192697319-7); paper $13.95 (978-19269731-8-0). An engaging introduction to a complex subject, with clear explanations, first-person sidebars, and graphic elements. ℮ (Rev: BL 5/1/12; LMC 8–9/12; SLJ 4/12) [332.4]

Health and the Human Body

General and Miscellaneous

11456 Apel, Melanie Ann. *Coping with Stuttering* (6–10). Series: Coping. 2000, Rosen LB $31.95 (978-0-8239-2970-2). Practical advice for stutterers and for listeners is accompanied by information on celebrities who have conquered this problem. (Rev: SLJ 4/00) [616.85]

11457 Costello, Patricia. *Female Fitness Stars of TV and the Movies* (7–12). Series: Legends of Health and Fitness. 2000, Mitchell Lane LB $25.70 (978-1-58415-050-3). Cher, Goldie Hawn, and Demi Moore are among the actors profiled here as examples of professionals who put fitness high on their list of priorities. (Rev: SLJ 2/01)

11458 Foley, Ronan. *World Health: The Impact on Our Lives* (5–8). Series: 21st Century Debates. 2003, Raintree LB $28.56 (978-0-7398-5507-2). A thorough and thought-provoking exploration of the health status of countries around the world and the reasons for the wide disparity between wealthy and poor nations. (Rev: BL 8/03; HBG 10/03; SLJ 7/03) [362.1]

11459 Jukes, Mavis. *The Guy Book: An Owner's Manual* (6–12). 2002, Crown paper $12.95 (978-0-679-89028-7). Jukes takes an appealing, frank-talking approach to sex, health, and hygiene for young men, covering everything from dating and birth control to choosing clothes and slow dancing. (Rev: BL 1/1–15/02; HBG 10/02; SLJ 3/02; VOYA 6/02) [305.235]

11460 Powell, Phelan. *Trailblazers of Physical Fitness* (7–12). Series: Legends of Health and Fitness. 2000, Mitchell Lane LB $25.70 (978-1-58415-024-4). Jack LaLanne and Richard Simmons are among the individuals profiled here as leading proponents of physical fitness. (Rev: SLJ 2/01)

11461 Rebman, Renee C. *Addictions and Risky Behaviors: Cutting, Bingeing, Snorting, and Other Dangers* (7–12). 2006, Enslow LB $31.93 (978-0-7660-2165-5). The many behaviors associated with addiction — alcohol, smoking, eating problems, drugs, inhalants, self-mutilation, Internet — are defined and the risks are clearly stated; resources include Web sites and related organizations. (Rev: SLJ 6/06)

11462 Sommers, Annie Leah. *Everything You Need to Know About Looking and Feeling Your Best: A Guide for Girls* (6–12). Series: Need to Know Library. 2000, Rosen LB $27.95 (978-0-8239-3079-1). This book aims to boost girls' self-images as well as their knowledge of health and hygiene. (Rev: HBG 9/00; SLJ 3/00) [613]

11463 Spalding, Frank. *Erasing the Ink: Getting Rid of Your Tattoo* (7–10). Illus. Series: Tattooing. 2011, Rosen LB $30.60 (978-144884615-3). Spalding presents frankly the reasons why a tattoo may be a bad idea — and one you may regret — in this volume in a series that deals with the art of tattooing and what to expect if you set out to get one, and to have one removed. (Rev: BL 9/15/11; SLJ 12/1/11) [617.4]

11464 Winner, Cherie. *Circulating Life: Blood Transfusions from Ancient Superstition to Modern Medicine* (6–9). Series: Discovery! 2007, Lerner LB $29.27 (978-0-8225-6606-9). A fascinating look at the history of blood transfusion and the ways in which the safety and efficacy of this technique have improved as medical knowledge has increased and superstition has (generally) decreased. (Rev: BL 4/15/07; SLJ 6/07) [615]

Aging and Death

11465 Colman, Penny. *Corpses, Coffins, and Crypts: A History of Burial* (7–12). 1997, Henry Holt $19.95 (978-0-8050-5066-0). Customs associated with death and burial traditions in various cultures and times are covered in a text enlivened with many photographs. (Rev: BL 11/1/97; HBG 3/98; SLJ 12/97*) [393]

11466 Digiulio, Robert, and Rachel Kranz. *Straight Talk About Death and Dying* (7–12). Series: Straight Talk. 1995, Facts on File $27.45 (978-0-8160-3078-1). Among the topics covered in this book about death and dying are Kubler-Ross's five psychological stages experienced by the dying and various aspects of mourning. (Rev: BL 9/15/95; SLJ 12/95) [155.9]

11467 Giddens, Sandra, and Owen Giddens. *Coping with Grieving and Loss* (6–10). 2000, Rosen LB $25.25 (978-0-8239-2894-1). Practical advice about the process of grieving and funerals is accompanied by personal teen stories. (Rev: SLJ 4/00) [155.9]

11468 Gootman, Marilyn E. *When a Friend Dies: A Book for Teens About Grieving and Healing. Rev. ed.* (6–12). 2005, Free Spirit paper $9.95 (978-1-57542-170-4). An updated edition of a guide first published in 1994, this volume offers sound advice and reassurance for teenagers suffering the loss of a friend or peer, including quotes from bereaved teens. (Rev: SLJ 10/05) [155.9]

11469 Grollman, Earl A. *Straight Talk About Death for Teenagers: How to Cope with Losing Someone You Love* (7–12). 1993, Beacon paper $13.00 (978-0-8070-2501-7). Grollman validates the painful feelings teens experience following the death of a loved one, conveying a sense of the grief as well as the need to get on with life. (Rev: BL 4/1/93; SLJ 6/93; VOYA 8/93) [155.9]

11470 Hyde, Margaret O., and Lawrence E. Hyde. *Meeting Death* (5–8). 1989, Walker LB $15.85 (978-0-8027-6874-2). After a history of how various cultures regard death, the authors discuss this phenomenon, the concept of grieving, and how to face death. (Rev: BL 1/1/90; SLJ 11/89) [306.9]

11471 Krementz, Jill. *How It Feels When a Parent Dies* (4–7). 1988, Knopf paper $15.00 (978-0-394-75854-1). Eighteen experiences of parental death are recounted.

11472 Marcovitz, Hal. *Suicide* (7–10). Series: Essential Issues. 2010, ABDO LB $32.79 (978-1-60453-958-5). After a history of suicide this volume looks at risk factors, the contribution of mental disorders, the right to die, and how to prevent these deaths. (Rev: LMC 10/10; SLJ 4/1/10) [362.2]

11473 Myers, Edward. *When Will I Stop Hurting? Teens, Loss, and Grief* (7–12). Illus. by Kelly Adams. Series: It Happened to Me. 2004, Scarecrow $34.50 (978-0-8108-4921-1). Firsthand accounts from teens add to this discussion of the stages of grief and of warning signs that should be monitored. (Rev: SLJ 11/04) [155.9]

11474 Wolfelt, Alan D. *Healing a Teen's Grieving Heart: 100 Practical Ideas* (6–12). 2001, Companion paper $11.95 (978-1-879651-24-1). Teens who have suffered a loss will find practical reassurance and com-

fort in the suggestions offered here. (Rev: SLJ 9/01; VOYA 8/01)

Alcohol, Drugs, and Smoking

11475 Alagna, Magdalena. *Everything You Need to Know About the Dangers of Binge Drinking* (6–10). Series: Need to Know Library. 2001, Rosen LB $27.95 (978-0-8239-3289-4). Warnings about the physical and psychological dangers of alcohol are interwoven with fictional examples. (Rev: BL 5/1/02) [362.292]

11476 Aretha, David. *Cocaine and Crack* (6–9). Series: Drugs. 2005, Enslow LB $25.26 (978-0-7660-5276-5). Focuses on cocaine and its derivative, crack, examining how they are produced, their effects, and the dangers they pose to users. Also use *Ecstasy and Other Party Drugs* (2005). (Rev: SLJ 6/05) [362.29]

11477 Aretha, David. *On the Rocks: Teens and Alcohol* (6–8). 2006, Watts LB $30.50 (978-0-531-16792-2). Binge drinking and other forms of alcohol abuse are covered in this volume that also discusses the efficacy of various strategies to solve these problems. (Rev: SLJ 3/07) [613.81]

11478 Aretha, David. *Steroids and Other Performance-Enhancing Drugs* (6–9). Series: MyReportLinks.com. 2005, Enslow LB $25.26 (978-0-7660-5277-2). Explores the dangers of steroids and other performance-enhancing drugs, with password access to Web sites that are regularly monitored. (Rev: BL 6/1–15/05; SLJ 6/05) [362.29]

11479 Aue, Pamela Willwerth, ed. *Teen Drug Abuse* (8–12). Series: Opposing Viewpoints. 2006, Gale LB $34.95 (978-0-7377-3335-8). Cigarettes, alcohol, marijuana, inhalants, ritalin — they're all discussed in pro and con essays that will be particularly helpful for reports and debates. (Rev: SLJ 3/07) [362.2]

11480 Bailey, Jacqui. *Taking Action Against Drugs* (5–8). Series: Taking Action. 2010, Rosen LB $26.50 (978-1-4358-5492-5). Bailey discusses the dangers of illegal drugs and the reasons why people choose to take them, along with their social and physical effects. (Rev: LMC 1–2/10)

11481 Banfield, Susan. *Inside Recovery: How the Twelve-Step Program Can Work for You* (7–10). Series: Drug Abuse Prevention Library. 1998, Rosen LB $27.95 (978-0-8239-2634-3). A look at the 12-steps to recovery and the many problems one can face going through this program, which has been a successful route for many addicts. (Rev: VOYA 2/99) [613.8]

11482 Barter, James. *Hallucinogens* (8–12). Series: Drug Education Library. 2002, Gale LB $32.45 (978-1-56006-915-7). This absorbing and comprehensive book explains the effects of hallucinogens on the body, traces their use — in ancient rituals, in medical treatments, and as a recreational drug — and looks at the debates over their legalization. Also in this series is *Marijuana*. (Rev: BL 6/1–15/02; SLJ 6/02) [362.29]

11483 Beal, Eileen. *Ritalin: Its Use and Abuse* (7–10). Series: Drug Abuse Prevention Library. 1999, Rosen LB $17.95 (978-0-8239-2775-3). This book explores the drug Ritalin, widely used for attention deficit disorder, and presents the controversies surrounding it. (Rev: BL 5/15/99; VOYA 4/00) [616.85]

11484 Bellenir, Karen, ed. *Tobacco Information for Teens: Health Tips about the Hazards of Using Cigarettes, Smokeless Tobacco, and Other Nicotine Products* (7–12). Series: Teen Health. 2007, Omnigraphics $65.00 (978-0-7808-0976-5). Full of facts and statistics, this book covers types of tobacco, addiction, the impact on health, and ways to stop using the substance. (Rev: SLJ 9/07) [362.2]

11485 Berne, Emma Carlson. *Methamphetamine* (7–10). Series: Compact Research: Drugs. 2007, Reference Point LB $24.95 (978-1-60152-004-3). A look at the dangerous drug that is used in rural as well as urban areas in what some are calling an epidemic. Quotations from officials and former users will be useful to report writers. (Rev: BL 4/1/07; LMC 11/07; SLJ 5/07) [362.29]

11486 Bjornlund, Lydia. *Marijuana* (8–12). Illus. Series: Compact Research: Drugs. 2011, ReferencePoint LB $27.95 (978-160152160-6). This volume provides facts and statistics on marijuana and its use and discusses its legalization and the impact on the economy and society. (Rev: BL 2/15/12) [362.29]

11487 Bjornlund, Lydia. *Oxycodone* (8–12). Illus. Series: Compact Research: Drugs. 2011, ReferencePoint LB $27.95 (978-160152161-3). Discusses oxcodone abuse and its effects on health. (Rev: BL 2/15/12) [615]

11488 Clayton, Lawrence. *Working Together Against Drug Addiction* (6–10). 1996, Rosen LB $27.95 (978-0-8239-2263-5). In addition to discussing drugs and addiction, this work takes an activist approach by providing ways for teens to locate drug and alcohol counselors and programs and ways they can become involved and make a difference. (Rev: SLJ 5/97) [362]

11489 Croft, Jennifer. *Drugs and the Legalization Debate* (6–10). Series: Drug Abuse Prevention Library. 1997, Rosen LB $17.95 (978-0-8239-2509-4). A well-balanced presentation of the pros and cons of legalizing drugs, along with a discussion of drug abuse and penalties and a brief look at how other countries deal with the issue. (Rev: SLJ 5/98) [362.29]

11490 Croft, Jennifer. *PCP: High Risk on the Streets* (7–10). Series: Drug Abuse Prevention Library. 1998, Rosen LB $27.95 (978-0-8239-2774-6). This book provides readers with important information about phen-

cyclidine, or angel dust, the behavior it produces, and its dangers. (Rev: BL 11/15/98; SLJ 12/98) [362.29]

11491 Deeugenio, Deborah, and Debra Henn. *Diet Pills* (6–9). Series: Drugs, The Straight Facts. 2005, Chelsea House LB $30.00 (978-0-7910-8198-3). The authors explore the pitfalls of using drugs to lose weight. (Rev: SLJ 11/05)

11492 Dolmetsch, Paul, and Gail Mauricette, eds. *Teens Talk about Alcohol and Alcoholism* (6–9). 1986, Doubleday paper $15 (978-0-385-23084-1). Eighteen students from a junior high school in Bennington, Vermont, tell about the effects of alcohol on their lives. (Rev: BL 2/15/87) [362.2]

11493 Egendorf, Laura K. *Heroin* (8–10). Series: Compact Research. 2007, Reference Point LB $24.95 (978-1-60152-002-9). This compact volume provides lots of information for report writers, with illustrations, quotations from primary sources, lists of facts, statistical charts, and brief timelines. (Rev: SLJ 5/07) [363.29]

11494 Egendorf, Laura K. *Performance-Enhancing Drugs* (7–10). Series: Compact Research. 2007, Reference Point LB $24.95 (978-1-60152-003-6). A well-organized look at the drugs used to enhance sports performance and the dangers involved. (Rev: LMC 11–12/07; SLJ 9/07) [362.29]

11495 Glass, George. *Drugs and Fitting In* (6–9). Series: Drug Abuse Prevention Library. 1998, Rosen LB $27.95 (978-0-8239-2554-4). After a description of teen culture and its pressures to conform and be popular, this book presents alternatives and advice on how to remain drug-free. (Rev: BL 3/15/98; VOYA 6/98) [362.29]

11496 Glass, George. *Narcotics: Dangerous Painkillers* (6–9). Series: Drug Abuse Prevention Library. 1998, Rosen LB $17.95 (978-0-8239-2719-7). This book explains the dangers of abusing prescribed painkilling drugs and their street derivatives and discusses issues relating to addiction and treatment. (Rev: BL 5/15/98; SLJ 10/98) [616.8632]

11497 Goldstein, Margaret J. *Legalizing Drugs: Crime Stopper or Social Risk?* (7–10). Series: USA Today's Debate: Voices and Perspectives. 2010, Lerner LB $35.93 (978-0-7613-5116-0). After a history of the war on drugs (since Prohibition), this attractive volume draws on *USA Today* to discuss the effectiveness of this battle and review arguments for and against legalization. (Rev: BL 4/1/10; LMC 10/10; SLJ 6/10) [364.1]

11498 Gottfried, Ted. *The Facts About Alcohol* (7–12). Series: Drugs. 2004, Benchmark LB $37.07 (978-0-7614-1805-4). A history of alcohol use plus discussion of its effects on the body and impact on society. (Rev: SLJ 3/05) [613.8]

11499 Gottfried, Ted, and Lisa Harkrader. *Marijuana* (6–12). Series: Benchmark Rockets. 2010, Marshall Cavendish LB $28.50 (978-0-7614-4351-3). With information about marijuana's history, the ways in which it is consumed, the dangers it poses, the legal problems involved in its use, and some sidebar accounts of teen usage, this title is useful for reports and for young people who have a more personal interest;. (Rev: LMC 3–4/10) [362.29]

11500 Green, Carl R. *Nicotine and Tobacco* (4–8). Series: Drugs. 2005, Enslow LB $25.26 (978-0-7660-5283-3). Fictional scenarios are combined with information on the addictive qualities of nicotine and the dangers of smoking and other forms of tobacco use; Web links extend the text. (Rev: SLJ 11/05) [362.2]

11501 Grosshandler-Smith, Janet. *Working Together Against Drinking and Driving* (4–8). Series: The Library of Social Activism. 1996, Rosen LB $16.95 (978-0-8239-2259-8). With an emphasis on prevention, the author presents a general discussion on drinking and driving and its consequences, followed by pointers on how to avoid embarrassing situations, how to handle peer pressure about drinking. (Rev: SLJ 2/97) [613.8]

11502 Hanan, Jessica. *When Someone You Love Is Addicted* (5–9). Series: Drug Abuse Prevention Library. 1999, Rosen LB $27.95 (978-0-8239-2831-6). A short book that begins with teenage case histories and then discusses treatments and resources for young people with drug problems. (Rev: SLJ 7/99) [362.29]

11503 Hyde, Margaret O. *Drug Wars* (7–12). 1990, Walker LB $12.85 (978-0-8027-6901-5). This account discusses the violence and despair that crack cocaine has brought to America and ways in which its production and distribution can be halted. (Rev: SLJ 6/90; VOYA 6/90) [616.86]

11504 Hyde, Margaret O. *Know About Drugs. 4th ed.* (5–8). 1995, Walker LB $15.85 (978-0-8027-8395-0). An introduction to drugs including marijuana, alcohol, PCP, inhalants, crack/cocaine, heroin, and nicotine. (Rev: BL 7/90; SLJ 3/96) [362.2]

11505 Hyde, Margaret O., and John F. Setaro. *Alcohol 101: An Overview for Teens* (5–10). 1999, Twenty-First Century LB $24.90 (978-0-7613-1274-1). Kinds of alcohol and their effects are described, with material on alcoholism and binge drinking. (Rev: HBG 3/00; SLJ 3/00; VOYA 12/00) [613.8]

11506 Hyde, Margaret O., and John F. Setaro. *Drugs 101: An Overview for Teens* (7–12). 2003, Twenty-First Century LB $25.90 (978-0-7613-2608-3). This well-researched and accessible introduction to the nature of addiction, illicit drugs, and the harmful results of their use features useful photographs, diagrams, and charts. (Rev: BL 5/15/03; HBG 10/03; SLJ 5/03; VOYA 10/03) [362.29]

11507 Hyde, Margaret O., and John K. Setaro. *Smoking 101: An Overview for Teens* (7–12). 2005, Twenty-First Century LB $26.60 (978-0-7613-2835-3). A nonjudgmental account of the physical effects of smoking,

with information on tobacco advertising, the kinds of products marketed, and the industry both in the United States and around the world. (Rev: SLJ 1/06) [362.29]

11508 Jeffrey, Laura S. *Marijuana = Busted* (6–9). Series: Busted! 2006, Enslow LB $23.95 (978-0-7660-2796-1). Scary stories of lives ruined, as well as facts about what marijuana does to the body and mind, will make readers think twice about using it. (Rev: BL 3/15/07) [613.8]

11509 Jones, Ralph. *Straight Talk: Answers to Questions Young People Ask About Alcohol* (7–9). 1989, TAB paper $4.95 (978-0-8306-9005-3). Fifty questions concerning alcohol and physical and psychological effects are answered in this short, straightforward book. (Rev: VOYA 12/89) [661]

11510 Kittleson, Mark J., ed. *The Truth About Alcohol* (8–12). Series: Truth About. 2004, Facts on File $35.00 (978-0-8160-5298-1). Discusses the effects and dangers of alcohol use, including binge drinking, alcoholism, unsafe sexual behavior, and impaired driving. (Rev: SLJ 4/05) [613.8]

11511 Klosterman, Lorrie. *The Facts about Depressants* (7–12). Series: Drugs. 2005, Benchmark LB $25.95 (978-0-7614-1976-1). A helpful guide to depressants with some basic information about the various kinds on the market, their medical uses, how they are abused, and how they affect the body. (Rev: SLJ 5/06) [362.29]

11512 Laliberte, Michelle. *Marijuana* (6–9). Series: Drugs. 2005, Enslow LB $25.26 (978-0-7660-5281-9). Presents the hard facts about marijuana and its effects on the body, along with links to related online resources. (Rev: SLJ 10/05) [362.29]

11513 Landau, Elaine. *Hooked: Talking About Addiction* (5–10). 1995, Millbrook LB $22.90 (978-1-56294-469-8). This account defines addiction broadly — from use of alcohol and drugs to various forms of compulsive behavior — and gives suggestions for recovery. (Rev: BL 1/1–15/96; SLJ 1/96) [362.29]

11514 Landau, Elaine. *Meth: America's Drug Epidemic* (7–12). 2007, Twenty-First Century LB $30.60 (978-0-8225-6808-7). This cautionary book should scare readers away from methamphetamine by the photos alone and stories of users damaged by the drug serve as additional deterrents; the history of meth use, efforts to stop the current epidemic, and scientific details are also provided. (Rev: BL 10/15/07; SLJ 10/07) [362.29]

11515 Lawton, Sandra Augustyn, ed. *Drug Information for Teens: Health Tips about the Physical and Mental Effects of Substance Abuse. 2nd ed.* (7–12). Series: Teen Health. 2006, Omnigraphics $65 (978-0-7808-0862-1). Updating an earlier edition, this is a comprehensive, well-organized guide to substance abuse — drugs, chemicals, alcohol, and tobacco and including herbal supplements and caffeine and energy drinks — that

743

covers treatment and drug testing as well as places to go to get help. (Rev: SLJ 12/06)

11516 Lee, Mary Price, and Richard S. Lee. *Drugs and Codependency* (6–10). Series: Drug Abuse Prevention Library. 1995, Rosen LB $17.95 (978-0-8239-2065-5). The vulnerability of teens who live in a household where drugs are abused is the focus of this volume. (Rev: BL 9/15/95; SLJ 10/95) [616.869]

11517 Levert, Suzanne. *The Facts about LSD and Other Hallucinogens* (7–12). Series: Drugs. 2005, Benchmark LB $25.95 (978-0-7614-1974-7). A helpful guide to LSD and other hallucinogens, with some history and basic information about the various kinds on the market, their medical uses, how they are abused, and how they affect the body. (Rev: SLJ 5/06) [362.29]

11518 Levert, Suzanne. *The Facts About Steroids* (7–12). Series: Drugs. 2004, Benchmark LB $37.07 (978-0-7614-1808-5). Examines the effects of steroids on users, the health risks, and the laws governing steroid use. (Rev: SLJ 3/05) [362.29]

11519 LeVert, Suzanne, and Jeff Hendricks. *Ecstasy* (6–12). Series: Benchmark Rockets. 2010, Marshall Cavendish LB $28.50 (978-0-7614-4349-0). With information about the history of this drug, the ways in which it is consumed, the dangers it poses, the legal problems involved in its use, and some sidebar accounts of teen usage, this title is useful for reports and for young people who have a more personal interest;. Also use *Steroids* (2010). (Rev: LMC 3–4/10) [362.29]

11520 Littell, Mary Ann. *Heroin Drug Dangers* (5–8). Series: Drug Dangers. 1999, Enslow LB $27.93 (978-0-7660-1156-4). A short, well-illustrated book that describes the physiological effects of heroin, the dangers of its use, and how to resist its temptations. (Rev: BL 9/15/99; HBG 3/00) [362.29]

11521 Lookadoo, Justin. *The Dirt on Drugs: A Dateable Book* (6–10). Series: The Dirt. 2005, Revell paper $9.99 (978-0-8007-5919-3). A former Texas probation officer writes frankly about the dangers of drugs. (Rev: SLJ 7/05) [616.8]

11522 McMillan, Daniel. *Teen Smoking: Understanding the Risk* (6–12). Series: Issues in Focus. 1998, Enslow LB $20.95 (978-0-89490-722-7). An interesting, informative account that discusses nicotine addiction, secondhand smoke, health hazards, smoking prevention, and treatments for people who want to stop. (Rev: VOYA 8/98) [362.2]

11523 McMullin, Jordan, ed. *Marijuana* (6–9). Series: History of Drugs. 2005, Gale LB $36.20 (978-0-7377-1957-4). Excerpts from previously published materials — going back as far as the 16th century — chronicle the history of marijuana, focusing in particular on the controversy surrounding its use in Western society. (Rev: BL 4/1/05) [615]

11524 Marcovitz, Hal. *Should the Drinking Age Be Lowered?* (8–11). Illus. Series: In Controversy. 2011, ReferencePoint LB $26.95 (978-160152144-6). Are teenagers mature enough to drink? Can other countries serve as a model? This book looks at the pros and cons of these and other questions relating to teens and alcohol. (Rev: BL 6/1/11) [362.292]

11525 Menhard, Francha Roffe. *The Facts about Amphetamines* (7–12). Series: Drugs. 2005, Benchmark LB $25.95 (978-0-7614-1972-3). This guide gives a brief history of these drugs and basic information about the various kinds on the market, their medical uses, how they are abused, and how they affect the body. (Rev: SLJ 5/06) [362.29]

11526 Menhard, Francha Roffe. *The Facts About Inhalants* (7–12). Series: Drugs. 2004, Benchmark LB $37.07 (978-0-7614-1809-2). Explores the dangers associated with the use of inhalants. (Rev: SLJ 3/05) [362.29]

11527 Menhard, Francha Roffe, and Lisa Harkrader. *Inhalants* (6–12). Series: Benchmark Rockets. 2010, Marshall Cavendish LB $28.50 (978-0-7614-4350-6). With information about inhalants' history, the ways in which they are consumed, the dangers posed, and the legal problems involved, plus some sidebar accounts of teen usage, this title is useful for reports and for young people who have a more personal interest;. (Rev: LMC 3–4/10) [362.29]

11528 Monroe, Judy. *Antidepressants* (7–10). Series: Drug Library. 1997, Enslow LB $26.60 (978-0-89490-848-4). Current information is given about these frequently abused drugs, actual case studies are cited, and discussion questions are provided. (Rev: BL 5/15/97) [616.85]

11529 Monroe, Judy. *Nicotine* (7–10). Series: Drug Library. 1995, Enslow LB $26.60 (978-0-89490-505-6). A concise, easy-to-use look at nicotine, where it is found, its effects, and how to avoid its use. (Rev: BL 7/95; SLJ 9/95) [613.85]

11530 Naff, Clay Farris. *Nicotine and Tobacco* (7–10). Series: Compact Research. 2007, Reference Point LB $24.95 (978-1-60152-006-7). A well-organized look at the use of nicotine and tobacco and the dangers involved. (Rev: LMC 11–12/07; SLJ 9/07) [613.85]

11531 Nakaya, Andrea C. *Marijuana* (8–10). Series: Compact Research. 2007, Reference Point LB $24.95 (978-1-60152-000-5). This compact volume provides lots of information for report writers, with illustrations, quotations from primary sources, lists of facts, statistical charts, and brief timelines. (Rev: SLJ 5/07) [362.29]

11532 Nolan, Meghan, ed. *Let's Clear the Air: 10 Reasons Not to Start Smoking* (5–8). Illus. by Deanna Staffo. 2007, Lobster paper $14.95 (978-1-897073-66-7). In personal essays, young people reveal the reasons why they don't smoke — reasons ranging from the deaths of loved ones to the smell and the cost. (Rev: BL 1/1–15/08; LMC 2/08; SLJ 3/08) [613.85]

11533 Olive, M. Foster. *Prescription Pain Relievers* (6–9). Series: Drugs, The Straight Facts. 2005, Chelsea House LB $30.00 (978-0-7910-8199-0). Describes how drugs work to relieve pain and the growing problems of abuse of such drugs. (Rev: SLJ 11/05) [613.8]

11534 Packard, Helen C. *Prozac: The Controversial Cure* (6–9). Series: Drug Abuse Prevention Library. 1998, Rosen LB $27.95 (978-0-8239-2551-3). This book explores the controversy around this antidepressant, called the miracle drug of the 1990s, and gives teens sound advice concerning its use and misuse. (Rev: BL 5/15/98; SLJ 10/98) [616.8527061]

11535 Packer, Alex J. *Highs! Over 150 Ways to Feel Really, REALLY Good . . . Without Alcohol or Other Drugs* (6–12). 2000, Free Spirit paper $15.95 (978-1-57542-074-5). Grouped into three areas (serenity, physical improvement, and creativity), the author describes 150 ways teenagers can feel good about themselves. (Rev: BL 11/1/00; SLJ 9/00) [158]

11536 Palenque, Stephanie Maher. *Crack and Cocaine = Busted!* (6–8). Series: Busted! 2005, Enslow LB $31.93 (978-0-7660-2169-3). A useful overview of cocaine and crack and the dangers these drugs pose to individual users and the community at large. (Rev: SLJ 9/05) [362.29]

11537 Sanders, Pete. *Smoking* (4–7). Series: What Do You Know About. 1996, Millbrook LB $23.90 (978-0-7613-0536-1). Covers the effects of smoking and ways in which youngsters can avoid getting hooked. (Rev: SLJ 3/97) [362.2]

11538 Sanders, Pete, and Steve Myers. *Drinking Alcohol* (4–8). Series: What Do You Know About. 1997, Millbrook LB $23.90 (978-0-7613-0573-6). An introduction to alcohol use and abuse, with material on how alcohol affects the body and behavior. (Rev: SLJ 10/97) [613.8]

11539 Santamaria, Peggy. *Drugs and Politics* (6–10). Series: Drug Abuse Prevention Library. 1994, Rosen LB $27.95 (978-0-8239-1703-7). A discussion of the influence of drugs on politics, such as in Colombia, where the government is involved with and intimidated by powerful drug interests. (Rev: BL 3/15/95; SLJ 3/95) [363.4]

11540 Shannon, Joyce Brennfleck, ed. *Alcohol Information for Teens: Health Tips About Alcohol and Alcoholism* (7–12). Series: Teen Health. 2005, Omnigraphics $58.00 (978-0-7808-0741-9). Authoritative information about the effects of alcohol on the mind and body and the dangers of alcohol dependency. (Rev: SLJ 7/05) [613.8]

11541 Sherman, Jill. *Drug Trafficking* (7–10). Series: Essential Issues. 2010, ABDO LB $32.79 (978-1-60453-953-0). After a history of drug trafficking this volume looks at the issue from the perspectives of producers, smugglers, dealers, and users and discusses the various approaches to law enforcement. (Rev: LMC 10/10) [363.4]

11542 Sherry, Clifford J. *Drugs and Eating Disorders* (5–10). Series: Drug Abuse Prevention Library. 1994, Rosen LB $17.95 (978-0-8239-1540-8). Shows how diet pills and other weight-loss products can lead to drug abuse and, in some cases, addiction. (Rev: BL 6/1–15/94; SLJ 6/94) [616.85]

11543 Sherry, Clifford J. *Inhalants* (5–10). 1994, Rosen LB $17.95 (978-0-8239-1704-4). A look at inhalants, where they are found, and how they affect the body. (Rev: BL 2/15/95; SLJ 3/95) [362.29]

11544 Shuker, Nancy. *Everything You Need to Know About an Alcoholic Parent. Rev. ed.* (7–12). 1998, Rosen LB $27.95 (978-0-8239-2869-9). After a general discussion of alcoholism, Shuker explains how it changes human relationships and how young people can cope with it. (Rev: BL 1/15/90; VOYA 4/90) [362.29]

11545 Strazzabosco-Hayn, Gina. *Drugs and Sleeping Disorders* (7–12). Series: Drug Abuse Prevention Library. 1996, Rosen LB $27.95 (978-0-8239-2144-7). An exploration of sleep disorders and potential problems and dangers of using drugs for sleep. (Rev: SLJ 3/96) [362.2]

11546 Trapani, Margi. *Inside a Support Group: Help for Teenage Children of Alcoholics* (6–9). Series: Drug Abuse Prevention Library. 1997, Rosen LB $27.95 (978-0-8239-2508-7). Teens with alcoholic parents get helpful information from this inside look at Alateen, an organization designed to help teens cope with a loved one's addiction to alcohol. (Rev: BL 12/15/97; SLJ 1/98) [362.292]

11547 Van Tuyl, Christine, ed. *Drunk Driving* (7–10). Series: Issues That Concern You. 2006, Gale $32.45 (978-0-7377-3239-9). Article excerpts present various points of view regarding legal drinking ages, blood-alcohol levels, the punishment of offenders, and so forth. (Rev: BL 10/15/06) [363.12]

11548 Webb, Margot. *Drugs and Gangs* (7–12). Series: Drug Abuse Prevention Library. 1996, Rosen LB $17.95 (978-0-8239-2059-4). This book describes the connections between gangs and drugs, in both selling and using, and provides teens with tips on how to avoid these dangers. (Rev: SLJ 3/96; VOYA 6/96) [362.29]

11549 Weitzman, Elizabeth. *Let's Talk About Smoking* (4–8). Series: Let's Talk. 1996, Rosen LB $19.95 (978-0-8239-2307-6). This book explains why people smoke, its effects, and ways to avoid starting, with tips on how to give up. (Rev: BL 3/15/97; SLJ 1/97) [362.29]

11550 Wilkins, Jessica. *Street Pharma* (6–10). Illus. Series: Dealing with Drugs. 2011, Crabtree LB $30.60 (978-077875512-8). Discusses teens' use of prescription medications and provides breakdowns of types of drugs as well as resources for those seeking treatment. (Rev: BL 4/1/12) [362.29]

11551 Wilkinson, Beth. *Drugs and Depression* (6–12). Series: Drug Abuse Prevention Library. 1994, Rosen LB $27.95 (978-0-8239-3004-3). Some young people turn to drugs to deal with their depression. This book shows the dangers in this approach and offers positive ways of handling depression and places to get assistance. (Rev: BL 6/1–15/94) [616.86]

Bionics and Transplants

11552 Beecroft, Simon. *Super Humans: A Beginner's Guide to Bionics* (5–7). Illus. by Ian Thompson and Stephen Sweet. Series: Future Files. 1998, Millbrook LB $23.40 (978-0-7613-0621-4). This work explores such futuristic topics as cloning humans, gene manipulation, electronic body parts, and life extension. (Rev: HBG 10/98; SLJ 10/98) [617.9]

11553 McClellan, Marilyn. *Organ and Tissue Transplants: Medical Miracles and Challenges* (7–12). Series: Issues in Focus. 2003, Enslow LB $26.60 (978-0-7660-1943-0). The story of a critically injured teen draws readers into this discussion of transplants of organs and tissues and the ethical issues involved. (Rev: HBG 10/03; SLJ 5/03) [617.9]

11554 Schwartz, Tina P. *Organ Transplants: A Survival Guide for the Entire Family: The Ultimate Teen Guide* (7–12). Series: It Happened to Me. 2005, Scarecrow $36.50 (978-0-8108-4924-2). A clear explanation, in question-and-answer format, of the complex problems relating to medical transplants, with discussion of the hazards and the emotional upheaval to be expected. (Rev: SLJ 10/05) [617.9]

Diseases and Illnesses

11555 Abramovitz, Melissa. *Lou Gehrig's Disease* (7–12). 2006, Gale LB $31.20 (978-1-59018-676-5). Sidebars, diagrams, and photographs help teens understand the causes, symptoms, and diagnosis of ALS, or Lou Gehrig's disease; potential future treatments are also discussed. (Rev: SLJ 7/06)

11556 Abrams, Liesa. *Chronic Fatigue Syndrome* (5–7). Series: Diseases and Disorders. 2003, Gale LB $32.45 (978-1-59018-039-6). The symptoms of and treatments for this mysterious condition and related medical problems are covered here, along with the research being undertaken. (Rev: SLJ 7/03) [616]

11557 Ambrose, Marylou. *Investigating Diabetes: Real Facts for Real Lives* (7–10). Series: Investigating Diseases. 2010, Enslow LB $34.60 (978-0-7660-3338-2). Symptoms, diagnosis, treatment, and current research are all covered in this book that also tells the stories of children coping with the disease and provides historical background. (Rev: LMC 10/10) [616.4]

11558 Ambrose, Marylou, and Veronica Deisler. *Investigating Eating Disorders (Anorexia, Bulimia and Binge Eating): Real Facts for Real Lives* (7–10). Series: Investigating Diseases. 2010, Enslow LB $34.60 (978-0-7660-3339-9). Symptoms, diagnosis, treatment, and current research are all covered in this book that also tells the stories of children coping with these problems and provides historical background. (Rev: LMC 10/10) [616.85]

11559 Anderson, Judith. *Fighting Disease* (4–7). Series: Working for Our Future. 2010, Black Rabbit LB $28.50 (978-1-59771-194-4). This volume explains why the United Nations chose fighting disease as one of its eight Millennium Development goals and looks at the various reasons why people are deprived of good medical care and what can be done to improve the situation. (Rev: BL 6/10; LMC 10/10; SLJ 4/10) [362.196]

11560 Anonymous. *Quicksand: HIV/AIDS In Our Lives* (4–7). 2009, Candlewick $16.99 (978-076361589-5). Part Q&A, part memoir, this book provides frank and supportive information about HIV/AIDS, dispelling myths in an age-appropriate manner. (Rev: BL 12/1/09; LMC 11–12/09; SLJ 11/09) [616.97]

11561 Bakewell, Lisa, and Karen Bellenir, eds. *Cancer Information for Teens: Health Tips About Cancer Awareness, Prevention, Diagnosis, and Treatment* (8–12). Series: Teen Health. 2009, Omnigraphics $69 (978-0-7808-1085-3). Provides current information on cancer's warning signs, risk factors, and treatment. (Rev: SLJ 3/10)

11562 Balkin, Karen F., ed. *Food-Borne Illness* (7–12). Series: At Issue. 2004, Gale LB $29.95 (978-0-7377-1334-3); paper $21.20 (978-0-7377-1335-0). A collection of previously published articles that examine the dangers of food-borne illness and what can be done to protect consumers. (Rev: SLJ 4/05) [615.9]

11563 Ballard, Carol. *AIDS and Other Epidemics* (5–8). Illus. Series: What If We Do Nothing? 2009, Gareth Stevens LB $31.00 (978-1-4339-0085-3). HIV/AIDS, SARS, and malaria are among the diseases addressed in this volume that looks at the past, the current status, and the future outlook. (Rev: BL 4/15/09; SLJ 6/09) [614.5]

11564 Ballard, Carol. *Explaining Food Allergies* (7–12). Series: Explaining . . . 2010, Smart Apple Media LB $34.25 (978-1-59920-316-4). Well designed and written, these books about common illnesses affecting children include ways to help kids cope with the various conditions (glossary, index). (Rev: BL 10/1/09; LMC 1–2/10)

11565 Barnard, Bryn. *Outbreak! Plagues That Changed History* (5–8). Illus. by author. 2005, Crown LB $19.99 (978-0-375-92986-1). Information on microbes and the study of microorganisms precedes details of specific epidemics. (Rev: SLJ 2/06) [614.4]

11566 Bellenir, Karen, ed. *Allergy Information for Teens: Health Tips About Allergic Reactions Such as Anaphylaxis, Respiratory Problems, and Rashes* (7–12). 2006, Omnigraphics $65 (978-0-7808-0799-0). Readers learn about allergy symptoms, tests, treatments, and management strategies with short Q&A sections, diagrams, and sidebars. (Rev: SLJ 7/06)

11567 Bellenir, Karen, ed. *Asthma Information for Teens: Health Tips About Managing Asthma and Related Concerns* (8–12). Series: Teen Health. 2005, Omnigraphics LB $65.00 (978-0-7808-0770-9). Information-packed but readable, this volume covers all aspects of asthma. (Rev: SLJ 9/05) [616.2]

11568 Bjorklund, Ruth. *Asthma* (4–7). Series: Health Alert. 2004, Benchmark LB $28.50 (978-0-7614-1803-0). In addition to describing the causes and treatment of asthma, this attractive title opens with a case history and also includes lists of famous people who suffer from the condition. (Rev: SLJ 5/05)

11569 Bjorklund, Ruth. *Food-Borne Illnesses* (4–7). Series: Health Alert. 2005, Marshall Cavendish LB $19.95 (978-0-7614-1917-4). This is a wide-ranging exploration of illnesses that can be caused by contaminated food — including those resulting from bacteria, poor hygiene, poor handling, and terrorism — and the treatments and preventions available. (Rev: SLJ 6/06) [615.9]

11570 Bowman-Kruhm, Mary. *Everything You Need to Know About Down Syndrome* (4–7). Series: Need to Know Library. 2000, Rosen LB $25.25 (978-0-8239-2949-8). Describes the causes, symptoms, and treatment of Down syndrome, and looks at the education and family life of individuals with this condition. (Rev: HBG 10/00; SLJ 3/00) [362.1]

11571 Brill, Marlene Targ. *Alzheimer's Disease* (4–7). Series: Health Alert. 2004, Benchmark LB $28.50 (978-0-7614-1799-6). In addition to describing the diagnosis and treatment of Alzheimer's disease, this attractive title opens with a case history and also includes lists of famous people who suffer from the condition. (Rev: SLJ 5/05) [362.19]

11572 Brill, Marlene Targ. *Tourette Syndrome* (6–12). Series: Twenty-First Century Medical Library. 2002, Millbrook LB $26.90 (978-0-7613-2101-9). This volume provides historical and medical information on the disorder named for neurologist Georges Gilles de la Tourette, presenting the stories of three teenagers who suffer from it. (Rev: BL 3/1/02; HBG 10/02; SLJ 4/02) [375]

11573 Bueche, Shelley. *The Ebola Virus* (4–7). Series: Parasites. 2003, Gale LB $24.95 (978-0-7377-1780-8). Although it's part of the Parasites series, this book focuses on the Ebola virus, which causes an infectious illness and is found widely in Central Africa. (Rev: BL 3/1/04; SLJ 6/04) [616.9]

11574 Burby, Liza N. *Bulimia Nervosa: The Secret Cycle of Bingeing and Purging* (6–10). Series: Teen Health Library of Eating Disorder Prevention. 1998, Rosen LB $27.95 (978-0-8239-2762-3). Bulimia is an eating disorder characterized by bingeing and purging. This book describes various eating disorders, then focuses on bulimia, its causes, physical and psychological effects, the roles of peer pressure, media images, family relationships, genetics, and treatment and recovery. (Rev: SLJ 1/99) [616.85]

11575 Bush, Jenna. *Ana's Story: A Journey of Hope* (8–11). 2007, HarperCollins $18.99 (978-0-06-137908-6). Bush worked for UNICEF in Latin America and this story highlights the impact of HIV/AIDS in the area, recounting Ana's birth with the disease, the death of both her parents, the struggle to find an accepting home, her eventual success in finding love, and her hope for the future when she gives birth to a disease-free baby. ∩ (Rev: BL 8/07; HB 11–12/07; SLJ 10/07) [362]

11576 Cain, Barbara. *Autism, the Invisible Cord: A Sibling's Diary* (4–7). 2012, Magination $14.95 (978-143381191-3); paper $9.95 (978-14338119-2-0). Fourteen-year-old Jenny describes her experiences with her autistic 11-year-old brother Ezra in this fictional story that is classified as nonfiction and includes pages of tips for siblings. (Rev: BL 11/15/12; SLJ 1/13) [618.92]

11577 Cefrey, Holly. *Coping with Cancer* (6–12). Series: Coping. 2000, Rosen LB $26.50 (978-0-8239-2849-1). As well as discussing how cancer develops in various parts of the body, this book gives self-help advice for anyone who is diagnosed with the disease. (Rev: BL 1/1–15/01; SLJ 12/00) [616.99]

11578 Cefrey, Holly. *Syphilis and Other Sexually Transmitted Diseases* (5–8). Series: Epidemics. 2001, Rosen LB $27.95 (978-0-8239-3488-1). Cefrey describes historic outbreaks and treatments, as well as the symptoms and cure, of syphilis and other sexually transmitted diseases. (Rev: BL 3/15/02) [616.95]

11579 Cefrey, Holly. *Yellow Fever* (5–8). Series: Epidemics. 2002, Rosen LB $27.95 (978-0-8239-3489-8). Yellow fever, spread by mosquitoes, was the cause of several epidemics in American cities during the 19th century before a cure was found by dedicated doctors who risked their lives. (Rev: BL 8/02) [616]

11580 Chilman-Blair, Kim, and John Taddeo. *Medikidz Explain HIV* (5–8). Series: Superheroes on a Medical Mission. 2010, Rosen LB $29.25 (978-143589458-7). Using cartoon illustrations and a graphic novel format, this volume — and the Medikidz superheroes — explain the HIV virus and its dangers. Also use *Medikidz*

Explain Swine Flu, Medikidz Explain Depression, and *Medikidz Explain Sleep Apnea* (all 2010). (Rev: BL 3/15/11; SLJ 5/1/11) [614.5]

11581 Chilman-Blair, Kim, and John Taddeo. *What's Up with Max? Medikidz Explain Asthma* (4–7). Series: Superheroes on a Medical Mission. 2010, Rosen LB $29.25 (978-1-4358-3534-4). Multicultural young "superheroes" explain about asthma and its treatment and show readers around the relevant parts of the body. Also use *What's Up with Pam? Medikidz Explain Childhood Obesity, What's Up with Paulina? Medikidz Explain Food Allergies,* and *What's Up with Sean? Medikidz Explain Scoliosis* (all 2010) (Rev: LMC 10/10) [616.2]

11582 Clarke, Julie M., and Ann Kirby- Payne. *Understanding Weight and Depression* (7–10). Series: Teen Eating Disorder Prevention. 1999, Rosen LB $31.95 (978-0-8239-2994-8). This book discusses the psychological origins of eating disorders such as anorexia and bulimia and suggests ways to develop a healthy self-image. [616.8]

11583 Currie-McGhee, Leanne K. *Sexually Transmitted Diseases* (6–12). Illus. Series: Compact Research. 2008, ReferencePoint $25.95 (978-160152045-6). Using a blend of text, diagrams, primary sources, and bullet points this volume delivers sobering information on a variety of STDs, including HPV. (Rev: BL 10/15/08; LMC 8–9/09) [614.5]

11584 DiConsiglio, John. *When Birds Get Flu and Cows Go Mad!* (5–7). Illus. Series: 24/7 Science Behind the Scenes: Medical Files. 2007, Scholastic LB $26.00 (978-0-531-12069-9); paper $7.95 (978-0-531-17528-6). A lively discussion of bird flu, mad cow disease, E. coli bacteria, and other food-borne and headline-grabbing illnesses. (Rev: BL 12/1/07; LMC 3/08) [616.9]

11585 Dillon, Erin, ed. *Obesity* (7–12). Series: Issues That Concern You. 2006, Gale LB $32.45 (978-0-7377-2194-2). Colorful photographs underline the importance of this problem being discussed in this helpful volume that presents essays giving different points of view. (Rev: SLJ 2/07)

11586 Dittmer, Lori. *Parkinson's Disease* (7–9). Illus. Series: Living with Disease. 2011, Creative Education $23.95 (978-160818076-9). In addition to discussing the disease, its possible causes, typical symptoms, and treatments, this volume features celebrities who suffer from the disease, including actor Michael J. Fox. (Rev: BL 10/1/11) [616.8]

11587 Donnelly, Karen. *Coping with Lyme Disease* (6–12). Series: Coping. 2001, Rosen LB $31.95 (978-0-8239-3199-6). This introduction to the symptoms, diagnosis, treatment, and prevention of Lyme disease includes personal stories. (Rev: SLJ 7/01) [616.9]

11588 Donnelly, Karen. *Everything You Need to Know About Lyme Disease* (5–8). Series: Need to Know Library. 2000, Rosen LB $27.95 (978-0-8239-3216-0).

This book explains how Lyme disease was discovered, how it is transmitted, its symptoms, and its treatments. (Rev: BL 12/1/00) [616.9]

11589 Donnelly, Karen. *Leprosy (Hansen's Disease)* (5–8). Series: Epidemics. 2002, Rosen LB $27.95 (978-0-8239-3498-0). This is the story of leprosy, the disease that created social outcasts of its victims, and of a man named Hansen who discovered an effective treatment. (Rev: BL 8/02) [616.9]

11590 Edelson, Edward. *The Immune System* (6–12). Series: 21st Century Health and Wellness. 2000, Chelsea LB $36.00 (978-0-7910-5525-0). A revised edition of Edelson's presentation on the immune system and what happens when it fails to function. (Rev: BL 4/15/00; HBG 9/00; SLJ 6/00) [616.07]

11591 Ellis, Deborah. *Our Stories, Our Songs: African Children Talk About AIDS* (6–9). 2005, Fitzhenry & Whiteside $18.95 (978-1-55041-913-9). First-person accounts from children in Malawi and Zambia whose lives have been touched by AIDS paint a heartbreaking portrait of the devastation wrought by the disease in sub-Saharan Africa. (Rev: BL 10/1/05*; SLJ 11/05*) [362.1]

11592 Frankenberger, Elizabeth. *Food and Love: Dealing with Family Attitudes About Weight* (7–12). Series: Teen Health Library of Eating Disorder Prevention. 1998, Rosen LB $27.95 (978-0-8239-2760-9). This book explores the role the family plays in developing a healthy self-image and affecting a teenager's attitudes toward food. (Rev: VOYA 4/99) [616.85]

11593 Fredericks, Carrie, ed. *Autism* (7–10). Series: Perspectives on Diseases and Disorders. 2008, Gale LB $34.95 (978-0-7377-3869-8). Readers whose lives are affected by autism will be interested in this look at the disorder and its spectrum of symptoms; personal accounts by those with autism and parents of autistic children add to the presentation. (Rev: BL 4/1/08) [616.85]

11594 Frissell, Susan, and Paula Harney. *Eating Disorders and Weight Control* (7–10). 1998, Enslow LB $26.60 (978-0-89490-919-1). This book covers anorexia, bulimia, binge eating disorders, and weight control issues with material on how to cope with them in a healthy, realistic manner. (Rev: BL 4/15/98; HBG 9/98; SLJ 3/98) [616.85]

11595 Gay, Kathlyn, and Sean McGarrahan. *Epilepsy: The Ultimate Teen Guide* (7–12). Series: Ultimate Teen Guide. 2003, Scarecrow LB $32.50 (978-0-8108-4339-4). This informative look at this seizure disease and its impact on typical teen activities (sports, jobs, driving, and so forth) includes the personal experiences of co-author McGarrahan, who was diagnosed with epilepsy at the age of 16. (Rev: BL 10/15/03; SLJ 10/03) [616]

11596 Gilman, Laura Anne. *Coping with Cerebral Palsy* (5–9). Series: Coping. 2001, Rosen LB $31.95 (978-0-8239-3150-7). This is a self-help book that looks at ways to deal with school, work, and travel as well as coping with other people and their attitudes. (Rev: SLJ 2/02) [616.836]

11597 Goldsmith, Connie. *Battling Malaria: On the Front Lines Against a Global Killer* (8–12). 2010, Lerner LB $37.27 (978-0-8225-8580-0). Goldsmith emphasizes the devastating impact of malaria on nations around the world and provides facts about its transmission, treatment, and methods of control; with personal stories and interesting sidebars. (Rev: LMC 11–12/10; SLJ 11/1/10)

11598 Goldsmith, Connie. *Hepatitis* (7–12). Series: USA Today Health Reports: Diseases and Disorders. 2010, Lerner LB $34.60 (978-0-8225-6787-5). Hepatitis is not sufficiently recognized as a health problem, and this succinct and accessible volume discusses symptoms, transmission, prevention, treatment, and research. (Rev: BL 6/10; LMC 11–12/10) [616.3]

11599 Goldsmith, Connie. *Influenza* (7–12). Series: USA Today Health Reports: Diseases and Disorders. 2010, Lerner LB $34.60 (978-0-7613-5881-7). This succinct and accessible volume discusses symptoms, transmission, prevention, and treatment of influenza as well as outbreaks of bird flu and swine flu. (Rev: BL 6/10; LMC 11–12/10) [616.2]

11600 Goldsmith, Connie. *Influenza: The Next Pandemic?* (6–9). 2006, Lerner $27.93 (978-0-7613-9457-0). Covers the history of the flu, past and present outbreaks, treatments, and new research being done to prevent the potentially deadly disease. (Rev: BL 9/1/06; SLJ 1/07) [614.5]

11601 Goldsmith, Connie. *Invisible Invaders: Dangerous Infectious Diseases* (7–10). Series: Discovery! 2006, Lerner LB $27.93 (978-0-8225-3416-7). This clearly written and well-illustrated book provides information on infectious diseases including SARS, Ebola, mad cow disease, and E.coli. (Rev: BL 5/1/06; SLJ 5/06) [362.196]

11602 Goldstein, Margaret J. *Everything You Need to Know About Multiple Sclerosis* (5–8). Series: Need to Know Library. 2001, Rosen LB $27.95 (978-0-8239-3292-4). An introduction to multiple sclerosis, its symptoms and treatment, and how it affects the nervous system, along with information on the importance of treating the emotional impact of this disease. (Rev: SLJ 5/01) [616]

11603 Goodfellow, Gregory. *Epilepsy* (7–9). Series: Diseases and Disorders. 2001, Lucent LB $32.45 (978-1-56006-701-6). The author describes the causes of epilepsy, how it is currently being treated, and how people live with this condition. (Rev: BL 1/1–15/02; SLJ 4/01) [616.8]

11604 Grady, Denise. *Deadly Invaders: Virus Outbreaks around the World, from Marburg Fever to Avian Flu* (7–10). 2006, Kingfisher $16.95 (978-0-7534-5995-9).

New York Times reporter Grady recalls her trip to Angola during the deadly outbreak of Marburg fever and describes the challenges faced in a community with few basic services; she also discusses other viral diseases including HIV and AIDS, West Nile, avian flu, SARS, and Hantavirus. (Rev: BL 10/1/06; LMC 4–5/07; SLJ 12/06*) [614.5]

11605 Grossberg, Blythe. *Asperger's Rules! How to Make Sense of School and Friends* (5–8). 2012, Magination $14.95 (978-1-4338-1128-9); paper $9.95 (978-1-4338-1-127-2). This helpful guide offers a selection of formats for young people interested in learning more about dealing with Asperger's, offering bulleted lists, quizzes, sample dialogues, multiple-choice and other tests, advice on body language, tips on making friends and coping with bullies, and so forth. (Rev: BL 8/12; SLJ 10/12) [618.92]

11606 Hardman, Lizabeth. *Plague* (6–10). Series: Diseases and Disorders. 2010, Lucent $32.45 (978-1-4205-0145-2). With real-life examples and many illustrations, this book describes epidemics of plague through the centuries. (Rev: LMC 5–6/10) [616.9232]

11607 Harris, Jacqueline. *Sickle Cell Disease* (6–10). 2001, Twenty-First Century LB $26.90 (978-0-7613-1459-2). After introducing three young victims of this disease, the author describes its symptoms and treatment and traces its history. (Rev: BL 9/15/01; HBG 3/02; SLJ 12/01) [616.1]

11608 Harris, Nancy, ed. *AIDS in Developing Countries* (6–12). Series: At Issue. 2004, Gale LB $29.95 (978-0-7377-1789-1). Through a series of essays that express different points of view, the AIDS situation in countries in Africa, Asia, and South America is explored. (Rev: BL 2/15/04) [616]

11609 Hawkins, Trisha. *Everything You Need to Know About Measles and Rubella* (4–8). Series: Need to Know Library. 2001, Rosen LB $27.95 (978-0-8239-3322-8). Simple text and photographs describe the diseases and methods of prevention and treatment, and discuss public-health issues. Also use *Everything You Need to Know About Chicken Pox and Shingles* (2001). (Rev: SLJ 8/01) [616.9]

11610 Hayhurst, Chris. *Cholera* (5–9). Series: Epidemics. 2001, Rosen LB $27.95 (978-0-8239-3345-7). In a readable style, Hayhurst discusses the history of cholera, formerly a deadly disease, and explains how its treatment was developed. Also use *Polio* and *Smallpox* (both 2001). (Rev: SLJ 7/01) [616.9]

11611 Hicks, Terry Allan. *Allergies* (4–8). Series: Health Alert. 2005, Benchmark LB $19.95 (978-0-7614-1918-1). All about what allergies are, what brings them on, and how they are treated, with colorful sidebars and features that add to the text. (Rev: SLJ 5/06) [616.97]

11612 Hirschmann, Kris. *The Ebola Virus* (6–8). Series: Diseases and Disorders. 2006, Gale LB $31.20 (978-1-

59018-672-5). Hirschmann gives an overview of the infectious disease discovered in 1976, for which no cure has yet been found. (Rev: SLJ 2/07)

11613 Hirschmann, Kris. *Salmonella* (4–7). Series: Parasites. 2003, Gale LB $24.95 (978-0-7377-1785-3). This fascinating examination of Salmonella bacteria, responsible for a wide variety of illnesses in the United States and elsewhere, is supplemented with numerous photos and microscopic views of the title bacteria. (Rev: BL 3/1/04) [615.4]

11614 Hoffmann, Gretchen. *Mononucleosis* (4–8). Series: Health Alert. 2005, Benchmark LB $19.95 (978-0-7614-1915-0). All about what "mono" is, its symptoms, and its treatment, with graphic features that add to the text. (Rev: SLJ 5/06) [616.9]

11615 Isle, Mick. *Everything You Need to Know About Food Poisoning* (4–8). Series: Need to Know Library. 2001, Rosen LB $27.95 (978-0-8239-3396-9). Safe ways to prepare food are the main focus of this book, which also describes the symptoms and treatment of food poisoning. (Rev: SLJ 10/01) [615.954]

11616 James, Otto. *AIDS* (7–9). Series: Voices. 2010, Smart Apple Media LB $34.25 (978-1-59920-282-2). In chapters titled with questions such as "What helped AIDS to increase in poorer countries?," "Should everyone be tested?," and "Could governments do more?," this title explores causes and solutions and includes various perspectives. (Rev: LMC 5–6/10; SLJ 11/1/09) [606.65]

11617 Johannsson, Phillip. *Heart Disease* (7–12). Series: Diseases and People. 1998, Enslow LB $20.95 (978-0-7660-1051-2). The causes and types of heart disease are described, along with an overview of current treatments and potential future advances. (Rev: BL 7/98) [616.1]

11618 Jurmain, Suzanne. *The Secret of the Yellow Death: A True Story of Medical Sleuthing* (5–8). 2009, Houghton Mifflin $19 (978-0-618-96581-6). As compelling as good fiction, this well-illustrated true story chronicles the fascinating methods used by scientists to discover the cause of yellow fever. (Rev: BL 9/15/09; HB 11–12/09; LMC 1–2/10; SLJ 9/09) [614.5]

11619 Kelly, Evelyn B., and Ian Wilker, et al. *Investigating Tuberculosis and Superbugs: Real Facts for Real Lives* (7–10). Illus. Series: Investigating Diseases. 2010, Enslow LB $34.60 (978-076603343-6). A thorough overview of diseases — tuberculosis, malaria, and so forth — that are becoming resistant to today's treatments, with discussion of options for the future. (Rev: BL 12/1/10) [616.9]

11620 Kittleson, Mark J., ed. *The Truth About Eating Disorders* (8–12). Series: Truth About. 2004, Facts on File $35.00 (978-0-8160-5300-1). Causes, diagnosis, and treatment are all covered in this user-friendly guide that looks at emotions along with physical symptoms

and does not neglect adolescent males with eating problems. (Rev: SLJ 4/05) [[616.85]

11621 Kittredge, Mary. *The Common Cold* (7–12). Series: 21st Century Health and Wellness. 2000, Chelsea House LB $24.95 (978-0-7910-5985-2). An interesting history of cold cures introduces this overview of the causes, prevention, and treatment of this perennial nuisance. (Rev: BL 11/15/00; HBG 10/01; SLJ 3/01) [616.1]

11622 Kowalski, Kathiann M. *Attack of the Superbugs: The Crisis of Drug-Resistant Diseases* (7–12). 2005, Enslow LB $31.93 (978-0-7660-2400-7). With full-color photographs and diagrams, this book show how viruses and diseases become resistant to drug treatments and mutate, resulting in the return of diseases that were thought extinct. (Rev: SLJ 6/06)

11623 Landau, Elaine. *Allergies* (4–7). Series: Understanding Illness. 1994, Twenty-First Century LB $24.90 (978-0-8050-2989-5). After a case history that explores allergies in personal terms, an objective presentation is given of their causes, effects, and treatment. (Rev: BL 12/15/94; SLJ 2/95) [616.97]

11624 Landau, Elaine. *Alzheimer's Disease: A Forgotten Life* (7–10). Series: Health and Human Disease. 2006, Scholastic LB $26.00 (978-0-531-16755-7). Symptoms, diagnosis, treatment, and prognosis are all covered here, plus a question-and-answer "ask the doctor" feature that adds pertinent information. (Rev: BL 12/1/05; SLJ 1/06) [616.8]

11625 Landau, Elaine. *Cancer* (4–7). Series: Understanding Illness. 1994, Twenty-First Century LB $24.90 (978-0-8050-2990-1). This book explains the many types of cancer, their causes, present-day treatments, and possible developments in the future. (Rev: BL 12/15/95; SLJ 2/95) [616.99]

11626 Landau, Elaine. *Food Poisoning and Foodborne Diseases* (7–12). Series: USA Today Health Reports: Diseases and Disorders. 2010, Lerner LB $34.60 (978-0-8225-7290-9). This succinct and accessible volume discusses symptoms, transmission, prevention, and treatment of illnesses caused by contaminated food and water. (Rev: BL 6/10; LMC 11–12/10) [615.9]

11627 Lawton, Sandra Augustyn, ed. *Eating Disorders Information for Teens: Health Tips About Anorexia, Bulimia, Binge Eating, and Other Eating Disorders* (7–12). Series: Teen Health. 2005, Omnigraphics $65.00 (978-0-7808-0783-9). This title explores all aspects of eating disorders as well as such related topics as body image, nutrition, self-esteem, and athleticism. (Rev: SLJ 12/05; VOYA 4/06)

11628 Lynette, Rachel. *Leprosy* (5–8). Series: Understanding Diseases and Disorders. 2005, Gale LB $26.20 (978-0-7377-3172-9). Straightforward text discusses the plight of leprosy patients around the world and through history; causes, treatments, and transmission are also discussed. (Rev: SLJ 6/06) [616.9]

11629 Manning, Karen. *AIDS: Can This Epidemic Be Stopped?* (6–8). Series: Issues of Our Time. 1995, Twenty-First Century LB $22.90 (978-0-8050-4240-5). A frank, unbiased look at AIDS, its causes, effects on society, and perspectives for the future. (Rev: BL 2/1/96; SLJ 2/96; VOYA 4/96) [616.97]

11630 Margulies, Phillip. *Creutzfeldt-Jakob Disease* (4–7). Series: Epidemics. 2004, Rosen LB $27.95 (978-0-8239-4199-5). Examines the history and current state of knowledge about this rare disorder that affects the brain and is related to Mad Cow Disease. Also use *West Nile Virus* (2004). (Rev: SLJ 8/04) [616.8]

11631 Margulies, Phillip. *Down Syndrome* (6–8). Series: Genetic Diseases and Disorders. 2006, Rosen LB $26.50 (978-1-4042-0695-3). This guide to Down syndrome — covering the history of the disorder and our contemporary understanding — will be useful for researchers; it includes a chapter on daily living that touches on issues such as sex. (Rev: SLJ 2/07) [362.1]

11632 Margulies, Phillip. *Everything You Need to Know About Rheumatic Fever* (5–8). Series: The Need to Know Library. 2004, Rosen LB $27.95 (978-0-8239-4509-2). After a brief history of the disease and the discovery of its cause, this volume discusses symptoms, treatment, and the concern that the disease may become more prevalent as bacteria develop resistance to antibiotics. (Rev: SLJ 4/05)

11633 Marisco, Katie. *HIV/AIDS* (7–10). Series: Essential Issues. 2010, ABDO LB $32.79 (978-1-60453-955-4). After a history of this disease, readers learn about its global impact, the medications available, continuing research, and the misconceptions and prejudices that have contributed to its spread. (Rev: LMC 10/10) [362.196]

11634 Markle, Sandra. *Leukemia: True Survival Stories* (5–8). Series: Powerful Medicine. 2010, Lerner LB $27.93 (978-0-8225-8700-2). Arresting full-color photographs, cross-sections, and personal stories are combined with facts about procedures and information about the medical personnel involved, (Rev: LMC 11–12/10) [616.99]

11635 Massari, Francesca. *Everything You Need to Know About Cancer* (5–9). Series: Need to Know Library. 2000, Rosen LB $27.95 (978-0-8239-3164-4). This book defines what cancer is and looks at its causes, prevention, symptoms, diagnosis, and treatment. (Rev: HBG 10/00; SLJ 8/00) [616.99]

11636 Miller, Debra A. *Pandemics* (8–12). Series: Hot Topics. 2006, Gale LB $31.20 (978-1-59018-965-8). A thoughtful exploration of infectious diseases and our ability to prevent and control outbreaks. (Rev: SLJ 4/07) [618.92]

11637 Moe, Barbara. *Coping with Eating Disorders* (7–10). 1999, Rosen $31.95 (978-0-8239-2974-0). Ac-

tual case histories are used to explain the characteristics of bulimia, anorexia, and compulsive-eating patterns. Practical coping suggestions are also offered. (Rev: BL 7/91; SLJ 11/91) [616.85]

11638 Moe, Barbara. *Coping with PMS* (7–12). Series: Coping. 1998, Rosen LB $25.25 (978-0-8239-2716-6). Supplemented by personal accounts, this book explains how PMS can be a manageable problem, with material on physiology, diet, lifestyle, attitude, and the relationship between nutrition and PMS control (recipes are included). (Rev: BL 5/15/98; SLJ 5/98) [618.172]

11639 Moe, Barbara. *Coping with Tourette Syndrome and Tic Disorders* (6–10). 2000, Rosen LB $26.50 (978-0-8239-2976-4). Solid information and many case studies are used in this examination of Tourette's syndrome, tic disorders, and related problems with material on how they affect moods, learning, activities, and sleep. (Rev: BL 7/00) [616.8]

11640 Moe, Barbara. *Everything You Need to Know About Migraines and Other Headaches* (7–12). Series: Need to Know Library. 2000, Rosen LB $27.95 (978-0-8239-3291-7). An accessible and thorough exploration of the symptoms, treatment, and prevention of migraines and other headaches. (Rev: HBG 10/01; SLJ 4/01) [616.8]

11641 Moe, Barbara. *Inside Eating Disorder Support Groups* (6–10). Series: Teen Health Library of Eating Disorder Prevention. 1998, Rosen LB $27.95 (978-0-8239-2769-2). After a general discussion of eating disorders and available treatments, this book explains the dynamics of support groups and how they can help teens recover from eating disorders and come to terms with their problems. (Rev: SLJ 1/99) [616.85]

11642 Moehn, Heather. *Everything You Need to Know When Someone You Know Has Leukemia* (5–10). Series: Need to Know Library. 2000, Rosen LB $27.95 (978-0-8239-3121-7). The basic facts about leukemia are covered with material on its various types and treatments, possible causes, and the emotional aspects of the illness. (Rev: SLJ 9/00) [616.99]

11643 Moehn, Heather. *Understanding Eating Disorder Support Groups* (7–12). Series: Teen Eating Disorder Prevention Library. 2000, Rosen LB $31.95 (978-0-8239-2992-4). Extensive information on the diagnosis, symptoms, and treatment of eating disorders precedes discussion of the types of support available; case studies appear throughout. (Rev: HBG 10/01; SLJ 2/01)

11644 Moragne, Wendy. *Allergies* (5–8). Series: Twenty-First Century Medical Library. 1999, Twenty-First Century LB $26.90 (978-0-7613-1359-5). After general material on allergies, their causes and treatment, this account describes specific allergies involving food, skin, rhinitis, drugs, and insects. (Rev: HBG 3/00; SLJ 3/00) [616.97]

11645 Mulcahy, Robert. *Diseases: Finding the Cure* (7–9). 1996, Oliver LB $21.95 (978-1-881508-28-1). After a general introduction on disease fighting, single chapters explore the breakthroughs of such scientists as Edward Jenner, Louis Pasteur, Alexander Fleming, and Jonas Salk, with a special afterword on AIDS. (Rev: SLJ 10/96) [616]

11646 Murphy, Jim, and Alison Blank. *Invincible Microbe: Tuberculosis and the Never-Ending Search for a Cure* (6–10). Illus. 2012, Clarion $17.99 (978-0-618-53574-3). With concise text, many images, and interesting anecdotes, this well-researched book traces the history of this devastating infectious disease. Outstanding Science Trade Books for Students K–12. ℮ Lexile 1200L (Rev: BL 7/12*; LMC 5–6/13; SLJ 7/12*; VOYA 4/12)

11647 Murphy, Wendy. *Asthma* (7–12). Series: Millbrook Medical Library. 1998, Millbrook LB $26.90 (978-0-7613-0364-0). Beginning with the causes of asthma, this book describes what happens during an attack, how the disease is controlled, and various avenues of medical treatment. (Rev: BL 1/1–15/99; HBG 3/99; SLJ 1/99) [616.2]

11648 Murphy, Wendy. *Orphan Diseases: New Hope for Rare Medical Conditions* (7–12). 2002, Millbrook LB $26.90 (978-0-7613-1919-1). Autism, cystic fibrosis, and dwarfism are among the conditions discussed, with information on origin, causes, treatment, and how patients cope with the condition. (Rev: BL 10/15/02; HBG 3/03) [362.1]

11649 Nakaya, Andrea C., ed. *Obesity* (8–12). Series: Opposing Viewpoints. 2005, Gale LB $36.20 (978-0-7377-3233-7). The causes of the soaring rates of obesity are discussed from various viewpoints, as well as who is responsible and what can be done to reduce this health problem. (Rev: SLJ 1/06) [616.3]

11650 Newton, David E. *Sick! Diseases and Disorders, Injuries and Infections* (8–12). 1999, U.X.L $247.00 (978-0-7876-3922-8). Arranged alphabetically, this volume covers 140 illnesses, disorders, and injuries with material on symptoms, causes, diagnosis, prevention, and treatment. (Rev: BL 10/1/00) [616]

11651 Nye, Bill, and Kathleen W. Zoehfeld. *Bill Nye the Science Guy's Great Big Book of Tiny Germs* (4–7). Illus. by Bryn Barnard. 2005, Hyperion $16.99 (978-0-7868-0543-3). Solid information on bacteria and viruses is presented in an appealing and lively format. (Rev: BL 6/1–15/05; SLJ 7/05) [579]

11652 Orr, Tamra. *When the Mirror Lies: Anorexia, Bulimia, and Other Eating Disorders* (7–12). 2006, Watts LB $30.50 (978-0-531-16791-5); paper $17.95 (978-0-531-17977-2). Case studies help to draw readers into this friendly account of eating disorders and their impact. ⌂ (Rev: SLJ 11/06)

11653 Ouriou, Katie. *Love Ya Like a Sister: A Story of Friendship* (8–12). 1999, Tundra paper $7.95 (978-0-88776-454-7). After her death from leukemia when only 16 years old, Katie Ouriou's life and thoughts during her last months were reconstructed from journal entries and e-mail correspondence with her many friends. (Rev: SLJ 5/99; VOYA 6/99) [616.95]

11654 Panno, Joseph. *Cancer: The Role of Genes, Lifestyle and Environment* (7–12). Series: The New Biology. 2004, Facts on File $35.00 (978-0-8160-4950-9). In this title from the New Biology series, author Joseph Panno explores the role of genetics, lifestyle choices, and the environment in cancer. (Rev: SLJ 2/05; VOYA 8/04)

11655 Parks, Peggy J. *Brain Tumors* (7–12). Illus. Series: Compact Research: Diseases and Disorders. 2011, ReferencePoint LB $26.95 (978-160152138-5). Looks at the causes, symptoms, and treatment of these tumors, with lots of graphs, tables, and diagrams. (Rev: BL 10/15/11) [616.99]

11656 Parks, Peggy J. *HPV* (7–12). Illus. Series: Compact Research: Diseases and Disorders. 2008, ReferencePoint LB $25.95 (978-160152070-8). Recent developments in the understanding and prevention of human papillomavirus (HPV) make this an interesting book on a hot health topic. (Rev: BL 4/1/09; SLJ 6/1/09) [362.196]

11657 Parks, Peggy J. *Influenza* (7–12). Illus. Series: Compact Research: Diseases and Disorders. 2010, ReferencePoint LB $26.95 (978-160152118-7). Looks at the causes, treatment, and prevention of influenza and at the danger of epidemics. (Rev: BL 2/1/11) [616.2]

11658 Parks, Peggy J. *Schizophrenia* (7–12). Illus. Series: Compact Research: Diseases and Disorders. 2011, ReferencePoint LB $26.95 (978-160152140-8). Looks at the symptoms and treatment of this disorder, with lots of graphs, tables, and diagrams. (Rev: BL 10/15/11) [616.89]

11659 Peters, Stephanie True. *The Battle Against Polio* (6–10). Series: Epidemic! 2004, Benchmark LB $29.93 (978-0-7614-1635-7). The history of polio, the toll it took on young lives, and the ultimately successful search for a vaccine are related in a compelling presentation. (Rev: BL 12/15/04; SLJ 2/05) [614.54]

11660 Pincus, Dion. *Everything You Need to Know About Cerebral Palsy* (4–7). Series: Need to Know Library. 2000, Rosen LB $27.95 (978-0-8239-2960-3). The causes and characteristics of cerebral palsy are discussed with material on the treatments and the daily life of those affected. (Rev: HBG 10/00; SLJ 3/00) [618.92]

11661 Pipher, Mary. *Hunger Pains: The Modern Woman's Tragic Quest for Thinness* (7–12). 1997, Ballantine paper $12.00 (978-0-345-41393-2). This book explains eating disorders, probes into their basic causes, and offers suggestions for help, with separate chapters on bulimia, anorexia, obesity, and diets. (Rev: VOYA 8/97) [616.95]

11662 Ramen, Fred. *Sleeping Sickness and Other Parasitic Tropical Diseases* (5–8). Series: Epidemics. 2002, Rosen LB $27.95 (978-0-8239-3499-7). After a history of parasitic diseases around the globe and the role played by bloodsucking killers like the tsetse fly, this account describes the treatments now available. (Rev: BL 8/02; SLJ 7/02) [616]

11663 Ray, Kurt. *Typhoid Fever* (5–8). Series: Epidemics. 2002, Rosen LB $27.95 (978-0-8239-3572-7). An introduction to the history and treatment of typhoid fever, including coverage of Typhoid Mary. (Rev: BL 3/15/02) [614.5]

11664 Reingold, Adam. *Smallpox: Is It Over?* (4–7). Illus. 2010, Bearport LB $25.27 (978-193608802-7). This well-organized book presents a clear and balanced view of smallpox, from the biology of the virus itself, to symptoms, to its long and eventful history and purported "defeat" in 1980. (Rev: BL 10/1/10) [614.5]

11665 Ridgway, Tom. *Mad Cow Disease: Bovine Spongiform Encephalopathy* (6–8). Series: Epidemics. 2002, Rosen LB $27.95 (978-0-8239-3487-4). A fascinating account of how this disease affects its victims, how it spreads, and how scientists raced to discover more about it. (Rev: BL 8/02; SLJ 6/02) [616.8]

11666 Rocha, Toni L. *Understanding Recovery from Eating Disorders* (6–10). Series: Teen Eating Disorder Prevention Library. 1999, Rosen $31.95 (978-0-8239-2884-2). This book offers first-person accounts of survivors of various types of eating disorders and also offers advice for teens who are in recovery programs. (Rev: BL 10/15/99; HBG 9/00; SLJ 7/00) [616.85]

11667 Romano, Amy. *Germ Warfare* (5–8). Series: Germs: The Library of Disease-Causing Organisms. 2004, Rosen LB $26.50 (978-0-8239-4493-4). An informative, illustrated overview of the history and current status of germ warfare, with discussion of what we can do to protect ourselves. (Rev: SLJ 1/05) [358]

11668 Rosaler, Maxine. *Botulism* (4–7). Series: Epidemics. 2004, Rosen LB $27.95 (978-0-8239-4197-1). A look at outbreaks of botulism and their causes and prevention. (Rev: SLJ 8/04) [614.5]

11669 Rosaler, Maxine. *Cystic Fibrosis* (6–8). Series: Genetic Diseases and Disorders. 2006, Rosen LB $26.50 (978-1-4042-0696-0). This guide to cystic fibrosis — covering history of our knowledge of the disorder and contemporary understanding — will be useful for researchers; (Rev: SLJ 2/07)

11670 Sanders, Pete, and Steve Myers. *Anorexia and Bulimia* (4–8). Illus. by Mike Lacy and Liz Sawyer. Series: What Do You Know About. 1999, Millbrook LB $23.90 (978-0-7613-0914-7). Using an actual case study as a beginning, this book explores the causes, ef-

fects, and treatment of these eating disorders and covers the behavioral patterns of those afflicted. (Rev: HBG 10/99; SLJ 10/99) [618.92]

11671 Schwartz, Robert H., and Peter M. G. Deane. *Coping with Allergies* (4–7). Series: Coping. 1999, Rosen LB $31.95 (978-0-8239-2511-7). After a rundown of the types and causes of allergies, this account describes their physical and emotional impact and current treatments. (Rev: BL 2/15/00) [616.97]

11672 Silverstein, Alvin. *The Asthma Update* (5–8). 2006, Enslow LB $31.93 (978-0-7660-2482-3). A thorough look at asthma, its symptoms, history, treatments, and the research being done in hopes of finding a cure. (Rev: BL 12/1/06) [616.2]

11673 Silverstein, Alvin. *Cancer: Conquering a Deadly Disease* (8–12). Series: Twenty-First Century Medical Library. 2005, Twenty-First Century LB $27.93 (978-0-7613-2833-9). Using case studies to introduce topics, this is a thorough exploration of new developments in the fight against cancer. (Rev: SLJ 3/06)

11674 Silverstein, Alvin. *The Food Poisoning Update* (5–8). Series: Disease Update. 2007, Enslow LB $23.95 (978-0-7660-2748-0). A clear introduction to what causes food poisoning, how it affects the body, and how it can be avoided. (Rev: BL 12/1/07; SLJ 2/08) [615.9]

11675 Silverstein, Alvin. *Mononucleosis* (7–10). Series: Diseases and People. 1994, Enslow LB $20.95 (978-0-89490-466-0). Examines this disease's history, causes, treatment, prevention, and societal response. (Rev: BL 1/15/95; HBG 10/01; SLJ 3/95) [616.9]

11676 Silverstein, Alvin. *Parkinson's Disease* (7–10). Series: Diseases and People. 2001, Enslow LB $26.60 (978-0-7660-1593-7). Parkinson's disease is described, with information on its causes, symptoms. diagnosis, and treatment. (Rev: HBG 3/03) [616.8]

11677 Silverstein, Alvin, and Virginia Silverstein. *The Breast Cancer Update* (5–9). Illus. Series: Disease Update. 2007, Enslow LB $31.93 (978-0-7660-2747-3). Symptoms, treatment, history, and new research are all included in this concise discussion of breast cancer. (Rev: SLJ 2/08)

11678 Silverstein, Alvin, and Virginia Silverstein. *The STDs Update* (6–12). Series: Disease Update. 2006, Enslow LB $23.95 (978-0-7660-2484-7). A question-and-answer format and personal accounts of STD infections make this a useful resource. (Rev: SLJ 9/06)

11679 Silverstein, Alvin, et al. *The Flu and Pneumonia Update* (5–8). Illus. Series: Disease Update. 2006, Enslow LB $31.93 (978-0-7660-2480-9). Symptoms, treatment, history, and new research are all included in this discussion of flu and pneumonia. (Rev: BL 4/1/06; SLJ 9/06) [616.2]

11680 Silverthorne, Elizabeth. *Anorexia and Bulimia* (6–10). Series: Diseases and Disorders. 2010, Lucent

$32.45 (978-1-4205-0141-4). With real-life examples and many illustrations, this book describes the causes, diagnosis, and treatment of these eating disorders. (Rev: LMC 5–6/10) [616.85]

11681 Simpson, Carolyn. *Coping with Sleep Disorders* (7–12). Series: Coping. 1995, Rosen LB $31.95 (978-0-8239-2068-6). This book discusses sleeping disorders from snoring to insomnia and offers a wide range of possible solutions. (Rev: SLJ 6/96; VOYA 8/96) [613.7]

11682 Simpson, Carolyn. *Everything You Need to Know About Asthma* (5–10). Series: Need to Know Library. 1998, Rosen LB $27.95 (978-0-8239-2567-4). Vital background information is given about the causes and effects, symptoms, and treatments of asthma. (Rev: SLJ 10/98) [616.2]

11683 Smart, Paul. *Everything You Need to Know About Mononucleosis* (5–9). Series: Need to Know Library. 1998, Rosen LB $27.95 (978-0-8239-2550-6). A straightforward presentation about the "kissing disease," which is often undiagnosed or mistaken for the flu and which requires long periods of rest for recovery. (Rev: SLJ 10/98) [616]

11684 Smith, Erica. *Anorexia Nervosa: When Food Is the Enemy* (6–10). Series: Teen Health Library of Eating Disorder Prevention. 1998, Rosen LB $27.95 (978-0-8239-2766-1). The author describes anorexia nervosa and its symptoms and treatment, and discusses what to do if you suspect someone is suffering from the eating disorder. Society's attitudes toward weight and body image and the role of peer pressure, media images, family relationships, and genetics are examined, along with how to deal with these influences. (Rev: SLJ 1/99) [616.85]

11685 Smith, Terry L. *Breast Cancer: Current and Emerging Trends in Detection and Treatment* (6–10). Series: Cancer and Modern Science. 2005, Rosen LB $29.25 (978-1-4042-0386-0). With photographs, diagrams, and sidebar features, this volume offers information on the diagnosis, treatment, and future issues of breast cancer, as well as ways to cope with the disease and survivor stories. (Rev: SLJ 5/06) [616.99]

11686 Sparks, Beatrice, ed. *It Happened to Nancy* (7–12). 1994, Avon paper $6.99 (978-0-380-77315-2). In diary format, this is the story of 14-year-old Nancy, who was raped by her boyfriend and infected with the HIV virus. (Rev: BL 6/1–15/94; SLJ 6/94; VOYA 10/94) [362.196]

11687 Spray, Michelle. *Growing Up with Scoliosis: A Young Girl's Story* (5–9). Illus. by author. 2002, Book Shelf paper $12.95 (978-0-9714160-3-1). An autobiographical account of the treatment of scoliosis and the emotional impact on the patient, with clear illustrations. (Rev: SLJ 12/02) [362.19673]

11688 Stanley, Debbie. *Understanding Anorexia Nervosa* (6–12). Series: Teen Eating Disorder Prevention Library. 1999, Rosen LB $31.95 (978-0-8239-2877-4). Why people get anorexia, how to get help for it, the dangers of this condition, and some of the myths surrounding it are all covered in this volume. (Rev: HBG 9/00; SLJ 2/00) [616.85]

11689 Stanley, Debbie. *Understanding Bulimia Nervosa* (6–10). Series: Teen Eating Disorder Prevention Library. 1999, Rosen $31.95 (978-0-8239-2878-1). A look at this eating disorder, in which a person binges and purges, with material on contributing factors and guidance to help recovery. (Rev: BL 10/15/99; HBG 9/00; SLJ 7/00) [616.85]

11690 Stewart, Gail B. *Teens with Cancer* (7–10). Photos by Carl Franzn. Series: The Other America. 2001, Gale LB $29.95 (978-1-56006-884-6). The first-person stories of four young people with life-threatening cancers reveal the hard realities such teens face. (Rev: SLJ 12/01)

11691 Stimola, Aubrey. *Ebola* (7–10). Illus. Series: Epidemics and Society. 2010, Rosen LB $30.60 (978-143589433-4). A brief but informative exploration of this disease, its discovery, the reasons why it is so deadly, and how it is treated. (Rev: BL 12/1/10) [614.57]

11692 Stokes, Mark. *Colon Cancer: Current and Emerging Trends in Detection and Treatment* (6–10). Series: Cancer and Modern Science. 2005, Rosen LB $29.25 (978-1-4042-0387-7). With photographs, diagrams, and sidebar features, this volume offers information on the diagnosis, treatment, and future issues of colon cancer, as well as ways to cope with the disease and survivor stories. Also use *Prostate Cancer* (2005). (Rev: SLJ 5/06)

11693 Stone, Tanya Lee. *Medical Causes* (5–10). Series: Celebrity Activists. 1997, Twenty-First Century LB $25.90 (978-0-8050-5233-6). The contributions of such celebrity activists as Elizabeth Taylor, Elton John, Paul Newman, Jerry Lewis, and Linda Ellerbee to various medical causes are highlighted, with material on each of their causes. (Rev: SLJ 1/98) [616]

11694 Storad, Conrad J. *Inside AIDS: HIV Attacks the Immune System* (8–12). 1998, Lerner LB $27.93 (978-0-8225-2857-9). An unusual book about the HIV virus that tells about the cellular structure of the body, its immune system, and how the virus tricks the host cells into replicating it. (Rev: BL 12/15/98; HBG 3/99; SLJ 1/99) [616.97]

11695 Susman, Edward. *Multiple Sclerosis* (4–7). Series: Diseases and People. 1999, Enslow LB $26.60 (978-0-7660-1185-4). A description of this debilitating disease that attacks the nervous system. (Rev: HBG 3/00; SLJ 2/00) [616]

11696 Viegas, Jennifer. *Parasites* (5–8). Series: Germs: The Library of Disease-Causing Organisms. 2004,

Rosen LB $26.50 (978-0-8239-4494-1). An informative, illustrated discussion of parasites, covering how they survive and the dangers they pose to humans. (Rev: SLJ 1/05) [574.5]

11697 Vogel, Carole G. *Breast Cancer: Questions and Answers for Young Women* (6–12). 2001, Twenty-First Century LB $25.90 (978-0-7613-1855-2). Teen readers will find clear answers to both emotional and physiological questions about breasts, breast development, and breast cancer. (Rev: HBG 10/01; SLJ 5/01; VOYA 8/01) [616.99]

11698 Wainwright, Tabitha. *You and an Illness in Your Family* (5–8). Series: Family Matters. 2001, Rosen LB $26.50 (978-0-8239-3352-5). Concise, readable advice is accompanied by full-page photographs of young teens and the recommendation to seek help when necessary. (Rev: SLJ 8/01) [610]

11699 Walker, Pamela. *Everything You Need to Know About Body Dysmorphic Disorder: Dealing with a Distorted Body Image* (6–9). Series: Need to Know Library. 1999, Rosen LB $27.95 (978-0-8239-2954-2). Body dysmorphic disorder usually hits boys and girls in adolescence; symptoms, warning signs, ways of detection, and treatment are all covered here. (Rev: HBG 9/00; SLJ 8/00) [616.89]

11700 Weeldreyer, Laura. *Body Blues: Weight and Depression* (6–12). Series: Teen Health Library of Eating Disorder Prevention. 1998, Rosen LB $27.95 (978-0-8239-2761-6). This book uses case studies of three teenagers who are trying to come to terms with food and their bodies to explore the relationship between weight and depression, and encourages teenagers to learn to accept their bodies rather than aspiring to some media ideal. (Rev: SLJ 2/99) [155.5]

11701 Yancey, Diane. *STDs: What You Don't Know Can Hurt You* (6–12). 2002, Millbrook LB $26.90 (978-0-7613-1957-3). The facts on common sexually transmitted diseases are combined with stories of teenagers with STDs, a section on prevention, and tests to help the reader determine his or her risk of becoming infected. (Rev: BL 4/1/02; HBG 10/02; SLJ 5/02) [616.95]

11702 Yancey, Diane. *Tuberculosis* (7–12). Series: Twenty-First Century Medical Library. 2001, Twenty-First Century LB $26.90 (978-0-7613-1624-4). Interesting illustrations and case studies draw the reader into this account of the historical and contemporary incidence of this disease. (Rev: HBG 10/01; SLJ 5/01) [616]

Doctors, Hospitals, and Medicine

11703 Ballard, Carol. *From Cowpox to Antibiotics: Discovering Vaccines and Medicines* (6–9). Series: Chain Reactions. 2006, Heinemann LB $34.29 (978-1-4034-

8839-8). Ballard discusses vaccines and medicines and their development over time. (Rev: SLJ 3/07) [615.372]

11704 Billitteri, Thomas J. *Alternative Medicine* (7–10). Series: Twenty-First Century Medical Library. 2001, Twenty-First Century LB $26.90 (978-0-7613-0965-9). This overview of alternative therapies such as hypnosis, acupuncture, and homeopathy balances success stories with solid information on the lack of rigorous scientific investigation and of FDA oversight. (Rev: HBG 3/02; SLJ 12/01; VOYA 4/02) [615.5]

11705 Campbell, Andrew. *Cosmetic Surgery* (6–12). Series: Science in the News. 2010, Smart Apple Media LB $34.25 (978-1-59920-322-5). A look at developments in the field of cosmetic surgery and its benefits and pitfalls. (Rev: LMC 1–2/10)

11706 Davis, Sampson. *We Beat the Street: How a Friendship Led to Success* (7–10). 2005, Dutton $16.99 (978-0-525-47407-4). Draper recounts the inspiring story of three young men who grew up in a tough neighborhood of Newark, New Jersey, escaped the mean streets of their childhood, and went on to become doctors. (Rev: BL 4/1/05; SLJ 5/05) [610]

11707 Dawson, Ian. *Renaissance Medicine* (6–9). Series: History of Medicine. 2005, Enchanted Lion LB $19.95 (978-1-59270-038-7). An informative, well-illustrated overview of medical developments in Europe from the mid-15th to mid-18th centuries. (Rev: BL 4/1/05; SLJ 11/05; VOYA 2/06) [610.9]

11708 de la Bédoyère, Guy. *The Discovery of Penicillin* (6–9). Series: Milestones in Modern Science. 2005, World Almanac LB $31.00 (978-0-8368-5852-5). Suitable for reports, this volume provides a good overview of the discovery of penicillin and its impact on public health. Also use *The First Polio Vaccine* (2005). (Rev: SLJ 1/06) [509]

11709 Farndon, John. *From Laughing Gas to Face Transplants: Discovering Transplant Surgery* (6–9). Series: Chain Reactions. 2006, Heinemann LB $34.29 (978-1-4034-8840-4). Farndon looks at transplant surgery from its inception to today's applications, with personal stories and quotations from specialists in the field. (Rev: SLJ 3/07)

11710 Fleischman, John. *Phineas Gage: A Gruesome But True Story About Brain Science* (7–10). 2002, Houghton Mifflin $16.00 (978-0-618-05252-3). This riveting story of the amiable man whose personality changed when an iron rod shot through his brain presents lots of information on brain science and medical knowledge in the 19th century. (Rev: BL 3/1/02; HB 5–6/02; HBG 10/02; SLJ 3/02; VOYA 6/02) [362.1]

11711 Giddens, Sandra, and Owen Giddens. *Future Techniques in Surgery* (6–9). Series: Library of Future Medicine. 2003, Rosen LB $29.25 (978-0-8239-3667-0). A look at the new techniques and equipment that make less invasive procedures possible and reduce recovery time. (Rev: BL 10/15/03; LMC 10/03; SLJ 5/03) [617]

11712 Gilpin, Daniel. *Medicine* (6–9). Series: History of Invention. 2004, Facts on File $35.00 (978-0-8160-5442-8). A slim introductory overview of advances in medicine from prehistoric times to today, with maps, illustrations, and profiles of key figures. (Rev: SLJ 12/04) [610.9]

11713 Goldsmith, Connie. *Superbugs Strike Back: When Antibiotics Fail* (7–10). 2007, Lerner LB $29.27 (978-0-8225-6607-6). Discusses bacteria that have becoming resistant to antibiotics, how antibiotics work, their presence in the food chain, and what can be done to deal with the problem. (Rev: BL 6/1–15/07; SLJ 8/07) [615]

11714 Ichord, Loretta Frances. *Toothworms and Spider Juice: An Illustrated History of Dentistry* (5–8). 2000, Millbrook LB $24.90 (978-0-7613-1465-3). A history of dentistry that reveals many of the barbaric treatments of the past and how superstition and ignorance gradually gave way to modern practices. (Rev: BCCB 2/00; BL 2/15/00; HBG 10/00; SLJ 2/00) [617.6]

11715 Jefferis, David. *Bio Tech: Frontiers of Medicine* (4–8). Series: Megatech. 2001, Crabtree paper $8.95 (978-0-7787-0061-6). An eye-catching look at future medical possibilities such as artificial body parts, enhanced use of robots, special foods, and so forth. (Rev: SLJ 6/02) [660.6]

11716 Kowalski, Kathiann M. *Alternative Medicine: Is It for You?* (7–9). Series: Issues in Focus. 1998, Enslow LB $26.60 (978-0-89490-955-9). After explaining the differences between traditional and alternative medicine, this book describes homeopathy, chiropractic medicine, medical practices from India and China, nutritional therapies, biofeedback, and healing based on prayer and meditation. (Rev: BL 10/1/98; SLJ 12/98) [615.5]

11717 Lawton, Sandra Augustyn, ed. *Complementary and Alternative Medicine Information for Teens: Health Tips about Non-Traditional and Non-Western Medical Practices* (7–12). Series: Teen Health. 2006, Omnigraphics LB $65.00 (978-0-7808-0966-6). The full subtitle of this book tells it all: Health Tips About Non-Traditional and Non-Western Medical Practices Including Information About Acupuncture, Chiropractic Medicine, Dietary and Herbal Supplements, Hypnosis, Massage Therapy, Prayer and Spirituality, Reflexology, Yoga, and More. (Rev: SLJ 5/07) [610]

11718 Lusted, Marcia Amidon. *Cosmetic Surgery* (7–10). Illus. Series: Essential Viewpoints. 2009, ABDO LB $32.79 (978-1-60453-530-3). An informative discussion — drawing on published sources — of the origins, popularity, and pros and cons of cosmetic surgery. (Rev: BL) 10/27/09; SLJ 1/10) [617.9]

11719 Marcovitz, Hal. *Health Care* (7–12). Series: Gallup Major Trends and Events. 2007, Mason Crest LB

$22.95 (978-1-59084-964-4). A useful, chronological survey of developments in health care over the last century, looking at such topics as polio, AIDS, smoking, and obesity. (Rev: SLJ 10/07) [362.1]

11720 Merino, Noel, ed. *Vaccines* (7–10). Illus. Series: Introducing Issues with Opposing Viewpoints. 2011, Greenhaven LB $35.75 (978-073775204-5). Presents pro and con arguments on such topics as vaccines' efficacy, safety, and public health policies. (Rev: BL 12/1/11) [615]

11721 Miller, Brandon Marie. *Just What the Doctor Ordered: The History of American Medicine* (5–8). Series: People's History. 1997, Lerner LB $30.35 (978-0-8225-1737-5). A history of American medicine from early Indian ceremonies and remedies to today's use of laser surgery, placing medical developments in a historical context, such as the role disease played in the Revolutionary and Civil Wars. (Rev: SLJ 5/97*) [610.9]

11722 Moe, Barbara. *The Revolution in Medical Imaging* (6–9). Series: Library of Future Medicine. 2003, Rosen LB $29.25 (978-0-8239-3672-4). A look at breakthroughs such as CAT, PET, and MRI scans and the benefits they offer to both diagnostician and patient. (Rev: BL 10/15/03; SLJ 5/03) [61]

11723 Morley, David. *Healing Our World: Inside Doctors Without Borders* (7–10). 2007, Fitzhenry & Whiteside $18.95 (978-1-55041-565-0). An introduction to the organization that helps the sick around the world, with information on global health problems and what is being done to try to solve them. (Rev: BL 3/1/07; SLJ 5/07) [610]

11724 Murphy, Patricia J. *Everything You Need to Know About Staying in the Hospital* (5–8). Series: Need to Know Library. 2001, Rosen LB $27.95 (978-0-8239-3325-9). This volume explains the basic hospital process from admission to discharge and follows a patient through a typical day. (Rev: SLJ 5/01) [362.1]

11725 Sherrow, Victoria. *Medical Imaging* (7–10). Series: Great Inventions. 2007, Marshall Cavendish LB $27.95 (978-0-7614-2231-0). From X-rays to ultrasound to MRI to the future, this is a review of medical imaging and its benefits. (Rev: SLJ 11/07) [616.07]

11726 Townsend, John. *Bedpans, Blood and Bandages: A History of Hospitals* (6–9). Series: A Painful History of Medicine. 2005, Raintree LB $32.86 (978-1-4109-1334-0). The graphic illustrations in sometimes-unsettling history of hospitals from medieval times to the present will attract readers. Other volumes are *Pills, Powders and Potions: A History of Medication* and *Pox, Pus and Plague: A History of Disease and Infection* (both 2005). (Rev: SLJ 7/05) [610]

11727 Townsend, John. *Scalpels, Stitches and Scars: A History of Surgery* (4–7). Series: A Painful History of Medicine. 2005, Raintree LB $32.86 (978-1-4109-1332-6). Gory it may be but this title conveys accurate facts and the eye-catching illustrations will entice browsers. (Rev: BL 5/15/05; SLJ 7/05) [617]

11728 Waters, Sophie. *Seeing the Gynecologist* (6–12). Series: Girls' Health. 2007, Rosen LB $19.95 (978-1-4042-1948-9). Girls who don't know what to expect when visiting a gynecologist will be reassured by this straightforward book. (Rev: BL 10/15/07; LMC 2/08) [618.1]

11729 Woods, Michael, and Mary B. Woods. *Ancient Medical Technology: From Herbs to Scalpels* (6–9). Illus. Series: Technology in Ancient Cultures. 2011, Lerner/Twenty-First Century LB $31.93 (978-076136522-8). This thought-provoking volume explores health from early man forward, with a concentration on ancient Egypt, India, China, Americas, Greece, and Rome, and discusses tools and techniques. (Rev: BL 4/1/11; VOYA 6/11) [610.938]

11730 Woods, Michael, and Mary B. Woods. *The History of Medicine* (5–8). Series: Major Inventions Through History. 2005, Twenty-First Century LB $26.60 (978-0-8225-2336-9). An attractive look at medical developments through time and their impact on our lives. (Rev: SLJ 1/06) [610]

Genetics

11731 Boskey, Elizabeth. *America Debates Genetic DNA Testing* (5–8). Series: America Debates. 2007, Rosen LB $29.25 (978-1-4042-1926-7). Presents facts and opinions on both sides of issues including prenatal and adult genetic testing. (Rev: LMC 2/08; SLJ 11/07) [362.196]

11732 Cohen, Daniel. *Cloning* (7–10). 1998, Millbrook $22.90 (978-0-7613-0356-5). A balanced examination of the social and ethical concerns raised by the recent cloning of a sheep named Dolly, including the history and scientific background of this area of research and a discussion of genetic engineering. (Rev: SLJ 3/99) [575.1]

11733 de la Bédoyère, Camilla. *The Discovery of DNA* (6–9). Series: Milestones in Modern Science. 2005, World Almanac LB $31.00 (978-0-8368-5851-8). Suitable for reports, this volume provides a good overview of the discovery of DNA. (Rev: SLJ 1/06) [574.87]

11734 Freedman, Jeri. *Stem Cell Research* (5–8). Illus. Series: America Debates. 2007, Rosen LB $21.95 (978-1-4042-1928-1). A technical and detailed examination of the issues surrounding stem cell research and the ethical questions that it provokes. (Rev: BL 12/1/07; LMC 1/08; SLJ 2/08) [616]

11735 Hyde, Margaret O., and John F. Setaro. *Medicine's Brave New World: Bioengineering and the New Genetics* (7–12). 2001, Millbrook LB $29.90 (978-0-

7613-1706-7). Cloning, stem cell research, and other breakthroughs in genetics are explored in this accessible book that also discusses the ethical issues faced by scientists in this field. (Rev: BL 12/15/01; HBG 10/02; SLJ 12/01; VOYA 2/02) [610]

11736 Jefferis, David. *Cloning: Frontiers of Genetic Engineering* (5–7). Series: Megatech. 1999, Crabtree LB $25.27 (978-0-7787-0048-7). This account discusses the history of genetic discoveries and theories, cell reproduction, and the present and possible future of genetic engineering with plants, animals, and humans. (Rev: SLJ 9/99) [174.957]

11737 Judson, Karen. *Genetic Engineering: Debating the Benefits and Concerns* (6–9). Series: Issues in Focus. 2001, Enslow LB $26.60 (978-0-7660-1587-6). An exploration of the pros and cons of genetic engineering, cloning, gene therapy, genetic testing, and the implications of genetic discrimination. (Rev: HBG 10/02; SLJ 12/01) [660.6]

11738 Kafka, Tina. *DNA on Trial* (6–12). Series: Overview. 2004, Gale LB $29.95 (978-1-59018-337-3). Stories of DNA's use in solving criminal cases are accompanied by discussion of the technology's potential flaws and of the process involved in DNA testing. (Rev: SLJ 3/05) [614]

11739 Marcovitz, Hal. *Gene Therapy Research* (7–12). Illus. Series: Inside Science. 2010, ReferencePoint LB $26.95 (978-160152108-8). From "What is gene therapy" to "What is the future of gene therapy?," this is a thorough guide to research in the areas of cloning, stem cells, and methods of delivery of therapy. ℮ (Rev: BL 10/1/10) [615.8]

11740 Marcovitz, Hal. *Genetic Testing* (7–10). Illus. Series: Compact Research: Current Issues. 2010, ReferencePoint LB $26.95 (978-160152115-6). Examines how genetic testing for diseases can have both positive and negative results. (Rev: BL 4/1/11) [616]

11741 Meany, John. *Is Genetic Research a Threat?* (7–12). Series: What Do You Think? 2008, Heinemann LB $32.86 (978-1-4329-1674-9). After an explanation of the nature of genetic research, this volume discusses the topic as it relates to the individual and to society at large, crime and the law, health, and nonhuman life. (Rev: SLJ 1/1/09) [174.957]

11742 Moore, Pete. *Stem Cell Research* (8–11). Illus. Series: Ethical Debates. 2012, Rosen LB $27.95 (978-144886021-0). A balanced review of the nature of stem cells, current and past research, future possibilities, and the ethical questions involved. (Rev: BL 5/1/12) [174.2]

11743 Morgan, Sally. *From Mendel's Peas to Genetic Fingerprinting: Discovering Inheritance* (6–9). Series: Chain Reactions. 2006, Heinemann LB $34.29 (978-1-4034-8837-4). Morgan traces the evolution of genetic science from Mendel's peas to today's genetic fingerprinting, ends with brief biographies of key individuals in the field. (Rev: SLJ 2/07)

11744 Morgan, Sally. *From Sea Urchins to Dolly the Sheep: Discovering Cloning* (6–9). Series: Chain Reactions. 2006, Heinemann LB $34.29 (978-1-4034-8838-1). Morgan traces developments in the field of cloning, from sea urchins in the 1890s to Dolly the sheep in 2003; ends with brief biographies of key individuals in the field. (Rev: SLJ 2/07)

11745 Phelan, Glen. *Double Helix: The Quest to Uncover the Structure of DNA* (5–8). Series: Science Quest. 2006, National Geographic $17.95 (978-0-7922-5541-3). From Mendel's early experiments with pea plants through Crick and Watson's race to solve the mystery of DNA, this is an accessible and informative history that also looks at the wide range of social and scientific areas influenced by the discovery. (Rev: SLJ 4/07) [572.8]

11746 Seiple, Samantha, and Todd Seiple. *Mutants, Clones, and Killer Corn: Unlocking the Secrets of Biotechnology* (6–9). 2005, Lerner $29.27 (978-0-8225-4860-7). After explaining the basic concepts of genes, DNA, and cloning, the Seiples discuss advances in biotechnology, presenting both sides of controversial techniques. (Rev: BL 6/1–15/05; SLJ 7/05) [660.6]

11747 Walker, Denise. *Inheritance and Evolution* (7–10). Series: Basic Biology. 2006, Smart Apple Media LB $23.95 (978-1-58340-989-3). This is a well-designed introduction to the basics of genetics, inheritance, natural selection, cloning, evolution, and extinction. (Rev: BL 10/15/06) [576]

11748 Yount, Lisa. *Biotechnology and Genetic Engineering. Rev. ed.* (8–12). Series: Library in a Book. 2004, Facts on File $45.00 (978-0-8160-5059-8). An overview of genetic engineering and biotechnology, with chapters on scientific achievements, ethical concerns, court battles, health issues, and scientific problems. (Rev: SLJ 2/05) [303.48]

Grooming, Personal Appearance, and Dress

11749 Bergamotto, Lori. *Skin: The Bare Facts* (6–12). Illus. by Kunkamon Taweenuch. 2009, Zest paper $18.95 (978-0-9800732-5-6). An eye-catching layout adds appeal to this useful guide to skin care, which covers skin types, acne and other problems, makeup, and sunscreens. (Rev: SLJ 5/10; VOYA 4/10) [646.7]

11750 Brashich, Audrey D. *All Made Up: A Girl's Guide to Seeing Through Celebrity Hype . . . and Celebrating Real Beauty* (6–9). Illus. by Shawn Banner. 2006, Walker paper $9.95 (978-0-8027-7744-7). Written by a former model, this book discusses the marketing hype surrounding female celebrities and reassures readers that the stars' physical perfection is only an illusion. (Rev: BL 6/1–15/06; LMC 1–2/08*; SLJ 6/06) [305.235]

11751 Dawson, Mildred L. *Beauty Lab: How Science Is Changing the Way We Look* (5–10). 1997, Silver Moon $14.95 (978-1-881889-84-7). This work on health and hygiene contains chapters on skin, eyes, teeth, fitness, and hair. (Rev: SLJ 3/97) [613.7]

11752 Espejo, Roman, ed. *The Culture of Beauty* (8–12). Illus. Series: Opposing Viewpoints. 2010, Gale/Greenhaven LB $38.50 (978-073774508-5); paper $26.75 (9780737745092). A collection of essays and article excerpts explore today's standards of beauty from various perspectives, looking at topics such as the advantages of beauty, cosmetics and cosmetic surgery, and the fashion industry. (Rev: BL 5/1/10) [306.4]

11753 Graydon, Shari. *In Your Face: The Culture of Beauty and You* (7–12). 2004, Annick paper $14.95 (978-1-55037-856-6). Graydon offers commonsense advice and reassurance to teenagers who may feel overwhelmed by the seemingly ubiquitous message that beauty is all-important. (Rev: BL 12/15/04; SLJ 3/05) [391.6/3]

11754 Hirschmann, Kris. *Reflections of Me: Girls and Body Image* (5–8). Series: What's the Issue? 2009, Compass Point $27.99 (978-0-7565-4132-3). A compelling mix of direct quotes, real-life scenarios, quizzes, and short glossaries enhance this book about girls' body image problems; suitable for reluctant readers. (Rev: LMC 10/09; SLJ 10/09) [155.3]

11755 Libal, Autumn. *Can I Change the Way I Look? A Teen's Guide to the Health Implications of Cosmetic Surgery, Makeovers, and Beyond* (7–12). Series: The Science of Health. 2005, Mason Crest LB $24.95 (978-1-59804-843-8). Libal clearly lays out the pitfalls of obsessing about body image, as well as the risks involved in piercing, tattooing, eating disorders, cosmetic surgery, and even common cosmetic products. (Rev: SLJ 7/05) [613.4]

11756 Mason, Linda. *Teen Makeup: Looks to Match Your Every Mood* (6–12). 2004, Watson-Guptill paper $16.95 (978-0-8230-2980-8). A photograph-filled how-to guide to the basics of skin care and makeup. (Rev: SLJ 11/04)

11757 Sommers, Michael A. *Everything You Need to Know About Looking and Feeling Your Best: A Guide for Guys* (6–9). Series: Need to Know Library. 1999, Rosen LB $27.95 (978-0-8239-3080-7). Good hygiene and grooming are not difficult or time-consuming, according to this book that also looks at the benefits of exercise and diet. (Rev: SLJ 8/00) [613]

11758 Sutherland, Adam. *Body Decoration* (5–8). Illus. Series: On the Radar: Street Style. 2012, Lerner LB $26.60 (978-076137769-6). With a history of body decoration since ancient times, this is an interesting survey of the various forms that are popular today. (Rev: BLO 3/15/12; SLJ 4/1/12) [391.6]

11759 Warrick, Leanne. *Hair Trix for Cool Chix: The Real Girl's Guide to Great Hair* (6–12). Illus. by Debbie Boon. 2004, Watson-Guptill paper $9.95 (978-0-8230-2179-6). From quizzes and practical tips to step-by-step directions for different styles and accessories, this is a reader-friendly guide to hair care. (Rev: SLJ 7/04) [391.5]

11760 Weiss, Stefanie Iris. *Coping with the Beauty Myth: A Guide for Real Girls* (7–12). Series: Coping. 2002, Rosen LB $31.95 (978-0-8239-3757-8). Readers are urged to ignore unrealistic images presented in the media and to accept their own attributes and deficiencies as well as those of others. (Rev: SLJ 8/00) [155.5]

The Human Body

General and Miscellaneous

11761 Allison, Linda. *Blood and Guts: A Working Guide to Your Own Little Insides* (5–8). 1976, Little, Brown paper $14.99 (978-0-316-03443-2). An off-putting title but a fine explanation of the functions of the human body.

11762 Basher, Simon, and Dan Green. *Human Body: A Book with Guts* (5–8). Illus. by Simon Basher. 2011, Kingfisher $14.99 (978-0-7534-6628-5); paper $8.99 (978-0-7534-6-501-1). An irreverent and entertaining look at the inner workings of the human body with Basher's cartoon illustrations. (Rev: BL 3/1/11; SLJ 9/1/11) [612]

11763 Brynie, Faith Hickman. *101 Questions About Your Immune System You Felt Defenseless to Answer . . . Until Now* (7–12). 2000, Twenty-First Century $27.90 (978-0-7613-1569-8). A question-and-answer format is used to explain the functioning and vulnerabilities of the immune system. (Rev: BL 6/1–15/00; HBG 9/00; SLJ 9/00; VOYA 4/01) [616.07]

11764 Brynie, Faith Hickman. *101 Questions About Your Skin* (7–12). Illus. by Sharon Lane Holm. Series: 101 Questions. 1999, Twenty-First Century LB $27.90 (978-0-7613-1259-8). This comprehensive, well-illustrated look at the composition, care, and diseases of the skin also includes information on tattooing, the effects of the sun, and aging and will attract both report writers and browsers. (Rev: HBG 4/00; SLJ 11/99) [612.7]

11765 Calabresi, Linda. *Human Body* (4–7). Series: Insiders. 2008, Simon & Schuster $16.99 (978-1-4169-3861-3). Cross-sections, computer-aided graphics, and other visual wonders offer amazing views of the body in this large-format book that provides text information

in snippets and sidebars. (Rev: BL 3/1/08; SLJ 5/08) [612]

11766 Donovan, Sandy. *Hawk and Drool: Gross Stuff in Your Mouth* (4–8). Illus. by Michael Slack. Series: Gross Body Science. 2010, Lerner LB $29.27 (978-0-8225-8966-2). Cavities, canker sores, bacteria, and saliva are among the gross items causing smelly breath that are discussed here with close-up pictures. (Rev: LMC 1–2/10)

11767 Ganeri, Anita. *Alive: The Living, Breathing Human Body Book* (5–7). Illus. 2007, DK $24.99 (978-0-7566-3211-3). Visual and audio effects accompany amazing graphics and text in this comprehensive and attention-grabbing pop-up anatomy book. (Rev: SLJ 3/08)

11768 Kim, Melissa L. *The Endocrine and Reproductive Systems* (5–10). Series: Human Body Library. 2003, Enslow LB $23.93 (978-0-7660-2020-7). Kim uses a conversational style to introduce detailed facts about these two body systems, with useful graphics and some practical advice. (Rev: BL 4/15/03; HBG 10/03) [612.4]

11769 Klosterman, Lorrie. *Immune System* (6–9). Illus. Series: Amazing Human Body. 2008, Marshall Cavendish LB $23.95 (978-076143054-4). After explaining the nature and organs of the immune system, this volume covers related illnesses and diseases and proper diet and hygiene. (Rev: BL 12/1/08; LMC 8–9/09) [616.07]

11770 Macaulay, David. *The Way We Work: Getting to Know the Amazing Human Body* (7–12). Illus. by author. 2008, Houghton Mifflin $35.00 (978-061823378-6). Whimsically illustrated, this book provides a broad, accessible tour of the human body and the myriad complex systems that make it work. Boston Globe–Horn Book Honor 2009; ALA Notable Books 2009. (Rev: BL 10/15/08; HB 9–10/08; LMC 5–6/09; SLJ 10/1/08*; VOYA 1008) [610]

11771 McNally, Robert Aquinas, ed. *Skin Health Information for Teens: Health Tips About Dermatological Concerns and Skin Cancer Risks* (7–12). Series: Teen Health. 2003, Omnigraphics $58.00 (978-0-7808-0446-3). Detailed information is provided on health problems and risks including acne, cosmetics, tanning, tattoos, and piercing. (Rev: SLJ 1/04; VOYA 2/04) [616.5]

11772 Parker, Steve. *Digestion and Reproduction* (6–9). Series: Understanding the Human Body. 2004, Gareth Stevens LB $26.00 (978-0-8368-4205-0). An attractive format is used to present solid information on the digestive and reproductive systems and the diseases that can affect them. Also use *Heart, Blood, and Lungs* (2004). (Rev: SLJ 4/05) [612]

11773 Parker, Steve. *The Human Body Book* (6–9). 2007, DK $35.00 (978-0-7566-2856-9). Extraordinary pictures and illustrations provide great detail of the human body's systems and processes in this coffee-table-sized book that (along with clear, informative text) includes a CD containing many of the illustrations, charts, and diagrams. (Rev: SLJ 7/07) [612]

11774 Parker, Steve. *Human Body: An Interactive Guide to the Inner Workings of the Body* (4–7). Series: Discoverology. 2008, Barron's $18.99 (978-0-7641-6083-7). Pop-ups, pullouts, gatefolds, cutaways, X-ray images, spinning wheels, and other visual elements make this guide to anatomy effective and interesting. (Rev: BL 6/1–15/08; SLJ 8/08) [612]

11775 Reilly, Kathleen M. *The Human Body: 25 Fantastic Projects* (5–9). Illus. by Shawn Braley. Series: Focus on Science. 2008, Nomad paper $15.95 (978-1-9346702-4-8). Experiments (many of which need adult supervision) show how various processes of the human body work and are accompanied by excellent descriptions. (Rev: SLJ 2/09) [611]

11776 Rosen, Marvin. *Sleep and Dreaming* (6–12). Series: Gray Matter. 2005, Chelsea House LB $35.00 (978-0-7910-8639-1). Snoring, sleepwalking, and night terrors are among the topics covered in this survey of our sleep processes and our dreams; Freudian and Jungian theories are also addressed. (Rev: SLJ 3/06) [616]

11777 Simon, Seymour. *The Human Body* (4–7). Illus. 2008, HarperCollins $19.99 (978-006055541-2); LB $20.89 (978-006055542-9). Drawing on earlier books, Simon presents a detailed overview of the human body with vivid illustrations and clear captions. (Rev: BL 10/15/08; HB 9–10/08; SLJ 11/1/08) [612]

11778 VanCleave, Janice. *The Human Body for Every Kid: Easy Activities That Make Learning Science Fun* (5–7). Series: Science for Every Kid. 1995, Wiley paper $12.95 (978-0-471-02408-8). The various systems in the human body are introduced and decribed, with many projects and experiments. (Rev: BL 4/15/95; SLJ 5/95) [612]

11779 Walker, Richard. *Body* (4–7). 2005, DK $19.99 (978-0-7566-1371-6). With a spiral binding, acetate overlays, and computer-generated 3-D images, this volume gives an in-depth view of the human body; there is an accompanying CD. (Rev: BL 12/1/05; SLJ 3/06) [611]

11780 Walker, Richard. *Human Body* (5–9). Series: DK/Google e.guides. 2005, DK $17.99 (978-0-7566-1009-8). This highly illustrated guide introduces readers to the human body and provides a link to a Web site that serves as a gateway to additional resources. (Rev: SLJ 8/05) [612]

11781 Walker, Richard. *Ouch! How Your Body Makes It Through a Very Bad Day* (5–8). Illus. 2007, DK $16.99 (978-0-7566-2536-8). Wonderfully gross, this day starts with some sneezes and progresses through a variety of events including urinating, sweating, vomiting, and being stung by a bee; the accompanying CD-ROM

adds an inside view to these processes. (Rev: LMC 10/07; SLJ 7/07)

11782 Weiss, Marisa C., and Isabel Friedman. *Taking Care of Your "Girls": A Breast Health Guide for Girls, Teens, and In-Betweens* (6–12). Illus. 2008, Three Rivers $15.95 (978-030740696-5). Health, beauty, fashion, and personal aspects of breasts and bras are discussed in a conversational tone. ℮ (Rev: BLO 10/7/08) [618.1]

11783 Wiese, Jim. *Head to Toe Science: Over 40 Eye-Popping, Spine-Tingling, Heart-Pounding Activities That Teach Kids* (4–8). 2000, Wiley paper $12.95 (978-0-471-33203-9). A collection of experiments and projects that is arranged by body systems (e.g., nervous, digestive), accompanied by good instructions and scientific explanations. (Rev: BL 7/00; SLJ 7/00) [612]

Brain and Nervous System

11784 Brynie, Faith Hickman. *101 Questions About Sleep and Dreams that Kept You Awake Nights . . . Until Now* (8–11). 2006, Lerner LB $27.93 (978-0-7613-2312-9). This is a sleep information handbook for teens, answering questions about dreaming, stages of sleep, the effect of sleep on the brain and body, and related topics. (Rev: BL 5/15/06) [612.8]

11785 Garfield, Patricia. *The Dream Book: A Young Person's Guide to Understanding Dreams* (5–8). 2002, Tundra paper $9.95 (978-0-88776-594-0). The author, a psychologist, explains the meanings of common (and uncommon) dreams and suggests how to use dreams to good effect. (Rev: BL 9/15/02; SLJ 9/02; VOYA 8/02) [154.6]

11786 Newquist, H. P. *The Great Brain Book: An Inside Look at the Inside of Your Head* (5–8). Illus. by Keith Kasnot. 2005, Scholastic $18.95 (978-0-439-45895-5). The structure of the brain, its inner workings, and the history of our knowledge of this organ are all discussed in detail; interesting anecdotes add to the presentation. (Rev: BL 6/1–15/05; SLJ 9/05) [612.8]

11787 Parker, Steve. *The Brain and Nervous System* (5–9). Series: Our Bodies. 2004, Raintree LB $28.56 (978-0-7398-6619-1). Details of the human body's brain and nervous system are accompanied by information on keeping them healthy. (Rev: BL 8/04)

11788 Policoff, Stephen P. *The Dreamer's Companion: A Beginner's Guide to Understanding Dreams and Using Them Creatively* (8–12). 1997, Chicago Review paper $12.95 (978-1-55652-280-2). This book covers mastering the art of lucid dreaming, the causes of dreams, how to analyze them, and how to keep a dream journal. (Rev: BL 5/15/98; SLJ 6/98) [154.63]

11789 Saab, Carl Y. *The Spinal Cord* (6–12). Series: Gray Matter. 2005, Chelsea House LB $35.00 (978-0-7910-8511-0). Explores the importance of the spinal cord to the whole nervous system and discusses the impact of disorders and injuries. (Rev: SLJ 3/06)

Circulatory System

11790 Markle, Sandra. *Faulty Hearts: True Survival Stories* (5–8). Series: Powerful Medicine. 2010, Lerner LB $27.93 (978-0-8225-8699-9). Arresting full-color photographs, cross-sections, and personal stories are combined with facts about procedures and information about the medical personnel involved, (Rev: LMC 11–12/10; VOYA 10/10) [612.1]

11791 Newquist, H. P. *The Book of Blood: From Legends and Leeches to Vampires and Veins* (5–8). Illus. 2012, Houghton Harcourt $17.99 (978-0-547-31584-3). A lively review of all things relating to blood, covering everything from ancient cultures' understanding of the body to modern knowledge about both human and animal blood and its amazing properties. (Rev: HB 9–10/12; SLJ 10/12) [612.1]

11792 Romanek, Trudee. *Squirt! The Most Interesting Book You'll Ever Read About Blood* (4–7). Illus. by Rose Cowles. Series: Mysterious You. 2006, Kids Can $14.95 (978-1-55337-776-4); paper $7.95 (978-1-55337-777-1). This fascinating book with an engaging format discusses the human circulatory system, with information about other animals and their blood, too. (Rev: BL 5/15/06; HBG 10/06) [612.1]

11793 Silverstein, Alvin, and Virginia Silverstein. *Heart Disease* (8–12). 2006, Twenty-First Century LB $27.93 (978-0-7613-3420-0). This informative and easy-to-understand book explains the causes, treatment, and prevention of heart disease, using true stories as examples and incorporating medical information and photographs. (Rev: SLJ 8/06)

Digestive and Excretory Systems

11794 Brynie, Faith Hickman. *101 Questions About Food and Digestion That Have Been Eating at You . . . Until Now* (5–8). 2002, Millbrook LB $27.90 (978-0-7613-2309-9). A question-and-answer format succeeds in conveying lots of food for thought, with details on digestive functions, digestive disorders, food safety, fat cells, Mad Cow disease, vitamins, and so forth. (Rev: BL 1/1–15/03; HBG 3/03; SLJ 3/03) [612.3]

11795 Magee, Elaine. *Tell Me What to Eat if I Have Irritable Bowel Syndrome* (8–12). 2008, Rosen LB $23.95 (978-140421836-9). This book provides a wealth of information — and debunks some pervasive IBS myths — in an approachable, matter-of-fact manner. (Rev: BL 10/15/08) [616.3]

11796 Monroe, Judy. *Coping with Ulcers, Heartburn, and Stress-Related Stomach Disorders* (7–12). Series: Coping. 2000, Rosen LB $31.95 (978-0-8239-2971-9). Fictional case histories convey lots of information

about a variety of uncomfortable stomach conditions, stressing the importance of prevention and early treatment. (Rev: SLJ 6/00) [616.3]

11797 Parker, Steve. *Digestion* (5–9). Series: Our Bodies. 2004, Raintree LB $28.56 (978-0-7398-6620-7). Details of the human body's digestive system are accompanied by information on keeping them healthy. (Rev: BL 8/04) [612]

11798 Simon, Seymour. *Guts: Our Digestive System* (5–8). 2005, HarperCollins LB $17.89 (978-0-06-054652-6). Photographs and straightforward yet fascinating text present the digestive system. (Rev: BL 3/1/05; SLJ 4/05) [612.3]

11799 Toriello, James. *The Stomach: Learning How We Digest* (5–9). Series: 3-D Library of the Human Body. 2002, Rosen LB $27.95 (978-0-8239-3536-9). Using outstanding diagrams and clear explanations, the digestive system is highlighted with material on each of its parts and their functions. (Rev: BL 7/02; SLJ 7/02) [612.3]

Musculoskeletal System

11800 Brynie, Faith Hickman. *101 Questions About Muscles: To Stretch Your Mind and Flex Your Brain* (7–12). Series: 101 Questions. 2007, Lerner LB $30.60 (978-0-8225-6380-8). Entertaining and interesting, this book uses a question-and-answer format to explore questions of interest to athletes, browsers, and researchers. (Rev: BL 12/1/07; SLJ 6/08) [612.7]

11801 Parker, Steve. *The Skeleton and Muscles* (5–9). Series: Our Bodies. 2004, Raintree LB $28.56 (978-0-7398-6622-1). Details of the human body's skeletal and muscular systems are accompanied by information on keeping them healthy. (Rev: BL 8/04) [612.7]

TEETH

11802 Lee, Jordan. *Coping with Braces and Other Orthodontic Work* (4–9). Series: Coping. 1998, Rosen LB $31.95 (978-0-8239-2721-0). A book about braces, their purposes, and the problems they can cause. (Rev: SLJ 11/98) [612.3]

Respiratory System

11803 Hayhurst, Chris. *The Lungs: Learning How We Breathe* (5–9). Series: 3-D Library of the Human Body. 2002, Rosen LB $27.95 (978-0-8239-3534-5). Amazing computer graphics are used to explain the composition of the lungs, how they work, and what keeps them healthy. (Rev: BL 7/02) [612.6]

11804 Siy, Alexandra. *Sneeze!* (6–9). Illus. by Dennis Kunkel. 2007, Charlesbridge $16.95 (978-1-57091-653-3). Students will no longer need to be reminded to cover their sneezes after seeing the close-up photographs in this book; scientific information about germs, allergies, the flu, and the human body's immune system rounds out the book. (Rev: BL 7/07; HB 11–12/07; LMC 1/08; SLJ 9/07) [612.2]

11805 Whittemore, Susan. *The Respiratory System* (7–12). Series: The Human Body: How It Works. 2009, Chelsea House $35 (978-1-60413-375-2). The functioning of the respiratory system is clearly explained, and there is discussion of diseases affecting it. (Rev: LMC 5–6/10) [612.2]

Senses

11806 Cobb, Vicki. *How to Really Fool Yourself: Illusions for All Your Senses* (7–9). 1999, Wiley paper $12.95 (978-0-471-31592-6). A book about perception, how illusions are created, and how they are present in everyday life. [152.1]

11807 Jackson, Donna M. *Phenomena: Secrets of the Senses* (6–9). Illus. 2008, Little, Brown $16.99 (978-031616649-2). Exploring such intriguing phenomena as "sixth sense," synthesia, and intuition, Jackson offers up a compelling glimpse into the inner workings of the brain. ℮ Lexile 1190L (Rev: BL 10/1/08; HB 11–12/08; LMC 5–6/09; SLJ 10/1/08; VOYA 12/08) [152.1]

11808 Light, Douglas B. *The Senses* (7–12). Series: The Human Body: How It Works. 2009, Chelsea House $35 (978-1-60413-362-2). Sight, smell, taste, touch, and hearing are all examined here, as well as thirst and hunger, with interesting factboxes and clear illustrations. (Rev: LMC 5–6/10) [612.8]

11809 Markle, Sandra. *Lost Sight: True Survival Stories* (5–8). Series: Powerful Medicine. 2010, Lerner LB $27.93 (978-0-8225-8701-9). Arresting full-color photographs, cross-sections, and personal stories are combined with facts about procedures and information about the medical personnel involved, (Rev: BL 10/1/10; LMC 11–12/10) [612.8]

11810 Martin, Paul D. *Messengers to the Brain: Our Fantastic Five Senses* (6–9). 1984, National Geographic LB $12.50 (978-0-87044-504-0). A well-illustrated introduction to the five senses and how they work. [612]

11811 Parker, Steve. *The Senses* (5–9). Series: Our Bodies. 2004, Raintree LB $28.56 (978-0-7398-6624-5). Details of the human senses are accompanied by information on keeping them healthy. (Rev: BL 8/04) [612]

11812 Viegas, Jennifer. *The Eye: Learning How We See* (5–9). Series: 3-D Library of the Human Body. 2002, Rosen LB $27.95 (978-0-8239-3530-7). This volume on the anatomy and function of the human eye includes illustrations, diagrams, a glossary, and other aids. (Rev: BL 7/02) [612.8]

Hygiene and Physical Fitness

11813 Crump, Marguerite. *Don't Sweat It! Every Body's Answers to Questions You Don't Want to Ask: A Guide for Young People* (5–9). Illus. by Chris Sharp. 2002, Free Spirit paper $12.95 (978-1-57542-114-8). Crump tackles potentially embarrassing questions about personal hygiene. (Rev: SLJ 1/03; VOYA 2/03) [613.0433]

11814 Finney, Sumukhi. *The Yoga Handbook* (8–12). Illus. 2009, Rosen LB $39.95 (978-143585359-1). For beginners, this is a clear introduction to the physical, mental, and spiritual aspects of yoga, with information on breathing, diet, and meditation plus step-by-step directions for poses. (Rev: BL 4/1/10) [613.7]

11815 Johnson, Marlys. *Understanding Exercise Addiction* (7–12). Series: Teen Eating Disorder Prevention Library. 2000, Rosen LB $31.95 (978-0-8239-2990-0). This book offers teens the opportunity to assess whether attitudes toward exercise, eating, and the human body are normal. (Rev: SLJ 7/00) [616.86]

11816 Kaminker, Laura. *Exercise Addiction: When Fitness Becomes an Obsession* (6–10). Series: Teen Health Library of Eating Disorder Prevention. 1998, Rosen LB $27.95 (978-0-8239-2759-3). Some teens become addicted to exercise and exercise too much for the wrong reasons. This book defines the problem, risks, and causes, describes the symptoms, and tells where to get help and support if needed. (Rev: BL 3/1/89; SLJ 1/99) [613.7]

11817 Kenney, Karen Latchana. *Strength Training for Teen Athletes: Exercises to Take Your Game to the Next Level* (6–9). Illus. Series: Sports Training Zone. 2012, Capstone LB $31.32 (978-142967678-6); paper $7.95 (9781429679992). With clear, easy-to-follow instructions and many photographs, this book focuses in turn on shoulders and arms, core, chest, and legs and hips. (Rev: BL 4/1/12) [613.711]

11818 Vedral, Joyce L. *Toning for Teens: The 20-Minute Workout That Makes You Look Good and Feel Great!* (7–12). 2002, Warner paper $15.95 (978-0-446-67815-5). Three sets of dumbbells and a bench or step are the only items required for this daily workout; nutritional and fitness tips are included. (Rev: SLJ 8/02)

Mental Disorders and Emotional Problems

11819 Abeel, Samantha. *What Once Was White* (5–8). Illus. by Charles R. Murphy. 1993, Village $19.95 (978-0-941653-13-8). The author is a 13-year-old learning-disabled student who can't tell time but writes sensitive interpretations of a group of watercolor paintings. (Rev: SLJ 9/93*) [618.62]

11820 Allman, Toney. *Autism* (6–10). Series: Diseases and Disorders. 2010, Lucent $32.45 (978-1-4205-0143-8). With real-life examples and many illustrations, this book describes the causes, diagnosis, and treatment of autism and discusses the prospects of finding a cure. (Rev: LMC 5–6/10) [616.8]

11821 Beckelman, Laurie. *Body Blues* (6–9). Series: Hot Line. 1994, Silver Burdett LB $17.95 (978-0-89680-842-3). This book is designed to help adolescents understand the changes that are occurring to their body and give reassurance through interviews with other teenagers experiencing the same changes. (Rev: BL 2/15/95) [155.5]

11822 Bellenir, Karen, ed. *Mental Health Information for Teens: Health Tips About Mental Wellness and Mental Illness. 2nd ed.* (6–12). Series: Teen Health. 2006, Omnigraphics $58 (978-0-7808-0863-8). A revised edition of this comprehensive and easy-to-use overview of topics relating to mental health — specific disorders, coping mechanisms, treatment, and so forth — with a new emphasis on self-injury and bullying. (Rev: SLJ 12/06)

11823 Bonnice, Sherry, and Carolyn Hoard. *Drug Therapy and Cognitive Disorders* (6–10). Series: Psychiatric Disorders: Drugs and Psychology for the Mind and Body. 2003, Mason Crest LB $24.95 (978-1-59084-562-2). Diagrams and charts reinforce the easily read text, which includes discussion of the nature of these disorders and how they are treated plus personal anecdotes from one of the authors. (Rev: SLJ 5/04)

11824 Bowman-Kruhm, Mary, and Claudine G. Wirths. *Everything You Need to Know About Learning Disabilities* (6–12). Series: Need to Know Library. 1999, Rosen LB $27.95 (978-0-8239-2956-6). An introduction to learning disabilities and how people cope with them at school and in everyday life, with fictionalized case studies and information on getting help. (Rev: SLJ 1/00; VOYA 4/00) [616.85]

11825 Chesner, Jonathan. *ADHD in HD: Brains Gone Wild* (6–9). Illus. 2012, Free Spirit paper $14.99 (978-1-57542-386-9). Covering such topics as school, authority figures, food, and social life, this is a digestible guide written by a man who has coped with ADHD since childhood. (Rev: BL 4/15/12; SLJ 10/12) [618.92]

11826 Cobain, Bev. *When Nothing Matters Anymore: A Survival Guide for Depressed Teens* (7–12). 1998, Free Spirit paper $13.95 (978-1-57542-036-3). The author, a psychiatric nurse who works with teens, discusses the types, causes, and warning signs of depression, the dangers of addictions and eating disorders, and the relationship between depression and suicide, and provides information on treatment options and suggestions for developing good mental and physical health. (Rev: SLJ 3/99; VOYA 2/99) [155]

11827 Corman, Catherine A., and Edward M. Hallowell. *Positively ADD: Real Success Stories to Inspire Your Dreams* (7–10). 2006, Walker $16.95 (978-0-8027-8988-4). Aimed at children with attention deficit disorder, this book includes profiles of successful adults who had ADD beginning in childhood. (Rev: BL 6/1–15/06; LMC 11–12/06; SLJ 9/06) [616.85]

11828 Davis, Brangien. *What's Real, What's Ideal: Overcoming a Negative Body Image* (7–12). Series: Teen Health Library of Eating Disorder Prevention. 1998, Rosen LB $27.95 (978-0-8239-2771-5). Because teenager's bodies are changing so quickly, many become confused about an ideal figure. This book describes why teens develop negative body images and offers suggestions for overcoming self-defeating perceptions. (Rev: VOYA 4/99) [305.23]

11829 Dendy, Chris A. Zeigler, and Alex Zeigler. *A Bird's-Eye View of Life with ADD and ADHD: Advice from Young Survivors* (5–9). 2003, Cherish the Children paper $19.95 (978-0-9679911-3-9). A guide to ADD and ADHD, written by a dozen teenagers with these disorders with the aim of helping others cope, with advice on succeeding in school, medication, driving, and so forth. (Rev: SLJ 4/04) [618.9]

11830 Donnelly, Karen. *Coping with Dyslexia* (6–9). Series: Coping. 2000, Rosen LB $31.95 (978-0-8239-2850-7). This volume offers short profiles of celebrities who have dyslexia as well as guidance on coping with this problem and choosing careers. (Rev: HBG 3/01; SLJ 12/00) [616.85]

11831 Farrell, Courtney. *Mental Disorders* (7–10). Series: Essential Issues. 2010, ABDO LB $32.79 (978-1-60453-956-1). The nature of mental disorders and their impact on society, treatment, and associated stigma are all discussed here along with the role of medical professionals and various key pieces of legislation. (Rev: LMC 10/10; SLJ 4/1/10) [362.2]

11832 Fisher, Gary L., and Rhoda Woods Cummings. *The Survival Guide for Kids with LD (Learning Differences)* (5–8). 1990, Free Spirit paper $9.95 (978-0-915793-18-1). A book that explains various kinds of learning disabilities and how to cope with them. (Rev: BL 7/90; SLJ 6/90) [371.9]

11833 Fox, Annie, and Ruth Kirschner. *Too Stressed to Think? A Teen Guide to Staying Sane When Life Makes You Crazy* (7–12). 2005, Free Spirit paper $14.95 (978-1-57542-173-5). A handy review of stress, how to reduce it and how to prevent the external forces that cause it, with tips and various scenarios that illustrate relevant situations. (Rev: SLJ 6/06)

11834 Giacobello, John. *Everything You Need to Know About Anxiety and Panic Attacks* (5–9). Series: Need to Know Library. 2000, Rosen LB $27.95 (978-0-8239-3219-1). This book explains anxiety attacks' causes, symptoms, and treatments in a reassuring tone. (Rev: SLJ 1/01) [616]

11835 Giacobello, John. *Everything You Need to Know About the Dangers of Overachieving: A Guide for Relieving Pressure and Anxiety* (6–9). Series: Need to Know Library. 2000, Rosen $27.95 (978-0-8239-3107-1). Stress-reduction techniques are among the strategies here for limiting the disadvantages of a compelling desire to achieve. (Rev: SLJ 9/00) [155.9]

11836 Grollman, Earl A., and Max Malikow. *Living When a Young Friend Commits Suicide: Or Even Starts Talking About It* (6–12). 1999, Beacon paper $12.00 (978-0-8070-2503-1). Using simple prose and a compassionate attitude, this book examines suicide from many standpoints and gives good advice on the grieving process. (Rev: BL 11/1/99; SLJ 1/00; VOYA 2/00) [368.28]

11837 Hermes, Patricia. *A Time to Listen: Preventing Youth Suicide* (8–12). 1987, Harcourt $13.95 (978-0-15-288196-2). Through questions and answers plus many case studies, the author explores many aspects of suicidal behavior and its causes. (Rev: BL 4/1/88; SLJ 3/88; VOYA 6/88) [362.2]

11838 Huddle, Lorena, and Jay Schleifer. *Teen Suicide* (7–10). Illus. Series: Teen Mental Health. 2011, Rosen LB $27.95 (978-144884586-6). With information about warning signs of impending suicide, prevention and intervention, and coping with grief, this book will be helpful for report writers and those seeking personal guidance. (Rev: BL 11/15/11) [302.3]

11839 Hyde, Margaret O., and Elizabeth H. Forsyth. *Stress 101: An Overview for Teens* (7–10). Series: Teen Overviews. 2008, Lerner LB $26.60 (978-0-8225-6788-2). A thorough survey of the kinds of stress we suffer, their origins, their impact on our body, and ways to reduce and deal with stress. (Rev: BL 1/1–15/08; SLJ 4/08) [616.9]

11840 Hyman, Bruce M., and Cherry Pedroch. *Obsessive-Compulsive Disorder* (7–10). 2003, Millbrook LB $26.90 (978-0-7613-2758-5). Profiles of teens with OCD introduce a discussion of the condition that will aid understanding and will be useful for teens experiencing anxieties. (Rev: BL 12/15/03; HBG 4/04; SLJ 1/04; VOYA 2/04) [616.85]

11841 Irwin, Cait. *Monochrome Days: A Firsthand Account of One Teenager's Experience with Depression* (8–12). Series: Adolescent Mental Health Initiative. 2007, Oxford Univ $30.00 (978-0-19-531004-7); paper $9.95 (978-0-19-531005-4). Irwin chronicles her own experience with depression — which began in 8th grade and included suicidal thoughts and inpatient treatment — and her co-authors add practical information about symptoms, treatment, and so forth. (Rev: SLJ 7/07) [616.85]

11842 Kent, Deborah. *Snake Pits, Talking Cures, and Magic Bullets: A History of Mental Illness* (6–12). 2003, Millbrook LB $26.90 (978-0-7613-2704-2). The madhouses of old, shock treatments, psychotherapy, psychoanalysis, and today's effective drug therapies are among the topics discussed in this volume. (Rev: BL 5/1/03; HBG 4/04; SLJ 7/03) [616.89]

11843 Levin, Judith. *Anxiety and Panic Attacks* (7–10). Illus. Series: Teen Mental Health. 2008, Rosen LB $19.95 (978-140421797-3). Teens curious about — or perhaps afflicted by — anxiety disorders will find much practical, comforting advice and information in this helpful guide. (Rev: BL 10/15/08) [616.85]

11844 Levine, Mel. *Keeping a Head in School: A Student's Book About Learning Abilities and Learning Disorders* (8–12). 1990, Educators Publg. paper $24.75 (978-0-8388-2069-8). This account deals with all sorts of learning disorders, how they affect the learning process, and how they can be treated. (Rev: BL 6/15/90) [371.9]

11845 Libal, Autumn. *Runaway Train: Youth with Emotional Disturbance* (7–12). Series: Youth with Special Needs. 2004, Mason Crest LB $24.95 (978-1-59084-732-9). The story of a disturbed high school student who resorts to cutting herself is combined with facts about the causes, symptoms, and treatment of severe emotional disturbance. (Rev: SLJ 12/04)

11846 Marcovitz, Hal. *Bipolar Disorders* (6–10). Illus. Series: Compact Research. 2009, ReferencePoint $25.95 (978-1-60152-066-1). Marcovitz provides a thorough and readable guide to the causes, symptoms, and treatment of bipolar disorders. (Rev: SLJ 6/1/09) [516]

11847 Meisel, Abigail. *Investigating Depression and Bipolar Disorder: Real Facts for Real Lives* (7–10). Series: Investigating Diseases. 2010, Enslow LB $34.60 (978-0-7660-3340-5). Symptoms, diagnosis, treatment, and current research are all covered in this book that also tells the stories of children coping with these problems and provides historical background. (Rev: LMC 10/10) [616.85]

11848 Metcalf, Tom, and Gena Metcalf. *Phobias* (6–10). Series: Perspectives on Diseases and Disorders. 2008, Gale/Greenhaven $34.95 (978-0-7377-4027-1). A collection of articles that discuss the symptoms, causes, and treatment of phobias, with interesting first-person accounts. (Rev: SLJ 2/1/09) [616.85]

11849 Miller, Allen R. *Living with Depression* (6–12). Series: Teen's Guides. 2007, Facts on File LB $34.95 (978-0-8160-6345-1). This guide to recognizing and treating depression will help teenagers with the disease and those who know others who suffer with it. (Rev: BL 10/15/07) [618.92]

11850 Moe, Barbara. *Coping with Mental Illness* (7–10). Series: Coping. 2001, Rosen LB $31.95 (978-0-8239-3205-4). The diagnosis, symptoms, and treatment of major forms of mental illness are discussed, along with the types of professionals who can help. Also use *Schizophrenia* (2001). (Rev: SLJ 8/01) [616.89]

11851 Moehn, Heather. *Social Anxiety* (7–12). 2001, Rosen LB $31.95 (978-0-8239-3363-1). A strong fear of social situations often manifests itself during adolescence, and Moehn combines case studies and coping strategies with an overview of the condition itself and a look at treatment alternatives. (Rev: BL 3/1/02; SLJ 5/02) [616.85]

11852 Mooney, Carla. *Mental Illness Research* (8–11). Illus. Series: Inside Science. 2012, ReferencePoint LB $27.95 (978-160152234-4). Discusses the causes, diagnosis, and treatment of mental disorders, with a focus on future techniques. (Rev: BL 7/12) [362.196]

11853 Mooney, Carla. *Mood Disorders* (7–12). Illus. Series: Compact Research: Diseases and Disorders. 2010, ReferencePoint LB $26.95 (978-160152119-4). Unipolar and bipolar mood disorders are introduced with statistics, primary source quotations, and information on treatment and support. (Rev: BL 2/1/11) [616.85]

11854 Moragne, Wendy. *Depression* (7–12). Series: Medical Library. 2001, Twenty-First Century LB $24.90 (978-0-7613-1774-6). Signs, symptoms, diagnosis, and treatment of depression are introduced clearly and concisely with case histories of seven teenagers. (Rev: BL 5/15/01; HBG 10/01; SLJ 4/01; VOYA 10/01) [616.85]

11855 Nakaya, Andrea C. *ADHD* (7–12). Illus. Series: Compact Research: Diseases and Disorders. 2009, ReferencePoint LB $25.95 (978-160152062-3). A balanced overview of attention deficit hyperactivity disorder and its symptoms and treatment. (Rev: BL 4/1/09; SLJ 6/1/09) [618.92]

11856 Paquette, Penny Hutchins, and Cheryl Gerson Tuttle. *Learning Disabilities: The Ultimate Teen Guide* (7–12). Series: It Happened to Me. 2003, Scarecrow LB $32.50 (978-0-8108-4261-8). Teens suffering from conditions including ADHD and dyslexia will find practical information on these disabilities, success stories, and advice on career and employment choices and strategies. (Rev: SLJ 10/03) [371.9]

11857 Parks, Peggy J. *Alzheimer's Disease* (6–10). Illus. Series: Compact Research: Diseases and Disorders. 2009, ReferencePoint $25.95 (978-1-60152-061-6). This accessible, illustrated book provides a thorough and readable guide to the causes, symptoms, and treatment of Alzheimer's disease. (Rev: SLJ 6/1/09) [616.831]

11858 Parks, Peggy J. *Autism* (7–12). Illus. Series: Compact Research: Diseases and Disorders. 2008, ReferencePoint LB $25.95 (978-160152058-6). "What causes autism?" and "How effective are autism treatments?" are among the questions discussed in this thoughtful and attractive volume. (Rev: BL 4/1/09; LMC 8–9/09) [616.85]

11859 Parks, Peggy J. *Down Syndrome* (7–12). Series: Compact Research. 2009, ReferencePoint $25.95 (978-

1-60152-065-4). In this broad overview of Down syndrome, Parks focuses on the genetic causes and ethical considerations surrounding the disorder, also discussing technology that may prevent it in the future. (Rev: SLJ 6/1/09) [362.1]

11860 Parks, Peggy J. *Obsessive-Compulsive Disorder* (7–12). Illus. Series: Compact Research: Diseases and Disorders. 2010, ReferencePoint LB $26.95 (978-160152120-0). The causes and symptoms of OCD are introduced with statistics, primary source quotations, and information on treatment and support. (Rev: BL 2/1/11)

11861 Parks, Peggy J. *Self-Injury Disorder* (7–12). Illus. Series: Compact Research: Diseases and Disorders. 2010, ReferencePoint LB $26.95 (978-160152112-5). The reasons for self-mutilation are introduced with statistics, primary source quotations, and information on treatment and support. (Rev: BL 2/1/11) [618.92]

11862 Porterfield, Kay Marie. *Straight Talk About Learning Disabilities* (6–12). 1999, Facts on File $27.45 (978-0-8160-3865-7). Using three fictional case studies, the author discusses various kinds of learning disabilities, their symptoms, methods of diagnosis, and available treatments. (Rev: BL 2/15/00; HBG 4/00; SLJ 2/00; VOYA 4/00) [371.92]

11863 Powell, Mark. *Stress Relief: The Ultimate Teen Guide* (7–12). Illus. by Kelly Adams. Series: Ultimate Teen Guide. 2003, Scarecrow LB $32.50 (978-0-8108-4433-9). Typical causes of teen stress — relationships, homework, money, and so forth — are examined and practical suggestions for dealing with them are spelled out. (Rev: BL 10/15/03; SLJ 7/03; VOYA 4/03) [155.5]

11864 Quinn, Patricia O. *Adolescents and ADD: Gaining the Advantage* (6–12). 1996, Magination paper $12.95 (978-0-945354-70-3). As well as citing many case studies, this book on teens and attention deficit disorder provides useful background information plus tips on how to adjust to this condition and how to create a lifestyle that accommodates it. (Rev: BL 1/1–15/96; SLJ 3/96; VOYA 8/96) [371.94]

11865 Quinn, Patricia O. *Attention, Girls! A Guide to Learn All About Your AD/HD* (3–8). Illus. by Carl Pearce. 2009, Magination $16.95 (978-1-4338-0447-2); paper $12.95 (978-1-4338-0448-9). A readable, girl-centered look at ADHD with advice and tips from the author who is a physician living with ADHD. (Rev: BL 7/09; SLJ 10/09) [618.92]

11866 Rashkin, Rachel. *Feeling Better: A Kid's Book About Therapy* (4–8). Illus. by Bonnie Adamson. 2005, Magination paper $9.95 (978-1-59147-238-4). Presented in journal format, this volume uses 12-year-old Maya's experiences with a therapist to offer useful insights into the process and its value. (Rev: SLJ 11/05) [618.92]

11867 Rosaler, Maxine. *Coping with Asperger Syndrome* (6–9). Series: Coping. 2004, Rosen LB $31.95 (978-0-8239-4482-8). This straightforward title provides valuable information on Asperger syndrome and its symptoms and treatment. (Rev: BL 3/1/05; SLJ 12/04) [616.89]

11868 Rosenberg, Marsha Sarah. *Coping When a Brother or Sister Is Autistic* (7–12). Series: Coping. 2001, Rosen LB $31.95 (978-0-8239-3194-1). Siblings of autistic children will find facts about the diagnosis and treatment of the disorder, as well as sympathetic, nononsense advice on dealing with the pressures of the situation. (Rev: SLJ 9/01) [618.92]

11869 Rosenberg, Marsha Sarah. *Everything You Need to Know When a Brother or Sister Is Autistic* (5–9). Series: Need to Know Library. 2000, Rosen LB $27.95 (978-0-8239-3123-1). Autism is defined and described, with material on its diagnosis and treatment plus coverage of how this condition can affect other members of the family. (Rev: SLJ 8/00) [616.8]

11870 Sanders, Pete, and Steve Myers. *Dyslexia* (4–8). Illus. by Mike Lacy and Liz Sawyer. Series: What Do You Know About. 1999, Millbrook LB $23.90 (978-0-7613-0915-4). Using a case study, this book explores one boy's problems with dyslexia, its causes, symptoms, and treatment. (Rev: HBG 10/99; SLJ 10/99) [617.7]

11871 Scowen, Kate. *My Kind of Sad: What It's Like to Be Young and Depressed* (7–12). Illus. by Jeff Szuc. 2006, Firefly $19.95 (978-1-55037-941-9); paper $10.95 (978-1-55037-940-2). Describes depression and how to tell between normal moods and feelings and what could be harmful; additional information on treatments and medications is included. (Rev: BL 9/15/06; SLJ 2/07) [616.85.5]

11872 Shields, Charles J. *Mental Illness and Its Effects on School and Work Environments* (6–10). Series: Encyclopedia of Psychological Disorders. 2000, Chelsea $35.00 (978-0-7910-5318-8). As well as giving a general introduction to the nature of mental illness, this work discusses how the mentally ill affect American society. (Rev: BL 11/1/00) [616.8]

11873 Simpson, Carolyn, and Dwain Simpson. *Coping with Post-Traumatic Stress Disorder* (7–10). Series: Coping. 1997, Rosen LB $25.25 (978-0-8239-2080-8). Post-traumatic stress disorder (PTSD) affects people who have experienced natural disasters, rape, war, or other traumatic events. This book explains the causes and primary signs of PTSD and how it affects family and friends, as well as the victim, and provides useful information on treatment. (Rev: SLJ 10/97) [362]

11874 Stewart, Gail B. *People with Mental Illness* (7–12). Series: The Other America. 2003, Gale LB $29.95 (978-1-59018-237-6). Personal stories of individuals with different conditions show how they cope with

daily life and the impact on the families as well as the patients. (Rev: SLJ 6/03) [616.89]

11875 Verdick, Elizabeth, and Elizabeth Reeve. *The Survival Guide for Kids with Autism Spectrum Disorders (and Their Parents)* (4–8). Illus. by Nick Kobyluch. 2012, Free Spirit paper $16.99 (978-15754238-5-2). This straightforward book provides background information on autism and famous people who have suffered from autism, and gives guidance on improving life at home and at school. (Rev: BL 4/15/12; SLJ 5/1/12; VOYA 6/12) [618.92]

11876 Zeinert, Karen. *Suicide: Tragic Choice* (6–12). Series: Issues in Focus. 1999, Enslow LB $26.60 (978-0-7660-1105-2). All aspects of suicide are covered including history, demographic patterns, causes, the grief of survivors, cluster suicide, and assisted suicide. (Rev: BL 12/15/99; HBG 4/00; VOYA 4/00) [362.28]

Nutrition and Diet

11877 Alters, Sandra. *Obesity* (7–12). Series: Introducing Issues with Opposing Viewpoints. 2006, Gale LB $32.45 (978-0-7377-3545-1). Fourteen articles look at the causes and nature of obesity and examine possible ways to deal with this epidemic; fact boxes, charts, photographs, and cartoon strips highlight key points. (Rev: SLJ 4/07) [616.3]

11878 Ballard, Carol. *Food for Feeling Healthy* (6–9). Series: Making Healthy Food Choices. 2006, Heinemann LB $32.86 (978-1-4034-8571-7). Using the new food pyramid, Ballard examines important factors in eating properly and discusses advertising, peer pressure, and food labels. (Rev: SLJ 4/07) [613.2]

11879 Bellenir, Karen, ed. *Diet Information for Teens: Health Tips About Diet and Nutrition, Including Facts About Nutrients, Dietary Guidelines, Breakfasts, School Lunches, Snacks, Party Food, Weight Control, Eating Disorders, and More* (7–12). 2001, Omnigraphics $48.00 (978-0-7808-0441-8). General nutrition information is amplified by topics of particular interest to teens, such as snacking, school lunches, and eating disorders. (Rev: SLJ 6/01; VOYA 8/01) [613.2]

11880 Bijlefeld, Marjolijn, and Sharon K. Zoumbaris. *Food and You: A Guide to Healthy Habits for Teens* (7–12). 2001, Greenwood $59.95 (978-0-313-31108-6). A comprehensive guide to healthy eating, weight, and exercise that provides lots of information for report writers. (Rev: SLJ 11/01; VOYA 2/02) [613.7]

11881 Currie-McGhee, Leanne K. *Childhood Obesity* (7–12). Illus. Series: Nutrition and Health. 2012, Gale/Lucent LB $30.95 (978-1-4205-0723-2). With statistics, fact boxes, and anecdotes, this is an informative introduction to the causes and treatment of childhood obesity. (Rev: BL 11/1/12; SLJ 12/12) [618.92]

766

11882 D'Aluisio, Faith. *What the World Eats* (4–8). 2008, Tricycle $22.99 (978-1-5824-6246-2). What do people eat around the world? This is a fascinating survey of expenses, ingredients, and meals shared with 25 families in 21 countries; with statistics on obesity, access to water, and other key factors. (Rev: BL 7/08*; SLJ 7/08) [641.300]

11883 Drohan, Michele I. *Weight-Loss Programs: Weighing the Risks and Realities* (6–10). Series: Teen Health Library of Eating Disorder Prevention. 1998, Rosen LB $27.95 (978-0-8239-2770-8). This book explores weight-loss programs, sheds light on potential dangers, and discusses safe and sensible approaches to weight loss. (Rev: BL 3/1/99; SLJ 1/99) [616.85]

11884 Edwards, Hazel, and Goldie Alexander. *Talking About Your Weight* (4–7). Illus. Series: Healthy Living. 2010, Gareth Stevens LB $26 (978-143393655-5). Loaded topics such as eating disorders and obesity are presented in a clear, nonjudgmental fashion with emphasis on making better choices. (Rev: BL 4/1/10) [613]

11885 Favor, Lesli J. *Weighing In: Nutrition and Weight Management* (8–11). Series: Food and Fitness. 2007, Marshall Cavendish LB $25.95 (978-0-7614-2555-7). Information on dieting, healthy weight, general and specialized nutrition, and eating disorders is provided in text, statistics, charts, sidebar features, and photographs. (Rev: BL 1/1–15/08; SLJ 6/08) [613.2]

11886 Favor, Lesli J., and Kira Freed. *Food as Foe: Nutrition and Eating Disorders* (6–8). Series: Food and You. 2009, Marshall Cavendish $19.95 (978-0-7614-4364-3). Geared towards younger teens, this accessible, nonjudgmental guide presents information on weight management, nutrition, and eating disorders, complete with tips, dos and don'ts, and true-life stories. (Rev: LMC 4–5/08; SLJ 3/10)

11887 Fredericks, Carrie. *Obesity* (6–12). Illus. Series: Compact Research: Current Issues. 2008, ReferencePoint LB $24.95 (978-160152040-1). This fact-filled volume examines the causes, dangers, and treatment of obesity, including a section on how personal choices influence health. (Rev: BL 8/08) [616.3]

11888 Gay, Kathlyn. *Am I Fat? The Obesity Issue for Teens* (7–12). 2006, Enslow LB $31.93 (978-0-7660-2527-1). Obesity and the health issues associated with it are discussed, as well as strategies for living better and avoiding the wrong dieting decisions that many teens make. (Rev: SLJ 6/06)

11889 Gay, Kathlyn. *The Scoop on What to Eat: What You Should Know About Diet and Nutrition* (6–10). Illus. Series: Issues in Focus Today. 2009, Enslow LB $23.95 (978-076603066-4). A realistic and readable approach to choosing healthy foods, with a chapter on exercise. (Rev: BL 4/15/09; SLJ 10/09) [613.2]

11890 Gordon, Sherri Mabry. *Peanut Butter, Milk, and Other Deadly Threats: What You Should Know About Food Allergies* (5–9). Series: Issues in Focus Today. 2006, Enslow LB $31.93 (978-0-7660-2529-5). This information-packed survey of food allergies identifies common culprit foods, explains the mechanics of allergic reactions, and also reports on medical research to find better treatments. (Rev: SLJ 11/06) [616.97]

11891 Hillstrom, Kevin. *Food Allergies* (7–12). Illus. Series: Nutrition and Health. 2012, Gale/Lucent LB $30.95 (978-142050720-1). With statistics, fact boxes, and anecdotes, this is an informative introduction to food allergies and their treatment. (Rev: BL 11/1/12; SLJ 12/12) [616.97]

11892 Hillstrom, Kevin. *Genetically Modified Foods* (7–12). Illus. Series: Nutrition and Health. 2012, Gale/Lucent LB $30.95 (978-142050722-5). With statistics, fact boxes, and anecdotes, this is an informative introduction to the rise of GM foods and their benefits and dangers. (Rev: BL 11/1/12; SLJ 12/12) [664]

11893 Ingram, Scott. *Want Fries with That? Obesity and the Supersizing of America* (8–11). 2005, Scholastic LB $26.00 (978-0-531-16756-4). Examines the relationship between America's burgeoning fast-food business and the country's obesity epidemic. (Rev: BL 11/15/05; SLJ 1/06) [362.196]

11894 Klimecki, Zachary, and Karen Bellenir, eds. *Diet Information for Teens* (7–12). Illus. Series: Teen Health. 2011, Omnigraphics $62 (978-078081156-0). An updated guide to nutrition and diet, incorporating the new MyPlate Food Guidance System. (Rev: BL 3/1/12) [613.2083]

11895 Lankford, Ronnie D., ed. *Can Diets Be Harmful?* (7–12). Series: At Issue: Health. 2007, Gale LB $28.70 (978-0-7377-3397-6); paper $19.95 (978-0-7377-3398-3). Essays about nutrition and healthy weight tackle such issues as fad diets, eating disorders, and fast food, with some personal stories. (Rev: BL 1/1–15/08) [613.2]

11896 Loonin, Meryl. *Overweight America* (7–12). Series: Hot Topics. 2006, Gale LB $31.20 (978-1-59018-744-9). Covering the reasons why Americans are overweight, the way we eat and think about food. (Rev: SLJ 2/07)

11897 Moe, Barbara. *Understanding Negative Body Image* (6–10). Series: Teen Eating Disorder Prevention Library. 1999, Rosen $31.95 (978-0-8239-2865-1). Our culture stresses body weight and shape, and this book explores the many causes and harmful consequences of a negative body image. (Rev: BL 10/15/99; HBG 9/00; SLJ 1/00; VOYA 2/00) [613.4]

11898 Monroe, Judy. *Understanding Weight-Loss Programs* (6–10). Series: Teen Eating Disorder Prevention Library. 1999, Rosen LB $31.95 (978-0-8239-2866-8). This book discusses good and bad weight loss programs, how to evaluate them, and how to be on guard for bogus products. (Rev: BL 10/15/99; HBG 9/00; SLJ 1/00) [613.7]

11899 Morris, Neil. *Do You Know What's in Your Food?* (6–10). Series: Making Healthy Food Choices. 2006, Heinemann LB $32.86 (978-1-4034-8574-8). Morris challenges teens to look at the questionable components of the foods they eat — bacteria, fat, chemicals, additives, and so forth. Also use *Food for Sports* (2006). (Rev: SLJ 2/07)

11900 Pierson, Stephanie. *Vegetables Rock! A Complete Guide for Teenage Vegetarians* (7–12). 1999, Bantam paper $13.95 (978-0-553-37924-2). Animal rights and health issues are touched on in this book that describes philosophical and practical aspects of vegetarianism and provides a guide to good foods and balancing nutritional needs. (Rev: BL 3/1/99) [613.2]

11901 Pollan, Michael. *The Omnivore's Dilemma: The Secrets Behind What You Eat* (6–10). Adapted by Richie Chevat. Illus. 2009, Dial $17.99 (978-0-8037-3415-9). For young adults, this condensed version of Pollan's groundbreaking work offers an attractive and accessible take on the importance of choosing your food carefully. (Rev: BL 10/15/09*; HB 11–12/09; LMC 11–12/09; SLJ 10/09) [338.10973.]

11902 Rau, Dana Meachen. *Going Organic: A Healthy Guide to Making the Switch* (6–9). Illus. Series: Food Revolution. 2012, Compass Point $33.99 (978-075654523-9); paper $8.95 (978-07565452-8-4). Discusses the benefits of eating organic foods and the ways in which they are marketed. (Rev: BL 4/1/12) [613]

11903 Schlosser, Eric, and Charles Wilson. *Chew on This: Everything You Don't Want to Know About Fast Food* (6–9). 2006, Houghton Mifflin $16.00 (978-0-618-71031-7). An unsettling but informative discussion of fast food and its attractions. (Rev: BL 3/1/06*; SLJ 5/06) [394.1]

11904 Schwartz, Ellen. *I'm a Vegetarian: Amazing Facts and Ideas for Healthy Vegetarians* (5–8). Illus. by Farida Zaman. 2002, Tundra paper $9.95 (978-0-88776-588-9). The social aspects of being a vegetarian are handled here with humor and sensitivity. (Rev: BL 7/02; SLJ 9/02) [613.2]

11905 Tattersall, Clare. *Understanding Food and Your Family* (6–10). Series: Teen Eating Disorder Prevention Library. 1999, Rosen $31.95 (978-0-8239-2860-6). Using many facts and references to case studies, this book describes family dynamics and how eating patterns are developed within the family structure. (Rev: BL 10/15/99; HBG 9/00; SLJ 11/99; VOYA 2/00) [616.85]

11906 Thornhill, Jan. *Who Wants Pizza? The Kids' Guide to the History, Science and Culture of Food* (5–8). 2010, Maple Tree paper $10.95 (978-1-897349-97-7). Taking pizza as an example, this appealingly busy and well-illustrated book discusses the nutrients that

food provides to the body and looks at various scientific (the chemistry of fertilizers, for example) and cultural aspects (a Bushman eating caterpillars) of food. (Rev: BL 12/1/10; LMC 11–12/10) [641.3]

11907 Traugh, Susan M. *Vegetarianism* (6–9). Illus. Series: Nutrition and Health. 2010, Gale/Lucent LB $30.85 (978-142050272-5). An attractive guide to the history of vegetarianism, the current availability of this diet, and the various diet choices. (Rev: BL 9/1/11; SLJ 4/11) [641.5]

11908 VanCleave, Janice. *Janice VanCleave's Food and Nutrition for Every Kid: Easy Activities That Make Learning Science Fun* (4–8). Series: Science for Every Kid. 1999, Wiley paper $12.95 (978-0-471-17665-7). Each of the 25 chapters in this book contains information about food, including food groups, the relationship between energy and food, how to read nutrition labels, and vitamins and minerals, plus dozens of easily performed projects that demonstrate these facts and concepts. (Rev: SLJ 8/99) [641.3]

11909 Watson, Stephanie. *Mystery Meat: Hot Dogs, Sausages, and Lunch Meats: The Incredibly Disgusting Story* (4–7). Illus. Series: Incredibly Disgusting Food. 2011, Rosen LB $26.50 (978-1-4488-1268-4); paper $11.75 (978-1-4488-2284-3). Discusses the ingredients of "mystery meats" and the impact they can have on our bodies and minds, with some eye-catchingly off-putting photographs. Lexile 1220L (Rev: BL 4/1/11; SLJ 6/11) [664]

11910 Weiss, Stefanie Iris. *Everything You Need to Know About Being a Vegan* (5–8). Series: Need to Know Library. 1999, Rosen LB $27.95 (978-0-8239-2958-0). This book discusses vegans, people who do not eat or use animal products (usually for religious reasons), their lifestyles, diets, and possible social problems. (Rev: SLJ 1/00; VOYA 4/00) [613.2]

11911 Williams, Kara. *Frequently Asked Questions About MyPyramid: Eating Right* (5–8). Illus. 2007, Rosen LB $20.95 (978-1-4042-1974-8). Introduces the 2005 version of the food pyramid as well as information on diet, nutrition, the human body, and exercise. (Rev: BL 6/1–15/07; LMC 10/07) [613.2]

11912 Zahensky, Barbara A. *Diet Fads* (4–8). Series: Danger Zone. Dieting and Eating Disorders. 2007, Rosen LB $27.95 (978-1-4042-1999-1). Fad and crash diets and the dangers of overeating and excessive weight loss are the focus of this practical guide. (Rev: LMC 10/07; SLJ 9/07) [613.2]

Physical Disabilities and Problems

11913 Costello, Elaine. *Signing: How to Speak with Your Hands* (7–9). 1995, Bantam paper $19.95 (978-0-553-

37539-8). A simple explanation of and a guide to the use of sign language for the deaf. [001.56]

11914 Laney, Dawn, ed. *People with Disabilities* (8–12). Series: History of Issues. 2008, Gale/Greenhaven $36.20 (978-0-7377-3972-5). Laney presents articles supporting and opposing issues relating to people with disabilities, addressing such topics as legal rights, education, and new technologies. (Rev: SLJ 2/1/09) [362.40973]

11915 Stewart, Gail B. *Teens with Disabilities* (8–12). Photos by Carl Franzén. Series: The Other America. 2000, Lucent LB $29.95 (978-1-56006-815-0). The personal — and positive — stories of four teens with physical disabilities show how people with these problems can be accommodated in family and social settings. (Rev: SLJ 3/01)

11916 Thornton, Denise. *Physical Disabilities: The Ultimate Teen Guide* (5–10). Series: It Happened to Me. 2007, Scarecrow $42.00 (978-0-8108-5300-3). In interviews, teens with disabilities describe how they cope at school, with technology and tools, getting around, sports, and so forth. (Rev: SLJ 10/07) [362.40835]

Reproduction and Child Care

11917 Almond, Lucinda, ed. *The Abortion Controversy* (8–12). Series: Current Controversies. 2007, Gale $23.70 (978-0-7377-3273-3). An updated collection of articles expressing many views on abortion and related issues including stem cell research and the rights of activists in general. (Rev: BL 12/1/07) [363.46]

11918 Anderson, Judith. *Healthy Mothers* (4–7). Series: Working for Our Future. 2010, Black Rabbit LB $28.50 (978-1-59771-197-5). This volume explains why the United Nations chose promoting healthy mothers as one of its eight Millennium Development goals. (Rev: BL 6/10; LMC 10/10; SLJ 4/10) [306.874.]

11919 Brynie, Faith Hickman. *101 Questions About Reproduction: Or How 1 + 1 = 3 or 4 or More . . . .* (6–10). Illus. by Sharon Lane Holm. 2005, Twenty-First Century LB $27.93 (978-0-7613-2311-2). Information on conception, pregnancy, childbirth, contraception (including a pill for males), abortion, reproductive disorders, and other issues of importance to teens is provided in a question-and-answer format with detailed black-and-white illustrations. (Rev: SLJ 1/06) [612]

11920 Byers, Ann. *Teens and Pregnancy: A Hot Issue* (6–12). Series: Hot Issues. 2000, Enslow LB $27.93 (978-0-7660-1365-0). Various aspects of teen pregnancy are discussed, from social factors that put teens at risk to the financial ramifications of single parenthood to ways in which teens can avoid pregnancy. (Rev: HBG 3/01; SLJ 1/01) [306.874]

11921 Coles, Robert. *The Youngest Parents* (8–12). 1997, Norton $27.50 (978-0-393-04082-1). The first two-thirds of this adult book consists of interviews by the author, a child psychiatrist, with teenagers who are or about to be parents, and the last part is a moving photoessay featuring many rural, underprivileged teen parents and their children. (Rev: BL 2/1/97; VOYA 6/98) [306.85]

11922 *Daycare and Diplomas: Teen Mothers Who Stayed in School* (7–12). 2001, Fairview paper $9.95 (978-1-57749-098-2). A group of young women who attend an unusual school that offers childcare relate the difficulties they have experienced in combining parenthood and education. (Rev: BL 5/15/01; VOYA 4/01) [306.874]

11923 Fisanick, Christina, ed. *Childbirth* (8–12). Series: Opposing Viewpoints. 2008, Gale/Greenhaven LB $37.40 (978-0-7377-4196-4); paper $25.95 (978-0-7377-4197-1). A collection of articles showing various points of view on aspects of childbirth practices. (Rev: SLJ 5/1/09) [618.2]

11924 Gottfried, Ted. *Teen Fathers Today* (8–12). 2001, Twenty-First Century LB $24.90 (978-0-7613-1901-6). Real-life stories add immediacy to this practical guide to the challenges of becoming a father during the teen years. (Rev: HBG 3/02; SLJ 12/01; VOYA 2/02) [306.874]

11925 Heller, Tania. *Pregnant! What Can I Do? A Guide for Teenagers* (6–12). 2002, McFarland $29.95 (978-0-7864-1169-6). Valuable information about pregnancy, abortion, adoption, prenatal care, and parenting is provided in this thoughtful and reassuring volume. (Rev: SLJ 6/02; VOYA 6/02) [306.874/]

11926 MacDonald, Fiona. *The First "Test-Tube Baby"* (6–12). Series: Days that Changed the World. 2004, World Almanac LB $31.00 (978-0-8368-5567-8); paper $11.95 (978-0-8368-5574-6). The science and ethics of in-vitro fertilization are explored in this overview of the 1978 birth of the world's first "test-tube baby." (Rev: BL 4/1/04; SLJ 7/04) [618.1]

11927 Parks, Peggy J. *Teenage Sex and Pregnancy* (7–12). Illus. Series: Compact Research: Teenage Problems. 2011, ReferencePoint LB $27.95 (978-160152168-2). Looks at topics ranging from abstinence and contraception to sex education and the consequences of teen pregnancy. (Rev: BL 4/1/12) [306.874]

11928 Powers, Meghan, ed. *The Abortion Rights Movement* (8–11). Series: American Social Movements. 2006, Gale LB $36.20 (978-0-7377-1947-5). This collection of 18 articles, speeches, first-person accounts, and interviews lays out the case for abortion. (Rev: BL 2/15/06) [363.46]

11929 Rosenthal, Beth, ed. *Birth Control* (7–12). Series: Opposing Viewpoints. 2008, Gale/Greenhaven $37.40 (978-073774194-0); paper $25.95 (978-073774195-7).

Questions such as "How does birth control affect society?" and "Who should control access to birth control?" are tackled in this collection of articles offering various perspectives. (Rev: BL 4/1/09; SLJ 5/1/09) [363.9]

11930 Sterngass, Jon. *Reproductive Technology* (7–10). Illus. Series: Controversy! 2011, Marshall Cavendish LB $25.95 (978-160870494-1). A balanced discussion of issues relating to reproductive technology such as genetic engineering, abortion, sperm and egg donation, and stem cell research. (Rev: BL 5/1/12; VOYA 10/12) [174.2]

11931 Trapani, Margi. *Listen Up: Teenage Mothers Speak Out* (6–12). Series: Teen Pregnancy Prevention Library. 1997, Rosen LB $23.95 (978-0-8239-2254-3). Young women speak candidly about why they had children at an early age and the impact this has had on their lives. (Rev: BL 6/1–15/97; SLJ 6/97; VOYA 10/97) [306.874]

11932 Trapani, Margi. *Reality Check: Teenage Fathers Speak Out* (7–10). 1997, Rosen LB $23.95 (978-0-8239-2255-0). Case studies of teenage fathers who did not plan on becoming parents are discussed in this book that does not shun the hardships of being a teenage parent. (Rev: BL 6/1–15/97; SLJ 6/97; VOYA 10/97) [306.85]

11933 Wilks, Corinne Morgan, ed. *Dear Diary, I'm Pregnant: Teenagers Talk About Their Pregnancy* (7–12). 1997, Annick paper $9.95 (978-1-55037-440-7). Ten teenage girls talk about how they got pregnant, what they decided to do, and how the pregnancy has changed their lives. (Rev: BL 2/1/98; SLJ 8/97; VOYA 12/97) [306.874]

11934 Williams, Kara. *Fertility Technology: The Baby Debate* (6–8). Series: Focus on Science and Society. 2000, Rosen LB $26.50 (978-0-8239-3210-8). An interesting exploration of the types of fertility treatment available, the science behind them, and the controversies surrounding their use. (Rev: SLJ 1/01) [618.1]

11935 Zerucha, Ted. *Human Development* (7–12). Series: The Human Body: How It Works. 2009, Chelsea House $35 (978-1-60413-371-4). Zerucha describes the development of a human being from the initial single cell. (Rev: LMC 5–6/10) [612.64]

Safety and First Aid

11936 Arnold, Caroline. *Coping with Natural Disasters* (7–10). 1988, Walker LB $14.85 (978-0-8027-6717-2). Natural disasters such as earthquakes, hurricanes, and blizzards are discussed, with information on how to react in these emergencies. (Rev: BCCB 6/88; BL 6/15/88; SLJ 6/88; VOYA 10/88) [904]

11937 Chaiet, Donna, and Francine Russell. *The Safe Zone: A Kid's Guide to Personal Safety* (4–7). 1998, Morrow paper $6.95 (978-0-688-16091-3). This book alerts youngsters to danger signs, gives advice on body language and self-esteem, and offers tips on how to avoid threatening situations. (Rev: BL 4/1/98; HBG 10/98) [613.6]

11938 Claybourne, Anna. *100 Deadliest Things on the Planet* (4–7). Illus. 2012, Scholastic paper $7.99 (978-05454343-7-9). Dangerous animals, natural catastrophes, deadly diseases, poisonous plants — they're all here, with danger ratings. (Rev: BL 12/1/12) [591.65]

11939 Gutman, Bill. *Be Aware of Danger* (5–8). Series: Focus on Safety. 1996, Twenty-First Century LB $24.90 (978-0-8050-4142-2). Situations that could be dangerous to young people are highlighted and preventive measures outlined. (Rev: BL 2/1/97; SLJ 2/97) [613.6]

11940 Gutman, Bill. *Recreation Can Be Risky* (4–8). Series: Focus on Safety. 1996, Henry Holt LB $24.90 (978-0-8050-4143-9). The author gives practical suggestions for enjoying such activities as baseball, biking, or hiking while also keeping safe through warm-up exercises, proper equipment, correct clothing, etc. (Rev: BL 7/96; SLJ 9/96; VOYA 10/96) [790]

11941 Hurley, Michael. *Surviving the Wilderness* (4–7). Series: Extreme Survival. 2011, Heinemann LB $33.50 (978-1-4109-3972-2). Hurley explores the dangers posed in the mountains, forest, outback, desert, jungle, and wilderness as well as those we face at sea, and offers survival tips and advice. (Rev: SLJ 8/11) [613.6]

11942 Kyi, Tanya Lloyd. *Fifty Poisonous Questions: A Book with Bite* (4–7). Illus. by Ross Kinnaird. 2011, Annick $21.95 (978-1-55451-281-2); paper $12.95 (978-1-55451-280-5). This luridly illustrated volume offers considerable information on poisons of all kinds, with humorous illustrations, interesting sidebars, and "Foul Facts." (Rev: LMC 11–12/11; SLJ 9/1/11) [615.9]

11943 Long, Denise. *Survivor Kid: A Practical Guide to Wilderness Survival* (5–8). Illus. 2011, Chicago Review paper $12.95 (978-15697670-8-5). Personal anecdotes bolster the sensible advice presented here about staying safe in the woods. e (Rev: BL 6/1/11) [613.6]

11944 Orndorff, John C., and Suzanne Harper. *Terrorists, Tornados, and Tsunamis: How to Prepare for Life's Danger Zones* (7–12). 2007, Abrams $16.95 (978-0-8109-5767-1). A practical guide to preparing for all kinds of disasters, from storms to Internet predators. (Rev: BL 4/15/07; SLJ 5/07) [613.6]

11945 Parker, Steve, and David West. *Human-Made Disasters* (5–8). Illus. by David West. Series: Science of Catastrophe. 2011, Crabtree LB $26.60 (978-077877575-1). Not for the faint-hearted, this is a survey of events including the *Challenger* explosion, the

Chernobyl meltdown, and the collapse of a bridge in Mississippi in 2007. (Rev: BL 4/1/12) [904]

11946 Wells, Donna K., and Bruce C. Morris. *Live Aware, Not in Fear: The 411 After 9-11 — A Book For Teens* (6–12). 2002, Health Communications paper $9.95 (978-0-7573-0013-4). The authors offer practical advice for teenagers who want to feel safe again, such as preparing escape routes and keeping a survival kit handy. (Rev: BL 5/15/02; VOYA 6/02) [363.3]

Sex Education and Sexual Identity

11947 Bailey, Jacqui. *Sex, Puberty and All That Stuff: A Guide to Growing Up* (5–10). Illus. by Jan McCafferty. 2004, Barron's paper $12.99 (978-0-7641-2992-6). In this comprehensive volume full of lighthearted illustrations, Bailey covers the wide range of changes that affect young people, emphasizing the individual's right to choose and the need to resist peer pressure. (Rev: SLJ 1/05) [613.9]

11948 Bily, Cynthia A., ed. *Homosexuality* (7–12). Series: Opposing Viewpoints. 2008, Gale/Greenhaven $37.40 (978-073774214-5); paper $25.95 (978-073774215-2). Questions such as "Should gay men and women serve in the military?" and "Should same-sex couples be allowed to marry?" are tackled in this collection of articles offering various perspectives. (Rev: BL 4/1/09) [306.76]

11949 Brynie, Faith Hickman. *101 Questions About Sex and Sexuality: With Answers for the Curious, Cautious, and Confused* (6–12). Series: 101 Questions. 2003, Twenty-First Century LB $27.90 (978-0-7613-2310-5). Information on abstinence, contraception, sexually transmitted diseases, and other issues of importance to teens is provided in a question-and-answer format with detailed black-and-white illustrations. (Rev: HBG 10/03; SLJ 6/03; VOYA 4/04) [306.7]

11950 Diamond, Shifra N. *Everything You Need to Know About Going to the Gynecologist* (7–12). Series: Need to Know Library. 1999, Rosen LB $27.95 (978-0-8239-2839-2). This book explains what a gynecologist does, when teenage girls should see one, and how to find one. There is helpful information on menstruation, breast self-examinations, treatments for common reproductive problems, contraception, myths, and what to expect from a pelvic examination. (Rev: SLJ 5/99; VOYA 8/99) [612]

11951 Dunham, Kelli. *The Boy's Body Book: Everything You Need to Know for Growing Up YOU* (4–7). Illus. by Steven Björkman. 2007, Sterling paper $9.95 (978-1-933662-74-9). This is a straightforward review of the changes to expect during puberty; it also discusses stress, friendship, peer pressure, and family problems such as divorce. (Rev: LMC 2/08; SLJ 10/07) [612.6]

11952 Feinmann, Jane. *Everything a Girl Needs to Know About Her Periods* (5–9). 2003, Ronnie Sellers paper $14.95 (978-1-56906-555-6). This useful and reassuring guide to the female body changes of puberty focuses largely on the menstrual cycle. (Rev: BL 2/1/04) [618.083]

11953 Feinstein, Stephen. *Sexuality and Teens: What You Should Know About Sex, Abstinence, Birth Control, Pregnancy, and STDs* (7–9). Series: Issues in Focus Today. 2009, Enslow LB $31.93 (978-0-7660-3312-2). Feinstein provides a thorough discussion of teen sexuality issues, including setting boundaries, birth control, and STDs. (Rev: SLJ 3/10)

11954 Gowen, L. Kris. *Making Sexual Decisions: The Ultimate Teen Guide* (7–12). Series: It Happened to Me. 2003, Scarecrow $32.50 (978-0-8108-4647-0). Puberty, safe sex, birth control, and rape are among the topics raised in this volume, which stresses the value of being fully informed about one's options. (Rev: SLJ 11/03) [306.7]

11955 Gravelle, Karen, and Nick Castro. *What's Going on Down There? Answers to Questions Boys Find Hard to Ask* (5–10). Illus. by Robert Leighton. 1998, Walker paper $8.95 (978-0-8027-7540-5). Straightforward information for boys covers such topics as physical changes, sexual intercourse, peer pressure, and pregnancy and birth. (Rev: BL 11/1/98; HB 1–2/99; HBG 3/99; SLJ 12/98) [613]

11956 Hoch, Dean, and Nancy Hoch. *The Sex Education Dictionary for Today's Teens and Pre-Teens* (7–12). 1990, Landmark paper $12.95 (978-0-9624209-0-0). A dictionary of 350 words relating to sex, sexuality, and reproduction all given clear, concise definitions. (Rev: BL 8/90) [306.7]

11957 Hyde, Margaret O., and Elizabeth H. Forsyth. *Safe Sex 101* (8–11). 2006, Lerner $26.60 (978-0-8225-3439-6). Straightforward and well-written, this book includes important information for teens on how to protect themselves from STDs and pregnancy, covering contraception as well as abstinence. (Rev: BL 5/1/06; SLJ 6/06) [613.9]

11958 Johnson, Eric W. *People, Love, Sex, and Families: Answers to Questions That Preteens Ask* (5–8). 1985, Walker LB $14.85 (978-0-8027-6605-2). Based on the results of a survey of 1,000 preteens, this book covers a broad range of topics, from sexual abuse to venereal disease to divorce and incest. (Rev: BL 3/15/86) [306.707]

11959 Jukes, Mavis. *Growing Up: It's a Girl Thing: Straight Talk About First Bras, First Periods and Your Changing Body* (4–8). 1998, Knopf paper $10.00 (978-0-679-89027-0). Essential information about the changes girls experience during puberty, with half the book devoted to what to expect and how to plan for their first period, presented in an easy, big-sister style. (Rev: BL 11/1/98; SLJ 11/98) [612]

11960 Jukes, Mavis. *It's a Girl Thing: How to Stay Healthy, Safe, and in Charge* (5–9). 1996, Knopf paper $12.00 (978-0-679-87392-1). This guide to puberty for girls discusses such topics as menstruation, drinking and drugs, body changes, contraceptives, sexually transmitted diseases, and sexual abuse and harassment. (Rev: SLJ 6/96*) [612.6]

11961 Katz, Anne. *Girl in the Know: Your Inside-and-Out Guide to Growing Up* (4–8). Illus. by Monika Melnychuk. 2010, Kids Can $18.95 (978-1-55453-303-9). A straightforward, conversational, and wide-ranging introduction to the physical and emotional changes that accompany puberty. (Rev: BL 4/1/10; LMC 8–9/10; SLJ 5/10) [613]

11962 Larimore, Walt. *The Ultimate Guys' Body Book: Not-So-Stupid Questions About Your Body* (5–8). Illus. by Guy Francis. 2012, Zondervan paper $7.99 (978-03107232-3-3). Answering such questions as "I've got BO — what's a guy to do?" and "My acne is scary! What's wrong with my face?," this book offers a Christian perspective on puberty. (Rev: BL 4/15/12; SLJ 5/1/12; VOYA 6/12) [613]

11963 Loulan, JoAnn, and Bonnie Worthen. *Period: A Girl's Guide to Menstruation with a Parent's Guide.* Rev. ed. (5–7). 2001, Book Peddlers paper $9.99 (978-0-916773-96-0). This practical guide to menstruation is arranged by such questions as "What do I do when I get my first period?" and "What kind of exercise can I do?" (Rev: BL 2/1/01; HBG 10/01) [612.6]

11964 Mar, Jonathan, and Grace Norwich. *The Body Book for Boys* (5–8). Illus. by Ming Sung Ku. 2010, Scholastic paper $8.99 (978-05452375-1-2). This straightforward book presents information on subjects of concern to middle-school boys, from hygiene to the opposite sex. (Rev: BL 12/1/10) [613]

11965 Marcovitz, Hal. *Teens and Gay Issues* (7–10). Series: The Gallup Youth Survey, Major Issues and Trends. 2005, Mason Crest LB $22.95 (978-1-59084-873-9). An attractive volume documenting Gallup findings on gay teens' attitudes toward coming out, homophobia, the nature/nurture debate, and gay marriage and adoption. (Rev: SLJ 1/06) [305.9]

11966 Marcus, Eric. *What If Someone I Know Is Gay? Answers to Questions About What It Means to Be Gay and Lesbian* (7–12). 2007, Simon & Schuster paper $8.99 (978-1-4169-4970-1). This update of the title first published in 2001 uses new terminology and addresses questions that teenagers may have about their own sexuality as well as that of someone they know. (Rev: BL 10/1/07; SLJ 1/08) [306.766]

11967 Movsessian, Shushann. *Puberty Girl* (4–7). 2005, Allen & Unwin paper $15.95 (978-1-74114-104-7). A frank and friendly guide covering such topics as body changes, conflict resolution, and personal boundaries, as well as the changes that puberty brings in the oppo-site sex. (Rev: BL 10/15/05; SLJ 10/05; VOYA 10/05) [612.6]

11968 O'Grady, Kathleen, and Paula Wansbrough, eds. *Sweet Secrets: Telling Stories of Menstruation* (6–10). 1997, Second Story paper $9.95 (978-0-929005-33-1). Following an interesting review of attitudes and rituals relating to menstruation in various cultures throughout history, the main body of the book recounts 20 anecdotes about young teens and their first periods, interspersed with boxes providing information on topics including tampons, toxic shock syndrome, and breast examinations. (Rev: VOYA 6/98) [530.8]

11969 Pfeifer, Kate Gruenwald. *Boy's Guide to Becoming a Teen* (4–7). 2006, Jossey-Bass paper $12.95 (978-0-7879-8343-7). A guide to handling the physical, emotional, and social changes that accompany puberty in boys. (Rev: BL 5/15/06; SLJ 5/07) [613]

11970 Pfeifer, Kate Gruenwald. *Girl's Guide to Becoming a Teen* (4–7). Ed. by Amy B. Middleman. 2006, Jossey-Bass paper $12.95 (978-0-7879-8344-4). A guide to handling the physical, emotional, and social changes that accompany puberty in girls. (Rev: BL 5/15/06; SLJ 5/07) [613]

11971 Pogany, Susan Browning. *Sex Smart: 501 Reasons to Hold Off on Sex* (8–12). 1998, Fairview paper $14.95 (978-1-57749-043-2). The author uses quotations from teenagers, "Dear Abby," and other sources to explore emotional issues involved in making sexual choices and to argue for abstinence. (Rev: VOYA 4/99) [613.9]

11972 Price, Geoff. *Puberty Boy* (5–8). 2006, Allen & Unwin paper $15.95 (978-1-74114-563-2). A frank and friendly guide with an Australian accent that covers the important physical and emotional changes that accompany puberty. (Rev: BL 7/06; SLJ 9/06; VOYA 8/06) [612]

11973 Rooney, Frances, ed. *Hear Me Out: True Stories of Teens Confronting Homophobia* (8–12). 2005, Second Story paper $9.95 (978-1-896764-87-0). Young people who are volunteers in a Toronto organization called T.E.A.C.H. (Teens Educating and Confronting Homophobia) talk about prejudice they've experienced because of their sexual orientation. (Rev: BL 8/05; SLJ 5/05; VOYA 4/05) [306.76]

11974 White, Joe. *Pure Excitement: A Radical Righteous Approach to Sex, Love, and Dating* (7–12). 1996, Family paper $10.99 (978-1-56179-483-6). Taking a conservative approach, this book, written by a minister and using many conversations with teens, proposes that premarital sex is harmful to young adults. (Rev: VOYA 8/97) [613.9]

Sex Problems
(Abuse, Harassment, etc.)

11975 Chaiet, Donna. *Staying Safe at School* (7–12). Series: Get Prepared Library. 1995, Rosen LB $23.95 (978-0-8239-1864-5). How to stay alert and protect oneself while at school, plus tips for girls on avoiding violent crimes on or near school campuses. (Rev: BL 11/15/95; SLJ 2/96) [613.6]

11976 Foltz, Linda Lee. *Kids Helping Kids: Break the Silence of Sexual Abuse* (4–9). 2003, Lighthouse Point $21.95 (978-0-9637966-8-4); paper $14.95 (978-0-9637966-9-1). Personal stories from young people and adults who suffered abuse as children illustrate the guilt and shame typically experienced and show how to get help. (Rev: SLJ 9/03) [362.7]

11977 Gordon, Sherri Mabry. *Beyond Bruises: The Truth About Teens and Abuse* (7–12). Series: Issues in Focus Today. 2009, Enslow LB $31.93 (978-0-7660-3064-0). This book explores the causes and consequences of various forms of abuse through firsthand accounts, photos, and concise sidebars. (Rev: BL 4/15/09; SLJ 10/09) [362.76083]

11978 Lehman, Carolyn. *Strong at the Heart: How It Feels to Heal from Sexual Abuse* (8–11). 2005, Farrar $16.00 (978-0-374-37282-8). First-person accounts reveal the damage caused by sexual abuse and present strategies for healing. (Rev: BL 9/15/05; SLJ 11/05; VOYA 10/05) [362.76]

11979 McFarland, Rhoda. *Working Together Against Sexual Harassment* (7–12). Series: Library of Social Activism. 1996, Rosen LB $27.95 (978-0-8239-1775-4). Following a review of the history of sexual harassment (of females) and recent scandals, the book emphasizes how teens can combat sexual harassment by responding politically, from fighting for official policies against it at school to organizing chapters of NOW or other organizations. (Rev: SLJ 4/97; VOYA 6/97) [344.73]

11980 Munson, Lulie, and Karen Riskin. *In Their Own Words: A Sexual Abuse Workbook for Teenage Girls* (7–12). 1997, Child Welfare League of America paper $10.95 (978-0-87868-596-7). This manual (for use in therapy situations) helps girls who have been sexually abused work through their problems and plan for the future. (Rev: VOYA 10/97) [382.88]

11981 Reinert, Dale R. *Sexual Abuse and Incest* (7–12). Series: Teen Issues. 1997, Enslow LB $17.95 (978-0-89490-916-0). After a general explanation of what constitutes sexual abuse and incest, this work explains how to identify potential abusive situations and what to do about them. (Rev: BL 12/1/97; HBG 3/98; SLJ 12/97; VOYA 6/98) [362.76]

Human Development and Behavior

General and Miscellaneous

11982 Smith, Larry, and Rachel Fershleiser, eds. *I Can't Keep My Own Secrets: Six-Word Memoirs by Teens Famous and Obscure* (6–10). Illus. 2009, HarperTeen paper $8.99 (978-006172684-2). A fascinating and moving collection of more than 600 six-word teen memoirs such as "Born 1992. Unhappy. Adopted 2007. Happy." and "You're the parent, act like one." Includes a subject index. (Rev: BL 7/09; SLJ 8/09) [808]

Psychology and Human Behavior

General and Miscellaneous

11983 Acker, Kerry. *Everything You Need to Know About the Goth Scene* (7–12). 2000, Rosen LB $27.95 (978-0-8239-3223-8). An informative and reliable guide to the origins, fashions, preferences, and behavior associated with the "Goth" movement. (Rev: BL 12/1/00; SLJ 3/01) [306]

11984 Allenbaugh, Kay. *Chocolate for a Teen's Dreams: Heartwarming Stories About Making Your Wishes Come True* (8–12). Series: Chocolate. 2003, Fireside paper $12.00 (978-0-7432-3703-1). A collection of stories by teens and older women about their dreams and desires, and how they came true. (Rev: SLJ 9/03) [305.235]

11985 Balog, Cyn, and Lise Bernier, et al. *Dear Bully: Seventy Authors Tell Their Stories* (7–12). Ed. by Megan Kelley Hall and Carrie Jones. 2011, HarperTeen $17.99 (978-0-06-206098-3). Top children's authors offer stories from the points-of-view of perpetrators, bystanders, and victims in various formats — fiction, poems, letters, and so forth. **e** (Rev: BL 7/11; SLJ 8/11) [302.3]

11986 Carlson, Dale, and Hannah Carlson. *Where's Your Head? Teenage Psychology* (8–12). 1998, Bick paper $14.95 (978-1-884158-19-3). This book explores in readable format the basic elements of psychological thought concerning personality, influences on beliefs and behavior, the stages of adolescence, and mental illness. (Rev: VOYA 8/98) [150]

11987 Gardner, Robert, and Barbara Gardner Conklin. *Health Science Projects About Psychology* (7–12). 2002, Enslow LB $26.60 (978-0-7660-1439-8). Interesting activities that illustrate psychological concepts are extended by suggestions for further investigation. (Rev: HBG 10/02; SLJ 7/02) [150]

11988 Hernández, Roger K. *Teens and Relationships* (7–10). Series: The Gallup Youth Survey, Major Issues and Trends. 2005, Mason Crest LB $22.95 (978-1-59084-875-3). An attractive volume documenting Gallup findings on teens' attitudes toward parents, divorce, blended families, friendship, and dating the opposite sex. (Rev: SLJ 1/06)

11989 Musgrave, Susan, ed. *Nerves Out Loud: Critical Moments in the Lives of Seven Teen Girls* (8–12). 2001, Annick $19.95 (978-1-55037-693-7); paper $9.95 (978-1-55037-692-0). Seven adult women look back at events and problems that absorbed them as teenagers. (Rev: BL 10/1/01; HBG 3/02; SLJ 10/01; VOYA 2/02) [305.235]

11990 Naik, Anita. *Read the Signals: The Body Language Handbook* (4–8). Series: Really Useful Handbooks. 2009, Crabtree LB $29.27 (978-0-7787-4388-0); paper $9.95 (978-0-7787-4401-6). This positive, often humorous book provides information on handling and interpreting a variety of tricky social situations — from bullying to shyness to flirtation — presented in digestible, bullet-point format. (Rev: BL 4/1/09; LMC 10/09; SLJ 6/1/09) [153.6]

11991 O'Halloran, Barbara Collopy. *Creature Comforts: People and Their Security Objects* (6–12). Illus. by Betty Udesen. 2002, Houghton Mifflin $17.00 (978-0-618-11864-9). First-person accounts, accompanied by photographs, explain why objects such as "blankies" prove invaluable to both children and adults. (Rev: BL 5/1/02; HBG 10/02; SLJ 3/02) [155.4]

11992 Spilsbury, Louise. *Together As a Team!* (6–10). Series: Life Skills. 2008, Heinemann LB $32.86 (978-1-4329-1363-2). With practical tips and quizzes at the ends of chapters, this volume discusses the benefits of teamwork and how to achieve it. (Rev: SLJ 3/1/09)

Emotions and Emotional Behavior

11993 Jackson, Donna M. *What's So Funny? Making Sense of Humor* (3–7). Illus. by Ted Stearn. 2011, Viking $16.99 (978-0-670-01244-2). Jackson looks at the origins of humor, the physiology of laughter, animals and humor, and various other aspects of being funny. (Rev: BLO 8/11; SLJ 7/11) [152.4]

11994 Spilsbury, Louise. *Cool That Anger!* (6–10). Series: Life Skills. 2008, Heinemann LB $32.86 (978-1-4329-1365-6). With tips on handling anger and quizzes at the ends of chapters, this volume discusses the causes of anger and physical reactions to it. (Rev: SLJ 3/1/09)

Ethics and Moral Behavior

11995 Altman, Linda J. *Bioethics: Who Lives, Who Dies, and Who Decides* (7–12). Series: Issues in Focus Today. 2007, Enslow LB $23.95 (978-0-7660-2546-2). Both sides of moral issues in bioethics (such as cloning, abortion, and organ transplants) are presented fairly. (Rev: BL 3/15/07; SLJ 8/07) [174]

11996 Canfield, Jack, and Mark Victor Hansen. *Chicken Soup for the Teenage Soul II: 101 More Stories of Life, Love and Learning* (7–12). 1998, Health Communications $24.00 (978-1-55874-615-2); paper $14.95 (978-1-55874-616-9). A new collection of personal stories from teens that supply inspiration and guidance. (Rev: BL 11/1/98; HBG 3/99) [158.1]

Etiquette and Manners

11997 Cabot, Meg. *Princess Lessons* (5–7). Illus. by Chesley McLaren. Series: Princess Diaries. 2003, HarperCollins $12.99 (978-0-06-052677-1). Princess Mia gives lighthearted tips and often quite practical tips on behaving like a real princess. (Rev: BL 5/15/03; HBG 10/03; VOYA 10/03) [646.7]

11998 Holyoke, Nancy. *A Smart Girl's Guide to Manners* (4–7). Illus. by Cathi Mingus. 2005, Pleasant paper

$9.95 (978-1-58485-983-3). A nice mix of good manners that ranges from introductions to cell phone etiquette to how and when to write real thank-you notes. (Rev: BL 11/1/05; SLJ 1/06; VOYA 12/05) [395]

11999 Hoving, Walter. *Tiffany's Table Manners for Teenagers* (7–12). 1989, Random House $17.00 (978-0-394-82877-0). A practical guide to good table manners. (Rev: SLJ 6/89) [395]

12000 James, Elizabeth, and Carol Barkin. *Social Smarts: Manners for Today's Kids* (4–7). 1996, Clarion paper $7.95 (978-0-395-81312-6). Table manners and responsible, appropriate public behavior are two topics covered. (Rev: BL 9/1/96; SLJ 9/96) [395]

12001 Lundsten, Apry. *A Smart Girl's Guide to Parties: How to Be a Great Guest, Be a Happy Hostess, and Have Fun at Any Party* (4–7). Illus. by Angela Martini. Series: Be Your Best. 2010, American Girl paper $9.95 (978-1-59369-645-0). With a light and breezy tone, this book outlines party etiquette for both hosts and guests at affairs formal and informal, with advice on invitations, gifts, and so forth. (Rev: SLJ 7/10)

12002 Packer, Alex J. *How Rude! The Teenagers' Guide to Good Manners, Proper Behavior, and Not Grossing People Out* (6–12). 1997, Free Spirit paper $19.95 (978-1-57542-024-0). A candid, often humorous guide to good manners for teenagers that stresses common sense and covers situations ranging from inline skating to computer hacking. (Rev: BL 2/1/98; SLJ 2/98; VOYA 6/98) [395.1]

12003 Senning, Cindy Post, and Peggy Post. *Emily Post's Table Manners for Kids* (4–8). Illus. by Steve Björkman. 2009, HarperCollins $15.99 (978-0-06-111709-1). When can you eat with your fingers? Which fork do I use? Everything today's child needs to know about proper meal etiquette and just why these things matter. (Rev: BL 4/1/09) [395.5]

12004 Stewart, Marjabelle Young, and Ann Buchwald. *What to Do When and Why* (4–7). 1988, Luce $14.95 (978-0-88331-105-9). An easily read introduction to the basics of good manners and behavior.

Intelligence and Thinking

12005 Nikola-Lisa, W. *How We Are Smart* (4–7). Illus. by Scan Quails. 2006, Lee & Low $16.95 (978-1-58430-254-4). A picture book for older readers that looks at different kinds of intelligence, using double-page spreads about 12 famous people to illustrate these concepts. (Rev: BL 4/1/06; SLJ 6/06) [811]

Personal Guidance

12006 Allenbaugh, Kay. *Chocolate for a Teen's Soul: Life-Changing Stories for Young Women About Growing Wise and Growing Strong* (6–12). 2000, Simon &

Schuster $12.00 (978-0-684-87081-6). Inspiring essays explore a wide array of issues, including first love, disabilities, beauty pageants, friendship, first jobs, and family relations. (Rev: VOYA 4/01) [152.4]

12007 Allman, Toney. *Mean Behind the Screen: What You Need to Know About Cyberbullying* (5–8). Illus. Series: What's the Issue? 2008, Compass Point LB $20.99 (978-0-7565-4145-3). A solid introduction to cyberbullying and its consequences. (Rev: BL 4/1/09; SLJ 10/09) [302.3]

12008 Amblard, Odile. *Privacy, Please! Gaining Independence from Your Parents* (6–9). Ed. by Kate O'Dare. Illus. by Celine Guyot. Series: Sunscreen. 2009, Abrams paper $10.95 (978-081098357-1). This attractive and accessible volume looks at teenagers' desire for privacy and freedom and recommends communication with parents. (Rev: BLO 6/19/09; SLJ 7/1/09) [155.5]

12009 Arredia, Joni. *Sex, Boys, and You: Be Your Own Best Girlfriend* (5–9). 1998, Perc paper $15.95 (978-0-9653203-2-0). A self-help book for younger teen girls with advice on how to accept oneself, when to say "no" to sex, how to assess one's strengths and weaknesses, and how to develop healthy relationships with boys. (Rev: SLJ 10/98) [305.23]

12010 Asgedom, Mawi. *The Code: The Five Secrets of Teen Success* (7–12). 2003, Little, Brown paper $9.99 (978-0-316-73689-3). Asgedom, a motivational speaker who was a refugee before coming to the United States and later attending Harvard, advises teens on strategies for success. (Rev: HBG 4/04; SLJ 11/03; VOYA 12/03)

12011 Bachel, Beverly K. *What Do You Really Want? How to Set a Goal and Go for It!* (6–12). 2001, Free Spirit paper $12.95 (978-1-57542-085-1). Bachel lays out ways to define and achieve goals, supported by quotations from teens who have tried them; reproducible forms are included. (Rev: BL 5/15/01; VOYA 8/01) [153.8]

12012 Blatt, Jessica. *The Teen Girl's Gotta-Have-It Guide to Boys: From Getting Them to Getting Over Them* (6–10). Illus. by Cynthia Frenette. 2007, Watson-Guptill paper $8.95 (978-0-8230-1725-6). Complete with self-quizzes, this is an entertaining, well-written guide for girls about dating and relationships. (Rev: SLJ 7/07)

12013 Blatt, Jessica. *The Teen Girl's Gotta-Have-It Guide to Embarrassing Moments: How to Survive Life's Cringe-Worthy Situations!* (6–10). Illus. by Cynthia Frenette. 2007, Watson-Guptill paper $8.95 (978-0-8230-1724-9). This is a lighthearted book that teaches girls how to overcome embarrassing situations with grace and humor. (Rev: SLJ 7/07)

12014 Bolden, Tonya, ed. *33 Things Every Girl Should Know: Stories, Songs, Poems and Smart Talk by 33 Extraordinary Women* (6–12). 1998, Crown paper $13.00 (978-0-517-70936-8). A collection of highly readable

pieces by well-known and successful women on the difficult transition from childhood to adulthood. (Rev: BL 5/15/98; HBG 9/98; SLJ 5/98) [810.8092827]

12015 Bridgers, Jay. *Everything You Need to Know About Having an Addictive Personality* (7–12). Series: Need to Know Library. 1998, Rosen LB $27.95 (978-0-8239-2777-7). The author examines the social, psychological, and biochemical aspects of an "addictive personality," explains why some people are more susceptible to addiction than others, and offers sound advice on how teens can cope with addiction. (Rev: SLJ 1/99) [157]

12016 Brown, Bobbi, and Annemarie Iverson. *Bobbi Brown Teenage Beauty: Everything You Need to Look Pretty, Natural, Sexy and Awesome* (8–12). 2000, Cliff St $25.00 (978-0-06-019636-3). As well as supplying beauty tips, this book stresses the importance of diet and exercise. (Rev: SLJ 12/00) [646.7]

12017 Buchholz, Rachel. *How to Survive Anything: Shark Attack, Lightning, Embarrassing Parents, Pop Quizzes, and Other Perilous Situations* (4–8). Illus. by Chris Philpot. 2011, National Geographic paper $14.95 (978-1-4263-0-774-4). Full of humor, this survival guide covers everything from truly dangerous situations to public humiliation. (Rev: BLO 8/11; SLJ 7/11) [646.7]

12018 Burningham, Sarah O'Leary. *Boyology: A Crash Course in All Things Boy* (7–12). Illus. by Keri Smith. 2009, Chronicle paper $12.99 (978-0-8118-6436-7). This chatty, approachable book provides guidance on everything from making the boy friend–boyfriend transition to kissing and setting sexual boundaries. (Rev: SLJ 6/1/09; VOYA 4/10) [306.7]

12019 Burton, Bonnie. *Girls Against Girls: Why We Are Mean to Each Other and How We Can Change* (7–10). Illus. 2009, Zest paper $12.95 (978-097901736-0). The author calls on "mean girls" and their targets to understand why girls can be cruel and what can be done about it. Lexile 860L (Rev: BL 2/15/09; SLJ 5/1/09; VOYA 4/09) [300]

12020 Camron, Roxanne. *60 Clues About Guys: A Guide to Feelings, Flirting, and Falling in Like* (6–10). Illus. by Ariane Elsammak. Series: 60 Clues About. 2002, Lunchbox paper $8.95 (978-0-9678285-5-8). For girls, this is a how-to manual for coping with relationships with the opposite sex, with a personal dating diary at the end. (Rev: SLJ 7/02)

12021 Canfield, Jack, and Mark Victor Hansen, comps. *Chicken Soup for the Teenage Soul — The Real Deal: School: Cliques, Classes, Clubs and More* (7–12). Series: Chicken Soup for the Soul. 2005, Health Communications paper $14.95 (978-0-7573-0255-8). Written for teenagers by teenagers, this collection of essays addresses many problems that confront high school students today. (Rev: SLJ 11/05) [158]

12022 Canfield, Jack, ed. *Chicken Soup for the Christian Teenage Soul: Stories of Faith, Love, Inspiration and Hope* (6–12). 2003, Health Communications paper $14.95 (978-0-7573-0095-0). Stories, poems, and cartoons of particular relevance to teens are grouped in thematic chapters. (Rev: BL 10/1/03) [242]

12023 Carlson, Dale, and Hannah Carlson. *Girls Are Equal Too: How to Survive — For Teenage Girls* (6–9). 1998, Bick paper $14.95 (978-1-884158-18-6). This work tells girls that it is okay to be smart, successful, a leader, and feel good. (Rev: VOYA 10/98) [305.23]

12024 Chopra, Deepak. *Fire in the Heart: A Spiritual Guide for Teens* (8–12). 2004, Simon & Schuster $14.95 (978-0-689-86216-8). In this book of spiritual advice for teens, the author uses the device of having a wise old man named Baba give self-help information. (Rev: BL 5/15/04; SLJ 8/04) [204]

12025 Chopra, Deepak. *Teens Ask Deepak: All the Right Questions* (7–10). 2006, Simon & Schuster $12.95 (978-0-689-86218-2). The popular spiritual guru turns his attention to teenage concerns — friendship, success, health, religion, and so forth. (Rev: BL 1/1–15/06; SLJ 1/06) [616]

12026 Choron, Sandra, and Harry Choron. *The Book of Lists for Teens* (7–12). 2002, Houghton Mifflin paper $13.95 (978-0-618-17907-7). More than 300 lists cover a wide range of topics of interest to teens, such as music videos, sports, eating disorders, substance abuse, and bullying. (Rev: SLJ 1/03; VOYA 4/03) [031.02]

12027 Cohen-Posey, Kate. *How to Handle Bullies, Teasers and Other Meanies: A Book That Takes the Nuisance out of Name Calling and Other Nonsense* (4–7). 1995, Rainbow paper $8.95 (978-1-56825-029-8). A practical book that offers useful suggestions on how to handle bullies. (Rev: BCCB 12/95; BL 11/15/95) [646.7]

12028 Cordes, Helen. *Girl Power in the Classroom: A Book About Girls, Their Fears, and Their Future* (5–8). 2000, Lerner LB $30.35 (978-0-8225-2693-3). This book of personal guidance for girls describes how to conquer fears and cope with difficult situations at school. (Rev: BL 5/15/00; HBG 10/00; SLJ 5/00) [373.1822]

12029 Cordes, Helen. *Girl Power in the Mirror: A Book About Girls, Their Bodies, and Themselves* (5–8). 2000, Lerner LB $30.35 (978-0-8225-2691-9). This book for girls explains proper attitudes about appearance and gives coping strategies concerning pressures about one's looks. (Rev: BL 5/15/00; HBG 10/00; SLJ 5/00) [306.4]

12030 Corriveau, Danielle, ed. *Trail Mix: Stories of Youth Overcoming Adversity* (7–12). 2001, Corvo Communications $14.95 (978-0-9702366-0-9). Fourteen teens tell inspiring first-person stories about hard times and the value of spending time in an outdoor program. (Rev: BL 12/1/01; SLJ 1/02) [158.1]

12031 Covey, Sean. *The 6 Most Important Decisions You'll Ever Make: A Guide for Teens* (8–12). 2006, Fireside paper $15.95 (978-0-7432-6504-1). Advice on education, friendship, family, dating and sex, avoiding addiction, and nurturing healthy self-esteem is presented in lively text with lots of graphics, charts, cartoons, and so forth. (Rev: SLJ 2/07)

12032 Crist, James J. *What to Do When You're Scared and Worried: A Guide for Kids* (5–8). Illus. by Michael Chesworth. 2004, Free Spirit paper $9.99 (978-1-57542-153-7). Reassuring words and sound advice for young people troubled by such diverse issues as school exams, bullies, terrorism, nightmares, monsters, and the dark. (Rev: SLJ 7/04) [152.4]

12033 Daldry, Jeremy. *The Teenage Guy's Survival Guide: The Real Deal on Girls, Growing Up, and Other Guy Stuff* (6–9). 1999, Little, Brown paper $8.99 (978-0-316-17824-2). From pimples to pornography, this guide book for boys is humorous, frank, and truthful about such subjects as dating, masturbation, drugs, mood swings, and homosexuality. (Rev: BL 5/15/99; SLJ 7/99; VOYA 10/99) [305.235]

12034 Dee, Catherine, ed. *The Girls' Book of Wisdom: Empowering, Inspirational Quotes from Over 400 Fabulous Females* (5–8). Illus. by Lou M. Pollack. 1999, Little, Brown paper $8.95 (978-0-316-17956-0). A collection of quotations from more than 400 famous women grouped by such subjects as "Friends," "Happiness," and "Leadership." (Rev: SLJ 12/99; VOYA 4/00) [305.23]

12035 Dentemaro, Christine, and Rachel Kranz. *Straight Talk About Student Life* (6–10). Series: Straight Talk. 1993, Facts on File $27.45 (978-0-8160-2735-4). This book explores problems that students are likely to experience, including communication with teachers and other students, parental pressures, homework, and developing a healthy social life. (Rev: BL 9/1/93) [373.18]

12036 Desetta, Al. *The Courage to Be Yourself: True Stories by Teens About Cliques, Conflicts, and Overcoming Peer Pressure* (8–11). 2005, Free Spirit paper $13.99 (978-1-57542-185-8). Teens from a wide variety of backgrounds offer personal accounts of how they overcame adversities such as bullying, cliques, prejudice, and peer pressure. (Rev: BL 2/1/06; SLJ 6/06; VOYA 4/06) [305.235]

12037 Devillers, Julia. *GirlWise: How to Be Confident, Capable, Cool, and in Control* (8–12). 2002, Prima paper $12.95 (978-0-7615-6363-1). Topics covered in this accessible volume of advice from experts range from fashion and diet to car repair and doing laundry. (Rev: SLJ 12/02) [646.7]

12038 Doeden, Matt. *Conflict Resolution Smarts: How to Communicate, Negotiate, Compromise, and More* (8–12). Illus. Series: USA Today Teen Wise Guides. 2012, Lerner/Twenty-First Century LB $31.93 (978-076137020-8). This accessible guide offers strategies for dealing with conflict and learning how to listen and negotiate. (Rev: BL 4/1/12) [303.6]

12039 Drew, Naomi. *The Kids' Guide to Working Out Conflicts: How to Keep Cool, Stay Safe, and Get Along* (6–10). Illus. by Chris Sharp. 2004, Free Spirit paper $13.95 (978-1-57542-150-6). Misunderstandings, teasing, bullying, and sexual harassment are all discussed in this guide that includes scenarios and offers strategies for improving self-control plus many quotations from middle school students. (Rev: SLJ 9/04) [303.6]

12040 Drill, Esther. *Deal with It! A Whole New Approach to Your Body, Brain and Life as a Gurl* (8–12). 1999, Pocket paper $15.00 (978-0-671-04157-1). Much of the flavor of the popular Gurl.com site is duplicated in this eye-catching book full of frank information about sex, adolescent development and behavior, and succeeding in life. (Rev: BL 10/1/99) [305.235]

12041 Dunham, Kelli. *The Girl's Body Book: Everything You Need to Know for Growing Up You* (4–7). Illus. by Laura Tallardy. 2008, Applesauce paper $9.95 (978-1-60433-004-5). This friendly introduction to puberty covers physical and emotional changes and offers practical guidance. (Rev: LMC 1/09; SLJ 11/08) [612]

12042 Ellis, Deborah. *We Want You to Know: Kids Talk About Bullying* (6–10). Illus. 2010, Coteau $21.95 (978-155050417-0). Teens describe their experiences as victims, witnesses, and perpetrators of bullying. (Rev: BL 9/1/10; LMC 5–6/11; SLJ 9/10; VOYA 12/10) [302.3]

12043 Erlbach, Arlene. *The Middle School Survival Guide* (5–7). Illus. by Helen Flook. 2003, Walker $16.95 (978-0-8027-8852-8); paper $8.95 (978-0-8027-7657-0). The author offers tips on a wide variety of topics of interest to this age group (homework, drugs, sex, and so forth), interspersed with advice from students themselves. (Rev: BL 9/15/03; SLJ 9/03) [373.18]

12044 Espeland, Pamela. *Life Lists for Teens: Tips, Steps, Hints, and How-tos for Growing Up, Getting Along, Learning, and Having Fun* (8–12). 2003, Free Spirit paper $11.95 (978-1-57542-125-4). Lists of suggestions, tips, and resources cover all topics of interest to teens — health, school, homework, safety, bullying, pregnancy, abuse, and so forth. (Rev: LMC 11–12/03; SLJ 5/03; VOYA 6/03) [646.7]

12045 Flaherty, Somer. *The Book of Styling: An Insider's Guide to Creating Your Own Look* (8–12). Illus. 2012, Zest $16.99 (978-098273224-3). An accessible guide to identifying your body type and face shape, plus closet-organization tips and the basics of building a wardrobe. (Rev: BL 12/1/12; SLJ 10/12) [746.9]

12046 Ford, Amanda. *Be True to Yourself: A Daily Guide for Teenage Girls* (6–12). 2001, Conari paper $17.95 (978-1-57324-189-2). Drawing on her own experiences, Amanda Ford offers daily inspirational nuggets of wisdom for girls making the difficult passage to womanhood. (Rev: VOYA 6/01) [158.1]

12047 Fox, Annie. *Can You Relate? Real-World Advice for Teens on Guys, Girls, Growing Up, and Getting Along* (6–12). 2000, Free Spirit paper $15.95 (978-1-57542-066-0). This guidance book tells teens how to form relationships with family, peers, and girl or boy friends, with material on how to understand oneself. (Rev: BL 4/15/00; SLJ 7/00) [305.235]

12048 Fox, Annie. *Real Friends vs the Other Kind* (5–8). Series: Middle School Confidential. 2009, Free Spirit paper $9.99 (978-1-57542-319-7). The intricacies of middle school friendships, allegiances, and romances are examined here, with advice from real tweens about handing difficult situations. (Rev: SLJ 8/09) [177.62]

12049 Galbraith, Judy, and Jim Delisle. *The Gifted Teen Survival Guide: Smart, Sharp, and Ready For (Almost) Anything* (8–11). 2011, Free Spirit $15.99 (978-157542381-4). With quizzes, stories, and quotations from gifted teens, this is a helpful guide for gifted teens who may feel distant from their peers. (Rev: BL 11/1/11; SLJ 1/12; VOYA 2/12) [155.5087]

12050 Goldstein, Mark A., and Myrna Chandler Goldstein. *Boys to Men: Staying Healthy Through the Teen Years* (7–12). 2000, Greenwood $59.95 (978-0-313-30966-3). This book is divided into three age groups between 12 and 21, and for each there are descriptions of changes that occur and how to adjust to them. (Rev: SLJ 6/01; VOYA 4/01) [613]

12051 Hantman, Clea. *30 Days to Finding and Keeping Sassy Sidekicks and BFFs: A Friendship Field Guide* (7–10). 2009, Delacorte paper $7.99 (978-038573623-7). An upbeat approach to making lifelong friends, with practical tips and activities that will make the effort easier. (Rev: BL 7/09; VOYA 4/09) [158.2]

12052 Harlan, Judith. *Girl Talk: Staying Strong, Feeling Good, Sticking Together* (6–10). 1977, Walker paper $8.95 (978-0-8027-7524-5). A breezy, lighthearted guide to approaching everyday problems faced by adolescent girls, with practical tips on how to solve them. (Rev: BL 12/1/97; VOYA 2/98) [305.23]

12053 Harris-Johnson, Debrah. *The African-American Teenagers' Guide to Personal Growth, Health, Safety, Sex and Survival: Living and Learning in the 21st Century* (6–12). 2000, Amber paper $19.95 (978-0-9655064-4-1). This guide for young African Americans growing up in America today covers such topics as family structure, friendships, sexual orientation, work, and spirituality. (Rev: BL 2/15/00; VOYA 6/02) [646.7]

12054 Hartman, Holly, ed. *Girlwonder: Every Girl's Guide to the Fantastic Feats, Cool Qualities, and Remarkable Abilities of Women and Girls* (4–8). 2003, Houghton Mifflin paper $9.95 (978-0-618-31939-8). A browsable look at famous women and their accomplishments, interspersed with information and advice on topics ranging from romance to fashion. (Rev: SLJ 5/04) [305.235]

12055 Hugel, Bob. *I Did It Without Thinking: True Stories About Impulsive Decisions That Changed Lives* (6–10). Series: Scholastic Choices. 2008, Watts LB $27 (978-0-531-13868-7); paper $8.95 (978-0-531-20526-6). Teens share their own stories of impulsive behavior and how the results changed their lives. (Rev: SLJ 10/1/08; VOYA 12/08)

12056 Jacobs, Tom. *Teen Cyberbullying Investigated: Where Do Your Rights End and Consequences Begin?* (7–12). 2010, Free Spirit paper $15.99 (978-1-57542-339-5). Jacobs encourages teens to think critically and consider every situation from the perspective of victim, bystander, and perpetrator. (Rev: BL 3/1/10; SLJ 3/10; VOYA 8/10) [345.73]

12057 Johnston, Marianne. *Let's Talk About Being Shy* (4–8). Series: Let's Talk. 1996, Rosen LB $19.95 (978-0-8239-2304-5). The causes and possible cures of shyness are covered in this straightforward discussion. Also use *Let's Talk About Being Afraid* (1996). (Rev: BL 3/15/97) [155.4]

12058 Judson, Karen. *Resolving Conflicts: How to Get Along When You Don't Get Along* (6–12). Series: Issues in Focus Today. 2005, Enslow LB $31.93 (978-0-7660-2359-8). "Dealing with Difficult People" and "Turning Conflict into Collaboration" are two of the chapters in this thorough volume that also covers bullying and gives historical examples of effective conflict resolution. (Rev: SLJ 5/06) [303.6]

12059 Kaywell, Joan F., ed. *Dear Author: Letters of Hope* (8–11). 2007, Philomel $14.99 (978-0-399-23705-8). A collection of letters to YA authors from teens, many with serious problems. Readers with problems of their own will find reassurance and some good advice. (Rev: BCCB 6/07; BL 2/15/07; SLJ 5/07) [028.5]

12060 King, Bart. *The Big Book of Girl Stuff* (4–8). Illus. by Jennifer Kalis. 2006, Gibbs Smith paper $19.99 (978-1-58685-819-3). A lighthearted, lightly organized guide to a great many topics of interest to growing girls, including why boys smell bad, etiquette, dieting, how to shop, and how to get a boy's attention. (Rev: SLJ 1/07) [646.7]

12061 Kirberger, Kimberly. *On Relationships: A Book for Teenagers* (7–12). Series: Teen Love. 1999, Health Communications paper $14.95 (978-1-55874-734-0). Letters, stories, and poems tackle problems that arise in romantic relationships. (Rev: BL 10/15/99; SLJ 1/00) [306.7]

12062 Kirberger, Kimberly, and Colin Mortensen. *On Friendship: A Book for Teenagers* (6–10). Series: Teen Love. 2000, Health Communications paper $12.95 (978-1-55874-815-6). This comforting overview of the meaning of friendship features writings by teenagers. (Rev: BL 1/1–15/01; SLJ 4/01) [302.3]

12063 Kirberger, Kimberly, ed. *No Body's Perfect: Stories by Teens About Body Image, Self-Acceptance, and*

the Search for Identity* (7–12). 2003, Scholastic paper $12.95 (978-0-439-42638-1). Mostly written by girls, these stories are intended to help teens grapple with problems of identity and image. (Rev: SLJ 6/03; VOYA 4/03)

12064 Kreiner, Anna. *Creating Your Own Support System* (7–10). Series: Need to Know Library. 1996, Rosen LB $27.95 (978-0-8239-2215-4). An easy-to-read account that teaches how to create a support system of friends, neighbors, relatives, clergy members, and teachers, if support is not available at home. (Rev: SLJ 1/97) [305.23]

12065 Lewis, Barbara A. *What Do You Stand For? A Kid's Guide to Building Character* (6–9). 1997, Free Spirit paper $19.95 (978-1-57542-029-5). This book explores the topic of character building through self-assessment, recommended readings, and activities that explore one's attitudes and reactions to real-life situations. (Rev: SLJ 1/00; VOYA 8/98) [305.23]

12066 Lound, Karen. *Girl Power in the Family: A Book About Girls, Their Rights, and Their Voice* (5–10). Series: Girl Power. 2000, Lerner LB $30.35 (978-0-8225-2692-6). A book that explores the problems of growing up female today with material on gender roles, biases, and relationships. (Rev: HBG 10/00; SLJ 6/00) [303.6]

12067 McCune, Bunny, and Deb Traunstein. *Girls to Women: Sharing Our Stories* (7–10). 1998, Celestial Arts paper $14.95 (978-0-89087-881-1). Arranged under thematic chapters that deal with self-esteem, friendships, menstruation, sexuality, and mother-daughter relations, this collection of essays, stories, and poems explores various aspects of being young and female. (Rev: SLJ 4/99) [305.23]

12068 McIntyre, Tom. *The Behavior Survival Guide for Kids: How to Make Good Choices and Stay out of Trouble* (4–7). Illus. by Chris Sharp. 2003, Free Spirit paper $14.95 (978-1-57542-132-2). This accessible guide offers concrete suggestions for dealing with behavior disorders and improving relations with teachers, family members, and friends. (Rev: SLJ 1/04) [649]

12069 Moehn, Heather. *Everything You Need to Know About Cliques* (5–8). Series: Need to Know Library. 2001, Rosen LB $27.95 (978-0-8239-3326-6). Moehn uses first-person narratives to introduce such topics as making friends, peer pressure, bullies, insecurity, and popularity, with a look at how cliques continue after high school. (Rev: SLJ 12/01) [158.25]

12070 Morgenstern, Julie, and Jessi Morgenstern-Colon. *Organizing from the Inside Out for Teens: The Foolproof System for Organizing Your Room, Your Time, and Your Life* (7–12). 2002, Henry Holt paper $15.00 (978-0-8050-6470-4). Strategies for managing the time, space, and responsibilities of typical teens are presented in this practical manual. (Rev: BL 1/1–15/03) [646.7]

12071 Morgenstern, Mindy. *The Real Rules for Girls* (8–12). 2000, Girl $14.95 (978-0-9659754-5-2). Advice on life, love, friends, and more is presented in an attractive, conversational way. (Rev: SLJ 3/00; VOYA 4/00)

12072 Morrison, Betsy S., and Ruth Ann Ruiz. *Self-Esteem* (7–10). Illus. Series: Teen Mental Health. 2011, Rosen LB $27.95 (978-144884587-3). With information about building self-confidence and setting goals, this book will be helpful for report writers and those seeking personal guidance. (Rev: BL 11/15/11; LMC 5–6/12) [155.5]

12073 Moss, Wendy L. *Being Me: A Kid's Guide to Boosting Confidence and Self-Esteem* (5–8). Illus. 2011, Magination $14.95 (978-143380883-8); paper $9.95 (978-14338088-4-5). "Stand Up for Yourself" and "Hang Out with a Group" are two of the chapters in this book full of helpful and practical advice for building social confidence. (Rev: BL 1/1–15/11; SLJ 3/1/11) [155.4]

12074 Musgrave, Susan, ed. *You Be Me: Friendship in the Lives of Teen Girls* (7–12). 2002, Annick $18.95 (978-1-55037-739-2); paper $7.95 (978-1-55037-738-5). Stories of girls' experiences show the sometimes difficult realities of teenage friendships. (Rev: BL 12/15/02; HBG 3/03; SLJ 1/03; VOYA 12/02) [305.235]

12075 Noel, Carol. *Get It? Got It? Good! A Guide for Teenagers* (7–12). 1996, Serious Business paper $7.95 (978-0-9649479-0-0). A teen self-help guide that discusses such topics as self-esteem, sex, health, relations with others, goals, and violence. (Rev: BL 6/1–15/96) [361.8]

12076 Packard, Gwen K. *Coping When a Parent Goes Back to Work* (8–12). Series: Coping. 1995, Rosen LB $31.95 (978-0-8239-1698-6). Gives children whose parents return to work tips on adapting to the new situation. Includes real-life examples. (Rev: BL 7/95) [306.874]

12077 Piquemal, Michel, and Melissa Daly. *When Life Stinks: How to Deal with Your Bad Moods, Blues, and Depression* (6–10). Illus. by Olivier Tossan. Series: Sunscreen. 2004, Abrams paper $9.95 (978-0-8109-4932-4). Sensible advice for adolescents suffering from normal anxieties and frustrations and for those who need to recognize that their problems are more deepseated and professional help is necessary. (Rev: SLJ 4/05) [616.85]

12078 Rechner, Amy. *The In Crowd: Dealing with Peer Pressure* (5–8). Series: What's the Issue? 2009, Compass Point $27.99 (978-0-7565-1891-2). A compelling mix of direct quotes, real-life scenarios, quizzes, and short glossaries enhance this book about coping with peer pressure; suitable for reluctant readers. (Rev: LMC 10/09; SLJ 10/09) [303.3]

12079 Rutledge, Jill Zimmerman. *Dealing with the Stuff That Makes Life Tough: The 10 Things That Stress Girls Out and How to Cope with Them* (8–10). 2003, Contemporary paper $15.95 (978-0-07-142326-7). Body image, boys, homosexuality, smoking and drinking, divorce — these and other sources of stress are addressed with sensible advice and helpful anecdotes. (Rev: SLJ 1/04)

12080 Ryan, Peter. *Online Bullying* (7–10). Illus. 2011, Rosen LB $27.95 (978-144884588-0). With information about bullies and their victims — and the laws governing such behavior, this book will be helpful for report writers and those seeking personal guidance. (Rev: BL 11/15/11) [302.3]

12081 Schwager, Tina, and Michele Schuerger. *The Right Moves: A Girl's Guide to Getting Fit and Feeling Good* (6–12). 1998, Free Spirit paper $15.95 (978-1-57542-035-6). Topics including self-esteem, diet, and exercise are covered in this upbeat guide for girls that promotes a positive, healthy lifestyle. (Rev: BL 1/1–15/99; SLJ 1/99*; VOYA 8/99) [613.7]

12082 Schwartz, John. *Short: Walking Tall When You're Not Tall at All* (4–8). 2010, Flash Point $16.99 (978-1-59643-323-6). Short himself, journalist Schwartz explores various aspects of the importance of height (in terms of popularity, business success, and so forth); provides information on such topics as genetics and growth hormones; and takes aim at the media in this funny book that's part memoir, part self-help book. (Rev: BL 2/15/10; LMC 5–6/10; SLJ 3/10) [921]

12083 Shapiro, Ouisie. *Bullying and Me: Schoolyard Stories* (4–7). Illus. by Steven Vote. 2010, Whitman $16.99 (978-0-8075-0921-0). A baker's dozen of stories describe physical abuse, verbal abuse, and online bullying, each followed by advice on how to deal with such situations. Lexile 740L (Rev: BL 8/10; LMC 11–12/10*; SLJ 10/1/10) [371.5]

12084 Shipp, Josh. *The Teen's Guide to World Domination: Advice on Life, Liberty, and the Pursuit of Awesomeness* (8–11). Illus. 2010, St. Martin's paper $14.99 (978-03126415-4-2). Motivational speaker Shipp offers thought-provoking advice for teens seeking to boost their self-esteem, to deal with crises at home and at school, and generally to succeed. (Rev: BL 8/10; VOYA 10/10) [646.7]

12085 Spinelli, Eileen, and Jerry Spinelli. *Today I Will: A Year of Quotes, Notes, and Promises to Myself* (5–8). Illus. by Julia Rothman. 2009, Knopf $15.99 (978-0-375-84057-9); LB $18.99 (978-0-375-96230-1). In this page-a-day advice book, the Spinellis offer accessible, often humorous quotes, advice, and affirmations from celebrities, historical figures, and popular literature. (Rev: BL 11/15/09; SLJ 10/09) [082]

12086 Stillman, Sarah. *Soul Searching: A Girl's Guide to Finding Herself* (7–12). 2012, Simon & Schuster $17.99 (978-1-5827-0342-8); paper $9.99 (978-1-5827-0303-9). An updated edition of the guide that covers everything relating to self-improvement and now includes cyberbullying, sexting, social media, and healthy eating. **℮** (Rev: LMC 8–9/12; SLJ 3/12; VOYA 12/11) [158.0835]

12087 Tarshis, Thomas Paul. *Living with Peer Pressure and Bullying* (6–12). Series: Teen's Guides. 2010, Facts on File LB $34.95 (978-143813074-3). "What is peer pressure?" "Who are your friends, really?" This practical guide answers these and other questions relating to problems facing many teens. **℮** (Rev: BLO 8/10; SLJ 9/10) [303.3]

12088 Taylor, Julie. *The Girls' Guide to Friends* (7–12). 2002, Three Rivers paper $12.00 (978-0-609-80857-3). A lighthearted look at getting and keeping friends, with quizzes and other entertaining features. (Rev: BL 12/15/02) [158.2]

12089 Tym, Kate, and Penny Worms. *Coping with Your Emotions: A Guide to Taking Control of Your Life* (6–10). Series: Get Real. 2004, Raintree LB $29.93 (978-1-4109-0575-8). The magazine-style layout, case studies, quizzes, photos, and advice will draw teens to this discussion of issues including depression, peer pressure, love interests, schoolwork, and teacher conflicts. Also use *School Survival: A Guide to Taking Control of Your Life* (2004). (Rev: SLJ 3/05) [646]

12090 Weinstein, Bruce. *Is It Still Cheating if I Don't Get Caught?* (8–12). Illus. by Harriet Russell. 2009, Flash Point paper $9.95 (978-159643306-9). The author gives readers five "life principles" to help guide them in making ethical decisions: "Do no harm," "Make things better," "Respect others," "Be fair," and "Be loving." He then gives examples of times when teens may have to make tough decisions. Lexile 1080L (Rev: BL 4/1/09; LMC 10/09; SLJ 4/1/09; VOYA 6/09) [300]

12091 Wesson, Carolyn McLenahan. *Teen Troubles* (7–12). 1988, Walker $17.95 (978-0-8027-1011-6); paper $11.95 (978-0-8027-7310-4). A candid, sometimes humorous self-help book on teenage problems and how to face them. (Rev: VOYA 12/88) [155.5]

12092 Weston, Carol. *For Girls Only: Wise Words, Good Advice* (6–9). 2004, HarperCollins paper $8.99 (978-0-06-058318-7). An update of the earlier edition, adding quotations from contemporary celebrities to the mix that ranges from Aesop and Socrates to Oprah Winfrey and Madonna. (Rev: BL 11/1/04) [305.23]

12093 White, Lee, and Mary Ditson. *The Teenage Human Body Operator's Manual* (6–10). 1999, Northwest Media paper $9.95 (978-1-892194-01-5). Using an appealing layout and cartoon illustrations, this is an overview of teenagers' physical and psychological needs, touching on hygiene, nutrition, disease, pregnancy and birth control, and mental health. (Rev: SLJ 11/98) [305.23]

12094 Williams, Venus, and Serena Williams. *Venus and Serena: Serving from the Hip* (5–8). 2005, Houghton Mifflin paper $14.00 (978-0-618-57653-1). The successful Williams sisters offer practical advice on self-respect, friendship, financial security, and other pertinent topics. (Rev: BL 5/15/05; SLJ 4/05) [796.342]

12095 Winkler, Kathleen. *Bullying: How to Deal with Taunting, Teasing, and Tormenting* (6–10). Series: Issues in Focus Today. 2005, Enslow $31.93 (978-0-7660-2355-0). Including a chapter on girls who bully, this is an accessible look at the problem that draws on discussions with both teens and professionals. (Rev: SLJ 12/05)

12096 Wirths, Claudine G., and Mary Bowman-Kruhm. *Coping with Confrontations and Encounters with the Police* (7–12). Series: Coping. 1997, Rosen LB $31.95 (978-0-8239-2431-8). This book gives teens essential and realistic information that will help them deal successfully with police encounters and minimize potential risks. (Rev: SLJ 4/98; VOYA 2/98) [364.3]

12097 Wolfelt, Alan D. *Healing Your Grieving Heart for Teens: 100 Practical Ideas* (6–12). 2001, Companion paper $11.95 (978-1-879651-23-4). The author, a teacher and grief counselor, offers 100 practical tips on accepting and dealing with grief and provides tasks that will help teens identify their needs. (Rev: BL 3/15/01; SLJ 9/01; VOYA 8/01)

12098 *Yikes! A Smart Girl's Guide to Surviving Tricky, Sticky, Icky Situations* (4–8). Illus. by Bonnie Timmons. Series: American Girl Library. 2002, Pleasant paper $8.95 (978-1-58485-530-9). Advice on everything from dealing with teachers and friends to coping with embarrassing situations and dangerous incidents. (Rev: SLJ 12/02) [305.23]

12099 Youngs, Bettie B., and Jennifer Leigh Youngs, eds. *More Taste Berries for Teens: A Second Collection of Inspirational Short Stories Encouragement on Life, Love, Friendship and Tough Issues* (6–12). Series: Taste Berries for Teens. 2000, Health Communications paper $12.95 (978-1-55874-813-2). Written almost exclusively by teens, the inspiring stories and essays in this collection touch on such varied issues of teen concern as love and relationships, family relations, friendship, deciding on a career, and getting into college. (Rev: VOYA 2/01)

12100 Zimmerman, Bill. *100 Things Guys Need to Know* (5–9). 2005, Free Spirit paper $13.95 (978-1-57542-167-4). Effective graphic design will draw teenage boys into this self-help guide that touches on a wide variety of topics, including body image, dating, school, friendship, and family. (Rev: SLJ 11/05) [305.235]

Social Groups

Family and Family Problems

12101 Brondino, Jeanne. *Raising Each Other* (7–12). 1988, Hunter House paper $8.95 (978-0-89793-044-4). This book, written and illustrated by a high school class, is about parent-teen relationships, problems, and solutions. (Rev: SLJ 1/89; VOYA 4/89) [306.1]

12102 Buscemi, Karen. *Split in Two: Keeping It Together When Your Parents Live Apart* (7–12). Illus. by Corinne Mucha. 2009, Zest paper $14.95 (978-098007321-8). For children of divorce, this is a practical guide to creating your own living space in both houses, synchronizing schedules, packing and hauling, and negotiating with two sets of adults. (Rev: BL 7/09; VOYA 8/09) [300]

12103 Cooper, Kay. *Where Did You Get Those Eyes? A Guide to Discovering Your Family History* (5–7). Illus. by Anthony Accardo. 1988, Walker LB $14.85 (978-0-8027-6803-2). A helpful guide for researching the family tree. (Rev: BCCB 11/88; BL 1/15/89; SLJ 2/89)

12104 Dudevszky, Szabinka. *Close-Up* (6–8). Trans. by Wanda Boeke. 1999, Front St $15.95 (978-1-886910-40-9). The stories of 15 teens from the Netherlands who left their homes and lived in foster homes, reform schools, alone, or with friends. (Rev: HBG 4/00; SLJ 9/99; VOYA 12/99) [306]

12105 Fakhrid-Deen, Tina. *Let's Get This Straight: The Ultimate Handbook for Youth with LGBTQ Parents* (5–10). 2010, Seal $15.95 (978-1-58005-333-4). This insightful book discusses the various challenges children with LGBTQ parents will face and offers excerpts from interviews, questionnaires, and a good list of resources. (Rev: SLJ 3/1/11) [306.8]

12106 Fields, Julianna. *Foster Families* (6–12). Illus. Series: The Changing Face of Modern Families. 2009, Mason Crest $22.95 (978-142221497-8). Fields explores the history of foster care and the reasons why children end up in foster homes, with real-life examples and discussion of potential problems. Also use *Gay and Lesbian Parents*, *Kids Growing Up Without a Home*, *Multiracial Families*, and *Teen Parents* (all 2009). (Rev: LMC 5–6/10; SLJ 2/10) [306.874]

12107 Flaming, Allen, and Kate Scowen, eds. *My Crazy Life: How I Survived My Family* (8–12). 2002, Annick paper $9.95 (978-1-55037-732-3). Ten teen narratives describe how each managed to deal with family problems such as abuse, addiction, AIDS, divorce, and homosexuality. (Rev: BL 9/1/02; HBG 10/02; SLJ 7/02) [306.87]

12108 Ford, Judy, and Amanda Ford. *Between Mother and Daughter: A Teenager and Her Mom Share the Secrets of a Strong Relationship* (6–12). 1999, Conari paper $14.95 (978-1-57324-164-9). Alternate chapters written by mother and daughter reveal the power of communication. (Rev: BL 8/99; VOYA 2/00) [306.874]

12109 Fox, Annie. *What's Up with My Family?* (5–8). Series: Middle School Confidential. 2010, Free Spirit paper $9.99 (978-1-57542-333-3). Stories of children in difficult family situations alternate with advice for dealing with family issues and staying positive; a blend of fictional graphic novel stories and practical advice. (Rev: LMC 8–9/10; SLJ 4/10) [646.7]

12110 Gardner, Richard. *Boys and Girls Book About Divorce* (5–8). 1992, Bantam paper $6.99 (978-0-553-27619-0). A self-help book written for adolescents trying to cope with parental marriage problems. [306.8]

12111 Gardner, Richard. *The Boys and Girls Book About Stepfamilies* (6–9). 1985, Creative Therapeutics paper $6.50 (978-0-933812-13-0). Written from a youngster's view, this is a frank discussion of the problems that can exist in stepfamilies. [306.8]

12112 Gravelle, Karen, and Susan Fischer. *Where Are My Birth Parents? A Guide for Teenage Adoptees* (7–12). 1993, Walker LB $15.85 (978-0-8027-8258-8). Includes firsthand experiences of young people who searched for their birth families with varied success. (Rev: BL 9/1/93; SLJ 7/93; VOYA 10/93) [362.7]

12113 Haugen, David M., and Matthew J. Box, eds. *Adoption* (8–12). Series: Social Issues Firsthand. 2005, Gale LB $29.95 (978-0-7377-2881-1). Personal accounts from adoptees, birth parents, and adoptive parents give moving perspectives on the process of adoption; gay parents, transracial adoptions, custody battles, and the search for adoptees and birth parents are all covered. (Rev: SLJ 2/06) [362.7]

12114 Hyde, Margaret O. *Know About Abuse* (7–12). Series: Know About. 1992, Walker LB $14.85 (978-0-8027-8177-2). Provides facts on child abuse, reasons, symptoms, examples, and solutions, covering a wide range of abuse, from obvious to subtle. (Rev: BL 11/1/92; SLJ 9/92) [362.7]

12115 Kaminker, Laura. *Everything You Need to Know About Being Adopted* (7–12). Series: Need to Know Library. 1999, Rosen $27.95 (978-0-8239-2834-7). As well as the legal aspects of adoption, this account explores the problems young people may face when they are adopted. [362.7]

12116 Krementz, Jill. *How It Feels to Be Adopted* (5–8). 1988, Knopf paper $15.00 (978-0-394-75853-4). Interviews with 19 young people, ages 8 to 16, on how it feels to be adopted. [362.7]

12117 Krementz, Jill. *How It Feels When Parents Divorce* (4–8). 1988, Knopf paper $15.00 (978-0-394-75855-8). Boys and girls, ages 8 to 16, share their experiences with divorced parents. [306.8]

12118 Krohn, Katherine. *Everything You Need to Know About Birth Order* (5–9). Series: Need to Know Library. 2000, Rosen LB $27.95 (978-0-8239-3228-3). An interesting book that looks at a number of theories about how birth order affects people. (Rev: SLJ 12/00) [306.85]

12119 Krohn, Katherine. *You and Your Parents' Divorce* (5–8). Series: Family Matters. 2001, Rosen LB $26.50 (978-0-8239-3354-9). Krohn writes about the practicalities and emotional problems of divorce in a style suitable for reluctant readers. (Rev: SLJ 8/01) [155.44]

12120 Lanchon, Anne. *All About Adoption* (6–9). Illus. by Monika Czarnecki. Series: Sunscreen. 2006, Abrams paper $9.95 (978-0-8109-9227-6). Lanchon offers commonsense advice and reassurance for teens who are adopted. (Rev: BL 4/1/06; SLJ 4/06) [649]

12121 Leibowitz, Julie. *Finding Your Place: A Teen Guide to Life in a Blended Family* (5–8). 2000, Rosen LB $27.95 (978-0-8239-3114-9). This book explores possible problems and solutions for members of blended families. (Rev: SLJ 6/00) [645.7]

12122 MacGregor, Cynthia. *The Divorce Helpbook for Kids* (4–7). 2001, Impact paper $13.95 (978-1-886230-39-2). In this candid, honest book, a divorced mother gives advice to children about how to survive their parent's divorce. (Rev: BL 2/1/02; SLJ 3/02) [306.89]

12123 MacGregor, Cynthia. *Jigsaw Puzzle Family: The Stepkids' Guide to Fitting It Together* (5–8). Series: Rebuilding Books. 2005, Impact paper $12.95 (978-1-886230-63-7). Offers reassuring, practical advice — with an emphasis on talking through problems and seeking solutions — for stepchildren who are having difficulty adjusting to life in a blended family. (Rev: BL 9/1/05; SLJ 10/05) [306.874]

12124 Meyer, Don, ed. *The Sibling Slam Book: What It's Really Like to Have a Brother or Sister with Special Needs* (7–12). 2005, Woodbine paper $15.95 (978-1-890627-52-2). Young people with special-needs siblings share their hopes, joys, fears, frustrations, and triumphs in this slam book. (Rev: SLJ 6/05)

12125 Mufson, Susan, and Rachel Kranz. *Straight Talk About Child Abuse* (7–12). Series: Straight Talk. 1991, Facts on File $27.45 (978-0-8160-2376-9). Beginning with a general discussion of child abuse, this book describes the common signs of physical, emotional, and sexual abuse, gives some case studies, and offers some solutions. (Rev: BL 4/1/91; SLJ 3/91) [362.7]

12126 Ryan, Elizabeth A. *Straight Talk About Parents* (7–12). 1989, Facts on File $27.45 (978-0-8160-1526-9). A self-help manual to help teens sort out their feelings about parents. (Rev: BL 8/89; SLJ 9/89; VOYA 2/90) [306.8]

12127 Sanders, Pete, and Steve Myers. *Divorce and Separation* (4–8). Series: What Do You Know About. 1997, Millbrook LB $23.90 (978-0-7613-0574-3). An introduction to separation and divorce, with an emphasis on tips to help youngsters adjust and cope. (Rev: SLJ 10/97) [306.8]

12128 Simons, Rae. *Blended Families* (5–8). Illus. Series: The Changing Face of Modern Families. 2009, Mason Crest $22.95 (978-1-4222-1492-3). This book about blended families provides statistics, information, and advice through graphs, newspaper articles, and questions for discussion. Also use *Grandparents Raising Kids* and *Single Parents*. (Rev: LMC 5–6/10; SLJ 3/10)

12129 Simpson, Carolyn. *Everything You Need to Know About Living with a Grandparent or Other Relatives* (8–12). 1995, Rosen LB $27.95 (978-0-8239-1872-0). This book explores the various situations that may cause teenagers to move in with grandparents, how to adjust, ways to maintain privacy, and the emotions involved on both sides. (Rev: VOYA 2/96) [306]

12130 Snow, Judith E. *How It Feels to Have a Gay or Lesbian Parent: A Book by Kids for Kids of All Ages* (5–8). 2004, Haworth $19.95 (978-1-56023-419-7); paper $12.95 (978-1-56023-420-3). Diverse reflections on what it means to have a gay or lesbian parent come from children, young adults, and adults (up to age 31). (Rev: BL 1/1–15/05; SLJ 10/04) [306.874]

12131 Stewart, Sheila. *What Is a Family?* (5–8). Illus. Series: The Changing Face of Modern Families. 2009, Mason Crest $22.95 (978-1-4222-1528-9). Exploring what, exactly, makes a family a family, this book provides statistics, information, and advice through graphs, newspaper articles, and questions for discussion. Also use *Celebrity Families*. (Rev: LMC 5–6/10; SLJ 3/10)

12132 Trueit, Trudi. *Surviving Divorce* (7–10). Series: Scholastic Choices. 2006, Scholastic LB $22.50 (978-0-531-12368-3). Personal stories add to the facts and quizzes in this book and will reassure readers whose parents are divorcing. (Rev: BL 1/1–15/07) [306.89]

12133 Tym, Kate, and Penny Worms. *Coping with Families: A Guide to Taking Control of Your Life* (5–8). Series: Get Real. 2004, Raintree LB $28.56 (978-1-4109-0574-1). Expert advice and case studies are presented in an appealing format, plus a list of hotline numbers. Also use *Coping with Friends* (2004). (Rev: SLJ 5/05)

12134 Weiss, Ann E. *Adoptions Today: Questions and Controversy* (7–12). 2001, Twenty-First Century LB $24.90 (978-0-7613-1914-6). This comprehensive and informative overview covers such topics as international adoptions, adoption by unconventional couples, open adoption, and privacy. (Rev: BL 12/15/01; HBG 3/02; VOYA 12/01) [362.73]

12135 Williams, Mary E., ed. *Adoption* (7–12). Series: Opposing Viewpoints. 2006, Gale LB $34.95 (978-0-7377-3301-3). Essays present both sides of various topics relating to adoption: gay adoptions, international adoptions, transracial adoptions, protection of identity, and so forth. (Rev: SLJ 11/06)

12136 Winchester, Elizabeth Siris. *Sisters and Brothers: The Ultimate Guide to Understanding Your Siblings and Yourself* (6–10). Series: Scholastic Choices. 2008, Watts LB $27 (978-0-531-13870-0); paper $8.95 (978-0-531-20528-0). Teens share stories about coping with siblings, including topics such as birth order, step and foster siblings, and being an only child. (Rev: SLJ 10/1/08)

Physical and Applied Sciences

General and Miscellaneous

12137 Aaseng, Nathan. *Yearbooks in Science: 1930–1939* (5–8). Series: Yearbooks in Science. 1995, Twenty-First Century LB $22.90 (978-0-8050-3433-2). An overview of the accomplishments in science in the 1930s arranged by such divisions as physics and chemistry. (Rev: BL 12/1/95; SLJ 1/96) [609]

12138 Aaseng, Nathan. *Yearbooks in Science: 1940–1949* (5–8). Series: Yearbooks in Science. 1995, Twenty-First Century LB $22.90 (978-0-8050-3434-9). An important decade in scientific discovery is chronicled, with emphasis on the impact of these advances on society. (Rev: BL1/1–15/96; SLJ 5/96) [609]

12139 Arnold, Nick. *The Stunning Science of Everything: Science with the Squishy Bits Left In!* (4–8). Illus. by Tony De Saulles. 2006, Scholastic $10.99 (978-0-439-87777-0). This lighthearted look at science, brightly illustrated with cartoons, examines such diverse topics as the Big Bang theory, atoms, insects, humans, dinosaurs, and the universe. (Rev: HBG 4/07; LMC 3/07; SLJ 2/07; VOYA 2/07) [500]

12140 Bjornlund, Lydia. *Natural Disaster Research* (8–11). Illus. Series: Inside Science. 2012, ReferencePoint LB $27.95 (978-160152236-8). With many quotations and interesting sidebars, this visually appealing book presents an overview of research into tsunamis, earthquakes, volcanic eruptions, tornadoes, floods, and hurricanes. (Rev: BL 7/12) [363.34]

12141 Bryson, Bill. *A Really Short History of Nearly Everything* (5–8). Illus. 2009, Delacorte $19.99 (978-0-385-73810-1). A junior edition of his popular book for adults, this volume tackles many scientific topics with humor and cheer. ℮ Lexile 1190L (Rev: BL 11/15/09; SLJ 2/10) [900]

12142 Carlson, Dale. *In and Out of Your Mind: Teen Science: Human Bites* (8–12). Illus. by Carol Nicklaus. 2002, Bick paper $14.95 (978-1-884158-27-8). Teens with a curious, contemplative nature will find food for thought in this look at the wonders of science, humankind, and the universe that touches on topics including evolution, environmental concerns, and medicine. (Rev: SLJ 9/02) [500]

12143 Crump, Donald J., ed. *On the Brink of Tomorrow: Frontiers of Science* (7–9). 1982, National Geographic $12.95 (978-0-87044-414-2). With many color illustrations, this account covers recent advances in such areas as physics, astronomy, and medicine. [500]

12144 Fradin, Dennis Brindell. *With a Little Luck: Surprising Stories of Amazing Discovery* (6–9). 2006, Dutton $17.99 (978-0-525-47196-7). Among the 11 serendipitous discoveries described here are Alexander Fleming's accidental invention of penicillin and Jocelyn Bell's discovery of pulsars. (Rev: BL 2/1/06*; SLJ 6/06) [509]

12145 Gutfreund, Geraldine M. *Yearbooks in Science: 1970–1979* (5–8). Series: Yearbooks in Science. 1995, Twenty-First Century LB $22.90 (978-0-8050-3437-0). A decade of new scientific concepts and inventions is discussed, with profiles of the scientists behind them. (Rev: BL 1/1–15/96; SLJ 5/96) [609]

12146 Hakim, Joy. *The Story of Science: Newton at the Center* (7–10). Series: Smithsonian's Story of Science. 2005, Smithsonian $24.95 (978-1-58834-161-7). In the second volume of the series, Hakim introduces readers to the discoveries of Copernicus, Galileo, Newton, and others. (Rev: BL 12/1/05; SLJ 12/05*; VOYA 2/05) [590]

12147 Hoyt, Beth Caldwell, and Erica Ritter. *The Ultimate Girls' Guide to Science: From Backyard Experiments to Winning the Nobel Prize!* (4–8). 2004, Beyond Words paper $9.95 (978-1-58270-092-2). Designed to pique girls' interest in the study of science, this attractive title offers brief profiles of famous female scientists as well as the major branches of science and also provides instructions for a number of scientific experiments. (Rev: SLJ 8/04) [500]

12148 McGowen, Tom. *The Beginnings of Science* (5–8). 1998, Twenty-First Century LB $26.90 (978-0-7613-3016-5). Beginning with primitive people and their use of magic, fire, counting, writing, and astronomy, this book traces the history of science up to the 16th century. (Rev: BL 12/1/98; HBG 3/99) [509]

12149 McGowen, Tom. *Yearbooks in Science: 1900–1919* (5–8). Series: Yearbooks in Science. 1995, Twenty-First Century LB $22.90 (978-0-8050-3431-8). An overview of human achievements in science and technology during the first 20 years of the 20th century, how they helped humanity, and the men and women involved. (Rev: BL 12/1/95; SLJ 1/96) [609]

12150 McGowen, Tom. *Yearbooks in Science: 1960–1969* (5–8). Series: Yearbooks in Science. 1996, Twenty-First Century LB $22.90 (978-0-8050-3436-3). Developments in the history of science and technology during the 1960s are covered in an exciting step-by-step approach. (Rev: BL 1/1–15/96; SLJ 5/96) [609]

12151 McGrayne, Sharon Bertsch. *Blue Genes and Polyester Plants: 365 More Surprising Scientific Facts, Breakthroughs and Discoveries* (8–12). 1997, Wiley paper $16.95 (978-0-471-14575-2). A compendium of strange and unusual facts from various branches of science. [500]

12152 Martin, Paul D. *Science: It's Changing Your World* (5–8). 1985, National Geographic LB $12.50 (978-0-87044-521-7). An overview of the science field today, crediting computers and lasers with the vast growth of scientific information. (Rev: BL 9/15/85; SLJ 10/85) [500]

12153 Masoff, Joy. *Oh, Yuck! The Encyclopedia of Everything Nasty* (4–8). Illus. by Terry Sirrell. 2001, Workman paper $14.95 (978-0-7611-0771-2). This unsavory, fact-filled look at smells, noises, creepy-crawlies, toilets, and other fascinating topics even includes some suitably gross experiments. (Rev: SLJ 5/01) [031.02]

12154 Newton, David E. *Yearbooks in Science: 1920–1929* (5–8). Series: Yearbooks in Science. 1995, Twenty-First Century LB $22.90 (978-0-8050-3432-5). The history of scientific advances in the 1920s, with chapters on various fields that explain the breakthroughs, how they helped humanity, and the scientists involved. (Rev: BL 12/1/95; SLJ 1/96) [609]

12155 Nye, Bill. *Bill Nye the Science Guy's Big Blast of Science* (5–8). 1993, Addison-Wesley paper $16.00 (978-0-201-60864-9). Matter, heat, light, electricity, magnetism, weather, and space are among the topics introduced in this quick and entertaining tour of the world of science. (Rev: BL 2/15/94) [507.8]

12156 Parker, Steve. *What About . . . Science and Technology?* (5–8). Illus. Series: Answering Q&A Questions. 2009, Mason Crest $19.95 (978-1-4222-1565-4). Using a question-and-answer format, two-page spreads look at subjects ranging from matter and magnetism to sound and transportation. (Rev: LMC 5–6/10; SLJ 4/10) [500]

12157 Richardson, Gillian. *Kaboom! Explosions of All Kinds* (4–7). 2009, Annick $22.95 (978-1-55451-204-1); paper $12.95 (978-1-55451-203-4). Loud noises of all kinds are covered here — natural explosions (in the earth and outer space, in plants and animals) and man-made explosions (dynamite, fireworks, internal combustion engine, and so forth). (Rev: BL 12/1/09; SLJ 12/09) [541]

12158 Schwartz, David M. *Q Is for Quark: A Science Alphabet Book* (4–9). Illus. by Kim Doner. 2001, Tricycle $15.95 (978-1-58246-021-5). An entertaining and informative alphabet book from atom to Zzzzzzzz that doesn't hesitate to tackle difficult topics. (Rev: HBG 3/02; SLJ 11/01) [500]

12159 Shields, Carol Diggory. *BrainJuice: Science, Fresh Squeezed!* (4–7). Illus. by Richard Thompson. 2003, Handprint $14.95 (978-1-59354-005-0). A humorous, rhyming look at grade-school science with appealing illustrations and useful mnemonic devices. (Rev: SLJ 3/04) [500]

12160 Silverstein, Herma. *Yearbooks in Science: 1990 and Beyond* (5–8). Series: Yearbooks in Science. 1995, Twenty-First Century LB $22.90 (978-0-8050-3439-4). The final volume in this series not only traces recent developments in science and technology but also presents the challenges of the future. (Rev: BL 1/1–15/96) [609]

12161 Spangenburg, Ray, and Diane Kit Moser. *The Birth of Science: Ancient Times to 1699*. Rev. ed. (6–10). Series: The History of Science. 2004, Facts on File $40.00 (978-0-8160-4851-9). A survey of the development of scientific knowledge from ancient times through the seventeenth century, with brief profiles of major scientists plus discussion of discoveries that didn't pan out. Also use *The Rise of Reason: 1700–1799*, *The Age of Synthesis: 1800–1895*, *Modern Science: 1896–1945*, and *Science Frontiers: 1946 to the Present* (all 2004). (Rev: SLJ 12/04) [509]

12162 Stein, Sara Bonnett. *The Science Book* (4–8). Illus. by author. 1980, Workman paper $9.95 (978-0-89480-120-4). A whole-earth approach to strange and fascinating science facts.

12163 Sullivan, Navin. *Time* (4–7). Series: Measure Up! 2006, Marshall Cavendish LB $20.95 (978-0-7614-2321-8). This entertaining volume provides a history of the way humans have measured time, up to the present day and including the new rule for Daylight Saving Time. (Rev: LMC 8–9/07; SLJ 6/07) [529]

12164 Sussman, Art. *Dr. Art's Guide to Science: Connecting Atoms, Galaxies, and Everything in Between* (6–12). 2006, Jossey-Bass $22.95 (978-0-7879-8326-0). The author makes understanding science fun, using colorful illustrations, chapter overviews, activities, Web links to experiments, a "Glindex" (combining glossary and index), and "Stop & Think" pages. (Rev: SLJ 6/06)

12165 Wollard, Kathy. *How Come?* (5–9). 1993, Workman paper $12.95 (978-1-56305-324-5). Provides answers to some common and not-so-common questions about ordinary things. (Rev: BL 5/1/94) [500]

12166 Wollard, Kathy. *How Come Planet Earth?* (4–7). Illus. by Debra Solomon. 1999, Workman paper $12.95 (978-0-7611-1239-6). This book contains 125 science questions asked by children involving subjects such as warts, dust, cholesterol, and volcanoes. (Rev: SLJ 5/00) [500]

Experiments and Projects

12167 Bardhan-Quallen, Sudipta. *Championship Science Fair Projects: 100 Sure-to-Win Experiments* (5–9). 2005, Sterling $19.95 (978-1-4027-1138-1). Clearly defined science projects (more than 100 at varying levels of difficulty) are accompanied by lists of materials, illustrations, and extension activities. (Rev: BL 8/05; SLJ 9/05; VOYA 8/05) [507]

12168 Bardhan-Quallen, Sudipta. *Kitchen Science Experiments: How Does Your Mold Garden Grow?* (4–7). Illus. by Edward Miller. Series: Mad Science. 2010, Sterling $12.95 (978-140272413-8). Eighteen activities introduce basics of biology and chemistry through recipes that can be used in everyday kitchens. (Rev: BL 12/1/10; LMC 5–6/11; SLJ 2/1/11) [579]

12169 Bardhan-Quallen, Sudipta. *Last-Minute Science Fair Projects* (4–7). Illus. 2007, Sterling $19.95 (978-1-4027-1690-4). A guide to science experiments that can be done in a short amount of time using common household materials. (Rev: BL 5/15/07) [507.8]

12170 Boring, Mel, and Leslie Dendy. *Guinea Pig Scientists: Bold Self-Experimenters in Science and Medicine* (5–9). Illus. by C. B. Mordan. 2005, Henry Holt $19.95 (978-0-8050-7316-4). Scientists who served as their own guinea pigs — demonstrating their passion for science and often their foolhardiness — are the topic of this appealing volume. (Rev: BL 7/05*; SLJ 7/05*; VOYA 6/05) [616]

12171 Brown, Jordan D. *Crazy Concoctions: A Mad Scientist's Guide to Messy Mixtures* (4–7). Illus. by Anthony Owsley. 2012, Imagine $14.95 (978-193614051-0). For budding scientists with a love of glop and viscosity, this volume proposes a number of experiments involving such ingredients as cornstarch and raisins and with names such as "bogus barf." (Rev: BL 2/15/12; SLJ 4/12) [540.76]

12172 Brown, Robert J. *333 Science Tricks and Experiments* (7–12). 1984, McGraw-Hill $15.95 (978-0-8306-0825-6). Basic scientific principles are demonstrated in experiments and projects. (Rev: BL 4/1/89) [507]

12173 Calhoun, Yael. *Plant and Animal Science Fair Projects Using Beetles, Weeds, Seeds, and More* (5–8). Series: Biology! Best Science Projects. 2005, Enslow LB $26.60 (978-0-7660-2368-0). Great ideas for biology-based science fair projects, with plenty of information for performing and presenting each activity correctly plus helpful charts and graphs. (Rev: SLJ 7/06) [570]

12174 Calhoun, Yael. *Plant and Animal Science Fair Projects, Revised and Expanded Using the Scientific Method* (5–8). Series: Science Projects Using the Scientific Method. 2010, Enslow LB $34.60 (978-0-7660-3421-1). With a focus on the basics of scientific investigation, this well-organized and attractive volume gives an overview of the topic and provides experiments that support various hypotheses. (Rev: LMC 8–9/10; SLJ 9/1/10) [570.78]

12175 Cobb, Vicki. *The Secret Life of Hardware: A Science Experiment Book* (7–9). 1982, HarperCollins LB $13.89 (978-0-397-32000-4). A book of science activities and experiments that involve a hammer, saw, soaps, paints, and other commonly found items. [670]

12176 Cobb, Vicki, and Kathy Darling. *We Dare You! Hundreds of Science Bets, Challenges, and Experiments You Can Do at Home* (3–7). Illus. by True Kelley and Meredith Johnson. 2008, Skyhorse $19.95 (978-1-60239-225-0). More than 200 well-explained experiments are presented in chapters with headings such as "Energy Entrapments" and "Mathematical Duplicity." (Rev: SLJ 9/08) [507.8]

12177 Connolly, Sean. *The Book of Potentially Catastrophic Science: 50 Experiments for Daring Young Scientists* (5–8). Illus. 2010, Workman $13.95 (978-0-7611-5687-1). Each chapter of this compelling book presents a scientific milestone, starting with Stone Age tools and ending with the Hadron Collider, and provides the historical context and related activities. (Rev: BL 6/10; HB 3–4/11; SLJ 9/1/10) [507.8]

12178 Duensing, Edward. *Talking to Fireflies, Shrinking the Moon: Nature Activities for All Ages* (5–9). 1997, Fulcrum paper $15.95 (978-1-55591-310-6). More than 40 nature activities are included in this volume, including how to hypnotize a frog, weave a daisy chain, and whistle for woodchucks. (Rev: VOYA 10/97) [507]

12179 Fox, Tom. *Snowball Launchers, Giant-Pumpkin Growers, and Other Cool Contraptions* (5–8). Illus. by Joel Holland. 2006, Sterling paper $9.95 (978-0-8069-5515-5). A collection of 20 creative projects with clear instructions and explanations of scientific principles. (Rev: BL 1/1–15/07; SLJ 3/07)

12180 Gardner, Robert. *Genetics and Evolution Science Fair Projects, Revised and Expanded Using the Scientific Method* (5–8). Series: Biology Science Projects Using the Scientific Method. 2010, Enslow LB $34.60 (978-0-7660-3422-8). With a focus on the basics of scientific investigation, this well-organized and attractive volume gives an overview of the topic and provides experiments that support various hypotheses. (Rev: LMC 8–9/10; SLJ 9/1/10) [576.078]

12181 Gardner, Robert, and Dennis Shortelle. *Slam Dunk! Science Projects with Basketball* (6–9). 2010, Enslow LB $31.93 (978-0-7660-3366-5). Blending physics and sports, this volume is part of a series that offers practical experiments. (Rev: LMC 1–2/10) [374]

12182 Harris, Elizabeth Snoke. *First Place Science Fair Projects for Inquisitive Kids* (4–7). 2005, Sterling LB $19.95 (978-1-57990-493-7). Project ideas in biology, chemistry, and physics mostly involve everyday materials and are presented in accessible text with an eight-week schedule and clear photographs. (Rev: SLJ 3/06) [507]

12183 Harris, Elizabeth Snoke. *Yikes! Wow! Yuck! Fun Experiments for Your First Science Fair* (4–7). Illus. by Nora Thompson. 2008, Sterling $12.95 (978-1-57990-930-7). The breezy, lighthearted tone of this book will appeal to young scientists looking for simple but interesting projects. (Rev: BL 4/15/08; SLJ 6/08) [507.8]

12184 Iritz, Maxine Haren. *Blue-Ribbon Science Fair Projects* (7–12). 1991, McGraw-Hill paper $9.95 (978-0-07-157629-1). A variety of science fair projects for the novice are presented, with charts, graphs, photographs, and a chapter on choosing a topic. (Rev: BL 9/15/91) [507.8]

12185 Iritz, Maxine Haren. *Science Fair: Developing a Successful and Fun Project* (8–12). 1987, TAB $16.95 (978-0-8306-0936-9). A thorough step-by-step introduction to doing a science project. (Rev: BL 4/15/88) [507]

12186 Lempke, Donald B., and Thomas K. Adamson. *Lessons in Science Safety with Max Axiom, Super Sci-*entist (5–8). Illus. by Tod Smith. Series: Graphic Science. 2006, Capstone LB $18.95 (978-0-7368-6834-1). This graphic-novel approach to teaching safe science procedures features an appealing adult. (Rev: BL 3/15/07) [507.8]

12187 Margles, Samantha. *Mythbusters Science Fair Book* (4–8). Illus. 2011, Scholastic paper $9.99 (978-05452374-5-1). A collection of science projects that answer common questions (can we believe the five-second rule?) using proper scientific methods. (Rev: BL 4/15/11) [507.8]

12188 Mercer, Bobby. *The Leaping, Sliding, Sprinting, Riding Science Book: 50 Super Sports Science Activities* (4–7). Illus. by Tom LaBaff. 2007, Sterling $14.95 (978-1-57990-785-3). Sports moves are used to illustrate scientific principles in this activity book with step-by-step instructions, discussions of the science, and lots of lively illustrations. (Rev: BL 5/1/07; SLJ 5/07) [796]

12189 Murphy, Pat. *Exploratopia* (4–7). Illus. 2006, Little, Brown $29.99 (978-0-316-61281-4). From San Francisco's Exploratorium, this is an interesting selection of facts, activities, and hands-on experiments that encourage students to learn about and explore the world around them. (Rev: BL 12/1/06; SLJ 1/07) [507.8]

12190 Newcomb, Rain, and Bobby Mercer. *Crash It! Smash It! Launch It!* (5–8). Illus. by Rain Newcomb. 2006, Sterling $14.95 (978-1-57990-795-2). More than 40 experiments provide great entertainment as well as scientific knowledge. (Rev: BL 11/1/06; SLJ 12/06) [507.8]

12191 Rainis, Kenneth G. *Blood and DNA Evidence: Crime-Solving Science Experiments* (8–11). Series: Forensic Science Projects. 2006, Enslow LB $23.95 (978-0-7660-1958-4). Contains accounts of real-life crime cases and challenges the reader with step-by-step forensic science experiments to solve the case just as real detectives do. (Rev: BL 10/15/06; SLJ 5/07) [363.25]

12192 Rosner, Marc Alan. *Science Fair Success Using the Internet* (8–12). Series: Science Fair Success. 1999, Enslow LB $26.60 (978-0-7660-1172-4). As well as an explanation of how to use Internet resources, this book explains how the Internet can enhance science projects. [507.8]

12193 *Science Fairs: Ideas and Activities* (4–8). 1998, World Book $15.00 (978-0-7166-4498-9). Using many diagrams and logical step-by-step explanations, this work offers science projects in such areas as space, earth science, geology, botany, and machines. (Rev: SLJ 1/99) [507]

12194 Tomecek, Stephen M. *Music* (6–9). Series: Experimenting with Everyday Science. 2010, Chelsea House $35 (978-1-60413-169-7). Twenty-five activities illustrate various musical concepts, with safety tips and explanations for results. (Rev: LMC 11–12/10; SLJ 11/1/10)

12195 Tomecek, Stephen M. *Tools and Machines* (6–9). Series: Experimenting with Everyday Science. 2010, Chelsea House $35 (978-1-60413-171-0). Twenty-five activities illustrate various uses for levers, pulleys, meters, and other basic tools and machines, with safety tips and explanations for results. (Rev: LMC 11–12/10; SLJ 11/1/10)

12196 UNESCO. *700 Science Experiments for Everyone* (5–8). 1964, Doubleday $19.95 (978-0-385-05275-7). An excellent collection of experiments, noted for its number of entries and breadth of coverage.

12197 VanCleave, Janice. *Janice VanCleave's A+ Projects in Chemistry: Winning Experiments for Science Fairs and Extra Credit* (6–10). 1993, Wiley paper $12.95 (978-0-471-58630-2). Thirty experiments that investigate such topics as calories, acids, and electrolytes, among others. (Rev: BL 12/1/95; SLJ 4/94) [930]

12198 VanCleave, Janice. *Janice VanCleave's Biology for Every Kid: 101 Easy Experiments That Really Work* (4–7). 1989, Wiley paper $12.95 (978-0-471-50381-1). This book outlines simple experiments that use readily available equipment and supplies. (Rev: BL 2/15/90) [574]

12199 VanCleave, Janice. *Janice VanCleave's Guide to More of the Best Science Fair Projects* (4–8). 2000, Wiley paper $14.95 (978-0-471-32627-4). After general information about the scientific method, research, and presentation, this book outlines about 50 projects in the areas of astronomy, biology, earth science, engineering, physical science, and mathematics. (Rev: SLJ 5/00) [509]

12200 VanCleave, Janice. *Janice VanCleave's 203 Icy, Freezing, Frosty, Cool and Wild Experiments* (4–7). 1999, Wiley paper $12.95 (978-0-471-25223-8). An excellent book filled with easily performed experiments in such areas as biology, chemistry, earth science, and physics. (Rev: SLJ 4/00) [507.8]

12201 Vancleave, Janice. *Step-By-Step Science Experiments in Ecology* (5–8). Series: Janice VanCleave's First-Place Science Fair Projects. 2012, Rosen Central LB $33.25 (978-1-4488-6980-0). An updated volume with step-by-step instructions for 22 experiments mostly using easily found materials. (Rev: SLJ 10/12) [577.078]

12202 Vecchione, Glen. *Blue Ribbon Science Fair Projects* (6–9). 2006, Sterling $19.95 (978-1-4027-1073-5). Ideas for projects in a wide range of subject areas are clearly presented, with background information, list of materials, hypothesis, steps to take, and so forth. (Rev: BL 2/1/06; SLJ 6/06) [507]

12203 Vickers, Tanya M. *Teen Science Fair Sourcebook: Winning School Science Fairs and National Competitions* (6–10). Illus. 2009, Enslow LB $25.95 (978-076602711-4). In chapters such as "The Research Plan and the Scientific Method," "The Rules: Safety, Originality, and Consent," and "The Project Notebook: A Scientist's Cookbook," Vickers lays out the various stages of project creation and provides useful tips. (Rev: BL 7/09; LMC 10/09) [507.8]

Astronomy and Space Science

General and Miscellaneous

12204 Banqueri, Eduardo. *The Night Sky* (6–10). Series: Field Guides. 2007, Enchanted Lion LB $16.95 (978-1-59270-066-0). An informative introduction to the night sky and how best to view it. (Rev: BL 5/15/07; LMC 11/07; SLJ 9/07) [523.80]

12205 Brake, Mark. *Really, Really Big Questions About Space and Time* (4–7). Illus. by Nishant Choksi. 2010, Kingfisher $16.99 (978-075346502-8). Presents lighthearted and thoughtful answers to questions children ask about space and time, with a section on "How to Think Like a Scientist and Apply the Scientific Method." (Rev: BL 11/1/10; LMC 3–4/11) [523.1]

12206 Campbell, Ann-Jeanette. *The New York Public Library Amazing Space: A Book of Answers for Kids* (5–8). 1997, Wiley paper $12.95 (978-0-471-14498-4). This question-and-answer book introduces space exploration, the solar system, individual planets, galaxies, and related phenomena. (Rev: SLJ 7/97) [523]

12207 Cole, Michael D. *Eye on the Universe: The Incredible Hubble Space Telescope* (5–8). Illus. Series: American Space Missions: Astronauts, Exploration, and Discovery. 2012, Enslow LB $23.93 (978-076604077-9). This volume looks at how the telescope works (and why), the problems it encountered initially, and the images it has sent home since then and what we can learn from them. (Rev: BL 11/15/12; LMC 5–6/13; SLJ 12/12) [522]

12208 Cole, Michael D. *Hubble Space Telescope: Exploring the Universe* (4–7). Series: Countdown to Space. 1999, Enslow LB $23.93 (978-0-7660-1120-5). This close-up look at the Hubble space telescope covers its parts, uses, problems, and photographs that the telescope has sent back to earth. (Rev: BL 2/1/99; HBG 10/99) [522]

12209 Couper, Heather, and Nigel Henbest. *The History of Astronomy* (8–12). 2007, Firefly $59.95 (978-1-55407-325-2). From Stonehenge and other ancient monuments forward, this attractive volume documents man's interest in the skies and the scientific advances in studying them. (Rev: BL 12/1/07) [520]

12210 Dyer, Alan. *Space* (5–8). Illus. Series: Insiders. 2007, Simon & Schuster $16.99 (978-1-4169-3860-6). An introduction to the big bang, the solar system, stars and nebulas, galaxies, and so forth, with eye-catching illustrations. (Rev: LMC 10/07; SLJ 12/07) [520]

12211 Hope, Terry. *Spacecam: Photographing the Final Frontier from Apollo to Hubble* (6–12). 2005, Fitzhenry & Whiteside $24.99 (978-0-7153-2164-5). Images captured from space — many never before published — offer fantastic views of Earth and beyond. (Rev: BL 12/15/05) [778.35]

12212 Jackson, Ellen. *The Mysterious Universe: Supernovae, Dark Energy, and Black Holes* (5–8). Series: Scientists in the Field. 2008, Houghton Mifflin $18.00 (978-0-618-56325-8). Astronomer Alex Filippenko and his work at key observatories is the focus of this book that also describes such phenomena as supernovae and black holes in accessible text with informative diagrams and spectacular photographs. (Rev: BL 6/1–15/08; SLJ 6/08) [523.8]

12213 Jefferis, David. *Black Holes and Other Bizarre Space Objects* (5–8). Illus. Series: Science Frontiers. 2006, Crabtree LB $26.60 (978-0-7787-2856-6); paper $8.95 (978-0-7787-2870-2). Double-page spreads with color photographs and informative sidebars explore the life of stars, black holes, gamma-ray bursts, space telescopes, and so forth. (Rev: BL 4/1/06) [523.8]

12214 Macy, Sue. *Are We Alone? Scientists Search for Life in Space* (4–8). 2004, National Geographic $18.95 (978-0-7922-6567-2). Modern scientific efforts to find extraterrestrial life are discussed along with the popularity of flying saucers, crop circles, and other theories. (Rev: BL 10/1/04; SLJ 12/04*) [001.9]

12215 Miller, Ron. *Extrasolar Planets* (7–12). Series: Worlds Beyond. 2002, Millbrook LB $25.90 (978-0-7613-2354-9). A handsome and accessible overview of the planets in our solar system and elsewhere in the universe that includes historical information, biographies of scientists, basic concepts, and many attention-grabbing illustrations. (Rev: BL 2/15/02; HBG 10/02; SLJ 3/02) [523]

12216 Mitchell, Mark G. *Seeing Stars: The McDonald Observatory and Its Astronomers* (6–10). 1997, Sunbelt Media $17.95 (978-1-57168-117-1). This is a history of the famous observatory operated by the University of Texas in Austin, with material on the equipment used and the day-to-day operation. (Rev: HBG 9/98; SLJ 5/98) [523]

12217 Schorer, Lonnie Jones. *Kids to Space: A Space Traveler's Guide* (5–9). Illus. 2006, Apogee paper $29.95 (978-1-894959-42-1). Organized in almost 100 categories, this volume includes thousands of questions about space posed by children and answered by experts including NASA engineers, former astronauts, and astronomy professors. (Rev: SLJ 12/06) [500.5]

12218 Scott, Elaine. *Space, Stars, and the Beginning of Time: What the Hubble Telescope Saw* (5–8). Illus. 2011, Clarion $17.99 (978-0-547-24189-0). This inspiring tribute to the Hubble Space Telescope features a discussion of the history of astronomy, and how the Hubble contributed to our understanding of the universe. ALA Notable Books 2012. (Rev: HB 3–4/11; SLJ 3/1/11) [522]

12219 Stott, Carole, and Clint Twist. *1001 Facts About Space* (7–12). Series: Backpack Books. 2002, DK paper $8.99 (978-0-7894-8450-5). A handy-sized overview full of illustrations that presents useful facts about the universe, galaxies, stars, solar system, and planets as well as pulsars, space history, and stellar classification. (Rev: BL 3/15/02) [590]

12220 Taschek, Karen. *Death Stars, Weird Galaxies, and a Quasar-Spangled Universe: The Discoveries of the Very Large Array Telescope* (7–10). 2006, Univ. of New Mexico $17.95 (978-0-8263-3211-0). Compelling images of space captured from New Mexico's VLA (Very Large Array) telescope are combined with readable descriptions of recent discoveries in astronomy and an overview of the problems that still plague astronomers. (Rev: BL 5/1/06; SLJ 7/06) [522]

12221 Vancleave, Janice. *Step-By-Step Science Experiments in Astronomy* (5–8). Series: Janice VanCleave's First-Place Science Fair Projects. 2012, Rosen Central LB $33.25 (978-1-4488-6978-7). An updated volume with step-by-step instructions for 22 experiments mostly using easily found materials. (Rev: SLJ 10/12) [520.78]

12222 Vogt, Gregory L. *Deep Space Astronomy* (5–8). 1999, Twenty-First Century LB $25.90 (978-0-7613-1369-4). This look beyond our own star system covers such topics as the development of space-based detectors, information-gathering techniques, and recent discoveries. (Rev: BL 1/1–15/00; HBG 3/00; SLJ 2/00) [520]

12223 Williams, Brian. *What About . . . the Universe?* (5–8). Illus. Series: Answering Q&A Questions. 2009, Mason Crest $19.95 (978-1-4222-1566-1). Using a question-and-answer format, two-page spreads look at subjects ranging from the Big Bang to space missions and the solar system. (Rev: LMC 5–6/10; SLJ 4/10) [520]

12224 Wills, Susan, and Steven Wills. *Astronomy: Looking at the Stars* (5–8). Series: Innovators. 2001, Oliver $21.95 (978-1-881508-76-2). A good starting point for research into astronomy, with profiles of individuals including Ptolemy, Copernicus, Galileo, and Newton. (Rev: HBG 10/02; SLJ 2/02) [520.922]

12225 Wittenstein, Vicki Oransky. *Planet Hunter: Geoff Marcy and the Search for Other Earths* (6–8). 2010, Boyds Mills $17.95 (978-1-59078-592-8). Wittenstein introduces astronomer Marcy and his work hunting for planets in other solar systems; large photographs and artists' images add interest to this large-format volume. Lexile 1080L (Rev: BL 5/15/10; LMC 8–9/10; SLJ 3/10) [523.2]

Astronautics and Space Exploration

12226 Angliss, Sarah. *Cosmic Journeys: A Beginner's Guide to Space and Time Travel* (5–7). Illus. by Alex Pang, et al. Series: Future Files. 1998, Millbrook LB $23.90 (978-0-7613-0620-7). This book explores such topics as traveling to other solar systems, time travel, black holes, and parallel universes. (Rev: HBG 10/98; SLJ 10/98) [629.4]

12227 Barbree, Jay. *Live from Cape Canaveral: Covering the Space Race, from Sputnik to Today* (8–12). 2007, Smithsonian $26.95 (978-0-06-123392-0). Journalist Barbree offers a behind-the-scenes look at the great events and personalities of space flight, from 1957 onward. (Rev: BL 9/1/07) [629.450973]

12228 Barter, James. *Space Stations* (5–8). Series: Lucent Library of Science and Technology. 2005, Gale LB $29.95 (978-1-59018-106-5). Explores the space stations that have been used for many years as medical laboratories and platforms for space study. (Rev: BL 1/05)

12229 Bortz, Fred. *Seven Wonders of Space Technology* (5–8). Illus. 2011, Lerner LB $33.26 (978-076135453-6). Observatories, satellites, the International Space Station, and the Mars Rovers are among the pieces of space technology covered in this volume that also looks at the future. (Rev: BL 3/1/11) [629.4]

12230 Carlisle, Rodney P. *Exploring Space* (6–10). Series: Discovery and Exploration. 2004, Facts on File $40.00 (978-0-8160-5265-3). The motivations for exploring space are examined in clear, informative text plus photographs, illustrations, and excerpts from primary sources. (Rev: SLJ 12/04) [629.5]

12231 Chaikin, Andrew, and Victoria Kohl. *Mission Control, This is Apollo: The Story of the First Voyages to the Moon* (5–8). Illus. by Alan Bean. 2009, Viking $23.99 (978-0-670-01156-8). A compelling wide-format account of the Apollo program, with interesting anecdotes, informative sidebars, excellent photographs, and paintings by former astronaut Bean. (Rev: BL 5/1/09; HB 7/09*; SLJ 5/09; VOYA 6/09) [900]

12232 Collins, Martin. *After Sputnik: 50 Years of the Space Age* (8–12). 2007, HarperCollins $35.00 (978-0-06-089781-9). With photographs accompanied by essays, this volume uses approximately 200 artifacts — John Glenn's space suit and a lunar rover, for example — to tell the story of the first 50 years of space exploration. (Rev: SLJ 7/07) [629.409]

12233 Duggins, Pat. *Final Countdown: NASA and the End of the Space Shuttle Program* (8–12). 2007, Univ. Press of Florida $24.95 (978-0-8130-3146-0). Duggins tells the story of the space shuttle from initial inception to the planning of the final missions, with information on shuttle astronauts and on the two shuttle disasters. (Rev: BL 9/1/07) [629.45]

12234 Dyer, Alan. *Mission to the Moon* (5–7). 2009, Simon & Schuster $19.99 (978-1-4169-7935-7). This well-organized package of clear narrative, color photographs, quotations, and DVD of video clips presents a good overview of the space race and the U.S. Apollo missions. (Rev: LMC 10/09; SLJ 4/09) [629.45]

12235 Dyson, Marianne J. *Home on the Moon: Living on a Space Frontier* (5–8). 2003, National Geographic $18.95 (978-0-7922-7193-2). Dyson, a former NASA mission controller, discusses the resources available on the moon, explores the possibilities of building facilities there, and suggests activities. (Rev: BL 7/03; HBG 10/03; SLJ 9/03) [919.91]

12236 Dyson, Marianne J. *Space Station Science: Life in Free Fall* (4–7). 1999, Scholastic paper $16.95 (978-0-590-05889-6). Written by a former member of a NASA control team, this work explores living and working in space including details on a space station bathroom. (Rev: BL 11/15/99; HBG 10/00; SLJ 12/99) [629.45]

12237 English, June A., and Thomas D. Jones. *Mission: Earth: Voyage to the Home Planet* (4–7). 1996, Scholastic paper $16.95 (978-0-590-48571-5). The space program is introduced, with special coverage of the flights of the shuttle *Endeavor* in 1994 and its environmental studies. (Rev: BL 10/15/96; SLJ 10/96) [550]

12238 Fallen, Anne-Catherine. *USA from Space* (4–7). 1997, Firefly LB $19.95 (978-1-55209-159-3); paper $7.95 (978-1-55209-157-9). Excellent satellite pictures of parts of the earth are contained in this book, which also explains the value of satellite imagery in tracking pollution, population, and natural disasters. (Rev: BL 3/1/98; SLJ 12/97) [917.3]

12239 Gaffney, Timothy R. *Secret Spy Satellites: America's Eyes in Space* (4–7). Series: Countdown to Space. 2000, Enslow LB $23.93 (978-0-7660-1402-2). With sharp illustrations and a strong narrative, this book describes U.S. spy satellites, their purposes, and findings. (Rev: BL 9/15/00; HBG 10/01) [629.4]

12240 Goldsmith, Mike. *Space* (4–7). Series: Kingfisher Voyages. 2005, Kingfisher $14.95 (978-0-7534-5910-2). An appealing overview of space exploration, with concise text, good photographs, and a foreword and comments by astronaut Sally Ride. (Rev: BL 10/15/05) [629.45]

12241 Green, Carl R. *Spacewalk: The Astounding Gemini 4 Mission* (5–8). Illus. Series: American Space Missions: Astronauts, Exploration, and Discovery. 2012, Enslow LB $23.93 (978-076604075-5). Tells the story of the first American to walk in space and the technology that made this possible. (Rev: BL 11/15/12; LMC 5–6/13; SLJ 12/12)

12242 Holden, Henry M. *The Coolest Job in the Universe: Working Aboard the International Space Station* (5–8). Illus. Series: American Space Missions: Astronauts, Exploration, and Discovery. 2012, Enslow LB $23.93 (978-076604074-8). The dangers and wonders of the International Space Station are explained in this review of how it was built, what life is like onboard, and the kinds of work performed there. (Rev: BL 11/15/12; LMC 5–6/13; SLJ 12/12) [629.44]

12243 Holden, Henry M. *Danger in Space: Surviving the Apollo 13 Disaster* (5–8). Illus. Series: American Space Missions: Astronauts, Exploration, and Discovery. 2012, Enslow LB $23.93 (978-076604072-4). What went wrong? This straightforward volume lays out the mission and the problems that occurred. (Rev: BL 11/15/12; LMC 5–6/13; SLJ 12/12) [629.45]

12244 Holden, Henry M. *The Tragedy of the Space Shuttle Challenger* (4–8). Series: Space Flight Adventures and Disasters. 2004, Enslow LB $25.26 (978-0-7660-5165-2). An account of the ill-fated *Challenger* mission, backed up by a list of Web sites that provide additional information. (Rev: BL 10/1/04; SLJ 2/05) [629.5]

12245 Kennedy, Gregory P. *Apollo to the Moon* (6–9). Series: World Explorers. 1992, Chelsea LB $32.00 (978-0-7910-1322-9). A chronicle of the Apollo moon landing expedition and descriptions of the astronauts involved. (Rev: BL 9/1/92; SLJ 7/92) [629.45]

12246 Kerrod, Robin. *Dawn of the Space Age* (5–7). Series: The History of Space Exploration. 2005, World Almanac LB $31.00 (978-0-8368-5705-4). A well-illustrated history of space exploration, from the ideas of Cyrano de Bergerac to the modern Mars probes. Also recommended in this series are *Space Probes*, *Space Shuttles*, and *Space Stations* (all 2004). (Rev: SLJ 3/05) [629.4]

12247 Kuhn, Betsy. *The Race for Space: The United States and the Soviet Union Compete for the New Frontier* (6–9). 2006, Lerner $29.27 (978-0-8225-5984-9). Follows the historical aspects of the space race between the United States and the former Soviet Union from the 1950's to the early 90's. (Rev: BL 8/06; SLJ 2/07) [629.45]

12248 Kupperberg, Paul. *Spy Satellites* (4–8). Series: Library of Satellites. 2003, Rosen LB $26.50 (978-0-8239-3854-4). The author discusses the history of U.S. spy satellites and how the country has used the information they have gleaned. (Rev: BL 5/15/03; SLJ 1/04) [327.1273]

12249 Markle, Sandra. *Pioneering Space* (5–8). 1992, Atheneum LB $14.95 (978-0-689-31748-4). A look at space travel and how people may succeed in living in space. (Rev: BL 9/1/92; SLJ 2/93) [629.4]

12250 Miller, Ron. *Satellites* (7–10). Series: Space Innovations. 2007, Lerner LB $31.93 (978-0-8225-7154-4). How do satellites get up there? Which country was the first to launch one? What do they do? Do they ever fall back to Earth? This well-designed book answers these questions and more, providing lots of relevant history. (Rev: BL 12/1/07) [629.44]

12251 Ottaviani, Jim. *T-Minus: The Race to the Moon* (6–8). Illus. by Zander Cannon. 2009, Aladdin paper $12.99 (978-141694960-2). In graphic-novel/count-down format, this book details the work that went into the first flight to the moon, crediting the efforts of engineers, designers, and scientists in both Russia and the United States. (Rev: BL 7/09; HB 9–10/09; LMC 10/09; SLJ 9/09)

12252 Parks, Peggy J. *Space Research* (8–11). Illus. Series: Inside Science. 2010, ReferencePoint LB $26.95 (978-160152111-8). A slim but informative overview of the kinds of research being conducted in space, the challenges of living and working in space, and the importance of this work for mankind as a whole. (Rev: BL 12/1/10) [500.5]

12253 Rusch, Elizabeth. *The Mighty Mars Rovers: The Incredible Adventures of Spirit and Opportunity* (5–8). Illus. Series: Scientists in the Field. 2012, Houghton Mifflin $18.99 (978-0-547-47881-4). With profiles of the scientists involved, and of the rovers *Spirit* and *Opportunity*, and their joint achievements, this is an ef-fective and informative celebration of NASA's efforts on Mars. (Rev: BL 6/12*; HB 9–10/12*; LMC 1–2/13; SLJ 7/12*) [523.43]

12254 Siy, Alexandra. *Cars on Mars: Roving the Red Planet* (5–8). Illus. by author. 2009, Charlesbridge $18.95 (978-1-57091-462-1). The fascinating story of the Mars rovers built to last for three months but still exploring the Martian terrain more than five years later. (Rev: BL 8/09*; LMC 11/09; SLJ 7/09) [919.9]

12255 Stone, Jerry. *One Small Step: Celebrating the First Men on the Moon* (4–8). 2009, Roaring Brook $24.95 (978-1-59643-491-2). This "scrapbook" offers a wealth of perspectives on the first moon landing. (Rev: SLJ 6/09)

12256 Sullivan, George. *The Day We Walked on the Moon: A Photo History of Space Exploration* (5–8). 1990, Scholastic paper $4.95 (978-0-685-58532-0). The history of U.S. space exploration, showing the ac-complishments of both the United States and the Soviet Union. (Rev: BL 9/1/90; SLJ 2/91) [629.4]

12257 Thimmesh, Catherine. *Team Moon: How 400,000 People Landed Apollo 11 on the Moon* (5–10). 2006, Houghton Mifflin $19.95 (978-0-618-50757-3). A breathless account of all the behind-the-scenes work that went into the Apollo space program, with plenty of photographs. Sibert Medal 2007. (Rev: SLJ 6/06) [629.45]

12258 Vogt, Gregory L. *Disasters in Space Exploration* (5–8). 2001, Millbrook LB $25.90 (978-0-7613-1920-7). Accidents and failures that have marred the success rates of the American and Soviet space programs are covered in interesting detail with many photographs. (Rev: BL 10/1/01; HBG 3/02; SLJ 8/01*) [363.12]

12259 Vogt, Gregory L. *Disasters in Space Exploration. Rev. ed.* (5–8). 2003, Millbrook LB $25.90 (978-0-7613-2895-7). An illustrated survey of serious accidents that have befallen the U.S. and Soviet space programs, what caused them, and what was learned from them. This revised edition includes the *Columbia* space shuttle disaster of February 2003. (Rev: SLJ 3/04) [363.12]

12260 Vogt, Gregory L. *Spacewalks: The Ultimate Adventures in Orbit* (4–7). Series: Countdown to Space. 2000, Enslow LB $23.93 (978-0-7660-1305-6). This gives a history of spacewalks, tells who were the pioneers, and explains their purpose. (Rev: BL 8/00; HBG 10/00) [629.4]

12261 Voit, Mark. *Hubble Space Telescope: New Views of the Universe* (8–12). 2000, Abrams paper $19.95 (978-0-8109-2923-4). With an accompanying text, this book includes more than 100 photographs taken by the Hubble Space Telescope. (Rev: SLJ 4/01) [520]

Comets, Meteors, and Asteroids

12262 Koppes, Steven N. *Killer Rocks from Outer Space: Asteroids, Comets, and Meteorites* (7–10). 2003, Lerner LB $27.93 (978-0-8225-2861-6). Koppes examines the science and history of planetary impacts by asteroids, comets, and meteorites and looks at steps being taken to protect the Earth from such impacts in the future. (Rev: BL 1/1–15/04; SLJ 3/04) [523.5]

12263 Miller, Ron. *Asteroids, Comets, and Meteors* (7–10). Series: Worlds Beyond. 2005, Twenty-First Century LB $27.93 (978-0-7613-2363-1). Using color photographs, vivid paintings, and helpful diagrams, this title introduces readers to asteroids, comets, and meteors. (Rev: SLJ 12/05)

12264 Nardo, Don. *Asteroids and Comets* (7–10). Illus. Series: Extreme Threats. 2009, Morgan Reynolds LB $28.95 (978-159935121-6). With chapters including "The Day the Sky Exploded," "Giant Impacts and Mass Extinctions," and "Recent Strikes and Near Misses," this book discusses past collisions with Earth and the likelihood of future disasters. (Rev: BL 4/1/10; VOYA 12/09) [523.44]

12265 Sherman, Josepha. *Asteroids, Meteors, and Comets* (5–7). Series: Space! 2009, Marshall Cavendish LB $22.95 (978-0-7614-4252-3). Good for research, this volume presents facts clearly and concisely with many photos and other illustrations. (Rev: LMC 3–4/10; SLJ 2/10) [523]

Earth and the Moon

12266 Goldsmith, Mike. *Earth: The Life of Our Planet* (4–7). Illus. by Mark A. Garlick. 2011, Kingfisher $17.99 (978-075346625-4). This broad overview of the big events that have shaped Earth's climate and topography begins with the planet's formation and ends with space exploration and possibilities for the future. (Rev: BLO 10/15/11; LMC 5–6/12) [550]

12267 Hicks, Terry Allan. *Earth and the Moon* (4–8). Series: Space! 2010, Marshall Cavendish LB $32.79 (978-0-7614-4254-7). After an overview of Earth and its moon, Hicks looks at our growing understanding over time and the missions to explore our moon. Also use *Saturn* (2010). ❷ (Rev: LMC 3–4/10; SLJ 2/10) [525]

12268 Miller, Ron. *Earth and the Moon* (5–7). Series: Worlds Beyond. 2003, Twenty-First Century LB $25.90 (978-0-7613-2358-7). NASA photographs and computer-generated images are used throughout this account of the origin, composition, and evolution the Earth and its moon. (Rev: HBG 10/03; SLJ 8/03) [525]

Stars

12269 Abramson, Andra Serlin, and Mordecai-Mark Mac Low. *Inside Stars* (5–8). Illus. 2011, Sterling paper $9.95 (978-14027816-2-9). A dramatic presentation of information about the Big Bang, the formation and death of stars, the sun, and so forth, with many photographs and gatefolds. (Rev: BL 11/1/11) [523.8]

12270 Aguilar, David A. *Super Stars: The Biggest, Hottest, Brightest, Most Explosive Stars in the Milky Way* (4–8). 2010, National Geographic LB $25.90 (978-1-4263-0602-0). An exciting, engaging look at different types of stars (for example, G Stars, planetary nebulae, and brown dwarfs), with beautiful photographs and art. Lexile NC1160L (Rev: BL 4/15/10; LMC 8–9/10; SLJ 4/10) [523.8]

12271 Asimov, Isaac. *The Life and Death of Stars* (5–8). Series: Isaac Asimov's 21st Century Library of the Universe. 2005, Gareth Stevens LB $26.00 (978-0-8368-3967-8). A revised, well-illustrated edition of a previously published book, this discusses the birth of stars, profiles different types of stars, and looks at the future of our Sun. Also in this series: *Black Holes, Pulsars, and Quasars, The Milky Way and Other Galaxies, Our Planetary System*, and *Comets and Meteors* (all 2005). (Rev: BL 3/1/05; SLJ 8/05)

12272 Croswell, Ken. *The Lives of Stars* (5–8). Illus. 2009, Boyds Mills $19.95 (978-159078582-9). Using easy-to-understand language and striking images, Croswell describes the different kinds of stars and how they are formed, live, and eventually die. (Rev: BLO 11/1/09; LMC 11–12/09; SLJ 11/09) [523.8]

12273 Croswell, Ken. *See the Stars* (4–8). 2000, Boyds Mills $16.95 (978-1-56397-757-2). Twelve constellations are introduced in double-page spreads, with material on where and when to look for them. (Rev: BL 11/1/00; HBG 3/01; SLJ 10/00) [523]

12274 Kerrod, Robin. *The Star Guide: Learn How to Read the Night Sky Star by Star. 2nd ed.* (8–12). 2005, Wiley $29.95 (978-0-471-70617-5). This guide to identifying heavenly bodies is well organized for novices and includes a removable sky map. (Rev: BL 4/15/05) [523.8]

12275 Miller, Ron. *Seven Wonders Beyond the Solar System* (5–8). Series: Seven Wonders. 2011, Twenty-First Century LB $33.26 (978-0-7613-5454-3). Miller discusses how stars and galaxies are formed and looks at significant nebulas and superclusters as well as the search for an Earthlike planet; readers are challenged to choose an eighth wonder. **e** (Rev: BL 3/1/11; SLJ 2/1/11) [523.8]

12276 Pearce, Q. L. *The Stargazer's Guide to the Galaxy* (4–8). Illus. by Mary Ann Fraser. 1991, Tor paper $6.99 (978-0-8125-9423-2). In this introduction to star gazing in the Northern Hemisphere, material covered includes a look at the night sky in each of the four seasons. (Rev: SLJ 12/91) [523]

12277 Rey, H. A. *Find the Constellations* (5–7). 1976, Houghton Mifflin LB $20.00 (978-0-395-24509-5); paper $9.95 (978-0-395-24418-0). Through clear text and illustrations, the reader is helped to recognize stars and constellations in the northern United States. Also use *The Stars: A New Way to See Them* (1973).

12278 VanCleave, Janice. *Janice VanCleave's Constellations for Every Kid: Easy Activities That Make Learning Science Fun* (8–12). 1997, Wiley paper $12.95 (978-0-471-15979-7). An excellent guide to the heavens, with each chapter presenting a different constellation with concise facts, new concepts, simple activities, and solutions to problems. (Rev: BL 12/1/97; HBG 3/98; SLJ 10/97) [523.8]

Sun and the Solar System

12279 Aguilar, David A. *11 Planets: A New View of the Solar System* (5–8). 2008, National Geographic $16.95 (978-1-4263-0236-7). The author includes the eight planets and three dwarf planets in his calculation of the main celestial bodies in the solar system; attractive color paintings and photographs accompany the text. (Rev: BL 5/1/08; SLJ 9/08) [523]

12280 Benson, Michael. *Beyond: A Solar System Voyage* (6–9). Illus. 2009, Abrams $19.95 (978-081098322-9). A fascinating combination of eye-catching photographs taken from unmanned spacecraft and interesting information about the space probes and astronomy. Lexile 1270 (Rev: BL 4/1/09; SLJ 6/1/09; VOYA 4/09) [523.2]

12281 Bjorklund, Ruth. *Venus* (4–8). Series: Space! 2010, Marshall Cavendish LB $32.79 (978-0-7614-4251-6). In chapters covering the discovery of Venus, its features, missions to the planet, and handy quick facts, this accessible title features useful, well-presented material. **e** (Rev: LMC 3–4/10; SLJ 2/10) [523.42]

12282 Bortolotti, Dan. *Exploring Saturn* (4–8). 2003, Firefly $19.95 (978-1-55297-766-8); paper $9.95 (978-1-55297-765-1). This highly visual volume with readable text presents facts about Saturn, explains how and when we acquired this knowledge, and looks at the Cassini-Huygens mission, scheduled to reach the planet in 2004. (Rev: BL 12/1/03; SLJ 5/04) [523.46]

12283 Capaccio, George. *Jupiter* (4–8). Series: Space! 2010, Marshall Cavendish LB $32.79 (978-0-7614-4244-8). Capaccio looks at the physical features of Jupiter, the history of its discovery and what we have since learned about it, and speculates about future missions. Also use *The Sun* and *Neptune* (both 2010). **e** (Rev: LMC 3–4/10; SLJ 2/10) [523.45]

12284 Colligan, L. H. *Mercury* (4–8). Series: Space! 2010, Marshall Cavendish LB $32.79 (978-0-7614-4239-4). Colligan looks at how planets were formed, the history of Mercury's discovery and what we have since learned about it, and speculates about its future importance. **e** (Rev: LMC 3–4/10; SLJ 2/10) [523.41]

12285 Farndon, John. *Exploring the Solar System* (4–9). Series: Why Science Matters. 2009, Heinemann-Raintree $32.86 (978-1-4329-2484-3). This appealing guide to the solar system emphasizes the importance of scientific understanding to everyday life. (Rev: LMC 11–12/09) [523.4]

12286 Feinstein, Stephen. *Saturn* (4–7). Series: Solar System. 2005, Enslow LB $25.26 (978-0-7660-5304-5). Useful for reports, this clearly written title includes links to Web sites for further research. (Rev: SLJ 12/05) [523.46]

12287 Gustafson, John. *Planets, Moons and Meteors: The Young Stargazer's Guide to the Galaxy* (4–8). 1992, Simon & Schuster LB $12.95 (978-0-671-72534-1); paper $6.95 (978-0-671-72535-8). This guidebook tells how and when to observe the solar system and provides basic information about the planets. (Rev: BL 11/1/92) [523]

12288 Lew, Kristi. *The Dwarf Planet Pluto* (4–8). Series: Space! 2010, Marshall Cavendish LB $32.79 (978-0-7614-4243-1). The author discusses Pluto's composition, its new status as a dwarf planet, missions to Pluto, and pertinent facts. **e** (Rev: LMC 3–4/10; SLJ 2/10) [523.482]

12289 Miller, Ron. *Jupiter* (5–8). Series: Worlds Beyond. 2002, Millbrook LB $25.90 (978-0-7613-2356-3). An excellent oversize volume that explores the largest of the planets with amazing full-page color illustrations and a detailed text. Also use *Venus* (2002). (Rev: BL 8/02; HBG 3/03; SLJ 8/02) [523.4]

12290 Miller, Ron. *Mars* (7–10). Series: Worlds Beyond. 2005, Twenty-First Century LB $27.93 (978-0-7613-2362-4). Introduces readers to the planet Mars in a blend of easy-to-understand narrative and colorful space photos. (Rev: SLJ 12/05)

12291 Miller, Ron. *Saturn* (5–8). Series: Worlds Beyond. 2003, Millbrook LB $25.90 (978-0-7613-2360-0). A colorful volume that describes the discovery of the solar system and supplies details about the planet Saturn and its many rings. (Rev: BL 11/15/03; SLJ 12/03) [523.4]

12292 Miller, Ron. *Seven Wonders of the Gas Giants and Their Moons* (5–8). Illus. Series: Seven Wonders. 2011, Twenty-First Century LB $33.26 (978-0-7613-5449-9). Saturn's rings, the great red spot of Jupiter, and the auroras of Saturn are among the seven wonders explored in this interesting volume. Also use *Seven Wonders of the Rocky Planets and Their Moons* (2011). **e** (Rev: BL 3/1/11; SLJ 2/1/11) [523.4]

12293 Miller, Ron. *The Sun* (5–8). Series: Worlds Beyond. 2002, Millbrook LB $25.90 (978-0-7613-2355-6). Miller explores the nature and structure of the sun and the importance of solar energy. (Rev: BL 4/1/02; HBG 10/02; SLJ 5/02) [523.7]

12294 Miller, Ron. *Uranus and Neptune* (5–7). Series: Worlds Beyond. 2003, Twenty-First Century LB $25.90 (978-0-7613-2357-0). NASA photographs and computer-generated images are used throughout this account of the discovery and exploration of these two planets and what we know about their origin, composition, and evolution. (Rev: HBG 10/03; SLJ 8/03) [523.47]

12295 O'Connell, Kim A. *Mercury* (4–7). Series: Solar System. 2005, Enslow LB $25.26 (978-0-7660-5209-3). A blend of easy-to-understand narrative, vivid color photographs, and links to related online resources introduce Mercury. Also use *Pluto* (2005). (Rev: SLJ 12/05) [523.4]

12296 Scott, Elaine. *Mars and the Search for Life* (5–8). Illus. 2008, Clarion $17.00 (978-0-618-76695-6). Is there water on the Red Planet? Scott addresses this and other questions while discussing what we know about the planet, the various explorations that have already taken place, and possible future missions. (Rev: BCCB 12/08; BL 12/1/08; HB 1/09; SLJ 1/09) [576.8]

12297 Sherman, Josepha. *Neptune* (5–7). Series: Space! 2009, Marshall Cavendish LB $22.95 (978-0-7614-4246-2). Good for research, this volume presents facts clearly and concisely with many photos and other illustrations. (Rev: LMC 3–4/10; SLJ 2/10) [523.4]

12298 Sherman, Josepha. *Uranus* (4–8). Series: Space! 2010, Marshall Cavendish LB $32.79 (978-0-7614-4248-6). The author discusses the discovery of this planet, mysteries surrounding it, Voyager 2's expedition, and other key facts in this easily understood volume. Also use *Mars* (2010). **e** (Rev: LMC 3–4/10; SLJ 2/10) [523.47]

12299 Spence, Pam. *Sun Observer's Guide* (7–12). 2004, Firefly paper $14.95 (978-1-55297-941-9). A useful guide to the sun and the equipment that ensures safe observation of it. (Rev: BL 11/1/04) [522]

12300 Tourville, Amanda Doering. *Exploring the Solar System* (4–7). Illus. Series: Let's Explore Science. 2010, Rourke LB $32.79 (978-161590323-8). With information on the sun and moon, planets, comets, and asteroids, this is an introduction to the solar system and how scientists study it. (Rev: BL 9/1/10) [523.2]

Universe

12301 Asimov, Isaac. *The Birth of Our Universe* (5–8). Series: Isaac Asimov's 21st Century Library of the Universe. 2005, Gareth Stevens LB $26.00 (978-0-8368-3964-7). This is an update of a 1995 edition on the origins of the universe, with illustrations and photographs. (Rev: BL 3/1/05) [523.1]

12302 Fleisher, Paul. *The Big Bang* (5–8). Series: Great Ideas in Science. 2005, Twenty-First Century LB $27.93 (978-0-8225-2133-4). Students with a real interest in science will benefit most from this overview of theories about the creation of the universe, from creation myths onward. (Rev: BL 12/1/05; SLJ 12/05) [523.1]

12303 Goldsmith, Mike. *Universe: Journey into Deep Space* (4–7). Illus. by Mark A. Garlick. 2012, Kingfisher $17.99 (978-075346876-0). A visually pleasing and accessible introduction to the Milky Way and other galaxies. (Rev: BL 12/15/12) [523.1]

12304 Miller, Ron. *Stars and Galaxies* (7–10). Series: Worlds Beyond. 2005, Twenty-First Century LB $27.93 (978-0-7613-3466-8). A comprehensive overview of the universe, discussing theories and facts about neighboring stars and distant galaxies alike, with wonderful NASA photos mixed with original art. (Rev: BL 12/1/05; SLJ 12/05) [523.8]

12305 Perricone, Mike. *The Big Bang* (6–12). Series: Science Foundations. 2009, Chelsea House $35 (978-1-60413-015-7). This volume covers the pioneering work of Hubble and other key scientists before discussing what we now know about the origins of the universe and the implications of the Big Bang. (Rev: LMC 11–12/09) [523.1]

12306 Villard, Ray, and Lynette Cook. *Infinite Worlds: An Illustrated Voyage to Planets Beyond Our Sun* (8–12). 2005, Univ. of California $39.95 (978-0-520-23710-0). Using known data, the author and illustrator speculate about the likely appearance of planets in other solar systems. (Rev: BL 6/1–15/05) [523.21]

Biological Sciences

General and Miscellaneous

12307 Bottone, Frank G, Jr. *The Science of Life: Projects and Principles for Beginning Biologists* (5–8). 2001, Chicago Review paper $14.95 (978-1-55652-382-3). Twenty-five projects introduce readers to the basics of biology and the rigors of scientific research. (Rev: SLJ 11/01) [570.78]

12308 Brooks, Bruce. *The Red Wasteland* (6–10). 1995, Henry Holt $15.95 (978-0-8050-4495-9). A fine anthology of essays, stories, poems, and book excerpts by some of the best nature writers, who raise themes and questions about crucial issues relating to the environment. (Rev: BL 8/98; HBG 3/99; SLJ 6/98; VOYA 8/98) [808]

12309 Collard, Sneed B. *Science Warriors: The Battle Against Invasive Species* (5–8). Series: Scientists in the Field. 2008, Houghton Mifflin $17 (978-0-618-75636-0). Collard balances often grotesque images with weighty scientific fact in this examination of invasive species — plant and animal — that cost the United States $137 billion annually. Lexile 1110L (Rev: BL 12/1/08; HB 1–2/09; SLJ 1/1/09) [578.6]

12310 *DK Nature Encyclopedia* (5–8). 1998, DK paper $29.99 (978-0-7894-3411-1). A browsable reference book that covers topics including classification of living things, ecology, the origins and evolution of life, specific animal and plant groups, and the inner workings of plants and animals, all in a series of beautifully illustrated double-page spreads. (Rev: BL 12/1/98; SLJ 2/99) [574]

12311 Fullick, Ann. *Adaptation and Competition* (6–9). Series: Life Science in Depth. 2006, Heinemann LB $24.00 (978-1-4034-7518-3). Explores living organisms' ability to adapt to a wide array of climates and habitats and how these organisms compete with one another to survive. (Rev: BL 4/1/06) [587.4]

12312 Gallant, Roy A. *The Wonders of Biodiversity* (5–8). Series: The Story of Science. 2002, Benchmark $29.93 (978-0-7614-1427-8). Gallant discusses the importance of biodiversity, the plight of species that are affected by loss of habitat and other environmental factors, and species interdependence. (Rev: HBG 3/03; SLJ 2/03) [578]

12313 Johnson, Rebecca L. *Mighty Animal Cells* (5–7). Illus. by Jack Desrocher. Series: Microquests. 2007, Lerner LB $29.27 (978-0-8225-7137-7). Animal cell structure and cell division, followed by human cells, are discussed in chapters such as "Meet the Organelles," "What Cells Do," and "Cells with Special Talents" in this reader-friendly but information-packed book with cartoon illustrations to spice up the text. (Rev: BL 10/15/07; HB 1/08*; SLJ 11/07) [571.6]

12314 Kelsey, Elin. *Strange New Species: Astonishing Discoveries of Life on Earth* (5–8). 2005, Maple Tree $24.95 (978-1-897066-31-7). A large-format, well-illustrated introduction to plant and animal classification and to newly discovered species. (Rev: BL 10/15/05; SLJ 2/06) [578]

12315 Quinlan, Susan E. *The Case of the Monkeys That Fell from the Trees: And Other Mysteries in Tropical Nature* (5–8). 2003, Boyds Mills $15.95 (978-1-56397-902-6). Quinlan introduces plant and animal mysteries in South and Central American tropical forests and shows how scientists approached solving them. (Rev: BL 3/1/03; HBG 10/03; SLJ 3/03; VOYA 10/03) [508.313]

12316 Raham, R. Gary. *Dinosaurs in the Garden: An Evolutionary Guide to Backyard Biology* (6–10). 1988, Plexus $22.95 (978-0-937548-10-3). The author uses common creatures to explain how they fit into the scheme of nature and overall patterns of evolution. (Rev: BL 12/1/88) [575]

12317 Silverstein, Alvin. *Adaptation* (6–9). Series: Science Concepts. 2007, Lerner LB $31.93 (978-0-8225-3434-1). This volume looks at evolution and adaptation and explores the factors involved. (Rev: BL 12/1/07; SLJ 4/08) [578.4]

12318 Triefeldt, Laurie. *Plants and Animals* (4–8). Illus. Series: World of Wonder. 2007, Quill Driver $19.95 (978-1-884956-72-0). By the author of a nationally syndicated newspaper column called World of Wonder, this book, a companion to *People and Places*, covers a huge amount of material and will be helpful to report writers. (Rev: BL 4/1/08) [570]

12319 Turner, Pamela S. *Life on Earth — and Beyond* (5–8). 2008, Charlesbridge $19.95 (978-1-58089-133-2); paper $11.95 (978-1-58089-134-9). Readers follow NASA astrobiologist Chris McKay as he searches for microbes in extreme environments on Earth — in hopes of determining if life can survive in extreme environments in space. (Rev: BL 2/1/08; SLJ 3/08) [571.0919]

12320 VanCleave, Janice. *Janice VanCleave's A+ Projects in Biology: Winning Experiments for Science Fairs and Extra Credit* (6–10). 1993, Wiley paper $12.95 (978-0-471-58628-9). Offers a variety of experiments in botany, zoology, and the human body. (Rev: BL 1/15/94; SLJ 11/93) [574]

12321 Vancleave, Janice. *Step-By-Step Science Experiments in Biology* (5–8). Series: Janice VanCleave's First-Place Science Fair Projects. 2012, Rosen Central LB $33.25 (978-1-4488-6982-4). An updated volume with step-by-step instructions for 22 experiments mostly using easily found materials. (Rev: SLJ 10/12) [570]

12322 Walker, Pam, and Elaine Wood. *Ecosystem Science Fair Projects Using Worms, Leaves, Crickets, and Other Stuff* (6–12). Series: Biology! Best Science Projects. 2005, Enslow LB $26.60 (978-0-7660-2367-3). Biology science projects are clearly presented with background information necessary to full understanding of the underlying principles. (Rev: SLJ 7/05) [570]

12323 Wallace, Holly. *Classification* (4–7). Series: Life Processes. 2006, Heinemann LB $20.50 (978-1-4034-8845-9). A clear and colorful introduction to the classification of plants and animals. (Rev: BL 10/15/06) [570.1]

12324 Winston, Robert. *Life As We Know It* (3–7). Illus. 2012, DK $16.99 (978-075669169-1). Covering everything from cells to the six kingdoms, evolution, photosynthesis, habitats, migration, and ecosystems, this is a visually appealing book organized into five sections such as "Living Together" and "Secrets of Survival." (Rev: BL 6/12; SLJ 8/1/12) [001]

Botany

General and Miscellaneous

12325 Lincoff, Gary. *The Audubon Society Field Guide to North American Mushrooms* (7–12). 1981, Knopf $19.95 (978-0-394-51992-0). More than 700 species are introduced and pictured in color photographs. [589.2]

12326 Patent, Dorothy Hinshaw. *Plants on the Trail with Lewis and Clark.* (5–8). Photos by William Muñoz. 2003, Clarion $18.00 (978-0-618-06776-3). This introduction to the trees and plants seen by Lewis and Clark also discusses Lewis's training as a botanist and his contributions to the field. (Rev: BL 3/1/03; HBG 10/03; SLJ 5/03) [581.978]

12327 Silverstein, Alvin. *Photosynthesis* (5–9). Series: Science Concepts. 1998, Twenty-First Century LB $26.90 (978-0-7613-3000-4). Photosynthesis is explained, with a history of the discoveries about the process and material on related issues including acid rain and the greenhouse effect. (Rev: HBG 3/99; SLJ 2/99) [581.1]

Foods, Farms, and Ranches

GENERAL AND MISCELLANEOUS

12328 Artley, Bob. *Once Upon a Farm* (4–9). Illus. by author. 2000, Pelican $21.95 (978-1-56554-753-7). Fine watercolors accompany a readable look at the seasons as experienced by the author while growing up on a farm in Iowa. (Rev: SLJ 12/00) [630]

12329 *Bound for Glory: America in Color, 1939–43* (8–12). 2004, Abrams $35.00 (978-0-8109-4348-3). American farm life during the late 1930s and early 1940s is beautifully captured in these color photographs taken under the auspices of the Farm Security Administration, best known for earlier black-and-white collections. (Rev: BL 6/1–15/04) [779]

12330 Busenberg, Bonnie. *Vanilla, Chocolate and Strawberry: The Story of Your Favorite Flavors* (6–9). Series: Discovery! 1994, Lerner LB $23.93 (978-0-8225-1573-9). With the generous use of maps, diagrams, and photographs, this is the breezy overview of three popular flavors, how they are produced, and how they are used. (Rev: BL 6/1–15/94) [664.5]

12331 Chandler, Gary, and Kevin Graham. *Natural Foods and Products* (4–8). Series: Making a Better World. 1996, Twenty-First Century LB $25.90 (978-0-8050-4623-6). This work discusses genetically engineered foods, safe eco-friendly methods of growing crops, and companies that engage in safe practices. (Rev: BL 12/15/96; SLJ 1/97) [333.76]

12332 Chapman, Garry, and Gary Hodges. *Coffee* (5–8). Illus. Series: World Commodities. 2010, Black Rabbit LB $28.50 (978-159920584-7). Explores the cultural, environmental, and political story of coffee. (Rev: BL 10/1/10; LMC 5–6/11) [338.1]

12333 Damerow, Gail. *Your Chickens: A Kid's Guide to Raising and Showing* (4–7). 1993, Storey paper $14.95 (978-0-88266-823-9). A straightforward, practical guide on raising prize-winning chickens that is both thorough and filled with information. (Rev: BL 5/15/94; SLJ 1/94) [636.5]

12334 Damerow, Gail. *Your Goats: A Kid's Guide to Raising and Showing* (4–7). 1993, Storey paper $14.95 (978-0-88266-825-3). This is a complete guide to raising, breeding, and showing goats, with many useful tips and helpful illustrations. (Rev: BL 5/15/94; SLJ 1/94) [636.3]

12335 Dunn-Georgiou, Elisha. *Everything You Need to Know About Organic Foods* (6–10). Series: Need to Know Library. 2002, Rosen LB $27.95 (978-0-8239-3551-2). An examination of the techniques that produce organic foods and the benefits of eating foods that are free of certain additives. (Rev: BL 5/1/02; SLJ 6/02) [641.3]

12336 Dyer, Hadley. *Potatoes on Rooftops: Farming in the City* (4–7). Illus. 2012, Annick $24.95 (978-1-55451-425-0); paper $14.95 (978-1-55451-424-3). An appealing overview of the various — environmental, psychological, health — benefits of rooftop and container gardening and of school and community gardens. Lexile 1090L (Rev: BL 12/1/12; SLJ 12/12*) [630]

12337 Eagen, Rachel. *The Biography of Bananas* (4–7). Series: How Did That Get Here? 2005, Crabtree LB $26.60 (978-0-7787-2483-4). This richly illustrated title offers a wealth of information about the science and business of producing bananas. (Rev: BL 3/1/06) [634]

12338 Freedman, Jeri. *Genetically Modified Food: How Biotechnology Is Changing What We Eat* (7–12). 2009, Rosen LB $29.95 (978-1-4358-5025-5). This balanced, thorough book provides insight into the history, challenges, issues, and risks of genetic modification of the foods we eat. (Rev: LMC 10/09) [363.1]

12339 Gay, Kathlyn. *Food: The New Gold* (8–12). Illus. 2012, Lerner/Twenty-First Century LB $31.93 (978-0-7613-4607-4). From global hunger and food distribution to trends in farming, the impact of climate change, genetic modification of plants and animals, food safety, and food policy, this informative book provides clear text and interesting sidebars. (Rev: BL 12/1/12*; LMC 5–6/13; SLJ 9/12) [338.1]

12340 Hayhurst, Chris. *Everything You Need to Know About Food Additives* (6–10). Series: Need to Know Library. 2002, Rosen LB $27.95 (978-0-8239-3548-2). An examination of the kinds of additives used in foods, their benefits and disadvantages, and the alternatives available to people seeking a healthier diet. (Rev: BL 5/1/02) [664]

12341 Hughes, Meredith S. *Glorious Grasses: The Grains* (5–8). Series: Plants We Eat. 1999, Lerner LB $26.60 (978-0-8225-2831-9). A description of the history, cultivation, processing, and dietary importance of wheat, rice, corn, millet, barley, oats, and rye, plus recipes and activities. (Rev: BL 7/99; HBG 10/99; SLJ 8/99) [633.1]

12342 Jango-Cohen, Judith. *The History of Food* (5–8). Series: Major Inventions Through History. 2005, Twenty-First Century LB $26.60 (978-0-8225-2484-7). Addresses inventions in the food industry such as canning, pasteurization, and genetically modified crops. (Rev: SLJ 2/06)

12343 Lasky, Kathryn. *Sugaring Time* (4–7). 1998, Center for Applied Research paper $4.95 (978-0-87628-350-9). Through photographs and text, the process of maple sugar production in New England is described.

12344 Maestro, Betsy. *How Do Apples Grow?* (5–8). Illus. by Giulio Maestro. Series: Let's-Read-and-Find-Out. 1992, HarperCollins LB $16.89 (978-0-06-020056-5). The development of the apple from bud to fruit. (Rev: BL 12/15/91; HB 1–2/92; SLJ 2/92) [582]

12345 Morris, Neil. *Do You Know Where Your Food Comes From?* (4–7). Illus. 2006, Heinemann LB $32.86 (978-1-4034-8575-5). In this informative book students learn all about the global food market, where and how their food is produced, and how to make good food choices. (Rev: BL 12/1/06; SLJ 4/07) [363.8]

12346 Olney, Ross R. *The Farm Combine* (4–8). 1984, Walker LB $10.85 (978-0-8027-6568-0). The development of the reaper and thrasher is discussed, with information on today's combine harvester.

12347 Reynolds, Jan. *Cycle of Rice, Cycle of Life: A Story of Sustainable Farming* (4–7). Illus. 2009, Lee & Low $19.95 (978-1-60060-254-2). This photo-essay describes Balinese rice farming and its importance to the community. (Rev: BL 6/1–15/09; SLJ 6/09) [633.1]

12348 Rosen, Michael J. *Our Farm: Four Seasons with Five Kids on One Family's Farm* (3–7). Photos by author. 2008, Darby Creek $18.95 (978-1-58196-067-9). An interesting photo-essay covering a year on an Ohio family farm. (Rev: SLJ 9/08) [630]

12349 Vogel, Julia. *Local Farms and Sustainable Food* (3–7). Series: Language Arts Explorer: Save the Planet. 2010, Cherry Lake LB $27.07 (978-1-60279-660-7). Students are given a mission at the beginning of the book and must use creative thinking and problem solving to gather facts as they travel on a virtual trip through the process of growing and distributing organic food. (Rev: LMC 8–9/10; SLJ 4/10) [630]

12350 Webber, Desiree Morrison. *Bone Head: Story of the Longhorn* (4–7). Illus. by Sandy Shropshire. 2003,

Eakin $16.95 (978-1-57168-763-0). The longhorn's characteristics and the reasons for its early success but decline with the arrival of the railroad are explored in appealing text and archival photographs. (Rev: SLJ 2/04) [636.2]

VEGETABLES

12351 Hughes, Meredith S. *Cool as a Cucumber, Hot as a Pepper* (5–8). Series: Foods We Eat. 1999, Lerner LB $26.60 (978-0-8225-2832-6). This lively book on vegetables gives botanical information, details on growing and harvesting, the history of many of these plants, and a number of mouth-watering recipes. (Rev: BL 7/99; HBG 10/99; SLJ 8/99) [635]

Forestry and Trees

12352 Bjornlund, Lydia. *Deforestation* (7–12). Series: Compact Research. 2009, ReferencePoint LB $25.95 (978-1-60152-075-3). Answering questions including "What Are the Consequences of Deforestation?," Bjornlund describes how the world's forests are being destroyed and discusses sustainable solutions for the future. (Rev: LMC 1–2/10)

12353 Little, Elbert L. *The Audubon Society Field Guide to North American Trees: Eastern Region* (7–12). 1980, Knopf $19.95 (978-0-394-50760-6). This volume describes through text and pictures of leaves, needles, and so on, the trees found east of the Rocky Mountains. [582.16]

12354 Little, Elbert L. *The Audubon Society Field Guide to North American Trees: Western Region* (7–12). 1980, Knopf $19.95 (978-0-394-50761-3). Trees west of the Rockies are identified and pictured in photographs and drawings. [582.16]

12355 Petrides, George A. *A Field Guide to Trees and Shrubs* (7–12). 1973, Houghton Mifflin paper $19.00 (978-0-395-35370-7). A total of 646 varieties found in northern United States and southern Canada are described and illustrated. [582.1]

12356 Spilsbury, Richard. *Deforestation* (6–8). Series: Development or Destruction? 2012, Rosen Central LB $27.95 (978-1-4488-6989-3); paper $11.75 (978-1-4488-6996-1). With a focus on palm oil in Indonesia and the pulp industry in Finland among others, this volume takes a look at deforestation in various countries and the prospects for a sustainable future. (Rev: LMC 10/12; SLJ 9/12) [338.1]

12357 Whitman, Ann H., and Jane Friedman, eds. *Familiar Trees of North America: Eastern Region* (8–12). 1986, Knopf paper $9.00 (978-0-394-74851-1). As well as pictures and descriptions, this guide supplies historical information, habitats, and uses for 80 trees commonly found in the eastern parts of North America. [582.16]

12358 Whitman, Ann H., and Jane Friedman, eds. *Familiar Trees of North America: Western Region* (8–12). 1986, Knopf paper $9.00 (978-0-394-74852-8). This pocket guide covers 80 trees found commonly in the western United States. [582.16]

12359 Zim, Herbert S., and Alexander C. Martin. *Trees* (5–8). 1991, Western paper $21.27 (978-0-307-64056-7). A small, handy volume packed with information and color illustrations that help identify our most important trees. [582.16]

Plants and Flowers

12360 Dowden, Anne O. *From Flower to Fruit* (6–9). 1984, HarperCollins $14.95 (978-0-690-04402-7). A description of seeds, how they are scattered, and how fruit is produced. [582]

12361 Hood, Susan, and National Audubon Society, eds. *Wildflowers* (5–8). 1998, Scholastic paper $17.95 (978-0-590-05464-5). Fifty common wildflowers are pictured and described, along with information on what equipment to use and what to look for to observe and study wildflowers (leaves, blooms, habitat, height, range). (Rev: BL 8/98; SLJ 8/98) [583]

12362 Johnson, Sylvia A. *Morning Glories* (4–7). 1985, Lerner LB $22.60 (978-0-8225-1462-6). Color photographs display the stages of this plant's development. (Rev: BCCB 3/86; BL 4/15/86; SLJ 4/86)

12363 Lerner, Carol. *Cactus* (4–7). 1992, Morrow LB $14.89 (978-0-688-09637-3). After explaining the parts of the cactus and how it can exist in near-waterless environments, this account describes different species. (Rev: BCCB 10/92; HB 1–2/93; SLJ 12/92) [635.7]

12364 Mooney, Carla. *Sunscreen for Plants* (4–7). Illus. Series: A Great Idea! Going Green. 2009, Norwood LB $18.95 (978-159953344-5). Discusses how exposure to the sun affects plants and posits potential inventions that could reduce the problem of sun damage. (Rev: BL 2/15/10) [632]

12365 Silverstein, Alvin. *Plants* (7–10). Series: Kingdoms of Life. 1996, Twenty-First Century LB $25.90 (978-0-8050-3519-3). The classification system of plants is explained, from simple plants through ferns and on to flowering plants. (Rev: BL 6/1–15/96; SLJ 7/96) [581]

12366 Silvey, Anita. *The Plant Hunters: True Stories of Their Daring Adventures to the Far Corners of the Earth* (5–8). Illus. 2012, Farrar $19.99 (978-037430908-4). A fascinating account of the work of botanists around the world, mainly during the 19th and 20th centuries. Lexile 1170L (Rev: BL 4/15/12; LMC 10/12; SLJ 6/12) [580.75]

12367 Spellenberg, Richard. *Familiar Flowers of North America: Eastern Region* (8–12). 1986, Knopf paper

$9.00 (978-0-394-74843-6). Photographs, diagrams, and descriptions are found in this guide to 80 wildflowers found in the eastern regions of North America. Also use *Familiar Flowers of North America: Western Region*. [582.13]

Seeds

12368 Burns, Diane L. *Berries, Nuts and Seeds* (4–7). Illus. by John F. McGee. 1996, NorthWord paper $7.95 (978-1-55971-573-7). Each page in this guide is devoted to a description of a single berry, nut, or seed. (Rev: BL 2/15/97) [582.13]

Zoology

General and Miscellaneous

12369 Aaseng, Nathan. *Nature's Poisonous Creatures* (5–9). Series: Scientific American Sourcebooks. 1997, Twenty-First Century LB $28.90 (978-0-8050-4690-8). After a general introduction to animal poisons, why they are produced, and their composition, this book devotes separate chapters to such venom-bearing vertebrates and invertebrates as sea wasps, blue-ringed octopi, African killer bees, and marine toads. (Rev: BL 2/1/98; SLJ 8/98) [591.6]

12370 Bloom, Steve. *Untamed: Animals Around the World* (4–7). Illus. by Emmanuelle Zicot. 2005, Abrams $18.95 (978-0-8109-5956-9). Enthralling photographs of wild animals are accompanied by brief facts and an environmentalist message. (Rev: BL 12/1/05) [636]

12371 Burnie, David. *How Animals Work: Why and How Animals Do the Things They Do* (5–8). Illus. 2010, DK $24.99 (978-0-7566-5897-7). This highly visual, oversize volume covers everything from animal anatomy, locomotion, diet, and habitat to evolution and communication. (Rev: BL 9/1/10; SLJ 12/1/10) [571.1]

12372 Cobb, Allan B. *Super Science Projects About Animals and Their Habitats* (4–8). Series: Psyched for Science. 2000, Rosen LB $26.50 (978-0-8239-3175-0). Six hand-on activities are introduced to help children observe animals and to study their adjustments to climate, habitat, and food. (Rev: SLJ 9/00) [591]

12373 Doris, Ellen. *Meet the Arthropods* (4–7). 1996, Thames & Hudson $16.95 (978-0-500-19010-4). Such arthropods as the horseshoe crab, potato beetle, and praying mantis are introduced with photographs and activities. (Rev: BL 10/15/96) [595.2]

12374 Ganeri, Anita. *Animals* (4–7). Series: Inside and Outside Guide. 2006, Heinemann LB $29.29 (978-1-4034-9084-1). This attractive guide provides in-depth introductions to 12 animals, with double-page spreads

focusing on each animal's identifying characteristics and behaviors. (Rev: BL 10/15/06) [571.3]

12375 Grayson, Robert. *Military* (4–7). Series: Working Animals. 2010, Marshall Cavendish LB $19.95 (978-1-60870-164-3). Describes the varied roles that animals — ranging from rats and pigeons to dogs, dolphins, and horses — have played in military operations. (Rev: SLJ 12/1/10) [355.424]

12376 Haven, Kendall. *Animal Mummies* (4–8). 2010, Scholastic $19.99 (978-0-545-03460-9). A fascinating overview of the practice of mummifying animals, with large, eye-catching photographs. (Rev: LMC 10/10)

12377 Hile, Lori. *Animal Survival* (4–7). Series: Extreme Survival. 2011, Heinemann LB $33.50 (978-1-4109-3973-9). Hile tells stories of animals that have beaten the odds and survived disasters. (Rev: SLJ 8/11)

12378 Hodgkins, Fran. *Animals Among Us: Living with Suburban Wildlife* (5–8). 2000, Linnet LB $19.50 (978-0-208-02478-7). This book discusses the behavior and lifestyles of animals such as deer, coyotes, bears, skunks, and bats that live in suburbs, close to their original haunts. (Rev: BL 6/1–15/00; HB 7–8/00; HBG 10/00; SLJ 9/00; VOYA 12/00) [591.7]

12379 Johnson, Sylvia A. *Silkworms* (4–7). 1982, Lerner paper $5.95 (978-0-8225-9557-1). The life cycle of the silkworm, told in text and striking color pictures. [595.78]

12380 Kneidel, Sally. *Slugs, Bugs, and Salamanders: Discovering Animals in Your Garden* (5–7). Illus. by Anna-Maria L. Crum. 1997, Fulcrum paper $16.95 (978-1-55591-313-7). As well as introducing backyard insects and other small creatures, this account gives a number of tips on growing healthy flowers and vegetables. (Rev: SLJ 10/97) [595.7]

12381 Lauber, Patricia. *Fur, Feathers, and Flippers: How Animals Live Where They Do* (4–8). 1994, Scholastic paper $4.95 (978-0-590-45072-0). Using various habitats such as the grasslands of East Africa as examples, this photoessay describes how animals have adapted to their different environments. (Rev: BL 12/1/94*; SLJ 12/94) [591.5]

12382 *Mammal Anatomy: An Illustrated Guide* (8–12). 2010, Marshall Cavendish LB $99.80 (978-0-7614-7882-9). This detailed yet accessible volume (a repackaging of an earlier multivolume set) examines the anatomy and physiology of mammals including chimpanzees, dolphins, elephants, giraffes, gray whales, grizzly bears, kangaroos, lions, manatees, seals, squirrels, wolves, and zebras. (Rev: BLO 1/21/10; LMC 1–2/10) [571.3]

12383 Marrin, Albert. *Little Monsters: The Creatures That Live on Us and in Us* (4–7). Illus. 2011, Dutton $19.99 (978-052542262-4). Not for the faint of heart, this book discusses — and shows in graphic detail —

parasites that live on or in the human body (leeches, tapeworms, and so forth). (Rev: BLO 2/15/12) [578.6]

12384 Martin, Claudia. *Farming* (4–7). Series: Working Animals. 2010, Marshall Cavendish LB $19.95 (978-1-60870-162-9). Animals' varied roles in agriculture are described in this attractive, informative book. Also use *Helpers* (2010), about animals that help the blind and deaf. (Rev: SLJ 12/1/10) [636]

12385 Mezzanotte, Jim. *Police* (4–7). Series: Working Animals. 2010, Marshall Cavendish LB $19.95 (978-1-60870-166-7). Animals' varied roles in police operations — search-and-rescue, tracking, bomb sniffing, and so forth — are described in this attractive, informative book. (Rev: SLJ 12/1/10) [363.2]

12386 Noyes, Deborah. *One Kingdom: Our Lives with Animals* (7–10). 2006, Houghton $18.00 (978-0-618-49914-4). The bond between humans and animals is the topic of this thoughtful photo-essay that looks in particular at zoos and conservation. (Rev: BL 10/15/06; HB 9–10/06; LMC 10/06; SLJ 11/06) [590]

12387 Palazzo, Tony. *The Biggest and the Littlest Animals* (4–7). Illus. by author. 1973, Lion LB $13.95 (978-0-87460-225-8). Many ways of comparing animals, including size and mobility, are explored.

Amphibians and Reptiles

GENERAL AND MISCELLANEOUS

12388 Behler, John. *National Audubon Society First Field Guide: Reptiles* (4–8). 1999, Scholastic $17.95 (978-0-590-05467-6); paper $11.95 (978-0-590-05487-4). This richly illustrated manual discusses common characteristics of North American reptiles, then presents individual species under four groups: crocodiles, turtles, lizards, and snakes. (Rev: BL 3/15/99; SLJ 7/99) [597.9]

12389 Crump, Marty. *Amphibians, Reptiles, and Their Conservation* (6–12). 2002, Linnet LB $25.00 (978-0-208-02511-1). After describing these animals and giving the pertinent scientific information, the author describes the challenges to their survival and what can be done to save them. (Rev: BL 12/1/02; HBG 3/03; SLJ 1/03; VOYA 6/03) [597.9]

12390 Dennard, Deborah. *Reptiles* (5–7). Illus. by Jennifer Owings Dewey. Series: Our Wild World. 2004, NorthWord $16.95 (978-1-55971-880-6). A compilation of four shorter books published by NorthWord in 2003, this volume examines the physical characteristics, natural habitat, diet, and behavior of alligators, crocodiles, lizards, snakes, and turtles. (Rev: SLJ 8/04) [597.9]

12391 Gibbons, Whit. *Their Blood Runs Cold: Adventures with Reptiles and Amphibians* (7–12). 1983, Univ. of Alabama paper $15.95 (978-0-8173-0133-0).

An informal guide, geographically arranged, to snakes, crocodiles, turtles, salamanders, and toads. [597.6]

12392 Hutchinson, Mark. *Reptiles* (4–7). Illus. Series: Insiders. 2011, Simon & Schuster $16.99 (978-144243276-5). With dramatic 3-D illustrations, this volume offers a general overview of reptiles and then focuses on 12 specific animals, exploring their anatomy, behavior, and other characteristics. (Rev: BL 9/15/11; LMC 1–2/12) [597.9]

12393 Wilkes, Sarah. *Amphibians* (5–9). Series: World Almanac Library of the Animal Kingdom. 2006, World Almanac LB $31.00 (978-0-8368-6208-9). This colorful guide identifies common species of amphibians and examines their physical characteristics, habitats, diets, behaviors, and life cycles. (Rev: SLJ 12/06) [597.5]

12394 Zabludoff, Marc. *The Reptile Class* (5–9). Series: Family Trees. 2005, Benchmark LB $32.79 (978-0-7614-1820-7). Habits, habitats, and other aspects of this varied class of animals; an engaging book with plenty of facts for report-writers. (Rev: SLJ 6/06) [597.9]

ALLIGATORS AND CROCODILES

12395 Hamilton, Sue. *Attacked by a Crocodile* (4–7). Series: Close Encounters of the Wild Kind. 2010, ABDO LB $27.07 (978-1-60453-929-5). Exciting stories and graphic photographs add high-interest appeal to the information about crocodiles and advice on avoiding and surviving such an attack. (Rev: LMC 10/10; SLJ 5/10) [597.98]

12396 Jango-Cohen, Judith. *Crocodiles* (5–8). Series: AnimalWays. 2000, Marshall Cavendish LB $31.36 (978-0-7614-1136-9). This book examines the habitat, range, classification, evolution, anatomy, behavior, and endangered status of the crocodile. (Rev: BL 1/1–15/01; HBG 3/01) [597.98]

12397 Scherer, Glenn, and Marty Fletcher. *The American Crocodile: Help Save This Endangered Species!* (5–7). Illus. Series: Saving Endangered Species. 2007, Enslow $33.27 (978-1-59845-041-5). Report writers will welcome the information included in this volume and at the recommended Web links. (Rev: SLJ 11/07) [597.98]

12398 Snyder, Trish. *Alligator and Crocodile Rescue: Changing the Future for Endangered Wildlife* (4–8). Series: Firefly Animal Rescue. 2006, Firefly LB $19.95 (978-1-55297-920-4); paper $9.95 (978-1-55297-919-8). Examines the work being done to protect alligators and crocodiles in their natural habitats and also looks at the physical characteristics, diets, behaviors, and life cycles of these reptiles. (Rev: SLJ 12/06) [597.98]

FROGS AND TOADS

12399 Turner, Pamela S. *The Frog Scientist* (5–9). Photos by Andy Comins. Series: Scientists in the Field.

2009, Houghton Mifflin $18 (978-0-618-71716-3). Why are frog populations disappearing at an alarming rate? This fascinating book recounts the research of African American biologist Tyrone Hayes and explains the advances he has made in this environmentally sensitive field. ALA Notable Books 2010. Lexile 950L (Rev: BL 8/09*; HB 9–10/09; SLJ 9/09) [597.8]

SNAKES AND LIZARDS

12400 Blobaum, Cindy. *Awesome Snake Science! 40 Activities for Learning About Snakes* (5–8). Illus. 2012, Chicago Review paper $14.95 (978-1-56976-807-5). Students learn about snakes and their biology through text, experiments, art projects, and games. e (Rev: LMC 5–6/13; SLJ 7/12) [597.96071]

12401 Coates, Jennifer. *Lizards* (7–12). Illus. Series: Our Best Friends. 2009, Eldorado Ink LB $26.95 (978-193290431-4). An in-depth review of the benefits and responsibilities of owning a lizard, covering choosing the best lizard, potential health problems, and how to make an attractive terrarium. (Rev: BL 6/1–15/09) [639.3]

12402 Collard, Sneed B. *Lizards* (4–7). Illus. 2012, Charlesbridge $16.95 (978-158089324-4); paper $7.95 (978-15808932-5-1). A clear, well-designed introduction to lizards and their life cycle, habitats, diets, and so forth, with plenty of close-up photographs. e (Rev: BL 1/1/12; LMC 11–12/12; SLJ 5/1/12) [597.95]

12403 Gaywood, Martin, and Ian Spellerberg. *Snakes* (6–12). Series: WorldLife Library. 1999, Voyageur paper $16.95 (978-0-89658-449-5). Facts about snakes and their ability to adapt to their environment are accompanied by discussion of their relationship with humans and eye-catching full-color photographs. (Rev: SLJ 4/00) [597.96]

12404 Gish, Melissa. *Komodo Dragons* (5–8). Illus. Series: Living Wild. 2011, Creative Education LB $23.95 (978-160818080-6). Gish looks at komodo dragons' habitats, physical characteristics, behaviors, relationships with humans, endangered status, and role in folklore. (Rev: BL 12/1/11) [597.95]

12405 Greenaway, Theresa. *Snakes* (4–7). Series: The Secret World of . . . 2001, Raintree LB $18.98 (978-0-7368-3510-7). A look at the world of snakes with material on their structure, habitats, behavior, food, mating habits, and enemies. (Rev: BL 10/15/01) [597.96]

12406 Hamilton, Sue. *Bitten by a Rattlesnake* (4–7). Series: Close Encounters of the Wild Kind. 2010, ABDO LB $27.07 (978-1-60453-930-1). Exciting stories and graphic photographs add high-interest appeal to the information about these snakes and advice on avoiding and surviving such an attack. (Rev: LMC 10/10; SLJ 5/10) [597.96]

12407 Montgomery, Sy. *The Snake Scientist* (5–8). Series: Scientists in the Field. 1999, Houghton Mifflin

$16.00 (978-0-395-87169-0). This account captures the excitement of scientific discovery by focusing on a zoologist and young students who are studying the red-sided garter snake in Canada. (Rev: BCCB 4/99; BL 2/15/99; HB 7–8/99; HBG 9/99; SLJ 5/99) [597.96]

12408 Pipe, Jim. *The Giant Book of Snakes and Slithery Creatures* (4–8). 1998, Millbrook LB $27.90 (978-0-7613-0804-1). This richly illustrated, oversize volume contains details about snakes, lizards, and amphibians. (Rev: BL 8/98; HBG 9/98; SLJ 12/98) [597.9]

12409 Roever, J. M. *Snake Secrets* (6–9). 1979, Walker LB $11.85 (978-0-8027-6333-4). An in-depth look at snakes, their behavior, and how people react to them. [597.96]

12410 Simon, Seymour. *Poisonous Snakes* (6–9). 1981, Macmillan $11.95 (978-0-590-07513-8). An explanation of venom and fangs is given and an introduction to the world's most famous poisonous snakes. [597.9]

TORTOISES AND TURTLES

12411 Hickman, Pamela. *Turtle Rescue: Changing the Future for Endangered Wildlife* (4–8). Series: Firefly Animal Rescue. 2006, Firefly $19.95 (978-1-55297-916-7); paper $9.95 (978-1-55297-915-0). Hickman provides a detailed but accessible overview of the dangers facing turtles around the world and what is being done to protect them. (Rev: SLJ 6/06) [597.92]

12412 Lockwood, Sophie. *Sea Turtles* (4–7). Illus. Series: World of Reptiles. 2006, Child's World LB $29.93 (978-1-59296-550-2). In addition to the kind of information needed for reports, Lockwood discusses conservation, how scientists track turtles, and the turtle's appearances in folklore and art. (Rev: BL 4/1/06) [597.92]

12413 Stefoff, Rebecca. *Turtles* (4–8). Illus. Series: AnimalWays. 2007, Marshall Cavendish LB $23.95 (978-0-7614-2539-7). Report writers will find plenty of valuable information about turtles' anatomy, habitat, evolution, and appearances in literature and legend as well as discussion of conservation efforts and many attractive photographs. (Rev: BL 2/8/08) [597.92]

Animal Behavior

GENERAL AND MISCELLANEOUS

12414 Allman, Toney. *Animal Life in Groups* (5–8). Series: Animal Behavior. 2009, Chelsea House $32.95 (978-1-60413-142-0). Examining the reasons why animals choose to live in groups, this volume discusses safety in numbers and various ways animals can cooperate, looking in particular at colonies, schools and flocks, herds, predator groups, and primate societies. (Rev: LMC 11–12/09) [591.5]

12415 Crump, Donald J., ed. *How Animals Behave: A New Look at Wildlife* (5–8). 1984, National Geographic LB $12.50 (978-0-87044-505-7). A general, colorful introduction to why and how animals perform such functions as courting, living together, and caring for their young. [591.5]

12416 Crump, Donald J., ed. *Secrets of Animal Survival* (4–8). 1983, National Geographic LB $12.50 (978-0-87044-431-9). The survival tactics of animals in five geographical environments are discussed.

12417 Flegg, Jim. *Animal Movement* (4–7). Illus. by David Hosking. Series: Wild World. 1991, Millbrook LB $17.90 (978-1-878137-21-0). Various ways animals move and at what speeds are discussed in this well-illustrated book. (Rev: BL 1/1/91; SLJ 2/92) [591.18]

12418 Goldstein, Natalie. *Animal Hunting and Feeding* (5–8). Series: Animal Behavior. 2009, Chelsea House $32.95 (978-1-60413-143-7). Examining the ways in which animals hunt and feed, this volume discusses waiting for food, sharing and taking, plant-eating animals, generalists and specialists, and scavengers and decomposers. (Rev: LMC 11–12/09) [591.5]

12419 Johnson, Rebecca L. *Zombie Makers: True Stories of Nature's Undead* (4–8). Illus. 2012, Millbrook LB $30.60 (978-0-7613-8633-9). A variety of different parasitic creatures that turn their hosts into some form of "zombie" are profiled in this fascinating title. ALA Notable Books 2013. **e** (Rev: BLO 10/1/12; SLJ 10/12*; VOYA 2/13) [578.6]

12420 McGrath, Susan. *The Amazing Things Animals Do* (4–7). 1989, National Geographic $8.95 (978-0-87044-709-9). Unusual animal behavior is shown in such areas as communication, motion, raising young, and survival. (Rev: SLJ 2/90) [591.5]

12421 Markle, Sandra. *Animal Heroes: True Rescue Stories* (4–7). 2009, Lerner LB $29.27 (978-0-8225-7884-0). A compelling collection of stories of animals saving human lives — from a dog on 9/11 to a gorilla, a cat, and dolphins; with factual information about each animal. (Rev: BL 7/08; LMC 3–4/09) [636.088]

12422 Rodriguez, Ana María. *Secret of the Puking Penguins . . . and More!* (5–7). Illus. Series: Animal Secrets Revealed! 2008, Enslow LB $17.95 (978-0-7660-2955-2). Unusual habits of a variety of animals are revealed along with the ways in which scientists establish these facts. (Rev: BL 12/1/08; SLJ 3/09) [597.9]

12423 Settel, Joanne. *Exploding Ants: Amazing Facts About How Animals Adapt* (4–8). 1999, Simon & Schuster $16.00 (978-0-689-81739-7). Lurid details of animal life, such as predatory fireflies, regurgitating birds, and bloodsuckers, are presented in this attention-getting collection of biological facts. (Rev: BCCB 3/99; BL 4/15/99; HBG 10/99; SLJ 4/99) [591.5]

12424 Singer, Marilyn. *Venom* (5–8). Illus. 2007, Darby Creek $19.95 (978-1-58196-043-3). Poisonous animals

and insects of the land, sea, and air are featured in this book, with plenty of strange facts and weird photographs. (Rev: BL 10/1/07; SLJ 11/07) [592.16]

12425 Thimmesh, Catherine. *Friends: True Stories of Extraordinary Animal Friendships* (4–8). Illus. 2011, Houghton Mifflin $16.99 (978-0-547-39010-9). Thirteen short real-life stories of unlikely animal friendships — a basset hound and an owl, for example. (Rev: BL 9/1/11; SLJ 7/11) [591.5]

COMMUNICATION

12426 Sayre, April Pulley. *Secrets of Sound: Studying the Calls and Songs of Whales, Elephants, and Birds* (4–7). 2002, Houghton Mifflin $17.00 (978-0-618-01514-6). Fascinating profiles of scientists who study animal sounds serve to introduce readers to a number of scientific concepts. (Rev: BL 12/1/02; HB 9–10/02; HBG 3/03; SLJ 10/02) [559.159]

MIGRATION

12427 Schueller, Gretel H., and Sheila K. Schueller. *Animal Migration* (5–8). Series: Animal Behavior. 2009, Chelsea House $32.95 (978-1-60413-127-7). Examining how and why animals migrate, this volume discusses birds, whales and other marine animals, animals that migrate on foot, sea turtles and salmon, and so forth. (Rev: LMC 11–12/09) [591.5]

TRACKS

12428 Murie, Olaus J. *A Field Guide to Animal Tracks*. 2nd ed. (7–12). 1996, Houghton Mifflin paper $8.95 (978-0-395-58297-8). This important volume in the Peterson Field Guide series first appeared in 1954 and now has become a classic in the area of identifying animal tracks and droppings. [591.5]

Animal Species

GENERAL AND MISCELLANEOUS

12429 Alden, Peter. *Peterson First Guide to Mammals of North America* (8–12). 1988, Houghton Mifflin paper $5.95 (978-0-395-91181-5). An uncluttered basic guide to mammal identification with many illustrations and useful background material. (Rev: BL 5/15/87) [599]

12430 Carson, Mary Kay. *The Bat Scientists* (7–10). Photos by Tom Uhlman. Series: Scientists in the Field. 2010, Houghton Mifflin $18.99 (978-0-547-19956-6). A fascinating photo-filled overview of bats, the environmental challenges they face, and the ways in which scientists study them. ALA Notable Books 2011. (Rev: BL 10/15/10*; SLJ 11/1/10) [599.4]

12431 Carson, Mary Kay. *Emi and the Rhino Scientist* (5–8). Illus. Series: Scientists in the Field. 2007, Houghton $18.00 (978-0-618-64639-5). Emi, a rhinoceros at the Cincinnati Zoo, gives birth in captivity (which is unusual for a rhino) thanks to the help of scientist Terri Roth in this exciting and informative account. (Rev: BL 12/1/07; HB 11/07; SLJ 11/07) [599.66]

12432 Crump, Donald J., ed. *Amazing Animals of Australia* (6–9). 1984, National Geographic LB $12.50 (978-0-87044-520-0). A colorful introduction to such animals as the kangaroo and platypus. (Rev: BL 6/1/85) [591.9]

12433 Fenton, M. Brock. *Just Bats* (7–12). 1983, Univ. of Toronto paper $15.95 (978-0-8020-6464-6). An introduction to this frequently misunderstood and very useful flying rodent. [599.4]

12434 Gish, Melissa. *Bison* (5–8). Illus. Series: Living Wild. 2011, Creative Education LB $23.95 (978-1-60818-077-6). Gish looks at the bison's habitats, physical characteristics, behaviors, relationships with humans, protected status, importance to Native Americans, and status as a symbol of the American West. (Rev: BL 12/1/11; SLJ 11/1/11) [599.64]

12435 Green, Jen, and David Burnie. *Mammal* (5–9). Series: DK/Google e.guides. 2005, DK $17.99 (978-0-7566-1139-2). This highly illustrated guide introduces readers to the evolution and diversity of mammals and provides a link to a Web site that serves as a gateway to additional resources. (Rev: SLJ 8/05) [599]

12436 Halls, Kelly Milner. *Wild Horses: Galloping Through Time* (4–7). Illus. by Mark Hallet. 2008, Darby Creek $18.95 (978-1-58196-065-5). Gorgeous photographs and clear text tell the history of horses and document the presence of wild horses worldwide. (Rev: BLO 7/29/08; SLJ 10/1/08) [599.665]

12437 Jarrow, Gail, and Paul Sherman. *The Naked Mole-Rat Mystery: Scientific Sleuths at Work* (6–8). Series: Discovery! 1996, Lerner LB $28.75 (978-0-8225-2853-1). This is a thorough exploration of what we know, and how we found out about, the naked mole-rat, which is a mammal but has a reptilian body temperature and lives in colonies like social insects. (Rev: BL 9/1/96; SLJ 8/96) [599.32]

12438 Laidlaw, Rob. *Wild Animals in Captivity* (4–7). Illus. 2008, Fitzhenry & Whiteside $19.95 (978-1-55455-025-8). Animal rights emerge front and center in this passionate, well-researched and convincing case for replacing zoos with wildlife sanctuaries and conservation centers. (Rev: BLO 2/5/09; SLJ 7/08) [636.088]

12439 Marrin, Albert. *Saving the Buffalo* (5–7). 2006, Scholastic $18.99 (978-0-439-71854-7). This well-written, well-illustrated history traces the fortunes of the American bison from the days when huge herds covered the plains to near extinction at the end of the 19th century and then to an amazing recovery over the past century or so. (Rev: SLJ 12/06*) [599.64]

12440 Momatiuk, Yva, and John Eastcott. *Face to Face with Wild Horses* (5–8). Illus. Series: Face to Face with

Animals. 2009, National Geographic $16.95 (978-1-4263-0466-8). Riveting close-up photographs show wild horses in their own environment; back matter includes sections on How You Can Help, It's Your Turn, and Facts at a Glance. (Rev: BL 4/1/09) [599.665]

12441 Murray, Peter. *Rhinos* (4–7). Series: The World of Mammals. 2005, Child's World LB $29.93 (978-1-59296-502-1). Arresting photographs and engaging text introduce the anatomy, behavior, habitat, and life cycle of the rhinoceros as well as the threats to the animal's survival in the wild. (Rev: SLJ 3/06) [599.72]

12442 Read, Nicholas. *City Critters: Wildlife in the Urban Jungle* (6–9). 2012, Orca paper $19.95 (978-1-55469-394-8). From rats and raccoons to insects and spiders, birds, and more exotic animals, this interesting survey discusses how wild animals adapt to life in our cities. ℮ (Rev: LMC 11–12/12; SLJ 5/1/12; VOYA 8/12) [591.75]

12443 Ross, Mark C., and David Reesor. *Predator: Life and Death in the African Bush* (7–12). 2007, Abrams $35.00 (978-0-8109-9301-3). Lions, cheetahs, hyenas, crocodiles, and leopards are shown in various activities in their native habitats, with accompanying text that discusses their daily lives, anatomy, behavior, and so forth. (Rev: BL 9/15/07) [599.7096]

12444 Siwanowicz, Igor. *Animals Up Close* (4–8). Illus. by author. 2009, DK $16.99 (978-0-7566-4513-7). Dramatic close-up photographs display the features of small creatures of all kinds; fascinating for browsing, this book also offers enough information for reports. (Rev: BLO 5/27/09; SLJ 8/09) [500]

12445 Webber, Desiree Morrison. *The Buffalo Train Ride* (4–7). Illus. by Sandy Shropshire. 1999, Eakin $14.95 (978-1-57168-275-8). This is a history of the American buffalo, how it was hunted to near extinction, and the modern efforts to make sure it survives, with special attention to the work of William Hornaday. (Rev: HBG 3/00; SLJ 3/00) [591.52]

APE FAMILY

12446 Goodall, Jane. *The Chimpanzees I Love: Saving Their World and Ours* (5–8). 2001, Scholastic paper $18.95 (978-0-439-21310-3). Jane Goodall combines details of her own life researching chimpanzees with fact-filled descriptions of the animals' behavior and a cry for chimpanzee protection. (Rev: BL 12/1/01; HB 1–2/02; HBG 3/02; SLJ 9/01*) [599]

12447 Lewin, Ted, and Betsy Lewin. *Gorilla Walk* (4–8). 1999, Lothrop LB $17.89 (978-0-688-16510-9). A beautifully illustrated book about the Lewins' trip to Uganda to study mountain gorillas. (Rev: BL 8/99; HBG 4/00; SLJ 9/99) [599.8]

12448 Lockwood, Sophie. *Baboons* (4–7). Series: The World of Mammals. 2005, Child's World LB $29.93 (978-1-59296-497-0). Arresting photographs and engaging text introduce the anatomy, behavior, habitat, and life cycle of the baboon as well as the threats to the animal's survival in the wild. (Rev: SLJ 3/06) [599.8]

12449 Pimm, Nancy Roe. *The Heart of the Beast: Eight Great Gorilla Stories* (4–7). 2007, Darby Creek $18.95 (978-1-58196-054-9). True stories about famous gorillas provide information on their mental and physical development, behavior, and diet. (Rev: BL 6/1–15/07; SLJ 12/07) [599.884]

12450 Powzyk, Joyce. *In Search of Lemurs: My Days and Nights in a Madagascar Rain Forest* (4–7). 1998, National Geographic $17.95 (978-0-7922-7072-0). The author describes and illustrates her journey into the wilds of Madagascar and the many animals, plants, and birds she encountered, culminating in the elusive lemur. (Rev: BL 9/15/98; HBG 3/99; SLJ 10/98) [599.8]

12451 Stefoff, Rebecca. *The Primate Order* (5–9). Series: Family Trees. 2005, Benchmark LB $32.79 (978-0-7614-1816-0). Habits, habitats, and human-like aspects of this order of animals; an engaging book with plenty of facts for report-writers. (Rev: SLJ 6/06) [599.8]

BEARS

12452 Calabro, Marian. *Operation Grizzly Bear* (5–8). 1989, Macmillan $13.95 (978-0-02-716241-7). An account by two naturalists on a 12-year study of silvertip bears in Yellowstone Park. (Rev: BL 3/15/90; VOYA 4/90) [599.74]

12453 Hamilton, Sue. *Mauled by a Bear* (4–7). Series: Close Encounters of the Wild Kind. 2010, ABDO LB $27.07 (978-1-60453-932-5). Exciting stories and graphic photographs add high-interest appeal to the information about bears and advice on avoiding and surviving such an attack. (Rev: LMC 10/10; SLJ 5/10) [599.7]

12454 Hunt, Joni Phelps. *A Band of Bears: The Rambling Life of a Lovable Loner* (5–8). Series: Jean-Michel Cousteau Presents. 2007, London Town paper $8.95 (978-0-9766134-5-9). With eye-catching photographs and stories of close encounters with these animals, this book looks at bears' characteristics, behavior, intelligence, and the threats to their survival. (Rev: SLJ 11/07) [599.78]

12455 Lockwood, Sophie. *Polar Bears* (5–8). Series: World of Mammals. 2005, Child's World LB $29.93 (978-1-59296-501-4). This slim but richly illustrated title looks at polar bears' physical characteristics, behavior, diet, relationship with the Inuit people, and the growing threats to their survival. (Rev: BL 10/15/05) [599.786]

12456 Lourie, Peter. *The Polar Bear Scientists* (7–10). Illus. Series: Scientists in the Field. 2012, Houghton Mifflin $18.99 (978-054728305-0). Lourie provides a fascinating look at the work of scientists studying Alaskan polar bears and the threats to their survival. **e** (Rev: BL 4/15/12; HB 3–4/12; LMC 8–9/12; SLJ 3/12) [599.786]

12457 McAllister, Ian, and Nicholas Read. *The Salmon Bears: Giants of the Great Bear Rainforest* (5–8). Illus. by Ian McAllister. 2010, Orca paper $18.95 (978-15546920-5-7). Introduces grizzly, black, and spirit bears as they experience the seasons in the Great Bear Rainforest of British Columbia, and their relationship with the salmon in the rivers. (Rev: BL 6/10; SLJ 7/10) [599.78]

12458 Milse, Thorsten. *Little Polar Bears* (7–12). 2006, Prestel $45.00 (978-3-7658-1586-7). As newly born polar bear cubs frolic and explore their surroundings in Hudson Bay, Manitoba, photographer Milse captures their every move amid a vast landscape, following the journey with their mother from birthing den to hunting grounds. (Rev: BL 11/15/06) [779.9599786]

12459 Montgomery, Sy. *Search for the Golden Moon Bear: Science and Adventure in the Asian Tropics* (5–9). 2004, Houghton Mifflin $17.00 (978-0-618-35650-8). Nature writer Montgomery describes her search across war-torn Southeast Asia for the elusive golden moon bear. (Rev: BL 12/1/04; SLJ 12/04) [599.78]

12460 Thomas, Keltie. *Bear Rescue: Changing the Future for Endangered Wildlife* (4–8). Series: Firefly Animal Rescue. 2006, Firefly LB $19.95 (978-1-55297-922-8); paper $9.95 (978-1-55297-921-1). Focuses on work that's being done on behalf of threatened bear species, including Indian sloth bears, Chinese black bears, and polar bears. (Rev: SLJ 12/06) [599.78]

12461 Turbak, Gary. *Grizzly Bears* (6–10). Series: World Life Library. 1997, Voyageur paper $14.95 (978-0-89658-334-4). High-quality photographs and concise, readable text are used to introduce the grizzly bear's life cycle, origin, habits, anatomy, and future. (Rev: SLJ 10/97) [599.74]

CATS (LIONS, TIGERS, ETC.)

12462 Adamson, Joy. *Born Free: A Lioness of Two Worlds* (7–12). 1987, Pantheon $11.95 (978-0-679-56141-5). First published in 1960, this is an account of a young lioness growing up in captivity in Kenya. [599.74]

12463 Becker, John E. *Wild Cats: Past and Present* (5–8). Illus. by Mark Hallett. 2008, Darby Creek $18.95 (978-1-58196-052-5). Lions, tigers, jaguars, and cheetahs are among the wild cats covered in this well-illustrated, large-format book that covers history, environmental threats, and conservation and will attract both researchers and browsers. (Rev: BL 3/15/08; SLJ 6/08) [599.75]

12464 Gamble, Cyndi. *Leopards: Natural History and Conservation* (7–10). Photos by Rodney Griffiths. Series: WorldLife Library. 2004, Voyageur paper $12.95 (978-0-89658-656-7). Introduces readers to the three leopard species of the world, their habitats, and the threats they face. (Rev: SLJ 4/05) [599.74]

12465 Hamilton, Sue. *Ambushed by a Cougar* (4–7). Series: Close Encounters of the Wild Kind. 2010, ABDO LB $27.07 (978-1-60453-928-8). Exciting stories and graphic photographs add high-interest appeal to the information about cougars and advice on avoiding and surviving such an attack. (Rev: LMC 10/10; SLJ 5/10) [599.73]

12466 Joubert, Beverly, and Dereck Joubert. *Face to Face with Lions* (4–8). Illus. by author. 2008, National Geographic $16.95 (978-142630207-7). Lions' biology, habitat, diet, and reproduction are vividly portrayed in this photographic guide that also provides engaging firsthand experiences, Lexile 820L (Rev: BL 11/15/08) [599.757]

12467 Montgomery, Sy. *Saving the Ghost of the Mountain: An Expedition Among Snow Leopards in Mongolia* (4–7). Photos by Nic Bishop. Series: Scientists in the Field. 2009, Houghton Mifflin $18 (978-0-618-91645-0). This compelling and thoughtful account of an (ultimately unsuccessful) expedition to find a snow leopard features eye-catching photographs and a handsome layout. (Rev: BLO 8/09; HB 11–12/09; SLJ 10/09) [599.75]

12468 Schneider, Jost. *Lynx* (4–7). 1994, Carolrhoda LB $28.75 (978-0-87614-844-0). The life cycle, habits, and behavior of the lynx are described. (Rev: BL 1/15/95; SLJ 3/95) [599.74]

12469 Seidensticker, John, and Susan Lumpkin. *Cats: Smithsonian Answer Book* (8–12). 2004, Smithsonian paper $24.95 (978-1-58834-126-6). From the characteristics of the common tabby to the exotic puma, researchers and browsers will find a wealth of information in this book, which is arranged in question-and-answer format and includes many color photographs. (Rev: BL 10/1/04) [599.75]

12470 Sinha, Vivek R. *The Vanishing Tiger* (8–12). 2004, Trafalgar $29.95 (978-1-84065-441-7). A wonderful photographic record of an expedition to locate and photograph India's massive Bengal tiger. (Rev: BL 3/1/04) [599.7]

12471 Thompson, Sharon E. *Built for Speed: The Extraordinary, Enigmatic Cheetah* (5–8). 1998, Lerner LB $27.93 (978-0-8225-2854-8). The habits and lifestyle of this endangered animal are introduced with full-color illustrations. (Rev: BL 6/1–15/98; HBG 10/98) [599.75]

COYOTES, FOXES, AND WOLVES

12472 Johnson, Sylvia A., and Alice Aamodt. *Wolf Pack: Tracking Wolves in the Wild* (5–8). 1985, Lerner paper $27.93 (978-0-8225-9526-7). Fascinating details

of the lives of these animals that travel in packs and share hunting, raising the young, and protection. (Rev: BCCB 12/85; BL 2/1/86; SLJ 1/86) [599.74442]

12473 McAllister, Ian. *The Last Wild Wolves: Ghosts of the Rain Forest* (7–12). 2007, Univ. of California $39.95 (978-0-520-25473-2). Beautiful photographs document the lives of wolves living on the Pacific Coast. (Rev: BL 12/15/07) [599.77309711]

12474 Silverstein, Alvin. *The Red Wolf* (4–8). Series: Endangered Species. 1994, Millbrook LB $24.90 (978-1-56294-416-2). The story of the red wolf, once thought to have become extinct in the United States, and the recent efforts to reintroduce it in North Carolina. (Rev: BL 4/15/95) [333.95]

DEER FAMILY

12475 Cox, Daniel, and John Ozoga. *Whitetail Country* (8–12). 1988, Willow Creek $39.00 (978-0-932558-43-5). Wonderful photographs complement this account of the life and living habits of the deer. [599.73]

ELEPHANTS

12476 Groning, Karl, and Martin Saller. *Elephants: A Cultural and Natural History* (8–12). 1999, Konemann $15.33 (978-3-8290-1752-7). Both the scientific and mythological aspects of elephants are covered, with material on behavior, anatomy, and habitats. (Rev: BL 6/1–15/99; SLJ 5/00) [599.67]

12477 Morgan, Jody. *Elephant Rescue: Changing the Future for Endangered Wildlife* (4–7). Series: Firefly Animal Rescue. 2005, Firefly $19.95 (978-1-55297-595-4); paper $9.95 (978-1-55297-594-7). This photo-filled book documents the many threats facing the world's remaining herds of African and Asian elephants, and discusses elephant physiology, behavior, and habitat. (Rev: BL 2/15/05; SLJ 5/05) [599.67]

12478 O'Connell, Caitlin, and Donna M. Jackson. *The Elephant Scientist* (6–9). Illus. by Caitlin O'Connell. Series: Scientists in the Field. 2011, Houghton Mifflin $17.99 (978-0-547-05344-8). Explore the world of elephants in Africa with a scientist who shares her knowledge and enthusiasm. Boston Globe–Horn Book Honor 2012; Sibert Honor 2012; ALA Notable Books 2012. (Rev: BL 9/15/11; HB 11–12/11; LMC 3–4/12; SLJ 11/1/11*) [599.67]

12479 Overbeck, Cynthia. *Elephants* (4–7). 1981, Lerner LB $22.60 (978-0-8225-1452-7). Elephants and their life cycle and habitats are discussed in this well-illustrated volume. [599]

MARSUPIALS

12480 Collard, Sneed B. *Pocket Babies and Other Amazing Marsupials* (4–7). Illus. 2007, Darby Creek $18.95 (978-1-58196-046-4). A large-format introduction to marsupials around the world — including the opossum, kangaroo, koala, and wombat — and to the efforts being made to save the many endangered marsupials. (Rev: BL 9/15/07; SLJ 10/07) [599.2]

12481 Montgomery, Sy. *Quest for the Tree Kangaroo: An Expedition to the Cloud Forest of New Guinea* (5–8). Illus. by Nic Bishop. 2006, Houghton $18.00 (978-0-618-49641-9). Join researchers on a challenging expedition to the cloud forests of Papua New Guinea to learn more about the rare Matschie's tree kangaroo. Sibert Honor 2007. (Rev: BL 12/1/06; SLJ 12/06*) [599.2]

12482 Murray, Peter. *Kangaroos* (4–7). Series: The World of Mammals. 2005, Child's World LB $29.93 (978-1-59296-499-4). Arresting photographs and engaging text introduce the anatomy, behavior, habitat, and life cycle of the kangaroo as well as the threats to the animal's survival in the wild. (Rev: SLJ 3/06) [599.2]

PANDAS

12483 Jiguang, Xin, and Markus Kappeler. *The Giant Panda* (5–7). Trans. by Noel Simon. 1984, China Books paper $9.95 (978-0-8351-1388-5). China's giant panda is introduced in its natural habitat. (Rev: BL 12/15/86; HB 1–2/87; SLJ 12/86) [599]

Birds

GENERAL AND MISCELLANEOUS

12484 Aziz, Laurel. *Hummingbirds: A Beginner's Guide* (5–8). 2002, Firefly LB $19.95 (978-1-55209-487-7); paper $9.95 (978-1-55209-374-0). This heavily illustrated book offers a great deal of information about hummingbirds, including their bills, metabolism, flight, nesting, and migration. (Rev: BL 6/1–15/02; HBG 10/02) [598.7]

12485 Bateman, Robert. *Bateman's Backyard Birds* (4–7). 2005, Barron's $14.99 (978-0-7641-5882-7). Wildlife artist Bateman introduces readers to numerous North American species of birds and the joys of birding in this beautifully illustrated guide. (Rev: BL 10/15/05) [598]

12486 Doris, Ellen. *Ornithology* (4–7). Series: Real Kids Real Science. 1994, Thames & Hudson $16.95 (978-0-500-19008-1). An excellent manual on how to study birds in their natural habitats, with accompanying activities for all seasons. (Rev: BL 9/1/94) [598]

12487 Gish, Melissa. *Hummingbirds* (5–8). Illus. Series: Living Wild. 2011, Creative Education LB $23.95 (978-160818078-3). Gish looks at hummingbirds' habitats, physical characteristics, behaviors, relationships with humans, and symbolic importance in some cultures. (Rev: BL 12/1/11) [598.7]

12488 Helget, Nicole. *Swans* (4–7). Series: Living Wild. 2008, Smart Apple LB $32.80 (978-1-58341-659-4). With excellent color photographs and extensive explanatory text this book looks at the seven species of swans, including humanity's influence on and involvement with the birds. (Rev: SLJ 2/09) [598.4]

12489 Hoose, Phillip. *Moonbird: A Year on the Wind with the Great Survivor B95* (7–12). Illus. 2012, Farrar $21.99 (978-0-374-30468-3). The remarkable migration of a single rufa red knot — an endangered species that winters in Argentina and breeds in the Canadian Arctic — is chronicled here. ⌒ Lexile 1150L (Rev: BL 6/12*; HB 7–8/12; LMC 11–12/12; SLJ 10/12*; VOYA 8/12) [598.072]

12490 Hoose, Phillip. *The Race to Save the Lord God Bird* (5–8). 2004, Farrar $20.00 (978-0-374-36173-0). The sad tale of the ivory-billed woodpecker's decline is interwoven with discussion of the scientific and sociological implications. (Rev: BL 6/1–15/04; SLJ 9/04) [598.7]

12491 Julivert, Maria Angeles. *Birds* (6–9). Series: Field Guides. 2006, Enchanted Lion $16.95 (978-1-59270-058-5). This guide to bird watching provides information on different types of birds, their characteristics, behavior, and where they make their homes; its format as a naturalist's journal makes clear the joys of this activity. (Rev: BL 10/15/06; SLJ 1/07) [598]

12492 Kenyon, Linda. *Rainforest Bird Rescue: Changing the Future for Endangered Wildlife* (4–8). Series: Firefly Animal Rescue. 2006, Firefly LB $19.95 (978-1-55407-153-1); paper $9.95 (978-1-55407-152-4). This book discusses the threats to the tropical bird species that live in the world's rain forests, habitat that is rapidly disappearing, and profiles the men and women who are crusading to save them. (Rev: SLJ 12/06) [598.1734]

12493 Martin, Gilles. *Birds* (5–8). 2005, Abrams $18.95 (978-0-8109-5878-4). An oversize book full of color photographs of birds, plus watercolor sketches and brief, quite advanced text that comments on various aspects of the birds. (Rev: BL 5/1/05; SLJ 5/05) [598.22]

12494 Montgomery, Sy. *Kakapo Rescue: Saving the World's Strangest Parrot* (4–7). Illus. by Nic Bishop. 2010, Houghton Mifflin $18 (978-061849417-0). The quest to save New Zealand's endangered Kakapo parrot is the focus of this inspiring conservation book. Sibert Medal 2011; ALA Notable Books 2011. (Rev: BL 4/15/10*; SLJ 6/10) [639.9]

12495 Peterson, Roger Tory, and Virginia Marie Peterson. *A Field Guide to the Birds of Eastern and Central North America. 5th ed.* (8–12). 2002, Houghton Mifflin $30.00 (978-0-395-74047-7). This book identifies birds found east of the Rockies with both verbal and pictorial descriptions. [598]

12496 Stokes, Donald, and Lillian Stokes. *The Bird Feeder Book: An Easy Guide to Attracting, Identifying, and Understanding Your Feeder Birds* (8–12). 1987, Little, Brown paper $12.95 (978-0-316-81733-2). A manual that describes, with color photographs, 72 backyard birds, plus tips on how to attract and feed them. (Rev: BL 2/1/88) [598]

12497 Taylor, Kenny. *Puffins* (5–9). Series: WorldLife Library. 1999, Voyageur paper $16.95 (978-0-89658-419-8). Outstanding photographs and conservation awareness are highlights of this introduction to puffins, their characteristics, habitats, and habits. (Rev: BL 8/99) [598.3]

12498 Vogel, Carole G. *The Man Who Flies with Birds* (4–8). 2009, Kar-Ben $18.95 (978-0-8225-7643-3). This is the fascinating story of Yossi Leshem, an Israeli ornithologist whose research on bird migration resulted in air space restrictions that reduce the number of bird-airplane collisions. (Rev: HB 11–12/09; LMC 1–2/10; SLJ 12/09) [598.0956]

12499 Wolf, Sallie. *The Robin Makes a Laughing Sound: A Birder's Journal* (4–8). Illus. by author. 2010, Charlesbridge $11.95 (978-1-58089-318-3). The author's journal — with sketches, watercolors, poems, and notes — documents bird visitors throughout the year, from geese to woodpeckers, robins, and cardinals. (Rev: SLJ 6/10) [598]

12500 Zim, Herbert S., and Ira N. Gabrielson. *Birds* (5–8). 1991, Western paper $21.27 (978-0-307-64053-6). A guide to the most commonly seen birds, with accompanying illustrations and basic materials. [598]

BEHAVIOR

12501 Elphick, Jonathan, ed. *Atlas of Bird Migration: Tracing the Great Journeys of the World's Birds* (8–12). 2007, Firefly $35.00 (978-1-55407-248-4). This handsome atlas presents the latest research into migration and the impact of climate change, with breeding/migration calendars, fact boxes on species, and much more for the bird watcher and researcher. (Rev: SLJ 6/07) [598.156]

12502 Leveille, Jean. *Birds in Love: The Secret Courting and Mating Rituals of Extraordinary Birds* (8–12). 2007, Voyageur $20.00 (978-0-7603-2807-1). Essays and photographs reveal a lot about the behavior of bird couples and bird families. (Rev: BL 12/15/07) [598.156]

12503 Read, Marie. *Secret Lives of Common Birds: Enjoying Bird Behavior Through the Seasons* (8–12). 2005, Houghton Mifflin paper $14.95 (978-0-618-55872-8). Beautiful photographs and season-by-season discussion of bird behavior make this satisfying both for browsers and report writers. (Rev: BL 12/15/05) [598.15]

EAGLES, HAWKS, AND OTHER BIRDS OF PREY

12504 Laubach, Christyna. *Raptor! A Kid's Guide to Birds of Prey* (4–7). 2002, Storey paper $14.95 (978-1-58017-445-9). A large-format treasure trove of facts about raptors, with information on individual species, identification, habits, habitat, range maps, and so forth. (Rev: BL 12/1/02; HBG 3/03; SLJ 10/02) [598.9]

12505 Patent, Dorothy Hinshaw. *The Bald Eagle Returns* (4–8). 2000, Clarion $16.00 (978-0-395-91416-8). This book not only discusses the successful efforts to save the bald eagle but also gives material on its anatomy, habitats, mating, and behavior. (Rev: BCCB 1/01; BL 10/15/00; HBG 10/01; SLJ 11/00) [598.9]

12506 Snyder, Noel, and Helen Snyder. *Raptors of North America* (8–12). 2006, MBI $50.00 (978-0-7603-2582-7). Equally suitable for reference and browsing, this book contains a wealth of information about the more than 50 species of North America's birds of prey. (Rev: BL 11/1/06) [598.9097]

OWLS

12507 Gish, Melissa. *Owls* (5–8). Illus. Series: Living Wild. 2011, Creative Education LB $23.95 (978-160818081-3). Gish looks at owls' habitats, physical characteristics, behaviors, relationships with humans, protected status, and role in folklore. (Rev: BL 12/1/11) [598.9]

12508 Mowat, Farley. *Owls in the Family* (7–9). 1989, Tundra paper $6.99 (978-0-7710-6693-1). Two seemingly harmless owls turn a household upside down when they are adopted as pets. [598]

PENGUINS

12509 Hanel, Rachael. *Penguins* (4–7). Series: Living Wild. 2008, Smart Apple LB $32.80 (978-1-58341-658-7). With excellent color photographs and extensive explanatory text this book looks at the 17 species of penguins, including humanity's influence on and involvement with the birds. (Rev: SLJ 2/09) [598.47]

12510 Johnson, Sylvia A. *Penguins* (4–7). 1981, Lerner LB $22.60 (978-0-8225-1453-4). Handsome photographs enliven the text of this introduction to penguins and their habitats. [598]

12511 Lynch, Wayne. *Penguins!* (4–7). 1999, Firefly LB $19.95 (978-1-55209-421-1); paper $9.95 (978-1-55209-424-2). An appealing book that introduces penguins and their various species with coverage of their evolution, food, life cycle, habits, and habitats. (Rev: BCCB 12/99; BL 9/15/99; HBG 3/00) [598.47]

12512 Pringle, Laurence. *Penguins!* (3–7). Series: Strange and Wonderful. 2007, Boyds Mills $16.95 (978-1-59078-090-9). Report writers will find plenty of material in this book that covers the 17 species of penguins and their behavior, with realistic double-page watercolor illustrations. (Rev: BL 2/15/07; SLJ 4/07) [516]

12513 Stefoff, Rebecca. *Penguins* (4–8). Series: Animal-Ways. 2005, Benchmark LB $21.95 (978-0-7614-1743-9). Beautiful photographs enrich this well-organized volume that provides basic information on the penguin's characteristics, habits, and habitat. (Rev: SLJ 5/06) [598.4]

12514 Webb, Sophie. *My Season with Penguins: An Antarctic Journal* (4–8). Illus. by author. 2000, Houghton Mifflin $15.00 (978-0-395-92291-0). Journal entries plus effective drawings show the joys and tribulations of a two-month stay in the Antarctic studying penguins and their behavior. (Rev: HB 11–12/00; HBG 3/01; SLJ 12/00) [598]

Environmental Protection and Endangered Species

12515 Barker, David. *Top 50 Reasons to Care About Great Apes* (5–8). Series: Top 50 Reasons to Care About Endangered Animals. 2010, Enslow LB $31.93 (978-0-7660-3456-3). Readers learn about apes' biology and habitat, behavior, and threats to their survival; activities in which young people can contribute to apes' welfare are listed. (Rev: LMC 3–4/10) [599.88]

12516 Barnes, Simon. *Planet Zoo* (4–7). 2001, Orion $29.95 (978-1-85881-488-9). An overview of 100 endangered species that conveys information in a conversational manner. (Rev: BL 8/01; SLJ 8/01) [578.68]

12517 Christopherson, Sara Cohen. *Top 50 Reasons to Care About Marine Turtles* (5–8). Series: Top 50 Reasons to Care About Endangered Animals. 2010, Enslow LB $31.93 (978-0-7660-3455-6). Threats to marine turtles' survival are the main focus of this volume that also discusses the animals' biology, habitat, and behavior. Also use *Top 50 Reasons to Care About Whales and Dolphins* (2010). (Rev: LMC 3–4/10) [597.928]

12518 Feinstein, Stephen. *The Jaguar: Help Save This Endangered Species!* (4–7). Series: Saving Endangered Species. 2008, Enslow LB $24.95 (978-1-59845-065-1). Part of the MyReportLinks.com series, this introduction to jaguars and the threats they face features Web sites that report writers can access for more information. (Rev: BL 2/15/08) [599.75]

12519 Firestone, Mary. *Top 50 Reasons to Care About Elephants* (5–8). Series: Top 50 Reasons to Care About Endangered Animals. 2010, Enslow LB $31.93 (978-0-7660-3454-9). Readers learn about elephants' biology and habitat, behavior, and threats to their survival; activities in which young people can contribute to elephant welfare are listed. Also in this series by this author are *Top 50 Reasons to Care About Giant Pandas, Top 50 Reasons to Care About Rhinos,* and *Top 50*

Reasons to Care About Tigers (all 2010). (Rev: LMC 3–4/10) [599.67]

12520 Fletcher, Marty, and Glenn Scherer. *The Green Sea Turtle: Help Save This Endangered Species!* (5–7). Series: Saving Endangered Species. 2006, Enslow LB $33.27 (978-1-59845-033-0). A well-illustrated look at the plight of the endangered green sea turtle, with an overview of its physical characteristics, diet, habitat, and behavior. (Rev: SLJ 9/06) [597.92]

12521 Hirsch, Rebecca. *Helping Endangered Animals* (3–7). Series: Language Arts Explorer: Save the Planet. 2010, Cherry Lake LB $27.07 (978-1-60279-658-4). Students are given a mission at the beginning of the book and must use creative thinking and problem solving to gather facts as they travel on a virtual trip researching the plight of animals including pandas and elephants. (Rev: LMC 8–9/10; SLJ 4/10) [591.68]

12522 Hirsch, Rebecca. *Top 50 Reasons to Care About Polar Bears* (5–8). Series: Top 50 Reasons to Care About Endangered Animals. 2010, Enslow LB $31.93 (978-0-7660-3458-7). Threats to polar bears' survival are the main focus of this volume that also discusses the animals' biology, habitat, and behavior. (Rev: LMC 3–4/10) [599.74]

12523 McClung, Robert M. *Last of the Wild: Vanished and Vanishing Giants of the Animal World* (8–12). 1997, Shoe String LB $27.50 (978-0-208-02452-7). Moving from continent to continent, this account gives historical and geographical background material on 60 animal species that have already disappeared or are currently in extreme danger of extinction. (Rev: BL 7/97; HBG 3/98; SLJ 11/97; VOYA 10/97) [591.51]

12524 Nirgiotis, Nicholas, and Theodore Nigiortis. *No More Dodos: How Zoos Help Endangered Wildlife* (5–8). 1996, Lerner LB $23.93 (978-0-8225-2856-2). An introduction to the many organizations that are trying to protect and preserve endangered wildlife worldwide. (Rev: BCCB 2/97; BL 2/15/97; SLJ 2/97) [639.9]

12525 Salmansohn, Pete, and Stephen W. Kress. *Saving Birds: Heroes Around the World* (4–7). 2003, Tilbury House $16.95 (978-0-88448-237-6). Efforts to save endangered bird species are detailed in informative text and arresting, full-color photographs. (Rev: BL 3/15/03; HBG 10/03; SLJ 5/03) [333.95]

12526 Sheehan, Sean. *Endangered Species* (5–8). Illus. Series: What If We Do Nothing? 2009, Gareth Stevens LB $31.00 (978-1-4339-0086-0). The threats to both plants and animals, along with factors such as ecotourism and the exotic pet market, are addressed in this volume that looks at the past, the current status, and the future outlook. (Rev: BL 4/15/09; SLJ 6/09) [333.95]

12527 Silhol, Sandrine, and Gaelle Guerive. *Extraordinary Endangered Animals* (5–8). Illus. by Marie Doucedame. 2011, Abrams $24.95 (978-1-4197-0034-7). Two-page spreads introduce species in six geographical groupings and describe habitat, location, feeding, hibernation, reproduction, and adaptations to the environment; with maps, large photographs, and discussion of threats to survival. (Rev: BL 11/15/11; LMC 3–4/12; SLJ 11/1/11) [333.95]

12528 Thomas, Peggy. *Big Cat Conservation* (5–8). Series: Science of Saving Animals. 2000, Twenty-First Century LB $25.90 (978-0-7613-3231-2). This book focuses on seven species, including panthers, cheetahs, and tigers, and discusses wildlife conservation programs, challenges, and successes. (Rev: BL 6/1–15/00; HBG 10/00; SLJ 7/00) [333.95]

12529 Thomas, Peggy. *Bird Alert* (5–8). Series: The Science of Saving Animals. 2000, Twenty-First Century LB $25.90 (978-0-7613-1457-8). This book discusses conservation programs designed to save endangered bird species and tells how youngsters can get involved in saving birds. (Rev: BL 10/15/00; HBG 10/01; SLJ 12/00) [591.52]

Insects and Arachnids

GENERAL AND MISCELLANEOUS

12530 Beccaloni, George. *Biggest Bugs Life-Size* (3–7). Illus. 2010, Firefly $19.95 (978-155407699-4). Thirty-five bugs of unusual sizes are presented in this fascinating book full of close-up photographs. (Rev: BL 12/1/10; SLJ 12/1/10) [595.714]

12531 Burnie, David. *Insect* (5–9). Series: DK/Google e.guides. 2005, DK $17.99 (978-0-7566-1010-4). This highly illustrated guide introduces readers to the life cycle, behavior, diet, and habitat of insects and provides a link to a Web site that serves as a gateway to additional resources. (Rev: SLJ 8/05)

12532 *Discovery Channel Insects and Spiders: An Explore Your World Handbook* (8–12). 2000, Discovery paper $14.95 (978-1-56331-841-2). About 160 insects and spiders are identified in text and pictures, with material on their anatomy, behavior, evolution, and the possibility of keeping them as pets. [595.7]

12533 Greenaway, Theresa. *Ants* (4–7). Series: The Secret World of . . . 2001, Raintree LB $18.98 (978-0-7368-3511-4). After presenting interesting and unusual facts about ants, this book examines their structure, homes, behavior, and enemies. (Rev: BL 10/15/01) [595.79]

12534 Markle, Sandra. *Mites: Master Sneaks* (4–7). Illus. Series: Arachnid World. 2012, Lerner LB $29.27 (978-076135046-0). With large color photographs and concise text, this book introduces the life cycle, characteristics, and behavior of the mite. (Rev: BL 3/1/12; SLJ 2/12) [595.4]

12535 Milne, Lorus, and Margery Milne. *The Audubon Society Field Guide to North American Insects and Spiders* (7–12). 1980, Knopf $19.95 (978-0-394-50763-7).

An extensive use of color photographs makes this a fine guide for identifying insects. [595.7]

12536 Pascoe, Elaine. *Ant Lions and Lacewings* (4–8). Photos by Dwight Kuhn. Series: Nature Close-Up. 2005, Gale LB $24.95 (978-1-4103-0310-3). Eye-catching close-ups illustrate information on these insects' life cycles and eating habits. Also use *Mantids and Their Relatives* (2005). (Rev: SLJ 6/05)

12537 Pipe, Jim. *The Giant Book of Bugs and Creepy Crawlies* (4–8). 1998, Millbrook LB $27.90 (978-0-7613-0716-7). Exotic and common insects and spiders are presented in this oversize book with eye-catching pictures and fascinating text. (Rev: BL 8/98) [595.7]

12538 Waldbauer, Gilbert. *Insights from Insects: What Bad Bugs Can Teach Us* (8–12). 2005, Prometheus paper $20.98 (978-1-59102-277-0). Friend or foe? Waldbauer profiles 20 insects that most humans consider pests and their roles in the natural world. (Rev: BL 3/15/05) [632]

12539 Wangberg, James K. *Do Bees Sneeze? And Other Questions Kids Ask About Insects* (7–10). 1997, Fulcrum paper $18.95 (978-1-55591-963-4). Full, interesting answers to more than 200 questions about insects on such subjects as physical characteristics, anatomical features, locomotion, behavior, habitat, and human health and safety. (Rev: BL 1/1–15/98; SLJ 4/98) [595.7]

12540 Wilkes, Sarah. *Insects* (5–9). Series: World Almanac Library of the Animal Kingdom. 2006, World Almanac LB $31.00 (978-0-8368-6211-9). A helpful introduction to members of the insect kingdom, this guide looks at physical characteristics that help to define this group as a whole, as well as specific species, habitats, diets, behaviors, and life cycles. (Rev: SLJ 12/06) [595.7]

12541 Young, Karen Romano. *Bug Science: 20 Projects and Experiments About Arthropods: Insects, Arachnids, Algae, Worms, and Other Small Creatures* (4–8). Illus. by David Goldin. Series: Science Fair Winners. 2009, National Geographic LB $24.90 (978-1-4263-0520-7); paper $12.95 (978-1-4263-0519-1). Divided into workshops that focus on specific bugs, this is an appealing compendium of projects that are properly documented and explained. (Rev: LMC 3–4/10; SLJ 3/10; VOYA 4/10) [595.7]

12542 Zabludoff, Marc. *The Insect Class* (5–9). Series: Family Trees. 2005, Benchmark LB $29.93 (978-0-7614-1819-1). Habits, habitats, and other aspects of this varied class of animals; an engaging book with plenty of facts for report-writers. (Rev: SLJ 6/06) [595.7]

BEES AND WASPS

12543 Hamilton, Sue. *Swarmed by Bees* (4–7). Series: Close Encounters of the Wild Kind. 2010, ABDO LB $27.07 (978-1-60453-933-2). Exciting stories and graphic photographs add high-interest appeal to the information about bees and advice on avoiding and surviving such an attack. (Rev: LMC 10/10; SLJ 5/10) [595.79]

BUTTERFLIES, MOTHS, AND CATERPILLARS

12544 Pyle, Robert Michael. *The Audubon Society Field Guide to North American Butterflies* (7–12). 1981, Knopf $19.95 (978-0-394-51914-2). An introduction to more than 600 species of butterflies in about 1,000 color photographs and text. [595.7]

12545 Schappert, Phil. *The Last Monarch Butterfly: Conserving the Monarch Butterfly in a Brave New World* (8–12). 2004, Firefly paper $19.95 (978-1-55297-969-3). The fascinating story of the monarch butterfly and its incredible migrations is told with an emphasis on the threats it faces. (Rev: BL 12/15/04) [595.78]

12546 Schlaepfer, Gloria G. *Butterflies* (4–8). Series: AnimalWays. 2005, Benchmark LB $21.95 (978-0-7614-1745-3). Beautiful photographs of butterfly specimens enrich this well-organized volume that provides basic information on the butterfly's characteristics, habits, and habitat. (Rev: SLJ 5/06) [595.78]

12547 Stewart, Melissa. *Butterflies* (4–7). Illus. by Andrew Recher. Series: Our Wild World. 2007, NorthWord LB $10.95 (978-1-55971-966-7); paper $7.95 (978-1-55971-967-4). The behavior, physical characteristics and life cycles of butterflies are presented in great detail with many photographs. (Rev: SLJ 7/07) [595.78]

SPIDERS AND SCORPIONS

12548 Allman, Toney. *From Spider Webs to Man-Made Silk* (4–7). Series: Imitating Nature. 2005, Gale LB $24.95 (978-0-7377-3124-8). An introduction to scientists' attempts to replicate spider silk in the laboratory. (Rev: BL 10/15/05; LMC 3/06) [595.4]

12549 Greenaway, Theresa. *Spiders* (4–7). Series: The Secret World of . . . 2001, Raintree LB $18.98 (978-0-7368-3509-1). An information-crammed text and attractive illustrations introduce spiders, how and where they live, and their behavior. (Rev: BL 10/15/01) [595.4]

12550 Lasky, Kathryn. *Silk and Venom: Searching for a Dangerous Spider* (5–8). Photos by Christopher G. Knight. 2011, Candlewick $16.99 (978-0-7636-4222-8). A scientist's research trips to study the dangerous brown recluse spider are documented in this compelling book, which includes plenty of photographs and factual material about spiders. Lexile 1050L (Rev: BL 2/15/11; HB 3–4/11; LMC 5–6/11; SLJ 3/1/11) [595.4]

12551 Markle, Sandra. *Wind Scorpions: Killer Jaws* (4–7). Illus. Series: Arachnid World. 2012, Lerner LB $29.27 (978-076135048-4). With large color photographs and concise text, this book introduces the life

cycle, characteristics, and behavior of the wind scorpion. Also use *Tarantulas: Supersized Predators* (2012). **e** (Rev: BL 3/1/12; SLJ 2/12) [595.4]

12552 Montgomery, Sy. *The Tarantula Scientist* (4–7). Photos by Nic Bishop. Series: Scientists in the Field. 2004, Houghton Mifflin $18.00 (978-0-618-14799-1). This informative, photo-filled book chronicles the day-to-day field work of arachnologist Sam Marshall as he searches for tarantulas in the French Guianan rain forest. (Rev: BL 3/15/04; HB 7–8/04; SLJ 5/04) [595.4]

12553 Zabludoff, Marc. *Spiders* (4–8). Series: Animal-Ways. 2005, Benchmark LB $21.95 (978-0-7614-1747-7). Beautiful photographs enrich this well-organized volume that provides basic information on the insect's characteristics, habits, and habitat. (Rev: SLJ 5/06) [595.4]

Marine and Freshwater Life

GENERAL AND MISCELLANEOUS

12554 Cerullo, Mary M. *Sea Soup: Zooplankton* (4–7). Illus. by Bill Curtsinger. 2001, Tilbury House $16.95 (978-0-88448-219-2). An inviting introduction to the world of tiny drifting animals known as zooplankton, with intriguing photographs. (Rev: BL 7/01; HBG 10/01; SLJ 8/01) [592.1776.]

12555 Collard, Sneed B, III. *On the Coral Reefs* (4–7). Series: Science Adventures. 2005, Marshall Cavendish LB $25.64 (978-0-7614-1953-2). In addition to a profile of a marine biologist who studies fish that eat parasites living on other fish, Collard presents information on scientific research methods and on global warming and other environmental threats. (Rev: BL 2/1/06; SLJ 5/06) [577.7]

12556 Halfmann, Janet. *Life in the Sea* (5–7). Series: LifeViews. 2000, Creative LB $22.60 (978-1-58341-074-5). All life in the sea is discussed with a focus on the tiniest — plankton, algae, sea spiders, coral, and worms. (Rev: SLJ 8/00) [591.92]

12557 Johnson, Jinny. *Simon and Schuster Children's Guide to Sea Creatures* (4–7). 1998, Simon & Schuster $19.95 (978-0-689-81534-8). This book contains broad coverage of the invertebrates, birds, mammals, and fish found in various parts of the oceans and their shores. (Rev: HBG 10/98; SLJ 5/98) [591]

12558 Johnson, Rebecca L. *Journey into the Deep: Discovering New Ocean Creatures* (5–8). 2010, Millbrook $31.93 (978-0-7613-4148-2). Documenting the Census of Marine Life, which was conducted between 2000 and 2001, this book provides facts, pithy quotes, and vivid photographs captured from the mission. Lexile 920L (Rev: BL 12/1/10; LMC 1–2/11; SLJ 10/1/10) [591.77]

12559 Meinkoth, Norman A. *The Audubon Society Field Guide to North American Seashore Creatures* (7–12).

1981, Knopf $19.95 (978-0-394-51993-7). This is a guide to such invertebrates as sponges, corals, urchins, and anemones. [592]

12560 Moore, Heidi. *Ocean Food Chains* (4–7). Series: Protecting Food Chains. 2010, Heinemann LB $32 (978-1-4329-3859-8); paper $8.99 (978-1-4329-3866-6). With chapter headings that ask questions such as "What Are the Producers in Oceans?" and "What Are the Decomposers in Oceans?," this volume explores food chains within an ocean habitat and discusses why we need to protect them. (Rev: SLJ 11/1/10) [577.7]

12561 Newquist, H. P. *Here There Be Monsters: The Legendary Kraken and the Giant Squid* (5–8). Illus. 2010, Houghton Mifflin $18 (978-0-547-07678-2). Explores the history and mystery of the giant squid, with many illustrations, historical maps, and scientific facts. (Rev: BL 9/1/10; HB 11–12/10; SLJ 9/1/10) [594]

12562 O'Neill, Michael Patrick. *Wild Waters Photo Journal* (6–12). 2010, Batfish Books $29.95 (978-0-9728653-6-4). A wonderful collection of color photographs and brief descriptions of marine life in ecosystems as varied as Komodo National Park, Bali, the Palm Beach coral reefs, and the Everglades. (Rev: LMC 11–12/10; SLJ 8/10) [591.77]

12563 Parker, Steve. *Ocean and Sea* (4–7). Illus. Series: Scholastic Discover More. 2012, Scholastic paper $15.99 (978-05453302-2-0). In five chapters — "All About Oceans," "Oceans of the World," "Life in the Ocean," "People and Oceans," and "Oceans Under Threat" — this attractive print book offers bright images and succinct text; an accompanying digital companion, *Shark Spotter,* offers additional detail on that species and includes videos. (Rev: BL 3/1/12) [551.46]

12564 Rehder, Harold A. *The Audubon Society Field Guide to North American Seashells* (7–12). 1981, Knopf $19.95 (978-0-394-51913-5). Seven hundred of the most common seashells from our coasts are pictured in color photographs and described in the text. [594]

12565 Rizzo, Johnna. *Oceans: Dolphins, Sharks, Penguins, and More!* (4–7). 2010, National Geographic $14.95 (978-1-4263-0686-0). This large-format volume full of eye-catching photographs and easy-to-find factoids covers 15 types of marine animals and will inspire browsers to investigate further. (Rev: BLO 6/10; LMC 10/10; SLJ 6/10) [551.46]

12566 Treat, Rose. *The Seaweed Book: How to Find and Have Fun with Seaweed* (4–7). 1995, Star Bright paper $5.95 (978-1-887724-00-5). The identification, collection, and preservation of various kinds of seaweed. (Rev: BL 2/1/96) [589.45]

12567 Waller, Geoffrey. *SeaLife: A Complete Guide to the Marine Environment* (8–12). 1996, Smithsonian $55.00 (978-1-56098-633-1). A comprehensive reference to marine biology, including profiles of more than 600 species of marine animals, this guide is written in easy-to-understand language and includes numerous illustrations and maps. [591.7]

12568 Zabludoff, Marc. *The Protoctist Kingdom* (5–9). Series: Family Trees. 2005, Benchmark LB $32.79 (978-0-7614-1818-4). Habits, habitats, and other aspects of this newly classified kingdom of animals that includes algae; an engaging book with plenty of facts for report-writers. (Rev: SLJ 6/06) [579]

CORALS AND JELLYFISH

12569 Walker, Pam, and Elaine Wood. *The Coral Reef* (8–11). Series: Life in the Seas. 2005, Facts on File $35.00 (978-0-8160-5703-0). An excellent introduction to the world's coral reefs, looking at how they were formed, the creatures that thrive within them, and the threats they face. (Rev: BL 1/1–15/06) [5/8.77]

FISHES

12570 Eschmeyer, William N., and Earl S. Herald. *A Field Guide to Pacific Coast Fishes* (7–12). 1983, Houghton Mifflin $20.00 (978-0-618-00212-2). In this volume in the Peterson Field Guide series, about 500 fish are described and illustrated. [597]

12571 Filisky, Michael. *Peterson First Guide to Fishes of North America* (7–12). 1989, Houghton Mifflin paper $4.95 (978-0-393-91179-4). This is a concise version of the parent Peterson guide that gives basic material on common fish but with less detail. (Rev: BL 6/1/89) [597]

12572 Pascoe, Elaine. *Freshwater Fish* (4–8). Photos by Dwight Kuhn. Series: Nature Close-Up. 2005, Gale LB $24.95 (978-1-4103-0308-0). Eye-catching close-ups illustrate information on the life cycles and eating habits of freshwater fish. (Rev: SLJ 6/05)

12573 Schweid, Richard. *Consider the Eel* (8–12). 2002, Univ. of North Carolina $24.95 (978-0-8078-2693-5). A fascinating profile of the eel, with information on its history, life cycle, importance as a food product, and appearances in folklore, along with a selection of eel recipes. (Rev: BL 3/15/02) [597]

12574 Walker, Sally M. *Fossil Fish Found Alive: Discovering the Coelacanth* (5–8). 2002, Carolrhoda LB $17.95 (978-1-57505-536-7). An engaging look at the search for and study of coelacanths, a fish believed to be extinct until 1938. (Rev: BL 3/15/02; HB 1–2/03; HBG 3/03; SLJ 5/02*) [597.3]

12575 Wilkes, Sarah. *Fish* (5–9). Series: World Almanac Library of the Animal Kingdom. 2006, World Almanac LB $31.00 (978-0-8368-6210-2). This brightly illustrated guide to fish introduces specific species, physical characteristics, habitats, diets, behaviors, and life cycles. (Rev: SLJ 12/06) [597]

12576 Zim, Herbert S., and Hurst H. Shoemaker. *Fishes* (5–8). Illus. by James G. Irving. 1991, Western paper

$21.27 (978-0-307-64059-8). This is a basic guide to both fresh and saltwater species.

SHARKS

12577 Brusha, Joe. *Top 10 Deadliest Sharks* (4–7). Illus. by Anthony Spay. 2010, Silver Dragon paper $9.99 (978-09827507-2-8). Facts about sharks are presented along with assessments of their threats to humans. (Rev: BL 3/15/11) [741.5]

12578 Capuzzo, Michael. *Close to Shore: The Terrifying Shark Attacks of 1916* (7–12). 2003, Crown $16.95 (978-0-375-82231-5). Photographs and newspaper clippings enhance this true story of a shark's brief and dangerous detour into a New Jersey creek in 1916. (Rev: BL 5/15/03; HBG 10/03; SLJ 4/03) [597.3]

12579 Cerullo, Mary M. *The Truth About Great White Sharks* (4–7). 2000, Chronicle $14.95 (978-0-8118-2467-5). A fascinating account with excellent underwater photographs that explores such topics about sharks as physical characteristics, behavior, feeding habits, and the difficulty of studying them. (Rev: BL 4/1/00; SLJ 7/00) [597.3]

12580 Hamilton, Sue. *Eaten by a Shark* (4–7). Series: Close Encounters of the Wild Kind. 2010, ABDO LB $27.07 (978-1-60453-931-8). Exciting stories and graphic photographs add high-interest appeal to the information about sharks and advice on avoiding and surviving such an attack. (Rev: LMC 10/10; SLJ 5/10) [597.3]

12581 McMillan, Beverly, and John A. Musick. *Sharks* (3–7). Illus. Series: Insiders. 2008, Simon & Schuster $16.99 (978-1-4169-3867-5). Close-up views introduce everything shark delivered in an easy conversational tone, with double-page spreads, detailed diagrams, photographs, and a glossary. (Rev: BL 9/15/08; SLJ 9/08) [597.3]

12582 Pope, Joyce. *1001 Facts About Sharks* (7–12). Series: Backpack Books. 2002, DK paper $8.99 (978-0-7894-8449-9). More than 550 illustrations and photographs are used to present basic facts about sharks, their anatomy, habits, and varieties. (Rev: BL 3/15/02) [597]

12583 Reader's Digest, ed. *Sharks: Silent Hunters of the Deep* (8–12). 1987, Reader's Digest $19.95 (978-0-86438-014-2). This handsomely illustrated account describes the ways of sharks, gives material on famous encounters, and identifies all 344 species. (Rev: BL 5/15/87; SLJ 1/88; VOYA 8/87) [597]

12584 Smith, Miranda. *Sharks* (4–7). Illus. Series: Kingfisher Knowledge. 2010, Kingfisher paper $8.99 (978-07534640-5-2). An eye-catching overview of sharks' physical characteristics, habit, diet, and behavior, with spreads on *Jaws* and on shark attacks as well as information on their history and myths about these animals. (Rev: BL 2/15/10; SLJ 9/1/08) [597.3]

WHALES, DOLPHINS, AND OTHER SEA MAMMALS

12585 Chadwick, Douglas H. *The Grandest of Lives: Eye to Eye with Whales* (8–12). Illus. by author. 2006, Sierra Club $24.95 (978-1-57805-126-7). Chadwick followed scientists on their whale observations as he compiled this compelling overview of five species and their behavior, intelligence, and the threats they face. (Rev: BL 6/1–15/06) [599.5]

12586 Darling, Jim. *Gray Whales* (6–12). Series: World Life Library. 1999, Voyageur paper $16.95 (978-0-89658-447-1). Physiology, behavior, habitat, migration, and relations with humans are all discussed in this volume that contains lots of full-color photographs. (Rev: SLJ 4/00) [599.5]

12587 Hall, Howard. *A Charm of Dolphins: The Threatened Life of a Flippered Friend* (5–8). Series: Jean-Michel Cousteau Presents. 2007, London Town paper $8.95 (978-0-9766134-8-0). With eye-catching photographs and stories of close encounters with these animals, this book looks at dolphins' characteristics, behavior, intelligence, and the threats to their survival. (Rev: SLJ 11/07) [599.53]

12588 Hodgkins, Fran. *The Whale Scientists: Solving the Mystery of Whale Strandings* (5–8). Illus. Series: Scientists in the Field. 2007, Houghton Mifflin $18.00 (978-0-618-55673-1). A look at scientists' efforts to understand why whales sometimes strand themselves on beaches, seemingly waiting for death; with accounts of efforts to rescue these huge mammals. (Rev: BL 12/1/07; HB 1–2/08; SLJ 12/07) [599.5]

12589 Kelsey, Elin. *Finding Out About Whales* (4–8). Series: Science Explorers. 1998, Owl $19.95 (978-1-895688-79-5); paper $9.95 (978-1-895688-80-1). This book discusses how information is gathered about whales and introduces five different species: blue, humpback, beluga, gray, and killer. (Rev: BL 3/1/99; SLJ 3/99) [595.5]

12590 Leon, Vicki. *A Pod of Killer Whales: The Mysterious Life of the Intelligent Orca* (5–8). Series: Jean-Michel Cousteau Presents. 2007, London Town paper $8.95 (978-0-9766134-7-3). With eye-catching photographs and stories of close encounters with these animals, this book looks at killer whales' characteristics, behavior, intelligence, and the threats to their survival. (Rev: SLJ 11/07) [599.53]

12591 Leon, Vicki. *A Raft of Sea Otters: The Playful Life of a Furry Survivor.* 2nd ed. (4–7). 2005, London Town paper $7.95 (978-0-9666490-4-8). This accessible introduction to the sea otter and its physical characteristics, behavior, diet, habitat, life cycle, and conservation threats is a picture-book-size revision of an earlier edition and contains excellent photographs. (Rev: BL 7/05) [599.7695]

12592 Lockwood, Sophie. *Whales* (4–7). Series: World of Mammals. 2008, Child's World LB $20.95 (978-1-59296-930-2). Well-suited to report writers, this surprisingly comprehensive title discusses whale behavior and physiology and includes information on conservation. (Rev: BLO 6/17/08; SLJ 6/08) [599.5]

12593 Lourie, Peter. *The Manatee Scientists: Saving Vulnerable Species* (4–7). Illus. Series: Scientists in the Field. 2011, Houghton Mifflin $18.99 (978-0-547-15254-7). Lourie looks at research scientists' work on manatees around the world, where these mammals face quite different dangers depending on the environment and priorities of the human population. (Rev: BL 5/1/11; SLJ 7/11) [599.55092]

12594 Lourie, Peter. *Whaling Season: A Year in the Life of an Arctic Whale Scientist* (4–8). Series: Scientists in the Field. 2009, Houghton Mifflin $18 (978-0-618-77709-9). Lourie follows the work of Arctic whale scientist John Craighead George (son of the well-known children's author) in this fascinating account of George's everyday work, the research process, his subjects, and his ways of relaxing at the end of the day. Lexile NC1150L (Rev: BL 12/1/09*; SLJ 2/10) [599.5]

12595 Nuzzolo, Deborah. *Bottlenose Dolphin Training and Interaction* (6–9). Series: SeaWorld Education. 2003, Sea World paper $7.99 (978-1-893698-03-1). An attractive introduction to this dolphin's habitat, physiology, and behavior, and to the ways in which they are trained at Sea World. (Rev: BL 6/1–15/03) [636.]

12596 Read, Andrew. *Porpoises* (5–8). Series: World-Life Library. 1999, Voyageur paper $16.95 (978-0-89658-420-4). With many color illustrations and large print, this book introduces porpoises, their characteristics, behavior, habitats, and how humans study them. (Rev: BL 8/99; VOYA 2/00) [599.53]

12597 Rinard, Judith E. *Amazing Animals of the Sea* (5–8). 1981, National Geographic LB $12.50 (978-0-87044-387-9). Whales, dolphins, sea otters, sea lions, seals, manatees, and other marine mammals are described.

12598 Silverstein, Alvin. *The Manatee* (4–7). Series: Endangered in America. 1995, Millbrook LB $24.90 (978-1-56294-551-0). A profile of this sea creature, its lifestyle and habits, and how it became an endangered species. (Rev: BL 10/15/95; SLJ 1/96) [599.5]

12599 Simmonds, Mark. *Whales and Dolphins of the World* (8–12). 2005, MIT $29.95 (978-0-262-19519-5). This photo-filled volume introduces readers to the cetaceans — whales, dolphins, and porpoises — and to their relationship with humans. (Rev: BL 3/15/05) [599.5]

Microscopes, Microbiology, and Biotechnology

12600 Aldridge, Susan. *Cloning* (7–10). Illus. Series: Cutting-Edge Science. 2010, Black Rabbit LB $34.25 (978-184898326-7). After introducing the basics of cloning and the story of Dolly the sheep, this volume looks in turn at the structure of cells, cloning and DNA, the history and current status of cloning, cloning in plants and animals, the ethics of cloning and various challenges to the practice, and the future of cloning. (Rev: BL 12/1/10; LMC 5–6/11) [571.8]

12601 Farrell, Jeanette. *Invisible Allies: Microbes That Shape Our Lives* (6–9). 2005, Farrar $17.00 (978-0-374-33608-0). The beneficial role of microbes (in food production, digestion, waste removal, and so forth) is the focus of this engaging title by the author of *Invisible Enemies* (1998). (Rev: BL 4/15/05*; SLJ 5/05; VOYA 8/05) [579]

12602 Kramer, Stephen. *Hidden Worlds: Looking Through a Scientist's Microscope* (4–7). Series: Scientists in the Field. 2001, Houghton Mifflin $16.00 (978-0-618-05546-3). Striking photographs, mostly taken with electron microscopes by scientist Dennis Kunkel, serve to illustrate this explanation of how scientists use microscopes in their work. (Rev: BL 8/01; HB 1–2/02; HBG 3/02; SLJ 9/01*) [570]

12603 Latta, Sara L. *The Good, the Bad, the Slimy: The Secret Life of Microbes* (5–8). Photos by Dennis Kunkel. 2006, Enslow LB $31.93 (978-0-7660-1294-3). Bright photography and clear explanations will engage browsers and please report writers. (Rev: LMC 4–5/07; SLJ 8/07)

12604 Levine, Shar, and Leslie Johnstone. *The Ultimate Guide to Your Microscope* (5–9). 2008, Sterling paper $9.95 (978-1-4027-4329-0). After covering the basics of using a microscope, this volume presents 41 hands-on activities. (Rev: LMC 10/08; SLJ 11/08) [570.28]

12605 Morgan, Sally. *From Microscopes to Stem Cell Research: Discovering Regenerative Medicine* (6–9). Series: Chain Reactions. 2006, Heinemann LB $34.29 (978-1-4034-8836-7). Morgan looks at ways in which the development of microscopes contributed to our knowledge of stem cells, ends with brief biographies of key individuals in the field. (Rev: SLJ 2/07)

12606 Rainis, Kenneth G. *Cell and Microbe Science Fair Projects Using Microscopes, Mold, and More* (6–12). Series: Biology! Best Science Projects. 2005, Enslow LB $26.60 (978-0-7660-2369-7). This introduction to the study of cells and microbes contains step-by-step instructions for a number of related experiments and projects. (Rev: SLJ 9/05) [578]

12607 Silverstein, Alvin. *Cells* (4–8). Series: Science Concepts. 2002, Millbrook LB $26.90 (978-0-7613-2254-2). The functions and components of plant and animal cells are discussed along with such topics as cloning, cell fusion, and stem cell research. (Rev: BL 9/15/02; HBG 3/03) [574.87]

12608 Stefoff, Rebecca. *Microscopes and Telescopes* (7–10). Series: Great Inventions. 2007, Marshall Cavendish LB $27.95 (978-0-7614-2230-3). From early spectacles through the invention of refractors and reflectors to space telescopes and on into the future, this history of microscopes and telescopes offers lots of hard scientific information. (Rev: SLJ 11/07) [502.8]

12609 Thomas, Peggy. *Bacteria and Viruses* (5–8). Series: Lucent Library of Science and Technology. 2005, Gale LB $29.95 (978-1-59018-438-7). Introduces the scientists who discovered bacteria and viruses and how we fight ones that harm us and attempt to use others to our benefit. (Rev: BL 1/05)

12610 Walker, Richard. *Microscopic Life* (4–8). Series: Kingfisher Knowledge. 2004, Kingfisher $11.95 (978-0-7534-5778-8). A well-illustrated look at the tiniest living things — bacteria, viruses, mites, fungi, and molds, for example — and how we study them and attempt to use them to our benefit. (Rev: BL 9/1/04; SLJ 1/05) [579]

Pets

GENERAL AND MISCELLANEOUS

12611 Albrecht, Kat. *The Lost Pet Chronicles: Adventures of a K-9 Cop Turned Pet Detective* (8–12). 2004, Bloomsbury $23.95 (978-1-58234-379-2). This is a memoir of a former police officer who has become a pet detective and a solver of such crimes as dognapping. (Rev: BL 3/1/04) [363.28]

12612 Moberg, Julia. *Presidential Pets: The Weird, Wacky, Little, Big, Scary, Strange Animals That Have Lived in the White House* (4–7). Illus. by Jeff Albrecht Studios. 2012, Charlesbridge $14.95 (978-193614079-4). With poems, bulleted facts, and lively illustrations, this is a solid introduction to animal residents of the White House from Washington to Obama. Lexile NC920L (Rev: BL 7/12; LMC 3–4/13; SLJ 7/12) [973]

12613 Sullivant, Holly J. *Hamsters* (7–12). Illus. Series: Our Best Friends. 2009, Eldorado Ink LB $26.95 (978-193290430-7). Everything you need to know about caring for a pet hamster, with interesting sidebars and eye-catching images. (Rev: BL 6/1–15/09) [636.935]

CATS

12614 Arnold, Caroline. *Cats: In from the Wild* (4–7). Photos by Richard Hewett. 1993, Carolrhoda LB $19.93 (978-0-87614-692-7). Domestic and wild cats are highlighted with comparisons and contrasts. (Rev: BL 8/93) [636.8]

12615 Gerstenfeld, Sheldon L. *The Cat Care Book: All You Need to Know to Keep Your Cat Healthy and Happy. Rev. ed.* (8–12). 1989, Addison-Wesley paper $17.50 (978-0-201-09569-2). Tips on how to choose a cat and detailed information on taking care of cats as pets. (Rev: BL 9/15/89) [636.8]

12616 Mattern, Joanne. *The American Shorthair Cat* (4–7). Series: Learning About Cats. 2002, Capstone LB $23.93 (978-0-7368-1300-6). Beautiful photographs of frisky felines are accompanied by data about the physical characteristics and personality, with a glossary, bibliography, and lists of addresses and Web sites. Also use *The Manx Cat* (2002). (Rev: BL 12/1/02; HBG 3/03) [636.8]

12617 Morris, Desmond. *Catwatching* (8–12). 1987, Crown paper $8.95 (978-0-517-88053-1). Using a question-and-answer approach, the author explores many facets of cat behavior. (Rev: BL 4/1/87) [636.8]

12618 Singer, Marilyn. *Cats to the Rescue* (4–7). Illus. by Jean Cassels. 2006, Henry Holt $16.95 (978-0-8050-7433-8). This collection of true cat stories focuses on feats ranging from catching tens of thousands of mice to detecting a gas leak. (Rev: BL 9/15/06; SLJ 11/06) [636.8]

12619 Whitehead, Sarah. *How to Speak Cat!* (4–8). 2008, Scholastic paper $6.99 (978-0-545-02079-4). Amply illustrated, this book offers advice on building a relationship with a pet cat through body language cues and mutual respect. (Rev: SLJ 6/1/09) [599.75]

DOGS

12620 American Kennel Club. *The Complete Dog Book. 19th ed.* (7–12). 1998, Book House $32.95 (978-0-87605-148-1). The standard manual for dog owners and guide to every AKC-recognized breed. (Rev: BL 6/15/85) [636.7]

12621 Bain, Terry. *You Are a Dog (Life Through the Eyes of Man's Best Friend)* (8–12). 2004, Harmony $16.00 (978-1-4000-5242-4). A humorous dog's-eye view of the world. (Rev: SLJ 1/05) [636.7]

12622 Bial, Raymond. *Rescuing Rover: Saving America's Dogs* (4–7). Illus. 2011, Houghton Mifflin $16.99 (978-0-547-34125-5). Cruelty to animals, puppy mills, dogfighting, dog rescue services, and animal shelters are all discussed in this wide-ranging survey that also includes a personal account of adopting a rescue dog. Lexile NC1230L (Rev: BL 6/1/11; LMC 1–2/12; SLJ 7/11) [636.08]

12623 Bolan, Sandra. *Caring for Your Mutt* (7–12). Series: Our Best Friend. 2008, Eldorado Ink LB $25.95 (978-1-932904-20-8). Readers who own mixed-breed (and no-breed) dogs will enjoy this book, which gives information on basic care and explains that mutts are sometimes puzzling and often pleasant surprises. (Rev: BL 4/1/08) [636.7]

12624 Fennell, Jan. *The Dog Listener: Learn How to Communicate with Your Dog for Willing Cooperation* (8–12). 2004, HarperResource paper $16.95 (978-0-06-008946-7). This comprehensive guide tells how one can peacefully coexist with one's dog and how successful training can be accomplished without violent behavior. (Rev: BL 1/1–15/04) [636.7]

12625 Gerstenfeld, Sheldon L. *The Dog Care Book: All You Need to Know to Keep Your Dog Healthy and Happy. Rev. ed.* (8–12). 1989, Addison-Wesley paper $17.00 (978-0-201-09667-5). Tips on selecting a dog plus extensive material on care and feeding. (Rev: BL 9/15/89) [636.7]

12626 Gewirtz, Elaine Waldorf. *The Chihuahua* (4–8). Illus. Series: Our Best Friends. 2011, Eldorado Ink LB $34.95 (978-193290475-8). An attractive introduction to these small dogs and their pros and cons as pets. (Rev: BL 4/15/11) [636.76]

12627 Gewirtz, Elaine Waldorf. *Fetch This Book: Train Your Dog to Do Almost Anything* (4–8). Series: Our Best Friends. 2010, Eldorado Ink $34.95 (978-1-932904-60-4). In clearly written chapters such as "What Your Dog Thinks About Training," "Establishing Who's in Charge," and "Making Your Dog a Champion," this is a practical guide to dog training from the basics to advanced opportunities in service roles. (Rev: BL 8/10*; SLJ 9/1/10) [636.7]

12628 Gorrell, Gena K. *Working Like a Dog: The Story of Working Dogs Through History* (4–8). 2003, Tundra $16.95 (978-0-88776-589-6). A comprehensive and very appealing look at dogs' services to man throughout history — as hunters and trackers, bomb sniffers, guide dogs, and companions, to name but a few. (Rev: BL 11/1/03; SLJ 12/03) [636.73]

12629 Grogan, John. *Marley: A Dog Like No Other* (4–7). Illus. 2007, HarperCollins $16.99 (978-0-06-124033-1). An adaptation of Grogan's book for adults, *Marley & Me*, this story of a hopelessly out-of-control but lovable dog who dies too soon will touch young readers. ◯ (Rev: BL 7/07; SLJ 7/07) [636.752]

12630 Halls, Kelly Milner. *Wild Dogs: Past and Present* (4–7). 2005, Darby Creek $18.95 (978-1-58196-027-3). A wide-ranging introduction to dogs and their history, with attractive design, many photographs, and lots of factboxes about dogs both wild and domestic. (Rev: BL 12/1/05; SLJ 11/05) [599.77]

12631 Hampl, Patricia. *The Nature of Dogs* (7–12). Illus. by Mary Ludington. 2007, Simon & Schuster $35.00

(978-1-4165-4287-2). Beautiful photographs accompany well-written informative text about various breeds of dogs. (Rev: BL 9/15/07) [636.7]

12632 Houston, Dick. *Bulu: African Wonder Dog* (5–8). 2010, Random House LB $18.99 (978-0-375-94720-9). The true story of an African terrier with an unusual personality and a protective attitude toward other animals. Lexile 700L (Rev: BL 3/15/10; LMC 8–9/10; SLJ 5/10) [636.7]

12633 Mehus-Roe, Kristin. *Dogs for Kids! Everything You Need to Know About Dogs* (4–7). Illus. 2007, Bowtie paper $14.95 (978-1-931993-83-8). From a history of dogs to information on breeds, anatomy, and behavior to advice on care and training — as the title says, this book is all you need. (Rev: BL 2/15/08; SLJ 6/07) [636.7]

12634 Morn, September. *The Doberman Pinscher* (4–7). Illus. Series: Our Best Friends. 2011, Eldorado Ink LB $34.95 (978-193290477-2). An attractive introduction to these popular dogs and their pros and cons as pets. (Rev: BL 4/15/11) [636.73]

12635 Murphy, Claire Rudolf, and Jane G. Haigh. *Gold Rush Dogs* (6–12). 2001, Alaska Northwest $16.95 (978-0-88240-534-6). Nine dogs that played important roles in the Yukon are profiled here with many sidebars that provide background historical detail. (Rev: BL 9/1/01; SLJ 9/01) [636.7]

12636 Page, Jake. *Dogs: A Natural History* (6–12). 2007, Smithsonian $24.95 (978-0-06-113259-9). Owner of six dogs, Page shares his extensive knowledge of doggy history, behavior, breeds, and relationship with humans. (Rev: BL 9/1/07) [636.7]

12637 Paulsen, Gary. *My Life in Dog Years* (5–10). 1998, Delacorte $15.95 (978-0-385-32570-7). The famous novelist tells about eight wonderful dogs that he has known and loved over the years. (Rev: BCCB 3/98; BL 1/1–15/98; SLJ 3/98; VOYA 4/98) [636.7]

12638 Rogers, Tammie. *4-H Guide to Dog Training and Dog Tricks* (5–12). 2010, Voyageur paper $18.99 (978-0-7603-3629-8). Learn how to train your dog to master the basics and then move on to competition skills and even emptying the dryer! (Rev: SLJ 5/10) [636.7]

12639 Rosenthal, Lisa. *A Dog's Best Friend: An Activity Book for Kids and Their Dogs* (4–7). Illus. by Bonnie Matthews. 1999, Chicago Review paper $12.95 (978-1-55652-362-5). This book that gives hints on how to choose a dog and care for a puppy offers 60 projects related to these subjects including crafts, recipes, and games. (Rev: SLJ 1/00) [636.7]

12640 Schweitzer, Karen. *The Cocker Spaniel* (4–7). Illus. Series: Our Best Friends. 2011, Eldorado Ink LB $34.95 (978-193290476-5). An attractive introduction to these dogs and their pros and cons as pets. (Rev: BL 4/15/11) [636.752]

12641 Silverstein, Alvin. *Different Dogs* (4–7). Series: What a Pet! 2000, Twenty-First Century LB $23.90 (978-0-7613-1371-7). Several different breeds of dogs are introduced in pictures and text plus information on cost, food, housing, and training. (Rev: HBG 10/00; SLJ 5/00) [636.7]

FISHES

12642 Turner, Pamela S. *Project Seahorse* (5–8). Illus. by Scott Tuason. Series: Scientists in the Field. 2010, Houghton Mifflin $18 (978-0-547-20713-1). Sea horses and the scientists who study these beguiling creatures are the focus of this book, which contains the story of fishermen and biologists working together to protect a reef where they live. (Rev: BL 7/10; HB 9–10/10; SLJ 8/10) [596]

HORSES

12643 Budd, Jackie. *Seasons of the Horse: A Practical Guide to Year-Round Equine Care* (5–12). 2007, T.F.H. $29.95 (978-0-7938-0611-9). Well-organized and visually pleasing, this book provides a complete guide to caring for a horse, including nutrition and exercise. (Rev: SLJ 3/08)

12644 Budiansky, Stephen. *The World According to Horses: How They Run, See, and Think* (4–8). 2000, Henry Holt $17.95 (978-0-8050-6054-6). This book explores horses' behavior — such as their sight and thinking powers — and goes on to explain how this knowledge was gained through observation and experiments. (Rev: BCCB 5/00; BL 3/1/00; HB 5–6/00; HBG 10/00; SLJ 7/00; VOYA 6/00) [636.1]

12645 Frydenborg, Kay. *Wild Horse Scientists* (7–9). Illus. Series: Scientists in the Field. 2012, Houghton Mifflin $18.99 (978-0-547-51831-2). The efforts of two wildlife veterinarians involved with studying and protecting the wild horses of Assateague island are profiled in this well-written volume and compelling photographs. (Rev: BL 12/1/12*; HB 1–2/13; SLJ 12/12*)

12646 Henry, Marguerite. *Album of Horses* (5–8). Illus. by Wesley Dennis. 1951, Macmillan paper $11.99 (978-0-689-71709-3). A beautifully illustrated guide to 20 breeds of horses.

12647 Joyce, Gare. *Northern Dancer: King of the Racetrack* (5–8). Illus. 2012, Fitzhenry & Whiteside $22.95 (978-155455163-7); paper $9.95 (978-1-55041-496-7). An interesting biography of the racehorse that overcame an inauspicious appearance to win the Derby and Preakness and sire many other winners. (Rev: BL 7/12; SLJ 7/12) [798.40092]

12648 Jurmain, Suzanne. *Once Upon a Horse: A History of Horses and How They Shaped Our History* (5–9). 1989, Lothrop $15.95 (978-0-688-05550-9). A history of the horse and how it has been domesticated and used by humans. (Rev: BL 12/15/89; SLJ 1/90; VOYA 4/90) [636.1]

12649 Ransford, Sandy. *The Kingfisher Illustrated Horse and Pony Encyclopedia* (4–8). Photos by Bob Langrish. 2004, Kingfisher $24.95 (978-0-7534-5781-8). After describing the history and various breeds of horses, this comprehensive and highly illustrated volume explains how to care for horses and how to ride them well and safely. (Rev: BL 3/1/05; SLJ 1/05) [636.1]

12650 Richter, Judy. *Riding for Kids* (4–8). 2003, Storey $23.95 (978-1-58017-511-1); paper $16.95 (978-1-58017-510-4). An introduction to horsemanship, from caring for horses and riding equipment to advice on safety, showing, and jumping. (Rev: BL 1/1–15/04; SLJ 3/04) [798.2]

12651 Scanlan, Lawrence. *The Big Red Horse: The Story of Secretariat and the Loyal Groom Who Loved Him* (4–8). Photos by Raymond Woolfe. 2010, HarperTrophy paper $7.99 (978-0-00-639352-8). Prized racehorse Secretariat's inspiring story is portrayed in this biography, which features a variety of compelling anecdotes and black-and-white pictures. (Rev: SLJ 3/1/11)

12652 Stefoff, Rebecca. *Horses* (5–8). Series: AnimalWays. 2000, Marshall Cavendish LB $31.36 (978-0-7614-1139-0). A well-illustrated account that describes the physical and behavioral characteristics of horses, their place in the classification system, and their relationships with humans. (Rev: BL 1/1–15/01) [599.884]

12653 Stromberg, Tony. *Spirit Horses* (8–12). 2005, New World Library $40.00 (978-1-57731-499-8). A photographic celebration of horses in a large-format album, accompanied by quotes from diverse sources. (Rev: BL 11/1/05) [636.1]

12654 van der Linde, Laurel. *From Mustangs to Movie Stars: Five True Horse Legends of Our Time* (4–7). 1995, Millbrook LB $24.40 (978-1-56294-456-8). Biographies of five famous horses are recounted, from the racer Native Dancer to Cass Olé, who was the star of the film *The Black Stallion*. (Rev: BCCB 12/95; SLJ 12/95) [636.1]

12655 Wilsdon, Christina. *For Horse-Crazy Girls Only: Everything You Want to Know About Horses* (3–8). Illus. by Alecia Underhill. 2010, Feiwel & Friends $14.99 (978-0-312-60323-6). A lighthearted survey of all things horse, from horse jokes and lore to information on markings and ailments to practical tips on working with horses. (Rev: SLJ 4/11) [636.1]

Zoos, Aquariums, and Animal Care

12656 Balliet, Gay L. *Lions and Tigers and Mares . . . Oh My!* (8–12). 2004, RDR paper $17.95 (978-1-57143-105-9). In humorous, appealing text, the wife of a Pennsylvania veterinarian sheds new light on the day-to-day challenges facing a vet who treats large and exotic animals. (Rev: BL 9/15/04) [636.089]

12657 Brown, Bradford B. *While You're Here, Doc: Farmyard Adventures of a Maine Veterinarian* (8–12). 2006, Tilbury House paper $15.00 (978-0-88448-279-6). Entertaining stories about life as a veterinarian in rural Maine. (Rev: BL 3/15/06) [636.0]

12658 Halls, Kelly Milner, and William Sumner. *Saving the Baghdad Zoo: A True Story of Hope and Heroes* (4–7). Illus. by William Sumner. 2010, Greenwillow $17.99 (978-0-06-177202-3). American soldiers work together with Iraqi citizens to protect and provide for the animals of the Baghdad zoo in this inspiring story of cooperation. (Rev: BL 2/15/10; SLJ 6/10) [590.73]

12659 Rinard, Judith E. *Zoos Without Cages* (5–8). 1981, National Geographic LB $12.50 (978-0-87044-340-4). A description of the new zoos that strive to reproduce the natural habitat of the enclosed animals. [590.74]

Chemistry

General and Miscellaneous

12660 Angliss, Sarah. *Gold* (4–8). Series: The Elements. 1999, Marshall Cavendish LB $25.64 (978-0-7614-0887-1). Easy-to-follow diagrams, fact boxes, and color illustrations accompany an informative text that introduces gold, where it is mined and processed, its properties, value, and uses. (Rev: BL 2/15/00; HBG 10/00) [546]

12661 Baxter, Roberta. *Chemical Reaction* (4–8). Series: The Kidhaven Science Library. 2004, Gale LB $26.20 (978-0-7377-2072-3). Clear, concise text, supported by full-color photographs and diagrams, describes many types of reactions — oxidation and photosynthesis, for example — and discusses their uses. (Rev: SLJ 6/05)

12662 Beatty, Richard. *Copper* (4–8). Series: The Elements. 2000, Marshall Cavendish LB $25.64 (978-0-7614-0945-8). This book identifies the element copper, defines its properties and describes its uses in everyday life, especially in electrical cables. (Rev: BL 1/1–15/01; HBG 10/01; SLJ 2/01) [546]

12663 Beatty, Richard. *The Lanthanides* (4–8). Series: The Elements. 2007, Marshall Cavendish LB $19.95 (978-0-7614-2687-5). This detailed and thorough overview of the 15 metal elements in the Lanthanides provides fact boxes and clear explanations in a graphically pleasing format. (Rev: SLJ 3/08)

12664 Beatty, Richard. *Phosphorus* (4–8). Series: The Elements. 2000, Marshall Cavendish LB $25.64 (978-0-7614-0946-5). This book describes this nonmetallic element, lists its properties, tells how it behaves, and discusses such uses as matches and fertilizers. (Rev: BL 1/1–15/01; HBG 10/01; SLJ 2/01) [546]

12665 Beatty, Richard. *Sulfur* (4–8). Series: The Elements. 2000, Marshall Cavendish LB $25.64 (978-0-7614-0948-9). Introduces this nonmetallic element, its characteristics, various compounds, and uses in everyday life, with color photographs, easy-to-follow diagrams, fact boxes, and a clear text. (Rev: BL 1/1–15/01; HBG 10/01; SLJ 2/01) [546]

12666 Brandolini, Anita. *Fizz, Bubble and Flash! Element Explorations and Atom Adventures for Hands-On Science Fun!* (4–7). Illus. by Michael Kline. Series: Kids Can! 2003, Williamson paper $14.25 (978-1-885593-83-2). A friendly narrative and cartoon-style drawing present activities that illustrate basic scientific concepts. (Rev: BL 1/1–15/04; SLJ 11/03) [546]

12667 Cobb, Allan B. *Cadmium* (4–8). Series: The Elements. 2007, Marshall Cavendish LB $19.95 (978-0-7614-2686-8). This well-designed overview of cadmium is thorough and also includes a section on how the element relates to the health of human beings. (Rev: SLJ 3/08)

12668 Cobb, Allan B. *Earth Chemistry* (8–12). Illus. Series: Essential Chemistry. 2009, Chelsea House $35 (978-0-7910-9677-2). Colorful illustrations and informative sidebars punctuate this comprehensive book on the chemical interactions between the four spheres — the atmosphere, hydrosphere, lithosphere, and biosphere — of the Earth. (Rev: SLJ 5/1/09)

12669 Cobb, Vicki. *Chemically Active! Experiments You Can Do at Home* (6–9). 1985, HarperCollins LB $14.89 (978-0-397-32080-6). A group of scientific experiments that demonstrate chemical principles and can be performed with common household items. (Rev: SLJ 8/85; VOYA 12/85) [507]

12670 Cooper, Chris. *Arsenic* (4–8). Illus. Series: The Elements. 2006, Benchmark LB $19.95 (978-0-7614-2203-7). A basic guide to arsenic's properties and uses (including as a poison and in industrial applications). (Rev: SLJ 5/07) [546]

12671 Farndon, John. *Aluminum* (4–8). Series: The Elements. 2000, Marshall Cavendish LB $25.64 (978-0-

7614-0947-2). This silvery, metallic element is introduced, with material on its individual characteristics, how it behaves, and its many uses in everyday life. (Rev: BL 1/1–15/01; HBG 10/01) [546]

12672 Farndon, John. *Oxygen* (5–8). Series: The Elements. 1998, Benchmark LB $25.64 (978-0-7614-0879-6). Oxygen, its properties, uses, and various chemical combinations are covered in this informative text that also discusses the ozone layer. (Rev: HBG 10/99; SLJ 2/99) [540]

12673 Goodstein, Madeline. *Plastics and Polymers Science Fair Projects: Using Hair Gel, Soda Bottles, and Slimy Stuff* (7–12). Series: Chemistry! Best Science Projects. 2004, Enslow LB $26.60 (978-0-7660-2123-5). Introduced by a discussion of the concept of polymers and a model of a hydrocarbon chain, subsequent projects build on this knowledge. (Rev: SLJ 7/04) [507]

12674 Gray, Leon. *Iodine* (5–8). Series: Elements (Group 7). 2004, Marshall Cavendish $25.64 (978-0-7614-1812-2). 2004, Marshall Cavendish $25.64 (978-0-7614-1812-2). This introduction to iodine examines the importance of this substance to body chemistry, as well as how it was discovered, where it is found, and its physical characteristics. (Rev: BL 12/1/04) [546]

12675 Green, Dan. *The Elements* (7–10). Illus. Series: Discover More. 2012, Scholastic $15.99 (978-054533019-0). A visually attractive survey of the periodic table, this volume also comes with a downloadable ebook supplement. (Rev: BL 4/1/12; SLJ 4/12) [546]

12676 Jackson, Tom. *Lithium* (4–8). Illus. Series: The Elements. 2006, Benchmark LB $19.95 (978-0-7614-2199-3). A basic guide to lithium's properties and uses in batteries and pharmaceuticals. (Rev: SLJ 5/07) [546]

12677 Lepora, Nathan. *Molybdenum* (4–8). Illus. Series: The Elements. 2006, Benchmark LB $19.95 (978-0-7614-2201-3). A basic guide to molybdenum's properties and uses (including its medical applications). (Rev: SLJ 5/07) [546]

12678 Lew, Kristi. *Acids and Bases* (8–12). Illus. Series: Essential Chemistry. 2009, Chelsea House $35 (978-0-7910-9783-0). Colorful illustrations and informative sidebars punctuate this comprehensive book on acids and bases and their importance. (Rev: SLJ 5/1/09)

12679 Miller, Ron. *The Elements: What You Really Want to Know* (7–12). Illus. by author. 2005, Twenty-First Century LB $29.27 (978-0-7613-2794-3). After historical information and profiles of key scientists, Miller provides information on each element in order of atomic number. (Rev: SLJ 3/06) [540]

12680 O'Daly, Anne. *Sodium* (4–8). Series: The Elements. 2001, Marshall Cavendish LB $25.64 (978-0-7614-1271-7). Diagrams and full-color illustrations are used to introduce sodium and its characteristics and importance in everyday life. (Rev: BL 3/15/02; HBG 3/02) [546]

12681 Oxlade, Chris. *Acids and Bases. Rev. ed.* (6–8). Series: Chemicals in Action. 2007, Heinemann LB $31.43 (978-1-4329-0050-2). After explaining the nature of acids and bases, this attractively arranged volume looks at reactions that take place around us and provides a few experiments. Also use *Atoms, Elements and Compounds,* and *States of Matter* (all 2007). (Rev: SLJ 10/07) [546]

12682 Roza, Greg. *Calcium* (5–8). Illus. Series: Understanding the Elements of the Periodic Table. 2007, Rosen LB $26.50 (978-1-4042-1963-2). This reader-friendly volume contains a full overview of calcium, including basic information and interesting sidebar features such as the amount of calcium found in different foods. (Rev: SLJ 3/08)

12683 Saucerman, Linda. *Chlorine* (5–8). Illus. Series: Understanding the Elements of the Periodic Table. 2007, Rosen LB $26.50 (978-1-4042-1962-5). Little-known facts interspersed among basic details make this book about chlorine an interesting read. (Rev: SLJ 3/08)

12684 Sommers, Michael A. *Phosphorus* (5–8). Illus. 2007, Rosen LB $26.50 (978-1-4042-1960-1). An easy to understand overview of phosphorus, including attractive graphics and interesting, little known facts (includes charts, diagrams, illustrations, photos, reproductions, bibliography, further reading, glossary, index and Web sites). (Rev: SLJ 3/08)

12685 Stimola, Aubrey. *Sulfur* (5–8). Illus. 2007, Rosen LB $26.50 (978-1-4042-1961-8). This basic overview of sulfur is well-organized and easy to understand, and contains interesting facts such as the use of sulfur in medicine (includes charts, diagrams, illustrations, photos, reproductions, bibliography, further reading, glossary, index and Web sites). (Rev: SLJ 3/08)

12686 Uttley, Colin. *Magnesium* (4–8). Series: The Elements. 1999, Marshall Cavendish LB $25.64 (978-0-7614-0889-5). This book explores magnesium, a silvery metallic element important in living organisms, and explains its place in the periodic table, as well as its forms, uses, and properties. (Rev: BL 2/15/00; HBG 10/00) [546]

12687 Vancleave, Janice. *Step-By-Step Science Experiments in Chemistry* (5–8). Series: Janice VanCleave's First-Place Science Fair Projects. 2012, Rosen Central LB $33.25 (978-1-4488-6981-7). An updated volume with step-by-step instructions for 22 experiments mostly using easily found materials. (Rev: SLJ 10/12) [540.78]

12688 Watt, Susan. *Cobalt* (4–8). Illus. Series: The Elements. 2006, Benchmark LB $19.95 (978-0-7614-2200-6). A basic guide to cobalt's properties and uses. (Rev: SLJ 5/07) [546]

12689 Watt, Susan. *Lead* (4–8). Series: The Elements. 2001, Marshall Cavendish LB $25.64 (978-0-7614-

1273-1). Explores the history, origins, discovery, characteristics, and uses of this heavy metallic element in everyday life. (Rev: BL 3/15/02; HBG 3/02) [546]

12690 Watt, Susan. *Zirconium* (4–8). Series: The Elements. 2007, Marshall Cavendish LB $19.95 (978-0-7614-2688-2). This volume covers all aspects of zirconium including its use in dating some rocks and minerals. (Rev: SLJ 3/08)

12691 West, Krista. *Bromine* (4–8). Series: The Elements. 2007, Marshall Cavendish LB $19.95 (978-0-7614-2685-1). The element bromine is covered in detail in this attractively designed volume. (Rev: SLJ 3/08)

Geology and Geography

Earth and Geology

12692 Blashfield, Jean F., and Richard P. Jacobs. *When Ice Threatened Living Things: The Pleistocene* (6–9). Series: Prehistoric North America. 2005, Heinemann LB $37.14 (978-1-4034-7662-3). Provides information on the geology of North America during the Pleistocene era, when much of the continent was covered in ice. Also use *When Land, Sea, and Life Began: The Precambrian, When Dinosaurs Ruled: The Mesozoic Era,* and *When Life Flourished in Ancient Seas: The Early Paleozoic Era* (all 2005). (Rev: SLJ 5/06)

12693 Calhoun, Yael. *Earth Science Fair Projects Using Rocks, Minerals, Magnets, Mud, and More* (5–8). Series: Earth Science! Best Science Projects. 2005, Enslow LB $26.60 (978-0-7660-2363-5). More than 20 geology-related projects are introduced with clear instructions and interesting background information. (Rev: BL 11/1/05) [550]

12694 Campbell, Ann-Jeanette, and Ronald Rood. *The New York Public Library Incredible Earth: A Book of Answers for Kids* (4–7). 1996, Wiley paper $14.95 (978-0-471-14497-7). Questions and answers involving science, collected from the reference department of the New York Public Library. (Rev: BL 9/15/96; SLJ 1/97) [550]

12695 Gardner, Robert. *Planet Earth Science Fair Projects Using the Moon, Stars, Beach Balls, Frisbees, and Other Far-Out Stuff* (6–12). Series: Earth Science! Best Science Projects. 2005, Enslow LB $26.60 (978-0-7660-2362-8). Earth science projects are clearly presented with background information necessary to give full understanding of the underlying principles. (Rev: SLJ 7/05) [551]

12696 Gardner, Robert. *Planet Earth Science Fair Projects, Revised and Expanded Using the Scientific Method* (5–8). Series: Earth Science Projects Using the Scientific Method. 2010, Enslow LB $34.60 (978-0-7660-3423-5). With a focus on the basics of scientific investigation, this well-organized and attractive volume gives an overview of the topic and provides experiments that support various hypotheses. (Rev: LMC 8–9/10) [550]

12697 Gilpin, Dan. *Planet Earth: What Planet Are You On?* (5–8). Illus. by Simon Basher. 2010, Kingfisher paper $8.99 (978-0-7534-6412-0). Geological features of the Earth (such as the core, crust, and volcanoes) are personified as cartoon characters in this informational and entertaining overview of earth science. (Rev: BL 5/15/10; LMC 8–9/10) [550]

12698 Hehner, Barbara Embury. *Blue Planet* (7–12). Series: Wide World. 1992, Harcourt $17.95 (978-0-15-200423-1). An examination of the interdependent systems that make up our planet, including plate tectonics, volcanoes, weather, satellites, and the ozone layer. (Rev: BL 11/15/92; SLJ 10/92) [508]

12699 O'Neill, Catherine. *Natural Wonders of North America* (7–12). 1984, National Geographic LB $12.50 (978-0-87044-519-4). Excellent color photographs complement the text and maps that describe such natural wonders as tundra regions, volcanoes, glaciers, and the Badlands of South Dakota. [557]

12700 Patent, Dorothy Hinshaw. *Shaping the Earth* (4–7). 2000, Clarion $18.00 (978-0-395-85691-8). The evolution of the earth is traced in this compelling book that describes how the surface has changed and continues to change, with coverage of plate tectonics, ice ages, natural disasters, and descriptions of its natural wonders. (Rev: BL 3/15/00; HBG 10/00; SLJ 4/00) [550]

12701 Redfern, Martin. *The Kingfisher Young People's Book of Planet Earth* (4–8). 1999, Kingfisher $21.95 (978-0-7534-5180-9). A useful, enjoyable look at the earth's geology, atmosphere, and weather. (Rev: HBG 10/00; SLJ 2/00) [525]

12702 VanCleave, Janice. *Janice VanCleave's A+ Projects in Earth Science: Winning Experiments for Science Fairs and Extra Credit* (5–10). 1999, Wiley paper $12.95 (978-0-471-17770-8). Thirty projects varying in complexity are included in this exploration of topography, minerals, atmospheric composition, the ocean floor, and erosion. (Rev: BL 12/1/98; SLJ 6/99) [550]

12703 Vancleave, Janice. *Step-By-Step Science Experiments in Earth Science* (5–8). Series: Janice VanCleave's First-Place Science Fair Projects. 2012, Rosen Central LB $33.25 (978-1-4488-6983-1). An updated volume with step-by-step instructions for 22 experiments mostly using easily found materials. (Rev: SLJ 10/12) [550.78]

12704 Vogt, Gregory L. *Earth's Core and Mantle: Heavy Metal, Moving Rock* (6–9). Series: Earth's Spheres. 2007, Twenty-First Century LB $29.27 (978-0-7613-2837-7). Vogt explores the makeup of the universe, the creation of the Earth and its moon, and the planet's core and mantle. Also use *The Lithosphere* (2007), which examines the crust, plate tectonics, volcanoes, and geysers. (Rev: SLJ 5/07) [551.1]

Earthquakes and Volcanoes

12705 Burleigh, Robert. *Volcanoes: Journey to the Crater's Edge* (5–9). Adapted by Robert Burleigh. Illus. by David Giraudon. Photos by Philippe Bourseiller. 2003, Abrams $14.95 (978-0-8109-4590-6). Volcanoes, lava lakes, ash plumes, and other related phenomena are beautifully illustrated in this oversized photoessay. (Rev: BL 1/1–15/04; SLJ 12/03) [550]

12706 Christian, Spencer, and Antonia Felix. *Shake, Rattle and Roll: The World's Most Amazing Natural Forces* (6–10). Series: Spencer Christian's World of Wonders. 1997, Wiley paper $13.95 (978-0-471-15291-0). This book supplies good information and suitable projects involving earthquakes and volcanoes, with material on topics including plate tectonics, seismic waves, geysers, and hot springs. (Rev: SLJ 6/98) [551.2]

12707 Clarkson, Peter. *Volcanoes* (8–12). Series: World Life Library. 2000, Voyageur paper $16.95 (978-0-89658-502-7). Illustrated with color photographs and diagrams, this account gives general information about volcanoes and presents a tour of the world's most famous ones. [551.2]

12708 Harper, Kristine C. *The Mount St. Helens Volcanic Eruptions* (5–8). Series: Environmental Disasters. 2005, Facts on File $35.00 (978-0-8160-5757-3). The environment impact of Mount St. Helens' eruptions is examined in this title from the Environmental Disasters series. (Rev: SLJ 11/05)

12709 Reed, Jennifer. *Earthquakes: Disaster and Survival, 2005* (4–7). Series: Disaster and Survival. 2005, Enslow LB $23.93 (978-0-7660-2381-9). Major earthquakes and their effects are detailed in text and personal accounts, with a chapter devoted to the December 2004 Asian tsunami. (Rev: BL 5/1/05; SLJ 10/05) [363.34]

12710 Rubin, Ken. *Volcanoes and Earthquakes* (4–7). Illus. Series: Insiders. 2007, Simon & Schuster $16.99 (978-1-4169-3862-0). Vivid illustrations accompany informative text, charts, and graphs introducing earthquakes and volcanoes and some of the important disasters that have taken place. (Rev: SLJ 10/07) [551.21]

12711 Stewart, Melissa. *Inside Earthquakes* (5–8). Illus. by Cynthia Shaw. Series: Inside. 2011, Sterling $16.95 (978-140275877-5); paper $9.95 (978-14027816-3-6). A dramatic presentation of information about what causes earthquakes and their impact on the population and environment, with many photographs and gatefolds. (Rev: BL 11/1/11) [551.22]

12712 Stewart, Melissa. *Inside Volcanoes* (5–8). Illus. by Cynthia Shaw. Series: Inside. 2011, Sterling $16.95 (978-140275876-8); paper $9.95 (978-14027816-4-3). A dramatic presentation of information about the different kinds of volcanoes and eruptions and their impact on the population and environment, with many photographs and gatefolds. (Rev: BL 11/1/11) [551.21]

12713 VanCleave, Janice. *Janice VanCleave's Volcanoes: Mind-Boggling Experiments You Can Turn into Science Fair Projects* (4–7). 1994, Wiley paper $10.95 (978-0-471-30811-9). Twenty experiments that explore the properties of erupting volcanoes using simple materials that can often be found around the house. (Rev: BL 7/94; SLJ 8/94) [551.2]

12714 Watson, Nancy. *Our Violent Earth* (4–8). 1982, National Geographic LB $12.50 (978-0-87044-388-6). A discussion of such phenomena as earthquakes, volcanoes, and floods. [363.3]

12715 Winchester, Simon. *The Day the World Exploded: The Earthshaking Catastrophe at Krakatoa* (5–8). Adapted by Dwight Jon Zimmerman. Illus. by Jason Chin. 2008, HarperCollins $22.99 (978-0-06-123982-3). After looking at volcanoes and the reasons for eruptions plus the culture and economy of the region at the time, Winchester describes the 1883 disaster and its aftermath; an adaptation of a book for adults titled *Krakatoa* (2003). (Rev: SLJ 11/08; VOYA 8/08) [363.3495]

12716 Worth, Richard. *The San Francisco Earthquake* (5–8). Series: Environmental Disasters. 2005, Facts on File $35.00 (978-0-8160-5756-6). Worth examines how the San Francisco earthquake of 1906 affected the region's environment. (Rev: SLJ 11/05) [363.34]

Physical Geography

General and Miscellaneous

12717 Casil, Amy Sterling. *The Creation of Canyons* (5–9). Series: Land Formation: The Shifting, Moving, Changing Earth. 2010, Rosen LB $29.95 (978-1-4358-5296-8). Part of a series that addresses how landforms are created and the ways in which scientists seek to understand them, this volume includes useful examples and provides interesting career information. (Rev: LMC 1–2/10)

12718 Moore, Peter D. *Tundra* (6–10). Illus. by Richard Garratt. 2006, Chelsea House $39.50 (978-0-8160-5325-4). This interesting volume discusses not only the geography, geology, ecosystem, and biodiversity of tundras around the world but also history related to the tundra, uses of the tundra, and the future of the tundra in terms of climate change and conservation. (Rev: SLJ 12/06)

12719 Warhol, Tom. *Chaparral and Scrub* (5–8). Series: Earth's Biomes. 2006, Marshall Cavendish LB $32.79 (978-0-7614-2195-5). Report writers will appreciate this attractive introduction to the characteristics of this biome and its plants and animals; also use *Tundra* (2006). (Rev: LMC 8–9/07; SLJ 8/07) [577.3]

Deserts

12720 Allaby, Michael. *Deserts* (6–10). Illus. by Richard Garratt. Series: Biomes of the Earth. 2006, Chelsea House $39.50 (978-0-8160-5320-9). This interesting volume discusses not only the geography, geology, climates, and flora and fauna of deserts around the world but also history related to deserts, desert exploration, desert industries (oil, solar energy, minerals, and tourism), threats to deserts, and efforts to manage deserts. (Rev: LMC 1/07; SLJ 12/06)

12721 Patent, Dorothy Hinshaw. *Life in a Desert* (5–8). Series: Ecosystems in Action. 2003, Lerner LB $26.60 (978-0-8225-2140-2). This account explores the plant and animal life in deserts and how human intervention has changed this ecosystem. (Rev: BL 9/15/03; HBG 10/03) [574.5]

12722 Sayre, April Pulley. *Desert* (4–7). Series: Exploring Earth's Biomes. 1994, Twenty-First Century LB $25.90 (978-0-8050-2825-6). After a general introduction to deserts, a specific one is explored in brief chapters with excellent illustrations. (Rev: BL 1/1/95*; SLJ 1/95) [574.5]

12723 Silverman, Buffy. *Desert Food Chains* (4–7). Series: Protecting Food Chains. 2010, Heinemann LB $32 (978-1-4329-3856-7); paper $8.99 (978-1-4329-3863-5). With chapter headings that ask questions such as "What Are the Producers in Deserts?" and "What Are the Decomposers in Deserts?," this volume explores species and food chains in deserts and discusses why we need to protect them. (Rev: SLJ 11/1/10) [577.5]

12724 Warhol, Tom. *Desert* (5–8). Series: Earth's Biomes. 2006, Marshall Cavendish LB $32.79 (978-0-7614-2194-8). Report writers will appreciate this attractive introduction to the characteristics of this biome and its plants and animals. (Rev: SLJ 8/07) [577.54]

Forests and Rain Forests

12725 Chinery, Michael. *Poisoners and Pretenders* (5–8). Series: Secrets of the Rainforests. 2000, Crabtree LB $25.27 (978-0-7787-0219-1); paper $7.95 (978-0-7787-0229-0). After a brief description of a rain forest, this book looks at animals found there and their mimicry, camouflage, venom, natural selection, and adaptation to the environment. Also use *Predators and Prey* (2000). (Rev: SLJ 2/01) [574.5]

12726 Jackson, Kay. *Rain Forests* (4–7). Illus. Series: Our Environment. 2007, Gale LB $23.70 (978-0-7377-3624-3). This well-illustrated volume explores why rain forests are important; what people, plants, and animals live there; why these areas are endangered; and what their future may hold. (Rev: BL 12/1/07) [577.34]

12727 Lasky, Kathryn. *The Most Beautiful Roof in the World: Exploring the Rainforest Canopy* (5–8). 1997, Harcourt paper $9.00 (978-0-15-200897-0). The canopy of plants and animals found in the rain forest of Belize is explored by the author, a biologist, who also explains the methods scientists use to conduct research in this environment, sometimes under extremely difficult conditions. (Rev: BL 4/1/97; SLJ 4/97) [574.5]

12728 Lewington, Anna. *Atlas of the Rain Forests* (6–12). 1997, Raintree $22.98 (978-0-8172-4756-0). Enhanced by maps and photographs, this work contains information on the plant and animal life found in rain forests, the cultures of the people who live in them, and how these environments are changed by economic development. (Rev: BL 5/15/97; SLJ 8/97) [574.5]

12729 McLeish, Ewan. *Rain Forest Destruction* (7–12). Series: What If We Do Nothing? 2007, World Almanac LB $30.60 (978-0-8368-7758-8). McLeish looks at the causes and potentially catastrophic results of deforestation in the rain forests and discusses what we can do to stop the destruction. (Rev: LMC 11–12/07; SLJ 5/07) [578.734]

12730 MacMillan, Dianne M. *Life in a Deciduous Forest* (5–8). Series: Ecosystems in Action. 2003, Lerner LB $26.60 (978-0-8225-4684-9). This book explores the ecosystem, its flora and fauna, where trees shed their leaves in autumn. (Rev: BL 9/15/03; HBG 10/03) [574.5]

12731 Montgomery, Sy. *Encantado: Pink Dolphin of the Amazon* (5–8). Illus. by Diane Taylor Snow. 2002,

Houghton Mifflin $18.00 (978-0-618-13103-7). The author describes the flora and fauna of the South American rain forest seen in her unsuccessful journey to locate the encantado, the elusive pink dolphin. (Rev: BL 4/1/02; HB 7–8/02; HBG 10/02; SLJ 5/02*) [599.53]

12732 Moore, Heidi. *Rain Forest Food Chains* (4–7). Series: Protecting Food Chains. 2010, Heinemann LB $32 (978-1-4329-3860-4); paper $8.99 (978-1-4329-3867-3). With chapter headings that ask questions such as "What Are the Producers in Rain Forests?" and "What Are the Decomposers in Rain Forests?," this volume explores species and food chains within rain forests and discusses why we need to protect them. (Rev: SLJ 11/1/10) [577.3]

12733 Mutel, Cornelia F., and Mary M. Rodgers. *Our Endangered Planet: Tropical Rain Forests* (4–7). Series: Our Endangered Planet. 1991, Lerner LB $27.15 (978-0-8225-2503-5); paper $8.95 (978-0-8225-9629-5). Describes tropical rain forests and the environmental threats they face. (Rev: BL 6/15/91; SLJ 5/91) [333]

12734 Rapp, Valerie. *Life in an Old Growth Forest* (5–8). Series: Ecosystems in Action. 2002, Lerner LB $26.60 (978-0-8225-2135-8). In pictures and text, this book introduces life in an established forest with material on the interdependence of organisms there, and how human intervention has changed this ecosystem. (Rev: BL 12/15/02; HBG 3/03; SLJ 2/03) [574.5]

12735 Sayre, April Pulley. *Tropical Rain Forest* (4–7). Series: Exploring Earth's Biomes. 1994, Twenty-First Century LB $25.90 (978-0-8050-2826-3). The structure and contents of rain forests are explored with information on the plants, animals, and people that exist in this habitat. (Rev: BL 1/1/95; SLJ 1/95) [574.5]

12736 Welsbacher, Anne. *Life in a Rainforest* (5–8). Series: Ecosystems in Action. 2003, Lerner LB $26.60 (978-0-8225-4685-6). This illustrated account covers the plant and animal life in rain forests and explains how human intervention has changed, and often endangered, this ecosystem. (Rev: BL 9/15/03; HBG 10/03) [574.5]

Mountains

12737 Tocci, Salvatore. *Alpine Tundra: Life on the Tallest Mountain* (4–7). Series: Biomes and Habitats. 2005, Watts LB $25.50 (978-0-531-12365-2). Introduces the climate, flora, and fauna found high above sea level on the world's highest mountains. Also use *Arctic Tundra: Life at the North Pole* (2005). (Rev: SLJ 7/05) [577.5]

Ponds, Rivers, and Lakes

12738 Beck, Gregor Gilpin. *Watersheds: A Practical Handbook for Healthy Water* (7–12). 1999, Firefly $19.95 (978-1-55037-330-1). This account highlights the importance of water in our lives, with special attention to pollution, flooding, and other environmental problems. (Rev: BL 9/1/99) [333.73]

12739 Castaldo, Nancy F. *River Wild: An Activity Guide to North American Rivers* (4–7). Illus. 2006, Chicago Review $14.95 (978-1-55652-585-8). From a general introduction to the water cycle and watersheds, this volume narrows in on specific rivers in North America and the flora and fauna found there, even offering profiles of riverkeepers. (Rev: BL 3/1/06; SLJ 6/06) [372.8991]

12740 Gray, Leon. *The Missouri River* (4–8). Series: Rivers of North America. 2003, Gareth Stevens LB $26.00 (978-0-8368-3758-2). A trip along the Missouri, the longest river in the United States, from its source to its confluence with the Mississippi, with a look at the history that has been made on its banks. (Rev: SLJ 3/04)

12741 Harris, Tim. *The Mackenzie River* (4–8). Series: Rivers of North America. 2003, Gareth Stevens LB $26.00 (978-0-8368-3756-8). A visit to the Mackenzie River in Canada's Northwest Territories and the people, plants, and animals who have lived along it. (Rev: SLJ 3/04)

12742 Hawkes, Steve. *The Tennessee River* (4–8). Series: Rivers of North America. 2003, Gareth Stevens LB $26.00 (978-0-8368-3763-6). A trip along the length of the Tennessee River, with information on its history, natural attributes, and its effect on the people who live along its path. (Rev: SLJ 3/04)

12743 Jackson, Tom. *The Arkansas River* (4–8). Series: Rivers of North America. 2003, Gareth Stevens LB $26.00 (978-0-8368-3752-0). Tracing the Arkansas River its entire length of nearly 1,500 miles, with coverage of the people who have lived along it over the centuries and its importance to them. (Rev: SLJ 3/04)

12744 Jackson, Tom. *The Ohio River* (4–8). Series: Rivers of North America. 2003, Gareth Stevens LB $26.00 (978-0-8368-3759-9). Following the Ohio River from Pittsburgh to its confluence with the Mississippi at Cairo, Illinois, with material on the people and places found along its banks. (Rev: SLJ 3/04)

12745 Rapp, Valerie. *Life in a River* (5–8). Series: Ecosystems in Action. 2002, Lerner LB $26.60 (978-0-8225-2136-5). The first title in a new series about ecosystems, this volume uses the example of the Columbia River to explain the concept and the interrelationship of rivers, animals, and humans. (Rev: BL 10/15/02; HBG 3/03; SLJ 1/03; VOYA 2/03) [577.6]

12746 Sayre, April Pulley. *Lake and Pond* (4–7). Series: Exploring Earth's Biomes. 1996, Twenty-First Century LB $25.90 (978-0-8050-4089-0). A colorful introduction to lake and pond habitats and the life forms found within them. (Rev: BL 6/1–15/96; SLJ 6/96) [574.05]

12747 Sayre, April Pulley. *River and Stream* (4–7). Series: Exploring Earth's Biomes. 1996, Twenty-First Century LB $25.90 (978-0-8050-4088-3). In a clearly written, informative style, this book presents material on rivers and streams, their ecology, and the various creatures and plants living in and around them. (Rev: BL 6/1–15/96; SLJ 6/96) [574.5]

12748 Stewart, Melissa. *Life in a Lake* (5–8). Series: Ecosystems in Action. 2002, Lerner LB $26.60 (978-0-8225-2138-9). The diversity and interdependence of life in a typical lake are introduced with material on how this ecosystem works and how man's interference has changed the balance of nature. (Rev: BL 12/15/02; HBG 3/03) [551.48]

12749 Walker, Sally M. *Life in an Estuary* (5–8). Series: Ecosystems in Action. 2002, Lerner LB $26.60 (978-0-8225-2137-2). A look at life at the tidal mouths of rivers and the diversity of life in these areas, its interdependence, the balance of nature, and how human interaction has changed this ecosystem. (Rev: BL 12/15/02; HBG 3/03; SLJ 2/03) [574]

Prairies and Grasslands

12750 Collard, Sneed B. *The Prairie Builders: Reconstructing America's Lost Grasslands* (5–8). 2005, Houghton Mifflin $17.00 (978-0-618-39687-0). This wide-format look at a project to regenerate tallgrass prairie and populate it with native plants and animals includes excellent photographs. (Rev: BL 6/1–15/05; SLJ 8/05*) [635.9]

12751 Lynch, Wayne. *Prairie Grasslands* (6–9). Photos by Wayne Lynch. Series: Our Wild World Ecosystems. 2006, NorthWord $16.95 (978-1-55971-946-9); paper $8.95 (978-1-55971-947-6). Grasslands, wetlands, badlands, and the connections between climate, soil, and plant and animal inhabitants are the focus of this well-illustrated title. (Rev: SLJ 1/07)

12752 Patent, Dorothy Hinshaw. *Life in a Grassland* (5–8). Series: Ecosystems in Action. 2002, Lerner LB $26.60 (978-0-8225-2139-6). Using excellent pictures and a clear text, this volume explores the flora and fauna of different kinds of grasslands, with material on conservation. (Rev: BL 12/15/02; HBG 3/03) [574.5]

12753 Sayre, April Pulley. *Grassland* (4–7). Series: Exploring Earth's Biomes. 1994, Twenty-First Century LB $25.90 (978-0-8050-2827-0). A well-organized, clearly written account that explains what grasslands are and where they exist and the interaction of the creatures who live in this biome. (Rev: BL 1/15/95; SLJ 2/95) [574.5]

12754 Toupin, Laurie Peach. *Life in the Temperate Grasslands* (4–7). Series: Biomes and Habitats. 2005, Watts LB $25.50 (978-0-531-12385-0). Introduces the climatic conditions, plants, and wildlife of the world's temperate grasslands. Also use *Savannas: Life in the Tropical Grasslands* (2005). (Rev: SLJ 7/05) [577.4]

Rocks, Minerals, and Soil

12755 Chesterman, Charles W., and Kurt E. Lowe. *The Audubon Society Field Guide to North American Rocks and Minerals* (7–12). 1978, Knopf $19.95 (978-0-394-50269-4). A basic guide that includes color illustrations of nearly 800 rocks and minerals. [549]

12756 Davis, Barbara J. *Minerals, Rocks, and Soil* (6–9). Series: Sci-Hi: Earth Science. 2010, Heinemann-Raintree $31.34 (978-1-4109-3347-8). In chapters on igneous rocks, sedimentary rocks, metamorphic rocks, and the nature of minerals and soil, this well-organized book provides plenty of facts with colorful graphics. (Rev: LMC 1–2/10)

12757 Downs, Sandra. *Earth's Hidden Treasures* (6–9). Series: Exploring Planet Earth. 1999, Twenty-First Century LB $24.90 (978-0-7613-1411-0). All about the planet's rocks and minerals and how they have been used by humans. (Rev: HBG 4/00; SLJ 2/00) [549]

12758 Farndon, John. *Rock and Mineral* (5–9). Series: DK/Google e.guides. 2005, DK $17.99 (978-0-7566-1140-8). This highly illustrated guide introduces readers to the basics of geology and provides a link to a Web site that serves as a gateway to additional resources. (Rev: SLJ 8/05) [552]

12759 Friend, Sandra. *Sinkholes* (4–7). 2002, Pineapple $18.95 (978-1-56164-258-8). This volume uncovers the geological and ecological causes of sinkholes, holes in the earth's surface that occur naturally, sometimes with devastating consequences. (Rev: BL 8/02; HBG 10/02) [551.44]

12760 Green, Dan, and Simon Basher. *Rocks and Minerals: A Gem of a Book!* (5–8). Illus. by Simon Basher. Series: Basher Science. 2009, Kingfisher paper $8.99 (978-0-7534-6314-7). Friendly cartoon characters narrate this informative and appealing introduction to rocks, gems, crystals, fossils, and so forth. (Rev: BL 9/15/09; SLJ 10/09) [500]

12761 Pough, Frederick H. *A Field Guide to Rocks and Minerals. 4th ed.* (7–12). 1976, Houghton Mifflin paper $20.00 (978-0-395-91096-2). This volume in the Peterson Field Guide series gives photographs and identifying information on 270 rocks and minerals. [549]

12762 Ricciuti, Edward R., ed. *National Audubon Society First Field Guide: Rocks and Minerals* (5–8). 1998, Scholastic paper $17.95 (978-0-590-05463-8). A guide to equipment and techniques for observation and general information on geology, followed by an examination of 50 common rocks, their composition, texture, color, and environment. (Rev: BL 8/98; SLJ 8/98) [552]

12763 Staedter, Tracy. *Rocks and Minerals* (4–8). Series: Reader's Digest Pathfinders. 1999, Reader's Digest $16.99 (978-1-57584-290-5). An outstanding introduction to geology is organized in three sections

— "Rocks," "Minerals," and "Collecting Rocks and Minerals" — with "discovery paths" featuring personal accounts, hands-on activities, vocabulary, and facts. (Rev: SLJ 11/99) [552]

12764 VanCleave, Janice. *Janice VanCleave's Rocks and Minerals: Mind-Boggling Experiments You Can Turn Into Science Fair Projects* (6–8). Series: Spectacular Science Projects. 1996, Wiley paper $10.95 (978-0-471-10269-4). In easy-to-follow steps, a series of experiments and projects are outlined that illustrate the properties and uses of a number of rocks and minerals. (Rev: BL 3/15/96; SLJ 3/96) [552]

Mathematics

General and Miscellaneous

12765 Ellis, Julie. *Pythagoras and the Ratios* (4–7). Illus. by Phyllis Hornung Peacock. 2010, Charlesbridge $16.95 (978-1-57091-775-2); paper $7.95 (978-1-57091-776-9). An entertaining picture book that explains ratios as young Pythagoras establishes that Octavius's pipes are the wrong length to make melodious music. (Rev: LMC 10/10; SLJ 2/10) [516.2]

12766 Formichelli, Linda, and W. Eric Martin. *Timekeeping: Explore the History and Science of Telling Time with 15 Projects* (4–7). Illus. by Samuel Carbaugh. Series: Build It Yourself. 2012, Nomad $21.95 (978-161930136-8); paper $15.95 (978-16193003-3-0). Projects that range in difficulty bolster readers' understanding of time and how we measure it. (Rev: BL 12/1/12) [529]

12767 Frederick, Shane. *Football: The Math of the Game* (6–10). Illus. Series: Sports Math. 2011, Capstone LB $22.99 (978-142966567-4); paper $7.95 (9781429673198). Shows how important a role math plays in the game of football, giving clear examples and appealing illustrations. (Rev: BL 10/1/11) [796.332]

12768 Haven, Kendall. *Marvels of Math: Fascinating Reads and Awesome Activities* (5–8). 1998, Teacher Ideas paper $23.50 (978-1-56308-585-7). This book chronicles 16 turning points in the history of mathematics, including the discovery of zero and the story of the first female to become a professor of mathematics. (Rev: VOYA 4/99) [510]

12769 Hense, Mary. *How Astronauts Use Math* (4–8). Illus. Series: Math in the Real World. 2009, Chelsea Clubhouse $28 (978-1-60413-610-4). A look at how astronauts use math in their everyday activities. Also use *How Fighter Pilots Use Math* (2009). (Rev: SLJ 4/10) [629.45]

12770 Hershey, Robert L. *How to Think with Numbers* (7–9). 1987, Janson paper $7.95 (978-0-939765-14-0). Elementary mathematical concepts such as percentage and interest are explained through a series of puzzles and problems. [510]

12771 Jenkins, Steve. *Just a Second* (4–7). Illus. by author. 2011, Houghton Mifflin $16.99 (978-0-618-70896-3). Jenkins explores time, looking at the amazing things that can take place in a second, a minute, an hour, a month, and a year. (Rev: BL 11/1/11; SLJ 12/1/11) [529]

12772 Kummer, Patricia K. *The Calendar* (5–8). Series: Inventions That Shaped the World. 2005, Watts LB $30.50 (978-0-531-12340-9). Traces the development of calendars from prehistoric times, with period and contemporary illustrations, lists of recommended resources, and a calendar. (Rev: BL 5/15/05) [529]

12773 Leech, Bonnie Coulter. *Mesopotamia: Creating and Solving Word Problems* (4–8). Series: Math for the Real World. 2007, Rosen LB $23.95 (978-1-4042-3357-7). Ancient number systems are among the mathematical concepts highlighted in this overview of the civilization of Mesopotamia that covers its people, buildings, writings, and calendars. (Rev: SLJ 2/07) [510]

12774 Long, Lynette. *Great Graphs and Sensational Statistics: Games and Activities That Make Math Easy and Fun* (4–7). 2004, Wiley paper $12.95 (978-0-471-21060-3). The games and activities in this large-format paperback will give new insights into the value of statistics and graphs and how the latter can be used to visually represent the former. (Rev: BL 5/1/04; SLJ 11/04) [372.7]

12775 Orr, Tamra. *Wildfires* (5–8). Illus. Series: Real World Math: Natural Disasters. 2012, Cherry Lake LB $27.07 (978-161080329-8). Math problems ranging in difficulty are integrated into this account of wildfires and their causes and impact. (Rev: BL 4/1/12) [363.37]

12776 Robbins, Ken. *For Good Measure: The Ways We Say How Much, How Far, How Heavy, How Big, How Old* (4–7). 2010, Flash Point $17.99 (978-1-59643-344-1). Robbins takes an unusual, highly illustrated approach to explaining various measurements, including the metric system. (Rev: BLO 4/1/10; HB 5–6/10; LMC 5–6/10; SLJ 4/10) [510]

12777 Schwartz, David M. *G Is for Googol: A Math Alphabet Book* (6–10). 1998, Tricycle $15.95 (978-1-883672-58-4). A humorous romp through mathematical terms and concepts using an alphabetical approach and cartoon illustrations. (Rev: BL 10/15/98; HBG 3/99; SLJ 11/98) [510]

12778 Shea, Therese. *America's Electoral College: Choosing the President: Comparing and Analyzing Charts, Graphs, and Tables* (4–8). Series: Math for the Real World. 2007, Rosen LB $23.95 (978-1-4042-3358-4). Results of various elections, including the controversial 2000 polls, are used to demonstrate fundamental mathematical principles. (Rev: SLJ 2/07) [324.6097]

12779 Shea, Therese. *The Great Barrier Reef: Using Graphs and Charts to Solve Word Problems* (4–8). Series: Math for the Real World. 2007, Rosen LB $23.95 (978-1-4042-3359-1). Charts and graphs are used to show the number of species found on the reef, the percentages of coral, the number of visitors, and so forth. (Rev: SLJ 2/07) [510]

12780 Shea, Therese. *The Transcontinental Railroad: Using Proportions to Solve Problems* (4–8). Series: Math for the Real World. 2007, Rosen LB $23.95 (978-1-4042-3361-4). The cost of laying the track, number of rails laid in a period, and other interesting aspects of construction of the railroad are considered using ratios, proportions, and other mathematical techniques. (Rev: SLJ 2/07) [513.24]

12781 Sullivan, Navin. *Area, Distance, and Volume* (4–7). Illus. Series: Measure Up. 2006, Marshall Cavendish LB $20.95 (978-0-7614-2323-2). Includes information on the history of measuring area, distance, and volume along with how to measure each and the devices used. (Rev: BL 2/15/07; SLJ 6/07) [598.47]

12782 Whiting, Jim. *Space and Time* (5–8). Illus. Series: Mysteries of the Universe. 2012, Creative Education LB $24.95 (978-160818192-6). "Is space expanding or contracting?" "Is time travel possible?" Whiting answers these and many other questions as he considers our strategies for keeping time. Lexile NC1270L (Rev: BL 12/1/12; LMC 5–6/13) [530.11]

12783 Wingard-Nelson, Rebecca. *Graphing and Probability Word Problems: No Problem!* (5–8). Illus. Series: Math Busters Word Problems. 2010, Enslow LB $27.93 (978-076603372-6). Bar graphs, histograms, line graphs, circle graphs, Venn diagrams — they are all covered here with explanations of how data, graphs, and probability are used in word problems. (Rev: BL 4/1/11) [519.2]

12784 Woods, Mary B., and Michael Woods. *Ancient Computing: From Counting to Calendars* (5–8). Series: Ancient Technologies. 2000, Runestone LB $25.26 (978-0-8225-2997-2). From the invention of the abacus and sundials to the creation of calculators and computers, this is a history of counting with material on the development of the calendar. (Rev: BL 9/15/00; HBG 3/01; SLJ 1/01) [510]

Algebra, Numbers, and Number Systems

12785 Schwartz, Joanne. *City Numbers* (3–7). Illus. by Matt Beam. 2011, Groundwood $18.95 (978-1-55498-081-9). An unusual look at numbers of all kinds seen in an urban landscape. (Rev: BL 6/1/11; LMC 11–12/11; SLJ 5/1/11) [971.3]

12786 Wingard-Nelson, Rebecca. *Algebra Word Problems* (6–10). Series: Math Busters Word Problems. 2010, Enslow LB $27.93 (978-0-7660-3367-2). A step-by-step guide to understanding basic algebra concepts and how they can be applied in real-life situations. Also use *Fraction and Decimal Word Problems* (2010). (Rev: LMC 11–12/10) [512.0076]

Mathematical Games and Puzzles

12787 Ball, Johnny. *Go Figure! A Totally Cool Book About Numbers* (4–7). 2005, DK $15.99 (978-0-7566-1374-7). A fascinating volume for math-minded youngsters and adults, introducing number-related games and puzzles as well as more sophisticated mathematical disciplines, such as chaos theory, fractals, and topology. (Rev: BL 10/15/05; SLJ 1/06) [510]

12788 Burns, Marilyn. *The I Hate Mathematics! Book* (5–8). Illus. by Martha Hairston. 1975, Little, Brown paper $14.99 (978-0-316-11741-8). A lively collection of puzzles and other mind stretchers that illustrate mathematical concepts.

12789 Burns, Marilyn. *Math for Smarty Pants: Or Who Says Mathematicians Have Little Pig Eyes* (6–9). 1982, Little, Brown paper $14.99 (978-0-316-11739-5). A series of games, puzzles, and tricks that use numbers. (Rev: BL 4/15/90) [513]

12790 Gardner, Martin. *Perplexing Puzzles and Tantalizing Teasers* (4–7). Illus. by Laszlo Kubinyi. 1988, Dover paper $7.95 (978-0-486-25637-5). An assortment of math problems, visual teasers, and tricky questions to challenge young, alert minds; perky drawings. [793.73]

12791 Salvadori, Mario, and Joseph P. Wright. *Math Games for Middle School: Challenges and Skill-Builders for Students at Every Level* (5–8). 1998, Chicago Review paper $14.95 (978-1-55652-288-8). After explaining the concepts involved in such mathematical areas as geometry, arithmetic, graphing, and linear equa-

tions, this work presents a series of puzzles for readers to solve. (Rev: BL 11/1/98) [510]

12792 Sharp, Richard M., and Seymour Metzner. *The Sneaky Square and 113 Other Math Activities for Kids* (4–8). 1990, TAB $15.95 (978-0-8306-8474-8); paper $8.95 (978-0-8306-3474-3). Readers are challenged to solve classic as well as new math and logic problems. (Rev: BL 1/1/91) [793.7]

Meteorology

General and Miscellaneous

12793 Allaby, Michael. *Fog, Smog and Poisoned Rain* (7–12). Illus. by Richard Garratt. Series: Dangerous Weather. 2003, Facts on File $40.00 (978-0-8160-4789-5). Natural sources of pollution such as volcanoes are included in this survey of dangerous weather phenomena. (Rev: SLJ 10/03) [363.739]

12794 Brezina, Corona. *Climate Change* (6–9). Series: In the News. 2007, Rosen LB $21.95 (978-1-4042-1913-7). Just what changes may be in store for the planet, what caused these changes, and what they mean for us. (Rev: BL 10/15/07) [363.738]

12795 Malone, Peter. *Close to the Wind: The Beaufort Scale* (4–8). Illus. by author. 2007, Putnam $16.99 (978-0-399-24399-8). An informative picture book that explains the history and use of the Beaufort scale that measures wind force at sea. (Rev: BL 6/1–15/07; LMC 11/07; SLJ 5/07) [551.51]

12796 Sullivan, Navin. *Temperature* (4–7). Series: Measure Up! 2006, Marshall Cavendish LB $20.95 (978-0-7614-2322-5). This well-designed book about temperature includes at-home experiments and easy-to-follow charts. (Rev: LMC 8–9/07; SLJ 6/07)

12797 Vogt, Gregory L. *The Atmosphere: Planetary Heat Engine* (5–8). Illus. Series: Earth's Spheres. 2007, Lerner $29.27 (978-0-7613-2841-4). Examines a wide array of topics, including the composition of our air, weather and climate, and the use of satellites and other tools to study the atmosphere. (Rev: BL 4/1/07; SLJ 5/07) [551.5]

Air

12798 Friend, Sandra. *Earth's Wild Winds* (5–8). Series: Exploring Planet Earth. 2002, Twenty-First Century LB $24.90 (978-0-7613-2673-1). Report writers will find good material in this attractively presented coverage of all kinds of winds that also looks at the ways in which humans have attempted to harness wind power. (Rev: HBG 3/03; SLJ 10/02) [551.518]

12799 Hoff, Mary, and Mary M. Rodgers. *Atmosphere* (4–7). Series: Our Endangered Planet. 1995, Lerner LB $27.15 (978-0-8225-2509-7). This account describes the atmosphere and current threats including the ozone layer problem. (Rev: BL 8/95; SLJ 12/95) [363.73]

Storms

12800 Allaby, Michael. *Tornadoes* (7–12). Series: Dangerous Weather. 1997, Facts on File $35.00 (978-0-8160-3517-5). This excellent book on tornadoes describes how they begin, their structure, travel patterns, interiors, historic tornadoes, and when and where tornadoes occur. (Rev: SLJ 4/98) [551.55]

12801 Carson, Mary Kay. *Inside Hurricanes* (5–8). Illus. 2010, Sterling $16.95 (978-140275880-5); paper $9.95 (978-14027778-0-6). Inventive, eye-catching fold-outs and dramatic photographs enhance this engaging book about hurricanes. (Rev: BL 10/1/10; LMC 1–2/11; SLJ 12/1/10*) [551.552]

12802 Ceban, Bonnie J. *Tornadoes: Disaster and Survival* (4–7). Series: Deadly Disasters. 2005, Enslow LB $23.93 (978-0-7660-2383-3). Explores the science behind tornadoes and offers advice about how to prepare for and survive such natural disasters. (Rev: SLJ 10/05) [551.5]

12803 Cerveny, Randy. *Freaks of the Storm: From Flying Cows to Stealing Thunder* (8–12). 2006, Thunder's Mouth paper $16.95 (978-1-56025-801-8). Cerveny chronicles bizarre weather phenomena — from fish falling from the sky to chickens plucked bare by hurricane winds — and extremes of heat, cold, rainfall, and so forth. (Rev: BL 12/1/05) [551.5]

12804 De Hahn, Tracee. *The Blizzard of 1888* (7–12). Series: Great Disasters: Reforms and Ramifications. 2000, Chelsea $21.95 (978-0-7910-5787-2). Exciting illustrations and eyewitness accounts enhance this exploration of the impact of this famous blizzard and of the changes in infrastructure and services that resulted from it. (Rev: BL 4/15/01; HBG 10/01; SLJ 6/01) [974.7]

12805 Dudley, William, ed. *Hurricane Katrina* (6–10). Series: At Issue. 2006, Gale LB $28.70 (978-0-7377-3551-2). An examination of the governmental, social, and natural forces that affected the victims of Hurricane Katrina and the city of New Orleans, this collection of articles will help students to see that there were many differing opinions on what action to take. (Rev: SLJ 9/06)

12806 Harper, Kristine C. *Hurricane Andrew* (5–8). Series: Environmental Disasters. 2005, Facts on File $35.00 (978-0-8160-5759-7). The impact of 1992's Hurricane Andrew on Florida's wetlands is seen as a warning about the need to be more prepared. (Rev: SLJ 11/05) [551.5]

12807 McGrath, Barbara Barbieri, comp. *The Storm: Students of Biloxi, Mississippi, Remember Hurricane Katrina* (3–8). Illus. 2006, Charlesbridge $18.95 (978-1-58089-172-1). Artwork and writings show the impact of the storm on K–12 students in Biloxi; the book is divided into four sections: "Evacuation," "Storm," "Aftermath," and "Hope." (Rev: SLJ 12/06) [976.2]

12808 Miller, Debra A. *Hurricane Katrina: Devastation on the Gulf Coast* (6–8). Series: Overview. 2006, Gale LB $28.70 (978-1-59018-936-8). Miller faults the government for not responding quickly enough to the disaster, and offers quotations from eyewitnesses and survivors to back up her opinion. Also covered are the rebuilding efforts and the relocation of many storm victims. (Rev: SLJ 9/06) [363.34]

12809 Miller, Mara. *Hurricane Katrina Strikes the Gulf Coast* (5–8). Series: Deadly Disasters. 2006, Enslow LB $23.93 (978-0-7660-2803-6). The story of Hurricane Katrina and its disastrous impact on the Gulf Coast in 2005 is accompanied by personal stories plus information on other deadly storms. (Rev: BL 7/06; SLJ 9/06) [363.34]

12810 Palser, Barb. *Hurricane Katrina: Aftermath of Disaster* (7–10). Series: Snapshots in History. 2006, Compass Point LB $31.93 (978-0-7565-2101-1). An interesting yet detailed look at how Katrina affected residents of New Orleans, and at the rescue and restoration efforts that followed the storm. (Rev: BL 12/1/06) [976]

12811 Simon, Seymour. *Tornadoes* (4–8). 1999, Morrow LB $16.89 (978-0-688-14647-4). Well-organized text discusses the weather conditions that give rise to tornadoes, how they form, where they are most likely to occur, and how scientists predict and track them, supplemented by large, riveting photographs showing meteorologists at work, a variety of tornadoes, and the devastation caused by major tornadoes. (Rev: BCCB 4/99; BL 5/99; HBG 9/99; SLJ 6/99) [551.55]

12812 Stewart, Melissa. *Inside Lightning* (5–8). Illus. by Cynthia Shaw. Series: Inside. 2011, Sterling $16.95 (978-140275878-2). A dramatic presentation of information about what causes lightning and its impact on the population and environment, with many photographs and gatefolds. (Rev: BL 11/1/11*) [551.55]

12813 Torres, John A. *Hurricane Katrina and the Devastation of New Orleans* (4–7). Series: Monumental Milestones. 2006, Mitchell Lane $29.95 (978-1-58415-473-0). An interview with a newlywed couple who lost everything in the storm draws readers into this account of the devastation. (Rev: BL 9/1/06) [363.34]

12814 Treaster, Joseph B. *Hurricane Force: In the Path of America's Deadliest Storms* (7–10). Series: New York Times Book. 2007, Kingfisher $16.95 (978-0-7534-3086-3). A reporter for the *New York Times* who witnessed firsthand the devastation wrought by Hurricane Katrina discusses that storm and hurricanes in general; with photographs and other visuals. (Rev: BL 3/1/07; SLJ 5/07) [551.55]

12815 Woods, Michael, and Mary B. Woods. *Tornadoes* (5–8). Illus. Series: Disasters Up Close. 2006, Lerner $27.93 (978-0-8225-4714-3). Eyewitness accounts add to this well-illustrated overview of tornadoes and the destruction they can cause. (Rev: BL 10/15/06) [551.55]

Water

12816 Gallant, Roy A. *Water: Our Precious Resource* (4–8). Series: Earthworks. 2003, Marshall Cavendish $29.93 (978-0-7614-1365-3). A thought-provoking and well-presented overview of the sources of water; the ways in which we use, misuse, and recycle water; and efforts to preserve this vital natural resource. (Rev: BL 3/15/03; HBG 3/03; SLJ 2/03) [553.7]

12817 Morgan, Sally, and Adrian Morgan. *Water* (4–7). Series: Designs in Science. 1994, Facts on File $23.00 (978-0-8160-2982-2). The importance and uses of water are described, with information on water storage, filtering, and conservation, plus activities and experiments. (Rev: BL 7/94) [533.7]

Weather

12818 Arnold, Caroline. *El Niño: Stormy Weather for People and Wildlife* (4–8). 1998, Clarion $16.00 (978-0-395-77602-5). A brief overview of El Niño, its causes and history, and how tracking and forecasting are used to make predictions. (Rev: BL 10/1/98; HBG 10/99; SLJ 12/98) [551.6]

12819 Banqueri, Eduardo. *Weather* (4–8). Illus. by Estudio Marcel Socías and Gabi Marfil. Series: Field Guides. 2006, Enchanted Lion $16.95 (978-1-59270-059-2). This information-packed guide explores a broad array of weather-related topics, including seasonal change, climatic zones, the science of meteorology, clouds, winds, storms, and the atmosphere. (Rev: SLJ 1/07) [551.5]

12820 Bredeson, Carmen. *El Niño and La Niña: Deadly Weather* (4–8). Series: American Disasters. 2002, Enslow LB $23.93 (978-0-7660-1551-7). A well-researched account of these two weather phenomena, their effects, and how they can be traced. (Rev: BL 6/1–15/02; HBG 10/02; SLJ 6/02) [551.6]

12821 Burt, Christopher C. *Extreme Weather: A Guide and Record Book* (8–12). 2004, Norton paper $24.95 (978-0-393-32658-1). An overview of weather at its worst, this richly illustrated volume contains a wealth of meteorological data on extreme events, including heat, drought, cold, floods, thunderstorms, windstorms, tornadoes, and fog. (Rev: SLJ 2/05) [551.6]

12822 Carson, Mary Kay. *Weather Projects for Young Scientists* (4–7). 2007, Chicago Review paper $14.95 (978-1-55652-629-9). A detailed look at weather basics is intertwined with more than 40 projects, many appropriate for science fairs, and a few career profiles. (Rev: BL 12/1/06; SLJ 3/08) [551.5078]

12823 Dickinson, Terence. *Exploring the Sky by Day: The Equinox Guide to Weather and the Atmosphere* (7–10). 1988, Camden House paper $9.95 (978-0-920656-71-6). A book about weather that explores such subjects as types of clouds and kinds of precipitation. (Rev: BL 3/1/89; SLJ 1/89) [551.6]

12824 Gardner, Robert. *Weather Science Fair Projects, Revised and Expanded Using the Scientific Method* (5–8). Series: Earth Science Projects Using the Scientific

Method. 2010, Enslow LB $34.60 (978-0-7660-3424-2). With a focus on the basics of scientific investigation, this well-organized and attractive volume gives an overview of the topic and provides experiments that support various hypotheses. (Rev: LMC 8–9/10) [551.63]

12825 Kahl, Jonathan D. *Weather Watch: Forecasting the Weather* (5–8). Series: How's the Weather? 1996, Lerner LB $21.27 (978-0-8225-2529-5). This work provides basic information on weather systems, maps, and forecasting tools, the history of weather forecasting and keeping weather records, and directions for making a weather station. (Rev: BL 6/1–15/96; SLJ 6/96) [551.6]

12826 Ramsey, Dan. *Weather Forecasting: A Young Meteorologist's Guide* (8–12). 1990, TAB $19.95 (978-0-8306-8338-3); paper $10.95 (978-0-8306-3338-8). A detailed and often technical examination of the techniques of weather forecasting with many tables, charts, and diagrams. (Rev: BL 10/15/90) [551.6]

12827 Rupp, Rebecca. *Weather! Watch How Weather Works* (4–8). 2003, Storey paper $14.95 (978-1-58017-420-6). A well-illustrated and appealing introduction to the science of weather, with numerous experiments and projects. (Rev: SLJ 5/04) [551.6]

12828 Sayre, April Pulley. *El Niño and La Niña: Weather in the Headlines* (4–8). 2000, Twenty-First Century LB $25.90 (978-0-7613-1405-9). An exploration of this complex Pacific Ocean phenomenon that produces unusual weather conditions that affect the entire world. (Rev: BL 9/15/00; HBG 3/01) [551.6]

12829 Silverstein, Alvin. *Weather and Climate* (4–7). Series: Science Concepts. 1998, Twenty-First Century LB $26.90 (978-0-7613-3223-7). This book introduces weather by explaining earth's atmosphere, rotation, and different climates with material on air and water movements, cloud formation, and recent climate changes. (Rev: BL 5/1/99; HBG 10/99) [551.5]

12830 Stein, Paul. *Forecasting the Climate of the Future* (5–7). Series: The Library of Future Weather and Climate. 2001, Rosen LB $29.25 (978-0-8239-3413-3). A fascinating, well-organized account that looks at long-range weather predictions and at the use and accuracy of computer models in forecasting future weather patterns, especially with regard to global warming. Also use *Storms of the Future* (2001), which looks at whether global warming might cause stronger storms. (Rev: SLJ 4/02) [551.5]

12831 Stein, Paul. *Ice Ages of the Future* (5–7). Series: The Library of Future Weather and Climate. 2001, Rosen LB $29.25 (978-0-8239-3415-7). A look at the possibility that the greenhouse effect and other factors could in fact cause a wave of colder rather than warmer air. (Rev: SLJ 11/01) [551.6]

Oceanography

General and Miscellaneous

12832 Burns, Loree Griffin. *Tracking Trash: Flotsam, Jetsam, and the Science of Ocean Motion* (7–10). Series: Scientists in the Field. 2007, Houghton Mifflin $18.00 (978-0-618-58131-3). Trash in the ocean can help scientists study currents as well as posing a threat to animals and ecosystems, according to this attractive book. Boston Globe–Horn Book Honor 2007; ALA Notable Books 2008. (Rev: BCCB 5/07; BL 4/1/07; HB 3–4/07; LMC 11/07; SLJ 3/07*) [551.46]

12833 Cobb, Allan B. *Super Science Projects About Oceans* (4–7). Series: Psyched for Science. 2000, Rosen LB $26.50 (978-0-8239-3174-3). Although the format is unattractive, this book contains six fine experiments that explore concepts involving the ocean. (Rev: SLJ 7/00) [551.46]

12834 Desonie, Dana. *Oceans: How We Use the Seas* (8–12). Series: Our Fragile Planet. 2007, Chelsea House LB $35.00 (978-0-8160-6216-4). An overview of oceanography with an emphasis on environmental protection and a no-frills format. (Rev: BL 10/15/07; SLJ 4/08) [551.46]

12835 Dinwiddie, Robert. *Ocean: The World's Last Wilderness Revealed* (7–12). 2006, DK $50.00 (978-0-7566-2205-3). With many eye-catching images and lots of information on the ocean environment (tides, waves, shallow seas, polar seas, and so forth) and the life found therein, this well-designed volume is useful both for browsers and researchers. (Rev: BL 11/15/06) [551.46]

12836 Friedman, Lauri S., ed. *Oceans* (7–10). Illus. Series: Introducing Issues with Opposing Viewpoints. 2011, Greenhaven LB $36.82 (978-073775200-7). Presents pro and con arguments on such topics as how our oceans are changing, the threats they face, and the

measures that can be taken to protect them. (Rev: BL 12/1/11) [551.46]

12837 Hague, Bradley. *Alien Deep: Revealing the Mysterious Living World at the Bottom of the Ocean* (4–7). Illus. 2012, National Geographic $17.95 (978-142631067-6); LB $26.90 (978-142631068-3). Hague explores hydrothermal vents and the creatures that live in them in this engaging volume. Outstanding Science Trade Book for Students K–12 2013. (Rev: BL 10/15/12; SLJ 4/13) [551.2]

12838 Hutchinson, Stephen, and Lawrence E. Hawkins. *Oceans: A Visual Guide* (8–12). 2005, Firefly $29.95 (978-1-55407-069-5). With dramatic photographs and highly readable text, oceanographers Hutchinson and Hawkins introduce readers to the oceans of the world and the qualities that clearly distinguish one from the other. (Rev: BL 10/15/05; VOYA 4/06) [551.46]

12839 McMillan, Beverly, and John A. Musick. *Oceans* (5–8). Illus. Series: Insiders. 2007, Simon & Schuster $16.99 (978-1-4169-3859-0). An introduction to Earth's oceans, marine life, ocean migrations, sea vents, coastal and polar seas, and so forth, with eye-catching illustrations. (Rev: LMC 10/07; SLJ 12/07) [551.46]

12840 VanCleave, Janice. *Janice VanCleave's Oceans for Every Kid: Easy Activities That Make Learning Science Fun* (5–7). Series: Science for Every Kid. 1996, Wiley paper $12.95 (978-0-471-12453-5). This book gives good background information about oceans plus a number of entertaining and instructive projects and activities. (Rev: BL 4/15/96; SLJ 5/96) [551.46]

12841 Young, Karen Romano. *Across the Wide Ocean: The Why, How, and Where of Navigation for Humans and Animals at Sea* (5–7). Illus. by author. 2007, HarperCollins $18.99 (978-0-06-009086-9). Before satellite global positioning technology, humans had to use many different methods to navigate at sea, and this book creatively explores many of these methods as well as those of sea creatures including turtles and whales. (Rev: SLJ 7/07) [623.89]

12842 Zim, Herbert S., and Lester Ingle. *Seashores* (5–8). 1991, Western $21.27 (978-0-307-64496-1). This is a guide to animals and plants found along the beaches.

Underwater Exploration and Sea Disasters

12843 Allen, Judy. *Higher Ground* (5–8). 2006, Chrysalis paper $8.99 (978-1-84458-581-6). First-person accounts of survivors and rescue workers mixed with fictional treatments based on fact portray the impact on children of the deadly Indian Ocean tsunami of December 2004. (Rev: BCCB 5/06; BL 2/1/06; SLJ 3/06) [363.349]

12844 Karwoski, Gail Langer. *Tsunami: The True Story of an April Fools' Day Disaster* (4–7). Illus. by John MacDonald. 2006, Darby Creek $17.95 (978-1-58196-044-0). Karwoski tells the story of a devastating 1946 tsunami, and expands the coverage to other destructive waves and their causes, effects, and the measures being taken to alert residents to their arrival. (Rev: SLJ 1/07) [363.34]

12845 Kusky, Timothy. *Tsunamis: Giant Waves from the Sea* (8–11). Series: Hazardous Earth. 2008, Facts on File $39.50 (978-0-8160-6464-9). Kusky explains the causes and behavior of these destructive waves, describes some particularly tragic occurrences, and looks at efforts to give people advance warning. (Rev: BL 4/1/08) [551.46]

12846 Lindop, Laurie. *Venturing the Deep Sea* (4–8). Series: Science on the Edge. 2005, Twenty-First Century LB $27.93 (978-0-7613-2701-1). A behind-the-scenes look at the technology employed by modern-day undersea explorers, with a clear explanation of the types of knowledge these researchers are seeking. (Rev: SLJ 8/06; VOYA 4/06) [551.46]

12847 Mallory, Kenneth. *Adventure Beneath the Sea: Living in an Underwater Science Station* (5–8). Illus. by Brian Skerry. 2010, Boyds Mills $18.95 (978-1-59078607-9). This readable book describes life in an underwater science station on a reef off the Florida Keys, with discussion of the training required, the living conditions, and the tasks performed. (Rev: BL 12/1/10; LMC 1–2/11; SLJ 11/1/10) [551.46]

12848 Mallory, Kenneth. *Diving to a Deep-Sea Volcano* (4–7). Illus. 2006, Houghton Mifflin $17.00 (978-0-618-33205-2). Take a dive with marine biologists as they explore deep-sea volcanoes and the creatures that live and thrive around them; scientific method, adventure, biography, and insight into a career are intertwined in this portrait of a marine biologist's work in an underwater habitat. (Rev: BL 12/1/06; SLJ 2/07) [551.2]

12849 Platt, Richard. *Shipwreck* (4–9). Series: Eyewitness Books. 1997, Knopf LB $20.99 (978-0-679-98569-3). An overview of the causes and consequences of the world's most famous maritime disasters. (Rev: BL 12/15/97) [387.2]

12850 Stewart, Gail B. *Catastrophe in Southern Asia: The Tsunami of 2004* (5–8). Series: Overview. 2005, Gale LB $29.95 (978-1-59018-831-6). An information-packed review of the tsunami itself, the human costs of the disaster, and the reconstruction efforts. (Rev: SLJ 12/05)

12851 *Sunk! Exploring Underwater Archaeology* (5–8). Series: Buried Worlds. 1994, Lerner LB $28.75 (978-0-8225-3205-7). Provides a general overview of how archaeologists interpret underwater discoveries to learn about aspects of ancient trade, commerce, and history. (Rev: BL 10/15/94; SLJ 9/94) [930.1]

12852 Torres, John A. *Disaster in the Indian Ocean: Tsunami 2004* (5–8). Series: Monumental Milestones: Great Events of Modern Times. 2005, Mitchell Lane LB $29.95 (978-1-58415-344-3). This slim volume, uneven in its coverage, nonetheless offers a chilling overview of the devastating Indian Ocean tsunami of December 2004 and includes a number of eyewitness accounts. (Rev: BL 10/15/05; SLJ 12/05) [909]

Physics

General and Miscellaneous

12853 Barnett, Lincoln. *The Universe of Dr. Einstein* (8–12). 1980, Amereon $18.95 (978-0-8488-0146-5). A lucid explanation of Einstein's theory of relativity and how it has changed our ideas of the universe. [530.1]

12854 Bortz, Fred. *The Quark* (7–10). Series: The Library of Subatomic Particles. 2004, Rosen LB $27.95 (978-0-8239-4533-7). Suitable for reluctant readers, this is a clear explanation of the quark, featuring large text and many color illustrations. Also recommended in this series are *The Proton, The Photon,* and *The Electron* (all 2004). (Rev: SLJ 10/04)

12855 Cook, Trevor. *Experiments with States of Matter* (3–7). Series: Science Lab. 2009, Rosen LB $25.25 (978-1-4358-2805-6). A variety of science experiments using simple materials from around the house; each one illustrates a key concept pertaining to the varying states of matter. (Rev: LMC 11–12/09) [530.4]

12856 Field, Andrea R., ed. *The Science of Physics* (7–10). Illus. Series: Introduction to Physics. 2012, Britannica LB $31.70 (978-161530676-3). Straightforward and clearly written text accompanies appealing graphics in this guide to the basic principles of physics. Also in this series: *Electricity, Energy,* and *Electronics* (all 2012). (Rev: BL 8/12) [530]

12857 Fleisher, Paul. *Liquids and Gases: Principles of Fluid Mechanics* (6–12). Series: Secrets of the Universe. 2001, Lerner LB $25.26 (978-0-8225-2988-0). Archimedes's principle, Pascal's law, and Bernoulli's principle are among the topics covered in this volume adapted from an adult title. (Rev: HBG 3/02; SLJ 12/01) [532]

12858 Fleisher, Paul. *Matter and Energy: Principles of Matter and Thermodynamics* (7–12). Series: Secrets of the Universe. 2001, Lerner LB $25.26 (978-0-8225-

2986-6). The periodic tables and the basic principles of thermodynamics and matter are explained in conversational language with clear diagrams and simple experiments. (Rev: BL 8/01; HBG 3/02; SLJ 1/02) [530.11]

12859 Fleisher, Paul. *Relativity and Quantum Mechanics: Principles of Modern Physics* (6–9). Series: Secrets of the Universe. 2001, Lerner LB $25.26 (978-0-8225-2989-7). The basic principles of modern physics are presented in clear text with helpful graphics and explanations of terms and concepts. (Rev: HBG 3/02; SLJ 1/02) [530.11]

12860 Gardner, Robert. *Easy Genius Science Projects with Light: Great Experiments and Ideas* (6–10). Illus. Series: Easy Genius Science Projects. 2008, Enslow LB $23.95 (978-076602926-2). Gardner provides fascinating physics experiments and mind-benders in this approachable, well-organized book. (Rev: BL 10/15/08) [537.078]

12861 Hakim, Joy. *Einstein Adds a New Dimension* (7–12). Series: Story of Science. 2007, Smithsonian $27.95 (978-1-58834-162-4). Not just about Einstein, this book also covers the giants upon whose shoulders Einstein stood and the many other factors in history and society that led to quantum theory; readable and compelling. (Rev: BL 12/1/07; SLJ 12/07) [509]

12862 Hammond, Richard. *Can You Feel the Force?* (5–8). Illus. 2006, DK $15.99 (978-0-7566-2033-2). Light, matter, friction, gravity, velocity — these and other basic physics principles are explained in a reader-friendly format that includes experiments, captions, sidebars, and other eye-catching elements. (Rev: SLJ 10/06) [530]

12863 Jerome, Kate Boehm. *Atomic Universe: The Quest to Discover Radioactivity* (5–8). Series: Science Quest. 2006, National Geographic $17.95 (978-0-7922-5543-7). An attractive and informative history of radioactivity, profiling key figures and placing the discovery and subsequent developments in scientific and social context. (Rev: SLJ 4/07) [539.7]

12864 Juettner, Bonnie. *Molecules* (4–8). 2004, Gale LB $26.20 (978-0-7377-2076-1). Clear, concise text, supported by full-color photographs and diagrams, describes the characteristics of atoms and molecules. (Rev: SLJ 6/05)

12865 Kagayame, Johnny, and Josepha Sherman. *Discovering the Construct of Time* (7–9). Illus. Series: Scientist's Guide to Physics. 2011, Rosen LB $33.25 (978-144884703-7). Describes the history of time measurement from ancient times to the present day. (Rev: BL 10/1/11) [529]

12866 Karam, P. Andrew, and Ben P. Stein. *Radioactivity* (6–12). Series: Science Foundations. 2009, Chelsea House $35 (978-1-60413-016-4). Providing an overview of radiation and its characteristics, this volume looks at its uses in warfare, medicine, and other areas. (Rev: LMC 11–12/09) [539.2]

12867 McGrath, Susan. *Fun with Physics* (5–9). 1986, National Geographic LB $12.50 (978-0-87044-581-1). An introduction to physics that uses everyday situations as examples and supplies a smattering of experiments. (Rev: SLJ 6/87) [530]

12868 Morgan, Sally, and Adrian Morgan. *Materials* (4–7). Series: Designs in Science. 1994, Facts on File $23.00 (978-0-8160-2985-3). Basic properties of matter and materials are explored in a series of experiments using everyday materials. (Rev: BL 7/94) [620.1]

12869 Silverstein, Alvin, and Virginia Silverstein. *Forces and Motion* (4–8). Illus. Series: Science Concepts, Second Series. 2008, Twenty-First Century LB $31.93 (978-0-8225-7514-6). With photographs, diagrams, and examples that attract young readers, this volume provides clear explanations of forces, motion, gravity, and simple machines. Also use *Matter* (2008). (Rev: SLJ 12/08) [531]

12870 Solway, Andrew. *Sports Science* (4–9). Series: Why Science Matters. 2009, Heinemann-Raintree $32.86 (978-1-4329-2480-5). Geared towards illuminating science's role in our everyday lives, this title provides a thorough, well-researched look at the science of sports. (Rev: LMC 11–12/09)

12871 Sonneborn, Liz. *Forces in Nature: Understanding Gravitational, Electrical, and Magnetic Force* (7–12). Series: Library of Physics. 2005, Rosen LB $26.50 (978-1-4042-0332-7). Explores a wide variety of forces, including gravitational, electrical, magnetic, and electromagnetic, using clear narrative with diagrams and photographs. (Rev: SLJ 12/05)

12872 Stille, Darlene R. *Physical Change: Reshaping Matter* (5–8). Series: Exploring Science. 2005, Compass Point LB $27.93 (978-0-7565-1257-6). An attractive format with plenty of graphics adds to the appeal of this brief discussion of the states of matter. (Rev: SLJ 7/06) [530]

12873 Stwertka, Albert. *The World of Atoms and Quarks* (7–12). Series: Scientific American Sourcebooks. 1995, Twenty-First Century LB $28.90 (978-0-8050-3533-9). Using profiles of important scientists, this work traces humankind's quest for an understanding of matter and its building blocks. (Rev: BL 12/1/95; SLJ 2/96) [539.7]

12874 Sullivan, Navin. *Weight* (4–7). Illus. Series: Measure Up! 2006, Marshall Cavendish LB $20.95 (978-0-7614-2324-9). Topics such as gravity and buoyancy are covered in this well-designed book about weight. (Rev: LMC 8–9/07; SLJ 6/07)

12875 Vancleave, Janice. *Step-By-Step Science Experiments in Energy* (5–8). Series: Janice VanCleave's First-Place Science Fair Projects. 2012, Rosen Central LB $33.25 (978-1-4488-6972-4). An updated volume with step-by-step instructions for 22 experiments mostly using easily found materials. (Rev: SLJ 10/12) [531.6078]

12876 Willett, Edward. *The Basics of Quantum Physics: Understanding the Photoelectric Effect and Line Spectra* (7–12). Series: Library of Physics. 2005, Rosen LB $26.50 (978-1-4042-0334-1). Examines the nature of light and the atom, key elements in the study of quantum physics, using clear narrative with diagrams and photographs. (Rev: SLJ 12/05)

Energy and Motion

General and Miscellaneous

12877 Asimov, Isaac. *How Did We Find Out About Solar Power?* (5–8). Illus. by David Wool. 1981, Walker LB $12.85 (978-0-8027-6423-2). An explanation of how man has benefited from solar power from the earliest time until today. [621.47]

12878 Ballard, Carol. *From Steam Engines to Nuclear Fusion* (6–9). Series: Chain Reactions. 2007, Heinemann LB $24.00 (978-1-4034-9554-9). The uses of energy, from the basic to the advanced, are covered, as well as the scientists who have contributed to this field and what the future advancements in energy theory may entail. (Rev: BL 4/1/07; SLJ 7/07) [621.042]

12879 Cruden, Gabriel. *Energy Alternatives* (5–8). Series: Lucent Library of Science and Technology. 2005, Gale LB $29.95 (978-1-59018-530-8). A look at the importance of finding alternatives to existing energy sources, covering such technologies as solar, wind, and geothermal power. (Rev: BL 1/05)

12880 Doeden, Matt. *Green Energy: Crucial Gains or Economic Strains?* (7–10). Series: USA Today's Debate: Voices and Perspectives. 2010, Lerner LB $35.93

(978-0-7613-5112-2). After a history of energy and a discussion of global warming, this attractive volume that draws on *USA Today* looks at nuclear, solar, and wind power as well as biomass and biofuel, and electric cars, hybrids, and fuel cells. (Rev: LMC 10/10; SLJ 6/10) [163.25]

12881 Doherty, Paul, and Don Rathjen. *The Spinning Blackboard and Other Dynamic Experiments on Force and Motion* (4–8). Series: Exploratorium Science Snackbook. 1996, Wiley paper $13.95 (978-0-471-11514-4). The many activities in this well-organized, attractive book reveal important characteristics of force and motion. (Rev: BL 4/15/96; SLJ 6/96) [531]

12882 Egendorf, Laura K., ed. *Energy Alternatives* (5–9). Series: Introducing Issues with Opposing Viewpoints. 2006, Gale LB $33.70 (978-0-7377-3458-4). Presents basic information about alternatives to fossil fuel-driven energy, along with diverse views on the feasibility and practicality of these alternative energy sources. (Rev: SLJ 8/06) [333.79]

12883 Farrell, Courtney. *Using Alternative Energies* (3–7). Series: Language Arts Explorer: Save the Planet. 2010, Cherry Lake LB $27.07 (978-1-60279-663-8). Students are given a mission at the beginning of the book and must use creative thinking and problem solving to gather facts as they travel on a virtual trip researching solar power, wind power, and other alternatives. (Rev: LMC 8–9/10) [333.79]

12884 Friedman, Lauri S., ed. *Energy Alternatives* (7–10). Illus. Series: Introducing Issues with Opposing Viewpoints. 2011, Greenhaven $36.82 (978-073775198-7). Presents pro and con arguments on such topics as the remaining oil reserves, climate change, the benefits and shortfalls of renewables, nuclear energy, and passenger cars of the future. (Rev: BL 12/1/11) [333.79]

12885 Gardner, Robert. *Energy Experiments: Using Ice Cubes, Springs, Magnets, and More* (4–7). Series: Last Minute Science Projects. 2012, Enslow LB $23.93 (978-076603959-9). Eighteen projects that use everyday objects demonstrate basic concepts of energy and how matter changes from a solid to a liquid to a gas. (Rev: BL 12/1/12; LMC 5–6/13)

12886 Gardner, Timothy. *Oil* (7–12). Illus. Series: Diminishing Resources. 2009, Morgan Reynolds LB $28.95 (978-159935117-9). Direct quotes and hard-hitting facts add drama and appeal to this title discussing America's dependence on oil, efforts to find alternative fuels, pollution problems, and relationship with the Middle East. (Rev: BL 1/1–15/10; VOYA 6/10) [333.8]

12887 Goodman, Polly. *Understanding Wind Power* (5–8). Illus. Series: The World of Energy. 2010, Gareth Stevens LB $31.95 (978-143394133-7). Different kinds of wind power, and pros and cons of their construction and use, are discussed in this slim volume. (Rev: BLO 2/14/11; LMC 5–6/11) [621.4]

12888 Jakab, Cheryl. *Renewable Energy* (4–7). Series: Global Issues. 2009, Smart Apple Media LB $28.50 (978-1-59920-453-6). Offering a global perspective, this volume discusses the benefits of renewable energy and the various challenges the technology faces. (Rev: SLJ 2/10) [333.79]

12889 Juettner, Bonnie. *Energy* (5–8). Series: Our Environment. 2004, Gale LB $26.20 (978-0-7377-1821-8). Answers such questions as "How is energy managed?" and "Are we running out of energy?" in four chapters that feature many illustrations and large type. (Rev: SLJ 4/05) [333.79]

12890 Kallen, Stuart A. *World Energy Crisis* (8–12). Series: Compact Research. 2007, Reference Point LB $24.95 (978-1-60152-011-1). This compact volume provides lots of information for report writers, with illustrations, quotations from primary sources, lists of facts, statistical charts, and brief timelines. (Rev: SLJ 5/07) [333.79]

12891 Landau, Elaine. *The History of Energy* (5–8). Series: Major Inventions Through History. 2005, Twenty-First Century LB $26.60 (978-0-8225-3806-6). An attractive look at developments through time in the use of various forms of energy (fire, wind, water, coal, steam, oil and gasoline, electricity, and so forth) and their application in transportation and other sectors. (Rev: SLJ 1/06)

12892 Lew, Kristi. *Goodbye, Gasoline: The Science of Fuel Cells* (5–7). Series: Headline Science. 2008, Compass Point LB $27.93 (978-0-7565-3521-6). Understandable text and helpful charts educate readers as they delve into the science of fuel cells as alternative, clean energy and learn about the negative impact that gasoline has on our environment. (Rev: LMC 5/09*; SLJ 2/09) [621.31]

12893 McLeish, Ewan. *Challenges to Our Energy Supply* (4–8). Series: Can the Earth Survive? 2010, Rosen LB $26.50 (978-1-4358-5357-7). With case studies and suggested strategies for the future, this volume looks at energy shortages around the world and the impact on everyday life. (Rev: LMC 3–4/10; SLJ 1/10) [333.79]

12894 Marrin, Albert. *Black Gold: The Story of Oil in Our Lives* (7–12). Illus. 2012, Knopf $19.99 (978-037586673-9); LB $22.99 (978-037596673-6). A thought-provoking overview of oil deposits through history and our increasing dependence on them even as they dwindle. Outstanding Science Trade Books for Students K–12. e Lexile 1070L (Rev: BLO 7/12; HB 5–6/12; LMC 10/12; SLJ 4/12) [553.2]

12895 Mooney, Carla. *What Is the Future of Biofuels?* (7–10). Illus. Series: Future of Renewable Energy. 2012, ReferencePoint $27.95 (978-160152272-6). Presenting opposing viewpoints, this volume looks at various questions relating to biofuels: are they affordable; do they impact the environment; can they replace fossil fuels; and should the government be involved in biofuel development. (Rev: BL 2/15/13; LMC 5–6/13) [662]

12896 Morgan, Sally. *From Windmills to Hydrogen Fuel Cells: Discovering Alternative Energy* (6–9). Series: Chain Reactions. 2007, Heinemann LB $34.29 (978-1-4034-9555-6). Clear text and interesting graphics will draw readers into this overview of alternative energy sources, including solar, wind, and fuel cells. (Rev: SLJ 7/07)

12897 Morris, Neil. *Biomass Power* (7–12). 2010, Smart Apple Media LB $34.25 (978-1-59920-337-9). A look at the technology of biomass power, with discussion of economic and environmental factors. Also use *The Energy Mix, Fossil Fuels, Geothermal Power, Nuclear Power, Solar Power, Water Power,* and *Wind Power* (all 2010). (Rev: LMC 1–2/10) [333.95]

12898 Nakaya, Andrea C. *Energy Alternatives* (8–12). Series: Compact Research. 2007, Reference Point LB $24.95 (978-1-60152-017-3). What alternative energy sources should be pursued? Can alternative energy be used for transportation? These and other questions are discussed from various points of view, with facts, profiles, and illustrations. (Rev: SLJ 1/08)

12899 Silverstein, Alvin. *Energy* (4–7). Series: Science Concepts. 1998, Twenty-First Century LB $26.90 (978-0-7613-3222-0). Photographs, diagrams, and illustrations help to introduce six types of energy: electrical, magnetic, light, heat, sound, and nuclear. (Rev: BL 5/1/99; HBG 10/99) [621.042]

12900 Spilsbury, Louise. *Dams and Hydropower* (6–8). Series: Development or Destruction? 2012, Rosen Central LB $27.95 (978-1-4488-6990-9); paper $11.75 (978-1-4488-6994-7). A useful overview of the pros and cons of dams and hydropower, with discussion of possible future developments. (Rev: LMC 10/12; SLJ 9/12)

12901 Stille, Darlene R. *Waves: Energy on the Move* (5–8). Series: Exploring Science. 2005, Compass Point LB $27.93 (978-0-7565-1259-0). An attractive format with plenty of graphics adds to the appeal of this brief discussion of waves in water, light, air, and other media. (Rev: SLJ 7/06) [531]

12902 Sullivan, Navin. *Speed* (4–7). Illus. Series: Measure Up! 2006, Marshall Cavendish LB $20.95 (978-0-7614-2325-6). In addition to providing an overview of the science of speed, this volume includes high-quality graphics, information about historical versus modern methods, and at-home experiments. (Rev: LMC 8–9/07; SLJ 6/07)

12903 Viegas, Jennifer. *Kinetic and Potential Energy: Understanding Changes Within Physical Systems* (7–12). Series: Library of Physics. 2005, Rosen LB $26.50 (978-1-4042-0333-4). Examines the distinction between potential and kinetic energy, as well as momentum, mechanical energy, and the laws of energy,

using clear narrative with diagrams and photographs. (Rev: SLJ 12/05)

12904 Walker, Niki. *Generating Wind Power* (5–8). Illus. Series: Energy Revolution. 2007, Crabtree LB $25.20 (978-0-7787-2913-6); paper $8.95 (978-0-7787-2927-3). Wind is explored as an alternative energy source in this well-designed volume. Also use *Harnessing Power from the Sun* and *Biomass: Fueling Change* (both 2007). (Rev: SLJ 7/07)

12905 Woodford, Chris. *Energy* (4–7). Illus. Series: See for Yourself. 2007, DK $14.99 (978-0-7566-2561-0). This introductory guide to energy provides an easy-to-understand definition, offers examples of both kinetic and potential energy, identifies major energy sources, explains the processes through which energy is released, and discusses the problems inherent in energy usage. (Rev: BL 4/1/07) [333.79]

12906 Woodford, Chris. *Power and Energy* (6–9). Series: History of Invention. 2004, Facts on File $35.00 (978-0-8160-5440-4). A slim introductory overview of advances in power and energy from prehistoric times to today, with illustrations, and profiles of key figures. (Rev: SLJ 12/04)

Nuclear Energy

12907 Bortz, Fred. *Meltdown! The Nuclear Disaster in Japan and Our Energy Future* (7–10). Illus. 2012, Lerner/Twenty-First Century $31.93 (978-076138660-5). Tells the story of the March 2011 earthquake in Japan and the disastrous impact on the Fukushima nuclear plant, and includes discussion of alternative sources of energy. (Rev: BL 2/1/12; LMC 10/12; SLJ 5/1/12; VOYA 6/12) [363.17]

12908 Daley, Michael J. *Nuclear Power: Promise or Peril?* (7–12). Series: Pro/Con Issues. 1997, Lerner LB $30.35 (978-0-8225-2611-7). This book examines conflicting opinions about nuclear power, the possibility of nuclear accidents, the demand for energy, and the problems involving storage of nuclear waste. (Rev: BL 11/1/97; SLJ 12/97) [333.792]

12909 Lusted, Marcia Amidon, and Greg Lusted. *A Nuclear Power Plant* (8–12). Series: Building History. 2005, Gale LB $32.45 (978-1-59018-392-2). Explores the history of nuclear power generation and considers the arguments for and against the construction of more nuclear power plants in the United States and elsewhere. (Rev: SLJ 6/05) [333.792]

Light, Color, and Laser Science

12910 Gardner, Robert. *Science Projects About Light* (4–8). Series: Science Projects. 1994, Enslow LB

$26.60 (978-0-89490-529-2). This project book contains a wealth of demonstrations that explain the basic principles of light. (Rev: SLJ 1/95) [535]

12911 Kirkland, Kyle. *Light and Optics* (8–12). Series: Physics in Our World. 2007, Facts on File $35.00 (978-0-8160-6114-3). A good explanation of the physics of light is followed by a look at real-world examples and applications of light put to use. (Rev: BL 4/15/07) [535]

12912 Sitarski, Anita. *Cold Light: Creatures, Discoveries, and Inventions that Glow* (4–7). Illus. 2007, Boyds Mills $16.95 (978-1-59078-468-6). An interesting introduction to the phenomenon of luminescence — found in animals that glow but also in light-emitting diodes — this will appeal to report writers and browsers. (Rev: BL 12/1/07; LMC 1/08; SLJ 10/07) [535.35]

12913 Stille, Darlene R. *Manipulating Light: Reflection, Refraction, and Absorption* (5–8). Series: Exploring Science. 2005, Compass Point LB $27.93 (978-0-7565-1258-3). An attractive format with plenty of graphics adds to the appeal of this brief discussion of the nature of light. (Rev: SLJ 7/06) [535]

Magnetism and Electricity

12914 Dreier, David. *Electrical Circuits: Harnessing Electricity* (5–7). Illus. Series: Exploring Science: Physical Science. 2007, Compass Point LB $19.95 (978-0-7565-3267-3). A user-friendly introduction to electricity and how we use it, with good graphics and interesting sidebar features. (Rev: BL 12/1/07; LMC 2/08) [537]

12915 Fleisher, Paul. *Waves: Principles of Light, Electricity, and Magnetism* (6–12). Series: Secrets of the Universe. 2001, Lerner LB $25.26 (978-0-8225-2987-3). Optics, electric current, and electromagnetism are among the topics covered in this volume adapted from an adult title. (Rev: HBG 3/02; SLJ 12/01) [539.2]

12916 Solway, Andrew. *Generating and Using Electricity* (4–9). Series: Why Science Matters. 2009, Heinemann-Raintree $32.86 (978-1-4329-2481-2). This ap-

pealing guide offers a look at the key role electricity plays in our lives. (Rev: LMC 11–12/09) [537]

12917 VanCleave, Janice. *Janice VanCleave's Electricity: Mind-Boggling Experiments You Can Turn into Science Fair Projects* (5–7). 1994, Wiley paper $10.95 (978-0-471-31010-5). As well as providing a discussion on the nature of electricity, this book offers 20 informative experiments that move from the very simple to the more complex. (Rev: BL 12/1/94; SLJ 11/94) [537]

Nuclear Physics

12918 Morgan, Sally. *From Greek Atoms to Quarks: Discovering Atoms* (6–9). Series: Chain Reactions. 2007, Heinemann LB $34.29 (978-1-4034-9551-8). With clear text and excellent graphics, this volume chronicles the history of humans' understanding of atoms and describes current subatomic research. (Rev: SLJ 7/07)

Sound

12919 Morgan, Sally, and Adrian Morgan. *Using Sound* (4–7). Series: Designs in Science. 1994, Facts on File $23.00 (978-0-8160-2981-5). The properties of sound and their relation to everyday life are covered in the text and a number of experiments using readily available materials. (Rev: BL 7/94) [534]

12920 Parker, Steve. *The Science of Sound: Projects and Experiments with Music and Sound Waves* (4–7). Series: Tabletop Scientist. 2005, Heinemann LB $29.29 (978-1-4034-7281-6). The 12 experiments and projects in this collection demonstrate the basic scientific principles of sound waves. (Rev: SLJ 12/05)

12921 Wright, Lynne. *The Science of Noise* (5–8). Series: Science World. 2000, Raintree LB $25.69 (978-0-7398-1324-9). This account describes how sound is produced, how it travels, how we hear it, and how it can be changed. (Rev: BL 9/1/00; HBG 10/00; SLJ 8/00) [534]

Technology and Engineering

General Works and Miscellaneous Industries

12922 *CDs, Super Glue, and Salsa Series 2: How Everyday Products Are Made* (5–10). 1996, Gale LB $126.00 (978-0-7876-0870-5). This two-volume set tells how 30 everyday products are made, including air bags, bungee cords, contact lenses, ketchup, pencils, soda bottles, and umbrellas. (Rev: SLJ 8/97) [658.5]

12923 Cobb, Vicki. *Fireworks* (4–8). Photos by Michael Gold. Series: Where's the Science Here? 2005, Lerner LB $23.93 (978-0-7613-2771-4). A well-illustrated, engaging text covers the history and science of pyrotechnics; experiments require adult supervision. Also recommended in this series are *Junk Food* and *Sneakers* (both 2005). (Rev: SLJ 2/06)

12924 Colman, Penny. *Toilets, Bathtubs, Sinks, and Sewers: A History of the Bathroom* (5–8). 1994, Atheneum $16.00 (978-0-689-31894-8). A fascinating look at sanitation systems and inventions related to personal hygiene from ancient times to the present. (Rev: BCCB 2/95; BL 1/1/95; SLJ 3/95) [643]

12925 Crompton, Samuel Willard. *The Printing Press* (7–10). Series: Transforming Power of Technology. 2003, Chelsea House LB $30.00 (978-0-7910-7451-0). This interesting volume explores the impact of the invention of the printing press on literacy and general social and economic conditions. (Rev: SLJ 6/04)

12926 Crump, Donald J., ed. *How Things Are Made* (6–9). 1981, National Geographic LB $12.50 (978-0-87044-339-8). An inquiry into how such objects as baseballs and light bulbs are made. [670]

12927 Crump, Donald J., ed. *How Things Work* (5–7). 1984, National Geographic LB $12.50 (978-0-87044-430-2). A handsome volume that explains the mechanics of a variety of objects from toasters to space shuttles. [600]

12928 Crump, Donald J., ed. *Small Inventions That Make a Big Difference* (6–9). 1984, National Geographic LB $12.50 (978-0-87044-503-3). A book on inventions and inventors that covers such common items as the zipper. [608]

12929 *Fantastic Feats and Failures* (4–8). Illus. by Jane Kurisu. 2004, Kids Can paper $9.95 (978-1-55337-634-7). Highs and lows of engineering (the Brooklyn Bridge in the first category, for example, and the Tacoma Narrows in the latter) are reviewed in this fascinating large-format book. (Rev: BL 9/15/04) [624.1]

12930 Goldberg, Jan. *Earth Imaging Satellites* (5–9). Series: The Library of Satellites. 2003, Rosen LB $26.50 (978-0-8239-3853-7). A survey of the various satellites and how their images of the earth's surface measure pollution, locate forest fires, find earthquake faults, and measure the size of polar caps. (Rev: BL 11/15/03) [629.46]

12931 Harrison, Ian. *The Book of Inventions* (8–12). 2004, National Geographic $30.00 (978-0-7922-8296-9). A photo-filled review of some eclectic and entertaining inventions, including sliced bread and the lava lamp. (Rev: BL 12/1/04) [609]

12932 Kassinger, Ruth G. *Iron and Steel: From Thor's Hammer to the Space Shuttle* (5–7). Series: Material World. 2003, Millbrook LB $25.90 (978-0-7613-2111-8). The different ways in which humans have used and processed iron and steel through the ages is the focus of this book. (Rev: BL 5/15/03; HBG 10/03; SLJ 1/04) [669]

12933 Kent, Peter. *Technology* (4–7). Illus. Series: Navigators. 2009, Kingfisher $12.99 (978-075346307-9). For browsers and those interested in learning about exciting technologies — everything from new developments in computers and electronics to nanotechnology, wave farming, and superstructures, this is a well-designed informative volume. (Rev: BLO 11/1/09; LMC 1–2/10) [500]

12934 Landau, Elaine. *The History of Everyday Life* (5–8). Series: Major Inventions Through History. 2005, Twenty-First Century LB $26.60 (978-0-8225-3808-0). Fireplaces, washing machines, and microwave ovens are among the inventions discussed here that have improved our everyday lives. (Rev: SLJ 2/06)

12935 Laxer, James. *Oil* (7–10). 2008, Groundwood $18.95 (978-0-88899-815-6); paper $10.00 (978-0-88899-816-3). An illuminating overview of the oil industry, with information on major oil companies, the industry's history, and its impact on the environment and politics. (Rev: BL 6/1–15/08) [333.8]

12936 Levy, Matthys, and Richard Panchyk. *Engineering the City* (6–12). 2000, Chicago Review $14.95 (978-1-55652-419-6). There are many curriculum connections in this book that includes information and activities relating to electricity, garbage, transportation, and other urban infrastructure issues. (Rev: BL 2/15/01) [624]

12937 Macaulay, David, and Neil Ardley. *The New Way Things Work* (6–12). 1998, Houghton Mifflin $35.00 (978-0-395-93847-8). With an emphasis on visual cutaways, this revision of a fascinating 1988 introduction to modern machines now includes more material on computers. (Rev: BL 12/1/98; HBG 9/99; SLJ 12/98) [600]

12938 *Machines and Inventions* (5–9). Series: Understanding Science and Nature. 1993, Time-Life $17.95 (978-0-8094-9704-1). Using a question-and-answer format, double-page spreads look at a variety of inventions including the box camera, printing press, and dynamite. (Rev: BL 1/15/94; SLJ 6/94) [621.8]

12939 Mara, Wil. *From Locusts to . . . Automobile Anti-Collision Systems* (4–7). Illus. Series: 21st Century Skills Innovation Library: Innovations from Nature. 2012, Cherry Lake LB $28.50 (978-161080501-8). An interesting exploration of how the science of biomimicry can be put to practical application, in this case in the design of collision avoidance systems based on locusts' swarming strategies. (Rev: BL 10/1/12; SLJ 11/1/12) [629.2]

12940 Martin, Russell, and Lydia Nibley. *The Mysteries of Beethoven's Hair* (6–9). 2009, Charlesbridge $15.95 (978-157091714-1). The journey of a locket containing a lock of Beethoven's hair takes readers from Germany to Nazi-occupied Denmark to the United States. Based on the adult book *Beethoven's Hair: An Extraordinary Historical Odyssey and Scientific Mystery Solved*. Lexile NC1400L (Rev: BLO 5/27/09; HB 5–6/09; SLJ 3/1/09) [780.92]

12941 Scott, Elaine. *Buried Alive! How 33 Miners Survived 69 Days Deep under the Chilean Desert* (4–7).

Illus. 2012, Clarion $17.99 (978-054770778-5). Scott recounts the experiences of the miners trapped deep beneath the ground in 2010, the ways in which they collaborated, the rescue efforts, and the intense media coverage. Lexile 1060L (Rev: BL 5/1/12; LMC 11–12/12; SLJ 5/1/12) [363.11]

12942 Skurzynski, Gloria. *Almost the Real Things: Simulation in Your High Tech World* (5–8). 1991, Macmillan LB $16.95 (978-0-02-778072-7). Skurzynski explains how engineers and scientists simulate events from weightlessness to complex animation. (Rev: BCCB 10/91; BL 10/15/91; HB 11–12/91; SLJ 10/91) [620]

12943 Slavin, Bill. *Transformed: How Everyday Things Are Made* (4–7). 2005, Kids Can $24.95 (978-1-55337-179-3). A behind-the-scenes look at the manufacturing process for a wide array of everyday products. (Rev: BL 10/15/05; SLJ 1/06) [670]

12944 Smith, Elizabeth Simpson. *Paper* (4–8). 1984, Walker LB $10.85 (978-0-8027-6569-7). An exploration of the manufacture and use of paper.

12945 Taylor, Barbara. *Be an Inventor* (5–9). 1987, Harcourt $11.95 (978-0-15-205950-7); paper $7.95 (978-0-15-205951-4). A discussion of the process of invention and some examples plus coverage of entries in a *Weekly Reader* invention contest. (Rev: BL 12/15/87; SLJ 3/88) [608]

12946 Thimmesh, Catherine. *Girls Think of Everything* (4–7). 2000, Houghton Mifflin $16.00 (978-0-395-93744-0). A fresh, breezy account about women whose inventions include the windshield wiper, chocolate chip cookies, and Glo-paper. (Rev: BCCB 5/00; BL 3/15/00; HB 5–6/00; HBG 10/00; SLJ 4/00) [609.2]

12947 Vare, Ethlie Ann, and Greg Ptacek. *Women Inventors and Their Discoveries* (6–10). 1993, Oliver LB $19.95 (978-1-881508-06-9). A review of women who are known in the world of industry and technology for their unusual inventions. (Rev: BL 10/15/93; SLJ 1/94; VOYA 2/94) [609.2]

12948 Whiting, Jim. *James Watt and the Steam Engine* (5–8). Series: Uncharted, Unexplored, and Unexplained: Scientific Advancements of the 19th Century. 2006, Mitchell Lane LB $29.95 (978-1-58415-371-9). Brief biographical information about Watt is accompanied by a more detailed discussion of his invention and its importance. (Rev: SLJ 5/06) [621]

12949 Woodford, Chris. *Cool Stuff and How It Works* (8–12). 2005, DK $24.99 (978-0-7566-1465-2). The inner workings of products ranging from the digital camera to the microwave oven are explained in clear text with lots of bright, often high-tech illustrations. (Rev: BL 12/1/05) [600]

12950 Woodford, Chris, and Jon Woodcock. *Cool Stuff 2.0 and How It Works* (4–8). Illus. by Darren Awuah, et al. 2007, DK $24.99 (978-0-7566-3207-6). More than

100 new "cool" items are featured in this updated edition full of things that appeal to kids, such as robot cars and "silent flight" aircraft. (Rev: SLJ 3/08)

12951 Woods, Michael, and Mary B. Woods. *The History of Communication* (5–8). Series: Major Inventions Through History. 2005, Twenty-First Century LB $26.60 (978-0-8225-3807-3). An attractive look at developments through time in methods of communication — the printing press, telephone, radio, television, and the Internet — and the impact on our lives. (Rev: SLJ 1/06) [302.2]

12952 Ye, Ting-Xing. *The Chinese Thought of It: Amazing Inventions and Innovations* (5–8). Illus. 2009, Annick LB $19.95 (978-155451196-9); paper $9.95 (978-155451195-2). Famous inventions from 37 centuries of Chinese history are presented in this well-organized book. (Rev: BLO 11/15/09) [609.51]

Building and Construction

12953 Aldridge, Rebecca. *The Hoover Dam* (5–8). Series: Building America: Then and Now. 2009, Chelsea House $35 (978-1-60413-069-0). This book about the Hoover Dam includes illustrative maps, primary source documents, Web sites, a timeline, and glossary. (Rev: LMC 10/09) [627]

12954 Barker, Geoff. *Incredible Skyscrapers* (5–7). Illus. Series: Superstructures. 2010, Amicus LB $19.95 (978-160753133-3). Sky-scraping structures from around the world are profiled in this book, which offers technical explanations of the engineering feats required in building such a structure. (Rev: BL 7/11) [720]

12955 Caney, Steven. *Steven Caney's Ultimate Building Book* (4–8). Illus. by Lauren House. 2006, Running Pr $29.95 (978-0-7624-0409-4). Starting with a history of construction and the basic techniques involved, Caney looks at the ways design and technology intersect and suggests a wide range of kid-tested building projects. (Rev: SLJ 1/07*) [624]

12956 Dreyer, Francis. *Lighthouses* (4–7). Photos by Philip Plisson. 2005, Abrams $18.95 (978-0-8109-5958-3). A fascinating and strikingly beautiful overview of lighthouses — of the past and present — and of the courage and loneliness of the men and women who tend them. (Rev: BL 1/1–15/06) [387.1]

12957 DuTemple, Lesley A. *The Hoover Dam* (4–7). Series: Great Building Feats. 2003, Lerner LB $27.93 (978-0-8225-4691-7). This story traces the dam's construction from the planning stages through its technically difficult and dangerous construction and places this impressive structure in historical context. (Rev: BL 11/15/03; HBG 10/03; SLJ 11/03) [627]

12958 DuTemple, Lesley A. *The Panama Canal* (6–9). Series: Great Building Feats. 2002, Lerner LB $27.93 (978-0-8225-0079-7). An attractive and absorbing overview of this massive and challenging project. (Rev: HBG 10/03; LMC 2/03; SLJ 1/03*) [972.87]

12959 Gonzales, Doreen. *Seven Wonders of the Modern World* (4–7). Series: Seven Wonders of the World. 2005, Enslow LB $25.26 (978-0-7660-5292-5). Profiles seven marvels of modern construction, including the Panama Canal, Toronto's CN Tower, and the Empire State Building in New York City; the text is extended by constantly updated links to Web sites. (Rev: SLJ 11/05)

12960 Jackson, Tom, ed. *Buildings and Structures* (7–10). Illus. Series: Facts at Your Fingertips: Invention and Technology. 2012, Black Rabbit LB $35.65 (978-193633341-7). A fascinating introduction to structural engineering and design and the various elements that must be taken into consideration, with a timeline of developments and profiles of key characters including Gustav Eiffel and Frank Lloyd Wright. (Rev: BL 10/1/12) [690]

12961 Kirkwood, Jon. *The Fantastic Cutaway Book of Giant Buildings* (4–7). 1997, Millbrook paper $9.95 (978-0-7613-0629-0). Using double-page spreads, outstanding graphics, and many fact boxes, this book features a wide variety of structures including the Statue of Liberty, the pyramids, the Colosseum, churches, operas houses, Grand Central Station, Munich's Olympic stadium, and skyscrapers. (Rev: BL 4/1/98; HBG 10/98) [720]

12962 Korres, Manolis. *The Stones of the Parthenon* (7–12). Trans. by D. Turner. 2001, Getty paper $14.95 (978-0-89236-607-1). The construction of the Parthenon is described in text and detailed drawings in this small-format book, which includes notes, a glossary, and a bibliography. (Rev: BL 2/1/01) [622]

12963 Macaulay, David. *Building Big* (7–12). 2000, Houghton Mifflin $30.00 (978-0-395-96331-9). This companion book to a set of videos explains the problems posed by ambitious construction projects such as tunnels, bridges, dams, domes, and skyscrapers. (Rev: BL 12/15/00*; HB 1–2/01; HBG 3/01; SLJ 11/00; VOYA 4/01) [720]

12964 Macaulay, David. *Unbuilding* (5–8). Illus. by author. 1980, Houghton Mifflin $19.00 (978-0-395-29457-4); paper $6.95 (978-0-395-45360-5). A book that explores the concept of tearing down the Empire State Building.

12965 Macaulay, David. *Underground* (5–10). Illus. by author. 1983, Houghton Mifflin $19.00 (978-0-395-24739-6); paper $9.95 (978-0-395-34065-3). An exploration in text and detailed drawings of the intricate network of systems under city streets. [624]

12966 Mann, Elizabeth. *The Brooklyn Bridge* (4–7). Series: Wonders of the World. 1996, Mikaya $19.95

(978-0-9650493-0-6). The story of the building of the Brooklyn Bridge is told through the eyes of a family. (Rev: BL 2/1/97; SLJ 6/97*) [624]

12967 Owens, Thomas S. *Football Stadiums* (5–8). Series: Sports Palaces. 2001, Millbrook LB $25.90 (978-0-7613-1764-7). Rather than highlighting individual stadiums, this book covers general topics such as their design, replacement, funding, amenities, and history. (Rev: BL 4/1/01; HBG 10/01; SLJ 4/01) [796.332]

12968 Roberts, Russell. *Building the Panama Canal* (7–10). Series: Monumental Milestones. 2009, Mitchell Lane LB $29.95 (978-1-58415-692-5). Both interesting and informative, this book focuses on the historic and technological factors relevant to the construction of the Panama Canal. (Rev: SLJ 6/1/09) [386.44]

12969 Sullivan, George. *Built to Last: Building America's Amazing Bridges, Dams, Tunnels, and Skyscrapers* (5–8). 2005, Scholastic $18.99 (978-0-439-51737-9). Seventeen marvels of American engineering — including the Erie Canal, Hoover Dam, Brooklyn Bridge, and Boston's "Big Dig" — are presented in chronological chapters with good illustrations and fact boxes that add historical and technological context. (Rev: BL 12/1/05; SLJ 3/06*; VOYA 8/06) [624]

12970 Vogel, Jennifer. *A Library Story: Building a New Central Library* (4–7). 2006, Lerner $26.60 (978-0-8225-5916-0). The construction of the new central library in Minneapolis is the topic of this lively, well-illustrated book that looks at the reasons for the building, architectural and engineering concerns, and artistic choices that were made. (Rev: BL 8/06; SLJ 9/06)

12971 Wearing, Judy, and Tom Riddolls. *Golden Gate Bridge* (4–7). Illus. Series: Structural Wonders. 2009, Weigl LB $18.20 (978-160596136-1). Looks at the history, construction, and design of the bridge, with period photographs and information on key individuals. (Rev: BL 9/15/09; SLJ 11/09) [624.2]

Clothing, Textiles, and Jewelry

12972 Behnke, Alison. *The Little Black Dress and Zoot Suits: Depression and Wartime Fashions from the 1930s to the 1950s* (7–10). Illus. Series: Dressing a Nation: The History of U.S. Fashion. 2011, Lerner/Twenty-First Century LB $31.93 (978-076135892-3). This visually appealing offering offers readers a glimpse into the innovative realm of fashion in America in the 1930s through 1950s. e (Rev: BL 10/1/11; LMC 1–2/12) [391.00973]

12973 Bell, Alison. *Fearless Fashion* (6–10). 2005, Lobster paper $14.95 (978-1-894222-86-0). From preppy to punk to goth to boho, this volume analyzes seven hot fashion trends, looks at trends in history, and gives tips on developing one's own style. (Rev: SLJ 3/05) [391]

12974 Kyi, Tanya Lloyd. *The Blue Jean Book: The Story Behind the Seams* (6–9). 2005, Annick $24.95 (978-1-55037-917-4); paper $12.95 (978-1-55037-916-7). The colorful history of blue jeans — and their cultural and economic impact — is chronicled in this accessible volume. (Rev: BL 11/1/05; SLJ 1/06; VOYA 4/06) [391]

12975 Kyi, Tanya Lloyd. *The Lowdown on Denim* (5–8). Illus. by Clayton Hanmer. 2011, Annick $21.95 (978-155451355-0); paper $12.95 (978-15545135-4-3). A history of denim is accompanied by a graphic-novel story of two students investigating dungarees as part of their detention project. (Rev: BLO 11/15/11; SLJ 2/12) [391]

12976 MacFarlane, Katherine. *The Jeweler's Art* (7–12). Series: Eye on Art. 2007, Gale LB $32.45 (978-1-59018-984-9). This book reviews the history of jewelry from ancient times through the Renaissance, Baroque and Rococo periods to the Victorians and Edwardians and contemporary styles and techniques. (Rev: LMC 2/08; SLJ 12/07) [739.27]

12977 Shaskan, Kathy. *How Underwear Got Under There: A Brief History* (5–8). Illus. by Regan Dunnick. 2007, Dutton $16.99 (978-0-525-47178-3). Shaskan takes a lighthearted look at the history of nether garments, looking at their various roles (protection, warmth, modesty, support, and so forth) and at changes in fashion and social attitudes; a lack of sources makes this most suitable for browsing. (Rev: BCCB 9/07; LMC 11–12/07; SLJ 8/07) [391.4]

12978 Smith, Elizabeth Simpson. *Cloth* (5–8). 1985, Walker LB $10.85 (978-0-8027-6577-2). The discovery of fiber and how cloth is made. (Rev: BL 8/85; SLJ 11/85) [677.02864]

12979 Weaver, Janice. *From Head to Toe: Bound Feet, Bathing Suits, and Other Bizarre and Beautiful Things* (5–8). Illus. by Francis Blake. 2003, Tundra paper $16.95 (978-0-88776-654-1). History and culture are interwoven in this account of fashion fads over the years, mostly in the West. (Rev: SLJ 2/04) [391]

Computers, Automation, and the Internet

12980 Allman, Toney. *Internet Predators* (6–9). Series: Ripped from the Headlines. 2007, Erickson LB $23.95 (978-1-60217-000-1). Straightforward and practical advice about how to avoid the scary stuff that can happen to young people who surf the wrong sites and trust the wrong people on the Internet. (Rev: BL 4/1/07) [364.16]

12981 Baker, Christopher W. *Robots Among Us: The Challenges and Promises of Robotics* (5–8). Series: New Century Technology. 2002, Millbrook LB $23.90

(978-0-7613-1969-6). A lavishly illustrated account that describes the science of robotics, current developments, and what might be expected in the future. (Rev: BL 6/1–15/02; HBG 10/02; SLJ 9/02) [629.8]

12982 Baker, Christopher W. *Scientific Visualization: The New Eyes of Science* (5–8). Series: New Century Technology. 2000, Millbrook LB $23.90 (978-0-7613-1351-9). This book explores the ways in which computers enable scientists to study the universe and simulate events such as the creation of a black hole. (Rev: BL 4/1/00; HBG 3/01; SLJ 6/00) [507.2]

12983 Billings, Charlene W. *Supercomputers: Shaping the Future* (7–12). Series: Science Sourcebooks. 1995, Facts on File $25.00 (978-0-8160-3096-5). A history of the silicon revolution — focusing on the megamachines that are the most powerful computers in the world. (Rev: BL 10/15/95; SLJ 4/96; VOYA 4/96) [004.1]

12984 Billings, Charlene W., and Sean M. Grady. *Supercomputers: Charting the Future of Cybernetics. Rev. ed.* (8–12). Series: Science and Technology in Focus. 2004, Facts on File $35.00 (978-0-8160-4730-7). This revised and expanded edition covers the history of computing devices from ancient clay tablets onward and looks forward to the future potential of optical and quantum computers. (Rev: SLJ 6/04) [004.1]

12985 Bingham, Jane. *Internet Freedom: Where Is the Limit?* (5–8). Series: Behind the News. 2006, Heinemann LB $32.86 (978-1-4034-8833-6). Short news stories highlight the problems involved in the freedom we find on the Internet and chapters discuss how to evaluate the stories behind the news and the pros and cons of Internet regulation. (Rev: SLJ 4/07)

12986 Brasch, Nicolas. *The Technology Behind the Internet* (5–8). Illus. 2011, Black Rabbit LB $28.50 (978-159920567-0). This thorough, well-designed book addresses such pertinent subjects as how the Internet works, email, blogs, Web pages, Twitter, and chat-room safety. (Rev: BL 4/1/11) [004.67]

12987 Burns, Michael. *Digital Fantasy Painting: A Step-by-Step Guide to Creating Visionary Art on Your Computer* (7–12). 2002, Watson-Guptill paper $24.95 (978-0-8230-1574-0). Eye-catching illustrations make this an attractive volume for browsing as well as for use as a manual of graphic design. (Rev: SLJ 3/03; VOYA 2/03) [760]

12988 Cindrich, Sharon. *A Smart Girl's Guide to the Internet* (3–7). Illus. by Ali Douglass. 2009, American Girl paper $9.95 (978-1-59369-599-6). This colorful and appealing volume is subtitled *How to Connect with Friends, Find What You Need, and Stay Safe Online* and provides relevant guidance to games, blogs, games, music, and so forth along with quizzes, lists, and other features. (Rev: LMC 1–2/10; SLJ 11/09) [004.67]

12989 de la Bédoyère, Guy. *The First Computers* (6–9). Series: Milestones in Modern Science. 2005, World Al-

manac LB $31.00 (978-0-8368-5854-9). Suitable for reports, this volume provides a good overview of the development of the first computers and the possibilities these offered. (Rev: SLJ 1/06) [004.6]

12990 German, Dave. *Dave Gorman's Googlewhack! Adventure* (8–12). 2004, Overlook $24.95 (978-1-58567-614-9). Gorman, a British stand-up comic, writes about his global quest to find googlewhacks — two-word Google search queries that yield a single, solitary hit — in the process of which he successfully put off writing a contracted novel. (Rev: BL 9/15/04) [910.4]

12991 Gordon, Sherri Mabry. *Downloading Copyrighted Stuff from the Internet: Stealing or Fair Use?* (7–10). Series: Issues in Focus Today. 2005, Enslow LB $31.93 (978-0-7660-2164-8). In concise, accessible text, Gordon defines fair use and copyright and examines issues involving downloading of text, music, games, and so forth. (Rev: BL 11/1/05; SLJ 11/05) [346.730]

12992 Graham, Ian. *Robot Technology* (4–7). Illus. Series: New Technology. 2011, Black Rabbit LB $34.25 (978-159920533-5). Describes the kinds of robots being used in various environments (space, military, factories, hospitals) and the technology evolutions taking place. (Rev: BL 10/15/11) [629.8]

12993 Herumin, Wendy. *Censorship on the Internet: From Filters to Freedom of Speech* (5–12). Series: Issues in Focus. 2004, Enslow LB $26.60 (978-0-7660-1946-1). A look at the various ways we restrict the free exchange of information over the Internet and the pros and cons of doing so. (Rev: SLJ 4/04) [303.48]

12994 Jefferis, David. *Internet: Electronic Global Village* (4–8). Series: Megatech. 2001, Crabtree paper $8.95 (978-0-7787-0062-3). An eye-catching look at the development of the Internet and the World Wide Web and their uses in communication and commerce. (Rev: SLJ 6/02) [4.678]

12995 Jones, David. *Mighty Robots: Mechanical Marvels That Fascinate and Frighten* (5–8). Illus. 2006, Annick $24.95 (978-1-55037-929-7); paper $14.95 (978-1-55037-928-0). Artificial intelligence, mobility, and various robot roles are discussed in this look at the past, present, and future of robots. (Rev: BL 2/1/06) [629.8]

12996 Kling, Andrew A. *Web 2.0* (7–10). Illus. Series: Technology 360. 2011, Gale/Lucent LB $33.45 (978-142050171-1). A clear discussion of the history of the Internet, the development of Web 2.0, and some of the groundbreaking sites; useful for report writers. (Rev: BL 11/1/11) [006.7]

12997 Knittel, John, and Michael Soto. *Everything You Need to Know About the Dangers of Computer Hacking* (5–8). 2000, Rosen LB $25.25 (978-0-8239-3034-0). This book points out the differences between a hacker and a cracker and, through this, discusses beneficial and harmful computer actions and how to avoid the latter. (Rev: BL 4/1/00; SLJ 5/00) [364.16]

12998 Lindsay, Dave. *Dave's Quick 'n' Easy Web Pages: An Introductory Guide to Creating Web Sites. 2nd ed.* (5–9). Illus. by Sean Lindsay. 2001, Erin $11.95 (978-0-9690609-8-7). Young Dave, Webmaster of the popular Redwall site, gives good, basic information on HTML coding and Web page design. (Rev: SLJ 8/01) [005.7]

12999 Lindsay, Dave. *Dave's Quick 'n' Easy Web Pages 2: A Guide to Creating Multi-page Web Sites* (6–10). Illus. by Sean Lindsay. 2004, Erin paper $11.95 (978-0-9690609-9-4). Readers with little prior knowledge will learn such techniques as creating frames and cascading style sheets as this straightforward title introduces concepts clearly with graphics and advice boxes. (Rev: SLJ 11/04) [005.7]

13000 McQuade, Samuel C., and Sarah E. Gentry, et al. *Internet Addiction and Online Gaming* (7–12). Illus. Series: Cybersafety. 2012, Chelsea House LB $39.95 (978-160413696-8). This volume examines the dangers of excessive use of social computing, online shopping, and Internet gambling. Also use *Living with the Internet* (2012). (Rev: BL 9/15/12) [616.85]

13001 Mason, Adrienne, ed. *Robots: From Everyday to Out of This World* (3–7). Illus. 2008, Kids Can $16.95 (978-1-55453-203-2). A fascinating introduction to robots at work and at play with snappy text, easy reading sidebars, cartoon graphics, and color photographs. (Rev: BL 9/1/08) [629.8]

13002 Menhard, Francha Roffe. *Internet Issues: Pirates, Censors, and Cybersquatters* (6–12). Series: Issues in Focus. 2001, Enslow LB $26.60 (978-0-7660-1687-3). Menhard's effective overview of problems concerning filtering, copyright, privacy, and piracy uses clear examples, many of which involve young people. (Rev: BL 2/1/02; HBG 10/02; SLJ 2/02) [384.3]

13003 Mooney, Carla. *Online Predators* (6–12). Illus. Series: Issues in the Digital Age. 2011, ReferencePoint LB $27.95 (978-160152193-4). Scary case studies add interest to this guide to the kinds of dangers that lurk online. (Rev: BL 10/1/11) [004.67]

13004 Otfinoski, Steven. *Computers* (6–9). Series: Great Inventions. 2007, Marshall Cavendish LB $27.95 (978-0-7614-2597-7). This history of computers is told in accessible, interesting text with effective illustrations and details of key personalities. (Rev: BL 12/15/07) [004]

13005 Oxlade, Chris. *Gaming Technology* (4–7). Illus. Series: New Technology. 2011, Black Rabbit LB $34.25 (978-159920531-1). An attractive (if soon dated) introduction to the technology used in creating video games. (Rev: BL 10/15/11) [794.8]

13006 Parks, Peggy J. *Online Addiction* (7–12). Illus. Series: Cybersafety. 2012, ReferencePoint LB $27.95 (978-160152270-2). Is online addiction real? Can peo-

ple get addicted to social networking? With primary source quotes, facts, and illustrations, Parks addresses these and other questions. (Rev: BL 10/1/12; LMC 5–6/13; SLJ 11/1/12) [616.85]

13007 Parks, Peggy J. *Online Social Networking* (7–10). Series: Compact Research: Current Issues. 2011, ReferencePoint LB $26.95 (978-160152116-3). With primary source quotes plus "Facts and Illustrations" this book examines how online social networking affects human interaction, associated dangers and potential addiction, and whether more regulation is necessary. (Rev: BL 4/1/11) [006.7]

13008 Pearce, Q. L. *Artificial Intelligence* (7–10). Illus. Series: Technology 360. 2011, Gale/Lucent LB $34.62 (978-142050384-5). A clear discussion of the history, future, and ethical issues surrounding artificial intelligence, with a chapter on robots, a timeline, and "Bits & Bytes" statistics. (Rev: BL 11/1/11) [006.3]

13009 Rooney, Anne. *Computers: Faster, Smaller, and Smarter* (5–9). Series: The Cutting Edge. 2005, Heinemann LB $32.86 (978-1-4034-7426-1). Looks at the technology behind computers of the past, present, and future; a high-tech design completes the package. (Rev: SLJ 6/06) [004]

13010 Rothman, Kevin F. *Coping with Dangers on the Internet: Staying Safe On-Line* (7–12). Series: Coping. 2001, Rosen LB $31.95 (978-0-8239-3201-6). Readers will find practical advice on safe use of Web sites, e-mail, chat rooms, newsgroups, and so forth, with a useful list of acronyms and emoticons. (Rev: SLJ 8/01) [025.04]

13011 Sandler, Corey. *Living with the Internet and Online Dangers* (6–10). Series: Teen's Guides. 2010, Facts on File LB $34.95 (978-143812971-6). A practical guide to safe use of the Internet, covering such topics as social networking, shopping, scams, file sharing, text messaging, wireless security, and protecting one's identity. e (Rev: BLO 8/10; SLJ 9/10) [004.67]

13012 Selfridge, Benjamin, and Peter Selfridge. *A Kid's Guide to Creating Web Pages for Home and School* (5–10). 2004, Chicago Review paper $19.95 (978-1-56976-180-9). Simple instructions on creating Web pages using HTML are accompanied by helpful illustrations and sample finished pages. (Rev: SLJ 2/05) [005.7]

13013 Spangenburg, Ray, and Kit Moser. *Savvy Surfing on the Internet: Searching and Evaluating Web Sites* (5–8). Series: Issues in Focus. 2001, Enslow LB $26.60 (978-0-7660-1590-6). Readers are encouraged to view much of the information on the Internet with healthy suspicion and are given advice on efficient searching for and assessment of Web sites. (Rev: HBG 3/02; SLJ 12/01) [004.6]

13014 Thomas, Peggy. *Artificial Intelligence* (5–8). Series: Lucent Library of Science and Technology. 2005,

Gale LB $29.95 (978-1-59018-437-0). An interesting overview of progress in efforts to create machines that can think like humans. (Rev: BL 1/05) [004]

13015 Vacca, John, and Mary E. Vacca. *Identity Theft* (7–12). Illus. Series: Cybersafety. 2012, Chelsea House LB $39.95 (978-160413700-2). "Types and Methods of Identity Theft," "Minimizing Risk," and "Protecting Identity Information" are three of the chapters in this useful volume. (Rev: BL 9/15/12) [332.024]

13016 Wan, Guofang. *Virtually True: Questioning Online Media* (4–7). Illus. Series: Fact Finders. Media Literacy. 2006, Capstone LB $22.60 (978-0-7368-6767-2). Designed to awaken skepticism about online media, this book discusses the motivations of those who produce online content and the influence this media has on society. (Rev: SLJ 6/07)

13017 Weber, Sandra. *The Internet* (7–10). Series: Transforming Power of Technology. 2003, Chelsea House LB $30.00 (978-0-7910-7449-7). A look at the influence of the Internet on areas ranging from the economy to society to health care and at the implications for schools and libraries. (Rev: SLJ 6/04) [004.6]

13018 Wolinsky, Art. *Internet Power Research Using the Big6 Approach* (4–8). Series: The Internet Library. 2002, Enslow LB $22.60 (978-0-7660-2094-8). Readers accompany young researchers as they conduct searches using the Big6 method. (Rev: HBG 3/03; SLJ 12/02) [025.04]

13019 Wolinsky, Art. *Safe Surfing on the Internet* (4–8). 2003, Enslow LB $22.60 (978-0-7660-2030-6). Wolinksy presents information on safe use of the Internet and topics including proper use of language, copyright, privacy, and plagiarism. (Rev: HBG 10/03; LMC 8–9/03; SLJ 7/03) [004.67]

13020 Woodford, Chris. *Digital Technology* (4–7). Series: Science in Focus. 2006, Chelsea House LB $27.00 (978-0-7910-8861-6). A clear introduction to the world of digital technology, covering topics including smart cards, computer-aided design, mobile phones, and so forth in easy-to-understand language. (Rev: BL 10/15/06) [621.381]

Electronics

13021 Oxlade, Chris. *Electronics: MP3s, TVs, and DVDs* (5–9). Series: The Cutting Edge. 2005, Heinemann LB $32.86 (978-1-4034-7427-8). Looks at the technology behind popular electronic devices and at predictions about gadgets of the future; a high-tech design completes the package. (Rev: SLJ 6/06)

Telecommunications

13022 Byers, Ann. *Communications Satellites* (5–9). Series: The Library of Satellites. 2003, Rosen LB $26.50 (978-0-8239-3851-3). From the first important communications satellites launched in 1962, this account traces the growth of this technology and its possible future developments. (Rev: BL 11/15/03; SLJ 1/04) [001.51]

13023 Gardner, Robert. *Communication* (6–9). Series: Yesterday's Science, Today's Technology. 1994, Twenty-First Century LB $25.90 (978-0-8050-2854-6). Today's electronic methods of communication are introduced with about 20 activities that would make good science fair projects. (Rev: BL 3/15/95) [303.48]

13024 Hegedus, Alannah, and Kaitlin Rainey. *Bleeps and Blips to Rocket Ships: Great Inventions in Communications* (5–9). Illus. by Bill Slavin. 2001, Tundra paper $17.95 (978-0-88776-452-3). This is a fact-packed and appealing look at the field of communications, with information on history and inventors and inventions as well as suggested activities. (Rev: SLJ 8/01) [609.71]

13025 Hillstrom, Laurie Collier. *Global Positioning Systems* (7–10). Illus. Series: Technology 360. 2011, Gale/Lucent LB $33.45 (978-142050325-8). A clear discussion of the history and importance of these satellites, with a timeline, and "Bits & Bytes" statistics. (Rev: BL 11/1/11) [910.285]

13026 Kling, Andrew A. *Cell Phones* (8–12). Series: Technology 360. 2009, Lucent $32.45 (978-1-4205-0164-3). An attractive and informative look at cell phone technology with a glossary and lists of material for further research. e (Rev: LMC 8–9/10; SLJ 1/1/11) [621.3845]

13027 Maddison, Simon. *Telecoms: Present Knowledge, Future Trends* (5–9). Series: 21st Century Science. 2003, Smart Apple Media LB $27.10 (978-1-58340-352-5). Numerous diagrams, photographs, and drawings add to this overview of the history of telecommunications and the status of current technology. (Rev: SLJ 1/04) [384]

13028 Streissguth, Thomas. *Communications: Sending the Message* (5–8). Series: Innovators. 1997, Oliver LB $21.95 (978-1-881508-41-0). A compact, easy-to-understand history of communication from earliest times, through Gutenberg, Edison, and Marconi, to the present "information highway." (Rev: SLJ 2/98) [001.51]

13029 Szumski, Bonnie, and Jill Karson. *Are Cell Phones Dangerous?* (7–10). Illus. Series: Controversy. 2012, ReferencePoint LB $27.95 (978-160152232-0). After a history of cell phone technology, this volume looks at potential risks ranging from a decline in male fertility to texting while driving. (Rev: BL 10/15/12) [615.9]

Television, Motion Pictures, Radio, and Recording

13030 Hamilton, Jake. *Special Effects: In Film and Television* (4–8). 1998, DK $17.95 (978-0-7849-2813-4). This is an intriguing glimpse at special effects in film and television, using double-page spreads that each focus on a different aspect of production, such as storyboards, makeup, and stunts. (Rev: BCCB 9/98; BL 8/98; VOYA 10/98) [791.43]

13031 Kinney, Jeff. *The Wimpy Kid Movie Diary: How Greg Heffley Went Hollywood* (4–8). Illus. 2010, Abrams $14.95 (978-081099616-8). Kinney offers a behind-the-scenes glimpse at the making of *Diary of a Wimpy Kid: The Movie* in this engrossing book. Lexile 1000L (Rev: BLO 3/15/10) [791.43]

13032 Spilsbury, Richard. *Cartoons and Animation* (4–7). Illus. Series: Art off the Wall. 2006, Heinemann LB $23.00 (978-1-4034-8287-7). Surveys the history, techniques, and movie applications of cartooning and animation, and includes bold color illustrations of familiar characters and animators at work. (Rev: BL 1/1–15/07; SLJ 5/07) [741.5]

Transportation

General and Miscellaneous

13033 *Go! The Whole World of Transportation* (5–10). Illus. 2006, DK $26.99 (978-0-7566-2224-4). This wide-ranging, visually fascinating journey through the world of transportation touches on everything from buses and ferries to speedboats and fighter jets. (Rev: SLJ 2/07*) [388]

13034 Hamilton, John. *Transportation: A Pictorial History of the Past One Thousand Years* (4–7). Series: The Millennium. 2000, ABDO LB $25.65 (978-1-57765-361-5). A history of 1,000 years of transportation that includes animals, ships, trains, bicycles, motorcycles, cars, airplanes, and spacecraft. (Rev: BL 7/00; HBG 10/00; SLJ 10/00) [388.21]

13035 Herbst, Judith. *The History of Transportation* (5–8). Series: Major Inventions Through History. 2005, Twenty-First Century LB $26.60 (978-0-8225-2496-0). From the wheel to the airplane, technological innovations involving transport have had a profound impact on our lives as shown in this attractive, well-written volume. (Rev: SLJ 2/06) [973]

Airplanes, Aeronautics, and Ballooning

13036 Berliner, Don. *Aviation: Reaching for the Sky* (5–8). Series: Innovators. 1997, Oliver LB $21.95 (978-1-881508-33-5). A thorough history of aviation, beginning with early hot-air balloons and dirigibles and continuing through the Wright Brothers and Sikorsky's helicopter to supersonic jets. (Rev: BL 5/1/97; SLJ 7/97) [629.133]

13037 Carson, Mary Kay. *The Wright Brothers for Kids: How They Invented the Airplane: 21 Activities Exploring the Science and History of Flight* (4–8). Illus. by Laura D'Argo. 2003, Chicago Review paper $14.95 (978-1-55652-477-6). After an account of the achievements of the Wrights and other early airplane enthusiasts, 21 activities allow readers to investigate some of the basic principles and to learn about equipment and means of communication. (Rev: SLJ 6/03) [629.13]

13038 De Angelis, Gina. *The Hindenburg* (6–8). Series: Great Disasters: Reforms and Ramifications. 2000, Chelsea LB $30.00 (978-0-7910-5272-3). A description of the Hindenburg disaster precedes discussion of how this tragedy has influenced safety regulations. (Rev: HBG 3/01; SLJ 1/01) [363.12]

13039 Finkelstein, Norman H. *Three Across: The Great Transatlantic Air Race of 1927* (5–8). Illus. 2008, Boyds Mills $17.95 (978-159078462-4). Finkelstein focuses on the first three fliers to make it across the Atlantic Ocean in this interesting account that conveys the flavor of the Roaring Twenties. (Rev: BL 9/1/08; LMC 11–12/08; SLJ 11/1/08; VOYA 12/08) [629.130]

13040 Friedrich, Belinda. *The Explosion of TWA Flight 800* (8–10). Series: Great Disasters: Reforms and Ramifications. 2001, Chelsea LB $30.00 (978-0-7910-6325-5). An account of this tragedy over Long Island in 1996, detailing the recovery efforts, the investigation, and the many theories about the cause of the disaster. (Rev: HBG 10/02; SLJ 5/02) [363.12]

13041 Gaffney, Timothy R. *Hurricane Hunters* (4–7). Series: Aircraft. 2001, Enslow LB $23.93 (978-0-7660-1569-2). Information on the planes that investigate hurricanes is accompanied by quotations from the pilots and scientists who fly in them. (Rev: HBG 3/02; SLJ 2/02) [551.55]

13042 Gitlin, Martin. *The Hudson Plane Landing* (7–10). Illus. Series: Essential Events. 2012, ABDO LB $23.95 (978-161783309-0). This concise account of pilot Sullenberger's successful landing on the Hudson River in 2009, saving the lives of 150 passengers, includes information on "Sully" himself and on the dangers birds pose to aircraft. (Rev: BL 7/12; SLJ 6/12) [363.12]

13043 Hansen, Ole Steen. *Amazing Flights: The Golden Age* (4–7). Series: The Story of Flight. 2003, Crabtree LB $25.27 (978-0-7787-1202-2); paper $8.95 (978-0-

7787-1218-3). Double-page spreads present text, feature sidebars, color photographs, and paintings on the people and events of flying after World War I — air races, barnstormers, Lindbergh, and more. (Rev: BL 10/15/03) [629.13]

13044 Hansen, Ole Steen. *Commercial Aviation* (4–7). Series: The Story of Flight. 2003, Crabtree $25.27 (978-0-7787-1205-3). The history and development of airlines and other forms of commercial aviation are discussed with coverage of present-day problems. (Rev: BL 10/15/03) [629.13]

13045 Hansen, Ole Steen. *Modern Military Aircraft* (4–7). Series: The Story of Flight. 2003, Crabtree LB $25.27 (978-0-7787-1204-6); paper $8.95 (978-0-7787-1220-6). A highly visual overview of military aircraft since World War II, with a spotter's guide. (Rev: BL 10/15/03) [623.]

13046 Homan, Lynn M., and Thomas Reilly. *Women Who Fly* (5–8). Illus. by Rosalie M. Shepherd. 2004, Pelican $14.95 (978-1-58980-160-8). Women's efforts to establish a foothold in the male-dominated field of aviation are recounted in this book that is suitable for browsers. (Rev: BL 7/04; SLJ 9/04) [629.13]

13047 Maynard, Chris. *Aircraft* (5–8). Series: Need for Speed. 1999, Lerner LB $23.93 (978-0-8225-2485-4); paper $7.95 (978-0-8225-9855-8). Using double-page spreads, this work introduces high-speed aircraft. (Rev: BL 1/1–15/00; HBG 3/00; SLJ 2/00) [629.133]

13048 Millspaugh, Ben. *Aviation and Space Science Projects* (5–8). 1992, TAB paper $9.95 (978-0-8306-2156-9). The principles of flight are explored in 19 projects that vary in difficulty and complexity. (Rev: BL 1/15/92; SLJ 6/92) [629.1]

13049 Mooney, Carla. *Pilotless Planes* (5–7). Illus. Series: A Great Idea. 2010, Norwood LB $25.27 (978-1-59953-381-0). An interesting account of the development and potential uses of "drones" in military and civilian situations. (Rev: BL 11/1/10; SLJ 1/1/11) [623.74]

13050 Oxlade, Chris. *Airplanes: Uncovering Technology* (4–8). Illus. Series: Uncovering. 2006, Firefly $16.95 (978-1-55407-134-0). A well-illustrated survey of developments in air travel, with four overlay pages and a look at future possibilities. (Rev: SLJ 2/07) [629.133]

13051 Santella, Andrew. *Air Force One* (4–7). 2003, Millbrook LB $24.90 (978-0-7613-2617-5). An overview of the aircraft that have transported United States presidents, with an inside look at today's Air Force One. (Rev: BL 2/15/03; HBG 10/03; SLJ 8/03) [387.7]

13052 Sherman, Jill. *The Hindenburg Disaster* (6–8). Series: Essential Events. 2010, ABDO LB $32.79 (978-1-60453-944-8). In a compelling narrative, Sherman describes the development of airships, their roles in peace and war, and theories about the cause of this tragedy. (Rev: BL 5/1/10; LMC 10/10; SLJ 5/10) [363.12]

Automobiles and Trucks

13053 Bearce, Stephanie. *All About Electric and Hybrid Cars and Who's Driving Them* (4–7). Series: Tell Your Parents. 2010, Mitchell Lane LB $29.95 (978-1-58415-763-2). With photographs and graphics, this is an attractive introduction to the mechanics and benefits of hybrid and electric cars. (Rev: BL 10/1/09; LMC 1–2/10)

13054 Edmonston, Phil, and Maureen Sawa. *Car Smarts: Hot Tips for the Car Crazy* (7–10). Illus. by Gordon Sauve. 2003, Tundra paper $15.95 (978-0-88776-646-6). Attractive and lively, this is a large-format compendium of facts and advice about cars — their history, how they work, and their purchase and maintenance. (Rev: BL 4/1/04; SLJ 7/04; VOYA 10/04) [629.222]

13055 *In the Driver's Seat: A Girl's Guide to Her First Car* (8–11). 2009, Zest paper $14.995 (978-09800732-4-9). From choosing your car to learning about maintenance, insurance, and troubleshooting problems and dealing with auto mechanics, this is a useful and eye-catching guide. Lexile 1360L (Rev: BLO 2/1/10; VOYA 6/10) [380]

13056 Italia, Bob. *Great Auto Makers and Their Cars* (6–10). Series: Profiles. 1993, Oliver LB $19.95 (978-1-881508-08-3). This is a history of automobiles with coverage of famous cars and biographies of famous engineers and automakers. (Rev: BL 10/15/93; SLJ 11/93) [629.2]

13057 Juettner, Bonnie. *Hybrid Cars* (4–7). Illus. Series: A Great Idea!: Going Green. 2009, Norwood House LB $18.95 (978-1-59953-193-9). Juettner places the development of hybrid cars in historical context and discusses research into alternative fuels; the photographs will attract browsers. (Rev: BL 4/1/09) [629.22]

13058 McKenna, A. T. *Corvette* (5–7). Series: Ultimate Car. 2000, ABDO LB $24.21 (978-1-57765-127-7). This introduction to this famous sports car includes material on its design, construction, and records it has broken. Similar material appears in companion books *Ferrari, Jaguar, Lamborghini, Mustang,* and *Porsche* (all 2000). (Rev: BL 3/1/01; HBG 10/01) [629]

13059 Mueller, Mike, and Bob Woods. *Corvette* (6–9). 2006, MBI paper $9.95 (978-0-7603-3231-3). A look at the corvette and its history with information on its evolvement over the years, showing up to the 2005 model. Color photographs included throughout. (Rev: BL 9/1/06)

13060 Murphy, John. *The Eisenhower Interstate System* (5–8). Series: Building America: Then and Now. 2009, Chelsea House $35 (978-1-60413-067-6). This book about the Eisenhower Interstate System includes illustrative maps, primary source documents, Web sites, a timeline, and glossary. (Rev: LMC 10/09)

13061 Nakaya, Andrea C., ed. *Cars in America* (7–12). Series: Opposing Viewpoints. 2006, Gale LB $34.95 (978-0-7377-3307-5); paper $23.70 (978-0-7377-3308-2). Opposing points of view are offered on everything from seatbelt laws to SUVs to urban sprawl. (Rev: SLJ 12/06)

13062 Whitman, Sylvia. *Get Up and Go! The History of American Road Travel* (5–8). 1996, Lerner LB $30.35 (978-0-8225-1735-1). From primitive pathways to modern superhighways, this is a history of American roads and the vehicles that traveled them. (Rev: BL 10/15/96; SLJ 10/96; VOYA 2/97) [388.1]

Motorcycles

13063 Smedman, Lisa. *From Boneshakers to Choppers: The Rip-Roaring History of Motorcycles* (5–8). Illus. 2007, Annick $24.95 (978-1-55451-016-0); paper $14.95 (978-1-55451-015-3). Covering all types of motorcycles, as well as all types of riders, this well-illustrated book will be popular with fans of transportation, extreme sports, history, and American popular culture. (Rev: BL 11/15/07) [629.227]

Railroads

13064 Murphy, Jim. *Across America on an Emigrant Train* (6–12). 1993, Clarion $18.00 (978-0-395-63390-8). A cross-country train trip by Robert Louis Stevenson in 1879 is the backdrop for information on the history of railroads. (Rev: BCCB 1/94; BL 12/1/93*; SLJ 12/93*) [625.2]

13065 Sandler, Martin W. *The Secret Subway: The Fascinating Tale of an Amazing Feat of Engineering* (6–12). Illus. 2009, National Geographic $17.95 (978-142630462-0); LB $26.90 (978-142630463-7). Sandler tells the compelling story of engineer Alfred Beach who in the late 1860s hoped to build an air-powered subway system in New York City without the knowledge of Tammany Hall boss William Tweed. (Rev: BL 6/1–15/09; LMC 8–9/09) [388.4]

13066 Weitzman, David. *A Subway for New York* (4–7). 2005, Farrar $17.00 (978-0-374-37284-2). The story behind the early-20th-century construction of New York City's first subway is presented in picture-book format. (Rev: BL 12/1/05; SLJ 2/06) [625.4]

13067 Weitzman, David. *Superpower: The Making of a Steam Locomotive* (6–9). 1987, Godine $35.00 (978-0-87923-671-7). A step-by-step guide to the parts of a locomotive and how they are assembled. (Rev: SLJ 1/88) [625.2]

13068 Wormser, Richard. *The Iron Horse: How Railroads Changed America* (6–9). 1993, Walker LB $19.85 (978-0-8027-8222-9). The economic and social impact of the railroad between 1830 and 1900, from the robber barons to the Gold Rush and massive influx of immigrants. (Rev: BL 12/15/93; SLJ 1/94; VOYA 4/94) [385]

13069 Yancey, Diane. *Camels for Uncle Sam* (4–7). 1995, Hendrick-Long $16.95 (978-0-937460-91-7). The story of the experiment that involved importing camels to the Southwest in the 1850s to help in railroad construction. (Rev: BL 9/15/95) [357]

13070 Zimmermann, Karl. *All Aboard! Passenger Trains Around the World* (4–7). Illus. 2006, Boyds Mills $19.95 (978-1-59078-325-2). Photo-filled double-page spreads show the excitement of travel by train and interweave history, geography, commerce, and technology. (Rev: BL 2/15/06; SLJ 6/06) [385]

13071 Zimmermann, Karl. *Steam Locomotives: Whistling, Chugging, Smoking Iron Horses of the Past* (4–8). 2004, Boyds Mills $19.95 (978-1-59078-165-4). Informative and photo-filled, this is an appealing history of steam engines. (Rev: BL 2/1/04; SLJ 7/04) [625.26]

Ships and Boats

13072 Bornhoft, Simon. *High Speed Boats* (5–8). Series: Need for Speed. 1999, Lerner LB $23.93 (978-0-8225-2488-5). Using a jazzy, attention-getting format with action photographs, sidebars with statistics and interesting facts, and different type sizes, this book covers present and future speedboats. (Rev: BL 1/1–15/00; HBG 3/00) [629.222]

13073 Burgan, Michael. *Titanic* (3–8). Illus. by Eldon Doty. Series: Truth and Rumors. 2010, Capstone LB $25.32 (978-1-4296-3951-4). Burgan clarifies certain aspects of the construction and final voyage of the *Titanic*, answering questions like "Was the *Titanic* disaster predicted before 1912?" and "Did an officer kill a passenger?," and finishes with a chapter on how to tell the difference between fact and fiction. (Rev: LMC 11–12/10) [910.45]

13074 Butler, Daniel Allen. *Unsinkable: The Full Story of the RMS Titanic* (8–12). 1998, Stackpole $21.95 (978-0-8117-1814-1). First-person accounts add to the tension of this narrative. (Rev: BL 5/1/98) [910.4]

13075 Cerullo, Mary M. *Shipwrecks: Exploring Sunken Cities Beneath the Sea* (5–8). 2009, Dutton $18.99 (978-0-525-47968-0). Cerullo looks at two well-preserved shipwrecks, describing the sinkings themselves, the state of the wrecks today which are home to a variety of marine life, and the technology used to explore these environments. (Rev: BL 12/1/09; SLJ 1/10; VOYA 12/09) [930.1028]

13076 Denenberg, Barry. *Titanic Sinks!* (5–8). Illus. 2011, Viking $19.99 (978-0-670-01243-5). Blending fact and fiction, this oversize volume infuses real information about the sinking with imagined sensationalistic newspaper articles, written by a victim of the disaster, that add energy and drama. (Rev: BL 10/15/11*; HB 3–4/12; LMC 3–4/12; SLJ 11/1/11*) [910.9163]

13077 Hopkinson, Deborah. *Titanic: Voices from the Disaster* (4–8). Illus. 2012, Scholastic $17.99 (978-054511674-9). With diagrams, maps, charts, and period photographs, this account also draws on survivor letters as well as newspaper and other reports. Sibert Honor 2013; ALA Notable Books 2013. ☊ (Rev: BL 12/1/11; HB 3–4/12; LMC 5–6/12; SLJ 2/12*; VOYA 4/12) [910.9163]

13078 Macaulay, David. *Ship* (5–8). 1993, Houghton Mifflin $19.95 (978-0-395-52439-8). A fictional caravel is featured in this exploration of historical seagoing vessels and the work of underwater archaeologists. (Rev: BCCB 11/93; BL 10/15/93*; SLJ 11/93) [387.2]

13079 McPherson, Stephanie Sammartino. *Iceberg, Right Ahead! The Tragedy of the Titanic* (6–10). Illus. 2011, Lerner/Twenty-First Century LB $33.26 (978-076136756-7). This is a compelling account of the disaster, giving information on the ship itself, newspaper and primary source accounts, and details of regulations and explorations that followed. ALA Notable Books 2013. ℮ (Rev: BL 12/15/11; HB 3–4/12; LMC 3–4/12; SLJ 11/1/11*; VOYA 12/11) [910.9163]

13080 Mayell, Hillary. *Shipwrecks* (5–8). Series: Man-Made Disasters. 2004, Gale LB $29.95 (978-1-59018-058-7). Period photographs enhance the impact of stories of shipwrecks of all kinds — from fishing boats to luxury liners — during the 19th and 20th centuries. (Rev: SLJ 7/04) [910.4]

13081 Whiting, Jim. *The Sinking of the Titanic* (6–9). 2006, Mitchell Lane LB $19.95 (978-1-58415-472-3). A brief, chronological account covering the building of the *Titanic* and its sister ships, the maiden voyage, the sinking, and the discovery of the wreck, with a review of current thinking on the cause of the accident. (Rev: SLJ 11/06)

13082 Wilkinson, Philip. *Ships* (4–7). 2000, Kingfisher $16.95 (978-0-7534-5280-6). Straightforward text and handsome illustrations cover maritime history from the earliest sailing ships and discuss piracy, the slave trade, and superstitions about the sea. (Rev: BL 2/1/01; HBG 10/01; SLJ 1/01) [623.8]

13083 Zimmermann, Karl. *Steamboats: The Story of Lakers, Ferries, and Majestic Paddle-Wheelers* (4–7). Illus. 2007, Boyds Mills $19.95 (978-1-59078-434-1). Carefully researched by an aficionado, this detailed examination of the history, purpose, and engineering of steamboats contains biographical information and excellent archival and modern illustrations. (Rev: BL 1/1–15/07; SLJ 4/07) [623.82]

Weapons, Submarines, and the Armed Forces

13084 Boos, Ben. *Swords: An Artist's Devotion* (4–7). Illus. by author. 2008, Candlewick $24.99 (978-076363148-2). In this large-format book, masterfully crafted swords used by everyone from peasants to sultans and in many countries over many centuries are illustrated and described in detail. (Rev: BLO 11/1/08; LMC 3–4/09; SLJ 10/1/08) [623.4]

13085 Byers, Ann. *America's Star Wars Program* (5–7). Series: The Library of Weapons of Mass Destruction. 2005, Rosen LB $27.95 (978-1-4042-0287-0). Photographs and text document the development of 20th-century missiles and America's controversial "Star Wars" strategy. (Rev: SLJ 11/05) [623]

13086 Egan, Tracie. *Weapons of Mass Destruction and North Korea* (5–7). Series: The Library of Weapons of Mass Destruction. 2005, Rosen LB $27.95 (978-1-4042-0296-2). Explores what the West knows about North Korea's efforts to build stockpiles of biological, chemical, and — potentially — nuclear weapons. (Rev: SLJ 11/05) [623]

13087 Ermey, R. Lee. *Mail Call* (8–12). 2005, Hyperion paper $17.95 (978-1-4013-0779-0). History Channel personality offers facts and figures about military weaponry, modern warfare, and other military trivia. (Rev: BL 12/15/04) [355.009]

13088 Friedman, Lauri S. *Nuclear Weapons and Security* (8–12). Series: Compact Research. 2007, Reference Point LB $24.95 (978-1-60152-021-0). Is the United States likely to be attacked with nuclear weapons? Could the world survive a nuclear war? These and other questions are discussed from various points of view, with facts, profiles, and illustrations. (Rev: SLJ 1/08)

13089 Gifford, Clive. *The Arms Trade* (6–9). Series: World Issues. 2004, Chrysalis LB $28.50 (978-1-59389-154-1). This thought-provoking title uses a question-and-answer format to examine the dimensions and ethics of the international arms trade. (Rev: BL 1/1–15/05)

13090 Gonen, Rivka. *Charge! Weapons and Warfare in Ancient Times* (5–8). 1993, Lerner LB $23.93 (978-0-8225-3201-9). A look at the development of weapons from sticks and stones to battering rams. (Rev: BCCB 12/93; BL 2/1/94; SLJ 2/94) [355.8]

13091 Graham, Ian. *Military Technology* (7–10). Illus. Series: New Technology. 2008, Smart Apple Media LB $22.95 (978-159920165-8). Unmanned spy planes, body armor, lasers, robots, and many other kinds of high-tech military equipment are examined in this accessible volume that includes many illustrations and thought-provoking ("What's Next?") sidebars. (Rev: BL 10/15/08; LMC 5–6/09) [355]

13092 Gurstelle, William. *The Art of the Catapult: Build Greek Ballistae, Roman Onagers, English Trebuchets, and More Ancient Artillery* (5–12). 2004, Chicago Review paper $14.95 (978-1-55652-526-1). Information on history, physics, and military tactics, plus step-by-step instructions for the construction of 10 working catapults. (Rev: SLJ 11/04) [623.4]

13093 Hamilton, John. *Armed Forces* (4–7). Series: War on Terrorism. 2002, ABDO LB $25.65 (978-1-57765-674-6). An introduction to the U.S. military and the roles these services play in protecting the country, with color photographs, a glossary, and list of Web sites. (Rev: BL 8/02; HBG 10/02) [355]

13094 Hamilton, John. *Weapons of War* (4–7). Series: War on Terrorism. 2002, ABDO LB $25.65 (978-1-57765-673-9). This account describes the weapons currently available to U.S. military personnel, including fighter planes, bombers, helicopters, bombs, missiles, and ships. (Rev: BL 5/1/02; HBG 10/02) [623.4]

13095 Hamilton, John. *Weapons of War: A Pictorial History of the Past One Thousand Years* (4–7). Series: The Millennium. 2000, ABDO LB $25.65 (978-1-57765-362-2). In a short space, this book traces 1,000 years of weapons including small weaponry, ships, firearms, military airplanes, tanks, missiles, and bombs. (Rev: BL 7/00; HBG 10/00; SLJ 10/00) [623.4]

13096 Hasan, Tahara. *Anthrax Attacks Around the World* (4–8). Series: Terrorist Attacks. 2003, Rosen LB $27.95 (978-0-8239-3859-9). Examines the use of anthrax as a terrorist weapon and includes accounts of its use in Japan, the Soviet Union, and the United States. (Rev: SLJ 2/04) [303.6]

13097 Herbst, Judith. *The History of Weapons* (5–8). Series: Major Inventions Through History. 2005, Twenty-First Century LB $26.60 (978-0-8225-3805-9). An attractive look at the evolution of weapons from rocks and sticks to today's weapons of mass destruction. (Rev: SLJ 1/06) [623.4]

13098 Landau, Elaine. *The New Nuclear Reality* (6–12). 2000, Twenty-First Century LB $22.90 (978-0-7613-1555-1). This account chronicles the post-war growth of countries that have nuclear arms including Russia, North Korea, Pakistan, and India. (Rev: BL 7/00; HBG 9/00; SLJ 9/00) [327.1]

13099 Lefkowitz, Arthur. *Bushnell's Submarine: The Best Kept Secret of the American Revolution* (7–10). 2006, Scholastic $16.99 (978-0-439-74352-5). The little-known story of the *Turtle*, America's first submarine, which was launched during the closing days of the American Revolution. (Rev: BL 2/15/06; SLJ 4/06) [973.3]

13100 Marcovitz, Hal. *Biological and Chemical Warfare* (7–10). Series: Essential Issues. 2010, ABDO LB $32.79 (978-1-60453-951-6). The characteristics of biological, chemical, and radiological substances are explained here and there is discussion of their use as weapons and measures that can be taken to guard against this. (Rev: BL 10/1/10; LMC 10/10; SLJ 4/1/10) [358.3]

13101 Regan, Paul, ed. *Weapon: A Visual History of Arms and Armor* (8–12). 2006, DK $40.00 (978-0-7566-2210-7). In the usual DK style, the history of handheld weapons is displayed with silhouetted images and captions, covering everything from the most primitive — such as a rock — to the automatic guns of today. (Rev: BL 11/1/06) [623.4]

13102 Richie, Jason. *Weapons: Designing the Tools of War* (5–10). 2000, Oliver LB $21.95 (978-1-881508-60-1). Using separate chapters for different categories of weapons — for example, submarines, battleships, and tanks — this is a history of the development of weaponry from 300 B.C. to today. (Rev: BL 5/1/00; HBG 10/00; SLJ 8/00) [623]

13103 Streissguth, Thomas. *Nuclear Weapons: More Countries, More Threats* (6–12). Series: Issues in Focus. 2000, Enslow LB $26.60 (978-0-7660-1248-6). An overview of nuclear weapons, who controls the technology to produce them, and the efforts to control this threat to human survival. (Rev: BL 9/15/00; HBG 3/01) [355.02]

13104 Sullivan, Edward T. *The Ultimate Weapon: The Race to Develop the Atomic Bomb* (6–9). 2007, Holiday $24.95 (978-0-8234-1855-8). In addition to an overall account of the creation of the bomb, this book takes a behind-the-scenes look at activities at the three sites (Los Alamos; Oak Ridge, Tennessee; and Hanford, Washington) where the Manhattan Project came to fruition. (Rev: BCCB 9/07; BL 7/07; SLJ 8/07) [355.8]

13105 Torr, James D., ed. *Weapons of Mass Destruction* (7–10). Series: Opposing Viewpoints. 2004, Gale LB $36.20 (978-0-7377-2250-5); paper $24.95 (978-0-7377-2251-2). Terrorist attacks using nuclear or biological weapons, the threat from "rogue" nations, U.S. policies regarding its own weapons of mass destruction, and national defense are all discussed in essays introduced by focus questions. (Rev: SLJ 4/05) [355.02]

13106 Walker, Sally M. *Secrets of a Civil War Submarine: Solving the Mysteries of the H. L. Hunley* (7–10). 2005, Carolrhoda $18.95 (978-1-57505-830-6). Walker chronicles the story of the Confederate submarine *H. L. Hunley* from its design and construction through its successful attack on the *USS Housatonic* in 1864 to its discovery on the bottom of Charleston Harbor in 1995. Sibert Medal, 2006. (Rev: BL 4/15/05*; SLJ 5/05) [973.7]

13107 Wolny, Philip. *Weapons Satellites* (5–9). Series: The Library of Satellites. 2003, Rosen LB $26.50 (978-0-8239-3855-1). This account explores the growing technology of weapon satellites that are capable of knocking out enemies' satellites, and launching attacks from outer space. (Rev: BL 11/15/03; SLJ 1/04) [629.46]

Recreation and Sports

Crafts, Hobbies, and Pastimes

13108 Bell, Alison. *Let's Party!* (6–10). Illus. by Kun-Sung Chung. Series: What's Your Style? 2005, Lobster paper $14.95 (978-1-894222-99-0). Eight theme parties are suggested, complete with invitations, decorations, food, music, and so forth; particularly useful may be the tips on keeping parents at bay and dealing with crashers. (Rev: SLJ 3/06) [793.2]

13109 Birdseye, Tom. *A Kids' Guide to Building Forts* (5–8). Illus. by Bill Klein. 1993, Harbinger paper $11.95 (978-0-943173-69-6). A guide to the building of 19 kinds of forts, from the very simple to the more complex, some of which can be turned into clubhouses. (Rev: SLJ 9/93) [745.5]

13110 Boonyadhistarn, Thiranut. *Fingernail Art: Dazzling Fingers and Terrific Toes* (4–8). Illus. Series: Snap Books: Crafts. 2006, Capstone LB $25.26 (978-0-7368-6474-9). This colorful, well-thought-out guide offers interesting tips on decorating nails. (Rev: SLJ 2/07) [646.7]

13111 Boonyadhistarn, Thiranut. *Stamping Art: Imprint Your Designs* (4–8). Illus. Series: Snap Books: Crafts. 2006, Capstone LB $25.26 (978-0-7368-6477-0). Simple, step-by-step instructions guide readers through a variety of stamping projects that use accessible materials. (Rev: SLJ 2/07) [761]

13112 Brownrigg, Sheri. *Hearts and Crafts* (4–8). 1995, Tricycle paper $9.95 (978-1-883672-28-7). Clear instructions show how to complete a variety of Valentine's Day projects, including making necklaces and candles. (Rev: BL 3/1/96; SLJ 3/96) [745.5]

13113 Dickins, Rosie. *Art Treasury: Pictures, Paintings, and Projects* (4–7). 2007, Usborne LB $19.99 (978-0-7945-1452-5). Each of the art projects in this exciting

collection is inspired by an existing work of art. (Rev: BL 4/1/07) [709]

13114 Dickinson, Gill, and Cheryl Owen. *Creative Crafts for Kids: Over 100 Projects for Two to Ten Year Olds* (4–10). 2007, Sterling LB $24.95 (978-0-600-61590-3). Paper crafts, jewelry, holiday decorations, food crafts, and even good-smelling crafts for children and their teachers or adult friends are presented in a pleasant format. Materials lists and step-by-step instructions make this user-friendly. (Rev: SLJ 5/07)

13115 Glenn, Joshua, and Elizabeth Foy Larsen. *Unbored: The Essential Field Guide to Serious Fun* (5–8). Illus. 2012, Bloomsbury $25.00 (978-1-60819-641-8). Bursting with creative ideas, this book encourages kids to make fun happen inside, outside, and in the community. (Rev: SLJ 9/12) [790]

13116 Griffith, Saul, and Nick Dragotta. *Howtoons: The Possibilities Are Endless* (5–8). Illus. by Nick Dragotta. 2007, HarperCollins paper $15.99 (978-0-06-076158-5). A comic book and a project book in one, this will appeal to readers who are reluctant to pick up ordinary craft books; the "crafts" go beyond origami and include a marshmallow shooter, a tree swing, a rocket, and a flute. (Rev: BL 12/15/07; SLJ 5/08) [741.5]

13117 Hendry, Linda. *Making Gift Boxes* (4–8). Illus. by author. Series: Kids Can! 1999, Kids Can paper $5.95 (978-1-55074-503-0). The 14 boxes included in this fine craft book with clear instructions include a photo box, a garden box to grow seeds, a box for storing CDs, and a treasure box with false compartments. (Rev: SLJ 12/99) [745]

13118 Hennessy, Alena. *Alter This!* (8–12). 2007, Sterling $14.95 (978-1-57990-948-2). Books can be craft material! This unusual book encourages teens to use books to create art or practical objects — hardbacks can be purses or clocks, for example, or words can be cut out to create poetry or stories. (Rev: BL 12/15/07; SLJ 9/07) [745.593]

13119 Henry, Sally, and Trevor Cook. *Eco-Crafts* (4–8). Photos by authors. Series: Make Your Own Art. 2011, Rosen LB $25.25 (978-1-4488-1582-1); paper $11.75 (978-1-4488-1611-8). Craft projects here — glow jars, a bird feeder, cat bookends, and so forth — feature natural or reused materials or support wildlife in some way. Also recommended in this series: *Making Mosaics* (2011). (Rev: SLJ 7/11) [745.5]

13120 Jennings, Lynette. *Have Fun with Your Room: 28 Cool Projects for Teens* (6–10). 2001, Simon & Schuster paper $12.00 (978-0-689-82585-9). The author offers a number of affordable ways to decorate bedrooms, with suggestions for walls, windows, headboards, bulletin boards, and so forth. (Rev: SLJ 11/01)

13121 Jovinelly, Joann, and Jason Netelkos. *The Crafts and Culture of a Medieval Monastery* (4–8). Illus. Series: Crafts of the Middle Ages. 2006, Rosen LB $29.25 (978-1-4042-0759-2). Crafts and history are interwoven in this interesting that looks at the history of monasteries, life within them, and the work that took place in scriptoria, gardens, and hospitals; crafts include prayer beads and a plague mask. Also use *The Crafts and Culture of a Medieval Town* (2006). (Rev: SLJ 4/07) [271.0094]

13122 Latno, Mark. *The Paper Boomerang Book: Build Them, Throw Them, and Get Them to Return Every Time* (5–8). 2010, Chicago Review paper $12.95 (978-1-56976-282-0). Everything you need to know about boomerangs and their construction and use, with a surprising depth of kid-friendly physics. **e** (Rev: SLJ 7/10; VOYA 12/10) [629.133]

13123 McGraw, Sheila. *Gifts Kids Can Make* (4–8). Photos by Sheila McGraw and Joy von Tiedemann. 1994, Firefly paper $9.95 (978-1-895565-35-5). A craft book that gives directions for making 14 simple gifts, such as a cotton sock doll and a hobby horse, using easily obtainable materials. (Rev: SLJ 12/94) [745]

13124 Martin, Laura C. *Nature's Art Box: From T-Shirts to Twig Baskets, 65 Cool Projects for Crafty Kids to Make with Natural Materials You Can Find Anywhere* (4–8). Illus. by David Cain. 2003, Storey paper $16.95 (978-1-58017-490-9). These projects use natural materials such as twigs, moss, gourds, stones, shells, flowers, and leaves to make articles including wreaths, necklaces, and a chess set. (Rev: HBG 10/03; SLJ 8/03*) [745.5]

13125 Merrill, Yvonne Y. *Hands-On Latin America: Art Activities for All Ages* (4–8). Series: Hands-On. 1998, Kits paper $20.00 (978-0-9643177-1-0). A collection of 30 interesting, affordable arts and crafts projects inspired by the ancient cultures of Latin America. (Rev: BL 9/1/98; SLJ 8/98) [980.07]

13126 Monaghan, Kathleen, and Hermon Joyner. *You Can Weave! Projects for Young Weavers* (4–7). 2001, Sterling $19.95 (978-0-87192-493-3). Step-by-step instructions and photographs guide young crafters through weaving projects of varying complexity. (Rev: BL 11/1/01) [746.41]

13127 Mooney, Carla. *Amazing Africa Projects You Can Build Yourself* (4–7). Illus. by Megan Stearns. Series: Build It Yourself. 2010, Nomad paper $15.95 (978-1-9346704-1-5). Full of information about all aspects of Africa, this volume includes 25 projects — such as a mask, a basket, and rock paintings — made with everyday materials. **e** Lexile IG930L (Rev: BL 5/15/10; SLJ 10/1/10) [745.5096]

13128 Murillo, Kathy Cano. *The Crafty Diva's Lifestyle Makeover: Awesome Ideas to Spice Up Your Life!* (5–12). Illus. by Carrie Wheeler. 2005, Watson-Guptill paper $12.95 (978-0-8230-1008-0). The Crafty Diva is back with this collection of easy-to-follow instructions for 50 projects that cover everything from room makeovers to fashion accessories. (Rev: SLJ 9/05)

13129 Powell, Michelle, and Judy Balchin. *Crafty Activities: Over 50 Fun and Easy Things to Make* (4–7). Illus. 2007, Search paper $19.95 (978-1-84448-250-4). Fifty crafts involving mosaics, printing, lettering, papier-mâché, card-making, and origami, attractively and clearly presented for the young crafter. (Rev: BL 12/15/07; SLJ 1/08) [745]

13130 Ralston, Birgitta. *Snow Play: How to Make Forts and Slides and Winter Campfires, Plus the Coolest Loch Ness Monster and 23 Other Brrrilliant Projects in the Snow* (4–12). Photos by Vegard Fimland. 2010, Artisan $14.95 (978-1-57965-405-4). Ralston presents a variety of compelling snow projects, ranging from small ornaments to an LED-illuminated birthday cake to a snow cave. (Rev: SLJ 4/11) [796.9]

13131 Rhodes, Vicki. *Pumpkin Decorating* (4–8). 1997, Sterling $10.95 (978-0-8069-9574-8). Clear directions and full-color photographs demonstrate more than 80 designs for pumpkins. (Rev: SLJ 12/97) [745.5]

13132 Schwarz, Renee. *Funky Junk* (4–7). Series: Kids Can Do It! 2002, Kids Can $12.95 (978-1-55337-387-2); paper $5.95 (978-1-55337-388-9). Using easily found materials, this craft book supplies details on how to make unusual conversation pieces. (Rev: BL 3/15/03; HBG 10/03; SLJ 4/03) [745.5]

13133 Shannon, George W., and Pat Torlen. *The Stained Glass Home: Projects and Patterns* (8–12). 2007, Sterling $24.95 (978-1-895569-59-9). Two talented stained glass artists provide 23 projects, each one complete with patterns, directions, materials lists, and photographs, suitable for beginners as well as experienced crafters. (Rev: BL 12/15/06) [748.5]

13134 Simons, Robin. *Recyclopedia: Games, Science Equipment and Crafts from Recycled Materials* (5–8).

Illus. by author. 1976, Houghton Mifflin paper $13.95 (978-0-395-59641-8). Clear directions complemented by good illustrations characterize this book of interesting projects using waste materials.

13135 Taylor, Maureen. *Through the Eyes of Your Ancestors: A Step-by-Step Guide to Uncovering Your Family's History* (5–9). 1999, Houghton Mifflin paper $8.95 (978-0-395-86982-6). Budding researchers learn how to investigate family history, from conducting interviews to visiting genealogical libraries. (Rev: BCCB 5/99; BL 3/1/99; HB 5–6/99; HBG 10/99; SLJ 5/99) [929.1]

13136 Taylor, Terry. *Altered Art: Techniques for Creating Altered Books, Boxes, Cards and More* (8–12). 2004, Lark $19.95 (978-1-57990-550-7). Terry Taylor provides a fascinating introduction into the world of altered art. (Rev: BL 12/15/04; SLJ 4/05)

13137 Temko, Florence. *Traditional Crafts from China* (5–7). Series: Culture Crafts. 2001, Lerner LB $23.93 (978-0-8225-2939-2). After a few words about crafts in general, this volume carefully outlines a number of projects relating to Chinese culture, including instructions for picture scrolls and tanagrams. (Rev: BL 2/15/01; HBG 10/01; SLJ 4/01) [745]

13138 Temko, Florence. *Traditional Crafts from the Caribbean* (5–7). Series: Culture Crafts. 2001, Lerner LB $23.93 (978-0-8225-2937-8). Step-by-step instructions with clear diagrams are given for a number of craft projects relating to Caribbean culture including yarn dolls, Puerto Rican masks, and metal cutouts. (Rev: BL 2/15/01; HBG 10/01; SLJ 4/01) [745]

13139 Trusty, Brad, and Cindy Trusty. *The Kids' Guide to Balloon Twisting* (4–8). Illus. Series: Kids' Guides. 2012, Capstone LB $26.65 (978-142965444-9). A variety of twisted-balloon projects are presented with easy-to-follow directions. (Rev: BL 9/1/11) [745.594]

13140 Wagner, Lisa. *Cool Melt and Pour Soap* (4–7). Photos by Kelly Doudna. Series: Cool Crafts. 2005, ABDO LB $22.78 (978-1-59197-741-4). Coloring, fragrance, and packaging are all covered in this guide to projects using soap. (Rev: SLJ 7/05)

13141 Weaver, Janice, and Frieda Wishinsky. *It's Your Room: A Decorating Guide for Real Kids* (6–10). Illus. by Claudia Dávila. 2006, Tundra paper $14.95 (978-0-88776-711-1). A step-by-step guide to room decoration, with tips on practical things like creating a budget and storage organization. (Rev: SLJ 6/06)

13142 White, Linda. *Haunting on a Halloween* (5–7). Illus. by Fran Lee. 2002, Gibbs Smith paper $9.95 (978-1-58685-112-5). Everything young party planners need to host a Halloween get-together, with instructions for crafts, food, decorations, and costumes. (Rev: BL 9/15/02) [745.594]

13143 Winters, Eleanor. *1-2-3 Calligraphy* (7–10). 2006, Sterling $14.95 (978-1-4027-1839-7). A com-

panion to the author's *Calligraphy for Kids* (2004), this instructional book helps beginners gather the correct tools, learn different styles of calligraphy, and choose projects to practice their art. (Rev: BL 12/15/06; SLJ 1/07) [745.6]

American Historical Crafts

13144 Anderson, Maxine. *Great Civil War Projects You Can Build Yourself* (7–10). 2005, Nomad paper $16.95 (978-0-9749344-1-9). Craft projects explore various aspects of life on the Civil War battlefield and home front — making cornbread, a pinhole camera, a rag doll, and so forth. (Rev: BL 11/1/05; SLJ 11/05) [745.5]

13145 Beard, D. C. *The American Boys' Handy Book: What to Do and How to Do It* (5–7). 1983, Godine paper $12.95 (978-0-87923-449-2). A facsimile edition of a manual first published in 1882. [790.194]

13146 Merrill, Yvonne Y. *Hands-On Rocky Mountains: Art Activities About Anasazi, American Indians, Settlers, Trappers, and Cowboys* (4–8). 1996, Kits paper $16.95 (978-0-9643177-2-7). Historical groups from the Rocky Mountain region — early people, American Indians, trappers, settlers, and cowboys — are introduced and, for each, a series of craft projects is outlined. (Rev: BL 1/1–15/97; SLJ 4/97) [745.5]

Clay Modeling and Ceramics

13147 Belcher, Judy. *Polymer Clay Creative Traditions: Techniques and Projects Inspired by the Fine and Decorative Arts* (8–12). 2006, Watson-Guptill paper $21.95 (978-0-8230-4065-0). Step-by-step instructions for more than 30 items that can be crafted from polymer clay. (Rev: BL 12/15/05) [745.57]

13148 Scheunemann, Pam. *Cool Clay Projects* (4–7). Photos by Anders Hanson. Series: Cool Crafts. 2005, ABDO LB $22.78 (978-1-59197-740-7). Clear, step-by-step instructions for a number of clay projects are accompanied by full-color photos and tips about safety. (Rev: SLJ 7/05) [731.4]

Cooking

13149 Amari, Suad. *Cooking the Lebanese Way. Rev. ed.* (5–10). Series: Easy Menu Ethnic Cookbooks. 2003, Lerner LB $25.26 (978-0-8225-4116-5). Revised to include low-fat and vegetarian foods, this introduction to Lebanese cooking contains about 40 recipes, clearly explained and well-illustrated. (Rev: BL 9/15/02; HBG 3/03) [641.5]

13150 Behnke, Alison, and Ehramjian Vartkes. *Cooking the Middle Eastern Way* (7–10). Series: Easy Ethnic Menu Cookbooks. 2005, Lerner LB $25.26 (978-0-8225-1238-7). An introduction to the basics of Middle East cooking plus a number of authentic recipes from the region. (Rev: BL 5/15/05) [641.5956]

13151 Bisignano, Alphonse. *Cooking the Italian Way. Rev. ed.* (5–10). Series: Easy Menu Ethnic Cookbooks. 2001, Lerner $25.26 (978-0-8225-4113-4); paper $7.95 (978-0-8225-4161-5). A revised edition that now includes vegetarian and low-fat recipes as well as an expanded introductory section on the country, the people, and the culture. (Rev: HBG 3/02; SLJ 9/01) [641]

13152 Blaxland, Wendy. *Middle Eastern Food* (5–8). Illus. Series: I Can Cook! 2011, Black Rabbit LB $28.50 (978-159920672-1). With recipes that will need adult supervision, this book places Middle Eastern food and ingredients in historical and cultural perspective. (Rev: BL 1/1/12; SLJ 12/1/11) [641.5956]

13153 Carle, Megan, and Jill Carle. *Teens Cook: How to Cook What You Want to Eat* (7–12). 2004, Ten Speed paper $19.95 (978-1-58008-584-7). A witty and practical cookbook that introduces varied recipes used by teenage siblings Megan and Jill Carle. (Rev: SLJ 10/04; VOYA 12/04) [641]

13154 Chung, Okwha, and Judy Monroe. *Cooking the Korean Way. Rev. ed.* (5–10). Series: Easy Menu Ethnic Cookbooks. 2003, Lerner LB $25.26 (978-0-8225-4115-8). Tempting recipes and a brief look at where they come from. (Rev: BL 8/88; HBG 3/03; SLJ 9/88) [641.59519]

13155 Cornell, Kari. *Holiday Cooking Around the World. Rev. ed.* (5–10). Series: Easy Menu Ethnic Cookbooks. 2002, Lerner LB $25.26 (978-0-8225-4128-8); paper $7.95 (978-0-8225-4159-2). Beginning cooks will appreciate the clear instructions and varied options in this appealing book that includes cultural and social information. (Rev: BL 1/1–15/02; HBG 10/02; SLJ 5/02) [641.5]

13156 Coronado, Rosa. *Cooking the Mexican Way. Rev. ed.* (5–10). Series: Easy Menu Ethnic Cookbooks. 2002, Lerner LB $25.26 (978-0-8225-4117-2). Recipes organized by type of meal are preceded by a section that covers the geography, culture, and festivals and by information on equipment, ingredients, and eating customs. Other titles in this series include *Cooking the East African Way* and *Cooking the Spanish Way* (both 2001). (Rev: HBG 3/02; SLJ 2/02) [641]

13157 D'Amico, Joan, and Karen Eich Drummond. *The Science Chef Travels Around the World: Fun Food Experiments and Recipes for Kids* (4–8). 1996, Wiley paper $12.95 (978-0-471-11779-7). An entertaining combination of simple science experiments and inter-national cooking, with recipes from 14 countries and activities that demonstrate scientific principles of various cooking and baking processes. (Rev: BL 2/1/96; SLJ 3/96) [641.5]

13158 Dunnington, Rose. *Bake It Up! Desserts, Breads, Entire Meals and More* (6–12). Photos by Steven Mann. 2007, Sterling $9.95 (978-1-57990-778-5). Mouthwatering recipes are presented in an appealing and straightforward manner. Also use *Super Sandwiches: Wrap 'em, Stack 'em, Stuff 'em* (2007). (Rev: SLJ 2/07)

13159 Dunnington, Rose. *Big Snacks, Little Meals: After School, Dinnertime, Anytime* (6–9). 2006, Sterling $9.95 (978-1-57990-780-8). This spiral-bound cookbook is easy for teens to use and contains appealing recipes along with helpful photos to guide novice cooks. (Rev: BL 7/06; SLJ 8/06) [641.5]

13160 Dunnington, Rose. *The Greatest Cookies Ever: Dozens of Delicious, Chewy, Chunky, Fun and Foolproof Recipes* (4–8). Photos by Stewart O'Shields. 2005, Sterling $9.95 (978-1-57990-627-6). More than 70 recipes are included in this spiral-bound guide to cookie making, with useful information about measuring, substitutions, types of mixers, and safety. (Rev: BL 1/1–15/06; SLJ 2/06) [641.8]

13161 Gillies, Judi, and Jennifer Glossop. *The Jumbo Vegetarian Cookbook* (4–8). 2002, Kids Can paper $14.95 (978-1-55074-977-9). An introduction to the vegetarian lifestyle, including nutrition and recipes. (Rev: BCCB 7–8/02; BL 3/1/02; SLJ 7/02) [641.5]

13162 Gillies, Judi, and Jennifer Glossop. *The Kids Can Press Jumbo Cookbook* (5–8). 2000, Kids Can paper $14.95 (978-1-55074-621-1). After a few cooking tips, this book provides recipes that range from the simple (scrambled eggs) to the difficult (crepes and carrot cake). (Rev: BL 5/1/00; SLJ 6/00) [641.8]

13163 Gioffre, Rosalba. *The Young Chef's French Cookbook* (4–7). Series: I'm the Chef! 2001, Crabtree LB $25.27 (978-0-7787-0282-5); paper $8.95 (978-0-7787-0296-2). This oversize book uses double-page spreads to present 15 appetizing French recipes along with good background material, clear directions, and excellent illustrations. (Rev: BL 10/15/01) [641]

13164 Greenwald, Michelle. *The Magical Melting Pot: The All-Family Cookbook That Celebrates America's Diversity* (7–12). 2003, Cherry $29.95 (978-0-9717565-0-2). Chefs from ethnic restaurants around the country contribute favorite recipes and cultural explanations. (Rev: SLJ 11/03)

13165 Hargittai, Magdolna. *Cooking the Hungarian Way. Rev. ed.* (5–10). Series: Easy Menu Ethnic Cookbooks. 2002, Lerner LB $25.26 (978-0-8225-4132-5). After an introduction to Hungary and its cuisine, there are about 40 clearly presented recipes from appetizers through desserts. (Rev: BL 9/15/02; HBG 3/03) [641.5]

13166 Harrison, Supenn, and Judy Monroe. *Cooking the Thai Way. Rev. ed.* (5–10). Series: Easy Menu Ethnic Cookbooks. 2002, Lerner LB $25.26 (978-0-8225-4124-0); paper $7.95 (978-0-8225-0608-9). The country of Thailand is introduced followed by general information on its foods and several easy-to-follow recipes. (Rev: BL 9/15/02) [641.5]

13167 Hill, Barbara W. *Cooking the English Way. Rev. ed.* (5–10). Series: Easy Menu Ethnic Cookbooks. 2002, Lerner LB $25.26 (978-0-8225-4105-9). The land and people of England are briefly introduced followed by material on their favorite dishes and easy-to-follow recipes. (Rev: BL 9/15/02) [641.5]

13168 Ichord, Loretta Frances. *Double Cheeseburgers, Quiche, and Vegetarian Burritos: American Cooking from the 1920s Through Today* (5–8). Illus. by Jan Davey Ellis. 2007, Lerner $25.26 (978-0-8225-5969-6). This title traces American cuisine from 1920 to the present, with chapters highlighting such trends as TV dinners, fast food, and the rise of organic foods; recipes round out a volume useful for both reports and browsing. (Rev: BL 1/1–15/07; SLJ 5/07) [394.1]

13169 Lagasse, Emeril. *Emeril's There's a Chef in My Soup: Recipes for the Kid in Everyone* (5–8). Illus. by Charles Yuen. 2002, HarperCollins $22.99 (978-0-688-17706-5). The famed TV chef presents a series of simple recipes for main dishes, pasta, desserts, breakfast and lunch items, and salads. (Rev: BL 5/1/02; HBG 10/02) [641.5]

13170 Lagasse, Emeril. *Emeril's There's a Chef in My World!* (5–8). Illus. 2006, HarperCollins $22.99 (978-0-06-073926-3). The famous chef adds to his successful series with a basic introduction to sandwiches, meals, snacks, and more from around the world, with sections on basic skills, safety, and equipment for beginners; cultural facts accompany each recipe. (Rev: BL 12/1/06; SLJ 2/07) [641.59]

13171 Lee, Frances. *The Young Chef's Chinese Cookbook* (4–7). Series: I'm the Chef! 2001, Crabtree LB $25.27 (978-0-7787-0280-1); paper $8.95 (978-0-7787-0294-8). Fifteen child-friendly recipes for Chinese dishes are presented with step-by-step directions and photographs. (Rev: BL 10/15/01; SLJ 11/01) [641.5951]

13172 Lewis, Sara. *Kids' Baking: 60 Delicious Recipes for Children to Make* (4–7). 2006, Sterling $12.95 (978-0-600-61561-3). Well-illustrated recipes for cakes, cookies, and breads are suitable for children working with adult help. (Rev: BL 12/1/06) [641.8]

13173 Llewellyn, Claire, and Clare O'Shea. *Cooking with Fruits and Vegetables* (5–8). Series: Cooking Healthy. 2011, Rosen LB $27.95 (978-1-4488-4844-7). Basic cooking terms and techniques are defined and illustrated in this accessible guide to cooking fruits and vegetables. Also use *Cooking with Meat and Fish* (2011). (Rev: SLJ 12/1/11) [641.3]

13174 Locricchio, Matthew. *The Cooking of France* (7–12). Series: Superchef. 2002, Marshall Cavendish $29.93 (978-0-7614-1216-8). Recipes are accompanied by details on technique and equipment and by information about the country's traditions and festivals. Also use *The Cooking of Mexico* (2002). (Rev: BL 12/15/02; HBG 3/03; SLJ 2/03) [641.5944]

13175 Locricchio, Matthew. *The Cooking of Italy* (7–12). Series: Superchef. 2002, Marshall Cavendish LB $29.93 (978-0-7614-1215-1). The different regional cuisines of Italy are described and a number of traditional recipes clearly outlined and colorfully illustrated. (Rev: BL 3/15/03; HBG 3/03; SLJ 4/03) [641]

13176 Madavan, Vijay. *Cooking the Indian Way* (5–8). 1985, Lerner LB $19.93 (978-0-8225-0911-0). Cultural information is detailed plus both vegetarian and non-vegetarian recipes. (Rev: SLJ 9/85) [641.5954]

13177 Mattern, Joanne. *Recipe and Craft Guide to China* (4–7). Illus. Series: World Crafts and Recipes. 2010, Mitchell Lane LB $24.50 (978-158415937-7). Mattern looks at foods and crafts found in various geographic regions around China, with recipes and activities; a glossary and vocabulary words are included. (Rev: BL 1/1/10) [641.591]

13178 Mendez, Sean. *One World Kids Cookbook: Easy, Healthy and Affordable Family Meals* (5–8). 2011, Interlink $20 (978-1-56656-866-1). Recipes from around the world are presented alongside snippets of trivia and relevant food proverbs. (Rev: SLJ 12/1/11) [641.5]

13179 Montgomery, Bertha Vining, and Constance Nabwire. *Cooking the West African Way. Rev. ed.* (5–10). Series: Easy Menu Ethnic Cookbooks. 2002, Lerner LB $25.26 (978-0-8225-4163-9). An appealing introduction to West African cuisine, with information on the land, people, and culture, and several low-fat and vegetarian recipes. (Rev: HBG 10/02; SLJ 5/02) [641.5966]

13180 Orr, Tamra. *The Food of China* (4–7). Illus. Series: Flavors of the World. 2011, Marshall Cavendish LB $21.95 (978-160870234-3). Introduces the five major cuisines of China, the kinds of foods that are eaten and the way they are cooked, and festive dishes, with recipes and photographs. (Rev: BL 10/1/11) [394.1]

13181 Osseo-Asare, Fran. *A Good Soup Attracts Chairs: A First African Cookbook for American Kids* (5–9). 1993, Pelican $18.95 (978-0-88289-816-2). A basic cookbook for youngsters that explores African cooking past and present and gives more than 35 recipes. (Rev: BL 10/15/93; SLJ 8/93) [641.5966]

13182 Parnell, Helga. *Cooking the German Way. Rev. ed.* (5–10). Series: Easy Menu Ethnic Cookbooks. 1988, Lerner LB $25.26 (978-0-8225-4107-3). Includes such treats as Black Forest torte and apple cake. (Rev: BL 8/88) [641.5943]

13183 Parnell, Helga. *Cooking the South American Way. Rev. ed.* (5–10). Series: Easy Menu Ethnic Cookbooks.

2002, Lerner LB $25.26 (978-0-8225-4121-9). The continent of South America is introduced followed by about 40 clearly presented recipes from several countries. (Rev: BL 9/15/02; HBG 3/03) [641.5]

13184 Paul, Anthea. *Girlosophy: Real Girls Eat* (8–12). 2006, Allen & Unwin paper $19.95 (978-1-74114-142-9). This colorful cookbook and healthy eating guide takes a holistic approach, giving suggestions on nurturing both the mind and body. (Rev: SLJ 6/06)

13185 Plotkin, Gregory, and Rita Plotkin. *Cooking the Russian Way. Rev. ed.* (5–10). Series: Easy Menu Ethnic Cookbooks. 2002, Lerner LB $25.26 (978-0-8225-4120-2). Included along with history and information are such recipes as Russian honey spice cake. (Rev: BL 10/15/86) [641.5947]

13186 Ralph, Judy, and Ray Gompf. *The Peanut Butter Cookbook for Kids* (5–7). 1995, Hyperion paper $10.95 (978-0-7868-1028-4). An amazing collection of recipes involving peanut butter, including soups, snacks, and main dishes. (Rev: BL 10/1/95; SLJ 9/95) [641.6]

13187 Shaw, Maura D., and Synda Altschuler Byrne. *Foods from Mother Earth* (6–10). 1994, Shawangunk paper $9.95 (978-1-885482-02-0). A vegetarian cookbook in which most of the recipes can be prepared in three or four easy steps. (Rev: BL 1/15/95; SLJ 2/95) [641.5]

13188 Sheen, Barbara. *Foods of Italy* (4–8). Series: A Taste of Culture. 2005, Gale LB $27.45 (978-0-7377-3034-0). Cultural and historical notes add to the simple, traditional recipes provided. Also use *Foods of Mexico* (2005). (Rev: SLJ 2/06) [641]

13189 Stern, Sam, and Susan Stern. *Cooking Up a Storm: The Teen Survival Cookbook* (6–9). 2006, Candlewick $16.99 (978-0-7636-2988-5). Filled with attractive photographs and clear recipes, this cookbook authored by a British teenage boy encourages young people to become independent in the kitchen. (Rev: BL 7/06) [641.5]

13190 Walker, Barbara M. *The Little House Cookbook* (5–7). Illus. by Garth Williams. 1979, HarperCollins paper $9.99 (978-0-06-446090-3). Frontier food, such as green pumpkin pie from the Little House books, served up in tasty, easily used recipes.

13191 Weston, Reiko. *Cooking the Japanese Way. Rev. ed.* (5–8). Series: Easy Menu Ethnic Cookbooks. 2002, Lerner LB $25.26 (978-0-8225-4114-1). Directions for preparing traditional foods are given along with lists of terms, ingredients, and utensils. (Rev: HBG 3/02) [641.5952]

13192 Whitman, Sylvia. *What's Cooking? The History of American Food* (7–10). 2001, Lerner LB $22.60 (978-0-8225-1732-0). An absorbing account of how American nutrition and tastes have changed over the years, with discussion of methods of food preparation and preservation, the impact of outside forces such as transportation and war, the use of pesticides, and the advent of fast food. (Rev: BCCB 7–8/01; BL 8/01; HBG 10/01; SLJ 7/01; VOYA 8/01) [394.1]

13193 Wolke, Robert L. *What Einstein Told His Cook: Further Adventures in Kitchen Science, Vol. 2* (8–12). 2005, Norton $25.95 (978-0-393-05963-2). Frequently asked culinary questions are answered in this collection of essays on food and food preparation. (Rev: BL 3/15/05) [641.5]

13194 Zanzarella, Marianne. *The Good Housekeeping Illustrated Children's Cookbook* (5–8). 1997, Morrow $17.95 (978-0-688-13375-7). A visually appealing cookbook containing a number of excellent recipes, some of which require adult supervision. (Rev: BL 12/15/97; HBG 3/98; SLJ 1/98) [641.5]

Costume and Jewelry Making, Dress, and Fashion

13195 Aveline, Erick, and Joyce Chargueraud. *Temporary Tattoos* (6–12). 2001, Firefly LB $19.95 (978-1-55209-609-3); paper $9.95 (978-1-55209-601-7). A book of body art designs that provides plenty of practical tips and guidance on the use of cosmetics. (Rev: BL 11/15/01; HBG 3/02; SLJ 11/01; VOYA 4/02) [391.65]

13196 Baskett, Mickey. *Jazzy Jeans* (8–12). 2007, Sterling $24.95 (978-1-4027-3513-4). How to jazz up your jeans with appliqués, embroidery, painting, and so forth. (Rev: BL 1/1–15/07) [746.4]

13197 Boonyadhistarn, Thiranut. *Beading: Bracelets, Barrettes, and Beyond* (4–8). Illus. Series: Snap Books: Crafts. 2006, Capstone LB $25.26 (978-0-7368-6472-5). Simple, step-by-step instructions guide readers through a variety of fashion accessories that use accessible materials. (Rev: SLJ 2/07) [745.58]

13198 Campbell, Jean, ed. *The Art of Beaded Beads: Exploring Design, Color and Technique* (8–12). 2006, Sterling $24.95 (978-1-57990-825-6). Learn to make projects using beaded beads — beads made out of other seed beads using a variety of knots and stitches; detailed instructions are accompanied by color photographs. (Rev: BL 11/1/06) [745.58]

13199 Carnegy, Vicky. *Fashions of a Decade: The 1980s* (7–12). Series: Fashions of a Decade. 1990, Facts on File $25.00 (978-0-8160-2471-1). This elegantly illustrated volume traces styles and trends in fashion for this decade, linking them to social and political developments. There are volumes in this set for each decade from the 1920s to the 1990s. (Rev: BL 2/15/91; SLJ 5/91) [391]

13200 Cindrich, Sharon. *A Smart Girl's Guide to Style: How to Have Fun with Fashion, Shop Smart, and Let Your Personal Style Shine Through* (4–7). Illus. by

Shannon Laskey. Series: Be Your Best. 2010, American Girl paper $9.95 (978-1-59369-648-1). With a light and breezy tone, this book outlines plenty of fashion dos and don'ts in chapters that define the difference between fashion and style, lay out the basics, and give shopping and storage advice. (Rev: SLJ 7/10) [562]

13201 Di Salle, Rachel, and Ellen Warwick. *Junk Drawer Jewelry* (4–7). Photos by Ray Boudreau. Illus. by Jane Kurisu. Series: Kids Can Do It. 2006, Kids Can $12.95 (978-1-55337-965-2); paper $6.95 (978-1-55337-966-9). This innovative craft book offers step-by-step instructions for making jewelry using odds and ends found in the junk drawer at home. (Rev: SLJ 11/06) [745.5]

13202 Haab, Sherri. *Designer Style Handbags: Techniques and Projects for Unique, Fun, and Elegant Designs from Classic to Retro* (7–12). Photos by Dan Haab. 2005, Watson-Guptill paper $19.95 (978-0-8230-1288-6). Projects suitable for every skill level are accompanied by advice on choosing materials and include bags made from objects such as cigar boxes and candy tins as well as a variety of fabrics and yarns. (Rev: SLJ 1/06; VOYA 12/05) [646.4]

13203 Haab, Sherri, and Michelle Haab. *Dangles and Bangles: 25 Funky Accessories to Make and Wear* (6–9). 2005, Watson-Guptill paper $9.95 (978-0-8230-0064-7). Ideas for stylish accessories are accompanied by guidance on techniques and materials. (Rev: BL 7/05; SLJ 10/05; VOYA 10/05) [745.5]

13204 Hantman, Clea. *I Wanna Make My Own Clothes* (7–12). Illus. by Azadeh Houshyar. 2006, Simon & Schuster paper $9.99 (978-0-689-87462-8). Nearly 50 sewing projects are featured in this guide to making your own unique apparel, including black-and-white illustrations and ideas to spark creativity. (Rev: SLJ 6/06)

13205 Haxell, Kate. *Customizing Cool Clothes: From Dull to Divine in 30 Projects* (8–12). 2006, Interweave paper $21.95 (978-1-59668-015-9). With the help of photographs and easy-to-follow instructions, this guide shows you how to get creative and embellish your bland wardrobe. (Rev: BL 11/15/06) [746]

13206 Litherland, Janet, and Sue McAnally. *Broadway Costumes on a Budget: Big Time Ideas for Amateur Producers* (7–12). 1996, Meriwether paper $15.95 (978-1-56608-021-7). Information about period costumes is given in this helpful manual with instructions for making costumes for nearly 100 Broadway plays and musicals. (Rev: BL 12/1/96) [792.6]

13207 Newcomb, Rain. *Girls' World Book of Jewelry: 50 Cool Designs to Make* (5–8). Series: Kids Crafts. 2004, Lark Books paper $14.95 (978-1-57990-473-9). Up-to-date designs are accompanied by well-thought-out instructions and advice in this large-format volume. (Rev: BL 12/15/04; SLJ 4/05)

13208 Sadler, Judy Ann. *Beading: Bracelets, Earrings, Necklaces and More* (4–8). Series: Kids Can! 1998, Kids Can paper $6.95 (978-1-55074-338-8). Using photographs and simple instructions, directions are given for making a simple beading loom and creating necklaces and bracelets. (Rev: BL 5/15/98) [745.594]

13209 Sadler, Judy Ann. *Hemp Jewelry* (4–7). Series: Kids Can Do It! 2005, Kids Can $12.95 (978-1-55337-774-0); paper $6.95 (978-1-55337-775-7). Sixteen projects for boys and girls using hemp, with drawings and photographs to illustrate the steps and the results. (Rev: BL 3/15/05; SLJ 5/05) [746.4]

13210 Scheunemann, Pam. *Cool Beaded Jewelry* (4–7). Photos by Anders Hanson. Series: Cool Crafts. 2005, ABDO LB $22.78 (978-1-59197-739-1). Step-by-step instructions and full-color photographs guide the user through beaded jewelry projects. (Rev: SLJ 7/05) [745]

13211 Warrick, Leanne. *Style Trix for Cool Chix: Your One-Stop Guide to Finding the Perfect Look* (7–10). Illus. by Debbie Boon. Photos by Shona Wood. 2005, Watson-Guptill paper $9.95 (978-0-8230-4940-0). A useful collection of tips on shopping, color coordination, closet organization, accessories, and finding clothes that fit. (Rev: SLJ 8/05; VOYA 8/05) [391]

Dolls and Other Toys

13212 Aronzo, Aranzi. *Cute Dolls* (6–10). Trans. by Rui Munakata. Series: Let's Make Cute Stuff. 2007, Vertical paper $14.95 (978-1-932234-78-7). A compact guide to making rag dolls that will appeal to manga fans. (Rev: BL 12/15/07) [745.59]

13213 Henry, Sally, and Trevor Cook. *Making Puppets* (4–8). Photos by authors. Series: Make Your Own Art. 2011, Rosen LB $25.25 (978-1-4488-1584-5); paper $11.75 (978-1-4488-1615-6). Color photographs and clear instructions add appeal to this book detailing a variety of creative puppet projects. (Rev: BL 12/15/11; SLJ 7/11) [791.5]

13214 Sadler, Judy Ann. *Beanbag Buddies and Other Stuffed Toys* (4–7). Illus. by June Bradford. Series: Kids Can! 1999, Kids Can paper $5.95 (978-1-55074-590-0). Using clear directions and many step-by-step illustrations, this book offers many ideas on how to create a variety of stuffed toys. (Rev: SLJ 10/99) [745]

13215 Stone, Tanya Lee. *The Good, the Bad, and the Barbie: A Doll's History and Her Impact on Us* (7–10). Illus. 2010, Viking $19.99 (978-067001187-2). Stone tells a fascinating story of a controversial doll and her evolution. Lexile 1120L (Rev: BL 11/15/10*; HB 11–12/10; SLJ 10/1/10*) [688.7]

Drawing and Painting

13216 Ames, Lee J. *Draw Fifty Cats* (4–7). 1986, Doubleday paper $8.95 (978-0-385-24640-8). Step-by-step ways of drawing different breeds and poses of cats. Also use *Draw Fifty Holiday Decorations* (1987). (Rev: BL 11/15/86) [743.69752]

13217 Baron, Nancy. *Getting Started in Calligraphy* (5–8). 1979, Sterling paper $13.95 (978-0-8069-8840-5). This well-organized text shows how to draw letters with beauty and grace. [745.6]

13218 Bergin, Mark. *How to Draw Pets* (4–7). Illus. Series: How to Draw. 2011, Rosen LB $25.25 (978-144884511-8). Cats, dogs, and rabbits are among the animals featured in this slim volume that shows how to use pencils, ink, charcoal, and pastels. (Rev: BL 11/1/11) [743.6]

13219 Bergin, Mark. *Robots* (5–8). Illus. by author. Series: How to Draw. 2008, PowerKids LB $18.95 (978-1-4358-2521-5). After discussion of perspective, tools, and materials, Bergin shows how to draw droids and robots, showing the progression of a drawing from its basic shape and form to the final detailing and shading. Lexile IG1140L (Rev: BLO 10/7/08) [743]

13220 Bohl, Al. *Guide to Cartooning* (6–12). 1997, Pelican paper $14.95 (978-1-56554-177-1). Though actually a textbook, this work is a splendid guide to the history of cartooning as well as a practical guide to all the basics. (Rev: BL 9/15/97) [741.5]

13221 Butterfield, Moira. *Fun with Paint* (4–8). Series: Creative Crafts. 1994, Random House paper $6.99 (978-0-679-83942-2). This simple introduction to painting covers various media and a number of creative projects, including making your own paints. (Rev: SLJ 3/94) [745]

13222 ComicsKey Staff. *How to Draw Kung Fu Comics* (4–8). 2004, ComicsOne paper $19.95 (978-1-58899-394-6). Cheung's instructions on creating architecture and perspective are particularly valuable. (Rev: BL 8/04) [741.5]

13223 DuBosque, Doug. *Draw! Grassland Animals: A Step-by-Step Guide* (4–7). Illus. by author. 1996, Peel paper $8.99 (978-0-939217-25-0). A step-by-step description of how to draw 31 animals from grasslands around the world. (Rev: SLJ 9/96) [741]

13224 DuBosque, Doug. *Draw Insects* (4–8). 1997, Peel paper $8.99 (978-0-939217-28-1). A carefully constructed drawing book that gives simple directions for drawing more than 80 insects, including millipedes, ticks, and spiders. (Rev: SLJ 6/98) [741.2]

13225 DuBosque, Doug. *Draw 3-D: A Step-by-Step Guide to Perspective Drawing* (4–9). Illus. by author. 1999, Peel paper $8.99 (978-0-939217-14-4). Using easy-to-follow sketches, the author introduces the techniques of 3-D drawing, beginning with basic concepts involving depth and progressing to more difficult areas such as multiple vanishing points. (Rev: SLJ 5/99; VOYA 8/99) [741.2]

13226 DuBosque, Doug. *Learn to Draw Now!* (5–8). Illus. by author. Series: Learn to Draw. 1991, Peel paper $8.99 (978-0-939217-16-8). A simple, easily followed manual on how to draw that contains many interesting practice exercises. (Rev: SLJ 8/91) [743]

13227 Gordon, Louise. *How to Draw the Human Figure: An Anatomical Approach* (7–10). 1979, Penguin paper $18.00 (978-0-14-046477-1). This is both a short course on anatomy and a fine manual on how to draw the human body. [743]

13228 Gray, Peter. *Heroes and Villains* (5–8). Series: Kid's Guide to Drawing. 2006, Rosen LB $25.25 (978-1-4042-3330-0). Shows clearly how to draw manga heroes and villains and offers guidance on getting facial expressions just right. (Rev: BL 9/1/06; SLJ 9/06) [741.5]

13229 Hart, Christopher. *Drawing on the Funny Side of the Brain* (7–12). 1998, Watson-Guptill paper $19.95 (978-0-8230-1381-4). This book describes how to create single and multipanel comic strips, with tips on joke writing, pacing, framing, color, and dialogue. (Rev: BL 7/98) [741.5]

13230 Hart, Christopher. *Drawing the New Adventure Cartoons: Cool Spies, Evil Guys and Action Heroes* (4–8). Illus. by author. 2008, Sixth & Spring paper $19.95 (978-1-933027-60-9). Both entertaining and educational, this book gives detailed instructions, and amusing side notes, that show how to create adventure characters. (Rev: SLJ 2/09) [741.5]

13231 Hart, Christopher. *Kids Draw Anime* (4–8). 2002, Watson-Guptill paper $10.95 (978-0-8230-2690-6). Instructions on how to draw anime (Japanese cartoons) characters, with many colorful examples. (Rev: BL 2/1/03; SLJ 11/02) [741.5]

13232 Hart, Christopher. *Manga Mania: How to Draw Japanese Comics* (5–9). 2001, Watson-Guptill paper $19.95 (978-0-8230-3035-4). Hart looks at the techniques for drawing typical Japanese comic characters and animals, providing examples of published manga along with an introduction to the various genres of manga and an interview with a manga publisher. (Rev: BL 7/01; SLJ 7/01) [741.5]

13233 Hart, Christopher. *Manga Mania Chibi and Furry Characters: How to Draw the Adorable Mini-People and Cool Cat-Girls of Japanese Comics* (5–12). Illus. 2006, Watson-Guptill paper $19.95 (978-0-8230-2977-8). Fans of these super-cute manga characters will appreciate the step-by-step directions in this informative book. (Rev: SLJ 5/06) [741.5]

13234 Hart, Christopher. *Mecha Mania: How to Draw the Battling Robots, Cool Spaceships, and Military Vehicles of Japanese Comics* (4–8). 2002, Watson-Guptill paper $19.95 (978-0-8230-3056-9). Instructions on how to draw the high-tech, scary, fanciful machines and weapons that fill the pages of Japanese comic books. (Rev: BL 2/1/03; SLJ 4/03) [741.5]

13235 Janson, Klaus. *The DC Comics Guide to Pencilling Comics* (7–12). 2002, Watson-Guptill paper $19.95 (978-0-8230-1028-8). This practical guide for budding comics creators also contains lots of material for comics fans. (Rev: BL 5/1/02) [741.5]

13236 Lewis, Amanda. *Lettering: Make Your Own Cards, Signs, Gifts and More* (4–8). 1997, Kids Can paper $6.95 (978-1-55074-232-9). This book describes calligraphy and gothic lettering techniques, covering such topics as typefaces, displays, types of pens to purchase, how to determine pen size, and how to use pens, as well as explaining how to make letterhead stationery and newsletters on the computer. (Rev: BL 10/15/97; SLJ 1/98) [745.6]

13237 Nagatomo, Haruno. *Draw Your Own Manga: Beyond the Basics* (7–12). Trans. from Japanese by Françoise White. Illus. by author. 2005, Kodansha paper $19.95 (978-4-7700-2304-9). Written and illustrated by Japanese manga artists, this is an entertaining yet professional guide to drawing in this style. (Rev: SLJ 9/05; VOYA 12/04) [741.5]

13238 Okum, David. *Manga Madness* (7–12). 2004, North Light paper $19.99 (978-1-58180-534-5). This is an excellent guide for would-be cartoonists and *manga* fans with step-by-step directions on how to produce your own art. (Rev: BL 3/15/04) [741.5]

13239 Peffer, Jessica. *DragonArt: How to Draw Fantastic Dragons and Fantasy Creatures* (5–12). Illus. by author. 2005, Impact paper $19.99 (978-1-58180-657-1). Beautiful creatures from the author's imagination fill the pages of this well-written book and will inspire young artists to develop their own fantasy style. (Rev: SLJ 5/06) [743]

13240 Reinagle, Damon J. *Draw! Medieval Fantasies* (4–8). 1995, Peel paper $8.99 (978-0-939217-30-4). A how-to drawing book that gives simple instructions on creating such medieval subjects as dragons and castles. (Rev: BL 1/1–15/96; SLJ 3/96) [743]

13241 Reinagle, Damon J. *Draw Sports Figures* (4–8). 1997, Peel paper $8.99 (978-0-939217-32-8). In six chapters arranged by sport or sports category, the author gives easy-to-follow instructions on how to draw action figures. (Rev: SLJ 6/98) [742]

13242 Roche, Art. *Art for Kids: Comic Strips: Create Your Own Comic Strips from Start to Finish* (4–8). Illus. by author. 2007, Sterling LB $17.95 (978-1-57990-788-4). This is a practical guide to creating a comic strip, with tips on story ideas, design, creating characters, and

writing jokes. (Rev: BCCB 5/07; LMC 8–9/07; SLJ 5/07) [741.5]

13243 Scott, Damian, and Kris Ex. *How to Draw Hip Hop* (7–12). 2006, Watson-Guptill paper $19.95 (978-0-8230-1446-0). This guide to drawing bright graffiti-style art with a manga flavor includes lots of back-and-forth between the authors, revealing a passion for hip-hop culture. (Rev: SLJ 7/06)

13244 Self, Caroline, and Susan Self. *Chinese Brush Painting: A Hands-on Introduction to the Traditional Art* (6–12). 2007, Tuttle $16.95 (978-0-8048-3877-1). An attractive introduction to Chinese calligraphy and brush painting, with history as well as step-by-step instructions. (Rev: BL 12/15/07) [751.4]

13245 Stephens, Jay. *Heroes!* (4–7). Illus. by author. 2007, Sterling $12.95 (978-1-57990-934-5). How to draw superheroes, masks, action moves, and so forth, with lots of great examples. (Rev: BL 12/1/07; SLJ 8/07) [741.5]

13246 Stephens, Jay. *Heroes!* (4–7). Illus. by author. 2007, Sterling $12.95 (978-1-57990-934-5). How to draw superheroes, masks, action moves, and so forth, with lots of great examples. (Rev: BL 12/1/07; SLJ 8/07) [741.5]

13247 Temple, Kathryn. *Drawing* (5–8). Series: Art for Kids. 2005, Sterling $17.95 (978-1-57990-587-3). A comprehensive and clearly written guide to equipment and techniques, with useful illustrations and practical exercises at the end of each section. (Rev: BL 5/1/05; SLJ 9/05) [741.2]

13248 Wallace, Mary. *I Can Make Art* (4–8). Series: I Can Make. 1997, Firefly paper $6.95 (978-1-895688-65-8). Art and crafts are combined in these 12 projects involving such techniques as watercolor, still life, chalk drawing, print making, and collage. (Rev: SLJ 12/97) [741.2]

13249 Wheeler, Annie. *Painting on a Canvas: Art Adventures for Kids* (5–8). Illus. by Debra Spina Dixon. 2006, Gibbs Smith $9.95 (978-1-58685-839-1). These projects are designed to get children's creative juices flowing and to introduce them to some of the techniques used by such world-famous artists as Matisse, Michelangelo, and Picasso. (Rev: SLJ 11/06) [701]

Gardening

13250 Barker, David. *Compost It* (3–7). Series: Language Arts Explorer: Save the Planet. 2010, Cherry Lake LB $27.07 (978-1-60279-656-0). Students are given a mission at the beginning of the book and must use creative thinking and problem solving to gather facts as they travel on a virtual trip researching how gardeners create and use compost. (Rev: BL 4/1/10; LMC 8–9/10; SLJ 4/10) [631.8]

13251 Hirsch, Rebecca. *Growing Your Own Garden* (3–7). Series: Language Arts Explorer: Save the Planet. 2010, Cherry Lake LB $27.07 (978-1-60279-657-7). Readers use creative thinking and problem solving to gather facts as they travel on a virtual trip researching vegetable gardening. (Rev: LMC 8–9/10; SLJ 4/10) [635]

13252 Houle, Michelle E. *Lindsey Williams: Gardening for Impoverished Families* (4–7). Illus. Series: Young Heroes. 2007, Gale LB $27.45 (978-0-7377-3867-4). Young author Williams has won many awards for her agricultural activism; here she talks about ways to have good food without spending a fortune and about the importance and rewards of volunteering. (Rev: BL 2/15/08) [363.8]

13253 Klindienst, Patricia. *The Earth Knows My Name: Food, Culture, and Sustainability in the Gardens of Ethnic Americans* (8–12). 2006, Beacon $26.95 (978-0-8070-8562-2). A tour of 15 American gardens that represent the culture and ethnicity of their immigrant designers. (Rev: BL 4/1/06) [635.09]

13254 Leavitt, Amie Jane. *A Backyard Vegetable Garden for Kids* (4–7). Illus. Series: Gardening for Kids. 2008, Mitchell Lane LB $20.95 (978-158415634-5). Young people learn to reap the rewards of their very own backyard garden — or container garden — in this helpful volume that offers simple, practical advice. (Rev: BL 10/15/08) [635]

Magic Tricks and Optical Illusions

13255 Becker, Helaine. *Magic Up Your Sleeve: Amazing Illusions, Tricks, and Science Facts You'll Never Believe* (4–7). Illus. by Claudia Dávila. 2010, Maple Tree paper $10.95 (978-1-897349-76-2). Thirty sleights of hand incorporating various scientific properties are collected in this clear, easy-to-follow book. (Rev: BLO 5/15/10; SLJ 4/10) [793.8]

13256 Cobb, Vicki. *Magic . . . Naturally! Science Entertainments and Amusements* (7–9). 1976, HarperCollins $12.95 (978-0-397-31631-1). Thirty magic acts are described, each involving a scientific principle. [507]

13257 Colbert, David. *The Magical Worlds of Harry Potter: A Treasury of Myths, Legends, and Fascinating Facts* (5–9). 2001, Lumina $14.95 (978-0-9708442-0-0). Information on more than 50 topics in Harry's universe — such as alchemy, Grindylows, and Voldemort — arranged in alphabetical order. (Rev: SLJ 2/02) [823]

13258 Keable, Ian. *The Big Book of Magic Fun* (5–9). Photos by Steve Tanner. 2005, Barron's paper $14.99 (978-0-7641-3222-3). Step-by-step instructions, with photographs, are given for 40 tricks plus discussion of suitable props and a history of different kinds of magic and famous performers. (Rev: SLJ 3/06) [793.8]

13259 Mandelberg, Robert. *Mind-Reading Card Tricks* (6–9). Illus. by Ferruccio Sardella. 2004, Sterling paper $5.95 (978-1-4027-0948-7). Tricks that convince others that you are reading their minds are explained in detail, with difficulty ratings. (Rev: SLJ 3/05) [795.4]

13260 Tarr, Bill. *Now You See It, Now You Don't! Lessons in Sleight of Hand* (7–9). 1976, Random House paper $19.95 (978-0-394-72202-3). More than 100 easy tricks to mystify one's friends. Each is graded by level of difficulty. [793.8]

13261 Wenzel, Angela. *Do You See What I See? The Art of Illusion* (5–8). Trans. from German by Rosie Jackson. 2001, Prestel $14.95 (978-3-7913-2488-3). Tricks with perspective and color, coded messages, and hidden images are all presented in this attractive volume that makes for excellent browsing. (Rev: HBG 3/02; SLJ 2/02) [152]

13262 *Wizardology: The Book of the Secrets of Merlin* (5–8). 2005, Candlewick $19.99 (978-0-7636-2895-6). This follow-up to *Dragonology* offers a variety of information for wannabe wizards. (Rev: BL 10/15/05)

13263 Zenon, Paul. *Simple Sleight-of-Hand: Card and Coin Tricks for the Beginning Magician* (4–7). Illus. 2007, Rosen LB $21.95 (978-1-4042-1070-7). Written by a practicing magician, this book walks the reader through 13 tricks that will astound and amaze; photographs provide additional explanation. (Rev: BL 11/15/07; SLJ 1/08) [793.8]

Masks and Mask Making

13264 Henry, Sally, and Trevor Cook. *Making Masks* (4–8). Photos by authors. Series: Make Your Own Art. 2011, Rosen LB $25.25 (978-1-4488-1583-8); paper $11.75 (978-1-4488-1613-2). Color photographs and clear instructions add appeal to this book detailing a variety of creative mask projects. (Rev: SLJ 7/11) [731.785]

Paper Crafts

13265 Boursin, Didier. *Origami Paper Airplanes* (6–8). 2001, Firefly $19.95 (978-1-55209-626-0); paper $9.95 (978-1-55209-616-1). Paper airplane devotees will love the origami models offered here, which are categorized by difficulty of construction. Also use *Origami Paper*

Animals (2001). (Rev: BCCB 12/01; BL 1/1–15/02; HBG 3/02; SLJ 12/01) [745.592]

13266 Castleforte, Brian. *Papertoy Monsters: 50 Cool Papertoys You Can Make Yourself!* (4–7). Illus. by Robert James. 2011, Workman paper $16.95 (978-0-7611-5882-0). Fifty different paper craft projects are contained within this punch-out-and-assemble collection. (Rev: BL 12/15/10; SLJ 4/11) [745]

13267 Harbo, Christopher L. *The Kids' Guide to Paper Airplanes* (4–7). Illus. 2009, Capstone LB $23.93 (978-1-4296-2274-5). Detailed, step-by-step directions show how to make a variety of arrows, missiles, and planes, with tips on increasing flight time. (Rev: BL 12/15/08; SLJ 5/09) [745.592]

13268 Henry, Sally, and Trevor Cook. *Origami* (4–8). Photos by authors. Series: Make Your Own Art. 2011, Rosen LB $25.25 (978-1-4488-1586-9); paper $11.75 (978-1-4488-1619-4). Color photographs and clear instructions detail a variety of origami projects such as a bird, a lotus flower, a windmill, and a butterfly. Also use *Papier-Mâché* (2011). (Rev: SLJ 7/11) [745.592]

13269 Nguyen, Duy. *Monster Origami* (5–7). Illus. 2007, Sterling paper $9.95 (978-1-4027-4014-5). This how-to origami book provides easy-to-understand instructions on creating amazing paper monsters. (Rev: SLJ 3/08)

13270 Nguyen, Duy. *Origami Birds* (6–9). 2006, Sterling $19.95 (978-1-4027-1932-5). The folding techniques required to create 19 species of birds are presented in black-and-white instructions; color photographs of the finished products show how beautiful origami can be. (Rev: BL 1/1–15/07) [736.9]

13271 Ransom, Candice. *Scrapbooking Just for You! How to Make Fun, Personal, Save-Them-Forever Keepsakes* (4–9). Illus. 2010, Sterling $14.95 (978-1-4027-4096-1). Plenty of innovative ideas for a variety of different scrapbooking projects — including magnets, frames, and cards — are collected in this well-designed title that also has instructions for hosting a scrapbooking party. (Rev: BLO 11/15/10; SLJ 6/10) [745.5]

Photography, Video, and Film Making

13272 Bidner, Jenni. *The Kids' Guide to Digital Photography: How to Shoot, Save, Play with and Print Your Digital Photos* (7–10). 2004, Sterling $14.95 (978-1-57990-604-7). A user-friendly guide to digital photography and the transfer of the results to the Web and other applications. (Rev: BL 1/1–15/05; SLJ 5/05) [775]

13273 Gaines, Thom. *Digital Photo Madness! 50 Weird and Wacky Things to Do with Your Digital Camera* (7–10). 2006, Sterling paper $9.95 (978-1-57990-624-

5). The fun part of digital photography is altering the images, and this guide explains how, after first covering the basics. (Rev: BL 12/15/06; SLJ 8/06) [773]

13274 Morgan, Terri, and Shmuel Thaler. *Photography: Take Your Best Shot* (5–8). Series: Media Workshop. 1991, Lerner LB $21.27 (978-0-8225-2302-4). A comprehensive and well-put-together guide to photography that covers cameras, film, developing, composition, lighting, and special effects, as well as discussing career opportunities. (Rev: BL 10/1/91; SLJ 11/91) [771]

13275 Price, Susanna, and Tim Stephens. *Click! Fun with Photography* (4–8). 1997, Sterling $14.95 (978-0-8069-9541-0). A fine introduction to photography that covers both beginning and advanced subjects, including the operation of various cameras, exposure, lighting, different types of photography, and filters. (Rev: SLJ 8/97) [771]

13276 Shulman, Mark, and Hazlitt Korg. *Attack of the Killer Video Book: Tips and Tricks for Young Directors* (5–8). Illus. by Martha Newbigging. 2004, Annick $24.95 (978-1-55037-841-2); paper $12.95 (978-1-55037-840-5). Practical advice on all aspects of movie making will be helpful for aspiring directors. (Rev: BL 5/15/04; SLJ 6/04) [778.59]

13277 Shulman, Mark, and Hazlitt Krog. *Attack of the Killer Video Book, Take 2: Tips and Tricks for Young Directors* (6–10). Illus. by Martha Newbigging. 2012, Annick $24.95 (978-155451367-3); paper $14.95 (978-155451366-6). A revised edition that brings up to date (well, to early 2012) the key techniques and resources used in film creation. (Rev: BLO 7/12) [778.59]

13278 Sullivan, George. *Click Click Click! Photography for Children* (5–8). Illus. 2012, Prestel $14.95 (978-379137079-8). A brief history of photography begins this user-friendly guide to getting started taking effective, well-composed pictures. (Rev: BL 1/1/12; SLJ 2/12) [771]

Sewing and Other Needle Crafts

13279 Barnden, Betty. *Very Easy Crazy Patchwork* (7–12). 2007, Reader's Digest $24.95 (978-0-7621-0671-4); paper $19.95 (978-0-7621-0672-1). From a potholder to an evening purse or even a quilt, this book shows how to make attractive patchwork projects using hand techniques and sewing machines. (Rev: SLJ 5/07) [746.46]

13280 Brack, Heather, and Shannon Okey. *Felt Frenzy: 26 Projects for All Forms of Felting* (8–12). 2007, Interweave paper $21.95 (978-1-59668-009-8). For beginners and experts, this book contains projects creating purses, scarves, hats, and so forth through felting. (Rev: SLJ 7/07) [746]

13281 Doherty, Elisabeth A. *Amigurumi! Super Happy Crochet Cute* (8–12). 2007, Sterling paper $14.95 (978-1-60059-017-7). Doherty provides patterns and clear instructions for 14 crocheted or knitted doll projects. (Rev: BL 9/15/07) [746.43]

13282 Eckman, Edie. *The Crochet Answer Book: Solutions to Every Problem You'll Ever Face, Answers to Every Question You'll Ever Ask* (7–12). 2005, Storey paper $12.95 (978-1-58017-598-2). For novice crocheters, this is a well-organized and comprehensive guide. (Rev: BL 12/15/05) [746.43]

13283 Hantman, Clea. *I Wanna Re-Do My Room* (7–12). Illus. by Azadeh Houshyar. 2006, Simon & Schuster paper $9.99 (978-0-689-87463-5). More than 50 projects are featured in this guide to room decoration, such as wall décor, box adornment, pillows, curtains, furniture, and storage ideas; illustrated with black-and-white photographs. (Rev: SLJ 6/06)

13284 Ivarsson, Anna-Stina Linden. *Second-Time Cool: The Art of Chopping Up a Sweater* (7–10). Trans. by Maria Lundin. 2005, Annick $24.95 (978-1-55037-911-2); paper $12.95 (978-1-55037-910-5). Adventurous clothes recycling for the ambitious teen with too much old wool lying around. (Rev: BL 1/1–15/06; SLJ 1/06) [646.4]

13285 Okey, Shannon. *Knitgrrl: Learn to Knit with 15 Fun and Funky Projects* (5–8). Photos by Shannon Fagan. 2005, Watson-Guptill paper $9.95 (978-0-8230-2618-0). Up-to-date designs are shown clearly and explained in detail. (Rev: BL 12/15/05*; SLJ 11/05; VOYA 12/05) [746.43]

13286 Okey, Shannon. *Knitgrrl 2: Learn to Knit with 16 All-New Patterns* (4–7). 2006, Watson-Guptill paper $9.99 (978-0-8230-2619-7). This sequel to *Knitgrrl* (2005) offers step-by-step instructions for 16 new projects, including bracelets, a sports bottle holder, and a cardigan. (Rev: BL 6/1–15/06; SLJ 6/06) [746]

13287 Percival, Kris. *Speed Knitting: 24 Quick and Easy Projects* (8–12). 2006, Chronicle paper $19.95 (978-0-8118-5245-6). Beginners will appreciate these simple projects that can be quickly accomplished. (Rev: BL 11/15/06) [746.32]

13288 Radcliffe, Margaret. *The Knitting Answer Book* (8–12). 2005, Storey paper $12.95 (978-1-58017-599-9). This well-organized volume introduces newcomers to knitting and also provides expert guidance for long-time knitters. (Rev: BL 12/15/05) [746.43]

13289 Ronci, Kelli. *Kids Crochet: Projects for Kids of All Ages* (4–8). Illus. by Lena Corwin. Photos by John Gruen. 2005, Stewart, Tabori & Chang $19.95 (978-1-58479-413-4). A poncho, a quilt, and a tool pouch are among the 15 crocheting projects presented, which are introduced by detailed coverage of techniques. (Rev: BL 5/15/04; SLJ 6/05) [745.5]

13290 Sadler, Judy Ann. *Corking* (4–8). Series: Kids Can! 1998, Kids Can paper $5.95 (978-1-55074-265-7). Provides directions for a handmade knitting device that is used to create knit tubes or corks popular in toys and headbands. (Rev: BL 5/15/98) [746.4]

13291 Sadler, Judy Ann. *The Jumbo Book of Needlecrafts* (4–7). Illus. by Esperança Melo, et al. 2005, Kids Can paper $16.95 (978-1-55337-793-1). After advice on getting started, step-by-step directions guide readers through a range of needlecraft projects. (Rev: SLJ 5/05)

13292 Sadler, Judy Ann. *Quick Knits* (5–8). Illus. by Esperanca Melo. 2006, Kids Can $12.95 (978-1-55337-963-8); paper $6.95 (978-1-55337-964-5). Clear instructions, appealing projects, and suggestions for personalizing these are features of this introduction to knitting. (Rev: BL 1/1–15/07; SLJ 12/06) [746.43]

13293 Storms, Biz. *All-American Quilts* (4–7). Illus. by June Bradford. Series: Kids Can Do It! 2003, Kids Can paper $6.95 (978-1-55337-539-5). Instructions are provided for making quilts with American themes — eagles, flags, and so forth. (Rev: BL 12/15/03; SLJ 1/04) [746.46]

13294 Turner, Sharon. *Find Your Style and Knit It Too* (6–9). 2007, Wiley paper $14.99 (978-0-470-13987-5). Knitters can make fresh, fashionable projects using this book geared to middle- and high-schoolers that gives basic instructions. (Rev: BL 12/15/07) [746.43]

13295 Warwick, Ellen. *Injeanuity* (5–8). Illus. by Bernice Lum. 2006, Kids Can $12.95 (978-1-55337-681-1). Seventeen projects involving jeans and a sewing machine are shown with clear directions. (Rev: BL 6/1–15/06; SLJ 6/06) [746.9]

13296 Wenger, Jennifer. *Teen Knitting Club: Chill Out and Knit Some Cool Stuff* (5–9). 2004, Artisan $17.95 (978-1-57965-244-9). Children who already know how to know will derive the most benefit from this collection of 35 appealing projects. (Rev: BL 12/15/04; SLJ 2/05)

13297 Werker, Kim. *Crochet Me: Designs to Fuel the Crochet Revolution* (8–12). 2007, Interweave paper $21.95 (978-1-59668-044-9). Not for beginners, this is a collection of crochet designs with information on designers and technical aspects. (Rev: BL 12/15/07) [746.43]

13298 Werker, Kim. *Get Hooked Again: Simple Steps to Crochet More Cool Stuff* (6–9). 2007, Watson-Guptill paper $11.95 (978-0-8230-5110-6). A second volume of crochet projects — a scarf, hat, choker, tote, and so forth — with clear explanations and helpful photographs. (Rev: BL 12/15/07; SLJ 2/08) [746.43]

13299 Willing, Karen Bates, and Julie Bates Dock. *Fabric Fun for Kids: Step-by-Step Projects for Children (and Their Grown-ups)* (4–9). 1997, Now & Then LB $17.95 (978-0-9641820-4-2); paper $12.95 (978-0-9641820-5-9). From simple sewing projects to more complex quilting work, this book gives good step-by-step instructions, provides a rundown on necessary sewing tools and materials, and discusses methods for putting designs on fabrics. (Rev: SLJ 4/98) [746.46]

13300 Wilson, Sule Greg C. *African American Quilting: The Warmth of Tradition* (4–7). Series: Library of African American Arts and Culture. 1999, Rosen LB $27.95 (978-0-8239-1854-6). This book traces African influences on textile patterns and techniques particularly as they have been applied to quilting by African Americans. (Rev: BL 2/15/00; SLJ 9/99) [746.46]

13301 Worrall, Jocelyn. *Simple Gifts to Stitch: 30 Elegant and Easy Projects* (8–12). 2007, Potter paper $19.95 (978-0-307-34756-5). Provides easy-to-follow patterns for scarves, bags, hats, aprons, pillows, and so forth. (Rev: SLJ 8/07) [746]

Stamp, Coin, and Other Types of Collecting

13302 Mackay, James. *The Guinness Book of Stamps, Facts and Feats* (7–12). 1989, Guinness $34.95 (978-0-85112-351-6). All sorts of curiosities about postage stamps such as the most valuable, the largest, and so on. (Rev: BL 4/15/89) [769.56]

13303 Owens, Thomas S. *Collecting Comic Books: A Young Person's Guide* (5–8). 1995, Millbrook LB $26.90 (978-1-56294-580-0). A beginner's guide to comic book collecting, with sections on kinds of collections, sources, and organizations. (Rev: BL 2/1/96; SLJ 1/96) [741.5]

13304 Owens, Thomas S. *Collecting Stock Car Racing Memorabilia* (4–8). 2001, Millbrook LB $26.90 (978-0-7613-1853-8). NASCAR fans in particular will

appreciate this practical and detailed guide to collecting, which includes extensive lists of useful addresses. (Rev: BL 12/15/01; HBG 3/02; SLJ 11/01) [796.72]

13305 *The Postal Service Guide to U.S. Stamps* (7–12). 1988, U.S. Postal Service $5.00 (978-0-9604756-8-1). A well-illustrated history of U.S. postage stamps. [769.56]

Woodworking and Carpentry

13306 Ellenwood, Everett. *Woodcarving* (4–7). Illus. Series: Kidcrafts. 2009, Fox Chapel paper $14.95 (978-1-56523-366-9). A succinct look at this craft and the wood, tools, and techniques involved, with seven woodcarving projects. (Rev: SLJ 7/09) [736]

13307 Freuchtel-Dearing, Erin. *Natural Wooden Toys: 75 Easy-to-Make and Kid-Safe Designs to Inspire Imaginations and Creative Play* (6–9). Illus. 2011, Fox Chapel paper $19.95 (978-15652352-4-3). Seventy-five different wooden toy projects are organized according to themes, such as "Fairy tale," and "City" in this accessible book intended for adults but suitable for younger people. (Rev: BLO 11/15/11) [745.592]

13308 Schwarz, Renee. *Birdhouses* (4–7). Series: Kids Can Do It! 2005, Kids Can $12.95 (978-1-55337-549-4); paper $6.95 (978-1-55337-550-0). Nine different birdhouse projects for children to tackle, with illustrated instructions and photographs of the finished products. (Rev: BL 4/1/05; SLJ 5/05) [690]

13309 Walker, Lester. *Housebuilding for Children* (4–7). 1977, Overlook paper $16.95 (978-0-87951-332-0). The construction of six different kinds of houses, including a tree house, is clearly described in text and pictures.

Jokes, Puzzles, Riddles, and Word Games

13310 Becker, Helaine. *Funny Business: Clowning Around, Practical Jokes, Cool Comedy, Cartooning, and More* (5–8). Illus. by Claudia Dávila. 2005, Maple Tree $21.95 (978-1-897066-40-9). Tips on body language, stand-up routines, clowning, and so forth are accompanied by discussion of various types of humor, a self-quiz, and recipes for delights including "Moose Droppings." (Rev: SLJ 1/06) [808.7]

13311 Rosenbloom, Joseph. *Biggest Riddle Book in the World* (6–9). 1977, Sterling paper $6.95 (978-0-8069-8884-9). Very clever riddles collected by a children's librarian. [808.7]

13312 Rosenbloom, Joseph. *Dr. Knock-Knock's Official Knock-Knock Dictionary* (6–9). 1977, Sterling paper $4.95 (978-0-8069-8936-5). This very humorous collection includes more than 500 knock-knock jokes. [808.7]

13313 Rosenbloom, Joseph. *The Gigantic Joke Book* (6–9). 1978, Sterling paper $6.95 (978-0-8069-7514-6). A large collection of jokes that span time from King Arthur to the space age. Also use *Funniest Joke Book Ever* (1986). [808.7]

Mysteries, Curiosities, and Controversial Subjects

13314 Aaseng, Nathan. *The Bermuda Triangle* (7–10). Series: Mystery Library. 2001, Lucent LB $27.45 (978-1-56006-769-6). Using a variety of sources, this book explores the past and present of this controversial phenomenon. (Rev: BL 9/15/01) [001.9]

13315 Abrams, Dennis. *The Lost World of Atlantis* (6–9). Series: Lost Worlds and Mysterious Civilizations. 2012, Chelsea House LB $35 (978-1-60413-969-3). Abrams presents the legends surrounding this missing continent and debunks many of the facts. (Rev: BL 7/12; SLJ 6/12) [398.23]

13316 Allman, Toney. *Werewolves* (4–7). Series: Monsters. 2004, Gale LB $26.20 (978-0-7377-2620-6). An examination of the origins of the werewolf, with references to and illustrations from movie and TV appearances by these monsters. (Rev: SLJ 4/05) [398]

13317 Bardhan-Quallen, Sudipta. *The Real Monsters* (5–8). Illus. by Josh Cochran. Series: Mysteries Unwrapped. 2008, Sterling paper $5.95 (978-1-4027-3776-3). This volume looks into stories about ghosts, werewolves, vampires, mummies, zombies, and other monsters. (Rev: SLJ 6/09) [001.944]

13318 Belanger, Jeff. *What It's Like to Climb Mount Everest, Blast Off into Space, Survive a Tornado, and Other Extraordinary Stories* (5–8). Illus. 2011, Sterling paper $9.95 (978-14027671-1-1). First-person accounts describe a variety of exciting, extreme adventures in this compilation that will appeal to reluctant readers. Lexile 1250 (Rev: BL 4/15/11) [179]

13319 Campbell, Guy. *The Boys' Book of Survival: How to Survive Anything, Anywhere* (4–7). Illus. by Simon Ecob. 2009, Scholastic paper $9.99 (978-0-545-08536-6). How to deal with everything from avalanches to zombie invasions. (Rev: BLO 3/16/09) [796.54]

13320 Campbell, Peter A. *Alien Encounters* (5–7). 2000, Millbrook LB $23.90 (978-0-7613-1402-8). An over-view of eight supposed encounters between humans and aliens. (Rev: BL 7/00; HBG 10/00; SLJ 4/00) [001.9]

13321 Cohen, Daniel. *Prophets of Doom: The Millennium Edition* (6–8). 1999, Millbrook LB $24.90 (978-0-7613-1317-5). An updated edition of the 1992 volume on individuals and groups who have predicted the end of the world, with additions including David Koresh of the Heaven's Gate cult and Shoko Ashara, the cultist who released nerve gas into a Tokyo subway. (Rev: BL 5/15/99; SLJ 6/99) [133.3]

13322 Crisp, Tony. *Super Minds: People with Amazing Mind Power* (4–7). Illus. by Mary Kuper. 1999, Element Books paper $4.95 (978-1-901881-03-5). A survey of near-death experiences, feral children's case histories, and instances of strange mental powers. (Rev: SLJ 5/99) [001.9]

13323 Curran, Robert. *The Zombie Handbook: An Essential Guide to Zombies and More Importantly, How to Avoid Them* (6–8). Illus. 2011, Barron's $14.99 (978-076416409-5). A handy guide to the nature, history, and mythology of zombies, with practical tips on how to identify them and how to behave if confronted by them. ⌒ ℮ (Rev: BL 8/11) [398.45]

13324 Dugan, Ellen. *Elements of Witchcraft: Natural Magick for Teens* (8–12). 2003, Llewellyn paper $14.94 (978-1-73870-393-7). A practicing witch introduces teens to the basics of witchcraft, with tips on proper casting of spells and a discussion of ethical concerns. (Rev: BL 6/1–15/03) [133.4]

13325 Dumont-Le Cornec, Elisabeth. *Wonders of the World: Natural and Man-Made Majesties* (5–9). Illus. by Laureen Topalian. 2007, Abrams $24.95 (978-0-8109-9417-1). Seventy-one striking sites around the world, both natural and man-made and featured on the UNESCO World Heritage list, are shown in beautiful photographs. (Rev: BL 12/15/07) [031.02]

13326 Feldman, David. *Why Do Clocks Run Clockwise? And Other Imponderables: Mysteries of Everyday Life* (8–12). 1987, Harper & Row paper $12.95 (978-0-06-091515-5). Questions about everyday occurrences and objects, like "Why do nurses wear white?" are answered in this book of curiosities. [031.02]

13327 Genge, N. E. *The Book of Shadows: The Unofficial Charmed Companion* (7–12). 2000, Three Rivers $14.00 (978-0-609-80652-4). A guide to some of the basic tenets of witchcraft that form the basis for *Charmed,* the popular TV series about teen witches. (Rev: SLJ 2/01; VOYA 6/01)

13328 Gibson, Marley, and Dave Schrader, et al. *The Other Side: A Teen's Guide to Ghost Hunting and the Paranormal* (7–10). Illus. 2009, Graphia paper $10.99 (978-0-547-25829-4). This concise, often witty guide doesn't glamorize ghost-hunting — the authors stress that it's a hobby, not a career — but it does contain much in the way of practical advice for teens interested in paranormal investigation. (Rev: SLJ 3/10; VOYA 2/10)

13329 Gray, Amy. *How to Be a Vampire: A Fangs-on Guide for the Newly Undead* (7–12). Illus. by Scott Erwert. 2009, Candlewick $14.99 (978-0-7636-4915-9). The ultimate guide to all things vampire, covering feeding, etiquette, fashion, pets, dating mortals, and so forth. Lexile 1070L (Rev: SLJ 1/10; VOYA 4/10) [398.4]

13330 Halls, Kelly Milner. *Alien Investigation: Searching for the Truth About UFOs and Aliens* (5–8). Illus. by Rick C. Spears. 2012, Millbrook $20.95 (978-0-7613-6204-3). Halls explores reports of alien encounters, with interviews of witnesses and discussion of hoaxes. ℮ (Rev: BL 4/1/12; LMC 10/12*; SLJ 10/12; VOYA 6/12) [001.942]

13331 Halls, Kelly Milner. *Tales of the Cryptids: Mysterious Creatures That May or May Not Exist* (4–7). Illus. by Rick Spears. 2006, Darby Creek $18.95 (978-1-58196-049-5). A fun, close-up look at cryptozoology, the study of legendary animals (that may or may not be real) such as the Loch Ness Monster and Bigfoot. (Rev: BL 11/15/06; SLJ 12/06) [001.944]

13332 Hirschmann, Kris. *Demons* (5–8). Illus. Series: Monsters and Mythical Creatures. 2011, ReferencePoint $26.95 (978-160152147-7). Demons and evil spirits' prevalence throughout world cultures is explored here, with eye-catching illustrations and discussion of topics such as exorcism and demonic possession. (Rev: BL 8/11; SLJ 4/11) [133.4]

13333 Holt, David, retel. *The Exploding Toilet: Modern Urban Legends* (7–12). Retold by Bill Mooney. Illus. by Kevin Pope. 2004, August House $16.95 (978-0-87483-754-4); paper $6.95 (978-0-87483-715-5). Amazing, often funny, shocking stories, many of which have appeared on the Internet. (Rev: SLJ 8/04) [398.2]

13334 Huang, Chungliang Al. *The Chinese Book of Animal Powers* (5–7). 1999, HarperCollins LB $16.89 (978-0-06-027729-1). The 12 animals of the Chinese zodiac are introduced in double-page spreads, and the characteristics and powers of each are outlined. (Rev: BCCB 12/99; BL 1/1–15/00; HBG 3/00) [133.5]

13335 Johnson, Julie Tallard. *Teen Psychic: Exploring Your Intuitive Spiritual Powers* (8–12). 2003, Inner Traditions paper $14.95 (978-0-89281-094-9). An introduction to investigating and developing one's intuitive powers, with quizzes, exercises, mediations, and many personal stories from teens. (Rev: BL 1/1–15/04; VOYA 4/04) [131]

13336 Kallen, Stuart A. *Atlantis* (4–7). Illus. Series: Mysterious Encounters. 2011, Kidhaven LB $27.50 (978-073775534-3). Kallen covers the legend of Atlantis in readable text with relevant illustrations. (Rev: BL 3/1/12) [398.23]

13337 Kallen, Stuart A. *Communication with the Dead* (7–12). Series: The Library of Ghosts and Hauntings. 2010, ReferencePoint LB $31.19 (978-1-60152-089-0). Well-written and filled with sources and documentation, this book allows students to examine claims of the paranormal in a straightforward, scholarly way. (Rev: LMC 1–2/10)

13338 Kallen, Stuart A. *Fortune-Telling* (4–8). Series: Mystery Library. 2004, Gale LB $29.95 (978-1-59018-289-5). This exploration of the history and mystery of fortune-telling separates fact from fiction. (Rev: BL 5/15/04) [133.3]

13339 Kallen, Stuart A. *Witches* (7–10). Series: Mystery Library. 2000, Lucent LB $29.95 (978-1-56006-688-0). A history of witchcraft precedes discussion of the beliefs and rituals of today's Wiccans. (Rev: BL 9/1/00; HBG 3/01; SLJ 9/00) [133.4]

13340 Kerns, Ann. *Wizards and Witches* (4–7). Illus. Series: Fantasy Chronicles. 2009, Lerner LB $27.93 (978-0-8225-9983-8). Kerns touches on everything from King Arthur's court to Middle Earth in her tour of primarily European and American witches and wizards. (Rev: BL 10/1/09; LMC 11–12/09; SLJ 1/10) [133.4]

13341 Krensky, Stephen. *Frankenstein* (4–7). Illus. Series: Monster Chronicles. 2006, Lerner LB $26.60 (978-0-8225-5923-8). A survey of the folklore and fiction featuring Frankenstein's monster, including excerpts from the famous Mary Shelley novel. Also use *Vampires* and *Werewolves* (both 2006). (Rev: SLJ 2/07) [823]

13342 Kyi, Tanya Lloyd. *Fifty Underwear Questions: A Bare-All History* (4–7). Illus. by Ross Kinnaird. 2011, Annick $21.95 (978-155451353-6); paper $12.95 (978-15545135-2-9). Everything you wanted to know about underwear through the ages, with some fascinating pieces of trivia — all delivered with humor and even some games. (Rev: BL 12/15/11; SLJ 2/12) [391.4]

13343 Lake, Matt, and Randy Fairbanks. *Weird U.S.: A Freaky Field Trip Through the 50 States* (6–9). Illus. 2011, Sterling $14.95 (978-1-4027-5462-3). Lake and Fairbanks take readers on a cross-country tour of some of the most interesting and bizarre attractions, including a house shaped like a mushroom and a cursed highway. (Rev: BL 11/1/11; SLJ 8/11) [973]

13344 Lynette, Rachel. *Curses* (4–7). Illus. Series: Mysterious Encounters. 2011, Greenhaven LB $27.50 (978-073775422-3). Lynette presents details of various famous curses (the Chicago Cubs' curse, the Hope diamond, to name just two) in readable text with relevant illustrations. (Rev: BL 3/1/12) [398]

13345 Miller, Raymond H. *Vampires* (4–7). Series: Monsters. 2004, Gale LB $26.20 (978-0-7377-2619-0). An examination of the origins of the vampire, with references to and illustrations from movie and TV appearances by these monsters. (Rev: SLJ 4/05) [398]

13346 Murphy, Glenn. *How Loud Can You Burp? More Extremely Important Questions (and Answers!)* (4–7). Illus. by Mike Phillips. 2009, Flash Point paper $10.99 (978-1-59643-506-3). Bizarre and often funny questions gleaned from Murphy's Web site are answered in a casual and engaging manner in this compendium of facts and trivia. (Rev: BLO 8/09; SLJ 10/09) [500]

13347 Murphy, Jim. *The Giant and How He Humbugged America* (5–8). Illus. 2012, Scholastic $19.99 (978-0-439-69184-0). Murphy chronicles the story of the Cardiff Giant, a hoax in 1869 upstate New York involving the body of a 10-foot-tall figure. Lexile 1210L (Rev: BL 6/12*; SLJ 9/12*) [974.7]

13348 Myers, Janet Nuzum. *Strange Stuff: True Stories of Odd Places and Things* (5–8). 1999, Linnet LB $19.50 (978-0-208-02405-3). A collection of curiosities — items about zombies, quicksand, scorpions, poisonous snakes, black holes, Bigfoot, mermaids, voodoo, the Bermuda Triangle, and feral children raised by wolves. (Rev: HBG 3/00; SLJ 7/99; VOYA 2/00) [001.9]

13349 Nardo, Don. *Atlantis* (5–8). Series: The Mystery Library. 2004, Gale LB $29.95 (978-1-59018-287-1). The author examines whether the ancient story of the lost continent of Atlantis — as described by Plato — could be true. (Rev: BL 5/15/04; SLJ 4/04) [001.94]

13350 Nardo, Don, and Bradley Steffens. *Medusa* (4–7). Series: Monsters. 2004, Gale LB $26.20 (978-0-7377-2617-6). Describes the mythological personage, telling the story of Perseus killing Medusa, and showing her role in paintings, sculptures, movie stills, and computer games. Also use *Cyclops* (2004). (Rev: SLJ 4/05) [398.2]

13351 Netzley, Patricia D. *Haunted Houses* (7–10). Series: Mystery Library. 2000, Lucent LB $29.95 (978-1-56006-685-9). A balanced account that examines specific cases of hauntings and discusses such topics as ghosts, poltergeists, seances, and mediums. (Rev: BL 9/1/00; HBG 3/01; SLJ 9/00; VOYA 4/01) [133.1]

13352 O'Connell, Margaret F. *The Magic Cauldron: Witchcraft for Good and Evil* (7–9). 1976, Phillips $38.95 (978-0-87599-187-0). In this history of witchcraft, the reader learns that witches can be agents of both good and evil. [133]

13353 O'Meara, Stephen James. *Are You Afraid Yet? The Science Behind Scary Stuff* (5–8). Illus. by Jeremy Kaposy. 2009, Kids Can $17.95 (978-1-55453-294-0); paper $9.95 (978-1-55453-295-7). A humorous yet macabre exploration of "mysteries" that include vampires, werewolves, ghosts, UFOs — with scientific explanations. (Rev: BL 3/15/09; LMC 10/09; SLJ 8/09) [001.944]

13354 O'Neill, Catherine. *Amazing Mysteries of the World* (7–12). 1983, National Geographic LB $12.50 (978-0-87044-502-6). UFOs, Bigfoot, and Easter Island are only three of the many mysteries explored. [001.9]

13355 Pearce, Q. L. *Ghost Hunters* (5–7). Illus. Series: Mysterious Encounters. 2011, Kidhaven LB $27.50 (978-073775290-8). Case studies, historical facts, and scientific explorations ground this satisfying book about haunted houses and the people who investigate them. (Rev: BL 8/11) [133.1]

13356 Pearce, Q. L. *Mysterious Disappearances* (4–7). Illus. Series: Mysterious Encounters. 2011, Kidhaven LB $27.50 (978-073775840-5). Roanoke and Amelia Earhart are among the mysteries presented here in readable text with relevant illustrations. (Rev: BL 3/1/12) [001.94]

13357 *Pick Me Up* (4–8). Illus. 2006, DK $29.99 (978-0-7566-2159-9). This attractive, child-friendly compilation of facts and figures offers information on a wide variety of topics, including nature, fashion, math, politics, popular culture, geography, music, movies, and technology. (Rev: SLJ 12/06) [900]

13358 Redmond, Shirley Raye. *Oak Island Treasure Pit* (4–7). Illus. Series: Mysterious Encounters. 2011, Kidhaven LB $27.50 (978-073775140-6). Redmond presents details of the pit in Nova Scotia that is reputed to house Captain Kidd's gold. (Rev: BL 3/1/12) [971.6]

13359 Regan, Sally. *The Vampire Book: The Legends, the Lore, the Allure* (7–12). 2009, DK $19.99 (978-0-7566-5551-8). Regan surveys the various myths and stories that exist about vampires and similar beings around the world and throughout history, with details of vampires in literature and on the screen; with eye-catching illustrations. (Rev: LMC 1–2/10; SLJ 12/09) [398.21]

13360 Reis, Ronald A. *Easter Island* (8–12). Illus. Series: Lost Worlds and Mysterious Civilizations. 2011, Chelsea House LB $39.95 (978-160413972-3). A thorough overview of what we know about the mysteries of Easter Island. (Rev: BL 4/1/12; SLJ 5/1/12) [996.1]

13361 Roberts, Nancy. *Southern Ghosts* (6–9). 1979, Sandlapper paper $7.95 (978-0-87844-075-7). Thirteen ghostly tales from the South are retold with photographs of their locales. [133]

13362 Robson, David. *Encounters with Vampires* (7–10). Illus. Series: Vampire Library. 2010, ReferencePoint LB $26.95 (978-160152133-0). A compelling survey of vampire tales from around the world, covering both legend and real incidents. ℮ Lexile 1130L (Rev: BL 10/1/10; LMC 3–4/11) [398]

13363 Rosen, Michael J. *Balls! Round 2* (4–7). Illus. by John Margeson. Series: Balls! 2008, Darby Creek $18.95 (978-1-58196-066-2). This sequel to *Balls!* (2006) introduces even more balls — bocce, croquet, meatballs, even the Magic Eight ball — with all kinds of facts, puzzles, experiments, and fun. (Rev: BLO 6/17/08; SLJ 7/08) [796.3]

13364 Savage, Candace. *Wizards: An Amazing Journey Through the Last Great Age of Magic* (5–8). 2003, Greystone $17.95 (978-1-55054-943-0). An appealing, oversize book full of information on witchcraft and wizardry in the late 17th century, when science and sorcery were not far apart. (Rev: BL 6/1–15/03; VOYA 8/03) [133]

13365 Schroeder, Andreas. *Duped! True Stories of the World's Best Swindlers* (4–7). Illus. by Remy Simard. 2011, Annick $21.95 (978-155451351-2); paper $12.95 (978-15545135-0-5). With graphic-novel flair, this is a lighthearted but informative exploration of hoaxes in modern times. (Rev: BL 12/15/11; SLJ 1/12) [364.16]

13366 Shaw, Maria. *Maria Shaw's Book of Love: Horoscopes, Palmistry, Numbers, Candles, Gemstones and Colors* (8–12). 2005, Llewellyn paper $14.95 (978-0-7387-0545-3). A lighthearted guide to unscientific methods of predicting the course of true love. (Rev: SLJ 2/05) [133.3]

13367 Shuker, Karl P. N. *Mysteries of Planet Earth: An Encyclopedia of the Inexplicable* (6–12). 1999, Carlton $22.95 (978-1-85868-802-2). A well-illustrated exploration of unusual — and mostly unexplained — phenomena including the Loch Ness monster, the Shroud of Turin, green polar bears, pea-soup fog, and the dodo bird. (Rev: VOYA 4/00) [001.94]

13368 Shulman, Mark. *Are You "Normal"? More Than 100 Questions That Will Test Your Weirdness* (5–8). 2011, National Geographic paper $12.95 (978-1-4263-0837-6). Can you roll your tongue? Where do you bite a chocolate bunny first? Which ice cream flavor do you like best? These and many other questions are posed

here with subliminal statistical lessons hidden in the final answers. Lexile 570L (Rev: BL 12/1/11; SLJ 3/12) [155.2]

13369 Slade, Arthur. *Monsterology: Fabulous Lives of the Creepy, the Revolting, and the Undead* (5–8). Illus. by Derek Mah. 2005, Tundra paper $8.95 (978-0-88776-714-2). Dracula, Medusa, Dr. Jekyll/ Mr. Hyde, and Sasquatch are among the characters profiled in this entertaining volume, each with a list of loves and hates, favorite saying, and fashion rating. (Rev: SLJ 2/06; VOYA 2/06)

13370 Tibballs, Geoff. *Ripley's Believe It or Not! Enter If You Dare!* (5–7). 2010, Ripley Entertainment $28.95 (978-1-893951-63-1). A compendium of odd information organized in such chapters as "Animal Antics," "Extreme Sports," "Incredible Feats," "Fantastic Food," and "Amazing Science." (Rev: BL 11/1/10; SLJ 12/1/10) [031.02]

13371 Valentino, Serena. *How to Be a Zombie: The Essential Guide for Anyone Who Craves Brains* (7–10). Illus. by Scott Erwert. 2010, Candlewick $14.99 (978-076364934-0). This tongue-in-cheek title offers up everything from "Decor for the Decaying" to makeup and behavioral advice for young zombie wannabes. (Rev: BL 8/10; VOYA 4/11) [398]

13372 Van Praagh, James. *Looking Beyond: A Teen's Guide to the Spiritual World* (8–12). 2003, Simon & Schuster paper $12.00 (978-0-7432-2942-5). Psychic Van Praagh tells teens what his contacts with the spirit world have taught him about the meaning of life and what we can do to make the most of it. (Rev: BL 1/1–15/04) [133.9]

13373 Wand, Kelly, ed. *Ape-Men: Fact or Fiction?* (6–12). 2005, Gale LB $29.95 (978-0-7377-1892-8). This volume consists of ten essays about large, legendary apelike creatures (known variously as Bigfoot, Sasquatch, and Yeti) sighted from the Himalayas to North America; half of the essays refute their existence and the others conversely offer proof. (Rev: SLJ 6/06)

13374 Wetzel, Charles. *Haunted U.S.A* (5–8). Illus. by Josh Cochran. Series: Mysteries Unwrapped. 2008, Sterling paper $5.95 (978-1-4027-3735-0). An eerie look at ghosts and apparitions, haunted houses, and mysteries across the United States, including on the Hollywood screen. (Rev: SLJ 6/09) [133.1]

13375 Windham, Kathryn Tucker. *Jeffrey Introduces 13 More Southern Ghosts* (7–10). 1978, Univ. of Alabama paper $13.95 (978-0-8173-0381-5). A total of 13 ghosts tell their weird stories. [133]

Sports and Games

General and Miscellaneous

13376 Aaseng, Nathan. *The Locker Room Mirror: How Sports Reflect Society* (7–10). 1993, Walker LB $15.85 (978-0-8027-8218-2). Aaseng argues that problems in professional sports today — cheating, drug abuse, violence, commercialization, discrimination — are reflections of society at large. (Rev: BL 6/1–15/93; SLJ 5/93) [306.4]

13377 Bell-Rehwoldt, Sheri. *The Kids' Guide to Jumping Rope* (4–8). Illus. Series: Kids' Guides. 2012, Capstone LB $26.65 (978-142965443-2). A variety of jump rope tricks and rhymes are presented with easy-to-follow directions. (Rev: BL 9/1/11) [796.2]

13378 Berman, Len. *The Greatest Moments in Sports* (6–9). 2009, Sourcebooks $16.99 (978-1-4022-2099-9). In this compendium, Berman draws on his 40-year career as a sportscaster to bring to life 24 of the greatest sports moments through lively narration, quality photographs, and an accompanying CD. Lexile 820L (Rev: BL 11/1/09; HB 1–2/11; SLJ 1/10) [796]

13379 Birkemoe, Karen. *Strike a Pose: The Planet Girl Guide to Yoga* (5–10). Illus. by Heather Collett. Series: Planet Girl. 2007, Kids Can paper $12.95 (978-155337004-8). This is a practical, easy-going guide to yoga poses, breathing, meditation, and uses in sports. (Rev: SLJ 8/07) [613.7]

13380 Blumenthal, Karen. *Let Me Play: The Story of Title IX: The Law That Changed the Future of Girls in America* (6–10). 2005, Simon & Schuster $17.95 (978-0-689-85957-1). Personal anecdotes, political cartoons, and profiles of female athletes add to the story of the 1972 passage of Title IX, which bans sex discrimination in U.S. schools. (Rev: BL 7/05; SLJ 7/05*) [796]

13381 Catel, Patrick. *Surviving Stunts and Other Amazing Feats* (4–7). Series: Extreme Survival. 2011, Heinemann LB $33.50 (978-1-4109-3969-2). Catel describes amazing feats performed by stuntmen and daredevils. (Rev: SLJ 8/11) [613.6]

13382 Ching, Jacqueline. *Adventure Racing* (7–10). Series: Ultra Sports. 2002, Rosen LB $26.50 (978-0-8239-3555-0). This is a fine introduction to this new, outdoor, multidiscipline sport that involves biking, paddling, and climbing plus survival skills and outdoor savvy. (Rev: BL 9/1/02) [796.5]

13383 Cleare, John. *Epic Climbs* (5–8). Illus. Series: Epic Adventures. 2011, Kingfisher $19.99 (978-0-7534-6473-8). The Eiger, K2, Everest, McKinley, and the Matterhorn are featured in this browsable volume full of photographs, maps, diagrams, and details of climbs, equipment, and so forth. (Rev: BL 4/1/11; SLJ 5/11; VOYA 6/11) [796.52]

13384 Corbett, Doris, and John Cheffers, eds. *Unique Games and Sports Around the World: A Reference Guide* (4–9). 2001, Greenwood $85.00 (978-0-313-29778-6). More than 300 games and sports are organized by continent and then by country, with details of the number of players, equipment, rules, and so forth, and indications of whether this is a suitable game for the classroom or playground. (Rev: SLJ 8/01) [790.1]

13385 Crossingham, John. *Cheerleading in Action* (4–7). Series: Sports in Action. 2003, Crabtree LB $25.27 (978-0-7787-0333-4); paper $6.95 (978-0-7787-0353-2). This is a colorful, attractive introduction to cheerleading, the cheers, costumes, duties, and its importance in sports. (Rev: BL 11/15/03) [791]

13386 Crossingham, John. *In-Line Skating in Action* (4–7). Series: Sports in Action. 2002, Crabtree LB $25.27 (978-0-7787-0328-0); paper $6.95 (978-0-7737-0348-3). A fine introduction to this fast-growing sport with easy-to-follow descriptions of moves and techniques. (Rev: BL 1/1–15/03; SLJ 10/03) [796.9]

13387 Crossingham, John. *Lacrosse in Action* (4–7). Series: Sports in Action. 2002, Crabtree LB $25.27 (978-0-7787-0329-7); paper $6.95 (978-0-7737-0349-0). A clear, concise introduction to lacrosse that discusses techniques, equipment, rules, and safety precautions. (Rev: BL 1/1–15/03) [796.34]

13388 Crossingham, John. *Wrestling in Action* (4–7). Series: Sports in Action. 2003, Crabtree LB $25.27 (978-0-7787-0336-5); paper $6.95 (978-0-7787-0356-3). This introduction to wrestling describes basic moves, skills, and rules. (Rev: BL 11/15/03) [796.8]

13389 Edwardes, Dan. *Parkour* (4–7). Illus. 2009, Crabtree LB $19.95 (978-0-7787-3821-3); paper $8.95 (978-0-7787-3842-8). A fascinating look at the athletes who use urban environments as their gyms. (Rev: BL 6/1–15/09) [796.04]

13390 Gay, Kathlyn. *They Don't Wash Their Socks! Sports Superstitions* (6–9). 1990, Walker LB $14.85 (978-0-8027-6917-6). A compendium of myths and superstitions that helps explain some of the unusual behavior of players and coaches. (Rev: VOYA 8/90) [796]

13391 Green, Sara. *Cheerleading Camp* (4–7). Illus. Series: Kick, Jump, Cheer! 2011, Children's Press LB $22.95 (978-160014647-3). This breezy book offers a behind-the-scenes glimpse into what takes place at cheerleading camp. (Rev: BL 10/1/11) [791.6]

13392 Gryski, Camilla. *Cat's Cradle, Owl's Eyes: A Book of String Games* (4–7). Illus. by Tom Sankey. 1984, Morrow LB $15.93 (978-0-688-03940-0); paper $6.95 (978-0-688-03941-7). Explanations of 21 string figures, plus variations. [793.9]

13393 Gurtler, Janet. *Small Game* (5–8). Illus. Series: Outdoor Hunting Guide. 2012, Weigl LB $27.13 (978-161913504-8). Covering the history of this sport as well as tracking, equipment, safety, and ethics, this is a useful volume for those contemplating hunting everything from skunks and woodchucks to grouse and beavers. (Rev: BL 10/1/12) [799.2]

13394 Hastings, Penny. *Sports for Her: A Reference Guide for Teenage Girls* (7–12). 1999, Greenwood $57.95 (978-0-313-30551-1). The basics of many individual sports are covered, with tips on playing sports in general for the young female athlete. (Rev: SLJ 7/00; VOYA 6/00) [796]

13395 Hayhurst, Chris. *Wakeboarding! Throw a Tantrum* (4–8). Series: Extreme Sports. 2000, Rosen LB $26.50 (978-0-8239-3008-1). This new water sport is described with material on the equipment needed and the necessary safety precautions. (Rev: BL 6/1–15/00; SLJ 8/00) [797.1]

13396 Hile, Lori. *Surviving Extreme Sports* (4–7). Series: Extreme Survival. 2011, Heinemann LB $33.50 (978-1-4109-3968-5). Starting with a chapter titled "Are You Nuts!?," Hile tells stories of extreme sports including diving, skateboarding, mountaineering, and skydiving. (Rev: SLJ 8/11) [796.046]

13397 Howes, Chris. *Caving* (4–8). Series: Radical Sports. 2003, Heinemann LB $25.64 (978-1-58810-626-1). Technique, safety, gear, and other vital aspects are covered in this introduction to the sport. (Rev: BL 2/15/03; HBG 3/03) [796.52]

13398 Hunter, Nick. *Money in Sports* (7–10). Illus. Series: Ethics of Sports. 2012, Heinemann $34 (978-143295977-7); paper $9 (978-14329598-2-1). Hunter reviews the history of sports before focusing on money's role in today's competitions. (Rev: BL 4/1/12*) [338.47796]

13399 Judson, Karen. *Sports and Money: It's a Sellout!* (7–12). Series: Issues in Focus. 1995, Enslow LB $20.95 (978-0-89490-622-0). A straightforward presentation that uses first-person accounts concerning the financial side of being in the sports business. (Rev: BL 11/15/95; SLJ 6/96) [796.0619]

13400 Kalman, Bobbie. *Extreme Wakeboarding* (3–10). Illus. Series: Extreme Sports: No Limits! 2006, Crabtree LB $25.27 (978-0-7787-1680-8); paper $6.95 (978-0-7787-1726-3). The history wakeboarding is covered here, as well as the fundamental techniques, equipment, and safety considerations. (Rev: SLJ 2/07) [797.3]

13401 Kalman, Bobbie, and John Crossingham. *Extreme Skydiving* (3–10). Illus. Series: Extreme Sports: No Limits! 2006, Crabtree LB $25.27 (978-0-7787-1684-6); paper $6.95 (978-0-7787-1730-0). This colorful introduction to skydiving chronicles the sport's long history, which can be traced back to the late 18th century, and describes its different disciplines and required equipment. (Rev: SLJ 2/07)

13402 Kalman, Bobbie, and John Crossingham. *Extreme Sports* (4–8). Series: Extreme Sports No Limits! 2004, Crabtree LB $25.27 (978-0-7787-1673-0). All manner of extreme sports are covered in this overview. (Rev: BL 9/1/04)

13403 Kaminker, Laura. *In-Line Skating! Get Aggressive* (5–8). Series: Extreme Sports. 1999, Rosen LB $26.50 (978-0-8239-3012-8). This book provides information for both beginning and advanced inline skaters and covers topics including equipment, history, techniques, and safety tips. (Rev: SLJ 4/00) [796]

13404 Lamovsky, Jesse, and Matthew Rosetti. *The Worst of Sports: Chumps, Cheats, and Chokers from the Games We Love* (8–12). 2007, Ballantine paper $13.95 (978-0-345-49891-5). Reluctant readers and sports fans will be drawn to this irreverent compilation of sorry facts about various sports. (Rev: BL 9/1/07; SLJ 12/07) [796.02]

13405 Li, WenFang. *Extreme Sports* (7–10). Illus. Series: Getting the Edge: Conditioning, Injuries, and Legal and Illicit Drugs. 2010, Mason Crest LB $24.95

(978-142221729-0). Mental and physical preparation are a focus of this book that also covers injuries, nutrition and supplements, and the dangers of performance-enhancing drugs. (Rev: BL 12/15/10) [796.04]

13406 Luby, Thia. *Yoga for Teens: How to Improve Your Fitness, Confidence, Appearance, and Health — and Have Fun Doing It* (6–12). 2000, Clear Light $14.95 (978-1-57416-032-1). The benefits of yoga, particularly in the teen years, are presented with eye-catching photographs and clear instructions for achieving the poses. (Rev: SLJ 5/00) [613.7]

13407 Maddox, Jake, and Lisa Trumbauer. *Kart Crash* (4–7). Illus. by Sean Tiffany. Series: Jake Maddox Sports Story. 2008, Stone Arch $16.95 (978-143420777-7). Austin learns the value of teamwork and determination in this fast-paced tale set on the go-kart track. Lexile 470L (Rev: BL 11/15/08)

13408 Morris, Neil. *Should Substance-Abusing Athletes Be Banned for Life?* (7–12). Series: What Do You Think? 2008, Heinemann LB $32.86 (978-1-4329-1676-3). After a discussion of the use of drugs in sports, this volume discusses drug tests, penalties for abuse, and so forth; it includes a case study that looks at the Tour de France. (Rev: SLJ 1/1/09) [362.29]

13409 Peters, Craig. *Chants, Cheers, and Jumps* (5–8). Series: Let's Go Team. 2003, Mason Crest $19.95 (978-1-59084-535-6). Readers will learn the difference between cheers and chants and how to do various jumps. Also use *Competitive Cheerleading* (2003). (Rev: BL 10/15/03; SLJ 9/03) [791.6]

13410 Peters, Craig. *Cheerleading Stars* (5–8). Series: Let's Go Team. 2003, Mason Crest LB $19.95 (978-1-59084-533-2). This book highlights the careers and accomplishments of a select group of star cheerleaders. (Rev: BL 10/15/03; HBG 4/04) [791]

13411 Roberts, Jeremy. *Rock and Ice Climbing! Top the Tower* (4–8). Series: Extreme Sports. 2000, Rosen LB $26.50 (978-0-8239-3009-8). This book on climbing covers the dangers, different climbing styles, equipment, techniques, and venues, and profiles some young climbers. (Rev: BL 3/15/00; SLJ 8/00) [796.52]

13412 Rosen, Michael J. *Balls!* (4–7). 2006, Darby Creek $18.95 (978-1-58196-030-3). Balls used in all sorts of sports and their history, choice of shape, and method of construction are the topic of lighthearted discussion. (Rev: BL 6/1–15/06) [796.3]

13413 Ross, Stewart. *Sports Technology* (4–7). Illus. Series: New Technology. 2011, Black Rabbit LB $34.25 (978-159920534-2). Technology's importance in all aspects of sports — equipment, judging and timing, surfaces and stadiums, clothing, machinery, training and cheating — is discussed in this attractive book. (Rev: BL 10/15/11) [688.76]

13414 Savage, Jeff. *A Sure Thing? Sports and Gambling* (7–12). Series: Sports Issues. 1996, Lerner LB $28.75

(978-0-8225-3303-0). After a brief history of gambling, this book looks at the many forms of gambling available today, from church bingo games to horse racing to Las Vegas casinos, with a focus on the connection between gambling and sports and emphasis on the dangers of gambling addiction. (Rev: BL 7/97; HBG 3/98; SLJ 11/97) [796]

13415 Scheppler, Bill. *The Ironman Triathlon* (7–10). 2002, Rosen LB $26.50 (978-0-8239-3556-7). Scheppler provides tips on training body and mind for the challenge of these races that combine running, swimming, and biking. (Rev: BL 9/1/02; VOYA 8/02) [796.42]

13416 Schwartz, Ellen. *I Love Yoga: A Guide for Kids and Teens* (5–12). Illus. by Ben Hodson. 2003, Tundra paper $9.95 (978-0-88776-598-8). Illustrated instructions for 18 basic poses are accompanied by breathing and relaxation exercises, discussion of the benefits of yoga, and a description of the different types of yoga practiced around the world. (Rev: SLJ 12/03; VOYA 10/03) [613.7]

13417 Shannon, Joyce Brennfleck, ed. *Sports Injuries Information for Teens: Health Tips About Sports Injuries and Injury Prevention* (8–12). Series: Teen Health. 2003, Omnigraphics $58.00 (978-0-7808-0447-0). Basic information on sports injuries and treatment is provided in separate sections on such topics as emergency treatment, common injuries affecting teens, rehabilitation and physical therapy, injury prevention, and sports nutrition. (Rev: SLJ 7/04; VOYA 10/04) [617.1]

13418 Sheely, Robert, and Louis Bourgeois. *Sports Lab: How Science Has Changed Sports* (4–7). Series: Science Lab. 1994, Silver Moon $14.95 (978-1-881889-49-6). Traces the effect on sports of applying findings from such branches of science as aerodynamics, psychology, and medicine. (Rev: SLJ 9/94) [617.1]

13419 Smolka, Bo. *Lacrosse* (5–8). Illus. Series: Girls Play to Win. 2011, Norwood LB $27.93 (978-159953463-3). Along with the history and rules of the sport, this volume discusses how women's lacrosse differs from men's. (Rev: BL 12/15/11) [796.34]

13420 Stark, Peter, and Steven M. Krauzer. *Winter Adventure: A Complete Guide to Winter Sports* (8–12). Series: Trailside Guide. 1995, Norton $17.95 (978-0-393-31400-7). This is a complete guide to winter sports including sledding, dogsledding, curling, ice skating, and cross-country skiing with additional material on organizations, safety tips, and information sources. [796.9]

13421 Steiner, Andy. *Girl Power on the Playing Field: A Book About Girls, Their Goals, and Their Struggles* (5–10). Series: Girl Power. 2000, Lerner LB $30.35 (978-0-8225-2690-2). This book explains women's roles in sports with good personal guidance for young girls on participation and goals. (Rev: HBG 10/00; SLJ 6/00) [796]

13422 Steiner, Andy. *A Sporting Chance: Sports and Gender* (4–8). Series: Sports Issues. 1995, Lerner LB $28.75 (978-0-8225-3300-9). An overview of the hurdles that female athletes have had to overcome and the persistent inequality between men and women in sports at all levels, from Little League to the pros. (Rev: BL 1/1–15/96; SLJ 1/96) [796]

13423 Sullivan, George. *Any Number Can Play: The Numbers Athletes Wear* (4–8). 2000, Millbrook LB $23.90 (978-0-7613-1557-5). A fascinating glimpse at players' devotion to their assigned numbers, along with information on retired and banned numbers and who uses the number 13. (Rev: BL 12/15/00; HBG 3/01; SLJ 2/01; VOYA 2/01) [796]

13424 Takeda, Pete. *Climb! Your Guide to Bouldering, Sport Climbing, Trad Climbing, Ice Climbing, Alpinism, and More* (4–9). Series: Extreme Sports. 2002, National Geographic paper $8.95 (978-0-7922-6744-7). An attractive guide to climbing of all types — sport, wall, ice, alpine, and so forth — and to the equipment, techniques, and dangers. (Rev: SLJ 1/03) [796.5223]

13425 Valliant, Doris. *The History of Cheerleading* (5–8). Series: Let's Go Team. 2003, Mason Crest LB $19.95 (978-1-59084-534-9). Using many illustrations, this slim volume describes the history and function of cheerleading at various levels in this country. (Rev: BL 10/15/03; HBG 4/04; SLJ 1/04) [791]

13426 Willker, Joshua D. G. *Everything You Need to Know About the Dangers of Sports Gambling* (5–10). Series: Need to Know Library. 2000, Rosen LB $27.95 (978-0-8239-3229-0). This brief, well-written book surveys the world of gambling on sports, its legal and illegal aspects, and how it has ruined the careers of many fine athletes. (Rev: BL 1/1–15/01) [796]

13427 Wurdinger, Scott, and Leslie Rapparlie. *Ice Climbing* (5–9). Series: Adventure Sports. 2006, Creative Education LB $31.35 (978-1-58341-393-7). This well-designed guide to ice climbing familiarizes readers with the sport's history, equipment, competitions, and safety measures. (Rev: SLJ 12/06) [796.52]

Automobile Racing

13428 Blackwood, Gary. *The Great Race: The Amazing Round-the-World Auto Race of 1908* (6–9). 2008, Abrams $19.95 (978-0-8109-9489-8). The epic race is described in detail with numerous photographs to help readers see what an undertaking it was for the six international teams that competed. (Rev: BL 4/15/08; SLJ 6/08) [796.72]

13429 Buckley, James. *NASCAR* (5–8). Series: Eyewitness Books. 2005, DK LB $19.99 (978-0-7566-1193-4). A visual pleasure for NASCAR fans, full of informa-

tion about people, places, individual races, engineering advances, and so forth. (Rev: BL 9/1/05) [796.72]

13430 Caldwell, Dave. *Speed Show: How NASCAR Won the Heart of America* (5–8). 2006, Kingfisher $16.95 (978-0-7534-6011-5). The history of NASCAR, the basics of stock car racing, its famous drivers, its fans, and so forth are all described in this very readable book by a *New York Times* sports writer. (Rev: BL 11/15/06; SLJ 3/07) [796.720973]

13431 Eagen, Rachel. *NASCAR* (4–7). Series: Automania. 2006, Crabtree $26.60 (978-0-7787-3007-1). An excellent, photo-filled overview of NASCAR's history, rules, safety measures, cars, and leading drivers. (Rev: BL 9/1/06) [796.720973]

13432 Gifford, Clive. *Racing: The Ultimate Motorsports Encyclopedia* (6–12). 2006, Kingfisher $19.95 (978-0-7534-6040-5). Racing of all sorts — from motorbikes to stock cars, rally cars, and Formula One — is covered in this well-illustrated volume that also profiles 60 famous drivers. (Rev: SLJ 5/07) [796.72092]

13433 Kelley, K. C. *Hottest NASCAR Machines* (5–7). Series: Wild Wheels! 2007, Enslow LB $23.93 (978-0-7660-2869-2). Colorful photographs and helpful fact boxes highlight interesting information on cars used on the NASCAR circuit. Also use *Hottest Muscle Cars* and *Hottest Sports Cars* (both 2007). (Rev: SLJ 4/08)

13434 Parr, Danny. *Lowriders* (4–7). Series: Wild Rides! 2001, Capstone LB $23.93 (978-0-7368-0928-3). This volume on "lowrider" cars discusses the types of vehicles that are popular, the history of this trend, and the competitions that are held. (Rev: BL 10/15/01; HBG 3/02) [628.28]

13435 Pearce, Al. *Famous Tracks* (4–8). Series: Race Car Legends: Collector's Edition. 2005, Chelsea House LB $25.00 (978-0-7910-8692-6). Four well-known racetracks are the focus of this readable title full of photographs. (Rev: SLJ 5/06; VOYA 4/06) [796.72]

13436 Pimm, Nancy Roe. *The Daytona 500: The Thrill and Thunder of the Great American Race* (5–8). Series: Spectacular Sports. 2011, Millbrook $29.27 (978-0-7613-6677-5). This visually appealing book features lots of information about the early days of NASCAR racing, including tragedies and rivalries. ℮ (Rev: BL 3/1/11; SLJ 5/11) [796.7]

Baseball

13437 Aretha, David. *Power in Pinstripes: The New York Yankees* (4–7). Series: Sensational Sports Teams. 2007, Enslow LB $24.95 (978-1-59845-044-6). Fans of this winning team will enjoy this book that includes the ball club's history, its top players, its World Series achievements, and lots of links to Web sites. (Rev: BL 7/07) [796.357]

13438 Bissinger, Buzz. *Three Nights in August: Strategy, Heartbreak, and Joy Inside the Heart of a Manager* (8–12). 2005, Houghton Mifflin $25.00 (978-0-618-40544-2). Bissinger dissects a three-game August 2003 series between baseball's St. Louis Cardinals and Chicago Cubs. (Rev: BL 3/1/05) [796.357]

13439 Buckley, James, Jr. *Ultimate Guide to Baseball* (4–7). Illus. by Mike Arnold. Series: Scholastic Ultimate Guides. 2010, Scholastic LB $30 (978-0-531-20750-5). An appealing review of key events, teams, athletes, slang, and all other aspects of baseball. (Rev: BL 6/10; SLJ 5/10; VOYA 8/10) [796.357]

13440 Collins, Ace, and John Hillman. *Blackball Superstars: Legendary Players of the Negro Baseball Leagues* (6–9). 1999, Avisson LB $19.95 (978-1-888105-38-4). This book profiles 12 stars of the Negro Baseball Leagues, including Satchel Paige and Josh Gibson, all of whom are now in the National Baseball Hall of Fame. (Rev: SLJ 8/99) [796.357]

13441 Dreier, David. *Baseball: How It Works* (6–9). Illus. Series: Sports Illustrated: The Science of Sports. 2010, Capstone LB $29.32 (978-142964020-6). Subjects such as pitching, equipment, injury risks, and the grass vs. turf question are examined from a physics standpoint in this well-designed book that also introduces individual players and their achievements. (Rev: BL 9/1/10) [796.357]

13442 Forker, Dom. *Baseball Brain Teasers* (7–12). 1986, Sterling paper $6.95 (978-0-8069-6284-9). A baseball trivia book in which baseball situations are described and questions are asked about them. (Rev: SLJ 12/86) [796.357]

13443 Fuerst, Jeffrey B. *The Kids' Baseball Workout: A Fun Way to Get in Shape and Improve Your Game* (5–8). Illus. by Anne Canevari Green. 2002, Millbrook LB $24.90 (978-0-7613-2307-5). This book offers exercises, stretches, and skills that will help young baseball players improve their game. (Rev: BL 9/1/02; HBG 10/02; SLJ 7/02) [796.357]

13444 Gardner, Robert, and Dennis Shortelle. *The Forgotten Players: The Story of Black Baseball in America* (5–8). 1993, Walker LB $13.85 (978-0-8027-8249-6). A discussion of the challenges that faced the players of the Negro Leagues. (Rev: BL 2/15/93; SLJ 4/93) [769.357]

13445 Glaser, Jason. *Catcher* (4–7). Illus. Series: Play Ball: Baseball. 2011, Gareth Stevens LB $31.95 (978-143394483-3). Explaining the difficult role of catcher — which demands intellectual qualities as well as physical strength and flexibility — this book also profiles well-known catchers and gives tips on how to ace the position. (Rev: BL 4/1/11; SLJ 4/1/11) [796.357]

13446 Goodman, Michael E. *The Story of the Boston Red Sox* (5–8). Illus. 2011, Creative Education LB $23.95 (978-160818034-9). The star-studded history of the Boston Red Sox is chronicled in this statistics-filled title full of archival and contemporary photographs. (Rev: BL 2/1/12)

13447 Goodman, Michael E. *The Story of the San Francisco Giants* (5–8). Illus. 2011, Creative Education LB $23.95 (978-160818055-4). The city-hopping history of the San Francisco Giants is chronicled in this statistics-filled title full of archival and contemporary photographs. (Rev: BL 2/1/12)

13448 Hample, Zack. *Watching Baseball Smarter: A Professional Fan's Guide for Beginners, Semi-Experts, and Deeply Serious Geeks* (8–12). 2007, Vintage paper $13.95 (978-0-307-28032-9). A guide to all aspects of baseball, from management to technique to trivia. (Rev: BL 2/1/07) [796.357]

13449 Kellogg, David. *True Stories of Baseball's Hall of Famers* (4–8). 2000, Bluewood $8.95 (978-0-912517-41-4). Using a chronological approach, this book profiles 60 Hall of Famers and tells why each is there. (Rev: BL 10/15/00; VOYA 8/01) [796.357]

13450 Kisseloff, Jeff. *Who Is Baseball's Greatest Pitcher?* (5–7). 2003, Cricket $15.95 (978-0-8126-2685-8). The author presents profiles of 33 pitchers, with relevant statistics, and challenges the reader to choose the best and justify this decision. (Rev: BL 7/03; HBG 10/03; SLJ 5/03) [796.359]

13451 Krasner, Steven. *Play Ball like the Hall of Famers: Tips for Kids from 19 Baseball Greats* (6–9). Illus. by Keith Neely. 2005, Peachtree paper $14.95 (978-1-56145-339-9). Using a question-and-answer format, notable baseball players give advice on different topics — pitching, fielding, base-running, and so forth. (Rev: BL 5/1/05; SLJ 6/05) [796.357]

13452 Krasner, Steven. *Play Ball Like the Pros: Tips for Kids from 20 Big League Stars* (5–9). 2002, Peachtree paper $12.95 (978-1-56145-261-3). Each chapter features a professional player talking about the position he plays and giving tips to the young athlete. (Rev: BL 5/1/02; SLJ 6/02; VOYA 10/03) [796.357]

13453 LeBoutillier, Nate. *The Story of the Los Angeles Dodgers* (5–8). Illus. 2011, Creative Education LB $23.95 (978-160818045-5). The city-hopping history of the Los Angeles Dodgers is chronicled in this statistics-filled title full of archival and contemporary photographs. (Rev: BL 2/1/12)

13454 McGuire, Mark, and Michael Sean Gormley. *The 100 Greatest Baseball Players of the 20th Century Ranked* (8–12). 2000, McFarland $30.00 (978-0-7864-0914-3). Using a variety of measuring techniques, the 100 greatest baseball players are ranked by importance. [796.357]

13455 Mackin, Bob. *Record-Breaking Baseball Trivia* (5–8). 2000, Douglas & McIntyre $6.95 (978-1-55054-757-3). Questions, answers, and quizzes cover topics including baseball history, team play, World Series facts, and trivia from the plate and mound. (Rev: BL 9/15/00) [796.357]

13456 Nelson, Kadir. *We Are the Ship: The Story of Negro League Baseball* (5–8). Illus. by author. 2008, Hyperion $18.99 (978-0-7868-0832-8). Beautiful illustrations accompany a history of the league told by an anonymous but proud former player. (Rev: BL 2/1/08; SLJ 1/08) [796.357]

13457 Preller, James. *McGwire and Sosa: A Season to Remember* (4–7). 1998, Simon & Schuster paper $5.99 (978-0-689-82871-3). An oversize paperback that traces the baseball season that brought Sosa and McGwire to the nation's attention and made them sports heroes. (Rev: BL 1/1–15/99) [796.357]

13458 Skipper, John C. *Umpires: Classic Baseball Stories from the Men Who Made the Calls* (8–12). 1997, McFarland paper $29.95 (978-0-7864-0364-6). Great, memorable moments in the careers of 19 umpires. (Rev: VOYA 12/97) [796.323]

13459 Stewart, John. *The Baseball Clinic: Skills and Drills for Better Baseball: A Handbook for Players and Coaches* (6–10). 1999, Burford paper $12.95 (978-1-58080-073-0). Written by a major league scout, this book contains useful tips for young baseball players in the areas of pitching, fielding, hitting, base running, and catching. (Rev: SLJ 7/99) [796.357]

13460 Teitelbaum, Michael. *Baseball* (4–7). Illus. Series: Innovation in Sports. 2008, Cherry Lake LB $18.95 (978-160279255-5). Teitelbaum tells the story of baseball by focusing not on the athletes but on the development of the rules, equipment, and training and profiling lesser-known figures — such as the man who invented box scoring — who made important contributions. (Rev: BL 9/1/08) [796.357]

13461 Wong, Stephen. *Baseball Treasures* (4–7). Illus. by Susan Einstein. 2007, HarperCollins $16.99 (978-0-06-114464-6). An inside look at the Smithsonian Institution's collection of baseball memorabilia, revealing how much the equipment has changed since the early days of the game. (Rev: BL 12/15/07) [796.3570]

13462 Young, Robert. *A Personal Tour of Camden Yards* (4–7). Series: How It Was. 1999, Lerner LB $30.35 (978-0-8225-3578-2). Designed to remind fans of famous old ballparks, this book visits Camden Yards, home of the Baltimore Orioles. The reader inspects the field, visits the old warehouse, and views the game from a skybox. (Rev: BL 6/1–15/99; HBG 10/99) [796.357]

Basketball

13463 Glenn, Mike. *Lessons in Success from the NBA's Top Players* (5–7). 1998, Visions 3000 paper $14.95 (978-0-9649795-5-0). This noted sportsman tells about his career in the NBA while introducing each of the NBA teams and its strengths. (Rev: BL 7/98) [796.323]

13464 Joravsky, Ben. *Hoop Dreams: A True Story of Hardship and Triumph* (8–12). 1995, Turner paper $13.95 (978-0-06-097689-7). Based on the movie documentary, this book explores the dream on inner-city kids to play in the NBA. [796.323]

13465 Klein, Leigh, and Matt Masiero, eds. *My Favorite Moves: Shooting Like the Stars* (6–12). Series: Five Star Basketball. 2003, Wish paper $12.95 (978-1-930546-58-5). Best for readers already familiar with the game, this drill book includes advice from five professional women players. Also use *My Favorite Moves: Making the Big Plays* (2003). (Rev: SLJ 1/04) [796.323]

13466 Lannin, Joanne. *A History of Basketball for Girls and Women: From Bloomers to the Big Leagues* (5–9). Series: Sports Legacy. 2000, Lerner LB $26.63 (978-0-8225-3331-3); paper $9.95 (978-0-8225-9863-3). From the creation of basketball in 1891 to today, this account describes women's roles. (Rev: BL 1/1–15/01; HBG 3/01; SLJ 2/01; VOYA 4/01) [796.323]

13467 Lazenby, Roland. *The Show: The Inside Story of the Spectacular Los Angeles Lakers in the Words of Those Who Lived It* (8–12). 2006, McGraw-Hill $27.95 (978-0-07-143034-0). This excellent volume traces the NBA team's fortunes from its inauspicious beginnings in Minneapolis in the early 1950s through its most recent string of championships. (Rev: BL 11/15/05) [796.323]

13468 Lieberman-Cline, Nancy, and Robin Roberts. *Basketball for Women* (7–12). 1995, Kinetics paper $19.95 (978-0-87322-610-3). After a brief history of women's basketball, Lieberman-Cline, who has played in college, Olympics, and professional women's basketball, discusses the commitment required of a serious basketball player, how to formulate a plan for skill development, the recruitment process, and other concerns, and devotes seven chapters to more than 100 drill exercises. (Rev: VOYA 6/96) [796.323]

13469 Morris, Greggory. *Basketball Basics* (7–9). 1976, TreeHouse $6.95 (978-0-13-072256-0). A fine book for the beginner that explains basic moves, shots, and skills. [796.32]

13470 Palmer, Chris. *Streetball: All the Ballers, Moves, Slams, and Shine* (8–12). 2004, Harper Resource paper $16.95 (978-0-06-072444-3). A celebration of urban playground basketball and the talented young people who enjoy it. (Rev: BL 11/15/04) [796.323]

13471 Silverman, Steve. *The Story of the Indiana Pacers* (5–8). Illus. Series: The NBA: A History of Hoops. 2010, Creative Education $23.95 (978-158341946-5). With plenty of action-packed photographs this volume tells the story of this team, its key players, and best games. (Rev: BL 9/1/10) [796.323]

13472 Stewart, Mark. *The Georgetown Hoyas* (4–7). Illus. Series: Team Spirit: College Basketball. 2010, Norwood LB $26.60 (978-159953364-3). A look at the history of university's basketball team, the key players and coaches, uniform, and so forth, with lots of photographs and statistics. (Rev: BL 9/1/10) [796.323]

13473 Stewart, Mark, and Mike Kennedy. *Swish: The Quest for Basketball's Perfect Shot* (5–8). Illus. 2009, Millbrook LB $25.26 (978-0-8225-8752-1). This wide-ranging volume covers basketball history, famous shots, key players, remarkable plays, scoring, and so forth. (Rev: BL 1/1–15/09; SLJ 5/09) [796.3230973]

13474 Thomas, Keltie. *How Basketball Works* (5–8). 2005, Maple Tree $16.95 (978-1-897066-18-8); paper $6.95 (978-1-897066-19-5). A lively overview of basketball's history, equipment, training, and skills, with interesting anecdotes and factoids. (Rev: BL 5/15/05) [796.323]

13475 Weatherspoon, Teresa. *Teresa Weatherspoon's Basketball for Girls* (6–10). 1999, Wiley paper $15.95 (978-0-471-31784-5). This manual, by the famous basketball star and Olympic gold medalist, gives wonderful, practical information about playing the game and becoming a healthy, happy athlete. (Rev: BL 7/99; SLJ 8/99) [796.323]

13476 Yancey, Diane. *Basketball* (5–10). Series: Science Behind Sports. 2011, Gale/Lucent LB $33.45 (978-1-4205-0293-0). This volume looks at all aspects of the sport, focusing in particular on the physics involved and the mental attitude required for success. **e** (Rev: SLJ 9/1/11) [796.3]

Bicycling, Motorcycling, etc.

13477 Buckley, Annie. *Be a Better Biker* (5–6). Series: Girls Rock! 2006, The Child's World LB $25.64 (978-1-59296-741-4). As well as advice on safety and maintenance, this volume (which is suitable for boys too) covers the history of bicycles and the various types available today. (Rev: SLJ 2/07) [796.6]

13478 Deady, Kathleen W. *BMX Bikes* (4–7). Series: Wild Rides! 2001, Capstone LB $23.93 (978-0-7368-0925-2). Bicycle motocross fans will enjoy the color

photographs and concise text that explains the equipment and skills needed for BMX (bicycle motocross) racing. (Rev: BL 10/15/01; HBG 3/02) [629.22]

13479 Haduch, Bill. *Go Fly a Bike! The Ultimate Book About Bicycle Fun, Freedom, and Science* (4–8). Illus. by Chris Murphy. 2004, Dutton $16.99 (978-0-525-47024-3). Packed with facts and cartoon illustrations, this comprehensive guide covers everything from the history of bicycling to practical tips for bike care and repair. (Rev: BL 2/1/04; SLJ 3/04) [796.6]

13480 Hayhurst, Chris. *Bicycle Stunt Riding!* (4–8). Series: Extreme Sports. 2000, Rosen LB $26.50 (978-0-8239-3011-1). In this book, readers will learn about stunts like the vert and mega spin as well as finding out about the bikes and the safety equipment needed to start this sport. (Rev: BL 6/1–15/00) [629]

13481 Hayhurst, Chris. *Mountain Biking: Get on the Trail* (4–8). Series: Extreme Sports. 2000, Rosen LB $26.50 (978-0-8239-3013-5). Stressing safety throughout, this book covers topics including the history of mountain biking, why mountain bikes are different than others, and riding techniques. (Rev: BL 3/15/00; SLJ 8/00) [796.6]

13482 Pavelka, Ed. *Bicycling Magazine's Basic Maintenance and Repair: Simple Techniques to Make Your Bike Ride Better and Last Longer* (8–12). 1999, Rodale paper $9.99 (978-1-57954-170-5). This book clearly explains how to maintain and repair a bicycle so it remains in tip-top condition. [629.28]

13483 Raby, Philip, and Simon Nix. *Motorbikes* (5–8). Series: Need for Speed. 1999, Lerner LB $23.93 (978-0-8225-2486-1); paper $23.93 (978-0-8225-9854-1). A variety of motorbikes are introduced including dirt, motorcross, and land speed bikes. (Rev: BL 1/1–15/00; HBG 3/00; SLJ 2/00) [629.227]

13484 Sidwells, Chris. *Complete Bike Book* (8–12). 2005, DK paper $17.95 (978-0-7566-1427-0). History, technology, training, and maintenance are all covered in this volume for all levels of riders that also includes a stunning section of color photographs. (Rev: BL 9/1/05) [796.6]

13485 Turner, Chérie. *Marathon Cycling* (7–10). Series: Ultra Sports. 2002, Rosen LB $26.50 (978-0-8239-3553-6). Long-distance cycling competitions are described with material on tips and tricks, safety, gear, and racing events. (Rev: BL 9/1/02; SLJ 9/02) [796.6]

13486 Wurdinger, Scott, and Leslie Rapparlie. *Mountain Biking* (5–9). Series: Adventure Sports. 2006, Creative Education LB $31.35 (978-1-58341-396-8). Using many eye-catching photographs this slim volume introduces the popular sport's history, equipment, competitions, and safety measures. (Rev: SLJ 12/06) [796.6]

Boxing and Wrestling

13487 Jarman, Tom, and Reid Hanley. *Wrestling for Beginners* (7–12). 1983, Contemporary paper $15.95 (978-0-8092-5656-3). From a history of wrestling, this book moves on to skills, strategies, moves, and holds. [796.8]

13488 Lewin, Ted. *At Gleason's Gym* (4–7). Illus. by author. 2007, Roaring Brook $17.95 (978-159643231-4). The history of the famous Gleason's Gym (where Muhammad Ali and Jake La Motta trained) is told as readers follow the progress of 9-year-old Sugar Boy Younan, already showing great promise as a boxer. ALA Notable Books 2008. (Rev: BL 9/1/07*; SLJ 10/07) [796.83]

Camping, Hiking, Backpacking, and Mountaineering

13489 Athans, Sandra K. *Tales from the Top of the World: Climbing Mount Everest with Pete Athans* (5–8). Illus. 2012, Millbrook LB $31.93 (978-0-7613-6506-8). Author Athans describes her mountaineer brother Pete's various climbs up Mount Everest and the risks and physical effort involved. e Lexile 860L (Rev: BL 8/12; LMC 3–4/13; SLJ 9/12) [796.5]

13490 Berger, Karen. *Hiking and Backpacking: A Complete Guide* (8–12). Series: Trailside Guide. 1995, Norton paper $18.95 (978-0-393-31334-5). A complete guide to outdoor hiking and backpacking with material on techniques, equipment, safety, camping, and related topics. [796.51]

13491 Brunelle, Lynn. *Camp Out! The Ultimate Kids' Guide* (5–12). Illus. by Brian Biggs and Elara Tanguy. 2007, Workman paper $11.95 (978-0-7611-4122-8). This volume is packed with information about camping out, covering equipment, planning, and skills, and offering games, activities, recipes, nature tips, and so forth. (Rev: SLJ 2/08)

13492 Champion, Neil. *Finding Your Way* (4–7). Illus. 2010, Amicus LB $28.50 (978-1-60753-038-1). Plenty of interactive quizzes and eye-catching photographs enhance this survival guide with an emphasis on navigation techniques — both technological and natural. (Rev: BL 10/1/10; SLJ 11/1/10) [613.6]

13493 Drake, Jane, and Ann Love. *The Kids Campfire Book* (4–8). 1998, Kids Can paper $12.95 (978-1-55074-539-9). This manual describes how to select a location, build safe campfires, and later douse them, suggests fireside activities, including some science demonstrations, and offers safe cooking tips. (Rev: BL 3/15/98; HBG 9/98; SLJ 4/98) [796.54]

13494 George, Jean Craighead, and Twig C. George. *Pocket Guide to the Outdoors: Based on My Side of the Mountain* (5–8). 2009, Dutton paper $9.99 (978-0-525-42163-4). This companion piece to George's *My Side of the Mountain* provides information on identifying edible plants, building shelters, catching fish, orienteering, and so forth. (Rev: SLJ 3/10; VOYA 6/10)

13495 Kalman, Bobbie, and John Crossingham. *Extreme Climbing* (4–8). Series: Extreme Sports No Limits! 2004, Crabtree LB $25.27 (978-0-7787-1671-6). Explores the full spectrum of climbing sports, looking at the specific challenges of each and offering readers valuable advice about equipment, climbing techniques, locations, and difficulty ratings, as well as profiles of notable climbers. (Rev: BL 9/1/04)

13496 Oxlade, Chris. *Rock Climbing* (4–8). Series: Extreme Sports. 2003, Lerner LB $22.60 (978-0-8225-1240-0). An appealing introduction to the history, equipment, techniques, safety concerns, and challenges of this sport. (Rev: BL 3/1/04; SLJ 5/04) [790.52]

13497 Venables, Stephen. *Voices from the Mountains: 40 True-Life Stories of Unforgettable Adventure, Drama, and Human Endurance* (8–12). 2006, Reader's Digest $26.95 (978-0-7621-0810-7). Eye-catching photographs add to these tales of mountain climbing, stories of determination and courage ranging from 1889 to 2005. (Rev: BL 2/1/07; SLJ 3/07) [796.552]

13498 Wurdinger, Scott, and Leslie Rapparlie. *Rock Climbing* (5–9). Series: Adventure Sports. 2006, Creative Education LB $31.35 (978-1-58341-394-4). Using many eye-catching photographs, this slim volume introduces rock climbing and examines the sport's history, equipment, competitions, and safety measures. (Rev: SLJ 12/06) [796.5]

Chess, Checkers, and Other Board and Card Games

13499 Basman, Michael. *Chess for Kids* (4–8). 2001, DK paper $12.99 (978-0-7894-6540-5). A guide to the game of chess that includes everything from the basic moves and important strategies to information on the game's origins and the roles the game has played in arenas ranging from literature to history. (Rev: BL 7/01; HBG 10/01) [794.1]

13500 Kidder, Harvey. *The Kids' Book of Chess* (4–8). Illus. by Kimberly Bulcken. 1990, Workman paper $15.95 (978-0-89480-767-1). Using their origins in the Middle Ages as a focus, this book explains the role of each chess piece and the basics of the game. (Rev: SLJ 2/91) [794.1]

13501 Sheinwold, Alfred. *101 Best Family Card Games* (5–12). 1993, Sterling paper $5.95 (978-0-8069-8635-

7). A book filled with games enjoyed by many age groups. (Rev: BL 2/15/93) [795.4]

Fishing and Hunting

13502 Mason, Bill. *Sports Illustrated Fly Fishing: Learn from a Master. Rev. ed.* (8–12). 1994, Sports Illustrated paper $14.95 (978-1-56800-033-6). Equipment and techniques are emphasized in this illustrated introduction to fly fishing. [799.1]

13503 Schmidt, Gerald D. *Let's Go Fishing: A Book for Beginners* (4–7). Illus. by Brian W. Payne. 1990, Roberts Rinehart paper $11.95 (978-0-911797-84-8). This practical guide to freshwater fishing includes material on tackle and kinds of fish. (Rev: BL 3/1/91; SLJ 5/91) [799.1]

Football

13504 Anderson, Lars. *Carlisle vs. Army: Jim Thorpe, Dwight Eisenhower, Pop Warner, and the Forgotten Story of Football's Greatest Battle* (8–12). 2007, Random House $24.95 (978-1-4000-6600-1). In 1912, the Carlisle Indian School football team, led by Jim Thorpe and coached by Pop Warner, played against the Army team, led by Dwight D. Eisenhower; the story of this exciting game is retold in historical context, with background on Thorpe's achievements, the rules of the Indian School, and other details. (Rev: BL 9/1/07) [796.332]

13505 Devaney, John. *Winners of the Heisman Trophy. Rev. ed.* (5–8). 1990, Walker LB $15.85 (978-0-8027-6907-7). A history of the award is given, with profiles of 15 past winners. (Rev: SLJ 6/90) [796.332]

13506 LeBoutillier, Nate. *The Story of the Chicago Bears* (5–8). Illus. 2009, Creative Education LB $22.95 (978-158341750-8). With eye-catching photographs and a pleasing design and interesting text, this is a fascinating history of a football team. (Rev: BL 10/1/09*) [796.323]

13507 McDonnell, Chris, ed. *The Football Game I'll Never Forget: 100 NFL Stars' Stories* (8–12). 2004, Firefly paper $24.95 (978-1-55297-850-4). One hundred football stars talk about the games they remember. (Rev: BL 9/1/04; VOYA 4/05) [796.332]

13508 Madden, John, and Bill Gutman. *John Madden's Heroes of Football: The Story of America's Game* (5–8). 2006, Dutton $18.99 (978-0-525-47698-6). The former NFL coach and popular football commentator chronicles the history of professional football, looking at how the game has changed over the years and profil-

ing some of its best-known players and coaches. (Rev: BL 9/1/06; SLJ 2/07) [796.332092]

13509 Price, Christopher. *The Blueprint: How the New England Patriots Beat the System to Create the Last Great NFL Superpower* (8–12). 2007, St. Martin's $24.95 (978-0-312-36838-8). This is a compelling history of the Patriots with lots of behind-the-scenes information and interesting anecdotes. (Rev: BL 9/1/07) [796.332]

13510 Stewart, Mark, and Mike Kennedy. *Touchdown: The Power and Precision of Football's Perfect Play* (5–8). 2009, Lerner LB $27.93 (978-0-8225-8751-4). Full of action photographs, trading cards, and period prints, this engaging book provides a history of American football, its heroes, bloopers, and most thrilling moments. (Rev: BL 9/1/09; SLJ 1/10) [796.33]

Golf

13511 Gifford, Clive. *Golf: From Tee to Green — The Essential Guide for Young Golfers* (5–8). Illus. 2010, Kingfisher $16.99 (978-075346399-4). This informative guide covers everything from gear and techniques to clothing and the achievements of golfing greats. (Rev: BL 9/1/10) [796.352]

Gymnastics

13512 Kalman, Bobbie, and John Crossingham. *Gymnastics in Action* (4–7). Series: Sports in Action. 2002, Crabtree LB $25.27 (978-0-7787-0330-3); paper $6.95 (978-0-7737-0350-6). Various branches of gymnastics are introduced in text and pictures with coverage of techniques, equipment, and basic movements. (Rev: BL 1/1–15/03) [796.44]

13513 McIntosh, J. S. *Gymnastics* (7–10). Illus. Series: Getting the Edge: Conditioning, Injuries, and Legal and Illicit Drugs. 2010, Mason Crest LB $24.95 (978-142221734-4). Mental and physical preparation are a focus of this book that also covers injuries, nutrition and supplements, and the dangers of performance-enhancing drugs. (Rev: BL 12/15/10) [796.44]

13514 Schwartz, Heather E. *Gymnastics* (7–10). Illus. Series: Science Behind Sports. 2011, Gale/Lucent LB $33.45 (978-142050277-0). After a history of gymnastics, this useful book looks at training and conditioning, explores basic scientific principles involved in gymnastics movements, discusses injuries and diet and exercise, and introduces the importance of competitors' psychological approach. (Rev: BL 10/1/11; SLJ 9/1/11) [796.4]

Hockey

13515 Adelson, Bruce. *Hat Trick Trivia: Secrets, Statistics, and Little-Known Facts About Hockey* (4–7). 1998, Lerner LB $23.93 (978-0-8225-3315-3). History, statistics, and trivia are combined in this lively discussion of hockey and its players. (Rev: BL 1/1–15/99) [796.962]

13516 Connolly, Helen. *Field Hockey: Rules, Tips, Strategy, and Safety* (4–8). Series: Sports from Coast to Coast. 2005, Rosen LB $26.50 (978-1-4042-0182-8). This title puts the spotlight on field hockey, including a brief history of the sport as well as a look at its rules, equipment, training, and so forth. (Rev: SLJ 10/05)

13517 McFarlane, Brian. *Real Stories from the Rink* (5–8). Illus. by Steve Nease. 2002, Tundra paper $14.95 (978-0-88776-604-6). Entertaining true stories give insight into ice hockey's history, rules, and players. (Rev: BL 2/15/03; SLJ 4/03) [796.962]

13518 McKinley, Michael, and Suzanne Levesque. *Ice Time: The Story of Hockey* (5–8). Illus. 2006, Tundra $18.95 (978-0-88776-762-3). This history of ice hockey focuses mainly on the development and current status of the game in Canada, also covering international stars. (Rev: BL 12/1/06; SLJ 1/07) [796.962]

13519 Stewart, Mark, and Mike Kennedy. *Score! The Action and Artistry of Hockey's Magnificent Moment* (5–8). Illus. 2010, Millbrook LB $29.27 (978-0-8225-8753-8). Not for beginning players, this is a book about strategy and technique, with information about key players. ℮ (Rev: BL 9/1/10; SLJ 4/11) [796.355]

13520 Vanderhoof, Gabrielle. *Hockey* (7–10). Illus. Series: Getting the Edge: Conditioning, Injuries, and Legal and Illicit Drugs. 2010, Mason Crest LB $24.95 (978-142221735-1). Mental and physical preparation are a focus of this book that also covers injuries, nutrition and supplements, and the dangers of performance-enhancing drugs. (Rev: BL 12/15/10) [796.355]

13521 Wiseman, Blaine. *Stanley Cup* (4–7). Series: Sporting Championships. 2011, Weigl $26 (978-1-61690-128-8). This is an appealing, colorful introduction to the sport of ice hockey and to its premier event. (Rev: LMC 11–12/10) [796.962]

Horse Racing and Horsemanship

13522 Haas, Jessie. *Safe Horse, Safe Rider: A Young Rider's Guide to Responsible Horsekeeping* (4–7). 1994, Storey paper $16.95 (978-0-88266-700-3). This guide to horsemanship stresses safety and covers such topics as understanding horse behavior. (Rev: BL 1/1/95) [636.1]

13523 Kimball, Cheryl. *Horse Showing for Kids* (4–8). 2004, Storey paper $16.95 (978-1-58017-501-2). A comprehensive guide to showing horses, covering preparations for both horse and rider/handler, plus advice on safety, sportsmanship, and appropriate attire (for animals and humans). (Rev: SLJ 2/05) [798.2]

13524 Kirksmith, Tommie. *Ride Western Style: A Guide for Young Riders* (4–8). 1991, Howell Book House $16.95 (978-0-87605-895-4). Background information and step-by-step instructions for young people interested in learning to ride Western style. (Rev: BL 4/1/92; SLJ 7/92) [798.2]

13525 Mickle, Shelley Fraser. *Barbaro: America's Horse* (4–8). 2007, Simon & Schuster LB $16.89 (978-1-4169-4866-7); paper $8.99 (978-1-4169-4865-0). The tragic story of racehorse Barbaro is told in straightforward but moving text, with lots of details about horses, racing, and genetic choices, plus many photographs. (Rev: SLJ 7/07) [636.1]

13526 Tate, Nikki. *Behind the Scenes: The Racehorse* (5–8). 2008, Fitzhenry & Whiteside $22.95 (978-1-55455-018-0); paper $12.95 (978-1-55455-032-6). Readers get an inside look at horse racing — breeding, training, jockeys and grooms, and so forth — and learn about both the glamor and the sometimes dangerous and harsh realities. (Rev: BL 2/1/08; SLJ 2/08) [798]

13527 Wiseman, Blaine. *Kentucky Derby* (4–7). Illus. Series: Sporting Championships. 2011, Weigl LB $27.13 (978-161690121-9); paper $10.95 (9781616901226). This is an appealing, colorful introduction to the sport of thoroughbred racing and to its premier event. (Rev: BL 4/1/11; LMC 11–12/10) [798.4]

Ice Skating

13528 Wilkes, Debbi. *The Figure Skating Book: A Young Person's Guide to Figure Skating* (4–8). 2000, Firefly LB $19.95 (978-1-55209-444-0); paper $12.95 (978-1-55209-445-7). The author, an Olympic silver medalist, gives practical advice on figure skating from buying skates to simple and complicated skating techniques. (Rev: BL 7/00; SLJ 4/00) [796.9]

In-Line Skating

13529 Werner, Doug. *In-Line Skater's Start-Up: A Beginner's Guide to In-Line Skating and Roller Hockey* (6–12). 1995, Tracks paper $9.95 (978-1-884654-04-6). Using many black-and-white photographs, this book is both a guide to inline skating basics for beginners and an introduction to the growing sport of roller hockey. (Rev: BL 2/1/96) [796.2]

Martial Arts

13530 Atwood, Jane. *Capoeira: A Martial Art and a Cultural Tradition* (5–8). Series: The Library of African American Arts and Culture. 1999, Rosen LB $27.95 (978-0-8239-1859-1). Capoeira, a unique martial art developed by African slaves in Brazil, is described, along with its history and preparations for its debut in the 2004 Olympic games. (Rev: SLJ 8/99) [796.8]

13531 Ellis, Carol. *Judo and Jujitsu* (5–7). Illus. 2011, Marshall Cavendish LB $20.95 (978-076144933-1). This title offers information about the history, practice, and philosophy of judo and jujitsu. (Rev: BL 2/1/12; SLJ 4/12)

13532 Haney-Withrow, Anna. *Tae Kwon Do* (5–7). Illus. 2011, Marshall Cavendish LB $20.95 (978-076144940-9). This interesting title covers the history, practice, and philosophy of tae kwon do. (Rev: BL 2/1/12; SLJ 4/12)

13533 Konzak, Burt. *Samurai Spirit: Ancient Wisdom for Modern Life* (6–12). 2002, Tundra paper $8.95 (978-0-88776-611-4). Martial arts are the focus of this combination of traditional tales, historical and cultural information, and advice from the author, a teacher of martial arts. (Rev: SLJ 6/03) [813]

13534 Mack, Gail. *Kickboxing* (5–7). Illus. 2011, Marshall Cavendish LB $20.95 (978-076144936-2). This title offers information about the history, practice, and philosophy of kickboxing. (Rev: BL 2/1/12; SLJ 4/12)

13535 Pawlett, Ray. *The Karate Handbook* (7–12). Series: Martial Arts. 2008, Rosen LB $29.95 (978-1-4042-1394-4). The basics about karate as well as its history and philosophy, accompanied by many helpful photographs. (Rev: BL 4/1/08) [796.815]

13536 Rielly, Robin L. *Karate for Kids* (5–8). Series: The Martial Arts for Kids. 2004, Tuttle paper $13.95 (978-0-8048-3534-3). After an overview of the history of karate, this appealing volume with clear illustrations looks at the moves, rules and etiquette, uniform and belts, and so forth. (Rev: BL 9/1/04; SLJ 2/05) [796.815]

13537 Tegner, Bruce. *Bruce Tegner's Complete Book of Jujitsu* (7–12). 1978, Thor paper $14.00 (978-0-87407-027-9). A master in the martial arts introduces this ancient Japanese form of self-defense and gives basic information on stances and routines. [796.8]

13538 Tegner, Bruce. *Bruce Tegner's Complete Book of Self-Defense* (7–12). 1975, Thor paper $14.00 (978-0-87407-030-9). A basic primer on ways to defend oneself including hand blows and restraints. [796.8]

13539 Tegner, Bruce. *Karate: Beginner to Black Belt* (7–12). 1982, Thor paper $14.00 (978-0-87407-040-8). Techniques for both the novice and the experienced practitioner are explained in this account that stresses safety and fitness. [796.8]

13540 Tegner, Bruce, and Alice McGrath. *Self-Defense and Assault Prevention for Girls and Women* (7–12). 1977, Thor paper $10.00 (978-0-87407-026-2). Various defensive and offensive techniques are introduced in situations where they would be appropriate. [796.8]

13541 Wiseman, Blaine. *Ultimate Fighting* (4–7). Series: Sporting Championships. 2011, Weigl $26 (978-1616901301). This is an appealing, colorful introduction to the world of mixed martial arts and the championship competition that features athletes trained in boxing, wrestling, karate, and so forth. (Rev: LMC 11–12/10) [796.815]

Olympic Games

13542 Bobrick, Benson. *A Passion for Victory: The Story of the Olympics in Ancient and Early Modern Times* (6–9). Illus. 2012, Knopf $19.99 (978-0-375-86869-6); LB $22.99 (978-0-375-96869-3). An attractive overview of the games from ancient Greece through the end of World War II, with many photographs, illustrations, and quotations. e (Rev: BL 6/12*; LMC 3–4/13; SLJ 7/12) [796.4]

13543 Coffey, Wayne. *The Boys of Winter: The Untold Story of a Coach, a Dream, and the 1980 U.S. Olympic Hockey Team* (8–12). 2005, Crown $23.95 (978-1-4000-4765-9). In this inspiring look back at the 1980 Winter Olympics victory of the U.S. men's hockey team, sportswriter Coffey introduces readers to the players and coach who pulled off this miracle on ice. (Rev: BL 11/15/04; SLJ 5/05) [796.962]

13544 Macy, Sue. *Freeze Frame: A Photographic History of the Winter Olympics* (6–9). 2005, National Geographic $18.95 (978-0-7922-7887-0). A vivid overview of the Winter Games, looking at the various events and the challenges of these winter sports. (Rev: BL 12/15/05; SLJ 2/06) [796.98]

Running and Jogging

13545 Hayhurst, Chris. *Ultra Marathon Running* (7–10). Series: Ultra Sports. 2002, Rosen LB $26.50 (978-0-8239-3557-4). This work looks at different long running races, the athletes that engage in this sport, and the mind-boggling distances they run. (Rev: BL 9/1/02; SLJ 9/02) [796.4]

13546 Manley, Claudia B. *Competitive Track and Field for Girls* (4–7). Series: Sportsgirl. 2001, Rosen LB $26.50 (978-0-8239-3408-9). An introduction to the rules of track and field competitions, the training necessary, and the special opportunities for girls, with material on nutrition and the dangers of overtraining. (Rev: SLJ 3/02) [796.42]

13547 Wiseman, Blaine. *Boston Marathon* (4–7). Illus. Series: Sporting Championships. 2011, Weigl LB $27.13 (978-161690124-0); paper $10.95 (9781616901257). This is an appealing, colorful introduction to the the sport of long-distance running and the history and modern technology of one of the key races in the United States. (Rev: BL 4/1/11; LMC 11–12/10) [796.425]

Sailing, Boating, and Canoeing

13548 Wurdinger, Scott, and Leslie Rapparlie. *Kayaking* (7–10). Series: Adventure Sports. 2006, Creative Education LB $21.95 (978-1-58341-397-5). Outlines the history of kayaking as well as the different types of boats, equipment used, the techniques and skills involved, competitions, and the dangers of the sport. (Rev: BL 10/15/06; SLJ 12/06) [797.122]

Skateboarding

13549 Badillo, Steve, and Doug Werner. *Skateboarding: Book of Tricks* (7–12). 2003, Tracks paper $12.95 (978-1-884654-19-0). Basic and advanced moves are well illustrated in black-and-white photographs although Badillo is shown without protective gear. (Rev: SLJ 5/04) [796.2]

13550 Burke, L. M. *Skateboarding! Surf the Pavement* (5–8). Series: Extreme Sports. 1999, Rosen LB $26.50 (978-0-8239-3014-2). This book supplies information for beginning and advanced skateboarders with coverage of history, techniques, equipment, and safety considerations. (Rev: SLJ 4/00) [796]

13551 Horsley, Andy. *Skateboarding* (4–7). Series: To the Limit. 2001, Raintree LB $25.69 (978-0-7398-3163-2). A brief history of skateboarding is included here along with material on equipment, moves, and some advice on turning pro. (Rev: BL 6/1–15/01) [796.22]

13552 Loizos, Constance. *Skateboard! Your Guide to Street, Vert, Downhill, and More* (4–9). Series: Extreme Sports. 2002, National Geographic paper $8.95 (978-0-7922-8229-7). An attractive guide to skateboarding equipment, technique, rules, etiquette, jargon, and safety. (Rev: SLJ 1/03) [796.22]

13553 Stutt, Ryan. *The Skateboarding Field Manual* (7–12). 2009, Firefly $29.95 (978-1-55407-467-9); paper $19.95 (978-1-55407-362-7). Stutt focuses on various skateboarding tricks and skills in this irreverent, nicely illustrated book; safety warnings are included, but are not prominent. (Rev: SLJ 6/1/09) [796.22]

Skiing and Snowboarding

13554 Barr, Matt, and Chris Moran. *Snowboarding* (4–8). Series: Extreme Sports. 2003, Lerner LB $22.60 (978-0-8225-1242-4). An appealing introduction to the history, equipment, techniques, safety concerns, and stars of this increasingly popular sport. (Rev: BL 3/1/04; SLJ 5/04; VOYA 6/04) [790.9]

13555 Cazeneuve, Brian. *Cross-Country Skiing: A Complete Guide* (8–12). Series: Trailside Guide. 1995, Norton $18.95 (978-0-393-31335-2). An illustrated manual that covers equipment, techniques, clothing, safety and other topics relating to cross-country skiing. [796.93]

13556 Hayhurst, Chris. *Snowboarding! Shred the Powder* (5–8). Series: Extreme Sports. 1999, Rosen LB $26.50 (978-0-8239-3010-4). The book supplies both beginning and advanced information on this sport, including material on history, equipment, techniques, and safety considerations. (Rev: SLJ 4/00; VOYA 6/00) [796.9]

13557 Herran, Joe, and Ron Thomas. *Snowboarding* (5–8). Series: Action Sports. 2003, Chelsea LB $28.00 (978-0-7910-7003-1). Basic information on this sport's gear and performance is accompanied by biographical details about snowboarding champions. (Rev: BL 4/15/03; HBG 10/03) [796.9]

13558 Kleh, Cindy. *Snowboarding Skills: The Back-to-Basics Essentials for All Levels* (7–12). 2002, Annick paper $16.95 (978-1-55297-626-5). Tips from an expert, with photographs and a glossary, make this a hip title for enthusiasts. (Rev: BL 12/15/02; SLJ 1/03) [796.9]

13559 MacAulay, Kelley, and Bobbie Kalman. *Extreme Skiing* (3–9). Illus. Series: Extreme Sports: No Limits! 2006, Crabtree LB $25.27 (978-0-7787-1682-2); paper $6.95 (978-0-7787-1728-7). This slim, well-illustrated volume looks at freestyle skiing, offering a brief history of the sport and touching on such topics as skiing styles, equipment, and competition rules. (Rev: SLJ 2/07) [797.937]

13560 Schwartz, Heather E. *Snowboarding* (5–10). Series: Science Behind Sports. 2011, Gale/Lucent LB $33.45 (978-1-4205-0322-7). After reviewing the history of snowboarding, this book discusses training and other preparations, glides and turns, jumps and rails, and aerial moves before looking at psychological aspects. **e** (Rev: SLJ 9/1/11) [796.9]

13561 Stiefer, Sandy. *Marathon Skiing* (7–10). Series: Ultra Sports. 2002, Rosen LB $26.50 (978-0-8239-3554-3). This work describes the sport of marathon skiing — cross-country skiing pushed to its limits. (Rev: BL 9/1/02) [796.95]

Soccer

13562 Buxton, Ted. *Soccer Skills: For Young Players* (6–12). 2000, Firefly paper $14.95 (978-1-55209-329-0). A practical guide to training and technique that will be useful for beginners and advanced players. (Rev: SLJ 10/00; VOYA 12/00) [796.344]

13563 Coleman, Lori. *Soccer* (5–9). Series: Play-by-Play. 2000, Lerner paper $23.93 (978-0-8225-9876-3). A fine introduction to the rules, equipment, and tactics of soccer with historical coverage through 1999. (Rev: SLJ 9/00) [796.334]

13564 Gifford, Clive. *The Kingfisher Book of Soccer Skills* (5–8). Illus. 2012, Kingfisher $15.99 (978-075346873-9). A practical guide to various soccer moves, techniques of offense and defense, types of passes, and so forth, with color photographs. (Rev: BL 6/12; SLJ 6/12) [796.334]

13565 Gifford, Clive. *The Kingfisher Soccer Encyclopedia* (6–10). 2006, Kingfisher $19.95 (978-0-7534-5928-7). Covers all aspects of the sport, including basic rules, skills, legends, famous games, and winning teams. (Rev: SLJ 5/06) [796.334]

13566 Herbst, Dan. *Sports Illustrated Soccer: The Complete Player* (7–12). 1988, Sports Illustrated for Kids paper $9.95 (978-1-56800-038-1). Basic and advanced skills are explained plus a variety of game strategies. [796.334]

13567 Radnedge, Keir, and Mark Bushell. *The Treasures of the World Cup* (7–12). 2006, Trafalgar $50.00 (978-1-84442-321-7). A scrapbook-like collection of all kinds of goodies connected to the World Cup soccer competitions dating from 1930 to 2002. Stickers, letters, posters, tickets and other souvenirs will thrill soccer fans. (Rev: BL 8/06) [796.334668]

13568 Stewart, Mark, and Mike Kennedy. *Goal! The Fire and Fury of Soccer's Greatest Moment* (5–8). 2010, Millbrook LB $27.93 (978-0-8225-8754-5). Famous goals are the main focus of this book that also

explores the history of the game and the scoring rules. (Rev: BL 3/1/10; SLJ 5/10) [796.334]

Surfing, Water Skiing, and Other Water Sports

13569 Crossingham, John, and Niki Walker. *Swimming in Action* (4–7). Series: Sports in Action. 2002, Crabtree LB $25.27 (978-0-7787-0331-0); paper $6.95 (978-0-7737-0351-3). Color photographs and many diagrams are used with a clear text to describe swimming basics, with tips on various strokes and safety. (Rev: BL 1/1–15/03; SLJ 10/03) [977.2]

13570 Egan, Tracie. *Water Polo: Rules, Tips, Strategy, and Safety* (4–8). Series: Sports from Coast to Coast. 2005, Rosen LB $26.50 (978-1-4042-0186-6). Introduces readers to the sport of water polo, along with its rules, training, and equipment. (Rev: SLJ 10/05)

13571 Gigliotti, Jim. *Barefoot Waterskiing* (5–8). Illus. Series: Extreme Sports. 2011, Child's World LB $27.07 (978-160973177-9). This extreme sports offering boasts dynamic photographs alongside historical and safety information about barefoot waterskiing. (Rev: BL 1/1/12) [797.3]

13572 Lourie, Peter. *First Dive to Shark Dive* (5–8). Illus. 2006, Boyds Mills $17.95 (978-1-59078-068-8). This attractive, interesting photoessay documents a 12-year-old girl's introduction to scuba diving among sharks. (Rev: BL 2/15/06; SLJ 6/06) [797.2]

13573 Manley, Claudia B. *Ultra Swimming* (7–10). Series: Ultra Sports. 2002, Rosen LB $26.50 (978-0-8239-3558-1). An introduction to the history of this demanding new sport that gives tips on improving performance, maintaining safety, and training both body and mind for the challenges. (Rev: BL 9/1/02) [797.2]

13574 Werner, Doug. *Surfer's Start-Up: A Beginner's Guide to Surfing. 2nd ed.* (7–12). 1999, Tracks paper $11.95 (978-1-884654-12-1). A new edition of this standard instructional guide that covers basic instruction, surfing gear, safety, etiquette, and history. (Rev: SLJ 9/99) [797]

Tennis and Other Racquet Games

13575 Kaiman, Bobbie, and Sarah Dann. *Badminton in Action* (4–7). Series: Sports in Action. 2003, Crabtree LB $25.27 (978-0-7787-0334-1); paper $6.95 (978-0-7787-0354-9). This basic introduction to badminton includes material on racquets, courts, rules, and strategies. (Rev: BL 11/15/03) [796.34]

13576 MacCurdy, Doug, and Shawn Tully. *Sports Illustrated Tennis: Strokes for Success! Rev. ed.* (8–12). 1994, Sports Illustrated paper $12.95 (978-1-56800-006-0). Using many illustrations, this volume covers topics like rules, equipment, techniques, and competitions. [796.342]

13577 Muskat, Carrie. *The Composite Guide to Tennis* (5–7). Series: Composite Guide. 1998, Chelsea LB $12.95 (978-0-7910-4728-6). Past and present tennis stars are mentioned along with a general introduction to the game. (Rev: HBG 10/98; SLJ 9/98) [796.342]

13578 Rutledge, Rachel. *The Best of the Best in Tennis* (4–7). 1998, Millbrook LB $24.90 (978-0-7613-1303-8). Using a lively text and many color photographs, this work gives a history of women in tennis and a rundown of today's most important female players. (Rev: BL 2/15/99; HBG 10/99; SLJ 3/99) [796.342]

13579 Sherrow, Victoria. *Tennis* (6–12). Series: History of Sports. 2003, Gale LB $29.95 (978-1-56006-959-1). The origins and evolution of the game are followed by information on recreational and competitive tennis and on outstanding players. (Rev: SLJ 9/03) [796.342]

Video Games

13580 Frederick, Shane. *Gamers Unite! The Video Game Revolution* (6–10). Illus. Series: Pop Culture Revolutions. 2010, Compass Point LB $31.99 (978-0-7565-4244-3). Looks at the history of video games, starting with Pong, and discusses the growth in their popularity of issues of violence and ratings. (Rev: SLJ 5/10) [794.8]

13581 Hile, Kevin. *Video Games* (5–8). Series: Technology 360. 2009, Lucent $32.45 (978-1-4205-0170-4). An attractive and informative look at video games and how they are created, with discussion of their history and impact on culture plus a glossary and lists of material for further research. (Rev: BL 4/1/10; LMC 8–9/10) [794.8]

13582 Parks, Peggy J. *Video Games* (6–9). Illus. Series: Compact Research. 2008, ReferencePoint LB $25.95 (978-1-60152-053-1). Parks answers such questions as "Do Video Games Cause Violent Crime?" and "Should Video Games Be Regulated?" and provides varying perspectives, data, and pages of quotations. (Rev: SLJ 1/1/09) [794.8]

Volleyball

13583 Giddens, Sandra, and Owen Giddens. *Volleyball: Rules, Tips, Strategy, and Safety* (4–8). Series: Sports from Coast to Coast. 2005, Rosen LB $26.50 (978-1-4042-0185-9). Introduces the sport of volleyball — including its rules, equipment, and strategies. (Rev: SLJ 10/05) [796.32]

Author Index

Authors are arranged alphabetically by last name. Authors' and joint authors' names are followed by book titles — which are also arranged alphabetically — and the text entry number. Book titles may refer to those that appear as a main entry or as an internal entry mentioned in the text. Fiction titles are indicated by (F) following the entry number.

Aamodt, Alice. *Wolf Pack*, 12472
Aaron, Chester. *Lackawanna*, 1(F)
Out of Sight, Out of Mind, 2(F)
Aaseng, Nathan. *American Dinosaur Hunters*, 9186
The Bermuda Triangle , 13314
Business Builders in Broadcasting, 8409
Business Builders in Computers, 8410
Business Builders in Fast Food, 8411
Business Builders in Oil, 8412
Business Builders in Sweets and Treats, 11222
Construction, 8413
The Locker Room Mirror, 13376
Michael Jordan, 8712
Nature's Poisonous Creatures, 12369
The O. J. Simpson Trial, 10672
The Peace Seekers, 8784
Treacherous Traitors, 11062
The White House, 10425
Yearbooks in Science, 12137
Yearbooks in Science, 12138
You Are the Corporate Executive, 11237
You Are the Explorer, 9257
You Are the General, 10737
You Are the General II, 9258
You Are the Juror, 10673
You Are the President, 10643
You Are the President II, 10644
You Are the Senator, 10655
You Are the Supreme Court Justice, 10674
Abadzis, Nick. *Laika*, 3836(F)
Abbott, David. *The Twin Towers*, 11187
Abbott, Ellen Jensen. *Watersmeet*, 2556(F)
Abbott, Hailey. *The Bridesmaid*, 1213(F)

Abbott, Tony. *City of the Dead*, 5341(F)
Firegirl, 1657(F)
Kringle, 2557(F)
Lunch-Box Dream, 5086(F)
The Postcard, 5839(F)
Abdel-Fattah, Randa. *Does My Head Look Big in This?*, 1046(F)
Ten Things I Hate About Me, 1047(F)
Where the Streets Had a Name, 4358(F)
Abe, Yoshitoshi. *New Feathers*, 3837(F)
Abeel, Samantha. *What Once Was White*, 11819
Abelove, Joan. *Go and Come Back*, 2482(F)
Abouzeid, Chris. *Anatopsis*, 2558(F)
Abraham, Denise Gonzales. *Cecilia's Year*, 1048(F)
Surprising Cecilia, 1049(F)
Abraham, Susan Gonzales. *Cecilia's Year*, 1048(F)
Surprising Cecilia, 1049(F)
Abrahams, Peter. *Down the Rabbit Hole*, 5840(F)
Into the Dark, 5841(F)
Reality Check, 5842(F)
Robbie Forester and the Outlaws of Sherwood Street, 450(F)
Up All Night, 6860(F)
Abrahams, Roger D. (ed.). *African Folktales*, 7207
Abramovitz, Melissa. *Lou Gehrig's Disease*, 11555
Abrams, Dennis. *Anthony Horowitz*, 7776
Ernesto "Che" Guevara, 8939
H. G. Wells, 7856
Hamid Karzai, 8846
Hillary Rodham Clinton, 8264
Julia Child, 8963
The Lost World of Atlantis, 13315
Nicolas Sarkozy, 8920

Rachael Ray, 8617
Abrams, Judith Z. *The Secret World of Kabbalah*, 10579
Abrams, Liesa. *Chronic Fatigue Syndrome*, 11556
Abramson, Andra Serlin. *Inside Stars*, 12269
Abramson, Jill. *Obama*, 8196
Acampora, Paul. *Defining Dulcie*, 5643(F)
Aciman, André. *Baby*, 1214(F)
Acker, Kerry. *Everything You Need to Know About the Goth Scene*, 11983
Ackerman, Jane. *Louis Pasteur and the Founding of Microbiology*, 8610
Ackermann, Joan. *In the Space Left Behind*, 1215(F)
Ackley, Amy. *Sign Language*, 451(F)
Adair, Gene. *Alfred Hitchcock*, 7937
Adair, Rick (ed.). *Critical Perspectives on Politics and the Environment*, 10958
Adam, Paul. *Max Cassidy*, 5843(F)
Adams, John Joseph (ed.). *Under the Moons of Mars*, 6409(F)
Adams, Lenora. *Baby Girl*, 1824(F)
Adams, Richard. *Tales from Watership Down*, 2559(F)
Watership Down, 2560(F)
Adams, Sean. *Tim Duncan*, 8707
Adams, Simon. *Alexander*, 8860
Adams, W. Royce. *Me and Jay*, 3(F)
Adamson, Joy. *Born Free*, 12462
Adamson, Thomas K. *Lessons in Science Safety with Max Axiom, Super Scientist*, 12186
Adare, Sierra. *Mohawk*, 10912
Adeleke, Tunde. *Songhay*, 9653
Adelson, Bruce. *Hat Trick Trivia*, 13515
Adkins, Jan. *Frank Lloyd Wright*, 7702

Arthus-Bertrand, Yann. *Our Living Earth*, 9262
Artley, Bob. *Once Upon a Farm*, 12328
Asai, Carrie. *The Book of the Sword*, 12(F)
Asamiya, Kia. *Dark Angel*, 3846(F)
Asgedom, Mawi. *The Code*, 12010
Ashabranner, Brent. *A Date with Destiny*, 10427
The Lion's Whiskers and Other Ethiopian Tales, 7209
Ashby, Amanda. *Fairy Bad Day*, 2595(F)
Zombie Queen of Newbury High, 2596(F)
Ashby, John. *Sea Gift*, 13(F)
Ashby, Ruth. *Franklin and Eleanor Roosevelt*, 8224
James and Dolley Madison, 8192
John and Abigail Adams, 8138
Steve Case, 8488
Woodrow and Edith Wilson, 8248
Young Charles Darwin and the Voyage of the Beagle, 8503
Asher, Dana. *Epidemiologists*, 11410
Asher, Jay. *The Future of Us*, 469(F)
Asher, Sandy. *Where Do You Get Your Ideas? Helping Young Writers Begin*, 11260
Asher, Sandy (ed.). *Dude! Stories and Stuff for Boys*, 6861(F)
Ashley, Bernard. *All My Men*, 1837(F)
Break in the Sun, 14(F)
A Kind of Wild Justice, 15(F)
Little Soldier, 1838(F)
Terry on the Fence, 1839(F)
Ashton, Victoria. *Confessions of a Teen Nanny*, 470(F)
Ashworth, Leon. *Winston Churchill*, 8878
Asimov, Isaac. *The Birth of Our Universe*, 12301
Caves of Steel, 6417(F)
Fantastic Voyage, 6418(F)
How Did We Find Out About Solar Power?, 12877
The Life and Death of Stars, 12271
Norby and the Invaders, 6422(F)
Norby and Yobo's Great Adventure, 6423(F)
Norby Finds a Villain, 6424(F)
Asimov, Isaac (ed.). *Young Extraterrestrials*, 6419(F)
Young Witches and Warlocks, 5349(F)
Asimov, Janet. *Norby and the Invaders*, 6422(F)
Norby and the Terrified Taxi, 6420(F)
Norby and Yobo's Great Adventure, 6423(F)
Norby Finds a Villain, 6424(F)
The Package in Hyperspace, 6421(F)
Aspinwall, Margaret. *Alexander Calder and His Magical Mobiles*, 7621
Athans, Sandra K. *Tales from the Top of the World*, 13489
Atkin, S. Beth. *Gunstories*, 10937

Atkins, Jeannine. *Borrowed Names*, 6997
Atkinson, Elizabeth. *From Alice to Zen and Everyone in Between*, 1840(F)
I, Emma Freke, 1232(F)
Atlema, Martha. *A Time to Choose*, 5192(F)
Attie, Alice. *Harlem on the Verge*, 10428
Atwater-Rhodes, Amelia. *Hawksong*, 2597(F)
Midnight Predator, 2598(F)
Persistence of Memory, 5350(F)
Token of Darkness, 5351(F)
Atwood, Jane. *Capoeira*, 13530
Atwood, Megan. *The Haunting of Apartment 101*, 5352(F)
Auch, M. J. *Guitar Boy*, 1233(F)
Auch, Mary Jane. *Seven Long Years Until College*, 1841(F)
Aue, Pamela Willwerth (ed.). *Teen Drug Abuse*, 11479
Auerbacher, Inge. *I Am a Star*, 9485
Augarde, Steve. *Celandine*, 2599(F)
Celandine, 2601(F)
Leonardo da Vinci, 7636
The Various, 2600(F)
The Various, 2601(F)
Winter Wood, 2601(F)
X-Isle, 2602(F)
Augustin, Byron. *Iraq*, 9898
Auseon, Andrew. *Alienated*, 6640(F)
Austen, Catherine. *Walking Backward*, 1234(F)
Auxier, Jonathan. *Peter Nimble and His Fantastic Eyes*, 2603(F)
Avakian, Monique. *A Historical Album of Massachusetts*, 10429
Aveline, Erick. *Temporary Tattoos*, 13195
Avi. *Beyond the Western Sea*, 4725(F)
Bright Shadow, 2604(F)
Captain Grey, 16(F)
City of Light, City of Dark, 3847(F)
City of Orphans, 4931(F)
Crispin, 4205(F)
Crispin, 4361(F)
Devil's Race, 5353(F)
The Fighting Ground, 4692(F)
Iron Thunder, 4785(F)
The Man Who Was Poe, 2605(F)
Midnight Magic, 5857(F)
Murder at Midnight, 5857(F)
Night Journeys, 4651(F)
A Place Called Ugly, 1842(F)
Punch with Judy, 5650(F)
Romeo and Juliet, 5651(F)
The Seer of Shadows, 5354(F)
Something Upstairs, 5355(F)
Sophia's War: A , 4693(F)
Strange Happenings, 2606(F)
The Traitors' Gate, 4362(F)
The True Confessions of Charlotte Doyle, 4726(F)
Who Was That Masked Man, Anyway?, 5193(F)
Windcatcher, 17(F)

Avi, sel. *Best Shorts*, 6862(F)
Avila, Kat (ed.). *Mexican Ghost Tales of the Southwest*, 7302
Axelrod, Amy. *Your Friend in Fashion, Abby Shapiro*, 1843(F)
Axelrod, Toby. *Hans and Sophie Scholl*, 8921
Axelrod-Contrada, Joan. *Women Who Led Nations*, 8785
Ayer, Eleanor H. *The Anasazi*, 10084
Aykroyd, Clarissa. *Julia Alvarez*, 7707
Refugees, 10829
Ayodo, Awuor. *Luo*, 9593
Aziz, Laurel. *Hummingbirds*, 12484
Azuonye, Chukwuma. *Dogon*, 9634
Edo, 9654

Babbitt, Natalie. *The Search for Delicious*, 2607(F)
Baccalario, Pierdomenico. *City of Wind*, 18(F)
Ring of Fire, 18(F)
Star of Stone, 18(F)
Bach, Shelby. *Of Giants and Ice*, 2608(F)
Bachel, Beverly K. *What Do You Really Want? How to Set a Goal and Go for It!*, 12011
Bachmann, Stefan. *The Peculiar*, 2609(F)
Bacigalupi, Paolo. *Ship Breaker*, 6425(F)
Badcott, Nicholas. *Pocket Timeline of Islamic Civilizations*, 9263
Badillo, Steve. *Skateboarding*, 13549
Badoe, Adwoa. *Between Sisters*, 4252(F)
Baer, Marianna. *Frost*, 5356(F)
Baer, Nadja. *The United States Constitution*, 10623
Bagert, Brod. *Hormone Jungle*, 1844(F)
Baggott, Julianna. *The Prince of Fenway Park*, 2610(F)
Bagnold, Enid. *National Velvet*, 323(F)
Bailey, Diane. *How Markets Work*, 11223
Suzanne Collins, 7729
Venus and Serena Williams, 8749
Bailey, Em. *Shift*, 471(F)
Bailey Hutchinson, Kay. *Leading Ladies*, 8011
Bailey, Jacqui. *Sex, Puberty and All That Stuff*, 11947
Taking Action Against Drugs, 11480
Bailey, LaWanda. *Miss Myrtle Frag, the Grammar Nag*, 7443
Bailey, Ronald H. *The Bloodiest Day*, 10237
Bailey-Williams, Nicole. *A Little Piece of Sky*, 1056(F)
Bain, Terry. *You Are a Dog (Life Through the Eyes of Man's Best Friend)*, 12621
Baird, Thomas. *Finding Fever*, 19(F)

Barnaby, Hannah. *Wonder Show*, 5020(F)

Barnard, Bryn. *The Genius of Islam*, 9264

Outbreak! Plagues That Changed History, 11565

Barnden, Betty. *Very Easy Crazy Patchwork*, 13279

Barnes, Derrick. *We Could Be Brothers*, 1057(F)

Barnes, Jennifer Lynn. *Enthralled*, 5358(F)

Every Other Day, 5357(F)

Fate, 2628(F)

Nobody, 2629(F)

Tattoo, 2628(F)

Tattoo, 2630(F)

Barnes, Rachel. *Abstract Expressionists*, 7583

Barnes, Simon. *Planet Zoo*, 12516

Barnes, Trevor. *Islam*, 10567

Barnett, Lincoln. *The Universe of Dr. Einstein*, 12853

Barney, William L. *The Civil War and Reconstruction*, 10238

Barnhill, Kelly. *Iron Hearted Violet*, 2631(F)

The Mostly True Story of Jack, 2632(F)

Barnholdt, Lauren. *The Secret Identity of Devon Delaney*, 1845(F)

Barnhouse, Rebecca. *The Coming of the Dragon*, 2633(F)

Peaceweaver, 2633(F)

Barnum, P. T. *Barnum's Own Story*, 8004

Baroin, Catherine. *Tubu*, 9584

Baron, Kathi. *Shattered*, 1238(F)

Baron, Nancy. *Getting Started in Calligraphy*, 13217

Barr, Matt. *Snowboarding*, 13554

Barraclough, Lindsey. *Long Lankin*, 5359(F)

Barratt, Mark. *Joe Rat*, 4368(F)

Barrett, Paul. *National Geographic Dinosaurs*, 9188

Barrett, Tracy. *The Ancient Greek World*, 9397

Cold in Summer, 5360(F)

Dark of the Moon, 2634(F)

King of Ithaka, 2635(F)

On Etruscan Time, 2636(F)

Virginia, 10486

Barrett, William E. *The Lilies of the Field*, 1058(F)

Barrie, J. M. *Peter Pan*, 407(F)

Peter Pan, 408(F)

Barron, T. A. , 2638(F)

The Ancient One, 2637(F)

Doomraga's Revenge, 2645(F)

Doomraga's Revenge, 2639(F)

The Eternal Flame, 2640(F)

The Fires of Merlin, 2641(F)

The Great Tree of Avalon, 2642(F)

The Lost Years of Merlin, 2643(F)

The Merlin Effect, 2644(F)

Merlin's Dragon, 2645(F)

The Mirror of Merlin, 2646(F)

The Seven Songs of Merlin, 2647(F)

Shadows on the Stars, 2648(F)

Tree Girl, 2649(F)

The Wings of Merlin, 2650(F)

Barrow, Randi. *Saving Zasha*, 5194(F)

Barrowman, Carole E. *Hollow Earth*, 2651(F)

Barrowman, John. *Hollow Earth*, 2651(F)

Barry, Dave. *Peter and the Secret of Rundoon*, 2652(F)

Peter and the Shadow Thieves, 2653(F)

Science Fair, 5653(F)

Barshaw, Ruth McNally. *Ellie McDoodle*, 475(F)

Bartek, Mary. *Funerals and Fly Fishing*, 1846(F)

Barter, James. *Abraham Lincoln*, 8177

The Ancient Persians, 9323

Hallucinogens, 11482

A Medieval Knight, 9423

Space Stations, 12228

Barth-Grozinger, Inge. *Something Remains*, 1059(F)

Bartoletti, Susan Campbell. *The Boy Who Dared*, 5195(F)

Growing Up in Coal Country, 10316

Hitler Youth, 9787

Kids on Strike!, 10317

They Called Themselves the K.K.K., 10854

Barton, Chris. *Can I See Your I.D.? True Stories of False Identities*, 11065

Barwin, Gary. *Seeing Stars*, 1239(F)

Barwin, Steven. *Icebreaker*, 6712(F)

Slam Dunk, 6713(F)

Basel, Roberta. *Sequoyah*, 8338

Basher, Simon. *Human Body*, 11762

Rocks and Minerals, 12760

Baskett, John. *The Horse in Art*, 9068

Baskett, Mickey. *Jazzy Jeans*, 13196

Baskin, Nora Raleigh. *All We Know of Love*, 1847(F)

Anything But Typical, 1659(F)

Basketball (or Something Like It), 6714(F)

The Summer Before Boys, 1848(F)

The Truth about My Bat Mitzvah, 1060(F)

Basman, Michael. *Chess for Kids*, 13499

Bass, Ruth. *Sarah's Daughter*, 4932(F)

Bassis, Volodymyr. *Ukraine*, 9826

Bastedo, Jamie. *Tracking Triple Seven*, 324(F)

Basye, Dale E. *Blimpo*, 2654(F)

Fibble: The Fourth Circle of Heck, 2654(F)

Rapacia, 2655(F)

Snivel, 2656(F)

Bat-Ami, Miriam. *Two Suns in the Sky*, 6292(F)

Batalden, Sandra L. *The Newly Independent States of Eurasia*, 9827

Batalden, Stephen K. *The Newly Independent States of Eurasia*, 9827

Bateman, Colin. *Running with the Reservoir Pups*, 2657(F)

Bateman, Robert. *Bateman's Backyard Birds*, 12485

Bateson, Catherine. *The Boyfriend Rules of Good Behavior*, 1849(F)

Stranded in Boringsville, 476(F)

Bath, K. P. *Escape from Castle Cant*, 5654(F)

Batmanglij, Najmieh. *Happy Nowruz*, 10515

Batson, Wayne Thomas. *The Rise of the Wyrm Lord*, 2658(F)

Batten, Jack. *The Man Who Ran Faster Than Everyone*, 8753

Silent in an Evil Time, 8876

Batten, Mary. *Anthropologist*, 9213

Bauer, A. C. E. *Come Fall*, 2659(F)

Gil Marsh, 477(F)

No Castles Here, 1850(F)

Bauer, Cat. *Harley, Like a Person*, 1240(F)

Bauer, Hans. *Fishtale*, 21(F)

Bauer, Joan. *Almost Home*, 1241(F)

Backwater, 1242(F)

Best Foot Forward, 478(F)

Close to Famous, 1851(F)

Hope Was Here, 479(F)

Peeled, 5861(F)

Rules of the Road, 1243(F)

Stand Tall, 1244(F)

Bauer, Marion Dane. *Killing Miss Kitty and Other Sins*, 5091(F)

Land of the Buffalo Bones, 4848(F)

On My Honor, 480(F)

Our Stories, 7461

Shelter from the Wind, 1245(F)

Touch the Moon, 2660(F)

What's Your Story? A Young Person's Guide to Writing Fiction, 11261

A Writer's Story from Life to Fiction, 11262

Bauer, Marion Dane (ed.). *Am I Blue?*, 6863(F)

Baum, L. Frank. *The Wonderful Wizard of Oz*, 2661(F)

The Wonderful Wizard of Oz, 2662(F)

Bausum, Ann. *Denied, Detained, Deported*, 10831

Dragon Bones and Dinosaur Eggs, 8459

Freedom Riders, 10760

Marching to the Mountaintop, 10374

Muckrakers, 7484

Our Country's First Ladies, 8013

Our Country's Presidents, 10645

Unraveling Freedom, 10340

With Courage and Cloth, 10761

Bavati, Robyn. *Dancing in the Dark*, 1061(F)

Bawden, Nina. *Carrie's War*, 5196(F)

908

Coakley, Lena. *Witchlanders*, 2807(F)
Coates, Jennifer. *Lizards*, 12401
Cobain, Bev. *When Nothing Matters Anymore*, 11826
Cobb, Allan B. *Cadmium*, 12667
Earth Chemistry, 12668
Super Science Projects About Animals and Their Habitats, 12372
Super Science Projects About Oceans, 12833
Cobb, Katie. *Happenings*, 551(F)
Cobb, Vicki. *Chemically Active! Experiments You Can Do at Home*, 12669
Fireworks, 12923
How to Really Fool Yourself, 11806
Magic . . . Naturally! Science Entertainments and Amusements, 13256
The Secret Life of Hardware, 12175
We Dare You! Hundreds of Science Bets, Challenges, and Experiments You Can Do at Home, 12176
Coben, Harlan. *Seconds Away*, 5902(F)
Shelter, 5903(F)
Coburn, Ann. *Glint*, 5904(F)
Coburn, Broughton. *Triumph on Everest*, 7547
Cochran, Molly. *Legacy*, 5393(F)
Cochrane, Mick. *Fitz*, 552(F)
The Girl Who Threw Butterflies, 553(F)
Cocke, William. *A Historical Album of Virginia*, 10488
Cody, Matthew. *The Dead Gentleman*, 5394(F)
Powerless, 2808(F)
Super, 2809(F)
Coerr, Eleanor. *Mieko and the Fifth Treasure*, 5210(F)
Cofer, Judith Ortiz. *Call Me María*, 1075(F)
If I Could Fly, 1076(F)
An Island Like You, 1077(F)
Cofer, Judith Ortiz (ed.). *Riding Low on the Streets of Gold*, 10901
Coffelt, Nancy. *Listen*, 1676(F)
Coffey, Jan. *Tropical Kiss*, 6304(F)
Coffey, Wayne. *The Boys of Winter*, 13543
Cohen, Charles D. *The Seuss, the Whole Seuss, and Nothing but the Seuss*, 7764
Cohen, Daniel. *Cloning*, 11732
Cults, 10590
Prophets of Doom, 13321
Southern Fried Rat and Other Gruesome Tales, 7304
Yellow Journalism, 7487
Cohen, Miriam. *Robert and Dawn Marie 4Ever*, 1919(F)
Cohen, Tish. *The Invisible Rules of the Zoe Lama*, 554(F)
Little Black Lies, 555(F)

Cohen-Posey, Kate. *How to Handle Bullies, Teasers and Other Meanies*, 12027
Cohn, Rachel. *Pop Princess*, 1920(F)
The Steps, 1293(F)
Two Steps Forward, 1294(F)
You Know Where to Find Me, 1295(F)
Cohon, Rhody. *Hot Pursuit*, 10769
Colasanti, Susane. *Take Me There*, 1921(F)
Waiting for You, 6305(F)
Colbert, David. *Anne Frank*, 8890
The Magical Worlds of Harry Potter, 13257
Michelle Obama, 8204
Colbert, Nancy. *The Firing on Fort Sumter*, 10244
Cole, Barbara. *Alex the Great*, 1677(F)
Cole, Brock. *The Goats*, 1922(F)
Cole, Carolyn Kozo. *Shades of L.A.*, 10856
Cole, Harriette. *Coming Together*, 10868
Cole, Joanna (ed.). *Best-Loved Folktales of the World*, 7172
Cole, Melanie. *Famous People of Hispanic Heritage*, 10902
Cole, Michael D. *Eye on the Universe*, 12207
Hubble Space Telescope, 12208
Cole, Stephen. *Thieves Like Us*, 556(F)
Thieves till We Die, 49(F)
Cole, Steve. *Z. Rex*, 5395(F)
Coleman, Alice Scovell. *Engraved in Stone*, 2810(F)
Coleman, Evelyn. *Freedom Train*, 5098(F)
Coleman, Janet Wyman. *Secrets, Lies, Gizmos, and Spies*, 11070
Coleman, Lori. *Soccer*, 13563
Vietnamese in America, 10891
Coleman, Rowan. *Ruby Parker Hits the Small Time*, 1923(F)
Coleman, Wim. *The Alamo*, 10505
The Amazing Erie Canal and How a Big Ditch Opened Up the West, 10208
Colonial Williamsburg, 10489
What Made the Wild West Wild, 10279
Coleridge, Samuel Taylor. *Samuel Taylor Coleridge*, 7084
Coles, Robert. *The Youngest Parents*, 11921
Coley, Mary McIntyre. *Environmentalism*, 10978
Colfer, Eoin. *The Arctic Incident*, 2811(F)
Artemis Fowl, 2812(F)
Artemis Fowl, 2813(F)
Artemis Fowl, 3868(F)
The Atlantis Complex, 2814(F)
Benny and Babe, 557(F)
Benny and Omar, 558(F)
The Eternity Code, 2815(F)
The Lost Colony, 2816(F)

The Opal Deception, 2817(F)
The Supernaturalist, 3869(F)
The Supernaturalist, 6460(F)
The Time Paradox, 2818(F)
The Wish List, 5396(F)
Collard, Sneed B. *Double Eagle*, 5905(F)
Global Warming, 10979
The Governor's Dog Is Missing!, 5906(F)
Hangman's Gold, 5907(F)
Lizards, 12402
Pocket Babies and Other Amazing Marsupials, 12480
The Prairie Builders, 12750
Science Warriors, 12309
Collard, Sneed B, III. *Dog Sense*, 1924(F)
Flash Point, 559(F)
On the Coral Reefs, 12555
Collier, Christopher. *My Brother Sam Is Dead*, 4697(F)
With Every Drop of Blood, 4790(F)
Collier, James Lincoln. *The Corn Raid*, 4655(F)
The Dreadful Revenge of Ernest Gallen, 5908(F)
Me and Billy, 4855(F)
My Brother Sam Is Dead, 4697(F)
Outside Looking In, 1296(F)
Wild Boy, 4856(F)
With Every Drop of Blood, 4790(F)
Collier, Kristi. *Throwing Stones*, 1925(F)
Colligan, L. H. *Mercury*, 12284
Collins, Ace. *Blackball Superstars*, 13440
Collins, Amberly. *Final Touch*, 5909(F)
Collins, Brandilyn. *Final Touch*, 5909(F)
Collins, David R. *Casimir Pulaski*, 8915
Grover Cleveland, 8149
Tiger Woods, Golfing Champion, 8779
Washington Irving, 7782
Write a Book for Me, 7773
Zachary Taylor, 8232
Collins, Martin. *After Sputnik*, 12232
Collins, Mary. *Airborne*, 8645
Collins, Pat Lowery. *The Fattening Hut*, 2491(F)
Hidden Voices, 4385(F)
Collins, Paul. *The Skyborn*, 6461(F)
Collins, Ross. *Medusa Jones*, 5675(F)
Collins, Suzanne. *Gregor and the Code of Claw*, 2819(F)
Gregor and the Marks of Secret, 2820(F)
Gregor the Overlander, 2821(F)
The Hunger Games, 6462(F)
Mockingjay, 2822(F)
Collins, Terry. *King of Pop*, 7943
Collins, Yvonne. *The Black Sheep*, 1297(F)
Introducing Vivien Leigh Reid, 560(F)

Geary, Rick. *The Case of Madeleine Smith*, 3911(F)
Great Expectations. Rev. ed., 3912(F)
Gedney, Mona. *The Life and Times of Buddha*, 8835
Gee, Maurice. *Salt*, 2992(F)
Geiger, Beth. *Clean Water*, 11043
Geiger, John. *Buried in Ice*, 9943
Geithner, Carole. *If Only*, 1373(F)
Gelber, Carol. *Love and Marriage Around the World*, 11180
Masks Tell Stories, 9281
Gelletly, LeeAnne. *Gift of Imagination*, 7741
Gendell, Megan. *The Spanish Missions of California*, 10469
The Spanish Misssions of Texas, 10506
Genge, N. E. *The Book of Shadows*, 13327
Gentry, Sarah E, et al. *Internet Addiction and Online Gaming*, 13000
Living with the Internet, 13000
George, Charles. *Maya Civilization*, 9330
Pyramids, 9032
George, Charles (ed.). *Living through the Civil Rights Movement*, 10780
George, Elizabeth. *The Edge of Nowhere*, 5976(F)
George, Jean Craighead. *The Cry of the Crow*, 336(F)
Frightful's Mountain, 337(F)
Julie of the Wolves, 81(F)
Julie's Wolf Pack, 82(F)
Pocket Guide to the Outdoors, 13494
Shark Beneath the Reef, 83(F)
The Talking Earth, 84(F)
Water Sky, 85(F)
George, Jessica Day. *Dragon Flight*, 2993(F)
Dragon Flight, 2995(F)
Dragon Slippers, 2994(F)
Dragon Slippers, 2995(F)
Dragon Spear, 2995(F)
Princess of the Midnight Ball, 2996(F)
Sun and Moon, Ice and Snow, 2997(F)
Tuesdays at the Castle, 2998(F)
George, Kristine O'Connell. *Swimming Upstream*, 7009
George, Linda. *Maya Civilization*, 9330
George, Madeleine. *The Difference between You and Me*, 2021(F)
Looks, 655(F)
George, Twig C. *Pocket Guide to the Outdoors*, 13494
George-Kanentiio, Douglas M. *Skywoman*, 7294
George-Warren, Holly. *The Cowgirl Way*, 8024
Shake, Rattle and Roll, 9121
Gephart, Donna. *How to Survive Middle School*, 2022(F)

Olivia Bean, Trivia Queen, 2023(F)
Gerardi, Dave. *Careers in the Computer Game Industry*, 11430
Geras, Adele. *Pictures of the Night*, 6326(F)
The Tower Room, 6327(F)
Gerber, Larry. *The Second Amendment*, 10632
Gerber, Linda. *Death by Bikini*, 5977(F)
Death by Bikini, 5978(F)
Death by Denim, 5978(F)
Death by Latte, 5978(F)
Gerberg, Mort. *The U.S. Constitution for Everyone*, 10633
Gerdes, Louise I. (ed.). *The Cold War*, 9572
Gangs, 11073
Rogue Nations, 10608
German, Carol. *A Midsummer Night's Dork*, 656(F)
German, Dave. *Dave Gorman's Googlewhack! Adventure*, 12990
Gerrold, David. *Blood and Fire*, 6494(F)
Chess with a Dragon, 6495(F)
Gerson, Corrine. *My Grandfather the Spy*, 5979(F)
Gerson, Mary-Joan. *Fiesta Feminina*, 7276
Gerstenfeld, Sheldon L. *The Cat Care Book*, 12615
The Dog Care Book, 12625
Gervay, Susanne. *Butterflies*, 2024(F)
Getzinger, Donna. *Antonio Vivaldi and the Baroque Tradition*, 7895
George Frideric Handel and Music for Voices, 7888
Johann Sebastian Bach and the Art of Baroque Music, 7876
Geus, Mireille. *Piggy*, 1708(F)
Gewirtz, Elaine Waldorf. *The Chihuahua*, 12626
Fetch This Book, 12627
Ghent, Natale. *No Small Thing*, 338(F)
Piper, 339(F)
Gherman, Beverly. *Anne Morrow Lindbergh*, 7553
Norman Rockwell, 7684
Sparky, 7687
Ghislain, Gary. *How I Stole Johnny Depp's Alien Girlfriend*, 6496(F)
Giacobello, John. *Bodyguards*, 11399
Careers in the Fashion Industry, 11323
Everything You Need to Know About Anxiety and Panic Attacks, 11834
Everything You Need to Know About the Dangers of Overachieving, 11835
Giallongo, Zack. *Broxo*, 3913(F)
Gibbons, Whit. *Their Blood Runs Cold*, 12391
Gibbs, Stuart. *Belly Up*, 5980(F)
The Last Musketeer, 2999(F)
Spy School, 5981(F)

Giblin, James Cross. *Charles A. Lindbergh*, 7555
Good Brother, Bad Brother, 8362
The Life and Death of Adolf Hitler, 8902
The Many Rides of Paul Revere, 8392
The Rise and Fall of Senator Joe McCarthy, 8317
Secrets of the Sphinx, 9363
Gibsen, Cole. *Katana*, 3000(F)
Gibson, Karen Bush. *Ancient Babylon*, 9906
Jovita Idar, 8101
The Life and Times of Eli Whitney, 8643
Native American History for Kids, 10098
Gibson, Marley. *The Awakening*, 5431(F)
The Other Side, 13328
Gibson, Phil. *Natural Selection*, 9217
Gibson, Terri R. *Natural Selection*, 9217
Giddens, Owen. *Coping with Grieving and Loss*, 11467
Future Techniques in Surgery, 11711
Volleyball, 13583
Giddens, Sandra. *Coping with Grieving and Loss*, 11467
Future Techniques in Surgery, 11711
Volleyball, 13583
Gideon, Melanie. *Pucker*, 6497(F)
Gidwitz, Adam. *In a Glass Grimmly*, 5689(F)
A Tale Dark and Grimm, 5432(F)
A Tale Dark and Grimm, 5689(F)
Gier, Kerstin. *Ruby Red*, 3001(F)
Gies, Miep. *Anne Frank Remembered*, 9510
Gifaldi, David. *Yours Till Forever*, 5433(F)
Giff, Patricia Reilly. *Don't Tell the Girls*, 7765
Hunter Moran Saves the Universe, 5690(F)
Lily's Crossing, 5225(F)
Pictures of Hollis Woods, 1374(F)
R My Name Is Rachel, 5040(F)
Storyteller, 4704(F)
Water Street, 4951(F)
Giffen, Keith. *Road Trip*, 4123(F)
Gifford, Clive. *The Arms Trade*, 13089
Child Labor, 10781
Golf, 13511
The Kingfisher Book of Soccer Skills, 13564
The Kingfisher Soccer Encyclopedia, 13565
1000 Years of Famous People, 7502
Pollution, 11044
Poverty, 11137
Racing, 13432
Spies, 11080
10 Explorers Who Changed the World, 7509
10 Kings and Queens Who Changed the World, 8794

Hades, 4023

Hera, 4024(F)

O'Connor, Frances. *The History of Islam*, 10575

O'Connor, Jane. *If the Walls Could Talk*, 8055

An Inconvenient Truth, 10984

O'Connor, Sheila. *Keeping Safe the Stars*, 5146(F)

O'Connor, Barbara. *Leonardo da Vinci*, 7641

O'Connor, Sheila. *Sparrow Road*, 1543(F)

O'Connor, George. *Zeus*, 4025

O'Daly, Anne. *Sodium*, 12680

O'Dell, Kathleen. *The Aviary*, 3458(F)

O'Dell, Scott. *The Black Pearl*, 221(F)

Black Star, Bright Dawn, 222(F)

The Captive, 4596(F)

Island of the Blue Dolphins, 223(F)

The King's Fifth, 4597(F)

Sarah Bishop, 4713(F)

Sing Down the Moon, 4636(F)

Streams to the River, River to the Sea, 4907(F)

Thunder Rolling in the Mountains, 4637(F)

Odinoski, Steve. *Georgia*, 10497

O'Donnell, Liam. *Max Finder Mystery*, 4026(F)

Soccer Sabotage, 4027(F)

Odyssey, Shawn Thomas. *The Wizard of Dark Street*, 6135(F)

Ogbaa, Kalu. *Igbo*, 9663

Ogier, Susan. *Objects and Meanings*, 9063

People in Action, 9063

A Sense of Place, 9063

Talking Textiles, 9063

O'Grady, Kathleen (ed.). *Sweet Secrets*, 11968

O'Halloran, Barbara Collopy. *Creature Comforts*, 11991

O'Hara, Mary. *My Friend Flicka*, 376(F)

O'Hearn, Kate. *Kira*, 3459(F)

O'Hearn, Claudine Chiawei (ed.). *Half and Half*, 10861

Ojo, Onukaba A. *Mbuti*, 9616

Okamoto, Kazuhiro. *Translucent, Vol. 1*, 4028(F)

O'Kane, Bernard. *Treasures of Islam*, 9017

Oke, Janette. *Dana's Valley*, 1767(F)

O'Keefe, Sherry. *Aung San Suu Kyi*, 8829

O'Keefe, Susan Heyboer. *My Life and Death by Alexandra Canarsie*, 868(F)

Okeke, Chika. *Kongo*, 9617

Okey, Shannon. *Felt Frenzy*, 13280

Knitgrrl, 13285

Knitgrrl 2, 13286

Okimoto, Jean D. *Talent Night*, 1161(F)

Okorafor, Nnedi. *Akata Witch*, 3462(F)

Okorafor-Mbachu, Nnedi. *The Shadow Speaker*, 3460(F)

Zahrah the Windseeker, 3461(F)

Okum, David. *Manga Madness*, 13238

Oldfield, Jenny, comp. *The Kingfisher Book of Horse and Pony Stories*, 6918(F)

Oldham, June. *Found*, 6610(F)

Oleksy, Walter. *Business and Industry*, 11235

Olive, M. Foster. *Prescription Pain Relievers*, 11533

Oliver, Andrew. *If Photos Could Talk*, 6136(F)

Oliver, Lauren. *Liesl and Po*, 3463(F)

The Spindlers, 3464(F)

Ollhoff, Jim. *Hazmat*, 11333

Indian Mythology, 7340

Japanese Mythology, 7341

Mayan and Aztec Mythology, 7342

Middle Eastern Mythology, 7343

Olmstead, Kathleen. *Jacques Cousteau*, 8492

Matthew Henson, 7546

Olmstead, Mary. *Tito Puente*, 7983

Olney, Ross R. *The Farm Combine*, 12346

Olsen, Sylvia. *The Girl with a Baby*, 1162(F)

White Girl, 1163(F)

Olshan, Matthew. *Finn*, 224(F)

Olson, Arielle North. *More Bones*, 5526(F)

Olson, Arielle North (ed.). *Ask the Bones*, 5527(F)

Olson, Gretchen. *Call Me Hope*, 1544(F)

Olson, Steven P. *The Trial of John T. Scopes*, 10712

Olson, Tod. *How to Get Rich in the California Gold Rush*, 4757(F)

How to Get Rich on the Oregon Trail, 4908(F)

Olster, Fredi. *A Midsummer Night's Dream*, 7430

Romeo and Juliet, 7431

The Taming of the Shrew, 7432

Oluikpe, Benson O. *Swazi*, 9645

O'Meara, Stephen James. *Are You Afraid Yet? The Science Behind Scary Stuff*, 13353

Omololu, C. J. *Dirty Little Secrets*, 1545(F)

Omoto, Susan. *Hmong Milestones in America*, 10894

O'Neal, Eilis. *The False Princess*, 3465(F)

O'Neill, Catherine. *Amazing Mysteries of the World*, 13354

O'Neill, Joseph R. *The Bolshevik Revolution*, 9840

O'Neill, Thomas. *Lakes, Peaks, and Prairies*, 9936

O'Neill, Catherine. *Natural Wonders of North America*, 12699

O'Neill, Michael Patrick. *Wild Waters Photo Journal*, 12562

Ono, Fuyumi. *Ghost Hunt, Vol. 3*, 4029(F)

Oodgeroo. *Dreamtime*, 7241

Opie, Iona. *I Saw Esau*, 7093

Opie, Iona (ed.). *The Classic Fairy Tales*, 7194

Opie, Mary-Jane. *Sculpture*, 9078

Opie, Peter. *I Saw Esau*, 7093

Opie, Peter (ed.). *The Classic Fairy Tales*, 7194

Oppel, Kenneth. *Airborn*, 3466(F)

Darkwing, 377(F)

Half Brother, 869(F)

Skybreaker, 3466(F)

Skybreaker, 6611(F)

Starclimber, 3466(F)

This Dark Endeavor, 5528(F)

Oppenheim, Joanne. *Dear Miss Breed*, 10895

Oppenheim, Shulamith. *The Fish Prince and Other Stories*, 7201

O'Reilly, Bill. *Lincoln's Last Days*, 10265

Orenstein, Denise Gosliner. *The Secret Twin*, 6137(F)

Orgad, Dorit. *The Boy from Seville*, 4503(F)

Orgel, Doris. *The Princess and the God*, 3467(F)

Orlev, Uri. *The Island on Bird Street*, 5265(F)

The Lady with the Hat, 4504(F)

The Man from the Other Side, 5266(F)

Run, Boy, Run, 5267(F)

The Song of the Whales, 870(F)

Orndorff, John C. *Terrorists, Tornados, and Tsunamis*, 11944

Orr, Tamra. *Bangladesh*, 9701

California, 10476

Egyptian Islamic Jihad, 9881

The Food of China, 13180

Great Hispanic-Americans, 8058

How'd They Do That in Ancient Egypt?, 9382

The Korean Americans, 10845

The Life and Times of Susan B. Anthony, 8072

The Sirens, 7379

Ways to Help the Elderly, 11061

When the Mirror Lies, 11652

Wildfires, 12775

Orr, Wendy. *Peeling the Onion*, 1768(F)

Ortiz, Michael J. *Swan Town*, 4505(F)

Osa, Nancy. *Cuba 15*, 1164(F)

Osborne, Linda Barrett. *Miles to Go for Freedom*, 10883

Traveling the Freedom Road, 10330

Traveling the Freedom Road, 10883

Osborne, Mary Pope. *Haunted Waters*, 3468(F)

Osborne, Robert A. *75 Years of the Oscar*, 9166

O'Shea, Clare. *Cooking with Fruits and Vegetables*, 13173

Cooking with Meat and Fish, 13173

979

981

Tamar, Erika. *Good-bye, Glamour Girl*, 5294(F)
The Things I Did Last Summer, 2392(F)

Tan, Shaun. *The Arrival*, 4109(F)
The Bird King, 9020
Lost and Found, 2393(F)
The Red Tree, 1796(F)
Tales from Outer Suburbia, 4110(F)

Tanaka, Shelley. *Climate Change*, 11031
Mummies, 9255

Tanen, Sloane. *Are You Going to Kiss Me Now?*, 969(F)

Tanguay, Bridget. *Kenya*, 9627

Taniguchi, Tomoko. *Call Me Princess*, 4111(F)

Tanner, Lian. *Museum of Thieves*, 3689(F)

Tanzman, Carol M. *dancergirl*, 970(F)

Tarnowska, Wafa'. *The Arabian Nights*, 7236

Tarr, Bill. *Now You See It, Now You Don't! Lessons in Sleight of Hand*, 13260

Tarrant-Reid, Linda. *Discovering Black America*, 10073

Tarshis, Lauren. *Emma-Jean Lazarus Fell in Love*, 2394(F)
I Survived the Shark Attacks of 1916, 5076(F)

Tarshis, Thomas Paul. *Living with Peer Pressure and Bullying*, 12087

Taschek, Karen. *The Civil War*, 10274
Death Stars, Weird Galaxies, and a Quasar-Spangled Universe, 12220

Tashjian, Janet. *Fault Line*, 1797(F)
The Gospel According to Larry, 971(F)
Larry and the Meaning of Life, 972(F)
My Life as a Book, 973(F)
Vote for Larry, 974(F)

Tate, Eleanora E. *African American Musicians*, 7608
Celeste's Harlem Renaissance, 5077(F)

Tate, Nikki. *Behind the Scenes*, 13526

Tattersall, Clare. *Understanding Food and Your Family*, 11905

Taudte, Jeca. *MySpace/OurPlanet*, 11032

Taus-Bolstad, Stacy. *Pakistan in Pictures*. Rev. ed., 9743

Tayler, Kassy. *Ashes of Twilight*, 3690(F)

Tayleur, Karen. *Chasing Boys*, 6398(F)

Taylor, Barbara. *Be an Inventor*, 12945

Taylor, C. J. *Peace Walker*, 10122

Taylor, Charles A. *Juneteenth*, 11186

Taylor, Cora. *Murder in Mexico*, 6238(F)

Taylor, Dereen. *Nigeria*, 9667

Taylor, G. P. *Mariah Mundi*, 6239(F)
The Shadowmancer Returns, 3691(F)

Taylor, Greg. *Killer Pizza*, 3692(F)

Taylor, Joanne. *There You Are*, 4606(F)

Taylor, Julie. *The Girls' Guide to Friends*, 12088

Taylor, Kenny. *Puffins*, 12497

Taylor, Kim. *Bowery Girl*, 5009(F)
Cissy Funk, 5078(F)

Taylor, Kimberly H. *Black Abolitionists and Freedom Fighters*, 8062
Black Civil Rights Champions, 8063

Taylor, Laini. *Blackbringer*, 3696(F)
Daughter of Smoke and Bone, 3693(F)
Daughter of Smoke and Bone, 3694(F)
Days of Blood and Starlight, 3694(F)
Faeries of Dreamdark, 3695(F)
Lips Touch Three Times, 5606(F)
Silksinger, 3696(F)

Taylor, Marilyn. *Faraway Home*, 5295(F)

Taylor, Maureen. *Through the Eyes of Your Ancestors*, 13135

Taylor, Michelle A. *The Angel of Barbican High*, 1798(F)

Taylor, Mildred D. *The Land*, 5010(F)
The Road to Memphis, 1193(F)

Taylor, Peter Lane. *The Secret of Priest's Grotto*, 9850

Taylor, Robert. *The History of Terrorism*, 11219

Taylor, Sarah Stewart. *Amelia Earhart*, 5079(F)

Taylor, Terry. *Altered Art*, 13136

Taylor, Theodore. *Air Raid — Pearl Harbor*, 9555
Billy the Kid, 4919(F)
The Cay, 284(F)
Ice Drift, 285(F)
The Odyssey of Ben O'Neal, 286(F)
Tuck Triumphant, 393(F)

Tchana, Katrin Hyman. *Changing Woman and Her Sisters*, 7350
The Serpent Slayer and Other Stories of Strong Women, 7219

Te Kanawa, Kiri. *Land of the Long White Cloud*, 7242

Teague, Mark. *The Doom Machine*, 6672(F)

Tebbetts, Chris. *Middle School*, 2259(F)

Teeters, Peggy. *Jules Verne*, 7855

Tegner, Bruce. *Bruce Tegner's Complete Book of Jujitsu*, 13537
Bruce Tegner's Complete Book of Self-Defense, 13538
Karate, 13539
Self-Defense and Assault Prevention for Girls and Women, 13540

Tehanetorens. *Roots of the Iroquois*, 10123

Teichmann, Iris. *Immigration and the Law*, 10853

Teitelbaum, Michael. *Baseball*, 13460
Chinese Immigrants, 10897
Jackie Robinson, 8697
The Scary States of America, 5607(F)

Telep, Trisha (ed.). *The Eternal Kiss*, 3697(F)

Telgemeier, Raina. *Drama*, 4113(F)

Telgen, Diane. *Brown v. Board of Education*, 10722

Teller, Janne. *Nothing*, 975(F)

Temko, Florence. *Traditional Crafts from China*, 13137
Traditional Crafts from the Caribbean, 13138

Temple, Frances. *The Beduins' Gazelle*, 4243(F)
Grab Hands and Run, 2550(F)
The Ramsay Scallop, 4244(F)
Taste of Salt, 4607(F)
Tonight, by Sea, 2551(F)

Temple, Kathryn. *Drawing*, 13247

TenNapel, Doug. *Bad Island*, 4114(F)
Cardboard, 4115(F)
Ghostopolis, 4116(F)

Tennyson, Alfred Lord. *The Lady of Shalott*, 7094

Terban, Marvin. *The Dove Dove*, 7458

Terhune, Albert Payson. *Lad*, 394(F)

Testa, Dom. *The Cassini Code*, 6673(F)
The Comet's Curse, 6676(F)
The Comet's Curse, 6674(F)
The Galahad Legacy, 6675(F)
The Web of Titan, 6676(F)

Testa, Maria. *Something About America*, 10932

Tetzner, Lisa. *The Black Brothers*, 4117(F)

Thal, Lilli. *Mimus*, 4245(F)

Thaler, Shmuel. *Chris Mullin*, 8720
Photography, 13274

Tharp, Tim. *Knights of the Hill Country*, 6840(F)
The Spectacular Now, 2395(F)

Thayer, Ernest L. *Casey at the Bat*, 7161
Casey at the Bat, 7162

Thesman, Jean. *Cattail Moon*, 2396(F)
Couldn't I Start Over?, 2397(F)
In the House of the Queen's Beasts, 976(F)
The Last April Dancers, 1609(F)
Molly Donnelly, 5296(F)
The Other Ones, 3698(F)
Rachel Chance, 6240(F)
Who Said Life Is Fair?, 6399(F)

Thimmesh, Catherine. *Friends*, 12425
Girls Think of Everything, 12946
Lucy Long Ago, 9229
Madam President, 8064
The Sky's the Limit, 8451
Team Moon, 12257

Thomas, Carroll. *Blue Creek Farm*, 4841(F)

Thomas, Dylan. *A Child's Christmas in Wales*, 7095

Thomas, Elizabeth. *We Live in China*, 9686

Thomas, Jane Resh. *Behind the Mask*, 8887
Blind Mountain, 287(F)

998

Title Index

This index contains both main entry and internal titles cited in the entries. References are to entry numbers, not page numbers. All fiction titles are indicated by (F), following the entry number.

Subject/Grade Level Index

All entries are listed by subject and then according to grade level suitability (see the key at the foot of pages for grade level designations). Subjects are arranged alphabetically and subject heads may be subdivided into nonfiction (e.g., "Africa") and fiction (e.g. "Africa — Fiction"). References to entries are by entry number, not page number.

A

Aaron, Hank
IJ: 8677–88

Abandoned children — Fiction
IJ: 142
J: 1515
JS: 1248

Abbott, Berenice
J: 7611

Abdul, Paula
IJ: 7896

Abenaki Indians — Fiction
IJ: 1440, 5881

Abolitionists
JS: 10217

Abolitionists — Biography
IJ: 8077, 8086, 8102, 8122–23
J: 8084
JS: 8078, 8085

Abolitionists — Fiction
IJ: 4752
J: 4731

Aborigines — Folklore
J: 7241

Abortion
JS: 11917, 11928

Abortion — Fiction
JS: 2147

Abuse
JS: 11977

Abuse — Fiction
JS: 2037

Academic guidance
JS: 11301

Academy of Motion Picture Arts and Sciences
JS: 9166

Acadia — Fiction
J: 4588

Accidents
J: 12907

Accidents — Fiction
IJ: 1009, 1497
J: 2332, 6757
JS: 1761, 2010, 2024

Acting
IJ: 6960, 11374
J: 6950, 9181
JS: 6948, 6953, 6957, 9180

Acting — Biography
IJ: 7920, 7923, 7927, 7959, 7961, 7967, 7989
J: 7586, 7897–98, 7907, 7931–32, 7942, 7948, 7950, 7958, 7975, 7977, 7984–85
JS: 7929, 7976

Acting — Fiction
IJ: 748, 4998
J: 14, 528, 560–61, 1044, 1127, 1923, 5650
JS: 530, 562, 939, 1894, 2174, 2427, 6100

Activism
IJ: 10939, 11167, 11172–73, 11176
J: 10618, 10976, 11693
JS: 11160

Activism — Biography
IJ: 8959
J: 7950

Activism — Careers
JS: 11308

Activism — Fiction
IJ: 978
J: 876, 2535, 5799

Adams, Abigail
IJ: 8135, 8138

Adams, Ansel
J: 7612

Adams, John
IJ: 8138
J: 8137
JS: 8136

Adams, Samuel
IJ: 8249
J: 8250

Addams, Jane
IJ: 8070, 10413
J: 8071

Addictions
J: 11513
JS: 11461, 12015, 12015

Adoption
IJ: 12116
J: 12120
JS: 12112–13, 12115, 12134–35

Adoption — Fiction
See also Foster care
IJ: 393, 1341, 1377, 1494, 2153, 2449, 4485, 4905, 5029, 6040, 6805
J: 886, 1159, 1206, 1247, 1399, 1410, 1417, 1420, 1436, 1446, 1475, 2469, 4550, 5322
JS: 1314, 1445, 1615, 1656, 2499, 6522

Adventure stories — Fiction
See also Mystery stories — Fiction; Sea stories — Fiction; Survival stories — Fiction
IJ: 3, 6–7–8, 10, 17–18, 20, 27, 29, 33, 38, 45–46, 50, 53, 55, 58, 60, 63–64, 67–68, 72–73–74, 76, 81, 89, 93–94–95–96–97, 102–03, 107, 110, 113–14–15–16–17, 120, 122, 130, 139–40–41, 148, 150, 152, 156, 158, 160–61, 163, 169–70–71–72, 175, 177, 182, 189–90, 202–03, 205–06, 209, 211, 215, 219–20, 222–23, 225, 227, 240–41, 243–44, 247, 249–50, 254–55, 260, 264, 268–69, 271–72–73–74–75, 278, 280, 288, 291, 295, 297, 299–00, 305, 307, 313, 318, 320, 480, 492,

IJ = Upper Elementary/Lower Middle School; J = Middle School/Junior High; JS = Junior High/Senior High

1101

4730, 4751, 4771, 4786, 4790, 4805, 4909, 4963, 5082, 5135, 5139–40, 5159, 5290, 5447, 5518, 6008, 6722, 6785, 6804
JS: 448, 601, 702, 780, 782, 847, 999, 1056, 1058, 1083, 1086, 1099, 1110, 1119, 1126, 1133, 1141, 1148–49, 1154, 1191, 1193, 1199, 1204, 1207, 1349, 1487, 1700, 1735, 1759, 1981, 2098, 2175, 2191, 2234, 2426, 2450–51, 4686, 4718, 4759, 4875, 5010, 5096, 5116, 5141, 5340, 6803, 6912

African Americans — Folklore
IJ: 7305–06
JS: 7275

African Americans — Poetry
IJ: 7067, 7109, 7133, 7148, 7152–53
J: 7097, 7124, 7134
JS: 1191, 7103, 7117–18–19, 7155, 7165

African Burial Ground (New York City)
JS: 10875

Agassi, Andre
IJ: 8746

Agikuyu (African people)
J: 9610

Aging — Fiction
J: 2092
JS: 431

Agriculture
See also Farms and farm life
IJ: 12349, 12364

Ahmadinejad, Mahmoud
JS: 8826

AIDS
See also HIV (virus)
IJ: 11560, 11563
J: 11591, 11616, 11629, 11633
JS: 11575, 11608, 11686, 11694

AIDS — Fiction
IJ: 4255
J: 1172, 1359, 1534, 1787, 2527
JS: 2409, 2499, 4153

Air
IJ: 12799

Air Force
J: 10748

Air Force — Careers
IJ: 11318

Air Force (U.S.)
IJ: 9520, 10746
J: 11315

Air Force (U.S.) — Careers
J: 11315

Air Force (U.S.) — Fiction
J: 11

Air pollution
IJ: 11041, 12799
J: 11047, 12882

JS: 12793

Aircraft bird strikes
IJ: 12498

Airplane accidents
J: 13040, 13042

Airplane accidents — Fiction
J: 52, 1783

Airplane pilots
IJ: 7532, 8044, 13046
J: 9539

Airplane pilots — Biography
IJ: 7531, 7539–40–41–42, 8645, 8647–48, 8650, 8953
J: 7553, 7563, 8036
JS: 7505, 7554–55, 8646, 8649

Airplane pilots — Careers
JS: 11337

Airplane pilots — Fiction
IJ: 3880, 5079, 5319
J: 4261, 5290

Airplanes
IJ: 8429, 9471, 9474, 13036–37, 13041, 13044, 13044, 13047, 13049–50–51

Airplanes — Fiction
IJ: 1336, 4939

Airships
J: 13038

Akamba (African people)
J: 9631

Al Qaeda
IJ: 11213
J: 9731

Al-Haytham, Ibn
JS: 8456

Alabama
JS: 10763

Alabama — Fiction
IJ: 1084
JS: 2314

Alamo (TX) — Biography
IJ: 8949

Alamo, Battle of the
IJ: 10222, 10225, 10512
J: 10505

Alamo, Battle of the — Fiction
IJ: 4739

Alaska
IJ: 10466, 10474
JS: 7518, 10465

Alaska — Fiction
IJ: 29, 81, 222, 247, 365, 483, 3802, 4623, 4968, 6244
J: 79, 85, 134, 208, 265, 495, 5102
JS: 132

Alateen
J: 11546

Albania — Fiction
J: 5333

Alberta (Canada) — Fiction
IJ: 1611

Albinos — Fiction
J: 1697

Albright, Madeleine
J: 8251

Alcatraz Island
IJ: 10475

Alcatraz Island — Fiction
IJ: 39, 5028

Alchemy — Fiction
JS: 3603, 5528

Alcohol and alcohol abuse
IJ: 1526, 11501, 11538
J: 11475, 11477, 11481, 11488, 11492, 11492, 11502, 11505, 11505, 11509, 11509, 11546
JS: 2184, 11498, 11510, 11515, 11524, 11535, 11540, 11544

Alcohol and alcohol abuse — Biography
IJ: 8406

Alcohol and alcohol abuse — Fiction
IJ: 1316, 1380, 1507, 1980, 1996, 2035, 5022
J: 478, 1137, 1243, 1245, 1268, 1326, 1364, 1432, 1715, 1988, 5147
JS: 1043, 1370

Aleutian Islands (Alaska)
IJ: 9550

Alexander the Great
IJ: 8860, 8862–63–64, 8866–67
J: 8865
JS: 8861

Alexander the Great — Fiction
JS: 4187

Alexandria (Egypt)
J: 9379

Alexandrian Library
IJ: 9404

Algebra
J: 12786

Algeria — Fiction
JS: 4071

Algonquin Indians
IJ: 10117

Ali, Muhammad
IJ: 8725–26
J: 8724

Ali, Rubina
J: 7897

Aliens — Fiction
IJ: 6621

Allen, Ethan
IJ: 8252

IJ = Upper Elementary/Lower Middle School; J = Middle School/Junior High; JS = Junior High/Senior High

IJ = Upper Elementary/Lower Middle School; J = Middle School/Junior High; JS = Junior High/Senior High

IJ = Upper Elementary/Lower Middle School; J = Middle School/Junior High; JS = Junior High/Senior High

Asperger's syndrome
J: 11867
IJ: 11605

Asperger's syndrome — Fiction
IJ: 707, 1669, 1696

Assassinations — Fiction
J: 6189

Assassinations (U.S.)
IJ: 8178, 8181, 8305, 11122
J: 10260, 10377–78

Assisted suicide — Fiction
J: 616, 1752

Asteroids
IJ: 12265, 12298
J: 12262–63

Asthma
IJ: 11568, 11581, 11672
J: 11682
JS: 11567, 11647

Asthma — Fiction
J: 6336

Astrology
IJ: 13334
JS: 13366

Astronautics
J: 12247, 12247

Astronauts
IJ: 12236, 12769

Astronauts — Biography
IJ: 7522, 7564, 7570, 7572–73
J: 7510, 7520, 7571
JS: 8570

Astronomy
IJ: 12206, 12206, 12206, 12208,
12208, 12210, 12212–13, 12218,
12221–22–23–24, 12273, 12276–77,
12287, 12301
J: 8414, 12204, 12216, 12220, 12225,
12262, 12280
JS: 12209, 12215, 12219, 12261,
12274

Astronomy — Biography
IJ: 8477, 8491, 8549–50, 8566
J: 8414, 8454, 8476, 8548, 8551,
8560–61, 8567, 8577

Astronomy — Experiments and projects
JS: 12278

Astronomy — Fiction
IJ: 1554

Atalanta (Greek mythology)
JS: 7386

Athena (Greek deity) — Fiction
IJ: 4022

Athens (Greece)
IJ: 9818

Athletes
JS: 8658

Atlanta (GA)
IJ: 10502

Atlanta (GA) — Fiction
IJ: 5098

Atlantis
IJ: 13336, 13349

Atlantis (legendary place)
J: 13315

Atlases
J: 9183

Atmosphere
IJ: 12797, 12799
J: 12823

Atomic bomb
IJ: 9511, 9523
J: 9533, 10370, 13104
JS: 9490, 9493

Atomic bomb — Biography
J: 8608–09
JS: 8535

Atomic bomb — Fiction
IJ: 5210, 5317

Atoms
IJ: 12864
J: 12918
JS: 12873

Attention deficit hyperactivity disorder
IJ: 11865
J: 11825, 11827, 11829
JS: 11855, 11864

Attention deficit hyperactivity disorder — Fiction
IJ: 1284, 1367, 1705
J: 1399, 1769, 6769

Attila the Hun
IJ: 8828

Attorney General (U.S.)
J: 10660

Auditions
IJ: 11374

Audubon, John James
IJ: 7613

Aung San Suu Kyi
IJ: 8830
JS: 8829

Aunts — Fiction
IJ: 2080
J: 1428
JS: 737

Austen, Jane
J: 7711
JS: 7710

Austin, Stephen F.
IJ: 8257

Australia
IJ: 9751–52, 9754, 9756–57
J: 12432

Australia — Fiction
IJ: 472, 476, 490, 608, 1011, 1190,
2108, 2160, 4292, 4331, 4345
J: 145, 147, 183, 485, 1046–47, 1287,
1403, 1698, 1849, 2052, 2064, 2190,
2456, 2870, 4287, 4291, 4296, 4302,
4316, 4319, 4406, 5493, 5913, 5985,
6085, 6307
JS: 168, 184–85–86–87, 314, 509,
514, 801, 841, 1531, 1911, 2024, 2178,
2224, 3262, 3371–72, 4288, 4301,
4341, 5480, 5729

Australia — Folklore
JS: 7240

Austria
IJ: 9792

Austria — Biography
IJ: 8930

Austria — Fiction
IJ: 385, 4449, 4469
JS: 4408

Authors
IJ: 7417, 7478
J: 7589
JS: 7744, 7780, 7826, 7873

Authors — Biography
IJ: 7585, 7587–88, 7595, 7599–00,
7674, 7708, 7712, 7714, 7720–21,
7727–28, 7733, 7735, 7738, 7745,
7749–50, 7755, 7759, 7765–66, 7774,
7782, 7788–89, 7791, 7793–94–95,
7804–05, 7808, 7813, 7815, 7821–22,
7825, 7831, 7836, 7839–40–41–42–43,
7849, 7851–52, 7854–55, 7858–59–
60–61, 7865–66–67, 7869, 7875, 8132,
8320
J: 7553, 7584, 7601, 7606, 7706,
7709, 7711, 7713, 7715–16, 7718,
7722–23, 7726, 7729–30–31–32, 7734,
7741–42–43, 7747–48, 7754, 7756–57,
7767, 7772–73, 7776, 7779, 7784,
7786, 7790, 7792, 7799, 7801–02,
7814, 7817–18, 7820, 7824, 7827,
7832–33–34–35, 7837, 7844, 7847–48,
7856–57, 7868, 7871, 8083
JS: 7581, 7602, 7607, 7710, 7724,
7739–40, 7744, 7752–53, 7758, 7760,
7763–64, 7768, 7771, 7777–78,
7781, 7783, 7785, 7787, 7797–98,
7807, 7816, 7819, 7826, 7830, 7838,
7845–46, 7850, 7853, 7864, 7870,
7872, 13064

Authors — Criticism
JS: 7419

Authors — Fiction
IJ: 5704
J: 1286, 1525, 1983
JS: 4577

Autism
IJ: 11576, 11875
J: 11593, 11820, 11869
JS: 11858, 11868

Autism — Biography
IJ: 8373

Autism — Fiction
IJ: 799, 850, 1659, 5028
J: 1689, 1708

Autobiography
IJ: 7825
J: 11982

Automobile accidents — Fiction
J: 2189
JS: 1768, 2105, 6284

Automobile racing
IJ: 13304, 13433, 13435
J: 13428
JS: 13432

Automobile racing — Biography
IJ: 8670–71–72–73, 8675–76
J: 8674

Automobile racing — Fiction
J: 6755, 6769
JS: 6707, 6773, 6786, 6849, 6851

Automobile travel — Fiction
IJ: 1284, 1430
J: 25, 568, 906, 5643, 6391
JS: 743, 1663, 2360

Automobiles
IJ: 13057–58, 13062, 13434
J: 13054, 13056
JS: 13055, 13061

Automobiles — Biography
IJ: 8467, 8539

Avalanches — Fiction
IJ: 4589

Avalon — Fiction
IJ: 3425

Avery, Oswald
IJ: 8462

Avi (author)
IJ: 7712, 7714
J: 7713

Aviation
IJ: 13036, 13039, 13043, 13045–46, 13050

Aviation — Fiction
J: 1209

Azerbaijan
JS: 9844

Aztecs
IJ: 9335, 9965, 9970–71
J: 9327, 9338, 9349

Aztecs — Fiction
J: 4590

Aztecs — Folklore
J: 7203

Aztecs — Mythology
IJ: 7342
J: 4146, 7278, 7321

B

Babies — Fiction
IJ: 1219
J: 1886

Baboons
IJ: 12448

Baboons — Fiction
J: 3181

Babylon
IJ: 9906

***Babylon 5* (television series)**
JS: 9174

Babysitting
IJ: 11443, 11445–46–47
JS: 11444

Babysitting — Fiction
IJ: 3800, 5740, 6174
J: 1080, 1594, 2180, 5705
JS: 5437

Bach, Johann Sebastian
JS: 7876

Backpacking
JS: 13490

Bacon, Roger — Fiction
IJ: 4238

Bacteria
IJ: 11613, 11651, 12609

Badgers — Fiction
IJ: 3162
J: 334

Badminton
IJ: 13575

Baghdad (Iraq)
IJ: 12658

Bagpipes — Fiction
IJ: 5949

Baha'i (religion)
J: 10526
JS: 6980

Bahrain
JS: 9913

Baker, Ella
JS: 8074

Baking
JS: 13158

Baking — Fiction
IJ: 932, 1851
J: 621

Balanchine, George
J: 7904
JS: 7903

Bald eagles
IJ: 12505

Bali
IJ: 12347

Ball games
IJ: 13363, 13412

Ballet
IJ: 9151–52, 9156
JS: 9149, 9154–55

Ballet — Biography
IJ: 7900, 7994
J: 7899, 7904, 7924, 7965, 7978
JS: 7903, 7930

Ballet — Fiction
IJ: 1858, 2290, 4467, 6372
J: 643, 3979, 5155, 5370
JS: 1061, 1732, 1991, 2116

Balloon twisting
IJ: 13139

Balloons and ballooning
J: 10253

Ballroom dancing — Fiction
JS: 5925

Balls (sporting equipment)
IJ: 13363, 13412

Baltimore (MD) — Fiction
J: 5060

Baltimore Orioles (baseball team)
IJ: 13462

Bama, James
JS: 7614, 7614

Bananas
IJ: 12337

Bands (music)
IJ: 9123
J: 9111

Bands (music) — Fiction
JS: 5616

Bangladesh
J: 9701, 9706
JS: 9704

Bar mitzvah
IJ: 10588

Bar Mitzvah — Fiction
IJ: 508, 1011
J: 917

Barakat, Ibtisam
J: 8958

Barbarians
IJ: 9435

Barbaro (race horse)
IJ: 13525

Barber, Ronde — Fiction
IJ: 6709

Barber, Tiki — Fiction
IJ: 6709

Barbie dolls
J: 13215

Barnum, P. T.
IJ: 8005, 8005–06

JS: 8004

Barrie, J. M.
J: 7715

Barton, Clara
IJ: 8351–52
J: 8349–50

Baseball
IJ: 8662, 10676, 13437, 13439,
13443–44–45–46–47, 13450, 13453,
13455–56–57, 13460–61–62
J: 13440–41, 13451–52, 13459
JS: 13438, 13442, 13448, 13454,
13458

Baseball — Biography
IJ: 8652, 8655, 8662, 8677–78, 8680,
8682–83–84–85–86–87–88–89–90–
91–92–93, 8696–97, 8699–00, 8702,
8704–05, 8733, 13449–50
J: 8679, 8681, 8694, 8701, 8703
JS: 8657, 8668, 8695, 8698

Baseball — Fiction
IJ: 533, 912, 1325, 1570, 2610, 2701,
3027–28, 3031, 5221, 5692, 5959,
6727–28, 6733–34, 6738, 6764, 6770,
6775, 6778, 6787–88, 6805, 6810–11,
6813–14, 6818, 6822–23, 6825–26–27,
6832, 6843, 6858, 6889
J: 553, 766, 1129, 1790, 2194, 2232,
2399, 2990, 3881, 6729, 6746, 6757,
6765–66, 6789, 6800, 6824, 6841–42,
6845, 6854–55
JS: 2409, 4102, 6741, 6816, 6828,
6848, 6850

Baseball — Poetry
IJ: 7044, 7162
J: 7161

Baseball cards — Fiction
IJ: 6000

Baseball Hall of Fame
IJ: 13449

Basketball
IJ: 13463, 13471–72–73–74, 13476
J: 13466, 13469, 13475
JS: 13464–65, 13468, 13470

Basketball — Biography
IJ: 8261, 8663, 8706–07–08–09,
8712–13, 8715–16–17, 8720, 8722–23
J: 8262, 8710, 8714, 8718, 8721
JS: 8711, 8719

Basketball — Fiction
IJ: 1479, 2862, 5721, 6713, 6715,
6718–19–20, 6723, 6736, 6774, 6791,
6797, 6831, 6836
J: 1188, 1495, 1925, 2145, 2230, 6714,
6722, 6739, 6758, 6792, 6804, 6812
JS: 538, 1116, 1154, 1907, 4018,
6748–49, 6781, 6803, 6839

Basketball — Poetry
IJ: 7066
JS: 7108

Basotho (African people)
IJ: 9650

Basque separatists
IJ: 9864

Bass, Tom
IJ: 8762

Bat mitzvah
IJ: 10588

Bates, Daisy
JS: 8075

Bath — Fiction
J: 2763

Bathrooms
IJ: 12924

Batman (fictitious character)
JS: 4017, 4055

Bats (animal)
J: 12430
JS: 12433

Batswana (African people)
J: 9639

Battles (military)
See specific battles, e.g., Antietam,
Battle of
J: 9258
JS: 9273

Bauer, Marion Dane
IJ: 11262

Bay of Pigs
JS: 9978

Beads and beadwork
IJ: 13208
JS: 13198

Beagles — Fiction
IJ: 373

Bears
See also Polar bears
IJ: 12452–53–54, 12457, 12460
J: 12459, 12461

Bears — Fiction
IJ: 33, 140, 148, 351, 364, 5293

Beatles (musical group)
J: 7906
JS: 7905

Beaufort scale
IJ: 12795

Beauty
J: 11750
JS: 11752, 11760

Beauty — Fiction
J: 1156, 1444, 4147
JS: 5997

Beauty contests — Fiction
IJ: 1019
J: 595
JS: 32, 2314, 5711

Beck, Glenn
J: 8353

Beckwourth, James
IJ: 8354

Bees
IJ: 12543

Bees — Fiction
JS: 3255

Beethoven, Ludwig Van
IJ: 7877
J: 12940

Behavior
IJ: 12068
JS: 11991

Behavior — Fiction
J: 1774, 1889, 2183
JS: 662

Beijing (China)
IJ: 9675–76, 9684–85

Belize
IJ: 12727

Bell, Alexander Graham
IJ: 8463–64
J: 8465
JS: 8466

Bell, Cool Papa
IJ: 8680

Ben-Gurion, David
J: 9888

Benin
IJ: 9653

Benin — Folklore
IJ: 7217

Benjamin of Tudela — Fiction
IJ: 4241

Benz, Karl
IJ: 8467

Beowulf **— Adaptations**
IJ: 7265
J: 7256
JS: 7264

Berlin (Germany)
IJ: 9786

Berlin (Germany) — Fiction
IJ: 4507

Berlin Airlift
IJ: 9565

Berlin, Irving
J: 7878

Berlioz, Hector
IJ: 7879

Bermuda Triangle
J: 13314

Berners-Lee, Tim
IJ: 8468

Bernstein, Leonard
IJ: 7880
J: 7882
JS: 7881

Berry, Halle
J: 7907

IJ = Upper Elementary/Lower Middle School; J = Middle School/Junior High; JS = Junior High/Senior High

JS: 8474

Braces (dental)
IJ: 11802

Braces (dental) — Fiction
J: 2077

Bradbury, Ray
J: 7716

Bradford, William
IJ: 10143
J: 8260

Bradley, Bill
IJ: 8261
J: 8262

Brady, Mathew
J: 7618, 10230

Brahe, Tycho
IJ: 8477
J: 8476

Braille, Louis
IJ: 8870

Brain and nervous system
IJ: 11786
J: 11710, 11787
JS: 11800

Brain damage — Fiction
IJ: 1233, 2054
JS: 509

Brain tumors
JS: 11655

Branson, Richard
IJ: 8478

Brazil
IJ: 7320, 9990
J: 9991

Brazil — Biography
IJ: 8950
J: 8772

Brazil — Fiction
IJ: 4584, 6092

Brazil — Folklore
IJ: 7317

Bread and Roses Strike
J: 10315

Breast cancer
J: 11677, 11685
JS: 11697

Breasts
JS: 11782

Breazeal, Cynthia
J: 8479

Bridges
IJ: 12959, 12966
J: 10914

Bridgman, Laura
IJ: 8364

Brin, Sergey
J: 8432, 8453

JS: 8446

British Columbia
IJ: 12457

British Columbia — Fiction
IJ: 722, 4589

Broadcasting — Biography
J: 7594, 8409

Broadcasting — Careers
J: 11381
JS: 11312

Broadway — Fiction
JS: 752

Broadwick, Georgia "Tiny"
IJ: 8365

Bromine
IJ: 12691

Brontë family
J: 7717–18

Brontë family — Fiction
J: 4508, 5420

Bronte, Charlotte
JS: 7413

Bronx (NY) — Fiction
J: 2446

Bronze Age — Fiction
IJ: 234

Brooklyn (NY) — Fiction
IJ: 450, 935, 6764
J: 821, 983, 5128
JS: 4967

Brooklyn Bridge
IJ: 12966

Brooklyn Bridge — Fiction
IJ: 4951

Brooklyn Dodgers (baseball team) — Fiction
J: 6845

Brooks, Gwendolyn
J: 7719

Brothers — Biography
J: 7800

Brothers — Fiction
IJ: 502
J: 708, 2481, 2706
JS: 2419

Brothers and sisters — Fiction
IJ: 850, 985, 1284, 1342, 1529, 1600, 1917, 2254, 2281, 2290, 2663, 5028, 5432
J: 551, 644, 889, 954, 1166, 1257, 1282, 1397, 1444, 1541, 1557, 1592, 1629, 1633, 4282, 4340, 4417, 4506, 4868, 4959, 5128, 5321, 5338, 5914, 6108, 6755
JS: 575, 752, 760, 977, 1433, 1628, 2005, 5118, 5937, 5946

Brown v. Board of Education
IJ: 10698

JS: 10690, 10722

Brown, Helen Gurley
IJ: 8480

Brown, John
IJ: 8077
JS: 8078

Brown, John — Fiction
J: 4731
JS: 4766

Browning, Robert
JS: 7087

Bryan, Ashley
IJ: 7619

Bryant, Kobe
IJ: 8706

Bubonic plague — Fiction
IJ: 4412, 4444

Buddha
IJ: 8835

Buddhism
J: 10549, 10552
JS: 10530, 10536, 10540

Buddhism — Fiction
IJ: 4352

Buddhism — Folklore
IJ: 7223

Buffaloes
IJ: 12445

Buffaloes — Fiction
J: 4921

Buffett, Warren
JS: 8481

Building and construction
See also Architecture
IJ: 9024, 9026–27, 9034, 9356, 12929, 12959, 12961, 12964, 12970, 13309
J: 9033, 9035, 10914, 11314
JS: 10971, 12963

Building and construction — Biography
J: 8413

Building and construction — Careers
JS: 11343, 11391

Building and construction — Experiments and projects
IJ: 12955

Bulimia
IJ: 11670
J: 11574, 11594, 11637, 11680, 11689
JS: 11661

Bulimia — Fiction
J: 759, 1717, 1749

Bull-riding — Fiction
J: 1644

Bullets
IJ: 11125

Bullfighting — Fiction
IJ: 2461

Bullies and bullying
See also Cyberbullying
IJ: 11937, 12007, 12027, 12083
J: 12019, 12042, 12080, 12095
JS: 11985, 12036, 12087

Bullies and bullying — Fiction
IJ: 220, 492, 517, 540, 754, 961, 1492,
1969, 1979, 2007, 2035, 2262, 2288,
2292, 2312, 2354, 2381, 2472, 6822,
6836
J: 455, 603, 622, 703, 755, 773, 802,
889, 968, 1203, 1565, 1695, 1733,
1769, 1826, 1865, 1992, 2006, 2018,
2039, 2082, 2134, 2177, 2294, 2351,
2410, 5175
JS: 676, 696, 1707, 1737, 2229, 2258,
2424, 6742, 6864

Bunyan, Paul
J: 7314

Burial customs
J: 9227
JS: 11465

Buried treasure
IJ: 9247, 10414, 10444

Buried treasure — Fiction
IJ: 17, 75, 297–98, 307, 5952

Burma — Fiction
IJ: 4327, 5289

Burr, Aaron
J: 8059

Burroughs, John
IJ: 8482

Burton, Richard Francis
J: 7526

Bush, George H. W.
JS: 8139

Bush, George W.
IJ: 8140–41–42–43–44
JS: 10650

Bush, Laura Welch
IJ: 8145

Business — Biography
IJ: 7947, 8478
J: 8259, 8571
JS: 8471, 8481, 8636, 8651

Butler, Jerry
IJ: 9097

Butlers — Fiction
IJ: 5824

Butterflies and moths
IJ: 12546–47
JS: 12544

Byars, Betsy
IJ: 7720–21

Byrd, Admiral Richard Evelyn
IJ: 7527

C

Cabeza de Vaca, Alvar Nunez
IJ: 7528

Cactus
IJ: 12363

Cadmium
IJ: 12667

Caesar, Julius
IJ: 8871, 8873
J: 8872

Cahokia Mounds (IL)
IJ: 10093

Cairo (Egypt)
IJ: 9880

Cairo (Egypt) — Fiction
JS: 4509

Cajuns — Folklore
J: 7308

Calcines, Eduardo F.
J: 8933

Calcium
IJ: 12682

Calculation (mathematics)
IJ: 12784

Caldecott Medal
IJ: 7599

Caldecott, Randolph
J: 7620

Calder, Alexander
J: 7621

Calendars
IJ: 12772, 12784

California
IJ: 10463–64, 10467, 10469, 10476,
10478, 10482–83–84
J: 9140

California — Biography
IJ: 7575, 8344, 8937

California — Fiction
IJ: 39, 223, 1104, 1540, 4859, 4867,
4888, 5163
J: 1147, 2168, 2934, 4861, 4896, 6303,
6929
JS: 199, 523, 818, 854, 2436

California Indians
IJ: 10107

Calligraphy
IJ: 13217, 13236
J: 13143
JS: 13244

Calusa Indians — Fiction
IJ: 46

Cambodia
IJ: 9738
J: 9741

Cambodia — Biography
JS: 8975

Cambodia — Fiction
IJ: 4339
J: 4303–04

Cambodian Americans
IJ: 10840

Cambodian Americans — Fiction
J: 1130, 2332

Camden Yards (Baltimore)
IJ: 13462

Camels — Fiction
IJ: 4884

Cameroon
J: 9659
JS: 9600

Campbell, Ben Nighthorse
IJ: 8263

Campfires
IJ: 13493

Camps and camping
IJ: 13493
J: 13491

Camps and camping — Fiction
IJ: 73, 148, 482, 768, 1926, 1979,
4969, 5769
J: 308, 667, 776, 1922, 2053, 2399,
5175, 5406, 5763, 6002, 6131
JS: 42, 586, 2286

Canada
IJ: 9278, 9943
J: 9944, 9946, 9949–50–51–52
JS: 4762, 9936, 9945, 12458

Canada — Biography
IJ: 8659, 8745, 8774
J: 7801, 8752
JS: 8447, 8753

Canada — Fiction
IJ: 58, 64, 277, 660, 1036, 1200, 1202,
1509, 1601, 2078, 4566, 4569–70,
4573, 4582–83, 4587, 4606, 4608,
5057, 5739, 6267
J: 26, 212, 228, 1163, 1523, 1616,
1668, 1826, 2299, 4417, 4563–64,
4571, 4586, 4588, 4598, 4602, 4604–
05, 4609, 4611, 4653, 5241, 6875
JS: 78, 128, 392, 576, 1808, 1871,
4595, 5711, 6296

Canada, Geoffrey
JS: 8962

Canaletto
JS: 7622

Canals
J: 12968

Canals — Fiction
IJ: 4745

Cancer
IJ: 8760, 11625
J: 11635, 11690

IJ = Upper Elementary/Lower Middle School; J = Middle School/Junior High; JS = Junior High/Senior High

IJ = Upper Elementary/Lower Middle School; J = Middle School/Junior High; JS = Junior High/Senior High

IJ = Upper Elementary/Lower Middle School; J = Middle School/Junior High; JS = Junior High/Senior High

and specific civil righs, e.g., Human rights; Women's rights
IJ: 8106, 10373–74, 10376, 10765, 10769, 10775–76, 10778, 10785, 10791, 10810, 10812, 10819, 10821, 10826
J: 9144, 9946, 10375, 10681, 10687, 10757, 10760, 10764, 10773–74, 10790, 10794, 10796, 10798, 10806, 10814, 10818, 10883
JS: 10372, 10385, 10677, 10717, 10758–59, 10763, 10768, 10770, 10780, 10783, 10788–89, 10795, 10800–01–02, 10804, 10808–09, 10811, 10824–25, 10865

Civil rights — Biography
IJ: 8098, 8103, 8107, 8111, 8113, 8115, 8121, 8401, 8726
J: 8083, 8089, 8093, 8095–96, 8105, 8112, 8116–17, 8119, 8131, 8310
JS: 8031, 8063, 8074–75, 8094, 8104, 8109, 8367

Civil rights — Fiction
IJ: 5093, 5153
J: 1136, 5087, 5109, 5135, 5144
JS: 1148, 5096, 5116

Civil rights — Poetry
IJ: 7063, 7426

Civil War — Fiction
J: 4805

Civil War (U.S.)
See also specific battles, e.g., Antietam, Battle of; and names of specific individuals, e.g., Lincoln, Abraham
IJ: 8178, 8371, 10228, 10231–32–33–34–35–36, 10239, 10243, 10245, 10247–48, 10250–51–52, 10256, 10258, 10261–62, 10267–68, 10270–71–72, 10276, 10797
J: 8183, 10229–30, 10253, 10255, 10259–60, 10263–64, 10269, 10330, 13106, 13144
JS: 10237–38, 10242, 10244, 10246, 10257, 10266, 10274–75, 10277

Civil War (U.S.) — Biography
IJ: 8088, 8125, 8160, 8162, 8272, 8295–96, 8307, 8351–52, 8362, 8402
J: 8294, 8308–09, 8349–50, 8403
JS: 8161, 8363

Civil War (U.S.) — Fiction
IJ: 2714, 3076, 4785, 4787, 4791–92–93, 4797, 4799, 4801, 4804, 4812, 4816–17–18, 4824, 4826, 4833, 4835, 4838, 4840–41
J: 4636, 4786, 4788, 4790, 4795–96, 4798, 4802–03, 4806–07, 4810–11, 4813–14, 4819, 4823, 4828–29–30, 4832, 4834, 4836–37, 4842–43–44–45, 5996
JS: 435, 4794, 4808, 4820, 4822, 4825, 4839

Civil War (U.S.) — Poetry
J: 7123

Clairvoyance — Fiction
J: 5050

Clark, William
JS: 7552

Clay modeling
IJ: 13148
JS: 13147, 13147

Cleisthenes
J: 8881

Clemente, Roberto
IJ: 8682–83

Cleopatra
IJ: 8815
J: 8813, 9378
JS: 8814

Cleopatra — Fiction
IJ: 4177, 4201
J: 4188

Cleveland, Grover
J: 8149

Climate
IJ: 12829

Climate change
IJ: 9274, 10997, 11018, 11024, 11026
J: 10983, 10992, 12794
JS: 10968, 10982, 10984, 10995

Clinton, Bill
IJ: 8150–51–52

Clinton, Hillary Rodham
IJ: 8266–67, 10735
J: 8264–65

Cliques — Fiction
IJ: 2386, 3867
JS: 1884, 5512

Clones and cloning
IJ: 11552, 11736
J: 11732, 11737, 11744, 12600
JS: 11735

Clones and cloning — Fiction
IJ: 5673, 6521, 6589
J: 6571

Close, Chuck
IJ: 7635

Clothing and dress
See also Fashion
IJ: 9324, 9454, 9797, 10070, 12977–78, 13200, 13295
J: 9283, 11000, 12972–73–74, 13211, 13284
JS: 9429–30, 9465–66–67, 10165, 10274, 10292, 13196, 13199, 13204–05

Clowns
IJ: 7953

Clowns — Fiction
J: 2090

Clubs — Fiction
IJ: 5652
J: 600, 637

CNN
IJ: 11226

Coaches (sports) — Careers
JS: 11375

Coal and coal mining
IJ: 10316
JS: 11020

Coal and coal mining — Fiction
IJ: 4949
J: 5089

Coast Guard (U.S.)
IJ: 10740

Cobain, Kurt
J: 7917
JS: 7916

Cobalt
IJ: 12688

Coca industry — Fiction
IJ: 4576
J: 4575

Cocaine
J: 11476, 11536
JS: 11503

Cochran, Jacqueline
IJ: 7531

Codes and ciphers
IJ: 7445, 7453, 9269
J: 10101

Codes and ciphers — Careers
J: 11345

Codes and ciphers — Fiction
J: 5200

Cody, Buffalo Bill — Fiction
IJ: 4635, 4922

Coelacanths
IJ: 12574

Coen, Ethan — Criticism
JS: 9161

Coen, Joel — Criticism
JS: 9161

Coffee
IJ: 12332

Cold (disease)
JS: 11621

Cold War
IJ: 9581, 10389
J: 10387
JS: 9572, 10386

Cold War — Fiction
IJ: 5174, 6057
J: 3390, 5120

Coleman, Bessie
IJ: 7532

Coleridge, Samuel Taylor
J: 7084

Collections and collecting
IJ: 13304

IJ = Upper Elementary/Lower Middle School; J = Middle School/Junior High; JS = Junior High/Senior High

**Colleges and universities —
Fiction**
J: 5882, 6400
JS: 1748, 2205, 5459, 6356

Collins, Suzanne
J: 7729–30

Colombia
IJ: 9989, 9992

Colombia — Fiction
JS: 309

Colon cancer
J: 11692

Colonial period (U.S.)
IJ: 9246, 10047, 10140–41, 10143–
44–45, 10148–49–50–51, 10153,
10155–56, 10159–60, 10163–64,
10170, 10489, 10494, 10498
J: 10139, 10142, 10147, 10152,
10166–67–68, 10199
JS: 9231, 10165

**Colonial period (U.S.) —
Biography**
IJ: 7859, 8281, 8322, 8393, 8398
J: 7579, 8260, 8275, 8277, 8327,
8347–48
JS: 8092, 8279–80

Colonial period (U.S.) — Fiction
IJ: 2939, 4654, 4659–60, 4662,
4665–66–67, 4669, 4672, 4674
J: 4651, 4656, 4658, 4661, 4668, 4670,
4677, 4680, 4684, 4687
JS: 4671

Colorado — Fiction
IJ: 4863
J: 2206
JS: 2311

Colorado River
IJ: 10314, 12957

Colosseum (Rome)
IJ: 9411, 9416

Coltrane, John
IJ: 7918

Columbia (space shuttle)
IJ: 12259

Columbine High School
IJ: 11086
J: 11081

Columbus, Christopher
IJ: 7533

Colvin, Claudette
JS: 8367

Comanche Indians — Fiction
IJ: 4850
J: 4642
JS: 4900

Comas — Fiction
IJ: 1471
J: 2067
JS: 936

Comedy — Biography
IJ: 7919, 7987
J: 7931
JS: 7915

Comets
IJ: 12265, 12298
J: 12262–63–64

Comic books
IJ: 4088, 5823, 6507, 7494, 10870,
13222, 13231, 13234, 13303
J: 4081, 7481, 11359, 13232
JS: 3945, 3972, 4017, 4055, 4086,
4096, 4154, 7490, 13235

Comic books — Careers
IJ: 11358

Comic books — Fiction
All: 3918
IJ: 3165, 3887–88, 3917, 4042
J: 5928
JS: 3840, 3890, 3956, 4104, 4137,
4139

Comic strips
IJ: 13242
JS: 7493, 7497–98

Comic strips — Biography
IJ: 7658

Comic strips — Fiction
J: 3847
JS: 4043

Coming of age — Biography
J: 9008
JS: 11157

Coming of age — Fiction
IJ: 496, 508, 520, 842, 1323, 1496,
1604, 1657, 1713, 1823, 1975, 1977,
2125, 2176, 2211, 2350, 2441, 4483,
5105, 5164
J: 30, 495, 542, 580, 583, 627, 630,
823, 894, 902, 906, 1034, 1037, 1082,
1228, 1258, 1829–30, 1847, 1902,
1925, 1939, 1968, 2088, 2094, 2151,
2238, 2275, 2291, 2309, 2338, 2344,
2397, 2405, 2413, 2429, 2438, 2445,
2464, 2504, 2877, 3844, 4065, 4275,
4611, 5157, 5241, 5668, 5781, 6332,
6389, 6812, 6894, 6925, 6939
JS: 470, 700, 775, 787, 806, 818, 854,
883, 936, 945, 1067, 1086, 1096, 1606,
1808, 1876, 1899, 1910, 1958, 2031,
2057, 2060, 2069, 2085, 2107, 2116,
2148, 2159, 2173, 2196, 2221, 2224,
2240, 2328, 2361, 2387, 2459, 2480,
3655, 4338, 4595, 5092, 6278, 6342,
6488, 6837, 6840

Communication
IJ: 7441, 9337, 13028
J: 13024

Communications
IJ: 12951

Communications — Careers
J: 11342

**Communications —
Experiments and projects**
J: 13023

Communications satellites
J: 13022

Communism
J: 9848
JS: 9833–34, 10381, 10386

Communism — Biography
J: 8933

Communism — Fiction
IJ: 4484, 5125
JS: 4480

Composers — Biography
IJ: 7598, 7877, 7879, 7883, 7885,
7889–90–91, 7893–94, 7991
J: 7888, 7895
JS: 7876, 7892

Compost
IJ: 13250

Compulsive behavior — Fiction
J: 1545

Computer games — Careers
J: 11340

Computer games — Fiction
See also Online games
IJ: 6622
J: 994, 2508, 3251, 6455

Computer graphics
JS: 12987

Computer hacking — Fiction
J: 6273
JS: 6274

Computers
IJ: 12152, 12784, 12982, 12997,
13013, 13020
J: 8423, 12989, 12998–99, 13004,
13009, 13011–12
JS: 11235, 11438, 12983–84

Computers — Biography
IJ: 8410, 8439, 8448, 8458, 8469,
8472, 8488, 8513, 8530, 8532, 8553,
8555, 8574, 8631, 8644
J: 8423, 8552, 8554, 8572, 8575,
8632–33

Computers — Careers
IJ: 11427, 11431, 11433–34
J: 11432, 11436
JS: 11424, 11428–29, 11435, 11438

Computers — Fiction
IJ: 3887, 6508, 6548
J: 145–46, 5893, 6510
JS: 1010

Concept books
IJ: 7460

Condors — Fiction
J: 6255

Conduct of life
JS: 11984

Conduct of life — Fiction
J: 498
JS: 6899

Cone, Claribel
JS: 9053

Cone, Etta
JS: 9053

Conestoga wagons — Fiction
IJ: 4903

Conflict management
J: 12039
JS: 12038, 12058

Confucianism
J: 10529

Congo
JS: 9600, 9617

Congress (U.S.)
J: 10391
JS: 10657

Congress (U.S.) — Biography
J: 8050, 8095, 8262
JS: 8314

Congress of Vienna
JS: 9458

Connecticut — Fiction
IJ: 3275, 3296, 4736, 4745
J: 4680, 4697

Connor, Eugene
JS: 10766

Conquistadors
IJ: 9931

Conservation
See also Ecology and environment;
Wildlife conservation
IJ: 10442, 10492, 10507, 10964,
10981, 10988, 11001, 11004, 11010,
11036, 12331, 12524, 12528
J: 10976

Conservation — Biography
IJ: 8486, 8584, 8950
J: 8419, 8484
JS: 8600

Conservation — Careers
IJ: 11422

Conservation — Fiction
IJ: 2462, 6020
J: 61, 5926

Conservation — Folklore
IJ: 7171

Conspiracies — Fiction
IJ: 5871

Constantine I, Emperor
J: 8882

Constellations
IJ: 12273
JS: 12278

Constitution
J: 10625

Constitution (U.S.)
IJ: 10623, 10627, 10629–30, 10632,
10634–35, 10639, 10641, 10791
J: 10626, 10628, 10636, 10638
JS: 10633, 10637, 10640, 10642,
10809

Constitution (U.S.) — Biography
IJ: 8021
J: 8030

Consumer credit
JS: 11451

Consumer guidance
J: 11017

**Consumer protection —
Biography**
JS: 8318

Consumerism — Fiction
J: 971
JS: 2241, 6270

Contests — Fiction
IJ: 619, 689, 932, 2023

Cook, Captain James
JS: 7534

Cook, Captain James — Fiction
IJ: 113

Cook, Frederick
JS: 10016

Cookbooks
IJ: 10515, 13157, 13160, 13162,
13169, 13186, 13188, 13190, 13194
J: 13159, 13181, 13187, 13189
JS: 13153, 13158, 13164, 13184

Cookbooks — Ethnic
IJ: 13163, 13171, 13176, 13191
J: 13149–50–51, 13154–55–56, 13165–
66–67, 13179, 13182–83, 13185
JS: 13175

Cookbooks — France
JS: 13174

**Cookbooks — Hispanic
Americans**
IJ: 1321

Cookbooks — Vegetarian
IJ: 13161

Cookies
IJ: 13160

Cooking
IJ: 9696, 9712, 9782, 11615, 13152,
13168, 13170, 13172–73, 13177–78
J: 13192
JS: 13193

Cooking — Africa
J: 13181

Cooking — Biography
IJ: 8379

Cooking — Careers
IJ: 11349

Cooking — Ethnic
IJ: 13180

Cooking — Fiction
J: 1947, 3842

Cooks — Biography
IJ: 8981
J: 8617, 8963, 8994

Cooks — Fiction
IJ: 6237

Cooperation
J: 11992

Cooperation — Fiction
IJ: 3239

Copernicus
IJ: 8491

Copper
IJ: 12662

Copyright
J: 12991

Coral reefs
IJ: 12555
JS: 12569

Coretta Scott King Award
IJ: 8103

Corking (knitting)
IJ: 13290

Cornwall (England) — Fiction
IJ: 4473

Corporations
J: 11237

Corsica (France) — Fiction
JS: 3123

Corvette automobile
J: 13059

Cosby, Bill
IJ: 7919

Cosmetic surgery
J: 11718

Cosmetics
JS: 11756

Cosmetics — Biography
J: 8434

Costumes and costume making
JS: 13206

Cotton
IJ: 10057

Cotton gin — Biography
IJ: 8643

Cougars
IJ: 12465

Cougars — Fiction
IJ: 2486

Country life — Fiction
J: 2036

Country music
IJ: 9118
J: 9122

IJ = Upper Elementary/Lower Middle School; J = Middle School/Junior High; JS = Junior High/Senior High

IJ = Upper Elementary/Lower Middle School; J = Middle School/Junior High; JS = Junior High/Senior High

IJ = Upper Elementary/Lower Middle School; J = Middle School/Junior High; JS = Junior High/Senior High

Dred Scott Case
IJ: 10710
J: 10223, 10706

Dred Scott Case — Fiction
JS: 4753

Drinker, Edward
IJ: 8436

Drinking age
JS: 11524

Drinking and driving
IJ: 11501
J: 11547

Drinking and driving — Fiction
J: 1692

Driving
JS: 13055

Drought
IJ: 10996

Droughts — Fiction
IJ: 5049

Drug testing
JS: 10815

Drugs and drug abuse
IJ: 11504, 11520
J: 10661, 11476, 11478, 11481, 11483, 11485, 11488–89, 11489–90, 11493–94–95–96–97, 11502, 11508, 11516, 11521, 11528, 11531, 11533–34, 11536, 11539, 11539, 11541–42–43, 11550, 11726, 11823
JS: 11479, 11503, 11506, 11511, 11514–15, 11517, 11525, 11535, 11545, 11548, 11551, 13408

Drugs and drug abuse — Fiction
IJ: 848, 1340
J: 125–26, 603, 1074, 1826, 1961, 1968, 2445, 4435
JS: 427, 494, 696, 1154, 1199, 1295, 1378, 1677, 1741, 1759, 1775, 2296, 2304, 2320, 2516, 5323, 6747, 6883

Druids — Fiction
IJ: 2798

Du Bois, W. E. B.
J: 8089–90

Ducks and geese — Fiction
JS: 335

Duncan, Tim
IJ: 8707–08

Dunkerque, Battle of
JS: 335

Dust Bowl
IJ: 10347, 10353, 10357
J: 10360

Dust Bowl — Fiction
IJ: 4036, 5067

Dvorak, Antonin
JS: 7884

Dwarfs — Biography
J: 7998

Dwarfs — Fiction
J: 4486

Dylan, Bob
JS: 7925

Dysgraphia
IJ: 7712

Dyslexia
IJ: 11832, 11870
J: 11830

Dyslexia — Fiction
IJ: 4578

Dyson, Esther
IJ: 8513

Dystopias — Fiction
JS: 173, 263, 2989

E

Eagles
IJ: 12505

Earhart, Amelia
IJ: 7539–40–41–42

Earhart, Amelia — Fiction
IJ: 5079

Earle, Sylvia
IJ: 8514–15

Earnhardt, Dale, Jr.
IJ: 8670

Earth
IJ: 12266, 12268, 12694, 12700–01
J: 12704
JS: 12211, 12698

Earth (planet)
IJ: 12267

Earth imaging satellites
J: 12930

Earth science
IJ: 9192, 12696–97, 12703
JS: 12668

Earth science — Experiments and projects
J: 12702
JS: 12695

Earthquakes
IJ: 12709–10–11, 12714
J: 12706

Earthquakes — Fiction
IJ: 257

East Germany — Fiction
J: 2243

East Indian Americans
JS: 10847

Easter — Poetry
IJ: 7016

Easter Island
IJ: 9750
J: 9755
JS: 13360

Eastern Europe
J: 9845
JS: 9776

Eating disorders
See also specific disorders, e.g., Anorexia nervosa
IJ: 11670
J: 11542, 11558, 11574, 11582, 11594, 11637, 11641, 11666, 11684, 11886
JS: 11592, 11620, 11627, 11643, 11652, 11661, 11688, 11700

Eating disorders — Fiction
J: 655, 1702
JS: 514

eBay
J: 11227

Ebola
J: 11612, 11691

Ecology and environment
See also Conservation; Pollution
IJ: 10023, 10442, 10492, 10507, 10509, 10959, 10962, 10967, 10973, 10978, 10981, 10987, 10991, 10994, 11005, 11008, 11010–11, 11025–26, 11028–29–30, 11033, 11035, 11037, 11049, 12201, 12312, 12490, 12708, 12745, 12806, 12879, 12889, 12893, 12905, 13057, 13119
J: 10019, 10960, 10976, 10985, 10993, 11000, 11003, 11017, 11019, 11022, 12308, 12356, 12399, 12880, 12882, 12895
JS: 9262, 10479, 10711, 10958, 10961, 10965–66, 10969–70–71–72, 10975, 10984, 10986, 11002, 11009, 11009, 11012–13, 11016, 11020–21, 11023, 11027, 11032, 11038–39–40, 11048, 11346, 11654, 12352, 12538, 12729, 12834, 12886

Ecology and environment — Biography
IJ: 8485, 8616, 9004
J: 8419, 8445

Ecology and environment — Careers
IJ: 11335, 11397
J: 11332, 11332

Ecology and environment — Experiments and projects
IJ: 10974, 11014, 11034

Ecology and environment — Fiction
IJ: 57, 302, 636, 711–12, 2505, 2830, 3878, 5844, 5853, 6869
J: 559, 2506, 2637, 6479
JS: 2241, 2494, 2498, 2532, 2676, 3335, 3996, 6559

IJ = Upper Elementary/Lower Middle School; J = Middle School/Junior High; JS = Junior High/Senior High

Ellabad, Mohieddin
J: 7645

Ellington, Duke
J: 7926

Ellis Island
IJ: 10334
JS: 10433, 10851

Ellis Island — Fiction
IJ: 5006

Ellison, Larry
IJ: 8530

Elmolo (African people)
J: 9604

Elves — Fiction
IJ: 2873, 3391

Emancipation Proclamation
IJ: 10249, 10256
J: 10240

Emergency personnel — Careers
J: 11398

Emerson, Ralph Waldo
J: 7754

Emotions
JS: 11845

Emotions — Fiction
IJ: 663
J: 1682, 1690, 1970, 2279
JS: 1676, 1746, 1768, 2038, 5883, 6079

Empire State Building
IJ: 12964

Employment
J: 11242
JS: 12076

Employment — Fiction
JS: 2178

Endangered species
IJ: 12398, 12404, 12411, 12434, 12445, 12460, 12471, 12474, 12492, 12515–16–17–18–19–20–21–22, 12524–25–26, 12526–27–28–29, 12529
JS: 12389, 12523, 12545

Endangered species — Fiction
IJ: 1784, 2553

Endocrine system
J: 11768

Energy
IJ: 12875, 12885

Energy (physics)
IJ: 12889, 12891, 12899
J: 12878, 12895, 12906
JS: 12903

Energy (physics)
J: 12856

Energy (sources)
See also Renewable energy
IJ: 12879, 12883, 12893, 12904–05, 13053

J: 11000, 11003, 11019, 12880, 12882, 12884, 12896
JS: 11012, 12352, 12890, 12897–98

Engel *v.* Vitale
J: 10686

Engineering
IJ: 12929
J: 12960

England
IJ: 8887, 8960
J: 9436–37–38, 9554, 9800, 9811
JS: 9444, 9796

England — Biography
IJ: 7750, 8886
J: 7569, 7718, 7725, 8565, 8888
JS: 7710

England — Cookbooks
J: 13167

England — Fiction
IJ: 6, 163, 240, 329, 417, 2909–10, 2943, 3230, 3758, 4238, 4360, 4373, 4395–96, 4399, 4429, 4468, 4481, 4536, 4552, 4558–59, 4780, 5545, 5820, 5967, 6070, 6093, 6480
J: 5, 286, 386, 418, 867, 873, 981, 1493, 1830, 1923, 2028, 2294, 2442, 2538, 3637, 4210–11, 4220, 4247, 4362, 4376, 4405, 4415, 4446, 4458, 4462, 4482, 4508, 4512, 4520, 4524, 4533, 4543, 4546, 5726, 5738, 5787, 5789, 5802, 6171, 6247–48
JS: 409, 419, 426, 447, 1100, 1260, 2559, 3889, 4204, 4248, 4359, 4366, 4391, 4398, 4400, 4402, 4424, 4491, 4532, 5359, 6118, 6172, 6326–27, 6347, 6370, 6488

England — Folklore
IJ: 7253, 7265
J: 7246, 7254, 7256–57, 7259, 7270, 7273
JS: 7260–61, 7264

England — Poetry
J: 7085

English language
IJ: 7448
J: 11276
JS: 7452

Entertainment industry — Biography
IJ: 7934, 7936

Entertainment industry — Careers
J: 11360
JS: 11367, 11387

Entitlement spending (U.S.)
J: 10658

Entomology
JS: 12538

Entomology — Experiments and projects
IJ: 12541

Entrepreneurs
IJ: 11439

Entrepreneurs — Biography
JS: 8442

Entrepreneurs — Careers
JS: 11357

Environmental chemistry
IJ: 11028

Epidemics
IJ: 11565
J: 11610
JS: 11636

Epidemics — Fiction
IJ: 4936, 4987

Epidemiology — Careers
J: 11410

Epilepsy
J: 11603
JS: 11595

Epilepsy — Fiction
JS: 1801, 5997

Equal rights
IJ: 10756

Equality (U.S.)
JS: 11053

Erie Canal
IJ: 10208, 10447

Erie Canal — Fiction
IJ: 4743
J: 4754

Eritrea
IJ: 9623
J: 9614

Eritrean Americans
IJ: 10832

Escapes
J: 9311

Essays
IJ: 6887
J: 7398
JS: 6893, 7395, 11272

Estonia
J: 9841, 9847

Estuaries
IJ: 12749

ETA (Spain)
IJ: 9864

Ethics
JS: 12090

Ethiopia
IJ: 9601, 9603
J: 9608, 9624

Ethiopia — Fiction
IJ: 4259, 4280

Ethiopia — Folklore
IJ: 7209

IJ = Upper Elementary/Lower Middle School; J = Middle School/Junior High; JS = Junior High/Senior High

Ethnic cleansing
J: 10602

Ethnic groups
IJ: 10855
JS: 10856, 10859, 10863

Ethnic groups — Fiction
IJ: 1088, 6908

Ethnography
IJ: 9297

Etiquette
IJ: 11997–98, 12000–01, 12003–04
JS: 11999, 11999, 12002

Etiquette — Fiction
JS: 2314

Etymology
IJ: 7444

Euclid
J: 8531

Eurasia
JS: 9827

Europe
IJ: 9298, 9763

Europe — Fiction
J: 4388
JS: 740

European Community
JS: 9766

Euthanasia — Fiction
J: 1804

Evans, Walker
J: 7646

Everglades
IJ: 10495

Everglades — Fiction
IJ: 57, 6204
J: 84

Everyday life
IJ: 6872

Everyday life — Fiction
J: 479

Evolution
IJ: 8502, 9221, 9225, 9233, 12180
J: 9228, 9230, 11747, 12316
JS: 9217, 9219, 9223, 9226

Evolution — Biography
IJ: 8503, 8505–06, 8509–10
J: 8504, 8507–08
JS: 8511

Evolution — Fiction
J: 498, 5026

Evolution — Trials
IJ: 10712

Ex-convicts — Fiction
JS: 760

Exercise
IJ: 13443
J: 11816–17

JS: 11815, 12081

Explosions
IJ: 12157

Expressionism
J: 7583, 7596

Extinct species
JS: 12523

Extrasensory perception (ESP) — Fiction
J: 5549

Extrasensory perception (ESP) — Fiction
IJ: 2565, 3208, 3599, 5492
J: 2, 802, 2599, 2668, 3654, 5942, 6432
JS: 5187

Extraterrestrial life
IJ: 12214, 13320, 13330

Extraterrestrial life — Fiction
IJ: 3642, 4032, 6498, 6554
J: 105, 6419, 6560, 6656, 6679
JS: 6572, 6644, 6692

Extreme sports
All: 13400–01
IJ: 13389, 13396, 13402, 13495, 13559, 13571
J: 13405, 13427

***Exxon Valdez* oil spill**
IJ: 11045

Eyeglasses — Fiction
IJ: 805

Eyes
J: 11812

F

Fables
IJ: 7410
JS: 7353

Facebook
IJ: 11226
JS: 8651

Fairies
IJ: 7337, 9807

Fairies — Fiction
IJ: 2609, 2613, 2659
J: 2586, 2601, 2618, 3193, 3304, 3515, 3696, 3832
JS: 3068, 3206, 3384, 3633

Fairy godmothers — Fiction
JS: 810

Fairy tales
IJ: 2653, 2663, 2865, 3374, 3548, 3615, 3695, 3894, 3899, 4056–57, 5432, 7173, 7179–80, 7252, 7266, 7272
J: 2599, 2864, 2917, 2932, 3042, 3194–95, 3290, 3484, 3524, 3807–08, 7175
JS: 2049, 2707, 3337, 3366, 3385,

7245

Fairy tales — Fiction
IJ: 2608, 3829, 5689
J: 2616, 2718, 6379, 7205
JS: 3716, 5530

Falcons — Fiction
IJ: 337

Fame
JS: 7503

Family histories
J: 13135

Family life
See also specific topics, e.g., Adoption; Divorce
IJ: 4334, 12109
J: 11905, 11988, 12118
JS: 6895, 12106

Family life — Fiction
IJ: 63, 211, 343, 348, 359, 454, 476, 483–84, 516, 520, 541, 554, 564, 634, 642, 653–54, 660–61, 674, 688–89, 705, 707, 716, 718, 722, 727, 734, 741, 748, 800, 808, 817, 856, 878, 900, 914, 956, 958, 979, 984, 1009, 1020, 1054, 1070, 1150, 1183, 1210, 1218–19, 1225–26–27, 1230, 1232–33, 1236, 1244, 1246, 1250–51, 1253, 1255, 1265–66, 1269, 1271, 1278–79, 1293, 1299–00–01, 1307, 1309, 1311, 1316, 1320–21, 1323, 1325, 1330, 1332–33–34, 1341, 1347, 1351–52, 1355, 1357, 1368, 1371–72, 1376, 1382, 1385–86, 1388–89, 1391, 1394–95–96, 1398, 1404, 1407–08, 1412, 1415–16, 1422, 1430–31, 1434, 1437, 1439–40, 1448, 1450–51, 1455–56–57, 1463, 1468–69, 1471, 1482–83, 1490–91, 1494, 1496–97–98–99–00, 1502, 1504–05, 1507, 1509–10, 1516–17–18, 1521–22, 1526, 1535–36, 1538–39–40, 1543, 1547, 1550, 1553–54, 1559, 1564, 1570–71–72, 1574, 1576, 1579–80, 1583, 1585, 1587–88–89, 1593, 1595, 1601–02, 1604–05, 1608, 1610–11, 1618, 1620–21, 1625, 1627, 1630–31, 1640–41–42, 1646–47–48, 1654, 1659, 1664, 1788, 1885, 1891, 1954, 2008, 2034, 2079, 2138, 2245, 2253–54, 2257, 2322, 2350, 2359, 2370, 2380, 2463, 2474, 2479, 2486, 2553, 2574, 3277, 3641, 3915, 4156, 4331–32, 4369, 4382, 4389, 4399, 4413, 4513, 4519, 4529, 4562, 4580–81–82, 4589, 4591, 4594, 4736, 4777, 4856, 4858, 4871, 4877, 4905, 4916–17, 4924, 4933, 4940, 4943, 4955, 4972, 4995, 5024, 5027, 5052, 5072, 5080, 5097, 5103–04, 5112, 5114, 5119, 5132–33–34, 5160, 5164, 5169, 5171, 5232, 5399, 5552, 5604, 5633, 5702, 5717–18, 5757, 5764, 5812, 5860, 6208, 6712, 6759, 6764, 6801, 6892, 6936, 12110, 12116–17, 12121, 12133
J: 79, 200, 239, 349, 380, 432, 474, 478, 497, 512, 525, 543, 550, 602–03, 610–11–12, 629, 632, 664, 710, 736,

738, 742, 744, 753, 759, 764, 832, 853, 862, 868, 886, 890, 894, 905–06, 911, 931, 947, 950, 952, 976, 981, 983, 1000, 1017, 1037, 1041, 1085, 1128, 1132, 1137, 1139, 1145, 1163, 1172, 1212, 1220, 1223, 1234–35, 1237–38, 1240, 1242–43, 1245, 1247, 1254, 1256, 1258–59, 1261, 1264, 1268, 1270, 1272, 1274, 1281, 1286–87–88–89–90–91, 1294, 1296, 1298, 1302–03–04–05, 1308, 1310, 1312–13, 1318–19, 1322, 1326–27, 1335, 1338–39, 1348, 1350, 1356, 1358–59, 1361, 1364–65, 1369, 1383, 1387, 1397, 1401, 1403, 1409–10, 1413, 1420–21, 1424–25, 1427, 1436, 1442, 1458, 1460, 1465–66, 1472, 1474–75–76–77, 1477, 1480, 1484, 1488–89, 1493, 1501, 1503, 1508, 1511–12–13–14–15, 1520, 1523, 1525, 1530, 1534, 1542, 1545–46, 1548, 1551–52, 1555–56–57–58, 1560–61–62, 1566, 1573, 1577–78, 1581–82, 1584, 1591–92, 1598–99, 1609, 1612, 1614, 1616, 1622–23–24, 1632, 1636–37–38–39, 1651–52, 1668, 1689, 1714, 1717, 1724, 1758, 1765, 1807, 1830, 1849, 1862, 1866–67, 1880, 1889, 1905, 1908, 1921, 1923, 1952, 1970, 1973, 1987, 2000, 2011, 2014, 2051, 2062, 2064, 2071, 2093, 2099, 2129, 2142, 2190, 2195, 2202, 2210, 2222, 2235, 2237, 2239, 2246, 2291, 2299, 2324, 2334, 2344, 2348, 2392, 2397, 2405, 2412, 2414, 2439, 2445, 2471, 2476, 2485, 2538, 3264, 4289, 4316, 4329, 4383, 4388, 4524, 4544, 4563–64, 4602–03, 4677, 4754, 4849, 4932, 4959, 4959, 4961, 5018, 5033, 5036, 5060, 5064, 5078, 5137, 5145, 5147, 5151, 5156, 5213, 5556, 5609, 5755, 5765, 5876, 5882, 5969, 6068, 6148, 6176, 6230, 6428, 6618, 6714, 6809, 6855, 12104

JS: 503, 544, 555, 563, 571, 625, 646, 658, 662, 666, 687, 701, 739, 743, 763, 806, 810, 830, 854–55, 875, 907, 946, 991, 1002, 1043, 1063, 1093, 1103, 1110, 1157, 1169, 1221, 1224, 1239, 1248, 1262, 1277, 1280, 1295, 1297, 1315, 1317, 1329, 1349, 1353, 1370, 1378, 1392, 1392–93, 1402, 1433, 1467, 1528, 1531, 1569, 1575, 1590, 1596–97, 1606, 1613, 1619, 1649, 1656, 1693, 1735, 1742, 1746, 1800, 1821, 1857, 1861, 1871, 1893, 1934, 1962, 1964, 2031, 2057, 2063, 2102, 2130, 2182, 2240, 2303, 2328, 2361, 2384, 2401, 2451, 2460, 2495, 3863, 3982, 4257, 4343, 4403, 4463, 4599, 5017, 5048, 5091–92, 5130, 5168, 5192, 5284, 5480, 5488, 5809, 6113, 6141, 6214, 6299, 6311, 6382–83, 6717, 6748, 6837, 11544, 12101, 12107, 12112, 12126, 12129

Family life — Poetry
IJ: 7007, 7007, 7067, 7110
JS: 7167

Famines
IJ: 10996

Famines — Fiction
IJ: 4901

Fanning, Shawn
IJ: 8532

Fantasy — Biography
IJ: 7588
J: 7601

Fantasy — Fiction
See also Science fiction; Supernatural; Time travel; Vampires; Werewolves; Zombies
All: 2823, 3571
IJ: 361, 407–08, 412–13–14, 416, 423, 443, 468, 925, 1670, 2355, 2431, 2557, 2561–62, 2565, 2570–71–72, 2574, 2577–78, 2583–84–85, 2587–88–89–90, 2600, 2604, 2606–07–08–09–10–11–12, 2614–15, 2617, 2620–21–22–23–24, 2631–32, 2649, 2651–52–53–54, 2656, 2659, 2670, 2672, 2675, 2678, 2691–92–93, 2698, 2701–02–03–04, 2713–14, 2717, 2719–20–21–22, 2725, 2732–33, 2741, 2743, 2749, 2752, 2756–57, 2762, 2764, 2766, 2776, 2780, 2782, 2785, 2787–88, 2790, 2796, 2802, 2808, 2810, 2813–14, 2818, 2820–21, 2824, 2828, 2830–31, 2833–34–35, 2838–39–40–41–42, 2847, 2853, 2857, 2860, 2863, 2873–74–75, 2883, 2886, 2888, 2891–92–93, 2899–00, 2903, 2906, 2908–09–10–11–12–13–14, 2919–20, 2923, 2926, 2933, 2938–39, 2942–43, 2953–54, 2956–57–58, 2960–61, 2964, 2970–71, 2975, 2981, 2986–87, 2991, 2998, 3005–06, 3009–10, 3015, 3017, 3023–24, 3027–28–29–30–31, 3033, 3038, 3046, 3054, 3056, 3058–59, 3064, 3066, 3069–70, 3075, 3080–81–82, 3093, 3096–97–98, 3101, 3104, 3107, 3110, 3115, 3119, 3122, 3130, 3134, 3138–39–40, 3143, 3145–46–47–48–49–50–51–52–53–54–55–56–57–58–59–60–61–62–63–64–65–66, 3168, 3170–71, 3173, 3175–76, 3178, 3188, 3207–08, 3211, 3215–16–17, 3219, 3221–22–23, 3225–26, 3230–31–32, 3239, 3242–43, 3246, 3248–49, 3253, 3257–58, 3260–61, 3265–66–67–68–69–70–71, 3275, 3277, 3283–84, 3287–88, 3291–92–93, 3296–97, 3300–01, 3305, 3308, 3311, 3316–17, 3319, 3323, 3325, 3331–32, 3341, 3343–44, 3347, 3349–50, 3356, 3369, 3374–75–76–77, 3379–80, 3382–83, 3388–89, 3391–92, 3395–96–97, 3399–00, 3408, 3413, 3417, 3422–23–24–25, 3432, 3434, 3437, 3439–40–41–42–43, 3445–46–47, 3449, 3454, 3456–57, 3460–61, 3463–64, 3469, 3472, 3479, 3485, 3493, 3496–97–98–99, 3519, 3525–26–27–28, 3531, 3535, 3540,

3542, 3544, 3546, 3549, 3551, 3553, 3555–56–57–58–59, 3561–62, 3564, 3567, 3569, 3572–73–74, 3576, 3578–79–80–81–82–83–84–85–86–87–88–89–90–91–92, 3594, 3597–98–99–00, 3606–07, 3609, 3612–13, 3615, 3631, 3638, 3644, 3646–47–48, 3650–51–52–53, 3658–59–60–61–62–63–64–65–66–67, 3669, 3675, 3677–78–79–80–81, 3689, 3695, 3703–04, 3706, 3710, 3712, 3717–18, 3720, 3722, 3725–26–27, 3729–30–31–32–33–34–35–36–37–38, 3740–41–42–43, 3746–47–48–49, 3752–53, 3755–56, 3758–59, 3761, 3764–65–66–67, 3774, 3776, 3781, 3786–87, 3791–92–93–94–95, 3797–98–99–00, 3802, 3805–06, 3809, 3813–14, 3816–17, 3819, 3822, 3827–28–29–30–31, 3853, 3855, 3866, 3868, 3886–87–88, 3892, 3903, 3909–10, 3917, 3921, 3943, 3959–60–61–62, 3969, 3971, 4020–21, 4037, 4042, 4046, 4077, 4092, 4138, 4164, 4552, 5344, 5346–47, 5383, 5385, 5394–95, 5425, 5435, 5445, 5463, 5467–68, 5470, 5474, 5478, 5487, 5531, 5543, 5547, 5561–62, 5573, 5577, 5583, 5598, 5604, 5626, 5844, 5953, 6245, 6474, 6493, 6686, 7204, 7206, 7244, 7352

J: 4, 47, 415, 2556, 2558, 2566–67–68–69, 2576, 2593, 2595, 2597–98–99, 2601–02–03, 2605, 2618–19, 2626, 2628, 2633, 2637–38, 2640–41, 2643–44–45–46–47–48, 2650, 2664–65–66–67–68, 2671, 2673–74, 2677, 2681–82–83, 2685–86–87, 2689–90, 2695–96, 2699–00, 2709, 2723–24, 2727, 2731, 2734–35–36–37, 2740, 2745–46–47–48, 2750–51, 2753–54–55, 2759, 2761, 2763, 2767, 2769, 2772–73, 2775, 2777, 2786, 2791–92–93–94, 2803, 2805, 2807, 2811–12, 2815–16–17, 2819, 2825–26, 2829, 2832, 2836–37, 2846, 2848–49–50, 2852, 2854–55, 2858, 2868, 2871, 2876–77–78–79, 2881, 2885, 2889–90, 2897, 2901–02, 2904–05, 2907, 2916–17, 2921, 2925, 2930, 2932, 2934–35–36–37, 2941, 2944, 2946, 2966, 2968–69, 2974, 2976, 2979, 2982–83, 2985, 2988, 2990, 2992–93–94–95–96–97, 3000, 3002, 3004, 3007–08, 3011–12–13–14, 3016, 3018–19–20, 3022, 3026, 3032, 3035–36, 3039, 3041, 3043–44–45, 3048–49–50–51, 3053, 3055, 3057, 3060–61–62–63, 3071, 3074, 3079, 3083–84–85–86–87–88, 3091–92, 3094–95, 3099–00, 3103, 3109, 3114, 3120–21, 3124–25–26, 3137, 3141, 3144, 3172, 3181–82–83–84–85, 3187, 3189–90–91–92–93–94–95–96, 3199, 3201, 3203–04–05, 3210, 3212, 3214, 3220, 3228–29, 3233, 3235–36, 3240, 3245, 3247, 3250, 3256, 3259, 3278, 3280, 3289, 3299,

IJ = Upper Elementary/Lower Middle School; J = Middle School/Junior High; JS = Junior High/Senior High

IJ = Upper Elementary/Lower Middle School; J = Middle School/Junior High; JS = Junior High/Senior High

IJ = Upper Elementary/Lower Middle School; J = Middle School/Junior High; JS = Junior High/Senior High

Gettysburg Address
J: 10263

Gettysburg, Battle of
IJ: 10241, 10252
J: 10255
JS: 10273

Gettysburg, Battle of — Fiction
IJ: 4789
J: 4814

Ghana
IJ: 9655

Ghana — Biography
IJ: 9010

Ghana — Fiction
J: 759
JS: 4252

Ghosts
IJ: 75, 1216, 2838, 3139, 5355, 5385,
5445, 5470, 5531, 5568, 5634, 9280,
10431, 13317, 13355, 13374
J: 13351, 13361, 13375

Ghosts — Fiction
IJ: 1670, 3226, 3274, 3347, 3434,
4116, 5341, 5344, 5354, 5360,
5365–66, 5388, 5403, 5408, 5438–39,
5442–43, 5451, 5466, 5481, 5496,
5506, 5510, 5517, 5519, 5521,
5544–45, 5585, 5593, 5604, 5610–11–
12, 5633, 5848–49, 5991, 6003, 6092,
6161, 6259, 6813, 7309
J: 566, 590, 1008, 2068, 2242, 2396,
2593, 3011, 3189, 3516, 3541, 3950,
4976, 5351–52, 5382, 5384, 5392,
5402, 5426–27–28, 5431, 5448, 5457,
5500, 5509, 5518, 5523, 5556–57,
5560, 5592, 5594–95, 5601, 5609,
5619, 5637, 5640, 5658, 5990, 6022,
6160, 6876
JS: 599, 1485, 2715, 3857, 3923, 5348,
5371, 5391, 5404, 5430, 5452, 5472,
5475, 5488, 5636, 5639, 6117, 6938

Ghosts — Folklore
IJ: 5458, 7312
J: 7302, 7313

Ghosts — Poetry
IJ: 7075

Giant pandas
IJ: 12483, 12519

Giant squids
IJ: 12561

Giants
IJ: 7337

Giants — Fiction
J: 1714

Gibson, Josh
IJ: 8686

Gideon v. Wainwright
J: 10687

Giff, Patricia Reilly
IJ: 7765

Gifted teenagers
JS: 12049

Gilbreth family
JS: 8954

Girls — Fiction
J: 750, 2074–75

Giuliani, Rudolph W.
J: 8283

Glacier National Park — Fiction
IJ: 6205

Gladiators — Fiction
IJ: 4202

Gladiators (Rome)
IJ: 9412

Glass making
JS: 9108

Glenn, Mike
IJ: 13463

Global positioning systems
J: 13025

Global warming
IJ: 10023, 10963, 10977, 10980,
10990, 11006–07, 11011, 12830
J: 10979, 11015, 11031, 12794
JS: 10968–69, 10998, 11002, 11298

Global warming — Fiction
IJ: 204
J: 2699–00, 3237

Globe Theatre (London)
IJ: 7828, 9031

Globe Theatre (London) —
Fiction
IJ: 4371, 4557

Goats
IJ: 12334

Goats — Fiction
J: 744

Goblins — Fiction
J: 3047

God — Fiction
IJ: 924

Goddard, Robert
IJ: 8556

Gods and goddesses
IJ: 7338, 7350

Gogh, Vincent van
J: 9081

Goh, Chan Hon
JS: 7930

Gold
IJ: 12660

Gold Rush (Alaska and Yukon)
IJ: 9947
JS: 7518, 12635

Gold Rush (Alaska and Yukon)
— Fiction
J: 131, 4612

Gold Rush (California)
IJ: 10482

Gold Rush (California) —
Fiction
IJ: 4729, 4757, 4872, 4888, 4928

Goldberg, Whoopi
J: 7931–32

Golden Gate Bridge
IJ: 12971

Golem — Fiction
IJ: 5631

Golf
IJ: 13511

Golf — Biography
IJ: 8771, 8779–80
J: 8769, 8778

Golf — Fiction
J: 679, 1481

Gómez de Avellaneda y Arteaga,
Gertrudis — Fiction
JS: 4577

Gonzalez, Henry B.
J: 8095

Goodall, Jane
J: 8557
JS: 8558

Google (company)
IJ: 11230
JS: 8446

Gordon, Jeff
IJ: 8671

Gorillas
IJ: 8634, 12447, 12449

Gorillas — Fiction
IJ: 6487

Gorman, R. C.
IJ: 7648

Gossip — Fiction
JS: 587

Goths
J: 9333
JS: 11983

Governesses — Fiction
IJ: 1650

Government and politics
IJ: 10592
JS: 10385

Government and politics —
Biography
IJ: 8064, 8313
J: 8334, 8348, 8804, 8849
JS: 8304, 8328

IJ = Upper Elementary/Lower Middle School; J = Middle School/Junior High; JS = Junior High/Senior High

IJ = Upper Elementary/Lower Middle School; J = Middle School/Junior High; JS = Junior High/Senior High

7362, 7364–65–66–67–68

Greece — Mythology — Fiction
IJ: 3733, 5675, 5804
J: 5803
JS: 2973

Greek Americans
IJ: 10923

Green movement — Fiction
IJ: 674

Greenberg, Hank
IJ: 8687

Greene, Nathanael
IJ: 8284

Greenhouse effect
IJ: 11011

Greenland — Fiction
IJ: 3249, 3662

Greenpeace
IJ: 10595, 11008

Greitens, Eric
JS: 8968

Grey, Lady Jane — Fiction
J: 4520

Grief
JS: 11468, 11473, 12097

Grief — Biography
JS: 9007

Grief — Fiction
IJ: 375, 513, 893, 1307, 1373, 1464,
1537, 1586, 1959, 2155, 2176, 5110
J: 66, 451, 553, 904, 1134, 1234, 1282,
1343, 1429, 1449, 1459, 1565, 1599,
1766, 1777, 1779, 2383, 2554, 6322,
6599
JS: 779, 1418, 1445, 1462, 1533, 1656,
1658, 1693, 1798, 1819, 1896, 1918,
2422, 2448, 3521, 6054, 6388

Grief — Poetry
IJ: 7018

Griffiths, Frances
IJ: 9807

Grimberg, Tina
JS: 8969

Grimm brothers
IJ: 7766

Grizzly bears
IJ: 12452
J: 12461

Grizzly bears — Fiction
IJ: 324, 6205

Grooming
J: 11751, 11757

Gross, Elly Berkovits
IJ: 8899

Group homes — Fiction
J: 2137

Groupon
J: 8587

Growing up
See also Coming of age
JS: 2001, 11989

Growing up — Fiction
IJ: 284, 688, 856, 961, 1855, 2033,
2212, 2219, 2368, 2380, 4292, 4309,
5163, 5757, 5759
J: 911, 983, 2062, 2222, 2366, 5763
JS: 224, 830, 1861, 1893, 2045, 2096,
2283, 2315, 2336, 2371, 2433, 2460

Guadeloupe — Fiction
J: 3844

Guam — Fiction
J: 1423

Guantanamo Bay — Fiction
JS: 2537

Guardian angels — Fiction
JS: 2742

Guatemala
J: 9963

Guatemala — Biography
IJ: 8945, 9964
JS: 8944, 8946–47

Guatemala — Fiction
J: 1168, 2489
JS: 4593

Guenevere, Queen — Fiction
J: 4229

Guernica (Spain)
IJ: 9094

Guernica (Spain) — Fiction
IJ: 4421

Guevara, Che
J: 8939, 8941–42
JS: 8940, 8943

Guide dogs — Fiction
IJ: 572
J: 820

Guilt — Fiction
IJ: 1583
J: 2032
JS: 858

Guitars
JS: 9131

Gulf War (1991)
IJ: 8331, 10749
J: 9577

Gulf War (1991) — Biography
J: 8330, 8337

Gun control
J: 10937
JS: 10950

Guns
J: 10937, 11091

Guns — Fiction
J: 2192

Gutenberg, Johannes
IJ: 8559

Guthrie, Woody
J: 7887
JS: 7886

Guyana
IJ: 9998

Gymnastics
IJ: 13512
J: 13513–14

Gymnastics — Biography
IJ: 8667, 8737

Gymnastics — Fiction
IJ: 6762

Gynecology
JS: 11728, 11950

Gypsies — Fiction
IJ: 5012
J: 4415

H

Habitat for Humanity
JS: 11168

Hackers (computers)
IJ: 12997

Hackers (computers) — Fiction
JS: 1010

**Hades (Greek deity) —
Mythology**
J: 4023

Haiku
IJ: 7003
J: 7029

Hairdressing
JS: 11325

Haiti
IJ: 9984

Haiti — Biography
IJ: 8951

Haiti — Fiction
IJ: 4572
J: 2551
JS: 4607

Haiti — Folklore
J: 7282

Haitian Americans — Fiction
IJ: 618
J: 1085, 1195

Hale, Nathan
IJ: 8285

Hale, Sarah Josepha Buell
J: 8374

Haley, Alex
J: 7767

IJ = Upper Elementary/Lower Middle School; J = Middle School/Junior High; JS = Junior High/Senior High

IJ = Upper Elementary/Lower Middle School; J = Middle School/Junior High; JS = Junior High/Senior High

IJ = Upper Elementary/Lower Middle School; J = Middle School/Junior High; JS = Junior High/Senior High

Hughes, Langston
JS: 7777–78

Hull House
IJ: 10413

Human body
See also specific parts and systems, e.g., Circulatory system
IJ: 11761–62, 11765–66–67, 11774, 11777, 11779, 11781
J: 11773, 11780, 13227
JS: 11770

Human body — Experiments and projects
IJ: 11778, 11783
J: 11775

Human development and behavior
JS: 11986

Human rights
See also civil rights
IJ: 10771, 10784, 10793
J: 11216
JS: 10594

Human rights — Biography
J: 8919
JS: 8802, 8821, 8829, 8944, 8946–47, 8961

Human rights — Fiction
J: 4260

Human trafficking
JS: 2520

Human-animal relations
J: 12386

Human-animal relations — Fiction
IJ: 3547

Humanitarians — Biography
IJ: 8928
JS: 8857

Hummingbirds
IJ: 12484, 12487

Humor
IJ: 11993
JS: 7394–95, 12990, 13404

Humor — Fiction
IJ: 10, 36–37, 75, 96, 144, 171, 379, 626, 653–54, 711–12, 717, 771–72, 815, 842, 1246, 1309, 1368, 1482, 1547, 1641, 1926, 2127, 2265, 2267, 2323, 2572, 2621, 2654–55–56, 2975, 3286, 3578, 3902, 3905, 4124–25, 4131, 4164, 4399, 4580, 4863, 4993, 5123, 5148, 5193, 5441, 5545, 5644–45–46–47–48–49, 5653, 5656, 5659–60, 5663, 5672–73, 5681, 5683–84–85–86–87–88–89–90, 5692–93–94–95, 5700, 5702–03–04, 5706, 5709–10, 5712, 5714–15–16–17–18–19–20–21, 5724–25, 5731–32–33, 5735–36, 5739–40, 5743, 5747, 5754, 5757, 5759, 5766–67–68, 5770–71, 5773–74, 5777–78, 5780, 5784, 5791–

92, 5794–95–96–97–98, 5801, 5804, 5807–08, 5811, 5813–14, 5822–23–24–25–26–27, 5830, 5834–35, 5854, 5981, 6194, 6272, 6434, 6478, 6540, 6573, 6584, 6646, 6650, 7179–80
J: 70, 467, 478, 512, 683, 844, 861, 887, 941, 965, 1348, 1990, 2083, 2132, 2145, 2238, 2374, 3516, 3595, 3674, 4211, 5603, 5643, 5650–51, 5654–55, 5658, 5661–62, 5665, 5668–69, 5674, 5676, 5678–79–80, 5682, 5697–98–99, 5701, 5705, 5707–08, 5713, 5722–23, 5726–27–28, 5730, 5734, 5741–42, 5744–45, 5749, 5751–52–53, 5755–56, 5758, 5772, 5775–76, 5779, 5781–82, 5785–86–87–88–89–90, 5793, 5799–00, 5802–03, 5805–06, 5821, 5829, 5831, 5833, 6366, 6560, 6783, 6856
JS: 32, 445, 462, 763, 798, 991–92, 1966, 2107, 2400, 2596, 4511, 5657, 5671, 5711, 5729, 5737, 5746, 5783, 5809–10, 5828, 5832, 5836–37, 6100, 6323

Humorous poetry
I: 7437

Hundred Years War
J: 8904

Hungarian Americans — Fiction
IJ: 5097

Hungary
IJ: 8928, 9771

Hungary — Cookbooks
J: 13165

Hungary — Fiction
J: 4383, 4534
JS: 4556, 5207

Hungary — Folklore
IJ: 7255

Hunger
IJ: 11133
J: 9589, 11134
JS: 11136

Huns
J: 9333

Hunter, Clementine
JS: 7652

Hunters and hunting
IJ: 13393

Hunters and hunting — Fiction
IJ: 2431
J: 1731

Hurricane Andrew
IJ: 12806

Hurricane Katrina
IJ: 12807, 12809, 12813
J: 12805, 12808, 12810, 12814

Hurricane Katrina — Fiction
IJ: 310, 378, 909
J: 464
JS: 296, 1818

Hurricane Mitch — Fiction
IJ: 4610

Hurricanes
IJ: 12801
JS: 9310

Hurricanes — Fiction
IJ: 80, 4737
J: 235, 583, 4961

Hurston, Zora Neale
J: 7779
JS: 7780–81

Hurston, Zora Neale — Fiction
IJ: 4935

Hussein, Saddam
IJ: 8844
J: 10405
JS: 8845

Hutu (African people)
J: 9628

Hydropower
J: 12900

Hydrothermal vents
IJ: 12837, 12848

Hygiene
J: 11751, 11757, 11813, 12093
JS: 11462

Hyperactivity — Fiction
IJ: 754, 1704, 1706

I

Ice — Fiction
IJ: 866

Ice — Poetry
IJ: 7168

Ice ages
J: 9215

Ice climbing
IJ: 13411, 13495
J: 13427

Ice hockey
IJ: 13515, 13517–18–19, 13521
J: 13520
JS: 13543

Ice hockey — Biography
IJ: 8741, 8745

Ice hockey — Fiction
IJ: 6721, 6723–24–25, 6751, 6759, 6806, 6838
JS: 6763

Ice mummies
IJ: 9240

Ice skating
IJ: 13528

Ice skating — Biography
IJ: 8666, 8738

IJ = Upper Elementary/Lower Middle School; J = Middle School/Junior High; JS = Junior High/Senior High

IJ = Upper Elementary/Lower Middle School; J = Middle School/Junior High; JS = Junior High/Senior High

Irish potato famine — Fiction
J: 4510

Iron
IJ: 12932
JS: 11020

Iroquois Indians
J: 10122–23

Irritable colon
JS: 11795

Irvin, Monte
IJ: 8689

Irving, Washington
IJ: 7782

Irwin, Bindi
IJ: 9004

Irwin, Steve
IJ: 9004

Islam
IJ: 10547, 10566–67, 10569, 10575, 10577
J: 9264, 10568, 10571
JS: 9017, 9072, 9263, 9704, 9746, 9832, 9835, 9844, 9875, 9918, 10570, 10573, 10576, 10578, 11208

Islam — Biography
IJ: 8852

Islam — Fiction
IJ: 4393

Islamic art
IJ: 9015, 9046
JS: 9072

Islamic empire
IJ: 9293, 9306

Islands
IJ: 10478

Islands — Fiction
IJ: 223, 297, 1793, 4397
J: 292, 2268, 2341, 6704
JS: 90

Israel
IJ: 9885, 9892–93–94
J: 9871, 9873–74, 9884, 9887–88–89
JS: 9895

Israel — Biography
IJ: 8850
JS: 9012

Israel — Fiction
IJ: 870, 2277, 2488
J: 1339, 2523, 4190
JS: 4475

Israeli-Arab relations
See also Arab-Israeli relations
J: 9886, 9897

Israeli-Arab relations — Fiction
JS: 2555

Istanbul
IJ: 9760

Italian Americans
IJ: 10916, 10918
JS: 10915

Italian Americans — Biography
JS: 7737, 8535

Italian Americans — Fiction
IJ: 1311, 4966, 4986, 4992, 5114
J: 4989–90

Italy
IJ: 9054, 9824
J: 9820

Italy — Biography
IJ: 7664, 8550, 8910, 8912
J: 7743

Italy — Cookbooks
IJ: 13188
J: 13151
JS: 13175

Italy — Fiction
IJ: 1382, 2636, 2942, 4390, 4485, 5264, 6808
J: 473, 536, 3610, 4117, 4370, 4385, 4434, 4515, 4530
JS: 690, 2387

Ive, Jonathan
IJ: 8568

Iwo Jima, Battle of
IJ: 9514

J

Jackson, Andrew
IJ: 8038, 8163, 10214
J: 8164

Jackson, Bo
IJ: 8733

Jackson, Michael
IJ: 7943–44

Jackson, Shirley Ann
IJ: 8569

Jackson, Stonewall
IJ: 8295–96
J: 8294

Jacobs, Harriet A.
IJ: 8102

Jacobs, Jane
JS: 8377

Jacobsen, Ruth
JS: 8972

Jaguars
IJ: 12518

Jamaica — Biography
J: 7972, 8750

Jamaica — Fiction
IJ: 1404, 4594
JS: 1249

James, LeBron
JS: 8711

Jamestown (VA)
IJ: 10156
J: 10142

Jamestown (VA) — Fiction
IJ: 4647, 4667
J: 4655
JS: 4652

Jane Eyre — Adaptations
J: 410

Janitors — Fiction
J: 5643

Japan
IJ: 4334, 9087, 9343, 9707, 9712–13
J: 9533, 9708–09, 9711, 12907

Japan — Biography
IJ: 8704
JS: 8695

Japan — Cookbooks
IJ: 13191

Japan — Fiction
IJ: 119, 3383, 4111, 4308, 4323–24, 4326, 4328, 4351, 5210
J: 731, 3938, 3979, 4285, 4306–07, 4340, 6932
JS: 3106, 3986, 4061–62, 4121, 4298, 4300

Japan — Folklore
IJ: 7233
J: 7226

Japan — Mythology
IJ: 7331, 7341
JS: 7346

Japanese — Fiction
JS: 4761

Japanese Americans
IJ: 10365, 10368, 10892, 10923
J: 10895
JS: 10364

Japanese Americans — Biography
IJ: 7685
J: 8293, 8743
JS: 7670

Japanese Americans — Fiction
IJ: 1415, 5221, 5243, 5283, 5285
J: 1082, 1107, 1142, 1161, 1194, 3938, 5238, 5256, 5270–71, 6854
JS: 5118

Japanese Canadians — Fiction
IJ: 1200

Jason (mythology)
IJ: 7356

Jay-Z
IJ: 7945–46–47

Jazz
J: 9119
JS: 9125

IJ = Upper Elementary/Lower Middle School; J = Middle School/Junior High; JS = Junior High/Senior High

Jujitsu
JS: 13537

Julius Caesar — **Adaptations**
JS: 4072

Julius Caesar (play)
IJ: 6972

Juneteenth
IJ: 11186

Jupiter (planet)
IJ: 12283, 12289

Jury system
J: 10673
JS: 10678

Justice
J: 10681

Justice — Fiction
IJ: 450, 6058

Justice — Folklore
IJ: 7184

Juvenile court
JS: 10705

Juvenile delinquents — Fiction
J: 123–24–25–26, 2137, 2162, 2233
JS: 258, 1414, 2384

K

Kahlo, Frida — Fiction
J: 3086

Kahlo, Frida — Poetry
JS: 7653

Kander, Lizzie
IJ: 8379

Kangaroos
IJ: 12482

Kansas
IJ: 10410
J: 10227

Kansas — Fiction
IJ: 331, 680, 4841, 4938
J: 4894, 5678

Karate
IJ: 13536
JS: 13535, 13539

Karate — Fiction
IJ: 6798, 6844, 6852

Karting — Fiction
IJ: 13407

Karzai, Hamid
JS: 8846

Kayaks and kayaking
IJ: 10466
J: 13548
JS: 10465

Kayaks and kayaking — Fiction
JS: 309

Kazakhstan
J: 9842
JS: 9830, 9832

Keat, Nawuth
JS: 8975

Keckley, Elizabeth
J: 10254

Kellar, Harry
IJ: 7952

Keller, Helen
IJ: 8383
J: 8380
JS: 8381–82, 8382

Keller, Helen — Fiction
JS: 1760

Kelly, Emmett, Sr.
IJ: 7953

Kennedy, Edward M.
IJ: 8302
J: 8303

Kennedy, John F.
IJ: 8037, 8173–74, 10383
J: 8175–76

Kennedy, Robert F.
IJ: 8305
J: 10377
JS: 8304

Kennewick Man
J: 9211

Kent State University
IJ: 10399

Kentucky — Fiction
IJ: 1253, 5100, 5103
J: 1016

Kentucky Derby
IJ: 13527

Kenya
IJ: 9593–94, 9618–19, 9626–27, 9632
J: 9598–99, 9604, 9606, 9608, 9610,
9630–31, 9633

Kenya — Biography
J: 8983
JS: 7752, 9595

Kenya — Fiction
IJ: 4268, 6184
JS: 4269

Kenya — Folklore
J: 7214

Kepler, Johannes
J: 8577

Kerr, M. E. — Criticism
JS: 7783

Kerry, John
J: 8306

Key West (FL) — Fiction
J: 1950

Keys, Alicia
J: 7954

Khamenei, Ali
JS: 8847

Kherdian, Jeron
J: 8976

Khmer Rouge
J: 9741

Kidd, Jason
IJ: 8715

Kidnapping
IJ: 11122
J: 10957

Kidnapping — Fiction
IJ: 95, 110, 159, 1895, 1957, 2835,
3288, 4280, 4993, 5827, 5870, 6051,
6145, 6174, 6272
J: 19, 106, 569, 648, 1304, 2039, 2282,
3333, 4236, 4282, 5845, 5876, 5904,
5941, 5943, 5995, 6159, 6240, 6655
JS: 193, 552, 922, 5909, 5983, 6036,
6105, 6164

Kidney failure — Fiction
J: 1754

Killer whales
IJ: 12590

Kim Jong II
J: 8849
JS: 8848

Kindertransport
J: 9519

King Arthur — Fiction
J: 3656

King Lear — **Adaptations**
J: 3926, 4150

King, Coretta Scott
IJ: 8103
JS: 8104

King, Martin Luther, Jr.
IJ: 8106, 10374
J: 8105

King, Stephen
J: 7784

Kings and queens
IJ: 9265

Kings and queens — Biography
IJ: 8793, 8801

Kings and queens — Fiction
IJ: 3906, 4253

Kipsigis (African people)
IJ: 9594

Kirby, Jack
IJ: 7655

KISS (rock group)
IJ: 7955

Kissing — Fiction
J: 6871

IJ = Upper Elementary/Lower Middle School; J = Middle School/Junior High; JS = Junior High/Senior High

IJ = Upper Elementary/Lower Middle School; J = Middle School/Junior High; JS = Junior High/Senior High

IJ = Upper Elementary/Lower Middle School; J = Middle School/Junior High; JS = Junior High/Senior High

IJ = Upper Elementary/Lower Middle School; J = Middle School/Junior High; JS = Junior High/Senior High

Mangrove trees
IJ: 9623

Manhattan Project
IJ: 9511
J: 13104

Manic depression
J: 11846

Manitoba — Fiction
J: 2453

Manjiro — Fiction
JS: 4761

Manning, Peyton
J: 8734

Mantle, Mickey
IJ: 8693

Manufacturing
IJ: 12943
J: 12922, 12926

Manzano, Juan Francisco
J: 7796

Maori (people) — Fiction
IJ: 4305
JS: 1174

Maori (people) — Folklore
JS: 7242

Maple sugar and syrup
IJ: 12343

Maps and globes
IJ: 7026, 9182, 10220
J: 9183–84

Maps and globes — Biography
J: 8597

Marathon (race)
J: 13545

Marcy, Geoff
J: 12225

Marijuana
J: 11508, 11512, 11523, 11531
JS: 11482, 11486, 11499

Marine animals
See also specific species, e.g., Sharks
IJ: 12556–57, 12597
JS: 12562, 12567

Marine animals — Poetry
IJ: 7002

Marine biology
IJ: 12555–56, 12565, 12839, 12848
JS: 10965, 12569, 12835

Marine biology — Biography
IJ: 8514–15

Marine Corps (U.S.)
IJ: 10738

Marine Corps (U.S.) — Careers
IJ: 11406–07

Marine ecology
IJ: 12560

Marine life
IJ: 12558, 12563

Marketing — Careers
J: 11388

Markham, Beryl
J: 7563

Markham, Beryl — Fiction
J: 4261

Marley, Bob
IJ: 7971
J: 7972

Marriage — Fiction
IJ: 4332

Mars (planet)
IJ: 12253–54, 12296, 12298
J: 12290

Marsh, Othniel Charles
IJ: 8436

Marshall Plan
JS: 9305

Marshall, Thurgood
JS: 8312

Marsupials
IJ: 12480

Martial arts
IJ: 13530, 13541
JS: 13533, 13537–38–39–40

Martial arts — Biography
JS: 7962

Martial arts — Fiction
IJ: 6852
J: 1883, 3862, 4175, 4344
JS: 1260, 3989, 6354

Martians — Fiction
JS: 6695

Martinez, Pedro
J: 8694

Mary Magdalene — Fiction
JS: 4176

Mary, Mother of Jesus
IJ: 10559

Mary, Queen of Scots
J: 8911

Mary, Queen of Scots — Fiction
IJ: 4470
J: 4448, 4494

Maryland
J: 10499

Maryland — Fiction
J: 1552, 1623, 4795

Masada — Fiction
J: 4184

Masai (African people)
IJ: 9632

Masai (African people) — Biography
J: 8983

Masks and mask making
IJ: 9281, 13264

Mason, Andrew
J: 8587

Mass media
IJ: 7485, 7495, 9176, 10793, 12985, 13016
JS: 7499

Massachusetts
IJ: 10429–30
J: 9422

Massachusetts — Fiction
IJ: 4763, 4782, 4992
J: 4684, 4747, 4764

Mastodons
IJ: 9187

Materials
IJ: 12868

Mathematics
See also specific branches, e.g., Algebra
IJ: 9306, 12768–69, 12773, 12775, 12778–79–80, 12783, 12787–88, 12790–91–92
J: 8417, 11452, 12767, 12770, 12770, 12777, 12789

Mathematics — Biography
IJ: 8460, 8525
J: 8417, 8420, 8461, 8531, 8548, 8633
JS: 8526

Mathematics — Careers
JS: 11415

Mathematics — Fiction
IJ: 5795
J: 793–94, 5888
JS: 5138

Matisse, Henri
IJ: 7661
JS: 9053

Matsui, Hideki
JS: 8695

Matter (physics)
IJ: 12855, 12868–69, 12872
JS: 12858

Mayan Indians
IJ: 9245, 9249, 9340, 9960
J: 9327, 9330, 9962
JS: 9334

Mayan Indians — Biography
IJ: 8945

Mayan Indians — Fiction
IJ: 3753, 4574
J: 105, 2489, 4596, 5995, 7277

Mayan Indians — Folklore
IJ: 7280

Mayan Indians — Mythology
IJ: 7330, 7342

J: 4146, 7321

Mayer, Maria Goeppert
JS: 8588

Mayflower (ship)
IJ: 10138
J: 10129

Mayflower (ship) — Fiction
IJ: 4672, 4675

Mayflower Compact
IJ: 10138

Mayors — Biography
J: 8283

Mbundu (African people)
JS: 9644

Mbuti (African people)
J: 9616

McCain, John
IJ: 8313, 8316
J: 8315
JS: 8314

McCarthy, Joseph
J: 10391
JS: 8317, 10381

McCarthyism
JS: 10386

McCarthyism — Fiction
J: 2220

McCartney, Paul
S: 7973

McCartney, Paul — Criticism
JS: 9128

McClintock, Barbara
IJ: 8591
JS: 8589

McGwire, Mark
IJ: 13457

McKinley, William
J: 8193

Mead, Margaret
IJ: 8592
J: 8593

Meaning (philosophy) — Fiction
JS: 975

Measures and measurement
IJ: 12781

Meat
IJ: 11909

Media
JS: 11088

Medical imaging
J: 11722

Medici, Lorenzo de
IJ: 8912

Medicine
IJ: 9306, 9445, 11552, 11715, 11721, 11727, 11730
J: 9292, 11645, 11693, 11703,

11707, 11710, 11712, 11716, 11723, 11725–26, 11729
JS: 10095, 11717

Medicine — Biography
IJ: 8421, 8441, 8579, 8601, 8622

Medicine — Careers
J: 11706
JS: 11356, 11415

Medicine — Fiction
J: 4379
JS: 4538

Medusa
IJ: 13350

Melville, Herman
JS: 7797

Memoirs
All: 8982
IJ: 7695, 7746, 7994, 8270, 8899, 8945, 8970, 8999, 9009
J: 7645, 7800, 8764, 8933, 8958, 8977, 8988, 9003, 9008, 9011, 9525
JS: 8957, 8962, 8968–69, 8973, 8975, 8984–85, 8989–90–91, 8996–97, 9005, 9007, 9012, 9517, 9595, 11989, 12656–57

Memory — Fiction
JS: 6141

Menchu, Rigoberta
IJ: 8945, 9964
JS: 8944, 8946–47

Mendel, Gregor
IJ: 8594
J: 8595

Mendeleyev, Dmitri
IJ: 8596

Mendelssohn, Fanny
JS: 7892

Mennonites — Fiction
IJ: 2078, 2330
JS: 1872

Menominee Indians
IJ: 10096
J: 10086

Menstruation
IJ: 11963
J: 11952, 11968

Menstruation — Fiction
JS: 1701

Mental disabilities
JS: 11914

Mental disabilities — Fiction
IJ: 1605
J: 4981, 5447

Mental health
JS: 11822

Mental illness
See also specific disorders, e.g., Schizophrenia
J: 11823, 11831, 11850, 11872, 11872

JS: 11842, 11852–53, 11874

Mental illness — Fiction
IJ: 1422
J: 525, 1466, 1473, 1484, 1519, 1690, 1698, 1716, 1720, 1722, 1726, 1763, 1765, 1786, 2014, 4598, 4676, 5943
JS: 471, 687, 996, 1262, 1676, 1683, 1687, 1735, 1773, 1812, 1820, 2221, 3179, 6113

Mental problems
IJ: 11832
JS: 12124

Mental problems — Biography
IJ: 8660

Mental problems — Fiction
IJ: 1671, 1789, 1791
J: 41, 1424, 1668, 1675, 1758
JS: 1815

Mercator, Gerardus
J: 8597

The Merchant of Venice —
Adaptations
JS: 3927

Mercury (planet)
IJ: 12284, 12295

Merina (African people)
JS: 9640

Merlin (legendary character) —
Fiction
IJ: 3820, 3822
J: 2638, 2643–44–45

Mermaids and mermen —
Fiction
IJ: 465, 2909–10, 3101, 3221, 3223, 3266
J: 3352, 3520
JS: 4199

Mermaids and mermen —
Folklore
JS: 7201

Mesa Verde National Park
IJ: 10126

Mesa Verde National Park —
Fiction
IJ: 264

Mesopotamia
IJ: 9355, 12773
J: 9358
JS: 9381, 9384

Mesopotamia — Folklore
JS: 7328

Messiaen, Olivier
IJ: 7893

Metals
IJ: 12932

Meteorites — Fiction
IJ: 227

Meteorology
IJ: 12797, 12819

IJ = Upper Elementary/Lower Middle School; J = Middle School/Junior High; JS = Junior High/Senior High

IJ = Upper Elementary/Lower Middle School; J = Middle School/Junior High; JS = Junior High/Senior High

Mime
JS: 9179

Minerals
IJ: 12760, 12763

Mines and mining
IJ: 9987, 12941

Mines and mining — Fiction
JS: 494

Ming, Yao
IJ: 8717
J: 8718
JS: 8719

Minik
J: 4978

Minnesota
IJ: 10418, 12970

Minnesota — Fiction
IJ: 2264, 4848, 5146
J: 1558

Minotaur (Greek mythology) — Fiction
J: 2634

Miracles — Fiction
JS: 1035

Mirrors — Fiction
IJ: 3009

Missing persons — Fiction
IJ: 307, 2884, 5860, 6271
J: 789, 1040, 1223, 1421
JS: 1014, 1402, 5887, 5946, 6429

Missionaries — Biography
IJ: 7580

Missionaries — Fiction
IJ: 247
J: 4262

Missions
IJ: 10134, 10469, 10503, 10506, 10510

Mississippi (state)
IJ: 10769

Mississippi (state) — Fiction
IJ: 21, 4983, 5022, 5131
J: 1195

Mississippi River — Fiction
J: 4868
JS: 445

Missouri (state)
IJ: 10408

Missouri (state) — Fiction
J: 4807
JS: 5075

Missouri River
IJ: 12740

Mites
IJ: 12534

Modern art
J: 9071, 9074

Modoc Indian War — Fiction
IJ: 4893

Moeyaert, Bart
J: 7800

Mohammed
IJ: 8852

Mohapatra, Jyotirmayee
IJ: 8987

Mohawk Indians
IJ: 10912
J: 10914

Mohawk Indians — Fiction
J: 4619

Moldova
J: 9846

Mole-rats
J: 12437

Moles — Fiction
IJ: 423

Moles — Folklore
IJ: 7318

Molnar, Haya Leah
J: 8988

Molybdenum
IJ: 12677

Monaque, Mathilde
JS: 8989

Monarch butterfly
JS: 12545

Monet, Claude
IJ: 7665, 7667
J: 7666

Monetary policy (U.S.)
J: 11238

Money
IJ: 11231, 11453
J: 11455

Money-making ideas
IJ: 11439, 11441, 11453
J: 11234, 11442
JS: 11440

Money-making ideas — Fiction
IJ: 949, 2267, 2455, 5773–74, 5791
J: 692

Mongolia
IJ: 9736, 12467
J: 9726

Mongolia — Biography
IJ: 8841

Mongols
IJ: 9671

Mongols — Biography
IJ: 8842

Monkeys — Fiction
J: 350

Monologues
IJ: 6958, 6960, 6977

J: 6961
JS: 6940, 6942–43, 6945, 6991

Mononucleosis
IJ: 11614
J: 11675, 11683

Monplaisir, Sharon
IJ: 8770

Monroe, Marilyn
J: 7975, 7977
JS: 7976

Monsters
See also Fantasy; Folklore; Mythology; Supernatural
IJ: 7337, 13317, 13331, 13341, 13369

Monsters — Fiction
IJ: 3078, 3692, 3831, 5422, 5583, 5881
J: 2573, 4044

Montagnier, Luc
J: 8599

Montgomery bus boycott
IJ: 10778
J: 10757

Montgomery, L. M.
J: 7801

Monuments
J: 9028

Moon
IJ: 12231, 12234–35, 12256, 12267–68
J: 12245

Moon — Fiction
JS: 6692

Moore, Wes
JS: 8990

Mormons
IJ: 10306, 10409

Mormons — Biography
IJ: 8408

Mormons — Fiction
J: 6391
JS: 899

Morrison, Toni
J: 7802
JS: 7803

Mortgage loans
IJ: 11450

Mosaics
IJ: 13119

Mosques
JS: 9037

Moss, Randy
IJ: 8729

Mothers — Fiction
IJ: 5173
J: 880

Mothers and daughters
JS: 12108

IJ = Upper Elementary/Lower Middle School; J = Middle School/Junior High; JS = Junior High/Senior High

N

National Guard (U.S.) — Careers
J: 11400

National parks (U.S.)
IJ: 10468

National parks (U.S.) — Fiction
IJ: 94

National security
JS: 11205

Native Americans
See also Inuit; and specific Indian tribes, e.g., Cherokee Indians
IJ: 4638, 9101, 10083, 10092, 10096, 10099–00, 10107, 10109, 10112, 10114, 10114, 10116, 10118, 10120–21, 10124, 10124, 10126–27–28, 10136
J: 9220, 9241, 9933, 10084, 10086, 10090, 10090, 10097–98, 10101, 10101, 10103, 10113, 10119, 10123, 10924
JS: 9100, 10088, 10094–95, 10111, 10132, 10538, 13504

Native Americans — Biography
See also Nez Perce Indians — Biography
IJ: 7648, 8263, 8269–70, 8282, 8338–39, 8356, 8366, 8404, 8407, 8756, 8758–59
J: 8023, 8341, 8345, 10102
JS: 7607, 8268, 8301, 8753, 8757

Native Americans — Fiction
IJ: 33–34, 46, 169, 1200, 4617, 4624, 4635, 4641, 4643, 4645–46, 4649, 4669, 4922, 4941, 4945, 5378, 5881, 6726
J: 79, 127, 230, 265–66, 836–37, 1095, 1127, 1138, 1163, 1192, 1208, 1827, 1883, 1898, 2050, 2142, 4604–05, 4609, 4618, 4620–21, 4627–28, 4631, 4637, 4640, 4642, 4650, 4658, 4668, 4679, 4681–82, 4764, 4846, 4870, 4882, 4890, 4909, 4913, 4920, 5102, 5223, 6754, 6782
JS: 35, 434, 576, 1126, 2676, 4595, 4632, 4639, 4644, 4900, 6165

Native Americans — Folklore
IJ: 7284, 7287, 7294, 7299
J: 7295, 7298, 7301
JS: 3884, 7283, 7292–93, 7297, 7336

Native Americans — Mythology
IJ: 7349

Natural disasters
IJ: 11938, 12844
J: 11936
JS: 9310, 12140

Natural disasters — Fiction
J: 1938, 6618
JS: 4999

Natural history
IJ: 9592, 9940, 9942
JS: 12835

Naturalists — Biography
IJ: 8482
J: 7844, 8557
JS: 8558, 8600

Nature
IJ: 9285, 10513, 12310
JS: 10445

Nature — Fiction
IJ: 757, 4972

Nature — Poetry
IJ: 7021

Nature study
J: 12308

Nauvoo (IL)
IJ: 10409

Navajo Arts and Crafts Enterprise (NACE)
J: 11239

Navajo Indians
IJ: 10089
J: 10105, 11239

Navajo Indians — Fiction
IJ: 1171, 2780, 4614
J: 127, 4636, 5200, 5223, 5994, 6241
JS: 4630

Navigation
IJ: 12841

Navy (U.S.)
IJ: 10746
J: 10743

Navy (U.S.) — Biography
IJ: 8297, 8299
J: 8298

Navy (U.S.) — Careers
IJ: 11403

Navy SEALS — Biography
JS: 8968

Naylor, Phyllis Reynolds
IJ: 7804

Nazi Germany — Biography
JS: 8901

Nazi Germany — Fiction
IJ: 5247, 5311

Nazis and Nazism
J: 9787
JS: 9462, 9790

Nazis and Nazism — Fiction
IJ: 4553, 5226, 5311
JS: 4465, 5208

Ndebele (African people)
JS: 9647

Nebraska — Fiction
IJ: 2040, 4944

Needlecrafts
J: 13284

Nefertiti
JS: 8823

Negro League baseball
IJ: 8691, 13444, 13456
J: 13440
JS: 4102

Negro League baseball — Biography
IJ: 8680, 8686, 8689, 8692

Neo-Nazis — Fiction
JS: 2543

Nepal
IJ: 9719

Nepal — Biography
IJ: 9006

Neptune (planet)
IJ: 12283, 12294, 12297

Neruda, Pablo — Fiction
IJ: 4601

Netherlands
JS: 9510

Netherlands — Biography
J: 8995

Netherlands — Fiction
IJ: 249, 4397, 4419
J: 1951, 5301
JS: 4392, 4463, 5192

Nevada
IJ: 10424

Nevada — Fiction
IJ: 382
JS: 5056

New Amsterdam
IJ: 8398

New Deal
IJ: 10343, 10356
J: 10359

New England
IJ: 10048, 10444

New England — Fiction
J: 1562, 2121, 4981, 4985, 5557

New England Patriots (football team)
JS: 13509

New France (Colony)
J: 9320

New Hampshire — Fiction
J: 4728
JS: 1214

New Jersey
IJ: 10435, 10449
JS: 12578

New Jersey — Fiction
IJ: 1850, 2335, 5656, 5791

New Mexico — Biography
IJ: 7525

New Mexico — Fiction
IJ: 1048, 1070, 5952
J: 1049, 7301

IJ = Upper Elementary/Lower Middle School; J = Middle School/Junior High; JS = Junior High/Senior High

New Orleans, Battle of
IJ: 10214

New Stone Age
IJ: 9222

New York (NY)
IJ: 8398, 10434, 10446, 10455–56, 10458, 11158, 12964, 13066
J: 10838
JS: 10428, 10454, 10875, 13065

New York (NY) — Biography
J: 8259, 8283

New York (NY) — Fiction
IJ: 158, 201, 379, 959, 1468, 1972, 1999, 3381, 3615, 4678, 4930–31, 4971, 4977, 5052, 6103, 6110, 6169, 6198
J: 136, 715, 1074, 1144, 1146, 1151, 1155, 1166, 1912, 1945, 2246, 2684, 4937, 4996–97, 5008, 5035, 5064, 5074, 5136, 6364
JS: 470, 713, 1199, 1204, 2218, 2329, 2385, 2507, 2524, 2869, 4822, 5009

New York (state)
IJ: 10452
JS: 10445

New York (state) — Fiction
IJ: 3139, 4659, 4743, 4988
J: 4732

New York State
IJ: 10460

New York State — Fiction
IJ: 5160

New York Yankees (baseball team)
IJ: 13437

New Zealand
IJ: 9753

New Zealand — Fiction
IJ: 122
J: 1256, 2190
JS: 1317, 1870

New Zealand — Folklore
JS: 7242

Newbery Medal
J: 7584

Newfoundland — Fiction
IJ: 103, 141
J: 41

Newspapers
IJ: 11260

Newspapers — Fiction
IJ: 614
J: 2216, 5677, 5861

Newton, John
IJ: 8388

Newton, Sir Isaac
IJ: 8604–05–06
J: 8602
JS: 8603

Nez Perce Indians
JS: 10088

Nez Perce Indians — Biography
IJ: 8300
JS: 8301

Nez Perce Indians — Fiction
J: 4637

Nezahualcoyotl
IJ: 8948

Ngoni (African people)
JS: 9615

Nicaragua
IJ: 9956
JS: 9958

Nicaraguan Americans
JS: 10900

Nicotine
IJ: 11500
J: 11529

Niger
IJ: 9653, 9664
JS: 9584

Nigeria
IJ: 9660, 9664, 9667
J: 9654, 9659, 9663, 9668
JS: 9657

Nigeria — Folklore
IJ: 7216

Nightmares — Fiction
IJ: 5626
J: 5964
JS: 6227

1900s
IJ: 9461, 10327

1910s
IJ: 9461, 10327

1910s — Fiction
J: 4950

1918 — Fiction
J: 4976

1920s
IJ: 9461
JS: 9465

1920s — Fiction
J: 5081
JS: 5041, 5075

1930s
IJ: 9461
J: 12972
JS: 9465

1930s — Fiction
IJ: 1572, 5055, 5080

1940s
J: 10033, 12972

1940s — Fiction
IJ: 5088, 5123
J: 4317, 4564, 5108, 6005
JS: 4599

1950s
J: 10033, 10390, 12972
JS: 9466

1950s — Fiction
IJ: 5148, 5150, 5158
J: 1639, 5113, 5121, 5155
JS: 4288, 5126, 5359, 6004

1960s
IJ: 10373
JS: 9466, 10385

1960s — Fiction
IJ: 389, 1036, 2249, 4484, 5093, 5104–05–06, 5131, 5162, 5167, 5172
J: 1094, 1136, 5102, 5136, 5147, 5156, 5175

1968
JS: 9464

1970s
IJ: 10388
J: 9576

1970s — Fiction
IJ: 5117, 5146

1980s
J: 9576
JS: 9467

1980s — Fiction
J: 3977, 5151

1990s
J: 9576
JS: 9467

1990s — Fiction
JS: 5143

19th century
J: 9815

19th century — Fiction
IJ: 4772, 4938
J: 4374, 4902
JS: 4366, 4973, 6347

Ninjas — Fiction
IJ: 119, 4351
JS: 3254, 3870

Nixon, Joan Lowery
IJ: 7805

Nixon, Richard M.
IJ: 8040, 8194
J: 8195, 10688

Noah's Ark — Fiction
J: 4183

Nobel Peace Prize — Biography
J: 8788

Nobel Prize
IJ: 8784, 9964

Nobel Prize — Biography
JS: 8588–89

Noguchi, Isamu
JS: 7670

Nonindigenous pests
IJ: 12309

IJ = Upper Elementary/Lower Middle School; J = Middle School/Junior High; JS = Junior High/Senior High

Nonviolence
IJ: 11167

Noor, Queen
J: 8853

Norman Conquest
J: 9798

North America
See also Canada, Mexico, United States
IJ: 7528, 7537, 7568, 9942, 10159, 12739
JS: 10130, 10285, 12699

North Carolina
IJ: 10501, 10504
J: 1546, 10491

North Carolina — Fiction
IJ: 1333, 4744, 5132–33–34
J: 1308, 5140
JS: 1148

North Korea
IJ: 13086
JS: 9728, 9737

North Korea — Biography
J: 8849
JS: 8848

North Pole
J: 7565, 11015
JS: 10016

Northeast (U.S.)
IJ: 10144

Northern Dancer (racehorse)
IJ: 12647

Northern Ireland
IJ: 9810

Northern Ireland — Fiction
IJ: 4438
J: 1970, 2341, 5202

Northup, Solomon
IJ: 8389

Northwest Passage
IJ: 9943

Norway
IJ: 9854
JS: 9508

Norway — Fiction
IJ: 5204, 5251
J: 683, 5278

Norwegian Americans — Fiction
J: 1358

Nova Scotia — Fiction
J: 4585

Nowruz (Persian New Year)
IJ: 10515

Nubia (African empire)
IJ: 9350

Nuclear energy
J: 12907
JS: 12908–09

Nuclear physics
JS: 12873

Nuclear power plants
IJ: 10989

Nuclear war — Fiction
J: 2056
JS: 199, 2536

Nuclear waste — Fiction
J: 2511, 6065

Nuclear weapons
JS: 13088, 13098, 13103

Numbers
IJ: 12785

Nunez, Tommy
J: 8721

Nureyev, Rudolf
J: 7978

Nurses
IJ: 9526

Nurses — Biography
IJ: 8352
J: 8876

Nurses — Fiction
JS: 5178, 5337

Nursing homes — Fiction
JS: 1597

Nutrition and diet
IJ: 11794, 11882, 11884, 11911–12, 12345
J: 11878, 11886, 11889, 11899, 11901–02–03
JS: 11795, 11880, 11885, 11894, 12338, 13184

Nzingha (African queen) — Fiction
IJ: 4264

O

O'Brien, Soledad
J: 7806

O'Connor, Sandra Day
J: 8319

O'Keeffe, Georgia — Fiction
J: 5053

O'Neal, Shaquille
IJ: 8722

Oak Island
IJ: 13358

Oakley, Annie
IJ: 7979

Oakley, Annie — Fiction
IJ: 4974

Obama, Barack
IJ: 8196–97, 8200, 8202

J: 8198–99, 8201

Obama, Michelle
IJ: 8203–04

Obesity
IJ: 11581
J: 11491
JS: 11585, 11649, 11877, 11881, 11887–88, 11893, 11896

Obesity — Fiction
J: 719, 1678, 1720, 1733, 2119, 2210, 2389
JS: 1709, 2924

Observatories
J: 12216

Obsessive-compulsive disorder
J: 582, 11840
JS: 11860

Obsessive-compulsive disorder — Biography
J: 8965

Obsessive-compulsive disorder — Fiction
J: 1661, 1674, 1721
JS: 555

Occupations and work
IJ: 9145, 9513

Occupations and work — Fiction
IJ: 493
J: 478, 2280
JS: 2038, 6127

Oceanography
IJ: 12846
J: 12832
JS: 12834–35

Oceanography — Biography
J: 8443

Oceanography — Experiments and projects
IJ: 12833

Oceans
IJ: 12557, 12563, 12565, 12839, 12841
J: 12836
JS: 12838

Oceans — Experiments and projects
IJ: 12840

Oceans — Fiction
IJ: 273

Ochoa, Ellen
IJ: 7564

Odysseus
IJ: 7377

Odysseus — Fiction
IJ: 7378

Odyssey
J: 7384

IJ = Upper Elementary/Lower Middle School; J = Middle School/Junior High; JS = Junior High/Senior High

Of Mice and Men — Criticism
J: 7424

Oglethorpe, James
IJ: 10146

Ohio
IJ: 10415, 12348

Ohio — Fiction
IJ: 1395

Ohio River
IJ: 12744

Ohno, Apolo Anton
J: 8742–43–44

Oil industry
IJ: 9573
J: 12935
JS: 10999

Oil industry — Biography
IJ: 8412, 8620

Ojibwa Indians
JS: 10091

Ojibwa Indians — Fiction
IJ: 4625–26
J: 1898

Oklahoma
IJ: 10407, 10415

Oklahoma — Fiction
IJ: 371, 1496, 1626
J: 2050, 4902

Olympic Games
J: 11194, 13542, 13544
JS: 13543

Olympic Games — Biography
IJ: 8659, 8745, 8774

Omidyar, Pierre
IJ: 8607

Online games — Fiction
J: 822

Online relationships — Fiction
J: 2171

Online social networks
J: 13007

Ontario — Fiction
J: 311

Opera
IJ: 9130

Operation Iraqi Freedom
IJ: 9569, 10749
J: 10405
JS: 9567, 9922, 9922, 10393

Operation Iraqi Freedom — Fiction
JS: 5340

Oppenheimer, J. Robert
J: 8608–09

Optical illusions
IJ: 13261
J: 11806

Oracle (computers) — Biography
IJ: 8530

Orchestras
IJ: 9132–33

Oregon — Fiction
IJ: 140, 366, 1544, 2257, 4874, 4885
J: 2637, 5073

Oregon Trail
JS: 10280

Oregon Trail — Fiction
IJ: 4869, 4891, 4908
JS: 4883

Organ donation — Fiction
JS: 615

Organ transplants
JS: 11554

Organ transplants — Fiction
See also Heart transplants — Fiction
J: 521, 1816

Organic foods
J: 12335

Orienteering
IJ: 13492

Origami
IJ: 13268–69
J: 13265, 13270

Origami — Fiction
IJ: 1415

Orkney Islands
IJ: 9234

Orphan Train — Biography
IJ: 8955

Orphan Train — Fiction
J: 4946

Orphans
J: 9803
JS: 11059

Orphans — Fiction
IJ: 53, 579, 892, 935, 2719, 2884, 3535, 4205, 4295, 4361, 4584, 4678, 4797, 4857, 4867, 4980, 4995, 5031, 5146, 5170, 5304, 5435, 5474, 5813, 6195
J: 191, 235, 237, 303, 755, 784, 1257, 1354, 1584, 1617, 2398, 2442, 2994, 3415, 3541, 3654, 3673, 4166, 4178, 4251, 4385, 4568, 4758, 4855, 5002, 5020, 5181, 5650, 6149
JS: 3889, 4276, 4599, 4774

Orwell, George
JS: 7807

Orwell, George — Criticism
J: 7414

Oscars (motion picture awards)
JS: 9166

Outdoor life
IJ: 13494
J: 13382

Overpopulation
IJ: 11055

Overweight persons — Fiction
IJ: 1969
J: 649, 6857
JS: 499

Owen, Wilfred
JS: 6999

Owens, Jesse
IJ: 8755
J: 8754

Owls
IJ: 12507
J: 12508

Owls — Fiction
IJ: 2512, 3265

Oxycodone
JS: 11487

Oxygen
IJ: 12672

Ozarks — Fiction
JS: 5639

P

Pacific Coast (U.S.)
IJ: 10220
JS: 10479

Pacific Islands
IJ: 9752

Pacific Islands — Folklore
JS: 7240

Pacific Ocean
J: 9758
JS: 9537, 9759

Pacific Rim
JS: 9674

Pacifists and pacifism
IJ: 7188, 8784

Pacifists and pacifism — Biography
IJ: 8790

Pacifists and pacifism — Fiction
IJ: 5233

Page, Larry
J: 8432, 8453
JS: 8446

Paige, Satchel — Fiction
IJ: 6843

Paige, Satchel — Graphic novels
JS: 4102

Pain
J: 11533

Paine, Thomas
IJ: 8320, 8322

IJ = Upper Elementary/Lower Middle School; J = Middle School/Junior High; JS = Junior High/Senior High

J: 8321

Pak, Se Ri
IJ: 8771

Pakistan
IJ: 9700, 9732
J: 9703, 9739, 9743
JS: 9693, 9697

Pakistan — Biography
J: 8832

Pakistan — Fiction
IJ: 2496
J: 4282, 4317, 4329
JS: 4343

Pakistani Americans — Fiction
J: 887, 1115

Palenque
IJ: 9248

Paleontology
IJ: 9187, 9189–90–91–92–93–94,
9202, 9204, 9206–07, 9209–10
J: 9186, 9188, 9201
JS: 9195, 9208

Paleontology — Biography
IJ: 8436, 8459

Paleontology — Fiction
J: 4169, 4876

Palestine
J: 9886, 9897
JS: 9891

Palestine — Biography
J: 8958
JS: 8827

Palestine — Fiction
IJ: 2488, 4358
J: 2523, 4504
JS: 2490, 4381

Palin, Sarah
J: 8323

Paluxet Indians
IJ: 11178

Panama
J: 9961

Panama Canal
J: 9961, 12958, 12968

Panic attacks
J: 11834, 11843

***Panther* (motion picture)**
JS: 10889

Paper
IJ: 12944

Paper airplanes
IJ: 13267

Paper crafts
IJ: 13266
J: 13265

Papier-mâché
IJ: 13268

Papillomavirus
JS: 11656

Parachutists — Biography
IJ: 8365

Paraguay
IJ: 9999–00

Paranormal phenomena
JS: 13372

Parasites
IJ: 12383, 12419

Parasites (biology)
IJ: 11696

Paredes, Americo
IJ: 7808

Parenting
JS: 11921

Parents
JS: 12126

Parents — Fiction
J: 1254, 1298, 1350, 1578, 1869, 1915,
1944, 1983, 2119
JS: 1262

Paris (France)
IJ: 9780, 9785

Paris (France) — Fiction
IJ: 758, 1521, 3009, 3787, 4527, 6195

Parker, Cynthia Ann — Fiction
JS: 4900

Parkinson's disease
J: 11676, 11586

Parkour
IJ: 13389

Parks, Rosa
IJ: 8111, 8113, 10778, 10810
J: 8112

Parrots
IJ: 12494

Parthenon (Greece)
IJ: 9029
J: 9030, 9400
JS: 12962

Parties
IJ: 12001, 13142
J: 13108

Passover
IJ: 10587

Passover — Fiction
JS: 5318

Pasteur, Louis
IJ: 8612
JS: 8610–11

Paterson, Katherine
IJ: 7809–10

Patrick, Danica
IJ: 8673
J: 8674

Patriot Act (U.S.)
JS: 10820

Patriotism
J: 10935

Patton, George S.
J: 8324

Paulsen, Gary
IJ: 7811–12–13

Pavlov, Ivan
J: 8613

Payne, Lucille M. W.
JS: 8992

PCP (drug)
J: 11490

Peace
IJ: 11176
J: 10618

Peace — Folklore
IJ: 7188

Peace — Poetry
JS: 7073

Peace Corps
IJ: 10595

Peace movements
IJ: 8811
JS: 10610

Peace movements — Fiction
J: 2526

Peanut butter
IJ: 13186

Pearl Harbor
IJ: 9555, 10366, 10369
J: 9480
JS: 10367

Pearl Harbor — Fiction
J: 5255

Peary, Marie Ahnighito
IJ: 8993

Peary, Robert E.
J: 7565
JS: 10016

Peary, Robert E. — Fiction
J: 4978

Peer pressure
IJ: 12078
JS: 12036, 12087

Peer pressure — Fiction
IJ: 1975

Pei, I. M.
J: 7671

Pele (soccer player)
J: 8772

Pelosi, Nancy
IJ: 8326
J: 8325

Pen pals — Fiction
IJ: 724

IJ = Upper Elementary/Lower Middle School; J = Middle School/Junior High; JS = Junior High/Senior High

Penguins
IJ: 12509–10–11–12–13–14

Penicillin
J: 11708

Penmanship — Fiction
IJ: 4735

Penn, William
IJ: 10148
J: 8327

Pennsylvania
IJ: 10148, 10443, 10462
J: 10436

Pennsylvania — Fiction
IJ: 4711, 4949
J: 4651, 4904
JS: 494

Perception
J: 11806

Periodic table
IJ: 12663, 12667, 12682–83–84–85, 12690–91

Perkins, Frances
JS: 8328

Persia
IJ: 9323
J: 9405

Persia — Biography
IJ: 7823

Persia — Fiction
J: 5181

Persian New Year
IJ: 10515

Personal appearance
JS: 11753, 11759

Personal finance
J: 11234, 11452, 11455
JS: 11448–49

Personal freedom
J: 10625

Personal guidance
IJ: 11252, 11256, 11256, 11951, 11959, 11961, 11998, 12017, 12028–29, 12032, 12034, 12043, 12048, 12060, 12069, 12085, 12094, 12098, 12109, 12123, 12988, 13200
J: 9127, 11960, 12008–09, 12013, 12019–20, 12023, 12025, 12033, 12035, 12052, 12055, 12064–65–66–67, 12077, 12079, 12089, 12092–93, 12100, 12120, 12136
JS: 10530, 10540, 10888, 10888, 11301, 11459, 11828, 11833, 11996, 12006, 12010–11, 12014, 12016, 12018, 12021–22, 12024, 12026, 12031, 12037, 12040, 12044, 12046–47, 12050, 12053, 12053, 12063, 12070–71, 12074–75, 12081, 12084, 12086–87–88, 12090–91, 12099

Personal guidance — Fiction
J: 2420

Personal problems
IJ: 12069, 12133
JS: 12030

Personal problems — Fiction
IJ: 80, 327, 411, 515, 585, 670, 688, 878, 885, 989, 1189, 1263, 1306, 1337, 1360, 1375, 1391, 1443, 1517–18, 1537, 1549, 1593, 1625, 1664, 1704, 1706, 1729, 1757, 1825, 1841, 1843, 1855, 1858, 1868, 1888, 1891, 1900, 1913, 1926, 1928, 1948, 1972, 1974, 1994, 1997, 1999, 2007, 2030, 2035, 2040, 2046–47–48, 2061, 2065, 2073, 2079, 2081, 2114–15, 2124, 2146, 2153, 2157, 2163–64, 2197–98, 2249, 2253, 2262, 2271, 2302, 2310, 2318, 2335, 2352, 2355, 2362, 2368, 2376, 2382, 2404, 2407, 2431, 2455, 2461, 2474, 2479, 2561, 3277, 4212, 4312, 4382, 4443, 4583, 4735, 4801, 4856, 4867, 4971, 5023, 5071, 5084, 5158, 5176, 5577, 6125, 6716, 6721, 6873, 6908
J: 54, 164, 311, 380, 965, 1107, 1121, 1192, 1240, 1274, 1289, 1296, 1454, 1582, 1594, 1632, 1666, 1715, 1725, 1754, 1817, 1824, 1826, 1837, 1839, 1842, 1847, 1852, 1856, 1862, 1873, 1875, 1886–87, 1903–04, 1914–15, 1919, 1922, 1927, 1931, 1933, 1936–37, 1944, 1961, 1963, 1971, 1973, 1976, 1982, 1986, 1992, 2004, 2006, 2012, 2018, 2026, 2028–29, 2042, 2050, 2056, 2059, 2071, 2084, 2090–91–92, 2104, 2112–13, 2121–22, 2129, 2132, 2139, 2142, 2144, 2150, 2167–68–69, 2187–88, 2192, 2199–00, 2202, 2204, 2213, 2217, 2220, 2226, 2236, 2261, 2263, 2268, 2307, 2324, 2331, 2333–34, 2349, 2372, 2375, 2377, 2392, 2396–97, 2399, 2408, 2411, 2418, 2435, 2453, 2456, 2465, 2475, 2477, 2497, 2754, 2791, 4256, 4270, 4526, 4567, 5296, 5397, 5661, 5677, 5738, 5745, 5756, 5760, 5762, 5790, 6402, 6722, 6817
JS: 133, 251, 578, 907, 1099, 1154, 1204, 1370, 1414, 1619, 1730, 1748, 1801, 1810, 1815, 1834, 1853, 1872, 1881–82, 1896, 1911, 1929, 1932, 1940–41, 1966, 1985, 1989, 1998, 2025, 2049, 2058, 2087, 2103, 2117, 2120, 2215, 2218, 2234, 2247, 2272, 2304, 2306, 2308, 2311, 2329, 2343, 2358, 2365, 2385, 2400, 2427, 2437, 2444, 2450–51, 2458, 2480, 2536, 2542, 2716, 4281, 4593, 5003, 5284, 5452, 5810, 6395, 6816, 6850

Personal problems — Poetry
IJ: 7110

Peru
IJ: 9993, 10006

Peru — Fiction
J: 217, 2482

Peru — Folklore
IJ: 7318

Peruvian Indians — Fiction
J: 2482

Petroleum
IJ: 12892
JS: 12886, 12894

Pets
See also Cats; Dogs
IJ: 12421, 12618, 12630
JS: 12611

Pharaohs — Fiction
J: 4174

Philadelphia (PA)
IJ: 10461
JS: 10196

Philadelphia (PA) — Fiction
J: 4689, 4702
JS: 2423

Philadelphia Centennial Exhibition — Fiction
JS: 4973

Philanthropy — Biography
J: 8554
JS: 8809

Philippines — Biography
JS: 8854

Philosophy
IJ: 10514

Philosophy — Biography
IJ: 8923

Phobias
J: 11848

Phobias — Fiction
IJ: 1745, 5681
J: 44, 2012, 5890, 6888

Phosphorus
IJ: 12664, 12684

Photography
IJ: 9067, 13274–75, 13278
J: 8183, 9098, 9104, 13272–73
JS: 9059–60, 9083, 9100, 9262, 9932, 10851, 12211

Photography — Biography
J: 7611–12, 7618, 7646, 7649, 7656, 7691
JS: 7617, 7819

Photography — Careers
J: 11382

Photography — Fiction
IJ: 5354
J: 951, 2091
JS: 963

Photojournalism
JS: 9060

Photojournalism — Biography
JS: 7686

Photojournalism — Fiction
J: 456

IJ = Upper Elementary/Lower Middle School; J = Middle School/Junior High; JS = Junior High/Senior High

IJ = Upper Elementary/Lower Middle School; J = Middle School/Junior High; JS = Junior High/Senior High

Poland
J: 9773

Poland — Biography
IJ: 8922

Poland — Fiction
J: 4439, 4457, 4504, 4560, 5216, 5265–66, 5287
JS: 4480

Polar bears
IJ: 12455, 12522
J: 12456
JS: 12458

Polar regions
IJ: 7527, 10026
J: 10030
JS: 10011

Police
JS: 10693, 10693, 11108, 12096

Police — Fiction
J: 1933, 3500

Polio
J: 11610, 11659

Polio — Fiction
IJ: 1672, 5107, 5237
J: 5115, 5121

Polio vaccine
J: 11708

Polish Americans
IJ: 10923

Polish Americans — Fiction
IJ: 4930
J: 5073

Politi, Leo
IJ: 7674

Political activism
IJ: 11173

Political activism — Biography
JS: 8807

Political activism — Fiction
JS: 2021

Political corruption — Fiction
J: 2531

Political parties
IJ: 10727

Political parties (U.S.)
J: 10726
JS: 10728

Politicians (U.S.) — Biography
J: 8265

Politics
JS: 10725

Polk, James K.
IJ: 8039

Pollution
See also Air pollution; Water pollution
IJ: 11042, 11044, 13053
JS: 10986, 11016, 11040, 11046

Polo, Marco
IJ: 7566
J: 7567

Polo, Marco — Fiction
IJ: 468

Polygamy — Fiction
J: 6277

Polynesia — Fiction
IJ: 273

Pompeii (Italy)
IJ: 9254, 9410, 9824

Pompeii (Italy) — Fiction
J: 4180

Ponce de Leon, Juan
IJ: 7568

Ponds
IJ: 12746

Ponies — Fiction
J: 381

Pony Express
J: 10297
JS: 10298

Pony Express — Fiction
J: 4783, 4870, 4897

Pop art
IJ: 9043
J: 7596, 9071

Pop-up books
IJ: 2662, 9031

Popes — Biography
J: 8907–08

Popular culture
J: 10379

Popular music — Biography
J: 7610

Popular music — Fiction
J: 1912

Popularity — Fiction
IJ: 472, 1959, 2022, 2070, 2126, 2140–41, 2225, 2472
J: 522, 590, 594, 699, 746, 898, 918, 970, 1016, 1908, 2250, 2414, 2478, 6799, 6857
JS: 471, 838, 855, 964, 1821, 3801

Population
IJ: 11052, 11056–57

Pornography
JS: 11147

Porpoises
IJ: 12596
JS: 12599

Portraits — Fiction
JS: 431

Portugal
IJ: 9866, 9869

Possums — Fiction
IJ: 326

Post-impressionism
J: 9081

Post-traumatic stress disorder
J: 11873

Post-traumatic stress disorder — Fiction
J: 1762, 5115

Potter, Harry
J: 13257

Pottery — Biography
IJ: 8369

Pottery — Fiction
IJ: 4321

Poverty
IJ: 10996, 11133, 11138, 11141
J: 11135, 11137, 11140
JS: 10080, 11139, 11143, 11145, 11174

Poverty — Biography
IJ: 8401

Poverty — Fiction
IJ: 516, 1187, 1306, 1371, 1468, 1478, 1850, 4428, 5065, 5068, 5071, 5132–33–34, 5169
J: 1089, 1097, 1261, 1520, 1652, 1875, 2531, 4319, 4386, 4937, 4962, 5047, 6785
JS: 720, 1030, 1177, 1349, 1649, 1649, 2517, 4451

Powell, Colin
IJ: 8329, 8331–32
J: 8330, 8333

Powell, John Wesley
IJ: 10314

Practical jokes — Fiction
IJ: 5652
J: 671

Prague (Czech Republic) — Fiction
IJ: 4454

Prairies
IJ: 12750

Prayers
IJ: 10533
J: 10542

Predictions
J: 13321
JS: 11163

Pregnancy
IJ: 11918
JS: 8997, 11927, 11933

Pregnancy — Fiction
IJ: 2153
J: 1270, 1534, 1886, 1982, 5036
JS: 586, 937, 1506, 1656, 1981, 2043, 2066, 2147, 2251, 2357, 2391, 5126

Prehistoric animals — Fiction
J: 377

IJ = Upper Elementary/Lower Middle School; J = Middle School/Junior High; JS = Junior High/Senior High

IJ = Upper Elementary/Lower Middle School; J = Middle School/Junior High; JS = Junior High/Senior High

Puerto Ricans — Fiction
J: 1050, 1076, 1144–45–46, 1166, 5136
JS: 1619

Puerto Rico
IJ: 9983
JS: 9977, 9985

Puerto Rico — Fiction
IJ: 1062, 2289, 4562
JS: 1165

Puffins
J: 12497

Pujols, Albert
IJ: 8696

Pulaski, Casimir
IJ: 8915

Pulitzer, Joseph
IJ: 8615

Pullman strike (1894)
JS: 11243

Pullman, Philip
J: 7818

Pumpkin decorating
IJ: 13131

Punic Wars — Fiction
J: 4194

Puppets and marionettes
IJ: 13213

Puppets and marionettes — Fiction
All: 2823
IJ: 4323, 5399, 7244
J: 3019

Puritans
J: 9422

Putin, Vladimir
J: 8916

Puzzles — Fiction
IJ: 489, 619–20, 5795, 5868

Puzzles — Poetry
IJ: 7070

Pyramids
IJ: 9356, 9361, 9367, 9369, 9376
J: 9032, 9377
JS: 9038

Pythagoras
IJ: 12765

Q

Quadrino, James
IJ: 8616

Quadruplets — Fiction
IJ: 1337

Quakers — Fiction
J: 1345

Quantum mechanics — Fiction
J: 6657

Quebec (province)
J: 9951

Quilts and quilting
IJ: 13293, 13299–00

Quilts and quilting — Fiction
IJ: 4860
J: 4677

Quinceañera (coming-of-age ritual)
JS: 11184

Quinceañera (coming-of-age ritual) — Fiction
J: 1050, 1052, 1071, 1164

Quinn, Anthony
J: 7984

Quotations
IJ: 11264
J: 7473

R

Rabbits — Fiction
IJ: 3275
JS: 2559–60

Rabies — Fiction
JS: 5056

Raccoons
JS: 8991

Raccoons — Fiction
IJ: 331

Race discrimination
J: 10371

Race relations
J: 10884–85
JS: 10800, 10863

Race relations — Fiction
IJ: 849, 4979, 5039, 5131
J: 609, 2161, 5140
JS: 1182, 4269, 5118, 5130, 5168

Race relations (U.S.)
JS: 10863

Race riots
JS: 10804

Racial prejudice
IJ: 8368, 10684

Racial prejudice — Fiction
JS: 5851

Racial profiling
J: 10860

Racially mixed people
JS: 10857, 10861–62

Racially mixed people — Biography
IJ: 7908
J: 7806, 7907, 7954, 7982, 8090, 8129

Racially mixed people — Fiction
IJ: 935, 1135, 1390, 1571, 2016, 4485
J: 821, 1134, 1162, 1172, 1328, 1530, 1567, 2161, 2440, 4783, 5238
JS: 1486, 4822

Racism
IJ: 10799, 10855
JS: 10779, 10865, 10877, 11278

Racism — Fiction
IJ: 727, 1084, 1276, 3030, 4553, 5038, 5098, 5149
J: 1112, 1137, 1195, 1198, 1205, 1651, 2428, 2501, 2510, 4790, 5061
JS: 702, 1093, 1116, 1934, 4825, 5010, 5045, 5099

Radiation
JS: 12866

Radio — Biography
J: 8353

Radio — Careers
JS: 11386

Radio — Fiction
IJ: 5193
JS: 825

Radioactivity
IJ: 12863
JS: 12866

Radium
IJ: 8499

Railroads and trains
IJ: 10291, 10312, 13069–70–71
J: 13067–68
JS: 11243, 13064

Railroads and trains — Fiction
J: 4927, 5161

Rain forests
IJ: 7320, 12492, 12725, 12725–26–27, 12731–32–33, 12735–36
JS: 12728–29

Rain forests — Fiction
J: 217, 1403

Rains Retreat
IJ: 10516

Raleigh, Sir Walter
J: 7569

Raleigh, Sir Walter — Fiction
IJ: 4360

Rama (Hindu deity) — Fiction
J: 3084

Ramadan
IJ: 10574

Ramadan — Fiction
J: 1179

Ramon, Ilan
IJ: 7570

IJ = Upper Elementary/Lower Middle School; J = Middle School/Junior High; JS = Junior High/Senior High

Ramsay, Gordon
J: 8994

Ramses II
J: 8824

**Ranches and ranch life —
Fiction**
IJ: 2281, 2310
J: 231
JS: 1414

Randolph, A. Philip
J: 8114

Rankin, Jeannette
J: 8334

Rap music — Biography
IJ: 7945–46, 7966, 7993
J: 7958
JS: 7992

Rap music — Fiction
J: 1161
JS: 2191

Rape
JS: 11071

Rape — Fiction
J: 1688, 1836, 1939, 2346, 6799
JS: 1119, 1834, 5937

Rasputin, Grigory
J: 8917

Ratio and proportion
IJ: 12765

Rats — Fiction
IJ: 423, 2721, 2824, 2842, 3457

Rattlesnakes
IJ: 12406

Ravens — Poetry
J: 7140

Ray, Rachael
J: 8617

Reagan, Ronald
IJ: 8040, 8206
J: 8207–08

Reality television — Fiction
IJ: 711
J: 162, 529, 532, 1254, 5914, 6702
JS: 752, 1297, 1694

Ream, Vinnie — Fiction
J: 4837

Recession (economy) — Fiction
IJ: 2521

Reconstruction
IJ: 10327

Reconstruction (U.S.)
IJ: 10323, 10336, 10338
J: 10321
JS: 10238, 10324, 10332

Reconstruction (U.S.) — Fiction
IJ: 4974, 5000
J: 4963, 4985
JS: 4831

Recreation
IJ: 13115

Recreation — Careers
J: 11369

Recycling
IJ: 11001
J: 11050, 13284

Red Cross — Biography
J: 8350

Red knot
JS: 12489

Reece, Gabrielle
IJ: 8773

Reeve, Christopher
J: 7985

Reeves, Bass — Fiction
IJ: 4911

Reform school — Fiction
J: 756

Reformation
IJ: 9450

Refugees
IJ: 9927, 10600, 10614
J: 9519, 10601–02, 10850, 10921, 10932
JS: 9512, 9968, 10598, 10605, 10829, 10896, 10900

Refugees — Biography
JS: 8975

Refugees — Fiction
IJ: 2500, 2544, 4350, 4431, 4587, 5105, 5305
J: 957, 1117, 1168, 2551, 4303, 5181, 5206, 5333
JS: 2492, 2502, 2550

Reggae music — Biography
IJ: 7971
J: 7972

Reincarnation — Fiction
IJ: 1448
J: 3775, 5473, 6082
JS: 3401–02

Reiss, Johanna
J: 8995

Relativity (physics)
IJ: 8524
JS: 12853

Religion
IJ: 9447, 10078, 10078, 10141, 10519–20–21, 10523, 10551
J: 9426, 10525, 10535, 10622, 10638, 10686
JS: 10517, 10517–18, 10518, 10522, 10536, 10545–46, 10941

Religion — Biography
IJ: 8808, 8856

Religion — Fiction
IJ: 1347, 2170
J: 864, 1426, 2084, 2122, 2439, 5033,

5699, 6824, 6928

Religion — Poetry
J: 7081
JS: 7072

Remarriage — Fiction
IJ: 1540

Rembert, Winfred
IJ: 7675

Rembrandt van Rijn
IJ: 7676
J: 7677
JS: 7678

Rembrandt van Rijn — Fiction
IJ: 4419
JS: 4392

Renaissance
IJ: 9054, 9428, 9450
J: 9077, 9424, 9440, 11707

Renaissance — Biography
IJ: 7637–38–39–40–41, 8550, 8910, 8912
J: 7663, 8551

Renaissance — Fiction
IJ: 4453, 5857
J: 4370, 4434
JS: 4440, 6373

Rendille (African people)
IJ: 9618

Renewable energy
IJ: 12888
J: 11311, 11314

Renoir, Pierre-Auguste
IJ: 7679

Report writing
J: 11277, 11293

Reproduction
J: 11768, 11772, 11919, 11930, 11934
JS: 11935

Reptiles
See also Alligators and crocodiles
IJ: 12388, 12390, 12392, 12422
J: 12394
JS: 12389, 12391

Reptiles — Fiction
JS: 980

Republican Party
IJ: 10337, 10724

**Resistance movement (World
War II) — Fiction**
J: 5229

Respiratory system
J: 11772, 11803
JS: 11805

Responsibility — Fiction
J: 5691

Revenge — Fiction
IJ: 2186
J: 4364
JS: 962

Revere, Paul
IJ: 8392

Revere, Paul — Fiction
IJ: 5725

Revolutionaries — Biography
J: 8932, 8939, 8941

Revolutionary period (U.S.)
IJ: 10047, 10169, 10193–94
JS: 10173

Revolutionary period (U.S.) — Biography
IJ: 8135, 8284, 8286
J: 8059, 8276, 8278
JS: 8136, 8279

Revolutionary period (U.S.) — Fiction
IJ: 4701
J: 4702, 4709, 4720

Revolutionary War (U.S.)
IJ: 8249, 10174–75–76, 10178–79–80, 10182, 10185–86, 10189, 10191, 10197–98, 10200, 10202–03
J: 9460, 10157, 10171, 10177, 10187, 13099
JS: 10190, 10192, 10195

Revolutionary War (U.S.) — Biography
IJ: 8238, 8252–53, 8255–56, 8285, 8288–89, 8297, 8299, 8320, 8392, 8394–95, 8915
J: 8250, 8254, 8298, 8321, 8980

Revolutionary War (U.S.) — Fiction
IJ: 4038, 4685, 4690, 4695–96, 4700, 4704–05–06, 4711, 4715
J: 2712, 4621, 4688, 4692–93, 4697, 4703, 4707–08, 4710, 4713–14, 4716, 4719
JS: 4067

Revolutions
See also specific revolutions, e.g., French Revolution; Industrial Revolution
J: 9678

Revolutions — Fiction
JS: 157

Rheumatic fever
IJ: 11632

Rhinoceroses
IJ: 12431, 12441, 12519

Rhode Island
IJ: 9036
J: 10437

Rhode Island — Biography
J: 8347

Rhode Island — Fiction
IJ: 5355
J: 6081

Rhodes-Courter, Ashley
JS: 8996

Rhodesia — Fiction
IJ: 4265

Rhythm and blues (music)
J: 9126

Rice
IJ: 12347

Rice, Condoleezza
IJ: 8335–36

Rice, Jerry
IJ: 8735

Ride, Sally
IJ: 7572–73
J: 7571

Rihanna
IJ: 7986

Riis, Jacob
JS: 7819

Rikers Island (NY) — Fiction
JS: 2426

Ringelblum, Emmanuel
IJ: 8918

Ringling Brothers
IJ: 8618

Rio de Janeiro — Fiction
JS: 720

Riordan, Rick
J: 7820

Riot Grrrl movement
J: 10822

Riots — Fiction
J: 986
JS: 4822

Ritalin (drug)
J: 11483

Ritalin (drug) — Fiction
J: 1769

Rivera, Diego
IJ: 7680
J: 7681–82–83

Rivers
IJ: 10136, 12739–40–41–42–43–44, 12747, 12749

Rizal, Jose
JS: 8854

Road trips — Fiction
IJ: 881
JS: 693

Roanoke Colony
IJ: 10160

Roanoke Colony — Fiction
IJ: 6523
J: 4681, 6349

Robbers and robbery
IJ: 11113

Robbers and robbery — Fiction
IJ: 4323
J: 4236

JS: 523

Roberts, Edward
IJ: 8619

Robin Hood
J: 7246, 7254, 7259, 7270

Robin Hood — Fiction
IJ: 274–75, 4227
J: 4208–09
JS: 4248

Robinson, Jackie
IJ: 8697, 8699
JS: 8698

Robinson, Jackie — Fiction
IJ: 3030

Robinson, Mary
J: 8919

Robots
IJ: 12981, 12992, 12995, 13001, 13219

Robots — Fiction
IJ: 2971, 3887, 6422–23–24, 6660
J: 6182, 6541, 6599
JS: 4135, 6181

Rock carvings — Fiction
J: 2506

Rock music
J: 9124, 9127, 9129
JS: 9117, 9120

Rock music — Biography
IJ: 7943, 7955, 9121
J: 7610, 7917, 7935, 7964, 7980–81
JS: 7905, 7916, 7960, 7970
S: 7973

Rock music — Criticism
JS: 9128

Rock music — Fiction
IJ: 3896, 5801
J: 610, 1298, 5701
JS: 872, 1920, 2031, 2419, 3986

Rock, Chris
IJ: 7987

Rockefeller, John D.
IJ: 8620

Rockets
IJ: 8556
J: 8449

Rocks and minerals
IJ: 12760, 12762–63
J: 12757–58
JS: 11020, 12755, 12761

Rocks and minerals — Experiments and projects
J: 12764

Rockwell, Norman
IJ: 7684

Rocky Mountains
IJ: 10421

Rodeos — Fiction
J: 1644

IJ = Upper Elementary/Lower Middle School; J = Middle School/Junior High; JS = Junior High/Senior High

Rodriguez, Robert
J: 7988

Rogers, Robert
IJ: 8393

Rogers, Will
IJ: 7989

Roller hockey
JS: 13529

Roman Empire
J: 9418

Roman Empire — Biography
IJ: 8871, 8873

Roman Empire — Fiction
IJ: 4201
J: 4197
JS: 4203

Romance — Fiction
IJ: 249, 993, 2394, 3875, 4111, 4736, 4780, 4863, 4923, 5112, 5663, 6321
J: 71, 317, 461, 521, 567, 624, 627, 873, 876, 941, 1217, 1274, 1454, 1609, 1753, 1813, 1887, 1902, 1963, 1971, 1987, 2062, 2064, 2094, 2133, 2188, 2326, 2364, 2413, 2456, 2476, 2511, 2686, 2829, 2894, 2934, 3039, 3044, 3079, 3116, 3289, 3345, 3491, 3872, 4059, 4302, 4436, 4488, 4498, 4568, 4588, 4732, 4798, 4811, 4852, 4948, 5205, 5384, 5535, 5537, 5559, 5635, 5651, 5662, 5674, 5679, 5726–27, 5734, 5734, 5793, 5977, 6119, 6289, 6291, 6293–94, 6302–03, 6306, 6308, 6313–14, 6319–20, 6322, 6324–25, 6334, 6334–35, 6338, 6341, 6343, 6349, 6353, 6357, 6359, 6361–62– 63–64–65–66, 6368–69, 6375, 6377, 6379–80, 6386–87, 6389–90–91–92– 93–94, 6396–97, 6399–00, 6402–03– 04–05–06, 6408, 6452, 7176
JS: 78, 895, 1870, 1907, 1910, 1935, 2019, 2058, 2103, 2109, 2203, 2207, 2215, 2215, 2224, 2304, 2336, 2436, 2513, 2543, 2697, 2715, 2940, 3202, 3676, 3904, 3934, 3968, 4122, 4128, 4475, 4480, 4518, 5138, 5657, 5737, 6118, 6292, 6295–96–97–98, 6300–01, 6304, 6309–10, 6312, 6315, 6317–18, 6323, 6326–27, 6331, 6333, 6337, 6339, 6345, 6347, 6355–56, 6358, 6367, 6373–74, 6376, 6378, 6381–82– 83–84, 6388, 6395, 6398, 6407, 6617

Romance — Poetry
JS: 7164

Romania — Biography
J: 8988

Romania — Fiction
J: 7267

Rome
IJ: 9407–08, 9408, 9411–12, 9414, 9416, 9419–20, 9819, 9822–23
J: 9378, 9409, 9413, 9415, 9417–18
JS: 9406

Rome — Biography
J: 8872, 8882

Rome — Crafts
IJ: 9414

Rome — Fiction
IJ: 4192–93, 4202, 4365
J: 4194

Rome — Mythology
JS: 7358, 7388

Romeo and Juliet (play)
J: 6973

Romeo and Juliet (play) —
Adaptations
J: 6976

Romeo and Juliet (play) —
Criticism
J: 7429
JS: 7431, 7433

Romeo and Juliet (play) —
Fiction
J: 3610

Roosevelt, Eleanor
IJ: 8212–13–14–15–16, 10356
J: 8209–10–11

Roosevelt, Franklin D.
IJ: 8217–18, 8220–21, 10343
J: 8219, 8222–23, 10359

Roosevelt, Franklin D. and Eleanor
IJ: 8224

Roosevelt, Theodore
IJ: 8039, 8227–28
J: 8225–26, 8229, 8231
JS: 8230

Rope jumping
IJ: 13377

Rosenberg, Isaac
JS: 6999

Rosenfeld, Fanny Bobbie
IJ: 8774

Ross, Betsy
IJ: 8394–95

Round the world travel — Fiction
J: 25

Rowling, J. K.
IJ: 7821–22

Royalty
IJ: 9451

Royalty — Biography
IJ: 8794

Royalty — Fiction
IJ: 2875
J: 1417, 4251, 4437, 4462, 4520, 6703
JS: 447

Rulers
IJ: 9295

Rumi
IJ: 7823

Rumors — Fiction
JS: 669

Runaways — Fiction
IJ: 1019, 1320, 1605, 1785, 1841, 1949, 3380, 4945
J: 99, 650, 1245, 1328, 1384, 1950, 2150, 2244, 2425, 2468, 4368, 4506, 5926
JS: 588, 796, 801, 922, 946, 1207, 1331, 1353, 2218, 2400, 2491

Running and jogging
J: 13545

Running and jogging — Biography
JS: 8753

Running and jogging — Fiction
IJ: 169, 1400, 6819, 13547
J: 649, 2067

Runyan, Brent
JS: 8998

Rural life
See also Farms and farm life

Rural life — Fiction
IJ: 812, 882, 4267

Rural youth
IJ: 10922

Russia
IJ: 8979, 9829
J: 9840, 9848, 9852
JS: 9843

Russia — Biography
J: 8874, 8916–17
JS: 8875

Russia — Cookbooks
J: 13185

Russia — Fiction
IJ: 4426, 4466, 4489, 5042, 5194
J: 262, 2740, 4514, 4547, 5312, 5922
JS: 4407, 4442

Russia — Folklore
IJ: 7258, 7263
JS: 7243

Russia — Mythology
IJ: 7327

Russian Americans
IJ: 10933

Russian Americans — Fiction
J: 1055, 4991

Russian Revolution
JS: 9833

Russian Revolution — Biography
J: 8909

Russian Revolution — Fiction
IJ: 4489

IJ = Upper Elementary/Lower Middle School; J = Middle School/Junior High; JS = Junior High/Senior High

IJ = Upper Elementary/Lower Middle School; J = Middle School/Junior High; JS = Junior High/Senior High

IJ = Upper Elementary/Lower Middle School; J = Middle School/Junior High; JS = Junior High/Senior High

Seti I
IJ: 9370

1700s — Fiction
J: 4682

1770s — Fiction
J: 4585

1790s — Fiction
J: 5987

17th century — Fiction
IJ: 65

Sewing
IJ: 13291, 13295, 13299
JS: 13204, 13279, 13301

Sex — Fiction
J: 2052, 2093, 2238, 2383, 2392, 6334
JS: 2427, 2459, 5671, 6301

Sex education
IJ: 11958–59
J: 11955, 11960, 12033, 12093
JS: 11459, 11949–50, 11954, 11956–57, 11971, 11974

Sex education — Fiction
J: 938

Sex roles
J: 11152
JS: 11973

Sex roles — Fiction
J: 491

Sexism
JS: 10747

Sexual abuse
IJ: 11958, 11976
JS: 11978, 11980–81

Sexual abuse — Fiction
J: 581, 1335, 1381, 1778, 1813, 2305
JS: 1229, 1280, 1283, 1569, 1643, 1711, 1740, 1756, 2297

Sexual harassment
JS: 11979

Sexual orientation
JS: 11154

Sexually transmitted diseases
JS: 11583, 11678, 11701

Shackleton, Sir Ernest
IJ: 7577, 10018
J: 7576
JS: 7578

Shakers (religion)
IJ: 10555
J: 10554

Shakers (religion) — Fiction
IJ: 4980

Shakespeare, William
IJ: 6967, 7828, 7831, 9031
J: 7829, 7832
JS: 7433, 7830

Shakespeare, William — Adaptations
J: 4073–74–75, 4148–49–50, 6971, 6973
JS: 4072

Shakespeare, William — Criticism
J: 6975
JS: 7430–31–32

Shakespeare, William — Fiction
IJ: 597, 4371–72, 4557, 6090
J: 4505
JS: 690, 4432, 4471, 4491, 4516

Shakespeare, William — Plays
IJ: 6965–66, 6968–69, 6978

Shakespeare, William — Plays — Criticism
J: 7429

Shakespeare, William — Poetry
IJ: 6978

Shakur, Tupac
IJ: 7993
JS: 7992

Shakur, Tupac — Fiction
J: 1034

Shamans — Fiction
J: 4348

Shanghai, China
IJ: 9691

Shape shifting — Fiction
JS: 2922, 3565

Sharks
IJ: 9191, 12577, 12579–80–81, 12584, 13572
JS: 12578, 12582–83

Sharks — Biography
J: 8764

Sharks — Fiction
IJ: 5076
JS: 325

Sharpton, Al
JS: 8340

Sheba, Queen of
JS: 8855

Sheep — Fiction
IJ: 3578
J: 231, 3320

Shelley, Mary Wollstonecraft
IJ: 13341
J: 7833

Shepard, Matthew — Fiction
JS: 2534

Sherlock Holmes — Fiction
JS: 420, 3841

Shetland Islands — Fiction
J: 3137

Ships and boats
See also Warships; *Titanic* (ship)

IJ: 7812, 9882, 9954, 13072, 13078, 13080, 13082–83

Ships and boats — Fiction
IJ: 17, 278, 288, 4785
J: 233, 5252
JS: 1941

Shipwrecks
IJ: 12849, 13075, 13078, 13080

Shipwrecks — Fiction
IJ: 177, 502
J: 181, 292, 406, 4296, 4592

Shona (African people)
IJ: 9651

Shoplifting — Fiction
JS: 891

Shopping — Fiction
J: 1807

Shopping malls — Fiction
J: 1978

Short stories — Fiction
IJ: 441, 1185–86–87, 2271, 2606, 2840, 2865, 3447, 3814, 3905, 4353, 5388, 5408, 5490–91, 5496, 5526, 5553, 5579, 5600, 5607, 5696, 5739, 5796, 6834, 6861, 6865, 6867, 6869, 6878, 6881–82, 6882, 6887, 6890–91–92, 6896–97, 6904–05, 6908, 6911, 6918–19, 6930–31, 6934, 6936
J: 433, 440, 1087, 1108, 1124, 1152, 1181, 1903–04, 2366, 2418, 2983, 3121, 3190, 3334, 3338, 3770, 3826, 4487, 4802, 5349, 5377, 5398, 5462, 5493, 5500, 5509, 5514, 5524, 5565–66, 5613, 5638, 5742, 5775, 6290, 6369, 6419, 6451, 6625, 6705, 6752, 6800, 6862, 6868, 6875–76, 6885, 6888, 6894, 6898, 6909–10, 6913–14, 6916, 6920, 6924–25–26–27, 6927–28–29, 6932–33, 6939, 7205, 7267
JS: 251, 402, 420–21–22, 578, 1067–68, 1086, 1092, 1182, 1191, 1249, 1871, 1882, 1946, 2214, 2356, 2358, 2388, 2480, 2541–42, 2564, 2694, 3298, 3697, 3713, 4041, 4127, 5358, 5364, 5436–37, 5525, 5539, 5606, 5620, 5636, 5639, 5809, 5901, 6409, 6412, 6437, 6444, 6530, 6730, 6860, 6863–64, 6866, 6874, 6877, 6879–80, 6883–84, 6893, 6899–00–01–02–03, 6906, 6912, 6915, 6917, 6921–22–23, 6937, 7404

Shoshoni Indians — Fiction
J: 4628, 4870

Shrubs
JS: 12355

Shuttlesworth, Fred L.
JS: 10766

Shyness
IJ: 12057

Shyness — Fiction
IJ: 452, 2048, 6776

IJ = Upper Elementary/Lower Middle School; J = Middle School/Junior High; JS = Junior High/Senior High

Siberia — Biography
JS: 8971

Siblings
J: 12136
JS: 12124

Siblings — Fiction
IJ: 1470, 1757, 3246, 6751
J: 124, 1288, 1296, 1305, 1552, 1561, 1577, 1594, 1635, 1675, 1716, 2179, 2504, 6657
JS: 214, 1985, 3494

Sickle cell anemia
J: 11607

Siegal, Aranka
IJ: 8999

Siegel, Siena Cherson
IJ: 7994

Sight
IJ: 11809

Sign language
J: 11913

Sikhism
J: 10528, 10544
JS: 10536

Silk
IJ: 12548

Silk — Fiction
J: 4355

Silk Road
IJ: 9329

Silkworms
IJ: 12379

Silva, Marina
IJ: 8950

Simmons, Philip
IJ: 7689

Simmons, Russell
J: 9000

Simple machines
J: 12195

Simpson, O. J.
J: 10672

Simulation (computers)
IJ: 12942, 12982

Sinclair, Upton
J: 7484

Singapore
IJ: 9717, 9729

Singer, Isaac Bashevis
J: 7834

Singers and singing — Biography
IJ: 7582, 7896, 7901, 7908, 7956, 7967–68, 7986, 7999
J: 7902, 7928, 7941–42, 7954, 7982, 8936
JS: 7970

Singers and singing — Fiction
IJ: 675
J: 1551, 3673

Single parents — Fiction
IJ: 457, 1851
JS: 1030, 1649, 4451

Sinkholes
IJ: 12759

Sirens (mythology) — Fiction
J: 2684, 3095

Sís, Peter
J: 7835

Sisters — Fiction
IJ: 597, 1537, 1645, 5173
J: 732, 994, 1421, 1960, 2412, 3404, 4436, 6146, 6408
JS: 524, 936, 1014, 1435, 1506, 1532, 1773, 5887

Sistine Chapel
J: 9093

Sitting Bull (Sioux chief)
J: 8341

Sitting Bull (Sioux chief) — Fiction
IJ: 4615

Six-Day War
J: 9871

1600s — Fiction
J: 4488

16th century — Fiction
J: 4486
JS: 4402, 4422

Skara Brae
IJ: 9234

Skateboarding
IJ: 13550–51–52
JS: 13549, 13553

Skateboarding — Biography
JS: 8765–66

Skateboarding — Fiction
IJ: 5506, 6833
J: 6761, 6853

Skiing
IJ: 13559
J: 13561
JS: 13555

Skiing — Fiction
J: 6830

Skin
JS: 11749, 11764

Skin care
JS: 11764, 11771

Skin disorders
JS: 11771

Sky diving
All: 13401

Skyscrapers
IJ: 9024, 12954

J: 10914

Slavery
See also related topics, e.g., African Americans; Underground Railroad
IJ: 9313, 10053, 10059, 10176, 10183, 10204, 10216, 10224, 10228, 10710, 10784, 10797
J: 10221, 10223, 10226–27, 10330, 10706, 10818, 10871
JS: 10081, 10207, 10209–10, 10217, 10246, 10872, 10874

Slavery — Biography
IJ: 8102, 8123, 8388
J: 8062, 8126, 8384
JS: 8092

Slavery — Fiction
IJ: 4474, 4772
J: 2161, 4894
JS: 4686

Slavery (U.S.)
IJ: 10256
J: 9290, 10206, 10215
JS: 10184

Slavery (U.S.) — Biography
IJ: 8077, 8087, 8389
J: 8120, 8127
JS: 8078

Slavery (U.S.) — Fiction
IJ: 3790, 4263–64, 4690, 4721–22–23, 4733–34, 4740, 4744, 4749, 4756, 4773, 4776, 4784, 4800, 4815, 4817, 4827, 4964
J: 245, 1123, 4260, 4571, 4688, 4694, 4712, 4724, 4730–31–32, 4738, 4748, 4750, 4770–71, 4786, 4806–07, 5518, 5987
JS: 3279, 4234, 4565, 4717–18, 4753, 4759, 4762, 4774, 4831, 5010

Slavery (U.S.) — Folk songs
IJ: 9137
J: 9136

Slavery (U.S.) — Poetry
JS: 7136

Sled dogs — Fiction
IJ: 222, 261, 483, 1618
J: 79
JS: 1214

Sleep
JS: 11776, 11784, 11788

Sleep — Fiction
IJ: 3166

Sleep apnea
IJ: 11580

Sleep disorders
JS: 11681

Sleep disorders — Fiction
JS: 6210

Sleeping sickness
IJ: 11662

Sleepwalking — Fiction
JS: 5423

IJ = Upper Elementary/Lower Middle School; J = Middle School/Junior High; JS = Junior High/Senior High

Slovakia
IJ: 9837

Slovenia
IJ: 9851

Slugs — Fiction
JS: 6495

Smallpox
IJ: 11664

Smallpox — Fiction
JS: 4898

Smith, John
J: 7579

Smoking
IJ: 11500, 11532, 11537, 11549
J: 11529–30
JS: 11484, 11507, 11522

Smoking — Fiction
J: 1937

Smuggling
IJ: 11069

Smuggling — Fiction
IJ: 5251, 5820

Snakes
IJ: 12400, 12405, 12407–08
J: 12409–10
JS: 12403

Sneakers (shoes)
IJ: 12923

Sneezing
J: 11804

Snow
IJ: 13130

Snow leopards
IJ: 12467

Snowboarding
IJ: 13554, 13556–57, 13560
JS: 13558

Snowboarding — Biography
IJ: 8776

Snowboarding — Fiction
IJ: 6716, 6735, 6829
JS: 701

Snowmen
IJ: 13130

Soccer
IJ: 13564, 13568
J: 13563, 13565
JS: 13562, 13566–67

Soccer — Biography
J: 8772

Soccer — Fiction
IJ: 2143, 4027, 5822, 6708, 6731,
6760, 6771, 6776, 6779, 6808, 6835,
6846
J: 1862, 6754, 6772, 6794, 6799
JS: 700, 977, 1606, 2128, 3518, 4279

Social action
IJ: 11165

JS: 11136, 11164

Social action — Fiction
J: 2470

Social change — Biography
IJ: 8630

Social concerns
IJ: 11172
J: 10762

Social networks
IJ: 10043

Social problems
JS: 10944

Social work — Biography
IJ: 8070
J: 8071

Socrates
IJ: 8923

Sodium
IJ: 12680

Softball — Fiction
IJ: 6795
J: 910

Software engineers — Careers
IJ: 11433

Solar eclipses — Fiction
IJ: 2211

Solar energy
IJ: 12877

Solar system
See also names of specific bodies, e.g.,
Mars (planet)
IJ: 12206, 12279, 12285, 12300
J: 12280, 12290

Soldiers
IJ: 9295, 10175

Soldiers — Fiction
IJ: 4191
JS: 4475

Solon
J: 8924

Somalia
JS: 9607

Somalia — Fiction
J: 4522

Son Thi Anh, Tuyet
IJ: 9001–02

Songhay (African people)
IJ: 9653

Songs
IJ: 9138, 9143, 9145
J: 9139–40, 9144

Soninke (African people)
IJ: 9662

Sonoran Desert
IJ: 10509

Sosa, Sammy
IJ: 13457

J: 8703

Sotomayor, Sonia
IJ: 8342–43

Sound
IJ: 12921

**Sound — Experiments and
projects**
IJ: 12919–20

South (U.S.)
IJ: 10492
JS: 10344

South (U.S.) — Fiction
IJ: 1888, 5032, 5152
J: 384
JS: 1119, 1193

South (U.S.) — Folklore
J: 7310

South Africa
IJ: 9638, 9646, 9648, 9650
J: 9637
JS: 9636, 9645, 9647

South Africa — Biography
J: 8819
JS: 8820–21, 9636

South Africa — Fiction
IJ: 3589
J: 306, 1147, 4258, 4270, 6913
JS: 563, 991–92, 2495, 2541, 4257

South America
IJ: 9940, 12731
J: 9997

South America — Cookbooks
J: 13183

South America — Crafts
IJ: 13125

South America — Fiction
J: 4567, 4579

South America — Mythology
JS: 7323

South Carolina
IJ: 10493, 10500

South Carolina — Fiction
IJ: 4816, 5012

South Dakota — Fiction
J: 1290

South Korea
IJ: 9742

South Korea — Cookbooks
J: 13154

Southeast Asia
IJ: 9747

Southwest (U.S.)
IJ: 10126, 10507, 10513
JS: 10511

Soviet Republics
J: 9839

IJ = Upper Elementary/Lower Middle School; J = Middle School/Junior High; JS = Junior High/Senior High

Soviet Union
J: 9840, 9845
JS: 9575, 9834, 9838, 9849

Soviet Union — Biography
J: 8909
JS: 8969

Soviet Union — Fiction
J: 4561

Space and time
IJ: 12205, 12782
JS: 12211

Space biology
IJ: 12319

Space exploration
IJ: 12206, 12208, 12222, 12226,
12229, 12231, 12234–35–36, 12238,
12240–41–42–43, 12246, 12249,
12253–54–55–56, 12258, 12260,
12267, 12281, 12283–84, 12288
J: 12217, 12230, 12245, 12257
JS: 12227, 12232

Space exploration — Biography
J: 8444

Space exploration — Careers
IJ: 11354
JS: 11337

Space exploration — Fiction
IJ: 5122
JS: 3836

Space exploration — Poetry
IJ: 7065

Space flight — Fiction
IJ: 5088

Space race
J: 12251

Space race — Fiction
IJ: 5119

Space research
JS: 12252

Space satellites
IJ: 12239, 12248

Space shuttles
JS: 12233

Space stations
IJ: 12228, 12236

Space stations — Fiction
IJ: 6463

Space travel
IJ: 12237, 12240, 12254, 12258–59
J: 8449, 12217

Space travel — Fiction
IJ: 3969, 6434, 6469

Spacewalks
IJ: 12260

Spain
IJ: 9801, 9864–65, 9867
J: 9868, 9937
JS: 9870

Spain — Biography
IJ: 7528
JS: 7672

Spain — Fiction
IJ: 399, 2461, 4410, 4421
J: 2095, 3264, 4244, 4554

Spain — Folklore
J: 7203

Spanish Armada — Fiction
J: 4378

Spanish Harlem (NY)
JS: 10428

Spanish Inquisition
J: 9868, 9868

Spanish Inquisition — Fiction
IJ: 4238
J: 4503
JS: 4555

Spanish language
IJ: 352, 8494

Spanish language — Folklore
IJ: 7318

Spanish language — Poetry
IJ: 6996, 7156
J: 7113
JS: 7098

Spanish Main
J: 9937

Sparta (extinct city) — Fiction
IJ: 4191

Speaking skills
IJ: 11291

Special education — Fiction
IJ: 1006
JS: 1673

Special effects (motion pictures)
IJ: 13030

Speeches
JS: 7397, 7399, 9572, 10654

Speed skating — Biography
J: 8742–43–44

Speedboats
IJ: 13072

Spelling — Fiction
IJ: 803

Spelling bees — Fiction
JS: 1103

Spenser (fictitious character) — Fiction
J: 6138

Sphinx
JS: 9363

Spiders
IJ: 12537, 12549–50, 12553
JS: 12532, 12535

Spiders — Fiction
IJ: 1994

Spiders — Folklore
IJ: 7208

Spielberg, Steven
IJ: 7995–96

Spies and spying
IJ: 9552, 10604, 10611, 11075, 11077,
11112
J: 9887, 10171, 10612, 11070, 11080
JS: 10275, 10613, 11078

Spies and spying — Biography
IJ: 8371, 8402, 8798
J: 11062

Spies and spying — Fiction
IJ: 36, 117, 5979, 5981, 6025, 6207
J: 118, 137, 262, 681, 2167, 3931,
4813, 5202, 5278, 5894, 6026–27,
6032, 6083, 6218, 6438
JS: 6031, 6097–98, 6210

Spinal cord
JS: 11789

Spinelli, Jerry
IJ: 7836

Spiritualism — Fiction
IJ: 6075
J: 4445
JS: 4767

Sports
See also Extreme sports; individual
sports, e.g., Baseball
IJ: 8659, 8664, 8783, 11302, 11940,
12870, 13241, 13384, 13412–13,
13418, 13423
J: 6907, 13376, 13376, 13376, 13376,
13378, 13380, 13390, 13398, 13421,
13426, 13544
JS: 8658, 8781–82, 11304, 13394,
13399, 13404, 13408, 13420, 13420

Sports — Biography
See also under specific sports, e.g.,
Baseball — Biography
IJ: 8653, 8660–61, 8665, 8669, 8756,
8774
J: 8656, 8752
JS: 8757, 8777, 8781–82

Sports — Careers
IJ: 11384
J: 11369, 11380
JS: 11366, 11375

Sports — Experiments and projects
IJ: 12188
J: 12181

Sports — Poetry
IJ: 7050
J: 6907
JS: 7121

Sports cars
IJ: 13058

Sports injuries
JS: 13417

IJ = Upper Elementary/Lower Middle School; J = Middle School/Junior High; JS = Junior High/Senior High

Sports medicine
IJ: 13418

Sports nutrition
J: 11899

Sports stories — Fiction
IJ: 2254, 6732, 6795, 6821, 6827, 6834, 6931
J: 1614, 2429, 5961, 6752, 6907
JS: 578, 6742

Spy satellites
IJ: 12239, 12248

Squanto
IJ: 11178

Sri Lanka
IJ: 9745
JS: 9749

Sri Lanka — Fiction
JS: 2342

Stadiums
IJ: 12967

Stained glass
JS: 13133

Stalingrad, Battle of — Fiction
J: 5312

Stalkers — Fiction
J: 970

Stalking
JS: 11129

Stamps
JS: 13302, 13305

Standardized testing — Fiction
J: 2546

Standish, Myles
J: 8396

Stanley Cup
IJ: 13521

Stanton, Elizabeth Cady
J: 8017, 8117

***Star Wars* (TV and motion picture series)**
IJ: 9167–68
J: 6546, 9164
JS: 6667, 9158–59, 9173

Stars
IJ: 12269–70–71–72–73, 12275–76–77, 12287
J: 12304
JS: 12274, 12278

Stars — Folklore
IJ: 7291

State birds (U.S.)
IJ: 10040

State flags (U.S.)
IJ: 10040, 10052

States (U.S.)
JS: 10044

Statistics
IJ: 12774

Statue of Liberty
IJ: 10440

Stature
IJ: 12082

Stealing — Fiction
IJ: 651, 1269, 4536, 5949, 6024
J: 804, 2113
JS: 2300

Steam engines
IJ: 12948

Steamboats — Biography
IJ: 8546

Steamboats — Fiction
J: 4868

Steel
IJ: 12932

Steffens, Lincoln
J: 7484

Steinbeck, John
IJ: 7839
J: 7837
JS: 7838

Steinbeck, John — Criticism
J: 7424

Steinbeck, John — Fiction
IJ: 2766

Steinem, Gloria
IJ: 8118

Steiner, Matthew
J: 9003

Stem cells
IJ: 11734
J: 12605
JS: 11742

Stepfamilies
IJ: 12121, 12121, 12123
J: 12111

Stepfamilies — Fiction
IJ: 1266–67, 1411, 1431, 1564, 4858, 5445
J: 22, 467, 525, 566, 736, 1327, 1363, 1513, 2398, 2468, 4832, 5444, 5761, 6176, 7174

Stepfathers — Fiction
J: 1778

Stepmothers — Fiction
J: 511

Stepsisters — Fiction
JS: 3716

Stereotypes
JS: 11155

Steroids (drugs)
J: 11478
JS: 11518

Steroids (drugs) — Fiction
J: 1495, 6765, 6847

JS: 6740, 6747

Stevenson, Robert Louis
JS: 13064

Stewart, Bridgett
JS: 8397

Stewart, Martha
J: 8624

Stewart, Tony
IJ: 8675

Stine, R. L.
IJ: 7840

Stock markets
IJ: 11241

Stock markets — Crash of 1929
JS: 10342, 11240

Stomach
J: 11799

Stone, Biz
JS: 8450

Stonehenge — Fiction
IJ: 2943

Stores — Fiction
IJ: 3325

Stories without words — Fiction
J: 4015
JS: 4109, 4135

Storks — Fiction
IJ: 4397

Storms — Fiction
IJ: 74, 288

Storytelling
IJ: 11270–71, 11283
JS: 7189

Storytelling — Fiction
IJ: 2663
J: 2718, 3002, 3428

Stowe, Harriet Beecher
IJ: 7841–42

Strauss, Levi
J: 8625

Strawberries
J: 12330

Stress (mental state)
J: 11835, 11839
JS: 11833, 11863

String games
IJ: 13392

Strokes — Fiction
J: 1755

Student rights
JS: 10717

Study skills
J: 11259
JS: 11258, 11285

Stuttering
J: 11456

IJ = Upper Elementary/Lower Middle School; J = Middle School/Junior High; JS = Junior High/Senior High

1176

IJ = Upper Elementary/Lower Middle School; J = Middle School/Junior High; JS = Junior High/Senior High

Swine flu
IJ: 11580

Swing music
J: 9119

Switzerland
IJ: 9793

Switzerland — Fiction
J: 294

Swords
IJ: 13084

Sydney (Australia)
IJ: 9754

Syphilis
IJ: 11578

Syria — Fiction
J: 4551

Systems analysis
J: 11305

T

Taiwan — Fiction
IJ: 4353

Taj Mahal
IJ: 9692, 9695

Tajikistan
JS: 9830

Tajiri, Satoshi
IJ: 8627

Talent shows — Fiction
IJ: 680

Taliban
J: 9731

Tall people — Fiction
IJ: 1244

Tall tales — Fiction
IJ: 3213

Tamang, Jhalak Man
IJ: 9006

The Taming of the Shrew —
Criticism
JS: 7432

Tan, Shaun
JS: 9020

Tanks
IJ: 9528

Tanzania
IJ: 9596, 9621, 9632
J: 9612

Taoism
IJ: 8851
J: 10527

Tarantulas
IJ: 12551–52

Tarbell, Ida
J: 7484

Tattoos
IJ: 11758
J: 11463

Tattoos — Fiction
IJ: 5818
JS: 2728

Taylor, Marshall B.
IJ: 8775

Taylor, Mildred D.
IJ: 7843

Taylor, Mildred D. — Criticism
JS: 7416

Taylor, Zachary
IJ: 8232

Tea — Fiction
IJ: 928

Teachers — Biography
IJ: 8399, 8952

Teachers — Fiction
IJ: 549, 659, 803, 884, 2515
J: 2009, 6196, 6397
JS: 1001, 2443, 4984, 5737

Teamwork
JS: 11347

Teapot Dome Scandal
IJ: 10350

Tebe
JS: 7652

Technical writing
J: 11320

Technology and engineering
IJ: 10262, 11083, 12156, 12927,
12927, 12932–33, 12939, 12942,
12942, 12950, 12969, 13005, 13020,
13413
J: 12926, 12940
JS: 9160, 11438, 12936, 12936–37,
12949

**Technology and engineering —
Biography**
IJ: 8438

**Technology and engineering —
Careers**
JS: 11429, 11438

**Technology and engineering —
Fiction**
IJ: 6025

**Tecumseh (Shawnee chief) —
Fiction**
J: 4913

Teddy bears — Fiction
JS: 4967

Teenagers
IJ: 11959
J: 11821
JS: 11986

**Teenagers — Alcohol use —
Fiction**
J: 1692

Teenagers — Authors
J: 11982

Teenagers — Authors — Essays
JS: 7403, 11272

Teenagers — Authors — Fiction
JS: 6902, 7403

Teenagers — Civil rights
J: 10794
JS: 10788

Teenagers — Crime — Fiction
J: 1978
JS: 2444

Teenagers — Essays
JS: 7400–01–02

Teenagers — Everyday life
JS: 10879

Teenagers — Fatherhood
J: 11932
JS: 11924

Teenagers — Fiction
JS: 888, 7400–01, 7406, 7462

Teenagers — Homeless
JS: 11144

Teenagers — Japan
J: 9709

Teenagers — Motherhood
JS: 8997, 11922

**Teenagers — Motherhood —
Fiction**
J: 1162

Teenagers — Parenthood
J: 11932
JS: 11921, 11931

**Teenagers — Parenthood —
Fiction**
J: 1982
JS: 1487, 1568, 1649, 2097, 2306

Teenagers — Poetry
JS: 7400–01–02, 7406, 7462

Teenagers — Pregnancy
JS: 11920, 11925, 11931, 11933

**Teenagers — Pregnancy —
Fiction**
J: 1465, 1546, 1824, 1836, 2239
JS: 1854, 1965, 2058, 2066, 2086,
2147, 2303, 2306, 3263

Teenagers — Problems
JS: 10879, 10938, 12036, 12059,
12099

**Teenagers — Problems —
Fiction**
J: 2011

Teenagers — Romance
JS: 12061

IJ = Upper Elementary/Lower Middle School; J = Middle School/Junior High; JS = Junior High/Senior High

Tikal (Guatemala)
IJ: 9960

Till, Emmett
J: 8400, 10814
JS: 10758, 10768

Timbuktu
IJ: 9656

Timbuktu — Fiction
JS: 154

Time and clocks
IJ: 9289, 12163, 12205, 12766, 12771, 12782
J: 12865

Time and clocks — Poetry
IJ: 7020

Time management
JS: 11255, 11334

Time travel
IJ: 2622, 2680, 2714, 2893, 2939, 3025, 3028, 3030, 3037, 3295, 3317, 3409, 3498, 3602, 3641, 3769, 3799, 3802, 3805, 5792, 6000, 6420, 6423, 6650
J: 286, 2637, 2829, 2897, 3026, 3387, 3541, 3750, 3757, 5259, 5507, 6306, 6563–64, 6624
JS: 446, 2856, 3252, 5318, 5855, 6608, 6694

Time travel — Fiction
See also Fantasy; Science fiction
IJ: 254, 987, 2575, 2636, 2679, 2765, 2857, 2962, 2999, 3027, 3031, 3076, 3180, 3224, 3274, 3356, 3359, 3376, 3421, 3479, 3525, 3563, 3585, 3652, 3742, 3771, 3787–88–89–90, 3828, 5394, 6478, 6523–24, 6588, 6770
J: 2753, 3001, 3074, 3116, 3141, 3264, 3406, 3473, 3543, 3610, 3803, 5198, 6438, 6441
JS: 2869, 3403, 3495, 3870, 6522, 6671

Times Square (New York, NY)
IJ: 10061

***Titanic* (ship)**
IJ: 3274, 13073, 13076–77
J: 13079, 13081
JS: 13074

***Titanic* (ship) — Fiction**
IJ: 987, 4975
J: 40, 5015
JS: 4545

Tobacco
IJ: 11500
J: 11530
JS: 11484, 11515

Toilets
IJ: 9259

Tokyo
J: 9711

Tolerance — Fiction
J: 2556

Tolkien, J. R. R.
J: 7847

Tools
J: 12195

Tornadoes
IJ: 12802, 12811, 12815
JS: 12800

Tornadoes — Fiction
IJ: 680
J: 256
JS: 1043, 1854

Toronto (ON) — Fiction
J: 2199

Torture
J: 10607, 10616

Torture — Fiction
JS: 6274

Torvalds, Linus
IJ: 8631

Tour guides — Careers
J: 11350

Tourette's syndrome
J: 11639
JS: 11572

Tourette's syndrome — Biography
J: 8965

Tourism
IJ: 10967

Toussaint l'Ouverture, François-Dominique
IJ: 8951

Toy making
IJ: 13214

Toys — Fiction
IJ: 2660, 3093

Track and field
IJ: 13546

Track and field — Biography
IJ: 8755, 8758–59, 8783
J: 8750–51, 8754

Track and field — Fiction
J: 6782, 6785, 6815
JS: 477

Trade
JS: 11246

Trail of Tears
J: 10108, 10119, 10125

Trail of Tears — Fiction
IJ: 4617

Tramps (U.S.)
JS: 10080

Tranquilizing drugs
JS: 11511

Transcontinental Railroad
IJ: 10291, 12780

Transgender people — Fiction
JS: 2424

Transplants
JS: 11553

Transportation
IJ: 13034–35, 13060, 13062
J: 11022, 13033

Transvestism — Fiction
JS: 1665

Travel
IJ: 13070
JS: 7396, 12990

Travel — Careers
J: 11344

Travel — Fiction
IJ: 691, 2080
J: 605
JS: 740

Treason — Biography
J: 11062

Treasure sites
IJ: 13358

Tree kangaroos
IJ: 12481

Trees
IJ: 12326, 12359
JS: 12353–54–55, 12357–58

Trees — Fiction
IJ: 4878

Trials
J: 10774, 10805
JS: 10758, 10768

Trials — Fiction
JS: 4671

Triangle Shirtwaist Factory fire
J: 10328
JS: 10329

Triangle Shirtwaist Factory fire — Fiction
IJ: 4960
J: 4947

Triathlons
J: 13415

Triathlons — Fiction
JS: 6742

Trinidad — Poetry
IJ: 7170

Trivia
IJ: 13346

Trivia — Biography
JS: 8043

Trojan War
IJ: 7375

Trojan War — Fiction
J: 2898, 7351

Truman, Harry S
JS: 8233

IJ = Upper Elementary/Lower Middle School; J = Middle School/Junior High; JS = Junior High/Senior High

U

IJ = Upper Elementary/Lower Middle School; J = Middle School/Junior High; JS = Junior High/Senior High

IJ = Upper Elementary/Lower Middle School; J = Middle School/Junior High; JS = Junior High/Senior High

Vermont
IJ: 10453
J: 10438

Vermont — Fiction
IJ: 1054, 1225–26–27, 3599, 4674, 4993, 5044, 5230
J: 1562, 2121, 4758, 4959, 4970, 5642

Verne, Jules
IJ: 7854–55

Veterinarians
JS: 12656

Veterinarians — Biography
JS: 12657

Veterinarians — Careers
IJ: 11326–27, 11336
J: 11353

Veterinarians — Fiction
IJ: 5852
J: 5018

Vice Presidents (U.S.) — Biography
J: 8258

Victoria, Queen of England
J: 9813

Victoria, Queen of England — Fiction
IJ: 4459
JS: 4479

Victorian Age
J: 9813

Victorian Age — Fiction
IJ: 3493, 4525
J: 286, 386, 2894, 4368, 4435, 4445, 5428
JS: 4367, 4511, 6077

Video games
IJ: 13005, 13581
J: 13580, 13582

Video games — Biography
IJ: 8627

Video games — Careers
JS: 11363, 11426, 11430

Video games — Fiction
J: 4087, 6108

Video recordings
IJ: 13276
J: 13277

Vietnam
IJ: 9744
J: 9721, 10404

Vietnam — Fiction
IJ: 1190, 4309, 4350
J: 2530
JS: 4310

Vietnam — Folklore
IJ: 7230, 7237

Vietnam Veterans Memorial
J: 7660

Vietnam War
IJ: 9566, 9568, 9580, 10376, 10394, 10399, 10401, 10406
J: 9571, 9721, 10395, 10397, 10402–03–04
JS: 9574, 9583, 10385, 10396, 10400, 10691

Vietnam War — Biography
IJ: 8313, 9001–02
JS: 8314

Vietnam War — Fiction
IJ: 1553, 1608, 5095, 5325, 5331, 5339
J: 2263, 4297, 5322, 5326–27, 5335–36, 5338, 5856
JS: 5323, 5328–29, 5332, 5334, 5337

Vietnamese Americans
IJ: 10891

Vietnamese Americans — Biography
J: 9003

Vietnamese Americans — Fiction
JS: 1093

Vikings
IJ: 9246, 9341, 9853, 9857
J: 9333, 9339, 9347, 9859, 9861
JS: 9321

Vikings — Fiction
IJ: 4416, 4501
J: 2937, 4173
JS: 4186

Village life
IJ: 9449

Vincent, Erin
JS: 9007

Violence
J: 10940, 10953, 11116
JS: 11058, 11088

Violence — Biography
JS: 8962

Violence — Fiction
IJ: 4373
J: 1542, 2545, 2554
JS: 775, 1995, 2103

Violins — Fiction
IJ: 1330
JS: 827

Virginia
IJ: 10486, 10488, 10496, 10498

Virginia — Fiction
IJ: 4701
J: 2068, 4656

Virtual reality — Fiction
J: 994, 6455, 6684

Viruses
IJ: 11573, 11651, 12609
J: 11604
JS: 11622

Viruses — Fiction
J: 6603

Visions — Fiction
J: 5465

Visual disabilities — Fiction
IJ: 5859

Visualization (computers)
IJ: 12982

Vivaldi, Antonio
J: 7895

Vocational guidance
JS: 11334, 11347

Volcanoes
IJ: 9410, 9824, 10468, 12708, 12710, 12712–13, 12715, 12848
J: 11419, 12705–06
JS: 9310, 12707

Volcanoes — Fiction
IJ: 4156
J: 3818
JS: 404

Volleyball
IJ: 13583

Volleyball — Biography
IJ: 8773

Volunteerism
IJ: 11161, 11165, 13252
J: 11166
JS: 10671, 11021, 11159, 11162, 11164, 11168–69–70–71

Volunteerism — Fiction
J: 1984, 2497, 2527

Voodooism — Fiction
J: 5603

Voting
JS: 10733

Voting rights
J: 10805

Voting Rights Act
JS: 10759

W

Wagon trains — Fiction
IJ: 4860

Wakeboarding
All: 13400
IJ: 13395

Waksman, Selman
IJ: 8635

Walden Pond
IJ: 10448

Waldman, Neil
IJ: 7695

Wales
IJ: 9034
J: 9799

IJ = Upper Elementary/Lower Middle School; J = Middle School/Junior High; JS = Junior High/Senior High

IJ = Upper Elementary/Lower Middle School; J = Middle School/Junior High; JS = Junior High/Senior High

IJ = Upper Elementary/Lower Middle School; J = Middle School/Junior High; JS = Junior High/Senior High

IJ = Upper Elementary/Lower Middle School; J = Middle School/Junior High; JS = Junior High/Senior High

1186

Yellow fever
IJ: 11579, 11618
JS: 10196

Yellow fever — Fiction
J: 4689, 4702

Yellowstone National Park
IJ: 12452
J: 10420

Yellowstone National Park — Fiction
IJ: 6206

Yemen
IJ: 9911, 9929

Yep, Laurence — Criticism
JS: 7419

Yeti
JS: 13373

Yetis — Fiction
JS: 100

Yoga
J: 13379, 13416
JS: 11814, 13406

Yom Kippur
IJ: 10516

Yom Kippur — Fiction
J: 2112

Yorktown, Battle of
IJ: 10203

Yosemite National Park
J: 10473

Young adult literature — Biography
JS: 7744, 7826

Young adult literature — Criticism
JS: 7415, 7783

Young, Brigham
IJ: 8408

Yu, Chun
J: 9011

Yukon
JS: 7518

Z

Zaharias, Babe Didrikson
IJ: 8783
JS: 8781–82

Zaire
J: 9616, 9622
JS: 9600, 9617

Zambia — Biography
IJ: 12632

Zamora, Pedro
JS: 4153

Zedong, Mao
J: 8859

Zenatti, Valérie
JS: 9012

Zenger, John Peter
J: 10702

Zeus (mythology)
J: 4025

Zhang, Ange
IJ: 7705

Zimbabwe
IJ: 9651–52

Zimbabwe — Fiction
IJ: 3588
J: 6485
JS: 4273, 4279

Zindel, Paul
IJ: 7875

Zirconium
IJ: 12690

Zombies
J: 13323, 13371

Zombies — Fiction
IJ: 2896, 3105, 3238, 5414, 5511, 5646
J: 3032, 3739, 5367–68, 5485–86, 5495, 5501, 5534, 5554
JS: 2596, 3623, 5362

Zoo animals — Fiction
IJ: 4431

Zoos
IJ: 12658–59

Zoos — Fiction
IJ: 161, 5980

Zuckerberg, Mark
JS: 8651

Zuñi Indians — Folklore
IJ: 7289

IJ = Upper Elementary/Lower Middle School; J = Middle School/Junior High; JS = Junior High/Senior High

About the Author

CATHERINE BARR is the coauthor of other volumes in the Best Books series (*Best Books for Children* and *Best Books for High School Readers*) and of *Popular Series Fiction for K–6 Readers, Popular Series Fiction for Middle School and Teen Readers,* and *High/Low Handbook: Best Books and Web Sites for Reluctant Teen Readers*, 4th Edition.